THE EUROPEAN FOOTBALL YEARBOOK 2016/17

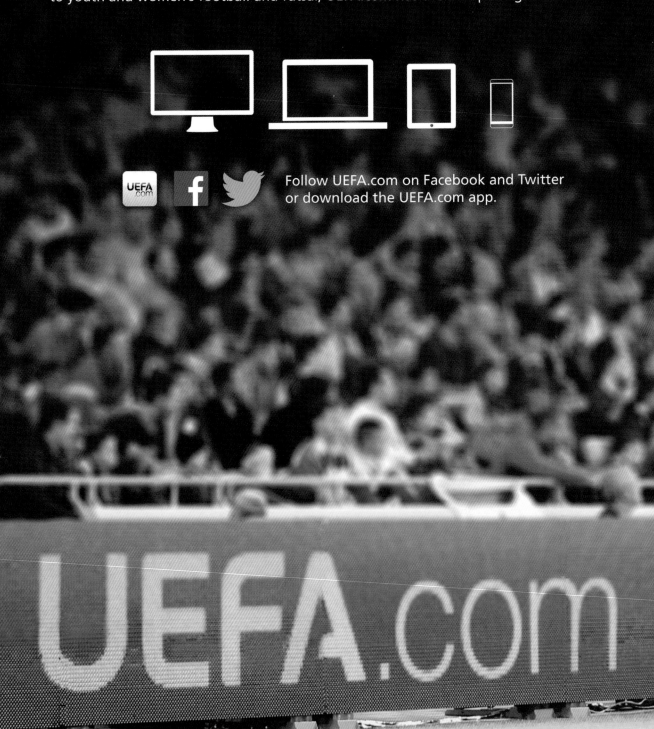

The official channel for European football

From the UEFA Champions League, UEFA Europa League and UEFA EURO 2016, to youth and women's football and futsal, UEFA.com has the European game covered.

Follow UEFA.com on Facebook and Twitter or download the UEFA.com app.

THE EUROPEAN FOOTBALL YEARBOOK 20 16 17

General Editor
Mike Hammond

The only authoritative annual on the European game

Further copies of The European Football Yearbook 2016/17
are available from:
www.carltonbooks.co.uk
hotline number +44 (0) 141 306 3100

The European Football Yearbook 2016/17

First published by Carlton Books Ltd, England in 2016

Printed by mpress ltd, England

ISBN 978-1-78097-845-1

UEFA – the Union of European Football Associations – is the governing body of football on the continent of Europe. UEFA's core mission is to promote, protect and develop European football at every level of the game, to promote the principles of unity and solidarity, and to deal with all questions relating to European football.

UEFA is an association of associations based on representative democracy, and is the governing body of European football.

UEFA
Route de Genève 46
Case postale
CH-1260 Nyon 2
Switzerland

Tel: +41 (0) 848 00 2727
Web: UEFA.com

Media Desk
Tel: +41 (0) 848 04 2727

All views expressed in the European Football Yearbook do not necessarily reflect those of UEFA. Every effort has been made to ensure the accuracy of the data in the European Football Yearbook, official and unofficial.

Front cover image: Cristiano Ronaldo, the captain of UEFA EURO 2016 winners Portugal, prepares to raise the Henri Delaunay Cup in front of jubilant team-mates at the Stade de France

The European Football Yearbook 2012/13, 2013/14, 2014/15, 2015/16
are available from:
www.calmproductions.com
orders@calmproductions.com
UK hotline 0845 408 2606

THE EUROPEAN FOOTBALL YEARBOOK 2016 / 17

General Editor
Mike Hammond

Assistant Editor
Jesper Krogshede Sørensen

Nation-by-nation

Correspondents and Researchers

Nikolai Belov (Russia), Sílvia Casals (Andorra), José Del Olmo (Spain), Sean DeLoughry (Republic of Ireland), Tamás Dénes (Hungary), Mike Farrugia (Malta), Arno Funck (Luxembourg), Stoyan Georgiev (Bulgaria), GFT (Julian Fortuna, Aaron Payas, Sean Mascarenhas, Ryan Gonzalez) (Gibraltar), Marshall Gillespie (Northern Ireland), Clas Glenning (France, Sweden), Miron Goihman (Moldova), Elia Gorini (San Marino), Marcel Haisma (Netherlands), Michael Hansen (Denmark), Kobi Hayat (Israel), Romeo Ionescu (Romania), Mikael Kirakosyan (Armenia), Jesper Krogshede Sørensen (Faroe Islands, Italy), Fuad & Fedja Krvavac (Bosnia & Herzegovina), Zdeněk Kučera (Czech Republic), Ambrosius Kutschera (Austria), Almantas Laužadis (Lithuania), Tarmo Lehiste (Estonia), John Leonidou (Cyprus), Dag Lindholm (Norway), Ewan Macdonald (Scotland), Ivica Madžarović (Montenegro), Erlan Manashev (Kazakhstan), Goran Mancevski (FYR Macedonia), Rasim Mövsümov (Azerbaijan), Giovanni Nappi (Albania), Kazimierz Oleszek (Poland), Olexandr Pauk (Belarus, Ukraine), Luca Pelliccioni (San Marino), Humberto Pereira Silva (Portugal), Ivan Reić (Croatia), Mike Ritter & Silvia Schäfer (Germany), Grega Sever (Slovenia), Revaz Shengelia (Georgia), Vídir Sigurdsson (Iceland), Erdinç Sivritepe (Turkey), Edouard Stutz (Switzerland), Matej Széher (Slovakia), Mel Thomas (Wales), Vesa Tikander (Finland), Serge Van Hoof (Belgium), Victor Vassallo (Malta), Georgios J Vassalos (Greece), Sergey Vorobyov (Latvia); additional assistance Charlie Hammond, Gabriel Mantz, Emil Gasevski, Sveinur Tróndarson

Photography

Getty Images, Sportsfile, Getty Images/AFP, Getty Images/Bongarts; additional assistance Fernando Galindo, C Correa Photography, Lato Klodian, Joe Borg, Domenic Aquilina, TASR/Radovan Stoklasa, propaganda-photo.com

UEFA

Editorial

Jim Foulerton, Wayne Harrison, Michael Harrold, Patrick Hart, Andrew Haslam, Conrad Leach, Richard Martin, Paul Saffer

Data

Andy Lockwood, Rob Esteva, Jim Agnew, Craig Steeples

Production

Print
m press ltd, England; Cliff Moulder

Distribution
Carlton Books Ltd; Martin Corteel, Jim Greenhough

Design
Keith Jackson

Graphics
Mikhail Sipovich

Data extraction
Delta3 (Emiliano Borello, Stefano Strignano, Paolo Calva, Edoardo Masci)

Foreword

Fernando Santos

National three-letter codes

There are many instances throughout the European Football Yearbook where country names are abbreviated using three-letter codes. These codes are shown below, listed alphabetically by nation and divided into Europe and the Rest of the World.

Europe

ALB	Alb	Albania
AND	And	Andorra
ARM	Arm	Armenia
AUT	Aut	Austria
AZE	Aze	Azerbaijan
BLR	Blr	Belarus
BEL	Bel	Belgium
BIH	Bih	Bosnia & Herzegovina
BUL	Bul	Bulgaria
CRO	Cro	Croatia
CYP	Cyp	Cyprus
CZE	Cze	Czech Republic
DEN	Den	Denmark
ENG	Eng	England
EST	Est	Estonia
FRO	Fro	Faroe Islands
FIN	Fin	Finland
FRA	Fra	France
GEO	Geo	Georgia
GER	Ger	Germany
GIB	Gib	Gibraltar
GRE	Gre	Greece
HUN	Hun	Hungary
ISL	Isl	Iceland
ISR	Isr	Israel
ITA	Ita	Italy
KAZ	Kaz	Kazakhstan
KOS	Kos	Kosovo
LVA	Lva	Latvia
LIE	Lie	Liechtenstein
LTU	Ltu	Lithuania
LUX	Lux	Luxembourg
MKD	Mkd	Former Yugoslav Republic of Macedonia
MLT	Mlt	Malta
MDA	Mda	Moldova
MNE	Mne	Montenegro
NED	Ned	Netherlands
NIR	Nir	Northern Ireland
NOR	Nor	Norway
POL	Pol	Poland
POR	Por	Portugal
IRL	Irl	Republic of Ireland
ROU	Rou	Romania
RUS	Rus	Russia
SMR	Smr	San Marino
SCO	Sco	Scotland
SRB	Srb	Serbia
SVK	Svk	Slovakia
SVN	Svn	Slovenia
ESP	Esp	Spain
SWE	Swe	Sweden
SUI	Sui	Switzerland
TUR	Tur	Turkey
UKR	Ukr	Ukraine
WAL	Wal	Wales

Rest of the World

AFG	Afg	Afghanistan
ALG	Alg	Algeria
ANG	Ang	Angola
ATG	Atg	Antigua & Barbuda
ARG	Arg	Argentina
ARU	Aru	Aruba
AUS	Aus	Australia
BAH	Bah	Bahamas
BHR	Bhr	Bahrain
BAN	Ban	Bangladesh
BRB	Brb	Barbados
BEN	Ben	Benin
BER	Ber	Bermuda
BOL	Bol	Bolivia
BOT	Bot	Botswana
BRA	Bra	Brazil
BFA	Bfa	Burkina Faso
BDI	Bdi	Burundi
CMR	Cmr	Cameroon
CAN	Can	Canada
CPV	Cpv	Cape Verde Islands
CAY	Cay	Cayman Islands
CTA	Cta	Central African Republic
CHA	Cha	Chad
CHI	Chi	Chile
CHN	Chn	China
TPE	Tpe	Chinese Taipei
COL	Col	Colombia
COM	Com	Comoros
CGO	Cgo	Congo
COD	Cod	Congo DR
CRC	Crc	Costa Rica
CUB	Cub	Cuba
CUW	Cuw	Curacao
DJI	Dji	Djibouti
DOM	Dom	Dominican Republic
ECU	Ecu	Ecuador
EGY	Egy	Egypt
SLV	Slv	El Salvador
EQG	Eqg	Equatorial Guinea
ERI	Eri	Eritrea
ETH	Eth	Ethiopia
FIJ	Fij	Fiji
GAB	Gab	Gabon
GAM	Gam	Gambia
GHA	Gha	Ghana
GRN	Grn	Grenada
GUM	Gum	Guam
GUA	Gua	Guatemala
GUI	Gui	Guinea
GNB	Gnb	Guinea-Bissau
GUY	Guy	Guyana
HAI	Hai	Haiti
HON	Hon	Honduras
HKG	Hkg	Hong Kong
IND	Ind	India
IDN	Idn	Indonesia
IRN	Irn	Iran
IRQ	Irq	Iraq
CIV	Civ	Ivory Coast
JAM	Jam	Jamaica
JPN	Jpn	Japan
JOR	Jor	Jordan
KEN	Ken	Kenya
KUW	Kuw	Kuwait
KGZ	Kgz	Kyrgyzstan

LIB	Lib	Lebanon
LBR	Lbr	Liberia
LBY	Lby	Libya
MAD	Mad	Madagascar
MWI	Mwi	Malawi
MAS	Mas	Malaysia
MLI	Mli	Mali
MTQ	Mtq	Martinique
MTN	Mtn	Mauritania
MRI	Mri	Mauritius
MEX	Mex	Mexico
MSR	Msr	Montserrat
MAR	Mar	Morocco
MOZ	Moz	Mozambique
NAM	Nam	Namibia
ANT	Ant	Netherlands Antilles
NCL	Ncl	New Caledonia
NZL	Nzl	New Zealand
NCA	Nca	Nicaragua
NIG	Nig	Niger
NGA	Nga	Nigeria
PRK	Prk	North Korea
OMA	Oma	Oman
PAK	Pak	Pakistan
PLE	Ple	Palestine
PAN	Pan	Panama
PAR	Par	Paraguay
PER	Per	Peru
PHI	Phi	Philippines
PUR	Pur	Puerto Rico
QAT	Qat	Qatar
RWA	Rwa	Rwanda
STP	Stp	Sao Tome & Principe
KSA	Ksa	Saudi Arabia
SEN	Sen	Senegal
SLE	Sle	Sierra Leone
SIN	Sin	Singapore
SOL	Sol	Solomon Islands
SOM	Som	Somalia
RSA	Rsa	South Africa
KOR	Kor	South Korea
SKN	Skn	St Kitts & Nevis
VIN	Vin	St Vincent & Grenadines
SDN	Sdn	Sudan
SUR	Sur	Surinam
SYR	Syr	Syria
TAH	Tah	Tahiti
TJK	Tjk	Tajikistan
TAN	Tan	Tanzania
THA	Tha	Thailand
TOG	Tog	Togo
TRI	Tri	Trinidad & Tobago
TUN	Tun	Tunisia
TKM	Tkm	Turkmenistan
UGA	Uga	Uganda
UAE	Uae	United Arab Emirates
USA	Usa	United States
URU	Uru	Uruguay
UZB	Uzb	Uzbekistan
VEN	Ven	Venezuela
VIE	Vie	Vietnam
YEM	Yem	Yemen
ZAM	Zam	Zambia
ZIM	Zim	Zimbabwe

Contents

THE EUROPEAN FOOTBALL YEARBOOK 20 16 17

Foreword

I am delighted to have been asked to write the foreword for the European Football Yearbook – a long-running publication that remains the most authoritative and attractive annual reference on this great game of ours.

This 2016/17 edition is, of course, a very special one for me as it chronicles Portugal's success at UEFA EURO 2016. To see the joyous expressions on the faces of my players on the front cover of the book, with my magnificent captain Cristiano Ronaldo at the forefront holding aloft the Henri Delaunay Cup, is an image that will stay with me for the rest of my days.

It is very difficult to sum up in a few words the extent of the pride and joy that comes from leading a team to a victory of such magnitude – especially when it means so much to so many. The people of Portugal have waited a long time to savour such intensely happy emotions, and it goes without saying that what we achieved would not have been possible without the incredible backing of our loyal and passionate fans.

They followed us everywhere around France for the whole month, and to reward them and all the people back home in Portugal for their support with the ultimate prize of being crowned European champions gives me, my players and everyone associated with the team an enormous glow of satisfaction.

And what can I say about my players? They were amazing. They fought like warriors in the qualifying competition, and they continued to give their heart and soul at the finals. I always told them that we had enough talent in our squad to win the tournament, that if we worked hard, played to our strengths and never lost our resolve, we could do it. They were superb, and I shall forever be grateful for the extraordinary application and ability they demonstrated in every game.

None of our opponents could break us down and beat us, not even France, the host nation, in the final – and with our talismanic skipper injured and off the pitch.

To win that match was a heroic effort from everyone involved and should be a lesson to every sportsman and woman that if you believe, stay focused and work hard for each other, you can make the most of your talent and achieve the goals you set out for yourselves. No dream is impossible.

Portugal's is just one of many success stories featured in this edition of the European Football Yearbook. While my country's historic first UEFA European Championship victory is afforded comprehensive coverage within these pages, so too are the successes and achievements of many champions, cup winners and leading players from all over Europe.

The European Football Yearbook, now in its 29th year, is a vast mine of information – statistical, narrative and pictorial – and I know for certain that, like a successful football team, it only comes together after a lot of diligence, organisation, patience and hard work. I will treasure this special edition and look forward to seeing many more in the years to come.

Fernando Santos
Head coach
Portugal
UEFA EURO 2016 winners

Introduction

From the General Editor

A very warm welcome to the 2016/17 edition of the European Football Yearbook.

The publication is now 29 years old, and this edition marks a distinctive anniversary as it is the tenth year that it has been produced with the co-operation and support of UEFA.

As ever, the Yearbook's aim is to provide a comprehensive, attractive and readable review of the past European football season, chronicling in statistics, graphics and words not only the performances and achievements of the big, high-profile teams and players but also those across the entire continental spectrum, from Iceland to Kazakhstan and all points in between.

This year, because of our extensive coverage of UEFA EURO 2016, the book has been expanded by 16 pages, giving you even more information than before – and for the same cover price.

It should be mentioned that the admission of Kosovo as the 55th member of UEFA in May came too late for inclusion this year, but rest assured that Kosovo will be afforded the same coverage as every other nation in next year's edition and beyond.

Regular purchasers of the Yearbook will be familiar with its contents, and I am pleased to report that this 2016/17 edition has maintained the structure and layout that has proved so popular in the past two years. Changes have been minimal, although readers will probably notice – and appreciate – a less formal style within the general narrative of the club names (e.g. Arsenal rather than Arsenal FC, Atlético Madrid rather than Club Atlético de Madrid etc).

UEFA EURO 2016 heads the opening section of the book devoted to UEFA competitions, with the full story of the finals in France supplemented by a review of the latter stages of the qualifying competition. The UEFA Champions League and UEFA Europa League also get the same in-depth treatment, and they are followed by chapters on all the various youth, women's and futsal competitions.

The Top 100 Players of the Season section, now in its 12th year and seemingly more talked-about than ever, follows next.

At the heart of the Yearbook is the nation-by-nation section, in which we provide a round-up of the season's events in each UEFA member association, listing domestic league results, scorers, appearances and goals for every top-division club as well as detailed national team and European data. A map with club locations, a concise review of the season and an at-a-glance domestic summary head each chapter.

Finally, the book looks forward to the 2016/17 season with a UEFA calendar of events and a complete list of fixtures for the 2018 FIFA World Cup European Qualifiers.

* * * * *

Two years ago, on this very page, I wrote of my beloved Leicester City after their promotion to the Premier League: "I don't expect there will be another [season] quite like it."

Well, how wrong – how wonderfully wrong – I was. You would not be reading this if you didn't know what my team went and did in 2015/16. Suffice to say that for me – and, I'm sure, for all LCFC fans – that truly was the season without compare. Whatever happens next is a bonus. The joy of experiencing Leicester City defy all odds and become the champions of England for the first time in the club's history will never be matched.

Of course, I never imagined in my wildest dreams that such a thing could happen, but it just goes to show – as Portugal coach Fernando Santos proclaims on the opposite page – that nothing in football, or indeed sport in general, is impossible. The unpredictability of sport is its beauty, complacency and entitlement its enemy, and we were reminded of that repeatedly at UEFA EURO 2016 – by

Portugal and other teams such as Wales, Iceland and Hungary. As one of my favourite sayings goes, where there's a will, there's a way.

* * * * *

My thanks, as always, go to everyone who has helped to bring this edition of the European Football Yearbook to fruition. Special gratitude is reserved for my trusty lieutenants Jesper and Keith, while the loving support of my family – Sue, Rebecca and Charlie – never fails to be appreciated.

I would also like to pay my special respects here to Chris Nawrat, former Sunday Times sports editor, mentor, friend and avid reader and collector of this Yearbook, who so sadly passed away before his time in December 2015. Chris, this one's for you.

Mike Hammond
1 August, 2016

2015/16 season summary

After eight years at the summit of European football, 2016 proved to be the year Spain's national team – if not their club sides – fell from their perch. Italy claimed the honour of knocking out the champions in the round of 16, yet the ultimate triumph at UEFA EURO 2016 was Portugal's. Fernando Santos's men started the tournament slowly but finished with the trophy in their hands thanks to substitute Éder's strike 11 minutes from the end of extra time in the final against France in Saint-Denis.

Éder may have been an unlikely hero for Portugal but, then again, nothing went entirely to script at the first 24-team EURO. The underdogs had their day, with Iceland eliminating England to reach the quarter-finals and Wales overcoming Belgium en route to the semi-finals. If France's passage to the final was more predictable – Les Bleus had won both the 1984 UEFA European Championship and the 1998 FIFA World Cup on home soil – Portugal ensured one last late twist.

That was the second major success of the summer for Cristiano Ronaldo and Pepe, who had helped Real Madrid to an 11th European Champion Clubs' Cup triumph less than six weeks previously. It was Ronaldo – sadly injured during the UEFA EURO 2016 final – who had the last word in Milan against neighbours Atlético Madrid, converting the winning penalty in a shoot-out after a 1-1 draw.

It was the second time in three years that the Madrid rivals had met in the UEFA Champions League decider, and there was another familiar face in the UEFA Europa League final in Basel as, for the third campaign running, Spanish sides claimed Europe's two major club honours. Sevilla overturned a half-time deficit against Liverpool as Kevin Gameiro equalised 18 seconds after the restart before two Coke goals made sure of the Andalusian club's third straight UEFA Europa League crown and, UEFA Cups included, record fifth in all.

The UEFA Youth League witnessed its own successful title defence, with Chelsea overcoming Paris Saint-Germain in the Nyon final to clinch their second consecutive title. In the UEFA Women's Champions League, however, Lyon were grateful to avoid a case of déjà vu. In front of over 15,000 spectators in Reggio Emilia, they avenged their 2013 final defeat by Wolfsburg, winning 4-3 on spot-kicks after a 1-1 draw.

That was Lyon's third European women's crown and it was not the only French hat-trick as Les Petits Bleus prevailed for the third time at the UEFA European Under-19 Championship, beating Italy 4-0 in the final. As for the U17 event, that ended with an all-Iberian affair won by Portugal who overcame Spain 5-4 on spot-kicks after a 1-1 draw.

The Spanish boys' female counterparts suffered the same fate at the Women's Under-17 finals, succumbing 3-2 on penalties to five-time winners Germany after a goalless draw in front of a competition-record crowd of 10,200 in Borisov. There would be further heartbreak for Spain at the Women's U19 finals in Slovakia as they lost 2-1 to France in a final interrupted for over two hours by a fierce thunderstorm.

There was a sunnier outcome for Spain's representatives at UEFA Futsal EURO 2016. Having lost to Russia in the 2014 semi-finals, Spain beat the same nation 7-3 in the final to clinch their seventh title – and sixth in eight tournaments. A record aggregate attendance of 113,820 across the 20 matches in Belgrade was proof of the sport's rising profile, and there were more sell-outs at the UEFA Futsal Cup in Guadalajara, Spain where this time a Russian side had the upper hand, Ugra Yugorsk beating hosts Inter 4-3 in the final.

| Hosts France defeated 1-0 after extra time in final | Injured skipper Cristiano Ronaldo lifts the trophy | Wales and Iceland enjoy fairytale EURO debuts |

EURO glory for Portugal

The final tournament of UEFA EURO 2016, the first in the competition's 56-year history to feature 24 teams, produced an unexpected winner as Portugal, who had never previously captured a major international trophy, defeated host nation France 1-0 after extra time in the final.

The outcome at the Stade de France mirrored that of 12 years earlier when Portugal, playing at home and strongly fancied, lost 1-0 in Lisbon to Greece. That UEFA EURO 2004 final featured a young Cristiano Ronaldo, who provided one of the tournament's abiding images with his tears of sorrow at the end of the match.

What goes around in sport, however, so often comes around, and in 2016 Ronaldo was able at last to erase those unhappy memories as he and his Portugal team, skilfully commanded by coach Fernando Santos, conquered Europe after a month-long adventure of dramatic twists and turns. It was a shame – a crying shame, indeed – that Ronaldo was injured so early in the final and had to leave the field on a stretcher, his eyes once again moist with tears, this time of frustration. But after a heroic

effort from his team-mates, capped with a tremendous extra-time goal from unheralded substitute Éder, the final tears for Portugal's captain were those of unrestrained joy as he hobbled up the Stade de France steps to collect and hoist aloft the Henri Delaunay Cup.

Portugal's victory enabled them to become the tenth different nation to claim the famous trophy, following Iberian neighbours Spain, victors in 2008 and 2012, on to the UEFA European Championship roll of honour. France, like Spain, had been eager to win the competition for the third time - and match (West) Germany's record – but after the holders were convincingly eliminated by Italy in the round of 16, the hosts too could have few complaints about the outcome of a final in which they underperformed, even if defeat was difficult to digest for a nation so accustomed to home-soil victory after previous triumphs at EURO '84 and the 1998 FIFA World Cup.

Antoine Griezmann did his best to emulate the feats of past French greats Michel Platini and Zinédine Zidane, but he ended up as a recipient only of individual prizes for his month's

endeavour, adding the Player of the Tournament tag to the Golden Boot. He top-scored with six goals – twice as many as any other player, Ronaldo included – and as five of those came in the knockout phase, including two in the semi-final victory over world champions Germany, he was entitled to the national hero worship that came his way.

That Germany-France encounter in Marseille was the pick of the 15 knockout matches in a tournament that will probably be remembered more for the excellent defending on show than for any sustained attacking brilliance. While drama of some description was never too far away, caution defined several encounters, which undoubtedly contributed to a lower than average figure of 108 goals in 51 games.

Against that, the expanded format enabled fairytales to be written by a number of first-time participants who, backed by thousands of noisy and enthusiastic followers, had the time of their lives – notably Iceland, who beat England to reach the last eight, and Wales, who overcame Belgium to go even further before Ronaldo and co dashed their dreams in the semi-finals.

Opposite: Portugal captain Cristiano Ronaldo, flanked by UEFA EURO 2016 final man of the match Pepe, raises the Henri Delaunay Cup at the Stade de France

Group A

Tournament hosts France kicked off UEFA EURO 2016 against Romania following a colourful choreographed opening ceremony at the Stade de France. After a hesitant start during which they came close to conceding a fourth-minute goal to Bogdan Stancu, Didier Deschamps' team regained their composure and began to dictate play, with Dimitri Payet, high on confidence after a superb debut season in England with West Ham United, coming repeatedly to the fore. On 57 minutes he created the opening goal, swinging in a finely judged cross for Olivier Giroud to nod home. The home supporters' joy did not last long, however, as a foul by Patrice Evra on Nicolae Stanciu gifted Romania a penalty, which Stancu coolly converted. A draw looked likely but Payet had other ideas, drilling the ball into the top corner with a perfectly executed left-foot drive in the 89th minute to give France a wildly celebrated opening 2-1 victory.

Switzerland joined France on three points by beating Albania 1-0 in Lens, Fabian Schär exploiting a lapse from goalkeeper Etrit Berisha to head in after five minutes. Albania's hopes of a comeback were compromised when captain Lorik Cana was dismissed

shortly before the break. However, their noisy supporters spurred them on, and it took several fine saves from Yann Sommer to preserve Switzerland's lead, with substitute Shkëlzen Gashi spurning one glorious one-on-one opportunity near the end.

Next up for France was a return to Deschamps' old stomping ground of Marseille to face Albania. The coach's decision to drop Paul Pogba and Antoine Griezmann, however, looked ill-conceived after a barren first half that ended with the crowd making their feelings known. It was a different story after the break as France piled on the pressure, only to meet dogged resistance from a defiant Albanian defence. Intense French pressure finally told, though, as Griezmann, on as a sub, headed home in the 90th minute. It was cruel on Albania after such a gutsy performance, but they were punished further in stoppage time by Payet, who burst into the area and rounded a defender before firing home.

Earlier the same day Switzerland could only draw 1-1 with Romania despite unleashing 19 shots at goal. Anghel Iordănescu's side went ahead against the run of play on 18 minutes from another Stancu spot-kick after Stephan

Lichtsteiner had been penalised for shirt-tugging. After repeatedly banging on the door, Switzerland finally levelled with 57 minutes gone through a powerful Admir Mehmedi strike. They dominated the remainder of the game but were unable to find a winner.

Albania finally got something to show for their spirit and endeavour as they overcame Romania in Lyon, triumphing 1-0 to send their winless opponents home. Armando Sadiku, a forlorn figure up front in previous games, headed in at the far post just before the break, thus saving the blushes of team-mate Emir Lenjani, who had missed an earlier sitter. The travelling masses of Albanian supporters celebrated long into the night even though they knew their three-point tally might not be enough to take them through. Three days later, the team's elimination was confirmed.

Meanwhile, on a patchy surface in Lille, a much-changed France struck the crossbar three times against unadventurous Switzerland but were unable to make it three wins out of three. The goalless draw, however, was no bad result for either team as it meant the hosts topped the group while Switzerland, also undefeated, qualified in second place.

Group B

EURO debutants Slovakia and Wales got Group B underway with an entertaining encounter in Bordeaux. Slovakia nearly got off to a dream start when Marek Hamšík zipped his way thrillingly through the Wales defence, only to be denied by Ben Davies's goal-line clearance. The significance of that intervention was, literally, hammered home a few minutes later as Gareth Bale drove in a trademark free-kick to put Wales ahead. Slovakia retaliated well after the break, though, and Ondrej Duda deservedly pulled them level just seconds after his introduction from the bench. Chris Coleman's side then rallied strongly and with nine minutes to go another substitute, Hal Robson-Kanu, found the net with a mishit shot to give Wales the lead – and ultimately the three points.

A youthful England side got their campaign underway against Russia in Marseille, and for the first half, with Wayne Rooney operating diligently in midfield, they outplayed their opponents with fluent, incisive football.

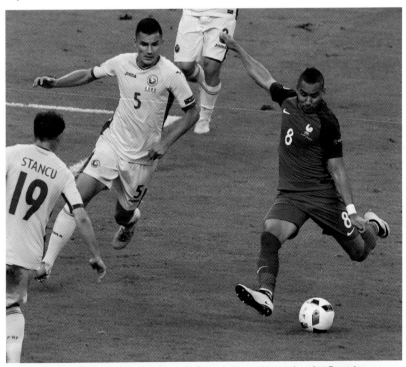

Dimitri Payet lets fly to score a superb late winner for France in the opening match against Romania

Vladimír Weiss fires Slovakia ahead against Russia in Lille

Unfortunately, they could not turn their superiority into goals. The momentum appeared to be stalling in the second half when, out of the blue, Rooney forced a brilliant save from Igor Akinfeev. A couple of minutes later, though, the Russia 'keeper could do nothing to stop a thunderbolt free-kick from Eric Dier. It gave England a deserved lead, but just as their curse of never having won an opening EURO finals game looked set to be lifted, inattentive defending allowed Russia captain Vasili Berezutski to leap high and equalise with a looping header. Moments later the whistle sounded, leaving Roy Hodgson's team in utter bewilderment that they had failed to see the job through.

Russia had escaped with a lucky draw, but the inadequacies of Leonid Slutski's team were exposed four days later as Slovakia defeated them 2-1 in Lille with a fine attacking display highlighted by two excellent goals at the end of the first half. Vladimír Weiss scored the first, controlling a long ball from Hamšík before blasting home. Weiss then returned the compliment to Hamšík, playing a short corner to his skipper, who slammed the ball in off the far post to double Slovakia's lead. As against England, Russia managed a late response, reducing the deficit through Denis Glushakov's superb header, but despite a late siege they could not find an equaliser and Slovakia held on for a first EURO victory.

Wales went into the all-British affair with England in Lens full of confidence, and although Hodgson's team again dominated possession and should have scored early on when Raheem Sterling fired a good chance wide, it was Wales who went ahead, and the inevitable Bale who scored, his long-range free-kick struck powerfully and accurately enough to escape the clutches of a floundering Hart before nestling in the bottom corner. Sensing a galling defeat, Hodgson looked to his bench for solutions and his half-time substitutes duly delivered, Jamie Vardy turning the ball home from close range after 56 minutes and, following an intense bout of attack-versus-defence, Daniel Sturridge snatching a dramatic injury-time winner as he pierced the crowded Welsh defence with a sharp right-footed toe-poke.

Hodgson surprisingly made six changes to his side against Slovakia in Saint-Etienne, and although England created plenty of openings, Slovakia, in all-out defence mode, stood strong to earn the 0-0 draw that would also take them through. Wales, meanwhile, leapfrogged England into top spot with an irresistible 3-0 win against Russia. Aaron Ramsey opened the scoring with a confident dink from Joe Allen's measured pass, and Wales were 2-0 up after 20 minutes when left-back Neil Taylor netted at the second attempt for his first international goal. In the second half the outstanding

Bale got in on the act too, converting Ramsey's pass to make it 3-0 and become only the seventh player to score in every group game at a EURO finals.

Group C

Poland, competing at their third EURO, claimed their first ever victory by beating tournament debutants Northern Ireland 1-0 in their opener and thus ending their opponents' 12-game unbeaten run. Despite the backing of fervent support in Nice, Northern Ireland struggled to impose themselves in attack and were generally second best. Robert Lewandowski was successfully kept quiet, but it was his strike partner Arkadiusz Milik who won the game with a skimming left-foot drive after 51 minutes.

Germany joined Poland on three points by beating Ukraine 2-0 in Lille, although it was far from plain sailing for the world champions, who needed Jérôme Boateng to clear the ball acrobatically off the line after Shkrodan Mustafi had given Germany an early lead with a glancing header from a Toni Kroos free-kick. Germany controlled the game in the second half, pinning Ukraine back, but it was not until added time that they cemented their victory, substitute Bastian Schweinsteiger finishing off a swift counterattack with a sweet far-post half-volley.

Northern Ireland manager Michael O'Neill made numerous changes to the team that had underwhelmed against Poland, and his new-look side outfought Ukraine in the pouring rain of Lyon to earn a vital first EURO win. Although in-vogue chants of 'Will Grigg is on fire' reverberated around the stadium, it was defender Gareth McAuley who scored first, leaping at the far post to head home Oliver Norwood's free-kick. Play was then briefly halted to shelter the players from a ferocious hailstorm, and on the resumption Northern Ireland survived a barrage of Ukraine attempts before substitute Niall McGinn scored with the last kick of the game to clinch a historic win.

Ukraine became the tournament's first eliminated team when Poland and Germany played out the first goalless draw of the tournament later that evening in Saint-Denis. The two sides, who had each beaten the other at home in the qualifiers, traded blows at the

Stade de France but two excellent defences held firm, Poland twice allowing their opponents off the hook with bad misses from Milik.

Ukraine had only pride to play for against Poland. They put on a brave face but were beaten by a classy goal from Jakub Błaszczykowski, who thus confirmed his country's first qualification for a EURO knockout phase. There was just one goal also at the Parc des Princes, where Mario Gomez's deflected effort was all Germany had to show for 90 minutes of relentless attack against Northern Ireland. The world champions chalked up 26 attempts but found themselves up against an outstanding goalkeeper in Michael McGovern, who had the game of his life, pulling off a succession of high-quality saves. Germany still finished top ahead of Poland on goals scored, and it would later be confirmed that McGovern's heroics had done enough for Northern Ireland's even goal difference to send them through as well in third place.

Group D

Luka Modrić got Croatia off to a winning start in Group D with a stunning volley to beat Turkey 1-0. Both sets of supporters made a racket inside the Parc des Princes despite the persistent rain, and Modrić capped an excellent display from his team by connecting beautifully with a high ball from 25 metres out and drilling it into the bottom corner. Croatia continued to demonstrate their quality after the break but could not add the additional goals their performance merited, with effervescent captain Darijo Srna and the equally lively Ivan Perišić both striking the crossbar.

Holders Spain kicked off their bid for an unprecedented third EURO triumph against Czech Republic in Toulouse, but despite dominating possession, Vicente Del Bosque's team created few genuine openings against opponents who had little ambition other than keeping their goal intact. Andrés Iniesta was nonetheless exceptional in his ability to keep probing patiently for holes in the Czech defence and with three minutes left he finally found one, sending over a pin-point cross for Barcelona team-mate Gerard Piqué to nod in unmarked from six metres out.

Spain moved on to six points by easily beating Turkey 3-0 four days later in

Nice. Their display had all the hallmarks of their 2008 and 2012 title-winning teams, with Iniesta once again the ubiquitous conductor-in-chief. It was newcomer Nolito, however, who was most influential in giving Spain a 2-0 half-time lead, serving up the cross for Álvaro Morata's opener before clipping in a neat half-volleyed finish himself. Morata netted again just after the break as Spain cruised through to the last 16.

Earlier in the day Croatia looked on course to secure further progress when they took a deserved 2-0 lead against Czech Republic thanks to an excellent individual strike from Perišić and a clever chip from Ivan Rakitić. Their lead was halved, however, by a powerful header from substitute Milan Škoda, and after a brief stoppage caused by some Croatian fans throwing flares and firecrackers on to the pitch, suddenly the Czechs gained momentum. A handball by Domagoj Vida gave Pavel Vrba's side a late penalty, and Tomáš Necid leathered his shot past Danijel Subašić to leave Croatia stunned.

Further late drama was to follow when Croatia met Spain in Bordeaux. Ante Čačić's side were missing the influential Modrić and they must have feared the worst when Morata turned in Cesc Fàbregas's cross after just six minutes, but Croatia showed they were made of sterner stuff than Spain's previous opponents. Rakitić hit the post before Nikola Kalinić levelled on the stroke of

half-time by deftly flicking in a Perišić cross. Spain looked set to restore their lead when they were awarded a 72nd-minute penalty, but the imposing Subašić saved from Sergio Ramos. Then, with three minutes remaining, Perišić snatched top spot from the holders, beating David de Gea at his near post after a pacy gallop down the left.

Turkey finally turned up in their final group game, claiming a resounding 2-0 win over Czech Republic to take third place. Showing an attacking verve hitherto unseen, they took an early lead when nifty teenager Emre Mor teed up Burak Yılmaz. Ozan Tufan later finished off a well-worked free-kick to the delight of Turkey's travelling army of supporters, although the victory would ultimately prove hollow when, 24 hours later, the Republic of Ireland denied them their best third-place spot.

Group E

The Stade de France was a sea of green and yellow as the Republic of Ireland took on Sweden. Martin O'Neill's men were on top in the first half, with John O'Shea missing an easy chance and Jeff Hendrick rattling the crossbar from distance. Ireland got the goal their efforts warranted, however, through a lovely strike on the half-volley from Wes Hoolahan at the beginning of the second half. They were denied the win, though, as Ciaran Clark panicked into diverting Zlatan Ibrahimović's cross into his own

Joy and a sense of disbelief are etched on Luka Modrić's face after his wonder goal for Croatia against Turkey

net, earning Sweden a point despite the fact they had not conjured a single shot on target.

Star-studded Belgium were predicted by many to prevail against an Italy side allegedly lacking bite in attack. The Azzurri, however, were superbly set up by coach Antonio Conte to counter the Belgian threat, and they went ahead on 32 minutes when Emanuele Giaccherini skilfully controlled an exquisite long pass from Leonardo Bonucci before tucking the ball home. Italy then protected their lead in characteristically assured fashion, executing their game plan to perfection, before clinching the points with a fluent breakaway goal in injury time as Graziano Pellè explosively volleyed home Antonio Candreva's cross.

Belgium took out their frustrations on Ireland in Bordeaux five days later, capping their 90-minute domination with three goals in a ruthless second-half display after somehow failing to score before the break. Kevin De Bruyne was the architect of the first goal, freeing himself from two markers before teeing up Romelu Lukaku, so ineffective against Italy, to slam the ball with accuracy inside the near post. Thomas Meunier then planted the ball on to Axel Witsel's head for a second goal before a livewire Eden Hazard made the third, racing down the right touchline past Clark's lunging challenge and squaring for Lukaku to round off a dominant win.

By contrast, Italy lacked sparkle a day earlier against Sweden, but they still managed to win, Éder galloping his way past three defenders before rifling in an unstoppable shot two minutes from time. It was a goal out of keeping with what had gone before, with a cautious Sweden once again failing to register a shot on target, but it was enough to take Italy through as group winners with a game to spare.

With all of Italy's group stage objectives safely accomplished, Conte fielded virtually a second-string XI against Ireland in Lille, making eight changes from the Sweden game. An additional advantage for Martin O'Neill's men was that, with Group E finishing last, they knew exactly what they needed to progress. It was a case of win or bust, and they duly went about their business with desire and ambition against opponents whose key aim, it seemed, was to protect their unbeaten

Forty-year-old goalkeeper Gábor Király helped Hungary finish on top of Group F

competitive record under Conte. When Hoolahan spurned a glorious late opening, Ireland's last chance appeared to have gone, but in their next attack the midfielder redeemed himself by crossing for Robbie Brady to head past Salvatore Sirigu, sending Ireland into the next round and their noisy fans into raptures.

Belgium needed a point to progress against Sweden, for whom, like Ireland, only victory was good enough. Ibrahimović had announced beforehand that he would retire from international football once Sweden were eliminated, and the game in Nice would duly turn out to be his swansong. He and his colleagues were again powerless in attack, and Belgium, though well stifled by the smothering Swedish defence, eventually got the winning goal their efforts merited when Radja Nainggolan found the net with a deflected drive six minutes from time, sending his team through as group runners-up.

Group F

Hungary had waited 30 years to make it to a major tournament, and they were nearly behind after only 30 seconds of their return as Austria's David Alaba smashed a shot against the post. However, having survived that early scare, Bernd Storck's side found their rhythm. They needed 40-year-old

goalkeeper Gabor Kiraly, the oldest-ever EURO participant, to keep the scoresheet blank at half-time, but 17 minutes after the interval they went in front, Ádám Szalai sliding in to finish off an intricate one-two with László Kleinheisler before jumping into the crowd to celebrate his first goal in 41 games for club or country with Hungary's boisterous supporters. Aleksandar Dragovic's red card four minutes later complicated matters further for Austria, and substitute Zoltán Stieber killed them off on the counterattack with a marvellous chip.

With just 330,000 inhabitants, Iceland comfortably set a new record for the smallest nation to compete at a EURO finals, with an estimated 8% of their population (27,000 fans) present in France. Their hard-working players honoured the supporters with a 1-1 draw against Portugal in Saint-Etienne, Birkir Bjarnason's emphatic 50th-minute far-post volley cancelling out Nani's first-half strike.

More frustration awaited Portugal against Austria at the Parc des Princes, and on the night he surpassed Luís Figo as his country's most-capped player, it proved to be a particularly tough experience for Cristiano Ronaldo. The Portugal skipper failed to find the net with all ten of his shots, which included a 79th-minute penalty that he struck against the post. The 0-0 draw was due reward for a resilient defensive performance from Austria, a first point keeping alive their hopes of further progress even though they remained bottom of the table following an earlier 1-1 draw between Iceland and Hungary. Iceland looked to be on their way to a first EURO victory after Gylfi Sigurdsson's perfectly executed 40th-minute penalty in Marseille, but Hungary's second-half onslaught bore fruit late on when Birkir Sævarsson put a dangerous cross from substitute Nemanja Nikolić into his own net.

Hungary were assured of qualification by the time they faced Portugal in Lyon, but they would still play their part in one of the most thrilling contests of the group stage. Fernando Santos's side, who had to get a point at least to progress, got off to a bad start when Zoltán Gera scored with a beautiful left-foot half-volley, but they were back on level terms before the interval when Nani converted Ronaldo's pass. Portugal's nerves were only temporarily eased, however, as Balázs Dzsudzsák restored Hungary's lead on 47 minutes with a deflected free-kick. With his side facing elimination, Ronaldo finally came to the party. First he equalised with a sumptuous back-heel – thus becoming the first player to score in four consecutive EURO finals – and then, after Dzsudzsák had rifled in another deflected goal, he again rose to the occasion, quite literally, heading in his team's third equaliser of the night.

There were no further goals in Lyon, but late drama in the other game affected the final placings as Iceland struck on the breakaway, through Arnór Ingvi Traustason, to beat Austria with the last kick of the game and go through as runners-up, sending Portugal, with their three successive draws, down to third place. Jón Dadi Bödvarsson had put Iceland in front with a neat finish on the turn following a throw-in, but they were let off when Dragovic, back from suspension, smacked a penalty against the post. Austria dominated the second half and duly equalised through substitute Alessandro Schöpf, but as they threw caution to the wind in search of a second goal that would put them into the next round, they allowed Iceland to break, score, seal their first major tournament win and send their supporters into dreamland.

Round of 16

Switzerland and Poland got the ball rolling in the EURO's first round of 16 tie on a roasting afternoon in Saint-Etienne. Poland could hardly believe their luck when the ball landed at the feet of Milik with the goal gaping in the opening minute, but the Ajax forward wastefully blazed over. It was Błaszczykowski who eventually put Poland ahead, latching on to a fine pass from Kamil Grosicki, dummied by Milik, before tucking the ball through Sommer's legs.

Błaszczykowski was denied a second goal after the break by a splendid save from Sommer, whose opposite number Łukasz Fabiański later preserved Poland's lead by tipping over Ricardo Rodriguez's free-kick before Haris Seferović struck the bar. It required a magnificently acrobatic effort from Xherdan Shaqiri to draw Switzerland level, the striker conjuring a brilliant bicycle kick on the edge of the area to send the ball in off the post and puncture Poland's defence for the first time in the tournament. Switzerland looked more likely to grab a winner in extra-time, but again Fabiański came to Poland's rescue to deny substitute Eren Derdiyok.

Respective captains Lewandowski and Lichtsteiner both nervelessly showed the way with successful opening penalties in the shoot-out but Granit Xhaka completely missed the target with Switzerland's second. Both sides

continued to convert their remaining kicks, leaving Grzegorz Krychowiak to smash the ball into the roof of the net with Poland's fifth and send them through to the quarter-finals.

Wales were favourites to defeat Northern Ireland after overwhelming Russia, but it was Michael O'Neill's side who were the more impressive outfit overall in a disappointing clash at the Parc des Princes. Northern Ireland had the better chances in the first half, Stuart Dallas and Jamie Ward each forcing Wayne Hennessey into saves. Wales did not test McGovern until after the interval when he repelled Bale's venomous free-kick. The Real Madrid forward was being effectively neutered but eventually he would have his moment, driving over a dangerous cross from the left that McAuley turned into his own net. It was the only goal of the game and it sent Northern Ireland home, while Wales celebrated their greatest achievement in a major tournament for 58 years.

Portugal and Croatia spent much of their tie in Lens sizing each other up, and sadly, given the vast potential for entertainment in both teams, it resulted in another lacklustre contest. Fernando Santos set his side up to minimise space for creative midfielders Rakitić and Modrić, but Croatia seemed hindered by caution too. There was not one shot on target from either side in the regular 90 minutes, and extra time was equally unadventurous, enlivened only by the

Gareth Bale celebrates in the distance as the Welshman's cross is turned into his own net by Northern Ireland's Gareth McAuley (front right)

belated introduction of effervescent Croatia sub Marko Pjaca. A dramatic finale was in store, however. Vida went agonisingly close with a header and, a minute later, Perišić, his hair dyed in red and white checks for the occasion, glanced against the near post. The breakthrough finally arrived 30 seconds later - at the other end. Nifty substitute Renato Sanches charged through the middle and gave the ball to Nani, who picked out Cristiano Ronaldo at the far post. Subašić got a glove to the Portugal captain's shot, but could only send it spinning across the goalmouth for Ricardo Quaresma to nod home and put his country into the quarter-finals for the sixth EURO in a row.

Ireland had left it late to qualify for the last 16, but they took a shock early lead against France in Lyon thanks to the same man who had got them out of the group. After a clumsy foul by Pogba on Shane Long, Brady slammed the resulting penalty in off the post with exactly two minutes gone. Martin O'Neill's side defended resolutely in the first half, but the 15-minute break served France well, and they came out with renewed purpose, Laurent Koscielny and Blaise Matuidi each going close. Griezmann eventually found a way through, powering Bacary Sagna's looping cross into the far corner with an excellent header beyond the outstretched Darren Randolph. It took just three minutes after that equaliser for France to take control, Giroud winning a header and opening up space for Griezmann to drive into the area and drill the ball under Randolph. The Atlético Madrid striker might have grabbed a third had he not been upended on his way to goal by Shane Duffy, who was duly sent off. France pressed for a third against by now bedraggled opponents, but the two goals sufficed to see them safely though to the last eight

Germany set out to finish Slovakia off as early as possible in Lille, laying siege to their opponents' goalmouth from the first whistle. Boateng's crisp, deflected volley – his first international goal – put them ahead after eight minutes and soon afterwards they were awarded a penalty. Özil, however, failed to take advantage, Matúš Kozáčik athletically swatting his misdirected effort away. Slovakia could not muster a shot on goal until the 40th minute, when Juraj Kucka forced a brilliant tip-over from Neuer, but moments later Germany

Yannick Carrasco (right) completes the scoring against Hungary with Belgium's fourth goal in Toulouse

doubled their lead, the lively Julian Draxler expertly teeing up Gomez. Draxler eventually got the goal his all-action display merited, swivelling to hook the ball into the top corner on 63 minutes and crown an utterly dominant display from a Germany side that had still to concede a goal.

Hungary's hopes of causing an upset against Belgium in Toulouse were hit when playmaker Kleinheisler pulled up injured in the warm-up. Marc Wilmots' side went for the jugular early, Toby Alderweireld meeting De Bruyne's free-kick to head them into a 10th-minute lead. They did not stop there, peppering the Hungary goal for the remainder of the half and forcing Király to make seven saves, the best of them a brilliant tip on to the bar from a De Bruyne piledriver. Hungary, having somehow kept the score down to 1-0, began to create chances of their own in the second half of what had become a riveting, end-to-end contest. Hazard was in top form for Belgium, though, and the Chelsea winger would cap arguably the individual performance of the tournament in the final dozen minutes. First he outpaced the Hungary defence to lay the ball on a plate for substitute Michy Batshuayi to score with his first touch. Then he finished Hungary off himself with a dazzling third goal, racing across from the left before curling

an unstoppable right-foot shot into the far corner. Seconds into injury time, Yannick Carraso made the final score 4-0, which was tough on Hungary, who had played their part in a highly entertaining encounter.

The Stade de France was a suitable setting for a re-run of the UEFA EURO 2012 final, where Spain had outclassed Italy and won 4-0. Italy, though, had learned from the experience and Conte, prowling his technical area in a rain jacket and cap to counter the persistent downpour, served up a repeat of the tactical masterclass that had defeated Belgium. Spain could barely breathe in the first half and would have been several goals behind but for the heroics of David de Gea, although the goalkeeper was unable to hold on to a 33rd-minute free-kick from Éder, enabling Giorgio Chiellini to pounce and scramble the loose ball home.

De Gea kept the score at 1-0 with further saves, but as the second half progressed it was Gianluigi Buffon who became the busier 'keeper, repelling a stinging volley from Andrés Iniesta and two efforts from Gerard Piqué. The second of those, in added time, was swiftly followed by a match-clinching second goal for Italy, who, as against Belgium, finished off their opponents on the counterattack with an emphatic close-range finish from Pellè. Italy were through to the quarter-final, and Spain's eight-year European reign was at an end.

In the last of the round of 16 encounters Rooney gave England an early lead against Iceland from the penalty spot, but it proved to be a false dawn for Hodgson's team. Just 34 seconds after the restart, throw-in expert Aron Gunnarsson hurled the ball goalwards, Kári Árnason flicked it on and his fellow centre-back Ragnar Sigurdsson lunged forward to volley past Hart. England were stunned, not least Hart, who 12 minutes later was caught out by a hopeful edge-of-the-area strike from Kolbeinn Sigthórsson that he allowed to squirm under his body and give Iceland an unfathomable lead. Hodgson and his players visibly tensed up from that moment onwards as the unthinkable scenario of being knocked out by the North Atlantic minnows began to gnaw at their senses. Bereft of ideas, they struggled to give the well-protected Icelandic goalkeeper Hannes Halldórsson any work to do during a dreadful second-half performance. No sooner had the final whistle gone than Hodgson announced his resignation. Iceland, meanwhile, advanced into the last eight with the most glorious victory in their history.

Quarter-finals

Portugal and Poland had both toiled for 120 minutes to reach the quarter-finals, and they would do so again when they met in Marseille, Portugal eventually prevailing on penalties after another attritional encounter. Lewandowski's inability to find the net had been one of the talking points of the tournament but the striker did not take long to end his drought, side-footing home Grosicki's low cross after precisely 100 seconds to score the second fastest goal at a EURO final tournament.

Cristiano Ronaldo failed to trouble Fabiański with Portugal's first effort but they equalised before half-time through a fine goal from rising star Renato Sanches, who played a one-two with Nani and collected the winger's delightful back-heel to fire a slightly deflected left-foot shot into the near corner. There were no further goals in the second period, with Ronaldo missing the best chance as he failed to connect with an inviting ball over the top

Manuel Neuer saves from Leonardo Bonucci to help Germany defeat Italy on penalties in the quarter-final

from substitute João Moutinho and thus leaving Portugal level-pegging at 90 minutes for the fifth successive game. Extra time was goalless too, giving Poland their second consecutive shoot-out. Sanches showed his maturity by confidently converting Portugal's second penalty after Ronaldo had scored his, and the balance tipped the way of Fernando Santos's side when Błaszczykowski's kick – Poland's fourth – was expertly saved by Rui Patrício. That allowed Quaresma, the last-16 match-winner against Croatia, to have the final say again, and he smashed his shot into the roof of the net to propel Portugal into the semi-finals.

Belgium looked destined to avenge their defeat to Wales in the qualifying competition as they made a fast start in Lille, spurning a triple opportunity in the opening minutes, in which only some stout Welsh defending prevented a goal, before taking the lead soon afterwards through Nainggolan's brilliant first-time thunderbolt from 30 metres. On the ropes at that stage, Wales came back strongly against a Belgium side handicapped by the loss of several key defenders, and they levelled on 31 minutes when Ashley Williams powered home a header from Ramsey's corner, prompting manic celebrations on the Wales bench. Hazard came close to restoring Belgium's lead early in the second half but then Wales pounced again. Bale's lofted pass from deep

found Ramsey, who again delivered a key pass, this time to Robson-Kanu. The Wales striker had his back to goal but freed himself of two defenders with a brilliant turn before driving left-footed past Thibaut Courtois. Marouane Fellaini could have equalised with one of two headed opportunities, but at the other end substitute Sam Vokes was more clinical with his finish, skillfully nodding Chris Gunter's cross beyond the outstretched Courtois to make it 3-1 and seal Wales' place in the last four of a major tournament for the first time.

Germany and Italy renewed one of the great rivalries in Bordeaux, where the Nationalmannschaft were looking for a first major tournament win over the Azzurri. Joachim Löw shuffled his pack by swapping Draxler for Benedikt Höwedes in a remodelled 3-5-2 formation, and he was forced to bring on Schweinsteiger for the injured Sami Khedira after just 16 minutes. A slow, ultra-cautious encounter ensued, and although Germany were the more adventurous team, opportunities were sparse. The game finally came alive in the 65th minute, when Özil appeared at the near post to knock Jonas Hector's cutback past Buffon after clever play from Gomez. Only a miraculous save from Buffon three minutes later prevented Gomez from putting the game to bed, and its significance was highlighted when a stray arm from Boateng at the other end offered Italy a lifeline from the spot.

Up stepped the unlikely figure of defender Leonardo Bonucci, who had never taken a regulation-play penalty in his career, to coolly convert, forcing Neuer to pick the ball out of his net for the first time at the tournament.

That took the game to extra time, during which very little goalmouth action took place, and then to penalties, where the pressure of the occasion clearly got to both sides as no fewer than seven players missed from the spot – Simone Zaza, Pellè, Bonucci and Matteo Darmian for Italy and Thomas Müller, Özil and Schweinsteiger for Germany. The outcome was finally settled as Hector squeezed his effort under Buffon, giving Germany that long-awaited first tournament win over Italy at the ninth attempt.

The next stop on Iceland's incredible journey was their toughest test yet, and it proved to be their last as France finally hit their stride, producing a devastating attacking display to illuminate a wet and gloomy Stade de France. Deschamps' men had a two-goal lead before 20 minutes had elapsed through Giroud's precise low strike and Pogba's header from a Griezmann corner. That lead was doubled before the break with two quick-fire goals – a low left-footer from Payet and then a delicious chip by Griezmann, facilitated by Giroud's dummy, which brought up 100 goals for the tournament. Sigthórsson slid in to convert Gylfi Sigurdsson's cross early in the second half, but a header from Giroud promptly made it 5-1. Iceland were not yet ready to lay down their arms, though, and Birkir Bjarnason headed in their eighth goal of an unforgettable tournament debut. France, meanwhile, toasted a comfortable, confidence-building passage through to the semi-finals.

Semi-finals

The newly-constructed Stade de Lyon was the setting for the first semi-final, between Portugal and Wales. Inevitably, the game was billed as a battle between Bale and Ronaldo, Real Madrid strike partners and their respective teams' talismen. Wales were without star midfielder Ramsey, suspended along with defender Davies, while Portugal were also without key personnel – centre-back Pepe through injury and midfield anchorman William Carvalho through suspension. Defences were largely on top in an opening period of few chances, although Bale tested Rui Patrício with a couple of shots from distance. Fernando Santos's tactic of denying Wales room for manoeuvre was bearing fruit, but Portugal showed more ambition after the break and they were to kill the game as a contest with two goals in three minutes. Ronaldo, inevitably, was the first to strike, freeing himself at a short corner and soaring above James Chester to power Raphael Guerreiro's cross home with a towering header, equalling Michel Platini's record of nine EURO finals goals in the process.

Wales barely had time to recover when another lapse of concentration led to a second goal in Portugal's next attack. Ronaldo misdirected a low shot across the area and Nani reacted instinctively to divert the ball past a wrong-footed Hennessey. Coleman's men tried their best to respond, but Portugal were too canny and collectively organised to allow them back into the game. The Welsh fans bellowed out their adopted chant of 'Don't take me home' but it was to no avail. Their magical journey had come to an end, while Portugal, with their first victory in 90 minutes, marched confidently into the final.

France and Germany met the next day in Marseille to determine Portugal's opponents in the final. The Stade Velodrome had proved a happy hunting ground for France in the past, Les Bleus beating Portugal there in the semi-final of EURO '84, but they had not defeated Germany in a tournament since 1958. The world champions were in a fifth consecutive major tournament semi-final, but they had to make do without Gomez and Khedira, both injured, and the suspended Mats Hummels. France made a bold start, the rampant Griezmann playing a one-two with Matuidi before bearing down on Neuer, but the goalkeeper got down impressively to fingertip the shot away. Germany reacted well to that early scare and began to dominate possession and force France backwards in what was becoming a fascinating contest. Löw's team looked likelier to take the lead, with Müller – still seeking his first EURO finals goal, on his tenth appearance – going close and Emre Can drawing a low save from Hugo Lloris, but they gifted France a golden opportunity to break the deadlock on the stroke of half-time when Schweinsteiger was adjudged by referee Nicola Rizzoli to have deliberately blocked a cross with his hand. Griezmann cast aside the unhappy memories of missing from the spot for Atlético Madrid in the UEFA Champions

Cristiano Ronaldo celebrates putting Portugal 1-0 up against Wales in Lyon

League final a few weeks earlier to blast France into the lead.

Germany looked determined after the break and continued to control the play, but with Müller out of form and no recognised striker on the field, they struggled to test Lloris. Then, at the other end, with defensive leader Boateng injured and substituted, another lapse in concentration cost them dear. Joshua Kimmich was caught in possession as Germany tried to play the ball out, and Pogba then held the ball up on the left while he waited for support. Neuer reached the midfielder's cross but could only claw it into the path of Griezmann, who gratefully prodded it back into the net through the 'keeper's legs for his sixth goal of the tournament. Kimmich tried to make up for his earlier blunder with a couple of impressive efforts, but he was denied first by the woodwork, then by a brilliant Lloris save. That was the closest Löw's side would get as their hopes of adding the continental title to their World Cup triumph were extinguished in arguably the best game of the championship. The buoyant hosts, on the other hand, were just one step away from a third tournament triumph on home soil.

Final

An electric atmosphere enveloped the Stade de France – as did an unwelcome swarm of moths – for the final of UEFA EURO 2016. France were on a mission to emulate their home victories of 1984 and 1998, while Portugal were intent on spoiling the hosts' party and lifting a first major trophy after so many near-misses, foremost among them the UEFA EURO 2004 final defeat on home soil against Greece.

Portugal engineered the first attempt of the game, a wayward shot from Nani, but the first real flashpoint arrived in the eighth minute when Cristiano Ronaldo was seen writhing with pain after a robust challenge from Payet. The only survivor in the starting XI from that 2004 final in Lisbon, Ronaldo did everything he could to stay on the pitch until he was finally forced to admit defeat to the pain in his left knee and stretchered off midway through the half – to the sound of sympathetic applause from Portuguese and French supporters alike. With his departure, all the pre-game plans and narratives had gone out of the window. Portugal were

Celebration time for Portugal after their UEFA EURO 2016 final victory over France

now without their captain, leader and all-time goalscorer, and although neutrals far and wide also bemoaned his premature departure, France had suddenly been presented with a massive boost to their title pretensions.

The new darling of the home fans, Griezmann, had a big opportunity to score early on when he headed Payet's floated cross towards the far corner, but Rui Patrício made a brilliant save with his outstretched palm. The lively Moussa Sissoko also drew a fine intervention from the impressive Portugal 'keeper before the break, then another after it, before Griezmann missed a gilt-edged chance on 66 minutes, uncharacteristically heading substitute Kingsley Coman's header over from close range.

Portugal were not asking too many questions at the other end, although Lloris was forced to tip away a cross-shot from Nani before Quaresma acrobatically volleyed the rebound back at the goalkeeper. Sissoko forced another fine save from Rui Patrício, but the closest France came to breaking the deadlock came in added time when substitute André-Pierre Gignac twisted his way past the hitherto outstanding Pepe but scuffed his shot against the foot of the post. At the blast of referee Mark Clattenburg's final whistle, the score was still 0-0 – the first UEFA

European Championship final to end goalless at 90 minutes.

Reprieved and refreshed, and with a bandaged-up Ronaldo there to offer support and inspiration, Portugal came out stronger in extra time and nearly took the lead as substitute Éder headed a Quaresma corner straight at Lloris. Fernando Santos had raised eyebrows when he brought the Lille forward on at the expense of Renato Sanches, but the move would prove a masterstroke. Barely a minute after Raphael Guerreiro had rattled the bar with a thunderous free-kick, Éder received the ball in the opposition half. There appeared little danger to the France defence, but the lanky striker had only one thing on his mind as he shuffled past Koscielny 25 metres from goal and drilled a right-foot shot low, hard and just beyond the outstretched fingertips of Lloris's right hand to put Portugal ahead.

Just 11 minutes separated Portugal from their first major trophy. It was a period of high anxiety, but with cheerleader-in-chief Ronaldo cajoling his team-mates from the touchline, the men in red and green defended for their lives, preventing France from making any further inroads. Les Bleus' dream was over, and as the final whistle sounded, an ecstatic Portugal rejoiced. The final act belonged, fittingly, to the great Ronaldo as he hoisted the Henri Delaunay Cup into the Parisian sky.

Group stage

Group A

10/06/16, Stade de France, Saint-Denis (att: 75,113)
France 2-1 Romania
Goals: 1-0 Giroud 57, 1-1 Stancu 65(p), 2-1 Payet 89
Referee: Kassai (HUN)
France: Lloris; Sagna, Rami, Koscielny, Evra; Pogba (Martial 77), Kanté, Matuidi; Griezmann (Coman 66), Giroud, Payet (Sissoko 90+2). Coach: Didier Deschamps (FRA)
Romania: Tătăruşanu; Săpunaru, Chiricheş, Grigore, Raţ; Hoban, Pintilii; Popa (Torje 82), Stanciu (Chipciu 72), Stancu; Andone (Alibec 61). Coach: Anghel Iordanescu (ROU)
Yellow cards: Chiricheş 32 (Romania), Raţ 45 (Romania), Giroud 69 (France), Popa 78 (Romania)

11/06/16, Stade Bollaert-Delelis, Lens (att: 33,805)
Albania 0-1 Switzerland
Goal: 0-1 Schär 5
Referee: Velasco Carballo (ESP)
Albania: Berisha; Hysaj, Cana, Mavraj, Agolli; Roshi (Çikalleshi 73), Abrashi, Kukeli, Xhaka (Kaçe 61), Lenjani; Sadiku (Gashi 82). Coach: Gianni De Biasi (ITA)
Switzerland: Sommer; Lichtsteiner, Schär, Djourou, Rodríguez; Behrami, Xhaka; Shaqiri (Fernandes 88), Džemaili (Frei 75), Mehmedi (Embolo 61); Seferovic. Coach: Vladimir Petković (SUI)
Red card: Cana 36 (Albania)
Yellow cards: Schär 14 (Switzerland), Cana 23 (Albania), Cana 36 (Albania), Kaçe 63 (Albania), Behrami 66 (Switzerland), Kukeli 89 (Albania), Mavraj 90+2 (Albania)

15/06/16, Parc des Princes, Paris (att: 43,576)
Romania 1-1 Switzerland
Goals: 1-0 Stancu 18(p), 1-1 Mehmedi 57
Referee: Karasev (RUS)
Romania: Tătăruşanu; Săpunaru, Chiricheş, Grigore, Raţ (Filip 62); Prepeliţă, Pintilii (Hoban 46); Torje, Stancu (Andone 84), Chipciu; Keşerü. Coach: Anghel Iordănescu (ROU)
Switzerland: Sommer; Lichtsteiner, Schär, Djourou, Rodríguez; Behrami, Xhaka; Shaqiri (Tarashaj 90+1), Džemaili (Lang 83), Mehmedi; Seferovic (Embolo 63). Coach: Vladimir Petković (SUI)
Yellow cards: Prepeliţă 22 (Romania), Chipciu 24 (Romania), Keşerü 37 (Romania), Xhaka 50 (Switzerland), Grigore 76 (Romania), Embolo 90+4 (Switzerland)

15/06/16, Stade Vélodrome, Marseille (att: 63,670)
France 2-0 Albania
Goals: 1-0 Griezmann 90, 2-0 Payet 90+6
Referee: Collum (SCO)
France: Lloris; Sagna, Rami, Koscielny, Evra; Kanté, Payet, Matuidi; Coman (Griezmann 68), Giroud (Gignac 77), Martial (Pogba 46). Coach: Didier Deschamps (FRA)
Albania: Berisha; Hysaj, Ajeti (Veseli 85), Mavraj, Agolli; Lila (Roshi 71), Abrashi, Kukeli (Xhaka 74), Memushaj, Lenjani; Sadiku. Coach: Gianni De Biasi (ITA)
Yellow cards: Kukeli 55 (Albania), Abrashi 81 (Albania), Kanté 88 (France)

19/06/16, Stade Pierre Mauroy, Lille (att: 45,616)
Switzerland 0-0 France
Referee: Skomina (SVN)
Switzerland: Sommer; Lichtsteiner, Schär, Djourou, Rodríguez; Behrami, Xhaka; Shaqiri (Fernandes 79), Džemaili, Mehmedi (Lang 86); Embolo (Seferovic 74). Coach: Vladimir Petković (SUI)
France: Lloris; Sagna, Rami, Koscielny, Evra; Sissoko, Cabaye, Pogba; Griezmann (Matuidi 77), Gignac, Coman (Payet 63). Coach: Didier Deschamps (FRA)
Yellow cards: Rami 25 (France), Koscielny 83 (France)

19/06/16, Stade de Lyon, Lyon (att: 49,752)
Romania 0-1 Albania
Goal: 0-1 Sadiku 43
Referee: Královec (CZE)
Romania: Tătăruşanu; Săpunaru, Chiricheş, Grigore, Măţel; Prepeliţă (Sânmărtean 46), Hoban, Popa (Andone 68), Stanciu, Stancu; Alibec (Torje 57). Coach: Anghel Iordănescu (ROU)
Albania: Berisha; Hysaj, Ajeti, Mavraj, Agolli; Lila, Memushaj, Basha (Cana 83), Abrashi, Lenjani (Roshi 77); Sadiku (Balaj 59). Coach: Gianni De Biasi (ITA)
Yellow cards: Basha 6 (Albania), Măţel 54 (Romania), Săpunaru 85 (Romania), Memushaj 85 (Albania), Torje 90+3 (Romania), Hysaj 90+4 (Albania)

Group B

11/06/16, Stade de Bordeaux, Bordeaux (att: 37,831)
Wales 2-1 Slovakia
Goals: 1-0 Bale 10, 1-1 Duda 61, 2-1 Robson-Kanu 81
Referee: Moen (NOR)
Wales: Ward; Gunter, Chester, A Williams, Davies, Taylor; Edwards (Ledley 69), Allen; Ramsey (Richards 88), J Williams (Robson-Kanu 71); Bale. Coach: Chris Coleman (WAL)

Armando Sadiku heads in the goal that gives Albania a 1-0 victory against Romania

Slovakia: Kozáčik; Pekarík, Škrtel, Ďurica, Švento; Hrošovský (Duda 60); Mak, Kucka, Hamšík, Weiss (Stoch 83); Ďuriš (Nemec 59). Coach: Ján Kozák (SVK)
Yellow cards: Hrošovský 31 (Slovakia), Mak 78 (Slovakia), Weiss 80 (Slovakia), Kucka 83 (Slovakia), Škrtel 90+2 (Slovakia)

11/06/16, Stade Vélodrome, Marseille (att: 62,343)
England 1-1 Russia
Goals: 1-0 Dier 73, 1-1 V Berezutski 90+2
Referee: Rizzoli (ITA)
England: Hart; Walker, Cahill, Smalling, Rose; Dier, Alli, Rooney (Wilshere 78); Lallana, Kane, Sterling (Milner 87). Coach: Roy Hodgson (ENG)
Russia: Akinfeev; Smolnikov, V Berezutski, Ignashevich, Schennikov; Neustädter (Glushakov 80), Golovin (Shirokov 77); Kokorin, Shatov, Smolov (Mamaev 85); Dzyuba. Coach: Leonid Slutski (RUS)
Yellow cards: Cahill 62 (England), Schennikov 72 (Russia)

Hal Robson-Kanu scuffs in Wales' winning goal against Slovakia

15/06/16, Stade Pierre Mauroy, Lille (att: 38,989)
Russia 1-2 Slovakia
Goals: 0-1 Weiss 32, 0-2 Hamšík 45,
1-2 Glushakov 80
Referee: Skomina (SVN)
Russia: Akinfeev; Smolnikov, V Berezutski,
Ignashevich, Schennikov; Neustädter (Glushakov
46), Golovin (Mamaev 46); Kokorin (Shirokov 75),
Shatov, Smolov; Dzyuba. Coach: Leonid Slutski
(RUS)
Slovakia: Kozáčik; Pekarík, Škrtel, Ďurica,
Hubočan; Pečovský; Mak (Ďuriš 80), Kucka,
Hamšík, Weiss (Švento 72); Duda (Nemec 67).
Coach: Ján Kozák (SVK)
Yellow card: Ďurica 46 (Slovakia)

16/06/16, Stade Bollaert-Delelis, Lens (att: 34,033)
England 2-1 Wales
Goals: 0-1 Bale 42, 1-1 Vardy 56,
2-1 Sturridge 90+2
Referee: Brych (GER)
England: Hart; Walker, Cahill, Smalling, Rose; Dier;
Alli, Rooney; Lallana (Rashford 73), Kane (Vardy 46),
Sterling (Sturridge 46). Coach: Roy Hodgson (ENG)
Wales: Hennessey; Gunter, Chester, A Williams,
Davies, Taylor; Allen, Ledley (Edwards 67);
Ramsey, Bale; Robson-Kanu (J Williams 72).
Coach: Chris Coleman (WAL)
Yellow card: Davies 61 (Wales)

*20/06/16, Stade Geoffroy Guichard, Saint-Etienne
(att: 39,051)*
Slovakia 0-0 England
Referee: Velasco Carballo (ESP)
Slovakia: Kozáčik; Pekarík, Škrtel, Ďurica,
Hubočan; Pečovský (Gyömber 66); Mak, Kucka,
Hamšík, Weiss (Škriniar 78); Duda (Švento 57).
Coach: Ján Kozák (SVK)
England: Hart; Clyne, Cahill, Smalling, Bertrand;
Dier; Henderson, Wilshere (Rooney 55); Lallana
(Alli 60), Vardy, Sturridge (Kane 75). Coach: Roy
Hodgson (ENG)
Yellow cards: Pečovský 23 (Slovakia), Bertrand
51 (England)

*20/06/16, Stadium de Toulouse, Toulouse
(att: 28,840)*
Russia 0-3 Wales
Goals: 0-1 Ramsey 11, 0-2 Taylor 20, 0-3 Bale 67
Referee: Eriksson (SWE)
Russia: Akinfeev; Smolnikov, V Berezutski (A
Berezutski 46), Ignashevich, Kombarov; Glushakov,
Mamaev; Kokorin, Shirokov (Golovin 52), Smolov
(Samedov 70); Dzyuba. Coach: Leonid Slutski (RUS)
Wales: Hennessey; Gunter, Chester, A Williams,
Davies, Taylor; Allen (Edwards 74), Ledley (King
76); Ramsey, Bale (Church 83); Vokes. Coach:
Chris Coleman (WAL)
Yellow cards: Vokes 16 (Wales), Mamaev 64 (Russia)

Group C

12/06/16, Stade de Nice, Nice (att: 33,742)
Poland 1-0 Northern Ireland
Goal: 1-0 Milik 51
Referee: Haţegan (ROU)
Poland: Szczęsny; Piszczek, Glik, Pazdan,
Jędrzejczyk; Błaszczykowski (Grosicki 80),
Krychowiak, Mączyński (Jodłowiec 78), Kapustka
(Peszko 88); Milik; Lewandowski. Coach: Adam
Nawałka (POL)
Northern Ireland: McGovern; Cathcart, McAuley,
J Evans, Baird (Ward 76); C McLaughlin, McNair
(Dallas 46); Davis, Norwood, Ferguson (Washington
66); K Lafferty. Coach: Michael O'Neill (NIR)
Yellow cards: Kapustka 65 (Poland), Cathcart 69
(Northern Ireland), Piszczek 89 (Poland)

Substitute Niall McGinn celebrates his added-time strike that wraps up Northern Ireland's 2-0 win against Ukraine

12/06/16, Stade Pierre Mauroy, Lille (att: 43,035)
Germany 2-0 Ukraine
Goals: 1-0 Mustafi 19, 2-0 Schweinsteiger 90+2
Referee: Atkinson (ENG)
Germany: Neuer; Höwedes, Boateng, Mustafi,
Hector; Khedira, Kroos; Müller, Özil, Draxler
(Schürrle 78); Götze (Schweinsteiger 90). Coach:
Joachim Löw (GER)
Ukraine: Pyatov; Fedetskiy, Khacheridi, Rakitskiy,
Shevchuk; Sydorchuk, Stepanenko; Yarmolenko,
Kovalenko (Zinchenko 73), Konoplyanka; Zozulya
(Seleznyov 66). Coach: Mykhailo Fomenko (UKR)
Yellow card: Konoplyanka 68 (Ukraine)

16/06/16, Stade de Lyon, Lyon (att: 51,043)
Ukraine 0-2 Northern Ireland
Goals: 0-1 McAuley 49, 0-2 McGinn 90+6
Referee: Královec (CZE)
Ukraine: Pyatov; Fedetskiy, Khacheridi,
Rakitskiy, Shevchuk; Sydorchuk (Garmash 76),
Stepanenko; Yarmolenko, Kovalenko (Zinchenko
83), Konoplyanka; Seleznyov (Zozulya 71). Coach:
Mykhailo Fomenko (UKR)
Northern Ireland: McGovern; Hughes, McAuley,
Cathcart, J Evans; Norwood; Ward (McGinn 69),
C Evans (McNair 90+3), Davis, Dallas; Washington
(Magennis 84). Coach: Michael O'Neill (NIR)
Yellow cards: Seleznyov 40 (Ukraine), Ward 63
(Northern Ireland), Sydorchuk 67 (Ukraine), Dallas 87
(Northern Ireland), J Evans 90+5 (Northern Ireland)

*16/06/16, Stade de France, Saint-Denis
(att: 73,648)*
Germany 0-0 Poland
Referee: Kuipers (NED)
Germany: Neuer; Höwedes, Boateng, Hummels,
Hector; Khedira, Kroos; Müller, Özil, Draxler
(Gomez 71); Götze (Schürrle 66). Coach: Joachim
Löw (GER)

Poland: Fabiański; Piszczek, Glik, Pazdan,
Jędrzejczyk; Błaszczykowski (Kapustka 80),
Krychowiak, Mączyński (Jodłowiec 76), Grosicki
(Peszko 87); Milik; Lewandowski. Coach: Adam
Nawałka (POL)
Yellow cards: Khedira 3 (Germany), Özil 34
(Germany), Mączyński 45 (Poland), Grosicki 55
(Poland), Boateng 67 (Germany), Peszko 90+3
(Poland)

21/06/16, Parc des Princes, Paris (att: 44,125)
Northern Ireland 0-1 Germany
Goal: 0-1 Gomez 30
Referee: Turpin (FRA)
Northern Ireland: McGovern; Hughes, McAuley,
Cathcart, J Evans; Norwood; Ward (Magennis 70),
C Evans (McGinn 84), Davis, Dallas; Washington (K
Lafferty 59). Coach: Michael O'Neill (NIR)
Germany: Neuer; Kimmich, Boateng (Höwedes
76), Hummels, Hector; Khedira (Schweinsteiger
69), Kroos; Müller, Özil, Götze (Schürrle 55);
Gomez. Coach: Joachim Löw (GER)

21/06/16, Stade Vélodrome, Marseille (att: 58,874)
Ukraine 0-1 Poland
Goal: 0-1 Błaszczykowski 54
Referee: Moen (NOR)
Ukraine: Pyatov; Fedetskiy, Khacheridi,
Kucher, Butko, Rotan, Stepanenko; Yarmolenko,
Zinchenko (Kovalenko 73), Konoplyanka;
Zozulya (Tymoshchuk 90+2). Coach: Mykhailo
Fomenko (UKR)
Poland: Fabiański; Cionek, Glik, Pazdan,
Jędrzejczyk; Zieliński (Błaszczykowski 46),
Krychowiak, Jodłowiec, Kapustka (Grosicki 71);
Milik (Starzyński 90+3); Lewandowski. Coach:
Adam Nawałka (POL)
Yellow cards: Rotan 25 (Ukraine), Kucher 38
(Ukraine), Kapustka 60 (Poland)

Group D

12/06/16, Parc des Princes, Paris (att: 43,842)
Turkey 0-1 Croatia
Goal: 0-1 Modrić 41
Referee: Eriksson (SWE)
Turkey: Volkan Babacan; Gökhan Gönül, Mehmet Topal, Hakan Balta, Caner Erkin; Selçuk İnan; Hakan Çalhanoğlu, Ozan Tufan, Oğuzhan Özyakup (Volkan Şen 46), Arda Turan (Burak Yılmaz 65); Cenk Tosun (Emre Mor 69). Coach: Fatih Terim (TUR)
Croatia: Subašić; Srna, Ćorluka, Vida, Strinić; Modrić, Badelj; Brozović, Rakitić (Schildenfeld 90), Perišić (Kramarić 87); Mandžukić (Pjaca 90+3). Coach: Ante Čačić (CRO)
Yellow cards: Cenk Tosun 31 (Turkey), Hakan Balta 48 (Turkey), Strinić 80 (Croatia), Volkan Şen 90+1 (Turkey)

13/06/16, Stadium de Toulouse, Toulouse (att: 29,400)
Spain 1-0 Czech Republic
Goal: 1-0 Piqué 87
Referee: Marciniak (POL)
Spain: De Gea; Juanfran, Piqué, Sergio Ramos, Jordi Alba; Fàbregas (Thiago Alcántara 70), Busquets, Iniesta; Silva, Morata (Aduriz 62), Nolito (Pedro 82). Coach: Vicente del Bosque (ESP)
Czech Republic: Čech; Kadeřábek, Sivok, Hubník, Limberský; Plašil, Darida; Gebre Selassie (Šural 86), Rosický (Pavelka 88), Krejčí; Necid (Lafata 75). Coach: Pavel Vrba (CZE)
Yellow card: Limberský 61 (Czech Republic)

17/06/16, Stade Geoffroy Guichard, Saint-Etienne (att: 38,376)
Czech Republic 2-2 Croatia
Goals: 0-1 Perišić 37, 0-2 Rakitić 59, 1-2 Škoda 76, 2-2 Necid 89(p)
Referee: Clattenburg (ENG)
Czech Republic: Čech; Kadeřábek, Sivok, Hubník, Limberský; Plašil (Necid 86), Darida; Skalák (Šural 67), Rosický, Krejčí; Lafata (Škoda 67). Coach: Pavel Vrba (CZE)
Croatia: Subašić; Srna, Ćorluka, Vida, Strinić (Vrsaljko 90+1); Modrić (Kovačić 62), Badelj; Brozović, Rakitić (Schildenfeld 90+2), Perišić; Mandžukić. Coach: Ante Čačić (CRO)
Yellow cards: Badelj 14 (Croatia), Sivok 72 (Czech Republic), Brozović 74 (Croatia), Vida 88 (Croatia)

Álvaro Morata taps in Spain's third goal against Turkey

Graziano Pellè (right) turns away to celebrate after completing Italy's 2-0 win over Belgium in Lyon

17/06/16, Stade de Nice, Nice (att: 33,409)
Spain 3-0 Turkey
Goals: 1-0 Morata 34, 2-0 Nolito 37, 3-0 Morata 48
Referee: Mažić (SRB)
Spain: De Gea; Juanfran, Piqué, Sergio Ramos, Jordi Alba (Azpilicueta 81); Fàbregas (Koke 71), Busquets, Iniesta; Silva (Bruno Soriano 64), Morata, Nolito. Coach: Vicente del Bosque (ESP)
Turkey: Volkan Babacan; Gökhan Gönül, Mehmet Topal, Hakan Balta, Caner Erkin; Selçuk İnan (Yunus Mallı 70); Hakan Çalhanoğlu (Nuri Şahin 46), Ozan Tufan, Oğuzhan Özyakup (Olcay Şahan 62), Arda Turan; Burak Yılmaz. Coach: Fatih Terim (TUR)
Yellow cards: Sergio Ramos 2 (Spain), Burak Yılmaz 9 (Turkey), Ozan Tufan 41 (Turkey)

21/06/16, Stade de Bordeaux, Bordeaux (att: 37,245)
Croatia 2-1 Spain
Goals: 0-1 Morata 7, 1-1 N Kalinić 45, 2-1 Perišić 87
Referee: Kuipers (NED)
Croatia: Subašić; Srna, Ćorluka, Jedvaj, Vrsaljko; Rog (Kovačić 82), Badelj; Pjaca (Čop 90+2), Rakitić, Perišić (Kramarić 90+4); N Kalinić. Coach: Ante Čačić (CRO)
Spain: De Gea; Juanfran, Piqué, Sergio Ramos, Jordi Alba; Fàbregas (Thiago Alcántara 84), Busquets, Iniesta; Silva, Morata (Aduriz 67), Nolito (Bruno Soriano 60). Coach: Vicente del Bosque (ESP)
Yellow cards: Rog 29 (Croatia), Srna 70 (Croatia), Vrsaljko 70 (Croatia), Perišić 88 (Croatia)

21/06/16, Stade Bollaert-Delelis, Lens (att: 32,836)
Czech Republic 0-2 Turkey
Goals: 0-1 Burak Yılmaz 10, 0-2 Ozan Tufan 65
Referee: Collum (SCO)
Czech Republic: Čech; Kadeřábek, Sivok, Hubník, Pudil; Pavelka (Škoda 57); Dočkal (Šural 71), Plašil (Kolář 90), Darida, Krejčí; Necid. Coach: Pavel Vrba (CZE)
Turkey: Volkan Babacan; Gökhan Gönül, Mehmet Topal, Hakan Balta, İsmail Köybaşı; Selçuk İnan; Emre Mor (Olcay Şahan 69), Ozan Tufan, Arda Turan, Volkan Şen (Oğuzhan Özyakup 61); Burak Yılmaz (Cenk Tosun 90). Coach: Fatih Terim (TUR)
Yellow cards: İsmail Köybaşı 35 (Turkey), Plašil 36 (Czech Republic), Pavelka 39 (Czech Republic), Hakan Balta 50 (Turkey), Šural 87 (Czech Republic)

Group E

13/06/16, Stade de France, Saint-Denis (att: 73,419)
Republic of Ireland 1-1 Sweden
Goals: 1-0 Hoolahan 48, 1-1 Clark 71(og)
Referee: Mažić (SRB)
Republic of Ireland: Randolph; Coleman, O'Shea, Clark, Brady; McCarthy (McGeady 85), Whelan, Hoolahan (Keane 78), Hendrick; Walters (McClean 64); Long. Coach: Martin O'Neill (NIR)
Sweden: Isaksson; Lustig (Johansson 45), Nilsson-Lindelöf, Granqvist, Olsson; Larsson, Lewicki (Ekdal 86), Källström, Forsberg; Ibrahimović, Berg (Guidetti 59). Coach: Erik Hamrén (SWE)
Yellow cards: McCarthy 43 (Republic of Ireland), Nilsson-Lindelöf 61 (Sweden), Whelan 77 (Republic of Ireland)

13/06/16, Stade de Lyon, Lyon (att: 55,408)
Belgium 0-2 Italy
Goals: 0-1 Giaccherini 32, 0-2 Pellè 90+3
Referee: Clattenburg (ENG)
Belgium: Courtois; Ciman (Carrasco 76), Alderweireld, Vermaelen, Vertonghen; Witsel, Nainggolan (Mertens 62); De Bruyne, Fellaini, Hazard; R Lukaku (Origi 73). Coach: Marc Wilmots (BEL)
Italy: Buffon; Barzagli, Bonucci, Chiellini; Candreva, Parolo, De Rossi (Thiago Motta 78), Giaccherini, Darmian (De Sciglio 58); Pellè, Éder (Immobile 75). Coach: Antonio Conte (ITA)
Yellow cards: Chiellini 65 (Italy), Éder 75 (Italy), Bonucci 78 (Italy), Thiago Motta 84 (Italy), Vertonghen 90+2 (Belgium)

17/06/16, Stadium de Toulouse, Toulouse (att: 29,600)
Italy 1-0 Sweden
Goal: 1-0 Éder 88
Referee: Kassai (HUN)
Italy: Buffon; Barzagli, Bonucci, Chiellini; Candreva, Parolo, De Rossi (Thiago Motta 74), Giaccherini, Florenzi (Sturaro 85); Pellè (Zaza 60), Éder. Coach: Antonio Conte (ITA)
Sweden: Isaksson; Nilsson-Lindelöf, Johansson, Granqvist, Olsson; Larsson, Ekdal (Lewicki 79), Källström, Forsberg (Durmaz 79); Ibrahimović, Guidetti (Berg 85). Coach: Erik Hamrén (SWE)
Yellow cards: De Rossi 69 (Italy), Olsson 89 (Sweden), Buffon 90+3 (Italy)

18/06/16, Stade de Bordeaux, Bordeaux (att: 39,493)
Belgium 3-0 Republic of Ireland
Goals: 1-0 R Lukaku 48, 2-0 Witsel 61,
3-0 R Lukaku 70
Referee: Çakır (TUR)
Belgium: Courtois; Meunier, Alderweireld,
Vermaelen, Vertonghen; Witsel, Dembélé
(Nainggolan 57); Carrasco (Mertens 64), De
Bruyne, Hazard; R Lukaku (Benteke 83). Coach:
Marc Wilmots (BEL)
Republic of Ireland: Randolph; Coleman, O'Shea,
Clark, Ward; McCarthy (McClean 62), Whelan;
Hendrick, Hoolahan (McGeady 71), Brady; Long
(Keane 79). Coach: Martin O'Neill (NIR)
Yellow cards: Hendrick 42 (Republic of Ireland),
Vermaelen 49 (Belgium)

22/06/16, Stade de Nice, Nice (att: 34,011)
Sweden 0-1 Belgium
Goal: 0-1 Nainggolan 84
Referee: Brych (GER)
Sweden: Isaksson; Nilsson-Lindelöf, Johansson,
Granqvist, Olsson; Larsson (Durmaz 70), Ekdal,
Källström, Forsberg (Zengin 82); Ibrahimović, Berg
(Guidetti 63), Coach: Erik Hamrén (SWE)
Belgium: Courtois; Meunier, Alderweireld,
Vermaelen, Vertonghen; Nainggolan, Witsel;
Carrasco (Mertens 71), De Bruyne, Hazard (Origi
90+3); R Lukaku (Benteke 87). Coach: Marc
Wilmots (BEL)
Yellow cards: Meunier 30 (Belgium),
Ekdal 33 (Sweden), Johansson 36 (Sweden),
Witsel 45+1 (Belgium)

22/06/16, Stade Pierre Mauroy, Lille (att: 44,268)
Italy 0-1 Republic of Ireland
Goal: 0-1 Brady 85
Referee: Hațegan (ROU)
Italy: Sirigu; Barzagli, Bonucci, Ogbonna;
Bernardeschi (Darmian 60), Sturaro, Thiago
Motta, Florenzi, De Sciglio (El Shaarawy 81); Zaza,
Immobile (Insigne 74). Coach: Antonio Conte (ITA)
Republic of Ireland: Randolph; Coleman, Duffy,
Keogh, Ward; McCarthy (Hoolahan 77); Hendrick,
Brady, McClean; Long (Quinn 90), Murphy
(McGeady 70). Coach: Martin O'Neill (NIR)
Yellow cards: Long 39 (Republic of Ireland),
Sirigu 39 (Italy), Ward 73 (Republic of Ireland),
Barzagli 78 (Italy), Zaza 87 (Italy), Insigne 90+1 (Italy)

Robbie Brady gestures to the Republic of Ireland
fans after scoring his team's late winner against Italy

Group F

14/06/16, Stade de Bordeaux, Bordeaux (att: 34,424)
Austria 0-2 Hungary
Goals: 0-1 Szalai 62, 0-2 Stieber 87
Referee: Turpin (FRA)
Austria: Almer; Klein, Dragovic, Hinteregger,
Fuchs; Alaba, Baumgartlinger; Harnik (Schöpf 77),
Junuzovic (Sabitzer 59), Arnautovic; Janko (Okotie
65). Coach: Marcel Koller (SUI)
Hungary: Király; Fiola, Guzmics, Lang, Kádár;
Nagy; Dzsudzsák, Gera, Kleinheisler (Stieber 80),
Németh (Pintér 89); Szalai (Priskin 69). Coach:
Bernd Storck (GER)
Red card: Dragovic 66 (Austria)
Yellow cards: Dragovic 33 (Austria), Dragovic 66
(Austria), Németh 80 (Hungary)

*14/06/16, Stade Geoffroy Guichard, Saint-Etienne
(att: 38,742)*
Portugal 1-1 Iceland
Goals: 1-0 Nani 31, 1-1 B Bjarnason 50
Referee: Çakır (TUR)
Portugal: Rui Patrício; Vieirinha, Pepe,
Ricardo Carvalho, Raphael Guerreiro; André
Gomes (Éder 84), Danilo Pereira, João Moutinho
(Renato Sanches 71), João Mário (Ricardo
Quaresma 76); Nani, Cristiano Ronaldo. Coach:
Fernando Santos (POR)
Iceland: Halldórsson; Sævarsson, R Sigurdsson,
Árnason, A Skúlason; Gudmundsson (T Bjarnason
90), Gunnarsson, G Sigurdsson, B Bjarnason;
Bödvarsson, Sigthórsson (A Finnbogason
81). Coach: Lars Lagerbäck (SWE) & Heimir
Hallgrímsson (ISL)
Yellow cards: B Bjarnason 55 (Iceland), A
Finnbogason 90+4 (Iceland)

18/06/16, Stade Vélodrome, Marseille (att: 60,842)
Iceland 1-1 Hungary
Goals: 1-0 G Sigurdsson 40(p),
1-1 Sævarsson 88(og)
Referee: Karasev (RUS)
Iceland: Halldórsson; Sævarsson, R Sigurdsson,
Árnason, A Skúlason; Gudmundsson, Gunnarsson
(Hallfredsson 65), G Sigurdsson, B Bjarnason;
Bödvarsson (A Finnbogason 69), Sigthórsson
(Gudjohnsen 84). Coach: Lars Lagerbäck (SWE)
& Heimir Hallgrímsson (ISL)
Hungary: Király; Lang, Juhász (Szalai 84),
Guzmics, Kádár; Nagy; Dzsudzsák, Gera,
Kleinheisler, Stieber (Nikolić 66); Priskin (Böde 66).
Coach: Bernd Storck (GER)
Yellow cards: Gudmundsson 42 (Iceland), A
Finnbogason 75 (Iceland), Sævarsson 77 (Iceland),
Kádár 81 (Hungary), Kleinheisler 83 (Hungary),
Nagy 90+1 (Hungary)

18/06/16, Parc des Princes, Paris (att: 44,291)
Portugal 0-0 Austria
Referee: Rizzoli (ITA)
Portugal: Rui Patrício; Vieirinha, Pepe, Ricardo
Carvalho, Raphael Guerreiro; João Moutinho,
William Carvalho, André Gomes (Éder 83);
Ricardo Quaresma (João Mário 71), Nani (Rafa
Silva 89), Cristiano Ronaldo. Coach: Fernando
Santos (POR)
Austria: Almer; Klein, Prödl, Hinteregger, Fuchs;
Baumgartlinger, Ilsanker (Wimmer 87); Sabitzer
(Hinterseer 85), Alaba (Schöpf 65), Arnautovic;
Harnik. Coach: Marcel Koller (SUI)
Yellow cards: Ricardo Quaresma 31 (Portugal),
Pepe 40 (Portugal), Harnik 47 (Austria), Fuchs
60 (Austria), Hinteregger 78 (Austria), Schöpf 86
(Austria)

*22/06/16, Stade de France, Saint-Denis
(att: 68,714)*
Iceland 2-1 Austria
Goals: 1-0 Bödvarsson 18, 1-1 Schöpf 60,
2-1 Traustason 90+4
Referee: Marciniak (POL)
Iceland: Halldórsson; Sævarsson, R Sigurdsson,
Árnason, A Skúlason; Gudmundsson (Ingason
86), Gunnarsson, G Sigurdsson, B Bjarnason;
Bödvarsson (T Bjarnason 71), Sigthórsson
(Traustason 80). Coach: Lars Lagerbäck (SWE) &
Heimir Hallgrímsson (ISL)
Austria: Almer; Klein, Prödl (Schöpf 46), Dragovic,
Hinteregger, Fuchs; Baumgartlinger, Ilsanker
(Janko 46); Alaba, Arnautovic; Sabitzer (Jantscher
78). Coach: Marcel Koller (SUI)
Yellow cards: A Skúlason 36 (Iceland),
Sigthórsson 51 (Iceland), Janko 70 (Austria),
Árnason 78 (Iceland), Halldórsson 82 (Iceland)

Arnór Ingvi Traustason scores Iceland's dramatic last-gasp winner against Austria in the Stade de France

22/06/16, Stade de Lyon, Lyon (att: 55,514)

Hungary 3-3 Portugal

Goals: 1-0 Gera 19, 1-1 Nani 42, 2-1 Dzsudzsák 47, 2-2 Cristiano Ronaldo 50, 3-2 Dzsudzsák 55, 3-3 Cristiano Ronaldo 62

Referee: Atkinson (ENG)

Hungary: Király; Lang, Juhász, Guzmics, Korhut; Gera (Bese 46); Lovrencsics (Stieber 83), Elek, Pintér, Dzsudzsák; Szalai (Németh 71). Coach: Bernd Storck (GER)

Portugal: Rui Patrício; Vieirinha, Pepe, Ricardo Carvalho, Eliseu; William Carvalho; João Mário, João Moutinho (Renato Sanches 46), André Gomes (Ricardo Quaresma 61); Nani (Danilo Pereira 81), Cristiano Ronaldo. Coach: Fernando Santos (POR)

Yellow cards: Guzmics 13 (Hungary), Juhász 28 (Hungary), Gera 34 (Hungary), Dzsudzsák 56 (Hungary)

Final group tables

Group A

	Pld	W	D	L	F	A	Pts
1 France	3	2	1	0	4	1	7
2 Switzerland	3	1	2	0	2	1	5
3 Albania	3	1	0	2	1	3	3
4 Romania	3	0	1	2	2	4	1

Group B

	Pld	W	D	L	F	A	Pts
1 Wales	3	2	0	1	6	3	6
2 England	3	1	2	0	3	2	5
3 Slovakia	3	1	1	1	3	3	4
4 Russia	3	0	1	2	2	6	1

Group C

	Pld	W	D	L	F	A	Pts
1 Germany	3	2	1	0	3	0	7
2 Poland	3	2	1	0	2	0	7
3 Northern Ireland	3	1	0	2	2	2	3
4 Ukraine	3	0	0	3	0	5	0

Group D

	Pld	W	D	L	F	A	Pts
1 Croatia	3	2	1	0	5	3	7
2 Spain	3	2	0	1	5	2	6
3 Turkey	3	1	0	2	2	4	3
4 Czech Republic	3	0	1	2	2	5	1

Group E

	Pld	W	D	L	F	A	Pts
1 Italy	3	2	0	1	3	1	6
2 Belgium	3	2	0	1	4	2	6
3 Republic of Ireland	3	1	1	1	2	4	4
4 Sweden	3	0	1	2	1	3	1

Group F

	Pld	W	D	L	F	A	Pts
1 Hungary	3	1	2	0	6	4	5
2 Iceland	3	1	2	0	4	3	5
3 Portugal	3	0	3	0	4	4	3
4 Austria	3	0	1	2	1	4	1

Grzegorz Krychowiak converts the decisive penalty past Yann Sommer in Poland's shoot-out victory against Switzerland

Round of 16

25/06/16, Stade Geoffroy Guichard, Saint-Etienne (att: 38,842)

Switzerland 1-1 Poland (aet; 4-5 on pens)

Goals: 0-1 Błaszczykowski 39, 1-1 Shaqiri 82

Penalties: 1-0 Lichtsteiner, 1-1 Lewandowski, 1-2 Milik, 2-2 Shaqiri, 2-3 Glik, 3-3 Schär, 3-4 Błaszczykowski, 4-4 Rodríguez, 4-5 Krychowiak

Referee: Clattenburg (ENG)

Switzerland: Sommer; Lichtsteiner, Schär, Djourou, Rodríguez; Behrami (Fernandes 77), Xhaka; Shaqiri, Džemaili (Embolo 58), Mehmedi (Derdiyok 70); Seferovic. Coach: Vladimir Petković (SUI)

Poland: Fabiański; Piszczek, Glik, Pazdan, Jędrzejczyk; Błaszczykowski, Krychowiak, Mączyński (Jodłowiec 101), Grosicki (Peszko 104); Milik; Lewandowski. Coach: Adam Nawałka (POL)

Yellow cards: Schär 55 (Switzerland), Jędrzejczyk 58 (Poland), Pazdan 111 (Poland), Djourou 117 (Switzerland)

25/06/16, Parc des Princes, Paris (att: 44,342)

Wales 1-0 Northern Ireland

Goal: 1-0 McAuley 75(og)

Referee: Atkinson (ENG)

Wales: Hennessey; Gunter, Chester, A Williams, Davies, Taylor; Allen, Ledley (J Williams 63); Ramsey, Bale, Vokes (Robson-Kanu 55). Coach: Chris Coleman (WAL)

Northern Ireland: McGovern; Hughes, McAuley (Magennis 84), Cathcart, J Evans; C Evans; Ward (Washington 69), Davis, Norwood (McGinn 79), Dallas; K Lafferty. Coach: Michael O'Neill (NIR)

Yellow cards: Dallas 44 (Northern Ireland), Taylor 58 (Wales), Davis 67 (Northern Ireland), Ramsey 90+4 (Wales)

25/06/16, Stade Bollaert-Delelis, Lens (att: 33,523)

Croatia 0-1 Portugal (aet)

Goal: 0-1 Ricardo Quaresma 117

Referee: Velasco Carballo (ESP)

Croatia: Subašić; Srna, Ćorluka (Kramarić 120), Vida, Strinić; Modrić, Badelj; Brozović, Rakitić (Pjaca 110), Perišić; Mandžukić (N Kalinić 88). Coach: Ante Čačić (CRO)

Portugal: Rui Patrício; Cédric, Pepe, José Fonte, Raphael Guerreiro; William Carvalho; João Mário (Ricardo Quaresma 87), Adrien Silva (Danilo Pereira 108), André Gomes (Renato Sanches 50); Nani, Cristiano Ronaldo. Coach: Fernando Santos (POR)

Yellow card: William Carvalho 78 (Portugal)

Ricardo Quaresma is a happy man after scoring Portugal's extra-time winner against Croatia

Julian Draxler hooks in Germany's third goal against Slovakia

26/06/16, Stade de Lyon, Lyon (att: 56,279)
France 2-1 Republic of Ireland
Goals: 0-1 Brady 2(p), 1-1 Griezmann 58, 2-1 Griezmann 61
Referee: Rizzoli (ITA)
France: Lloris; Sagna, Rami, Koscielny, Evra; Matuidi, Kanté (Coman 46; Sissoko 93), Pogba; Griezmann, Giroud (Gignac 73), Payet. Coach: Didier Deschamps (FRA)
Republic of Ireland: Randolph; Coleman, Duffy, Keogh, Ward; McCarthy (Hoolahan 71); Hendrick, Brady, McClean (O'Shea 68); Long, Murphy (Walters 65). Coach: Martin O'Neill (NIR)
Red card: Duffy 66 (Republic of Ireland)
Yellow cards: Coleman 25 (Republic of Ireland), Kanté 27 (France), Hendrick 41 (Republic of Ireland), Rami 44 (France), Long 72 (Republic of Ireland)

26/06/16, Stade Pierre Mauroy, Lille (att: 44,312)
Germany 3-0 Slovakia
Goals: 1-0 Boateng 8, 2-0 Gomez 43, 3-0 Draxler 63
Referee: Marciniak (POL)
Germany: Neuer; Kimmich, Boateng (Höwedes 72), Hummels, Hector; Khedira (Schweinsteiger 76), Kroos; Müller, Özil, Draxler (Podolski 72); Gomez. Coach: Joachim Löw (GER)
Slovakia: Kozáčik; Pekarík, Škrtel, Ďurica, Gyömber (Saláta 84); Škriniar; Kucka, Hrošovský, Hamšík, Weiss (Greguš 46); Ďuriš (Šesták 64). Coach: Ján Kozák (SVK)
Yellow cards: Škrtel 13 (Slovakia), Kimmich 46 (Germany), Hummels 67 (Germany), Kucka 90+1 (Slovakia)

26/06/16, Stadium de Toulouse, Toulouse (att: 28,921)
Hungary 0-4 Belgium
Goals: 0-1 Alderweireld 10, 0-2 Batshuayi 78, 0-3 Hazard 80, 0-4 Carrasco 90+1
Referee: Mažić (SRB)
Hungary: Király; Lang, Juhász (Böde 79), Guzmics, Kádár; Nagy; Dzsudzsák, Gera (Elek 46), Pintér (Nikolić 75), Lovrencsics; Szalai. Coach: Bernd Storck (GER)
Belgium: Courtois; Meunier, Alderweireld, Vermaelen, Vertonghen; Nainggolan, Witsel; Mertens (Carrasco 70), De Bruyne, Hazard (Fellaini 81); R Lukaku (Batshuayi 76). Coach: Marc Wilmots (BEL)
Yellow cards: Kádár 34 (Hungary), Lang 47 (Hungary), Elek 61 (Hungary), Vermaelen 67 (Belgium), Batshuayi 89 (Belgium), Szalai 90+2 (Hungary), Fellaini 90+2 (Belgium)

27/06/16, Stade de France, Saint-Denis (att: 76,165)
Italy 2-0 Spain
Goals: 1-0 Chiellini 33, 2-0 Pellè 90+1
Referee: Çakır (TUR)
Italy: Buffon; Barzagli, Bonucci, Chiellini; Florenzi (Darmian 84), Parolo, De Rossi (Thiago Motta 54), Giaccherini, De Sciglio; Pellè, Éder (Insigne 82). Coach: Antonio Conte (ITA)
Spain: De Gea; Juanfran, Piqué, Sergio Ramos, Jordi Alba; Fàbregas, Busquets, Iniesta; Silva, Morata (Lucas Vázquez 70), Nolito (Aduriz 46; Pedro 81). Coach: Vicente del Bosque (ESP)
Yellow cards: De Sciglio 24 (Italy), Nolito 41 (Spain), Pellè 54 (Italy), Jordi Alba 89 (Spain), Busquets 89 (Spain), Thiago Motta 89 (Italy), Silva 90+4 (Spain)

27/06/16, Stade de Nice, Nice (att: 33,901)
England 1-2 Iceland
Goals: 1-0 Rooney 4(p), 1-1 R Sigurdsson 6, 1-2 Sigthórsson 18
Referee: Skomina (SVN)
England: Hart; Walker, Cahill, Smalling, Rose; Dier (Wilshere 46); Alli, Rooney (Rashford 87); Sturridge, Kane, Sterling (Vardy 60). Coach: Roy Hodgson (ENG)
Iceland: Halldórsson; Sævarsson, R Sigurdsson, Árnason, A Skúlason; Gudmundsson, Gunnarsson, G Sigurdsson, B Bjarnason; Bödvarsson (Traustason 89), Sigthórsson (T Bjarnason 76). Coach: Lars Lagerbäck (SWE) & Heimir Hallgrímsson (ISL)
Yellow cards: G Sigurdsson 38 (Iceland), Sturridge 47 (England), A Gunnarsson 65 (Iceland)

Quarter-finals

30/06/16, Stade Vélodrome, Marseille (att: 62,940)
Poland 1-1 Portugal (aet; 3-5 on pens)
Goals: 1-0 Lewandowski 2, 1-1 Renato Sanches 33
Penalties: 0-1 Cristiano Ronaldo, 1-1 Lewandowski, 1-2 Renato Sanches, 2-2 Milik, 2-3 João Moutinho, 3-3 Glik, 3-4 Nani, 3-5 Ricardo Quaresma
Referee: Brych (GER)

Poland: Fabiański; Piszczek, Glik, Pazdan, Jędrzejczyk; Błaszczykowski, Krychowiak, Mączyński (Jodłowiec 98), Grosicki (Kapustka 82); Milik; Lewandowski. Coach: Adam Nawałka (POL)
Portugal: Rui Patrício; Cédric, Pepe, José Fonte, Eliseu; William Carvalho (Danilo Pereira 96); Renato Sanches, Adrien Silva (João Moutinho 73), João Mário (Ricardo Quaresma 80); Nani, Cristiano Ronaldo. Coach: Fernando Santos (POR)
Yellow cards: Jędrzejczyk 42 (Poland), Glik 66 (Poland), Adrien Silva 70 (Portugal), Kapustka 89 (Poland), William Carvalho 90+2 (Portugal)

01/07/16, Stade Pierre Mauroy, Lille (att: 45,936)
Wales 3-1 Belgium
Goals: 0-1 Nainggolan 13, 1-1 A Williams 31, 2-1 Robson-Kanu 55, 3-1 Vokes 86
Referee: Skomina (SVN)
Wales: Hennessey; Gunter, Chester, A Williams, Davies, Taylor; Allen, Ledley (King 78); Ramsey (Collins 90), Bale; Robson-Kanu (Vokes 80). Coach: Chris Coleman (WAL)
Belgium: Courtois; Meunier, Alderweireld, Denayer, J Lukaku (Mertens 75), Witsel; Carrasco (Fellaini 46), De Bruyne, Hazard; R Lukaku (Batshuayi 83). Coach: Marc Wilmots (BEL)
Yellow cards: Davies 5 (Wales), Chester 16 (Wales), Gunter 24 (Wales), Fellaini 59 (Belgium), Ramsey 75 (Wales), Alderweireld 85 (Belgium)

02/07/16, Stade de Bordeaux, Bordeaux (att: 38,764)
Germany 1-1 Italy (aet; 6-5 on pens)
Goals: 1-0 Özil 65, 1-1 Bonucci 78(p)
Penalties: 0-1 Insigne, 1-1 Kroos, 1-2 Barzagli, 2-2 Draxler, 2-3 Giaccherini, 3-3 Hummels, 3-4 Parolo, 4-4 Kimmich, 4-5 De Sciglio, 5-5 Boateng, 6-5 Hector
Referee: Kassai (HUN)
Germany: Neuer; Höwedes, Boateng, Hummels; Kimmich, Khedira (Schweinsteiger 16), Kroos, Hector; Müller; Özil; Gomez (Draxler 72). Coach: Joachim Löw (GER)
Italy: Buffon; Barzagli, Bonucci, Chiellini (Zaza 120+1); Florenzi (Darmian 86), Sturaro, Parolo, Giaccherini, De Sciglio; Pellè, Éder (Insigne 108). Coach: Antonio Conte (ITA)
Yellow cards: Sturaro 56 (Italy), De Sciglio 57 (Italy), Parolo 59 (Italy), Hummels 90 (Germany), Pellè 91 (Italy), Giaccherini 103 (Italy), Schweinsteiger 112 (Germany)

Sam Vokes beats Thibaut Courtois with a brilliant header to complete the scoring in Wales' 3-1 quarter-final victory over Belgium

Éder drives in the extra-time goal that gives Portugal a 1-0 victory over France in the UEFA EURO 2016 final

03/07/16, Stade de France, Saint-Denis (att: 76,833)
France 5-2 Iceland
Goals: 1-0 Giroud 12, 2-0 Pogba 20, 3-0 Payet 43, 4-0 Griezmann 45, 4-1 Sigthórsson 56, 5-1 Giroud 59, 5-2 B Bjarnason 84
Referee: Kuipers (NED)
France: Lloris; Sagna, Umtiti, Koscielny (Mangala 72), Evra; Pogba, Matuidi; Sissoko, Griezmann, Payet (Coman 80); Giroud (Gignac 60). Coach: Didier Deschamps (FRA)
Iceland: Halldórsson; Sævarsson, R Sigurdsson, Árnason (Ingason 46), A Skúlason; Gudmundsson, Gunnarsson, G Sigurdsson, B Bjarnason; Bödvarsson (A Finnbogason 46), Sigthórsson (Gudjohnsen 83). Coach: Lars Lagerbäck (SWE) & Heimir Hallgrímsson (ISL)
Yellow cards: B Bjarnason 58 (Iceland), Umtiti 75 (France)

Semi-finals

06/07/16, Stade de Lyon, Lyon (att: 55,679)
Portugal 2-0 Wales
Goals: 1-0 Cristiano Ronaldo 50, 2-0 Nani 53
Referee: Eriksson (SWE)
Portugal: Rui Patrício; Cédric, José Fonte, Bruno Alves, Raphael Guerreiro; Danilo Pereira; Renato Sanches (André Gomes 74), Adrien Silva (João Moutinho 79), João Mário; Nani (Ricardo Quaresma 86), Cristiano Ronaldo. Coach: Fernando Santos (POR)
Wales: Hennessey; Gunter, Chester, A Williams, Collins (J Williams 66), Taylor; Allen, Ledley (Vokes 58); King, Bale; Robson-Kanu (Church 63). Coach: Chris Coleman (WAL)
Yellow cards: Allen 8 (Wales), Chester 62 (Wales), Bruno Alves 71 (Portugal), Cristiano Ronaldo 72 (Portugal), Bale 88 (Wales)

07/07/16, Stade Vélodrome, Marseille (att: 64,078)
Germany 0-2 France
Goals: 0-1 Griezmann 45+2(p), 0-2 Griezmann 72
Referee: Rizzoli (ITA)
Germany: Neuer; Kimmich, Höwedes, Boateng (Mustafi 61), Hector; Schweinsteiger (Sané 79); Özil, Can (Götze 67), Kroos, Draxler; Müller. Coach: Joachim Löw (GER)
France: Lloris; Sagna, Umtiti, Koscielny, Evra; Pogba, Matuidi; Sissoko, Griezmann (Cabaye 90+2), Payet (Kanté 71); Giroud (Gignac 78). Coach: Didier Deschamps (FRA)
Yellow cards: Can 36 (Germany), Evra 43 (France), Özil 45+1 (Germany), Schweinsteiger 45+1 (Germany), Draxler 50 (Germany), Kanté 75 (France)

Final

10/07/16, Stade de France, Saint-Denis (att: 75,868)
Portugal 1-0 France (aet)
Goal: 1-0 Éder 109
Referee: Clattenburg (ENG)
Portugal: Rui Patrício; Cédric, Pepe, José Fonte, Raphael Guerreiro; William Carvalho; Renato Sanches (Éder 79), Adrien Silva (João Moutinho 66), João Mário; Nani, Cristiano Ronaldo (Ricardo Quaresma 25), Coach: Fernando Santos (POR)
France: Lloris; Sagna, Umtiti, Koscielny, Evra; Pogba, Matuidi; Sissoko (Martial 110), Griezmann, Payet (Coman 58); Giroud (Gignac 78). Coach: Didier Deschamps (FRA)
Yellow cards: Cédric 34 (Portugal), João Mário 62 (Portugal), Umtiti 80 (France), Raphael Guerreiro 95 (Portugal), Matuidi 97 (France), William Carvalho 98 (Portugal), Koscielny 107 (France), Pogba 115 (France), José Fonte 119 (Portugal), Rui Patrício 123 (Portugal)

Top goalscorers

6	Antoine Griezmann (France)
3	Olivier Giroud (France)
	Dimitri Payet (France)
	Cristiano Ronaldo (Portugal)
	Nani (Portugal)
	Álvaro Morata (Spain)
	Gareth Bale (Wales)

Squads/Appearances/Goals

Albania

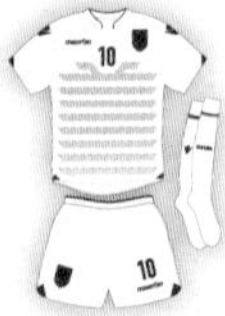

No	Name	DoB	Aps	(s)	Gls	Club
Goalkeepers						
1	Etrit Berisha	10/03/89	3			Lazio (ITA)
23	Alban Hoxha	23/11/87				Partizani
12	Orges Shehi	25/09/77				Skënderbeu
Defenders						
7	Ansi Agolli	11/10/82	3			Qarabağ (AZE)
18	Arlind Ajeti	25/09/93	2			Frosinone (ITA)
17	Naser Aliji	27/12/93				Basel (SUI)
5	Lorik Cana	27/07/83	1	(1)		Nantes (FRA)
4	Elseid Hysaj	20/02/94	3			Napoli (ITA)
15	Mërgim Mavraj	09/06/86	3			Köln (GER)
6	Frederic Veseli	20/11/92		(1)		Lugano (SUI)
Midfielders						
22	Amir Abrashi	27/03/90	3			Freiburg (GER)
8	Migjen Basha	05/01/87	1			Como (ITA)
20	Ergys Kaçe	08/07/93		(1)		PAOK (GRE)
13	Burim Kukeli	16/01/84	2			Zürich (SUI)
3	Ermir Lenjani	05/08/89	3			Rennes (FRA)
2	Andi Lila	12/02/86	2			Giannina (GRE)
9	Ledian Memushaj	07/12/86	2			Pescara (ITA)
21	Odhise Roshi	22/05/91	1	(2)		Rijeka (CRO)
14	Taulant Xhaka	28/03/91	1	(1)		Basel (SUI)
Forwards						
19	Bekim Balaj	11/01/91		(1)		Rijeka (CRO)
16	Sokol Çikalleshi	27/07/90		(1)		İstanbul Başakşehir (TUR)
11	Shkëlzen Gashi	15/07/88		(1)		Colorado Rapids (USA)
10	Armando Sadiku	27/05/91	3		1	Vaduz (LIE)

Austria

No	Name	DoB	Aps	(s)	Gls	Club
Goalkeepers						
1	Robert Almer	20/03/84	3			Austria Wien
12	Heinz Lindner	17/07/90				Eintracht Frankfurt (GER)
23	Ramazan Özcan	28/06/84				Ingolstadt (GER)
Defenders						
3	Aleksandar Dragovic	06/03/91	2			Dynamo Kyiv (UKR)
5	Christian Fuchs	07/04/86	3			Leicester (ENG)
2	György Garics	08/03/84				Darmstadt (GER)
4	Martin Hinteregger	07/09/92	3			Mönchengladbach (GER)
17	Florian Klein	17/11/86	3			Stuttgart (GER)
15	Sebastian Prödl	21/06/87	2			Watford (ENG)
13	Markus Suttner	16/04/87				Ingolstadt (GER)
16	Kevin Wimmer	15/11/92		(1)		Tottenham (ENG)
Midfielders						
8	David Alaba	24/06/92	3			Bayern (GER)
7	Marko Arnautovic	19/04/89	3			Stoke (ENG)
14	Julian Baumgartlinger	02/01/88	3			Mainz (GER)
11	Martin Harnik	10/06/87	2			Stuttgart (GER)
6	Stefan Ilsanker	18/05/89	2			RB Leipzig (GER)
22	Jakob Jantscher	08/01/89		(1)		Luzern (SUI)
10	Zlatko Junuzovic	26/09/87	1			Bremen (GER)
20	Marcel Sabitzer	17/03/94	2	(1)		RB Leipzig (GER)
18	Alessandro Schöpf	07/02/94		(3)	1	Schalke (GER)
Forwards						
19	Lukas Hinterseer	28/03/91		(1)		Ingolstadt (GER)
21	Marc Janko	25/06/83	1	(1)		Basel (SUI)
9	Rubin Okotie	06/06/87		(1)		1860 München (GER)

Belgium

No	Name	DoB	Aps	(s)	Gls	Club
Goalkeepers						
1	Thibaut Courtois	11/05/92	5			Chelsea (ENG)
13	Jean-François Gillet	31/05/79				Mechelen
12	Simon Mignolet	06/03/88				Liverpool (ENG)
Defenders						
2	Toby Alderweireld	02/03/89	5		1	Tottenham (ENG)
23	Laurent Ciman	05/08/85	1			Montreal Impact (USA)
15	Jason Denayer	28/06/95	1			Galatasaray (TUR)
18	Christian Kabasele	24/02/91				Genk
21	Jordan Lukaku	25/07/94	1			Oostende
16	Thomas Meunier	12/09/91	4			Club Brugge
3	Thomas Vermaelen	14/11/85	4			Barcelona (ESP)
5	Jan Vertonghen	24/04/87	4			Tottenham (ENG)
Midfielders						
11	Yannick Carrasco	04/09/93	3	(2)	1	Atlético (ESP)
7	Kevin De Bruyne	28/06/91	5			Man. City (ENG)
19	Mousa Dembélé	16/07/87	1			Tottenham (ENG)
8	Marouane Fellaini	22/11/87	1	(2)		Man. United (ENG)
10	Eden Hazard	07/01/91	5		1	Chelsea (ENG)
14	Dries Mertens	06/05/87	1	(4)		Napoli (ITA)
4	Radja Nainggolan	04/05/88	4	(1)	2	Roma (ITA)
6	Axel Witsel	12/01/89	5		1	Zenit (RUS)
Forwards						
22	Michy Batshuayi	02/10/93		(2)	1	Marseille (FRA)
20	Christian Benteke	03/12/90		(2)		Liverpool (ENG)
9	Romelu Lukaku	13/05/93	5		2	Everton (ENG)
17	Divock Origi	18/04/95		(2)		Liverpool (ENG)

Croatia

No	Name	DoB	Aps	(s)	Gls	Club
Goalkeepers						
12	Lovre Kalinić	03/04/90				Hajduk Split
23	Danijel Subašić	27/10/84	4			Monaco (FRA)
1	Ivan Vargić	15/03/87				Rijeka
Defenders						
5	Vedran Ćorluka	05/02/86	4			Lokomotiv Moskva (RUS)
6	Tin Jedvaj	28/11/95	1			Leverkusen (GER)
13	Gordon Schildenfeld	18/03/85		(2)		Dinamo Zagreb
11	Darijo Srna	01/05/82	4			Shakhtar Donetsk (UKR)
3	Ivan Strinić	17/07/87	3			Napoli (ITA)
21	Domagoj Vida	29/04/89	3			Dynamo Kyiv (UKR)
2	Šime Vrsaljko	10/01/92	1	(1)		Sassuolo (ITA)
Midfielders						
19	Milan Badelj	25/02/89	4			Fiorentina (ITA)
14	Marcelo Brozović	16/11/92	3			Internazionale (ITA)
18	Ante Ćorić	14/04/97				Dinamo Zagreb
8	Mateo Kovačić	06/05/94		(2)		Real Madrid (ESP)
10	Luka Modrić	09/09/85	3		1	Real Madrid (ESP)
4	Ivan Perišić	02/02/89	4		2	Internazionale (ITA)
20	Marko Pjaca	06/05/95	1	(2)		Dinamo Zagreb
7	Ivan Rakitić	10/03/88	4		1	Barcelona (ESP)
15	Marko Rog	19/07/95	1			Dinamo Zagreb
Forwards						
22	Duje Čop	01/02/90		(1)		Málaga (ESP)
16	Nikola Kalinić	05/01/88	1	(1)	1	Fiorentina (ITA)
9	Andrej Kramarić	19/06/91		(3)		Hoffenheim (GER)
17	Mario Mandžukić	21/05/86	3			Juventus (ITA)

Czech Republic

No	Name	DoB	Aps	(s)	Gls	Club
Goalkeepers						
1	Petr Čech	20/05/82	3			Arsenal (ENG)
23	Tomáš Koubek	26/08/92				Liberec
16	Tomáš Vaclík	29/03/89				Basel (SUI)
Defenders						
4	Theodor Gebre Selassie	24/12/86	1			Bremen (GER)
5	Roman Hubník	06/06/84	3			Plzeň
2	Pavel Kadeřábek	25/04/92	3			Hoffenheim (GER)
3	Michal Kadlec	13/12/84				Fenerbahçe (TUR)
8	David Limberský	06/10/83	2			Plzeň
11	Daniel Pudil	27/09/85	1			Sheffield Wednesday (ENG)
6	Tomáš Sivok	15/09/83	3			Bursaspor (TUR)
17	Marek Suchý	29/03/88				Basel (SUI)
Midfielders						
22	Vladimír Darida	08/08/90	3			Hertha (GER)
9	Bořek Dočkal	30/09/88	1			Sparta Praha
14	Daniel Kolář	27/10/85		(1)		Plzeň
19	Ladislav Krejčí	05/07/92	3			Sparta Praha
15	David Pavelka	18/05/91	1	(1)		Kasımpaşa (TUR)
13	Jaroslav Plašil	05/01/82	3			Bordeaux (FRA)
10	Tomáš Rosický	04/10/80	2			Arsenal (ENG)
20	Jiří Skalák	12/03/92	1			Brighton (ENG)
18	Josef Šural	30/05/90		(3)		Sparta Praha
Forwards						
21	David Lafata	18/09/81	1	(1)		Sparta Praha
7	Tomáš Necid	13/08/89	2	(1)	1	Bursaspor (TUR)
12	Milan Škoda	16/01/86		(2)	1	Slavia Praha

England

No	Name	DoB	Aps	(s)	Gls	Club
Goalkeepers						
13	Fraser Forster	17/03/88				Southampton
1	Joe Hart	19/04/87	4			Man. City
23	Tom Heaton	15/04/86				Burnley
Defenders						
21	Ryan Bertrand	05/08/89	1			Southampton
5	Gary Cahill	19/12/85	4			Chelsea
12	Nathaniel Clyne	05/04/91	1			Liverpool
3	Danny Rose	02/07/90	3			Tottenham
6	Chris Smalling	22/11/89	4			Man. United
16	John Stones	28/05/94				Everton
2	Kyle Walker	28/05/90	3			Tottenham
Midfielders						
20	Dele Alli	11/04/96	3	(1)		Tottenham
19	Ross Barkley	05/12/93				Everton
17	Eric Dier	15/01/94	4		1	Tottenham
14	Jordan Henderson	17/06/90	1			Liverpool
8	Adam Lallana	10/05/88	3			Liverpool
4	James Milner	04/01/86		(1)		Liverpool
10	Wayne Rooney	24/10/85	3	(1)	1	Man. United
18	Jack Wilshere	01/01/92	1	(2)		Arsenal
Forwards						
9	Harry Kane	28/07/93	3	(1)		Tottenham
22	Marcus Rashford	31/10/97		(2)		Man. United
7	Raheem Sterling	08/12/94	3			Man. City
15	Daniel Sturridge	01/09/89	2	(1)	1	Liverpool
11	Jamie Vardy	11/01/87	1	(2)	1	Leicester

France

No	Name	DoB	Aps	(s)	Gls	Club
Goalkeepers						
23	Benoît Costil	03/07/87				Rennes
1	Hugo Lloris	26/12/86	7			Tottenham (ENG)
16	Steve Mandanda	28/03/85				Marseille
Defenders						
17	Lucas Digne	20/07/93				Roma (ITA)
3	Patrice Evra	15/05/81	7			Juventus (ITA)
2	Christophe Jallet	31/10/83				Lyon
21	Laurent Koscielny	10/09/85	7			Arsenal (ENG)
13	Eliaquim Mangala	13/02/91		(1)		Man. City (ENG)
4	Adil Rami	27/12/85	4			Sevilla (ESP)
19	Bacary Sagna	14/02/83	7			Man. City (ENG)
22	Samuel Umtiti	14/11/93	3			Lyon
Midfielders						
6	Yohan Cabaye	14/01/86	1	(1)		Crystal Palace (ENG)
5	N'Golo Kanté	29/03/91	3	(1)		Leicester (ENG)
14	Blaise Matuidi	09/04/87	6	(1)		Paris
8	Dimitri Payet	29/03/87	6	(1)	3	West Ham (ENG)
15	Paul Pogba	15/03/93	6	(1)	1	Juventus (ITA)
12	Morgan Schneiderlin	08/11/89				Man. United (ENG)
18	Moussa Sissoko	16/08/89	4	(2)		Newcastle (ENG)
Forwards						
20	Kingsley Coman	13/06/96	2	(4)		Bayern (GER)
10	André-Pierre Gignac	05/12/85	1	(5)		Tigres (MEX)
9	Olivier Giroud	30/09/86	6		3	Arsenal (ENG)
7	Antoine Griezmann	21/03/91	6	(1)	6	Atlético (ESP)
11	Anthony Martial	05/12/95	1	(2)		Man. United (ENG)

Hungary

No	Name	DoB	Aps	(s)	Gls	Club
Goalkeepers						
12	Dénes Dibusz	16/11/90				Ferencváros
22	Péter Gulácsi	06/05/90				RB Leipzig (GER)
1	Gábor Király	01/04/76	4			Haladás
Defenders						
21	Barnabás Bese	06/05/94		(1)		MTK
5	Attila Fiola	17/02/90	1			Puskás Akadémia
20	Richárd Guzmics	16/04/87	4			Wisła Kraków (POL)
23	Roland Juhász	01/07/83	3			Videoton
4	Tamás Kádár	14/03/90	3			Lech (POL)
3	Mihály Korhut	01/12/88	1			Debrecen
2	Ádám Lang	17/01/93	4			Videoton
Midfielders						
7	Balázs Dzsudzsák	23/12/86	4		2	Bursaspor (TUR)
6	Ákos Elek	21/07/88	1	(1)		Diósgyőr
10	Zoltán Gera	22/04/79	4		1	Ferencváros
15	László Kleinheisler	08/04/94	2			Bremen (GER)
14	Gergő Lovrencsics	01/09/88	2			Lech (POL)
8	Ádám Nagy	17/06/95	3			Ferencváros
11	Krisztián Németh	05/01/89	1	(1)		Al-Gharafa (QAT)
16	Ádám Pintér	12/06/88	2	(1)		Ferencváros
18	Zoltán Stieber	16/10/88	1	(2)	1	Nürnberg (GER)
Forwards						
13	Dániel Böde	24/10/86		(2)		Ferencváros
17	Nemanja Nikolić	31/12/87		(2)		Legia (POL)
19	Tamás Priskin	27/09/86	1	(1)		Slovan Bratislava (SVK)
9	Ádám Szalai	09/12/87	3	(1)	1	Hannover (GER)

Italy

No	Name	DoB	Aps	(s)	Gls	Club
Goalkeepers						
1	Gianluigi Buffon	28/01/78	4			Juventus
13	Federico Marchetti	07/02/83				Lazio
12	Salvatore Sirigu	12/01/87				Paris (FRA)
Defenders						
15	Andrea Barzagli	08/05/81	5			Juventus
19	Leonardo Bonucci	01/05/87	5		1	Juventus
3	Giorgio Chiellini	14/08/84	4			Juventus
4	Matteo Darmian	02/12/89	1	(3)		Man. United (ENG)
2	Mattia De Sciglio	20/10/92	3	(1)		Milan
5	Angelo Ogbonna	23/05/88	1			West Ham (ENG)
Midfielders						
21	Federico Bernardeschi	16/02/94	1			Fiorentina
6	Antonio Candreva	28/02/87	2			Lazio
16	Daniele De Rossi	24/07/83	3			Roma
8	Alessandro Florenzi	11/03/91	4			Roma
23	Emanuele Giaccherini	05/05/85	4		1	Bologna
10	Lorenzo Insigne	04/06/91		(3)		Napoli
18	Marco Parolo	25/01/85	4			Lazio
14	Stefano Sturaro	09/03/93	2	(1)		Juventus
10	Thiago Motta	28/08/82	1	(3)		Paris (FRA)
Forwards						
17	Éder	15/11/86	4		1	Internazionale
22	Stephan El Shaarawy	27/10/92		(1)		Roma
11	Ciro Immobile	20/02/90	1	(1)		Torino
9	Graziano Pellè	15/07/85	4		2	Southampton (ENG)
7	Simone Zaza	25/06/91	1	(2)		Juventus

Germany

No	Name	DoB	Aps	(s)	Gls	Club
Goalkeepers						
12	Bernd Leno	04/03/92				Leverkusen
1	Manuel Neuer	27/03/86	6			Bayern
22	Marc-André ter Stegen	30/04/92				Barcelona (ESP)
Defenders						
17	Jérôme Boateng	03/09/88	6		1	Bayern
3	Jonas Hector	27/05/90	6			Köln
4	Benedikt Höwedes	29/02/88	4	(2)		Schalke
5	Mats Hummels	16/12/88	4			Dortmund
21	Joshua Kimmich	08/02/95				Bayern
2	Shkodran Mustafi	17/04/92	1	(1)	1	Valencia (ESP)
16	Jonathan Tah	11/02/96				Leverkusen
Midfielders						
14	Emre Can	12/01/94	1			Liverpool (ENG)
11	Julian Draxler	20/09/93	4	(1)		Wolfsburg
6	Sami Khedira	04/04/87	5			Juventus (ITA)
18	Toni Kroos	04/01/90	6			Real Madrid (ESP)
8	Mesut Özil	15/10/88	6		1	Arsenal (ENG)
20	Leroy Sané	11/01/96		(1)		Schalke
9	André Schürrle	06/11/90		(3)		Wolfsburg
7	Bastian Schweinsteiger	01/08/84	1	(4)	1	Man. United (ENG)
15	Julian Weigl	08/09/95				Dortmund
Forwards						
23	Mario Gomez	10/07/85	3	(1)	2	Beşiktaş (TUR)
19	Mario Götze	03/06/92	3	(1)		Bayern
13	Thomas Müller	13/09/89	6			Bayern
10	Lukas Podolski	04/06/85		(1)		Galatasaray (TUR)

Iceland

No	Name	DoB	Aps	(s)	Gls	Club
Goalkeepers						
1	Hannes Thór Halldórsson	27/04/84	5			Boðo/Glimt (NOR)
13	Ingvar Jónsson	18/10/89				Sandefjord (NOR)
12	Ögmundur Kristinsson	19/06/89				Hammarby (SWE)
Defenders						
14	Kári Árnason	13/10/82	5			Malmö (SWE)
2	Haukur Heidar Hauksson	01/09/91				AIK (SWE)
4	Hjörtur Hermannsson	08/02/95				Göteborg (SWE)
5	Sverrir Ingi Ingason	05/08/93		(2)		Lokeren (BEL)
19	Hördur Björgvin Magnússon	11/02/93				Cesena (ITA)
6	Ragnar Sigurdsson	19/06/86	5		1	Krasnodar (RUS)
23	Ari Freyr Skúlason	14/05/87	5			OB (DEN)
2	Birkir Már Sævarsson	11/11/84	5			Hammarby (SWE)
Midfielders						
10	Birkir Bjarnason	27/05/88	5		2	Basel (SUI)
18	Theódór Elmar Bjarnason	04/03/87		(3)		AGF (DEN)
7	Jóhann Berg Gudmundsson	27/10/90	5			Charlton (ENG)
17	Aron Einar Gunnarsson	22/04/89	5			Cardiff (ENG)
20	Emil Hallfredsson	29/06/84		(1)		Udinese (ITA)
10	Gylfi Thór Sigurdsson	08/09/89	5		1	Swansea (ENG)
16	Rúnar Már Sigurjónsson	18/06/90				Sundsvall (SWE)
21	Arnór Ingvi Traustason	30/04/93		(1)		Norrköping (SWE)
Forwards						
15	Jón Dadi Bödvarsson	25/05/92	5		1	Kaiserslautern (GER)
11	Alfred Finnbogason	01/02/89		(3)		Augsburg (GER)
22	Eidur Smári Gudjohnsen	15/09/78		(2)		Molde (NOR)
9	Kolbeinn Sigthórsson	14/03/90	5		2	Nantes (FRA)

Northern Ireland

No	Name	DoB	Aps	(s)	Gls	Club
Goalkeepers						
12	Roy Carroll	30/09/77				Notts County (ENG)
23	Alan Mannus	19/05/82				St Johnstone (SCO)
1	Michael McGovern	12/07/84	4			Hamilton (SCO)
Defenders						
20	Craig Cathcart	06/02/89	4			Watford (ENG)
3	Jonny Evans	03/01/88	4			West Brom (ENG)
2	Shane Ferguson	12/07/91	1			Millwall (ENG)
12	Lee Hodson	02/10/91				MK Dons (ENG)
18	Aaron Hughes	08/11/79	3			Melbourne City (AUS)
4	Gareth McAuley	05/12/79	4		1	West Brom (ENG)
15	Luke McCullough	15/02/94				Doncaster (ENG)
2	Conor McLaughlin	26/07/91	1			Fleetwood (ENG)
Midfielders						
6	Chris Baird	25/02/82	1			Derby (ENG)
14	Stuart Dallas	19/04/91	3	(1)		Leeds (ENG)
8	Steven Davis	01/01/85	4			Southampton (ENG)
13	Corry Evans	30/07/90	3			Blackburn (ENG)
7	Niall McGinn	20/07/87		(3)	(1)	Aberdeen (SCO)
17	Paddy McNair	27/04/95	1	(1)		Man. United (ENG)
12	Oliver Norwood	12/04/91	4			Reading (ENG)
19	Jamie Ward	12/05/86	3	(1)		Nottingham Forest (ENG)
Forwards						
9	Will Grigg	03/07/91				Wigan (ENG)
10	Kyle Lafferty	16/09/87	2	(1)		Norwich (ENG)
21	Josh Magennis	15/08/90		(3)		Kilmarnock (SCO)
11	Conor Washington	18/05/92	2	(2)		QPR (ENG)

UEFA EURO 2016

Poland

No	Name	DoB	Aps	(s)	Gls	Club
Goalkeepers						
12	Artur Boruc	20/02/80				Bournemouth (ENG)
22	Łukasz Fabiański	18/04/85	4			Swansea (ENG)
1	Wojciech Szczęsny	18/04/90	1			Roma (ITA)
Defenders						
4	Thiago Cionek	21/04/86	1			Palermo (ITA)
15	Kamil Glik	03/02/88	5			Torino (ITA)
3	Artur Jędrzejczyk	04/11/87	5			Legia
2	Michał Pazdan	21/09/87	5			Legia
20	Łukasz Piszczek	03/06/85	4			Dortmund (GER)
18	Bartosz Salamon	01/05/91				Cagliari (ITA)
14	Jakub Wawrzyniak	07/07/83				Lechia
Midfielders						
16	Jakub Błaszczykowski	14/12/85	4	(1)	2	Fiorentina (ITA)
11	Kamil Grosicki	08/06/88	3	(2)		Rennes (FRA)
6	Tomasz Jodłowiec	08/09/85	1	(4)		Legia
21	Bartosz Kapustka	23/12/96	2	(2)		Cracovia
10	Grzegorz Krychowiak	29/01/90	5			Sevilla (ESP)
8	Karol Linetty	02/02/95				Lech
5	Krzysztof Mączyński	23/05/87	4			Wisła Kraków
17	Sławomir Peszko	19/02/85		(3)		Lechia
23	Filip Starzyński	27/05/91		(1)		Zagłębie
19	Piotr Zieliński	20/05/94	1			Empoli (ITA)
Forwards						
9	Robert Lewandowski	21/08/88	5		1	Bayern (GER)
7	Arkadiusz Milik	28/02/94	5		1	Ajax (NED)
13	Mariusz Stępiński	12/05/95				Ruch

Republic of Ireland

No	Name	DoB	Aps	(s)	Gls	Club
Goalkeepers						
16	Shay Given	20/04/76				Stoke (ENG)
23	Darren Randolph	12/05/87	4			West Ham (ENG)
1	Keiren Westwood	23/10/84				Sheffield Wednesday (ENG)
Defenders						
15	Cyrus Christie	30/09/92				Derby (ENG)
3	Ciaran Clark	26/09/89	2			Aston Villa (ENG)
2	Séamus Coleman	11/10/88	4			Everton (ENG)
12	Shane Duffy	01/01/92	2			Blackburn (ENG)
5	Richard Keogh	11/08/86	2			Derby (ENG)
4	John O'Shea	30/04/81	2	(1)		Sunderland (ENG)
17	Stephen Ward	20/08/85	3			Burnley (ENG)
Midfielders						
19	Robbie Brady	14/01/92	4		2	Norwich (ENG)
13	Jeff Hendrick	31/01/92	4			Derby (ENG)
20	Wes Hoolahan	20/05/82	2	(2)	1	Norwich (ENG)
8	James McCarthy	12/11/90	4			Everton (ENG)
11	James McClean	22/04/89	2	(2)		West Brom (ENG)
7	Aiden McGeady	04/04/86		(3)		Everton (ENG)
18	David Meyler	29/05/89				Hull (ENG)
22	Stephen Quinn	01/04/86		(1)		Reading (ENG)
6	Glenn Whelan	13/01/84	2			Stoke (ENG)
Forwards						
10	Robbie Keane	08/07/80		(2)		LA Galaxy (USA)
9	Shane Long	22/01/87	4			Southampton (ENG)
21	Daryl Murphy	15/03/83	2			Ipswich (ENG)
14	Jonathan Walters	20/09/83	1	(1)		Stoke (ENG)

Russia

No	Name	DoB	Aps	(s)	Gls	Club
Goalkeepers						
1	Igor Akinfeev	08/04/86	3			CSKA Moskva
16	Guilherme	12/12/85				Lokomotiv Moskva
12	Yuri Lodygin	26/05/90				Zenit
Defenders						
6	Aleksei Berezutski	20/06/82		(1)		CSKA Moskva
14	Vasili Berezutski	20/06/82	3		1	CSKA Moskva
4	Sergei Ignashevich	14/07/79	3			CSKA Moskva
23	Dmitri Kombarov	22/01/87	1			Spartak Moskva
21	Georgi Schennikov	27/04/91	2			CSKA Moskva
2	Roman Shishkin	27/01/87				Lokomotiv Moskva
3	Igor Smolnikov	08/08/88	3			Zenit
Midfielders						
8	Denis Glushakov	27/01/87	1	(2)	1	Spartak Moskva
13	Aleksandr Golovin	30/05/96	2	(1)		CSKA Moskva
18	Oleg Ivanov	04/08/86				Terek
11	Pavel Mamaev	17/09/88	1	(2)		Krasnodar
5	Roman Neustädter	18/02/88	2			Schalke (GER)
19	Aleksandr Samedov	19/07/84		(1)		Lokomotiv Moskva
17	Oleg Shatov	29/07/90	2			Zenit
15	Roman Shirokov	06/07/81	1	(2)		CSKA Moskva
20	Dmitri Torbinski	28/04/84				Krasnodar
7	Artur Yusupov	01/09/89				Zenit
Forwards						
22	Artem Dzyuba	22/08/88	3			Zenit
9	Aleksandr Kokorin	19/03/91	3			Zenit
10	Fedor Smolov	09/02/90	3			Krasnodar

Portugal

No	Name	DoB	Aps	(s)	Gls	Club
Goalkeepers						
12	Anthony Lopes	01/10/90				Lyon (FRA)
22	Eduardo	19/09/82				Dinamo Zagreb (CRO)
1	Rui Patrício	15/02/88	7			Sporting
Defenders						
2	Bruno Alves	27/11/81	1			Fenerbahçe (TUR)
21	Cédric	31/08/91	4			Southampton (ENG)
19	Eliseu	01/10/83	2			Benfica
4	José Fonte	22/12/83	4			Southampton (ENG)
3	Pepe	26/02/83	6			Real Madrid (ESP)
5	Raphael Guerreiro	22/12/93	5			Lorient (FRA)
6	Ricardo Carvalho	18/05/78	3			Monaco (FRA)
11	Vieirinha	24/01/86	3			Wolfsburg (GER)
Midfielders						
23	Adrien Silva	15/03/89	4			Sporting
15	André Gomes	30/07/93	4	(1)		Valencia (ESP)
13	Danilo Pereira	09/09/91	2	(3)		Porto
10	João Mário	19/01/93	6	(1)		Sporting
8	João Moutinho	08/09/86	3	(3)		Monaco (FRA)
18	Rafa Silva	17/05/93		(1)		Braga
16	Renato Sanches	18/08/97	3	(3)	1	Benfica
14	William Carvalho	07/04/92	5			Sporting
Forwards						
7	Cristiano Ronaldo	05/02/85	7		3	Real Madrid (ESP)
9	Éder	22/12/87		(3)	1	LOSC (FRA)
17	Nani	17/11/86	7		3	Fenerbahçe (TUR)
20	Ricardo Quaresma	26/09/83	1	(6)	1	Beşiktaş (TUR)

Romania

No	Name	DoB	Aps	(s)	Gls	Club
Goalkeepers						
23	Silviu Lung	04/06/89				Astra
1	Costel Pantilimon	01/02/87				Watford (ENG)
12	Ciprian Tătăruşanu	09/02/86	3			Fiorentina (ITA)
Defenders						
6	Vlad Chiricheş	14/11/89	3			Napoli (ITA)
16	Steliano Filip	15/05/94		(1)		Dinamo Bucureşti
15	Valerică Găman	25/02/89				Astra
21	Dragoş Grigore	07/09/86	3			Al-Sailiya (QAT)
2	Alexandru Măţel	17/10/89	1			Dinamo Zagreb (CRO)
4	Cosmin Moţi	03/12/84				Ludogorets (BUL)
3	Răzvan Raţ	26/05/81	2			Rayo Vallecano (ESP)
22	Cristian Săpunaru	05/04/84	3			Pandurii
Midfielders						
7	Alexandru Chipciu	18/05/89	1	(1)		Steaua
5	Ovidiu Hoban	27/12/82	2	(1)		H. Beer Sheva (ISR)
8	Mihai Pintilii	09/11/84	2			Steaua
20	Adrian Popa	24/07/88	2			Steaua
18	Andrei Prepeliţă	08/12/85	2			Ludogorets (BUL)
17	Lucian Sânmărtean	13/03/80		(1)		Al-Ittihad (KSA)
10	Nicolae Stanciu	07/05/93	2			Steaua
19	Bogdan Stancu	28/06/87	3		2	Gençlerbirliği (TUR)
11	Gabriel Torje	22/11/89	1	(2)		Osmanlıspor (TUR)
Forwards						
9	Denis Alibec	05/01/91	1	(1)		Astra
14	Florin Andone	11/04/93	1	(2)		Córdoba (ESP)
13	Claudiu Keşerü	02/12/86	1			Ludogorets (BUL)

Slovakia

No	Name	DoB	Aps	(s)	Gls	Club
Goalkeepers						
23	Matúš Kozáčik	27/12/83	4			Plzeň (CZE)
1	Ján Mucha	05/12/82				Slovan Bratislava
12	Ján Novota	29/11/83				Rapid Wien (AUT)
Defenders						
4	Ján Ďurica	10/12/81	4			Lokomotiv Moskva (RUS)
5	Norbert Gyömber	03/07/92	1	(1)		Roma (ITA)
15	Tomáš Hubočan	17/09/85	2			Dinamo Moskva (RUS)
2	Peter Pekarík	30/10/86	4			Hertha (GER)
16	Kornel Saláta	24/01/85		(1)		Slovan Bratislava
14	Milan Škriniar	11/02/95	1	(1)		Sampdoria (ITA)
3	Martin Škrtel	15/12/84	4			Liverpool (ENG)
18	Dušan Švento	01/08/85	1	(2)		Köln (GER)
Midfielders						
8	Ondrej Duda	05/12/94	2	(1)	1	Legia (POL)
6	Ján Greguš	29/01/91		(1)		Jablonec (CZE)
17	Marek Hamšík	27/07/87	4		1	Napoli (ITA)
13	Patrik Hrošovský	22/04/92	2			Plzeň (CZE)
19	Juraj Kucka	26/02/87	4			Milan (ITA)
20	Róbert Mak	08/03/91	3			PAOK (GRE)
22	Viktor Pečovský	24/05/83	2			Žilina
10	Miroslav Stoch	19/10/89		(1)		Bursaspor (TUR)
7	Vladimír Weiss	30/11/89	4		1	Al-Gharafa (QAT)
Forwards						
21	Michal Ďuriš	01/06/88	2	(1)		Plzeň (CZE)
11	Adam Nemec	02/09/85		(2)		Willem II (NED)
9	Stanislav Šesták	16/12/82		(1)		Ferencváros (HUN)

Spain

No	Name	DoB	Aps	(s)	Gls	Club
Goalkeepers						
1	Iker Casillas	20/05/81				Porto (POR)
13	David de Gea	07/11/90	4			Man. United (ENG)
23	Sergio Rico	01/09/93				Sevilla
Defenders						
2	César Azpilicueta	28/08/89		(1)		Chelsea (ENG)
4	Marc Bartra	15/01/91				Barcelona
12	Héctor Bellerín	19/03/95				Arsenal (ENG)
18	Jordi Alba	21/03/89	4			Barcelona
16	Juanfran	09/01/85	4			Atlético
3	Gerard Piqué	02/02/87	4		1	Barcelona
17	Mikel San José	30/05/89				Athletic
15	Sergio Ramos	30/03/86	4			Real Madrid
Midfielders						
19	Bruno Soriano	12/06/84		(2)		Villarreal
5	Sergio Busquets	16/07/88	4			Barcelona
10	Cesc Fàbregas	04/05/87	4			Chelsea (ENG)
6	Andrés Iniesta	11/05/84	4			Barcelona
8	Koke	08/01/92		(1)		Atlético
21	David Silva	08/01/86	4			Man. City (ENG)
14	Thiago Alcántara	11/04/91		(2)		Bayern (GER)
Forwards						
20	Aritz Aduriz	11/02/81		(3)		Athletic
9	Lucas Vázquez	01/07/91		(1)		Real Madrid
7	Álvaro Morata	23/10/92	4		3	Juventus (ITA)
22	Nolito	15/10/86	4		1	Celta
11	Pedro Rodríguez	28/07/87		(2)		Chelsea (ENG)

Switzerland

No	Name	DoB	Aps	(s)	Gls	Club
Goalkeepers						
21	Roman Bürki	14/11/90				Dortmund (GER)
12	Marwin Hitz	18/09/87				Augsburg (GER)
1	Yann Sommer	17/12/88	4			Mönchengladbach (GER)
Defenders						
20	Johan Djourou	18/01/87	4			Hamburg (GER)
4	Nico Elvedi	30/09/96				Mönchengladbach (GER)
6	Michael Lang	08/02/91		(2)		Basel
2	Stephan Lichtsteiner	16/01/84	4			Juventus (ITA)
3	François Moubandje	21/06/90				Toulouse (FRA)
13	Ricardo Rodriguez	25/08/92	4			Wolfsburg (GER)
22	Fabian Schär	20/12/91	4		1	Hoffenheim (GER)
5	Steve von Bergen	10/06/83				Young Boys
Midfielders						
11	Valon Behrami	19/04/85	4			Watford (ENG)
15	Blerim Džemaili	12/04/86	4			Genoa (ITA)
16	Gelson Fernandes	02/09/86		(3)		Rennes (FRA)
8	Fabian Frei	08/01/89		(1)		Mainz (GER)
18	Admir Mehmedi	16/03/91	4		1	Leverkusen (GER)
23	Xherdan Shaqiri	10/10/91	4		1	Stoke (ENG)
10	Granit Xhaka	27/09/92	4			Mönchengladbach (GER)
14	Denis Zakaria	20/11/96				Young Boys
Forwards						
19	Eren Derdiyok	12/06/88		(1)		Kasımpaşa (TUR)
7	Breel Embolo	14/02/97	1	(3)		Basel
9	Haris Seferovic	22/02/92	3	(1)		Eintracht Frankfurt (GER)
17	Shani Tarashaj	07/02/95		(1)		Grasshoppers

Ukraine

No	Name	DoB	Aps	(s)	Gls	Club
Goalkeepers						
1	Denys Boyko	29/01/88				Beşiktaş (TUR)
12	Andriy Pyatov	28/06/84	3			Shakhtar Donetsk
23	Mykyta Shevchenko	26/01/93				Zorya
Defenders						
2	Bohdan Butko	13/01/91	1			Amkar (RUS)
17	Artem Fedetskiy	26/04/85	3			Dnipro
3	Yevhen Khacheridi	28/07/87	3			Dynamo Kyiv
5	Olexandr Kucher	22/10/82	1			Shakhtar Donetsk
20	Yaroslav Rakitskiy	03/08/89	2			Shakhtar Donetsk
13	Vyacheslav Shevchuk	13/05/79	2			Shakhtar Donetsk
Midfielders						
19	Denys Garmash	19/04/90		(1)		Dynamo Kyiv
22	Olexandr Karavaev	02/06/92				Zorya
10	Yevhen Konoplyanka	29/09/89	3			Sevilla (ESP)
9	Viktor Kovalenko	14/02/96	2	(1)		Shakhtar Donetsk
14	Ruslan Rotan	29/10/81	1			Dnipro
18	Serhiy Rybalka	01/04/90				Dynamo Kyiv
6	Taras Stepanenko	08/08/89	3			Shakhtar Donetsk
16	Serhiy Sydorchuk	02/05/91	2			Dynamo Kyiv
4	Anatoliy Tymoshchuk	30/03/79		(1)		Kairat (KAZ)
7	Andriy Yarmolenko	23/10/89	3			Dynamo Kyiv
21	Olexandr Zinchenko	15/12/96	1	(2)		Ufa (RUS)
Forwards						
15	Pylyp Budkivskiy	10/03/92				Zorya
11	Yevhen Seleznyov	20/07/85	1	(1)		Shakhtar Donetsk
8	Roman Zozulya	17/11/89	2	(1)		Dnipro

Sweden

No	Name	DoB	Aps	(s)	Gls	Club
Goalkeepers						
23	Patrik Carlgren	08/01/92				AIK
1	Andreas Isaksson	03/10/81	3			Kasımpaşa (TUR)
12	Robin Olsen	08/01/90				København (DEN)
Defenders						
17	Ludwig Augustinsson	21/04/94				København (DEN)
4	Andreas Granqvist	16/04/85	3			Krasnodar (RUS)
13	Pontus Jansson	13/02/91				Torino (ITA)
3	Erik Johansson	30/12/88	2	(1)		København (DEN)
2	Mikael Lustig	13/12/86	1			Celtic (SCO)
14	Victor Nilsson-Lindelöf	17/07/94	3			Benfica (POR)
5	Martin Olsson	17/05/88	3			Norwich (ENG)
Midfielders						
21	Jimmy Durmaz	22/03/89		(2)		Olympiacos (GRE)
8	Albin Ekdal	28/07/89	2	(1)		Hamburg (GER)
6	Emil Forsberg	23/10/91	3			RB Leipzig (GER)
15	Oscar Hiljemark	28/06/92				Palermo (ITA)
9	Kim Källström	24/08/82	3			Grasshoppers (SUI)
7	Sebastian Larsson	06/06/85	3			Sunderland (ENG)
18	Oscar Lewicki	14/07/92	1	(1)		Malmö
16	Pontus Wernbloom	25/06/86				CSKA Moskva (RUS)
22	Erkan Zengin	05/08/85		(1)		Trabzonspor (TUR)
Forwards						
11	Marcus Berg	17/08/86	2	(1)		Panathinaikos (GRE)
20	John Guidetti	15/04/92	1	(2)		Celta (ESP)
10	Zlatan Ibrahimović	03/10/81	3			Man. United (ENG)
19	Emir Kujovic	22/06/88				Norrköping

Turkey

No	Name	DoB	Aps	(s)	Gls	Club
Goalkeepers						
23	Harun Tekin	17/06/89				Bursaspor
12	Onur Kıvrak	01/01/88				Trabzonspor
1	Volkan Babacan	11/08/88	3			İstanbul Başakşehir
Defenders						
4	Ahmet Çalık	26/02/94				Gençlerbirliği
18	Caner Erkin	04/10/88	2			Fenerbahçe
7	Gökhan Gönül	04/01/85	3			Fenerbahçe
3	Hakan Balta	23/03/83	3			Galatasaray
13	İsmail Köybaşı	10/07/89	1			Beşiktaş
15	Mehmet Topal	03/03/86	3			Fenerbahçe
2	Semih Kaya	24/02/91				Galatasaray
22	Şener Özbayraklı	23/01/90				Fenerbahçe
Midfielders						
10	Arda Turan	30/01/87	3			Barcelona (ESP)
21	Emre Mor	24/07/97	1	(1)		Nordsjælland (DEN)
6	Hakan Çalhanoğlu	08/02/94	2			Leverkusen (GER)
5	Nuri Şahin	05/09/88	1			Dortmund (GER)
14	Oğuzhan Özyakup	23/09/92	2	(1)		Beşiktaş
11	Olcay Şahan	26/05/87		(2)		Beşiktaş
20	Ozan Tufan	23/03/95	3		1	Fenerbahçe
8	Selçuk İnan	10/02/85	3			Galatasaray
17	Volkan Şen	07/07/87	1	(1)		Fenerbahçe
9	Yunus Mallı	24/02/92				Mainz (GER)
Forwards						
17	Burak Yılmaz	15/07/85	2	(1)	1	Beijing Guoan (CHN)
9	Cenk Tosun	07/06/91	1	(1)		Beşiktaş

Wales

No	Name	DoB	Aps	(s)	Gls	Club
Goalkeepers						
1	Wayne Hennessey	24/01/87	5			Crystal Palace (ENG)
13	Danny Ward	22/06/93	1			Liverpool (ENG)
12	Owain Fon Williams	17/03/87				Inverness (SCO)
Defenders						
5	James Chester	23/01/89	6			West Brom (ENG)
19	James Collins	23/08/83	1	(1)		West Ham (ENG)
4	Ben Davies	24/04/93	5			Tottenham (ENG)
2	Chris Gunter	21/07/89	6			Reading (ENG)
15	Ashley Richards	12/04/91		(1)		Fulham (ENG)
3	Neil Taylor	07/02/89	6		1	Swansea (ENG)
6	Ashley Williams	23/08/84	6		1	Swansea (ENG)
Midfielders						
7	Joe Allen	14/03/90	6			Liverpool (ENG)
17	David Cotterill	04/12/87				Birmingham (ENG)
14	David Edwards	03/02/86	1	(2)		Wolves (ENG)
8	Andy King	29/10/88	1	(2)		Leicester (ENG)
16	Joe Ledley	23/01/87	5	(1)		Crystal Palace (ENG)
10	Aaron Ramsey	26/12/90	5		1	Arsenal (ENG)
22	David Vaughan	18/02/83				Nottingham Forest (ENG)
13	George Williams	07/09/95				Fulham (ENG)
20	Jonathan Williams	09/10/93	1	(3)		Crystal Palace (ENG)
Forwards						
11	Gareth Bale	16/07/89	6		3	Real Madrid (ESP)
23	Simon Church	10/12/88		(2)		MK Dons (ENG)
9	Hal Robson-Kanu	21/05/89	3	(2)	2	Reading (ENG)
18	Sam Vokes	21/10/89	2	(2)	1	Burnley (ENG)

EUROPEAN QUALIFIERS ™

First-timers take centre stage

The expansion of the UEFA European Championship final tournament to 24 teams ensured an eventful and exciting qualifying competition. Encouraged by the easier access, a number of countries that had never previously participated at the European finals – or indeed the FIFA World Cup – found the strength and resolve to make UEFA EURO 2016 a tournament to remember.

No fewer than six countries reached the EURO finals for the first time. Northern Ireland even managed it as group winners, while Iceland, Wales, Slovakia and Albania all went through as runners-up, with Hungary sealing their place in France via

the play-offs. Two other nations, Austria and Ukraine, also achieved a first successful qualification for the finals, their only previous involvement having been as tournament co-hosts.

Austria were one of the standout teams of the qualifying competition. Marcel Koller's side drew their opening fixture but won each of the next nine to complete their campaign with 28 points out of a possible 30. England surpassed even that tally, Roy Hodgson's team winning all ten of their Group E fixtures and scoring 31 goals – a figure bettered only by Group D runners-up Poland, whose final haul of 33 included 13 for captain Robert Lewandowski, which equalled the qualifying competition record.

England and Austria were two of four undefeated qualifiers, the others being Group H winners Italy and Group F runners-up Romania, who, with just two goals conceded, boasted the competition's best defence. Two other nations also ended the competition on hot streaks, with holders Spain heading for France on a run of eight successive Group C victories and Portugal on a roll of seven straight wins in Group I.

Not all of the established powers prospered. The biggest shock of all was the non-qualification of 1988 winners and 2014 World Cup semi-finalists the Netherlands, who could finish only fourth in Group A behind the Czech Republic, Iceland and Turkey, the latter dramatically seizing the automatic qualifying place reserved for the best third-placed team with a late winner in their final game. Other former European champions absent from the 2016 party were Denmark, defeated in a play-off by neighbours Sweden, and Greece, who sensationally finished bottom of Group F. There was misery too for Scotland. They fell away at the end to finish fourth in Group D behind the Republic of Ireland, whose subsequent play-off win enabled them to make the short journey to France alongside fellow British Isles qualifiers England, Northern Ireland and Wales.

Gareth Bale (centre) leads the celebrations in Cardiff as Wales qualify for UEFA EURO 2016

Group A

On top of the Group A table going into the final four fixtures, Iceland faced a major test of their qualifying credentials when they travelled to the Netherlands in early September. They would pass it with flying colours, Gylfi Sigurdsson's 51st-minute penalty adding another three points to their total from a game that summed up the two teams' contrasting fortunes, with the Oranje having defender Bruno Martins Indi red-carded for a reckless challenge in the first half. While Iceland won on matchday seven, so did the Czech Republic, two late headers from substitute Milan Škoda enabling them to defeat Kazakhstan 2-1 in Plzen. With Turkey conceding a stoppage-time equaliser at home to Latvia, things were looking good for the top two, and, sure enough, three days later they were both celebrating their qualification.

Iceland needed only a point at home to Kazakhstan, and that is what they got, in a cagey 0-0 draw, to secure a place at a major tournament for the first time. Jubilation in Reykjavik was matched in Riga, where a brilliant long-range strike from Vladimír Darida proved decisive as Czech Republic downed Latvia 2-1 while the Netherlands' nightmare continued against Turkey in Konya. Danny Blind's side were beaten 3-0, enabling their conquerors to leapfrog them into third place.

Buoyed by that big win, Fatih Terim's side would claim another three points on their next outing, beating the Czech Republic 2-0 in Prague, and although the Netherlands kept their hopes alive with a 2-1 win in Kazakhstan, their inferior head-to-head record against Turkey meant their only chance of survival was to beat the Czechs at home in their final fixture and hope for a home defeat for Turkey against Iceland. In the event, neither outcome occurred. Instead, the Oranje suffered another calamity in Amsterdam, losing 3-2, while ten-man Turkey snatched a dramatic 1-0 win with a brilliant 89th-minute free-kick from Selçuk İnan. Not only did that clinch third place, it also secured Turkey's automatic qualification thanks to Kazakhstan's 1-0 victory in Latvia, which meant those two teams swapped places at the foot of the table and Turkey's six points against Kazakhstan (rather than the two gained against Latvia) now entered the equation in the ranking of the nine third-placed teams, putting them top of the table ahead of Hungary.

Burak Yılmaz (No17) completes the scoring for Turkey in a crucial 3-0 win at home to the Netherlands

Group B

Wales' first qualification for a major tournament in 58 years seemed almost a foregone conclusion after they had beaten Belgium in Cardiff and built up a five-point gap between themselves and third place. They reinforced their position by defeating Cyprus in Nicosia, the talismanic Gareth Bale proving to be the match-winning hero once again with a thumping late header – his sixth goal of the competition. However, needing a win at home to Israel to clinch their ticket to France, they disappointed a capacity crowd in the Cardiff City Stadium by only drawing 0-0. Ironically, and perhaps with a sense of anti-climax, it was after their first defeat, 2-0 away to Bosnia & Herzegovina a month later, that their qualification was confirmed.

It was Israel's simultaneous 2-1 home defeat to Cyprus that assured Wales of a top-two finish, which they celebrated back home three days later with a closing 2-0 win against Andorra. Belgium also confirmed their place in France on matchday nine, with a 4-1 win in Andorra, before beating Wales to top spot with a 3-1 home win over Israel, in which Eden Hazard scored for the fourth successive qualifier, all of those goals contributing to victories.

That result in Brussels ended Israel's hopes of taking third spot, which would go to Cyprus if they could beat Bosnia & Herzegovina in Nicosia. They actually came from behind to lead, but only for three minutes, as Haris Medunjanin equalised with his second well-taken goal of the evening before substitute Milan Djurić's 67th-minute header won the game and carried Bosnia & Herzegovina into the play-offs.

Group C

Slovakia's 100 % record ended on matchday seven – as did their lengthy stint as group leaders – with a 2-0 defeat to Spain in Oviedo, first-half goals from Jordi Alba – a header – and Andrés Iniesta – a penalty – giving the holders their fifth successive victory. They would stretch that run to eight on the trot by overcoming FYR Macedonia, Luxembourg and Ukraine – all without conceding a goal – as they headed to France in style. Confirmation of their qualification as group winners came on matchday nine, when two goals apiece from Santi Cazorla and Paco Alcácer disposed of Luxembourg in Logrono.

After their dynamic early burst of wins, Slovakia's first EURO qualification looked inevitable, but Ján Kozák's side struggled to get the job done. A 0-0 draw at home to Ukraine was a decent outcome as it kept them three points ahead of their direct rivals for the runners-up spot and with a superior head-to-head record, but a subsequent 1-0 defeat to Belarus kept their supporters on edge, and it was only on matchday ten, with a Marek Hamšík-inspired 4-2 win in Luxembourg, that Slovakia's safe passage to France was secured.

Ukraine needed to beat Spain at home in any case to put pressure on Slovakia, but on a night of inspired goalkeeping – mostly from Spain's David de Gea but also from Ukraine's Andriy Pyatov, who saved a Cesc Fàbregas penalty – it was a first-half header from Spain's debutant right-back Mario Gaspar that won the day.

Group D

Poland went into the last stretch of the qualifying campaign on top of Group D, but they were replaced there after matchday seven by Germany, who avenged their 2-0 defeat in Warsaw by overcoming Adam Nawałka's side 3-1 in Frankfurt. All four scorers were Bayern München players, with Thomas Müller opening the scoring for Germany, Mario Götze adding a double and Robert Lewandowski finding the net for Poland. Indeed, another Bayern player, Manuel Neuer, also distinguished himself, pulling off a fantastic save from Lewandowski with the score at 2-1.

Germany would score three goals again a few days later as they inflicted a second damaging defeat in a week on Scotland. Gordon Strachan's side had lost 1-0 to Georgia in Tbilisi, but they could not redeem themselves in front of their own fans despite twice coming from behind to cancel out goals from Müller, who also set up İlkay Gündoğan's winner. To deepen the Glaswegian gloom, the Republic of Ireland followed up a routine win in Gibraltar by defeating Scotland's conquerors Georgia 1-0 in Dublin – thanks to a Jonathan Walters goal superbly set up by Jeff Hendrick.

All was still to play for, but matchday nine ended Scotland's interest as they conceded a scrappy late equaliser to Poland at Hampden – Lewandowski bundling home for his second goal of the evening after two superb strikes from Matt Ritchie and Steven Fletcher had given the home side the lead – while Ireland sensationally beat the world champions 1-0 in Dublin. Shane Long scored the goal that inflicted a second defeat of the competition on Germany, latching on to a long punt from goalkeeper Darren Randolph before smashing the ball past Neuer.

A late sitter missed by Müller in Dublin left Germany still unsure of their place in France. However, with a one-point lead over both Poland and Ireland, who faced off in Warsaw, they needed only one further point at home to Georgia. Unsurprisingly, they got all three, Max Kruse's calmly converted strike giving

Joachim Löw's side a 2-1 win and first place in the group. That was also the final scoreline in the Polish capital, where a brilliant Lewandowski header – his 13th goal of the competition – secured all three points for Poland after a Walters penalty had cancelled out a fine early Grzegorz Krychowiak strike. A second equaliser would have lifted the visitors above their hosts on the head-to-head rule but Poland held firm to reach their third EURO finals in succession and send Martin O'Neill's men into the play-offs.

Group E

England became the first team to book a place at the finals alongside hosts France with a routine 6-0 win over San Marino on matchday seven. Captain Wayne Rooney opened the scoring with a penalty that matched Bobby Charlton's all-time record of 49 goals for England, and he claimed the distinction all for himself when, three days later, against Switzerland at Wembley, he converted another spot kick to reach the magical half-century. That historic goal doubled England's lead, following a well-struck opener from Harry Kane, and wrapped up an eighth successive win for Roy Hodgson's team. The Three Lions had never previously won every game in a qualifying campaign, but further victories – without the injured Rooney – over Estonia (2-0 at home) and Lithuania (3-0 away) ensured that they qualified for France with a flawless record.

Switzerland's 2-0 defeat at Wembley was not as costly as it might have been, because three days earlier Vladimir

Petković's side had snatched victory from the jaws of defeat at home to their main challengers for second place, Slovenia. Two goals down with 10 minutes remaining, they fought back to win 3-2, with substitute Josip Drmic's winning goal not arriving until deep into added time.

Slovenia's subsequent 1-0 win against Estonia in Maribor kept them in contention, but the following month they could only draw 1-1 in Ljubljana against Lithuania, and that allowed Switzerland to book their qualifying spot with a game to spare as they put San Marino to the sword in St Gallen, six second-half goals bringing seven in total – their opponents' heaviest defeat of the competition. Slovenia would only score twice against the group's bottom team three days later, but it was more than enough to guarantee their play-off place.

Group F

The Faroe Islands had provided one of the upsets of the qualifying campaign by twice defeating Greece, but they were unable to halt the charge of Northern Ireland when they hosted Michael O'Neill's side on matchday six. The night belonged to visiting defender Gareth McAuley, who headed in twice before Kyle Lafferty concluded a 3-1 win with his sixth goal of the competition. Three days later the big striker would be called upon again, deep into injury time, to salvage a last-gasp 1-1 draw with ten men at home to Hungary.

Victory in that Windsor Park encounter would have clinched Northern Ireland's qualification, and the same scenario

Wayne Rooney scores his record-breaking 50th goal for England with a penalty against Switzerland at Wembley

Group H

A mere 12,551 spectators were present in Florence to see Italy go top of Group H with a 1-0 win over Malta on matchday seven. It was a poor game, decided by an appropriately scrappy goal that went in off Graziano Pellè's knee, but with Croatia surprisingly drawing 0-0 in Azerbaijan – a team they had beaten 6-0 at home – the three points enabled Antonio Conte's side to leapfrog their rivals into first place. It was a position they protected three days later in Palermo with another low-key 1-0 win, during which long-serving midfielder Daniele De Rossi scored the winning penalty and was also sent off.

Croatia's campaign went from bad to worse when they lost 2-0 to Norway in Oslo, Jo Inge Berget scoring the first goal with a neat turn and strike and then seeing another shot deflected in off Vedran Ćorluka. The victory enabled Norway, victorious also in Bulgaria three days earlier, to go second in the table, prompting Croatia to sack coach Niko Kovač and replace him with the more experienced Ante Čačić. The new man duly got the team back on track with a 3-0 home win over Bulgaria, although there were no spectators there to see it – a legacy of previous misdemeanours by the Zagreb public. Ivan Perišić, Ivan Rakitić and Nikola Kalinic scored the goals that kept Croatia two points adrift of Norway, who beat Malta 2-0 in Oslo, while Italy wrapped up qualification with a game to spare thanks to a 3-1 win in Azerbaijan.

Croatia needed help from Italy on the final matchday to join them in France. If Norway won in Rome, they would take the runners-up spot, whereas Čačić's men had to win in Malta and hope that the Azzurri's unbeaten record would be preserved. For over an hour in the Stadio Olimpico, following Alexander Tettey's rasping left-footed half-volley, Norway were on course for a fourth straight win and qualification. But a defensive misunderstanding allowed Alessandro Florenzi to equalise, and as Norway pressed forward, Italy won the game with a late breakaway strike from Pellè. The final whistle in Rome was greeted with joy a few hundred kilometers to the south by Croatia, who had got the win they needed thanks to a deflected early strike from Perišić.

Group I

The qualifying competition's only five-team section had begun with a shock home defeat for Portugal against Albania, but coach Fernando Santos

Austria's Zlatko Junuzovic pounces to score against Moldova in Vienna

presented itself when they returned there to face Greece a month later. This time the men in green seized the day, with skipper Steven Davis stealing the limelight in the absence of the suspended Lafferty with two vital goals in a superb 3-1 win that secured the country's first major tournament qualification for 30 years.

Romania, who drew 0-0 against both Hungary and Greece in September, finally ended a goal drought lasting 429 minutes when Ovidiu Hoban tapped in a last-gasp equaliser in their penultimate fixture, against Finland in Bucharest. It was a crucial goal as it kept qualification in Romania's hands, a one-point lead over Hungary – who came from behind to beat the Faroe Islands with two Dániel Böde goals – enabling them to travel to Torshavn knowing that a win would take them through. They duly got it, with Constantin Budescu's two first-half goals firing them towards France as Hungary, defeated 4-3 in a dead rubber against Greece, were forced to wait to see if their 15 points against the teams placed first, second, fourth and fifth in the group would be enough to bring automatic qualification as the best third-placed team. Alas, two results in Group A two days later conspired to despatch them into the play-offs instead.

Group G

There was no stopping Austria as they won their last four matches to make it nine victories on the spin in Group G and finish eight points clear. The country's first successful UEFA European Championship qualifying campaign peaked with the result that confirmed their place in France – a brilliant 4-1 victory over Sweden at the Friends Arena on matchday eight. David Alaba's early penalty set the tone for an extraordinary one-sided display. Austria would add another six goals to their total the following month in overcoming Montenegro and Liechtenstein, the comeback 3-2 win in Podgorica sealed late on thanks to a clinical strike from substitute Marcel Sabitzer.

That result ended Montenegro's hopes of finishing in the top three, but although they were out, their matchday ten hosts Russia still needed a point in Moscow to guarantee a second-place finish ahead of Sweden. With CSKA Moskva boss Leonid Slutski having replaced Fabio Capello as coach, Russia had won three games in a row, the first of them a crucial 1-0 victory against Sweden in which centre-forward Artem Dzyuba struck the decisive goal. Dzyuba scored four more in a 7-0 win over Liechtenstein later that week plus another in a 2-1 victory away to Moldova, but it was defender Oleg Kuzmin, on his first international start, who opened the scoring against Montenegro before Aleksandr Kokorin sealed victory shortly afterwards from the penalty spot.

Russia's 2-0 win rendered Sweden's victory by the same scoreline at home to Moldova academic – Erik Hamrén's side had already secured third place and their opponents were guaranteed to finish sixth – but it gave Zlatan Ibrahimović the opportunity to score his eighth goal of the campaign and get his shooting boots ready for the play-offs.

and his players would exact appropriate revenge a year to the day later in Elbasan as midfielder Miguel Veloso powered in a stoppage-time header to give Portugal their fifth successive victory and strengthen their position at the top of the Group I table.

Needing just one more point to secure a sixth successive appearance at the EURO finals, Portugal were to qualify in style, with a game to spare, João Moutinho's excellent strike defeating Denmark in Braga and maintaining his team's winning run. That was Denmark's final group fixture, and coming after goalless draws against Albania and Armenia, it left automatic qualification out of their hands.

The onus was on Albania to seize the opportunity to qualify for their first major tournament. They could not do it at home, losing not only to Portugal but also to Serbia, where again they conceded in added time, not once but twice. The third and last chance for Gianni De Biasi's side to make history was away to bottom-of-the-table Armenia. A point behind Denmark, who held the head-to-head advantage, Albania had to win, and win they did, in emphatic fashion, putting three goals without reply past their hosts, with striker Armando Sadiku wrapping up a momentous victory 14 minutes from time. As Albania rejoiced and Denmark despaired, Portugal concluded their campaign with yet another win, 2-1 in Belgrade, thanks to another pearler from Moutinho.

Play-offs

The draw for the play-offs yielded four well-balanced ties, with the fate of the eight teams, and the allocation of the final four spots at UEFA EURO 2016, to be decided over six tension-filled evenings in mid-November.

The Ullevaal Stadion in Oslo was the setting for the first of the eight matches, and it would result in a 1-0 win for visitors Hungary. If the outcome was a surprise, so too was the identity of the match-winner, László Kleinheisler. It took the energetic young midfielder just 26 minutes of his first international to lash an instinctive left-foot shot past Norway 'keeper Ørjan Håskjold Nyland and give Hungary the lead, and although the home side created several chances to draw level, they could not score. Three days later in Budapest, an expectant capacity crowd in the Groupama Aréna were lifted from their seats 14 minutes in as Tamás Priskin received a long ball on the left and cut inside before smashing a brilliant

shot into the far corner. With a two-goal cushion, Hungary just needed to defend well to reach their first final tournament since the 1986 World Cup. With veteran custodian Gábor Király in fine form, they kept the Norwegian attack at bay, and although they conceded late on, to Markus Henriksen, that goal arrived four minutes after the Norway striker had put through his own net to increase Hungary's lead. The final whistle was greeted with an eruption of joy as a nation's 30 years of hurt came to an end.

The closing stages of Bosnia & Herzegovina's home leg against the Republic of Ireland in Celje were played in a thick mist, yet that was when the game's two goals were scored – the first, on 82 minutes, from Ireland midfielder Robbie Brady, the second, three minutes later, from local hero Edin Džeko, his eighth of the competition. The 1-1 scoreline gave Ireland the advantage going into the Dublin return, and Martin O'Neill's side made it count in front of a capacity crowd, with Walters scoring both goals in a hard-fought 2-0 win – the first from a rather fortuitous penalty, the second from a neat far-post volley.

The Scandinavian derby between Sweden and Denmark was, as expected, keenly contested, but it was the team in yellow and blue who emerged triumphant after the two legs, the second of them, in Copenhagen, settled by a brilliant double from Swedish goal king Ibrahimović. The Paris Saint-Germain striker scored his first goal of the tie from the penalty spot to give Sweden a 2-0 lead at the Friends

Arena, Emil Forsberg having opened the scoring with a sweeping cross-shot just before the interval. A late Nicolai Jørgensen strike made the final score 2-1, giving Denmark considerable hope for the return three days later. However, Ibrahimović would strengthen Sweden's grip, opening the scoring with a neat flick from a well-rehearsed corner routine and then, 14 minutes from time, curling in a wonderful free-kick to beat Danish 'keeper Kasper Schmeichel – who had made an amazing save from a similar effort in the first leg – and seal Sweden's place in France. Denmark scored twice in the closing minutes, but it was too little too late in what would be Morten Olsen's last game as coach after over 15 years' service.

Ukraine had lost all five of their previous qualifying play-offs, but they would finally make it sixth time lucky, seeing off Slovenia, one of their previous play-off conquerors, after a 2-0 win in Lviv and a last-gasp 1-1 draw in Maribor. A goal from Andriy Yarmolenko – converted, unusually, with his right foot – was supplemented by a second, tapped in by Yevhen Seleznyov, as Mykhailo Fomenko's side took control in the first leg, but there were to be many anxious moments for Ukraine three days later following Slovenia skipper Boštjan Cesar's early close-range header. However, with the home side down to ten men and becoming increasingly desperate to level the tie, Ukraine broke away in the seventh minute of added time, with Artem Kravets unselfishly laying the ball square for Yarmolenko to knock the ball into the empty net and take his country to UEFA EURO 2016.

Zlatan Ibrahimović celebrates a brilliant free-kick that gives Sweden a 2-0 lead against Denmark in Copenhagen

Qualifying round

Group A

09/09/14
Iceland 3-0 Turkey
Czech Republic 2-1 Netherlands
Kazakhstan 0-0 Latvia

10/10/14
Netherlands 3-1 Kazakhstan
Latvia 0-3 Iceland
Turkey 1-2 Czech Republic

13/10/14
Iceland 2-0 Netherlands
Latvia 1-1 Turkey
Kazakhstan 2-4 Czech Republic

16/11/14
Netherlands 6-0 Latvia
Czech Republic 2-1 Iceland
Turkey 3-1 Kazakhstan

28/03/15
Czech Republic 1-1 Latvia
Netherlands 1-1 Turkey
Kazakhstan 0-3 Iceland

12/06/15
Iceland 2-1 Czech Republic
Latvia 0-2 Netherlands
Kazakhstan 0-1 Turkey

03/09/15, Doosan Arena, Plzen (att: 10,572)
Czech Republic 2-1 Kazakhstan
Goals: 0-1 Logvinenko 21, 1-1 Škoda 74,
2-1 Škoda 86
Referee: Strömbergsson (SWE)
Czech Republic: Čech, Kadeřábek, Procházka,
Limberský, Dočkal, Skalák (Škoda 46), Pavelka,
Suchý, Krejčí (Kopic 84), Lafata, Darida (Šural
68). Coach: Pavel Vrba (CZE)
Kazakhstan: Pokatilov, Maliy, Gurman, Kuat,
Konysbayev (Kukeyev 88), Smakov, Islamkhan
(Suyumbayev 78), Nuserbayev (Khizhnichenko
72), Shomko, Dzholchiev, Logvinenko. Coach:
Yuri Krasnozhan (RUS)

*03/09/15, Amsterdam ArenA, Amsterdam
(att: 50,275)*
Netherlands 0-1 Iceland
Goal: 0-1 G Sigurdsson 51(p)
Referee: Mažić (SRB)
Netherlands: Cillessen, Van der Wiel, De Vrij,
Martins Indi, Blind, Klaassen, Depay, Wijnaldum
(Promes 80), Huntelaar (Bruma 40), Sneijder,
Robben (Narsingh 31). Coach: Danny Blind (NED)
Iceland: Halldórsson, Sævarsson, R Sigurdsson,
Gudmundsson, B Bjarnason, Sigthórsson
(Gudjohnsen 64), G Sigurdsson, Árnason,
Bödvarsson (Kjartansson 78), Gunnarsson
(Ó Skúlason 86), A Skúlason. Coach: Lars
Lagerbäck (SWE) & Heimir Hallgrímsson (ISL)
Red card: Martins Indi 33 (Netherlands)

*03/09/15, Konya Büyükşehir
Stadyumu, Konya (att: 35,900)*
Turkey 1-1 Latvia
Goals: 1-0 Selçuk İnan 77, 1-1 Šabala 90+1
Referee: Johannesson (SWE)
Turkey: Volkan Babacan, Şener Özbayraklı,
Hakan Balta, Serdar Aziz, Hakan Çalhanoğlu,
Selçuk İnan, Arda Turan,
Gökhan Töre (Şener Özbayraklı 58), Ozan Tufan,
Burak Yılmaz (Mehmet Topal 84), Volkan Şen
(Umut Bulut 56). Coach: Fatih Terim
(TUR)
Latvia: Vaņins, Maksimenko, Dubra, Laizāns
(E Višņakovs 82), Gabovs, A Višņakovs, Cauņa
(Zjuzins 60), Karašausks (Šabala 85), Rakels,
Tarasovs, Jagodinskis. Coach: Marians Pahars
(LVA)

Pavel Kadeřábek – on target for the Czech Republic
in Amsterdam against the Netherlands

06/09/15, Laugardalsvöllur, Reykjavik (att: 9,767)
Iceland 0-0 Kazakhstan
Referee: Aranovskiy (UKR)
Iceland: Halldórsson, Sævarsson, R Sigurdsson,
Gudmundsson, B Bjarnason, Sigthórsson, G
Sigurdsson, Árnason, Bödvarsson (Kjartansson
85), Gunnarsson, A Skúlason. Coach: Lars
Lagerbäck (SWE) & Heimir Hallgrímsson (ISL)
Kazakhstan: Pokatilov, Maliy, Gurman, Kuat,
Konysbayev, Smakov, Islamkhan, Suyumbayev,
Nuserbayev (Shchetkin 76), Dzholchiev (Merkel
46), Logvinenko. Coach: Yuri Krasnozhan (RUS)
Red card: Gunnarsson 89 (Iceland)

06/09/15, Skonto Stadions, Riga (att: 7,913)
Latvia 1-2 Czech Republic
Goals: 0-1 Limberský 13, 0-2 Darida 25,
1-2 Zjuzins 73
Referee: Aytekin (GER)
Latvia: Vaņins, Maksimenko, Dubra, Karašausks
(Cauņa 66), Gorkšs, Kamešs (A Višņakovs 29),
Rakels, Tarasovs, Zjuzins, Fertovs, Freimanis
(Gabovs 33). Coach: Marians Pahars (LVA)
Czech Republic: Čech, Kadeřábek, Procházka,
Limberský, Dočkal, Gebre Selassie 90), Škoda,
Pavelka, Kolář (Krejčí 54), Suchý, Šural (Vaněk
77), Darida. Coach: Pavel Vrba (CZE)

*06/09/15, Konya Büyükşehir Belediyesi
Stadyumu, Konya (att: 41,007)*
Turkey 3-0 Netherlands
Goals: 1-0 Oğuzhan Özyakup 8,
2-0 Arda Turan 26, 3-0 Burak Yılmaz 86
Referee: Mateu Lahoz (ESP)
Turkey: Volkan Babacan, Şener Özbayraklı,
Hakan Balta, Serdar Aziz, Hakan Çalhanoğlu
(Mehmet Topal 65), Oğuzhan Özyakup (Olcay
Şahan 83), Selçuk İnan, Arda Turan (Volkan Şen
57), Ozan Tufan, Burak Yılmaz, Caner Erkin.
Coach: Fatih Terim (TUR)
Netherlands: Cillessen, Van der Wiel, De Vrij
(Wijnaldum 46), Bruma, Riedewald, Blind (De
Jong 74), Depay, Klaassen, Van Persie, Sneijder,
Narsingh (Promes 69). Coach: Danny Blind (NED)

10/10/15, Stadion Letná, Prague (att: 17,190)
Czech Republic 0-2 Turkey
Goals: 0-1 Selçuk İnan 62(p),
0-2 Hakan Çalhanoğlu 79
Referee: Atkinson (ENG)
Czech Republic: Vaclík, Kadeřábek, Procházka,
Dočkal (Petržela 78), Pavelka, Suchý, Šural
(Škoda 67), Krejčí (Skalák 54), Novák, Lafata,
Darida. Coach: Pavel Vrba (CZE)

10/10/15, Laugardalsvöllur, Reykjavik (att: 9,767)
Iceland 2-2 Latvia
Goals: 1-0 Sigthórsson 5, 2-0 G Sigurdsson 27,
2-1 Cauņa 49, 2-2 Šabala 68
Referee: Eskov (RUS)
Iceland: Halldórsson, Sævarsson, R Sigurdsson,
Gudmundsson, B Bjarnason, Sigthórsson, G
Sigurdsson, A Finnbogason (Gudjohnsen 65),
Árnason (Ottesen 18), Hallfredsson, A Skúlason.
Coach: Lars Lagerbäck (SWE) & Heimir
Hallgrímsson (ISL)
Latvia: Vaņins, Maksimenko, Dubra, Gabovs,
A Višņakovs (Karašausks 65), Cauņa, Šabala,
Gorkšs, Rakels, Tarasovs (Laizāns 77), Zjuzins
(J Ikaunieks 85). Coach: Marians Pahars (LVA)

10/10/15, Astana Arena, Astana (att: 20,716)
Kazakhstan 1-2 Netherlands
Goals: 0-1 Wijnaldum 33, 0-2 Sneijder 50,
1-2 Kuat 90+6
Referee: Turpin (FRA)
Kazakhstan: Pokatilov, Maliy, Kuat, Konysbayev,
Smakov, Islamkhan (Geteriev 16), Engel,
Shchetkin (Khizhnichenko 63), Suyumbayev,
Dosmagambetov (Nurgaliyev 81), Logvinenko.
Coach: Yuri Krasnozhan (RUS)
Netherlands: Krul (Zoet 81), Tete, Bruma, Van
Dijk, Riedewald, Blind, Depay, Wijnaldum,
Huntelaar (Van Persie 87), Sneijder (Afellay 80), El
Ghazi. Coach: Danny Blind (NED)

13/10/15, Skonto Stadions, Riga (att: 7,027)
Latvia 0-1 Kazakhstan
Goal: 0-1 Kuat 65
Referee: McLean (SCO)
Latvia: Vaņins, Maksimenko, Dubra, Laizāns,
Gabovs, A Višņakovs (Karašausks 57), Cauņa (E
Višņakovs 72), Šabala, Gorkšs, Rakels, Zjuzins
(J Ikaunieks 83). Coach: Marians Pahars (LVA)
Kazakhstan: Pokatilov, Maliy, Kuat, Smakov,
Engel, Suyumbayev, Nuserbayev (Gurman 82),
Shomko, Dosmagambetov (Konysbayev 68),
Khizhnichenko (Shchetkin 90), Logvinenko.
Coach: Yuri Krasnozhan (RUS)

*13/10/15, Amsterdam ArenA, Amsterdam
(att: 48,000)*
Netherlands 2-3 Czech Republic
Goals: 0-1 Kadeřábek 24, 0-2 Šural 35, 0-3 Van
Persie 66 (og), 1-3 Huntelaar 70, 2-3 Van Persie 83
Referee: Skomina (SVN)
Netherlands: Zoet, Tete, Bruma, Van Dijk (Dost
64), Riedewald (Van Persie 39), Blind, Depay,
Wijnaldum, Huntelaar, Sneijder, El Ghazi (Lens
69). Coach: Danny Blind (NED)
Czech Republic: Čech, Kadeřábek, Kadlec,
Gebre Selassie, Necid (Procházka 46), Skalák,
Pavelka, Plašil (Škoda 86), Suchý, Šural (Kalas
71), Darida. Coach: Pavel Vrba (CZE)
Red card: Suchý 43 (Czech Republic)

*13/10/15, Konya Büyükşehir Belediyesi
Stadyumu, Konya (att: 39,404)*
Turkey 1-0 Iceland
Goal: 1-0 Selçuk İnan 89
Referee: Rocchi (ITA)
Turkey: Volkan Babacan, Şener Özbayraklı,
Hakan Balta, Serdar Aziz, Hakan Çalhanoğlu
(Cenk Tosun 72), Selçuk İnan, Arda Turan,
Oğuzhan Özyakup (Gökhan Töre 62), Ozan Tufan,
Caner Erkin, Volkan Şen (Umut Bulut 75). Coach:
Fatih Terim (TUR)
Iceland: Kristinsson, Sævarsson, R Sigurdsson,
Gudmundsson, B Bjarnason, Sigthórsson (A
Finnbogason 88), G Sigurdsson, Árnason,
Bödvarsson (Kjartansson 82), Gunnarsson,
A Skúlason. Coach: Lars Lagerbäck (SWE) &
Heimir Hallgrímsson (ISL)
Red card: Gökhan Töre 78 (Turkey)

Group B

09/09/14
Andorra 1-2 Wales
Bosnia & Herzegovina 1-2 Cyprus

10/10/14
Wales 0-0 Bosnia & Herzegovina
Belgium 6-0 Andorra
Cyprus 1-2 Israel

13/10/14
Wales 2-1 Cyprus
Andorra 1-4 Israel
Bosnia & Herzegovina 1-1 Belgium

16/11/14
Belgium 0-0 Wales
Cyprus 5-0 Andorra
Israel 3-0 Bosnia & Herzegovina

28/03/15
Israel 0-3 Wales
Andorra 0-3 Bosnia & Herzegovina
Belgium 5-0 Cyprus

31/03/15
Israel 0-1 Belgium

12/06/15
Wales 1-0 Belgium
Andorra 1-3 Cyprus
Bosnia & Herzegovina 3-1 Israel

03/09/15, King Baudouin Stadium, Brussels (att: 42,975)
Belgium 3-1 Bosnia & Herzegovina
Goals: 0-1 Džeko 15, 1-1 Fellaini 23, 2-1 De Bruyne 44, 3-1 Hazard 78(p)
Referee: Manuel De Sousa (POR)
Belgium: Courtois, Alderweireld, Kompany, Vertonghen, Witsel, De Bruyne (Mertens 89), Fellaini, R Lukaku (Origi 82), Hazard, Nainggolan, Vermaelen. Coach: Marc Wilmots (BEL)
Bosnia & Herzegovina: Begović, Spahić (Šunjić 56), Kolašinac (Hajrovic 72), Vranješ, Bešić, Medunjanin (Ibišević 80), Pjanić, Džeko, Mujdža, Lulić, Višća. Coach: Mehmed Baždarević (BIH)

03/09/15, GSP, Nicosia (att: 14,492)
Cyprus 0-1 Wales
Goal: 0-1 Bale 82
Referee: Marciniak (POL)
Cyprus: Georgallides, Dossa Júnior, Demetriou, Oikonomidis, Mytidis (Kolokoudias 65), Charalambides (Englezou 74), Makrides, Antoniades, Laifis, Makris (Sotiriou 84), Nicolaou. Coach: Pambos Christodoulou (CYP)
Wales: Hennessey, Gunter, Taylor, Richards, A Williams, Edwards, King, Robson-Kanu (Vokes 68), Ramsey (MacDonald 90+3), Bale (Church 90), Davies. Coach: Chris Coleman (WAL)

03/09/15, Sammy Ofer Stadium, Haifa (att: 22,650)
Israel 4-0 Andorra
Goals: 1-0 Zahavi 3, 2-0 N Biton 22, 3-0 Hemed 26(p), 4-0 Dabbur 38
Referee: Bognar (HUN)
Israel: Marciano, Ben Haim I (Melikson 46), N Biton, Natcho, Zahavi (Buzaglo 46), Dabbur, Hemed (Kayal 75), Ben Haim II, Dasa, Tibi, Rikan. Coach: Eli Gutman (ISR)
Andorra: Pol, C Martínez, San Nicolás, E Garcia, Lima, Vieira, A Sánchez, Moreno (Jordi Rubio 72), Rebés (Llovera 81), M Garcia, Rodríguez (Sonejee 55). Coach: Koldo Alvarez (AND)

06/09/15, Stadion Bilino polje, Zenica (att: 6,830)
Bosnia & Herzegovina 3-0 Andorra
Goals: 1-0 Bičakčić 14, 2-0 Džeko 30, 3-0 Lulić 45
Referee: Hunter (NIR)

Bosnia & Herzegovina: Begović, Zec, Bičakčić, Spahić, Kolašinac (Vrančić 79), Bešić, Ibišević, Pjanić (Hadžić 45), Džeko (Djurić 68), Šunjić, Lulić. Coach: Mehmed Baždarević (BIH)
Andorra: Pol, C Martínez (A Sánchez 76), San Nicolás, Sonejee, Lima, Vieira, Riera (Alves 87), Rebés, Ayala (Peppe 81), M Garcia, Rodríguez. Coach: Koldo Alvarez (AND)
Red cards: Bešić 63 (Bosnia & Herzegovina), Rodríguez 64 (Andorra)

06/09/15, GSP, Nicosia (att: 11,866)
Cyprus 0-1 Belgium
Goal: 0-1 Hazard 86
Referee: Bezborodov (RUS)
Cyprus: Georgallides, Dossa Júnior, Demetriou, Oikonomidis, Mytidis (Sotiriou 11), Charalambides (Laban 53), Makrides, Antoniades, Laifis, Makris, Nicolaou (Artymatas 84). Coach: Pambos Christodoulou (CYP)
Belgium: Courtois, Alderweireld, Vertonghen, Witsel, De Bruyne, Fellaini (Mertens 64), Benteke (Origi 46), Hazard, Nainggolan, Vermaelen. Coach: Marc Wilmots (BEL)

06/09/15, Cardiff City Stadium, Cardiff (att: 32,653)
Wales 0-0 Israel
Referee: Bebek (CRO)
Wales: Hennessey, Gunter, Taylor, Richards, A Williams, Edwards, King (Vokes 86), Robson-Kanu (Church 79), Ramsey, Bale, Davies. Coach: Chris Coleman (WAL)
Israel: Marciano, Ben Haim I, N Biton, Natcho, Zahavi (Sahar 90+3), Kayal (Ben Haim II 46), Dabbur (Hemed 46), Dasa, Dgani, Ben Harush, Tibi. Coach: Eli Gutman (ISR)

10/10/15, Estadi Nacional, Andorra la Vella (att: 3,032)
Andorra 1-4 Belgium
Goals: 0-1 Nainggolan 19, 0-2 De Bruyne 42, 1-2 Lima 51(p), 1-3 Hazard 56(p), 1-4 Depoitre 64
Referee: Gil (POL)
Andorra: Pol, San Nicolás, Sonejee (Rodrigues 62), Rebés, Lima, Vieira (Peppe 86), A Sánchez Moreira (Riera 73), Llovera, M Garcia, Jordi Rubio. Coach: Koldo Alvarez (AND)

Belgium: Mignolet, Alderweireld, Vertonghen, Witsel, De Bruyne, Hazard (Bakkali 79), Mertens (Chadli 72), Nainggolan, Meunier (Cavanda 81), Depoitre, J Lukaku. Coach: Marc Wilmots (BEL)

10/10/15, Stadion Bilino polje, Zenica (att: 10,250)
Bosnia & Herzegovina 2-0 Wales
Goals: 1-0 Djurić 71, 2-0 Ibišević 90
Referee: Undiano Mallenco (ESP)
Bosnia & Herzegovina: Begović, Spahić (Cocalić 46), Ibišević, Pjanić, Mujdža, Šunjić, Lulić, Zukanović, Višća (Djurić 61), Hadžić (Bičakčić 89), Salihović. Coach: Mehmed Baždarević (BIH)
Wales: Hennessey, Gunter, Taylor, Richards, Davies, A Williams, Allen (Edwards 85), Robson-Kanu (Church 84), Ramsey, Bale, Ledley (Vokes 75). Coach: Chris Coleman (WAL)

10/10/15, Itztadion Teddy, Jerusalem (att: 25,300)
Israel 1-2 Cyprus
Goals: 0-1 Dossa Júnior 58, 1-1 N Biton 76, 1-2 Demetriou 80
Referee: Manuel De Sousa (POR)
Israel: Marciano, Dasa (Dgani 54), Ben Haim I, N Biton, Zahavi, Kayal, Dabbur, Ben Haim II, Vermouth (Hemed 65), Ben Harush (Melikson 71), Tibi. Coach: Eli Gutman (ISR)
Cyprus: Georgallides, Dossa Júnior, Demetriou, Mytidis, Makrides (Oikonomidis 84), Laban, Antoniades, Efrem (Merkis 86), Laifis, Makris (Charalambides 46), Nicolaou. Coach: Pambos Christodoulou (CYP)

13/10/15, King Baudouin Stadium, Brussels (att: 39,773)
Belgium 3-1 Israel
Goals: 1-0 Mertens 64, 2-0 De Bruyne 78, 3-0 Hazard 84, 3-1 Hemed 88
Referee: Sidiropoulos (GRE)
Belgium: Mignolet, Alderweireld, Lombaerts, Kompany (Meunier 58), Vertonghen, De Bruyne, Fellaini (Witsel 66), R Lukaku (Origi 65), Hazard, Mertens, Nainggolan. Coach: Marc Wilmots (BEL)
Israel: Marciano, Ben Haim I, Peretz, Zahavi, Kayal (Damari 66), Hemed, Ben Haim II (Rikan 59), Yeini (Vermouth 77), Dgani, Ben Harush, Tibi. Coach: Eli Gutman (ISR)

A debut strike from Laurent Depoitre completes the scoring for Belgium in Andorra

13/10/15, GSP, Nicosia (att: 17,687)
Cyprus 2-3 Bosnia & Herzegovina
Goals: 0-1 Medunjanin 13, 1-1 Charalambides 32, 2-1 Mytidis 41, 2-2 Medunjanin 44, 2-3 Djurić 67
Referee: Taylor (ENG)
Cyprus: Georgallides, Dossa Júnior, Demetriou, Mytidis, Charalambides (Kolokoudias 83), Makrides, Laban (Aloneftis 75), Antoniades, Efrem, Laifis, Nicolaou (Oikonomidis 65). Coach: Charalampos Christodoulou (CYP)
Bosnia & Herzegovina: Begović, Spahić, Vranješ, Medunjanin, Ibišević, Pjanić (Salihović 85), Mujdža, Šunjić, Lulić, Zukanović (Djurić 60), Višća (Bičakčić 79). Coach: Mehmed Baždarević (BIH)

13/10/15, Cardiff City Stadium, Cardiff (att: 33,280)
Wales 2-0 Andorra
Goals: 1-0 Ramsey 50, 2-0 Bale 86
Referee: Blom (NED)
Wales: Hennessey, Gunter, Davies, A Williams, Robson-Kanu (Edwards 23; Lawrence 46), Ramsey, Bale, J Williams (Church 86), Vokes, Chester, Vaughan. Coach: Chris Coleman (WAL)
Andorra: Pol, San Nicolás, Sonejee (Ayala 70), Llovera, Lima, Vieira, A Sánchez, Rodrigues, Moreira (Riera 12), Lorenzo (M Garcia 81), Jordi Rubio. Coach: Koldo Alvarez (AND)

Group C

08/09/14
Luxembourg 1-1 Belarus
Spain 5-1 FYR Macedonia
Ukraine 0-1 Slovakia

09/10/14
FYR Macedonia 3-2 Luxembourg
Slovakia 2-1 Spain
Belarus 0-2 Ukraine

12/10/14
Ukraine 1-0 FYR Macedonia
Luxembourg 0-4 Spain
Belarus 1-3 Slovakia

15/11/14
Luxembourg 0-3 Ukraine
FYR Macedonia 0-2 Slovakia
Spain 3-0 Belarus

27/03/15
FYR Macedonia 1-2 Belarus
Slovakia 3-0 Luxembourg
Spain 1-0 Ukraine

14/06/15
Ukraine 3-0 Luxembourg
Slovakia 2-1 FYR Macedonia
Belarus 0-1 Spain

05/09/15, Stade Josy Barthel, Luxembourg (att: 1,657)
Luxembourg 1-0 FYR Macedonia
Goal: 1-0 S Thill 90+2
Referee: Evans (WAL)
Luxembourg: Joubert, Chanot, Delgado, Philipps, Gerson, Martins (S Thill 72), Da Mota, Payal, Joachim, Jans, Deville (Bensi 64). Coach: Luc Holtz (LUX)
FYR Macedonia: Pacovski, Mojsov (Ristevski 37), Sikov, Trajkovski (Ilijoski 74), Ibraimi (Askovski 80), Ristovski, Gligorov, Petrovic, Zhuta, Abdurahimi, Ivanovski. Coach: Ljubinko Drulović (SRB)

05/09/15, Nuevo Carlos Tartiere, Oviedo (att: 19,874)
Spain 2-0 Slovakia
Goals: 1-0 Jordi Alba 5, 2-0 Iniesta 30(p)
Referee: Skomina (SVN)

Santi Cazorla – a double goalscorer for Spain against Luxembourg

Spain: Casillas, Piqué, Busquets, Iniesta (Koke 85), Fàbregas (Santi Cazorla 67), Pedro Rodríguez, Sergio Ramos, Juanfran, Jordi Alba, Diego Costa (Paco Alcácer 75), Silva. Coach: Vicente del Bosque (ESP)
Slovakia: Kozáčik, Pekarík, Gyömbér, Tesák, Greguš, Hrošovský (Sabo 73), Hubočan, Saláta, Hamšík (Duda 61), Švento, Mak (Ďuriš 46). Coach: Ján Kozák (SVK)

05/09/15, Arena Lviv, Lviv (att: 32,648)
Ukraine 3-1 Belarus
Goals: 1-0 Kravets 7, 2-0 Yarmolenko 30, 3-0 Konoplyanka 40(p), 3-1 Kornilenko 62(p)
Referee: Liany (ISR)
Ukraine: Pyatov, Khacheridi, Stepanenko, Yarmolenko (Gusev 69), Konoplyanka, Shevchuk, Rotan (Rybalka 75), Fedetskiy, Garmash, Rakitskiy, Kravets (Gladkiy 86). Coach: Mykhailo Fomenko (UKR)
Belarus: Gorbunov, Martynovich, Shitov, Kornilenko, Stasevich, Hleb (Renan Bressan 86), M Volodko, Sivakov (Gordeichuk 46), Mayevski, Filipenko, Kalachev (Signevich 72). Coach: Aleksandr Khatskevich (BLR)
Red card: Garmash 90+2 (Ukraine)

08/09/15, Borisov Arena, Borisov (att: 3,482)
Belarus 2-0 Luxembourg
Goals: 1-0 Gordeichuk 34, 2-0 Gordeichuk 62
Referee: Vinčić (SVN)
Belarus: Zhevnov, Dragun, Shitov, Renan Bressan, Kornilenko (Signevich 84), Hleb (Kislyak 58), Gordeichuk (Kalachev 75), Sivakov, Nekhaichik, Bordachev, Filipenko. Coach: Aleksandr Khatskevich (BLR)
Luxembourg: Joubert, Chanot, Jänisch, Schnell, Philipps, Gerson, Payal (Da Mota 46), Joachim (Bensi 64), Mutsch, Jans, Deville (Turpel 69). Coach: Luc Holtz (LUX)

08/09/15, Filip II Arena, Skopje (att: 28,843)
FYR Macedonia 0-1 Spain
Goal: 0-1 Pacovski 8(og)
Referee: Tagliavento (ITA)
FYR Macedonia: Pacovski, Brdarovski, Sikov, Hasani, Ristevski, Gligorov, Petrovic, Zhuta, Radeski (Ibraimi 84), Ivanovski (Trajkovski 68), Askovski (Bardi 76). Coach: Ljubinko Drulović (SRB)
Spain: De Gea, Piqué, Busquets, Juan Mata, Bernat, Sergio Ramos, Carvajal, Diego Costa (Paco Alcácer 61), Santi Cazorla (Koke 68), Silva, Isco (Iniesta 78). Coach: Vicente del Bosque (ESP)

08/09/15, Štadión MŠK Žilina, Zilina (att: 10,648)
Slovakia 0-0 Ukraine
Referee: Atkinson (ENG)
Slovakia: Kozáčik, Pekarík (Saláta 51), Škrtel, Gyömbér, Vittek (Jakubko 66), Hubočan, Hamšík, Kucka, Mak (Stoch 84), Ďuriš, Pečovský. Coach: Ján Kozák (SVK)
Ukraine: Pyatov, Khacheridi, Stepanenko, Yarmolenko, Konoplyanka, Shevchuk, Rotan, Fedetskiy, Rybalka, Rakitskiy, Kravets (Gladkiy 90+1). Coach: Mykhailo Fomenko (UKR)

09/10/15, Filip II Arena, Skopje (att: 4,821)
FYR Macedonia 0-2 Ukraine
Goals: 0-1 Seleznyov 59(p), 0-2 Kravets 87
Referee: Haţegan (ROU)
FYR Macedonia: Pacovski, Brdarovski, Zhuta, Petrovic, Sikov, Alimi, Ibraimi, Hasani (Abdurahimi 22), Ristevski, Ilijoski (Ivanovski 64), Askovski (Nestorovski 78). Coach: Ljubinko Drulović (SRB)
Ukraine: Pyatov, Khacheridi, Yarmolenko (Karavayev 86), Konoplyanka, Seleznyov (Kravets 74), Shevchuk, Rotan (Malinovskiy 90), Sydorchuk, Fedetskiy, Rybalka, Rakitskiy. Coach: Mykhailo Fomenko (UKR)

09/10/15, Štadión MŠK Žilina, Zilina (att: 9,859)
Slovakia 0-1 Belarus
Goal: 0-1 Dragun 34
Referee: Göçek (TUR)
Slovakia: Kozáčik, Škrtel, Weiss (Stoch 71), Hubočan, Saláta, Hamšík, Švento, Kucka, Mak (Duda 79), Ďuriš, Pečovský (Nemec 60). Coach: Ján Kozák (SVK)
Belarus: Gorbunov, Dragun, Martynovich, Polyakov, Renan Bressan, Stasevich, Gordeichuk, Nekhaichik (Politevich 69), Sivakov, Bordachev (M Volodko 40), Signevich (Kislyak 72). Coach: Aleksandr Khatskevich (BLR)
Red card: Martynovich 65 (Belarus)

09/10/15, Estadio Municipal Las Gaunas, Logrono (att: 14,472)
Spain 4-0 Luxembourg
Goals: 1-0 Santi Cazorla 42, 2-0 Paco Alcácer 67, 3-0 Paco Alcácer 80, 4-0 Santi Cazorla 85
Referee: Delferiere (BEL)
Spain: Casillas, Piqué, Bartra, Busquets, Morata (Paco Alcácer 33), Fàbregas, Pedro Rodríguez (Nolito 77), Juanfran, Jordi Alba, Santi Cazorla, Silva (Juan Mata 11). Coach: Vicente del Bosque (ESP)
Luxembourg: Joubert, Chanot, Delgado, Gerson, Martins (Da Mota 79), Payal, Bensi (Deville 64), Joachim (Turpel 90), Malget, Mutsch, Jans. Coach: Luc Holtz (LUX)

12/10/15, Borisov Arena, Borisov (att: 1,545)
Belarus 0-0 FYR Macedonia
Referee: Dingert (GER)
Belarus: Gorbunov, Dragun (Putilo 73), Polyakov, Politevich, Renan Bressan, Stasevich, Gordeichuk, M Volodko, Nekhaichik (Kislyak 61), Sivakov, Signevich. Coach: Aleksandr Khatskevich (BLR)
FYR Macedonia: Mitov Nilson, Brdarovski (Abdurahimi 73), Zhuta, Petrovic, Mojsov, Sikov, Trickovski, Trajkovski, Ibraimi (Nestorovski 86), Ristovski, Stjepanovic (Alimi 84). Coach: Ljubinko Drulović (SRB)

12/10/15, Stade Josy Barthel, Luxembourg (att: 2,512)
Luxembourg 2-4 Slovakia
Goals: 0-1 Hamšík 24, 0-2 Nemec 29, 0-3 Mak 30, 1-3 Mutsch 61, 2-3 Gerson 65(p), 2-4 Hamšík 90+1
Referee: Drachta (AUT)
Luxembourg: Joubert, Chanot, Delgado (Turpel 81), Philipps, Gerson, Martins, Payal (Malget 57), Bensi (S Thill 66), Joachim, Mutsch, Jans. Coach: Luc Holtz (LUX)
Slovakia: Kozáčik, Škrtel, Gyömbér, Weiss (Šesták 72), Nemec (Jakubko 79), Hubočan, Hamšík, Švento, Kucka, Mak (Sabo 87), Pečovský. Coach: Ján Kozák (SVK)

12/10/15, NSK Olimpiyskiy, Kyiv (att: 61,248)
Ukraine 0-1 Spain
Goal: 0-1 Mario 22
Referee: Mažić (SRB)
Ukraine: Pyatov, Kucher, Stepanenko, Yarmolenko, Konoplyanka, Shevchuk, Rotan (Zinchenko 87), Fedetskiy, Garmash (Rybalka 58), Rakitskiy, Kravets (Seleznyov 87). Coach: Mykhailo Fomenko (UKR)
Spain: De Gea, Azpilicueta, San José, Thiago Alcántara, Paco Alcácer (Busquets 85), Fàbregas (Juan Mata 64), Etxeita, Nacho, Mario, Nolito (Jordi Alba 75), Isco. Coach: Vicente del Bosque (ESP)

Group D

07/09/14
Gibraltar 0-7 Poland
Georgia 1-2 Republic of Ireland
Germany 2-1 Scotland

11/10/14
Republic of Ireland 7-0 Gibraltar
Scotland 1-0 Georgia
Poland 2-0 Germany

14/10/14
Gibraltar 0-3 Georgia
Germany 1-1 Republic of Ireland
Poland 2-2 Scotland

14/11/14
Scotland 1-0 Republic of Ireland
Germany 4-0 Gibraltar
Georgia 0-4 Poland

29/03/15
Scotland 6-1 Gibraltar
Republic of Ireland 1-1 Poland
Georgia 0-2 Germany

13/06/15
Republic of Ireland 1-1 Scotland
Poland 4-0 Georgia
Gibraltar 0-7 Germany

04/09/15, Boris Paichadze Dinamo Arena, Tbilisi (att: 23,000)
Georgia 1-0 Scotland
Goal: 1-0 Kazaishvili 38
Referee: Hațegan (ROU)
Georgia: Revishvili, Lobjanidze, Kverkvelia, Kashia, Amisulashvili, Kankava, Kazaishvili, Okriashvili (Merebashvili 71), Ananidze (Daushvili 82), Navalovski, Mchedlidze (Vatsadze 90+3). Coach: Kakhaber Tskhadadze (GEO)
Scotland: Marshall, Hutton, Robertson (Hanley 59), R Martin, Mulgrew, Maloney, Morrison, Brown, S Fletcher, Naismith (Forrest 59), Anya (Griffiths 75). Coach: Gordon Strachan (SCO)

04/09/15, Commerzbank Arena, Frankfurt am Main (att: 48,500)
Germany 3-1 Poland
Goals: 1-0 Müller 12, 2-0 Götze 19, 2-1 Lewandowski 37, 3-1 Götze 82
Referee: Rizzoli (ITA)
Germany: Neuer, Hector, Hummels, Schweinsteiger, Özil, Müller, Can, Bellarabi (Gündoğan 53), Boateng, Kroos, Götze (Podolski 90+1). Coach: Joachim Löw (GER)
Poland: Fabiański, Szukała, Mączyński (Błaszczykowski 63), Jodłowiec, Milik, Krychowiak, Lewandowski, Grosicki (Peszko 83), Rybus, Glik, Piszczek (Olkowski 43). Coach: Adam Nawałka (POL)

04/09/15, Estádio Algarve, Faro (att: 5,393)
Gibraltar 0-4 Republic of Ireland
Goals: 0-1 Christie 26, 0-2 Keane 49, 0-3 Keane 51(p), 0-4 Long 79
Referee: Strahonja (CRO)
Gibraltar: J Perez, J Chipolina, Sergeant (Guiling 85), R Chipolina, L Casciaro, K Casciaro (Gosling 61), Walker, Barnett, Bardon, JP Duarte (Yome 73), Garcia. Coach: Jeff Wood (ENG)
Republic of Ireland: Given, O'Shea, Clark, Whelan, McCarthy (Quinn 70), Keane (Long 71), Walters, Christie, Brady, Hoolahan (McGeady 77), Hendrick. Coach: Martin O'Neill (NIR)

07/09/15, Stadion Narodowy, Warsaw (att: 27,763)
Poland 8-1 Gibraltar
Goals: 1-0 Grosicki 8, 2-0 Grosicki 15, 3-0 Lewandowski 18, 4-0 Lewandowski 29, 5-0 Milik 56, 6-0 Błaszczykowski 59(p), 7-0 Milik 72, 8-0 Kapustka 73, 8-1 Gosling 87
Referee: Mažeika (LTU)
Poland: Fabiański, Szukała, Mączyński, Milik, Krychowiak, Lewandowski (Zieliński 66), Grosicki, Rybus, Olkowski (Mila 87), Glik, Błaszczykowski (Kapustka 62). Coach: Adam Nawałka (POL)
Gibraltar: J Perez, J Chipolina, R Chipolina, L Casciaro (Lopez 79), Walker, Gosling, Barnett, Bardon, JP Duarte (Bosio 68), J Coombes (K Casciaro 46), Garcia. Coach: Jeff Wood (ENG)

07/09/15, Aviva Stadium, Dublin (att: 27,200)
Republic of Ireland 1-0 Georgia
Goal: 1-0 Walters 69
Referee: Vad (HUN)
Republic of Ireland: Given, Coleman, O'Shea, Clark, Whelan, McCarthy, Keane (Long 46), Walters, Brady, Hoolahan (McClean 75), Hendrick. Coach: Martin O'Neill (NIR)
Georgia: Revishvili, Lobjanidze, Kverkvelia, Kashia (Tsintsadze 76), Amisulashvili, Khizanishvili (Kenia 81), Kankava, Kazaishvili (Papunashvili 64), Okriashvili, Navalovski, Mchedlidze. Coach: Kakhaber Tskhadadze (GEO)

07/09/15, Hampden Park, Glasgow (att: 50,753)
Scotland 2-3 Germany
Goals: 0-1 Müller 18, 1-1 Hummels 28(og), 1-2 Müller 34, 2-2 McArthur 43, 2-3 Gündoğan 54
Referee: Kuipers (NED)
Scotland: Marshall, Hutton, Mulgrew, R Martin, Hanley, McArthur, Morrison, Brown (C Martin 81), S Fletcher, Forrest (Ritchie 81), Maloney (Anya 60). Coach: Gordon Strachan (SCO)
Germany: Neuer, Hector, Hummels, Schweinsteiger, Özil (Kramer 90+2), Müller, Can, Boateng, Kroos, Götze (Schürrle 86), Gündoğan. Coach: Joachim Löw (GER)

08/10/15, Boris Paichadze Dinamo Arena, Tbilisi (att: 11,330)
Georgia 4-0 Gibraltar
Goals: 1-0 Vatsadze 30, 2-0 Okriashvili 35(p), 3-0 Vatsadze 45, 4-0 Kazaishvili 87
Referee: Boiko (UKR)
Georgia: Revishvili, Kashia, Amisulashvili, Kankava (Palavandishvili 58), Kazaishvili, Okriashvili (Dzalamidze 58), Vatsadze (Tskhadadze 73), Kvekveskiri, Grigalava, Kobakhidze, Kakabadze. Coach: Kakhaber Tskhadadze (GEO)
Gibraltar: J Perez, J Chipolina, R Casciaro, R Chipolina, L Casciaro (JP Duarte 76), K Casciaro (Yome 85), Walker, Gosling, Cabrera (B Perez 46), Bardon, Garcia. Coach: Jeff Wood (ENG)

08/10/15, Aviva Stadium, Dublin (att: 50,604)
Republic of Ireland 1-0 Germany
Goal: 1-0 Long 70
Referee: Velasco Carballo (ESP)
Republic of Ireland: Given (Randolph 43), O'Shea, McCarthy, Hoolahan, Walters, Christie, Ward (Meyler 69), Murphy (Long 65), Brady, Hendrick, Keogh. Coach: Martin O'Neill (NIR)
Germany: Neuer, Hector, Hummels, Ginter (Bellarabi 77), Özil, Reus, Müller, Boateng, Kroos, Götze (Schürrle 35), Gündoğan (Volland 85). Coach: Joachim Löw (GER)

08/10/15, Hampden Park, Glasgow (att: 49,359)
Scotland 2-2 Poland
Goals: 0-1 Lewandowski 3, 1-1 Ritchie 45, 2-1 S Fletcher 62, 2-2 Lewandowski 90+4
Referee: Kassai (HUN)
Scotland: Marshall, Hutton, Whittaker, R Martin, Hanley, Forrest (Dorrans 84), D Fletcher (McArthur 74), Brown, S Fletcher, Naismith (Maloney 69), Ritchie. Coach: Gordon Strachan (SCO)
Poland: Fabiański, Mączyński, Milik (Jodłowiec 63), Krychowiak, Lewandowski, Grosicki, Rybus (Wawrzyniak 71), Glik, Błaszczykowski (Olkowski 83), Piszczek, Pazdan. Coach: Adam Nawałka (POL)

Thomas Müller heads in his second goal for Germany against Scotland at Hampden Park

11/10/15, Red Bull Arena, Leipzig (att: 43,630)
Germany 2-1 Georgia
Goals: 1-0 Müller 50(p), 1-1 Kankava 53,
2-1 Kruse 79
Referee: Královec (CZE)
Germany: Neuer, Hector, Hummels, Ginter, Özil,
Schürrle (Kruse 76), Reus (Bellarabi 90), Müller,
Boateng, Kroos, Gündoğan. Coach: Joachim
Löw (GER)
Georgia: Revishvili, Lobjanidze, Kverkvelia,
Kashia, Amisulashvili, Kankava, Kazaishvili
(Kobakhidze 90), Gelashvili (Vatsadze 46),
Okriashvili, Kvekveskiri (Khizanishvili 78),
Navalovski. Coach: Kakhaber Tskhadadze (GEO)

11/10/15, Estádio Algarve, Faro (att: 12,401)
Gibraltar 0-6 Scotland
Goals: 0-1 C Martin 25, 0-2 Maloney 39,
0-3 S Fletcher 52, 0-4 S Fletcher 56,
0-5 S Fletcher 85, 0-6 Naismith 90+1
Referee: Kulbakov (BLR)
Gibraltar: J Robba, J Chipolina, R Casciaro, R
Chipolina, L Casciaro (JP Duarte 82), K Casciaro
(Yome 89), Walker, D Duarte (B Perez 57),
Barnett, Bardon, Garcia. Coach: Jeff Wood (ENG)
Scotland: A McGregor, Hutton, Robertson, Berra,
Greer, Maloney, Dorrans, Brown (D Fletcher 63), S
Fletcher, C Martin (Naismith 76), Ritchie (Russell
63). Coach: Gordon Strachan (SCO)

11/10/15, Stadion Narodowy, Warsaw (att: 57,497)
Poland 2-1 Republic of Ireland
Goals: 1-0 Krychowiak 13, 1-1 Walters 16(p),
2-1 Lewandowski 42
Referee: Çakır (TUR)
Poland: Fabiański, Mączyński (Szukała 78),
Olkowski (Błaszczykowski 63), Krychowiak,
Lewandowski, Linetty, Grosicki (Peszko 85),
Wawrzyniak, Glik, Piszczek, Pazdan. Coach:
Adam Nawałka (POL)
Republic of Ireland: Randolph, Coleman,
O'Shea, Keogh, Whelan (McGeady 58),
McCarthy, Long (Keane 55), McClean (Hoolahan
73), Walters, Brady, Hendrick. Coach: Martin
O'Neill (NIR)
Red card: O'Shea 90+2 (Republic of Ireland)

Group E

08/09/14
San Marino 0-2 Lithuania
Switzerland 0-2 England
Estonia 1-0 Slovenia

09/10/14
England 5-0 San Marino
Slovenia 1-0 Switzerland
Lithuania 1-0 Estonia

12/10/14
Estonia 0-1 England
Lithuania 0-2 Slovenia
San Marino 0-4 Switzerland

15/11/14
England 3-1 Slovenia
San Marino 0-0 Estonia
Switzerland 4-0 Lithuania

27/03/15
England 4-0 Lithuania
Slovenia 6-0 San Marino
Switzerland 3-0 Estonia

14/06/15
Slovenia 2-3 England
Estonia 2-0 San Marino
Lithuania 1-2 Switzerland

England's Raheem Sterling (right) thanks Jamie
Vardy for setting him up to score against Estonia at
Wembley

05/09/15, A. Le Coq Arena, Tallinn (att: 6,621)
Estonia 1-0 Lithuania
Goal: 1-0 Vassiljev 71
Referee: Drachta (AUT)
Estonia: Aksalu, Lindpere (Kallaste 67), Pikk,
Dmitrijev, Purje (Puri 86), Zenjov, Vassiljev (Luts
90+3), Klavan, Jääger, Mets, Teniste. Coach:
Magnus Pehrsson (SWE)
Lithuania: Arlauskis, L Klimavičius, Žaliūkas,
Česnauskis (Freidgeimas 79), Vaitkūnas,
Matulevičius (Novikovas 73), Novikovas, Slivka,
Žulpa, Panka (Petravičius 78), Černych. Coach:
Igoris Pankratjevas (LTU)

*05/09/15, San Marino Stadium, Serravalle
(att: 4,378)*
San Marino 0-6 England
Goals: 0-1 Rooney 13(p), 0-2 Brolli 30(og),
0-3 Barkley 46, 0-4 Walcott 68, 0-5 Kane 77,
0-6 Walcott 78
Referee: Trattou (CYP)
San Marino: A Simoncini, Bonini (Tosi 72),
Berardi, Brolli, D Simoncini (Alessandro Della
Valle 81), Palazzi, Hirsch, Battistini, Chiaruzzi,
Selva (Rinaldi 75), M Vitaioli. Coach: Pierangelo
Manzaroli (SMR)
England: Hart, Clyne, Shaw, Shelvey, Stones,
Jagielka, Milner (Delph 58), Barkley, Vardy,
Rooney (Kane 58), Oxlade-Chamberlain (Walcott
67). Coach: Roy Hodgson (ENG)

05/09/15, St Jakob-Park, Basel (att: 25,750)
Switzerland 3-2 Slovenia
Goals: 0-1 Novkovič 45, 0-2 Cesar 48, 1-2
Drmic 80, 2-2 Stocker 84, 3-2 Drmic 90+4
Referee: Královec (CZE)
Switzerland: Sommer, Lichtsteiner, Klose,
Seferovic (Embolo 56), Xhaka, Behrami, Kasami,
Rodriguez, Dzemaili (Drmic 64), Mehmedi
(Embolo 56), Schär, Shaqiri. Coach: Vladimir
Petković (SUI)
Slovenia: Handanović, Stevanović, Cesar, Ilič,
Iličič (Samardžič 90), Kurtić, Birsa (Krhin 83),
Novkovič (Pečnik 58), Jokič, Andraž Struna,
Kampl. Coach: Srečko Katanec (SVN)

08/09/15, Wembley Stadium, London (att: 75,751)
England 2-0 Switzerland
Goals: 1-0 Kane 67, 2-0 Rooney 84(p)
Referee: Rocchi (ITA)
England: Hart, Clyne (Stones 68), Shaw, Shelvey
(Kane 58), Cahill, Smalling, Milner, Delph (Barkley
3), Sterling, Rooney, Oxlade-Chamberlain.
Coach: Roy Hodgson (ENG)
Switzerland: Sommer, Lichtsteiner, Klose,
Inler, Xhaka, Behrami (Dzemaili 79), Rodriguez,
Stocker (Seferovic 71), Drmic (Embolo 63), Schär,
Shaqiri. Coach: Vladimir Petković (SUI)

08/09/15, LFF stadionas, Vilnius (att: 2,856)
Lithuania 2-1 San Marino
Goals: 1-0 Černych 7, 1-1 M Vitaioli 55, 2-1
Spalvis 90+2
Referee: Pisani (MLT)
Lithuania: Arlauskis, L Klimavičius, Freidgeimas,
Slavickas (Matulevičius 73), Žaliūkas, Novikovas,
Pilibaitis (Chvedukas 82), Slivka (Černiauskas
53), Žulpa, Spalvis, Černych. Coach: Igoris
Pankratjevas (LTU)
San Marino: Benedettini, Battistini, Palazzi, F
Vitaioli, Alessandro Della Valle, M Vitaioli
(Selva 80), L Gasperoni (Berretti 68), Stefanelli
(Hirsch 73), Chiaruzzi, Rinaldi. Coach: Pierangelo
Manzaroli (SMR)
Red cards: Arlauskis 50 (Lithuania), Chiaruzzi 88
(San Marino)

08/09/15, Stadion Ljudski vrt, Maribor (att: 6,068)
Slovenia 1-0 Estonia
Goal: 1-0 Berič 63
Referee: Sidiropoulos (GRE)
Slovenia: Handanović, Cesar, Ilič, Iličič
(Ljubijankič 55), Kurtić, Birsa, Jokič, Andraž
Struna, Kampl, Krhin (Rotman 88), Berič
(Lazarevič 77). Coach: Srečko Katanec (SVN)
Estonia: Aksalu, Lindpere (Teever 84), Pikk,
Purje, Zenjov (Puri 46), Vassiljev, Klavan, Jääger,
Mets, Kallaste (Luts 88), Teniste. Coach: Magnus
Pehrsson (SWE)

09/10/15, Wembley Stadium, London (att: 75,427)
England 2-0 Estonia
Goals: 1-0 Walcott 45, 2-0 Sterling 85
Referee: Vad (HUN)
England: Hart, Clyne, Bertrand, Milner, Cahill,
Smalling, Walcott (Vardy 82), Barkley (Alli 88),
Sterling, Kane, Lallana (Oxlade-Chamberlain 73).
Coach: Roy Hodgson (ENG)
Estonia: Aksalu, Pikk, Dmitrijev (Lindpere 70),
Purje (Puri 70), Zenjov, Vassiljev, Klavan, Jääger,
Mets, Kallaste (Luts 88), Teniste. Coach: Magnus
Pehrsson (SWE)

09/10/15, Stadion Stožice, Ljubljana (att: 10,498)
Slovenia 1-1 Lithuania
Goals: 1-0 Birsa 45+1(p), 1-1 Novikovas 79(p)
Referee: Kuipers (NED)
Slovenia: Handanović, Cesar, Ilič, Iličič (Matavž
90), Kurtić, Birsa, Jokič, Lazarevič (Pečnik 73),
Andraž Struna, Berič (Ljubijankič 62), Krhin.
Coach: Srečko Katanec (SVN)
Lithuania: Zubas, L Klimavičius, Freidgeimas,
Slavickas (Žaliūkas (Mikuckis 90), Slivka
(Petravičius 69), Novikovas, Žulpa, Panka,
Spalvis, Černych (Česnauskis 63). Coach: Igoris
Pankratjevas (LTU)

09/10/15, AFG Arena, St Gallen (att: 16,200)
Switzerland 7-0 San Marino
Goals: 1-0 Lang 17, 2-0 Inler 55(p), 3-0 Mehmedi
65, 4-0 Djourou 72(p), 5-0 Kasami 75, 6-0
Embolo 80(p), 7-0 Derdiyok 89
Referee: Gestranius (FIN)
Switzerland: Bürki, Lang, Embolo, Inler,
Rodriguez (Moubandje 62), Zuffi, Kasami,
Mehmedi (Derdiyok 68), Drmic (Steffen 78),
Djourou, Schär. Coach: Vladimir Petković (SUI)
San Marino: A Simoncini, Alessandro Della Valle,
D Simoncini, L Gasperoni (Coppini 64), Palazzi,
M Vitaioli, Cesarini (F Vitaioli 78), Berardi, E
Golinucci (Hirsch 83), Tosi, Stefanelli. Coach:
Pierangelo Manzaroli (SMR)

EUROPEAN
QUALIFIERS

12/10/15, A. Le Coq Arena, Tallinn (att: 7,304)
Estonia 0-1 Switzerland
Goal: 0-1 Klavan 90+4(og)
Referee: Van Boekel (NED)
Estonia: Aksalu, Pikk, Puri (Lindpere 67), Zenjov (Purje 61), Vassiljev, Klavan, Antonov, Jääger, Mets, Kallaste (Luts 80), Teniste. Coach: Magnus Pehrsson (SWE)
Switzerland: Hitz, Lang, Moubandje, Lustenberger, Inler, Derdiyok, Xhaka (Kasami 80), Dzemaili, Mehmedi (Steffen 71), Djourou, Shaqiri (Embolo 46). Coach: Vladimir Petković (SUI)

12/10/15, LFF stadionas, Vilnius (att: 5,051)
Lithuania 0-3 England
Goals: 0-1 Barkley 29, 0-2 Arlauskis 35(og), 0-3 Oxlade-Chamberlain 62
Referee: Hansen (DEN)
Lithuania: Arlauskis, L Klimavičius, Freidgeimas, Mikuckis, Slivka, Novikovas (Petravičius 63), Žulpa, Panka, Spalvis (Matulevičius 86), Černych, Andriuškevičius (Vaitkūnas 82). Coach: Igoris Pankratjevas (LTU)
England: Butland, Walker, Gibbs, Shelvey, Jones, Jagielka, Oxlade-Chamberlain, Barkley (Townsend 73), Vardy, Kane (Ings 59), Lallana (Alli 67). Coach: Roy Hodgson (ENG)

12/10/15, San Marino Stadium, Serravalle (att: 781)
San Marino 0-2 Slovenia
Goals: 0-1 Cesar 54, 0-2 Pečnik 75
Referee: Stavrev (MKD)
San Marino: A Simoncini, Valentini (Alessandro Della Valle 73), Brolli, D Simoncini, M Vitaioli (Mazza 90), Hirsch, Palazzi, Selva (Rinaldi 71), Chiaruzzi, Battistini, A Gasperoni. Coach: Pierangelo Manzaroli (SMR)
Slovenia: Oblak, Samardžić, Cesar, Iličič (Pečnik 46), Kurtić, Birsa, Berić (Matavž 46), Jokić, Andraž Struna, Kirm (Lazarevič 70), Krhin. Coach: Srečko Katanec (SVN)

Group F

07/09/14
Hungary 1-2 Northern Ireland
Faroe Islands 1-3 Finland
Greece 0-1 Romania

11/10/14
Romania 1-1 Hungary
Northern Ireland 2-0 Faroe Islands
Finland 1-1 Greece

14/10/14
Faroe Islands 0-1 Hungary
Finland 0-2 Romania
Greece 0-2 Northern Ireland

14/11/14
Hungary 1-0 Finland
Greece 0-1 Faroe Islands
Romania 2-0 Northern Ireland

29/03/15
Northern Ireland 2-1 Finland
Romania 1-0 Faroe Islands
Hungary 0-0 Greece

13/06/15
Finland 0-1 Hungary
Northern Ireland 0-0 Romania
Faroe Islands 2-1 Greece

04/09/15, Tórsvøllur, Torshavn (att: 4,513)
Faroe Islands 1-3 Northern Ireland
Goals: 0-1 McAuley 12, 1-1 Edmundsson 36, 1-2 McAuley 71, 1-3 K Lafferty 75
Referee: Zwayer (GER)
Faroe Islands: Nielsen, Næs, Nattestad, Hansson, Benjaminsen (Baldvinsson 87), B Olsen (K Olsen 83), Sørensen, Holst (P Justinussen 76), Edmundsson, Vatnhamar, Færø. Coach: Lars Olsen (DEN)

Steven Davis (centre) wheels away in jubilation after securing Northern Ireland's qualification for France with the team's third goal at home to Greece

Northern Ireland: McGovern, C McLaughlin (Magennis 70), McAuley, J Evans, Baird, McGinn, Davis, K Lafferty (McNair 78), Brunt (Ferguson 83), Dallas, Norwood. Coach: Michael O'Neill (NIR)
Red card: Edmundsson 65 (Faroe Islands)

04/09/15, Stadio Georgios Karaiskakis, Piraeus (att: 17,358)
Greece 0-1 Finland
Goal: 0-1 Pohjanpalo 75
Referee: Boiko (UKR)
Greece: Karnezis, Tziolis, Mitroglou, Fortounis, Vyntra, Papadopoulos, Karelis (Fountas 77), Papastathopoulos, Holebas, Aravidis (Kone 68), Samaris (Tachtsidis 86). Coach: Kostas Tsanas (GRE)
Finland: L Hradecky, Arajuuri, Toivio, P Hetemaj, Pukki (Pohjanpalo 67), Arkivuo, Sparv, Halsti, Uronen, Ring, Hämäläinen (Sadik 46; Mattila 81). Coach: Markku Kanerva (FIN)

04/09/15, Groupama Aréna, Budapest (att: 22,060)
Hungary 0-0 Romania
Referee: Brych (GER)
Hungary: Király, Leandro, Kádár, Fiola, Elek, Dzsudzsák, Tőzsér, Szalai, Nikolić (Németh 70), Stieber (Priskin 88), Juhász (Guzmics 24). Coach: Bernd Storck (GER)
Romania: Tătărușanu, Papp , Rat, Hoban, Chircheș, Torje (Maxim 90), Keșerü, Sânmărtean (Budescu 78), Prepeliță, Grigore, Popa (Chipciu 68). Coach: Anghel Iordanescu (ROU)

07/09/15, Olympiastadion, Helsinki (att: 9,477)
Finland 1-0 Faroe Islands
Goal: 1-0 Pohjanpalo 23
Referee: Borski (POL)
Finland: L Hradecky, Arajuuri, P Hetemaj, Riku Riski (Väyrynen 74), Arkivuo, Sparv, Halsti, Lam (Mattila 84), Uronen, Ring, Pohjanpalo (Hämäläinen 90+3). Coach: Markku Kanerva (FIN)
Faroe Islands: Nielsen, Næs, Gregersen, Nattestad, Hansson, Benjaminsen (Baldvinsson 84), B Olsen, Sørensen, Holst (Bartalsstovu 84), K Olsen (F Justinussen 75), Vatnhamar. Coach: Lars Olsen (DEN)

07/09/15, Windsor Park, Belfast (att: 10,200)
Northern Ireland 1-1 Hungary
Goals: 0-1 Guzmics 74, 1-1 K Lafferty 90+3
Referee: Çakır (TUR)

Northern Ireland: McGovern, C McLaughlin, McAuley, J Evans, Baird, Davis, K Lafferty, Brunt, C Evans (McGinn 56), Dallas (Ferguson 84), Norwood (Magennis 75). Coach: Michael O'Neill (NIR)
Hungary: Király, Leandro, Kádár, Fiola, Elek (Nagy 22), Dzsudzsák, Szalai (Priskin 68), Gera, Németh (Vanczák 89), Kalmár, Guzmics. Coach: Bernd Storck (GER)
Red card: Baird 81 (Northern Ireland)

07/09/15, Arena Națională, Bucharest (att: 38,153)
Romania 0-0 Greece
Referee: Kulbakov (BLR)
Romania: Tătărușanu, Papp, Rat, Hoban (Andone 80), Chircheș, Pintilii, Maxim (Popa 64), Torje, Keșerü, Budescu (Sânmărtean 64), Grigore. Coach: Anghel Iordanescu (ROU)
Greece: Karnezis, Manolas, Tziolis, Mitroglou (Karelis 87), Fortounis (Kone 54), Kitsiou, Fetfatzidis (Vyntra 46), Papastathopoulos, Holebas, Aravidis, Samaris. Coach: Kostas Tsanas (GRE)

08/10/15, Groupama Aréna, Budapest (att: 16,500)
Hungary 2-1 Faroe Islands
Goals: 0-1 Jakobsen 11, 1-1 Böde 63, 2-1 Böde 71
Referee: Schörgenhofer (AUT)
Hungary: Király, Kádár, Fiola, Dzsudzsák, Tőzsér (Németh 46), Gera, Nagy, Nikolić (Priskin 75), Guzmics, Bódi (Böde 46), Juhász. Coach: Bernd Storck (GER)
Faroe Islands: Nielsen, Næs, V Davidsen, Gregersen, Nattestad (Færø 84), Edmundsson, Vatnhamar, Bartalsstovu, Baldvinsson, Jakobsen (P Justinussen 62), Joensen (Sørensen 78). Coach: Lars Olsen (DEN)
Red card: Gregersen 90+4 (Faroe Islands)

08/10/15, Windsor Park, Belfast (att: 11,700)
Northern Ireland 3-1 Greece
Goals: 1-0 Davis 35, 2-0 Magennis 49, 3-0 Davis 58, 3-1 Aravidis 87
Referee: Nijhuis (NED)
Northern Ireland: McGovern, McAuley, Davis, Brunt, C Evans, Dallas, Norwood, McNair (McCullough 85), Ward (McGinn 81), Cathcart, Magennis (Boyce 78). Coach: Michael O'Neill (NIR)

Greece: Karnezis, Moras, Tziolis, Kone (Pelkas 71), Mitroglou (Athanasiadis 76), Torosidis, Karelis (Mantalos 65), Papastathopoulos, Holebas, Aravidis, Samaris. Coach: Kostas Tsanas (GRE)

08/10/15, Arena Naţională, Bucharest (att: 47,987)
Romania 1-1 Finland
Goals: 0-1 Pohjanpalo 67, 1-1 Hoban 90+1
Referee: Thomson (SCO)
Romania: Tătăruşanu, Papp , Raţ, Hoban, Chiricheş, Chipciu (Maxim 60), Torje (Popa 87), Keşerü, Sânmărtean, Stancu (Andone 69), Grigore. Coach: Anghel Iordanescu (ROU)
Finland: L Hradecky, Arajuuri (Toivio 62), N Moisander, Schüller, P Hetemaj, Pukki, Arkivuo (Jalasto 64), Halsti, Uronen, Ring, Pohjanpalo (Hämäläinen 77). Coach: Markku Kanerva (FIN)

11/10/15, Tórsvøllur, Torshavn (att: 3,941)
Faroe Islands 0-3 Romania
Goals: 0-1 Budescu 4, 0-2 Budescu 45+1, 0-3 Maxim 83
Referee: Kružliak (SVK)
Faroe Islands: Nielsen, Næs, Nattestad (Baldvinsson 84), Hansson, B Olsen, Sørensen, Holst (A Olsen 69), Edmundsson, Vatnhamar (Frederiksberg 69), Færø, Bartalsstovu. Coach: Lars Olsen (DEN)
Romania: Tătăruşanu, Raţ, Hoban, Chiricheş, Pintilii, Torje (Maxim 78), Mǎţel, Stancu (Alibec 90), Budescu (Prepeliţă 88), Grigore, Popa. Coach: Anghel Iordanescu (ROU)

11/10/15, Olympiastadion, Helsinki (att: 14,550)
Finland 1-1 Northern Ireland
Goals: 0-1 Cathcart 31, 1-1 Arajuuri 87
Referee: Karasev (RUS)
Finland: L Hradecky, Arajuuri, Jalasto, Schüller (Hämäläinen 79), Ojala, Sadik (Pukki 66), Sparv, Mattila, Uronen, Ring (Lod 44), Pohjanpalo. Coach: Markku Kanerva (FIN)
Northern Ireland: McGovern, McAuley, Baird, McGinn (Ferguson 71), Davis, K Lafferty (Magennis 79), Brunt, Dallas, Norwood, McNair (C McLaughlin 51), Cathcart. Coach: Michael O'Neill (NIR)

11/10/15, Stadio Georgios Karaiskakis, Piraeus (att: 9,500)
Greece 4-3 Hungary
Goals: 1-0 Stafylidis 5, 1-1 Lovrencsics 26, 1-2 Németh 55, 2-2 Tachtsidis 57, 2-3 Németh 75, 3-3 Mitroglou 79, 4-3 Kone 86
Referee: Bebek (CRO)
Greece: Karnezis, Kitsiou, Stafylidis (Holebas 35), Moras, Pelkas, Mitroglou, Fortounis, Tachtsidis, Mantalos (Kone 72), Papastathopoulos (Tzanetopoulos 64), Samaris. Coach: Kostas Tsanas (GRE)
Hungary: Király, Kádár, Fiola, Elek, Dzsudzsák (Kalmár 71), Németh, Gera (Nagy 71), Böde, Lovrencsics (Nikolić 62), Leandro, Juhász. Coach: Bernd Storck (GER)

Group G

08/09/14
Russia 4-0 Liechtenstein
Austria 1-1 Sweden
Montenegro 2-0 Moldova

09/10/14
Liechtenstein 0-0 Montenegro
Sweden 1-1 Russia
Moldova 1-2 Austria

12/10/14
Austria 1-0 Montenegro
Russia 1-1 Moldova
Sweden 2-0 Liechtenstein

15/11/14
Austria 1-0 Russia
Moldova 0-1 Liechtenstein
Montenegro 1-1 Sweden

27/03/15
Liechtenstein 0-5 Austria
Montenegro 0-3(f) Russia
Moldova 0-2 Sweden

14/06/15
Liechtenstein 1-1 Moldova
Russia 0-1 Austria
Sweden 3-1 Montenegro

05/09/15, Ernst-Happel-Stadion, Vienna (att: 48,500)
Austria 1-0 Moldova
Goal: 1-0 Junuzovic 52
Referee: Stavrev (MKD)
Austria: Almer, Dragovic, Fuchs, Arnautovic, Alaba (Ilsanker 90+2), Junuzovic, Harnik (Jantscher 76), Baumgartlinger, Prödl, Klein, Janko (Okotie 86). Coach: Marcel Koller (SUI)
Moldova: Cebanu, Armas, Patras, Erhan, Golovatenco, Jardan, Cojocari, Cebotari (Ginsari 79), G Andronic (Racu 55), Dedov, Milinceanu (Carp 87). Coach: Alexandru Curteian (MDA)

05/09/15, Gradski Stadion Podgorica, Podgorica (att: 150)
Montenegro 2-0 Liechtenstein
Goals: 1-0 Bećiraj 38, 2-0 Jovetić 56
Referee: Estrada (ESP)
Montenegro: Poleksić, Volkov, N Vukčević, Baša, Tomašević, Jovetic (Mugoša 69), Vučinić (Damjanović 59), Bećiraj, Savić, Boljević, Marušić (Zverotić 69). Coach: Branko Brnović (MNE)
Liechtenstein: Jehle, Kaufmann, Christen, Wieser (Salanovic 66), Frick, Burgmeier (Kieber 76), Martin Büchel (Gubser 86), Yildiz, Rechsteiner, Hasler, Polverino. Coach: René Pauritsch (AUT)

05/09/15, Otkrytie Arena, Moscow (att: 43,768)
Russia 1-0 Sweden
Goal: 1-0 Dzyuba 38
Referee: Clattenburg (ENG)
Russia: Akinfeev, Ignashevich, Denisov, Kokorin, Dzagoev, V Berezutski, Shirokov (A Berezutski 83), Shatov, Zhirkov (Kuzmin 71), Smolnikov, Dzyuba (Ionov 79). Coach: Leonid Slutsky (RUS)
Sweden: Isaksson, Bengtsson (Berg 60), Antonsson, Granqvist, M Olsson, Forsberg, Larsson, Ekdal (Kiese Thelin 82), Ibrahimović (Toivonen 46), Wernbloom, Durmaz. Coach: Erik Hamrén (SWE)

08/09/15, Rheinpark Stadion, Vaduz (att: 2,874)
Liechtenstein 0-7 Russia
Goals: 0-1 Dzyuba 21, 0-2 Kokorin 40(p), 0-3 Dzyuba 45, 0-4 Dzyuba 73, 0-5 Smolov 77, 0-6 Dzagoev 85, 0-7 Dzyuba 90
Referee: Madden (SCO)
Liechtenstein: Jehle, Kaufmann, Kieber (M Sele 77), Frick, Burgmeier, Martin Büchel (Gubser 84), Yildiz, Rechsteiner, Hasler, Salanovic (Christen 88), Polverino. Coach: René Pauritsch (AUT)
Russia: Akinfeev, Ignashevich, Denisov (Glushakov 46), Kokorin, Dzagoev, V Berezutski, Shirokov (Smolov 75), Shatov (Mamaev 65), Smolnikov, Dzyuba, Kombarov. Coach: Leonid Slutski (RUS)
Red card: Kaufmann 40 (Liechtenstein)

08/09/15, Stadionul Zimbru, Chisinau (att: 6,243)
Moldova 0-2 Montenegro
Goals: 0-1 Savić 9, 0-2 Racu 65(og)
Referee: Delferiere (BEL)
Moldova: Cebanu, Armas, Patras (Ginsari 71), Erhan, Golovatenco, Jardan, Cojocari, Gatcan, Cebotari (Racu 36), Dedov, Milinceanu. Coach: Alexandru Curteian (MDA)
Montenegro: Poleksić, N Vukčević, Baša, Tomašević, Jovetic (Kašćelan 88), Damjanović (Mugoša 46), Bećiraj, Savić, Boljević, Simić, Marušić (Mandić 69). Coach: Branko Brnović (MNE)

Artem Dzyuba (right) completes his hat-trick in Russia's 7-0 rout of Liechtenstein

European Qualifiers

08/09/15, Friends Arena, Solna (att: 48,355)
Sweden 1-4 Austria
Goals: 0-1 Alaba 9(p), 0-2 Harnik 38, 0-3 Janko 77, 0-4 Harnik 88, 1-4 Ibrahimović 90+1
Referee: Velasco Carballo (ESP)
Sweden: Isaksson, Antonsson, Granqvist, M Olsson (Durmaz 82), Forsberg, Larsson, Ekdal (Khalili 86), Källström, Ibrahimović, Berg, Erkan Zengin (Kiese Thelin 62). Coach: Erik Hamrén (SWE)
Austria: Almer, Dragovic, Fuchs, Arnautovic (Jantscher 88), Alaba, Junuzovic (Sabitzer 80), Harnik, Baumgartlinger, Prödl, Klein, Janko (Ilsanker 84). Coach: Marcel Koller (SUI)

09/10/15, Rheinpark Stadion, Vaduz (att: 4,740)
Liechtenstein 0-2 Sweden
Goals: 0-1 Berg 18, 0-2 Ibrahimović 55
Referee: Liany (ISR)
Liechtenstein: Jehle, Christen (Kieber 83), Marcel Büchel, Wieser, Kühne (Yildiz 72), Frick, Burgmeier, Martin Büchel, Oehri, Rechsteiner, Polverino (Gubser 59). Coach: René Pauritsch (AUT)
Sweden: Isaksson, Lustig, Antonsson, Granqvist, M Olsson, Ekdal (Lewicki 66), Källström, Ibrahimović, Berg (Guidetti 62), Durmaz (Larsson 69), Zengin. Coach: Erik Hamrén (SWE)

09/10/15, Stadionul Zimbru, Chisinau (att: 10,244)
Moldova 1-2 Russia
Goals: 0-1 Ignashevich 58, 0-2 Dzyuba 78, 1-2 Cebotaru 85
Referee: Koukoulakis (GRE)
Moldova: Coselev, Armas, Jardan, Cebotari, Bordian, Antoniuc, Milinceanu (Istrati 88), Spataru, Burghiu, Onica (Ambros 79), Carp (Vremea 70). Coach: Ştefan Stoica (ROU)
Russia: Akinfeev, Smolnikov (Kuzmin 27), Ignashevich, Mamaev, A Berezutski, Denisov, Kokorin, Shirokov (Glushakov 76), Shatov, Dzyuba (Smolov 88), Kombarov. Coach: Leonid Slutski (RUS)

09/10/15, Gradski Stadion Podgorica, Podgorica (att: 7,107)
Montenegro 2-3 Austria
Goals: 1-0 Vučinić 32, 1-1 Janko 55, 2-1 Bećiraj 68, 2-2 Arnautovic 81, 2-3 Sabitzer 90+2
Referee: Orsato (ITA)
Montenegro: Poleksić, Rodić, N Vukčević, Tomašević (Balić 74), Vučinić, Bećiraj, Savić, Boljević (Zverotić 56), Mugoša (Mandić 64), Simić, Marušić. Coach: Branko Brnović (MNE)
Austria: Almer, Dragovic, Fuchs, Arnautovic, Alaba (Jantscher 82), Junuzovic (Sabitzer 82), Harnik, Baumgartlinger, Prödl, Klein, Janko (Okotie 82). Coach: Marcel Koller (SUI)
Red card: Vučinić 87 (Montenegro)

12/10/15, Ernst-Happel-Stadion, Vienna (att: 48,500)
Austria 3-0 Liechtenstein
Goals: 1-0 Arnautovic 12, 2-0 Janko 54, 3-0 Janko 57
Referee: Zelinka (CZE)
Austria: Almer, Dragovic, Fuchs, Arnautovic, Alaba (Sabitzer 64), Junuzovic, Harnik, Baumgartlinger (Ilsanker 71), Prödl, Klein, Janko (Okotie 64). Coach: Marcel Koller (SUI)
Liechtenstein: Jehle, Kaufmann, Marcel Büchel, Wieser, Frick (Kühne 90), Burgmeier, Martin Büchel (Brändle 46), Rechsteiner, Kieber (Yildiz 62), Polverino. Coach: René Pauritsch (AUT)

12/10/15, Otkrytie Arena, Moscow (att: 35,604)
Russia 2-0 Montenegro
Goals: 1-0 Kuzmin 33, 2-0 Kokorin 37(p)
Referee: Moen (NOR)
Russia: Akinfeev, Kuzmin, Ignashevich, A Berezutski, Denisov, Kokorin, Dzagoev (Cheryshev 86), Shirokov, Shatov (Mamaev 69), Dzyuba (Smolov 84), Kombarov. Coach: Leonid Slutski (RUS)
Montenegro: Mijatović, Balić, Rodić (Marušić 67), N Vukčević (Boljević 85), Mandić, Bećiraj, Saveljić, Savić, Kašćelan, Nikolić (Mugoša 46), Simić. Coach: Radislav Dragićević (MNE)

Matteo Darmian puts Italy 3-1 up against Azerbaijan in Baku

12/10/15, Friends Arena, Solna (att: 25,351)
Sweden 2-0 Moldova
Goals: 1-0 Ibrahimović 23, 2-0 Zengin 47
Referee: Banti (ITA)
Sweden: Isaksson, Lustig (Tinnerholm 83), Antonsson, Granqvist, M Olsson, Lewicki, Larsson (Källström 57), Ibrahimović (Toivonen 57), Guidetti, Zengin. Coach: Erik Hamrén (SWE)
Moldova: Cebanu, Erhan (Armas 63), Golovatenco, Jardan (Spataru 80), Cebotari, Bordian, Burghiu, Patras (A Antoniuc 61), Istrati, Vremea, Potirniche. Coach: Ştefan Stoica (ROU)

Group H

09/09/14
Croatia 2-0 Malta
Norway 0-2 Italy
Azerbaijan 1-2 Bulgaria

10/10/14
Italy 2-1 Azerbaijan
Malta 0-3 Norway
Bulgaria 0-1 Croatia

13/10/14
Croatia 6-0 Azerbaijan
Malta 0-1 Italy
Norway 2-1 Bulgaria

16/11/14
Italy 1-1 Croatia
Azerbaijan 0-1 Norway
Bulgaria 1-1 Malta

28/03/15
Croatia 5-1 Norway
Azerbaijan 2-0 Malta
Bulgaria 2-2 Italy

12/06/15
Croatia 1-1 Italy
Malta 0-1 Bulgaria
Norway 0-0 Azerbaijan

03/09/15, Bakcell Arena, Baku (att: 10,000)
Azerbaijan 0-0 Croatia
Referee: Buquet (FRA)
Azerbaijan: K Ağayev, Qarayev, Mirzäbäyov, Hüseynov, M Qurbanov (R A Sadiqov 63), R Qurbanov (Nadirov 79), Nazarov (İsrafilov 90), R F Sadiqov, Ämirquliyev, Daşdämirov, İsmayılov. Coach: Robert Prosinečki (CRO)
Croatia: Subašić, Vrsaljko, Pranjić, Perišić (N Kalinić 83), Ćorluka, Rakitić, Pjaca, Modrić (Brozović 71), Mandžukić, Badelj (Kovačić 59), Vida. Coach: Niko Kovač (CRO)

03/09/15, Natsionalen Stadion Vasil Levski, Sofia (att: 12,913)
Bulgaria 0-1 Norway
Goal: 0-1 Forren 57
Referee: Nijhuis (NED)
Bulgaria: Mitrev, Bandalovski, A Alexandrov, Bodurov, Y Minev, I Popov, Manolev (Tonev 61), Chochev, G Milanov (Nedelev 78), Micanski (Rangelov 68), Dyakov. Coach: Ivaylo Petev (BUL)
Norway: Nyland, Høgli, Hovland, Tettey, Johansen (Strandberg 87), Søderlund, Henriksen, Samuelsen (Skjelbred 64), Elabdellaoui, Berget, Forren (Nordtveit 75). Coach: Per-Mathias Høgmo (NOR)

03/09/15, Artemio Franchi, Florence (att: 12,551)
Italy 1-0 Malta
Goal: 1-0 Pellè 69
Referee: Kružliak (SVK)
Italy: Buffon, Chiellini, Darmian, Bertolacci (Parolo 55), Verratti (Soriano 77), Éder, Bonucci, Pellè, Pirlo, Gabbiadini (Candreva 64), Pasqual. Coach: Antonio Conte (ITA)
Malta: Hogg, A Muscat, Agius, P Fenech, Failla, R Briffa (Sciberras 90+1), R Muscat, Schembri (Kristensen 73), S Borg, Effiong (Mifsud 90+3), Z Muscat. Coach: Pietro Ghedin (ITA)

06/09/15, Renzo Barbera, Palermo (att: 21,000)
Italy 1-0 Bulgaria
Goal: 1-0 De Rossi 6(p)
Referee: Karasev (RUS)
Italy: Buffon, De Sciglio, Chiellini, Darmian, Candreva (Éder 86), Verratti, El Shaarawy (Florenzi 72), De Rossi, Parolo, Bonucci, Pellè (Zaza 73). Coach: Antonio Conte (ITA)

Bulgaria: Mitrev, A Alexandrov, Bodurov, Y Minev (Bandalovski 64), I Popov (Rangelov 71), V Minev, Chochev, G Milanov, Micanski, Dyakov, Nedelev (M Alexandrov 67). Coach: Ivaylo Petev (BUL)
Red cards: De Rossi 55 (Italy), Micanski 55 (Bulgaria)

06/09/15, National Stadium, Ta' Qali (att: 5,266)
Malta 2-2 Azerbaijan
Goals: 0-1 Ämirquliyev 36, 1-1 Mifsud 55, 2-1 Effiong 71, 2-2 Ämirquliyev 80
Referee: Lechner (AUT)
Malta: Hogg, A Muscat, Agius, Failla (S Pisani 85), R Briffa, Mifsud (Cohen 62), R Muscat, Schembri, S Borg, Camilleri (Zerafa 80), Effiong. Coach: Pietro Ghedin (ITA)
Azerbaijan: K Ağayev, Qarayev, Mirzäbäyov, Hüseynov, R Qurbanov (Äliyev 81), Nazarov (R A Sadıqov 70), R F Sadıqov, Ämirquliyev, Tağıyev, Daşdämirov, İsmayılov (Abdullayev 72). Coach: Robert Prosinečki (CRO)

06/09/15, Ullevaal Stadion, Oslo (att: 26,751)
Norway 2-0 Croatia
Goals: 1-0 Berget 51, 2-0 Ćorluka 69(og)
Referee: Kassai (HUN)
Norway: Nyland, Høgli, Hovland, Tettey, Johansen (Nordtveit 90+2), Søderlund (Valon Berisha 90+4), Henriksen, Elabdellaoui, Skjelbred (Nielsen 90+1), Berget, Forren. Coach: Per-Mathias Høgmo (NOR)
Croatia: Subašić, Vrsaljko, Perišić, Ćorluka, Rakitić (N Kalinić 72), Pjaca (Olić 63), Modrić, Srna, Brozović, Mandžukić, Vida. Coach: Niko Kovač (CRO)

10/10/15, Bakı Olimpiya Stadionu, Baku (att: 48,000)
Azerbaijan 1-3 Italy
Goals: 0-1 Éder 11, 1-1 Nazarov 31, 1-2 El Shaarawy 43, 1-3 Darmian 65
Referee: Collum (SCO)
Azerbaijan: K Ağayev, Qarayev, Hüseynov, Medvedev, İsrafilov (R A Sadıqov 66), R Qurbanov (Erat 74), Nazarov, R F Sadıqov, Ämirquliyev, Daşdämirov, İsmayılov (Mirzäbäyov 90+1). Coach: Robert Prosinečki (CRO)
Italy: Buffon, De Sciglio, Chiellini, Darmian, Candreva (Montolivo 88), Pellè, Verratti, El Shaarawy (Florenzi 74), Parolo, Éder (Giovinco 79), Bonucci. Coach: Antonio Conte (ITA)
Red card: Hüseynov 88 (Azerbaijan)

10/10/15, Stadion Maksimir, Zagreb (att: 150)
Croatia 3-0 Bulgaria
Goals: 1-0 Perišić 2, 2-0 Rakitić 42, 3-0 N Kalinić 81
Referee: Artur Dias (POR)
Croatia: Subašić, Perišić, Ćorluka, Rakitić, Pjaca (Čop 60), Modrić (Badelj 46), Srna, N Kalinić (Kramarić 85), Kovačić, Vida, Pivarić. Coach: Ante Čačić (CRO)
Bulgaria: Mitrev, S Popov, A Alexandrov, Terziev (Ivanov 46), Rangelov, I Popov (M Alexandrov 71), Slavchev, Tonev, Z Milanov, Nedelev (G Milanov 46), Zlatinski. Coach: Ivaylo Petev (BUL)
Red card: Čop 89 (Croatia)

10/10/15, Ullevaal Stadion, Oslo (att: 27,120)
Norway 2-0 Malta
Goals: 1-0 Tettey 19, 2-0 Søderlund 52
Referee: Hunter (NIR)
Norway: Nyland, Hovland, Tettey, Johansen, Søderlund (King 77), Henriksen, Elabdellaoui, Skjelbred (Ødegaard 53), Aleesami, Berget (Valon Berisha 84), Forren. Coach: Per-Mathias Høgmo (NOR)
Malta: Hogg, A Muscat (Zerafa 56), Agius, P Fenech, Failla, R Briffa, R Muscat, Schembri (Kristensen 81), S Borg (Camilleri 83), Effiong, Z Muscat. Coach: Pietro Ghedin (ITA)

13/10/15, Natsionalen Stadion Vasil Levski, Sofia (att: 2,500)
Bulgaria 2-0 Azerbaijan
Goals: 1-0 M Alexandrov 20, 2-0 Rangelov 56
Referee: Bognar (HUN)
Bulgaria: Mitrev, A Alexandrov, Ivanov, Y Minev, M Alexandrov (Slavchev 80), Rangelov (Nedelev 88), I Popov (Hristov 65), Z Milanov, G Milanov, Dyakov, Zlatinski. Coach: Ivaylo Petev (BUL)
Azerbaijan: K Ağayev, Qarayev (İsrafilov 82), Medvedev (Daşdämirov 63), R Qurbanov, Nazarov, R F Sadıqov, Abışov, Cäfärov (Erat 67), Ämirquliyev, Mirzäbäyov, İsmayılov. Coach: Robert Prosinečki (CRO)

13/10/15, Olimpico, Rome (att: 30,000)
Italy 2-1 Norway
Goals: 0-1 Tettey 23, 1-1 Florenzi 73, 2-1 Pellè 82
Referee: Brych (GER)
Italy: Buffon, De Sciglio, Chiellini, Darmian, Soriano, Pellè, Barzagli (Candreva 72), Florenzi, Éder (Giovinco 62), Montolivo (Bertolacci 68), Bonucci. Coach: Antonio Conte (ITA)
Norway: Nyland, Hovland, Tettey, Johansen, Søderlund (King 60), Henriksen, Elabdellaoui, Skjelbred (Samuelsen 51), Aleesami, Berget (Valon Berisha 78), Forren. Coach: Per-Mathias Høgmo (NOR)

13/10/15, National Stadium, Ta' Qali (att: 5,835)
Malta 0-1 Croatia
Goal: 0-1 Perišić 25
Referee: Clattenburg (ENG)
Malta: Hogg, Zerafa, Agius, Failla, R Briffa (P Fenech 79), R Muscat, Schembri (Cohen 90+2), S Borg, Kristensen, Effiong (Mifsud 75), Z Muscat. Coach: Pietro Ghedin (ITA)
Croatia: Subašić, Perišić, Ćorluka, Rakitić (Brozović 77), Pjaca (Olić 83), Srna, N Kalinić (Kramarić 46), Badelj, Kovačić, Vida, Pivarić. Coach: Ante Čačić (CRO)

Group I

07/09/14
Denmark 2-1 Armenia
Portugal 0-1 Albania

11/10/14
Armenia 1-1 Serbia
Albania 1-1 Denmark

Miguel Veloso struck late to give Portugal a 1-0 victory in Albania

14/10/14
Denmark 0-1 Portugal
Serbia 0-3(f) Albania

14/11/14
Portugal 1-0 Armenia
Serbia 1-3 Denmark

29/03/15
Albania 2-1 Armenia
Portugal 2-1 Serbia

13/06/15
Armenia 2-3 Portugal
Denmark 2-0 Serbia

04/09/15, Telia Parken, Copenhagen (att: 35,648)
Denmark 0-0 Albania
Referee: Collum (SCO)
Denmark: Schmeichel, Kjær, Agger, Durmisi, Jacobsen, Kvist (J Poulsen 46), Krohn-Dehli, Bendtner, Sisto (Y Poulsen 46), N Jørgensen, Højbjerg. Coach: Morten Olsen (DEN)
Albania: Berisha, Lenjani (Sadiku 64), Cana, Djimsiti, Agolli, Gashi (Roshi 83), Kukeli, Xhaka, Ajeti, Çikalleshi, Abrashi (Basha 64). Coach: Gianni De Biasi (ITA)

04/09/15, Karađjordje, Novi Sad (att: 150)
Serbia 2-0 Armenia
Goals: 1-0 Hayrapetyan 22(og), 2-0 Ljajić 53
Referee: Zelinka (CZE)
Serbia: Stojković, Tomović, Ivanović, A Mitrović, Kolarov, Spajić, Matić, Brašanac, Kostić (Tadić 84), A Živković (Z Tošić 59), Ljajić (Fejsa 73). Coach: Radovan Ćurčić (SRB)
Armenia: Kasparov, Andonyan, Arzumanyan, Mkrtchyan, Pizzelli (Koryan 65), Ghazaryan (Simonyan 82), Movsisyan, Mkoyan, Mkhitaryan, Hayrapetyan, Özbiliz (Hovhannisyan 59). Coach: Sargis Hovsepyan (ARM)

07/09/15, Elbasan Arena, Elbasan (att: 12,121)
Albania 0-1 Portugal
Goal: 0-1 Miguel Veloso 90+2
Referee: Eriksson (SWE)
Albania: Berisha, Lenjani, Cana, Djimsiti, Agolli, Gashi (Roshi 70), Kukeli, Xhaka, Ajeti, Çikalleshi (Balaj 86), Abrashi (Basha 54). Coach: Gianni De Biasi (ITA)
Portugal: Rui Patrício, Pepe, Miguel Veloso, Ricardo Carvalho, Cristiano Ronaldo, Danny (Éder 76), Vieirinha (Cédric 54), Danilo Pereira, Bernardo Silva (Ricardo Quaresma 90), Nani, Eliseu. Coach: Fernando Santos (POR)

07/09/15, Vazgen Sargsyan anvan Hanrapetakan Marzadasht, Yerevan (att: 7,500)
Armenia 0-0 Denmark
Referee: Moen (NOR)
Armenia: Kasparov, Andonyan, Haroyan, Arzumanyan, Mkrtchyan, Pizzelli (Koryan 62), Ghazaryan, Hovhannisyan (Simonyan 87), Movsisyan (Özbiliz 83), Mkoyan, Mkhitaryan. Coach: Sargis Hovsepyan (ARM)
Denmark: Schmeichel, Kjær (Sviatchenko 80), Agger, Durmisi, Jacobsen, Krohn-Dehli (Delaney 56), Bendtner, J Poulsen, N Jørgensen (Braithwaite 64), Y Poulsen, Højbjerg. Coach: Morten Olsen (DEN)

08/10/15, Elbasan Arena, Elbasan (att: 12,330)
Albania 0-2 Serbia
Goals: 0-1 Kolarov 90+1, 0-2 Ljajić 90+4
Referee: Rizzoli (ITA)
Albania: Berisha, Lila (Kaçe 46), Lenjani (Meha 83), Hysaj, Cana, Djimsiti, Agolli, Basha, Memushaj , Xhaka, Balaj (Çikalleshi 69). Coach: Gianni De Biasi (ITA)
Serbia: Stojković, Tomović, Ivanović (D Tošić 65), Z Tošić, A Mitrović, Tadić (Sulejmani 54), Kolarov, S Mitrović, Milivojević, Matić (Fejsa 73), Ljajić. Coach: Radovan Ćurčić (SRB)

08/10/15, Estádio Municipal de Braga, Braga (att: 29,860)
Portugal 1-0 Denmark
Goal: 1-0 João Moutinho 66
Referee: Clattenburg (ENG)
Portugal: Rui Patrício, Bruno Alves, Fábio Coentrão, Ricardo Carvalho, Cristiano Ronaldo, João Moutinho (José Fonte 90+1), Danilo Pereira, Bernardo Silva (Danny 76), Nani (Ricardo Quaresma 82), Tiago, Cédric. Coach: Fernando Santos (POR)
Denmark: Schmeichel, Wass (N Jørgensen 69), Kjær, Agger, Durmisi, Jacobsen, Braithwaite, Krohn-Dehli, Eriksen (Y Poulsen 82), Bendtner, Højbjerg (Kvist 46). Coach: Morten Olsen (DEN)

11/10/15, Vazgen Sargsyan anvan Hanrapetakan Marzadasht, Yerevan (att: 4,700)
Armenia 0-3 Albania
Goals: 0-1 Hovhannisyan 9(og), 0-2 Djimsiti 23, 0-3 Sadiku 76
Referee: Marciniak (POL)
Armenia: Kasparov, Andonyan, Haroyan, Arzumanyan, Mkrtchyan, Pizzelli, Ghazaryan (Poghosyan 83), Hovhannisyan, Movsisyan (Sarkisov 59), Yusbashyan (Özbiliz 46), Mkhitaryan. Coach: Sargis Hovsepyan (ARM)
Albania: Berisha, Hysaj, Cana, Djimsiti, Aliji, Basha (Abrashi 87), Memushaj (Kukeli 72), Gashi, Xhaka, Çikalleshi (Sadiku 58), Roshi. Coach: Gianni De Biasi (ITA)

11/10/15, Stadion FK Partizan, Belgrade (att: 7,485)
Serbia 1-2 Portugal
Goals: 0-1 Nani 5, 1-1 Z Tošić 65, 1-2 João Moutinho 78
Referee: Fernández Borbalán (ESP)
Serbia: Stojković, D Tošić, Tomović, Z Tošić (Sulejmani 84), A Mitrović (Škuletić 85), Tadić, Kolarov (Obradović 77), S Mitrović, Milivojević, Matić, Ljajić. Coach: Radovan Ćurčić (SRB)
Portugal: Rui Patrício, Bruno Alves (Luís Neto 46), Miguel Veloso (João Moutinho 70), Danny (Éder 57), André André, Danilo Pereira, José Fonte, Nani, Eliseu, Ricardo Quaresma, Nélson Semedo. Coach: Fernando Santos (POR)
Red cards: Kolarov 80 (Serbia), Matić 81 (Serbia)

Final tables

Group A

	Pld	Home W D L F A	Away W D L F A	Total W D L F A	Pts
1 Czech Republic	10	3 1 1 7 6	4 0 1 12 8	7 1 2 19 14	22
2 Iceland	10	3 2 0 9 3	3 0 2 8 3	6 2 2 17 6	20
3 Turkey	10	3 1 1 9 4	2 2 1 5 5	5 3 2 14 9	18
4 Netherlands	10	2 1 2 12 6	2 0 3 5 8	4 1 5 17 14	13
5 Kazakhstan	10	0 1 4 3 10	1 1 3 4 8	1 2 7 7 18	5
6 Latvia	10	0 1 4 2 9	0 4 1 4 10	0 5 5 6 19	5

Group B

	Pld	Home W D L F A	Away W D L F A	Total W D L F A	Pts
1 Belgium	10	4 1 0 17 2	3 1 1 7 3	7 2 1 24 5	23
2 Wales	10	3 2 0 5 1	3 1 1 6 3	6 3 1 11 4	21
3 Bosnia & Herzegovina	10	3 1 1 10 4	2 1 2 7 8	5 2 3 17 12	17
4 Israel	10	2 0 3 8 6	2 1 2 8 8	4 1 5 16 14	13
5 Cyprus	10	1 0 4 8 7	3 0 2 8 10	4 0 6 16 17	12
6 Andorra	10	0 0 5 4 16	0 0 5 0 20	0 0 10 4 36	0

Group C

	Pld	Home W D L F A	Away W D L F A	Total W D L F A	Pts
1 Spain	10	5 0 0 15 1	4 0 1 8 2	9 0 1 23 3	27
2 Slovakia	10	3 1 1 7 3	4 0 1 10 5	7 1 2 17 8	22
3 Ukraine	10	3 0 2 7 3	3 1 1 7 1	6 1 3 14 4	19
4 Belarus	10	1 1 3 3 6	2 1 2 5 8	3 2 5 8 14	11
5 Luxembourg	10	1 1 3 4 12	0 0 5 2 15	1 1 8 6 27	4
6 FYR Macedonia	10	1 0 4 4 9	0 1 4 2 9	1 1 8 6 18	4

Group D

	Pld	Home W D L F A	Away W D L F A	Total W D L F A	Pts
1 Germany	10	4 1 0 12 4	3 0 2 12 5	7 1 2 24 9	22
2 Poland	10	4 1 0 18 4	2 2 1 15 6	6 3 1 33 10	21
3 Republic of Ireland	10	3 2 0 11 2	2 1 2 8 5	5 3 2 19 7	18
4 Scotland	10	3 1 1 12 6	1 2 2 10 6	4 3 3 22 12	15
5 Georgia	10	2 0 3 6 8	1 0 4 4 8	3 0 7 10 16	9
6 Gibraltar	10	0 0 5 0 27	0 0 5 2 29	0 0 10 2 56	0

Group E

	Pld	Home W D L F A	Away W D L F A	Total W D L F A	Pts
1 England	10	5 0 0 16 1	5 0 0 15 2	10 0 0 31 3	30
2 Switzerland	10	4 0 1 17 4	3 0 2 7 4	7 0 3 24 8	21
3 Slovenia	10	3 1 1 11 4	2 0 3 7 7	5 1 4 18 11	16
4 Estonia	10	3 0 2 4 2	0 1 4 0 7	3 1 6 4 9	10
5 Lithuania	10	2 0 3 4 8	1 1 3 3 10	3 1 6 7 18	10
6 San Marino	10	0 1 4 0 14	0 0 5 1 22	0 1 9 1 36	1

Group F

	Pld	Home W D L F A	Away W D L F A	Total W D L F A	Pts
1 Northern Ireland	10	3 2 0 8 3	3 1 1 8 5	6 3 1 16 8	21
2 Romania	10	2 3 0 5 2	3 2 0 6 0	5 5 0 11 2	20
3 Hungary	10	2 2 1 4 3	2 2 1 7 6	4 4 2 11 9	16
4 Finland	10	1 2 2 3 5	2 1 2 6 5	3 3 4 9 10	12
5 Faroe Islands	10	1 0 4 4 11	1 0 4 2 6	2 0 8 6 17	6
6 Greece	10	1 0 4 4 8	0 3 2 3 6	1 3 6 7 14	6

Group G

	Pld	Home W D L F A	Away W D L F A	Total W D L F A	Pts
1 Austria	10	4 1 0 7 1	5 0 0 15 4	9 1 0 22 5	28
2 Russia	10	3 1 1 8 2	3 1 1 13 3	6 2 2 21 5	20
3 Sweden	10	3 1 1 9 6	2 2 1 6 3	5 3 2 15 9	18
4 Montenegro	10	2 1 2 7 7	1 1 3 3 6	3 2 5 10 13	11
5 Liechtenstein	10	0 2 3 1 15	1 0 4 1 11	1 2 7 2 26	5
6 Moldova	10	0 0 5 2 9	0 2 3 2 7	0 2 8 4 16	2

Group H

	Pld	Home W D L F A	Away W D L F A	Total W D L F A	Pts
1 Italy	10	4 1 0 7 3	3 2 0 9 4	7 3 0 16 7	24
2 Croatia	10	4 1 0 17 2	2 1 3 3	6 3 1 20 5	20
3 Norway	10	3 1 1 6 3	3 0 2 7 7	6 1 3 13 10	19
4 Bulgaria	10	1 2 2 5 5	2 0 3 4 7	3 2 5 9 12	11
5 Azerbaijan	10	1 1 3 4 6	0 2 3 3 12	1 3 6 7 18	6
6 Malta	10	0 1 4 2 8	0 1 4 1 8	0 2 8 3 16	2

NB Croatia – 1 pt deducted.

Group I

	Pld	Home W D L F A	Away W D L F A	Total W D L F A	Pts
1 Portugal	8	3 0 1 4 2	4 0 0 7 3	7 0 1 11 5	21
2 Albania	8	1 1 2 3 5	3 1 0 7 0	4 2 2 10 5	14
3 Denmark	8	2 1 1 4 2	1 2 1 4 3	3 3 2 8 5	12
4 Serbia	8	0 2 3 4 8	1 1 2 4 5	2 1 5 8 13	4
5 Armenia	8	0 2 2 3 7	0 0 4 2 7	0 2 6 5 14	2

NB Serbia – 3 pts deducted.

Play-offs

12/11/15, Ullevaal Stadion, Oslo (att: 27,182)
Norway 0-1 Hungary
Goal: 0-1 Kleinheisler 26
Referee: Clattenburg (ENG)
Norway: Nyland, Høgli, Hovland, Tettey, Johansen, Søderlund (Pedersen 61), Henriksen, Elabdellaoui, Skjelbred (Helland 86), Berget (Elyounoussi 74), Forren. Coach: Per-Mathias Høgmo (NOR)
Hungary: Király, Lang, Kádár, Fiola, Elek, Dzsudzsák (Lovrencsics 76), Szalai (Priskin 90+2), Gera, Németh, Kleinheisler (Nagy 72), Guzmics. Coach: Bernd Storck (GER)

15/11/15, Groupama Aréna, Budapest (att: 22,189)
Hungary 2-1 Norway
Goals: 1-0 Priskin 14, 2-0 Henriksen 83(og), 2-1 Henriksen 87
Referee: Velasco Carballo (ESP)
Hungary: Király, Lang, Kádár, Fiola, Elek (Pintér 46), Dzsudzsák, Nagy, Lovrencsics, Kleinheisler (Németh 75), Priskin (Böde 62), Guzmics. Coach: Bernd Storck (GER)
Norway: Nyland, Hovland, Tettey, Johansen, Henriksen, Ødegaard (Helland 46), Elyounoussi (Pedersen 46), Elabdellaoui, Skjelbred (Berget 80), Aleesami, Forren. Coach: Per-Mathias Høgmo (NOR)

Aggregate: 3-1; Hungary qualify.

13/11/15, Stadion Bilino polje, Zenica (att: 12,000)
Bosnia & Herzegovina 1-1 Republic of Ireland
Goals: 0-1 Brady 82, 1-1 Džeko 85
Referee: Brych (GER)
Bosnia & Herzegovina: Begović, Cocalić, Spahić, Ibišević, Pjanić, Džeko, Mudžža (Vranješ 51), Šunjić, Lulić (Hajrovic 88), Zukanović, Višća (Djuric 73). Coach: Mehmed Baždarević (BIH)
Republic of Ireland: Randolph, Coleman, Keogh, Whelan, McCarthy, Murphy, Clark, Ward (Wilson 67), Brady (McGeady 86), Hoolahan (McClean 60), Hendrick. Coach: Martin O'Neill (NIR)

16/11/15, Aviva Stadium, Dublin (att: 50,500)
Republic of Ireland 2-0 Bosnia & Herzegovina
Goals: 1-0 Walters 24(p), 2-0 Walters 70
Referee: Kuipers (NED)
Republic of Ireland: Randolph, Coleman, Keogh, Whelan (O'Shea 90), McCarthy, Clark, Murphy (Long 55), Walters, Brady, Hoolahan (McClean 55), Hendrick. Coach: Martin O'Neill (NIR)
Bosnia & Herzegovina: Begović, Cocalić (Bešić 46), Spahić, Kolašinac, Vranješ, Medunjanin (Djuric 69), Pjanić, Džeko, Lulić (Ibišević 80), Zukanović, Višća. Coach: Mehmed Baždarević (BIH)

Aggregate: 3-1; Republic of Ireland qualify.

14/11/15, Friends Arena, Solna (att: 49,053)
Sweden 2-1 Denmark
Goals: 1-0 Forsberg 45, 2-0 Ibrahimović 50(p), 2-1 N Jørgensen 80
Referee: Rizzoli (ITA)
Sweden: Isaksson, Lustig, Antonsson (Johansson 29), Granqvist, M Olsson, Forsberg, Lewicki, Källström, Ibrahimović (Guidetti 82), Berg, Durmaz (Larsson 68). Coach: Erik Hamrén (SWE)
Denmark: Schmeichel, Kjær, Agger, Durmisi, Jacobsen, Kvist, Braithwaite (Y Poulsen 71), Eriksen, Bendtner, Kahlenberg (N Jørgensen 54), Fischer (Højbjerg 54). Coach: Morten Olsen (DEN)

17/11/15, Telia Parken, Copenhagen (att: 36,051)
Denmark 2-2 Sweden
Goals: 0-1 Ibrahimović 19, 0-2 Ibrahimović 76, 1-2 Y Poulsen 82, 2-2 Vestergaard 90+1
Referee: Atkinson (ENG)
Denmark: Schmeichel, Kjær, Agger, Durmisi (Vestergaard 84), Jacobsen, Eriksen, Bendtner (Rasmussen 60), Delaney (Krohn-Dehli 46), N Jørgensen, Y Poulsen, Højbjerg. Coach: Morten Olsen (DEN)
Sweden: Isaksson, Lustig, Granqvist, Forsberg, Larsson (Hiljemark 81), Lewicki, Källström (Svensson 69), Ibrahimović, Johansson, Bengtsson (M Olsson 86), Berg. Coach: Erik Hamrén (SWE)

Aggregate: 3-4; Sweden qualify.

14/11/15, Arena Lviv, Lviv (att: 32,592)
Ukraine 2-0 Slovenia
Goals: 1-0 Yarmolenko 22, 2-0 Seleznyov 54
Referee: Eriksson (SWE)
Ukraine: Pyatov, Khacheridi, Yarmolenko (Karavayev 90), Konoplyanka, Seleznyov (Kravets 84), Shevchuk, Sydorchuk, Fedetskiy, Rybalka, Garmash (Malinovskyi 79), Rakitskiy. Coach: Mykhailo Fomenko (UKR)
Slovenia: Handanovič, Brečko, Cesar, Ilič, Iličič (Bezjak 63), Kurtič, Birsa (Pečnik 73), Novakovič (Ljubijankič 90), Jokič, Kampl, Krhin. Coach: Srečko Katanec (SVN)

17/11/15, Stadion Ljudski vrt, Maribor (att: 12,702)
Slovenia 1-1 Ukraine
Goals: 1-0 Cesar 11, 1-1 Yarmolenko 90+7
Referee: Çakır (TUR)
Slovenia: Handanovič, Brečko, Cesar, Ilič, Birsa (Lazarevič 80), Novakovič, Jokič, Pečnik (Iličič 67), Kampl, Krhin, Bezjak (Ljubijankič 68). Coach: Srečko Katanec (SVN)
Ukraine: Pyatov, Khacheridi, Stepanenko, Yarmolenko, Konoplyanka (Tymoshchuk 90+6), Seleznyov (Kravets 80), Shevchuk, Sydorchuk (Garmash 61), Fedetskiy, Rybalka, Rakitskiy. Coach: Mykhailo Fomenko (UKR)
Red card: Brečko 90+3 (Slovenia)

Aggregate: 1-3; Ukraine qualify.

Top goalscorers

13	Robert Lewandowski (Poland)
11	Zlatan Ibrahimović (Sweden)
9	Thomas Müller (Germany)
8	Edin Džeko (Bosnia & Herzegovina)
	Artem Dzyuba (Russia)
7	Marc Janko (Austria)
	Wayne Rooney (England)
	Kyle Lafferty (Northern Ireland)
	Steven Fletcher (Scotland)
	Gareth Bale (Wales)
6	Ivan Perišić (Croatia)
	Danny Welbeck (England)
	Gylfi Sigurdsson (Iceland)
	Arkadiusz Milik (Poland)
	Milivoje Novakvič (Slovenia)
	Andriy Yarmolenko (Ukraine)

Jonathan Walters is pursued in celebration by Richard Keogh after scoring his second goal of the evening to wrap up Ireland's play-off win over Bosnia & Herzegovina

Real Madrid reclaim their crown

Two years after winning the European Cup for a historic tenth time – the much coveted Décima – Real Madrid were triumphant again. As in 2014, their opponents in the final were city rivals Atlético. Defeated in extra time in Lisbon, Diego Simeone's gallant team suffered further heartbreak in Milan, going down 5-3 on penalties after another hard-fought encounter on European club football's biggest stage. The glory, however, belonged to the men in white and their coach, Zinédine Zidane, who took over from Rafael Benítez midway through the campaign and guided the club to victory in a competition he had previously graced as a player, winning the trophy in 2002 after scoring a glorious goal in the Glasgow final against Bayer Leverkusen.

The hero of the hour for Madrid in Milan was Cristiano Ronaldo, who, despite a relatively subdued evening, struck the winning penalty in the shoot-out. Nobody deserved their winner's medal more than three-time Ballon d'Or winner, who scored 16 goals during his team's run to the final, including a record haul of 11 in the group stage and three hat-tricks, the last of which turned around a tricky quarter-final tie against Wolfsburg. The total may have fallen one short of his record tally for a single UEFA Champions League campaign recorded two years earlier, but the spot kick in the San Siro was more than ample consolation. It brought him a third winner's medal in the competition and enabled Madrid to maintain their 100% success rate in UEFA Champions League finals – five out of five and all of them, curiously, in even-numbered years (1998, 2000, 2002, 2014 and 2016).

Although the plaudits went to Real, sympathy was widespread for Atlético, who yet again came so close to lifting the biggest club prize of all for the first time only to be denied at the last. They may have needed a penalty triumph themselves to knock out PSV Eindhoven in the round of 16, but the application and fortitude, not to mention tactical and technical expertise, that enabled them to eliminate the competition's two most fancied sides, Barcelona and Bayern München, in successive knockout rounds earned the team and their charismatic coach Diego Simeone a whole legion of new admirers.

Luis Enrique's Barça, equipped with their deadly three-pronged South American strikeforce of Lionel Messi, Luis Suárez and Neymar, became the latest holders struck by the curse that has prevented any club from making a successful defence of the UEFA Champions League, while Bayern, with their former Barcelona boss Pep Guardiola in charge, exited at the semi-final stage for the third year running. Both clubs extended long winning runs at home, but defeats in the Estadio Vicente Calderón proved costly.

Manchester City did their best to revive flagging English fortunes in the competition by reaching the semi-finals for the first time, but a lack of adventure against Real Madrid, the former club of their departing coach Manuel Pellegrini, undid a lot of good work that had gone before. City actually won their group despite losing home and away to Juventus, whose bid to reach a second successive final was cut short prematurely in an epic round of 16 contest with Bayern. That was also the drop-off point for London clubs Chelsea and Arsenal – the latter for the sixth year in a row – while Paris Saint-Germain failed once again to conquer their quarter-final jinx and Manchester United, back in the competition after a year away, could not make it out of their group.

Qualifying rounds

The first qualifying round of the 2015/16 UEFA Champions League started on 30 June – just 24 days after the conclusion of the previous season's competition – with first-leg matches staged in locations as far flung as Torshavn, Belfast, Yerevan and Gibraltar.

None of the four teams who came through those opening jousts – Crusaders, Lincoln, Pyunik or The New Saints – made it past the second qualifying round, although the champions of Wales pushed Videoton all the way into extra time. Celtic posted the biggest aggregate victory of the round, overcoming Stjarnan 6-1 over the two legs, while Molde ran up the most convincing on-the-night win, 5-0 against Pyunik.

Remarkably, five of the 16 winners in the second qualifying round – FC Astana, BATE Borisov, Dinamo Zagreb, Maccabi Tel-Aviv and Malmö FF – would go on to reach the group stage. They all survived tight engagements in the third qualifying round before using that experience to positive effect in the play-offs.

Malmö were the qualifying phase's comeback kings, reaching the group stage for the second season in a row after rallying from first-leg defeats against Salzburg and Celtic to claim decisive wins in the Swedbank Stadion. Dinamo, BATE and Maccabi all exploited the away goals rule to their advantage, with the prolific Eran Zahavi scoring all three of the Israeli champions' goals in their two play-off draws against FC Basel, while Astana scored a decisive late goal in Cyprus against APOEL to become the first team from Kazakhstan to reach the competition proper.

Elsewhere, there were a number of heavyweight casualties, with Fenerbahçe and Panathinaikos falling in the third qualifying round before Lazio, Monaco and Sporting Clube de Portugal joined them as play-off losers. Manchester United ensured a return to the group stage after a year's sabbatical with a thumping 7-1 aggregate win over Club Brugge, with new signing Memphis Depay scoring twice at Old Trafford and skipper Wayne Rooney three times in Bruges. However, apart from that tie and Dinamo Zagreb's 6-2 aggregate triumph against surprise Albanian qualifiers Skënderbeu, the play-offs were all closely contested, with the identity of the winner uncertain in most cases until the final whistle.

6

On matchday one Rafael Benítez joined his predecessor at Real Madrid, Carlo Ancelotti, in becoming only the second coach to lead six different clubs in the UEFA Champions League, having previously been in charge of Valencia, Liverpool, Internazionale, Chelsea and Napoli.

Group stage

Real Madrid and Paris Saint-Germain were the two seeded teams in **Group A** and, as expected, both coasted through to the knockout phase. Madrid did so for a record 19th successive season, and although they were unable to repeat their 100% success rate of 12 months earlier, they still ended up with the best record of all 32 teams, signing off – and, as it turned out, bidding farewell to coach Rafael Benítez – with a record-equalling 8-0 win over Malmö at the Estadio Santiago Bernabéu. Four of the goals were scored by Cristiano Ronaldo, who thus broke his own record tally in a UEFA Champions League group stage as he increased his haul to 11.

Ronaldo was not the only star to shine. His ex-Madrid team-mate, Ángel Di María, not only scored the very first goal of the group stage – in Paris's opening 2-0 win at home to Malmö – but also struck the UEFA Champions League's 7000th goal in the return fixture against the Swedish champions – a 5-0 win that secured his team's safe passage into the round of 16. Not that Laurent Blanc's side ever looked likely to miss out. They failed to score in both games against Madrid, but only conceded once over the six-match schedule – a freakish strike from Nacho at the Bernabéu in a game they largely dominated – and therefore equalled another group stage record.

The section's most exciting encounter came on matchday five when Madrid went 4-0 up with 20 minutes remaining against Shakhtar Donetsk in Lviv only to concede three times thereafter and end up clinging on nervously to their three points in a frantic finale. Shakhtar's long-serving Romanian coach, Mircea Lucescu, became only the fifth man to take charge of 100 UEFA Champions League matches on the night his team lost 1-0 to Malmö,

Memphis Depay (centre) gets in on the goalscoring act as Manchester United make light work of Club Brugge in the play-offs

but a 4-0 win in the reverse fixture would prove enough to take the Ukrainian club into the UEFA Europa League, their final three-point tally the lowest of all the third-place finishers.

Group B produced a turn-up for the books as Manchester United, beneficiaries by common consent of a favourable draw, failed to make further progress. Louis van Gaal's side got off to a bad start, with left-back Luke Shaw suffering a terrible leg break in a 2-1 defeat at PSV Eindhoven after the returning Depay had given his new club the lead. But although United staged a comeback 2-1 win of their own next time out, at home to Wolfsburg, and bagged a further four points from their two games against CSKA Moskva, they stumbled at the finish, drawing 0-0 at home to PSV on matchday five and losing a game they had to win, 3-2 away to Wolfsburg, in their final fixture.

That result alone was not enough to relegate United to the UEFA Europa League, but while they were conceding a late winner to Wolfsburg – with Brazilian defender Naldo grabbing his second goal of the game – PSV simultaneously recovered from falling behind to a 75th-minute penalty at home to CSKA, two late goals from Luuk de Jong and Davy Pröpper transforming defeat into victory and hoisting them above United into second place.

Wolfsburg and PSV both won all three home games, which meant that United's goalless draw against the Dutch champions at Old Trafford proved decisive. The only away win in the section was recorded by Dieter Hecking's side, 2-0 at CSKA, while the Russian club's sole victory came at home to PSV. Not that it ultimately mattered to Phillip Cocu and his players as they celebrated the club's first qualification for the knockout phase in nine years.

Benfica made the early running in **Group C**, winning their opening two UEFA Champions League fixtures for the first time at the 11th attempt, the first of them with a routine 2-0 home win over competition debutants Astana, the second with a wholly unexpected 2-1 success at Atlético Madrid's Vicente Calderón fortress, where Gonçalo Guedes made himself a hero with a delightful winner.

While that result was not quite a flash in the pan, it did assume an increasingly unorthodox profile as the group

Kevin De Bruyne rifles in Manchester City's late winner at home to Sevilla

progressed. For while Benfica won only won of their remaining four fixtures, Atlético claimed ten points out of the final 12 on offer, gradually closing the gap on their fellow Iberians until they got their revenge – both on Benfica and their stadium, venue of their 2014 UEFA Champions League final defeat – with a 2-1 win of their own. It was a result that enabled Diego Simeone's side to finish top of the group by three points, the two teams having already clinched qualification a fortnight earlier, when Benfica came from two goals down to draw 2-2 at Astana and deny their hosts a first UEFA Champions League victory and Antoine Griezmann scored both Atlético goals in a 2-0 win against Galatasaray – exactly as he had done in the opening game of the group.

Group D provided several tales of the unexpected, not least on matchday one when Manchester City, going well in the Premier League with victories in each of their opening five fixtures, lost 2-1 at home to a Juventus side that had taken just a single point from their first three matches of the new Serie A season. More remarkably still, three matchdays later City would find themselves qualified for the knockout phase with two games

to spare. Furthermore, Manuel Pellegrini's team would go on to top the group – something they had never managed in four previous campaigns – despite losing a second time to the Italian champions, 1-0 in Turin.

The key to City's success was a knack of scoring late goals. A 90th-minute Sergio Agüero penalty brought three points at group stage debutants Borussia Mönchengladbach – after Joe Hart had saved an earlier spot kick from Raffael – and that was backed up by an even later winning goal, sumptuously scored by new signing Kevin De Bruyne, in another 2-1 win, at home to Sevilla. The Spanish side were defeated again two weeks later, 3-1 in Andalusia, and all of a sudden, with Mönchengladbach holding Juventus to a pair of draws, City's nine points were enough to guarantee them a top-two placing.

A single goal from Mario Mandžukić, who had also scored in Manchester, enabled Juventus to do the double over City, clinch qualification and move two points clear at the top of the table with a game to play. A draw in Seville was enough for the Serie A champions to lock up top spot, but the home side required victory to give themselves a chance of prolonging their European campaign in the UEFA Europa League, a competition they had won in each of the previous two seasons. Although Juve lost 1-0, at the time they conceded the goal, to Fernando Llorente, they were still heading through as group winners. That was because City were losing 2-1 at home to Gladbach. But the late goal specialists struck again, not once but three times in the last ten minutes, to win the game 4-2 and return to the top of the table for good.

There were goals galore in **Group E** – 44 in total – as defending champions Barcelona romped undefeated into the last 16. Rarely, if ever, had they dominated a group quite so emphatically, with their margin of victory in the final table standing at a whopping eight points – even after they had been held to a draw in their final fixture.

The absence of the injured Lionel Messi for three of their fixtures made no difference to Barça's superiority. Indeed, they won all three, coming from behind to defeat Bayer Leverkusen 2-1 at the Camp Nou before doing the double over BATE Borisov. The Argentinian maestro had

made his 100th UEFA Champions League appearance on matchday one, failing to score for once in a 1-1 draw at Roma that featured an astonishing goal from near the touchline in his own half by Italian international Alessandro Florenzi, but when he returned he struck twice as Barça overwhelmed the Serie A side 6-1, with Luis Suárez also helping himself to a memorable brace.

That resounding win confirmed the Catalans' place in the last 16, but remarkably it did no lasting damage to Roma's hopes of joining their victors in the knockout phase. With Barcelona subsequently protecting their unbeaten record in a 1-1 draw at Leverkusen, Roma were able to draw their final fixture 0-0 at home to BATE and still take second place, on the head-to-head rule over Leverkusen (4-4 away, 3-2 at home), despite ending up with a measly six points and a goals-against figure of 16 – the worst record of any group stage qualifier in UEFA Champions League history.

If Roma's progress was unusual, Arsenal's advancement from **Group F** bordered on the miraculous. Arsène Wenger's side had qualified from their group in each of the previous 15

seasons, but when they suffered shock defeats in their opening two fixtures – 2-1 away to Dinamo Zagreb, a club without a group stage win for 16 years, and 3-2 at home to Olympiacos, who had lost on all of their previous 12 visits to England – hope of maintaining that extraordinary run seemed forlorn, not least because their next two games were against one of the favourites to win the competition, Bayern München.

Arsenal won the first game, 2-0 in north London, but they were easily beaten 5-1 by Pep Guardiola's side in the Munich return – the club's heaviest UEFA Champions League defeat. With Olympiacos turning the knife by grabbing a last-minute winner at home to Dinamo, the Gunners had a six-point deficit to make up on the Greek champions. That was down to three points after matchday five as Arsenal won 3-0 at home to Dinamo and Bayern confirmed their qualification as group winners with another big home win (4-0) against Olympiacos. Although qualification was still in the English club's hands, they travelled to Piraeus knowing that unless they won by a two-goal margin or by scoring at least three times, their proud record would be at an end. It was a challenge to which they fronted up in breathtaking style, with striker Olivier Giroud scoring all of the goals in a momentous 3-0 win.

As the Frenchman, who had been red-carded in the opening defeat in Zagreb, celebrated an extremely timely first hat-trick for the club, Bayern signed off with a 2-0 win at the Maksimir Stadium thanks to a double from Robert Lewandowski that enabled him to move ahead of team-mate Thomas Müller as his club's leading marksman for the competition with seven goals. Bayern's total as a team for the group stage was 19, the same as Real Madrid's and one short of the all-time record, which would have been theirs to share had Müller not struck the post with a late penalty in Zagreb.

Qualification from **Group G** would go down to the wire, with any combination of two from three teams still possible going into the final round of games. Chelsea, FC Porto and Dynamo Kyiv were the three clubs still in contention, all of them having taken their full quota of points off Maccabi Tel-Aviv – whose only crumb of comfort in a calamitous campaign was a consolation penalty at the end of a 3-1 home defeat by Porto – while sharing around the points in the fixtures among themselves.

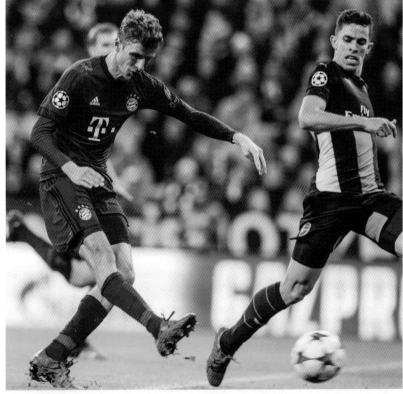
Thomas Müller completes the scoring as Bayern beat Arsenal 5-1 in Munich

Chelsea, who were enduring a dreadful time on the domestic front in defence of their Premier League title, lost 2-1 on manager José Mourinho's return to former club Porto but repaired some of the damage by collecting four points from their two games against Dynamo, with Brazilian winger Willian scoring a brilliant free-kick to win the game at Stamford Bridge after a goalless stalemate in Kyiv. Porto, on the other hand, surrendered the advantage they had given themselves with that win over Chelsea by losing 2-0 at home to Dynamo, opponents they had previously held to a 2-2 draw on Ukrainian soil.

Dynamo's win at the Estádio do Dragão meant that they would be sure of reaching the last 16 – after a 16-year wait – if they beat Maccabi at home as one of their rivals would have to drop points in their head-to-head at Stamford Bridge. Unfortunately, they had to go about their task in an empty stadium – a punishment for earlier misdeeds by their fans – but an early goal from Denys Garmash would suffice to see Dynamo through. In London, where Chelsea needed only a draw against Porto to progress, a full house assembled, and the vast majority of those in attendance would go home happy as Mourinho's men not only avoided defeat but won the game, 2-0, to top the group, Willian crowning the victory with his fifth goal of the campaign.

It was another Brazilian winger, Hulk, who set the ball rolling in **Group H**, scoring two brilliant goals to give Zenit an opening 3-2 win at Valencia – the club's first victory in Spain after defeats on all of their previous seven visits. André Villas-Boas's team took great confidence from that display and went on to win their next four matches as well, with another fantastic strike from Hulk embellishing a 3-1 home win over Olympique Lyonnais

Danijel Milicevic strikes Gent's winning goal at home to Group H winners Zenit

before his strike partner Artem Dzyuba struck both goals in the return fixture to seal the Russian side's place in the round of 16 with two matches still to play.

Another victory over Valencia, 2-0 in St Petersburg, made it five wins out of five, but the more significant result of that particular matchday occurred later that evening when Gent, appearing in their first UEFA Champions League group stage, scored a stoppage-time winner to defeat Lyon 2-1 in what would be the final European game to be staged in the Stade Gerland as the French side crashed out of the competition.

The Belgian champions had picked up just two points from their opening three games, but now, with back-to-back wins over Valencia (1-0 at home) and Lyon, knew that another, at home to Zenit, would carry them through to the knockout phase, where no previous Belgian club had dared to tread. In the event, with Valencia losing at home to Lyon, Gent could have allowed Zenit their sixth win and still qualified alongside them, but instead they treated their fans to another memorable victory, with Swiss midfielder Danijel Milicevic's sumptuous left-footed half-volley

winning the game and also, as the last goal scored in the group stage, providing a suitably spectacular ending to a gripping autumn campaign.

Round of 16

There were a record ten nations still represented in the knockout phase (the previous highest number had been nine in 2012/13), but as ever the big guns from England, Germany, Spain and Italy were out in force, those four countries accounting for ten of the remaining 16 participants, with Belgium, France, the Netherlands, Portugal, Russia and Ukraine supplying one club apiece.

There was something of a lop-sided look to the round of 16 draw, with knockout phase debutants Wolfsburg and Gent being paired together while Juventus, the previous season's runners-up, were punished for failing to win their group with a heavyweight match-up against Bayern. Paris Saint-Germain and Chelsea were drawn together for the third season running, while Arsenal's late qualifying heroics found scant reward as they were pitted against bogey team Barcelona, the holders and competition favourites.

The Juve-Bayern clash was the tie of the round, both on paper and on the pitch. Both legs developed along similar lines, with the away side utterly dominant for most of the contest and taking a deserved 2-0 lead, only for the hosts to stage late rallies and level the scores. Juventus were especially imperious as they built up a 4-2 aggregate lead with a magnificent first-half performance in Munich, well-taken goals from Paul Pogba – after a Manuel Neuer error – and Juan Cuadrado – following a devastating run from Álvaro Morata – reflecting their superiority. But further chances were spurned by Cuadrado (just before half-time) and Morata (three times in three second-half minutes) and Bayern made them pay, with two headed goals from Robert Lewandowski and – in the 91st minute – Thomas Müller, before completing an extraordinary comeback with two further goals, from substitutes Thiago Alcántara and Kingsley Coman, in extra time. Bayern thus progressed to a record 15th UEFA Champions League quarter-final – and ninth in a row – while a frustrated Juventus crashed out, ending Italian interest in the competition for another year.

Eight days earlier Roma had also been sent packing as they lost 4-0 on aggregate to Real Madrid, now coached by Zinédine Zidane following the winter departure of Benítez. The Giallorossi were guilty of spurning numerous chances in both games, but Cristiano Ronaldo maintained his prolific form of the group stage to open the scoring in both matches and send Madrid through in relative comfort. That was far from the case for their city rivals Atlético, who needed a penalty shoot-out win to progress after two goalless draws against PSV Eindhoven. Repeatedly denied by PSV 'keeper Jeroen Zoet, Atlético ultimately found the target when it mattered most, scoring all eight of their spot kicks, the last of them from Juanfran, after Luciano Narsingh had struck the bar, to prevail in the longest shoot-out in UEFA Champions League history.

Barcelona ensured a 100% success rate for Spanish clubs by overpowering Arsenal and thus consigning the Gunners to their sixth successive round of 16 exit. Lionel Messi effectively killed the tie by scoring twice in a first-leg 2-0 win in north London, his first goal a collective work of art involving his illustrious strike

partners Neymar and Luis Suárez. Each of the three amigos found the net in the Camp Nou return as Barça matched Bayern with their tenth successive home win in the competition to wrap up a 5-1 aggregate victory. Arsenal were not the only English club to lose both games, with Chelsea going down 2-1 to Paris Saint-Germain both at the Parc des Princes and Stamford Bridge. The west Londoners had been unbeaten under interim boss Guus Hiddink – the replacement for the sacked José Mourinho – before the first leg, but the runaway Ligue 1 leaders clinched victory with a late Edinson Cavani strike before

Zlatan Ibrahimović, scorer of the tie's opening goal, added a second-leg assist and winner at the venue where he had been sent off 12 months earlier to knock Chelsea out in the round of 16 for the second year running.

A second successive season without an English presence in the quarter-finals was averted by Manchester City, who progressed to that stage for the first time after disposing of Dynamo Kyiv. A sumptuous Yaya Touré strike sealed an excellent 3-1 win in the Ukrainian capital following first-half goals by Sergio Agüero and David Silva, and that effectively was that, the second leg proving uneventful – and ultimately goalless – as City contented themselves with keeping their first clean sheet of the competition.

Benfica and Wolfsburg both worked their way into the quarter-finals with victories home and away against, respectively, Zenit and Gent. The Portuguese champions were indebted in both matches to added-time winners, their prolific Brazilian marksman Jonas heading home with 91 minutes on the clock in Lisbon and his fellow countryman Talisca striking even later in St Petersburg after Nicolas Gaitán's out-of-the-blue 85th-minute equaliser had completely transformed a tie that was heading for extra time with the

Lionel Messi celebrates the first of his two goals for Barcelona away to Arsenal

Russian side in the ascendancy. Wolfsburg, on the other hand, were always in full control against Gent after two excellent goals from Julian Draxler and another from fellow German international Max Kruse propelled them into a 3-0 lead in Belgium. Gent managed to pull two goals back before the final whistle, but an André Schürrle strike in the return – set up by Draxler – ensured a stress-free climax to the tie for the followers of the Bundesliga club as they celebrated a first appearance in a UEFA Champions League quarter-final.

Quarter-finals

There were three Spanish clubs in the last eight for the fourth successive season, but the pairing of Barcelona with Atlético Madrid guaranteed that not all of them would make further progress. Real Madrid appeared to have been favoured by the draw as they pulled out quarter-final novices Wolfsburg, while the other club treading new ground, Manchester City, were handed the task of avenging Premier League rivals Chelsea in the shape of Paris Saint-Germain. Bayern, meanwhile, were charged with the task of adding the scalp of Benfica to that of Juventus.

The all-Spanish tie was a repeat of the quarter-final two years previously, when Diego Simeone's Atlético had surprisingly eliminated Gerardo Martino's Barcelona. The Catalans were out for revenge under Luis Enrique, but it was the visitors who opened the scoring at the Camp Nou as Fernando Torres converted Koke's measured pass – before handing the initiative straight back to Barça by getting himself sent off for two reckless yellow-card offences. The second half was an unrelenting onslaught from Barcelona, and although Luis Suárez might have been red-carded himself for a reckless challenge on Filipe Luís, the Uruguayan striker stayed on the field to score twice and send his team to Madrid for the second leg with a handy lead.

The intensity of the first game rose a notch or two in the Vicente Calderón as Atlético treated their fans to a heroic defensive display that was rewarded with two tie-deciding goals from French ace Griezmann. His first, a brilliant 36th-minute header, came when Atlético were on top, his second, from the penalty spot after Andrés Iniesta had handled, when his team were hanging on for dear life as Barcelona launched wave after wave of

Cristiano Ronaldo beats Diego Benaglio to score the first of his three goals in Real Madrid's 3-0 win at home to Wolfsburg

attack in a continuous siege on Jan Oblak's goal. Fortunately the young Slovenian goalkeeper had the game of his life, and with defiant assistance from those in front of him, Atlético held out – even surviving a last-minute penalty appeal when skipper Gabi handled. So, once again, the curse of the UEFA Champions League holders had struck – and while Atlético marched on to the semi-finals, Barcelona's title defence was at an end.

Real Madrid were close to going out too, but after falling to a shock 2-0 defeat in the first leg away to Wolfsburg – just days

after beating Barcelona at the Camp Nou in El Clásico – they did what only two teams had ever previously managed in the UEFA Champions League by coming back from that scoreline to win the tie. Inevitably, it was Cristiano Ronaldo who saved their blushes, breaking Wolfsburg hearts with all three goals in Madrid's second-leg 3-0 win. It was the Portuguese superstar's fifth hat-trick in the competition and third of the 2015/16 campaign – not to mention 37th in all for Madrid – and could hardly have been more opportune. Goals from Ricardo Rodriguez and Maximilian Arnold had stunned the Spanish side in the first leg – and ended Madrid keeper Keylor Navas's remarkable record of never having conceded a goal in eight previous UEFA Champions League outings – but Ronaldo took just 17 minutes to level things up in the Bernabéu, and it was he who, with the tie on a knife edge, supplied the coup de grace from a free kick 13 minutes from time.

A day after Wolfsburg's elimination, Bayern ensured a continued German presence in the competition – and a fifth successive qualification for the semi-finals – with a 2-2 draw against Benfica in Lisbon. That followed another home win, 1-0 in Munich, in which Arturo Vidal struck with an early header but the anticipated floodgates never opened. It was a Benfica side decimated by injuries and suspensions that went into the second leg hoping to turn the tie around, but although they went ahead, with Raúl Jiménez exploiting an error of judgment from Neuer, another Vidal goal, struck with venom from the edge of the area, soon re-established Bayern's authority before Müller's close-range effort left Benfica with too much to do. Talisca's equalising free-kick reduced the deficit but two additional goals were still needed and Bayern saw out the game in some comfort.

Curiously, all four ties would end with 3-2 aggregates, Manchester City also prevailing by that outcome against Paris Saint-Germain and thus ending the French side's challenge at the quarter-final stage for the fourth year in a row while becoming semi-finalists themselves for the very first time. The opening encounter, at the Parc des Princes, ended 2-2, with City taking the lead through De Bruyne after Hart had saved an Ibrahimović penalty, then relinquishing it with two defensive mistakes before the Paris defence also got in a mix-up, allowing Fernandinho to score a deflected equaliser. Laurent Blanc raised eyebrows by fielding a three-man defence in the second leg – something he had never done before – and it was a gamble that did not pay off as PSG rarely looked like getting the goal they required to progress and ended up losing the game 1-0 to a superb 76th-minute strike from De Bruyne after Agüero had missed a first-half penalty.

Semi-finals

The semi-final draw kept apart the two Madrid clubs and also spared Bayern boss Guardiola the awkwardness of facing Manchester City, the club he had already agreed to take charge of in 2016/17. City, the only newcomers to the UEFA Champions League's last four, were instead up against Real Madrid, while Bayern were tasked with eliminating Barcelona's conquerors Atlético as Guardiola sought to avoid ending his three-year stay in Bavaria with a hat-trick of semi-final defeats.

There was a terrific atmosphere on a cold night at the City of Manchester Stadium as home-team boss Manuel Pellegrini took on his old club Madrid, who received a devastating blow just before kick-off when it was announced that Ronaldo had failed a late fitness test. That should have been a source of encouragement for City to go all-out for a first-leg victory, but with Madrid defending in numbers they barely fashioned a single worthwhile opportunity all evening. After an uneventful but absorbing first half, Madrid began to attack more, but Hart denied Casemiro and the excellent Pepe with two fine saves, and so the stalemate remained.

By avoiding an away goal, City had a good opportunity to reach their first final of Europe's premier club competition, but even after conceding early in the Bernabéu – a scrappy effort credited as a Fernando own goal – they never looked likely to breach the Madrid defence and score the goal that would put them in control of the tie. Madrid circulated the ball at their leisure and would have doubled their lead in the second half but for the efforts of Hart and his defenders – and indeed the intervention of the crossbar that kept out a Gareth Bale header. By the final whistle City had failed to muster a single shot on target, going out with a whimper. Madrid,

Atlético's Saúl Ñíguez (centre) gets the better of the Bayern defence to score a brilliant winning goal in the first leg of the semi-final

though far from their best and with Ronaldo still seemingly short of full fitness, were never fully stretched as they sauntered through to the final for the second time in three years.

There, in Milan, the men in white would be reacquainted with their opponents in the 2014 final, Atlético, who a day earlier claimed their second major scalp of the competition by knocking out Bayern. It was an away-goals success that took Simeone's side through and, as against Barcelona in the previous round, it was a colossal effort of teamwork, stamina and, above all, defensive fortitude that brought about their success.

It was a piece of individual magic, however, from rising star Saúl Ñíguez, that enabled them to win the first leg at a raucous Vicente Calderón. The

21-year-old slalomed his way past several Bayern defenders before beating Neuer with an exquisite left-foot shot that cannoned into the net via the inside of the post. A goal to the good and on top at the interval, Atlético then fell back into all-out defence as Bayern pressed hard for an equaliser. The closest they came was a David Alaba long-ranger that struck the crossbar. Few clear-cut chances were created as Simeone's brilliantly organised unit continually stymied them, even creating a counterattacking chance of their own which came so close to doubling their lead as Fernando Torres's shot came back off the inside of the post and Koke's follow-up shot was saved.

There was no change to the pattern of play six days later in Munich as Bayern attacked and Atlético defended. Guardiola's side were rewarded for their pressure on 31 minutes when a Xabi Alonso free-kick was deflected off the wall past a helpless Oblak. Just three minutes later, though, the Slovenian goalkeeper kept the tie level with a brilliant penalty save from Müller. That let-off seemed to re-energise the visitors and nine minutes after the interval they scored a vital away goal, Griezmann skillfully beating Neuer in a one-on-one contest after being set free by a fine Torres pass. Now Bayern had to score twice. It took them 20 minutes before Lewandowski headed them back into the lead on the night, but another goal would not come. Indeed, the home side were only still in contention at the finish because of the second penalty save of the night, by Neuer from Torres's weak 85th-minute spot kick. The final whistle sounded and although Bayern won the game, the tie belonged to Atlético, the third different Spanish team to defeat Guardiola's Bayern in successive UEFA Champions League semi-finals.

Final

A re-run of the 2014 final in Lisbon brought Madrid rivals Real and Atlético back into the UEFA Champions League spotlight at the Stadio San Siro in Milan. It was the first final to be held in the stadium since 2001, when Bayern and Valencia had drawn 1-1 before the German club took the trophy in a penalty shoot-out. Fifteen years on, the pattern and the outcome of the match would be spookily similar.

Although traditionally the poor relation of the two Madrid clubs, with no European Cup wins to Real's ten, Atlético had no reason to feel inferior as they took the field in Milan. Not only had Diego Simeone's men knocked out the two favourites, Barcelona and Bayern München, they had also had much the better of their meetings with Real since their agonising defeat in Lisbon, winning five and drawing four of those ten matches. If either of the two sides had reason to be fearful of stepping on to the San Siro turf, it was Real, who had never won there in 14 previous visits.

After a delayed kick-off, the match began at a brisk, entertaining pace. Both teams threatened an early goal, but it was Real who forced the first save as Oblak athletically kept out Casemiro's effort with his foot following a brilliant Bale free-kick. Less then ten minutes later Real took the lead, another set piece, delivered by Toni Kroos, causing problems in the Atlético rearguard as Bale flicked the ball on and Sergio Ramos, the man whose last-gasp equaliser had turned the 2014 final, poked it home from close range. For the remainder of the half, Zinédine Zidane's side ran the show, their midfield, anchored by the excellent Casemiro, keeping the ball and denying Atlético an approach route to their goalmouth.

The second period was barely a minute old, however, when Pepe was adjudged to have fouled Fernando Torres and Atlético were awarded a penalty. Up stepped Griezmann, but the Frenchman,

1

In guiding Real Madrid to victory, Zinédine Zidane became the first French coach to win the UEFA Champions League. He also became the first player to have scored in a UEFA Champions League final (2002 for Madrid against Bayer Leverkusen) and won one as a coach.

who had missed a spot kick against Real earlier in the season, smashed his left-foot strike against the bar. It was a ghastly moment for Atlético, and as a spell of pressure in the 15 minutes thereafter came to nought, it looked as if their chance had gone. Twelve minutes from time an excellent run from Bale resulted in a chance for the otherwise anonymous Cristiano Ronaldo. But his effort was brilliantly saved by Oblak and almost immediately Atlético charged up to the other end and scored, Yannick Carrasco, a lively half-time substitute, sliding in to convert Juanfran's immaculate volleyed cross from the right. As in Lisbon, the score was 1-1, and the match went into extra time.

Carrasco was the outstanding player on the field in the additional 30 minutes as

players from both sides began to cramp up in the heat and humidity. But neither he nor anyone else could find the crucial breakthrough, so for the 11th time since the European Cup became the UEFA Champions League its decisive fixture had to be settled by a penalty shoot-out. Real Madrid won the toss so skipper Sergio Ramos chose the end where his team's supporters were gathered. Surprisingly, Gabi, his Atlético counterpart, elected to go second. Equally surprisingly, the relatively inexperienced Lucas Vázquez was first up to the spot. He scored, though, and so did the six who followed him – Marcelo, Bale and Ramos for Real, Griezmann, Gabi and Saúl for Atlético. But then Juanfran, one of Atlético's better performers on the night, miscued his effort against the foot of the post and the stage was set for Ronaldo. In regular play the Real Madrid talisman had seldom looked like scoring the goal that would have equalled his record of 17 for a single UEFA Champions League campaign, but in the defining moment of the entire season, with the world watching on, he delivered, drilling an unstoppable shot past Oblak before wheeling away and ripping his shirt in joyous celebration.

The biggest prize in European club football belonged once again, for the 11th time in their history, to the mighty Real Madrid.

Real Madrid's Pepe (in white) tangles with Atlético's Yannick Carrasco in the UEFA Champions League final

UEFA Champions League

First qualifying round

30/06/15, Seaview, Belfast
Crusaders FC 0-0 FC Levadia Tallinn
07/07/15, A. Le Coq Arena, Tallinn
FC Levadia Tallinn 1-1 Crusaders FC
Aggregate: 1-1; Crusaders FC qualify on away goal.

30/06/15, Victoria Stadium, Gibraltar
Lincoln FC 0-0 FC Santa Coloma
07/07/15, Estadi Comunal, Andorra la Vella
FC Santa Coloma 1-2 Lincoln FC
Aggregate: 1-2; Lincoln FC qualify.

30/06/15, Vazgen Sargsyan anvan Hanrapetakan Marzadasht, Yerevan
FC Pyunik 2-1 SS Folgore
07/07/15, San Marino Stadium, Serravalle
SS Folgore 1-2 FC Pyunik
Aggregate: 2-4; FC Pyunik qualify.

01/07/15, Tórsvøllur, Torshavn
B36 Tórshavn 1-2 The New Saints FC
07/07/15, Park Hall, Oswestry
The New Saints FC 4-1 B36 Tórshavn
Aggregate: 6-2; The New Saints FC qualify.

Second qualifying round

14/07/15, Ventspils Olimpiskais Centrs, Ventspils
FK Ventspils 1-3 HJK Helsinki
21/07/15, Helsinki Football Stadium, Helsinki
HJK Helsinki 1-0 FK Ventspils
Aggregate: 4-1; HJK Helsinki qualify.

14/07/15, Park Hall, Oswestry
The New Saints FC 0-1 Videoton FC
22/07/15, Sóstói, Szekesfehervar
Videoton FC 1-1 The New Saints FC (aet)
Aggregate: 2-1; Videoton FC qualify

14/07/15, Arena Herning, Herning
FC Midtjylland 1-0 Lincoln FC
21/07/15, Victoria Stadium, Gibraltar
Lincoln FC 0-2 FC Midtjylland
Aggregate: 0-3; FC Midtjylland qualify.

14/07/15, Hibernians Stadium, Paola
Hibernians FC 2-1 Maccabi Tel-Aviv FC
21/07/15, Bloomfield, Tel-Aviv
Maccabi Tel-Aviv FC 5-1 Hibernians FC
Aggregate: 6-3; Maccabi Tel-Aviv FC qualify.

14/07/15, GSP, Nicosia
APOEL FC 0-0 FK Vardar
21/07/15, Nacionalna Arena Filip II Makedonski, Skopje
FK Vardar 1-1 APOEL FC
Aggregate: 1-1; APOEL FC qualify on away goal.

14/07/15, Molde Stadion, Molde
Molde FK 5-0 FC Pyunik
21/07/15, Vazgen Sargsyan anvan Hanrapetakan Marzadasht, Yerevan
FC Pyunik 1-0 Molde FK
Aggregate: 1-5; Molde FK qualify.

14/07/15, Skënderbeu, Korca
KF Skënderbeu 4-1 Crusaders FC
21/07/15, Seaview, Belfast
Crusaders FC 3-2 KF Skënderbeu
Aggregate: 4-6; KF Skënderbeu qualify.

14/07/15, Stadion Ljudski vrt, Maribor
NK Maribor 1-0 FC Astana
22/07/15, Astana Arena, Astana
FC Astana 3-1 NK Maribor
Aggregate: 3-2; FC Astana qualify.

14/07/15, Štadión MŠK Žilina, Zilina
FK AS Trenčín 0-2 FC Steaua Bucureşti
22/07/15, Arena Naţională, Bucharest
FC Steaua Bucureşti 2-3 FK AS Trenčín
Aggregate: 4-3; FC Steaua Bucureşti qualify.

14/07/15, Stadion FK Partizan, Belgrade
FK Partizan 1-0 FC Dila Gori
21/07/15, Tengiz Burjanadze Stadioni, Gori
FC Dila Gori 0-2 FK Partizan
Aggregate: 0-3; FK Partizan qualify.

14/07/15, Ludogorets Arena, Razgrad
PFC Ludogorets Razgrad 0-1 FC Milsami Orhei
21/07/15, District Sport Complex, Orhei
FC Milsami Orhei 2-1 PFC Ludogorets Razgrad
Aggregate: 3-1; FC Milsami Orhei qualify.

14/07/15, Asim Ferhatović Hase Stadion, Sarajevo
FK Sarajevo 0-2 KKS Lech Poznań
22/07/15, Stadion Miejski, Poznan
KKS Lech Poznań 1-0 FK Sarajevo
Aggregate: 3-0; KKS Lech Poznań qualify.

15/07/15, Malmö New Stadium, Malmo
Malmö FF 0-0 FK Žalgiris Vilnius
21/07/15, LFF stadionas, Vilnius
FK Žalgiris Vilnius 0-1 Malmö FF
Aggregate: 0-1; Malmö FF qualify.

15/07/15, Celtic Park, Glasgow
Celtic FC 2-0 Stjarnan
22/07/15, Stjörnuvöllur, Gardabaer
Stjarnan 1-4 Celtic FC
Aggregate: 1-6; Celtic FC qualify.

15/07/15, Borisov-Arena, Borisov
FC BATE Borisov 2-1 Dundalk FC
22/07/15, Oriel Park, Dundalk
Dundalk FC 0-0 FC BATE Borisov
Aggregate: 1-2; FC BATE Borisov qualify.

15/07/15, Stadion Maksimir, Zagreb
GNK Dinamo Zagreb 1-1 CS Fola Esch
22/07/15, Stade Josy Barthel, Luxembourg
CS Fola Esch 0-3 GNK Dinamo Zagreb
Aggregate: 1-4; GNK Dinamo Zagreb qualify.

15/07/15, Tofiq Bähramov Republican stadium, Baku
Qarabağ FK 0-0 FK Rudar Pljevlja
22/07/15, Pod Malim Brdom, Petrovac
FK Rudar Pljevlja 0-1 Qarabağ FK
Aggregate: 0-1; Qarabağ FK qualify.

Action from Ireland as Dundalk's Darren Meenan holds off BATE Borisov's Filip Mladenović

Third qualifying round

28/07/15, Arena Herning, Herning
FC Midtjylland 1-2 APOEL FC
04/08/15, GSP, Nicosia
APOEL FC 0-1 FC Midtjylland
Aggregate: 2-2; APOEL FC qualify on away goals.

28/07/15, Arena Khimki, Khimki
PFC CSKA Moskva 2-2 AC Sparta Praha
05/08/15, Stadion Letná, Prague
AC Sparta Praha 2-3 PFC CSKA Moskva
Aggregate: 4-5; PFC CSKA Moskva qualify.

28/07/15, Stadionul Zimbru, Chisinau
FC Milsami Orhei 0-2 KF Skënderbeu
05/08/15, Elbasan Arena, Elbasan
KF Skënderbeu 2-0 FC Milsami Orhei
Aggregate: 4-0; KF Skënderbeu qualify.

28/07/15, Stade de Suisse, Berne
BSC Young Boys 1-3 AS Monaco FC
04/08/15, Stade Louis II, Monaco
AS Monaco FC 4-0 BSC Young Boys
Aggregate: 7-1; AS Monaco FC qualify.

28/07/15, Bloomfield, Tel-Aviv
Maccabi Tel-Aviv FC 1-2 FC Viktoria Plzeň
05/08/15, Doosan Arena, Plzen
FC Viktoria Plzeň 0-2 Maccabi Tel-Aviv FC
Aggregate: 2-3; Maccabi Tel-Aviv FC qualify.

28/07/15, Sóstói, Szekesfehervar
Videoton FC 1-1 FC BATE Borisov
05/08/15, Borisov-Arena, Borisov
FC BATE Borisov 1-0 Videoton FC
Aggregate: 2-1; FC BATE Borisov qualify.

28/07/15, Stadion Maksimir, Zagreb
GNK Dinamo Zagreb 1-1 Molde FK
04/08/15, Molde Stadion, Molde
Molde FK 3-3 GNK Dinamo Zagreb
Aggregate: 4-4; GNK Dinamo Zagreb qualify on away goals.

28/07/15, Apostolos Nikolaidis, Athens
Panathinaikos FC 2-1 Club Brugge KV
05/08/15, Jan Breydelstadion, Bruges
Club Brugge KV 3-0 Panathinaikos FC
Aggregate: 4-2; Club Brugge KV qualify.

28/07/15, Şükrü Saracoğlu, Istanbul
Fenerbahçe SK 0-0 FC Shakhtar Donetsk
05/08/15, Arena Lviv, Lviv
FC Shakhtar Donetsk 3-0 Fenerbahçe SK
Aggregate: 3-0; FC Shakhtar Donetsk qualify.

29/07/15, Helsinki Football Stadium, Helsinki
HJK Helsinki 0-0 FC Astana
05/08/15, Astana Arena, Astana
FC Astana 4-3 HJK Helsinki
Aggregate: 4-3; FC Astana qualify.

29/07/15, Stadion Salzburg, Salzburg
FC Salzburg 2-0 Malmö FF
05/08/15, Malmö New Stadium, Malmo
Malmö FF 3-0 FC Salzburg
Aggregate: 3-2; Malmö FF qualify.

29/07/15, Celtic Park, Glasgow
Celtic FC 1-0 Qarabağ FK
05/08/15, Tofiq Bähramov Republican stadium, Baku
Qarabağ FK 0-0 Celtic FC
Aggregate: 0-1; Celtic FC qualify.

29/07/15, Stadion Miejski, Poznan
KKS Lech Poznań 1-3 FC Basel 1893
05/08/15, St Jakob-Park, Basel
FC Basel 1893 1-0 KKS Lech Poznań
Aggregate: 4-1; FC Basel 1893 qualify.

29/07/15, Ernst-Happel-Stadion, Vienna
SK Rapid Wien 2-2 AFC Ajax
04/08/15, Amsterdam ArenA, Amsterdam
AFC Ajax 2-3 SK Rapid Wien
Aggregate: 4-5; SK Rapid Wien qualify.

29/07/15, Arena Naţională, Bucharest
FC Steaua Bucureşti 1-1 FK Partizan
05/08/15, Stadion FK Partizan, Belgrade
FK Partizan 4-2 FC Steaua Bucureşti
Aggregate: 5-3; FK Partizan qualify.

Play-offs

18/08/15, Old Trafford, Manchester
Manchester United FC 3-1 Club Brugge KV
Goals: 0-1 Carrick 8(og), 1-1 Depay 13,
2-1 Depay 43, 3-1 Fellaini 90+4
26/08/15, Jan Breydelstadion, Bruges
Club Brugge KV 0-4 Manchester United FC
Goals: 0-1 Rooney 20, 0-2 Rooney 49,
0-3 Rooney 57, 0-4 Ander Herrera 63
Aggregate: 1-7; Manchester United FC qualify.

18/08/15, José Alvalade, Lisbon
Sporting Clube de Portugal 2-1 PFC CSKA Moskva
Goals: 1-0 Gutiérrez 12, 1-1 Doumbia 40,
2-1 Slimani 82
26/08/15, Arena Khimki, Khimki
PFC CSKA Moskva 3-1 Sporting Clube de Portugal
Goals: 0-1 Gutiérrez 36, 1-1 Doumbia 49,
2-1 Doumbia 72, 3-1 Musa 85
Aggregate: 4-3; PFC CSKA Moskva qualify.

18/08/15, Stadio Olimpico, Rome
SS Lazio 1-0 Bayer 04 Leverkusen
Goal: 1-0 Baldé 77
26/08/15, BayArena, Leverkusen
Bayer 04 Leverkusen 3-0 SS Lazio
Goals: 1-0 Hakan Çalhanoğlu 40,
2-0 Mehmedi 48, 3-0 Bellarabi 88
Aggregate: 3-1; Bayer 04 Leverkusen qualify.

18/08/15, Borisov-Arena, Borisov
FC BATE Borisov 1-0 FK Partizan
Goal: 1-0 Gordeichuk 75
26/08/15, Stadion FK Partizan, Belgrade
FK Partizan 2-1 FC BATE Borisov
Goals: 0-1 Stasevich 25, 1-1 Zhavnerchik 74(og),
2-1 Šaponjić 90+3
Aggregate: 2-2; FC BATE Borisov qualify on away goal.

18/08/15, Astana Arena, Astana
FC Astana 1-0 APOEL FC
Goal: 1-0 Dzholchiev 14
26/08/15, GSP, Nicosia
APOEL FC 1-1 FC Astana
Goals: 1-0 Štilić 60, 1-1 Maksimović 84
Aggregate: 1-2; FC Astana qualify.

19/08/15, Celtic Park, Glasgow
Celtic FC 3-2 Malmö FF
Goals: 1-0 Griffiths 3, 2-0 Biton 10, 2-1 Berget 52,
3-1 Griffiths 61, 3-2 Berget 90+5
25/08/15, Malmö New Stadium, Malmo
Malmö FF 2-0 Celtic FC
Goals: 1-0 Rosenberg 23, 2-0 Boyata 54(og)
Aggregate: 4-3; Malmö FF qualify.

19/08/15, Elbasan Arena, Elbasan
KF Skënderbeu 1-2 GNK Dinamo Zagreb
Goals: 1-0 Shkëmbi 37, 1-1 Soudani 66,
1-2 Pivarić 90+3
25/08/15, Stadion Maksimir, Zagreb
GNK Dinamo Zagreb 4-1 KF Skënderbeu
Goals: 1-0 Soudani 9, 1-1 Esquerdinha 10,
2-1 Hodžić 15, 3-1 Taravel 55, 4-1 Soudani 80
Aggregate: 6-2; GNK Dinamo Zagreb qualify.

Hakan Çalhanoğlu celebrates after putting Leverkusen 1-0 up at home against Lazio

19/08/15, St Jakob-Park, Basel
FC Basel 1893 2-2 Maccabi Tel-Aviv FC
Goals: 0-1 Zahavi 31, 1-1 Delgado 39(p),
2-1 Embolo 88, 2-2 Zahavi 90+6
25/08/15, Bloomfield, Tel-Aviv
Maccabi Tel-Aviv FC 1-1 FC Basel 1893
Goals: 0-1 Zuffi 11, 1-1 Zahavi 24
Aggregate: 3-3; Maccabi Tel-Aviv FC qualify on away goals.

19/08/15, Ernst-Happel-Stadion, Vienna
SK Rapid Wien 0-1 FC Shakhtar Donetsk
Goal: 0-1 Marlos 44
25/08/15, Arena Lviv, Lviv
FC Shakhtar Donetsk 2-2 SK Rapid Wien
Goals: 1-0 Marlos 10, 1-1 Schaub 13,
1-2 S Hofmann 22, 2-2 Gladkiy 27
Aggregate: 3-2; FC Shakhtar Donetsk qualify.

19/08/15, Estadi de Mestalla, Valencia
Valencia CF 3-1 AS Monaco FC
Goals: 1-0 Rodrigo 4, 1-1 Pašalić 49, 2-1 Parejo
59, 3-1 Feghouli 86
25/08/15, Stade Louis II, Monaco
AS Monaco FC 2-1 Valencia CF
Goals: 0-1 Negredo 4, 1-1 Raggi 17,
2-1 Echiéjilé 75
Aggregate: 3-4; Valencia CF qualify.

Group stage

Group A

15/09/15, Parc des Princes, Paris (att: 46,612)
Paris Saint-Germain 2-0 Malmö FF
Goals: 1-0 Di María 4, 2-0 Cavani 61
Referee: Karasev (RUS)

15/09/15, Estadio Santiago Bernabéu, Madrid (att: 66,389)
Real Madrid CF 4-0 FC Shakhtar Donetsk
Goals: 1-0 Benzema 30, 2-0 Cristiano Ronaldo
55(p), 3-0 Cristiano Ronaldo 63(p), 4-0 Cristiano
Ronaldo 81
Referee: Bebek (CRO)

30/09/15, Malmö New Stadium, Malmo (att: 20,500)
Malmö FF 0-2 Real Madrid CF
Goals: 0-1 Cristiano Ronaldo 29,
0-2 Cristiano Ronaldo 90
Referee: Çakır (TUR)

30/09/15, Arena Lviv, Lviv (att: 32,730)
FC Shakhtar Donetsk 0-3 Paris Saint-Germain
Goals: 0-1 Aurier 7, 0-2 David Luiz 23,
0-3 Srna 90(og)
Referee: Aytekin (GER)

21/10/15, Malmö New Stadium, Malmo (att: 20,500)
Malmö FF 1-0 FC Shakhtar Donetsk
Goal: 1-0 Rosenberg 17
Referee: Sidiropoulos (GRE)

21/10/15, Parc des Princes, Paris (att: 46,858)
Paris Saint-Germain 0-0 Real Madrid CF
Referee: Rizzoli (ITA)

03/11/15, Estadio Santiago Bernabéu, Madrid (att: 78,300)
Real Madrid CF 1-0 Paris Saint-Germain
Goal: 1-0 Nacho 35
Referee: Clattenburg (ENG)

03/11/15, Arena Lviv, Lviv (att: 24,055)
FC Shakhtar Donetsk 4-0 Malmö FF
Goals: 1-0 Gladkiy 29, 2-0 Srna 48(p),
3-0 Eduardo 55, 4-0 Alex Teixeira 73
Referee: Haţegan (ROU)

25/11/15, Malmö New Stadium, Malmo (att: 20,500)
Malmö FF 0-5 Paris Saint-Germain
Goals: 0-1 Rabiot 3, 0-2 Di María 14,
0-3 Ibrahimović 50, 0-4 Di María 68, 0-5 Lucas 82
Referee: Collum (SCO)

25/11/15, Arena Lviv, Lviv (att: 33,990)
FC Shakhtar Donetsk 3-4 Real Madrid CF
Goals: 0-1 Cristiano Ronaldo 18, 0-2 Modrić 50,
0-3 Carvajal 52, 1-3 Cristiano Ronaldo 70, 1-4 Alex
Teixeira 77(p), 2-4 Dentinho 83, 3-4 Alex Teixeira 88
Referee: Nijhuis (NED)

08/12/15, Parc des Princes, Paris (att: 44,408)
Paris Saint-Germain 2-0 FC Shakhtar Donetsk
Goals: 1-0 Lucas 57, 2-0 Ibrahimović 86
Referee: Taylor (ENG)

08/12/15, Estadio Santiago Bernabéu, Madrid (att: 60,663)
Real Madrid CF 8-0 Malmö FF
Goals: 1-0 Benzema 12, 2-0 Benzema 24,
3-0 Cristiano Ronaldo 39, 4-0 Cristiano Ronaldo 47,
5-0 Cristiano Ronaldo 50, 6-0 Cristiano Ronaldo 59,
7-0 Kovačić 70, 8-0 Benzema 74
Referee: Orsato (ITA)

Group B

15/09/15, VfL Wolfsburg Arena, Wolfsburg (att: 20,126)
VfL Wolfsburg 1-0 PFC CSKA Moskva
Goal: 1-0 Draxler 40
Referee: Moen (NOR)

15/09/15, PSV Stadion, Eindhoven (att: 35,000)
PSV Eindhoven 2-1 Manchester United FC
Goals: 0-1 Depay 41, 1-1 Moreno 45+2,
2-1 Narsingh 57
Referee: Rizzoli (ITA)

30/09/15, Old Trafford, Manchester (att: 74,811)
Manchester United FC 2-1 VfL Wolfsburg
Goals: 0-1 Caligiuri 4, 1-1 Mata 34(p),
2-1 Smalling 53
Referee: Kassai (HUN)

30/09/15, Arena Khimki, Khimki (att: 16,152)
PFC CSKA Moskva 3-2 PSV Eindhoven
Goals: 1-0 Musa 7, 2-0 Doumbia 21, 3-0 Doumbia 36(p), 3-1 Lestienne 60, 3-2 Lestienne 68
Referee: Buquet (FRA)

21/10/15, VfL Wolfsburg Arena, Wolfsburg (att: 23,375)
VfL Wolfsburg 2-0 PSV Eindhoven
Goals: 1-0 Dost 46, 2-0 Kruse 57
Referee: Undiano Mallenco (ESP)

21/10/15, Arena Khimki, Khimki (att: 18,457)
PFC CSKA Moskva 1-1 Manchester United FC
Goals: 1-0 Doumbia 15, 1-1 Martial 65
Referee: Velasco Carballo (ESP)

03/11/15, Old Trafford, Manchester (att: 75,165)
Manchester United FC 1-0 PFC CSKA Moskva
Goal: 1-0 Rooney 79
Referee: Marciniak (POL)

03/11/15, PSV Stadion, Eindhoven (att: 35,000)
PSV Eindhoven 2-0 VfL Wolfsburg
Goals: 1-0 Locadia 55, 2-0 De Jong 86
Referee: Eriksson (SWE)

25/11/15, Old Trafford, Manchester (att: 75,321)
Manchester United FC 0-0 PSV Eindhoven
Referee: Královec (CZE)

25/11/15, Arena Khimki, Khimki (att: 16,450)
PFC CSKA Moskva 0-2 VfL Wolfsburg
Goals: 0-1 Akinfeev 67(og), 0-2 Schürrle 88
Referee: Rocchi (ITA)

08/12/15, VfL Wolfsburg Arena, Wolfsburg (att: 26,400)
VfL Wolfsburg 3-2 Manchester United FC
Goals: 0-1 Martial 10, 1-1 Naldo 13, 2-1 Vieirinha 29, 2-2 Guilavogui 82(og), 3-2 Naldo 84
Referee: Mažić (SRB)

08/12/15, PSV Stadion, Eindhoven (att: 34,000)
PSV Eindhoven 2-1 PFC CSKA Moskva
Goals: 0-1 Ignashevich 76(p), 1-1 De Jong 78, 2-1 Pröpper 86
Referee: Fernández Borbalán (ESP)

Group C

15/09/15, Estádio do Sport Lisboa e Benfica, Lisbon (att: 32,799)
SL Benfica 2-0 FC Astana
Goals: 1-0 Gaitán 51, 2-0 Mitroglou 62
Referee: Sidiropoulos (GRE)

15/09/15, Ali Sami Yen Spor Kompleksi, Istanbul (att: 33,469)
Galatasaray AŞ 0-2 Club Atlético de Madrid
Goals: 0-1 Griezmann 18, 0-2 Griezmann 25
Referee: Marciniak (POL)

30/09/15, Estadio Vicente Calderón, Madrid (att: 40,938)
Club Atlético de Madrid 1-2 SL Benfica
Goals: 1-0 Correa 23, 1-1 Gaitán 36, 1-2 Gonçalo Guedes 51
Referee: Rocchi (ITA)

30/09/15, Astana Arena, Astana (att: 27,264)
FC Astana 2-2 Galatasaray AŞ
Goals: 0-1 Bilal Kısa 31, 1-1 Hakan Balta 77(og), 1-2 Erić 86(og), 2-2 Carole 89(og)
Referee: Strömbergsson (SWE)

Astana's Aleksei Shchetkin (left) contests an aerial duel with Benfica's Gonçalo Guedes

21/10/15, Estadio Vicente Calderón, Madrid (att: 33,853)
Club Atlético de Madrid 4-0 FC Astana
Goals: 1-0 Saúl Ñíguez 23, 2-0 Martínez 29, 3-0 Óliver Torres 63, 4-0 Dedechko 89(og)
Referee: Kulbakov (BLR)

21/10/15, Ali Sami Yen Spor Kompleksi, Istanbul (att: 33,615)
Galatasaray AŞ 2-1 SL Benfica
Goals: 0-1 Gaitán 2, 1-1 Selçuk İnan 19(p), 2-1 Podolski 33
Referee: Collum (SCO)

03/11/15, Estádio do Sport Lisboa e Benfica, Lisbon (att: 35,726)
SL Benfica 2-1 Galatasaray AŞ
Goals: 1-0 Jonas 52, 1-1 Podolski 58, 2-1 Luisão 67
Referee: Mažić (SRB)

03/11/15, Astana Arena, Astana (att: 29,231)
FC Astana 0-0 Club Atlético de Madrid
Referee: Taylor (ENG)

25/11/15, Estadio Vicente Calderón, Madrid (att: 35,753)
Club Atlético de Madrid 2-0 Galatasaray AŞ
Goals: 1-0 Griezmann 13, 2-0 Griezmann 65
Referee: Rizzoli (ITA)

25/11/15, Astana Arena, Astana (att: 15,089)
FC Astana 2-2 SL Benfica
Goals: 1-0 Twumasi 19, 2-0 Aničić 31, 2-1 Jiménez 40, 2-2 Jiménez 72
Referee: Buquet (FRA)

08/12/15, Estádio do Sport Lisboa e Benfica, Lisbon (att: 47,360)
SL Benfica 1-2 Club Atlético de Madrid
Goals: 0-1 Saúl Ñíguez 33, 0-2 Vietto 55, 1-2 Mitroglou 75
Referee: Haţegan (ROU)

08/12/15, Ali Sami Yen Spor Kompleksi, Istanbul (att: 26,464)
Galatasaray AŞ 1-1 FC Astana
Goals: 0-1 Twumasi 62, 1-1 Selçuk İnan 64
Referee: Thomson (SCO)

Group D

15/09/15, City of Manchester Stadium, Manchester (att: 50,363)
Manchester City FC 1-2 Juventus FC
Goals: 1-0 Chiellini 57(og), 1-1 Mandžukić 70, 1-2 Morata 81
Referee: Skomina (SVN)

15/09/15, Estadio Ramón Sánchez Pizjuán, Seville (att: 36,959)
Sevilla FC 3-0 VfL Borussia Mönchengladbach
Goals: 1-0 Gameiro 47(p), 2-0 Banega 66(p), 3-0 Konoplyanka 84
Referee: Královec (CZE)

30/09/15, Borussia-Park, Mönchengladbach (att: 46,127)
VfL Borussia Mönchengladbach 1-2 Manchester City FC
Goals: 1-0 Stindl 54, 1-1 Demichelis 65, 1-2 Agüero 90(p)
Referee: Turpin (FRA)

30/09/15, Juventus FC Stadium, Turin (att: 36,640)
Juventus FC 2-0 Sevilla FC
Goals: 1-0 Morata 41, 2-0 Zaza 87
Referee: Eriksson (SWE)

21/10/15, City of Manchester Stadium, Manchester (att: 45,595)
Manchester City FC 2-1 Sevilla FC
Goals: 1-0 Konoplyanka 30, 1-1 Rami 36(og), 2-1 De Bruyne 90+1
Referee: Nijhuis (NED)

21/10/15, Juventus FC Stadium, Turin (att: 40,940)
Juventus FC 0-0 VfL Borussia Mönchengladbach
Referee: Thomson (SCO)

03/11/15, Borussia-Park, Mönchengladbach (att: 46,217)
VfL Borussia Mönchengladbach 1-1 Juventus FC
Goals: 1-0 Johnson 18, 1-1 Lichtsteiner 44
Referee: Kuipers (NED)

03/11/15, Estadio Ramón Sánchez Pizjuán, Seville (att: 39,261)
Sevilla FC 1-3 Manchester City FC
Goals: 0-1 Sterling 8, 0-2 Fernandinho 11, 1-2 Trémoulinas 25, 1-3 Bony 36
Referee: Moen (NOR)

25/11/15, Juventus FC Stadium, Turin (att: 38,193)
Juventus FC 1-0 Manchester City FC
Goal: 1-0 Mandžukić 18
Referee: Brych (GER)

25/11/15, Borussia-Park, Mönchengladbach (att: 45,177)
VfL Borussia Mönchengladbach 4-2 Sevilla FC
Goals: 1-0 Stindl 29, 2-0 Johnson 68, 3-0 Raffael 78, 3-1 Vitolo 82, 4-1 Stindl 83, 4-2 Éver Banega 90+1(p)
Referee: Skomina (SVN)

08/12/15, City of Manchester Stadium, Manchester (att: 41,829)
Manchester City FC 4-2 VfL Borussia Mönchengladbach
Goals: 1-0 Silva 16, 1-1 Korb 19, 1-2 Raffael 42, 2-2 Sterling 80, 3-2 Sterling 81, 4-2 Bony 85
Referee: Makkelie (NED)

08/12/15, Estadio Ramón Sánchez Pizjuán, Seville (att: 35,583)
Sevilla FC 1-0 Juventus FC
Goal: 1-0 Llorente 65
Referee: Marciniak (POL)

Group E

16/09/15, BayArena, Leverkusen (att: 24,280)
Bayer 04 Leverkusen 4-1 FC BATE Borisov
Goals: 1-0 Mehmedi 4, 1-1 Milunović 13,
2-1 Hakan Çalhanoğlu 47, 3-1 Hernández 59,
4-1 Hakan Çalhanoğlu 76(p)
Referee: Makkelie (NED)

16/09/15, Stadio Olimpico, Rome (att: 57,836)
AS Roma 1-1 FC Barcelona
Goals: 0-1 Suárez 21, 1-1 Florenzi 31
Referee: Kuipers (NED)

29/09/15, Camp Nou, Barcelona (att: 68,694)
FC Barcelona 2-1 Bayer 04 Leverkusen
Goals: 0-1 Papadopoulos 22, 1-1 Sergi Roberto 80,
2-1 Suárez 82
Referee: Atkinson (ENG)

29/09/15, Borisov-Arena, Borisov (att: 12,767)
FC BATE Borisov 3-2 AS Roma
Goals: 1-0 Stasevich 8, 2-0 Mladenović 12,
3-0 Mladenović 30, 3-1 Gervinho 66,
3-2 Torosidis 82
Referee: Clattenburg (ENG)

20/10/15, BayArena, Leverkusen (att: 29,412)
Bayer 04 Leverkusen 4-4 AS Roma
Goals: 1-0 Hernández 4(p), 2-0 Hernández 19,
2-1 De Rossi 29, 2-2 De Rossi 38, 2-3 Pjanić 54,
2-4 Iago Falqué 73, 3-4 Kampl 84,
4-4 Mehmedi 86
Referee: Kassai (HUN)

20/10/15, Borisov-Arena, Borisov (att: 13,074)
FC BATE Borisov 0-2 FC Barcelona
Goals: 0-1 Rakitić 48, 0-2 Rakitić 64
Referee: Manuel De Sousa (POR)

04/11/15, Camp Nou, Barcelona (att: 68,506)
FC Barcelona 3-0 FC BATE Borisov
Goals: 1-0 Neymar 30(p), 2-0 Suárez 60,
3-0 Neymar 83
Referee: Vad (HUN)

Olivier Giroud scores the second of his three goals in Arsenal's crucial 3-0 win at Olympiacos

04/11/15, Stadio Olimpico, Rome (att: 38,361)
AS Roma 3-2 Bayer 04 Leverkusen
Goals: 1-0 Salah 2, 2-0 Džeko 29,
2-1 Mehmedi 46, 2-2 Hernández 51,
3-2 Pjanić 80(p)
Referee: Karasev (RUS)

24/11/15, Borisov-Arena, Borisov (att: 12,601)
FC BATE Borisov 1-1 Bayer 04 Leverkusen
Goals: 1-0 Gordeichuk 2, 1-1 Mehmedi 68
Referee: Turpin (FRA)

24/11/15, Camp Nou, Barcelona (att: 71,433)
FC Barcelona 6-1 AS Roma
Goals: 1-0 Suárez 15, 2-0 Messi 18, 3-0 Suárez 44,
4-0 Piqué 56, 5-0 Messi 60, 6-0 Adriano 77,
6-1 Džeko 90+1
Referee: Çakır (TUR)

09/12/15, BayArena, Leverkusen (att: 29,412)
Bayer 04 Leverkusen 1-1 FC Barcelona
Goals: 0-1 Messi 20, 1-1 Hernández 23
Referee: Clattenburg (ENG)

09/12/15, Stadio Olimpico, Rome (att: 29,489)
AS Roma 0-0 FC BATE Borisov
Referee: Atkinson (ENG)

Group F

16/09/15, Stadion Maksimir, Zagreb (att: 17,840)
GNK Dinamo Zagreb 2-1 Arsenal FC
Goals: 1-0 Pivarić 24, 2-0 Fernandes 58,
2-1 Walcott 79
Referee: Haţegan (ROU)

16/09/15, Stadio Georgios Karaiskakis, Piraeus (att: 31,688)
Olympiacos FC 0-3 FC Bayern München
Goals: 0-1 Müller 52, 0-2 Götze 89,
0-3 Müller 90+2(p)
Referee: Velasco Carballo (ESP)

29/09/15, Arsenal Stadium, London (att: 59,428)
Arsenal FC 2-3 Olympiacos FC
Goals: 1-0 Pardo 33, 1-1 Walcott 35,
1-2 Ospina 40(og), 2-2 Alexis Sánchez 65,
2-3 Finnbogason 66
Referee: Nijhuis (NED)

29/09/15, Fußball Arena München, Munich (att: 70,000)
FC Bayern München 5-0 GNK Dinamo Zagreb
Goals: 1-0 Douglas Costa 13, 2-0 Lewandowski
21, 3-0 Götze 25, 4-0 Lewandowski 28,
5-0 Lewandowski 55
Referee: Kulbakov (BLR)

20/10/15, Arsenal Stadium, London (att: 59,824)
Arsenal FC 2-0 FC Bayern München
Goals: 1-0 Giroud 77, 2-0 Özil 90+4
Referee: Çakır (TUR)

20/10/15, Stadion Maksimir, Zagreb (att: 13,678)
GNK Dinamo Zagreb 0-1 Olympiacos FC
Goal: 0-1 Ideye 79
Referee: Tagliavento (ITA)

04/11/15, Fußball Arena München, Munich (att: 70,000)
FC Bayern München 5-1 Arsenal FC
Goals: 1-0 Lewandowski 10, 2-0 Müller 29,
3-0 Alaba 44, 4-0 Robben 55, 4-1 Giroud 69,
5-1 Müller 89
Referee: Rocchi (ITA)

04/11/15, Stadio Georgios Karaiskakis, Piraeus (att: 31,473)
Olympiacos FC 2-1 GNK Dinamo Zagreb
Goals: 0-1 Hodžić 21, 1-1 Pardo 65, 2-1 Pardo 90
Referee: Mateu Lahoz (ESP)

24/11/15, Arsenal Stadium, London (att: 58,978)
Arsenal FC 3-0 GNK Dinamo Zagreb
Goals: 1-0 Özil 29, 2-0 Alexis Sánchez 33,
3-0 Alexis Sánchez 69
Referee: Kassai (HUN)

24/11/15, Fußball Arena München, Munich (att: 70,000)
FC Bayern München 4-0 Olympiacos FC
Goals: 1-0 Douglas Costa 8, 2-0 Lewandowski 16,
3-0 Müller 20, 4-0 Coman 69
Referee: Eriksson (SWE)

09/12/15, Stadion Maksimir, Zagreb (att: 19,681)
GNK Dinamo Zagreb 0-2 FC Bayern München
Goals: 0-1 Lewandowski 61, 0-2 Lewandowski 64
Referee: Strömbergsson (SWE)

09/12/15, Stadio Georgios Karaiskakis, Piraeus (att: 31,388)
Olympiacos FC 0-3 Arsenal FC
Goals: 0-1 Giroud 29, 0-2 Giroud 49,
0-3 Giroud 67(p)
Referee: Rizzoli (ITA)

Group G

16/09/15, Stamford Bridge, London (att: 40,684)
Chelsea FC 4-0 Maccabi Tel-Aviv FC
Goals: 1-0 Willian 15, 2-0 Oscar 45+4(p),
3-0 Diego Costa 58, 4-0 Fàbregas 78
Referee: Zwayer (GER)

16/09/15, NSK Olimpiyskyi, Kyiv (att: 52,369)
FC Dynamo Kyiv 2-2 FC Porto
Goals: 1-0 Gusev 20, 1-1 Aboubakar 23,
1-2 Aboubakar 81, 2-2 Buyalskiy 89
Referee: Brych (GER)

29/09/15, Estádio do Dragão, Porto (att: 46,120)
FC Porto 2-1 Chelsea FC
Goals: 1-0 André André 39, 1-1 Willian 45+2,
2-1 Maicon 52
Referee: Mateu Lahoz (ESP)

29/09/15, Sammy Ofer Stadium, Haifa (att: 27,104)
Maccabi Tel-Aviv FC 0-2 FC Dynamo Kyiv
Goals: 0-1 Yarmolenko 4, 0-2 Júnior Moraes 50
Referee: Fernández Borbalán (ESP)

20/10/15, Estádio do Dragão, Porto (att: 35,209)
FC Porto 2-0 Maccabi Tel-Aviv FC
Goals: 1-0 Aboubakar 37, 2-0 Brahimi 41
Referee: Turpin (FRA)

20/10/15, NSK Olimpiyskyi, Kyiv (att: 60,291)
FC Dynamo Kyiv 0-0 Chelsea FC
Referee: Skomina (SVN)

04/11/15, Stamford Bridge, London (att: 41,421)
Chelsea FC 2-1 FC Dynamo Kyiv
Goals: 1-0 Dragovic 34(og), 1-1 Dragovic 78,
2-1 Willian 83
Referee: Královec (CZE)

04/11/15, Sammy Ofer Stadium, Haifa (att: 26,745)
Maccabi Tel-Aviv FC 1-3 FC Porto
Goals: 0-1 Tello 19, 0-2 André André 49,
0-3 Layún 72, 1-3 Zahavi 75(p)
Referee: Sidiropoulos (GRE)

24/11/15, Estádio do Dragão, Porto (att: 31,220)
FC Porto 0-2 FC Dynamo Kyiv
Goals: 0-1 Yarmolenko 35(p), 0-2 González 64
Referee: Velasco Carballo (ESP)

24/11/15, Sammy Ofer Stadium, Haifa (att: 29,121)
Maccabi Tel-Aviv FC 0-4 Chelsea FC
Goals: 0-1 Cahill 20, 0-2 Willian 73, 0-3 Oscar 77,
0-4 Zouma 90+1
Referee: Undiano Mallenco (ESP)

09/12/15, Stamford Bridge, London (att: 41,096)
Chelsea FC 2-0 FC Porto
Goals: 1-0 Marcano 12(og), 2-0 Willian 52
Referee: Çakır (TUR)

09/12/15, NSK Olimpiyskyi, Kyiv (att: 475)
FC Dynamo Kyiv 1-0 Maccabi Tel-Aviv FC
Goal: 1-0 Garmash 16
Referee: Kuipers (NED)

Group H

16/09/15, Estadi de Mestalla, Valencia (att: 27,975)
Valencia CF 2-3 FC Zenit
Goals: 0-1 Hulk 9, 0-2 Hulk 44,
1-2 João Cancelo 55, 2-2 André Gomes 73,
2-3 Witsel 76
Referee: Thomson (SCO)

16/09/15, KAA Gent Stadium, Ghent (att: 19,601)
KAA Gent 1-1 Olympique Lyonnais
Goals: 0-1 Jallet 58, 1-1 Milicevic 68
Referee: Collum (SCO)

29/09/15, Stade de Gerland, Lyon (att: 33,534)
Olympique Lyonnais 0-1 Valencia CF
Goal: 0-1 Feghouli 42
Referee: Mažić (SRB)

29/09/15, Stadion Petrovski, St Petersburg (att: 18,095)
FC Zenit 2-1 KAA Gent
Goals: 1-0 Dzyuba 35, 1-1 Matton 56, 2-1 Shatov 67
Referee: Jug (SVN)

20/10/15, Estadi de Mestalla, Valencia (att: 38,207)
Valencia CF 2-1 KAA Gent
Goals: 1-0 Feghouli 15, 1-1 Foket 40,
2-1 Mitrović 72(og)
Referee: Zwayer (GER)

20/10/15, Stadion Petrovski, St Petersburg (att: 17,517)
FC Zenit 3-1 Olympique Lyonnais
Goals: 1-0 Dzyuba 3, 1-1 Lacazette 49, 2-1 Hulk
56, 3-1 Danny 82
Referee: Atkinson (ENG)

04/11/15, Stade de Gerland, Lyon (att: 30,173)
Olympique Lyonnais 0-2 FC Zenit
Goals: 0-1 Dzyuba 25, 0-2 Dzyuba 57
Referee: Brych (GER)

04/11/15, KAA Gent Stadium, Ghent (att: 19,542)
KAA Gent 1-0 Valencia CF
Goal: 1-0 Kums 49(p)
Referee: Orsato (ITA)

24/11/15, Stadion Petrovski, St Petersburg (att: 17,002)
FC Zenit 2-0 Valencia CF
Goals: 1-0 Shatov 15, 2-0 Dzyuba 74
Referee: Moen (NOR)

24/11/15, Stade de Gerland, Lyon (att: 30,206)
Olympique Lyonnais 1-2 KAA Gent
Goals: 1-0 Ferri 7, 1-1 Milicevic 32, 1-2 Coulibaly
90+5
Referee: Karasev (RUS)

09/12/15, Estadi de Mestalla, Valencia (att: 32,494)
Valencia CF 0-2 Olympique Lyonnais
Goals: 0-1 Cornet 37, 0-2 Lacazette 76
Referee: Jug (SVN)

09/12/15, KAA Gent Stadium, Ghent (att: 19,978)
KAA Gent 2-1 FC Zenit
Goals: 1-0 Depoitre 18, 1-1 Dzyuba 65, 2-1
Milicevic 78
Referee: Manuel De Sousa (POR)

Final group tables

Group A

		Pld	Home W	D	L	F	A	Away W	D	L	F	A	Total W	D	L	F	A	Pts
1	Real Madrid CF	6	3	0	0	13	0	2	1	0	6	3	5	1	0	19	3	16
2	Paris Saint-Germain	6	2	1	0	4	0	2	0	1	8	1	4	1	1	12	1	13
3	FC Shakhtar Donetsk	6	1	0	2	7	7	0	0	3	0	7	1	0	5	7	14	3
4	Malmö FF	6	1	0	2	1	7	0	0	3	0	14	1	0	5	1	21	3

Group B

		Pld	Home W	D	L	F	A	Away W	D	L	F	A	Total W	D	L	F	A	Pts
1	VfL Wolfsburg	6	3	0	0	6	2	1	0	2	3	4	4	0	2	9	6	12
2	PSV Eindhoven	6	3	0	0	6	2	0	1	2	2	5	3	1	2	8	7	10
3	Manchester United FC	6	2	1	0	3	1	0	1	2	4	6	2	2	2	7	7	8
4	PFC CSKA Moskva	6	1	1	1	4	5	0	0	3	1	4	1	1	4	5	9	4

Group C

		Pld	Home W	D	L	F	A	Away W	D	L	F	A	Total W	D	L	F	A	Pts
1	Club Atlético de Madrid	6	2	0	1	7	2	2	1	0	4	1	4	1	1	11	3	13
2	SL Benfica	6	2	0	1	5	3	1	1	1	5	5	3	1	2	10	8	10
3	Galatasaray AŞ	6	1	1	1	3	4	0	1	2	3	6	1	2	3	6	10	5
4	FC Astana	6	0	3	0	4	4	0	1	2	1	7	0	4	2	5	11	4

Group D

		Pld	Home W	D	L	F	A	Away W	D	L	F	A	Total W	D	L	F	A	Pts
1	Manchester City FC	6	2	0	1	7	5	2	0	1	5	3	4	0	2	12	8	12
2	Juventus FC	6	2	1	0	3	0	1	1	1	3	3	3	2	1	6	3	11
3	Sevilla FC	6	2	0	1	5	3	0	0	3	3	8	2	0	4	8	11	6
4	VfL Borussia Mönchengladbach	6	1	1	1	6	5	0	1	2	2	7	1	2	3	8	12	5

Group E

		Pld	Home W	D	L	F	A	Away W	D	L	F	A	Total W	D	L	F	A	Pts
1	FC Barcelona	6	3	0	0	11	4	1	2	0	4	2	4	2	0	15	4	14
2	AS Roma	6	1	2	0	4	3	0	1	2	7	13	1	3	2	11	16	6
3	Bayer 04 Leverkusen	6	1	2	0	9	6	0	1	2	4	6	1	3	2	13	12	6
4	FC BATE Borisov	6	1	1	1	4	5	0	1	2	1	7	1	2	3	5	12	5

Group F

		Pld	Home W	D	L	F	A	Away W	D	L	F	A	Total W	D	L	F	A	Pts
1	FC Bayern München	6	3	0	0	14	1	2	0	1	5	2	5	0	1	19	3	15
2	Arsenal FC	6	2	0	1	7	3	1	0	2	5	7	3	0	3	12	10	9
3	Olympiacos FC	6	1	0	2	2	7	2	0	1	4	6	3	0	3	6	13	9
4	GNK Dinamo Zagreb	6	1	0	2	2	4	0	0	3	1	10	1	0	5	3	14	3

Group G

		Pld	Home W	D	L	F	A	Away W	D	L	F	A	Total W	D	L	F	A	Pts
1	Chelsea FC	6	3	0	0	8	1	1	1	1	5	2	4	1	1	13	3	13
2	FC Dynamo Kyiv	6	1	2	0	3	2	2	0	1	5	2	3	2	1	8	4	11
3	FC Porto	6	2	0	1	4	3	1	1	1	5	5	3	1	2	9	8	10
4	Maccabi Tel-Aviv FC	6	0	0	3	1	9	0	0	3	0	7	0	0	6	1	16	0

Group H

		Pld	Home W	D	L	F	A	Away W	D	L	F	A	Total W	D	L	F	A	Pts
1	FC Zenit	6	3	0	0	7	2	2	0	1	6	4	5	0	1	13	6	15
2	KAA Gent	6	2	1	0	4	2	1	0	2	4	5	3	1	2	8	7	10
3	Valencia CF	6	1	0	2	4	6	1	0	2	1	3	2	0	4	5	9	6
4	Olympique Lyonnais	6	0	0	3	1	5	1	1	1	4	4	1	1	4	5	9	4

André Schürrle points the way forward for Wolfsburg against Gent

Round of 16

16/02/16, Estádio do Sport Lisboa e Benfica, Lisbon (att: 48,615)
SL Benfica 1-0 FC Zenit
Goal: 1-0 Jonas 90+1
Referee: Rocchi (ITA)
09/03/16, Stadion Petrovski, St Petersburg (att: 17,688)
FC Zenit 1-2 SL Benfica
Goals: 1-0 Hulk 69, 1-1 Gaitán 85, 1-2 Talisca 90+6
Referee: Kassai (HUN)
Aggregate: 1-3; SL Benfica qualify.

16/02/16, Parc des Princes, Paris (att: 46,505)
Paris Saint-Germain 2-1 Chelsea FC
Goals: 1-0 Ibrahimović 39, 1-1 Mikel 45+1, 2-1 Cavani 78
Referee: Velasco Carballo (ESP)
09/03/16, Stamford Bridge, London (att: 37,591)
Chelsea FC 1-2 Paris Saint-Germain
Goals: 0-1 Rabiot 16, 1-1 Diego Costa 27, 1-2 Ibrahimović 67
Referee: Brych (GER)
Aggregate: 2-4; Paris Saint-Germain qualify.

17/02/16, KAA Gent Stadium, Ghent (att: 19,978)
KAA Gent 2-3 VfL Wolfsburg
Goals: 0-1 Draxler 44, 0-2 Draxler 54, 0-3 Kruse 60, 1-3 Kums 80, 2-3 Coulibaly 89
Referee: Moen (NOR)
08/03/16, VfL Wolfsburg Arena, Wolfsburg (att: 23,457)
VfL Wolfsburg 1-0 KAA Gent
Goal: 1-0 Schürrle 74
Referee: Skomina (SVN)
Aggregate: 4-2; VfL Wolfsburg qualify.

17/02/16, Stadio Olimpico, Rome (att: 55,612)
AS Roma 0-2 Real Madrid CF
Goals: 0-1 Cristiano Ronaldo 57, 0-2 Jesé 86
Referee: Královec (CZE)
08/03/16, Estadio Santiago Bernabéu, Madrid (att: 76,654)
Real Madrid CF 2-0 AS Roma
Goals: 1-0 Cristiano Ronaldo 64, 2-0 James Rodríguez 68
Referee: Marciniak (POL)
Aggregate: 4-0; Real Madrid CF qualify.

23/02/16, Arsenal Stadium, London (att: 59,889)
Arsenal FC 0-2 FC Barcelona
Goals: 0-1 Messi 71, 0-2 Messi 83(p)
Referee: Çakır (TUR)
16/03/16, Camp Nou, Barcelona (att: 76,092)
FC Barcelona 3-1 Arsenal FC
Goals: 1-0 Neymar 18, 1-1 Elneny 51, 2-1 Suárez 65, 3-1 Messi 88
Referee: Karasev (RUS)
Aggregate: 5-1; FC Barcelona qualify.

23/02/16, Juventus FC Stadium, Turin (att: 41,332)
Juventus FC 2-2 FC Bayern München
Goals: 0-1 Müller 43, 0-2 Robben 55, 1-2 Dybala 63, 2-2 Sturaro 76
Referee: Atkinson (ENG)
16/03/16, Fußball Arena München, Munich (att: 70,000)
FC Bayern München 4-2 Juventus FC (aet)
Goals: 0-1 Pogba 5, 0-2 Cuadrado 28, 1-2 Lewandowski 73, 2-2 Müller 90+1, 3-2 Thiago 108, 4-2 Coman 110
Referee: Eriksson (SWE)
Aggregate: 6-4; FC Bayern München qualify after extra time.

24/02/16, PSV Stadion, Eindhoven (att: 34,948)
PSV Eindhoven 0-0 Club Atlético de Madrid
Referee: Orsato (ITA)
15/03/16, Estadio Vicente Calderón, Madrid (att: 50,135)
Club Atlético de Madrid 0-0 PSV Eindhoven (aet)
Referee: Clattenburg (ENG)
Aggregate: 0-0; Club Atlético de Madrid qualify 8-7 on penalties.

24/02/16, NSK Olimpiyskyi, Kyiv (att: 53,691)
FC Dynamo Kyiv 1-3 Manchester City FC
Goals: 0-1 Agüero 15, 0-2 Silva 40, 1-2 Buyalskyi 59, 1-3 Touré 90
Referee: Mateu Lahoz (ESP)
15/03/16, City of Manchester Stadium, Manchester (att: 43,630)
Manchester City FC 0-0 FC Dynamo Kyiv
Referee: Haţegan (ROU)
Aggregate: 3-1; Manchester City FC qualify.

Quarter-finals

05/04/16, Fußball Arena München, Munich (att: 70,000)
FC Bayern München 1-0 SL Benfica
Goal: 1-0 Vidal 2
Referee: Marciniak (POL)
13/04/16, Estádio do Sport Lisboa e Benfica, Lisbon (att: 63,265)
SL Benfica 2-2 FC Bayern München
Goals: 1-0 Jiménez 27, 1-1 Vidal 38, 1-2 Müller 52, 2-2 Talisca 76
Referee: Kuipers (NED)
Aggregate: 2-3; FC Bayern München qualify.

05/04/16, Camp Nou, Barcelona (att: 88,534)
FC Barcelona 2-1 Club Atlético de Madrid
Goals: 0-1 Fernando Torres 25, 1-1 Suárez 63, 2-1 Suárez 74
Referee: Brych (GER)
13/04/16, Estadio Vicente Calderón, Madrid (att: 52,851)
Club Atlético de Madrid 2-0 FC Barcelona
Goals: 1-0 Griezmann 36, 2-0 Griezmann 88(p)
Referee: Rizzoli (ITA)
Aggregate: 3-2; Club Atlético de Madrid qualify.

06/04/16, VfL Wolfsburg Arena, Wolfsburg (att: 26,400)
VfL Wolfsburg 2-0 Real Madrid CF
Goals: 1-0 R Rodriguez 18(p), 2-0 Arnold 25
Referee: Rocchi (ITA)
12/04/16, Estadio Santiago Bernabéu, Madrid (att: 76,684)
Real Madrid CF 3-0 VfL Wolfsburg
Goals: 1-0 Cristiano Ronaldo 15, 2-0 Cristiano Ronaldo 17, 3-0 Cristiano Ronaldo 77
Referee: Kassai (HUN)
Aggregate: 3-2; Real Madrid CF qualify.

06/04/16, Parc des Princes, Paris (att: 47,228)
Paris Saint-Germain 2-2 Manchester City FC
Goals: 0-1 De Bruyne 38, 1-1 Ibrahimović 41, 2-1 Rabiot 59, 2-2 Fernandinho 72
Referee: Mažić (SRB)
12/04/16, City of Manchester Stadium, Manchester (att: 53,039)
Manchester City FC 1-0 Paris Saint-Germain
Goal: 1-0 De Bruyne 76
Referee: Velasco Carballo (ESP)
Aggregate: 3-2; Manchester City FC qualify.

Atlético Madrid's Antoine Griezmann scores from the penalty spot to seal holders Barcelona's fate in the quarter-finals

UEFA Champions League

Semi-finals

26/04/16, City of Manchester Stadium, Manchester (att: 52,221)
Manchester City FC 0-0 Real Madrid CF
Referee: Çakır (TUR)
04/05/16, Estadio Santiago Bernabéu, Madrid (att: 78,300)
Real Madrid CF 1-0 Manchester City FC
Goal: 1-0 Fernando 20(og)
Referee: Skomina (SVN)
Aggregate: 1-0; Real Madrid CF qualify.

27/04/16, Estadio Vicente Calderón, Madrid (att: 52,127)
Club Atlético de Madrid 1-0 FC Bayern München
Goal: 1-0 Saúl Ñíguez 11
Referee: Clattenburg (ENG)
03/05/16, Fußball Arena München, Munich (att: 70,000)
FC Bayern München 2-1 Club Atlético de Madrid
Goals: 1-0 Xabi Alonso 31, 1-1 Griezmann 54, 2-1 Lewandowski 74
Referee: Çakır (TUR)
Aggregate: 2-2; Club Atlético de Madrid qualify on away goal.

Final

28/05/16, Stadio San Siro, Milan (att: 71,942)
Real Madrid CF 1-1 Club Atlético de Madrid (aet; 5-3 on pens)
Goals: 1-0 Sergio Ramos 15, 1-1 Carrasco 79
Referee: Clattenburg (ENG)
Real Madrid: Navas, Pepe, Sergio Ramos, Cristiano Ronaldo, Kroos (Isco 72), Benzema (Lucas Vázquez 77), Bale, Marcelo, Casemiro, Carvajal (Danilo 52), Modrić. Coach: Zinédine Zidane (FRA)
Atlético: Oblak, Godín, Filipe Luís (Hernández 109), Koke (Partey 116), Griezmann, Fernando Torres, Fernández (Carrasco 46), Gabi, Savić, Saúl Ñíguez, Juanfran. Coach: Diego Simeone (ARG)
Yellow cards: Carvajal 11 (Real Madrid), Navas 47 (Real Madrid), Fernando Torres 61 (Atlético), Casemiro 79 (Real Madrid), Sergio Ramos 90+3 (Real Madrid), Gabi 90+3 (Atlético), Danilo 93 (Real Madrid), Pepe 112 (Real Madrid)

Top goalscorers

16	Cristiano Ronaldo (Real Madrid)
9	Robert Lewandowski (Bayern)
8	Luis Suárez (Barcelona)
	Thomas Müller (Bayern)
7	Antoine Griezmann (Atlético)
6	Lionel Messi (Barcelona)
	Artem Dzyuba (Zenit)
5	Olivier Giroud (Arsenal)
	Javier Hernández (Leverkusen)
	Willian (Chelsea)
	Zlatan Ibrahimović (Paris)

Squads/Appearances/Goals

Arsenal FC

No	Name	Nat	DoB	Aps	(s)	Gls
Goalkeepers						
33	Petr Čech	CZE	20/05/82	5		
13	David Ospina	COL	31/08/88	3		
Defenders						
24	Héctor Bellerín	ESP	19/03/95	6		
21	Calum Chambers		20/01/95		(3)	
2	Mathieu Debuchy	FRA	28/07/85	2	(1)	
5	Gabriel	BRA	26/11/90	4		
6	Laurent Koscielny	FRA	10/09/85	7		
4	Per Mertesacker	GER	29/09/84	5	(1)	
18	Nacho Monreal	ESP	26/02/86	6		
Midfielders						
8	Mikel Arteta	ESP	26/03/82	1		
34	Francis Coquelin	FRA	13/05/91	4	(2)	
35	Mohamed Elneny	EGY	11/07/92	1		1
20	Mathieu Flamini	FRA	07/03/84	3	(1)	
3	Kieran Gibbs		26/09/89	2	(3)	
15	Alex Oxlade-Chamberlain		15/08/93	3	(2)	
11	Mesut Özil	GER	15/10/88	8		2
14	Aaron Ramsey	WAL	26/12/90	3	(2)	
19	Santi Cazorla	ESP	13/12/84	5		
Forwards						
17	Alexis Sánchez	CHI	19/12/88	7		3
28	Joel Campbell	CRC	26/06/92	3	(2)	
12	Olivier Giroud	FRA	30/09/86	5	(2)	5
45	Alex Iwobi	NGA	03/05/96	1	(1)	
14	Theo Walcott		16/03/89	3	(3)	2
23	Danny Welbeck		26/11/90	1	(1)	

FC Astana

No	Name	Nat	DoB	Aps	(s)	Gls
Goalkeepers						
1	Nenad Erić		26/05/82	6		
Defenders						
2	Eldos Akhmetov		01/06/90	1		
5	Marin Aničić	BIH	17/08/89	5		1
15	Abzal Beysebekov		30/11/92	1	(2)	
33	Branko Ilič	SVN	06/02/83	6		
28	Birzhan Kulbekov		22/04/94		(1)	
12	Igor Pikalkin		19/03/92		(1)	
44	Evgeni Postnikov		16/04/86	6		
77	Dmitri Shomko		19/03/90	5		
Midfielders						
88	Roger Cañas	COL	27/03/90	5		
24	Denys Dedechko	UKR	02/07/87	1	(2)	
10	Foxi Kéthévoama	CTA	30/05/86	6		
20	Zhakyp Kozhamberdy		26/02/92		(1)	
6	Nemanja Maksimović	SRB	26/01/95	5		
11	Serikzhan Muzhikov		17/06/89	4	(1)	
8	Georgi Zhukov		19/11/94	3	(3)	
Forwards						
22	Baurzhan Dzholchiev		08/05/90	3	(1)	
89	Junior Kabananga	COD	04/04/89	6		
17	Tanat Nuserbayev		01/01/87		(2)	
9	Aleksei Shchetkin		21/05/91	1	(4)	
23	Patrick Twumasi	GHA	09/05/94	2		2

Real Madrid captain Sergio Ramos opens the scoring against Atlético in the UEFA Champions League final

Club Atlético de Madrid

No	Name	Nat	DoB	Aps	(s)	Gls
Goalkeepers						
13	Jan Oblak	SVN	07/01/93	13		
Defenders						
3	Filipe Luís	BRA	09/08/85	10		
24	José María Giménez	URU	20/01/95	7	(1)	
2	Diego Godín	URU	16/02/86	12		
18	Jesús Gámez		10/04/85	1		
19	Lucas Hernández	FRA	14/02/96	2	(2)	
20	Juanfran		09/01/85	12		
15	Stefan Savić	MNE	08/01/91	5	(2)	
4	Guilherme Siqueira	BRA	28/04/86	3		
Midfielders						
21	Yannick Carrasco	BEL	04/09/93	6	(3)	1
12	Augusto Fernández	ARG	10/04/86	5	(1)	
14	Gabi		10/07/83	12	(1)	
6	Koke		08/01/92	11		
8	Matías Kranevitter	ARG	21/05/93		(1)	
10	Óliver Torres		10/11/94	2	(5)	1
22	Thomas Partey	GHA	13/06/93		(5)	
17	Saúl Ñíguez		21/11/94	11	(2)	3
5	Tiago	POR	02/05/81	5		
Forwards						
16	Ángel Correa	ARG	09/03/95	1	(4)	1
9	Fernando Torres		20/03/84	6	(6)	1
7	Antoine Griezmann	FRA	21/03/91	13		7
11	Jackson Martínez	COL	03/10/86	3	(1)	
23	Luciano Vietto	ARG	05/12/93	3	(2)	1

FC BATE Borisov

No	Name	Nat	DoB	Aps	(s)	Gls
Goalkeepers						
16	Sergei Chernik		20/07/88	6		
Defenders						
4	Kaspars Dubra	LVA	20/12/90	2	(1)	
3	Vitali Gaiduchik		12/07/89	2		
19	Nemanja Milunović	SRB	31/05/89	6		1
25	Filip Mladenović	SRB	15/08/91	6		2
33	Denis Polyakov		17/04/91	6		
15	Maksim Zhavnerchik		09/02/85	2		
Midfielders						
9	Ilya Aleksiyevich		10/02/91	1		
55	Dmitri Baga		04/01/90	1		
81	Aleksandr Hleb		01/05/81	3	(2)	
7	Aleksandr Karnitski		14/02/89		(4)	
10	Nemanja Nikolić	MNE	01/01/88	3	(2)	
17	Aleksei Rios		14/05/87	1	(2)	
22	Igor Stasevich		21/10/85	5		1
8	Aleksandr Volodko		18/06/86	3	(2)	
42	Maksim Volodko		10/11/92	3	(3)	
5	Evgeni Yablonski		10/05/95	4	(1)	
Forwards						
62	Mikhail Gordeichuk		23/10/89	6		1
18	Dmitri Mozolevski		30/04/85	3	(1)	
13	Nikolai Signevich		20/02/92	3		

FC Bayern München

No	Name	Nat	DoB	Aps	(s)	Gls
Goalkeepers						
1	Manuel Neuer		27/03/86	11		
26	Sven Ulreich		03/08/88	1		
Defenders						
27	David Alaba	AUT	24/06/92	10		1
28	Holger Badstuber		13/03/89	1		
5	Medhi Benatia	MAR	17/04/87	2	(4)	
18	Juan Bernat	ESP	01/03/93	6	(2)	
17	Jérôme Boateng		03/09/88	6	(1)	
21	Philipp Lahm		11/11/83	12		
13	Rafinha	BRA	07/09/85	2	(2)	
Midfielders						
29	Kingsley Coman	FRA	13/06/96	4	(4)	2
11	Douglas Costa	BRA	14/09/90	11		2
19	Mario Götze		03/06/92	1	(3)	2
8	Javi Martínez	ESP	02/09/88	5	(3)	
32	Joshua Kimmich		08/02/95	6	(3)	
7	Franck Ribéry	FRA	07/04/83	5	(2)	
10	Arjen Robben	NED	23/01/84	2	(1)	2
20	Sebastian Rode		11/10/90	1		
6	Thiago Alcántara	ESP	11/04/91	8	(1)	1
23	Arturo Vidal	CHI	22/05/87	9	(2)	2
14	Xabi Alonso	ESP	25/11/81	8		1
Forwards						
37	Julian Green	USA	06/06/95	1		
9	Robert Lewandowski	POL	21/08/88	11	(1)	9
25	Thomas Müller		13/09/89	9	(3)	8

FC Barcelona

No	Name	Nat	DoB	Aps	(s)	Gls
Goalkeepers						
1	Marc-André ter Stegen	GER	30/04/92	10		
Defenders						
21	Adriano	BRA	26/10/84	2	(1)	1
15	Marc Bartra		15/01/91	2	(2)	
6	Dani Alves	BRA	06/05/83	8		
18	Jordi Alba		21/03/89	8	(1)	
14	Javier Mascherano	ARG	08/06/84	7	(1)	
24	Jérémy Mathieu	FRA	29/10/83	3		
3	Gerard Piqué		02/02/87	7		1
23	Thomas Vermaelen	BEL	14/11/85	3		
Midfielders						
7	Arda Turan	TUR	30/01/87		(3)	
5	Sergio Busquets		16/07/88	9		
27	Juan Cámara		13/02/94		(1)	
28	Gerard Gumbau		18/12/94		(3)	
8	Andrés Iniesta		11/05/84	7		
34	Wilfrid Kaptoum	CMR	07/07/96	1		
12	Rafinha		12/02/93		(2)	
4	Ivan Rakitić	CRO	10/03/88	9	(1)	2
20	Sergi Roberto		07/02/92	4	(4)	1
26	Sergi Samper		20/01/95	1	(1)	
Forwards						
10	Lionel Messi	ARG	24/06/87	7		6
17	Munir El Haddadi		01/09/95	2	(2)	
7	Neymar	BRA	05/02/92	9		3
19	Sandro Ramírez		09/07/95	2	(1)	
9	Luis Suárez	URU	24/01/87	9		8

Bayer 04 Leverkusen

No	Name	Nat	DoB	Aps	(s)	Gls
Goalkeepers						
1	Bernd Leno		04/03/92	6		
Defenders						
2	André Ramalho	BRA	16/02/92	1		
26	Giulio Donati	ITA	05/02/90	4		
13	Roberto Hilbert		16/10/84	2	(1)	
21	Ömer Toprak	TUR	21/07/89	3		
5	Kyriakos Papadopoulos	GRE	23/02/92	4	(1)	1
4	Jonathan Tah		11/02/96	6		
18	Wendell	BRA	20/07/93	6		
Midfielders						
38	Karim Bellarabi		08/04/90	5	(1)	
8	Lars Bender		27/04/89	2		
19	Julian Brandt		02/05/96		(6)	
10	Hakan Çalhanoğlu	TUR	08/02/94	6		2
44	Kevin Kampl	SVN	09/10/90	6		1
23	Christoph Kramer		19/02/91	4	(2)	
35	Vladlen Yurchenko	UKR	22/01/94		(2)	
Forwards						
7	Javier Hernández	MEX	01/06/88	6		5
11	Stefan Kiessling		25/01/84	1	(3)	
14	Admir Mehmedi	SUI	16/03/91	4	(1)	4

SL Benfica

No	Name	Nat	DoB	Aps	(s)	Gls
Goalkeepers						
1	Ederson	BRA	17/08/93	3		
12	Júlio César	BRA	03/09/79	7		
Defenders						
19	Eliseu		01/10/83	10		
33	Jardel	BRA	29/03/86	9		
2	Lisandro López	ARG	01/09/89	2		
4	Luisão	BRA	13/02/81	4		1
50	Nélson Semedo		16/11/93	3		
14	Victor Nilsson-Lindelöf	SWE	17/07/94	4		
28	Silvio		28/09/87	3		
Midfielders						
34	André Almeida		10/09/90	7	(1)	
39	Mehdi Carcela-González	BEL	01/07/89	1	(3)	
24	Bryan Cristante	ITA	03/03/95		(2)	
5	Ljubomir Fejsa	SRB	14/08/88	4	(2)	
10	Nicolás Gaitán	ARG	23/02/88	8		4
20	Gonçalo Guedes		29/11/96	6	(1)	1
21	Pizzi		06/10/89	6	(4)	
85	Renato Sanches		18/08/97	6		
18	Eduardo Salvio	ARG	13/07/90	1	(2)	
7	Andreas Samaris	GRE	13/06/89	6	(1)	
30	Talisca	BRA	01/02/94	2	(3)	2
31	Victor Andrade	BRA	30/09/95		(1)	
Forwards						
9	Raúl Jiménez	MEX	05/05/91	5	(5)	3
17	Jonas	BRA	01/04/84	9		2
35	Luka Jović	SRB	23/12/97		(1)	
11	Kostas Mitroglou	GRE	12/03/88	4	(3)	2

VfL Borussia Mönchengladbach

No	Name	Nat	DoB	Aps	(s)	Gls
Goalkeepers						
1	Yann Sommer	SUI	17/12/88	6		
Defenders						
15	Álvaro Domínguez	ESP	16/05/89	3		
4	Roel Brouwers	NED	28/11/81	1		
3	Andreas Christensen	DEN	10/04/96	5		
30	Nico Elvedi	SUI	30/09/96	1	(1)	
24	Tony Jantschke		07/04/90	1		
27	Julian Korb		21/03/92	5		1
18	Marvin Schulz		15/01/95		(2)	
17	Oscar Wendt	SWE	24/10/85	6		
Midfielders						
8	Mahmoud Dahoud		01/01/96	5	(1)	
28	André Hahn		13/08/90	1	(2)	
10	Thorgan Hazard	BEL	29/03/93	1	(3)	
7	Patrick Herrmann		12/02/91	1		
19	Fabian Johnson		11/12/87	5		2
6	Håvard Nordtveit	NOR	21/06/90	4	(2)	
14	Nico Schulz		01/04/93		(1)	
16	Ibrahima Traoré	GUI	21/04/88	4	(1)	
34	Granit Xhaka	SUI	27/09/92	5		
Forwards						
9	Josip Drmic	SUI	08/08/92		(3)	
11	Raffael	BRA	28/03/85	6		2
13	Lars Stindl		26/08/88	6		3

PFC CSKA Moskva

No	Name	Nat	DoB	Aps	(s)	Gls
Goalkeepers						
35	Igor Akinfeev		08/04/86	6		
Defenders						
6	Aleksei Berezutski		20/06/82	4	(1)	
24	Vasili Berezutski		20/06/82	2		
4	Sergei Ignashevich		14/07/79	6		1
2	Mário Fernandes	BRA	19/09/90	5		
14	Kirill Nababkin		08/09/86	2		
42	Georgi Schennikov		27/04/91	4		
5	Viktor Vasin		06/10/88		(1)	
Midfielders						
19	Aleksandrs Cauņa	LVA	19/01/88	1	(1)	
10	Alan Dzagoev		17/06/90	6		
25	Roman Eremenko	FIN	19/03/87	2	(1)	
60	Aleksandr Golovin		30/05/96		(1)	
23	Georgi Milanov	BUL	19/02/92	2	(2)	
66	Bebras Natcho	ISR	18/02/88	4	(1)	
7	Zoran Tošić	SRB	28/04/87	6		
3	Pontus Wernbloom	SWE	25/06/86	6		
Forwards						
88	Seydou Doumbia	CIV	31/12/87	4	(2)	3
18	Ahmed Musa	NGA	14/10/92	6		1
8	Kirill Panchenko		16/10/89		(4)	

FC Dynamo Kyiv

No	Name	Nat	DoB	Aps	(s)	Gls
Goalkeepers						
23	Olexandr Rybka		10/04/87	1		
1	Olexandr Shovkovskiy		02/01/75	7		
Defenders						
5	Antunes	POR	01/04/87	6		
2	Danilo Silva	BRA	24/11/86	6		
6	Aleksandar Dragovic	AUT	06/03/91	8		1
34	Yevhen Khacheridi		28/07/87	8		
27	Yevhen Makarenko		21/05/91		(1)	
24	Domagoj Vida	CRO	29/04/89	4	(1)	
Midfielders						
90	Younes Belhanda	FRA	25/02/90		(2)	
29	Vitaliy Buyalskiy		06/01/93	4	(3)	2
19	Denys Garmash		19/04/90	5	(2)	1
25	Derlis González	PAR	20/03/94	7	(1)	1
20	Oleh Gusev		25/04/83	2	(1)	1
4	Miguel Veloso	POR	11/05/86	3	(2)	
17	Serhiy Rybalka		01/04/90	7		
16	Serhiy Sydorchuk		02/05/91	5	(1)	
7	Olexandr Yakovenko		23/06/87		(1)	
10	Andriy Yarmolenko		23/10/89	7		2
Forwards						
11	Júnior Moraes	BRA	04/04/87	4	(3)	1
22	Artem Kravets		03/06/89	2	(2)	
91	Łukasz Teodorczyk	POL	03/06/91	2	(2)	

Chelsea FC

No	Name	Nat	DoB	Aps	(s)	Gls
Goalkeepers						
1	Asmir Begović	BIH	20/06/87	5		
13	Thibaut Courtois	BEL	11/05/92	3		
Defenders						
28	César Azpilicueta	ESP	28/08/89	8		
24	Gary Cahill		19/12/85	6	(1)	1
2	Branislav Ivanović	SRB	22/02/84	4		
6	Abdul Baba Rahman	GHA	02/07/94	4		
26	John Terry		07/12/80	4		
5	Kurt Zouma	FRA	27/10/94	5	(1)	
Midfielders						
4	Cesc Fàbregas	ESP	04/05/87	7		1
10	Eden Hazard	BEL	07/01/91	6	(2)	
16	Kenedy	BRA	08/02/96	1	(1)	
36	Ruben Loftus-Cheek		23/01/96	1		
21	Nemanja Matić	SRB	01/08/88	4	(1)	
12	John Obi Mikel	NGA	22/04/87	3	(1)	1
8	Oscar	BRA	09/09/91	4	(3)	2
7	Ramires	BRA	24/03/87	4	(1)	
14	Bertrand Traoré	BFA	06/09/95		(2)	
22	Willian	BRA	09/08/88	8		5
Forwards						
19	Diego Costa	ESP	07/10/88	7	(1)	2
17	Pedro Rodríguez	ESP	28/07/87	3	(3)	
18	Loïc Rémy	FRA	02/01/87	1	(2)	

GNK Dinamo Zagreb

No	Name	Nat	DoB	Aps	(s)	Gls
Goalkeepers						
34	Eduardo	POR	19/09/82	6		
Defenders						
26	Filip Benković		13/07/97	1	(1)	
6	Ivo Pinto	POR	07/01/90	3		
77	Alexandru Mățel	ROU	17/10/89	4		
3	Mario Musa		06/07/90		(1)	
19	Josip Pivarić		30/01/89	5		1
22	Leonardo Sigali	ARG	29/05/87	3	(1)	
87	Jérémy Taravel	FRA	17/04/87	6		
Midfielders						
16	Arijan Ademi	MKD	29/05/91	2		
8	Domagoj Antolić		30/06/90	6		
24	Ante Ćorić		14/04/97	1	(3)	
13	Gonçalo	POR	15/11/86	4	(1)	
10	Paulo Machado	POR	31/03/86	5	(1)	
18	Domagoj Pavičić		09/03/94		(1)	
20	Marko Pjaca		06/05/95	4	(2)	
30	Marko Rog		19/07/95	4	(2)	
Forwards						
11	Júnior Fernandes	CHI	10/04/88	6		1
9	Ángelo Henríquez	CHI	13/04/94		(4)	
15	Armin Hodžić	BIH	17/11/94	2		1
2	El Arabi Hillel Soudani	ALG	25/11/87	4	(1)	

Galatasaray AŞ

No	Name	Nat	DoB	Aps	(s)	Gls
Goalkeepers						
1	Fernando Muslera	URU	16/06/86	6		
Defenders						
23	Lionel Carole	FRA	12/04/91	3		
21	Aurélien Chedjou	CMR	20/06/85	4		
64	Jason Denayer	BEL	28/06/95	4		
22	Hakan Balta		23/03/83	6		
55	Sabri Sarıoğlu		26/07/84	5	(1)	
26	Semih Kaya		24/02/91	4		
Midfielders						
5	Bilal Kısa		22/06/83	4		1
52	Emre Çolak		20/05/91	1	(1)	
6	Jem Karacan		21/02/89	1		
14	José Rodríguez	ESP	16/12/94		(3)	
29	Olcan Adın		30/09/85	2	(2)	
8	Selçuk İnan		10/02/85	5		2
18	Sinan Gümüş		15/01/94		(3)	
10	Wesley Sneijder	NED	09/06/84	6		
7	Yasin Öztekin		19/03/87	4	(2)	
Forwards						
17	Burak Yılmaz		15/07/85	3	(1)	
11	Lukas Podolski	GER	04/06/85	6		2
9	Umut Bulut		15/03/83	2	(4)	

KAA Gent

No	Name	Nat	DoB	Aps	(s)	Gls
Goalkeepers						
1	Matz Sels		26/02/92	8		
Defenders						
21	Nana Asare	GHA	11/07/86	8		
55	Rami Gershon	ISR	12/08/88	1		
13	Stefan Mitrović	SRB	22/05/90	7		
23	Lasse Nielsen	DEN	08/01/88	8		
4	Rafinha	BRA	29/06/82	3	(3)	
Midfielders						
19	Brecht Dejaegere		29/05/91	5	(1)	
32	Thomas Foket		25/09/94	6	(1)	1
14	Sven Kums		26/02/88	8		2
8	Thomas Matton		24/10/85	3	(2)	1
77	Danijel Milicevic	SUI	05/01/86	8		3
10	Renato Neto	BRA	27/09/91	8		
15	Kenny Saief	ISR	17/12/93	4	(3)	
Forwards						
7	Kalifa Coulibaly	MLI	21/08/91		(6)	2
9	Laurent Depoitre		07/12/88	7		1
28	Nicklas Pedersen	DEN	10/10/87		(1)	
26	Benito Raman		07/11/94		(4)	
27	Moses Simon	NGA	12/07/95	4	(1)	

Olympique Lyonnais

No	Name	Nat	DoB	Aps	(s)	Gls
Goalkeepers						
1	Anthony Lopes	POR	01/10/90	6		
Defenders						
3	Henri Bedimo	CMR	04/06/84	3		
5	Milan Biševac	SRB	31/08/83	2		
13	Christophe Jallet		31/10/83	3	(1)	1
4	Bakary Koné	BFA	27/04/88		(1)	
15	Jérémy Morel		02/04/84	4		
20	Rafael	BRA	09/07/90	4	(1)	
14	Samuel Umtiti		14/11/93	4		
2	Mapou Yanga-Mbiwa		15/05/89	5		
Midfielders						
14	Sergi Darder	ESP	22/12/93	3	(1)	
12	Jordan Ferri		12/03/92	3	(2)	1
11	Rachid Ghezzal	ALG	09/05/92	1	(3)	
21	Maxime Gonalons		10/03/89	5		
7	Clément Grenier		07/01/91	1		
17	Steed Malbranque		06/01/80	1	(1)	
8	Corentin Tolisso		03/08/94	6		
19	Mathieu Valbuena		28/09/84	5		
Forwards						
9	Claudio Beauvue		16/04/88	2	(4)	
27	Maxwel Cornet		27/09/96	1	(3)	1
26	Aldo Kalulu		21/01/96	1	(1)	
10	Alexandre Lacazette		28/05/91	6		2

Malmö FF

No	Name	Nat	DoB	Aps	(s)	Gls
Goalkeepers						
1	Johan Wiland		24/01/81	6		
Defenders						
21	Kári Árnason	ISL	13/10/82	5		
17	Rasmus Bengtsson		26/06/86	5		
31	Franz Brorsson		30/01/96	1		
25	Felipe Carvalho	URU	18/09/93	2	(1)	
2	Pa Konate		25/04/94	3		
3	Anton Tinnerholm		26/02/91	6		
13	Yoshimar Yotún	PER	07/04/90	3	(1)	
Midfielders						
8	Enoch Kofi Adu	GHA	14/09/90	6		
19	Magnus Wolff Eikrem	NOR	08/08/90		(3)	
7	Simon Kroon		16/06/93		(2)	
6	Oscar Lewicki		14/07/92	6		
5	Erdal Rakip		13/02/96	1	(4)	
20	Vladimir Rodić	MNE	07/09/93	4	(2)	
22	Tobias Sana		11/07/89	1		
Forwards						
23	Jo Inge Berget	NOR	11/09/90	6		
28	Nikola Djurdjić	SRB	01/04/86	6		
11	Agon Mehmeti	ALB	20/11/89		(2)	
9	Markus Rosenberg		27/09/82	5		1

Juventus FC

No	Name	Nat	DoB	Aps	(s)	Gls
Goalkeepers						
1	Gianluigi Buffon		28/01/78	8		
Defenders						
12	Alex Sandro	BRA	26/01/91	4	(1)	
15	Andrea Barzagli		08/05/81	6	(2)	
19	Leonardo Bonucci		01/05/87	8		
3	Giorgio Chiellini		14/08/84	6		
33	Patrice Evra	FRA	15/05/81	5	(1)	
26	Stephan Lichtsteiner	SUI	16/01/84	6		1
24	Daniele Rugani		29/07/94		(1)	
Midfielders						
16	Juan Cuadrado	COL	26/05/88	5	(3)	1
11	Hernanes	BRA	29/05/85	4	(1)	
6	Sami Khedira	GER	04/04/87	4		
18	Mario Lemina	GAB	01/09/93		(1)	
8	Claudio Marchisio		19/01/86	5		
37	Roberto Pereyra	ARG	07/01/91		(2)	
10	Paul Pogba	FRA	15/03/93	8		1
27	Stefano Sturaro		09/03/93	4	(2)	1
Forwards						
21	Paulo Dybala	ARG	15/11/93	5	(2)	1
17	Mario Mandžukić	CRO	21/05/86	4	(1)	2
9	Álvaro Morata	ESP	23/10/92	6	(2)	2
7	Simone Zaza		25/06/91		(2)	1

Maccabi Tel-Aviv FC

No	Name	Nat	DoB	Aps	(s)	Gls
Goalkeepers						
95	Predrag Rajković	SRB	31/10/95	6		
Defenders						
26	Tal Ben Haim (I)		31/03/82	5		
20	Omri Ben Harush		07/03/90	5		
31	Carlos García	ESP	29/04/84	4		
2	Eli Dasa		03/12/92	3		
3	Yuval Shpungin		03/04/87	1		
18	Eitan Tibi		16/11/87	5		
Midfielders						
6	Gal Alberman		17/04/83	6		
16	Shlomi Azulay		30/03/90		(1)	
40	Emmanuel Nosa Igiebor	NGA	09/11/90	3	(1)	
15	Dor Micha		02/03/92	2	(2)	
24	Nikola Mitrović	SRB	02/01/87	3	(1)	
42	Dor Peretz		17/05/95	4	(2)	
22	Avi Rikan		10/09/88	5	(1)	
28	Gil Vermouth		05/08/85	2	(2)	
7	Eran Zahavi		25/07/87	6		1
Forwards						
9	Eden Ben Basat		08/09/86	1	(2)	
11	Tal Ben Haim (II)		05/08/89	5	(1)	
10	Barak Itzhaki		25/09/84		(4)	
99	Dejan Radonjić	CRO	23/07/90		(1)	

Manchester City FC

No	Name	Nat	DoB	Aps	(s)	Gls
Goalkeepers						
13	Willy Caballero	ARG	28/09/81		(1)	
1	Joe Hart		19/04/87	12		
Defenders						
22	Gaël Clichy	FRA	26/07/85	8		
26	Martín Demichelis	ARG	20/12/80	2	(2)	1
11	Aleksandar Kolarov	SRB	10/11/85	4	(2)	
4	Vincent Kompany	BEL	10/04/86	6	(1)	
20	Eliaquim Mangala	FRA	13/02/91	5	(2)	
30	Nicolás Otamendi	ARG	12/02/88	11	(1)	
3	Bacary Sagna	FRA	14/02/83	10	(1)	
5	Pablo Zabaleta	ARG	16/01/85	2	(1)	
Midfielders						
17	Kevin De Bruyne	BEL	28/06/91	8	(2)	3
18	Fabian Delph		21/11/89	1	(4)	
25	Fernandinho	BRA	04/05/85	12		2
6	Fernando	BRA	25/07/87	8	(2)	
15	Jesús Navas	ESP	21/11/85	8	(2)	
8	Samir Nasri	FRA	26/06/87	1		
21	David Silva	ESP	08/01/86	8		2
42	Yaya Touré	CIV	13/05/83	9	(1)	1
Forwards						
10	Sergio Agüero	ARG	02/06/88	8	(1)	2
14	Wilfried Bony	CIV	10/12/88	3	(2)	2
72	Kelechi Iheanacho	NGA	03/10/96		(4)	
7	Raheem Sterling		08/12/94	6	(4)	3

Manchester United FC

No	Name	Nat	DoB	Aps	(s)	Gls
Goalkeepers						
1	David de Gea	ESP	07/11/90	6		
Defenders						
17	Daley Blind	NED	09/03/90	5	(1)	
43	Cameron Borthwick-Jackson		02/02/97		(1)	
36	Matteo Darmian	ITA	02/12/89	4		
4	Phil Jones		21/02/92	1	(1)	
5	Marcos Rojo	ARG	20/03/90	3	(1)	
23	Luke Shaw		12/07/95	1		
12	Chris Smalling		22/11/89	6		1
30	Guillermo Varela	URU	24/03/93	1		
Midfielders						
21	Ander Herrera	ESP	14/08/89	2	(1)	
44	Andreas Pereira	BRA	01/01/96	1	(1)	
16	Michael Carrick		28/07/81	1	(1)	
27	Marouane Fellaini	BEL	22/11/87	1	(4)	
35	Jesse Lingard		15/12/92	4		
8	Juan Mata	ESP	28/04/88	4	(1)	1
22	Nick Powell		23/03/94		(1)	
28	Morgan Schneiderlin	FRA	08/11/89	3		
31	Bastian Schweinsteiger	GER	01/08/84	6		
25	Antonio Valencia	ECU	04/08/85	2	(1)	
18	Ashley Young		09/07/85	2	(2)	
Forwards						
7	Memphis Depay	NED	13/02/94	4	(2)	1
9	Anthony Martial	FRA	05/12/95	6		2
10	Wayne Rooney		24/10/85	4		1

Paris Saint-Germain

No	Name	Nat	DoB	Aps	(s)	Gls
Goalkeepers						
16	Kevin Trapp	GER	08/07/90	10		
Defenders						
19	Serge Aurier	CIV	24/12/92	5		1
32	David Luiz	BRA	22/04/87	7		1
20	Layvin Kurzawa		04/09/92	1		
5	Marquinhos	POR	14/05/94	6		
17	Maxwell	BRA	27/08/81	9		
2	Thiago Silva	BRA	22/09/84	9		
23	Gregory van der Wiel	NED	03/02/88	4	(2)	
Midfielders						
11	Ángel Di María	ARG	14/02/88	9	(1)	3
7	Lucas	BRA	13/08/92	3	(6)	2
14	Blaise Matuidi		09/04/87	9		
33	Christopher Nkunku		14/11/97		(1)	
27	Javier Pastore	ARG	20/06/89		(6)	
25	Adrien Rabiot		03/04/95	5	(2)	3
4	Benjamin Stambouli		13/08/90	1	(1)	
8	Thiago Motta	ITA	28/08/82	9		
6	Marco Verratti	ITA	05/11/92	5		
Forwards						
29	Jean-Kévin Augustin		16/06/97		(1)	
9	Edinson Cavani	URU	14/02/87	7	(3)	2
10	Zlatan Ibrahimović	SWE	03/10/81	10		5
22	Ezequiel Lavezzi	ARG	03/05/85	1	(3)	

PSV Eindhoven

No	Name	Nat	DoB	Aps	(s)	Gls
Goalkeepers						
1	Jeroen Zoet		06/01/91	8		
Defenders						
4	Santiago Arias	COL	13/01/92	6		
20	Joshua Brenet		20/03/94	6	(1)	
5	Jeffrey Bruma		13/11/91	8		
30	Jordy de Wijs		08/01/95		(1)	
2	Nicolas Isimat-Mirin	FRA	15/11/91	2	(3)	
3	Héctor Moreno	MEX	17/01/88	8		1
14	Simon Busk Poulsen	DEN	07/10/84	1	(1)	
15	Jetro Willems		30/03/94	2		
Midfielders						
18	Andrés Guardado	MEX	28/09/86	7		
29	Jorrit Hendrix		06/02/95	5	(2)	
10	Adam Maher		20/07/93	3		
7	Gastón Pereiro	URU	11/06/95	2	(4)	
6	Davy Pröpper		02/09/91	8		1
8	Stijn Schaars		11/01/84		(1)	
28	Marco van Ginkel		01/12/92	2		
23	Rai Vloet		08/05/95		(1)	
Forwards						
27	Steven Bergwijn		08/10/97		(1)	
9	Luuk de Jong		27/08/90	6		2
16	Maxime Lestienne	BEL	17/06/92	2	(2)	2
19	Jürgen Locadia		07/11/93	6	(2)	1
11	Luciano Narsingh		13/09/90	6	(1)	1

Olympiacos FC

No	Name	Nat	DoB	Aps	(s)	Gls
Goalkeepers						
16	Roberto	ESP	10/02/86	6		
Defenders						
3	Alberto Botía	ESP	27/01/89	3		
6	Manuel da Costa	MAR	06/05/86	3	(2)	
14	Omar Elabdellaoui	NOR	05/12/91	6		
30	Leandro Salino	BRA	22/04/85	2	(2)	
26	Arthur Masuaku	FRA	07/11/93	5		
23	Dimitrios Siovas		16/09/88	6		
29	Praxitelis Vouros		05/05/95		(1)	
Midfielders						
91	Esteban Cambiasso	ARG	18/08/80	3		
10	Alejandro Domínguez	ARG	10/06/81	1	(2)	
7	Kostas Fortounis		16/10/92	4	(2)	
11	Pajtim Kasami	SUI	02/06/92	6		
5	Luka Milivojević	SRB	07/04/91	4		
Forwards						
9	Alfred Finnbogason	ISL	01/02/89		(3)	1
77	Hernâni	POR	20/08/91	1	(4)	
99	Brown Ideye	NGA	10/10/88	6		1
90	Felipe Pardo	COL	17/08/90	5	(1)	3
92	Sebá	BRA	08/06/92	5	(1)	

FC Porto

No	Name	Nat	DoB	Aps	(s)	Gls
Goalkeepers						
12	Iker Casillas	ESP	20/05/81	6		
Defenders						
21	Miguel Layún	MEX	25/06/88	5	(1)	1
4	Maicon	BRA	14/09/88	3		1
5	Iván Marcano	ESP	23/06/87	5		
3	Bruno Martins Indi	NED	08/02/92	6		
2	Maxi Pereira	URU	08/06/84	6		
Midfielders						
20	André André		26/08/89	4	(1)	2
8	Yacine Brahimi	ALG	08/02/90	5		1
22	Danilo Pereira		09/09/91	5	(1)	
15	Evandro	BRA	23/08/86	1	(1)	
16	Héctor Herrera	MEX	19/04/90	2	(2)	
25	Giannelli Imbula	FRA	12/09/92	4	(1)	
6	Rúben Neves		13/03/97	5	(1)	
Forwards						
9	Vincent Aboubakar	CMR	22/01/92	5	(1)	3
17	Jesús Corona	MEX	06/01/93	2	(2)	
10	Pablo Osvaldo	ITA	12/01/86		(3)	
11	Cristian Tello	ESP	11/08/91	2	(3)	1
7	Silvestre Varela		02/02/85		(1)	

Real Madrid CF

No	Name	Nat	DoB	Aps	(s)	Gls
Goalkeepers						
13	Kiko Casilla		02/10/86	2		
1	Keylor Navas	CRC	15/12/86	11		
Defenders						
17	Álvaro Arbeloa		17/01/83	2		
2	Daniel Carvajal		11/01/92	8		1
23	Danilo	BRA	15/07/91	5	(2)	
12	Marcelo	BRA	12/05/88	10	(1)	
6	Nacho		18/01/90	3	(2)	1
3	Pepe	POR	26/02/83	8	(1)	
4	Sergio Ramos		30/03/86	10		1
2	Raphaël Varane	FRA	25/04/93	6	(1)	
Midfielders						
14	Casemiro	BRA	23/02/92	10	(1)	
21	Denis Cheryshev	RUS	26/12/90		(3)	
22	Isco		21/04/92	8	(3)	
10	James Rodríguez	COL	12/07/91	3	(2)	1
16	Mateo Kovačić	CRO	06/05/94	3	(5)	1
8	Toni Kroos	GER	04/01/90	11	(1)	
18	Lucas Vázquez		01/07/91	2	(5)	
19	Luka Modrić	CRO	09/09/85	10	(2)	1
Forwards						
11	Gareth Bale	WAL	16/07/89	8		
9	Karim Benzema	FRA	19/12/87	8	(1)	4
7	Cristiano Ronaldo	POR	05/02/85	12		16
20	Jesé		26/02/93	3	(6)	1

AS Roma

No	Name	Nat	DoB	Aps	(s)	Gls
Goalkeepers						
26	Morgan De Sanctis		26/03/77		(1)	
25	Wojciech Szczęsny	POL	18/04/90	8		
Defenders						
3	Lucas Digne	FRA	20/07/93	8		
24	Alessandro Florenzi		11/03/91	8		1
13	Maicon	BRA	26/07/81	1	(2)	
44	Kostas Manolas	GRE	14/06/91	8		
2	Antonio Rüdiger	GER	03/03/93	6		
35	Vasilios Torosidis	GRE	10/06/85	1	(3)	1
87	Ervin Zukanović	BIH	11/02/87	1		
Midfielders						
16	Daniele De Rossi		24/07/83	5	(1)	2
14	Iago Falqué	ESP	04/01/90	3	(2)	1
20	Seydou Keita	MLI	16/01/80	3		
4	Radja Nainggolan	BEL	04/05/88	7		
8	Diego Perotti	ARG	26/07/88	2		
15	Miralem Pjanić	BIH	02/04/90	7		2
48	Salih Uçan	TUR	06/01/94		(2)	
21	William Vainqueur	FRA	19/11/88	2	(2)	
Forwards						
9	Edin Džeko	BIH	17/03/86	5	(2)	2
22	Stephan El Shaarawy		27/10/92	2		
27	Gervinho	CIV	27/05/87	3		1
7	Juan Manuel Iturbe	ARG	04/06/93	2	(4)	
11	Mohamed Salah	EGY	15/06/92	6	(1)	1
92	Edoardo Soleri		19/10/97		(1)	
10	Francesco Totti		27/09/76		(2)	

FC Shakhtar Donetsk

No	Name	Nat	DoB	Aps	(s)	Gls
Goalkeepers						
32	Anton Kanibolotskiy		16/05/88	2		
30	Andriy Pyatov		28/06/84	4		
Defenders						
31	Ismaily	BRA	11/01/90	2		
14	Vasyl Kobin		24/05/85	1		
5	Olexandr Kucher		22/10/82	3		
66	Márcio Azevedo	BRA	05/02/86	3		
18	Ivan Ordets		08/07/92	1		
44	Yaroslav Rakitskiy		03/08/89	6		
13	Vyacheslav Shevchuk		13/05/79	1		
33	Darijo Srna	CRO	01/05/82	5		1
Midfielders						
29	Alex Teixeira	BRA	06/01/90	6		3
10	Bernard	BRA	08/09/92	3	(3)	
9	Dentinho	BRA	19/01/89		(3)	1
8	Fred	BRA	05/03/93	6		
74	Viktor Kovalenko		14/02/96		(5)	
17	Maksym Malyshev		24/12/92	1	(1)	
11	Marlos	BRA	07/06/88	6		
6	Taras Stepanenko		08/08/89	5		
Forwards						
22	Eduardo	CRO	25/02/83	1	(2)	1
19	Facundo Ferreyra	ARG	14/03/91		(1)	
21	Olexandr Gladkiy		24/08/87	5		1
28	Taison	BRA	13/01/88	3	(2)	

VfL Wolfsburg

No	Name	Nat	DoB	Aps	(s)	Gls
Goalkeepers						
1	Diego Benaglio	SUI	08/09/83	8		
28	Koen Casteels	BEL	25/06/92	2		
Defenders						
18	Dante	BRA	18/10/83	9		
24	Sebastian Jung		22/06/90	2	(2)	
5	Timm Klose	SUI	09/05/88	1	(1)	
31	Robin Knoche		22/05/92	2		
25	Naldo	BRA	10/09/82	8		2
34	Ricardo Rodriguez	SUI	25/08/92	9		1
4	Marcel Schäfer		07/06/84	1	(4)	
15	Christian Träsch		01/09/87	7	(1)	
Midfielders						
27	Maximilian Arnold		27/05/94	8	(2)	1
7	Daniel Caligiuri	ITA	15/01/88	5	(3)	1
10	Julian Draxler		20/09/93	8	(1)	3
23	Josuha Guilavogui	FRA	19/09/90	8	(1)	
22	Luiz Gustavo	BRA	23/07/87	7		
17	André Schürrle		06/11/90	6	(4)	2
8	Vieirinha	POR	24/01/86	5	(3)	1
Forwards						
3	Nicklas Bendtner	DEN	16/01/88		(4)	
16	Bruno Henrique	BRA	30/12/90	2		
12	Bas Dost	NED	31/05/89	5	(1)	1
11	Max Kruse		19/03/88	7	(2)	2
32	Leandro Putaro		07/01/97		(1)	

Sevilla FC

No	Name	Nat	DoB	Aps	(s)	Gls
Goalkeepers						
1	Sergio Rico		01/09/93	6		
Defenders						
17	Marco Andreolli	ITA	10/06/86	2		
23	Coke		26/04/87	6		
5	Timothée Kolodziejczak	FRA	01/10/91	6		
25	Mariano	BRA	23/06/86		(4)	
3	Adil Rami	FRA	27/12/85	4		
2	Benoît Trémoulinas	FRA	28/12/85	6		1
Midfielders						
19	Éver Banega	ARG	29/06/88	5		2
8	Vicente Iborra		16/01/88	2	(1)	
22	Yevhen Konoplyanka	UKR	29/09/89	5	(1)	2
7	Michael Krohn-Dehli	DEN	06/06/83	2	(4)	
4	Grzegorz Krychowiak	POL	29/01/90	6		
15	Steven N'Zonzi	FRA	15/12/88	3	(2)	
10	José Antonio Reyes		01/09/83	2		
20	Vitolo		02/11/89	5		1
Forwards						
9	Kevin Gameiro	FRA	09/05/87	4	(1)	1
11	Ciro Immobile	ITA	20/02/90		(3)	
30	Juan Muñoz		12/11/95		(1)	
24	Fernando Llorente		26/02/85	2	(1)	1

Valencia CF

No	Name	Nat	DoB	Aps	(s)	Gls
Goalkeepers						
24	Jaume Doménech		05/11/90	6		
Defenders						
23	Aymen Abdennour	TUN	06/08/89	4		
4	Aderlan Santos	BRA	09/04/89	2	(1)	
19	Antonio Barragán		12/06/87	1		
14	José Gayá		25/05/95	5		
2	João Cancelo	POR	27/05/94	5	(1)	1
5	Shkodran Mustafi	GER	17/04/92	5		
6	Lucas Orbán		03/02/89	1		
3	Rúben Vezo	POR	25/04/94	1		
Midfielders						
21	André Gomes	POR	30/07/93	2	(2)	1
12	Danilo	BRA	28/02/96	1	(3)	
8	Sofiane Feghouli	ALG	26/12/89	5		2
18	Javi Fuego		04/01/84	4	(1)	
10	Daniel Parejo		16/04/89	6		
15	Enzo Pérez	ARG	22/02/86	5		
Forwards						
20	Rodrigo de Paul	ARG	24/05/94	1	(1)	
37	Rafael Mir		18/06/97	1		
7	Álvaro Negredo		20/08/85	2	(1)	
9	Paco Alcácer		30/08/93	4	(1)	
11	Pablo Piatti	ARG	31/03/89	2	(3)	
17	Rodrigo		06/03/91		(3)	
22	Santi Mina		07/12/95	3	(1)	

FC Zenit

No	Name	Nat	DoB	Aps	(s)	Gls
Goalkeepers						
41	Mikhail Kerzhakov		28/01/87	2		
1	Yuri Lodygin		26/05/90	6		
Defenders						
2	Aleksandr Anyukov		28/09/82	7		
4	Domenico Criscito	ITA	30/12/86	6		
24	Ezequiel Garay	ARG	10/10/86	6		
6	Nicolas Lombaerts	BEL	20/03/85	8		
13	Luís Neto	POR	26/05/88	4	(3)	
19	Igor Smolnikov		08/08/88	3	(2)	
Midfielders						
10	Danny	POR	07/08/83	8		1
94	Aleksei Evseev		30/03/94		(1)	
20	Viktor Fayzulin		22/04/86		(1)	
21	Javi García	ESP	08/02/87	6		
8	Maurício	BRA	21/10/88	1	(1)	
5	Aleksandr Ryazantsev		05/09/86	1	(4)	
17	Oleg Shatov		29/07/90	5	(2)	2
79	Konstantin Troyanov		18/11/95		(1)	
28	Axel Witsel	BEL	12/01/89	7		1
14	Artur Yusupov		01/09/89	1	(5)	
81	Yuri Zhirkov		20/08/83	1	(1)	
Forwards						
70	Dmitri Bogaev		24/01/94		(1)	
92	Pavel Dolgov		16/08/96		(1)	
22	Artem Dzyuba		22/08/88	8		6
7	Hulk	BRA	25/07/86	7		4
9	Aleksandr Kokorin		19/03/91	1	(1)	

Unai Emery's side make history in Basel

Second-half comeback rocks Liverpool

Fifth Spanish triumph in seven years

Stunning hat-trick for Sevilla

Sevilla FC's love affair with the UEFA Europa League continued in 2015/16 as they lifted the trophy for the third year in a row – an unprecedented achievement in both the new competition and its forerunner, the UEFA Cup. Having won finals against Benfica and Dnipro Dnipropetrovsk in each of the previous two years, Unai Emery's side completed the hat-trick at the expense of Liverpool, coming from behind to defeat their English opponents 3-1 at St Jakob-Park in Basel.

With back-to-back UEFA Cup wins, in 2005 and 2006, also on their roll of honour, Sevilla's pedigree in the competition is second to none. The reward for their victory over Liverpool was a free pass into the group stage of the 2016/17 UEFA Champions League. Indeed, their 2015/16 European campaign had also begun in the more established event, with a third-place finish in their group enabling them to cross over and defend their trophy. Molde, Basel, Athletic Club and Shakhtar Donetsk were all eliminated, with varying degrees of efficiency, before the Andalusians made history with their victory over Jürgen Klopp's side in Switzerland, three second-half goals swinging the game their way after they had trailed 1-0 at the interval.

Kevin Gameiro, who scored the equaliser, and captain Coke, author of the second and third goals, proved to be Sevilla's match-winners, which was fitting as they were two of the four players who had appeared in all three of the team's victorious finals, Daniel Carriço and Vitolo being the others. Emery was also in charge on all three occasions, enabling him to match the achievement of Giovanni Trapattoni, the only other coach with three UEFA Cups or UEFA Europa Leagues – in his case the former – on his CV.

Gameiro contributed eight goals to Sevilla's success plus the winning penalty in the quarter-final shoot-out against fellow Spaniards Athletic, who provided the competition's leading marksman in ten-goal Aritz Aduriz. African strikers Pierre-Emerick Aubameyang (Borussia Dortmund) and Cédric Bakambu (Villarreal) also made their mark, spearheading their clubs' challenge with a plethora of goals until Liverpool blocked their route to Basel with a couple of stirring performances at Anfield.

The Merseysiders' epic 4-3 comeback win over Klopp's ex-club Dortmund in the quarter-finals was the stuff of dreams and legends, with the winning goal, from Dejan Lovren, coming in added time in front of the Kop. With arch-rivals Manchester

United having been emphatically eliminated the round before, it was a campaign of many highlights for the Liverpool fans. Their team went 12 games unbeaten – as did their semi-final opponents Villarreal, which was the most in a single UEFA Europa League campaign, while Sparta Praha also avoided defeat all the way from the group stage to the quarter-finals, where they were well beaten by a Villarreal side victorious in all seven of their home matches.

Apart from Sevilla, the best of the eight teams that entered the knockout phase from the UEFA Champions League were Shakhtar Donetsk, who won five games out of six and drew the other until they met the holders in the last four, while the stand-out performers of the group stage were Napoli, the only side to win all six matches while also setting a new scoring record of 22 goals.

There would be no first UEFA Europa League finalist from Italy, however – nor indeed from Germany, or France, or the Netherlands. The seven years of the competition have been dominated by one country, Spain, and in 2015/16 Sevilla eclipsed the achievement of inaugural and two-time winners Atlético Madrid with their extraordinary hat-trick of triumphs.

Opposite: Club captain José Antonio Reyes lifts the trophy as Sevilla win the UEFA Europa League for the third year in a row

Group stage

A new breakdown of the qualification routes into the group stage of the 2015/16 UEFA Europa League meant that as many as a third of the 48-team field were afforded direct entry, with the remaining participants making their way through from the play-offs of either the UEFA Europa League (the 22 winners) or the UEFA Champions League (the ten losers).

One of the 16 teams exempt from pre-qualifying were 2014/15 semi-finalists Napoli, and they were to set new records for the group stage of the competition as they cruised through to the round of 32 in **Group D**. New coach Maurizio Sarri led the Serie A side to six wins out of six, their three home games all bringing five-goal victories – against Club Brugge, FC Midtjylland and Legia Warszawa – that resulted in a new group stage record haul of 22 goals, beating FC Salzburg's previous mark (set in 2014/15) by one. Napoli became the seventh team to progress with a 100% record, with their goal difference of +19 making them the most convincing of the lot. Indeed, Napoli's 18 points were two more than the other three teams in the section could muster put together, but one of them had to qualify and it was Midtjylland – surprise play-off conquerors of Southampton and the only one of the eight UEFA Europa League newcomers in 2015/16 to win their opening two matches – who squeezed through after ending a run of three successive defeats by holding competition regulars Club Brugge to a 1-1 draw in Denmark on the final matchday.

Another Italian club, Lazio, went through with an unbeaten record, winning four and drawing two of their six **Group G** encounters and in the process prompting the elimination of Napoli's conquerors in the previous season's semi-finals, Dnipro Dnipropetrovsk. The Ukrainian side snatched a stoppage-time draw on matchday one at home to their Serie A visitors, but a 3-1 loss in Rome a couple of months later proved fatal after home and away defeats by Saint-Étienne, for whom a 1-1 draw away to Rosenborg – a rare survivor from the competition's first qualifying round – proved sufficient to book their place in the knockout phase as runners-up to Lazio with a game to spare.

Fiorentina, who, like Napoli, entered the competition eager to atone for semi-final elimination in 2014/15, made it three Italian qualifiers out of three after recovering in **Group I** from an opening 2-1 home defeat by FC Basel, the club from whom they had just acquired their new coach, Paulo Sousa. The Viola maintained their fine away form of the previous two campaigns to see off the modest threat of Belenenses and Lech Poznań, although Basel, whose major incentive for further progress was the selection of their St Jakob-Park home as the venue for the final, outdid them by winning all three of their road fixtures and securing round of 32 qualification as a group winner for the first time.

Another Swiss team, FC Sion, marked their debut in the UEFA Europa League by taking seven points from their first three fixtures in **Group B**, wins against Rubin and Bordeaux sandwiching an impressive 1-1 draw against Liverpool at Anfield. That early burst would take Sion through, but a 0-0 home draw against the Merseysiders in freezing conditions on matchday six meant that their opponents, now led by new coach Jürgen Klopp, maintained not just their unbeaten record but their place at the top of the standings. Liverpool's progress was of the pragmatic rather than crowd-pleasing variety as they drew four of their matches and scored only six goals – the fewest of any of the 12 group winners. However, it was the third time they had topped a UEFA Europa League group, which equalled a competition record.

Sion's Moussa Konaté celebrates a goal against Rubin

3

Lazio completed a UEFA Europa League group stage undefeated for the third time to share the competition record with PSV Eindhoven and FC Salzburg. Liverpool, meanwhile, joined PSV, Salzburg and Sporting Clube de Portugal on a record three qualifications for the knockout phase as a group winner, repeating the feat they had previously managed in 2010/11 and 2012/13.

With FairPlay qualifiers West Ham United having dropped out of the competition even before Southampton exited in the play-offs, there were just two Premier League teams in the group stage, but Tottenham, like Liverpool, restored some English pride by going through to the knockout phase as section winners, taking the spoils in **Group J** ahead of fellow qualifiers Anderlecht, the only team to beat them. Mauricio Pochettino's side struck 12 goals, nine of them at White Hart Lane, where they claimed maximum points, with Erik Lamela becoming the fourth Spurs player to score a UEFA Europa League hat-trick with a first-half treble in a closing 4-1 victory over Monaco, whose disappointing campaign left them with just two points more than bottom-placed Qarabağ.

A faster hat-trick than Lamela's was provided by his fellow Argentine, Franco Di Santo, who scored three times in the space of 16 minutes as Schalke routed Asteras Tripolis 4-0 at home on matchday two in **Group K**. The German club would go on to win the section, their only dropped points coming in home and away draws against Sparta Praha as both teams qualified with unbeaten records. Sparta striker David Lafata scored half of his team's ten goals, including one in each game against Schalke and a late winning double against APOEL in Cyprus on matchday six.

Lafata's goal haul was one shy of the competition's leading tally, with Aritz Aduriz's half-dozen including a double in each of Athletic Club's two **Group L** victories against Augsburg. It looked as if Germany's European debutants were out for the count as they fell 1-0 behind to FK Partizan in Belgrade on matchday six in a game they needed not only to win but also by scoring a minimum three goals. The Serbian side, who had won the earlier meeting 3-1 in south Germany, looked poised to join Athletic in the next round but the nightmare scenario unfolded and they duly conceded the three goals they could ill afford, the last of them after a number of defensive errors in the 89th minute as Augsburg's Raúl Bobadilla, who had scored a matchday four hat-trick against AZ Alkmaar, pounced to fire his team through at Partizan's expense and in the process join Aduriz on six goals for the competition.

With UEFA Europa League holders Sevilla having taken their place alongside four other Spanish clubs in the UEFA Champions League, Athletic were one of only two Liga entrants in the competition, the other being Villarreal, who despite amassing 13 points in **Group E** did not finish on top of their section. That honour went, somewhat unexpectedly, to Rapid Wien, who won each of their first four fixtures to ensure an early passage through to the round of 32, Villarreal joining them after they punctured the Austrian club's perfect record thanks to a single Bruno Soriano goal at El Madrigal on matchday five. The only wins for group also-rans Viktoria Plzeň and Dinamo Minsk were against each other.

Rapid were not the only surprise group winners, with perhaps the unlikeliest of all being Norway's Molde, who found themselves among illustrious company in **Group A** alongside Ajax, Celtic and Fenerbahçe. Remarkably, though, the underdogs from Scandinavia were already guaranteed a round of 32 place after just four of their six matches, which yielded ten points, six of them at the expense of Celtic and their Norwegian coach Ronny Deila. The 2-1 win in Glasgow also featured a goal from Molde's veteran skipper Daniel Berg Hestad, who thus, at the age of 40 years and 98 days, became the UEFA Europa League's oldest scorer. Fenerbahçe joined Molde in the next round, which meant that for the first time in its seven seasons the competition's knockout phase would not feature Ajax. As for Celtic, they stretched their winless run in the competition to 11 matches – one short of the unwanted record held jointly by Partizan and Slovan Bratislava.

There were unlikely Russian table-toppers in **Group C**, where FC Krasnodar edged

Teenage striker Marcus Rashford scored twice on his Manchester United debut against Midtjylland in the round of 32

highly-fancied Borussia Dortmund, who had qualified with ease after four matches, into second place on the final day, and in **Group H**, where Lokomotiv Moskva kicked off their campaign by becoming the first UEFA Europa League visitors to beat Sporting Clube de Portugal in Lisbon. That 3-1 win ended the Lions' record run as new coach Jorge Jesus, twice a runner-up with Benfica, returned to the competition with a defeat. Sporting's woes continued when they lost 3-0 away to Skënderbeu – the first victory in the competition proper by a team from Albania – but a revenge 4-2 win in Moscow and an exciting matchday six comeback triumph over Beşiktaş (3-1) ensured extended involvement at their Turkish opponents' expense.

By the time Sporting made it through, Portuguese rivals Braga had already secured their berth in the round of 32, the 2011 runners-up eventually pipping Olympique Marseille to top spot in **Group F** thanks to a perfect home record and a last-day draw at winless FC Groningen. Marseille needed a point away to Slovan Liberec in their final fixture to prevent their hosts from leapfrogging them into second place but the Czech side, who had earlier won 1-0 at the Stade Vélodrome with their only shot on target, recoiled under the pressure, falling 3-0 behind before Marseille, struggling in Ligue 1 at the time, wrapped up a much-needed 4-2 win – and a place in the round of 32 – with the last kick of the game.

Round of 32

The arrival of eight teams from the UEFA Champions League swelled German and Spanish ranks in the round of 32 to four clubs apiece, with England and Portugal both increasing their number to match Italy's tally of three. For the first time in the competition's seven seasons there were no participants from the Netherlands, while Molde's presence enabled Norway to become the 24th nation to feature in the UEFA Europa League knockout phase.

Anderlecht, Liverpool, Napoli and Sporting were all playing post-Christmas football in the revamped competition for the fifth time, but only the first two advanced into the round of 16, the Brussels club after two extra-time goals from Frank Acheampong against Olympiacos in Piraeus, the Merseysiders thanks to a lone James Milner penalty against Augsburg. Sporting lost home and away to new arrivals Bayer Leverkusen, while Napoli were the victims of two long-range Villarreal strikes, the first at El Madrigal a sumptuous free-kick from Denis Suárez, the decisive second at the Stadio San Paolo a fortuitous effort from Tomás Pina.

Sevilla, back in the competition via the UEFA Champions League and bidding to lift the trophy for a third successive year, effectively ended Molde's hopes with a 3-0 win in Andalusia, although the Norwegians exited on a high by beating the holders 1-0 in the return. Rapid Wien, on the other hand, were shown no mercy by their Spanish opponents as Valencia, coached by English novice Gary Neville, broke a whole host of competition records, not least that of the highest aggregate win in the knockout phase, by pummeling them 6-0 at home and 4-0 away. The only other team to score half that many in the round were Neville's former club, Manchester United, who avoided an improbable elimination at the hands of Midtjylland thanks to a brace of goals from debutant teenage striker Marcus Rashford as they recovered from a 3-1 aggregate deficit to triumph 5-1 at Old Trafford.

Tottenham made it three English qualifiers out of three by reaping their revenge on Fiorentina, the team that had knocked them out at the same stage a year earlier, an excellent 3-0 second-leg win in north London building on the

UEFA Europa League

Pierre-Emerick Aubameyang outjumps Ben Davies to score for Dortmund against Tottenham

KEY FACT

50

In the second leg of the round of 32 Daniel Carriço became the first player to make 50 UEFA Europa League appearances, although his half-century was spoiled by a defeat – with Sevilla losing 1-0 at Molde – and a yellow card. He ended the season on 54 appearances (28 for Sevilla and 26 for Sporting Clube de Portugal) – ten more than the second-ranked player on the all-time list, Óscar Cardozo.

foundation of a fine 1-1 draw in Tuscany. That left Lazio, 4-2 aggregate conquerors of Galatasaray, as the lone remaining Italian team, while France lost both of their participants, Marseille failing to recover from a wonder goal in the Vélodrome from Athletic's ever-prolific Aduriz and St-Étienne falling victim to the away goals rule after Luca Zuffi's dramatic added-time decider for Basel in the St Jakob-Park.

Russian involvement ended too as group winners Lokomotiv Moskva and Krasnodar succumbed, respectively, to group runners-up Fenerbahçe and Sparta Praha, while there were differing fortunes for the two rivals from Germany's Ruhr as Schalke lost 3-0 on aggregate to Shakhtar Donetsk, with all the goals coming in Gelsenkirchen, and Dortmund prevailed by the same score over the two legs against FC Porto in a tie that did nothing for the lasting reputation of former Real Madrid goalkeeper Iker Casillas. Braga, however, preserved Portuguese interest by edging home against Sion.

Round of 16

There were four Spanish clubs in the round of 16 for the first time, but the pairing of Athletic and Valencia ensured that the full compliment could advance no further. It turned out to be one of the most keenly contested ties of the round. Both teams won their home leg, Athletic 1-0 on a sodden pitch in Bilbao before Valencia conceded late on to a heavily contested Aduriz goal that transformed their 2-1 victory on the night into an aggregate away-goal defeat and ultimately ended Neville's short reign as coach.

The other tie between two teams from the same country brought together English rivals Liverpool and Manchester United. It was the first time the two clubs had ever been paired together in Europe, and the first leg at Anfield suggested that it meant a lot more to the Merseysiders, who dominated throughout and would have constructed a bigger lead than the 2-0 scoreline provided by Daniel Sturridge and Roberto Firmino but for a typically resilient display from United goalkeeper David de Gea. A week later at Old Trafford, where a UEFA Europa League record crowd of 75,180 spectators gathered, the tie was effectively settled by a clever equaliser from Philippe Coutinho on the stroke of half-time, United's only consolation having been to deny Liverpool a record-equalling fifth consecutive UEFA Europa League clean sheet thanks to Anthony Martial's early penalty.

United were accompanied out of the competition by Tottenham, who paid the price for manager Mauricio Pochettino's audacious gamble to field weakened teams in both legs against Borussia Dortmund. Striker Pierre-Emerick Aubameyang struck three times as the German club made light work of their depleted opponents, winning 5-1 on aggregate. That was the largest margin of victory in the round, although Sevilla, Sparta Praha and Shakhtar Donetsk all ran Thomas Tuchel's side close.

Sevilla were too strong for Basel in a battle between the holders and the final hosts, setting a new competition record by registering their 11th successive home win, 3-0, after a goalless draw in Switzerland. Sparta extended their unbeaten run to ten matches by shocking Lazio with three first-half strikes in the Stadio Olimpico, although the pick of their four goals in the tie was a spectacular opener from Martin Frýdek in the 1-1 first-leg draw in Prague. Shakhtar also claimed a 4-1 aggregate win, seeing off Anderlecht home and away, while that was the scoreline of the second-leg encounter between Braga and Fenerbahçe, with the Portuguese side coming back from a 1-0 defeat in Istanbul against a Turkish team that ended the second contest with eight men.

Quarter-finals

Having seen off Valencia in the round of 16, Athletic were handed another familiar opponent in the quarter-final draw as Sevilla, through to the last eight for the third year running, joined them in the UEFA Europa League's eighth all-Spanish tie – and the fourth involving the Andalusian club. The first leg, in a damp Bilbao, looked to be going the way of the home side when Aduriz headed home Iker Muniain's cross for his ninth goal of the campaign, but Sevilla, who had not won on their travels in either Europe or the Spanish league all season, were handed a lifeline when a Muniain error gifted a goal to defender Timothée Kolodziejczak. Seven minutes from time the San Mamés was stunned into silence as Vicente Iborra deflected in a second to give Sevilla a precious 2-1 win.

Athletic's chances of a comeback appeared remote, but that was not how Aduriz saw it as yet again he put his team in front to become only the fourth scorer in the UEFA Europa League to reach double figures in a single campaign. Kevin Gameiro restored Sevilla's overall advantage soon afterwards, but with ten minutes to go Raúl García's looping header levelled up the tie at 3-3. Markel Susaeta squandered a huge chance to give the visitors a decisive lead in extra time, and he was made to pay as Sevilla prevailed in the ensuing penalty shoot-out, Beñat Etxeberria missing Athletic's fourth kick before Gameiro's perfectly-struck decider gave the Andalusians their third win in as many UEFA Europa League shoot-outs.

Villarreal, Spain's third quarter-finalist, negotiated a comparatively straightforward passage into the last four, ending Sparta Praha's long unbeaten run with a narrow but deserved 2-1 home win before finishing off their Czech adversaries 4-2 in Prague. Four goals from DR Congo striker Bakambu did most of the damage as he lifted his tally in the competition to nine – one behind Aduriz. It was plain sailing also for Shakhtar as they brushed aside Braga. The Portuguese side surrendered their unbeaten home record in the first leg, losing 2-1, before Shakhtar skipper Darijo Srna took centre stage in the Lviv return, marking his record-breaking 486th club appearance with a penalty and two assists as the last team to win the UEFA Cup breezed to a 4-0 win.

Billed as the tie of the round, Dortmund against Liverpool more than lived up to expectations. The first leg brought Liverpool boss Jürgen Klopp back to his former club and to a sold-out BVB Stadion. Although the welcome was warm, the challenge was a tough one against in-form opponents. Liverpool played well and were good value for the 1-1 draw that stretched their unbeaten run in the competition to 11 games, with Divock Origi giving the visitors a first-half lead before Mats Hummels headed Dortmund level from Henrikh Mkhitaryan's cross shortly after the interval.

All square at the start of the second leg, the German side were 2-0 up after less than ten minutes, Mikhitaryan and Aubameyang striking to put Dortmund firmly in control. Liverpool needed three goals to get back in front and although they got one, through Origi again, Marco Reus made it 3-1 not long afterwards to re-establish the differential. The final 25 minutes, however, would enter Anfield legend as Klopp's team pounded the Dortmund defence, pulling one back, through Coutinho, adding another, from Mamadou Sakho's stooping header, and then, in the first minute of added time, winning the match and the tie with another header, from Sakho's central defensive partner Dejan Lovren, to send the Kop into raptures of joy and leave the Dortmund players and fans looking on in bemused disbelief.

Semi-finals

Liverpool's remarkable tide-turning display against Dortmund was followed by another comeback triumph in the semi-finals against Villarreal. The Spanish club, who had lost each of their

Adam Lallana turns the ball home to put Liverpool 3-0 up at Anfield in the semi-final second leg against Villarreal

previous three European semi-finals, were a touch fortunate to extend their 100% record at El Madrigal – and end Liverpool's record 12-game unbeaten run for a single UEFA Europa League campaign – when substitute Adrián López scored the only goal of the first leg with virtually the last kick of the game. But there was only one team in it at an electric Anfield seven days later. Gifted an early pick-me-up by Bruno's freakish 7th-minute own goal, Klopp's team took a while to establish their authority, but once Sturridge had converted Firmino's pass – via the goalkeeper and post – to put Liverpool ahead in the tie, Villarreal caved in. Defender Víctor Ruiz was red-carded and Adam Lallana flicked the ball home from close range to make it 3-0 and take Liverpool through to the final in style, ending Villarreal's own 12-game unbeaten run in the process.

An all-Spanish final was averted by Liverpool's triumph, but Sevilla duly made it through to join Klopp's men in Basel as they convincingly ended the

hopes of Shakhtar in a contest between two teams that had started their European campaign in the UEFA Champions League. Ahead early in the first leg at Arena Lviv when Vitolo put the finishing touch to a lethal counterattack, Sevilla then fell 2-1 behind, to Marlos's exquisite half-volley and Taras Stepanenko's powerful header, before a late Gameiro penalty levelled things up at 2-2. The following week's return at the Estadio Ramón Sánchez Pizjuán would belong to the French striker as he struck twice – once with his right foot, once with his left – to inspire his team into a third successive UEFA Europa League final. Eduardo's equaliser just before half-time kept things interesting in between Gameiro's two goals, but a stunning third from Sevilla full-back Mariano that swerved in off the outside of his right foot ended Shakhtar's hopes of emulating their domestic rivals Dnipro and bringing a Ukrainian presence to the final for the second year running.

Final

The stakes were high as Liverpool and Sevilla met in Basel's St Jakob-Park. Not only was there a major European trophy to win, but both teams knew that victory would bring the bonus of a place in the group stage of the 2016/17 UEFA Champions League. For Liverpool, having finished eighth in the Premier League, defeat would mean no European football at all the following season, whereas Sevilla, seventh in the Liga, at least had the insurance of another UEFA Europa League qualification.

The Spanish club were also, of course, seeking to make history by winning the competition for a third successive year. They had won each of their previous four European finals, all of recent vintage, and while Liverpool had the continental pedigree, with 11 UEFA trophies to their name, none of those had come in the past decade. Furthermore, Klopp, the Reds' manager, was on a run of four successive defeats in major finals.

Liverpool's 63rd game of a busy season began well. Backed by their fervent support, which far outnumbered that of their Andalusian adversaries, they made the first attacking inroads of the match, and although it was Sevilla who manufactured the first moment of genuine goalmouth excitement, with Gameiro trying an overhead kick that went fractionally wide, it was the Premier League side who scored first. It was a magnificent goal, Sturridge finding enough space in a crowded area to curl home a delightful shot with the outside of his left foot. The remainder of the first half had Liverpool repeatedly testing the Sevilla defence in an attempt to hammer home their advantage, but Lovren had a goal disallowed and a couple of other decent openings went begging, so 1-0 it remained at the interval.

Within just 18 seconds of the start of the second half, however, the score was 1-1, Gameiro tapping home after Sevilla full-back Mariano had skipped past his opposite number (and ex-Sevilla player) Alberto Moreno to the byline. From that moment on there was a complete momentum switch, with all the action now concentrated at the same end Liverpool had been attacking in the first half – almost as if the pitch were somehow tilted in that direction. Gameiro missed a couple of big chances to put Sevilla ahead, first Kolo Touré then

KEY FACT

4

Coke became the fourth player to score twice in a UEFA Europa League final – after Diego Forlán (2010, Atlético Madrid v Fulham), Radamel Falcao (2012, Atlético Madrid v Athletic Club) and Carlos Bacca (2015, Sevilla v Dnipro Dnipropetrovsk).

Simon Mignolet denying him with decisive interventions, but a second goal from the holders was coming and, sure enough, on 64 minutes their captain Coke delivered it, despatching a sweet right-foot shot on the run after a brisk forward break led by Vitolo.

Sevilla now had the lead and six minutes later they were 3-1 up, Coke scoring again as Liverpool failed to clear their lines and a fortunate ricochet enabled him to gather the ball in space and drive it home off Mignolet. The goalkeeper and his team-mates complained that the scorer was offside, but the ball had come to Coke off a Liverpool player so the goal was correctly allowed to stand. Sevilla were now in complete control as Liverpool began to disintegrate, their minds and bodies spent.

It was a magnificent second-half display by the Spanish side, with Emery outsmarting his opposite number in much the same way that his white-shirted players were overrunning those in red on the pitch. The final whistle put Liverpool out of their misery and brought unbridled joy to Sevilla, who had achieved a landmark triumph, winning a record fifth UEFA Cup/UEFA Europa League and an unprecedented third in a row.

Sevilla skipper Coke rifles in his second goal of the game to put Sevilla 3-1 up against Liverpool in Basel

First qualifying round

30/06/15, Hibernians Stadium, Paola
Balzan FC 0-2 FK Željezničar
09/07/15, Asim Ferhatović Hase Stadion, Sarajevo
FK Željezničar 1-0 Balzan FC
Aggregate: 3-0; FK Željezničar qualify.

30/06/15, Stade Municipal de Differdange, Differdange
FC Progrès Niederkorn 0-0 Shamrock Rovers FC
07/07/15, Tallaght Stadium, Dublin
Shamrock Rovers FC 3-0 FC Progrès Niederkorn
Aggregate: 3-0; Shamrock Rovers FC qualify.

30/06/15, Nacionalna Arena Filip II Makedonski, Skopje
KF Renova 0-1 FC Dacia Chisinau
09/07/15, District Sport Complex, Orhei
FC Dacia Chisinau 4-1 KF Renova
Aggregate: 5-1; FC Dacia Chisinau qualify.

02/07/15, Gyumri City, Gyumri
FC Shirak 2-0 HŠK Zrinjski
09/07/15, NK Zrinjski, Mostar
HŠK Zrinjski 2-1 FC Shirak
Aggregate: 2-3; FC Shirak qualify.

02/07/15, Laçi, Lac
KF Laçi 1-1 İnter Bakı PİK
09/07/15, Shafa, Baku
İnter Bakı PİK 0-0 KF Laçi
Aggregate: 1-1; İnter Bakı PİK qualify on away goal.

02/07/15, Stadiumi Kombëtar Qemal Stafa, Tirana
FK Kukësi 2-0 FC Torpedo Zhodino
09/07/15, Torpedo, Zhodino
FC Torpedo Zhodino 0-0 FK Kukësi
Aggregate: 0-2; FK Kukësi qualify.

02/07/15, Asim Ferhatović Hase Stadion, Sarajevo
FK Olimpic Sarajevo 1-1 FC Spartak Trnava
09/07/15, Štadión FC ViOn, Zlate Moravce
FC Spartak Trnava 0-0 FK Olimpic Sarajevo
Aggregate: 1-1; FC Spartak Trnava qualify on away goal.

02/07/15, Kazhimukan Munaytpasov, Shymkent
FC Ordabasy Shymkent 0-0 Beitar Jerusalem FC
09/07/15, Itztadion Teddy, Jerusalem
Beitar Jerusalem FC 2-1 FC Ordabasy Shymkent
Aggregate: 2-1; Beitar Jerusalem FC qualify.

02/07/15, Estadi Comunal, Andorra la Vella
UE Sant Julià 0-1 Randers FC
09/07/15, Viborg Stadion, Viborg
Randers FC 3-0 UE Sant Julià
Aggregate: 4-0; Randers FC qualify.

02/07/15, Šiauliai central stadium, Siauliai
FK Kruoja 0-1 Jagiellonia Białystok
09/07/15, Miejski, Bialystok
Jagiellonia Białystok 8-0 FK Kruoja
Aggregate: 9-0; Jagiellonia Białystok qualify.

02/07/15, Debrecen Stadion, Debrecen
Debreceni VSC 3-0 FK Sutjeska
09/07/15, Gradski, Niksic
FK Sutjeska 2-0 Debreceni VSC
Aggregate: 2-3; Debreceni VSC qualify.

02/07/15, Nantporth, Bangor
AUK Broughton FC 1-3 NK Lokomotiva Zagreb
09/07/15, Zagreb, Zagreb
NK Lokomotiva Zagreb 2-2 AUK Broughton FC
Aggregate: 5-3; NK Lokomotiva Zagreb qualify.

02/07/15, Vazgen Sargsyan anvan Hanrapetakan Marzadasht, Yerevan
Alashkert FC 1-0 Saint Johnstone FC
09/07/15, McDiarmid Park, Perth
Saint Johnstone FC 2-1 Alashkert FC
Aggregate: 2-2; Alashkert FC qualify on away goal.

02/07/15, Zemgales Olympic Centre, Jelgava
FK Jelgava 1-1 PFC Litex Lovech
09/07/15, Lovech Stadion, Lovech
PFC Litex Lovech 2-2 FK Jelgava
Aggregate: 3-3; FK Jelgava qualify on away goals.

02/07/15, Stade Municipal de Differdange, Differdange
FC Differdange 03 3-1 Bala Town FC
09/07/15, Belle Vue, Rhyl
Bala Town FC 2-1 FC Differdange 03
Aggregate: 3-4; FC Differdange 03 qualify.

02/07/15, Toftir, Toftir
Víkingur 0-2 Rosenborg BK
09/07/15, Lerkendal Stadion, Trondheim
Rosenborg BK 0-0 Víkingur
Aggregate: 2-0; Rosenborg BK qualify.

02/07/15, Helsinki Football Stadium, Helsinki
SJK Seinäjoki 0-1 FH Hafnarfjördur
09/07/15, Kaplakrikavöllur, Hafnarfjördur
FH Hafnarfjördur 1-0 SJK Seinäjoki
Aggregate: 2-0; FH Hafnarfjördur qualify.

02/07/15, Brøndby, Brondby
Brøndby IF 9-0 AC Juvenes/Dogana
09/07/15, San Marino Stadium, Serravalle
AC Juvenes/Dogana 0-2 Brøndby IF
Aggregate: 0-11; Brøndby IF qualify.

02/07/15, Skonto Stadions, Riga
Skonto FC 2-1 Saint Patrick's Athletic FC
09/07/15, Richmond Park, Dublin
Saint Patrick's Athletic FC 0-2 Skonto FC
Aggregate: 1-4; Skonto FC qualify.

02/07/15, Lahti Stadium, Lahti
FC Lahti 2-2 IF Elfsborg
09/07/15, Borås Arena, Boras
IF Elfsborg 5-0 FC Lahti
Aggregate: 7-2; IF Elfsborg qualify.

02/07/15, Klaipédosmiesto Centrinis, Klaipeda
FK Atlantas 0-2 PFC Beroe Stara Zagora
09/07/15, Beroe, Stara Zagora
PFC Beroe Stara Zagora 3-1 FK Atlantas
Aggregate: 5-1; PFC Beroe Stara Zagora qualify.

02/07/15, A. Le Coq Arena, Tallinn
FC Flora Tallinn 1-0 FK Rabotnicki
09/07/15, Nacionalna Arena Filip II Makedonski, Skopje
FK Rabotnicki 2-0 FC Flora Tallinn
Aggregate: 2-1; FK Rabotnicki qualify.

02/07/15, Raatti, Oulu
VPS Vaasa 2-2 AIK Solna
09/07/15, Friends Arena, Solna
AIK Solna 4-0 VPS Vaasa
Aggregate: 6-2; AIK Solna qualify.

02/07/15, Marienlyst, Drammen
Strømsgodset IF 3-1 FK Partizani
09/07/15, Stadiumi Kombëtar Qemal Stafa, Tirana
FK Partizani 0-1 Strømsgodset IF
Aggregate: 1-4; Strømsgodset IF qualify.

02/07/15, Víkingsvöllur, Reykjavik
Víkingur Reykjavik 0-1 FC Koper
09/07/15, ŠRC Bonifika, Koper
FC Koper 2-2 Víkingur Reykjavik
Aggregate: 3-2; FC Koper qualify.

Diafra Sakho of West Ham (right) takes on Eduardo Moya of Lusitans

02/07/15, Latham Park, Newtown
Newtown AFC 2-1 Valletta FC
09/07/15, Hibernians Stadium, Paola
Valletta FC 1-2 Newtown AFC
Aggregate: 2-4; Newtown AFC qualify.

02/07/15, Rakvere, Rakvere
JK Sillamäe Kalev 1-1 HNK Hajduk Split
09/07/15, SC Hrvatskih vitezova, Dugopolje
HNK Hajduk Split 6-2 JK Sillamäe Kalev
Aggregate: 7-3; HNK Hajduk Split qualify.

02/07/15, Victoria Stadium, Gibraltar
Europa FC 0-6 ŠK Slovan Bratislava
09/07/15, Štadión Pasienky, Bratislava
ŠK Slovan Bratislava 3-0 Europa FC
Aggregate: 9-0; ŠK Slovan Bratislava qualify.

02/07/15, Boleyn Ground, London
West Ham United FC 3-0 FC Lusitans
09/07/15, Estadi Comunal, Andorra la Vella
FC Lusitans 0-1 West Ham United FC
Aggregate: 0-4; West Ham United FC qualify.

02/07/15, Mourneview Park, Lurgan
Glenavon FC 1-2 FC Shakhtyor Soligorsk
09/07/15, Stroitel, Soligorsk
FC Shakhtyor Soligorsk 3-0 Glenavon FC
Aggregate: 5-1; FC Shakhtyor Soligorsk qualify.

02/07/15, Windsor Park, Belfast
Linfield FC 2-0 NSÍ Runavík
09/07/15, Toftir, Toftir
NSÍ Runavík 4-3 Linfield FC
Aggregate: 4-5; Linfield FC qualify.

02/07/15, Turner's Cross, Cork
Cork City FC 1-1 KR Reykjavík
09/07/15, KR-völlur, Reykjavik
KR Reykjavík 2-1 Cork City FC (aet)
Aggregate: 3-2; KR Reykjavík qualify after extra time.

02/07/15, Belfield Bowl, UCD, Dublin
University College Dublin AFC 1-0 F91 Dudelange
09/07/15, Jos Nosbaum, Dudelange
F91 Dudelange 2-1 University College Dublin AFC
Aggregate: 2-2; University College Dublin AFC qualify on away goals.

02/07/15, Stadionul Sheriff, Tiraspol
FC Sheriff 0-3 Odds BK
09/07/15, Odd, Skien
Odds BK 0-0 FC Sheriff
Aggregate: 3-0; Odds BK qualify.

02/07/15, Boris Paichadze Dinamo Arena, Tbilisi
FC Dinamo Tbilisi 2-1 Qäbälä FK
09/07/15, Qäbälä Şähär Stadionu, Qäbälä
Qäbälä FK 2-0 FC Dinamo Tbilisi
Aggregate: 3-2; Qäbälä FK qualify.

02/07/15, Stadionul Zimbru, Chisinau
FC Saxan 0-2 Apollon Limassol FC
09/07/15, Antonis Papadopoulos, Larnaca
Apollon Limassol FC 2-0 FC Saxan
Aggregate: 4-0; Apollon Limassol FC qualify.

02/07/15, David Abashidze, Zestaponi
FC Dinamo Batumi 1-0 AC Omonia
09/07/15, GSP, Nicosia
AC Omonia 2-0 FC Dinamo Batumi
Aggregate: 2-1; AC Omonia qualify.

02/07/15, Jens Vesting Stadium, Emmen
Go Ahead Eagles 1-1 Ferencvárosi TC
09/07/15, Groupama Aréna, Budapest
Ferencvárosi TC 4-1 Go Ahead Eagles
Aggregate: 5-2; Ferencvárosi TC qualify.

02/07/15, Dariaus ir Giréno stadionas, Kaunas
FK Trakai 3-0 HB Tórshavn
09/07/15, Tórsvøllur, Torshavn
HB Tórshavn 1-4 FK Trakai
Aggregate: 1-7; FK Trakai qualify.

02/07/15, Športni park, Domzale
NK Domžale 0-1 FK Čukarički
09/07/15, FK Čukarički, Belgrade
FK Čukarički 0-0 NK Domžale
Aggregate: 1-0; FK Čukarički qualify.

02/07/15, The Oval, Belfast
Glentoran FC 1-4 MŠK Žilina
09/07/15, Štadión MŠK Žilina, Zilina
MŠK Žilina 3-0 Glentoran FC
Aggregate: 7-1; MŠK Žilina qualify.

02/07/15, Arena Petrol, Celje
NK Celje 0-1 WKS Śląsk Wrocław
09/07/15, Municipal Stadium Wroclaw, Wroclaw
WKS Śląsk Wrocław 3-1 NK Celje
Aggregate: 4-1; WKS Śląsk Wrocław qualify.

02/07/15, Municipal, Botosani
FC Botoşani 1-1 FC Tskhinvali
09/07/15, Mikheil Meskhi Stadioni, Tbilisi
FC Tskhinvali 1-3 FC Botoşani
Aggregate: 2-4; FC Botoşani qualify.

02/07/15, Ferenc Szusza Stadion, Budapest
MTK Budapest 0-0 FK Vojvodina
09/07/15, Karadjordje, Novi Sad
FK Vojvodina 3-1 MTK Budapest
Aggregate: 3-1; FK Vojvodina qualify.

02/07/15, Gradski Stadion Podgorica, Podgorica
FK Budućnost Podgorica 1-3 FK Spartaks Jūrmala
09/07/15, Zemgales Olympic Centre, Jelgava
FK Spartaks Jūrmala 0-0 FK Budućnost Podgorica
Aggregate: 3-1; FK Spartaks Jūrmala qualify.

02/07/15, San Marino Stadium, Serravalle
SP La Fiorita 0-5 FC Vaduz
09/07/15, Rheinpark Stadion, Vaduz
FC Vaduz 5-1 SP La Fiorita
Aggregate: 10-1; FC Vaduz qualify.

02/07/15, Stadion FK Crvena zvezda, Belgrade
FK Crvena zvezda 0-2 FC Kairat Almaty
09/07/15, Almaty Ortalyk Stadion, Almaty
FC Kairat Almaty 2-1 FK Crvena zvezda
Aggregate: 4-1; FC Kairat Almaty qualify.

02/07/15, Hibernians Stadium, Paola
Birkirkara FC 0-0 Ulisses FC
09/07/15, Vazgen Sargsyan anvan Hanrapetakan Marzadasht, Yerevan
Ulisses FC 1-3 Birkirkara FC
Aggregate: 1-3; Birkirkara FC qualify.

02/07/15, Tsentralniy, Aktobe
FC Aktobe 0-1 Nõmme Kalju FC
09/07/15, A. Le Coq Arena, Tallinn
Nõmme Kalju FC 0-0 FC Aktobe
Aggregate: 1-0; Nõmme Kalju FC qualify.

02/07/15, Bakcell Arena, Baku
Neftçi PFK 2-2 FK Mladost Podgorica
09/07/15, Gradski Stadion Podgorica, Podgorica
FK Mladost Podgorica 1-1 Neftçi PFK
Aggregate: 3-3; FK Mladost Podgorica qualify on away goals.

02/07/15, Nacionalna Arena Filip II Makedonski, Skopje
KF Shkëndija 1-1 Aberdeen FC
09/07/15, Pittodrie, Aberdeen
Aberdeen FC 0-0 KF Shkëndija
Aggregate: 1-1; Aberdeen FC qualify on away goal.

Second qualifying round

16/07/15, Randers Stadium, Randers
Randers FC 0-0 IF Elfsborg
21/07/15, Borås Arena, Boras
IF Elfsborg 1-0 Randers FC (aet)
Aggregate: 1-0; IF Elfsborg qualify after extra time.

16/07/15, Zemgales Olympic Centre, Jelgava
FK Jelgava 1-0 FK Rabotnicki
23/07/15, Nacionalna Arena Filip II Makedonski, Skopje
FK Rabotnicki 2-0 FK Jelgava
Aggregate: 2-1; FK Rabotnicki qualify.

16/07/15, Stockholms, Stockholm
AIK Solna 2-0 FC Shirak
23/07/15, Gyumri City, Gyumri
FC Shirak 0-4 AIK Solna
Aggregate: 0-4; AIK Solna qualify.

16/07/15, Stadionul Zimbru, Chisinau
FC Dacia Chisinau 1-2 MŠK Žilina
23/07/15, Štadión MŠK Žilina, Zilina
MŠK Žilina 4-2 FC Dacia Chisinau
Aggregate: 6-3; MŠK Žilina qualify.

16/07/15, Mestský, Mlada Boleslav
FK Mladá Boleslav 1-2 Strømsgodset IF
23/07/15, Marienlyst, Drammen
Strømsgodset IF 0-1 FK Mladá Boleslav
Aggregate: 2-2; Strømsgodset IF qualify on away goals.

16/07/15, ŠRC Bonifika, Koper
FC Koper 3-2 HNK Hajduk Split
23/07/15, Stadion Poljud, Split
HNK Hajduk Split 4-1 FC Koper
Aggregate: 6-4; HNK Hajduk Split qualify.

16/07/15, Skonto Stadions, Riga
Skonto FC 2-2 Debreceni VSC
23/07/15, Debrecen Stadion, Debrecen
Debreceni VSC 9-2 Skonto FC
Aggregate: 11-4; Debreceni VSC qualify.

16/07/15, KR-völlur, Reykjavik
KR Reykjavík 0-1 Rosenborg BK
23/07/15, Lerkendal Stadion, Trondheim
Rosenborg BK 3-0 KR Reykjavík
Aggregate: 4-0; Rosenborg BK qualify.

16/07/15, Kaplakrikavöllur, Hafnarfjördur
FH Hafnarfjördur 1-2 İnter Bakı PİK
23/07/15, Shafa, Baku
İnter Bakı PİK 2-2 FH Hafnarfjördur (aet)
Aggregate: 4-3; İnter Bakı PİK qualify after extra time.

16/07/15, Stadiumi Kombëtar Qemal Stafa, Tirana
FK Kukësi 0-1 FK Mladost Podgorica
23/07/15, Gradski Stadion Podgorica, Podgorica
FK Mladost Podgorica 2-4 FK Kukësi
Aggregate: 3-4; FK Kukësi qualify.

16/07/15, Stroitel, Soligorsk
FC Shakhtyor Soligorsk 0-1 Wolfsberger AC
23/07/15, Wörthersee, Klagenfurt
Wolfsberger AC 2-0 FC Shakhtyor Soligorsk
Aggregate: 3-0; Wolfsberger AC qualify.

16/07/15, Pays de Charleroi, Charleroi
R. Charleroi SC 5-1 Beitar Jerusalem FC
23/07/15, Itztadion Teddy, Jerusalem
Beitar Jerusalem FC 1-4 R. Charleroi SC
Aggregate: 2-9; R. Charleroi SC qualify.

16/07/15, Rheinpark Stadion, Vaduz
FC Vaduz 3-1 Nõmme Kalju FC
23/07/15, A. Le Coq Arena, Tallinn
Nõmme Kalju FC 0-2 FC Vaduz
Aggregate: 1-5; FC Vaduz qualify.

16/07/15, Boleyn Ground, London
West Ham United FC 1-0 Birkirkara FC
23/07/15, National Stadium, Ta' Qali
Birkirkara FC 1-0 West Ham United FC (aet)
Aggregate: 1-1; West Ham United FC qualify 5-3 on penalties.

16/07/15, Tulloch Caledonian Stadium, Inverness
Inverness Caledonian Thistle FC 0-1 FC Astra Giurgiu
23/07/15, Marin Anastasovici, Giurgiu
FC Astra Giurgiu 0-0 Inverness Caledonian Thistle FC
Aggregate: 1-0; FC Astra Giurgiu qualify.

16/07/15, Telia Parken, Copenhagen
FC København 2-0 Newtown AFC
23/07/15, Latham Park, Newtown
Newtown AFC 1-3 FC København
Aggregate: 1-5; FC København qualify.

Slovan Bratislava's Boris Sekulić (left) gets the better of UCD's Jamie Doyle

16/07/15, Zagreb, Zagreb
NK Lokomotiva Zagreb 2-1 PAOK FC
23/07/15, Stadio Toumba, Salonika
PAOK FC 6-0 NK Lokomotiva Zagreb
Aggregate: 7-2; PAOK FC qualify.

16/07/15, Beroe, Stara Zagora
PFC Beroe Stara Zagora 0-1 Brøndby IF
23/07/15, Brøndby, Brondby
Brøndby IF 0-0 PFC Beroe Stara Zagora
Aggregate: 1-0; Brøndby IF qualify.

16/07/15, Tallaght Stadium, Dublin
Shamrock Rovers FC 0-2 Odds BK
23/07/15, Odd, Skien
Odds BK 2-1 Shamrock Rovers FC
Aggregate: 4-1; Odds BK qualify.

16/07/15, Itztadion Teddy, Jerusalem
Hapoel Beer Sheva FC 1-1 FC Thun
23/07/15, Arena Thun, Thun
FC Thun 2-1 Hapoel Beer Sheva FC
Aggregate: 3-2; FC Thun qualify.

16/07/15, Ludogorets Arena, Razgrad
PFC Cherno More Varna 1-1 FC Dinamo Minsk
23/07/15, Traktor, Minsk
FC Dinamo Minsk 4-0 PFC Cherno More Varna
Aggregate: 5-1; FC Dinamo Minsk qualify.

16/07/15, Antonis Papadopoulos, Larnaca
Apollon Limassol FC 4-0 FK Trakai
23/07/15, LFF stadionas, Vilnius
FK Trakai 0-0 Apollon Limassol FC
Aggregate: 0-4; Apollon Limassol FC qualify.

16/07/15, Štadión FC ViOn, Zlate Moravce
FC Spartak Trnava 2-1 Linfield FC
23/07/15, Windsor Park, Belfast
Linfield FC 1-3 FC Spartak Trnava
Aggregate: 2-5; FC Spartak Trnava qualify.

16/07/15, Štadión Pasienky, Bratislava
ŠK Slovan Bratislava 1-0 University College Dublin AFC
23/07/15, Belfield Bowl, UCD, Dublin
University College Dublin AFC 1-5 ŠK Slovan Bratislava
Aggregate: 1-6; ŠK Slovan Bratislava qualify.

16/07/15, Groupama Aréna, Budapest
Ferencvárosi TC 0-1 FK Željezničar
23/07/15, Asim Ferhatović Hase Stadion, Sarajevo
FK Željezničar 2-0 Ferencvárosi TC
Aggregate: 3-0; FK Željezničar qualify.

16/07/15, Karadjordje, Novi Sad
FK Vojvodina 3-0 FK Spartaks Jūrmala
23/07/15, Zemgales Olympic Centre, Jelgava
FK Spartaks Jūrmala 1-1 FK Vojvodina
Aggregate: 1-4; FK Vojvodina qualify.

16/07/15, Miejski, Bialystok
Jagiellonia Białystok 0-0 AC Omonia
23/07/15, GSP, Nicosia
AC Omonia 1-0 Jagiellonia Białystok
Aggregate: 1-0; AC Omonia qualify.

16/07/15, FK Čukarički, Belgrade
FK Čukarički 1-0 Qäbälä FK
23/07/15, Bakcell Arena, Baku
Qäbälä FK 2-0 FK Čukarički
Aggregate: 2-1; Qäbälä FK qualify.

16/07/15, Municipal Stadium Wroclaw, Wroclaw
WKS Śląsk Wrocław 0-0 IFK Göteborg
23/07/15, Gamla Ullevi, Gothenburg
IFK Göteborg 2-0 WKS Śląsk Wrocław
Aggregate: 2-0; IFK Göteborg qualify.

16/07/15, Almaty Ortalyk Stadion, Almaty
FC Kairat Almaty 3-0 Alashkert FC
23/07/15, Vazgen Sargsyan anvan Hanrapetakan Marzadasht, Yerevan
Alashkert FC 2-1 FC Kairat Almaty
Aggregate: 2-4; FC Kairat Almaty qualify.

16/07/15, Stadion Wojska Polskiego, Warsaw
Legia Warszawa 1-0 FC Botoşani
23/07/15, Municipal, Botosani
FC Botoşani 0-3 Legia Warszawa
Aggregate: 0-4; Legia Warszawa qualify.

16/07/15, Hüseyin Avni Aker Stadyumu, Trabzon
Trabzonspor AŞ 1-0 FC Differdange 03
23/07/15, Stade Josy Barthel, Luxembourg
FC Differdange 03 1-2 Trabzonspor AŞ
Aggregate: 1-3; Trabzonspor AŞ qualify.

16/07/15, Kantrida, Rijeka
HNK Rijeka 0-3 Aberdeen FC
23/07/15, Pittodrie, Aberdeen
Aberdeen FC 2-2 HNK Rijeka
Aggregate: 5-2; Aberdeen FC qualify.

Third qualifying round

29/07/15, Strelnice Stadion, Jablonec nad Nisou
FK Jablonec 0-1 FC København
06/08/15, Telia Parken, Copenhagen
FC København 2-3 FK Jablonec
Aggregate: 3-3; FK Jablonec qualify on away goals.

30/07/15, Borås Arena, Boras
IF Elfsborg 2-1 Odds BK
06/08/15, Odd, Skien
Odds BK 2-0 IF Elfsborg
Aggregate: 3-2; Odds BK qualify.

30/07/15, Stadion Graz Liebenau, Graz
SK Sturm Graz 2-3 FC Rubin
06/08/15, Centralniy Stadion, Kazan
FC Rubin 1-1 SK Sturm Graz
Aggregate: 4-3; FC Rubin qualify.

30/07/15, U Nisy, Liberec
FC Slovan Liberec 2-1 Hapoel Kiryat Shmona FC
06/08/15, Netanya Municipal Stadium, Netanya
Hapoel Kiryat Shmona FC 0-3 FC Slovan Liberec
Aggregate: 1-5; FC Slovan Liberec qualify.

30/07/15, Friends Arena, Solna
AIK Solna 1-3 Atromitos FC
06/08/15, Peristeri, Athens
Atromitos FC 1-0 AIK Solna
Aggregate: 4-1; Atromitos FC qualify.

30/07/15, Tivoli Neu, Innsbruck
SCR Altach 2-1 Vitória SC
06/08/15, Estádio D. Afonso Henriques, Guimaraes
Vitória SC 1-4 SCR Altach
Aggregate: 2-6; SCR Altach qualify.

30/07/15, Stadion Letzigrund, Zurich
FC Zürich 0-1 FC Dinamo Minsk
06/08/15, Brestsky, Brest
FC Dinamo Minsk 1-1 FC Zürich (aet)
Aggregate: 2-1; FC Dinamo Minsk qualify after extra time.

30/07/15, Štadión MŠK Žilina, Zilina
MŠK Žilina 3-1 FC Vorskla Poltava
06/08/15, Stadion Vorskla im. Olexiy Butovskiy, Poltava
FC Vorskla Poltava 3-1 MŠK Žilina (aet)
Aggregate: 3-3; MŠK Žilina qualify on away goal.

Zorya's Ruslan Malinovskiy (left) is congratulated after scoring against Charleroi

30/07/15, AZ Stadion, Alkmaar
AZ Alkmaar 2-0 İstanbul Başakşehir
06/08/15, Başakşehir Fatih Terim Stadyumu, Istanbul
İstanbul Başakşehir 1-2 AZ Alkmaar
Aggregate: 1-4; AZ Alkmaar qualify.

30/07/15, Arena Thun, Thun
FC Thun 0-0 FC Vaduz
06/08/15, Rheinpark Stadion, Vaduz
FC Vaduz 2-2 FC Thun
Aggregate: 2-2; FC Thun qualify on away goals.

30/07/15, Boleyn Ground, London
West Ham United FC 2-2 FC Astra Giurgiu
06/08/15, Marin Anastasovici, Giurgiu
FC Astra Giurgiu 2-1 West Ham United FC
Aggregate: 4-3; FC Astra Giurgiu qualify.

30/07/15, Stadio Toumba, Salonika
PAOK FC 1-0 FC Spartak Trnava
06/08/15, Štadión FC ViOn, Zlate Moravce
FC Spartak Trnava 1-1 PAOK FC
Aggregate: 1-2; PAOK FC qualify.

30/07/15, Debrecen Stadion, Debrecen
Debreceni VSC 2-3 Rosenborg BK
06/08/15, Lerkendal Stadion, Trondheim
Rosenborg BK 3-1 Debreceni VSC
Aggregate: 6-3; Rosenborg BK qualify.

30/07/15, Estádio do Restelo, Lisbon
Os Belenenses 2-1 IFK Göteborg
06/08/15, Gamla Ullevi, Gothenburg
IFK Göteborg 0-0 Os Belenenses
Aggregate: 1-2; Os Belenenses qualify.

30/07/15, Stadiumi Kombëtar Qemal Stafa, Tirana
FK Kukësi 0-3(f) Legia Warszawa
06/08/15, Stadion Wojska Polskiego, Warsaw
Legia Warszawa 1-0 FK Kukësi
Aggregate: 4-0; Legia Warszawa qualify.

30/07/15, Antonis Papadopoulos, Larnaca
Apollon Limassol FC 1-1 Qäbälä FK
06/08/15, Bakcell Arena, Baku
Qäbälä FK 1-0 Apollon Limassol FC
Aggregate: 2-1; Qäbälä FK qualify.

30/07/15, Nacionalna Arena Filip II Makedonski, Skopje
FK Rabotnicki 1-0 Trabzonspor AŞ
06/08/15, Hüseyin Avni Aker Stadyumu, Trabzon
Trabzonspor AŞ 1-1 FK Rabotnicki (aet)
Aggregate: 1-2; FK Rabotnicki qualify after extra time.

30/07/15, Brøndby, Brondby
Brøndby IF 0-0 AC Omonia
06/08/15, GSP, Nicosia
AC Omonia 2-2 Brøndby IF
Aggregate: 2-2; Brøndby IF qualify on away goals.

30/07/15, Kuban, Krasnodar
FC Krasnodar 2-0 ŠK Slovan Bratislava
06/08/15, Štadión Pasienky, Bratislava
ŠK Slovan Bratislava 3-3 FC Krasnodar
Aggregate: 3-5; FC Krasnodar qualify.

30/07/15, St Mary's Stadium, Southampton
Southampton FC 3-0 Vitesse
06/08/15, Gelredome, Arnhem
Vitesse 0-2 Southampton FC
Aggregate: 0-5; Southampton FC qualify.

30/07/15, Stade de Bordeaux, Bordeaux
FC Girondins de Bordeaux 3-0 AEK Larnaca FC
06/08/15, Antonis Papadopoulos, Larnaca
AEK Larnaca FC 0-1 FC Girondins de Bordeaux
Aggregate: 0-4; FC Girondins de Bordeaux qualify.

30/07/15, Pays de Charleroi, Charleroi
R. Charleroi SC 0-2 FC Zorya Luhansk
06/08/15, Stadion Dynamo im. Valeriy Lobanovskiy, Kyiv
FC Zorya Luhansk 3-0 R. Charleroi SC
Aggregate: 5-0; FC Zorya Luhansk qualify.

30/07/15, Stade Maurice Dufrasne, Liege
R. Standard de Liège 2-1 FK Željezničar
06/08/15, Asim Ferhatović Hase Stadion, Sarajevo
FK Željezničar 0-1 R. Standard de Liège
Aggregate: 1-3; R. Standard de Liège qualify.

30/07/15, Almaty Ortalyk Stadion, Almaty
FC Kairat Almaty 2-1 Aberdeen FC
06/08/15, Pittodrie, Aberdeen
Aberdeen FC 1-1 FC Kairat Almaty
Aggregate: 2-3; FC Kairat Almaty qualify.

30/07/15, Estadio de San Mamés, Bilbao
Athletic Club 2-0 İnter Bakı PİK
06/08/15, Shafa, Baku
İnter Bakı PİK 0-0 Athletic Club
Aggregate: 0-2; Athletic Club qualify.

30/07/15, Trans-Sil, Targu Mures
ASA Tîrgu Mureş 0-3 AS Saint-Étienne
06/08/15, Stade Geoffroy Guichard, Saint-Étienne
AS Saint-Étienne 1-2 ASA Tîrgu Mureş
Aggregate: 4-2; AS Saint-Étienne qualify.

30/07/15, Stadio Olimpico, Turin
UC Sampdoria 0-4 FK Vojvodina
06/08/15, Karadjordje, Novi Sad
FK Vojvodina 0-2 UC Sampdoria
Aggregate: 4-2; FK Vojvodina qualify.

30/07/15, Stadion Poljud, Split
HNK Hajduk Split 2-0 Strømsgodset IF
06/08/15, Marienlyst, Drammen
Strømsgodset IF 0-2 HNK Hajduk Split
Aggregate: 0-4; HNK Hajduk Split qualify.

30/07/15, Wörthersee, Klagenfurt
Wolfsberger AC 0-1 Borussia Dortmund
06/08/15, BVB Stadion Dortmund, Dortmund
Borussia Dortmund 5-0 Wolfsberger AC
Aggregate: 6-0; Borussia Dortmund qualify.

UEFA Europa League

Play-offs

20/08/15, Amsterdam ArenA, Amsterdam
AFC Ajax 1-0 FK Jablonec
27/08/15, Strelnice Stadion, Jablonec nad Nisou
FK Jablonec 0-0 AFC Ajax
Aggregate: 0-1; AFC Ajax qualify.

20/08/15, Molde Stadion, Molde
Molde FK 2-0 R. Standard de Liège
27/08/15, Stade Maurice Dufrasne, Liege
R. Standard de Liège 3-1 Molde FK
Aggregate: 3-3; Molde FK qualify on away goal.

20/08/15, Brestsky, Brest
FC Dinamo Minsk 2-0 FC Salzburg
27/08/15, Stadion Salzburg, Salzburg
FC Salzburg 2-0 FC Dinamo Minsk (aet)
Aggregate: 2-2; FC Dinamo Minsk qualify 3-2 on penalties.

20/08/15, U Nisy, Liberec
FC Slovan Liberec 1-0 HNK Hajduk Split
27/08/15, Stadion Poljud, Split
HNK Hajduk Split 0-1 FC Slovan Liberec
Aggregate: 0-2; FC Slovan Liberec qualify.

20/08/15, Marin Anastasovici, Giurgiu
FC Astra Giurgiu 3-2 AZ Alkmaar
27/08/15, AZ Stadion, Alkmaar
AZ Alkmaar 2-0 FC Astra Giurgiu
Aggregate: 4-3; AZ Alkmaar qualify.

20/08/15, Stadion Letná, Prague
AC Sparta Praha 3-1 FC Thun
27/08/15, Arena Thun, Thun
FC Thun 3-3 AC Sparta Praha
Aggregate: 4-6; AC Sparta Praha qualify.

20/08/15, Stadion Dynamo im. Valeriy Lobanovskiy, Kyiv
FC Zorya Luhansk 0-1 Legia Warszawa
27/08/15, Stadion Wojska Polskiego, Warsaw
Legia Warszawa 3-2 FC Zorya Luhansk
Aggregate: 4-2; Legia Warszawa qualify.

20/08/15, Stade de Suisse, Berne
BSC Young Boys 0-1 Qarabağ FK
27/08/15, Tofiq Bähramov Republican stadium, Baku
Qarabağ FK 3-0 BSC Young Boys
Aggregate: 4-0; Qarabağ FK qualify.

20/08/15, Stadio Toumba, Salonika
PAOK FC 5-0 Brøndby IF
27/08/15, Brøndby, Brondby
Brøndby IF 1-1 PAOK FC
Aggregate: 1-6; PAOK FC qualify.

20/08/15, Nacionalna Arena Filip II Makedonski, Skopje
FK Rabotnicki 1-1 FC Rubin
27/08/15, Centralniy Stadion, Kazan
FC Rubin 2-0 FK Rabotnicki
Aggregate: 2-1; FC Rubin qualify.

20/08/15, St Mary's Stadium, Southampton
Southampton FC 1-1 FC Midtjylland
27/08/15, Arena Herning, Herning
FC Midtjylland 1-0 Southampton FC
Aggregate: 2-1; FC Midtjylland qualify.

20/08/15, Kuban, Krasnodar
FC Krasnodar 5-1 HJK Helsinki
27/08/15, Helsinki Football Stadium, Helsinki
HJK Helsinki 0-0 FC Krasnodar
Aggregate: 1-5; FC Krasnodar qualify.

20/08/15, Štadión MŠK Žilina, Zilina
MŠK Žilina 3-2 Athletic Club
27/08/15, Estadio de San Mamés, Bilbao
Athletic Club 1-0 MŠK Žilina
Aggregate: 3-3; Athletic Club qualify on away goals.

Mats Hummels enthuses over one of Dortmund's 11 goals against Odd

20/08/15, Tivoli Neu, Innsbruck
SCR Altach 0-1 Os Belenenses
27/08/15, Estádio do Restelo, Lisbon
Os Belenenses 0-0 SCR Altach
Aggregate: 1-0; Os Belenenses qualify.

20/08/15, Stadionul Zimbru, Chisinau
FC Milsami Orhei 1-1 AS Saint-Étienne
27/08/15, Stade Geoffroy Guichard, Saint-Etienne
AS Saint-Étienne 1-0 FC Milsami Orhei
Aggregate: 2-1; AS Saint-Étienne qualify.

20/08/15, Stade de Bordeaux, Bordeaux
FC Girondins de Bordeaux 1-0 FC Kairat Almaty
27/08/15, Almaty Ortalyk Stadion, Almaty
FC Kairat Almaty 2-1 FC Girondins de Bordeaux
Aggregate: 2-2; FC Girondins de Bordeaux qualify on away goal.

20/08/15, Odd, Skien
Odds BK 3-4 Borussia Dortmund
27/08/15, BVB Stadion Dortmund, Dortmund
Borussia Dortmund 7-2 Odds BK
Aggregate: 11-5; Borussia Dortmund qualify.

20/08/15, Doosan Arena, Plzen
FC Viktoria Plzeň 3-0 FK Vojvodina
27/08/15, Karadjordje, Novi Sad
FK Vojvodina 0-2 FC Viktoria Plzeň
Aggregate: 0-5; FC Viktoria Plzeň qualify.

20/08/15, Arena Naţională, Bucharest
FC Steaua Bucureşti 0-3 Rosenborg BK
27/08/15, Lerkendal Stadion, Trondheim
Rosenborg BK 0-1 FC Steaua Bucureşti
Aggregate: 3-1; Rosenborg BK qualify.

20/08/15, Stadion Miejski, Poznan
KKS Lech Poznań 3-0 Videoton FC
27/08/15, Sóstói, Szekesfehervar
Videoton FC 0-1 KKS Lech Poznań
Aggregate: 0-4; KKS Lech Poznań qualify.

20/08/15, Peristeri, Athens
Atromitos FC 0-1 Fenerbahçe SK
27/08/15, Şükrü Saracoğlu, Istanbul
Fenerbahçe SK 3-0 Atromitos FC
Aggregate: 4-0; Fenerbahçe SK qualify.

20/08/15, Bakcell Arena, Baku
Qäbälä FK 0-0 Panathinaikos FC
27/08/15, Apostolos Nikolaidis, Athens
Panathinaikos FC 2-2 Qäbälä FK
Aggregate: 2-2; Qäbälä FK qualify on away goals.

Group stage

Group A

17/09/15, Amsterdam ArenA, Amsterdam
AFC Ajax 2-2 Celtic FC
Goals: 0-1 Biton 8, 1-1 Fischer 25, 1-2 Lustig 42, 2-2 Schöne 84

17/09/15, Şükrü Saracoğlu, Istanbul
Fenerbahçe SK 1-3 Molde FK
Goals: 0-1 Høiland 36(p), 1-1 Nani 42, 1-2 Elyounoussi 53, 1-3 Linnes 65

01/10/15, Celtic Park, Glasgow
Celtic FC 2-2 Fenerbahçe SK
Goals: 1-0 Griffiths 28, 2-0 Commons 32, 2-1 Fernandão 43, 2-2 Fernandão 48

01/10/15, Molde Stadion, Molde
Molde FK 1-1 AFC Ajax
Goals: 1-0 Hestad 8, 1-1 Fischer 19

22/10/15, Molde Stadion, Molde
Molde FK 3-1 Celtic FC
Goals: 1-0 Kamara 11, 2-0 Forren 18, 2-1 Commons 55, 3-1 Elyounoussi 56

22/10/15, Şükrü Saracoğlu, Istanbul
Fenerbahçe SK 1-0 AFC Ajax
Goal: 1-0 Fernandão 89

05/11/15, Celtic Park, Glasgow
Celtic FC 1-2 Molde FK
Goals: 0-1 Elyounoussi 21, 1-1 Commons 26, 1-2 Berg Hestad 37

05/11/15, Amsterdam ArenA, Amsterdam
AFC Ajax 0-0 Fenerbahçe SK

26/11/15, Celtic Park, Glasgow
Celtic FC 1-2 AFC Ajax
Goals: 1-0 McGregor 4, 1-1 Milik 22, 1-2 Černý 88

26/11/15, Molde Stadion, Molde
Molde FK 0-2 Fenerbahçe SK
Goals: 0-1 Fernandão 68, 0-2 Ozan Tufan 84

10/12/15, Amsterdam ArenA, Amsterdam
AFC Ajax 1-1 Molde FK
Goals: 1-0 Van de Beek 14, 1-1 Singh 29

10/12/15, Şükrü Saracoğlu, Istanbul
Fenerbahçe SK 1-1 Celtic FC
Goals: 1-0 Marković 39, 1-1 Commons 75

Group B

17/09/15, Stade de Bordeaux, Bordeaux
FC Girondins de Bordeaux 1-1 Liverpool FC
Goals: 0-1 Lallana 65, 1-1 Jussiè 81

17/09/15, Tourbillon, Sion
FC Sion 2-1 FC Rubin
Goals: 1-0 Konaté 11, 1-1 Kanunnikov 65, 2-1 Konaté 82

01/10/15, Anfield, Liverpool
Liverpool FC 1-1 FC Sion
Goals: 1-0 Lallana 4, 1-1 Assifuah 18

01/10/15, Centralniy Stadion, Kazan
FC Rubin 0-0 FC Girondins de Bordeaux

22/10/15, Anfield, Liverpool
Liverpool FC 1-1 FC Rubin
Goals: 0-1 Dević 15, 1-1 Can 37

22/10/15, Stade de Bordeaux, Bordeaux
FC Girondins de Bordeaux 0-1 FC Sion
Goal: 0-1 Lacroix 21

05/11/15, Tourbillon, Sion
FC Sion 1-1 FC Girondins de Bordeaux
Goals: 0-1 Touré 67, 1-1 Chantôme 90+4(og)

05/11/15, Kazan Arena, Kazan
FC Rubin 0-1 Liverpool FC
Goal: 0-1 Ibe 52

26/11/15, Kazan Arena, Kazan
FC Rubin 2-0 FC Sion
Goals: 1-0 Georgiev 72, 2-0 Dević 90

26/11/15, Anfield, Liverpool
Liverpool FC 2-1 FC Girondins de Bordeaux
Goals: 0-1 Saivet 33, 1-1 Milner 38(p), 2-1 Benteke 45+1

10/12/15, Stade de Bordeaux, Bordeaux
FC Girondins de Bordeaux 2-2 FC Rubin
Goals: 0-1 Kanunnikov 31, 1-1 Laborde 58, 2-1 Rolán 63, 2-2 Ustinov 76

10/12/15, Tourbillon, Sion
FC Sion 0-0 Liverpool FC

Group C

17/09/15, BVB Stadion Dortmund, Dortmund
Borussia Dortmund 2-1 FC Krasnodar
Goals: 0-1 Mamaev 12, 1-1 Ginter 45+1, 2-1 Park 90+3

17/09/15, Bakcell Arena, Baku
Qäbälä FK 0-0 PAOK FC

01/10/15, Kuban, Krasnodar
FC Krasnodar 2-1 Qäbälä FK
Goals: 1-0 Wanderson 8, 1-1 Dodô 51, 2-1 Smolov 84

01/10/15, Stadio Toumba, Salonika
PAOK FC 1-1 Borussia Dortmund
Goals: 1-0 Mak 34, 1-1 Castro 72

22/10/15, Bakcell Arena, Baku
Qäbälä FK 1-3 Borussia Dortmund
Goals: 0-1 Aubameyang 31, 0-2 Aubameyang 38, 0-3 Aubameyang 72, 1-3 Dodô 90+3

22/10/15, Stadio Toumba, Salonika
PAOK FC 0-0 FC Krasnodar

05/11/15, BVB Stadion Dortmund, Dortmund
Borussia Dortmund 4-0 Qäbälä FK
Goals: 1-0 Reus 28, 2-0 Aubameyang 45, 3-0 Zenjov 67(og), 4-0 Mkhitaryan 70

05/11/15, Kuban, Krasnodar
FC Krasnodar 2-1 PAOK FC
Goals: 1-0 Ari 33, 2-0 Joãozinho 67(p), 2-1 Mak 90+1

26/11/15, Kuban, Krasnodar
FC Krasnodar 1-0 Borussia Dortmund
Goal: 1-0 Mamaev 2(p)

26/11/15, Stadio Toumba, Salonika
PAOK FC 0-0 Qäbälä FK

10/12/15, BVB Stadion Dortmund, Dortmund
Borussia Dortmund 0-1 PAOK FC
Goal: 0-1 Mak 33

10/12/15, Bakcell Arena, Baku
Qäbälä FK 0-3 FC Krasnodar
Goals: 0-1 Sigurdsson 26, 0-2 Pereyra 41, 0-3 Wanderson 76

Group D

17/09/15, Arena Herning, Herning
FC Midtjylland 1-0 Legia Warszawa
Goal: 1-0 Rasmussen 60

17/09/15, Stadio San Paolo, Naples
SSC Napoli 5-0 Club Brugge KV
Goals: 1-0 Callejón 5, 2-0 Mertens 19, 3-0 Mertens 25, 4-0 Hamšík 53, 5-0 Callejón 77

01/10/15, Jan Breydelstadion, Bruges
Club Brugge KV 1-3 FC Midtjylland
Goals: 0-1 Sisto 51, 0-2 Onuachu 67, 0-3 Novák 74, 1-3 Meunier 79

01/10/15, Stadion Wojska Polskiego, Warsaw
Legia Warszawa 0-2 SSC Napoli
Goals: 0-1 Mertens 53, 0-2 Higuaín 84

22/10/15, Stadion Wojska Polskiego, Warsaw
Legia Warszawa 1-1 Club Brugge KV
Goals: 0-1 De Fauw 39, 1-1 Kucharczyk 51

22/10/15, Arena Herning, Herning
FC Midtjylland 1-4 SSC Napoli
Goals: 0-1 Callejón 19, 0-2 Gabbiadini 31, 0-3 Gabbiadini 40, 1-3 Pusic 43, 1-4 Higuaín 90+4

05/11/15, Jan Breydelstadion, Bruges
Club Brugge KV 1-0 Legia Warszawa
Goal: 1-0 Meunier 38

05/11/15, Stadio San Paolo, Naples
SSC Napoli 5-0 FC Midtjylland
Goals: 1-0 El Kaddouri 13, 2-0 Gabbiadini 23, 3-0 Gabbiadini 38, 4-0 Maggio 54, 5-0 Callejón 77

26/11/15, Stadion Wojska Polskiego, Warsaw
Legia Warszawa 1-0 FC Midtjylland
Goal: 1-0 Prijovic 35

26/11/15, Jan Breydelstadion, Bruges
Club Brugge KV 0-1 SSC Napoli
Goal: 0-1 Chiricheş 41

10/12/15, Arena Herning, Herning
FC Midtjylland 1-1 Club Brugge KV
Goals: 1-0 Sisto 27, 1-1 Vossen 68

10/12/15, Stadio San Paolo, Naples
SSC Napoli 5-2 Legia Warszawa
Goals: 1-0 Chalobah 32, 2-0 Insigne 39, 3-0 Callejón 57, 3-1 Vranješ 62, 4-1 Mertens 65, 5-1 Mertens 90+1, 5-2 Prijovic 90+2

Group E

17/09/15, Ernst-Happel-Stadion, Vienna
SK Rapid Wien 2-1 Villarreal CF
Goals: 0-1 Léo Baptistão 45, 1-1 Schwab 50, 2-1 S Hofmann 53(p)

17/09/15, Doosan Arena, Plzen
FC Viktoria Plzeň 2-0 FC Dinamo Minsk
Goals: 1-0 Hořava 36, 2-0 Petržela 75

01/10/15, Estadio El Madrigal, Villarreal
Villarreal CF 1-0 FC Viktoria Plzeň
Goal: 1-0 Léo Baptistão 54

01/10/15, Borisov-Arena, Borisov
FC Dinamo Minsk 0-1 SK Rapid Wien
Goal: 0-1 S Hofmann 54

22/10/15, Estadio El Madrigal, Villarreal
Villarreal CF 4-0 FC Dinamo Minsk
Goals: 1-0 Bakambu 17, 2-0 Bakambu 32, 3-0 Soldado 61, 4-0 Bailly 71

22/10/15, Ernst-Happel-Stadion, Vienna
SK Rapid Wien 3-2 FC Viktoria Plzeň
Goals: 0-1 Ďuriš 12, 1-1 S Hofmann 34, 2-1 Schaub 52, 3-1 Petsos 68, 3-2 Hrošovský 76

05/11/15, Doosan Arena, Plzen
FC Viktoria Plzeň 1-2 SK Rapid Wien
Goals: 0-1 Schobesberger 13, 1-1 Holenda 71, 1-2 Schobesberger 77

05/11/15, Borisov-Arena, Borisov
FC Dinamo Minsk 1-2 Villarreal CF
Goals: 1-0 Vitus 69, 1-1 Soldado 72(p), 1-2 Politevich 86(og)

26/11/15, Borisov-Arena, Borisov
FC Dinamo Minsk 1-0 FC Viktoria Plzeň
Goal: 1-0 Adamović 90+3

26/11/15, Estadio El Madrigal, Villarreal
Villarreal CF 1-0 SK Rapid Wien
Goal: 1-0 Bruno Soriano 78

10/12/15, Ernst-Happel-Stadion, Vienna
SK Rapid Wien 2-1 FC Dinamo Minsk
Goals: 1-0 M Hofmann 29, 2-0 Jelić 59, 2-1 El Monir 65

10/12/15, Doosan Arena, Plzen
FC Viktoria Plzeň 3-3 Villarreal CF
Goals: 1-0 Kolář 8(p), 1-1 Bakambu 40, 1-2 Jonathan dos Santos 62, 2-2 Kovařík 65, 3-2 Hořava 90, 3-3 Bruno Soriano 90+4

Rapid Wien's Steffen Hofmann (right) attempts to evade Villarreal defender Bojan Jokič

UEFA Europa League

Group F

17/09/15, U Nisy, Liberec
FC Slovan Liberec 0-1 SC Braga
Goal: 0-1 Rafa Silva 60

17/09/15, Euroborg, Groningen
FC Groningen 0-3 Olympique de Marseille
Goals: 0-1 N'Koudou 25, 0-2 Ocampos 40,
0-3 Alessandrini 61

01/10/15, Estádio Municipal de Braga, Braga
SC Braga 1-0 FC Groningen
Goal: 1-0 Hassan 5

01/10/15, Stade Vélodrome, Marseille
Olympique de Marseille 0-1 FC Slovan Liberec
Goal: 0-1 Coufal 84

22/10/15, Estádio Municipal de Braga, Braga
SC Braga 3-2 Olympique de Marseille
Goals: 1-0 Hassan 61, 2-0 Wilson Eduardo 77,
2-1 Alessandrini 84, 2-2 Batshuayi 87, 3-2 Alan 88

22/10/15, U Nisy, Liberec
FC Slovan Liberec 1-1 FC Groningen
Goals: 1-0 Luckassen 87, 1-1 Hoesen 90+6

05/11/15, Stade Vélodrome, Marseille
Olympique de Marseille 1-0 SC Braga
Goal: 1-0 N'Koudou 39

05/11/15, Euroborg, Groningen
FC Groningen 0-1 FC Slovan Liberec
Goal: 0-1 Padt 81(og)

26/11/15, Estádio Municipal de Braga, Braga
SC Braga 2-1 FC Slovan Liberec
Goals: 0-1 Efremov 35, 1-1 Ricardo Ferreira 42,
2-1 Crislan 90+2

26/11/15, Stade Vélodrome, Marseille
Olympique de Marseille 2-1 FC Groningen
Goals: 1-0 N'Koudou 28, 1-1 Maduro 50,
2-1 Batshuayi 88

10/12/15, U Nisy, Liberec
FC Slovan Liberec 2-4 Olympique de Marseille
Goals: 0-1 Batshuayi 14, 0-2 N'Koudou 43,
0-3 Barrada 48, 1-3 Bakoš 75(p), 2-3 Šural 76,
2-4 Ocampos 90+4

10/12/15, Euroborg, Groningen
FC Groningen 0-0 SC Braga

Group G

17/09/15, Stade Geoffroy Guichard, Saint-Etienne
AS Saint-Étienne 2-2 Rosenborg BK
Goals: 1-0 Berič 4, 1-1 Mikkelsen 16,
1-2 Svensson 78, 2-2 Roux 87(p)

17/09/15, Dnipro Arena, Dnipropetrovsk
FC Dnipro Dnipropetrovsk 1-1 SS Lazio
Goals: 0-1 Milinković-Savić 34, 1-1 Seleznyov 90+4

01/10/15, Lerkendal Stadion, Trondheim
Rosenborg BK 0-1 FC Dnipro Dnipropetrovsk
Goal: 0-1 Seleznyov 80

01/10/15, Stadio Olimpico, Rome
SS Lazio 3-2 AS Saint-Étienne
Goals: 0-1 Bayal Sall 6, 1-1 Onazi 22,
2-1 Hoedt 48, 3-1 Biglia 80, 3-2 Monnet-Paquet 84

22/10/15, Stadio Olimpico, Rome
SS Lazio 3-1 Rosenborg BK
Goals: 1-0 Matri 28, 2-0 Felipe Anderson 54,
2-1 Søderlund 69, 3-1 Candreva 79

Filip Djordjević finds the net for Lazio against Dnipro

22/10/15, Dnipro Arena, Dnipropetrovsk
FC Dnipro Dnipropetrovsk 0-1 AS Saint-Étienne
Goal: 0-1 Hamouma 44

05/11/15, Lerkendal Stadion, Trondheim
Rosenborg BK 0-2 SS Lazio
Goals: 0-1 Djordjević 9, 0-2 Djordjević 29

05/11/15, Stade Geoffroy Guichard, Saint-Etienne
AS Saint-Étienne 3-0 FC Dnipro Dnipropetrovsk
Goals: 1-0 Monnet-Paquet 38, 2-0 Berič 52,
3-0 Hamouma 65

26/11/15, Stadio Olimpico, Rome
SS Lazio 3-1 FC Dnipro Dnipropetrovsk
Goals: 1-0 Candreva 4, 1-1 Bruno Gama 65, 2-1
Parolo 68, 3-1 Djordjević 90+3

26/11/15, Lerkendal Stadion, Trondheim
Rosenborg BK 1-1 AS Saint-Étienne
Goals: 1-0 Søderlund 40, 1-1 Roux 80(p)

10/12/15, Stade Geoffroy Guichard, Saint-Etienne
AS Saint-Étienne 1-1 SS Lazio
Goals: 0-1 Matri 52, 1-1 Eysseric 76

10/12/15, Dnipro Arena, Dnipropetrovsk
FC Dnipro Dnipropetrovsk 3-0 Rosenborg BK
Goals: 1-0 Matheus 35, 2-0 Matheus 60, 3-0
Shakhov 79

Group H

17/09/15, José Alvalade, Lisbon
**Sporting Clube de Portugal 1-3 FC Lokomotiv
Moskva**
Goals: 0-1 Samedov 12, 1-1 Montero 50,
1-2 Samedov 56, 1-3 Niasse 65

17/09/15, Elbasan Arena, Elbasan
KF Skënderbeu 0-1 Beşiktaş JK
Goal: 0-1 Sosa 28

01/10/15, Atatürk Olimpiyat Stadium, Istanbul
Beşiktaş JK 1-1 Sporting Clube de Portugal
Goals: 0-1 Ruiz 16, 1-1 Gökhan Töre 61

01/10/15, Stadion Lokomotiv, Moscow
FC Lokomotiv Moskva 2-0 KF Skënderbeu
Goals: 1-0 Niasse 35, 2-0 Samedov 73

22/10/15, José Alvalade, Lisbon
Sporting Clube de Portugal 5-1 KF Skënderbeu
Goals: 1-0 Aquilani 38(p), 2-0 Montero 41(p),
3-0 Matheus Pereira 64, 4-0 Tobias Figueiredo 69,
5-0 Matheus Pereira 77, 5-1 Jashanica 89

22/10/15, Stadion Lokomotiv, Moscow
FC Lokomotiv Moskva 1-1 Beşiktaş JK
Goals: 1-0 Maicon 54, 1-1 Gomez 64

05/11/15, Atatürk Olimpiyat Stadium, Istanbul
Beşiktaş JK 1-1 FC Lokomotiv Moskva
Goals: 1-0 Ricardo Quaresma 58, 1-1 Niasse 76

05/11/15, Elbasan Arena, Elbasan
KF Skënderbeu 3-0 Sporting Clube de Portugal
Goals: 1-0 Lilaj 15, 2-0 Lilaj 19(p), 3-0 Nimaga 55

26/11/15, Atatürk Olimpiyat Stadium, Istanbul
Beşiktaş JK 2-0 KF Skënderbeu
Goals: 1-0 Cenk Tosun 35, 2-0 Cenk Tosun 78

26/11/15, Stadion Lokomotiv, Moscow
**FC Lokomotiv Moskva 2-4 Sporting Clube de
Portugal**
Goals: 1-0 Maicon 5, 1-1 Montero 20, 1-2 Ruiz 38,
1-3 Gelson Martins 43, 1-4 Matheus Pereira 60,
2-4 Miranchuk 86

10/12/15, José Alvalade, Lisbon
Sporting Clube de Portugal 3-1 Beşiktaş JK
Goals: 0-1 Gomez 58, 1-1 Slimani 67, 2-1 Ruiz 72,
3-1 Gutiérrez 78

10/12/15, Elbasan Arena, Elbasan
KF Skënderbeu 0-3 FC Lokomotiv Moskva
Goals: 0-1 Tarasov 18, 0-2 Niasse 89,
0-3 Samedov 90

Group I

17/09/15, Stadio Artemio Franchi, Florence
ACF Fiorentina 1-2 FC Basel 1893
Goals: 1-0 Kalinić 4, 1-1 Bjarnason 71, 1-2 Elneny 79

17/09/15, Stadion Miejski, Poznan
KKS Lech Poznań 0-0 Os Belenenses

01/10/15, Estádio do Restelo, Lisbon
Os Belenenses 0-4 ACF Fiorentina
Goals: 0-1 Bernardeschi 18, 0-2 Babacar 45+1,
0-3 Tonel 83(og), 0-4 Rossi 90

01/10/15, St. Jakob-Park, Basel
FC Basel 1893 2-0 KKS Lech Poznań
Goals: 1-0 Bjarnason 55, 2-0 Embolo 90

22/10/15, St. Jakob-Park, Basel
FC Basel 1893 1-2 Os Belenenses
Goals: 1-0 Lang 15, 1-1 Luís Leal 27, 1-2 Kuca 45+1

22/10/15, Stadio Artemio Franchi, Florence
ACF Fiorentina 1-2 KKS Lech Poznań
Goals: 0-1 Kownacki 65, 0-2 Gajos 82, 1-2 Rossi 90

05/11/15, Estádio do Restelo, Lisbon
Os Belenenses 0-2 FC Basel 1893
Goals: 0-1 Janko 45+1(p), 0-2 Embolo 64

05/11/15, Stadion Miejski, Poznan
KKS Lech Poznań 0-2 ACF Fiorentina
Goals: 0-1 Iličić 42, 0-2 Iličić 83

26/11/15, Estádio do Restelo, Lisbon
Os Belenenses 0-0 KKS Lech Poznań

26/11/15, St. Jakob-Park, Basel
FC Basel 1893 2-2 ACF Fiorentina
Goals: 0-1 Bernardeschi 23, 0-2 Bernardeschi 36,
1-2 Suchý 40, 2-2 Elneny 74

10/12/15, Stadio Artemio Franchi, Florence
ACF Fiorentina 1-0 Os Belenenses
Goal: 1-0 Babacar 67

10/12/15, Stadion Miejski, Poznan
KKS Lech Poznań 0-1 FC Basel 1893
Goal: 0-1 Boëtius 50

Group J

17/09/15, White Hart Lane, London
Tottenham Hotspur FC 3-1 Qarabağ FK
Goals: 0-1 Richard 7(p), 1-1 Son 28, 2-1 Son 30,
3-1 Lamela 86

*17/09/15, Constant Vanden Stock Stadium,
Brussels*
RSC Anderlecht 1-1 AS Monaco FC
Goals: 1-0 Gillet 11, 1-1 L Traoré 85

01/10/15, Stade Louis II, Monaco
AS Monaco FC 1-1 Tottenham Hotspur FC
Goals: 0-1 Lamela 35, 1-1 El Shaarawy 81

*01/10/15, Tofiq Bähramov Republican stadium,
Baku*
Qarabağ FK 1-0 RSC Anderlecht
Goal: 1-0 Richard 36

22/10/15, Stade Louis II, Monaco
AS Monaco FC 1-0 Qarabağ FK
Goal: 1-0 L Traoré 70

*22/10/15, Constant Vanden Stock Stadium,
Brussels*
RSC Anderlecht 2-1 Tottenham Hotspur FC
Goals: 0-1 Eriksen 4, 1-1 Gillet 13, 2-1 Okaka 75

*05/11/15, Tofiq Bähramov Republican stadium,
Baku*
Qarabağ FK 1-1 AS Monaco FC
Goals: 1-0 Armenteros 39, 1-1 Ivan Cavaleiro 72

05/11/15, White Hart Lane, London
Tottenham Hotspur FC 2-1 RSC Anderlecht
Goals: 1-0 Kane 29, 1-1 Ezekiel 72, 2-1 Dembélé 87

26/11/15, Stade Louis II, Monaco
AS Monaco FC 0-2 RSC Anderlecht
Goals: 0-1 Gillet 45+1, 0-2 Acheampong 78

*26/11/15, Tofiq Bähramov Republican stadium,
Baku*
Qarabağ FK 0-1 Tottenham Hotspur FC
Goal: 0-1 Kane 78

10/12/15, White Hart Lane, London
Tottenham Hotspur FC 4-1 AS Monaco FC
Goals: 1-0 Lamela 2, 2-0 Lamela 15,
3-0 Lamela 38, 3-1 El Shaarawy 61, 4-1 Carroll 78

*10/12/15, Constant Vanden Stock Stadium,
Brussels*
RSC Anderlecht 2-1 Qarabağ FK
Goals: 0-1 Dani Quintana 26, 1-1 Najar 28,
2-1 Okaka 31

Group K

17/09/15, GSP, Nicosia
APOEL FC 0-3 FC Schalke 04
Goals: 0-1 Matip 28, 0-2 Huntelaar 35,
0-3 Huntelaar 71

*17/09/15, Stadio Theodoros Kolokotronis, Tripoli
Arkadia*
Asteras Tripolis FC 1-1 AC Sparta Praha
Goals: 1-0 Mazza 2, 1-1 Lafata 56

01/10/15, Stadion Letná, Prague
AC Sparta Praha 2-0 APOEL FC
Goals: 1-0 Fatai 24, 2-0 Brabec 60

01/10/15, Arena AufSchalke, Gelsenkirchen
FC Schalke 04 4-0 Asteras Tripolis FC
Goals: 1-0 Di Santo 28, 2-0 Di Santo 37,
3-0 Di Santo 44(p), 4-0 Huntelaar 84

22/10/15, Arena AufSchalke, Gelsenkirchen
FC Schalke 04 2-2 AC Sparta Praha
Goals: 1-0 Di Santo 6, 1-1 Fatai 50,
1-2 Lafata 63, 2-2 Sané 73

22/10/15, GSP, Nicosia
APOEL FC 2-1 Asteras Tripolis FC
Goals: 0-1 Lluy 8, 1-1 Cavenaghi 45+9(p),
2-1 Carlão 59

05/11/15, Stadion Letná, Prague
AC Sparta Praha 1-1 FC Schalke 04
Goals: 1-0 Lafata 6, 1-1 Geis 20(p)

*05/11/15, Stadio Theodoros Kolokotronis, Tripoli
Arkadia*
Asteras Tripolis FC 2-0 APOEL FC
Goals: 1-0 Bertoglio 2, 2-0 Giannou 45+1

26/11/15, Arena AufSchalke, Gelsenkirchen
FC Schalke 04 1-0 APOEL FC
Goal: 1-0 Choupo-Moting 86

26/11/15, Stadion Letná, Prague
AC Sparta Praha 1-0 Asteras Tripolis FC
Goal: 1-0 Brabec 33

10/12/15, GSP, Nicosia
APOEL FC 1-3 AC Sparta Praha
Goals: 1-0 Cavenaghi 6, 1-1 Juliš 63,
1-2 Lafata 77, 1-3 Lafata 87

*10/12/15, Stadio Theodoros Kolokotronis, Tripoli
Arkadia*
Asteras Tripolis FC 0-4 FC Schalke 04
Goals: 0-1 Di Santo 29, 0-2 Choupo-Moting 37,
0-3 Choupo-Moting 78, 0-4 Meyer 86

Group L

17/09/15, Stadion FK Partizan, Belgrade
FK Partizan 3-2 AZ Alkmaar
Goals: 1-0 Oumarou 11, 1-1 Van der Linden 34,
2-1 Oumarou 40, 3-1 A Živković 89,
3-2 Henriksen 90+3

17/09/15, Estadio de San Mamés, Bilbao
Athletic Club 3-1 FC Augsburg
Goals: 0-1 Halil Altıntop 15, 1-1 Aduriz 55,
2-1 Aduriz 66, 3-1 Susaeta 90

01/10/15, Augsburg Arena, Augsburg
FC Augsburg 1-3 FK Partizan
Goals: 0-1 A Živković 31, 0-2 Fabrício 54,
1-2 Bobadilla 58, 1-3 A Živković 62

01/10/15, AZ Stadion, Alkmaar
AZ Alkmaar 2-1 Athletic Club
Goals: 1-0 Henriksen 55, 2-0 Bóveda 65(og),
2-1 Aduriz 75

22/10/15, AZ Stadion, Alkmaar
AZ Alkmaar 0-1 FC Augsburg
Goal: 0-1 Trochowski 43

22/10/15, Stadion FK Partizan, Belgrade
FK Partizan 0-2 Athletic Club
Goals: 0-1 Raúl García 32, 0-2 Beñat Etxebarria 85

05/11/15, Augsburg Arena, Augsburg
FC Augsburg 4-1 AZ Alkmaar
Goals: 1-0 Bobadilla 24, 2-0 Bobadilla 33,
2-1 Janssen 45+1, 3-1 Ji 66, 4-1 Bobadilla 74

05/11/15, Estadio de San Mamés, Bilbao
Athletic Club 5-1 FK Partizan
Goals: 1-0 Iñaki Williams 15, 1-1 Oumarou 17,
2-1 Iñaki Williams 19, 3-1 Beñat Etxebarria 40,
4-1 Aduriz 71, 5-1 Elustondo 81

26/11/15, AZ Stadion, Alkmaar
AZ Alkmaar 1-2 FK Partizan
Goals: 1-0 Dos Santos 48, 1-1 Oumarou 65,
1-2 A Živković 89

26/11/15, Augsburg Arena, Augsburg
FC Augsburg 2-3 Athletic Club
Goals: 0-1 Susaeta 10, 1-1 Trochowski 41,
2-1 Bobadilla 59, 2-2 Aduriz 83, 2-3 Aduriz 86

10/12/15, Stadion FK Partizan, Belgrade
FK Partizan 1-3 FC Augsburg
Goals: 1-0 Oumarou 11, 1-1 Hong 45+2,
1-2 Verhaegh 51, 1-3 Bobadilla 89

10/12/15, Estadio de San Mamés, Bilbao
Athletic Club 2-2 AZ Alkmaar
Goals: 0-1 Van Overeem 26, 1-1 Kike Sola 43,
2-1 San José 47(p), 2-2 Enric Saborit 88(og)

Franco Di Santo (in blue) scores the first of his three goals for Schalke at home to Asteras Tripolis

UEFA Europa League

Final group tables

Group A

	Pld	Home W D L F A		Away W D L F A		Total W D L F A		Pts
1 Molde FK	6	1 1 1 4 4		2 1 0 6 3		3 2 1 10 7		11
2 Fenerbahçe SK	6	1 1 1 3 4		1 2 0 4 2		2 3 1 7 6		9
3 AFC Ajax	6	0 3 0 3 3		1 1 1 3 3		1 4 1 6 6		7
4 Celtic FC	6	0 1 2 4 6		0 2 1 4 6		0 3 3 8 12		3

Group B

	Pld	Home W D L F A		Away W D L F A		Total W D L F A		Pts
1 Liverpool FC	6	1 2 0 4 3		1 2 0 2 1		2 4 0 6 4		10
2 FC Sion	6	1 2 0 3 2		1 1 1 2 3		2 3 1 5 5		9
3 FC Rubin	6	1 1 1 2 1		0 2 1 4 5		1 3 2 6 6		6
4 FC Girondins de Bordeaux	6	0 2 1 3 4		0 2 1 2 3		0 4 2 5 7		4

Group C

	Pld	Home W D L F A		Away W D L F A		Total W D L F A		Pts
1 FC Krasnodar	6	3 0 0 5 2		1 1 1 4 2		4 1 1 9 4		13
2 Borussia Dortmund	6	2 0 1 6 2		1 1 1 4 3		3 1 2 10 5		10
3 PAOK FC	6	0 3 0 1 1		1 1 1 2 2		1 4 1 3 3		7
4 Qäbälä FK	6	0 1 2 1 6		0 1 2 1 6		0 2 4 2 12		2

Group D

	Pld	Home W D L F A		Away W D L F A		Total W D L F A		Pts
1 SSC Napoli	6	3 0 0 15 2		3 0 0 7 1		6 0 0 22 3		18
2 FC Midtjylland	6	1 1 1 3 5		1 0 2 3 7		2 1 3 6 12		7
3 Club Brugge KV	6	1 0 2 2 4		0 2 1 2 7		1 2 3 4 11		5
4 Legia Warszawa	6	1 1 1 2 3		0 0 3 2 7		1 1 4 4 10		4

Group E

	Pld	Home W D L F A		Away W D L F A		Total W D L F A		Pts
1 SK Rapid Wien	6	3 0 0 7 4		2 0 1 3 2		5 0 1 10 6		15
2 Villarreal CF	6	3 0 0 6 0		1 1 1 6 6		4 1 1 12 6		13
3 FC Viktoria Plzeň	6	1 1 1 6 5		0 0 3 2 5		1 1 4 8 10		4
4 FC Dinamo Minsk	6	1 0 2 2 3		0 0 3 1 8		1 0 5 3 11		3

Group F

	Pld	Home W D L F A		Away W D L F A		Total W D L F A		Pts
1 SC Braga	6	3 0 0 6 3		1 1 1 1 1		4 1 1 7 4		13
2 Olympique de Marseille	6	2 0 1 3 2		2 0 1 9 5		4 0 2 12 7		12
3 FC Slovan Liberec	6	0 1 2 3 6		2 0 1 3 2		2 1 3 6 8		7
4 FC Groningen	6	0 1 2 0 4		0 1 2 2 4		0 2 4 2 8		2

Group G

	Pld	Home W D L F A		Away W D L F A		Total W D L F A		Pts
1 SS Lazio	6	3 0 0 9 4		1 2 0 4 2		4 2 0 13 6		14
2 AS Saint-Étienne	6	1 2 0 6 3		1 1 1 4 4		2 3 1 10 7		9
3 FC Dnipro Dnipropetrovsk	6	1 1 1 4 2		1 0 2 2 6		2 1 3 6 8		7
4 Rosenborg BK	6	0 1 2 1 4		0 1 2 3 8		0 2 4 4 12		2

Group H

	Pld	Home W D L F A		Away W D L F A		Total W D L F A		Pts
1 FC Lokomotiv Moskva	6	1 1 1 5 5		2 1 0 7 2		3 2 1 12 7		11
2 Sporting Clube de Portugal	6	2 0 1 9 5		1 1 1 5 6		3 1 2 14 11		10
3 Beşiktaş JK	6	1 2 0 4 2		1 1 1 3 4		2 3 1 7 6		9
4 KF Skënderbeu	6	1 0 2 3 4		0 0 3 1 9		1 0 5 4 13		3

Group I

	Pld	Home W D L F A		Away W D L F A		Total W D L F A		Pts
1 FC Basel 1893	6	1 1 1 5 4		3 0 0 5 1		4 1 1 10 5		13
2 ACF Fiorentina	6	1 0 2 3 4		2 1 0 8 2		3 1 2 11 6		10
3 KKS Lech Poznań	6	0 1 2 0 3		1 1 1 2 3		1 2 3 2 6		5
4 Os Belenenses	6	0 1 2 0 6		1 1 1 2 2		1 2 3 2 8		5

Group J

	Pld	Home W D L F A		Away W D L F A		Total W D L F A		Pts
1 Tottenham Hotspur FC	6	3 0 0 9 3		1 1 1 3 3		4 1 1 12 6		13
2 RSC Anderlecht	6	2 1 0 5 3		1 0 2 3 3		3 1 2 8 6		10
3 AS Monaco FC	6	1 1 1 2 3		0 2 1 3 6		1 3 2 5 9		6
4 Qarabağ FK	6	1 1 1 2 2		0 0 3 2 6		1 1 4 4 8		4

Group K

	Pld	Home W D L F A		Away W D L F A		Total W D L F A		Pts
1 FC Schalke 04	6	2 1 0 7 2		2 1 0 8 1		4 2 0 15 3		14
2 AC Sparta Praha	6	2 1 0 4 1		1 2 0 6 4		3 3 0 10 5		12
3 Asteras Tripolis FC	6	1 1 1 3 5		0 0 3 1 7		1 1 4 4 12		4
4 APOEL FC	6	1 0 2 3 7		0 0 3 0 5		1 0 5 3 12		3

Group L

	Pld	Home W D L F A		Away W D L F A		Total W D L F A		Pts
1 Athletic Club	6	2 1 0 10 4		2 0 1 6 4		4 1 1 16 8		13
2 FC Augsburg	6	1 0 2 7 7		2 0 1 5 4		3 0 3 12 11		9
3 FK Partizan	6	1 0 2 4 7		2 0 1 6 7		3 0 3 10 14		9
4 AZ Alkmaar	6	1 0 2 3 4		0 1 2 5 9		1 1 4 8 13		4

Round of 32

16/02/16, Şükrü Saracoğlu, Istanbul (att: 36,195)
Fenerbahçe SK 2-0 FC Lokomotiv Moskva
Goals: 1-0 Souza 18, 2-0 Souza 72
Referee: Strömbergsson (SWE)
25/02/16, Stadion Lokomotiv, Moscow (att: 15,695)
FC Lokomotiv Moskva 1-1 Fenerbahçe SK
Goals: 1-0 Samedov 45, 1-1 Mehmet Topal 83
Referee: Kružliak (SVK)
Aggregate: 1-3; Fenerbahçe SK qualify.

18/02/16, Stadio Artemio Franchi, Florence (att: 15,200)
ACF Fiorentina 1-1 Tottenham Hotspur FC
Goals: 0-1 Chadli 37(p), 1-1 Bernardeschi 59
Referee: Zwayer (GER)

25/02/16, White Hart Lane, London (att: 34,880)
Tottenham Hotspur FC 3-0 ACF Fiorentina
Goals: 1-0 Mason 25, 2-0 Lamela 63, 3-0 Gonzalo Rodríguez 81(og)
Referee: Haţegan (ROU)
Aggregate: 4-1; Tottenham Hotspur FC qualify.

18/02/16, BVB Stadion Dortmund, Dortmund (att: 65,851)
Borussia Dortmund 2-0 FC Porto
Goals: 1-0 Piszczek 6, 2-0 Reus 71
Referee: Banti (ITA)
25/02/16, Estádio do Dragão, Porto (att: 32,707)
FC Porto 0-1 Borussia Dortmund
Goal: 0-1 Casillas 23(og)
Referee: Clattenburg (ENG)
Aggregate: 0-3; Borussia Dortmund qualify.

18/02/16, Constant Vanden Stock Stadium, Brussels (att: 15,397)
RSC Anderlecht 1-0 Olympiacos FC
Goal: 1-0 Mbodji 67
Referee: Bebek (CRO)
25/02/16, Stadio Georgios Karaiskakis, Piraeus (att: 31,005)
Olympiacos FC 1-2 RSC Anderlecht (aet)
Goals: 1-0 Fortounis 29(p), 1-1 Acheampong 102, 1-2 Acheampong 111
Referee: Hunter (NIR)
Aggregate: 1-3; RSC Anderlecht qualify after extra time.

18/02/16, Arena Herning, Herning (att: 9,182)
FC Midtjylland 2-1 Manchester United FC
Goals: 0-1 Depay 37, 1-1 Sisto 44, 2-1 Onuachu 77
Referee: Artur Dias (POR)
25/02/16, Old Trafford, Manchester (att: 58,609)
Manchester United FC 5-1 FC Midtjylland
Goals: 0-1 Sisto 28, 1-1 Bodurov 32(og),
2-1 Rashford 64, 3-1 Rashford 75,
4-1 Ander Herrera 88(p), 5-1 Depay 90
Referee: Vad (HUN)
Aggregate: 6-3; Manchester United FC qualify.

*18/02/16, Estadio Ramón Sánchez Pizjuán,
Seville (att: 28,920)*
Sevilla FC 3-0 Molde FK
Goals: 1-0 Llorente 35, 2-0 Llorente 49,
3-0 Gameiro 72
Referee: Mažeika (LTU)
25/02/16, Molde Stadion, Molde (att: 7,284)
Molde FK 1-0 Sevilla FC
Goal: 1-0 Hestad 43
Referee: Madden (SCO)
Aggregate: 1-3; Sevilla FC qualify.

18/02/16, Estadio El Madrigal, Villarreal (att: 17,686)
Villarreal CF 1-0 SSC Napoli
Goal: 1-0 Denis Suárez 82
Referee: Nijhuis (NED)
25/02/16, Stadio San Paolo, Naples (att: 23,928)
SSC Napoli 1-1 Villarreal CF
Goals: 1-0 Hamšík 17, 1-1 Pina 59
Referee: Aytekin (GER)
Aggregate: 1-2; Villarreal CF qualify.

*18/02/16, Stade Geoffroy Guichard,
Saint-Etienne (att: 27,013)*
AS Saint-Étienne 3-2 FC Basel 1893
Goals: 1-0 Bayal Sall 9, 2-0 Monnet-Paquet 39,
2-1 Samuel 44, 2-2 Janko 56(p), 3-2 Bahebeck 77
Referee: Sidiropoulos (GRE)
25/02/16, St Jakob-Park, Basel (att: 20,976)
FC Basel 1893 2-1 AS Saint-Étienne
Goals: 1-0 Zuffi 15, 1-1 Sall 90, 2-1 Zuffi 90+2
Referee: Makkelie (NED)
Aggregate: 4-4; FC Basel 1893 qualify on away
goals.

18/02/16, José Alvalade, Lisbon (att: 26,201)
**Sporting Clube de Portugal 0-1 Bayer 04
Leverkusen**
Goal: 0-1 Bellarabi 26
Referee: Kuipers (NED)
25/02/16, BayArena, Leverkusen (att: 26,585)
**Bayer 04 Leverkusen 3-1 Sporting Clube de
Portugal**
Goals: 1-0 Bellarabi 30, 1-1 João Mário 38,
2-1 Bellarabi 65, 3-1 Hakan Çalhanoğlu 87
Referee: Buquet (FRA)
Aggregate: 4-1; Bayer 04 Leverkusen qualify.

*18/02/16, Estadi de Mestalla, Valencia
(att: 28,831)*
Valencia CF 6-0 SK Rapid Wien
Goals: 1-0 Santi Mina 4, 2-0 Parejo 10, 3-0 Santi
Mina 25, 4-0 Negredo 29, 5-0 André Gomes 35,
6-0 Rodrigo 89
Referee: Zelinka (CZE)
*25/02/16, Ernst-Happel-Stadion, Vienna
(att: 39,800)*
SK Rapid Wien 0-4 Valencia CF
Goals: 0-1 Rodrigo 59, 0-2 Feghouli 64,
0-3 Piatti 72, 0-4 Rúben Vezo 88
Referee: Tagliavento (ITA)
Aggregate: 0-10; Valencia CF qualify.

*18/02/16, Augsburg Arena, Augsburg
(att: 25,000)*
FC Augsburg 0-0 Liverpool FC
Referee: Fernández Borbalán (ESP)
25/02/16, Anfield, Liverpool (att: 43,081)
Liverpool FC 1-0 FC Augsburg
Goal: 1-0 Milner 5(p)
Referee: Turpin (FRA)
Aggregate: 1-0; Liverpool FC qualify.

Sparta Praha's Lukáš Mareček puts his team in
command of their round of 32 tie against Krasnodar

18/02/16, Stadion Letná, Prague (att: 14,120)
AC Sparta Praha 1-0 FC Krasnodar
Goal: 1-0 Juliš 64
Referee: Vinčić (SVN)
25/02/16, Kuban, Krasnodar (att: 14,850)
FC Krasnodar 0-3 AC Sparta Praha
Goals: 0-1 Mareček 51, 0-2 Frýdek 57, 0-3 Fatai 70
Referee: Johannesson (SWE)
Aggregate: 0-4; AC Sparta Praha qualify.

18/02/16, Tourbillon, Sion (att: 9,000)
FC Sion 1-2 SC Braga
Goals: 0-1 Stoiljković 13, 1-1 Konaté 53,
1-2 Rafa Silva 61
Referee: Aranovskiy (UKR)
*24/02/16, Estádio Municipal de Braga, Braga
(att: 6,759)*
SC Braga 2-2 FC Sion
Goals: 0-1 Gekas 16, 1-1 Josué 27(p),
1-2 Gekas 29, 2-2 Stoiljković 48
Referee: Liany (ISR)
Aggregate: 4-3; SC Braga qualify.

*18/02/16, Stade Vélodrome, Marseille
(att: 29,727)*
Olympique de Marseille 0-1 Athletic Club
Goal: 0-1 Aduriz 54
Referee: Thomson (SCO)
*25/02/16, Estadio de San Mamés, Bilbao
(att: 38,259)*
Athletic Club 1-1 Olympique de Marseille
Goals: 0-1 Batshuayi 40, 1-1 Merino 81
Referee: Kulbakov (BLR)
Aggregate: 2-1; Athletic Club qualify.

*18/02/16, Ali Sami Yen Spor Kompleksi, Istanbul
(att: 33,353)*
Galatasaray AŞ 1-1 SS Lazio
Goals: 1-0 Sabri Sarıoğlu 12,
1-1 Milinković-Savić 21
Referee: Oliver (ENG)
25/02/16, Stadio Olimpico, Rome (att: 14,019)
SS Lazio 3-1 Galatasaray AŞ
Goals: 1-0 Parolo 59, 2-0 Felipe Anderson 61,
2-1 Yasin Öztekin 62, 3-1 Klose 72
Referee: Bezborodov (RUS)
Aggregate: 4-2; SS Lazio qualify.

18/02/16, Arena Lviv, Lviv (att: 23,615)
FC Shakhtar Donetsk 0-0 FC Schalke 04
Referee: Göçek (TUR)
*25/02/16, Arena AufSchalke, Gelsenkirchen
(att: 45,308)*
FC Schalke 04 0-3 FC Shakhtar Donetsk
Goals: 0-1 Marlos 27, 0-2 Ferreyra 63,
0-3 Kovalenko 77
Referee: Jug (SVN)
Aggregate: 0-3; FC Shakhtar Donetsk qualify.

Round of 16

10/03/16, St Jakob-Park, Basel (att: 22,403)
FC Basel 1893 0-0 Sevilla FC
Referee: Taylor (ENG)
*17/03/16, Estadio Ramón Sánchez Pizjuán, Seville
(att: 35,546)*
Sevilla FC 3-0 FC Basel 1893
Goals: 1-0 Rami 35, 2-0 Gameiro 44,
3-0 Gameiro 45
Referee: Aytekin (GER)
Aggregate: 3-0; Sevilla FC qualify.

*10/03/16, BVB Stadion Dortmund, Dortmund
(att: 65,848)*
Borussia Dortmund 3-0 Tottenham Hotspur FC
Goals: 1-0 Aubameyang 30, 2-0 Reus 61,
3-0 Reus 70
Referee: Çakır (TUR)
17/03/16, White Hart Lane, London (att: 34,943)
Tottenham Hotspur FC 1-2 Borussia Dortmund
Goals: 0-1 Aubameyang 24, 0-2 Aubameyang 71,
1-2 Son 74
Referee: Rizzoli (ITA)
Aggregate: 1-5; Borussia Dortmund qualify.

10/03/16, Arena Lviv, Lviv (att: 23,621)
FC Shakhtar Donetsk 3-1 RSC Anderlecht
Goals: 1-0 Taison 21, 2-0 Kucher 24, 2-1
Acheampong 69, 3-1 Eduardo 79
Referee: Artur Dias (POR)
*17/03/16, Constant Vanden Stock Stadium,
Brussels (att: 13,785)*
RSC Anderlecht 0-1 FC Shakhtar Donetsk
Goal: 0-1 Eduardo 90+3
Referee: Mateu Lahoz (ESP)
Aggregate: 1-4; FC Shakhtar Donetsk qualify.

10/03/16, Şükrü Saracoğlu, Istanbul (att: 40,197)
Fenerbahçe SK 1-0 SC Braga
Goal: 1-0 Mehmet Topal 82
Referee: Turpin (FRA)
*17/03/16, Estádio Municipal de Braga, Braga
(att: 16,431)*
SC Braga 4-1 Fenerbahçe SK
Goals: 1-0 Hassan 11, 1-1 Alper Potuk 45+3,
2-1 Josué 69(p), 3-1 Stoiljković 74, 4-1 Rafa Silva 83
Referee: Bebek (CRO)
Aggregate: 4-2; SC Braga qualify.

10/03/16, Anfield, Liverpool (att: 43,228)
Liverpool FC 2-0 Manchester United FC
Goals: 1-0 Sturridge 20(p), 2-0 Roberto Firmino 73
Referee: Velasco Carballo (ESP)
17/03/16, Old Trafford, Manchester (att: 75,180)
Manchester United FC 1-1 Liverpool FC
Goals: 1-0 Martial 32(p), 1-1 Coutinho 45
Referee: Mažić (SRB)
Aggregate: 1-3; Liverpool FC qualify.

*10/03/16, Estadio El Madrigal, Villarreal
(att: 16,211)*
Villarreal CF 2-0 Bayer 04 Leverkusen
Goals: 1-0 Bakambu 4, 2-0 Bakambu 56
Referee: Rocchi (ITA)
17/03/16, BayArena, Leverkusen (att: 23,409)
Bayer 04 Leverkusen 0-0 Villarreal CF
Referee: Collum (SCO)
Aggregate: 0-2; Villarreal CF qualify.

UEFA Europa League

10/03/16, Estadio de San Mamés, Bilbao (att: 35,765)
Athletic Club 1-0 Valencia CF
Goal: 1-0 Raúl García 20
Referee: Kuipers (NED)
17/03/16, Estadi de Mestalla, Valencia (att: 31,681)
Valencia CF 2-1 Athletic Club
Goals: 1-0 Santi Mina 13, 2-0 Aderlan Santos 37, 2-1 Aduriz 76
Referee: Orsato (ITA)
Aggregate: 2-2; Athletic Club qualify on away goal.

10/03/16, Stadion Letná, Prague (att: 17,482)
AC Sparta Praha 1-1 SS Lazio
Goals: 1-0 Frýdek 13, 1-1 Parolo 38
Referee: Undiano Mallenco (ESP)
17/03/16, Stadio Olimpico, Rome (att: 18,827)
SS Lazio 0-3 AC Sparta Praha
Goals: 0-1 Dočkal 10, 0-2 Krejčí 12, 0-3 Juliš 44
Referee: Buquet (FRA)
Aggregate: 1-4; AC Sparta Praha qualify.

Quarter-finals

07/04/16, Estádio Municipal de Braga, Braga (att: 21,645)
SC Braga 1-2 FC Shakhtar Donetsk
Goals: 0-1 Rakitskiy 45, 0-2 Ferreyra 75, 1-2 Wilson Eduardo 89
Referee: Eriksson (SWE)
14/04/16, Arena Lviv, Lviv (att: 33,617)
FC Shakhtar Donetsk 4-0 SC Braga
Goals: 1-0 Srna 25(p), 2-0 Ricardo Ferreira 43(og), 3-0 Kovalenko 50, 4-0 Ricardo Ferreira 73(og)
Referee: Královec (CZE)
Aggregate: 6-1; FC Shakhtar Donetsk qualify.

07/04/16, Estadio El Madrigal, Villarreal (att: 15,803)
Villarreal CF 2-1 AC Sparta Praha
Goals: 1-0 Bakambu 3, 1-1 Brabec 45+4, 2-1 Bakambu 63
Referee: Haţegan (ROU)
14/04/16, Stadion Letná, Prague (att: 18,201)
AC Sparta Praha 2-4 Villarreal CF
Goals: 0-1 Bakambu 16, 0-2 Samu Castillejo 43, 0-3 Lafata 45+1(og), 0-4 Bakambu 49, 1-4 Dočkal 65, 2-4 Krejčí 71
Referee: Atkinson (ENG)
Aggregate: 3-6; Villarreal CF qualify.

07/04/16, Estadio de San Mamés, Bilbao (att: 40,856)
Athletic Club 1-2 Sevilla FC
Goals: 1-0 Aduriz 48, 1-1 Kolodziejczak 56, 1-2 Iborra 83
Referee: Clattenburg (ENG)
14/04/16, Estadio Ramón Sánchez Pizjuán, Seville (att: 38,567)
Sevilla FC 1-2 Athletic Club (aet)
Goals: 0-1 Aduriz 57, 1-1 Gameiro 59, 1-2 Raúl García 80
Referee: Skomina (SVN)
Aggregate: 3-3; Sevilla FC qualify 5-4 on penalties.

07/04/16, BVB Stadion Dortmund, Dortmund (att: 65,848)
Borussia Dortmund 1-1 Liverpool FC
Goals: 0-1 Origi 36, 1-1 Hummels 48
Referee: Velasco Carballo (ESP)
14/04/16, Anfield, Liverpool (att: 42,984)
Liverpool FC 4-3 Borussia Dortmund
Goals: 0-1 Mkhitaryan 5, 0-2 Aubameyang 9, 1-2 Origi 48, 1-3 Reus 57, 2-3 Coutinho 66, 3-3 Sakho 78, 4-3 Lovren 90+1
Referee: Çakır (TUR)
Aggregate: 5-4; Liverpool FC qualify.

Semi-finals

28/04/16, Estadio El Madrigal, Villarreal (att: 21,606)
Villarreal CF 1-0 Liverpool FC
Goal: 1-0 Adrián López 90+2
Referee: Skomina (SVN)
05/05/16, Anfield, Liverpool (att: 43,074)
Liverpool FC 3-0 Villarreal CF
Goals: 1-0 Bruno Soriano 7(og), 2-0 Sturridge 63, 3-0 Lallana 81
Referee: Kassai (HUN)
Aggregate: 3-1; Liverpool FC qualify.

28/04/16, Arena Lviv, Lviv (att: 34,267)
FC Shakhtar Donetsk 2-2 Sevilla FC
Goals: 0-1 Vitolo 6, 1-1 Marlos 23, 2-1 Stepanenko 36, 2-2 Gameiro 82(p)
Referee: Marciniak (POL)
05/05/16, Estadio Ramón Sánchez Pizjuán, Seville (att: 41,286)
Sevilla FC 3-1 FC Shakhtar Donetsk
Goals: 1-0 Gameiro 9, 1-1 Eduardo 44, 2-1 Gameiro 47, 3-1 Mariano 59
Referee: Kuipers (NED)
Aggregate: 5-3; Sevilla FC qualify.

Final

18/05/16, St Jakob-Park, Basel (att: 34,429)
Liverpool FC 1-3 Sevilla FC
Goals: 1-0 Sturridge 35, 1-1 Gameiro 46, 1-2 Coke 64, 1-3 Coke 70
Referee: Eriksson (SWE)
Liverpool: Mignolet, Clyne, Touré (Benteke 82), Lovren, Milner, Coutinho, Roberto Firmino (Origi 69), Sturridge, Moreno, Lallana (Allen 73), Can. Coach: Jürgen Klopp (GER)
Sevilla: Soria, Rami (Kolodziejczak 78), Krychowiak, Daniel Carriço, Gameiro (Iborra 89), N'Zonzi, Sergio Escudero, Éver Banega (Cristóforo 90+3), Vitolo, Coke, Mariano. Coach: Unai Emery (ESP)
Yellow cards: Lovren 30 (Liverpool), Vitolo 56 (Sevilla), Éver Banega 57 (Sevilla), Origi 72 (Liverpool), Rami 77 (Sevilla), Mariano 84 (Sevilla), Clyne 90+4 (Liverpool)

Top goalscorers

10	Aritz Aduriz (Athletic)
9	Cédric Bakambu (Villarreal)
8	Pierre-Emerick Aubameyang (Dortmund)
	Kevin Gameiro (Sevilla)
6	Raúl Bobadilla (Augsburg)
	Erik Lamela (Tottenham)
5	Marco Reus (Dortmund)
	Aleksandr Samedov (Lokomotiv Moskva)
	José Callejón (Napoli)
	Dries Mertens (Napoli)
	Abubakar Oumaru (Partizan)
	Franco Di Santo (Schalke)
	David Lafata (Sparta Praha)

Squads/Appearances/Goals

AFC Ajax

No	Name	Nat	DoB	Aps	(s)	Gls
Goalkeepers						
1	Jasper Cillessen		22/04/89	6		
Defenders						
35	Mitchell Dijks		09/02/93	5		
22	Jaïro Riedewald		09/09/96	6		
23	Kenny Tete		09/10/95	4	(1)	
4	Mike van der Hoorn		15/10/92	1		
2	Ricardo van Rhijn		13/06/91	2		
3	Joël Veltman		15/01/92	5		
26	Nick Viergever		03/08/89	1		
Midfielders						
6	Riechedly Bazoer		12/10/96	3	(1)	
27	Nemanja Gudelj	SRB	16/11/91	6		
10	Davy Klaassen		21/02/93	6		
20	Lasse Schöne	DEN	27/05/86	2	(3)	1
25	Thulani Serero	RSA	11/04/90		(3)	
8	Daley Sinkgraven		04/07/95	1	(1)	
30	Donny van de Beek		18/04/97	1	(1)	1
11	Amin Younes	GER	06/08/93	3	(3)	
Forwards						
32	Václav Černý	CZE	17/10/97		(1)	1
21	Anwar El Ghazi		03/05/95	4	(1)	
7	Viktor Fischer	DEN	09/06/94	6		2
9	Arkadiusz Milik	POL	28/02/94	4	(1)	1
19	Yaya Sanogo	FRA	27/01/93		(1)	

RSC Anderlecht

No	Name	Nat	DoB	Aps	(s)	Gls
Goalkeepers						
1	Silvio Proto		23/05/83	10		
Defenders						
28	Alexander Büttner	NED	11/02/89	2		
3	Olivier Deschacht		16/02/81	10		
30	Guillaume Gillet		09/03/84	6		3
24	Michaël Heylen		03/01/94		(1)	
4	Serigne Mbodji	SEN	11/11/89	9		1
21	Fabrice N'Sakala	COD	21/07/90	3		
14	Bram Nuytinck	NED	04/05/90	2	(2)	
37	Ivan Obradović	SRB	25/07/88	3		
Midfielders						
18	Frank Acheampong	GHA	16/10/93	5	(4)	4
8	Stéphane Badji	SEN	18/01/90	4		
17	Ibrahima Conté	GUI	03/04/91		(3)	
16	Steven Defour		15/04/88	8	(1)	
32	Leander Dendoncker		15/04/95	6		
31	Filip Djuričić	SRB	30/01/92	2	(1)	
27	Mahmoud Hassan	EGY	01/10/94		(1)	
7	Andy Najar	HON	16/03/93	9		1
10	Dennis Praet		14/05/94	9		
31	Youri Tielemans		07/05/97	5	(4)	
Forwards						
93	Imoh Ezekiel	NGA	24/10/93	4	(3)	1
38	Andy Kawaya		23/08/96		(1)	
46	Dodi Lukebakio		24/09/97		(1)	
99	Stefano Okaka	ITA	09/08/89	10		2
9	Matías Suárez	ARG	09/05/88	3	(4)	
26	Idrissa Sylla	GUI	03/12/90		(4)	

APOEL FC

No	Name	Nat	DoB	Aps	(s)	Gls
Goalkeepers						
99	Boy Waterman	NED	24/01/84	6		
Defenders						
11	Nektarios Alexandrou		19/12/83	1	(1)	
25	Rafael Anastasiou		09/06/97	1		
15	Marios Antoniades		14/05/90	5		
5	Carlão	BRA	19/01/86	6		1
23	Iñaki Astiz	ESP	05/11/83	2	(2)	
3	João Guilherme	BRA	21/04/86	3		
28	Mário Sérgio	POR	28/07/81	5		
Midfielders						
4	Kostakis Artymatas		15/04/93	5	(1)	
10	Kostas Charalambides		25/07/81	1	(3)	
8	Tomás De Vincenti	ARG	09/02/89	3		
7	Georgios Efrem		05/07/89	2	(1)	
13	Konstantinos Makrides		13/01/82	2	(1)	
26	Nuno Morais	POR	29/01/84	6		
17	Semir Štilić	BIH	08/10/87	3	(2)	
77	Vander	BRA	03/10/88	5	(1)	
16	Vinícius	BRA	16/05/86	4	(1)	
Forwards						
79	Fernando Cavenaghi	ARG	21/09/83	2	(3)	2
27	Mateusz Piątkowski	POL	22/11/84	2	(2)	
20	Pieros Sotiriou		13/01/93	2		

Athletic Club

No	Name	Nat	DoB	Aps	(s)	Gls
Goalkeepers						
13	Iago Herrerín		25/01/88	12		
Defenders						
24	Mikel Balenziaga		29/02/88	9		
2	Eneko Bóveda		14/12/88	6	(2)	
25	Enric Saborit		27/04/92	1		
16	Xabier Etxeita		31/10/87	9		
4	Aymeric Laporte	FRA	27/05/94	9		
30	Iñigo Lekue		04/05/93	4	(2)	
6	Mikel San José		30/05/89	9		1
Midfielders						
23	Ager Aketxe		30/12/93	1	(1)	
7	Beñat Etxebarria		19/02/87	8		2
10	Óscar De Marcos		14/04/89	8	(1)	
3	Gorka Elustondo		18/03/87	2	(4)	1
5	Javier Eraso		22/03/90	5	(1)	
18	Carlos Gurpegui		19/08/80	3	(1)	
8	Ander Iturraspe		08/03/89	3	(4)	
17	Mikel Rico		04/11/84	3	(4)	
19	Iker Muniain		19/12/92	3	(2)	
22	Raúl García		11/07/86	7	(2)	3
14	Markel Susaeta		14/12/87	8	(2)	2
Forwards						
20	Aritz Aduriz		11/02/81	10	(1)	10
11	Ibai Gómez		11/11/89	1		
15	Iñaki Williams		15/06/94	4	(2)	2
9	Kike Sola		25/02/86	2		1
27	Sabín Merino		04/01/92	4	(4)	1
21	Borja Viguera		26/03/87	1	(3)	

AZ Alkmaar

No	Name	Nat	DoB	Aps	(s)	Gls
Goalkeepers						
16	Gino Coutinho		05/08/82	5		
1	Sergio Rochet	URU	23/03/93	1		
Defenders						
5	Rajko Brežančić	SRB	21/08/89	2		
3	Jeffrey Gouweleeuw		10/07/91	6		
24	Ridgeciano Haps		12/06/93	3		
33	Pantelis Hatzidiakos		18/01/97		(1)	
2	Mattias Johansson	SWE	16/02/92	6		
23	Derrick Luckassen		03/07/95	4	(1)	
14	Jop van der Linden		17/07/90	4		1
Midfielders						
19	Dabney dos Santos		31/07/96	3	(1)	1
20	Thom Haye		09/02/95	2	(3)	
10	Markus Henriksen	NOR	25/07/92	5		2
6	Celso Ortíz	PAR	26/01/89	2	(1)	
38	Thomas Ouwejan		24/06/96	1		
17	Ben Rienstra		05/06/90	5		
8	Joris van Overeem		01/06/94	6		1
Forwards						
7	Guus Hupperts		25/04/92	2	(3)	
9	Alireza Jahanbakhsh	IRN	11/08/93	2	(1)	
18	Vincent Janssen		15/06/94	6		1
21	Robert Mühren		18/05/89		(3)	
11	Muamer Tankovic	SWE	22/02/95	1	(4)	

Asteras Tripolis FC

No	Name	Nat	DoB	Aps	(s)	Gls
Goalkeepers						
1	Tomáš Košický	SVK	11/03/86	1		
21	Konstantinos Theodoropoulos		27/03/90	5		
Defenders						
6	Fernando Alloco	ARG	30/04/86	2	(1)	
18	Konstantinos Giannoulis		09/12/87	4		
30	Dorin Goian	ROU	12/12/80	3		
25	Dimitrios Kourbelis		02/11/93	3	(1)	
27	Braian Lluy	ARG	25/04/89	6		1
3	Athanasios Panteliadis		06/09/87	2	(1)	
15	Khalifa Sankaré	SEN	15/08/84	5		
Midfielders						
23	Facundo Bertoglio	ARG	30/06/90	3	(1)	1
8	Elini Dimoutsos		18/06/88	1	(3)	
86	Ederson	BRA	14/03/86	2		
11	Nicolás Fernández	ARG	17/11/86	2	(2)	
20	Taxiarhis Fountas		04/09/95	2	(2)	
54	Rachid Hamdani	MAR	08/04/85	2	(2)	
62	Walter Iglesias	ARG	18/04/85	6		
10	Manuel Lanzarote	ESP	20/01/84	2	(2)	
19	Anastasios Tsokanis		02/05/91	1	(1)	
13	Georgios Zisopoulos		23/05/84	3	(1)	
Forwards						
99	Apostolos Giannou	AUS	25/01/90	6		1
7	Pablo Mazza	ARG	21/12/87	5		1
12	Vasil Shkurtaj	ALB	27/02/92		(1)	

FC Augsburg

No	Name	Nat	DoB	Aps	(s)	Gls
Goalkeepers						
35	Marwin Hitz	SUI	18/09/87	8		
Defenders						
18	Jan-Ingwer Callsen-Bracker		23/09/84	4		
20	Hong Jeong-ho	KOR	12/08/89	1	(1)	1
16	Christoph Janker		14/02/85	5		
5	Ragnar Klavan	EST	30/10/85	6		
31	Philipp Max		30/09/93	2	(2)	
3	Kostas Stafylidis	GRE	02/12/93	4		
2	Paul Verhaegh	NED	01/09/83	8		1
Midfielders						
10	Daniel Baier		18/05/84	6		
30	Caiuby	BRA	14/07/88	3	(3)	
11	Alexander Esswein		25/03/90	4	(2)	
8	Markus Feulner		12/02/82	3	(2)	
7	Halil Altıntop	TUR	08/12/82	5		1
3	Dominik Kohr		31/01/94	5	(1)	
19	Koo Ja-cheol	KOR	27/02/89	4	(4)	
14	Jan Morávek	CZE	01/11/89		(1)	
15	Piotr Trochowski		22/03/84	3	(2)	2
13	Tobias Werner		19/07/85	3	(2)	
Forwards						
25	Raúl Bobadilla	PAR	18/06/87	5	(2)	6
22	Ji Dong-won	KOR	28/05/91	5	(1)	1
23	Tim Matavž	SVN	13/01/89	4		
9	Shawn Parker		07/03/93		(1)	

FC Basel 1893

No	Name	Nat	DoB	Aps	(s)	Gls
Goalkeepers						
23	Mirko Salvi		14/02/94		(1)	
1	Tomáš Vaclík	CZE	29/03/89	7		
18	Germano Vailati		30/08/80	3		
Defenders						
37	Adonis Ajeti		26/02/97		(1)	
16	Manuel Akanji		19/07/95	1		
26	Daniel Høegh	DEN	06/01/91	2	(1)	
5	Michael Lang		08/02/91	10		1
19	Behrang Safari	SWE	09/02/85	7		
6	Walter Samuel	ARG	23/03/78	6		1
17	Marek Suchý	CZE	29/03/88	9		1
3	Adama Traoré	CIV	03/02/90	1	(2)	
Midfielders						
8	Birkir Bjarnason	ISL	27/05/88	9	(1)	2
77	Jean-Paul Boëtius	NED	22/03/94	3	(1)	1
39	Davide Callà		06/10/84	2	(3)	
10	Matías Delgado	ARG	15/12/82	4	(1)	
33	Mohamed Elneny	EGY	11/07/92	5		2
15	Alexander Fransson	SWE	02/04/94		(3)	
28	Robin Huser		24/01/98		(1)	
22	Zdravko Kuzmanović	SRB	22/09/87	1	(1)	
24	Renato Steffen		03/11/91	3	(1)	
34	Taulant Xhaka	ALB	28/03/91	10		
7	Luca Zuffi		27/03/90	9	(1)	2
Forwards						
38	Albian Ajeti		26/02/97	1	(1)	
36	Breel Embolo		14/02/97	7	(1)	2
11	Shkelzen Gashi	ALB	15/07/88	1	(1)	
30	Cédric Itten		27/12/96		(1)	
21	Marc Janko	AUT	25/06/83	9		2

Bayer 04 Leverkusen

No	Name	Nat	DoB	Aps	(s)	Gls
Goalkeepers						
1	Bernd Leno		04/03/92	4		
Defenders						
2	André Ramalho	BRA	16/02/92		(2)	
13	Roberto Hilbert		16/10/84		(1)	
16	Tin Jedvaj	CRO	28/11/95	3		
21	Ömer Toprak	TUR	21/07/89	1		
5	Kyriakos Papadopoulos	GRE	23/02/92	3	(1)	
4	Jonathan Tah		11/02/96	4		
18	Wendell	BRA	20/07/93	4		
Midfielders						
38	Karim Bellarabi		08/04/90	4		3
19	Julian Brandt		02/05/96	4		
37	Marlon Frey		24/03/96	1	(1)	
10	Hakan Çalhanoğlu	TUR	08/02/94	4		1
39	Benjamin Henrichs		23/02/97		(1)	
23	Christoph Kramer		19/02/91	4		
35	Vladlen Yurchenko	UKR	22/01/94		(1)	
Forwards						
7	Javier Hernández	MEX	01/06/88	3		
11	Stefan Kiessling		25/01/84	3		
27	Robbie Kruse	AUS	05/10/88		(3)	
14	Admir Mehmedi	SUI	16/03/91	2	(2)	

Beşiktaş JK

No	Name	Nat	DoB	Aps	(s)	Gls
Goalkeepers						
29	Tolga Zengin		10/10/83	6		
Defenders						
32	Andreas Beck	GER	13/03/87	6		
22	Ersan Gülüm		17/05/87	5		
3	İsmail Köybaşı		10/07/89	6		
44	Rhodolfo	BRA	11/08/86	6		
6	Duško Tošić	SRB	19/01/85	1	(1)	
Midfielders						
7	Gökhan Töre		20/01/92	4	(1)	1
4	Atiba Hutchinson	CAN	08/02/83	6		
21	Kerim Koyunlu		19/11/93	2	(3)	
20	Necip Uysal		24/01/91	3	(3)	
2	Olcay Şahin		26/05/87	2	(1)	
15	Oğuzhan Özyakup		23/09/92	4	(1)	
17	Ricardo Quaresma	POR	26/09/83	4	(2)	1
5	José Sosa	ARG	19/06/85	5		1
Forwards						
23	Cenk Tosun		07/06/91	2	(4)	2
33	Mario Gomez	GER	10/07/85	4	(1)	2
11	Mustafa Pektemek		11/08/88		(1)	

Borussia Dortmund

No	Name	Nat	DoB	Aps	(s)	Gls
Goalkeepers						
38	Roman Bürki	SUI	14/11/90	2		
1	Roman Weidenfeller		06/08/80	10		
Defenders						
37	Erik Durm		12/05/92	2	(1)	
28	Matthias Ginter		19/01/94	6	(3)	1
15	Mats Hummels		16/12/88	10		1
25	Sokratis Papastathopoulos	GRE	09/06/88	5	(1)	
3	Park Joo-ho	KOR	16/01/87	4		1
26	Łukasz Piszczek	POL	03/06/85	8	(1)	1
29	Marcel Schmelzer		22/01/88	9	(2)	
35	Pascal Stenzel		20/03/96	1		
4	Neven Subotić	SRB	10/12/88	3	(2)	
Midfielders						
6	Sven Bender		27/04/89	7	(1)	
27	Gonzalo Castro		11/06/87	8		1
8	İlkay Gündoğan		24/10/90	4	(2)	
7	Jonas Hofmann		14/07/92	3		
9	Adnan Januzaj	BEL	05/02/95	3	(2)	
23	Shinji Kagawa	JPN	17/03/89	5	(3)	
14	Moritz Leitner		08/12/92		(3)	
10	Henrikh Mkhitaryan	ARM	21/01/89	10	(1)	2
18	Nuri Şahin	TUR	05/09/88	1	(2)	
22	Christian Pulisic	USA	18/09/98		(3)	
11	Marco Reus		31/05/89	10		5
33	Julian Weigl		08/09/95	10	(2)	
Forwards						
17	Pierre-Emerick Aubameyang	GAB	18/06/89	9	(1)	8
20	Adrián Ramos	COL	22/01/86	2	(6)	

Os Belenenses

No	Name	Nat	DoB	Aps	(s)	Gls
Goalkeepers						
24	Ventura		14/01/88	6		
Defenders						
19	André Geraldes		02/05/91	3		
20	Filipe Ferreira		27/09/90	5		
28	Gonçalo Brandão		09/10/86	5		
37	Gonçalo Silva		04/06/91	2	(1)	
13	João Afonso		11/02/82	2		
2	João Amorim		26/07/92	4		
4	Tonel		13/04/80	3	(1)	
Midfielders						
8	André Sousa		09/07/90	5		
22	Carlos Martins		29/04/82	3	(1)	
7	Miguel Rosa		13/01/89	1		
18	Ricardo Dias		25/02/91	2	(2)	
6	Rúben Pinto		24/04/92	6		
10	Tiago Silva		02/06/93	3		
Forwards						
14	Dálcio		22/05/96		(3)	
92	Fábio Nunes		24/07/92		(3)	
17	Fábio Sturgeon		04/02/94	6		
12	Kuca	CPV	02/08/89	4	(2)	1
99	Luís Leal		29/05/87	5	(1)	1
9	Tiago Caeiro		29/03/84	1	(4)	

FC Girondins de Bordeaux

No	Name	Nat	DoB	Aps	(s)	Gls
Goalkeepers						
16	Cédric Carrasso		30/12/81	5		
30	Jérôme Prior		08/08/95	1		
Defenders						
3	Diego Contento	GER	01/05/90	3		
2	Milan Gajić	SRB	28/01/96	1		
26	Frédéric Guilbert		24/12/94	2	(1)	
4	Pablo	BRA	21/06/91	1		
5	Nicolas Pallois		19/09/87	4		
29	Maxime Poundjé		16/08/92	3		
6	Lamine Sané	SEN	22/03/87	3	(1)	
21	Cédric Yambéré		06/11/90	4		
Midfielders						
17	André Biyogo Poko	GAB	01/01/93	5	(1)	
11	Clément Chantôme		11/09/87	5		
24	Wahbi Khazri	TUN	08/02/91	1	(3)	
31	Robin Maulun		23/11/96	1		
19	Nicolas Maurice-Belay		19/04/85	2	(2)	
37	Adam Ounas		11/11/96		(2)	
18	Jaroslav Plašil	CZE	05/01/82	3	(1)	
10	Henri Saivet		26/10/90	4	(1)	1
28	Kévin Soni	CMR	17/04/98		(1)	
7	Abdou Traoré	MLI	17/01/88	1		
23	Valentin Vada	ARG	06/03/96	1		
Forwards						
27	Enzo Crivelli		06/02/95	3	(3)	
14	Cheick Diabaté	MLI	25/04/88	2	(1)	
20	Jussiê	BRA	19/09/83	3	(1)	1
12	Isaac Kiese Thelin	SWE	24/06/92	1		
15	Gaëtan Laborde		03/05/94	1		1
9	Diego Rolán	URU	24/03/93	4		1
13	Thomas Touré	CIV	27/12/93	2		1

SC Braga

No	Name	Nat	DoB	Aps	(s)	Gls
Goalkeepers						
92	Matheus	BRA	29/03/92	12		
Defenders						
6	André Pinto		05/10/89	5	(2)	
32	Arghus	BRA	19/01/88	1		
15	Baiano	BRA	23/02/87	8		
5	Willy Boly	FRA	03/02/91	11	(1)	
16	Djavan	BRA	31/12/87	5		
87	Marcelo Goiano	BRA	13/10/87	10		
24	Ricardo Ferreira		25/11/92	7	(2)	1
Midfielders						
30	Alan	BRA	19/09/79	7		1
21	Filipe Augusto	BRA	12/08/93		(3)	
27	Josué		17/09/90	4	(1)	2
8	Luíz Carlos	BRA	05/07/85	8	(2)	
63	Mauro	BRA	31/10/90	5	(2)	
23	Pedro Santos		22/04/88	1	(7)	
4	Rafa Silva		17/05/93	12		3
35	Nikola Vukčević	MNE	13/12/91	11		
Forwards						
9	Crislan	BRA	13/03/92	1	(4)	1
20	Ahmed Hassan	EGY	05/03/93	11		3
17	Rui Fonte		23/04/90	5	(2)	
19	Nikola Stoiljković	SRB	17/08/92	4	(2)	3
7	Wilson Eduardo		08/07/90	4	(6)	2

Celtic FC

No	Name	Nat	DoB	Aps	(s)	Gls
Goalkeepers						
1	Craig Gordon		31/12/82	6		
Defenders						
4	Efe Ambrose	NGA	18/10/88	2	(1)	
2	Tyler Blackett	ENG	02/04/94		(3)	
20	Dedryck Boyata	BEL	28/11/90	6		
3	Emilio Izaguirre	HON	10/05/86	2	(1)	
22	Saidy Janko	SUI	22/10/95		(1)	
23	Mikael Lustig	SWE	13/12/86	6		1
21	Charlie Mulgrew		06/03/86		(1)	
5	Jozo Šimunović	CRO	04/08/94	4		
63	Kieran Tierney		05/06/97	4		
Midfielders						
19	Scott Allan		28/11/91	1	(1)	
14	Stuart Armstrong		30/03/92	4	(1)	
6	Nir Biton	ISR	30/10/91	5		1
8	Scott Brown		25/06/85	3		
15	Kris Commons		30/08/83	4	(1)	4
49	James Forrest		07/07/91	3	(2)	
25	Stefan Johansen	NOR	08/01/91	5		
16	Gary Mackay-Steven		31/08/90	1	(1)	
42	Callum McGregor		14/06/93	2		1
18	Tom Rogic	AUS	16/12/92	2	(2)	
Forwards						
9	Leigh Griffiths		20/08/90	5		1
7	Nadir Çiftçi	TUR	12/02/92	1	(2)	

Club Brugge KV

No	Name	Nat	DoB	Aps	(s)	Gls
Goalkeepers						
16	Sébastien Bruzzese		01/03/89	5		
38	Sinan Bolat	TUR	03/09/88	1		
Defenders						
28	Laurens De Bock		07/11/92	3	(1)	
2	Davy De Fauw		08/07/81	4	(1)	1
24	Stefano Denswil	NED	07/05/93	4		
4	Óscar Duarte	CRC	03/06/89	2		
40	Björn Engels		15/09/94		(1)	
44	Brandon Mechele		28/01/93	6		
7	Thomas Meunier		12/09/91	5	(1)	2
Midfielders						
63	Boli Bolingoli-Mbombo		01/07/95	2	(1)	
6	Claudemir	BRA	27/03/88	2	(1)	
18	Felipe Gedoz	BRA	12/07/93	3		
8	Lior Refaelov	ISR	26/04/86		(1)	
3	Timmy Simons		11/12/76	5		
20	Hans Vanaken		24/08/92	2	(2)	
7	Víctor Vázquez	ESP	20/01/87	4		
25	Ruud Vormer	NED	11/05/88	4		
Forwards						
10	Abdoulay Diaby	MLI	21/05/91	4	(1)	
55	Tuur Dierckx		09/05/95		(2)	
22	José Izquierdo	COL	07/07/92	4	(1)	
17	Leandro Pereira	BRA	13/07/91	3	(3)	
9	Jelle Vossen		22/03/89	3	(2)	1

FC Dinamo Minsk

No	Name	Nat	DoB	Aps	(s)	Gls
Goalkeepers						
30	Aleksandr Gutor		18/04/89	5		
35	Sergei Ignatovich		29/06/92	1		
Defenders						
17	Umaru Bangura	SLE	07/10/87	6		
22	Roman Begunov		22/03/93	6		
32	Mohamed El Monir	LBY	08/04/92	1	(4)	1
6	Sergei Politevich		09/04/90	6		
20	Oleg Veretilo		10/07/88	1	(1)	
3	Maksim Vitus		11/02/89	4	(1)	1
Midfielders						
88	Nenad Adamović	SRB	12/01/89	4	(2)	1
10	Vladimir Korytko		06/07/79	5	(1)	
18	Nikita Korzun		06/03/95	5		
9	Sergiu Neacşa	ROU	03/09/91	1		
5	Kirill Premudrov		11/06/92	4		
28	Yan Tigorev		10/03/84		(1)	
15	Chigozie Udoji	NGA	16/07/86	5		
2	Ihor Voronkov	UKR	24/04/81	3	(2)	
23	Yaroslav Yarotski		28/03/96		(1)	
77	Artur Yedigaryan	ARM	26/06/87		(1)	
Forwards						
21	Fatos Bećiraj	MNE	05/05/88	6		
19	Vitali Bulyga		12/01/80		(1)	
8	Hleb Rassadkin		05/04/95	3	(2)	

FC Dnipro Dnipropetrovsk

No	Name	Nat	DoB	Aps	(s)	Gls
Goalkeepers						
71	Denys Boyko		29/01/88	6		
Defenders						
36	Anderson Pico	BRA	04/11/88	1	(2)	
15	Dmytro Chygrynskiy		07/11/86	2		
23	Douglas	BRA	04/04/90	5		
44	Artem Fedetskiy		26/04/85	6		
30	Papa Gueye	SEN	07/06/84	6		
12	Léo Matos	BRA	02/04/86	6		
Midfielders						
10	Roman Bezus		26/09/90	1	(3)	
20	Bruno Gama	POR	15/11/87	2	(4)	1
14	Yevhen Cheberyachko		19/06/83	2	(1)	
6	Danilo	BRA	13/01/90	1	(1)	
8	Edmar		16/06/80	5		
25	Valeriy Fedorchuk		05/10/88	3		
24	Valeriy Luchkevych		11/01/96		(3)	
29	Ruslan Rotan		29/10/81	4		
7	John Jairo Ruiz	CRC	10/01/94	1	(1)	
28	Yevhen Shakhov		30/11/90	1	(1)	1
22	Ivan Tomečak	CRO	07/12/89	3	(1)	
Forwards						
99	Matheus	BRA	15/01/83	6		2
11	Yevhen Seleznyov		20/07/85	5		2
18	Roman Zozulya		17/11/89		(1)	

Fenerbahçe SK

No	Name	Nat	DoB	Aps	(s)	Gls
Goalkeepers						
40	Fabiano	BRA	29/02/88	7		
1	Volkan Demirel		27/10/81	3		
Defenders						
53	Abdoulaye Ba	SEN	01/01/91	2	(1)	
22	Bruno Alves	POR	27/11/81	9		
88	Caner Erkin		04/10/88	5	(1)	
77	Gökhan Gönül		04/01/85	6		
3	Hasan Ali Kaldırım		09/12/89	5		
24	Michal Kadlec	CZE	13/12/84	1	(4)	
4	Simon Kjær	DEN	26/03/89	8		
19	Şener Özbayraklı		23/01/90	4	(1)	
Midfielders						
26	Alper Potuk		08/04/91	5	(4)	1
10	Diego	BRA	28/02/85	5	(1)	
50	Lazar Marković	SRB	02/03/94	2		1
5	Mehmet Topal		03/03/86	9		2
8	Ozan Tufan		23/03/95	6	(3)	1
14	Raul Meireles	POR	17/03/83	2	(1)	
6	Souza	BRA	11/02/89	8		2
15	Uygar Mert Zeybek		04/06/95		(1)	
20	Volkan Şen		07/07/87	5	(3)	
Forwards						
9	Fernandão	BRA	27/03/87	2	(7)	4
17	Nani	POR	17/11/86	8	(1)	1
11	Robin van Persie	NED	06/08/83	8	(1)	

ACF Fiorentina

No	Name	Nat	DoB	Aps	(s)	Gls
Goalkeepers						
33	Luigi Sepe		08/05/91	6		
12	Ciprian Tătăruşanu	ROU	09/02/86	2		
Defenders						
28	Marcos Alonso	ESP	28/12/90	6	(1)	
13	Davide Astori		07/01/87	8		
3	Gilberto	BRA	07/03/93	1	(1)	
2	Gonzalo Rodríguez	ARG	10/04/84	5		
23	Manuel Pasqual		13/03/82	2	(1)	
32	Facundo Roncaglia	ARG	10/02/87	3		
4	Nenad Tomović	SRB	30/08/87	6	(2)	
Midfielders						
5	Milan Badelj	CRO	25/02/89	4	(3)	
16	Jakub Błaszczykowski	POL	14/12/85	3	(2)	
20	Borja Valero	ESP	12/01/85	6		
14	Matías Fernández	CHI	15/05/86	4	(1)	
72	Josip Iličić	SVN	29/01/88	5	(1)	2
21	Joan Verdú	ESP	05/05/83	2	(1)	
18	Mario Suárez	ESP	24/02/87	3		
6	Tino Costa	ARG	09/01/85	1		
8	Matías Vecino	URU	24/08/91	4	(3)	
Forwards						
30	Khouma Babacar	SEN	17/03/93	3	(2)	2
10	Federico Bernardeschi		16/02/94	5	(2)	4
9	Nikola Kalinić	CRO	05/01/88	3	(2)	1
11	Ante Rebić	CRO	21/09/93	2		
22	Giuseppe Rossi		01/02/87	4		2
7	Mauro Zárate	ARG	18/03/87	1	(1)	

UEFA Europa League

Galatasaray AŞ

No	Name	Nat	DoB	Aps	(s)	Gls
Goalkeepers						
1	Fernando Muslera	URU	16/06/86	2		
Defenders						
23	Lionel Carole	FRA	12/04/91	2		
21	Aurélien Chedjou	CMR	20/06/85	2		
64	Jason Denayer	BEL	28/06/95	2		
28	Koray Günter	GER	16/08/94	1		
22	Hakan Balta		23/03/83	2		
Midfielders						
5	Bilal Kısa		22/06/83		(1)	
15	Ryan Donk	NED	30/03/86	2		
29	Olcan Adın		30/09/85		(2)	
55	Sabri Sarıoğlu		26/07/84	2		1
8	Selçuk İnan		10/02/85	2		
10	Wesley Sneijder	NED	09/06/84	2		
7	Yasin Öztekin		19/03/87	1	(1)	1
Forwards						
11	Lukas Podolski	GER	04/06/85	2		
9	Umut Bulut		15/03/83		(2)	

FC Krasnodar

No	Name	Nat	DoB	Aps	(s)	Gls
Goalkeepers						
31	Andriy Dykan		16/07/77	7		
88	Andrei Sinitsin		23/06/88	1		
Defenders						
6	Andreas Granqvist	SWE	16/04/85	8		
5	Artur Jędrzejczyk	POL	04/11/87	4		
17	Vitali Kaleshin		03/10/80	7		
98	Sergei Petrov		02/01/91	5		
27	Ragnar Sigurdsson	ISL	19/06/86	5		1
3	Stefan Strandberg	NOR	25/07/90	4		
Midfielders						
10	Odil Akhmedov	UZB	25/11/87	8		
13	Vladimir Bystrov		31/01/84		(1)	
8	Yuri Gazinski		20/07/89	1	(6)	
22	Joãozinho	BRA	25/12/88	4	(2)	1
77	Charles Kaboré	BFA	09/02/88	7		
21	Ricardo Laborde	COL	16/02/88	2	(4)	
7	Pavel Mamaev		17/09/88	6	(2)	2
33	Mauricio Pereyra	URU	15/03/90	5		1
4	Dmitri Torbinski		28/04/84	2	(2)	
Forwards						
9	Ari	BRA	11/12/85	5	(2)	1
90	Fedor Smolov		09/02/90	5	(3)	1
14	Wanderson	BRA	18/02/86	2	(2)	2

KKS Lech Poznań

No	Name	Nat	DoB	Aps	(s)	Gls
Goalkeepers						
1	Jasmin Burić	BIH	18/02/87	5		
33	Maciej Gostomski		27/09/88	1		
Defenders						
23	Paulus Arajuuri	FIN	15/06/88	3		
21	Kebba Ceesay	GAM	14/11/87	2		
3	Barry Douglas	SCO	04/09/89	1		
15	Dariusz Dudka		09/12/83	4		
5	Tamás Kádár	HUN	14/03/90	6		
35	Marcin Kamiński		15/01/92	5		
4	Tomasz Kędziora		11/06/94	4		
Midfielders						
14	Maciej Gajos		19/03/91	3	(2)	1
19	Kasper Hämäläinen	FIN	08/08/86	1	(5)	
20	Dávid Holman	HUN	17/03/93	1		
10	Darko Jevtic	SUI	08/02/93	2		
24	Dawid Kownacki		14/03/97	3	(1)	1
7	Karol Linetty		02/02/95	4	(1)	
8	Szymon Pawłowski		04/11/86	2	(2)	
55	Abdul Aziz Tetteh	GHA	25/05/90	3	(2)	
6	Łukasz Trałka		11/05/84	5	(1)	
Forwards						
28	Dariusz Formella		21/10/95	5	(1)	
11	Gergő Lovrencsics	HUN	01/09/88	3	(2)	
18	Denis Thomalla	GER	16/08/92	3	(1)	

FC Groningen

No	Name	Nat	DoB	Aps	(s)	Gls
Goalkeepers						
1	Sergio Padt		06/06/90	6		
Defenders						
5	Lorenzo Burnet		11/01/91	1		
33	Hans Hateboer		09/01/94	5	(1)	
2	Johan Kappelhof		05/08/90	6		
3	Kasper Larsen	DEN	25/01/93	4	(1)	
21	Rasmus Lindgren	SWE	29/11/84	1		
6	Etiënne Reijnen		05/04/87	5		
28	Abel Tamata	COD	05/12/90	5		
Midfielders						
38	Juninho Bacuna		07/08/97		(1)	
17	Jesper Drost		11/01/93		(3)	
23	Hedwiges Maduro		13/02/85	6		1
14	Mimoun Mahi		13/03/94	2	(1)	
10	Albert Rusnák	SVK	07/07/94	6		
22	Simon Tibbling	SWE	07/09/94	5	(1)	
Forwards						
7	Jarchinio Antonia		27/12/90	2	(3)	
8	Michael de Leeuw		07/10/86	2	(2)	
9	Danny Hoesen		15/01/91	4	(2)	1
11	Bryan Linssen		08/10/90	6		

SS Lazio

No	Name	Nat	DoB	Aps	(s)	Gls
Goalkeepers						
99	Etrit Berisha	ALB	10/03/89	5		
22	Federico Marchetti		07/02/83	5		
Defenders						
8	Dušan Basta	SRB	18/08/84	2	(1)	
13	Milan Biševac	SRB	31/08/83	3		
18	Santiago Gentiletti		09/01/85	3	(2)	
2	Wesley Hoedt	NED	06/03/94	8		1
29	Abdoulay Konko	FRA	09/03/84	9		
33	Maurício	BRA	20/09/88	6	(2)	
26	Ştefan Radu	ROU	22/10/86	8		
Midfielders						
20	Lucas Biglia	ARG	30/01/86	5		1
87	Antonio Candreva		28/02/87	5	(4)	2
32	Danilo Cataldi		06/08/94	4	(1)	
10	Felipe Anderson	BRA	15/04/93	6	(1)	2
70	Chris Ikonomidis	AUS	04/05/95	1		
19	Senad Lulić	BIH	18/01/86	3	(3)	
6	Stefano Mauri		08/01/80	3	(3)	
21	Sergej Milinković-Savić	SRB	27/02/95	5	(2)	2
7	Ravel Morrison	ENG	02/02/93	1	(1)	
23	Ogenyi Onazi	NGA	25/12/92	4		1
16	Marco Parolo		25/01/85	7		3
Forwards						
14	Keita Baldé	SEN	08/03/95	3	(2)	
9	Filip Djordjević	SRB	28/09/87	2	(1)	3
88	Ricardo Kishna	NED	04/01/95	3		
11	Miroslav Klose	GER	09/06/78	2	(2)	1
17	Alessandro Matri		19/08/84	7	(3)	

Legia Warszawa

No	Name	Nat	DoB	Aps	(s)	Gls
Goalkeepers						
12	Dušan Kuciak	SVK	21/05/85	5		
1	Arkadiusz Malarz		19/06/80	1		
Defenders						
19	Bartosz Bereszyński		12/07/92	5		
28	Łukasz Broź		17/12/85	3		
17	Tomasz Brzyski		10/01/82	4		
17	Igor Lewczuk		30/05/85	6		
47	Rafał Makowski		05/08/96		(2)	
2	Michał Pazdan		21/09/87	4		
25	Jakub Rzeźniczak		26/10/86	4		
Midfielders						
8	Ondrej Duda	SVK	05/12/94	3	(2)	
37	Dominik Furman		06/07/92	2		
6	Guilherme	BRA	21/05/91	4	(2)	
3	Tomasz Jodłowiec		08/09/85	5		
7	Pablo Dyego	BRA	08/03/94		(1)	
20	Ivan Trickovski	MKD	18/04/87	3	(3)	
23	Stojan Vranješ	BIH	11/10/86	4		1
33	Michał Żyro		20/09/92		(1)	
Forwards						
18	Michał Kucharczyk		20/03/91	5	(1)	
11	Nemanja Nikolić	HUN	31/12/87	4	(1)	
99	Aleksandar Prijovic	SUI	21/04/90	3	(3)	2
9	Marek Saganowski		31/10/78	1	(1)	

Liverpool FC

No	Name	Nat	DoB	Aps	(s)	Gls
Goalkeepers						
22	Simon Mignolet	BEL	06/03/88	15		
Defenders						
2	Nathaniel Clyne		05/04/91	14		
12	Joe Gomez		23/05/97	2		
6	Dejan Lovren	CRO	05/07/89	10		1
18	Alberto Moreno	ESP	05/07/92	12	(1)	
17	Mamadou Sakho	FRA	13/02/90	9	(1)	1
37	Martin Škrtel	SVK	15/12/84	1	(1)	
44	Brad Smith	AUS	09/04/94	1		
4	Kolo Touré	CIV	19/03/81	8		
Midfielders						
24	Joe Allen	WAL	14/03/90	5	(6)	
32	Cameron Brannagan		09/05/96		(2)	
23	Emre Can	GER	12/01/94	13	(1)	1
68	Pedro Chirivella	ESP	23/05/97		(1)	
10	Philippe Coutinho	BRA	12/06/92	11	(2)	2
14	Jordan Henderson		17/06/90	6		
33	Jordon Ibe		08/12/95	4	(2)	1
53	João Carlos Teixeira	POR	18/01/93		(1)	
20	Adam Lallana		10/05/88	11	(2)	3
21	Lucas Leiva	BRA	09/01/87	3	(4)	
7	James Milner		04/01/86	12		2
11	Roberto Firmino	BRA	02/10/91	11	(2)	1
46	Jordan Rossiter		24/03/97	2	(1)	
Forwards						
9	Christian Benteke	BEL	03/12/90	2	(5)	1
28	Danny Ings		23/07/92	1	(1)	
27	Divock Origi	BEL	18/04/95	6	(6)	2
15	Daniel Sturridge		01/09/89	6	(2)	3

Manchester United FC

No	Name	Nat	DoB	Aps	(s)	Gls
Goalkeepers						
1	David de Gea	ESP	07/11/90	2		
40	Sergio Romero	ARG	22/02/87	2		
Defenders						
17	Daley Blind	NED	09/03/90	4		
36	Matteo Darmian	ITA	02/12/89		(1)	
37	Donald Love	SCO	02/12/94	1		
33	Paddy McNair	NIR	27/04/95	1		
41	Regan Poole	WAL	18/06/98		(1)	
49	Joe Riley		06/12/96	1		
5	Marcos Rojo	ARG	20/03/90	2	(1)	
12	Chris Smalling		22/11/89	3		
30	Guillermo Varela	URU	24/03/93	3		
Midfielders						
21	Ander Herrera	ESP	14/08/89	2	(1)	1
44	Andreas Pereira	BEL	01/01/96		(2)	
16	Michael Carrick		28/07/81	3	(1)	
27	Marouane Fellaini	BEL	22/11/87	2		
35	Jesse Lingard		15/12/92	3		
8	Juan Mata	ESP	28/04/88	4		
28	Morgan Schneiderlin	FRA	08/11/89	2	(1)	
31	Bastian Schweinsteiger	GER	01/08/84		(2)	
25	Antonio Valencia	ECU	04/08/85		(1)	
Forwards						
7	Memphis Depay	NED	13/02/94	3		2
9	Anthony Martial	FRA	05/12/95	3		1
39	Marcus Rashford		31/10/97	3		2

FC Midtjylland

No	Name	Nat	DoB	Aps	(s)	Gls
Goalkeepers						
31	Mikkel Andersen		17/12/88	8		
Defenders						
32	Kristian Bach Bak		20/10/82	2		
26	Patrick Banggaard		04/04/94	1		
4	Nikolay Bodurov	BUL	30/05/86	2		
2	Kian Hansen		03/03/89	8		
15	Jesper Lauridsen		27/03/91		(1)	
70	Filip Novák	CZE	26/06/90	8		1
28	André Rømer		18/07/93	6	(1)	
4	Erik Sviatchenko		04/10/91	6		
Midfielders						
8	Petter Andersson	SWE	20/02/85	1		
22	Mikkel Duelund		29/06/97	1		
36	Rilwan Hassan	NGA	09/02/91	2		
19	Marco Larsen		15/05/93		(1)	
45	Awer Mabil	AUS	15/09/95		(2)	
17	Kristoffer Olsson	SWE	30/06/95	6	(1)	
7	Jakob Poulsen		07/07/83	7		
77	Daniel Royer	AUT	22/05/90	6	(1)	
26	Pione Sisto		04/02/95	6	(1)	4
3	Tim Sparv	FIN	20/02/87	8		
Forwards						
14	Václav Kadlec	CZE	20/05/92	1	(1)	
33	Ebere Paul Onuachu	NGA	28/05/94	1	(7)	2
10	Martin Pusic	AUT	24/10/87	3	(4)	1
9	Morten "Duncan" Rasmussen		31/01/85	4		1
11	Marcos Ureña	CRC	05/03/90	1	(4)	

FC Lokomotiv Moskva

No	Name	Nat	DoB	Aps	(s)	Gls
Goalkeepers						
1	Guilherme		12/12/85	8		
Defenders						
14	Vedran Ćorluka	CRO	05/02/86	4		
29	Vitali Denisov	UZB	23/02/87	7		
28	Ján Ďurica	SVK	10/12/81	4	(2)	
15	Arseni Logashov		20/08/91	1		
17	Taras Mikhalik	UKR	28/10/83	3	(3)	
5	Nemanja Pejčinović	SRB	04/11/87	5		
49	Roman Shishkin		27/01/87	5		
55	Renat Yanbaev		07/04/84	3		
Midfielders						
9	Maksim Grigoryev		06/07/90		(3)	
3	Alan Kasaev		08/04/86	3	(2)	
18	Aleksandr Kolomeytsev		21/02/89	5	(2)	
4	Manuel Fernandes	POR	05/02/86	7		
59	Aleksei Miranchuk		17/10/95	1	(5)	1
88	Delvin N'Dinga	CGO	14/03/88	7	(1)	
19	Aleksandr Samedov		19/07/84	8		5
23	Dmitri Tarasov		18/03/87	5		1
Forwards						
7	Maicon	BRA	18/02/90	5	(2)	2
21	Oumar Niasse	SEN	18/04/90	6		4
32	Petar Škuletić	SRB	29/06/90	1	(3)	
96	Rifat Zhemaletdinov		20/09/96		(1)	

Olympique de Marseille

No	Name	Nat	DoB	Aps	(s)	Gls
Goalkeepers						
30	Steve Mandanda		28/03/85	8		
Defenders						
25	Paolo De Ceglie	ITA	17/09/86		(1)	
26	Brice Dja Djédjé	CIV	23/12/90	2	(1)	
2	Javi Manquillo	ESP	05/05/94	3	(1)	
23	Benjamin Mendy		17/07/94	7		
3	Nicolas N'Koulou	CMR	27/03/90	5		
4	Karim Rekik	NED	02/12/94	5		
6	Rolando	POR	31/08/85	4	(1)	
15	Stéphane Sparagna		17/02/95	2	(2)	
Midfielders						
11	Romain Alessandrini		03/04/89	4	(2)	2
19	Abdelaziz Barrada	MAR	19/06/89	3	(3)	1
13	Rémy Cabella		08/03/90	5	(1)	
10	Lassana Diarra		10/03/85	4		
18	Mauricio Isla	CHI	12/06/88	8		
14	Lucas Silva	BRA	16/02/93	4	(2)	
14	Georges-Kévin N'Koudou		13/02/95	6	(1)	4
20	Lucas Ocampos	ARG	11/07/94	4	(2)	2
20	Alaixys Romao	TGO	18/01/84	5		
17	Bouna Sarr		31/01/92		(3)	
24	Florian Thauvin		26/01/93		(2)	
29	André Zambo Anguissa	CMR	16/11/95	1		
Forwards						
22	Michy Batshuayi	BEL	02/10/93	6	(1)	4
9	Steven Fletcher	SCO	26/03/87	2		

Molde FK

No	Name	Nat	DoB	Aps	(s)	Gls
Goalkeepers						
1	Ethan Horvath	USA	09/06/95	8		
Defenders						
15	Per-Egil Flo		18/01/89	3	(1)	
25	Vegard Forren		16/02/88	8		1
4	Ruben Gabrielsen		10/03/92	5	(2)	
14	Martin Linnes		20/09/91	6		1
23	Knut Olav Rindarøy		17/07/85	5		
51	Kristian Strande		03/10/97		(1)	
5	Joona Toivio	FIN	10/03/88	6	(2)	
Midfielders						
17	Fredrik Aursnes		10/12/95	2		
6	Daniel Berg Hestad		30/07/75	7	(1)	1
3	Amidou Diop	SEN	25/02/92		(1)	
19	Eirik Hestad		26/06/95	3	(5)	2
16	Etzaz Hussain		27/01/93	5	(1)	
9	Mattias Moström	SWE	25/02/83	7		
7	Harmeet Singh		12/11/90	6		1
31	Petter Strand		24/08/91		(1)	
Forwards						
21	Agnaldo	BRA	11/03/94		(1)	
27	Mushaga Bakenga		08/08/92		(1)	
30	Pape Paté Diouf	SEN	04/04/86	2		
24	Mohamed Elyounoussi		04/08/94	7		3
8	Fredrik Gulbrandsen		10/09/92	2	(1)	
20	Tommy Høiland		11/04/89	3		1
11	Ola Kamara		15/10/89	2	(4)	1
32	Sander Svendsen		06/08/97	2	(2)	

UEFA Europa League

AS Monaco FC

No	Name	Nat	DoB	Aps	(s)	Gls
Goalkeepers						
1	Danijel Subašić	CRO	27/10/84	6		
Defenders						
42	Raphaël Diarra		27/05/95		(1)	
21	Elderson Echiéjilé	NGA	20/01/88	2	(2)	
2	Fabinho	BRA	23/10/93	5		
4	Fábio Coentrão	POR	11/03/88	3		
24	Andrea Raggi	ITA	24/06/84	5		
6	Ricardo Carvalho	POR	18/05/78	4		
38	Almamy Touré	MLI	28/04/96	1	(1)	
13	Wallace	BRA	14/10/94	4		
Midfielders						
14	Tiémoué Bakayoko		17/08/94	1		
10	Bernardo Silva	POR	10/08/94	6		
7	Nabil Dirar	MAR	25/02/86	1	(2)	
8	João Moutinho	POR	08/09/86	6		
27	Thomas Lemar		12/11/95	2	(2)	
20	Mario Pašalić	CRO	09/02/95	4	(1)	
28	Jérémy Toulalan		10/09/83	5		
23	Adama Traoré	MLI	28/06/95	1		
Forwards						
11	Guido Carrillo	ARG	25/05/91		(4)	
22	Stephan El Shaarawy	ITA	27/10/92	4	(2)	2
17	Ivan Cavaleiro	POR	18/10/93	1	(1)	1
39	Kylian Mbappé Lottin		20/12/98		(1)	
19	Lacina Traoré	CIV	20/08/90	5	(1)	2

SSC Napoli

No	Name	Nat	DoB	Aps	(s)	Gls
Goalkeepers						
22	Gabriel	BRA	27/09/92	3		
25	Pepe Reina	ESP	31/08/82	5		
Defenders						
33	Raúl Albiol	ESP	04/09/85	2	(1)	
21	Vlad Chiricheş	ROU	14/11/89	7		1
31	Faouzi Ghoulam	ALG	01/02/91	3	(1)	
2	Elseid Hysaj	ALB	20/02/94	3	(2)	
26	Kalidou Koulibaly	SEN	20/06/91	7		
96	Sebastiano Luperto		06/09/96		(1)	
11	Christian Maggio		11/02/82	5	(1)	1
3	Ivan Strinić	CRO	17/07/87	5	(1)	
Midfielders						
5	Allan	BRA	08/01/91	2	(4)	
7	José Callejón	ESP	11/02/87	5	(2)	5
94	Nathaniel Chalobah	ENG	12/12/94	2	(1)	1
19	David López	ESP	09/10/89	8		
77	Omar El Kaddouri	MAR	21/08/90	4	(1)	1
17	Marek Hamšík	SVK	27/07/87	5	(1)	2
8	Jorginho		20/12/91	1	(1)	
14	Dries Mertens	BEL	06/05/87	5		5
6	Mirko Valdifiori		21/04/86	7		
Forwards						
23	Manolo Gabbiadini		26/11/91	4	(2)	4
9	Gonzalo Higuaín	ARG	10/12/87	2	(3)	2
24	Lorenzo Insigne		04/06/91	3	(2)	1

Olympiacos FC

No	Name	Nat	DoB	Aps	(s)	Gls
Goalkeepers						
16	Roberto	ESP	10/02/86	2		
Defenders						
3	Alberto Botía	ESP	27/01/89	1		
14	Omar Elabdellaoui	NOR	05/12/91	1		
30	Leandro Salino	BRA	22/04/85	1		
6	Manuel da Costa	MAR	06/05/86	2		
26	Arthur Masuaku	FRA	07/11/93	2		
Midfielders						
91	Esteban Cambiasso	ARG	18/08/80	1		
10	Alejandro Domínguez	ARG	10/06/81		(2)	
21	Jimmy Durmaz	SWE	22/03/89	2		
7	Kostas Fortounis		16/10/92	2		1
11	Pajtim Kasami	SUI	02/06/92	1	(1)	
5	Luka Milivojević	SRB	07/04/91	2		
44	Saša Zdjelar	SRB	20/03/95	1	(1)	
Forwards						
99	Brown Ideye	NGA	10/10/88	2		
17	Alan Pulido	MEX	08/03/91	1	(1)	
92	Sebá	BRA	08/06/92	1	(1)	

PAOK FC

No	Name	Nat	DoB	Aps	(s)	Gls
Goalkeepers						
71	Panagiotis Glykos		10/10/86	4		
25	Robin Olsen	SWE	08/01/90	2		
Defenders						
70	Stilianos Kitsiou		28/09/93	2	(1)	
22	Dimitrios Konstantinidis		02/06/94	2		
4	Marin Leovac	CRO	07/08/88		(2)	
13	Stilianos Malezas		11/03/85	4		
15	Miguel Vítor	POR	30/06/89	3		
20	Ricardo Costa	POR	16/05/81	4		
2	Ioannis Skondras		21/02/90	4		
31	Georgios Tzavellas		26/11/87	5		
Midfielders						
21	Charilaos Charisis		12/01/95	1	(1)	
16	Gojko Cimirot	BIH	19/12/92	1		
7	Eyal Golasa	ISR	07/10/91	1	(1)	
26	Ergys Kaçe	ALB	08/07/93	4		
24	Garry Mendes Rodrigues	CPV	27/11/90	5	(1)	
27	Ioannis Mystakidis		07/12/94	1	(1)	
77	Dimitrios Pelkas		26/10/93	3	(2)	
52	Erik Sabo	SVK	22/11/91	4	(2)	
6	Alexandros Tziolis		13/02/85	5		
Forwards						
33	Stefanos Athanasiadis		24/12/88	2	(2)	
10	Dimitar Berbatov	BUL	30/01/81	3	(2)	
9	Jairo	BRA	06/05/92	1	(2)	
11	Róbert Mak	SVK	08/03/91	5	(1)	3

FK Partizan

No	Name	Nat	DoB	Aps	(s)	Gls
Goalkeepers						
12	Filip Kljajić		16/08/90	2		
1	Živko Živković		14/04/89	4		
Defenders						
6	Gregor Balažic	SVN	12/02/88	3		
2	Ivan Bandalovski	BUL	23/11/86	2		
13	Lazar Ćirković		22/08/92	2	(1)	
44	Fabrício	BRA	20/02/90	5		1
3	Nikola Leković		19/12/89	2		
40	Miloš Ostojić		03/08/91	1	(1)	
5	Nemanja Petrović		17/04/92	1	(2)	
19	Aleksandar Subić	BIH	27/09/93	4		
4	Miroslav Vulićević		29/05/85	5		
Midfielders						
10	Stefan Babović		07/01/87	5		
8	Darko Brašanac		12/02/92	4		
14	Petar Grbić	MNE	07/08/88	1	(3)	
22	Saša Ilić		30/12/77		(2)	
21	Marko Jevtović		24/07/93	5		
20	Saša Lukić		13/08/96	2		
11	Nikola Ninković		19/12/94	3	(2)	
91	Alen Stevanović		07/01/91	3		
92	Nikola Trujić		14/04/92	1	(1)	
17	Andrija Živković		11/07/96	5		4
Forwards						
86	Valeri Bozhinov	BUL	15/02/86	1	(3)	
15	Aboubakar Oumarou	CMR	04/01/87	5		5
33	Ivan Šaponjić		02/08/97	1	(2)	

FC Porto

No	Name	Nat	DoB	Aps	(s)	Gls
Goalkeepers						
1	Iker Casillas	ESP	20/05/81	2		
Defenders						
14	José Ángel	ESP	05/09/89	2		
21	Miguel Layún	MEX	25/06/88	2		
5	Iván Marcano	ESP	23/06/87	1		
3	Bruno Martins Indi	NED	08/02/92	1		
2	Maxi Pereira	URU	08/06/84	1		
Midfielders						
20	André André		26/08/89		(1)	
8	Yacine Brahimi	ALG	08/02/90	1	(1)	
22	Danilo Pereira		09/09/91	1		
15	Evandro	BRA	23/08/86	1	(1)	
16	Héctor Herrera	MEX	19/04/90	1	(1)	
6	Rúben Neves		13/03/97	2		
13	Sérgio Oliveira		02/06/92	1		
Forwards						
9	Vincent Aboubakar	CMR	22/01/92	2		
7	Moussa Marega	MLI	14/04/91	2		
39	Suk Hyun-jun	KOR	29/06/91		(2)	
7	Silvestre Varela		02/02/85	2		

Qarabağ FK

No	Name	Nat	DoB	Aps	(s)	Gls
Goalkeepers						
13	Ibrahim Šehić	BIH	02/09/88	6		
Defenders						
25	Ansi Agolli	ALB	11/10/82	5		
55	Bädavi Hüseynov		11/07/91	6		
5	Maksim Medvedev		29/09/89	6		
18	İlqar Qurbanov		25/04/86	1		
14	Räşad F Sadıqov		16/06/82	6		
32	Elvin Yunuszadä		22/08/92		(1)	
Midfielders						
70	Chumbinho	BRA	21/09/86	1	(3)	
10	Dani Quintana	ESP	08/03/87	6		1
91	Coşqun Diniyev		13/09/95		(1)	
67	Alharbi El Jadeyaoui	MAR	08/08/86	3	(1)	
22	Äfran İsmayılov		08/10/88	5	(1)	
11	Elvin Mämmädov		18/07/88		(2)	
8	Míchel	ESP	08/11/85		(2)	
2	Qara Qarayev		12/10/92	6		
20	Richard	BRA	20/03/89	6		2
77	Cavid Tağıyev		22/07/92	2	(1)	
Forwards						
90	Samuel Armenteros	SWE	27/05/90	4	(2)	1
29	Rydell Poepon	NED	28/08/87	1	(3)	
9	Reynaldo	BRA	24/08/89	2		

SK Rapid Wien

No	Name	Nat	DoB	Aps	(s)	Gls
Goalkeepers						
1	Ján Novota	SVK	29/11/83	5		
30	Richard Strebinger		14/02/93	3	(1)	
Defenders						
24	Stephan Auer		11/01/91	1	(1)	
17	Christopher Dibon		02/11/90	5		
20	Maximilian Hofmann		07/08/93	5	(2)	1
22	Mario Pavelic		19/09/93	8		
6	Mario Sonnleitner		08/10/86	6		
23	Stefan Stangl		20/10/91	6	(1)	
39	Maximilian Wöber		04/02/98	1		
Midfielders						
15	Srdjan Grahovac	BIH	19/09/92	3	(4)	
11	Steffen Hofmann	GER	09/09/80	7		3
18	Philipp Huspek		05/02/91		(2)	
14	Florian Kainz		24/10/92	7		
29	Thomas Murg		14/11/94	1	(1)	
5	Thanos Petsos	GRE	05/06/91	6		1
10	Louis Schaub		29/12/94	3	(1)	1
7	Philipp Schobesberger		10/12/93	3	(3)	2
8	Stefan Schwab		27/09/90	8		1
Forwards						
33	Deni Alar		18/01/90	2	(2)	
9	Matej Jelić	CRO	05/11/90	3	(4)	1
38	Philipp Prosenik		03/03/93	5	(2)	

FC Rubin

No	Name	Nat	DoB	Aps	(s)	Gls
Goalkeepers						
1	Sergei Ryzhikov		19/09/80	6		
Defenders						
21	Guillermo Cotugno	URU	12/03/95	1	(1)	
88	Ruslan Kambolov		01/01/90	6		
2	Oleg Kuzmin		09/05/81	4		
5	Solomon Kverkvelia	GEO	06/02/92	6		
3	Elmir Nabiullin		08/03/95	6		
49	Vitali Ustinov		03/05/91	1	(2)	1
Midfielders						
85	Ilzat Akhmetov		31/12/97		(2)	
14	Diniyar Bilyaletdinov		27/02/85	1	(3)	
10	Carlos Eduardo	BRA	18/07/87	6		
77	Blagoy Georgiev	BUL	21/12/81	5		1
61	Gökdeniz Karadeniz	TUR	11/01/80	3		
15	Sergei Kislyak	BLR	06/08/87	4		
27	Magomed Ozdoev		05/11/92	4	(2)	
Forwards						
11	Marko Dević	UKR	27/10/83	5	(1)	2
22	Vladimir Dyadyun		12/07/88		(5)	
99	Maksim Kanunnikov		14/07/91	6		2
7	Igor Portnyagin		07/01/89	2	(1)	

Qäbälä FK

No	Name	Nat	DoB	Aps	(s)	Gls
Goalkeepers						
22	Dmytro Bezotosniy	UKR	15/11/83	4		
33	Dawid Pietrzkiewicz	POL	09/02/88	1		
1	Andrey Popoviç		04/04/92	1		
Defenders						
21	Arif Daşdämirov		10/02/87	6		
8	Mähämmäd Mirzäbäyov		16/11/90		(1)	
44	Rafael Santos	BRA	10/11/84	3		
20	Ricardinho	BRA	09/09/84	6		
3	Vojislav Stanković	SRB	22/09/87	6		
15	Vitaliy Vernydub	UKR	17/10/87	4		
Midfielders						
4	Elvin Camalov		04/02/95		(2)	
70	Vaqif Cavadov		25/05/89		(1)	
10	Dodô	BRA	16/10/87	5		2
19	Olexiy Gai	UKR	06/11/82	6		
88	David Meza	PAR	15/08/88	5		
32	Facundo Pereyra	ARG	03/09/87	3	(2)	
6	Räşad A Sadiqov		08/10/83	1	(3)	
66	Samir Zärgärov		29/08/86	1	(5)	
Forwards						
69	Olexiy Antonov	UKR	08/05/86	6		
7	Ermin Zec	BIH	18/02/88	2	(3)	
9	Sergei Zenjov	EST	20/04/89	6		

Rosenborg BK

No	Name	Nat	DoB	Aps	(s)	Gls
Goalkeepers						
1	André Hansen		17/12/89	5		
12	Alexander Lund Hansen		06/10/82	1		
Defenders						
14	Johan Lædre Bjørdal		05/05/86	3	(1)	
3	Mikael Dorsin	SWE	06/10/81	2		
5	Hólmar Örn Eyjólfsson	ISL	06/08/90	5		
4	Tore Reginiussen		10/04/86	1		
16	Jørgen Skjelvik		05/07/91	6		
22	Jonas Svensson		06/03/93	6		1
Midfielders						
7	Mike Jensen	DEN	19/02/88	5	(1)	
24	Anders Konradsen		18/07/90	3	(3)	
21	Fredrik Midtsjø		11/08/93	5		
20	Ole Kristian Selnæs		07/07/94	6		
32	John Hou Sæter		13/01/98		(1)	
Forwards						
19	Yann-Erik de Lanlay		14/05/92	2	(3)	
23	Pål André Helland		04/01/90	5		
11	Tobias Mikkelsen	DEN	18/09/86	4	(2)	1
15	Alexander Søderlund		03/08/87	6		2
10	Matthías Vilhjálmsson	ISL	30/01/87	1	(3)	

AS Saint-Étienne

No	Name	Nat	DoB	Aps	(s)	Gls
Goalkeepers						
30	Jessy Moulin		13/01/86	1		
16	Stéphane Ruffier		27/09/86	7		
Defenders						
32	Benoît Assou-Ekotto	CMR	24/03/84	4		
26	Moustapha Bayal Sall	SEN	30/11/85	4	(1)	3
20	Jonathan Brison		07/02/83	1		
29	François Clerc		18/04/83	5		
39	Benjamin Karamoko		17/05/95	1		
24	Loïc Perrin		07/08/85	5		
17	Florentin Pogba	GUI	19/08/90	5		
3	Pierre-Yves Polomat		27/12/93	3	(1)	
2	Kévin Théophile-Catherine		28/10/89	2		
Midfielders						
7	Jean-Christophe Bahebeck		01/05/93	2	(3)	1
17	Jonathan Bamba		26/03/96		(2)	
6	Jérémy Clément		26/08/84	5	(1)	
10	Renaud Cohade		29/09/84	3		
8	Benjamin Corgnet		06/04/87	2	(2)	
28	Ismaël Diomandé	CIV	28/08/92	1	(3)	
15	Erin Pinheiro	CPV	15/07/97		(1)	
15	Valentin Eysseric		25/03/92	4	(1)	1
18	Fabien Lemoine		16/03/87	6		
5	Neal Maupay		14/08/96	1	(1)	
5	Vincent Pajot		19/08/90	4	(2)	
13	Franck Tabanou		30/01/89	2		
Forwards						
27	Robert Berič	SVN	17/06/91	3		2
21	Romain Hamouma		29/03/87	3	(3)	2
22	Kévin Monnet-Paquet		19/08/88	6	(1)	3
9	Nolan Roux		01/03/88	6	(1)	2
4	Oussama Tannane	MAR	23/03/94	2		

FC Schalke 04

No	Name	Nat	DoB	Aps	(s)	Gls
Goalkeepers						
1	Ralf Fährmann		27/09/88	8		
Defenders						
15	Dennis Aogo		14/01/87	3	(2)	
2	Marvin Friedrich		13/12/95		(1)	
4	Benedikt Höwedes		29/02/88	3		
3	Júnior Caiçara	BRA	27/04/89	7		
24	Kaan Ayhan	TUR	10/11/94	2	(2)	
6	Sead Kolašinac	BIH	20/06/93	5	(1)	
32	Joël Matip	CMR	08/08/91	5		1
33	Roman Neustädter	RUS	18/02/88	7		
27	Sascha Riether		23/03/83	1	(1)	
Midfielders						
11	Younes Belhanda	MAR	25/02/90	2		
5	Johannes Geis		17/08/93	7	(1)	1
8	Leon Goretzka		06/02/95	7		
12	Marco Höger		16/09/89		(1)	
23	Pierre Højbjerg	DEN	05/08/95	4	(2)	
7	Max Meyer		18/09/95	3	(4)	1
18	Sidney Sam		31/01/88	1	(3)	
19	Leroy Sané		11/01/96	6	(1)	1
21	Alessandro Schöpf	AUT	07/02/94	1	(1)	
Forwards						
13	Eric Maxim Choupo-Moting	CMR	23/03/89	5	(1)	3
9	Franco Di Santo	ARG	07/04/89	5	(2)	5
25	Klaas-Jan Huntelaar	NED	12/08/83	6	(1)	3

FC Shakhtar Donetsk

No	Name	Nat	DoB	Aps	(s)	Gls
Goalkeepers						
30	Andriy Pyatov		28/06/84	8		
Defenders						
31	Ismaily	BRA	11/01/90	8		
38	Serhiy Kryvtsov		15/03/91	1	(1)	
5	Olexandr Kucher		22/10/82	6		1
18	Ivan Ordets		08/07/92	2	(1)	
44	Yaroslav Rakitskiy		03/08/89	7		1
33	Darijo Srna	CRO	01/05/82	8		1
Midfielders						
10	Bernard	BRA	08/09/92		(5)	
9	Dentinho	BRA	19/01/89		(5)	
74	Viktor Kovalenko		14/02/96	8		2
17	Maksym Malyshev		24/12/92	8		
11	Marlos	BRA	07/06/88	8		2
6	Taras Stepanenko		08/08/89	7		1
Forwards						
41	Andriy Boryachuk		23/04/96		(1)	
22	Eduardo	CRO	25/02/83	2	(6)	3
19	Facundo Ferreyra	ARG	14/03/91	6		2
21	Olexandr Gladkiy		24/08/87	1		
28	Taison	BRA	13/01/88	8		1
7	Wellington Nem	BRA	06/02/92		(5)	

KF Skënderbeu

No	Name	Nat	DoB	Aps	(s)	Gls
Goalkeepers						
1	Orges Shehi		25/09/77	6		
Defenders						
11	Leonit Abazi	KOS	05/07/93	5	(1)	
20	Ademir	BRA	20/09/85	2		
3	Renato Arapi		28/08/86	2	(3)	
5	Bajram Jashanica	KOS	25/09/90	5		1
19	Tefik Osmani		08/06/85	1		
33	Marko Radaš	CRO	26/10/83	5		
32	Kristi Vangjeli		05/09/85	4	(1)	
Midfielders						
23	Bernard Berisha	KOS	24/10/91	6		
87	Djair	BRA	10/02/91		(2)	
30	Esquerdinha	BRA	16/11/90	5		
27	Liridon Latifi		06/02/94	5	(1)	
88	Sabien Lilaj		18/02/89	6		2
8	Bakary Nimaga	MLI	06/12/94	3	(1)	1
7	Gerhard Progni		06/11/86	1	(4)	
10	Bledi Shkëmbi		13/08/79	1	(3)	
Forwards						
99	Peter Olayinka	NGA	18/11/95	5		
14	Hamdi Salihi		19/01/84	4	(1)	

Sevilla FC

No	Name	Nat	DoB	Aps	(s)	Gls
Goalkeepers						
31	David Soria		04/04/93	9		
Defenders						
23	Coke		26/04/87	5	(2)	2
40	Federico Fazio	ARG	17/03/87	1	(1)	
41	Diogo Figueiras	POR	01/07/91		(1)	
5	Timothée Kolodziejczak	FRA	01/10/91	6	(1)	1
25	Mariano	BRA	23/06/86	6		1
3	Adil Rami	FRA	27/12/85	7		1
18	Sergio Escudero		02/09/89	5	(2)	
2	Benoît Trémoulinas	FRA	28/12/85	4		
Midfielders						
14	Sebastián Cristóforo	URU	23/08/93	3	(3)	
6	Daniel Carriço	POR	04/08/88	4	(1)	
19	Éver Banega	ARG	29/06/88	8		
8	Vicente Iborra		16/01/88	3	(4)	1
22	Yevhen Konoplyanka	UKR	29/09/89	2	(4)	
7	Michael Krohn-Dehli	DEN	06/06/83	5	(2)	
4	Grzegorz Krychowiak	POL	29/01/90	5	(1)	
15	Steven N'Zonzi	FRA	15/12/88	7		
10	José Antonio Reyes		01/09/83	2		
20	Vitolo		02/11/89	7		1
Forwards						
9	Kevin Gameiro	FRA	09/05/87	7	(2)	8
24	Fernando Llorente		26/02/85	2	(2)	2

FC Sion

No	Name	Nat	DoB	Aps	(s)	Gls
Goalkeepers						
1	Andris Vaņins	LVA	30/04/80	8		
Defenders						
4	Léo Lacroix		27/02/92	7		1
34	Birama N'Doye	SEN	27/03/94	5	(2)	
22	Vincent Rüfli		22/01/88	5		
20	Vilmos Vanczák	HUN	20/06/83	1		
3	Reto Ziegler		16/01/86	7		
31	Elsad Zverotić	MNE	31/10/86	6		
Midfielders						
10	Carlitos	POR	06/09/82	8		
7	Edimilson Fernandes		15/04/96	8		
94	Daniel Follonier		18/01/94		(4)	
92	Joaquim Adão	ANG	14/07/92		(1)	
8	Xavier Kouassi	CIV	28/12/89	3		
17	Pa Modou	GAM	26/12/89	6		
63	Geoffrey Mujangi Bia	BEL	12/08/89	1	(5)	
8	Veroljub Salatic		14/11/85	8		
11	Martin Zeman	CZE	28/03/89		(2)	
Forwards						
21	Ebenezer Assifuah	GHA	03/07/93	7	(1)	1
33	Theofanis Gekas	GRE	23/05/80	1	(1)	2
12	Grégory Karlen		30/01/95		(2)	
14	Moussa Konaté	SEN	03/04/93	7		3

FC Slovan Liberec

No	Name	Nat	DoB	Aps	(s)	Gls
Goalkeepers						
21	Tomáš Koubek		26/08/92	6		
Defenders						
26	Lukáš Bartošák		03/07/90	6		
5	Vladimír Coufal		22/08/92	6		1
11	David Hovorka		07/08/93	4		
18	Jan Mudra		22/01/90		(1)	
29	Lukáš Pokorný		05/07/93	5		
13	Ondřej Švejdík		03/12/82	4		
Midfielders						
24	Daniel Bartl		05/07/89	1	(2)	
15	Dmitri Efremov	RUS	01/04/95	5		1
10	Zdeněk Folprecht		01/07/91	4		
17	Milan Kerbr		10/09/89	1	(4)	
8	David Pavelka		18/05/91	5		
12	Isaac Sackey	GHA	04/04/94		(1)	
9	Herolind Shala	ALB	01/02/92	6		
22	Soune Soungole	CIV	26/02/95	1		
23	Josef Šural		30/05/90	4	(1)	1
6	Jan Sýkora		29/12/93	2	(3)	
Forwards						
27	Marek Bakoš	SVK	15/04/83	5	(1)	1
19	Kevin Luckassen	NED	27/07/93		(1)	1
7	Michael Rabušic		17/09/89	1	(4)	

AC Sparta Praha

No	Name	Nat	DoB	Aps	(s)	Gls
Goalkeepers						
35	David Bičík		06/04/81	11		
1	Marek Štěch		28/01/90	1		
Defenders						
5	Jakub Brabec		06/08/92	10		3
25	Mario Holek		28/10/86	7	(2)	
29	Matěj Hybš		03/01/93	4		
15	Radoslav Kováč		27/11/79	1	(1)	
11	Lukáš Mareček		17/04/90	11	(1)	1
26	Costa Nhamoinesu	ZIM	06/01/86	11		
17	Markus Steinhöfer	GER	07/03/86		(1)	
16	Ondřej Zahustel		18/06/91	4		
Midfielders						
9	Bořek Dočkal		30/09/88	12		2
14	Martin Frýdek		24/03/92	9		2
22	Josef Hušbauer		16/03/90	1	(1)	
24	Petr Jiráček		02/03/86	4	(1)	
18	Tiémoko Konaté	CIV	03/03/90	4	(6)	
23	Ladislav Krejčí		05/07/92	11		2
20	Francis Litsingi	CGO	10/09/86		(1)	
8	Marek Matějovský		20/12/81	6	(4)	
6	Lukáš Vácha		13/05/89	6		
Forwards						
7	Kehinde Fatai	NGA	19/02/90	8	(4)	3
30	Lukáš Juliš		02/12/94	5	(4)	3
21	David Lafata		18/09/81	6	(3)	5

Tottenham Hotspur FC

No	Name	Nat	DoB	Aps	(s)	Gls
Goalkeepers						
1	Hugo Lloris	FRA	26/12/86	9		
13	Michel Vorm	NED	20/10/83	1		
Defenders						
4	Toby Alderweireld	BEL	02/03/89	10		
33	Ben Davies	WAL	24/04/93	8		
3	Danny Rose		02/07/90	2	(1)	
16	Kieran Trippier		19/09/90	10		
5	Jan Vertonghen	BEL	24/04/87	4		
27	Kevin Wimmer	AUT	15/11/92	6		
Midfielders						
20	Dele Alli		11/04/96	7	(2)	
6	Nabil Bentaleb	FRA	24/11/94		(2)	
28	Tom Carroll		28/05/92	4	(3)	1
22	Nacer Chadli	BEL	02/08/89	5	(1)	1
19	Mousa Dembélé	BEL	16/07/87	1	(3)	1
15	Eric Dier		15/01/94	8	(1)	
23	Christian Eriksen	DEN	14/02/92	7		1
11	Erik Lamela	ARG	04/03/92	7	(1)	6
8	Ryan Mason		13/06/91	6		1
25	Josh Onomah		27/04/97	2	(5)	
17	Andros Townsend		16/07/91	2	(1)	
29	Harry Winks		02/02/96		(2)	
Forwards						
10	Harry Kane		28/07/93	3	(4)	2
14	Clinton Njié	CMR	15/08/93	2	(3)	
7	Son Heung-min	KOR	08/07/92	6	(1)	3

FC Viktoria Plzeň

No	Name	Nat	DoB	Aps	(s)	Gls
Goalkeepers						
13	Petr Bolek		13/06/84	2		
1	Matúš Kozáčik	SVK	27/12/83	4		
Defenders						
22	Jan Baránek		26/06/93	5		
2	Lukáš Hejda		09/03/90	3	(1)	
8	David Limberský		06/10/83	6		
3	Aleš Matějů		03/06/96	2		
21	Václav Procházka		08/05/84	4	(1)	
27	František Rajtoral		12/03/86	4	(1)	
Midfielders						
7	Tomáš Hořava		29/05/88	5		2
17	Patrik Hrošovský	SVK	22/04/92	5		1
26	Daniel Kolář		27/10/85	3	(1)	1
10	Jan Kopic		04/06/90	5	(1)	
19	Jan Kovařík		19/06/88	6		1
29	Tomáš Kučera		20/07/91	2	(1)	
11	Milan Petržela		19/06/83	2	(3)	1
9	Ondřej Vaněk		05/07/90	2		
23	Egon Vůch		01/02/91		(1)	
Forwards						
12	Michal Ďuriš	SVK	01/06/88	4	(1)	1
16	Jan Holenda		22/08/85	1	(4)	1
25	Aidin Mahmutović	BIH	06/04/86	1	(3)	

Sporting Clube de Portugal

No	Name	Nat	DoB	Aps	(s)	Gls
Goalkeepers						
22	Marcelo	BRA	28/11/84	1	(1)	
1	Rui Patrício		15/02/88	7		
Defenders						
13	Sebastián Coates	URU	07/10/90	1		
5	Ewerton	BRA	23/03/89	4	(1)	
4	Jefferson	BRA	05/07/88	4		
21	João Pereira		25/02/84	5		
44	Naldo	BRA	25/08/88	4		
15	Paulo Oliveira		08/01/92	2	(1)	
47	Ricardo Esgaio		16/05/93	3		
35	Rúben Semedo		04/04/94	1		
3	Jonathan Silva	ARG	29/06/94	4		
55	Tobias Figueiredo		02/02/94	4		1
Midfielders						
23	Adrien Silva		15/03/89	4	(2)	
28	André Martins		21/01/90	1	(2)	
6	Alberto Aquilani	ITA	07/07/84	5	(1)	1
11	Bruno César	BRA	03/11/88	1		
30	Bruno Paulista	BRA	21/08/95	2		
36	Carlos Mané		11/03/94	6		
60	Gelson Martins		11/05/95	2	(4)	1
17	João Mário		19/01/93	4	(1)	1
8	William Carvalho		07/04/92	4	(1)	
Forwards						
19	Teófilo Gutiérrez	COL	17/05/85	4	(1)	1
73	Matheus Pereira	BRA	05/05/96	4	(1)	3
10	Fredy Montero	COL	26/07/87	5		3
20	Bryan Ruiz	CRC	18/08/85	4	(2)	3
9	Islam Slimani	ALG	18/06/88	1	(6)	1
8	Junya Tanaka	JPN	15/07/87			

Valencia CF

No	Name	Nat	DoB	Aps	(s)	Gls
Goalkeepers						
25	Mathew Ryan	AUS	08/04/92	4		
Defenders						
23	Aymen Abdennour	TUN	06/08/89	1		
4	Aderlan Santos	BRA	09/04/89	2		1
19	Antonio Barragán		12/06/87	2	(1)	
16	José Gayà		25/05/95	4		
2	João Cancelo	POR	27/05/94	1		
36	Lato		21/11/97		(1)	
5	Shkodran Mustafi	GER	17/04/92	3		
3	Rúben Vezo	POR	25/04/94	3		1
Midfielders						
21	André Gomes	POR	30/07/93	2	(1)	1
12	Danilo	BRA	28/02/96	4		
8	Sofiane Feghouli	ALG	26/12/89	1	(2)	1
18	Javi Fuego		04/01/84	3	(1)	
10	Daniel Parejo		16/04/89	2	(1)	1
28	Tropi		12/05/95		(1)	
Forwards						
37	Rafael Mir		18/06/97		(1)	
7	Álvaro Negredo		20/08/85	4		1
9	Paco Alcácer		30/08/93		(2)	
11	Pablo Piatti	ARG	31/03/89	3		1
17	Rodrigo		06/03/91	3	(1)	2
22	Santi Mina		07/12/95	2		3

Villarreal CF

No	Name	Nat	DoB	Aps	(s)	Gls
Goalkeepers						
13	Alphonse Areola	FRA	27/02/93	5		
1	Sergio Asenjo		28/06/89	3		
25	Mariano Barbosa	ARG	27/07/84	6		
Defenders						
27	Adrián Marín		09/01/97		(2)	
24	Eric Bailly	CIV	12/04/94	7		1
23	Daniele Bonera	ITA	31/05/81	1	(1)	
11	Jaume Costa		18/03/88	7	(1)	
3	Bojan Jokič	SVN	17/05/86	4		
2	Mario Gaspar		24/11/90	10		
5	Mateo Musacchio	ARG	26/08/90	4	(1)	
22	Antonio Rukavina	SRB	26/01/84	10		
6	Víctor Ruiz		25/01/89	14		
Midfielders						
21	Bruno Soriano		12/06/84	12		2
10	Denis Suárez		06/01/94	11	(2)	1
8	Jonathan dos Santos	MEX	26/04/90	7	(3)	1
26	Nahuel		22/11/96	2	(4)	
28	Alfonso Pedraza		09/04/96		(1)	
7	Tomás Pina		14/10/87	6	(1)	1
19	Samu Castillejo		18/01/95	8	(5)	1
7	Samuel		13/07/90	4	(2)	
14	Manu Trigueros		17/10/91	6	(6)	
Forwards						
20	Adrián López		08/01/88	1	(6)	1
17	Cédric Bakambu	COD	11/04/91	11	(2)	9
10	Léo Baptistão	BRA	26/08/92	3	(3)	2
9	Roberto Soldado		27/05/85	12	(1)	6

West London club enjoy repeat triumph in Nyon

Paris Saint-Germain defeated 2-1 in final

Expanded competition incorporates 64 teams

Chelsea retain the trophy

Chelsea FC created an early piece of UEFA Youth League history by becoming the first team to retain the Lennart Johansson Trophy, thanks to a 2-1 victory over Paris Saint-Germain in the Nyon final.

That the Blues accomplished the feat in only the competition's third season – one in which the field doubled in size to 64 teams to include the domestic youth champions of UEFA's 32 best-ranked associations – spoke volumes about the quality of the London club's academy and Adi Viveash's squad.

For four of the starting XI against Paris (Bradley Collins, Jake Clarke-Salter, Temitayo Aina and captain Charlie Colkett) it was a second UEFA Youth League success, the quartet having also featured from the off against Shakhtar Donetsk 12 months earlier.

The result extended Chelsea's run without defeat in the tournament to 15 matches, a sequence dating back to November 2014. Returning semi-finalists Anderlecht seldom threatened to interrupt that run as the Blues eased to a 3-0 victory courtesy of strikes from Kasey Palmer, Colkett and Tammy Abraham, but Paris, who overcame Real Madrid 3-1 in the other last-four tie at

Colovray Sports Centre, offered a sterner test of Chelsea's credentials in the final.

Jean-Kévin Augustin, on target against Madrid, had a first-half penalty saved, the spot kick awarded for a foul by the scorer of the game's opening goal, Fikayo Tomori. Although the French side equalised that 10th-minute strike just before the hour through Yakou Meïté, François Rodrigues' charges conceded again a mere four minutes later when Palmer tucked away Ali Mukhtar's through ball to score what proved to be the trophy-winning goal for the west London side.

Chelsea lift the UEFA Youth League trophy for the second year in a row

Anderlecht were the only one of the semi-finalists whose journey to Switzerland had started in the Domestic Champions path, which featured entrants from Scotland to Kazakhstan and many countries in between, bringing the total number of competing nations to 37. The well-supported team from Brussels survived two autumn knockout rounds along with seven others to make it to round three in February, where those teams hosted the runners-up from the eight UEFA Champions League groups in one-off ties.

Barcelona and Benfica, like Chelsea, were unbeaten in the group stage, from which the eight section winners qualified directly for the round of 16. Indeed, the Lisbon outfit registered 29 goals in their six matches, demolishing Galatasaray 11-1 and Astana 8-0, but their scoring touch deserted them thereafter as they succumbed 2-0 to Madrid after edging out Příbram on penalties in the round of 16.

Atlético Madrid managed 25 goals of their own, but while the Spanish side's campaign ended in a shoot-out defeat to FC Midtjylland in the third round, Roberto Núñez finished the campaign as the competition's leading marksman thanks to a haul of nine goals in his first five games – one more than the final tallies of Chelsea's Abraham and Real Madrid's Borja Mayoral.

Group stage

Group A

15/09/15, Stade Georges-Lefèvre, Saint-Germain-en-Laye
Paris Saint-Germain 0-0 Malmö FF

15/09/15, Estadio Alfredo Di Stéfano, Madrid
Real Madrid CF 4-0 FC Shakhtar Donetsk

30/09/15, Medyk, Morshyn
FC Shakhtar Donetsk 1-4 Paris Saint-Germain

30/09/15, Malmö Idrottsplats, Malmo
Malmö FF 1-0 Real Madrid CF

21/10/15, Stade Georges-Lefèvre, Saint-Germain-en-Laye
Paris Saint-Germain 4-1 Real Madrid CF

21/10/15, Malmö Idrottsplats, Malmo
Malmö FF 5-5 FC Shakhtar Donetsk

03/11/15, Medyk, Morshyn
FC Shakhtar Donetsk 3-1 Malmö FF

03/11/15, Estadio Alfredo Di Stéfano, Madrid
Real Madrid CF 2-0 Paris Saint-Germain

25/11/15, Medyk, Morshyn
FC Shakhtar Donetsk 2-6 Real Madrid CF

25/11/15, Malmö Idrottsplats, Malmo
Malmö FF 0-3 Paris Saint-Germain

08/12/15, Stade Georges-Lefèvre, Saint-Germain-en-Laye
Paris Saint-Germain 5-2 FC Shakhtar Donetsk

08/12/15, Estadio Alfredo Di Stéfano, Madrid
Real Madrid CF 3-0 Malmö FF

		Pld	W	D	L	F	A	Pts
1	Paris Saint-Germain	6	4	1	1	16	6	13
2	Real Madrid CF	6	4	0	2	16	7	12
3	Malmö FF	6	1	2	3	7	14	5
4	FC Shakhtar Donetsk	6	1	1	4	13	25	4

Group B

15/09/15, Sportcomplex de Herdgang, Eindhoven
PSV Eindhoven 0-3 Manchester United FC

15/09/15, AOK stadium, Wolfsburg
VfL Wolfsburg 2-4 PFC CSKA Moskva

30/09/15, Stadium «Oktyabr», Moscow
PFC CSKA Moskva 0-0 PSV Eindhoven

30/09/15, Leigh Sports Village Company, Leigh
Manchester United FC 1-1 VfL Wolfsburg

21/10/15, Stadium «Oktyabr», Moscow
PFC CSKA Moskva 4-0 Manchester United FC

21/10/15, AOK stadium, Wolfsburg
VfL Wolfsburg 4-1 PSV Eindhoven

03/11/15, Leigh Sports Village Company, Leigh
Manchester United FC 0-0 PFC CSKA Moskva

03/11/15, Sportcomplex de Herdgang, Eindhoven
PSV Eindhoven 2-1 VfL Wolfsburg

25/11/15, Stadium «Oktyabr», Moscow
PFC CSKA Moskva 1-2 VfL Wolfsburg

25/11/15, Leigh Sports Village Company, Leigh
Manchester United FC 0-5 PSV Eindhoven

08/12/15, AOK stadium, Wolfsburg
VfL Wolfsburg 0-2 Manchester United FC

08/12/15, Sportcomplex de Herdgang, Eindhoven
PSV Eindhoven 2-1 PFC CSKA Moskva

Christopher Nkunku helped Paris to top Group A

		Pld	W	D	L	F	A	Pts
1	PSV Eindhoven	6	3	1	2	10	9	10
2	PFC CSKA Moskva	6	2	2	2	10	6	8
3	Manchester United FC	6	2	2	2	6	10	8
4	VfL Wolfsburg	6	2	1	3	10	11	7

Group C

15/09/15, Caixa Futebol Campus, Seixal
SL Benfica 8-0 FC Astana

15/09/15, Bahçelievler İl Özel İdare Stadı, Istanbul
Galatasaray AŞ 1-3 Club Atlético de Madrid

30/09/15, Ciudad Deportiva Cerro Del Espino, Majadahonda
Club Atlético de Madrid 1-2 SL Benfica

30/09/15, Kazhimukan Munaytpasov, Astana
FC Astana 0-3 Galatasaray AŞ

21/10/15, Ciudad Deportiva Cerro Del Espino, Majadahonda
Club Atlético de Madrid 7-1 FC Astana

21/10/15, Bahçelievler İl Özel İdare Stadı, Istanbul
Galatasaray AŞ 1-11 SL Benfica

03/11/15, Astana Arena, Astana
FC Astana 0-9 Club Atlético de Madrid

03/11/15, Caixa Futebol Campus, Seixal
SL Benfica 2-0 Galatasaray AŞ

25/11/15, Ciudad Deportiva Cerro Del Espino, Majadahonda
Club Atlético de Madrid 4-0 Galatasaray AŞ

25/11/15, Astana Arena, Astana
FC Astana 0-5 SL Benfica

08/12/15, Bahçelievler İl Özel İdare Stadı, Istanbul
Galatasaray AŞ 3-0 FC Astana

08/12/15, Caixa Futebol Campus, Seixal
SL Benfica 1-1 Club Atlético de Madrid

		Pld	W	D	L	F	A	Pts
1	SL Benfica	6	5	1	0	29	3	16
2	Club Atlético de Madrid	6	4	1	1	25	5	13
3	Galatasaray AŞ	6	2	0	4	8	20	6
4	FC Astana	6	0	0	6	1	35	0

Group D

15/09/15, José Ramón Cisneros Palacios, Seville
Sevilla FC 4-2 VfL Borussia Mönchengladbach

15/09/15, Mini-Stadium, Manchester
Manchester City FC 4-1 Juventus

30/09/15, Fohlenplatz, Monchengladbach
VfL Borussia Mönchengladbach 1-2 Manchester City FC

30/09/15, Stadio Silvio Piola, Vercelli
Juventus 0-1 Sevilla FC

21/10/15, Stadio Silvio Piola, Vercelli
Juventus 2-1 VfL Borussia Mönchengladbach

21/10/15, Mini-Stadium, Manchester
Manchester City FC 1-1 Sevilla FC

03/11/15, Fohlenplatz, Monchengladbach
VfL Borussia Mönchengladbach 3-2 Juventus

03/11/15, Estadio Municipal Manuel Leonardo Ventura, Pilas
Sevilla FC 0-2 Manchester City FC

25/11/15, Stadio Silvio Piola, Vercelli
Juventus 2-1 Manchester City FC

25/11/15, Fohlenplatz, Monchengladbach
VfL Borussia Mönchengladbach 2-2 Sevilla FC

08/12/15, Mini-Stadium, Manchester
Manchester City FC 1-1 VfL Borussia Mönchengladbach

08/12/15, Estadio Municipal Manuel Leonardo Ventura, Pilas
Sevilla FC 1-0 Juventus

		Pld	W	D	L	F	A	Pts
1	Manchester City FC	6	3	2	1	11	6	11
2	Sevilla FC	6	3	2	1	9	7	11
3	Juventus	6	2	0	4	7	11	6
4	VfL Borussia Mönchengladbach	6	1	2	3	10	13	5

Group E

16/09/15, Ulrich Haberland Stadion, Leverkusen
Bayer 04 Leverkusen 1-0 FC BATE Borisov

16/09/15, Campo Agostino Di Bartolomei, Rome
AS Roma 0-0 FC Barcelona

29/09/15, Mini Estadi, Barcelona
FC Barcelona 1-1 Bayer 04 Leverkusen

29/09/15, Gorodskoi Stadion, Borisov
FC BATE Borisov 0-0 AS Roma

20/10/15, Gorodskoi Stadion, Borisov
FC BATE Borisov 0-3 FC Barcelona

20/10/15, Ulrich Haberland Stadion, Leverkusen
Bayer 04 Leverkusen 2-1 AS Roma

04/11/15, Campo Agostino Di Bartolomei, Rome
AS Roma 5-1 Bayer 04 Leverkusen

04/11/15, Mini Estadi, Barcelona
FC Barcelona 2-0 FC BATE Borisov

24/11/15, Mini Estadi, Barcelona
FC Barcelona 3-3 AS Roma

24/11/15, Gorodskoi Stadion, Borisov
FC BATE Borisov 1-1 Bayer 04 Leverkusen

09/12/15, Ulrich Haberland Stadion, Leverkusen
Bayer 04 Leverkusen 0-1 FC Barcelona

09/12/15, Campo Agostino Di Bartolomei, Rome
AS Roma 3-0 FC BATE Borisov

		Pld	W	D	L	F	A	Pts
1	FC Barcelona	6	3	3	0	10	4	12
2	AS Roma	6	2	3	1	12	6	9
3	Bayer 04 Leverkusen	6	2	2	2	6	9	8
4	FC BATE Borisov	6	0	2	4	1	10	2

Group F

16/09/15, Olympiacos FC Training Centre, Piraeus
Olympiacos FC 1-0 FC Bayern München

16/09/15, Hitrec-Kacijan, Zagreb
GNK Dinamo Zagreb 0-2 Arsenal FC

29/09/15, an der Grünwalderstrasse, Munich
FC Bayern München 1-2 GNK Dinamo Zagreb

29/09/15, Meadow Park, Borehamwood
Arsenal FC 3-2 Olympiacos FC

20/10/15, Meadow Park, Borehamwood
Arsenal FC 2-0 FC Bayern München

20/10/15, Hitrec-Kacijan, Zagreb
GNK Dinamo Zagreb 2-2 Olympiacos FC

04/11/15, an der Grünwalderstrasse, Munich
FC Bayern München 1-1 Arsenal FC

04/11/15, Olympiacos FC Training Centre, Piraeus
Olympiacos FC 1-3 GNK Dinamo Zagreb

24/11/15, Meadow Park, Borehamwood
Arsenal FC 1-2 GNK Dinamo Zagreb

24/11/15, an der Grünwalderstrasse, Munich
FC Bayern München 0-1 Olympiacos FC

09/12/15, Hitrec-Kacijan, Zagreb
GNK Dinamo Zagreb 0-1 FC Bayern München

09/12/15, Olympiacos FC Training Centre, Piraeus
Olympiacos FC 2-0 Arsenal FC

		Pld	W	D	L	F	A	Pts
1	GNK Dinamo Zagreb	6	3	1	2	9	8	10
2	Arsenal FC	6	3	1	2	9	7	10
3	Olympiacos FC	6	3	1	2	9	8	10
4	FC Bayern München	6	1	1	4	3	7	4

Group G

16/09/15, Chelsea FC Training Ground, Surrey
Chelsea FC 3-0 Maccabi Tel-Aviv FC

16/09/15, Stadion Dynamo im. Valeriy Lobanovskiy, Kyiv
FC Dynamo Kyiv 2-1 FC Porto

29/09/15, Grundman, Ramat Ha Sharon
Maccabi Tel-Aviv FC 1-1 FC Dynamo Kyiv

29/09/15, Centro de Treinos e Formação Desportiva, Vila Nova de Gaia (Porto)
FC Porto 3-3 Chelsea FC

20/10/15, Centro de Treinos e Formação Desportiva, Vila Nova de Gaia (Porto)
FC Porto 2-0 Maccabi Tel-Aviv FC

20/10/15, Stadion Dynamo im. Valeriy Lobanovskiy, Kyiv
FC Dynamo Kyiv 0-2 Chelsea FC

04/11/15, Chelsea FC Training Ground, Surrey
Chelsea FC 3-1 FC Dynamo Kyiv

04/11/15, Bloomfield, Tel-Aviv
Maccabi Tel-Aviv FC 1-2 FC Porto

24/11/15, Centro de Treinos e Formação Desportiva, Vila Nova de Gaia (Porto)
FC Porto 0-1 FC Dynamo Kyiv

24/11/15, Netanya Municipal Stadium, Netanya
Maccabi Tel-Aviv FC 0-4 Chelsea FC

09/12/15, Chelsea FC Training Ground, Surrey
Chelsea FC 0-0 FC Porto

09/12/15, Stadion Dynamo im. Valeriy Lobanovskiy, Kyiv
FC Dynamo Kyiv 2-0 Maccabi Tel-Aviv FC

		Pld	W	D	L	F	A	Pts
1	Chelsea FC	6	4	2	0	15	4	14
2	FC Dynamo Kyiv	6	3	1	2	7	7	10
3	FC Porto	6	2	2	2	8	7	8
4	Maccabi Tel-Aviv FC	6	0	1	5	2	14	1

Group H

16/09/15, PGB Stadion, Ghent
KAA Gent 0-3 Olympique Lyonnais

16/09/15, Estadio Antonio Puchades, Valencia
Valencia CF 2-0 FC Zenit

29/09/15, Stadion Petrovski, St Petersburg
FC Zenit 0-1 KAA Gent

29/09/15, Plaine des Jeux de Gerland, Lyon
Olympique Lyonnais 1-0 Valencia CF

20/10/15, Minor Sport Arena Petrovsiy, St Petersburg
FC Zenit 3-1 Olympique Lyonnais

20/10/15, Estadio Antonio Puchades, Valencia
Valencia CF 5-1 KAA Gent

04/11/15, PGB Stadion, Ghent
KAA Gent 0-4 Valencia CF

04/11/15, Plaine des Jeux de Gerland, Lyon
Olympique Lyonnais 6-0 FC Zenit

24/11/15, Minor Sport Arena Petrovski, St Petersburg
FC Zenit 0-1 Valencia CF

24/11/15, Plaine des Jeux de Gerland, Lyon
Olympique Lyonnais 4-0 KAA Gent

09/12/15, Estadio Antonio Puchades, Valencia
Valencia CF 1-1 Olympique Lyonnais

09/12/15, PGB Stadion, Ghent
KAA Gent 0-2 FC Zenit

		Pld	W	D	L	F	A	Pts
1	Olympique Lyonnais	6	4	1	1	16	4	13
2	Valencia CF	6	4	1	1	13	3	13
3	FC Zenit	6	2	0	4	5	11	6
4	KAA Gent	6	1	0	5	2	18	3

Rafael Mir was Valencia's top scorer in the competition with six goals

First round

29/09/15, FK Senica, Senica
FK Senica 0-0 Torino FC
21/10/15, Stadio Olimpico, Turin
Torino FC 2-1 FK Senica
Aggregate: 2-1; Torino FC qualify.

29/09/15, FC Minsk, Minsk
FC Minsk 2-2 FC Viitorul
21/10/15, Central Stadium Hagi Academy, Ovidiu
FC Viitorul 5-1 FC Minsk
Aggregate: 7-3; FC Viitorul qualify.

30/09/15, Mini-Estadi - Ciudad Deportiva, Villarreal
Villarreal CF 2-3 Servette FC
21/10/15, Stade de Genève, Geneva
Servette FC 1-2 Villarreal CF
Aggregate: 4-4; Servette FC qualify on away goals.

30/09/15, FK Rad, Belgrade
FK Rad 0-1 NK Domžale
20/10/15, Športni park, Domzale
NK Domžale 0-1 FK Rad (aet)
Aggregate: 1-1; FK Rad qualify 3-2 on penalties.

30/09/15, "Spartak" Academy, Moscow
FC Spartak Moskva 4-0 Ravan
21/10/15, Dalga Stadium, Baku
Ravan 0-0 FC Spartak Moskva
Aggregate: 0-4; FC Spartak Moskva qualify.

30/09/15, Makarion, Nicosia
APOEL FC 3-3 Puskás Akadémia Felcsút
21/10/15, Pancho stadium, Felcsut
Puskás Akadémia Felcsút 6-1 APOEL FC
Aggregate: 9-4; Puskás Akadémia Felcsút qualify.

30/09/15, Stimberg-Stadion, Erkenschwick
FC Schalke 04 2-3 AFC Ajax
21/10/15, De Toekomst, Duivendrecht
AFC Ajax 2-0 FC Schalke 04
Aggregate: 5-2; AFC Ajax qualify.

30/09/15, Na Litavce, Pribram
1. FK Příbram 2-0 FC Zimbru Chisinau
21/10/15, Stadionul Zimbru, Chisinau
FC Zimbru Chisinau 1-2 1. FK Příbram
Aggregate: 1-4; 1. FK Příbram qualify.

30/09/15, Borås Arena, Boras
IF Elfsborg 2-0 Stjarnan
21/10/15, Stjörnuvöllur, Gardabaer
Stjarnan 1-0 IF Elfsborg
Aggregate: 1-2; IF Elfsborg qualify.

30/09/15, Untersberg Arena, Grodig
FC Salzburg 4-0 FK Željezničar
14/10/15, Grbavica, Sarajevo
FK Željezničar 2-1 FC Salzburg
Aggregate: 2-5; FC Salzburg qualify.

30/09/15, Arena Herning, Herning
FC Midtjylland 3-1 FC Saburtalo
21/10/15, Mikheil Meskhi Stadioni, Tbilisi
FC Saburtalo 1-2 FC Midtjylland
Aggregate: 2-5; FC Midtjylland qualify.

30/09/15, Tsentralniy, Aktobe
FC Aktobe 0-2 Beşiktaş JK
21/10/15, Maltepe, Istanbul
Beşiktaş JK 4-0 FC Aktobe
Aggregate: 6-0; Beşiktaş JK qualify.

30/09/15, Helsinki Football Stadium, Helsinki
HJK Helsinki 0-5 Celtic FC
20/10/15, Livingston Arena, Livingston
Celtic FC 1-1 HJK Helsinki
Aggregate: 6-1; Celtic FC qualify.

30/09/15, Auguste-Delaune, Reims
Stade de Reims 5-3 Middlesbrough FC
21/10/15, Riverside, Middlesbrough
Middlesbrough FC 3-0 Stade de Reims
Aggregate: 6-5; Middlesbrough FC qualify.

30/09/15, Brann, Bergen
SK Brann 1-1 RSC Anderlecht
07/10/15, Constant Vanden Stock Stadium, Brussels
RSC Anderlecht 5-0 SK Brann
Aggregate: 6-1; RSC Anderlecht qualify.

30/09/15, Lovech Stadion, Lovech
PFC Litex Lovech 1-2 Legia Warszawa
20/10/15, Wycieczka, Nowy Dwor Mazowiecki
Legia Warszawa 3-1 PFC Litex Lovech
Aggregate: 5-2; Legia Warszawa qualify.

Second round

04/11/15, "Spartak" Academy, Moscow
FC Spartak Moskva 0-3 AFC Ajax
25/11/15, De Toekomst, Duivendrecht
AFC Ajax 2-1 FC Spartak Moskva
Aggregate: 5-1; AFC Ajax qualify.

04/11/15, FK Rad, Belgrade
FK Rad 0-1 IF Elfsborg
25/11/15, Borås Arena, Boras
IF Elfsborg 0-0 FK Rad
Aggregate: 1-0; IF Elfsborg qualify.

04/11/15, Maltepe, Istanbul
Beşiktaş JK 1-0 FC Salzburg
24/11/15, Untersberg Arena, Grodig
FC Salzburg 5-1 Beşiktaş JK
Aggregate: 5-2; FC Salzburg qualify.

04/11/15, Na Litavce, Pribram
1. FK Příbram 2-0 FC Viitorul
25/11/15, Central Stadium Hagi Academy, Ovidiu
FC Viitorul 0-0 1. FK Příbram
Aggregate: 0-2; 1. FK Příbram qualify.

04/11/15, Pancho stadium, Felcsut
Puskás Akadémia Felcsút 1-0 Celtic FC
25/11/15, Livingston Arena, Livingston
Celtic FC 3-0 Puskás Akadémia Felcsút
Aggregate: 3-1; Celtic FC qualify.

04/11/15, Arena Herning, Herning
FC Midtjylland 2-0 Legia Warszawa
24/11/15, Wycieczka, Nowy Dwor Mazowiecki
Legia Warszawa 1-3 FC Midtjylland
Aggregate: 1-5; FC Midtjylland qualify.

05/11/15, Riverside, Middlesbrough
Middlesbrough FC 3-0 Torino FC
24/11/15, Stadio Olimpico, Turin
Torino FC 3-3 Middlesbrough FC
Aggregate: 3-6; Middlesbrough FC qualify.

02/12/15, Stade de Genève, Geneva
Servette FC 1-2 RSC Anderlecht
06/12/15, Van Roy Stadium, Denderleeuw
RSC Anderlecht 2-2 Servette FC
Aggregate: 4-3; RSC Anderlecht qualify.

Third round

09/02/16, De Toekomst, Duivendrecht
AFC Ajax 3-1 Sevilla FC
Goals: 1-0 Dekker 14, 1-1 Nané 36,
2-1 Van de Beek 49, 3-1 Nouri 79

*09/02/16, Constant Vanden Stock Stadium,
Brussels*
RSC Anderlecht 2-0 Arsenal FC
Goals: 1-0 Vancamp 8, 2-0 Vancamp 28

09/02/16, Riverside, Middlesbrough
Middlesbrough FC 5-0 FC Dynamo Kyiv
Goals: 1-0 C Cooke 8, 2-0 Pattison 31,
3-0 Jakupovic 49, 4-0 Coulson 68, 5-0 Wheatley 78

10/02/16, Stadion Salzburg, Salzburg
FC Salzburg 0-4 AS Roma
Goals: 0-1 Marchizza 8(p), 0-2 Umar 17,
0-3 Soleri 39, 0-4 Di Livio 72

Chelsea's Kasey Palmer (right) enjoys his winning
goal in the final

10/02/16, Na Litavce, Pribram
1. FK Příbram 2-2 PFC CSKA Moskva (aet)
Goals: 1-0 Chaluš 13, 1-1 Kuchaev 46,
1-2 Gordyushenko 56, 2-2 Januška 71(p)
1. FK Příbram qualify 5-4 on penalties.

10/02/16, Celtic Park, Glasgow
Celtic FC 1-1 Valencia CF (aet)
Goals: 1-0 Aitchison 40, 1-1 I Martinez 87
Valencia CF qualify 4-3 on penalties.

10/02/16, Arena Herning, Herning
FC Midtjylland 4-4 Club Atlético de Madrid (aet)
Goals: 1-0 Thychosen 32, 1-1 Juan Moreno 37,
1-2 Theo 41, 2-2 Anderson 43, 2-3 Mohedano 51,
3-3 J Thomsen 56, 4-3 Madsen 67, 4-4 Ferni 90+1
FC Midtjylland qualify 5-4 on penalties.

10/02/16, Borås Arena, Boras
IF Elfsborg 1-3 Real Madrid CF
Goals: 0-1 Mayoral 48, 1-1 Kabashi 63,
1-2 Febas 72, 1-3 Mayoral 84

Round of 16

23/02/16, Mini Estadi, Barcelona
FC Barcelona 3-1 FC Midtjylland
Goals: 0-1 Montes 34(og), 1-1 Chendri 51,
2-1 Seungwoo Lee 90, 3-1 Aleñá 90+2

23/02/16, Chelsea FC Training Ground, Surrey
Chelsea FC 1-1 Valencia CF (aet)
Goals: 1-0 Jay DaSilva 44, 1-1 Soler 45+1(p)
Chelsea FC qualify 5-3 on penalties.

23/02/16, Estadio Alfredo Di Stéfano, Madrid
Real Madrid CF 3-1 Manchester City FC
Goals: 1-0 Mayoral 36, 2-0 Mayoral 41,
2-1 Buckley-Ricketts 63, 3-1 Hakimi 87

23/02/16, Constant Vanden Stock Stadium, Brussels
RSC Anderlecht 3-0(f) GNK Dinamo Zagreb

24/02/16, Sportcomplex de Herdgang, Eindhoven
PSV Eindhoven 2-2 AS Roma (aet)
Goals: 1-0 Bergwijn 14, 1-1 Marchizza 49(p),
1-2 Soleri 68, 2-2 Verreth 73
AS Roma qualify 3-1 on penalties.

*24/02/16, Stade Georges-Lefèvre,
Saint-Germain-en-Laye*
Paris Saint-Germain 1-0 Middlesbrough FC
Goal: 1-0 Augustin 41

24/02/16, Na Litavce, Pribram
1. FK Příbram 1-1 SL Benfica (aet)
Goals: 0-1 Sarkic 34, 1-1 Ayong 85
SL Benfica qualify 5-3 on penalties.

24/02/16, Plaine des Jeux de Gerland, Lyon
Olympique Lyonnais 0-3 AFC Ajax
Goals: 0-1 Van de Beek 18, 0-2 Nouri 25,
0-3 Bergsma 51

Quarter-finals

08/03/16, Estadio Alfredo Di Stéfano, Madrid
Real Madrid CF 2-0 SL Benfica
Goals: 1-0 Febas 66, 2-0 Salto 77

08/03/16, Van Roy Stadium, Denderleeuw
RSC Anderlecht 2-0 FC Barcelona
Goals: 1-0 Vancamp 53, 2-0 Bernier 88

*09/03/16, Stade Georges-Lefèvre,
Saint-Germain-en-Laye*
Paris Saint-Germain 3-1 AS Roma
Goals: 1-0 Toure 26, 2-0 Meïté 39, 2-1 Tumminello
75, 3-1 Nkunku 90

15/03/16, Chelsea FC Training Ground, Surrey
Chelsea FC 1-0 AFC Ajax
Goal: 1-0 Scott 44

Semi-finals

15/04/16, Colovray Sports Centre, Nyon (att: 3,280)
Chelsea FC 3-0 RSC Anderlecht
Goals: 1-0 Palmer 21, 2-0 Colkett 56,
3-0 Abraham 75

15/04/16, Colovray Sports Centre, Nyon (att: 4,000)
Real Madrid CF 1-3 Paris Saint-Germain
Goals: 0-1 Hakimi 5(og), 1-1 Mayoral 33(p),
1-2 Kanga 84, 1-3 Augustin 90

Final

18/04/16, Colovray Sports Centre, Nyon (att: 4,000)
Paris Saint-Germain 1-2 Chelsea FC
Goals: 0-1 Tomori 10, 1-1 Meïté 58, 1-2 Palmer 61
Referee: Siebert (GER)
Paris: Descamps, Georgen, Toure, Eboa Eboa,
Doucoure, Demoncy, Nkunku, Edouard (Ikone 62),
Meïté, Augustin (Kanga 71), Bernede (Giacomini
85). Coach: François Rodrigues (FRA)
Chelsea: Collins, Sterling, Tomori, Clarke-Salter,
Aina, Colkett, Maddox, Mukhtar, Abraham, Palmer
(Wakefield 86), Scott (Mount 59). Coach: Adi
Viveash (ENG)
Yellow cards: Tomori 12 (Chelsea), Eboa Eboa
23 (Paris), Scott 40 (Chelsea), Aina 64 (Chelsea),
Clarke-Salter 73 (Chelsea), Meïté 81 (Paris),
Mukhtar 90+3 (Chelsea)

Top goalscorers

9	Roberto Núñez (Atlético)
8	Tammy Abraham (Chelsea)
	Borja Mayoral (Real Madrid)
7	Diogo Gonçalves (Benfica)
	José Gomes (Benfica)
6	Jorn Vancamp (Anderlecht)
	Carles Aleñá (Barcelona)
	Rafael Mir (Valencia)

Pedro strikes in extra time to defeat Sevilla

Bumper crowd in Tbilisi enjoy nine-goal thriller

Record-equalling fifth win for Catalan club

More silverware for Barcelona

2014/15 treble winners FC Barcelona supplemented their trophy collection under coach Luis Enrique as they defeated UEFA Europa League holders Sevilla in an all-Spanish UEFA Super Cup, substitute Pedro Rodríguez scoring in the 115th minute to seal a pulsating 5-4 victory in front of a record 51,490 crowd in Tbilisi.

Pedro, Barcelona's extra-time match-winner against Shakhtar Donetsk in the same fixture six years earlier, repeated the feat after a Lionel Messi free-kick had been blocked and a second shot parried by Sevilla goalkeeper Beto. Nine days later the scorer would leave the Catalan club for Chelsea.

It was Sevilla who took the lead, with the fastest-ever UEFA Super Cup goal. Javier Mascherano brought down José Antonio Reyes and Éver Banega's free-kick was too good for Marc-André ter Stegen. Messi wasted little time in bringing the scores level, converting another free-kick after Grzegorz Krychowiak had fouled Luis Suárez, and on 16 minutes the Argentinian did it again, with another set piece, after Banega had brought down former Sevilla man Ivan Rakitić.

Suárez had a strike ruled out for offside, but before the break Rafinha made it 3-1, sliding the ball in after Suárez had recovered it when his original effort was blocked by Beto. Barça did not relent in the second half and appeared to be out of sight in the 52nd minute when Suárez got his goal, played through after Sergio Busquets had intercepted a defensive pass.

Reyes pulled one back five minutes later, set up by Vitolo, and shortly after the scorer was replaced by new signing Yevhen Konoplyanka, Sevilla reduced the deficit to 4-3, Jérémy Mathieu bringing down Vitolo in the area and Kevin Gameiro smashing in the penalty. Another Sevilla debutant, Ciro Immobile, came on for Gameiro in the 80th minute and soon crossed for Konoplyanka to level and complete the Andalusians' astonishing comeback.

Messi nearly prevented extra time, hitting the post in the final minute with another free-kick. Instead the stage was set for Pedro, enabling Barcelona to claim the trophy for a record-equalling fifth time (alongside AC Milan), while Sevilla finished empty-handed for the second year in a row.

Final

11/08/15, Boris Paichadze Dinamo Arena, Tbilisi (att: 51,940)
FC Barcelona 5-4 Sevilla FC (aet)
Goals: 0-1 Éver Banega 3, 1-1 Messi 7, 2-1 Messi 16, 3-1 Rafinha 44, 4-1 Suárez 52, 4-2 Reyes 57, 4-3 Gameiro 72(p), 4-4 Konoplyanka 81, 5-4 Pedro 115
Referee: Collum (SCO)
Barcelona: Ter Stegen, Piqué, Rakitić, Busquets, Dani Alves, Iniesta (Sergi Roberto 63), Suárez, Messi, Rafinha (Bartra 78), Mascherano (Pedro 93), Mathieu. Coach: Luis Enrique (ESP)
Sevilla: Beto, Trémoulinas, Rami, Krychowiak, Krohn-Dehli, Iborra (Mariano 80), Gameiro (Immobile 80), Reyes (Konoplyanka 68), Éver Banega, Vitolo, Coke. Coach: Unai Emery (ESP)
Yellow cards: Krychowiak 14 (Sevilla), Mathieu 71 (Barcelona), Coke 87 (Sevilla), Éver Banega 90+2 (Sevilla), Immobile 92 (Sevilla), Pedro 94 (Barcelona), Busquets 117 (Barcelona), Dani Alves 120 (Barcelona), Krohn-Dehli 120 (Sevilla)

Barcelona skipper Andrés Iniesta lifts the UEFA Super Cup

Nine automatic qualifying places up for grabs

Germany and Portugal top groups with perfect record

Holders Sweden among six other unbeaten teams

Road to Poland takes shape

Germany and Portugal entered the summer break with perfect records in 2017 UEFA European Under-21 Championship qualifying.

The two teams ended the season with six-point leads over the second-placed nations in their respective sections and were well on the way to becoming the first of the nine group winners to secure automatic places at the finals in Poland, where there will be a 12-strong field for the first time, the final two places being contested in play-offs by the four best runners-up.

Portugal, beaten on penalties in the 2015 final by Sweden, accumulated maximum points from their first six **Group 4** fixtures, registering 23 goals and conceding just one. Rui Jorge's side knew they would qualify by beating Israel, the only country capable of overhauling them, when their campaign resumed on 2 September.

Germany made it a perfect seven in **Group 7**, scoring 26 times, with Leroy Sané, Max Meyer and Davie Selke contributing five goals apiece. Austria, three points adrift in second place, had a game in hand, however, and were still to host the leaders in a potentially decisive final encounter on 11 October.

Austria boasted the competition's leading marksman in Michael Gregoritsch, the Hamburg forward having plundered nine goals in six games, the highlight a hat-trick in a 7-0 defeat of Azerbaijan. Gregoritsch's tally left him one clear of the Czech Republic's Patrik Schick, also the author of a hat-trick, recorded in a 7-0 triumph away to Malta in the pacesetters' last pre-summer assignment in **Group 1**.

Holders Sweden faced Georgia in the season's concluding match on 3 June. Otar Kiteishvili's 89th-minute equaliser looked set to have earned the visitors a 2-2 draw, only for Jordan Larsson, son

Leroy Sané, one of Germany's three five-goal marksmen, in action against the Faroe Islands

of Henrik, to stab in an added-time winner seconds after coming off the bench for his U21 debut. The result left Sweden two points in arrears of **Group 6** frontrunners Croatia, having played a game less.

Like the Czechs, Germany, Portugal and Sweden, four other teams – Italy, Iceland, Denmark and England – also ended the season unbeaten. Italy headed **Group 2,** with third-ranked Serbia – six points behind but with a game in hand – due to be hosted on the early-September resumption. Iceland were also undefeated in **Group 3**. Two points adrift of France in second place, their next outing was a visit to the leaders on 6 September.

In **Group 5**, Denmark held a three-point advantage over nearest challengers Romania, who had played one match more, while Gareth Southgate's England were setting the pace with three wins and two draws from their opening five matches in **Group 9**, one of the two five-team sections. In the other, **Group 8**, Slovakia looked well placed. Although defeated 1-0 by Belarus in their opening game, Pavel Hapal's charges managed to build a three-point advantage over the Netherlands, having prevailed 3-1 away from home in the sides' first meeting.

UEFA European Under-21 Championship

Qualifying round

Group 1

30/03/15, Den Dreef, Louvain
Belgium 2-1 Moldova
Goals: 1-0 Tielemans 14, 2-0 Castagne 45,
2-1 Spataru 50

11/06/15, Stadionul Zimbru, Chisinau
Moldova 0-0 Malta

15/06/15, Gradski Stadion Podgorica, Podgorica
Montenegro 1-0 Moldova
Goal: 1-0 Savićević 40

16/06/15, Daugava, Liepaja
Latvia 1-2 Malta
Goals: 1-0 Stuglis 43, 1-1 Camenzuli 55,
1-2 Montebello 78

04/09/15, District Sport Complex, Orhei
Moldova 1-0 Montenegro
Goal: 1-0 Spataru 31

04/09/15, Strelnice Stadion, Jablonec nad Nisou
Czech Republic 4-1 Malta
Goals: 1-0 Schick 10, 2-0 Schick 21,
2-1 Montebello 37, 3-1 Čermák 40, 4-1 Hrubý 56

04/09/15, Zemgales Olympic Centre, Jelgava
Latvia 0-2 Belgium
Goals: 0-1 Kabasele 5, 0-2 Praet 18

08/09/15, Zemgales Olympic Centre, Jelgava
Latvia 1-1 Czech Republic
Goals: 1-0 Šadčins 53, 1-1 Klobása 85

08/09/15, Gradski Stadion Podgorica, Podgorica
Montenegro 0-0 Malta

09/10/15, Den Dreef, Louvain
Belgium 2-0 Malta
Goals: 1-0 Tielemans 75(p), 2-0 J De Sart 78

11/10/15, District Sport Complex, Orhei
Moldova 0-3 Latvia
Goals: 0-1 Klimaševičs 26, 0-2 Kazačoks 45(p),
0-3 Gutkovskis 54

13/10/15, City Stadium, Uherske Hradiste
Czech Republic 3-3 Montenegro
Goals: 1-0 Havlík 42, 2-0 Čermák 44,
2-1 Raspopović 51, 3-1 Černý 57,
3-2 Janković 65, 3-3 Jovović 81

12/11/15, Strelnice Stadion, Jablonec nad Nisou
Czech Republic 1-0 Belgium
Goal: 1-0 Schick 11

13/11/15, Gradski Stadion Podgorica, Podgorica
Montenegro 3-3 Latvia
Goals: 0-1 Kazačoks 17, 0-2 Kazačoks 52,
1-2 Djordjević 60, 1-3 Gutkovskis 62,
2-3 Djordjević 69(p), 3-3 Savićević 85

16/11/15, District Sport Complex, Orhei
Moldova 1-3 Czech Republic
Goals: 1-0 Havel 13(og), 1-1 Souček 37,
1-2 Rozgoniuc 53(og), 1-3 Barák 81

23/03/16, Stadionul Zimbru, Chisinau
Moldova 0-2 Belgium
Goals: 0-1 Heylen 72, 0-2 Kayembe 90+4

23/03/16, Hibernians Stadium, Paola
Malta 0-1 Montenegro
Goal: 0-1 Kartal 18

25/03/16, City Stadium, Uherske Hradiste
Czech Republic 2-1 Latvia
Goals: 1-0 Schick 22, 1-1 D Ikaunieks 33,
2-1 Schick 48

28/03/16, Den Dreef, Louvain
Belgium 1-2 Montenegro
Goals: 0-1 Lagator 6, 0-2 Savićević 41,
1-2 Bongonda 45

29/03/16, National Stadium, Ta' Qali
Malta 0-7 Czech Republic
Goals: 0-1 Schick 20(p), 0-2 Čermák 25,
0-3 Černý 36, 0-4 Schick 42, 0-5 Havel 57,
0-6 Čermák 75, 0-7 Schick 89

		Pld	W	D	L	F	A	Pts
1	Czech Republic	7	5	2	0	21	7	17
2	Montenegro	7	3	3	1	10	8	12
3	Belgium	6	4	0	2	9	4	12
4	Malta	7	1	2	4	3	15	5
5	Latvia	6	1	2	3	9	10	5
6	Moldova	7	1	1	5	3	11	4

Remaining fixtures

01/09/16
Montenegro - Czech Republic
02/09/16
Malta - Belgium
Latvia - Moldova
06/09/16
Belgium - Czech Republic
Latvia - Montenegro

07/10/16
Czech Republic - Moldova
Montenegro - Belgium
Malta - Latvia
11/10/16
Belgium - Latvia
Malta - Moldova

Group 2

26/03/15, Regional Sports Centre, Waterford
Republic of Ireland 1-0 Andorra
Goal: 1-0 Connolly 31

08/06/15, Mestni, Ajdovscina
Slovenia 4-0 Andorra
Goals: 1-0 Šporar 14, 2-0 Kastrevec 21,
3-0 Zahovič 29, 4-0 Stankovič 74

16/06/15, Estadi Comunal, Andorra la Vella
Andorra 1-0 Lithuania
Goal: 1-0 A Sánchez 51(p)

04/09/15, Arena Petrol, Celje
Slovenia 3-0 Lithuania
Goals: 1-0 Hotič 31, 2-0 Šporar 65, 3-0 Štulac 81

08/09/15, Estadi Comunal, Andorra la Vella
Andorra 0-2 Republic of Ireland
Goals: 0-1 Hoban 13, 0-2 Cullen 21

08/09/15, Giglio, Reggio Emilia
Italy 1-0 Slovenia
Goal: 1-0 Bernardeschi 51(p)

08/09/15, FK Metalac, Gornji Milanovac
Serbia 5-0 Lithuania
Goals: 1-0 Djurdjević 29, 2-0 Djurdjević 36(p),
3-0 S Milinković-Savić 44, 4-0 Ožegović 49,
5-0 S Milinković-Savić 75

07/10/15, Karadjordje, Novi Sad
Serbia 5-0 Andorra
Goals: 1-0 Luković 9, 2-0 Ožegović 38(p),
3-0 Ožegović 47, 4-0 Luković 52, 5-0 Mulić 64

08/10/15, ŠRC Bonifika, Koper
Slovenia 0-3 Italy
Goals: 0-1 Monachello 71, 0-2 Monachello 84,
0-3 Benassi 87

09/10/15, Regional Sports Centre, Waterford
Republic of Ireland 3-0 Lithuania
Goals: 1-0 O'Dowda 27, 2-0 Wilkinson 30,
3-0 Browne 77

13/10/15, Romeo Menti, Vicenza
Italy 1-0 Republic of Ireland
Goal: 1-0 Parigini 66

13/10/15, Estadi Comunal, Andorra la Vella
Andorra 0-5 Slovenia
Goals: 0-1 Stankovič 6, 0-2 Štulac 48,
0-3 Štulac 52, 0-4 Kastrevec 55, 0-5 Kastrevec 81

13/10/15, Dariaus ir Girėno stadionas, Kaunas
Lithuania 0-2 Serbia
Goals: 0-1 Čavrić 19, 0-2 Čavrić 44

13/11/15, Karadjordje, Novi Sad
Serbia 1-1 Italy
Goals: 1-0 S Milinković-Savić 47, 1-1 Cataldi 56

13/11/15, LFF stadionas, Vilnius
Lithuania 3-1 Republic of Ireland
Goals: 1-0 Spalvis 22, 1-1 Wilkinson 44,
2-1 Stankevičius 45, 3-1 D Kazlauskas 73

17/11/15, ŠRC Bonifika, Koper
Slovenia 2-0 Serbia
Goals: 1-0 Šporar 61, 2-0 Hotič 83

17/11/15, Teofilo Patini, Castel Di Sangro
Italy 2-0 Lithuania
Goals: 1-0 Berardi 2, 2-0 Benassi 24

24/03/16, Regional Sports Centre, Waterford
Republic of Ireland 1-4 Italy
Goals: 1-0 Mandragora 17(og), 1-1 Benassi 28,
1-2 Rosseti 36, 1-3 Romagnoli 59,
1-4 Lenihan 82(og)

25/03/16, Estadi Comunal, Andorra la Vella
Andorra 0-4 Serbia
Goals: 0-1 Babić 29, 0-2 Djurdjević 40,
0-3 Ožegović 59(p), 0-4 Maraš 87

28/03/16, ŠRC Bonifika, Koper
Slovenia 3-1 Republic of Ireland
Goals: 1-0 Krajnc 14, 2-0 Bajde 55(p),
2-1 O'Dowda 65, 3-1 Zajc 72

29/03/16, Estadi Comunal, Andorra la Vella
Andorra 0-1 Italy
Goal: 0-1 Cerri 79

		Pld	W	D	L	F	A	Pts
1	Italy	7	6	1	0	13	2	19
2	Slovenia	7	5	0	2	17	5	15
3	Serbia	6	4	1	1	17	3	13
4	Republic of Ireland	7	3	0	4	9	11	9
5	Andorra	8	1	0	7	1	22	3
6	Lithuania	7	1	0	6	3	17	3

Remaining fixtures

01/09/16
Lithuania - Andorra
02/09/16
Italy - Serbia
Republic of Ireland - Slovenia
06/09/16
Italy - Andorra
Serbia - Republic of Ireland

07/10/16
Republic of Ireland - Serbia
Lithuania - Slovenia
11/10/16
Serbia - Slovenia
Lithuania - Italy

Group 3

11/06/15, Hlíðarendi, Reykjavik
Iceland 3-0 FYR Macedonia
Goals: 1-0 E Ómarsson 55, 2-0 Gunnlaugsson 61,
3-0 Gunnlaugsson 67

05/09/15, Kópavogsvöllur, Kopavogur
Iceland 3-2 France
Goals: 1-0 Sigurjónsson 10, 1-1 Laporte 39,
2-1 Hermannsson 48, 3-1 Sigurjónsson 85(p),
3-2 Kyei 90

05/09/15, Mourneview Park, Lurgan
Northern Ireland 1-2 Scotland
Goals: 1-0 Kennedy 7, 1-1 Christie 33,
1-2 Fraser 61

05/09/15, FFM Training Centre, Skopje
FYR Macedonia 1-0 Ukraine
Goal: 1-0 Radeski 90+3

08/09/15, Fylkisvöllur, Reykjavik
Iceland 1-1 Northern Ireland
Goals: 0-1 Johnson 2, 1-1 Thrándarson 37

08/10/15, KP Tcentralnyi, Cherkassy
Ukraine 0-1 Iceland
Goal: 0-1 Vilhjálmsson 71

10/10/15, Pittodrie, Aberdeen
Scotland 1-2 France
Goals: 0-1 Kingsley 11(og), 0-2 Tolisso 53, 1-2 King 90+1

13/10/15, Mourneview Park, Lurgan
Northern Ireland 1-2 FYR Macedonia
Goals: 1-0 Doherty 43, 1-1 Bardi 46, 1-2 Markoski 85

13/10/15, Pittodrie, Aberdeen
Scotland 0-0 Iceland

13/10/15, La Meinau, Strasbourg
France 2-0 Ukraine
Goals: 1-0 Lemar 70, 2-0 Rabiot 77

12/11/15, Roudourou, Guingamp
France 1-0 Northern Ireland
Goal: 1-0 Crivelli 82

13/11/15, Saint Mirren Park, Paisley
Scotland 2-2 Ukraine
Goals: 0-1 Khlyobas 26, 1-1 Cummings 31, 2-1 Paterson 37, 2-2 Svatok 83

15/11/15, FFM Training Centre, Skopje
FYR Macedonia 2-2 France
Goals: 1-0 Angelov 19, 2-0 Radeski 40, 2-1 Haller 65, 2-2 N'Koudou 72

17/11/15, Mourneview Park, Lurgan
Northern Ireland 1-2 Ukraine
Goals: 1-0 McCartan 53, 1-1 Kovalenko 64, 1-2 Kovalenko 73

24/03/16, FFM Training Centre, Skopje
FYR Macedonia 0-0 Iceland

24/03/16, Jean-Bouin, Angers
France 2-0 Scotland
Goals: 1-0 Haller 69, 2-0 Haller 74

28/03/16, MMArena, Le Mans
France 1-1 FYR Macedonia
Goals: 0-1 Angelov 15, 1-1 Bejtulai 27(og)

29/03/16, Saint Mirren Park, Paisley
Scotland 3-1 Northern Ireland
Goals: 0-1 McCartan 13, 1-1 McBurnie 58, 2-1 Cummings 64, 3-1 Cummings 78

27/05/16, Stadion Dynamo im. Valeriy Lobanovskiy, Kyiv
Ukraine 0-2 FYR Macedonia
Goals: 0-1 Radeski 18, 0-2 Demiri 56

	Pld	W	D	L	F	A	Pts
1 France	7	4	2	1	12	7	14
2 Iceland	6	3	3	0	8	3	12
3 FYR Macedonia	7	3	3	1	8	7	12
4 Scotland	6	2	2	2	8	8	8
5 Ukraine	6	1	1	4	4	9	4
6 Northern Ireland	6	0	1	5	5	11	1

Remaining fixtures

02/09/16	*05/10/16*
Scotland - FYR Macedonia	Iceland - Scotland
Northern Ireland - Iceland	*06/10/16*
Ukraine - France	Ukraine - Northern Ireland
06/09/16	*08/10/16*
France - Iceland	FYR Macedonia - Scotland
Ukraine - Scotland	*11/10/16*
FYR Macedonia - Northern Ireland	Iceland - Ukraine
	Northern Ireland - France

Group 4

28/03/15, Sportpark Eschen-Mauren, Eschen
Liechtenstein 0-2 Albania
Goals: 0-1 Latifi 31, 0-2 Manaj 52

07/06/15, Rheinpark Stadion, Vaduz
Liechtenstein 0-4 Israel
Goals: 0-1 Kinda 5, 0-2 Altman 49, 0-3 Abu Abaid 58, 0-4 Altman 62

03/09/15, Stadiumi Kombëtar Qemal Stafa, Tirana
Albania 1-1 Israel
Goals: 0-1 Hugy 29, 1-1 Çekiçi 84(p)

03/09/15, Sportpark Eschen-Mauren, Eschen
Liechtenstein 0-6 Hungary
Goals: 0-1 Márkvárt 29, 0-2 Prosser 39, 0-3 Forgács 45, 0-4 Kleinheisler 59, 0-5 Prosser 68, 0-6 Sallai 90

07/09/15, Sportpark Eschen-Mauren, Eschen
Liechtenstein 0-2 Greece
Goals: 0-1 Ioannidis 43, 0-2 Ioannidis 75

08/09/15, Stadiumi Kombëtar Qemal Stafa, Tirana
Albania 1-6 Portugal
Goals: 0-1 Rúben Neves 31, 0-2 Marcos Lopes 36, 0-3 André Silva 43, 0-4 André Silva 45, 0-5 André Silva 62, 0-6 Ricardo Horta 70, 1-6 Rashica 83

09/10/15, Municipal 25 de Abril, Penafiel
Portugal 2-0 Hungary
Goals: 1-0 Bruno Fernandes 35, 2-0 Gonçalo Paciência 56

13/10/15, Xanthis, Xanthi
Greece 0-4 Portugal
Goals: 0-1 Gonçalo Guedes 44, 0-2 Gelson Martins 50, 0-3 João Cancelo 87, 0-4 Gonçalo Paciência 90+3

13/10/15, Pancho stadium, Felcsut
Hungary 2-2 Albania
Goals: 1-0 Manaj 24, 1-1 Prosser 28, 1-2 Latifi 43, 2-2 Prosser 85

12/11/15, Kallithea, Athens
Greece 5-0 Liechtenstein
Goals: 1-0 Mavrias 20, 2-0 Fountas 32, 3-0 Mavrias 37, 4-0 Vergos 60, 5-0 Ioannidis 70

12/11/15, Arouca Municipal Stadium, Arouca
Portugal 4-0 Albania
Goals: 1-0 Ricardo Horta 43, 2-0 Carlos Mané 47, 3-0 Rúben Vezo 60, 4-0 Gonçalo Paciência 82

12/11/15, Ha Moshava, Petach-Tikva
Israel 3-0 Hungary
Goals: 1-0 David 60, 2-0 Gozlan 85, 3-0 Ohana 90+2

16/11/15, Gyirmóti Stadion, Gyor
Hungary 2-1 Greece
Goals: 1-0 Kalmár 45, 1-1 Ioannidis 75(p), 2-1 Bese 78

16/11/15, Elbasan Arena, Elbasan
Albania 2-0 Liechtenstein
Goals: 1-0 Latifi 18, 2-0 Laci 83

17/11/15, Ha Moshava, Petach-Tikva
Israel 0-3 Portugal
Goals: 0-1 Bruno Fernandes 28(p), 0-2 André Silva 35, 0-3 Ricardo Horta 87

24/03/16, São Miguel, Ponta Delgada
Portugal 4-0 Liechtenstein
Goals: 1-0 Ruben Semedo 8, 2-0 Tobias Figueiredo 10, 3-0 Gonçalo Paciência 13, 4-0 Bruma 24

24/03/16, Elbasan Arena, Elbasan
Albania 0-0 Greece

24/03/16, Gyirmóti Stadion, Gyor
Hungary 0-0 Israel

28/03/16, Peristeri, Athens
Greece 0-1 Israel
Goal: 0-1 Gozlan 74

28/03/16, Elbasan Arena, Elbasan
Albania 2-1 Hungary
Goals: 0-1 Gera 55, 1-1 Manaj 69, 2-1 Prenga 79

		Pld	W	D	L	F	A	Pts
1	Portugal	6	6	0	0	23	1	18
2	Albania	8	3	3	2	10	14	12
3	Israel	6	3	2	1	9	4	11
4	Hungary	7	2	2	3	11	10	8
5	Greece	6	2	1	3	8	7	7
6	Liechtenstein	7	0	0	7	0	25	0

Remaining fixtures

01/09/16	*06/10/16*
Hungary - Liechtenstein	Israel - Greece
02/09/16	Hungary - Portugal
Portugal - Israel	*10/10/16*
Greece - Albania	Israel - Albania
06/09/16	Greece - Hungary
Portugal - Greece	*11/10/16*
Israel - Liechtenstein	Liechtenstein - Portugal

Group 5

31/03/15, Cardiff City Stadium, Cardiff
Wales 3-1 Bulgaria
Goals: 1-0 O'Sullivan 9, 2-0 O'Sullivan 13, 3-0 Yorwerth 25, 3-1 Kolev 51

16/06/15, Trans-Sil, Targu Mures
Romania 3-0 Armenia
Goals: 1-0 Puşcaş 16, 2-0 Păun 32, 3-0 F Tănase 90+2

04/09/15, La Frontière, Esch-sur-Alzette
Luxembourg 1-3 Wales
Goals: 0-1 Burns 35, 0-2 Wilson 63, 0-3 Burns 72, 1-3 Sinani 90+2

04/09/15, Trans-Sil, Targu Mures
Romania 0-2 Bulgaria
Goals: 0-1 Minchev 16, 0-2 Kolev 89

08/09/15, FFA Academy Stadium, Yerevan
Armenia 2-3 Romania
Goals: 0-1 Păun 35, 0-2 Păun 38, 1-2 G Malakyan 47, 1-3 Puşcaş 60, 2-3 Simonyan 90+2

08/09/15, Ludogorets Arena, Razgrad
Bulgaria 3-0 Luxembourg
Goals: 1-0 B Tsonev 17, 2-0 Vutov 35, 3-0 Despodov 78

09/10/15, Stade Municipal de Differdange, Differdange
Luxembourg 0-1 Romania
Goal: 0-1 Puşcaş 36

09/10/15, Aalborg Stadion, Aalborg
Denmark 0-0 Wales

09/10/15, Beroe, Stara Zagora
Bulgaria 2-0 Armenia
Goals: 1-0 Malinov 68, 2-0 Minchev 81

13/10/15, FFA Academy Stadium, Yerevan
Armenia 1-1 Luxembourg
Goals: 0-1 Ricardo Pinto 23(p),
1-1 Shakhnazaryan 67

13/10/15, Aalborg Stadion, Aalborg
Denmark 1-0 Bulgaria
Goal: 1-0 Hjulsager 71

13/11/15, Nantporth, Bangor
Wales 2-1 Armenia
Goals: 1-0 Harrison 9(p), 1-1 G Malakyan 59,
2-1 Wilson 90+1

13/11/15, Marin Anastasovici, Giurgiu
Romania 0-3 Denmark
Goals: 0-1 Børsting 8, 0-2 Børsting 30,
0-3 Zohore 79

17/11/15, The Racecourse Ground, Wrexham
Wales 1-1 Romania
Goals: 0-1 Nedelcearu 2, 1-1 Burns 14

17/11/15, Aalborg Stadion, Aalborg
Denmark 2-0 Armenia
Goals: 1-0 Banggaard 49, 2-0 Ingvartsen 82

25/03/16, Stade Municipal de Differdange, Differdange
Luxembourg 0-1 Denmark
Goal: 0-1 Nielsen 90

25/03/16, Beroe, Stara Zagora
Bulgaria 0-0 Wales

29/03/16, Henri Dunant, Beggen
Luxembourg 0-0 Bulgaria

29/03/16, Gaz Metan, Medias
Romania 2-1 Wales
Goals: 1-0 Hodorogea 37, 2-0 Ioniță 58,
2-1 Charles 90+2

29/03/16, Republican Stadium, Yerevan
Armenia 1-3 Denmark
Goals: 0-1 Fischer 28, 0-2 Andersen 30,
1-2 G Malakyan 35(p), 1-3 Nielsen 90+2

	Pld	W	D	L	F	A	Pts
1 Denmark	6	5	1	0	10	1	16
2 Romania	7	4	1	2	10	9	13
3 Wales	7	3	3	1	10	6	12
4 Bulgaria	7	3	2	2	8	4	11
5 Luxembourg	6	0	2	4	2	9	2
6 Armenia	7	0	1	6	5	16	1

Remaining fixtures

02/09/16
Wales - Denmark
Romania - Luxembourg
06/09/16
Denmark - Romania
Armenia - Bulgaria
Wales - Luxembourg

07/10/16
Bulgaria - Denmark
Luxembourg - Armenia
11/10/16
Armenia - Wales
Bulgaria - Romania
Denmark - Luxembourg

Group 6

03/06/15, San Marino Stadium, Serravalle
San Marino 0-3 Georgia
Goals: 0-1 Kacharava 44, 0-2 Kacharava 58,
0-3 Papunashvili 81

16/06/15, Haapsalu, Haapsalu
Estonia 0-0 San Marino

02/09/15, A. Le Coq Arena, Tallinn
Estonia 0-2 Spain
Goals: 0-1 Gayá 82, 0-2 Deulofeu 90+2(p)

03/09/15, Gradski stadion Koprivnica, Koprivnica
Croatia 1-0 Georgia
Goal: 1-0 A Milić 23

03/09/15, Strandvallen Mjällby, Solvesborg
Sweden 3-0 San Marino
Goals: 1-0 Olsson 22, 2-0 Tankovic 69,
3-0 Mrabti 87

07/09/15, Tartu Tamme, Tartu
Estonia 0-4 Croatia
Goals: 0-1 A Milić 22, 0-2 Pašalić 35,
0-3 Pašalić 66(p), 0-4 Radošević 80

07/10/15, San Marino Stadium, Serravalle
San Marino 0-3 Croatia
Goals: 0-1 Marić 7, 0-2 Pašalić 12, 0-3 Marić 32

07/10/15, Mikheil Meskhi Stadioni, Tbilisi
Georgia 2-5 Spain
Goals: 0-1 Munir 2, 1-1 Tsintsadze 4,
2-1 Lobjanidze 60, 2-2 Marco Asensio 62,
2-3 Borja Mayoral 67, 2-4 Munir 73,
2-5 Dani Ceballos 90

09/10/15, Studentarnas Idrottspark, Uppsala
Sweden 5-0 Estonia
Goals: 1-0 Engvall 10, 2-0 Hallberg 13,
3-0 Engvall 31, 4-0 Ayaz 81, 5-0 Ayaz 90+1

13/10/15, Heliodoro Rodríguez López, Santa Cruz de Tenerife
Spain 1-1 Sweden
Goals: 1-0 Óliver Torres 20, 1-1 Engvall 60

13/10/15, Mikheil Meskhi Stadioni, Tbilisi
Georgia 3-0 Estonia
Goals: 1-0 Kakabadze 11, 2-0 Kacharava 20,
3-0 Kiteishvili 36

11/11/15, Šubicevac, Sibenik
Croatia 4-0 San Marino
Goals: 1-0 Manuel Battistini 12(og), 2-0 A Milić 44,
3-0 Perić 47, 4-0 Pjaca 51

12/11/15, Estadio del Mediterráneo, Almeria
Spain 5-0 Georgia
Goals: 1-0 Deulofeu 17, 2-0 Deulofeu 33,
3-0 Iñaki Williams 56, 4-0 Dani Ceballos 65,
5-0 Deulofeu 84

15/11/15, San Marino Stadium, Serravalle
San Marino 1-2 Estonia
Goals: 0-1 Käit 26, 0-2 Cesarini 48(og),
1-2 Cesarini 50

17/11/15, Tengiz Burjanadze Stadioni, Gori
Georgia 0-1 Sweden
Goal: 0-1 Mrabti 72

17/11/15, Stadion HNK Rijeka, Rijeka
Croatia 2-3 Spain
Goals: 0-1 Deulofeu 19(p), 0-2 Marco Asensio 41,
0-3 Deulofeu 54, 1-3 Pašalić 64,
2-3 Radošević 81(p)

23/03/16, Mikheil Meskhi Stadioni, Tbilisi
Georgia 4-0 San Marino
Goals: 1-0 Kharaishvili 10, 2-0 Kacharava 33(p),
3-0 Kacharava 48, 4-0 Shengelia 81

24/03/16, Municipal El Plantío, Burgos
Spain 0-3 Croatia
Goals: 0-1 Ćaleta-Car 36, 0-2 Perica 42,
0-3 Perica 46

27/03/16, San Marino Stadium, Serravalle
San Marino 0-2 Sweden
Goals: 0-1 Fransson 37, 0-2 Gustafsson 81

28/03/16, NK Inter Zaprešić, Zapresic
Croatia 2-1 Estonia
Goals: 1-0 Pavičić 5, 2-0 Perica 41, 2-1 Kirss 53

03/06/16, Rimnersvallen, Udevalla
Sweden 3-2 Georgia
Goals: 1-0 Olsson 27(p), 1-1 Arabuli 35,
2-1 Krafth 77, 2-2 Kiteishvili 89, 3-2 Larsson 90+5

	Pld	W	D	L	F	A	Pts
1 Croatia	7	6	0	1	19	4	18
2 Sweden	6	5	1	0	15	3	16
3 Spain	6	4	1	1	16	8	13
4 Georgia	8	3	0	5	14	15	9
5 Estonia	7	1	1	5	3	17	4
6 San Marino	8	0	1	7	1	21	1

Remaining fixtures

01/09/16
Croatia - Sweden
Estonia - Georgia
Spain - San Marino
05/09/16
Sweden - Spain
06/09/16
Georgia - Croatia

05/10/16
San Marino - Spain
06/10/16
Estonia - Sweden
10/10/16
Spain - Estonia
Sweden - Croatia

Group 7

17/06/15, Toftir, Toftir
Faroe Islands 0-1 Azerbaijan
Goal: 0-1 Salahlı 81

04/09/15, Arto Tolsa Areena, Kotka
Finland 2-0 Russia
Goals: 1-0 Lassas 17, 2-0 Mero 36

04/09/15, Dalga Stadium, Baku
Azerbaijan 0-2 Austria
Goals: 0-1 Gregoritsch 14, 0-2 Gregoritsch 45(p)

08/09/15, NV Arena, St Polten
Austria 4-3 Russia
Goals: 1-0 Gregoritsch 9, 2-0 Schaub 21,
2-1 Sheydaev 41, 2-2 Tashaev 49, 3-2 Schöpf 53,
3-3 Sheydaev 64(p), 4-3 Schöpf 79

08/09/15, ISS, Vantaa
Finland 3-0 Faroe Islands
Goals: 1-0 Yaghoubi 24(p), 2-0 Skrabb 31,
3-0 Yaghoubi 39

08/09/15, Dalga Stadium, Baku
Azerbaijan 0-3 Germany
Goals: 0-1 Selke 33, 0-2 Kimmich 88(p),
0-3 Selke 90+3

09/10/15, NV Arena, St Polten
Austria 7-0 Azerbaijan
Goals: 1-0 Grillitsch 45+1, 2-0 Gregoritsch 49(p),
3-0 Friesenbichler 60, 4-0 Gregoritsch 74,
5-0 Schöpf 75, 6-0 Gregoritsch 88,
7-0 Wydra 90+5(p)

09/10/15, Georg-Meiches, Essen
Germany 4-0 Finland
Goals: 1-0 Sané 13, 2-0 Selke 16,
3-0 Kimmich 27, 4-0 Sané 90+1

13/10/15, Tórsvøllur, Torshavn
Faroe Islands 0-6 Germany
Goals: 0-1 Meyer 8, 0-2 Arnold 13, 0-3 Meyer 40,
0-4 Süle 45+2, 0-5 Sané 73, 0-6 Gnabry 75

13/10/15, Dalga Stadium, Baku
Azerbaijan 0-1 Finland
Goal: 0-1 Lassas 80

12/11/15, Kuban, Krasnodar
Russia 2-0 Faroe Islands
Goals: 1-0 Sheydaev 54, 2-0 Panyukov 77

13/11/15, Continental Arena, Regensburg
Germany 3-1 Azerbaijan
Goals: 0-1 İsayev 30, 1-1 Werner 37,
2-1 Arnold 43, 3-1 Werner 63

13/11/15, Austria Arena, Vienna
Austria 2-0 Finland
Goals: 1-0 Gregoritsch 77, 2-0 Friesenbichler 90+1

17/11/15, Bayil stadium , Baku
Azerbaijan 3-0 Russia
Goals: 1-0 Behnke 11, 2-0 Behnke 39,
3-0 E Abdullayev 69(p)

17/11/15, Playmobil, Furth
Germany 4-2 Austria
Goals: 0-1 Gregoritsch 21(p), 1-1 Meyer 39,
2-1 Goretzka 42, 3-1 Selke 50, 4-1 Sané 76,
4-2 Gregoritsch 86

24/03/16, Olimp 2, Rostov-na-Donu
Russia 2-2 Azerbaijan
Goals: 0-1 Mädätov 46, 1-1 Zuev 51,
2-1 Barinov 56, 2-2 R Mämmädov 59

24/03/16, Bornheimer Hang, Frankfurt am Main
Germany 4-1 Azerbaijan
Goals: 1-0 Sané 17, 1-1 Dam 43,
2-1 Nattestad 59(og), 3-1 Meyer 63(p),
4-1 Brandt 74

29/03/16, Austria Arena, Vienna
Austria 1-0 Faroe Islands
Goal: 1-0 Sallahi 28

29/03/16, Olimp 2, Rostov-na-Donu
Russia 0-2 Germany
Goals: 0-1 Selke 11, 0-2 Meyer 79

02/06/16, Tórsvøllur, Torshavn
Faroe Islands 1-6 Finland
Goals: 0-1 Tuominen 18, 1-1 Edmundsson 35,
1-2 Lassas 38, 1-3 D O'Shaughnessy 42,
1-4 Hambo 45, 1-5 Hambo 73, 1-6 T Olsen 90+2(og)

		Pld	W	D	L	F	A	Pts
1	Germany	7	7	0	0	26	4	21
2	Austria	6	5	0	1	18	7	15
3	Finland	6	4	0	2	12	7	12
4	Azerbaijan	8	2	1	5	7	18	7
5	Russia	6	1	1	4	7	13	4
6	Faroe Islands	7	0	0	7	2	23	0

Remaining fixtures

01/09/16
Faroe Islands - Russia
02/09/16
Finland - Austria
06/09/16
Russia - Austria
Finland - Germany
Azerbaijan - Faroe Islands

07/10/16
Germany - Russia
Finland - Azerbaijan
10/10/16
Faroe Islands - Austria
11/10/16
Russia - Finland
Austria - Germany

Group 8

04/09/15, De Adelaarshorst, Deventer
Netherlands 4-0 Cyprus
Goals: 1-0 Hateboer 4, 2-0 Janssen 23,
3-0 Bazoer 53, 4-0 Janssen 66

06/09/15, City Stadium, Slutsk
Belarus 1-0 Slovakia
Goal: 1-0 Yarotski 39

08/09/15, Recep Tayyip Erdoğan, Istanbul
Turkey 0-1 Netherlands
Goal: 0-1 Boëtius 35

08/10/15, Spartak Myjava, Myjava
Slovakia 2-0 Cyprus
Goals: 1-0 Mihalík 62, 2-0 Zrelǎk 70

09/10/15, City Stadium, Slutsk
Belarus 0-2 Turkey
Goals: 0-1 Cenk Şahin 27, 0-2 Kenan Karaman 79

11/10/15, De Goffert, Nijmegen
Netherlands 1-3 Slovakia
Goals: 1-0 Janssen 16, 1-1 Chrien 44,
1-2 Škriniar 64, 1-3 Bero 69

13/10/15, Ammochostos, Larnaca
Cyprus 0-1 Belarus
Goal: 0-1 Klimovich 84

12/11/15, Ammochostos, Larnaca
Cyprus 0-3 Turkey
Goals: 0-1 Bilal Başaçıkoğlu 33,
0-2 Kaan Ayhan 53, 0-3 Mouktaris 67(og)

12/11/15, Willem II, Tilburg
Netherlands 1-0 Belarus
Goal: 1-0 Janssen 25

17/11/15, Spartak Myjava, Myjava
Slovakia 4-2 Netherlands
Goals: 0-1 Janssen 16, 0-2 Janssen 23,
1-2 Mihalík 50, 2-2 Rusnák 64, 3-2 Chrien 83,
4-2 Zrelǎk 90+4(p)

17/11/15, Gorodskoi Stadion, Borisov
Belarus 2-2 Cyprus
Goals: 0-1 Antoniou 6, 1-1 Rassadkin 10,
1-2 Makris 42, 2-2 Savitski 48

29/03/16, Spartak Myjava, Myjava
Slovakia 5-0 Turkey
Goals: 1-0 Zrelǎk 10, 2-0 Rusnák 23,
3-0 Mihalík 75, 4-0 Zrelǎk 79(p), 5-0 Zrelǎk 85

		Pld	W	D	L	F	A	Pts
1	Slovakia	5	4	0	1	14	4	12
2	Netherlands	5	3	0	2	9	7	9
3	Belarus	5	2	1	2	4	5	7
4	Turkey	4	2	0	2	5	6	6
5	Cyprus	5	0	1	4	2	12	1

Remaining fixtures

01/09/16
Turkey - Cyprus
02/09/16
Belarus - Netherlands
05/09/16
Cyprus - Slovakia
06/09/16
Turkey - Belarus

06/10/16
Netherlands - Turkey
07/10/16
Slovakia - Belarus
10/10/16
Cyprus - Netherlands
11/10/16
Turkey - Slovakia

Group 9

13/06/15, Marienlyst, Drammen
Norway 2-0 Bosnia & Herzegovina
Goals: 1-0 Elyounoussi 45, 2-0 Aursnes 88

02/09/15, Asim Ferhatović Hase Stadion, Sarajevo
Bosnia & Herzegovina 1-2 Kazakhstan
Goals: 0-1 Tuliyev 27, 0-2 Aimbetov 43,
1-2 Hajradinović 58

07/09/15, Marienlyst, Drammen
Norway 0-1 England
Goal: 0-1 Ward-Prowse 45+1(p)

07/09/15, Almaty Ortalyk Stadion, Almaty
Kazakhstan 0-1 Switzerland
Goal: 0-1 Tarashaj 85(p)

08/10/15, Biel/Bienne, Biel
Switzerland 3-1 Bosnia & Herzegovina
Goals: 1-0 Tarashaj 12(p), 2-0 Tabakovic 63,
3-0 Tarashaj 76, 3-1 Ćerimagić 80

08/10/15, Marienlyst, Drammen
Norway 2-1 Kazakhstan
Goals: 1-0 Elyounoussi 14, 1-1 Zhalmukan 50,
2-1 Sørloth 69

09/10/15, City Stadium, Slutsk

12/10/15, Biel/Bienne, Biel
Switzerland 1-1 Norway
Goals: 0-1 Trondsen 19, 1-1 Tabakovic 30

13/10/15, Ricoh Arena, Coventry
England 3-0 Kazakhstan
Goals: 1-0 Loftus-Cheek 53, 2-0 Redmond 70,
3-0 Akpom 90+4

12/11/15, Asim Ferhatović Hase Stadion, Sarajevo
Bosnia & Herzegovina 0-0 England

16/11/15, American Express Community Stadium, Brighton
England 3-1 Switzerland
Goals: 1-0 Tarashaj 45, 1-1 Ward-Prowse 82(p),
2-1 Watmore 85, 3-1 Akpom 90+1

25/03/16, Astana Arena, Astana
Kazakhstan 0-0 Bosnia & Herzegovina

26/03/16, Arena Thun, Thun
Switzerland 1-1 England
Goals: 0-1 Akpom 47, 1-1 Kamberi 76

		Pld	W	D	L	F	A	Pts
1	England	5	3	2	0	8	2	11
2	Switzerland	5	2	2	1	7	6	8
3	Norway	4	2	1	1	5	3	7
4	Kazakhstan	5	1	1	3	3	7	4
5	Bosnia & Herzegovina	5	0	2	3	2	7	2

Remaining fixtures

02/09/16
Switzerland - Kazakhstan
Bosnia & Herzegovina - Norway
06/09/16
England - Norway
Bosnia & Herzegovina - Switzerland

06/10/16
Kazakhstan - England
07/10/16
Norway - Switzerland
11/10/16
England - Bosnia & Herzegovina
Kazakhstan – Norway

Top goalscorers

9	Michael Gregoritsch (Austria)
8	Patrik Schick (Czech Republic)
6	Vincent Janssen (Netherlands)
	Gerard Deulofeu (Spain)
5	Nika Kacharava (Georgia)
	Max Meyer (Germany)
	Davie Selke (Germany)
	Leroy Sané (Germany)
	Adam Zrelǎk (Slovakia)

Italy defeated by record-breaking 4-0 margin in final

Group winners England and Portugal ousted in semi-finals

Hosts Germany win play-off to claim U-20 World Cup place

Third title for free-scoring France

France won the UEFA European Under-19 Championship for the third time in 2015/16, producing their best performances at the business end of the final tournament in Germany. They racked up 12 goals in their last three games, concluding proceedings with a 4-0 win against Italy at the Rhein-Neckar-Arena in Sinsheim – a record-breaking margin of victory for a U19 final.

Ludovic Batelli's side lost their opening game of the tournament, against England, but they hit top form when it mattered most, brushing aside the Netherlands with a 5-1 win to reach the semi-finals, where they disposed of Portugal 3-1. Their very best was saved until last, though, as two early goals from Jean-Kévin Augustin and Ludovic Blas put them in control of the final before captain Lucas Tousart and Issa Diop struck late on to put the seal on a comprehensive victory.

England, who surprisingly eliminated holders and seven-time winners Spain in the elite round, took that impressive form to Germany, scoring twice in the first nine minutes of their opening victory over France. That was the first of three successive 2-1 wins for Aidy Boothroyd's team that placed them on top of Group B.

France, meanwhile, responded strongly to that opening setback, wins against Croatia (2-0) and the Netherlands giving them the runners-up spot. Augustin struck five of France's group stage goals – en route to a record-equalling six in the finals overall – with Kylian Mbappé Lottin grabbing the other three.

Group A opened with hosts Germany playing Italy in front of a U19 record crowd of 54,689 at the VfB Arena in Stuttgart. The majority of the spectators went home disappointed, however, after Federico Dimarco's late penalty earned Italy a 1-0 win. Germany's hopes of further progress

European Under-19 champions France show off their medals

were then dashed by a 4-3 defeat against Portugal despite Phillipp Ochs' hat-trick, with their conquerors going on to clinch first place in the section thanks to a 1-1 draw against Italy that also put their opponents through.

Germany finished third in the group with a 3-0 win against Austria, which set the hosts up in a play-off against the Netherlands for a place alongside the four semi-finalists in the 2017 FIFA U-20 World Cup. Three late goals made it 2-2 after 90 minutes, with both sides then permitted to use a fourth substitute during extra time under an experimental new UEFA rule. Germany, true to tradition, prevailed on penalties after a 3-3 draw.

Italy, whose group stage goals had come from two penalties and a free-kick, further demonstrated their set-piece prowess in the first semi-final, Dimarco converting another spot kick and a wonderful curling free-kick to give the Azzurrini a 2-1 win against England. Portugal struck first in the second semi-final, against France, through Pedro Pacheco's early header, before Mbappé Lottin took centre stage, the Monaco forward setting up his team's tenth-minute equaliser for Blas before scoring twice himself from close range in the second half to clinch his team's place in the final.

Qualifying round

Group 1

13-18/11/15 Limerick, Galway
Scotland 2-0 Latvia, Republic of Ireland 0-1 Slovenia, Slovenia 1-0 Scotland, Republic of Ireland 3-0 Latvia, Scotland 4-0 Republic of Ireland, Latvia 0-0 Slovenia

		Pld	W	D	L	F	A	Pts
1	Slovenia	3	2	1	0	2	0	7
2	Scotland	3	2	0	1	6	1	6
3	Republic of Ireland	3	1	0	2	3	5	3
4	Latvia	3	0	1	2	0	5	1

Group 2

18-23/09/15 Porec, Pula
Hungary 4-0 Kazakhstan, Croatia 3-1 Montenegro, Montenegro 3-0 Hungary, Croatia 1-0 Kazakhstan, Hungary 1-1 Croatia, Kazakhstan 1-2 Montenegro

		Pld	W	D	L	F	A	Pts
1	Croatia	3	2	1	0	5	2	7
2	Montenegro	3	2	0	1	6	4	6
3	Hungary	3	1	1	1	5	4	4
4	Kazakhstan	3	0	0	3	1	7	0

Group 3

11-16/11/15 Paphos
Bulgaria 0-1 Poland, Cyprus 1-2 Luxembourg, Bulgaria 2-1 Luxembourg, Poland 3-0 Cyprus, Cyprus 3-3 Bulgaria, Luxembourg 2-2 Poland

		Pld	W	D	L	F	A	Pts
1	Poland	3	2	1	0	6	2	7
2	Bulgaria	3	1	1	1	5	5	4
3	Luxembourg	3	1	1	1	5	5	4
4	Cyprus	3	0	1	2	4	8	1

Group 4

08-13/10/15 Skopje
Italy 1-1 Finland, England 2-0 FYR Macedonia, Finland 0-1 England, Italy 3-2 FYR Macedonia, England 0-0 Italy, FYR Macedonia 1-2 Finland

		Pld	W	D	L	F	A	Pts
1	England	3	2	1	0	3	0	7
2	Italy	3	1	2	0	4	3	5
3	Finland	3	1	1	1	3	4	4
4	FYR Macedonia	3	0	0	3	3	7	0

Group 5

10-15/11/15 Baku
Turkey 1-2 Bosnia & Herzegovina, Ukraine 4-0 Azerbaijan, Bosnia & Herzegovina 1-3 Ukraine, Turkey 1-0 Azerbaijan, Ukraine 3-4 Turkey, Azerbaijan 1-0 Bosnia & Herzegovina

		Pld	W	D	L	F	A	Pts
1	Turkey	3	2	0	1	6	5	6
2	Ukraine	3	2	0	1	10	5	6
3	Azerbaijan	3	1	0	2	1	5	3
4	Bosnia & Herzegovina	3	1	0	2	3	5	3

Group 6

10-15/11/15 Hamrun, Paola
Israel 3-1 Malta, Denmark 1-1 Iceland, Israel 4-1 Iceland, Malta 0-3 Denmark, Denmark 0-0 Israel, Iceland 1-0 Malta

		Pld	W	D	L	F	A	Pts
1	Israel	3	2	1	0	7	2	7
2	Denmark	3	1	2	0	4	1	5
3	Iceland	3	1	1	1	3	5	4
4	Malta	3	0	0	3	1	7	0

Group 7

10-15/11/15 Santa Comba Dao, Nelas, Mangualde, Viseu
Greece 1-0 Lithuania, Portugal 1-0 Moldova, Greece 2-1 Moldova, Lithuania 0-5 Portugal, Portugal 4-0 Greece, Moldova 0-1 Lithuania

		Pld	W	D	L	F	A	Pts
1	Portugal	3	3	0	0	10	0	9
2	Greece	3	2	0	1	3	5	6
3	Lithuania	3	1	0	2	1	6	3
4	Moldova	3	0	0	3	1	4	0

Group 8

12-17/11/15 Tbilisi
Austria 3-0 Albania, Georgia 0-3 Wales, Austria 2-0 Wales, Albania 0-3 Georgia, Georgia 0-0 Austria, Wales 2-3 Albania

		Pld	W	D	L	F	A	Pts
1	Austria	3	2	1	0	5	0	7
2	Georgia	3	1	1	1	3	3	4
3	Albania	3	1	0	2	3	8	3
4	Wales	3	1	0	2	5	5	3

Group 9

12-16/11/15 Sochi
Russia 1-1 Slovakia, Norway 1-2 Northern Ireland, Slovakia 2-2 Norway, Russia 1-1 Northern Ireland, Norway 1-1 Russia, Northern Ireland 0-2 Slovakia

		Pld	W	D	L	F	A	Pts
1	Slovakia	3	1	2	0	5	3	5
2	Northern Ireland	3	1	1	1	3	4	4
3	Russia	3	0	3	0	3	3	3
4	Norway	3	0	2	1	4	5	2

Group 10

07-12/10/15 St-Paul lès Dax, Mont-de-Marsan
France 3-1 Liechtenstein, Netherlands 9-0 Gibraltar, Netherlands 2-0 Liechtenstein, Gibraltar 0-9 France, France 1-1 Netherlands, Liechtenstein 1-1 Gibraltar

		Pld	W	D	L	F	A	Pts
1	France	3	2	1	0	13	2	7
2	Netherlands	3	2	1	0	12	1	7
3	Liechtenstein	3	0	1	2	2	6	1
4	Gibraltar	3	0	1	2	1	19	1

Group 11

12-17/11/15 Oradea, Paleu
Switzerland 1-0 Andorra, Romania 2-0 Faroe Islands, Faroe Islands 0-4 Switzerland, Romania 2-0 Andorra, Switzerland 3-1 Romania, Andorra 1-1 Faroe Islands

		Pld	W	D	L	F	A	Pts
1	Switzerland	3	3	0	0	8	1	9
2	Romania	3	2	0	1	5	3	6
3	Andorra	3	0	1	2	1	4	1
4	Faroe Islands	3	0	1	2	1	7	1

Group 12

08-13/10/15 Tallinn
Czech Republic 4-0 Armenia, Serbia 5-0 Estonia, Armenia 0-4 Serbia, Czech Republic 2-1 Estonia, Serbia 2-4 Czech Republic, Estonia 2-0 Armenia

		Pld	W	D	L	F	A	Pts
1	Czech Republic	3	3	0	0	10	3	9
2	Serbia	3	2	0	1	11	4	6
3	Estonia	3	1	0	2	3	7	3
4	Armenia	3	0	0	3	0	10	0

Group 13

07-12/10/15 St. Nicolas, Deinze
Sweden 2-0 Belarus, Belgium 9-0 San Marino, San Marino 0-1 Sweden, Belgium 2-2 Belarus, Sweden 0-2 Belgium, Belarus 6-1 San Marino

		Pld	W	D	L	F	A	Pts
1	Belgium	3	2	1	0	13	2	7
2	Sweden	3	2	0	1	3	2	6
3	Belarus	3	1	1	1	8	5	4
4	San Marino	3	0	0	3	1	16	0

Elite round

Group 1

24-29/03/16 Lepe, Cartaya
Spain 2-0 Greece, England 2-1 Georgia, Spain 1-1 Georgia, Greece 1-1 England, England 2-0 Spain, Georgia 1-2 Greece

		Pld	W	D	L	F	A	Pts
1	England	3	2	1	0	5	2	7
2	Spain	3	1	1	1	3	3	4
3	Greece	3	1	1	1	3	4	4
4	Georgia	3	0	1	2	3	5	1

Group 2

25-30/03/16 Caldogno, Padova, Vicenza
Switzerland 1-4 Turkey, Israel 0-4 Italy, Turkey 1-0 Israel, Switzerland 0-2 Italy, Israel 2-0 Switzerland, Italy 2-2 Turkey

		Pld	W	D	L	F	A	Pts
1	Italy	3	2	1	0	8	2	7
2	Turkey	3	2	1	0	7	3	7
3	Israel	3	1	0	2	2	5	3
4	Switzerland	3	0	0	3	1	8	0

Group 3

24-29/03/16 Bad Waltersdorf, Rohrbach an der Lafnitz, Gleisdorf
Czech Republic 3-0 Romania, Austria 3-1 Slovakia, Czech Republic 1-2 Slovakia, Romania 0-4 Austria, Austria 3-1 Czech Republic, Slovakia 3-1 Romania

		Pld	W	D	L	F	A	Pts
1	Austria	3	3	0	0	10	2	9
2	Slovakia	3	2	0	1	6	5	6
3	Czech Republic	3	1	0	2	5	5	3
4	Romania	3	0	0	3	1	10	0

Group 4

24-29/03/16 Uden, Groesbeek
Poland 2-1 Northern Ireland, Netherlands 3-2 Ukraine, Ukraine 0-0 Poland, Netherlands 1-0 Northern Ireland, Poland 0-0 Netherlands, Northern Ireland 0-2 Ukraine

		Pld	W	D	L	F	A	Pts
1	Netherlands	3	2	1	0	4	2	7
2	Poland	3	1	2	0	2	1	5
3	Ukraine	3	1	1	1	4	3	4
4	Northern Ireland	3	0	0	3	1	5	0

Group 5

23-25/03/16 Kostrena, Rijeka
Belgium 2-0 Scotland, Croatia 1-0 Bulgaria, Belgium 1-0 Bulgaria, Scotland 0-3 Croatia, Croatia 4-0 Belgium, Bulgaria 1-2 Scotland

		Pld	W	D	L	F	A	Pts
1	Croatia	3	3	0	0	8	0	9
2	Belgium	3	2	0	1	3	4	6
3	Scotland	3	1	0	2	2	6	3
4	Bulgaria	3	0	0	3	1	4	0

Group 6

24-29/03/16 Fao, Vila do Conde, Povoa do Varzim, Barcelos
Slovenia 1-0 Russia, Portugal 4-0 Sweden,
Sweden 1-3 Slovenia, Portugal 1-1 Russia,
Slovenia 1-3 Portugal, Russia 2-1 Sweden

		Pld	W	D	L	F	A	Pts
1	Portugal	3	2	1	0	8	2	7
2	Slovenia	3	2	0	1	5	4	6
3	Russia	3	1	1	1	3	3	4
4	Sweden	3	0	0	3	2	9	0

Group 7

24-29/03/16 Jagodina, Kragujevac, Gornji Milanovac
France 1-0 Montenegro, Serbia 2-2 Denmark,
France 4-0 Denmark, Montenegro 1-4 Serbia,
Serbia 0-1 France, Denmark 7-1 Montenegro

		Pld	W	D	L	F	A	Pts
1	France	3	3	0	0	6	0	9
2	Denmark	3	1	1	1	9	7	4
3	Serbia	3	1	1	1	6	4	4
4	Montenegro	3	0	0	3	2	12	0

Top goalscorers (Qualifying/Elite rounds)

6	Ivan Šaponjić (Serbia)
5	Nany Dimata (Belgium)
	Jean-Kévin Augustin (France)
	Anas Mahamid (Israel)
	Karol Swiderski (Poland)
	Luka Jović (Serbia)

Final tournament

Group A

11/07/16, VfB Arena, Stuttgart
Germany 0-1 Italy
Goal: 0-1 Dimarco 78(p)
Referee: Hernández (ESP)

11/07/16, Arena Grossaspach, Großaspach
Portugal 1-1 Austria
Goals: 0-1 Jakupovic 10, 1-1 Pedro Empis 53
Referee: Reinshreiber (ISR)

14/07/16, Stadion an der Kreuzeiche, Reutlingen
Italy 1-1 Austria
Goals: 0-1 Schlager 21, 1-1 Locatelli 24
Referee: Aghayev (AZE)

14/07/16, Arena Grossaspach, Großaspach
Germany 3-4 Portugal
Goals: 1-0 Ochs 12, 1-1 Abubakar 37,
1-2 Gonçalo Rodrigues 48, 2-2 Ochs 68(p),
2-3 Alex Silva 70, 2-4 Buta 73, 3-4 Ochs 90+3(p)
Referee: Vertenten (BEL)

17/07/16, Stadion an der Kreuzeiche, Reutlingen
Austria 0-3 Germany
Goals: 0-1 Neumann 50, 0-2 Teuchert 52,
0-3 Gül 87
Referee: Zhabchenko (UKR)

17/07/16, Stadion auf der Waldau, Stuttgart
Italy 1-1 Portugal
Goals: 1-0 Dimarco 15(p), 1-1 Buta 86
Referee: Petrescu (ROU)

		Pld	W	D	L	F	A	Pts
1	Portugal	3	1	2	0	6	5	5
2	Italy	3	1	2	0	3	2	5
3	Germany	3	1	0	2	6	5	3
4	Austria	3	0	2	1	2	5	2

Group B

12/07/16, Donaustadion, Ulm
Croatia 1-3 Netherlands
Goals: 0-1 Bergwijn 17, 0-2 Lammers 33,
1-2 Brekalo 43, 1-3 Bergwijn 85
Referee: Zhabchenko (UKR)

12/07/16, Albstadion, Heidenheim
France 1-2 England
Goals: 0-1 Michelin 3(og), 0-2 Solanke 9,
1-2 Augustin 33
Referee: Petrescu (ROU)

15/07/16, Donaustadion, Ulm
Netherlands 1-2 England
Goals: 1-0 Lammers 10, 1-1 Solanke 36,
1-2 Brown 90+2
Referee: Reinshreiber (ISR)

15/07/16, Wald Stadion, Aalen
Croatia 0-2 France
Goals: 0-1 Augustin 37, 0-2 Mbappé Lottin 69
Referee: Hernández (ESP)

18/07/16, Albstadion, Heidenheim
England 2-1 Croatia
Goals: 1-0 Brown 4, 2-0 Anočić 10(og),
2-1 Moro 58
Referee: Aghayev (AZE)

18/07/16, Wald Stadion, Aalen
Netherlands 1-5 France
Goals: 0-1 Mbappé Lottin 10, 0-2 Augustin 29,
1-2 Nouri 36(p), 1-3 Augustin 48,
1-4 Mbappé Lottin 63, 1-5 Augustin 75
Referee: Vertenten (BEL)

		Pld	W	D	L	F	A	Pts
1	England	3	3	0	0	6	3	9
2	France	3	2	0	1	8	3	6
3	Netherlands	3	1	0	2	5	8	3
4	Croatia	3	0	0	3	2	7	0

Play-off for FIFA U-20 World Cup

21/07/16, Hardtwaldstadion, Sandhausen
Germany 3-3 Netherlands (aet; 5-4 on pens)
Goals: 1-0 Ochs 44, 1-1 Nouri 81,
1-2 Van der Heijden 88, 2-2 Serdar 90+3,
3-2 Mehlem 96, 3-3 Lammers 111
Referee: Hernández (ESP)

Semi-finals

21/07/16, Carl-Benz, Mannheim
England 1-2 Italy
Goals: 0-1 Dimarco 27(p), 0-2 Dimarco 60,
1-2 Picchi 85(og)
Referee: Reinshreiber (ISR)

21/07/16, Carl-Benz, Mannheim
Portugal 1-3 France
Goals: 1-0 Pedro Pacheco 3, 1-1 Blas 10, 1-2
Mbappé Lottin 67, 1-3 Mbappé Lottin 75
Referee: Petrescu (ROU)

Final

24/07/16, Rhein-Neckar-Arena, Sinsheim (att: 25,100)
France 4-0 Italy
Goals: 1-0 Augustin 6, 2-0 Blas 19, 3-0 Tousart 82,
4-0 Diop 90+2
Referee: Aghayev (AZE)
France: Bernardoni, Onguene, Diop, Augustin,
Tousart, Mbappé Lottin, Blas (Gelin 81), Michelin,
Harit (Fuchs 90+1), Maouassa, Poha (Thuram 85).
Coach: Ludovic Batelli (FRA).
Italy: Meret, Vitturini, Dimarco, Barella, Romagna,
Locatelli, Picchi (Cutrone 46), Favilli, Minelli (Edera
56), Coppolaro, Ghiglione (Cassata 78). Coach:
Paolo Vanoli (ITA).
Yellow cards: Barella 33 (Italy), Vitturini 41 (Italy),
Diop 49 (France), Locatelli 80 (Italy), Favilli 84
(Italy), Michelin 84 (France), Cassata 86 (Italy)

Top goalscorers (Final tournament)

6	Jean-Kévin Augustin (France)
5	Kylian Mbappé Lottin (France)
4	Phillipp Ochs (Germany)
	Federico Dimarco (Italy)
3	Sam Lammers (Netherlands)

Squads/Appearances/Goals

Austria

No	Name	DoB	Aps	(s)	Gls	Club
Goalkeepers						
1	Paul Gartler	10/03/97	3			Rapid Wien
21	Tobias Schützenauer	19/05/97				Sturm
Defenders						
20	Sandro Ingolitsch	18/04/97				Liefering
5	Benjamin Kaufmann	14/06/97	3			Liefering
15	Manuel Maranda	09/07/97	1			Admira
3	Stefan Peric	13/02/97	2			Stuttgart (GER)
6	Stefan Posch	14/05/97	3			Hoffenheim (GER)
14	Maximilian Wöber	04/02/98	3			Rapid Wien
Midfielders						
8	Albin Gashi	25/01/97	1	(1)		Rapid Wien
4	Marco Krainz	17/05/97	3			Austria Lustenau
7	Sandi Lovric	28/03/98	2	(1)		Sturm
10	Philipp Malicsek	03/06/97	3			Rapid Wien
11	Simon Pirkl	03/04/97	2	(1)		Wacker
2	Xaver Schlager	28/09/97	3		1	Liefering
16	Wilhelm Vorsager	29/06/97	1			Admira
Forwards						
17	Fabian Gmeiner	27/01/97		(3)		Stuttgart (GER)
19	Patrick Hasenhüttl	20/05/97		(2)		Ingolstadt (GER)
9	Arnel Jakupovic	29/05/98	3		1	Middlesbrough (ENG)

Croatia

No	Name	DoB	Aps	(s)	Gls	Club
Goalkeepers						
1	Karlo Letica	11/02/97	2			Hajduk Split
12	Ivan Nevistić	31/07/98	1			Rijeka
Defenders						
3	Silvio Anočić	10/09/97	2			Roma (ITA)
15	Marijan Čabraja	25/02/97	1	(1)		Dinamo Zagreb
4	Martin Erlić	24/01/98	2			Sassuolo (ITA)
2	Matej Hudeček	27/12/98	3			Dinamo Zagreb
5	Vinko Soldo	02/03/98	3			Dinamo Zagreb
Midfielders						
10	Andrija Balić	11/08/97	2	(1)		Udinese (ITA)
17	Matija Fintić	12/06/97	1			Dinamo Zagreb
14	Luka Ivanušec	26/11/98	2	(1)		Lokomotiva Zagreb
18	Kristijan Jakić	14/05/97	1			Split
8	Bojan Knežević	28/01/97	2	(1)		Dinamo Zagreb
16	Nikola Moro	12/03/98	2	(1)	1	Dinamo Zagreb
6	Karlo Plantak	11/11/97	2			Dinamo Zagreb
Forwards						
13	Ivan Božić	08/06/97	1	(2)		Dinamo Zagreb
7	Josip Brekalo	23/06/98	3		1	Wolfsburg (GER)
9	Fran Brodić	08/01/97	1	(2)		Club Brugge (BEL)
11	Davor Lovren	03/10/98	3			Dinamo Zagreb

UEFA European Under-19 Championship

England

No	Name	DoB	Aps	(s)	Gls	Club
Goalkeepers						
13	Sam Howes	10/11/97				West Ham
1	Freddie Woodman	04/03/97	4			Newcastle
Defenders						
3	Callum Connolly	23/09/97	1			Everton
6	Dael Fry	30/08/97	1			Middlesbrough
2	Jonjoe Kenny	15/03/97	3			Everton
19	Tafari Moore	05/07/97				Arsenal
5	Taylor Moore	12/05/97	3			Lens (FRA)
15	Fikayo Tomori	19/12/97	3			Chelsea
12	Kyle Walker-Peters	13/04/97	3	(1)		Tottenham
Midfielders						
14	Ryan Ledson	19/08/97	1	(1)		Everton
18	Ainsley Maitland-Niles	29/08/97	3	(1)		Ipswich
10	Sheyi Ojo	19/06/97	2	(2)		Liverpool
8	Josh Onomah	27/04/97	4			Tottenham
16	Reece Oxford	16/12/98	3			West Ham
4	Jordan Rossiter	24/03/97	3			Rangers (SCO)
Forwards						
7	Tammy Abraham	02/10/97	2	(1)		Chelsea
11	Isaiah Brown	07/01/97	3	(1)	2	Chelsea
17	Ademola Lookman	20/10/97	2	(1)		Charlton
9	Dominic Solanke	14/09/97	3		2	Chelsea

Germany

No	Name	DoB	Aps	(s)	Gls	Club
Goalkeepers						
12	Florian Müller	13/11/97	2			Mainz
23	Moritz Nicolas	21/10/97				Mönchengladbach
1	Dominik Reimann	18/06/97	2			Dortmund
21	Markus Schubert	12/06/98				Dresden
Defenders						
4	Lukas Boeder	18/04/97	1	(1)		Leverkusen
5	Benedikt Gimber	19/02/97	4			Sandhausen
14	Gökhan Gül	17/07/98	3		1	Bochum
15	Jannes Horn	06/02/97	2			Wolfsburg
3	Maximilian Mittelstädt	18/03/97	3			Hertha
2	Phil Neumann	08/07/97	4		1	Schalke
Midfielders						
10	Max Besuschkow	31/05/97	3			Stuttgart
18	Amara Conde	06/01/97	2			Wolfsburg
6	Gino Fechner	05/09/97	3			RB Leipzig
8	Benjamin Henrichs	23/02/97	4			Leverkusen
17	Marvin Mehlem	11/09/97		(3)	1	Karlsruhe
13	Fabian Reese	29/11/97	1	(2)		Schalke
7	Suat Serdar	11/04/97	2	(2)	1	Mainz
Forwards						
19	Emmanuel Iyoha	11/10/97		(1)		Düsseldorf
11	Philipp Ochs	17/04/97	4		4	Hoffenheim
16	Janni Serra	13/03/98	2	(2)		Dortmund
9	Cedric Teuchert	14/01/97	2	(2)	1	Nürnberg

Netherlands

No	Name	DoB	Aps	(s)	Gls	Club
Goalkeepers						
16	Maarten Paes	14/05/98				NEC
1	Yanick van Osch	24/03/97	4			PSV
Defenders						
13	Jurich Carolina	15/07/98		(2)		PSV
12	Julian Lelieveld	24/11/97	2			Vitesse
3	Pablo Rosario	07/01/97	4			Almere
4	Hidde ter Avest	20/05/97	4			Twente
5	Calvin Verdonk	26/04/97	4			Zwolle
2	Deyovaisio Zeefuik	11/03/98	2			Ajax
Midfielders						
6	Laros Duarte	28/02/97	4			PSV
14	Carel Eiting	11/02/98	1	(2)		Ajax
8	Abdelhak Nouri	02/04/97	4		2	Ajax
10	Jari Schuurman	22/02/97	4			Willem II
18	Michel Vlap	02/06/97		(2)		Heerenveen
Forwards						
7	Steven Bergwijn	08/10/97	4		2	PSV
15	Gino Dekker	22/03/97	1	(2)		Ajax
9	Sam Lammers	30/04/97	3	(1)	3	PSV
11	Kenneth Paal	24/06/97	3			PSV
17	Dennis van der Heijden	17/02/97		(3)	1	Den Haag

France

No	Name	DoB	Aps	(s)	Gls	Club
Goalkeepers						
1	Paul Bernardoni	18/04/97	5			Bordeaux
16	Quentin Braat	06/07/97				Nantes
Defenders						
3	Olivier Boscagli	18/11/97	2			Nice
5	Issa Diop	09/01/97	5		1	Toulouse
6	Jérémy Gelin	24/04/97		(2)		Rennes
2	Enock Kwateng	09/04/97	1	(1)		Nantes
15	Faitout Maouassa	06/07/98	4			Nancy
13	Clément Michelin	11/05/97	4			Toulouse
4	Jérôme Onguene	22/12/97	4			Sochaux
Midfielders						
12	Ludovic Blas	31/12/97	4	(1)	2	Guingamp
18	Jeando Fuchs	11/10/97		(5)		Sochaux
11	Kylian Mbappé Lottin	20/12/98	5		5	Monaco
17	Denis Will Poha	28/05/97	5			Rennes
8	Lucas Tousart	29/04/97	5		1	Lyon
Forwards						
7	Jean-Kévin Augustin	16/06/97	5		6	Paris
9	Florian Aye	19/01/97	1	(1)		Auxerre
14	Amine Harit	18/06/97	5			Nantes
10	Marcus Thuram	06/08/97		(5)		Sochaux

Italy

No	Name	DoB	Aps	(s)	Gls	Club
Goalkeepers						
1	Alex Meret	22/03/97	5			Udinese
22	Andrea Zaccagno	27/05/97				Torino
Defenders						
15	Mauro Coppolaro	10/03/97	5			Udinese
3	Federico Dimarco	10/11/97	4		4	Empoli
13	Giuseppe Pezzella	29/11/97	1	(3)		Palermo
5	Filippo Romagna	26/05/97	5			Juventus
2	Davide Vitturini	21/02/97	5			Pescara
Midfielders						
4	Nicolò Barella	07/02/97	4			Cagliari
11	Francesco Cassata	16/07/97		(4)		Juventus
7	Simone Edera	09/01/97	1	(1)		Torino
18	Paolo Ghiglione	02/02/97	5			Genoa
6	Manuel Locatelli	08/01/98	4		1	Milan
8	Alberto Picchi	12/08/97	4			Empoli
14	Simone Pontisso	20/03/97	2	(1)		SPAL
Forwards						
16	Patrick Cutrone	03/01/98		(4)		Milan
9	Andrea Favilli	17/05/97	4			Livorno
10	Simone Minelli	08/01/97	2	(2)		Fiorentina
17	Giuseppe Panico	10/05/97	4			Genoa

Portugal

No	Name	DoB	Aps	(s)	Gls	Club
Goalkeepers						
12	Diogo Costa	19/09/99				Porto
1	Pedro Silva	13/02/97	4			Sporting
Defenders						
15	Diogo Dalot	18/03/99	3			Porto
4	Francisco Ferreira	26/03/97	4			Benfica
2	Pedro Empis	01/02/97	1	(1)	1	Sporting
13	Pedro Pacheco	27/01/97	1	(2)	1	Basel (SUI)
3	Rúben Dias	14/05/97	3			Benfica
5	Yuri Ribeiro	24/01/97	4			Benfica
Midfielders						
16	Bruno Xadas	02/12/97	1	(1)		Braga
8	Gonçalo Rodrigues	18/07/97	3		1	Benfica
10	João Carvalho	09/03/97	4			Benfica
14	Pedro Delgado	07/04/97	3			Internazionale (ITA)
6	Pedro Rodrigues	20/05/97	4			Benfica
Forwards						
9	Alex Silva	16/03/97	1	(3)	1	Guimarães
17	Asumah Abubakar	10/05/97	1	(1)	1	Willem II (NED)
11	Buta	10/02/97	3	(1)	2	Benfica
7	Diogo Gonçalves	06/02/97	2	(2)		Benfica
18	Ricardo Almeida	09/05/97	2			Moreirense

UEFA UNDER17™ CHAMPIONSHIP

Spot kicks decide all-Iberian final in Baku	**Record-equalling second title for champions**	**Holders France exit without scoring**

Portugal pip Spain on penalties

Just as they did in 2003, Portugal got the better of Spain in the final to win the UEFA European Under-17 Championship and claim the trophy for the second time.

Thirteen years after a squad featuring João Moutinho, Miguel Veloso and Vieirinha triumphed on home soil, Hélio Sousa's class of 2016 came out on top in Azerbaijan, defeating their Iberian counterparts on penalties after a 1-1 draw at Baku's 8KM Stadium. In doing so, Portugal became the joint most successful nation in U17 history, alongside England, France, the Netherlands, Russia and Spain.

The finals got off to a mixed start for the enthusiastic hosts. While 33,000 fans converged on Baku Olympic Stadium – the biggest crowd for any UEFA youth fixture since the inaugural U17 and U19 seasons in 2001/02 – Azerbaijan's 5-0 reverse against Portugal left Tabriz Hasanov's side up against it from the outset. They responded admirably to that setback, drawing 1-1 with Belgium and beating Scotland 1-0, but it was not enough to carry them into the knockout phase.

Second victories for Austria, who had beaten Azerbaijan's fellow U17 finals debutants Bosnia & Herzegovina 2-0 in their curtain-raiser, and Portugal meant they both qualified for the quarter-finals with a game to spare. Belgium and Germany joined them on matchday three, when Sweden, England, Spain and the Netherlands all claimed closing victories to fill the top two places in Groups C and D respectively. Holders France, meanwhile, went home without a goal to their name.

Portugal eased to another 5-0 win, against Austria, in the last eight, with José Gomes registering the first three goals. In completing his hat-trick, the Benfica forward surpassed Spain's Paco Alcácer

Joy for 2015/16 European U17 champions Portugal

as the 15-goal top scorer in the competition's history. The other quarter-finals were much tighter affairs, with Germany (v Belgium), Spain (v England) and the Netherlands (v Sweden) all recording 1-0 victories.

Gomes's seventh goal of the tournament, and his fifth header, put Portugal ahead against the Netherlands in the semi-finals before right-back Diogo Dalot rounded things off in the second half. For long periods of the second match of the day at Baku's Dalga Stadium it appeared that Germany would be Portugal's opponents in the final, with Renat Dadashov, a player of Azerbaijani extraction, having fired the 2015 runners-up in front. However, goals inside the last 16 minutes from Abel Ruiz and Brahim Díaz tipped the balance of the contest Spain's way.

Dalot struck again in the final, on 27 minutes, only for Díaz to head La Roja level shortly afterwards and end Portugal's run of five successive clean sheets. There were no further goals in normal or extra time, so the tournament had to be decided from the penalty spot. Nine kicks had been successfully converted when Spain captain Manu Morlanes clipped the outside of Diogo Costa's left-hand post, enabling Portugal's youngsters to make the long journey back home with the trophy.

Qualifying round

Group 1

22-27/10/15 Newport
Netherlands 1-2 Wales, Switzerland 2-0 Albania, Albania 0-5 Netherlands, Switzerland 1-0 Wales, Netherlands 4-1 Switzerland, Wales 1-1 Albania

	Pld	W	D	L	F	A	Pts
1 Netherlands	3	2	0	1	10	3	6
2 Switzerland	3	2	0	1	4	4	6
3 Wales	3	1	1	1	3	3	4
4 Albania	3	0	1	2	1	8	1

Group 2

30/09-05/10/15 Orsha, Mogilev
Belarus 1-1 Montenegro, Russia 6-0 Cyprus, Belarus 2-3 Cyprus, Montenegro 0-2 Russia, Russia 2-0 Belarus, Cyprus 0-1 Montenegro

	Pld	W	D	L	F	A	Pts
1 Russia	3	3	0	0	10	0	9
2 Montenegro	3	1	1	1	2	3	4
3 Cyprus	3	1	0	2	3	9	3
4 Belarus	3	0	1	2	3	6	1

Group 3

24-29/09/15 Tammela, Lohja
Sweden 5-1 Malta, Republic of Ireland 1-0 Finland, Malta 0-6 Republic of Ireland, Sweden 1-1 Finland, Republic of Ireland 1-1 Sweden, Finland 4-2 Malta

	Pld	W	D	L	F	A	Pts
1 Republic of Ireland	3	2	1	0	8	1	7
2 Sweden	3	1	2	0	7	3	5
3 Finland	3	1	1	1	5	4	4
4 Malta	3	0	0	3	3	15	0

Group 4

24-29/10/15 Telki, Dabas, Felcsut
Hungary 1-2 Romania, Georgia 3-4 Slovakia, Hungary 1-1 Slovakia, Romania 0-3 Georgia, Georgia 2-2 Hungary, Slovakia 1-1 Romania

	Pld	W	D	L	F	A	Pts
1 Slovakia	3	1	2	0	6	5	5
2 Georgia	3	1	1	1	8	6	4
3 Romania	3	1	1	1	3	5	4
4 Hungary	3	0	2	1	4	5	2

Group 5

24-29/10/15 Consdorf, Mensdorf, Beggen
Serbia 6-1 Luxembourg, Austria 2-0 Lithuania, Serbia 0-0 Lithuania, Luxembourg 1-2 Austria, Austria 1-1 Serbia, Lithuania 2-0 Luxembourg

	Pld	W	D	L	F	A	Pts
1 Austria	3	2	1	0	5	2	7
2 Serbia	3	1	2	0	7	2	5
3 Lithuania	3	1	1	1	2	2	4
4 Luxembourg	3	0	0	3	2	10	0

Group 6

25-30/10/15 Riga
Spain 2-0 Andorra, Poland 4-0 Latvia, Poland 1-0 Andorra, Latvia 0-2 Spain, Spain 2-1 Poland, Andorra 0-3 Latvia

	Pld	W	D	L	F	A	Pts
1 Spain	3	3	0	0	6	1	9
2 Poland	3	2	0	1	6	2	6
3 Latvia	3	1	0	2	3	6	3
4 Andorra	3	0	0	3	0	6	0

João Filipe of Portugal – the top scorer in the qualifying competition

Group 7

26-31/10/15 Eschen, Balzers
Croatia 4-1 Gibraltar, Czech Republic 4-0 Liechtenstein, Gibraltar 1-9 Czech Republic, Croatia 2-0 Liechtenstein, Czech Republic 2-2 Croatia, Liechtenstein 3-0 Gibraltar

	Pld	W	D	L	F	A	Pts
1 Czech Republic	3	2	1	0	15	3	7
2 Croatia	3	2	1	0	8	3	7
3 Liechtenstein	3	1	0	2	3	6	3
4 Gibraltar	3	0	0	3	2	16	0

Group 8

22-27/09/15 Keflavik, Grindavik, Hafnarfjördur, Reykjavik
Denmark 0-0 Greece, Iceland 5-0 Kazakhstan, Denmark 4-1 Kazakhstan, Greece 1-0 Iceland, Iceland 0-2 Denmark, Kazakhstan 0-6 Greece

	Pld	W	D	L	F	A	Pts
1 Denmark	3	2	1	0	6	1	7
2 Greece	3	1	2	0	7	1	5
3 Iceland	3	1	1	1	6	3	4
4 Kazakhstan	3	0	0	3	1	15	0

Group 9

29/09-04/10/15 Febres, Luso, Pampilhosa, Tocha, Coimbra
England 8-0 San Marino, Portugal 7-0 Armenia, England 5-0 Armenia, San Marino 0-5 Portugal, Portugal 1-1 England, Armenia 1-1 San Marino

	Pld	W	D	L	F	A	Pts
1 England	3	2	1	0	14	1	7
2 Portugal	3	2	1	0	13	1	7
3 Armenia	3	0	1	2	1	13	1
4 San Marino	3	0	1	2	1	14	1

Group 10

24-29/09/15 Bakovci, Lendava
Turkey 3-0 Faroe Islands, Belgium 2-1 Slovenia, Turkey 1-1 Slovenia, Faroe Islands 1-4 Belgium, Belgium 0-0 Turkey, Slovenia 1-0 Faroe Islands

	Pld	W	D	L	F	A	Pts
1 Belgium	3	2	1	0	6	2	7
2 Turkey	3	1	2	0	4	1	5
3 Slovenia	3	1	1	1	3	3	4
4 Faroe Islands	3	0	0	3	1	8	0

Group 11

20-25/10/15 Petach-Tikva, Shefayim
Norway 1-3 Israel, France 1-0 Northern Ireland, Norway 1-1 Northern Ireland, Israel 0-3 France, France 1-0 Norway, Northern Ireland 1-2 Israel

	Pld	W	D	L	F	A	Pts
1 France	3	3	0	0	5	0	9
2 Israel	3	2	0	1	5	5	6
3 Northern Ireland	3	0	1	2	2	4	1
4 Norway	3	0	1	2	2	5	1

Group 12

21-26/10/15 Sozopol, Burgas
Italy 3-0 Bulgaria, Scotland 3-0 FYR Macedonia, Italy 0-0 FYR Macedonia, Bulgaria 2-0 Scotland, Scotland 1-1 Italy, FYR Macedonia 0-0 Bulgaria

	Pld	W	D	L	F	A	Pts
1 Italy	3	1	2	0	4	1	5
2 Bulgaria	3	1	1	1	2	3	4
3 Scotland	3	1	1	1	4	3	4
4 FYR Macedonia	3	0	2	1	0	3	2

Group 13

26-31/10/15 Orhei, Vadul lui Voda
Ukraine 1-1 Moldova, Bosnia & Herzegovina 2-1 Estonia, Ukraine 2-0 Estonia, Moldova 0-5 Bosnia & Herzegovina, Bosnia & Herzegovina 0-3 Ukraine, Estonia 1-0 Moldova

	Pld	W	D	L	F	A	Pts
1 Ukraine	3	2	1	0	6	1	7
2 Bosnia & Herzegovina	3	2	0	1	7	4	6
3 Estonia	3	1	0	2	2	4	3
4 Moldova	3	0	1	2	1	7	1

Elite round

Group 1

28/03-02/04/16 Zlin, Uherske Hradiste, Stare Mesto
Denmark 4-0 Scotland, Czech Republic 2-2 Switzerland, Switzerland 1-2 Denmark, Czech Republic 0-2 Scotland, Denmark 2-3 Czech Republic, Scotland 1-1 Switzerland

	Pld	W	D	L	F	A	Pts
1 Denmark	3	2	0	1	8	4	6
2 Scotland	3	1	1	1	3	5	4
3 Czech Republic	3	1	1	1	5	6	4
4 Switzerland	3	0	2	1	4	5	2

Group 2

24-29/03/16 Leek, Chesterfield, Burton-on-Trent
Ukraine 3-0 Finland, England 3-1 Turkey, England 1-0 Finland, Turkey 0-3 Ukraine, Ukraine 1-1 England, Finland 1-3 Turkey

	Pld	W	D	L	F	A	Pts
1 Ukraine	3	2	1	0	7	1	7
2 England	3	2	1	0	5	2	7
3 Turkey	3	1	0	2	4	7	3
4 Finland	3	0	0	3	1	7	0

Group 3

15-20/03/16 Tbilisi
Bosnia & Herzegovina 2-1 Georgia, Russia 0-4 Italy, Russia 1-0 Georgia, Italy 0-1 Bosnia & Herzegovina, Bosnia & Herzegovina 1-2 Russia, Georgia 0-1 Italy

	Pld	W	D	L	F	A	Pts
1 Italy	3	2	0	1	5	1	6
2 Bosnia & Herzegovina	3	2	0	1	4	3	6
3 Russia	3	2	0	1	3	5	6
4 Georgia	3	0	0	3	1	4	0

UEFA European Under-17 Championship

Group 4

24-29/03/16 Buderich, Dusseldorf, Ratingen
**Netherlands 0-0 Bulgaria, Germany 5-1
Slovakia, Slovakia 0-2 Netherlands, Germany
1-1 Bulgaria, Netherlands 0-1 Germany,
Bulgaria 0-3 Slovakia**

		Pld	W	D	L	F	A	Pts
1	Germany	3	2	1	0	7	2	7
2	Netherlands	3	1	1	1	2	1	4
3	Slovakia	3	1	0	2	4	7	3
4	Bulgaria	3	0	2	1	1	4	2

Group 5

16-21/03/16 Pula, Rovinj
**Portugal 2-0 Sweden, Croatia 0-2 Wales,
Portugal 1-0 Wales, Sweden 2-1 Croatia,
Croatia 2-4 Portugal, Wales 0-1 Sweden**

		Pld	W	D	L	F	A	Pts
1	Portugal	3	3	0	0	7	2	9
2	Sweden	3	2	0	1	3	3	6
3	Wales	3	1	0	2	2	2	3
4	Croatia	3	0	0	3	3	8	0

Group 6

29/03-03/04/16 Anglet, Saint-Jean-de-Luz, Biarritz
**France 1-0 Greece, Austria 1-0 Iceland, France
1-0 Iceland, Greece 0-0 Austria, Austria 2-1
France, Iceland 1-0 Greece**

		Pld	W	D	L	F	A	Pts
1	France	3	2	0	1	3	2	6
2	Austria	3	1	2	0	2	1	5
3	Iceland	3	1	1	1	1	1	4
4	Greece	3	0	1	2	0	2	1

Group 7

28/03-02/04/16 Pruszkow, Warsaw, Siedlce
**Republic of Ireland 0-2 Serbia, Poland
2-0 Montenegro, Republic of Ireland 3-0
Montenegro, Serbia 2-1 Poland, Poland 0-0
Republic of Ireland, Montenegro 0-2 Serbia**

		Pld	W	D	L	F	A	Pts
1	Serbia	3	3	0	0	6	1	9
2=	Poland	3	1	1	1	3	2	4
	Republic of Ireland	3	1	1	1	3	2	4
4	Montenegro	3	0	0	3	0	7	0

Group 8

11-16/03/16 Tubize, Overijse, Merchtem
**Spain 1-0 Israel, Belgium 0-0 Slovenia, Spain
0-0 Slovenia, Israel 0-1 Belgium, Belgium 0-0
Spain, Slovenia 1-1 Israel**

		Pld	W	D	L	F	A	Pts
1=	Belgium	3	1	2	0	1	0	5
	Spain	3	1	2	0	1	0	5
3	Slovenia	3	0	3	0	1	1	3
4	Israel	3	0	1	2	1	3	1

Top goalscorers (Qualifying/Elite rounds)

7	João Filipe (Portugal)
6	Reiss Nelson (England)
5	Jens Odgaard (Denmark)
	Dylan Vente (Netherlands)
	José Gomes (Portugal)
	Teddy Bergqvist (Sweden)

Final tournament

Group A

05/05/16, 8KM Stadium, Baku
**Belgium 2-0 Scotland
Goals:** 1-0 Corryn 45, 2-0 Openda 60
Referee: Kralović (SVK)

05/05/16, Bakı Olimpiya Stadionu, Baku
**Azerbaijan 0-5 Portugal
Goals:** 0-1 José Gomes 4, 0-2 José Gomes 16,
0-3 Asadov 24(og), 0-4 Miguel Luis 44,
0-5 Gedson Fernandes 76
Referee: Frankowski (POL)

08/05/16, Dalga Stadium, Baku
**Portugal 2-0 Scotland
Goals:** 1-0 Quina 15, 2-0 José Gomes 55
Referee: Jónsson (ISL)

08/05/16, 8KM Stadium, Baku
**Azerbaijan 1-1 Belgium
Goals:** 0-1 Bongiovanni 72, 1-1 Mahmudov 77
Referee: Ardeleanu (CZE)

11/05/16, 8KM Stadium, Baku
**Scotland 0-1 Azerbaijan
Goal:** 0-1 Nabiyev 79
Referee: Edvartsen (NOR)

11/05/16, Dalga Stadium, Baku
**Portugal 0-0 Belgium
Referee:** Nevalainen (FIN)

		Pld	W	D	L	F	A	Pts
1	Portugal	3	2	1	0	7	0	7
2	Belgium	3	1	2	0	3	1	5
3	Azerbaijan	3	1	1	1	2	6	4
4	Scotland	3	0	0	3	0	5	0

Group B

05/05/16, 8KM Stadium, Baku
**Austria 2-0 Bosnia & Herzegovina
Goals:** 1-0 Baumgartner 18, 2-0 Baumgartner 35
Referee: Ardeleanu (CZE)

05/05/16, Bakı Olimpiya Stadionu, Baku
**Ukraine 2-2 Germany
Goals:** 1-0 Yanakov 33, 1-1 Y Otto 37,
2-1 Buletsa 67, 2-2 Schreck 74
Referee: Jónsson (ISL)

08/05/16, 8KM Stadium, Baku
**Ukraine 0-2 Austria
Goals:** 0-1 Schmid 7, 0-2 V Müller 21
Referee: Edvartsen (NOR)

08/05/16, Dalga Stadium, Baku
**Germany 3-1 Bosnia & Herzegovina
Goals:** 0-1 Baack 2(og), 1-1 Akkaynak 17(p),
2-1 Y Otto 66, 3-1 Y Otto 72
Referee: Kralović (SVK)

11/05/16, 8KM Stadium, Baku
**Bosnia & Herzegovina 2-1 Ukraine
Goals:** 1-0 Hadžić 38, 2-0 Hadžić 40+1,
2-1 Kulakov 69
Referee: Jović (CRO)

11/05/16, Dalga Stadium, Baku
**Germany 4-0 Austria
Goals:** 1-0 Meisl 7(og), 2-0 Akkaynak 25,
3-0 Havertz 32, 4-0 Dadashov 80+1
Referee: Žganec (SVN)

		Pld	W	D	L	F	A	Pts
1	Germany	3	2	1	0	9	3	7
2	Austria	3	2	0	1	4	4	6
3	Bosnia & Herzegovina	3	1	0	2	3	6	3
4	Ukraine	3	0	1	2	3	6	1

Group C

06/05/16, Dalga Stadium, Baku
**France 0-0 Denmark
Referee:** Nevalainen (FIN)

06/05/16, Karabakh Stadium, Baku
**England 1-2 Sweden
Goals:** 0-1 Asoro 4, 0-2 Asoro 59, 1-2 Nelson 62
Referee: Edvartsen (NOR)

Abel Ruiz (left), Spain's leading marksman in
Azerbaijan, takes on the Netherlands' Pascal Struijk

09/05/16, Bakı Olimpiya Stadionu, Baku
**Denmark 1-0 Sweden
Goal:** 1-0 Buch Jensen 80+3
Referee: Žganec (SVN)

09/05/16, Karabakh Stadium, Baku
**France 0-2 England
Goals:** 0-1 Morris 15, 0-2 Nelson 43(p)
Referee: Jović (CRO)

12/05/16, Karabakh Stadium, Baku
**Sweden 1-0 France
Goal:** 1-0 Bergqvist 45
Referee: Frankowski (POL)

12/05/16, Bakı Olimpiya Stadionu, Baku
**Denmark 1-3 England
Goals:** 0-1 Nelson 30, 0-2 Mount 51, 0-3 Hirst 78,
1-3 Odgaard 80+1
Referee: Kralović (SVK)

		Pld	W	D	L	F	A	Pts
1	Sweden	3	2	0	1	3	2	6
2	England	3	2	0	1	6	3	6
3	Denmark	3	1	1	1	2	3	4
4	France	3	0	1	2	0	3	1

Group D

06/05/16, Karabakh Stadium, Baku
**Italy 2-1 Serbia
Goals:** 1-0 Scamacca 9, 2-0 Kean 32,
2-1 Maksimović 77
Referee: Žganec (SVN)

06/05/16, Dalga Stadium, Baku
**Netherlands 0-2 Spain
Goals:** 0-1 Mboula 16, 0-2 Ruiz 52
Referee: Jović (CRO)

09/05/16, Karabakh Stadium, Baku
**Italy 0-1 Netherlands
Goal:** 0-1 Nunnely 78
Referee: Frankowski (POL)

09/05/16, Bakı Olimpiya Stadionu, Baku
**Serbia 1-1 Spain
Goals:** 0-1 Ruiz 4, 1-1 Joveljić 59(p)
Referee: Nevalainen (FIN)

12/05/16, Karabakh Stadium, Baku
**Spain 4-2 Italy
Goals:** 1-0 Díaz 44, 2-0 García 59,
2-1 Olivieri 65(p), 2-2 Pinamonti 72, 3-2 Ruiz 76,
4-2 Lozano 80+1
Referee: Ardeleanu (CZE)

12/05/16, Bakı Olimpiya Stadionu, Baku
**Serbia 0-2 Netherlands
Goals:** 0-1 M Ilić 72(og), 0-2 Vente 80+1
Referee: Jónsson (ISL)

		Pld	W	D	L	F	A	Pts
1	Spain	3	2	1	0	7	3	7
2	Netherlands	3	2	0	1	3	2	6
3	Italy	3	1	0	2	4	6	3
4	Serbia	3	0	1	2	2	5	1

Quarter-finals

14/05/16, Dalga Stadium, Baku
Portugal 5-0 Austria
Goals: 1-0 José Gomes 7(p), 2-0 José Gomes 18,
3-0 José Gomes 47, 4-0 Mesaque Dju 51,
5-0 Miguel Luis 77
Referee: Jović (CRO)

14/05/16, Dalga Stadium, Baku
Germany 1-0 Belgium
Goal: 1-0 Dadashov 46
Referee: Jónsson (ISL)

15/05/16, 8KM Stadium, Baku
Spain 1-0 England
Goal: 1-0 García 11
Referee: Edvartsen (NOR)

15/05/16, 8KM Stadium, Baku
Sweden 0-1 Netherlands
Goal: 0-1 Chong 62
Referee: Nevalainen (FIN)

Semi-finals

18/05/16, Dalga Stadium, Baku
Portugal 2-0 Netherlands
Goals: 1-0 José Gomes 25, 2-0 Diogo Dalot 56
Referee: Kralović (SVK)

18/05/16, Dalga Stadium, Baku
Germany 1-2 Spain
Goals: 1-0 Dadashov 10, 1-1 Ruiz 64, 1-2 Díaz 78
Referee: Frankowski (POL)

Final

21/05/16, 8KM Stadium, Baku (att: 7,253)
Portugal 1-1 Spain (aet; 5-4 on pens)
Goals: 1-0 Diogo Dalot 27, 1-1 Díaz 32
Referee: Ardeleanu (CZE)
Portugal: Diogo Costa, Diogo Dalot, Diogo
Queirós, Rúben Vinagre, Gedson Fernandes,
João Filipe, José Gomes, Quina (Rafael Leão
79), Mesaque Dju (Miguel Luis 55), Diogo Leite,
Florentino. Coach: Hélio Sousa (POR)
Spain: Peña (Adrián 80+2), Robles, García (Martín
70), Brandariz, Zabarte, Busquets, Mboula (Lozano
80), Morlanes, Ruiz, Díaz, Subias. Coach: Santi
Denia (ESP)

Top goalscorers (Final tournament)

7	José Gomes (Portugal)
4	Abel Ruiz (Spain)
3	Reiss Nelson (England)
	Renat Dadashov (Germany)
	Yari Otto (Germany)
	Brahim Díaz (Spain)

Squads/Appearances/Goals

Austria

No	Name	DoB	Aps	(s)	Gls
Goalkeepers					
21	Semir Karalic	03/05/99	1		
1	Benjamin Ozegovic	09/08/99	3		
Defenders					
4	Alexandar Borkovic	11/06/99	1		
3	Alexander Burgstaller	12/07/99	3		
12	Lukas Malicsek	06/06/99	3		
14	Dario Maresic	29/09/99	4		
5	Luca Meisl	04/03/99	4		
20	Christian Müller	10/02/99		(2)	
2	Leonardo Zottele	16/04/99	1	(1)	
Midfielders					
10	Christoph Baumgartner	01/08/99	4		2
13	Dominik Fitz	16/06/99		(4)	
17	Maurice Mathis	09/05/99	1	(1)	
9	Nicolas Meister	28/09/99	1	(3)	
6	Valentino Müller	19/01/99	4		1
7	Philipp Sittsam	16/02/99	3	(1)	
16	Jörg Wagnes	29/01/99	3		
Forwards					
18	Kelvin Arase	15/01/99	4		
11	Romano Schmid	27/01/00	4		1

Azerbaijan

No	Name	DoB	Aps	(s)	Gls
Goalkeepers					
1	Mammad Huseynov	29/05/99	2		
12	Kamran Ibrahimov	07/06/99		(1)	
22	Murad Popov	05/03/99	1		
Defenders					
19	Ege Atlam	01/05/99		(1)	
3	Rijat Garayev	07/09/99	3		
4	Yusif Hasanov	30/11/99	1		
14	Ismayil Karakash	08/01/99	3		
2	Huseyin Seylighli	19/01/99	3		
Midfielders					
18	Suleyman Ahmadov	25/11/99	2	(1)	
5	Elchin Asadov	03/08/99	3		
17	Baris Ekinjier	24/03/99	2		
6	Ibrahim Gadirzade	21/03/99	2		
8	Metin Güler	10/09/99	3		
13	Bahadur Haziyev	26/03/99			
10	Pilagha Mehdiyev	25/05/99	2	(1)	
15	Jeyhun Mukhtarli	30/09/99	1		
7	Farid Nabiyev	22/07/99	3		1
Forwards					
11	Nadir Kasumov	27/08/99		(2)	
16	Murad Mahmudov	07/05/00		(2)	1
9	Dogukan Oksuz	25/02/99	2		

Belgium

No	Name	DoB	Aps	(s)	Gls
Goalkeepers					
12	Ilias Moutha-Sebtaoui	01/04/99			
1	Mile Svilar	27/08/99	4		
Defenders					
2	Sebastiaan Bornauw	22/03/99	3		
4	Hannes Delcroix	28/02/99	4		
5	Daam Foulon	23/03/99	4		
17	Soufiane Karkache	02/07/99	1		
3	Zinho Vanheusden	29/07/99	4		
Midfielders					
10	Francesco Antonucci	20/06/99	3		
8	Milan Corryn	04/04/99	3	(1)	1
14	Xian Emmers	20/07/99	4		
13	Natanaël Frenoy	08/01/99			
6	Daouda Peeters	26/01/99	3		
7	Thibaud Verlinden	09/07/99	2	(2)	
15	Louis Verstraete	04/05/99		(3)	
Forwards					
11	Adrien Bongiovanni	20/09/99	3	(1)	1
18	Indy Boonen	04/01/99	2	(2)	
16	Loïs Openda	16/02/00	3	(1)	1
9	Jules Vanhaecke	17/03/99	1	(1)	

Bosnia & Herzegovina

No	Name	DoB	Aps	(s)	Gls
Goalkeepers					
12	Filip Dujmović	12/03/99	1		
1	Filip Vasilj	22/11/99	2		
Defenders					
3	Amar Beširević	08/08/99	2	(1)	
6	Milan Mirić	12/03/99	3		
2	Saša Perić	29/06/99	2	(2)	
7	Ševkija Resić	04/12/99	2	(1)	
16	Rijad Sadiku	18/01/99	2		
5	Amir Velić	28/03/99	2		
15	Nikola Vuletić	18/01/99	1	(1)	
Midfielders					
4	Jasmin Čeliković	07/01/99	3		
8	Stefan Kovač	14/01/99	3		
14	Anel Šabanadžović	22/05/99		(1)	
10	Demirel Veladžić	15/05/99	2		
17	Predrag Vladić	04/02/99	2		
Forwards					
9	Tomas Dadić	02/04/99	2	(1)	
18	Benjamin Hadžić	04/03/99	3		2
13	Nedim Hadžić	19/03/99	1	(1)	
11	Edis Smajić	10/09/99	2	(1)	

Denmark

No	Name	DoB	Aps	(s)	Gls
Goalkeepers					
16	Casper Hauervig	03/04/99			
1	Oskar Snorre	26/01/99	3		
Defenders					
4	Christian Bech	17/05/99			
17	Nicolai Damkjær	02/04/99			
5	Andreas Poulsen	13/10/99	3		
13	Luka Racic	08/05/99	3		
2	Mads Roerslev	24/06/99	3		
3	Niklas Vesterlund	06/06/99	3		
Midfielders					
14	Sebastian Buch Jensen	28/01/99	2	(1)	1
11	Carlo Holse	02/06/99	3		
18	Mads Mikkelsen	11/12/99	1	(1)	
7	Jeppe Okkels	27/07/99		(2)	
6	Nicklas Strunck	17/08/99	3		
12	Lasse Sørensen	21/10/99		(3)	
8	Victor Torp	30/07/99	3		
10	Jonas Wind	07/02/99	3		
Forwards					
15	Wessam Abou Ali	04/01/99		(1)	
9	Jens Odgaard	31/03/99	3		1

France

No	Name	DoB	Aps	(s)	Gls
Goalkeepers					
16	Didier Desprez	13/03/99	1	(1)	
1	Gaëtan Poussin	13/01/99	2		
Defenders					
13	Loïc Bessile	19/02/99			
15	Mahamadou Dembele	10/04/99	1		
4	Boubacar Kamara	23/11/99	2		
6	Aurélien Nguiamba	18/01/99	3		
3	Malang Sarr	23/01/99	3		
2	Yann Valery	22/02/99	2		
5	Dan-Axel Zagadou	03/06/99	3		
Midfielders					
11	Antoine Bernede	26/05/99	2	(1)	
8	Mickaël Cuisance	16/08/99	3		
7	Hakim El Mokkedem	15/02/99	2	(1)	
12	Paul Fargeas	21/03/99	1		
10	Rafik Guitane	26/05/99	3		
17	Raouf Mroivili	14/01/99		(1)	
18	Ervin Taha	14/03/99	2	(1)	
Forwards					
14	Yassin Fortune	30/01/99	1	(2)	
9	Amine Karraoui	09/06/99	2	(1)	

Italy

No	Name	DoB	Aps	(s)	Gls
Goalkeepers					
12	Gabriel Manuel Meli	05/02/99			
1	Alessandro Plizzari	12/03/00	3		
Defenders					
5	Alessandro Bastoni	13/04/99	3		
2	Raoul Bellanova	17/05/00	3		
4	Edoardo Bianchi	30/04/99	3		
3	Luca Pellegrini	07/03/99	1	(1)	
7	Carmine Setola	13/01/99		(1)	
6	Alessandro Tripaldelli	09/02/99	2	(1)	
Midfielders					
15	Fabrizio Caligara	12/04/00			
19	Christian Capone	28/04/99		(1)	
13	Davide Frattesi	22/09/99	3		
10	Matteo Gabbia	21/10/99	3		
14	Alessandro Mallamo	22/03/99	1	(1)	
8	Andrea Marcucci	07/02/99	2	(1)	
11	Alessio Militari	15/01/99	3		
Forwards					
17	Moise Kean	28/02/00	2		1
9	Marco Olivieri	30/06/99	1	(2)	1
16	Andrea Pinamonti	19/05/99	2	(1)	1
18	Gianluca Scamacca	01/01/99	1		1

England

No	Name	DoB	Aps	(s)	Gls
Goalkeepers					
21	Nicholas Hayes	10/04/99			
13	Ryan Sandford	21/02/99			
1	Jared Thompson	23/02/99	4		
Defenders					
14	Tolaji Bola	04/01/99	1		
3	Jaden Brown	24/01/99	1	(1)	
5	Trevoh Chalobah	05/07/99	4		
18	Morgan Feeney	08/02/99	3	(1)	
12	Edward Francis	11/09/99		(1)	
15	Ryan Sessegnon	18/05/00	4		
2	Dujon Sterling	24/10/99	4		
Midfielders					
6	Dennis Adeniran	02/01/99	3		
4	Marcus McGuane	02/02/99	4		
10	Mason Mount	10/01/99	4		1
11	Reiss Nelson	10/12/99	4		3
Forwards					
17	Joshua Bohui	03/03/99		(2)	
8	Andre Dozzell	02/05/99	4		
9	George Hirst	15/02/99	2	(2)	1
7	Ben Morris	06/07/99	2	(2)	1
16	Samuel Shashoua	13/05/99		(3)	

Germany

No	Name	DoB	Aps	(s)	Gls
Goalkeepers					
1	Jan-Christoph Bartels	13/01/99	5		
12	Lennart Grill	25/01/99		(1)	
Defenders					
2	Alfons Amade	12/11/99	3		
4	Tom Baack	13/03/99	5		
5	Florian Baak	18/03/99	4		
14	Mika Hanraths	04/06/99	2		
18	Davide Itter	05/01/99	2		
3	Gian-Luca Itter	05/01/99	5		
15	Sven Sonnenberg	19/01/99		(2)	
Midfielders					
6	Atakan Akkaynak	05/01/99	4		2
13	Jan-Niklas Beste	04/01/99	3	(2)	
7	Kai Havertz	11/06/99	5		1
16	Jannis Kübler	25/05/99		(4)	
8	Arne Maier	08/01/99	5		
10	Sam Francis Schreck	29/01/99	2	(1)	1
Forwards					
11	Jano Baxmann	18/01/99	1	(4)	
9	Renat Dadashov	17/05/99	5		3
17	Yari Otto	27/05/99	4	(1)	3

Netherlands

No	Name	DoB	Aps	(s)	Gls
Goalkeepers					
1	Mike van de Meulenhof	11/05/99	5		
16	Menno Vink	03/04/99			
Defenders					
2	Navajo Bakboord	29/01/99	4		
3	Matthijs de Ligt	12/08/99	5		
15	Tyrell Malacia	17/08/99	4		
12	Boyd Reith	05/05/99	1	(1)	
4	Pascal Struijk	11/08/99	1	(1)	
13	Jordan Teze	30/09/99		(2)	
5	Owen Wijndal	28/11/99	5		
Midfielders					
8	Leandro Fernandes	25/12/99	4		
14	Ferdi Kadioglu	07/10/99	2	(3)	
10	Donyell Malen	19/01/99	5		
18	Tommie van de Looi	02/07/99		(1)	
6	Jordy Wehrmann	25/03/99	5		
Forwards					
11	Tahith Chong	04/12/99	4		1
7	Justin Kluivert	05/05/99	2	(3)	
17	Che Nunnely	04/02/99	4	(1)	1
9	Dylan Vente	09/05/99	4		

Portugal

No	Name	DoB	Aps	(s)	Gls
Goalkeepers					
1	Diogo Costa	19/09/99	6		
12	João Virginia	10/10/99			
22	Luis Maximiano	05/01/99			
Defenders					
2	Diogo Dalot	18/03/99	5		2
13	Diogo Leite	23/01/99	5		
3	Diogo Queirós	05/01/99	6		
4	Luis Silva	18/02/99	1	(1)	
5	Rúben Vinagre	09/04/99	5		
15	Thierry Correia	09/03/99	2	(1)	
Midfielders					
14	Florentino	19/08/99	5		
6	Gedson Fernandes	09/01/99	5	(1)	1
16	João Lameira	19/04/99	1	(2)	
8	Miguel Luis	27/02/99	2	(3)	2
10	Quina	18/11/99	5	(1)	1
Forwards					
7	João Filipe	30/03/99	6		
9	José Gomes	08/04/99	5	(1)	7
11	Mesaque Dju	18/03/99	5	(1)	1
18	Mickael Almeida	27/01/99	1	(2)	
17	Rafael Leão	10/06/99	1	(4)	

Serbia

No	Name	DoB	Aps	(s)	Gls
Goalkeepers					
1	Miloš Čupić	24/04/99			
12	Aleksandar Popović	27/09/99	3		
Defenders					
6	Strahinja Bošnjak	18/02/99	3		
3	Mladen Devetak	12/03/99	2		
5	Marko Ilić	24/09/99	3		
2	Julijan Popović	15/06/99	3		
15	Aleksa Terzić	17/08/99	1	(2)	
14	Ranko Veselinović	24/03/99		(3)	
Midfielders					
16	Armin Djerlek	15/07/00	1	(2)	
10	Igor Maksimović	31/07/99	2	(1)	1
18	Njegoš Petrović	18/07/99	3		
13	Lazar Nikolić	01/08/99			
4	Miloš Nikolić	08/04/99			
8	Veljko Nikolić	29/08/99	3		
Forwards					
7	Luka Ilić	02/07/99	2		
17	Stefan Ilić	24/09/99	3		
9	Djordje Jovanović	15/02/99	2		
11	Dejan Joveljić	07/08/99	2	(1)	1

Sweden

No	Name	DoB	Aps	(s)	Gls
Goalkeepers					
1	Pontus Dahlberg	21/01/99	4		
12	Malte Påhlsson	02/06/99			
Defenders					
18	Anel Ahmedhodzic	26/03/99	3		
3	Hugo Andersson	01/01/99	4		
4	Joseph Colley	13/04/99	4		
5	Johan Stenmark	26/02/99	2	(1)	
13	Filip Örnblom	11/03/99	1		
Midfielders					
6	Henrik Bellman	24/03/99	4		
2	Emre Erdogdu	06/08/99	2	(1)	
16	Mirad Garza	14/02/99		(2)	
7	Niclas Holgersson	26/06/99		(1)	
11	Simon Marklund	14/09/99	4		
10	Nebiyou Perry	02/10/99	3	(1)	
17	Oscar Petersson	26/02/99	1	(3)	
8	Mattias Svanberg	05/01/99	4		
Forwards					
9	Joel Asoro	27/04/99	4		2
14	Teddy Bergqvist	16/03/99	4		1
15	Adrian Edqvist	20/05/99		(3)	

Scotland

No	Name	DoB	Aps	(s)	Gls
Goalkeepers					
1	Aidan McAdams	23/03/99	2		
12	Kieran Wright	01/04/99	1		
Defenders					
5	Daniel Baur	06/05/99	3		
3	Kieran Freeman	30/03/00			
18	Liam Hegarty	12/02/99	3		
2	Dan Meredith	14/09/99	3		
4	Aidan Wilson	02/01/99	3		
Midfielders					
7	Jack Aitchison	05/03/00	2		
10	Liam Burt	01/02/99	3		
11	Lee Connelly	18/10/99	1	(1)	
8	Fraser Hornby	13/09/99	3		
14	Kyle McAllister	21/01/99	3		
6	Glenn Middleton	01/01/00		(3)	
9	Lewis Morrison	12/03/99		(3)	
Forwards					
15	Jack Adamson	07/01/99	1		
16	Connor McLennan	05/10/99	2		
13	Zak Rudden	06/02/00	3		
17	Broque Watson	05/02/99		(2)	

Spain

No	Name	DoB	Aps	(s)	Gls
Goalkeepers					
13	Adrián	09/01/99		(1)	
1	Ignacio Peña	02/03/99	6		
Defenders					
18	Jose Carlos Aliaga	18/01/99	1	(2)	
4	Juan Brandariz	02/03/99	6		
2	Alejandro Robles	28/01/99	6		
15	David Subias	06/03/99	5		
12	Alex Ujía	09/06/99		(1)	
5	Gorka Zabarte	09/01/99	6		
Midfielders					
6	Oriol Busquets	20/01/99	6		
14	Martín Calderón	01/03/99		(2)	
3	Francisco García	14/08/99	3	(2)	2
16	Pol Lozano	06/10/99		(6)	1
11	Iván Martín	14/02/99	3	(2)	
8	Manu Morlanes	12/01/99	6		
Forwards					
10	Brahim Díaz	03/08/99	6		3
7	Jordi Mboula	16/03/99	6		1
17	Alejandro Millán	07/11/99		(2)	
9	Abel Ruiz	28/01/00	6		4

Ukraine

No	Name	DoB	Aps	(s)	Gls
Goalkeepers					
1	Vladyslav Kucheruk	14/02/99			
12	Andriy Lunin	11/02/99	3		
Defenders					
3	Olexandr Avramenko	22/03/99			
2	Valeriy Bondar	27/02/99	3		
5	Vitaliy Mykolenko	29/05/99	3		
4	Denys Popov	17/02/99	3		
17	Olexiy Sich	30/03/99	2	(1)	
18	Tymofiy Sukhar	04/02/99	1	(1)	
Midfielders					
11	Serhiy Buletsa	16/02/99	3		1
6	Maxym Chekh	03/01/99	3		
9	Olexiy Khakhlov	06/02/99	2	(1)	
16	Mykola Musolitin	21/01/99	1	(2)	
21	Vladyslav Naumets	07/03/99		(1)	
Forwards					
10	Yaroslav Deda	28/05/99		(1)	
8	Olexiy Kashchuk	29/06/00	3		
20	Yuriy Kozyrenko	27/11/99	1	(1)	
7	Andriy Kulakov	28/04/99	3		1
19	Denys Yanakov	01/01/99	2	(1)	1

Three-year German
dominance comes to an end

Wolfsburg denied on
penalties in Reggio Emilia

Mammoth 13-goal haul for
Lyon's Ada Hegerberg

Third title for Lyon

**Olympique Lyonnais claimed a third
UEFA Women's Champions League title,
but what appeared to be a
straightforward final victory against
Wolfsburg turned into an epic.**

Wolfsburg had ended Lyon's previous
two-year reign as champions in 2013,
but Ada Hegerberg's early goal in Reggio
Emilia – her 13th of the competition, seven
more than any other player – looked set to
reverse the scoreline from that previous
final at London's Stamford Bridge. However,
with two minutes left Alex Popp equalised
and Wolfsburg even led the ensuing
penalty shoot-out before the trophy
returned to France.

A record 56 clubs from 47 nations had
begun the competition, including three
from Germany as 2015 winners Frankfurt
had finished behind both Bayern München
and Wolfsburg in the league. Luxembourg
had their first entry since 2011/12 while
Chelsea, Atlético Madrid and Ferencváros
made their debuts.

Like Faroese champions KÍ Klaksvík, the
only team to have participated in all 15
editions, Ferencváros fell in the qualifying
round, beaten by FC Twente, who then
pulled off one of the competition's biggest
surprises, winning on away goals against

Bayern. The Dutch side lost in the last 16 to
newly-professional Barcelona, while
Wolfsburg knocked out Chelsea and Anja
Mittag scored for new club Paris Saint-
Germain against KIF Örebro to reach 49
European goals, one ahead of Conny
Pohlers' record.

Making the quarter-finals for the first time
were Slavia Praha, but there they were
routed 9-1 in the first women's match at the
new Stade de Lyon.

Frankfurt had needed penalties to keep their
campaign alive in the round of 16 against
LSK Kvinner, and again at Rosengård's
expense in the quarter-finals, but the
holders' luck eventually ran out in the semis
with a 4-0 loss at Wolfsburg, rendering their
1-0 second-leg win academic.

The other semi-final was also a one-nation
affair, with Lyon avenging their 2014/15
round of 16 defeat by Paris thanks to a
brilliant 7-0 victory in front of 22,050 fans,
more than had ever previously attended a
women's game in France. Lyon won the
second leg 1-0 to set up a rematch with
Wolfsburg, the sixth Franco-German final in
seven seasons.

In front of more than 15,000 fans at the home
of Italian Serie A side Sassuolo, Norwegian

striker Hegerberg gave Lyon a 12th-minute
lead with her 13th goal of the season, one
short of the competition record.

Lyon remained dominant but Gérard
Prêcheur's normally free-scoring side could
not double their lead and with two minutes
left they paid the price as Popp headed in
an equaliser.

Penalties were needed for only the second
time in the fixture. Lyon had lost the
previous shoot-out to Turbine Potsdam in
2010 and they fell behind as Almuth Schult
saved from Hegerberg. But Lyon's Sarah
Bouhaddi denied both Nilla Fischer and
Élise Bussaglia before Saki Kumagai coolly
converted the winning penalty, just as she
had done for Japan in the 2011 FIFA
Women's World Cup final.

Kumagai was rewarded with the Player of
the Match award by the UEFA technical
team, who included ten Lyon players in their
18-strong Squad of the Season.

Referring to the celebrated trio of Louisa
Necib, Amandine Henry and Lotta Schelin,
who were all set to leave Lyon after
participating in each of the club's nine
European campaigns, Kumagai said:
"Before the game we swore we had to win it
– for us, but especially for them."

Opposite: Lyon captain Wendie Renard raises the UEFA Women's Champions League trophy

UEFA Women's Champions League

Qualifying round

Group 1

11-16/08/15 Sarajevo

WFC SFK 2000 Sarajevo 5-0 Vllaznia, Konak Belediyespor 1-10 ZFK Minsk, ZFK Minsk 3-0 WFC SFK 2000 Sarajevo, Konak Belediyespor 5-1 Vllaznia, WFC SFK 2000 Sarajevo 3-1 Konak Belediyespor, Vllaznia 0-3 ZFK Minsk

	Pld	W	D	L	F	A	Pts
1 ZFK Minsk	3	3	0	0	16	1	9
2 WFC SFK 2000 Sarajevo	3	2	0	1	8	4	6
3 Konak Belediyespor	3	1	0	2	7	14	3
4 Vllaznia	3	0	0	3	1	13	0

Group 2

11-16/08/15 Belfast

FC NSA Sofia 6-0 ŽFK Dragon 2014, FC PAOK Thessaloniki 4-0 Glentoran Belfast United, FC PAOK Thessaloniki 10-0 ŽFK Dragon 2014, Glentoran Belfast United 1-2 FC NSA Sofia, FC NSA Sofia 0-4 FC PAOK Thessaloniki, ŽFK Dragon 2014 0-2 Glentoran Belfast United

	Pld	W	D	L	F	A	Pts
1 FC PAOK Thessaloniki	3	3	0	0	18	0	9
2 FC NSA Sofia	3	2	0	1	8	5	6
3 Glentoran Belfast United	3	1	0	2	3	6	3
4 ŽFK Dragon 2014	3	0	0	3	0	18	0

Group 3

11-16/08/15 Paphos

Apollon Ladies FC 2-0 Klaksvíkar Ítrottarfelag, Stjarnan 5-0 Hibernians FC, Klaksvíkar Ítrottarfelag 0-4 Stjarnan, Apollon Ladies FC 8-0 Hibernians FC, Stjarnan 2-0 Apollon Ladies FC, Hibernians FC 3-3 Klaksvíkar Ítrottarfelag

	Pld	W	D	L	F	A	Pts
1 Stjarnan	3	3	0	0	11	0	9
2 Apollon Ladies FC	3	2	0	1	10	2	6
3 Klaksvíkar Ítrottarfelag	3	0	1	2	3	9	1
4 Hibernians FC	3	0	1	2	3	16	1

Group 4

11-16/08/15 Hengelo, Oldenzaal

FC Twente 2-0 Ferencvárosi TC, ASA Tel-Aviv University SC 5-1 FC Jeunesse Jonglënster, FC Twente 10-0 FC Jeunesse Jonglënster, Ferencvárosi TC 2-1 ASA Tel-Aviv University SC, ASA Tel-Aviv University SC 0-7 FC Twente, FC Jeunesse Jonglënster 0-11 Ferencvárosi TC

	Pld	W	D	L	F	A	Pts
1 FC Twente	3	3	0	0	19	0	9
2 Ferencvárosi TC	3	2	0	1	13	3	6
3 ASA Tel-Aviv University SC	3	1	0	2	6	10	3
4 FC Jeunesse Jonglënster	3	0	0	3	1	26	0

Jennifer Hermoso helped Barcelona through to the quarter-finals

Group 5

11-16/08/15 Beltinci, Lendava

Olimpia Cluj Napoca 4-0 Pärnu Jalgpalliklubi, ŽNK Pomurje 4-0 Ekonomist, Olimpia Cluj Napoca 6-1 Ekonomist, Pärnu Jalgpalliklubi 1-2 ŽNK Pomurje, ŽNK Pomurje 0-2 Olimpia Cluj Napoca, Ekonomist 1-2 Pärnu Jalgpalliklubi

	Pld	W	D	L	F	A	Pts
1 Olimpia Cluj Napoca	3	3	0	0	12	1	9
2 ŽNK Pomurje	3	2	0	1	6	3	6
3 Pärnu Jalgpalliklubi	3	1	0	2	3	7	3
4 Ekonomist	3	0	0	3	2	12	0

Group 6

11-16/08/15 Osijek, Vinkovci

ZFK Spartak Subotica 2-1 CF Benfica, ŽNK Osijek 4-0 FC Noroc Nimoreni, ZFK Spartak Subotica 4-1 FC Noroc Nimoreni, CF Benfica 3-0 ŽNK Osijek, ŽNK Osijek 0-3 ZFK Spartak Subotica, FC Noroc Nimoreni 0-3 CF Benfica

	Pld	W	D	L	F	A	Pts
1 ZFK Spartak Subotica	3	3	0	0	9	2	9
2 CF Benfica	3	2	0	1	7	2	6
3 ŽNK Osijek	3	1	0	2	4	6	3
4 FC Noroc Nimoreni	3	0	0	3	1	11	0

Group 7

11-16/08/15 Kleczew, Konin

Gintra Universitetas 0-1 Wexford Youths Women's AFC, KKPK Medyk Konin 5-0 Cardiff Met Ladies FC, Gintra Universitetas 5-1 Cardiff Met Ladies FC, Wexford Youths Women's AFC 0-6 KKPK Medyk Konin, KKPK Medyk Konin 4-0 Gintra Universitetas, Cardiff Met Ladies FC 1-5 Wexford Youths Women's AFC

	Pld	W	D	L	F	A	Pts
1 KKPK Medyk Konin	3	3	0	0	15	0	9
2 Wexford Youths Women's AFC	3	2	0	1	6	7	6
3 Gintra Universitetas	3	1	0	2	5	6	3
4 Cardiff Met Ladies FC	3	0	0	3	2	15	0

Group 8

11-16/08/15 Vantaa, Helsinki

WFC Kharkiv 4-1 Rīgas Futbola skola, PK-35 Vantaa 9-0 FC Union Nové Zámky, FC Union Nové Zámky 0-5 WFC Kharkiv, PK-35 Vantaa 9-0 Rīgas Futbola skola, WFC Kharkiv 1-2 PK-35 Vantaa, Rīgas Futbola skola 3-2 FC Union Nové Zámky

	Pld	W	D	L	F	A	Pts
1 PK-35 Vantaa	3	3	0	0	20	1	9
2 WFC Kharkiv	3	2	0	1	10	3	6
3 Rīgas Futbola skola	3	1	0	2	4	15	3
4 FC Union Nové Zámky	3	0	0	3	2	17	0

Round of 32

07/10/15, BIIK Stadium, Shymkent
FC BIIK-Kazygurt 1-1 FC Barcelona
Goals: 0-1 Ruth 57, 1-1 Woods 82
Referee: Radzik-Johan (POL)
14/10/15, Mini Estadi, Barcelona
FC Barcelona 4-1 FC BIIK-Kazygurt
Goals: 1-0 Hermoso 11, 2-0 Melanie 20, 3-0 Unzue 52, 4-0 Hermoso 65, 4-1 Gabelia 90
Referee: Karagiorgi (CYP)
Aggregate: 5-2; FC Barcelona qualify.

07/10/15, ISS, Vantaa
PK-35 Vantaa 0-2 FC Rosengård
Goals: 0-1 Ilestedt 10, 0-2 Nilsson 75
Referee: Lampadariou (GRE)
14/10/15, Malmö Idrottsplats, Malmo
FC Rosengård 7-0 PK-35 Vantaa
Goals: 1-0 Belanger 2, 2-0 Van de Ven 6, 3-0 Belanger 25, 4-0 N Andonova 31, 5-0 Marta 45+1, 6-0 Van de Ven 52, 7-0 Belanger 76
Referee: Bastos (POR)
Aggregate: 9-0; FC Rosengård qualify.

07/10/15, Stadio Toumba, Salonika
FC PAOK Thessaloniki 0-3 KIF Örebro DFF
Goals: 0-1 Talonen 47, 0-2 Pettersson-Engström 60(p), 0-3 Abrahamsson 89
Referee: Kurtes (GER)
14/10/15, Behrn, Orebro
KIF Örebro DFF 5-0 FC PAOK Thessaloniki
Goals: 1-0 Michael 10, 2-0 Markou 15(og), 3-0 Talonen 24, 4-0 Chukwudi 50, 5-0 Spetsmark 76
Referee: Kováčová (SVK)
Aggregate: 8-0; KIF Örebro DFF qualify.

07/10/15, Eden Stadium, Prague
SK Slavia Praha 4-1 Brøndby IF
Goals: 0-1 L Kristiansen 6, 1-1 Divišová 8, 2-1 Divišová 13, 3-1 Budošová 24, 4-1 Chlastáková 52
Referee: Daly (IRL)
14/10/15, Brøndby, Brondby
Brøndby IF 1-0 SK Slavia Praha
Goal: 1-0 Boye Sørensen 2
Referee: Hussein (GER)
Aggregate: 2-4; SK Slavia Praha qualify.

07/10/15, Stade Maurice Dufrasne, Liege
Standard de Liège 0-2 1. FFC Frankfurt
Goals: 0-1 Schmidt 10(p), 0-2 Garefrekes 86
Referee: Budimir (CRO)
15/10/15, Am Brentano Bad, Frankfurt am Main
1. FFC Frankfurt 6-0 Standard de Liège
Goals: 1-0 Islacker 6, 2-0 Garefrekes 44,
3-0 Bartusiak 48(p), 4-0 Ogimi 68,
5-0 Crnogorčević 86, 6-0 Linden 86
Referee: Pirie (SCO)
Aggregate: 8-0; 1. FFC Frankfurt qualify.

07/10/15, Voithplatz, St Polten
FSK St.Pölten-Spratzern 4-5 ASD Verona CF
Goals: 0-1 Larsen 21, 0-2 Bonetti 24, 1-2 Pöltl 29,
2-2 Sipos 31, 3-2 Vágó 37(p), 3-3 Pirone 41,
3-4 Pirone 73, 4-4 Pinther 77, 4-5 Gabbiadini 82(p)
Referee: Frias Acedo (ESP)
15/10/15, Marc'Antonio Bentegodi, Verona
ASD Verona CF 2-2 FSK St.Pölten-Spratzern
Goals: 0-1 Vágó 8, 1-1 Gabbiadini 12(p),
1-2 Vágó 69, 2-2 Gabbiadini 87(p)
Referee: Staubli (SUI)
Aggregate: 7-6; ASD Verona CF qualify.

07/10/15, Stjörnuvöllur, Gardabaer
Stjarnan 1-3 WFC Zvezda 2005
Goals: 0-1 Boychenko 5, 0-2 Apanaschenko 13,
1-2 Stefánsdóttir 28, 1-3 Kurochkina 32
Referee: Albon (ROU)
15/10/15, Zvezda, Perm
WFC Zvezda 2005 3-1 Stjarnan
Goals: 1-0 Kurochkina 45, 2-0 Apanaschenko 62,
2-1 Makarenko 78(p), 3-1 Apanaschenko 90(p)
Referee: Adámková (CZE)
Aggregate: 6-2; WFC Zvezda 2005 qualify.

07/10/15, Åråsen, Lillestrom
LSK Kvinner FK 1-0 FC Zürich Frauen
Goal: 1-0 Bachor 63
Referee: Pustovoitova (RUS)
14/10/15, Stadion Letzigrund, Zurich
FC Zürich Frauen 1-1 LSK Kvinner FK (aet)
Goals: 1-0 Humm 87, 1-1 Mykjåland 99
Referee: Guillemin (FRA)
Aggregate: 1-2; LSK Kvinner FK qualify after extra time.

07/10/15, FC Twente Stadion, Enschede
FC Twente 1-1 FC Bayern München
Goals: 1-0 R Jansen 14, 1-1 Leupolz 85
Referee: Kulcsár (HUN)
14/10/15, an der Grünwalderstrasse, Munich
FC Bayern München 2-2 FC Twente
Goals: 0-1 Roord 13, 1-1 Erman 29(og),
1-2 Roetgering 56(p), 2-2 Behringer 75(p)
Referee: Monzul (UKR)
Aggregate: 3-3; FC Twente qualify on away goals.

07/10/15, Ciudad Deportiva Cerro Del Espino, Majadahonda
Club Atlético de Madrid 0-2 Zorky
Goals: 0-1 Slonova 18, 0-2 Slonova 71
Referee: Sørø (NOR)
15/10/15, Rodina, Khimki
Zorky 0-3 Club Atlético de Madrid
Goals: 0-1 Esther 9, 0-2 Beltrán 84,
0-3 D Garcia 87
Referee: Vitulano (ITA)
Aggregate: 2-3; Club Atlético de Madrid qualify.

07/10/15, Mario Rigamonti, Brescia
ACF Brescia Calcio Femminile 1-0 Liverpool Ladies FC
Goal: 1-0 Gama 28
Referee: Persson (SWE)

14/10/15, Stobart Halton, Widnes
Liverpool Ladies FC 0-1 ACF Brescia Calcio Femminile
Goal: 0-1 Bonansea 26
Referee: Frappart (FRA)
Aggregate: 0-2; ACF Brescia Calcio Femminile qualify.

08/10/15, Gradski, Subotica
ZFK Spartak Subotica 0-0 VfL Wolfsburg
Referee: Gaál (HUN)
14/10/15, AOK stadium, Wolfsburg
VfL Wolfsburg 4-0 ZFK Spartak Subotica
Goals: 1-0 Faisst 30, 2-0 Simic 44, 3-0 Dickenmann 54, 4-0 Graham Hansen 62
Referee: Spinelli (ITA)
Aggregate: 4-0; VfL Wolfsburg qualify.

08/10/15, Miejski Im. Złotej Jedenastki, Konin
KKPK Medyk Konin 0-6 Olympique Lyonnais
Goals: 0-1 Ada Hegerberg 19, 0-2 Le Sommer 35,
0-3 Ada Hegerberg 37, 0-4 Bremer 73,
0-5 Bremer 81, 0-6 Renard 84
Referee: Larsson (SWE)
14/10/15, Stade de Gerland, Lyon
Olympique Lyonnais 3-0 KKPK Medyk Konin
Goals: 1-0 Le Sommer 2, 2-0 Ada Hegerberg 69,
3-0 Ada Hegerberg 89
Referee: Poxhofer (AUT)
Aggregate: 9-0; Olympique Lyonnais qualify.

08/10/15, FC Minsk, Minsk
ZFK Minsk 0-2 Fortuna Hjørring
Goals: 0-1 Nadim 33, 0-2 Nadim 61(p)
Referee: Clark (SCO)
14/10/15, Hjørring Stadion, Hjørring
Fortuna Hjørring 4-0 ZFK Minsk
Goals: 1-0 Olar 20, 2-0 Nadim 29, 3-0 Jensen 46,
4-0 Olar 90+2(p)
Referee: Minić (SRB)
Aggregate: 6-0; Fortuna Hjørring qualify.

Paris striker Cristiane plundered five goals in the round of 32 tie against Olimpia Cluj Napoca

08/10/15, Cluj Arena, Cluj-Napoca
Olimpia Cluj Napoca 0-6 Paris Saint-Germain
Goals: 0-1 Mittag 38, 0-2 Cristiane 43, 0-3 Cristiane 54, 0-4 Mittag 71, 0-5 Cruz Traña 79, 0-6 Sarr 90+1
Referee: Azzopardi (MLT)
14/10/15, Charlety, Paris
Paris Saint-Germain 9-0 Olimpia Cluj Napoca
Goals: 1-0 Delannoy 21(p), 2-0 Cristiane 42, 3-0 Cristiane 49, 4-0 Dahlkvist 53, 5-0 Cristiane 63, 6-0 Horan 65, 7-0 Horan 66, 8-0 Olar 70(og), 9-0 Sarr 84
Referee: Lehtovaara (FIN)
Aggregate: 15-0; Paris Saint-Germain qualify.

08/10/15, Wheatsheaf Park, Staines-upon-Thames
Chelsea LFC 1-0 Glasgow City FC
Goal: 1-0 Kirby 39
Referee: Zadinová (CZE)
14/10/15, Excelsior Stadium, Airdrie
Glasgow City FC 0-3 Chelsea LFC
Goals: 0-1 Aluko 22, 0-2 Kirby 57, 0-3 Flaherty 61
Referee: Steinhaus (GER)
Aggregate: 0-4; Chelsea LFC qualify.

Round of 16

11/11/15, Åråsen, Lillestrom
LSK Kvinner FK 0-2 1. FFC Frankfurt
Goals: 0-1 Islacker 37, 0-2 Garefrekes 56
Referee: Spinelli (ITA)
18/11/15, Am Brentano Bad, Frankfurt am Main
1. FFC Frankfurt 0-2 LSK Kvinner FK (aet)
Goals: 0-1 Lundh 12, 0-2 Lund 70
Referee: Gaál (HUN)
Aggregate: 2-2; 1. FFC Frankfurt qualify 5-4 on penalties.

11/11/15, FC Twente Stadion, Enschede
FC Twente 0-1 FC Barcelona
Goal: 0-1 García 76
Referee: Larsson (SWE)
18/11/15, Mini Estadi, Barcelona
FC Barcelona 1-0 FC Twente
Goal: 1-0 García 25
Referee: Staubli (SUI)
Aggregate: 2-0; FC Barcelona qualify.

11/11/15, Wheatsheaf Park, Staines-upon-Thames
Chelsea LFC 1-2 VfL Wolfsburg
Goals: 0-1 C Rafferty 3(og), 1-1 Peter 54(og),
1-2 Graham Hansen 78
Referee: Kulcsár (HUN)
18/11/15, AOK stadium, Wolfsburg
VfL Wolfsburg 2-0 Chelsea LFC
Goals: 1-0 Bernauer 12, 2-0 C Rafferty 68(og)
Referee: Persson (SWE)
Aggregate: 4-1; VfL Wolfsburg qualify.

11/11/15, Behrn, Orebro
KIF Örebro DFF 1-1 Paris Saint-Germain
Goals: 1-0 Talonen 3, 1-1 Mittag 71
Referee: Vitulano (ITA)
18/11/15, Charlety, Paris
Paris Saint-Germain 0-0 KIF Örebro DFF
Referee: Bastos (POR)
Aggregate: 1-1; Paris Saint-Germain qualify on away goal.

UEFA Women's Champions League

11/11/15, Ciudad Deportiva Cerro Del Espino, Majadahonda
Club Atlético de Madrid 1-3 Olympique Lyonnais
Goals: 0-1 Necib 22, 0-2 Ada Hegerberg 45+1, 1-2 Calderón 71, 1-3 Ada Hegerberg 90+3
Referee: Hussein (GER)
18/11/15, Stade de Gerland, Lyon
Olympique Lyonnais 6-0 Club Atlético de Madrid
Goals: 1-0 Ada Hegerberg 23, 2-0 Schelin 25, 3-0 Kumagai 45+1(p), 4-0 Schelin 47, 5-0 Ada Hegerberg 57, 6-0 Thomis 72
Referee: Monzul (UKR)
Aggregate: 9-1; Olympique Lyonnais qualify.

11/11/15, Mario Rigamonti, Brescia
ACF Brescia Calcio Femminile 1-0 Fortuna Hjørring
Goal: 1-0 Sabatino 2
Referee: Steinhaus (GER)
18/11/15, Hjørring Stadion, Hjorring
Fortuna Hjørring 1-1 ACF Brescia Calcio Femminile
Goals: 1-0 Nadim 58, 1-1 Boattin 89
Referee: Mitsi (GRE)
Aggregate: 1-2; ACF Brescia Calcio Femminile qualify.

12/11/15, Eden Stadium, Prague
SK Slavia Praha 2-1 WFC Zvezda 2005
Goals: 1-0 Divišová 5, 1-1 Nahi 19, 2-1 Necidová 54
Referee: Azzopardi (MLT)
19/11/15, Zvezda, Perm
WFC Zvezda 2005 0-0 SK Slavia Praha
Referee: Pirie (SCO)
Aggregate: 1-2; SK Slavia Praha qualify.

12/11/15, Marc'Antonio Bentegodi, Verona
ASD Verona CF 1-3 FC Rosengård
Goals: 0-1 Marta 6, 1-1 Pirone 30, 1-2 Carissimi 37(og), 1-3 Gunnarsdóttir 77
Referee: Adámková (CZE)
19/11/15, Malmö Idrottsplats, Malmo
FC Rosengård 5-1 ASD Verona CF
Goals: 0-1 Gabbiadini 20, 1-1 Belanger 38, 2-1 Marta 50, 3-1 Fuselli 65(og), 4-1 Marta 67, 5-1 Marta 87
Referee: Albon (ROU)
Aggregate: 8-2; FC Rosengård qualify.

Quarter-finals

23/03/16, AOK stadium, Wolfsburg
VfL Wolfsburg 3-0 ACF Brescia Calcio Femminile
Goals: 1-0 Wullaert 32, 2-0 Popp 52, 3-0 Graham Hansen 61
Referee: Frappart (FRA)
30/03/16, Mario Rigamonti, Brescia
ACF Brescia Calcio Femminile 0-3 VfL Wolfsburg
Goals: 0-1 Jakabfi 7, 0-2 Jakabfi 33, 0-3 Bachmann 62
Referee: Zadinová (CZE)
Aggregate: 0-6; VfL Wolfsburg qualify.

23/03/16, Mini Estadi, Barcelona
FC Barcelona 0-0 Paris Saint-Germain
Referee: Kulcsár (HUN)
30/03/16, Charlety, Paris
Paris Saint-Germain 1-0 FC Barcelona
Goal: 1-0 Cristiane 86
Referee: Hussein (GER)
Aggregate: 1-0; Paris Saint-Germain qualify.

Lyon's Saki Kumagai celebrates her winning penalty in the final shoot-out against Wolfsburg

23/03/16, Stade de Lyon, Lyon
Olympique Lyonnais 9-1 SK Slavia Praha
Goals: 1-0 Necib 18, 2-0 Le Sommer 24, 3-0 Ada Hegerberg 35, 4-0 M'Bock Bathy 39, 4-1 Svitková 42, 5-1 M'Bock Bathy 53, 6-1 Majri 56, 7-1 Abily 64, 8-1 Abily 80, 9-1 Ada Hegerberg 86
Referee: Larsson (SWE)
30/03/16, Eden Stadium, Prague
SK Slavia Praha 0-0 Olympique Lyonnais
Referee: Mitsi (GRE)
Aggregate: 1-9; Olympique Lyonnais qualify.

23/03/16, Malmö Idrottsplats, Malmo
FC Rosengård 0-1 1. FFC Frankfurt
Goal: 0-1 Marozsán 71(p)
Referee: Dorcioman (ROU)
30/03/16, Am Brentano Bad, Frankfurt am Main
1. FFC Frankfurt 0-1 FC Rosengård (aet)
Goal: 0-1 Gunnarsdóttir 28
Referee: Vitulano (ITA)
Aggregate: 1-1; 1. FFC Frankfurt qualify 5-4 on penalties.

Semi-finals

24/04/16, Stade de Lyon, Lyon
Olympique Lyonnais 7-0 Paris Saint-Germain
Goals: 1-0 Ada Hegerberg 18, 2-0 Le Sommer 28, 3-0 Ada Hegerberg 40, 4-0 Le Sommer 43, 5-0 Abily 45+1, 6-0 Necib 73, 7-0 Schelin 76
Referee: Steinhaus (GER)
02/05/16, Parc des Princes, Paris
Paris Saint-Germain 0-1 Olympique Lyonnais
Goal: 0-1 Schelin 44
Referee: Staubli (SUI)
Aggregate: 0-8; Olympique Lyonnais qualify.

24/04/16, AOK stadium, Wolfsburg
VfL Wolfsburg 4-0 1. FFC Frankfurt
Goals: 1-0 I Kerschowski 7, 2-0 Popp 28, 3-0 Peter 42, 4-0 Bachmann 58
Referee: Albon (ROU)
01/05/16, Am Brentano Bad, Frankfurt am Main
1. FFC Frankfurt 1-0 VfL Wolfsburg
Goal: 1-0 Priessen 90
Referee: Monzul (UKR)
Aggregate: 1-4; VfL Wolfsburg qualify.

Final

26/05/16, Stadio Città del Tricolore, Reggio Emilia (att: 15,117)
VfL Wolfsburg 1-1 Olympique Lyonnais (aet; 3-4 on pens)
Goals: 0-1 Ada Hegerberg 12, 1-1 Popp 88
Referee: Kulcsár (HUN)
Wolfsburg: Schult, Jakabfi (Bachmann 59), Fischer, Peter, Blässe (Bunte 113), Popp, Bernauer (Wullaert 73), Dickenmann, I Kerschowski, Goessling, Bussaglia. Coach: Ralf Kellermann (GER)
Lyon: Bouhaddi, Renard, Kumagai, Henry, Majri, Le Sommer (Schelin 79), Necib, Ada Hegerberg, Bremer (Thomis 86), Abily, M'Bock Bathy. Coach: Gérard Prêcheur (FRA)
Yellow cards: Necib 22 (Lyon), Kumagai 44 (Lyon), Abily 101 (Lyon)

Top goalscorers

13	Ada Hegerberg (Lyon)
6	Cristiane (Paris)
5	Eugénie Le Sommer (Lyon)
	Marta (Rosengård)
4	Nadia Nadim (Fortuna Hjørring)
	Lotta Schelin (Lyon)
	Josee Belanger (Rosengård)
	Melania Gabbiadini (Verona)

WOMEN'S EURO 2017
THE NETHERLANDS

| France and holders Germany qualify without conceding | Finals debut guaranteed for Switzerland | England, Spain and Norway also book their places |

Six through to the Netherlands

UEFA Women's EURO 2017 in the Netherlands will be the largest tournament of its kind, the first to feature 16 finalists, and with September's final batch of qualifiers still to go, holders Germany, England, France, Norway, Spain and Switzerland had already booked their places alongside the hosts in the finals, which take place from 16 July to 6 August, 2017.

For Switzerland, qualification means a first participation in a UEFA Women's EURO finals, which comes hot on the heels of a FIFA Women's World Cup debut in 2015. They began Group 6 brilliantly with a 3-0 win in Italy and followed that up with home victories against both the Czech Republic and the Azzurre. A 5-0 win in the Czech Republic on 4 June clinched first place, leaving their hosts, perennial qualifiers Italy and outsiders Northern Ireland battling it out for second place.

The first teams through in April were Germany and France, both on maximum points without having conceded a goal. That was also true of Sweden, although going into the summer break they could still be caught in Group 4 by neighbours Denmark, with neither of those confirmed top two yet certain of being one of the six best runners-up that would avoid the October play-off between the remaining pair of hopefuls.

There were no such concerns for the competition's last two beaten finalists,

England and Norway, or Spain. Although none of the three had clinched first place in their respective groups, they were all safe in the knowledge that they would at worst end up among the six runners-up with the best records against the sides placed first, third and fourth in their sections. Unlike Norway and Spain, 2015 World Cup bronze-medallists England did not boast a perfect record, having drawn 1-1 at home to Belgium, who, thanks in part to that result, were certain of a top-two finish in Group 7 and well placed to earn a first qualification for a senior women's tournament.

Also assured of at least a play-off place in their quest for a first qualification were Austria, buoyed by an impressive 2-2 draw in Norway, and Scotland. The Scots have suffered play-off heartbreak for the past two

tournaments, but despite losing their perfect Group 1 record with a 4-0 loss at home to flawless Iceland, Anna Signeul's side still had every chance of qualifying directly as one of the best runners-up. Iceland's Harpa Thorsteinsdóttir became the first player to reach ten goals in the qualifying competition after she hit hat-tricks against Belarus and FYR Macedonia.

Finland were still able to catch Spain in Group 2 but also uncertain of a play-off place after being held 0-0 at home by Portugal, their hosts in the return fixture on 16 September. Behind Germany in Group 5, Russia were also sure of a top-two finish, while Ukraine and Romania were tussling for second place behind France in Group 3.

Germany players celebrate a goal against Croatia on their way to early qualification

Qualifying round

Group 1

22/09/15, Mestni, Ajdovscina
Slovenia 0-3 Scotland
Goals: 0-1 Little 28, 0-2 Little 49, 0-3 Little 59

22/09/15, Laugardalsvöllur, Reykjavik
Iceland 2-0 Belarus
Goals: 1-0 Magnúsdóttir 30, 2-0 Brynjarsdóttir 73

19/10/15, Stanko Mlakar, Kranj
Slovenia 3-0 Belarus
Goals: 1-0 Tibaut 16, 2-0 Zver 65,
3-0 Linnik 68(og)

22/10/15, FFM Training Centre, Skopje
FYR Macedonia 0-4 Iceland
Goals: 0-1 M Vidarsdóttir 9, 0-2 Viggósdóttir 12,
0-3 Thorsteinsdóttir 17, 0-4 M Vidarsdóttir 29

23/10/15, Fir Park, Motherwell
Scotland 7-0 Belarus
Goals: 1-0 J Ross 44, 2-0 Weir 46, 3-0 Corsie 53,
4-0 J Ross 67, 5-0 Evans 69, 6-0 Love 89,
7-0 Love 90+2

26/10/15, Športni park, Lendava
Slovenia 0-6 Iceland
Goals: 0-1 Brynjarsdóttir 15,
0-2 Thorsteinsdóttir 20, 0-3 Thorsteinsdóttir 65,
0-4 M Vidarsdóttir 70, 0-5 Jessen 80,
0-6 Brynjarsdóttir 86

27/10/15, FFM Training Centre, Skopje
FYR Macedonia 1-4 Scotland
Goals: 0-1 Little 22, 0-2 Corsie 27, 0-3 Corsie 28,
0-4 Weir 31, 1-4 Rochi 44

26/11/15, FFM Training Centre, Skopje
FYR Macedonia 0-2 Belarus
Goals: 0-1 Slesarchik 67, 0-2 Avkhimovich 90+3

29/11/15, Saint Mirren Park, Paisley
Scotland 10-0 FYR Macedonia
Goals: 1-0 J Ross 3, 2-0 Love 8, 3-0 Beattie 24,
4-0 Lauder 27, 5-0 Evans 35, 6-0 Love 40,
7-0 Love 53, 8-0 J Ross 59, 9-0 J Ross 61,
10-0 J Ross 87

08/04/16, Saint Mirren Park, Paisley
Scotland 3-1 Slovenia
Goals: 1-0 J Ross 19, 1-1 Erman 42,
2-1 J Ross 45, 3-1 Little 52(p)

12/04/16, FC Minsk, Minsk
Belarus 0-5 Iceland
Goals: 0-1 M Vidarsdóttir 14,
0-2 Thorsteinsdóttir 24, 0-3 Thorsteinsdóttir 34,
0-4 Thorsteinsdóttir 54, 0-5 Brynjarsdóttir 86

12/04/16, Športni park, Lendava
Slovenia 8-1 FYR Macedonia
Goals: 1-0 Tibaut 6, 2-0 Ivanuša 47,
3-0 Prašnikar 50, 4-0 Kralj 60, 4-1 Jakovska 71,
5-1 Tibaut 75, 6-1 Prašnikar 81, 7-1 Kos 86,
8-1 Rogan 90+3(p)

03/06/16, FFM Training Centre, Skopje
FYR Macedonia 0-9 Slovenia
Goals: 0-1 Eržen 2, 0-2 Eržen 18,
0-3 Prašnikar 23, 0-4 Zver 26, 0-5 Tibaut 29,
0-6 Kralj 31, 0-7 Prašnikar 57, 0-8 Tibaut 81,
0-9 Kralj 88

03/06/16, Falkirk Stadium, Falkirk
Scotland 0-4 Iceland
Goals: 0-1 Gísladóttir 10, 0-2 Thorsteinsdóttir 62,
0-3 Jónsdóttir 65, 0-4 M Vidarsdóttir 69

07/06/16, FC Minsk, Minsk
Belarus 0-1 Scotland
Goal: 0-1 Love 15

07/06/16, Laugardalsvöllur, Reykjavik
Iceland 8-0 FYR Macedonia
Goals: 1-0 Fridriksdóttir 15, 2-0 Thorsteinsdóttir 17,
3-0 Jensen 25, 4-0 Gunnarsdóttir 27, 5-0
Thorsteinsdóttir 34, 6-0 Thorsteinsdóttir 42,
7-0 Fridriksdóttir 50, 8-0 Brynjarsdóttir 81

		Pld	W	D	L	F	A	Pts
1	Iceland	6	6	0	0	29	0	18
2	Scotland	7	6	0	1	28	6	18
3	Slovenia	6	3	0	3	21	13	9
4	Belarus	6	1	0	5	2	18	3
5	FYR Macedonia	7	0	0	7	2	45	0

Remaining fixtures

15/09/16
Belarus - FYR Macedonia
16/09/16
Iceland - Slovenia

20/09/16
Iceland - Scotland
Belarus - Slovenia

Group 2

17/09/15, Turku Stadium, Turku
Finland 1-0 Montenegro
Goal: 1-0 Öling 67

21/09/15, Tallaght Stadium, Dublin
Republic of Ireland 0-2 Finland
Goals: 0-1 Koivisto 13, 0-2 Sällström 71

*27/10/15, Joaquim de Almeida Freitas,
Moreira de Conegos*
Portugal 1-2 Republic of Ireland
Goals: 1-0 Carole Costa 16, 1-1 Quinn 22,
1-2 O'Gorman 40

27/10/15, Helsinki Football Stadium, Helsinki
Finland 1-2 Spain
Goals: 0-1 Alexia 4, 1-1 Kuikka 25, 1-2 Virginia 29

26/11/15, Tallaght Stadium, Dublin
Republic of Ireland 0-3 Spain
Goals: 0-1 Losada 30, 0-2 Hermoso 44(p),
0-3 Perry 90+3(og)

26/11/15, António Coimbra Da Mota, Estoril
Portugal 6-1 Montenegro
Goals: 1-0 Cláudia Neto 7, 1-1 Kuć 20,
2-1 Cláudia Neto 28, 3-1 Carolina Mendes 31,
4-1 Ana Borges 40, 5-1 Dolores Silva 61(p),
6-1 Edite Fernandes 90+1

01/12/15, Estadio Nuevo Vivero, Badajoz
Spain 2-0 Portugal
Goals: 1-0 Losada 8, 2-0 Sonia 25

24/01/16, Pod Malim Brdom, Petrovac
Montenegro 0-7 Spain
Goals: 0-1 Losada 15, 0-2 Verónica Boquete 22,
0-3 Alexia 42(p), 0-4 Losada 62, 0-5 Hermoso 69,
0-6 Sampedro 74, 0-7 Virginia 77

07/04/16, Pod Malim Brdom, Petrovac
Montenegro 0-5 Republic of Ireland
Goals: 0-1 Quinn 3, 0-2 O'Gorman 24,
0-3 Littlejohn 26(p), 0-4 D O'Sullivan 73,
0-5 Roche 84

*08/04/16, Estádio Complexo Desportivo Covilhã,
Covilha*
Portugal 1-4 Spain
Goals: 0-1 Virginia 36, 0-2 Alexia 40,
1-2 Dolores Silva 66, 1-3 Sampedro 87,
1-4 Verónica Boquete 89

12/04/16, Pod Malim Brdom, Petrovac
Montenegro 1-7 Finland
Goals: 1-0 Bulatović 8, 1-1 Djurković 15(og),
1-2 Alanen 21, 1-3 Danielsson 27, 1-4 Saari 68,
1-5 Sällström 73, 1-6 Saarinen 83,
1-7 Heroum 90+3

*12/04/16, Pabellón de la Ciudad del Fútbol 1,
Madrid*
Spain 3-0 Republic of Ireland
Goals: 1-0 Verónica Boquete 58,
2-0 Verónica Boquete 65, 3-0 Hermoso 86

03/06/16, Tehtaan Kenttä, Valkeakoski
Finland 4-1 Republic of Ireland
Goals: 1-0 Alanen 32, 2-0 Danielsson 39,
3-0 Kuikka 70, 3-1 Roche 76, 4-1 Sällström 87

03/06/16, Pod Malim Brdom, Petrovac
Montenegro 0-3 Portugal
Goals: 0-1 Edite Fernandes 7,
0-2 Edite Fernandes 29, 0-3 Edite Fernandes 54

07/06/16, Helsinki Football Stadium, Helsinki
Finland 0-0 Portugal

07/06/16, Tallaght Stadium, Dublin
Republic of Ireland 9-0 Montenegro
Goals: 1-0 Connolly 3, 2-0 O'Gorman 11,
3-0 Roche 45, 4-0 O'Gorman 53, 5-0 O'Gorman 58,
6-0 Quinn 62, 7-0 Roche 65, 8-0 Roche 69,
9-0 F O'Sullivan 83

		Pld	W	D	L	F	A	Pts
1	Spain	6	6	0	0	21	2	18
2	Finland	6	4	1	1	15	4	13
3	Republic of Ireland	7	3	0	4	17	13	9
4	Portugal	6	2	1	3	11	9	7
5	Montenegro	7	0	0	7	2	38	0

Remaining fixtures

15/09/16
Spain - Montenegro
16/09/16
Portugal - Finland

20/09/16
Spain - Finland
Republic of Ireland - Portugal

Group 3

22/09/15, MMArena, Le Mans
France 3-0 Romania
Goals: 1-0 Delie 16, 2-0 Le Sommer 35,
3-0 Le Sommer 48

22/10/15, Loni Papuçiu, Fier
Albania 1-4 Greece
Goals: 0-1 Zani 14(og), 1-1 Kurbogaj 23,
1-2 Kydonaki 27, 1-3 Sidira 37, 1-4 Markou 90+2

22/10/15, Arena Lviv, Lviv
Ukraine 2-2 Romania
Goals: 0-1 Voicu 13, 1-1 Andrushchak 63,
2-1 Romanenko 71, 2-2 Giurgiu 82

Camille Abily (right) bursts through the Ukraine defence to score in France's 4-0 win in Valenciennes

27/10/15, Mogosoaia, Bucharest
Romania 3-0 Albania
Goals: 1-0 Lunca 9, 2-0 Corduneanu 24,
3-0 Giurgiu 74

27/10/15, Arena Lviv, Lviv
Ukraine 0-3 France
Goals: 0-1 Delie 42, 0-2 Bussaglia 59, 0-3 Majri 68

27/11/15, FC Katerini, Katerini
Greece 1-3 Romania
Goals: 0-1 Rus 10, 0-2 Voicu 45+1, 1-2 Sarri 65,
1-3 Olar 90+1

27/11/15, Stadiumi Kombëtar Qemal Stafa, Tirana
Albania 0-6 France
Goals: 0-1 Houara-D'Hommeaux 12,
0-2 Houara-D'Hommeaux 15, 0-3 Le Sommer 25,
0-4 Le Bihan 63, 0-5 Le Bihan 73,
0-6 Le Sommer 81

01/12/15, FC Katerini, Katerini
Greece 0-3 France
Goals: 0-1 Bilbault 12, 0-2 Le Bihan 72,
0-3 Le Sommer 75

26/01/16, Trikala, Trikala
Greece 3-2 Albania
Goals: 1-0 Sidira 6(p), 2-0 Kongouli 10,
3-0 Panteliadou 15, 3-1 Velaj 26, 3-2 Hashani 41

04/03/16, Elbasan Arena, Elbasan
Albania 0-4 Ukraine
Goals: 0-1 Apanaschenko 14(p), 0-2 Kozyrenko 30,
0-3 Bajraktari 67(og), 0-4 Kravets 84

08/03/16, Aharnaikos, Athens
Greece 1-3 Ukraine
Goals: 0-1 Apanaschenko 31(p),
1-1 Kravets 64(og), 1-2 Kalinina 68,
1-3 Boychenko 80

08/04/16, Arena Lviv, Lviv
Ukraine 2-0 Albania
Goals: 1-0 Apanaschenko 15,
2-0 Apanaschenko 74(p)

08/04/16, Nicolae Dobrin, Pitesti
Romania 0-1 France
Goal: 0-1 Bussaglia 16(p)

11/04/16, Nungesser, Valenciennes
France 4-0 Ukraine
Goals: 1-0 Hamraoui 8, 2-0 Abily 27,
3-0 Vasylyuk 60(og), 4-0 Majri 89

02/06/16, Elbasan Arena, Elbasan
Albania 0-3 Romania
Goals: 0-1 Vătafu 43, 0-2 Vătafu 67, 0-3 Vătafu 77

03/06/16, Stade de la Route-de-Lorient, Rennes
France 1-0 Greece
Goal: 1-0 Le Sommer 36

07/06/16, Arena Lviv, Lviv
Ukraine 2-0 Greece
Goals: 1-0 Apanaschenko 2(p), 2-0 Boychenko 44

	Pld	W	D	L	F	A	Pts
1 France	7	7	0	0	21	0	21
2 Ukraine	7	4	1	2	13	10	13
3 Romania	6	3	1	2	11	7	10
4 Greece	7	2	0	5	9	15	6
5 Albania	7	0	0	7	3	25	0

Remaining fixtures

15/09/16
Romania - Ukraine

20/09/16
France - Albania
Romania - Greece

Group 4

17/09/15, District Sport Complex, Orhei
Moldova 0-3 Sweden
Goals: 0-1 Schough 1, 0-2 Schelin 42(p),
0-3 Hammarlund 88

22/09/15, Gamla Ullevi, Gothenburg
Sweden 3-0 Poland
Goals: 1-0 Hurtig 21, 2-0 Schough 52, 3-0 Diaz 72

22/10/15, Stadion Miejski Tychy, Tychy
Poland 2-0 Slovakia
Goals: 1-0 Chudzik 18, 2-0 Grabowska 63

22/10/15, Viborg Stadion, Viborg
Denmark 4-0 Moldova
Goals: 1-0 S Troelsgaard 24, 2-0 Harder 35,
3-0 Nadim 52, 4-0 Nadim 89

26/10/15, National Training Centre, Senec
Slovakia 4-0 Moldova
Goals: 1-0 Bíróová 50, 2-0 Fecková 81,
3-0 Škorvánková 85, 4-0 Vojteková 87(p)

27/10/15, Gamla Ullevi, Gothenburg
Sweden 1-0 Denmark
Goal: 1-0 Seger 59

26/11/15, National Training Centre, Senec
Slovakia 0-1 Denmark
Goal: 0-1 S Troelsgaard 34

27/11/15, District Sport Complex, Orhei
Moldova 1-3 Poland
Goals: 0-1 Pajor 56, 0-2 Daleszczyk 63,
0-3 Grabowska 81, 1-3 Andone 90+3

01/12/15, District Sport Complex, Orhei
Moldova 0-4 Slovakia
Goals: 0-1 Fecková 28, 0-2 Ondrušová 32,
0-3 Fecková 54, 0-4 Bíróová 86

07/04/16, Stadion Miejski Tychy, Tychy
Poland 0-0 Denmark

08/04/16, The National Training Centre, Poprad
Slovakia 0-3 Sweden
Goals: 0-1 Appelquist 27, 0-2 Sembrant 55,
0-3 Blackstenius 63

12/04/16, The National Training Centre, Poprad
Slovakia 2-1 Poland
Goals: 0-1 Daleszczyk 30, 1-1 Vojteková 76(p),
2-1 Hmírová 90+3

02/06/16, LKS, Lodz
Poland 0-4 Sweden
Goals: 0-1 Ilestedt 40, 0-2 Schelin 60, 0-3 Asllani
70, 0-4 Rolfö 87

02/06/16, Viborg Stadion, Viborg
Denmark 4-0 Slovakia
Goals: 1-0 Harder 28, 2-0 Nadim 49,
3-0 Nadim 60(p), 4-0 S Troelsgaard 90+2

06/06/16, Gamla Ullevi, Gothenburg
Sweden 6-0 Moldova
Goals: 1-0 Munteanu 34(og), 2-0 Asllani 41,
3-0 Rolfö 48, 4-0 Asllani 61, 5-0 Rolfö 88,
6-0 Berglund 90+3

07/06/16, Viborg Stadion, Viborg
Denmark 6-0 Poland
Goals: 1-0 S Troelsgaard 18, 2-0 Harder 24,
3-0 S Troelsgaard 27, 4-0 Harder 41,
5-0 Rasmussen 53, 6-0 S Troelsgaard 62

	Pld	W	D	L	F	A	Pts
1 Sweden	6	6	0	0	20	0	18
2 Denmark	6	4	1	1	15	1	13
3 Slovakia	7	3	0	4	10	11	9
4 Poland	7	2	1	4	6	16	7
5 Moldova	6	0	0	6	1	24	0

Remaining fixtures

15/09/16
Sweden - Slovakia
Moldova - Denmark

20/09/16
Poland - Moldova
Denmark - Sweden

Group 5

17/09/15, Kazım Karabekir Stadium, Erzurum
Turkey 1-4 Croatia
Goals: 1-0 Yağmur Uraz 17, 1-1 Landeka 29,
1-2 Joščak 71, 1-3 Šundov 80, 1-4 Šalek 90+2

18/09/15, Erdgas Sportpark, Halle
Germany 12-0 Hungary
Goals: 1-0 Popp 7, 2-0 Maier 9, 3-0 Kemme 16,
4-0 Behringer 19(p), 5-0 Bremer 28,
6-0 Goessling 33, 7-0 Goessling 39,
8-0 Laudehr 63, 9-0 Popp 66, 10-0 Bremer 70,
11-0 Leupolz 72, 12-0 Bremer 84

22/09/15, Zagreb, Zagreb
Croatia 0-1 Germany
Goal: 0-1 Popp 4

21/10/15, Groupama Aréna, Budapest
Hungary 1-0 Turkey
Goal: 1-0 Szuh 46

22/10/15, BRITA-Arena, Wiesbaden
Germany 2-0 Russia
Goals: 1-0 Islacker 8, 2-0 Maier 48

25/10/15, Hardtwaldstadion, Sandhausen
Germany 7-0 Turkey
Goals: 1-0 Islacker 6, 2-0 Mittag 29,
3-0 Behringer 37(p), 4-0 Däbritz 69, 5-0 Magull 78,
6-0 Magull 86, 7-0 Däbritz 90+3

25/10/15, Gradski vrt, Osijek
Croatia 1-1 Hungary
Goals: 0-1 Jakabfi 45(p), 1-1 Joščak 68

25/11/15, Fethiye İlçe Stadı, Fethiye
Turkey 0-0 Russia

29/11/15, Pancho stadium, Felcsut
Hungary 0-1 Russia
Goal: 0-1 Makarenko 55

30/11/15, Stadion HNK Rijeka, Rijeka
Croatia 3-0 Turkey
Goals: 1-0 Šundov 29, 2-0 Joščak 39,
3-0 Andrlić 88

08/04/16, Recep Tayyip Erdoğan, Istanbul
Turkey 0-6 Germany
Goals: 0-1 I Kerschowski 29, 0-2 Mittag 40,
0-3 I Kerschowski 60, 0-4 Popp 78, 0-5 Popp 86,
0-6 I Kerschowski 90+3

08/04/16, Gyirmóti Stadion, Gyor
Hungary 2-0 Croatia
Goals: 1-0 Jakabfi 43, 2-0 Jakabfi 86

12/04/16, Bremer Brücke, Osnabruck
Germany 2-0 Croatia
Goals: 1-0 Marozsán 32, 2-0 Mittag 50

*12/04/16, Minor Sport Arena Petrovsky,
St Petersburg*
Russia 3-3 Hungary
Goals: 1-0 Terekhova 13, 1-1 Vágó 19,
1-2 Zeller 66, 1-3 Jakabfi 76, 2-3 Terekhova 85(p),
3-3 Dmitrenko 90+2

02/06/16, Arena Khimki, Khimki
Russia 2-0 Turkey
Goals: 1-0 Pantyukhina 47, 2-0 Karpova 64

06/06/16, Akdeniz Üniversitesi Stadyumu, Antalya
Turkey 2-1 Hungary
Goals: 1-0 Ece Türkoğlu 4, 2-0 Mosdóczi 27(og),
2-1 Jakabfi 40

Switzerland's top scorer Ana-Maria Crnogorčević
on the mark against Italy

06/06/16, Gradski stadion Koprivnica, Koprivnica
Croatia 0-3 Russia
Goals: 0-1 Žigić 10(og), 0-2 Karpova 21,
0-3 Kozhnikova 38

		Pld	W	D	L	F	A	Pts
1	Germany	6	6	0	0	30	0	18
2	Russia	6	3	2	1	9	5	11
3	Hungary	7	2	2	3	8	19	8
4	Croatia	7	2	1	4	8	10	7
5	Turkey	8	1	1	6	3	24	4

Remaining fixtures

16/09/16
Russia - Germany

20/09/16
Russia - Croatia
Hungary - Germany

Group 6

18/09/15, Stadium Alberto Picco, La Spezia
Italy 6-1 Georgia
Goals: 0-1 Gabelia 3, 1-1 Cernoia 13,
2-1 Giugliano 23, 3-1 Manieri 42, 4-1 Sabatino 58,
5-1 Girelli 79, 6-1 Girelli 83

22/09/15, Mikheil Meskhi Stadioni, Tbilisi
Georgia 0-3 Czech Republic
Goals: 0-1 I Martínková 69, 0-2 Voňková 73,
0-3 I Martínková 88

24/10/15, Dino Manuzzi, Cesena
Italy 0-3 Switzerland
Goals: 0-1 Bachmann 59, 0-2 Bachmann 62,
0-3 Crnogorčević 87

24/10/15, Mikheil Meskhi Stadioni, Tbilisi
Georgia 0-3 Northern Ireland
Goals: 0-1 Nelson 3, 0-2 Bergin 29, 0-3 Bergin 56

27/10/15, FC Chomutov, Chomutov
Czech Republic 0-3 Italy
Goals: 0-1 Mauro 19, 0-2 Manieri 42(p),
0-3 Bartoli 78

27/10/15, Biel/Bienne, Biel
Switzerland 4-0 Georgia
Goals: 1-0 Skhirtladze 9(og), 2-0 Crnogorčević 34,
3-0 Dickenmann 50, 4-0 Humm 74

27/11/15, Mourneview Park, Lurgan
Northern Ireland 1-8 Switzerland
Goals: 0-1 Humm 14, 0-2 Kiwic 28,
0-3 Moser 33, 0-4 Humm 35, 0-5 Ismaili 36,
1-5 Furness 37, 1-6 Crnogorčević 59,
1-7 Deplazes 74, 1-8 Dickenmann 85

01/12/15, La Maladière, Neuchatel
Switzerland 5-1 Czech Republic
Goals: 1-0 Bürki 23, 2-0 Humm 28,
3-0 Bachmann 33, 4-0 Crnogorčević 42,
4-1 Svitková 73, 5-1 Terchoun 84

09/04/16, Biel/Bienne, Biel
Switzerland 2-1 Italy
Goals: 1-0 Bachmann 7, 2-0 Terchoun 36,
2-1 Parisi 65

12/04/16, Mestský fotbalovy, Opava
Czech Republic 4-1 Georgia
Goals: 1-0 L Martínková 3, 2-0 Zakaidze 13(og),
2-1 Skhirtladze 45+1, 3-1 Voňková 51,
4-1 L Martínková 57

12/04/16, Stadio Città del Tricolore, Reggio Emilia
Italy 3-1 Northern Ireland
Goals: 0-1 Magill 62, 1-1 Sabatino 71,
2-1 Mauro 86, 3-1 Stracchi 90+3

03/06/16, Solitude, Belfast
Northern Ireland 4-0 Georgia
Goals: 1-0 Magill 1, 2-0 Callaghan 21,
3-0 Callaghan 40, 4-0 Furness 90+5

04/06/16, Strelnice Stadion, Jablonec nad Nisou
Czech Republic 0-5 Switzerland
Goals: 0-1 Humm 4, 0-2 Moser 35,
0-3 Crnogorčević 40, 0-4 Crnogorčević 66(p),
0-5 Moser 90+3

07/06/16, Tengiz Burjanadze Stadioni, Gori
Georgia 0-7 Italy
Goals: 0-1 Manieri 7, 0-2 Bonansea 21,
0-3 Sabatino 41, 0-4 Bonansea 59, 0-5 Mauro 75,
0-6 Girelli 79(p), 0-7 Girelli 90

07/06/16, Strelnice Stadion, Jablonec nad Nisou
Czech Republic 3-0 Northern Ireland
Goals: 1-0 Voňková 3, 2-0 Cahynová 34,
3-0 Bartoňová 65

		Pld	W	D	L	F	A	Pts
1	Switzerland	6	6	0	0	27	3	18
2	Italy	6	4	0	2	20	7	12
3	Czech Republic	6	3	0	3	11	14	9
4	Northern Ireland	5	2	0	3	9	14	6
5	Georgia	7	0	0	7	2	31	0

Remaining fixtures

03/08/16
**Northern Ireland -
Czech Republic**

15/09/16
Georgia - Switzerland

16/09/16
**Northern Ireland -
Italy**

20/09/16
**Italy - Czech Republic
Switzerland -
Northern Ireland**

Group 7

17/09/15, Tartu Tamme, Tartu
Estonia 0-1 Serbia
Goal: 0-1 Mijatović 43

21/09/15, A. Le Coq Arena, Tallinn
Estonia 0-8 England
Goals: 0-1 Carter 2, 0-2 Potter 34, 0-3 Kirby 40, 0-4 J Scott 53, 0-5 Christiansen 74, 0-6 Kirby 81, 0-7 Carter 83, 0-8 Carter 90+2

22/09/15, Den Dreef, Louvain
Belgium 6-0 Bosnia & Herzegovina
Goals: 1-0 Dijaković 7(og), 2-0 De Gernier 20, 3-0 Zeler 33, 4-0 Cayman 35, 5-0 Zeler 41(p), 6-0 Coutereels 72(p)

23/10/15, FF BH Football Training Centre, Zenica
Bosnia & Herzegovina 4-0 Estonia
Goals: 1-0 Nikolić 6, 2-0 Nikolić 36, 3-0 Nikolić 43, 4-0 Radeljić 73

27/10/15, Suvača, Pecinci
Serbia 3-0 Estonia
Goals: 1-0 Čubrilo 17, 2-0 Čubrilo 61, 3-0 Radojičić 82

27/10/15, FF BH Football Training Centre, Zenica
Bosnia & Herzegovina 0-5 Belgium
Goals: 0-1 Biesmans 25, 0-2 Biesmans 65, 0-3 Wullaert 73, 0-4 Wullaert 83, 0-5 Demoustier 90+2

25/11/15, Sports Center of FA of Serbia, Stara Pazova
Serbia 0-1 Bosnia & Herzegovina
Goal: 0-1 Nikolić 88

29/11/15, Ashton Gate, Bristol
England 1-0 Bosnia & Herzegovina
Goal: 1-0 J Scott 69

30/11/15, Den Dreef, Louvain
Belgium 1-1 Serbia
Goals: 1-0 Yuceil 17, 1-1 Damnjanović 39

08/04/16, AESSEAL New York Stadium, Rotherham
England 1-1 Belgium
Goals: 0-1 Cayman 18, 1-1 J Scott 84

12/04/16, FF BH Football Training Centre, Zenica
Bosnia & Herzegovina 0-1 England
Goal: 0-1 Carney 86

12/04/16, Den Dreef, Louvain
Belgium 6-0 Estonia
Goals: 1-0 Coutereels 11, 2-0 De Caigny 21, 3-0 Wullaert 30, 4-0 De Caigny 50, 5-0 Wullaert 63, 6-0 Schrijvers 67

03/06/16, Tartu Tamme, Tartu
Estonia 0-5 Belgium
Goals: 0-1 Zlidnis 10(og), 0-2 Zeler 38, 0-3 Van Gorp 60, 0-4 Cayman 65, 0-5 Cayman 70

04/06/16, Adams Park, Wycombe
England 7-0 Serbia
Goals: 1-0 Greenwood 16, 2-0 Carney 34(p), 3-0 Daly 43, 4-0 White 51, 5-0 Christiansen 52, 6-0 Carney 60, 7-0 Carney 64

06/06/16, Tartu Tamme, Tartu
Estonia 0-1 Bosnia & Herzegovina
Goal: 0-1 Nikolić 57

07/06/16, Sports Center of FA of Serbia, Stara Pazova
Serbia 0-7 England
Goals: 0-1 J Scott 13, 0-2 White 28, 0-3 Davison 41, 0-4 Davison 46, 0-5 Damjanović 53(og), 0-6 Parris 69, 0-7 Parris 90

		Pld	W	D	L	F	A	Pts
1	England	6	5	1	0	25	1	16
2	Belgium	6	4	2	0	24	2	14
3	Bosnia & Herzegovina	7	3	0	4	6	13	9
4	Serbia	6	2	1	3	5	16	7
5	Estonia	7	0	0	7	0	28	0

Remaining fixtures

15/09/16
England - Estonia
Serbia - Belgium

20/09/16
Belgium - England
Bosnia & Herzegovina - Serbia

Group 8

17/09/15, BIIK Stadium, Shymkent
Kazakhstan 0-2 Austria
Goals: 0-1 Billa 45+1, 0-2 Billa 89

22/09/15, Kazhimukan Munaytpasov, Astana
Kazakhstan 0-4 Norway
Goals: 0-1 Ada Hegerberg 19, 0-2 Ada Hegerberg 27, 0-3 Haavi 51, 0-4 Haavi 61

22/09/15, NV Arena, St Polten
Austria 3-0 Wales
Goals: 1-0 Schiechtl 25, 2-0 Puntigam 73, 3-0 Burger 86

22/10/15, Lod Municipal, Lod
Israel 0-0 Kazakhstan

23/10/15, Aalesund Stadion, Aalesund
Norway 4-0 Wales
Goals: 1-0 Herlovsen 30, 2-0 Ada Hegerberg 39, 3-0 Herlovsen 71, 4-0 Mjelde 90+3

25/10/15, Lod Municipal, Lod
Israel 0-1 Austria
Goal: 0-1 Prohaska 48

26/11/15, Bridge Meadow, Haverfordwest
Wales 4-0 Kazakhstan
Goals: 1-0 Harding 48, 2-0 Lander 60, 3-0 Lander 62, 4-0 Lander 83

01/12/15, Itztadion Ramat Gan, Ramat Gan
Israel 2-2 Wales
Goals: 1-0 Falkon 25, 1-1 Harding 59, 1-2 Harding 80, 2-2 Shelina 83

06/04/16, Itztadion Ramat Gan, Ramat Gan
Israel 0-1 Norway
Goal: 0-1 Ada Hegerberg 25

06/04/16, Vorwärts Steyr, Steyr
Austria 6-1 Kazakhstan
Goals: 1-0 Schiechtl 13, 2-0 Billa 15, 3-0 Aschauer 18, 4-0 Zadrazil 32, 5-0 Burger 36, 5-1 Kirgizbaeva 79, 6-1 Billa 88

10/04/16, Vorwärts Steyr, Steyr
Austria 0-1 Norway
Goal: 0-1 Mykjåland 23(p)

12/04/16, BIIK Stadium, Shymkent
Kazakhstan 0-4 Wales
Goals: 0-1 K Green 15, 0-2 K Green 23, 0-3 Lander 60(p), 0-4 Lander 81(p)

02/06/16, BIIK Stadium, Shymkent
Kazakhstan 1-0 Israel
Goal: 1-0 Yalova 69

02/06/16, Ullevaal Stadion, Oslo
Norway 2-2 Austria
Goals: 0-1 Burger 13, 1-1 Mjelde 23, 2-1 Herlovsen 56, 2-2 Feiersinger 85

06/06/16, Horn, Niederosterreich
Austria 4-0 Israel
Goals: 1-0 Burger 4, 2-0 Burger 19, 3-0 Barqui 41(og), 4-0 Kirchberger 78

07/06/16, Newport, Newport
Wales 0-2 Norway
Goals: 0-1 Ada Hegerberg 69, 0-2 Ada Hegerberg 81

		Pld	W	D	L	F	A	Pts
1	Norway	6	5	1	0	14	2	16
2	Austria	7	5	1	1	18	4	16
3	Wales	6	2	1	3	10	11	7
4	Kazakhstan	7	1	1	5	2	20	4
5	Israel	6	0	2	4	2	9	2

Remaining fixtures

15/09/16
Norway - Kazakhstan
Wales - Israel

19/09/16
Norway - Israel

20/09/16
Wales - Austria

Top goalscorers

10	Harpa Thorsteinsdóttir (Iceland)
8	Jane Ross (Scotland)
6	Sanne Troelsgaard (Denmark)
	Ada Hegerberg (Norway)
	Joanne Love (Scotland)
	Ana-Maria Crnogorčević (Switzerland)

Spain defeated 2-1 in rain-interrupted final

Six-goal haul for France striker Katoto

Switzerland and Netherlands ousted in semi-finals

France splash to victory

It may have seemed like business as usual with France winning their fourth UEFA European Women's Under-19 Championship – and Spain reaching, and losing, a third final in a row – but the match that decided the destination of the trophy, in the Slovakian town of Senec, was more than a little out of the ordinary.

The game began in sunshine, but by the time Grace Geyoro had given France the lead, on 36 minutes, the predicted heavy rain was already falling. By half-time it was a thunderous downpour and play had to be suspended. For two hours attempts were made to clear the pitch, with tentative arrangements underway to re-schedule for the following day. Finally, however, the pitch was declared playable, with rain still falling, and the game began again.

Not long after the re-start France goalkeeper Mylène Chavas saved Nahikari García's penalty and, assisted by the puddle-strewn surface, Marie-Antoinette Katoto made it 2-0 with her top-scoring sixth goal at the finals. Lucía García pulled one back, finishing off a shot from Nahikari, who so nearly equalised at the death only to kick water as she went to make contact with the ball.

It was the second weather-disrupted match of a tournament played largely in warm sunshine, the group game between Norway and Slovakia having been abandoned early in the second half at 0-0 because of a waterlogged pitch. Since France's simultaneous 2-1 victory over the Netherlands ensured that both of those teams would qualify from Group A, the result of the other game was confirmed as goalless, giving hosts Slovakia their first point in a UEFA women's final tournament. The hosts had earlier lost 6-0 to both the Netherlands and France, who began with a 1-0 defeat against Norway. A subsequent 1-0 loss to the Netherlands would prove Norway's undoing.

France's players gather on the winner's podium to celebrate their Women's U19 victory

Spain dominated Group B, beating Germany 1-0, finals debutants Austria 4-0 and Switzerland 5-0. By then Switzerland were already through as well, having defeated Austria 4-0 and Germany 4-2. Germany did manage to overcome Austria 3-1 and take third place but it was a fifth successive Women's U19 tournament without a title for the record six-time winners.

With an aggregate of 11 goals, the semi-finals were the highest-scoring the competition had ever witnessed. France trailed Switzerland at half-time but a double substitution changed the game, Clara Mateo coming on to score twice and set up another goal in a nine-minute spell for a 3-1 win. Spain, meanwhile, overcame the Netherlands 4-3 in an entertaining encounter that featured several long-range goals.

However, for the third year running – and fifth time in six appearances – Spain lost the final. In defeat Nuria Garrote, Nahikari and Andrea Sánchez had the consolation of playing in an unprecedented fourth UEFA youth final, while Nahikari's 22 UEFA youth tournament appearances and Sánchez's 40 overall, qualifying included, also constituted new records.

Qualifying round

Group 1

15-20/09/15 Nyon
Iceland 6-1 Georgia, Switzerland 7-0 Greece, Greece 2-1 Iceland, Switzerland 23-0 Georgia, Iceland 0-2 Switzerland, Georgia 0-7 Greece

	Pld	W	D	L	F	A	Pts
1 Switzerland	3	3	0	0	32	0	9
2 Greece	3	2	0	1	9	8	6
3 Iceland	3	1	0	2	7	5	3
4 Georgia	3	0	0	3	1	36	0

Group 2

15-20/09/15 Bijeljina
France 2-0 Bosnia & Herzegovina, Czech Republic 4-1 Faroe Islands, France 7-0 Faroe Islands, Bosnia & Herzegovina 0-5 Czech Republic, Czech Republic 0-6 France, Faroe Islands 0-1 Bosnia & Herzegovina

	Pld	W	D	L	F	A	Pts
1 France	3	3	0	0	15	0	9
2 Czech Republic	3	2	0	1	9	7	6
3 Bosnia & Herzegovina	3	1	0	2	1	7	3
4 Faroe Islands	3	0	0	3	1	12	0

Group 3

15-20/09/15 Oswestry, Broughton
Wales 1-4 Azerbaijan, Belgium 4-0 Croatia, Croatia 3-2 Wales, Belgium 0-3 Azerbaijan, Wales 0-6 Belgium, Azerbaijan 2-1 Croatia

	Pld	W	D	L	F	A	Pts
1 Azerbaijan	3	3	0	0	9	2	9
2 Belgium	3	2	0	1	10	3	6
3 Croatia	3	1	0	2	4	8	3
4 Wales	3	0	0	3	3	13	0

Group 4

15-20/09/15 Tammela, Hameenlinna
Poland 5-0 Lithuania, Finland 1-0 Turkey, Finland 8-0 Lithuania, Turkey 0-4 Poland, Poland 3-7 Finland, Lithuania 0-1 Turkey

	Pld	W	D	L	F	A	Pts
1 Finland	3	3	0	0	16	3	9
2 Poland	3	2	0	1	12	7	6
3 Turkey	3	1	0	2	1	5	3
4 Lithuania	3	0	0	3	0	14	0

Group 5

15-20/09/15 Szombathely, Buk
Germany 2-0 Hungary, Serbia 2-0 Kazakhstan, Germany 7-0 Kazakhstan, Hungary 1-0 Serbia, Serbia 1-6 Germany, Kazakhstan 0-5 Hungary

	Pld	W	D	L	F	A	Pts
1 Germany	3	3	0	0	15	1	9
2 Hungary	3	2	0	1	6	2	6
3 Serbia	3	1	0	2	3	7	3
4 Kazakhstan	3	0	0	3	0	14	0

Group 6

15-20/09/15 Skopje
Sweden 3-0 FYR Macedonia, Northern Ireland 0-0 Montenegro, Sweden 5-0 Montenegro, FYR Macedonia 0-5 Northern Ireland, Northern Ireland 0-4 Sweden, Montenegro 4-1 FYR Macedonia

Sippie Folkertsma of the Netherlands – the nine-goal top scorer in qualifying

	Pld	W	D	L	F	A	Pts
1 Sweden	3	3	0	0	12	0	9
2 Northern Ireland	3	1	1	1	5	4	4
3 Montenegro	3	1	1	1	4	6	4
4 FYR Macedonia	3	0	0	3	1	12	0

Group 7

15-20/09/15 Heerenveen, Assen
Italy 9-0 Moldova, Netherlands 9-0 Cyprus, Cyprus 0-11 Italy, Netherlands 12-0 Moldova, Italy 1-1 Netherlands, Moldova 2-1 Cyprus

	Pld	W	D	L	F	A	Pts
1 Netherlands	3	2	1	0	22	1	7
2 Italy	3	2	1	0	21	1	7
3 Moldova	3	1	0	2	2	22	3
4 Cyprus	3	0	0	3	1	22	0

Group 8

15-20/09/15 Seia, Fornos de Algodres, Guarda
Norway 6-0 Estonia, Portugal 2-1 Israel, Norway 7-0 Israel, Estonia 0-4 Portugal, Portugal 2-2 Norway, Israel 2-2 Estonia

	Pld	W	D	L	F	A	Pts
1 Norway	3	2	1	0	15	2	7
2 Portugal	3	2	1	0	8	3	7
3 Israel	3	0	1	2	3	11	1
4 Estonia	3	0	1	2	2	12	1

Group 9

15-20/09/15 Orsha, Mogilev
Denmark 2-1 Belarus, Romania 8-0 Latvia, Denmark 8-0 Latvia, Belarus 3-1 Romania, Romania 0-1 Denmark, Latvia 0-7 Belarus

	Pld	W	D	L	F	A	Pts
1 Denmark	3	3	0	0	11	1	9
2 Belarus	3	2	0	1	11	3	6
3 Romania	3	1	0	2	9	4	3
4 Latvia	3	0	0	3	0	23	0

Group 10

15-20/09/15 Gornja Radgona, Bakovci
Republic of Ireland 3-0 Slovenia, Russia 4-0 Bulgaria, Republic of Ireland 6-0 Bulgaria, Slovenia 1-7 Russia, Russia 2-1 Republic of Ireland, Bulgaria 0-3 Slovenia

	Pld	W	D	L	F	A	Pts
1 Russia	3	3	0	0	13	2	9
2 Republic of Ireland	3	2	0	1	10	2	6
3 Slovenia	3	1	0	2	4	10	3
4 Bulgaria	3	0	0	3	0	13	0

Group 11

15-20/09/15 Lindabrunn, Bad Erlach, St Polten
Scotland 3-2 Ukraine, Austria 8-1 Albania, Scotland 4-2 Albania, Ukraine 0-1 Austria, Austria 1-2 Scotland, Albania 1-3 Ukraine

	Pld	W	D	L	F	A	Pts
1 Scotland	3	3	0	0	9	5	9
2 Austria	3	2	0	1	10	3	6
3 Ukraine	3	1	0	2	5	5	3
4 Albania	3	0	0	3	4	15	0

Elite round

Group 1

05-10/04/16 Dublin
Azerbaijan 0-0 Poland, Germany 1-0 Republic of Ireland, Germany 3-1 Poland, Republic of Ireland 3-0 Azerbaijan, Azerbaijan 1-5 Germany, Poland 0-2 Republic of Ireland

	Pld	W	D	L	F	A	Pts
1 Germany	3	3	0	0	9	2	9
2 Republic of Ireland	3	2	0	1	5	1	6
3 Poland	3	0	1	2	1	5	1
4 Azerbaijan	3	0	1	2	1	8	1

Group 2

05-10/04/16 Linkoping, Norrkoping
England 1-0 Austria, Sweden 2-1 Belgium, England 0-1 Belgium, Austria 1-0 Sweden, Sweden 0-0 England, Belgium 0-2 Austria

	Pld	W	D	L	F	A	Pts
1 Austria	3	2	0	1	3	1	6
2 Sweden	3	1	1	1	2	2	4
3 England	3	1	1	1	1	1	4
4 Belgium	3	1	0	2	2	4	3

Group 3

05-10/04/16 Eibergen, Hengelo
Finland 2-1 Belarus, Netherlands 7-2 Czech Republic, Finland 1-2 Czech Republic, Belarus 0-3 Netherlands, Netherlands 1-1 Finland, Czech Republic 2-0 Belarus

	Pld	W	D	L	F	A	Pts
1 Netherlands	3	2	1	0	11	3	7
2 Czech Republic	3	2	0	1	6	8	6
3 Finland	3	1	1	1	4	4	4
4 Belarus	3	0	0	3	1	7	0

Group 4

05-10/04/16 Hobro, Viborg, Skive
Spain 3-0 Italy, Denmark 5-0 Northern Ireland, Spain 7-1 Northern Ireland, Italy 1-1 Denmark, Denmark 1-3 Spain, Northern Ireland 0-3 Italy

	Pld	W	D	L	F	A	Pts
1 Spain	3	3	0	0	13	2	9
2 Denmark	3	1	1	1	7	4	4
3 Italy	3	1	1	1	4	4	4
4 Northern Ireland	3	0	0	3	1	15	0

Group 5

05-10/04/16 Lagos, Ferreiras, Parchal, Faro-Loule
**Scotland 1-0 Greece, France 3-0 Portugal,
France 6-0 Greece, Portugal 1-1 Scotland,
Scotland 0-2 France, Greece 0-2 Portugal**

		Pld	W	D	L	F	A	Pts
1	France	3	3	0	0	11	0	9
2	Portugal	3	1	1	1	3	4	4
3	Scotland	3	1	1	1	2	3	4
4	Greece	3	0	0	3	0	9	0

Group 6

05-10/04/16 Buk, Szombathely
**Switzerland 2-2 Norway, Russia 1-1 Hungary,
Switzerland 4-0 Hungary, Norway 1-0 Russia,
Russia 0-1 Switzerland, Hungary 0-1 Norway**

		Pld	W	D	L	F	A	Pts
1	Switzerland	3	2	1	0	7	2	7
2	Norway	3	2	1	0	4	2	7
3	Russia	3	0	1	2	1	3	1
4	Hungary	3	0	1	2	1	6	1

Top goalscorers (Qualifying/Elite rounds)

9 Sippie Folkertsma (Netherlands)

8 Heidi Kollanen (Finland)

7 Marina Fedorova (Russia)
Julia Glaser (Switzerland)

5 Stefanie Sanders (Germany)
Megan Connolly (Republic of Ireland)
Céline Imhof (Switzerland)
Lesley Ramseier (Switzerland)

Final tournament

Group A

19/07/16, National Training Centre, Senec
Slovakia 0-6 Netherlands
Goals: 0-1 Folkertsma 23(p), 0-2 Roord 37,
0-3 Deszathová 40(og), 0-4 Roord 57, 0-5 Hendriks
69, 0-6 Roord 74

19/07/16, Štadión FC ViOn, Zlate Moravce
France 0-1 Norway
Goal: 0-1 Jørgensen 36

22/07/16, Štadión FC ViOn, Zlate Moravce
Netherlands 1-0 Norway
Goal: 1-0 Folkertsma 56

22/07/16, National Training Centre, Senec
Slovakia 0-6 France
Goals: 0-1 Katoto 49, 0-2 Mateo 51,
0-3 Katoto 53, 0-4 Morroni 65, 0-5 Katoto 68,
0-6 D Cascarino 90

25/07/16, Štadión FC ViOn, Zlate Moravce
Norway 0-0 Slovakia *(match abandoned; result
stood)*

25/07/16, National Training Centre, Senec
Netherlands 1-2 France
Goals: 0-1 Katoto 18, 0-2 Geyoro 24(p),
1-2 Roord 60

		Pld	W	D	L	F	A	Pts
1	France	3	2	0	1	8	2	6
2	Netherlands	3	2	0	1	8	2	6
3	Norway	3	1	1	1	1	1	4
4	Slovakia	3	0	1	2	0	12	1

Group B

19/07/16, FK Senica, Senica
Spain 1-0 Germany
Goal: 1-0 N García 62

19/07/16, Spartak Myjava, Myjava
Austria 0-4 Switzerland
Goals: 0-1 Zehnder 19, 0-2 Mégroz 60,
0-3 Jenzer 77, 0-4 Zehnder 88

22/07/16, Spartak Myjava, Myjava
Spain 4-0 Austria
Goals: 1-0 Sánchez 5, 2-0 Sánchez 29,
3-0 L García 69, 4-0 Bonmati 83(p)

22/07/16, FK Senica, Senica
Germany 2-4 Switzerland
Goals: 1-0 Sanders 3, 1-1 Mégroz 6,
1-2 Surdez 64, 2-2 Freigang 70, 2-3 Surdez 72,
2-4 Zehnder 90+1

25/07/16, Spartak Myjava, Myjava
Switzerland 0-5 Spain
Goals: 0-1 N García 15, 0-2 Hernández 36,
0-3 N García 47, 0-4 L García 52, 0-5 L García 74

25/07/16, FK Senica, Senica
Germany 3-1 Austria
Goals: 1-0 Ehegötz 43, 2-0 Freigang 58,
3-0 Sanders 73, 3-1 Feric 84

		Pld	W	D	L	F	A	Pts
1	Spain	3	3	0	0	10	0	9
2	Switzerland	3	2	0	1	8	7	6
3	Germany	3	1	0	2	5	6	3
4	Austria	3	0	0	3	1	11	0

Semi-finals

28/07/16, National Training Centre, Senec
France 3-1 Switzerland
Goals: 0-1 Reuteler 44, 1-1 Mateo 46,
2-1 Katoto 50, 3-1 Mateo 54

28/07/16, National Training Centre, Senec
Spain 4-3 Netherlands
Goals: 0-1 Admiraal 22, 1-1 Hernández 25,
1-2 Roord 59, 2-2 Hernández 68, 3-2 Cazalla 73,
4-2 Hernández 81, 4-3 Hendriks 84

Final

31/07/16, National Training Centre, Senec
(att: 1,024)
France 2-1 Spain
Goals: 1-0 Geyoro 36, 2-0 Katoto 66,
2-1 L García 84
Referee: Urbán (HUN)
France: Chavas, Mansuy, Greboval, Cissoko,
E Cascarino, D Cascarino, Condon, Mateo, Geyoro,
Morroni, Katoto (Couturier 84). Coach: Gilles
Eyquem (FRA)
Spain: Peña, Beltrán, Bonmati (L García 46), Cazalla
(María Vázquez 87), N Garrote, N García, Guijarro,
Sánchez, Menayo, Hernández, Oroz (Carrión 69).
Coach: Pedro López (ESP)
Yellow card: D Cascarino 54 (France)

Top goalscorers (Final tournament)

6 Marie-Antoinette Katoto (France)

5 Jill Roord (Netherlands)

4 Lucía García (Spain)
Sandra Hernández (Spain)

3 Clara Mateo (France)
Nahikari García (Spain)
Cinzia Zehnder (Switzerland)

Squads/Appearances/Goals

Austria

No	Name	DoB	Aps	(s)	Gls
Goalkeepers					
1	Carolin Grössinger	10/05/97	3		
21	Isabella Kresche	28/11/98			
Defenders					
18	Anna Egretzberger	06/01/97	1		
10	Marina Georgieva	13/04/97	2		
6	Adina Hamidovic	26/04/98	1	(1)	
9	Katharina Naschenweng	16/12/97	3		
11	Nina Wasserbauer	06/11/98	3		
4	Anna Zimmerebner	16/10/98	2		
Midfielders					
8	Katharina Aufhauser	16/01/97	3		
17	Ivana Feric	25/08/97		(3)	1
13	Duygu Karkac	19/05/97		(1)	
16	Teresa Knauseder	07/03/97	3		
14	Julia Kofler	02/09/98	3		
20	Sandrine Sobotka	08/10/98	3		
Forwards					
7	Barbara Dunst	25/09/97	3		
12	Sarah Lackner	02/06/97		(1)	
15	Viktoria Pinther	16/10/98	3		
19	Melissa Schmid	02/11/98		(2)	

France

No	Name	DoB	Aps	(s)	Gls
Goalkeepers					
1	Mylène Chavas	07/01/98	5		
16	Jade Lebastard	03/05/98			
Defenders					
4	Hawa Cissoko	10/04/97	4		
13	Elisa De Almeida	11/01/98	1	(1)	
12	Pauline Dechilly	07/04/98	1		
5	Estelle Cascarino	05/02/97	3	(1)	
3	Théa Greboval	05/04/97	5		
2	Héloïse Mansuy	13/02/97	4	(1)	
Midfielders					
7	Delphine Cascarino	05/02/97	4	(1)	1
8	Laura Condon	18/03/97	4		
6	Cathy Couturier	08/01/97	3	(1)	
10	Grace Geyoro	02/07/97	5		2
14	Elise Legrout	12/08/97	2		
11	Perle Morroni	15/10/97	3	(2)	1
15	Julie Thibaud	20/04/98	1		
Forwards					
17	Anna Clerac	02/06/97	2	(2)	
19	Louise Fleury	08/08/97		(1)	
18	Marie-Antoinette Katoto	01/11/98	4	(1)	6
9	Clara Mateo	28/11/97	4	(1)	3

Germany

No	Name	DoB	Aps	(s)	Gls
Goalkeepers					
12	Vanessa Fischer	18/04/98	1		
1	Lena Pauels	02/02/98	2		
Defenders					
5	Melissa Friedrich	06/05/97	1	(1)	
3	Anna Gerhardt	17/04/98	2		
13	Isabella Hartig	12/08/97	3		
2	Lisa Karl	15/01/97	1		
15	Isabella Möller	04/02/98	1	(2)	
19	Katja Nicola Orschmann	08/01/98	1		
4	Michaela Specht	15/02/97	2		
Midfielders					
9	Nina Ehegötz	22/02/97	2	(1)	1
16	Jana Feldkamp	15/03/98	3		
8	Lina Hausicke	30/12/97	3		
6	Saskia Matheis	06/06/97	1		
14	Melanie Ott	13/04/97	1	(1)	
7	Pia-Sophie Wolter	13/11/97	2		
Forwards					
10	Laura Freigang	01/02/98	2	(1)	2
18	Stefanie Sanders	12/06/98	2	(1)	2
11	Lea Schüller	12/11/97	1	(2)	
17	Jasmin Sehan	16/06/97	2		

Norway

No	Name	DoB	Aps	(s)	Gls
Goalkeepers					
1	Ida Norstrøm	11/06/97	3		
12	Hildegunn Sævik	09/01/98			
Defenders					
5	Ingrid Elvebakken	28/04/97	3		
2	Tuva Hansen	04/08/97	3		
17	Mariken Kleppe	21/11/97			
3	Svanhild Sand	20/10/98	3		
4	Sarah Suphellen	10/07/98	3		
Midfielders					
14	Vilde Hasund	27/06/97	1	(1)	
15	Karoline Haugland	23/02/98	2	(1)	
6	Maria Hiim	06/10/97	2		
16	Katrine W. Jørgensen	22/01/97	2		1
13	Gabrielle Lie	08/02/98		(1)	
8	Nora Eide Lie	22/04/97	3		
7	Ingrid Syrstad Engen	29/04/98	1	(1)	
Forwards					
9	Siw Døvle	28/04/98	3		
11	Vilde Fjelldal	23/09/97	3		
10	Ingrid Kvernvolden	01/05/98	1	(2)	
18	Marie Markussen	15/02/97		(1)	

Spain

No	Name	DoB	Aps	(s)	Gls
Goalkeepers					
1	Yolanda Aguirre	23/10/98		(1)	
13	Amaia Peña	22/11/98	5		
Defenders					
3	Beatriz Beltrán	10/12/97	4		
5	Marta Cazalla	05/04/97	4		1
12	María Vázquez	17/11/97	1	(3)	
11	Carmen Menayo	14/04/98	5		
6	Nuria Garrote	10/06/97	5		
2	Andrea Sierra	15/05/98	1	(2)	
Midfielders					
4	Aitana Bonmati	18/01/98	4	(1)	1
15	Maria Ángeles Carrión	22/02/97	1	(3)	
9	Laura Domínguez	12/08/97	1		
8	Patricia Guijarro	17/05/98	4		
14	Sandra Hernández	25/05/97	5		4
16	Maite Oroz	25/03/98	3	(1)	
Forwards					
17	Lucía García	14/07/98	3	(2)	4
18	Laura María Pérez	15/06/98		(1)	
7	Nahikari García	10/03/97	5		3
10	Andrea Sánchez	28/02/97	4		2

Netherlands

No	Name	DoB	Aps	(s)	Gls
Goalkeepers					
16	Lize Kop	17/03/98			
1	Paulina Quaye	22/07/97	4		
Defenders					
12	Kay-Lee de Sanders	06/01/98	1	(3)	
5	Maureen Sanders	18/07/97		(1)	
4	Vera ten Westeneind	20/03/98	3		
3	Vita van der Linden	04/01/97	4		
2	Yvonne van Schijndel	20/08/97	4		
13	Ashleigh Weerden	07/06/99	4		
Midfielders					
8	Michelle Hendriks	10/02/97	4		2
14	Pleun Raaijmakers	15/04/97	3	(1)	
10	Jill Roord	22/04/97	4		5
15	Cheyenne van den Goorbergh	06/09/97			
6	Nurija van Schoonhoven	08/02/98	1	(2)	
Forwards					
7	Suzanne Admiraal	30/01/97	4		1
18	Esmee De Graaf	02/08/97		(3)	
9	Sisca Folkertsma	21/05/97	4		2
17	Nadine Noordam	29/07/98			
11	Soraya Verhoeve	28/12/97	4		

Slovakia

No	Name	DoB	Aps	(s)	Gls
Goalkeepers					
12	Patrícia Chládeková	04/04/97	2		
1	Veronika Matušková	29/08/98	1		
Defenders					
2	Natália Botková	21/01/98			
3	Stephanie Deszathová	03/03/97	3		
5	Terézia Kulová	02/04/97	3		
16	Michaela Moťovská	24/09/97	3		
9	Alexandra Tóthová	31/12/97	1	(1)	
Midfielders					
14	Adriana Briššová	28/02/98	3		
2	Juliána Čahojová	28/07/97	1		
8	Klaudia Fabová	12/09/98	3		
11	Veronika Galarovičová	21/08/98			
4	Monika Havranová	04/04/97	2	(1)	
18	Katarína Košlabová	27/11/98		(2)	
13	Terézia Kovaľbová	12/02/98	3		
17	Mária Mikolajová	13/06/99	3		
7	Martina Šurnovská	10/02/99	3		
Forwards					
6	Stanislava Lišková	15/03/97	2		
15	Martina Švecová	18/04/97		(1)	

Switzerland

No	Name	DoB	Aps	(s)	Gls
Goalkeepers					
12	Nadja Furrer	30/04/98	1		
1	Natascha Honegger	27/09/97	3		
Defenders					
2	Lorena Baumann	11/02/97	4		
17	Jana Brunner	20/01/97	4		
5	Carola Fasel	27/06/97	4		
14	Sina Spieser	06/07/97	1	(2)	
8	Julia Stierli	03/04/97	3	(1)	
Midfielders					
16	Julia Glaser	07/10/97	1	(1)	
11	Yara Hofmann	29/09/98	1	(2)	
7	Lara Jenzer	05/08/98	3	(1)	1
10	Naomi Mégroz	06/08/98	3		2
6	Lesley Ramseier	05/06/97	4		
9	Marilena Widmer	07/08/97	3	(1)	
13	Cinzia Zehnder	04/08/97	4		3
Forwards					
4	Kim Dubs	22/09/98	1	(1)	
3	Géraldine Reuteler	21/04/99	2	(1)	1
18	Camille Surdez	13/01/98	1	(2)	2
15	Elena Van Niekerk	04/08/97	1		

Spain edged out on penalties after goalless draw

Five-figure crowd present for Borisov final

Goals galore for third-placed England

Spot-kick success for Germany

The ninth UEFA European Women's Under-17 Championship was the biggest yet, featuring 47 countries, and appropriately ended with an eight-team final tournament – the third in the competition's history – that broke records on and off the pitch.

For Belarus, it was a second UEFA tournament after the 2009 Women's Under-19s, and the 16 matches attracted an unprecedented aggregate attendance of 44,653, including a championship-high 10,200 for the final. Moreover, the crowds that flocked to Minsk, Zhodino, Borisov and Slutsk witnessed a championship-record 58 goals.

The group stage action showcased three newcomers in Belarus, Czech Republic and Serbia, but the highlight of matchday one was the 2-2 draw between traditional heavyweights Germany and holders Spain, two nations who between them had won seven of the previous eight Women's U17 tournaments. Three days later England inflicted a 12-0 defeat on Belarus, which was a UEFA tournament record, while that second set of games was notable also for the first of Spaniard Lorena Navarro's five goals that would earn her a share of the golden shoe.

The group stage culminated with all eight teams, arithmetically at least, in

contention. Anouschka Bernhard's Germany stepped up to beat Czech Republic 4-0, but Spain maintained pole position in Group B, overcoming Italy 3-1. The Group A honours went to England, who made it nine points from nine as they came from behind to oust Serbia 4-1, leaving Norway second thanks to their two unanswered goals against Belarus.

Norway's reward was a semi-final against Spain. The Scandinavians started well but eight minutes after the restart Silvia Rubio struck from distance and, as Norway tired, Spain conjured three goals in six late minutes to reach a record sixth final. The second semi-final, between England and Germany, was a classic. Either side of half-time, England swiftly equalised twice after falling behind, with Vanessa Ziegler, Ellie Brazil, Klara Bühl

Germany celebrate a fifth European Women's U17 title

and Alessia Russo all on target. Germany then pulled clear as Tanja Pawollek and Ziegler both found the net, but even at 4-2 down England mustered one last Russo goal, putting her on five for the tournament alongside Navarro.

England subsequently claimed the consolation prize of FIFA U-17 Women's World Cup qualification, pipping Norway 2-1 in the third-place play-off with a double from Niamh Charles to join the two semi-final victors in Jordan in September.

The immediate business for Spain and Germany was the Borisov-Arena final. María Antonia Is, aka 'Toña', was seeking to mastermind a fourth Spanish title, and her troops dominated the first 25 minutes. The clearer chances, though, went to Germany as Janina Minge, Pawollek and Bühl all rattled the woodwork. With their speed, fitness and physicality, the Germans just about edged the 80 minutes but they could not score and eventually prevailed only on penalties, winning the shoot-out 3-2 thanks to successful conversions from Giulia Gwinn, Minge and Caroline Siems. It was Germany's fifth triumph from as many final appearances, and a second (after 2014) achieved on spot kicks at Spain's expense.

Qualifying round

Group 1

15-20/10/15 Izmir
Turkey 5-0 Andorra, Republic of Ireland 3-0 Ukraine, Republic of Ireland 7-0 Andorra, Ukraine 1-0 Turkey, Turkey 0-3 Republic of Ireland, Andorra 0-11 Ukraine

		Pld	W	D	L	F	A	Pts
1	Republic of Ireland	3	3	0	0	13	0	9
2	Ukraine	3	2	0	1	12	3	6
3	Turkey	3	1	0	2	5	4	3
4	Andorra	3	0	0	3	0	23	0

Group 2

11-16/10/15 Shymkent
Scotland 0-0 Latvia, Austria 2-0 Kazakhstan, Austria 1-0 Latvia, Kazakhstan 0-4 Scotland, Scotland 0-3 Austria, Latvia 1-1 Kazakhstan

		Pld	W	D	L	F	A	Pts
1	Austria	3	3	0	0	6	0	9
2	Scotland	3	1	1	1	4	3	4
3	Latvia	3	0	2	1	1	2	2
4	Kazakhstan	3	0	1	2	1	7	1

Group 3

23-28/10/15 Abrantes, Torres Novas, Entroncamento, Fatima
Spain 9-0 Armenia, Greece 1-0 Portugal, Armenia 0-8 Greece, Spain 4-1 Portugal, Greece 0-6 Spain, Portugal 1-0 Armenia

		Pld	W	D	L	F	A	Pts
1	Spain	3	3	0	0	19	1	9
2	Greece	3	2	0	1	9	6	6
3	Portugal	3	1	0	2	2	5	3
4	Armenia	3	0	0	3	0	18	0

Group 4

01-06/10/15 Tallinn, Rakvere
Poland 10-0 Estonia, England 13-0 Croatia, Poland 5-0 Croatia, Estonia 0-13 England, Croatia 0-0 Estonia, England 2-2 Poland

		Pld	W	D	L	F	A	Pts
1	England	3	2	1	0	28	2	7
2	Poland	3	2	1	0	17	2	7
3	Croatia	3	0	1	2	0	18	1
4	Estonia	3	0	1	2	0	23	1

Group 5

28/09-03/10/15 Skopje
Italy 5-0 Bosnia & Herzegovina, Northern Ireland 3-0 FYR Macedonia, Italy 4-0 FYR Macedonia, Bosnia & Herzegovina 0-0 Northern Ireland, Northern Ireland 0-5 Italy, FYR Macedonia 1-1 Bosnia & Herzegovina

		Pld	W	D	L	F	A	Pts
1	Italy	3	3	0	0	14	0	9
2	Northern Ireland	3	1	1	1	3	5	4
3	Bosnia & Herzegovina	3	0	2	1	1	6	2
4	FYR Macedonia	3	0	1	2	1	8	1

Group 6

29/09-04/10/15 Liege, Eupen
Czech Republic 4-1 Azerbaijan, Belgium 15-0 Georgia, Georgia 0-13 Czech Republic, Belgium 1-0 Azerbaijan, Azerbaijan 5-0 Georgia, Czech Republic 2-4 Belgium

England's Alessia Russo scored 14 goals over the whole competition

		Pld	W	D	L	F	A	Pts
1	Belgium	3	3	0	0	20	2	9
2	Czech Republic	3	2	0	1	19	5	6
3	Azerbaijan	3	1	0	2	6	5	3
4	Georgia	3	0	0	3	0	33	0

Group 7

10-15/10/15 Szombathely, Buk
Denmark 5-0 Israel, Hungary 2-1 Wales, Denmark 3-0 Wales, Israel 0-3 Hungary, Hungary 0-1 Denmark, Wales 4-0 Israel

		Pld	W	D	L	F	A	Pts
1	Denmark	3	3	0	0	9	0	9
2	Hungary	3	2	0	1	5	2	6
3	Wales	3	1	0	2	5	5	3
4	Israel	3	0	0	3	0	12	0

Group 8

12-17/10/15 Buftea, Bucharest
Sweden 3-1 Slovakia, Russia 4-0 Romania, Slovakia 0-3 Russia, Sweden 13-0 Romania, Russia 0-2 Sweden, Romania 0-5 Slovakia

		Pld	W	D	L	F	A	Pts
1	Sweden	3	3	0	0	18	1	9
2	Russia	3	2	0	1	7	2	6
3	Slovakia	3	1	0	2	6	6	3
4	Romania	3	0	0	3	0	22	0

Group 9

16-21/10/15 Jakovo, Stara Pazova
Switzerland 6-1 Lithuania, Serbia 3-0 Slovenia, Switzerland 0-1 Slovenia, Lithuania 1-5 Serbia, Serbia 0-3 Switzerland, Slovenia 2-1 Lithuania

		Pld	W	D	L	F	A	Pts
1	Switzerland	3	2	0	1	9	2	6
2	Serbia	3	2	0	1	8	4	6
3	Slovenia	3	2	0	1	3	4	6
4	Lithuania	3	0	0	3	3	13	0

Group 10

23-28/10/15 Kavarna, Albena
Norway 14-0 Moldova, Netherlands 6-0 Bulgaria, Norway 8-0 Bulgaria, Moldova 0-8 Netherlands, Netherlands 1-1 Norway, Bulgaria 4-0 Moldova

		Pld	W	D	L	F	A	Pts
1	Norway	3	2	1	0	23	1	7
2	Netherlands	3	2	1	0	15	1	7
3	Bulgaria	3	1	0	2	4	14	3
4	Moldova	3	0	0	3	0	26	0

Group 11

22-27/10/15 Podgorica, Danilovgrad
Iceland 3-0 Montenegro, Finland 11-0 Faroe Islands, Iceland 8-0 Faroe Islands, Montenegro 0-5 Finland, Finland 2-0 Iceland, Faroe Islands 1-3 Montenegro

		Pld	W	D	L	F	A	Pts
1	Finland	3	3	0	0	18	0	9
2	Iceland	3	2	0	1	11	2	6
3	Montenegro	3	1	0	2	3	9	3
4	Faroe Islands	3	0	0	3	1	22	0

Elite round

Group 1

19-24/03/16 Lindabrunn, Rohrendorf
Germany 2-0 Switzerland, Austria 4-0 Russia, Germany 3-0 Russia, Switzerland 3-3 Austria, Austria 1-4 Germany, Russia 1-4 Switzerland

		Pld	W	D	L	F	A	Pts
1	Germany	3	3	0	0	9	1	9
2	Austria	3	1	1	1	8	7	4
3	Switzerland	3	1	1	1	7	6	4
4	Russia	3	0	0	3	1	11	0

Group 2

22-27/03/16 Belfast, Castledawson
Denmark 4-0 Northern Ireland, Spain 4-0 Ukraine, Ukraine 0-7 Denmark, Spain 5-0 Northern Ireland, Denmark 0-2 Spain, Northern Ireland 0-0 Ukraine

		Pld	W	D	L	F	A	Pts
1	Spain	3	3	0	0	11	0	9
2	Denmark	3	2	0	1	11	2	6
3	Northern Ireland	3	0	1	2	0	9	1
4	Ukraine	3	0	1	2	0	11	1

Group 3

19-24/03/16 Flers, Bayeux, Saint-Lo
France 1-1 Czech Republic, Republic of Ireland 2-1 Hungary, France 2-0 Hungary, Czech Republic 1-0 Republic of Ireland, Republic of Ireland 1-0 France, Hungary 0-2 Czech Republic

		Pld	W	D	L	F	A	Pts
1	Czech Republic	3	2	1	0	4	1	7
2	Republic of Ireland	3	2	0	1	3	2	6
3	France	3	1	1	1	3	2	4
4	Hungary	3	0	0	3	1	6	0

Group 4

15-20/03/16 Cervia, Ravenna, San Zaccaria
Finland 0-2 Netherlands, Italy 4-1 Greece, Finland 1-0 Greece, Netherlands 0-2 Italy, Italy 2-2 Finland, Greece 0-2 Netherlands

		Pld	W	D	L	F	A	Pts
1	Italy	3	2	1	0	8	3	7
2	Netherlands	3	2	0	1	4	2	6
3	Finland	3	1	1	1	3	4	4
4	Greece	3	0	0	3	1	7	0

UEFA European Women's Under-17 Championship

Group 5

03-08/03/16 Algard, Klepp
**Sweden 2-2 Poland, Norway 6-0 Scotland,
Sweden 1-0 Scotland, Poland 0-4 Norway,
Norway 6-0 Sweden, Scotland 0-3 Poland**

	Pld	W	D	L	F	A	Pts
1 Norway	3	3	0	0	16	0	9
2 Poland	3	1	1	1	5	6	4
3 Sweden	3	1	1	1	3	8	4
4 Scotland	3	0	0	3	0	10	0

Group 6

25-29/03/16 Pecinci, Stara Pazova, Novi Sad
**Belgium 1-2 Iceland, England 3-1 Serbia,
Belgium 0-2 Serbia, Iceland 0-5 England,
England 2-0 Belgium, Serbia 5-1 Iceland**

	Pld	W	D	L	F	A	Pts
1 England	3	3	0	0	10	1	9
2 Serbia	3	2	0	1	8	4	6
3 Iceland	3	1	0	2	3	11	3
4 Belgium	3	0	0	3	1	6	0

Top goalscorers (Qualifying/Elite rounds)

9 Alessia Russo (England)
Georgia Stanway (England)
Lorena Navarro (Spain)

8 Jutta Rantala (Finland)
Andrea Norheim (Norway)
Nicole Eckerle (Poland)
Allegra Poljak (Serbia)

Final tournament

Group A

04/05/16, Traktor, Minsk
Belarus 1-5 Serbia
Goals: 0-1 Poljak 7, 0-2 Agbaba 30, 0-3 Ivanović 48, 0-4 Filipović 57, 1-4 Zhitko 68, 1-5 Burkert 79

04/05/16, Torpedo, Zhodino
England 3-2 Norway
Goals: 1-0 Charles 16, 2-0 Russo 36, 2-1 Haug 59, 2-2 Haug 62, 3-2 Filbey 69

07/05/16, City Stadium, Slutsk
Belarus 0-12 England
Goals: 0-1 Toone 5, 0-2 Filbey 7, 0-3 Russo 15, 0-4 Filbey 19, 0-5 Russo 23, 0-6 Stanway 29, 0-7 Toone 38, 0-8 Cain 71, 0-9 Smith 74, 0-10 Cain 75, 0-11 Brazil 80+1, 0-12 Smith 80+5

07/05/16, Gorodskoi Stadion, Borisov
Serbia 0-1 Norway
Goal: 0-1 Maanum 54

10/05/16, City Stadium, Slutsk
Norway 2-0 Belarus
Goals: 1-0 Olsen 18, 2-0 Ruud 40

10/05/16, Traktor, Minsk
Serbia 1-4 England
Goals: 1-0 Ivanović 40, 1-1 Stanway 47(p), 1-2 Brazil 68, 1-3 Charles 71, 1-4 Cain 76

	Pld	W	D	L	F	A	Pts
1 England	3	3	0	0	19	3	9
2 Norway	3	2	0	1	5	3	6
3 Serbia	3	1	0	2	6	6	3
4 Belarus	3	0	0	3	1	19	0

Group B

04/05/16, Gorodskoi Stadion, Borisov
Italy 0-0 Czech Republic

04/05/16, City Stadium, Slutsk
Germany 2-2 Spain
Goals: 0-1 Rubio 43, 1-1 Bühl 44, 1-2 Kleinherne 45(og), 2-2 Bühl 74

07/05/16, Torpedo, Zhodino
Italy 0-0 Germany

07/05/16, Traktor, Minsk
Czech Republic 0-1 Spain
Goal: 0-1 L Navarro 54

10/05/16, Torpedo, Zhodino
Spain 3-1 Italy
Goals: 1-0 Blanco 10, 2-0 L Navarro 29, 3-0 L Navarro 58, 3-1 Glionna 62

10/05/16, Gorodskoi Stadion, Borisov
Czech Republic 0-4 Germany
Goals: 0-1 Ziegler 7, 0-2 Ziegler 22, 0-3 Müller 36, 0-4 Müller 51

	Pld	W	D	L	F	A	Pts
1 Spain	3	2	1	0	6	3	7
2 Germany	3	1	2	0	6	2	5
3 Italy	3	0	2	1	1	3	2
4 Czech Republic	3	0	1	2	0	5	1

Semi-finals

13/05/16, Torpedo, Zhodino
Spain 4-0 Norway
Goals: 1-0 Rubio 48, 2-0 Natalia Ramos 71, 3-0 L Navarro 73, 4-0 L Navarro 76

13/05/16, Torpedo, Zhodino
England 3-4 Germany
Goals: 0-1 Ziegler 29, 1-1 Brazil 31, 1-2 Bühl 41, 2-2 Russo 42, 2-3 Pawollek 57, 2-4 Ziegler 70, 3-4 Russo 77

Third place play-off

16/05/16, Traktor, Minsk (att: 4,180)
Norway 1-2 England
Goals: 0-1 Charles 8, 1-1 Haug 52, 1-2 Charles 57

Final

16/05/16, Borisov-Arena, Borisov (att: 10,200)
Spain 0-0 Germany (2-3 on pens)
Referee: Antoniou (GRE)
Spain: Noelia Ramos, Batlle, Pujadas, Aleixandri, Natalia Ramos, Rubio (Monente 74), L Navarro, Fernández, Rodríguez, Andújar, Blanco. Coach: María Antonia Is (ESP)
Germany: Doege, Linder, Siems, Kleinherne, Pawollek, Gwinn, Kögel (Ziegler 51), Minge, Müller, Wieder (Stolze 63), Bühl. Coach: Anouschka Bernhard (GER)
Yellow card: Batlle 73 (Spain)

Top goalscorers (Final tournament)

5 Alessia Russo (England)
Lorena Navarro (Spain)

4 Niamh Charles (England)
Vanessa Ziegler (Germany)

3 Hannah Cain (England)
Ellie Brazil (England)
Anna Filbey (England)
Klara Bühl (Germany)
Sophie Haug (Norway)

Squads/Appearances/Goals

Belarus

No	Name	DoB	Aps	(s)	Gls
Goalkeepers					
12	Maria Svidunovich	20/05/00		(1)	
1	Darya Vinograd	15/04/99	3		
Defenders					
5	Kristina Kiyanka	10/11/99	3		
2	Alina Koneva	09/04/99	2	(1)	
18	Daria Pismenkova	14/01/99	2	(1)	
6	Anastasia Savko	03/11/00	2		
13	Alina Scherbo	18/06/00		(1)	
15	Polina Shilyonok	11/05/00	1		
Midfielders					
10	Maria Belobrovina	03/03/99	2	(1)	
9	Yana Benkevich	05/05/99	2	(1)	
7	Ksenia Kubichnaya	06/03/99	3		
19	Anastasia Miranovich	07/09/99	2		
8	Yulia Shalupenko	28/12/99		(1)	
4	Anastasia Shlapakova	06/03/00	2	(1)	
11	Karolina Zhitko	22/11/99	3		1
Forwards					
3	Alina Lodyga	25/08/99	3		
17	Darya Maysyuk	03/04/00		(1)	
14	Karina Olkhovik	17/06/00	3		

Czech Republic

No	Name	DoB	Aps	(s)	Gls
Goalkeepers					
1	Gabriela Lipková	20/07/99	3		
16	Kateřina Zuchová	18/03/99			
Defenders					
2	Lucie Dudová	29/08/00			
6	Natálie Kavalová	07/04/99	3		
5	Markéta Klímová	08/06/99	3		
7	Kristýna Příkaská	03/03/99	3		
3	Kristýna Siváková	14/06/00	1		
4	Natálie Valášková	04/05/00	2		
Midfielders					
10	Kristýna Čiperová	19/03/99	1	(2)	
8	Kamila Dubcová	17/01/99	3		
9	Michaela Dubcová	17/01/99	3		
14	Michaela Khýrová	03/02/00	2	(1)	
18	Natálie Kodadová	05/05/00		(3)	
12	Adéla Radová	16/02/99		(2)	
13	Gabriela Šlajsová	07/04/00	3		
10	Olívie Valentová	10/11/99		(1)	
Forwards					
17	Andrea Stašková	12/05/00	3		
11	Kateřina Vojtková	01/08/99	3		

England

No	Name	DoB	Aps	(s)	Gls
Goalkeepers					
1	Ellie Roebuck	23/09/99	4		
13	Katie Startup	28/01/99	1		
Defenders					
2	Florence Allen	13/08/99	2		
3	Taylor Hinds	25/04/99	4	(1)	
15	Lois Kathleen Joel	02/06/99	3	(1)	
12	Anna Patten	20/04/99	5		
14	Kelsey Pearson	10/10/99	2		
5	Grace Smith	20/01/99	3	(1)	2
6	Carlotte Wubben-Moy	11/01/99	2		
Midfielders					
17	Hannah Cain	11/02/99	2	(2)	3
18	Anna Filbey	11/10/99	4	(1)	3
8	Laura Hooper	05/07/99	2	(2)	
4	Hollie Olding	03/01/99	4		
7	Alessia Russo	08/02/99	5		5
10	Georgia Stanway	03/01/99	4		2
Forwards					
9	Ellie Brazil	10/01/99	3	(2)	3
11	Niamh Charles	21/06/99	4	(1)	4
16	Ella Ann Toone	02/09/99	1	(1)	2

Italy

No	Name	DoB	Aps	(s)	Gls
Goalkeepers					
12	Roberta Aprile	22/11/00			
1	Nicole Lauria	24/12/99	3		
Defenders					
14	Chiara Cecotti	17/01/99	2		
13	Maria Luisa Filangeri	28/01/00			
3	Beatrice Merlo	23/02/99	3		
2	Vanessa Panzeri	22/06/00	1	(1)	
8	Erika Santoro	03/09/99	3		
5	Federica Veritti	06/07/99	3		
Midfielders					
15	Benedetta Brignoli	04/10/99		(1)	
7	Arianna Caruso	06/11/99	3		
10	Giada Greggi	18/02/00	3		
4	Maddalena Porcarelli	06/03/00		(3)	
6	Alice Regazzoli	15/03/99	3		
17	Angelica Soffia	02/07/00			
Forwards					
11	Sofia Cantore	30/09/99	3		
18	Benedetta Glionna	26/07/99	3		1
9	Camilla Labate	02/05/99	2	(1)	
16	Elisa Polli	27/08/00	1	(1)	

Serbia

No	Name	DoB	Aps	(s)	Gls
Goalkeepers					
12	Sara Cetinja	16/04/00			
1	Tanja Djapić	04/07/99	3		
Defenders					
2	Teodora Burkert	11/12/99	2	(1)	1
18	Andjela Frajtović	08/07/00	3		
4	Aida Kardović	22/01/00	3		
17	Milana Knežević	05/05/99		(1)	
6	Jovana Miladinović	16/04/00	1	(2)	
5	Dunja Mostarac	25/02/00	3		
15	Anastasija Nikolić	18/04/00			
14	Jelena Spasojević	19/03/00	1	(1)	
3	Isidora Vučković	09/05/99		(3)	
Midfielders					
10	Tijana Filipović	26/05/99	3		1
13	Andjela Kričak	13/02/99			
16	Sara Savanović	12/08/00	2	(1)	
8	Ivana Trbojević	26/07/00	3		
Forwards					
11	Jovana Agbaba	11/03/00	3		1
9	Miljana Ivanović	17/05/00	3		2
7	Allegra Poljak	05/02/99	3		1

Germany

No	Name	DoB	Aps	(s)	Gls
Goalkeepers					
1	Leonie Doege	20/02/99	5		
12	Janina Leitzig	16/04/99			
12	Tilda Novotny	21/11/99			
Defenders					
13	Anna Hausdorff	26/04/00	1		
4	Sophia Kleinherne	12/04/00	5		
2	Sarai Linder	26/10/99	4		
14	Jessica May	02/12/99		(1)	
5	Tanja Pawollek	18/01/99	5		1
16	Annalena Rieke	10/01/99		(3)	
3	Caroline Siems	09/05/99	5		
Midfielders					
7	Giulia Gwinn	02/07/99	5		
15	Sydney Lohmann	19/06/00	2		
10	Janina Minge	11/06/99	4		
11	Marie Müller	25/07/00	4	(1)	2
17	Verena Wieder	26/06/00	4		
6	Vanessa Ziegler	16/01/99	1	(4)	4
Forwards					
18	Klara Bühl	07/12/00	5		3
8	Kristin Kögel	21/09/99	5		
9	Anna-Lena Stolze	08/07/00		(4)	

Norway

No	Name	DoB	Aps	(s)	Gls
Goalkeepers					
1	Linn-Mari Nilsen	24/02/99	5		
12	Frida Bergmann Thomas	18/04/99			
Defenders					
18	Joanna Aalstad Bækkelund	10/12/00	4		
2	Vilde Gullhaug Birkeli	07/10/00	4	(1)	
13	Silje Bjørneboe	25/02/00		(1)	
4	Malin Brenn	13/03/99	1	(1)	
5	Marte Bjelde Hjelmehaug	02/04/99	5		
3	Camilla Huseby	12/04/99	5		
Midfielders					
14	Emilie Raaum Closs	26/03/99		(1)	
15	Noor Hoelsbrekken Eckhoff	06/12/99	4		
9	Sophie Haug	04/06/99	4		3
7	Camilla Linberg	19/02/99		(3)	
8	Frida Maanum	16/07/99	5		1
10	Andrea Norheim	30/01/99	5		
17	Ingrid Olsen	16/03/99	2	(1)	1
6	Emilia Ruud	22/07/99	3		1
Forwards					
16	Emilie Nautnes	13/01/99	5		
11	Elise Isolde Stenevik	09/09/99	3	(1)	

Spain

No	Name	DoB	Aps	(s)	Gls
Goalkeepers					
13	Catalina Coll	23/04/01		(1)	
1	Noelia Ramos	10/02/99	5		
Defenders					
4	Laia Aleixandri	25/08/00	5		
2	Ona Batlle	10/06/99	5		
5	Natalia Ramos	10/02/99	2	(3)	1
3	Berta Pujadas	09/04/00	4		
12	Lucía Rodríguez	24/05/99	5		
Midfielders					
14	Damaris Egurrola	26/08/99	1		
16	Nerea Eizaguirre	04/01/00		(2)	
10	Paula Fernández	01/07/99	5		
11	Laura Gutiérrez	18/04/00		(2)	
8	Leyre Monente	15/02/00	3	(1)	
6	Silvia Rubio	12/10/00	5		2
Forwards					
15	Candela Andújar	26/03/00	5		
17	María Blanco	15/08/99	5		1
18	Eva Maria Navarro	27/01/01		(2)	
9	Lorena Navarro	11/10/00	5		5
7	Laia Muñoz	07/05/99		(2)	

Seventh triumph for Spain

A record number of goals were scored at UEFA Futsal EURO 2016 in Belgrade, but it was their spectacular nature, and the dominant manner in which Spain reclaimed the title, that will mostly live in the memory.

Qualifying threw up no shortage of drama, with Kazakhstan earning a finals berth for the first time and Hungary pipping Romania in the play-offs with a last-second extra-time goal. There was also a spectacular start to the finals as 11,000 fans, the most ever assembled at an opening game, saw hosts Serbia come from behind to beat Slovenia 5-1.

Serbia's next game was watched by a capacity 11,161, and while the home team beat Portugal 3-1, the consolation strike by Ricardinho was so spectacular that it earned an ovation from the home fans and subsequently went viral on social media. That result gave Serbia first place in Group A and meant they avoided favourites Spain in the quarter-finals. Instead the dubious honour of meeting the comfortable Group B winners went to Portugal, and despite another spectacular Ricardinho goal, Spain routed their Iberian neighbours 6-2. Serbia, meanwhile, overcame Ukraine 2-1 after Miloš Simić struck with the last kick of the game.

Elsewhere, Kazakhstan – with the same coach, Cacau, and most of the squad that had helped Kairat Almaty to victory in two of the last three UEFA Futsal Cups – came through their group behind Russia, while holders Italy struck ten goals without reply in Group D, with Azerbaijan accompanying them through after edging the Czech Republic in an 11-goal thriller.

Russia had been unconvincing in their group, but they improved to beat Azerbaijan 6-2, and an exciting sequence of quarter-finals was capped when Kazakhstan dethroned Italy 5-2. However, there was a sting in the tail for

the debutants as their influential goalkeeper Higuita was booked and therefore suspended for the semi-final with Spain.

Although depleted, Kazakhstan became the only team to lead Spain in the tournament, going 1-0 up on three minutes. They also mounted a late rally from 4-1 down but were eventually defeated 5-3. Serbia fell 3-2 after extra time to Russia and were then beaten 5-2 for third place by Kazakhstan.

The fifth Spain v Russia final was somewhat one-sided. Spain, aiming to avenge the semi-final loss in 2014 that had ended their previous nine-year reign, stormed into a 4-0 half-time lead, and their eventual 7-3 victory amounted to a record margin for a final. It also completed a hat-trick of final defeats for Russia.

Spain's six-goal Miguelín and Mario Rivillos shared the Golden Shoe on assists, ahead of team-mate Alex, Ricardinho and Serik Zhamankulov of Kazakhstan. They all helped contribute to a tournament-record goal tally of 129, watched by a tournament-best total attendance of 113,820, with five of the ten double-header matchdays selling out. Spain's victory was their seventh in the ten editions of the competition and, by common consent, the most convincing of the lot.

Spain celebrate their UEFA Futsal EURO 2016 win

Play-offs

15/09/15, Romeo Iamandi, Buzau
Romania 2-2 Hungary
22/09/15, Fönix Arena, Debrecen
Hungary 4-3 Romania (aet)
Aggregate: 6-5; Hungary qualify.

15/09/15, Sparta Praha, Prague
Czech Republic 2-1 Belarus
22/09/15, Sport Palace, Minsk
Belarus 1-1 Czech Republic
Aggregate: 2-3; Czech Republic qualify.

15/09/15, İdman Sarayı, Baku
Azerbaijan 3-1 Slovakia
22/09/15, Mestskaya Sportova Hala, Trnava
Slovakia 1-1 Azerbaijan
Aggregate: 2-4; Azerbaijan qualify.

15/09/15, City Arena, Zenica
Bosnia & Herzegovina 0-5 Kazakhstan
22/09/15, Baluan Sholak Sport Palace, Almaty
Kazakhstan 4-0 Bosnia & Herzegovina
Aggregate: 9-0; Kazakhstan qualify.

Final tournament

Group stage

Group A

02/02/16, Arena Belgrade, Belgrade
Serbia 5-1 Slovenia
Goals: 0-1 Osredkar 2, 1-1 Janjić 13 penalty
second mark, 2-1 Kocić 20, 3-1 Rajčević 26,
4-1 Kocić 29, 5-1 Pršić 33

04/02/16, Arena Belgrade, Belgrade
Slovenia 2-6 Portugal
Goals: 1-0 Čujec 2, 1-1 Fábio Cecílio 4,
1-2 Ricardinho 15, 2-2 Vrhovec 19,
2-3 Ricardinho 23, 2-4 Pedro Cary 30,
2-5 Ricardinho 32, 2-6 Fábio Cecílio 39

06/02/16, Arena Belgrade, Belgrade
Portugal 1-3 Serbia
Goals: 0-1 Kocić 7, 1-1 Ricardinho 14,
1-2 Rajčević 36, 1-3 Simić 39

	Pld	W	D	L	F	A	Pts
1 Serbia	2	2	0	0	8	2	6
2 Portugal	2	1	0	1	7	5	3
3 Slovenia	2	0	0	2	3	11	0

Group B

02/02/16, Arena Belgrade, Belgrade
Spain 5-2 Hungary
Goals: 1-0 Németh 7(og), 2-0 Bebe 14,
3-0 Miguelín 19, 3-1 Dróth 23, 4-1 Miguelín 28,
5-1 Andresito 35, 5-2 Dróth 37

04/02/16, Arena Belgrade, Belgrade
Hungary 3-6 Ukraine
Goals: 0-1 D Sorokin 1, 0-2 Bondar 6,
1-2 Dróth 7, 1-3 Ovsyannikov 24, 2-3 Trencsényi 29,
2-4 Mykola Grytsyna 29, 3-4 Dróth 33,
3-5 Bondar 34, 3-6 Valenko 35

06/02/16, Arena Belgrade, Belgrade
Ukraine 1-4 Spain
Goals: 0-1 Alex 19, 0-2 Mario Rivillos 29,
0-3 Alex 33, 1-3 Mykola Grytsyna 37,
1-4 Mario Rivillos 39

	Pld	W	D	L	F	A	Pts
1 Spain	2	2	0	0	9	3	6
2 Ukraine	2	1	0	1	7	7	3
3 Hungary	2	0	0	2	5	11	0

Group C

03/02/16, Arena Belgrade, Belgrade
Russia 2-1 Kazakhstan
Goals: 1-0 Romulo 11, 2-0 Romulo 11,
2-1 Zhamankulov 12

05/02/16, Arena Belgrade, Belgrade
Kazakhstan 4-2 Croatia
Goals: 1-0 Douglas Jr 5, 1-1 Matošević 6,
2-1 Suleimenov 6, 3-1 Zhamankulov 16,
4-1 Zhamankulov 26, 4-2 Suton 32

07/02/16, Arena Belgrade, Belgrade
Croatia 2-2 Russia
Goals: 1-0 Robinho 8(og), 1-1 Abramov 11,
2-1 Novak 24, 2-2 Pereverzev 38

	Pld	W	D	L	F	A	Pts
1 Russia	2	1	1	0	4	3	4
2 Kazakhstan	2	1	0	1	5	4	3
3 Croatia	2	0	1	1	4	6	1

Group D

03/02/16, Arena Belgrade, Belgrade
Italy 3-0 Azerbaijan
Goals: 1-0 Alex Merlim 19, 2-0 Alex Merlim 20,
3-0 Giasson 28

05/02/16, Arena Belgrade, Belgrade
Azerbaijan 6-5 Czech Republic
Goals: 1-0 Farzaliyev 5, 2-0 Borisov 6,
2-1 Záruba 9, 3-1 Fineo 11, 3-2 Holý 11,
3-3 Rešetár 15, 4-3 Eduardo 19, 4-4 Novotný 23,
5-4 Augusto 26, 5-5 Kovács 30, 6-5 Rafael 39

07/02/16, Arena Belgrade, Belgrade
Czech Republic 0-7 Italy
Goals: 0-1 Fortino 0, 0-2 Gabriel Lima 10,
0-3 Alex Merlim 20, 0-5 Koudelka 21(og),
0-4 Fortino 21, 0-6 Honorio 23, 0-7 Patias 32

	Pld	W	D	L	F	A	Pts
1 Italy	2	2	0	0	10	0	6
2 Azerbaijan	2	1	0	1	6	8	3
3 Czech Republic	2	0	0	2	5	13	0

Quarter-finals

08/02/16, Arena Belgrade, Belgrade
Serbia 2-1 Ukraine
Goals: 1-0 Kocić 1, 1-1 Mykola Grytsyna 23,
2-1 Simić 39

08/02/16, Arena Belgrade, Belgrade
Portugal 2-6 Spain
Goals: 0-1 Miguelín 12(p), 0-2 Mario Rivillos 14,
0-3 Alex 17, 1-4 Raúl Campos 22,
1-3 Ricardinho 22, 2-4 Ricardinho 25, 2-5 Alex 34,
2-6 Mario Rivillos 39

09/02/16, Arena Belgrade, Belgrade
Russia 6-2 Azerbaijan
Goals: 1-0 Abramov 6, 1-1 Augusto 7,
2-1 Romulo 14, 3-1 Eder Lima 24,
4-1 Abramov 25, 4-2 Augusto 28, 5-2 Eder Lima 38,
6-2 Eder Lima 39

09/02/16, Arena Belgrade, Belgrade
Kazakhstan 5-2 Italy
Goals: 1-0 Leo 15, 2-0 Zhamankulov 18,
3-1 Yesenamanov 22, 2-1 Fortino 22, 3-2 Canal 36,
4-2 Nurgozhin 36, 5-2 Leo 39

Alex of Spain (left) shapes to shoot past Russia's
Romulo in the final

Semi-finals

11/02/16, Arena Belgrade, Belgrade
Serbia 2-3 Russia (aet)
Goals: 0-1 Eder Lima 12, 1-1 Kocić 25,
1-2 Abramov 32, 2-2 Simić 35, 2-3 Romulo 43

11/02/16, Arena Belgrade, Belgrade
Spain 5-3 Kazakhstan
Goals: 0-1 Dovgan 3, 1-1 Bebe 7, 2-1 Miguelín 16,
3-1 Raúl Campos 17, 4-1 Alex 26, 4-2 Leo 35,
4-3 Zhamankulov 37, 5-3 Raúl Campos 38

Third place play-off

13/02/16, Arena Belgrade, Belgrade (att: 11,161)
Serbia 2-5 Kazakhstan
Goals: 0-1 Douglas Jr 19, 0-2 Zhamankulov 20,
0-3 Douglas Jr 29, 0-4 Higuita 31,
0-5 Douglas Jr 33, 1-5 Rakić 37, 2-5 Rajčević 39

Final

13/02/16, Arena Belgrade, Belgrade (att: 8,350)
Russia 3-7 Spain
Goals: 0-1 Alex 8, 0-2 Pola 15, 0-3 Mario Rivillos
16, 0-4 Pola 16, 1-4 Romulo 19, 1-5 Miguelín 30,
2-5 Robinho 31, 2-6 Miguelín 34,
2-7 Mario Rivillos 35, 3-7 Milovanov 39
Referee: Bogdan Sorescu (ROU) / Alessandro
Malfer (ITA)
Russia: Gustavo, Vikulov, Shayakhmetov,
Abramov, Robinho, Romulo, Pereverzev, Lyskov,
Sergeev, Kutuzov, Milovanov, Shakirov. Coach:
Sergei Skorovich (RUS)
Spain: Juanjo, Paco Sedano, Jesús Herrero, Ortiz,
Mario Rivillos, Pola, Raúl Campos, José Ruiz,
Bebe, Rafa Usín, Lin, Alex. Coach: José Venancio
López (ESP)
Yellow cards: Shayakhmetov 15 (Russia),
Kutuzov 17 (Russia), Ortiz 20 (Spain),
Robinho 35 (Russia)

Top goalscorers

6	Serik Zhamankulov (Kazakhstan)
	Ricardinho (Portugal)
	Alex (Spain)
	Mario Rivillos (Spain)
	Miguelín (Spain)
5	Romulo (Russia)
	Mladen Kocić (Serbia)

Ugra return trophy to Russia

Russia's eight-year wait for a third UEFA Futsal Cup victory came to an end as debutants Ugra Yugorsk pipped Spanish hosts Inter FS to round off a thrilling final tournament in Guadalajara.

Ugra proved their credentials when they eliminated holders Kairat Almaty 5-2 in the elite round – only the second time since the introduction of the current format in 2006/07 that the reigning champions had missed out on the finals. But Ugra's squad were far from inexperienced. Not only had Vladislav Shayakhmetov and Andrei Afanasyev been part of the last Russian success, in 2008 with Sinara Ekaterinburg; Robinho had also won the trophy back in 2005 with Action 21 Charleroi.

Benfica, the 2010 winners, were Ugra's semi-final opponents and the 40 minutes of normal time flew by, the Eagles having to equalise late to make it 3-3. Ugra goalkeeper and captain Zviad Kupatadze had been sent off at 1-1 for handling a shot outside the area but Sergei Slemzin proved a worthy replacement. After both teams had scored once in extra time, the goalkeeper saved Rafael Henmi's kick in the penalty shoot-out and Robinho coolly converted to fire Ugra into the final.

Record three-time winners Inter were cheered on by a capacity crowd against another debutant team, Pescara, the first

ever to plot a successful course from the preliminary round to the finals. The Italian side led through Mauro Canal before Ricardinho and Cardinal turned the game for the hosts. Rafael made it 3-1 in the first minute of the second half, but there was a tight finish after Adolfo Salas pulled one back, only for Mario Rivillos to settle matters at the death and seal a 4-2 win.

Pescara looked on course for a bronze medal when they led Benfica 2-0, but their lead was to be wiped out and the Portuguese side eventually prevailed on penalties, their former Murcia FS goalkeeper Juanjo now having been involved in five of the nine shoot-outs in the competition's history. Preceded by three edge-of-the-seat thrillers, the final

would also go to the wire. Ricardinho, injured against Pescara, played but was not his normal self for Inter, however goalkeeper Slemzin impressed again for Ugra. Both sides took the lead in the first half and it was 2-2 from the 18th until the 38th minute, when Afanasyev finished off an Ugra corner move. With 55 seconds left Katata bundled the ball into an empty net to make it 4-2.

Inter were not finished, though, and Daniel Shiraishi pulled one back as Ugra's Ivan Chishkala was red-carded. The hosts even had time to hit the woodwork in a dramatic finale, but Ugra held on to emulate compatriots Dynamo (2007) and Ekaterinburg (2008) and return the UEFA Futsal Cup to Russia.

Ugra Yugorsk of Russia claimed the UEFA Futsal Cup for the first time

Preliminary round

Group A

25-28/08/15 Vienna
Kremlin Bicêtre United 7-1 FK Inkaras, Stella Rossa Wien 3-2 Istanbul Üniversitesi SK, Istanbul Üniversitesi SK 0-3 Kremlin Bicêtre United, Stella Rossa Wien 4-1 FK Inkaras, FK Inkaras 1-6 Istanbul Üniversitesi SK, Kremlin Bicêtre United 2-0 Stella Rossa Wien

	Pld	W	D	L	F	A	Pts
1 Kremlin Bicêtre United	3	3	0	0	12	1	9
2 Stella Rossa Wien	3	2	0	1	7	5	6
3 Istanbul Üniversitesi SK	3	1	0	2	8	7	3
4 FK Inkaras	3	0	0	3	3	17	0

Group B

26-29/08/15 Andorra la Vella
Pescara 9-0 St Andrews FC, FC Encamp 2-3 JB Futsal Gentofte, JB Futsal Gentofte 0-3 Pescara, FC Encamp 3-5 St Andrews FC, St Andrews FC 5-5 JB Futsal Gentofte, Pescara 6-0 FC Encamp

	Pld	W	D	L	F	A	Pts
1 Pescara	3	3	0	0	18	0	9
2 JB Futsal Gentofte	3	1	1	1	8	10	4
3 St Andrews FC	3	1	1	1	10	17	4
4 FC Encamp	3	0	0	3	5	14	0

Group C

26-29/08/15 Podgorica
FC Nacional Zagreb 11-0 Cardiff University, Titograd 5-1 Blue Magic, Blue Magic 0-15 FC Nacional Zagreb, Titograd 3-1 Cardiff University, Cardiff University 1-2 Blue Magic, FC Nacional Zagreb 4-1 Titograd

	Pld	W	D	L	F	A	Pts
1 FC Nacional Zagreb	3	3	0	0	30	1	9
2 Titograd	3	2	0	1	9	6	6
3 Blue Magic	3	1	0	2	3	21	3
4 Cardiff University	3	0	0	3	2	16	0

Group D

26-29/08/15 Gibraltar
Grorud 6-0 FC Santos, Lynx FC 3-8 Sievi Futsal, Sievi Futsal 7-2 Grorud, Lynx FC 7-4 FC Santos, FC Santos 1-6 Sievi Futsal, Grorud 4-4 Lynx FC

	Pld	W	D	L	F	A	Pts
1 Sievi Futsal	3	3	0	0	21	6	9
2 Grorud	3	1	1	1	12	11	4
3 Lynx FC	3	1	1	1	14	16	4
4 FC Santos	3	0	0	3	5	19	0

Group E

25-28/08/15 Olafsvík
Hamburg Panthers 6-2 FC Differdange 03, Víkingur Ólafsvík 1-5 KF Flamurtari Vlorë, KF Flamurtari Vlorë 0-3 Hamburg Panthers, Víkingur Ólafsvík 8-5 FC Differdange 03, FC Differdange 03 2-3 KF Flamurtari Vlorë, Hamburg Panthers 5-3 Víkingur Ólafsvík

Rogério da Silva of Pescara takes on the Benfica defence in the third place play-off

	Pld	W	D	L	F	A	Pts
1 Hamburg Panthers	3	3	0	0	14	5	9
2 KF Flamurtari Vlorë	3	2	0	1	8	6	6
3 Víkingur Ólafsvík	3	1	0	2	12	15	3
4 FC Differdange 03	3	0	0	3	9	17	0

Group F

27-29/08/15 Skopje
KMF Zelezarec Skopje 4-0 SK Augur, SK Augur 1-4 ASA Ben Gurion, ASA Ben Gurion 2-3 KMF Zelezarec Skopje

	Pld	W	D	L	F	A	Pts
1 KMF Zelezarec Skopje	2	2	0	0	7	2	6
2 ASA Ben Gurion	2	1	0	1	6	4	3
3 SK Augur	2	0	0	2	1	8	0

Group G

27-29/08/15 Ciorescu
FC Progress Chisinau 4-1 ASUE, ASUE 0-6 FP Halle-Gooik, FP Halle-Gooik 8-1 FC Progress Chisinau

	Pld	W	D	L	F	A	Pts
1 FP Halle-Gooik	2	2	0	0	14	1	6
2 FC Progress Chisinau	2	1	0	1	5	9	3
3 ASUE	2	0	0	2	1	10	0

Group H

27-29/08/15 Berne
Mobulu Futsal UNI Bern 2-5 Göteborg Futsal Club, Göteborg Futsal Club 1-13 MNK Centar Sarajevo, MNK Centar Sarajevo 11-2 Mobulu Futsal UNI Bern

	Pld	W	D	L	F	A	Pts
1 MNK Centar Sarajevo	2	2	0	0	24	3	6
2 Göteborg Futsal Club	2	1	0	1	6	15	3
3 Mobulu Futsal UNI Bern	2	0	0	2	4	16	0

Main round

Group 1

01-04/10/15 Nicosia
FC APOEL Nicosia 1-5 Georgians Tbilisi, Ugra Yugorsk 5-0 Kremlin Bicêtre United, Georgians Tbilisi 2-13 Ugra Yugorsk, FC APOEL Nicosia 3-4 Kremlin Bicêtre United, Kremlin Bicêtre United 3-0 Georgians Tbilisi, Ugra Yugorsk 10-3 FC APOEL Nicosia

	Pld	W	D	L	F	A	Pts
1 Ugra Yugorsk	3	3	0	0	28	5	9
2 Kremlin Bicêtre United	3	2	0	1	7	8	6
3 Georgians Tbilisi	3	1	0	2	7	17	3
4 FC APOEL Nicosia	3	0	0	3	7	19	0

Group 2

30/09-03/10/15 Podčetrtek
SL Benfica 8-2 MNK Centar Sarajevo, KMN Dobovec 7-2 FC Grand Pro Varna, FC Grand Pro Varna 2-9 SL Benfica, KMN Dobovec 5-2 MNK Centar Sarajevo, MNK Centar Sarajevo 5-6 FC Grand Pro Varna, SL Benfica 6-1 KMN Dobovec

	Pld	W	D	L	F	A	Pts
1 SL Benfica	3	3	0	0	23	5	9
2 KMN Dobovec	3	2	0	1	13	10	6
3 FC Grand Pro Varna	3	1	0	2	10	21	3
4 MNK Centar Sarajevo	3	0	0	3	9	19	0

Group 3

30/09-03/10/15 Targu Mures
Lokomotiv Kharkiv 7-1 Hamburg Panthers, City'US Târgu Mureş 3-8 Pescara, Pescara 5-1 Lokomotiv Kharkiv, City'US Târgu Mureş 9-1 Hamburg Panthers, Hamburg Panthers 0-11 Pescara, Lokomotiv Kharkiv 5-3 City'US Târgu Mureş

	Pld	W	D	L	F	A	Pts
1 Pescara	3	3	0	0	24	4	9
2 Lokomotiv Kharkiv	3	2	0	1	13	9	6
3 City'US Târgu Mureş	3	1	0	2	15	14	3
4 Hamburg Panthers	3	0	0	3	2	27	0

UEFA Futsal Cup

Group 4

30/09-03/10/15 Bratislava
FC Eindhoven 3-5 Sievi Futsal, Slov-Matic Bratislava 5-3 KMF Zelezarec Skopje, KMF Zelezarec Skopje 6-3 FC Eindhoven, Slov-Matic Bratislava 6-1 Sievi Futsal, Sievi Futsal 5-6 KMF Zelezarec Skopje, FC Eindhoven 1-8 Slov-Matic Bratislava

		Pld	W	D	L	F	A	Pts
1	Slov-Matic Bratislava	3	3	0	0	19	5	9
2	KMF Zelezarec Skopje	3	2	0	1	15	13	6
3	Sievi Futsal	3	1	0	2	11	15	3
4	FC Eindhoven	3	0	0	3	7	19	0

Group 5

01-04/10/15 Riga
FK EP Chrudim 2-4 FP Halle-Gooik, FK Nikars Riga 4-1 Athina '90, Athina '90 0-6 FK EP Chrudim, FK Nikars Riga 6-4 FP Halle-Gooik, FP Halle-Gooik 8-1 Athina '90, FK EP Chrudim 5-2 FK Nikars Riga

		Pld	W	D	L	F	A	Pts
1	FK EP Chrudim	3	2	0	1	13	6	6
2	FP Halle-Gooik	3	2	0	1	16	9	6
3	FK Nikars Riga	3	2	0	1	12	10	6
4	Athina '90	3	0	0	3	2	18	0

Group 6

29/09-02/10/15 Gyor
Baku United FC 4-5 FC Nacional Zagreb, Győri ETO FC 3-4 Lidselmash Lida, Lidselmash Lida 4-2 Baku United FC, Győri ETO FC 5-4 FC Nacional Zagreb, FC Nacional Zagreb 0-1 Lidselmash Lida, Baku United FC 1-5 Győri ETO FC

		Pld	W	D	L	F	A	Pts
1	Lidselmash Lida	3	3	0	0	9	5	9
2	Győri ETO FC	3	2	0	1	13	9	6
3	FC Nacional Zagreb	3	1	0	2	9	10	3
4	Baku United FC	3	0	0	3	7	14	0

Elite round

Group A

12-15/11/15 Torrejon de Ardoz
Lidselmash Lida 4-2 Kremlin Bicêtre United, Inter FS 8-0 KMN Dobovec, KMN Dobovec 2-7 Lidselmash Lida, Inter FS 10-2 Kremlin Bicêtre United, Kremlin Bicêtre United 1-2 KMN Dobovec, Lidselmash Lida 2-4 Inter FS

		Pld	W	D	L	F	A	Pts
1	Inter FS	3	3	0	0	22	4	9
2	Lidselmash Lida	3	2	0	1	13	8	6
3	KMN Dobovec	3	1	0	2	4	16	3
4	Kremlin Bicêtre United	3	0	0	3	5	16	0

Group B

11-14/11/15 Pescara
Astana-Tulpar 2-2 FP Halle-Gooik, Pescara 2-0 KMF Zelezarec Skopje, KMF Zelezarec Skopje 6-4 Astana-Tulpar, Pescara 4-2 FP Halle-Gooik, FP Halle-Gooik 0-4 KMF Zelezarec Skopje, Astana-Tulpar 0-4 Pescara

		Pld	W	D	L	F	A	Pts
1	Pescara	3	3	0	0	10	2	9
2	KMF Zelezarec Skopje	3	2	0	1	10	6	6
3	Astana-Tulpar	3	0	1	2	6	12	1
4	FP Halle-Gooik	3	0	1	2	4	10	1

Ugra's Andrei Afanasyev (right) takes to his knees to celebrate one of his two goals in the final against Spanish hosts Inter

Group C

10-13/11/15 Gyor
Kairat Almaty 2-5 Ugra Yugorsk, Győri ETO FC 3-3 FK EP Chrudim, FK EP Chrudim 1-4 Kairat Almaty, Győri ETO FC 2-5 Ugra Yugorsk, Ugra Yugorsk 6-0 FK EP Chrudim, Kairat Almaty 5-4 Győri ETO FC

		Pld	W	D	L	F	A	Pts
1	Ugra Yugorsk	3	3	0	0	16	4	9
2	Kairat Almaty	3	2	0	1	11	10	6
3	Győri ETO FC	3	0	1	2	9	13	1
4	FK EP Chrudim	3	0	1	2	4	13	1

Group D

10-13/11/15 Bratislava
KMF Ekonomac Kragujevac 0-3 SL Benfica, Slov-Matic Bratislava 0-2 Lokomotiv Kharkiv, Lokomotiv Kharkiv 6-1 KMF Ekonomac Kragujevac, Slov-Matic Bratislava 5-4 SL Benfica, SL Benfica 2-0 Lokomotiv Kharkiv, KMF Ekonomac Kragujevac 2-2 Slov-Matic Bratislava

		Pld	W	D	L	F	A	Pts
1	SL Benfica	3	2	0	1	9	5	6
2	Lokomotiv Kharkiv	3	2	0	1	8	3	6
3	Slov-Matic Bratislava	3	1	1	1	7	8	4
4	KMF Ekonomac Kragujevac	3	0	1	2	3	11	1

Semi-finals

22/04/16, Palacio Multiusos Guadalajara, Guadalajara
Ugra Yugorsk 4-4 SL Benfica (aet; 3-2 on pens)
Goals: 0-1 Chaguinha 14, 1-1 Lyskov 20, 2-1 Signev 29, 3-2 Afanasyev 31, 2-2 Patias 31, 3-3 Jefferson 37, 4-4 Katata 41, 3-4 Patias 45+35

22/04/16, Palacio Multiusos Guadalajara, Guadalajara
Pescara 2-4 Inter FS
Goals: 1-0 Canal 5, 1-1 Ricardinho 8, 1-2 Cardinal 11, 1-3 Rafael 20, 2-3 Salas 37, 2-4 Mario Rivillos 39

Third place play-off

24/04/16, Palacio Multiusos Guadalajara, Guadalajara
SL Benfica 2-2 Pescara (aet; 2-0 on pens)
Goals: 0-1 Canal 19, 0-2 Borruto 20, 1-2 Ré 33, 2-2 Bruno Coelho 38

Final

24/04/16, Palacio Multiusos Guadalajara, Guadalajara (att: 5,300)
Ugra Yugorsk 4-3 Inter FS
Goals: 1-0 Afanasyev 5, 1-1 Cardinal 5, 1-2 Pola 13, 2-2 Marcênio 17, 3-2 Afanasyev 37, 4-3 Shiraishi 39, 4-2 Katata 39
Referee: Bogdan Sorescu (ROU)/ Saša Tomić (CRO)
Ugra: Slemzin, Shayakhmetov, Afanasyev, Marcênio, Davydov, Lyskov, Eder Lima, Robinho, Katata, Chishkala, Niyazov, Signev. Coach: Kakà (BRA)
Inter: Luis Amado, Jesús Herrero, Gonzalez, Ortiz, Shiraishi, Mario Rivillos, Borja, Humberto, Lolo, Pola, Ricardinho, Darlan. Coach: Jesús Velasco (ESP)
Red card: Chishkala 39 (Ugra)
Yellow cards: Chishkala 8 (Ugra), Humberto 19 (Inter), Shayakhmetov 21 (Ugra), Davydov 32 (Ugra), Mario Rivillos 37 (Inter), Chishkala 39 (Ugra), Gonzalez 39 (Inter), Caio 39 (Ugra)

Top goalscorers (Final tournament)

3	Andrei Afanasyev (Ugra)
2	Alessandro Patias (Benfica)
	Cardinal (Inter)
	Mauro Canal (Pescara)
	Katata (Ugra)

THE EUROPEAN FOOTBALL YEARBOOK 2016 2017

TOP 100 PLAYERS

Welcome to the Top 100 Players of the Season chapter.

Listed overleaf, in alphabetical order, are the names of the players who have been selected in the 2016/17 European Football Yearbook's Top 100.

On the pages that follow, each of those players is given a short narrative profile describing and explaining his particular achievements during the 2015/16 season. That is supplemented by a rundown of historical career statistics and the season's key appearances/goals figures.

This is the 12th successive year in which the Top 100 Players of the Season section has featured in the Yearbook. While the list has no official UEFA backing, it has developed a little history and prestige of its own.

It should be stressed that players are only included on merit – not for any other reason. In many cases selection is obvious. For example, the players pictured on this page were always going to make it. In others, though, lengthy consideration was required before the final decision was made as to who was in and who was out.

Should you wish to have your say on the choices we have made, do not hesitate to make contact using either of the email addresses below.

Please be aware that the deadline for statistical data in the profiles is 1 August 2016.

Mike Hammond
General Editor
efyhammond@gmail.com
mike.hammond@uefa.ch

Top 100 players

Aritz Aduriz (Athletic Club/Spain)
Sergio Agüero (Manchester City FC/Argentina)
Toby Alderweireld (Tottenham Hotspur FC/Belgium)
Alex Teixeira (FC Shakhtar Donetsk/Brazil)
Dele Alli (Tottenham Hotspur FC/England)
Pierre-Emerick Aubameyang (Borussia Dortmund/Gabon)
Gareth Bale (Real Madrid CF/Wales)
Andrea Barzagli (Juventus FC/Italy)
Michy Batshuayi (Olympique de Marseille/Belgium)
Héctor Bellerín (Arsenal FC/Spain)
Hatem Ben Arfa (OGC Nice/France)
Karim Benzema (Real Madrid CF/France)
Leonardo Bonucci (Juventus FC/Italy)
Bruno Soriano (Villarreal CF/Spain)
Gianluigi Buffon (Juventus FC/Italy)
Petr Čech (Arsenal FC/Czech Republic)
Giorgio Chiellini (Juventus FC/Italy)
Kingsley Coman (FC Bayern München/France)
Cristiano Ronaldo (Real Madrid CF/Portugal)
Steven Davis (Southampton FC/Northern Ireland)
Kevin De Bruyne (Manchester City FC/Belgium)
David de Gea (Manchester United FC/Spain)
Luuk de Jong (PSV Eindhoven/Netherlands)
Ousmane Dembélé (Stade Rennais FC/France)
Ángel Di María (Paris Saint-Germain/Argentina)
Eric Dier (Tottenham Hotspur FC/England)
Douglas Costa (FC Bayern München/Brazil)
Danny Drinkwater (Leicester City FC/England)
Paulo Dybala (Juventus FC/Argentina)
Alan Dzagoev (PFC CSKA Moskva/Russia)
Christian Eriksen (Tottenham Hotspur FC/Denmark)
Filipe Luís (Club Atlético de Madrid/Brazil)
Alessandro Florenzi (AS Roma/Italy)
Kostas Fortounis (Olympiacos FC/Greece)
Gabi (Club Atlético de Madrid/Spain)
Kevin Gameiro (Sevilla FC/France)
Zoltán Gera (Ferencvárosi TC/Hungary)
Diego Godín (Club Atlético de Madrid/Uruguay)
Mario Gomez (Beşiktaş JK/Germany)
Antoine Griezmann (Club Atlético de Madrid/France)
Marek Hamšík (SSC Napoli/Slovakia)
Gonzalo Higuaín (SSC Napoli/Argentina)
Hulk (FC Zenit/Brazil)
Mats Hummels (Borussia Dortmund/Germany)
Elseid Hysaj (SSC Napoli/Albania)
Zlatan Ibrahimović (Paris Saint-Germain/Sweden)
Josip Iličič (ACF Fiorentina/Slovenia)
Andrés Iniesta (FC Barcelona/Spain)
Vincent Janssen (AZ Alkmaar/Netherlands)
João Mário (Sporting Clube de Portugal/Portugal)
Jonas (SL Benfica/Brazil)
Juanfran (Club Atlético de Madrid/Spain)
Harry Kane (Tottenham Hotspur FC/England)
N'Golo Kanté (Leicester City FC/France)
Davy Klaassen (AFC Ajax/Netherlands)
Koke (Club Atlético de Madrid/Spain)

Toni Kroos (Real Madrid CF/Germany)
Grzegorz Krychowiak (Sevilla FC/Poland)
Philipp Lahm (FC Bayern München/Germany)
Robert Lewandowski (FC Bayern München/Poland)
Hugo Lloris (Tottenham Hotspur FC/France)
Riyad Mahrez (Leicester City FC/Algeria)
Blaise Matuidi (Paris Saint-Germain/France)
Lionel Messi (FC Barcelona/Argentina)
Henrikh Mkhitaryan (Borussia Dortmund/Armenia)
Luka Modrić (Real Madrid CF/Croatia)
Álvaro Morata (Juventus FC/Spain)
Wes Morgan (Leicester City FC/Jamaica)
Thomas Müller (FC Bayern München/Germany)
Radja Nainggolan (AS Roma/Belgium)
Nani (Fenerbahçe SK/Portugal)
Manuel Neuer (FC Bayern München/Germany)
Neymar (FC Barcelona/Brazil)
Nolito (RC Celta de Vigo/Spain)
Jan Oblak (Club Atlético de Madrid/Slovenia)
Mesut Özil (Arsenal FC/Germany)
Dimitri Payet (West Ham United FC/France)
Pepe (Real Madrid CF/Portugal)
Ivan Perišić (FC Internazionale Milano/Croatia)
Gerard Piqué (FC Barcelona/Spain)
Miralem Pjanić (AS Roma/Bosnia & Herzegovina)
Paul Pogba (Juventus FC/France)
Ivan Rakitić (FC Barcelona/Croatia)
Aaron Ramsey (Arsenal FC/Wales)
Renato Sanches (SL Benfica/Portugal)
Rui Patrício (Sporting Clube de Portugal/Portugal)
Saúl Ñíguez (Club Atlético de Madrid/Spain)
Kasper Schmeichel (Leicester City FC/Denmark)
Sergio Ramos (Real Madrid CF/Spain)
Gylfi Thór Sigurdsson (Swansea City AFC/Iceland)
Chris Smalling (Manchester United FC/England)
Darijo Srna (FC Shakhtar Donetsk/Croatia)
Luis Suárez (FC Barcelona/Uruguay)
Thiago Silva (Paris Saint-Germain/Brazil)
Virgil van Dijk (Celtic FC & Southampton FC/Netherlands)
Jamie Vardy (Leicester City FC/England)
Ashley Williams (Swansea City AFC/Wales)
Willian (Chelsea FC/Brazil)
Granit Xhaka (VfL Borussia Mönchengladbach/Switzerland)
Andriy Yarmolenko (FC Dynamo Kyiv/Ukraine)

NB Clubs indicated are those the players belonged to in the 2015/16 season.

Key to competitions:

WCF = FIFA World Cup final tournament
WCQ = FIFA World Cup qualifying round
ECF = UEFA EURO final tournament
ECQ = UEFA EURO qualifying round
CC = FIFA Confederations Cup
CA = Copa América
ANF = Africa Cup of Nations final tournament
ANQ = Africa Cup of Nations qualifying round
CGC = CONCACAF Gold Cup

Aritz Aduriz

Striker, Height 182cm
Born 11/02/81, San Sebastian, Spain

At the age of 35, Aduriz enjoyed the finest season of his career. The Basque-born striker had certainly never found goals quite so easy to come by. He started the season by netting a hat-trick against Barcelona in the Spanish Super Cup and ended it with 36 goals in all competitions for Athletic, including a top-scoring tally of ten in the UEFA Europa League, the pick of them an amazing long-range match-winning strike against Marseille in the Stade Vélodrome. His 20 Liga goals also persuaded Vicente Del Bosque to include the in-form striker in Spain's squad for UEFA EURO 2016 – his first major tournament.

International career

SPAIN
Debut 08/10/10 v Lithuania (h, Salamanca, ECQ), won 2-1
First goal 24/03/16 v Italy (a, Udine, friendly), drew 1-1
Caps 9 Goals 1
Major tournaments UEFA EURO 2016

Club career

Clubs 99-00 CD Aurrerá; 00-02 Bilbao Athletic; 02-04 Athletic Club; 03-04 Burgos CF (loan); 04-05 Real Valladolid CF; 06-08 Athletic Club; 08-10 RCD Mallorca; 10-12 Valencia CF; 12- Athletic Club

2015/16 appearances/goals

Domestic league Spanish Liga 30(4)/20
Europe UEFA Europa League 10(1)/10; UEFA Europa League qualifying/play-offs 3/-
National team UEFA EURO 2016 finals (3)/-; Friendlies 3(2)/1

Sergio Agüero

Striker, Height 172cm
Born 02/06/88, Quilmes, Argentina

Several Manchester City players went missing in 2015/16 as the club struggled to sustain a challenge for the Premier League title, but not Agüero. The Argentinian striker supplied more evidence to strengthen his reputation as the number one attraction in England's top division, scoring 24 goals, five of them in a 6-1 home win over Newcastle United in October, and then taking his all-time Premier League tally to 100 against the same opposition six months later. He also helped City into the semi-finals of the UEFA Champions League and the final of the League Cup, which they won on penalties against Liverpool.

International career

ARGENTINA
Debut 03/09/06 v Brazil (n, London, friendly), lost 0-3
First goal 17/11/07 v Bolivia (h, Buenos Aires, WCQ), won 3-0
Caps 77 **Goals** 33
Major tournaments FIFA World Cup 2010; Copa América 2011; FIFA World Cup 2014; Copa América 2015; Copa América 2016

Club career

Major honours *UEFA Europa League (2010); UEFA Super Cup (2010); English League (2012, 2014); English League Cup (2014, 2016)*
Clubs 02-06 CA Independiente; 06-11 Club Atlético de Madrid (ESP); 11- Manchester City FC (ENG)

2015/16 appearances/goals

Domestic league English Premier League 29(1)/24
Europe UEFA Champions League 8(1)/2
National team FIFA World Cup 2018 qualifying 2(1)/-; Copa América 2016 1(4)/1; Friendlies 1(2)/3

Toby Alderweireld

Centre-back, Height 187cm
Born 02/03/89, Antwerp, Belgium

Alderweireld joined Tottenham from Atlético Madrid on a five-year contract in July 2015, having got to grips with the particular demands of the Premier League during a season-long loan spell at Southampton. His first season at White Hart Lane established the versatile defender as one of the most accomplished centre-backs in England. He started all 38 league games for Spurs, scoring four goals, and formed an excellent partnership with fellow Belgian international – and ex-Ajax team-mate – Jan Vertonghen. He was also ever-present at UEFA EURO 2016 and scored Belgium's opener in the 4-0 win against Hungary.

International career

BELGIUM
Debut 29/05/09 v Chile (n, Chiba, Kirin Cup), drew 1-1
First goal 19/11/13 v Japan (h, Brussels, friendly), lost 2-3
Caps 61 **Goals** 2
Major tournaments FIFA World Cup 2014; UEFA EURO 2016

Club career

Major honours *Dutch League (2011, 2012, 2013); Spanish League (2014); Dutch Cup (2010)*
Clubs 08-13 AFC Ajax (NED); 13-15 Club Atlético de Madrid (ESP); 14-15 Southampton FC (ENG) (loan); 15- Tottenham Hotspur FC (ENG)

2015/16 appearances/goals

Domestic league English Premier League 38/4
Europe UEFA Europa League 10/-
National team UEFA EURO 2016 finals 5/1; UEFA EURO 2016 qualifying 4/-; Friendlies 4/-

Alex Teixeira

Attacking midfielder, Height 173cm
Born 06/01/90, Duque de Caxias, Brazil

The joint top scorer in the 2014/15 Ukrainian Premier League with 17 goals, Alex Teixeira had the prize all to himself in 2015/16 – despite leaving Shakhtar Donetsk halfway through the season to join Chinese Super League side Jiangsu Suning for an Asian record fee of €50m. The goal-hungry Brazilian found the net a remarkable 22 times in just 15 league appearances, including two in the top-of-the-table clash with Dynamo Kyiv – one of nine doubles. He also added a UEFA Champions League brace against Real Madrid before ending his six-year stay at Shakhtar, which brought him eight domestic winner's medals.

International career

BRAZIL
Uncapped

Club career

Major honours *Ukrainian League (2010, 2011, 2012, 2013, 2014); Ukrainian Cup (2011, 2012, 2013)*
Clubs 08-09 CR Vasco da Gama; 10-16 FC Shakhtar Donetsk (UKR); 16- Jiangsu Suning FC (CHN)

2015/16 appearances/goals

Domestic league Ukrainian Premier League 15/22
Europe UEFA Champions League 6/3; UEFA Champions League qualifying/play-offs 4/1

Dele Alli

Midfielder, Height 188cm
Born 11/04/96, Milton Keynes, England

Alli's transfer to Tottenham from third-tier MK Dons in the summer of 2015 (after a half-season loan back to the League One club) did not raise much interest outside White Hart Lane, but it was not long before Premier League observers came to realise that the £5m Spurs had paid for the 19-year-old represented an outrageous bargain. A tall, imposing midfielder who combines silk with steel, he scored a brilliant goal on his first start for England, against France at Wembley, and eclipsed that with the Premier League's goal of the season – a sublime turn and volley from the edge of the penalty area against Crystal Palace.

International career

ENGLAND
Debut 09/10/15 v Estonia (h, London, ECQ), won 2-0
First goal 17/11/15 v France (h, London, friendly), won 2-0
Caps 12 **Goals** 1
Major tournaments UEFA EURO 2016

Club career

Clubs 11-15 Milton Keynes Dons FC; 15- Tottenham Hotspur FC

2015/16 appearances/goals

Domestic league English Premier League 28(5)/10
Europe UEFA Europa League 7(2)/-
National team UEFA EURO 2016 finals 3(1)/-; UEFA EURO 2016 qualifying (2)/-; Friendlies 4(2)/1

Pierre-Emerick Aubameyang

Striker, Height 187cm
Born 18/06/89, Laval, France

The first player from Gabon to be voted CAF African Footballer of the Year, Aubameyang had scored 18 league goals for Dortmund when he collected that trophy in January, and he would add seven more in the spring to finish second to Bayern München's Robert Lewandowski in the German Bundesliga's goalscoring charts. The jet-heeled French-born striker, who extended his Dortmund contract at the start of the campaign, also made waves in Europe, scoring 11 goals in the various phases of the UEFA Europa League, including four in as many knockout games against English clubs Tottenham and Liverpool.

International career

GABON
Debut 28/03/09 v Morocco (a, Casablanca, WCQ), won 2-1
First goal 28/03/09 v Morocco (a, Casablanca, WCQ), won 2-1
Caps 47 **Goals** 20
Major tournaments Africa Cup of Nations 2010; Africa Cup of Nations 2012; Africa Cup of Nations 2015

Club career

Major honours French League Cup (2013)
Clubs 08-11 AC Milan (ITA); 08-09 Dijon FCO (FRA) (loan); 09-10 LOSC Lille (FRA) (loan); 10-11 AS Monaco FC (FRA) (loan); 11-13 AS Saint-Étienne (FRA); 13- Borussia Dortmund (GER)

2015/16 appearances/goals

Domestic league German Bundesliga 28(3)/25
Europe UEFA Europa League 9(1)/8; UEFA Europa League qualifying/play-offs 3(1)/3
National team FIFA World Cup 2018 qualifying 1/-; Friendlies 4/3

Gareth Bale

Attacking midfielder/Striker, Height 183cm
Born 16/07/89, Cardiff, Wales

The inspirational figure behind Wales' astonishing performance at UEFA EURO 2016, Bale not only struck six vital goals in qualifying but also found the net in all three of his country's group games in France, twice with trademark free-kicks. Losing to England clearly hurt his pride, but he could not contain his glee as Wales eventually topped the group and outlasted their British rivals all the way into the semi-finals. The 26-year-old had a mixed season with Real Madrid but he scored frequently in the Spanish Liga and helped the team to a second UEFA Champions League victory in his third season at the club.

International career

WALES
Debut 27/05/06 v Trinidad & Tobago (n, Graz, friendly), won 2-1
First goal 07/10/06 v Slovakia (h, Cardiff, ECQ), lost 1-5
Caps 61 **Goals** 22
Major tournaments UEFA EURO 2016

Club career

Major honours UEFA Champions League (2014, 2016); UEFA Super Cup (2014); FIFA Club World Cup (2014); Spanish Cup (2014)
Clubs 06-07 Southampton FC (ENG); 07-13 Tottenham Hotspur FC (ENG); 13- Real Madrid CF (ESP)

2015/16 appearances/goals

Domestic league Spanish Liga 21(2)/19
Europe UEFA Champions League 8/-
National team UEFA EURO 2016 finals 6/3; UEFA EURO 2016 qualifying 4/2; Friendlies (1)/-

Andrea Barzagli

Centre-back, Height 186cm
Born 08/05/81, Fiesole, Italy

After spending most of the 2014/15 campaign on the sidelines recovering from injury, Barzagli bounced back with one of the most satisfying seasons of his career. The 35-year-old defender re-established the 'BBC' three-man central-defensive unit alongside Leonardo Bonucci and Giorgio Chiellini – both for Juventus and the Italian national team – and was every bit as influential as his illustrious partners in the Bianconeri's second successive Serie A/ Coppa Italia double triumph. Three days after making his 150th Serie A appearance for Juve, he signed a new contract extending his stay in Turin for two more years.

International career

ITALY
Major honours FIFA World Cup (2006)
Debut 17/11/04 v Finland (h, Messina, friendly), won 1-0
Caps 61 **Goals** 0
Major tournaments FIFA World Cup 2006; UEFA EURO 2008; UEFA EURO 2012; FIFA Confederations Cup 2013; FIFA World Cup 2014; UEFA EURO 2016

Club career

Major honours German League (2009); Italian League (2012, 2013, 2014, 2015, 2016); Italian Cup (2015, 2016)
Clubs 98-01 Rondinella Calcio; 00 AC Pistoiese (loan); 01-03 Piacenza Calcio; 01-03 Ascoli Calcio (loan); 03-04 AC Chievo Verona; 04-08 US Città di Palermo; 08-11 VfL Wolfsburg (GER); 11- Juventus FC

2015/16 appearances/goals

Domestic league Italian Serie A 31/1
Europe UEFA Champions League 6(2)/-
National team UEFA EURO 2016 finals 5/-; UEFA EURO 2016 qualifying 1/-; Friendlies 3(1)/-

Michy Batshuayi

Striker, Height 182cm
Born 02/10/93, Brussels, Belgium

Marseille endured a largely forgettable 2015/16 season, but Batshuayi enjoyed an exceptional campaign from an individual viewpoint, scoring 23 goals in all competitions, the last of them in the final of the Coupe de France against Paris Saint-Germain. After playing – and scoring, with his first touch, against Hungary – for Belgium at UEFA EURO 2016, he left the Stade Vélodrome for Stamford Bridge, becoming new Chelsea boss Antonio Conte's first signing at a cost of €40m. Twelve years earlier a player with similar attacking strengths, Didier Drogba, joined the Blues from Marseille. Comparisons will be unfair but inevitable.

International career

BELGIUM
Debut 28/03/15 v Cyprus (h, Brussels, ECQ), won 5-0
First goal 28/03/15 v Cyprus (h, Brussels, ECQ), won 5-0
Caps 7 **Goals** 3
Major tournaments UEFA EURO 2016

Club career

Clubs 11-14 R. Standard de Liège; 14-16 Olympique de Marseille (FRA); 16- Chelsea FC (ENG)

2015/16 appearances/goals

Domestic league French Ligue 1 32(4)/17
Europe UEFA Europa League 6(1)/4
National team UEFA EURO 2016 finals (2)/1; Friendlies 1(3)/1

Héctor Bellerín

Right-back, Height 177cm
Born 19/03/95, Barcelona, Spain

A graduate of the FC Barcelona academy, Bellerín left for Arsenal at 16 and in 2015/16, his second season in the Gunners' first team, established himself as the club's first-choice right-back. The 21-year-old was also voted into the PFA Premier League Team of the Year in that position – due reward for a season in which he started 36 league games, scored one goal and set up another six – the most assists in the division by a defender. Blessed with remarkable natural speed, he has a bright future at both club and international level, having made his senior debut for Spain just before UEFA EURO 2016, where he was an unused squad member.

International career

SPAIN
Debut 29/05/16 v Bosnia & Herzegovina (n, St Gallen, friendly), won 3-1
Caps 3 **Goals** 0
Major tournaments UEFA EURO 2016

Club career

Major honours English FA Cup (2015)
Clubs 13- Arsenal FC (ENG); 13-14 Watford FC (loan)

2015/16 appearances/goals

Domestic league English Premier League 36/1
Europe UEFA Champions League 6/-
National team Friendlies 2(1)/-

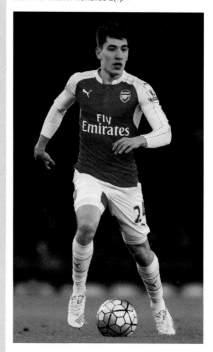

Hatem Ben Arfa

Attacking midfielder, Height 178cm
Born 07/03/87, Clamart, France

After six months on the sidelines following a troubled spell in England, Ben Arfa returned to action with a bang at Nice. His batteries fully recharged, the skilful left-footed winger revived memories of the exciting early years of his career, at Lyon and Marseille, with a series of quality performances, many of them adorned with spectacular goals, such as his magnificent slalom run through the Saint-Étienne defence in a 4-1 win at the Stade Geoffroy-Guichard. Having helped Nice into Europe, but disappointingly missed out on a place in France's UEFA EURO 2016 squad, he left in the summer for champions Paris Saint-Germain.

International career
FRANCE
Debut 13/10/07 v Faroe Islands (a, Torshavn, ECQ), won 6-0
First goal 13/10/07 v Faroe Islands (a, Torshavn, ECQ), won 6-0
Caps 15 **Goals** 2
Major tournaments UEFA EURO 2012

Club career
Major honours French League (2005, 2006, 2007, 2008, 2010); French Cup (2008); French League Cup (2010)
Clubs 04-08 Olympique Lyonnais; 08-11 Olympique de Marseille; 11-15 Newcastle United FC (ENG); 14-15 Hull City AFC (ENG) (loan); 15-16 OGC Nice; 16- Paris Saint-Germain

2015/16 appearances/goals
Domestic league French Ligue 1 33(1)/17
National team Friendlies 1(1)/-

Karim Benzema

Striker, Height 183cm
Born 17/12/87, Lyon, France

Denied a place in France's UEFA EURO 2016 squad for non-footballing reasons, Benzema had to content himself with another excellent season as the main central striker for Real Madrid, his seventh at the club. The 28-year-old rattled in 24 goals in the Spanish Liga – only Luis Suárez, Cristiano Ronaldo and Lionel Messi scored more – and also contributed four goals to the club's second UEFA Champions League victory in three seasons, bringing his grand total in the competition to 46, eighth in the competition's all-time rankings and just four behind the top-scoring Frenchman, Thierry Henry.

International career
FRANCE
Debut 28/03/07 v Austria (h, Saint-Denis, friendly), won 1-0
First goal 28/03/07 v Austria (h, Saint-Denis, friendly), won 1-0
Caps 81 **Goals** 27
Major tournaments UEFA EURO 2008; UEFA EURO 2012; FIFA World Cup 2014

Club career
Major honours UEFA Champions League (2014, 2016); UEFA Super Cup (2014); FIFA Club World Cup (2014); French League (2005, 2006, 2007, 2008); Spanish League (2012); French Cup (2008); Spanish Cup (2011, 2014)
Clubs 04-09 Olympique Lyonnais; 09- Real Madrid CF (ESP)

2015/16 appearances/goals
Domestic league Spanish Liga 26(1)/24
Europe UEFA Champions League 8(1)/4
National team Friendlies 2(1)/2

Leonardo Bonucci

Centre-back, Height 190cm
Born 01/05/87, Viterbo, Italy

At 29, Bonucci is widely considered to be one of the best defenders in the world. His consistency of performance stood out once again in 2015/16, with Juventus benefiting from his class and experience to win the domestic double for the second successive season under coach Massimiliano Allegri. A fifth scudetto in a row with the Bianconeri was followed by a trip to France with his ex-Juve boss Antonio Conte for UEFA EURO 2016, where he was one of the Azzurri's most prominent performers, his immaculate defending supplemented by a delightful assist against Belgium and a nerveless penalty against Germany.

International career
ITALY
Debut 03/03/10 v Cameroon (n, Monaco, friendly), drew 0-0
First goal 03/06/10 v Mexico (n, Brussels, friendly), lost 1-2
Caps 62 **Goals** 4
Major tournaments FIFA World Cup 2010; UEFA EURO 2012; FIFA Confederations Cup 2013; FIFA World Cup 2014; UEFA EURO 2016

Club career
Major honours Italian League (2006, 2012, 2013, 2014, 2015, 2016); Italian Cup (2015, 2016)
Clubs 05-07 FC Internazionale Milano; 07-09 FC Treviso; 09 AC Pisa (loan); 09-10 AS Bari; 10- Juventus FC

2015/16 appearances/goals
Domestic league Italian Serie A 35(1)/3
Europe UEFA Champions League 8/-
National team UEFA EURO 2016 finals 5/1; UEFA EURO 2016 qualifying 4/-; Friendlies 6/-

Bruno Soriano

Midfielder, Height 184cm
Born 12/06/84, Artana, Spain

Six years after making his international debut for Spain, Bruno finally got to play for his country at a major tournament. The Villarreal captain earned his call-up for UEFA EURO 2016 with a season of sustained excellence for his club, which helped the Yellow Submarine travel all the way to the semi-finals of the UEFA Europa League and claim a UEFA Champions League play-off berth with an impressive fourth-place finish in the Spanish Liga. The 2015/16 season was the one-club midfielder's tenth in succession at El Madrigal. Like the previous nine, it brought no silverware, but it did raise his profile to a new level.

International career

SPAIN
Debut 11/08/10 v Mexico (a, Mexico City, friendly), drew 1-1
Caps 10 **Goals** 0
Major tournaments UEFA EURO 2016

Club career

Clubs 06- Villarreal CF

2015/16 appearances/goals

Domestic league Spanish Liga 28(3)/5
Europe UEFA Europa League 12/2
National team UEFA EURO 2016 finals (2)/-;
Friendlies 2/-

Gianluigi Buffon

Goalkeeper, Height 191cm
Born 28/01/78, Carrara, Italy

Italy's most-capped international made it to an unprecedented 11th major tournament at UEFA EURO 2016, and the veteran goalkeeper proved in France that he is perfectly capable of going on for another two years and appearing for the Azzurri at the age of 40 in a sixth FIFA World Cup. His seventh scudetto with Juventus came at the end of a season in which his inspirational captaincy came to the fore and he also set new Serie A records for successive clean sheets (ten) and consecutive minutes without conceding a goal (974). Although he had many rivals, he was officially voted by Juve fans as their player of the season.

International career

ITALY
Major honours FIFA World Cup (2006)
Debut 29/10/97 v Russia (a, Moscow, WCQ), drew 1-1
Caps 161 **Goals** 0
Major tournaments FIFA World Cup 1998; FIFA World Cup 2002; UEFA EURO 2004; FIFA World Cup 2006; UEFA EURO 2008; FIFA Confederations Cup 2009; FIFA World Cup 2010; UEFA EURO 2012; FIFA Confederations Cup 2013; FIFA World Cup 2014; UEFA EURO 2016

Club career

Major honours UEFA Cup (1999); Italian League (2002, 2003, 2012, 2013, 2014, 2015, 2016); Italian Cup (1999, 2015, 2016)
Clubs 95-01 Parma FC; 01- Juventus FC

2015/16 appearances/goals

Domestic league Italian Serie A 35/-
Europe UEFA Champions League 8/-
National team UEFA EURO 2016 finals 4/-; UEFA EURO 2016 qualifying 4/-; Friendlies 5/-

Petr Čech

Goalkeeper, Height 197cm
Born 20/05/82, Plzeň, Czech Republic

After 11 seasons with Chelsea, Čech moved from west to north London, where he became the new first-choice goalkeeper at Arsenal. It had come to be perceived by many as a problem position for the Gunners, but with the imposing Czech Republic international between the posts that was no longer the case. After helping Arsenal defeat Chelsea 1-0 in the pre-season FA Community Shield on his debut, he went on to star time and again in the Premier League and ended the campaign with 16 clean sheets in his 34 appearances, which earned the 34-year-old the division's Golden Glove for the fourth time in his career.

International career

CZECH REPUBLIC
Debut 12/02/02 v Hungary (n, Larnaca, friendly), won 2-0
Caps 124 **Goals** 0
Major tournaments UEFA EURO 2004; FIFA World Cup 2006; UEFA EURO 2008; UEFA EURO 2012; UEFA EURO 2016

Club career

Major honours UEFA Champions League (2012); UEFA Europa League (2013); English League (2005, 2006, 2010, 2015); English FA Cup (2007, 2009, 2010, 2012); English League Cup (2005, 2007, 2015)
Clubs 99-01 FK Chmel Blšany; 01-02 AC Sparta Praha; 02-04 Stade Rennais FC (FRA); 04-15 Chelsea FC (ENG); 15- Arsenal FC (ENG)

2015/16 appearances/goals

Domestic league English Premier League 34/-
Europe UEFA Champions League 5/-
National team UEFA EURO 2016 finals 3/-; UEFA EURO 2016 qualifying 3/-; Friendlies 4/-

Giorgio Chiellini

Centre-back, Height 186cm
Born 14/08/84, Pisa, Italy

The second half of the 2015/16 season was one of disruption for Chiellini as he was repeatedly sidelined with injury niggles, one of which kept him out of the UEFA Champions League last-16 tie against Bayern München, but he was back at the end of the campaign to join in Juventus's celebrations as they completed a second successive Italian double. He made his 400th appearance for the Bianconeri in the final game of the Serie A campaign and skippered the club to victory over AC Milan in the Coppa Italia final a week later before turning his mind to UEFA EURO 2016, where he starred – and scored (against Spain) – for Italy.

International career

ITALY
Debut 17/11/04 v Finland (h, Messina, friendly), won 1-0
First goal 21/11/07 v Faroe Islands (h, Modena, ECQ), won 3-1
Caps 88 **Goals** 7
Major tournaments UEFA EURO 2008; FIFA Confederations Cup 2009; FIFA World Cup 2010; UEFA EURO 2012; FIFA Confederations Cup 2013; FIFA World Cup 2014; UEFA EURO 2016

Club career

Major honours Italian League (2012, 2013, 2014, 2015, 2016); Italian Cup (2015, 2016)
Clubs 00-04 AS Livorno Calcio; 04-05 ACF Fiorentina; 05- Juventus FC

2015/16 appearances/goals

Domestic league Italian Serie A 21(3)/1
Europe UEFA Champions League 6/-
National team UEFA EURO 2016 finals 4/1; UEFA EURO 2016 qualifying 4/-; Friendlies 4/-

Kingsley Coman

Winger, Height 178cm
Born 13/06/96, Paris, France

Before Coman turned 20, in June 2016, the French winger had already won seven major trophies, including league titles in France, Italy and Germany. However, it was only in winning the 2015/16 league and cup double with Bayern München, in the first half of a two-year loan from Juventus, that he could consider himself a key contributor. Standing in for injured compatriot Franck Ribéry, he dazzled on the wing with his explosive speed and ability to get to the byline. Called up to France's UEFA EURO 2016 squad, he appeared in six games, the last of them in the final, but could not add to his formidable trophy haul.

International career

FRANCE
Debut 13/11/15 v Germany (h, Saint-Denis, friendly), won 2-0
First goal 29/03/16 v Russia (h, Saint-Denis, friendly), won 4-2
Caps 11 **Goals** 1
Major tournaments UEFA EURO 2016

Club career

Major honours French League (2013, 2014); Italian League (2015); German League (2016); Italian Cup (2015); German Cup (2016); French League Cup (2014)
Clubs 13-14 Paris Saint-Germain; 14- Juventus FC (ITA); 15- FC Bayern München (GER) (loan)

2015/16 appearances/goals

Domestic league German Bundesliga 20(3)/4
Europe UEFA Champions League 4(4)/2
National team UEFA EURO 2016 finals 2(4)/-; Friendlies 2(3)/1

Cristiano Ronaldo

Striker, Height 184cm
Born 05/02/85, Funchal, Madeira, Portugal

There has never been a dull moment in the brilliant career of Cristiano Ronaldo, but none can have filled him with as much elation as the final whistle of the UEFA EURO 2016 final, which added a first major international honour with Portugal to the reams of trophies and individual prizes he had won at club level. Victory with his country came just a few weeks after he had conquered Europe again with his club, scoring the decisive penalty in the UEFA Champions League final against Atlético Madrid after driving Real Madrid to the San Siro showdown with 16 goals in 12 games – remarkable figures for most but not for the great Ronaldo.

International career

PORTUGAL
Major honours UEFA European Championship (2016)
Debut 20/08/03 v Kazakhstan (h, Chaves, friendly), won 1-0
First goal 12/06/04 v Greece (h, Porto, ECF), lost 1-2
Caps 133 **Goals** 61
Major tournaments UEFA EURO 2004; FIFA World Cup 2006; UEFA EURO 2008; FIFA World Cup 2010; UEFA EURO 2012; FIFA World Cup 2014; UEFA EURO 2016

Club career

Major honours UEFA Champions League (2008, 2014, 2016); UEFA Super Cup (2014); FIFA Club World Cup (2008, 2014); English League (2007, 2008, 2009); Spanish League (2012); English FA Cup (2004); Spanish Cup (2011, 2014); English League Cup (2006, 2009)
Clubs 02-03 Sporting Clube de Portugal; 03-09 Manchester United FC (ENG); 09- Real Madrid CF (ESP)

2015/16 appearances/goals

Domestic league Spanish Liga 36/35
Europe UEFA Champions League 12/16
National team UEFA EURO 2016 finals 7/3; UEFA EURO 2016 qualifying 2/-; Friendlies 4/3

Steven Davis

Midfielder, Height 178cm
Born 01/01/85, Ballymena,
Northern Ireland

Northern Ireland's first tournament appearance for 30 years was clinched with a 3-1 victory at home to Greece, and it was fitting that the team's captain should mark the occasion by scoring two of the goals – his first international double in 78 appearances. Davis went on to lead his country into the UEFA EURO 2016 knockout phase, starting all four matches in France. The 31-year-old crossed the Channel after an excellent season in the English Premier League with Southampton, highlighted by a winning brace at Tottenham as the Saints marched into the UEFA Europa League thanks to their sixth-place finish.

International career

NORTHERN IRELAND
Debut 09/02/05 v Canada (h, Belfast, friendly), lost 0-1
First goal 08/10/05 v Wales (h, Belfast, WCQ), lost 2-3
Caps 87 **Goals** 8
Major tournaments UEFA EURO 2016

Club career

Major honours Scottish League (2009, 2010, 2011); Scottish Cup (2008, 2009); Scottish League Cup (2008, 2010, 2011)
Clubs 04-07 Aston Villa FC (ENG); 07-08 Fulham FC (ENG); 08 Rangers FC (SCO) (loan); 08-12 Rangers FC (SCO); 12- Southampton FC (ENG) (loan)

2015/16 appearances/goals

Domestic league English Premier League 31(3)/5
Europe UEFA Europa League qualifying/ play-offs 3/-
National team UEFA EURO 2016 finals 4/-; UEFA EURO 2016 qualifying 4/2; Friendlies 5/1

Kevin De Bruyne

Attacking midfielder, Height 181cm
Born 28/06/91, Drongen, Belgium

Manchester City broke their transfer record to sign De Bruyne from Wolfsburg, but the £55m they splashed out on the 2014/15 Bundesliga player of the year proved to be money well spent on the evidence of his first season. Unfortunately, he was out of action in February and March, when City's Premier League challenge collapsed without him, but he was back to score vital goals in each leg of the UEFA Champions League quarter-final against Paris Saint-Germain, supplementing a crucial late winner he had struck in a group game against Sevilla. The classy schemer-cum-winger went on to start all of Belgium's five matches at UEFA EURO 2016.

International career

BELGIUM
Debut 11/08/10 v Finland (a, Turku, friendly), lost 0-1
First goal 12/10/12 v Serbia (a, Belgrade, WCQ), won 3-0
Caps 46 **Goals** 13
Major tournaments FIFA World Cup 2014; UEFA EURO 2016

Club career

Major honours Belgian League (2011); German Cup (2015); English League Cup (2016)
Clubs 08-12 KRC Genk; 12-14 Chelsea FC (ENG); 12 KRC Genk (loan); 12-13 SV Werder Bremen (GER) (loan); 14-15 VfL Wolfsburg (GER); 15- Manchester City FC (ENG)

2015/16 appearances/goals

Domestic league English Premier League 22(3)/7
Europe UEFA Champions League 8(2)/3
National team UEFA EURO 2016 finals 5/-; UEFA EURO 2016 qualifying 4/3; Friendlies 4/2

David de Gea

Goalkeeper, Height 190cm
Born 07/11/90, Madrid, Spain

Manchester United's player of the year award was won by De Gea for an unprecedented third successive season. At the start of the 2015/16 campaign it looked as if he was about to join Real Madrid, but a transfer deadline-day hiccup prevented the deal from taking place and he signed a new contract before proceeding to see out a fifth season at Old Trafford that many United fans considered his very best. It ended with an FA Cup winner's medal and a first major tournament as Spain's No1 goalkeeper, his excellent performances at UEFA EURO 2016 justifying the decision to promote him ahead of the legendary Iker Casillas.

International career

SPAIN
Debut 07/06/14 v El Salvador (n, Landover, USA, friendly), won 2-0
Caps 13 **Goals** 0
Major tournaments FIFA World Cup 2014; UEFA EURO 2016

Club career

Major honours UEFA Europa League (2010); UEFA Super Cup (2010); English League (2013); English FA Cup (2016)
Clubs 09-11 Club Atlético de Madrid; 11- Manchester United FC (ENG)

2015/16 appearances/goals

Domestic league English Premier League 34/-
Europe UEFA Champions League 6/-; UEFA Europa League 2/-
National team UEFA EURO 2016 4/-; UEFA EURO 2016 qualifying 2/-; Friendlies 2/-

Luuk de Jong

Striker, Height 188cm
Born 27/08/90, Aigle, Switzerland

De Jong's second season at PSV Eindhoven ended just like the first one – with a Dutch Eredivisie winner's medal. The striker never settled properly in Germany with Borussia Mönchengladbach or England with Newcastle United, but a return to the comforts of home rekindled the talent first unearthed at FC Twente, and he compiled a personal-best tally of 26 league goals in 2015/16 to fire his team to a second successive title. It was the most scored by a PSV player in the Eredivisie for 13 years, and he added two more in the UEFA Champions League as well as a couple for the Netherlands in friendlies against France and the Republic of Ireland.

International career

NETHERLANDS
Debut 09/02/11 v Austria (h, Eindhoven, friendly), won 3-1
First goal 06/09/11 v Finland (a, Helsinki, ECQ), won 2-0
Caps 12 **Goals** 3
Major tournaments UEFA EURO 2012

Club career

Major honours Dutch League (2010, 2015, 2016); Dutch Cup (2011)
Clubs 08-09 De Graafschap; 09-12 FC Twente; 12-14 VfL Borussia Mönchengladbach (GER); 14 Newcastle United FC (ENG) (loan); 14- PSV Eindhoven

2015/16 appearances/goals

Domestic league Dutch Eredivisie 32(1)/26
Europe UEFA Champions League 6/2
National team UEFA EURO 2016 qualifying (1)/-; Friendlies 1(2)/2

Ousmane Dembélé

Attacking midfielder, Height 177cm
Born 15/05/97, Vernon, France

Dembélé did not sign his first professional contract until 1 October 2015. A month later he had made his debut for Rennes, with his first goal following soon afterwards. By the turn of the year news of the 18-year-old's exceptional talent was already spreading fast across France and by the spring, after a breathtaking hat-trick in the Breton derby against Nantes, the whole of Europe was getting to know his name. The dazzling two-footed youngster ended a remarkable debut campaign as Rennes' top scorer, with 12 goals, plus official recognition as Ligue 1's best young player, before signing a five-year contract with Borussia Dortmund.

International career

FRANCE
Uncapped

Club career

Clubs 15-16 Stade Rennais FC; 16- Borussia Dortmund (GER)

2015/16 appearances/goals

Domestic league French Ligue 1 22(4)/12

Ángel Di María

Attacking midfielder/Winger, Height 180cm
Born 14/02/88, Rosario, Argentina

Things did not go to plan for Ángel Di María at Manchester United, so after just a year at Old Trafford the ex-Real Madrid winger returned to the European mainland to join Paris Saint-Germain, for another substantial fee. This time the €63m price tag proved no hindrance as he produced some of the best form of his career. With 18 assists in Ligue 1, he set a new record for France's top division, and he also scored ten goals, including an astonishing long-distance volley against Angers of which his team-mate Zlatan Ibrahimović would have been proud. He also scored the winning goal against Lille in the League Cup final.

International career

ARGENTINA
Debut 06/09/08 v Paraguay (h, Buenos Aires, WCQ), drew 1-1
First goal 24/05/10 v Canada (h, Buenos Aires, friendly), won 5-0
Caps 76 **Goals** 17
Major tournaments FIFA World Cup 2010; Copa América 2011; FIFA World Cup 2014; Copa América 2015; Copa América 2016

Club career

Major honours UEFA Champions League (2014); UEFA Super Cup (2014); Portuguese League (2010); Spanish League (2012); French League (2016); Spanish Cup (2011, 2014); French Cup (2016); French League Cup (2016)
Clubs 05-07 Rosario Central; 07-10 SL Benfica (POR); 10-14 Real Madrid CF (ESP); 14-15 Manchester United FC (ENG); 15- Paris Saint-Germain (FRA)

2015/16 appearances/goals

Domestic league French Ligue 1 26(3)/10
Europe UEFA Champions League 9(2)/3
National team FIFA World Cup 2018 qualifying 6/1; Copa América 2016 3/1; Friendlies 1/-

Eric Dier

Midfielder, Height 188cm
Born 15/01/94, Cheltenham, England

Born in England but brought up in Portugal, Dier left Lisbon for London when Tottenham tracked him down and recruited him in August 2014. His first season at White Hart Lane was spent chiefly in central defence, but in 2015/16 Spurs manager Mauricio Pochettino switched him to a holding midfield position. The 22-year-old performed the role with such authority that Roy Hodgson elected to deploy him there for England, and he not only proved a success there too but also displayed other qualities besides, scoring a last-minute headed winner against Germany in a Berlin friendly and a powerful free-kick against Russia at UEFA EURO 2016.

International career

ENGLAND
Debut 13/11/15 v Spain (a, Alicante), lost 0-2
First goal 26/03/16 v Germany (a, Berlin, friendly), won 3-2
Caps 11 **Goals** 2
Major tournaments UEFA EURO 2016

Club career

Clubs 12-14 Sporting Clube de Portugal (POR); 14- Tottenham Hotspur FC

2015/16 appearances/goals

Domestic league English Premier League 37/3
Europe UEFA Europa League 8(1)/-
National team UEFA EURO 2016 finals 4/1; Friendlies 4(3)/-

Douglas Costa

Winger, Height 170cm
Born 14/09/90, Sapucaia do Sul, Brazil

A €30m purchase from Shakhtar Donetsk, Douglas Costa enjoyed a fabulous first season at Bayern München, his speed, elusiveness and all-round left-footed trickery making him a perpetual nuisance for opposition full-backs. The 25-year-old Brazilian had won five national championships and three domestic cups with Shakhtar, and he added one more of each with Bayern, where Arjen Robben's injury problems allowed him more game time than he might have expected. It was his decisive penalty that enabled coach Pep Guardiola to leave Bayern on a high with a shoot-out victory over Borussia Dortmund in the German Cup final.

International career

BRAZIL
Debut 12/11/14 v Turkey (a, Istanbul, friendly, won 4-0)
First goal 14/06/15 v Peru (n, Temuco, Copa América), won 2-1
Caps 17 **Goals** 3
Major tournaments Copa América 2015

Club career

Major honours Ukrainian League (2010, 2011, 2012, 2013, 2014); German League (2016); Ukrainian Cup (2011, 2012, 2013); German Cup (2016)
Clubs 08-10 Grêmio FBPA; 10-15 FC Shakhtar Donetsk (UKR); 15- FC Bayern München (GER)

2015/16 appearances/goals

Domestic league German Bundesliga 23(4)/4
Europe UEFA Champions League 11/2
National team FIFA World Cup 2018 qualifying 5(1)/2; Friendlies 2/-

Danny Drinkwater

Midfielder, Height 178cm
Born 05/03/90, Manchester, England

Leicester's player of the year when they won promotion to the Premier League in 2013/14, Drinkwater made little impact in the top flight the following season, but the departure of Esteban Cambiasso and a long-term injury to Matty James enabled him to become a regular in central midfield under new boss Claudio Ranieri. The consistent quality of his performances, including one magnificent display in a 3-1 win at Manchester City, played an important part in helping Leicester to their remarkable Premier League title triumph. It was a surprise to many that the in-form 26-year-old was excluded from England's UEFA EURO 2016 squad.

International career

ENGLAND
Debut 29/03/16 v Netherlands (h, London, friendly), lost 1-2
Caps 3 **Goals** 0

Club career

Major honours English League (2016)
Clubs 08-12 Manchester United FC; 09-10 Huddersfield Town AFC (loan); 10-11 Cardiff City FC (loan); 11 Watford FC (loan); 11-12 Barnsley FC (loan); 12- Leicester City FC

2015/16 appearances/goals

Domestic league English Premier League 35/2
National team Friendlies 2(1)/-

Paulo Dybala

Striker, Height 179cm
Born 15/11/93, Cordoba, Argentina

A €32m signing from Palermo, Dybala did everything expected of him during his first season at Juventus, filling the boots of his departed compatriot Carlos Tévez and finishing as the Bianconeri's leading marksman in Serie A with 19 goals. A lithe, technically gifted left-footer whose best position is just off the central striker – in the mould of former Juve greats Roberto Baggio and Alessandro Del Piero – the 22-year-old was a key factor in the club's second successive league and cup double. Among his most memorable Serie A goals were the winning strikes at home to Milan, Roma and Sassuolo and an absolute gem away to Lazio.

International career

ARGENTINA
Debut 13/10/15 v Paraguay (a, Asunción, WCQ), drew 0-0
Caps 3 **Goals** 0

Club career

Major honours *Italian League (2016); Italian Cup (2016)*
Clubs 11-12 Instituto de Córdoba; 12-15 US Città di Palermo (ITA); 15- Juventus FC (ITA)

2015/16 appearances/goals

Domestic league Italian Serie A 29(5)/19
Europe UEFA Champions League 5(2)/1
National team FIFA World Cup 2018 qualifying (3)/-

Alan Dzagoev

Attacking midfielder, Height 180cm
Born 17/06/90, Beslan, Russia

Dzagoev's eighth season at CSKA Moskva brought him a third Russian championship winner's medal in four years. The 2015/16 triumph was particularly special to the 26-year-old because he was so influential in bringing it about. Back to his best as CSKA's conductor-in-chief in central midfield, he registered eight assists and six goals, the last of those bringing his side the 1-0 final-day victory at Rubin that sealed the title. Unfortunately he broke a toe in that game and was therefore ruled out of UEFA EURO 2016– a major setback for Russia, who struggled for creativity without him and failed to win a game in France.

International career

RUSSIA
Debut 11/10/08 v Germany (a, Dortmund, WCQ), lost 1-2
First goal 08/10/10 v Republic of Ireland (a, Dublin, ECQ), won 3-2
Caps 49 **Goals** 9
Major tournaments UEFA EURO 2012; FIFA World Cup 2014

Club career

Major honours *Russian League (2013, 2014, 2016); Russian Cup (2008, 2009, 2011, 2013)*
Clubs 06-07 FC Krylya Sovetov-SOK Dimitrovgrad; 08- PFC CSKA Moskva

2015/16 appearances/goals

Domestic league Russian Premier-Liga 29/6
Europe UEFA Champions League 6/-
National team UEFA EURO 2016 qualifying 3/1; Friendlies 2/-

Christian Eriksen

Midfielder, Height 180cm
Born 14/02/92, Middelfart, Denmark

A winner of the Danish footballer of the year award for an unprecedented third year running in 2015, Eriksen was unable to help his country qualify for UEFA EURO 2016 but he treated supporters of Tottenham Hotspur to a succession of top-class midfield displays – and some quality goals – during the club's quest for the 2015/16 Premier League title. His third season at White Hart Lane did not have the happy ending he and his team-mates craved, but he cheered himself up by journeying to Japan with his country in June and scoring his first international hat-trick – in a 4-0 Kirin Cup victory over Bulgaria.

International career

DENMARK
Debut 03/03/10 v Austria (a, Vienna, friendly), lost 1-2
First goal 04/06/11 v Iceland (a, Reykjavik, ECQ), won 2-0
Caps 61 **Goals** 9
Major tournaments FIFA World Cup 2010; UEFA EURO 2012

Club career

Major honours *Dutch League (2011, 2012, 2013); Dutch Cup (2010)*
Clubs 10-13 AFC Ajax (NED); 13- Tottenham Hotspur FC (ENG)

2015/16 appearances/goals

Domestic league English Premier League 33(2)/6
Europe UEFA Europa League 7/1
National team UEFA EURO 2016 qualifying 3/-; Friendlies 5/3

Filipe Luís

Left-back, Height 182cm
Born 09/08/85, Jaragua do Sul, Brazil

Unable to command a regular place in Chelsea's 2014/15 Premier League-winning side under José Mourinho, Filipe Luís opted to return whence he had come and re-sign for Atlético Madrid, the club with whom he had won the Spanish title in 2013/14. Diego Simeone and the Atlético fans welcomed him back with open arms, and the nifty Brazilian international left-back performed as if he had never been away, saving some of his best efforts for the UEFA Champions League, where he defended and attacked with equal alacrity in helping the team reach the final – his second in successive seasons with the club.

International career

BRAZIL
Major honours FIFA Confederations Cup (2013)
Debut 14/10/09 v Venezuela (h, Campo Grande, WCQ), drew 0-0
First goal 17/11/15 v Peru (h, Salvador, WCQ), won 3-0
Caps 26 **Goals** 1
Major tournaments FIFA Confederations Cup 2013; Copa América 2015; Copa América 2016

Club career

Major honours UEFA Europa League (2012); UEFA Super Cup (2010, 2012); Spanish League (2014); English League (2015); Spanish Cup (2013); English League Cup (2015)
Clubs 03-05 Figueirense FC; 05-08 CA Rentistas (URU); 05-06 Real Madrid CF (ESP) (loan); 06-08 RC Deportivo La Coruña (ESP) (loan); 08-10 RC Deportivo La Coruña (ESP); 10-14 Club Atlético de Madrid (ESP); 14-15 Chelsea FC (ENG); 15- Club Atlético de Madrid (ESP)

2015/16 appearances/goals

Domestic league Spanish Liga 32/1
Europe UEFA Champions League 10/-
National team FIFA World Cup 2018 qualifying 5/1; Copa América 2016 3/-

Alessandro Florenzi

Midfielder/Full-back, Height 173cm
Born 11/03/91, Rome, Italy

There were many outstanding goals scored in the 2015/16 UEFA Champions League but none quite so spectacular as the one Florenzi launched into the Barcelona net from his own half to earn Roma a 1-1 home draw against the holders on matchday one. It earned him a nomination for the FIFA Puskás award for the goal of 2015 and it set the tone for what would be the best season of the 25-year-old's career – one in which he became a highly versatile and indispensable performer for both club and country, helping Roma finish third in Serie A and making his international tournament bow for Italy at UEFA EURO 2016.

International career

ITALY
Debut 14/11/12 v France (h, Parma, friendly), lost 1-2
First goal 15/10/13 v Armenia (h, Naples, WCQ), drew 2-2
Caps 21 **Goals** 2
Major tournaments UEFA EURO 2016

Club career

Clubs 11- AS Roma; 11-12 FC Crotone (loan)

2015/16 appearances/goals

Domestic league Italian Serie A 31(2)/7
Europe UEFA Champions League 8/1
National team UEFA EURO 2016 finals 4/-; UEFA EURO 2016 qualifying 1(2)/1; Friendlies 5(1)/-

Kostas Fortounis

Attacking midfielder, Height 183cm
Born 16/10/92, Trikala, Greece

Greek football hit a low during an ill-starred UEFA EURO 2016 qualifying campaign, but encouragement for the future was provided by the outstanding form during the 2015/16 season of Fortounis. The Olympiacos midfielder topped both the goal and the assists charts at the end of a Superleague campaign in which the perennial champions dropped only five points and won it by 30. A set-piece specialist with excellent vision and awareness, the 23-year-old was watched by an increasing number of foreign scouts as the season progressed. In June, however, Olympiacos persuaded him to remain in Piraeus for four more years.

International career

GREECE
Debut 29/02/12 v Belgium (h, Heraklion, friendly), drew 1-1
First goal 29/03/16 v Iceland (h, Piraeus, friendly), lost 2-3
Caps 19 **Goals** 2
Major tournaments UEFA EURO 2012

Club career

Major honours Greek League (2015, 2016); Greek Cup (2015)
Clubs 08-10 Trikala FC; 10-11 Asteras Tripolis FC; 11-14 1. FC Kaiserslautern (GER); 14- Olympiacos FC

2015/16 appearances/goals

Domestic league Greek Superleague 22(5)/18
Europe UEFA Champions League 4(2)/-; UEFA Europa League 2/1
National team UEFA EURO 2016 qualifying 3/-; Friendlies 3/2

Gabi

Midfielder, Height 180cm
Born 10/07/83, Madrid, Spain

At the age of 33 the prospect of playing international football for Spain appears to have passed him by, but Gabi's achievements at Atlético Madrid since he returned there for a second spell in 2011 have made him one of the most influential figures in the Spanish club game. In 2015/16 he skippered Atlético to a second UEFA Champions League final in three years, playing brilliantly against Barcelona and Bayern München en route to the San Siro, where he again stood out with his diligent midfield play before smashing home his penalty in the shoot-out. Sadly for him, though, it was his Real Madrid counterpart Sergio Ramos who got to lift the trophy instead.

International career

SPAIN
Uncapped

Club career

Major honours UEFA Europa League (2012); UEFA Super Cup (2012); Spanish League (2014); Spanish Cup (2013)
Clubs 02-04 Club Atlético de Madrid B; 04-07 Club Atlético de Madrid; 04-05 Getafe CF (loan); 07-11 Real Zaragoza; 11- Club Atlético de Madrid

2015/16 appearances/goals

Domestic league Spanish Liga 34(1)/1
Europe UEFA Champions League 12(1)/-

Kevin Gameiro

Striker, Height 172cm
Born 09/05/87, Senlis, France

Gameiro was the principal figure in Sevilla's third successive UEFA Europa League triumph. The fleet-footed French striker found the net in every round of the knockout phase, scoring eight goals, including at least one in every home game and the equaliser in the Basel final against Liverpool. A member of all three trophy-winning teams, he enjoyed his best domestic season for Sevilla in 2015/16, scoring 16 times in the Liga and four in the Copa del Rey to help his club into another final. Although his name was mentioned in despatches, there was no recall for the 29-year-old to the France squad for UEFA EURO 2016.

International career

FRANCE
Debut 03/09/10 v Belarus (h, Saint-Denis, ECQ), lost 0-1
First goal 06/06/11 v Ukraine (a, Donetsk, friendly), won 4-1
Caps 8 **Goals** 1

Club career

Major honours UEFA Europa League (2014, 2015, 2016); French League (2013)
Clubs 05-08 RC Strasbourg; 08-11 FC Lorient; 11-13 Paris Saint-Germain; 13-16 Sevilla FC (ESP); 16- Club Atlético de Madrid (ESP)

2015/16 appearances/goals

Domestic league Spanish Liga 22(9)/16
Europe UEFA Champions League 4(1)/1; UEFA Europa League 7(2)/8

Zoltán Gera

Midfielder, Height 183cm
Born 22/04/79, Pecs, Hungary

No one was more excited about representing Hungary at UEFA EURO 2016 than 37-year-old Zoltán Gera. The first major tournament of his career finally arrived 14 years after his debut, and he made the most of it, starting all four games and scoring a spectacular goal against Portugal – left-footed on the half-volley from the edge of a crowded penalty area – that was voted as the goal of the tournament in an official online poll. The veteran midfielder travelled to France on a high after helping Ferencváros capture the Hungarian double, his late winning goal in the cup final against arch-rivals Újpest sealing the deal.

International career

HUNGARY
Debut 13/02/02 v Switzerland (n, Limassol, friendly), lost 1-2
First goal 16/10/02 v San Marino (h, Budapest, ECQ), won 3-0
Caps 93 **Goals** 25
Major tournaments UEFA EURO 2016

Club career

Major honours Hungarian League (2001, 2004, 2016); Hungarian Cup (2003, 2004, 2015, 2016)
Clubs 96-97 Harkány SE; 97-00 Pécsi MFC; 00-04 Ferencvárosi TC; 04-08 West Bromwich Albion FC (ENG); 08-11 Fulham FC (ENG); 11-14 West Bromwich Albion FC (ENG); 14- Ferencvárosi TC

2015/16 appearances/goals

Domestic league Hungarian NB I 29(1)/4
Europe UEFA Europa League qualifying 4/2
National team UEFA EURO 2016 finals 4/1; UEFA EURO 2016 qualifying 4/-; Friendlies 1(2)/-

Diego Godín

Centre-back, Height 186cm
Born 16/02/86, Rosario, Uruguay

Six Atlético Madrid players made it into the 18-man UEFA Champions League Squad of the Season and Godín was one of them. Excluding him would have been a travesty after a succession of outstanding displays from the Uruguayan in both the run to the final and the match in Milan itself. The 30-year-old further enhanced his growing reputation as one of the world's best centre-backs in the Spanish Liga, where he was a major factor in giving Atlético the best defensive figures in the division. A busy man also for his country in 2015/16, he scored four competitive goals, thus doubling his international tally, and also won his 100th cap.

International career

URUGUAY
Major honours Copa América (2011)
Debut 26/10/05 v Mexico (a, Guadalajara, friendly), lost 1-3
First goal 27/05/06 v Serbia & Montenegro (a, Belgrade, friendly), drew 1-1
Caps 100 **Goals** 8
Major tournaments Copa América 2007; FIFA World Cup 2010; Copa América 2011; FIFA Confederations Cup 2013; FIFA World Cup 2014; Copa América 2015; Copa América 2016

Club career

Major honours UEFA Europa League (2012); UEFA Super Cup (2010, 2012); Spanish League (2014); Spanish Cup (2013)
Clubs 03-06 CA Cerro; 06-07 Club Nacional; 07-10 Villarreal CF (ESP); 10- Club Atlético de Madrid (ESP)

2015/16 appearances/goals

Domestic league Spanish Liga 32/1
Europe UEFA Champions League 12/-
National team FIFA World Cup 2018 qualifying 4/3; Copa América 2016 3/1; Friendlies 2/-

Mario Gomez

Striker, Height 189cm
Born 10/07/85, Riedlingen, Germany

After two inconspicuous seasons at Fiorentina, Gomez rediscovered the form that had made him such a lethal weapon in the attacks of VfB Stuttgart and Bayern München after moving on loan to Beşiktaş. The strapping striker took an immediate liking to the Turkish Süper Lig and powered his club to the title with a golden boot-winning tally of 26 goals. It was a return to form that caught the eye of Germany boss Joachim Löw, who recalled him to the side after a lengthy absence. He scored twice at UEFA EURO 2016 but his presence up front was badly missed when he sat out the semi-final defeat against France with an injured thigh muscle.

International career

GERMANY
Debut 07/02/07 v Switzerland (h, Dusseldorf, friendly), won 3-1
First goal 07/02/07 v Switzerland (h, Dusseldorf, friendly), won 3-1
Caps 68 **Goals** 29
Major tournaments UEFA EURO 2008; FIFA World Cup 2010; UEFA EURO 2012; UEFA EURO 2016

Club career

Major honours UEFA Champions League (2013); German League (2007, 2010, 2013); Turkish League (2016); German Cup (2010, 2013)
Clubs 03-09 VfB Stuttgart; 09-13 FC Bayern München; 13- ACF Fiorentina (ITA); 15-16 Beşiktaş JK (TUR) (loan)

2015/16 appearances/goals

Domestic league Turkish Süper Lig 31(2)/26
Europe UEFA Europa League 4(1)/2
National team UEFA EURO 2016 finals 3(1)/2; Friendlies 3(1)/2

Antoine Griezmann

Striker/Attacking midfielder, Height 176cm
Born 21/03/91, Macon, France

The 2015/16 season will be remembered as the season in which Griezmann became a global star thanks to his brilliant performances for Atlético Madrid and the French national team. On the other hand, it will probably be recalled by the player himself as one of immense frustration as missed chances in the UEFA Champions League final against Real Madrid and the UEFA EURO 2016 final against Portugal denied the 25-year-old the first major honours of his career. He did, however, scoop a couple of individual prizes at UEFA EURO 2016, claiming the Golden Boot with his six goals and also being officially named as the Player of the Tournament.

International career

FRANCE
Debut 05/03/14 v Netherlands (h, Saint-Denis, friendly), won 2-0
First goal 01/06/14 v Paraguay (h, Nice, friendly), drew 1-1
Caps 34 **Goals** 13
Major tournaments FIFA World Cup 2014; UEFA EURO 2016

Club career

Clubs 09-14 Real Sociedad de Fútbol (ESP); 14- Club Atlético de Madrid (ESP)

2015/16 appearances/goals

Domestic league Spanish Liga 36(2)/22
Europe UEFA Champions League 13/7
National team UEFA EURO 2016 finals 6(1)/6; Friendlies 6(3)/2

Marek Hamšík

Attacking midfielder, Height 180cm
Born 27/07/87, Banska Bystrica, Slovakia

Hamšík's ninth season at Napoli ended with a runners-up spot in Serie A. The spiky-haired schemer started every one of the club's 38 games as he passed the milestone of 300 appearances for the club. Many of striker Gonzalo Higuaín's record-breaking 36 goals were sourced by his skipper, who also found the net half a dozen times himself, taking his all-time Serie A tally to 81. The captain also of Slovakia, he clinched his country's qualification for UEFA EURO 2016 with a timely brace in Luxembourg and also scored one of the most eye-catching goals at the finals to help the team to a crucial 2-1 win against Russia in Lille.

International career

SLOVAKIA
Debut 07/02/07 v Poland (n, Jerez, friendly), drew 2-2
First goal 13/10/07 v San Marino (h, Dubnica, ECQ), won 7-0
Caps 91 **Goals** 19
Major tournaments FIFA World Cup 2010; UEFA EURO 2016

Club career

Major honours Italian Cup (2012, 2014)
Clubs 04 ŠK Slovan Bratislava; 04-07 Brescia Calcio (ITA); 07- SSC Napoli (ITA)

2015/16 appearances/goals

Domestic league Italian Serie A 38/6
Europe UEFA Europa League 5(1)/2
National team UEFA EURO 2016 finals 4/1; UEFA EURO 2016 qualifying 4/2; Friendlies 5/1

Gonzalo Higuaín

Striker, Height 184cm
Born 10/12/87, Brest, France

Italian football had a new record-breaker in 2015/16 as Higuaín scored 36 goals for Napoli to set a new all-time Serie A high. It was not just the record itself that made Higuaín's feat so special but the way that he achieved it, scoring a hat-trick on the final day in a match Napoli had to win to secure the runners-up spot and completing it with one of the goals of the Serie A season – a magnificent chest-and-volley strike into the roof of the net with several Frosinone defenders gathered around him. To the immense sorrow of the locals, that would be his final act in a Napoli shirt as he departed for champions Juventus in July.

International career

ARGENTINA
Debut 10/10/09 v Peru (h, Buenos Aires, WCQ), won 2-1
First goal 10/10/09 v Peru (h, Buenos Aires, WCQ), won 2-1
Caps 63 **Goals** 30
Major tournaments FIFA World Cup 2010; Copa América 2011; FIFA World Cup 2014; Copa América 2015; Copa América 2016

Club career

Major honours Spanish League (2007, 2008, 2012); Spanish Cup (2011); Italian Cup (2014)
Clubs 04-06 CA River Plate; 07-13 Real Madrid CF (ESP); 13-16 SSC Napoli (ITA); 16- Juventus FC (ITA)

2015/16 appearances/goals

Domestic league Italian Serie A 35/36
Europe UEFA Europa League 2(3)/2
National team FIFA World Cup 2018 qualifying 3(1)/-; Copa América 2016 6/4; Friendlies 1/1

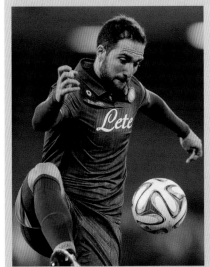

Hulk

Winger/Striker, Height 180cm
Born 25/07/86, Campina Grande, Brazil

Hulk did all he could to help Zenit retain the Premier-Liga title in 2015/16, scoring 17 goals and thrilling the St Petersburg locals with his fabulous strength, speed and ferocious left-footed shooting. Ultimately, though, he and his team had to make do with third place and victory in the Russian Cup. The barrel-chested Brazilian scored two penalties in the final – a 4-1 win over champions CSKA Moskva – and was also prominent for the club as they charged through the group stage of the UEFA Champions League, but 2015/16 would be his final season in Russia as in June he signed a lucrative deal to join Chinese Super League side Shangai SIPG.

International career

BRAZIL
Major honours FIFA Confederations Cup (2013)
Debut 14/11/09 v England (n, Doha, friendly), won 1-0
First goal 26/05/12 v Denmark (n, Hamburg, friendly), won 3-1
Caps 48 **Goals** 11
Major tournaments FIFA Confederations Cup 2013; FIFA World Cup 2014; Copa América 2016

Club career

Major honours UEFA Europa League (2011); Portuguese League (2009, 2011, 2012); Russian League (2015); Portuguese Cup (2009, 2010, 2011); Russian Cup (2016)
Clubs 04 SC Vitória; 05-08 Kawasaki Frontale (JPN); 06 Consadole Sapporo (JPN) (loan); 07 Tokyo Verdy (JPN) (loan); 08 Tokyo Verdy (JPN); 08-12 FC Porto (POR); 12-16 FC Zenit (RUS); 16- Shanghai SIPG FC (CHN)

2015/16 appearances/goals

Domestic league Russian Premier-Liga 26(1)/17
Europe UEFA Champions League 7/4
National team FIFA World Cup 2018 qualifying 1(2)/-; Copa América 2016 (1)/-; Friendlies 2(1)/2

Mats Hummels

Centre-back, Height 192cm
Born 16/12/88, Bergisch Gladbach, Germany

One of the world's most elegant and dependable central defenders, Hummels was as good as ever in 2015/16, but his ninth season with Borussia Dortmund turned out to be his last. Even before his club faced Bayern München in the German Cup final – a game in which he was injured and substituted – it was announced that he would be leaving for Bayern, the club where he began his career. Sidelined for Germany's opener at UEFA EURO 2016, he started the next four matches, but in winning his 50th cap against Italy he picked up a yellow card that suspended him for the semi-final against France, in which his calming presence was sorely missed.

International career

GERMANY
Major honours FIFA World Cup (2014)
Debut 13/05/10 v Malta (h, Aachen, friendly), won 3-0
First goal 26/05/12 v Switzerland (a, Basel, friendly), lost 3-5
Caps 50 **Goals** 4
Major tournaments UEFA EURO 2012; FIFA World Cup 2014; UEFA EURO 2016

Club career

Major honours German League (2011, 2012); German Cup (2012)
Clubs 07-09 FC Bayern München; 08-09 Borussia Dortmund (loan); 09-16 Borussia Dortmund; 16- FC Bayern München

2015/16 appearances/goals

Domestic league German Bundesliga 29(1)/2
Europe UEFA Europa League 10/1; UEFA Europa League qualifying/play-offs 4/-
National team UEFA EURO 2016 finals 4/-; UEFA EURO 2016 qualifying 4/-; Friendlies 3/-

Elseid Hysaj

Right-back, Height 182cm
Born 20/02/94, Rec, Albania

Having starred in his debut Serie A campaign for Empoli in 2014/15, Hysaj followed his coach Maurizio Sarri to Napoli, and the young Albanian international played even better for his new club in 2015/16, making the right-back berth his own and finding his way into most Serie A pundits' composite team of the season. Eagerly anticipated at UEFA EURO 2016, where Albania were making their international tournament debut, he did not let anyone down, his accurate passing and crossing from the right proving to be one of the team's most productive attacking outlets – even if he could not help the team progress beyond the opening round.

International career

ALBANIA
Debut 06/02/13 v Georgia (h, Tirana, friendly), lost 1-2
Caps 22 **Goals** 0
Major tournaments UEFA EURO 2016

Club career

Clubs 12-15 Empoli FC (ITA); 15- SSC Napoli (ITA)

2015/16 appearances/goals

Domestic league Italian Serie A 37/-
Europe UEFA Europa League 3(2)/-
National team UEFA EURO 2016 finals 3/-; UEFA EURO 2016 qualifying 2/-; Friendlies 3/-

Zlatan Ibrahimović

Striker, Height 192cm
Born 03/10/81, Malmo, Sweden

A career full of extravagant highs peaked for Ibrahimović at the age of 34 with a wonderful 2015/16 season for Paris Saint-Germain. The Swedish superstar played 51 games and scored 50 goals, becoming the club's all-time top marksman in the process. His 38 in Ligue 1 constituted a club record, and he also signed off in style with a double in the Coupe de France final, helping to complete the club's second successive domestic clean sweep. He retired from international duty after a lacklustre UEFA EURO 2016 with Sweden, but his decision to pursue his club career at Manchester United guarantees that his name will be up in lights a little while longer.

International career

SWEDEN
Debut 31/01/01 v Faroe Islands (h, Vaxjo, friendly), drew 0-0
First goal 07/10/01 v Azerbaijan (h, Solna, WCQ), won 3-0
Caps 116 **Goals** 62
Major tournaments FIFA World Cup 2002; UEFA EURO 2004; FIFA World Cup 2006; UEFA EURO 2008; UEFA EURO 2012; UEFA EURO 2016

Club career

Major honours UEFA Super Cup (2009); FIFA Club World Cup (2009); Dutch League (2002, 2004); Italian League (2007, 2008, 2009, 2011); Spanish League (2010); French League (2013, 2014, 2015, 2016); Dutch Cup (2002); French Cup (2015, 2016); French League Cup (2014, 2015, 2016)
Clubs 99-01 Malmö FF; 01-04 AFC Ajax (NED); 04-06 Juventus FC (ITA); 06-09 FC Internazionale Milano (ITA); 09-11 FC Barcelona (ESP); 10-11 AC Milan (ITA) (loan); 11-12 AC Milan (ITA); 12-16 Paris Saint-Germain (FRA); 16- Manchester United FC (ENG)

2015/16 appearances/goals

Domestic league French Ligue 1 29(2)/38
Europe UEFA Champions League 10/5
National team UEFA EURO 2016 finals 3/-; UEFA EURO 2016 qualifying 6/6; Friendlies 2/-

Josip Iličič

Attacking midfielder, Height 190cm
Born 29/01/88, Prijedor, Bosnia & Herzegovina

Iličič's third season with Fiorentina was his best yet. An influential figure in Paulo Sousa's Viola side that raced to the top of the Serie A table at the start of the campaign, the tall, skilful Slovenian international playmaker maintained his form for its duration, ending up with 13 league goals as his team finished fifth to re-qualify for the UEFA Europa League. A free-kick and penalty specialist, he scored one double during the season and that came in a 3-1 win at former club Palermo, whose fans sportingly acknowledged his feat with a round of applause. The 28-year-old played in all ten of Slovenia's internationals in 2015/16.

International career

SLOVENIA
Debut 11/08/10 v Australia (h, Ljubljana, friendly), won 2-0
First goal 10/09/13 v Cyprus (a, Nicosia, WCQ), won 2-0
Caps 39 **Goals** 2

Club career

Clubs 07-08 SC Bonifika; 08-10 NK IB Ljubljana; 10 NK Maribor; 10-13 US Città di Palermo (ITA); 13- ACF Fiorentina (ITA)

2015/16 appearances/goals

Domestic league Italian Serie A 24(6)/13
Europe UEFA Europa League 5(1)/2
National team UEFA EURO 2016 qualifying 5(1)/-; Friendlies 4/-

Andrés Iniesta

Midfielder, Height 170cm
Born 11/05/84, Fuentealbilla, Spain

Spain's most popular footballer of recent times added four more winner's medals to his bulging treasure chest as he skippered Barcelona to victories in the UEFA Super Cup, FIFA Club World Cup, Spanish Liga and Copa del Rey. Iniesta scored just one goal in all those competitions but it was a rather special one, in a 4-0 league victory over Real Madrid at the Santiago Bernabéu, and led to the home fans doing what they had only ever done to two previous Barça players – Diego Maradona and Ronaldinho – and applauding him from the field. The 32-year-old schemer was equally impressive in Spain's opening two matches of UEFA EURO 2016.

International career

SPAIN
Major honours FIFA World Cup (2010); UEFA European Championship (2008, 2012)
Debut 27/05/06 v Russia (h, Albacete, friendly), drew 0-0
First goal 07/02/07 v England (a, Manchester, friendly), won 1-0
Caps 113 **Goals** 12
Major tournaments FIFA World Cup 2006; UEFA EURO 2008; FIFA World Cup 2010; UEFA EURO 2012; FIFA Confederations Cup 2013; FIFA World Cup 2014; UEFA EURO 2016

Club career

Major honours UEFA Champions League (2006, 2009, 2011, 2015); UEFA Super Cup (2009, 2011, 2015); FIFA Club World Cup (2009, 2011, 2015); Spanish League (2005, 2006, 2009, 2010, 2011, 2013, 2015, 2016); Spanish Cup (2009, 2012, 2015, 2016)
Clubs 00- FC Barcelona

2015/16 appearances/goals

Domestic league Spanish Liga 25(3)/1
Europe UEFA Champions League 7/-
National team UEFA EURO 2016 finals 4/-; UEFA EURO 2016 qualifying 1(1)/1; Friendlies 2(1)/-

Vincent Janssen

Striker, Height 180cm
Born 15/06/94, Heesch, Netherlands

With their failure to qualify for UEFA EURO 2016 still fresh in the memory, the Netherlands went into a series of spring friendlies in need of a pick-me-up. They got it from the man who had taken the Eredivisie by storm in his debut season at that level, eventually topping the golden boot standings with 27 goals for AZ Alkmaar and also winning the Johan Cruyff trophy as the country's young player of the year. Janssen scored the opening goal in three successive Oranje wins, away to England, Poland and Austria, and can expect more call-ups from Bondscoach Danny Blind following his €20m summer move to Tottenham.

International career

NETHERLANDS
Debut 25/03/16 v France (h, Amsterdam, friendly), lost 2-3
First goal 29/03/16 v England (a, London, friendly), won 2-1
Caps 5 **Goals** 3

Club career

Clubs 13-15 Almere City; 15-16 AZ Alkmaar; 16- Tottenham Hotspur FC (ENG)

2015/16 appearances/goals

Domestic league Dutch Eredivisie 32(2)/27
Europe UEFA Europa League 6/1; UEFA Europa League qualifying/play-offs 4/2
National team Friendlies 4(1)/3

João Mário

Midfielder, Height 177cm
Born 19/01/93, Porto, Portugal

A frustrated runner-up with Portugal at the 2015 UEFA European Under-21 Championship, João Mário became a winner with his country a year later at UEFA EURO 2016. Handed the prestigious No10 shirt by coach Fernando Santos, he played in all seven games – six from the start – of Portugal's history-making triumph in France, his dogged midfield work and tireless running proving crucial in an outstanding team effort. The 23-year-old travelled to the tournament encouraged by an excellent season in the Portuguese Primeira Liga, in which he furthered his reputation with some memorable displays for Jorge Jesus's Sporting side.

International career

PORTUGAL
Major honours UEFA European Championship (2016)
Debut 11/10/14 v France (a, Saint-Denis, friendly), lost 1-2
Caps 18 **Goals** 0
Major tournaments UEFA EURO 2016

Club career

Major honours Portuguese Cup (2015)
Clubs 11- Sporting Clube de Portugal; 14 Vitória FC (loan)

2015/16 appearances/goals

Domestic league Portuguese Liga 31(2)/6
Europe UEFA Champions League play-offs 2/-; UEFA Europa League 4(1)/1
National team UEFA EURO 2016 finals 6(1)/-; Friendlies 7(1)/-

Jonas

Striker, Height 181cm
Born 01/01/84, Sao Paulo, Brazil

Lisbon rivals Benfica and Sporting enjoyed a terrific ding-dong battle for the 2015/16 Portuguese league title, but although it was his strike partner Kostas Mitroglou who scored the crucial winning goal at the Estádio José Alvalade that effectively gave Benfica the title, the 32-goal contribution of Brazilian striker Jonas was arguably the decisive factor in the Eagles' triumph over the season as a whole. It earned him a second successive player of the year crown as well as the Primeira Liga's top scorer prize. A call-up by Brazil for the Copa América was further reward for the 32-year-old at the end of an exceptional club campaign.

International career

BRAZIL
Debut 27/03/11 v Scotland (n, London, friendly), won 2-0
First goal 14/11/11 v Egypt (n, Al-Rayyan, friendly), won 2-0
Caps 12 **Goals** 3
Major tournaments Copa América 2016

Club career

Major honours Portuguese League (2015, 2016)
Clubs 05-06 Guarani FC; 06-07 Santos FC; 07-11 Grêmio FBPA; 08-09 Portuguesa (loan); 11-14 Valencia CF (ESP); 14- SL Benfica (POR)

2015/16 appearances/goals

Domestic league Portuguese Liga 33(1)/32
Europe UEFA Champions League 9/2
National team FIFA World Cup 2018 qualifying (1)/-; Copa América 2016 2/-; Friendlies 1/1

Juanfran

Right-back, Height 180cm
Born 09/01/85, Crevillent, Spain

Atlético Madrid ended the 2015/16 season empty-handed but they enthralled partisans and neutrals alike with their UEFA Champions League exploits. Right-back Juanfran was one of the most consistently impressive performers in Diego Simeone's side, both as a defender and in attack with his link-up play and measured crosses, one of which, on the volley, set up Yannick Carrasco's equaliser in the final against Real Madrid. It was rough justice on the 31-year-old Spanish international that his should be the only penalty missed in the shoot-out, especially as he had struck Atlético's decisive spot kick in an earlier penalty triumph against PSV Eindhoven.

International career

SPAIN
Major honours UEFA European Championship (2012)
Debut 26/05/12 v Serbia (n, St Gallen, friendly), won 2-0
First goal 16/11/13 v Equatorial Guinea (a, Malabo, friendly), won 2-1
Caps 22 **Goals** 1
Major tournaments UEFA EURO 2012; FIFA World Cup 2014; UEFA EURO 2016

Club career

Major honours UEFA Europa League (2012); UEFA Super Cup (2012); Spanish League (2014); Spanish Cup (2006, 2013)
Clubs 04-06 Real Madrid CF; 05-06 RCD Espanyol (loan); 06-11 CA Osasuna; 11- Club Atlético de Madrid

2015/16 appearances/goals

Domestic league Spanish Liga 34/1
Europe UEFA Champions League 12/-
National team UEFA EURO 2016 finals 4/-; UEFA EURO 2016 qualifying 2/-; Friendlies 2/-

Harry Kane

Striker, Height 188cm
Born 28/07/93, London, England

When Kane made a slow start to the 2015/16 Premier League campaign, failing to score in Tottenham's first six matches, the new England striker was belittled in some quarters as a one-season wonder. He proved to be anything but, a hat-trick at Bournemouth sparking him into life and offering a prelude to another prolific campaign in which he went on to score 25 times and win the golden boot. Goals in both games against Arsenal were particularly special, as were those he struck for his country against Switzerland and Germany. At UEFA EURO 2016, however, he looked exhausted and offered precious little in England's attack.

International career

ENGLAND
Debut 27/03/15 v Lithuania (h, London, ECQ), won 4-0
First goal 27/03/15 v Lithuania (h, London, ECQ), won 4-0
Caps 16 **Goals** 5
Major tournaments UEFA EURO 2016

Club career

Clubs 09- Tottenham Hotspur FC; 11 Leyton Orient FC (loan); 12 Millwall FC (loan); 12-13 Norwich City FC (loan); 13 Leicester City FC (loan)

2015/16 appearances/goals

Domestic league English Premier League 38/25
Europe UEFA Europa League 3(4)/2
National team UEFA EURO 2016 finals 3(1)/-;
UEFA EURO 2016 qualifying 2(2)/2;
Friendlies 5(1)/2

N'Golo Kanté

Midfielder, Height 169cm
Born 29/03/91, Paris, France

Leicester City's scouting team unearthed a gem when they bought Kanté from French club Caen. The diminutive midfielder was the heartbeat of Claudio Ranieri's Premier League-winning side, his ability to break up the play with finely-judged tackles and timely interceptions supplemented by an alertness and speed off the mark that enabled him to catch the opposition off guard and launch dangerous counterattacks. A call to international football was inevitable, and his first eight games for France all ended in victory, which begged the question why Didier Deschamps left the Chelsea-bound 25-year-old on the bench for the UEFA EURO 2016 final.

International career

FRANCE
Debut 25/03/16 v Netherlands (a, Amsterdam, friendly), won 3-2
First goal 29/03/16 v Russia (h, Saint-Denis, friendly), won 4-2
Caps 8 **Goals** 1
Major tournaments UEFA EURO 2016

Club career

Major honours *English League (2016)*
Clubs 11-13 US Boulogne; 13-15 SM Caen; 15-16 Leicester City FC (ENG); 16- Chelsea FC (ENG)

2015/16 appearances/goals

Domestic league English Premier League 33(4)/1
National team UEFA EURO 2016 finals 3(1)/-;
Friendlies 2(2)/1

Davy Klaassen

Attacking midfielder, Height 185cm
Born 22/02/93, Hilversum, Netherlands

An Ajax player since the age of 11, Klaassen has the famous Amsterdam club in his blood, so it was particularly galling for him when, at the end of his third season as a regular first-teamer and his first as club captain, the team blew their big chance of regaining the Dutch Eredivisie title from PSV Eindhoven with an unlikely last-day 1-1 draw at De Graafschap. Before that game the season had gone almost perfectly for the Ajax No10. He scored 13 league goals, skippered the team with authority, and had his efforts recognised with the Eredivisie player of the year award – two years after he had scooped the young player prize.

International career

NETHERLANDS
Debut 05/03/14 v France (a, Saint-Denis, friendly), lost 0-2
First goal 31/03/15 v Spain (h, Amsterdam, friendly), won 2-0
Caps 5 **Goals** 1

Club career

Major honours *Dutch League (2012, 2013, 2014)*
Clubs 11- AFC Ajax

2015/16 appearances/goals

Domestic league Dutch Eredivisie 30(1)/13
Europe UEFA Champions League qualifying 2/2; UEFA Europa League 6/-; UEFA Europa League play-offs 2/-
National team UEFA EURO 2016 qualifying 2/-; Friendlies 1/-

Koke

Midfielder, Height 178cm
Born 08/01/92, Madrid, Spain

Only two players set up more goals in the 2015/16 Spanish Liga than Koke. Barcelona duo Lionel Messi and Luis Suárez both added 16 assists to their multitude of goals, leaving the Atlético Madrid stalwart in third place with 14 – two more than another Barça striker, Neymar, and one more than Real Madrid's Cristiano Ronaldo. It was impressive company to be keeping, but the 24-year-old Spanish international has become something of a superstar in his own right – certainly to his adoring public at the Vicente Calderón – and in his sixth season as an Atleti regular, which culminated in a second UEFA Champions League final appearance, the figures backed him up.

International career

SPAIN
Debut 14/08/13 v Ecuador (a, Guayaquil, friendly), won 2-0
Caps 24 **Goals** 0
Major tournaments FIFA World Cup 2014; UEFA EURO 2016

Club career

Major honours UEFA Europa League (2012); UEFA Super Cup (2010, 2012); Spanish League (2014); Spanish Cup (2013)
Clubs 09- Club Atlético de Madrid

2015/16 appearances/goals

Domestic league Spanish Liga 34(1)/5
Europe UEFA Champions League 11/-
National team UEFA EURO 2016 finals (1)/-; UEFA EURO 2016 qualifying (2)/-; Friendlies 1(3)/-

Toni Kroos

Midfielder, Height 182cm
Born 04/01/90, Greifswald, Germany

Kroos became the 13th player to win the UEFA Champions League with more than one club, but having missed Bayern München's 2013 final victory at Wembley through injury, it was a particular pleasure for the 26-year-old German playmaker to claim the trophy again with Real Madrid – this time as an on-field participant in the game that mattered most, against Atlético Madrid in Milan. Stimulated by that victory, he went on to star for Germany at UEFA EURO 2016 as the world champions' elegant, unflustered orchestrator-in-chief, starting and finishing all six matches and barely putting a foot wrong in any of them.

International career

GERMANY
Major honours FIFA World Cup (2014)
Debut 03/03/10 v Argentina (h, Munich, friendly), lost 0-1
First goal 06/09/11 v Poland (a, Gdansk, friendly), drew 2-2
Caps 71 **Goals** 11
Major tournaments FIFA World Cup 2010; UEFA EURO 2012; FIFA World Cup 2014; UEFA EURO 2016

Club career

Major honours UEFA Champions League (2013, 2016); UEFA Super Cup (2013, 2014); FIFA Club World Cup (2013, 2014); German League (2008, 2013, 2014); German Cup (2008, 2013, 2014)
Clubs 07-14 FC Bayern München; 09-10 Bayer 04 Leverkusen (loan); 14- Real Madrid CF (ESP)

2015/16 appearances/goals

Domestic league Spanish Liga 32/1
Europe UEFA Champions League 11(1)/-
National team UEFA EURO 2016 finals 6/-; UEFA EURO 2016 qualifying 4/-; Friendlies 3/2

Grzegorz Krychowiak

Midfielder, Height 186cm
Born 29/01/90, Gryfice, Poland

A busy and productive 2015/16 season brought Krychowiak a second successive UEFA Europa League triumph with Sevilla and a first tournament appearance for Poland, at UEFA EURO 2016, where he was one of his country's most enterprising performers. His winning penalty in the last-16 shoot-out success against Switzerland was an obvious highlight, but the 26-year-old impressed throughout with his combination of industry and flair and was needed for all 510 minutes of Poland's campaign. Shortly after the tournament he followed Sevilla coach Unai Emery to Paris Saint-Germain, signing a five-year deal with the French champions.

International career

POLAND
Debut 14/12/08 v Serbia (n, Antalya, friendly), won 1-0
First goal 14/11/14 v Georgia (a, Tbilisi, ECQ), won 4-0
Caps 39 **Goals** 2
Major tournaments UEFA EURO 2016

Club career

Major honours UEFA Europa League (2015, 2016)
Clubs 08-12 FC Girondins de Bordeaux (FRA); 09-11 Stade de Reims (FRA) (loan); 11-12 FC Nantes (FRA) (loan); 12-14 Stade de Reims (FRA); 14-16 Sevilla FC (ESP); 16- Paris Saint-Germain (FRA)

2015/16 appearances/goals

Domestic league Spanish Liga 25(1)/-
Europe UEFA Champions League 6/-; UEFA Europa League 5(1)/-
National team UEFA EURO 2016 finals 5/-; UEFA EURO 2016 qualifying 4/1; Friendlies 4/-

Philipp Lahm

Full-back, Height 170cm
Born 11/11/83, Munich, Germany

Having quit the international game at 30 after captaining Germany to their 2014 FIFA World Cup triumph in Brazil, Lahm decided to devote himself exclusively to Bayern München, and the benefits to player and club – if not country – continued in 2015/16 as he won the sixth Bundesliga/DFB-Pokal double of his career. It was his second as club captain and, as ever, he was one of Bayern's most dependable performers. He was also active for every minute of Bayern's UEFA Champions League campaign, in the process overtaking Oliver Kahn as the German with the most appearances in the competition as he raised his all-time total to 105.

International career

GERMANY
Major honours FIFA World Cup (2014)
Debut 18/02/04 v Croatia (a, Split, friendly), won 2-1
First goal 28/04/04 v Romania (a, Bucharest, friendly), lost 1-5
Caps 113 **Goals** 5
Major tournaments UEFA EURO 2004; FIFA World Cup 2006; UEFA EURO 2008; FIFA World Cup 2010; UEFA EURO 2012; FIFA World Cup 2014

Club career

Major honours UEFA Champions League (2013); UEFA Super Cup (2013); FIFA Club World Cup (2013); German League (2006, 2008, 2010, 2013, 2014, 2015, 2016); German Cup (2006, 2008, 2010, 2013, 2014, 2016)
Clubs; 02- FC Bayern München; 03-05 VfB Stuttgart (loan)

2015/16 appearances/goals

Domestic league German Bundesliga 25(1)/1
Europe UEFA Champions League 12/-

Robert Lewandowski

Striker, Height 184cm
Born 21/08/88, Warsaw, Poland

Not since Dieter Müller scored 34 goals for Köln in 1976/77 had the 30-goal barrier been broken in a Bundesliga campaign, but Lewandowski finally managed it in 2015/16. Already a Bundesliga top scorer two seasons earlier with 20 goals for Borussia Dortmund, the Bayern München No9 reaffirmed his status as one of the world's deadliest marksmen – not just domestically but also in the UEFA Champions League, where he struck nine times. The 13-goal top scorer in UEFA EURO 2016 qualifying added just one more for Poland at the finals, but he was the only player to find the net in the knockout phase against eventual winners Portugal.

International career

POLAND
Debut 10/09/08 v San Marino (a, Serravalle, WCQ), won 2-0
First goal 10/09/08 v San Marino (a, Serravalle, WCQ), won 2-0
Caps 81 **Goals** 35
Major tournaments UEFA EURO 2012; UEFA EURO 2016

Club career

Major honours Polish League (2010); German League (2011, 2012, 2015, 2016); Polish Cup (2009); German Cup (2012, 2016)
Clubs 06-08 Znicz Pruszków; 08-10 KKS Lech Poznań; 10-14 Borussia Dortmund (GER); 14- FC Bayern München (GER)

2015/16 appearances/goals

Domestic league German Bundesliga 29(3)/30
Europe UEFA Champions League 11(1)/9
National team UEFA EURO 2016 finals 5/1; UEFA EURO 2016 qualifying 4/6; Friendlies 3(1)/2

Hugo Lloris

Goalkeeper, Height 188cm
Born 26/12/86, Nice, France

The dream of lifting the Henri Delaunay Cup at the Stade de France did not come true for Lloris, but the goalkeeper-captain of the UEFA EURO 2016 hosts had a starring role in Les Bleus' passage to the final, not least in the 2-0 semi-final win over Germany. During the tournament the 29-year-old overtook his coach Didier Deschamps as the French international with most appearances as captain, raising that total to 58 in the final. Appointed as the permanent skipper of Tottenham Hotspur at the start of the 2015/16 campaign, he missed just one league game en route to helping the team qualify for the UEFA Champions League.

International career

FRANCE
Debut 19/11/08 v Uruguay (h, Saint-Denis, friendly), drew 0-0
Caps 82 **Goals** 0
Major tournaments FIFA World Cup 2010; UEFA EURO 2012; FIFA World Cup 2014; UEFA EURO 2016

Club career

Major honours French Cup (2012)
Clubs 05-08 OGC Nice; 08-12 Olympique Lyonnais; 12- Tottenham Hotspur FC (ENG)

2015/16 appearances/goals

Domestic league English Premier League 37/-
Europe UEFA Europa League 9/-
National team UEFA EURO 2016 finals 7/-; Friendlies 8/-

Riyad Mahrez

Winger, Height 178cm
Born 21/02/91, Sarcelles, France

Mahrez became the first African player to win the PFA Player of the Year award in England, topping the poll thanks to a season of unremitting brilliance in the Premier League for champions Leicester City. Graceful, elusive and capable of extraordinary feats of skill with his precious jewel of a left foot, the 25-year-old Algerian had defences rocking and reeling all season long, scoring 17 goals and setting up another 11 as Leicester wrote one of the most uplifting chapters in the history of English football. If the highlight of his season was a hat-trick at Swansea, majestic strikes against Tottenham, Chelsea and Manchester City were not far behind.

International career

ALGERIA
Debut 31/05/14 v Armenia (n, Sion, friendly), won 3-1
First goal 15/10/14 v Malawi (h, Blida, ANQ), won 3-0
Caps 24 **Goals** 4
Major tournaments FIFA World Cup 2014; Africa Cup of Nations 2015

Club career

Major honours English League (2016)
Clubs 09-10 Quimper KFC (FRA); 10-14 Le Havre AC (FRA); 14- Leicester City FC (ENG)

2015/16 appearances/goals

Domestic league English Premier League 36(1)/17
National team Africa Cup of Nations 2017 qualifying 3/-; FIFA World Cup 2018 qualifying 2/1; Friendlies 2/-

Blaise Matuidi

Midfielder, Height 175cm
Born 09/04/87, Toulouse, France

To the casual observer his work may go unnoticed, but Matuidi is a coach's dream, a player who never stops working or running and invariably makes the right choice when the ball is at his feet. The 29-year-old midfielder had another effective season for club and country in 2015/16, helping Paris Saint-Germain to a second successive domestic clean sweep, for which he was recognised with a place in the Ligue 1 team of the season. He then played in all of France's seven matches at UEFA EURO 2016, including every one of the four knockout games from first whistle to last, collecting his 50th cap in the semi-final against Germany.

International career

FRANCE
Debut 07/09/10 v Bosnia & Herzegovina (a, Sarajevo, ECQ), won 2-0
First goal 05/03/14 v Netherlands (h, Saint-Denis, friendly), won 2-0
Caps 51 **Goals** 8
Major tournaments UEFA EURO 2012; FIFA World Cup 2014; UEFA EURO 2016

Club career

Major honours French League (2013, 2014, 2015, 2016); French Cup (2015, 2016); French League Cup (2014, 2015, 2016)
Clubs 04-07 ES Troyes AC; 07-11 AS Saint-Étienne; 11- Paris Saint-Germain

2015/16 appearances/goals

Domestic league French Ligue 1 23(7)/4
Europe UEFA Champions League 9/-
National team UEFA EURO 2016 finals 6(1)/-; Friendlies 9/4

Lionel Messi

Striker, Height 170cm
Born 24/06/87, Rosario, Argentina

Despite missing two months of the season with medial ligament damage to his left knee, Messi still notched up 41 goals and 23 assists for Barcelona while adding four more major honours to an already lengthy list. In January he collected the FIFA Ballon d'Or – the fifth time he had officially been named as the world's best player – and he also reached several personal milestones during the season, including a 500th career goal. There would be no first trophy for Argentina, however, as a second successive Copa América final defeat to Chile on penalties prompted the team's inconsolable skipper to announce his shock international retirement at just 29.

International career

ARGENTINA
Debut 17/08/05 v Hungary (a, Budapest, friendly), won 2-1
First goal 01/03/06 v Croatia (n, Basel, friendly), lost 2-3
Caps 113 **Goals** 55
Major tournaments FIFA World Cup 2006; Copa América 2007; FIFA World Cup 2010; Copa América 2011; FIFA World Cup 2014; Copa América 2015; Copa América 2016

Club career

Major honours UEFA Champions League (2006, 2009, 2011, 2015); UEFA Super Cup (2009, 2011, 2015); FIFA Club World Cup (2009, 2011, 2015); Spanish League (2005, 2006, 2009, 2010, 2011, 2013, 2015, 2016); Spanish Cup (2009, 2012, 2015, 2016)
Clubs 04- FC Barcelona (ESP)

2015/16 appearances/goals

Domestic league Spanish Liga 31(2)/26
Europe UEFA Champions League 7/6
National team FIFA World Cup 2018 qualifying 2/1; Copa América 2016 3(2)/5; Friendlies 2(1)/3

Henrikh Mkhitaryan

Attacking midfielder, Height 178cm
Born 21/01/89, Yerevan, Armenia

Armenian national team captain Mkhitaryan followed a frustrating, injury-curtailed second season at Borussia Dortmund with a brilliant third, at the end of which he was voted by his fellow players as the Bundesliga's player of the year. He also topped the league's assists chart with 15, supplementing those with 11 goals of his own, and was a star performer too for Thomas Tuchel's side in their run to the German Cup final and the last eight of the UEFA Europa League. Quick, beautifully balanced and a sharp finisher, he has now taken those qualities to England following a Dortmund club-record €42m transfer to Manchester United.

International career

ARMENIA
Debut 14/01/07 v Panama (n, Los Angeles, friendly), drew 1-1
First goal 28/03/09 v Estonia (h, Yerevan, WCQ), drew 2-2
Caps 59 **Goals** 19

Club career

Major honours Armenian League (2006, 2007, 2008, 2009); Ukrainian League (2011, 2012, 2013); Armenian Cup (2009); Ukrainian Cup (2011, 2012, 2013)
Clubs 06-09 FC Pyunik; 09-10 FC Metalurh Donetsk (UKR); 10-13 FC Shakhtar Donetsk (UKR); 13-16 Borussia Dortmund (GER); 16- Manchester United (ENG)

2015/16 appearances/goals

Domestic league German Bundesliga 28(3)/11
Europe UEFA Europa League 10(1)/2; UEFA Europa League qualifying/play-offs 4/5
National team UEFA EURO 2016 qualifying 3/-; Friendlies 4/3

Luka Modrić

Midfielder, Height 174cm
Born 09/09/85, Zadar, Croatia

There was no first Spanish Liga triumph for Modrić in 2015/16 as Real Madrid were beaten to the title on the final day by Barcelona, but the club's second UEFA Champions League victory in three seasons was more than ample compensation. As in 2013/14, the little Croatian schemer had a big role to play in Madrid's success, his ability to run the game from midfield with both technical prowess and an acute tactical awareness shining through on many occasions. He got off to a great start with Croatia at UEFA EURO 2016, scoring a spectacular winning volley against Turkey, but an injury reduced his effectiveness in the last-16 defeat against Portugal.

International career

CROATIA
Debut 01/03/06 v Argentina (n, Basel, friendly), won 3-2
First goal 16/08/06 v Italy (a, Livorno, friendly), won 2-0
Caps 93 **Goals** 11
Major tournaments FIFA World Cup 2006; UEFA EURO 2008; UEFA EURO 2012; FIFA World Cup 2014; UEFA EURO 2016

Club career

Major honours UEFA Champions League (2014, 2016); UEFA Super Cup (2014); FIFA Club World Cup (2014); Croatian League (2006, 2007, 2008); Croatian Cup (2007, 2008); Spanish Cup (2014)
Clubs 02-08 GNK Dinamo Zagreb; 03-04 HŠK Zrinjski (BIH) (loan); 04-05 NK Inter Zaprešić (loan); 08-12 Tottenham Hotspur FC (ENG); 12- Real Madrid CF (ESP)

2015/16 appearances/goals

Domestic league Spanish Liga 31(1)/2
Europe UEFA Champions League 10(2)/1
National team UEFA EURO 2016 finals 3/1; UEFA EURO 2016 qualifying 3/-; Friendlies 3/-

Álvaro Morata

Striker, Height 187cm
Born 23/10/92, Madrid, Spain

Morata started the 2015/16 season by scoring in a fourth and fifth successive UEFA Champions League game for Juventus, thus matching the legendary Alessandro Del Piero's club record, and ended it by netting the extra-time winner in the Coppa Italia final against AC Milan to complete the Bianconeri's second successive Italian double. As an epilogue the tall 23-year-old striker made his tournament bow for Spain, at UEFA EURO 2016, and left a positive impression, starting every game and scoring three goals – two against Turkey and one against Croatia. After the tournament, he re-signed for former club Real Madrid.

International career

SPAIN
Debut 15/11/14 v Belarus (h, Huelva, ECQ), won 3-0
First goal 27/03/15 v Ukraine (h, Seville, ECQ), won 1-0
Caps 13 **Goals** 6
Major tournaments UEFA EURO 2016

Club career

Major honours UEFA Champions League (2014); Spanish League (2012); Italian League (2015, 2016); Spanish Cup (2011, 2014); Italian Cup (2015, 2016)
Clubs 10-14 Real Madrid CF; 14-16 Juventus FC (ITA); 16- Real Madrid CF

2015/16 appearances/goals

Domestic league Italian Serie A 16(18)/7
Europe UEFA Champions League 6(2)/2
National team UEFA EURO 2016 finals 4/3; UEFA EURO 2016 qualifying 1/-; Friendlies 2(1)/2

Wes Morgan

Centre-back, Height 185cm
Born 21/01/84, Nottingham, England

A busy summer with Jamaica at the Copa América and CONCACAF Gold Cup meant that Morgan missed Leicester City's pre-season, but despite the lack of a break the Foxes captain went on to appear for every minute of the team's stunning Premier League triumph. A colossal figure in central defence alongside former German international Robert Huth, the 32-year-old led by example in every game with important blocks, interceptions and clearing headers. He also scored a couple of vital goals, against Southampton and Manchester United, before savouring the unimaginable thrill of hoisting aloft the Premier League trophy.

International career

JAMAICA
Debut 06/09/13 v Panama (a, Panama City, WCQ), drew 0-0
Caps 27 **Goals** 0
Major tournaments Copa América 2015; CONCACAF Gold Cup 2015; Copa América 2016

Club career

Major honours English League (2016)
Clubs 02-12 Nottingham Forest FC; 03 Kidderminster Harriers FC (loan); 12- Leicester City FC

2015/16 appearances/goals

Domestic league English Premier League 38/2
National team FIFA World Cup 2018 qualifying 4/-; Copa América 2016 2(1)/-

Thomas Müller

Attacking midfielder/Striker, Height 186cm
Born 13/09/89, Weilheim, Germany

The most prolific German goalscorer in the UEFA Champions League, Müller increased his all-time total by eight to 36 in 2015/16. He was equally prolific in the Bundesliga, finding the target 20 times – the highest tally of his career – and also added four more in the DFB-Pokal as Bayern München won the league and cup double for the fourth time during his seven seasons as a first-teamer. Having performed so well for his club, it was a mystery why the 26-year-old seemed so short of confidence at UEFA EURO 2016. Joachim Löw kept him on the field throughout Germany's six matches, yet for the second successive EURO he failed to find the net.

International career

GERMANY
Major honours FIFA World Cup (2014)
Debut 03/03/10 v Argentina (h, Munich, friendly), lost 0-1
First goal 13/06/10 v Australia (n, Durban, WCF), won 4-0
Caps 77 **Goals** 32
Major tournaments FIFA World Cup 2010; UEFA EURO 2012; FIFA World Cup 2014; UEFA EURO 2016

Club career

Major honours UEFA Champions League (2013); UEFA Super Cup (2013); FIFA Club World Cup (2013); German League (2010, 2013, 2014, 2015, 2016); German Cup (2010, 2013, 2014, 2016)
Clubs 08- FC Bayern München

2015/16 appearances/goals

Domestic league German Bundesliga 26(5)/20
Europe UEFA Champions League 9(3)/8
National team UEFA EURO 2016 finals 6/-; UEFA EURO 2016 qualifying 4/4; Friendlies 4/1

Radja Nainggolan

Midfielder, Height 175cm
Born 04/05/88, Antwerp, Belgium

Belgium's first appearance at the UEFA European Championship for 16 years enabled Nainggolan to make his international tournament debut, and the 28-year-old midfielder with the eye-catching hairstyle and tattoos gave his fellow countrymen a couple of moments to treasure with two ferociously struck long-range goals to put Belgium in front against Sweden and Wales. The feisty midfielder went to France on the back of an excellent third season in Italy with Roma, especially the second half under Luciano Spalletti, during which he struck six Serie A goals to help the Giallorossi climb the table all the way up to third place.

International career

BELGIUM
Debut 29/05/09 v Chile (n, Chiba, Kirin Cup), drew 1-1
First goal 05/03/14 v Ivory Coast (h, Brussels, friendly), drew 2-2
Caps 24 **Goals** 6
Major tournaments UEFA EURO 2016

Club career

Clubs 06-10 Piacenza Calcio (ITA); 10 Cagliari Calcio (ITA) (loan); 10-14 Cagliari Calcio (ITA); 14 AS Roma (ITA) (loan); 14- AS Roma (ITA)

2015/16 appearances/goals

Domestic league Italian Serie A 33(2)/6
Europe UEFA Champions League 7/-
National team UEFA EURO 2016 finals 4(1)/2; UEFA EURO 2016 qualifying 4/1; Friendlies 3/-

Nani

Winger/Striker, Height 177cm
Born 17/11/86, Praia, Cape Verde

A frustrating conclusion to an impressive first – and last – season for Nani in Turkey with Fenerbahçe, which brought runners-up spots behind Beşiktaş in the league and Galatasaray in the cup, was offset by Portugal's history-making triumph at UEFA EURO 2016. The 29-year-old winger generally operated up front alongside Cristiano Ronaldo in Fernando Santos's side, and the plan worked well as he scored three goals – against Iceland, Hungary and Wales – to help his country to a first major international tournament success. He also became only the fourth Portugal player to reach 100 caps when he took the field for the last-16 win against Croatia.

International career

PORTUGAL
Major honours UEFA European Championship (2016)
Debut 01/09/06 v Denmark (h, Copenhagen, friendly), lost 2-4
First goal 01/09/06 v Denmark (h, Copenhagen, friendly), lost 2-4
Caps 103 **Goals** 21
Major tournaments UEFA EURO 2008; UEFA EURO 2012; FIFA World Cup 2014; UEFA EURO 2016

Club career

Major honours UEFA Champions League (2008); FIFA Club World Cup (2008); English League (2008, 2009, 2011, 2013); Portuguese Cup (2007, 2015); English League Cup (2009, 2010)
Clubs 05-07 Sporting Clube de Portugal; 07-15 Manchester United FC (ENG); 14-15 Sporting Clube de Portugal (loan); 15-16 Fenerbahçe SK (TUR); 16- Valencia CF (ESP)

2015/16 appearances/goals

Domestic league Turkish Süper Lig 25(3)/8
Europe UEFA Champions League qualifying 2/-; UEFA Europa League 8(1); UEFA Europa League play-offs 2/-
National team UEFA EURO 2016 finals 7/3; UEFA EURO 2016 qualifying 3/1; Friendlies 5(2)/2

Manuel Neuer

Goalkeeper, Height 193cm
Born 27/03/86, Gelsenkirchen, Germany

There was no reason to dispute Neuer's status as the world's No1 goalkeeper after another season of excellence with Bayern München and an outstanding effort for Germany at UEFA EURO 2016. An ever-present in Pep Guardiola's Bundesliga-winning side, the 30-year-old conceded just 17 goals in his 34 games, keeping a record-breaking 21 clean sheets. A penalty shoot-out winner with Bayern against Borussia Dortmund in the DFB-Pokal final, he was at it again for his country a few weeks later as Germany defeated Italy for the first time in a tournament thanks to his spot-kick saves from Leonardo Bonucci and Matteo Darmian.

International career

GERMANY
Major honours FIFA World Cup (2014)
Debut 02/06/09 v United Arab Emirates (a, Dubai, friendly), won 7-2
Caps 71 **Goals** 0
Major tournaments FIFA World Cup 2010; UEFA EURO 2012; FIFA World Cup 2014; UEFA EURO 2016

Club career

Major honours UEFA Champions League (2013); UEFA Super Cup (2013); FIFA Club World Cup (2013); German League (2013, 2014, 2015, 2016); German Cup (2011, 2013, 2014, 2016)
Clubs 05-11 FC Schalke 04; 11- FC Bayern München

2015/16 appearances/goals

Domestic league German Bundesliga 34/-
Europe UEFA Champions League 11/-
National team UEFA EURO 2016 finals 6/-; UEFA EURO 2016 qualifying 4/-; Friendlies 3/-

Neymar

Striker, Height 174cm
Born 05/02/92, Mogi das Cruzes, Brazil

He may have ended the season a long way behind his team-mate Luis Suárez in the Pichichi charts, with 24 goals to the Uruguayan's 40, but at Christmas Neymar was actually leading that contest, having found the net 11 times in a storming seven-match run during October and November while the other member of Barcelona's holy trinity, Lionel Messi, was out injured. The 24-year-old's domestic season closed with a goal in the Copa del Rey final, and he was discharged from international duty at the Copa América in order to be kept fresh for the Rio Olympics as Brazil sought their elusive first men's football gold medal.

International career

BRAZIL
Major honours FIFA Confederations Cup (2013)
Debut 10/08/10 v United States (a, East Rutherford, friendly), won 2-0
First goal 10/08/10 v United States (a, East Rutherford, friendly), won 2-0
Caps 70 **Goals** 46
Major tournaments Copa América 2011; FIFA Confederations Cup 2013; FIFA World Cup 2014; Copa América 2015

Club career

Major honours UEFA Champions League (2015); Copa Libertadores (2011); Recopa Sudamericana (2012); UEFA Super Cup (2015); FIFA Club World Cup (2015); Spanish League (2015, 2016); Brazilian Cup (2010); Spanish Cup (2015, 2016)
Clubs 09-13 Santos FC; 13- FC Barcelona (ESP)

2015/16 appearances/goals

Domestic league Spanish Liga 34/24
Europe UEFA Champions League 9/3
National team FIFA World Cup 2018 qualifying 3/-; Friendlies (2)/2

Nolito

Winger/Striker, Height 175cm
Born 15/10/86, Sanlucar de
Barrameda, Spain

A former FC Barcelona B player under the tutelage of Luis Enrique, Nolito never made the grade for the first team under Pep Guardiola, but the 29-year-old will hope for more game time under the great man at Manchester City following his £13.8m summer move from Celta Vigo. His three seasons in Galicia were all productive, but it was a blistering man-of-the-match display in a 4-1 win over Barça in September 2015, during which he scored one goal and set up two others, that catapulted his career to a new level, making him a regular in the Spanish national side and a starter in all four matches for Vicente del Bosque's side at UEFA EURO 2016.

International career

SPAIN
Debut 18/11/14 v Germany (h, Vigo, friendly), lost 0-1
First goal 29/05/16 v Bosnia & Herzegovina (n, St Gallen, friendly), won 3-1
Caps 13 **Goals** 5
Major tournaments UEFA EURO 2016

Club career

Major honours Spanish League (2011)
Clubs 04-06 Atlético Sanluqueño CF; 06-08 Écija Balompié; 08-11 FC Barcelona B; 10-11 FC Barcelona; 11-13 SL Benfica (POR); 13 Granada CF (loan); 13-16 RC Celta de Vigo; 16- Manchester City FC (ENG)

2015/16 appearances/goals

Domestic league Spanish Liga 27(2)/12
National team UEFA EURO 2016 finals 4/1; UEFA EURO 2016 qualifying 1(1)/-; Friendlies 4(1)/4

Jan Oblak

Goalkeeper, Height 186cm
Born 07/01/93, Skofla Loka, Slovenia

Oblak did not just win the Spanish Liga's coveted Zamora trophy in 2015/16. By playing all 38 games for Atlético Madrid and conceding a mere 18 goals he became only the second goalkeeper in the 86-year-old history of the award to win it by conceding at a rate of less than a goal every two games, matching Francisco Liaño's figures for Deportivo La Coruña in 1993/94. The performances of the 23-year-old Slovenian in the UEFA Champions League were even more impressive as he kept clean sheets in eight of his 13 appearances and also made a vital penalty save from Thomas Müller in the semi-final second leg away to Bayern München.

International career

SLOVENIA
Debut 11/09/12 v Norway (a, Oslo, WCQ), lost 1-2
Caps 8 **Goals** 0

Club career

Major honours Portuguese League (2014); Portuguese Cup (2014)
Clubs 09-10 NK Olimpija Ljubljana; 10-14 SL Benfica (POR); 10 SC Beira Mar (POR) (loan); 11 SC Olhanense (POR) (loan); 11-12 UD Leiria (POR) (loan); 12-13 Rio Ave FC (POR) (loan); 14- Club Atlético de Madrid (ESP)

2015/16 appearances/goals

Domestic league Spanish Liga 38/-
Europe UEFA Champions League 13/-
National team UEFA EURO 2016 qualifying 1/-; Friendlies 2/-

Mesut Özil

Attacking midfielder, Height 182cm
Born 15/10/88, Gelsenkirchen, Germany

Özil was voted Arsenal's player of the season at the end of a 2015/16 campaign in which he set up 19 Premier League goals – a tally of assists surpassed only once before, when another Arsenal star, Thierry Henry, registered 20 in 2002/03. He also scored six goals as the Gunners pipped local rivals Tottenham to the runners-up spot on the final day. UEFA EURO 2016, his fourth tournament with Germany, was a bittersweet experience for the 27-year-old schemer. He played every minute and scored a fine goal in the quarter-final against Italy but also missed two penalties and was a losing EURO semi-finalist for the second time.

International career

GERMANY
Major honours FIFA World Cup (2014)
Debut 11/02/09 v Norway (h, Dusseldorf, friendly), lost 0-1
First goal 05/09/09 v South Africa (h, Leverkusen, friendly), won 2-0
Caps 79 **Goals** 20
Major tournaments FIFA World Cup 2010; UEFA EURO 2012; FIFA World Cup 2014; UEFA EURO 2016

Club career

Major honours Spanish League (2012); German Cup (2009); Spanish Cup (2011); English FA Cup (2014, 2015)
Clubs 06-08 FC Schalke 04; 08-10 SV Werder Bremen; 10-13 Real Madrid CF (ESP); 13- Arsenal FC (ENG)

2015/16 appearances/goals

Domestic league English Premier League 35/6
Europe UEFA Champions League 8/2
National team UEFA EURO 2016 finals 6/1; UEFA EURO 2016 qualifying 4/-; Friendlies 3/-

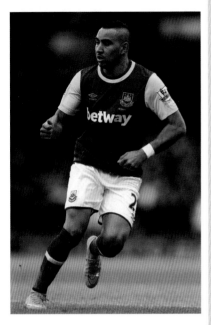

Dimitri Payet

Attacking midfielder, Height 175cm
Born 29/03/87, Saint-Pierre, Reunion

There was an inevitable place in the PFA Premier League Team of the Year for Payet at the end of a season in which he enchanted English football followers, especially those of West Ham United, with his dazzling array of skills. His free-kicks, above all, were something to behold. Those that found the net against Crystal Palace in the Premier League and Manchester United in the FA Cup were things of rare beauty from a true master of the genre. The 29-year-old carried his exquisite club form into UEFA EURO 2016, where he scored three goals for France, the first of them a left-footed screamer to win the opening game against Romania.

International career

FRANCE
Debut 09/10/10 v Romania (h, Saint-Denis, ECQ), won 2-0
First goal 07/06/15 v Belgium (h, Saint-Denis, friendly), lost 3-4
Caps 26 **Goals** 6
Major tournaments UEFA EURO 2016

Club career

Clubs 05-07 FC Nantes; 07-11 AS Saint-Étienne; 11-13 LOSC Lille; 13-15 Olympique de Marseille; 15- West Ham United FC (ENG)

2015/16 appearances/goals

Domestic league English Premier League 29(1)/9
Europe UEFA Europa League qualifying 1/-
National team UEFA EURO 2016 finals 6(1)/3; Friendlies 4(1)/2

Pepe

Centre-back, Height 187cm
Born 26/02/83, Maceio, Brazil

Cristiano Ronaldo was not the only player to achieve a UEFA Champions League/UEFA European Championship double in 2015/16. Pepe, his Real Madrid and Portugal team-mate, also conquered Europe with both club and country, scaling a new career peak at the age of 33. The rugged centre-back did himself no favours with some ill-advised simulation against Atlético Madrid in Milan, but he was at his absolute best in the UEFA EURO 2016 final against France, earning the official Man of the Match award with one of the finest performances of his life – and this after he had missed the semi-final with an injured thigh muscle.

International career

PORTUGAL
Major honours UEFA European Championship (2016)
Debut 21/11/07 v Finland (h, Porto, ECQ), drew 0-0
First goal 07/06/08 v Turkey (n, Geneva, ECF), won 2-0
Caps 77 **Goals** 3
Major tournaments UEFA EURO 2008; FIFA World Cup 2010; UEFA EURO 2012; FIFA World Cup 2014; UEFA EURO 2016

Club career

Major honours UEFA Champions League (2014, 2016); UEFA Super Cup (2014); European/South American Cup (2004); FIFA Club World Cup (2014); Portuguese League (2006, 2007); Spanish League (2008, 2012); Portuguese Cup (2006); Spanish Cup (2011, 2014)
Clubs 01-04 CS Marítimo; 04-07 FC Porto; 07- Real Madrid CF (ESP)

2015/16 appearances/goals

Domestic league Spanish Liga 21/1
Europe UEFA Champions League 8(1)/-
National team UEFA EURO 2016 finals 6/-; UEFA EURO 2016 qualifying 1/-; Friendlies 5/-

Ivan Perišić

Winger/Attacking midfielder, Height 187cm
Born 02/02/89, Split, Croatia

Excellent for Croatia at the 2014 FIFA World Cup, Perišić was again one of his country's star performers at UEFA EURO 2016. His ability to control the ball at speed with either foot is a special quality that the Czech Republic and Spain were unable to withstand as he pierced both defences with quality individual strikes, enabling Ante Čačić's entertaining team to top their group. The 27-year-old also scored the goal that qualified Croatia for France, in a 1-0 win against Malta, and enjoyed a productive debut season in Italy with Internazionale to help the Nerazzurri reach the Coppa Italia semi-finals and finish fourth in Serie A.

International career

CROATIA
Debut 26/03/11 v Georgia (a, Tbilisi, ECQ), lost 0-1
First goal 11/09/12 v Belgium (a, Brussels, WCQ), drew 1-1
Caps 51 **Goals** 15
Major tournaments UEFA EURO 2012; FIFA World Cup 2014; UEFA EURO 2016

Club career

Major honours German League (2012); German Cup (2012, 2015)
Clubs 07-09 FC Sochaux-Montbéliard (FRA); 09 KSV Roeselare (BEL) (loan); 09-11 Club Brugge KV (BEL); 11-13 Borussia Dortmund (GER); 13-15 VfL Wolfsburg (GER); 15- FC Internazionale Milano (ITA)

2015/16 appearances/goals

Domestic league Italian Serie A 26(8)/7
National team UEFA EURO 2016 finals 4/2; UEFA EURO 2016 qualifying 4/2; Friendlies 5/2

Gerard Piqué

Centre-back, Height 190cm
Born 02/02/87, Barcelona, Spain

While the big prizes of the UEFA Champions League and UEFA EURO 2016 eluded him, Piqué was still able to add third victories in the UEFA Super Cup and FIFA Club World Cup to his collection of international winner's medals. The big defender also played a prominent role in helping Barcelona claim a second straight Spanish double, which took his tally of domestic honours in eight seasons at the Camp Nou to six Liga titles and three victories in the Copa del Rey. Always a man for the big occasion, he scored at home to Real Madrid in El Clásico and also got Spain off to a winning start in France with the late winner against the Czech Republic.

International career

SPAIN
Major honours FIFA World Cup (2010); UEFA European Championship (2012)
Debut 11/02/09 v England (h, Seville, friendly), won 2-0
First goal 28/03/09 v Turkey (h, Madrid, WCQ), won 1-0
Caps 81 **Goals** 5
Major tournaments FIFA Confederations Cup 2009; FIFA World Cup 2010; UEFA EURO 2012; FIFA Confederations Cup 2013; FIFA World Cup 2014; UEFA EURO 2016

Club career

Major honours UEFA Champions League (2008, 2009, 2011, 2015); UEFA Super Cup (2009, 2011, 2015); FIFA Club World Cup (2009, 2011, 2015); English League (2008); Spanish League (2009, 2010, 2011, 2013, 2015, 2016); Spanish Cup (2009, 2012, 2015, 2016); English League Cup (2006)
Clubs 04-08 Manchester United FC (ENG); 06-07 Real Zaragoza (loan); 08- FC Barcelona

2015/16 appearances/goals

Domestic league Spanish Liga 30/2
Europe UEFA Champions League 7/1
National team UEFA EURO 2016 finals 4/1; UEFA EURO 2016 qualifying 3/-; Friendlies 5/-

Miralem Pjanić

Midfielder, Height 180cm
Born 02/04/90, Tuzla, Bosnia & Herzegovina

Pjanić's fifth season with Roma featured many memorable moments, most of them from his magnificent free-kicks as the 26-year-old midfielder firmly established himself as one of the game's finest set-piece practitioners. The first of his ten Serie A goals – his highest tally for the Giallorossi in a single campaign – came from a brilliant dead-ball strike in Roma's opening home game, a 2-1 win against Juventus that left Gianluigi Buffon rooted to the spot. Such memories die hard, and the Turin giants were quick to snap up the Bosnia & Herzegovina international at the end of the season, signing him on a five-year contract for a €32m fee.

International career

BOSNIA & HERZEGOVINA
Debut 20/08/08 v Bulgaria (h, Zenica, friendly), lost 1-2
First goal 03/03/10 v Ghana (h, Sarajevo, friendly), won 2-1
Caps 68 **Goals** 11
Major tournaments FIFA World Cup 2014

Club career

Clubs 07-08 FC Metz (FRA); 08-11 Olympique Lyonnais (FRA); 11-16 AS Roma (ITA); 16- Juventus FC (ITA)

2015/16 appearances/goals

Domestic league Italian Serie A 30(3)/10
Europe UEFA Champions League 7/2
National team UEFA EURO 2016 qualifying 6/-; Friendlies 2(1)/2

Paul Pogba

Midfielder, Height 186cm
Born 15/03/93, Lagny-sur-Marne, France

An Italian champion for the fourth time in as many seasons, Pogba was the pivotal figure in the Juventus midfield, the giant 23-year-old commanding the space around him and registering 12 assists – the joint highest figure in the league alongside Roma's Miralem Pjanić – and eight goals. A shirt number switch from six to ten seemed to inspire him as he became a more dynamic contributor to the Juve attack. Much was expected of him at UEFA EURO 2016, but while he undoubtedly had his moments in helping France to reach the final, he was not quite able to impose himself on the tournament to the extent that many had anticipated.

International career

FRANCE
Debut 22/03/13 v Georgia (h, Saint-Denis, WCQ), won 3-1
First goal 10/09/13 v Belarus (a, Gomel, WCQ), won 4-2
Caps 38 **Goals** 6
Major tournaments FIFA World Cup 2014; UEFA EURO 2016

Club career

Major honours Italian League (2013, 2014, 2015, 2016); Italian Cup (2015, 2016)
Clubs 11-12 Manchester United FC (ENG); 12- Juventus FC (ITA)

2015/16 appearances/goals

Domestic league Italian Serie A 33(2)/8
Europe UEFA Champions League 8/1
National team UEFA EURO 2016 finals 6(1)/1; Friendlies 7(1)/-

Ivan Rakitić

Midfielder, Height 184cm
Born 10/03/88, Mohlin, Switzerland

With Xavi departed, Rakitić embedded himself in the Barcelona midfield as Andrés Iniesta's partner and the principal creative link to the team's illustrious all-South American attack. The 28-year-old's second season at Camp Nou confirmed the quality of his first. It kicked off with a 5-4 win against ex-club Sevilla in the UEFA Super Cup and ended with a second successive Spanish league and cup double. His third UEFA European Championship promised much after he helped Croatia top their group ahead of Spain, scoring a fine goal against the Czech Republic, but ended in frustration with a tepid team display against Portugal in the round of 16.

International career

CROATIA
Debut 08/09/07 v Estonia (h, Zagreb, ECQ), won 2-0
First goal 12/09/07 v Andorra (a, Andorra la Vella, ECQ), won 6-0
Caps 80 **Goals** 12
Major tournaments UEFA EURO 2008; UEFA EURO 2012; FIFA World Cup 2014; UEFA EURO 2016

Club career

Major honours UEFA Champions League (2015); UEFA Europa League (2014); UEFA Super Cup (2015); FIFA World Club Cup (2015); Spanish League (2015, 2016); Swiss Cup (2007); Spanish Cup (2015, 2016)
Clubs 05-07 FC Basel 1893 (SUI); 07-11 FC Schalke 04 (GER); 11-14 Sevilla FC (ESP); 14- FC Barcelona (ESP)

2015/16 appearances/goals

Domestic league Spanish Liga 30(6)/7
Europe UEFA Champions League 9(1)/2
National team UEFA EURO 2016 finals 4/1; UEFA EURO 2016 qualifying 4/1; Friendlies 1/1

Aaron Ramsey

Midfielder, Height 177cm
Born 26/12/90, Caerphilly, Wales

With his hair bleached blond for the occasion, Ramsey made his first international tournament with Wales one to treasure, spurring the team far beyond what was reasonably expected of them with a series of top-class performances. A scorer against Russia, the all-action 25-year-old set up another four goals, registering the joint highest number of assists at the tournament alongside Belgium's Eden Hazard, whose efforts he eclipsed in Wales' 3-1 quarter-final win. Sadly, a second yellow card picked up in that game suspended the Arsenal player from the semi-final, which, shorn of his verve and creativity, Wales lost 2-0 to Portugal.

International career

WALES
Debut 19/11/08 v Denmark (a, Brondby, friendly), won 1-0
First goal 14/10/09 v Liechtenstein (a, Vaduz, WCQ), won 2-0
Caps 44 **Goals** 11
Major tournaments UEFA EURO 2016

Club career

Major honours English FA Cup (2014, 2015)
Clubs 06-08 Cardiff City FC (ENG); 08- Arsenal FC (ENG); 10-11 Nottingham Forest FC (ENG) (loan); 11 Cardiff City FC (ENG) (loan)

2015/16 appearances/goals

Domestic league English Premier League 29(2)/5
Europe UEFA Champions League 3(2)/-
National team UEFA EURO 2016 finals 5/1; UEFA EURO 2016 qualifying 4/1; Friendlies 1/-

Renato Sanches

Midfielder, Height 176cm
Born 18/08/97, Amadora, Portugal

Voted Young Player of the Tournament at UEFA EURO 2016, Renato Sanches demonstrated over the course of a month in France exactly why, at the age of 18, Bayern München had paid a small fortune to prise him away from Benfica. On the bench at the start of the tournament, the powerful, technically gifted young midfielder marked his first international start by scoring a crucial equaliser against Poland in the quarter-final. He then maintained his place in Fernando Santos's first XI through to the final, where victory against France wrapped up a phenomenal debut season in which he also won the Portuguese Primeira Liga.

International career

PORTUGAL
Major honours UEFA European Championship (2016)
Debut 25/03/16 v Bulgaria (h, Leiria, friendly), lost 0-1
First goal 30/06/16 v Poland (n, Marseille, ECF), drew 1-1 (won 5-3 on pens)
Caps 11 **Goals** 1
Major tournaments UEFA EURO 2016

Club career

Major honours Portuguese League (2016)
Clubs 14-15 SL Benfica B; 15-16 SL Benfica; 16- FC Bayern München (GER)

2015/16 appearances/goals

Domestic league Portuguese Liga 22(2)/2
Europe UEFA Champions League 6/-
National team UEFA EURO 2016 finals 3(3)/1; Friendlies (5)/-

Rui Patrício

Goalkeeper, Height 190cm
Born 15/02/88, Leiria, Portugal

The only Portugal player actively involved for every minute of the country's triumphant UEFA EURO 2016 campaign, qualifying and final tournament matches combined, Rui Patrício saved his best for the final, the Sporting 'keeper making excellent saves from Antoine Griezmann, Olivier Giroud and Moussa Sissoko to keep his eighth clean sheet of the 15-match campaign. Capped for the 50th time in the quarter-final against Poland, the 28-year-old celebrated it in style with a brilliant save from Jakub Błaszczykowski in the penalty shoot-out. His heroics were duly rewarded with a place in UEFA's official Team of the Tournament.

International career

PORTUGAL
Major honours UEFA European Championship (2016)
Debut 17/11/10 v Spain (h, Lisbon, friendly), won 4-0
Caps 52 **Goals** 0
Major tournaments UEFA EURO 2008; UEFA EURO 2012; FIFA World Cup 2014; UEFA EURO 2016

Club career

Major honours Portuguese Cup (2008, 2015)
Clubs 06- Sporting Clube de Portugal

2015/16 appearances/goals

Domestic league Portuguese Liga 34/-
Europe UEFA Champions League play-offs 2/-; UEFA Europa League 7/-
National team UEFA EURO 2016 finals 7/-; UEFA EURO 2016 qualifying 3/-; Friendlies 5/-

Saúl Ñíguez

Attacking midfielder, Height 182cm
Born 21/11/94, Elche, Spain

Capped by Spain at every age group from Under-16 to Under-21, Saúl was called up to the senior squad prior to UEFA EURO 2016 but cut from Vicente del Bosque's final 23 without having made his senior debut. That was a surprise to many as the 21-year-old had just completed a season of immense productivity with Atlético Madrid, especially in the UEFA Champions League, where his magnificent match-winning strike at home to Bayern München was one of the competition's outstanding goals. The young left-footer also converted his penalty in the final shoot-out against Real Madrid with the confidence and composure of a veteran.

International career

SPAIN
Uncapped

Club career

Major honours Spanish Cup (2013)
Clubs 10-13 Club Atlético de Madrid B; 12- Club Atlético de Madrid; 13-14 Rayo Vallecano de Madrid (loan)

2015/16 appearances/goals

Domestic league Spanish Liga 26(5)/4
Europe UEFA Champions League 11(2)/3

Kasper Schmeichel

Goalkeeper, Height 189cm
Born 05/11/86, Copenhagen, Denmark

One of the longest-serving players in the Leicester City ranks, Schmeichel played every minute of the club's historic 2015/16 Premier League title-winning campaign, keeping 15 clean sheets. Just as important as his saves and shut-outs were his quick and accurate kicks and throws to launch counterattacks. In a remarkable coincidence, the day on which Leicester's title was confirmed, 2 May, was the very date on which his famous father Peter had won his first Premier League title, also aged 29, with Manchester United. Like father like son again, the Leicester No1 is now the undisputed first-choice goalkeeper for Denmark.

International career

DENMARK
Debut 06/02/13 v FYR Macedonia (a, Skopje, friendly), lost 0-3
Caps 22 **Goals** 0

Club career

Major honours English League (2016)
Clubs 05-09 Manchester City FC (ENG); 06 Darlington FC (ENG) (loan); 06 Bury FC (ENG) (loan); 07 Falkirk FC (SCO) (loan); 07-08 Cardiff City FC (ENG) (loan); 08 Coventry City FC (ENG) (loan); 09-10 Notts County FC (ENG); 10-11 Leeds United FC (ENG); 11- Leicester City FC (ENG)

2015/16 appearances/goals

Domestic league English Premier League 38/-
National team UEFA EURO 2016 qualifying 5/-; Friendlies 5/-

Sergio Ramos

Centre-back, Height 183cm
Born 30/03/86, Seville, Spain

Sergio Ramos's first season as captain of Real Madrid ended with the 30-year-old defender lifting the UEFA Champions League trophy in Milan. Furthermore, he was voted Man of the Match in the final against Atlético Madrid, having scored his team's early goal – his second in two finals against the same opponents – and converted the crucial fourth penalty in the shoot-out. He also skippered Spain at UEFA EURO 2016 but with less success, missing a penalty against Croatia and ending up on the losing side in a UEFA European Championship fixture for the first time since October 2006, thus ending a remarkable 35-game unbeaten run.

International career

SPAIN
Major honours FIFA World Cup (2010); UEFA European Championship (2008, 2012)
Debut 26/03/05 v China (h, Salamanca, friendly), won 3-0
First goal 13/10/05 v San Marino (a, Serravalle, WCQ), won 6-0
Caps 136 **Goals** 10
Major tournaments FIFA World Cup 2006; UEFA EURO 2008; FIFA Confederations Cup 2009; FIFA World Cup 2010; UEFA EURO 2012; FIFA Confederations Cup 2013; FIFA World Cup 2014; UEFA EURO 2016

Club career

Major honours UEFA Champions League (2014, 2016); UEFA Super Cup (2014); FIFA Club World Cup (2014); Spanish League (2007, 2008, 2012); Spanish Cup (2011, 2014)
Clubs 02-05 Sevilla FC; 05- Real Madrid CF

2015/16 appearances/goals

Domestic league Spanish Liga 23/2
Europe UEFA Champions League 10/1
National team UEFA EURO 2016 finals 4/-; UEFA EURO 2016 qualifying 2/-; Friendlies 2/-

Gylfi Thór Sigurdsson

Midfielder, Height 186cm
Born 08/09/89, Reykjavik, Iceland

With nine goals in 14 Premier League games at the start of 2016, Sigurdsson saved Swansea City from a potentially fraught relegation battle. The cool-headed set-piece expert earned the right to be rested by Swansea boss Francesco Guidolin from the team's last two fixtures as he looked ahead to his first major international tournament. The 26-year-old had been one of the main reasons for Iceland's participation at UEFA EURO 2016, scoring six goals in qualifying, and he excelled again at the finals, adding to his tally with a penalty in a 1-1 draw against Hungary as the North Atlantic minnows sensationally reached the quarter-finals.

International career

ICELAND
Debut 29/05/10 v Andorra (h, Reykjavik, friendly), won 4-0
First goal 07/10/11 v Portugal (a, Porto, ECQ), lost 3-5
Caps 44 **Goals** 14
Major tournaments UEFA EURO 2016

Club career

Clubs 08-10 Reading FC (ENG); 08 Shrewsbury Town FC (ENG) (loan); 09 Crewe Alexandra FC (ENG) (loan); 10-12 TSG 1899 Hoffenheim (GER); 12 Swansea City AFC (ENG) (loan); 12-14 Tottenham Hotspur FC (ENG); 14- Swansea City AFC (ENG)

2015/16 appearances/goals

Domestic league English Premier League 32(4)/11
National team UEFA EURO 2016 finals 5/1; UEFA EURO 2016 qualifying 4/2; Friendlies 4(1)/2

Chris Smalling

Centre-back, Height 193cm
Born 22/11/89, Greenwich, England

Manchester United often struggled to make headway in attack during the 2015/16 Premier League season, but they were well served in defence, where Smalling was the linchpin and leading light of Louis van Gaal's backline. The 26-year-old's strength, awareness and aerial ability earned him recognition by his United team-mates as the club's player of the year. Red-carded in the team's FA Cup final win against Crystal Palace, his next visit to Wembley provided a happier memory when he headed in his first international goal to enable England to beat Portugal. He went on to start all four games for the Three Lions at UEFA EURO 2016.

International career

ENGLAND
Debut 02/09/11 v Bulgaria (a, Sofia, ECQ), won 3-0
First goal 02/06/16 v Portugal (h, London, friendly), won 1-0
Caps 29 **Goals** 1
Major tournaments FIFA World Cup 2014; UEFA EURO 2016

Club career

Major honours English League (2011, 2013); English FA Cup (2016)
Clubs 07-08 Maidstone United FC; 08-10 Fulham FC; 10- Manchester United FC

2015/16 appearances/goals

Domestic league English Premier League 35/-
Europe UEFA Champions League 6/1; UEFA Champions League play-offs 2/-; UEFA Europa League 3/-
National team UEFA EURO 2016 finals 4/-; UEFA EURO 2016 qualifying 2/-; Friendlies 5/1

Darijo Srna

Right-back, Height 178cm
Born 01/05/82, Metkovic, Croatia

Srna decided to end his 14-year international career after Croatia's elimination from UEFA EURO 2016. The captain of his country for seven years, he departed with a record 134 caps, the last four of them collected in France where, despite having to mourn the death of his father, he was one of his team's most effective players, his outswinging right-footed crosses as accurate and dangerous as ever. The 34-year-old completed a 13th successive season with Shakhtar Donetsk in 2015/16, during which he set a new club appearance mark, his record 486th outing in a UEFA Europa League win against Braga putting the Pitmen into the semi-finals.

International career

CROATIA
Debut 20/11/02 v Romania (a, Timisoara, friendly), won 1-0
First goal 29/03/03 v Belgium (h, Zagreb, ECQ), won 4-0
Caps 134 **Goals** 22
Major tournaments UEFA EURO 2004; FIFA World Cup 2006; UEFA EURO 2008; UEFA EURO 2012; FIFA World Cup 2014; UEFA EURO 2016

Club career

Major honours *UEFA Cup (2009); Croatian League (2001); Ukrainian League (2005, 2006, 2008, 2010, 2011, 2012, 2013, 2014); Croatian Cup (2000, 2003); Ukrainian Cup (2004, 2008, 2011, 2012, 2013, 2016)*
Clubs 99-03 HNK Hajduk Split; 03- FC Shakhtar Donetsk (UKR)

2015/16 appearances/goals

Domestic league Ukrainian Premier League 19/2
Europe UEFA Champions League 5/1; UEFA Champions League qualifying/play-offs 4/1; UEFA Europa League 8/1
National team UEFA EURO 2016 finals 4/-; UEFA EURO 2016 qualifying 3/-; Friendlies 3(1)/1

Luis Suárez

Striker, Height 181cm
Born 24/01/87, Salto, Uruguay

There was no stopping Suárez in 2015/16. The Uruguayan striker was in irrepressible form throughout a fantastic second season at Barcelona – his first in entirety following his post-2014 FIFA World Cup suspension. A final tally of 59 goals in 53 games elevated his marksmanship to the stratospheric level of Lionel Messi and Cristiano Ronaldo and included 40 in the Liga as he outscored that pair to win the Pichichi trophy. Additionally, he found the net against every one of the seven teams Barça met in international competition, which included five in two games at the FIFA Club World Cup, where he was named Player of the Tournament.

International career

URUGUAY
Major honours *Copa América (2011)*
Debut 07/02/07 v Colombia (a, Cucuta, friendly), won 3-1
First goal 13/10/07 v Bolivia (h, Montevideo, WCQ), won 5-0
Caps 84 **Goals** 44
Major tournaments FIFA World Cup 2010; Copa América 2011; FIFA Confederations Cup 2013; FIFA World Cup 2014; Copa América 2016

Club career

Major honours *UEFA Champions League (2015); UEFA Super Cup (2015); FIFA Club World Cup (2015); Uruguayan League (2006); Dutch League (2011); Spanish League (2015, 2016); Dutch Cup (2010); Spanish Cup (2015, 2016); English League Cup (2012)*
Clubs 05-06 Club Nacional; 06-07 FC Groningen (NED); 07-11 AFC Ajax (NED); 11-14 Liverpool FC (ENG); 14- FC Barcelona (ESP)

2015/16 appearances/goals

Domestic league Spanish Liga 35/40
Europe UEFA Champions League 9/8
National team FIFA World Cup 2018 qualifying 2/1

Thiago Silva

Centre-back, Height 183cm
Born 22/09/84, Rio de Janeiro, Brazil

Lifting trophies has become second nature to Thiago Silva during his time as Paris Saint-Germain captain, and the 31-year-old centre-back had four more to raise in 2015/16 as his team completed another domestic quadruple. For the fourth season running he was voted into Ligue 1's team of the year, the quality of his performances remaining consistently high as his perfect blend of technique and toughness helped his team to a succession of clean sheets. That PSG conceded just seven goals in 19 away league fixtures was thanks largely to their indomitable skipper, whose devotion was total during a year off from international football with Brazil.

International career

BRAZIL
Major honours *FIFA Confederations Cup (2013)*
Debut 12/10/08 v Venezuela (a, San Cristobal, WCQ), won 4-0
First goal 30/05/12 v United States (a, Landover, friendly), won 4-1
Caps 59 **Goals** 4
Major tournaments FIFA World Cup 2010; Copa América 2011; FIFA Confederations Cup 2013; FIFA World Cup 2014; Copa América 2015

Club career

Major honours *Italian League (2011); French League (2013, 2014, 2015, 2016); Brazilian Cup (2007); French Cup (2015, 2016); French League Cup (2014, 2015, 2016)*
Clubs 01-03 RS Futebol Clube; 04 EC Juventude; 04 FC Porto (POR); 05 FC Dinamo Moskva (RUS); 06-09 Fluminense FC; 09-12 AC Milan (ITA); 12- Paris Saint-Germain (FRA)

2015/16 appearances/goals

Domestic league French Ligue 1 29(1)/1
Europe UEFA Champions League 9/-

Virgil van Dijk

Centre-back, Height 193cm
Born 08/07/91, Breda, Netherlands

Van Dijk's successful two-year spell in Scotland with Celtic came to an end when the Premiership champions were knocked out of the UEFA Champions League play-offs by Malmö FF. A big hit in Glasgow, the tall Dutch centre-back headed to the south coast of England and became just as productive and popular at Southampton, where his compatriot Ronald Koeman was the manager. A Premier League ever-present following his early-September arrival, his performances were so commanding that he not only became a regular for the Netherlands but was also rewarded by the club at the season's end with a new six-year contract.

International career

NETHERLANDS
Debut 10/10/15 v Kazakhstan (a, Astana, ECQ), won 2-1
Caps 7 **Goals** 0

Club career

Major honours Scottish League (2014, 2015, 2016); Scottish League Cup (2015)
Clubs 11-13 FC Groningen; 13-15 Celtic FC (SCO); 15- Southampton FC (ENG)

2015/16 appearances/goals

Domestic league Scottish Premiership 5/-; English Premier League 34/3
Europe UEFA Champions League qualifying/play-offs 5/-
National team UEFA EURO 2016 qualifying 2/-; Friendlies 5/-

Jamie Vardy

Striker, Height 178cm
Born 11/01/87, Sheffield, England

At the centre of Leicester City's journey to Premier League paradise was the remarkable rags-to-riches tale of their former non-league striker – one so heartwarmingly improbable that it drew the interest of a team of Hollywood screenwriters. Jamie Vardy: the Movie, should it come about, will focus on a season of sustained brilliance from the rapid 29-year-old leader of the Leicester attack, one that yielded 24 Premier League goals, including a record-breaking stretch in the autumn during which he scored in 11 successive games. He also broke into the England team, scoring his first international goal with an exquisite back-heeled flick against Germany in Berlin.

International career

ENGLAND
Debut 07/06/15 v Republic of Ireland (a, Dublin, friendly), drew 0-0
First goal 26/03/16 v Germany (a, Berlin, friendly), won 3-2
Caps 11 **Goals** 4
Major tournaments UEFA EURO 2016

Club career

Major honours English League (2016)
Clubs 07-10 Stocksbridge Park Steels FC; 10-11 FC Halifax Town; 11-12 Fleetwood Town FC; 12- Leicester City FC

2015/16 appearances/goals

Domestic league English Premier League 36/24
National team UEFA EURO 2016 finals 1(2)/1; UEFA EURO 2016 qualifying 2(1)/-; Friendlies 3(1)/3

Ashley Williams

Centre-back, Height 183cm
Born 23/08/84, Wolverhampton, England

As the captain of the Wales team that ended the country's 58-year wait to participate in a major tournament, and then reached the semi-finals of the main event, Williams will forever have a place in the nation's heart. Like many of his international colleagues, the 32-year-old Swansea City centre-back was actually born and raised in England, qualifying for Wales only through his maternal grandfather, but the effort and commitment he repeatedly displayed throughout an unforgettable UEFA EURO 2016 campaign in which he played every minute – both of the qualifiers and the five games in France – was not just total but at times beyond the call of duty.

International career

WALES
Debut 26/03/08 v Luxembourg (a, Luxembourg, friendly), won 2-0
First goal 11/08/10 v Luxembourg (h, Llanelli, friendly), won 5-1
Caps 65 **Goals** 2
Major tournaments UEFA EURO 2016

Club career

Major honours English League Cup (2013)
Clubs 01-03 Hednesford Town FC (ENG); 03-08 Stockport County FC (ENG); 08 Swansea City AFC (ENG) (loan); 08- Swansea City AFC (ENG)

2015/16 appearances/goals

Domestic league English Premier League 36/2
National team UEFA EURO 2016 finals 6/1; UEFA EURO 2016 qualifying 4/-; Friendlies 4/-

Willian

Winger, Height 174cm
Born 09/08/88, Ribeirao Pires, Brazil

Chelsea endured a miserable 2015/16 season, not just failing to defend their Premier League title but declining so sharply that they had lost nine of their first 16 matches when manager José Mourinho was sacked just before Christmas. Even during a bleak autumn, however, Willian was in excellent form, the one player in the side living up to his reputation, indeed furthering it, especially in the UEFA Champions League, where he scored in five of the six group games, four of his goals from eye-catching free-kicks. At the end of the season the Brazilian winger duly won every Chelsea player award going and also penned a new four-year contract.

International career

BRAZIL
Debut 10/11/11 v Gabon (a, Libreville, friendly), won 2-0
First goal 16/11/13 v Honduras (n, Miami, friendly), won 5-0
Caps 38 **Goals** 6
Major tournaments FIFA World Cup 2014; Copa América 2015; Copa América 2016

Club career

Major honours UEFA Cup (2009); Ukrainian League (2008, 2010, 2011, 2012, 2013); English League (2015); Ukrainian Cup (2008, 2011, 2012, 2013); English League Cup (2015)
Clubs 06-07 SC Corinthians; 07-13 FC Shakhtar Donetsk (UKR); 13 FC Anji (RUS); 13- Chelsea FC (ENG)

2015/16 appearances/goals

Domestic league English Premier League 32(3)/5
Europe UEFA Champions League 8/5
National team FIFA World Cup 2018 qualifying 6/2; Copa América 2016 3/-; Friendlies 3/-

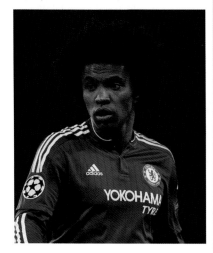

Granit Xhaka

Midfielder, Height 185cm
Born 27/09/92, Basel, Switzerland

Xhaka's fourth season as a Borussia Mönchengladbach player proved to be his last as he was transferred to Arsenal even before travelling to France to play for Switzerland at UEFA EURO 2016. His swansong campaign for the Bundesliga club started badly but improved dramatically after his compatriot Lucien Favre was replaced as coach by André Schubert and he was handed the captain's armband. The 23-year-old's leadership and left-footed playmaking skills inspired Gladbach's climb to fourth place, and he also impressed for his country in the summer before missing the vital spot kick in the round of 16 penalty shoot-out against Poland.

International career

SWITZERLAND
Debut 04/06/11 v England (a, London, ECQ), drew 2-2
First goal 15/11/11 v Luxembourg (a, Luxembourg, friendly), won 1-0
Caps 47 **Goals** 6
Major tournaments FIFA World Cup 2014; UEFA EURO 2016

Club career

Major honours Swiss League (2011, 2012); Swiss Cup (2012)
Clubs 10-12 FC Basel 1893; 12-16 VfL Borussia Mönchengladbach (GER); 16- Arsenal FC (ENG)

2015/16 appearances/goals

Domestic league German Bundesliga 28/3
Europe UEFA Champions League 5/-
National team UEFA EURO 2016 finals 4/-; UEFA EURO 2016 qualifying 3/-; Friendlies 4/-

Andriy Yarmolenko

Winger, Height 187cm
Born 23/10/89, St Petersburg, Russia

A frustratingly ineffective UEFA EURO 2016, where neither he nor any of his team-mates managed to score as Ukraine were eliminated without a goal or a point, could not detract from another outstanding season for Yarmolenko on the club front with Dynamo Kyiv. The tricky, powerful left-footer was once again the talismanic star of Serhiy Rebrov's team, scoring 13 goals in 23 games as the club retained the Ukrainian title for the first time in a dozen years. The 26-year-old also inspired Dynamo to their longest run in the UEFA Champions League since Rebrov the player helped the team reach the second group stage back in 1999/2000.

International career

UKRAINE
Debut 05/09/09 v Andorra (h, Kyiv, WCQ), won 5-0
First goal 05/09/09 v Andorra (h, Kyiv, WCQ), won 5-0
Caps 62 **Goals** 25
Major tournaments UEFA EURO 2012; UEFA EURO 2016

Club career

Major honours Ukrainian League (2009, 2015, 2016); Ukrainian Cup (2014, 2015)
Clubs 06 FC Desna Chernihiv; 07-08 FC Dynamo-2 Kyiv; 08- FC Dynamo Kyiv

2015/16 appearances/goals

Domestic league Ukrainian Premier League 23/13
Europe UEFA Champions League 7/2
National team UEFA EURO 2016 finals 3/-; UEFA EURO 2016 qualifying 6/3; Friendlies 4/3

Nation-by-nation

Welcome to the Nation-by-nation section of the European Football Yearbook.

Here you will find separate chapters, alphabetically arranged, on each UEFA member association containing the following information.

Association directory

The member association's official logo, name, address, contact details, senior officials, year of formation and, where applicable, national stadium as of July 2016.

Map/Club index

A map of the country illustrating the locations of its top-division clubs, which are listed in alphabetical order, plus any clubs promoted to the top division at the end of the 2015/16 (2015) season. Teams qualified for the 2016/17 UEFA Champions League and UEFA Europa League are indicated as such with colour coding, as are relegated teams. Official logos are set beside all clubs.

NB Locations are those where the club played all or the majority of their home matches during the 2015/16 (2015) season.

Review

A narrative review of the season, headed by an appropriate photo, is divided into four sections – Domestic league, Domestic cup, Europe and National team.

DOMESTIC SEASON AT A GLANCE

Domestic league final table

The final standings of the member association's top division including home, away and total records. The champions are indicated in bold type.

Key: Pld = matches played, W = matches won, D = matches drawn, L = matches lost, F = goals for (scored), A = goals against (conceded), Pts = points

··············· = play-off line

--------- = relegation line

Any peculiarities, such as the deduction of points, clubs withdrawn or relegation issues, are indicated as *NB* at the foot of the table.

European qualification

The clubs qualified for the 2016/17 UEFA Champions League and UEFA Europa League are indicated, together with (in brackets) the round for which they have qualified. Champions and Cup winners are highlighted.

The league's top scorer(s), promoted club(s), relegated club(s) and the result of the domestic cup final(s) are listed in summary.

Player of the season

Newcomer of the season

Team of the season

These are either official selections or personal choices of the correspondents.

NATIONAL TEAM

Home (left) and away (right) playing kits, international honours and major international tournament appearances head this section. Also included are the member association's top five all-time international cap-holders and goalscorers. Players active in 2015/16 are highlighted in bold.

Results 2015/16

Details on all senior international matches played between September 2015 and July 2016 with date, opponent, venue, result, scorer(s) and goal time(s).

Key: H = home, A = away, N = neutral, W = won, D = drawn, L = lost, *og* = own goal, *p* = penalty, *(aet)* = after extra time, (ECQ) = UEFA EURO 2016 qualification (ECF) – UEFA EURO 2016 final tournament

Appearances 2015/16

Details on all participants in the aforementioned matches (coaches and players), including name, date of birth and, for each player, club(s), match-by-match appearances and all-time international caps and goals scored.

Opponents are ranged across the top and abbreviated with the appropriate three-letter country code – capital letters identify a competitive match (i.e. UEFA EURO 2016).

Changes of national team coach are indicated with the appropriate appointment dates; temporary coaches are indicated in brackets.

Non-native coaches and clubs are indicated with the appropriate three-letter country code.

Key: G = goalkeeper, D = defender, M = midfielder, A = attacker, s = substitute, * = red card.

The number appearing after the letter indicates the minute in which a substitution took place. The number preceding an asterisk indicates the minute in which a red card occurred.

EUROPE

Details including opponent, result, scorers, goaltimes, lineups and red cards of all matches played by the member association's clubs in the 2015/16 UEFA Champions League and UEFA Europa League, including qualifying rounds and play-offs. Each team's entry is headed by home and away playing kits (those used in 2015/16) and the club logo. The home kit is on the left.

Key: *(aet)* = after extra time

DOMESTIC LEAGUE CLUB-BY-CLUB

Information on each top-division club, displayed in alphabetical order, is provided in six parts:

1) Club name and a circular swatch indicating shirt and short colours.

2) The year in which the club was founded, the home stadium(s) used during the season (with capacity) and, where applicable, the official club website.

3) Major honours, including European, international and domestic competitions. National 'super cups', secondary leagues and minor or age-restricted knockout competitions are not included.

4) The coach(es)/manager(s) used during the season and, in the case of new appointments, the dates on which they took place. Non-native coaches/ managers are indicated with the appropriate three-letter country code.

5) League fixtures chronologically listed, including dates, opponents, results and goalscorers.

Key: h = home, a = away, W = won, D = drawn, L = lost, *og* = own goal, *(p)* = penalty, *(w/o)* = walkover/forfeit

6) A list of all players used in the league campaign, including name, nationality (where non-native), date of birth, principal playing position, appearances and goals. Where applicable, squad numbers are also included.

Key: No = squad (shirt) number, Name = first name and family name, or, in some instances, 'football name', Nat = nationality (native unless listed with three-letter country code), DoB = date of birth, Pos = playing position, Aps = number of appearances in the starting lineup, (s) = number of appearances as a substitute, Gls = number of goals scored, G = goalkeeper, D = defender, M = midfielder, A = attacker.

Top goalscorers

A list of the top ten (and equal) goalscorers in the member association's top division. The figures refer to league goals only.

Promoted club(s)

Information on each promoted club is provided in four parts:

1) Club name and a circular swatch indicating shirt and short colours.

2) The year in which the club was founded, the home stadium(s) used during the season (with capacity) and, where applicable, the official club website.

3) Major honours, including European, international and domestic competitions. National 'super cups', secondary leagues and minor or age-restricted knockout competitions are not included.

4) The coach(es)/manager(s) used during the season and, in the case of new appointments, the dates on which they took place. Non-native coaches/ managers are indicated with the appropriate three-letter country code.

Second level final table

The final classification of the member association's second level (i.e. feeder league to the top division) table(s). Play-off details, where applicable, are also indicated.

Key: Pld = matches played, W = matches won, D = matches drawn, L = matches lost, F = goals for (scored), A = goals against (conceded), Pts = points.

- - - - - - - - = promotion line (at the top)

·············· = play-off line

- - - - - - - - = relegation line (at the bottom)

Any peculiarities, such as the deduction of points, clubs withdrawn or promotion issues, are indicated as *NB* at the foot of the final league table.

DOMESTIC CUP(S)

Results from the member association's principal domestic knockout competition, beginning at the round in which the top-division clubs (or some of them) enter.

Goalscorers and goaltimes are indicated from the quarter-final stage, with complete lineups, referees and red cards added for the final.

Details of the latter stages of significant secondary knockout competitions are also included for some member associations.

Key: *(aet)* = after extra time, *(w/o)* = walkover/forfeit

NB A complete key to all three-letter country codes can be found on page 6.

Page index

ALBANIA
Federata Shqiptarë e Futbollit (FShF)

Address	Rruga e Elbasanit AL-1000 Tiranë	**President**	Armand Duka
Tel	+355 42 346 605	**General secretary**	Ilir Shulku
Fax	+355 42 346 609	**Media officer**	Tritan Kokona
E-mail	fshf@fshf.org.al	**Year of formation**	1930
Website	fshf.org	**National stadium**	Elbasan Arena, Elbasan (15,000)

KATEGORIA SUPERIORE CLUBS

 ① **FK Bylis**

 ② **KS Flamurtari**

 ③ **FK Kukësi**

 ④ **KF Laçi**

 ⑤ **FK Partizani**

 ⑥ **KF Skënderbeu**

 ⑦ **KF Tërbuni**

 ⑧ **KF Teuta**

 ⑨ **KF Tirana**

 ⑩ **KF Vllaznia**

PROMOTED CLUBS

 ⑪ **KS Korabi**

 ⑫ **KS Luftëtari**

KEY:
- ● – UEFA Champions League
- ● – UEFA Europa League
- ● – Promoted
- ● – Relegated

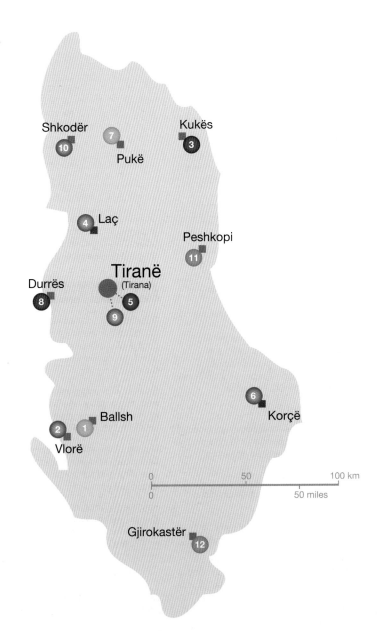

Six in a row for Skënderbeu

History was made by the Albanian national side as they reached a major tournament for the first time, qualifying for UEFA EURO 2016, but there was a familiar outcome in the domestic championship as KF Skënderbeu withstood a strong challenge from FK Partizani to win the title for a sixth straight season.

FK Kukësi ended a run of frustrating near-misses by edging out holders KF Laçi in the Albanian Cup final, while Skënderbeu emulated the national side by breaking new ground in Europe. The club from Korce would be banned, however, from continental competition in 2016/17.

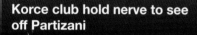

| Korce club hold nerve to see off Partizani | Kukës shed bridesmaid tag in cup triumph | Creditable showing from national team in France |

Domestic league

Mirel Josa's fourth season as Skënderbeu coach was to end in the same triumphant fashion as the previous three, but he and his players had to draw on all their reserves of stamina to end up as champions once again, with Partizani, seeking a first league title since 1993, pushing them hard all the way to the finish line.

Both challengers reeled off a string of wins in the early weeks, Skënderbeu claiming maximum points from their opening six fixtures while Partizani, back in the hands of their former defender Sulejman Starova, eclipsed them with nine successive three-pointers, including 2-1 at home to the defending champions.

By the time the two teams met again, in mid-December, they were dead level, but it was Skënderbeu who took a three-point lead into the winter break thanks to an early winning strike from Peter Olayinka. The Nigerian striker was second only to his team-mate, long-serving Albanian international Hamdi Salihi, in the mid-season top scorer standings, with ten goals, but those would be his last for Skënderbeu as he left for Belgian champions Gent. There was also a significant change at Partizani as Starova made way for Italian coach Andrea Agostinelli.

The second half of the season remained a tight affair, with Skënderbeu, and Salihi especially, continuing to score freely, while Partizani kept their points tally ticking over thanks in the main to an excellent defence, in which Arnbor Fejzullahu and goalkeeper Alban Hoxha were particularly prominent. With four games to go, Skënderbeu held a two-point lead, but when Partizani suffered a shock 2-1 home defeat to relegation strugglers Bylis – their first loss under Agostinelli – that appeared to be that. Remarkably, though, Partizani then staged some Friday 13th drama in Korce, a 90th-minute strike from Emiljano Vila silencing the 8,000 Skënderbeu fans who had come to celebrate another title coronation. Skënderbeu now had to win their final fixture, at Flamurtari, to retain the title. The pressure was on, but Josa's men held their nerve, winning 2-0 – just as they had at home to the same opponents when clinching the title a year earlier.

Domestic cup

Kukës, perpetual runners-up in the past three seasons, finally got their hands on some silverware as they gained revenge on 2015 cup final conquerors Laç by defeating them on penalties in Tirana. Further agony beckoned when they conceded a stoppage-time equaliser and had to play extra time with ten men, but at long last fate decided to smile on them as they came through to prevail in the shoot-out 5-3.

Europe

Skënderbeu became the first club to represent Albania in the group stage of a European competition when they came through two qualifying rounds of the UEFA Champions League to ensure themselves six additional matches in the UEFA Europa League. They would lose five of them, but a handsome 3-0 home win over Sporting Clube de Portugal made the experience worthwhile.

National team

Three games without a goal looked set to end Albania's hopes of automatic qualification for UEFA EURO 2016 until they closed their campaign with a famous 3-0 victory in Armenia that clinched the country's first ever participation in a major tournament. Gianni De Biasi and his players put up a decent effort in France, losing unluckily to both Switzerland and France before beating Romania 1-0 with a goal from the previously misfiring Armando Sadiku. That kept their hopes of further progress alive for a few days until it was confirmed that their record of three points and a minus-two goal difference would be insufficient to take them through as one of the best four third-placed teams.

DOMESTIC SEASON AT A GLANCE

Kategoria Superiore 2015/16 final table

		Pld	Home					Away					Total					Pts
			W	D	L	F	A	W	D	L	F	A	W	D	L	F	A	
1	KF Skënderbeu	36	15	1	2	46	12	10	3	5	27	15	25	4	7	73	27	79
2	FK Partizani	36	11	4	3	30	11	10	7	1	21	10	21	11	4	51	21	74
3	FK Kukësi	36	13	2	3	25	7	5	7	6	16	18	18	9	9	41	25	63
4	KF Teuta	36	9	5	4	21	10	9	4	5	22	18	18	9	9	43	28	63
5	KF Tirana	36	7	9	2	19	8	6	5	7	18	17	13	14	9	37	25	53
6	KF Vllaznia	36	8	4	6	23	16	3	2	13	13	26	11	6	19	36	42	39
7	KF Laçi	36	5	6	7	23	25	3	6	9	7	23	8	12	16	30	48	36
8	KS Flamurtari	36	6	6	6	19	12	3	5	10	15	32	9	11	16	34	44	35
9	FK Bylis	36	5	4	9	17	22	3	4	11	10	31	8	8	20	27	53	32
10	KF Tërbuni	36	2	4	12	14	34	2	2	14	8	47	4	6	26	22	81	18

NB KS Flamurtari – 3 pts deducted.

European qualification 2016/17

 CHAMPIONS LEAGUE

FK Partizani (second qualifying round)

NB Champion KF Skënderbeu banned.

EUROPA LEAGUE

Cup winner: FK Kukësi (first qualifying round)

KF Teuta (first qualifying round)

Top scorer	Hamdi Salihi (Skënderbeu), 27 goals
Relegated clubs	KF Tërbuni, FK Bylis
Promoted clubs	KS Korabi, KS Luftëtari
Cup final	FK Kukësi 1-1 KF Laçi *(aet; 5-3 on pens)*

Team of the season
(4-3-3)

Coach: Josa *(Skënderbeu)*

A Hoxha *(Partizani)*

Vangjeli *(Skënderbeu)* — Cicmil *(Vllaznia)* — Buljan *(Laç)* — Fejzullahu *(Partizani)*

Hasani *(Kukës)* — Musta *(Teuta)* — Lilaj *(Skënderbeu)*

Elis Bakaj *(Tirana)* — Sukaj *(Partizani)* — Salihi *(Skënderbeu)*

Player of the season

Sabien Lilaj
(KF Skënderbeu)

While the 27 goals of Hamdi Salihi, back in his homeland after eight years abroad, proved pivotal to Skënderbeu's Kategoria Superiore triumph, the all-round excellence of midfield mainstay Lilaj was equally valuable. Voted the league's player of the year for 2015 (helped by two goals in a UEFA Europa League win against Sporting Clube de Portugal), the 27-year-old native of the Korce region in eastern Albania continued to excel in the spring, eventually completing a personal hat-trick of domestic league title triumphs.

Newcomer of the season

Realdo Fili
(FK Partizani)

Relegated with his hometown club KF Apolonia in 2014/15, Fili returned to the Kategoria Superiore, aged 19, midway through the following campaign after being snapped up by title challengers Partizani. Although mostly deployed by coach Andrea Agostinelli as a substitute, the sprightly young winger-cum-central striker soon became a crowd favourite. Partizani were unable to win the title, but he scored three goals in the run-in and repeatedly caught the eye with his skill, speed and all-round enthusiasm.

NATIONAL TEAM

International tournament appearances
UEFA European Championship (1) 2016

Top five all-time caps
Lorik Cana (92); Altin Lala (78); Klodian Duro (76); Erjon Bogdani & Ervin Skela (75)

Top five all-time goals
Erjon Bogdani (18); Alban Bushi (14); Ervin Skela (13); Altin Rraklli & Hamdi Salihi (11)

Results 2015/16

Date	Opponent		Venue		Result	Scorers
04/09/15	Denmark (ECQ)	A	Copenhagen	D	0-0	
07/09/15	Portugal (ECQ)	H	Elbasan	L	0-1	
08/10/15	Serbia (ECQ)	H	Elbasan	L	0-2	
11/10/15	Armenia (ECQ)	A	Yerevan	W	3-0	Hovhannisyan (9og), Djimsiti (23), Sadiku (76)
16/11/15	Georgia	H	Tirana	D	2-2	Basha (89), Çikalleshi (90+3)
26/03/16	Austria	A	Vienna	L	1-2	Lenjani (47)
29/03/16	Luxembourg	A	Luxembourg	W	2-0	Sadiku (63), Çikalleshi (75)
29/05/16	Qatar	N	Hartberg (AUT)	W	3-1	Ajeti (23), Lenjani (40), Sadiku (64)
03/06/16	Ukraine	N	Bergamo (ITA)	L	1-3	Sadiku (12)
11/06/16	Switzerland (ECF)	N	Lens (FRA)	L	0-1	
15/06/16	France (ECF)	A	Marseille	L	0-2	
19/06/16	Romania (ECF)	N	Lyon (FRA)	W	1-0	Sadiku (43)

Appearances 2015/16

Coach: Gianni De Biasi (ITA)	16/06/56		DEN	POR	SRB	ARM	Geo	Aut	Lux	Qat	Ukr	SUI	FRA	ROU	Caps	Goals
Etrit Berisha	10/03/89	Lazio (ITA)	G	G	G	G	G75	G	G60	G	G	G	G	G	37	-
Berat Djimsiti	19/02/93	Zürich (SUI)/Atalanta (ITA)	D	D	D	D	s29		D						6	1
Lorik Cana	27/07/83	Nantes (FRA)	D	D	D	D		D		s61	D46	D 36*		s83	92	1
Arlind Ajeti	25/09/93	unattached/Frosinone (ITA)	D	D			D		D67	D	s46		D85	D	11	1
Ansi Agolli	11/10/82	Qarabağ (AZE)	D	D	D		D	D		s66	D	D	D	D	64	2
Burim Kukeli	16/01/84	Zürich (SUI)	M	M		s72		s86	M46			M	M74		17	-
Amir Abrashi	27/03/90	Freiburg (GER)	M64	M54		s87		M86			M46	M	M	M	21	-
Taulant Xhaka	28/03/91	Basel (SUI)	M	M	M	M	M57	M86			M46	M61	s74		13	-
Shkëlzen Gashi	15/07/88	Basel (SUI)/Colorado Rapids (USA)	M83	M70		M	M65		M	M46	s66	s82			14	1
Ermir Lenjani	05/08/89	Nantes (FRA)	M64	M	M83		M57	M79	s60	M46	M66		M	M77	21	3
Sokol Çikalleshi	27/07/90	İstanbul Başakşehir (TUR)	A	A86	s69	A58	s65	s46	A	A46	s59	s73			19	2
Migjen Basha	05/01/87	Luzern (SUI)/Como (ITA)	s64	s54	M	M87	s57		s86	M	M61	s46		M83	19	3
Armando Sadiku	27/05/91	Zürich (SUI)/Vaduz (SUI)	s64			s58	A		s79	s60	s46	A59	A82	A59	22	6
Odhise Roshi	22/05/91	Rijeka (CRO)	s83	s70		M	M65	s46	s67	M72	M	M73	s71	s77	34	1
Bekim Balaj	11/01/91	Rijeka (CRO)		s86	A69			A46			s46	s73		s59	16	1
Elseid Hysaj	20/02/94	Napoli (ITA)			D	D		D		D	D	D	D	D	22	-
Andi Lila	12/02/86	Giannina (GRE)		M46			D29	M46	M				M71	M	59	-
Ledian Memushaj	07/12/86	Pescara (ITA)			M	M72			M60		s46		M	M	15	-
Ergys Kaçe	08/07/93	PAOK (GRE)			s46			M 77*	s46		M73	s61			17	2
Alban Meha	26/04/86	Konyaspor (TUR)			s83										7	2
Naser Aliji	27/12/93	Basel (SUI)				D			D60	D66					4	-
Frederic Veseli	20/11/92	Lugano (SUI)					D		D				s85		3	-
Sabien Lilaj	18/02/89	Skënderbeu					M								12	-
Herolind Shala	01/02/92	Liberec (CZE)					s57		M60	s72					5	-
Rey Manaj	24/02/97	Internazionale (ITA)					s65								1	-
Alban Hoxha	23/11/87	Partizani					s75								1	-
Mërgim Mavraj	09/06/86	Köln (GER)						D		D	D	D	D	D	29	3
Orges Shehi	25/09/77	Skënderbeu							s60						6	-
Milot Rashica	28/06/96	Vitesse (NED)							s60	s46					2	-

EUROPE

KF Skënderbeu

Second qualifying round - Crusaders FC (NIR)

H 4-1 *Nimaga (15), Salihi (34, 83), Berisha (76)*
Shehi, Arapi, Progni (Latifi 74), Nimaga, Shkëmbi, Salihi (Abilaliaj 90+3), Hristov (Esquerdinha 79), Osmani, Berisha, Vangjeli, Radaš. Coach: Mirel Josa (ALB)

A 2-3 *Berisha (69), Latifi (77)*
Shehi, Arapi, Jashanica, Nimaga, Shkëmbi, Salihi (Hristov 90), Berisha, Latifi (Progni 85), Esquerdinha, Vangjeli, Radaš. Coach: Mirel Josa (ALB)

Red card: Arapi 11

Third qualifying round - FC Milsami Orhei (MDA)

A 2-0 *Salihi (49, 73p)*
Shehi, Jashanica, Nimaga, Shkëmbi, Salihi (Abilaliaj 90+1), Berisha (Ademir 90+2), Latifi (Progni 86), Esquerdinha, Vangjeli, Radaš, Lilaj. Coach: Mirel Josa (ALB)

H 2-0 *Salihi (16), Progni (55)*
Shehi, Jashanica, Progni (Ademir 75), Nimaga, Shkëmbi, Salihi (Hristov 78), Berisha, Esquerdinha (Abazi 46), Vangjeli, Radaš, Lilaj. Coach: Mirel Josa (ALB)

Play-offs - GNK Dinamo Zagreb (CRO)

H 1-2 *Shkëmbi (37)*
Shehi, Jashanica, Nimaga, Shkëmbi, Salihi, Berisha (Abazi 90), Latifi (Progni 79), Esquerdinha, Vangjeli (Ademir 87), Radaš, Lilaj. Coach: Mirel Josa (ALB)

A 1-4 *Esquerdinha (10)*
Shehi, Arapi, Jashanica, Progni (Nimaga 65), Shkëmbi, Berisha (Olayinka 58), Latifi (Hristov 78), Esquerdinha, Vangjeli, Radaš, Lilaj. Coach: Mirel Josa (ALB)

Group H

Match 1 - Beşiktaş JK (TUR)

H 0-1
Shehi, Arapi, Shkëmbi, Abazi, Ademir (Vangjeli 67), Berisha, Latifi (Nimaga 46), Esquerdinha, Radaš, Lilaj, Olayinka (Salihi 70). Coach: Mirel Josa (ALB)

Match 2 - FC Lokomotiv Moskva (RUS)

A 0-2
Shehi, Jashanica, Nimaga, Abazi (Arapi 77), Salihi, Berisha, Latifi (Shkëmbi 71), Vangjeli, Radaš, Lilaj, Olayinka (Progni 87). Coach: Mirel Josa (ALB)

Match 3 - Sporting Clube de Portugal (POR)

A 1-5 *Jashanica (89)*
Shehi, Arapi, Jashanica, Progni (Latifi 67), Nimaga (Shkëmbi 66), Salihi, Osmani, Berisha, Esquerdinha (Abazi 75), Vangjeli, Lilaj. Coach: Mirel Josa (ALB)

Red card: Salihi 24

Match 4 - Sporting Clube de Portugal (POR)

H 3-0 *Lilaj (15, 19p), Nimaga (55)*
Shehi, Jashanica, Nimaga, Abazi, Berisha (Arapi 90+2), Latifi (Progni 82), Esquerdinha (Shkëmbi 90), Vangjeli, Radaš, Lilaj, Olayinka. Coach: Mirel Josa (ALB)

Match 5 - Beşiktaş JK (TUR)

A 0-2
Shehi, Jashanica, Abazi, Salihi (Djair 83), Berisha (Arapi 46), Latifi (Progni 79), Esquerdinha, Vangjeli, Radaš, Lilaj, Olayinka. Coach: Mirel Josa (ALB)

Match 6 - FC Lokomotiv Moskva (RUS)

H 0-3
Shehi, Jashanica, Abazi, Salihi, Ademir, Berisha, Latifi (Progni 72), Esquerdinha (Djair 82), Radaš, Lilaj, Olayinka. Coach: Mirel Josa (ALB)

KF Laçi

First qualifying round - İnter Bakı PİK (AZE)

H 1-1 *Meto (20)*
Vujadinović, Çela, Sheta, Doku (Nimani 56), Adeniyi, Vuçaj, Sefgjini, Mustafa, Meto (Mitraj 78), Teqja, Veliaj. Coach: Armando Cungu (ALB)

A 0-0
Vujadinović, Çela, Sheta, Doku (Mitraj 76), Adeniyi, Vuçaj, Sefgjini, Meto, Nimani (Bardhi 82), Teqja, Veliaj. Coach: Armando Cungu (ALB)

FK Kukësi

First qualifying round - FC Torpedo Zhodino (BLR)

H 2-0 *Jean Carioca (9), Pejić (54)*
Stajila, Muça, Mici, Erick Flores, Hallaçi, Hasani (Musolli 46), Birungueta (Jefferson 68), Felipe Moreira (Hysa 60), Jean Carioca, Pejić, Malota. Coach: Marcello Troisi (BRA)

A 0-0
Stajila, Shameti (Hasani 56), Muça, Mici, Erick Flores, Hallaçi, Felipe Moreira (Birungueta 70), Jean Carioca, Pejić, Malota, Jefferson (Musolli 87). Coach: Marcello Troisi (BRA)

Second qualifying round - FK Mladost Podgorica (MNE)

H 0-1
Stajila, Muça, Mici, Erick Flores, Hallaçi, Birungueta (Hasani 36), Felipe Moreira (Semião Granado 61), Jean Carioca (Halili 89), Pejić, Malota, Jefferson. Coach: Marcello Troisi (BRA)

A 4-2 *Felipe Moreira (13), Pejić (19, 72), Erick Flores (32)*
Stajila, Muça, Mici, Erick Flores, Hallaçi, Hasani (Musolli 35), Felipe Moreira (Birungueta 60), Jean Carioca, Pejić (Semião Granado 79), Malota, Jefferson. Coach: Marcello Troisi (BRA)

Third qualifying round - Legia Warszawa (POL)

H 1-2 *Felipe Moreira (49)* (awarded as 0-3)
Stajila, Muça, Mici, Erick Flores, Hallaçi, Hasani, Birungueta, Felipe Moreira, Jean Carioca, Malota, Jefferson. Coach: Marcello Troisi (BRA)

A 0-1
Koçi, Muça, Mici, Erick Flores, Hallaçi, Hasani (Halili 50), Birungueta, Felipe Moreira (Qafa 90+2), Jean Carioca (Shameti 83), Musolli, Malota. Coach: Marcello Troisi (BRA)

FK Partizani

First qualifying round - Strømsgodset IF (NOR)

A 1-3 *Fazliu (68)*
A Hoxha (Xhika 30), Fejzullahu, Plaku (Fazliu 60), Batha, Bicaj, Račić (Tafili 89), Trashi, Ibrahimi, Vrapi, Vila, Kalari. Coach: Genc Tomorri (ALB)

H 0-1
A Hoxha, Fejzullahu, Fazliu, Plaku (Trashi 77), Batha, Mazrekaj (Nedzipi 61), Bicaj, Račić, Vrapi, Vila, Kalari (Bylykbashi 89). Coach: Genc Tomorri (ALB)

DOMESTIC LEAGUE CLUB-BY-CLUB

FK Bylis

1972 • Adush Muça (5,000) • no website
Coach: Agim Canaj;
(08/10/15) (Mauro De Vecchis (ITA));
(23/10/15) (Marenglen Kule);
(29/01/16) Adnan Zildžović (BIH)

2015
23/08	a	Kukës	L	0-2	
30/08	h	Tërbuni	L	0-2	
12/09	a	Tirana	D	0-0	
20/09	a	Laç	L	1-3	Mbella
26/09	h	Skënderbeu	L	1-4	Ronaille
04/10	a	Teuta	L	0-3	
17/10	h	Partizani	L	1-2	Peposhi
25/10	a	Flamurtari	D	0-0	
31/10	h	Vllaznia	W	3-1	Muçaj, Pepa, Gava
08/11	h	Kukës	D	1-1	Gava
18/11	a	Tërbuni	L	2-4	Pepa, Papa
23/11	h	Tirana	L	0-1	
28/11	h	Laç	W	1-0	Hyshmeri
03/12	a	Skënderbeu	L	0-4	
06/12	h	Teuta	W	2-1	Hoxhaj 2
12/12	a	Partizani	D	1-1	Hoxhaj
19/12	h	Flamurtari	L	2-3	Papa, Pepa
23/12	a	Vllaznia	L	2-3	Pepa, Hoxhaj
2016					
31/01	a	Kukës	L	0-3	
06/02	h	Tërbuni	W	4-0	Pepa, Hoxhaj, Brahja, Mbella
13/02	a	Tirana	L	0-2	
21/02	a	Laç	W	1-0	Bilali
28/02	h	Skënderbeu	D	1-1	Izuchukwuka
05/03	a	Teuta	L	0-1	
09/03	h	Partizani	L	0-2	
13/03	a	Flamurtari	D	0-0	
20/03	h	Vllaznia	L	0-1	
02/04	h	Kukës	L	0-3	
09/04	a	Tërbuni	W	1-0	Bilali
17/04	h	Tirana	D	0-0	
25/04	a	Laç	W	1-0	Varea
30/04	a	Skënderbeu	L	0-3	
04/05	h	Teuta	L	0-1	
08/05	a	Partizani	W	2-1	Hoxhaj 2
14/05	h	Flamurtari	D	0-0	
18/05	a	Vllaznia	L	0-1	

No	Name	Nat	DoB	Pos	Aps	(s)	Gls
20	Sulaimon Adekunle	NGA	26/10/90	D	12	(1)	
6	Albi Alla		01/02/93	D	16		
13	Dzelil Asani	MKD	12/09/95	D	9	(2)	
4	Elton Basriu		03/08/87	D	8	(3)	
3	Amir Bilali		15/04/94	D	11	(2)	2
4	Julian Brahja		06/12/80	D	14	(1)	1
16	Arvid Bregasi		04/09/97	A	1	(1)	
18	Abdelaye Diakité	FRA	08/01/97	D	5		
11	Elis Doksani		05/07/98	D	1		
2	Duško Dukić	SRB	21/06/85	D	16		
10	Edmilson	BRA	15/10/87	A	5	(1)	
14	Plarent Fejzaj		05/07/97	M	2	(2)	
1	Stivi Frasheri		29/08/90	G	16		
17	Orgest Gava		29/03/90	M	28	(2)	2
3	Serxhio Gjonbrati		06/12/93	D	4	(4)	
21	Ahmet Haliti		01/10/88	D	14		
7	Ardit Hoxhaj		20/07/94	A	26	(5)	7
29	Renato Hyshmeri		14/03/89	M	23	(5)	1
25	Solomonson Izuchukwuka	NGA	23/12/88	A	11	(4)	1
12	Mikel Kaloshi		16/06/93	G	1		
20	Amar Kaplanaj		09/09/98	D		(1)	
19	Bekim Kuli		19/09/82	M	1	(4)	
20	Bruno Lipi		07/04/94	M	1		
78	Emmanuel Mbella	FRA	18/06/92	M	16	(17)	2
5	Ledion Muçaj		04/06/92	M	11	(4)	1
1	Kushtrim Mushica		01/05/83	G	13		
14	Arbën Muskaj		27/06/94	M	8	(5)	
11	Qemal Mustafaraj		01/07/95	A		(6)	
67	Enriko Papa		12/03/93	M	13	(4)	2
9	Brunild Pepa		27/11/90	A	17	(8)	5
22	Ardit Peposhi		14/03/93	D	31	(1)	1
12	Ronaille	BRA	03/04/93	A	3	(3)	1
17	Shkëlzen Ruçi		01/07/92	G	6		
88	Samir Sahiti		15/08/88	D	1	(2)	
6	Marenglen Shoshi		29/01/87	D	10	(1)	
88	Borislav Šimić	SRB	15/05/87	D	23	(2)	
8	Flamur Tairi		24/11/90	M	12		
67	Juan Manuel Varea	ARG	23/03/86	A	7	(8)	1

KS Flamurtari

1923 • Flamurtari (9,000) • skflamurtari.com
Major honours
Albanian League (1) 1991; Albanian Cup (4) 1985, 1988, 2009, 2014
Coach: Stanislav Levý (CZE);
(31/10/15) Gentian Mezani;
(05/01/16) Zekirija Ramadani (MKD)

2015
22/08	h	Teuta	L	0-1	
28/08	a	Partizani	L	1-2	Trapp
13/09	h	Laç	D	0-0	
20/09	a	Vllaznia	W	2-0	Greca, Tskhadadze
27/09	a	Kukës	L	0-1	
04/10	h	Tërbuni	W	7-0	Greca, Nedzipi, Zeqiri, Tskhadadze, Telushi, Morina, Fuštar
17/10	a	Tirana	D	1-1	Tskhadadze
25/10	h	Bylis	D	0-0	
31/10	a	Skënderbeu	L	0-2	
07/11	a	Teuta	L	1-3	Tskhadadze
18/11	h	Partizani	L	0-1	
23/11	a	Laç	L	1-2	Fuštar
28/11	a	Vllaznia	L	0-1	
03/12	h	Kukës	L	0-1	
13/12	h	Tirana	L	0-2	
13/12	a	Bylis	W	3-2	Telushi (p), Lena, Hoxha
23/12	h	Skënderbeu	W	3-1	Lena, Greca, Telushi
2016					
31/01	h	Teuta	W	1-0	Greca
06/02	a	Partizani	D	1-1	Hoxha
13/02	h	Laç	L	0-1	
21/02	h	Vllaznia	W	2-0	Lushtaku, Telushi (p)
27/02	a	Kukës	L	0-4	
05/03	h	Tërbuni	D	1-1	Lacoste
09/03	a	Tirana	D	0-0	
13/03	h	Bylis	D	0-0	
20/03	a	Skënderbeu	L	1-5	Lushtaku (p)
02/04	a	Teuta	D	1-1	Danilo Alves
10/04	h	Partizani	D	1-1	Danilo Alves
16/04	a	Laç	W	2-1	Danilo Alves, João Henrique
24/04	a	Vllaznia	L	1-2	Dushku
29/04	h	Kukës	L	0-1	
04/05	a	Tërbuni	W	2-0	Telushi (p), Danilo Alves
10/05	h	Tirana	W	2-1	Telushi, Danilo Alves
14/05	a	Bylis	D	0-0	
18/05	h	Skënderbeu	L	0-2	

No	Name	Nat	DoB	Pos	Aps	(s)	Gls
4	Arbri Beqaj		29/09/98	M	4	(2)	
28	David Bocaj		28/03/98	M		(1)	
22	Dejvi Bregu		24/10/96	M	4	(3)	
12	Bedi Buval	FRA	16/06/86	A	1	(3)	
18	Dardan Çerkini		27/09/91	D	4	(6)	
6	Debatik Curri		28/12/83	D	7	(1)	
99	Danilo Alves	BRA	11/04/91	A	16		5
18	Rigers Dushku		08/09/91	M	1	(9)	1
5	Ivan Fuštar	CRO	18/08/89	D	13		2
14	Julian Gjinaj		24/10/96	D	4	(4)	
77	Bedri Greca		23/10/90	A	13	(4)	4
1	Argjend Halilaj		16/11/82	G	22		
8	Ylli Hoxha		26/12/91	A	30	(4)	2
13	Hektor Idrizaj		15/04/89	D	29		
87	João Henrique	BRA	13/01/87	A	12	(5)	1
2	Besnik Krasniqi		01/02/90	D	13	(3)	
20	Taulant Kuqi		11/05/95	D	14	(10)	
13	Pablo Lacoste	URU	15/01/88	D	17		1
24	Nijaz Lena	MKD	25/06/86	M	8	(1)	2
80	Ilion Lika		17/05/80	G	14		
97	Lucas	BRA	17/01/97	M	4	(6)	
8	Kushtrim Lushtaku		08/10/94	A	16	(5)	2
3	Kristi Marku		13/04/95	D	6	(4)	
19	Lorik Maxhuni		02/07/92	M	5	(6)	
10	Mario Morina		16/10/92	M	7	(1)	1
10	Nderim Nedzipi	MKD	22/05/84	M	10		1
8	Ignacio Nicolini	URU	30/09/88	M	18		
14	Entonio Pashaj		10/11/84	D	29		
2	Giorgi Popkhadze	GEO	25/09/86	D	10		
15	Ardi Qejvani		28/01/93	M	2	(2)	
5	Daniel Sadushi		23/09/90	A	10	(12)	
3	Ardit Shehaj		23/09/90	A	10	(12)	
9	Jurgen Sino		24/01/97	A		(4)	
17	Bruno Telushi		14/11/90	M	28		6
7	Petr Trapp	CZE	06/12/85	M	4		1
28	Bachana Tskhadadze	GEO	23/10/87	M	9	(2)	4
99	Valto Zeqaj		24/08/94	D	6		
18	Hair Zeqiri		11/10/88	M	5	(1)	1

FK Kukësi

1930 • Zeqir Ymeri (4,500) • fk-kukesi.al
Major honours
Albanian Cup (1) 2016
Coach: Marcello Troisi (BRA);
(24/11/15) Klodian Duro

2015
23/08	h	Bylis	W	2-0	Mateus, Erick Flores
29/08	a	Skënderbeu	L	0-1	
12/09	h	Teuta	W	3-0	Felipe Moreira, Jean Carioca, Erick Flores
19/09	a	Partizani	L	0-2	
27/09	h	Flamurtari	W	1-0	Mateus
03/10	a	Vllaznia	D	1-1	Mateus
17/10	h	Laç	W	1-0	Malota
25/10	h	Tërbuni	W	1-0	Mateus
01/11	a	Tirana	L	1-2	Mici
08/11	h	Bylis	D	1-1	Jean Carioca (p)
19/11	h	Skënderbeu	W	2-1	Mateus 2
23/11	a	Teuta	L	0-1	
28/11	h	Partizani	L	0-1	
03/12	a	Flamurtari	L	1-3	og (Fuštar)
06/12	h	Vllaznia	W	1-0	Hasani
12/12	a	Laç	D	1-1	Hasani
19/12	a	Tërbuni	W	1-0	Mateus
23/12	h	Tirana	L	0-1	
2016					
31/01	h	Bylis	W	3-0	Emini 2, Dvorneković
07/02	a	Skënderbeu	L	1-3	Dvorneković
13/02	h	Teuta	D	2-2	Emini, Erick Flores
22/02	a	Partizani	L	0-1	
27/02	h	Flamurtari	W	4-0	Emini, Hasani 2 (1p), Erick Flores
05/03	a	Vllaznia	W	2-1	Emini, Hasani
09/03	h	Laç	W	1-0	Emini
13/03	h	Tërbuni	W	1-0	Emini
20/03	a	Tirana	D	1-1	Erick Flores
02/04	a	Bylis	W	2-0	Dvorneković, Erick Flores
10/04	a	Skënderbeu	W	1-0	Shameti
16/04	a	Teuta	D	0-0	
25/04	h	Partizani	L	0-1	
29/04	a	Flamurtari	W	1-0	Dvorneković
04/05	h	Vllaznia	D	0-0	
08/05	a	Laç	D	1-1	Jean Carioca (p)
14/05	a	Tërbuni	W	2-1	Nika, Emini
18/05	h	Tirana	W	2-1	Emini 2

No	Name	Nat	DoB	Pos	Aps	(s)	Gls
17	Birungueta	BRA	18/07/93	M	6	(8)	
18	Eglantin Dhima		12/12/93	M		(4)	
21	Matija Dvorneković	CRO	01/01/89	A	11	(6)	4
8	Izair Emini	MKD	04/10/85	A	18		10
19	Erick Flores	BRA	30/04/88	M	30		6
25	Felipe Hereda	BRA	10/09/92	M		(1)	
15	Felipe Moreira	BRA	28/11/88	M	7	(1)	1
1	Nertil Ferraj		11/09/87	D	1	(7)	
13	Rrahman Hallaçi		12/11/83	D	30	(1)	
16	Edon Hasani		09/01/92	M	20	(2)	5
8	Eni Imami		19/12/92	M	1	(2)	
10	Jean Carioca	BRA	01/06/88	A	32	(2)	3
23	Jefferson	BRA	27/10/89	D	10	(4)	
20	Fjoart Jonuzi		09/07/96	M		(13)	
13	Resul Kastrati		20/03/94	D		(1)	
31	Ervis Koçi		13/11/84	G	24		
31	Enea Koliqi		13/12/86	G	12	(1)	
3	Leomir	BRA	05/07/87	M	6	(9)	
30	Lapidar Lladrovci		15/12/90	D	8	(6)	
24	Renato Malota		24/06/89	D	29		1
19	Mateus	BRA	18/01/93	A	18	(9)	7
7	Rexhep Memini		10/04/94	D	9	(2)	
7	Gledi Mici		06/02/91	D	34		1
18	Mario Mijatović	CRO	24/10/80	A	1	(6)	
18	Mario Morina		16/10/92	A	1	(6)	
23	Besar Musolli		28/02/89	M	33	(1)	
17	Kostandin Ndoni		31/03/89	D	4		
17	Ansi Nika		22/08/90	A	18	(10)	1
21	Edison Qafa		16/11/89	A		(2)	
21	Renaldo Rama		27/01/90	A	1	(3)	
4	Ylli Shameti		07/06/84	D	26		1
11	Franc Veliu		11/11/88	D	5	(3)	
25	Williams Recife	BRA	29/06/86	A	1		

KF Laçi

1960 • Laçi (5,000) • kflaci.com

Major honours
Albanian Cup (2) 2013, 2015

Coach: Armando Cungu;
(31/12/15) Stavri Nica;
(27/03/16) Eugent Zeka;
(13/04/16) Ramadan Ndreu

2015
21/08	a	Partizani	D	1-1	Çela
29/08	h	Tirana	D	1-1	Adeniyi
13/09	a	Flamurtari	D	0-0	
20/09	h	Bylis	W	3-1	Adeniyi, Meto 2
27/09	a	Vllaznia	W	1-0	Adeniyi
05/10	a	Skënderbeu	L	0-3	
17/10	a	Kukës	L	0-1	
25/10	h	Teuta	D	2-2	Gocaj, Adeniyi (p)
31/10	a	Tërbuni	D	1-1	Mustafa
08/11	h	Partizani	L	2-3	Gocaj, Adeniyi
19/11	a	Tirana	D	0-0	
23/11	h	Flamurtari	W	2-1	Nimani, Veliaj (p)
28/11	a	Bylis	L	0-1	
03/12	h	Vllaznia	W	2-0	Kruja, Nimani
06/12	a	Skënderbeu	L	0-4	
12/12	h	Kukës	D	1-1	Adeniyi
18/12	a	Teuta	W	1-0	Adeniyi
23/12	h	Tërbuni	W	4-0	Nimani, Adeniyi 2 (1p), Gocaj

2016
30/01	a	Partizani	L	0-2	
07/02	h	Tirana	L	0-3	
13/02	a	Flamurtari	W	1-0	Ćetković
21/02	h	Bylis	L	0-1	
27/02	a	Vllaznia	D	0-0	
05/03	h	Skënderbeu	L	0-2	
09/03	a	Kukës	L	0-1	
13/03	h	Teuta	L	1-2	Ademir
19/03	a	Tërbuni	D	1-1	Nimani
02/04	h	Partizani	D	0-0	
10/04	a	Tirana	L	0-1	
16/04	h	Flamurtari	L	1-2	Ćetković
25/04	a	Bylis	L	0-1	
30/04	h	Vllaznia	W	3-2	Nimani 2, Ćetković
04/05	a	Skënderbeu	L	1-6	Mustafa
08/05	h	Kukës	D	1-1	Mustafa
14/05	a	Teuta	L	0-3	
18/05	h	Tërbuni	D	0-0	

No	Name	Nat	DoB	Pos	Aps	(s)	Gls
6	Ademir	BRA	20/09/85	D	16		1
8	James Adeniyi	NGA	20/12/92	A	30		9
15	Kejvi Bardhi		07/08/96	A	1	(10)	
6	Mikelanxhelo Bardhi		08/01/95	D		(5)	
4	Stipe Buljan	CRO	21/09/83	D	30		
5	Ded Bushi		02/10/98	D	1		
3	Emiljano Çela		21/07/85	D	31	(1)	1
10	Marko Ćetković	MNE	10/07/86	M	14	(2)	3
2	Elton Doku		01/10/86	D	15		
7	Albi Dosti		13/09/91	M	10	(5)	
16	Eglantin Gjoni		02/12/92	M	9	(1)	
31	Luan Gjoni		23/07/97	M		(1)	
7	Olsi Gocaj		30/09/89	M	30	(1)	3
17	Arsid Kruja		08/06/93	A	11	(3)	1
18	Regi Lushkja		17/05/96	A	4	(3)	
17	Enco Malindi		15/01/88	A	5	(5)	
14	Agim Meto		02/02/86	M	15	(2)	2
9	Aldo Mitraj		12/01/87	A	13	(12)	
22	Endri Mucmata		24/03/92	M	1	(1)	
14	Drilon Musaj		11/09/94	M	8	(13)	
14	Argjend Mustafa		30/08/92	M	26	(2)	3
16	Edison Ndreca		05/07/94	M		(2)	
19	Valdano Nimani		05/03/87	A	15	(10)	6
11	Taulant Sefgjini		21/07/86	D	27	(2)	
1	Gentian Selmani		09/03/98	G	18	(1)	
5	Arjan Sheta		13/02/81	D	25	(2)	
28	Emiljano Veliaj		09/02/85	M	26	(2)	1
31	Miroslav Vujadinović	MNE	22/04/83	G	18		
20	Dardan Vuthaj		30/09/95	D	2	(3)	
22	Alfred Zefi		20/08/91	M	7	(3)	

FK Partizani

1946 • Qemal Stafa (16,230) • partizani.net

Major honours
Albanian League (15) 1947, 1948, 1949, 1954, 1957, 1958, 1959, 1961, 1963, 1964, 1971, 1979, 1981, 1987, 1993; Albanian Cup (15) 1948, 1949, 1957, 1958, 1961, 1964, 1966, 1968, 1970, 1973, 1980, 1991, 1993, 1997, 2004

Coach: Sulejman Starova;
(04/01/16) Andrea Agostinelli (ITA)

2015
21/08	h	Laç	D	1-1	Sukaj
28/08	h	Flamurtari	W	2-1	Trashi, Sukaj (p)
13/09	a	Vllaznia	W	2-1	Sukaj (p), Morini
19/09	h	Kukës	W	2-0	Plaku, Sukaj (p)
26/09	a	Tërbuni	W	2-1	Sukaj, Bicaj
03/10	h	Tirana	W	1-0	Sukaj
17/10	a	Bylis	W	2-1	Batha, Sukaj
25/10	h	Skënderbeu	W	2-1	Krasniqi, Ibrahimi
01/11	a	Teuta	W	1-0	Trashi
08/11	a	Laç	W	3-2	Fazliu, Sukaj, Mazrekaj
18/11	a	Flamurtari	D	0-0	
23/11	h	Vllaznia	W	1-0	Fazliu
28/11	a	Kukës	W	1-0	Mazrekaj
02/12	h	Tërbuni	W	4-0	Ibrahimi, Račić 2, Sukaj
06/12	a	Tirana	D	0-0	
12/12	h	Bylis	D	1-1	Račić
19/12	a	Skënderbeu	L	0-1	
23/12	h	Teuta	L	0-1	

2016
30/01	h	Laç	W	2-0	Račić, Vila
06/02	h	Flamurtari	D	1-1	Sukaj
13/02	a	Vllaznia	D	1-1	Račić
22/02	h	Kukës	W	2-0	Sukaj
27/02	a	Tërbuni	D	0-0	
04/03	h	Tirana	W	2-0	Sukaj, Fejzullahu
09/03	a	Bylis	W	2-0	Vila, Trashi
14/03	h	Skënderbeu	D	1-1	Račić
20/03	a	Teuta	W	2-0	Batha, Daja
02/04	a	Laç	D	0-0	
10/04	a	Flamurtari	D	1-1	Sukaj
17/04	h	Vllaznia	W	3-0	Sukaj 2, Fili
25/04	a	Kukës	W	1-0	Sukaj
30/04	h	Tërbuni	W	4-0	Sukaj 3, Vila
04/05	a	Tirana	D	2-2	Sukaj, Fili
08/05	h	Bylis	L	1-2	Fili
13/05	a	Skënderbeu	W	1-0	Vila
18/05	h	Teuta	L	1-2	Sukaj

No	Name	Nat	DoB	Pos	Aps	(s)	Gls
36	Sodiq Atanda	NGA	26/08/93	D	16		
18	Jurgen Bardhi		06/11/97	A	2	(15)	
10	Idriz Batha		28/03/92	M	32		2
15	Ditmar Bicaj		26/02/89	D	22	(1)	1
70	Dorjan Bylykbashi		08/08/80	M		(4)	
21	Asjon Daja		14/03/90	M	14	(12)	1
4	Astrit Fazliu		28/09/87	M	8	(8)	2
4	Arbnor Fejzullahu		08/04/93	D	33		1
6	Felipe Gomes	BRA	28/05/87	M	14	(1)	
28	Realdo Fili		04/05/96	A	4	(7)	3
30	Gabriel	BRA	12/04/90	A		(1)	
12	Alban Hoxha		23/11/87	G	32		
13	Nertil Hoxha		21/05/97	D	1		
22	Labinot Ibrahimi		25/06/86	D	20	(3)	2
8	Renaldo Kalari		25/06/84	D	23	(1)	
5	Gëzim Krasniqi		05/01/90	D	29	(1)	1
14	Mentor Mazrekaj		08/02/89	M	19	(1)	2
34	Emanuele Morini	ITA	31/01/82	A	3	(4)	1
9	Sebino Plaku		20/05/85	A	5	(3)	1
17	Stevan Račić	SRB	31/03/88	A	11	(14)	6
16	Ylber Ramadani		12/04/96	D		(3)	
11	Carlos Robles	COL	16/05/92	M	3	(2)	
20	Xhevahir Sukaj		05/10/87	A	26	(5)	21
8	Alsid Tafili		20/08/87	D	1	(7)	
27	Agustín Torassa	ARG	20/10/88	A	16	(1)	
18	Lorenc Trashi		19/05/92	M	33		3
11	Franc Veliu		11/11/88	D	1	(2)	
3	Marko Vidović	MNE	03/06/88	D	2	(1)	
88	Emiljano Vila		12/03/87	M	17	(1)	4
44	Endrit Vrapi		23/05/82	D	5	(1)	
1	Dashamir Xhika		23/05/89	G	4	(4)	

KF Skënderbeu

1909 • Skënderbeu (7,000) • kfskenderbeu.al

Major honours
Albanian League (7) 1933, 2011, 2012, 2013, 2014, 2015, 2016

Coach: Mirel Josa

2015
29/08	h	Kukës	W	1-0	Hristov
09/09	a	Vllaznia	W	1-0	Arapi
12/09	a	Tërbuni	W	2-0	Olayinka 2
21/09	h	Tirana	W	2-1	Berisha, Progni
26/09	a	Bylis	W	4-1	Olayinka, Lilaj, Salihi, Latifi
05/10	a	Laç	W	3-0	Salihi 2 (1p), Lilaj
16/10	a	Teuta	D	2-2	Salihi, Olayinka
25/10	a	Partizani	L	1-2	Salihi
31/10	a	Flamurtari	W	2-1	Salihi (p), Olayinka
08/11	h	Vllaznia	W	3-1	Salihi 2 (1p), Olayinka
19/11	a	Kukës	L	1-2	Olayinka
22/11	h	Tërbuni	W	4-0	Salihi, Berisha, Progni 2
30/11	a	Tirana	W	2-1	Salihi, Lilaj
03/12	h	Bylis	W	4-0	Progni, Abazi, Berisha, Salihi
06/12	h	Laç	W	4-0	Olayinka, Salihi 2, Berisha
14/12	a	Teuta	W	1-0	Salihi
19/12	h	Partizani	W	1-0	Olayinka
23/12	a	Flamurtari	L	1-3	Olayinka

2016
30/01	a	Vllaznia	L	0-1	
07/02	h	Kukës	W	3-1	Salihi 2, Adeniyi
13/02	a	Tërbuni	W	3-1	Salihi 2, Renatinho
22/02	h	Tirana	W	1-0	Salihi (p)
28/02	a	Bylis	W	1-0	Salihi (p)
05/03	h	Laç	W	2-0	Progni, Salihi
09/03	h	Teuta	W	1-0	Latifi
14/03	a	Partizani	D	1-1	Vangjeli
20/03	h	Flamurtari	W	5-1	Radaš, Salihi 3 (1p), Adeniyi
02/04	h	Vllaznia	W	2-1	Renatinho, Latifi
10/04	a	Kukës	L	0-1	
16/04	h	Tërbuni	L	2-3	Salihi (p), Plaku
25/04	a	Tirana	W	1-0	og (Hoxhallari)
30/04	h	Bylis	W	3-0	Salihi (p), Adeniyi 2
04/05	a	Laç	W	6-1	Abazi, Adeniyi 2, Esquerdinha 2, Salihi
08/05	a	Teuta	D	1-1	Latifi
15/05	h	Partizani	L	0-1	
18/05	a	Flamurtari	W	2-0	Latifi, Plaku

No	Name	Nat	DoB	Pos	Aps	(s)	Gls
11	Leonit Abazi	KOS	05/07/93	D	13	(12)	2
20	Ademir	BRA	20/09/85	D	5	(4)	
78	James Adeniyi	NGA	20/12/92	A	17		6
3	Renato Arapi		28/08/86	D	32	(2)	1
23	Bernard Berisha	KOS	24/10/91	A	16	(1)	4
6	Bekim Dema		30/03/93	M		(3)	
87	Djair	BRA	10/02/91	M	3		
30	Esquerdinha	BRA	16/11/90	A	15	(15)	2
17	Ventsislav Hristov	BUL	09/11/88	A	1	(3)	1
5	Bajram Jashanica	KOS	25/09/90	D	28	(2)	
27	Liridon Latifi		06/02/94	M	21	(7)	5
88	Sabien Lilaj		18/02/89	M	29	(1)	3
12	Erjon Llapanji		10/05/85	G	1	(1)	
4	Bruno Lulaj		02/04/95	D		(2)	
23	Valmir Nafiu	MKD	23/04/94	A		(1)	
8	Bakary Nimaga	MLI	06/12/94	M	6	(9)	
99	Peter Olayinka	NGA	18/11/95	A	18		10
88	Nurudeen Orelesi	NGA	10/04/89	M	12	(3)	
22	Ángel Orue	PAR	05/01/89	A		(1)	
19	Tefik Osmani		08/06/85	D	21	(1)	
9	Sebino Plaku		20/05/85	A	1	(6)	2
7	Gerhard Progni		06/11/86	M	27	(6)	5
33	Marko Radaš	CRO	26/10/83	D	23	(2)	1
24	Valdrin Rashica		14/12/92	M		(1)	
34	Renatinho	BRA	14/05/87	A	4	(8)	2
14	Hamdi Salihi		19/01/84	A	29	(1)	27
1	Orges Shehi		25/09/77	G	35		
10	Bledi Shkëmbi		13/08/79	M	13	(9)	
32	Kristi Vangjeli		05/09/85	D	26	(2)	1

KF Tërbuni

1936 • Ismail Xhemaili (1,950) • no website

Coach: Samuel Nikaj;
(05/10/15) (Alket Kruja);
(20/10/15) Gino Gargano (DOM);
(29/11/15) Viktor Gjoni

2015
23/08	h Tirana	L	1-2	Malindi
30/08	a Bylis	W	2-0	Danaj, Sulmataj
12/09	h Skënderbeu	L	0-2	
19/09	a Teuta	L	1-3	Dhrami
26/09	h Partizani	L	1-2	og (Bicaj)
04/10	a Flamurtari	L	0-7	
17/10	h Vllaznia	L	0-3	
25/10	a Kukës	L	0-1	
31/10	h Laç	D	1-1	Dhrami
07/11	a Tirana	L	0-3	
18/11	h Bylis	W	4-2	Tushe, Vatnikaj 2, T Marku
21/11	a Skënderbeu	L	0-4	
28/11	h Teuta	L	0-1	
02/12	a Partizani	L	0-4	
06/12	h Flamurtari	W	1-0	Malindi
12/12	a Vllaznia	L	0-2	
19/12	h Kukës	D	1-1	Dhrami
23/12	a Laç	L	0-4	

2016
30/01	h Tirana	L	1-3	H Marku
06/02	a Bylis	L	0-4	
13/02	h Skënderbeu	L	1-3	Jovanović
21/02	a Teuta	L	1-2	Karakaçi
27/02	h Partizani	D	0-0	
05/03	a Flamurtari	D	1-1	Lala
09/03	h Vllaznia	L	0-4	
13/03	a Kukës	L	0-1	
19/03	h Laç	D	1-1	Karakaçi
03/04	a Tirana	L	0-3	
09/04	h Bylis	L	0-3	
16/04	a Skënderbeu	W	3-2	Lala, Jovanović, Karakaçi
25/04	h Teuta	L	1-4	Kaçaj
30/04	a Partizani	L	0-4	
04/05	h Flamurtari	L	0-2	
08/05	a Vllaznia	L	0-2	
14/05	h Kukës	L	1-2	Kuka
18/05	a Laç	D	0-0	

No	Name	Nat	DoB	Pos	Aps	(s)	Gls
5	Dritmir Beci		09/06/96	M	13	(1)	
2	Ergi Borshi		09/08/95	D	9	(1)	
5	Julian Brahja		06/12/80	D	8		
4	Klaudio Çema		22/04/95	D	3	(2)	
4	Sadush Danaj		06/11/88	D	16	(3)	1
9	Martín Dedyn	ARG	18/06/88	M	17		
88	Arber Dhrami		23/06/88	A	14	(1)	3
21	Abdurraman Fangaj		12/10/97	D	12	(2)	
6	Alush Gavazaj		24/03/95	M	30	(2)	
2	Abel Gebor	LBR	27/08/90	M	4	(3)	
20	Julian Gërxho		22/01/85	M	10	(4)	
1	Gledar Haxho		10/11/88	G	24		
20	Ivan Jovanović	CRO	22/05/91	D	15	(2)	2
17	David Kaçaj		13/09/96	M	8	(3)	1
99	Abaz Karakaçi		25/08/92	M	16	(4)	3
9	Artan Karapici		19/04/80	M	15	(5)	
12	Klejdi Kuka		29/03/90	G	10		1
6	Andrea Kule		02/07/90	D	4		
19	Endri Lala		23/02/92	M	13	(1)	2
13	Vilson Lila		06/10/89	D	13		
11	Enco Malindi		15/01/88	A	9	(1)	2
18	Xhon Marinaj		12/10/97	M		(8)	
17	Herald Marku		18/05/96	M	14	(4)	1
14	Taulant Marku		14/06/94	A	5	(14)	1
3	Borko Milenković	SRB	07/10/84	D	13		
19	Liridon Mjekaj		14/04/94	M		(7)	
7	Arber Mone		08/06/88	M	17		
22	Roland Peqini		25/11/90	M	12	(4)	
2	Flavio Prendi		12/10/95	D	4	(3)	
33	Ervin Rexha		01/11/91	D	7	(3)	
5	Adrian Rudović	MNE	10/06/95	D	5	(4)	
22	Andi Selimaj		28/12/93	D	2	(1)	
21	Mergent Sulmataj		16/10/96	A		(5)	1
14	Klodian Sulollari		27/07/89	D	6		
14	Aleksandar Tašić	SRB	06/04/88	M	13	(1)	
8	Gerald Tushe		02/05/91	A	20	(4)	1
12	Eduin Ujka		10/04/95	G	2		
17	Jurgen Vatnikaj		08/08/95	M	6	(5)	2
7	Wilker	BRA	16/06/87	A	7	(8)	

KF Teuta

1920 • Niko Dovana (8,000) • kfteuta.com

Major honours
Albanian League (1) 1994; Albanian Cup (3) 1995, 2000, 2005

Coach: Gugash Magani

2015
22/08	a Flamurtari	W	1-0	Mihani
29/08	h Vllaznia	W	2-0	E Hoxha, Magani
12/09	h Kukës	L	0-3	
19/09	h Tërbuni	W	3-1	Lamçja, Magani, Gripshi
26/09	a Tirana	L	0-2	
04/10	h Bylis	W	3-0	Hila, Musta, Dita
16/10	a Skënderbeu	D	2-2	Dita, Musta
25/10	a Laç	D	2-2	Musta, Lamçja
01/11	h Partizani	L	0-1	
07/11	h Flamurtari	W	3-1	Magani 2, R Hoxha
18/11	a Vllaznia	W	1-0	Hodo (p)
23/11	h Kukës	W	1-0	Dita
28/11	h Tërbuni	W	1-0	Magani
03/12	h Tirana	D	0-0	
06/12	a Bylis	L	1-2	Musta
14/12	h Skënderbeu	L	0-1	
18/12	h Laç	L	0-1	
23/12	a Partizani	W	1-0	Lukić

2016
31/01	a Flamurtari	L	0-1	
07/02	h Vllaznia	W	1-0	Bernardo
13/02	h Kukës	D	2-2	Shkalla, og (Koçi)
21/02	h Tërbuni	W	2-1	Dita 2
27/02	a Tirana	D	0-0	
05/03	h Bylis	W	1-0	Musta
09/03	a Skënderbeu	L	0-1	
13/03	a Laç	W	2-0	Bernardo, Magani
20/03	h Partizani	L	0-2	
02/04	a Flamurtari	D	1-1	E Hoxha
09/04	a Vllaznia	W	2-0	Musta, Magani
16/04	h Kukës	D	0-0	
25/04	a Tërbuni	W	4-1	Magani 2, Musta, Hila
29/04	h Tirana	D	0-0	
04/05	a Bylis	W	1-0	Lukić
08/05	h Skënderbeu	D	1-1	Lena (p)
14/05	h Laç	W	3-0	Gripshi, Çyrbja, R Hoxha
18/05	a Partizani	W	2-1	Lamçja, Hila

No	Name	Nat	DoB	Pos	Aps	(s)	Gls
19	Fabio Beqja		15/02/94	M			
88	Bernardo	BRA	07/11/88	A	12	(5)	2
7	Arbër Çyrbja		18/09/93	M	13	(10)	1
22	Bruno Dita		18/02/93	D	25	(1)	5
7	Nertil Ferraj		11/11/87	M		(7)	
8	Nazmi Gripshi		05/07/94	M	1	(13)	2
27	Arjan Hila		06/01/93	M	28	(2)	3
30	Bledar Hodo		21/09/85	M	18	(9)	1
4	Erand Hoxha		25/04/85	D	14	(1)	2
5	Rustem Hoxha		04/07/91	D	34		2
11	Klejdi Hyka		13/06/97	A		(3)	
5	Klaudio Hyseni		15/07/89	M	5	(18)	
21	Jildemar	BRA	05/01/89	A		(1)	
18	Florijan Kadriu	MKD	29/08/96	A	3	(7)	
4	Resul Kastrati		20/03/94	D	1		
15	Blerim Kotobelli		10/08/92	D	34		
21	Viktor Kuka		25/06/90	M	4	(4)	
17	Eri Lamçja		10/03/94	A	24	(8)	3
16	Nijaz Lena	MKD	25/06/86	M	17	(1)	1
4	Slavko Lukić	SRB	14/03/89	D	29	(1)	2
16	Artur Magani		08/07/94	A	29	(5)	9
2	Meglid Mihani		01/09/83	M	11	(5)	1
12	Shpëtim Moçka		20/10/89	G	29	(1)	
29	Emiljano Musta		31/01/92	M	30	(1)	7
1	Bledian Rizvani		27/07/85	G	7		
4	Klaidi Shala		22/03/98	D	2		
2	Dajan Shehi		19/03/97	M		(1)	
3	Silvester Shkalla		10/08/95	D	26	(2)	1

KF Tirana

1920 • Qemal Stafa (16,230); Selman Stërmasi (9,600) • kftirana.al

Major honours
Albanian League (24) 1930, 1931, 1932, 1934, 1936, 1937, 1965, 1966, 1968, 1970, 1982, 1985, 1988, 1989, 1995, 1996, 1997, 1999, 2000, 2003, 2004, 2005, 2007, 2009; Albanian Cup (15) 1939, 1963, 1976, 1977, 1983, 1984, 1986, 1994, 1996, 1999, 2001, 2002, 2006, 2011, 2012

Coach: Shkëlqim Muça;
(18/10/15) (Emanuel Egbo (NGA));
(28/10/15) Ilir Daja

2015
23/08	a Tërbuni	W	2-1	Lika, Fukui
29/08	a Laç	D	1-1	Karabeci
12/09	h Bylis	D	0-0	
21/09	a Skënderbeu	L	1-2	Fukui
27/09	h Teuta	W	2-0	Muça, Karan
03/10	a Partizani	L	0-1	
17/10	h Flamurtari	D	1-1	Vucaj
25/10	a Vllaznia	D	1-1	Smajlaj
01/11	h Kukës	W	2-1	Muça, og (Veliu)
07/11	h Tërbuni	W	3-0	Karan, Elis Bakaj, Lika
19/11	h Laç	D	0-0	
23/11	a Bylis	W	1-0	Elis Bakaj
30/11	h Skënderbeu	L	1-2	Elis Bakaj (p)
03/12	a Teuta	D	0-0	
06/12	h Partizani	D	0-0	
13/12	a Flamurtari	W	2-0	Elis Bakaj 2
19/12	h Vllaznia	D	0-0	
23/12	a Kukës	W	1-0	Muça

2016
30/01	a Tërbuni	W	3-1	Elis Bakaj, Muzaka, Muça
07/02	a Laç	W	3-0	Elis Bakaj, Muzaka, Hugo Almeida
13/02	h Bylis	W	2-0	Muzaka (p), Peçi
22/02	a Skënderbeu	L	0-1	
27/02	h Teuta	D	0-0	
04/03	a Partizani	L	0-2	
09/03	h Flamurtari	D	0-0	
13/03	a Vllaznia	L	1-3	og (Cicmil)
19/03	h Kukës	D	1-1	Muzaka
03/04	a Tërbuni	W	3-0	Elis Bakaj 3
10/04	h Laç	W	1-0	Elis Bakaj
17/04	a Bylis	D	0-0	
25/04	h Skënderbeu	L	0-1	
29/04	a Teuta	D	0-0	
04/05	h Partizani	D	2-2	Muça, Elis Bakaj
08/05	a Flamurtari	L	1-2	Papa
14/05	h Vllaznia	W	1-0	Elis Bakaj
18/05	a Kukës	L	1-2	Elis Bakaj

No	Name	Nat	DoB	Pos	Aps	(s)	Gls
1	Ilir Avdyli		20/05/90	G	1		
22	Edvan Bakaj		09/10/87	G	29		
19	Elis Bakaj		25/09/87	A	26	(1)	14
8	Ervin Bulku		03/03/81	M	4		
14	Fjoralb Deliaj		04/04/97	M	4	(6)	
20	David Domgjoni		21/05/97	M		(1)	
2	Stivi Frashëri		29/08/92	G	6		
99	Masato Fukui	JPN	14/11/88	A	33	(1)	2
16	Ronald Gercaliu	AUT	12/02/86	D	15	(9)	
33	Gilberto	BRA	11/07/87	A	5	(3)	
9	Grent Halili		24/05/98	M		(12)	
29	Erjon Hoxhallari		15/10/95	D	27	(5)	
8	Hugo Almeida	BRA	06/01/86	A	2	(1)	1
3	Endrit Idrizaj		14/06/89	D	1	(1)	
24	Florijan Kadriu	MKD	29/08/96	A		(5)	
13	Erando Karabeci		06/09/88	M	33		1
5	Dejan Karan	SRB	25/08/88	D	21		2
3	Martin Kavdanski	BUL	13/02/87	D	2	(2)	
7	Dorjan Kërçiku		30/08/93	M	19	(6)	
7	Gilman Lika		13/01/87	M	31	(2)	2
23	Argjend Malaj		16/10/90	M	22	(6)	
8	Gentian Muça		13/05/87	D	24		5
20	Anxhelo Mumajezi		28/03/97	A		(1)	
17	Gjergji Muzaka		26/09/84	M	12	(7)	4
2	Enriko Papa		12/03/93	A	1	(11)	1
25	Majkëll Peçi		29/08/96	A	4	(8)	1
24	Kristjan Prendi		13/10/97	D		(2)	
24	Jetmir Sefa		30/01/87	M		(1)	
2	Dritan Smajlaj		12/02/85	D	26		1
21	Olsi Teqja		27/07/88	M	31		
10	Erjon Vucaj		25/12/90	M	1	(1)	1

 **ALBANIA**

KF Vllaznia

1919 • Ismail Xhemaili, Pukë (1,950);
Reshit Rusi (3,500); Loro Boriçi (16,000) • vllaznia.al

Major honours
Albanian League (9) 1945, 1946, 1972, 1974, 1978,
1983, 1992, 1998, 2001; Albanian Cup (6) 1965,
1972, 1979, 1981, 1987, 2008

Coach: Luan Zmijani;
(27/09/15) Armir Grima;
(09/01/16) Armando Cungu

2014
29/08	a	Teuta	L	0-2	
09/09	h	Skënderbeu	L	0-1	
13/09	h	Partizani	L	1-2	Krymi
20/09	a	Flamurtari	L	0-2	
26/09	a	Laç	L	0-1	
03/10	h	Kukës	D	1-1	Sefa
17/10	a	Tërbuni	W	3-0	Shtupina, Sosa, Pavićević
25/10	h	Tirana	D	1-1	Arbëri
31/10	a	Bylis	L	1-3	Sosa
08/11	a	Skënderbeu	L	1-3	Sosa
18/11	h	Teuta	L	0-1	
21/11	a	Partizani	L	0-1	
28/11	h	Flamurtari	W	4-0	Cicmil, Çinari 2, Sefa
03/12	a	Laç	L	0-2	
06/12	a	Kukës	L	0-1	
12/12	h	Tërbuni	W	2-0	Çinari, Ahmeti
19/12	a	Dinamo	D	0-0	
23/12	h	Bylis	W	3-2	Shtupina, Çinari 2
2015					
30/01	h	Skënderbeu	W	1-0	Kalaja
07/02	a	Teuta	L	0-1	
13/02	h	Partizani	D	1-1	Dibra
21/02	a	Flamurtari	L	0-2	
27/02	h	Laç	D	0-0	
05/03	h	Kukës	L	1-2	Vrapi
09/03	a	Tërbuni	W	4-0	Çinari, Dibra 2, Dyca
13/03	h	Tirana	W	3-1	Cicmil, Shtupina, Kalaja
20/03	a	Bylis	W	1-0	Kalaja
02/04	a	Skënderbeu	L	1-2	Shtupina
09/04	h	Teuta	L	0-2	
17/04	a	Partizani	L	0-3	
25/04	h	Flamurtari	W	2-1	Cicmil, Shtupina
30/04	a	Laç	L	2-3	Marku, Pjeshka
04/05	a	Kukës	D	0-0	
08/05	h	Tërbuni	W	2-0	Cicmil, Shtupina
14/05	a	Tirana	L	0-1	
18/05	h	Bylis	W	1-0	Kalaja

No	Name	Nat	DoB	Pos	Aps	(s)	Gls
8	Berat Ahmeti		26/01/95	M	7	(8)	1
13	Polizoi Arbëri		09/09/88	D	19		1
7	Florind Bardhulla		19/11/92	M	30		
7	Ergi Borshi		09/08/95	M	3	(1)	
59	Stefan Cicmil	MNE	16/08/90	D	29		4
19	Eraldo Çinari		11/10/96	M	19	(12)	6
9	Arenc Dibra		11/05/90	M	5	(10)	3
30	Andrija Dragojević	MNE	25/12/91	G	30		
17	Denis Dyca		11/01/96	M	1	(4)	1
14	Bekim Erkoçeviç		23/04/92	M		(5)	
22	Erdenis Gurishta		24/04/95	D	10	(3)	
16	Semir Hadžibulić	SRB	16/08/86	M	12	(2)	
4	Esin Hakaj		06/12/96	D	9	(14)	
5	Adnan Haxhaj		16/09/87	D	5	(1)	
14	Arlind Kalaja		27/12/95	A	28	(1)	4
16	Ambroz Kapaklija		30/11/96	M	5	(9)	
9	Mohammad Kdouh	LIB	04/05/93	M	3	(1)	
14	Fatjon Kiri		20/01/94	M		(1)	
6	Ardit Krymi		02/05/96	M	23	(1)	1
21	Kreshnik Lushtaku		20/07/94	M	2		
3	Antonio Marku		24/03/92	D	35		1
19	Santiago Martínez	PAR	16/08/95	M	2	(3)	
20	Darko Pavićević	MNE	27/12/86	M	1	(5)	1
23	Denis Pjeshka		28/05/95	D	16	(3)	1
18	Ronaldo Rudović	MNE	12/06/96	M	2	(4)	
24	Jetmir Sefa		30/01/87	M	21	(9)	2
31	Erind Selimaj		22/05/89	G	1	(1)	
30	Alen Sherri		15/12/97	G	2	(1)	
10	Ndriçim Shtupina		18/03/87	M	33		6
14	Sebastián Sosa	URU	13/03/94	A	5	(1)	3
5	Alsid Tafili		20/08/87	M	12	(2)	
8	Uendi Vecaj		18/02/97	M	7	(4)	
21	Endrit Vrapi		23/05/82	D	16		1

Top goalscorers

27	Hamdi Salihi (Skënderbeu)	
21	Xhevahir Sukaj (Partizani)	
15	James Adeniyi (Laç/Skënderbeu)	
14	Elis Bakaj (Tirana)	
10	Izair Emini (Kukës)	
	Peter Olayinka (Skënderbeu)	
9	Artur Magani (Teuta)	
7	Ardit Hoxhaj (Bylis)	
	Mateus (Kukës)	
	Emiljano Musta (Teuta)	

Promoted clubs

KS Korabi

1930 • Korabi (3,500) • no website
Coach: Dritan Mehmeti

KS Luftëtari

1929 • Gjirokastër (7,000) • no website
Coach: Mustafa Hysi;
(29/02/16) (Vasil Papa);
(03/03/16) Gerd Haxhiu

Second level final tables 2015/16

Group A	Pld	W	D	L	F	A	Pts
1 KS Korabi	27	20	2	5	43	16	62
2 KS Kastrioti	27	19	6	2	61	27	60
3 KS Besëlidhja	27	16	6	5	59	26	54
4 KF Erzeni	27	10	4	13	47	45	34
5 KS Burreli	27	10	4	13	29	38	34
6 FC Kamza	27	8	6	13	33	44	30
7 KS Besa	27	8	5	14	31	40	29
8 KF Iliria	27	8	4	15	34	45	28
9 KF Mamurrasi	27	6	7	14	22	42	25
10 KF Ada	27	5	6	16	29	65	21

NB KS Kastrioti – 3 pts deducted.

Group B	Pld	W	D	L	F	A	Pts
1 KS Luftëtari	27	21	5	1	53	9	68
2 KF Pogradeci	27	20	3	4	51	24	63
3 KF Apolonia	27	14	4	9	42	26	46
4 KS Lushnja	27	9	4	14	26	35	31
5 FK Dinamo Tirana	27	10	3	14	27	32	30
6 KF Elbasani	27	8	5	14	27	45	29
7 KS Shkumbini	27	8	5	14	19	40	29
8 KF Sopoti	27	8	4	15	30	33	28
9 KS Turbina	27	7	12	29	37	28	
10 KF Butrinti	27	6	6	15	15	38	24

NB KS Turbina & FK Dinamo Tirana – 3 pts deducted.

DOMESTIC CUP

Kupa e Shqipërisë 2015/16

FIRST ROUND
(06/09/15 & 09/10/15)
Tomori 0-3, 0-2 Skënderbeu *(0-5)*

(16/09/15 & 29/09/15)
Erzeni 0-1, 0-2 Tirana *(0-3)*
Korabi 0-5, 2-0 Partizani *(2-5)*

(16/09/15 & 30/09/15)
Ada 1-5, 1-6 Teuta *(2-11)*
Besa 1-3, 1-1 Laç *(2-4)*
Burreli 0-0, 0-2 Tërbuni *(0-2)*
Dinamo 0-1, 0-6 Bylis *(0-7)*
Iliria 1-0, 2-0 Mamurrasi *(3-0)*
Kamza 4-2, 1-1 Elbasan *(5-3)*
Kastrioti 1-0, 1-2 Besëlidhja *(2-2; Kastrioti on
away goal)*
Naftëtari 3-1, 1-4 Kukës *(aet; 4-5)*
Oriku 1-2, 2-3 Flamurtari *(3-5)*
Pograbec 1-1, 0-4 Vllaznia *(1-5)*
Shkumbini 2-2, 0-1 Apolonia *(2-3)*
Sopoti 5-0, 0-2 Butrinti *(5-2)*

SECOND ROUND
(12/10/15 & 15/11/15)
Sopoti 1-1, 0-2 Skënderbeu *(1-3)*

(21/10/15 & 11/11/15)
Bylis 0-0, 2-3 Laç *(2-3)*
Iliria 0-5, 1-3 Kukës *(1-8)*
Kamza 0-1, 0-3 Teuta *(0-4)*
Kastrioti 1-5, 1-2 Tirana *(2-7)*
Lushnja 1-3, 0-3 Partizani *(1-6)*
Tërbuni 0-1, 0-5 Flamurtari *(0-6)*

(28/10/15 & 04/11/15)
Apolonia 0-0, 1-2 Vllaznia *(1-2)*

QUARTER-FINALS
(23/01/16 & 17/02/16)
Laç 2-0 Partizani *(Adeniyi 49, 65)*
Partizani 1-0 Laç *(Sukaj 65)*
(Laç 2-1)

Teuta 1-0 Kukës *(Hila 20)*
Kukës 2-0 Teuta *(Shameti 35, Malota 88)*
(Kukës 2-1)

(24/01/16 & 17/02/16)
Flamurtari 0-1 Tirana *(Malaj 87)*
Tirana 1-2 Flamurtari *(Fukui 47; Telushi 16,
Lushtaku 67)*
(2-2; Flamurtari on away goals)

Vllaznia 0-0 Skënderbeu
Skënderbeu 2-1 Vllaznia *(Renatinho 42,
Adeniyi 56; Marku 88)*
(Skënderbeu 2-1)

SEMI-FINALS
(06/04/16 & 20/04/16)
Flamurtari 0-2 Kukës *(Hasani 11, Shameti 20)*
Kukës 2-0 Flamurtari *(Emini 69p, Erick Flores 82)*
(Kukës 4-0)

Laç 1-0 Skënderbeu *(Ćetković 50)*
Skënderbeu 2-1 Laç *(Progni 53, Plaku 79;
Ćetković 57)*
(2-2; Laç on away goal)

FINAL
(22/05/16)
Qemal Stafa, Tirana
FK KUKËSI 1 *(Jean Carioca 64)*
KF LAÇI 1 *(Mitraj 90+2)*
(aet; 5-3 on pens)
Referee: Guida (ITA)
KUKËS: Koliqi, Hallaçi, Malota (Lladrovci 46), Mici,
Shameti, Hasani (Felipe Moreira 44; Memini 80),
Nika, Musolli, Emini, Dvorneković, Jean Carioca
Red card: Nika (74)
LAÇ: Selmani, Ademir, Sheta, Buljan, Çela, Mustafa
(Zefi 44), Veliaj (Dosti 75), Sefgjini (Mitraj 67),
Ćetković, Gocaj, Nimani

ANDORRA
Federació Andorrana de Fútbol (FAF)

Address	c/ Batlle Tomàs, 4 Baixos AD-700 Escaldes-Engordany	**President**	Victor Manuel Domingos dos Santos
Tel	+376 805 830	**General secretary**	Tomás Gea
Fax	+376 862 006	**Media officer**	Teresa Figueras
E-mail	info@faf.ad	**Year of formation**	1934
Website	faf.ad	**National stadium**	Estadi Nacional, Andorra la Vella (3,306)

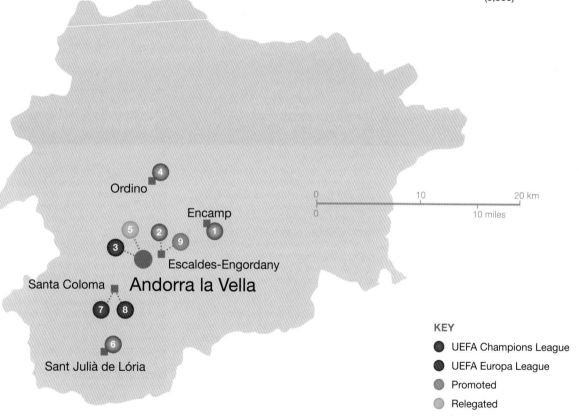

Ordino

Encamp

Escaldes-Engordany

Santa Coloma · Andorra la Vella

Sant Julià de Lória

0   10   20 km
0   10 miles

KEY
- ● UEFA Champions League
- ● UEFA Europa League
- ● Promoted
- ● Relegated

PRIMERA DIVISIÓ CLUBS

  1 FC Encamp

  **2 UE Engordany**

  3 FC Lusitans

 4 FC Ordino

 5 Penya Encarnada d'Andorra

 6 UE Sant Julià

 7 FC Santa Coloma

 8 UE Santa Coloma

PROMOTED CLUB

  9 CE Jenlai

FC Santa Coloma complete title treble

FC Santa Coloma captured the Andorran title for the third season running – and a record tenth time in all – as Richard Imbernón's side maintained their Primera Divisió supremacy in convincing style, losing only one of their 20 matches and conceding just eight goals.

Local rivals UE Santa Coloma rounded off an otherwise disappointing campaign by lifting the Copa Constitució following a 3-0 win in the final against giant-killing UE Engordany. The win earned them UEFA Europa League qualification alongside league runners-up FC Lusitans.

| **Runaway success for record champions** | **UE Santa Coloma lift domestic cup** | **Century of international caps for Ildefons Lima** |

Domestic league

FC Santa Coloma began the season on a mission to do what the club had never managed before and win three successive Primera Divisió crowns. The hat-trick had only ever been achieved once previously, by CE Principat from 1996/97-1998/99, and in coach Imbernón's third season at the helm confidence was high at the outset that history could be achieved in the year of the club's 30th anniversary.

An early 1-0 defeat by Lusitans came as something of a shock, but the defending champions appeared to use the setback as extra motivation, winning ten of their next 11 games – and drawing the other – to end the first phase of the competition with a handy seven-point lead.

For the seventh season in a row the same four teams – FC Santa Coloma, Lusitans, UE Santa Coloma and UE Sant Julià – made it through to the championship pool, but with just six matches remaining the chances of the league leaders being shifted from their perch were remote – especially as Imbernón's side had conceded just once in their previous nine matches.

The team's rock-solid defence would come even more prominently to the fore during the play-offs. In fact, FC Santa Coloma would score just three goals during those additional six matches, but with five clean sheets at the other end they actually increased their final margin of victory from seven points to eight. Fittingly, it was with a goalless draw against Lusitans, in round 18, that the title was mathematically sewn up. That stalemate also confirmed Lusitans as runners-up for the second season in a row.

Engordany topped the relegation pool, scoring 19 goals in the six games against their three group rivals, but there was a predictable return to second-tier football for newly-promoted Penya Encarnada, whose squad of Mexican and Portuguese immigrants were never competitive. FC Encamp finished next-to-last but were ultimately handed a play-off win by forfeit after an administrative error from their opponents CE Carrol, runners-up to runaway second division champions CE Jeniai.

Domestic cup

UE Santa Coloma failed to win any of their six games in the second phase of the league and finished fourth, but they made amends by reclaiming the Copa Constitució, which they had previously won three years earlier. Two goals from Spanish striker Víctor Bernat, the joint leading marksman in the Primera Divisió, completed a comfortable 3-0 win over Engordany, whose first final appearance was earned against the odds with a couple of stunning comeback wins in each of the previous rounds against Lusitans and holders Sant Julià.

Europe

Andorra's three European representatives all fell by the wayside in the first qualifying round, with FC Santa Coloma's exit arguably the most painful as they lost 2-1 at home to the champions of Gibraltar, Lincoln FC, after drawing the first game 0-0 at the other end of the Iberian peninsula.

National team

Defeats in each of their last four UEFA EURO 2016 qualifiers left the Andorran national team without a single point in 50 UEFA European Championship qualifying matches. A penalty from veteran defender Ildefons Lima at home to Belgium did, however, enable the team to score more goals (four) than in any of their previous campaigns in the competition – with Lima scoring three of them, all from the penalty spot, to lift his all-time record tally for the country into double figures. The FC Santa Coloma captain also won his 100th cap in a June friendly against Estonia, becoming the second Andorran player to reach the landmark after Óscar Sonejee, who had achieved the feat 12 months earlier.

DOMESTIC SEASON AT A GLANCE

Primera Divisió 2015/16 final tables

FIRST PHASE

		Pld	W	D	L	F	A	Pts
1	FC Santa Coloma	14	12	1	1	41	7	37
2	FC Lusitans	14	10	0	4	28	18	30
3	UE Santa Coloma	14	8	3	3	31	11	27
4	UE Sant Julià	14	7	3	4	30	14	24
5	UE Engordany	14	5	2	7	18	22	17
6	FC Encamp	14	3	2	9	15	41	11
7	FC Ordino	14	3	1	10	15	35	10
8	Penya Encarnada d'Andorra	14	1	2	11	6	36	5

SECOND PHASE
Championship Pool

		Pld	W	D	L	F	A	Pts
1	**FC Santa Coloma**	20	14	5	1	44	8	**47**
2	FC Lusitans	20	12	3	5	37	28	39
3	UE Sant Julià	20	9	5	6	41	20	32
4	UE Santa Coloma	20	8	6	6	34	20	30

Relegation Pool

		Pld	W	D	L	F	A	Pts
5	UE Engordany	20	9	2	9	37	34	29
6	FC Ordino	20	8	2	10	32	44	26
7	FC Encamp	20	4	4	12	22	50	16
8	Penya Encarnada d'Andorra	20	1	3	16	15	58	3

NB Penya Encarnada d'Andorra – 3 pts deducted.

European qualification 2016/17

Champion: FC Santa Coloma (first qualifying round)

Cup winner: UE Santa Coloma (first qualifying round)

FC Lusitans (first qualifying round)

Top scorer	José Antonio Aguilar (Lusitans) & Víctor Bernat (UE Santa Coloma), 12 goals
Relegated club	Penya Encarnada d'Andorra
Promoted club	CE Jenlai
Cup final	UE Santa Coloma 3-0 UE Engordany

Team of the season
(4-3-3)

Coach: Imbernón *(FC Santa Coloma)*

Casals
(FC Santa Coloma)

Jordi Rubio *(UE Santa Coloma)* — Ruiz *(Sant Julià)* — Lima *(FC Santa Coloma)* — Jesús Rubio *(UE Santa Coloma)*

Fernández *(Engordany)* — Pujol *(FC Santa Coloma)* — Noguerol *(FC Santa Coloma)*

C Martínez *(FC Santa Coloma)* — Bernat *(UE Santa Coloma)* — Villanueva *(Lusitans)*

Player of the season

Marc Pujol
(FC Santa Coloma)

Still going strong in the Andorran national team at 33 after over 16 years' service, Pujol may have become accustomed to ending up on the losing side in the international arena, but his three seasons on the home front with FC Santa Coloma have all brought Primera Divisió titles. The diminutive midfielder celebrated the hat-trick in 2015/16 with another excellent campaign in Richard Imbernón's championship-winning side, captaining the team to victory with decisive contributions in both defence and attack.

Newcomer of the season

Alejandro Fernández
(UE Engordany)

Introduced to Engordany in mid-season at a time when the team were struggling for goals, 19-year-old Fernández announced himself in grand style, scoring on his debut – a 3-0 win against UE Santa Coloma – before adding another seven strikes in the relegation pool to end the season with a goal-a-game record. The young Spaniard also found the net for his team in Copa Constitució wins against Lusitans and Sant Julià as Engordany qualified for the final of the competition for the first time in their history.

NATIONAL TEAM

Top five all-time caps
Óscar Sonejee (106); Ildefons Lima (100); Josep Manel Ayala (84); Manolo Jiménez (80); Koldo Alvarez (79)

Top five all-time goals
Ildefons Lima (10); Óscar Sonejee (4); Jesús Julián Lucendo (3); Emiliano González, **Marc Pujol**, Justo Ruiz & Fernando Silva (2)

Results 2015/16

Date	Opponent		Venue		Result	
03/09/15	Israel (ECQ)	A	Haifa	L	0-4	
06/09/15	Bosnia & Herzegovina (ECQ)	A	Zenica	L	0-3	
10/10/15	Belgium (ECQ)	H	Andorra la Vella	L	1-4	Lima (51p)
13/10/15	Wales (ECQ)	A	Cardiff	L	0-2	
12/11/15	St Kitts & Nevis	H	Andorra la Vella	L	0-1	
28/03/16	Moldova	N	Paola (MLT)	L	0-1	
26/05/16	Azerbaijan	N	Bad Erlach (AUT)	D	0-0	
01/06/16	Estonia	A	Tallinn	L	0-2	

Appearances 2015/16

Coach: Koldo Alvarez	04/09/70		ISR	BIH	BEL	WAL	Skn	Mda	Aze	Est	Caps	Goals
Ferran Pol	28/02/83	FC Andorra (ESP)	G	G	G	G		G		G	23	-
Moisés San Nicolás	17/09/93	Lusitans	D	D	D	D	D51	D86	s88	s64	20	-
Emili García	11/01/89	Le Pontet (FRA) /FC Andorra (ESP)	D					s80	D52	s76	32	1
Ildefons Lima	10/12/79	FC Santa Coloma	D	D	D	D	D	D	s52	D92	100	10
Marc García	21/03/88	Rubí (ESP)	D	D	D	s81		D	D	D	31	-
Cristian Martínez	16/10/89	FC Santa Coloma	M	M76			M	M67	M52	s47	38	1
Márcio Vieira	10/10/84	Atlético Monzón (ESP)	M	M	M86	M	M72	M80	M	M70	67	-
Marc Rebés	03/07/94	FC Santa Coloma	M81	D	M		M				6	-
Victor Rodríguez	07/09/87	FC Santa Coloma	M55	M 64*				M	M82		12	-
Sergio Moreno	25/11/87	Yeclano (ESP)	M72						s72		54	-
Aaron Sánchez	05/06/96	Lleida Esportiu (ESP)	A	s76	A	A			A65	s92	8	-
Óscar Sonejee	26/03/76	Lusitans /Sant Julià	s55	M	M62	M70	D27				106	4
Jordi Rubio	01/11/87	UE Santa Coloma	s72		M	D	D		D88	D	31	-
Max Llovera	08/01/97	Lleida Esportiu (ESP)	s81		D	D			D	D	5	-
Josep Manel Ayala	08/04/80	UE Santa Coloma		M81		s70	s27	s67		s70 86*	84	-
Gabriel Riera	05/06/85	FC Santa Coloma		A87	s73	s12	A60				34	1
Edu Peppe	28/01/83	Sant Julià		s81	s86		s51	s74			23	-
Leonel Alves	28/09/93	FC Andorra (ESP)		s87							3	-
Victor Hugo Moreira	05/10/82	FC Andorra (ESP)			M73	M12	M72	M84			16	-
Adrián Rodrigues	14/08/88	Villarrobledo (ESP)			s62	M		s86			15	-
Iván Lorenzo	15/04/86	Fraga (ESP)				M81			A86	A47	27	-
José Antonio Gomes	03/12/85	Illescas (ESP)					G		G		35	-
Marc Pujol	21/08/82	FC Santa Coloma					M51	M74		M76	68	2
Jesús Rubio	09/09/94	UE Santa Coloma					s51				1	-
Sebastián Gómez	01/11/83	FC Andorra (ESP)					s60				26	-
Juli Sánchez	20/06/78	FC Andorra (ESP)					s72				65	1
Ludovic Clemente	09/05/86	FC Andorra (ESP)					s72	s84	s82		14	-
Marc Vales	04/04/90	Hospitalet (ESP)						D	M	M	42	-
Carlos Gomes	18/10/93	Sant Julià						s86			1	-
Jordi Aláez	23/01/98	FC Andorra (ESP)							M72	s65	2	-
Alexandre Martínez	10/10/98	FC Andorra (ESP)							s52	M65	2	-
Andreu Matos	01/12/95	Engordany							s65	M64	2	-

EUROPE

DOMESTIC LEAGUE CLUB-BY-CLUB

FC Santa Coloma

First qualifying round - Lincoln FC (GIB)
A 0-0
Casals, Wagner, A Ramos, Rebés (Rodríguez 74), Lima, Pujol, Juvenal, C Martínez (J Toscano 83), Parra, Riera (Juanfer 61), R Ramos. Coach: Richard Imbernón (AND)
H 1-2 *Lima (44)*
Casals, Wagner (Mercadé 68), A Ramos, Rebés, Lima, Pujol, Juvenal, C Martínez (J Martínez 76), Parra, Juanfer (J Toscano 52), R Ramos. Coach: Richard Imbernón (AND)

UE Sant Julià

First qualifying round - Randers FC (DEN)
H 0-1
Coca, Ruiz, Rafael Brito, Girau (Peppe 67), Rodríguez, Fábio Serra, Quirino (Gándara 57), Vigo, Varela, Bruninho, Spano (Castellano 63). Coach: Raúl Cañete (ESP)
A 0-3
Coca, Ruiz, Rafael Brito, Girau (Peppe 62), Gándara, Rodríguez, Quirino (Castellano 71), Vigo, Varela, Bruninho, Spano (Fábio Serra 78). Coach: Raúl Cañete (ESP)

FC Lusitans

First qualifying round - West Ham United FC (ENG)
A 0-3
Gerardo Rubio, Acosta, M San Nicolás, Muñoz, Romero, Luís dos Reis, Aguilar (Alfi 46), Molina, L San Nicolás (Moya 46), Franklim Soares (Sonejee 54), Léo Maciel. Coach: Xavier Roura (ESP)
H 0-1
Gerardo Rubio, Acosta (Moya 52), M San Nicolás, Muñoz, Romero (Alfi 76), Luís dos Reis, Aguilar, Molina, L San Nicolás (Pinto 74), Franklim Soares, Léo Maciel. Coach: Xavier Roura (ESP)

Stadiums

Camp d'Esports d'Aixovall, Aixovall (520)
Estadi Comunal, Andorra la Vella (1,504)
Centre d'Entrenament FAF - Borda Mateu, Andorra la Vella (500)
Camp de Futbol Prada de Moles, Encamp (200)

FC Encamp

1950 • no website
Major honours
Andorran League (2) 1996, 2002
Coach: Óscar Guerrero

2015
27/09	Penya Encarnada	D	1-1	*Léo Correia*
04/10	Engordany	L	2-4	*Bueno 2*
18/10	Sant Julià	L	0-2	
25/10	FC Santa Coloma	L	1-5	*G Garcia (p)*
01/11	UE Santa Coloma	L	0-6	
08/11	Ordino	W	3-0	*Renato (p), Bueno, Prat*
15/11	Lusitans	L	0-6	
22/11	Penya Encarnada	W	1-0	*Prat*
29/11	Engordany	D	0-0	
09/12	Sant Julià	L	0-6	
13/12	FC Santa Coloma	L	0-6	

2016
31/01	UE Santa Coloma	L	1-2	*Bueno*
07/02	Ordino	W	4-0	*Léo Correia, Idris, Renato, Ramírez*
14/02	Lusitans	L	2-3	*Idris, Alanis*
20/03	Engordany	L	0-3	
03/04	Ordino	L	0-1	
10/04	Penya Encarnada	D	1-1	*Montobbio*
17/04	Engordany	L	3-4	*Bové, Renato, Alanis (p)*
24/04	Ordino	D	0-0	
29/04	Penya Encarnada	W	3-0	*(w/o; original result 0-3)*

No	Name	Nat	DoB	Pos	Aps	(s)	Gls
31	Diego Abdian	ARG	02/11/82	M	1	(1)	
10	Pablo Alanis	ARG	25/03/95	A	2	(3)	2
5	Helder Alves		25/01/94	D	9	(2)	
2	André Marinho	POR	26/03/93	D	17		
9	Aleix Bové		08/03/96	M	9	(3)	1
9	Victor Bueno		23/07/94	M	14		4
6	Marc Cabanes		13/04/99	D	1		
18	Facundo Cristos	ESP	28/05/94	M		(1)	
12	Ángel De la Fuente		29/12/97	G	2		
17	Roberto Dos Santos		20/04/94	M	14	(2)	
20	Gerard Escoda		04/08/00	A	1	(1)	
4	Yael Fontan	ESP	24/02/80	D	4		
6	Genís Garcia		18/05/78	M	10	(4)	1
22	Txema Garcia		04/12/74	D	14	(1)	
10	Sandro Gutiérrez		02/01/96	M	10	(6)	
33	Hugo Veloso	POR	11/07/79	D	3		
19	Rachid Idris	GHA	30/09/89	A	5	(2)	2
13	Marcos Lage		14/10/97	G		(1)	
21	Léo Correia	POR	10/07/83	A	15	(4)	2
54	Fernando Meilan		06/08/82	D	10	(1)	
20	Paulo Bruno Monteiro		24/09/95	M	2	(2)	
14	Ferran Montobbio		10/03/94	A	3	(7)	1
23	Xavier Moreno		03/12/90	D	16		
1	Israel Pérez-Serrano	ESP	08/02/75	G	14		
8	Xavier Prat		28/04/92	M	6	(5)	2
8	Albert Ramírez		05/02/87	M	5	(4)	1
7	Renato	POR	19/03/80	M	19		3
8	Albert Reyes		24/03/96	M	7		
13	David Ribolleda		13/02/85	D	1	(2)	
93	Jordi Rodríguez		01/12/93	A	4		
4	Rui Filipe Barroso	POR	13/09/97	D	1	(1)	
16	Sergi Suárez		02/07/98	M	1		
8	Albert Valero		04/08/99	A		(2)	
18	Oriol Vales		23/12/97	M		(1)	

UE Engordany

2001 • ueengordauny.jimdo.com
Coach: Josep Mengual

2015
27/09	Lusitans	L	2-4	*Jallow, Valera*
04/10	Encamp	W	4-2	*Villanueva, Sanguina 2, Jallow*
18/10	Penya Encarnada	W	2-0	*Jallow 2*
25/10	Sant Julià	D	1-1	*González*
01/11	FC Santa Coloma	L	1-3	*Oladymeji*
08/11	UE Santa Coloma	L	0-2	
15/11	Ordino	L	0-2	
22/11	Lusitans	L	0-1	
29/11	Encamp	D	0-0	
06/12	Penya Encarnada	W	1-0	*Vila*
13/12	Sant Julià	L	0-4	

2016
31/01	FC Santa Coloma	L	1-3	*Sanguina (p)*
07/02	UE Santa Coloma	W	3-0	*Matos, Sanguina, Fernández*
14/02	Ordino	W	3-0	*Sanguina 2, Matos*
20/03	Encamp	W	3-0	*Sanguina, Fernández, Jallow*
03/04	Penya Encarnada	W	5-2	*Pinto, Matos, Fernández 2, Sanguina*
10/04	Ordino	L	1-2	*Fernández*
17/04	Encamp	W	4-3	*Bacallao, Fernández, Matos 2*
24/04	Penya Encarnada	W	3-1	*Sanguina, Fernández 2*
08/05	Ordino	L	3-4	*Matos 2, Jallow*

No	Name	Nat	DoB	Pos	Aps	(s)	Gls
12	Erick Alejandro Aceves	MEX	24/03/95	M	1	(2)	
2	Carlos Alberto Bacallao	ESP	27/06/95	D	18	(1)	1
18	Bruno Miguel Cerqueira		11/12/97	A		(1)	
18	David Cervós		08/08/99	M		(1)	
23	Gabriel Fernandes		24/07/96	M	6	(3)	
10	Alejandro Fernández	ESP	17/12/96	M	8		8
14	Jonathan Ferreira		17/06/93	D	4	(4)	
3	Cristian González	ESP	19/04/96	D	10	(5)	1
9	Momodou Jallow	GAM	30/03/92	A	15	(1)	6
1	Eric Saúl León	MEX	10/11/94	G	3		
23	Rafa Martins		07/11/91	M	15	(4)	
7	Andreu Matos		01/12/95	A	6		7
17	Carles Medina		21/12/95	D	2	(7)	
21	Brian Mengual		30/06/94	D	3	(2)	
12	Alejandro Mireles	MEX	12/12/92	M		(1)	
6	Olajubu Oladymeji	IRL	02/08/94	M	5	(4)	1
15	Paulo Alexandre Silva	POR	08/02/98	M		(1)	
14	Jorge Pinto		15/05/94	M	14	(2)	1
16	Bryan Pubill		26/07/00	M		(1)	
6	Albert Puigdollers	ESP	30/10/80	M	5		
15	Fede Quiroz	ARG	05/10/95	A		(1)	
18	Isidro Fabián Rodríguez	PER	27/02/85	M	1	(2)	
6	Hamza Ryahi	ESP	11/03/94	M	5	(1)	
7	Carlos Javier Sanguina	PAR	22/06/95	A	17	(2)	9
1	Pol Serrat	ESP	20/05/96	G	6		
10	Gerard Suárez	ESP	22/02/96	M	9	(2)	
8	Brian André Teixeira		26/06/95	M	8		
1	Alberto Usubiaga		06/11/94	G	11		
5	Aitor Valera	ESP	09/10/92	M	19		1
8	Oriol Vila	ESP	23/03/79	M	10		1
4	David Villanueva	ESP	12/02/96	D	19		1

FC Lusitans

1999 • fclusitans.com
Major honours
Andorran League (2) 2012, 2013
Coach: Xavier Roura (ESP);
(27/01/16) Raúl Cañete (ESP)

2015

27/09	Engordany	W 4-2	*Aguilar 2 (1p), Luís dos Reis, João Lima*
04/10	Sant Julià	L 1-3	*Muñoz*
18/10	FC Santa Coloma	W 1-0	*Aguilar (p)*
25/10	UE Santa Coloma	L 0-2	
01/11	Ordino	W 1-0	*Lucas Maciel*
08/11	Penya Encarnada	W 2-0	*Aguilar 2 (1p)*
15/11	Encamp	W 6-0	*Aguilar 2, Pinto, Lopes, João Lima 2 (1p)*
22/11	Engordany	W 1-0	*Muñoz*
29/11	Sant Julià	L 0-2	
06/12	FC Santa Coloma	L 0-4	
13/12	UE Santa Coloma	W 3-2	*L San Nicolás, Fontan, Aguilar*

2016

31/01	Ordino	W 2-1	*Lucas Maciel, Villanueva*
07/02	Penya Encarnada	W 4-0	*Villanueva (p), Muñoz, Fábio Serra, Aguilar*
14/02	Encamp	W 3-2	*Aguilar, Pousa, Villanueva*
20/03	FC Santa Coloma	D 0-0	
03/04	UE Santa Coloma	D 1-1	*Villanueva*
10/04	Sant Julià	W 3-2	*Aguilar, Riera, Lucas Maciel*
17/04	FC Santa Coloma	D 0-0	
24/04	UE Santa Coloma	W 3-1	*Aguilar, L San Nicolás 2*
27/04	Sant Julià	L 2-6	*L San Nicolás, Villanueva (p)*

No	Name	Nat	DoB	Pos	Aps	(s)	Gls
2	Carlos Acosta	ESP	15/08/89	M	16		
11	José Antonio Aguilar	ESP	11/10/89	A	14	(2)	12
30	Andrés Benítez	PAR	01/01/83	G	6		
19	Samïr Bousenine		07/02/91	M	3	(2)	
22	Oumar Diop	CMR	23/06/94	M	4	(2)	
31	Fábio Serra	POR	24/08/84	A	17	(2)	1
23	Gabriel Fernandes		24/07/96	A	1	(2)	
12	Yael Fontan	ESP	24/02/80	D	3	(5)	1
15	Rui Filipe Gonçalves		17/08/91	D	1		
17	João Lima	POR	30/04/90	A		(9)	3
24	Léo Maciel	POR	02/07/82	D	13	(1)	
20	João Lopes		09/10/91	A	1	(5)	1
4	Lucas Maciel	POR	06/03/91	D	18	(1)	3
10	Luís dos Reis	POR	22/03/81	A	13	(4)	1
19	Miguel Ricardo Ferreira	POR	01/06/79	D		(1)	
14	Alberto Molina	ESP	21/04/88	M	12	(3)	
5	Pedro Muñoz	ESP	09/01/87	D	17		3
6	Joel Paredes	ESP	03/05/95	M	6		
1	Ricardo Paz	ESP	14/05/93	G	14		
8	Luis Pinto		05/03/87	M	10	(2)	1
23	Cristopher Pousa		29/06/92	M	5	(3)	1
21	Riera	POR	15/09/86	A	6		1
13	Mateo Rodríguez	URU	25/05/93	D	4		
9	José Manuel Romero	ESP	29/09/88	A	1		
7	Luigi San Nicolás		28/06/92	A	10	(4)	4
3	Moisés San Nicolás		17/09/93	D	17	(1)	
9	José Antonio Villanueva	ESP	16/08/85	A	8	(1)	5

FC Ordino

2010 • no website
Coach: Miguel Ángel Lozano (ESP)

2015

27/09	Sant Julià	L 0-4	
04/10	FC Santa Coloma	L 3-4	*Jefferson, Vázquez, Rubiralta*
18/10	UE Santa Coloma	D 1-1	*Damià (p)*
25/10	Penya Encarnada	L 0-2	
01/11	Lusitans	L 0-1	
08/11	Encamp	L 0-3	
15/11	Engordany	W 2-0	*Reyes (p), Bertran*
22/11	Sant Julià	W 4-3	*Bertran, Camí 2, Jiménez*
29/11	FC Santa Coloma	L 0-2	
06/12	UE Santa Coloma	L 1-6	*Jefferson*
13/12	Penya Encarnada	W 3-0	*Jiménez, Camí 2*

2016

31/01	Lusitans	L 1-2	*Camí*
07/02	Encamp	L 0-4	
14/02	Engordany	L 0-3	
20/03	Penya Encarnada	W 3-2	*Jefferson 2 (1p), Rubiralta*
03/04	Encamp	W 1-0	*Xarpell*
10/04	Engordany	W 2-1	*Rubiralta, Jefferson*
17/04	Penya Encarnada	W 7-3	*og (Esparza), Pereira, Aranyó 2, Luque, Rubiralta, Lozano*
24/04	Encamp	D 0-0	
08/05	Engordany	W 4-3	*Lozano 3, Gaeta*

No	Name	Nat	DoB	Pos	Aps	(s)	Gls
10	Marc Aranyó	ESP	13/01/93	A	7		2
8	Marc Baró		31/12/96	M		(1)	
17	Jordi Barra		10/07/78	M	8		
10	Sebastià Bertran		10/12/92	M	9	(1)	2
7	Jordi Camí	ESP	07/08/94	A	8	(5)	5
18	Germán Damià	ESP	18/01/90	M	6		1
99	Francisco José Domingo		12/02/99	G	1		
5	Cristian Ferreira		16/12/96	D	1	(2)	
4	Jonathan Ferreira		17/06/93	D	4	(3)	
22	Robert Flotats		11/11/97	M	1	(2)	
23	David Gaeta		24/08/82	A	3	(9)	1
20	Aaron García	ESP	21/08/94	M	9	(3)	
1	Aleix García	ESP	08/01/94	G	12		
3	Jonathan Gonçalves		21/02/96	D	8	(2)	
5	Francisco Hernández	ESP	08/01/86	M	1	(1)	
19	Jefferson	BRA	06/02/95	A	10	(3)	5
9	Jaime Jiménez	ESP	16/04/94	M	10		2
4	Jonathan Lorente	ESP	21/01/95	D	2		
21	Miguel Ángel Lozano	ESP	16/09/78	M	14	(4)	4
16	Daniel Luque	ESP	05/03/93	M	8	(1)	1
20	Matías Maturana	CHI	19/05/99	M		(1)	
8	Daniel Mejías		28/06/82	M	6	(4)	
9	Noham Pereira		30/09/98	M	5	(4)	1
22	Alex Ramírez	ESP	14/06/94	D	6		
3	Oscar Reyes	ESP	12/03/88	D	10		1
2	Daniel Ribeiro		09/01/92	D	7		
9	Axel Rubiralta	ESP	21/06/94	A	9	(4)	4
9	Tiago	POR	06/07/88	M	1	(3)	
12	Gil Tudó		26/03/99	A	1	(1)	
6	Oscar Vázquez	ESP	03/01/94	M	20		1
5	Pere Vilardell	ESP	08/01/86	D	18		
2	Jordi Xapell		01/06/98	D	3	(2)	
19	David Xarpell		20/04/94	M	5		1
13	Houssain Zain	MAR	20/01/96	G	7		

Penya Encarnada d'Andorra

2009 • penyaencarnada.com
Coach: Filipe António Busto (POR);
(29/01/16) Ruben Olivera (POR)

2015

27/09	Encamp	D 1-1	*Hernández*
04/10	UE Santa Coloma	L 0-3	
18/10	Engordany	L 0-2	
25/10	Ordino	W 2-0	*Huerta, Rivera*
01/11	Sant Julià	D 2-2	*Najera, Sérgio Paulo Carvalho*
08/11	Lusitans	L 0-2	
15/11	FC Santa Coloma	L 0-5	
22/11	Encamp	L 0-5	
29/11	UE Santa Coloma	L 0-5	
06/12	Engordany	L 0-1	
13/12	Ordino	L 0-3	

2016

31/01	Sant Julià	L 1-3	*Ulloa*
07/02	Lusitans	L 0-4	
14/02	FC Santa Coloma	L 0-4	
20/03	Ordino	L 2-3	*Vázquez, Joya*
03/04	Engordany	L 2-5	*Vázquez, Esparza*
10/04	Encamp	D 1-1	*Najera*
17/04	Ordino	L 3-7	*Vázquez, og (Rubiralta), Huerta*
24/04	Engordany	L 1-3	*Rojas*
29/04	Encamp	L 0-3	*(w/o; original result 3-0 Vázquez, Sandoval, Aguilera (p))*

No	Name	Nat	DoB	Pos	Aps	(s)	Gls
1	Antonio Aguilera	MEX	01/10/96	G	16		1
2	Antonio Aguilera	MEX	01/10/96	D	2		
21	Miguel Ángel Braz		01/10/97	M	1	(3)	
7	Carlos Miguel Braga	POR	20/07/93	D	5	(1)	
8	Cristian Carvalho		27/02/00	M	2		
10	Nuno Miguel Da Silva		26/01/92	A		(1)	
3	Daniel Filipe da Silva	POR	16/01/87	D	1	(1)	
3	Luis Vicente Esparza	MEX	31/03/89	D	5		1
6	Alexandre Fajardo		07/06/00	M	2		
15	Cristian Fernández		16/12/96	D		(2)	
3	Jonathan Gonçalves		21/02/96	M		(1)	
21	César Daniel González	MEX	17/10/94	A	2	(2)	
11	César Oswaldo Hernández	MEX	26/01/91	A	4		1
16	Emmanuel Huerta	MEX	15/02/96	M	17		2
16	José Manuel da Costa	POR	09/11/82	M	3		
14	Juan José Joya	MEX	18/03/92	D	19		1
25	Lazaro Manuel Silveira	POR	28/05/85	G	4	(2)	
1	Lucas	BRA	09/11/97	A	1		
23	Miguel Angelo Carvalho	MEX	04/10/97	M	1		
5	Milton dos Santos	POR	12/06/87	D	1		
19	Héctor Alejandro Muñoz	MEX	21/06/97	A		(1)	
9	Diego Alejandro Najera	MEX	11/12/94	A	20		2
22	Nuno Miguel Barros	POR	18/08/87	M	9	(1)	
4	Marc Pedascoll		19/10/99	D	2		
17	Pedro Miguel Gonçalves	POR	25/07/90	M	3	(1)	
8	Víctor Pérez	MEX	12/11/90	M	16		
18	Pedro Adán Puente	MEX	20/12/96	M	14		
20	José Maria Ramírez	MEX	21/09/95	D	9		
2	Ángel Giovanni Ramos	MEX	19/02/90	D	17		
4	Joshua Gabriel Razo	MEX	03/08/95	D	1		
11	Christian Regalo		08/03/99	M	2	(1)	
9	Yair Alberto Reyes	MEX	04/01/95	D		(1)	
12	Yael Sirvando Rivera	MEX	01/12/96	D	19		1
6	Sergio Rodrigo	ESP	31/07/85	M	2	(2)	
10	Fernando Rodríguez	MEX	20/02/97	A	2	(2)	
11	Daniel Alberto Rojas	COL	09/07/96	M	3		1
7	Sergio Sánchez		08/11/99	M	1	(3)	
17	Irving Asael Sandoval	MEX	18/10/95	A	1		1
19	Sérgio Paulo Carvalho	POR	06/07/84	D	6	(3)	1
7	Luis Francisco Ulloa	MEX	17/06/97	A	2		1
7	Joel Vázquez	MEX	22/11/90	A	6		4

UE Sant Julià

1982 • no website
Major honours
Andorran League (2) 2005, 2009; Andorran Cup (5)
2008, 2010, 2011, 2014, 2015
Coach: Raúl Cañete (ESP);
(24/11/15) Carlos Sánchez (ESP)

2015

Date	Opponent	Res	Scorers
27/09	Ordino	W 4-0	Gomes 2, Bruninho, Alfi
04/10	Lusitans	W 3-1	Luizão 2, og (Muñoz)
18/10	Encamp	W 2-0	Alfi, Rafael Brito
25/10	Engordany	D 1-1	Varela
01/11	Penya Encarnada	D 2-2	Peppe, Martín
08/11	FC Santa Coloma	L 0-1	
15/11	UE Santa Coloma	L 0-2	
22/11	Ordino	L 3-4	Luizão 3 (1p)
29/11	Lusitans	W 2-0	Luizão, Martín
09/12	Encamp	W 6-0	Sonejee 2, Rafael Brito 2, Spano, Bruninho
13/12	Engordany	W 4-0	Sonejee, Spano, Rafael Brito, Girau

2016

Date	Opponent	Res	Scorers
31/01	Penya Encarnada	W 3-1	Alfi, Gallego, og (Joya)
07/02	FC Santa Coloma	L 0-2	
14/02	UE Santa Coloma	D 0-0	
20/03	UE Santa Coloma	D 0-0	
03/04	FC Santa Coloma	L 0-1	
10/04	Lusitans	L 2-3	Gomes, Girau
17/04	UE Santa Coloma	W 3-0	Coca (p), Alfi, Bruninho
24/04	FC Santa Coloma	D 0-0	
27/04	Lusitans	W 6-2	Alfi 3, Bruninho 3

No	Name	Nat	DoB	Pos	Aps	(s)	Gls
9	Alfi	ESP	18/01/85	A	14	(1)	7
10	Luis Blanco		15/01/90	M	2	(1)	
30	Bruninho	POR	11/01/86	A	19	(1)	6
13	Jesús Coca	ESP	22/05/89	G	20		1
19	Juan Antonio Gallego	ESP	19/09/91	A	3	(1)	1
20	Roberto García	ESP	09/01/87	M	4		
7	Kiko Girau	ESP	03/06/85	M	6	(10)	2
11	Carlos Gomes		18/10/93	A	9	(7)	3
21	Rodrigo Guida		24/08/82	A		(5)	
20	Luizão	BRA	25/02/90	A	8	(3)	6
8	Aaron Martín	ESP	27/09/87	M	17	(2)	2
4	Edu Peppe		28/01/83	M	16	(1)	1
6	Rafael Brito	POR	06/07/86	D	17		4
14	Eric Rodríguez		02/04/93	D	16	(2)	
5	Miguel Ruiz	ESP	16/07/82	D	17	(1)	
26	Óscar Sonejee		26/03/76	D	9	(4)	3
32	Mario Valentín Spano	ITA	07/02/86	M	14	(2)	2
23	Sebas Varela	URU	23/09/80	D	17	(3)	1
22	Iván Vigo	ESP	07/09/86	D	12	(3)	

FC Santa Coloma

1986 • fclubsantacoloma.net
Major honours
Andorran League (10) 1995, 2001, 2003, 2004, 2008,
2010, 2011, 2014, 2015, 2016; Andorran Cup (8)
2001, 2003, 2004, 2005, 2006, 2007, 2009, 2012
Coach: Richard Imbernón

2015

Date	Opponent	Res	Scorers
27/09	UE Santa Coloma	W 2-0	Lima, Noguerol
04/10	Ordino	W 4-3	C Martínez 2, Riera, Lima
18/10	Lusitans	L 0-1	
25/10	Encamp	W 5-1	Rodríguez, C Martínez 2, J Toscano, Lima
01/11	Engordany	W 3-1	Rebés, J Toscano 2
08/11	Sant Julià	W 1-0	Riera
15/11	Penya Encarnada	W 5-0	Pujol, C Martínez, J Toscano, Riera, J Martínez
22/11	UE Santa Coloma	D 0-0	
29/11	Ordino	W 2-0	C Martínez 2 (1p)
06/12	Lusitans	W 4-0	C Martínez 2, Noguerol, Parra
13/12	Encamp	W 6-0	Pujol, Parra 2, Riera 3

2016

Date	Opponent	Res	Scorers
31/01	Engordany	W 3-1	Pujol (p), Parra 2
07/02	Sant Julià	W 2-0	Riera, Parra
14/02	Penya Encarnada	W 4-0	Pujol 2, Juanfer, Mercadé
20/03	Lusitans	D 0-0	
03/04	Sant Julià	W 1-0	Parra
10/04	UE Santa Coloma	W 1-0	og (Anton)
17/04	Lusitans	D 0-0	
24/04	Sant Julià	D 0-0	
06/05	UE Santa Coloma	D 1-1	Lima

No	Name	Nat	DoB	Pos	Aps	(s)	Gls
15	António José Marinho	POR	30/05/94	A	1	(2)	
1	Eloy Casals	ESP	22/10/82	G	13		
3	Oriol Fité		02/02/89	D	7	(2)	
22	Fernando González	ESP	07/04/88	M	7	(2)	
23	Juanfer	ESP	05/05/83	A	11	(8)	1
6	Ildefons Lima		10/12/79	D	17		4
16	Cristian Martínez		16/10/89	A	15	(1)	9
8	Joel Martínez		31/12/88	A	5	(6)	1
17	Andreu Matos		11/12/95	A		(2)	
11	Albert Mercadé	ESP	23/01/85	M	8	(6)	1
20	Jaime Noguerol	ESP	24/02/84	M	17	(1)	2
19	Iban Parra	ESP	18/10/77	A	12	(7)	7
7	Marc Pujol		21/08/82	M	16	(1)	5
4	Andreu Ramos	ESP	19/01/89	D	19		
24	Robert Ramos	ESP	11/12/92	D	5	(5)	
16	Marc Rebés		03/07/94	M	16		1
21	Gabriel Riera		05/06/85	A	13	(4)	7
25	Victor Rodríguez		07/09/87	M	13	(2)	1
17	Dinis Silva		30/03/95	A		(1)	
13	Francisco Toscano		05/02/83	G	7		
10	Juan Carlos Toscano		14/08/84	A	7	(4)	4
2	Walter Wagner	ARG	12/01/81	D	11	(3)	

UE Santa Coloma

1986 • uesantacoloma.com
Major honours
Andorran Cup (2) 2013, 2016
Coach: Emiliano González

2015

Date	Opponent	Res	Scorers
27/09	FC Santa Coloma	L 0-2	
04/10	Penya Encarnada	W 3-0	Anton, Bernat, Jordi Rubio
18/10	Ordino	D 1-1	Bernat
25/10	Lusitans	W 2-0	Amat, Bernat
01/11	Encamp	W 6-0	Crespo 3, Bernat, Anton, Jordi Rubio (p)
08/11	Engordany	W 2-0	Rodríguez, Crespo
15/11	Sant Julià	W 2-0	Bernat, Rodríguez
22/11	FC Santa Coloma	D 0-0	
29/11	Penya Encarnada	W 5-0	Bernat 2, Salomó, Jordi Rubio, Jesús Rubio
06/12	Ordino	W 6-1	Crespo 3, Salomó 2, Bernat
13/12	Lusitans	L 2-3	Crespo, Bernat

2016

Date	Opponent	Res	Scorers
31/01	Encamp	W 2-1	Bernat, Crespo
07/02	Engordany	L 0-3	
14/02	Sant Julià	D 0-0	
20/03	Sant Julià	D 0-0	
03/04	Lusitans	D 1-1	Bernat
10/04	FC Santa Coloma	L 0-1	
17/04	Sant Julià	L 0-3	
24/04	Lusitans	L 1-3	Pedro Reis
06/05	FC Santa Coloma	D 1-1	Bernat

No	Name	Nat	DoB	Pos	Aps	(s)	Gls
17	Gerard Aloy		17/04/89	M	14	(3)	
4	Marc Amat		26/06/93	M		(4)	1
9	Boris Anton		27/02/87	A	17	(1)	2
8	Josep Manel Ayala		08/04/80	M	18	(1)	
14	Víctor Bernat	ESP	17/05/87	A	19		12
24	Walid Bousenine		07/04/93	M	9	(5)	
22	Sergio Crespo		29/09/92	M	18	(1)	9
23	Adel Durán	CUB	29/01/93	M	2	(5)	
13	Ricard Fernández	ESP	26/05/75	G	3		
16	Luca Maciocia	ITA	28/05/97	M		(1)	
3	David Maneiro		16/02/89	D	2	(2)	
5	Alex Martínez		04/03/87	D	7	(1)	
16	Zacharie Moussa	CMR	07/01/96	A	1	(5)	
25	Cristian Orosa		12/12/90	D	15	(1)	
19	Pedro Reis	POR	08/02/85	A	5	(6)	1
19	Aitor Pereira		22/12/92	M		(5)	
1	Ivan Periánez		25/01/82	G	17		
6	Alex Roca		04/07/91	D	18	(1)	
18	Albert Rodríguez		12/02/86	M	4	(5)	2
2	Jesús Rubio		09/09/94	D	16	(1)	1
7	Jordi Rubio		01/11/87	D	18	(1)	3
11	Juan Salomó		20/12/83	A	17	(2)	3

 **ANDORRA**

Top goalscorers

12	José Antonio Aguilar (Lusitans)
	Víctor Bernat (UE Santa Coloma)
9	Carlos Javier Sanguina (Engordany)
	Cristian Martínez (FC Santa Coloma)
	Sergio Crespo (UE Santa Coloma)
8	Alejandro Fernández (Engordany)
7	Andreu Matos (Engordany)
	Alfi (Sant Julià)
	Iban Parra (FC Santa Coloma)
	Gabriel Riera (FC Santa Coloma)

Promoted club

CE Jenlai

2008 • no website
Coach: Llorenç Codoñes (ESP)

Second level final table 2015/16

		Pld	W	D	L	F	A	Pts
1	CE Jenlai	23	21	1	1	111	15	64
2	CE Carroi	23	19	1	3	73	23	58
3	Atlètic Club d'Escaldes	23	18	2	3	59	13	56
4	UE Extremenya	23	17	1	5	85	26	52
5	Inter Club d'Escaldes	23	13	4	6	71	28	43
6	FC Encamp B	23	9	5	9	44	42	32
7	CF Atlètic Amèrica	23	8	2	13	52	57	26
8	FS La Massana	23	7	3	13	48	58	24
9	FC Santa Coloma B	23	6	4	13	44	58	22
10	UE Santa Coloma B	23	6	4	13	40	74	22
11	Ranger's FC	23	4	0	19	35	98	12
12	FC Lusitans B	23	0	0	23	10	129	0
13	FC Ordino B	12	2	1	9	14	65	7

NB: FC Ordino B withdrew after round 12 and were placed last; their results stood.

Promotion/Relegation play-offs

(15/05/16 & 22/05/16)
Carroi 0-3 Encamp *(w/o; original result 0-0)*
Encamp w/o Carroi
(Encamp 3-0)

DOMESTIC CUP

Copa Constitució 2016

FIRST ROUND

(21/02/16)
Extremenya 0-5 Engordany
Inter 0-3 Encamp *(aet)*
Ordino 5-3 Jenlai *(aet)*
Penya Encarnada 7-0 Atlètic

QUARTER-FINALS

(28/02/16)
Lusitans 2-4 Engordany *(Rodríguez 50, Acosta 63; Fernandes 40, Jallow 84, 102, Fernández 115) (aet)*
Penya Encarnada 1-3 UE Santa Coloma *(Najera 4; Martínez 2, 47, Bernat 70)*
Sant Julià 1-0 Encamp *(Meilan 77og)*
FC Santa Coloma 2-0 Ordino *(Pujol 69p, Lima 87)*

SEMI-FINALS

(06/03/16)
Sant Julià 1-2 Engordany *(Vigo 79; Fernández 81, Sanguina 86)*
FC Santa Coloma 0-1 UE Santa Coloma *(Moussa 88)*

FINAL

(15/05/16)
Estadi Comunal, Andorra la Vella
UE SANTA COLOMA 3 *(Anton 4, Bernat 57, 65)*
UE ENGORDANY 0
Referee: *Villamayor*
UE SANTA COLOMA: *Periánez, Jesús Rubio, Martínez, Roca, Jordi Rubio (Pedro Reis 75), Ayala (Orosa 86), Aloy, Crespo (Bousenine 73), Anton, Salomó, Bernat*
ENGORDANY: *Serrat, Bacallao, Villanueva, González (Martins 69), Valera, Ryahi, Teixeira, Fernández, Matos, Sanguina, Fernandes (Jallow 54)*

UE Santa Coloma savour their Copa Constitució success after defeating Engordany 3-0 in the final

ARMENIA
Hayastani Futboli Federacia (HFF)

Address	Khanjyan Street 27	**President**	Ruben Hayrapetyan
	AM-0010 Yerevan	**Vice-president**	Armen Minasyan
Tel	+374 10 568883	**Media officer**	Tigran Israelyan
Fax	+374 10 547173	**Year of formation**	1992
E-mail	media@ffa.am	**National stadium**	Hanrapetakan,
Website	ffa.am		Yerevan (14,400)

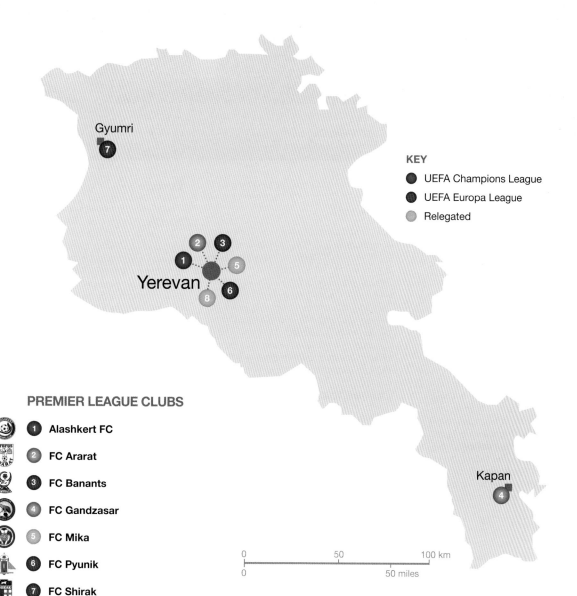

KEY

● UEFA Champions League
● UEFA Europa League
● Relegated

PREMIER LEAGUE CLUBS

1 Alashkert FC

2 FC Ararat

3 FC Banants

4 FC Gandzasar

5 FC Mika

6 FC Pyunik

7 FC Shirak

8 Ulisses FC

Alashkert edge to first title

Once the private preserve of FC Pyunik, the Armenian Premier Division title was claimed by a fifth different club in as many seasons in 2016 as Alashkert FC lifted the trophy for the first time. Front-runners throughout, Abraham Khashmanyan's free-scoring team recovered from a late stutter to hold off FC Shirak and triumph on the final day.

FC Banants, the last first-time champions before Alashkert, in 2014, captured the Armenian Cup with a 2-0 victory over FC Mika, defeated in the final for the second successive year.

Nerve-racking finale for long-time leaders

Fast-finishing Shirak take runners-up spot

Independence Cup glory for Banants

Domestic league

The last team to win promotion to Armenia's top division, in 2013, before it became a closed shop, Alashkert ended their debut season among the elite in bottom place before rising to fourth in 2014/15. The club's upward curve continued to rise steeply in coach Khashmanyan's first full season at the helm as the unlikely challengers powered to the top of the table.

Pyunik, the defending champions, were the only team to defeat Alashkert in the first half of the campaign, which ended with Ulisses FC, the 2011 champions and 2014/15 runners-up, pulling out of the league and, ultimately, going out of business. In fact, Pyunik would have entered the three-month winter break in pole position had they defeated the leaders at home in late November, but a 0-0 draw kept Alashkert two points in front, and there they would continue to reside for the remainder of the campaign.

Pyunik's challenge withered and died in the spring as they suddenly forgot how to win, and that appeared to leave the way clear for Alashkert to cruise home unopposed. But with the prize so close and just one point needed from their last three matches Khashmanyan's men suddenly got edgy, losing back-to-back home games against FC Ararat and Shirak, both to late winning goals, with Shirak's coming in the fourth minute of added time.

With that dramatic strike from Viulen Ayvazyan, Shirak had cut Alashkert's lead from nine points to three in just four days and could still take the title, in a play-off, if they won their final fixture and Alashkert lost again, away to Mika. But there would be no third successive defeat. Goals from Mihran Manasyan and Brazilian loanee Héber, which would leave the pair tied on 16 at the top of the division's scoring charts, ensured a victorious finale for a relieved and joyous Alashkert.

Domestic cup

Mika's last-day defeat left them last of the seven teams that completed the league campaign. One point and one place above them were Banants, and it was those two teams who met in the Armenian Cup final. Mika were eager to get their excellent record in the fixture back on track after losing for the first time in 2015 (3-1 to Pyunik) following six successful final appearances, but Banants, who had impressively eliminated Alashkert on the away goals rule in the semi-finals, took the trophy for the third time thanks to an early penalty from Brazilian hitman Laércio and a second goal from Russian striker Atsamaz Buraev.

Europe

Pyunik, Shirak and Alashkert – on their European debut – all came through their first qualifying round ties, only to exit a round later. Of the seven matches played on Armenian soil, however, five resulted in victory, with Pyunik and Alashkert winning both of theirs, the second albeit after suffering heavy first-leg defeats to Molde and Kairat Almaty, respectively.

National team

A difficult UEFA EURO 2016 campaign for Armenia closed with a 3-0 home defeat by Albania, leaving them last in Group I with just two points. Four games without a goal concluded record cap-holder Sargis Hovsepyan's short spell in charge, and although new boss Varuzhan Sukiasyan kicked off with another stalemate – a 0-0 draw in Yerevan against Belarus in which 41-year-old goalkeeper Roman Berezovski made a short farewell cameo – two end-of-term friendlies in the United States against Central American opposition yielded no fewer than 12 goals. Three of those, against Guatemala, were scored by star midfielder and perennial Armenian footballer of the year Henrikh Mkhitaryan, who thus ended a 21-month drought to increase his record haul to 19.

DOMESTIC SEASON AT A GLANCE

Premier League 2015/16 final table

		Pld	Home					Away					Total					
			W	D	L	F	A	W	D	L	F	A	W	D	L	F	A	Pts
1	**Alashkert FC**	28	9	2	3	28	11	7	5	2	22	13	16	7	5	50	24	55
2	FC Shirak	28	8	2	4	22	15	7	5	2	19	12	15	7	6	41	27	52
3	FC Pyunik	28	7	4	3	24	9	6	5	3	20	12	13	9	6	44	21	48
4	FC Gandzasar	28	7	7	0	21	9	4	5	5	14	18	11	12	5	35	27	45
5	FC Ararat	28	3	5	6	14	20	6	5	3	14	11	9	10	9	28	31	37
6	FC Banants	28	4	7	3	22	13	3	5	6	14	21	7	12	9	36	34	33
7	FC Mika	28	5	3	6	12	13	4	2	8	18	19	9	5	14	30	32	32
8	Ulisses FC	28	0	2	12	4	35	0	0	14	4	41	0	2	26	8	76	2

NB Ulisses FC withdrew after round 15 – their remaining matches were awarded as 0-3 defeats.

European qualification 2016/17

 Champion: Alashkert FC (first qualifying round)

 Cup winner: FC Banants (first qualifying round)
FC Shirak (first qualifying round)
FC Pyunik (first qualifying round)

Top scorer — Héber (Alashkert) & Mihran Manasyan (Alashkert), 16 goals
Relegated clubs — Ulisses FC (withdrew), FC Mika (withdrew)
Promoted clubs — none
Cup final — FC Banants 2-0 FC Mika

Team of the season
(4-4-2)

Coach: Khashmanyan (Alashkert)

Kasparov *(Alashkert)*

Haroyan *(Pyunik)* — A Hovhannisyan *(Shirak)* — Karapetyan *(Mika)* — Artak Yedigaryan *(Alashkert)*

Khachatryan *(Ararat)* — Tigran Barseghyan *(Gandzasar)* — Hakobyan *(Shirak)* — Satumyan *(Pyunik)*

Laércio *(Banants)* — Héber *(Alashkert)*

Player of the season

Tigran Barseghyan
(FC Gandzasar)

Alashkert had the best team in the 2015/16 Armenian Premier League and also the most fluent attack, but it was fourth-placed Gandzasar who boasted the division's most crowd-pleasing individual. A new signing from Mika, Barseghyan repeatedly wowed the crowds in Kapan and beyond with his dribbling, passing and all-round creativity. The 22-year-old left-footer was duly called up by new Armenia national team coach Varuzhan Sukiasyan and scored on his third appearance, a 4-0 win against El Salvador.

Newcomer of the season

Héber
(Alashkert FC)

As loan signings go, Alashkert could hardly have asked for more from their new temporary acquisition from Brazilian club Coimbra EC as Héber Araújo dos Santos lit up the Premier League and helped his club to their first Armenian title. A double on his debut in a 2-1 win at defending champions Pyunik was the perfect start, and the 24-year-old forward maintained a healthy output throughout the campaign, ending up with 16 goals – the same number as his equally proficient strike partner Mihran Manasyan.

NATIONAL TEAM

Top five all-time caps
Sargis Hovsepyan (131);
Roman Berezovski (94);
Robert Arzumanyan (74);
Artur Petrosyan (69); Harutyun Vardanyan (63)

Top five all-time goals
Henrikh Mkhitaryan (19);
Artur Petrosyan (11);
**Gevorg Ghazaryan, Edgar Manucharyan
& Yura Movsisyan** (9)

Results 2015/16

04/09/15	Serbia (ECQ)	A	Novi Sad	L	0-2	
07/09/15	Denmark (ECQ)	H	Yerevan	D	0-0	
08/10/15	France	A	Nice	L	0-4	
11/10/15	Albania (ECQ)	H	Yerevan	L	0-3	
25/03/16	Belarus	H	Yerevan	D	0-0	
28/05/16	Guatemala	N	Carson (USA)	W	7-1	Mkhitaryan (39, 60 ,70), Manucharyan (45), Kadimyan (50), Sarkisov (72), Badoyan (84)
01/06/16	El Salvador	N	Carson (USA)	W	4-0	García (3og), Hambardzumyan (9), Barseghyan (69), Kadimyan (76)

Appearances 2015/16

Coach: Sargis Hovsepyan /(10/12/15) Varuzhan Sukiasyan	02/11/72 05/08/56		SRB	DEN	Fra	ALB	Blr	Gua	Slv	Caps	Goals
Gevorg Kasparov	25/07/80	Alashkert	G	G	G	G				29	-
Hrayr Mkoyan	02/09/86	Esteghlal (IRN)	D	D			D78			36	1
Robert Arzumanyan	24/07/85	Amkar (RUS)	D	D		D				74	5
Gael Andonyan	07/02/95	Marseille (FRA) /Dijon (FRA)	D	D	D	D	D	D	D	9	-
Levon Hayrapetyan	17/04/89	Pyunik	D		D		D	D	D73	34	1
Aras Özbiliz	09/03/90	Spartak Moskva (RUS) /Rayo Vallecano (ESP)	M59	s83	s54	s46	M63	s61		24	4
Henrikh Mkhitaryan	21/01/89	Dortmund (GER)	M	M	M60	M	M	M	M	59	19
Marcos Pizzelli	03/10/84	Aktobe (KAZ) /Al-Raed (KSA)	M65	M62	s60	M	M68	M64	M53	49	8
Karlen Mkrtchyan	25/11/88	Anji (RUS)	M	M	M80	M				45	2
Gevorg Ghazaryan	05/04/88	Marítimo (POR)	M82	M	M67	M83				49	9
Yura Movsisyan	02/08/87	Spartak Moskva (RUS)	A	A83		A59			s71	34	9
Kamo Hovhannisyan	05/10/92	Pyunik	s59	M87	M61	D				27	-
Ruslan Koryan	15/06/88	Luch-Energia (RUS)	s65	s62						4	-
Artem Simonyan	20/02/95	Zürich (SUI)	s82	s87						3	-
Varazdat Haroyan	24/08/92	Pyunik		D		D	D	D71	s69	21	-
Hovhannes Hambardzumyan	04/10/90	Vardar (MKD)			D70		s78	D	D71	14	1
Taron Voskanyan	22/02/93	Pyunik			D			s71	D	15	-
Artur Yusbashyan	07/09/89	Pyunik			M	M46				11	-
Artur Sarkisov	19/01/87	Volga (RUS)			A54	s59	s63	s64		34	5
Vardan Poghosyan	08/03/92	Pyunik			s61	s83				2	-
Norayr Aslanyan	25/03/91	Almere (NED)			s67					8	-
Davit Manoyan	05/07/90	Pyunik			s70		M		s53	20	-
Artak Grigoryan	19/10/87	Alashkert			s80					2	-
Roman Berezovski	05/08/74	unattached					G8			94	-
Gor Malakyan	12/06/94	Stal (UKR)					M	M75	M69	3	-
Edgar Manucharyan	19/01/87	Ural (RUS)					A81	A61	A55	50	9
Arsen Beglaryan	18/02/93	Mika					s8	G	G	3	-
Gegam Kadimyan	19/10/92	Karpaty (UKR)					s68	M61	s55	3	2
Tigran Barseghyan	22/09/93	Gandzasar					s81	M75	M73	3	1
Artak Yedigaryan	18/03/90	Alashkert						s61	M	19	-
Zaven Badoyan	22/12/89	Banants						s75		6	1
Benik Hovhannisyan	01/05/93	Ararat						s75		1	-
Sergey Avagimyan	05/07/89	Ararat							s73	1	-
Davit Hakobyan	21/03/93	Shirak							s73	1	-

EUROPE

FC Pyunik

CHAMPIONS LEAGUE

First qualifying round - SS Folgore (SMR)
H 2-1 *Satumyan (45+2), Romero (48)*
Ayvazov, Haroyan, G Hovhannisyan (Shahinyan 79), K Hovhannisyan, Yusbashyan, Badoyan, Hayrapetyan, Hovsepyan (Romero 46), Jeremiah (Razmik Hakobyan 65), Satumyan, Voskanyan. Coach: Sargis Hovsepyan (ARM)
A 2-1 *K Hovhannisyan (6), Satumyan (41)*
Ayvazov, Haroyan, Romero, G Hovhannisyan (G Hovhannisyan 71), Romero, Gagik Poghosyan (Hovsepyan 65), Razmik Hakobyan (Jeremiah 73), Yusbashyan, Badoyan, Hayrapetyan, Satumyan, Voskanyan. Coach: Sargis Hovsepyan (ARM)

Second qualifying round - Molde FK (NOR)
A 0-5
Ayvazov, Haroyan, G Hovhannisyan (Jeremiah 59), K Hovhannisyan, Romero, Gagik Poghosyan (Manoyan 67), Yusbashyan, Badoyan (Razmik Hakobyan 77), Hayrapetyan, Satumyan, Voskanyan. Coach: Sargis Hovsepyan (ARM)
H 1-0 *Badoyan (74)*
Ayvazov, Haroyan, K Hovhannisyan, Gagik Poghosyan, Yusbashyan, Badoyan, Hayrapetyan, Hovsepyan (Manoyan 46), Jeremiah (Razmik Hakobyan 46), Satumyan (Ghukas Poghosyan 70), Voskanyan. Coach: Sargis Hovsepyan (ARM)

Ulisses FC

EUROPA LEAGUE

First qualifying round - Birkirkara FC (MLT)
A 0-0
Beglaryan, Chezhiya, Khurtsidze, Geperidze (Kalimulin 84), Piliev (Tshibamba 62), Aleksanyan, Mamakhanov, Dugalić, Morozov, Jarkava, Khubua (Belomitsev 79). Coach: Suren Chakhalyan (ARM)
H 1-3 *Morozov (71)*
Beglaryan, Paderin, Khurtsidze, Tshibamba (Piliev 53), Geperidze, Aleksanyan, Mamakhanov, Dugalić, Morozov, Dzharkava (Janashia 70), Khubua. Coach: Suren Chakhalyan (ARM)
Red card: Aleksanyan 81

FC Shirak

EUROPA LEAGUE

First qualifying round - HŠK Zrinjski (BIH)
H 2-0 *Bougouhi (18, 67)*
Ermakov, A Hovhannisyan, Davtyan, G Malakyan, Bougouhi (Muradyan 86), Hakobyan (Barikyan 59), Stamenković, G Hovhannisyan, E Malakyan, Davoyan, Diarrassouba (Ayvazyan 80). Coach: Vardan Bichakhchyan (ARM)
A 1-2 *Bougouhi (90+8)*
Ermakov, A Hovhannisyan, Davtyan (Aleksanyan 83), G Malakyan, Bougouhi, Hakobyan, Stamenković, G Hovhannisyan, E Malakyan, Davoyan, Diarrassouba (Barikyan 46). Coach: Vardan Bichakhchyan (ARM)

Second qualifying round - AIK Solna (SWE)
A 0-2
Ermakov, A Hovhannisyan, G Malakyan, Bougouhi (Ayvazyan 90+3), Hakobyan (Barikyan 78), Aleksanyan, Stamenković, G Hovhannisyan, E Malakyan, Davoyan, Diarrassouba (Davtyan 90). Coach: Vardan Bichakhchyan (ARM)
Red cards: A Hovhannisyan 69, G Malakyan 80, Barikyan 85
H 0-2
Ermakov, Mikaelyan, Davtyan, Bougouhi (Muradyan 76), Hakobyan (Ayvazyan 58), Aleksanyan (Kaba 70), Stamenković, G Hovhannisyan, E Malakyan, Davoyan, Diarrassouba. Coach: Vardan Bichakhchyan (ARM)

Alashkert FC

EUROPA LEAGUE

First qualifying round - Saint Johnstone FC (SCO)
H 1-0 *Manasyan (59)*
Kasparov, Fofana, Muradyan, Arakelyan, Veranyan, Gevorg Poghosyan, Bareghamyan, Usenya (Manasyan 57), Minasyan, Grigoryan (Hovsepyan 90+5), Norayr Gyozalyan (Héber 80). Coach: Abraham Khashmanyan (ARM)
A 1-2 *Norayr Gyozalyan (74)*
Kasparov, Fofana, Muradyan, Arakelyan, Veranyan (A Voskanyan 90+3), Gevorg Poghosyan, Bareghamyan (Héber 90+5), Usenya, Minasyan, Grigoryan, Norayr Gyozalyan (Manasyan 75). Coach: Abraham Khashmanyan (ARM)
Red card: Muradyan 65

Second qualifying round - FC Kairat Almaty (KAZ)
A 0-3
Kasparov, Fofana, Arakelyan, Manasyan (Ghazaryan 57), Veranyan, Gevorg Poghosyan, Bareghamyan, Usenya (Karapetyan 77), Usenya, Minasyan, Grigoryan, Norayr Gyozalyan (Héber 73). Coach: Abraham Khashmanyan (ARM)
H 2-1 *Arakelyan (28), Héber (90+3)*
Kasparov, Fofana, Héber, Muradyan (Hovsepyan 78), Arakelyan, Veranyan (Gevorg Poghosyan 58), Bareghamyan, Usenya, Minasyan, Grigoryan, Gyozalyan (Manasyan 58). Coach: Abraham Khashmanyan (ARM)

DOMESTIC LEAGUE CLUB-BY-CLUB

Alashkert FC

2012 • Nairi (2,500) • fcalashkert.am
Major honours
Armenian League (1) 2016
Coach: Abraham Khashmanyan

2015

01/08	a	Pyunik	W	2-1	*Héber 2 (1p)*
08/08	h	Gandzasar	D	0-0	
16/08	a	Banants	D	2-2	*Dukić, Manasyan*
22/08	h	Ulisses	W	4-0	*Manasyan, Loretsyan, Héber, Grigoryan*
29/08	a	Ararat	W	2-1	*Manasyan, Héber (p)*
12/09	h	Mika	W	2-0	*Manasyan 2*
19/09	a	Shirak	W	2-1	*Artak Yedigaryan, Héber*
27/09	h	Pyunik	L	1-4	*Manasyan*
03/10	a	Gandzasar	D	2-2	*Manasyan, Héber*
18/10	h	Banants	W	3-0	*Héber 2, Manasyan (p)*
25/10	a	Ulisses	W	3-0	*Manasyan 2, Héber*
31/10	a	Ararat	D	1-1	*Manasyan*
07/11	a	Mika	W	1-0	*Manasyan*
21/11	h	Shirak	W	2-0	*Héber, Hovsepyan*
28/11	a	Pyunik	D	0-0	

2016

02/03	h	Gandzasar	W	3-0	*Manasyan, Héber 2*
12/03	a	Banants	L	0-2	
19/03	h	Ulisses	W	3-0	*(w/o)*
02/04	h	Mika	W	2-1	*Grigoryan, Héber*
06/04	a	Ararat	D	0-0	
09/04	a	Shirak	L	1-2	*Manasyan*
16/04	h	Pyunik	W	3-0	*Manasyan, Arakelyan, Artak Yedigaryan*
23/04	a	Gandzasar	D	2-2	*Héber, Ghazaryan*
30/04	h	Banants	W	2-1	*Héber, Muradyan*
08/05	a	Ulisses	W	3-0	*(w/o)*
14/05	a	Ararat	L	0-1	
18/05	h	Shirak	L	2-3	*Avagyan, Minasyan*
22/05	a	Mika	W	2-0	*Manasyan, Héber (p)*

No	Name	Nat	DoB	Pos	Aps	(s)	Gls
6	Ararat Arakelyan		01/02/84	D	25		1
16	Artur Avagyan		04/07/87	D	7	(1)	1
35	Areg Azatyan		23/06/90	A		(1)	
21	Arsen Balabekyan		24/11/86	A	1	(11)	
14	Aram Bareghamyan		01/06/88	M	5	(7)	
17	Liparit Dashtoyan		18/11/97	M		(1)	
20	Duško Dukić	SRB	21/06/86	D	4	(1)	1
25	Mamadou Sekou Fofana	MLI	26/09/89	D	14		
4	Rafayel Ghazaryan		17/05/90	M		(6)	1
21	Artak G Grigoryan		19/10/87	M	19	(1)	2
32	Narek Gyozalyan		10/07/92	M		(1)	
22	Norayr Gyozalyan		15/03/90	A	12	(5)	
9	Héber	BRA	10/08/91	A	25	(1)	16
3	Grigor Hovhannisyan		08/12/93	D	2	(2)	
15	Aram Hovsepyan		06/06/91	M	10	(5)	1
1	Gevorg Kasparov		25/07/80	G	26		
18	Aram Loretsyan		07/03/93	M	1	(9)	1
7	Mihran Manasyan		13/06/89	A	20	(2)	16
19	Vahagn Minasyan		25/04/85	D	18		1
5	Karen Muradyan		01/11/92	M	17	(2)	1
34	Gagik Poghosyan		04/05/93	M		(1)	
13	Gevorg Poghosyan		26/08/86	D	14	(3)	
10	Khoren Veranyan		04/09/86	M	24	(1)	
8	Andranik Voskanyan		11/04/90	D	17	(2)	
17	Artak Yedigaryan		18/03/90	D	20	(2)	2
20	Artur Yedigaryan		26/07/87	M	5	(6)	

 **ARMENIA**

FC Ararat

1935 • Hrazdan (45,000) • fcararat.am

Major honours
USSR League (1) 1973; Armenian League (1) 1993;
USSR Cup (2) 1973, 1975; Armenian Cup (5) 1993,
1994, 1995, 1997, 2008

Coach: Varuzhan Sukiasyan

2015

02/08	h	Ulisses	W	2-0	Chueca, Orozco
09/08	a	Mika	W	1-0	De la Fuente
16/08	h	Pyunik	D	1-1	Rakić
23/08	a	Banants	L	0-3	
29/08	h	Alashkert	L	1-2	Bulut
12/09	h	Shirak	L	0-2	
20/09	a	Gandzasar	L	0-1	
26/09	a	Ulisses	W	2-1	De la Fuente 2
05/10	h	Mika	W	2-1	Nranyan 2
18/10	a	Pyunik	W	1-0	Nranyan
24/10	h	Banants	D	0-0	
31/10	a	Alashkert	D	1-1	Nranyan
08/11	a	Shirak	W	1-0	Hovhannisyan
21/11	h	Gandzasar	D	2-2	Hovsepyan, Orozco
28/11	h	Ulisses	W	3-1	og (Hunanyan), Nranyan, Sahakyan

2016

03/03	a	Mika	D	1-1	Kaina
13/03	h	Pyunik	L	1-2	Grigoryan
20/03	a	Banants	D	2-2	Orozco (p), De la Fuente
02/04	h	Shirak	D	1-1	De la Fuente
06/04	h	Alashkert	D	0-0	
10/04	a	Gandzasar	D	0-0	
17/04	h	Ulisses	W	3-0	(w/o)
23/04	h	Mika	L	0-4	
30/04	a	Pyunik	D	0-0	
08/05	h	Banants	L	1-2	Nwabueze
14/05	a	Alashkert	W	1-0	Koné
18/05	h	Gandzasar	L	0-2	
22/05	a	Shirak	L	1-2	Hovhannisyan

No	Name	Nat	DoB	Pos	Aps	(s)	Gls
3	Sergey Avagimyan		05/07/89	D	12		
2	Ruslan Avagyan		24/06/95	D	1	(5)	
15	Tamaz Avdalyan	UKR	03/02/94	A		(1)	
10	Areg Azatyan		29/06/90	A	1	(1)	
20	Zaven Bulut	FRA	05/04/92	M	10	(4)	1
7	Christian Chaney	USA	08/10/94	M		(1)	
5	Hayk Chilingaryan		01/02/89	D	1	(5)	
23	Carlo Chueca	PER	23/03/93	M	4	(4)	1
11	Bryan de la Fuente	MEX	01/07/92	M	26		5
21	David Ghandilyan		04/07/93	A		(3)	
6	Marin Glavaš	CRO	17/03/92	M	3	(1)	
3	Norayr Grigoryan		07/06/83	D	26		1
1	Aram Hayrapetyan		22/11/86	G	3		
6	Benik Hovhannisyan		01/05/93	M	19	(4)	2
3	Davit Hovsepyan		01/01/94	M	1	(4)	1
3	Juliano	BRA	04/12/84	D	6		
30	Oumarou Kaina	CMR	16/10/96	M	24		1
14	Sargis Karapetyan		24/04/90	M		(2)	
17	Raffi Kaya	FRA	08/06/94	D	16	(3)	
16	Gorik Khachatryan		16/06/88	M	19	(2)	
8	Giorgi Khubua	GEO	19/04/93	M	7		
4	Souleymane Koné	CIV	05/01/92	D	25		1
2	Vahe Martirosyan		19/01/88	M	24	(1)	
16	Arman Meliksetyan		21/07/95	G	3		
9	Gevorg Nranyan		08/03/86	A	19	(4)	5
11	Kieran Nwabueze	USA	12/11/92	A	8	(3)	1
19	Moises Orozco	USA	06/02/92	M	10	(3)	3
10	Paul Oshie	NGA	27/09/96	A		(3)	
2	Gevorg Prazyan		24/07/89	G	21		
7	Aleksandar Rakić	SRB	17/01/87	A	5	(1)	1
21	Mher Sahakyan		01/01/93	M	1	(17)	1
5	Aram Shahnazaryan		21/04/94	D	2	(3)	
24	Karen Yesayan		10/04/96	M		(2)	

FC Banants

1992 • Banants (3,500) • fcbanants.am

Major honours
Armenian League (1) 2014; Armenian Cup (3) 1992,
2007, 2016

Coach: Aram Voskanyan;
(10/10/15) Tito Ramallo (ESP)

2015

01/08	h	Mika	D	1-1	Jeremiah
08/08	a	Pyunik	L	1-5	Laércio (p)
16/08	h	Alashkert	D	2-2	Jeremiah 2
23/08	h	Ararat	W	3-0	Jeremiah, López, Minasyan
29/08	a	Shirak	D	1-1	Laércio
13/09	h	Gandzasar	L	0-1	
19/09	a	Ulisses	D	2-2	Avetisyan, López
27/09	a	Mika	L	0-1	
03/10	h	Pyunik	L	0-1	
18/10	a	Alashkert	L	0-3	
24/10	a	Ararat	D	0-0	
31/10	h	Shirak	D	1-1	Laércio
07/11	h	Gandzasar	D	1-1	Laércio
21/11	h	Ulisses	W	5-1	Laércio 3, Ayvazyan, Mihajlović
29/11	h	Mika	D	1-1	Ayvazyan

2016

02/03	a	Pyunik	W	2-1	Laércio, Badoyan
12/03	h	Alashkert	W	2-0	Badoyan, Avetisyan
20/03	h	Ararat	D	2-2	Laércio, Badoyan
03/04	a	Gandzasar	L	1-2	Laércio
06/04	h	Shirak	L	1-3	Avetisyan
09/04	a	Ulisses	W	3-0	(w/o)
17/04	a	Mika	D	0-0	
23/04	h	Pyunik	D	1-1	Badoyan
30/04	a	Alashkert	L	1-2	Ayvazyan
08/05	a	Ararat	W	2-1	Minasyan, Buraev
14/05	h	Shirak	L	0-1	
18/05	h	Ulisses	W	3-0	(w/o)
22/05	a	Gandzasar	D	0-0	

No	Name	Nat	DoB	Pos	Aps	(s)	Gls
4	Lionel Adams	RUS	09/08/94	D	8		
11	Petros Avetisyan		07/01/96	M	14	(7)	3
18	Vahagn Ayvazyan		16/04/92	M	14	(7)	3
2	Vladimir Babayan		06/05/97	A		(1)	
17	Zaven Badoyan		22/12/89	M	9	(1)	4
9	Sargis Baloyan		24/08/92	A	8	(3)	
90	Atsamaz Buraev	RUS	05/02/90	A	5	(1)	1
3	Vlatko Drobarov	MKD	02/11/92	D	23		
12	Stepan Ghazaryan		11/01/85	G	22		
12	Tigran Ghazaryan		14/02/97	A		(1)	
24	Hakob Hakobyan		29/03/97	D	12	(3)	
20	Karen Harutyunyan		05/08/86	M	7	(3)	
10	John Jeremiah	NGA	02/09/93	A	4	(4)	4
5	Soslan Kachmazov	RUS	14/07/91	D	4	(2)	
2	Aslan Kalmanov	RUS	05/06/94	D	4	(1)	
12	Soslan Kalmanov	RUS	05/06/94	D	5	(3)	
3	Gevorg Khuloyan		18/08/96	D	2	(1)	
29	Andranik Kocharyan		29/01/94	A	5	(1)	
14	Laércio	BRA	03/03/90	A	21	(1)	10
15	Miguel López	ARG	09/06/88	M	20	(2)	2
16	Gagik Maghakyan		07/02/96	D	1		
32	Denis Mahmudov	MKD	06/11/89	A	3	(4)	
1	Grigor Makaryan		19/04/95	G	1		
2	Armen Manucharyan		25/01/96	D	10	(3)	
17	Zhirayr Margaryan		13/09/97	D		(1)	
4	Jasmin Mecinovic	MKD	22/10/90	D	7	(2)	
22	Bojan Mihajlović	BIH	15/09/88	D	13	(1)	1
39	Nairi Minasyan		26/08/95	M	21	(2)	2
28	Edgar Movsisyan		09/09/98	A		(10)	
23	Vardan Movsisyan		18/08/91	D	10	(2)	
4	Aleksandr Oganesyan		20/07/96	M	4		
18	Narek Petrosyan		25/01/96	D	4	(2)	
8	Valter Poghosyan		16/05/92	M	8	(5)	
24	Aram Sargsyan		13/05/96	M	1		
4	Aram Shakhnazaryan		21/04/94	D	7		
1	Artur Toroyan		01/02/92	G	3		
14	Claudio Torrejón	PER	14/05/93	M	6	(1)	
23	Emil Yeghiazaryan		03/11/97	M		(14)	

FC Gandzasar

2002 • Lernagorts (3,500) • no website

Coach: Ashot Barseghyan

2015

02/08	a	Shirak	L	1-2	T Barseghyan
08/08	a	Alashkert	D	0-0	
15/08	h	Ulisses	W	3-0	Beglaryan 2, Buraev
22/08	a	Mika	W	3-2	Angulo, Memović, Buraev
30/08	h	Pyunik	D	1-1	Buraev (p)
13/09	a	Banants	W	1-0	Beglaryan
20/09	a	Ararat	W	1-0	T Barseghyan
26/09	h	Shirak	D	1-1	Memović
03/10	h	Alashkert	D	2-2	og (Dukić), Buraev
17/10	a	Ulisses	D	0-0	
25/10	h	Mika	W	2-1	Buraev, Gogatishvili
01/11	a	Pyunik	L	0-4	
07/11	a	Banants	D	1-1	Gogatishvili
21/11	a	Ararat	D	2-2	Beglaryan, Gogatishvili
29/11	a	Shirak	L	1-2	Harutyunyan

2016

02/03	a	Alashkert	L	0-3	
13/03	h	Ulisses	W	3-0	(w/o)
19/03	a	Mika	L	0-2	
03/04	h	Banants	W	2-1	Beglaryan, Harutyunyan
06/04	h	Pyunik	W	1-0	Kpodo
10/04	a	Ararat	D	0-0	
16/04	h	Shirak	D	0-0	
23/04	h	Alashkert	D	2-2	Ishkhanyan, T Barseghyan
30/04	a	Ulisses	W	3-0	(w/o)
08/05	h	Mika	W	3-1	Harutyunyan 2, Rakić
15/05	a	Pyunik	D	0-0	
18/05	a	Ararat	W	2-0	T Barseghyan, Harutyunyan
22/05	h	Banants	D	0-0	

No	Name	Nat	DoB	Pos	Aps	(s)	Gls
6	Wbeymar Angulo	COL	06/03/92	M	21		1
3	Hamlet Asoyan		13/06/95	D		(4)	
5	Artur Avagyan		04/07/87	M	11	(2)	
3	Artur Barseghyan		16/11/86	M		(3)	
11	Tigran Barseghyan		22/09/93	M	21		4
10	Narek Beglaryan		01/09/85	A	21	(3)	5
9	Atsamaz Buraev	RUS	05/02/90	A	12	(2)	5
17	Armen Durunts		01/11/90	D	4	(15)	
33	Gogita Gogatishvili	GEO	02/02/90	D	19	(7)	3
21	Hovhannes Grigoryan		09/03/85	D	5	(2)	
18	Alen Hambartsumyan		01/03/92	D	4	(5)	
22	Gegham Harutyunyan		23/08/90	D	7	(17)	5
7	Armen Hovhannisyan		25/11/96	M		(1)	
21	Hayk Ishkhanyan		24/07/89	D	14	(1)	1
16	Ara Khachatryan		21/10/81	M	22	(3)	
5	Edward Kpodo	GHA	14/07/90	D	6	(1)	1
1	Gor Martirosyan		04/04/93	G	1		
1	Grigor Meliksetyan		03/08/93	G	11		
13	Damir Memović	SRB	19/01/89	D	23		2
89	Lubambo Musonda	ZAM	01/01/95	M	23	(2)	
2	Joshua Otoo	GHA	06/04/90	D	2	(1)	
15	Alexander Petrosyan		28/05/86	D	15	(3)	
2	Armen S Petrosyan		26/09/85	M	23		
23	Arsen Petrosyan		27/09/91	G	14		
7	Aleksandar Rakić	SRB	17/01/87	A	7	(3)	1
35	Arkadi Safaryan		06/09/98	M		(4)	

FC Mika

1997 • Mika stadium (7,000) • no website

Major honours
Armenian Cup (6) 2000, 2001, 2003, 2005, 2006, 2011

Coach: Aram Voskanyan;
(29/07/15) Armen Adamyan;
(19/01/16) Sergei Yuran (RUS)

2015
01/08	a	Banants	D	1-1	Toboyev
09/08	h	Ararat	L	0-1	
16/08	a	Shirak	L	0-2	
22/08	h	Gandzasar	L	2-3	Toboyev (p), Inkin
30/08	a	Ulisses	W	2-0	Kozlov, Inkin
12/09	a	Alashkert	L	0-2	
20/09	h	Pyunik	W	1-0	Melkonyan
27/09	h	Banants	W	1-0	Talalay
05/10	a	Ararat	L	1-2	Melkonyan
17/10	h	Shirak	L	0-1	
25/10	a	Gandzasar	L	1-2	Toboyev
01/11	h	Ulisses	W	1-0	Melkonyan
07/11	h	Alashkert	L	0-1	
22/11	a	Pyunik	L	1-2	Kvekveskiri
29/11	a	Banants	D	1-1	Melkonyan

2016
03/03	h	Ararat	D	1-1	Melkonyan
12/03	a	Shirak	W	1-0	Gorelishvili
19/03	h	Gandzasar	W	2-0	Shumilin, Gorelishvili
27/03	a	Ulisses	W	3-0	(w/o)
02/04	a	Alashkert	L	1-2	Kpenia
10/04	h	Pyunik	D	0-0	
17/04	h	Banants	D	0-0	
23/04	a	Ararat	W	4-0	Gorelishvili, Chicherin, Kiselev, Voskanyan
30/04	h	Shirak	L	1-4	Čmajčanin
08/05	a	Gandzasar	L	1-3	Karapetyan
15/05	h	Ulisses	W	3-0	(w/o)
18/05	a	Pyunik	L	1-2	Shumilin
22/05	a	Alashkert	L	0-2	

No	Name	Nat	DoB	Pos	Aps	(s)	Gls
15	Ashot Adamyan		01/01/95	M		(1)	
12	Henri Avagyan		16/06/96	G	1	(1)	
16	Poghos Ayvazyan		09/06/95	G		(1)	
16	Narek Balayan	UKR	20/03/91	M	14		
1	Arsen Beglaryan		18/02/93	G	25		
10	Andrei Belomitsev	RUS	29/10/94	M	12		
13	Ioseb Chakhvashvili	GEO	03/08/93	A	4		
33	Nikita Chicherin	RUS	18/08/90	D	9		1
14	Dmitri Chistyakov	RUS	13/01/94	D	16		
32	Tarik Čmajčanin	SRB	18/07/94	M	6	(1)	1
30	Sayputin Dadydov	RUS	23/05/95	M		(1)	
6	Narek T Davtyan		24/08/88	M	1		
7	Mikheil Gorelishvili	RUS	29/05/93	M	9		3
20	Artur Grigoryan		07/07/93	M	9	(4)	
4	David G Grigoryan		12/09/87	D		(2)	
21	Arman Hakobyan		14/03/91	A		(2)	
7	Oleg Inkin	MDA	16/03/90	M	8	(5)	2
8	Ahmed Jindoyan		02/10/97	A		(1)	
7	Ashot Karapetyan		12/05/93	D	15	(4)	1
51	Aleksey Kiselev	RUS	01/05/92	M	8		1
55	Andranik Kocharyan		03/05/94	A	1	(1)	
42	Bruno Koné	CIV	01/01/92	M	5	(1)	
77	Viktor Kosachev	RUS	03/11/91	D	6		
38	Miloš Kovačević	MNE	31/03/91	D	8		
19	Anton Kozlov	RUS	02/06/88	M	6	(1)	1
36	Aaron Kpenia	CIV	01/01/93	M	5	(2)	1
24	Dmitriy Kudinov	RUS	25/08/85	D	10		
33	Irakli Kvekveskiri	GEO	12/03/90	M	12	(1)	1
23	Dmitriy Lushnikov	RUS	22/08/89	M	11		
2	Daniil Martinov	RUS	18/03/91	D	1	(1)	
6	Samvel Melkonyan		15/03/94	A	12	(4)	5
11	Yegor Mishura	RUS	09/04/95	M		(1)	
14	Edgar Mkrtchyan		14/07/94	A	2	(5)	
35	Mikhail Mochalov	RUS	29/06/94	M		(3)	
3	Vardan Movsisyan		18/08/91	D	7	(1)	
3	Goran Obradović	SRB	25/12/86	D	3		
5	Gor Poghosyan		11/06/88	D	8	(3)	
37	Konstantin Prokopyev	RUS	07/04/93	M	4	(3)	
10	Sergey Shumilin	RUS	21/02/90	A	7	(3)	2
12	Denis Talalay	RUS	02/02/92	M	11	(1)	1
9	Teymuraz Toboyev	RUS	09/03/95	M	12	(1)	3
	Vladimir Ulukhanyan		19/09/85	M		(1)	
21	Erik Vardanyan		08/03/99	M		(1)	
17	Hayk Voskanyan		23/06/96	A	4	(5)	1
6	Artem Yarmolitski	RUS	04/04/94	D	1	(3)	
8	Revik Yeghiazaryan		01/06/91	D	2		
24	Ramil Zaripov	RUS	03/05/92	D	14		
7	Albert Zohrabyan		01/10/94	M	1	(3)	

FC Pyunik

1992 • Armenian Football Academy (1,000); Hanrapetakan (14,400) • fcpyunik.am

Major honours
Armenian League (14) 1992 (shared), 1996, 1997, 2001, 2002, 2003, 2004, 2005, 2006, 2007, 2008, 2009, 2010, 2015; Armenian Cup (8) 1996, 2002, 2004, 2009, 2010, 2013, 2014, 2015

Coach: Sargis Hovsepyan

2015
01/08	h	Alashkert	L	1-2	Haroyan
08/08	h	Banants	W	5-1	Satumyan 2, Hovhannisyan, V Poghosyan, Yusbashyan
16/08	a	Ararat	D	1-1	Ghukas Poghosyan
23/08	h	Shirak	W	3-0	Hovhannisyan, Yusbashyan, V Poghosyan
30/08	a	Gandzasar	D	1-1	Arakelyan
13/09	h	Ulisses	W	2-0	Satumyan, V Poghosyan
20/09	a	Mika	L	0-1	
27/09	a	Alashkert	W	4-1	Ghukas Poghosyan 3, V Poghosyan
03/10	a	Banants	W	1-0	Hayrapetyan (p)
18/10	h	Ararat	L	0-1	
24/10	a	Shirak	W	2-0	V Poghosyan, Satumyan
01/11	h	Gandzasar	W	4-0	Manoyan (p), V Poghosyan, Razmik Hakobyan 2
08/11	a	Ulisses	W	4-1	Manoyan (p), V Poghosyan 2 (p), Hovhannisyan
22/11	h	Mika	W	2-1	Arakelyan, Satumyan
28/11	h	Alashkert	D	0-0	

2016
02/03	h	Banants	L	1-2	Ghukas Poghosyan
13/03	a	Ararat	W	2-1	Manucharyan, Kartashyan
20/03	h	Shirak	D	1-1	Manoyan
03/04	h	Ulisses	W	3-0	(w/o)
06/04	a	Gandzasar	L	0-1	
10/04	a	Mika	D	0-0	
16/04	a	Alashkert	L	0-3	
23/04	a	Banants	D	1-1	Petrosyan
30/04	h	Ararat	D	0-0	
08/05	a	Shirak	D	1-1	V Poghosyan
15/05	h	Gandzasar	D	0-0	
18/05	h	Mika	W	2-1	Satumyan 2
22/05	a	Ulisses	W	3-0	(w/o)

No	Name	Nat	DoB	Pos	Aps	(s)	Gls
18	Alik Arakelyan		21/05/96	M	18	(4)	2
5	Narek Aslanyan`		04/01/96	M	1	(3)	
1	Anatoli Ayvazov	RUS	08/06/96	G	12		
2	Serob Grigoryan		04/02/95	D	4	(2)	
26	Razmik Hakobyan		09/02/94	A	2	(11)	2
16	Robert Hakobyan		22/10/96	D	18	(4)	
3	Varazdat Haroyan		24/08/92	D	21	(1)	1
6	Hovhannes Harutyunyan		25/05/99	M		(3)	
16	Levon Hayrapetyan		17/04/89	D	16	(2)	1
5	Kamo Hovhannisyan		05/10/92	D	25	(1)	3
18	Artur Kartashyan		08/01/97	D	8	(4)	1
11	Davit Manoyan		05/07/90	M	17	(8)	3
12	Gor Manukyan		27/09/93	G	14		
26	Narek Mikaelyan		02/01/98	D		(1)	
7	Robert Minasyan		08/04/97	A	5		
19	Vaspurak Minasyan		29/06/94	M		(1)	
21	Artur Nadiryan		27/03/98	M		(9)	
26	Hovik Nersisyan		06/02/95	D		(3)	
15	Hovhannes Panosyan		25/03/89	A		(2)	
17	Erik Petrosyan		19/02/98	A		(5)	1
8	Gagik Poghosyan		04/05/93	M	6	(3)	
10	Ghukas Poghosyan		06/02/94	M	18	(2)	5
17	Vardan Poghosyan		08/03/92	A	16	(2)	9
30	Vardges Satumyan		07/02/90	A	16	(8)	7
24	Sargis Shahinyan		10/09/95	M	11	(8)	
33	Taron Voskanyan		22/02/93	D	24		
15	Artur Yusbashyan		07/09/89	M	24		2

FC Shirak

1958 • Gyumri City (4,500) • fcshirak.am

Major honours
Armenian League (4) 1992 (shared), 1994, 1999, 2013; Armenian Cup (1) 2012

Coach: Vardan Bichakhchyan

2015
02/08	h	Gandzasar	W	2-1	og (Arsen Petrosyan), Bougouhi
09/08	h	Ulisses	W	3-2	Hakobyan 2, Ayvazyan
15/08	h	Mika	W	2-0	Ayvazyan, G Malakyan
23/08	a	Pyunik	L	0-3	
29/08	a	Banants	D	1-1	Kouakou
12/09	a	Ararat	W	2-0	Hakobyan, E Malakyan
19/09	a	Alashkert	L	1-2	Kouakou
26/09	a	Gandzasar	D	1-1	G Hovhannisyan
04/10	a	Ulisses	W	1-0	Hakobyan
17/10	a	Mika	W	1-0	Kouakou
24/10	h	Pyunik	L	0-2	
31/10	a	Banants	D	1-1	Kouakou
08/11	h	Ararat	L	0-1	
21/11	a	Alashkert	L	0-2	
29/11	h	Gandzasar	W	2-1	Hakobyan, Ayvazyan

2016
03/03	a	Ulisses	W	3-0	(w/o)
12/03	h	Mika	L	0-1	
20/03	a	Pyunik	D	1-1	Hovsepyan
02/04	a	Ararat	D	1-1	Diarrassouba
06/04	h	Banants	W	3-1	Kouakou, Stošković, Ayvazyan
09/04	h	Alashkert	W	2-1	Diarrassouba 2
16/04	a	Gandzasar	D	0-0	
24/04	a	Ulisses	W	3-0	(w/o)
30/04	a	Mika	W	4-1	Kouakou, Stošković, Aleksanyan, Hovsepyan
08/05	h	Pyunik	D	1-1	Diarrassouba
14/05	a	Banants	W	1-0	og (Oganesyan)
18/05	a	Alashkert	W	3-2	Diarrassouba, og (Minasyan), Ayvazyan
22/05	h	Ararat	W	2-1	A Hovhannisyan, Hovsepyan

No	Name	Nat	DoB	Pos	Aps	(s)	Gls
1	Norayr Abrahamyan		30/10/85	G	3	(1)	
15	Karen Aleksanyan		17/06/80	M	15	(2)	1
13	Eder Areola	USA	13/11/91	D	5	(5)	
31	Arman Aslanyan		30/01/94	M	1	(6)	
7	Viulen Ayvazyan		01/01/95	A	4	(12)	5
12	Andranik Barikyan		11/09/80	A	5	(4)	
17	Vahan Bichakhchyan		01/01/97	M		(2)	
9	Jean-Jacques Bougouhi	CIV	12/09/92	A	1		1
2	Robert Darbinyan		04/10/95	D	6	(2)	
25	Aghvan Davoyan		21/03/90	D	19	(3)	
9	Drissa Diarrassouba	CIV	15/11/94	A	11		5
13	Gor Elazyan		01/06/91	G	12		
10	Davit Hakobyan		21/03/93	M	24	(1)	5
29	Arman Hovhannisyan		07/07/93	D	25		
21	Gevorg Hovhannisyan		16/06/83	D	26		1
7	Rumyan Hovsepyan		13/11/91	M	7	(3)	3
28	Mohamed Kaba	CIV	05/04/89	M	20	(5)	
1	Armen Khachatryan		25/09/84	G	11		
27	Konan Kouakou	CIV	18/04/96	A	19		6
22	Edgar Malakyan		22/09/90	M	8	(1)	1
8	Gor Malakyan		12/06/94	M	13		1
3	Artyom Mikaelyan		12/07/91	D	9	(2)	
18	Aram Muradyan		01/01/96	A	1	(13)	
4	Eduard Panosyan		11/10/92	M	7	(5)	
24	Shahen Shahinyan		12/02/95	M	1		
8	Miloš Stamenković	SRB	01/06/90	D	18		
4	Nemanja Stošković	SRB	21/02/90	M	7	(2)	2
22	Arman Tadevosyan		26/09/94	D	4	(2)	
25	Solomon Udo	NGA	15/07/95	M	5	(5)	

 **ARMENIA**

Ulisses FC

2006 • Hanrapetakan (14,400) • fculisses.com
Major honours
Armenian League (1) 2011
Coach: Suren Chakhalyan;
(01/09/15) (Gagik Simonyan)

2015
02/08	a	Ararat	L	0-2
09/08	a	Shirak	L	2-3	og (Stamenković), Ivanović
15/08	a	Gandzasar	L	0-3
22/08	a	Alashkert	L	0-4
30/08	h	Mika	L	0-2
13/09	h	Pyunik	L	0-2
19/09	h	Banants	D	2-2	Yushin, Chimakadze
26/09	h	Ararat	L	1-2	Ivanović
04/10	h	Shirak	L	0-1
17/10	h	Gandzasar	D	0-0
25/10	h	Alashkert	L	0-3
01/11	a	Mika	L	0-1
08/11	h	Pyunik	L	1-4	og (Robert Hakobyan)
21/11	a	Banants	L	1-5	Movsisyan
28/11	a	Ararat	L	1-3	V Avetisyan

2016
03/03	h	Shirak	L	0-3	(w/o)
13/03	a	Gandzasar	L	0-3	(w/o)
19/03	a	Alashkert	L	0-3	(w/o)
27/03	h	Mika	L	0-3	(w/o)
03/04	a	Pyunik	L	0-3	(w/o)
09/04	h	Banants	L	0-3	(w/o)
17/04	h	Ararat	L	0-3	(w/o)
24/04	a	Shirak	L	0-3	(w/o)
30/04	h	Gandzasar	L	0-3	(w/o)
08/05	h	Alashkert	L	0-3	(w/o)
15/05	a	Mika	L	0-3	(w/o)
18/05	a	Banants	L	0-3	(w/o)
22/05	h	Pyunik	L	0-3	(w/o)

No	Name	Nat	DoB	Pos	Aps	(s)	Gls
2	Artak Andrikyan		24/01/88	D	4		
3	Artashes Arakelyan		10/06/89	D	7		
29	Mikael Arustamyan		01/01/92	M	1	(1)	
4	Karen Avetisyan		04/07/93	D	3	(1)	
9	Vigen Avetisyan		12/01/93	A	2	(3)	1
13	Drilon Berisha	ALB	13/05/88	D	8	(1)	
10	Besik Chimakadze	GEO	24/06/88	A	9	(1)	1
14	Narek Davtyan		24/08/88	M	8	(1)	
24	Tatul Davtyan		08/04/96	M	1		
1	Tigran V Davtyan		30/03/92	G	1		
22	Zakhar Dilanyan	RUS	06/05/95	M		(1)	
15	Narek Gyozalyan		10/07/92	M	5	(1)	
2	Artur Hakobyan		13/09/88	D	2		
34	Orbeli Hambartsumyan		26/03/96	A	1	(3)	
16	Edgar Harutyunyan		09/02/95	A	5	(2)	
23	Mher Harutyunyan		16/09/92	M	2	(2)	
26	Samvel Hovhannisyan		01/01/95	M		(1)	
22	Hayk Hunanyan		21/05/92	D	3		
24	Milutin Ivanović	SRB	30/10/90	A	10		2
2	Aslan Kalmanov	RUS	05/01/94	A	7		
24	Soslan Kalmanov	RUS	05/01/94	D	1	(1)	
28	Tigran Kandikyan		11/03/93	G	8		
21	Giorgi Katchkatchishvili	GEO	08/08/90	D	8		
17	Pavel Kondrakhin	RUS	27/04/94	A	5		
30	Narek Makoyan		01/01/96	M	1		
12	Gor Martirosyan		04/04/93	G	5		
35	Garnik Movsisyan		23/03/96	D	2	(1)	1
7	Oleksandr Oganisyan		20/07/96	M	3	(1)	
37	Daniel Özbiliz	NED	29/04/87	M		(1)	
39	Narek Papoyan		01/01/97	M	1		
18	Melik Saradyan		19/07/94	D	2		
38	Erik Sargsyan		21/08/92	D	1	(1)	
24	Andrey Shahgeldyan		04/11/95	M	1	(6)	
31	Daniel Sserenkuma	UGA	14/12/93	A	9	(3)	
1	Papin Tevosyan		22/03/92	G	1		
19	Armen Tigranyan		27/11/85	M	3	(2)	
20	Claudio Torrejón	PER	14/05/93	M	9	(2)	
32	Arman Tutyan		20/12/92	M	1	(2)	
33	Solomon Udo	NGA	15/07/95	M	12		
26	Vardges Vardanyan		01/01/98	M		(1)	
29	Aleksandr Yushin	RUS	04/04/95	M	4	(2)	1
27	Ben Aziz Zagre	TUN	21/12/94	D	8		
17	Davit Zakaryan		19/04/94	M	1		

Top goalscorers

16 Héber (Alashkert)
 Mihran Manasyan (Alashkert)
10 Laércio (Banants)
9 Vardan Poghosyan (Pyunik)
7 Vardges Satumyan (Pyunik)
6 Atsamaz Buraev (Gandzasar/Banants)
 Konan Kouakou (Shirak)
5 Bryan de la Fuente (Ararat)
 Gevorg Nranyan (Ararat)
 Narek Beglaryan (Gandzasar)
 Gegham Harutyunyan (Gandzasar)
 Samvel Melkonyan (Mika)
 Ghukas Poghosyan (Pyunik)
 Viulen Ayvazyan (Shirak)
 Drissa Diarrassouba (Shirak)
 Davit Hakobyan (Shirak)

Second level

Second level final table 2015/16

		Pld	W	D	L	F	A	Pts
1	Alashkert FC-2	28	22	3	3	65	22	69
2	FC Mika-2	28	17	3	8	50	28	54
3	FC Banants-2	28	15	3	10	67	30	48
4	FC Pyunik-2	28	14	2	12	55	45	44
5	FC Ararat-2	28	13	2	13	37	39	41
6	FC Shirak-2	28	11	5	12	47	48	38
7	FC Gandzasar-2	28	5	4	19	25	80	19
8	FC Shengavit	28	3	2	23	34	88	11

NB No promotion.

DOMESTIC CUP

Armenian Independence Cup 2015/16

QUARTER-FINALS

(21/10/15 & 04/11/15)
Mika 1-1 Shirak *(Balayan 27; Kaba 65)*
Shirak 0-1 Mika *(A Grigoryan 2)*
(Mika 2-1)

Pyunik 1-3 Gandzasar *(Hayrapetyan 30; Beglaryan 41, 73, Musonda 62)*
Gandzasar 0-0 Pyunik
(Gandzasar 3-1)

(28/10/15 & 25/11/15)
Alashkert 1-0 Ararat *(Manasyan 17)*
Ararat 0-4 Alashkert *(Héber 41, 58, Manasyan 49, Balabekyan 84)*
(Alashkert 5-0)

Ulisses 0-3 Banants *(Laércio 69p, 77, Baloyan 90)*
Banants 1-2 Ulisses *(Laércio 19; V Avetisyan 31, Tutyan 37)*
(Banants 4-2)

SEMI-FINALS

(15/03/16 & 12/04/16)
Banants 0-1 Alashkert *(Héber 44)*
Alashkert 1-2 Banants *(Voskanyan 90; Badoyan 14, Laércio 75)*
(2-2; Banants on away goals)

(16/03/16 & 13/04/16)
Mika 0-1 Gandzasar *(Rakić 38)*
Gandzasar 0-1 Mika *(Kiselev 42) (aet)*
(1-1; Mika 6-5 on pens)

FINAL

(04/05/16)
Hanrapetakan, Yerevan
FC BANANTS 2 *(Laércio 3p, Buraev 38)*
FC MIKA 0
Referee: *Baliyan*
BANANTS: *S Ghazaryan, Adams, Drobarov, Hakobyan (E Movsisyan 90+1), Kachmazov, A Kalmanov, Badoyan (Mecinovic 83), Torrejón, López (Ayvazyan 78), Buraev (Mahmudov 86), Laércio*
MIKA: *Beglaryan, Kudinov, Movsisyan (Koné 46), Chicherin, Kovačević, Chistyakov, Kiselev, Lushnikov, Gorelishvili (Melkonyan 80), Shumilin (Chakhvashvili 80), Kpenia*

Banants enjoy their moment of triumph after defeating Mika 2-0 to win the Armenian Cup

AUSTRIA

Österreichischer Fussball-Bund (ÖFB)

Address	Ernst-Happel-Stadion Sektor A/F, Meiereistrasse 7 AT-1020 Wien	**President**	Leo Windtner
		General secretary	Alfred Ludwig
		Media officer	Wolfgang Gramann
Tel	+43 1 727 180	**Year of formation**	1904
Fax	+43 1 728 1632	**National stadium**	Ernst Happel-
E-mail	office@oefb.at		Stadion, Vienna
Website	oefb.at		(50,000)

KEY

- UEFA Champions League
- UEFA Europa League
- Promoted
- Relegated

Ried im Innkreis

Wien
(Vienna)

St Pölten

Mödling

Salzburg

Grödig

Mattersburg

Altach

Graz

Wolfsberg

0 — 100 — 200 km
0 — 100 miles

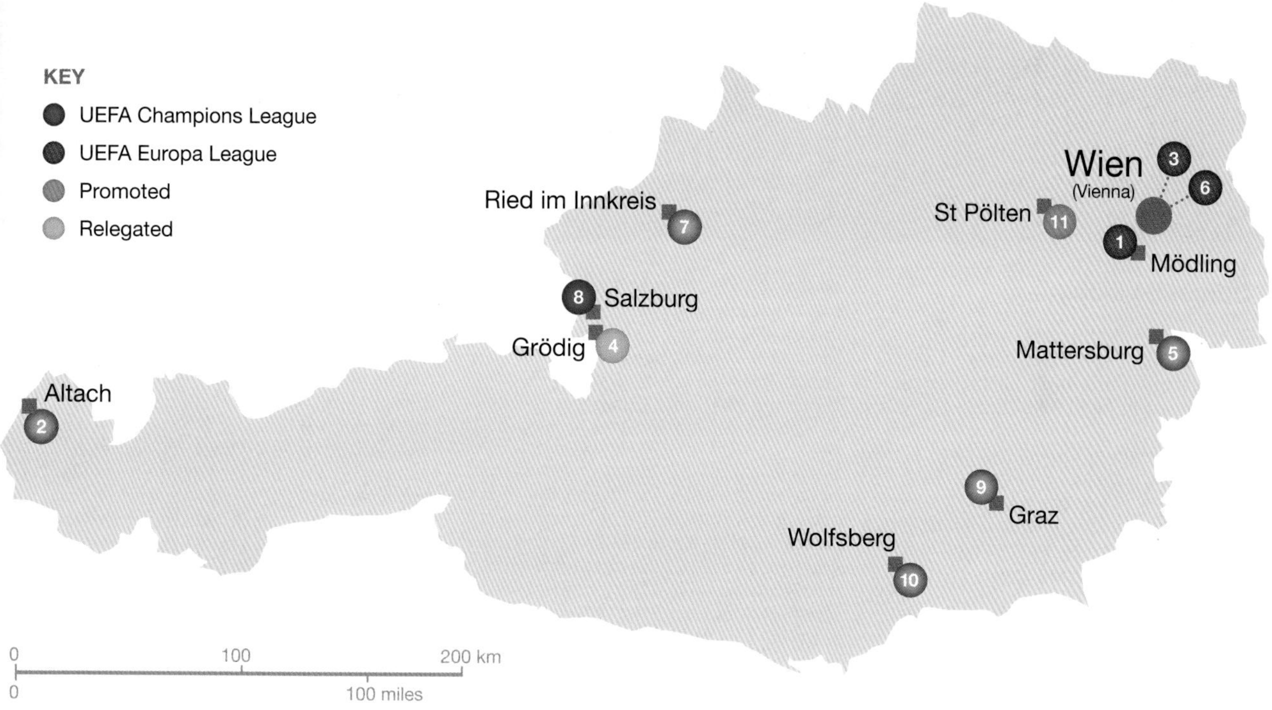

BUNDESLIGA CLUBS

 1 FC Admira Wacker Mödling

 2 SCR Altach

 3 FK Austria Wien

 4 SV Grödig

 5 SV Mattersburg

 6 SK Rapid Wien

 7 SV Ried

 8 FC Salzburg

 9 SK Sturm Graz

 10 Wolfsberger AC

PROMOTED CLUB

 11 SKN St Pölten

Salzburg go from strength to strength

The FC Salzburg bandwagon rolled on in 2015/16, with the dominant Austrian club of the decade adding to their trophy hoard with a fourth double in five seasons, all of them achieved under different head coaches. Spaniard Óscar García was the latest to lead the club to league and cup success, after assuming the reins in mid-campaign.

It was another season of disappointment, however, for Salzburg in Europe, and there was dismay too for the country as a whole at UEFA EURO 2016 as Austria, outstanding in the qualifying campaign, left France early after failing to win a game.

Youthful team claim back-to-back doubles

Rapid and Austria Wien fail to last the pace

EURO qualifying heroes fall short in France

Domestic league

With their 2014/15 double-winning coach Adi Hütter departed after a disagreement over the club's direction, Salzburg appointed Peter Zeidler, a German previously in charge of feeder side FC Liefering. It was supposed to be a seamless transition, but the team made a very shaky start, losing their first two Bundesliga games and winning just two of the first six to find themselves in the bottom half of the table.

With captain Jonatan Soriano eventually rediscovering his scoring boots, the points began to accumulate, enabling Salzburg to mount a challenge to early leaders Rapid Wien and FK Austria, an improving force under their new German boss Thorsten Fink. Salzburg went top after crushing Admira Wacker Mödling 8-0 in mid-October, but a subsequent form dip led to Zeidler's dismissal in early December and his replacement a few weeks later by Óscar, who had coached Maccabi Tel-Aviv to the Israeli title before working in England with Brighton and Watford.

Goals from Soriano and Naby Keïta enabled Salzburg, under caretaker coach Thomas Letsch, to defeat Rapid 2-0 at home in the last game before Christmas and go top at the winter break. In the spring, the main challenge would come from the green, rather than the violet, half of Vienna as Rapid rattled off five straight wins on the resumption. But when Zoran Barisic's side then went five games without a victory, Salzburg, resurgent under their new Spanish coach, took full advantage, eventually clinching their tenth Bundesliga title with two games to spare.

Soriano ended up with 21 goals – ten fewer than in 2014/15 but enough to complete a Bundesliga golden boot hat-trick, while Keïta struck 12 and Japanese import Takumino Minamino ten. No scorer for runners-up Rapid reached double figures, although schemer Florian Kainz bossed the assists chart with 17, more than twice as many as anyone else. Third-placed Austria's standout performer was another Austrian midfielder, 19-goal Alexander Gorgon.

Domestic cup

Admira, who finished fourth in the league, were already guaranteed UEFA Europa League qualification when they faced Salzburg in the ÖFB-Pokal final in Klagenfurt, but the underdogs were unable to celebrate the 50th anniversary of their last victory in the competition with another success. Instead they were torn apart by the champions, with Soriano taking his goal tally for the competition to ten with a hat-trick and Keïta and teenage talent Konrad Laimer adding further goals in a thumping 5-0 win.

Europe

Salzburg's dream of UEFA Champions League group stage participation died at the hands of Malmö FF for the second summer in succession with another depressing 3-0 defeat in Sweden. They even failed to reach the UEFA Europa League proper after losing on penalties to Dinamo Minsk, which allowed Rapid, shock conquerors of Ajax in a UEFA Champions League qualifier, to take centre stage. Barisic's men thundered through their UEFA Europa League group with four successive victories, only to be smashed 10-0 on aggregate by Valencia in the round of 32.

National team

Austria's first ever successful qualifying campaign for the UEFA European Championship bordered on perfection – nine victories, one draw and 22 goals, including four in a magnificent qualification-clinching win in Sweden. But when they got to France, Marcel Koller's team never remotely reached the same heights. After losing to Hungary and drawing with Portugal, they knew a win against Iceland would take them into the round of 16, but while they were pressing hard for a late winner at 1-1, following substitute Alessandro Schöpf's equaliser, their opponents raced up field to snatch a last-gasp winner of their own and send Austria home with just one point and one goal to their name.

DOMESTIC SEASON AT A GLANCE

Bundesliga 2015/16 final table

		Pld	Home					Away					Total					Pts
			W	D	L	F	A	W	D	L	F	A	W	D	L	F	A	
1	**FC Salzburg**	36	14	3	1	45	15	7	8	3	26	18	21	11	4	71	33	74
2	SK Rapid Wien	36	12	2	4	35	20	8	3	7	31	22	20	5	11	66	42	65
3	FK Austria Wien	36	8	5	5	30	25	9	3	6	35	23	17	8	11	65	48	59
4	FC Admira Wacker Mödling	36	6	6	6	18	21	7	5	6	27	30	13	11	12	45	51	50
5	SK Sturm Graz	36	7	9	2	26	16	5	3	10	14	24	12	12	12	40	40	48
6	Wolfsberger AC	36	9	5	4	25	17	2	5	11	8	19	11	10	15	33	36	43
7	SV Ried	36	10	2	6	17	17	1	7	10	19	35	11	9	16	36	52	42
8	SCR Altach	36	7	4	7	21	20	4	3	11	18	29	11	7	18	39	49	40
9	SV Mattersburg	36	6	4	8	20	38	4	5	9	20	32	10	9	17	40	70	39
10	SV Grödig	36	6	5	7	26	25	3	3	12	16	31	9	8	19	42	56	35

European qualification 2016/17

Champion/Cup winner: FC Salzburg (second qualifying round)

SK Rapid Wien (third qualifying round)
FK Austria Wien (second qualifying round)
FC Admira Wacker Mödling (first qualifying round)

Top scorer — Jonatan Soriano (Salzburg), 21 goals
Relegated club — SV Grödig
Promoted club — SKN St Pölten
Cup final — FC Salzburg 5-0 FC Admira Wacker Mödling

Team of the season
(4-5-1)

Coach: Pfeifenberger *(Wolfsberg)*

Walke *(Salzburg)*

Ebner *(Admira)* — Dibon *(Rapid)* — Ćaleta-Car *(Salzburg)* — Ulmer *(Salzburg)*

Schwab *(Rapid)* — Keïta *(Salzburg)* — Gorgon *(Austria)* — Berisha *(Salzburg)* — Kainz *(Rapid)*

Jonatan Soriano *(Salzburg)*

Player of the season

Naby Keïta
(FC Salzburg)

After a debut season of high promise in 2014/15, all-action Guinean midfielder Keïta confirmed his class with Salzburg in 2015/16, registering 12 goals and seven assists in the Austrian Bundesliga as his team successfully defended their title. They also retained the domestic cup, with the 21-year-old scoring one of their five goals in the final against Admira Wacker Mödling. Voted player of the season in June, he left Austria for Germany shortly afterwards, joining Salzburg's newly-promoted sister club RB Leipzig.

Newcomer of the season

Duje Ćaleta-Car
(FC Salzburg)

Aged 18 at the start of the season, Ćaleta-Car became a linchpin in the centre of the Salzburg defence under coach Peter Zeidler, who had previously worked with him at FC Liefering. Zeidler's successor, Óscar García, also placed great faith in the youngster, and by the end of term he not only had well-earned winner's medals in the league and cup to savour but was also called up to Croatia's provisional UEFA EURO 2016 squad. He did not make the final cut, but he had certainly laid down a marker for the future.

 **AUSTRIA**

NATIONAL TEAM

International tournament appearances

FIFA World Cup (7) 1934 (4th), 1954 (3rd), 1958, 1978 (2nd phase), 1982 (2nd phase), 1990, 1998
UEFA European Championship (2) 2008, 2016

Top five all-time caps

Andreas Herzog (103); Anton Polster (95); Gerhard Hanappi (93); Karl Koller (86); Friedl Koncilia & Bruno Pezzey (84)

Top five all-time goals

Anton Polster (44); Hans Krankl (34); Johann Horvath (29); Erich Hof (28); Anton Schall (27)

Results 2015/16

05/09/15	Moldova (ECQ)	H	Vienna	W	1-0	Junuzovic (52)
08/09/15	Sweden (ECQ)	A	Solna	W	4-1	Alaba (9p), Harnik (38, 88), Janko (77)
09/10/15	Montenegro (ECQ)	A	Podgorica	W	3-2	Janko (55), Arnautovic (81), Sabitzer (90+2)
12/10/15	Liechtenstein (ECQ)	H	Vienna	W	3-0	Arnautovic (12), Janko (54, 57)
17/11/15	Switzerland	H	Vienna	L	1-2	Alaba (13)
26/03/16	Albania	H	Vienna	W	2-1	Janko (6), Harnik (13)
29/03/16	Turkey	H	Vienna	L	1-2	Junuzovic (22)
31/05/16	Malta	H	Klagenfurt	W	2-1	Arnautovic (4), Schöpf (18)
04/06/16	Netherlands	H	Vienna	L	0-2	
14/06/16	Hungary (ECF)	N	Bordeaux (FRA)	L	0-2	
18/06/16	Portugal (ECF)	N	Paris (FRA)	D	0-0	
22/06/16	Iceland (ECF)	N	Saint-Denis (FRA)	L	1-2	Schöpf (60)

Appearances 2015/16

Coach: Marcel Koller (SUI) 11/11/60			MDA	SWE	MNE	LIE	Sui	Alb	Tur	Mlt	Ned	HUN	POR	ISL	Caps	Goals
Robert Almer	20/03/84	Austria Wien	G	G	G	G		G			G	G	G	G	31	-
Florian Klein	17/11/86	Stuttgart (GER)	D	D	D	D	D	D	D78	D	D	D	D	D	40	-
Aleksandar Dragovic	06/03/91	Dynamo Kyiv (UKR)	D	D	D	D	D	D	D59	D	D	D66*		D	49	1
Sebastian Prödl	21/06/87	Watford (ENG)	D	D	D	D	D3		s59		D79		D	D46	59	4
Christian Fuchs	07/04/86	Leicester (ENG)	D	D	D	D	D	D46	D		D	D	D	D	78	1
Julian Baumgartlinger	02/01/88	Mainz (GER)	M	M	M	M71	M82	M76		M46	M90	M	M	M	48	1
David Alaba	24/06/92	Bayern (GER)	M92	M	M82	M64	M	M87	M78		M64	s67	M77	M65	49	11
Martin Harnik	10/06/87	Stuttgart (GER)	M76	M	M	M		M		M64	s67	M77	A		60	14
Zlatko Junuzovic	26/09/87	Bremen (GER)	M	M80	M82	M			M	M73	M	M67	M59		49	7
Marko Arnautovic	19/04/89	Stoke (ENG)	M	M88	M	M	M	M87	M	M46	M82	M	M	M	55	11
Marc Janko	25/06/83	Basel (SUI)	A84	A84	A82	A64		A79	s67	A72	A67	A65		s46	56	26
Jakob Jantscher	08/01/89	Luzern (SUI)	s76	s88	s82		M58		s67		s82			s78	23	1
Rubin Okotie	06/06/87	1860 München (GER)	s84		s82	s64	A66	s79	A67	s72		s65			18	2
Stefan Ilsanker	18/05/89	RB Leipzig (GER)	s92	s84		s71	s46	s76	M	s46	s90		M87	M46	18	-
Marcel Sabitzer	17/03/94	RB Leipzig (GER)		s80	s82	s64	M46			s46	M82	s59	M85	A78	21	3
Ramazan Öczan	28/06/84	Ingolstadt (GER)					G		G	s46					7	-
Martin Hinteregger	07/09/92	Salzburg /Mönchengladbach (GER)					s3	D46	D	D	s79	D	D	D	17	-
Karim Onisiwo	17/03/92	Mattersburg					s58								1	-
Lukas Hinterseer	28/03/91	Ingolstadt (GER)					s66		s73	s64	s67		s85		11	-
Florian Kainz	24/10/92	Rapid Wien					s82								1	-
Kevin Wimmer	15/11/92	Tottenham (ENG)					s46						s87		4	-
Markus Suttner	16/04/87	Ingolstadt (GER)					s46			D					16	-
Alessandro Schöpf	07/02/94	Schalke (GER)					s87	s78	M64	s82	s77		s65	s46	7	2
Guido Burgstaller	29/04/89	Nürnberg (GER)					s87	M67							9	-
György Garics	08/03/84	Darmstadt (GER)						s78							41	2
Heinz Lindner	17/07/90	Eintracht Frankfurt (GER)							G46						8	-

EUROPE

FC Salzburg

Third qualifying round - Malmö FF (SWE)
H 2-0 *Ulmer (51), Hinteregger (89p)*
Stankovic, Schmitz, Paulo Miranda, Keïta, Djuricin (Nielsen 76), Berisha, Ulmer, Atanga (Lainer 90+2), Leitgeb, Hinteregger, Oberlin (Felipe Pires 63). Coach: Peter Zeidler (GER)
A 0-3
Stankovic, Schmitz, Paulo Miranda (Lainer 78), Keïta, Felipe Pires, Berisha, Ulmer, Atanga (Reyna 85), Leitgeb, Hinteregger, Oberlin (Prevljak 77). Coach: Peter Zeidler (GER)

Play-offs - FC Dinamo Minsk (BLR)
A 0-2
Walke, Paulo Miranda, Ćaleta-Car, Schwegler, Keïta, Berisha, Reyna, Ulmer, Minamino (Lazaro 74), Leitgeb, Oberlin (Atanga 59). Coach: Peter Zeidler (GER)
H 2-0 (aet; 2-3 on pens) *Minamino (11), Jonatan Soriano (58)*
Walke, Schmitz, Ćaleta-Car, Berisha, Reyna (Atanga 77), Ulmer (Sørensen 106), Minamino, Lainer, Leitgeb (Schwegler 91), Jonatan Soriano, Hinteregger. Coach: Peter Zeidler (GER)

SK Rapid Wien

Third qualifying round - AFC Ajax (NED)
H 2-2 *Kainz (48), Berić (76)*
Novota, Petsos, Sonnleitner, Schobesberger (Schaub 69), Schwab, Berić, S Hofmann (Grahovac 60), Kainz (Huspek 84), M Hofmann, Stangl, Auer. Coach: Zoran Barisic (AUT)
Red card: Schwab 59
A 3-2 *Berić (12), Schaub (39, 86)*
Novota, Petsos, Sonnleitner, Berić (Prosenik 90+4), Schaub (Alar 88), S Hofmann (Schobesberger 58), Kainz, Grahovac, Dibon, Stangl, Auer. Coach: Zoran Barisic (AUT)

Play-offs - FC Shakhtar Donetsk (UKR)
H 0-1
Novota, Petsos, Sonnleitner, Berić (Prosenik 89), Schaub, S Hofmann (Alar 84), Kainz (Schobesberger 80), Grahovac, Dibon, Pavelic, Auer. Coach: Zoran Barisic (AUT)
A 2-2 *Schaub (13), S Hofmann (22)*
Novota, Petsos, Sonnleitner, Berić, Schaub (Prosenik 85), S Hofmann (Schobesberger 63), Kainz, Grahovac (Schwab 70), Dibon, Pavelic, Auer. Coach: Zoran Barisic (AUT)
Red card: Sonnleitner 88

Group E
Match 1 - Villarreal CF (ESP)
H 2-1 *Schwab (50), S Hofmann (53p)*
Novota, Schwab, Schaub (Schobesberger 64), S Hofmann, Kainz (Huspek 72), Grahovac, Dibon, M Hofmann, Pavelic, Stangl (Auer 90+2), Prosenik. Coach: Zoran Barisic (AUT)
Match 2 - FC Dinamo Minsk (BLR)
A 1-0 *S Hofmann (54)*
Novota, Sonnleitner, Schwab, Jelić (Prosenik 86), Schaub (Schobesberger 46), S Hofmann (Alar 76), Kainz, Grahovac, Dibon, Pavelic, Stangl. Coach: Zoran Barisic (AUT)
Match 3 - FC Viktoria Plzeň (CZE)
H 3-2 *S Hofmann (34), Schaub (52), Petsos (68)*
Novota, Petsos, Schwab, Schaub (Huspek 80), S Hofmann (Grahovac 62), Kainz, Dibon, M Hofmann, Pavelic, Stangl, Prosenik (Jelić 68). Coach: Zoran Barisic (AUT)
Match 4 - FC Viktoria Plzeň (CZE)
A 2-1 *Schobesberger (13, 77)*
Novota, Petsos, Sonnleitner, Schobesberger, Schwab, S Hofmann (Grahovac 51), Kainz, Dibon (M Hofmann 67), Pavelic, Stangl, Prosenik (Jelić 79). Coach: Zoran Barisic (AUT)
Match 5 - Villarreal CF (ESP)
A 0-1
Novota (Strebinger 61), Petsos, Sonnleitner, Schobesberger, Schwab, S Hofmann, Kainz, Dibon (M Hofmann 6), Pavelic, Stangl, Prosenik (Jelić 86). Coach: Zoran Barisic (AUT)
Match 6 - FC Dinamo Minsk (BLR)
H 2-1 *M Hofmann (29), Jelić (59)*
Strebinger, Petsos, Sonnleitner, Schwab, Jelić (Prosenik 71), S Hofmann (Grahovac 65), Kainz, M Hofmann, Pavelic, Auer, Alar (Stangl 80). Coach: Zoran Barisic (AUT)

Round of 32 - Valencia CF (ESP)
A 0-6
Strebinger, Petsos, Sonnleitner, Schobesberger (Alar 87), Schwab, Jelić, S Hofmann (Grahovac 45+1), Kainz (Murg 46), M Hofmann, Pavelic, Stangl. Coach: Zoran Barisic (AUT)
H 0-4
Strebinger, Petsos, Sonnleitner, Schwab, Grahovac, M Hofmann, Pavelic, Murg (Schaub 82), Alar (Schobesberger 70), Prosenik (Jelić 65), Wöber. Coach: Zoran Barisic (AUT)

SCR Altach

Third qualifying round - Vitória SC (POR)
H 2-1 *Ngwat-Mahop (24), Aigner (50p)*
Lukse, Netzer, Lienhart, Zwischenbrugger, César Ortiz, Luxbacher, Zech, Aigner (Harrer 78), Seeger (Barrera 78), Prokopic (Jäger 90), Ngwat-Mahop. Coach: Damir Canadi (AUT)
A 4-1 *Netzer (31), Pedro Correia (59og), Prokopic (63), Lienhart (90+3)*
Lukse, Netzer (Roth 63), Lienhart, Zwischenbrugger, César Ortiz, Luxbacher (Hofbauer 86), Jäger, Zech, Seeger (Aigner 67), Prokopic, Ngwat-Mahop. Coach: Damir Canadi (AUT)

Play-offs - Os Belenenses (POR)
H 0-1
Lukse, Netzer, Lienhart, Salomon (Hofbauer 65), Zwischenbrugger, César Ortiz, Zech, Aigner (Harrer 72), Seeger (Barrera 80), Prokopic, Ngwat-Mahop. Coach: Damir Canadi (AUT)
A 0-0
Lukse, Pöllhuber, Netzer (Roth 64), Lienhart, Salomon (Aigner 57), Zwischenbrugger, César Ortiz (Harrer 83), Zech, Seeger, Prokopic, Ngwat-Mahop. Coach: Damir Canadi (AUT)

SK Sturm Graz

Third qualifying round - Rubin (RUS)
H 2-3 *Avdijaj (21), Piesinger (56)*
Esser, Hadžić (Horvath 75), Tadić (Kienast 63), Piesinger, Madl, Ehrenreich, Klem, Kamavuaka, Dobras, Schick (Gruber 68), Avdijaj. Coach: Franco Foda (GER)
Red card: Avdijaj 69
A 1-1 *Tadić (68)*
Esser, Tadić, Lykogiannis (Ehrenreich 45+1), Madl, Potzmann, Offenbacher, Spendlhofer, Schmerböck (Edomwonyi 46), Kamavuaka, Dobras (Kienast 81), Schick. Coach: Franco Foda (GER)

Wolfsberger AC

Second qualifying round - FC Shakhtyor Soligorsk (BLR)
A 1-0 *Jacobo (62)*
Kofler, Palla, Weber (Hüttenbrenner 90+3), Silvio (Trdina 71), Hellquist, Jacobo, Berger, Putsche, Sollbauer, Drescher, Zündel (Wernitznig 82). Coach: Dietmar Kühbauer (AUT)
H 2-0 *Sollbauer (19), Hellquist (90)*
Kofler, Palla, Weber (Tschernegg 45+2), Silvio, Hellquist, Jacobo, Berger, Putsche, Sollbauer, Drescher (Hüttenbrenner 59), Zündel (Wernitznig 85). Coach: Dietmar Kühbauer (AUT)

Third qualifying round - Borussia Dortmund (GER)
H 0-1
Kofler, Palla, Silvio, Hüttenbrenner, Berger, Putsche (Trdina 70), Seidl, Wernitznig (Jacobo 81), Standfest (Tschernegg 90), Sollbauer, Zündel. Coach: Dietmar Kühbauer (AUT)
A 0-5
Kofler, Palla, Weber, Silvio, Jacobo, Hüttenbrenner, Berger, Putsche (Trdina 67), Wernitznig (Zulj 74), Standfest (Tschernegg 85), Sollbauer. Coach: Dietmar Kühbauer (AUT)

DOMESTIC LEAGUE CLUB-BY-CLUB

FC Admira Wacker Mödling

1905 • BSFZ-Arena (12,000) • admirawacker.at

Major honours
Austrian League (9) 1927, 1928, 1932, 1934, 1936, 1937, 1939, 1947, 1966; Austrian Cup (6) 1928, 1932, 1934, 1947, 1964, 1966

Coach: Ernst Baumeister & Oliver Lederer

2015
25/07	a	Sturm	D	1-1	Starkl
01/08	h	Mattersburg	W	2-1	Knasmüller, Vastic
08/08	h	Salzburg	D	2-2	Starkl, Lackner
12/08	a	Grödig	W	3-2	Bajrami, og (Rasner), Vastic
15/08	h	Ried	W	3-1	Starkl 2, Schösswendter
23/08	a	Altach	W	2-1	Schösswendter, Blutsch
29/08	h	Austria Wien	L	0-1	
12/09	h	Wolfsberg	W	1-0	Schösswendter
20/09	a	Rapid	L	0-2	
27/09	a	Sturm	L	0-1	
03/10	a	Mattersburg	W	4-0	Zwierschitz, Sax, Starkl, Toth
17/10	a	Salzburg	L	0-8	
24/10	h	Grödig	D	0-0	
31/10	a	Ried	D	1-1	Schicker
07/11	h	Altach	D	1-1	Schösswendter (p)
21/11	a	Austria Wien	D	1-1	Spiridonovic
28/11	a	Wolfsberg	L	0-4	
02/12	h	Rapid	W	2-1	Zwierschitz, Spiridonovic (p)
05/12	a	Sturm	D	1-1	Zulj
12/12	h	Mattersburg	D	1-1	Schösswendter

2016
07/02	h	Salzburg	L	1-2	Spiridonovic
13/02	a	Grödig	D	2-2	Knasmüller, Schösswendter
20/02	h	Ried	D	0-0	
27/02	a	Altach	W	2-1	Ayyildiz, Schösswendter
02/03	h	Austria Wien	L	0-3	
05/03	h	Wolfsberg	L	0-2	
12/03	a	Rapid	W	4-0	Knasmüller 2, Grozurek (p), Spiridonovic
19/03	h	Sturm	W	1-0	Toth
02/04	a	Mattersburg	W	3-0	Grozurek 2, Malicsek
10/04	a	Salzburg	L	0-1	
16/04	h	Grödig	D	1-1	Spiridonovic (p)
23/04	a	Ried	L	0-1	
30/04	h	Altach	W	2-1	Malicsek, Monschein
07/05	a	Austria Wien	L	1-3	Wostry
11/05	a	Wolfsberg	W	2-1	Spiridonovic, Monschein
15/05	h	Rapid	L	1-3	Grozurek

No	Name	Nat	DoB	Pos	Aps	(s)	Gls
55	Ilter Ayyildiz		31/07/92	M	5	(5)	1
27	Eldis Bajrami	MKD	12/12/92	M	19	(13)	1
44	Markus Blutsch		01/06/95	M	17	(8)	1
5	Thomas Ebner		22/02/92	D	34		
45	Marvin Egho		09/05/94	A		(1)	
11	Lukas Grozurek		22/12/91	M	14	(11)	4
8	Christoph Knasmüller		30/04/92	M	17	(5)	4
29	Manuel Kuttin		17/12/93	G	1		
6	Markus Lackner		05/04/91	D	33		1
22	Marcus Maier		18/12/95	M		(3)	
12	Philipp Malicsek		03/06/97	M	14	(4)	2
15	Manuel Maranda		09/07/97	D	3		
14	Christopher Monschein		22/10/92	A	4	(7)	2
24	Florian Neuhold		06/07/93	D		(2)	
9	Issiaka Ouédraogo	BFA	19/08/88	A		(1)	
20	Markus Pavic		26/03/95	D	8	(1)	
32	Philipp Posch		09/01/94	D		(1)	
7	Maximilian Sax		22/11/92	A	12	(7)	1
18	Rene Schicker		28/09/84	A	9	(7)	1
3	Christoph Schösswendter		16/07/88	D	23	(1)	7
28	Jörg Siebenhandl		18/01/90	G	35		
93	Srdjan Spiridonovic		13/10/93	M	20	(5)	6
17	Dominik Starkl		06/11/93	A	22	(7)	5
10	Daniel Toth		10/06/87	M	26	(4)	2
77	Toni Vastic		17/01/93	A	3	(2)	2
25	Patrick Wessely		17/07/92	D	13		
21	Markus Wostry		19/07/92	D	35		1
99	Peter Zulj		09/06/93	M	2	(6)	1
4	Stephan Zwierschitz		17/09/90	D	27	(3)	2

SCR Altach

1929 • Cashpoint Arena (8,900) • scra.at

Coach: Damir Canadi

2015
25/07	a	Grödig	L	1-2	Aigner
02/08	a	Austria Wien	L	1-3	César Ortiz
09/08	h	Sturm	L	0-1	
12/08	h	Mattersburg	W	3-1	Prokopic, Pöllhuber, Seeger
15/08	a	Salzburg	L	0-2	
23/08	h	Admira	L	1-2	Ngwat-Mahop
30/08	a	Wolfsberg	W	2-0	Harrer, Hofbauer
12/09	h	Rapid	W	2-0	Harrer 2
19/09	a	Ried	L	0-2	
26/09	h	Grödig	W	1-0	Ngwat-Mahop
03/10	a	Austria Wien	L	1-2	Tajouri
17/10	a	Sturm	L	1-3	Aigner
24/10	a	Mattersburg	L	1-2	Luxbacher
31/10	h	Salzburg	W	1-0	Roth
07/11	a	Admira	D	1-1	Luxbacher
21/11	h	Wolfsberg	W	2-1	Salomon, Aigner
29/11	a	Rapid	L	1-3	Ngwat-Mahop
02/12	h	Ried	L	1-3	Hofbauer
05/12	a	Grödig	W	3-0	César Ortiz, Aigner 2
12/12	h	Austria Wien	W	2-1	Ngwat-Mahop 2

2016
06/02	h	Sturm	D	2-2	Harrer (p), Lucas Galvão
13/02	h	Mattersburg	L	1-2	Prokopic
20/02	a	Salzburg	L	0-2	
27/02	h	Admira	L	1-2	Aigner
01/03	a	Wolfsberg	L	0-1	
06/03	h	Rapid	D	0-0	
12/03	a	Ried	W	2-0	Salomon, Aigner
19/03	h	Grödig	W	1-0	Aigner
02/04	a	Austria Wien	W	2-0	Aigner (p), Schreiner
09/04	a	Sturm	L	1-4	Ngwat-Mahop
16/04	a	Mattersburg	D	0-0	
23/04	h	Salzburg	L	1-3	Aigner
30/04	a	Admira	L	1-2	Jäger
07/05	h	Wolfsberg	D	1-1	César Ortiz
11/05	h	Rapid	D	1-1	Netzer
15/05	h	Ried	D	0-0	

No	Name	Nat	DoB	Pos	Aps	(s)	Gls
25	Hannes Aigner		16/03/81	A	26	(1)	10
20	Juan Barrera	NCA	02/05/89	M	1	(1)	
4	Sebastian Brandner		08/02/83	G		(1)	
19	César Ortiz	ESP	30/01/89	D	23	(1)	3
9	Martin Harrer		19/05/92	A	14	(13)	4
8	Dominik Hofbauer		19/09/90	M	18	(8)	2
22	Lukas Jäger		12/02/94	D	24	(4)	1
1	Martin Kobras		19/06/86	G	10		
7	Andreas Lienhart		28/01/86	D	19	(1)	
3	Lucas Galvão	BRA	22/06/91	M	11	(3)	1
12	Andreas Lukse		08/11/87	G	26		
21	Daniel Luxbacher		13/03/92	M	10	(3)	2
5	Philipp Netzer		02/10/85	M	27		1
29	Louis Ngwat-Mahop	CMR	16/09/87	A	22	(4)	6
2	Alexander Pöllhuber		30/04/85	D	13	(4)	1
28	Boris Prokopic		29/03/88	M	17	(9)	2
11	Felix Roth	GER	13/11/87	M	10	(9)	1
10	Patrick Salomon		10/06/88	M	23	(3)	2
27	Christian Schilling		06/01/92	D	8	(3)	
16	Emanuel Schreiner		02/02/89	D	22	(4)	1
26	Patrick Seeger		25/08/86	A	5	(19)	1
30	Ismael Tajouri	LBY	27/03/94	M	13	(6)	1
31	Mihret Topčagić	BIH	21/08/88	A		(6)	
6	Stefan Umjenovic		11/08/95	D	1	(1)	
23	Benedikt Zech		03/11/90	D	28	(1)	
18	Jan Zwischenbrugger		16/06/90	D	25	(3)	

FK Austria Wien

1911 • Generali-Arena (13,400) • fk-austria.at

Major honours
Austrian League (24) 1924, 1926, 1949, 1950, 1953, 1961, 1962, 1963, 1969, 1970, 1976, 1978, 1979, 1980, 1981, 1984, 1985, 1991, 1992, 1993, 2003, 2006, 2013; Austrian Cup (27) 1921, 1924, 1925, 1926, 1933, 1935, 1936, 1948, 1949, 1960, 1962, 1963, 1967, 1971, 1974, 1977, 1980, 1982, 1986, 1990, 1992, 1994, 2003, 2005, 2006, 2007, 2009

Coach: Thorsten Fink (GER)

2015
26/07	a	Wolfsberg	W	2-0	Gorgon (p), Grünwald
02/08	h	Altach	W	3-1	Sikov, Kayode, Gorgon (p)
08/08	a	Grödig	D	2-2	Grünwald, og (Pichler)
12/08	h	Rapid	L	2-5	Gorgon 2
15/08	h	Mattersburg	W	5-1	Gorgon 2 (1p), Kayode 2, Meilinger
23/08	a	Salzburg	D	2-2	Grünwald, Kayode
29/08	a	Admira	W	1-0	Gorgon (p)
12/09	h	Ried	D	1-1	Holzhauser
19/09	a	Sturm	L	0-2	
26/09	h	Wolfsberg	W	1-0	Grünwald
03/10	h	Altach	W	2-1	Kayode, Koch
17/10	h	Grödig	W	2-1	Gorgon 2
25/10	a	Rapid	W	2-1	og (M Hofmann), Friesenbichler
01/11	a	Mattersburg	W	2-1	Kayode, Rotpuller
07/11	h	Salzburg	D	1-1	Friesenbichler
21/11	h	Admira	D	1-1	Kayode
29/11	a	Ried	L	2-4	Kehat, Gorgon (p)
02/12	h	Sturm	W	2-1	Kayode, Gorgon
05/12	a	Wolfsberg	L	0-2	
12/12	a	Altach	L	1-2	Vukojević

2016
06/02	a	Grödig	W	1-0	Gorgon
14/02	h	Rapid	L	0-3	
20/02	h	Mattersburg	D	2-2	og (Novak), Gorgon (p)
28/02	a	Salzburg	L	1-4	Kayode
02/03	a	Admira	W	3-0	Grünwald, Kayode, Friesenbichler
05/03	h	Ried	W	3-1	Rotpuller, Grünwald, Kayode
13/03	a	Sturm	D	1-1	Stryger
19/03	h	Wolfsberg	D	0-0	
02/04	a	Altach	L	0-2	
09/04	a	Grödig	L	0-2	
17/04	a	Rapid	L	0-1	
23/04	a	Mattersburg	W	9-0	Gorgon 2 (1p), Kayode, Grünwald 2, Friesenbichler 2, Lucas Venuto, De Paula
01/05	h	Salzburg	L	0-2	
07/05	h	Admira	W	3-1	Gorgon 2, Lucas Venuto
11/05	a	Ried	W	5-0	Gorgon 2, Holzhauser, Grünwald, Lucas Venuto
15/05	h	Sturm	W	3-0	Friesenbichler, Kayode, Holzhauser

No	Name	Nat	DoB	Pos	Aps	(s)	Gls
1	Robert Almer		20/03/84	G	22		
23	David De Paula	ESP	03/05/84	M	7	(13)	1
9	Kevin Friesenbichler		06/05/94	A	9	(22)	6
20	Alexander Gorgon		28/10/88	M	35		19
10	Alexander Grünwald		01/05/89	M	33		9
31	Osman Hadzikic		12/03/96	G	13		
26	Raphael Holzhauser		16/02/93	M	35		3
8	Olarenwaju Kayode	NGA	08/05/93	A	31	(3)	13
19	Roi Kehat	ISR	15/05/91	M	16	(12)	1
30	Fabian Koch		24/06/89	D	21	(1)	1
27	Marko Kvasina		20/12/96	A	1	(2)	
6	Mario Leitgeb		09/07/88	M		(1)	
11	Lucas Venuto	BRA	14/01/95	M	13	(2)	3
28	Christoph Martschinko		13/02/94	D	33		
7	Marco Meilinger		03/08/91	M	10	(8)	1
32	Patrick Pentz		02/01/97	G	1		
16	Dominik Prokop		02/06/97	M		(1)	
33	Lukas Rotpuller		31/03/91	D	32		2
25	Thomas Salamon		18/01/89	M	2	(1)	
15	Tarkan Serbest		02/05/94	M	6	(13)	
4	Vance Sikov	MKD	19/07/85	D	21	(5)	1
22	Marco Stark		05/01/93	D		(1)	
18	Patrizio Stronati	CZE	17/11/94	D	2	(1)	
17	Jens Stryger	DEN	21/02/91	D	10	(1)	1
5	Ognjen Vukojević	CRO	20/12/83	M	14	(5)	
3	Richard Windbichler		02/04/91	D	18	(7)	
16	Philipp Zulechner		12/04/90	A	11	(2)	

SV Grödig

1948 • DAS.GOLDBERG Stadion (4,128) • sv-groedig.at
Coach: Peter Schöttel

2015

25/07	h Altach	W	2-1	Brauer, Strobl
02/08	a Sturm	D	1-1	Maak
08/08	h Austria Wien	D	2-2	Sulimani, Lucas Venuto (p)
12/08	h Admira	L	2-3	Wallner, Pichler
15/08	a Wolfsberg	L	2-3	Wallner, Schütz
22/08	a Rapid	L	0-3	
29/08	h Ried	W	4-1	Derflinger, Lucas Venuto, Gschweidl, og (Reifeltshammer)
12/09	a Salzburg	L	2-4	Lucas Venuto, og (Ulmer)
19/09	h Mattersburg	D	1-1	Wallner
26/09	a Altach	L	0-1	
03/10	h Sturm	W	3-0	Sulimani 2, Lucas Venuto
17/10	a Austria Wien	L	1-2	Djuric
24/10	a Admira	D	0-0	
31/10	h Wolfsberg	W	1-0	Kainz
08/11	h Rapid	W	2-1	Lucas Venuto 2 (1p)
21/11	a Ried	L	0-1	
28/11	h Salzburg	D	1-1	Rasner
02/12	a Mattersburg	W	2-0	Derflinger, Lucas Venuto
05/12	h Altach	L	0-3	
12/12	a Sturm	L	0-2	

2016

06/02	h Austria Wien	L	0-1	
13/02	h Admira	D	2-2	Brauer, Wallner
20/02	a Wolfsberg	L	0-2	
28/02	a Rapid	L	2-3	Maak, Schütz
02/03	h Ried	D	2-2	Kainz 2
05/03	a Salzburg	L	0-3	
12/03	h Mattersburg	L	0-1	
19/03	h Altach	L	0-1	
02/04	h Sturm	L	1-3	Strobl
09/04	a Austria Wien	W	2-0	Sulimani, Ofosu
16/04	a Admira	D	1-1	Ofosu
23/04	h Wolfsberg	L	0-1	
30/04	h Rapid	W	2-0	Rasner, Kerschbaum
07/05	a Ried	L	0-2	
11/05	h Salzburg	L	1-2	Schütz
15/05	a Mattersburg	W	3-2	Derflinger (p), V Grubeck, Djuric (p)

No	Name	Nat	DoB	Pos	Aps	(s)	Gls
17	Dominik Baumgartner		20/07/96	D	6	(1)	
5	Timo Brauer	GER	30/05/90	M	30		2
19	Lukas Denner		19/06/91	D	20	(8)	
8	Christian Derflinger		02/02/94	M	10	(12)	3
10	Sandro Djuric		15/02/94	M	18	(3)	2
27	Thomas Goiginger		15/03/93	M	5	(11)	
30	Fabian Grubeck		12/03/96	M		(1)	
9	Valentin Grubeck		26/02/95	A	2	(5)	1
9	Bernd Gschweidl		08/09/95	A	2	(7)	1
21	Pascal Itter	GER	03/04/95	D	13	(2)	
22	Tobias Kainz		31/10/92	D	28		3
20	Roman Kerschbaum		19/01/94	M	14	(7)	1
23	Lucas Venuto	BRA	14/01/95	M	20		7
31	Matthias Maak		12/05/92	D	28	(1)	2
14	Reagy Ofosu	GER	20/09/91	M	12	(4)	2
13	Harald Pichler		18/06/87	D	26		1
18	Martin Rasner		18/05/95	M	32	(1)	2
33	Alexander Schlager		01/02/96	G	10		
11	Daniel Schütz		19/06/91	M	19	(8)	3
25	Pirmin Strasser		16/10/90	G	11		
2	Fabio Strauss		06/08/94	D	13		
12	Robert Strobl		24/10/85	D	23	(6)	2
32	Benjamin Sulimani		26/09/88	A	21	(6)	4
1	Rene Swete		01/06/90	G	15		
6	Robert Völkl		12/02/93	M	5	(6)	
7	Roman Wallner		04/02/82	A	13	(17)	4

SV Mattersburg

1922 • Pappelstadion (15,700) • svm.at
Coach: Ivica Vastic

2014

25/07	h Salzburg	W	2-1	Pink, Ibser
01/08	a Admira	L	1-2	Pink
08/08	h Ried	W	4-1	Grgic 2, Pink, Perlak
12/08	a Altach	L	1-3	Templ
15/08	a Austria Wien	L	1-5	Onisiwo
22/08	h Wolfsberg	W	1-0	Röcher
29/08	a Rapid	W	4-2	Perlak, Röcher, Pink, Mahrer
13/09	h Sturm	W	2-0	Farkas 2
19/09	a Grödig	D	1-1	Onisiwo
26/09	a Salzburg	L	2-4	Farkas, Jano
03/10	h Admira	L	0-4	
17/10	a Ried	W	1-0	Perlak
24/10	h Altach	W	2-1	Mahrer, Bürger
01/11	h Austria Wien	L	1-2	Templ
07/11	a Wolfsberg	L	1-2	Ibser
21/11	h Rapid	L	1-6	Bürger
28/11	a Sturm	D	0-0	
02/12	h Grödig	L	0-2	
06/12	h Salzburg	D	0-0	
12/12	a Admira	D	1-1	Pink

2015

06/02	h Ried	D	3-3	Pink, Malić, Prietl
13/02	a Altach	W	2-1	Bürger, Templ
20/02	a Austria Wien	D	2-2	Pink, Mahrer
27/02	h Wolfsberg	D	1-1	Bürger (p)
02/03	a Rapid	L	0-3	
05/03	h Sturm	W	1-0	Pink
12/03	a Grödig	W	1-0	Prietl
19/03	a Salzburg	L	1-2	Ibser
02/04	h Admira	L	0-3	
09/04	a Ried	L	0-1	
16/04	h Altach	D	0-0	
23/04	h Austria Wien	L	0-9	
30/04	a Wolfsberg	L	0-2	
08/05	h Rapid	L	0-2	
11/05	a Sturm	D	1-1	Malić
15/05	h Grödig	L	2-3	Bürger 2

No	Name	Nat	DoB	Pos	Aps	(s)	Gls
22	Markus Böcskör		01/10/82	G	2		
1	Thomas Borenitsch		19/12/80	G	2	(1)	
33	Patrick Bürger		27/06/87	A	9	(10)	6
14	Dominik Doleschal		09/05/89	M		(2)	
6	Philipp Erhardt		10/09/93	D	2	(3)	
23	Julius Ertlthaler		25/04/97	M		(7)	
17	Patrick Farkas		09/09/92	M	30	(2)	3
26	Fran	ESP	08/02/90	D	1	(2)	
16	Mario Grgic		10/09/91	M	3	(8)	2
8	Alois Höller		15/03/89	M	24	(7)	
11	Alexander Ibser		19/02/91	A	7	(14)	3
10	Jano	ESP	23/12/86	M	33		1
21	Markus Kuster		22/02/94	G	32		
31	Thorsten Mahrer		22/01/90	D	33		3
2	Vitālijs Maksimenko	LVA	08/12/90	D	15	(4)	
4	Nedeljko Malić	BIH	15/05/88	D	29		2
25	Michael Novak		30/12/90	D	18	(2)	
12	Karim Onisiwo		17/03/92	A	17	(1)	2
20	Michael Perlak		26/12/85	M	23	(5)	3
32	Markus Pink		24/02/91	A	28	(3)	8
19	Manuel Prietl		03/08/91	M	33	(1)	2
18	Lukas Rath		18/01/92	D	7	(3)	
27	Thorsten Röcher		11/06/91	M	25	(5)	2
15	Sven Sprangler		27/03/95	M	17	(4)	
13	Florian Templ		01/10/88	A	6	(21)	3

SK Rapid Wien

1899 • Ernst Happel-Stadion (50,000) • skrapid.at
Major honours
Austrian League (32) 1912, 1913, 1916, 1917, 1919, 1920, 1921, 1923, 1929, 1930, 1935, 1938, 1940, 1941, 1946, 1948, 1951, 1952, 1954, 1956, 1957, 1960, 1964, 1967, 1968, 1982, 1983, 1987, 1988, 1996, 2005, 2008; German League (1) 1941; Austrian Cup (14) 1919, 1920, 1927, 1946, 1961, 1968, 1969, 1972, 1976, 1983, 1984, 1985, 1987, 1995; German Cup (1) 1938
Coach: Zoran Barisic

2014

25/07	h Ried	W	3-0	Kainz, Berić, Schaub
01/08	a Salzburg	W	2-1	Petsos, Schwab
09/08	h Wolfsberg	W	2-1	Kainz 2
12/08	a Austria Wien	W	5-2	Stangl, Schobesberger, Schwab, S Hofmann, Berić
16/08	a Sturm	D	2-2	Berić, og (Madl)
22/08	h Grödig	W	3-0	Sonnleitner, Alar, Schobesberger
29/08	h Mattersburg	L	2-4	Alar, S Hofmann
12/09	a Altach	L	0-2	
20/09	h Admira	W	2-0	Schwab, Dibon
26/09	a Ried	W	1-0	Jelić
04/10	h Salzburg	L	1-2	Stangl
18/10	a Wolfsberg	L	1-2	Schaub
25/10	h Austria Wien	L	1-2	Prosenik
31/10	h Sturm	W	2-1	S Hofmann, Sonnleitner
08/11	h Grödig	L	1-2	Tomi Correa
21/11	a Mattersburg	W	6-1	Kainz 2, Stangl, Prosenik 2, Jelić
29/11	h Altach	W	3-1	Stangl, Grahovac, Nutz
02/12	a Admira	L	1-2	Alar
05/12	h Ried	W	2-1	Schwab, Schobesberger
13/12	a Salzburg	L	0-2	

2015

06/02	h Wolfsberg	W	3-0	Schobesberger, Pavelic, Jelić
14/02	a Austria Wien	W	3-0	Murg, S Hofmann (p), Jelić
21/02	a Sturm	W	2-0	Schobesberger 2
28/02	h Grödig	W	3-2	Jelić 2, Schwab
02/03	h Mattersburg	W	3-0	Schwab, Stangl, Kainz
06/03	a Altach	D	0-0	
12/03	h Admira	L	0-4	
20/03	a Ried	L	0-1	
03/04	h Salzburg	D	1-1	Schaub
09/04	a Wolfsberg	D	2-2	Tomi Correa, Schaub
17/04	a Austria Wien	W	1-0	Tomi Correa
24/04	h Sturm	W	2-0	Grahovac, Kainz
30/04	a Grödig	L	0-2	
08/05	a Mattersburg	W	2-0	Pavelic, Prosenik
11/05	h Altach	D	1-1	Schwab
15/05	a Admira	W	3-1	Schaub, Schwab, Sonnleitner

No	Name	Nat	DoB	Pos	Aps	(s)	Gls
33	Deni Alar		18/01/90	A	5	(14)	3
24	Stephan Auer		11/01/91	D	18	(1)	
9	Robert Berić	SVN	17/06/91	A	3	(2)	3
17	Christopher Dibon		02/11/90	D	22	(1)	1
15	Srdjan Grahovac	BIH	19/09/92	M	20	(6)	2
20	Maximilian Hofmann		07/08/93	D	21	(1)	
11	Steffen Hofmann	GER	09/09/80	M	22	(7)	4
18	Philipp Huspek		03/03/91	M	3	(3)	
9	Matej Jelić	CRO	05/11/90	A	16	(11)	6
14	Florian Kainz		24/10/92	M	31	(2)	7
21	Tobias Knoflach		30/12/93	G	1	(1)	
31	Dino Kovačec	CRO	27/12/93	D		(1)	
27	Andreas Kuen		24/03/95	M		(2)	
29	Thomas Murg		14/11/94	M	3	(4)	1
1	Ján Novota	SVK	29/11/83	G	12		
19	Stefan Nutz		15/02/92	M	7	(4)	1
22	Mario Pavelic		19/09/93	D	23	(3)	2
5	Thanos Petsos	GRE	05/06/91	M	18	(2)	1
38	Philipp Prosenik		03/03/93	A	10	(12)	4
10	Louis Schaub		29/12/94	M	15	(9)	5
36	Michael Schimpelsberger		12/02/91	D	2		
7	Philipp Schobesberger		10/12/93	M	23	(10)	6
4	Thomas Schrammel		05/09/87	D	4	(1)	
8	Stefan Schwab		27/09/90	M	34	(2)	8
6	Mario Sonnleitner		08/10/86	D	27		3
23	Stefan Stangl		21/10/91	D	25	(1)	5
30	Richard Strebinger		14/02/93	G	23		
40	Attila Szalai	HUN	20/01/98	D	1		
28	Tomi Correa	ESP	05/12/84	A	7	(5)	3

AUSTRIA

SV Ried

1912 • Keine Sorgen Arena (7,680) • svried.at
Major honours
Austrian Cup (2) 1998, 2011
Coach: Helgi Kolvidsson (ISL);
(16/08/15) Paul Gludovatz

2015
25/07	a	Rapid	L	0-3
02/08	h	Wolfsberg	D	0-0
08/08	a	Mattersburg	L	1-4	*Sikorski*
11/08	h	Salzburg	L	1-4	*Schubert*
15/08	a	Admira	L	1-3	*Schubert*
22/08	h	Sturm	W	1-0	*Sikorski*
29/08	a	Grödig	L	1-4	*Elsneg*
12/09	a	Austria Wien	D	1-1	*Trauner*
19/09	h	Altach	W	2-0	*Trauner, Bergmann*
26/09	h	Rapid	L	0-1	
03/10	a	Wolfsberg	D	1-1	*Kragl*
17/10	h	Mattersburg	L	0-1	
24/10	a	Salzburg	L	1-2	*Möschl*
31/10	h	Admira	D	1-1	*Trauner*
07/11	a	Sturm	L	2-3	*Sikorski, Elsneg*
21/11	h	Grödig	W	1-0	*Reifeltshammer*
29/11	h	Austria Wien	W	4-2	*Trauner, Murg 2, Elsneg (p)*
02/12	a	Altach	W	3-1	*Filipovic, Reifeltshammer, Elsneg*
05/12	a	Rapid	L	1-2	*Murg*
12/12	h	Wolfsberg	W	1-0	*Elsneg (p)*

2016
06/02	a	Mattersburg	D	3-3	*Möschl, Fröschl, Antonitsch*
13/02	h	Salzburg	W	1-0	*Fröschl*
20/02	a	Admira	D	0-0	
27/02	h	Sturm	L	0-1	
02/03	h	Grödig	D	2-2	*Reifeltshammer, Honsak*
05/03	a	Austria Wien	L	1-3	*Filipovic*
12/03	h	Altach	L	0-2	
20/03	h	Rapid	W	1-0	*Kreuzer*
02/04	a	Wolfsberg	L	0-1	
09/04	a	Mattersburg	W	1-0	*Fröschl*
16/04	a	Salzburg	L	1-2	*Elsneg*
23/04	a	Admira	W	1-0	*Elsneg*
30/04	a	Sturm	D	0-0	
07/05	h	Grödig	W	2-0	*Elsneg, Fröschl*
11/05	h	Austria Wien	L	0-5	
15/05	a	Altach	D	0-0	

No	Name	Nat	DoB	Pos	Aps	(s)	Gls
24	Alberto Prada	ESP	19/01/89	D	21	(6)	
3	Nico Antonitsch		30/09/91	D	6	(7)	1
14	Thomas Bergmann		20/09/89	D	25	(3)	1
13	Michael Brandner		13/02/95	M	6	(2)	
34	Reuf Duraković	BIH	21/03/94	G	1		
20	Dieter Elsneg		04/02/90	M	30	(1)	8
17	Petar Filipovic	GER	14/09/90	D	32		2
19	Thomas Fröschl		20/09/88	A	14	(1)	4
1	Thomas Gebauer	GER	30/06/82	G	35		
12	Florian Hart		11/05/90	D	24	(2)	
11	Matthias Honsak		20/12/96	M	3	(11)	1
5	Bernhard Janeczek		10/03/92	D	26	(2)	
11	Oliver Kragl	GER	12/05/90	M	19		1
29	Jakob Kreuzer		15/01/95	M	6	(7)	1
7	Manuel Gavilán	ESP	12/07/91	A	6	(12)	
25	Patrick Möschl		06/03/93	M	14	(6)	2
10	Thomas Murg		14/11/94	M	7	(4)	3
16	Michele Polverino	LIE	26/09/84	M	21	(3)	
28	Thomas Reifeltshammer		03/07/88	D	30	(1)	3
22	Fabian Schubert		29/08/94	A		(11)	2
9	Daniel Sikorski		02/11/87	A	10	(10)	3
6	Denis Streker	GER	06/04/91	M	8	(7)	
8	Gernot Trauner		25/03/92	M	28	(1)	4
33	Clemens Walch		10/07/87	A	12	(8)	
4	Marcel Ziegl		20/12/92	M	12	(3)	

FC Salzburg

1933 • Bullen Arena Wals-Siezenheim (30,900) • redbullsalzburg.at
Major honours
Austrian League (10) 1994, 1995, 1997, 2007, 2009, 2010, 2012, 2014, 2015, 2016; Austrian Cup (4) 2012, 2014, 2015, 2016
Coach: Peter Zeidler (GER);
(03/12/15) (Thomas Letsch (GER));
(28/12/15) Óscar García (ESP)

2015
25/07	a	Mattersburg	L	1-2	*Keïta*
01/08	h	Rapid	L	1-2	*Oberlin*
08/08	a	Admira	D	2-2	*Reyna, Keïta*
11/08	h	Ried	W	4-1	*Minamino 2, Damari 2*
15/08	h	Altach	W	2-0	*Damari, Keïta*
23/08	h	Austria Wien	D	2-2	*Prevljak, Lainer*
30/08	a	Sturm	W	3-2	*og (Spendlhofer), Reyna, Minamino*
12/09	h	Grödig	W	4-2	*Minamino 2, Keïta, Jonatan Soriano (p)*
19/09	a	Wolfsberg	D	1-1	*Minamino*
26/09	h	Mattersburg	W	4-2	*Jonatan Soriano 4 (1p)*
04/10	a	Rapid	W	2-1	*Minamino, Schwegler*
17/10	h	Admira	W	8-0	*Jonatan Soriano 2, Berisha 2, Keïta, Minamino, Damari, Mukhtar*
24/10	h	Ried	W	2-1	*Jonatan Soriano, Keïta*
31/10	a	Altach	L	0-1	
07/11	a	Austria Wien	D	1-1	*Paulo Miranda*
22/11	h	Sturm	W	3-1	*Jonatan Soriano 2, Keïta*
28/11	a	Grödig	W	1-0	*Jonatan Soriano*
01/12	h	Wolfsberg	D	1-1	*Jonatan Soriano*
06/12	h	Mattersburg	D	0-0	
13/12	h	Rapid	W	2-0	*Jonatan Soriano, Keïta*

2016
07/02	a	Admira	W	2-1	*Berisha, Jonatan Soriano*
13/02	a	Ried	L	0-1	
20/02	h	Altach	W	2-0	*Paulo Miranda, Oberlin*
28/02	h	Austria Wien	W	4-1	*Keïta 2, Jonatan Soriano, Minamino*
02/03	h	Sturm	D	0-0	
05/03	h	Grödig	W	3-0	*Jonatan Soriano, Minamino, Ulmer*
12/03	a	Wolfsberg	D	1-1	*Jonatan Soriano (p)*
19/03	h	Mattersburg	W	2-1	*Berisha, Jonatan Soriano (p)*
03/04	a	Rapid	D	1-1	*Ćaleta-Car*
10/04	h	Admira	W	1-0	*Jonatan Soriano*
16/04	h	Ried	W	2-1	*Keïta, Jonatan Soriano*
23/04	a	Altach	W	3-1	*Keïta, Ćaleta-Car, Laimer*
01/05	a	Austria Wien	W	2-0	*Lazaro, Reyna*
07/05	h	Sturm	D	1-1	*Berisha*
11/05	a	Grödig	W	2-1	*Minamino, Oberlin*
15/05	h	Wolfsberg	W	1-0	*Lazaro*

No	Name	Nat	DoB	Pos	Aps	(s)	Gls
20	David Atanga	GHA	25/12/96	M	3	(2)	
14	Valon Berisha	NOR	07/02/93	M	32	(1)	5
95	Bernardo	BRA	14/05/95	D	7	(6)	
5	Duje Ćaleta-Car	CRO	17/09/96	D	31		2
16	Omer Damari	ISR	24/03/89	A	15	(1)	4
9	Marco Djuricin		12/12/92	A	2	(1)	
11	Felipe Pires	BRA	18/04/95	M	2		
36	Martin Hinteregger		07/09/92	D	8		
48	Hwang Hee-chan	KOR	26/01/96	A	5	(8)	
26	Jonatan Soriano	ESP	24/09/85	A	25	(2)	21
8	Naby Keïta	GUI	10/02/95	M	24	(5)	12
27	Konrad Laimer		27/05/97	M	14	(4)	1
22	Stefan Lainer		27/08/92	D	14	(7)	1
10	Valentino Lazaro		24/03/96	M	9	(8)	2
24	Christoph Leitgeb		14/04/85	M	2	(1)	
18	Takumi Minamino	JPN	16/01/95	A	22	(10)	10
23	Hany Mukhtar	GER	21/03/95	M	3	(10)	1
19	Håvard Nielsen	NOR	15/07/93	A	4	(4)	
37	Dimitri Oberlin	SUI	27/09/97	A	5	(7)	3
3	Paulo Miranda	BRA	16/08/88	D	30		2
55	Yasin Pehlivan		05/01/89	M	10	(6)	
46	Smail Prevljak	BIH	10/05/95	A	3	(4)	1
15	Yordy Reyna	PER	17/09/93	A	9	(7)	3
47	Xaver Schlager		28/09/97	M	1	(1)	
2	Benno Schmitz	GER	17/11/94	D	22	(2)	
6	Christian Schwegler	SUI	06/06/84	D	23	(2)	1
1	Cican Stankovic		04/11/92	G	5		
28	Asger Sørensen	DEN	05/06/96	D		(2)	
17	Andreas Ulmer		30/10/85	D	33	(1)	1
4	Dayot Upamaneco	FRA	27/10/98	D	2		
33	Alexander Walke	GER	06/06/83	G	31		

SK Sturm Graz

1909 • UPC-Arena (15,400) • sksturm.at
Major honours
Austrian League (3) 1998, 1999, 2011; Austrian Cup (4) 1996, 1997, 1999, 2010
Coach: Franco Foda (GER)

2015
25/07	h	Admira	D	1-1	*Tadić*
02/08	h	Grödig	D	1-1	*Tadić*
09/08	a	Altach	W	1-0	*Piesinger*
12/08	a	Wolfsberg	D	2-2	*Tadić, Avdijaj*
16/08	h	Rapid	D	2-2	*Hadžić (p), Avdijaj*
22/08	a	Ried	L	0-1	
30/08	h	Salzburg	L	2-3	*Hadžić, Tadić*
13/09	a	Mattersburg	W	1-0	
19/09	h	Austria Wien	W	2-0	*Gruber, Horvath*
27/09	a	Admira	W	1-0	*Kienast*
03/10	a	Grödig	L	0-3	
17/10	h	Altach	W	3-1	*Kienast 2, Madl*
24/10	h	Wolfsberg	W	2-0	*Offenbacher, Kienast*
31/10	a	Rapid	L	1-2	*Kienast*
07/11	h	Ried	W	3-2	*Kienast 2, Schick*
22/11	a	Salzburg	L	1-3	*Lykogiannis*
28/11	h	Mattersburg	D	0-0	
02/12	h	Austria Wien	L	1-2	*Horvath*
05/12	h	Admira	D	1-1	*Horvath*
12/12	h	Grödig	W	2-0	*Stankovic, Edomwonyi*

2016
06/02	a	Altach	D	2-2	*Stankovic, Schick*
13/02	a	Wolfsberg	D	0-0	
21/02	h	Rapid	L	0-2	
27/02	a	Ried	W	1-0	*Kienast*
02/03	h	Salzburg	D	0-0	
05/03	a	Mattersburg	L	0-1	
13/03	h	Austria Wien	D	1-1	*Edomwonyi*
19/03	a	Admira	L	0-1	
02/04	a	Grödig	W	3-1	*Avdijaj, Gruber 2*
09/04	h	Altach	W	4-1	*Horvath, Edomwonyi 3*
16/04	h	Wolfsberg	W	1-0	*Edomwonyi*
24/04	a	Rapid	L	0-2	
30/04	h	Ried	D	0-0	
07/05	a	Salzburg	D	1-1	*Edomwonyi*
11/05	h	Mattersburg	D	1-1	*og (Prietl)*
15/05	a	Austria Wien	L	0-3	

No	Name	Nat	DoB	Pos	Aps	(s)	Gls
77	Donis Avdijaj	GER	25/08/96	A	17	(8)	3
4	Anastasios Avlonitis	GRE	01/01/90	D	16		
37	Kristijan Dobras		09/10/92	M	15	(15)	
34	Bright Edomwonyi	NGA	24/07/94	A	15	(12)	7
17	Martin Ehrenreich		10/05/83	D	5	(1)	
31	Michael Esser	GER	22/11/87	G	36		
22	Andreas Gruber		29/06/95	A	14	(15)	3
8	Anel Hadžić	BIH	16/08/89	M	14	(1)	2
29	Sascha Horvath		22/08/96	M	18	(7)	4
36	Wilson Kamavuaka	GER	29/03/90	D	29	(2)	
28	Tanju Kayhan		22/07/89	D	15	(1)	
42	Roman Kienast		29/03/84	A	15	(9)	8
25	Danijel Klarić	CRO	19/01/95	M		(3)	
27	Christian Klem		21/04/91	D	15	(2)	
30	Sandi Lovric		28/03/98	M	5	(3)	
14	Charalambos Lykogiannis	GRE	22/10/93	D	19	(1)	1
15	Michael Madl		21/03/88	D	18		1
20	Daniel Offenbacher		18/02/92	M	26	(4)	1
13	Simon Piesinger		13/05/92	M	13	(1)	1
19	Marvin Potzmann		07/12/93	D	20	(2)	
21	Benjamin Rosenberger		15/01/96	M		(1)	
44	Thorsten Schick		19/05/90	M	27	(3)	2
24	Marc-Andre Schmerböck		01/04/94	M		(1)	
23	Lukas Spendlhofer		02/06/93	D	28		
10	Marko Stankovic		17/02/86	M	10	(7)	2
11	Josip Tadić	CRO	22/08/87	A	6	(8)	4

Wolfsberger AC

1931 • Lavanttal Arena (7,300) •
rzpelletswac.at

**Coach: Dietmar Kühbauer;
(25/11/15) Heimo Pfeifenberger**

2015

26/07	h	Austria Wien	L	0-2	
02/08	a	Ried	D	0-0	
09/08	a	Rapid	L	1-2	Wernitznig
12/08	h	Sturm	L	0-2	
15/08	h	Grödig	W	3-2	Sílvio, Wernitznig, Hüttenbrenner
22/08	a	Mattersburg	L	0-1	
30/08	h	Altach	L	0-2	
12/09	a	Admira	L	0-1	
19/09	h	Salzburg	D	1-1	Ouédraogo
26/09	a	Austria Wien	L	0-1	
03/10	h	Ried	D	1-1	Drescher
18/10	h	Rapid	W	2-1	Jacobo, Ouédraogo
24/10	a	Sturm	L	0-2	
31/10	a	Grödig	L	0-1	
07/11	h	Mattersburg	W	2-1	Ouédraogo 2
21/11	a	Altach	L	1-2	Ouédraogo
28/11	h	Admira	W	4-0	Sílvio 2, og (Lackner), Standfest
01/12	a	Salzburg	D	1-1	Wernitznig
05/12	h	Austria Wien	W	2-0	Sílvio, Hüttenbrenner
12/12	a	Ried	L	0-1	

2016

06/02	h	Rapid	L	0-3	
13/02	h	Sturm	D	0-0	
20/02	h	Grödig	W	2-0	Ouédraogo 2
27/02	a	Mattersburg	D	1-1	Seidl
01/03	h	Altach	W	1-0	Schmerböck
05/03	a	Admira	W	2-0	Hellquist, Schmerböck
12/03	h	Salzburg	D	1-1	Jacobo (p)
19/03	a	Austria Wien	D	0-0	
02/04	h	Ried	W	1-0	Sílvio
09/04	h	Rapid	D	2-2	Ouédraogo, Schmerböck
16/04	a	Sturm	L	0-1	
23/04	a	Grödig	W	1-0	Jacobo
30/04	h	Mattersburg	W	2-0	Ouédraogo, Schmerböck
07/05	a	Altach	D	1-1	Standfest
11/05	h	Admira	L	1-2	Trdina
15/05	a	Salzburg	L	0-1	

No	Name	Nat	DoB	Pos	Aps	(s)	Gls
7	Dario Baldauf		27/03/85	D	11	(6)	
18	Michael Berger		01/12/90	D	4	(7)	
10	Ibrahim Bingöl		24/09/93	M	2		
1	Christian Dobnik		10/07/86	G	11		(2)
27	Daniel Drescher		07/10/89	D	15		1
9	Philip Hellquist	SWE	12/05/91	A	12	(14)	1
16	Boris Hüttenbrenner		23/09/85	M	30		2
11	Jacobo	ESP	04/02/84	M	26	(4)	3
31	Alexander Kofler		06/11/86	G	25		
33	Issiaka Ouédraogo	BFA	19/08/88	A	28	(1)	9
4	Stefan Palla	PHI	15/05/89	D	25	(1)	
19	Roland Putsche		22/03/91	M	5	(8)	
20	Christoph Rabitsch		10/04/96	M	14	(4)	
15	Nemanja Rnić	SRB	30/09/84	D	23		
29	Marc-Andre Schmerböck		01/04/94	M	9	(5)	4
22	Manuel Seidl		26/10/88	M	8	(7)	1
8	Sílvio	BRA	01/02/81	A	21	(10)	5
26	Michael Sollbauer		15/05/90	D	21	(4)	
25	Joachim Standfest		30/05/80	D	34		2
17	Tadej Trdina	SVN	25/01/88	A	2	(4)	1
23	Peter Tschernegg		23/07/92	M	25	(1)	
6	Manuel Weber		28/08/85	M	5	(2)	
24	Christopher Wernitznig		24/02/90	M	17	(15)	3
10	Peter Zulj		09/06/93	M	2	(4)	
28	Thomas Zündel		24/12/87	M	21	(3)	

Top goalscorers

21	Jonatan Soriano (Salzburg)
19	Alexander Gorgon (Austria)
13	Olarenwaju Kayode (Austria)
12	Naby Keïta (Salzburg)
10	Hannes Aigner (Altach)
	Lucas Venuto (Grödig/Austria)
	Takumi Minamino (Salzburg)
9	Alexander Grünwald (Austria)
	Issiaka Ouédraogo (Wolfsberg)
8	Markus Pink (Mattersburg)
	Stefan Schwab (Rapid)
	Dieter Elsneg (Ried)
	Roman Kienast (Sturm)

Promoted club

SKN St Pölten

2000 • NV-Arena (8,000) • skn-stpoelten.at
Coach: Karl Daxbacher

Second level final table 2015/16

		Pld	W	D	L	F	A	Pts
1	SKN St Pölten	36	26	2	8	68	34	80
2	LASK Linz	36	22	6	8	65	35	72
3	FC Wacker Innsbruck	36	17	8	11	61	47	59
4	FC Liefering	36	17	6	13	65	49	57
5	SC Austria Lustenau	36	16	9	11	56	40	57
6	Kapfenberger SV	36	14	8	14	63	62	50
7	SC Wiener Neustadt	36	12	9	15	39	49	45
8	Floridsdorfer AC	36	4	5	27	23	77	17
9	SK Austria Klagenfurt	36	8	10	18	43	62	34
10	SV Austria Salzburg	36	7	11	18	45	73	26

NB SK Austria Klagenfurt & SV Austria Salzburg did not obtain licence for 2016/17 and were placed last; SV Austria Salzburg – 6pts deducted.

DOMESTIC CUP

ÖFB-Cup 2015/16

FIRST ROUND

(17/07/15)
Allerheiligen 0-3 Kapfenberg
Amstetten 3-2 Kottingbrunn *(aet)*
Blau-Weiss Linz 1-1 Wacker Innsbruck *(aet; 4-5 on pens)*
Horn 2-0 Ritzing
Krems 8-1 Trausdorf
Lafnitz 1-2 Altach
Oberwart 0-3 Austria Wien
Parndorf 2-7 LASK
Sollenau 0-3 Mattersburg
SV Innsbruck 0-15 Ried
Vienna 0-1 Wiener Neustadt
Völkermarkt 2-2 Lendorf *(aet; 3-4 on pens)*
Wallern 2-1 Vorwärts Steyr
Weiz 1-5 Rapid

(18/07/15)
Bregenz 0-1 Wels
Deutschlandsberg 0-7 Salzburg
Dornbirn 0-2 St Pölten
Ebreichsdorf 4-0 Penzing
Eugendorf 2-4 Austria Salzburg *(aet)*
Golling 0-6 Floridsdorfer AC
Gurten 1-0 Grödig
Hartberg 0-6 Sturm Graz
Höchst 1-2 Seekirchen
Leobendorf 0-0 Wiener Sportklub *(aet; 4-5 on pens)*
Neumarkt 0-3 Hard
Schwechat 1-1 Admira *(aet; 2-4 on pens)*
St Johann 4-0 Kitzbühel
Stadl-Paura 1-5 Wattens

(19/07/15)
Annabichl 1-4 Stadlau
Köttmannsdorf 0-6 Wolfsberg
Lankowitz 3-1 Austria Lustenau
Reichenau 1-4 Austria Klagenfurt

SECOND ROUND

(22/09/15)
Ebreichsdorf 3-1 Wiener Neustadt
Gurten 1-3 Mattersburg
Hard 1-4 St Pölten
Horn 2-3 Salzburg *(aet)*
Krems 3-5 Wacker Innsbruck *(aet)*
Lankowitz 1-0 Floridsdorfer AC
Lendorf 0-5 Austria Salzburg
Seekirchen 0-7 Sturm Graz
St Johann 1-1 LASK *(aet; 4-5 on pens)*
Stadlau 2-1 Austria Klagenfurt *(aet)*
Wattens 0-0 Kapfenberg *(aet; 6-5 on pens)*
Wiener Sportklub 0-3 Altach

(23/09/15)
Amstetten 1-1 Rapid *(aet; 3-4 on pens)*
Ried 0-0 Wolfsberg *(aet; 5-3 on pens)*
Wallern 2-2 Admira *(aet; 2-4 on pens)*
Wels 0-7 Austria Wien

THIRD ROUND

(27/10/15)
Ebreichsdorf 2-3 Sturm Graz
Lankowitz 0-1 Admira
Salzburg 4-2 Ried
Stadlau 0-4 St Pölten
Wacker Innsbruck 0-2 LASK

(28/10/15)
Rapid 5-1 Austria Salzburg
Wattens 0-2 Mattersburg

(04/11/15)
Austria Wien 2-1 Altach

QUARTER-FINALS

(09/02/16)
Austria Wien 1-0 LASK
(Friesenbichler 21)
Mattersburg 1-2 St Pölten
(Röcher 88; Dober 8, Wisio 57)

(10/02/16)
Rapid 0-1 Admira *(Grozurek 87)*
Sturm Graz 0-1 Salzburg
(Lainer 29)

SEMI-FINALS

(19/04/16)
Admira 2-1 St Pölten *(Grozurek 52, Starkl 59; Hartl 50)*

(20/04/16)
Salzburg 5-2 Austria Wien
(Jonatan Soriano 57, Ulmer 60, Stryger 72og, Laimer 81, 87; Lucas Venuto 12, Grünwald 82)

FINAL

(19/05/16)
Wörthersee-Stadion, Klagenfurt
FC SALZBURG 5 *(Jonatan Soriano 7, 65, 86p, Keïta 28, Laimer 73)*
FC ADMIRA WACKER MÖDLING 0
Referee: Schörgenhofer
SALZBURG: Walke, Lainer, Paulo Miranda, Ćaleta-Car, Ulmer (Schmitz 16), Bernardo, Lazaro, Laimer, Keïta (Minamino 69), Berisha, Jonatan Soriano (Reyna 87)
ADMIRA: Siebenhandl, Zwierschitz, Lackner, Wostry, Wessely, Knasmüller (Bajrami 74), Toth, Grozurek (Maranda 87), Spiridonovic (Malicsek 68), Starkl, Monschein

AZERBAIJAN

Azärbaycan Futbol Federasiyaları Assosiasiyası (AFFA)

Address	Nobel Prospekti 2208 AZ-1025 Bakı	**President**	Rövnaq Abdullayev
Tel	+994 12 490 87 21	**General secretary**	Elkhan Mämmädov
Fax	+994 12 404 27 72	**Media officer**	Mikayıl Narimanoğlu
E-mail	info@affa.az	**Year of formation**	1992
Website	affa.az	**National stadium**	Baku National Stadium, Baku (68,700)

KEY

● UEFA Champions League
● UEFA Europa League
● Relegated

Qäbälä
6

Gäncä
2

Sumqayıt **8**   **4** Şüvälan
10 Zirä

1
Bakı
(Baku)
3
5
7

Länkäran
9

PREMYER LİQASI CLUBS

 1 İnter Bakı PİK

 2 Käpäz PFK

 3 Neftçi PFK

 4 Olimpik-Şüvälan PFK

 5 Qarabağ FK

 6 Qäbälä FK

 7 Rävan Bakı FK

 8 Sumqayıt FK

 9 Xäzär Länkäran FK

 10 Zirä FK

Double joy for classy Qarabağ

There was only one team in the race for Azerbaijan's Premyer Liqası title in 2015/16 as Qurban Qurbanov's Qarabağ FK coasted unopposed to their third championship crown in a row, finishing up 22 points clear of newly-promoted Zirä FK, the distant runners-up.

Qarabağ also beat Neftçi PFK in the cup final for the second successive year to land a repeat domestic double, and they were joined in the UEFA Europa League group stage by Qäbälä FK, who progressed all the way from the first qualifying round.

Qurbanov's fluent side claim hat-trick of titles

Last-gasp cup final win completes double double

Qäbälä put together extended European run

Domestic league

Qarabağ's title hat-trick was never in doubt at any stage. An opening draw at Qäbälä was followed by four straight wins, and although they lost at Neftçi and Sumgayıt before concluding the first half of the season with three successive draws, they were still able to go into the winter break cushioned by an eight-point lead, with İnter Bakı PİK heading a posse already resigned to the fact that the best they could hope for was second place.

With just domestic football to concentrate on in the spring, Qarabağ became even more dominant. A draw at İnter in late February was followed by 11 successive wins, the ninth of those, 2-0 at Zirä, wrapping up the title with four matches to spare. Qurbanov's side were simply in a different class from the other nine teams in the division, and although their sequence of victories was broken before the season's end, by relegated Rävan Bakı FK of all clubs, there was only celebration in the Qarabağ camp, with the team topping every statistical category and also boasting the Premyer Liqası's top scorer in 15-goal Dani Quintana.

The Spaniard snatched the golden boot from Zirä's El Salvador international striker Nelson Bonilla, who had 14 goals in the bank with six games to go but

failed to add any more as his club took just three points from those remaining fixtures. They still managed to finish second, three points ahead of Qäbälä, but neither Zirä nor fourth-placed İnter were permitted to qualify for Europe in 2016/17 – the former because they had not been in professional existence for three years, the latter for financial irregularities – so their UEFA Europa League qualifying spots were passed on to newly-promoted Käpäz PFK and record champions Neftçi, whose thoroughly underwhelming campaign was betrayed by end-of-season figures showing as many defeats as victories and the same number of goals conceded as scored.

Relegated alongside Rävan were Xäzär Länkäran FK, double winners in 2006/07 but doomed to the drop after failing to score for 15 successive matches in mid-campaign. With no teams promoted, the Premyer Liqası was to be reduced to just eight participants in 2016/17.

Domestic cup

Neftçi's bid to salvage their season in the Azerbaijan Cup met an untimely end when they lost the final to a 119th-minute goal from Qarabağ's Spanish midfielder Míchel, who had also scored three times in the semi-final against İnter. It was Neftçi's fifth successive appearance in the

final but their second straight defeat in the fixture, having gone down 3-1 to the same opponents 12 months earlier.

Europe

Premyer Liqası clubs enjoyed a bumper 2015/16 season in Europe. There was no breakthrough entry into the UEFA Champions League group stage, with Qarabağ losing narrowly to Celtic in the third qualifying round, but Qurbanov did lead his team back into the UEFA Europa League equivalent with a convincing 4-0 aggregate success over Young Boys. An even greater upset was that of Qäbälä, who overcame Greek giants Panathinaikos on away goals in the play-offs having already worked their way through all three qualifying rounds.

National team

Robert Prosinečki's first full season in charge of the Azerbaijan national side began positively with a goalless draw in the UEFA EURO 2016 qualifiers against the country he used to play for, Croatia, but that turned out to be the highlight, with just one win recorded over the next nine months – 2-1 in a Baku friendly against Moldova. The following fixture, a 1-0 defeat by Kazakhstan, was notable chiefly for the 100th cap collected by team captain Räşad F Sadıqov, the first player from Azerbaijan to reach that prestigious landmark.

DOMESTIC SEASON AT A GLANCE

Premyer Liqası 2015/16 final table

		Pld	Home					Away					Total					Pts
			W	D	L	F	A	W	D	L	F	A	W	D	L	F	A	
1	**Qarabağ FK**	36	15	3	0	40	6	11	3	4	26	15	26	6	4	66	21	84
2	Zirä FK	36	12	4	2	27	16	5	7	6	15	15	17	11	8	42	31	62
3	Qäbälä FK	36	6	8	4	22	13	10	3	5	22	15	16	11	9	44	28	59
4	İnter Bakı PİK	36	11	3	4	23	13	5	8	5	16	15	16	11	9	39	28	59
5	Käpäz PFK	36	8	6	4	24	14	7	5	6	24	26	15	11	10	48	40	56
6	Neftçi PFK	36	6	6	6	22	20	7	4	7	19	21	13	10	13	41	41	49
7	Olimpik-Şüvälan PFK	36	11	4	3	19	10	2	3	13	7	28	13	7	16	26	38	46
8	Sumqayıt FK	36	5	8	5	24	24	4	4	10	17	25	9	12	15	41	49	39
9	Rävan Bakı FK	36	4	3	11	11	30	1	6	11	16	33	5	9	22	27	63	18
10	Xäzär Länkäran FK	36	2	2	14	9	23	1	4	13	7	28	3	6	27	16	51	15

NB Rävan Bakı FK – 6 pts deducted.

European qualification 2016/17

Champion/Cup winner: Qarabağ FK (second qualifying round)

Qäbälä FK (first qualifying round)
Käpäz PFK (first qualifying round)
Neftçi PFK (first qualifying round)

Top scorer	Dani Quintana (Qarabağ), 15 goals
Relegated clubs	Xäzär Länkäran FK, Rävan Bakı FK
Promoted clubs	none
Cup final	Qarabağ FK 1-0 Neftçi PFK (aet)

Player of the season

Dani Quintana
(Qarabağ FK)

Although Qarabağ's 2015/16 double-winning side was packed with Azerbaijan internationals, the club was once again indebted to vital contributions from its foreign legion. Bosnian goalkeeper Ibrahim Šehić and Albanian international defender Ansi Agolli were among the most consistent performers, but it was winger Dani Quintana, a Canary Islander newly recruited from Saudi Arabian club Al Ahli, who took top honours, firing a league-best tally of 15 goals to spearhead Qarabağ to glory.

Newcomer of the season

Amil Yunanov
(Sumqayıt FK)

After an encouraging 2014/15 campaign in Azerbaijan's second tier with Rävan, which ended with the club being belatedly invited into the Premyer Liqası following the withdrawal of cash-strapped Simurq, Yunanov switched to Sumqayıt and became one of the revelations of the season. The classy striker scored 12 league goals, with four of his best strikes coming against Rävan, who would suffer immediate relegation without him. The 23-year-old ended the season by winning a first senior cap for Azerbaijan.

Team of the season
(4-5-1)

Coach: Qurbanov *(Qarabağ)*

Šehić *(Qarabağ)*

Agolli *(Qarabağ)* — Hüseynov *(Qarabağ)* — Stanković *(Qäbälä)* — Daşdämirov *(Qäbälä)*

Kvekveskiri *(İnter)* — Gai *(Qäbälä)* — Míchel *(Qarabağ)*

Dani Quintana *(Qarabağ)* — Juninho *(Käpäz)*

Bonilla *(Zirä)*

NATIONAL TEAM

Top five all-time caps
Räşad F Sadıqov (101); Aslan Kärimov (79); Mahir Şükürov (76); Tärlan Ähmädov (73); Mahmud Qurbanov (72)

Top five all-time goals
Qurban Qurbanov (12); Vaqif Cavadov (9); **Rauf Äliyev**, **Elvin Mämmädov** & Branimir Subašić (7)

Results 2015/16

Date	Opponent	H/A/N	Venue	Result	Score	Scorers
03/09/15	Croatia (ECQ)	H	Baku	D	0-0	
06/09/15	Malta (ECQ)	A	Ta' Qali	D	2-2	*Ämirquliyev (36, 80)*
10/10/15	Italy (ECQ)	H	Baku	L	1-3	*Nazarov (31)*
13/10/15	Bulgaria (ECQ)	A	Sofia	L	0-2	
17/11/15	Moldova	H	Baku	W	2-1	*Carp (32og), Ramazanov (49)*
26/03/16	Kazakhstan	N	Antalya (TUR)	L	0-1	
26/05/16	Andorra	N	Bad Erlach (AUT)	D	0-0	
29/05/16	FYR Macedonia	N	Bad Erlach (AUT)	L	1-3	*İsmayılov (72p)*
03/06/16	Canada	N	Rohrbach (AUT)	D	1-1	*Nazarov (58p)*

Appearances 2015/16

Coach: Robert Prosinečki (CRO)	12/01/69		CRO	MLT	ITA	BUL	Mda	Kaz	And	Mkd	Can	Caps	Goals
Kamran Ağayev	09/02/86	Karşıyaka (TUR) /İnter Bakı	G	G	G	G		G			G	59	-
Mähämmäd Mirzäbäyov	16/11/90	Qäbälä	D	D	s91	D		s46	D60	D	D	9	-
Bädavi Hüseynov	11/07/91	Qarabağ	D	D	88*	D	D	D		D		23	-
Räşad F Sadıqov	16/06/82	Qarabağ	D	D	D	D		D46		D		101	4
Arif Daşdämirov	10/02/87	Qäbälä	D	D	D	s63	D91	D				10	-
Qara Qarayev	12/10/92	Qarabağ	M	M	M	M82	M	M74		M	M92	24	-
Äfran İsmayılov	08/10/88	Qarabağ	M	M72	M91	M	M	M61		M	M46	29	2
Rahid Ämirquliyev	01/09/89	Xäzär Länkäran	M	M	M	M	M					48	3
Dimitrij Nazarov	04/04/90	Karlsruhe (GER)	M90	M70	M	M		M	M63	M	M88	18	5
Ruslan Qurbanov	12/09/91	Neftçi	M79	A81	A74	A	A46	A		A	s46	11	-
Mähämmäd Qurbanov	11/04/92	Neftçi	A63									3	-
Räşad Ä Sadıqov	08/10/83	Qäbälä	s63	s70	s66							24	-
Vüqar Nadirov	15/06/87	Xäzär Länkäran	s79									59	4
Eddy İsrafilov	02/08/92	Eibar (ESP) /Córdoba (ESP)	s90		M66	s82					M79	5	-
Cavid Tağıyev	22/07/92	Qarabağ		M				s46				2	-
Araz Abdullayev	18/04/92	Neftçi		s72				M69		M46	s55	19	-
Rauf Äliyev	12/02/89	İnter Bakı		s81								42	7
Maksim Medvedev	29/09/89	Qarabağ			D	D63	D	D46		D	D	35	-
Tuğrul Erat	17/06/92	Düsseldorf (GER)			s74	s67						4	-
Ruslan Abışov	10/10/87	Qäbälä				D		s74	M		s88	49	4
Elnur Cäfärov	28/03/97	Xäzär Länkäran				M67						1	-
Sälahät Ağayev	04/01/91	İnter Bakı /Sumqayıt					G46			G		8	-
Pavlo Paşayev	04/01/88	Metalurh Zaporizhya (UKR) /Qäbälä					D69		s60		D	3	-
Elvin Mämmädov	18/07/88	Qarabağ /Zirä					M75		s69	M		35	7
Rähman Hacıyev	25/07/93	Neftçi					M63			M46	s92	3	-
Aqil Mämmädov	01/05/89	Neftçi					s46					1	-
Ağabala Ramazanov	20/01/93	Sumqayıt					s46	A46	A	s46	A	6	1
Elşän Rzazadä	11/09/93	Xäzär Länkäran					s63					1	-
Ürfan Abbasov	14/10/92	Qäbälä					s69					1	-
Räşad Eyubov	03/12/92	Käpäz /Qäbälä					s75		s63			2	-
Tärlan Quliyev	19/04/92	Käpäz					s91	s46	D46		D	6	-
Namiq Äläsgärov	03/02/95	Käpäz						s61			M55	3	-
Anar Näzirov	08/09/85	Zirä							G			3	-
Adil Nağıyev	11/09/95	Zirä							D			1	-
Ufuk Budak	26/05/90	Gaziantep BB (TUR)							D			16	-
Budaq Näsirov	15/07/96	Käpäz							M			1	-
Murad Sättarlı	09/05/92	Olimpik-Şüvälan							M46			1	-
Vüqar Mustafayev	05/08/94	Zirä							s46			1	-
Amil Yunanov	06/01/93	Sumqayıt							s46			1	-
Coşqun Diniyev	13/09/95	Qarabağ								s46	s79	3	-

EUROPE

Qarabağ FK

Second qualifying round - FK Rudar Pljevlja (MNE)
H 0-0
Šehić, Qarayev (Diniyev 74), Medvedev, Reynaldo, Dani Quintana, Sadıqov, Richard, Agolli, Hüseynov, El Jadeyaoui, Tağıyev (Mämmädov 67). Coach: Qurban Qurbanov (AZE)
A 1-0 *Reynaldo (57)*
Šehić, Qarayev, Medvedev, Reynaldo, Dani Quintana, Sadıqov, Richard, Agolli (Qurbanov 64), Hüseynov, El Jadeyaoui (Tağıyev 56), Diniyev (Mämmädov 79). Coach: Qurban Qurbanov (AZE)

Third qualifying round - Celtic FC (SCO)
A 0-1
Šehić, Qarayev, Reynaldo, Dani Quintana (Diniyev 82), Sadıqov, Qurbanov, Richard, Agolli, Hüseynov, El Jadeyaoui (Poepon 86), Tağıyev (Mämmädov 73). Coach: Qurban Qurbanov (AZE)
H 0-0
Šehić, Qarayev, Reynaldo, Dani Quintana (Tağıyev 84), Sadıqov, Qurbanov, Richard, Agolli, Poepon (Ismayilov 64), Hüseynov, El Jadeyaoui (Mämmädov 74). Coach: Qurban Qurbanov (AZE)

Play-offs - BSC Young Boys (SUI)
A 1-0 *Richard (67)*
Šehić, Qarayev, Reynaldo, Dani Quintana (Diniyev 75), Sadıqov, Qurbanov, Richard, Agolli, Hüseynov, El Jadeyaoui (Yunuszadä 87), Tağıyev (Ismayilov 80). Coach: Qurban Qurbanov (AZE)
H 3-0 *Richard (4p), Reynaldo (43), Ismayilov (61)*
Šehić, Qarayev (Mustafayev 85), Reynaldo, Dani Quintana, Sadıqov, Qurbanov, Richard, Ismayilov (Poepon 71), Agolli, Hüseynov, Tağıyev (Diniyev 78). Coach: Qurban Qurbanov (AZE)

Group J
Match 1 - Tottenham Hotspur FC (ENG)
A 1-3 *Richard (7p)*
Šehić, Qarayev, Medvedev, Reynaldo, Dani Quintana (Míchel 79), Sadıqov, Richard, Ismayilov (El Jadeyaoui 79), Agolli, Hüseynov, Tağıyev (Armenteros 67). Coach: Qurban Qurbanov (AZE)
Match 2 - RSC Anderlecht (BEL)
H 1-0 *Richard (36)*
Šehić, Qarayev, Medvedev, Reynaldo, Dani Quintana (Diniyev 68), Sadıqov, Richard, Agolli, Hüseynov, El Jadeyaoui (Yunuszadä 77), Armenteros (Ismayilov 61). Coach: Qurban Qurbanov (AZE)
Match 3 - AS Monaco FC (FRA)
A 0-1
Šehić, Qarayev, Medvedev, Dani Quintana (Chumbinho 59), Sadıqov, Richard, Ismayilov (Poepon 71), Agolli, Hüseynov, El Jadeyaoui (Mämmädov 77), Armenteros. Coach: Qurban Qurbanov (AZE)

Match 4 - AS Monaco FC (FRA)
H 1-1 *Armenteros (39)*
Šehić, Qarayev, Medvedev, Dani Quintana (Chumbinho 68), Sadıqov, Richard, Ismayilov (Poepon 64), Agolli, Hüseynov, El Jadeyaoui, Armenteros. Coach: Qurban Qurbanov (AZE)
Match 5 - Tottenham Hotspur FC (ENG)
H 0-1
Šehić, Qarayev, Medvedev, Dani Quintana, Sadıqov, Richard, Ismayilov (Mämmädov 80), Agolli, Poepon (Armenteros 54), Hüseynov, Tağıyev (Chumbinho 65). Coach: Qurban Qurbanov (AZE)
Match 6 - RSC Anderlecht (BEL)
A 1-2 *Dani Quintana (26)*
Šehić, Qarayev (Poepon 75), Medvedev, Dani Quintana, Sadıqov, Qurbanov, Richard, Ismayilov (Tağıyev 63), Hüseynov, Chumbinho (Míchel 71), Armenteros. Coach: Qurban Qurbanov (AZE)

İnter Bakı PİK

First qualifying round - KF Laçi (ALB)
A 1-1 *Kvekveskiri (47)*
S Ağayev, Juanfran, Kasradze, Kvekveskiri, Äliyev (Nähävandi 90+3), Abbasov (Sadıqov 74), Khizanishvili, Seyidov, Fomenko (Hacıyev 43), Bayramov, Hüseynov. Coach: Zaur Svanadze (GEO)
H 0-0
S Ağayev, Juanfran, Kasradze, Kvekveskiri, Hacıyev(Sadıqov 81), Äliyev (Dênis Silva 90+1), Abbasov (Nahavandi 90+4), Khizanishvili, Seyidov, Bayramov, Hüseynov. Coach: Zaur Svanadze (GEO)

Second qualifying round - FH Hafnarfjördur (ISL)
A 2-1 *Kvekveskiri (54p), Dhiego Martins (61)*
S Ağayev, Juanfran, Kasradze, Kvekveskiri, Hacıyev (Poljak 80), Aliyev, Abbasov (Dhiego Martins 46), Khizanishvili, Seyidov, Bayramov (Dênis Silva 69), Hüseynov. Coach: Zaur Svanadze (GEO)
H 2-2 (aet) *Hüseynov (45+1), Äliyev (91)*
S Ağayev, Juanfran, Kasradze, Kvekveskiri, Hacıyev, Aliyev, Khizanishvili, Seyidov (Poljak 72), Dhiego Martins (Abbasov 55), Bayramov, Hüseynov (Qırtımov 87). Coach: Zaur Svanadze (GEO)

Third qualifying round - Athletic Club (ESP)
A 0-2
S Ağayev, Juanfran (Hüseynov 45), Kasradze, Dênis Silva, Kvekveskiri, Hacıyev, Aliyev, Khizanishvili, Poljak (Fomenko 46), Qırtımov (Abdullayev 87), Bayramov. Coach: Zaur Svanadze (GEO)
H 0-0
S Ağayev, Kasradze, Dênis Silva, Kvekveskiri, Hacıyev(Abdullayev 76), Aliyev, Khizanishvili, Seyidov, Qırtımov, Dhiego Martins (Fomenko 77), Bayramov. Coach: Zaur Svanadze (GEO)

Qäbälä FK

First qualifying round - FC Dinamo Tbilisi (GEO)
A 1-2 *C Hüseynov (74)*
Bezotosniy, Florescu (Sadıqov 72), Zenjov, C Hüseynov, Vernydub, Gai, Ricardinho, Daşdämirov (Dodô 73), Abbasov, Rafael Santos, Antonov. Coach: Roman Hryhorchuk (UKR)
H 2-0 *A Mämmädov (88), Antonov (90+3)*
Bezotosniy, Florescu (Dodô 77), Sadıqov (A Mämmädov 82), Zenjov, C Hüseynov, Vernydub, Gai, Ricardinho, Abbasov (Daşdämirov 86), Rafael Santos, Antonov. Coach: Roman Hryhorchuk (UKR)

Second qualifying round - FK Čukarički (SRB)
A 0-1
Bezotosniy, Florescu (Dodô 36), Sadıqov, Zenjov (A Mämmädov 88), C Hüseynov, Vernydub, Gai, Ricardinho, Abbasov, Rafael Santos, Antonov (Daşdämirov 46). Coach: Roman Hryhorchuk (UKR)
H 2-0 *Zenjov (39, 53)*
Bezotosniy, Stanković, Sadıqov, Zenjov, C Hüseynov, Gai, Ricardinho, Abbasov, Rafael Santos, Zärgärov (Daşdämirov 70), Antonov (Dodô 90). Coach: Roman Hryhorchuk (UKR)

Third qualifying round - Apollon Limassol FC (CYP)
A 1-1 *C Hüseynov (90+5p)*
Bezotosniy, Stanković, Sadıqov, Zenjov, C Hüseynov, Gai, Ricardinho, Abbasov (Daşdämirov 85), Rafael Santos, Zärgärov (Dodô 36), Antonov (Zec 76). Coach: Roman Hryhorchuk (UKR)
H 1-0 *C Hüseynov (80p)*
Bezotosniy, Stanković, Sadıqov, Zenjov, Dodô, C Hüseynov, Gai, Daşdämirov, Abbasov, Rafael Santos, Antonov (Zec 71). Coach: Roman Hryhorchuk (UKR)
Red card: Abbasov 90+1

Play-offs - Panathinaikos FC (GRE)
H 0-0
Bezotosniy, Stanković, Sadıqov, Zec (Zärgärov 58), Zenjov, Dodô, Gai, Ricardinho, Daşdämirov, Rafael Santos, Antonov (A Mämmädov 90). Coach: Roman Hryhorchuk (UKR)
A 2-2 *Dodô (6, 60)*
Bezotosniy, Stanković, Sadıqov, Zec (Camalov 86), Zenjov, Dodô, Vernydub, Gai, Ricardinho, Daşdämirov, Antonov. Coach: Roman Hryhorchuk (UKR)

Group C
Match 1 - PAOK FC (GRE)
H 0-0
Bezotosniy, Stanković, Zec (Pereyra 46), Zenjov, Dodô (Zärgärov 83), Vernydub, Gai, Ricardinho, Daşdämirov, Antonov, Meza. Coach: Roman Hryhorchuk (UKR)
Match 2 - FC Krasnodar (RUS)
A 1-2 *Dodô (51)*
Bezotosniy, Stanković, Zenjov, Dodô, Vernydub, Gai, Ricardinho, Daşdämirov, Pereyra, Antonov (Zec 74), Meza (Sadıqov 46; Zärgärov 90). Coach: Roman Hryhorchuk (UKR)

DOMESTIC LEAGUE CLUB-BY-CLUB

Match 3 - Borussia Dortmund (GER)
H 1-3 *Dodô (90+3)*
Bezotosniy, Stanković, Zenjov (Zec 79), Dodô, Vernydub, Gai, Ricardinho, Daşdämirov, Pereyra (Zärgärov 60), Antonov, Meza (Sadiqov 83). Coach: Roman Hryhorchuk (UKR)

Match 4 - Borussia Dortmund (GER)
A 0-4
Pietrzkiewicz, Stanković, Zenjov (Zärgärov 86), Dodô, Vernydub, Gai, Ricardinho, Daşdämirov, Rafael Santos, Antonov (Pereyra 68), Meza (Camalov 76). Coach: Roman Hryhorchuk (UKR)

Match 5 - PAOK FC (GRE)
A 0-0
Bezotosniy, Stanković, Sadiqov (Camalov 87), Zec, Zenjov (Cavadov 77), Gai, Ricardinho, Daşdämirov, Rafael Santos, Zärgärov (Mirzäbäyov 83), Antonov. Coach: Roman Hryhorchuk (UKR)

Match 6 - FC Krasnodar (RUS)
H 0-3
Popoviç, Stanković, Zenjov (Zärgärov 57), Dodô, Gai (Sadiqov 76), Ricardinho, Daşdämirov, Pereyra (Zec 61), Rafael Santos, Antonov, Meza. Coach: Roman Hryhorchuk (UKR)

Neftçi PFK

First qualifying round - FK Mladost Podgorica (MNE)
H 2-2 *K Qurbanov (36), A Abdullayev (55)*
A Mämmädov, Melli, Ailton, A Abdullayev (Abbasov 73), E Abdullayev (Näcäfzadä 77), R Qurbanov, M Qurbanov, Hacıyev, Mäsimov (N Qurbanov 80), K Qurbanov, Bädälov. Coach: Samir Äliyev (AZE)

A 1-1 *A Abdullayev (71)*
A Mämmädov, Melli, Ailton, A Abdullayev, R Qurbanov, M Qurbanov (E Abdullayev 63), Hacıyev, Cauê, Mäsimov (N Qurbanov 78), K Qurbanov, Bädälov. Coach: Samir Äliyev (AZE)

Red cards: Ailton 90+9, Vailo 90+9

İnter Bakı PİK

2004 • İnter Arena (6,500) • inter.az
Major honours
Azerbaijan League (2) 2008, 2010
Coach: Zaur Svanadze (GEO)

2015

09/08	a	Xäzär Länkäran	L	0-2	
17/08	h	Neftçi	W	1-0	*Dênis Silva*
24/08	a	Zirä	D	0-0	
12/09	h	Qäbälä	W	2-1	*Dhiego Martins 2*
19/09	a	Olimpik-Şüvälan	W	1-0	*Hacıyev*
25/09	h	Käpäz	W	1-0	*Dhiego Martins*
04/10	h	Qarabağ	L	0-2	
18/10	a	Sumqayıt	D	1-1	*Kvekveskiri*
24/10	h	Rävan	W	2-0	*Fomenko, Qırtımov*
28/10	a	Neftçi	D	1-1	*Hacıyev*
31/10	h	Zirä	D	0-0	
09/11	a	Qäbälä	D	1-1	*Dhiego Martins*
23/11	h	Olimpik-Şüvälan	W	2-0	*Dhiego Martins, Hüseynov*
27/11	a	Käpäz	D	0-0	
06/12	a	Qarabağ	L	0-1	
11/12	h	Sumqayıt	L	2-3	*Fomenko, Abdullayev*
15/12	a	Rävan	W	2-0	*Khizanishvili, Seydi*
20/12	h	Xäzär Länkäran	W	2-0	*Khizanishvili, Abdullayev*

2016

31/01	a	Zirä	L	1-2	*Hüseynov*
07/02	h	Qäbälä	L	0-1	
13/02	a	Olimpik-Şüvälan	D	0-0	
19/02	h	Käpäz	W	1-0	*Hacıyev*
27/02	h	Qarabağ	D	1-1	*Hacıyev*
05/03	a	Sumqayıt	W	1-0	*Hacıyev*
13/03	h	Rävan	W	3-1	*Khizanishvili, Abbasov, Kvekveskiri*
20/03	a	Xäzär Länkäran	W	1-0	*Kvekveskiri*
30/03	h	Neftçi	L	0-1	
03/04	a	Qäbälä	D	0-0	
09/04	h	Olimpik-Şüvälan	W	1-0	*Nadírov*
16/04	a	Käpäz	D	1-1	*Fomenko*
22/04	a	Qarabağ	L	0-2	
01/05	h	Sumqayıt	D	2-2	*Abbasov, Kvekveskiri*
07/05	a	Rävan	W	4-0	*Hüseynov, Abbasov 2, Hacıyev*
11/05	h	Xäzär Länkäran	W	2-1	*Äliyev, Fomenko*
15/05	a	Neftçi	L	2-4	*Abbasov 2*
20/05	h	Zirä	W	1-0	*Hüseynov*

No	Name	Nat	DoB	Pos	Aps	(s)	Gls
88	Abdulla Abatsiyev		16/08/93	M	9	(2)	
77	Mirsahib Abbasov		19/01/93	M	12	(9)	6
10	Elnur Abdullayev		16/02/86	M	13	(9)	2
1	Kamran Ağayev		09/02/86	G	14		
25	Sälahät Ağayev		04/01/91	G	13		
11	Rauf Äliyev		12/02/89	A	8	(2)	1
12	Ruslan Amircanov		01/02/85	D	10	(6)	
24	Fuad Bayramov		30/11/94	M	24	(3)	
3	Dênis Silva	BRA	28/12/85	D	35		1
23	Dhiego Martins	BRA	27/08/88	A	14	(1)	5
20	Yuriy Fomenko	UKR	31/12/86	M	20	(8)	4
8	Nizami Hacıyev		08/02/88	M	20	(5)	6
30	Abbas Hüseynov		13/06/95	D	20	(6)	4
3	Juanfran	ESP	10/01/86	D	5	(2)	
4	Lasha Kasradze	GEO	28/07/89	D	14	(6)	
14	Zurab Khizanishvili	GEO	06/10/81	D	24		3
7	Nika Kvekveskiri	GEO	29/05/92	M	28	(1)	4
79	Giorgi Lomaia	GEO	08/08/79	G	12	(2)	
23	César Meza	PAR	05/10/91	A	15		
17	Vüqar Nadírov		15/06/87	A	9	(4)	1
18	Mänsur Nähavändi		12/08/96	M	2	(1)	
96	Elşän Poladov		30/11/79	G	1		
15	Stjepan Poljak	CRO	17/11/83	M	8	(6)	
9	Qara İ Qarayev		05/03/98	A	1	(4)	
22	İlkin Qırtımov		04/11/90	D	28	(3)	1
33	Aqşin Quluzadä		31/08/98	M		(1)	
45	İlkin Sadiqov		12/09/97	A		(1)	
6	Lasha Salukvadze	GEO	21/12/81	D	22	(1)	
9	L'Imam Seydi	FRA	31/08/85	A	3	(4)	1
19	Mirhüseyn Seyidov		10/08/92	M	10	(6)	
2	Särtan Taşkın		08/10/97	D	5	(4)	
77	Emiljano Vila	ALB	12/03/88	M	1	(5)	

Käpäz PFK

1959 • Gäncä şähär stadionu (27,830) • kapazpfc.az
Major honours
Azerbaijan League (3) 1995, 1998, 1999; Azerbaijan Cup (4) 1994, 1997, 1998, 2000
Coach: Şahin Diniyev

2015

09/08	a	Neftçi	D	0-0	
16/08	h	Zirä	D	1-1	*Rähimov*
23/08	a	Qäbälä	L	0-1	
12/09	h	Olimpik-Şüvälan	W	1-0	*Dário Júnior*
20/09	h	Qarabağ	L	2-3	*Soltanov, Rähimov*
25/09	a	İnter	L	0-1	
04/10	h	Sumqayıt	W	3-1	*Juninho 2, Eyubov*
16/10	a	Rävan	W	2-0	*Ebah, Juninho*
24/10	h	Xäzär Länkäran	W	1-0	*Dário Júnior*
28/10	a	Zirä	D	2-2	*Soltanov, Juninho*
01/11	a	Qäbälä	W	2-1	*Sytnik, Dário Júnior*
07/11	a	Olimpik-Şüvälan	D	1-1	*Ebah*
21/11	a	Qarabağ	L	0-3	
27/11	h	İnter	D	0-0	
07/12	a	Sumqayıt	D	2-2	*Sytnik, Axundov (p)*
11/12	h	Rävan	D	0-0	
17/12	a	Xäzär Länkäran	W	1-0	*Rähimov*
20/12	h	Neftçi	D	1-1	*Quliyev*

2016

30/01	h	Qäbälä	W	3-0	*Ebah 2, Äläsgärov*
07/02	h	Olimpik-Şüvälan	W	2-0	*Näsirov, Ebah*
14/02	h	Qarabağ	L	1-2	*Äläsgärov*
19/02	a	İnter	L	0-1	
27/02	h	Sumqayıt	L	0-1	
06/03	a	Rävan	W	3-1	*Diniyev, Äläsgärov, Juninho*
13/03	h	Xäzär Länkäran	W	2-0	*Närimanov, Rzayev*
19/03	a	Neftçi	W	3-2	*Soltanov, Axundov (p), Rähimov*
30/03	h	Zirä	W	2-0	*Axundov (p), og (Mütällimov)*
03/04	a	Olimpik-Şüvälan	L	0-3	
08/04	a	Qarabağ	L	0-4	
16/04	h	İnter	D	1-1	*Axundov (p)*
24/04	a	Sumqayıt	W	3-2	*og (Fardjad-Azad), Juninho, Ebah*
30/04	h	Rävan	W	3-2	*Ebah, og (Müslümov), Axundov (p)*
07/05	a	Xäzär Länkäran	W	3-0	*Diniyev, Ebah, O Äliyev*
11/05	h	Neftçi	L	1-2	*Ebah*
15/05	a	Zirä	D	2-2	*O Äliyev, Soltanov*
20/05	h	Qäbälä	L	0-1	

No	Name	Nat	DoB	Pos	Aps	(s)	Gls
9	Murad Ağakişiyev		13/06/85	M		(4)	
18	Tural Axundov		01/08/88	D	35		5
9	Namiq Äläsgärov		03/02/95	M	15		3
1	Eyyub Äliyev		13/05/95	G		(1)	
19	Orxan Äliyev		21/12/95	M	7	(5)	2
25	Şähriyar Äliyev		25/12/92	D	33		
6	Ceyhun Cavadov		05/10/92	M	2	(15)	
6	Elvin Cäbrayıllı		04/02/92	M		(1)	
10	Dário Júnior	BRA	11/09/91	M	12		3
5	Kärim Diniyev		05/09/93	M	29	(1)	2
90	Julien Ebah	CMR	27/09/90	A	21	(7)	9
68	Räşad Eyubov		03/12/92	M	13		1
7	Juninho	BRA	07/07/82	M	33		6
15	Azad Kärimov		31/10/94	D	7	(17)	
23	Tural Närimanov		27/10/89	D	6	(5)	1
8	Budaq Näsirov		15/07/96	M	33		1
21	Xäzär Qäribov		24/02/92	M		(1)	
3	Tärlan Quliyev		19/04/92	D	35		4
13	Şähriyar Rähimov		06/04/89	M	35		4
80	Tural Elx. Rzayev		26/08/93	A	11	(20)	1
99	Äli Sämädov		06/09/97	M		(1)	
88	Tadas Simaitis	LTU	29/12/90	G	36		
27	Bäxtiyar Soltanov		21/06/89	A	23	(12)	4
19	Olexandr Sytnik	UKR	07/07/84	A	10	(7)	2

Neftçi PFK

1937 • Bakcell Arena (11,000); İsmät Qayıbov adına Bakıxanov qäsäbä stadionu (4,500); Älincä Arena (13,000) • neftchipfk.com

Major honours
Azerbaijan League (8) 1992, 1996, 1997, 2004, 2005, 2011, 2012, 2013; Azerbaijan Cup (7) 1995, 1996, 1999, 2002, 2004, 2013, 2014

Coach: Samir Äliyev;
(14/11/15) Äsgär Abdullayev;
(06/03/16) (Väli Qasımov)

2015
09/08	h Käpäz	D	0-0	
17/08	a İnter	L	0-1	
23/08	h Sumqayıt	W	2-1	A Abdullayev, Hacıyev
13/09	a Rävan	W	3-1	Muradbäyli 2, Hacıyev
20/09	a Xäzär Länkäran	D	1-1	A Abdullayev
26/09	a Qarabağ	D	1-1	Ramos
03/10	a Zirä	L	0-2	
17/10	h Qäbälä	L	0-1	
23/10	a Olimpik-Şüvälan	L	1-2	R Qurbanov
28/10	h İnter	L	1-2	R Qurbanov (p)
02/11	a Sumqayıt	W	2-1	Muradbäyli, R Qurbanov (p)
08/11	h Rävan	L	2-3	R Qurbanov 2
22/11	a Xäzär Länkäran	W	2-0	E Abdullayev, Muradbäyli
29/11	a Qarabağ	W	1-0	Hacıyev
06/12	h Zirä	D	1-1	R Qurbanov
13/12	h Qäbälä	W	1-0	Jairo
17/12	h Olimpik-Şüvälan	L	0-1	
20/12	a Käpäz	L	1-2	İmamverdiyev

2016
30/01	h Sumqayıt	W	1-0	R Qurbanov
05/02	h Rävan	D	1-1	Jairo
13/02	h Xäzär Länkäran	W	1-0	E Abdullayev
20/02	a Qarabağ	L	0-2	
27/02	a Zirä	L	0-3	
05/03	h Qäbälä	L	1-2	Añete
13/03	a Olimpik-Şüvälan	D	1-1	Canales
19/03	h Käpäz	L	2-3	A Abdullayev, R Qurbanov (p)
30/03	a İnter	W	1-0	R Qurbanov (p)
03/04	a Rävan	L	0-1	
10/04	a Xäzär Länkäran	W	1-0	R Qurbanov
14/04	h Qarabağ	L	1-2	Aílton
23/04	h Zirä	D	0-0	
01/05	a Qäbälä	D	2-2	R Qurbanov, E Abdullayev
07/05	h Olimpik-Şüvälan	W	3-1	Añete, A Abdullayev, Aílton
11/05	a Käpäz	W	2-1	Añete, R Qurbanov (p)
15/05	h İnter	W	4-2	R Qurbanov, A Abdullayev, E Abdullayev, Aílton
20/05	a Sumqayıt	L	1-2	A Abdullayev

No	Name	Nat	DoB	Pos	Aps	(s)	Gls
22	Mirabdulla Abbasov		27/04/95	A		(2)	
7	Araz Abdullayev		18/04/92	M	21	(5)	6
8	Elşän Abdullayev		05/02/94	M	19	(13)	4
6	Aílton	BRA	16/03/95	D	30	(2)	3
20	Añete	ESP	01/10/85	A	23	(3)	3
95	Elvin Bädälov		14/06/95	D	18	(1)	
9	Nicolás Canales	CHI	27/06/85	A	3	(4)	1
18	Cauê	BRA	24/05/89	M	13	(5)	
17	Rähman Hacıyev		25/07/93	M	29	(5)	3
10	Cavid İmamverdiyev		08/01/90	M	12	(10)	1
27	Mäqsäd İsayev		07/06/94	D	20	(2)	
3	Jairo	BRA	31/12/92	D	20		2
1	Aqil Mämmädov		01/05/89	G	28		
4	Rahil Mämmädov		24/11/95	D	18	(1)	
61	Täyyar Mämmädov		10/02/96	D		(2)	
21	Samir Mäsimov		25/08/95	M	4	(6)	
5	Melli	ESP	06/06/84	D	24	(2)	
9	Fähmin Muradbäyli		16/03/96	A	23	(8)	4
24	Michal Peškovič	SVK	08/02/82	G	2		
16	Äziz Quliyev		02/05/87	D	1	(1)	
41	Aqşin Qurbanlı		15/07/96	M		(1)	
26	Kamal Qurbanov		06/05/94	D	19	(4)	
14	Mähämmäd Qurbanov		11/04/92	A	4	(9)	
11	Ruslan Qurbanov		12/09/91	A	28	(3)	13
15	Éric Ramos	PAR	12/06/87	M	31		1
18	Elşän Rzazadä		11/09/93	M		(2)	
53	Maksym Vailo		13/05/95	G	6		

Olimpik-Şüvälan PFK

1996 • AZAL Arena (3,000); Dalğa Arena (6,700) • azalpfc.az
Coach: Tärlan Ähmädov

2015
09/08	a Zirä	L	0-1	
15/08	h Qäbälä	L	0-2	
23/08	h Qarabağ	L	0-2	
12/09	a Käpäz	L	0-1	
19/09	h İnter	L	0-1	
26/09	a Sumqayıt	D	1-1	Guruli
02/10	h Rävan	W	1-0	Kvirtia
18/10	a Xäzär Länkäran	L	1-3	Sättarlı
23/10	h Neftçi	W	2-1	Kvirtia (p), Guruli (p)
28/10	a Qäbälä	D	0-0	
31/10	a Qarabağ	L	0-2	
07/11	h Käpäz	D	1-1	Novruzov
23/11	a İnter	L	0-2	
28/11	h Sumqayıt	W	2-0	Sättarlı, Näsirli
07/12	a Rävan	D	0-0	
13/12	a Xäzär Länkäran	W	1-0	Sättarlı
17/12	a Neftçi	W	1-0	Näsirli
20/12	h Zirä	W	1-0	Novruzov (p)

2016
31/01	h Qarabağ	W	1-0	Kvirtia
07/02	a Käpäz	L	0-2	
13/02	h İnter	D	0-0	
20/02	a Sumqayıt	L	0-2	
27/02	h Rävan	W	1-0	Kvirtia
05/03	a Xäzär Länkäran	W	1-0	Guruli (p)
13/03	h Neftçi	D	1-1	Mirzäyev
20/03	a Zirä	L	2-4	Qasımov, Näsirli
30/03	h Qäbälä	W	2-1	Hümbätov, Sättarlı
03/04	h Käpäz	W	3-0	Qasımov, Ähmädov, Hüseynpur (p)
09/04	a İnter	L	0-1	
17/04	h Sumqayıt	W	1-0	Hümbätov
24/04	a Rävan	L	0-1	
30/04	a Xäzär Länkäran	W	1-0	Kvirtia
07/05	a Neftçi	L	1-3	Kvirtia
11/05	h Zirä	D	1-1	Kvirtia
15/05	a Qäbälä	L	0-2	
20/05	a Qarabağ	L	0-3	

No	Name	Nat	DoB	Pos	Aps	(s)	Gls
23	Hacı Ähmädov		23/11/93	M	13	(4)	1
14	İlqar Äläkbärov		06/10/93	M	32	(1)	
8	Seymur Äsädov		05/05/94	M	6		
19	Mähämmäd Bädälbäyli		27/04/92	A	7	(23)	
24	Emin Cäfärquliyev		17/06/90	D	34		
17	Elmin Çobanov		13/05/92	M		(3)	
77	Adan Coronado	USA	20/04/90	D	8	(6)	
42	Aleksandre Guruli	GEO	09/11/85	M	19	(6)	3
3	Tural Hümbätov		24/01/94	D	35		2
18	Eltun Hüseynov		27/02/93	D	1		
5	Kamil Hüseynov		04/02/92	M	18	(2)	
88	Mirzağa Hüseynpur		11/03/90	A	9	(2)	1
20	İsmayıl İbrahimli		13/02/98	M		(1)	
10	Nugzar Kvirtia	RUS	16/09/84	M	23	(10)	7
42	Elşad Manafov		08/03/92	D	1		
4	Qvanzav Maqomedov		08/06/94	D	16	(4)	
2	Rail Mälikov		18/12/85	D	33		
22	Kamal Mirzäyev		05/12/95	M	14	(7)	1
16	Stanislav Namasco	MDA	10/11/86	G	36		
11	Ruslan Näsirli		12/01/95	M	11	(12)	3
6	Taqim Novruzov		21/11/88	M	20	(1)	2
9	Aydın Qasımov		22/09/93	D	20	(4)	2
21	Murad Sättarlı		09/05/92	M	30	(1)	4
28	Müşfiq Teymurov		15/01/93	D	4	(11)	
7	Tärlan Xälilov		27/08/84	M	6	(8)	

Qarabağ FK

1987 • Dalğa Arena (6,700); Azärsun Arena (5,900); İnter Arena (6,500); Älincä Arena (13,000) • qarabagh.com

Major honours
Azerbaijan League (4) 1993, 2014, 2015, 2016; Azerbaijan Cup (5) 1993, 2006, 2009, 2015, 2016

Coach: Qurban Qurbanov

2015
10/08	a Qäbälä	D	2-2	Richard 2 (1p)
15/08	a Rävan	W	2-1	og (Ağakärimzadä), Qarayev
23/08	a Olimpik-Şüvälan	W	2-0	Mädätov, Dani Quintana
12/09	h Xäzär Länkäran	W	1-0	Armenteros
20/09	a Käpäz	W	3-2	Diniyev (p), Armenteros, Mämmädov (p)
26/09	h Neftçi	D	1-1	Richard (p)
04/10	a İnter	W	2-0	Dani Quintana, Reynaldo
17/10	h Zirä	W	4-1	Armenteros 2, Richard 2 (1p)
25/10	a Sumqayıt	L	0-1	
28/10	h Rävan	W	1-0	Mustafayev
31/10	h Olimpik-Şüvälan	W	2-0	İsmayılov, Poepon
08/11	a Xäzär Länkäran	W	1-0	İsmayılov
21/11	h Käpäz	W	3-0	Chumbinho, Dani Quintana, Richard
29/11	a Neftçi	W	1-0	
06/12	h İnter	W	1-0	Dani Quintana
13/12	a Zirä	D	0-0	
16/12	h Sumqayıt	D	2-2	Richard (p), Dani Quintana
19/12	h Qäbälä	D	1-1	İsmayılov

2016
31/01	a Olimpik-Şüvälan	L	0-1	
06/02	h Xäzär Länkäran	W	3-0	Dani Quintana, Richard (p), Armenteros
14/02	a Käpäz	W	2-1	Sadıqov, İsmayılov
20/02	h Neftçi	W	2-0	Armenteros, Dani Quintana
27/02	a İnter	D	1-1	Sadıqov
05/03	a Zirä	W	2-0	Muarem, Mädätov
13/03	a Sumqayıt	W	2-0	Dani Quintana, Míchel
19/03	a Qäbälä	W	2-1	Míchel, Mädätov
30/03	h Rävan	W	5-1	Míchel, Muarem, Richard, Reynaldo, Dani Quintana
03/04	a Xäzär Länkäran	W	2-1	Mädätov 2
08/04	h Käpäz	W	4-0	og (Axundov), Dani Quintana, Mädätov, Armenteros
16/04	a Neftçi	W	2-1	Dani Quintana, Reynaldo
22/04	h İnter	W	2-0	Reynaldo, Muarem
01/05	a Zirä	W	2-0	Dani Quintana, Reynaldo
07/05	h Sumqayıt	W	1-0	İsmayılov
11/05	h Qäbälä	W	2-0	Dani Quintana 2
15/05	a Rävan	L	1-2	İsmayılov (p)
20/05	h Olimpik-Şüvälan	W	3-0	Mädätov, Míchel, Dani Quintana

No	Name	Nat	DoB	Pos	Aps	(s)	Gls
25	Ansi Agolli	ALB	11/10/82	D	23	(1)	
90	Samuel Armenteros	SWE	27/05/90	A	14	(9)	7
15	Rahid Ämirquliyev		01/09/89	M		(2)	
70	Chumbinho	BRA	21/09/86	M	7	(2)	1
10	Dani Quintana	ESP	08/03/87	M	26	(6)	15
23	Vladimir Dimitrovski	MKD	30/11/88	D	3		
91	Coşqun Diniyev		13/09/95	M	24	(8)	1
67	Alharbi El Jadeyaoui	MAR	08/08/86	M	7	(2)	
55	Bädavi Hüseynov		11/07/91	D	30		
22	Äfran İsmayılov		08/10/88	M	16	(13)	6
97	Mahir Mädätov		01/07/97	D	12	(4)	7
63	Şahruddin Mähämmädäliyev		12/06/94	G	2		
11	Elvin Mämmädov		18/07/88	M	11	(2)	1
5	Maksim Medvedev		29/09/89	D	26		
8	Míchel	ESP	08/11/85	M	20	(4)	4
99	Muarem Muarem	MKD	22/10/88	M	9	(5)	3
6	Vüqar Mustafayev		05/08/94	M	6	(2)	1
29	Rydell Poepon	NED	28/08/87	A	10	(5)	1
2	Qara Qarayev		12/10/92	M	15	(11)	1
18	İlqar Qurbanov		25/04/86	D	16	(2)	
9	Reynaldo	BRA	24/08/89	A	8	(6)	5
20	Richard	BRA	20/03/89	M	25	(6)	2
14	Räşad F Sadıqov		16/06/82	D	19		2
19	Azär Salahlı		11/04/94	M	5	(1)	
13	Ibrahim Şehić	BIH	02/09/88	G	32		
77	Cavid Tağıyev		22/07/92	M	6	(9)	
1	Färhad Väliyev		01/11/80	G	2		
4	Eltun Yaqublu		19/08/91	D	3		
32	Elvin Yunuszadä		22/08/92	D	17	(2)	
7	Namiq Yusifov		14/08/86	M	2	(1)	

Qäbälä FK

2005 • Qäbälä şähär stadionu (4,350) •
gabalafc.az
Coach: Roman Hryhorchuk (UKR)

2015

10/08	h	Qarabağ	D	2-2	Zenjov, Zärgärov
15/08	a	Olimpik-Şüvälan	W	2-0	Gai (p), Antonov
23/08	h	Käpäz	W	1-0	Zec
12/09	a	İnter	L	1-2	Antonov
21/09	h	Sumqayıt	W	1-0	Gai (p)
25/09	a	Rävan	W	3-0	Dodô, Zärgärov, Gai
04/10	h	Xäzär Länkäran	W	6-0	Dodô, Pereyra 2, Gai, Antonov, Zec
17/10	a	Neftçi	W	1-0	Antonov
25/10	h	Zirä	D	0-0	
28/10	h	Olimpik-Şüvälan	D	0-0	
01/11	h	Käpäz	L	1-2	Pereyra
09/11	h	İnter	D	1-1	Antonov
21/11	a	Sumqayıt	D	2-2	og (Hacıyev), Zärgärov
30/11	h	Rävan	D	1-1	Pereyra
06/12	a	Xäzär Länkäran	W	1-0	Antonov
13/12	h	Neftçi	L	0-1	
16/12	a	Zirä	L	0-1	
19/12	a	Qarabağ	D	1-1	Zec

2016

30/01	a	Käpäz	L	0-3	
07/02	a	İnter	W	1-0	Zec
14/02	h	Sumqayıt	W	1-0	Zec
21/02	a	Rävan	W	1-0	Daşdämirov
27/02	h	Xäzär Länkäran	D	0-0	
05/03	a	Neftçi	W	2-1	Rafael Santos, Eyubov
13/03	h	Zirä	L	1-2	Gai
19/03	h	Qarabağ	L	1-2	Zenjov
30/03	a	Olimpik-Şüvälan	L	1-2	Gai (p)
03/04	h	İnter	D	0-0	
09/04	a	Sumqayıt	D	1-1	Gai
15/04	h	Rävan	W	2-0	Mämmädov, Antonov
23/04	a	Xäzär Länkäran	W	1-0	Gai
01/05	h	Neftçi	D	2-2	Gai (p), Sadiqov
07/05	a	Zirä	W	3-0	Rafael Santos, Zec 2
11/05	a	Qarabağ	L	0-2	
15/05	h	Olimpik-Şüvälan	W	2-0	Mämmädov, og (K Hüseynov)
20/05	a	Käpäz	W	1-0	Gai

No	Name	Nat	DoB	Pos	Aps	(s)	Gls
34	Ürfan Abbasov		14/10/92	D	18	(3)	
18	Vadim Abdullayev		17/12/94	M	1		
87	Ruslan Abışov		10/10/87	D	17		
17	Qismät Alıyev		24/10/96	M	5	(1)	
69	Olexiy Antonov	UKR	08/05/86	A	19	(13)	7
22	Dmytro Bezotosniy	UKR	15/11/83	G	28		
4	Elvin Camalov		04/02/95	M	29		
70	Vaqif Cavadov		25/05/89	M	2	(1)	
21	Arif Daşdämirov		08/08/87	D	27	(3)	1
10	Dodô	BRA	16/10/87	M	18	(1)	2
32	Räşad Eyubov		03/12/92	M	7	(10)	1
5	Gheorghe Florescu	ROU	21/05/84	M	1		
9	Olexiy Gai	UKR	06/11/82	M	34	(1)	10
97	Roman Hüseynov		26/12/97	M		(3)	
11	Asif Mämmädov		05/08/86	M	12	(7)	2
88	David Meza	PAR	15/08/88	M	2	(2)	
8	Mähämmäd Mirzäbäyov		16/11/90	D	18	(7)	
1	Murad Musayev		13/06/94	M	1		
5	Pavlo Paşayev		04/01/88	D	1		
32	Facundo Pereyra	ARG	03/09/87	M	7	(7)	4
33	Dawid Pietrzkiewicz	POL	09/02/88	G		(1)	
1	Andrey Popoviç		04/04/92	G	8		
44	Rafael Santos	BRA	10/11/84	D	20		2
20	Ricardinho	BRA	09/09/84	D	11	(5)	
6	Räşad Ä Sadiqov		08/10/83	M	23	(4)	1
3	Vojislav Stanković	SRB	22/09/87	D	22	(2)	
77	Ehtiram Şahverdiyev		01/10/96	A		(1)	
15	Vitaliy Vernydub	UKR	17/10/87	D	11		
66	Samir Zärgärov		28/08/86	M	16	(10)	3
7	Ermin Zec	BIH	18/02/88	A	16	(7)	7
9	Sergei Zenjov	EST	20/04/89	A	22	(4)	2

Rävan Bakı FK

2009 • Bayıl Arena (3,000) •
no website
**Coach: Emin Quliyev;
(17/10/15) Bähmän Häsänov**

2015

10/08	h	Sumqayıt	D	0-0	
15/08	h	Qarabağ	L	1-2	Qürbätov
22/08	a	Xäzär Länkäran	D	1-1	Abbasov
13/09	h	Neftçi	L	1-3	Muxtarov
19/09	a	Zirä	L	1-2	Qürbätov
25/09	h	Qäbälä	L	0-3	
02/10	a	Olimpik-Şüvälan	L	0-1	
16/10	h	Käpäz	L	0-2	
24/10	a	İnter	L	0-2	
28/10	a	Qarabağ	L	0-1	
02/11	h	Xäzär Länkäran	L	0-1	
08/11	a	Neftçi	W	3-2	Muxtarov, Ağakärimzadä, Tağızadä
22/11	h	Zirä	W	1-0	Qürbätov
30/11	a	Qäbälä	D	1-1	Qürbätov
07/12	a	Olimpik-Şüvälan	D	0-0	
11/12	a	Käpäz	D	0-0	
15/12	h	İnter	L	0-2	
19/12	a	Sumqayıt	D	3-3	Suma, Tağızadä, Abbasov (p)

2016

31/01	a	Xäzär Länkäran	D	0-0	
05/02	a	Neftçi	D	1-1	Abdullayev
15/02	a	Zirä	L	1-2	Ağakärimzadä
21/02	h	Qäbälä	L	0-1	
27/02	a	Olimpik-Şüvälan	L	0-1	
06/03	h	Käpäz	L	1-3	M Quliyev
13/03	a	İnter	L	1-1	Tağızadä
18/03	h	Sumqayıt	L	1-2	Tağızadä (p)
30/03	a	Qarabağ	L	1-5	Khamid
03/04	h	Neftçi	W	1-0	Häsänäliyev
10/04	h	Zirä	L	0-4	
15/04	a	Qäbälä	L	0-2	
24/04	h	Olimpik-Şüvälan	W	1-0	Khamid
30/04	a	Käpäz	L	2-3	Abbasov (p), Abdulov
07/05	h	İnter	L	0-4	
11/05	a	Sumqayıt	L	1-3	Khamid
15/05	h	Qarabağ	W	2-1	Abbasov (p), Abdulov
20/05	h	Xäzär Länkäran	D	2-2	Khamid, Abbasov (p)

No	Name	Nat	DoB	Pos	Aps	(s)	Gls
17	Ramazan Abbasov		22/09/83	M	31	(1)	5
15	Ceyhun Abdullayev		25/11/91	M	5	(7)	
11	Elnur Abdulov		18/09/92	M	5	(6)	2
92	Yamin Ağakärimzadä		25/07/92	D	25	(3)	2
22	Mähämmäd Alıyev		24/10/92	A	7	(3)	
55	Hüseyn Axundov		30/04/88	M	7	(5)	
14	Elvin Äliyev		21/08/84	D	9	(3)	
1	Räşad Äzizli		01/01/94	G	16		
25	Oruc Balaşlı		23/02/94	A		(2)	
18	Samuel Barlay	SLE	15/09/86	M	6		
9	Vüqar Bäybalayev		05/08/93	D	16	(2)	
5	Mirkamil Haşımlı		20/02/96	M	6	(5)	
7	Elvin Häsänäliyev		07/08/93	M	10	(6)	1
99	Äziz Hüseynov		21/03/92	M	9	(5)	
77	Cavad Kazımov		08/08/94	M		(7)	
86	Yasın Khamid	UKR	10/01/93	A	10	(5)	4
16	Orxan Lalayev		12/10/91	D	21	(4)	
32	Kostyantyn Makhnovskiy	UKR	01/01/89	G	18		
20	Känan Manafov		03/05/95	M	1		
13	Cämşid Mähärrämov		03/10/83	D	11	(9)	
39	Älibäy Mämmädli		01/05/97	M		(1)	
21	Novruz Mämmädov		20/03/90	D	32	(1)	
99	Nicat Muxtarov		01/06/95	M	14	(3)	2
4	Känan Müslümov		04/10/92	D	20	(2)	
29	Äziz Quliyev		02/05/87	D	3	(1)	
86	Färid Quliyev		06/01/86	A	4	(3)	
8	Mämmäd Quliyev		25/08/95	M	22	(3)	1
9	Nuran Qurbanov		10/08/93	M	5	(4)	
19	Tural Qürbätov		01/03/93	A	13	(2)	4
10	Alibobo Rakhmatullaev	UZB	08/02/91	M	1	(3)	
12	Elçin Sadiqov		14/06/89	G	2		
11	Sheriff Suma	SLE	12/10/86	D	17		1
2	Ruslan Tağızadä		12/09/93	D	28	(2)	4
3	Saşa Yunisoğlu		18/12/85	D	17	(1)	

Sumqayıt FK

2010 • Kapital Bank Arena (1,326) •
sumqayitpfc.az
**Coach: Aqil Mämmädov;
(08/10/15) Samir Abasov**

2015

10/08	a	Rävan	D	0-0	
16/08	h	Xäzär Länkäran	D	1-1	Häsänalizadä
23/08	a	Neftçi	L	1-2	Qurbanov
13/09	h	Zirä	D	0-0	
21/09	a	Qäbälä	L	0-1	
26/09	h	Olimpik-Şüvälan	D	1-1	Ramazanov
04/10	a	Käpäz	L	1-3	Pamuk
18/10	h	İnter	D	1-1	Fardjad-Azad
25/10	h	Qarabağ	W	1-0	Hüseynpur
28/10	a	Xäzär Länkäran	W	2-1	Mikayılov, Ramazanov
02/11	h	Neftçi	L	1-2	Pamuk
07/11	a	Zirä	L	2-3	Ramazanov, Fardjad-Azad
21/11	h	Qäbälä	D	2-2	Pamuk, Ramazanov
28/11	a	Olimpik-Şüvälan	L	0-2	
07/12	h	Käpäz	D	2-2	E Mehdiyev, Yunanov
11/12	a	İnter	W	3-2	Yunanov 2, Alxasov
16/12	a	Qarabağ	D	2-2	Yunanov, Rähimov
19/12	h	Rävan	D	3-3	Yunanov 2, Rähimov

2016

30/01	h	Neftçi	L	0-1	
06/02	h	Zirä	L	0-2	
14/02	a	Qäbälä	L	0-1	
20/02	h	Olimpik-Şüvälan	W	2-0	M Ağayev, Ramazanov
27/02	a	Käpäz	D	0-0	
05/03	a	İnter	L	0-2	
13/03	h	Qarabağ	L	0-2	
18/03	a	Rävan	W	2-1	og (Yunisoğlu), Yunanov
30/03	h	Xäzär Länkäran	W	2-1	og (Mämmädov), M Ağayev
03/04	a	Zirä	L	0-1	
09/04	h	Qäbälä	D	1-1	Fardjad-Azad (p)
17/04	a	Olimpik-Şüvälan	L	0-1	
24/04	h	Käpäz	L	2-3	M Ağayev, Yunanov
01/05	a	İnter	D	2-2	Cavadov, Yunanov
07/05	a	Qarabağ	L	0-1	
11/05	h	Rävan	W	3-1	Yunanov, Fardjad-Azad 2
15/05	a	Xäzär Länkäran	W	2-1	Cavadov, Yunanov
20/05	h	Neftçi	W	2-1	Cavadov, Yunanov

No	Name	Nat	DoB	Pos	Aps	(s)	Gls
16	Elnur Abdulov		18/09/92	M	1	(1)	
13	Murad Ağayev		09/02/93	M	33		3
1	Sälahät Ağayev		04/01/91	G	16		
2	Slavik Alxasov		06/02/93	D	33	(1)	1
94	Tärlan Ähmädli		21/11/94	G	7	(2)	
99	Äli Älimärdanlı		24/10/96	A		(3)	
27	İsmayıl Babayev		01/05/99	D	1		
70	Vaqif Cavadov		25/05/89	M	15	(1)	3
18	Aleksandr Chertopalov		08/02/80	M	20	(4)	
7	Pardis Fardjad-Azad		12/04/88	A	16	(9)	5
5	Cämil Hacıyev		24/08/94	D	21	(3)	
14	Bäxtiyar Häsänalizadä		29/12/92	D	29	(1)	1
3	Vurğun Hüseynov		25/04/88	D	33		
9	Mirzağa Hüseynpur		11/03/90	M	1	(8)	1
1	Şahruddin Mähämmädäliyev		12/06/94	G	13		
15	Nodar Mämmädov		03/06/88	D	7	(2)	
25	Ayaz Mehdiyev		22/02/93	M	6	(3)	
39	Emin Mehdiyev		22/09/92	D	17	(3)	1
22	Tofiq Mikayılov		11/04/86	M	11	(7)	1
8	Nicat Muxtarov		01/06/95	M	9	(5)	
97	Xäyal Näcäfov		19/12/97	M	5	(9)	
10	Uğur Pamuk		26/07/89	M	19	(6)	3
24	Amit Quluzadä		20/11/92	M	16	(6)	
9	Nuran Qurbanov		10/08/93	M	5	(6)	1
99	Rasim Ramaldanov		24/01/86	D	7	(2)	
55	Ağabala Ramazanov		20/01/93	M	31	(2)	5
6	Mikayıl Rähimov		11/05/87	D	6	(1)	2
23	Tural Elç. Rzayev		27/07/95	A	5	(4)	
29	Amil Yunanov		06/01/93	M	13	(11)	12

AZERBAIJAN

Xäzär Länkäran FK

2004 • Xäzär Länkäran märkäzi stadionu
(15,000) • lankaranfc.com

Major honours
Azerbaijan League (1) 2007; Azerbaijan Cup (3) 2007,
2008, 2011

Coach: Yunis Hüseynov;
(13/01/16) Elbrus Mämmädov;
(08/05/16) Ağadadaş Hämidov

2015

09/08	h	İnter	W	2-0	E Cäfärov, Ämirquliyev
16/08	a	Sumqayıt	D	1-1	Rzazadä
22/08	h	Rävan	D	1-1	Ämirquliyev (p)
12/09	a	Qarabağ	L	0-1	
20/09	a	Neftçi	D	1-1	Ämirquliyev
27/09	h	Zirä	L	0-1	
04/10	a	Qäbälä	L	0-6	
18/10	h	Olimpik-Şüvälan	W	3-1	Abdullazadä 2, Tounkara
24/10	a	Käpäz	L	0-1	
28/10	h	Sumqayıt	L	1-2	Ämirquliyev
02/11	a	Rävan	W	1-0	E Cäfärov
08/11	h	Qarabağ	L	0-1	
22/11	h	Neftçi	L	0-2	
28/11	a	Zirä	L	0-1	
06/12	h	Qäbälä	L	0-1	
13/12	a	Olimpik-Şüvälan	L	0-1	
17/12	h	Käpäz	L	0-1	
20/12	a	İnter	L	0-2	

2016

31/01	h	Rävan	D	0-0	
06/02	a	Qarabağ	L	0-3	
13/02	a	Neftçi	L	0-1	
21/02	h	Zirä	L	0-2	
27/02	a	Qäbälä	D	0-0	
05/03	h	Olimpik-Şüvälan	L	0-1	
13/03	a	Käpäz	L	0-2	
20/03	h	İnter	L	0-1	
30/03	a	Sumqayıt	L	1-2	Mirzäzadä (p)
03/04	h	Qarabağ	L	1-2	Qürbätov
10/04	h	Neftçi	L	0-1	
17/04	a	Zirä	L	0-1	
23/04	h	Qäbälä	L	0-1	
30/04	a	Olimpik-Şüvälan	L	0-1	
07/05	h	Käpäz	L	0-3	
11/05	a	İnter	L	1-2	Güläliyev
15/05	h	Sumqayıt	L	1-2	Qürbätov (p)
20/05	a	Rävan	D	2-2	Budaqov, Qädirzadä

No	Name	Nat	DoB	Pos	Aps	(s)	Gls
42	Kamran Abdullazadä		20/03/95	M	15	(1)	2
77	Äli Äliyev		14/03/97	M		(3)	
9	Orxan Äliyev		21/12/95	M	7	(1)	
14	Rahid Ämirquliyev		01/09/89	M	18		4
5	Färid Äsädov		30/06/96	M	2	(8)	
35	Elfad Balähmädov		07/10/97	A	6	(9)	
8	Vüqar Bäybalayev		05/08/93	D	16		
9	Bayram Budaqov		08/01/94	A	6	(7)	1
97	Elnur Cäfärov		28/03/97	A	18		2
4	Ruslan Cäfärov		26/01/93	D	15	(1)	
18	Tural Cälilov		28/11/86	D	35		
17	Vaquf Güläliyev		11/05/93	D	16		1
66	Känan Häsänov		09/01/99	M		(2)	
44	Yusif Häsänov		30/11/99	D	3	(2)	
11	Kazım Kazımlı		05/09/93	M	16	(1)	
15	Nodar Mämmädov		03/06/88	D	15		
6	Asif Mirili		10/12/91	M	15	(3)	
72	Elvin Mirzäyev		11/11/93	D	12	(2)	
32	Zaman Mirzäzadä		08/02/95	D	22	(10)	1
25	Tärlan Qasımzadä		01/01/95	G	6		
16	İbrahim Qädirzadä		21/03/99	M	15	(2)	1
99	Mahsum Qämbärli		25/10/96	D	20	(11)	
79	Namiq Qocayev		14/12/97	M		(5)	
10	Tural Qürbätov		01/03/93	A	14		2
3	Rasim Ramaldanov		24/01/86	D	7		
8	Elşän Rzazadä		11/09/93	M	16		1
1	Orxan Sadıqlı		19/03/93	G	30		
86	Xaqani Sadıqov		10/04/00	A		(1)	
12	İlyas Säfärzadä		20/01/96	D	17	(6)	
7	Orxan Säfiyaroğlu		22/02/90	M	13	(4)	
27	Adrian Scarlatache	ROU	05/12/86	D	9		
7	Sadio Tounkara	MLI	27/04/92	M	7	(2)	1
41	Hüseyn Xälilzadä		15/04/96	D	5	(3)	

Zirä FK

2014 • Zirä qäsäbä Olimpiya Kompleksinin
stadionu (1,512) • fczire.az

Coach: Adil Şükürov

2015

09/08	h	Olimpik-Şüvälan	W	1-0	Igbekoyi
16/08	a	Käpäz	D	1-1	Ivanović
24/08	h	İnter	D	0-0	
13/09	a	Sumqayıt	D	0-0	
19/09	h	Rävan	W	2-1	Abdullayev (p), Krneta
27/09	a	Xäzär Länkäran	W	1-0	Abdullayev (p)
03/10	h	Neftçi	W	2-0	Ivanović, Bonilla
17/10	a	Qarabağ	L	1-4	Ivanović
25/10	a	Qäbälä	D	0-0	
28/10	h	Käpäz	D	2-2	Bonilla 2
31/10	a	İnter	D	0-0	
07/11	h	Sumqayıt	W	3-2	og (Hacıyev), Nağıyev, Qurbanov
22/11	a	Rävan	L	0-1	
28/11	h	Xäzär Länkäran	W	1-0	og (Mirzäzadä)
06/12	a	Neftçi	D	1-1	Tato
13/12	h	Qarabağ	D	0-0	
16/12	h	Qäbälä	W	1-0	Qurbanov
20/12	a	Olimpik-Şüvälan	L	0-1	

2016

31/01	h	İnter	W	2-1	Tato, Novruzov
06/02	a	Sumqayıt	W	2-0	Bonilla, Abdullayev
15/02	h	Rävan	W	2-1	Bonilla 2 (1p)
21/02	a	Xäzär Länkäran	W	2-0	Krneta, Bonilla
27/02	h	Neftçi	W	3-0	Bonilla, Tato 2
05/03	a	Qarabağ	L	0-2	
13/03	a	Qäbälä	W	2-1	Bonilla 2
20/03	h	Olimpik-Şüvälan	W	4-2	Abdullayev, Mämmädov, Krneta, Novruzov
30/03	a	Käpäz	L	0-2	
03/04	h	Sumqayıt	W	1-0	Novruzov
10/04	a	Rävan	W	4-0	Tato, Bonilla 3
17/04	a	Xäzär Länkäran	W	1-0	Bonilla
23/04	a	Neftçi	D	0-0	
01/05	h	Qarabağ	L	0-2	
07/05	h	Qäbälä	L	0-3	
11/05	a	Olimpik-Şüvälan	D	1-1	Igbekoyi
15/05	h	Käpäz	D	2-2	Mämmädov, Qurbanov
20/05	a	İnter	L	0-1	

No	Name	Nat	DoB	Pos	Aps	(s)	Gls
27	Räşad Abdullayev		01/10/81	M	20	(4)	4
6	Hacı Ähmädov		23/11/93	M	1	(5)	
85	Kamal Bayramov		15/08/85	G	6		
9	Nelson Bonilla	SLV	11/09/90	A	28	(1)	14
8	Tärzin Cahangirov		17/01/92	M	7	(15)	
7	Diego Souza	BRA	12/09/88	M	7	(3)	
66	Eduardo	BRA	12/11/86	A		(2)	
23	Eltun Hüseynov		27/02/93	D	1		
11	Victor Igbekoyi	NGA	01/09/86	M	32	(2)	2
10	Igor Ivanović	MNE	09/09/90	M	23	(5)	3
90	Vüsal İsgändärli		03/11/95	M	1	(9)	
37	Jovan Krneta	SRB	04/05/92	D	30		3
60	Elvin Mämmädov		18/07/88	M	14	(1)	2
2	Chimezie Mbah	NGA	10/11/92	D	18	(1)	
7	Rihairo Meulens	CUW	03/06/88	A	6	(5)	
6	Vüqar Mustafayev		05/08/94	M	11	(3)	
14	Tellur Mütällimov		08/04/95	M	15		
5	Adil Nağıyev		11/09/95	D	21	(4)	1
1	Anar Näzirov		08/09/85	G	30		
19	Nurlan Novruzov		03/03/93	A	15	(8)	3
77	Ruslan Poladov		30/11/79	D	2		
39	Sadiq Quliyev		09/03/95	D	28	(1)	
12	Nicat Qurbanov		17/02/92	M	9	(16)	3
13	Aleksandr Şemonayev		04/01/85	D	33		
32	Tato	ESP	09/07/92	M	23	(9)	5
28	Tämkin Xälilzadä		06/08/93	M	15	(14)	

Top goalscorers

15	Dani Quintana (Qarabağ)
14	Nelson Bonilla (Zirä)
13	Ruslan Qurbanov (Neftçi)
12	Amil Yunanov (Sumqayıt)
10	Olexiy Gai (Qäbälä)
9	Julien Ebah (Käpäz)
	Richard (Qarabağ)
7	Nugzar Kvirtia (Olimpik-Şüvälan)
	Samuel Armenteros (Qarabağ)
	Mahir Mädätov (Qarabağ)
	Olexiy Antonov (Qäbälä)
	Ermin Zec (Qäbälä)

Second level

Second level final table 2015/16

		Pld	W	D	L	F	A	Pts
1	Neftçala FK	26	20	2	4	74	20	62
2	Qaradağ Lökbatan FK	26	18	4	4	59	28	58
3	Ağsu FK	30	13	8	5	46	29	47
4	MOİK Bakı PFK	26	14	5	7	53	24	47
5	Şämkir FK	26	10	8	8	30	24	38
6	Zaqatala PFK	26	9	9	8	47	36	36
7	Turan Tovuz İK	26	10	6	10	35	31	36
8	Mil-Muğan İmişli FK	26	8	8	10	28	26	32
9	Bakılı Bakı PFK	26	8	6	12	34	46	30
10	Şahdağ Qusar FK	26	8	6	12	31	54	30
11	Şärurspor PFK	26	8	4	14	45	44	28
12	Göyäzän Qazax FK	26	3	8	15	17	42	17
13	Energetik Mingäçevir FK	26	4	3	19	14	100	15
14	Bakı FK	26	9	3	14	33	42	15

NB No promotion; Bakı FK – 15 pts deducted.

DOMESTIC CUP

Azärbaycan kuboku 2015/16

1/8 FINALS

(02/12/15)
Neftçala 0-1 Sumqayıt
Neftçi 8-0 Qaradağ Lökbatan
Olimpik-Şüvälan 1-2 Zirä
Qarabağ 2-0 Şämkir
Turan Tovuz 1-3 İnter
Xäzär Länkäran 1-0 Käpäz

(03/12/15)
Rävan 1-0 Bakı
Qäbälä 7-0 Mil-Muğan

QUARTER-FINALS

(02/03/16 & 09/03/16)
Rävan 2-1 İnter *(Qurbanov 61, Abbasov 81; Meza 56)*
İnter 3-0 Rävan *(Kvekveskiri 31, Meza 65, Nadirov 85)*
(İnter 4-2)

Qarabağ 2-0 Sumqayıt *(Richard 52p, Mädätov 86)*
Sumqayıt 1-4 Qarabağ *(Näcäfov 65; Muarem 6, 50, Armenteros 10, 58)*
(Qarabağ 6-1)

Xäzär Länkäran 3-2 Neftçi *(Güläliyev 18, Qürbätov 19, Qädirzadä 52; R Qurbanov 22, Muradbäyli 39)*
Neftçi 2-0 Xäzär Länkäran *(R Qurbanov 60p, A Abdullayev 64)*
(Neftçi 4-3)

Zirä 1-2 Qäbälä *(Bonilla 77; Gai 75, Dodô 84)*
Qäbälä 5-1 Zirä *(Gai 5, 12, Sadiqov 17, Eyubov 65, Zec 79; Novruzov 36)*
(Qäbälä 7-2)

SEMI-FINALS

(27/04/16 & 04/05/16)
İnter 0-4 Qarabağ *(Míchel 19, 61, Dani Quintana 67, Reynaldo 85)*
Qarabağ 1-0 İnter *(Míchel 23)*
(Qarabağ 5-0)

Neftçi 1-1 Qäbälä *(Hacıyev 71; Gai 5)*
Qäbälä 1-1 Neftçi *(Zec 75; R Qurbanov 58) (aet)*
(2-2; Neftçi 4-3 on pens)

FINAL

(25/05/16)
Tofiq Bähramov adına Respublika stadionu, Baku
QARABAĞ FK 1 *(Míchel 119) (aet)*
NEFTÇİ PFK 0
Referee: Yusifov
QARABAĞ: Šehić, Medvedev, Sadıqov, Hüseynov, Mädätov (Diniyev 77), Agolli, Qarayev (İsmayılov 112), Míchel, Richard (Muarem 110), Dani Quintana, Reynaldo
Red card: Reynaldo (120+1)
NEFTÇİ: A Mämmädov, K Qurbanov, Jairo, R Mämmädov, İsayev (Melli 115), Bädälov, A Abdullayev (Canales 84), Ramos, E Abdullayev (Muradbäyli 111), Hacıyev, R Qurbanov
Red card: Ramos (120)

Qarabağ completed back-to-back domestic doubles with their last-gasp cup final win against Neftçi

BELARUS
Belorusskaja Federacija Futbola (BFF)

Address	Prospekt Pobeditelei 20/3 BY-220020 Minsk	**President**	Sergei Roumas
Tel	+375 17 2509 636	**General secretary**	Sergei Safaryan
Fax	+375 17 2544 483	**Media officer**	Aleksandr Aleinik
E-mail	info@bff.by	**Year of formation**	1989
Website	bff.by	**National stadium**	Borisov Arena, Borisov (13,126)

PREMIER LEAGUE CLUBS

1. FC BATE Borisov
2. FC Belshina Bobruisk
3. FC Dinamo Brest
4. FC Dinamo Minsk
5. FC Gomel
6. FC Granit Mikashevichi
7. FC Minsk
8. FC Naftan Novopolotsk
9. FC Neman Grodno
10. FC Shakhtyor Soligorsk
11. FC Slavia-Mozyr
12. SFC Slutsk
13. FC Torpedo Zhodino
14. FC Vitebsk

PROMOTED CLUBS

15. FC Isloch
16. FC Gorodeya
17. FC Krumkachy

KEY
- UEFA Champions League
- UEFA Europa League
- Promoted
- Relegated

BATE complete decade of dominance

A modification to the format of the Belarusian Premier League could not prevent another assured triumph for FC BATE Borisov, who brushed off the challenge of Dinamo Minsk to claim their tenth title in a row and record-extending 12th in all.

The league's top two clubs in 2015 both played group stage European football for the second year running, but BATE were unable to defend the Belarusian Cup, surprisingly losing out in the final on penalties to Torpedo Zhodino, who thus claimed their first major trophy.

Ten titles on the trot for Borisov club	Runners-up Dinamo Minsk 12 points adrift	Torpedo Zhodino shock champions in cup final

Domestic league

Increased from 12 to 14 teams but with a reduced workload of 26 matches, the 2015 Premier League opened with defending champions BATE bidding to prolong a competition-record unbeaten run. Aleksandr Yermakovich's side had lost their opening encounter in 2014 before avoiding defeat in the next 31, and that unblemished sequence was to be extended for another 14 matches as the title holders found top form right from the off.

The most impressive facet of their spring-heeled start was a defensive solidity that brought clean sheets in all ten opening fixtures. Goalkeeper Sergei Chernik and Serbian duo Filip Mladenović and Nemana Milunović, the latter newly recruited from FK Mladost Lučani, were the key contributors to that remarkable run, which laid the foundation for another routine championship triumph.

Dinamo Minsk, defeated 2-0 at home by BATE in round two – a result that served to make illustrious new coach Dušan Uhrin's stay in the Belarusian capital extremely brief – ended the perennial champions' unbeaten run when, under new Serbian boss Vuk Rašović, they won 1-0 at the Borisov Arena in the first match after the summer break. But although BATE dropped further points four days later in a goalless draw at

lowly FC Gomel, thus allowing Dinamo to move to within touching distance at the top, they responded with their biggest win of the season, 7-1 at home to Neman Grodno, while Dinamo, their resources tested by extended European involvement, suddenly fell apart, failing to win in five games.

BATE's 12th title was duly sealed with three games to spare thanks to a 2-0 win at FC Vitebsk, an assist and goal from Belarus international striker Dmitri Mozolevski on his comeback game after two years out through injury further embellishing a historic occasion.

Vitebsk narrowly avoided relegation, finishing one place higher than 2003 champions Gomel. With the Premier League set for further expansion in 2016, three clubs were promoted, all of them – Isloch, Gorodeya and Krumkachy – new to Belarus's top division.

Domestic cup

Easy winners against Torpedo when they routed them 5-0 in the 2010 cup final, BATE were firm favourites to stage an encore six years on, but the underdogs were to have their day in the first final staged in the western border town of Brest. Torpedo had needed a late extra-time goal to eliminate Dinamo Minsk in the quarter-finals, and Igor Kriushenko's side required an even greater display of brinkmanship to see off

BATE, winning 3-2 on penalties after a 0-0 draw, with substitute Denis Trapashko netting the decisive spot kick.

Europe

BATE and Dinamo Minsk both repeated their feats of the previous season by qualifying for the group stage of, respectively, the UEFA Champions League and UEFA Europa League. It was BATE's fifth qualification for the premier competition in eight seasons and they fared much better than in 2014, conceding half as many goals and registering four points against Roma, including a rousing 3-2 home win in which star midfielder Igor Stasevich scored once and Mladenović twice. Dinamo lost five of their six group games, their one win coming in stoppage time at home to Viktoria Plzeň.

National team

Although Belarus never challenged for a place at UEFA EURO 2016, their new coach Aleksandr Khatskevich, appointed in December 2014, ended the qualifying campaign with a positive personal ledger, the highlight a 1-0 win in Zilina against group runners-up Slovakia. The season also ended well as Belarus defeated another France-bound team away from home, goals from BATE duo Mikhail Gordeichuk and Maksim Volodko bringing an unexpected 2-1 friendly win over the Republic of Ireland in Cork.

DOMESTIC SEASON AT A GLANCE

Premier League 2015 final table

		Pld	Home					Away					Total					Pts
			W	D	L	F	A	W	D	L	F	A	W	D	L	F	A	
1	**FC BATE Borisov**	**26**	**10**	**2**	**1**	**26**	**6**	**10**	**3**	**0**	**18**	**5**	**20**	**5**	**1**	**44**	**11**	**65**
2	FC Dinamo Minsk	26	9	3	1	20	5	6	5	2	16	8	15	8	3	36	13	53
3	FC Shakhtyor Soligorsk	26	9	4	0	27	6	5	3	5	20	21	14	7	5	47	27	49
4	FC Belshina Bobruisk	26	7	3	3	19	8	5	4	4	20	11	12	7	7	39	19	43
5	FC Granit Mikashevichi	26	7	2	4	17	14	5	4	4	13	18	12	6	8	30	32	42
6	FC Minsk	26	9	1	3	21	12	3	3	7	8	16	12	4	10	29	28	40
7	FC Torpedo Zhodino	26	5	4	4	18	14	5	2	6	13	15	10	6	10	31	29	36
8	FC Neman Grodno	26	5	2	6	14	16	3	6	4	7	16	8	8	10	21	32	32
9	FC Naftan Novopolotsk	26	3	3	7	15	18	5	3	5	19	17	8	6	12	34	35	30
10	FC Slavia-Mozyr	26	4	3	6	21	26	3	2	8	12	24	7	5	14	33	50	26
11	SFC Slutsk	26	2	5	6	10	13	4	2	7	16	17	6	7	13	26	30	25
12	FC Dinamo Brest	26	6	2	5	15	18	1	1	11	8	24	7	3	16	23	42	24
13	FC Vitebsk	26	3	6	4	10	15	1	3	9	11	32	4	9	13	21	47	21
14	FC Gomel	26	4	2	7	14	18	1	1	11	8	23	5	3	18	22	41	18

European qualification 2016/17

 Champion: FC BATE Borisov (second qualifying round)

 Cup winner: FC Torpedo Zhodino (second qualifying round)
FC Dinamo Minsk (first qualifying round)
FC Shakhtyor Soligorsk (first qualifying round)

Top scorer	Nikolai Yanush (Shakhtyor), 15 goals
Relegated club	FC Gomel
Promoted clubs	FC Isloch, FC Gorodeya, FC Krumkachy
Cup final	FC Torpedo Zhodino 0-0 FC Bate Borisov *(aet; 3-2 on pens)*

Team of the season
(4-4-2)

Coach: Yermakovich *(BATE)*

Chernik *(BATE)*

Shagoiko *(Belshina)* — Bangura *(Dinamo Minsk)* — Milunović *(BATE)* — Mladenović *(BATE)*

Stasevich *(BATE)* — Starhorodskiy *(Shakhtyor)* — Zhukovski *(Naftan)* — Habovda *(Granit)*

Vasilyuk *(Dinamo Brest)* — Yanush *(Shakhtyor)*

Player of the season

Igor Stasevich
(FC BATE Borisov)

Back for a second spell at FC BATE after a three-season sojourn at rivals Dinamo Minsk, Stasevich did what was asked of him in Borisov and improved the quality of the team's midfield, notably with his speed and cunning on the right flank plus an assortment of useful goals, seven in the league plus another two in Europe, including the opener in a memorable 3-2 win at home to Roma. Furthermore, the 30-year-old continued to feature regularly as one of several BATE players in the Belarus national team.

Newcomer of the season

Nikita Korzun
(FC Dinamo Minsk)

Dinamo Minsk were unable to loosen BATE Borisov's grip on the Belarusian Premier League title, but there was a notable effort to do so from one of the team's younger members. Defensive midfielder Korzun returned from an extended spell on the sidelines to add grit and poise in equal measure to Vuk Rašović's side, and his consistent displays on both domestic and European fronts earned the youngster, 20 at the time, a dream January 2016 move to Ukrainian champions Dynamo Kyiv.

NATIONAL TEAM

Top five all-time caps
Aleksandr Kulchy (102); Sergei Gurenko (80); Sergei Omelyanchuk (74); Sergei Shtanyuk (71); **Aleksandr Hleb** & **Timofei Kalachev** (73)

Top five all-time goals
Maksim Romashchenko (20); **Sergei Kornilenko** (17); Vitali Kutuzov (13); Vyacheslav Hleb (12); Valentin Belkevich, **Timofei Kalachev**, Vitali Rodionov & Roman Vasilyuk (10)

Results 2015/16

05/09/15	Ukraine (ECQ)	A	Lviv	L	1-3	*Kornilenko (62p)*
08/09/15	Luxembourg (ECQ)	H	Borisov	W	2-0	*Gordeichuk (34, 62)*
09/10/15	Slovakia (ECQ)	A	Zilina	W	1-0	*Dragun (34)*
12/10/15	FYR Macedonia (ECQ)	H	Borisov	D	0-0	
25/03/16	Armenia	A	Yerevan	D	0-0	
29/03/16	Montenegro	A	Podgorica	D	0-0	
27/05/16	Northern Ireland	A	Belfast	L	0-3	
31/05/16	Republic of Ireland	A	Cork	W	2-1	*Gordeichuk (20), Volodko (63)*

Appearances 2015/16

Coach: Aleksandr Khatskevich	19/10/73		UKR	LUX	SVK	MKD	Arm	Mne	Nir	Irl	Caps	Goals
Andrei Gorbunov	25/05/83	Atromitos (GRE)	G		G	G			G	G	7	-
Igor Shitov	24/10/86	Mordovia (RUS)	D	D				D	D75	D78	50	1
Aleksandr Martynovich	26/08/87	Ural (RUS)	D		D65*			D	D	D	50	2
Yegor Filipenko	10/04/88	Málaga (ESP)	D	D			D		D38		43	1
Maksim Volodko	10/11/92	BATE	D		s40	D	s62	M	D	D	11	1
Ivan Mayevski	05/05/88	Anji (RUS)	M					M			5	-
Mikhail Sivakov	16/01/88	Zorya (UKR)	M46	D	D	D	D		s38	D	10	-
Timofei Kalachev	01/05/81	Rostov (RUS)	M72	s75			M62	M61			73	10
Aleksandr Hleb	01/05/81	BATE /Gençlerbirliği (TUR)	M86	M58					s60	M91	73	6
Igor Stasevich	21/10/85	BATE	M		M	M			M89	M93	29	2
Sergei Kornilenko	14/06/83	Krylya Sovetov (RUS)	A	A84			A	A 9*			72	17
Mikhail Gordeichuk	23/10/89	BATE	s46	M75	M	M			M	M76	13	4
Nikolai Signevich	20/02/92	BATE	s72	s84	A72	A					6	1
Renan Bressan	03/11/88	Rio Ave (POR)	s86	M	M	M	M80	s82			24	3
Yuri Zhevnov	17/04/81	Ural (RUS)		G							58	-
Maksim Bordachev	18/06/86	Tom (RUS)		D	D40						40	2
Stanislav Dragun	04/06/88	Krylya Sovetov (RUS) /Dinamo Moskva (RUS)		M	M	M73		M	s67		37	5
Pavel Nekhaichik	15/07/88	Tom (RUS)		M	M69	M61			s89	s93	19	1
Sergei Kislyak	06/08/87	Rubin (RUS)		s58	s72	s61	s62	M67	M	M	60	9
Denis Polyakov	17/04/91	BATE			D	D	D	D	s72	D	18	-
Sergei Politevich	09/04/90	Dinamo Minsk /Gençlerbirliği (TUR)			s69	D		D	s78	s76	10	-
Anton Putilo	10/06/87	Gaziantepspor (TUR)				s73					50	6
Sergei Chernik	20/07/88	BATE					G			G	8	-
Sergei Krivets	08/06/86	Metz (FRA)					M62	M82	M60	s91	35	4
Sergei Balanovich	29/08/87	Amkar (RUS)					M	s61			25	2
Nikolai Yanush	09/09/84	Shakhtyor Soligorsk					s80		A72	A	4	-
Roman Begunov	22/03/93	Dinamo Minsk						s75			1	-
Nikita Korzun	06/03/95	Dynamo Kyiv (UKR)							M	M	2	-

EUROPE

FC BATE Borisov

Second qualifying round - Dundalk FC (IRL)
H 2-1 *Karnitski (11), Yablonski (38)*
Chernik, Dubra, Yablonski, Karnitski, Zhavnerchik, Milunović, Rodionov, Stasevich, Mladenović, Baga (Nikolić 64), Gordeichuk (Rios 80). Coach: Aleksandr Yermakovich (BLR)
A 0-0
Chernik, Dubra, Karnitski (Signevich 90+1), Aleksiyevich (Nikolić 68), Zhavnerchik, Milunović, Rodionov, Stasevich, Mladenović, Baga, Gordeichuk (Rios 85). Coach: Aleksandr Yermakovich (BLR)

Third qualifying round - Videoton FC (HUN)
A 1-1 *Karnitski (56)*
Chernik, Dubra, Karnitski (Rios 64), Aleksiyevich, Nikolić, Zhavnerchik, Milunović, Rodionov (Signevich 75), Mladenović, Baga, Gordeichuk (M Volodko 85). Coach: Aleksandr Yermakovich (BLR)
H 1-0 *Nikolić (82)*
Chernik, Dubra, Karnitski (Baga 75), Aleksiyevich (Yablonski 65), Nikolić, Zhavnerchik, Milunović, Rodionov (Signevich 89), Mladenović, M Volodko, Gordeichuk. Coach: Aleksandr Yermakovich (BLR)

Play-offs - FK Partizan (SRB)
H 1-0 *Gordeichuk (75)*
Chernik, Yablonski (Signevich 71), Aleksiyevich, Zhavnerchik, Milunović, Rodionov, Mladenović, Polyakov, M Volodko (Stasevich 64), Gordeichuk, Hleb (Baga 86). Coach: Aleksandr Yermakovich (BLR)
A 1-2 *Stasevich (25)*
Chernik, A Volodko, Aleksiyevich, Zhavnerchik, Milunović, Rodionov (Signevich 16), Stasevich, Mladenović, Polyakov, Gordeichuk (Rios 90), Hleb (Karnitski 75). Coach: Aleksandr Yermakovich (BLR)

Group E
Match 1 - Bayer 04 Leverkusen (GER)
A 1-4 *Milunović (13)*
Chernik, Dubra, Aleksiyevich, Signevich, Milunović, Stasevich, Mladenović, Polyakov, Baga (Karnitski 60), Gordeichuk (M Volodko 78), Hleb (A Volodko 30). Coach: Aleksandr Yermakovich (BLR)
Match 2 - AS Roma (ITA)
H 3-2 *Stasevich (8), Mladenović (12, 30)*
Chernik, Dubra, Yablonski, Nikolić (A Volodko 87), Signevich, Milunović, Stasevich, Mladenović, Polyakov, M Volodko (Rios 85), Gordeichuk (Hleb 72). Coach: Aleksandr Yermakovich (BLR)
Match 3 - FC Barcelona (ESP)
H 0-2
Chernik, Gaiduchik, A Volodko, Nikolić (Yablonski 65), Signevich (Mozelevski 79), Milunović, Stasevich, Mladenović, Polyakov, M Volodko (Karnitski 62), Gordeichuk. Coach: Aleksandr Yermakovich (BLR)

Match 4 - FC Barcelona (ESP)
A 0-3
Chernik, Gaiduchik, Yablonski, A Volodko (Nikolić 68), Mozolevski (Hleb 60), Milunović, Stasevich, Mladenović, Polyakov, M Volodko (Rios 78), Gordeichuk. Coach: Aleksandr Yermakovich (BLR)
Match 5 - Bayer 04 Leverkusen (GER)
H 1-1 *Gordeichuk (2)*
Chernik, Yablonski, A Volodko (Nikolić 78), Zhavnerchik, Rios (M Volodko 46), Mozolevski, Milunović, Mladenović, Polyakov, Gordeichuk, Hleb (Karnitski 73). Coach: Aleksandr Yermakovich (BLR)
Match 6 - AS Roma (ITA)
A 0-0
Chernik, Yablonski, Nikolić (Karnitski 79), Zhavnerchik, Mozolevski (M Volodko 60), Milunović, Stasevich, Mladenović, Polyakov (Dubra 56), Gordeichuk, Hleb. Coach: Aleksandr Yermakovich (BLR)

FC Dinamo Minsk

Second qualifying round - PFC Cherno More Varna (BUL)
A 1-1 *Politevich (72)*
Gutor, Vitus, Politevich, Bykov, Rassadkin (Voronkov 87), Bangura, Korzun, Bećiraj, Begunov, Yedigaryan (Udoji 60), Adamović (Korytko 77). Coach: Vuk Rašović (SRB)
H 4-0 *Korytko (41), Adamović (58), Bećiraj (86, 90+2)*
Gutor, Vitus, Politevich, Rassadkin, Korytko (Voronkov 88), Bangura, Korzun, Bećiraj, Begunov, El Monir (Neacşa 58), Adamović (Bykov 63). Coach: Vuk Rašović (SRB)

Third qualifying round - FC Zürich (SUI)
A 1-0 *Bećiraj (63p)*
Gutor, Politevich, Rassadkin, Korytko (Neacşa 75), Bangura, Korzun, Veretilo, Bećiraj, Begunov, El Monir (Tigorev 55), Adamović (Vitus 90+1). Coach: Vuk Rašović (SRB)
H 1-1 (aet) *Bećiraj (118)*
Gutor, Politevich, Rassadkin, Korytko (Voronkov 102), Bangura, Korzun, Veretilo, Bećiraj, Begunov, Tigorev (Neacşa 36), Adamović (El Monir 81). Coach: Vuk Rašović (SRB)

Play-offs - FC Salzburg (AUT)
H 2-0 *Rassadkin (57), Adamović (90+3)*
Gutor, Vitus, Politevich, Rassadkin (Voronkov 90+1), Neacşa (El Monir 70), Korytko, Udoji (Adamović 53), Bangura, Korzun, Bećiraj, Begunov. Coach: Vuk Rašović (SRB)
A 0-2 (aet; 3-2 on pens)
Gutor, Voronkov (Veretilo 77), Vitus, Politevich, Rassadkin (El Monir 62), Neacşa (Premudrov 84), Korytko, Bangura, Bećiraj, Begunov, Adamović. Coach: Vuk Rašović (SRB)

Group E
Match 1 - FC Viktoria Plzeň (CZE)
A 0-2
Gutor, Voronkov (Tigorev 78), Vitus, Politevich, Neacşa (Rassadkin 73), Korytko (Yarotsli 61), Bangura, Korzun, Bećiraj, Begunov, Adamović. Coach: Vuk Rašović (SRB)

Match 2 - SK Rapid Wien (AUT)
H 0-1
Gutor, Voronkov (El Monir 66), Vitus, Politevich, Korytko, Udoji, Bangura, Korzun, Bećiraj, Begunov (Veretilo 90+2), Adamović (Rassadkin 72). Coach: Vuk Rašović (SRB)
Match 3 - Villarreal CF (ESP)
A 0-4
Gutor, Vitus, Premudrov, Politevich, Rassadkin, Korytko (Adamović 46), Udoji (Voronkov 74), Bangura, Korzun, Bećiraj (El Monir 66), Begunov. Coach: Vuk Rašović (SRB)
Match 4 - Villarreal CF (ESP)
H 1-2 *Vitus (69)*
Ignatovich, Voronkov (Korytko 73), Premudrov, Politevich, Rassadkin, Udoji (Yedigaryan 78), Bangura, Korzun, Bećiraj, Begunov, El Monir, Adamović (Vitus 67). Coach: Vuk Rašović (SRB)
Match 5 - FC Viktoria Plzeň (CZE)
H 1-0 *Adamović (90+3)*
Gutor, Premudrov, Politevich, Rassadkin (Adamović 76), Korytko (El Monir 66), Udoji, Bangura, Korzun, Veretilo, Bećiraj, Begunov. Coach: Vuk Rašović (SRB)
Red card: Veretilo 90
Match 6 - SK Rapid Wien (AUT)
A 1-2 *El Monir (65)*
Gutor, Vitus, Premudrov (Voronkov 61), Politevich, Korytko (Bulyga 85), Udoji, Bangura, Korzun, Bećiraj, Begunov, Adamović (El Monir 64). Coach: Vuk Rašović (SRB)

FC Shakhtyor Soligorsk

First qualifying round - Glenavon FC (NIR)
A 2-1 *Afanasiyev (2), Komarovski (30)*
Bushma, Matveichik, Yanushkevich, Yurevich, Afanasiyev (Čović 73), Yanush, Starhorodskiy, Mikoliūnas (Kovalev 52), Komarovski (Martynyuk 84), Rybak, Kuzmenok. Coach: Sergei Nikiforenko (BLR)
H 3-0 *Yurevich (8), Yanush (66), Komarovski (86)*
Bushma, Matveichik, Yanushkevich, Yurevich (Kozeka 75), Afanasiyev (Mikoliūnas 59), Yanush, Starhorodskiy, Komarovski, Rybak, Kuzmenok, Kovalev (Shibun 82). Coach: Sergei Nikiforenko (BLR)

Second qualifying round - Wolfsberger AC (AUT)
H 0-1
Bushma, Matveichik, Yanushkevich, Yurevich, Afanasiyev (Trubilo 63), Yanush, Starhorodskiy, Komarovski (Kozeka 80), Rybak, Kuzmenok, Kovalev (Mikoliūnas 72). Coach: Sergei Nikiforenko (BLR)
A 0-2
Bushma, Matveichik (Čović 82), Yanushkevich, Yurevich, Yanush, Starhorodskiy, Komarovski, Rybak, Kuzmenok, Martynyuk (Vergeichik 52), Kovalev (Afanasiyev 65). Coach: Sergei Nikiforenko (BLR)

DOMESTIC LEAGUE CLUB-BY-CLUB

FC Torpedo Zhodino

First qualifying round - FK Kukësi (ALB)

A 0-2
Stepanov, Serdyuk (Selyava 79), Melnyk, Burko, Pankovets, Kontsevoi (Vaskov 67), Yatskevich, Maximov, Datsenko, Platonov (Matveyenko 75), Hleb. Coach: Igor Kriushenko (BLR)

H 0-0
Chesnovski, Serdyuk, Melnyk, Burko, Pankovets, Selyava, Yatskevich (Platonov 59), Maximov (Kibuk 61), Vaskov (Kontsevoi 67), Datsenko, Hleb. Coach: Igor Kriushenko (BLR)

FC BATE Borisov

1996 • Borisov Arena (13,126) • fcbate.by

Major honours
Belarusian League (12) 1999, 2002, 2006, 2007, 2008, 2009, 2010, 2011, 2012, 2013, 2014, 2015; Belarusian Cup (3) 2006, 2010, 2015

Coach: Aleksandr Yermakovich

2015

Date		Opponent	Res	Score	Scorers
10/04	h	Slavia-Mozyr	W	1-0	Mladenović
19/04	a	Dinamo Minsk	W	2-0	M Volodko, Rodionov
25/04	h	Gomel	W	2-0	Stasevich, Rodionov
04/05	a	Neman	W	1-0	Stasevich
10/05	a	Belshina	W	1-0	Karnitski
16/05	a	Shakhtyor	D	0-0	
20/05	a	Torpedo	D	0-0	
30/05	h	Minsk	W	1-0	Gordeichuk
05/06	a	Granit	W	1-0	Rodionov
18/06	a	Vitebsk	W	4-0	Baga 2, Milunović, M Volodko
22/06	a	Naftan	W	2-1	Baga, Rodionov
28/06	h	Dinamo Brest	W	1-0	Rios
05/07	a	Slutsk	W	1-0	Rodionov
10/07	a	Slavia-Mozyr	W	5-3	Rodionov 2, Stasevich 2, Karnitski
10/08	h	Dinamo Minsk	L	0-1	
14/08	a	Gomel	D	0-0	
22/08	h	Neman	W	7-1	Signevich 2, Stasevich, A Volodko, Rios, Rodionov 2
31/08	h	Belshina	W	1-0	Mladenović
12/09	h	Shakhtyor	D	1-1	Stasevich
20/09	h	Torpedo	W	1-0	Jevtić
25/09	a	Minsk	W	2-1	Stasevich, Signevich
04/10	h	Granit	D	1-1	Milunović
16/10	a	Vitebsk	W	2-0	Rios, Mozolevski
25/10	h	Naftan	W	2-1	Mozolevski 2
31/10	a	Dinamo Brest	W	1-0	Gordeichuk
08/11	h	Slutsk	W	4-1	Rios 2, Nikolić (p), Karnitski

No	Name	Nat	DoB	Pos	Aps	(s)	Gls
9	Ilya Aleksiyevich		10/02/91	M	9	(4)	
55	Dmitri Baga		04/01/90	M	12	(6)	3
16	Sergei Chernik		20/07/88	G	24		
4	Kaspars Dubra	LVA	20/12/90	D	9		
49	Aleksandr Dzhygero		15/04/96	M		(1)	
3	Vitali Gaiduchik		12/07/89	D	3		
62	Mikhail Gordeichuk		23/10/89	A	18	(8)	2
81	Aleksandr Hleb		01/05/81	M	3	(1)	
11	Aleksandar Jevtić	SRB	30/03/85	A	3	(4)	1
7	Aleksandr Karnitski		14/02/89	M	14	(10)	3
2	Dmitri Likhtarovich		01/03/78	M	2	(2)	
19	Nemanja Milunović	SRB	31/05/89	D	23		2
25	Filip Mladenović	SRB	15/08/91	D	21		2
18	Dmitri Mozolevski		30/04/85	A	4		3
10	Nemanja Nikolić	MNE	01/01/88	M	7	(3)	1
23	Edgar Olekhnovich		17/05/87	M	7	(3)	
33	Denis Polyakov		17/04/91	D	22		
17	Aleksei Rios		14/05/87	M	13	(7)	5
20	Vitali Rodionov		11/12/83	A	15	(2)	9
13	Nikolai Signevich		20/02/92	A	6	(12)	3
34	Artem Soroko		01/04/92	G	2		
22	Igor Stasevich		21/10/85	M	20	(2)	7
8	Aleksandr Volodko		18/06/86	M	7	(1)	1
42	Maksim Volodko		10/11/92	M	13	(5)	2
5	Evgeni Yablonski		10/05/95	M	16	(4)	
15	Maksim Zhavnerchik		09/02/85	D	13		

FC Belshina Bobruisk

1976 • Spartak (3,700) • fcbelshina.by

Major honours
Belarusian League (1) 2001; Belarusian Cup (3) 1997, 1999, 2001

Coach: Aleksandr Sednev

2015

Date		Opponent	Res	Score	Scorers
10/04	a	Gomel	L	0-2	
19/04	h	Vitebsk	D	1-1	Galyuza
25/04	a	Neman	W	3-1	Bogunov, og (Anyukevich), Rozhok
04/05	h	Naftan	D	1-1	Karamushka
10/05	h	BATE	L	0-1	
16/05	h	Dinamo Brest	W	2-0	Gorbachev, Rozhok
20/05	a	Shakhtyor	D	0-0	
31/05	h	Slutsk	W	2-0	Turlin, Shramchenko
05/06	a	Torpedo	W	3-0	Shramchenko, Karamushka, Skvernyuk
17/06	h	Slavia-Mozyr	W	2-0	Galyuza, Rozhok
21/06	a	Minsk	L	1-2	Skvernyuk
27/06	a	Dinamo Minsk	D	0-0	
04/07	a	Granit	W	5-1	Rozhok, Turlin, Bogunov 2, Skvernyuk
11/07	a	Gomel	W	3-1	Rozhok 2, Galyuza
08/08	a	Vitebsk	D	1-1	Rozhok
15/08	h	Neman	D	0-0	
23/08	a	Naftan	W	2-0	Yatskevich 2
31/08	a	BATE	L	0-1	
14/09	a	Dinamo Brest	L	1-2	Yatskevich
20/09	h	Shakhtyor	W	3-1	Kozlov 2, Galyuza
27/09	a	Slutsk	D	0-0	
03/10	a	Torpedo	W	1-0	Galyuza
18/10	a	Slavia-Mozyr	W	4-1	Bogunov 2, Rozhok, Skvernyuk
24/10	h	Minsk	W	4-0	Shagoiko, Skvernyuk 2, Shramchenko
31/10	a	Dinamo Minsk	D	0-0	
08/11	h	Granit	L	0-1	

No	Name	Nat	DoB	Pos	Aps	(s)	Gls
9	Olexandr Batyshchev	UKR	14/09/91	M	24		
88	Artem Bobukh	UKR	04/12/88	D	14	(2)	
10	Yaroslav Bogunov	UKR	04/09/93	A	15	(9)	5
6	Anton Burko		16/02/95	M		(8)	
11	Illya Galyuza	UKR	16/11/79	M	23	(1)	5
4	Mikhail Gorbachev		29/07/83	D	18	(1)	1
15	Roman Gribovski		17/07/95	A		(6)	
99	Vitaliy Ivanko	UKR	09/04/92	A	6	(3)	
22	Oleh Karamushka	UKR	03/04/84	D	22		2
19	Vladimir Khilkevich		31/10/87	M	1	(5)	
14	Aleksei Kozlov		11/07/89	D	20		2
5	Pavel Nazarenko		20/01/95	D	1	(8)	
30	Boris Pankratov		30/12/82	G	25	(1)	
3	Pavel Plaskonny		29/01/85	D	10		
8	Serhiy Rozhok	UKR	25/04/85	M	24		8
2	Aleksandr Shagoiko		27/07/80	D	26		1
17	Kirill Shakurov		07/04/94	A		(3)	
1	Andrei Shcherbakov		31/01/91	G	1	(1)	
20	Anton Shramchenko		12/03/93	A	20	(4)	3
23	Aleksei Skvernyuk		13/10/85	M	21	(2)	6
7	Dmitri Turlin		08/09/85	M	8	(15)	2
13	Sergei Vodyanovich		02/05/95	M		(3)	
99	Aleksandr Yatskevich		04/01/85	A	7	(4)	3

BELARUS

FC Dinamo Brest

1960 • GOSK Brestski (10,080) •
dynamo-brest.by
Major honours
Belarusian Cup (1) 2007
Coach: Sergei Kovalchuk

2015

11/04	a	Torpedo	W	3-1	Premudrov 2, Vasilyuk	
20/04	h	Minsk	W	1-0	Premudrov	
25/04	a	Granit	L	0-1		
03/05	h	Vitebsk	W	3-2	Shcherbo, Premudrov, Vasilyuk	
10/05	a	Naftan	L	0-1		
16/05	a	Belshina	L	0-2		
23/05	h	Slutsk	D	1-1	Premudrov	
31/05	a	Slavia-Mozyr	L	0-3		
05/06	h	Dinamo Minsk	W	1-0	Shcherbo	
17/06	a	Gomel	L	0-2		
21/06	h	Neman	L	1-3	Vasilyuk (p)	
28/06	a	BATE	L	0-1		
06/07	h	Shakhtyor	W	3-2	Vasilyuk 2, Solovei	
12/07	h	Torpedo	W	2-1	Premudrov, Kovalevski	
09/08	a	Minsk	L	1-2	Solovei	
16/08	h	Granit	D	0-0		
23/08	a	Vitebsk	L	0-2		
29/08	h	Naftan	L	0-1		
14/09	h	Belshina	W	2-1	Vasilyuk, Rozhkov	
19/09	a	Slutsk	D	1-1	Vasilyuk	
27/09	h	Slavia-Mozyr	L	1-2	Perepechko	
05/10	a	Dinamo Minsk	L	1-4	Sedko	
19/10	h	Gomel	L	0-4		
26/10	a	Neman	L	1-2	Shcherbo	
31/10	h	BATE	L	0-1		
08/11	a	Shakhtyor	L	1-2	Vasilyuk (p)	

No	Name	Nat	DoB	Pos	Aps	(s)	Gls
93	Pavel Chelyadko		03/03/93	D	22	(1)	
9	Aleksandr Demeshko		07/11/86	M	19	(6)	
30	Dmitri Dudar		08/11/91	G	18		
23	Valeri Fomichev		23/03/88	G	8		
4	Evgeni Klopotski		12/08/93	D	5		
13	Sergei Kondratiev		02/02/90	D	18	(3)	
21	Boris Konevega		06/08/95	M	4	(8)	
8	Denis Kovalevski		02/05/92	D	21	(3)	1
25	Vadim Kurlovich		30/10/92	M	7	(3)	
16	Pavel Pampukha		26/06/95	A	1	(5)	
31	Yuri Pavlyukovets		24/06/94	M	16	(1)	
24	Aleksandr Perepechko		07/04/89	M	5	(7)	1
19	Yegor Pistyk		01/02/95	A		(4)	
6	Kirill Premudrov		11/06/92	M	14		6
33	Igor Rozhkov		24/06/81	M	24		1
17	Pavel Sedko		03/04/98	M	6	(2)	1
91	Serhiy Semenyuk	UKR	27/01/91	D	7	(1)	
18	Vladimir Shcherbo		01/04/86	D	18	(1)	3
70	Andrei Shemruk		27/04/94	A	5	(8)	
14	Andrei Solovei		13/12/94	M	16	(4)	2
6	Andriy Strinheus	UKR	18/08/95	M		(1)	
2	Igor Tymonyuk		31/03/94	D	2	(2)	
10	Roman Vasilyuk		23/11/78	A	24		8
7	Vladimir Yurchenko		26/01/89	A	2	(9)	
5	Eduard Zhevnerov		01/11/87	D	24	(1)	

FC Dinamo Minsk

1927 • Traktor (17,600) • dinamo-minsk.by
Major honours
USSR League (1) 1982; Belarusian League (7) 1992,
1993, 1994, 1995 (spring), 1995 (autumn), 1997,
2004; Belarusian Cup (3) 1992, 1994, 2003
Coach: Dušan Uhrin (CZE);
(01/05/15) Vuk Rašović (SRB)

2015

11/04	a	Neman	D	1-1	Udoji	
19/04	h	BATE	L	0-2		
25/04	a	Shakhtyor	D	0-0		
04/05	h	Torpedo	W	4-0	Nivaldo, Yedigaryan, Bećiraj 2	
11/05	a	Minsk	W	3-0	Bećiraj 2, Fajić	
16/05	h	Granit	W	1-0	Bećiraj	
23/05	a	Vitebsk	D	0-0		
31/05	h	Naftan	W	2-1	Adamović 2	
05/06	a	Dinamo Brest	L	0-1		
18/06	h	Slutsk	W	2-0	Adamović, Bećiraj	
22/06	a	Slavia-Mozyr	W	4-2	Rassadkin, Adamović, Yarotski, Udoji	
27/06	h	Belshina	W	2-0	Bećiraj (p), Bykov	
05/07	h	Gomel	W	1-0	Adamović	
12/07	h	Neman	W	2-0	Adamović, Bećiraj	
10/08	h	BATE	W	1-0	Rassadkin	
15/08	h	Shakhtyor	W	1-0	Neacşa	
23/08	a	Torpedo	L	0-1		
31/08	h	Minsk	D	1-1	Korytko	
12/09	a	Granit	D	0-0		
21/09	h	Vitebsk	D	0-0		
26/09	a	Naftan	D	2-2	Udoji 2	
05/10	h	Dinamo Brest	W	4-1	Udoji 2, Korytko (p), Premudrov	
17/10	a	Slutsk	W	1-0	Udoji	
26/10	h	Slavia-Mozyr	W	2-0	Udoji 2	
31/10	h	Belshina	D	0-0		
08/11	a	Gomel	W	2-1	Bećiraj, Udoji	

No	Name	Nat	DoB	Pos	Aps	(s)	Gls
88	Nenad Adamović	SRB	12/01/89	M	23		6
17	Umaru Bangura	SLE	07/10/87	D	22		
21	Fatos Bećiraj	MNE	05/05/88	A	22	(1)	9
22	Roman Begunov		22/03/93	D	8		
19	Vitali Bulyga		12/01/80	A	2	(7)	
7	Artem Bykov		19/10/92	M	6	(6)	1
32	Mohamed El Monir	LBY	08/04/92	D	7	(4)	
21	Nusmir Fajić	BIH	12/01/87	A	1	(7)	1
30	Aleksandr Gutor		18/04/89	G	22		
35	Sergei Ignatovich		29/06/92	G	2		
16	Sergei Karpovich		29/03/94	D	3	(2)	
	Vasili Khomutovski		30/08/78	G	2		
26	Sergei Kontsevoi		21/06/86	D	8		
10	Vladimir Korytko		06/07/79	M	8	(2)	2
18	Nikita Korzun		06/03/95	M	19		
7	Aleksandr Kucherov		22/01/95	A		(1)	
9	Sergiu Neacşa	ROU	03/09/91	M	4	(4)	1
10	Nemanja Nikolić	MNE	01/01/88	M	9		
21	Nivaldo	CPV	10/07/88	M	6	(2)	1
6	Sergei Politevich		09/04/90	D	22		
5	Kirill Premudrov		11/06/92	M	6	(2)	1
8	Hleb Rassadkin		05/04/95	A	11	(8)	2
14	Artur Saramakha		06/06/98	M		(1)	
28	Yan Tigorev		10/03/84	M	1	(1)	
15	Chigozie Udoji	NGA	16/07/86	M	12	(6)	10
20	Oleg Veretilo		10/07/88	D	20	(1)	
3	Maksim Vitus		11/02/89	D	18	(1)	
2	Ihor Voronkov	UKR	24/04/81	M	6	(5)	
23	Yaroslav Yarotski		28/03/96	M	4	(10)	1
77	Artur Yedigaryan	ARM	26/06/87	M	12	(2)	1

FC Gomel

1995 • Central Sportkomplex (CSK) (14,307) •
fcgomel.by
Major honours
Belarusian League (1) 2003; Belarusian Cup (2) 2002,
2011
Coach: Vladimir Golmak

2015

10/04	h	Belshina	W	2-0	Teslyuk, Sitko	
18/04	h	Neman	D	0-0		
25/04	a	BATE	L	0-2		
04/05	h	Shakhtyor	L	1-3	Sitko (p)	
10/05	a	Torpedo	L	0-3		
17/05	h	Minsk	W	3-0	Bliznyuk (p), Savostyanov, Sitko	
23/05	a	Granit	L	0-1		
30/05	h	Vitebsk	W	2-0	Teslyuk, Yanchenko	
05/06	a	Naftan	L	1-3	Gavrilovich	
17/06	h	Dinamo Brest	W	2-0	Sitko, Teslyuk	
21/06	a	Slutsk	D	0-2		
28/06	h	Slavia-Mozyr	D	0-2		
05/07	a	Dinamo Minsk	L	0-1		
11/07	a	Belshina	L	1-3	Bliznyuk	
09/08	a	Neman	L	0-2		
14/08	h	BATE	D	0-0		
23/08	a	Shakhtyor	L	1-4	Bliznyuk	
30/08	h	Torpedo	L	0-2		
14/09	a	Minsk	L	0-1		
20/09	h	Granit	L	1-2	Bliznyuk	
28/09	a	Vitebsk	L	0-1		
04/10	h	Naftan	L	1-4	Antanyuk	
19/10	a	Dinamo Brest	W	4-0	Bliznyuk 3 (1p), Teslyuk	
25/10	h	Slutsk	L	1-3	Sanets	
31/10	a	Slavia-Mozyr	L	1-3	Troyakov	
08/11	h	Dinamo Minsk	L	1-2	Teslyuk	

No	Name	Nat	DoB	Pos	Aps	(s)	Gls
11	Andrei Antanyuk		17/03/95	A	1	(6)	1
10	Gennadi Bliznyuk		30/07/80	A	23		7
33	Pavel Chernyshov		12/07/95	M	6	(9)	
3	Oleg Chmyrikov		08/02/96	D	6	(2)	
19	Aleksandr Danilov		10/09/80	D	24		
30	Artem Fedyanin		25/04/94	M	1	(3)	
28	Evgeni Fomin		14/05/94	D		(1)	
3	Aleksei Gavrilovich		05/01/90	D	13		1
71	Denis Holenko		13/06/96	M		(3)	
55	Dmitri Ignatenko		01/02/95	D	12	(1)	
4	Stanislav Izhakovski		22/08/94	D	16	(4)	
36	Oleg Kovalev		24/05/87	G	8	(1)	
18	Denis Medvedev		26/01/88	M	14	(3)	
95	Evgeni Milevski		14/01/95	M	20	(2)	
20	Vitali Novik		09/11/94	D	9	(2)	
16	Andrei Sakovich		15/04/92	G	18		
29	Maksim Sanets		04/04/97	A	1	(14)	1
9	Evgeni Savostyanov		30/01/88	M	12		1
23	Stanislav Sazonovich		06/03/92	D	20	(2)	
24	Pavel Sitko		17/12/85	M	12		4
8	Ivan Sulim		04/05/89	M	18	(1)	
22	Dmitri Sviridenko		20/08/97	M		(1)	
27	Anton Tereshchenko		20/09/95	M	6	(6)	
17	Aleksei Teslyuk		10/01/94	A	22	(3)	5
15	Yegor Troyakov		24/02/95	D	12		1
11	Denis Yakhno		20/11/92	A	1	(5)	
7	Aleksandr Yanchenko		14/02/95	M	11	(5)	1

FC Granit Mikashevichi

1978 • Polesiye, Luninets (3,090) • fcgranit.by
Coach: Valeri Bokhno

2015

11/04	h	Vitebsk	D	1-1	Ignatenko (p)
18/04	a	Naftan	D	0-0	
25/04	h	Dinamo Brest	W	1-0	Lutsevich
03/05	a	Slutsk	W	2-1	Lutsevich, Sheryakov
10/05	h	Slavia-Mozyr	W	3-2	Sheryakov, Ignatenko, Khlebosolov
16/05	a	Dinamo Minsk	L	0-1	
23/05	h	Gomel	W	1-0	Lutsevich
30/05	a	Neman	L	0-2	
05/06	h	BATE	L	0-1	
18/06	a	Shakhtyor	D	1-1	Sheryakov
22/06	h	Torpedo	W	2-1	Kirilchik, Karshakevich
28/06	a	Minsk	L	0-5	
04/07	h	Belshina	L	1-5	Nevmyvaka
11/07	a	Vitebsk	W	3-2	Kirilchik, Trukhov, Ignatenko (p)
08/08	h	Naftan	W	3-0	Habovda 2, Trukhov
16/08	a	Dinamo Brest	D	0-0	
24/08	h	Slutsk	W	1-0	Habovda
29/08	a	Slavia-Mozyr	L	0-2	
12/09	h	Dinamo Minsk	D	0-0	
20/09	a	Gomel	W	2-1	Lutsevich, Osipenko
27/09	h	Neman	L	0-1	
04/10	a	BATE	D	1-1	Timoshenko
17/10	h	Shakhtyor	L	2-3	Klimovich, Osipenko
24/10	a	Torpedo	W	3-2	Lutsevich, Habovda, Osipenko (p)
31/10	h	Minsk	W	2-0	Klimovich, Osipenko
08/11	a	Belshina	W	1-0	Habovda

No	Name	Nat	DoB	Pos	Aps	(s)	Gls
28	Pavel Baskakov		28/11/91	M		(5)	
1	Ilya Gavrilov	RUS	26/09/88	G	26		
19	Yuriy Habovda	UKR	06/05/89	M	22	(2)	5
7	Dmitri Ignatenko		24/10/88	A	26		3
21	Valeri Karshakevich		30/10/80	D	16	(5)	1
10	Dmitri Khlebosolov		07/10/90	A	4	(9)	1
6	Pavel Kirilchik		04/01/81	M	24		2
26	Dmitri Klimovich		09/02/84	D	23		2
14	Terenti Lutsevich		19/04/91	D	23	(1)	5
3	Dmytro Nevmyvaka	UKR	19/03/84	D	23	(1)	1
55	Dmytro Osadchiy	UKR	05/08/92	M	2	(16)	
8	Dmitri Osipenko		12/12/82	A	14	(4)	4
11	Andrei Sheryakov		10/11/82	A	18	(4)	3
18	Aleksei Timoshenko		09/12/86	M	24	(2)	1
15	Igor Trukhov		19/08/76	M	26		2
20	Igor Yasinski		04/07/90	M	1	(12)	
9	Pavel Yevseyenko		30/10/80	M	14	(6)	

FC Minsk

1995 • FC Minsk (3,000) • fcminsk.by
Major honours
Belarusian Cup (1) 2013
Coach: Andrei Pyshnik

2015

11/04	h	Naftan	D	0-0	
20/04	a	Dinamo Brest	L	0-1	
25/04	h	Slutsk	W	2-0	Khvashchinski, Rusak
03/05	a	Slavia-Mozyr	D	0-0	
11/05	h	Dinamo Minsk	L	0-3	
17/05	h	Gomel	L	0-3	
23/05	h	Neman	W	2-0	Khvashchinski 2
30/05	a	BATE	L	0-1	
05/06	h	Shakhtyor	W	1-0	Makas
17/06	a	Torpedo	L	0-2	
21/06	h	Belshina	W	2-1	Khvashchinski, Makas (p)
28/06	h	Granit	W	5-0	Khvashchinski, Ostroukh 2, Begunov, Gromyko
04/07	a	Vitebsk	W	4-0	Khvashchinski, Makas, Lukić, Pushnyakov
11/07	a	Naftan	W	1-0	Ostroukh
09/08	h	Dinamo Brest	W	2-1	Lukić, Kovel
16/08	a	Slutsk	W	1-0	Khvashchinski
22/08	h	Slavia-Mozyr	W	2-1	Khvashchinski 2
31/08	a	Dinamo Minsk	D	1-1	Pushnyakov
14/09	a	Gomel	W	1-0	Ostroukh
21/09	a	Neman	D	1-1	Bykov
25/09	h	BATE	L	1-2	Makas
04/10	a	Shakhtyor	L	0-1	
17/10	h	Torpedo	L	0-2	
24/10	a	Belshina	L	0-4	
01/11	a	Granit	L	0-2	
08/11	h	Vitebsk	W	3-2	Khvashchinski, og (Kashevski), Makas

No	Name	Nat	DoB	Pos	Aps	(s)	Gls
16	Ivan Bakhar		10/07/98	M		(2)	
2	Roman Begunov		22/03/93	D	14		1
15	Dmitri Bessmertnykh		03/01/97	M		(1)	
17	Artem Bykov		19/10/92	M	10		1
20	Andrei Chukhlei		02/10/87	M	6	(4)	
6	Valeri Gromyko		23/01/97	M	5	(14)	1
12	Aleksei Ivanov		19/02/97	D		(1)	
23	Vladimir Khvashchinski		10/05/90	A	23	(2)	10
1	Andrei Klimovich		27/08/88	G	26		
11	Leonid Kovel		29/07/86	A	14	(7)	1
10	Nikola Lukić	SRB	14/05/90	M	11	(2)	2
13	Aleksandr Makas		08/10/91	A	21	(3)	5
7	Sergei Omelyanchuk		08/08/80	D	20	(1)	
30	Yuri Ostroukh		21/01/88	D	25		4
8	Thomas Piermayr	AUT	02/08/89	M	10		
9	Sergei Pushnyakov		08/02/93	M	9	(9)	2
37	Sergei Rusak		03/09/93	M	5	(10)	1
22	Aleksandr Sachivko		05/01/86	D	22		
24	Fedor Sapon		18/03/93	A		(3)	
96	Evgeni Shevchenko		06/06/96	A		(5)	
27	Igor Shumilov		20/10/93	D	18	(1)	
4	Aleksandr Sverchinski		16/09/91	D	25		
14	Oleg Yevdokimov		25/02/94	M	14	(11)	
3	Dmitri Zinovich		29/03/95	D	8		

FC Naftan Novopolotsk

1995 • Atlant (5,300) • fcnaftan.com
Major honours
Belarusian Cup (2) 2009, 2012
Coach: Valeri Stripeikis

2015

11/04	a	Minsk	D	0-0	
18/04	h	Granit	D	0-0	
26/04	a	Vitebsk	W	3-1	Suchkov 2 (1p), Zhukovski
04/05	a	Belshina	D	1-1	Demidovich
10/05	h	Dinamo Brest	W	1-0	Zhukovski
18/05	a	Slutsk	W	1-0	Hunchak
23/05	h	Slavia-Mozyr	D	1-1	Suchkov
31/05	a	Dinamo Minsk	L	1-2	Demidovich
05/06	h	Gomel	W	3-1	Zhukovski, Demidovich 2
17/06	a	Neman	L	1-3	Shugunkov
22/06	h	BATE	L	1-2	Lebedev
27/06	a	Shakhtyor	L	0-1	
06/07	h	Torpedo	L	0-2	
11/07	h	Minsk	L	0-1	
08/08	a	Granit	L	0-3	
16/08	h	Vitebsk	W	3-0	Volkov 2, Yelezarenko
23/08	h	Belshina	L	0-2	
29/08	a	Dinamo Brest	W	1-0	Hunchak
13/09	a	Slutsk	L	0-1	
19/09	a	Slavia-Mozyr	W	3-0	Volkov 2, Teplov
26/09	h	Dinamo Minsk	D	2-2	Teverov, Teplov
04/10	a	Gomel	W	4-1	Volkov 2, Teverov, Naumov
18/10	h	Neman	L	1-2	Zhukovski
25/10	a	BATE	L	1-2	Hunchak
31/10	h	Shakhtyor	L	3-4	Volkov, Zyulev, Karpovich
08/11	a	Torpedo	D	3-3	Zyulev, Zhukovski, Volkov

No	Name	Nat	DoB	Pos	Aps	(s)	Gls
31	Evgeni Berezkin		05/07/96	M	3	(5)	
13	Vadim Demidovich		20/09/85	A	13		4
16	Igor Dovgyallo		17/07/85	G	3		
35	Ruslan Hunchak	UKR	09/08/79	D	24		3
3	Sergei Karpovich		29/03/94	D	11		1
30	Yegor Khatkevich		09/07/88	G	22	(1)	
9	Marat Khotov	RUS	02/06/87	M	22	(3)	
3	Anton Khromykh	UKR	25/05/82	D	10		
55	Vladislav Kosmynin		17/01/90	D	4	(12)	
4	Abdulaziz Lawal	NGA	20/12/92	M	4	(12)	1
25	Andrei Lebedev		01/02/91	M	4	(12)	1
7	Mohamed Muzayev	RUS	24/01/93	M		(1)	
23	Nikita Naumov		15/11/89	D	24		1
16	Vitali Ridlevich		12/04/91	G	1		
10	Oleg Shkabara		15/02/83	M	15	(2)	
18	Nikita Shugunkov		17/04/92	A	5	(11)	1
17	Aleksei Suchkov		10/06/81	M	21	(1)	3
37	Artem Teplov		14/01/92	D	4	(9)	2
99	Ruslan Teverov		01/05/94	A	6	(7)	2
19	Roman Volkov		08/01/87	A	14	(4)	8
71	Andrei Yakimov		17/11/89	M	3	(8)	
21	Evgeni Yelezarenko		04/07/93	M	22		1
11	Valeri Zhukovski		21/05/84	M	24	(1)	5
33	Igor Zyulev		05/01/84	D	23		2

FC Neman Grodno

1964 • Central Sportkomplex Neman (8,404) • fcneman.by

Major honours
Belarusian Cup (1) 1993

Coach: Sergei Solodovnikov

2015

11/04	h	Dinamo Minsk	D	1-1	*Bombel*
18/04	a	Gomel	D	0-0	
25/04	h	Belshina	L	1-3	*Bombel (p)*
04/05	h	BATE	L	0-1	
10/05	a	Shakhtyor	L	0-3	
16/05	h	Torpedo	L	0-1	
23/05	a	Minsk	L	0-2	
30/05	h	Granit	W	2-0	*og (Lutsevich), Yedeshko*
05/06	a	Vitebsk	D	0-0	
17/06	h	Naftan	W	3-1	*Legchilin 2, Kryvobok (p)*
21/06	a	Dinamo Brest	W	3-1	*Soro, Bombel (p), Zhurnevich*
28/06	h	Slutsk	L	0-4	
04/07	a	Slavia-Mozyr	D	0-0	
12/07	h	Dinamo Minsk	L	0-2	
09/08	h	Gomel	W	1-0	*Savitski*
15/08	a	Belshina	D	0-0	
22/08	a	BATE	L	1-7	*Savitski*
30/08	h	Shakhtyor	D	0-0	
13/09	a	Torpedo	D	0-0	
21/09	h	Minsk	D	1-1	*Kovalenok*
27/09	a	Granit	W	1-0	*Savitski*
03/10	h	Vitebsk	L	0-1	
18/10	a	Naftan	W	2-1	*Gorbach, Kontsevoi*
26/10	h	Dinamo Brest	W	2-1	*Savitski, Kontsevoi*
31/10	a	Slutsk	D	0-0	
08/11	h	Slavia-Mozyr	W	3-1	*Kontsevoi, Savitski, Bebey*

No	Name	Nat	DoB	Pos	Aps	(s)	Gls
14	Aleksandr Anyukevich		10/04/92	D	18		
8	Paul Bebey	CMR	09/11/86	D	16	(3)	1
29	Artur Bombel		14/12/92	A	14	(5)	3
9	Ivan Denisevich		09/11/84	A	3	(1)	
32	Andrei Gorbach		20/05/85	D	16	(6)	1
7	Andrei Khachaturyan		02/09/87	M	6	(1)	
77	Artem Kontsevoi		20/05/83	A	12		3
10	Dmitri Kovalenok		03/11/77	A	2	(13)	1
7	Sergei Kovalyuk		07/01/80	M	11		
77	Ihor Kryvobok	UKR	28/07/78	A	4	(2)	1
19	Sergei Kurganski		15/05/86	G	16		
46	Aleksei Legchilin		11/04/92	M	26		2
25	Evgeni Leshko		24/06/96	D	17	(2)	
21	Igor Lisitsa		10/04/88	M	18	(2)	
23	Aleksei Nosko		15/08/96	M	5	(4)	
6	Aleksandr Poznyak		23/07/94	D	23		
88	Pavel Savitski		12/07/94	M	13		5
33	Evgeni Savostyanov		30/01/88	M	11		
17	Yan Senkevich		18/02/95	M	1	(3)	
18	Andrei Shtygel		22/06/94	M		(3)	
34	Adama Soro	CIV	20/12/81	M	13		1
3	Sergei Sosnovski		14/08/81	D	25		
99	Vladislav Vasilyuchek		28/03/94	G	10		
13	Aleksandr Yedeshko		28/01/93	A		(5)	1
30	Pavel Zabelin		30/06/95	M	5	(16)	
11	Vasili Zhurnevich		21/02/95	A	1	(13)	1

FC Shakhtyor Soligorsk

1961 • Stroitel (4,200) • fcshakhter.by

Major honours
Belarusian League (1) 2005; Belarusian Cup (2) 2004, 2014

**Coach: Sergei Borovski;
(25/06/15) Sergei Nikiforenko**

2015

11/04	h	Slutsk	W	2-0	*Yanush 2*
19/04	a	Slavia-Mozyr	D	1-1	*Yanush*
25/04	h	Dinamo Minsk	D	0-0	
04/05	a	Gomel	W	3-1	*Kovalev, Yurevich, og (Milevski)*
10/05	h	Neman	W	3-0	*Yanush, Matveichik, Komarovski*
16/05	h	BATE	D	0-0	
20/05	h	Belshina	D	0-0	
30/05	h	Torpedo	W	3-1	*Kobin, Komarovski, Yanush*
05/06	a	Minsk	L	0-1	
18/06	h	Granit	D	1-1	*Starhorodskiy*
22/06	a	Vitebsk	D	2-2	*Čović, Vergeichik*
27/06	h	Naftan	W	1-0	*Rybak*
06/07	a	Dinamo Brest	L	2-3	*Starhorodskiy (p), Rybak*
12/07	a	Slutsk	W	2-0	*Komarovski 2*
10/08	h	Slavia-Mozyr	W	6-1	*Starhorodskiy (p), Yanush 4, Mikoliūnas*
15/08	a	Dinamo Minsk	L	0-1	
23/08	h	Gomel	W	4-1	*Komarovski, Yanush, Vergeichik, Kuzmenok*
30/08	a	Neman	W	1-0	*Kovalev*
12/09	a	BATE	D	1-1	*og (Milunović)*
20/09	a	Belshina	L	1-3	*Mikoliūnas*
26/09	a	Torpedo	L	0-3	
04/10	h	Minsk	W	1-0	*Mikoliūnas*
17/10	a	Granit	W	3-2	*Yanush, Starhorodskiy, Mikoliūnas*
25/10	h	Vitebsk	W	4-1	*Afanasiyev 2, Martynyuk, Yanush*
31/10	a	Naftan	W	4-3	*Starhorodskiy, Yanush 3 (1p)*
08/11	h	Dinamo Brest	W	2-1	*Starhorodskiy, Yanush (p)*

No	Name	Nat	DoB	Pos	Aps	(s)	Gls
8	Mikhail Afanasiyev		04/11/86	M	12	(5)	2
16	Vladimir Bushma		24/11/83	G	18		
7	Nemanja Čović	SRB	18/06/91	A	7	(8)	2
14	Vasyl Kobin	UKR	24/05/85	D	10	(1)	1
15	Dmitri Komarovski		10/10/86	A	22	(2)	5
1	Artur Kotenko	EST	20/08/81	G	8		
23	Yuri Kovalev		27/01/93	M	12	(9)	2
17	Sergei Kozeka		17/09/86	M	7	(3)	
19	Igor Kuzmenok		06/07/90	D	19	(2)	1
20	Yaroslav Martynyuk		20/02/89	M	8	(7)	1
3	Sergei Matveichik		05/06/88	D	16	(2)	1
13	Saulius Mikoliūnas	LTU	02/05/84	M	22	(3)	4
12	Filipp Rudik		22/03/87	M	2	(7)	
18	Pavel Rybak		11/09/83	D	25		2
2	Mikhail Shibun		01/01/96	M		(4)	
11	Artem Starhorodskiy	UKR	17/01/82	M	24	(1)	6
24	Vitali Trubilo		07/01/85	D	5	(3)	
29	Aleksei Vasilevski		02/06/93	M	2	(1)	
9	Kirill Vergeichik		23/08/91	A	2	(12)	2
10	Nikolai Yanush		09/09/84	A	23	(2)	15
4	Aleksei Yanushkevich		15/01/86	D	17	(2)	
5	Aleksandr Yurevich		08/08/79	D	25	(1)	1

FC Slavia-Mozyr

1987 • Yunost (5,253) • fcslavia.by

Major honours
Belarusian League (2) 1996, 2000; Belarusian Cup (2) 1996, 2000

Coach: Yuri Puntus

2015

10/04	a	BATE	L	0-1	
19/04	h	Shakhtyor	D	1-1	*Laptev*
27/04	a	Torpedo	W	1-0	*Laptev*
03/05	h	Minsk	D	0-0	
10/05	a	Granit	L	2-3	*Laptev, Strakhanovich*
16/05	h	Vitebsk	W	4-0	*Strakhanovich 2, Laptev, German*
23/05	a	Naftan	D	1-1	*Voronkov (p)*
31/05	h	Dinamo Brest	W	3-0	*Laptev 2, Tarasenko*
05/06	a	Slutsk	L	1-3	*Trapashko*
17/06	a	Belshina	L	0-2	
22/06	h	Dinamo Minsk	L	2-4	*Laptev 2*
28/06	a	Gomel	W	2-0	*Kotlyarov, Laptev*
04/07	h	Neman	D	0-0	
10/07	h	BATE	L	3-5	*Trapashko 2, Chigoyev*
10/08	a	Shakhtyor	L	1-6	*Kuzovkin*
17/08	h	Torpedo	L	1-2	*Voronkov*
22/08	a	Minsk	L	1-2	*Kotlyarov*
29/08	h	Granit	W	2-0	*Voronkov, Sitko*
13/09	a	Vitebsk	D	0-0	
19/09	h	Naftan	L	0-3	
27/09	a	Dinamo Brest	W	2-1	*Kotlyarov, Sitko*
03/10	h	Slutsk	L	1-6	*Sitko (p)*
18/10	h	Belshina	L	1-4	*Trapashko*
26/10	a	Dinamo Minsk	L	0-2	
31/10	h	Gomel	W	3-1	*Strakhanovich 2, Voronkov*
08/11	a	Neman	L	1-3	*German*

No	Name	Nat	DoB	Pos	Aps	(s)	Gls
30	Iakob Apkhazava	GEO	30/04/91	A	2	(6)	
6	David Chigoyev	GEO	28/09/94	M	2	(10)	1
1	Vladimir Gayev		28/01/77	G	10		
7	Dmitri German		12/06/88	M	10	(11)	2
5	Pavel Grechishko		23/03/89	D	23		
12	Vyacheslav Kaminski		05/07/88	G	2		
11	Dmitri Kobets		11/06/81	M	16	(5)	
14	Aleksandr Kotlyarov		30/01/93	M	21	(4)	3
99	Roman Kuzovkin	RUS	19/10/94	M		(3)	1
15	Denis Laptev		01/08/91	A	13		9
92	Maksim Pavlovets		08/08/96	M	2	(5)	
19	Aleksandr Rayevski		19/06/88	M	10	(7)	
84	Nikolai Romanyuk		02/06/84	G	14		
17	Sergei Shchegrikovich		19/12/90	D	21		
16	Yaroslav Shkurko		08/02/91	M	18	(5)	
27	Artem Shut		18/06/95	D	5	(1)	
9	Pavel Sitko		17/12/85	M	9		3
13	Artur Slabashevich		09/02/89	D	21	(2)	
8	Oleg Strakhanovich		13/10/79	M	19	(4)	5
90	Denis Trapashko		17/05/90	A	6	(8)	4
35	Valeri Tarasenko		01/09/81	D	23		1
77	Sergei Tikhonovski		26/06/90	M	18		
22	Ivan Vasilenok		17/05/89	D	5	(1)	
3	Andrei Voronkov		08/02/89	A	16	(5)	4

SFC Slutsk

1998 • City (1,896) • sfc-slutsk.by
Coach: Yuri Krot

2015

11/04	a	Shakhtyor	L	0-2	
19/04	h	Torpedo	D	1-1	Marakhovski
24/04	a	Minsk	L	0-2	
03/05	h	Granit	L	1-2	Tsvetinski
11/05	a	Vitebsk	L	0-1	
18/05	h	Naftan	L	0-1	
23/05	a	Dinamo Brest	D	1-1	Hlebko
31/05	a	Belshina	L	0-2	
05/06	h	Slavia-Mozyr	W	3-1	Bobko, Aliseiko, Zubovich
18/06	a	Dinamo Minsk	L	0-2	
21/06	h	Gomel	D	0-0	
28/06	a	Neman	W	4-0	Zubovich 2, Tsvetinski, Levitski
05/07	h	BATE	L	0-1	
12/07	h	Shakhtyor	L	0-2	
09/08	a	Torpedo	D	0-0	
16/08	h	Minsk	L	0-1	
24/08	a	Granit	L	0-1	
29/08	h	Vitebsk	W	4-2	Zubovich 2 (1p), Tsvetinski, Hlebko
13/09	a	Naftan	W	1-0	Milko
19/09	h	Dinamo Brest	D	1-1	Bamba
27/09	h	Belshina	D	0-0	
03/10	a	Slavia-Mozyr	W	6-1	Bamba 2, Zubovich 2, Levitski 2
17/10	h	Dinamo Minsk	L	0-1	
25/10	a	Gomel	W	3-1	Bamba, Zubovich, Sebai (p)
31/10	h	Neman	D	0-0	
08/11	a	BATE	L	1-4	Bobko

No	Name	Nat	DoB	Pos	Aps	(s)	Gls
16	Dmitri Aliseiko		28/08/92	D	26		1
11	Yacouba Bamba	CIV	30/11/91	M	12		4
23	Igor Bobko		09/09/85	M	25	(1)	2
15	Serhiy Garashchenkov	UKR	16/05/90	D	9	(3)	
20	Aleksei Gavrilovich		05/01/90	D	12		
8	Aleksandr Gavryushko		23/01/86	A		(2)	
29	Vyacheslav Grigorov		08/03/82	M	6	(2)	
17	Sergei Hlebko		23/08/92	A	24		2
2	Kouassi Kouadja	CIV	22/06/95	D	12		
7	Vadim Kurlovich		30/10/92	M	1	(8)	
27	Artur Lesko		25/05/84	G	20		
6	Sergei Levitski		17/03/90	M	3	(15)	3
10	Evgeni Loshankov		02/01/79	M	15	(4)	
5	Vitali Marakhovski	RUS	14/01/88	D	6	(2)	1
4	Vadym Milko	UKR	22/08/86	M	23	(1)	1
7	Aleksandr Perepechko		07/04/89	M	3	(4)	
1	Konstantin Rudenok		15/12/90	G	6		
9	Senin Sebai	CIV	18/12/93	A	2	(5)	1
18	Sergei Tsvetinski		22/02/84	D	21		3
9	Dmytro Yeremenko	UKR	20/06/90	M	1	(4)	
22	Aleksei Zaleski		07/10/94	D	14	(3)	
13	Andrei Zaleski		20/01/91	D	16	(1)	
19	Nikolai Zenko		11/03/89	A	8	(10)	
14	Yegor Zubovich		01/06/89	A	21	(5)	8

FC Torpedo Zhodino

1961 • Torpedo (6,542) • torpedo-belaz.by
Major honours
Belarusian Cup (1) 2016
Coach: Igor Kriushenko

2015

11/04	h	Dinamo Brest	L	1-3	Maximov
19/04	a	Slutsk	D	1-1	Platonov
27/04	h	Slavia-Mozyr	L	0-1	
04/05	a	Dinamo Minsk	L	0-4	
10/05	h	Gomel	W	3-0	Platonov 2, Hleb (p)
16/05	a	Neman	W	1-0	Kibuk
20/05	h	BATE	D	0-0	
30/05	a	Shakhtyor	L	1-3	Shchegrikovich
05/06	h	Belshina	L	0-3	
17/06	h	Minsk	W	2-0	Pankovets, Hleb
22/06	a	Granit	L	1-2	Burko
27/06	h	Vitebsk	W	3-1	Platonov, Hleb, Vaskov
06/07	a	Naftan	W	2-0	Kibuk, Maximov
12/07	a	Dinamo Brest	L	1-2	Platonov
09/08	h	Slutsk	D	0-0	
17/08	a	Slavia-Mozyr	W	2-1	Platonov, Hleb
23/08	h	Dinamo Minsk	W	1-0	Khachaturyan
30/08	a	Gomel	W	2-0	Skavysh, Hleb
13/09	h	Neman	D	0-0	
20/09	a	BATE	L	0-1	
26/09	h	Shakhtyor	W	3-0	Demidovich 2 (1p), Khachaturyan
03/10	a	Belshina	L	0-1	
17/10	a	Minsk	W	2-0	Serdyuk, Platonov
24/10	h	Granit	L	2-3	Burko, Demidovich
31/10	a	Vitebsk	D	0-0	
08/11	h	Naftan	D	3-3	Demidovich 2 (1p), Vaskov

No	Name	Nat	DoB	Pos	Aps	(s)	Gls
5	Igor Burko		08/09/88	D	20	(1)	2
2	Artem Chelyadinski		29/12/77	D	14		
1	Pavel Chesnovski		04/03/86	G	25		
23	Serhiy Datsenko	UKR	06/09/87	D	14	(1)	
7	Vadim Demidovich		20/09/85	A	8	(3)	5
99	Vyacheslav Hleb		12/02/83	M	16	(6)	5
24	Vitali Kazantsev	RUS	04/07/81	D	7	(2)	
10	Andrei Khachaturyan		02/09/87	M	12		2
20	Vitali Kibuk		07/01/89	A	4	(11)	2
7	Artem Kontsevoi		20/05/83	A	7	(4)	
18	Valeri Marov		17/11/93	M	1		
10	Anton Matveyenko		03/09/96	M	10	(1)	
17	Olexandr Maximov	UKR	13/02/85	M	11	(2)	2
4	Serhiy Melnyk	UKR	04/09/88	D	12		
6	Aleksei Pankovets		18/04/81	M	24		1
22	Aleksandr Pavlovets		13/08/96	D	8		
32	Dmitri Platonov		07/02/86	A	15	(9)	7
28	Pavlo Rebenok	UKR	23/07/85	M	12		
8	Aleksandr Selyava		17/05/92	M	20	(2)	
3	Vyacheslav Serdyuk	UKR	28/01/85	D	15	(4)	1
11	Dmitri Shchegrikovich		07/12/83	M	7	(10)	1
15	Maksim Skavysh		13/11/89	A	12	1	
13	Roman Stepanov		06/08/91	G	1		
19	Artem Vaskov		21/10/88	D	6	(15)	2
15	Aleksandr Yatskevich		04/01/85	A	6	(6)	

FC Vitebsk

1960 • Central (8,100) • fc.vitebsk.by
Major honours
Belarusian Cup (1) 1998
Coach: Sergei Vekhtev; (08/07/15) Sergei Yasinski

2015

11/04	a	Granit	D	1-1	Lebedev
19/04	a	Belshina	D	1-1	Kovb (p)
26/04	h	Naftan	L	1-3	Kozlov
03/05	a	Dinamo Brest	L	2-3	Kovb 2 (1p)
11/05	h	Slutsk	W	1-0	Kozlov
16/05	a	Slavia-Mozyr	L	0-4	
23/05	h	Dinamo Minsk	D	0-0	
30/05	a	Gomel	L	0-2	
05/06	h	Neman	D	0-0	
18/06	a	BATE	L	0-4	
22/06	h	Shakhtyor	D	2-2	Solovei, Korobka
27/06	a	Torpedo	L	1-3	Kashevski (p)
04/07	h	Minsk	L	0-4	
11/07	h	Granit	L	2-3	Kravchenko, Baranok
08/08	h	Belshina	D	1-1	Khlebosolov
16/08	a	Naftan	L	0-3	
23/08	h	Dinamo Brest	W	2-0	Kravchenko, Khlebosolov
29/08	a	Slutsk	L	2-4	Marakhovski, Khlebosolov (p)
13/09	h	Slavia-Mozyr	D	0-0	
21/09	a	Dinamo Minsk	D	0-0	
28/09	h	Gomel	W	1-0	Chukhlei
03/10	a	Neman	W	1-0	Solovei
16/10	h	BATE	L	0-2	
25/10	a	Shakhtyor	L	1-4	Solovei
31/10	h	Torpedo	D	0-0	
08/11	a	Minsk	L	2-3	Solovei, Khlebosolov

No	Name	Nat	DoB	Pos	Aps	(s)	Gls
30	Aleksandr Aleksandrovich		06/07/97	M	2	(6)	
22	Andrei Baranok		20/07/79	M	15	(7)	1
20	Andrei Chukhlei		02/10/87	M	11		1
26	Maksim Grechikha		10/06/93	M	1	(5)	
1	Dmitri Gushchenko		12/05/88	G	26		
13	Dmitri Ivanov		21/02/97	A		(1)	
8	Maksim Karpovich		27/02/86	M	8	(5)	
6	Nikolai Kashevski		05/10/80	D	22	(2)	1
10	Dmitri Khlebosolov		07/10/90	A	11		4
13	Aleksandr Komlev		26/06/94	A		(8)	
11	Volodymyr Korobka	UKR	22/07/89	A	1	(8)	1
99	Dmitri Kovb		20/01/87	A	6	(6)	3
17	Mikhail Kozlov		12/02/90	M	15	(3)	2
19	Aleksei Kravchenko		15/01/85	D	24	(1)	2
14	Evgeni Lebedev		29/12/94	M	10	(7)	1
5	Vitali Marakhovski	RUS	14/01/88	D	10	(1)	1
25	Sergei Melnik		05/07/95	M	9	(5)	
2	Serhiy Melnyk	UKR	04/09/88	D	12		
7	Vladyslav Pavlenko	UKR	05/04/94	M	21	(2)	
26	Filipp Postnikov	RUS	10/04/89	M		(1)	
5	Pavel Plaskonny		29/01/85	D	6		
4	Azam Radzhabov		21/03/93	M	20	(1)	
4	Artem Skitov		21/01/91	D	18		
15	Artem Solovei		01/11/90	M	24	(1)	4
3	Nikolai Zolotov		11/11/94	D	14	(2)	

BELARUS

Top goalscorers

15	Nikolai Yanush (Shakhtyor)
10	Chigozie Udoji (Dinamo Minsk)
	Vladimir Khvashchinski (Minsk)
9	Vitali Rodionov (BATE)
	Fatos Bećiraj (Dinamo Minsk)
	Vadim Demidovich (Naftan/Torpedo)
	Denis Laptev (Slavia-Mozyr)
8	Serhiy Rozhok (Belshina)
	Roman Vasilyuk (Dinamo Brest)
	Roman Volkov (Naftan)
	Yegor Zubovich (Slutsk)

Promoted clubs

FC Isloch

2007 • RCOP-BGU (1,500) • fcisloch.by
Coach: Vitali Zhukovski

FC Gorodeya

2004 • Gorodeya (1,020) • fcgorodeya.by
Coach: Sergei Yaromko

FC Krumkachy

2014 • SOK Olimpiysky (1,630) • krumka.by
**Coach: Aleksandr Bogaichuk;
(30/04/15) Oleg Dulub**

Second level final table 2015

		Pld	W	D	L	F	A	Pts
1	FC Isloch	30	20	9	1	76	24	69
2	FC Gorodeya	30	21	5	4	73	25	68
3	FC Krumkachy	30	19	3	8	67	45	60
4	FC Dnepr Mogilev	30	17	5	8	48	21	56
5	FC Smorgon	30	15	8	7	60	41	53
6	FC Lida	30	15	5	10	60	53	50
7	FC Smolevichi-STI	30	13	8	9	47	37	47
8	FC Gomelzheldortrans Gomel	30	12	8	10	45	39	44
9	FC Slonim	30	13	2	15	41	55	41
10	FC Zvezda-BGU Minsk	30	10	10	10	47	47	40
11	FC Bereza-2010	30	10	4	16	39	43	34
12	FC Khimik Svetlogorsk	30	9	7	14	42	50	34
13	FC Baranovichi	30	8	8	14	36	49	32
14	FC Orsha	30	3	8	19	24	70	17
15	FC Kobrin	30	4	3	23	23	77	15
16	FC Rechitsa-2014	30	2	5	23	14	66	11

DOMESTIC CUP

Kubok Belarusii 2015/16

SECOND ROUND

(16/07/15 & 01/08/15)
Dnepr 0-4, 2-3 Naftan *(2-7)*

(16/07/15 & 02/08/15)
Baranovichi 1-1, 0-2 Slavia-Mozyr *(1-3)*

(17/07/15 & 01/08/15)
Gomelzheldortrans 1-2, 2-2 Belshina *(3-4)*

(18/07/15 & 01/08/15)
Dinamo Brest 3-1, 2-3 Bereza-2010 *(5-4)*
Gorodeya 0-0, 0-2 Minsk *(0-2)*
Khimik Svetlogorsk 0-2, 2-3 Isloch *(2-5)*
Krumkachy 2-2, 0-4 Slutsk *(2-6)*
Lida 0-2, 3-3 Smorgon *(3-5)*
Oshmyany 1-3, 1-5 Granit *(2-8)*
Rechitsa-2014 0-0, 0-6 Neman *(0-6)*
Spartak Shklov 2-1, 0-7 BATE *(2-8)*
Volna 1-3, 0-2 Vitebsk *(1-5)*

(18/07/15 & 02/08/15)
Kobrin 0-2, 0-4 Gomel *(0-6)*

(19/07/15 & 02/08/15)
Dinamo Minsk 2-0, 5-2 Smolevichi-STI *(7-2)*
Orsha 0-5, 1-11 Torpedo *(1-16)*
Slonim 1-10, 1-8 Shakhtyor *(2-18)*

THIRD ROUND

(08/09/15 & 15/11/15)
Minsk 2-1, 2-3 Slavia-Mozyr *(4-4; Minsk on away goals)*

(12/11/15 & 16/11/15)
Naftan 3-1, 0-1 Dinamo Brest *(3-2)*

(14/11/15 & 18/11/15)
Vitebsk 1-1, 1-3 Shakhtyor *(2-4)*

(14/11/15 & 21/11/15)
Gomel 0-3, 0-2 Slutsk *(0-5)*

(19/11/15 & 23/11/15)
Belshina 3-0, 1-1 Isloch *(4-1)*

(19/11/15 & 25/11/15)
Smorgon 0-5, 1-4 Torpedo *(1-9)*

(20/11/15 & 29/11/15)
BATE 5-0, 3-1 Granit *(8-1)*

(21/11/15 & 30/11/15)
Dinamo Minsk 1-1, 1-0 Neman *(2-1)*

QUARTER-FINALS

(19/03/16 & 06/04/16)
BATE 1-0 Slutsk *(M Volodko 90+3)*
Slutsk 0-2 BATE *(Mozolevski 11, Ivanić 54)*
(BATE 3-0)

Minsk 2-0 Shakhtyor *(Kovel 52, Sachivko 76p)*
Shakhtyor 0-0 Minsk
(Minsk 2-0)

(20/03/16 & 06/04/16)
Dinamo Minsk 1-0 Torpedo *(Begunov 43)*
Torpedo 2-0 Dinamo Minsk *(Demidovich 12, Klopotski 113) (aet)*
(Torpedo 2-1)

Naftan 1-1 Belshina *(Shugunkov 85; Fameyeh 64)*
Belshina 1-3 Naftan *(Matveyenko 47; Teverov 32, 90+2, 113) (aet)*
(Naftan 4-2)

SEMI-FINALS

(20/04/16 & 04/05/16)
Naftan 2-2 BATE *(Gorbachev 27, Yakimov 81; Gordeichuk 23, 64p)*
BATE 0-0 Naftan
(2-2; BATE on away goals)

Torpedo 1-1 Minsk *(Skavysh 10; Bessmertnykh 49)*
Minsk 0-1 Torpedo *(Klopotski 16)*
(Torpedo 2-1)

FINAL

(21/05/16)
GOSK Brestski, Brest
FC TORPEDO ZHODINO 0
FC BATE BORISOV 0
(aet; 3-2 on pens)
Referee: Kulbakov
TORPEDO ZHODINO: Fomichev, Shcherbo, Pankovets, Chelyadinski, Chelyadko (Klopotski 91), Karshakevich, Shapoval, Chumak, Golenkov (Trapashko 116), Demidovich (Kvashuk 80), Skavysh
BATE: Chernik, Zhavnerchik, Dubra, Milunović, Polyakov, Yablonski, Ivanić, Rios (M Volodko 82), Stasevich, Gordeichuk (Antilevski 116), Kendysh (A Volodko 108)

Torpedo celebrate the club's first major trophy after their penalty shoot-out victory over BATE

BELGIUM

Union Royale Belge des Sociétés de Football Association (URBSFA) /
Koninklijke Belgische Voetbalbond (KBVB)

Address	145 Avenue Houba de Strooper BE-1020 Bruxelles
Tel	+32 2 477 1211
Fax	+32 2 478 2391
E-mail	urbsfa.kbvb@footbel.com
Website	footbel.com

President	François De Keersmaecker
Media officer	Pierre Cornez
Year of formation	1895
National stadium	King Baudouin, Brussels (47,350)

KEY

- UEFA Champions League
- UEFA Europa League
- Promoted
- Relegated

PRO LEAGUE CLUBS

 1 **RSC Anderlecht**

 2 **R. Charleroi SC**

 3 **Club Brugge KV**

 4 **KRC Genk**

 5 **KAA Gent**

 6 **KV Kortrijk**

 7 **KSC Lokeren OV**

 8 **KV Mechelen**

 9 **R. Excel Mouscron**

 10 **KV Oostende**

 11 **Oud-Heverlee Leuven**

 12 **K. Sint-Truidense VV**

 13 **R. Standard de Liège**

 14 **Waasland-Beveren**

 15 **KVC Westerlo**

 16 **SV Zulte Waregem**

PROMOTED CLUB

 17 **KAS Eupen**

Celebration time for Club Brugge

An uncomfortably long wait for a 14th Belgian championship title ended for Club Brugge in 2015/16 as coach Michel Preud'homme steered the team to their first national crown for 11 years.

Runners-up Anderlecht had a relatively quiet season, during which Standard Liège won the Belgian Cup, Gent reached the knockout stage of the UEFA Champions League, and the Belgian national team blew hot and cold at UEFA EURO 2016.

Pro League triumph ends 11-year title wait

Standard take the honours in Belgian Cup

Wilmots departs after EURO quarter-final exit

Domestic league

After a hectic schedule the previous season, which had involved 63 fixtures over three competitions, Club Brugge's main focus for 2015/16 was to become champions of Belgium again. They had not gone so long without a domestic league title since the early 1970s, and although the club had ended an eight-year trophy drought in 2014/15 by lifting the Belgian Cup, the prospect of being Pro League also-rans once again did not sit easily with either the club's board of directors or the ever-demanding Blauw-Zwart fans.

Preud-homme's mission was clear, but his team did not start well. Erratic early form brought maximum points at home but five defeats and a draw from their first seven away fixtures, leaving them well off the pace set by unlikely frontrunners Oostende. However, a run of six successive victories – during which new signing Jelle Vossen found his scoring touch – reinvigorated their challenge, and by early December they were on top of the table for the first time.

A couple of defeats, the second of them 4-1 at home to Anderlecht, quickly dislodged them from the summit, however, and at the short winter break they were back down in third place, with

Anderlecht a point above them and defending champions Gent, defeated only twice, sitting pretty on top with an additional two-point advantage. The three-week rest did Preud'homme's men a power of good, as did a pre-Christmas exit from Europe, because they won nine of their next ten games, including 1-0 at home to Gent in early February (four days after beating the same opposition in the cup semi-final), to arrive at the end of the regular season four points above Hein Vanhaezebrouck's reigning champions in first place.

That lead was halved before the ten-match play-off series, in which the top two were joined by Anderlecht, Oostende, Genk and – after leapfrogging Standard on the final day – Zulte Waregem. Although Club Brugge maintained their fine form with a couple of wins against Oostende and Gent, their fans must have feared the worst when a third defeat of the campaign against Besnik Hasi's Anderlecht, 1-0 in Brussels, was followed three days later by a comprehensive 4-2 loss at Genk (in which they were 4-0 down after 80 minutes). Fortunately, though, Club Brugge's home form was rock solid, and two big confidence-restoring wins over Zulte Waregem and Genk not only kept them in first place but also pumped them

up sufficiently for the next two all-important fixtures against Gent and Anderlecht, which they would win in fanfare style, 4-1 and 4-0 respectively, to claim the title with two games to spare.

Star midfielder Hans Vanaken scored twice away to Gent, while a first-half double from top-scoring Mali international striker Abdoulay Diaby led the rout of Anderlecht in front of a delirious capacity crowd at the Jan Breydelstadion, with Vanaken adding a third goal and veteran skipper Timmy Simons concluding matters from the penalty spot. It was the perfect way for Club Brugge to end their 11-year wait. Simons had been a Belgian champion twice before during his first spell with the club, in 2002/03 and 2004/05, while Preud'homme had led Standard to the title in 2007/08.

Club Brugge's prize for victory was a place in the group stage of the UEFA Champions League, from which they had also endured an 11-year absence, while Anderlecht, who finished second, seven points adrift, claimed a place in the third qualifying round of Europe's flagship competition. Hasi would not be there to lead them, however, having left to take charge of Polish double winners Legia Warszawa, with Swiss coach René Weiler coming in from Nürnberg to

replace him. The former Albanian international's last season in Brussels had its moments – they were unbeaten in all 20 league games at the Constant Vandenstock stadium – but the lack of a trophy deemed it unsatisfactory for most Mauves fans, with the team's inability to turn draws into wins during the regular season a particular source of frustration.

Gent's bid to defend the title they had won for the first time in 2014/15 was undone by a shaky spell in the spring, with just three wins in the play-offs dropping them down to third, just above Genk, whose form zigzagged all season but would finish on a high as they beat Charleroi 5-1 at home to recover from a 2-0 first-leg defeat and win the UEFA Europa League qualification play-off final. Charleroi had their new free-scoring French striker Jérémy Perbet to thank for taking them that far. He scored 24 goals in all phases of the league campaign to win the golden boot – and earn a summer move to Gent.

The promotion/relegation issue was complicated by the fact that second division winners White Star Bruxelles were denied a professional licence, which barred their access to the newly-named First Division A in 2016/17. Runners-up Eupen were therefore promoted instead, with just Oud-Heverlee Leuven – who had been relegated then promoted in the previous two seasons – going down from the top flight.

Domestic cup

Standard may have missed out on the championship play-offs, but a week after that disappointment they made amends by defeating holders Club Brugge 2-1 in the Belgian Cup final and taking the trophy for the seventh time. Yannick Ferrera became, at the age of 35 years and 178 days, the youngest coach to win the cup thanks to Croatian striker Ivan Santini's 88th-minute winner after Club Brugge had been reduced to ten men by Diaby's 52nd-minute red card.

Santini had set up Standard's opening goal for Jean-Luc Dompé before Lior Refaelov, the match-winning hero for Club Brugge against Anderlecht 12 months earlier, drew the holders level. The result enabled Les Rouches to gain revenge for their 1-0 defeat by the Blauw-Zwart in the 2007 final – the only time the two clubs had previously met in the fixture.

Europe

Gent's first experience of the UEFA Champions League proved to be a memorable one as they achieved what no previous Belgian club had managed and progressed into the competition's knockout phase. Vanhaezebrouck's side looked doomed to the same fate as those before them when they took just one point from their opening three games – and that after goalkeeper Matz Sels had saved a late Alexandre

Lacazette penalty at home to Lyon – but a successful spot kick from inspirational skipper Sven Kums brought them a first win, at home to Valencia, and they followed that up with two more, against Lyon and group winners Zenit, to defy the odds and reach the last 16, where their run ended against Wolfsburg.

Anderlecht and Club Brugge were both involved in the UEFA Europa League group stage – the latter after losing heavily to Manchester United in the UEFA Champions League play-offs – but only the Brussels side remained in the competition after Christmas, with Frank Acheampong ensuring further progress thanks to two extra-time goals away to Olympiacos in the round of 32 before Shakhtar Donetsk brought their involvement to an end.

National team

Having qualified for the UEFA European Championship for the first time in seven attempts, Belgium were expected to shine at the 2016 finals just across the border in France. That they went out, as in the 2014 FIFA World Cup, at the quarter-final stage was generally perceived as underachievement given the quality of playing personnel in their ranks, but while their attack, led by stand-in skipper Eden Hazard, turned on the style in the two matches against the Republic of Ireland and Hungary, dominating both games with their pace, skill and ingenuity and eventually cruising to victory in exhibition mode, they were well beaten in their first game by Italy and, more significantly, in their last one by Wales.

Although Wales had gleaned four points from Belgium in the qualifying campaign, Marc Wilmots' side were expected to beat them in nearby Lille and advance to their first major semi-final for 30 years, but a crisis in defence, where the injured Jan Vertonghen and suspended Thomas Vermaelen joined a list of pre-tournament absentees including captain Vincent Kompany and qualifying regular Nicolas Lombaerts, was exploited by their opponents, who ran out deserved 3-1 winners. Another hit-and-miss tournament was deemed one too many by the Belgian FA, who decided to relieve Wilmots of his duties after four years in charge.

Eden Hazard (right), Belgium's captain at UEFA EURO 2016, shields the ball from the Republic of Ireland's Séamus Coleman

DOMESTIC SEASON AT A GLANCE

Pro League 2015/16 final tables

Championship play-offs

		Pld	Home W	D	L	F	A	Away W	D	L	F	A	Total W	D	L	F	A	Pts
1	**Club Brugge KV**	10	4	1	0	16	3	3	0	2	9	6	7	1	2	25	9	54
2	RSC Anderlecht	10	5	0	0	8	1	1	1	3	7	15	6	1	3	15	16	47
3	KAA Gent	10	1	3	1	6	6	2	0	3	5	9	3	3	4	10	15	42
4	KRC Genk	10	4	0	1	16	6	1	1	3	4	7	5	1	4	20	13	40
5	KV Oostende	10	2	1	2	9	8	1	1	3	5	11	3	2	5	14	19	36
6	SV Zulte Waregem	10	1	0	4	7	10	0	2	3	4	13	1	2	7	11	23	27

Pro League final table

		Pld	Home W	D	L	F	A	Away W	D	L	F	A	Total W	D	L	F	A	Pts
1	Club Brugge KV	30	14	0	1	42	9	7	1	7	22	21	21	1	8	64	30	64
2	KAA Gent	30	10	4	1	35	14	7	5	3	21	15	17	9	4	56	29	60
3	RSC Anderlecht	30	10	5	0	29	13	5	5	5	22	16	15	10	5	51	29	55
4	KV Oostende	30	10	2	3	35	21	4	5	6	20	23	14	7	9	55	44	49
5	KRC Genk	30	11	1	3	32	16	3	5	7	10	14	14	6	10	42	30	48
6	SV Zulte Waregem	30	7	4	4	30	22	5	3	7	21	28	12	7	11	51	50	43
7	R. Standard de Liège	30	8	2	5	22	16	4	3	8	19	35	12	5	13	41	51	41
8	R. Charleroi SC	30	5	7	3	20	16	5	2	8	16	23	10	9	11	36	39	39
9	KV Kortrijk	30	8	5	2	19	12	2	4	9	12	23	10	9	11	31	35	39
10	KV Mechelen	30	7	4	4	28	20	3	3	9	20	30	10	7	13	48	50	37
11	KSC Lokeren OV	30	3	5	7	16	19	5	5	5	19	21	8	10	12	35	40	34
12	Waasland-Beveren	30	4	5	6	19	25	5	1	9	21	32	9	6	15	40	57	33
13	K. Sint-Truidense VV	30	4	4	7	17	23	4	2	9	11	24	8	6	16	28	47	30
14	R. Excel Mouscron	30	3	5	7	18	22	4	4	7	21	29	7	9	14	39	51	30
15	KVC Westerlo	30	5	4	6	17	22	2	5	8	18	37	7	9	14	35	59	30
16	Oud-Heverlee Leuven	30	6	2	7	23	22	1	6	8	19	31	7	8	15	42	53	29

NB After 30 rounds the top six clubs enter a championship play-off, carrying forward half of their points total (half points rounded upwards); clubs placed 7-14 enter two play-off groups.

European qualification 2016/17

Champion: Club Brugge KV (group stage)
RSC Anderlecht (third qualifying round)

Cup winner: R. Standard de Liège (group stage)
KAA Gent (third qualifying round)
KRC Genk (second qualifying round)

Top scorer	Jérémy Perbet (Charleroi), 24 goals
Relegated club	Oud-Heverlee Leuven
Promoted club	KAS Eupen
Cup final	R. Standard de Liège 2-1 Club Brugge KV

Team of the season
(4-4--2)

Coach: Preud'homme (Club Brugge)

Player of the season

Sofiane Hanni
(KV Mechelen)

The winner of the Belgian professional footballer of the year award for 2015/16 went to a player who was not even involved in the Pro League championship play-offs. Hanni's second season at Mechelen – following a three-year spell in Turkey – proved so impressive, however, that he was voted in ahead of any player from the title-chasing teams. The 25-year-old French-born Algerian international scored 17 goals in the league, adding several more assists, and was rewarded with a four-year contract at Anderlecht.

Newcomer of the season

Leon Bailey
(KRC Genk)

Jamaican wing wizard Bailey had only just turned 18 when he made his league debut for Genk in a 3-1 defeat at newly-promoted Sint-Truiden. It was a low-key start, but soon he was a regular in Peter Maes's team and by the end of the campaign he had not only become a huge local favourite but had also attracted sufficient admiration from elsewhere to pick up the Pro League young player of the year award. His exceptional pace and skill helped Genk to finish fourth and qualify for the UEFA Europa League via the play-offs.

NATIONAL TEAM

International tournament appearances

FIFA World Cup (12) 1930, 1934, 1938, 1954, 1970, 1982 (2nd phase), 1986 (4th), 1990 (2nd round), 1994 (2nd round), 1998, 2002 (2nd round), 2014 (qtr-finals)
UEFA European Championship (5) 1972 (3rd), 1980 (runners-up), 1984, 2000, 2016 (qtr-finals)

Top five all-time caps

Jan Ceulemans (96); Timmy Simons (93), Eric Gerets & Franky Van Der Elst (86); Daniel Van Buyten (85)

Top five all-time goals

Paul Van Himst & Bernard Voorhoof (30); Marc Wilmots (28); Jef Mermans (27); Raymond Braine & Robert De Veen (26)

Results 2015/16

03/09/15	Bosnia & Herzegovina (ECQ)	H	Brussels	W	3-1		Fellaini (23), De Bruyne (44), Hazard (78p)
06/09/15	Cyprus (ECQ)	A	Nicosia	W	1-0		Hazard (86)
10/10/15	Andorra (ECQ)	A	Andorra la Vella	W	4-1		Nainggolan (19), De Bruyne (42), Hazard (56p), Depoitre (64)
13/10/15	Israel (ECQ)	H	Brussels	W	3-1		Mertens (64), De Bruyne (78), Hazard (84)
13/11/15	Italy	H	Brussels	W	3-1		Vertonghen (13), De Bruyne (74), Batshuayi (83)
29/03/16	Portugal	A	Leiria	L	1-2		R Lukaku (62)
28/05/16	Switzerland	A	Geneva	W	2-1		R Lukaku (34), De Bruyne (83)
01/06/16	Finland	H	Brussels	D	1-1		R Lukaku (89)
05/06/16	Norway	H	Brussels	W	3-2		R Lukaku (3), Hazard (70), Ciman (73)
13/06/16	Italy (ECF)	N	Lyon (FRA)	L	0-2		
18/06/16	Republic of Ireland (ECF)	N	Bordeaux (FRA)	W	3-0		R Lukaku (48, 70), Witsel (61)
22/06/16	Sweden (ECF)	N	Nice (FRA)	W	1-0		Nainggolan (84)
26/06/16	Hungary (ECF)	N	Toulouse (FRA)	W	4-0		Alderweireld (10), Batshuayi (78), Hazard (80), Carrasco (90+1)
01/07/16	Wales (ECF)	N	Lille (FRA)	L	1-3		Nainggolan (13)

Appearances 2015/16

Coach: Marc Wilmots 22/02/69

Player	DOB	Club	BIH	CYP	AND	ISR	Ita	Por	Sui	Fin	Nor	ITA	IRL	SWE	HUN	WAL	Caps	Goals
Thibaut Courtois	11/05/92	Chelsea (ENG)	G	G				G	G	G	G	G	G	G	G	G	42	-
Toby Alderweireld	02/03/89	Tottenham (ENG)	D	D	D	D	D		D	D	D	D	D	D	D	D	61	2
Vincent Kompany	10/04/86	Man. City (ENG)	D	D		D58											72	4
Thomas Vermaelen	14/11/85	Barcelona (ESP)	D	D				D	D67	D		D	D	D	D		58	1
Jan Vertonghen	24/04/87	Tottenham (ENG)	D	D	D	D	D		D	D		D	D	D	D		83	6
Radja Nainggolan	04/05/88	Roma (ITA)	M	M	M	M	M	M			M	M62	s57	M	M	M	24	6
Axel Witsel	12/01/89	Zenit (RUS)	M	M	M	s66	M	M	D	M	M57	M	M	M	M	M	74	7
Kevin De Bruyne	28/06/91	Man. City (ENG)	M89	M	M	M	M		M	M	M	M	M	M	M	M	46	13
Marouane Fellaini	22/11/87	Man. United (ENG)	M	M64		M66		M79	M85	M79	s57	M		s81	s46		73	15
Eden Hazard	07/01/91	Chelsea (ENG)	M	M	M79	M	M		M	M	M84	M	M	M93	M81	M	71	14
Romelu Lukaku	13/05/93	Everton (ENG)	A82			A65	A63	A	A58	s79	A	A73	A83	A87	A76	A83	51	17
Divock Origi	18/04/95	Liverpool (ENG)	s82	s46		s65			s67	A58	s80	s73		s93			22	3
Dries Mertens	06/05/87	Napoli (ITA)	s89	s64	M72	M		M67	M67	s58	M80	s62	s64	s71	M70	s75	51	8
Christian Benteke	03/12/90	Liverpool (ENG)		A46					s85	s57				s83	s87		29	7
Simon Mignolet	06/03/88	Liverpool (ENG)			G	G	G										17	-
Thomas Meunier	12/09/91	Club Brugge			D81	s58							D	D	D	D	9	-
Jordan Lukaku	25/07/94	Oostende			D			s59	s67		D					D75	5	-
Laurent Depoitre	07/12/88	Gent			A												1	1
Nacer Chadli	02/08/89	Tottenham (ENG)			s72			M									32	4
Zakaria Bakkali	26/01/96	Valencia (ESP)			s79												2	-
Luis Cavanda	02/01/91	Trabzonspor (TUR)			s81	D63											2	-
Nicolas Lombaerts	20/03/85	Zenit (RUS)				D	D	D									39	3
Yannick Carrasco	04/09/93	Atlético (ESP)				M87						s76	M64	M71	s70	M46	9	1
Jason Denayer	28/06/95	Galatasaray (TUR)				s63	D86		D		D66					D	8	-
Michy Batshuayi	02/10/93	Marseille (FRA)				s63	s67		s58	A57				s76	s83		7	3
Kevin Mirallas	05/10/87	Everton (ENG)					s87										51	9
Guillaume Gillet	09/03/84	Nantes (FRA)						D59									22	1
Mousa Dembélé	16/07/87	Tottenham (ENG)						s79	M55		s84		M57				66	5
Dedryck Boyata	28/11/90	Celtic (SCO)							s86								2	-
Laurent Ciman	05/08/85	Montreal Impact (USA)							s55	s66	D76						12	1

EUROPE

KAA Gent

Group H

Match 1 - Olympique Lyonnais (FRA)
H 1-1 Milicevic (68)
Sels, Depoitre, Renato Neto, Mitrović, Kums, Dejaegere, Asare, Nielsen, Simon (Raman 69; Rafinha 90), Foket, Milicevic (Matton 82). Coach: Hein Vanhaezebrouck (BEL)
Red cards: Dejaegere 41, Foket 87

Match 2 - FC Zenit (RUS)
A 1-2 Matton (56)
Sels, Rafinha (Coulibaly 89), Matton (Raman 84), Depoitre, Renato Neto, Mitrović, Kums, Saief, Asare, Nielsen, Milicevic (Pedersen 80). Coach: Hein Vanhaezebrouck (BEL)

Match 3 - Valencia CF (ESP)
A 1-2 Foket (40)
Sels, Matton (Simon 84), Depoitre, Renato Neto, Mitrović, Kums, Saief, Asare, Nielsen, Foket, Milicevic. Coach: Hein Vanhaezebrouck (BEL)

Match 4 - Valencia CF (ESP)
H 1-0 Kums (49p)
Sels, Depoitre, Renato Neto, Mitrović, Kums, Saief (Raman 55; Rafinha 85), Dejaegere (Coulibaly 90+3), Asare, Nielsen, Foket, Milicevic. Coach: Hein Vanhaezebrouck (BEL)

Match 5 - Olympique Lyonnais (FRA)
A 2-1 Milicevic (32), Coulibaly (90+5)
Sels, Depoitre (Coulibaly 90), Renato Neto, Mitrović, Kums, Saief (Raman 67), Dejaegere (Rafinha 82), Asare, Nielsen, Foket, Milicevic. Coach: Hein Vanhaezebrouck (BEL)

Match 6 - FC Zenit (RUS)
H 2-1 Depoitre (18), Milicevic (78)
Sels, Rafinha, Depoitre (Coulibaly 90+3), Renato Neto, Mitrović, Kums, Asare, Nielsen, Simon (Saief 88), Foket, Milicevic (Dejaegere 82). Coach: Hein Vanhaezebrouck (BEL)

Round of 16 - VfL Wolfsburg (GER)
H 2-3 Kums (80), Coulibaly (89)
Sels, Depoitre (Coulibaly 80), Renato Neto, Mitrović, Kums, Dejaegere, Asare, Nielsen, Simon (Matton 60), Foket, Milicevic (Saief 61). Coach: Hein Vanhaezebrouck (BEL)
A 0-1
Sels, Rafinha (Foket 78), Matton (Saief 68), Renato Neto, Kums, Dejaegere, Asare, Nielsen, Simon (Coulibaly 70), Gershon, Milicevic. Coach: Hein Vanhaezebrouck (BEL)

Club Brugge KV

Third qualifying round - Panathinaikos FC (GRE)
A 1-2 Bolingoli-Mbombo (10)
Bruzzese, De Fauw (Cools 80), Simons, Duarte, Víctor Vázquez (Izquierdo 59), Diaby, Vanaken, Vormer, De Bock, Mechele, Bolingoli-Mbombo (De Sutter 71). Coach: Michel Preud'homme (BEL)
H 3-0 Cools (53), Víctor Vázquez (58), Oularé (82)
Bruzzese, Simons, Duarte, Víctor Vázquez (Vanaken 84), De Sutter (Oularé 77), Diaby, Cools, Vormer, De Bock, Mechele, Dierckx (Bolingoli-Mbombo 66). Coach: Michel Preud'homme (BEL)

Play-offs - Manchester United FC (ENG)
A 1-3 Carrick (80g)
Bruzzese, Simons (Claudemir 40), Duarte, Víctor Vázquez (Vanaken 78), Diaby (Oularé 56), Cools, Vormer, De Bock, Mechele, Dierckx, Bolingoli-Mbombo. Coach: Michel Preud'homme (BEL)
Red card: Mechele 80
H 0-4
Sinan Bolat, De Fauw, Duarte, Castelletto, Claudemir, Víctor Vázquez (Vanaken 62), De Sutter, Diaby (Dierckx 63), Vormer, De Bock, Bolingoli-Mbombo (Cools 77). Coach: Michel Preud'homme (BEL)

Group D
Match 1 - SSC Napoli (ITA)
A 0-5
Sinan Bolat, Simons, Duarte, Víctor Vázquez (De Fauw 69), Diaby (Claudemir 60), Leandro Pereira, Meunier, Vormer, De Bock, Mechele, Bolingoli-Mbombo (Izquierdo 46). Coach: Michel Preud'homme (BEL)

Match 2 - FC Midtjylland (DEN)
H 1-3 Meunier (79)
Bruzzese, De Fauw (Meunier 70), Duarte, Claudemir, Diaby (Vossen 63), Leandro Pereira, Vanaken, Izquierdo (Dierckx 70), Vormer, De Bock, Mechele. Coach: Michel Preud'homme (BEL)

Match 3 - Legia Warszawa (POL)
A 1-1 De Fauw (39)
Bruzzese, De Fauw, Simons, Vossen (Leandro Pereira 80), Diaby (Dierckx 71), Meunier, Vanaken, Izquierdo, Denswil, Mechele, Bolingoli-Mbombo (De Bock 67). Coach: Michel Preud'homme (BEL)

Match 4 - Legia Warszawa (POL)
H 1-0 Meunier (38)
Bruzzese, Simons, Claudemir, Víctor Vázquez (Vanaken 90), Diaby (Bolingoli-Mbombo 82), Leandro Pereira (Vossen 74), Felipe Gedoz, Meunier, Denswil, De Bock, Mechele. Coach: Michel Preud'homme (BEL)

Match 5 - SSC Napoli (ITA)
H 0-1
Bruzzese, De Fauw, Simons (Leandro Pereira 88), Víctor Vázquez (Vanaken 81), Vossen, Felipe Gedoz (Diaby 81), Meunier, Izquierdo, Denswil, Vormer, Mechele. Coach: Michel Preud'homme (BEL)

Match 6 - FC Midtjylland (DEN)
A 1-1 Vossen (68)
Bruzzese, De Fauw, Simons, Vázquez, Vossen, Felipe Gedoz (Refaelov 46), Meunier, Izquierdo (Leandro Pereira 62), Denswil, Vormer, Mechele (Engels 81). Coach: Michel Preud'homme (BEL)

RSC Anderlecht

Group J
Match 1 - AS Monaco FC (FRA)
H 1-1 Gillet (11)
Proto, Deschacht, Najar, Suárez (Acheampong 74), Praet, Defour (Heylen 84), Gillet, Tielemans, Dendoncker, Obradović, Okaka. Coach: Besnik Hasi (ALB)

Match 2 - Qarabağ FK (AZE)
A 0-1
Proto, Deschacht, Mbodji, Najar, Praet (Suárez 72), Defour, Gillet (Tielemans 72), Dendoncker, Obradović (Acheampong 65), Ezekiel, Okaka. Coach: Besnik Hasi (ALB)

Match 3 - Tottenham Hotspur FC (ENG)
H 2-1 Gillet (13), Okaka (75)
Proto, Deschacht, Mbodji, Praet (Conté 90+2), Defour, Gillet, Tielemans, Dendoncker, Obradović, Ezekiel (Acheampong 66), Okaka (Sylla 88). Coach: Besnik Hasi (ALB)

Match 4 - Tottenham Hotspur FC (ENG)
A 1-2 Ezekiel (72)
Proto, Deschacht, Mbodji, Najar, Defour, Acheampong (Sylla 89), N'Sakala (Conté 83), Gillet, Tielemans (Ezekiel 69), Dendoncker, Okaka. Coach: Besnik Hasi (ALB)

Match 5 - AS Monaco FC (FRA)
A 2-0 Gillet (45+1), Acheampong (78)
Proto, Deschacht, Mbodji, Najar (Ezekiel 65), Praet (Acheampong 76), Defour, N'Sakala, Gillet, Tielemans, Dendoncker, Okaka (Suárez 84). Coach: Besnik Hasi (ALB)

Match 6 - Qarabağ FK (AZE)
H 2-1 Najar (28), Okaka (31)
Proto, Deschacht, Mbodji, Najar, Suárez, Praet (Kawaya 90+1), N'Sakala, Gillet, Tielemans, Ezekiel (Lukebakio 66), Okaka (Sylla 81). Coach: Besnik Hasi (ALB)

Round of 32 - Olympiacos FC (GRE)
H 1-0 Mbodji (67)
Proto, Deschacht, Mbodji, Najar, Badji, Praet, Djuričić (Tielemans 74), Defour (Suárez 89), Acheampong, Büttner (Nuytinck 89), Okaka. Coach: Besnik Hasi (ALB)
A 2-1 (aet) Acheampong (102, 111)
Proto, Deschacht, Mbodji, Najar, Badji, Praet, Djuričić (Suárez 82), Acheampong, Büttner (Nuytinck 91), Dendoncker (Defour 97), Okaka. Coach: Besnik Hasi (ALB)

Round of 16 - FC Shakhtar Donetsk (UKR)
A 1-3 Acheampong (69)
Proto, Deschacht, Mbodji, Najar, Badji (Tielemans 74), Suárez (Djuričić 67), Praet (Conté 67), Nuytinck, Defour, Acheampong, Okaka. Coach: Besnik Hasi (ALB)
H 0-1
Proto, Deschacht, Mbodji, Najar, Badji (Tielemans 71), Praet, Nuytinck (Sylla 78), Defour, Acheampong, Ezekiel (Hassan 71), Okaka. Coach: Besnik Hasi (ALB)
Red card: Mbodji 86

DOMESTIC LEAGUE CLUB-BY-CLUB

R. Standard de Liège

Third qualifying round - FK Željezničar (BIH)
H 2-1 *Kosorić (16og), Knockaert (28)*
Thuram-Ulien, Faty, Milec, Knockaert (Yattara 86), Badibanga (Kasmi 67), Scholz, J De Sart (A De Sart 54), Santini, Enoh, Trebel, Van Damme. Coach: Slavoljub Muslin (SRB)
A 1-0 *Van Damme (68)*
Thuram-Ulien, El Messaoudi (J De Sart 59), Faty, Jorge Teixeira, Milec, Knockaert, Badibanga (Andrade 79), Santini (Yattara 70), Enoh, Trebel, Van Damme. Coach: Slavoljub Muslin (SRB)

Play-offs - Molde FK (NOR)
A 0-2
Thuram-Ulien, El Messaoudi (J De Sart 52), Faty, Jorge Teixeira, Milec (Yattara 46), Knockaert, Santini (Badibanga 65), Enoh, Trebel, Andrade, Van Damme. Coach: Slavoljub Muslin (SRB)
H 3-1 *Knockaert (26), Santini (48), Trebel (90+5)*
Thuram-Ulien, Faty, Knockaert, Yattara, Brüls (Legear 74), Santini, Enoh, Trebel, Fiore, Andrade, Van Damme. Coach: Slavoljub Muslin (SRB)

R. Charleroi SC

Second qualifying round - Beitar Jerusalem FC (ISR)
H 5-1 *Pollet (10, 68), Kebano (47, 90+3), Stevance (88)*
Penneteau, Dewaest, Tainmont, Martos, Pollet (Stevance 80), Marinos, Marcq, Saglik (Ferber 89), N'Ganga, Ndongala (François 90+1), Kebano. Coach: Felice Mazzu (BEL)
A 4-1 *Kebano (43), Saglik (53), Ndongala (76), Stevance (90+2)*
Penneteau, Dewaest, Martos, Pollet, Marinos, Galvez-Lopez (Geraerts 57), Marcq, Saglik (Stevance 78), N'Ganga, Ndongala, Kebano (Boulenger 68). Coach: Felice Mazzu (BEL)

Third qualifying round - FC Zorya Luhansk (UKR)
H 0-2
Penneteau, Dewaest, Martos, Stevance (Galvez-Lopez 74), Pollet, Marinos, Marcq, Saglik, N'Ganga, Ndongala (Ferber 79), Kebano. Coach: Felice Mazzu (BEL)
A 0-3
Penneteau, Willems, Boulenger (N'Ganga 57), Dewaest, Pollet, Marinos, Geraerts (Stevance 63), Marcq, Saglik, Ferber (Ndongala 42), Kebano. Coach: Felice Mazzu (BEL)

RSC Anderlecht

1908 • Constant Vanden Stock (28,063) • rsca.be
Major honours
UEFA Cup Winners' Cup (2) 1976, 1978; UEFA Cup (1) 1983; UEFA Super Cup (2) 1976, 1978; Belgian League (33) 1947, 1949, 1950, 1951, 1954, 1955, 1956, 1959, 1962, 1964, 1965, 1966, 1967, 1968, 1972, 1974, 1981, 1985, 1986, 1987, 1991, 1993, 1994, 1995, 2000, 2001, 2004, 2006, 2007, 2010, 2012, 2013, 2014; Belgian Cup (9) 1965, 1972, 1973, 1975, 1976, 1988, 1989, 1994, 2008
Coach: Besnik Hasi (ALB)

2015

26/07	h	Waasland-Beveren	W 3-2	Gillet, Sylla, Tielemans
02/08	a	Leuven	W 2-0	Sylla, Tielemans
09/08	h	Gent	D 1-1	Sylla
16/08	a	Oostende	L 1-3	og (Milić)
23/08	h	Lokeren	W 1-0	Praet
30/08	a	Westerlo	W 3-0	Okaka, Tielemans, Praet
13/09	h	Genk	D 0-0	
20/09	a	Charleroi	D 1-1	Okaka
27/09	h	Sint-Truiden	W 1-0	Okaka
04/10	h	Mechelen	D 1-1	Okaka
18/10	a	Zulte Waregem	W 4-0	Okaka 2, Defour (p), Dendoncker
25/10	h	Club Brugge	W 3-1	Okaka, Ezekiel, Praet
29/10	a	Kortrijk	D 1-1	Ezekiel
01/11	a	Mouscron	W 2-0	Najar 2
08/11	a	Standard	L 0-1	
29/11	h	Leuven	W 3-2	Suárez, Sylla 2
06/12	a	Genk	D 0-0	
13/12	h	Oostende	D 1-1	Suárez
20/12	a	Club Brugge	W 4-1	Okaka, Praet 2, Suárez (p)
23/12	a	Lokeren	D 1-1	Gillet
27/12	h	Westerlo	W 2-1	Okaka, Gillet

2016

17/01	a	Gent	L 0-2	
24/01	h	Charleroi	W 2-1	og (Baby), Okaka
29/01	a	Sint-Truiden	W 2-1	Tielemans (p), Sylla
05/02	a	Mechelen	D 2-2	Acheampong 2
13/02	h	Zulte Waregem	W 3-0	Acheampong, Büttner, Suárez
21/02	a	Waasland-Beveren	L 0-1	
28/02	h	Standard	D 3-3	Suárez, Okaka, Lukebakio
05/03	a	Mouscron	L 1-2	Okaka
13/03	h	Kortrijk	W 3-0	Okaka, Acheampong, Mbodji
03/04	h	Genk	W 1-0	og (Bizot)
10/04	a	Zulte Waregem	W 2-1	Praet, Okaka
17/04	h	Club Brugge	W 1-0	Tielemans
21/04	a	Gent	D 1-1	Nuytinck
24/04	h	Oostende	L 2-4	Defour, Sylla
01/05	h	Gent	W 2-0	Mbodji, Acheampong
08/05	h	Oostende	W 2-1	Tielemans, Okaka
15/05	a	Club Brugge	L 0-4	
19/05	a	Genk	L 2-5	Djuričić, Suárez
22/05	h	Zulte Waregem	W 2-0	Nuytinck, Praet

No	Name	Nat	DoB	Pos	Aps	(s)	Gls
18	Frank Acheampong	GHA	16/10/93	M	21	(7)	5
8	Stéphane Badji	SEN	18/01/90	M	13	(1)	
28	Alexander Büttner	NED	11/02/89	D	14		1
2	Maxime Colin	FRA	15/11/91	D		(1)	
17	Ibrahima Conté	GUI	03/04/91	M	4	(1)	
36	Nathan De Medina		08/10/97	D	2		
16	Steven Defour		15/04/88	M	32		2
32	Leander Dendoncker		15/04/95	M	22	(1)	1
3	Olivier Deschacht		16/02/81	D	28	(4)	
11	Filip Djuričić	SRB	30/01/92	M	11	(6)	1
93	Imoh Ezekiel	NGA	24/10/93	A	11	(9)	2
30	Guillaume Gillet		09/03/84	D	19		3
27	Mahmoud Hassan	EGY	01/10/94	M	1	(6)	
24	Michaël Heylen		03/01/94	D	6	(2)	
38	Andy Kawaya		23/08/96	A		(2)	
35	Aaron Leya Iseka		15/11/97	A		(3)	
46	Dodi Lukebakio		24/09/97	M	3	(14)	1
4	Serigne Mbodji	SEN	11/11/89	D	32		2
21	Fabrice N'Sakala	COD	21/07/90	D	5	(1)	
12	Andy Najar	HON	16/03/93	D	24	(3)	2
14	Bram Nuytinck	NED	04/05/90	D	13	(5)	2
37	Ivan Obradović	SRB	25/07/88	D	13		
99	Stefano Okaka	ITA	09/08/89	A	30	(7)	15
10	Dennis Praet		14/05/94	M	36	(1)	7
1	Silvio Proto		23/05/83	G	40		
2	Rafael Galhardo	BRA	30/10/91	D	1		
9	Matías Suárez	ARG	09/05/88	A	18	(9)	6
26	Idrissa Sylla	GUI	03/12/90	A	10	(20)	7
31	Youri Tielemans		07/05/97	M	29	(5)	6
39	Anthony Vanden Borre		24/10/87	D	2		

R. Charleroi SC

1904 • Pays de Charleroi (22,000) • sporting-charleroi.be

Coach: Felice Mazzu

2015

26/07	h	Mouscron	W	2-1	*Kebano (p), Marcq*
02/08	a	Lokeren	D	2-2	*Ferber, Ndongala*
09/08	h	Club Brugge	D	0-0	
16/08	a	Leuven	L	0-2	
22/08	h	Westerlo	D	0-0	
28/08	a	Genk	L	0-2	
13/09	a	Sint-Truiden	D	1-1	*Perbet*
20/09	h	Anderlecht	D	1-1	*Perbet*
26/09	a	Mechelen	W	1-0	*Perbet*
03/10	h	Zulte Waregem	W	3-0	*Pollet, Ndongala, Saglik*
18/10	a	Kortrijk	L	0-2	
25/10	h	Standard	L	2-3	*Perbet, Baby*
28/10	a	Waasland-Beveren	W	1-0	*Perbet*
31/10	h	Oostende	D	1-1	*Saglik*
08/11	a	Gent	W	3-1	*Perbet 2, og (Nielsen)*
28/11	h	Lokeren	L	1-2	*Ndongala*
06/12	a	Club Brugge	L	1-2	*Ferber*
12/12	h	Leuven	W	2-1	*Dessoleil, Perbet*
19/12	a	Westerlo	L	1-2	*Dessoleil*
22/12	a	Mouscron	W	1-0	*Perbet*
26/12	h	Genk	W	1-0	*Pollet*

2016

16/01	h	Sint-Truiden	D	0-0	
24/01	a	Anderlecht	L	1-2	*Perbet*
30/01	h	Mechelen	W	3-2	*Perbet, Baby, Benavente*
06/02	a	Zulte Waregem	W	3-2	*Pollet, Benavente, Ndongala*
13/02	h	Kortrijk	D	1-1	*Dessoleil*
20/02	a	Standard	L	0-3	
28/02	h	Waasland-Beveren	L	2-3	*Saglik (p), Perbet*
05/03	a	Oostende	L	1-2	*Perbet*
13/03	h	Gent	D	1-1	*Perbet*
02/04	a	Lokeren	L	0-1	
09/04	h	Sint-Truiden	D	1-1	*Baby*
16/04	a	Mechelen	W	3-2	*Perbet, Ndongala, Ninis*
23/04	h	Mechelen	W	4-0	*Ninis (p), Perbet 2, Baby*
30/04	h	Lokeren	D	2-2	*Perbet 2*
07/05	a	Sint-Truiden	W	3-0	*Baby, Ndongala, Perbet*
13/05	h	Kortrijk	W	1-0	*Perbet*
21/05	a	Kortrijk	W	2-1	*Perbet, Baby*
26/05	h	Genk	W	2-0	*Baby, Perbet*
29/05	a	Genk	L	1-5	*Perbet*

No	Name	Nat	DoB	Pos	Aps	(s)	Gls
18	Amara Baby	SEN	23/02/89	M	22	(9)	7
14	Cristian Benavente	PER	19/05/94	M	3	(8)	2
5	Benjamin Boulenger	FRA	01/03/90	D		(1)	
19	Clinton Mata	ANG	07/11/92	A	20	(6)	
24	Dorian Dessoleil		07/08/92	D	22	(2)	3
6	Sebastien Dewaest		27/05/91	D	3		
13	Christophe Diandy	SEN	25/11/90	M	26	(4)	
45	Roman Ferber		29/05/93	A	2	(9)	2
22	Guillaume François		03/06/90	A	1	(3)	
20	Jessy Galvez-Lopez		17/07/95	M		(4)	
23	Karel Geraerts		05/01/82	M	7	(6)	
92	Neeskens Kebano	COD	10/03/92	M	4	(1)	1
35	Parfait Mandanda	COD	10/10/89	G	8	(1)	
25	Damien Marcq	FRA	08/12/88	D	31	(3)	1
17	Stergos Marinos	GRE	17/09/87	D	20		
8	Martos	ESP	04/01/84	M	37		
41	Francis N'Ganga	CGO	16/06/85	D	35	(2)	
88	Dieumerci Ndongala	COD	14/06/91	A	32	(3)	6
29	Sotiris Ninis	GRE	03/04/90	M	9	(4)	2
1	Nicolas Penneteau	FRA	20/02/81	G	32		
21	Jérémy Perbet	FRA	12/12/84	A	32	(1)	24
10	David Pollet		12/08/88	A	18	(16)	3
28	Enes Saglik		08/07/91	M	34	(4)	3
9	Florent Stevance	FRA	08/10/88	A	4	(14)	
7	Clément Tainmont	FRA	12/02/86	M	14	(13)	
3	Steeven Willems	FRA	31/08/90	D	20		
6	Gjoko Zajkov	MKD	10/02/95	D	4	(3)	

Club Brugge KV

1891 • Jan Breydelstadion (29,042) • clubbrugge.be

Major honours

Belgian League (14) 1920, 1973, 1976, 1977, 1978, 1980, 1988, 1990, 1992, 1996, 1998, 2003, 2005, 2016; Belgian Cup (11) 1968, 1970, 1977, 1986, 1991, 1995, 1996, 2002, 2004, 2007, 2015

Coach: Michel Preud'homme

2015

24/07	a	Sint-Truiden	L	1-2	*De Sutter*
01/08	h	Mechelen	W	3-0	*og (Paulussen), Diaby (p), Dierckx*
09/08	a	Charleroi	D	0-0	
14/08	h	Kortrijk	W	2-1	*Vormer, Dierckx*
22/08	a	Zulte Waregem	L	0-2	
30/08	h	Standard	W	7-1	*Diaby 4, Vormer, Oularé, Claudemir*
11/09	a	Mouscron	L	1-2	*Vormer*
20/09	h	Waasland-Beveren	W	5-1	*Dierckx 2, og (Jans), Vossen, De Fauw*
27/09	a	Lokeren	W	1-0	*Vossen*
04/10	a	Gent	L	1-4	*Vormer*
18/10	h	Oostende	W	1-0	*Felipe Gedoz*
25/10	a	Anderlecht	L	1-3	*og (Proto)*
28/10	h	Leuven	W	2-0	*Diaby 2*
31/10	a	Westerlo	W	2-0	*Diaby, Claudemir*
08/11	h	Genk	W	1-0	*Vossen*
21/11	h	Zulte Waregem	W	3-0	*Vossen, Izquierdo, Vormer*
29/11	a	Mechelen	W	4-1	*Vossen 2, Dierckx, Vanaken*
06/12	h	Charleroi	W	2-1	*Vossen, Diaby*
13/12	a	Standard	L	0-2	
20/12	h	Anderlecht	L	1-4	*Denswil*
26/12	a	Kortrijk	W	4-1	*Izquierdo, Vanaken, Diaby, Refaelov*

2016

16/01	h	Mouscron	W	3-0	*Engels, Diaby, Vossen*
24/01	a	Waasland-Beveren	W	2-1	*Engels, Vossen*
31/01	h	Lokeren	W	2-1	*Refaelov 2*
07/02	h	Gent	W	1-0	*Refaelov (p)*
14/02	a	Oostende	W	2-0	*Refaelov, Vanaken*
19/02	h	Westerlo	W	6-0	*Izquierdo, Vanaken 2, Diaby, Wesley, og (Schuermans)*
28/02	a	Genk	L	2-3	*Meunier, Vanaken*
05/03	h	Sint-Truiden	W	3-0	*Simons, Izquierdo, Vossen*
13/03	a	Leuven	W	1-0	*Vossen*
02/04	a	Oostende	W	1-0	*og (Godeau)*
09/04	h	Gent	W	2-0	*og (Mitrović), Izquierdo*
17/04	a	Anderlecht	L	0-1	
20/04	a	Genk	L	2-4	*Vormer, Meunier*
23/04	h	Zulte Waregem	W	5-0	*Vanaken, Izquierdo, Diaby (p), Vossen 2*
01/05	h	Genk	W	3-1	*Denswil, Vormer, Refaelov*
08/05	a	Gent	W	4-1	*Vanaken 2, Izquierdo, og (Gershon)*
15/05	h	Anderlecht	W	4-0	*Diaby 2, Vanaken, Simons*
19/05	a	Zulte Waregem	W	2-0	*Vossen, Wesley*
22/05	h	Oostende	D	2-2	*Diaby, De Bock*

No	Name	Nat	DoB	Pos	Aps	(s)	Gls
30	Mikel Agu	NGA	27/05/93	M	2		
63	Boli Bolingoli-Mbombo		01/07/95	M	8	(6)	
16	Sébastien Bruzzese		01/03/89	G	19		
1	Ludovic Butelle	FRA	03/04/83	G	18		
5	Jean-Charles Castelletto	FRA	26/01/95	D	1	(2)	
6	Claudemir	BRA	27/03/88	M	21	(5)	2
21	Dion Cools		04/06/96	D	5		
43	Sander Coopman		02/08/95	M	3	(2)	
28	Laurens De Bock		07/11/92	D	31		1
2	Davy De Fauw		08/07/81	D	10	(10)	1
9	Tom De Sutter		03/07/85	A	1	(3)	1
24	Stefano Denswil	NED	07/05/93	D	26		2
10	Abdoulay Diaby	MLI	21/05/91	A	24	(8)	16
55	Tuur Dierckx		09/05/95	A	5	(20)	5
4	Óscar Duarte	CRC	03/06/89	D	14		
40	Björn Engels		15/09/94	D	16		2
18	Felipe Gedoz	BRA	12/07/93	M	13	(9)	1
22	José Izquierdo	COL	07/07/92	M	21	(3)	7
17	Leandro Pereira	BRA	13/07/91	A	7	(10)	
44	Brandon Mechele		28/01/93	D	17	(1)	
19	Thomas Meunier		12/09/91	D	30	(1)	2
58	Obbi Oularé		08/01/96	A	4	(2)	1
5	Benoît Poulain	FRA	24/07/87	D	6	(1)	
8	Lior Refaelov	ISR	26/04/86	M	11	(4)	6
3	Timmy Simons		11/12/76	M	33	(1)	2
38	Sinan Bolat	TUR	03/09/88	G	3		
42	Nikola Storm		30/09/94	A		(4)	
20	Hans Vanaken		24/08/92	M	34	(2)	10
7	Víctor Vázquez	ESP	20/01/87	M	10	(4)	
25	Ruud Vormer	NED	11/05/88	M	26	(2)	7
9	Jelle Vossen		22/03/89	A	19	(12)	14
7	Wesley	BRA	26/11/96	A	2	(6)	2

KRC Genk

1988 • Cristal Arena (25,010) • krcgenk.be

Major honours

Belgian League (3) 1999, 2002, 2011; Belgian Cup (4) 1998, 2000, 2009, 2013

Coach: Peter Maes

2015

25/07	h	Leuven	W	3-1	*De Camargo 2, Gorius*
31/08	a	Gent	L	0-1	
07/08	a	Zulte Waregem	D	0-0	
15/08	h	Westerlo	W	2-1	*Buyens, Buffel*
21/08	a	Sint-Truiden	L	1-3	*Buyens (p)*
28/08	h	Charleroi	W	2-0	*Gorius, Dewaest*
13/09	a	Anderlecht	D	0-0	
18/09	h	Mechelen	W	3-1	*De Camargo, Kebano, Buyens*
27/09	a	Kortrijk	L	0-1	
04/10	h	Standard	W	3-1	*Kabasele, De Camargo, Buffel*
17/10	a	Waasland-Beveren	W	1-0	*Buyens (p)*
23/10	h	Mouscron	L	0-4	
27/10	a	Oostende	L	2-3	*Enes, Buffel*
30/10	h	Lokeren	L	0-2	
08/11	a	Club Brugge	L	0-1	
21/11	a	Leuven	W	3-1	*Kebano, Bailey, De Camargo*
28/11	h	Gent	L	0-1	
06/12	h	Anderlecht	D	0-0	
11/12	a	Westerlo	D	0-0	
19/12	h	Sint-Truiden	W	3-0	*Bailey, Kebano (p), Dewaest*
26/12	a	Charleroi	L	0-1	

2016

15/01	h	Zulte Waregem	W	2-1	*Ndidi, Karelis*
23/01	a	Mechelen	D	1-1	*Kabasele*
30/01	h	Kortrijk	W	1-0	*Kabasele*
06/02	a	Mouscron	W	1-0	*Buffel*
13/02	h	Waasland-Beveren	W	6-1	*Karelis 2, Kebano (p), Bailey, Buffel, Kabasele*
20/02	a	Lokeren	D	0-0	
28/02	h	Club Brugge	W	3-2	*Karelis (p), Buffel, Samatta*
05/03	a	Standard	L	1-2	*Karelis*
13/03	h	Oostende	W	4-1	*Samatta, Bailey, Pozuelo, De Camargo*
03/04	a	Anderlecht	L	0-1	
08/04	h	Oostende	W	4-0	*Pozuelo, Buffel, Samatta, Kebano*
16/04	a	Zulte Waregem	W	2-1	*Samatta, og (Baudry)*
20/04	h	Club Brugge	W	4-2	*Ndidi, Pozuelo, og (Meunier), Uronen*
24/04	h	Gent	L	1-2	*Bailey*
01/05	a	Club Brugge	L	1-3	*Karelis*
06/05	h	Zulte Waregem	W	2-0	*Kebano, Ndidi*
15/05	a	Oostende	L	1-2	*Buffel*
19/05	h	Anderlecht	W	5-2	*Bailey, Buffel, Pozuelo, Ndidi, Karelis*
22/05	a	Gent	D	0-0	
26/05	a	Charleroi	L	0-2	
29/05	h	Charleroi	W	5-1	*Karelis 3, Samatta, Walsh*

No	Name	Nat	DoB	Pos	Aps	(s)	Gls
31	Leon Bailey	JAM	09/08/97	A	31	(6)	6
1	Marco Bizot	NED	13/11/91	G	26	(1)	
19	Thomas Buffel		19/02/81	A	38	(2)	9
71	Yoni Buyens		10/03/88	M	19	(11)	4
41	Timothy Castagne		05/12/95	D	21		
17	Aleksandar Čavric	SRB	18/05/94	A		(2)	
21	Sekou Cissé	CIV	23/05/85	A	2		
11	Igor De Camargo		12/05/83	A	17	(13)	6
6	Sebastien Dewaest		27/05/91	D	38		2
9	Enes Ünal	TUR	10/05/97	A	3	(9)	1
39	Pieter Gerkens		17/02/95	M		(2)	
10	Julien Gorius	FRA	17/03/85	M	8	(3)	2
4	Brian Hamalainen	DEN	29/05/89	D	12	(5)	
28	Bryan Heynen		06/02/97	M	5	(5)	
27	Christian Kabasele		24/02/91	D	42		4
7	Nikolaos Karelis	GRE	24/02/92	A	10	(8)	10
92	Neeskens Kebano	COD	10/03/92	M	30	(4)	6
26	László Köteles	HUN	01/09/84	G	16		
18	Ruslan Malinovskiy	UKR	04/05/93	M	9	(4)	
2	Serigne Mbodji	SEN	11/11/89	D	2		
25	Wilfred Ndidi	NGA	16/12/96	D	37	(1)	4
16	Anele Ngcongca	RSA	20/10/87	D		(1)	
7	Tornike Okriashvili	GEO	12/02/92	A	3	(8)	
24	Alejandro Pozuelo	ESP	20/09/91	M	27	(6)	4
77	Mbwana Samatta	TAN	13/12/92	A	10	(8)	5
18	Siebe Schrijvers		18/07/96	A	3	(8)	
3	Katuku Tshimanga		06/11/88	D	18	(1)	
21	Jere Uronen	FIN	13/07/94	D	12		1
5	Sandy Walsh	NED	14/03/95	D	21	(2)	1
15	Dries Wouters		28/01/97	D	1		
8	Bennard Yao Kumordzi	GHA	21/03/85	M	1	(12)	

KAA Gent

1898 • Ghelamco Arena (20,000) • kaagent.be
Major honours
Belgian League (1) 2015; Belgian Cup (3) 1964, 1984, 2010
Coach: Hein Vanhaezebrouck

2015
26/07	a Westerlo	D	1-1	Saief (p)
31/07	h Genk	W	1-0	Kums (p)
09/08	a Anderlecht	D	1-1	Depoitre
16/08	h Sint-Truiden	W	1-0	Depoitre
23/08	a Kortrijk	D	0-0	
29/08	h Mechelen	D	2-2	Depoitre 2
12/09	a Zulte Waregem	D	1-1	Raman (p)
20/09	h Standard	W	4-1	Kums, Milicevic, Matton 2
26/09	a Waasland-Beveren	W	3-1	Mitrović, Matton, Depoitre
04/10	h Club Brugge	W	4-1	Kums 3 (2p), Depoitre
16/10	a Mouscron	W	2-1	og (Oussalah), Kums (p)
24/10	h Oostende	D	2-2	Milicevic, Matton
27/10	a Lokeren	W	2-1	Raman, Renato Neto
31/10	a Leuven	W	2-0	Coulibaly, Dejaegere
08/11	h Charleroi	L	1-3	Saief
20/11	h Westerlo	W	5-0	Coulibaly, Dejaegere, Raman, Kums 2 (1p)
28/11	a Genk	W	1-0	Milicevic
04/12	h Zulte Waregem	D	2-2	Kums (p), Simon
13/12	a Sint-Truiden	W	2-0	Dejaegere, Van der Bruggen
20/12	h Kortrijk	W	3-0	Simon, Kums (p), Milicevic
26/12	a Mechelen	L	0-2	

2016
17/01	h Anderlecht	W	2-0	Depoitre 2
24/01	a Standard	W	3-0	Depoitre, Kums, Dejaegere
31/01	h Waasland-Beveren	W	2-1	Depoitre, Dejaegere
07/02	a Club Brugge	L	0-1	
12/02	h Mouscron	W	2-0	Boussoufa, Milicevic
21/02	a Oostende	L	2-5	Kums (p), Depoitre
26/02	h Lokeren	W	3-1	Renato Neto, Dejaegere, Depoitre
04/03	h Leuven	D	1-1	Boussoufa
13/03	a Charleroi	D	1-1	Dejaegere
01/04	h Zulte Waregem	D	1-1	Kums
09/04	a Club Brugge	L	0-2	
15/04	h Oostende	W	2-0	Matton, Simon
21/04	h Anderlecht	D	1-1	Saief (p)
24/04	a Genk	W	2-1	Depoitre, Renato Neto (p)
01/05	a Anderlecht	L	0-2	
08/05	h Club Brugge	L	1-4	Depoitre
15/05	a Zulte Waregem	L	2-4	Saief (p), Coulibaly
19/05	a Oostende	W	1-0	Coulibaly
22/05	h Genk	D	0-0	

No	Name	Nat	DoB	Pos	Aps	(s)	Gls
21	Nana Asare	GHA	11/07/86	D	34	(1)	
6	Mbark Boussoufa	MAR	15/08/84	M	6	(5)	2
7	Kalifa Coulibaly	MLI	21/08/91	A	10	(14)	4
18	Lucas Deaux	FRA	26/12/88	M	4	(1)	
19	Brecht Dejaegere		29/05/91	M	21	(4)	7
9	Laurent Depoitre		07/12/88	A	33	(2)	14
11	Simon Diedhiou	SEN	10/07/91	A	1	(3)	
4	Abed Hatem Elhamid	ISR	18/03/91	M		(1)	
32	Thomas Foket		25/09/94	M	37	(2)	
55	Rami Gershon	ISR	12/08/88	D	12		
5	Erik Johansson	SWE	30/12/88	D	7	(2)	
14	Sven Kums		26/02/88	M	39		13
8	Thomas Matton		27/10/85	M	9	(7)	5
77	Danijel Milicevic	SUI	05/01/86	M	29	(4)	5
13	Stefan Mitrović	SRB	22/05/90	D	23	(3)	1
23	Lasse Nielsen	DEN	08/01/88	D	38		
28	Nicklas Pedersen	DEN	10/10/87	A		(4)	
12	Marko Poletanović	SRB	20/07/93	M		(3)	
4	Rafinha	BRA	29/06/82	D	12	(5)	
26	Benito Raman		07/11/94	A	9	(4)	3
10	Renato Neto	BRA	27/09/91	M	33	(2)	3
15	Kenny Saief	ISR	17/12/93	M	20	(8)	4
16	Rob Schoofs		23/03/94	M	2	(3)	
1	Matz Sels		26/02/92	G	40		
27	Moses Simon	NGA	12/07/95	A	19	(13)	3
70	Yaya Soumahoro	CIV	28/09/89	A	1	(2)	
22	Serge Tabekou	CMR	15/10/96	M		(1)	
17	Hannes Van der Bruggen		01/04/93	M	1	(11)	1
3	Uroš Vitas	SRB	06/07/92	D		(1)	
22	Gustav Wikheim	NOR	18/03/93	A		(2)	

KV Kortrijk

1971 • Guldensporenstadion (9,500) • kvk.be
Coach: Johan Walem;
(08/02/16) Karim Belhocine (FRA);
(01/04/16) Patrick De Wilde

2015
25/07	h Standard	W	2-1	Chanot 2
01/08	a Waasland-Beveren	L	1-2	Rolland
09/08	h Lokeren	D	0-0	
14/08	a Club Brugge	L	1-2	Papazoglou
23/08	h Gent	D	0-0	
29/08	a Mouscron	W	1-0	Kagé
12/09	h Leuven	D	0-0	
19/09	a Oostende	L	0-1	
27/09	h Genk	W	1-0	De Smet
03/10	a Westerlo	D	1-1	Kiš
18/10	h Charleroi	W	2-0	Papazoglou, Kiš
25/10	a Sint-Truiden	L	1-2	Papazoglou
29/10	h Anderlecht	D	1-1	Marušić
01/11	a Zulte Waregem	D	2-2	Pavlović, Tomašević
07/11	h Mechelen	W	1-0	Tomašević
22/11	a Standard	D	1-1	Papazoglou
28/11	h Waasland-Beveren	W	3-1	Marušić, Papazoglou, De Smet
06/12	a Lokeren	L	1-3	D'Haene
12/12	h Mouscron	L	1-3	Tomašević
20/12	a Gent	L	0-3	
26/12	h Club Brugge	L	1-4	Tomašević

2016
16/01	a Leuven	L	0-1	
22/01	h Oostende	W	2-1	Mercier, Rolland
30/01	a Genk	L	0-1	
06/02	h Westerlo	D	1-1	Rolland
13/02	a Charleroi	D	1-1	Mercier
20/02	h Sint-Truiden	W	3-0	Papazoglou 2, Marušić (p)
27/02	a Mechelen	W	2-0	Tomašević, Rolland
05/03	h Zulte Waregem	W	1-0	Mercier
13/03	a Anderlecht	L	0-3	
02/04	h Mouscron	D	0-0	
10/04	a Standard	D	1-1	Papazoglou
16/04	a Waasland-Beveren	W	3-2	D'Haene, Marušić, Chanot
23/04	h Waasland-Beveren	W	5-0	De Smet, Kagé 2 (1p), Papazoglou, Rolland
30/04	h Standard	W	1-0	Sarr
07/05	a Mouscron	W	3-2	Kagé 2, De Smet
13/05	a Charleroi	L	0-1	
21/05	h Charleroi	L	1-2	Sarr

No	Name	Nat	DoB	Pos	Aps	(s)	Gls
3	Fabien Boyer	FRA	12/04/91	D	9	(4)	
2	Maxime Chanot	LUX	21/11/89	D	35		3
30	Kristof D'Haene		06/06/90	M	14	(10)	2
17	Gertjan De Mets		02/04/87	D	29		
7	Stijn De Smet		27/03/85	A	25	(5)	4
22	Samuel Gigot	FRA	12/10/93	D	24	(4)	
10	Hervé Kagé	COD	10/04/89	A	14	(14)	5
27	Aboubakar Kamara	FRA	07/03/95	A	3	(9)	
16	Darren Keet	RSA	05/08/89	G	30		
44	Tomislav Kiš	CRO	04/04/94	A	9	(8)	2
22	Michael Lallemand		11/02/93	A	1	(5)	
11	Adam Marušić	MNE	17/10/92	M	33	(4)	4
4	Xavier Mercier	FRA	25/07/89	M	10	(3)	3
99	Michael Olaitan	NGA	01/01/93	A	2	(5)	
9	Sakis Papazoglou	GRE	30/03/88	A	30	(6)	9
8	Nebojša Pavlović	SRB	09/04/81	M	25	(2)	1
6	Benoît Poulain	FRA	22/12/86	D	19		
26	Elohim Rolland	FRA	03/03/89	M	27	(4)	5
88	Sidy Sarr	SEN	05/06/96	M	1	(9)	2
13	Mihail Sifakis	GRE	09/09/84	G	8		
33	Marko Tomašević	MNE	22/02/90	D	32		5
23	Baptiste Ulens		24/07/87	M		(1)	
12	Lukas Van Eenoo		06/02/91	M	7	(6)	
31	Anthony Van Loo		05/10/88	D	15	(5)	
5	Birger Verstraete		16/04/94	M	16	(2)	

KSC Lokeren OV

1970 • Daknamstadion (9,271) • sporting.be
Major honours
Belgian Cup (2) 2012, 2014
Coach: Bob Peeters;
(25/10/15) Georges Leekens

2015
25/07	a Zulte Waregem	L	1-3	Patosi
02/08	h Charleroi	D	2-2	Ngolok, Bolbat
09/08	a Kortrijk	D	0-0	
15/08	h Mechelen	W	2-0	Maric, Ansah
23/08	a Anderlecht	L	0-1	
30/08	h Waasland-Beveren	L	1-2	Ngolok
13/09	a Standard	W	1-0	Maric
19/09	h Mouscron	L	1-2	Patosi
27/09	h Club Brugge	L	0-1	
02/10	a Oostende	L	0-2	
17/10	h Leuven	L	1-2	Patosi
24/10	a Westerlo	W	2-1	Ngolok, Mirić
27/10	h Gent	L	1-2	Mirić
30/10	a Genk	W	2-0	Ngolok, Patosi
07/11	h Sint-Truiden	D	1-1	Mirić
28/11	a Charleroi	W	2-1	Ngolok, Mirić
06/12	h Kortrijk	W	3-1	Enoh, Jajá, Patosi
12/12	a Mechelen	D	1-1	Maric
18/12	h Zulte Waregem	D	1-1	Jajá
23/12	h Anderlecht	D	1-1	Bolbat
26/12	a Waasland-Beveren	W	3-2	Patosi, Overmeire, Jajá

2016
17/01	h Standard	L	0-2	
23/01	a Mouscron	D	1-1	Harbaoui
31/01	a Club Brugge	L	1-2	Harbaoui
07/02	h Oostende	L	0-1	
13/02	a Leuven	D	3-3	Ingason, Odoi, Mirić
20/02	h Genk	D	0-0	
26/02	a Gent	L	1-3	Harbaoui
05/03	h Westerlo	W	2-1	Maric, Harbaoui
13/03	a Sint-Truiden	D	1-1	Harbaoui
02/04	h Charleroi	W	1-0	Harbaoui
09/04	a Mechelen	L	1-2	Enoh
16/04	h Sint-Truiden	W	1-0	Ticinović
23/04	a Sint-Truiden	D	2-2	Patosi, Bolbat
30/04	a Charleroi	D	2-2	Harbaoui 2
07/05	h Mechelen	W	5-1	Harbaoui 4, Galitsios

No	Name	Nat	DoB	Pos	Aps	(s)	Gls
18	Besart Abdurahimi	MKD	31/07/90	A	3	(6)	
23	Eugene Ansah	GHA	16/12/94	A	2	(9)	1
1	Boubacar Barry	CIV	30/12/79	G	7		
50	Serhiy Bolbat	UKR	13/06/93	A	16	(7)	3
17	Cyriel Dessers		08/12/94	A	2	(9)	
29	Lewis Enoh	CMR	23/10/92	A	10	(9)	2
11	Georgios Galitsios	GRE	06/07/86	D	10	(1)	1
9	Muhammad Ghadir	ISR	21/01/91	A	6	(2)	
9	Hamdi Harbaoui	TUN	05/01/85	A	16		12
15	Sverrir Ingi Ingason	ISL	05/08/93	D	31	(2)	1
70	Jajá	BRA	28/02/86	A	20		3
30	João Carlos	BRA	01/01/82	D	10		
5	Mijat Maric	SUI	30/04/84	D	22		4
21	Dario Melnjak	CRO	31/10/92	D	3	(6)	
21	Marko Mirić	SRB	26/03/87	A	27	(6)	5
28	Evariste Ngolok		15/11/88	M	12		5
25	Branislav Ninaj	SVK	17/05/94	D	9	(8)	
3	Denis Odoi		27/05/88	D	35		1
7	Killian Overmeire		06/12/85	M	34		1
10	Ayanda Patosi	RSA	31/10/92	A	29	(4)	7
8	Koen Persoons		12/07/83	M	13		
20	Joher Rassoul	SEN	31/12/95	M	9	(4)	
34	Filip Starzyński	POL	27/05/91	M	5	(4)	
14	Mehdi Terki	ALG	27/09/91	M	6	(4)	
19	Mario Ticinović	CRO	20/08/91	D	23	(8)	1
13	Davino Verhulst		25/11/87	G	29	(1)	

BELGIUM

KV Mechelen

1904 • Veolia Stadion (13,123) • kvmechelen.be

Major honours

UEFA Cup Winners' Cup (1) 1988; UEFA Super Cup (1) 1989; Belgian League (4) 1943, 1946, 1948, 1989; Belgian Cup (1) 1987

Coach: Aleksandar Janković (SRB)

2015					
25/07	a	Oostende	L	1-3	*Van Damme*
01/08	a	Club Brugge	L	0-3	
08/08	h	Mouscron	W	3-1	*Veselinović, Kosanović, Claes*
15/08	a	Lokeren	L	0-2	
22/08	h	Leuven	W	2-1	*Verdier, Kosanović (p)*
29/08	a	Gent	D	2-2	*Veselinović, Rits*
12/09	h	Westerlo	D	2-2	*Verdier, De Witte*
18/09	a	Genk	L	1-3	*Kosanović (p)*
26/09	h	Charleroi	L	0-1	
04/10	a	Anderlecht	D	1-1	*og (Mbodji)*
17/10	h	Sint-Truiden	W	3-0	*Kosanović (p), Matthys, Hanni*
24/10	h	Zulte Waregem	L	3-4	*De Petter, Hanni 2*
28/10	a	Standard	L	1-2	*Kosanović*
31/10	h	Waasland-Beveren	W	2-0	*Hanni, Matthys*
07/11	a	Kortrijk	L	0-1	
22/11	h	Oostende	W	2-1	*Hanni, Van Damme*
29/11	h	Club Brugge	L	1-4	*Naessens*
05/12	a	Mouscron	W	3-2	*Matthys, Hanni, Verdier*
12/12	h	Lokeren	D	1-1	*Hanni*
19/12	a	Leuven	L	1-3	*Hanni*
26/12	h	Gent	W	2-0	*Hanni, Matthys*
2016					
16/01	a	Westerlo	L	2-3	*Cocalić, Hanni*
23/01	h	Genk	D	1-1	*De Petter*
30/01	a	Charleroi	L	2-3	*Verdier, Matthys (p)*
05/02	h	Anderlecht	D	2-2	*Rits, Verdier*
14/02	a	Sint-Truiden	W	3-0	*De Petter, Hanni, Claes*
21/02	a	Zulte Waregem	W	3-2	*Verdier, Rits, Hanni*
27/02	h	Kortrijk	L	0-2	
05/03	a	Waasland-Beveren	D	0-0	
13/03	h	Standard	W	4-0	*Hanni 2, Verdier 2*
02/04	a	Sint-Truiden	W	1-0	*Matthys*
09/04	h	Lokeren	W	2-1	*Rits, Hanni*
16/04	h	Charleroi	L	2-3	*Hanni 2 (1p)*
23/04	a	Charleroi	L	0-4	
30/04	h	Sint-Truiden	D	1-1	*De Petter*
07/05	a	Lokeren	L	1-5	*De Petter*

No	Name	Nat	DoB	Pos	Aps	(s)	Gls
6	Sheldon Bateau	TRI	29/01/91	D	1	(1)	
17	Nassim Ben Khalifa	SUI	13/01/92	A		(7)	
16	Aleksandar Bjelica	SRB	07/01/94	D	13		
14	Xavier Chen	TPE	05/10/83	D	2	(2)	
44	Ibrahima Cissé		28/02/94	M	14	(1)	
77	Glen Claes		08/03/94	M	22	(11)	2
15	Edin Cocalić	BIH	05/12/87	D	22	(2)	1
18	Alexander Corryn		03/01/94	D		(1)	
6	Ljuban Crepulja	CRO	02/09/93	M		(4)	
12	Steven De Petter		22/11/85	M	23	(5)	5
4	Seth De Witte		18/10/87	D	27	(1)	1
33	Ahmed El Messaoudi	MAR	03/08/95	D	2	(3)	
1	Jean-François Gillet		31/05/79	G	35		
94	Sofiane Hanni	ALG	29/12/90	M	32	(3)	17
33	Miloš Kosanović	SRB	28/05/90	D	20		5
8	Randall Leal	CRC	14/01/97	M	1	(10)	
7	Tim Matthys		23/12/83	M	25	(1)	6
49	Anthony Moris	LUX	29/04/90	G	1		
17	Jens Naessens		01/04/91	M	9	(9)	1
2	Laurens Paulussen		19/07/90	D	28	(2)	
11	Mats Rits		18/07/93	M	25	(3)	4
5	Mourad Satli	FRA	29/01/90	D	1	(3)	
20	Joachim Van Damme		23/07/91	M	10	(4)	2
30	Jordi Vanlerberghe		27/03/96	M	7	(9)	
99	Nicolas Verdier	FRA	17/01/87	A	31	(2)	8
9	Dalibor Veselinović	SRB	21/09/87	A	16	(13)	2
23	Uroš Vitas	SRB	28/09/92	D	11		
3	Vladimir Volkov	MNE	06/06/86	D	13		
10	Rafał Wolski	POL	10/11/92	M	5	(6)	

R. Excel Mouscron

2010 • Le Canonnier (10,570) • rmp-foot.be

Coach: Cedomir Janevski (MKD); (20/01/16) Glen De Boeck

2015					
26/07	a	Charleroi	L	1-2	*Peyre*
01/08	h	Sint-Truiden	L	0-2	
08/08	a	Mechelen	L	1-3	*Dingomé*
15/08	h	Standard	D	1-1	*Peyre*
22/08	a	Waasland-Beveren	D	3-3	*Michel, Mézague, Šćepović*
29/08	h	Kortrijk	L	0-1	
11/09	h	Club Brugge	W	2-1	*Dussenne, Šćepović*
19/09	a	Lokeren	W	2-1	*og (Ingason), Dussenne*
26/09	h	Oostende	D	2-2	*Dussenne, Šćepović*
03/10	a	Leuven	D	1-1	*Michel (p)*
16/10	h	Gent	L	1-2	*Dussenne*
23/10	a	Genk	W	4-0	*Tózé Marreco, Badri, Vaccaro, Mohamed*
27/10	h	Westerlo	D	2-2	*Aksentijević, og (Schuermans)*
01/11	a	Anderlecht	L	0-2	
06/11	h	Zulte Waregem	D	2-2	*Hubert, Vaccaro*
28/11	a	Sint-Truiden	W	1-0	*Badri*
05/12	h	Mechelen	L	2-3	*og (Verdier), Marković*
12/12	a	Kortrijk	W	3-1	*Šćepović 2, Marković*
19/12	h	Waasland-Beveren	L	0-1	
22/12	h	Charleroi	L	0-1	
27/12	a	Standard	L	0-3	
2016					
16/01	a	Club Brugge	L	0-3	
23/01	h	Lokeren	D	1-1	*Mulić*
31/01	a	Oostende	D	3-3	*Dussenne, Viola, Marković*
06/02	h	Genk	L	0-1	
12/02	a	Gent	L	0-2	
20/02	h	Leuven	W	3-1	*Coulibaly, Badri 2*
27/02	a	Westerlo	D	2-2	*Dussenne, Oussalah*
05/03	h	Anderlecht	W	2-1	*Hubert, Badri*
13/03	a	Zulte Waregem	L	0-3	
02/04	a	Kortrijk	D	0-0	
09/04	h	Waasland-Beveren	D	0-0	
17/04	h	Standard	W	2-0	*Hubert, Šćepović*
22/04	a	Standard	L	1-4	*Marković*
30/04	a	Waasland-Beveren	L	0-1	
07/05	h	Kortrijk	L	2-3	*Michel 2*

No	Name	Nat	DoB	Pos	Aps	(s)	Gls
13	Nikola Aksentijević	SRB	09/03/93	D	14	(5)	1
21	Selim Amallah		15/11/96	M		(3)	
9	Anice Badri	FRA	18/09/90	M	16	(7)	5
7	Yahya Boumediene		23/05/90	A	3	(3)	
15	Jean-Charles Castelletto	FRA	26/01/95	D	9	(1)	
17	Elimane Coulibaly	SEN	15/03/80	A	8	(1)	1
15	Emir Dautovič	SVN	05/02/95	D	2		
33	Théo Defourny		25/04/92	G	1		
19	Tristan Dingomé	FRA	17/02/91	M	16	(2)	1
3	Noë Dussenne		07/04/92	D	34		6
27	Frédéric Maciel	POR	15/03/94	A	7	(8)	
24	Nikola Gulan	SRB	23/03/89	D	14	(1)	
22	Jérémy Houzé		28/10/96	M		(1)	
5	David Hubert		12/08/88	M	26		3
17	Marin Jakoliš	CRO	26/12/96	A	1	(10)	
14	Corentin Kocur		17/10/95	M	3		
55	Cristian Manea	ROU	09/08/97	D	6	(1)	
1	Ofir Marciano	ISR	07/10/89	G	6		
18	Filip Marković	SRB	03/03/92	M	23	(8)	4
8	François Marquet		17/04/95	M	23	(3)	
6	Teddy Mézague	FRA	27/05/90	D	33	(1)	1
10	Julian Michel	FRA	19/02/92	M	24	(4)	4
11	Dimitri Mohamed	FRA	11/06/89	M	12	(4)	1
5	Pieter-Jan Monteyne		01/01/83	D	2		
45	Fejsal Mulić	SRB	03/10/94	A	1	(4)	1
7	Melvin Neves		23/02/96	M		(1)	
98	Fabrice Olinga	CMR	12/05/96	A	1	(6)	
25	Mustapha Oussalah	MAR	19/02/82	M	23	(4)	1
30	Marko Pavlovski	SRB	07/02/94	M		(2)	
29	Thibault Peyre	FRA	03/10/92	D	12		2
44	Marko Šćepović	SRB	23/05/91	A	21	(3)	6
34	Kevin Tapoko	FRA	13/04/94	M	1		
23	Mickaël Tirpan		23/10/93	D	9	(2)	
90	Tózé Marreco	POR	25/07/87	A	3	(4)	1
26	Luigi Vaccaro		26/03/91	M	8	(11)	2
86	Vagner	BRA	06/06/86	G	29		
90	Benjamin Van Durmen		20/03/97	M		(1)	
16	Valentín Viola	ARG	28/08/91	A	5	(4)	1

KV Oostende

1981 • Albertparkstadion (8,125) • kvo.be

Coach: Yves Vanderhaeghe

2015					
25/07	h	Mechelen	W	3-1	*Jonckheere, Fernando Canesin, Siani*
01/08	h	Westerlo	W	2-1	*Musona, Lukaku*
08/08	a	Sint-Truiden	D	1-1	*Akpala*
16/08	h	Anderlecht	W	3-1	*Musona 2 (1p), Cyriac*
23/08	a	Standard	W	2-1	*Akpala, Musona*
29/08	h	Zulte Waregem	L	0-2	
12/09	a	Waasland-Beveren	W	5-1	*Akpala, Cyriac 3 (1p), Godwin*
19/09	h	Kortrijk	W	1-0	*Cyriac*
26/09	a	Mouscron	D	2-2	*og (Dussenne), Cyriac (p)*
02/10	h	Lokeren	W	2-0	*Cyriac, Fernando Canesin*
18/10	a	Club Brugge	L	0-1	
24/10	a	Gent	D	2-2	*Vandendriessche, Siani*
27/10	h	Genk	W	3-2	*Fernando Canesin 2, Cyriac*
31/10	a	Charleroi	D	1-1	*Cyriac*
07/11	h	Leuven	W	3-0	*Vandendriessche, Musona, Cyriac*
22/11	a	Mechelen	L	1-2	*Musona (p)*
29/11	a	Westerlo	W	1-0	*Akpala*
05/12	h	Sint-Truiden	L	1-2	*Vandendriessche*
13/12	a	Anderlecht	D	1-1	*Berrier*
20/12	h	Standard	W	4-1	*Berrier, Musona 2, Fernando Canesin*
27/12	a	Zulte Waregem	L	0-1	
2016					
17/01	h	Waasland-Beveren	D	3-3	*Akpala, Fernando Canesin, Musona*
22/01	a	Kortrijk	L	1-2	*Fernando Canesin*
31/01	h	Mouscron	D	3-3	*Cyriac (p), Musona, Lukaku*
07/02	a	Lokeren	W	1-0	*Jali*
14/02	h	Club Brugge	L	0-2	
21/02	h	Gent	W	5-2	*Jonckheere 2, Milić, Musona, El Ghanassy*
27/02	a	Leuven	L	1-4	*Milić*
05/03	h	Charleroi	W	2-1	*Cyriac 2 (1p)*
13/03	a	Genk	L	1-4	*Siani*
02/04	h	Club Brugge	L	0-1	
08/04	a	Genk	L	0-4	
15/04	a	Gent	L	0-2	
19/04	h	Zulte Waregem	D	3-3	*El Ghanassy, Akpala, Berrier (p)*
24/04	h	Anderlecht	W	4-2	*Akpala, Fernando Canesin, El Ghanassy 2*
29/04	a	Zulte Waregem	W	2-1	*El Ghanassy, Musona*
08/05	a	Anderlecht	L	1-2	*Godeau*
15/05	h	Genk	W	2-1	*Musona, Lukaku*
19/05	h	Gent	L	0-1	
22/05	a	Club Brugge	D	2-2	*Cyriac, Jonckheere*

No	Name	Nat	DoB	Pos	Aps	(s)	Gls
17	Joseph Akpala	NGA	24/08/86	A	20	(15)	7
4	Fabien Antunes	FRA	19/11/91	D	1	(6)	
27	Franck Berrier	FRA	02/02/84	M	25	(9)	3
25	Wouter Biebauw		21/05/84	G	10	(1)	
13	Frédéric Brillant	FRA	26/05/85	D	7	(4)	
27	Brecht Capon		24/04/88	D	29	(1)	
24	Mathieu Cornet		08/08/90	A		(1)	
16	Elimane Coulibaly	SEN	15/03/80	A		(1)	
9	Cyriac	CIV	15/08/90	A	23	(10)	14
3	Niels De Schutter		08/08/88	D	2	(3)	
8	Yassine El Ghanassy		12/07/90	M	8	(7)	5
55	Fernando Canesin	BRA	27/02/92	M	34	(2)	8
31	Bruno Godeau		10/05/92	D	12	(1)	1
30	Saviour Godwin	NGA	22/08/96	A		(6)	1
15	Andile Jali	RSA	10/04/90	M	30	(5)	1
20	Michiel Jonckheere		03/01/90	M	13	(16)	4
90	Yannick Loemba		21/04/90	A		(8)	
2	Xavier Luissint	FRA	13/01/84	D		(2)	
5	Jordan Lukaku		25/07/94	D	34		3
44	Antonio Milić	CRO	10/03/94	D	31	(2)	2
11	Knowledge Musona	ZIM	21/06/90	A	28	(7)	13
1	Didier Ovono	GAB	23/01/83	G	30		
19	Nicklas Pedersen	DEN	10/10/87	A	1	(6)	
14	David Rozehnal	CZE	05/07/80	D	36		
7	Sébastien Siani	CMR	21/12/86	M	37	(1)	3
26	Kevin Vandendriessche	FRA	07/08/89	M	29	(5)	3

242 | The European Football Yearbook 2016/17

Oud-Heverlee Leuven

2002 • Den Dreef (8,700) • ohl.be

Coach: Jacky Mathijssen; (26/10/15) Emilio Ferrera

2015

25/07	a Genk	L	1-3	*Kostovski*
02/08	h Anderlecht	L	0-2	
08/08	a Westerlo	L	2-3	*Kostovski 2*
16/08	h Charleroi	W	2-0	*Bostock, Trossard*
22/08	a Mechelen	L	1-2	*Houdret*
29/08	h Sint-Truiden	W	1-0	*Trossard*
12/09	a Kortrijk	D	0-0	
19/09	h Zulte Waregem	L	2-3	*Cerigioni, Trossard*
26/09	a Standard	D	2-2	*Croizet, Remacle*
03/10	h Mouscron	D	1-1	*Bostock (p)*
17/10	a Lokeren	W	2-1	*Croizet 2*
24/10	h Waasland-Beveren	L	0-2	
28/10	a Club Brugge	L	0-2	
31/10	h Gent	L	0-2	
07/11	a Oostende	L	0-3	
21/11	h Genk	L	1-3	*Cerigioni*
29/11	a Anderlecht	L	2-3	*Croizet, Trossard*
05/12	h Westerlo	W	5-1	*Kostovski 2, Bostock, Remacle, Trossard*
12/12	a Charleroi	L	1-2	*Remacle*
19/12	h Mechelen	W	3-1	*Croizet, Cerigioni, Bostock (p)*
26/12	a Sint-Truiden	D	2-2	*Asamoah, Ngawa*

2016

16/01	h Kortrijk	W	1-0	*Kostovski*
23/01	a Zulte Waregem	D	2-2	*Croizet, Azevedo*
30/01	h Standard	L	0-2	
06/02	a Waasland-Beveren	D	2-2	*Croizet, Trossard*
13/02	h Lokeren	D	3-3	*Kanu, Ojo, Bostock (p)*
20/02	a Mouscron	L	1-3	*Trossard*
27/02	h Oostende	W	4-1	*Bostock 2 (1p), Croizet 2*
04/03	a Gent	D	1-1	*Trossard*
13/03	h Club Brugge	L	0-1	

No	Name	Nat	DoB	Pos	Aps	(s)	Gls
22	Samuel Asamoah	GHA	22/03/94	M	8	(9)	1
14	Thomas Azevedo		31/08/91	M	2	(14)	1
15	John Bostock	ENG	15/01/92	M	24	(1)	7
11	Alessandro Cerigioni		30/09/92	A	9	(10)	3
10	Yohan Croizet	FRA	15/02/92	M	26	(2)	9
24	Nicolas Delporte		30/12/93	D	3	(1)	
12	Kenneth Houdret		09/08/93	M	8	(12)	1
25	Kanu	BRA	03/05/84	D	7		1
23	Jovan Kostovski	MKD	19/04/87	A	11	(4)	6
8	Flavien Le Postollec	FRA	19/02/84	M	28		
1	Yves Lenaerts		27/02/83	G	1	(1)	
29	Pieter-Jan Monteyne		01/01/83	D	25		
5	Pierre-Yves Ngawa		09/02/92	D	25		1
27	Kim Ojo	NGA	02/12/88	A	8	(4)	1
9	Romero Regales	CUW	07/11/86	A	4	(8)	
7	Jordan Remacle		14/02/87	M	27	(1)	3
4	Romain Reynaud	FRA	02/03/83	D	25		
26	Rudy Riou	FRA	22/01/80	G	29		
16	Konstantinos Rougalas	GRE	13/10/93	D	17		
20	Din Sula		02/03/98	A	1		
24	Kevin Tapoko	FRA	13/04/94	M	3	(2)	
19	Leandro Trossard		04/12/94	M	22	(8)	8
17	Slobodan Urošević	SRB	15/04/94	D		(2)	
3	David Vandenbroeck		12/07/85	D	3	(2)	
28	Olexandr Volovyk	UKR	28/10/85	D	14		

K. Sint-Truidense VV

1924 • Stayen (14,600) • stvv.com

Coach: Yannick Ferrera; (08/09/15) Chris O'Loughlin (NIR)

2015

24/07	h Club Brugge	W	2-1	*Rúben Fernandes, Edmilson Junior*
01/08	a Mouscron	W	2-0	*Mbombo, Boli*
08/08	h Oostende	D	1-1	*Edmilson Junior*
16/08	a Gent	L	0-1	
21/08	h Genk	W	3-1	*Edmilson Junior, Mbombo, Dompé*
29/08	a Leuven	L	0-1	
13/09	h Charleroi	D	1-1	*Schoofs*
19/09	a Westerlo	W	3-0	*og (Schuermans), Boli, Rúben Fernandes*
27/09	a Anderlecht	L	0-1	
03/10	h Waasland-Beveren	L	1-3	*Schoofs*
17/10	a Mechelen	L	0-3	
25/10	h Kortrijk	W	2-1	*Boli 2*
28/10	a Zulte Waregem	L	0-4	
01/11	h Standard	W	1-0	*Edmilson Junior*
07/11	a Lokeren	D	1-1	*Dutoît*
21/11	a Waasland-Beveren	L	1-2	*Cuevas*
28/11	h Mouscron	L	0-1	
05/12	a Oostende	W	2-1	*Tchité, Edmilson Junior (p)*
12/12	h Gent	L	0-2	
19/12	a Genk	L	0-3	
26/12	h Leuven	D	2-2	*Hendrickx, Mahlangu*

2016

16/01	a Charleroi	D	0-0	
23/01	h Westerlo	L	1-2	*Mahlangu*
30/01	h Anderlecht	L	1-2	*Rúben Fernandes*
07/02	a Standard	W	2-1	*Proschwitz 2*
14/02	h Mechelen	L	0-3	
20/02	a Kortrijk	L	0-3	
27/02	h Zulte Waregem	L	1-2	*Proschwitz*
05/03	a Club Brugge	L	0-3	
13/03	h Lokeren	D	1-1	*Boli*
02/04	h Mechelen	L	0-1	
09/04	a Charleroi	D	1-1	*Kotysch*
16/04	a Lokeren	L	0-1	
23/04	h Lokeren	D	2-2	*Raman, Gerkens*
30/04	a Mechelen	D	1-1	*Gerkens*
07/05	h Charleroi	L	0-3	

No	Name	Nat	DoB	Pos	Aps	(s)	Gls
22	Allan	BRA	03/03/97	M	6	(3)	
29	Victorien Angban	CIV	29/09/96	M	20	(3)	
5	Alfonso Artabe	ESP	18/08/88	M	7	(1)	
18	Mamadou Bagayoko	CIV	31/12/89	D	26	(1)	
4	Pierre-Baptiste Baherlé	FRA	07/07/91	M		(2)	
11	Yohan Boli	FRA	17/11/93	A	8	(8)	5
30	Alessio Castro Montes		17/05/97	M		(1)	
15	Cristian Cuevas	CHI	02/04/95	D	26	(2)	1
7	Casper De Norre		07/02/97	M		(2)	
5	Alexis De Sart		12/11/96	M	4	(2)	
1	Yves De Winter		25/08/87	G	3	(1)	
10	Jean-Luc Dompé	FRA	12/08/95	M	10	(3)	1
20	Damien Dussaut	FRA	08/11/94	D	9	(3)	
28	William Dutoît	FRA	18/09/88	G	32		1
22	Edmilson Junior		19/08/94	A	19		5
19	Yvan Erichot	FRA	25/03/90	D	30		
14	Pieter Gerkens		17/02/95	M	12		2
6	Gaëtan Hendrickx		30/03/95	M	8	(6)	1
23	Sascha Kotysch	GER	02/10/88	M	8	(1)	1
29	Panagiotis Kynigopoulos	GRE	24/09/96	A		(1)	
7	Mehdi Lazaar		09/03/93	M		(5)	
4	May Mahlangu	RSA	01/05/89	M	17	(1)	2
9	Yannis Mbombo		08/04/94	A	7	(2)	2
20	Hilaire Momi	CTA	16/03/90	A		(9)	
24	Salomon Nirisarike	RWA	23/03/93	D	6	(4)	
25	Yuji Ono	JPN	22/12/92	M	19	(7)	
33	Nick Proschwitz	GER	28/11/86	A	12		3
9	Benito Raman		07/11/94	A	8	(2)	1
14	Jordan Renson		14/05/96	D		(1)	
8	Faycal Rherras	MAR	07/04/93	D	26	(2)	
30	Joao Rodríguez	COL	19/05/96	A	1	(9)	
26	Rúben Fernandes	POR	06/05/86	D	26		3
21	Mathias Schils		01/05/93	M	4	(4)	
16	Rob Schoofs		23/03/94	M	23		2
12	Yaya Soumahoro	CIV	28/09/89	M	3	(2)	
27	Iebe Swers		27/12/96	M	5		
7	Fabien Tchenkoua	CMR	01/10/92	M	3	(5)	
10	Mohamed Tchité		31/01/84	A	7	(5)	1
13	Emil Velič	SVN	06/02/95	G	1		
2	Reno Wilmots		16/03/97	M		(2)	

R. Standard de Liège

1898 • Maurice Dufrasne (27,500) • standard.be

Major honours
Belgian League (10) 1958, 1961, 1963, 1969, 1970, 1971, 1982, 1983, 2008, 2009; Belgian Cup (7) 1954, 1966, 1967, 1981, 1993, 2011, 2016

Coach: Slavoljub Muslin (SRB); (28/08/15) (Éric Deflandre) (07/09/15) Yannick Ferrera

2015

25/07	a Kortrijk	L	1-2	*Knockaert (p)*
02/08	h Zulte Waregem	W	2-1	*Enoh, Santini*
08/08	h Waasland-Beveren	W	1-0	*Faty*
15/08	a Mouscron	D	1-1	*Knockaert*
23/08	h Oostende	L	1-2	*Brüls*
30/08	a Club Brugge	L	1-7	*Santini*
13/09	h Lokeren	L	0-1	
20/09	a Gent	L	1-4	*Knockaert*
26/09	h Leuven	D	2-2	*Emond, Santini*
04/10	a Genk	L	1-3	*Knockaert*
17/10	h Westerlo	L	1-2	*Tetteh*
25/10	a Charleroi	W	3-2	*Arslanagic, Van Damme, Emond*
28/10	h Mechelen	W	2-1	*Knockaert, Yattara*
01/11	a Sint-Truiden	L	0-1	
08/11	h Anderlecht	W	1-0	*Legear*
22/11	h Kortrijk	D	1-1	*Santini*
27/11	a Zulte Waregem	W	3-2	*og (Bossut), Jorge Teixeira, Dossevi*
05/12	a Waasland-Beveren	D	0-0	
13/12	h Club Brugge	W	2-0	*Van Damme, Dossevi*
20/12	a Oostende	L	1-4	*Milec*
27/12	h Mouscron	W	3-0	*Badibanga, Dossevi, Santini*

2016

17/01	a Lokeren	W	2-0	*Santini 2*
24/01	h Gent	L	0-3	
30/01	a Leuven	W	2-0	*Dossevi, Boschilia*
07/02	h Sint-Truiden	L	1-2	*Edmilson Junior*
14/02	a Westerlo	L	0-2	
20/02	h Charleroi	W	3-0	*Santini, Trebel, Dossevi*
28/02	a Anderlecht	D	3-3	*Santini, Kosanović, Edmilson Junior*
05/03	h Genk	W	2-1	*Santini, Dompé*
13/03	a Mechelen	L	0-4	
02/04	a Waasland-Beveren	W	1-0	*Legear*
10/04	h Kortrijk	D	1-1	*Maniatis (p)*
17/04	a Mouscron	L	0-2	
22/04	h Mouscron	W	4-1	*Miya, Maniatis, Boschilia, Tetteh*
30/04	a Kortrijk	L	0-1	
07/05	h Waasland-Beveren	W	2-0	*Santini, Edmilson Junior*

No	Name	Nat	DoB	Pos	Aps	(s)	Gls
35	Achraf Achaoui	MAR	10/12/96	D	1		
27	Darwin Andrade	COL	11/02/91	D	14	(2)	
36	Dino Arslanagic		24/04/93	D	16	(5)	1
12	Beni Badibanga		12/02/96	A	12	(11)	1
8	Boschilia	BRA	05/03/96	M	7	(3)	2
14	Christian Brüls		30/09/88	M	5	(5)	1
29	Hugo Cuypers		07/02/97	A		(1)	
15	Julien De Sart		23/12/94	M	7	(5)	
6	Jérôme Deom		19/04/99	M		(1)	
10	Jean-Luc Dompé	FRA	12/08/95	M	5	(3)	1
17	Mathieu Dossevi	TOG	12/02/88	M	25	(1)	5
19	Damien Dussaut	FRA	08/11/94	D	1		
22	Edmilson Junior		19/08/94	A	10	(1)	3
3	Ahmed El Messaoudi	MAR	03/08/95	D		(1)	
9	Renaud Emond		05/12/91	A	7	(14)	2
21	Eyong Enoh	CMR	23/03/86	M	14	(2)	1
32	Collins Fai	CMR	13/08/92	D	7		
4	Ricardo Faty	SEN	04/08/86	M	5		1
24	Corentin Fiore		24/03/95	D	16	(6)	
98	Fadel Gobitaka		16/01/98	M		(3)	
2	Réginal Goreux	HAI	31/12/87	D	17		
28	Guillaume Hubert		11/01/94	G	18		
5	Jorge Teixeira	POR	27/08/86	D	15	(1)	1
8	Faysel Kasmi		31/10/95	M	3	(1)	
7	Anthony Knockaert	FRA	20/11/91	M	19	(2)	5
33	Miloš Kosanović	SRB	28/05/90	D	14		1
30	Jonathan Legear		13/04/87	M	6	(4)	2
7	Ioannis Maniatis	GRE	12/10/86	M	5	(2)	2
6	Martin Milec	SVN	20/09/91	D	10	(2)	1
15	Faruka Miya	UGA	26/11/97	A	3	(1)	1
97	Ryan Mmaee A Nwambeben		01/04/97	A	2	(4)	
20	Samy Mmaee A Nwambeben		08/09/96	D	3		
77	Jonathan Okita		05/10/95	A	2		
44	Martin Remacle		16/05/97	M	2	(1)	
25	Rochinha	POR	03/05/95	M		(2)	
18	Ivan Santini	CRO	21/05/89	A	19	(8)	11
13	Alexander Scholz	DEN	24/10/92	D	15		
11	Benjamin Tetteh	GHA	10/07/97	A	6	(8)	2
16	Yohann Thuram-Ulien	FRA	31/10/88	G	12		
23	Adrien Trebel	FRA	03/03/91	M	30		1
37	Jelle Van Damme		10/10/83	M	17		2
1	Víctor Valdés	ESP	14/01/82	G	6		
60	Sambou Yatabaré	MLI	02/03/89	M	12	(1)	
10	Mohammed Yattara	GUI	28/07/93	A	8	(4)	1

 **BELGIUM**

Waasland-Beveren

2010 • Freethiel (12,930) •
waasland-beveren.be
Coach: Stijn Vreven

2015
26/07	a	Anderlecht	L 2-3	Langil, Vanzo
01/08	h	Kortrijk	W 2-1	Emond, Gano
08/08	a	Standard	L 0-1	
15/08	h	Zulte Waregem	W 2-1	Myny, Gano
22/08	h	Mouscron	D 3-3	Langil 2, Gano
30/08	a	Lokeren	W 2-1	Emond, Langil
12/09	h	Oostende	L 1-5	Langil
20/09	a	Club Brugge	L 1-5	Milošević
26/09	h	Gent	L 1-3	Milošević
03/10	a	Sint-Truiden	W 3-1	Milošević, Gano, Myny
17/10	h	Genk	L 0-1	
24/10	a	Leuven	W 2-0	Marić (p), Jans
28/10	h	Charleroi	L 0-1	
31/10	h	Mechelen	L 0-2	
07/11	h	Westerlo	D 2-2	Langil, Gano
21/11	h	Sint-Truiden	W 2-1	Gano, M'Sila
28/11	a	Kortrijk	L 1-3	Gano
05/12	h	Standard	D 0-0	
12/12	a	Zulte Waregem	L 1-2	Marić
19/12	a	Mouscron	W 1-0	Myny
26/12	h	Lokeren	L 2-3	Gano, Milošević

2016
17/01	a	Oostende	D 3-3	Schrijvers 2, Moulin (p)
24/01	h	Club Brugge	L 1-2	Cissé
31/01	a	Gent	L 1-2	Buatu
06/02	h	Leuven	D 2-2	Gano, Schrijvers
13/02	a	Genk	L 1-6	Gano
21/02	h	Anderlecht	W 1-0	Vanzo
28/02	a	Charleroi	W 3-2	Moulin 2 (2p), Nabab
05/03	h	Mechelen	D 0-0	
13/03	a	Westerlo	L 0-1	
02/04	h	Standard	L 0-1	
09/04	a	Mouscron	D 0-0	
16/04	h	Kortrijk	L 2-3	Caufriez, Hugo Sousa
23/04	a	Kortrijk	L 0-5	
30/04	h	Mouscron	W 1-0	Schrijvers
07/05	a	Standard	L 0-2	

No	Name	Nat	DoB	Pos	Aps	(s)	Gls
5	Jonathan Buatu	ANG	27/09/93	D	33	(1)	1
23	Maximiliano Caufriez		16/02/97	D	3	(1)	1
6	Ousseynou Cissé	SEN	06/04/91	M	12		1
8	Gary Coulibaly	FRA	30/03/86	D	28	(3)	
2	Erdin Demir	SWE	27/03/90	D	32		
17	David Destorme		30/08/79	M		(6)	
16	Renaud Emond		05/12/91	A	6		2
9	Zino Gano		13/10/93	A	33	(1)	10
18	Merveille Goblet		20/11/94	G	14		
1	Laurent Henkinet		14/09/92	G	22		
27	Hugo Sousa	POR	04/06/92	D	5	(2)	1
21	Laurent Jans	LUX	05/08/92	D	34		1
7	Steven Langil	FRA	04/03/88	M	33	(2)	6
	Tortol Lumanza		13/04/94	M	2	(4)	
55	Zakaria M'Sila	MAR	06/04/92	M	6	(13)	1
10	Miloš Marić	SRB	05/03/82	M	21	(4)	2
11	Deni Milošević	BIH	09/03/95	M	15	(8)	4
4	Valtteri Moren	FIN	15/06/91	D	11	(3)	
15	Thibault Moulin	FRA	13/01/90	M	31		3
32	Olivier Myny		10/11/94	A	23	(9)	3
97	Livio Nabab	FRA	14/06/88	A	2	(18)	1
12	Ebrahima Ibou Sawaneh	GAM	07/09/86	A		(4)	
14	Siebe Schrijvers		18/07/96	A	15		4
28	Floriano Vanzo		22/04/94	A	15	(18)	2

KVC Westerlo

1933 • Het Kuipje (8,035) • kvcwesterlo.be
Major honours
Belgian Cup (1) 2001
**Coach: Harm van Veldhoven (NED);
(26/11/15) Bob Peeters**

2015
26/07	h	Gent	D 1-1	Aoulad
01/08	a	Oostende	L 1-2	Gounongbe
08/08	h	Leuven	W 3-2	Apau, Petković, Gounongbe
15/08	a	Genk	L 1-2	Gounongbe
22/08	a	Charleroi	D 0-0	
30/08	h	Anderlecht	L 0-3	
12/09	h	Mechelen	D 2-2	og (Vanlerberghe), Višňakovs
19/09	h	Sint-Truiden	L 0-3	
25/09	a	Zulte Waregem	L 2-4	Cools, Schouterden
03/10	h	Kortrijk	D 1-1	Schuermans
17/10	a	Standard	W 2-1	De Ceulaer 2
24/10	h	Lokeren	L 1-2	Gounongbe (p)
27/10	a	Mouscron	D 2-2	Višňakovs, Aoulad
31/10	h	Club Brugge	L 0-2	
07/11	a	Waasland-Beveren	D 2-2	Gounongbe 2
20/11	a	Gent	L 0-5	
29/11	h	Oostende	L 0-1	
05/12	a	Leuven	L 1-5	Daems (p)
11/12	h	Genk	D 0-0	
19/12	h	Charleroi	W 2-1	Gounongbe 2 (1p)
27/12	a	Anderlecht	L 1-2	Cools

2016
16/01	h	Mechelen	W 3-2	Gounongbe, De Ceulaer, Vercauteren
23/01	a	Sint-Truiden	W 2-1	De Ceulaer, Gounongbe (p)
30/01	h	Zulte Waregem	L 1-2	Apau
06/02	a	Kortrijk	D 1-1	Gounongbe
14/02	h	Standard	W 2-0	De Ceulaer, Gounongbe (p)
19/02	a	Club Brugge	L 0-6	
27/02	h	Mouscron	D 2-2	Cools, Henkens
05/03	a	Lokeren	L 1-2	Gounongbe
13/03	h	Waasland-Beveren	W 1-0	Cools

No	Name	Nat	DoB	Pos	Aps	(s)	Gls
8	Maxime Annys		24/07/86	M	13	(4)	
14	Mohamed Aoulad		29/08/91	A	11	(8)	2
2	Mitch Apau	NED	27/04/90	D	30		2
24	Jens Cools		16/10/90	M	26	(2)	4
3	Filip Daems		31/10/78	D	22		1
10	Benjamin De Ceulaer		19/12/83	A	22	(1)	5
12	Frédéric Gounongbe	BEN	01/05/88	A	24	(4)	13
2	Robin Henkens		12/09/88	M	10	(1)	1
11	Khaleem Hyland	TRI	05/06/89	M	26	(3)	
9	Kevin Koffi	CIV	25/06/86	A	2	(12)	
7	Raphaël Lecomte	FRA	22/05/88	M	13	(6)	
23	Jarno Molenberghs		11/12/89	M	9	(12)	
16	Jordan Mustoe	ENG	28/01/91	D	16	(2)	
5	Nikola Petković	SRB	28/03/86	D	14	(1)	1
22	Gilles Ruyssen		18/06/94	D	12	(3)	
18	Nils Schouterden		14/12/88	M	14	(4)	1
17	Kenneth Schuermans		25/05/91	D	28	(1)	1
4	Jore Trompet		30/07/92	M	1		
1	Kristof Van Hout		09/02/87	G	1		
30	Koen Van Langendonck		09/06/89	G	29		
27	Julien Vercauteren		12/01/93	M		(3)	1
19	Arno Verschueren		08/04/97	M	1	(3)	
90	Eduards Višňakovs	LVA	10/05/90	A	6	(10)	2

SV Zulte Waregem

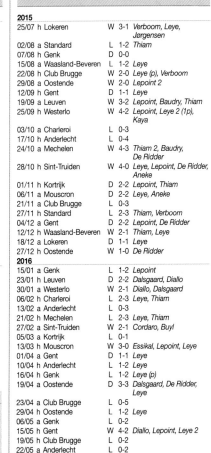

2001 • Regenboogstadion (8,500) •
essevee.be
Major honours
Belgian Cup (1) 2006
Coach: Francky Dury

2015
25/07	h	Lokeren	W 3-1	Verboom, Leye, Jørgensen
02/08	a	Standard	L 1-2	Thiam
07/08	h	Genk	D 0-0	
15/08	a	Waasland-Beveren	L 1-2	Leye
22/08	h	Club Brugge	W 2-0	Leye (p), Verboom
29/08	a	Oostende	W 2-0	Lepoint 2
12/09	h	Gent	D 1-1	Leye
19/09	a	Leuven	W 3-2	Lepoint, Baudry, Thiam
25/09	h	Westerlo	W 4-2	Lepoint, Leye 2 (1p), Kaya
03/10	a	Charleroi	L 0-3	
17/10	a	Anderlecht	L 0-4	
24/10	a	Mechelen	W 4-3	Thiam 2, Baudry, De Ridder
28/10	h	Sint-Truiden	W 4-0	Leye, Lepoint, De Ridder, Aneke
01/11	h	Kortrijk	D 2-2	Lepoint, Thiam
06/11	a	Mouscron	D 2-2	Leye, Aneke
21/11	a	Club Brugge	L 0-3	
27/11	h	Standard	L 2-3	Thiam, Verboom
04/12	a	Gent	D 2-2	Lepoint, De Ridder
12/12	h	Waasland-Beveren	W 2-1	Thiam, Leye
18/12	a	Leuven	D 1-1	Leye
27/12	h	Oostende	W 1-0	De Ridder

2016
15/01	a	Genk	L 1-2	Lepoint
23/01	h	Leuven	D 2-2	Dalsgaard, Diallo
30/01	a	Westerlo	W 2-1	Diallo, Dalsgaard
06/02	h	Charleroi	L 2-3	Leye, Thiam
13/02	a	Anderlecht	L 0-3	
21/02	h	Mechelen	L 2-3	Leye, Thiam
27/02	a	Sint-Truiden	W 2-1	Cordaro, Buyl
05/03	a	Kortrijk	L 0-1	
13/03	h	Mouscron	W 3-0	Essikal, Lepoint, Leye
01/04	a	Gent	D 1-1	Leye
10/04	h	Anderlecht	L 1-2	Leye
16/04	h	Genk	L 1-2	Leye (p)
19/04	a	Oostende	D 3-3	Dalsgaard, De Ridder, Leye
23/04	a	Club Brugge	L 0-5	
29/04	h	Oostende	L 1-2	Leye
06/05	a	Genk	L 0-2	
15/05	h	Gent	W 4-2	Diallo, Lepoint, Leye 2
19/05	h	Club Brugge	L 0-2	
22/05	a	Anderlecht	L 0-2	

No	Name	Nat	DoB	Pos	Aps	(s)	Gls
26	Chuks Aneke	ENG	03/07/93	M	10	(1)	2
3	Marvin Baudry	CGO	26/01/90	D	29	(3)	2
15	Jonathan Benteke		01/01/95	A	1	(14)	
1	Sammy Bossut		11/08/85	G	28		
33	Sébastien Brebels		05/05/95	M	1	(3)	
11	Stephen Buyl		02/09/92	A	9	(13)	1
29	Alessandro Cordaro		02/05/86	M	15	(9)	1
2	Cédric D'Ulivo		29/09/89	D	5	(1)	
14	Henrik Dalsgaard	DEN	27/07/89	D	19		3
10	Steve De Ridder		25/02/87	A	32	(5)	5
4	Abdou Diallo	FRA	04/05/96	D	33		3
35	Karim Essikal	MAR	08/02/96	M	16	(6)	1
14	Ghislain Gimbert	FRA	07/08/85	A		(1)	
21	Bruno Godeau		10/05/92	D	7	(1)	
8	Jesper Jørgensen	DEN	09/05/84	M	7	(5)	1
34	Onur Kaya		20/04/86	M	34	(4)	1
23	Christophe Lepoint		24/10/84	M	36	(1)	10
9	Mbaye Leye	SEN	01/12/82	A	38		20
17	Soualiho Meïté	FRA	17/03/94	M	11	(1)	
20	Formose Mendy	FRA	08/10/93	M	2	(5)	
8	Marko Poletanović	SRB	20/07/93	M	7	(1)	
6	Joël Sami	COD	13/11/84	D	25	(1)	
22	Kenny Steppe		14/11/88	G	12		
42	Nikola Storm		30/09/94	A	9	(8)	
7	Mame Baba Thiam	SEN	09/10/92	A	23	(5)	9
5	Bryan Verboom		30/01/92	D	31	(3)	3
44	Azzedine Zaidi		13/10/96	A		(1)	

Top goalscorers

24	Jérémy Perbet (Charleroi)
20	Mbaye Leye (Zulte Waregem)
17	Sofiane Hanni (Mechelen)
16	Abdoulay Diaby (Club Brugge)
15	Stefano Okaka (Anderlecht)
14	Jelle Vossen (Club Brugge)
	Laurent Depoitre (Gent)
	Cyriac (Oostende)
13	Sven Kums (Gent)
	Knowledge Musona (Oostende)
	Frédéric Gounongbe (Westerlo)

Promoted club

KAS Eupen

1945• Kehrwegstadion (8,363) • as-eupen.be
Coach: Jordi Condom Aulí (ESP)

Second level final table 2015/16

		Pld	W	D	L	F	A	Pts
1	R. White Star Bruxelles	32	19	6	7	53	28	63
2	KAS Eupen	32	18	8	6	69	34	62
3	R. Antwerp FC	32	18	8	6	52	20	62
4	AFC Tubize	32	17	6	9	51	34	57
5	Cercle Brugge KSV	32	14	12	6	56	35	54
6	R. Union Saint-Gilloise	32	15	6	11	50	34	51
7	K. Lierse SK	32	14	9	9	53	41	51
8	Lommel United	32	14	8	10	43	29	50
9	KSV Roeselare	32	14	8	10	46	47	50
10	KFC Dessel Sport	32	14	6	12	38	40	48
11	Seraing United	32	13	5	14	45	50	44
12	R. Excelsior Virton	32	8	10	14	40	55	44
13	AS Verbroedering Geel	32	6	13	13	40	56	31
14	KMSK Deinze	32	6	11	15	36	58	29
15	K. Patro Eisden Maasmechelen	32	5	9	18	33	63	24
16	KSK Heist	32	4	7	21	39	82	19
17	KVV Coxyde	32	2	10	20	29	67	16

NB R. White Star Bruxelles did not obtain licence for Pro League; KAS Eupen promoted instead.

Mid-table play-offs 2015/16

Play-off 2A final table		Home					Away					Total					
	Pld	W	D	L	F	A	W	D	L	F	A	W	D	L	F	A	Pts
1 KV Kortrijk	6	2	1	0	6	0	2	1	0	7	5	4	2	0	13	5	14
2 R. Standard de Liège	6	2	1	0	7	2	1	0	2	1	3	3	1	2	8	5	10
3 R. Excel Mouscron	6	1	1	1	4	3	0	1	2	1	5	1	2	3	5	8	5
4 Waasland-Beveren	6	1	0	2	3	4	0	1	2	0	7	1	1	4	3	11	4

Play-off 2B final table		Home					Away					Total					
	Pld	W	D	L	F	A	W	D	L	F	A	W	D	L	F	A	Pts
1 R. Charleroi SC	6	1	2	0	7	3	2	0	1	6	3	3	2	1	13	6	11
2 KSC Lokeren OV	6	3	0	0	7	1	0	2	1	5	6	3	2	1	12	7	11
3 KV Mechelen	6	1	1	1	5	5	1	0	2	2	9	2	1	3	7	14	7
4 K. Sint-Truidense VV	6	0	1	2	2	6	0	2	1	2	3	0	3	3	4	9	3

UEFA Europa League qualification play-offs

FIRST ROUND

(13/05/16 & 21/05/16)
Charleroi 1-0 Kortrijk
Kortrijk 1-2 Charleroi
(Charleroi 3-1)

SECOND ROUND

(26/05/16 & 29/05/16)
Charleroi 2-0 Genk
Genk 5-1 Charleroi
(Genk 5-3)

DOMESTIC CUP

Coupe de Belgique/Beker van België 2015/16

SIXTH ROUND

(22/09/15)
Westerlo 3-2 Cercle Brugge
Zulte Waregem 2-0 Union St-Gilloise

(23/09/15)
Anderlecht 3-1 Spouwen-Mopertingen
Charleroi 3-0 Wallonia Walhain
Coxyde 2-3 Standard
Deinze 0-2 Mouscron
Genk 5-2 Dessel Sport
Gent 3-0 Eupen
Kortrijk 5-0 Olsa Brakel
KV Mechelen 1-0 White Star Bruxelles
Leuven 3-2 Lommel
Lokeren 6-2 Acren
Oostende 0-2 Antwerp
Patro Eisden 0-4 Club Brugge
Sint-Truiden 1-0 Bocholt
Waasland-Beveren 2-1 Dender

SEVENTH ROUND

(01/12/15)
Gent 1-0 Zulte Waregem

(02/12/15)
Genk 1-1 Charleroi *(aet; 5-4 on pens)*
Kortrijk 4-2 Anderlecht
KV Mechelen 2-1 Waasland-Beveren
Mouscron 1-0 Leuven
Westerlo 1-1 Antwerp *(aet; 5-4 on pens)*
Standard 2-0 Sint-Truiden

(03/12/15)
Club Brugge 1-0 Lokeren

QUARTER-FINALS

(16/12/15)
Genk 2-1 Mouscron *(Kebano 36, 44; Hubert 90p)*
Gent 1-0 KV Mechelen *(Dejaegere 10)*
Westerlo 0-2 Club Brugge *(Diaby 18, 72p)*

(17/12/15)
Standard 2-0 Kortrijk *(Jorge Teixeira 8, Dossevi 35)*

SEMI-FINALS

(20/01/16 & 02/02/16)
Standard 2-0 Genk *(Edmilson Junior 6, Trebel 30)*
Genk 1-1 Standard *(Karelis 20; Trebel 28)*
(Standard 3-1)

(21/01/16 & 03/02/16)
Gent 2-1 Club Brugge *(Dejaegere 59, Kums 90; Diaby 38)*
Club Brugge 1-0 Gent *(Diaby 22)*
(2-2; Club Brugge on away goal)

FINAL

(20/03/16)
King Baudouin, Brussels
R. STANDARD DE LIÈGE 2 *(Dompé 17, Santini 88)*
CLUB BRUGGE KV 1 *(Refaelov 27)*
Referee: *Verbist*
STANDARD: Víctor Valdés, Fai, Scholz, Kosanović, Andrade, Trebel *(Emond 75)*, Maniatis, Dossevi, Dompé, Edmilson Junior *(Arslanagic 90)*, Santini *(Legear 90+2)*
CLUB BRUGGE: Butelle, Meunier, Engels, Poulain, De Bock, Simons, Vormer *(Vossen 89)*, Vanaken *(Felipe Gedoz 90)*, Izquierdo *(Dierckx 61)*, Refaelov, Diaby
Red card: *Diaby (52)*

BOSNIA&HERZEGOVINA
Nogometni / Fudbalski savez Bosne i Hercegovine (NFSBiH)

Address	Ulica Ferhadija 30
	BA-71000 Saarajevo
Tel	+387 33 276 660
Fax	+387 33 444 332
E-mail	elmir.pilav@nsbih.ba
Website	nfsbih.ba

President	Elvedin Begić
General secretary	Jasmin Baković
Media officer	Slavica Pecikoza
Year of formation	1992
National stadium	Bilino Polje, Zenica (13,000)

PREMIJER LIGA CLUBS

 1 **FK Borac Banja Luka**

 2 **NK Čelik Zenica**

 3 **FK Drina Zvornik**

 4 **FK Mladost Doboj Kakanj**

 5 **FK Olimpic Sarajevo**

 6 **FK Radnik Bijeljina**

 7 **FK Rudar Prijedor**

 8 **FK Sarajevo**

 9 **FK Slavija Sarajevo**

 10 **FK Sloboda Tuzla**

 11 **NK Široki Brijeg**

 12 **NK Travnik**

 13 **FK Velež**

 14 **NK Vitez**

 15 **HŠK Zrinjski**

 16 **FK Željezničar**

KEY

- ● UEFA Champions League
- ● UEFA Europa League
- ● Promoted
- ● Relegated

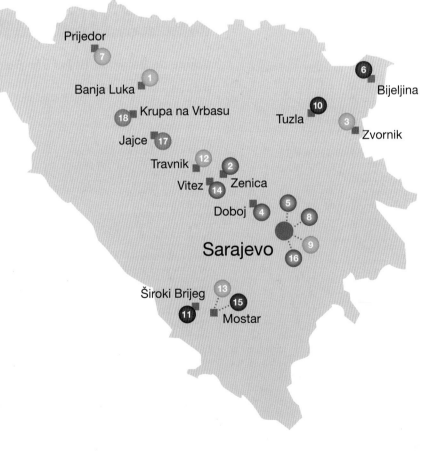

PROMOTED CLUBS

 17 **NK Metalleghe-BSI Jajce**

 18 **FK Krupa**

Fourth league crown for Zrinjski

Champions of Bosnia & Herzegovina in 2013/14, HŠK Zrinjski took just two years to regain the title thanks to a brilliant burst of form in the spring that saw off the dual challenge of Sloboda Tuzla and Široki Brijeg, enabling the Mostar club to finish seven points clear in the final standings.

Sloboda took the runners-up spot in the league and were also second best in the domestic cup – for the third time in as many finals – as Radnik Bijeljina defeated them 4-1 over two legs to pick up their first major trophy.

| **Mostar club regain title thanks to spring surge** | **Cup winners Radnik capture first major trophy** | **Sloboda finish runners-up in league and cup** |

Domestic league

Zrinjski's 2015/16 title-winning team bore little resemblance to the one of two years earlier, with only a handful of players having remained. It was under a new coach also that the Mostar club ascended once again to the Premijer Liga summit, former Yugoslavia international Vinko Marinović emulating the achievement of the club's former boss Branko Karačić.

Zrinjski were in the thick of the title race from day one, winning their opening four matches, the last of them at defending champions and pre-season favourites FK Sarajevo. It was not until round nine that they were beaten, 2-1 at Marinović's former club Borac Banja Luka, and although that triggered a mini-slump, Zrinjski were just one point in arrears of leaders Sloboda at the winter break.

With Sarajevo and their city rivals Željezničar too far back to pose a threat, and third-placed Široki Brijeg falling behind after losing a seven-goal thriller at home to Zrinjski, the race looked set to be restricted to just two runners. Marinović's men would soon overhaul Sloboda with five successive victories, all by a one-goal margin, and although they gave their rivals a glimmer of hope by drawing 0-0 at Željezničar, the challengers from Tuzla wasted the

opportunity, losing the next day at home to lowly Drina Zvornik.

That left the way clear for Zrinjski, and they wrapped up the title with a 3-0 win at Mladost Doboj Kakanj, ensuring that their final-day fixture at home to Sloboda – one which for so long had looked destined to be a title decider – would be of negligible significance. Zrinjski won it anyway, 2-1, thus completing a third successive season without a home defeat, but Husref Musemić's side still took second place, one point ahead of Široki Brijeg, whose seven wins in the last eight games enabled them to finish above both Sarajevo clubs and claim a UEFA Europa League spot.

There would be no clubs from the capital playing European football in 2016/17 and a reduced number in the Premijer Liga as Slavija were among six teams relegated to allow for the reduction in the top division to 12 clubs. Bottom of that particular pile were Zrinjski's city rivals Velež, who won just one game.

Domestic cup

The meeting of Radnik and Sloboda in the cup final guaranteed a new name on the trophy. It was the former's first final and the latter's third after previous losses in 2008 and 2009, but despite having the better of their opponents in the league,

Sloboda could not make it third time lucky. Radnik drew the away leg 1-1 before cruising to a 3-0 win in Bijeljina seven days later, with defenders Dušan Hodžić and Samir Memišević (two) scoring the goals.

Europe

Zrinjski were one of three Bosnian sides to suffer immediate elimination in Europe, the exception being Željezničar, who knocked out Maltese minnows Balzan and Hungarian heavyweights Ferencváros without conceding a goal before losing out to Standard Liège.

National team

An improvement in Bosnia & Herzegovina's UEFA EURO 2016 qualifying fortunes after the replacement of coach Safet Sušić with Mehmed Baždarević did not stretch to actually reaching the finals in France. Three successive wins, including one at home to Wales, ended the group stage, but Edin Džeko and co were second best in the play-offs to the Republic of Ireland. Baždarević's team did, however, win a trophy in the summer of 2016, landing the Kirin Cup in Japan with a 2-1 victory over the hosts following a semi-final penalty shoot-out win over Denmark. All four of the team's goals in the mini-tournament were scored by unheralded Italy-based striker Milan Djurić.

DOMESTIC SEASON AT A GLANCE

Premijer Liga 2015/16 final table

		Pld	Home					Away					Total					Pts
			W	D	L	F	A	W	D	L	F	A	W	D	L	F	A	
1	HŠK Zrinjski	30	11	4	0	28	6	10	2	3	24	11	21	6	3	52	17	69
2	FK Sloboda Tuzla	30	11	1	3	28	13	8	4	3	16	10	19	5	6	44	23	62
3	NK Široki Brijeg	30	10	4	1	35	10	8	3	4	21	11	18	7	5	56	21	61
4	FK Sarajevo	30	12	0	3	35	11	6	3	6	21	17	18	3	9	56	28	57
5	FK Željezničar	30	10	4	1	25	9	6	3	6	11	11	16	7	7	36	20	55
6	NK Čelik Zenica	30	11	4	0	24	7	1	6	8	11	21	12	10	8	35	28	46
7	FK Radnik Bijeljina	30	7	3	5	13	10	6	3	6	12	15	13	6	11	25	25	45
8	FK Olimpic Sarajevo	30	6	4	5	21	15	5	2	8	15	18	11	6	13	36	33	39
9	NK Vitez	30	8	2	5	25	13	3	4	8	11	28	11	6	13	36	41	39
10	FK Mladost Doboj Kakanj	30	8	4	3	20	15	2	5	8	9	24	10	9	11	29	39	39
11	FK Borac Banja Luka	30	6	4	5	17	15	4	2	9	10	18	10	6	14	27	33	36
12	FK Slavija Sarajevo	30	6	6	3	13	8	2	5	8	12	29	8	11	11	25	37	35
13	NK Travnik	30	7	2	6	28	23	1	3	11	8	24	8	5	17	36	47	29
14	FK Rudar Prijedor	30	4	5	6	14	11	1	5	9	10	27	5	10	15	24	38	25
15	FK Drina Zvornik	30	4	1	10	11	24	3	0	12	13	42	7	1	22	24	66	22
16	FK Velež	30	0	4	11	3	21	1	2	12	7	34	1	6	23	10	55	9

European qualification 2016/17

Champion: HŠK Zrinjski (second qualifying round)

Cup winner: FK Radnik Bijeljina (first qualifying round)
FK Sloboda Tuzla (first qualifying round)
FK Široki Brijeg (first qualifying round)

Top scorer   Leon Benko (Sarajevo), 18 goals
Relegated clubs   FK Velež, FK Drina Zvornik, FK Rudar Prijedor, NK Travnik, FK Slavija Sarajevo, FK Borac Banja Luka
Promoted clubs   NK Metalleghe-BSI Jajce, FK Krupa
Cup final   FK Sloboda Tuzla 1-1; 0-3 FK Radnik Bijeljina (agg 1-4)

Player of the season

Jasmin Mešanović
(HŠK Zrinjski)

After a decent 2014/15 season across the border in Croatia with Osijek, Mešanović returned to his homeland and turned out to be one of the Premijer Liga's decisive figures as he spearheaded Zrinjski's title challenge. He top-scored for the champions with 11 goals, the last two coming in the game that sealed the team's triumph, 3-0 at Mladost Doboj Kakanj. The striker might have been forgiven for having mixed feelings as Zrinjski's title came at the expense of his hometown and former club Sloboda.

Newcomer of the season

Goran Karačić
(HŠK Zrinjski)

Drafted into Zrinjski's first team at the start of the 2015/16 campaign, the giant 19-year-old goalkeeper proved to be a sturdy, at times acrobatic, last line of defence for the Mostar club, and as the clean sheets mounted up en route to a title-winning conclusion to his debut season, Karačić was being widely hailed as the best 'keeper in the Premijer Liga. His first season for Zrinjski would also be his last, however, as he left his hometown team in July for newly-promoted Turkish Süper Lig club Adanaspor.

Team of the season
(4-4-2)

Coach: Marinović *(Zrinjski)*

Karačić *(Zrinjski)*

Memija *(Željezničar)*   Memišević *(Radnik)*   Marković *(Široki Brijeg)*   Ivetić *(Sloboda)*

Duljević *(Sarajevo)*   Wagner *(Široki Brijeg)*   Zeba *(Sloboda)*   Zakarić *(Zrinjski)*

Mešanović *(Zrinjski)*   Benko *(Sarajevo)*

NATIONAL TEAM

International tournament appearances
FIFA World Cup (1) 2014

Top five all-time caps
Emir Spahić (89): Zvjezdan Misimović (83); **Edin Džeko** (79); **Vedad Ibišević** (73); **Miralem Pjanić** (68)

Top five all-time goals
Edin Džeko (46); **Vedad Ibišević** & Zvjezdan Misimović (25); Elvir Bolić (22); Sergej Barbarez (17)

Results 2015/16

Date	Opponent		Venue		Score	Scorers
03/09/15	Belgium (ECQ)	A	Brussels	L	1-3	Džeko (15)
06/09/15	Andorra (ECQ)	H	Zenica	W	3-0	Bičakčić (14), Džeko (30), Lulić (45)
10/10/15	Wales (ECQ)	H	Zenica	W	2-0	Djurić (71), Ibišević (90)
13/10/15	Cyprus (ECQ)	A	Nicosia	W	3-2	Medunjanin (13, 44), Djurić (67)
13/11/15	Republic of Ireland (ECQ)	H	Zenica	D	1-1	Džeko (85)
16/11/15	Republic of Ireland (ECQ)	A	Dublin	L	0-2	
25/03/16	Luxembourg	A	Luxembourg	W	3-0	Chanot (73og), Djurić (75), Pjanić (90+1)
29/03/16	Switzerland	A	Zurich	W	2-0	Džeko (14), Pjanić (57)
29/05/16	Spain	N	St Gallen (SUI)	L	1-3	Spahić (30)
03/06/16	Denmark	N	Toyota (JPN)	D	2-2	Djurić (52, 83) (4-3 on pens)
07/06/16	Japan	A	Suita	W	2-1	Djurić (29, 66)

Appearances 2015/16

Coach: Mehmed Baždarević 28/09/60

Player	DOB	Club	BEL	AND	WAL	CYP	IRL	IRL	Lux	Sui	Esp	Den	Jpn	Caps	Goals
Asmir Begović	20/06/87	Chelsea (ENG)	G	G	G	G	G	G	G46	G62	G			50	-
Mensur Mujdža	28/03/84	Freiburg (GER)	D		D	D	D51							37	-
Ognjen Vranješ	24/10/89	Gaziantepspor (TUR) /Sporting Gijón (ESP)	D			M	s51	D	D46	D	D90	D70*		25	-
Emir Spahić	18/08/80	Hamburg (GER)	D56	D	D46	D	D	D		D79	D	D45*		89	4
Sead Kolašinac	20/06/93	Schalke (GER)	D72	D79					D	D	D	D		13	-
Muhamed Bešić	10/09/92	Everton (ENG)	M	M63*			s46		M67	M	M			26	-
Haris Medunjanin	08/03/85	Deportivo (ESP)/ M. Tel-Aviv (ISR)	M80			M		M69			s67	M	M	51	7
Senad Lulić	18/01/86	Lazio (ITA)	M	M	M	M	M88	M80		M				48	2
Miralem Pjanić	02/04/90	Roma (ITA)	M	M45	M	M85	M	M	s67	M73	M			68	11
Edin Višća	17/02/90	İstanbul Başakşehir (TUR)	M		M61	M79	M73	M	M60	M51	M46			25	2
Edin Džeko	17/03/86	Roma (ITA)	A	A68			A	A	s46	A	A22			79	46
Toni Šunjić	15/12/88	Stuttgart (GER)	s56	D	D	D	D		D			D	D	23	-
Izet Hajrović	04/08/91	Eibar (ESP)	s72				s88				s46	M73	M90	20	3
Vedad Ibišević	06/08/84	Hertha (GER)	s80	A	A	A	A		s80	A46	A66			73	25
Ermin Bičakčić	24/01/90	Hoffenheim (GER)		D	s89	s79								14	2
Ermin Zec	18/02/88	Qäbälä (AZE)		M										10	1
Anel Hadžić	16/08/89	Sturm (AUT) /Eskişehirspor (TUR)		s45	M89					s66	M67	M46		13	-
Milan Djurić	22/05/90	Cesena (ITA)		s68	s61	s60	s73	s69	A	s22/78		A89	A76	10	7
Mario Vrančić	23/05/89	Darmstadt (GER)	s79							M	s46	M89		4	-
Ervin Zukanović	11/02/87	Sampdoria (ITA) /Roma (ITA)				D	D60	D	D	D85	D			15	-
Sejad Salihović	08/10/84	Guizhou Renhe (CHN)			M	s85								47	4
Edin Cocalić	05/12/87	Mechelen (BEL)			s46		M	M46		s79		D	D	7	-
Marin Aničić	17/08/89	Astana (KAZ)							D					1	-
Sanjin Prcić	20/11/93	Perugia (ITA)							M77					5	-
Ibrahim Šehić	02/09/88	Qarabağ (AZE)							s46			G	G	6	-
Mateo Sušić	18/11/90	Sheriff (MDA)							s46	s51		s73	D	4	-
Haris Duljević	16/11/93	Sarajevo							s60	s73	s57	M82	M66	5	-
Srdjan Grahovac	19/09/92	Rapid Wien (AUS)							s77		s78	M46		3	-
Jasmin Burić	18/02/87	Lech (POL)								s62				2	-
Daniel Graovac	08/08/93	Zrinjski								s85				1	-
Armin Hodžić	17/11/94	Dinamo Zagreb (CRO)								A57	s46	A		3	-
Samir Memišević	13/08/93	Radnik Bijeljina								s90				1	-
Miroslav Stevanović	29/07/90	Željezničar									s82	s66		12	1
Rade Krunić	07/10/93	Empoli (ITA)									s89			1	-
Almir Bekić	01/06/89	Sarajevo										D		1	-
Zvonimir Kožulj	15/11/93	Široki Brijeg										s76		1	-
Filip Arežina	08/11/92	Zrinjski										s89		1	-
Aleksandar Kosorić	30/01/87	Željezničar										s90		1	-

EUROPE

FK Sarajevo

Second qualifying round - KKS Lech Poznań (POL)
H 0-2
Oštraković, Stojčev (Alispahić 66), Velkoski (Almir Bekić 73), Hebibović, Stepanov, Duljević, Benko, Barbarić, Cimirot, Puzigaća, Radovac (Rustemović 78). Coach: Samer Naser (BIH)
A 0-1
Oštraković, Alispahić, Tatomirović, Stepanov, Duljević (Velkoski 54), Almir Bekić (Hebibović 85), Benko, Barbarić, Cimirot, Puzigaća, Radovac (Stojčev 77). Coach: Samer Naser (BIH)

FK Olimpic Sarajevo

First qualifying round - FC Spartak Trnava (SVK)
H 1-1 *Pandža (14)*
Hamzić, Merajić, Regoje, Brković, Muharemović, Pandža (Stefan 80), Bogičević, Gligorov, Handžić, Jusufović (Karić 80), Raščić. Coach: Edin Prljača (BIH)
A 0-0
Hamzić, Merajić, Regoje, Brković (Stefan 65), Muharemović, Pandža, Smajić (Karić 55), Bogičević, Gligorov, Handžić (Jusufović 80), Raščić. Coach: Edin Prljača (BIH)

FK Željezničar

First qualifying round - Balzan FC (MLT)
A 2-0 *Bajić (4p, 13)*
Antolović, Kvesić, Kosorić, Bajić, Blagojević, Djelmić, Livaja, Hadžiahmetović (E Sadiković 76), Beganović (D Sadiković 56), Bogdanović, Kokot (Diatta 84). Coach: Milomir Odović (BIH)
H 1-0 *D Sadiković (68)*
Antolović, Kvesić, Kosorić, Memija, Bajić, Blagojević (E Sadiković 69), Djelmić, Hadžiahmetović, Beganović (D Sadiković 64), Bogdanović, Kokot (Hiroš 84). Coach: Milomir Odović (BIH)

Second qualifying round - Ferencvárosi TC (HUN)
A 1-0 *Beganović (90)*
Antolović, Kvesić, Kosorić, Memija, Bajić, Blagojević, Djelmić (E Sadiković 71), Hadžiahmetović (Beganović 53), D Sadiković, Bogdanović, Kokot (Diatta 87). Coach: Milomir Odović (BIH)
H 2-0 *Kokot (23), Djelmić (90+1)*
Antolović, Kvesić, Kosorić, Memija, Bajić, Blagojević, Djelmić, Hadžiahmetović (E Sadiković 57), D Sadiković (Beganović 72), Bogdanović, Kokot (Stokić 86). Coach: Milomir Odović (BIH)

Third qualifying round - R. Standard de Liège (BEL)
A 1-2 *Djelmić (64)*
Antolović, Kosorić, Memija, Bajić, Blagojević, Djelmić, Mladenović, Hadžiahmetović (E Sadiković 90+3), D Sadiković (Diatta 90+1), Bogdanović, Kokot (Beganović 78). Coach: Milomir Odović (BIH)
H 0-1
Antolović, Kosorić, Memija, Bajić, Blagojević, Djelmić, Mladenović, Hadžiahmetović (E Sadiković 60), D Sadiković (Beganović 66), Bogdanović, Kokot (Stokić 76). Coach: Milomir Odović (BIH)

HŠK Zrinjski

First qualifying round - FC Shirak (ARM)
A 0-2
Dujković, Blaić, Graovac, Radeljić, Simeunović (Šćepanović 46), Muminović, Žeravica, Stojkić, Todorović, Nikolić (Aćimović 86), Filipović (Stojanović 71). Coach: Vinko Marinović (BIH)
H 2-1 *Mešanović (80p), Filipović (86)*
Dujković, Blaić, Radulović (Muminović 90+2), Graovac, Radeljić, Žeravica, Todorović (Filipović 69), Stojanović, Mešanović, Nikolić, Zakarić (Šćepanović 76). Coach: Vinko Marinović (BIH)

DOMESTIC LEAGUE CLUB-BY-CLUB

FK Borac Banja Luka

1926 • Gradski (10,000) • fkborac.net
Major honours
Bosnian-Herzegovinian League (1) 2011; Yugoslav Cup (1) 1988; Bosnian-Herzegovinian Cup (1) 2010
Coach: Vlado Jagodić;
(31/08/15) Petar Kurčubić (SRB);
(28/10/15) Željko Vranješ;
(20/01/16) Aleksandar Janjić (SRB);
(06/03/16) Borče Sredojević

2015
26/07	h	Željezničar	W	1-0	Ilić
01/08	a	Velež	D	1-1	T Jović
08/08	h	Mladost	D	1-1	Runić
14/08	a	Sloboda	D	1-1	T Jović
23/08	h	Olimpic	L	0-1	
29/08	a	Drina	L	0-1	
09/09	h	Travnik	W	2-1	Redžić, Saničanin
13/09	a	Sarajevo	L	0-2	
19/09	h	Zrinjski	W	2-1	Radinović, T Jović
26/09	a	Čelik	L	0-1	
03/10	h	Rudar	L	1-2	T Jović
18/10	a	Slavija	L	0-1	
24/10	h	Široki Brijeg	L	0-2	
31/10	h	Radnik	L	0-1	
07/11	a	Vitez	L	0-1	
23/11	a	Željezničar	L	0-1	
28/11	h	Velež	W	2-1	Redžić, Jandrić
05/12	a	Mladost	W	2-1	Radinović, Marjanović

2016
27/02	h	Sloboda	D	0-0	
05/03	a	Olimpic	L	0-3	
12/03	h	Drina	W	3-0	T Jović, Milosavljev, Marjanović (p)
19/03	a	Travnik	W	2-0	Mance, T Jović
02/04	h	Sarajevo	L	0-1	
09/04	a	Zrinjski	L	1-2	Maletić
16/04	h	Čelik	D	1-1	Radinović
23/04	a	Rudar	W	1-0	Radinović
30/04	h	Slavija	W	2-1	Radinović, Marjanović
04/05	a	Široki Brijeg	L	0-1	
07/05	a	Radnik	W	2-0	Milosavljev, Redžić
15/05	h	Vitez	D	2-2	Djokić, Popović

No	Name	Nat	DoB	Pos	Aps	(s)	Gls
22	Srdjan Bečelić	SRB	08/06/92	D	29		
28	Vladimir Djilas	SRB	03/03/83	A	5	(2)	
23	Željko Djokić	SRB	10/05/82	D	8		1
14	Stevan Djordjilović	SRB	12/05/94	D	1	(4)	
14	Miloš Dujković		09/10/90	M	2	(2)	
9	Petar Ilić	SRB	28/04/93	A	6	(5)	1
16	Damir Jakupović		16/02/96	A		(1)	
28	Srboljub Jandrić		04/03/91	M	15	(2)	1
12	Bojan Jović	SRB	01/04/82	G	9	(1)	
11	Toni Jović	CRO	02/09/92	M	23	(1)	6
8	Stojko Kikić		02/08/93	M	2	(2)	
8	Nenad Kiso		30/04/89	M	11	(1)	
17	Elvir Koljić	SVN	08/07/95	A	12	(2)	
13	Dušan Komljenović		24/05/95	D	1		
23	Miloš Kukić		10/03/98	A		(1)	
20	Mićo Kuzmanović		18/03/96	A		(3)	
33	Darko Maletić		20/10/80	M	9		1
27	Armando Mance	CRO	27/10/92	A	4	(2)	1
89	Lazar Marjanović	SRB	08/09/89	M	17	(6)	3
7	Vladan Milosavljev	SRB	01/02/87	M	6	(4)	2
27	Mile Paštar		22/02/92	D	10		
5	Dejan Popović		17/02/95	D	7	(2)	1
10	Fedor Predragović		08/04/95	M	10	(9)	
26	Marko Prljević	SRB	02/08/88	D	1		
24	Uglješa Radinović	SRB	25/08/93	M	22	(1)	5
17	Marko Rajović	SRB	10/06/88	D	2		
15	Boris Raspudić		11/10/82	D	6		
4	Ajdin Redžić	SVN	05/12/89	A	19	(2)	3
9	Filip Ristovski	MKD	03/01/90	D	6	(2)	
12	Nebojša Runić		18/09/92	D	11	(1)	1
1	Branislav Ružić		02/04/89	G	21		
5	Siniša Saničanin		24/04/95	D	18		1
7	Mihajlo Savanović		02/07/94	A	1	(7)	
19	Stefan Savić		09/01/95	M	2	(8)	
13	Milan Stojanović	SRB	10/05/88	M	6	(8)	
18	Aleksandar Subić		27/09/93	D	6		
16	Ognjen Škorić		02/03/93	M	5	(3)	
6	Nemanja Vidović		25/09/93	D	17	(2)	
21	Predrag Zekanović		22/07/97	M		(4)	

NK Čelik Zenica

1945 • Bilino Polje (13,000) • nkcelik.ba
Coach: Boris Pavić (CRO);
(02/11/15) Elvedin Beganović

2015
25/07	h	Sloboda	W	1-0	Karić
01/08	a	Olimpic	D	1-1	Čolić
08/08	h	Drina	W	2-1	Karić, Dedić
15/08	a	Travnik	L	2-3	Karić 2 (1p)
22/08	h	Sarajevo	D	1-1	og (Hebibović)
28/08	a	Zrinjski	D	0-0	
09/09	h	Široki Brijeg	W	2-1	Dedić, Salčinović
12/09	h	Rudar	D	0-0	
20/09	a	Slavija	L	1-2	Selimović
26/09	h	Borac	W	1-0	Kojić
03/10	a	Radnik	L	1-2	Selimović
17/10	h	Vitez	W	6-1	M Popović, Karić, Selimović, Bajraktarević 2, Čolić
25/10	a	Željezničar	L	0-4	
31/10	h	Velež	W	1-0	Karić
07/11	a	Mladost	L	0-1	
23/11	a	Sloboda	L	2-4	Jusić, Selimović
28/11	a	Olimpic	W	1-0	Dedić
05/12	a	Drina	W	2-0	Čolić, M Popović (p)

2016
27/02	h	Travnik	D	1-1	Kojić
05/03	a	Sarajevo	L	1-2	M Popović
12/03	h	Zrinjski	D	2-2	Dedić, Džidić
20/03	a	Široki Brijeg	D	0-0	
02/04	a	Rudar	D	0-0	
09/04	h	Slavija	W	2-0	Dedić 2
16/04	a	Borac	D	1-1	Karić
23/04	h	Radnik	W	2-1	Bajraktarević, Karić
29/04	a	Vitez	L	0-1	
04/05	h	Željezničar	W	1-0	Salčinović
07/05	a	Velež	D	0-0	
15/05	h	Mladost	W	1-0	Karić (p)

No	Name	Nat	DoB	Pos	Aps	(s)	Gls
25	Adi Adilović		20/02/83	G	27		
9	Hanan Adilović		08/08/96	A		(3)	
17	Amir Ajan	AUS	03/10/95	A	1	(3)	
16	Semir Bajraktarević		14/10/87	M	24	(1)	3
18	Stipe Barač	CRO	18/04/85	M	1	(4)	
26	Sead Bučan		08/03/81	M		(6)	
1	Semir Bukvić		21/05/91	G	3		
16	Dženan Bureković		29/05/95	D	26		
27	Benjamim Čolić		23/07/91	D	14	(3)	3
8	Anel Dedić		02/05/91	M	24		6
22	Anes Duraković		22/12/96	D		(5)	
5	Aldin Džidić		30/08/83	D	9		1
3	Vladimir Grahovac		12/01/95	M	15	(4)	
20	Haris Hećo		20/05/87	M	19	(7)	
17	Dženis Huseinspahić		30/09/91	A	1	(1)	
18	Armin Imamović		17/01/94	D		(2)	
26	Dušan Jevtić		29/03/92	A	1	(3)	
21	Emir Jusić		13/06/86	D	23	(1)	1
7	Mahir Karić		14/12/86	A	27		9
4	Zlatko Kazazić		10/02/89	D	10	(3)	
13	Jovo Kojić		08/08/88	D	27		2
19	Semir Pezer		18/08/92	A	15	(10)	
14	Goran Popović		11/01/88	D	10	(8)	
15	Marin Popović		18/08/94	M	25	(1)	3
9	Igor Radovanović		02/08/85	A		(2)	
10	Fenan Salčinović		26/06/87	M	10	(8)	2
11	Vernes Selimović		08/05/83	M	18	(2)	4
24	Emrad Šabanović		15/01/96	D		(5)	

FK Drina Zvornik

1945 • Gradski (5,000) • no website
Coach: Vladica Petrović (SRB);
(27/09/15) Aleksandar Vasić;
(05/10/15) Svetozar Vukašinović;
(20/10/15) Dragan Alimpić;
(25/11/15) Miljan Radonja;
(07/12/15) Cvijetin Blagojević

2015
27/07	a	Sarajevo	L	1-6	Djerić
01/08	h	Zrinjski	L	0-1	
08/08	a	Čelik	L	1-2	Ilić
15/08	h	Rudar	W	4-1	Jakšić 2, Stojanović, Ivanović
23/08	a	Slavija	L	0-1	
29/08	h	Borac	W	1-0	Jakšić
09/09	a	Radnik	L	0-1	
12/09	h	Vitez	L	1-2	Jakšić
20/09	a	Željezničar	L	2-3	Ilić, Jakšić
26/09	h	Velež	L	1-2	Jakšić
03/10	a	Mladost	L	2-4	Popović, Jakšić
17/10	h	Sloboda	L	1-2	Stojanović
24/10	a	Olimpic	L	0-4	
31/10	a	Široki Brijeg	L	1-5	A Nikolić
07/11	h	Travnik	W	1-0	Jakšić
21/11	h	Sarajevo	L	1-4	D Nikolić
28/11	a	Zrinjski	L	0-5	
05/12	h	Čelik	L	0-2	

2016
27/02	a	Rudar	W	1-0	Kuzmanović
05/03	h	Slavija	D	1-1	Ćulibrk
12/03	a	Borac	L	0-3	
19/03	h	Radnik	W	1-0	og (Obradović)
02/04	a	Vitez	L	0-4	
09/04	h	Željezničar	L	0-2	
16/04	a	Velež	W	1-0	Ivanović
23/04	h	Mladost	L	0-2	
30/04	a	Sloboda	W	2-0	Kuzmanović, Stefanović
04/05	h	Olimpic	L	0-3	
07/05	h	Široki Brijeg	L	0-3	
15/05	a	Travnik	L	2-4	Kuzmanović, Atić

No	Name	Nat	DoB	Pos	Aps	(s)	Gls
18	Goran Antelj	SRB	06/04/88	A	6	(4)	
11	Mladen Atić	SRB	13/05/96	M	7	(4)	1
13	Dejan Blagojević	SRB	18/01/90	D	9		
11	Stefan Čolović	SRB	02/07/94	M	9	(5)	
6	Slavko Ćulibrk	SRB	21/04/86	D	11	1	1
14	Danijel Čulum		19/08/89	A	13	(4)	
17	Boban Djerić		20/10/93	D	13		1
2	Zvezdan Djordjilović	SRB	12/05/94	D		(1)	
3	Borislav Erić		05/01/91	M	16		
18	Dušan Erić		04/06/98	A		(6)	
1	Filip Erić	SRB	10/10/94	G	18	(1)	
5	Aleksandar Ilić		08/04/94	A	20	(6)	2
5	Vlado Ivanović		24/01/94	D	28		2
9	Marko Jakšić	SRB	10/08/83	A	15	(2)	7
8	Miloš Jokić		20/04/93	D	7	(1)	
8	Aleksandar Kikić	SRB	15/03/83	M	24	(1)	
15	Darko Kostić		30/01/97	M		(3)	
6	Mićo Kuzmanović		18/03/96	A	11	(1)	3
6	Slobodan Lalić	SRB	18/02/92	D	7	(1)	
2	Elvir Majlović		06/06/97	M	3	(3)	
1	Goran Maksimović		04/05/80	G	3		
7	Novica Marković		15/02/94	M	1		
7	Miroslav Mitrović	SRB	09/12/94	M	1		
6	Ermin Musić		28/05/97	D	1	(1)	
16	Aleksandar Nikolić		25/06/91	A	2	(6)	1
9	Dragomir Nikolić	SRB	10/06/92	D	10	(1)	1
1	Srdjan Ostojić	SRB	10/01/83	G	9		
11	Mirza Palata		20/11/98	D		(1)	
4	Stefan Pečenica		29/02/96	D	2	(3)	
4	Novica Petrović	SRB	04/08/89	M	16	(9)	
6	Dejan Popović		17/02/96	D	6	(1)	1
11	Aleksandar Radović	MNE	30/03/87	D	7	(1)	
3	Velibor Simic	SUI	05/05/92	M	3	(5)	
18	Nikola Stefanović	SRB	25/03/91	A	7	(2)	1
4	Ognjen Stjepanović		09/08/98	M		(3)	
9	Nemanja Stojanović	SRB	09/04/87	M	12		2
13	Ognjen Šinik	SRB	27/10/86	D	9	(2)	
3	Ranko Torbica		22/01/94	M		(1)	
5	Saša Trifković		29/10/95	A	2	(1)	
10	Aleksandar Vasić		21/05/91	M	1	(2)	
18	Radovan Vasić		27/07/93	M	12	(6)	
11	Nikola Vasiljević		19/12/83	A		(1)	

FK Mladost Doboj Kakanj

1959 • Gradski (3,000); Kamberovića polje, Zenica (5,000) • no website
Coach: Ibro Rahimić

2015
25/07	a	Rudar	L	0-3	
01/08	h	Slavija	D	1-1	Dilaver
08/08	a	Borac	D	1-1	og (Runić)
15/08	h	Radnik	D	0-0	
22/08	a	Vitez	D	1-1	Šišić
30/08	h	Željezničar	W	2-1	Dilaver 2
09/09	a	Velež	D	0-0	
13/09	a	Široki Brijeg	L	0-3	
20/09	h	Sloboda	D	1-1	Bošković
28/09	a	Olimpic	D	0-0	
03/10	h	Drina	W	4-2	Dilaver, Šišić, Kovač 2
17/10	a	Travnik	W	2-1	Dilaver, Rizvanović
24/10	h	Sarajevo	W	2-1	Dilaver, Kovač
31/10	a	Zrinjski	L	0-4	
07/11	h	Čelik	W	1-0	Šišić
21/11	h	Rudar	W	2-1	Kovač, Kobilica
29/11	a	Slavija	D	1-1	Kobilica
05/12	h	Borac	L	1-2	A Husić

2016
27/02	a	Radnik	L	0-3	
05/03	h	Vitez	D	0-0	
13/03	a	Željezničar	L	1-2	Čović
19/03	h	Velež	W	1-0	Dilaver
03/04	h	Široki Brijeg	L	1-2	Dilaver
09/04	a	Sloboda	L	0-2	
16/04	h	Olimpic	W	2-0	Isaković, Šišić
23/04	a	Drina	W	2-0	Dilaver, Hodžić
30/04	a	Travnik	W	2-1	Dilaver, Kovač
04/05	a	Sarajevo	L	1-2	Dilaver
07/05	h	Zrinjski	L	0-3	
15/05	a	Čelik	L	0-1	

No	Name	Nat	DoB	Pos	Aps	(s)	Gls
90	Nemanja Asanović	MNE	23/09/90	A	1	(1)	
6	Darko Bošković	SRB	16/09/87	M	14	(4)	1
89	Mehmedalija Čović		16/03/86	D	15	(2)	1
23	Anel Ćurić		28/07/88	M		(4)	
22	Arnel Delić		13/02/92	D	12	(3)	
9	Haris Dilaver		16/12/90	A	28	(1)	11
4	Faruk Gačan		08/01/94	D	11	(6)	
88	Adnan Hadžić		15/01/88	G	28		
5	Almir Hasanović		06/11/81	D		(2)	
11	Šerif Hasić		07/01/88	M	6	(5)	
22	Adnan Hodžić		01/06/90	M	7	(1)	1
17	Adnan Hrelja		10/10/93	M	8	(6)	
2	Ibrahim Hrvat		19/11/92	M	1		
71	Anel Husić		12/12/94	M	8	(11)	1
42	Edin Husić		10/11/85	M	8	(6)	
99	Aladin Isaković		28/07/85	M	25		1
80	Senad Karahmet		23/02/92	D	19		
7	Belmin Kobilica		22/06/93	M	9	(4)	2
29	Ousman Koli	GAM	18/08/88	D			
8	Mirza Kovač		23/05/92	A	20	(5)	5
1	Vedin Kulović		12/12/95	M	2	(8)	
45	Franko Lalić	CRO	05/02/91	G	2		
16	Miloš Milisavljević	SRB	26/10/92	M	4	(2)	
11	Omer Musić		11/04/93	D	24		
21	Kenan Muslimovic	AUT	13/02/97	M		(1)	
23	Armin Pasagić	SWE	02/02/91	M	1	(1)	
90	Igor Poček	MNE	23/12/94	A	1	(2)	
77	Anis Rahimić		06/12/95	M		(1)	
20	Sinan Ramović		13/10/92	M	17	(4)	
21	Mirza Rizvanović		27/09/86	D	27		1
8	Anel Salković		25/03/93	A		(2)	
10	Pavle Sušić	SRB	15/04/88	M	9		
90	Aldin Šišić		29/09/90	M	23	(2)	4
6	Dženis Šuman		17/08/97	M		(1)	

FK Olimpic Sarajevo

1993 • Otoka (3,500); SC Slavija (4,000);
Olimpijski Asim Ferhatović Hase (34,600) •
olimpic.ba
Major honours
Bosnian-Herzegovinian Cup (1) 2015
**Coach: Mirza Varešanović;
(21/11/15) Edin Prljača;
(29/02/16) Milomir Odović;
(18/04/16) Faik Kolar**

2015
26/07	a	Zrinjski	L	0-2	
01/08	h	Čelik	D	1-1	og (Bajraktarević)
09/08	a	Rudar	D	0-0	
17/08	h	Slavija	L	2-3	Stefan, Muharemović
23/08	a	Borac	W	1-0	Pandža
31/08	h	Radnik	D	0-0	
09/09	a	Vitez	W	2-1	Muharemović, Pandža
14/09	h	Željezničar	L	0-1	
19/09	a	Velež	W	2-1	Muharemović, Karić
28/09	h	Mladost	D	0-0	
03/10	a	Sloboda	L	1-2	Stefan
18/10	h	Široki Brijeg	L	1-2	Muharemović
24/10	h	Drina	W	4-0	Stanić, Karić, Hadžić, Varešanović
31/10	a	Travnik	L	1-2	Muharemović
08/11	h	Sarajevo	L	1-3	Pandža
21/11	h	Zrinjski	L	0-3	
28/11	a	Čelik	L	0-1	
05/12	h	Rudar	W	6-2	Hadžić (p), Stefan (p), Brković 3, Pandža

2016
28/02	a	Slavija	L	0-1	
05/03	h	Borac	W	3-0	Muharemović, Andjušić, Uzelac
12/03	h	Radnik	D	0-0	
20/03	h	Vitez	D	0-0	
02/04	a	Željezničar	L	1-3	Hadžić
09/04	a	Velež	W	1-0	Hadžić
16/04	a	Mladost	L	0-1	
23/04	h	Sloboda	L	0-1	
30/04	h	Široki Brijeg	W	2-1	Zolj, Hebibović
04/05	a	Drina	W	3-0	Vukomanović, Brković, Hebibović
07/05	h	Travnik	W	1-0	Hebibović
15/05	a	Sarajevo	W	3-1	Handžić, og (Kovačević), Hebibović

No	Name	Nat	DoB	Pos	Aps	(s)	Gls
20	Nemanja Andjušić		17/10/96	M	5	(4)	1
1	Dejan Bandović		11/06/83	G	15		
26	Sead Begić		05/05/97	M		(1)	
15	Jadranko Bogičević		11/03/83	D	8	(1)	
7	Danijel Brković		03/06/91	A	17	(8)	4
12	Irfan Fejzić		01/07/86	G	6		
22	Filip Gligorov	MKD	31/07/93	D	9	(1)	
11	Emir Hadžić		19/07/84	A	16	(5)	4
30	Dino Hamzić		22/01/88	G	8		
24	Kenan Handžić		23/01/91	M	22	(1)	1
13	Anel Hebibović		07/07/90	M	11	(1)	4
11	Hugo Souza	BRA	14/05/89	M	2	(8)	
4	Ermin Imamović		30/04/95	D	13		
5	Branko Jovanović	SRB	07/04/95	D	1		
33	Ervin Jusufović		07/05/95	D	8	(1)	
9	Mahir Karić		05/03/92	M	18	(6)	2
9	Rijad Kobiljar		08/04/96	M	2	(2)	
80	Sanjin Lelić		11/01/97	A	1		
5	Armin Mahović		28/11/91	A	3	(5)	
2	Alem Merajić		04/02/94	D	11	(1)	
8	Djoko Milović		16/09/92	M	6		
26	Veldin Muharemović		05/12/84	M	25	(1)	6
9	Amer Osmanagić		07/05/89	M	1	(5)	
3	Dalibor Pandža		23/03/91	A	12	(3)	4
99	Slaviša Radović		08/10/93	D	9		
6	Admir Raščić		16/09/81	A	8	(5)	
10	Bojan Regoje		26/07/81	D	27		
9	Sulejman Smajić		13/08/84	D	14	(8)	
80	Srdjan Stanić		06/07/89	M	11	(1)	1
30	Stefan	BRA	16/04/88	M	9	(8)	3
15	Rasto Šuljagić	SRB	27/01/95	G			
21	Dejan Uzelac	SRB	29/11/93	D	6	(1)	1
20	Mak Varešanović		05/04/00	M	2	(6)	1
4	Predrag Videkanić	MNE	23/08/86	M	6	(1)	
33	Dejan Vukomanović		21/10/90	M	11		1
20	Faris Zeljković		09/08/93	D		(1)	
1	Amir Zolj		24/11/89	M	6	(5)	1

FK Radnik Bijeljina

1945 • Gradski (4,000) • fkradnik.net
Major honours
Bosnian-Herzegovinian Cup (1) 2016
Coach: Slavko Petrović (SRB)

2015
25/07	h	Vitez	W	1-0	Lazić
02/08	a	Željezničar	W	2-1	Obradović, Maksimović
08/08	h	Velež	D	0-0	
15/08	h	Mladost	D	0-0	
22/08	h	Sloboda	L	0-1	
31/08	h	Olimpic	D	0-0	
09/09	h	Drina	W	1-0	Obradović
13/09	a	Travnik	W	3-1	Krsmanović, Lazić 2
18/09	h	Sarajevo	L	0-3	
27/09	a	Zrinjski	D	0-0	
03/10	h	Čelik	W	2-1	Hodžić, Obradović
17/10	a	Rudar	W	1-0	Šećerović
24/10	h	Slavija	W	2-1	S Jakovljević, Lazić
31/10	a	Borac	W	1-0	Obradović
07/11	h	Široki Brijeg	L	0-1	
21/11	a	Vitez	W	1-0	Obradović
29/11	h	Željezničar	D	0-0	
05/12	a	Velež	W	2-0	Obradović, Maksimović

2016
27/02	h	Mladost	W	3-0	Stokić, Hodžić, Obradović
06/03	a	Sloboda	L	0-1	
12/03	h	Olimpic	D	0-0	
19/03	a	Drina	L	0-1	
02/04	h	Travnik	W	2-0	Memišević, Obradović
10/04	a	Sarajevo	L	1-2	D Beširović
16/04	h	Zrinjski	L	0-1	
24/04	a	Čelik	L	0-1	
30/04	h	Rudar	W	2-0	D Beširović, Obradović
04/05	a	Slavija	L	1-2	Maksimović
07/05	h	Borac	L	0-2	
15/05	a	Široki Brijeg	L	0-5	

No	Name	Nat	DoB	Pos	Aps	(s)	Gls
7	Sladjan Antić	SRB	11/01/92	D	6	(7)	
13	Asmir Avdukić		13/05/81	G	28		
20	Branko Bajić		04/06/98	D	1		
9	Adnan Bajrektarević		09/09/97	D	1		
3	Armel Berbić	SVK	03/02/96	A		(4)	
3	Abdurahman Beširović		05/06/97	M		(2)	
1	Dino Beširović		31/01/94	M	22		2
20	Miloš Djurković	SRB	23/09/87	G	2		
14	Aleksandar Glišić		03/09/92	M	2	(6)	
2	Ademin Hadžić		25/01/96	M	8	(1)	
4	Dušan Hodžić		31/10/93	D	26		2
21	Ivan Jakovljević	SRB	26/05/89	D	27		
17	Slobodan Jakovljević	SRB	26/05/89	D	23	(1)	
6	Dejan Janković	SRB	06/01/86	M	7	(1)	
15	Taulant Kadrija	SVN	18/05/93	D	1	(2)	
11	Željko Krsmanović		11/12/90	D	12	(4)	1
2	Milivoje Lazić		19/09/92	M	19	(1)	4
25	Dejan Maksimović		11/10/95	M	6	(11)	3
5	Eldin Mašić		02/01/87	M	15	(5)	
5	Samir Memišević		13/08/93	D	22		1
19	Nemanja Milinković		07/06/97	M	1		
19	Jovan Motika		11/09/98	A	2		
16	Momčilo Mrkajić		21/09/90	A	1	(10)	
18	Marko Obradović	MNE	30/06/91	A	26		9
18	Stanko Ostojić		15/01/85	M	22	(1)	
19	Stefan Rakić		16/06/98	M		(1)	
19	Ermin Seratlić	MNE	21/09/90	M	6	(6)	
10	Nenad Srećković	SRB	11/04/88	M	6		
10	Darko Stanojević	SRB	12/04/87	D		(2)	
10	Joco Stokić		07/04/87	M	5	(3)	1
9	Adnan Šećerović		01/12/91	A	20	(5)	1
12	Aleksandar Vasić		04/06/91	D	2	(4)	
8	Mladen Zeljković	SRB	18/11/87	D	3		
7	Mladen Žižović		27/12/80	M	8	(1)	

FK Rudar Prijedor

1928 • Gradski (4,000) • rudarprijedor.com
**Coach: Boris Gavran;
(28/10/15) Zlatko Jelisavac**

2015
25/07	h	Mladost	W	3-0	Radoja, Arežina 2 (1p)
01/08	a	Sloboda	L	1-2	Arežina
09/08	h	Olimpic	D	0-0	
15/08	a	Drina	L	1-4	Kojić
23/08	h	Travnik	W	2-1	Pekija, Džafić
30/08	a	Sarajevo	L	0-2	
09/09	a	Zrinjski	L	0-1	
12/09	a	Čelik	D	0-0	
19/09	h	Široki Brijeg	L	0-1	
26/09	h	Slavija	D	2-2	Arežina, Džafić
03/10	a	Borac	W	2-1	Džafić, Milutinović
17/10	h	Radnik	L	0-1	
24/10	a	Vitez	L	1-3	Milutinović
01/11	a	Željezničar	W	1-0	Mrkić
07/11	h	Velež	D	0-0	
21/11	a	Mladost	L	1-2	Radoja
28/11	h	Sloboda	L	0-1	
05/12	a	Olimpic	L	2-6	Kunić 2

2016
27/02	h	Drina	L	0-1	
05/03	a	Travnik	D	0-0	
12/03	h	Sarajevo	D	1-1	Burazor (p)
20/03	a	Zrinjski	L	1-2	Kantar
02/04	h	Čelik	D	0-0	
09/04	a	Široki Brijeg	L	0-2	
17/04	a	Slavija	D	0-0	
23/04	h	Borac	L	0-1	
30/04	a	Radnik	L	0-2	
04/05	h	Vitez	D	1-1	Jakupović
07/05	a	Željezničar	D	1-1	Rokvić
15/05	h	Velež	W	4-0	Rokvić, Jakupović 2, Milutinović (p)

No	Name	Nat	DoB	Pos	Aps	(s)	Gls
10	Ljuban Antonić		25/10/92	A	10	(1)	
10	Filip Arežina		08/11/92	M	15	(1)	4
4	Petar Bogdanović	SRB	11/06/94	D	1	(1)	
6	Bojan Burazor		25/12/92	M	28		1
14	Čedomir Ćelum		06/11/83	D	17		
8	Ognjen Davidović		17/08/98	M	1		
16	Mario Desnica		15/05/94	M		(2)	
25	Mirza Džafić		30/03/81	A	7	(4)	3
3	Borislav Erić		05/01/91	M	10		
44	Stefan Gavranović		14/06/97	D	1	(5)	
15	Edvin Hamzić		06/11/90	D	1	(4)	
19	Demir Jakupović		16/02/96	A	9	(3)	3
18	Aleksandar Jovičić		18/01/95	M	25		
11	Vedran Kantar		01/03/85	M	10		1
7	Dejan Kojić		31/05/86	A	12	(5)	1
12	Dalibor Kozić		10/02/88	G	29		
11	Amir Kukavica		12/03/94	M			
42	Petar Kunić		15/07/93	A	18	(8)	2
23	Nemanja Marić		20/02/95	D	7	(1)	
4	Armin Mešić		18/03/88	D		(1)	
11	Stipe Miloš		15/02/90	D	11		
30	Zoran Milutinović		01/03/88	M	19		3
30	Nebojša Mrkić		03/01/96	A	4	(7)	1
21	Jasper Nartey	GHA	21/01/95	M	2	(6)	
3	Boris Nišević		26/05/90	D	9	(1)	
20	George Owosu	GHA	16/04/96	M	1	(3)	
20	Nebojša Pejić		05/01/88	M	19	(6)	
8	Nemanja Pekija		27/10/92	D	25	(2)	1
25	Vladimir Petković		02/04/97	D		(5)	
1	Nemanja Petrović		02/01/94	G	1		
8	Siniša Radoja	SRB	25/09/86	D	10	(7)	2
15	Marinko Rastoka		10/06/91	D	5	(1)	
9	Rastko Rokvić		05/10/94	A	1	(5)	2
2	Nebojša Šodić		15/07/85	D	22		

FK Sarajevo

1946 • Olimpijski Asim Ferhatović Hase
(34,600) • fksarajevo.ba

Major honours
*Yugoslav League (2) 1967, 1985; Bosnian-
Herzegovinian League (2) 2007, 2015; Bosnian-
Herzegovinian Cup (4) 1998, 2002, 2005, 2014*

Coach: Dženan Uščuplić;
(10/09/15) Almir Hurtić;
(25/09/15) Miodrag Ješić (SRB);
(16/03/16) Almir Hurtić

2015
27/07	h	Drina	W	6-1	Benko 3, Alispahić, Velkoski, Okić
03/08	a	Travnik	L	0-1	
09/08	h	Široki Brijeg	W	2-1	Benko, Stojčev
14/08	h	Zrinjski	L	0-1	
22/08	a	Čelik	D	1-1	Benko
30/08	h	Rudar	W	2-0	Puzigaća, Okić
10/09	a	Slavija	L	0-1	
13/09	h	Borac	W	2-0	Amer Bekić, Velkoski
18/09	a	Radnik	W	3-0	Velkoski, Benko, Okić
27/09	h	Vitez	W	4-0	Barbarić, Hebibović, Kovačević, Benko
04/10	a	Željezničar	L	0-1	
18/10	h	Velež	W	4-1	Velkoski 2, Amer Bekić, Benko
24/10	a	Mladost	L	1-2	Barbarić
01/11	h	Sloboda	W	1-0	Amer Bekić
08/11	a	Olimpic	W	3-1	Benko 2, Velkoski
21/11	a	Drina	W	3-1	Rustemović, Okić, Duljević
29/11	h	Travnik	W	4-0	Benko, Duljević, Kovačević, Osmanović
05/12	a	Široki Brijeg	L	0-1	

2016
28/02	a	Zrinjski	D	2-2	Simeunović, Amer Bekić
05/03	h	Čelik	W	2-1	Benko, Harba
12/03	h	Rudar	D	1-1	Benko
20/03	a	Slavija	W	3-0	Benko, Amer Bekić, Čataković
02/04	a	Borac	W	1-0	Barbarić
10/04	h	Radnik	W	2-1	Amer Bekić 2
17/04	h	Vitez	W	3-1	Benko, Amer Bekić 2
24/04	h	Željezničar	L	0-1	
30/04	a	Velež	W	3-0	Harba, Okić, Duljević
04/05	h	Mladost	W	2-1	Benko 2
07/05	a	Sloboda	L	0-4	
15/05	h	Olimpic	L	1-3	Benko

No	Name	Nat	DoB	Pos	Aps	(s)	Gls
10	Mehmed Alispahić		24/11/87	A	4	(1)	1
25	Tomislav Barbarić	CRO	29/03/89	D	22	(1)	3
5	Mario Barić	CRO	15/04/85	D	5	(2)	
19	Almir Bekić		01/06/89	D	15	(5)	
8	Amer Bekić		05/08/92	A	16	(8)	9
21	Leon Benko	CRO	11/11/83	A	22	(4)	18
23	Džemal Berberović		05/11/81	D	6	(8)	
13	Cézar Augusto	BRA	13/03/86	A	3		
59	Gojko Cimirot		19/12/92	M	2		
99	Hamza Čataković		15/01/97	A		(3)	1
2	Matej Delač	CRO	20/08/92	G	11	(1)	
17	Haris Duljević		16/11/93	M	23	(3)	3
10	Emerson	BRA	04/01/86	A	6	(3)	
8	Vedad Gljiva		01/03/97	M		(3)	
28	Haris Harba		14/07/88	M	4	(6)	2
13	Anel Hebibović		07/07/90	M	7		1
97	Elvedin Herić		02/09/97	M		(4)	
70	Harmony Ikande	NGA	17/09/90	M	4	(2)	
3	Adnan Kadušić		14/10/97	D	13		
55	Ahmad Kallasi	SYR	18/07/90	D	8	(5)	
6	Adnan Kovačević		09/09/93	D	21		2
5	Denis Kramar	SVN	07/11/91	D	4	(1)	
16	Marko Mihojević		21/04/96	D	9	(6)	
9	Šefko Okić	CRO	26/07/88	M	20	(6)	5
18	Adnan Osmanović		20/03/97	M		(4)	1
32	Senedin Oštraković		13/04/87	G	2		
30	Bojan Pavlović	SRB	08/11/86	G	10		
1	Emir Plakalo		19/02/95	G	7		
77	Bojan Puzigaća		10/05/85	D	10		1
88	Samir Radovac		25/01/96	M	20	(4)	
4	Edin Rustemović		06/01/93	M	21	(3)	1
92	Deni Simeunović	CRO	12/02/92	M	3		1
15	Milan Stepanov	SRB	02/04/83	D	5		
7	Miloš Stojčev	MNE	19/01/87	M	1	(1)	1
14	Ivan Tatomirović	SRB	11/09/89	D	11		
69	Demirel Veladžić		15/09/99	M		(1)	
11	Krste Velkoski	MKD	20/02/88	A	15	(3)	6

FK Slavija Sarajevo

1908 • SC Slavija (4,500) • fkslavija.com

Major honours
Bosnian-Herzegovinian Cup (1) 2009

Coach: Milan Gutović;
(11/08/15) (Duško Petrović, Dragan Škrba &
Goran Simić);
(19/08/15) Darko Vojvodić;
(06/12/15) Veljko Dovedan (SRB);
(22/03/16) Milko Djurovski (MKD)

2015
26/07	h	Velež	D	1-1	Rovčanin
01/08	a	Mladost	D	1-1	Rovčanin
09/08	h	Sloboda	D	0-1	
17/08	h	Olimpic	W	3-2	Spalević, Barić, Vejnović
23/08	h	Drina	W	1-0	Kartal
30/08	a	Travnik	D	0-0	
10/09	h	Sarajevo	W	1-0	Spalević
13/09	a	Zrinjski	L	0-4	
20/09	h	Čelik	W	2-1	Spalević, N Pušara
26/09	a	Rudar	D	2-2	N Pušara, Spalević
04/10	h	Široki Brijeg	D	0-0	
18/10	h	Borac	W	3-0	Arsenijević, Spalević, N Pušara
24/10	a	Radnik	L	1-2	Rovčanin
01/11	h	Vitez	L	0-1	
08/11	a	Željezničar	D	0-0	
21/11	h	Velež	W	3-0	Spalević 2, Jovanović
29/11	h	Mladost	D	1-1	Barić
05/12	a	Sloboda	L	0-4	

2016
28/02	h	Olimpic	W	1-0	Spalević (p)
05/03	a	Drina	D	1-1	N Pušara
13/03	h	Travnik	D	0-0	
20/03	h	Sarajevo	L	0-3	
03/04	a	Zrinjski	L	0-1	
09/04	a	Čelik	L	0-2	
17/04	h	Rudar	D	0-0	
24/04	a	Široki Brijeg	L	0-4	
30/04	a	Borac	L	1-2	Marušić
04/05	h	Radnik	W	2-1	N Pušara, Simović
07/05	a	Vitez	L	0-2	
15/05	h	Željezničar	D	1-1	Spalević

No	Name	Nat	DoB	Pos	Aps	(s)	Gls
20	Branislav Arsenijević	SRB	02/08/82	D	24		1
22	Stefan Barić	SRB	17/02/91	M	26	(2)	2
21	Ljubiša Berjan		18/08/94	M		(8)	
22	Karlo Bilić	CRO	06/09/93	D	2		
7	Nikola Bjeloš		03/08/98	M		(1)	
10	Nemanja Bošković	SRB	05/08/90	M	11		
17	Denis Čomor		03/01/90	D	23	(1)	
7	Semir Djip		23/06/92	A	1	(2)	
11	Srdjan Grujičić	SRB	19/06/87	M	20	(3)	
27	Dino Hasković		28/10/95	M	1	(2)	
19	Ivan Jovanović	CRO	22/05/91	A	3	(3)	1
26	Nemanja Kartal	MNE	17/07/94	D	24		1
7	Igor Kartal	SRB	17/05/91	M	3	(4)	
12	Miloš Kubura		25/05/94	G	2		
2	Milan Lalović		11/11/97	M		(3)	
15	Mladen Lučić		06/07/85	G	28		
25	Bojan Marković		12/11/85	D	23	(1)	
4	Zoran Marušić	SRB	29/11/93	D	6	(1)	1
21	Predrag Papaz		20/01/97	A	4	(1)	
21	Toni Pervan		13/03/94	D		(2)	
19	Almir Pliska		12/08/87	A	2	(3)	
13	Aleksandar Pušara		29/11/95	M		(7)	
13	Nemanja Pušara		21/08/91	A	13	(8)	5
14	Igor Radovanović		02/08/85	A	5	(4)	
3	Marko Ristić		09/03/87	D	28		
10	Damir Rovčanin		12/03/88	A	13	(3)	3
16	Marko Simović		13/07/90	M	7	(15)	1
2	Luka Sindjić	SRB	13/02/93	M		(2)	
9	Darko Spalević	SRB	24/03/77	A	23	(2)	9
15	Nemanja Vejnović		04/04/92	D	24	(3)	1
8	Emir Zeba		10/06/89	M	13	(5)	
8	Momir Zečević		07/01/94	M	1		

FK Sloboda Tuzla

1919 • Tušanj (8,000) • fksloboda.ba

Coach: Husref Musemić

2015
25/07	a	Čelik	L	0-1	
01/08	h	Rudar	W	2-1	Ahmetović, Moranjkić
09/08	a	Slavija	W	1-0	Ahmetović
14/08	h	Borac	D	1-1	Ahmetović
22/08	h	Radnik	W	1-0	Ahmetović
29/08	h	Vitez	W	2-1	Zeba 2
09/09	a	Željezničar	D	0-0	
13/09	h	Velež	W	2-0	Ahmetović, Ordagić
20/09	a	Mladost	D	1-1	Kostić
27/09	a	Široki Brijeg	D	0-0	
03/10	h	Olimpic	W	2-1	Veselinović, Stjepanović
17/10	a	Drina	W	2-1	Kostić, Krpić
24/10	h	Travnik	W	2-0	Krpić, Ahmetović
01/11	a	Sarajevo	L	0-1	
08/11	h	Zrinjski	W	2-1	Zeba, Mehidić
23/11	h	Čelik	W	4-2	Ahmetović 2, Sarić, Zeba
28/11	a	Rudar	W	1-0	Zeba
05/12	h	Slavija	W	4-0	Ahmetović, Zeba (p), Ordagić, Krpić

2016
27/02	a	Borac	D	0-0	
06/03	h	Radnik	W	1-0	Sarić
12/03	h	Vitez	W	3-1	og (Novak), Ordagić, Zeba
19/03	h	Željezničar	L	0-1	
02/04	a	Velež	W	2-1	Kostić, Zeba
10/04	h	Mladost	W	2-0	Haurdić, Zeba
17/04	h	Široki Brijeg	L	0-3	
23/04	a	Olimpic	W	1-0	Mehidić
30/04	h	Drina	L	0-2	
04/05	a	Travnik	W	3-2	Krpić, Ivetić, Ordagić
07/05	h	Sarajevo	W	4-0	Zeba (p), og (Kovačević), Veselinović, Sarić
15/05	a	Zrinjski	L	1-2	Ahmetović (p)

No	Name	Nat	DoB	Pos	Aps	(s)	Gls
24	Mersudin Ahmetović		19/03/85	A	27	(2)	10
16	Mehmed Ćosić		25/06/97	M		(1)	
22	Samir Efendić		10/05/91	D	27		
22	Miljan Govedarica		26/05/94	M	9	(6)	
1	Mirza Hamzabegović		11/07/90	G	2		
20	Anes Haurdić		01/03/90	M	7	(2)	1
18	Perica Ivetić		28/11/92	D	28		1
18	Nenad Kiso		30/04/89	D	4	(6)	
3	Ivan Kostić	SRB	24/06/89	D	21		3
9	Sulejman Krpić		01/01/91	A	5	(20)	4
6	Slobodan Lakičević	MNE	12/01/88	D	3	(1)	
23	Damir Mehidić		07/01/92	M	10	(11)	2
7	Haris Mehmedagić		29/03/88	D	25		
28	Samir Merzić		29/06/84	M	1		
6	Jasmin Moranjkić		11/10/83	D	4		1
11	Muhamed Mujić		26/01/91	A		(1)	
13	Adnan Mujkić		27/10/95	D		(1)	
13	Azir Muminović		18/04/97	G	1		
18	Ermin Musić		28/05/97	M		(1)	
19	Amer Ordagić		05/05/93	M	25	(3)	4
14	Kenan Oruč		07/07/94	D	27	(1)	
7	Omar Pršeš		07/05/95	M	3	(3)	
5	Adnan Salihović		18/10/82	D	2	(5)	
5	Elvis Sarić	CRO	21/07/90	M	20	(4)	3
20	Nemanja Stjepanović	SRB	07/02/84	M	22	(2)	1
4	Ibrahim Škahić		25/10/93	D	5	(3)	
25	Darko Todorović		05/05/97	D	1	(1)	
27	Mladen Veselinović		04/01/93	M	21	(7)	2
10	Zajko Zeba		22/05/83	M	27		10

BOSNIA & HERZEGOVINA

NK Široki Brijeg

1948 • Pecara (7,000) • nk-sirokibrijeg.com
Major honours
*Bosnian-Herzegovinian League (2) 2004, 2006;
Bosnian-Herzegovinian Cup (2) 2007, 2013*
**Coach: Davor Mladina;
(10/09/15) Slaven Musa**

2015
26/07	a	Travnik	W	2-1	Wagner, Menalo
02/08	h	Vitez	W	5-1	Wagner 2, Menalo 2, Kožulj
09/08	a	Sarajevo	L	1-2	Wagner
16/08	h	Željezničar	D	1-1	Kožulj
23/08	a	Zrinjski	D	0-0	
30/08	h	Velež	W	1-0	Bralić
09/09	a	Čelik	L	1-2	Kresinger
13/09	h	Mladost	W	3-0	Wagner, Kresinger, Buhač
19/09	a	Rudar	W	1-0	Pehar
27/09	h	Sloboda	D	0-0	
04/10	a	Slavija	D	0-0	
18/10	h	Olimpic	W	2-1	Wagner, Krstanović
24/10	a	Borac	W	2-0	Wagner 2
31/10	h	Drina	W	5-1	Menalo, Krstanović, Wagner, Buhač 2
07/11	a	Radnik	W	1-0	Baraban
21/11	h	Travnik	D	2-2	Wagner, Krstanović
28/11	a	Vitez	L	1-2	Kresinger
06/12	h	Sarajevo	W	1-0	Kožulj

2016
28/02	a	Željezničar	L	0-2	
06/03	h	Zrinjski	L	3-4	Crnov, Krstanović, Pandža
12/03	a	Velež	W	3-0	Sesar, Krstanović (p), Ivanković
20/03	h	Čelik	D	0-0	
03/04	a	Mladost	W	2-1	Pandža, Krstanović
09/04	h	Rudar	W	2-0	Ajayi, og (Pekija)
17/04	a	Sloboda	W	3-0	Ajayi 2, Krstanović
24/04	h	Slavija	W	4-0	Kožulj, Crnov 2, Pehar
30/04	a	Olimpic	L	1-2	Kožulj
04/05	h	Borac	W	1-0	Ajayi
07/05	a	Drina	W	3-0	Wagner, Kožulj, Krstanović
15/05	h	Radnik	W	5-0	Krstanović 3, Wagner, Ajayi

No	Name	Nat	DoB	Pos	Aps	(s)	Gls
22	Goodness Ajayi	NGA	06/10/94	A	10	(5)	5
11	Ivan Baraban	CRO	22/01/88	A	11	(5)	1
6	Josip Barišić		12/08/83	D	14	(9)	
12	Luka Bilobrk		08/12/85	G	1		
28	Slavko Bralić	CRO	15/12/92	D	20		1
21	Slavko Brekalo		25/02/90	D	23	(1)	
19	Ivan Buhač		15/12/94	A	1	(7)	3
30	Ivan Crnov	CRO	14/08/88	M	24	(4)	3
9	Josip Čorluka		03/03/95	D	6	(5)	
7	Dino Čorić		30/06/90	D	20		
10	Jure Ivanković		15/11/85	M	8	(13)	1
24	Matej Karačić		01/08/94	M	6	(1)	
4	Danijel Kožul		01/08/88	M	1	(3)	
18	Zvonimir Kožulj		15/11/93	M	22		6
32	Dino Kresinger	CRO	20/03/82	A	4	(7)	3
9	Ivan Krstanović	CRO	05/01/83	A	19		11
14	Davor Landeka		18/09/84	M	2	(12)	
25	Stipo Marković		03/12/93	D	23	(2)	
17	Luka Menalo		22/07/96	M	11	(5)	4
5	Boris Pandža		15/12/86	D	9		2
8	Mate Pehar		25/02/88	M	21		2
19	Ivan Sesar		23/01/89	M	23	(3)	1
23	Antonio Soldo		12/01/88	G	29		
15	Wagner	BRA	01/01/78	A	22	(6)	12

NK Travnik

1922 • Pirota (3,000) • no website
**Coach: Almir Memić;
(08/01/16) Darko Vojvodić;
(21/03/16) Boris Gavran**

2015
26/07	h	Široki Brijeg	L	1-2	Smajić
03/08	h	Sarajevo	W	1-0	Kouadio
08/08	a	Zrinjski	L	0-1	
15/08	h	Čelik	W	3-2	Dudić, og (G Popović), Šivšić
23/08	a	Rudar	L	1-2	Dudić
30/08	h	Slavija	D	0-0	
09/09	a	Borac	L	1-2	Dudić
13/09	h	Radnik	L	1-3	Dudić
19/09	a	Vitez	L	0-2	
27/09	h	Željezničar	W	2-0	Aleksić, Šivšić
03/10	a	Velež	W	1-0	Kouadio
17/10	h	Mladost	L	1-2	Smajić
24/10	a	Sloboda	L	0-2	
31/10	h	Olimpic	W	2-1	Zajmović, Dudić
07/11	a	Drina	L	0-1	
21/11	a	Široki Brijeg	D	2-2	Dudić, Kouadio
29/11	a	Sarajevo	L	0-4	
05/12	h	Zrinjski	L	1-4	Nuhić

2016
27/02	h	Čelik	D	1-1	Kouadio
05/03	h	Rudar	D	0-0	
13/03	a	Slavija	D	0-0	
19/03	h	Borac	L	0-2	
02/04	a	Radnik	L	0-2	
09/04	h	Vitez	W	3-1	Zec 3
16/04	a	Željezničar	L	1-2	Zec
23/04	h	Velež	W	7-1	Jelić, Nuhić 2, Smajić, Kouadio 2, Varupa
30/04	a	Mladost	L	1-2	Zec
04/05	h	Sloboda	L	2-3	Anel Ćurić, Jelić
08/05	a	Olimpic	L	0-1	
15/05	h	Drina	W	4-2	Kouadio 3, og (Jokić)

No	Name	Nat	DoB	Pos	Aps	(s)	Gls
6	Radoslav Aleksić	SRB	06/03/86	D	26		1
16	Nemanja Andjušić		17/10/96	M	3	(3)	
23	Miloš Bakrač	MNE	25/02/92	D	1		
23	Muharem Čivić		04/01/93	D	14	(1)	
20	Daniel Ćulum		19/08/89	M	1	(3)	
7	Amel Ćurić		22/02/93	M	3	(13)	
11	Anel Ćurić		28/07/88	M	11		1
11	Selmin Djogić		28/03/97	A		(3)	
13	Fedja Dudić		01/02/83	A	17		6
24	Dženan Durak		04/02/91	A	3	(2)	
19	Nijaz Fazlić		08/09/93	M		(15)	
15	Sead Hadžibulić		30/01/83	A	1	(2)	
5	Emrah Hasanhodžić		09/08/93	D	16		
8	Irfan Jašarević		24/08/95	M	21	(4)	
18	Igor Jelić	SRB	28/12/89	M	11		2
15	Hrustan Kadrić		21/07/97	M	8	(2)	
17	Rijad Kobiljar		08/04/96	M	4	(5)	
6	Germain Kouadio	CIV	27/12/92	M	25	(1)	9
6	Sanel Kovač		31/10/96	D	27		
12	Željko Kuzmić	SRB	02/11/84	G	1		
24	Nedim Mekić		15/04/95	M	11	(2)	
5	Mario Mornar	CRO	07/07/90	D	4		
4	Ajdin Nuhić		01/11/91	M	14	(7)	3
1	Adis Nurković		28/04/86	G	26		
11	Hasib Peco		17/08/95	M	1		
18	Alem Plakalo		01/05/94	M	1	(6)	
20	Duško Radosavljević	SRB	16/06/88	M	6	(2)	
16	Fahret Selimović	LUX	26/09/93	M	2		
22	Irhan Smajić		08/09/90	A	26	(1)	3
12	Harun Strika		14/11/91	G	2		
11	Safet Šivšić		16/02/93	M	14	(1)	2
2	Sinbad Terzić		22/02/81	D	9	(2)	
18	Nermin Varupa		18/04/91	M	6	(2)	1
9	Dženan Zajmović		11/11/94	A	9	(5)	1
13	Asim Zec		23/01/94	A	8	2	5

FK Velež

1922 • Vrapčići (3,500) • fkvelez.ba
Major honours
Yugoslav Cup (2) 1981, 1986
**Coach: Dželaludin Muharemović;
(25/08/15) Adis Obad;
(17/09/15) Dženan Zaimović;
(20/10/15) Dragan Kanatlarovski (MKD);
(07/11/15) Dženan Zaimović;
(23/11/15) Zijo Tojaga**

2015
26/07	a	Slavija	D	1-1	Janković
01/08	h	Borac	D	1-1	Matić
08/08	a	Radnik	D	0-0	
15/08	h	Vitez	L	0-1	
23/08	a	Željezničar	L	1-2	Haurdić
30/08	a	Široki Brijeg	L	0-1	
09/09	h	Mladost	L	0-1	
13/09	a	Sloboda	L	0-2	
19/09	h	Olimpic	L	1-2	Zec
26/09	a	Drina	W	2-1	M Ćemalović, Merzić
03/10	h	Travnik	L	0-1	
18/10	a	Sarajevo	L	1-4	Maletić
24/10	h	Zrinjski	L	0-1	
31/10	a	Čelik	L	0-1	
07/11	h	Rudar	D	0-0	
21/11	h	Slavija	L	0-3	
28/11	a	Borac	L	1-2	D Ćemalović
05/12	h	Radnik	L	0-1	

2016
27/02	a	Vitez	L	0-6	
05/03	h	Željezničar	L	0-3	
12/03	h	Široki Brijeg	L	0-3	
19/03	a	Mladost	L	0-1	
02/04	h	Sloboda	L	1-2	Papaz
09/04	a	Olimpic	L	0-1	
16/04	h	Drina	L	0-1	
23/04	a	Travnik	L	1-7	D Ćemalović
30/04	h	Sarajevo	L	0-3	
04/05	a	Zrinjski	L	0-1	
07/05	h	Čelik	D	0-0	
15/05	a	Rudar	L	0-4	

No	Name	Nat	DoB	Pos	Aps	(s)	Gls
2	Amar Alikadić		15/06/98	D	7	(2)	
13	Tomislav Barišić		06/03/93	D	7	(3)	
6	Harun Benca		04/05/94	D	1		
12	Adnan Bobić		04/02/87	G	26		
4	Dragan Cadikovski	MKD	13/01/82	A	3	(4)	
15	Dino Ćemalović		16/04/95	A	10	(6)	2
11	Mirza Ćemalović		06/07/93	M	13	(3)	1
5	Riad Demić		17/11/93	M	16	(1)	
4	Dino Gavrić	CRO	11/04/89	D	5		
9	Aldin Dino Hajdarević		12/10/90	A	5	(1)	
20	Anes Haurdić		01/06/90	M	13	(2)	1
32	Irfan Husić		08/06/95	M	2		
27	Tarik Isić		03/05/96	M	8	(2)	
3	Nino Jakirović		22/04/95	D	7	(3)	
13	Sinan Jakupović		27/08/94	M	7	(3)	
17	Dejan Janković	SRB	06/01/86	M	10	(1)	1
5	Armin Jazvin		11/10/90	D	8		
7	Mustafa Kodro		29/08/81	M	13	(2)	
25	Selver Količić		13/05/95	D	6	(2)	
19	Benjamin Lukomirak		12/04/94	D	11		
14	Amer Mahinić		02/06/90	M	8	(3)	
33	Darko Maletić		20/10/80	D	15		1
22	Goran Matić	SRB	28/02/89	M	7	(5)	1
16	Meris Memić		16/03/95	D	2	(4)	
16	Samir Merzić		29/06/84	D	9	(2)	1
3	Hamza Mešanović		21/12/97	M	3		
23	Marko Nikolić	SRB	09/06/89	M	17		
18	Anes Nuspahić		10/07/93	M		(3)	
25	Damir Osmanković		12/09/93	D	4		
27	Novo Papaz		31/12/90	M	7	(2)	1
9	Damir Peco		21/07/96	D	8	(8)	
1	Nemanja Popović	SRB	20/05/84	G	1		
10	Miloš Reljić	SRB	12/06/89	A	7	(6)	
10	Damir Rovčanin		12/03/88	A	8		
8	Nedžad Serdarević		20/09/84	M	11	(1)	
6	Asim Škaljić		09/08/81	D	8	(2)	
28	Mario Tadejević	CRO	28/08/92	D	3		
20	Kerin Tatar		02/09/96	D		(4)	
18	Petar Vidović		20/06/97	A	1	(4)	
30	Haris Voloder		18/02/96	D	3		
24	Asim Zec		23/01/94	A	7	(6)	1
19	Amir Zolj		24/11/89	D	15		
14	Senad Zuhrić		03/03/92	M	4	(1)	

NK Vitez

1947 • Gradski (2,000) • nkvitez.com
Coach: Valentin Plavčić;
(05/08/15) Ivica Bonić;
(12/09/15) Branko Karačić (CRO)

2015

25/07	a	Radnik	L	0-1	
02/08	a	Široki Brijeg	L	1-5	Kantar
09/08	h	Željezničar	L	0-1	
15/08	h	Velež	W	1-0	Jusufbašić
22/08	h	Mladost	D	1-1	Djurić
29/08	a	Sloboda	L	1-2	Kapetan
09/09	a	Olimpic	L	1-2	Pilipović
12/09	a	Drina	W	2-0	Kapetan 2
19/09	a	Travnik	W	2-0	Anastasov, Muminović
27/09	a	Sarajevo	L	0-4	
03/10	h	Zrinjski	W	1-0	Pilipović
17/10	a	Čelik	L	1-6	Fajić
24/10	h	Rudar	W	3-1	Jevtić, Djurić, Basara
01/11	a	Slavija	W	1-0	og (Čomor)
07/11	h	Borac	W	1-0	Djurić
21/11	h	Radnik	L	0-1	
28/11	h	Široki Brijeg	D	1-1	Djurić
06/12	a	Željezničar	L	0-3	

2016

27/02	h	Velež	W	6-0	Radeljić, Šantić, Djurić, Mrkaić (p), Livančić 2
05/03	a	Mladost	D	0-0	
12/03	h	Sloboda	L	1-3	og (Kostić)
20/03	a	Olimpic	D	0-0	
02/04	h	Drina	W	4-0	Livančić 2, Jurić, Mrkaić
09/04	a	Travnik	L	1-3	Djurić
17/04	h	Sarajevo	L	1-3	Jevtić
23/04	a	Zrinjski	L	0-1	
29/04	h	Čelik	W	1-0	Mrkaić
04/05	a	Rudar	D	1-1	Anastasov
07/05	h	Slavija	W	2-0	Novak, Livančić
15/05	a	Borac	D	2-2	Djurić, Šantić

No	Name	Nat	DoB	Pos	Aps	(s)	Gls
3	Sanel Alić		20/11/91	D	4	(2)	
22	Aleksandar Anastasov	MKD	04/05/93	M	11	(8)	2
5	Mario Barić	CRO	15/04/85	D	11		
19	Hrvoje Barišić	CRO	03/02/91	M	24		
7	Marko Basara	SRB	29/07/84	A	9	(4)	1
13	Boban Djerić		20/08/93	A		(2)	
55	Velibor Djurić		05/05/82	M	23	(4)	7
30	Nusmir Fajić		12/01/87	A	5	(1)	1
8	Josip Grebenar		13/12/95	M		(3)	
5	Marko Jevtić	SRB	21/05/82	D	24		2
25	Dragan Jurčević		10/07/95	M		(1)	
4	Goran Jurić	CRO	22/08/83	M	12	(11)	1
45	Sabahudin Jusufbašić		13/01/90	A	5	(6)	1
11	Vedran Kantar		01/03/85	M	8	(7)	1
21	Armin Kapetan		11/03/86	A	12	(11)	3
7	Ivan Livaja		01/10/87	D	2	(4)	
15	Toni Livančić		11/12/94	A	28	(2)	5
10	Momčilo Mrkaić		21/09/90	A	10	1	3
6	Milan Muminović		02/10/83	M	23	(2)	1
18	Leopold Novak	CRO	03/12/90	A	9		1
9	Toni Pezo	CRO	14/02/87	D	9	(1)	
18	Borislav Pilipović		25/03/84	D	16	(1)	2
30	Anto Radeljić		31/12/90	D	8		1
20	Elvis Sadiković		29/10/83	D	20		
30	Jasmin Smriko		20/01/91	A	3	(1)	
2	Ivan Stanić		30/06/96	D	1	(8)	
10	Josip Šantić		29/12/93	M	21	(6)	2
1	Ivan Tirić		15/04/93	G	17		
17	Vedran Vidović		14/11/90	A	2	(3)	
87	Aleksandar Živković		18/06/87	G	13		

HŠK Zrinjski

1905 • Bijeli Brijeg (15,000) • hskzrinjski.ba
Major honours
Bosnian-Herzegovinian League (4) 2005, 2009,
2014, 2016; Bosnian-Herzegovinian Cup (1) 2008
Coach: Vinko Marinović

2015

26/07	h	Olimpic	W	2-0	Mešanović, Šćepanović
01/08	a	Drina	W	1-0	Laštro
08/08	h	Travnik	W	1-0	Nikolić
14/08	a	Sarajevo	W	1-0	Radulović
23/08	h	Široki Brijeg	D	0-0	
28/08	h	Čelik	D	0-0	
09/09	a	Rudar	W	1-0	Todorović
13/09	h	Slavija	W	4-0	Mešanović 2, Filipović 2
19/09	a	Borac	L	1-2	Šćepanović
27/09	h	Radnik	D	0-0	
03/10	a	Vitez	L	0-1	
17/10	h	Željezničar	W	2-1	Todorović, Filipović
24/10	a	Velež	W	1-0	Stojkić
31/10	h	Mladost	W	4-0	Nikolić, Todorović 2, Filipović
08/11	a	Sloboda	L	1-2	Šćepanović
21/11	a	Olimpic	W	3-0	og (Regoje), Zakarić, Petrak
28/11	h	Drina	W	5-0	Todorović, Mešanović 2, Nikolić, Vranjić
05/12	a	Travnik	W	4-1	Mešanović, Zakarić 2, Laštro

2016

28/02	h	Sarajevo	D	2-2	Todorović, Bilbija
06/03	a	Široki Brijeg	W	4-3	Mešanović (p), Petrak, Todorović, Arežina
12/03	h	Čelik	D	2-2	Graovac, Mešanović (p)
19/03	h	Rudar	W	2-1	Arežina, og (Pekija)
03/04	a	Slavija	W	1-0	Zakarić
09/04	h	Borac	W	2-1	Zakarić 2
16/04	a	Radnik	W	1-0	Zakarić
23/04	h	Vitez	W	1-0	Mešanović
29/04	a	Željezničar	D	0-0	
04/05	h	Velež	W	1-0	Bilbija
07/05	h	Mladost	W	3-0	Mešanović 2 (1p), Bilbija
15/05	h	Sloboda	W	2-1	Bilbija, Petrak

No	Name	Nat	DoB	Pos	Aps	(s)	Gls
19	Miloš Aćimović		06/07/97	A		(1)	
23	Filip Arežina		08/11/92	A	8	(2)	2
12	Krešimir Bandić		16/01/95	G		(1)	
99	Nemanja Bilbija		02/11/90	A	2	(7)	4
15	Zvonimir Blaić	CRO	02/01/91	D	25		
15	Benjamin Čolić		23/07/91	D	4		
55	Miloš Filipović	SRB	06/05/90	M	7	(15)	4
2	Daniel Graovac		08/08/93	D	24		1
22	Goran Karačić		18/08/96	G	24		
32	Matija Katanec	CRO	04/05/90	D	9		
9	Krešimir Kordić		03/09/81	A		(3)	
27	Neven Laštro		01/10/88	M	24	(1)	2
1	Filip Lončarić	CRO	17/09/86	G	3		
21	Jasmin Mešanović		21/06/92	A	28	(1)	11
24	Stevo Nikolić		05/12/84	A	9	(6)	3
4	Ivan Peko		05/01/90	A	6	(6)	
25	Oliver Petrak	CRO	06/02/91	M	23		3
6	Anto Radeljić		31/12/90	D	3		
8	Aleksandar Radulović		09/02/87	M	14	(3)	1
20	Danijel Stojanović	CRO	18/08/84	D	19	(4)	
16	Pero Stojkić		09/12/86	D	11	(9)	1
17	Vučina Šćepanović	SRB	17/11/82	M	6	(12)	3
17	Ognjen Todorović		24/03/89	D	23	(6)	7
7	Tomislav Tomić		16/11/90	M	10	(1)	
14	Nikola Vasilj		02/12/95	M		(1)	
14	Marin Vranjić		12/02/95	M		(1)	1
77	Goran Zakarić		07/11/92	M	25	(1)	7
10	Miloš Žeravica	SRB	22/07/88	M	20	(5)	

FK Željezničar

1921 • Grbavica (14,000) • fkzeljeznicar.ba
Major honours
Yugoslav League (1) 1972; Bosnian-Herzegovinian
League (5) 2001, 2002, 2010, 2012, 2013;
Bosnian-Herzegovinian Cup (5) 2000, 2001, 2003,
2011, 2012

Coach: Milomir Odović;
(10/09/15) Vlado Čapljić;
(28/09/15) Edis Mulalić;
(07/05/16) Haris Alihodžić

2015

26/07	a	Borac	L	0-1	
02/08	h	Radnik	L	1-2	D Sadiković
09/08	a	Vitez	W	1-0	E Sadiković
16/08	a	Široki Brijeg	D	1-1	Djelmić
23/08	h	Velež	W	2-1	Kokot, Djelmić
30/08	a	Mladost	D	1-1	Hadžiahmetović
09/09	h	Sloboda	D	0-0	
14/09	a	Olimpic	W	1-0	Kokot
20/09	h	Drina	W	3-2	Djelmić 2, Blagojević
27/09	a	Travnik	L	0-2	
04/10	h	Sarajevo	W	1-0	Tiago
17/10	a	Zrinjski	L	1-2	Tiago
25/10	h	Čelik	W	4-0	Kokot, Tiago 2, Mujagić
01/11	a	Rudar	L	0-1	
08/11	h	Slavija	D	0-0	
23/11	h	Borac	W	1-0	Tiago
29/11	a	Radnik	D	0-0	
06/12	h	Vitez	W	3-0	Beganović, Mujagić, Hadžiahmetović

2016

28/02	h	Široki Brijeg	W	2-0	Lendrić, Bekrić
05/03	a	Velež	W	1-0	Bekrić (p)
13/03	h	Mladost	W	2-1	Bogičević, Lendrić
19/03	a	Sloboda	W	1-0	Lendrić
02/04	h	Olimpic	W	3-1	Lendrić 3
09/04	a	Drina	W	2-0	M Stevanović, Lendrić
16/04	h	Travnik	W	1-0	M Stevanović, Bekrić
24/04	a	Sarajevo	W	1-0	M Stevanović
29/04	h	Zrinjski	D	0-0	
04/05	a	Čelik	L	0-1	
07/05	h	Rudar	D	1-1	Lendrić
15/05	a	Slavija	D	1-1	Djermanović

No	Name	Nat	DoB	Pos	Aps	(s)	Gls
1	Marijan Antolović	CRO	07/05/89	G	17		
8	Riad Bajić		06/05/94	A	7		
21	Dženis Beganović		23/05/96	A	10	(9)	1
10	Samir Bekrić		20/10/84	M	11		3
11	Jovan Blagojević	SRB	15/03/88	M	25	(1)	1
15	Jadaranko Bogičević		11/03/83	D	11		
22	Jasmin Bogdanović		10/05/90	D	14		
30	Aldin Čeman		05/05/95	G		(1)	
7	Secouba Diatta	SEN	21/12/92	A	1	(3)	
15	Ognjen Djelmić		18/08/88	M	16		4
24	Dejan Djermanović	SVN	17/06/88	A	1	(8)	1
1	Irfan Fejzić		01/07/86	G	3		
18	Amir Hadžiahmetović		08/03/97	M	14	(1)	2
17	Mirza Halvadzic	SWE	15/02/96	A	1	(1)	
4	Dino Hasanović		21/01/96	M		(7)	
23	Amer Hiroš		10/06/96	M	1		
37	Emir Hodžurda		12/11/90	D	9	(2)	
13	Vedran Kjosevski		22/05/95	G	10	(1)	
35	Zoran Kokot		28/06/85	A	15	(1)	3
5	Aleksandar Kosorić		30/01/87	D	25		
7	Mirko Kramarić	CRO	27/01/89	D	6	(1)	
24	Ivan Lendrić	CRO	08/08/91	A	12		8
17	Ivan Livaja		01/10/87	D	2		
90	Mailson	BRA	13/07/89	A		(1)	
6	Kerim Memija		06/01/96	D	21	(2)	
16	Dušan Mladenović	SRB	13/10/90	D	16		
29	Ajdin Mujagić		03/01/98	A		(7)	2
27	Kemal Osmanković		04/03/97	D	1		
20	Damir Sadiković		07/04/95	M	14	(2)	1
19	Enis Sadiković		21/03/95	M	6	(8)	1
16	Srđan Stanić		06/07/89	A	10		
88	Miroslav Stevanović		29/07/90	M	12		3
2	Siniša Stevanović	SRB	07/04/87	D	10		
14	Joco Stokić		07/04/87	M	6	(8)	
25	Tiago	BRA	30/05/89	A	13	(10)	5
14	Dejan Uzelac	SRB	27/08/93	D	1	(2)	
44	Adnan Zahirović		23/03/90	M	10	(2)	
8	Nermin Zolotić		07/07/93	M	4	(3)	
39	Denis Žerić		21/03/98	M	1		

Top goalscorers

18   Leon Benko (Sarajevo)

12   Wagner (Široki Brijeg)

11   Haris Dilaver (Mladost)

       Ivan Krstanović (Široki Brijeg)

       Jasmin Mešanović (Zrinjski)

10   Mersudin Ahmetović (Sloboda)

       Zajko Zeba (Sloboda)

9   Mahir Karić (Čelik)

      Marko Obradović (Radnik)

      Amer Bekić (Sarajevo)

      Darko Spalević (Slavija)

      Germain Kouadio (Travnik)

Promoted clubs

NK Metalleghe-BSI Jajce

2009 • Gradski stadion Mračaj (2,000) • nkmetalleghe-bsi.com
Coach: Nermin Bašić

FK Krupa

1983 • Stadion Krupa (1,500) • no website
Coach: Slobodan Starčević

Second level final tables 2015/16

Prva liga FBIH	Pld	W	D	L	F	A	Pts
1 NK Metalleghe-BSI Jajce	30	18	7	5	50	24	61
2 NK Zvijezda Gradačac	30	18	5	7	49	26	59
3 HNK Orašje	30	13	8	9	41	30	47
4 NK Bosna Visoko	30	15	2	13	47	36	47
5 HNK Čapljina	30	13	8	9	39	30	47
6 NK Bratstvo Gračanica	30	14	4	12	38	28	46
7 FK Budućnost Banovići	30	14	4	12	34	27	46
8 NK GOŠK Gabela	30	12	9	9	33	27	45
9 FK Rudar Kakanj	30	13	5	12	40	31	44
10 NK Jedinstvo Bihać	30	13	4	13	41	35	43
11 FK Goražde	30	13	3	14	30	30	42
12 NK Novi Travnik	30	12	5	13	51	43	41
13 FK Radnički Lukavac	30	10	8	12	38	46	38
14 HNK Branitelj Mostar	30	7	6	17	25	44	24
15 NK Sloga Ljubuški	30	4	9	17	17	39	21
16 NK Podgrmeč Sanski Most	30	5	5	20	17	94	20

NB NK Branitelj Mostar – 3 pts deducted.

Prva liga RS	Pld	W	D	L	F	A	Pts
1 FK Krupa	32	23	5	4	64	21	74
2 FK Mladost Velika Obarska	32	18	8	6	68	29	62
3 FK Tekstilac Derventa	32	13	12	7	45	29	51
4 FK Kozara Gradiška	32	14	7	11	44	36	49
5 FK Zvijezda 09 Stanišići	32	13	9	10	47	39	48
6 FK Borac Šamac	32	8	8	16	35	54	32
7 FK Sutjeska Foča	32	14	6	12	39	37	48
8 FK Sloboda Mrkonjić Grad	32	14	6	12	43	46	48
9 FK Leotar	32	14	6	12	40	43	48
10 FK Sloboda Bosanski Novi	32	11	6	15	40	43	39
11 FK Drina Višegrad	32	7	4	21	24	59	25
12 FK Vlasenica	32	3	3	26	27	80	12

NB League splits into top and bottom halves after 22 games, after which the clubs play exclusively against teams in their group

DOMESTIC CUP

Kup Bosne i Hercegovine 2015/16

1/16 FINALS

(22/09/15)
Mladost Gacko 0-1 Borac Banja Luka
Široki Brijeg 5-0 Rudar Prijedor
Velež 0-1 Sloboda Bosanski Novi

(23/09/15)
Čelik 1-0 Vitez
Drina Zvornik 0-1 Bratstvo Gračanica
Goražde 0-2 Sloboda Tuzla
Mladost Doboj Kakanj 2-0 Čapljina
Modriča 1-1 GOŠK Gabela *(4-5 on pens)*
Novi Travnik 1-5 Travnik
Orašje 3-2 TOŠK Tešanj
Radnički Lukavac 2-1 Olimpic Sarajevo
Radnik Bijeljina 3-0 Mladost Velika Obarska
Rudar Kakanj 2-0 Sloga Ljubuški
Slavija Sarajevo 4-0 Rudar Ugljevik
Željezničar 1-0 Krupa
Zrinjski 1-1 Sarajevo *(5-6 on pens)*

1/8 FINALS

(21/10/15 & 03/11/15)
Orašje 0-3, 0-6 Široki Brijeg *(0-9)*

(21/10/15 & 04/11/15)
Borac Banja Luka 1-0, 2-0 Bratstvo Gračanica *(3-0)*
Čelik 1-1, 1-2 Sloboda Tuzla *(2-3)*
Rudar Kakanj 1-3, 1-7 Radnik Bijeljina *(2-10)*
Slavija Sarajevo 1-4, 1-3 Sarajevo *(2-7)*
Sloboda Bosanski Novi 2-1, 0-7 Mladost Doboj Kakanj *(2-8)*
Travnik 0-2, 0-0 Radnički Lukavac *(0-2)*
Željezničar 3-0, 1-0 GOŠK Gabela *(4-0)*

QUARTER-FINALS

(09/03/16 & 15/03/16)
Sloboda Tuzla 2-1 Sarajevo *(Krpić 23, Zeba 52; Okić 82p)*
Sarajevo 0-3 Sloboda Tuzla *(Veselinović 11, 57, Ahmetović 72)*
(Sloboda 5-1)

(09/03/16 & 16/03/16)
Borac Banja Luka 0-2 Željezničar *(Bekrić 11, Lendrić 15)*
Željezničar 2-1 Borac Banja Luka *(M Stevanović 7, Djermanović 90 +3; Marjanović 88)*
(Željezničar 4-1)

Radnički Lukavac 0-2 Radnik Bijeljina *(Srećković 38, Obradović 86)*
Radnik Bijeljina 1-1 Radnički Lukavac *(Maksimović 26; Šuljić 46)*
(Radnik Bijeljina 3-1)

Široki Brijeg 3-1 Mladost Doboj Kakanj *(Ivanković 36p, 88, Krstanović 90; Kobilica 76)*
Mladost Doboj Kakanj 1-0 Široki Brijeg *(Šišić 86p)*
(Široki Brijeg 3-2)

SEMI-FINALS

(13/04/16 & 20/04/16)
Radnik Bijeljina 1-0 Široki Brijeg *(Obradović 9)*
Široki Brijeg 2-1 Radnik Bijelina *(Pandža 26, Kožulj 66; Šećerović 70p)*
(2-2; Radnik Bijeljina on away goal)

Željezničar 1-2 Sloboda Tuzla *(Bogićević 61; Krpić 2, Kostić 71)*
Sloboda Tuzla 3-1 Željezničar *(Merzić 28, Krpić 38, Kostić 79; Lendrić 90p)*
(Sloboda Tuzla 5-2)

FINAL

(11/05/16)
Stadion Tušanj, Tuzla
FK SLOBODA TUZLA 1 *(Merzić 37)*
FK RADNIK BIJELJINA 1 *(S Jakovljević 57)*
Referee: Šehović
SLOBODA: *Pirić, Kostić, Salihović, Efendić, Ivetić, Ordagić (Ahmetović 53), Zeba, Stjepanović, Mehidić, Merzić (Pršeš 89), Krpić (Govedarica 83)*
Red card: *Zeba (90+2)*
RADNIK : *Avdukić, Hodžić (Antić 82), S Jakovljević, I Jakovljević, Zeljković, D Beširović, Maksimović, Memišević, Lazić (Mašić 60), Obradović, Šećerović (Ostojić 80)*
Red card: *D Beširović (90+3)*

(18/05/16)
Gradski stadion, Bijeljina
FK RADNIK BIJELJINA 3 *(Hodžić 5, Memišević 65, 85)*
FK SLOBODA TUZLA 0
Referee: Valjić
RADNIK: *Avdukić, Hodžić, S Jakovljević, I Jakovljević (Ostojić 88), Zeljković, D Beširović, Maksimović (Vasić 76), Memišević, Lazić, Obradović, Šećerović (Mašić 63)*
SLOBODA: *Pirić, Kostić, Efendić, Ivetić, Sarić (Pršeš 88), Ordagić, Stjepanović, Mehidić, Veselinović (Govedarica 66), Merzić, Krpić (Ahmetović 46)*

(Radnik Bijeljina 4-1)

BULGARIA
Bulgarski Futbolen Soyuz (BFS)

Address	26 Tzar Ivan Assen II Street
	BG-1124 Sofia
Tel	+359 2 942 6253
Fax	+359 2 942 6200
E-mail	bfu@bfunion.bg
Website	bfunion.bg

President	Borislav Mihaylov
General secretary	Borislav Popov
Media officer	Yordan Grozdanov
Year of formation	1923
National stadium	Vasil Levski, Sofia
	(43,230)

Ruse
11

Razgrad
7

Montana
8

Lovech
12
5

Gorna Oryahovitsa

3
Varna

4 10 15

Sofia

14
Burgas

Stara Zagora
1   13

Plovdiv
2   6

9 Blagoevgrad

KEY
● UEFA Champions League
● UEFA Europa League
● Promoted
● Relegated
▨ New club

0 —————— 100 —————— 200 km
0 —————————— 100 miles

A GRUPA CLUBS

 ① **PFC Beroe Stara Zagora**

 ② **PFC Botev Plovdiv**

 ③ **PFC Cherno More Varna**

 ④ **PFC Levski Sofia**

 ⑤ **PFC Litex Lovech**

 ⑥ **PFC Lokomotiv Plovdiv 1936**

 ⑦ **PFC Ludogorets Razgrad**

 ⑧ **PFC Montana 1921**

 ⑨ **OFC Pirin Blagoevgrad**

 ⑩ **PFC Slavia Sofia**

PROMOTED CLUBS

 ⑪ **PFC Dunav 2010 Ruse**

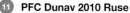 ⑫ **FC Lokomotiv Gorna Oryahovitsa**

 ⑬ **FC Vereya Stara Zagora**

 ⑭ **PFC Neftochimic Burgas**

NEW CLUB

 ⑮ **PFC CSKA-Sofia**

Five out of five for Ludogorets

The 2015/16 Bulgarian season was generally characterised by upheaval, but the one constant was provided by Ludogorets Razgrad, who won the A PFG championship for the fifth year in a row.

With Georgi Dermendzhiev restored as coach, the serial champions made easy work of a league that was initially reduced to ten teams then to nine following the mid-season expulsion of Litex Lovech. It would be back to 14 in 2016/17, with a newly formed CSKA-Sofia among the new intake.

Fifth title in as many years for Razgrad club

Litex Lovech expelled from league in mid-season

CSKA Sofia win cup as third division club

Domestic league

With the original CSKA and their city rivals Lokomotiv Sofia both refused an A PFG licence and banished to the lower leagues, the 2015/16 season kicked off with fewer participants than ever before. The plan was to have the ten teams play each other four times in a 36-match programme, and that was how things were progressing until 12 December when a top-of-the-table clash between Levski Sofa and Litex was abandoned just before half-time after Litex players walked off the field in protest at a series of unfavourable refereeing decisions. Punishment was severe, with the club thrown out of the league and all their results subsequently annulled.

This led to a reconfiguration of the league table as well as a reduced spring schedule. One of the beneficiaries were Ludogorets, who had taken just one point from their two meetings with Litex. The defending champions, who had reappointed 2014/15 title-winning boss Dermendzhiev in November after several poor showings under his successors Bruno Ribeiro and Eduard Eranosyan, thus wintered with a useful lead.

A 2-1 win at home to closest pursuers Levski on the spring resumption further strengthened Ludogorets' hand, and they would go on to win their next seven fixtures as well, building up an insurmountable lead. When Levski lost 3-2 at home to Lokomotiv Plovdiv on 10 May, the title race was run, and Ludogorets celebrated the next day by winning 4-1 at home to Pirin Blagoevgrad. Lokomotiv had been the only team to beat the champions at that juncture, but although Dermendzhiev's men lost their last two fixtures, they still boasted a 14-point lead in the final table. Levski finished runners-up, with Beroe Stara Zagora, second the previous season, ending up third.

From Vladislav Stoyanov in goal, through Cosmin Moți in defence, Svetoslav Dyakov and Marcelinho in midfield to Claudiu Keșerü in attack, Ludogorets possessed some of the league's most impressive performers. Keșerü, the Romanian international, was the Razgrad outfit's top scorer with 15 goals – three behind Lokomotiv's evergreen Martin Kamburov, who collected the A PFG golden boot for the fifth time, at the age of 35.

Post-season restructuring resulted in the relegation of no teams – ninth-placed Montana saved themselves in a play-off – and the promotion of five, all fulfilling new licensing criteria including a newly formed CSKA-Sofia (complete with hyphen), who, in a complex ownership reshuffle and merger arrangement, effectively assumed the identity of Litex Lovech, including their honours, while maintaining their traditional all-red colours.

Domestic cup

Before that took place the old CSKA Sofia (no hyphen) reminded everybody of their existence by winning the Bulgarian Cup despite residing in the country's third tier. In defeating Montana 1-0 before a bumper crowd of 33,345 in the Vasil Levski stadium, they denied their opponents a first major trophy while claiming the silverware themselves for the 20th time.

Europe

For the first time ever there were no clubs from Sofia representing Bulgaria in Europe, and it proved to be an uneventful experience without them as all four clubs departed early, with Ludogorets crashing out in the second qualifying round of the UEFA Champions League only a few months after competing in the group stage.

National team

Just as memories of a disappointing UEFA EURO 2016 qualifying campaign appeared to have been banished by a couple of encouraging friendly wins in March, the first of them away to Portugal in which Brazilian-born debutant Marcelinho scored the only goal, Bulgaria went to the Kirin Cup in June and suffered two crushing defeats, going down 7-2 to hosts Japan and 4-0 to Denmark. Suddenly a tough 2018 FIFA World Cup qualifying group seemed a whole lot tougher.

DOMESTIC SEASON AT A GLANCE

A PFG 2015/16 final table

		Pld	Home W	D	L	F	A	Away W	D	L	F	A	Total W	D	L	F	A	Pts
1	**PFC Ludogorets Razgrad**	32	12	3	1	30	10	9	4	3	25	11	21	7	4	55	21	70
2	PFC Levski Sofia	32	10	4	2	24	7	6	4	6	12	11	16	8	8	36	18	56
3	PFC Beroe Stara Zagora	32	7	7	2	20	12	7	4	5	17	15	14	11	7	37	27	53
4	PFC Slavia Sofia	32	6	5	5	14	11	8	2	6	22	18	14	7	11	36	29	49
5	PFC Lokomotiv Plovdiv 1936	32	12	2	2	29	15	3	2	11	11	30	15	4	13	40	45	49
6	PFC Cherno More Varna	32	7	3	6	18	19	3	5	8	18	26	10	8	14	36	45	38
7	PFC Botev Plovdiv	32	6	5	5	17	16	2	4	10	10	28	8	9	15	27	44	33
8	OFC Pirin Blagoevgrad	32	3	5	8	14	21	2	6	8	13	24	5	11	16	27	45	26
9	PFC Montana 1921	32	4	3	9	17	23	0	6	10	6	20	4	9	19	23	43	21
10	PFC Litex Lovech	0	0	0	0	0	0	0	0	0	0	0	0	0	0	0	0	0

NB PFC Litex Lovech excluded after round 20 – all their matches were annulled.

European qualification 2016/17

Champion: PFC Ludogorets Razgrad (second qualifying round)

PFC Levski Sofia (second qualifying round)
PFC Beroe Stara Zagora (first qualifying round)
PFC Slavia Sofia (first qualifying round)

NB Cup winner PFC CSKA Sofia banned.

Top scorer	Martin Kamburov (Lokomotiv), 18 goals
Relegated club	PFC Litex Lovech (expelled)
Promoted clubs	PFC Dunav 2010 Ruse, FC Lokomotiv Gorna Oryahovitsa, FC Vereya Stara Zagora, PFC Neftochimic Burgas, PFC CSKA-Sofia
Cup final	PFC CSKA Sofia 1-0 PFC Montana 1921

Team of the season
(4-2-3-1)

Coach: Dermendzhiev (Ludogorets)

Stoyanov (Ludogorets)

Procházka (Levski) — Moți (Ludogorets) — Ivanov (Beroe) — Natanael (Ludogorets)

Dyakov (Ludogorets) — Kostadinov (Levski)

Baldzhiyski (Montana/Slavia) — Marcelinho (Ludogorets) — Wanderson (Ludogorets)

Kamburov (Lokomotiv)

Player of the season

Vladislav Stoyanov
(PFC Ludogorets Razgrad)

The 2015/16 season was not the busiest of Stoyanov's career – injury and Ludogorets' early exit from both Europe and the Bulgarian Cup contributed to that – but when he played, the 29-year-old goalkeeper was invariably decisive. He kept clean sheets in over half of his A PFG appearances en route to winning a fourth successive title, and on his one international outing, against Portugal, he was the star of the show, making a succession of spectacular saves, including one from a Cristiano Ronaldo penalty, in Bulgaria's 1-0 win.

Newcomer of the season

Natanael
(PFC Ludogorets Razgrad)

Ludogorets added to their cluster of Brazilian players in July 2015 by recruiting left-back Natanael Batista Pimienta from Atlético Paranaense. Surrounded by his compatriots, he became one of the mainstays of the team, excelling in particular – along with the rest of the team – following the reappointment of coach Georgi Dermendzhiev. The 25-year-old's first season in Europe ended with a Bulgarian championship winner's medal and more credit in the bank for Ludogorets' scouting network.

BULGARIA

NATIONAL TEAM

International tournament appearances

FIFA World Cup (7) 1962, 1966, 1970, 1974, 1986 (2nd round), 1994 (4th), 1998
UEFA European Championship (2) 1996, 2004

Top five all-time caps

Stiliyan Petrov (106); Borislav Mihaylov (102); Hristo Bonev (96); Krasimir Balakov (92); Martin Petrov (91)

Top five all-time goals

Dimitar Berbatov (48); Hristo Bonev (47); Hristo Stoichkov (37); Emil Kostadinov (26); Lyubomir Angelov, Ivan Kolev & Petar Zhekov (25)

Results 2015/16

03/09/15	Norway (ECQ)	H	Sofia	L	0-1	
06/09/15	Italy (ECQ)	A	Palermo	L	0-1	
10/10/15	Croatia (ECQ)	A	Zagreb	L	0-3	
13/10/15	Azerbaijan (ECQ)	H	Sofia	W	2-0	M Alexandrov (20), Rangelov (56)
25/03/16	Portugal	A	Leiria	W	1-0	Marcelinho (19)
29/03/16	FYR Macedonia	A	Skopje	W	2-0	Rangelov (66), Tonev (88)
03/06/16	Japan	A	Toyota	L	2-7	M Alexandrov (59), Chochev (82)
07/06/16	Denmark	N	Suita (JPN)	L	0-4	

Appearances 2015/16

Coach: Ivaylo Petev	09/07/75		NOR	ITA	CRO	AZE	Por	Mkd	Jpn	Den	Caps	Goals
Bozhidar Mitrev	31/03/87	Sheriff (MDA)	G	G	G	G			G	G	9	-
Ivan Bandalovski	23/11/86	Partizan (SRB)	D	s64							16	-
Alexander D Alexandrov	13/04/86	Ludogorets /Levski	D	D	D	D		D	D46	D	12	-
Nikolay Bodurov	30/05/86	Fulham (ENG) /Midtjylland (DEN)	D	D				D	D		36	1
Yordan Minev	14/10/80	Ludogorets	D	D64		D					24	-
Svetoslav Dyakov	31/05/84	Ludogorets	M	M		M	M	M	M	M	31	-
Ivaylo Chochev	18/02/93	Palermo (ITA)	M				M	M	M	M	8	1
Stanislav Manolev	16/12/85	Kuban (RUS)	M61								46	4
Ivelin Popov	26/10/87	Spartak Moskva (RUS)	M	A71	A71	M65	A90	M90	M57	M81	63	12
Georgi Milanov	19/02/92	CSKA Moskva (RUS) /Grasshoppers (SUI)	M78	M	s46	M			s54	M67	30	2
Ilian Micanski	20/12/85	Suwon Bluewings (KOR)	A68	A 55*							17	4
Alexander Tonev	03/02/90	Frosinone (ITA)	s61		M		s84	s85			22	4
Dimitar Rangelov	09/02/83	Konyaspor (TUR)	s68	s71	A	A88	M	A85	A72	A61	39	5
Todor Nedelev	07/02/93	Mainz (GER)	s78	M67	M46	s88					10	-
Veselin Minev	14/10/80	Levski			D						25	-
Mihail Alexandrov	11/06/89	Ludogorets /Legia (POL)		s67	s71	M80	M65	M	M75	s67	15	2
Zhivko Milanov	15/07/84	Levski /APOEL (CYP)			D	D	D		D		27	-
Strahil Popov	31/08/90	Litex /Kasımpaşa (TUR)			D		D89	D	D62	s81	6	-
Georgi Terziev	18/04/92	Ludogorets			D46		s90	D	D		9	-
Hristo Zlatinski	22/01/85	U Craiova (ROU)			M	M					12	-
Simeon Slavchev	25/09/93	Apollon (CYP)			M	s80	s65 /90				7	-
Ivo Ivanov	11/03/85	Beroe			s46	D		s90	s46	D	6	-
Ventsislav Hristov	09/11/88	Skënderbeu (ALB) /Levski				s65			s72	s61	8	1
Vladislav Stoyanov	08/06/87	Ludogorets					G				15	-
Marcelinho	24/08/84	Ludogorets					M84	M75	M54	M76	4	1
Vasil Bozhikov	02/06/88	Kasımpaşa (TUR)					s89	D		D	3	-
Spas Delev	22/09/89	Beroe					s90	s75		s76	12	-
Stefan Velev	02/05/89	Lokomotiv Plovdiv							s57	s79	4	-
Ventsislav Vasilev	08/07/88	Beroe							s62	D79	3	-
Galin Ivanov	15/04/88	Samsunspor (TUR)							s75		1	-

EUROPE

PFC Ludogorets Razgrad

Second qualifying round - FC Milsami Orhei (MDA)
H 0-1
Stoyanov, M Alexandrov (Cicinho 63), Lucas Sasha, Juninho Quixadá (Chunchukov 46), Anicet Abel (Prepeliţă 46), A Alexandrov, Angulo, Dyakov, Minev, Moţi, Misidjan. Coach: Bruno Ribeiro (POR)
A 1-2 *Wanderson (25)*
Stoyanov, Juninho Quixadá (Chunchukov 72), A Alexandrov, Angulo, Dyakov, Minev, Moţi, Prepeliţă (Lukoki 63), Marcelinho, Wanderson, Misidjan. Coach: Bruno Ribeiro (POR)

PFC Beroe Stara Zagora

First qualifying round - FK Atlantas (LTU)
A 2-0 *Delev (60), Bozhilov (84)*
Makendzhiev, Ivanov, Mapuku (Andonov 81), Bozhilov, Zehirov, Milisavljević, Elias (Tom 87), Vasilev, Djoman, Penev, Delev (Kokonov 69). Coach: Petar Hubchev (BUL)
H 3-1 *Delev (7, 45, 67)*
Makendzhiev, Ivanov, Mapuku (Kostov 69), Bozhilov, Zehirov (Filipov 54), Milisavljević, Elias, Vasilev, Djoman (Tom 63), Penev, Delev. Coach: Petar Hubchev (BUL)

Second qualifying round - Brøndby IF (DEN)
H 0-1
Makendzhiev, Ivanov, Mapuku (Andonov 71), Bozhilov, Zehirov, Milisavljević (Kokonov 86), Elias, Vasilev, Djoman (Tom 89), Penev, Delev. Coach: Petar Hubchev (BUL)
A 0-0
Makendzhiev, Ivanov, Mapuku, Bozhilov (Kokonov 79), Zehirov, Milisavljević, Elias, Vasilev, Djoman, Penev, Delev. Coach: Petar Hubchev (BUL)

PFC Cherno More Varna

Second qualifying round - FC Dinamo Minsk (BLR)
H 1-1 *Coureur (11)*
Čanović, Venkov, Stanchev, Coulibaly, Klok, Raykov, Burkhardt (Sténio 67), Coureur (Vasev 72), Bizhev (Varea 58), Bourabia, Palankov. Coach: Nikola Spasov (BUL)
A 0-4
Čanović, Venkov, Stanchev, Coulibaly, Klok (Georgiev 46), Raykov, Burkhardt (Sténio 46), Coureur, Bizhev (Vasev 65), Bourabia, Palankov. Coach: Nikola Spasov (BUL)
Red card: Palankov 45+1

PFC Litex Lovech

First qualifying round - FK Jelgava (LVA)
A 1-1 *Bozhikov (50)*
Vinícius, Pérez, Johnsen, Bozhikov, Malinov, Popov, Rumenov (Boumal 57), Goranov, Asprilla (Georgiev 90), Arsénio (Angelov 77), Kolev. Coach: Dobromir Mitov (BUL)
H 2-2 *Johnsen (25, 56)*
Vinícius, Pérez, Johnsen, Bozhikov, Malinov (Angelov 86), Popov, Goranov, Asprilla, Arsénio (Diogo Viana 61), Kolev (Georgiev 72), Boumal. Coach: Krasimir Balakov (BUL)

DOMESTIC LEAGUE CLUB-BY-CLUB

PFC Beroe Stara Zagora

1916 • Beroe (15,000) • beroe.bg
Major honours
Bulgarian League (1) 1986; Bulgarian Cup (2) 2010, 2013
Coach: Petar Hubchev;
(07/04/16) Plamen Lipenski

2015

Date		Opponent	Res	Score	Scorers
19/07	h	Montana	D	0-0	
26/07	a	Lokomotiv	W	2-1	Djoman, Mapuku
02/08	h	Pirin	W	1-0	Bozhilov
09/08	a	Slavia	D	0-0	
17/08	h	Cherno More	D	1-1	Zehirov
22/08	h	Botev	D	0-0	
29/08	a	Litex	W	1-0	Delev (match annulled)
12/09	h	Ludogorets	D	0-0	
20/09	a	Levski	L	0-2	
27/09	a	Montana	L	0-1	
02/10	h	Lokomotiv	W	2-0	Delev, Isa
19/10	a	Pirin	W	1-0	Petkov
26/10	h	Slavia	L	1-2	Zehirov
03/11	a	Cherno More	W	3-0	Milisavljević, Tom, Isa
08/11	a	Botev	W	3-1	Andonov, Elias, Zehirov
21/11	h	Litex	D	3-3	Djoman, Isa, Elias (match annulled)
27/11	a	Ludogorets	L	0-5	
02/12	h	Levski	W	1-0	Delev
06/12	h	Montana	W	2-1	Isa, Andonov
13/12	a	Lokomotiv	D	1-1	Dinkov
2016					
20/02	h	Pirin	W	3-1	Vasilev, Milisavljević, Isa
28/02	a	Slavia	D	0-0	
03/03	h	Cherno More	D	0-0	
06/03	h	Botev	D	1-1	Andonov
19/03	h	Ludogorets	L	0-2	
02/04	a	Levski	L	0-1	
10/04	a	Montana	W	3-1	og (Kokonov), Kostov, Isa
16/04	a	Lokomotiv	W	5-2	Elias (p), Isa, Delev, Kostov, Milisavljević
24/04	a	Pirin	D	1-1	Elias
30/04	a	Slavia	D	1-1	Bozhilov
06/05	a	Cherno More	L	0-1	
11/05	h	Botev	W	1-0	Zehirov
22/05	a	Ludogorets	W	2-0	Ahmed, Vasilev
28/05	h	Levski	W	2-1	Elias, Ivanov

No	Name	Nat	DoB	Pos	Aps	(s)	Gls
13	Emin Ahmed		10/03/96	D	16		1
7	Georgi Andonov		28/06/83	M	11	(11)	3
16	Ivaylo Angelov		08/10/97	M		(1)	
14	Gegrpi Bozhilov		12/02/87	A	16	(13)	2
77	Spas Delev		22/09/89	A	27	(2)	4
15	Georgi Dinkov		20/05/91	D	15	(3)	1
27	Igor Djoman	FRA	01/05/86	M	25	(2)	2
21	Elias	BRA	04/09/81	A	29	(2)	5
4	Venelin Filipov		20/08/90	D	2	(7)	
19	Ivelin Iliev		08/08/97	M		(2)	
10	Ismail Isa		26/06/89	A	13	(12)	7
1	Ivo Ivanov		11/03/85	D	31		1
17	Ivan Kokonov		17/08/91	A		(4)	
9	Stanislav Kostov		02/10/91	A	4	(12)	2
22	Blagoy Makendzhiev		11/07/88	G	29		
30	Junior Mapuku	COD	07/01/90	A	3	(2)	1
71	Iliya Milanov		19/02/92	D	2	(2)	
11	Nemanja Milisavljević	SRB	01/11/84	M	25	(4)	3
87	Benjamin Morel	FRA	10/06/87	M		(3)	
7	Anton Ognyanov		30/06/88	M		(2)	
17	Pedro Marques	POR	31/03/88	M		(2)	
27	Veselin Penev		11/08/82	D	33		
73	Steven Petkov		07/05/95	M	18		1
23	Ilko Pirgov		23/05/86	G	5		
8	Georgi Sarmov		07/09/85	M	4		
70	Tom	BRA	18/03/86	M	17	(4)	1
23	Ventsislav Vasilev		08/07/88	D	24	(3)	2
3	Vladimir Zafirov		21/03/83	M	10	(3)	
18	Atanas Zehirov		13/02/89	M	15	(3)	4

BULGARIA

PFC Botev Plovdiv

1912 • Komatevo (3,300) • botevplovdiv.bg

Major honours
Bulgarian League (2) 1929, 1967; Bulgarian Cup (2) 1962, 1981

Coach: Petar Penchev;
(28/07/15) Ermin Šiljak (SVN);
(11/11/15) Nikolay Kostov

2015

18/07	h	Levski	D	1-1	Genov
25/07	a	Montana	L	0-6	
01/08	h	Lokomotiv	D	1-1	Kolev
09/08	h	Pirin	W	1-0	Kolev
16/08	h	Slavia	L	0-1	
22/08	h	Beroe	D	0-0	
29/08	h	Cherno More	W	2-1	Vasev, Varela (p)
12/09	h	Litex	L	0-2	(match annulled)
19/09	a	Ludogorets	L	1-2	Baltanov
28/09	a	Levski	L	0-1	
04/10	h	Montana	W	1-0	Varela
17/10	a	Lokomotiv	L	1-2	Hristov
23/10	a	Pirin	W	1-0	Nelson
30/10	a	Slavia	L	0-2	
08/11	h	Beroe	L	1-3	Vasev
22/11	a	Cherno More	W	2-1	Baltanov (p), Varela
28/11	h	Litex	L	2-4	Nelson 2 (match annulled)
02/12	h	Ludogorets	L	0-2	
05/12	a	Levski	D	0-0	
13/12	a	Montana	D	1-1	Baltanov

2016

20/02	h	Lokomotiv	W	1-0	Baltanov
28/02	h	Pirin	D	2-2	Nedelev, Milev
03/03	h	Slavia	L	0-1	
06/03	h	Beroe	D	1-1	Nelson
13/03	h	Cherno More	W	3-1	Gamakov, Baltanov 2 (1p)
03/04	a	Ludogorets	L	0-1	
09/04	a	Levski	L	0-3	
16/04	h	Montana	D	2-2	Baltanov, Nedelev
24/04	a	Lokomotiv	L	1-2	Marin
29/04	h	Pirin	D	2-2	og (Toshev), Nedelev
07/05	a	Slavia	L	0-2	
11/05	h	Beroe	L	0-1	
14/05	a	Cherno More	L	0-3	
27/05	h	Ludogorets	W	2-1	Vasev, K Dimitrov

No	Name	Nat	DoB	Pos	Aps	(s)	Gls
39	Dimitar Aleksiev		28/07/93	A		(4)	
26	Radoslav Apostolov		07/06/97	M	2	(2)	
2	Vladimir Aytov		12/04/96	D	1	(5)	
17	Lachezar Baltanov		11/07/88	M	30		7
5	Kristian Dimitrov		27/02/97	D	1	(2)	1
31	Martin Dimitrov		20/03/96	G	2		
28	Filip Filipov		02/08/88	D	18	(4)	
84	Valentin Galev		01/01/84	G	1		
38	Milen Gamakov		12/03/89	M	23	(4)	1
96	Daniel Genov		19/05/89	M	14	(5)	1
22	Milko Georgiev		03/08/98	M		(3)	
11	Yordan Hristov		12/02/84	D	32		1
89	Mihail Ivanov		07/08/89	G	2		
9	Emil Kamberov		07/04/96	A		(2)	
88	Hristiyan Kazakov		10/03/93	M		(3)	
91	Rahavi Kifoueti	CGO	12/03/89	A	15	(5)	
9	Alexander Kolev		08/12/92	M	12	(5)	2
24	Lazar Marin		09/02/94	D	19	(5)	1
45	Nasko Milev		18/07/96	A	9	(8)	1
8	Todor Nedelev		07/02/93	M	12		3
23	Gregory Nelson	NED	31/01/88	M	14	(1)	4
22	Plamen Nikolov		12/06/85	D	19		
7	Mariyan Ognyanov		30/07/88	M	13	(1)	
4	Ihor Oshchypko	UKR	25/10/85	D	10		
13	Ismet Ramadan		18/03/98	A		(2)	
66	Orlin Starokin		08/01/87	M	12	(3)	
18	Radoslav Terziev		06/08/94	D	14	(5)	
99	Joël Tshibamba	COD	22/09/88	A	3	(2)	
19	Boris Tyutyukov		28/10/97	M	1	(3)	
9	Nicolás Varela	URU	19/01/91	M	8	(7)	3
8	Bozhidar Vasev		14/03/93	M	15	(11)	3
9	Vítor Golas	BRA	27/12/90	G	29		
20	Serkan Yusein		31/03/96	M	22	(2)	
6	Daniel Zlatkov		06/03/89	D	21	(2)	

PFC Cherno More Varna

1945 • Ticha (8,000) • chernomorepfc.bg

Major honours
Bulgarian Cup (1) 2015

Coach: Nikola Spasov

2015

19/07	a	Pirin	D	1-1	Coureur
26/07	h	Ludogorets	L	2-3	Sténio, Coureur
02/08	a	Slavia	W	1-0	Bizhev
08/08	h	Levski	L	0-1	
17/08	a	Beroe	D	1-1	Petkov
22/08	h	Montana	W	1-0	og (A Georgiev)
29/08	a	Botev	L	1-2	Coureur
11/09	h	Lokomotiv	W	2-1	Varea, og (Kotev)
18/09	a	Litex	L	0-1	(match annulled)
26/09	h	Pirin	W	1-0	Raykov
03/10	a	Ludogorets	D	1-1	Coureur
17/10	h	Slavia	W	1-0	Coulibaly
23/10	a	Levski	L	0-1	
03/11	h	Beroe	L	0-3	
07/11	a	Montana	W	4-0	Bourabia, Coureur, Pedro Eugénio, Varea
22/11	h	Botev	L	1-2	Coureur
28/11	a	Lokomotiv	W	3-1	Coureur, Bourabia 2 (1p)
01/12	h	Litex	D	1-1	Raykov (match annulled)
06/12	a	Pirin	L	0-4	
12/12	h	Ludogorets	L	0-2	

2016

21/02	a	Slavia	D	0-0	
27/02	h	Levski	L	0-2	
03/03	a	Beroe	D	0-0	
06/03	h	Montana	D	1-1	Sténio
13/03	a	Botev	L	1-3	Raykov
20/03	h	Lokomotiv	D	1-1	Coureur
09/04	h	Pirin	D	1-1	Coureur
15/04	a	Ludogorets	L	1-2	Iliev
23/04	h	Slavia	W	3-2	Trayanov, Bacari 2
28/04	a	Levski	L	1-5	Georgiev
06/05	h	Beroe	W	1-0	Iliev
10/05	a	Montana	L	2-3	Raykov, Coureur
14/05	h	Botev	W	3-0	Bacari, Iliev, Coureur
22/05	a	Lokomotiv	L	1-2	Iliev

No	Name	Nat	DoB	Pos	Aps	(s)	Gls
9	Bubacar Bacari	ESP	14/03/88	A	7	(4)	3
20	Veliyan Bizhev		03/01/93	A	5	(7)	1
21	Mehdi Bourabia	FRA	07/08/91	M	19		3
18	Marcin Burkhardt	POL	25/09/83	D	3	(6)	
40	Aleksandar Čanović	SRB	18/02/83	G	1		
23	Mamoutou Coulibaly	MLI	23/02/84	D	17	(3)	1
19	Mathias Coureur	MTQ	22/03/88	A	33	(1)	11
3	Daniel Georgiev		06/11/82	M	21	(5)	1
22	Ginho	POR	08/07/85	D	9		
21	Georgi Iliev		05/09/81	M	14		4
33	Georgi Kitanov		06/03/95	M	33		
10	Marc Klok	NED	20/04/93	M	23	(1)	
17	Martin Kostadinov		13/05/96	M	1		
28	Ivan Marković	SRB	20/06/94	M		(1)	
11	Iliyan Nedelchev		01/03/96	A		(1)	
1	Ilia Nikolov		14/07/86	G		(1)	
22	Plamen Nikolov		12/06/85	D	14		
84	Todor Palankov		13/01/84	M	21	(5)	
70	Pedro Eugénio	POR	26/06/90	D	13	(4)	1
11	Zhivko Petkov		15/02/93	A	7	(13)	1
7	Bekir Rasim		26/12/94	M	3	(6)	
13	Simeon Raykov		11/11/89	M	20	(5)	4
73	Vladislav Romanov		07/02/88	M	8	(5)	
5	Stefan Stanchev		26/04/89	D	12	(1)	
8	Sténio	CPV	06/05/89	M	25	(3)	2
55	Borislav Stoychev		26/11/86	D	8		
15	Trayan Trayanov		03/08/87	D	13	(1)	1
35	Ivan Valchanov		28/09/91	M		(4)	
77	Juan Manuel Varea	ARG	23/03/86	A	3	(3)	2
8	Andreas Vasev		01/03/91	M	8	(12)	
4	Mihail Venkov		28/07/83	D	33		
98	Valentin Yoskov		05/06/98	A		(5)	

PFC Levski Sofia

1914 • Georgi Asparuhov (29,000) • levski.bg

Major honours
Bulgarian League (26) 1933, 1937, 1942, 1946, 1947, 1949, 1950, 1953, 1965, 1968, 1970, 1974, 1977, 1979, 1984, 1985, 1988, 1993, 1994, 1995, 2000, 2001, 2002, 2006, 2007, 2009; Bulgarian Cup (25) 1942, 1946, 1947, 1949, 1950, 1956, 1957, 1959, 1967, 1970, 1971, 1976, 1977, 1979, 1984, 1986, 1991, 1992, 1994, 1998, 2000, 2002, 2003, 2005, 2007

Coach: Stoycho Stoev;
(16/05/16) Ljupko Petrović (SRB)

2015

18/07	a	Botev	D	1-1	Kostadinov
25/07	h	Litex	D	2-2	Kraev, Procházka (match annulled)
01/08	a	Ludogorets	L	0-2	
08/08	a	Cherno More	W	1-0	B Tsonev
15/08	h	Montana	W	2-0	Kraev 2
23/08	a	Lokomotiv	L	0-1	
30/08	h	Pirin	D	0-0	
13/09	a	Slavia	W	1-0	Diaby
20/09	h	Beroe	W	2-0	Gadzhev, Procházka
28/09	h	Botev	W	1-0	Kostadinov
04/10	a	Litex	W	2-1	Belaïd, Procházka (match annulled)
18/10	h	Ludogorets	D	1-1	Milanov
23/10	h	Cherno More	W	1-0	Karner
02/11	a	Montana	W	2-0	Procházka (p), Kraev
08/11	h	Lokomotiv	W	1-0	Bedoya
22/11	a	Pirin	L	0-1	
29/11	h	Slavia	W	2-0	Procházka, De Nooijer
02/12	a	Beroe	L	0-1	
05/12	a	Botev	D	0-0	
12/12	h	Litex	L	0-1	(match abandoned after 45 minutes and annulled)

2016

21/02	a	Ludogorets	L	1-2	Procházka
27/02	a	Cherno More	W	2-0	Kostadinov, Bedoya
02/03	h	Montana	D	0-0	
05/03	a	Lokomotiv	D	1-1	Hristov
13/03	h	Pirin	W	3-1	Bedoya, Hristov, Narh
19/03	a	Slavia	D	0-0	
02/04	h	Beroe	W	1-0	Hristov (p)
09/04	h	Botev	W	3-0	Hristov, Procházka 2
23/04	a	Ludogorets	D	0-0	
28/04	h	Cherno More	W	5-1	Kraev, Hristov 3, Bedoya
06/05	a	Montana	W	1-0	Bedoya
10/05	h	Lokomotiv	L	2-3	Hristov, Bedoya
15/05	a	Pirin	W	1-0	Alexander D Alexandrov
22/05	h	Slavia	L	0-1	
28/05	a	Beroe	L	1-2	Kostadinov

No	Name	Nat	DoB	Pos	Aps	(s)	Gls
17	Tunde Adeniji	NGA	17/09/95	A	1	(11)	
5	Alexander Dragimirov Alexandrov		13/04/86	D	13		1
25	Alexander Emilov Alexandrov		30/07/86	D	12	(3)	
10	Miguel Bedoya	ESP	15/04/86	M	26	(3)	6
3	Aymen Belaïd	TUN	02/01/89	D	18	(1)	1
27	Mehdi Bourabia	FRA	07/08/91	M	7	(3)	
8	Jeremy de Nooijer	CUW	15/03/92	M	22	(7)	1
11	Omar Diaby	FRA	07/02/90	A	9	(2)	1
19	Iliya Dimitrov		10/07/96	A		(4)	
45	Vladimir Gadzhev		18/07/87	M	4	(3)	1
91	Ventsislav Hristov		09/11/88	A	12	(3)	8
39	Deyan Ivanov		12/04/96	D	5	(1)	
99	Stanislav Ivanov		12/04/98	M		(1)	
29	Bojan Jorgačević	SRB	12/02/82	G	35		
30	Maximilian Karner	AUT	03/01/90	D	20		1
99	Lynel Kitambala	FRA	26/10/88	A	3	(4)	
70	Georgi Kostadinov		07/09/90	M	29		4
52	Bozhidar Kraev		23/06/97	M	26	(3)	5
9	Atanas Kurdov		28/09/88	A	3	(5)	
2	Srdjan Luchin	ROU	04/03/86	D	11		
1	Denis Mahmudov	MKD	06/11/89	A	4	(6)	
11	Justin Mengolo	CMR	24/06/93	A	3	(4)	
20	Zhivko Milanov		15/07/84	D	12		1
55	Yordan Miliev		05/10/87	D	2		
14	Veselin Minev		14/10/80	D	32		
22	Vladislav Misyak		18/01/95	M		(3)	
4	Francis Narh	GHA	18/04/94	A	15		1
4	Miki Orachev		19/03/96	D	11	(12)	
5	Roman Procházka	SVK	14/03/89	D	33	(3)	8
20	Galin Tashev		02/02/97	D		(3)	
18	Borislav Tsonev		29/04/95	M	6	(2)	1
21	Radoslav Tsonev		29/04/95	M	11	(16)	
88	Georgi Yanev		04/01/98	M		(1)	

PFC Litex Lovech

1921• Gradski (7,000) • pfclitex.com

Major honours
Bulgarian League (4) 1998, 1999, 2010, 2011;
Bulgarian Cup (4) 2001, 2004, 2008, 2009

Coach: Krasimir Balakov;
(12/07/15) (Ljupko Petrović (SRB));
(07/08/15) Laurențiu Reghecampf (ROU);
(03/12/15) (Ljupko Petrović (SRB));
(22/01/16) Luboslav Penev

2015

18/07	h	Ludogorets	W	2-0	Asprilla, Diogo Viana
25/07	a	Levski	D	2-2	Pérez, Arsénio
03/08	h	Montana	W	2-1	Asprilla 2 (1p)
08/08	a	Lokomotiv	D	1-1	Rojas
14/08	h	Pirin	W	1-0	Asprilla
23/08	a	Slavia	D	0-0	
29/08	h	Beroe	L	0-1	
12/09	h	Botev	W	2-0	Arsénio, Johnsen
18/09	h	Cherno More	W	1-0	Johnsen
26/09	a	Ludogorets	D	1-1	Arsénio
04/10	a	Levski	L	1-2	Malinov
18/10	a	Montana	W	2-0	Asprilla, Johnsen
23/10	h	Lokomotiv	D	0-0	
30/10	a	Pirin	D	1-1	Johnsen
06/11	h	Slavia	W	4-0	Diogo Viana, Malinov, Johnsen, Asprilla
21/11	a	Beroe	D	3-3	Asprilla 2, Helton dos Reis
28/11	h	Botev	W	4-2	Asprilla 2, Rojas, Boumal
01/12	a	Cherno More	D	1-1	Johnsen
05/12	h	Ludogorets	D	1-1	Popov
12/12	a	Levski	W	1-0	Asprilla (match abandoned after 45 minutes)

NB Litex excluded after round 20 – all their matches were annulled.

No	Name	Nat	DoB	Pos	Aps	(s)	Gls
73	Milcho Angelov		02/01/95	A		(5)	
77	Arsénio	POR	30/08/89	M	19	(1)	3
70	Danilo Asprilla	COL	12/01/89	A	19		11
93	Petrus Boumal	CMR	20/04/93	M	16		1
17	Reyan Daskalov		10/02/89	M		(2)	
99	Kiril Despodov		11/11/96	A	1	(4)	
7	Diogo Viana	POR	22/02/90	M	3	(6)	2
28	Plamen Galabov		02/11/95	D	9	(1)	
8	Alexander Georgiev		10/10/97	M		(3)	
23	Ivan Goranov		10/06/92	D	9	(3)	
69	Helton dos Reis	FRA	01/05/88	D	12		1
11	Bjørn Johnsen	NOR	06/11/91	A	15	(5)	6
88	Nikola Kolev		06/06/95	M	7	(9)	
15	Kristiyan Malinov		30/03/94	M	14		2
7	Georgi Minchev		20/04/95	A	5	(3)	
3	Anton Nedyalkov		30/04/93	D	13	(2)	
5	Rafael Pérez	COL	09/01/90	D	19		1
16	Strahil Popov		30/08/90	D	19		1
10	Henry Rojas	COL	27/07/87	M	11	(4)	2
6	Krasimir Stanoev		14/09/94	M	9	(7)	
21	Alexander Tsvetkov		31/08/90	M		(2)	
31	Vinícius	BRA	19/07/85	G	20		

PFC Lokomotiv Plovdiv 1936

1936 • Lokomotiv (13,000) • lokomotivpd.com

Major honours
Bulgarian League (1) 2004

Coach: Hristo Kolev;
(26/02/16) Ilian Iliev

2015

17/07	a	Slavia	L	0-3	
26/07	h	Beroe	L	1-2	Kamburov (p)
01/08	a	Botev	D	1-1	Baldovaliev
08/08	h	Litex	D	1-1	Baldovaliev (match annulled)
16/08	a	Ludogorets	L	0-1	
23/08	h	Levski	W	1-0	Karageren
30/08	a	Montana	W	1-0	
11/09	a	Cherno More	L	1-2	Karageren
20/09	h	Pirin	W	2-1	Kamburov, Baldovaliev
27/09	a	Slavia	W	2-0	Kamburov 2
02/10	a	Beroe	L	0-2	
17/10	h	Botev	W	2-1	Baldovaliev, Kamburov
23/10	a	Litex	D	0-0	(match annulled)
02/11	h	Ludogorets	W	2-0	Bakalov, Gargorov
08/11	a	Levski	L	0-1	
20/11	h	Montana	W	1-0	Bakalov
28/11	h	Cherno More	L	1-3	Baldovaliev
03/12	a	Pirin	L	0-3	
07/12	a	Slavia	L	0-2	
13/12	h	Beroe	D	1-1	Kiki

2016

20/02	a	Botev	L	0-1	
01/03	a	Ludogorets	L	0-2	
05/03	h	Levski	D	1-1	Trajanov
12/03	a	Montana	W	1-0	Kamburov
20/03	a	Cherno More	W	1-0	Kamburov (p)
01/04	h	Pirin	W	4-2	Kamburov 3 (p), Kiki
10/04	h	Slavia	W	3-1	Kamburov 2, Paulo Teles
16/04	a	Beroe	L	2-5	Kamburov 2 (p)
24/04	h	Botev	W	2-1	Velev, Kotev
07/05	h	Ludogorets	W	2-1	Kamburov, Gargorov
10/05	a	Levski	W	3-2	og (Minev), Kamburov, Karageren
14/05	h	Montana	W	2-0	Kamburov, Gargorov
22/05	h	Cherno More	W	2-1	Kamburov, Kiki
28/05	a	Pirin	W	2-1	Marchev 2

No	Name	Nat	DoB	Pos	Aps	(s)	Gls
29	Yassine Amrioui	FRA	21/02/95	D	2		
27	Dimo Bakalov		19/12/88	A	11	(6)	2
28	Zoran Baldovaliev	MKD	04/03/83	A	14	(4)	5
90	Olivier Bonnes	NIG	07/02/90	M	11	(4)	
98	Georgi Chukalov		25/02/98	M		(1)	
9	Nikolay Dimitrov		15/06/90	D	2	(2)	
6	Ignat Dishliev		08/07/87	D	1	(1)	
22	Loïc Dufau	FRA	15/03/89	M	8	(1)	
23	Yassine El Kharroubi	MAR	29/03/90	G	28		
23	Emil Gargorov		15/02/81	M	14	(5)	3
99	Mansour Gueye	SEN	30/12/85	A	2		
9	Ivan Ivanov		25/02/88	D	9		
11	Martin Kamburov		13/10/80	A	30		18
21	Birsent Karageren		06/12/92	M	7	(11)	3
55	Martin Kavdanski		13/02/87	D		(1)	
23	Dani Kiki		08/01/88	M	12	(9)	3
6	Kiril Kotev		18/04/82	D	27		1
71	Plamen Krumov		04/11/85	D	28		
89	Yohann Lasimant	FRA	04/09/89	A	5	(5)	
10	Veselin Marchev		07/02/90	M	3	(8)	2
20	Paulo Teles	POR	30/09/93	M	7	(3)	1
18	Martin Raynov		25/04/92	M	12	(1)	
1	Teodor Skorchev		04/09/86	G	2		
18	Hristo Stamov		02/01/94	M	7		
25	Krum Stoyanov		15/04/89	D	26	(2)	
23	Vanco Trajanov	MKD	09/08/78	M	16	(4)	1
3	Alexander Tunchev		10/07/81	D	26	(2)	
5	Georgi Valchev		07/03/91	D	8	(10)	
22	Stefan Velev		02/05/89	M	23	(3)	1
19	Dimitar Velkovski		22/01/95	M	22		
1	Alexander Vitanov		01/05/92	G	4	(1)	
16	Aykut Yanakov		08/04/95	A	5	(3)	
10	Iliyan Yordanov		03/04/89	M		(2)	

PFC Ludogorets Razgrad

1945 • Ludogorets Arena (5,000) •
ludogorets.com

Major honours
Bulgarian League (5) 2012, 2013, 2014, 2015, 2016;
Bulgarian Cup (2) 2012, 2014

Coach: Bruno Ribeiro (POR);
(02/09/15) Eduard Eranosyan;
(06/11/15) Georgi Dermendzhiev

2015

18/07	a	Litex	L	0-2	(match annulled)
26/07	a	Cherno More	W	3-2	Marcelinho, Wanderson, og (Stanchev)
01/08	h	Levski	W	2-0	Marcelinho, Misidjan
07/08	a	Montana	D	1-1	Moți (p)
16/08	a	Lokomotiv	W	1-0	Marcelinho
21/08	a	Pirin	W	3-0	Vasilev, Keșerü 2
28/08	a	Slavia	D	1-1	Misidjan
12/09	a	Beroe	D	0-0	
19/09	h	Botev	W	2-0	Keșerü 2
26/09	h	Litex	D	1-1	Jonathan Cafu (match annulled)
03/10	h	Cherno More	D	1-1	Keșerü
18/10	a	Levski	D	1-1	Keșerü
24/10	h	Montana	W	2-0	Jonathan Cafu, Keșerü
02/11	a	Lokomotiv	L	0-2	
07/11	h	Pirin	D	0-0	
21/11	a	Slavia	W	1-0	Moți (p)
27/11	h	Beroe	W	5-0	Wanderson 2, Marcelinho, Terziev, Keșerü
02/12	a	Botev	W	1-0	Keșerü
05/12	a	Litex	D	1-1	Marcelinho (match annulled)
12/12	a	Cherno More	W	2-0	Jonathan Cafu, Keșerü

2016

21/02	h	Levski	W	2-1	Wanderson, Lucas Sasha
26/02	a	Montana	W	2-0	Keșerü
01/03	h	Lokomotiv	W	2-0	Marcelinho, Moți
05/03	a	Pirin	W	3-1	Jonathan Cafu 2, Keșerü
12/03	h	Slavia	W	3-1	Jonathan Cafu, Wanderson, Moți (p)
19/03	a	Beroe	W	2-0	Kerchev, Marcelinho
03/04	h	Botev	W	1-0	Marcelinho
15/04	h	Cherno More	W	4-0	Wanderson, Keșerü
23/04	a	Levski	D	0-0	
29/04	h	Montana	W	2-1	Jonathan Cafu, Juninho Quixadá
07/05	a	Lokomotiv	L	1-2	Wanderson
11/05	h	Pirin	W	4-1	Prepeliță, Keșerü, Moți, Wanderson
16/05	a	Slavia	W	5-0	Juninho Quixadá 2, Keșerü, Wanderson, Jonathan Cafu
21/05	h	Beroe	L	0-2	
27/05	a	Botev	L	1-2	Kerchev

No	Name	Nat	DoB	Pos	Aps	(s)	Gls
15	Alexander Dragomirov Alexandrov		13/04/86	D	2	(1)	
80	Denislav Alexandrov		19/07/97	A	2		
7	Mihail Alexandrov		11/06/89	M		(4)	
16	Brayan Angulo	COL	02/11/89	D	3	(3)	
12	Anicet Abel	MAD	16/03/90	M	5	(16)	
30	Georgi Argilashki		13/06/91	G	4	(1)	
1	Milan Borjan	CAN	23/10/87	G	9		
23	Tsvetelin Chunchukov		26/12/94	A	5	(5)	
4	Cicinho	BRA	26/12/88	D	10		
34	Oleg Dimitrov		06/03/96	M	1		
22	Svetoslav Dyakov		31/05/84	M	28	(1)	
22	Jonathan Cafu	BRA	10/07/91	A	23	(1)	8
11	Juninho Quixadá	BRA	12/12/85	A	7	(9)	3
37	Ventsislav Kerchev		02/06/97	D	26		2
28	Claudiu Keșerü	ROU	02/12/86	A	27	(1)	15
45	Ivaylo Klimentov		21/08/98	M		(1)	
98	Svetoslav Kovachev		14/03/98	M		(2)	
8	Lucas Sasha	BRA	01/03/90	M	20	(2)	1
92	Jody Lukoki	COD	15/11/92	A	3	(17)	
84	Marcelinho		24/08/84	M	29		8
25	Yordan Minev		14/10/80	D	25		
93	Virgil Misidjan	NED	24/07/93	M	12	(5)	2
27	Cosmin Moți	ROU	03/12/84	D	30		5
6	Natanael	BRA	25/12/90	D	26	(1)	
24	Preslav Petrov		01/05/95	D		(1)	
83	Hristo Popadiyn		06/01/94	D	1	(1)	
30	Andrei Prepeliță	ROU	08/12/85	M	12	(13)	1
71	Yanaki Smirnov		20/09/92	A		(1)	
21	Vladislav Stoyanov		08/06/87	G	22		
55	Georgi Terziev		18/04/92	D	10	(12)	1
19	Alexander Vasilev		27/04/95	D	9		1
77	Vitinha	POR	11/02/86	M	10	(2)	
88	Wanderson	BRA	02/01/88	M	23	(6)	9

NB Appearances and goals for all clubs include those from the annulled matches against PFC Litex Lovech.

 **BULGARIA**

PFC Montana 1921

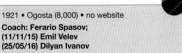

1921 • Ogosta (8,000) • no website
Coach: Ferario Spasov;
(11/11/15) Emil Velev;
(25/05/16) Dilyan Ivanov

2015

19/07	a	Beroe	D	0-0	
25/07	h	Botev	W	6-0	Minchev 3, A Iliev, Baldzhiyski, Y Angelov
03/08	a	Litex	L	1-2	Baldzhiyski (match annulled)
07/08	h	Ludogorets	D	1-1	A Iliev
15/08	h	Levski	L	0-2	
22/08	a	Cherno More	L	0-1	
30/08	h	Lokomotiv	W	2-0	S Georgiev, S Genchev
13/09	h	Pirin	D	0-0	
19/09	h	Slavia	L	1-2	Minchev
27/09	h	Beroe	W	1-0	Baldzhiyski
04/10	a	Botev	L	0-1	
18/10	h	Litex	L	0-2	(match annulled)
24/10	a	Ludogorets	L	0-2	
02/11	h	Levski	L	0-2	
07/11	h	Cherno More	L	0-4	
20/11	a	Lokomotiv	L	0-1	
29/11	h	Pirin	D	1-1	Minchev
03/12	a	Slavia	L	0-1	
06/12	h	Beroe	L	1-2	A Iliev
13/12	h	Botev	D	1-1	A Iliev

2016

26/02	h	Ludogorets	L	0-1	
02/03	a	Levski	D	0-0	
06/03	a	Cherno More	D	1-1	A Georgiev
12/03	h	Lokomotiv	L	0-1	
20/03	a	Pirin	D	0-0	
02/04	a	Slavia	L	0-3	
10/04	h	Beroe	L	1-3	Minchev
16/04	h	Botev	D	2-2	Michev (p), A Georgiev
29/04	a	Ludogorets	L	1-2	Pashov
06/05	h	Levski	L	0-1	
10/05	h	Cherno More	W	3-2	Kokonov, Stoyanov, A Iliev
14/05	a	Lokomotiv	L	0-2	
20/05	h	Pirin	L	0-1	
28/05	a	Slavia	L	1-3	S Georgiev

No	Name	Nat	DoB	Pos	Aps	(s)	Gls
17	Georgi Angelov		12/11/90	M	28	(1)	
18	Yanko Angelov		29/07/93	M	1	(4)	1
20	Petar Atanasov		13/10/90	M	12	(2)	
11	Borislav Baldzhiyski		12/10/90	M	17		3
90	Olivier Bonnes	NIG	07/02/90	M	10		
23	Borislav Damyanov		11/04/98	M		(1)	
10	Albi Dosti	ALB	13/09/91	M	2	(10)	
4	Nabil Ejenavi	ALG	16/02/94	M	1	(4)	
14	Lyubomir Genchev		13/04/86	M	1	(2)	
25	Stanislav Genchev		20/03/81	M	27	(1)	1
5	Asen Georgiev		09/07/93	M	33		2
22	Sergey Georgiev		05/05/92	A	15	(11)	2
6	Hristofor Hubchev		24/11/95	D	22		
8	Atanas Iliev		09/10/94	A	19	(11)	5
11	Hristiyan Iliev		31/03/98	M	1	(1)	
1	Hristo Ivanov		06/04/82	G	32		
17	Ivan Kokonov		17/08/91	A	11	(3)	1
76	Zdravko Lazarov		20/02/76	A	5	(14)	
16	Vladimir Michev		20/11/85	M	10	(7)	1
3	Ivan Mihov		08/06/91	D	22		
8	Ivan Minchev		28/05/91	A	27	(3)	6
13	Raif Muradov		10/12/93	D	5	(1)	
17	Georgi Pashov		04/03/90	D	19	(3)	1
19	Matej Poplatnik	SVN	15/07/92	A	4	(10)	
21	Hristiyan Popov		05/02/90	D	6	(3)	
14	Denislav Sergiev		01/03/97	M		(1)	
10	Ivan Stoyanov		24/07/83	M	11	(2)	1
7	Yordan Georgiev Todorov		12/11/81	M	3	(1)	
26	Yordan Valkov Todorov		27/07/81	D	27	(1)	
33	Ivaylo Vasilev		15/01/91	G	2		
19	Tsvetan Versanov		20/06/91	M	1	(3)	

OFC Pirin Blagoevgrad

1922 • Hristo Botev (11,000) • pirinfc.com
Coach: Nedelcho Matushev;
(29/09/15) (Vasil Petov);
(14/10/15) Naci Şensoy (TUR)

2015

19/07	h	Cherno More	D	1-1	Toshev
27/07	h	Slavia	L	0-3	
02/08	a	Beroe	L	0-1	
09/08	h	Botev	L	0-1	
14/08	h	Litex	L	0-1	(match annulled)
21/08	h	Ludogorets	L	0-3	
30/08	a	Levski	D	0-0	
13/09	h	Montana	D	0-0	
20/09	a	Lokomotiv	L	1-2	Karapetrov
26/09	a	Cherno More	L	0-1	
03/10	a	Slavia	D	0-0	
19/10	h	Beroe	L	0-1	
23/10	a	Botev	L	0-1	
30/10	h	Litex	D	1-1	Bashliev (match annulled)
07/11	a	Ludogorets	D	0-0	
22/11	h	Levski	W	1-0	Toshev
29/11	a	Montana	D	1-1	Trayanov
03/12	h	Lokomotiv	W	3-0	Toshev, Bashliev, Nakov
06/12	h	Cherno More	W	4-0	Sandanski, Trayanov, og (Georgiev), Toshev
11/02	h	Slavia	L	0-3	

2016

20/02	a	Beroe	L	1-3	Mladenov
28/02	h	Botev	D	2-2	Marquinhos, Dyulgerov
05/03	h	Ludogorets	L	1-3	og (Moți)
13/03	a	Levski	L	1-3	Nikolov
20/03	h	Montana	D	0-0	
01/04	a	Lokomotiv	L	2-4	Toshev 2 (1p)
09/04	a	Cherno More	D	1-1	Blagov
17/04	a	Slavia	W	2-1	Toshev 2
24/04	a	Beroe	D	1-1	Popev
29/04	a	Botev	D	2-2	Toshev, Marquinhos
11/05	a	Ludogorets	L	1-4	Genov
15/05	h	Levski	L	0-1	
20/05	a	Montana	W	1-0	Genov
28/05	h	Lokomotiv	L	1-2	Toshev

No	Name	Nat	DoB	Pos	Aps	(s)	Gls
21	Alexander Bashliev		16/11/89	D	24	(1)	2
16	Ventsislav Bengyuzov		22/01/91	M	10	(9)	
15	Dimitar Blagov		30/03/92	M	9	(11)	1
25	Vasil Bozhinov		08/12/96	D		(1)	
22	Bogomil Dyakov		12/04/84	D	6		
6	Kostadin Dyakov		22/08/85	M	11	(2)	
5	Alexander Dyulgerov		19/04/90	D	31	(1)	1
11	Edenilson	BRA	13/09/87	M	2	(1)	
8	Daniel Genov		19/05/89	M	6	(7)	2
4	Antonio Hadzhiivanov		16/01/90	A	1	(17)	
17	Iliya Karapetrov		29/04/92	D	13	(3)	1
24	Anton Kostadinov		24/06/82	D	25	(1)	
76	Krasimir Kostov		01/09/85	G	34		
28	Marquinhos		30/04/82	M	17	(14)	2
9	Daniel Mladenov		25/05/87	M	7	(1)	1
19	Blagoy Nakov		19/03/85	M	5	(10)	1
14	Stiliyan Nikolov		16/07/90	D	28		1
18	Yulian Popev		06/07/86	D	19		1
20	Yanko Sandanski		23/11/88	M	20	(2)	1
3	Rumen Sandev		19/11/88	D	28		
7	Toni Tasev		25/03/94	M	19	(9)	
10	Martin Toshev		15/08/90	A	29	(4)	10
23	Todor Trayanov		30/05/95	M	17		2
33	Emil Viyachki		18/05/90	D	6	(2)	
26	Alexander Yakimov		27/04/89	M	7	(2)	

PFC Slavia Sofia

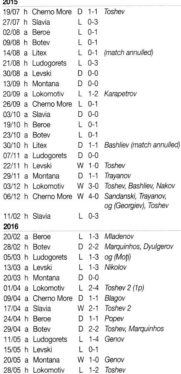

1913 • Slavia (15,000) • pfcslavia.com
Major honours
Bulgarian League (7) 1928, 1930, 1936, 1939, 1941, 1943, 1996; Bulgarian Cup (7) 1952, 1963, 1964, 1966, 1975, 1980, 1996

Coach: Ivan Kolev;
(01/12/15) (Vladimir Ivanov);
(18/12/15) Aleksandr Tarkhanov (RUS)

2015

17/07	h	Lokomotiv	W	3-0	Dimitrov 2, Valchanov
27/07	a	Pirin	W	3-0	Manzorro 2 (1p), Dimitrov
02/08	h	Cherno More	L	0-1	
09/08	h	Beroe	L	0-1	
16/08	h	Botev	W	1-0	Dimitrov
23/08	h	Litex	L	0-1	(match annulled)
28/08	a	Ludogorets	D	1-1	Karachanakov
13/09	h	Levski	L	0-1	
19/09	a	Montana	W	2-1	Karachanakov, Semerdzhiev
27/09	a	Lokomotiv	L	0-2	
03/10	h	Pirin	D	0-0	
17/10	a	Cherno More	L	0-1	
16/10	a	Beroe	W	2-1	Karachanakov 2
30/10	h	Botev	W	2-0	Dimitrov, Manzorro
06/11	a	Litex	L	0-4	(match annulled)
21/11	h	Ludogorets	L	0-1	
29/11	a	Levski	L	0-2	
03/12	h	Montana	W	1-0	Karachanakov (p)
07/12	h	Lokomotiv	W	3-0	N'Dongala 2, Manset (p)
11/12	a	Pirin	W	3-0	Karachanakov, Dimitrov, Valchanov

2016

21/02	h	Cherno More	D	0-0	
28/02	h	Beroe	D	0-0	
03/03	a	Botev	W	1-0	Serderov
12/03	a	Ludogorets	L	1-3	Moukanza
19/03	h	Levski	D	0-0	
02/04	h	Montana	W	3-0	Serderov, Yomov, N'Dongala
10/04	a	Lokomotiv	L	1-3	Dimitrov
17/04	h	Pirin	L	1-2	Baldzhiyski
23/04	a	Cherno More	L	2-3	Baldzhiyski, Pirgov
30/04	a	Beroe	D	1-1	Baldzhiyski
07/05	h	Botev	W	1-0	Baldzhiyski
14/05	h	Ludogorets	L	0-5	
22/05	a	Levski	W	1-0	Baldzhiyski
28/05	h	Montana	W	3-1	Yomov, Stankev, Stoev

No	Name	Nat	DoB	Pos	Aps	(s)	Gls
20	Petar Atanasov		13/10/90	A	8	(6)	
6	Zhivko Atanasov		03/02/91	D	8	(1)	
11	Borislav Baldzhiyski		12/10/90	M	12	(1)	5
5	Dimitar Burov		31/08/97	D	1		
2	Martin Dechev		20/03/90	D	7	(2)	
71	Diego	BRA	21/05/92	M	20	(3)	
14	Ivaylo Dimitrov		26/03/89	M	28	(6)	7
17	Kostadin Dyakov		22/08/85	M	11	(4)	
75	Yanis Karabelyov		08/03/96	M	24	(1)	
71	Anton Karachanakov		17/01/92	M	16	(3)	6
6	Aboud Omar Khamis	KEN	09/09/92	D	11		
13	Mario Kirev		15/08/89	G	16		
66	Plamen Krachunov		11/01/89	D	6	(2)	
16	Kaloyan Krastev		24/01/99	A	3	(7)	
9	Mathieu Manset	FRA	05/08/89	A	5	(4)	1
7	Jérémy Manzorro	FRA	11/11/91	M	12	(3)	3
27	Emil Martinov		18/03/92	M	22	(2)	
5	Franck Mbarga	GER	09/01/92	M	5	(3)	
9	Donnell Moukanza	FRA	27/02/91	A	1	(5)	1
11	Doude N'Dongala	FRA	06/09/94	A	10	(4)	3
25	Tsvetomir Panov		17/04/89	D	30	(1)	
1	Georgi Petkov		14/03/76	G	18		
3	Dimitar Pirgov		23/10/89	D	29	(1)	1
22	Vladimir Semerdzhiev		27/05/95	M	12	(9)	1
20	Serder Serderov	RUS	10/03/94	A	9	(2)	2
4	Nikita Sergeev	RUS	14/02/92	D	3		
24	Martin Stankev		29/07/89	M	1	(2)	1
23	Emil Stoev		17/01/96	M	11	(11)	1
35	Ivan Valchanov		28/09/91	M	4	(6)	2
24	Kitan Vasilev		19/02/97	A		(2)	
13	Stefan Velkov		12/12/96	D	22	(2)	
35	Georgi Yomov		06/07/97	M	9	(4)	2

Top goalscorers

18	Martin Kamburov (Lokomotiv)	
15	Claudiu Keşerü (Ludogorets)	
11	Mathias Coureur (Cherno More)	
	Danilo Asprilla (Litex)	
10	Martin Toshev (Pirin)	
9	Wanderson (Ludogorets)	
8	Ventsislav Hristov (Levski)	
	Roman Procházka (Levski)	
	Jonathan Cafu (Ludogorets)	
	Marcelinho (Ludogorets)	
	Borislav Baldzhiyski (Montana/Slavia)	

New club

PFC CSKA-Sofia

2016 • Bulgarska Armia (22,000) • cska.bg

Major honours
Bulgarian League (4) 1998, 1999, 2010, 2011
(as Litex Lovech); Bulgarian Cup (4) 2001, 2004,
2008, 2009 (as Litex Lovech)

Coach: Hristo Yanev

Promoted clubs

PFC Dunav 2010 Ruse

2010 • Gradski (15,000) • fcdunav.eu
Coach: Veselin Velikov

FC Lokomotiv Gorna Oryahovitsa

1932 • Lokomotiv (10,000) • no website
Coach: Sasho Angelov;
(24/03/16) Alexander Tomash

FC Vereya Stara Zagora

2001 • Trace Arena (1,714) • fcvereya.bg
Coach: Vladislav Yanush

PFC Neftochimic Burgas

1962 • Lazur (18,037) • neftochimic.com
Coach: Radostin Kishishev;
(12/08/15) Atanas Atanasov;
(30/09/15) Dian Petkov;
(10/05/16) Dimcho Nenov

Second level final table 2015/16

		Pld	W	D	L	F	A	Pts
1	PFC Dunav 2010 Ruse	30	18	10	2	53	19	64
2	OFC Pomorie	30	15	9	6	36	23	54
3	FC Lokomotiv Gorna Oryahovitsa	30	13	11	6	42	26	50
4	FC Sozopol	30	13	10	7	44	28	49
5	PFC Litex II Lovech	30	14	7	9	50	38	49
6	FC Botev Galabovo	30	12	5	13	32	47	41
7	PFC Ludogorets II Razgrad	30	12	5	13	41	41	41
8	FC Vereya Stara Zagora	30	10	10	10	33	27	40
9	FC Bansko 1951	30	11	6	13	42	38	39
10	FC Oborishte Panagyurishte	30	11	6	13	29	33	39
11	FC Pirin 2002 Razlog	30	10	8	12	31	41	38
12	PFC Neftochimic Burgas	30	8	14	8	31	39	38
13	PFC Spartak Pleven	30	9	9	12	35	42	36
14	PFC Dobrudzha 1919 Dobrich	30	8	10	12	27	33	34
15	FC Septemvri Simitli	30	6	5	19	26	50	23
16	FC Lokomotiv 2012 Mezdra	30	5	5	20	28	55	20

Promotion/Relegation play-off

(04/06/16)
Montana 2-1 Pomorie

NB FC Lokomotiv Gorna Oryahovitsa, FC Vereya Stara
Zagora & PFC Neftochimic Burgas subsequently invited
to top level for 2016/17 - as highest-ranked teams to
obtain license.

DOMESTIC CUP

Kupa na Bulgariya 2015/16

FIRST ROUND

(22/09/15)
Chernomorets Balchik 0-3 Lokomotiv Gorna
Oryahovitsa
Dunav 2010 Ruse 4-0 Botev Galabovo
Lokomotiv 2012 Mezdra 0-3 Litex Lovech
(23/09/15)
CSKA Sofia 3-1 Neftochimic Burgas
Etar Veliko Turnovo 1-1 Sozopol *(aet; 4-5 on pens)*
Lokomotiv 1929 Mezdra 0-5 Ludogorets Razgrad
Nesebar 1-0 OFC Pirin Blagoevgrad
Oborishte Panagyurishte 0-2 Lokomotiv Plovdiv
Pirin 2002 Razlog 1-7 Cherno More Varna
Pirin Gotse Delchev 1-3 Montana
Septemvri Simitli 0-4 Botev Plovdiv
Spartak Pleven 2-1 Slavia Sofia
Svetkavista Targovishte 0-4 Beroe Stara Zagora
Vereya Stara Zagora 1-3 Bansko
Vihar Stroevo 0-0 Dobrudzha *(aet; 5-3 on pens)*
(24/09/15)
Pomorie 0-0 Levski Sofia *(aet; 2-4 on pens)*

SECOND ROUND

(27/10/15)
Litex Lovech 4-2 Dunav 2010 Ruse
Sozopol 1-0 Botev Plovdiv
Spartak Pleven 0-2 CSKA Sofia
Vihar Stroevo 0-5 Cherno More Varna
(28/10/15)
Lokomotiv Plovdiv 1-1 Montana *(aet; 2-4 on pens)*
Nesebar 1-3 Levski Sofia
(29/10/15)
Beroe Stara Zagora 3-1 Bansko
Lokomotiv Gorna Oryahovitsa 1-0 Ludogorets
Razgrad

QUARTER-FINALS

(08/12/15)
Litex Lovech 3-0 Levski Sofia *(Arsénio 101,
Despodov 109, 112) (aet)*
(09/12/15)
Beroe Stara Zagora 0-0 Cherno More Varna
(aet; 5-3 on pens)
Lokomotiv Gorna Oryahovitsa 1-1 Montana
(Kunev 29; Michev 69) (aet; 3-4 on pens)
(10/12/15)
CSKA Sofia 3-0 Sozopol *(P Yordanov 78, 86,
Tsvetanov 90+7)*

SEMI-FINALS

(06/04/16 & 20/04/16)
Beroe Stara Zagora 0-2 CSKA Sofia *(Ayass 5,
Galchev 53)*
CSKA Sofia 2-0 Beroe Stara Zagora *(P Yordanov
3, Tsvetkov 41)*
(CSKA Sofia 4-0)

(06/04/16 & 21/04/16)
Montana 2-0 Litex Lovech *(S Georgiev 22, 70)*
Litex Lovech 1-0 Montana *(Malinov 33)*
(Montana 2-1)

FINAL

(24/05/16)
Vasil Levski, Sofia
PFC CSKA SOFIA 1 *(Malamov 12)*
PFC MONTANA 1921 0
Referee: *Todorov*
CSKA: *Gospodinov, Dinchev, Chorbadzhiyski,
Granchov, Kikarin, Y Yordanov, Malamov, Galchev,
Ayass (Vitanov 79), Tsvetanov (Tsvetkov 90+2),
P Yordanov (Hazurov 88)*
MONTANA: *Vasilev, Yordan V Todorov, A Georgiev,
Hubchev, G Angelov, S Genchev (Atanasov 83),
Michev (Minchev 38), Stoyanov, Bonnes,
S Georgiev, Kokonov (A Iliev 62)*

CROATIA
Hrvatski Nogometni Savez (HNS)

Address	Vukovarska 269A	**President**	Davor Šuker
	HR-10000 Zagreb	**General secretary**	Damir Vrbanović
Tel	+385 1 2361 555	**Media officer**	Tomislav Pacak
Fax	+385 1 2441 501	**Year of formation**	1912
E-mail	info@hns-cff.hr	**National stadium**	Maksimir, Zagreb
Website	hns-cff.hr		(35,123)

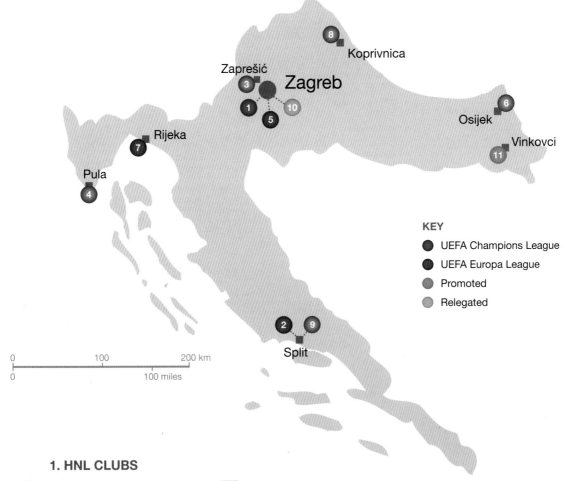

KEY

● UEFA Champions League
● UEFA Europa League
● Promoted
● Relegated

1. HNL CLUBS

  ① GNK Dinamo Zagreb

  ② HNK Hajduk Split

  ③ NK Inter Zaprešić

 ④ NK Istra 1961

 ⑤ NK Lokomotiva Zagreb

  ⑥ NK Osijek

  ⑦ HNK Rijeka

 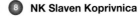 ⑧ NK Slaven Koprivnica

  ⑨ RNK Split

 ⑩ NK Zagreb

PROMOTED CLUB

  ⑪ HNK Cibalia

Tenth double for Dinamo Zagreb

Dinamo Zagreb's stranglehold on the Croatian national championship remained as tight as ever in 2015/16 as the club from the capital added another title to their collection. It was their 11th in succession and 18th overall, with victory over Slaven Koprivnica in the Croatian Cup final completing a tenth domestic double.

Rijeka gave Dinamo a run for their money in the league, losing just one of their 36 matches, and it was a solitary defeat for new national team coach Ante Čačić, after extra time against Portugal, that brought Croatia's impressive UEFA EURO 2016 campaign to a disappointingly premature conclusion.

Zagreb giants claim 11th league title in a row

Slaven Koprivnica defeated 2-1 in cup final

Last-16 EURO exit for enterprising national team

Domestic league

Armed with the same coach, Zoran Mamić, and practically the same playing staff that had won the 2014/15 league title undefeated, Dinamo were never likely to cede their crown. They did, however, make a stuttering start, drawing three of their opening five games, including one at home to each of their two main rivals, Hajduk Split and Rijeka.

The perennial champions managed to prolong their unbeaten run to exactly 50 matches before a last-minute winner from Rijeka's Anas Sharbini brought it to an end. Not untypically, that defeat was immediately followed by another, 1-0 at RNK Split, but Dinamo then collected maximum points from their next dozen games, a 3-0 win over Rijeka in late February levering them into a five-point lead that would provide them with sufficient comfort for the remainder of the campaign.

Exatraordinarily, that decisive defeat in Zagreb would be Rijeka's only one all season. Runners-up twice under Slovenian coach Matjaž Kek, Rijeka's bid to dethrone Dinamo was bold and relentless, but while they were virtually impossible to beat, they were too prone to draws. They ended up with 14 of them – twice as many as Dinamo – and it was after the 13th, a May Day stalemate at home to Split, that Dinamo were confirmed as champions.

Mamić's side were a fine blend of foreign experience and Croatian youth, with midfielders Marko Pjaca and Marko Rog particularly prominent in the latter category. Dinamo's top marksman was Bosnian youngster Armin Hodžić, with 13 goals, the same number as Rijeka's Slovenian Roman Bezjak, but the golden boot standings were topped by two Macedonians – Inter Zaprešić's Ilija Nestrovski, who scored 25 of his team's 39 goals, and Slaven's Muzafer Ejupi, on 16. The top Croatian in the list was Lokomotiva Zagreb's 12-goal Franko Andrijašević, with the only other homegrown player to reach double figures being Gabrijel Boban of relegated NK Zagreb.

Domestic cup

The Croatian Cup final was a repeat of the 2007 fixture, with Dinamo taking on Slaven, who had surprisingly overcome Rijeka in the semis. The Zagreb side had won that previous contest 2-1 over two legs, but this time the same outcome was achieved in 90 minutes, with Pjaca putting Dinamo ahead and Ejupi equalising before Rog, who had missed a penalty against Dinamo in the 2015 final shoot-out for previous club Split, struck a 77th-minute winner.

Europe

Dinamo had one of their better European campaigns in 2015/16, reaching the UEFA Champions League group stage for the fifth time and finally ending their long wait for a victory in the competition proper when they overcame Arsenal 2-1 at the Maksimir in their opening encounter. Unfortunately, they lost all of their other five fixtures as well as midfielder Arijan Ademi, banned for four years after he failed a drugs test following the Arsenal win.

National team

Niko Kovač lost his job as Croatia coach following a 2-0 defeat in Norway that placed UEFA EURO 2016 qualification in jeopardy, but Ante Čačić, 18 years his senior, came in and not only led the country to France but also succeeded in turning a collection of highly talented individuals into a fluent and entertaining team. Having prepared for the tournament with a record 10-0 win over San Marino, they then topped their group in style, memorably defeating holders Spain 2-1 in Bordeaux with a late winner from Ivan Perišić, one of several players to distinguish themselves. But just as Croatia were being talked up as potential European champions, they came across Portugal, who stymied their attack, took them to extra time, then cruelly knocked them out with a late breakaway goal.

DOMESTIC SEASON AT A GLANCE

1. HNL 2015/16 final table

		Home					Away					Total					
	Pld	W	D	L	F	A	W	D	L	F	A	W	D	L	F	A	Pts
1 **GNK Dinamo Zagreb**	36	16	2	0	41	9	10	5	3	26	10	26	7	3	67	19	85
2 HNK Rijeka	36	12	6	0	35	9	9	8	1	21	11	21	14	1	56	20	77
3 HNK Hajduk Split	36	10	5	3	27	12	7	5	6	19	16	17	10	9	46	28	61
4 NK Lokomotiva Zagreb	36	9	2	7	28	24	7	2	9	28	29	16	4	16	56	53	52
5 NK Inter Zaprešić	36	6	9	3	24	16	5	5	8	15	32	11	14	11	39	48	47
6 RNK Split	36	7	6	5	19	15	3	10	5	9	14	10	16	10	28	29	46
7 NK Slaven Koprivnica	36	7	6	5	23	15	3	6	9	18	27	10	12	14	41	42	42
8 NK Osijek	36	5	9	4	15	13	2	4	12	12	36	7	13	16	27	49	34
9 NK Istra 1961	36	4	6	8	15	22	0	6	12	8	36	4	12	20	23	58	24
10 NK Zagreb	36	2	4	12	17	31	1	4	13	10	33	3	8	25	27	64	17

European qualification 2016/17

 Champion/Cup winner: GNK Dinamo Zagreb (second qualifying round)

 HNK Rijeka (third qualifying round)
HNK Hajduk Split (second qualifying round)
NK Lokomotiva Zagreb (first qualifying round)

Top scorer	Ilija Nestorovski (Inter), 25 goals
Relegated club	NK Zagreb
Promoted club	HNK Cibalia
Cup final	GNK Dinamo Zagreb 2-1 NK Slaven Koprivnica

Team of the season
(3-4-3)

Coach: Mamić (Dinamo)

Player of the season

Marko Pjaca
(GNK Dinamo Zagreb)

Pjaca's second season at Dinamo was every bit as impressive as his first, the young winger not only helping the club to a second successive league and cup double but finishing the campaign so strongly that he was a shoo-in for Croatia's UEFA EURO 2016 squad. The skilful 21-year-old scored seven league goals in the spring plus a penalty in the cup final and although he did not have as many minutes on the field in France as he and his many admirers would have wished for, he certainly made the most of his limited opportunity.

Newcomer of the season

Ante Ćorić
(GNK Dinamo Zagreb)

Having made his breakthrough with Dinamo in 2014/15, Ćorić cemented his status as Croatia's top teenage talent with a string of eye-catching and productive displays that helped his team to win the domestic double for the second straight season. Bright, creative and difficult to dispossess, the 18-year-old attacking midfielder was rewarded for his excellent season with a place in Croatia's UEFA EURO 2016 squad, although the tournament turned out to be a look-and-learn experience as he never made it off the bench.

NATIONAL TEAM

International tournament appearances

FIFA World Cup (4) 1998 (3rd), 2002, 2006, 2014

UEFA European Championship (5) 1996 (qtr-finals), 2004, 2008 (qtr-finals), 2012, 2016 (round of 16)

Top five all-time caps

Darijo Srna (134); Stipe Pletikosa (114); Josip Šimunić (105); **Ivica Olić** (104); Dario Šimić (100)

Top five all-time goals

Davor Šuker (45); Eduardo (29); **Mario Mandžukić** (24); **Darijo Srna** (22); Ivica Olić (20)

Results 2015/16

03/09/15	Azerbaijan (ECQ)	A	Baku	D	0-0	
06/09/15	Norway (ECQ)	A	Oslo	L	0-2	
10/10/15	Bulgaria (ECQ)	H	Zagreb	W	3-0	Perišić (2), Rakitić (42), N Kalinić (81)
13/10/15	Malta (ECQ)	A	Ta'Qali	W	1-0	Perišić (25)
17/11/15	Russia	A	Rostov-na-Donu	W	3-1	N Kalinić (57), Brozović (60), Mandžukić (82)
23/03/16	Israel	H	Osijek	W	2-0	Perišić (4), Brozović (34)
26/03/16	Hungary	A	Budapest	D	1-1	Mandžukić (29)
27/05/16	Moldova	H	Koprivnica	W	1-0	Kramarić (9)
04/06/16	San Marino	H	Rijeka	W	10-0	Pjaca (20), Mandžukić (23, 36, 38), Srna (24), Perišić (40), Rakitić (50), N Kalinić (59, 73, 84)
12/06/16	Turkey (ECF)	N	Paris (FRA)	W	1-0	Modrić (41)
17/06/16	Czech Republic (ECF)	N	Saint-Etienne (FRA)	D	2-2	Perišić (37), Rakitić (59)
21/06/16	Spain (ECF)	N	Bordeaux (FRA)	W	2-1	N Kalinić (45), Perišić (87)
25/06/16	Portugal (ECF)	N	Lens (FRA)	L	0-1	(aet)

Appearances 2015/16

Coach: Niko Kovač /(22/09/15) Ante Čačić	15/10/71 29/09/53		AZE	NOR	BUL	MLT	Rus	Isr	Hun	Mda	Smr	TUR	CZE	ESP	POR	Caps	Goals
Danijel Subašić	27/10/84	Monaco (FRA)	G	G	G	G		G46		G	G	G	G	G	G	25	-
Šime Vrsaljko	10/01/92	Sassuolo (ITA)	D	D		s46	s44	D	D	D	s56		s91	D		21	-
Vedran Ćorluka	05/02/86	Lokomotiv Moskva (RUS)	D	D	D	D		D46	D	D		D	D	D	D120	92	4
Domagoj Vida	29/04/89	Dynamo Kyiv (UKR)	D	D	D	D	D	D	D	D46	D	D	D		D	41	1
Danijel Pranjić	02/12/81	Panathinaikos (GRE)	D													58	1
Milan Badelj	25/02/89	Fiorentina (ITA)	M59		s46	M	M	M50		M46	M76	M	M	M	M	24	1
Luka Modrić	09/09/85	Real Madrid (ESP)	M71	M	M46			M67	M		M46	M	M62		M	93	11
Marko Pjaca	06/05/95	Dinamo Zagreb	M	M63	M60	M83				M46	M75	s93		M92	s110	11	1
Ivan Rakitić	10/03/88	Barcelona (ESP)	M	M72	M	M77					M55	M90	M92	M	M110	80	12
Ivan Perišić	02/02/89	Internazionale (ITA)	M83	M	M	M	M	M	M	M46	M	M87	M	M94	M	51	15
Mario Mandžukić	21/05/86	Juventus (ITA)	A	A			A87	A	A		A56	A93	A		A88	69	24
Mateo Kovačić	06/05/94	Real Madrid (ESP)	s59		M	M		s56	M75		s46		s62	s82		29	1
Marcelo Brozović	16/11/92	Internazionale (ITA)	s71	M		s77	M	M	M	M46		M	M		M	20	4
Nikola Kalinić	05/01/88	Fiorentina (ITA)	s83	s72	A85	A60	A74	A56		A	s56		A	s88		31	12
Darijo Srna	01/05/82	Shakhtar Donetsk (UKR)	D	D	D	D46	M44	s75		D56	D	D	D	D	134	22
Ivica Olić	14/09/79	Hamburg (GER)		s63		s83										104	20
Josip Pivarić	30/01/89	Dinamo Zagreb			D	D	D									5	-
Duje Čop	01/02/90	Málaga (ESP)			s60 89*					s46			s92			5	-
Andrej Kramarić	19/06/91	Leicester (ENG) /Hoffenheim (GER)			s85	s60	s87			A46	s55	s87		s94	s120	14	4
Lovre Kalinić	03/04/90	Hajduk Split					G90	s46	G							4	-
Marko Lešković	27/04/91	Rijeka					D									3	-
Ivan Močinić	30/04/93	Rijeka					M									1	-
Goran Milović	29/01/89	Hajduk Split					s74									1	-
Ivan Vargić	15/03/87	Rijeka					s90									2	-
Dejan Lovren	05/07/89	Liverpool (ENG)						D								31	2
Gordon Schildenfeld	18/03/85	Dinamo Zagreb						s46	D	s46	D	s90	s92			29	1
Alen Halilović	18/06/96	Sporting Gijón (ESP)						s50		s46						9	-
Domagoj Antolić	30/06/90	Dinamo Zagreb						s67	M	s46						4	-
Ivan Strinić	17/07/87	Napoli (ITA)								D	D	D	D91		D	38	-
Marko Rog	19/07/95	Dinamo Zagreb								s46	s76		M82			4	-
Ante Ćorić	14/04/97	Dinamo Zagreb								s46	s75					2	-
Tin Jedvaj	28/11/95	Leverkusen (GER)												D		4	-

GNK Dinamo Zagreb

CHAMPIONS LEAGUE

Second qualifying round - CS Fola Esch (LUX)
H 1-1 *Henríquez (36)*
Eduardo, Soudani, Šimunović, Ivo Pinto, Henríquez, Paulo Machado (Pamić 59), Gonçalo (Çekiçi 68), Pivarić, Pjaca, Rog, Taravel (Hodžić 80). Coach: Damir Krznar (CRO)
A 3-0 *Pjaca (29, 40), Rog (75)*
Eduardo, Soudani (Fernandes 69), Šimunović, Henríquez (Rog 59), Paulo Machado, Ademi, Pivarić, Pjaca, Sigali (Benković 78), Mâţel, Taravel. Coach: Zoran Mamić (CRO)

Third qualifying round - Molde FK (NOR)
H 1-1 *Henríquez (18)*
Eduardo, Soudani, Šimunović, Henríquez, Paulo Machado (Rog 64), Ademi, Pivarić, Pjaca, Sigali, Mâţel (Ivo Pinto 56), Taravel (Fernandes 73). Coach: Zoran Mamić (CRO)
Red card: Paulo Machado 65
A 3-3 *Pjaca (17), Ademi (20), Rog (22)*
Eduardo, Soudani (Hodžić 62), Šimunović, Ivo Pinto, Henríquez (Antolić 54), Gonçalo, Ademi, Pivarić, Pjaca, Sigali, Rog (Ćorić 75). Coach: Zoran Mamić (CRO)

Play-offs - KF Skënderbeu (ALB)
A 2-1 *Soudani (66), Pivarić (90+3)*
Eduardo, Soudani (Fernandes 78), Ivo Pinto, Paulo Machado (Ćorić 61), Gonçalo, Hodžić, Pivarić, Pjaca, Sigali, Rog (Antolić 71), Taravel. Coach: Zoran Mamić (CRO)
H 4-1 *Soudani (9, 80), Hodžić (15), Taravel (55)*
Eduardo, Soudani, Ivo Pinto, Paulo Machado, Gonçalo, Hodžić (Antolić 52), Pivarić, Pjaca (Fernandes 77), Sigali, Ćorić (Rog 67), Taravel. Coach: Zoran Mamić (CRO)
Red card: Gonçalo 48

Group F
Match 1 - Arsenal FC (ENG)
H 2-1 *Pivarić (24), Fernandes (58)*
Eduardo, Soudani, Ivo Pinto, Antolić (Rog 82), Paulo Machado, Fernandes (Ćorić 74), Ademi, Pivarić, Pjaca (Benković 88), Sigali, Taravel. Coach: Zoran Mamić (CRO)
Match 2 - FC Bayern München (GER)
A 0-5
Eduardo, Soudani, Antolić, Paulo Machado (Rog 61), Fernandes, Ademi, Pivarić, Pjaca (Henríquez 69), Benković (Gonçalo 46), Mâţel, Taravel. Coach: Zoran Mamić (CRO)
Match 3 - Olympiacos FC (GRE)
H 0-1
Eduardo, Soudani, Antolić, Paulo Machado, Fernandes (Henríquez 73), Gonçalo, Hodžić (Pjaca 61), Pivarić, Rog (Ćorić 87), Mâţel, Taravel. Coach: Zoran Mamić (CRO)
Match 4 - Olympiacos FC (GRE)
A 1-2 *Hodžić (21)*
Eduardo, Antolić, Paulo Machado, Fernandes (Musa 88), Gonçalo, Hodžić (Henríquez 57), Pivarić, Pjaca (Sigali 80), Rog, Mâţel, Taravel. Coach: Zoran Mamić (CRO)
Red card: Pivarić 79

Match 5 - Arsenal FC (ENG)
A 0-3
Eduardo, Ivo Pinto, Antolić (Henríquez 68), Paulo Machado (Ćorić 84), Fernandes (Soudani 57), Gonçalo, Pjaca, Sigali, Rog, Mâţel, Taravel. Coach: Zoran Mamić (CRO)
Match 6 - FC Bayern München (GER)
H 0-2
Eduardo, Soudani, Ivo Pinto, Antolić, Fernandes (Paulo Machado 74), Gonçalo, Pivarić, Sigali, Ćorić (Pjaca 61), Rog (Pavičić 81), Taravel. Coach: Zoran Mamić (CRO)

HNK Rijeka

EUROPA LEAGUE

Second qualifying round - Aberdeen FC (SCO)
H 0-3
Vargić, Tomasov (Kvržić 46), Balaj, Sharbini, Tomečak, Lešković, Bradarić (Močinić 76), Samardžić, Leovac, Radošević (Bezjak 55), Moisés. Coach: Matjaž Kek (SVN)
A 2-2 *Tomasov (58), Kvržić (63)*
Sluga, Ristovski, Tomasov, Bezjak, Mitrović, Bradarić (Balaj 74), Samardžić, Leovac, Roshi (Kvržić 52), Radošević, Moisés. Coach: Matjaž Kek (SVN)

HNK Hajduk Split

EUROPA LEAGUE

First qualifying round - JK Sillamäe Kalev (EST)
A 1-1 *Caktaš (6p)*
Kalinić, Mikanović, Milović, Vlašić, Ohandza, Caktaš, Maloku (Radchenko 58), Nižić, Tudor, Roguljić (Biliy 74), Balić (Maglica 81). Coach: Damir Burić (CRO)
H 6-2 *Balić (15), Caktaš (45+1), Ohandza (56, 63), Vlašić (72), Maglica (88)*
Kalinić, Milović (Biliy 81), Vlašić (Kiš 87), Ohandza (Maglica 74), Caktaš, Maloku, Nižić, Pejić, Tudor, Roguljić, Balić. Coach: Damir Burić (CRO)

Second qualifying round - FC Koper (SVN)
A 2-3 *Milović (29), Nižić (90)*
Kalinić, Milović, Jefferson, Vlašić, Maglica (Radchenko 74), Caktaš, Nižić, Pejić, Tudor, Roguljić (Maloku 70), Balić (Kiš 46). Coach: Damir Burić (CRO)
H 4-1 *Kiš (2), Jefferson (40), Caktaš (62), Maglica (69)*
Kalinić, Milović, Jefferson, Vlašić, Caktaš, Nižić, Pejić, Tudor, Kiš (Maglica 69), Roguljić (Maloku 53), Balić (Sušić 77). Coach: Damir Burić (CRO)

Third qualifying round - Strømsgodset IF (NOR)
H 2-0 *Balić (67), Kiš (90+3)*
Kalinić, Milović, Jefferson, Vlašić, Ohandza (Kiš 78), Caktaš, Nižić, Pejić, Tudor, Roguljić (Maloku 61), Balić (Sušić 74). Coach: Damir Burić (CRO)
A 2-0 *Caktaš (55), Ohandza (77)*
Kalinić, Milović, Jefferson, Vlašić, Ohandza (Maglica 80), Caktaš (Sušić 83), Maloku, Nižić, Pejić, Tudor, Balić (Juranović 70). Coach: Damir Burić (CRO)
Red card: Nižić 53

Play-offs - FC Slovan Liberec (CZE)
A 0-1
Kalinić, Milić, Biliy, Milović, Jefferson, Vlašić, Ohandza, Juranović, Caktaš, Sušić, Balić (Maloku 66). Coach: Damir Burić (CRO)
H 0-1
Kalinić, Milić, Milović, Jefferson, Vlašić, Ohandza, Caktaš (Roguljić 49), Nižić, Sušić, Tudor (Juranović 73), Balić (Maloku 34). Coach: Damir Burić (CRO)

NK Lokomotiva Zagreb

EUROPA LEAGUE

First qualifying round - AUK Broughton FC (WAL)
A 3-1 *Šovšić (48), Marić (61), Kolar (68)*
Zelenika, Bartolec, Mrcela, Šovšić (Ćorić 84), Marić (Kolar 63), Bručić, Fiolić, Mišić (Gržan 75), Andrijašević, Leko, Capan. Coach: Ante Čačić (CRO)
H 2-2 *Fiolić (65), Šovšić (73)*
Zelenika, Bartolec, Mamić, Mrcela, Šovšić (Puljić 90+2), Begonja, Marić, Fiolić (Gržan 70), Mišić (Kolar 46), Andrijašević, Capan. Coach: Ante Čačić (CRO)

Second qualifying round - PAOK FC (GRE)
H 2-1 *Kolar (30), Andrijašević (45+1)*
Zelenika, Bartolec, Mrcela, Šovšić (Capan 90+3), Begonja, Marić (Mišić 73), Bručić, Prenga, Kolar (Doležal 65), Andrijašević, Leko. Coach: Ante Čačić (CRO)
A 0-6
Zelenika, Bartolec, Mrcela, Šovšić, Begonja, Marić (Capan 57), Bručić, Prenga (Mišić 25), Kolar, Andrijašević, Leko (Doležal 46). Coach: Ante Čačić (CRO)

DOMESTIC LEAGUE CLUB-BY-CLUB

GNK Dinamo Zagreb

1945 • Maksimir (35,123) • gnkdinamo.hr

Major honours
Inter Cities Fairs Cup (1) 1967;
Yugoslav League (4) 1948, 1954, 1958, 1982;
Croatian League (18) 1993, 1996, 1997, 1998, 1999, 2000, 2003, 2006, 2007, 2008, 2009, 2010, 2011, 2012, 2013, 2014, 2015, 2016;
Yugoslav Cup (7) 1951, 1960, 1963, 1965, 1969, 1980, 1983;
Croatian Cup (14) 1994, 1996, 1997, 1998, 2001, 2002, 2004, 2007, 2008, 2009, 2011, 2012, 2015, 2016

Coach: Zoran Mamić

2015

12/07	h	Hajduk	D	1-1	Soudani
19/07	a	Osijek	D	1-1	Soudani
25/07	h	Inter	W	5-1	Hodžić 3, Fernandes 2 (1p)
31/07	a	Zagreb	W	2-0	Hodžić 2
08/08	h	Rijeka	D	0-0	
15/08	h	Split	W	3-0	Soudani, Paulo Machado, Henríquez
22/08	a	Istra 1961	D	1-1	Ćorić
29/08	h	Slaven	D	3-0	og (Paracki), Henríquez, Mâţel
11/09	a	Lokomotiva	W	4-0	Henríquez 2, Fernandes, Sigali
19/09	a	Hajduk	D	0-0	
25/09	h	Osijek	W	4-1	Hodžić 2, Henríquez, Musa
03/10	a	Inter	D	2-2	Fernandes (p), Hodžić
16/10	h	Zagreb	W	4-1	Fernandes 2, Hodžić, Henríquez
25/10	a	Rijeka	L	1-2	Fernandes
30/10	a	Split	L	0-1	
08/11	h	Istra 1961	W	1-0	Fernandes
20/11	a	Slaven	W	2-1	Taravel, Henríquez
29/11	h	Lokomotiva	W	3-1	Rog 2, Ćorić
05/12	h	Hajduk	W	3-0	Henríquez, Soudani
13/12	a	Osijek	W	1-0	Pjaca
19/12	h	Inter	W	1-0	Soudani

2016

14/02	a	Zagreb	W	2-1	Fernandes, Hodžić (p)
21/02	h	Rijeka	W	3-0	Soudani 2, Sigali
28/02	h	Split	W	1-0	Pjaca
03/03	a	Istra 1961	W	1-0	Pjaca
06/03	h	Slaven	W	2-1	Ćorić, Hodžić
13/03	h	Lokomotiva	W	3-2	Pjaca 2, Ćorić
20/03	a	Hajduk	L	0-1	
03/04	h	Osijek	W	3-0	Taravel, Henríquez, Fernandes
10/04	a	Inter	W	1-0	Soudani
16/04	h	Zagreb	W	1-0	Taravel (p)
19/04	a	Rijeka	D	0-0	
23/04	a	Split	W	1-0	Pjaca
30/04	h	Istra 1961	W	1-0	Pjaca
06/05	a	Slaven	W	3-0	Pjaca, Sigali, Hodžić
14/05	a	Lokomotiva	W	4-0	Rog, Gojak, Hodžić, Fernandes

No	Name	Nat	DoB	Pos	Aps	(s)	Gls
16	Arijan Ademi	MKD	29/05/91	M	6	(2)	
8	Domagoj Antolić		30/06/90	M	21	(3)	
25	Borna Barišić		10/11/92	D	1		
26	Filip Benković		13/07/97	D	10	(3)	
29	Ivan Božić		08/06/97	A		(1)	
7	Josip Brekalo		23/09/98	A	1	(7)	
17	Endri Çekiçi	ALB	23/11/96	M		(1)	
24	Ante Ćorić		14/04/97	M	19	(9)	4
21	Dani Olmo	ESP	07/05/98	M		(1)	
34	Eduardo	POR	19/09/82	G	32		
11	Júnior Fernandes	CHI	10/04/88	A	24	(4)	12
14	Amer Gojak	BIH	13/02/97	M		(5)	1
13	Gonçalo	POR	15/11/86	M	11	(6)	
9	Ángelo Henríquez	CHI	13/04/94	A	23	(4)	8
15	Armin Hodžić	BIH	17/11/94	A	15	(9)	13
7	Said Husejinović	BIH	13/05/88	M	1	(1)	
6	Ivo Pinto	POR	07/01/90	D	13		
1	Antonio Ježina		05/06/89	G	3		
25	Bojan Knežević		28/01/97	M	1		
17	Davor Lovren		03/10/98	A		(1)	
71	Alexandru Mâţel	ROU	17/10/89	D	17	(4)	1
27	Nikola Moro		12/03/98	M	1		
27	Darick Kobie Morris		15/07/95	D		(1)	
3	Mario Musa		06/07/90	D	16	(1)	1
28	Zvonko Pamić		04/02/91	M	2		
10	Paulo Machado	POR	31/03/86	M	26	(2)	1
18	Domagoj Pavičić		09/03/94	M	3	(8)	
19	Josip Pivarić		30/01/89	D	15		
20	Marko Pjaca		06/05/95	M	21	(7)	8
30	Marko Rog		19/07/95	M	26	(8)	3
23	Gordon Schildenfeld		18/03/85	D	11		
22	Leonardo Sigali	ARG	29/05/87	D	21	(1)	3
6	Vinko Soldo		15/02/98	D		(1)	
28	Borna Sosa		21/01/98	D	2		
2	El Arabi Hillel Soudani	ALG	25/11/87	A	17	(4)	8
37	Petar Stojanović	SVN	07/10/95	M	10		
33	Adrian Šemper		12/01/98	G	1		
5	Jozo Šimunović		04/08/94	D	6		
5	Damir Šovšić		05/02/90	M	5	(9)	
87	Jérémy Taravel	FRA	17/04/87	D	15	(1)	3

HNK Hajduk Split

1911 • Poljud (34,200) • hajduk.hr

Major honours
Yugoslav League (9) 1927, 1929, 1950, 1952, 1955, 1971, 1974, 1975, 1979; Croatian League (6) 1992, 1994, 1995, 2001, 2004, 2005; Yugoslav Cup (9) 1967, 1972, 1973, 1974, 1976, 1977, 1984, 1987, 1991; Croatian Cup (6) 1993, 1995, 2000, 2003, 2010, 2013

Coach: Damir Burić

2015

12/07	a	Dinamo	D	1-1	Caktaš
19/07	h	Split	D	0-0	
26/07	a	Istra 1961	L	1-4	Kiš
02/08	h	Slaven	D	2-2	Maloku, Milović
10/08	a	Lokomotiva	W	2-1	Kiš, Balić
15/08	a	Rijeka	D	0-0	
23/08	h	Osijek	W	3-0	Maloku, Caktaš, Bencun
30/08	a	Inter	W	2-0	Balić, Ohandza
12/09	h	Zagreb	W	1-0	Caktaš
19/09	h	Dinamo	D	0-0	
27/09	a	Split	W	2-0	Vlašić, Caktaš
04/10	a	Istra 1961	W	3-0	og (Gojković), Jefferson, Caktaš (p)
18/10	a	Slaven	W	1-0	Sušić
24/10	h	Lokomotiva	W	2-1	Sušić, Tudor
01/11	h	Rijeka	L	0-3	
07/11	a	Osijek	L	0-1	
21/11	h	Inter	W	4-0	Sušić, Tudor, Bencun, Roguljić
28/11	a	Zagreb	W	2-0	Tudor, Bencun
05/12	a	Dinamo	L	1-2	Caktaš
12/12	h	Split	W	1-0	
19/12	a	Istra 1961	W	2-0	Milić, Sušić

2016

13/02	h	Slaven	W	2-0	Sušić, Nižić
20/02	a	Lokomotiva	L	1-2	Tudor
27/02	a	Rijeka	D	0-1	
01/03	h	Osijek	D	2-2	Sušić, Nižić
08/03	a	Inter	D	0-0	
13/03	h	Zagreb	W	1-0	Sušić (p)
20/03	h	Dinamo	W	1-0	Tudor
03/04	a	Split	D	0-0	
10/04	a	Istra 1961	W	3-0	Šimić, Sušić 2 (2p)
17/04	a	Slaven	D	0-0	
20/04	h	Lokomotiva	W	2-0	Sušić (p), Juranović
24/04	h	Rijeka	L	1-2	Sušić
01/05	a	Osijek	L	1-2	Sušić (p)
08/05	h	Inter	L	0-2	
14/05	a	Zagreb	W	3-2	T Bašić, Tudor 2 (1p)

No	Name	Nat	DoB	Pos	Aps	(s)	Gls
22	Manuel Arteaga	VEN	17/06/94	A	1	(1)	
99	Andrija Balić		11/08/97	M	14	(2)	2
30	Josip Bašić		02/03/96	M	4	(2)	
26	Toma Bašić		25/11/96	M	2	(2)	1
28	Marko Bencun		09/11/92	A	10	(6)	3
4	Maxym Biliy	UKR	21/06/90	D	25	(3)	
18	Mijo Caktaš		08/05/92	M	17		6
13	Ivo Grbić		18/01/96	G	4		
5	Ardian Ismajli	ALB	30/09/96	D	1		
17	Jefferson	BRA	14/04/93	M	33		1
17	Josip Juranović		16/08/95	M	27	(4)	1
20	Anthony Kalik	AUS	05/11/97	M	8	(3)	
91	Lovre Kalinić		03/04/90	G	31		
33	Tomislav Kiš		04/04/94	A	4	(2)	2
30	Josip Maganjić		06/01/99	A	1		
9	Anton Maglica		11/11/91	A	1	(15)	
19	Elvir Maloku		14/05/96	A	9	(13)	2
16	Ivan Mastelić		02/01/96	A	9	(3)	
3	Hrvoje Milić		10/05/89	D	28		1
5	Goran Milović		29/01/89	D	20		1
14	Tonći Mujan		19/07/95	A	4	(4)	
23	Zoran Nižić		11/10/89	D	16		2
11	Franck Ohandza	CMR	28/09/91	A	4	(4)	1
24	Marko Pejić		24/02/95	D	4	(3)	
21	Ivan Prskalo		29/03/95	M		(4)	
7	Artem Radchenko	UKR	02/01/95	A	1	(3)	
19	Hrvoje Relota		19/01/96	D	1		
44	Ante Roguljić		11/03/96	M	7	(12)	1
25	Dante Stipica		30/05/91	G	1		
31	Tino-Sven Sušić	BIH	13/02/92	M	27		12
5	Lorenco Šimić		15/07/96	D	6	(3)	1
32	Fran Tudor		27/09/95	M	31		7
2	Julián Velázquez	ARG	23/10/90	D	15	(2)	
9	Nicolás Vélez	ARG	04/07/90	A	3	(1)	
8	Nikola Vlašić		04/10/97	M	22	(1)	1
88	Frane Vojković		20/12/96	M	5	(5)	

 CROATIA

NK Inter Zaprešić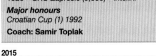

1929 • ŠRC Zaprešić (5,000) • inter.hr
Major honours
Croatian Cup (1) 1992
Coach: Samir Toplak

2015
10/07	h	Rijeka	D	0-0	
18/07	h	Zagreb	D	1-1	Nestorovski
25/07	a	Dinamo	L	1-5	Nestorovski
01/08	h	Split	D	0-0	
08/08	a	Istra 1961	D	0-0	
14/08	h	Slaven	W	2-1	Blažević, Nestorovski
21/08	a	Lokomotiva	W	2-1	Nestorovski, Ottochian
30/08	h	Hajduk	L	0-2	
13/09	a	Osijek	L	1-3	Čeliković (p)
19/09	a	Rijeka	D	0-0	
26/09	h	Zagreb	W	3-2	Nestorovski 3
03/10	h	Dinamo	D	2-2	Čabraja, Nestorovski
18/10	a	Split	L	1-3	Begić
24/10	h	Istra 1961	W	3-0	Nestorovski 2, Mazalović
01/11	a	Slaven	L	0-4	
06/11	h	Lokomotiva	L	1-2	Nestorovski
21/11	a	Hajduk	L	0-4	
27/11	h	Osijek	D	0-0	
04/12	h	Rijeka	D	0-0	
11/12	h	Zagreb	D	2-2	Nestorovski 2 (1p)
19/12	a	Dinamo	L	0-1	

2016
14/02	h	Split	D	1-1	Ottochian
20/02	a	Istra 1961	W	2-1	Nestorovski 2
26/02	h	Slaven	W	2-1	Puljić, Blažević
02/03	a	Lokomotiva	W	2-1	Ottochian, Nestorovski (p)
08/03	h	Hajduk	D	0-0	
11/03	a	Osijek	L	0-1	
19/03	h	Rijeka	L	0-4	
01/04	a	Zagreb	D	0-0	
10/04	h	Dinamo	L	0-1	
15/04	a	Split	D	0-0	
20/04	h	Istra 1961	W	3-0	Nestorovski 2, Puljić
25/04	a	Slaven	L	1-4	Nestorovski
29/04	h	Lokomotiva	W	3-1	Nestorovski (p), Ćosić, Glavina
08/05	a	Hajduk	W	2-1	Nestorovski 2 (1p)
13/05	h	Osijek	W	4-2	Nestorovski 3 (1p), Bočkaj

No	Name	Nat	DoB	Pos	Aps	(s)	Gls
4	Silvije Begić		03/06/93	D	16	(2)	1
10	Ivan Blažević		25/07/92	M	25	(8)	2
34	Petar Bočkaj		23/07/90	D	19	(11)	1
31	Driton Camaj	MNE	07/03/97	A		(2)	
14	Dejan Čabraja		22/08/93	A	4	(3)	1
33	Darijo Čavar		02/04/91	D			
13	Ivan Čeliković		10/07/89	D	32		1
25	Marko Ćosić		02/03/94	D	31	(1)	1
1	Ivan Čović		17/09/90	G	15		
19	Josip Filipović		08/05/96	D	4	(4)	
6	Bostjan Frelih	SVN	10/02/93	D	1		
26	Dominik Glavina		06/12/92	A	12	(16)	1
29	Tomislav Hanžek		31/05/96	D	10	(2)	
6	Jefthon	BRA	03/01/92	D	3	(9)	
20	Josip Jurjević		10/01/94	M	2	(1)	
15	Mislav Komorski		17/04/92	D	31		
31	Matheus Cassini	BRA	15/02/96	A		(6)	
11	Tomislav Mazalović		10/06/90	M	29		1
21	Ivan Mikulić		29/10/91	D	5		
21	Luka Miletić	BIH	04/10/94	D	1	(3)	
8	Frano Mlinar		30/03/92	M	25	(4)	
12	Ante Mrmić		06/08/92	G	1		
30	Ilija Nestorovski	MKD	12/03/90	A	33		25
27	Andrea Ottochian		28/06/88	M	33	(2)	3
22	Ivan Parlov		03/04/84	M		(2)	
32	Josip Posavec		10/03/96	G	20		
70	Jakov Puljić		04/08/93	A	12		2
9	Dominik Radić		26/07/96	A	1	(10)	
8	Nikola Šafarić		11/03/81	M		(1)	
7	Josip Šoljić		18/06/87	M	27	(5)	
19	Marin Zulim		26/10/91	A	4	(12)	

NK Istra 1961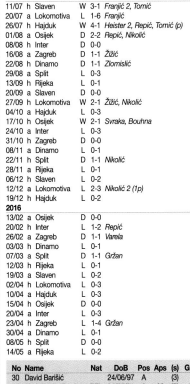

1961 • Aldo Drosina (8,923) • nkistra1961.hr
Coach: Igor Pamić;
(05/10/15) Robert Rubčić;
(04/01/16) Andrej Panadić

2015
11/07	h	Slaven	W	3-1	Franjić 2, Tomić
20/07	a	Lokomotiva	L	1-6	Franjić
26/07	h	Hajduk	W	4-1	Heister 2, Repić, Tomić (p)
01/08	a	Osijek	D	2-2	Repić, Nikolić
08/08	h	Inter	D	0-0	
16/08	a	Zagreb	D	1-1	Žižić
22/08	h	Dinamo	D	1-1	Zlomislić
29/08	a	Split	L	0-3	
13/09	h	Rijeka	L	0-1	
20/09	a	Slaven	D	0-0	
27/09	h	Lokomotiva	W	2-1	Žižić, Nikolić
04/10	a	Hajduk	L	0-3	
17/10	h	Osijek	W	2-1	Svraka, Bouhna
24/10	a	Inter	L	0-3	
31/10	h	Zagreb	D	0-0	
08/11	a	Dinamo	L	0-1	
22/11	h	Split	D	1-1	Nikolić
28/11	a	Rijeka	L	0-1	
06/12	h	Slaven	L	0-2	
12/12	a	Lokomotiva	L	2-3	Nikolić 2 (1p)
19/12	h	Hajduk	L	0-1	

2016
13/02	a	Osijek	D	0-0	
20/02	h	Inter	L	1-2	Repić
26/02	a	Zagreb	D	1-1	Varela
03/03	h	Dinamo	L	0-1	
07/03	a	Split	D	1-1	Gržan
12/03	h	Rijeka	L	0-1	
19/03	a	Slaven	L	0-2	
02/04	h	Lokomotiva	L	0-3	
10/04	a	Hajduk	L	0-3	
15/04	h	Osijek	L	0-1	
20/04	a	Inter	L	0-3	
23/04	h	Zagreb	L	1-4	Gržan
30/04	a	Dinamo	L	0-1	
08/05	h	Split	D	0-0	
14/05	a	Rijeka	L	0-2	

No	Name	Nat	DoB	Pos	Aps	(s)	Gls
30	David Barišić		24/06/97	A		(3)	
10	Abdelhakim Bouhna	BEL	24/05/91	A	20	(3)	1
1	Ivan Brkić		29/06/95	G	9	(1)	
8	Milan Djuric	SRB	10/03/87	M	24	(2)	
29	Luka Franić		10/03/93	D		(2)	
30	Petar Franjić		21/08/91	A			4
2	Renato Gojković	BIH	10/09/95	D	16	(2)	
2	Šime Gregov		08/07/89	D	1	(3)	
8	Toni Grković		29/12/90	D	3	(3)	
77	Šime Gržan		06/04/94	A	10	(2)	2
4	Adis Hadžanović	BIH	02/01/93	M		(1)	
25	Kenan Hadžić		07/05/94	D	16	(3)	
26	Marcel Heister	GER	29/07/92	D	29	(1)	2
9	Vanja Iveša		21/07/77	G	22		
33	Ivica Ivušić		01/02/95	G	5		
5	Ivica Jurkić		22/02/94	D	12		
99	Filip Kasalica	MNE	17/12/88	A	12	(2)	
30	Viktor Marić		18/03/98	M		(1)	
15	Marin Matoš		26/01/89	M	2	(3)	
4	Dominik Mihaljević		27/08/94	A	1	(4)	
20	Darko Mišić		27/06/91	D	25	(6)	
28	Stefan Nikolić	MNE	16/04/90	A	16	(2)	5
6	Branko Ojdanić	BIH	21/06/90	D	16		
22	Manuel Pamić		30/08/86	D	3	(6)	
16	Bojan Pavlović	SRB	01/02/85	D	6	(3)	
24	Antonio Repić		30/03/91	M	16	(14)	3
1	Dennis Salanovic	LIE	26/02/96	M	1	(1)	
29	Muamer Svraka	BIH	14/02/88	A	4	(11)	1
17	Dario Tomić		23/06/87	D	20	(2)	2
27	Marko Trojak		23/04/88	M	3	(3)	
9	Ignacio Varela	ARG	20/07/90	A	11		1
11	Victor da Silva	BRA	04/01/95	A	2	(11)	
7	Neven Vukman		11/04/88	M	1	(1)	
7	Josip Vuković		02/05/92	M	19	(2)	
21	Damir Zlomislić	BIH	20/07/91	M	27	(1)	1
27	Nermin Zolotić	BIH	07/07/93	M	10	(3)	
3	Nikola Žižić		23/01/88	D	30		1

NK Lokomotiva Zagreb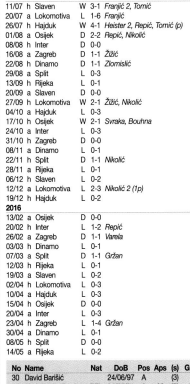

1914 • Maksimir (35,123);
Kranjčevićeva (8,850) • nklokomotiva.hr
Coach: Ante Čačić;
(22/09/15) Sreten Ćuk

2015
13/07	a	Split	L	1-2	Marić
20/07	h	Istra 1961	W	6-1	Šovšić 2 (1p), Doležal, Kolar, Bručić, Fiolić
27/07	a	Slaven	D	2-2	Marić, Fiolić
02/08	a	Rijeka	L	1-3	Andrijašević
10/08	h	Hajduk	L	1-2	Kolar
17/08	a	Osijek	W	1-0	Doležal
21/08	h	Inter	L	1-2	Ćorić
28/08	a	Zagreb	W	2-1	Mrcela, Marić
11/09	h	Dinamo	L	0-4	
20/09	h	Split	W	1-0	og (Vrgoč)
27/09	a	Istra 1961	L	1-2	Andrijašević
02/10	h	Slaven	D	1-1	Andrijašević
17/10	h	Rijeka	L	1-2	Perić
24/10	a	Hajduk	L	1-2	Andrijašević
31/10	a	Osijek	W	2-1	Marić 2 (1p)
06/11	a	Inter	W	2-1	Capan, Andrijašević
22/11	h	Zagreb	W	2-0	Grezda 2
29/11	a	Dinamo	L	1-3	Grezda
05/12	a	Split	D	1-1	Grezda
12/12	h	Istra 1961	W	3-2	Fiolić 2, Andrijašević
20/12	a	Slaven	D	3-0	Andrijašević, Grezda, Marić (p)

2016
12/02	a	Rijeka	L	0-2	
20/02	h	Hajduk	W	2-1	Grezda, Andrijašević
27/02	a	Osijek	W	3-1	Grezda 2, Andrijašević
02/03	h	Inter	L	1-2	Kolar (p)
05/03	a	Zagreb	W	3-1	Fiolić 2, Marić
13/03	a	Dinamo	L	1-3	Čekiçi, Fiolić
20/03	a	Split	D	1-1	Prenga
02/04	a	Istra 1961	W	3-0	Andrijašević 3
09/04	a	Slaven	D	2-0	Marić, Çekiçi
16/04	h	Rijeka	L	0-1	
20/04	a	Hajduk	L	0-2	
24/04	h	Osijek	W	2-0	Aralica, og (Arsenić)
29/04	a	Inter	L	1-3	Çekiçi
07/05	h	Zagreb	W	2-0	Grezda, Ćorić
14/05	h	Dinamo	L	0-4	

No	Name	Nat	DoB	Pos	Aps	(s)	Gls
24	Franko Andrijašević		22/06/91	M	27	(1)	12
21	Ante Aralica		23/07/96	A		(6)	1
17	Matko Babić		28/07/98	A		(1)	
3	Borna Barišić		10/11/92	D	17	(2)	
5	Karlo Bartolec		20/04/95	D	23	(1)	
8	Luka Begonja		23/05/92	M	2	(2)	
6	Karlo Bručić		17/04/92	D	28	(2)	1
31	Luka Capan		06/03/96	D	25	(1)	1
17	Endri Çekiçi	ALB	23/11/96	M	5	(7)	4
16	Josip Ćorić	BIH	09/11/88	M	11	(11)	2
25	Jan Doležal		12/02/93	A	15	(5)	2
12	Ivan Filipović		13/11/94	G	2		
10	Ivan Fiolić		29/04/96	M	26	(4)	7
8	Eros Grezda	ALB	15/04/95	M	24	(5)	9
30	Šime Gržan		06/04/94	M	1	(5)	
77	Said Husejinović	BIH	13/05/88	M	3		
32	Luka Ivanušec		26/11/98	M		(1)	
13	Robert Janjiš		03/12/94	M		(1)	
26	Fran Karačić		12/05/96	D	9	(1)	
22	Marko Kolar		31/05/95	A	12	(9)	3
2	Jerko Leko		09/04/80	M	25	(1)	
3	Petar Mamić		06/03/96	D			
9	Mirko Marić		16/05/95	A	19	(12)	8
33	Marko Mulić		30/01/94	G	1		
20	Petar Mišić		24/07/94	A	5		
5	Tomislav Mrcela	AUS	01/10/90	D	16	(4)	1
28	Zvonko Pamić		04/02/91	M	11	(5)	
15	Dino Perić		12/07/94	D	21	(1)	1
19	Herdi Prenga	ALB	31/08/94	D	24	(2)	1
10	Jakov Puljić		04/08/93	A	3	(10)	
7	Damir Šovšić		05/02/90	M	4	(1)	2
30	Ivan Šunjić		09/10/96	M	4	(6)	
1	Oliver Zelenika		14/05/93	G	33		

NK Osijek

1947 • Gradski vrt (19,500) • nk-osijek.hr
Major honours
Croatian Cup (1) 1999
Coach: Dražen Besek;
(01/09/15) Zoran Zekić

2015

11/07	a	Zagreb	W 1-0	Mandić
19/07	h	Dinamo	D 1-1	Radotić
25/07	a	Split	L 1-2	Šorša
01/08	a	Istra 1961	D 2-2	Perošević, Lukić
09/08	a	Slaven	L 0-3	
17/08	h	Lokomotiva	L 0-1	
23/08	a	Hajduk	L 0-3	
30/08	a	Rijeka	L 0-5	
13/09	h	Inter	W 3-1	Perošević 2 (2p), Roce
18/09	a	Zagreb	D 0-0	
25/09	a	Dinamo	L 1-4	Grgić
03/10	h	Split	L 0-1	
17/10	a	Istra 1961	L 1-2	Roce (p)
23/10	h	Slaven	D 0-0	
31/10	a	Lokomotiva	L 1-2	Škorić
07/11	h	Hajduk	W 1-0	Šarić
21/11	h	Rijeka	D 1-1	Škorić (p)
27/11	a	Inter	D 0-0	
06/12	a	Zagreb	W 1-0	Šarić
13/12	h	Dinamo	L 0-1	
20/12	a	Split	D 1-1	Grgić

2016

13/02	a	Istra 1961	D 0-0	
21/02	a	Slaven	L 0-1	
27/02	a	Lokomotiva	L 1-3	Perošević (p)
01/03	a	Hajduk	D 2-2	Šorša, Mioc
06/03	a	Rijeka	L 1-2	Perošević (p)
11/03	h	Inter	W 1-0	Grgić
18/03	h	Zagreb	W 2-0	Grgić 2
03/04	a	Dinamo	L 0-3	
08/04	h	Split	D 0-0	
15/04	a	Istra 1961	D 0-0	
21/04	h	Slaven	D 0-0	
24/04	a	Lokomotiva	L 0-2	
01/05	h	Hajduk	W 2-1	Knežević 2
07/05	h	Rijeka	D 1-1	Lukić
13/05	a	Inter	L 2-4	Perošević, Žaper

No	Name	Nat	DoB	Pos	Aps	(s)	Gls
11	Almir Aganspahić	BIH	12/09/96	A		(5)	
20	Lovro Anić		22/06/97	D	2	(2)	
15	Zoran Arsenić		02/06/94	D	19	(5)	
27	Tomislav Čuljak		25/05/87	D	13	(6)	
6	Ivica Džolan		11/10/88	D	8	(3)	
23	Alen Grgić		10/08/94	A	20	(6)	5
30	Josip Knežević		30/10/88	M	10	(2)	2
4	Hrvoje Kurtović		06/10/83	M	23		
19	Zoran Lesjak		01/02/88	D	28	(6)	
28	Andrej Lukić		02/04/94	M	26	(2)	2
13	Marko Malenica		08/02/94	G	8		
9	Nikola Mandić		19/03/95	A	13	(11)	1
7	Luka Marin		16/03/98	M	1		
17	Mario Maslać	SRB	09/09/90	D	7		
26	Nikola Matas		22/06/87	D	19	(7)	
29	Dominik Mihaljević		27/08/94	A	1	(3)	
1	Zvonimir Mikulić		05/02/90	G	24		
5	Benedikt Mioc		06/10/94	M	8	(3)	1
10	Antonio Perošević		06/03/92	A	19	(4)	6
16	Tomislav Radotić		13/12/81	D	15	(2)	1
11	Goran Roce		12/04/86	A	17	(7)	2
24	Tomislav Šarić		24/06/90	M	20	(6)	2
21	Mile Škorić		19/06/91	D	23		2
22	Tomislav Šorša		11/05/89	M	32		2
7	Matija Špičić		24/02/88	D	16	(1)	
77	Josip Špoljarić		05/01/97	M	4	(8)	
18	Tomislav Štrkalj		05/01/97	A	2	(9)	
5	Sandro Tsveiba	RUS	05/09/93	D	1		
14	Steven Ugarkovic	AUS	19/08/94	M	5	(6)	
8	Aljoša Vojnović		24/10/85	M	8	(2)	
3	Mihael Žaper		11/08/98	D		(1)	1
12	Borna Žitnjak		23/08/93	G	4		

HNK Rijeka

1946 • Kantrida (11,000); Rujevica (8,500) • nk-rijeka.hr
Major honours
Yugoslav Cup (2) 1978, 1979; Croatian Cup (3) 2005, 2006, 2014
Coach: Matjaž Kek (SVN)

2015

10/07	a	Inter	D 0-0	
19/07	h	Slaven	D 3-3	Bezjak 2, Balaj
26/07	a	Zagreb	D 3-3	Balaj 2, Bezjak
02/08	a	Lokomotiva	W 3-1	Leovac, Bezjak, Sharbini
08/08	a	Dinamo	D 0-0	
15/08	h	Hajduk	D 0-0	
22/08	a	Split	W 2-0	Tomasov 2
30/08	h	Osijek	W 5-0	Balaj 2, Bezjak, Mitrović, Sharbini
13/09	a	Istra 1961	W 1-0	Bezjak
19/09	h	Inter	W 1-0	
26/09	a	Slaven	D 0-0	
04/10	h	Zagreb	W 4-1	Moisés, Roshi, Radošević, Balaj
17/10	a	Lokomotiva	W 2-1	Maleš, Lešković
25/10	h	Dinamo	W 2-1	Samardžič, Sharbini
01/11	a	Hajduk	W 3-0	Bezjak, Tomasov, Balaj
08/11	h	Split	W 2-1	Samardžič, Bezjak
21/11	a	Osijek	D 1-1	Bezjak
28/11	h	Istra 1961	W 1-0	Tomasov
04/12	a	Inter	D 0-0	
13/12	a	Slaven	D 1-1	Tomasov
18/12	a	Zagreb	W 2-0	Bezjak 2

2016

12/02	h	Lokomotiva	W 2-0	Tomasov, Gavranovic
21/02	a	Dinamo	L 0-3	
27/02	h	Hajduk	W 1-0	Samardžič
02/03	a	Split	W 2-1	Gavranovic, Balaj
06/03	h	Osijek	W 2-1	Gavranovic, Bezjak
12/03	a	Istra 1961	W 1-0	Tomasov
19/03	h	Inter	W 4-0	Tomasov, Gavranovic, Samardžič, Balaj
02/04	a	Slaven	D 0-0	
09/04	h	Zagreb	W 3-0	Bradarić, Bezjak, Matei
16/04	a	Lokomotiva	W 1-0	Gavranovic
19/04	h	Dinamo	D 0-0	
24/04	a	Hajduk	W 2-1	Vešović, Gavranovic
01/05	h	Split	D 0-0	
07/05	a	Osijek	D 1-1	Gavranovic
14/05	h	Istra 1961	W 2-0	Vešović, Brezovec

No	Name	Nat	DoB	Pos	Aps	(s)	Gls
9	Bekim Balaj	ALB	11/01/91	A	20	(11)	9
24	Mateo Bertoša		10/08/88	D	3	(2)	
11	Roman Bezjak	SVN	21/02/89	A	30	(2)	13
18	Filip Bradarić		11/01/92	M	20	(6)	1
30	Josip Brezovec		12/03/86	M	7	(5)	1
40	Gerald Diyoke	NGA	11/03/96	M		(1)	
17	Mario Gavranovic	SUI	24/11/89	A	13		7
89	Vedran Jugović		31/07/89	M	5	(6)	
8	Zoran Kvržić	BIH	07/08/88	M		(1)	
22	Marin Leovac		07/08/88	D	5		1
13	Marko Lešković		27/04/91	D	20		1
26	Mate Maleš		13/01/89	M	25	(3)	1
10	Florentin Matei	ROU	15/04/93	M	10	(3)	1
21	Aleš Mejač	SVN	18/03/83	D	1	(1)	
24	Josip Mišić		28/06/94	M	1		
15	Matej Mitrović		10/11/93	D	20	(2)	1
16	Ivan Močinić		30/04/93	M	24	(7)	
88	Moisés	BRA	16/04/88	M	10	(4)	1
32	Andrej Prskalo		01/05/87	G	2		
33	Josip Radošević		03/04/94	M	7	(9)	1
23	Mihael Rebernik		06/08/96	D		(1)	
6	Stefan Ristovski	MKD	12/02/92	D	31	(1)	
23	Odhise Roshi	ALB	22/05/91	M	1	(19)	1
19	Miral Samardžić	SVN	17/02/87	D	30		4
10	Anas Sharbini		21/02/87	M	10	(2)	3
1	Simon Sluga		17/03/93	G	1		
7	Marin Tomasov		31/08/87	M	32	(4)	8
11	Ivan Tomečak		07/12/89	D	4	(1)	
1	Ivan Vargić		15/03/87	G	32		
29	Marko Vešović	MNE	28/08/91	D	6	(12)	2
20	Dario Vizinger		06/06/98	A	1	(1)	
8	Leonard Zhuta	MKD	09/08/92	D	24	(2)	

NK Slaven Koprivnica

1907 • Gradski (3,800) • nk-slaven-belupo.hr
Coach: Željko Kopić

2015

11/07	a	Istra 1961	L 1-3	Ejupi (p)
19/07	a	Rijeka	D 3-3	Ejupi 2 (1p), Križman
27/07	h	Lokomotiva	D 2-2	Križman, Savic
02/08	a	Hajduk	D 2-2	Crepulja, Ozobić
09/08	h	Osijek	W 3-0	Paracki, og (Radotić), Delić
14/08	a	Inter	L 1-2	Delić
23/08	h	Zagreb	W 2-1	Gregurina, Ejupi (p)
29/08	a	Dinamo	L 0-3	
12/09	h	Split	D 1-1	Ejupi
20/09	h	Istra 1961	D 0-0	
26/09	h	Rijeka	D 0-0	
02/10	a	Lokomotiva	D 1-1	Ejupi (p)
18/10	h	Hajduk	L 0-1	
23/10	a	Osijek	D 0-0	
01/11	h	Inter	W 4-0	Delić, Savic, Ozobić, Arap
07/11	a	Zagreb	L 0-2	
20/11	h	Dinamo	L 1-2	Delić
27/11	a	Split	L 0-2	
06/12	h	Istra 1961	W 2-0	Ejupi 2 (1p)
13/12	h	Rijeka	D 1-1	Arap
20/12	a	Lokomotiva	L 0-3	

2016

13/02	a	Hajduk	L 0-2	
21/02	h	Osijek	W 1-0	Ozobić
26/02	a	Inter	L 1-2	Ejupi (p)
01/03	h	Zagreb	W 3-0	Ejupi, Delić, Ozobić
06/03	a	Dinamo	L 1-2	Križman
12/03	h	Split	L 0-1	
19/03	h	Istra 1961	W 2-0	Ejupi 2 (1p)
02/04	h	Rijeka	D 0-0	
09/04	a	Lokomotiva	D 0-2	
17/04	h	Hajduk	D 0-0	
21/04	a	Osijek	D 0-0	
25/04	h	Inter	W 4-1	Pokrivač, Ejupi, Savic, Delić
30/04	a	Zagreb	W 3-0	Barić, Ejupi 2
06/05	h	Dinamo	L 0-3	
14/05	a	Split	W 2-0	Ejupi, og (Blagojević)

No	Name	Nat	DoB	Pos	Aps	(s)	Gls
13	David Arap		09/03/95	M	5	(8)	2
10	Gordan Barić		11/08/94	D	9	(3)	1
17	Mario Burić		25/10/91	M	1	(4)	
12	Goran Blažević		07/06/86	G	2		
10	Petar Brlek		29/01/94	M	19	(3)	
8	Søren Christensen	DEN	29/06/86	M	10	(2)	
6	Ljuban Crepulja		02/09/93	M	20	(1)	1
14	Mateas Delić		17/06/88	A	30	(3)	6
7	Edson Henrique	BRA	06/07/87	D	8	(3)	
9	Muzafer Ejupi	MKD	16/09/88	A	28	(4)	16
26	Nino Galović		06/07/92	D	11		
20	Mario Gregurina		23/03/88	M	12	(4)	1
21	Nikola Jambor		25/09/95	M	15	(11)	
19	Nikola Katić		10/10/96	D		(1)	
15	Sandi Križman		17/08/89	A	10	(9)	3
23	Marko Marciuš		24/03/95	A	2	(8)	
12	Antun Marković		04/07/92	G	1		
4	Vinko Medjimorec		01/06/96	D	21		
9	Filip Mihaljević		09/03/92	A		(5)	
5	Tomislav Mikulić		04/01/82	D	8	(1)	
26	Božo Musa		15/09/88	D	15		
30	Filip Ozobić		08/04/91	M	25	(6)	4
11	Goran Paracki		21/01/87	M	29		1
10	Nikola Pokrivač		26/11/85	M	5	(2)	1
22	Nejc Potokar	SVN	02/12/88	D	7		
16	Vedran Purić		16/03/86	M	27	(2)	
1	Matjaž Rozman	SVN	09/01/87	G	33	(1)	
5	Stefan Savic	AUT	03/01/94	M	13	(23)	4
24	Dino Štiglec		03/10/90	D	30	(2)	

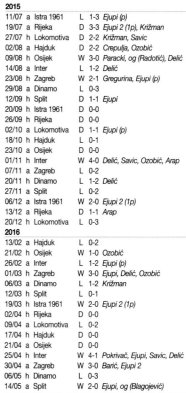

RNK Split

1912 • Park mladeži (8,000) • rnksplit.hr

Coach: Zoran Vulić;
(30/09/15) Goran Sablić

2015
13/07	h	Lokomotiva	W	2-1	Špehar, Blagojević (p)
19/07	a	Hajduk	D	0-0	
25/07	h	Osijek	W	2-1	Blagojević, Špehar
01/08	a	Inter	D	0-0	
07/08	h	Zagreb	W	3-0	Mršić (p), og (B Musa), Bagarić
15/08	a	Dinamo	L	0-3	
22/08	h	Rijeka	L	0-2	
29/08	h	Istra 1961	W	3-0	Bagarić 2, Blagojević
12/09	a	Slaven	D	1-1	Pešić
20/09	a	Lokomotiva	L	0-1	
27/09	h	Hajduk	L	0-2	
03/10	h	Osijek	W	1-0	Bagarić
18/10	h	Inter	D	1-1	Bagarić
25/10	a	Zagreb	W	2-1	Oremuš, Vidović
30/10	h	Dinamo	W	1-0	Franjić
08/11	a	Rijeka	L	1-2	Mršić (p)
22/11	a	Istra 1961	D	1-1	Bagarić
27/11	h	Slaven	W	2-0	Pešić, Bagarić
05/12	a	Lokomotiva	D	1-1	Mršić (p)
12/12	a	Hajduk	D	0-0	
20/12	h	Osijek	D	1-1	og (Matas)

2016
14/02	a	Inter	D	1-1	Pešić
19/02	h	Zagreb	W	1-0	Bagarić
28/02	h	Dinamo	L	0-1	
02/03	h	Rijeka	L	1-2	Rrahmani
07/03	a	Istra 1961	D	1-1	Mišić (p)
12/03	a	Slaven	W	1-0	Mišić (p)
20/03	a	Lokomotiva	D	1-1	Franjić
03/04	h	Hajduk	D	0-0	
08/04	a	Osijek	D	0-0	
15/04	h	Inter	D	0-0	
19/04	a	Zagreb	L	0-2	
23/04	h	Dinamo	L	0-1	
01/05	a	Rijeka	L	0-2	
08/05	a	Istra 1961	D	0-0	
14/05	h	Slaven	L	0-2	

No	Name	Nat	DoB	Pos	Aps	(s)	Gls
9	Abdiel Arroyo	PAN	13/12/93	A	10	(4)	
11	Dražen Bagarić		12/11/92	A	29	(1)	8
22	Édgar Bárcenas	PAN	23/10/93	M	4	(4)	
99	Nemanja Bilbija	BIH	02/11/90	A	5	(4)	
77	Slavko Blagojević		21/03/87	M	28		3
13	Chung Woon	KOR	30/06/89	D	12		
32	Miloš Djordević	SRB	07/06/92	A	1	(2)	
1	Tomislav Duka		07/09/92	G	8		
10	Ante Erceg		12/12/89	M	2	(2)	
23	Filip Faletar		02/04/95	M		(2)	
30	Petar Franjić		21/08/91	A	15	(8)	2
26	Nino Galović		07/06/92	D		(1)	
20	Luka Grubišić		09/11/97	M	8	(9)	
31	Kristijan Jakić		14/05/97	M	5	(2)	
7	Ivan Jukić		21/06/96	M	2	(1)	
7	Matej Jukić		07/04/97	M	1	(3)	
6	Frane Maglica		02/07/97	M	1	(2)	
4	Ante Majstorović		06/11/93	D	31	(1)	
88	Artem Milevskiy	UKR	12/01/85	A		(1)	
2	Aleksandar Miljković	SRB	26/02/90	D	14		
10	Petar Mišić		24/07/94	A	8	(1)	2
70	Tomislav Mrkonjić		22/02/94	A	1	(1)	
8	Antonio Mršić		05/06/87	M	15	(1)	3
44	Jure Obšivač		28/05/90	D	18	(6)	
33	Mirko Oremuš		06/09/88	M	15	(1)	1
22	Marko Pervan		04/04/96	M	6	(8)	
21	Ivan Pešić		06/04/92	A	22	(8)	3
3	Marin Roglić		16/06/97	A		(3)	
18	Amir Rrahmani	ALB	24/02/94	D	34		1
25	Dario Rugašević		29/01/91	D	13	(4)	
9	Marko Simonovski	MKD	02/01/92	A	5	(7)	
19	Miro Slavica		24/06/91	A		(1)	
17	Dino Špehar		08/02/94	A	11	(7)	2
15	Josip Tomašević		04/03/94	D		(2)	
8	Mateo Topić		13/04/96	M		(3)	
24	Miloš Vidović	SRB	03/10/89	M	24	(1)	1
3	Maksim Vitus	BLR	11/02/89	D	11		
5	Branko Vrgoč		18/12/91	D	9	(2)	
12	Danijel Zagorac		07/02/87	G	28		

NK Zagreb

1903 • Kranjčevićeva (8,850) • nkzagreb.hr

Major honours
Croatian League (1) 2002
Coach: Dražen Madunović

2015
11/07	h	Osijek	L	0-1	
18/07	a	Inter	D	1-1	Medić
26/07	h	Rijeka	D	3-3	G Boban 2, Krovinović
31/07	h	Dinamo	L	0-2	
07/08	a	Split	L	0-3	
16/08	a	Istra 1961	D	1-1	Krovinović
23/08	a	Slaven	L	1-2	Medić
28/08	h	Lokomotiva	L	1-2	Medić (p)
12/09	a	Hajduk	L	0-1	
18/09	a	Osijek	D	0-0	
26/09	h	Inter	L	2-3	G Boban 2
04/10	a	Rijeka	L	1-4	G Boban
16/10	a	Dinamo	L	1-4	G Boban
25/10	h	Split	L	1-2	Stepčić (p)
31/10	a	Istra 1961	D	0-0	
07/11	h	Slaven	W	2-0	Medić (p), G Boban (p)
22/11	a	Lokomotiva	L	0-2	
28/11	h	Hajduk	L	0-2	
06/12	h	Osijek	L	0-1	
11/12	a	Inter	D	2-2	G Boban, Stepčić
18/12	h	Rijeka	L	0-2	

2016
14/02	h	Dinamo	L	1-2	Medić
19/02	a	Split	L	0-1	
26/02	h	Istra 1961	D	1-1	Tešija
01/03	a	Slaven	L	0-3	
05/03	h	Lokomotiva	L	1-3	G Boban
13/03	a	Hajduk	L	0-1	
18/03	a	Osijek	L	0-2	
01/04	h	Inter	D	0-0	
09/04	a	Rijeka	L	0-3	
16/04	a	Dinamo	L	0-1	
19/04	h	Split	W	2-0	G Boban, Stepčić
23/04	a	Istra 1961	W	4-1	Medić, Stepčić 2, Šulc
30/04	h	Slaven	L	0-3	
07/05	a	Lokomotiva	L	0-2	
14/05	h	Hajduk	L	2-3	Medić 2 (1p)

No	Name	Nat	DoB	Pos	Aps	(s)	Gls
14	Dino Bevab	BIH	13/01/93	D	20	(4)	
99	Bruno Boban		12/08/92	A	3	(4)	
30	Gabrijel Boban		23/07/89	A	30	(1)	10
3	Damir Čavar		26/09/95	M	2	(3)	
12	Josip Čondrić		27/08/93	G	1		
24	Mario Čubel		20/03/90	M	6	(9)	
11	Anto Gudelj		12/08/92	A	12	(10)	
15	Jakša Herceg		15/02/89	G	3	(1)	
8	Alen Jurilj	BIH	07/03/96	D	10	(9)	
26	Vedran Jurjević		21/01/92	M	3		
20	Denis Kolinger		14/01/94	D	25		
9	Miroslav Konopek		28/03/91	A	4	(6)	
4	Dominik Kovačić		05/01/94	D	21	(2)	
10	Filip Krovinović		29/08/95	M	6		2
1	Dominik Livaković		09/01/95	G	32		
24	Ivan Ljubičić		17/01/92	M	17	(7)	
27	Bernardo Matić		27/07/94	D	21	(3)	
23	Filip Matijašević		08/01/96	M		(1)	
28	Lovro Medić		23/10/90	M	33	(1)	8
16	Robert Mudražija		05/05/97	M	16	(6)	
18	Domagoj Muić		05/09/93	M	12	(3)	
23	Božo Musa		15/09/88	D	6		
22	Petar Musa		04/03/98	A	2	(4)	
21	Valentino Stepčić		16/01/90	M	30	(3)	5
26	Rodney Strasser	SLE	30/03/90	M	12		
5	Roko Strika	AUS	12/02/94	A		(1)	
6	Stjepan Stubičan		04/06/92	D	5		
29	Edin Šehić	BIH	03/02/95	D	15	(4)	
19	Matias Šulc		28/07/92	D	28	(1)	4
7	Marko Tešija		14/01/92	M	21	(5)	4

Top goalscorers

25	Ilija Nestorovski (Inter)
16	Muzafer Ejupi (Slaven)
13	Armin Hodžić (Dinamo)
	Roman Bezjak (Rijeka)
12	Júnior Fernandes (Dinamo)
	Tino-Sven Sušić (Hajduk)
	Franko Andrijašević (Lokomotiva)
10	Gabrijel Boban (Zagreb)
9	Eros Grezda (Lokomotiva)
	Bekim Balaj (Rijeka)

Promoted club

HNK Cibalia

1919 • HNK Cibalia (10,000) • hnk-cibalia.hr

Coach: Damir Milinović
(08/09/15) Miroslav Bojko;
(06/04/16) (Siniša Sesar);
(12/04/16) Stanko Mršić

Second level final table 2015/16

		Pld	W	D	L	F	A	Pts
1	HNK Cibalia	33	20	10	3	54	20	70
2	HNK Šibenik	33	20	9	4	54	21	69
3	NK Sesvete	33	15	7	11	56	40	52
4	HNK Gorica	33	13	8	12	40	40	47
5	NK Rudeš	33	12	10	11	50	43	46
6	GNK Dinamo Zagreb II	33	11	10	12	34	37	43
7	NK Dugopolje	33	11	7	15	38	41	40
8	NK Lučko	33	11	7	15	40	47	40
9	NK Imotski	33	11	7	15	40	50	40
10	HNK Segesta	33	10	8	15	44	54	38
11	NK Hrvatski dragovoljac	33	10	7	16	28	42	37
12	NK Zadar	33	5	8	20	30	73	23

Promotion/Relegation play-off

(29/05/16 & 01/06/16)
Šibenik 1-1 Istra 1961
Istra 1961 1-1 Šibenik *(aet)*
(2-2; Istra 1961 5-4 on pens)

DOMESTIC CUP

Hrvatski Nogometni Kup 2015/16

SECOND ROUND

(22/09/15)
Duga Resa 1-3 Osijek
Jadran 0-3 Zadar
Oštrc 1-7 Dinamo
Zmaj 2-3 Inter

(23/09/15)
Bednja 0-10 Rijeka
Croatia 0-2 Istra 1961
Funtana 0-3 Zagreb
Gorica 0-0 Šibenik *(aet; 4-5 on pens)*
Lekenik 1-0 Vinogradar *(aet)*
Mladost 3-0 Varaždin
Nehaj 0-8 Lokomotiva
Omladinac 0-6 Cibalia
Opatija 4-0 Zelina
Pomorac 0-3 HAŠK
Sloga Nova Gradiška 0-7 Hajduk
Tehničar 0-3 Slaven

THIRD ROUND

(27/10/15)
Inter 0-0 Cibalia *(aet; 4-3 on pens)*
Mladost 1-3 Dinamo
Šibenik 0-2 Slaven

(28/10/15)
HAŠK 0-2 Osijek
Lekenik 1-5 Hajduk
Opatija 0-3 Rijeka
Zadar 2-2 Lokomotiva *(aet; 4-5 on pens)*
Zagreb 2-1 Istra 1961 *(aet)*

QUARTER-FINALS

(02/12/15)
Slaven 1-1 Osijek *(Savic 47; Lesjak 54) (aet; 4-1 on pens)*

Zagreb 1-2 Hajduk *(Juranović 18og; Jefferson 24, Bencun 32)*

(08/12/15)
Lokomotiva 0-1 Rijeka *(Bezjak 65)*

(10/02/16)
Inter 0-1 Dinamo *(Hodžić 10)*

SEMI-FINALS

(15/03/16 & 05/04/16)
Rijeka 2-1 Slaven *(Bezjak 10, Matei 15; Christensen 71)*
Slaven 3-0 Rijeka *(Ejupi 43, Ozobić 54, Pokrivač 72)*
(Slaven 4-2)

(16/03/16 & 06/04/16)
Hajduk 0-2 Dinamo *(Soudani 22, Ćorić 29)*
Dinamo 4-0 Hajduk *(Brekalo 2, Fernandes 24, 50, Soudani 67)*
(Dinamo 6-0)

FINAL

(10/05/16)
Gradski vrt, Osijek
GNK DINAMO ZAGREB 2 *(Pjaca 31p, Rog 77)*
NK SLAVEN KOPRIVNICA 1 *(Ejupi 61)*
Referee: Vučemilović
DINAMO: *Ježina, Mäţel, Sigali, Schildenfeld, Sosa, Paulo Machado (Hodžić 72), Ćorić (Henríquez 88), Antolić, Rog, Pjaca, Soudani (Fernandes 72)*
SLAVEN: *Rozman, Purić, Edson Henrique, Musa, Štiglec, Pokrivač, Jambor, Ozobić, Christensen, Delić (Križman 69), Ejupi*

Victorious Dinamo Zagreb players gather around the Croatian Cup

CYPRUS
Kypriaki Omospondia Podosfairon (KOP)/ Cyprus Football Association (CFA)

Address 10 Achaion Street
2413 Engomi, PO Box 25071
CY-1306 Nicosia
Tel +357 22 352 341
Fax +357 22 590 544
E-mail info@cfa.com.cy
Website cfa.com.cy

President Costakis Koutsokoumnis
General secretary Phivos Vakis
Media officer Kyriacos Giorgallis
Year of formation 1934
National stadium GSP, Nicosia (23,700)

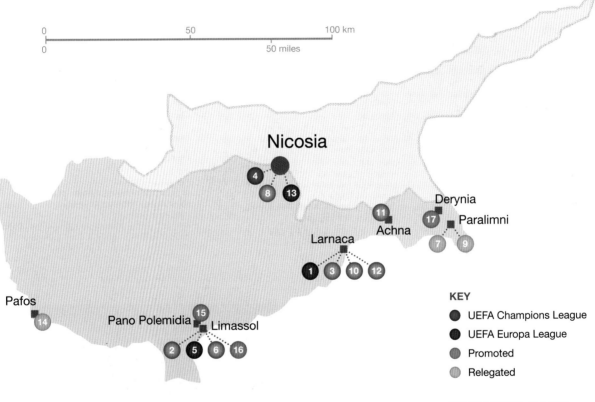

KEY
- UEFA Champions League
- UEFA Europa League
- Promoted
- Relegated

A KATIGORIA CLUBS

 1 **AEK Larnaca FC**

 2 **AEL Limassol FC**

 3 **Anorthosis Famagusta FC**

 4 **APOEL FC**

 5 **Apollon Limassol FC**

 6 **Aris Limassol FC**

 7 **Ayia Napa FC**

 8 **Doxa Katokopia FC**

 9 **Enosis Neon Paralimni FC**

 10 **Ermis Aradippou FC**

 11 **Ethnikos Achnas FC**

 12 **Nea Salamis Famagusta FC**

 13 **AC Omonia**

 14 **Pafos FC**

PROMOTED CLUBS

 15 **Karmiotissa Pano Polemidia FC**

 16 **AEZ Zakakiou FC**

 17 **Anagennisi Derynia FC**

APOEL hit the accelerator

APOEL FC raced to a record 25th Cypriot league triumph in 2015/16, running up 91 goals as they fended off a concerted challenge from AEK Larnaca to defend the title they had won in each of the previous three campaigns.

Disappointing results in other competitions meant that APOEL used three different coaches en route to their A Katigoria success, but Apollon Limassol kept faith in new Portuguese coach Pedro Emanuel, who led the team to third place in the league and an eighth victory in the Cypriot Cup.

Free-scoring Nicosia giants speed to 25th title

AEK Larnaca retain runners-up spot

Third-placed Apollon lift Cypriot Cup

Domestic league

APOEL's own new Portuguese boss, Domingos Paciência, lasted just one league match before he was sacked to make way for Temur Ketsbaia, and under the ex-Georgia midfielder and coach the team stormed to the top of the table. By the end of October they had not just won nine of their opening ten matches, drawing the other away to AEK, but amassed 41 goals – just 11 fewer than they had scored in their entire 2014/15 title-winning campaign.

It would take Ketsbaia's team another ten matches, however, to match and overtake that tally, by which stage they were no longer the league leaders. In fact, after the first fixture of 2016, APOEL were actually down in fourth position, a brutal run of four home defeats out of five having allowed three of their conquerors – Anorthosis, Apollon and AEK – to move above them in the standings.

Thomas Christiansen's AEK, with six wins on the trot and just one defeat in their 18 games, were now in pole position to land their first Cypriot title, but it was at this point that APOEL put their foot back on the gas and charged back into contention with a succession of victories that enabled them to overtake AEK and enter the play-off phase with a one-point

lead. Although handicapped by a serious injury to their 19-goal leading marksman Fernando Cavenaghi, a pre-season signing from River Plate, APOEL extended their winning sequence into the play-offs, their 12th three-pointer on the spin coming in the game that mattered most as they defeated AEK 3-0 in Larnaca with goals from in-form trio Tomás De Vincenti, Georgios Efrem and Pieros Sotiriou.

Draws in APOEL's next two games allowed AEK to close the gap back to two points, and with Ketsbaia then dismissed after a domestic cup exit that ended the Nicosia club's hopes of a third successive double, all eventualities seemed possible. The crunch fixture was AEK's visit to APOEL on 28 April. Realistically the visitors had to win to keep the contest alive, but it was the home side who dominated and grabbed all three points, with a first-half goal from Sotiriou and a second-half penalty from Giannis Giannotas, to go seven points clear and clinch the title with two games to go.

Domestic cup

Apollon defeated AC Omonia 2-1 in Nicosia on the final day of the league campaign to leapfrog their hosts into third place, and four days later history repeated itself, this time in Apollon's

Tsirion stadium, as the Limassol club avenged their Cypriot Cup final penalty shoot-out defeat to the same opponents five years earlier, goals from Fotios Papoulis and Angelis Angeli propelling Pedro Emanuel's side to another 2-1 victory.

Europe

A late goal conceded at home to FC Astana cost APOEL a quick return to the UEFA Champions League group stage – and coach Domingos his job – and there was a sense that the disappointment still lingered as they lost five of their six UEFA Europa League group games. The island's other three representatives – AEK, Apollon and Omonia – had all dropped out of the competition in the third qualifying round.

National team

Cyprus played just six games in 2015/16. The bad news was that they lost five of them, the good news that in every case defeat was by a single-goal margin. A 2-1 victory away to Israel in the team's penultimate UEFA EURO 2016 qualifier was the exception, but it was not enough to keep coach Pambos Christodoulou in situ. As he returned to club work at AEL Limassol, the man who had started the season there, Christakis Christoforou, was drafted in to replace him.

DOMESTIC SEASON AT A GLANCE

A Katigoria 2015/16 final table

		Pld	Home					Away					Total					Pts
			W	D	L	F	A	W	D	L	F	A	W	D	L	F	A	
1	**APOEL FC**	36	12	2	4	49	16	14	3	1	42	10	26	5	5	91	26	83
2	AEK Larnaca FC	36	12	2	4	35	21	11	4	3	26	13	23	6	7	61	34	75
3	Apollon Limassol FC	36	12	4	2	35	13	7	7	4	26	23	19	11	6	61	36	68
4	AC Omonia	36	10	5	3	38	18	10	2	6	25	16	20	7	9	63	34	67
5	Anorthosis Famagusta FC	36	9	6	3	32	18	7	5	6	25	23	16	11	9	57	41	59
6	Nea Salamis Famagusta FC	36	4	6	8	19	33	5	4	9	25	39	9	10	17	44	72	37
7	AEL Limassol FC	36	8	2	8	21	18	6	5	7	17	25	14	7	15	38	43	47
8	Ermis Aradippou FC	36	7	5	6	23	24	4	4	10	13	28	11	9	16	36	52	42
9	Aris Limassol FC	36	7	6	5	23	16	3	5	10	20	30	10	11	15	43	46	41
10	Doxa Katokopia FC	36	6	4	8	23	27	4	7	7	23	32	10	11	15	46	59	41
11	Ethnikos Achnas FC	36	6	7	5	23	19	3	5	10	20	38	9	12	15	43	57	39
12	Pafos FC	36	7	7	4	28	18	1	5	12	13	40	8	12	16	41	58	36
13	Enosis Neon Paralimni FC	26	2	5	6	13	24	2	3	8	15	23	4	8	14	28	47	20
14	Ayia Napa FC	26	0	2	11	9	33	0	4	9	8	31	0	6	20	17	64	6

NB After 26 matches the top 12 clubs split into two groups of six, after which they play exclusively against teams in their group;
AEL Limassol FC – 2 pts deducted

European qualification 2016/17

Champion: APOEL FC (second qualifying round)

Cup winner: Apollon Limassol FC (third qualifying round)
AEK Larnaca FC (first qualifying round)
AC Omonia (first qualifying round)

Top scorer	André Alves (AEK), Fernando Cavenaghi (APOEL) & Dimitar Makriev (Nea Salamis), 19 goals
Relegated clubs	Ayia Napa FC, Enosis Neon Paralimni FC, Pafos FC
Promoted clubs	Karmiotissa Pano Polemidia FC, AEZ Zakakiou FC, Anagennisi Derynia FC
Cup final	Apollon Limassol FC 2-1 AC Omonia

Team of the season
(4-3-3)

Coach: Christiansen (AEK)

N Michael (Nea Salamis)

Christoforou (Aris) — Laifis (Anorthosis) — David Català (AEK) — Hafez (Omonia)

Efrem (APOEL) — De Vincenti (APOEL) — Papoulis (Apollon)

Makriev (Nea Salamis) — Cavenaghi (APOEL) — André Alves (AEK)

Player of the season

Georgios Efrem
(APOEL FC)

A former stalwart of Nicosia rivals Omonia, Efrem doubled the number of Cypriot titles he won in five campaigns with his former club as he inspired APOEL to back-to-back league wins in his second season with the Yellow-and-Blues. The Cypriot international winger, who served as an apprentice with Arsenal and Rangers, scored a career-best tally of 11 league goals, including a match-winning double against Omonia, and was officially voted by the Cyprus Football Association in May as their player of the year.

Newcomer of the season

Neofytos Michael
(Nea Salamis Famagusta FC)

The first five places in the final table of the 2015/16 A Katigoria were filled by the very same clubs that had occupied them in 2014/15. Nea Salamis, who finished sixth, were the only newcomer to the championship pool, and for that they were grateful not just to the 19 goals of their golden boot-sharing Bulgarian striker Dimitar Makriev but also their spectacular young goalkeeper Michael, whose rapid development earned him a call-up to the Cyprus national side and the league's young player of the year award.

NATIONAL TEAM

Top five all-time caps
Ioannis Okkas (104); Michalis Konstantinou (87); **Kostas Charalambides** (83); Pambos Pittas (82); **Konstantinos Makrides** (77)

Top five all-time goals
Michalis Konstantinou (32); Ioannis Okkas (26); **Kostas Charalambides** (12); Marios Agathokleous & **Efstathios Aloneftis** (10)

Results 2015/16

03/09/15	Wales (ECQ)	H	Nicosia	L	0-1	
06/09/15	Belgium (ECQ)	H	Nicosia	L	0-1	
10/10/15	Israel (ECQ)	A	Jerusalem	W	2-1	*Dossa Júnior (58), Demetriou (80)*
13/10/15	Bosnia & Herzegovina (ECQ)	H	Nicosia	L	2-3	*Charalambides (32), Mytidis (41)*
24/03/16	Ukraine	A	Odessa	L	0-1	
25/05/16	Serbia	A	Uzice	L	1-2	*Nikola Maksimović (32og)*

Appearances 2015/16

Coach: Pambos Christodoulou /(02/12/15) Christakis Christoforou	17/10/67 26/01/64		WAL	BEL	ISR	BIH	Ukr	Srb	Caps	Goals
Antonis Georgallides	30/01/82	Omonia	G	G	G	G		G	64	-
Jason Demetriou	18/11/87	Walsall (ENG)	D	D	D	D	D		31	1
Konstantinos Laifis	19/05/93	Anorthosis	D	D	D	D	D	D	8	-
Dossa Júnior	28/07/86	Konyaspor (TUR) /Eskişehirspor (TUR)	D	D	D	D	D		20	1
Marios Antoniades	14/05/90	APOEL	D	D	D	D			12	-
Konstantinos Makrides	13/01/82	APOEL /Apollon	M	M	M84	M	M		77	6
Marios Nicolaou	04/10/83	Levadiakos (GRE) /Inter Turku (FIN)	M	M84	M	M65	s89	s90	53	1
Kostas Charalambides	25/07/81	APOEL	M74	M53	s46	M83	M77	M82	83	12
Georgios Oikonomidis	10/04/90	Omonia	M	M	s84	s65			6	-
Andreas Makris	27/11/95	Anorthosis	M84	M	M46		s58	s66	10	-
Nestoras Mytidis	01/06/91	AEK Larnaca	A65	A11	A	A	A70		21	4
Georgios Kolokoudias	03/05/89	Apollon	s65			s83			3	-
Nikos Englezou	11/07/93	AEK Larnaca	s74				s77	s82	3	-
Pieros Sotiriou	13/01/93	APOEL	s84	s11			s70	A	16	-
Vincent Laban	09/09/84	AEK Larnaca		s53	M	M75	M81	M	24	2
Kostakis Artymatas	15/04/93	APOEL		s84			M89	M90	8	-
Georgios Efrem	05/07/89	APOEL			M86	M	M58		32	3
Georgios Merkis	30/07/84	Apollon /APOEL			s86			D	33	1
Efstathios Aloneftis	29/03/83	APOEL				s75		s66	62	10
Konstantinos Panagi	08/10/94	Omonia					G		1	-
Nektarios Alexandrou	19/12/83	APOEL					D	M66	32	-
Charalambos Kyriakou	09/02/95	Apollon					s81	M66	3	-
Ilias Charalambous	25/09/80	AEK Larnaca						D	66	-
Marios Stylianou	23/09/93	Apollon						D90	3	-
Kypros Christoforou	23/04/93	Aris Limassol						s90	1	-

EUROPE

APOEL FC

CHAMPIONS LEAGUE

Second qualifying round - FK Vardar (MKD)
H 0-0
Waterman, Carlão (João Guilherme 41), De Vincenti, Luís Leal, Makrides (Efrem 60), Antoniades, Vinícius, Sotiriou (Piątkowski 66), Iñaki Astiz, Nuno Morais, Mário Sérgio. Coach: Domingos Paciência (POR)
A 1-1 De Vincenti (60)
Waterman, De Vincenti (Ioannou 85), Luís Leal, Makrides, Antoniades, Vinícius, Sotiriou (Štilić 57), Iñaki Astiz, Nuno Morais, Mário Sérgio, Vander (Alexandrou 72). Coach: Domingos Paciência (POR)

Third qualifying round - FC Midtjylland (DEN)
A 2-1 Hansen (30og), De Vincenti (33)
Waterman, Carlão, De Vincenti (Charalambides 84), Luís Leal (Efrem 78), Alexandrou, Makrides, Vinícius, Iñaki Astiz, Nuno Morais, Mário Sérgio, Vander (Sotiriou 63). Coach: Domingos Paciência (POR)
H 0-1
Waterman, Carlão, De Vincenti (Sotiriou 90), Luís Leal (Artymatas 83), Alexandrou, Makrides, Vinícius, Iñaki Astiz, Nuno Morais, Piątkowski (Vander 46), Mário Sérgio. Coach: Domingos Paciência (POR)
Red card: Vinícius 30

Play-offs - FC Astana (KAZ)
A 0-1
Waterman, Carlão, Efrem (Štilić 63), De Vincenti, Luís Leal, Alexandrou (Piątkowski 46), Makrides (Sotiriou 85), Antoniades, Iñaki Astiz, Nuno Morais, Mário Sérgio. Coach: Domingos Paciência (POR)
H 1-1 Štilić (60)
Waterman, Carlão (João Guilherme 83), De Vincenti, Luís Leal, Makrides (Charalambides 55), Antoniades (Piątkowski 85), Štilić, Iñaki Astiz, Nuno Morais, Mário Sérgio, Vander. Coach: Domingos Paciência (POR)

EUROPA LEAGUE

Group K
Match 1 - FC Schalke 04 (GER)
H 0-3
Waterman, Carlão, De Vincenti, Makrides, Antoniades (Artymatas 23), Vinícius (Štilić 61), Sotiriou (Cavenaghi 56), Iñaki Astiz, Nuno Morais, Mário Sérgio, Vander. Coach: Temur Ketsbaia (GEO)
Red card: De Vincenti 77
Match 2 - AC Sparta Praha (CZE)
A 0-2
Waterman, Artymatas, Carlão, Efrem, Makrides (Charalambides 80), Antoniades, Anastasiou, Nuno Morais, Piątkowski (Cavenaghi 67), Mário Sérgio, Vander (Štilić 53). Coach: Temur Ketsbaia (GEO)
Match 3 - Asteras Tripolis FC (GRE)
H 2-1 Cavenaghi (45+9p), Carlão (59)
Waterman, João Guilherme, Artymatas, Carlão, Efrem, Antoniades, Vinícius, Štilić (Iñaki Astiz 87), Nuno Morais, Vander (Charalambides 79), Cavenaghi (Piątkowski 63). Coach: Temur Ketsbaia (GEO)

Match 4 - Asteras Tripolis FC (GRE)
A 0-2
Waterman, Artymatas (Charalambides 90+1), Carlão, Antoniades (Alexandrou 64), Vinícius, Štilić, Iñaki Astiz, Nuno Morais, Piątkowski (Cavenaghi 46), Mário Sérgio, Vander. Coach: Temur Ketsbaia (GEO)
Match 5 - FC Schalke 04 (GER)
A 0-1
Waterman, João Guilherme, Artymatas, Carlão, De Vincenti, Charalambides (Vander 77), Antoniades (Iñaki Astiz 31), Vinícius, Sotiriou (Makrides 54), Nuno Morais, Mário Sérgio. Coach: Temur Ketsbaia (GEO)
Match 6 - AC Sparta Praha (CZE)
H 1-3 Cavenaghi (6)
Waterman, João Guilherme, Artymatas, Carlão (Vinícius 35), De Vincenti, Alexandrou, Štilić, Nuno Morais, Mário Sérgio, Vander (Efrem 60), Cavenaghi (Piątkowski 80). Coach: Temur Ketsbaia (GEO)

AEK Larnaca FC

EUROPA LEAGUE

Third qualifying round - FC Girondins de Bordeaux (FRA)
A 0-3
Toño, Marciniak, Mintikkis, David Català, Jorge Larena (Juanma Ortiz 57), André Alves (Mytides 69), Joan Tomàs, Tete (José Kanté 89), Boljević, Ninu, Monteiro. Coach: Thomas Christiansen (ESP)
H 0-1
Toño, David Català, Juanma Ortiz, Joan Tomàs, Tete, Boljević, Ninu (Jorge Larena 46), Mytides, Laban, Charalambides (André Alves 74), Monteiro (José Kanté 64). Coach: Thomas Christiansen (ESP)
Red card: Juanma Ortiz 82

Apollon Limassol FC

EUROPA LEAGUE

First qualifying round - FC Saxan (MDA)
A 2-0 João Pedro (33), Papoulis (89)
Bruno Vale, Elízio, Nuno Lopes, Freire, Sachetti, Marcos Gullón, João Pedro, Stojanović (Reynolds 72), C Kyriakou, Papoulis, Kolokoudias (Josephides 90+2). Coach: Pedro Emanuel (POR)
H 2-0 Stojanović (2), Papoulis (61)
Bruno Vale, Elízio, Nuno Lopes, Freire, Sachetti, Marcos Gullón, João Pedro (Wheeler 67), Stojanović (Farley 57), C Kyriakou, Papoulis, Kolokoudias (Josephides 82). Coach: Pedro Emanuel (POR)

Second qualifying round - FK Trakai (LTU)
H 4-0 Kolokoudias (21, 64p), Stojanović (52), Farley (87)
Bruno Vale, Elízio, Nuno Lopes (M Stylianou 80), Freire, Sachetti, Marcos Gullón, Jaime, João Pedro, Stojanović (Alex 72), Papoulis (Farley 68), Kolokoudias. Coach: Pedro Emanuel (POR)
A 0-0
Bruno Vale, Elízio, Freire, Sachetti, Marcos Gullón (Alex 63), Farley (Thuram 73), Jaime, João Pedro, Stojanović, M Stylianou, Kolokoudias (Josephides 87). Coach: Pedro Emanuel (POR)

Third qualifying round - Qäbälä FK (AZE)
H 1-1 Kolokoudias (14)
Bruno Vale, Elízio, Nuno Lopes, Freire, Sachetti, Marcos Gullón, Alex (Thuram 76), Jaime, João Pedro (M Stylianou 89), Papoulis, Kolokoudias (Gneki Guié 63). Coach: Pedro Emanuel (POR)
A 0-1
Bruno Vale, Elízio, Nuno Lopes (Thuram 61), Freire, Sachetti, Marcos Gullón, Alex, Jaime (Farley 81), João Pedro, Papoulis, Kolokoudias (Gneki Guié 61). Coach: Pedro Emanuel (POR)

AC Omonia

EUROPA LEAGUE

First qualifying round - FC Dinamo Batumi (GEO)
A 0-1
Georgallides, Lobjanidze, Cristóvão, Nuno Assis, Oikonomidis, Fofana (Kirm 58), Schembri (Okeuhie 70), Poté, Mendy (Renato Margaça 46), Runje, Goulon. Coach: Michael Sergiou (CYP)
H 2-0 Goulon (56), Schembri (62)
Panagi, Lobjanidze, Sheridan, Cristóvão, Nuno Assis (Pérez 87), Oikonomidis, Schembri (Okeuhie 78), Renato Margaça, Kirm (Fofana 46), Runje, Goulon. Coach: Kostas Kaiafas (CYP)

Second qualifying round - Jagiellonia Białystok (POL)
A 0-0
Panagi, Lobjanidze, Sheridan, Cristóvão, Nuno Assis (Luciano Bebê 89), Oikonomidis, Fofana (Demetriou 81), Schembri (Kirm 65), Renato Margaça, Runje, Goulon. Coach: Kostas Kaiafas (CYP)
H 1-0 Sheridan (8)
Panagi, Lobjanidze, Sheridan, Luciano Bebê (Fofana 56), Cristóvão, Nuno Assis, Oikonomidis, Schembri (Kirm 84), Renato Margaça, Runje, Goulon (Fylaktou 79). Coach: Kostas Kaiafas (CYP)

Third qualifying round - Brøndby IF (DEN)
A 0-0
Panagi, Lobjanidze, Sheridan, Luciano Bebê (Roushias 89), Cristóvão, Nuno Assis, Oikonomidis, Fofana (Fylaktou 75), Schembri (Kirm 61), Renato Margaça, Runje. Coach: Kostas Kaiafas (CYP)
H 2-2 Sheridan (16p, 45+3p)
Panagi, Lobjanidze, Demetriou (Mendy 90+5), Sheridan, Luciano Bebê, Nuno Assis, Oikonomidis (Fylaktou 86), Fofana (Roushias 69), Schembri, Renato Margaça, Runje. Coach: Kostas Kaiafas (CYP)
Red card: Nuno Assis 90+13

DOMESTIC LEAGUE CLUB-BY-CLUB

AEK Larnaca FC

1994 • Neo GSZ (13,032) • aek.com.cy

Major honours
Cypriot Cup (1) 2004

Coach: Thomas Christiansen (ESP); (29/04/16) (Demetris Demetriou)

2015					
22/08	a	Pafos	W	2-0	*Joan Tomàs 2*
29/08	a	Doxa	W	3-0	*Jorge Larena, Mytides, Englezou (p)*
12/09	h	APOEL	D	2-2	*José Kanté, Monteiro*
20/09	a	Aris	W	1-0	*Marciniak*
26/09	h	Paralimni	W	2-1	*Englezou, Marciniak*
04/10	a	AEL	W	1-0	*Joan Tomàs*
19/10	h	Nea Salamis	L	1-2	*Joan Tomàs*
25/10	a	Ethnikos	W	2-0	*Monteiro, André Alves*
01/11	h	Omonia	W	2-1	*André Alves 2*
07/11	a	Anorthosis	D	1-1	*André Alves*
22/11	h	Ayia Napa	W	3-1	*André Alves 2, José Kanté*
28/11	a	Apollon	D	0-0	
07/12	h	Ermis	W	2-0	*Joan Tomàs, André Alves*
12/12	h	Pafos	W	3-0	*André Alves 2, Englezou*
19/12	h	Doxa	W	2-0	*Joan Tomàs, Jorge Larena*
22/12	a	APOEL	W	2-1	*David Català, André Alves*
2016					
03/01	h	Aris	W	2-1	*André Alves, Tete*
09/01	a	Paralimni	W	1-0	*André Alves*
16/01	h	AEL	L	0-2	
24/01	a	Nea Salamis	D	0-0	
31/01	h	Ethnikos	W	1-0	*André Alves*
06/02	a	Omonia	L	1-3	*Tete*
14/02	h	Anorthosis	W	1-0	*Trickovski*
21/02	a	Ayia Napa	W	3-1	*David Català, Trickovski, André Alves (p)*
28/02	h	Apollon	W	6-1	*Tete, André Alves, Trickovski, og (Freire), Jorge Larena, Mytides*
02/03	a	Ermis	W	3-0	*Joan Tomàs (p), Mytides, og (Christofi)*
06/03	h	Apollon	D	2-2	*Jorge Larena, og (Pedro Monteiro)*
12/03	a	Anorthosis	W	1-0	*André Alves*
20/03	h	APOEL	L	0-3	
03/04	a	Omonia	W	1-0	*Trickovski*
09/04	h	Nea Salamis	W	2-0	*André Alves, Joan Tomàs (p)*
16/04	a	Apollon	D	2-2	*Trickovski, og (Nuno Lopes)*
23/04	h	Anorthosis	W	3-2	*Trickovski 2 (1p), og (Avraam)*
28/04	a	APOEL	L	0-2	
07/05	h	Omonia	L	1-3	*André Alves (p)*
14/05	a	Nea Salamis	L	2-3	*André Alves (p), Kaiserlides*

No	Name	Nat	DoB	Pos	Aps	(s)	Gls
9	André Alves	BRA	15/10/83	A	29	(4)	19
32	Constantinos Anthimou		20/07/97	A	1		
14	Vladimir Boljević	MNE	17/01/88	M	29	(2)	
33	Ilias Charalambous		25/09/80	D	14	(1)	
6	David Català	ESP	03/05/80	D	29		2
21	Nikos Englezou		11/07/93	M	19	(10)	3
70	Farley	BRA	14/01/94	M	5	(9)	
17	Vasilios Hadjiyiannakou		10/04/91	A	2	(2)	
10	Joan Tomàs	ESP	17/05/85	M	30		8
7	Jorge Larena	ESP	29/09/81	M	24	(3)	4
29	José Kanté	ESP	27/09/90	A	2	(10)	2
8	Juanma Ortiz	ESP	01/03/82	D	28	(4)	
34	Iacovos Kaiserlides		01/07/98	A		(1)	1
36	Andreas Kakoulis		08/01/97	D	1		
31	Konstantinos Konstantinou		08/10/99	M		(1)	
28	Christoforos Kourtis		05/11/96	A	1	(1)	
23	Dimitris Kyprianou		02/02/93	M	4	(4)	
20	Vincent Laban		09/09/84	M	13	(11)	
3	Adam Marciniak	POL	28/09/88	D	22	(2)	2
5	Konstantinos Mintikkis		08/06/89	D	7	(10)	
50	Daniel Mojsov	MKD	25/12/87	D	6	(1)	
77	Monteiro	POR	15/08/88	M	11	(5)	2
18	Ander Murillo	ESP	26/07/83	D	6	(1)	
27	Michael Music		04/02/99	M	1	(2)	
19	Nestoras Mytides		01/06/91	A	6	(15)	3
16	Emil Ninu	ROU	23/08/86	D	16	(3)	
13	Mikel Saizar	ESP	18/01/83	G	3	(1)	
4	Alberto Serrán	ESP	17/07/84	D	12		
1	Mateusz Taudul	POL	12/01/94	G	1		
11	Tete	ESP	26/05/85	M	29	(3)	3
25	Toño	ESP	23/11/86	G	32		
12	Ivan Trickovski	MKD	18/04/87	A	13	(1)	7

AEL Limassol FC

1930 • Tsirion (13,331) • ael-limassol.com.cy

Major honours
Cypriot League (6) 1941, 1953, 1955, 1956, 1968, 2012; Cypriot Cup (6) 1939, 1940, 1948, 1985, 1987, 1989

Coach: Christakis Christoforou; (27/10/15) Makis Chavos (GRE); (08/02/16) Pambos Christodoulou

2015					
23/08	a	Anorthosis	L	0-2	
30/08	h	Ayia Napa	W	1-0	*Adrián Sardinero*
13/09	a	Apollon	L	0-1	
19/09	h	Ermis	W	1-0	*Feltscher*
27/09	a	Pafos	D	0-0	
04/10	h	AEK	L	0-1	
17/10	a	APOEL	L	0-6	
25/10	h	Aris	L	1-2	*Niang*
31/10	a	Paralimni	D	2-2	*Adrián Sardinero 2*
08/11	a	Doxa	L	1-2	*Adrián Sardinero*
23/11	h	Nea Salamis	L	0-2	
29/11	a	Ethnikos	D	0-0	
06/12	h	Omonia	W	2-1	*Adrián Sardinero, Sema (p)*
12/12	h	Anorthosis	L	0-1	
20/12	a	Ayia Napa	W	1-0	*João Paulo*
23/12	h	Apollon	L	0-2	
2016					
04/01	a	Ermis	L	1-2	*Sielis (p)*
09/01	h	Pafos	D	0-0	
16/01	a	AEK	W	2-0	*Adrián Sardinero, Feltscher*
24/01	h	APOEL	L	0-1	
01/02	a	Aris	W	1-0	*Mavrou*
06/02	h	Paralimni	L	0-2	
13/02	h	Doxa	W	4-0	*Adrián Sardinero, Piech, Ohene, Mesca*
20/02	a	Nea Salamis	W	2-1	*Piech, Coutadeur*
28/02	h	Ethnikos	W	1-0	*Piech*
03/03	a	Omonia	L	2-4	*Piech, Aganović*
06/03	h	Ethnikos	W	5-2	*Piech 2, og (Ogungbe), Aganović, Adrián Sardinero*
11/03	a	Doxa	W	2-1	*Mesca, Piech*
20/03	h	Aris	D	2-2	*Aganović, Piech*
03/04	a	Pafos	D	1-1	*Piech*
10/04	h	Ermis	W	3-1	*Mesca, Adrián Sardinero, A Kyriakou*
17/04	a	Ethnikos	L	0-2	
24/04	h	Doxa	L	0-1	
27/04	a	Aris	W	1-0	*Aganović*
08/05	h	Pafos	W	1-0	*Mesca*
15/05	a	Ermis	D	1-1	*S Vasiliou*

No	Name	Nat	DoB	Pos	Aps	(s)	Gls
77	Adrián Sardinero	ESP	13/10/90	A	31	(1)	9
79	Adnan Aganović	CRO	03/10/87	M	15		4
6	John Arwuah	GHA	01/09/85	M	2	2)	
8	Mathieu Coutadeur	FRA	20/06/86	M	32		1
32	Matías Degra	ARG	18/06/83	G	23		
22	Mihai Dina	ROU	15/09/85	A		(5)	
27	Georgios Eleftheriou		30/09/84	M	18	(1)	
7	Frank Feltscher	VEN	17/05/88	M	12	(11)	2
81	Andreas Fragkou		19/01/97	M	2	(7)	
40	Evangelos Georgiou		01/01/95	G	3		
24	Giannis Gerolemou		27/01/00	M	1	(2)	
99	Evanthis Ioannou		01/10/97	D		(1)	
50	João Paulo	BRA	06/06/81	D	27	(1)	1
15	Vasilios Karagounis	GRE	18/01/94	D	3	(2)	
45	Andreas Kyriakou		05/02/94	D	9	(2)	1
66	Konstantinos Kyriakou		31/10/96	M	2		
21	Marco Airosa	ANG	06/08/84	D	25	(1)	
60	Marco Soares	CPV	16/06/84	M	29	(3)	
19	Ioannis Mavrou		19/07/94	A	5	(5)	1
17	Mesca	POR	06/05/93	M	20	(10)	4
98	Andreas Neophytou		07/07/98	M	2	(1)	
20	Mame Niang	SEN	20/03/84	A	4	(9)	1
94	Carlos Ohene	GHA	21/07/93	M	23	(7)	1
70	Stylianos Panteli		07/08/99	M		(3)	
29	Arkadiusz Piech	POL	07/06/85	A	12	(1)	9
3	Bertrand Robert	FRA	16/11/83	D	29	(1)	
23	Massamba Sambou	SEN	17/09/86	D	10	(1)	
9	Maic Sema	SWE	02/12/88	A	8	(2)	1
4	Valentinos Sielis		01/03/90	D	22	(2)	1
1	Łukasz Skowron	POL	17/03/91	G	10		
10	Andreas Stavrou		27/10/88	M	6	(16)	
33	Ostoja Stjepanovic	MKD	17/01/85	M	8	(5)	
56	Panos Theodorou		03/09/94	M	1	(1)	
28	Antonis Vasiliou		25/10/93	A		(3)	
87	Sotiris Vasiliou		29/12/95	M	2		1

Anorthosis Famagusta FC

1911 • Antonis Papadopoulos (10,230) • anorthosisfc.com.cy

Major honours
Cypriot League (13) 1950, 1957, 1958, 1960, 1962, 1963, 1995, 1997, 1998, 1999, 2000, 2005, 2008; Cypriot Cup (10) 1949, 1959, 1962, 1964, 1971, 1975, 1998, 2002, 2003, 2007

Coach: André Paus (NED); (18/02/16) Zoran Milinković (SRB); (23/03/16) Neophytos Larkou

2015					
23/08	h	AEL	W	2-0	*Ndlovu, Holgersson*
29/08	a	Nea Salamis	W	3-1	*Ndlovu 3 (1p)*
13/09	h	Ethnikos	W	3-0	*João Victor, Pelé, Ndlovu*
19/09	a	Omonia	D	0-0	
28/09	h	Doxa	W	2-1	*Holgersson, Makris*
04/10	h	Ayia Napa	D	2-2	*Pelé, Ndlovu (p)*
18/10	a	Apollon	L	0-3	*(w/o)*
24/10	h	Ermis	W	4-0	*Ndlovu, og (Fran González), Avraam, Schwechlen*
01/11	a	Pafos	W	2-1	*Avraam, Koulouris*
07/11	h	AEK	D	1-1	*Koulouris*
21/11	a	APOEL	W	2-0	*João Victor, Ndlovu (p)*
29/11	h	Aris	W	2-1	*Koulouris, Pelé*
05/12	a	Paralimni	W	2-0	*Ndlovu (p), Martínez*
12/12	a	AEL	W	1-0	*João Victor*
20/12	h	Nea Salamis	W	2-1	*Ndlovu (p), Avraam*
23/12	a	Ethnikos	D	1-1	*Ndlovu*
2016					
02/01	h	Omonia	D	0-0	
10/01	a	Doxa	D	1-1	*og (João Leonardo)*
16/01	a	Ayia Napa	W	7-1	*Schwechlen, Martínez, Pelé (p), Orlandi, Toni Calvo, Ndlovu, Makris (p)*
23/01	h	Apollon	W	3-2	*Holgersson, Laifis, Pelé (p)*
30/01	a	Ermis	L	0-2	
08/02	h	Pafos	W	5-1	*Ndlovu 2, Orlandi, Koulouris*
14/02	a	AEK	L	0-1	
21/02	h	APOEL	L	1-2	*Ndlovu*
27/02	a	Aris	D	0-0	
02/03	h	Paralimni	W	2-0	*Laifis, Ndlovu*
06/03	a	Omonia	L	0-3	
12/03	h	AEK	L	0-1	
19/03	a	Apollon	L	1-4	*Esmaël Gonçalves*
02/04	a	Nea Salamis	W	1-0	*Orlandi*
09/04	h	APOEL	D	1-1	*Laifis*
16/04	h	Omonia	L	0-3	
23/04	a	AEK	L	2-3	*Laifis, Ndlovu*
27/04	h	Apollon	D	1-1	*Tzanakakis*
07/05	h	Nea Salamis	D	1-1	*Orlandi*
15/05	a	APOEL	D	2-2	*Koulouris, Makris*

No	Name	Nat	DoB	Pos	Aps	(s)	Gls
8	Giorgi Aburjania	GEO	02/01/95	M	9	(3)	
30	Andreas Avraam		06/06/87	M	11	(14)	3
77	Esmaël Gonçalves	POR	25/06/91	A	5	(9)	1
2	Gabriel	BRA	18/06/88	D	30		
39	Christos Hadjipaschalis		01/08/99	M		(1)	
15	Markus Holgersson	SWE	16/04/85	D	30		3
19	João Victor	BRA	17/11/88	M	25		3
31	Andreas Kittos		09/09/90	G	2		
28	Panagiotis Konstantinou		06/08/86	M		(1)	
88	Jan Koprivec	SVN	15/07/88	G	33		
20	Efthimis Koulouris	GRE	06/03/96	A	7	(14)	6
38	Fytos Kyriakou		29/10/97	A	1	(1)	
34	Konstantinos Laifis		19/05/93	D	28		4
18	Irakli Maisuradze	GEO	22/08/88	M	21	(8)	
33	Andreas Makris		27/11/95	A	16	(11)	3
91	Jérémy Manzorro	FRA	11/11/91	M	3	(5)	
6	Christos Marangos		09/05/83	M	1	(3)	
10	Nicolás Martínez	ARG	25/09/87	M	31	(2)	2
9	Dino Ndlovu	RSA	15/02/90	A	25	(6)	17
5	Razak Nuhu	GHA	14/05/91	D	19		
22	Dimitris Oikonomou		10/11/92	D		(1)	
11	Andrea Orlandi	ESP	03/08/84	M	23	(3)	4
4	Pelé	POR	14/09/87	M	12	(10)	5
23	Léo Schwechlen	FRA	05/06/89	D	23	(1)	2
7	Toni Calvo	ESP	28/03/87	M	19	(4)	1
17	Manolis Tzanakakis	GRE	30/04/92	D	11	(4)	1

CYPRUS

APOEL FC

1926 • GSP (23,700) • apoelfc.com.cy

Major honours

Cypriot League (25) 1936, 1937, 1938, 1939, 1940, 1947, 1948, 1949, 1952, 1965, 1973, 1980, 1986, 1990, 1992, 1996, 2002, 2004, 2007, 2009, 2011, 2013, 2014, 2015, 2016; Cypriot Cup (21) 1937, 1941, 1947, 1951, 1963, 1968, 1969, 1973, 1976, 1978, 1979, 1984, 1993, 1995, 1996, 1997, 1999, 2006, 2008, 2014, 2015

Coach: Domingos Paciência (POR); (28/08/15) Temur Ketsbaia (GEO) (21/04/16) (Georgios Kostis) (GRE)

2015

22/08	a	Ermis	W	5-1	*De Vincenti, Luís Leal 2, Štilić, Charalambides*
30/08	h	Pafos	W	6-2	*Vinícius 2, De Vincenti, Charalambides, Cavenaghi 2*
12/09	a	AEK	D	2-2	*Vander, Cavenaghi*
21/09	a	Doxa	W	1-0	*Cavenaghi (p)*
26/09	h	Aris	W	4-0	*Cavenaghi (p), Efrem, De Vincenti 2*
05/10	a	Paralimni	W	5-0	*De Vincenti, Vander, Efrem, Cavenaghi 2 (1p)*
17/10	h	AEL	W	6-0	*Efrem 2, Cavenaghi 3 (1p), Artymatas*
26/10	a	Nea Salamis	W	9-0	*Efrem, Štilić, og (Žarković), De Vincenti 2, Vinícius, Cavenaghi 2, Piątkowski*
31/10	h	Ethnikos	W	3-0	*Charalambides, De Vincenti, Vinícius*
09/11	a	Omonia	D	2-2	*Cavenaghi 2*
21/11	h	Anorthosis	L	0-2	
30/11	a	Ayia Napa	W	1-0	*Cavenaghi (p)*
05/12	h	Apollon	L	0-1	
14/12	h	Ermis	W	2-0	*Cavenaghi (p), De Vincenti*
19/12	a	Pafos	W	1-0	*Vander*
22/12	h	AEK	L	1-2	*João Guilherme*

2016

03/01	h	Doxa	L	1-2	*Sotiriou*
10/01	a	Aris	W	2-1	*De Vincenti, Sotiriou*
17/01	h	Paralimni	W	3-0	*Nuno Morais, Cavenaghi (p), Giannotas*
24/01	a	AEL	W	1-0	*Nuno Morais*
30/01	h	Nea Salamis	W	6-1	*Sotiriou, De Vincenti 2, Vander, Vinícius, Cavenaghi*
07/02	a	Ethnikos	W	3-1	*Sotiriou 2, Cavenaghi*
13/02	h	Omonia	W	2-0	*Efrem 2*
21/02	a	Anorthosis	W	2-1	*De Vincenti, Sotiriou*
27/02	h	Ayia Napa	W	3-0	*Efrem, Vander, Aloneftis*
02/03	a	Apollon	W	1-0	*Efrem*
05/03	a	Nea Salamis	W	1-0	*Carlão*
12/03	h	Omonia	W	2-1	*Efrem, Vander*
20/03	a	AEK	W	3-0	*De Vincenti, Efrem, Sotiriou*
02/04	h	Apollon	D	2-2	*Carlão, Merkis*
09/04	a	Anorthosis	D	1-1	*Giannotas*
16/04	h	Nea Salamis	W	4-1	*Štilić, Sotiriou, Nuno Morais (p), Charalambides*
23/04	a	Omonia	W	2-0	*Giannotas 2*
28/04	h	AEK	W	2-0	*Sotiriou, Giannotas (p)*
07/05	a	Apollon	L	0-1	
15/05	h	Anorthosis	D	2-2	*Sotiriou, De Vincenti*

No	Name	Nat	DoB	Pos	Aps	(s)	Gls
11	Nektarios Alexandrou		19/12/83	D	14	(6)	
46	Efstathios Aloneftis		29/03/83	M	1	(9)	1
25	Rafael Anastasiou		09/06/97	D		(1)	
15	Marios Antoniades		14/05/90	D	14	(4)	
4	Kostakis Artymatas		15/04/93	M	23	(3)	1
32	Andreas Assiotis		06/02/96	D		(1)	
5	Carlão	BRA	19/01/86	D	24	(1)	2
79	Fernando Cavenaghi	ARG	21/09/83	A	14	(4)	19
10	Kostas Charalambides		25/07/81	M	8	(11)	4
19	Michalis Charalambous		29/01/99	A		(1)	
45	Georgios Christodoulou		17/08/97	M		(1)	
8	Tomás De Vincenti	ARG	09/02/89	M	26		15
7	Georgios Efrem		05/07/89	M	22	(2)	11
55	Estrela	POR	22/09/95	M		(1)	
70	Ioannis Gianniotas	GRE	29/04/93	M	17		5
23	Iñaki Astiz	ESP	05/11/83	D	15	(1)	
44	Nicholas Ioannou		10/11/95	D	2	(3)	
3	João Guilherme	BRA	21/04/86	D	16	(5)	1
88	Tasos Kissas		18/01/88	G	1		
9	Luís Leal	STP	29/05/87	A	1		2
13	Konstantinos Makrides		13/01/82	M	7	(7)	
28	Mário Sérgio	POR	28/07/81	D	20	(1)	
30	Georgios Merkis		30/07/84	D	12	(1)	1
21	Zhivko Milanov	BUL	15/07/84	D	16		
26	Nuno Morais	POR	29/01/84	M	34		3
31	Vasilios Papafotis		10/08/95	A		(2)	
27	Mateusz Piątkowski	POL	22/11/84	A	2	(12)	1
20	Pieros Sotiriou		13/01/93	A	19	(7)	10
17	Semir Štilić	BIH	08/10/87	M	9	(7)	3
78	Urko Pardo	ESP	28/01/83	G	16		
77	Vander	BRA	03/10/88	M	15	(15)	6
16	Vinícius	BRA	16/05/86	M	29		5
99	Boy Waterman	NED	24/01/84	G	19	(1)	

Apollon Limassol FC

1954 • Tsirion (13,331) • apollon.com.cy

Major honours

Cypriot League (3) 1991, 1994, 2006; Cypriot Cup (8) 1966, 1967, 1986, 1992, 2001, 2010, 2013, 2016

Coach: Pedro Emanuel (POR)

2015

23/08	h	Aris	W	2-1	*Thuram, Slavchev*
30/08	a	Paralimni	D	0-0	
13/09	h	AEL	W	1-0	*Papoulis*
20/09	a	Nea Salamis	L	0-2	
26/09	h	Ethnikos	W	5-2	*Elízio 2, Gneki Guié, Mezga, Papoulis*
03/10	a	Omonia	D	0-0	
18/10	h	Anorthosis	W	3-0	*(w/o)*
24/10	a	Ayia Napa	W	3-0	*Gneki Guié, Freire, Alex (p)*
31/10	h	Doxa	W	2-1	*Papoulis 2*
07/11	h	Ermis	D	0-0	
22/11	a	Pafos	D	0-0	
28/11	h	AEK	D	0-0	
05/12	a	APOEL	W	1-0	*Gneki Guié*
13/12	a	Aris	D	2-2	*Kolokoudias 2 (1p)*
20/12	h	Paralimni	W	2-1	*Kolokoudias (p), Gneki Guié*
23/12	a	AEL	W	2-0	*Stojanović, og (Sielis)*

2016

02/01	h	Nea Salamis	W	3-0	*Stojanović 2, Thuram*
11/01	a	Ethnikos	L	0-2	
16/01	h	Omonia	D	0-0	
23/01	a	Anorthosis	L	2-3	*Alex (p), og (Holgersson)*
31/01	h	Ayia Napa	W	4-0	*Stojanović 2, Maglica, Angeli*
07/02	a	Doxa	W	3-1	*Maglica, Alex (p), Stojanović*
15/02	a	Ermis	W	2-1	*Maglica, Alex (p)*
20/02	h	Pafos	W	3-1	*Maglica 3*
28/02	a	AEK	L	1-6	*João Pedro*
02/03	h	APOEL	L	0-1	
06/03	a	AEK	D	2-2	*Papoulis, Alex (p)*
12/03	h	Nea Salamis	W	2-1	*Freire, Papoulis (p)*
19/03	h	Anorthosis	W	4-1	*Gneki Guié, Mezga, Papoulis, Maglica*
02/04	a	APOEL	D	2-2	*Maglica, Alex*
09/04	h	Omonia	L	1-2	*Freire*
16/04	h	AEK	D	2-2	*Papoulis, Gneki Guié*
23/04	a	Nea Salamis	W	3-0	*Angeli, Alex (p), Stojanović*
27/04	a	Anorthosis	D	1-1	*Stojanović*
07/05	h	APOEL	W	1-0	*Stojanović*
14/05	a	Omonia	W	2-1	*Alex, Papoulis*

No	Name	Nat	DoB	Pos	Aps	(s)	Gls
10	Alex	BRA	15/08/83	M	29	(3)	8
27	Angelis Angeli		31/05/89	D	20		2
83	Bruno Vale	POR	08/04/83	G	35		
2	Elízio	BRA	22/11/88	D	31		2
8	Farley	BRA	14/01/94	M	1	(4)	
4	Freire	BRA	21/08/89	D	32		3
19	Abraham Gneki Guié	CIV	25/07/86	A	24	(4)	6
14	Jaime	POR	11/06/89	D	10		
17	João Pedro	POR	04/05/86	M	33		1
29	Georgios Kolokoudias		03/05/89	A	1	(11)	3
25	Charalambos Kyriakou		09/02/95	M	4	(5)	
99	Anton Maglica	CRO	11/11/91	A	10	(4)	8
20	Konstantinos Makrides		13/01/82	M	9	(2)	
6	Marcos Gullón	ESP	20/02/89	M	4	(4)	
11	Dejan Mezga	CRO	16/07/85	M	12	(13)	2
3	Nuno Lopes	POR	19/12/86	D	6	(1)	
26	Fotios Papoulis	GRE	22/01/85	M	19	(5)	9
33	Pedro Monteiro	POR	30/01/94	D	7	(1)	
52	Ioannis Pittas		10/07/96	M	2	(9)	
57	Petros Psychas		28/08/98	A	1		
5	Esteban Sachetti	ARG	21/11/85	M	21	(2)	
18	Simeon Slavchev	BUL	25/09/93	M	12	(8)	1
22	Luka Stojanović	SRB	04/01/94	M	26	(1)	9
28	Marios Stylianou		23/09/93	D	9	(1)	
9	Thuram	BRA	01/02/91	A	5	(14)	2
88	Georgios Vasiliou		12/06/84	D	20	(3)	
42	Christos Wheeler		29/06/97	D	2	(6)	

Aris Limassol FC

1930 • Tsirion (13,331) • no website

Coach: Jane Nikolovski (MKD); (21/07/15) Akis Agiomamitis; (15/09/15) Eugen Neagoe (ROU); (08/02/16) Kostas Kaiafas; (09/05/16) (Michalis Sergiou)

2015

23/08	a	Apollon	L	1-2	*Maragoudakis*
29/08	h	Ermis	D	1-1	*González*
12/09	a	Pafos	L	0-3	
20/09	h	AEK	L	0-1	
26/09	a	APOEL	L	0-4	
03/10	a	Doxa	L	1-2	*Maragoudakis*
17/10	h	Paralimni	W	2-1	*Boniface, Marco Aurélio*
25/10	a	AEL	W	2-1	*Bangura, Maragoudakis*
02/11	h	Nea Salamis	W	2-0	*Marco Aurélio, Maragoudakis*
07/11	a	Ethnikos	W	2-1	*Boniface, Borg*
22/11	h	Omonia	L	0-1	
29/11	a	Anorthosis	L	1-2	*Maragoudakis*
05/12	h	Ayia Napa	W	2-0	*Boniface, Marco Aurélio (p)*
13/12	h	Apollon	D	2-2	*Maragoudakis, González*
19/12	a	Ermis	D	0-0	
22/12	h	Pafos	W	1-0	*Douglas*

2016

03/01	a	AEK	L	1-2	*Randy*
10/01	h	APOEL	L	1-2	*Boniface*
17/01	h	Doxa	D	1-1	*Ranos*
23/01	a	Paralimni	D	2-2	*Ranos, Marco Aurélio (p)*
01/02	h	AEL	L	0-1	
06/02	a	Nea Salamis	D	0-0	
14/02	h	Ethnikos	W	2-0	*Ranos (p), Boniface*
20/02	a	Omonia	L	1-2	*Ranos*
27/02	h	Anorthosis	D	0-0	
02/03	a	Ayia Napa	W	4-0	*Douglas, Ranos 2, Maragoudakis*
06/03	a	Ermis	L	1-3	*Predescu*
11/03	h	Pafos	D	0-0	
20/03	a	AEL	D	2-2	*Boniface, Maragoudakis*
03/04	h	Ethnikos	D	2-2	*Ranos, Boniface*
10/04	a	Doxa	D	1-1	*Maragoudakis*
17/04	h	Ermis	W	3-0	*Ranos, Boniface, Kyprou*
24/04	a	Pafos	L	0-1	
27/04	h	AEL	L	0-1	
08/05	a	Ethnikos	L	1-2	*Kyprou*
15/05	h	Doxa	W	4-3	*Maragoudakis, A Charalambous (p), Kyprou, Predescu*

No	Name	Nat	DoB	Pos	Aps	(s)	Gls
22	Minas Antoniou		22/02/94	M	6	(7)	
10	Mustapha Bangura	SLE	24/10/89	M	9	(7)	1
19	Mathew Boniface	NGA	05/10/94	A	18	(10)	8
36	Steve Borg	MLT	15/05/88	D	31	(2)	1
16	Andreas Charalambous		12/05/98	A	1		1
20	Christos Charalambous		03/10/81	M	10	(4)	
4	Kypros Christoforou		24/04/93	D	34		
5	Douglas	BRA	07/05/91	D	21		2
3	Ioannis Efstathiou		14/02/93	D	27	(2)	
88	José Pedrosa Galán	ESP	02/02/86	M		(2)	
9	Silvio González	ARG	08/06/80	A	4	(15)	2
27	Ivica Guberac	SVN	05/07/88	M	5	(5)	
12	Christos Ierides		12/12/94	D	2	(2)	
33	Marián Kello	SVK	05/09/82	G	2		
17	Theodosis Kyprou		24/02/92	A	26	(2)	3
32	Evangelos Kyriakou		03/02/94	M	11	(10)	
1	Georgios Loizou		25/02/92	G	11		
28	Georgios Malekkidis		14/07/97	M	2	(4)	
11	Markos Maragoudakis	GRE	28/01/82	A	32	(1)	10
8	Marco Aurélio	BRA	27/03/83	M	32		4
15	Edin Nuredinoski	MKD	21/04/82	G	23		
44	Andreas Pachipis		16/12/94	M	4	(6)	
30	Kyriakos Panagi		22/04/96	M	18	(1)	
7	Valentinos Pastellis		30/01/91	D		(3)	
25	Cornel Predescu	ROU	21/12/87	M	11	(8)	2
18	Randy	EQG	02/06/87	M	16	(9)	1
93	Antonis Ranos	GRE	15/06/93	A	12	(4)	8
6	Roger Guerreiro	POL	25/05/82	M	4	(1)	
97	Giannis Stefanou		12/02/97	G		(1)	
21	Christos Theophilou		30/04/81	D	24	(2)	

Ayia Napa FC

1990 • Tasos Markou, Paralimni (8,000) •
aoanfc.com

**Coach: Georgios Kosma;
(28/01/15) (Antonis Mertakkas);
(16/02/15) Panikos Protopapas**

2015

24/08	h	Paralimni	L	0-2	
30/08	a	AEL	L	0-1	
13/09	h	Nea Salamis	L	1-3	Stojanov
19/09	a	Ethnikos	L	0-2	
27/09	h	Omonia	L	1-2	Maatsen
04/10	a	Anorthosis	D	2-2	Ibson, Antoniou
17/10	h	Doxa	D	2-2	Olatubosun, Antoniou
24/10	h	Apollon	L	0-3	
31/10	a	Ermis	D	0-0	
07/11	h	Pafos	D	1-1	Mguni
22/11	a	AEK	L	1-3	Stojanov
30/11	h	APOEL	L	0-1	
05/12	a	Aris	L	0-2	
13/12	a	Paralimni	D	2-2	Antolek, Lambropoulos
20/12	h	AEL	L	0-2	
23/12	a	Nea Salamis	D	2-2	Lambropoulos, Bamba

2016

02/01	h	Ethnikos	L	2-3	Georgiou, Felgate
09/01	a	Omonia	L	0-4	
16/01	h	Anorthosis	L	1-7	Loizides
25/01	a	Doxa	L	0-2	
31/01	a	Apollon	L	0-4	
06/02	h	Ermis	L	0-1	
14/02	a	Pafos	L	1-4	Moulazimis
21/02	h	AEK	L	1-3	Skopljak
27/02	a	APOEL	L	0-3	
02/03	h	Aris	L	0-4	

No	Name	Nat	DoB	Pos	Aps	(s)	Gls
97	Anastasios Anastasiou		16/03/97	G		(1)	
99	Kristis Andreou		12/08/94	A	8		
14	Ivan Antolek	CRO	27/01/93	A	5	(7)	1
24	Giannis Antoniou		21/01/90	D	16	(3)	2
28	Fousseni Bamba	CIV	19/04/90	D	14	(1)	1
3	Michael Felgate	ENG	01/04/91	D	18	(1)	1
18	Emiliano Fusco	ARG	02/03/86	M	15		
19	Ilias Georgiou		24/07/97	M	15	(3)	1
27	Ibson	BRA	08/11/89	A	13	(3)	1
77	Georgios Katsiati		04/02/96	A	7	(4)	
20	Antonis Katsis		06/09/89	M	9	(4)	
1	Andreas Kittos		09/09/90	G	13		
13	Symeon Kittos		11/05/96	D		(2)	
92	Elvis Kryukov		01/03/92	D	2	(1)	
5	Georgios Lambropoulos	GRE	26/10/84	M	20	(2)	2
35	Panagiotis Loizides		28/02/95	D	8	(2)	1
10	Anej Lovrečič	SVN	10/05/87	M	7	(4)	
91	Darren Maatsen	NED	30/01/91	A	2	(6)	1
26	Antonis Machattou		08/07/98	D	3	(4)	
16	Bojan Markoski	MKD	08/08/83	M	11		
7	Kostas Markou		27/03/88	M	7	(5)	
21	Daniel Mensah	GHA	28/08/97	D	1	(1)	
37	Eleftherios Mertakkas		16/03/85	D	21		
8	Musawengosi Mguni	ZIM	05/04/83	A	10	(3)	1
17	Antonis Moulazimis		14/09/96	A	2	(5)	1
11	Joseph Olatubosun	NGA	21/12/90	A	8	(1)	1
76	Marios Peratikos		08/09/99	A		(1)	
17	Marios Pierettis		21/11/98	M		(1)	
30	Marko Pridigar	SVN	18/05/85	G	12	(1)	
6	Alastair Reynolds	SCO	02/09/96	M	11	(3)	
4	Nebojša Skopljak	SRB	12/05/87	D	16		1
25	Alistair Slowe	ENG	16/10/88	M	1	(2)	
73	Konstantinos Stefani		26/01/98	G	1		
9	Uroš Stojanov	SRB	05/01/89	A	7	(5)	2
22	Nektarios Tziortzis		09/11/90	M	3	(1)	

Doxa Katokopia FC

1954 • Makario, Nicosia (16,000) •
doxafc.com .cy

Coach: Loukas Hadjiloukas

2015

23/08	a	Ethnikos	D	2-2	Ricardo Lobo (p), Edmar
29/08	h	AEK	L	0-3	
12/09	a	Omonia	D	1-1	Leandro
21/09	h	APOEL	L	0-1	
28/09	a	Anorthosis	L	1-2	Carlitos
03/10	h	Aris	W	2-1	Ricardo Fernandes, Ricardo Lobo
17/10	a	Ayia Napa	D	2-2	Edmar, og (Mertakkas)
25/10	h	Paralimni	W	2-1	Dani López, Ricardo Fernandes
31/10	a	Apollon	L	1-2	Edmar
08/11	h	AEL	W	2-1	Carlitos, Paulinho (p)
21/11	a	Ermis	D	2-2	Carlitos 2
28/11	h	Nea Salamis	L	1-2	Carlitos
06/12	a	Pafos	D	3-3	Ricardo Lobo, Carlitos, Fofana
12/12	h	Ethnikos	D	1-1	Dani López
19/12	a	AEK	L	0-2	
22/12	h	Omonia	L	0-1	

2016

03/01	h	APOEL	W	2-1	Edmar, Paulinho
10/01	h	Anorthosis	D	1-1	Dani López
17/01	a	Aris	D	1-1	Carlitos
25/01	h	Ayia Napa	W	2-0	Paulinho (p), Fofana (p)
30/01	a	Paralimni	D	1-1	Edmar
07/02	h	Apollon	L	1-3	Aguinaldo
13/02	a	AEL	L	0-4	
20/02	h	Ermis	W	2-1	Paulinho, Eninful
28/02	a	Nea Salamis	D	0-0	
02/03	h	Pafos	L	1-3	Diego León
06/03	a	Pafos	L	1-2	
11/03	h	AEL	L	1-2	Leandro
20/03	a	Ethnikos	W	2-1	João Leonardo 2
03/04	a	Ermis	L	1-3	Demetriou
10/04	h	Aris	D	1-1	Fofana
17/04	h	Pafos	W	3-1	Aguinaldo, Carlitos, Fofana
24/04	a	AEL	W	1-0	Aguinaldo
27/04	h	Ethnikos	L	1-2	Aguinaldo
08/05	h	Ermis	D	2-2	Wilson Kenidy, Aguinaldo
15/05	a	Aris	L	3-4	Fofana 2, Demetriou

No	Name	Nat	DoB	Pos	Aps	(s)	Gls
5	Abel Pereira	POR	15/04/90	D	9	(2)	
89	Aguinaldo	ANG	04/03/89	A	11	(3)	5
88	Georgios Aresti		02/09/94	M	2	(7)	
11	Carlitos	POR	09/03/93	M	26	(5)	8
21	Konstantinos Christodoulou		22/03/96	M		(2)	
8	Dani López	ESP	31/03/92	M	27	(8)	3
3	Stelios Demetriou		04/10/90	D	24	(5)	2
20	Diego León	ESP	16/01/84	M	10	(5)	1
19	Edmar	BRA	09/04/82	D	32	(2)	5
94	Andreas Efstathiou		22/01/94	G	2		
7	Richard Emmanuel	CMR	17/01/95	M	2	(14)	
30	Henri Eninful	TOG	21/07/92	M	15	(13)	1
26	Gaoussou Fofana	CIV	14/04/84	M	29	(4)	6
99	Evagoras Hadjifrangiskou		29/10/86	G	17		
25	João Leonardo	BRA	25/06/85	D	29	(2)	2
77	Alex Konstantinou		11/04/92	M	2	(3)	
34	Leandro	BRA	11/01/87	D	30	(2)	2
14	Aritz López Garai	ESP	06/11/80	M	12	(1)	
12	Michalis Morfis		15/01/79	G		(1)	
36	Dimitris Myrthianos	GRE	13/08/95	D	2	(1)	
1	Alexandre Negri		27/03/81	G	17		
2	Paulinho	BRA	04/08/83	D	28	(2)	4
6	Manuel Redondo	ESP	11/01/85	D	20	(3)	
10	Ricardo Fernandes	POR	21/04/78	M	13		2
9	Ricardo Lobo	BRA	20/03/84	A	6	(4)	3
23	Anthos Solomou		30/11/85	M	13	(2)	
15	Paolo Stylianou		11/06/97	D	2		
13	Wilson Kenidy	ANG	02/02/93	A	16	(11)	1
31	Georgios Xenofontos		01/03/96	D		(1)	

Enosis Neon Paralimni FC

1936 • Tasos Markou (8,000) • enpfc.com

**Coach: Nikos Karageorgiou (GRE);
(05/11/15) (Yiasoumis Yiasoumi);
(10/11/15) Ronny Van Geneugden (BEL)**

2015

24/08	a	Ayia Napa	W	2-0	Valianos, Dickson
30/08	h	Apollon	D	0-0	
14/09	a	Ermis	L	1-2	og (Frangeskou)
20/09	h	Pafos	W	2-1	Budimir, Bojović
26/09	a	AEK	L	1-2	Svojić
05/10	h	APOEL	L	0-5	
17/10	a	Aris	L	1-2	Bashov
25/10	a	Doxa	L	1-2	Vukčević
31/10	h	AEL	D	2-2	Budimir (p), Papadopoulos
08/11	a	Nea Salamis	L	1-3	Dickson
21/11	h	Ethnikos	W	2-1	Papadopoulos, og (Iacob)
29/11	a	Omonia	D	2-2	Bojović, Dickson
05/12	h	Anorthosis	L	0-2	
13/12	h	Ayia Napa	D	2-2	Froxylias, Bouwman
20/12	a	Apollon	L	1-2	Bojović
23/12	h	Ermis	L	0-1	

2016

02/01	a	Pafos	D	3-3	Svojić, Papadopoulos, Froxylias
09/01	h	AEK	L	0-1	
17/01	a	APOEL	L	0-3	
23/01	h	Aris	D	2-2	Papadopoulos, Bojović
30/01	h	Doxa	L	0-1	
06/02	a	AEL	W	2-0	Papadopoulos, Shalaj
13/02	h	Nea Salamis	D	2-2	Bouwman, Bojović
20/02	a	Ethnikos	D	0-0	
27/02	h	Omonia	L	1-4	Bukorac
02/03	a	Anorthosis	L	0-2	

No	Name	Nat	DoB	Pos	Aps	(s)	Gls
19	Georgios Ambaris	GRE	23/04/82	G	15		
9	Miloš Antić	SRB	28/10/94	M	2	(3)	
20	Amir Azmy	EGY	14/02/83	D	7		
7	Kostadin Bashov	BUL	26/11/82	A	8	(8)	1
21	Mijuško Bojović	MNE	09/08/88	D	19		5
8	Pim Bouwman	NED	30/01/91	M	20	(1)	2
33	Mario Budimir	CRO	12/02/86	A	17	(3)	2
31	Stefan Bukorac	SRB	15/02/91	M	4		1
16	Andreas Daniel		10/05/97	D	1	(1)	
84	Chris Dickson	GHA	28/12/84	A	12	(3)	3
4	Edson Silva	ANG	10/09/92	D	16	(2)	
80	Dimitris Froxylias		28/06/93	M	15	(4)	2
11	Michalis Giorkatzis		11/03/97	M	1	(5)	
22	Panagiotis Hadjiandreas		10/12/97	A		(5)	
1	Gavriel Konstantinou		05/07/89	G	3	(1)	
14	Loizos Kosma		25/01/95	M	11	(5)	
25	Antonis Koumis		11/02/97	M	7	(1)	
18	Vasilios Papadopoulos	GRE	28/01/95	A	13	(6)	5
5	Stelios Parpas		25/07/85	D	17	(2)	
3	Adamos Pierettis		22/11/82	D	9		
32	Krševan Santini	CRO	11/04/97	G	8		
90	Gezim Shalaj	SUI	28/07/90	M	5		1
23	Milan Svojić	SRB	09/10/90	M	9	(11)	2
24	Sadio Tounkara	MLI	27/04/92	M	5		
6	Angelos Tsiakklis		02/10/89	M	13	(4)	
2	Vasilios Valianos	GRE	11/09/88	D	26		1
94	Kenneth Van Ransbeeck	BEL	06/12/94	M	15	(5)	
10	Simon Vukčević	MNE	29/01/86	M	8	(7)	1

Ermis Aradippou FC

1958 • Ammochostos, Larnaca (4,000) • ermisfc.com.cy

Coach: Pavlos Dermitzakis (GRE);
(03/09/15) Apostolos Makrides;
(22/10/15) Nicos Panayiotou

2015
22/08	h	APOEL	L	1-5	Vasilogiannis
29/08	a	Aris	D	1-1	Quaynor
14/09	h	Paralimni	W	2-1	Vasilogiannis, Yenga
19/09	a	AEL	L	0-1	
26/09	h	Nea Salamis	L	1-2	Keita
04/10	a	Ethnikos	D	2-2	Yiangoudakis, Latorre
18/10	h	Omonia	L	0-1	
24/10	a	Anorthosis	L	0-4	
31/10	h	Ayia Napa	D	0-0	
07/11	a	Apollon	D	0-0	
21/11	h	Doxa	D	2-2	Mayele, Keita
28/11	h	Pafos	W	2-1	Keita, Mayele
07/12	a	AEK	L	0-2	
14/12	a	APOEL	L	0-2	
19/12	h	Aris	D	0-0	
23/12	a	Paralimni	W	1-0	Fran González

2016
04/01	h	AEL	W	2-1	Vasilogiannis, Keita
09/01	h	Nea Salamis	L	2-3	Keita 2 (2p)
17/01	h	Ethnikos	D	1-1	Keita (p)
23/01	a	Omonia	L	0-1	
30/01	h	Anorthosis	W	2-0	Dickson, Weeks
06/02	a	Ayia Napa	W	1-0	Dickson
15/02	a	Apollon	L	1-0	Dickson
20/02	a	Doxa	L	2-1	Keita
27/02	a	Pafos	L	0-2	
02/03	h	AEK	L	0-3	
06/03	h	Aris	W	3-1	Vasilogiannis, Keita (p), Fran González
12/03	a	Ethnikos	W	1-0	Weeks
20/03	h	Pafos	W	1-0	Dickson
03/04	h	Doxa	W	3-1	Keita (p), Dickson, Fran González
10/04	a	AEL	L	1-3	Mayele
17/04	a	Aris	L	0-3	
24/04	h	Ethnikos	D	1-1	Keita (p)
27/04	a	Pafos	W	1-0	Yiangoudakis
08/05	a	Doxa	D	2-2	Mayele, Keita
15/05	h	AEL	D	1-1	Keita

No	Name	Nat	DoB	Pos	Aps	(s)	Gls
92	Anastasios Andreou		26/05/98	A		(3)	
29	Femi Balogun	NGA	27/12/92	M	5	(5)	
10	Charles	BRA	11/03/84	M		(2)	
20	China	POR	15/04/82	D	1		
17	Martinos Christofi		26/07/93	D	26	(2)	
31	Athos Chrysostomou		08/07/81	G	2		
99	Anastasios Demetriou		18/10/99	A		(3)	
42	Chris Dickson	GHA	28/12/84	A	15	(1)	5
35	Diogo Rosado	POR	21/02/90	M	10	(3)	
5	Fran González	ESP	01/11/89	D	30	(4)	3
4	Panagiotis Frangeskou		12/04/91	D	11	(3)	
19	Alhassane Keita	GUI	16/04/92	A	36		13
22	Petros Kourou		03/06/94	A		(5)	
18	Christian Latorre	URU	17/04/87	M	26	(3)	1
14	Leandros Lillis		13/09/96	M	1	(7)	
91	Sérgio Marakis	RSA	11/11/91	M	2	(3)	
25	Jessy Mayele	NED	11/11/91	A	12	(17)	4
9	Cendrino Misidjan	NED	29/08/88	D	5	(3)	
55	Dimitris Moulazimis		15/01/92	A	16	(2)	
6	Ulysse Ndong	FRA	24/11/92	D	20	(3)	
90	Issouf Ouattara	BFA	07/10/88	A	1	(6)	
12	Leonidas Panagopoulos	GRE	03/01/87	G	28		
26	Paulo Pina	CPV	04/01/81	D	28		
8	Cristian Portilla	ESP	28/08/88	M	1		
24	Moustapha Quaynor	GHA	17/07/95	M	12	(4)	1
7	Rúben Brígido	POR	23/06/91	M	8	(2)	
16	Cristian Sirghi	ROU	23/11/86	D	16		
84	Dimitris Stylianou		05/07/84	G	6		
11	Andreas Vasilogiannis	GRE	21/02/91	M	26	(6)	4
27	Theo Weeks	LBR	19/01/90	M	24	(3)	2
23	Yannick Yenga	COD	10/04/85	A	6	(13)	1
21	Rafael Yiangoudakis		03/08/90	M	22	(4)	2

Ethnikos Achnas FC

1968 • Dasaki (5,000) • fcachna.com.cy

Coach: Borce Gjurev;
(24/11/15) Danilo Dončić (SRB)

2015
23/08	h	Doxa	D	2-2	Eduardo Pincelli, og (López Garai)
29/08	h	Omonia	W	1-0	Chatzivasilis
13/09	a	Anorthosis	L	0-3	
19/09	h	Ayia Napa	W	2-0	Elia, Carles Coto
26/09	a	Apollon	L	2-5	Eduardo Pincelli, Chatzivasilis
04/10	a	Ermis	D	2-2	Eduardo Pincelli (p), Obregón
18/10	a	Pafos	L	0-3	
25/10	h	AEK	L	0-3	
31/10	a	APOEL	L	0-3	
07/11	h	Aris	L	1-2	Carles Coto
21/11	a	Paralimni	L	1-2	Eduardo Pincelli
29/11	h	AEL	D	0-0	
06/12	a	Nea Salamis	D	2-2	Samuel Araújo, Obregón
12/12	a	Doxa	D	1-1	Obregón
19/12	a	Omonia	L	1-2	S Grigalashvili
23/12	h	Anorthosis	D	1-1	Carles Coto (p)

2016
02/01	h	Ayia Napa	W	3-2	Carles Coto 2 (2p), S Grigalashvili
11/01	h	Apollon	W	2-0	Ogungbe, Elia
17/01	a	Ermis	W	2-1	Ogungbe, Poutziouris
23/01	h	Pafos	D	1-1	Eduardo Pincelli
31/01	a	AEK	L	0-1	
07/02	h	APOEL	L	1-3	Elia
14/02	a	Aris	L	0-2	
20/02	h	Paralimni	D	0-0	
28/02	a	AEL	L	0-1	
02/03	h	Nea Salamis	D	2-2	Samuel Araújo, Carles Coto
06/03	a	AEL	L	2-5	Guilherme, Eduardo Pincelli
12/03	h	Ermis	L	0-1	
20/03	h	Doxa	L	1-2	Ogungbe
03/04	a	Aris	D	2-2	S Grigalashvili, Ogungbe
10/04	h	Pafos	W	3-0	Chatzivasilis 2, Iacob
17/04	a	AEL	W	2-1	E Grigalashvili, Chatzivasilis
24/04	a	Ermis	D	1-1	De Vriese
27/04	a	Doxa	W	2-1	Eduardo Pincelli 2
08/05	h	Aris	W	2-1	Ogungbe, E Grigalashvili
15/05	a	Pafos	D	1-1	Chatzivasilis

No	Name	Nat	DoB	Pos	Aps	(s)	Gls
77	Revaz Barabadze	GEO	04/10/88	A	5	(7)	
22	Martin Bogatinov	MKD	26/04/86	G	32		
83	Corrin Brooks-Meade	MSR	19/03/88	G	3		
6	Bruno Arrabal	BRA	22/02/92	M	25	(2)	
7	Carles Coto	ESP	11/02/88	M	31	(4)	6
13	Petros Chatziaros		10/08/82	D	5		
19	Giannis Chatzivasilis		26/04/90	A	24	(7)	6
11	Sebastian Cojocnean	ROU	11/07/89	M	8	(4)	
12	Alexandru Coman	ROU	16/10/91	M		(1)	
5	Emmerik De Vriese	BEL	14/02/85	M	23	(4)	1
5	Eduardo Pincelli	BRA	23/04/83	M	22	(5)	8
35	Marios Elia		19/05/96	A	12	(8)	3
3	Everton	BRA	15/06/84	D	21	(2)	
18	Elguja Grigalashvili	GEO	30/12/89	M	7	(5)	2
21	Shota Grigalashvili	GEO	21/06/86	M	19	(9)	3
31	Guilherme	BRA	09/11/86	A	2	(8)	1
4	Alexandru Iacob	ROU	14/04/89	D	28	(1)	1
30	Krasniqi Kreshnic	ENG	15/09/94	M		(1)	
40	Charalambos Kyriakou		15/10/89	D	33		
9	Jhon Obregón	COL	08/02/90	A	4	(7)	3
25	Ganiu Ogungbe	NGA	01/12/92	D	26	(1)	5
16	Michalis Panagiotou		31/08/96	G	1		
8	Marios Poutziouris		08/12/93	M	21	(9)	1
10	Christos Poyiatzis		27/04/78	M		(2)	
20	Thomas Prager	AUT	13/09/85	M	22	(5)	
41	Samuel Araújo	BRA	28/03/88	D	19	(5)	2
88	Beka Tugushi	GEO	24/01/89	A	3	(5)	

Nea Salamis Famagusta FC

1948 • Ammochostos (4,000) • neasalamina.com

Major honours
Cypriot Cup (1) 1990

Coach: Jan de Jonge (NED)
(22/04/16) (Georgios Langaditis);
(07/05/16) Eugen Neagoe (ROU)

2015
23/08	h	Omonia	L	3-5	Pavlou, Ćurjurić, Adorno
29/08	h	Anorthosis	L	1-3	Adorno
13/09	a	Ayia Napa	W	3-1	Makriev 2 (1p), Ćurjurić
20/09	h	Apollon	W	2-0	Makriev (p), Pavlou
26/09	a	Ermis	W	2-1	Ćurjurić, Makriev
03/10	h	Pafos	D	1-1	Ćurjurić
19/10	a	AEK	W	2-1	Makriev (p), Pavlou
26/10	h	APOEL	L	0-9	
02/11	a	Aris	L	0-2	
08/11	h	Paralimni	W	3-1	Makriev 2 (2p), Pedrito
23/11	a	AEL	W	2-0	Pavlou, Pedrito
28/11	h	Doxa	W	2-1	Pedrito, Pavlou
06/12	a	Ethnikos	D	2-2	Makriev, Pavlou
13/12	h	Omonia	L	0-2	
20/12	a	Anorthosis	L	1-2	Adorno
23/12	h	Ayia Napa	D	2-2	Pavlou, Marchev

2016
02/01	a	Apollon	L	0-3	
09/01	h	Ermis	W	3-2	Makriev, Ćurjurić, Cinquini
18/01	a	Pafos	D	2-2	Makriev 2 (2p)
24/01	h	AEK	D	0-0	
30/01	a	APOEL	L	1-6	Makriev (p)
06/02	h	Aris	D	0-0	
13/02	a	Paralimni	D	2-2	Makriev 2 (1p)
20/02	h	AEL	L	1-2	Ćurjurić
28/02	h	Doxa	D	0-0	
02/03	a	Ethnikos	D	2-2	Makriev, Adorno
05/03	h	APOEL	L	0-1	
12/03	a	Apollon	L	1-2	Makriev
19/03	h	Omonia	L	1-2	Makriev
02/04	h	Anorthosis	L	0-1	
09/04	a	AEK	L	0-2	
16/04	a	APOEL	L	1-4	Adorno
23/04	a	Apollon	L	0-3	
27/04	a	Omonia	L	0-2	
07/05	a	Anorthosis	D	1-1	Makriev
14/05	h	AEK	W	3-2	Makriev, Pavlou 2

No	Name	Nat	DoB	Pos	Aps	(s)	Gls
10	Aldo Adorno	PAR	08/04/82	A	10	(15)	5
2	Marko Andić	SRB	14/12/83	D	19	(1)	
6	Matthieu Bemba	FRA	03/03/88	M	12	(12)	
82	China	POR	15/04/82	D	28	(1)	
26	Christoforos Christofi		23/03/91	D	7	(11)	
90	Mattia Cinquini	ITA	11/05/90	D	31	(2)	1
23	Simón Colina	ESP	07/02/95	M	5	(6)	
8	Ivan Ćurjurić	CRO	29/09/89	M	28	(3)	6
15	Emiliano Fusco	ARG	02/03/86	M	7		
50	Solomon Grimes	LBR	24/07/87	D	19	(6)	
95	Arnaud Honoré	FRA	22/03/93	M		(4)	
21	Fotis Kezos		25/07/95	M	1	(2)	
17	Stavros Konstantinou		19/03/97	A	2	(2)	
30	Ioannis Kostis		17/03/00	A		(1)	
13	Giannis Kousoulos		14/06/96	D	26	(5)	
12	Kyriakos Kyriakou		20/06/92	D	5	(2)	
16	Andreas Lemesios		24/09/97	M	1	(3)	
25	Liliu	BRA	30/03/90	A	10	(4)	
9	Dimitar Makriev	BUL	07/01/84	A	35	(1)	19
3	Chrysanthos Mantzalos		04/05/96	D		(1)	
18	Veselin Marchev	BUL	07/02/90	M	3	(6)	1
19	Marcos Michael		13/06/91	A		(4)	
93	Neofytos Michael		16/12/93	G	20		
11	Koullis Pavlou		04/09/86	M	23	(4)	9
7	Pedrito	ESP	28/04/89	M	21	(7)	3
20	Giannis Skopelitis	GRE	02/05/78	M	29		
1	Pāvels Šteinbors	LVA	21/09/95	G	16		
22	Tiago Gomes	POR	18/08/85	M	12	(3)	
4	Dragan Žarković	SRB	16/04/86	D	26		

AC Omonia

1948 • GSP (23,700) • omonoia.com.cy

Major honours
*Cypriot League (20) 1961, 1966, 1972, 1974, 1975,
1976, 1977, 1978, 1979, 1981, 1982, 1983, 1984,
1985, 1987, 1989, 1993, 2001, 2003, 2010; Cypriot
Cup (14) 1965, 1972, 1974, 1980, 1981, 1982, 1983,
1988, 1991, 1994, 2000, 2005, 2011, 2012*

Coach: Kostas Kaiafas;
(11/11/15) Vladan Milojević (SRB)

2015

22/08	h	Nea Salamis	W	5-3	*Sheridan 2 (1p), Nuno Assis 2, Schembri*
29/08	a	Ethnikos	L	0-1	
12/09	h	Doxa	D	1-1	*Schembri*
19/09	h	Anorthosis	D	0-0	
27/09	a	Ayia Napa	W	2-1	*Badibanga 2*
03/10	h	Apollon	W	0-0	
18/10	h	Ermis	W	1-0	*Roushias*
24/10	h	Pafos	W	6-0	*Nuno Assis (p), Oikonomidis, Kirm, Schembri 2, Okeuhie*
01/11	a	AEK	L	1-2	*Schembri*
09/11	a	APOEL	D	2-2	*Renato Margaça, Sheridan (p)*
22/11	h	Aris	W	1-0	*Sheridan (p)*
29/11	h	Paralimni	D	2-2	*Schembri, Roushias*
06/12	a	AEL	L	1-2	*Sheridan*
13/12	a	Nea Salamis	W	2-0	*Kirm, Nuno Assis*
19/12	h	Ethnikos	W	2-1	*Sheridan (p), Schembri*
22/12	h	Doxa	W	1-0	*Nuno Assis*
2016					
02/01	h	Anorthosis	D	0-0	
09/01	h	Ayia Napa	W	4-0	*Sheridan, Nuno Assis, Schembri 2*
16/01	a	Apollon	D	0-0	
23/01	h	Ermis	W	1-0	*Sheridan (p)*
31/01	a	Pafos	W	2-1	
06/02	a	AEK	W	3-1	*Luciano Bebê, Schembri 2*
13/02	h	APOEL	L	0-2	
20/02	h	Aris	W	2-0	*Nuno Assis 2*
27/02	a	Paralimni	W	4-1	*Runje, Badibanga, Sheridan, Kirm*
03/03	h	AEL	W	4-2	*Kirm 2, Badibanga 2*
06/03	h	Anorthosis	W	3-0	*Badibanga, Sheridan 2*
12/03	a	APOEL	L	1-2	*Luciano Bebê*
19/03	a	Nea Salamis	W	2-1	*Schembri, Sheridan*
03/04	h	AEK	L	0-1	
09/04	a	Apollon	W	2-1	*Schembri 2*
16/04	a	Anorthosis	W	3-0	*Nuno Assis, Cristóvão, Sheridan*
23/04	h	APOEL	L	0-2	
27/04	h	Nea Salamis	W	2-0	*Sheridan, Schembri*
07/05	a	AEK	W	3-1	*Roushias, Christofi, Nuno Assis*
14/05	h	Apollon	L	1-2	*og (Pedro Monteiro)*

No	Name	Nat	DoB	Pos	Aps	(s)	Gls
39	Ziguy Badibanga	BEL	26/11/91	M	14	(10)	6
31	Laurențiu Brănescu	ROU	30/03/94	G	2		
4	Carlitos	CPV	23/04/85	D	16	(1)	
77	Dimitris Christofi		28/09/88	A	7	(3)	1
16	Cristóvão	POR	25/03/83	M	20	(4)	1
7	Marios Demetriou		25/12/92	A	2	(2)	
40	George Florescu	ROU	21/05/84	M	10	(2)	
20	Gerasimos Fylaktou		24/07/91	M	12	(1)	
33	Antonis Georgallides		30/01/82	G	3		
93	Hérold Goulon	FRA	12/06/88	D	7	(1)	
45	Karim Hafez	EGY	12/03/96	D	29		
24	Anastasios Kantoutsis	GRE	23/05/94	D	1	(2)	
88	Faysel Kasmi	BEL	31/10/95	M		(2)	
30	Andraž Kirm	SVN	06/09/84	M	21	(6)	5
3	Ucha Lobjanidze	GEO	23/02/87	D	10	(1)	
76	Luciano Bebê	BRA	11/03/81	M	17	(11)	2
76	Jackson Mendy	SEN	25/05/87	D	1	(1)	
21	Nuno Assis	POR	25/11/77	M	26	(2)	10
23	Georgios Oikonomidis		10/04/90	M	27	(5)	1
13	Eze Vincent Okeuhie	NGA	06/06/94	A	5	(8)	1
48	Marin Oršulić	CRO	25/08/87	D	7	(3)	
1	Konstantinos Panagi		08/10/94	G	31		
19	Andreas Panagiotou		31/05/95	D	1		
6	Matías Pérez	URU	20/07/85	D		(1)	
28	Renato Margaça	POR	17/07/85	D	16	(2)	1
5	Romaric	CIV	04/06/83	D	29	(1)	
8	Onisiforos Roushias		15/07/92	A	9	(13)	3
90	Ivan Runje	CRO	09/10/90	D	28	(2)	1
27	André Schembri	MLT	27/05/86	A	23	(7)	15
7	Cillian Sheridan	IRL	23/02/89	A	22	(9)	15

Pafos FC

2014 • Pafiako (7,650) • pafosfc.com.cy

Coach: Sofoklis Sofokleous;
(10/11/15) (Angelos Efthymiou);
(17/11/15) José Manuel Roca (ESP);
(16/12/15) Apostolos Makrides

2015

22/08	h	AEK	L	0-2	
30/08	a	APOEL	L	2-6	*Damahou, Grigalava*
12/09	h	Aris	W	3-0	*Gelashvili, Maachi, Damahou (p)*
20/09	a	Paralimni	L	1-2	*Maachi*
27/09	h	AEL	D	0-0	
03/10	a	Nea Salamis	D	1-1	*Maachi*
18/10	h	Ethnikos	W	3-0	*Gelashvili, Maachi, Grigalashvili*
24/10	a	Omonia	L	0-6	
01/11	h	Anorthosis	L	1-2	*Maachi*
07/11	a	Ayia Napa	D	1-1	*Grigalashvili*
11/11	h	Apollon	D	0-0	
28/11	a	Ermis	L	1-2	*Gelashvili*
06/12	h	Doxa	D	3-3	*Maachi, Khmaladze, Gelashvili*
12/12	a	AEK	D	0-0	
19/12	a	APOEL	L	0-1	
22/12	a	Aris	L	0-1	
2016					
02/01	h	Paralimni	D	3-3	*Khmaladze, Damahou, og (Bojović)*
09/01	a	AEL	D	0-0	
18/01	h	Nea Salamis	D	2-2	*Ayivi, Damahou*
23/01	a	Ethnikos	D	1-1	*Maachi*
31/01	h	Omonia	W	2-1	*Ibson, Maachi*
08/02	a	Anorthosis	L	1-5	*Matoukou*
14/02	h	Ayia Napa	W	4-1	*Okoye 2, Ayivi, Damahou (p)*
20/02	a	Apollon	L	1-3	*Maachi*
27/02	h	Ermis	W	2-0	*Alba, Okoye*
02/03	a	Doxa	W	3-1	*Alba, Maachi, Bodiong*
06/03	a	Doxa	W	2-1	*Alba, Maachi*
11/03	a	Aris	D	0-0	
20/03	a	Ermis	L	0-1	
03/04	h	AEL	D	1-1	*Grgec*
10/04	a	Ethnikos	L	0-3	
17/04	a	Doxa	L	1-3	*Okoye*
24/04	h	Aris	W	1-0	*Okoye*
27/04	a	Ermis	L	0-1	
08/05	a	AEL	L	0-1	
15/05	h	Ethnikos	D	1-1	*Demosthenous*

No	Name	Nat	DoB	Pos	Aps	(s)	Gls
2	Rasheed Alabi	NGA	09/01/86	D	24		
11	Miguel Alba	ARG	11/08/88	A	14		3
99	Hugues Ayivi	FRA	20/10/86	A	14	(18)	2
23	Hervé Bodiong	CMR	17/06/97	M		(7)	1
13	Carlos Marques	POR	06/02/83	D	9	(5)	
46	Jordi Codina	ESP	27/04/82	G	16		
3	Joël Damahou	CIV	28/01/87	M	32	(2)	5
56	Charalambos Demosthenous		16/04/90	M	21	(7)	1
9	Nikoloz Gelashvili	GEO	05/08/85	A	12	(2)	4
44	Jurica Grgec	CRO	01/09/92	M	25	(2)	1
30	Elguja Grigalashvili	GEO	30/12/89	M	6	(7)	2
5	Gia Grigalava	GEO	05/08/89	D	16		1
10	Hugo Moutinho	POR	01/01/82	M	13	(7)	
95	Ibson	BRA	08/11/89	A	17	(2)	1
21	Thomas Ioannou		19/07/95	D	33		
7	Ivan Forbes	POR	01/12/86	D	29	(3)	
88	Levan Khmaladze	GEO	06/04/85	M	29	(2)	2
1	Jānis Krūmiņš	LVA	09/01/92	G	5	(1)	
89	Roin Kvaskhvadze	GEO	31/05/89	G	15		
16	Nassir Maachi	NED	09/09/85	A	29	(2)	11
12	Anastasios Makris		29/07/92	M	9	(4)	
14	Eric Matoukou	CMR	08/07/83	D	13		1
97	Stefanos Miller		14/01/97	D	1	(1)	
31	Emmanuel Okoye	NGA	04/04/91	A	9	(23)	5
8	Georgios Sielis		23/10/86	M	1	(6)	
17	Panagiotis Zachariou		26/02/96	M	4	(4)	

Top goalscorers

André Alves

Fernando Cavenaghi

Dimitar Makriev

19	André Alves (AEK)
	Fernando Cavenaghi (APOEL)
	Dimitar Makriev (Nea Salamis)
17	Dino Ndlovu (Anorthosis)
15	Tomás De Vincenti (APOEL)
	André Schembri (Omonia)
	Cillian Sheridan (Omonia)
13	Alhassane Keita (Ermis)
11	Georgios Efrem (APOEL)
	Nassir Maachi (Pafos)

CYPRUS

Promoted clubs

Karmiotissa Pano Polemidia FC

1979 • Pano Polemidia Municipal (1,500) • karmiotissafc.com
Coach: Liasos Louka

AEZ Zakakiou FC

1956 • Zakaki Municipal (1,800) • no website
Coach: Nikolas Martides (GRE)

Anagennisi Derynia FC

1920 • Anagennisi (4,000) • no website
Coach: Adamos Adamou

Second level final table 2015/16

		Pld	W	D	L	F	A	Pts
1	Karmiotissa Pano Polemidia FC	26	20	1	5	54	19	61
2	AEZ Zakakiou FC	26	19	3	4	47	18	60
3	Anagennisi Derynia FC	26	17	8	1	50	18	59
4	Olympiakos Nicosia FC	26	20	2	4	51	19	59
5	Othellos Athienou FC	26	17	5	4	55	24	56
6	ENTHOI Lakatamia FC	26	11	2	13	44	48	35
7	ENAD Polis-Chrysochous FC	26	9	6	11	30	32	33
8	PAEEK FC	26	10	3	13	32	29	33
9	Omonia Aradippou FC	26	9	5	12	28	29	30
10	Enosis Neon Parekklisias FC	26	6	8	12	34	37	26
11	ASIL Lysi FC	26	6	7	13	31	36	25
12	Elpida Xylofagou FC	26	3	6	17	24	60	15
13	Nikos & Sokratis Erimis FC	26	2	3	21	13	79	9
14	AS Digenis Voroklinis	26	1	5	20	16	61	8

NB Olympiakos Nicosia FC – 3 pts deducted; Omonia Aradippou FC – 2 pts deducted.

DOMESTIC CUP

Cyprus Cup 2015/16

FIRST ROUND

(28/10/15)
AEZ 0-3 Ethnikos Achnas
Anagennisi Derynia 1-1 Digenis Voroklinis *(aet; 3-2 on pens)*
Anorthosis 9-0 Elpida Xylofagou
ASIL Lysi 4-3 Doxa *(aet)*
Ayia Napa 5-1 Karmiotissa
ENAD 0-2 Aris Limassol
ENTHOI 1-6 Apollon
Nicos & Sokratis 2-1 Othellos
Omonia 2-0 PAEEK

(04/11/15)
EN Parekklisias 1-5 Ermis
Paralimni 0-1 Olympiakos

(02/12/15)
Omonia Aradippou 0-3 Nea Salamis

Byes – AEK, AEL, APOEL, Pafos

SECOND ROUND

(06/01/16 & 13/01/16)
AEK 5-0, 8-1 Nicos & Sokratis *(13-1)*
Aris 1-0, 3-1 Olympiakos *(4-1)*

(06/01/16 & 20/01/16)
Anorthosis 2-1, 0-0 Anagennisi Derynia *(2-1)*
Omonia 2-0, 3-1 Ethnikos Achnas *(5-1)*

(06/01/16 & 26/01/16)
Pafos 3-0, 2-0 ASIL Lysi *(5-0)*

(13/01/16 & 20/01/16)
AEL 1-0, 2-1 Ayia Napa *(3-1)*

(13/01/16 & 27/01/16)
Nea Salamis 0-1, 2-3 APOEL *(2-4)*

(20/01/16 & 27/01/16)
Apollon 3-1, 1-0 Ermis *(4-1)*

QUARTER-FINALS

(03/02/16 & 17/02/16)
AEK 3-0 Anorthosis *(Joan Tomàs 30, Boljević 45, Mytides 51)*
Anorthosis 2-2 AEK *(Makris 55, 76; Trickovski 26, Mytides 34)*
(AEK 5-2)

Omonia 4-0 Pafos *(Schembri 26, Badibanga 29, 64, Christofi 79)*
Pafos 0-4 Omonia *(Kasmi 40, Okeuhie 42, Hafez 64, Kirm 68)*
(Omonia 8-0)

(10/02/16 & 17/02/16)
APOEL 1-1 Aris *(Cavenaghi 18p; Randy 15)*
Aris 1-3 APOEL *(Maragoudakis 63; Efrem 49, De Vincenti 77, Aloneftis 81)*
(APOEL 4-2)

(10/02/16 & 24/02/16)
Apollon 2-0 AEL *(Gneki Guié 81, Slavchev 83)*
AEL 0-1 Apollon *(Wheeler 90+4)*
(Apollon 3-0)

SEMI-FINALS

(06/04/16 & 20/04/16)
AEK 0-0 Omonia
Omonia 0-0 AEK *(aet)*
(0-0; Omonia 5-3 on pens)

APOEL 1-1 Apollon *(Sotiriou 29; Gneki Guié 20)*
Apollon 1-1 APOEL *(Alex 44; Efrem 45) (aet)*
(2-2; Apollon 5-4 on pens)

FINAL

(18/05/16)
Tsirion, Limassol
APOLLON LIMASSOL FC 2 *(Papoulis 5, Angeli 72)*
AC OMONIA 1 *(Renato Margaça 51)*
Referee: *Vučemilović (CRO)*
APOLLON: *Bruno Vale, Stylianou (Mezga 69), Angeli, Freire, Vasiliou, Sachetti, Kyriakou (Jaime 90), João Pedro (Nuno Lopes 87), Alex, Papoulis, Gneki Guié*
OMONIA: *Georgallides, Renato Margaça, Runje, Romaric, Hafez, Cristóvão (Christofi 80), Florescu, Nuno Assis (Roushias 87), Kirm (Carlitos 70), Schembri, Sheridan*

Apollon defeated Omonia 2-1 on home turf in Limassol to win the Cypriot Cup

CZECH REPUBLIC
Fotbalová asociace České republiky (FAČR)

Address	Diskařská 2431/4	**President**	Miroslav Pelta
	CZ-160 17 Praha	**General secretary**	Rudolf Řepka
Tel	+420 2 3302 9111	**Media officer**	Ondřej Lípa
Fax	+420 2 3335 3107	**Year of formation**	1901
E-mail	facr@fotbal.cz		
Website	fotbal.cz		

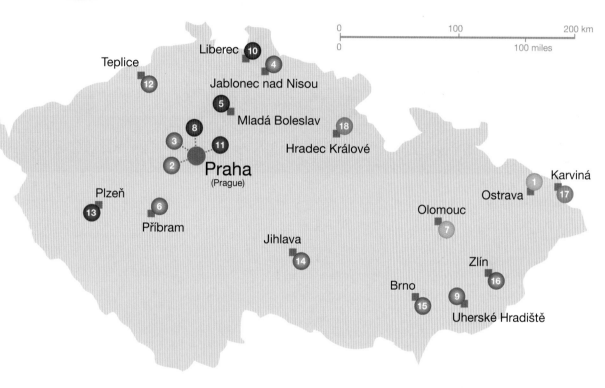

1. LIGA CLUBS

  1 FC Baník Ostrava

 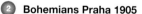 2 Bohemians Praha 1905

  3 FK Dukla Praha

  4 FK Jablonec

  5 FK Mladá Boleslav

  6 1. FK Příbram

  7 SK Sigma Olomouc

  8 SK Slavia Praha

 9 1. FC Slovácko

 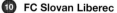 10 FC Slovan Liberec

  11 AC Sparta Praha

  12 FK Teplice

  13 FC Viktoria Plzeň

  14 FC Vysočina Jihlava

  15 FC Zbrojovka Brno

 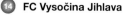 16 FC Zlín

PROMOTED CLUBS

 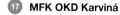 17 MFK OKD Karviná

  18 FC Hradec Králové

KEY

- ● UEFA Champions League
- ● UEFA Europa League
- ○ Promoted
- ○ Relegated

Viktoria Plzeň rule again

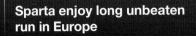

Viktoria Plzeň retained the 1. Liga title in 2015/16 to become champions of the Czech Republic for the fourth time in six seasons. A two-team tussle with Sparta Praha turned into a one-horse race as Karel Krejčí's side notched up 16 victories in a row to cross the line with three games to spare.

Sparta outran Plzeň in Europe, however, reaching the quarter-finals of the UEFA Europa League, while there was a second Czech Cup win for the league's top-scoring team Mladá Boleslav, who defeated Jablonec 2-0 in the Teplice final.

| **Record winning sequence brings fourth title** | **Sparta enjoy long unbeaten run in Europe** | **Vrba's national side struggle in France** |

Domestic league

There was a change in coach at Plzeň in the early weeks of the campaign as Miroslav Koubek, the 2014/15 title-winning boss, paid the price for a faulty start and was replaced by Krejčí, the assistant to Pavel Vrba in the club's first two championship-winning campaigns of 2010/11 and 2012/13. Under the new man Plzeň were a team transformed, Slovakian striker Michal Ďuriš scoring eight goals in six games – all victories – to send the defending champions soaring up the table. A surprise 1-0 defeat in Brno stopped them in their tracks, but seven days later they beat Sparta 2-1 to join them at the top of the table. When the league closed down for the winter, Plzeň held a three-point lead.

To the five straight wins that had carried them into the break Krejčí's side added another 11, setting a new Czech league record for consecutive victories. Better still, they ended any lingering doubts about the outcome of the title race by completing the double over Sparta with a sumptuous 3-0 victory at the Letná, where Zdeněk Ščasný's side had a 100% record. Six days later, with a routine 2-0 win at home to bottom club Baník Ostrava, Plzeň were champions.

Krejčí's men visibly eased off after completing the job and lost their final three games, the last of them 5-0 at Slavia

Praha, but even then seven points still separated them from runners-up Sparta, whose own 5-0 win on the final day, against Vysočina Jihlava, featured a full house from striker David Lafata, enabling him to overtake Ďuriš and scoop the league's top scorer prize for the fourth time in five seasons. Ďuriš was one of three Slovakian internationals – alongside goalkeeper Matúš Kozáčik and midfielder Patrik Hrošovský – who enjoyed memorable seasons for Plzeň, while Roman Hubník, who returned from a loan spell at Sigma Olomouc in mid-season, formed an excellent central-defensive alliance with Jan Baránek.

Olomouc would end up relegated alongside Moravian rivals Ostrava, while Slovan Liberec, Mladá Boleslav and Slavia all secured UEFA Europa League berths. Sparta's European prize was the same as Plzeň's – a third qualifying round spot in the UEFA Champions League.

Domestic cup

Plzeň and Sparta were both eliminated in the semi-finals of the Czech Cup, and it was the champions' conquerors, Mladá Boleslav, who went on to reclaim the trophy they had won five years earlier. Jablonec, their opponents, had beaten them on penalties in the 2013 final before losing in the same fashion to Liberec in 2015, but there would be no fourth successive final shoot-out thanks

to two goals in four second-half minutes, from Jan Chramosta and Jasmin Ščuk, which gave Mladá Boleslav's experienced coach Karel Jarolím his first cup success.

Europe

There were three Czech teams in the UEFA Europa League group stage – Plzeň, Sparta and Liberec – but only one stayed around to contest the knockout phase. Sparta, indeed, went all the way to the quarter-finals, remaining unbeaten until Villarreal defeated them home and away. Even then they retained their record of scoring in every game, with the three first-half goals they fired past Lazio in Rome standing out as their champagne moment.

National team

The Czech Republic qualified for UEFA EURO 2016 as group winners from a very competitive section, but the lustre had gone from Vrba's team when they reached France, and the only point they managed from their three group games came courtesy of a late equalising penalty against a Croatia team that had outplayed them for practically the entire game. After such an overwhelming experience, in which no Czech player excelled, Vrba was replaced by Jarolím for the 2018 FIFA World Cup qualifiers.

DOMESTIC SEASON AT A GLANCE

1. Liga 2015/16 final table

		Pld	Home					Away					Total					Pts
			W	D	L	F	A	W	D	L	F	A	W	D	L	F	A	
1	**FC Viktoria Plzeň**	30	13	1	1	32	10	10	1	4	25	15	23	2	5	57	25	71
2	AC Sparta Praha	30	14	0	1	41	9	6	4	5	20	15	20	4	6	61	24	64
3	FC Slovan Liberec	30	12	2	1	33	15	5	5	5	18	20	17	7	6	51	35	58
4	FK Mladá Boleslav	30	11	3	1	44	18	5	6	4	19	19	16	9	5	63	37	57
5	SK Slavia Praha	30	8	6	1	31	13	6	4	5	17	13	14	10	6	48	26	52
6	FC Zbrojovka Brno	30	11	2	2	23	12	3	3	9	14	26	14	5	11	37	38	47
7	FK Jablonec	30	6	7	2	25	13	4	4	7	21	26	10	11	9	46	39	41
8	1. FC Slovácko	30	9	2	4	26	20	3	2	10	11	31	12	4	14	37	51	40
9	Bohemians Praha 1905	30	6	6	3	18	12	2	7	6	17	25	8	13	9	35	37	37
10	FK Dukla Praha	30	7	2	6	25	13	1	9	5	19	28	8	11	11	44	41	35
11	FC Vysočina Jihlava	30	5	6	4	21	19	3	1	11	10	35	8	7	15	31	54	31
12	FK Teplice	30	4	7	4	17	17	3	2	10	20	35	7	9	14	37	52	30
13	FC Zlín	30	5	5	5	17	17	2	4	9	17	33	7	9	14	34	50	30
14	1. FK Příbram	30	3	3	9	20	29	4	3	8	13	24	7	6	17	33	53	27
15	SK Sigma Olomouc	30	5	6	4	26	18	1	3	11	9	31	6	9	15	35	49	27
16	FC Baník Ostrava	30	3	1	11	15	27	1	1	13	12	38	4	2	24	27	65	14

European qualification 2016/17

Champion: FC Viktoria Plzeň (third qualifying round)
AC Sparta Praha (third qualifying round)

Cup winner: FK Mladá Boleslav (third qualifying round)
FC Slovan Liberec (third qualifying round)
SK Slavia Praha (second qualifying round)

Top scorer	David Lafata (Sparta), 20 goals
Relegated clubs	FC Baník Ostrava, SK Sigma Olomouc
Promoted clubs	MFK OKD Karviná, FC Hradec Králové
Cup final	FK Mladá Boleslav 2-0 FK Jablonec

Team of the season
(4-4-2)

Coach: Krejčí (Plzeň)

Bičík (Sparta)

Deli (Slavia) — Hubník (Plzeň) — Baránek (Plzeň) — Pokorný (Liberec)

Dočkal (Sparta) — Čermák (Mladá Boleslav) — Souček (Slavia) — Krejčí (Sparta)

Ďuriš (Plzeň) — Lafata (Sparta)

Player of the season

Bořek Dočkal
(AC Sparta Praha)

Sparta went trophyless for the fifth time in six seasons, but it was not for the want of trying. They finished second to a relentless Viktoria Plzeň in the 1. Liga title race, reached the semi-finals of the Czech Cup and quarter-finals of the UEFA Europa League. Central to their efforts was Dočkal, who confirmed his status as the country's best midfielder with several top-notch displays. Having played such a key role in the Czech Republic's UEFA EURO 2016 qualification, it was a frustration that he saw so little action in France.

Newcomer of the season

Patrik Schick
(Bohemians Praha 1905)

Sent out on loan from Sparta Praha to Bohemians in 2015/16, Schick used the experience to good effect, scoring eight goals to finish as the Kangaroos' top scorer and help them into a comfortable mid-table position free of relegation worries. The gifted 20-year-old forward was handed his first senior cap for the Czech Republic – after many at various youth levels – and scored on his debut, against Malta. He was on Pavel Vrba's shortlist for UEFA EURO 2016 but just missed out on the final 23-man squad.

CZECH REPUBLIC

NATIONAL TEAM

International honours*
UEFA European Championship (1) 1976.

International tournament appearances*
FIFA World Cup (9) 1934 (runners-up), 1938 (qtr-finals), 1954, 1958, 1962 (runners-up), 1970, 1982, 1990 (qtr-finals), 2006
UEFA European Championship (9) 1960 (3rd), 1976 (Winners), 1980 (3rd), 1996 (runners-up), 2000, 2004 (semi-finals), 2008, 2012 (qtr-finals), 2016.

Top five all-time caps
Petr Čech (124); Karel Poborský (118); Tomáš Rosický (105); Jaroslav Plašil (103); Milan Baroš (93)

Top five all-time goals
Jan Koller (55); Milan Baroš (41); Antonín Puč (35); Zdeněk Nehoda (32); Oldřich Nejedlý & Pavel Kuka (29)

(* before 1996 as Czechoslovakia)

Results 2015/16

03/09/15	Kazakhstan (ECQ)	H	Plzen	W	2-1	Škoda (74, 86)
06/09/15	Latvia (ECQ)	A	Riga	W	2-1	Limberský (13), Darida (25)
10/10/15	Turkey (ECQ)	H	Prague	L	0-2	
13/10/15	Netherlands (ECQ)	A	Amsterdam	W	3-2	Kadeřábek (24), Šural (35), Van Persie (66og)
13/11/15	Serbia	H	Ostrava	W	4-1	Sivok (17), Necid (63p), Krejčí (82), Zahustel (90+3)
17/11/15	Poland	A	Wroclaw	L	1-3	Krejčí (41)
24/03/16	Scotland	H	Prague	L	0-1	
29/03/16	Sweden	A	Solna	D	1-1	Vydra (26)
27/05/16	Malta	N	Kufstein (AUT)	W	6-0	Plašil (15), Škoda (22), Hubník (40), Lafata (74), Necid (81), Schick (90+1)
01/06/16	Russia	N	Innsbruck (AUT)	W	2-1	Rosický (50), Necid (90)
05/06/16	South Korea	H	Prague	L	1-2	Suchý (46)
13/06/16	Spain (ECF)	N	Toulouse (FRA)	L	0-1	
17/06/16	Croatia (ECF)	N	Saint-Etienne (FRA)	D	2-2	Škoda (76), Necid (89p)
21/06/16	Turkey (ECF)	N	Lens (FRA)	L	0-2	

Appearances 2015/16

Pavel Vrba	06/12/63		KAZ	LVA	TUR	NED	Srb	Pol	Sco	Swe	Mlt	Rus	Kor	ESP	CRO	TUR	Caps	Goals
Petr Čech	20/05/82	Arsenal (ENG)	G	G		G		G			G46	G	G	G	G	G	124	-
Pavel Kadeřábek	25/04/92	Hoffenheim (GER)	D	D	D	D	D	s76	D		D66	s64	D46	D	D	D	21	2
Marek Suchý	29/03/88	Basel (SUI)	D	D	D	D 43*		D		D			s46				27	1
Václav Procházka	08/05/84	Plzeň	D	D	D	s46		D									15	-
David Limberský	06/10/83	Plzeň	D	D					D		D46	D64	s46	D	D		40	1
David Pavelka	18/05/91	Liberec /Kasımpaşa (TUR)	M	M	M	M	M				M66	M46	M46	s88		M57	10	-
Vladimír Darida	08/08/90	Hertha (GER)	M68	M	M	M	M86	s84	M87	M60	s46	M	M	M	M	M	39	1
Bořek Dočkal	30/09/88	Sparta Praha	M	M90	M78		M56		M65	s86		M41				M71	25	6
Jiří Skalák	12/03/92	Mladá Boleslav /Brighton (ENG)	M46		s54	M	M71	s57	s46	M60	s46	s41	s46		M67		11	-
Ladislav Krejčí	05/07/92	Sparta Praha	M84	s54	M54		s71	M58		M	M46	M	M70	M	M	M	26	4
David Lafata	18/09/81	Sparta Praha	A		A						s46	A46		s75	A67		41	9
Milan Škoda	16/01/86	Slavia Praha	s46	A	s67	s86	s80	A67			A46		s79		s67	s57	11	4
Josef Šural	30/05/90	Liberec /Sparta Praha	s68	M77	M67	M71	M71	s58	M78	s60	M46		M46	s86	s67	s71	14	1
Jan Kopic	04/06/90	Plzeň	s84														2	-
Daniel Kolář	27/10/85	Plzeň			M54				s65	M86	s66	s85				s90	29	2
Ondřej Vaněk	05/07/90	Plzeň			s77												8	-
Theodor Gebre Selassie	24/12/86	Bremen (GER)			s90		D			D	s46	D	D 60*	M86			37	1
Tomáš Vaclík	29/03/89	Basel (SUI)			G		G		G								6	-
Filip Novák	26/06/90	Midtjylland (DEN)			D												2	-
Milan Petržela	19/06/83	Plzeň			s78												17	-
Michal Kadlec	13/12/84	Fenerbahçe (TUR)				D	D		D			D	D46				65	8
Jaroslav Plašil	05/01/82	Bordeaux (FRA)			M86	s56	M				M46	s46	s46	M	M86	M90	103	7
Tomáš Necid	13/08/89	Bursaspor (TUR)			A46	A80	s67	A65	s72		s46	s46	A79	A75	s86	A	42	12
Tomáš Kalas	15/05/93	Middlesbrough (ENG)			s71		D76										3	-
Tomáš Sivok	15/09/83	Bursaspor (TUR)				D			D	D60	D		s46	D	D	D	58	5
Daniel Pudil	27/09/85	Sheffield Wednesday (ENG)				D	s76	s78	D				s70			D	33	2
Ondřej Zahustel	18/06/91	Mladá Boleslav				s71	M57										2	1
Kamil Vacek	18/05/87	Piast (POL)				s86	M	M78									9	-
Lukáš Bartošák	03/07/90	Liberec					D76										1	-
Martin Pospíšil	26/06/91	Jablonec					M84										3	-
Tomáš Koubek	26/08/92	Liberec							G		s46						2	-
Martin Frýdek	24/03/92	Sparta Praha							M46	s60							2	-
Matěj Vydra	01/05/92	Reading (ENG)							s65	A72							17	5
Lukáš Mareček	17/04/90	Sparta Praha							s78	M72	s66						3	-
Jakub Rada	05/05/87	Mladá Boleslav							s87	s72							2	-
Jakub Brabec	06/08/92	Sparta Praha								s60							1	-
Roman Hubník	06/06/84	Plzeň									D	D46		D	D	D	29	3
Tomáš Rosický	04/10/80	Arsenal (ENG)									M66	M85	M	M88	M		105	23
Patrik Schick	24/01/96	Bohemians 1905									s66						1	1

FC Viktoria Plzeň

Third qualifying round - Maccabi Tel-Aviv FC (ISR)
A 2-1 *Mahmutović (17), Petržela (21)*
Kozáčik, Hubník, Hořava, Limberský, Vaněk, Petržela (Kopic 86), Kovařík, Procházka, Mahmutović (Holenda 75), Kolář (Hrošovský 70), Rajtoral. Coach: Miroslav Koubek (CZE)
H 0-2
Kozáčik, Hubník, Hořava, Limberský, Vaněk, Petržela (Kopic 83), Kovařík, Procházka, Mahmutović (Ďuriš 58), Kolář (Holenda 84), Rajtoral. Coach: Miroslav Koubek (CZE)

Play-offs - FK Vojvodina (SRB)
H 3-0 *Kopic (25, 82), Vaněk (51)*
Kozáčik, Hubník, Limberský, Vaněk, Kopic, Ďuriš (Holenda 86), Hrošovský, Kovařík (Petržela 78), Procházka, Kolář (Hořava 69), Rajtoral. Coach: Karel Krejčí (CZE)
A 2-0 *Djurić (19og), Ďuriš (60)*
Kozáčik, Hubník, Baránek 54), Limberský, Vaněk, Kopic, Petržela (Vůch 72), Ďuriš, Hrošovský, Procházka, Kolář (Mahmutović 81), Rajtoral. Coach: Karel Krejčí (CZE)

Group E
Match 1 - FC Dinamo Minsk (BLR)
H 2-0 *Hořava (36), Petržela (59)*
Kozáčik, Hořava (Kučera 90+1), Limberský, Vaněk, Kopic, Ďuriš (Holenda 83), Hrošovský, Kovařík (Petržela 74), Procházka, Baránek, Rajtoral. Coach: Karel Krejčí (CZE)
Match 2 - Villarreal CF (ESP)
A 0-1
Kozáčik, Hořava, Limberský, Kopic (Hejda 81), Petržela (Mahmutović 75), Ďuriš, Hrošovský, Kovařík (Vůch 88), Procházka, Baránek, Rajtoral. Coach: Karel Krejčí (CZE)
Red card: Procházka 80
Match 3 - SK Rapid Wien (AUT)
A 2-3 *Ďuriš (12), Hrošovský (76)*
Kozáčik, Hejda, Hořava (Kolář 58), Limberský, Vaněk (Holenda 80), Kopic (Petržela 58), Ďuriš, Hrošovský, Kovařík, Baránek, Rajtoral. Coach: Karel Krejčí (CZE)
Match 4 - SK Rapid Wien (AUT)
H 1-2 *Holenda (71)*
Kozáčik, Hejda, Hořava, Limberský, Petržela (Kopic 63), Ďuriš, Hrošovský, Kovařík, Procházka, Kolář (Holenda 70), Rajtoral (Mahmutović 81). Coach: Karel Krejčí (CZE)
Match 5 - FC Dinamo Minsk (BLR)
A 0-1
Bolek, Matějů, Limberský, Kopic (Rajtoral 73), Hrošovský, Kovařík (Holenda 83), Procházka, Baránek, Mahmutović (Ďuriš 63), Kolář, Kučera. Coach: Karel Krejčí (CZE)
Match 6 - Villarreal CF (ESP)
H 3-3 *Kolář (8p), Kovařík (65), Hořava (90)*
Bolek, Hejda, Matějů, Hořava, Limberský, Kopic (Petržela 83), Holenda (Mahmutović 71), Kovařík, Baránek, Kolář, Kučera (Procházka 88). Coach: Karel Krejčí (CZE)

AC Sparta Praha

Third qualifying round - PFC CSKA Moskva (RUS)
A 2-2 *Fatai (15), Krejčí (57)*
Bičík, Vácha, Fatai (Konaté 57), Matějovský, Dočkal (Brabec 90+2), Mareček, Frýdek, Krejčí (Marco Paixão 84), Holek, Nhamoinesu, Hybš. Coach: Zdeněk Ščasný (CZE)
H 2-3 *Krejčí (6), Fatai (16)*
Bičík, Vácha, Fatai (Lafata 54), Matějovský, Dočkal, Mareček, Frýdek, Krejčí (Hušbauer 87), Holek (Konaté 64), Nhamoinesu, Hybš. Coach: Zdeněk Ščasný (CZE)
Red card: Matějovský 64

Play-offs - FC Thun (SUI)
H 3-1 *Nhamoinesu (43), Dočkal (45+1, 90+4)*
Bičík, Vácha (Frýdek 29), Fatai (Marco Paixão 72), Dočkal, Mareček, Lafata, Hušbauer (Konaté 55), Krejčí, Holek, Nhamoinesu, Hybš. Coach: Zdeněk Ščasný (CZE)
A 3-3 *Dočkal (10), Hušbauer (21), Nhamoinesu (71)*
Bičík, Dočkal, Mareček, Frýdek, Steinhöfer, Lafata (Fatai 82), Hušbauer (Litsingi 27), Krejčí, Holek, Nhamoinesu, Hybš (Breznaník 68). Coach: Zdeněk Ščasný (CZE)
Red card: Breznaník 85

Group K
Match 1 - Asteras Tripolis FC (GRE)
A 1-1 *Lafata (56)*
Bičík, Matějovský, Dočkal, Frýdek, Lafata, Hušbauer (Fatai 66), Krejčí, Jiráček (Mareček 83), Holek, Nhamoinesu, Hybš. Coach: Zdeněk Ščasný (CZE)
Match 2 - APOEL FC (CYP)
H 2-0 *Fatai (24), Brabec (60)*
Bičík, Brabec, Fatai (Konaté 86), Matějovský, Dočkal, Mareček, Frýdek, Lafata, Krejčí (Steinhöfer 90+1), Jiráček, Nhamoinesu. Coach: Zdeněk Ščasný (CZE)
Match 3 - FC Schalke 04 (GER)
A 2-2 *Fatai (50), Lafata (63)*
Bičík, Brabec, Fatai (Holek 88), Matějovský (Hušbauer 90+2), Dočkal, Mareček, Konaté (Lafata 62), Krejčí, Jiráček, Nhamoinesu, Hybš. Coach: Zdeněk Ščasný (CZE)
Match 4 - FC Schalke 04 (GER)
H 1-1 *Lafata (6)*
Bičík, Brabec, Fatai (Konaté 88), Matějovský, Dočkal, Mareček, Lafata (Juliš 90), Krejčí, Jiráček, Nhamoinesu, Hybš. Coach: Stanislav Hejkal (CZE)
Match 5 - Asteras Tripolis FC (GRE)
H 1-0 *Brabec (33)*
Bičík, Brabec, Vácha, Fatai (Konaté 80), Dočkal (Holek 86), Mareček, Frýdek (Juliš 90+2), Lafata, Krejčí, Nhamoinesu, Hybš. Coach: Zdeněk Ščasný (CZE)
Red card: Krejčí 82
Match 6 - APOEL FC (CYP)
A 3-1 *Juliš (63), Lafata (77, 87)*
Štěch, Brabec, Vácha (Lafata 74), Fatai (Matějovský 46), Dočkal, Mareček, Frýdek, Konaté, Holek, Nhamoinesu, Juliš (Litsingi 85). Coach: Zdeněk Ščasný (CZE)

Round of 32 - FC Krasnodar (RUS)
H 1-0 *Juliš (64)*
Bičík, Brabec, Vácha, Fatai (Jiráček 89), Dočkal (Matějovský 80), Mareček, Zahustel, Krejčí, Holek, Nhamoinesu, Juliš (Konaté 78). Coach: Zdeněk Ščasný (CZE)

A 3-0 *Mareček (51), Frýdek (57), Fatai (70)*
Bičík, Brabec, Vácha, Fatai (Juliš 76), Dočkal (Konaté 84), Mareček (Matějovský 79), Frýdek, Zahustel, Krejčí, Holek, Nhamoinesu. Coach: Zdeněk Ščasný (CZE)

Round of 16 - SS Lazio (ITA)
H 1-1 *Frýdek (13)*
Bičík, Brabec, Vácha, Dočkal (Fatai 59), Mareček, Frýdek, Zahustel, Lafata (Juliš 62), Krejčí, Holek, Nhamoinesu. Coach: Zdeněk Ščasný (CZE)
A 3-0 *Dočkal (10), Krejčí (12), Juliš (44)*
Bičík, Brabec, Vácha (Matějovský 70), Dočkal, Mareček, Frýdek, Zahustel, Krejčí (Fatai 83), Holek, Nhamoinesu, Juliš (Konaté 58). Coach: Zdeněk Ščasný (CZE)

Quarter-final - Villarreal CF (ESP)
A 1-2 *Brabec (45+4)*
Bičík, Brabec, Matějovský (Lafata 88), Dočkal, Mareček, Frýdek, Konaté, Krejčí, Holek (Kováč 28), Nhamoinesu, Juliš (Fatai 73). Coach: Zdeněk Ščasný (CZE)
H 2-4 *Dočkal (65), Krejčí (71)*
Bičík, Fatai, Matějovský, Dočkal, Mareček, Frýdek, Kováč, Konaté, Lafata, Krejčí, Juliš. Coach: Zdeněk Ščasný (CZE)

FC Slovan Liberec

Third qualifying round - Hapoel Kiryat Shmona FC (ISR)
H 2-1 *Delarge (43), Shala (84)*
Koubek, Coufal, Rabušic (Bakoš 73), Pavelka, Hovorka, Sackey, Švejdík, Kerbr (Shala 53), Šural, Bartošák, Delarge (Fleišman 86). Coach: Jindřich Trpišovský (CZE)
A 3-0 *Pavelka (33), Šural (44), Bakoš (52)*
Koubek, Coufal, Pavelka, Shala (Kerbr 82), Folprecht, Hovorka, Šural, Bartošák, Bakoš (Rabušic 80), Delarge (Sackey 76), Pokorný. Coach: Jindřich Trpišovský (CZE)

Play-offs - HNK Hajduk Split (CRO)
H 1-0 *Pokorný (79)*
Koubek, Coufal, Pavelka, Shala (Sackey 79), Folprecht, Hovorka, Šural, Bartošák, Bakoš (Rabušic 62), Delarge (Kerbr 90+1), Pokorný. Coach: Jindřich Trpišovský (CZE)
A 1-0 *Šural (23)*
Koubek, Coufal, Pavelka, Shala (Soungole 90), Hovorka, Sackey (Fleišman 75), Šural, Bartošák, Bakoš, Delarge (Kerbr 49), Pokorný. Coach: Jindřich Trpišovský (CZE)

Group F
Match 1 - SC Braga (POR)
H 0-1
Koubek, Coufal, Pavelka, Shala (Rabušic 65), Hovorka, Soungole (Sýkora 64), Šural, Bartl, Bartošák, Bakoš (Kerbr 75), Pokorný. Coach: Jindřich Trpišovský (CZE)
Match 2 - Olympique de Marseille (FRA)
A 1-0 *Coufal (84)*
Koubek, Coufal, Sýkora, Rabušic (Bakoš 46), Pavelka, Shala (Bartl 74), Hovorka, Efremov, Šural (Kerbr 90), Bartošák, Pokorný. Coach: Jindřich Trpišovský (CZE)
Match 3 - FC Groningen (NED)
H 1-1 *Luckassen (87)*
Koubek, Coufal, Pavelka, Shala (Bartl 84), Folprecht, Švejdík, Efremov, Šural (Sackey 89), Bartošák, Bakoš (Luckassen 61), Pokorný. Coach: Jindřich Trpišovský (CZE)

DOMESTIC LEAGUE CLUB-BY-CLUB

Match 4 - FC Groningen (NED)
A 1-0 *Padt (81og)*
Koubek, Coufal, Pavelka, Shala, Folprecht, Švejdík, Efremov (Kerbr 90+4), Šural, Bartošák (Sýkora 60), Bakoš (Rabušic 73), Pokorný. Coach: Jindřich Trpišovský (CZE)

Match 5 - SC Braga (POR)
A 1-2 *Efremov (35)*
Koubek, Coufal (Sýkora 85), Shala, Folprecht, Hovorka, Švejdík, Efremov (Rabušic 62), Kerbr (Mudra 76), Bartošák, Bakoš, Pokorný. Coach: Jindřich Trpišovský (CZE)

Match 6 - Olympique de Marseille (FRA)
H 2-4 *Bakoš (75p), Šural (76)*
Koubek, Coufal, Kerbr 89), Pavelka, Shala (Šural 66), Folprecht (Rabušic 60), Hovorka, Švejdík, Efremov, Bartošák, Bakoš. Coach: Jindřich Trpišovský (CZE)

FK Jablonec

Third qualifying round - FC København (DEN)
H 0-1
Hrubý, Hübschman, Pernica, Novák, Crnkić, Wágner (Doležal 77), Karavaev, Beneš, Greguš, Pospíšil (Trávník 62), Masopust (Tecl 62). Coach: Jaroslav Šilhavý (CZE)
Red card: Tecl 69
A 3-2 *Wágner (14), Greguš (53), Pospíšil (83)*
Hrubý, Hübschman, Pernica, Novák, Crnkić (Daniel Rossi 88), Wágner (Doležal 82), Karavaev, Beneš, Greguš, Pospíšil, Masopust (Mingazov 72). Coach: Jaroslav Šilhavý (CZE)

Play-offs - AFC Ajax (NED)
A 0-1
Hrubý, Hübschman, Pernica, Novák, Crnkić, Mingazov (Masopust 67), Wágner (Doležal 84), Karavaev, Beneš, Greguš, Pospíšil (Trávík 72). Coach: Jaroslav Šilhavý (CZE)
H 0-0
Hrubý, Hübschman, Pernica, Novák, Crnkić (Doležal 68), Mingazov, Wágner (Tecl 46), Karavaev, Beneš, Greguš (Trávník 75), Pospíšil. Coach: Jaroslav Šilhavý (CZE)

FK Mladá Boleslav

Second qualifying round - Strømsgodset IF (NOR)
H 1-2 *Bartl (39)*
Veselovský, Kúdela, Ščuk, Chramosta (Magera 64), Kysela, Zahustel, Rada, Klobása (Štohanzl 77), Mendy, Bartl (Čermák 64), Křapka. Coach: Karel Jarolím (CZE)
A 1-0 *Čermák (31)*
Veselovský, Čermák (Ščuk 79), Bořil, Kúdela, Magera, Kysela, Zahustel, Rada, Malpon (Chramosta 77), Klobása (Skalák 67), Křapka. Coach: Karel Jarolím (CZE)

FC Baník Ostrava

1922 • Stadion Bazaly (15,123) • fcb.cz
Major honours
Czechoslovakian/Czech League (4) 1976, 1980, 1981, 2004; Czechoslovakian/Czech Cup (4) 1973, 1978, 1991, 2005
Coach: Radomír Korytář;
(04/01/16) Vlastimil Petržela

2015
25/07	a Brno	L	1-2	Kukec
01/08	a Sparta	L	1-3	Kouřil
08/08	h Mladá Boleslav	D	2-2	Narh 2
15/08	a Zlín	L	0-2	
22/08	h Slavia	L	1-3	Mišák
14/09	a Dukla	L	1-4	Narh
19/09	h Jablonec	L	1-2	Kukec (p)
26/09	a Teplice	L	0-1	
02/10	h Sigma	W	1-0	Machovec
17/10	a Slovácko	L	1-2	Kukec
24/10	h Příbram	L	0-2	
31/10	a Liberec	L	1-2	Červenka
08/11	h Plzeň	L	0-4	
21/11	a Bohemians 1905	L	1-3	Dostál
28/11	h Jihlava	L	1-2	og (Krejčí)
06/12	h Sparta	L	0-1	

2016
14/02	a Mladá Boleslav	L	0-3	
20/02	h Zlín	W	3-0	Holzer, Mondek, Lásik
28/02	a Slavia	L	1-3	Dyjan
06/03	h Dukla	L	1-2	Hrubý
11/03	a Jablonec	D	1-1	Vraštil
19/03	h Teplice	L	1-2	Holzer
01/04	a Sigma	L	2-6	Holzer, og (Ševčík)
09/04	h Slovácko	W	2-1	Hrubý 2
16/04	a Příbram	W	2-1	Dyjan, og (Bednář)
23/04	h Liberec	L	0-2	
30/04	a Plzeň	L	0-2	
07/05	h Bohemians 1905	L	1-2	Hrubý (p)
11/05	a Jihlava	L	0-3	
14/05	h Brno	L	1-2	Meschaninov

No	Name	Nat	DoB	Pos	Aps	(s)	Gls
27	Namir Alispahić	BIH	16/04/95	A		(3)	
15	Zdeněk Behan		05/03/96	M		(1)	
24	Josef Celba		30/01/95	D	5	(2)	
26	Marek Červenka		17/12/92	A	10	(8)	1
16	František Chmiel		15/06/97	G	6		
14	Martin Dostál		23/09/89	D	18	(1)	1
7	Dyjan	BRA	23/06/91	M	16	(9)	2
9	Vojtěch Engelmann		04/07/89	M	4	(4)	
23	Martin Foltýn		17/08/93	M	2	(1)	
21	Michal Frydrych		27/02/90	D	4		
6	Denis Granečný		07/09/98	M	8	(1)	
2	Matěj Helešic		12/11/96	D	2	(4)	
21	Daniel Holzer		18/08/95	M	24	(3)	3
22	Martin Honiš		26/01/96	D	3		
8	Robert Hrubý		27/04/94	M	12		4
4	Václav Ježdík		03/07/87	D	14		
4	Adam Karčmář		08/10/96	M		(1)	
18	Filip Kaša		01/01/94	D	28		
18	Martin Kouřil		24/02/91	D	6	(2)	1
7	Davor Kukec	CRO	16/03/86	M	13	(2)	3
18	Richard Lásik	SVK	18/08/92	M	19		1
28	Luka Lučić	CRO	02/01/95	D	11		
20	Jaroslav Machovec	SVK	05/09/86	A	10		1
10	Jan Matěj		04/06/96	M	1	(3)	
28	Derrick Mensah	GHA	28/05/95	M	4		
32	Artem Meschaninov	RUS	19/02/96	D	7	(4)	1
25	Tomáš Mičola		26/09/88	M	5	(1)	
17	Patrik Mišák	SVK	29/03/91	A	7	(3)	1
17	Karol Mondek	SVK	02/06/91	M	23	(5)	1
15	Francis Narh	GHA	18/04/94	A	14	(1)	3
13	Daniel Ožvolda		11/01/96	M	7	(1)	
1	Jiří Pavlenka		14/04/92	G	16		
29	Radim Plesník		11/10/96	D		(1)	
31	Jakub Šašinka		02/10/95	A	4	(10)	
9	Ondřej Šašinka		21/03/98	A	3		
8	Marek Šichor		17/07/90	M		(3)	
30	Vojtěch Šrom		03/05/88	G	8		
9	Ondřej Sukup		08/12/88	D	2	(1)	
23	Jakub Švehlík		18/11/96	M		(1)	
29	Marek Szotkowski		18/01/96	A		(6)	
12	Tomáš Vengřínek		08/06/92	D	3	(2)	
27	Lukáš Vraštil		10/03/94	D	11	(1)	1

Bohemians Praha 1905

1905 • Ďolíček (5,000) • bohemians.cz
Major honours
Czechoslovakian League (1) 1983
Coach: Roman Pivarník

2015
26/07	h Zlín	L	0-1	
02/08	a Jablonec	D	2-2	Acosta, Čížek
08/08	h Sigma	D	1-1	Šmíd
15/08	a Dukla	D	2-2	Jindřišek (p), Zlámal
22/08	h Příbram	D	1-1	Bartek
12/09	a Teplice	L	1-2	Schick
20/09	h Plzeň	L	0-1	
26/09	a Slovácko	L	0-1	
04/10	a Liberec	L	1-3	Schick
17/10	h Brno	D	1-1	Hubínek
25/10	a Sparta	L	0-3	
31/10	h Jihlava	W	2-1	Jindřišek (p), Acosta
08/11	h Slavia	D	2-2	og (Deli), Jindřišek (p)
21/11	h Baník	W	3-1	Acosta, Schick 2
28/11	a Mladá Boleslav	D	1-1	Jirásek
05/12	h Jablonec	W	2-1	Bartek, Krch

2016
13/02	a Sigma	D	2-2	Schick, Acosta
20/02	h Dukla	W	1-0	Krch
27/02	a Příbram	D	0-0	
05/03	h Teplice	D	1-1	Schick
12/03	a Plzeň	L	0-2	
19/03	h Slovácko	W	2-0	Hubínek, Mosquera
02/04	a Liberec	L	0-1	
08/04	a Brno	L	1-2	Čížek
17/04	h Sparta	D	2-2	Acosta, Šmíd
23/04	a Jihlava	W	2-1	Šmíd, Hubínek
01/05	h Slavia	D	0-0	
07/05	a Baník	W	2-1	Schick, Bartek
11/05	h Mladá Boleslav	W	2-0	Lulić, Acosta
14/05	a Zlín	D	1-1	Schick

No	Name	Nat	DoB	Pos	Aps	(s)	Gls
16	Rafael Acosta	URU	02/10/90	M	22	(2)	6
9	Leonid Akulinin	UKR	07/03/93	A	4	(16)	
5	David Bartek		13/02/88	M	12	(8)	3
22	Tomáš Čížek		27/11/78	M	14	(8)	2
7	Peter Čögley	SVK	11/08/88	D	12		
30	Tomáš Fryšták		18/08/87	G	1		
13	Zoran Gajić	SRB	18/05/90	D	5	(10)	
25	Pavel Hašek		27/06/83	M	3	(1)	
24	Milan Havel		07/08/94	M	19	(2)	
20	Tomas Hradecky	FIN	13/10/92	M	1	(1)	
16	Michal Hubínek		10/11/94	M	16	(3)	3
7	Marek Jarolím		21/05/84	M		(2)	
4	Josef Jindřišek		14/02/81	M	16		3
4	Milan Jirásek		14/05/92	M	24		1
19	Dominik Kostka		04/05/96	M	1		
15	Daniel Krch		20/03/92	D	21		2
23	Karlo Lulić	CRO	19/05/96	A	5	(3)	1
18	Matúš Mikuš	SVK	08/07/91	A	3	(9)	
18	Jhon Mosquera	COL	08/05/90	M	24	(4)	1
3	Lukáš Pauschek	SVK	09/12/92	D	15		
12	Václav Prošek		08/04/93	M	1	(1)	
17	Patrik Schick		24/01/96	A	22	(5)	8
11	Radek Šírl		20/03/81	D	10		
28	Aleš Škerle		14/06/82	D	12	(2)	
14	Michal Šmíd		20/10/86	D	24	(4)	3
2	Michal Švec		19/03/87	D	14		
30	Zdeněk Zlámal		05/11/85	G	29		1

FK Dukla Praha

1958 • Na Julisce (8,150) • fkdukla.cz
Coach: Luboš Kozel

2015

25/07	a	Slovácko	L 3-4	Berger, Tetour, Krmenčík
01/08	h	Plzeň	W 1-0	Berger
10/08	a	Liberec	D 1-1	Berger (p)
15/08	h	Bohemians 1905	D 2-2	Berger 2
23/08	a	Sparta	L 0-2	
14/09	h	Baník	W 4-1	Přikryl, Vrzal, Berger, Hanousek
18/09	a	Jihlava	D 2-2	Přikryl, Krmenčík
26/09	h	Brno	L 1-2	Berger
04/10	a	Slavia	D 1-1	Krmenčík
16/10	h	Mladá Boleslav	D 1-1	Čajić
24/10	a	Jablonec	D 3-3	Krmenčík 2, Štětina
30/10	h	Zlín	W 1-0	Vrzal
07/11	h	Příbram	L 0-1	
21/11	a	Sigma	D 0-0	
27/11	h	Teplice	W 4-0	Čajić, Gorkšs 2, Přikryl
06/12	a	Plzeň	L 0-3	

2016

12/02	h	Liberec	W 2-0	Berger, og (Karafiát)
20/02	a	Bohemians 1905	L 0-1	
06/03	a	Baník	W 2-1	Vrzal, Berger
12/03	h	Jihlava	L 0-1	
19/03	h	Brno	L 0-3	
03/04	h	Slavia	L 0-1	
09/04	a	Mladá Boleslav	D 2-2	Mareš, Manzia
15/04	h	Jablonec	W 6-1	Vrzal, Gorkšs, Tetour, Mareš 2, Manzia
20/04	h	Sparta	L 1-2	Tetour
24/04	a	Zlín	D 2-2	Néstor Albiach 2
30/04	a	Příbram	D 2-2	Mareš, Néstor Albiach
06/05	h	Sigma	W 2-0	Štětina, Vrzal
11/05	a	Teplice	D 1-1	Berger
14/05	h	Slovácko	L 0-1	

No	Name	Nat	DoB	Pos	Aps	(s)	Gls
9	Jean-David Beauguel	FRA	21/03/92	A	8	(11)	
13	Tomáš Berger		22/08/85	M	26		10
21	David Bezdička		09/07/96	A		(1)	
6	Michal Bezpalec		19/08/96	M		(3)	
32	Michal Breznaník	SVK	16/12/85	M	5	(1)	
8	Aldin Čajić	BIH	11/09/92	M	17	(8)	2
31	Kaspars Gorkšs	LVA	06/11/81	D	23		3
5	Marek Hanousek		06/08/91	M	29		1
33	Marek Hlinka	SVK	04/10/90	M	1		
30	Lukáš Hroššo	SVK	19/04/87	G	1		
2	Michal Jeřábek		10/09/93	D	10	(3)	
17	Josip Jurendić	CRO	26/07/89	D	13	(4)	
16	Róbert Kovaľ	SVK	16/01/94	M	1	(1)	
11	Michael Krmenčík		15/03/93	A	8	(4)	5
21	Budje Manzia	COD	24/09/95	A	4	(5)	2
26	Jakub Mareš		26/01/87	M	18	(7)	4
20	Branislav Milošević	SRB	13/05/88	D	20		
10	Néstor Albiach	ESP	18/08/92	A	10	(8)	3
7	Jakub Považanec	SVK	31/01/91	M	29	(1)	
1	Dominik Preisler		20/09/95	D	1	(3)	
32	Tomáš Přikryl		04/07/92	M	8	(2)	3
1	Filip Rada		05/09/84	G	26		
22	Michal Smejkal		21/02/86	D		(5)	
19	Lukáš Štětina	SVK	24/07/91	D	25		2
15	Daniel Tetour		17/07/94	M	18	(11)	3
18	Václav Vašíček		10/02/91	A	4	(5)	
23	Ondřej Vrzal		01/03/87	D	22	(1)	5

FK Jablonec

1945 • Stadion Střelnice (6,108) • fkjablonec.cz
Major honours
Czech Cup (2) 1998, 2013
Coach: Jaroslav Šilhavý; (13/02/16) Zdenko Frťala

2015

25/07	a	Příbram	W 3-2	Karavaev, Greguš, Wágner
02/08	h	Bohemians 1905	D 2-2	Doležal, Masopust
10/08	a	Jihlava	L 0-1	
16/08	h	Liberec	D 1-1	Beneš
23/08	a	Brno	W 3-0	Greguš, Masopust, Doležal
13/09	h	Sparta	D 1-1	Wágner (p)
19/09	a	Baník	W 2-1	Crnkić, Mingazov
25/09	h	Mladá Boleslav	L 1-2	Tecl (p)
03/10	a	Zlín	D 2-2	Pospíšil, Masopust
17/10	h	Slavia	D 0-0	
24/10	h	Dukla	D 3-3	Pospíšil (p), Doležal, Wágner (p)
31/10	a	Slovácko	D 1-1	Pospíšil
06/11	h	Sigma	W 4-0	Doležal, Pernica, Tecl, Pospíšil
22/11	a	Teplice	D 2-2	Mingazov 2
30/11	h	Plzeň	L 0-1	
05/12	a	Bohemians 1905	L 1-2	Karavaev

2016

13/02	h	Jihlava	W 2-0	Pernica, Tecl (p)
20/02	a	Liberec	L 2-3	Tecl (p), Kysela
27/02	h	Brno	W 3-0	Tecl 2, Karavaev
06/03	a	Sparta	L 1-2	Greguš
11/03	h	Baník	D 1-1	Doležal
19/03	a	Mladá Boleslav	L 0-1	
02/04	h	Zlín	W 3-1	Masopust, Mihálik, Beneš
09/04	a	Slavia	D 0-0	
15/04	a	Dukla	L 1-6	Kysela
24/04	h	Slovácko	W 3-1	Tecl, Masopust, Doležal
30/04	a	Sigma	L 1-2	Mihálik
08/05	h	Teplice	W 1-0	Pernica
11/05	a	Plzeň	W 2-1	Mingazov 2
14/05	h	Příbram	D 0-0	

No	Name	Nat	DoB	Pos	Aps	(s)	Gls
20	Michal Bárta		23/12/89	G	9		
23	Vít Beneš		12/08/88	D	16	(1)	2
14	David Breda		04/01/96	M	3	(2)	
9	Nermin Crnkić	BIH	31/08/92	M	6	(2)	1
8	Daniel Rossi	BRA	04/01/81	M	11	(6)	
15	Martin Doležal		03/05/90	A	12	(14)	6
24	Ján Greguš	SVK	29/01/91	M	21	(4)	3
5	Matěj Hanousek		02/06/93	D	7	(5)	
30	Vlastimil Hrubý		21/02/85	G	20		
3	Tomáš Hübschman		04/09/81	M	25		
7	Matěj Hybš		03/01/93	D	10	(8)	
22	Vyacheslav Karavaev	RUS	20/05/95	D	27	(2)	3
27	Vojtěch Kubista		19/03/93	M	2		
6	Marek Kysela		10/07/92	D	17		2
28	Lukáš Masopust		12/02/93	M	15	(11)	5
17	Ondřej Mihálik		02/04/97	A	5	(2)	2
7	Ruslan Mingazov	TKM	23/11/91	M	14	(2)	5
7	Filip Novák		26/06/90	D	3		
4	Luděk Pernica		16/06/90	D	27		3
26	Martin Pospíšil		26/06/91	M	25	(3)	4
16	José Romera	ESP	08/09/87	D	13		
1	Michal Špit		09/04/75	G		(1)	
11	Stanislav Tecl		01/09/90	A	20	(6)	7
18	Michal Trávnik		17/05/94	M	11	(12)	
2	Roman Valeš		06/03/90	G	1		
19	Tomáš Wágner		06/03/90	A	10	(16)	3

FK Mladá Boleslav

1902 • Adidas Arena (5,000) • fkmb.cz
Major honours
Czech Cup (2) 2011, 2016
Coach: Karel Jarolím

2015

26/07	a	Liberec	L 2-4	Magera, Skalák
02/08	h	Brno	W 2-0	Čermák, Chramosta
08/08	a	Baník	D 2-2	og (Kouřil), Skalák
14/08	h	Sparta	L 2-4	Skalák, Zahustel
21/08	h	Zlín	W 5-2	Magera 2, Čermák, Zahustel, og (Holý)
12/09	a	Slavia	D 1-1	Skalák
19/09	h	Teplice	W 4-3	Magera (p), Zahustel, Čermák, Šćuk
25/09	a	Jablonec	W 2-1	Čermák, Magera (p)
03/10	h	Příbram	W 4-0	Skalák, Zahustel 2, Magera
16/10	a	Dukla	D 1-1	Magera (p)
24/10	a	Slovácko	W 4-1	Baroš 2, Skalák, og (Daníček)
31/10	a	Sigma	W 2-1	Magera 2 (1p)
07/11	h	Jihlava	W 6-1	Rada, Šćuk, Magera, Baroš, Chramosta, Zahustel
21/11	a	Plzeň	L 0-1	
28/11	h	Bohemians 1905	D 1-1	Zahustel
06/12	a	Brno	D 1-1	Chramosta

2016

14/02	h	Baník	W 3-0	Baroš 2, Čermák
21/02	a	Sparta	L 0-2	
27/02	a	Zlín	W 2-0	Magera (p), Čermák
05/03	h	Slavia	W 2-1	Magera (p), Rada
12/03	h	Teplice	D 0-0	
19/03	h	Jablonec	W 1-0	Kúdela
02/04	a	Příbram	W 3-2	Kalabiška, og (Zápotočný), Rada
09/04	h	Dukla	D 2-2	Klobása, Chramosta
16/04	a	Slovácko	W 2-0	Jánoš, Magera (p)
22/04	h	Sigma	W 4-1	Čmovš, Chramosta, Přikryl, Takács
29/04	a	Jihlava	D 1-1	Šćuk
07/05	h	Plzeň	W 2-0	Magera (p), Baroš
11/05	a	Bohemians 1905	L 0-2	
14/05	a	Liberec	D 2-2	Rada 2

No	Name	Nat	DoB	Pos	Aps	(s)	Gls
27	Milan Baroš		28/10/81	A	6	(15)	6
33	Daniel Bartl		05/07/89	M	3	(1)	
8	Jan Bořil		11/01/91	D	15		
7	Aleš Čermák		01/10/94	M	23	(3)	6
19	Jan Chramosta		12/10/90	A	12	(14)	5
24	Pavel Čmovš		29/06/90	D	11	(1)	1
23	Jakub Diviš		27/07/86	G	6		
3	Jiří Fleišman		02/10/84	D	18	(1)	
6	Adam Jánoš		20/07/92	M	13		1
9	Jan Kalabiška		22/12/86	M	10	(4)	1
31	Stanislav Klobása		07/03/94	A	1	(8)	1
34	Antonín Křapka		22/01/94	D	2		
22	Vojtěch Kubista		19/03/93	D			
11	Ondřej Kúdela		26/03/87	D	29		1
20	Jan Kysela		17/12/85	D	12	(3)	
18	Lukáš Magera		17/01/83	A	28		14
30	Kevin Malpon	FRA	01/03/96	M	5	(1)	
21	Lukáš Pauschek	SVK	09/12/92	D	5		
2	Roman Polom		11/01/92	D	9		
32	Tomáš Přikryl		04/07/92	M	5	(7)	1
25	Jakub Rada		05/05/87	M	26		5
17	Jasmin Šćuk	BIH	14/07/90	M	23	(4)	3
28	Jan Šeda		17/12/85	G	23		
24	Jan Šisler		24/04/88	M	3		
16	Rudolf Skácel		17/07/79	M		(2)	
10	Jiří Skalák		12/03/92	M	15	(1)	6
22	Laco Takács		15/07/96	D	5	(7)	1
29	Martin Toml		25/03/96	M	1		
26	Róbert Veselovský	SVK	02/09/85	G	1		
33	Jan Vodháněl		25/04/97	M	1		
13	Lukáš Vraštil		10/03/94	D	6		
21	Ondřej Zahustel		18/06/91	D	14	(1)	7

CZECH REPUBLIC

1. FK Příbram

1928 • Energon Arena (7,900) • fkpribram.cz
Coach: Pavel Tobiáš;
(03/05/16) Martin Pulpit

2015
25/07	h	Jablonec	L	2-3	Pilík, Bednář
01/08	a	Sigma	W	3-1	Bednář 2 (1p), Hnaníček
08/08	h	Teplice	W	3-2	Rezek, Bednář, Hnaníček
16/08	a	Slovácko	L	1-2	Rezek
22/08	a	Bohemians 1905	D	1-1	Rezek
13/09	h	Plzeň	L	0-4	
20/09	a	Liberec	L	0-3	
26/09	a	Jihlava	W	4-1	Hnaníček, Pilík 3
03/10	a	Mladá Boleslav	L	0-4	
18/10	h	Sparta	L	0-4	
24/10	a	Baník	W	2-0	Rezek, Barák
31/10	h	Brno	D	1-1	Barák
07/11	a	Dukla	W	1-0	og (Hanousek)
21/11	h	Zlín	L	1-2	Tregler
28/11	a	Slavia	L	1-2	Divišek
05/12	h	Sigma	W	3-0	Hnaníček, Barák, Bednář

2016
13/02	a	Teplice	L	0-2	
20/02	h	Slovácko	L	0-1	
27/02	h	Bohemians 1905	D	0-0	
06/03	a	Plzeň	L	0-4	
12/03	h	Liberec	L	0-1	
18/03	a	Jihlava	W	3-1	Tregler, Bednář, Suchan
02/04	a	Mladá Boleslav	L	2-3	og (Kúdela), Bednář
10/04	a	Sparta	L	1-2	Šabala
16/04	h	Baník	L	1-2	Šabala
24/04	a	Brno	L	0-2	
30/04	h	Dukla	D	2-2	Pilík (p), og (Hanousek)
07/05	a	Zlín	D	0-0	
11/05	h	Slavia	L	1-3	Brandner
14/05	a	Jablonec	D	0-0	

No	Name	Nat	DoB	Pos	Aps	(s)	Gls
3	Antonín Barák		03/12/94	M	8	(4)	3
19	Roman Bednář		26/03/83	A	25		7
7	Patrik Brandner		04/01/94	A		(15)	1
3	Matěj Chaluš		02/02/98	D	9	(2)	
24	Josef Divišek		24/09/90	D	20		1
18	Radek Dosoudil		20/06/83	D	9	(3)	
15	Vojtěch Hadaščok		08/01/92	A	2	(7)	
20	Tomáš Hájovský	SVK	10/12/82	D	6		
29	Josef Hnaníček		28/12/86	M	27		4
13	Aleš Hruška		23/11/85	G	30		
16	Jiří Januška		11/10/97	M		(5)	
12	David Kilián		07/12/94	M		(2)	
8	Matěj Končal		08/12/93	M	7	(2)	
23	Martin Krameš		17/08/93	M	15	(2)	
21	Jiří Mareš		16/02/92	M	1	(8)	
10	Jakub Moravec		10/02/96	M		(5)	
15	Jan Mudra		22/01/90	D	14		
22	Denis Laňka		13/05/97	A		(3)	
25	Tomáš Pilík		20/12/88	M	28	(1)	5
11	Jan Rezek		05/05/82	M	25	(1)	4
12	Petr Rys		15/01/96	M	1	(1)	
21	Valērijs Šabala	LVA	12/10/94	A	5	(2)	2
6	David Štípek		31/05/92	M	24	(1)	
14	Jan Suchan		18/01/96	M	10	(7)	1
4	Martin Sus		15/03/90	D	17		
30	Jaroslav Tregler		01/12/95	D	17	(4)	2
17	Jan Vošahlík		08/03/89	A	4	(3)	
5	Tomáš Zápotočný		13/09/80	D	26		

SK Sigma Olomouc

1919 • Andrův stadion (12,541) •
sigmafotbal.cz
Major honours
Czech Cup (1) 2012
Coach: Leoš Kalvoda;
(19/10/15) Václav Jílek

2015
25/07	a	Teplice	D	2-2	Petr, Hála
01/08	h	Příbram	L	1-3	Navrátil
08/08	a	Bohemians 1905	D	1-1	Vašíček
15/08	h	Brno	D	1-1	Chorý
23/08	a	Plzeň	L	0-2	
12/09	h	Jihlava	W	2-1	Plšek, Malec
20/09	a	Sparta	L	0-4	
26/09	h	Zlín	D	1-1	Ordoš
02/10	a	Baník	L	0-1	
17/10	h	Liberec	D	1-1	Houska
23/10	a	Slavia	W	2-0	Houska 2
31/10	h	Mladá Boleslav	L	1-2	Halenár
06/11	a	Jablonec	L	0-4	
21/11	h	Dukla	D	0-0	
28/11	a	Slovácko	W	2-0	Malec 2 (1p)
05/12	a	Příbram	L	0-3	

2016
13/02	h	Bohemians 1905	D	2-2	Ordoš, Mahmutović
20/02	a	Brno	L	0-2	
27/02	h	Plzeň	L	0-1	
05/03	a	Jihlava	L	1-2	Falta
13/03	h	Sparta	L	0-2	
19/03	a	Zlín	D	0-0	
01/04	h	Baník	W	6-2	Ordoš, Ševčík, Plšek (p), Navrátil, Petr, Malec
09/04	a	Liberec	L	1-2	Ševčík
16/04	h	Slavia	D	1-1	Navrátil
22/04	a	Mladá Boleslav	L	1-4	Falta
30/04	h	Jablonec	W	2-1	Šindelář, Ordoš
06/05	a	Dukla	L	0-2	
11/05	a	Slovácko	L	1-2	Navrátil
14/05	h	Teplice	W	6-0	Štěrba 2, Chorý, Ordoš, Navrátil, Mahmutović

No	Name	Nat	DoB	Pos	Aps	(s)	Gls
30	Miloš Buchta		19/07/80	G	25		
9	Denis Cana	MNE	08/10/87	M	6		
15	Tomáš Chorý		26/01/95	A	6	(12)	2
20	Šimon Falta		23/04/93	M	14	(6)	2
12	Martin Hála		24/03/92	D	28		1
14	Juraj Halenár	SVK	28/06/83	A	6	(4)	1
8	David Houska		29/06/93	M	22	(5)	3
44	Roman Hubník		06/06/84	D	7		
14	Aidin Mahmutović	BIH	06/04/86	A	5	(5)	2
29	Tomáš Malec	SVK	05/01/93	A	6	(9)	4
7	Pavel Moulis		07/04/91	A	8	(2)	
10	Jan Navrátil		13/04/90	M	28		5
7	Michal Ordoš		27/01/83	M	15	(7)	5
22	Jakub Petr		10/04/90	A	20	(8)	2
3	Jakub Plšek		13/12/93	M	18	(3)	2
26	Uroš Radaković	SRB	31/03/94	D	27		
17	Jan Rajnoch		30/09/81	D	12	(2)	
1	Milan Reichl		14/09/92	G	5		
27	Renārs Rode	LVA	06/04/89	D	2		
24	Petr Ševčík		04/05/94	M	11	(1)	2
13	Martin Šindelář		22/01/91	D	18	(3)	1
5	Vojtěch Štěpán		08/06/85	D	1	(7)	
12	Jan Štěrba		08/07/94	D	4	(3)	2
4	Jaroslav Svozil		09/09/93	D	1		
16	Václav Vašíček		10/02/91	A	8	(2)	1
21	Michal Vepřek		10/06/85	D	26		
23	Tomáš Zahradníček		11/08/93	M	1	(10)	

SK Slavia Praha

1892 • Eden Arena (20,800) • slavia.cz
Major honours
Czechoslovakian/Czech League (16) 1925, 1929,
1930, 1931, 1933, 1934, 1935, 1937, 1940, 1941,
1942, 1943, 1947, 1996, 2008, 2009; Czech Cup (3)
1997, 1999, 2002
Coach: Dušan Uhrin Jr

2015
24/07	h	Plzeň	L	1-2	Škoda
02/08	h	Liberec	D	2-2	Škoda, Mikula
07/08	a	Brno	L	0-1	
16/08	h	Jihlava	W	4-0	Škoda 2, Deli, Souček
22/08	a	Baník	W	3-1	Voltr, Škoda 2
12/09	h	Mladá Boleslav	D	1-1	og (Polom)
19/09	a	Zlín	W	2-0	Kenia, Souček
27/09	h	Sparta	W	1-0	Zmrhal
04/10	h	Dukla	D	1-1	Škoda
17/10	a	Jablonec	D	0-0	
23/10	h	Sigma	L	0-2	
01/11	a	Teplice	W	1-0	Bílek
08/11	h	Bohemians 1905	D	2-2	Škoda 2
21/11	a	Slovácko	W	2-0	Vukadinović, Zmrhal
28/11	h	Příbram	W	2-1	Škoda (p), Piták
06/12	a	Liberec	L	1-2	Zmrhal

2016
13/02	h	Brno	W	2-0	Mešanović, Bílek
19/02	a	Jihlava	D	0-0	
28/02	h	Baník	W	3-1	Souček 3
05/03	a	Mladá Boleslav	L	1-2	Mešanović
11/03	h	Zlín	W	1-0	Souček
20/03	a	Sparta	L	1-3	Škoda
03/04	a	Dukla	W	1-0	og (Štětina)
09/04	a	Jablonec	D	0-0	
16/04	a	Sigma	D	1-1	Zmrhal
23/04	h	Teplice	D	2-2	Škoda 2
01/05	a	Bohemians 1905	D	0-0	
08/05	h	Slovácko	W	5-1	Barák 2, Hušbauer, Bílek, Škoda
11/05	a	Příbram	W	3-1	Souček, Mešanović, Barák
14/05	h	Plzeň	W	5-0	Mihálik, Barák, Mešanović, Hušbauer, Vukadinović

No	Name	Nat	DoB	Pos	Aps	(s)	Gls
27	Antonín Barák		03/12/94	M	6	(3)	4
18	Josef Bazal		06/11/93	M	1	(4)	
12	Martin Berkovec		12/02/89	G	22	(1)	
20	Jan Bílek		04/11/83	D	16	(6)	3
8	Jan Bořil		11/01/91	D	11		
16	Milan Černý		16/03/88	M	8	(6)	
27	Marek Červenka		17/12/92	A		(1)	
19	Simon Deli	CIV	27/10/91	D	28		1
17	Dame Diop	SEN	15/03/93	A		(1)	
30	Martin Dostál		23/09/89	D	1		
25	Michal Frydrych		27/02/90	D	13	(2)	
15	Libor Holík		12/05/98	D		(1)	
4	Robert Hrubý		27/04/94	M	6	(3)	
10	Josef Hušbauer		16/03/90	M	13		2
6	Tomáš Jablonský		21/06/87	D	21		
11	Levan Kenia	GEO	18/10/90	M	7	(9)	1
10	Jan Kuchta		08/01/97	A		(1)	
28	Martin Latka		28/09/84	D	12	(1)	
24	Muris Mešanović	BIH	06/07/90	A	9	(4)	4
17	Jaroslav Mihálik	SVK	27/07/94	M	10	(1)	1
3	Jan Mikula		05/01/92	D	20	(2)	1
1	Jiří Pavlenka		14/04/92	G	8		
23	Karel Piták		28/01/80	M	10	(10)	1
21	Milan Škoda		16/01/86	A	24	(1)	14
22	Tomáš Souček		27/02/95	M	29		7
9	Jan Štohanzl		20/03/85	M	6	(4)	
2	Michal Švec		19/03/87	D	4	(2)	
24	Radek Voltr		28/11/91	A	9	(6)	1
14	Miljan Vukadinović	SRB	27/12/92	A	8	(8)	2
2	Lukáš Železník		18/06/90	A	4	(4)	
8	Jaromír Zmrhal		31/07/93	M	24	(3)	4

1. FC Slovácko

1894 • Městský fotbalový stadion
Miroslava Valenty (8,121) • fcslovacko.cz
Coach: Svatopluk Habanec

2015

25/07	h Dukla	W 4-3	Havlík, Došek 3
01/08	a Teplice	L 0-2	
09/08	a Plzeň	D 2-2	Došek, Daníček
16/08	h Příbram	W 2-1	Daníček, Kovář
22/08	a Jihlava	W 2-1	Valenta, Hlúpík
12/09	h Liberec	L 1-2	Havlík
19/09	a Brno	L 0-2	
26/09	h Bohemians 1905	W 1-0	Diviš
04/10	a Sparta	L 0-4	
17/10	h Baník	W 2-1	Diviš 2
23/10	a Mladá Boleslav	L 1-4	Došek
31/10	h Jablonec	D 1-1	Diviš
07/11	a Zlín	L 1-2	Došek
21/11	h Slavia	L 0-2	
28/11	a Sigma	L 0-2	
04/12	h Teplice	W 4-2	Diviš 2, Valenta, Sumulikoski

2015

14/02	h Plzeň	L 1-2	Kerbr (p)
20/02	a Příbram	W 1-0	Došek
27/02	a Jihlava	W 3-1	Sumulikoski, Koné, Havlík
06/03	a Liberec	D 0-0	
12/03	h Brno	W 2-1	Havlík (p), Košút
19/03	a Bohemians 1905	L 0-2	
02/04	h Sparta	W 2-0	Koné, Čivić
09/04	a Baník	L 1-2	Hofmann
16/04	h Mladá Boleslav	L 0-2	
23/04	a Jablonec	L 1-3	Došek
30/04	h Zlín	D 1-1	Koné
08/05	a Slavia	L 1-5	Diviš
11/05	h Sigma	W 2-1	Valenta (p), Diviš
14/05	a Dukla	W 1-0	

No	Name	Nat	DoB	Pos	Aps	(s)	Gls
15	Matěj Biolek		09/02/91	M	10	(2)	
19	Tomáš Břečka		12/05/94	D	9	(4)	
21	Juraj Chvátal	SVK	13/07/96	D	14	(4)	
24	Petr Chyla		05/05/94	D	4		
3	Eldar Čivić	BIH	28/05/96	M	21	(3)	1
25	Michal Daněk		06/07/83	G	1	(1)	
14	Vlastimil Daníček		15/07/91	D	15	(7)	2
9	Jaroslav Diviš		09/07/86	M	21	(5)	9
7	Libor Došek		24/04/78	A	18	(7)	8
20	Marek Havlík		08/07/95	M	29	(1)	4
29	Milan Heča		23/03/91	G	29		
8	Filip Hlúpík		30/04/91	M	7	(7)	1
6	Stanislav Hofmann		17/06/90	D	17	(2)	1
13	Milan Kerbr		10/09/89	A	4	(4)	1
26	Francis Koné	TOG	22/11/90	A	9	(8)	3
22	Tomáš Košút	SVK	13/01/90	D	17	1	
13	Marián Kovář		13/08/93	A	1	(8)	1
13	Filip Kubala		02/09/99	M		(1)	
11	Martin Kuncl		01/04/84	D	5	(4)	
1	Jakub Prajza		21/12/93	M		(1)	
4	Tomáš Rada		15/02/83	D	21	(3)	
23	Petr Reinberk		23/05/89	D	25		
18	Lukáš Sadílek		23/05/96	M	9	(8)	
16	Patrik Šimko	SVK	08/07/91	D	5		
5	Velice Sumulikoski	MKD	24/04/81	M	23	(1)	2
11	Jiří Valenta		14/02/88	M	16	(2)	3

FC Slovan Liberec

1958 • U Nisy (9,900) • fcslovanliberec.cz
Major honours
Czech League (3) 2002, 2006, 2012; Czech Cup (2) 2000, 2015
Coach: Jindřich Trpišovský

2015

26/07	h Mladá Boleslav	W 4-2	Šural (p), Bakoš, Bartošák, Švejdík
02/08	a Slavia	D 2-2	Bakoš, Šural
10/08	h Dukla	D 1-1	Šural
16/08	a Jablonec	D 1-1	Luckassen
23/08	h Teplice	W 2-0	Bakoš 2
12/09	a Slovácko	W 2-1	Bakoš, Šural
20/09	h Příbram	W 3-0	Pokorný, og (Dosoudil), Shala
26/09	a Plzeň	L 1-2	Shala
04/10	h Bohemians 1905	W 3-1	Kerbr, Coufal, Pavelka (p)
17/10	a Sigma	D 1-1	Kerbr
25/10	a Jihlava	D 1-1	Bartošák
31/10	h Baník	W 2-1	Bakoš, Šural
08/11	a Brno	L 1-3	Rabušic
22/11	h Sparta	W 1-0	Delarge
30/11	a Zlín	L 0-2	
06/12	h Slavia	W 2-1	Bakoš, Pavelka

2016

12/02	a Dukla	L 0-2	
20/02	h Jablonec	W 3-2	Bakoš 3
27/02	a Teplice	W 3-0	Shala, Vůch 2
06/03	h Slovácko	D 0-0	
12/03	a Příbram	W 1-0	Shala
20/03	h Plzeň	L 0-1	
02/04	a Bohemians 1905	W 1-0	Sackey
09/04	h Sigma	W 2-1	Luckassen, Folprecht
16/04	h Jihlava	W 2-0	Shala 2
23/04	a Baník	W 2-0	Sýkora, Bakoš
30/04	h Brno	W 4-2	Folprecht, Pulkrab, Bakoš, Bartl
07/05	a Sparta	L 0-3	
11/05	h Zlín	W 4-3	Pulkrab 2, Hovorka 2
14/05	a Mladá Boleslav	D 2-2	Breite, Pulkrab

No	Name	Nat	DoB	Pos	Aps	(s)	Gls
27	Marek Bakoš	SVK	15/04/83	A	22	(6)	12
24	Daniel Bartl		05/07/89	M	14	(6)	1
26	Lukáš Bartošák		03/07/90	D	14	(3)	2
14	Ondřej Bláha		22/08/96	M		(1)	
22	Radim Breite		10/08/89	M	13		1
5	Vladimír Coufal		16/08/92	D	27		1
28	Dzon Delarge	CGO	23/06/90	A	5	(2)	1
15	Dmitri Efremov	RUS	01/04/95	M	10	(7)	
25	Jiří Fleišman		02/10/84	D	2	(1)	
7	Zdeněk Folprecht		01/07/91	M	15	(5)	2
16	Václav Hladký		14/11/90	G	1		
11	David Hovorka		07/08/93	D	25		2
4	Ondřej Karafiát		01/12/94	D	4		
1	Milan Kerbr		10/09/89	M	9	(5)	2
21	Tomáš Koubek		26/08/92	G	25		
19	Kevin Luckassen	NED	27/07/93	A	5	(4)	2
3	Serhiy Lyulka	UKR	22/02/90	D	1		
31	Ondřej Machuča		13/04/96	M	5	(4)	
18	Jan Mudra		22/01/90	D	3	(2)	
20	Michal Obročník	SVK	04/06/91	M		(3)	
8	David Pavelka		18/05/91	M	14		2
29	Lukáš Pokorný		05/07/93	D	28		1
33	Matěj Pulkrab		23/05/97	A	1	(6)	4
7	Michael Rabušic		17/09/89	A	7	(12)	1
12	Isaac Sackey	GHA	04/04/94	M	6	(7)	1
9	Herolind Shala	ALB	01/02/92	M	21	(3)	6
22	Soune Soungole	CIV	26/02/95	M	2	(2)	
23	Josef Šural		30/05/90	M	11	(4)	5
13	Ondřej Švejdík		03/12/82	D	7	(3)	1
6	Jan Sýkora		29/12/93	M	17	(4)	1
23	Egon Vůch		01/02/91	M	12	(1)	2

AC Sparta Praha

1893 • Generali Arena (19,416) • sparta.cz
Major honours
Czechoslovakian/Czech League (33) 1926, 1927, 1932, 1936, 1938, 1939, 1944, 1946, 1948, 1952, 1954, 1965, 1967, 1984, 1985, 1987, 1988, 1989, 1990, 1991, 1993, 1994, 1995, 1997, 1998, 1999, 2000, 2001, 2003, 2005, 2007, 2010, 2014; Czechoslovakian/Czech Cup (14) 1964, 1972, 1976, 1980, 1984, 1988, 1989, 1992, 1996, 2004, 2006, 2007, 2008, 2014
Coach: Zdeněk Ščasný

2015

24/07	a Jihlava	D 0-0	
01/08	h Baník	W 3-1	Lafata, Dočkal, Fatai
09/08	a Zlín	W 3-0	Dočkal 2 (2p), Lafata
14/08	a Mladá Boleslav	W 4-2	Vácha, Lafata 2, Nhamoinesu
23/08	h Dukla	W 2-0	Krejčí, Lafata
13/09	a Jablonec	D 1-1	Lafata
20/09	h Sigma	W 4-0	Hušbauer, Lafata, Dočkal 2 (1p)
27/09	a Slavia	L 0-1	
04/10	h Slovácko	W 4-0	Fatai 2, og (Diviš), Krejčí
18/10	a Příbram	W 4-0	Lafata, Fatai 2, Konaté
25/10	h Bohemians 1905	W 3-0	Lafata, Fatai, Litsingi
01/11	a Plzeň	L 1-2	Juliš
08/11	h Teplice	W 3-1	Fatai 2, Krejčí
22/11	a Liberec	L 0-1	
30/11	h Brno	W 2-1	Juliš, Lafata
06/12	h Baník	W 1-0	Lafata

2016

13/02	a Zlín	W 2-1	Brabec, Šural
21/02	h Mladá Boleslav	W 2-0	Šural, Nhamoinesu
06/03	h Jablonec	W 2-1	Lafata, Vácha
13/03	a Sigma	W 2-0	Mareček, Juliš
20/03	h Slavia	W 3-1	Lafata, Nhamoinesu, Zahustel
02/04	a Slovácko	L 0-2	
10/04	h Příbram	W 2-1	Dočkal, Lafata
17/04	a Bohemians 1905	D 2-2	Lafata, Dočkal
20/04	a Dukla	W 2-1	Juliš, Dočkal (p)
24/04	h Plzeň	L 0-3	
01/05	a Teplice	D 1-1	Konaté
07/05	h Liberec	W 3-0	Krejčí, Juliš, Konaté
11/05	a Brno	L 0-1	
14/05	h Jihlava	W 5-0	Lafata 5

No	Name	Nat	DoB	Pos	Aps	(s)	Gls
35	David Bičík		06/04/81	G	27		
5	Jakub Brabec		06/08/92	D	19	(3)	1
3	Michal Breznaník	SVK	16/12/85	M	1	(2)	
16	David Čapek		07/05/97	A		(1)	
9	Bořek Dočkal		30/09/88	M	29		8
7	Kehinde Fatai	NGA	19/02/90	A	9	(15)	8
14	Martin Frýdek		24/03/92	M	21	(2)	
25	Mario Holek		28/10/86	D	14		
22	Josef Hušbauer		16/03/90	M	8	(4)	1
29	Matěj Hybš		03/01/93	D	10	(2)	
2	Petr Jiráček		02/03/86	M	14	(4)	
30	Lukáš Juliš		02/12/94	A	6	(14)	5
18	Tiémoko Konaté	CIV	03/03/90	M	10	(10)	3
15	Radoslav Kováč		27/11/79	D	4		
8	Ladislav Krejčí		05/07/92	M	24	(3)	4
21	David Lafata		18/09/81	A	24	(2)	20
20	Francis Litsingi	CGO	10/09/86	M		(5)	1
19	Marco Paixão	POR	07/04/84	A	2	(1)	
11	Lukáš Mareček		17/04/90	D	25	(3)	1
8	Marek Matějovský		20/12/81	M	21	(5)	
2	Ondřej Mazuch		15/03/89	D	4		
27	Miroslav Miller		19/08/80	G	1		
26	Costa Nhamoinesu	ZIM	06/01/86	D	25		3
34	Milan Piško		06/03/96	D	1		
17	Michal Sáček		19/09/96	M		(1)	
1	Marek Štěch		28/01/90	G	2		
17	Martin Steinhöfer	GER	07/03/86	D	5	(1)	
32	Josef Šural		30/05/89	A	8		2
6	Lukáš Vácha		13/05/89	M	10	(3)	2
28	Ondřej Zahustel		18/06/91	D	9		1

CZECH REPUBLIC

FK Teplice

1945 • Na Stínadlech (18,221) • fkteplice.cz
Major honours
Czech Cup (2) 2003, 2009
Coach: David Vavruška

2015

25/07	h	Sigma	D	2-2	*Fillo, Potočný*
01/08	h	Slovácko	W	2-0	*Fillo (p), Vondrášek*
08/08	a	Příbram	L	2-3	*Fillo 2 (1p)*
14/08	h	Plzeň	D	2-2	*Fillo (p), Lüftner*
23/08	a	Liberec	L	0-2	
12/09	h	Bohemians 1905	W	2-1	*Vachoušek, Ljevaković*
19/09	a	Mladá Boleslav	L	3-4	*Lüftner, Táborský, Fillo*
26/09	h	Baník	W	1-0	*Jablonský*
03/10	a	Brno	W	4-0	*Vachoušek 2, Vondrášek, Lüftner*
17/10	h	Jihlava	L	0-1	
24/10	a	Zlín	W	2-1	*Breite, Fillo*
01/11	h	Slavia	L	0-1	
08/11	a	Sparta	L	1-3	*Vachoušek*
22/11	h	Jablonec	D	2-2	*Ljevaković, Krob*
27/11	a	Dukla	L	0-4	
04/12	a	Slovácko	L	2-4	*Hora 2*

2016

13/02	h	Příbram	W	2-0	*Hora, Ljevaković*
19/02	a	Plzeň	L	0-1	
27/02	h	Liberec	L	0-3	
05/03	a	Bohemians 1905	D	1-1	*Potočný*
12/03	h	Mladá Boleslav	D	0-0	
19/03	a	Baník	W	2-1	*Fillo, Vachoušek*
02/04	h	Brno	L	0-1	
09/04	a	Jihlava	L	1-2	*Vachoušek*
16/04	h	Zlín	D	2-2	*og (Jugas), Vondrášek*
27/04	a	Slavia	D	2-2	*Kukec, Táborský*
01/05	h	Sparta	D	1-1	*Potočný*
08/05	a	Jablonec	L	0-1	
11/05	h	Dukla	D	1-1	*Fillo*
14/05	a	Sigma	L	0-6	

No	Name	Nat	DoB	Pos	Aps	(s)	Gls
25	Benjamin Balázs	HUN	26/04/90	M		(1)	
21	Elvis Bratanovič	SVN	21/08/92	A	3	(8)	
2	Radim Breite		10/08/89	M	16		1
16	Tomáš Česlák		08/06/93	M		(2)	
30	Martin Chudý	SVK	23/04/89	G	8		
12	Chukwudi Chukwuma	NGA	17/10/87	A	1	(4)	
3	Mahamadou Dramé	FRA	03/12/91	M	1	(1)	
15	Patrik Dressler		30/10/90	D	6	(3)	
7	Martin Fillo		07/02/86	M	28		9
16	Miroslav Gregáň	SVK	26/04/96	M	3	(4)	
30	Tomáš Grigar		01/02/83	G	17		
13	Jakub Hora		23/02/91	M	26	(2)	3
23	Jan Hošek		01/04/89	D	1	(2)	
18	David Jablonský		08/10/91	D	14		1
18	Michal Jeřábek		10/09/93	D	7		
11	Ulrich Kapolongo	CGO	31/07/89	A	4	(8)	
22	Petr Kodeš		31/01/96	M	12	(7)	
24	Jan Krob		27/04/87	D	28		1
14	Davor Kukec	CRO	16/03/86	M	8	(4)	1
5	Admir Ljevaković	BIH	07/08/84	M	23	(1)	3
8	Michael Lüftner		14/03/94	D	27		3
20	Milan Matula		22/04/84	D	2	(3)	
27	Nivaldo	CPV	10/07/88	D	5	(5)	
26	Roman Potočný		25/04/91	A	15	(8)	3
1	Martin Slavík		21/09/79	G	5	(1)	
19	Soune Soungole	CIV	26/02/95	M	8	(1)	
10	Ivo Táborský		10/05/85	A	1	(16)	2
23	Zurab Tsiskaridze	GEO	08/09/86	D	8	(1)	
8	Štěpán Vachoušek		26/07/79	M	30		6
28	David Vaněček		09/03/91	A	2	(1)	
17	Tomáš Vondrášek		26/10/87	D	21	(2)	3

FC Viktoria Plzeň

1911 • Doosan Arena (11,700) • fcviktoria.cz
Major honours
Czech League (4) 2011, 2013, 2015, 2016; Czech Cup (1) 2010
Coach: Miroslav Koubek;
(16/08/15) Karel Krejčí

2015

24/07	h	Slavia	W	2-1	*Kolář, Mahmutović*
01/08	a	Dukla	L	0-1	
09/08	h	Slovácko	D	2-2	*Hořava, Ďuriš*
14/08	a	Teplice	D	2-2	*Baránek, Kopic*
23/08	h	Sigma	W	2-0	*Ďuriš 2 (1p)*
13/09	a	Příbram	W	4-0	*Limberský 2, Ďuriš, Kovařík*
20/09	h	Bohemians 1905	W	1-0	*Ďuriš*
26/09	h	Liberec	W	2-1	*Ďuriš, Mahmutović*
04/10	a	Jihlava	W	4-2	*Kovařík, Ďuriš 2, Mahmutović*
17/10	a	Zlín	W	4-2	*Kopic, Ďuriš (p), Kovařík, Hořava*
25/10	a	Brno	L	0-1	
01/11	h	Sparta	W	2-1	*Baránek, Petržela*
08/11	h	Baník	W	4-0	*Hořava, Holenda, Petržela, Ďuriš*
21/11	h	Mladá Boleslav	W	1-0	*Ďuriš*
30/11	a	Jablonec	W	1-0	*Baránek*
06/12	h	Dukla	W	3-0	*Hořava, Baránek, Kovařík*

2016

14/02	a	Slovácko	W	2-1	*Kolář 2 (1p)*
19/02	h	Teplice	W	1-0	*Kolář*
27/02	a	Sigma	W	1-0	*Hořava*
06/03	a	Příbram	W	4-0	*Rajtoral, Ďuriš, Kovařík, Hořava*
12/03	h	Bohemians 1905	W	2-0	*Ďuriš 2*
20/03	a	Liberec	W	1-0	*Ďuriš*
02/04	h	Jihlava	W	2-0	*Kovařík, Kolář*
09/04	a	Zlín	W	2-1	*Petržela, Vaněk*
17/04	h	Brno	W	2-1	*Baránek, Kopic*
24/04	a	Sparta	W	3-0	*Vaněk (p), Krmenčík 2*
30/04	h	Baník	W	2-0	*Hrošovský (p), Kolář*
07/05	a	Mladá Boleslav	L	0-2	
11/05	h	Jablonec	L	1-2	*Ďuriš (p)*
14/05	a	Slavia	L	0-5	

No	Name	Nat	DoB	Pos	Aps	(s)	Gls
22	Jan Baránek		20/06/93	D	23	(2)	5
13	Petr Bolek		08/06/84	G	3		
12	Michal Ďuriš	SVK	01/06/88	A	22	(3)	16
5	Pavel Fořt		26/06/83	A		(4)	
2	Lukáš Hejda		09/03/90	D	16	(2)	
16	Jan Holenda		22/08/85	A	6	(12)	1
7	Tomáš Hořava		29/05/88	M	21	(1)	6
17	Patrik Hrošovský	SVK	22/04/92	M	26		1
4	Roman Hubník		06/06/84	D	13	(2)	
26	Daniel Kolář		27/10/85	M	26		6
10	Jan Kopic		04/06/90	M	19	(7)	3
19	Jan Kovařík		19/06/88	M	25	(5)	6
1	Matúš Kozáčik	SVK	27/12/83	G	27		
15	Michael Krmenčík		15/03/93	A	2	(5)	2
29	Tomáš Kučera		20/07/91	M	2	(4)	
8	David Limberský		06/10/83	D	27		2
25	Aidin Mahmutović	BIH	06/04/86	A		(9)	3
3	Aleš Matějů		03/06/96	D	17		
11	Milan Petržela		19/06/83	M	14	(13)	3
21	Václav Procházka		08/05/84	D	11	(3)	
27	František Rajtoral		12/03/86	D	16	(6)	1
14	Radim Řezník		20/01/89	D	2		
9	Ondřej Vaněk		05/07/90	M	13	(7)	2
23	Egon Vůch		01/02/91	M	1	(2)	

FC Vysočina Jihlava

1948 • Stadion v Jiráskově ulici (4,155) • fcvysocina.cz
Coach: Luděk Klusáček;
(16/09/15) (Milan Bokša);
(04/01/16) Michal Hipp (SVK)

2015

24/07	h	Sparta	D	0-0	
01/08	a	Zlín	L	0-1	
10/08	h	Jablonec	W	1-0	*Jungr*
16/08	a	Slavia	L	0-4	
22/08	h	Slovácko	L	1-2	*og (Heča)*
12/09	a	Sigma	L	1-2	*Mešanović*
18/09	h	Dukla	D	2-2	*Mešanović 2*
26/09	a	Příbram	L	1-4	*Mešanović*
04/10	h	Plzeň	L	2-4	*Mešanović, Mišůn*
17/10	a	Teplice	W	1-0	*Vaculík (p)*
25/10	h	Liberec	D	1-1	*Mešanović*
31/10	a	Bohemians 1905	L	1-2	*Nerad*
07/11	a	Mladá Boleslav	L	1-6	*Demeter*
20/11	h	Brno	W	2-0	*Vaculík (p), Batioja*
28/11	a	Baník	W	2-1	*Nerad, Mešanović*
06/12	h	Zlín	D	2-2	*Vaculík (p), Mešanović*

2016

13/02	a	Jablonec	L	0-2	
19/02	h	Slavia	D	0-0	
27/02	a	Slovácko	L	1-3	*Hronek*
05/03	h	Sigma	W	2-1	*Hronek 2*
12/03	a	Dukla	W	1-0	*og (Štětina)*
18/03	h	Příbram	L	1-3	*Nerad*
02/04	a	Plzeň	L	0-2	
09/04	h	Teplice	W	2-1	*Kučera, Vaculík (p)*
16/04	a	Liberec	L	0-2	
23/04	h	Bohemians 1905	L	1-2	*Hronek*
29/04	h	Mladá Boleslav	D	1-1	*Hronek*
06/05	a	Brno	D	1-1	*Urdinov*
11/05	h	Baník	W	3-0	*Bazal, Hronek, Dvořák (p)*
14/05	a	Sparta	L	0-5	

No	Name	Nat	DoB	Pos	Aps	(s)	Gls
24	Augusto Batioja	ECU	04/05/90	A	9	(3)	1
10	Josef Bazal		06/11/93	M	10	(2)	1
21	Patrik Demeter		02/01/94	M	7	(3)	1
28	Pavel Dvořák		19/02/89	A	8	(17)	1
22	Jakub Fulnek		26/04/94	M	9	(12)	
1	Jan Hanuš		24/04/88	G	27		
7	Petr Hronek		04/07/93	D	14		6
8	Adam Jánoš		20/07/92	M	10	(1)	
9	Marek Jungr		11/04/87	M	5	(12)	1
25	Jiří Klíma		05/01/97	A	1		
5	Jiří Krejčí		22/03/86	D	28		
15	Lukáš Kryštůfek		11/08/92	D	22	(1)	
16	Tomáš Kučera		20/07/91	M	12		1
30	Vladimír Kukoľ	SVK	08/05/86	M	19	(6)	
27	Matúš Marcin	SVK	06/04/94	A		(1)	
14	Tomáš Marek		20/04/81	M	16	(1)	
4	Muris Mešanović	BIH	04/07/90	A	14	(2)	8
23	Milan Mišůn		21/02/90	D	17	(3)	1
26	Petr Nerad		06/02/94	M	11	(7)	3
7	Vojtěch Přeučil		19/09/90	A		(3)	
34	Matej Rakovan	SVK	14/09/92	G	3	(1)	
6	Ondřej Šourek		26/04/83	D	12		
20	Peter Šulek	SVK	21/09/88	D	22	(2)	
17	Petr Tlustý		12/01/86	D	9		
11	Yani Urdinov	MKD	28/03/91	D	11	(1)	1
11	Lukáš Vaculík		06/06/83	M	25	(2)	4
24	Radek Voltr		28/11/91	A	10	(4)	

FC Zbrojovka Brno

1913 • Městský fotbalový stadion (12,550)
• fczbrno.cz
Major honours
Czechoslovakian League (1) 1978
Coach: Václav Kotal

2015
25/07	h Baník	W	2-1	Škoda, Zavadil (p)
02/08	a Mladá Boleslav	L	0-2	
07/08	h Slavia	W	1-0	Škoda
15/08	a Sigma	D	1-1	Zavadil
23/08	h Jablonec	L	0-3	
12/09	a Zlín	L	1-2	Chrien
19/09	h Slovácko	W	2-0	Řezníček 2
26/09	a Dukla	W	2-1	Řezníček 2
03/10	h Teplice	L	0-4	
17/10	h Bohemians 1905	D	1-1	Lutonský
25/10	h Plzeň	W	1-0	Řezníček (p)
31/10	a Příbram	D	1-1	Lutonský
08/11	h Liberec	W	3-1	Chrien, Řezníček, Zavadil
20/11	a Jihlava	L	0-2	
30/11	a Sparta	L	1-2	Řezníček
06/12	h Mladá Boleslav	D	1-1	Řezníček

2016
12/02	h Slavia	L	0-2	
20/02	h Sigma	W	2-0	Řezníček, Hyčka
27/02	a Jablonec	L	0-3	
05/03	h Zlín	W	2-0	Zavadil, Hyčka
12/03	a Slovácko	L	1-2	Škoda
19/03	a Dukla	W	3-0	Hyčka, P Buchta, Škoda
02/04	a Teplice	W	1-0	Řezníček (p)
08/04	h Bohemians 1905	W	2-1	og (Švec), Škoda
17/04	a Plzeň	L	1-2	Řezníček
24/04	h Příbram	W	2-1	Škoda, Řezníček
30/04	a Liberec	L	2-4	Zoubele 2
06/05	h Jihlava	D	1-1	Škoda
11/05	h Sparta	W	1-0	Hyčka
14/05	a Baník	W	2-1	Řezníček, Chrien

No	Name	Nat	DoB	Pos	Aps	(s)	Gls
9	Tomáš Brigant	SVK	18/10/94	A	5	(12)	
3	Petr Buchta		11/07/92	D	28		1
26	Radek Buchta		22/04/89	D	11	(7)	
18	Martin Chrien	SVK	08/09/95	M	9	(15)	3
1	Martin Doležal		18/12/80	G	7		
4	Boštjan Frelih	SVN	10/02/93	M	4	(1)	
24	Alois Hyčka		22/07/90	D	14		4
6	Mihailo Jovanović	SRB	14/02/89	D	6	(2)	
30	Miroslav Keresteš	SVK	30/07/89	D	24	(1)	
5	Václav Klán		07/09/93	A		(1)	
14	Pavel Košťál		17/09/80	D	28	(1)	
16	Jakub Kučera		28/01/97	M		(1)	
28	Matúš Lacko	SVK	14/04/87	M	25	(3)	
19	Milan Lutonský		10/08/93	M	23	(3)	2
8	Jan Malík		07/04/92	D	17	(8)	
1	Dušan Melichárek		29/11/83	G	23		
27	Donneil Moukanza	FRA	27/02/91	M		(7)	
25	David Pašek		27/10/89	A	16	(5)	
37	Jakub Řezníček		26/05/88	A	29		13
22	Aleš Schuster		26/10/81	D	1	(2)	
21	Michal Škoda		01/03/88	A	24		7
15	Jakub Šural		01/07/96	D	1	(2)	
11	Stanislav Vávra		20/07/93	A	6	(8)	
13	Tomáš Weber		26/05/96	M	1	(1)	
7	Pavel Zavadil		30/04/78	M	21	(1)	4
10	Lukáš Zoubele		20/12/85	M	7	(4)	2

FC Zlín

1919 • Stadion Letná (6,375) • fcfastavzlin.cz
Major honours
Czechoslovakian Cup (1) 1970
Coach: Bohumil Páník

2015
26/07	a Bohemians 1905	W	1-0	Pazdera
01/08	h Jihlava	W	1-0	Železník
09/08	a Sparta	L	0-3	
15/08	h Baník	W	2-0	Poznar 2
21/08	a Mladá Boleslav	L	2-5	Železník 2 (1p)
12/09	h Brno	W	2-1	Železník 2 (1p)
19/09	h Slavia	L	0-2	
26/09	a Sigma	D	1-1	Koreš
03/10	h Jablonec	D	2-2	Poznar, Koreš
17/10	a Plzeň	L	2-4	Železník 2 (1p)
24/10	h Teplice	L	1-2	Holík
30/10	a Dukla	L	0-1	
07/11	a Slovácko	W	2-1	Poznar, Vukadinović
21/11	a Příbram	W	2-1	Koreš, Jordan
30/11	h Liberec	W	2-0	Koreš, Poznar
06/12	a Jihlava	D	2-2	Železník, Koreš

2016
13/02	h Sparta	L	1-2	Hájek
20/02	a Baník	L	0-3	
27/02	h Mladá Boleslav	L	0-2	
05/03	a Brno	L	0-2	
11/03	a Slavia	L	0-1	
19/03	h Sigma	D	0-0	
02/04	a Jablonec	L	1-3	Holík
09/04	h Plzeň	L	1-2	Poznar
16/04	a Teplice	D	2-2	Koreš, Vukadinović
24/04	h Dukla	D	2-2	Koreš, Janíček
30/04	a Slovácko	D	1-1	Diop
07/05	h Příbram	D	0-0	
11/05	a Liberec	L	3-4	Poznar, Jordan, Vukadinović
14/05	h Bohemians 1905	D	1-1	Jordan

No	Name	Nat	DoB	Pos	Aps	(s)	Gls
25	Robert Bartolomeu		03/12/93	M	3	(12)	
21	Ladislav Benček		13/08/84	D		(1)	
7	Dame Diop	SEN	15/03/93	A	4	(3)	1
17	Stanislav Dostál		30/06/91	G	10		
19	Antonín Fantiš		15/04/92	A	5	(8)	
18	Tomáš Hájek		01/12/91	D	27		1
5	Lukáš Holík		23/08/92	M	19	(9)	2
1	Tomáš Holý		10/12/91	G	20		
4	David Hubáček		23/07/77	D	14	(5)	
13	Tomáš Janíček		07/09/82	D	24		1
29	Marko Jordan	CRO	27/10/90	A	2	(11)	3
24	Jakub Jugas		05/05/92	D	30		
23	Miloš Kopečný		26/12/93	M	4	(3)	
3	Štěpán Koreš		14/02/89	M	24	(1)	7
2	Michal Malý		29/05/87	D	1	(14)	
16	Róbert Matejov	SVK	05/07/88	M	26	(1)	
14	Lukáš Motal		06/03/90	M	4	(4)	
20	Lukáš Pazdera		06/03/87	D	28		1
10	Tomáš Poznar		27/09/88	A	27	(1)	7
26	Vukadin Vukadinović	SRB	14/12/90	M	19	(6)	3
7	Lukáš Železník		18/06/90	A	16		8
15	Diego Živulić	CRO	23/03/92	M	19	(4)	

Top goalscorers

20	David Lafata (Sparta)
16	Michal Ďuriš (Plzeň)
14	Lukáš Magera (Mladá Boleslav)
	Milan Škoda (Slavia)
13	Jakub Řezníček (Brno)
12	Muris Mešanović (Jihlava/Slavia)
	Marek Bakoš (Liberec)
10	Tomáš Berger (Dukla)
9	Jaroslav Diviš (Slovácko)
	Martin Fillo (Teplice)

Promoted clubs

MFK OKD Karviná

2003 • Městský stadion (8,000) • mfkkarvina.cz
Coach: Jozef Weber

FC Hradec Králové

1905 • Všesportovní stadion (7,100) • fchk.cz
Major honours
Czechoslovakian League (1) 1960;
Czech Cup (1) 1995
Coach: Milan Frimmel

Second level final table 2015/16

		Pld	W	D	L	F	A	Pts
1	MFK OKD Karviná	28	17	8	3	50	17	59
2	FC Hradec Králové	28	17	8	3	45	16	59
3	1. SC Znojmo	28	17	5	6	62	33	56
4	FK Baník Sokolov	28	10	11	7	32	26	41
5	FC MAS Táborsko	28	9	12	7	39	34	39
6	FK Pardubice	28	10	8	10	29	29	38
7	FC Vlašim	28	9	8	11	35	33	35
8	FK Ústí nad Labem	28	9	8	11	39	38	35
9	FK Varnsdorf	28	8	10	10	35	44	34
10	MFK Frýdek-Místek	28	8	9	11	30	37	33
11	SFC Opava	28	6	14	8	34	37	32
12	SK Dynamo České Budějovice	28	6	14	8	41	48	32
13	FK Fotbal Třinec	28	6	9	13	29	41	27
14	SK Sigma Olomouc B	28	6	3	17	23	49	21
15	FK Slavoj Vyšehrad	28	5	5	18	20	61	20

CZECH REPUBLIC

DOMESTIC CUP

Pohár České Pošty 2015/16

SECOND ROUND

(26/08/15)
Sokol Tasovice 1-3 Znojmo
Stará Říše 2-3 Vysočina Jihlava
Vyškov 1-1 Hanácká Slavia Kroměříž *(6-7 on pens)*

(27/08/15)
Jiskra Rýmařov 4-3 Baník Ostrava
Prostějov 0-0 Fotbal Třinec *(5-4 on pens)*
Slavoj Český Krumlov 0-4 České Budějovice

(28/08/15)
Klatovy 1-0 Baník Most
Loko Vltavín 1-9 Příbram
Neratovice-Byškovice 0-4 Dukla Praha
Union 2013 Nový Bydžov 0-7 Slavia Praha
Velké Meziříčí 1-2 Zbrojovka Brno

(29/08/15)
Dobrovice 1-2 Varnsdorf
Hlučín 0-1 Opava
Chrudim 0-5 Hradec Králové
Karlovy Vary 2-6 Táborsko
Králův Dvůr 1-1 Vlašim *(3-1 on pens)*
Mohelnice 1-2 Frýdek-Místek
Olympia Hradec Králové 1-2 Bohemians 1905
Slavičín 2-0 Slovácko
Tachov 2-2 Baník Sokolov *(5-3 on pens)*
Velké Karlovice 1-6 Zlín
Vítkovice 2-2 Karviná *(3-5 on pens)*

(30/08/15)
Čáslav 0-3 Slavoj Vyšehrad
Kolín 2-4 Ústí nad Labem
Převýšov 0-5 Pardubice
Štěchovice 1-4 Teplice

(02/09/15)
Slovan Rosice 0-5 Sigma Olomouc

Byes – Jablonec, Mladá Boleslav, Slovan Liberec, Sparta Praha, Viktoria Plzeň

THIRD ROUND

(22/09/15)
Prostějov 1-4 Zlín
Táborsko 1-2 Dukla Praha
Ústí nad Labem 4-2 Slavia Praha

(23/09/15)
Hanácká Slavia Kroměříž 0-1 Zbrojovka Brno
Králův Dvůr 1-1 Sparta Praha *(4-5 on pens)*
Pardubice 3-0 Teplice
Slavičín 1-2 Frýdek-Místek
Tachov 0-2 Viktoria Plzeň
Varnsdorf 2-2 Slovan Liberec *(2-3 on pens)*
Znojmo 0-5 Vysočina Jihlava

(29/09/15)
České Budějovice 2-5 Příbram
Klatovy 0-5 Mladá Boleslav
Opava 1-5 Sigma Olomouc
Slavoj Vyšehrad 0-2 Jablonec

(30/09/15)
Hradec Králové 1-0 Bohemians 1905

(06/10/15)
Jiskra Rýmařov 0-3 Karviná

FOURTH ROUND

(10/10/15 & 11/11/15)
Vysočina Jihlava 0-1, 2-2 Sigma Olomouc *(2-3)*

(20/10/15 & 03/11/15)
Frýdek-Místek 0-2, 0-3 Jablonec *(0-5)*

(20/10/15 & 10/11/15)
Ústí nad Labem 0-3, 0-3 Dukla Praha *(0-6)*

(27/10/15 & 11/11/15)
Hradec Králové 0-1, 5-1 Příbram *(5-2)*

(27/10/15 & 24/11/15)
Karviná 0-1, 0-3 Mladá Boleslav *(0-4)*

(14/11/15 & 03/12/15)
Slovan Liberec 1-0, 0-1 Zlín *(1-1;7-6 on pens)*

(15/11/15 & 03/12/15)
Viktoria Plzeň 2-1, 1-0 Zbrojovka Brno *(3-1)*

(17/11/15 & 03/12/15)
Pardubice 1-0, 1-3 Sparta Praha *(2-3)*

QUARTER-FINALS

(02/03/16 & 16/03/16)
Viktoria Plzeň 4-2 Sigma Olomouc *(Matějů 11, Holenda 31, Krmenčík 66, Kovařík 84; Ordoš 57, Plšek 75p)*
Sigma Olomouc 1-1 Viktoria Plzeň *(Ordoš 22; Kopic 63)*
(Viktoria Plzeň 5-3)

(03/03/16 & 15/03/16)
Dukla Praha 0-0 Jablonec
Jablonec 2-1 Dukla Praha *(Doležal 52, 59; Beauguel 33)*
(Jablonec 2-1)

(03/03/16 & 30/03/16)
Slovan Liberec 2-1 Sparta Praha *(Rabušic 45, Bakoš 79; Konaté 42)*
Sparta Praha 2-0 Slovan Liberec *(Jiráček 27, Fatai 80)*
(Sparta Praha 3-2)

(16/03/16 & 30/03/16)
Hradec Králové 1-4 Mladá Boleslav *(Pázler 41; Baroš 20p, Chramosta 66, 84, Takács 86)*
Mladá Boleslav 1-1 Hradec Králové
(Chramosta 84; Shejbal 54)
(Mladá Boleslav 5-2)

SEMI-FINALS

(05/04/16 & 13/04/16)
Mladá Boleslav 1-0 Viktoria Plzeň *(Čermák 74)*
Viktoria Plzeň 0-0 Mladá Boleslav
(Mladá Boleslav 1-0)

(27/04/16 & 04/05/16)
Jablonec 2-0 Sparta Praha *(Greguš 8, Trávník 50)*
Sparta Praha 1-2 Jablonec *(Turyna 54; Wágner 22, Doležal 39)*
(Jablonec 4-1)

FINAL

(18/05/16)
Na Stínadlech, Teplice
FK MLADÁ BOLESLAV 2 *(Chramosta 71, Ščuk 74)*
FK JABLONEC 0
Referee: *Hrubeš*
MLADÁ BOLESLAV: *Šeda, Kysela, Kúdela, Čmovš, Fleišman (Pauschek 87), Ščuk, Rada, Jánoš (Chramosta 68), Čermák, Kalabiška, Magera (Takács 90+1)*
JABLONEC: *Hrubý, Karavaev, Pernica, Daniel Rossi, Hybš, Hübschman, Greguš, Masopust, Pospíšil (Trávník 72), Mingazov (Wágner 78), Doležal (Mihálik 83)*

Two second-half goals in quick succession enabled Mladá Boleslav to claim the Czech Cup at Jablonec's expense in Teplice

DENMARK
Dansk Boldspil-Union (DBU)

Address	House of Football
	DBU Allé 1
	DK-2605 Brøndby
Tel	+45 43 262 222
Fax	+45 43 262 245
E-mail	dbu@dbu.dk
Website	dbu.dk

President	Jesper Møller
	Christensen
Chief executive	Claus Bretton-Meyer
Media officer	Jacob Høyer
Year of formation	1889
National stadium	Telia Parken (38,065)

SUPERLIGA CLUBS

 1 **Aalborg BK**

 2 **AGF Aarhus**

3 **Brøndby IF**

4 **Esbjerg fB**

 5 **Hobro IK**

 6 **FC København**

 7 **FC Midtjylland**

 8 **FC Nordsjælland**

 9 **Odense BK**

 10 **Randers FC**

 11 **SønderjyskE**

 12 **Viborg FF**

PROMOTED CLUBS

 13 **Lyngby BK**

 14 **Silkeborg IF**

 15 **AC Horsens**

KEY

● UEFA Champions League

● UEFA Europa League

● Promoted

● Relegated

FC København back in command

After two years in Jutland, the Superliga trophy made its way back to the Danish capital as FC København reclaimed it in dominant fashion, overtaking local rivals Brøndby in the all-time roll of honour with an 11th triumph.

It was the first league title in Ståle Solbakken's second spell at the club and the sixth in total under the Norwegian coach, who also led the team to their second straight Danish Cup triumph to complete FCK's third domestic double. On the international front, Denmark failed to qualify for UEFA EURO 2016, ending Morten Olsen's long stint in charge on a disappointing note.

DANMARKSMESTER 2016

Eleventh Superliga title and sixth for Solbakken	Cup win completes club's third domestic double	EURO play-off defeat by Sweden ends Olsen's reign

Domestic league

After finishing as runners-up to Aalborg BK and FC Midtjylland in Solbakken's first two seasons back in charge, FCK were determined to make it third time lucky. Although Midtjylland – now led by ex-Denmark Under-21 boss Jess Thorup following the shock resignation of title-winning coach Glen Riddersholm – threatened early on, with AaB following suit in the late autumn, it was a feat that the well-resourced club from the capital would ultimately achieve with a measure of comfort.

Once Solbakken's men had replaced Midtjylland at the top in late October, there was no shifting them. Although they led AaB by just a point at the winter break, they widened the gap in the spring, beating each of their chief rivals and forging clear thanks to the winning combination of a fluent attack, led by the prolific strike duo of Danish international Nicolai Jørgensen and Paraguayan forward Federico Santander, a solid defence, and some strong leadership from Solbakken and skipper Thomas Delaney. It was a double from Santander, one of several effective new signings, in a 2-0 home win over FC Nordsjælland that secured the title with three rounds still to play.

Midtjylland and AaB both fell away to such an extent that the runners-up spot was grabbed by surprise package SønderjyskE, who won seven of their last nine games to finish higher than ever before and claim a first ever qualification for Europe. Midtjylland took third place, one place above Brøndby, whose coach Thomas Frank had walked out in March following a fall-out with the club's chairman.

Village club Hobro were stranded at the bottom of the table, which meant that, with the Superliga increasing to 14 clubs in 2016/17 and just one club going down, there was no relegation battle. In contrast, excitement abounded in the promotion race, with Lyngby, Silkeborg and Horsens all returning to the big time after short spells away.

Domestic cup

AGF Aarhus had a tough time in the league, but although the mid-term appointment of Riddersholm lifted them no higher than tenth, the ex-Midtjylland boss did take them to the Danish Cup final thanks to an impressive derby win over AaB in the two-legged semis. FCK also overcame Brøndby at that stage thanks to a late Nicolai Jørgensen strike, and it was he who opened the scoring in the final, played in the Copenhagen club's Telia Parken home, only for AGF's Morten 'Duncan' Rasmussen to equalise on the stroke of half-time. A tight encounter was eventually won by a rare goal from Danish international defensive midfielder William Kvist, enabling FCK to win the trophy back-to-back for the first time.

Europe

The biggest headlines made by a Danish club in Europe belonged to Midtjylland – not in the UEFA Champions League as they might have hoped, but in the UEFA Europa League, where they won at home against two English Premier League clubs, knocking Southampton out of the play-offs and then taking a first-leg lead over Manchester United in the round of 32 before their 14-match European campaign ended at Old Trafford.

National team

Denmark failed to score in their last three UEFA EURO 2016 group qualifiers, which left them in third place. Forced into a play-off against Sweden, they were beaten fair and square by their Scandinavian neighbours and thus missed out on the European finals for only the second time since 1984. That spelt the end of the line for Olsen after over 15 years in the job – and exactly 150 matches. He was replaced the following month not by another Great Dane, Michael Laudrup, who turned the job down, but by a 62-year-old Norwegian, the vastly experienced Åge Hareide.

DOMESTIC SEASON AT A GLANCE

Superliga 2015/16 final table

		Pld	Home W	D	L	F	A	Away W	D	L	F	A	Total W	D	L	F	A	Pts
1	**FC København**	**33**	**14**	**3**	**0**	**43**	**14**	**7**	**5**	**4**	**19**	**14**	**21**	**8**	**4**	**62**	**28**	**71**
2	SønderjyskE	33	10	2	4	34	18	9	3	5	22	18	19	5	9	56	36	62
3	FC Midtjylland	33	11	3	3	32	13	6	5	5	25	20	17	8	8	57	33	59
4	Brøndby IF	33	8	4	5	14	13	8	2	6	29	24	16	6	11	43	37	54
5	Aalborg BK	33	8	3	6	34	18	7	2	7	22	26	15	5	13	56	44	50
6	Randers FC	33	7	5	5	24	19	6	3	7	21	24	13	8	12	45	43	47
7	Odense BK	33	7	3	6	29	23	7	1	9	21	29	14	4	15	50	52	46
8	Viborg FF	33	5	5	6	14	19	6	2	9	20	23	11	7	15	34	42	40
9	FC Nordsjælland	33	7	3	7	22	24	4	2	10	13	27	11	5	17	35	51	38
10	AGF Aarhus	33	7	5	4	25	17	1	8	8	22	32	8	13	12	47	49	37
11	Esbjerg fB	33	5	2	9	20	31	2	7	8	18	33	7	9	17	38	64	30
12	Hobro IK	33	2	4	10	15	34	2	2	13	11	36	4	6	23	26	70	18

European qualification 2016/17

 Champion/Cup winner: FC København (second qualifying round)

 SønderjyskE (second qualifying round)
FC Midtjylland (first qualifying round)
Brøndby IF (first qualifying round)

Top scorer Lukas Spalvis (AaB), 18 goals
Relegated club Hobro IK
Promoted clubs Lyngby BK, Silkeborg IF, AC Horsens
Cup final FC København 2-1 AGF Aarhus

Team of the season
(4-4-2)

Coach: Michelsen (SønderjyskE)

	Johnsson		
	(Randers)		
Ankersen	**Hansen**	**M Jørgensen**	**Durmisi**
(København)	(Midtjylland)	(København)	(Brøndby)
Falk	**Delaney**	**Kvist**	**Thomsen**
(OB)	(København)	(København)	(AaB)
	Spalvis	**Santander**	
	(AaB)	(København)	

Player of the season

Thomas Delaney
(FC København)

A Danish native with Irish-American roots, Delaney won his fourth Superliga title with FC København in 2015/16. It was more special than the previous three, however, because it was his first as club captain. An inspirational figure throughout the team's double-winning campaign, the 24-year-old midfielder was not only rewarded for his efforts with regular selection by new Denmark boss Åge Hareide but also by becoming the first FCK player to win the club's player of the season award two years in a row.

Newcomer of the season

Emre Mor
(FC Nordsjælland)

Danish Superliga supporters were treated to some extraordinary skills in the second half of the 2015/16 season from 18-year-old Emre Mor. Although he only started a dozen games for Nordsjælland, the diminutive schemer's breathtaking dribbling and left-footed artistry – very reminiscent of a young Lionel Messi – were enough to persuade Turkey, the team he chose over his native Denmark, to take him to UEFA EURO 2016 and Borussia Dortmund to lure him to the German Bundesliga. A glittering future beckons.

NATIONAL TEAM

International honours
UEFA European Championship (1) 1992

International tournament appearances
FIFA World Cup (4) 1986 (2nd round), 1998 (qtr-finals), 2002 (2nd round), 2010
UEFA European Championship (8) 1964 (4th), 1984 (semi-finals), 1988, 1992 (Winners), 1996, 2000, 2004 (qtr-finals), 2012

Top five all-time caps
Peter Schmeichel (129); Dennis Rommedahl (126); Jon Dahl Tomasson (112); Thomas Helveg (109); Michael Laudrup (104)

Top five all-time goals
Poul "Tist" Nielsen & Jon Dahl Tomasson (52); Pauli Jørgensen (44); Ole Madsen (42); Preben Elkjær (38)

Results 2015/16

04/09/15	Albania (ECQ)	H	Copenhagen	D	0-0	
07/09/15	Armenia (ECQ)	A	Yerevan	D	0-0	
08/10/15	Portugal (ECQ)	A	Braga	L	0-1	
11/10/15	France	H	Copenhagen	L	1-2	*Sviatchenko (90+1)*
14/11/15	Sweden (ECQ)	A	Solna	L	1-2	*N Jørgensen (80)*
17/11/15	Sweden (ECQ)	H	Copenhagen	D	2-2	*Y Poulsen (82), Vestergaard (90+1)*
24/03/16	Iceland	H	Herning	W	2-1	*N Jørgensen (50, 54)*
29/03/16	Scotland	A	Glasgow	L	0-1	
03/06/16	Bosnia & Herzegovina	N	Toyota (JPN)	D	2-2	*Kjær (22), Fischer (41) (3-4 on pens)*
07/06/16	Bulgaria	N	Suita (JPN)	W	4-0	*Rasmussen (39), Eriksen (72, 74, 82)*

Appearances 2015/16

Coach: Morten Olsen 14/08/49 /(10/12/15) Åge Hareide (NOR) 23/09/53			ALB	ARM	POR	Fra	SWE	SWE	Isl	Sco	Bih	Bul	Caps	Goals
Kasper Schmeichel	05/11/86	Leicester (ENG)	G	G	G	G	G	G	G	G46	G	G	22	-
Lars Jacobsen	20/09/79	Guingamp (FRA)	D	D	D	D	D	D					81	1
Daniel Agger	12/12/84	Brøndby	D	D	D	D85	D	D	D62	D64			75	12
Simon Kjær	26/03/89	Fenerbahçe (TUR)	D	D80	D	D73	D	D	D	D	D	D	60	3
Riza Durmisi	08/01/94	Brøndby	D	D	D	D	D	D84	M	M	M86	M	11	-
William Kvist Jørgensen	24/02/85	København	M46		s46	M	M		s83		s61	M	64	2
Pierre Højbjerg	05/08/95	Schalke (GER)	M	M	M46	s46	s54	M	M83	M	M61	M	17	1
Michael Krohn-Dehli	06/06/83	Sevilla (ESP)	M	M56	M	M56		s46					56	6
Nicolai Jørgensen	15/01/91	København	A	A64	s69	s56	s54	A	A62	A			16	3
Nicklas Bendtner	16/01/88	Wolfsburg (GER)	A	A	A	A	A	A60					74	29
Pione Sisto	04/02/95	Midtjylland	A46			s69							2	-
Yussuf Poulsen	15/06/94	RB Leipzig (GER)	s46	A	s82	s61	s71	A	A79	A46			13	2
Jakob Poulsen	07/07/83	Midtjylland	s46	M	M46								35	2
Thomas Delaney	03/09/91	København		s56				M46	M	M	M46	s69	9	-
Martin Braithwaite	05/06/91	Toulouse (FRA)		s64	A	A69	A71		s79	s46			14	1
Erik Sviatchenko	04/10/91	Midtjylland /Celtic (SCO)		s80		s73				s64			5	1
Daniel Wass	31/05/89	Celta (ESP)			M69								14	-
Christian Eriksen	14/02/92	Tottenham (ENG)			A82	A61	M	M	M62	M81	M	M86	61	9
Jannik Vestergaard	03/08/92	Bremen (GER)			s85			s84	s62		D	D	8	1
Thomas Kahlenberg	20/03/83	Brøndby				M54							47	5
Viktor Fischer	09/06/94	Ajax (NED)				A54					A61	A	10	2
Morten "Duncan" Rasmussen	31/01/85	Midtjylland /AGF						s60			A	A69	13	4
Andreas Christensen	10/04/96	Mönchengladbach (GER)							D	D	D	D	6	-
Henrik Dalsgaard	27/07/89	Zulte Waregem (BEL)							M	M	M		3	-
Lasse Schöne	27/05/86	Ajax (NED)							s62	s81	s61	s86	26	3
Lasse Vibe	22/02/87	Brentford (ENG)							s62				10	1
Jonas Lössl	01/02/89	Guingamp (FRA)								s46			1	-
Mike Jensen	19/02/88	Rosenborg (NOR)									s46		3	-
Peter Ankersen	22/09/90	København									s86	M	12	-

EUROPE

FC Midtjylland

CHAMPIONS LEAGUE

Second qualifying round - Lincoln FC (GIB)
H 1-0 *Rasmussen (33)*
Dahlin, Hansen, Sparv (Pusic 72), Sviatchenko, Poulsen, Rasmussen, Ureña (Sisto 56), Lauridsen, Larsen (Andersson 55), Rømer, Royer. Coach: Jess Thorup (DEN)
A 2-0 *Pusic (44), Duelund (89)*
Andersen, Hansen, Sparv, Sviatchenko (Banggaard 46), Poulsen, Pusic, Lauridsen, Olsson, Larsen (Duelund 69), Sisto (Gemmer 54), Rømer. Coach: Jess Thorup (DEN)

Third qualifying round - APOEL FC (CYP)
H 1-2 *Poulsen (88)*
Dahlin, Hansen, Sparv, Sviatchenko, Poulsen, Andersson (Royer 27), Pusic (Rasmussen 71), Lauridsen, Olsson (Ureña 63), Sisto, Rømer. Coach: Jess Thorup (DEN)
A 1-0 *Sviatchenko (3)*
Dahlin, Hansen, Sparv, Sviatchenko, Poulsen, Andersson (Larsen 89), Rasmussen, Lauridsen, Sisto, Bak (Onuachu 81), Royer (Pusic 66). Coach: Jess Thorup (DEN)

EUROPA LEAGUE

Play-offs - Southampton FC (ENG)
A 1-1 *Sparv (45)*
Dahlin, Hansen, Sparv, Sviatchenko, Poulsen, Andersson (Olsson 78), Rasmussen (Onuachu 89), Lauridsen, Sisto (Hassan 71), Rømer, Royer. Coach: Jess Thorup (DEN)
H 1-0 *Rasmussen (28)*
Dahlin, Hansen, Sparv, Sviatchenko, Poulsen, Andersson (Pusic 80), Rasmussen, Lauridsen, Sisto (Hassan 68), Bak (Rømer 83), Royer. Coach: Jess Thorup (DEN)

Group D
Match 1 - Legia Warszawa (POL)
H 1-0 *Rasmussen (60)*
Andersen, Hansen, Sparv, Sviatchenko, Poulsen, Andersson (Olsson 46), Rasmussen (Pusic 89), Sisto (Onuachu 81), Bak, Novák, Royer. Coach: Jess Thorup (DEN)
Match 2 - Club Brugge KV (BEL)
A 3-1 *Sisto (51), Onuachu (67), Novák (74)*
Andersen, Hansen, Sparv, Sviatchenko, Poulsen, Rasmussen (Onuachu 54), Olsson, Sisto (Ureña 78), Bak (Rømer 32), Novák, Royer. Coach: Jess Thorup (DEN)
Match 3 - SSC Napoli (ITA)
H 1-4 *Pusic (43)*
Andersen, Hansen, Sparv, Sviatchenko, Poulsen, Rasmussen (Larsen 73), Pusic (Onuachu 62), Duelund (Mabil 73), Rømer, Novák, Royer. Coach: Jess Thorup (DEN)
Match 4 - SSC Napoli (ITA)
A 0-5
Andersen, Hansen (Ureña 46), Sparv, Sviatchenko, Poulsen, Olsson (Sisto 69), Banggaard, Rømer, Onuachu (Pusic 62), Novák, Royer. Coach: Jess Thorup (DEN)

Match 5 - Legia Warszawa (POL)
A 0-1
Andersen, Hansen, Sparv, Sviatchenko, Poulsen, Rasmussen (Onuachu 36), Olsson (Pusic 69), Sisto (Mabil 46), Rømer, Novák, Royer. Coach: Jess Thorup (DEN)
Match 6 - Club Brugge KV (BEL)
H 1-1 *Sisto (27)*
Andersen, Hansen, Sparv, Sviatchenko, Poulsen, Pusic (Onuachu 83), Olsson (Lauridsen 90+2), Sisto (Ureña 74), Rømer, Novák, Royer. Coach: Jess Thorup (DEN)

Round of 32 - Manchester United FC (ENG)
H 2-1 *Sisto (44), Onuachu (77)*
Andersen, Hansen, Sparv, Bodurov, Pusic (Onuachu 60), Kadlec (Royer 85), Olsson, Sisto, Rømer, Hassan (Ureña 67), Novák. Coach: Jess Thorup (DEN)
A 1-5 *Sisto (28)*
Andersen, Hansen, Sparv, Bodurov, Poulsen, Ureña (Onuachu 46), Olsson (Pusic 79), Sisto, Rømer, Hassan (Kadlec 67), Novák. Coach: Jess Thorup (DEN)
Red card: Rømer 89

FC København

EUROPA LEAGUE

Second qualifying round - Newtown AFC (WAL)
H 2-0 *Verbič (3), Kusk (74)*
Andersen, Augustinsson, Nilsson, Verbič (B Olsen 90+3), Delaney, N Jørgensen, Kusk, Amartey, Ankersen, Pourie (Høgli 82), Toutouh. Coach: Ståle Solbakken (NOR)
A 3-1 *Pourie (28, 51), N Jørgensen (40p)*
Andersen, Augustinsson, Nilsson, Verbič, Delaney, N Jørgensen (Remmer 46), Kusk (B Olsen 65), Ankersen, Pourie, Toutouh (Høgli 46), M Jørgensen. Coach: Ståle Solbakken (NOR)

Third qualifying round - FK Jablonec (CZE)
A 1-0 *Verbič (51)*
Andersen, Augustinsson, Verbič (Kusk 81), Delaney, N Jørgensen, Antonsson, Amartey, Santander (Pourie 88), Ankersen, Toutouh (Kvist 63), M Jørgensen. Coach: Ståle Solbakken (NOR)
H 2-3 *N Jørgensen (72), Santander (88)*
Andersen, Augustinsson, Kvist (Kusk 61), Verbič, Delaney, N Jørgensen, Antonsson, Amartey, Santander, Ankersen (Nilsson 86), M Jørgensen. Coach: Ståle Solbakken (NOR)
Red card: Verbič 64

Brøndby IF

EUROPA LEAGUE

First qualifying round - AC Juvenes/Dogana (SMR)
H 9-0 *Elmander (6, 16), Da Silva (14), Pukki (22), Holst (23), Larsson (35), Rashani (55, 87), Corlu (66)*
Hradecky, Ørnskov, Szymanowski, Pukki (Stückler 63), Elmander (Rashani 46), Holst, Larsson, Phiri (Corlu 63), Dumic, Hjulsager, Da Silva. Coach: Thomas Frank (DEN)
A 2-0 *Elmander (49), Rashani (59)*
Hradecky, Albrechtsen, Szymanowski (Corlu 46), Pukki, Elmander, Larsson, Rashani, Durmisi, Phiri (Crone 82), Dumic, Hjulsager (Stückler 71). Coach: Thomas Frank (DEN)

Second qualifying round - PFC Beroe Stara Zagora (BUL)
A 1-0 *Albrechtsen (85)*
Hradecky, Albrechtsen, Ørnskov, Pukki, Elmander (Eriksson 73), Larsson, Rashani (Hjulsager 60), Durmisi, Phiri, Nørgaard (Holst 84), Dumic. Coach: Thomas Frank (DEN)
H 0-0
Hradecky, Albrechtsen, Ørnskov, Pukki (Holst 79), Elmander, Larsson, Rashani (Eriksson 58), Durmisi, Phiri, Nørgaard, Hjulsager. Coach: Thomas Frank (DEN)

Third qualifying round - AC Omonia (CYP)
H 0-0
Hradecky, Albrechtsen (Johansen 43), Pukki, Eriksson (Hjulsager 81), Elmander (Schwartz 62), Holst, Larsson, Rashani, Durmisi, Phiri, Dumic. Coach: Thomas Frank (DEN)
A 2-2 *Pukki (2, 39)*
Hradecky, Albrechtsen, Ørnskov, Pukki (Rashani 90+6), Eriksson, Elmander (Phiri 56), Holst, Larsson, Durmisi, Da Silva (Johansen 89). Coach: Thomas Frank (DEN)
Red card: Hradecky 90+8

Play-offs - PAOK FC (GRE)
A 0-5
Rønnow, Albrechtsen, Ørnskov, Pukki, Eriksson, Elmander (Schwartz 58), Holst (Dumic 42), Larsson, Durmisi, Phiri (Nørgaard 75), Agger. Coach: Thomas Frank (DEN)
H 1-1 *Rashani (27)*
Rønnow, Albrechtsen, Ørnskov, Eriksson (Pukki 72), Larsson, Rashani, Durmisi, Phiri (Holst 81), Nørgaard, Hjulsager, Schwartz (Elmander 60). Coach: Thomas Frank (DEN)

DENMARK

Randers FC

First qualifying round - UE Sant Julià (AND)
A 1-0 *Borring (22)*
Johnsson, Keller, Thomsen, Tverskov, Amini, Borring (Marxen 82), Fenger, Fischer, Lundberg, Poulsen (Allansson 62), Brock-Madsen (Thygesen 85). Coach: Colin Todd (ENG)
Red cards: Lundberg 17, Tverskov 81
H 3-0 *Amini (42), Babayan (72), Ishak (90+3)*
Johnsson, Keller, Thomsen (Bager 76), Amini, Borring, Ishak, Marxen, Fenger, Thygesen (Kallesøe 72), Allansson (Babayan 60), Fischer. Coach: Colin Todd (ENG)

Second qualifying round - IF Elfsborg (SWE)
H 0-0
Johnsson, Keller, Thomsen, Tverskov, Amini, Borring (Marxen 78), Ishak (Babayan 75), Fenger, Fischer, Poulsen, Brock-Madsen. Coach: Colin Todd (ENG)
A 0-1 (aet)
Johnsson, Keller, Thomsen, Tverskov, Amini, Borring (Thygesen 80), Marxen (Babayan 54), Fenger, Fischer, Poulsen, Brock-Madsen. Coach: Colin Todd (ENG)
Red card: Brock-Madsen 84

Aalborg BK

1885 • Nordjyske Arena (13,800) • fodbold.aabsport.dk
Major honours
Danish League (4) 1995, 1999, 2008, 2014; Danish Cup (3) 1966, 1970, 2014
Coach: Lars Søndergaard

2015
20/07	h Esbjerg	D	1-1	Abildgaard
24/07	a Hobro	W	1-0	Risgård
03/08	a Nordsjælland	L	1-2	Risgård
10/08	h Midtjylland	L	0-2	
15/08	a AGF	W	3-2	Spalvis 2, Jönsson
24/08	h OB	W	5-1	Enevoldsen, Risgård 2, Spalvis, Børsting
30/08	h Randers	L	0-2	
13/09	a København	L	2-4	Enevoldsen, Spalvis
20/09	h Brøndby	W	4-1	Spalvis 2, Jönsson, Thomsen
25/09	a Viborg	L	0-1	
04/10	h SønderjyskE	W	5-0	Spalvis 2, Thomsen, Enevoldsen, Børsting
19/10	h Esbjerg	W	2-1	Risgård, Spalvis
25/10	a Nordsjælland	L	0-3	
01/11	h Hobro	W	6-0	Pedersen, Spalvis 2, Enevoldsen, Thrane, Jönsson
06/11	a SønderjyskE	W	2-1	Enevoldsen 2
23/11	h Randers	W	3-2	Enevoldsen, Spalvis 2
29/11	a Brøndby	W	2-0	Enevoldsen, Spalvis
07/12	h Viborg	W	2-0	Jönsson, Enevoldsen

2016
29/02	a Midtjylland	D	1-1	Spalvis
04/03	h OB	L	0-1	
13/03	a København	L	2-6	Risgård, Enevoldsen
18/03	h AGF	D	2-2	Spalvis, og (Jönsson)
01/04	h Nordsjælland	W	1-0	Enevoldsen
10/04	a Hobro	W	2-0	Thomsen 2
17/04	h SønderjyskE	L	1-2	Jönsson
25/04	a Randers	D	0-0	
01/05	h Brøndby	W	3-0	Thomsen, Spalvis 2 (1p)
08/05	a Viborg	W	2-0	Risgård, Thomsen
12/05	h København	L	0-2	
17/05	a AGF	L	0-2	
22/05	h Esbjerg	L	1-2	Enevoldsen
26/05	h Midtjylland	D	0-0	
29/05	a OB	L	2-3	Pohl, Risgård

No	Name	Nat	DoB	Pos	Aps	(s)	Gls
27	Oliver Abildgaard		10/06/96	M	7	(7)	1
3	Jakob Ahlmann		18/01/91	D	10	(2)	
9	Thomas Augustinussen		20/03/81	M	2	(6)	
17	Christian Bassogog	CMR	18/10/95	M	1	(8)	
4	Jakob Blåbjerg		11/01/95	D	17	(9)	
30	Andreas Bruhn		17/02/94	M	2	(6)	
25	Frederik Børsting		13/02/95	M	15	(14)	2
20	Henrik Dalsgaard		27/07/89	D	17		
7	Thomas Enevoldsen		27/07/87	M	28	(2)	12
11	Nicklas Helenius		08/05/91	A	3	(7)	
10	Rasmus Jönsson	SWE	27/01/90	A	24	(8)	5
26	Robert Kakeeto	UGA	19/05/95	M	1		
2	Patrick Kristensen		28/04/87	D	21	(1)	
1	Nicolai Larsen		09/03/91	G	33		
32	Kasper Pedersen		13/01/93	D	27		1
5	Kenneth Emil Petersen		15/01/85	D	32		
79	Jannik Pohl		06/04/96	A	4	(3)	1
6	Jukka Raitala	FIN	15/09/88	D	3	(2)	
19	Marco Ramkilde		09/05/98	A		(1)	
21	Kasper Risgård		04/01/83	M	26	(3)	8
24	Morten Rokkedal		10/10/97	D	1		
33	Lukas Spalvis	LTU	27/07/94	A	24	(6)	18
15	Gilli Sørensen	FRO	11/08/92	A	4	(7)	
23	Nicolaj Thomsen		08/05/93	M	33		6
16	Mathias Thrane		04/09/93	M		(5)	1
8	Rasmus Würtz		18/09/83	M	28		

AGF Aarhus

1880 • Ceres Park (20,032) • agf.dk
Major honours
Danish League (5) 1955, 1956, 1957, 1960, 1986; Danish Cup (9) 1955, 1957, 1960, 1961, 1965, 1987, 1988, 1992, 1996
Coach: Morten Wieghorst;
(06/12/15) Glen Riddersholm

2015
19/07	h Brøndby	W	2-1	Vatsadze 2
27/07	a Viborg	D	0-0	
02/08	h Randers	W	3-2	Aabech 2 (1p), Petersen
07/08	a OB	D	2-2	Aabech, Vatsadze
15/08	h AaB	L	2-3	Elez, Yasin
23/08	a København	D	2-2	Andersen, Nordstrand
28/08	h Esbjerg	D	0-0	
11/09	a Hobro	W	3-0	(w/o; original result 1-2 og (Hansen))
18/09	h SønderjyskE	L	1-2	Vatsadze
27/09	a Nordsjælland	L	0-2	
04/10	a Midtjylland	L	0-2	
18/10	h Nordsjælland	W	3-0	Aabech 2, Vatsadze
23/10	a Hobro	W	1-3	Olsen
02/11	h SønderjyskE	D	0-0	
06/11	a Randers	L	1-4	Petersen
22/11	h Brøndby	D	1-1	Olsen
27/11	a Viborg	L	0-1	
04/12	h Midtjylland	W	2-1	Čavrić, Aabech (p)

2016
26/02	a OB	D	2-2	Bjarnason, Backman
06/03	h København	D	0-0	
11/03	a Esbjerg	L	1-2	Nielsen
18/03	a AaB	D	2-2	M Rasmussen, S Rasmussen
02/04	h Hobro	D	1-1	Olsen
09/04	a SønderjyskE	D	2-2	Elez, Lange
16/04	h Randers	L	0-2	
24/04	a Brøndby	L	1-2	Olsen
29/04	h Viborg	L	1-2	Lange
08/05	a Midtjylland	D	1-1	og (Sparv)
11/05	h Esbjerg	W	5-1	Olsen, Petersen, Andersen, M Rasmussen 2
17/05	h AaB	W	2-0	M Rasmussen 2
21/05	a Nordsjælland	D	3-3	M Rasmussen 3
26/05	h OB	W	2-1	M Rasmussen, Olsen
29/05	a København	L	1-2	M Rasmussen

No	Name	Nat	DoB	Pos	Aps	(s)	Gls
10	Kim Aabech		31/05/83	M	22	(10)	6
5	Alexander Juel Andersen		29/01/91	D	23	(3)	2
3	Niklas Backman	SWE	13/11/88	D	14		1
20	Theódór Elmar Bjarnason	ISL	04/03/87	M	26	(1)	1
17	Oskar Buur		31/03/98	D		(1)	
8	Aleksandar Čavrić	SRB	18/05/94	A	15	(4)	1
6	Daniel Christensen		19/09/88	D	32	(1)	
18	Josip Elez	CRO	25/04/94	D	22	(3)	2
16	Jens Jønsson		10/01/93	M	30	(1)	
28	Dzhamaldin Khodzhaniyazov	RUS	18/07/96	D	11	(4)	
11	Jesper Lange		11/01/86	A	8	(13)	2
2	Dino Mikanović	CRO	07/05/94	D	18	(1)	
15	Emil Nielsen		08/11/93	A	1	(3)	1
26	Morten Nordstrand		08/06/83	A		(10)	1
9	Danny Olsen		11/06/85	M	24	(3)	6
4	Daniel Pedersen		27/07/92	M	24		
7	Stephan Petersen		15/11/85	M	22	(7)	3
25	Piscu	ESP	25/02/87	D	5		
13	Morten "Duncan" Rasmussen		31/01/85	A	12	(1)	10
1	Steffen Rasmussen		30/09/82	G	33		1
22	Davit Skhirtladze	GEO	16/03/93	M		(6)	
14	Jens Stage		08/11/96	M	3	(3)	
21	Mate Vatsadze	GEO	17/12/88	A	14	(6)	5
14	Ahmed Yasin	IRQ	22/04/91	M	4	(13)	1
27	Michael Zacho		11/11/96	M		(3)	

Brøndby IF

1964 • Brøndby Stadion (28,000) •
brondby.com
Major honours
*Danish League (10) 1985, 1987, 1988, 1990, 1991,
1996, 1997, 1998, 2002, 2005; Danish Cup (6) 1989,
1994, 1998, 2003, 2005, 2008*
**Coach: Thomas Frank;
(09/03/15) (Aurelijus Skarbalius (LTU))**

2015

19/07 a AGF	L	1-2	Pukki
26/07 h OB	L	1-2	Pukki
02/08 h Hobro	L	0-2	
09/08 a Randers	D	3-3	Schwartz 2 (1p), Larsson
16/08 a Viborg	W	4-0	Pukki 2, Elmander, Phiri
23/08 h SønderjyskE	W	1-0	Rashani
30/08 a Nordsjælland	W	2-0	Schwartz (p), Pukki
13/09 h Midtjylland	D	0-0	
20/09 a AaB	L	1-4	Phiri
27/09 h København	W	1-0	Albrechtsen
04/10 h Esbjerg	D	1-1	Pukki
18/10 a Viborg	W	2-0	Eriksson, Elmander
25/10 h Midtjylland	W	2-1	Jakobsen, Elmander
01/11 a OB	W	5-2	Austin, Pukki, Kahlenberg, Elmander 2
08/11 h København	D	0-0	
22/11 a AGF	D	1-1	og (Jönsson)
29/11 h AaB	L	0-2	
06/12 h Nordsjælland	W	2-0	Agger, Schwartz

2016

28/02 h Hobro	W	1-0	Wilczek
06/03 a SønderjyskE	L	1-3	Eriksson
13/03 h Randers	W	1-0	Boysen
20/03 h Esbjerg	D	0-0	
03/04 a Midtjylland	L	0-2	
10/04 h OB	W	1-0	Phiri
17/04 a København	L	0-2	
24/04 h AGF	W	2-1	Wilczek 2
01/05 a AaB	L	0-3	
09/05 h Nordsjælland	W	2-1	Durmisi, Wilczek
12/05 a Randers	W	2-0	Boysen, Stückler
16/05 a Esbjerg	W	3-2	Pukki 2, Larsson
23/05 h Viborg	L	0-1	
26/05 a Hobro	W	2-0	Boysen, Wilczek
29/05 h SønderjyskE	L	1-2	Hjulsager

No	Name	Nat	DoB	Pos	Aps	(s)	Gls
22	Daniel Agger		12/12/84	D	24		1
5	Martin Albrechtsen		31/03/80	D	16	(1)	1
8	Rodolph Austin	JAM	01/06/85	M	16	(1)	1
15	David Boysen		30/04/91	M	14		3
32	Rezan Corlu		07/08/97	M		(1)	
27	Svenn Crone		20/05/95	D	1	(3)	
23	Patrick da Silva		23/10/94	D	2	(1)	
20	Dario Dumic		30/01/92	D	7		
17	Riza Durmisi		08/01/94	D	29		1
11	Johan Elmander	SWE	27/05/81	A	4	(24)	5
10	Magnus Eriksson	SWE	08/04/90	A	19	(3)	2
35	Nicklas Halse		03/05/97	D		(1)	
21	Andrew Hjulsager		15/01/95	M	16	(3)	1
12	Frederik Holst		24/09/94	D	11	(9)	
1	Lukas Hradecky	FIN	24/11/89	G	3		
25	Christian Jakobsen		27/03/93	M	10	(6)	1
2	Jesper Juelsgård		26/01/89	D	11	(4)	
7	Thomas Kahlenberg		20/03/83	M	9	(4)	1
19	Johan Larsson	SWE	05/05/90	D	32		2
19	Christian Nørgaard		10/03/94	M	10	(6)	
18	Lebogang Phiri	RSA	09/11/94	M	25	(3)	3
9	Teemu Pukki	FIN	29/03/90	A	28	(5)	9
14	Elbasan Rashani	KOS	09/05/93	M	7	(3)	1
1	Frederik Rønnow		04/08/92	G	29		
64	Ronnie Schwartz		29/08/89	A	10	(6)	4
34	Daniel Stückler		13/04/97	A	1	(6)	1
8	Alexander Szymanowski	ARG	13/10/88	M		(1)	
16	Mads Toppel		30/01/82	G	1		
20	Kamil Wilczek	POL	14/01/88	A	10	(3)	5
6	Martin Ørnskov		10/10/85	M	18	(4)	

Esbjerg fB

1924 • Blue Water Arena (16,942) • efb.dk
Major honours
*Danish League (5) 1961, 1962, 1963, 1965, 1979;
Danish Cup (3) 1964, 1976, 2013*
**Coach: Niels Frederiksen;
(10/08/15) (Michael Pedersen);
(20/10/15) Jonas Dal Andersen**

2015

20/07 a AaB	D	1-1	Van Buren (p)
26/07 h København	L	1-2	Vestergaard
31/07 a Viborg	L	1-2	Van Buren
09/08 h SønderjyskE	L	0-4	
16/08 a Nordsjælland	W	2-1	Söder, Rise
23/08 h Midtjylland	D	1-1	Söder
28/08 a AGF	D	0-0	
14/09 h OB	W	4-2	Söder, Bille Nielsen, Pálsson, Mensah
21/09 h Randers	L	0-2	
28/09 a Hobro	D	2-2	Bille Nielsen 2 (1p)
04/10 a Brøndby	D	1-1	Van Buren
19/10 h AaB	L	1-2	og (Larsen)
24/10 a Viborg	L	2-4	Mensah 2
30/10 h Nordsjælland	W	2-1	Bille Nielsen (p), Rise
08/11 h Midtjylland	L	1-5	Mensah
22/11 h Hobro	D	4-4	Söder, Lekven, Rise, Van Buren
30/11 a OB	L	1-2	Bille Nielsen
06/12 h SønderjyskE	L	0-1	

2016

28/02 a København	L	1-2	Paulsen
06/03 h Randers	W	1-0	Schwartz
11/03 h AGF	W	2-1	Hagelskjær, Lekven
20/03 a Brøndby	D	0-0	
04/04 h Viborg	W	1-0	Paulsen
11/04 a Nordsjælland	D	0-0	
18/04 h Midtjylland	L	0-2	
23/04 a Hobro	D	2-2	Schwartz 2
02/05 h OB	L	0-2	
06/05 h SønderjyskE	L	0-2	
11/05 a AGF	L	1-5	Paulsen
16/05 h Brøndby	L	2-3	Mensah, Van Buren
22/05 a AaB	W	2-1	Van Buren, Schwartz
26/05 h SønderjyskE	L	1-4	Mensah
29/05 a Randers	L	1-3	Brink

No	Name	Nat	DoB	Pos	Aps	(s)	Gls
19	Michael Almebäck	SWE	04/04/88	D	11	(2)	
8	Jeppe Andersen		06/12/92	M	13	(2)	
20	Hans Henrik Andreasen		10/01/79	M		(9)	
12	Søren Andreasen		13/03/96	A		(1)	
14	Nicki Bille Nielsen		07/02/88	A	17		5
25	Jeppe Brinch		30/04/95	D	11	(2)	
29	Mark Brink		15/03/98	M	3	(3)	1
30	Martin Dúbravka	SVK	15/01/89	G	18		
22	Mohammed Fellah	NOR	24/05/89	M	13	(5)	
32	Nikolaj Hagelskjær		06/05/90	D	14	(1)	1
16	Jeppe Højbjerg		30/04/95	G	15		
2	Michael Jakobsen		02/01/86	D	15		
18	Leon Jessen		11/06/86	D	15	(4)	
7	Jesper Jørgensen		09/05/84	M	13		
23	Jonas Knudsen		16/09/92	D	2		
26	Mathias Kristensen		21/03/97	M		(2)	
14	Jesper Lauridsen		27/03/91	D	15		
15	Ryan Laursen		14/04/92	D	4	(3)	
6	Magnus Lekven	NOR	13/01/88	M	27		2
21	Jerry Lucena	PHI	11/08/80	M	6	(3)	
24	Marco Lund		30/06/96	D	4	(3)	
10	Emil Lyng		03/08/89	M	5	(7)	
33	Kevin Mensah		15/05/91	A	13	(3)	6
17	Casper Nielsen		29/04/94	M	27	(4)	
4	Gudlaugur Victor Pálsson	ISL	30/04/91	M	3	(2)	1
5	Bjørn Paulsen		02/07/91	M	25		3
31	Jesper Rasmussen		04/01/92	M		(1)	
11	Lasse Rise		09/06/86	M	8	(16)	3
19	Ronnie Schwartz		29/08/89	A	11	(1)	4
3	Daniel Stenderup		31/05/89	D	28	(2)	
27	Robin Söder	SWE	01/04/91	A	10	(2)	4
9	Mick van Buren	NED	24/08/92	A	14	(11)	4
7	Mikkel Vestergaard		22/11/92	A	3	(8)	1

Hobro IK

1913 • DS Arena (7,500) • hikfodbold.dk
**Coach: Jonas Dal Andersen;
(20/10/15) (Lars Justesen);
(24/11/15) Ove Pedersen**

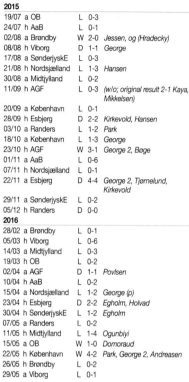

2015

19/07 a OB	L	0-3	
24/07 h AaB	L	0-1	
02/08 a Brøndby	W	2-0	Jessen, og (Hradecky)
08/08 h Viborg	D	1-1	George
17/08 a SønderjyskE	L	0-2	
21/08 h Nordsjælland	L	1-3	Hansen
30/08 a Midtjylland	L	0-2	
11/09 h AGF	L	0-3	(w/o; original result 2-1 Kaya, Mikkelsen)
20/09 a København	L	0-1	
28/09 h Esbjerg	D	2-2	Kirkevold, Hansen
03/10 a Randers	L	1-2	Park
18/10 a København	L	1-3	George
23/10 h AGF	W	3-1	George 2, Bøge
01/11 a AaB	L	0-6	
07/11 h Nordsjælland	L	0-2	
22/11 a Esbjerg	D	4-4	George 2, Tjørnelund, Kirkevold
29/11 h SønderjyskE	L	0-2	
05/12 h Randers	D	0-0	

2016

28/02 a Brøndby	L	0-1	
05/03 h Viborg	L	0-6	
14/03 a Midtjylland	L	0-3	
19/03 h OB	L	0-2	
02/04 a AGF	D	1-1	Povlsen
10/04 h AaB	L	0-2	
15/04 a Nordsjælland	L	1-2	George (p)
23/04 h Esbjerg	D	2-2	Egholm, Holvad
30/04 h SønderjyskE	L	1-2	Egholm
07/05 a Randers	L	0-2	
11/05 h Midtjylland	L	1-4	Ogunbiyi
15/05 a OB	W	1-0	Domoraud
22/05 h København	W	4-2	Park, George 2, Andreasen
26/05 h Brøndby	L	0-2	
29/05 a Viborg	L	0-1	

No	Name	Nat	DoB	Pos	Aps	(s)	Gls
7	Hans Henrik Andreasen		10/01/79	M	2	(7)	1
80	Quincy Antipas	ZIM	20/04/84	A	1	(4)	
9	Morten Beck		02/01/88	A	5	(8)	
20	Mathias Bersang		24/11/91	M	3	(12)	
2	Jonas Brix-Damborg		17/04/86	M	30		
3	Jesper Bøge		22/02/90	D	24		1
15	Tanaka Chinyahara	ZIM	12/10/95	M		(3)	
18	Michael Christensen		06/02/83	D	10	(1)	
5	Rasmus Lynge Christensen		12/08/91	M	4	(8)	
21	Wilfried Domoraud	FRA	18/08/88	M	11	(2)	1
2	Anders Egholm		15/03/83	D	13		2
21, 10	Mayron George	CRC	23/10/93	A	17	(6)	9
14	Thomas Hansen		18/01/83	D	13	(4)	2
17	Rune Hastrup		16/10/91	D	10	(4)	
19	Anders Holvad		14/10/89	M	16	(6)	1
11	Mads Jessen		14/10/89	A	16	(6)	1
13	Mads Justesen		31/12/82	D	26	(1)	
27	Gökcan Kaya		07/08/95	M	15	(7)	1
19, 9	Pål Alexander Kirkevold	NOR	10/11/90	A	11	(4)	2
26	Martin Mikkelsen		29/04/86	M	22	(5)	1
16	Alexander Nybo		27/04/95	G	2		
12	Babajide Ogunbiyi	USA	03/11/86	D	14		1
22	Park Jung-bin	KOR	22/02/94	A	21	(1)	2
25	Kasper Povlsen		26/09/89	M	21	(4)	1
1	Jesper Rask		28/07/88	G	31		
8	Tidiane Sane	SEN	10/07/85	M	9	(3)	
33	Adama Tamboura	MLI	18/05/85	D	8		
4	Jacob Tjørnelund		31/12/91	D	17	(1)	1
23	Christoffer Østergaard		22/05/93	M			

DENMARK

FC København

1992 • Telia Parken (38,065) • fck.dk

Major honours
Danish League (11) 1993, 2001, 2003, 2004, 2006, 2007, 2009, 2010, 2011, 2013, 2016; Danish Cup (7) 1995, 1997, 2004, 2009, 2012, 2015, 2016

Coach: Ståle Solbakken (NOR)

2015

26/07	a Esbjerg	W	2-1	*Pourie, N Jørgensen*
02/08	a SønderjyskE	W	3-1	*Delaney, N Jørgensen (p), Kvist*
09/08	h Nordsjælland	D	1-1	*M Jørgensen*
14/08	a Midtjylland	D	0-0	
23/08	h AGF	D	2-2	*Augustinsson, Delaney*
30/08	a OB	L	0-1	
13/09	h AaB	W	4-2	*Cornelius, Kusk, N Jørgensen, og (Pedersen)*
16/09	h Randers	W	3-0	*Verbič, Toutouh, Cornelius*
20/09	h Hobro	W	1-0	*Cornelius*
27/09	a Brøndby	L	0-1	
04/10	a Viborg	W	1-0	*Toutouh*
18/10	h Hobro	W	3-1	*Santander, Kusk 2*
25/10	a SønderjyskE	W	2-1	*Santander, Cornelius*
01/11	h Randers	W	4-0	*Kusk 2, Toutouh 2*
08/11	a Brøndby	D	0-0	
22/11	a Viborg	D	0-0	
06/12	h OB	W	4-1	*M Jørgensen 2, N Jørgensen, og (L Nielsen)*

2016

28/02	h Esbjerg	W	2-1	*Santander, N Jørgensen*
03/03	a Midtjylland	W	1-0	*N Jørgensen*
06/03	a AGF	D	0-0	
13/03	h AaB	W	6-2	*Santander 2, Kusk, N Jørgensen, Toutouh, Cornelius*
20/03	a Nordsjælland	L	0-2	
03/04	a SønderjyskE	W	1-0	*Verbič*
10/04	a Randers	D	1-1	*Santander*
17/04	h Brøndby	W	2-0	*N Jørgensen 2 (1p)*
24/04	a Viborg	D	1-1	*Delaney*
01/05	h Midtjylland	W	5-3	*Delaney, Santander, Verbič, N Jørgensen 2 (1p)*
08/05	a OB	W	1-0	*Santander*
12/05	a AaB	W	2-0	*Santander, N Jørgensen*
16/05	h Nordsjælland	W	2-0	*Santander 2*
22/05	a Hobro	L	2-4	*Kadrii, N Jørgensen*
26/05	a Esbjerg	W	4-1	*Santander 2, N Jørgensen 2 (1p)*
29/05	h AGF	W	2-1	*Delaney, Santander*

No	Name	Nat	DoB	Pos	Aps	(s)	Gls
32	Danny Amankwaa		30/01/94	M		(7)	
18	Daniel Amartey	GHA	21/12/94	M	15		
1	Stephan Andersen		26/11/81	G	17		
22	Peter Ankersen		22/09/90	D	27	(3)	
15	Mikael Antonsson	SWE	31/05/81	D	9	(4)	
3	Ludwig Augustinsson	SWE	21/04/94	D	31		1
11	Andreas Cornelius		16/03/93	A	11	(15)	5
8	Thomas Delaney		03/09/91	M	29		5
2	Tom Høgli	NOR	24/02/84	D	6	(2)	
5	Erik Johansson	SWE	30/12/88	D	13		
25	Mathias "Zanka" Jørgensen		23/04/90	D	31		3
10	Nicolai Jørgensen		15/01/91	A	30	(1)	15
9	Bashkim Kadrii		09/07/91	M	2	(16)	1
28	Thomas Kaminski	BEL	23/10/92	G	2		
35	Aboubakar Keita	CIV	05/11/97	M	1	(1)	
37	Julian Kristoffersen	NOR	10/05/97	A		(2)	
17	Kasper Kusk		10/11/91	M	22	(2)	6
6	William Kvist Jørgensen		24/02/85	M	25	(5)	
34	Marcus Mathisen		27/02/96	M		(3)	
4	Per Nilsson	SWE	15/09/82	D	4		
36	Brandur H Olsen	FRO	19/12/95	M		(1)	
31	Robin Olsen	SWE	08/01/90	G	14		
23	Marvin Pourie	GER	08/01/91	A	2		1
20	Christoffer Remmer		16/01/93	D	5	(12)	
19	Federico Santander	PAR	04/06/91	A	29	(1)	14
24	Youssef Toutouh	MAR	06/10/92	M	20	(8)	5
7	Benjamin Verbič	SVN	27/11/93	M	18	(8)	5

FC Midtjylland

1999 • MCH Arena (11,809) • fcm.dk

Major honours
Danish League (1) 2015

Coach: Jess Thorup

2015

18/07	h Viborg	W	2-0	*Sisto 2*
24/07	a SønderjyskE	W	2-1	*Duelund, Rasmussen*
31/07	h OB	W	1-0	*Rasmussen*
10/08	a AaB	W	2-0	*Royer, Onuachu*
14/08	h København	D	0-0	
23/08	a Esbjerg	D	1-1	*Onuachu*
30/08	h Hobro	W	2-0	*Pusic 2*
13/09	a Brøndby	D	0-0	
20/09	h Nordsjælland	L	0-1	
27/09	a Randers	W	2-0	*Banggaard, Rasmussen*
04/10	h AGF	W	2-0	*Royer, Ureña*
16/10	h Randers	W	2-1	*Sviatchenko, Pusic*
25/10	a Brøndby	L	1-2	*Poulsen*
31/10	h Viborg	W	2-0	*Duelund, Sviatchenko*
08/11	h Esbjerg	W	5-1	*Rasmussen, Novák, Duelund, Olsson, Poulsen*
20/11	a OB	D	1-1	*Rømer*
04/12	a AGF	L	1-2	*Duelund*

2016

29/02	h AaB	D	1-1	*Poulsen (p)*
03/03	h København	L	0-1	
07/03	a Nordsjælland	L	1-2	*Onuachu*
14/03	h Hobro	W	3-0	*Hassan, Pusic, Ureña*
20/03	a SønderjyskE	L	2-3	*Novák, Pusic*
03/04	h Brøndby	W	2-0	*Hassan, Pusic*
08/04	a Viborg	D	1-1	*Onuachu*
18/04	a Esbjerg	W	2-0	*Hassan 2*
22/04	h OB	W	2-0	*Pusic 2*
01/05	a København	L	3-5	*Pusic, Poulsen 2*
08/05	h AGF	D	1-1	*og (S Rasmussen)*
11/05	a Hobro	W	4-1	*og (M Christensen), Nissen, Hassan, Poulsen (p)*
14/05	h SønderjyskE	W	3-2	*Pusic, Onuachu, Sisto*
22/05	a Randers	W	2-1	*Duelund, Pusic (p)*
26/05	a AaB	D	0-0	
29/05	h Nordsjælland	W	4-1	*Onuachu, Pusic 2, Sisto*

No	Name	Nat	DoB	Pos	Aps	(s)	Gls
42	David Akintola	NGA	13/01/96	M		(1)	
31	Mikkel Andersen		17/12/88	G	29		
8	Petter Andersson	SWE	20/02/85	M	3	(1)	
32	Kristian Bach Bak		20/10/82	D	1		
26	Patrick Banggaard		04/04/94	D	12	(1)	1
4	Nikolay Bodurov	BUL	30/05/86	D	15		
16	Johan Dahlin	SWE	08/09/86	G	4		
20	Francis Dickoh	GHA	13/12/82	D		(1)	
22	Mikkel Duelund		29/06/97	M	13	(9)	5
29	Jonas Gemmer		31/01/96	M	2	(1)	
2	Kian Hansen		03/03/89	D	27	(1)	
36	Rilwan Hassan	NGA	09/02/91	M	16	(1)	5
14	Václav Kadlec	CZE	20/05/92	A	5	(1)	
19	Marco Larsen		15/05/93	M	1	(6)	
15	Jesper Lauritsen		27/03/91	D	6	(1)	
37	Rasmus Lauritsen		27/02/96	D		(1)	
45	Awer Mabil	AUS	15/09/95	M		(6)	
41	Alexander Munksgaard		13/12/97	D	1		
35	Frederik Møller		08/07/93	D	1		
43	Rasmus Nissen		07/07/97	M	9	(3)	1
70	Filip Novák	CZE	26/06/90	D	21	(2)	2
20	Daniel O'Shaughnessy	FIN	14/09/94	D		(1)	
17	Kristoffer Olsson	SWE	30/06/95	M	24	(3)	1
33	Ebere Paul Onuachu	NGA	28/05/94	A	8	(17)	6
7	Jakob Poulsen		07/07/83	M	31	(1)	6
10	Martin Pusic	AUT	24/10/87	A	18	(7)	13
9	Morten "Duncan" Rasmussen		31/01/85	A	10	(6)	4
77	Daniel Royer	AUT	22/05/90	M	15	(8)	2
28	André Rømer		18/07/93	D	26	(2)	1
27	Pione Sisto		04/02/95	M	20	(9)	4
3	Tim Sparv	FIN	20/02/87	M	31		
4	Erik Sviatchenko		04/10/91	D	13		2
24	Mads Døhr Thychosen		27/06/97	A		(1)	
11	Marcos Ureña	CRC	05/03/90	A	1	(7)	2

FC Nordsjælland

2003 • Right to Dream Park (10,300) • fcn.dk

Major honours
Danish League (1) 2012; Danish Cup (2) 2010, 2011

Coach: Ólafur Kristjánsson (ISL); (15/12/15) Kasper Hjulmand

2015

17/07	h SønderjyskE	L	0-2	
26/07	a Randers	L	0-3	
03/08	h AaB	W	2-1	*Bruninho, Ingvartsen*
09/08	a København	D	1-1	*Bruninho*
16/08	h Esbjerg	L	1-2	*Bruninho*
21/08	a Hobro	W	3-1	*Thórarinsson, Bruninho 2*
30/08	h Brøndby	L	0-2	
12/09	a Viborg	W	1-0	*Bruninho*
20/09	a Midtjylland	W	1-0	*Bruninho*
27/09	h AGF	W	2-0	*Thychosen, Ingvartsen*
02/10	h OB	L	1-5	*Vingaard*
18/10	a AGF	L	0-3	
25/10	h AaB	W	3-0	*Bruninho 2, John*
30/10	a Esbjerg	L	1-2	*Ingvartsen*
07/11	a Hobro	W	1-0	*John*
21/11	h SønderjyskE	L	1-2	*Mtiliga*
28/11	a Randers	L	0-1	
06/12	h Brøndby	L	0-2	

2016

28/02	a Viborg	D	1-1	*Emre*
07/03	h Midtjylland	W	2-1	*Moberg Karlsson, Marcondes*
13/03	a OB	L	1-3	*Mikkelsen*
20/03	h København	W	2-0	*Emre, Mikkelsen*
01/04	a AaB	L	0-1	
11/04	h Esbjerg	D	0-0	
15/04	h Hobro	W	2-1	*Mikkelsen, Maxsø*
24/04	a SønderjyskE	L	1-3	*Maxsø*
01/05	h Randers	D	2-2	*M Jensen, Køhler*
09/05	a Brøndby	L	1-2	*Marcondes*
12/05	h OB	L	0-1	
16/05	a København	L	0-2	
21/05	h AGF	D	3-3	*John, Maxsø, Ingvartsen*
26/05	a Viborg	W	1-0	*John*
29/05	a Midtjylland	L	1-4	*Ingvartsen*

No	Name	Nat	DoB	Pos	Aps	(s)	Gls
2	Adam Örn Arnarson	ISL	27/08/95	D	8		
11	Bruninho	BRA	29/09/89	A	12	(3)	9
14	Emil Damgaard		20/08/98	D	1		
27	Souheib Dhaflaoui		08/05/96	A	1	(7)	
31	Godsway Donyoh	GHA	14/10/94	A		(4)	
9	Emre Mor	TUR	24/07/97	A	12	(1)	2
3	Pascal Gregor		18/02/94	D	26	(3)	
19	Marcus Ingvartsen		04/01/96	A	13	(10)	5
1	David Jensen		25/03/92	G	30		
23	Mathias Jensen		01/01/96	M	1	(4)	1
12	Joshua John	NED	01/10/88	A	19	(4)	4
24	Christian Køhler		04/04/96	M	6	(1)	1
7	Stanislav Lobotka	SVK	25/11/94	M	26		
18	Emiliano Marcondes		09/03/95	M	19	(11)	2
4	Andreas Maxsø		18/03/94	D	32		3
13	Tobias Mikkelsen		18/03/86	A	6	(3)	3
5	David Moberg Karlsson	SWE	20/03/94	A	17	(6)	1
25	Adnan Mohammad		02/07/96	A		(1)	
20	Nicklas Mouritsen		15/03/95	D	3	(4)	
8	Patrick Mtiliga		28/01/81	D	16		1
34	Dominic Oduro	GHA	23/01/95	D		(1)	
22	Mads Pedersen		01/09/96	D	14	(2)	
6	Lasse Petry		19/09/92	M	11	(4)	
5	Ramón	BRA	22/08/90	M	18	(5)	
14	Mathias Hebo Rasmussen		02/08/96	M	1	(2)	
21	Johannes Ritter		15/02/95	A	1	(1)	
16	Rúnar Alex Rúnarsson	ISL	18/02/95	G	3		
17	Andreas Skovgaard		27/03/97	D	14	(1)	
33	Collins Tanor	GHA	04/01/98	M	3		
14	Gudmundur Thórarinsson	ISL	15/04/92	M	18	(2)	1
13	Oliver Thychosen		17/01/93	A	4	(10)	1
30	Jonathan Vervoort	BEL	13/08/93	D		(1)	
10	Martin Vingaard		20/03/85	M	28	(3)	1

Odense BK

1887 • TRE-FOR Park (15,790) • ob.dk
Major honours
Danish League (3) 1977, 1982, 1989; Danish Cup (5) 1983, 1991, 1993, 2002, 2007
Coach: Kent Nielsen

2015
19/07	h Hobro	W	3-0	Festersen, Greve, Falk
26/07	a Brøndby	W	2-1	Festersen 2
31/07	a Midtjylland	L	0-1	
07/08	h AGF	D	2-2	Festersen, Skúlason
16/08	h Randers	L	2-3	Skúlason, Zohore
24/08	a AaB	L	1-5	E Larsen
30/08	h København	W	1-0	Jacobsen
14/09	a Esbjerg	L	2-4	Zohore, El Makrini
19/09	h Viborg	W	2-0	Zohore, Kryger
25/09	a SønderjyskE	L	0-4	
02/10	a Nordsjælland	W	5-1	Festersen 3 (1p), Zohore, Greve
17/10	h SønderjyskE	L	1-2	Zohore
26/10	a Randers	D	1-1	Zohore
01/11	h Brøndby	L	2-5	Zohore, Jacobsen
08/11	a Viborg	W	1-0	Festersen
20/11	h Midtjylland	D	1-1	Festersen
30/11	h Esbjerg	W	2-1	Festersen, Falk
06/12	a København	L	1-4	Jacobsen

2016
26/02	h AGF	D	2-2	Jacobsen, Greve
04/03	a AaB	W	1-0	Festersen
13/03	h Nordsjælland	W	3-1	Jacobsen, Festersen, Falk
19/03	a Hobro	W	2-0	Jacobsen, Falk
03/04	h Randers	L	0-1	
10/04	a Brøndby	L	0-1	
17/04	h Viborg	W	5-1	Festersen (p), Falk, Jacobsen 3
22/04	a Midtjylland	L	0-2	
02/05	a Esbjerg	W	2-0	Jacobsen, Skúlason
08/05	h København	L	0-1	
12/05	a Nordsjælland	W	1-0	Festersen
15/05	h Hobro	L	0-1	
20/05	a SønderjyskE	L	1-3	Jacobsen
26/05	a AGF	L	1-2	Falk
29/05	h AaB	W	3-2	Tingager, Jacobsen, Busuladzic

No	Name	Nat	DoB	Pos	Aps	(s)	Gls
18	Azer Busuladzic		12/11/91	M	16	(9)	1
19	Mikkel Desler		19/02/95	M	16	(3)	
6	Mohammed Diarra	FRA	20/06/92	D	3	(2)	
26	Yao Dieudonne	CIV	14/02/97	M		(2)	
13	Vladimer Dvalishvili	GEO	20/04/86	A		(1)	
7	Jóan Símun Edmundsson	FRO	26/07/91	A	2	(3)	
8	Mohamed El Makrini	NED	06/07/87	M	30		1
9	Rasmus Falk		15/01/92	A	30	(1)	6
16	Michael Falkesgaard		09/04/91	G	4		
10	Rasmus Festersen		26/08/86	A	29	(1)	14
21	Mathias Greve		11/02/95	A	12	(14)	3
13	Sten Grytebust	NOR	25/10/89	G	15		
28	Anders Jacobsen		27/10/89	A	19	(5)	12
11	Lucas Jensen		08/10/94	M	1	(9)	
4	Hallgrímur Jónasson	ISL	04/05/86	D	33		
2	Mikkel Kirkeskov		05/09/91	D	8	(1)	
25	Maxym Koval	UKR	09/12/92	G	10		
15	Lasse Kryger		03/11/82	D	2	(9)	1
7	Emil Larsen		22/06/91	M	13	(3)	1
3	Kasper Larsen		25/01/93	D	4		
20	Jacob Barrett Laursen		17/11/94	D	12		
24	Oliver Lund		21/08/90	D	18	(7)	
5	Lasse Nielsen		03/03/87	D	21		
26	Matti Lund Nielsen		08/05/88	M		(2)	
30	Magnus Pedersen		23/11/96	D		(1)	
27	Casper Radza		26/02/94			(1)	
22	Ari Freyr Skúlason	ISL	14/05/87	D	28	(1)	3
14	Jens Jakob Thomasen		25/06/96	M	5	(13)	
3	Frederik Tingager		22/02/93	D	6		1
1	Michael Tørnes		08/01/86	G	4		
15	Izunna Uzochukwu	NGA	11/04/90	M	10	(4)	
17	Kenneth Zohore		31/01/94	A	12	(4)	7

Randers FC

2003 • BioNutria Park (10,300) • randersfc.dk
Major honours
Danish Cup (1) 2006
Coach: Colin Todd (ENG)

2015
26/07	h Nordsjælland	W	3-0	Lundberg 3
02/08	a AGF	L	2-3	Lundberg, Borring
09/08	h Brøndby	D	3-3	Borring 2, Lundberg
16/08	a OB	W	3-2	Tverskov, Brock-Madsen (p), Lundberg
23/08	h Viborg	L	0-1	
30/08	a AaB	W	2-0	Lundberg, Masango
13/09	h SønderjyskE	W	1-0	Ishak
16/09	a København	L	0-3	
21/09	a Esbjerg	W	2-0	Ishak, Poulsen
27/09	h Midtjylland	L	0-2	
03/10	h Hobro	W	2-1	Borring, Masango
16/10	a Midtjylland	L	1-2	Tverskov
26/10	h OB	D	1-1	Borring
01/11	a København	L	0-4	
06/11	h AGF	W	4-1	Ishak 2 (1p), Borring, Masango
23/11	a AaB	L	2-3	Marxen, og (Petersen)
28/11	h Nordsjælland	W	1-0	Parzyszek
05/12	a Hobro	D	0-0	

2016
27/02	h SønderjyskE	D	1-1	Kallesøe
06/03	a Esbjerg	L	0-1	
13/03	a Brøndby	L	0-1	
20/03	h Viborg	L	1-3	Masango
03/04	a OB	W	1-0	Ishak
10/04	h København	D	1-1	Fisker
16/04	a AGF	W	2-0	Fisker, Masango
25/04	a AaB	D	0-0	
01/05	a Nordsjælland	D	2-2	Fisker, Ishak
07/05	h Hobro	W	2-0	Maâzou, Ishak
12/05	h Brøndby	L	0-2	
16/05	a Viborg	W	3-2	og (Pallesen), Ishak 2
22/05	h Midtjylland	L	1-2	Masango
26/05	a SønderjyskE	D	1-1	Ishak
29/05	h Esbjerg	W	3-1	Ishak 2, Lundberg

No	Name	Nat	DoB	Pos	Aps	(s)	Gls
5	Mads Agesen		17/03/83	D	14		
20	Joel Allansson	SWE	03/11/92	M	6	(3)	
8	Mustafa Amini	AUS	20/04/93	M	23	(6)	
18	Edgar Babayan		28/10/95	M		(7)	
24	Jonas Bager		18/07/96	D	2	(1)	
9	Jonas Borring		04/01/85	M	19		6
44	Nicolai Brock-Madsen		09/01/93	A	4		1
15	Patrick da Silva		23/10/94	D	2	(2)	
22	Jack Duncan	AUS	19/04/93	G	1		
13	Mads Fenger		10/09/90	D	31	(1)	
21	Alexander Fischer		16/09/86	D	2	(2)	
16	Kasper Fisker		22/05/88	M	18	(4)	3
10	Mikael Ishak	SWE	31/03/93	A	23	(5)	12
1	Karl-Johan Johnsson	SWE	28/01/90	G	32		
14	Kasper Junker		05/03/94	A	1	(7)	
19	Mikkel Kallesøe		20/04/97	M		(12)	1
3	Christian Keller		17/08/80	M	19		
23	Viktor Lundberg	SWE	04/03/91	A	26	(2)	8
31	Moussa Maâzou	NIG	25/08/88	A	4	(6)	1
11	Erik Marxen		02/12/90	D	20	(2)	1
17	Mandla Masango	RSA	18/07/89	M	18	(9)	6
30	Piotr Parzyszek	POL	08/09/93	A	1	(7)	1
38	Nicolai Poulsen		15/08/93	M	30	(1)	1
4	Johnny Thomsen		26/02/82	D	28	(1)	
15	Mikkel Thygesen		22/10/84	M		(1)	
6	Jeppe Tverskov		12/03/93	M	19	(3)	2

SønderjyskE

2004 • Sydbank Park (10,000) • soenderjyske.dk
Coach: Jakob Michelsen

2015
17/07	a Nordsjælland	W	2-0	Dalgaard 2
24/07	h Midtjylland	L	1-2	Absalonsen
02/08	h København	L	1-3	Kanstrup
09/08	a Esbjerg	W	4-0	Absalonsen, Kløve, Madsen, Bechmann
17/08	h Hobro	W	3-0	Bechmann 2, Kløve
23/08	a Brøndby	L	0-1	
29/08	h Viborg	W	2-1	Bechmann 2
13/09	a Randers	L	0-1	
18/09	h AGF	W	2-1	Dalgaard, Simonsen
25/09	h OB	W	4-0	Madsen, Absalonsen, Pedersen, Dalgaard
04/10	a AaB	L	0-5	
17/10	a OB	W	2-1	Dalgaard, Absalonsen
25/10	h København	L	1-2	Absalonsen (p)
02/11	a AGF	D	0-0	
06/11	h AaB	L	1-2	Kanstrup
21/11	a Nordsjælland	W	2-1	Absalonsen 2 (1p)
29/11	h Hobro	W	2-1	Absalonsen 2 (1p)
06/12	a Esbjerg	W	1-0	Luijckx

2016
27/02	a Randers	D	1-1	Absalonsen
06/03	h Brøndby	W	3-1	Bechmann, Madsen 2
12/03	a Viborg	D	0-0	
20/03	h Midtjylland	W	3-2	Madsen 2, Hedegaard
03/04	a København	L	0-1	
09/04	h AGF	D	2-2	João Pereira, Guira
17/04	a AaB	W	3-1	Dal Hende, Bechmann
24/04	h Nordsjælland	W	3-1	Bechmann, Kanstrup, Madsen
30/04	a Hobro	W	2-1	Rømer, Absalonsen
06/05	h Esbjerg	W	2-0	Dal Hende, Kroon
11/05	h Viborg	W	2-1	Dal Hende, Simonsen
14/05	a Midtjylland	L	2-3	Dal Hende, Songani
20/05	h OB	W	3-1	Kroon, Bechmann, Absalonsen (p)
26/05	h Randers	D	1-1	Dickoh
29/05	a Brøndby	W	2-1	Madsen 2

No	Name	Nat	DoB	Pos	Aps	(s)	Gls
11	Johan Absalonsen		16/09/85	A	31		12
9	Tommy Bechmann		22/12/81	A	23	(7)	9
7	Marc Dal Hende		06/11/90	M	10	(6)	4
33	Thomas Dalgaard		13/04/84	A	10	(11)	6
20	Francis Dickoh	GHA	13/12/82	D	3	(2)	1
8	Janus Drachmann		11/05/88	M	28		
18	Adama Guira	BFA	24/04/88	M	31		1
14	Mikkel Hedegaard		03/07/96	M	2	(4)	1
2	João Pereira	POR	10/05/90	D	22	(2)	1
21	Pierre Kanstrup		21/02/89	D	33		3
15	Troels Kløve		23/10/90	M	9		2
6	Simon Kroon	SWE	16/06/93	M	15		2
5	Kees Luijckx	NED	11/02/86	D	15	(5)	1
10	Nicolaj Madsen		16/07/88	M	27	(2)	9
12	Søren Mussmann		29/06/93	D	15	(1)	
24	Andreas Oggesen		18/03/94	M	9	(8)	
25	Emmanuel Okwi	UGA	25/12/92	A		(2)	
13	Casper Olesen		10/05/96	A		(4)	
20	Bjørn Paulsen		02/07/91	D	7		
3	Marc Pedersen		31/07/89	D	28	(2)	1
30	Marcel Rømer		06/11/90	M	6	(6)	1
4	Baldur Sigurdsson	ISL	24/04/85	D	2	(5)	
21	Jeppe Simonsen		21/11/95	A	2	(11)	2
1	Marin Skender	CRO	12/08/79	G	33		
23	Silas Songani	ZIM	28/06/89	A	2	(13)	1

 **DENMARK**

Viborg FF

1896 • Energi Viborg Arena (10,000) • vff.dk
Major honours
Danish Cup (1) 2000
Coach: Johnny Mølby

2015

18/07	a Midtjylland	L	0-2	
27/07	h AGF	D	0-0	
31/07	h Esbjerg	W	2-1	*Curth 2*
08/08	a Hobro	D	1-1	*Veldmate*
16/08	h Brøndby	L	0-4	
23/08	a Randers	W	1-0	*Kamper*
29/08	h SønderjyskE	L	1-2	*Kamper*
12/09	h Nordsjælland	L	0-1	
19/09	a OB	L	0-2	
25/09	h AaB	W	1-0	*Curth*
04/10	a København	L	0-1	
18/10	h Brøndby	L	0-2	
24/10	h Esbjerg	W	4-2	*Curth, og (Van Buren), Deblé, Andersen*
31/10	a Midtjylland	W	4-2	*Akharraz 2, Deblé, og (Hansen)*
08/11	h OB	L	0-1	
22/11	a København	D	0-0	
27/11	h AGF	W	1-0	*Curth*
07/12	a AaB	L	0-2	

2016

28/02	h Nordsjælland	D	1-1	*Andersen*
05/03	a Hobro	W	6-0	*Curth 2, Thorsen, Deblé 2, Kamper*
12/03	h SønderjyskE	D	0-0	
20/03	a Randers	W	3-1	*Akharraz, Curth (p), Andersen*
04/04	a Esbjerg	L	0-1	
08/04	h Midtjylland	D	1-1	*Kamper*
17/04	h OB	L	1-5	*Curth*
24/04	h København	D	1-1	*Kamper*
29/04	a AGF	W	2-1	*Deblé, Curth*
08/05	h AaB	L	0-2	
11/05	h SønderjyskE	L	0-2	
16/05	h Randers	L	2-3	*Rask, Kamper*
23/05	a Brøndby	W	1-0	*Wichmann*
26/05	a Nordsjælland	L	0-1	
29/05	h Hobro	W	1-0	*Andersen*

No	Name	Nat	DoB	Pos	Aps	(s)	Gls
21	Osama Akharraz		26/11/90	M	15	(1)	3
27	Sebastian Andersen		23/12/88	M	10	(22)	4
10	Jeppe Curth		21/03/84	A	29	(1)	10
28	Serge Deblé	CIV	01/10/89	A	25		5
34	Sebastian Denius		08/06/95	M		(1)	
4	Jacob Egeris		19/05/90	D	3	(3)	
8	George Fochive	USA	24/03/92	M	4	(4)	
25	Søren Frederiksen		08/07/89	A	7	(6)	
17	Alhaji Gero	NGA	10/10/93	A		(8)	
13	Jeppe Grønning		24/05/91	M	24	(4)	
1	Peter Friis Jensen		02/05/88	G	33		
11	Jonas Kamper		03/05/83	M	32		6
12	Lukas Lerager		12/07/93	M	31		
19	Jeff Mensah		10/08/92	M		(4)	
14	Babajide Ogunbiyi	USA	03/11/86	D	3	(1)	
15	Kristoffer Pallesen		30/04/90	D	32		
6	Christopher Poulsen		11/09/81	D	10	(3)	
5	Mikkel Rask		22/06/83	D	26		1
20	Søren Reese		29/07/93	D	25	(1)	
9	Ante Rukavina	CRO	18/06/86	A	4	(1)	
8	Marcel Rømer		08/08/91	M	6	(4)	
23	Christian Sivebæk		19/02/88	M	4	(9)	
2	Jonas Thorsen		19/04/90	D	23	(1)	1
26	Jeroen Veldmate	NED	08/11/88	D	9		1
29	Mikkel Vestergaard		22/11/92	A		(2)	
7	Mathias Wichmann		06/08/91	M	8	(16)	1

Top goalscorers

18   Lukas Spalvis (AaB)

15   Nicolai Jørgensen (København)

14   Federico Santander (København)
      Morten "Duncan" Rasmussen
      (Midtjylland/AGF)
      Rasmus Festersen (OB)

13   Martin Pusic (Midtjylland)

12   Thomas Enevoldsen (AaB)
      Anders Jacobsen (OB)
      Mikael Ishak (Randers)
      Johan Absalonsen (SønderjyskE)

Promoted clubs

Lyngby BK

1921 • Lyngby Stadion (8,000) •
lyngby-boldklub.dk
Major honours
Danish League (2) 1983, 1992; Danish Cup (3) 1984,
1985, 1990
Coach: David Nielsen

Silkeborg IF

1917 • Mascot Park (10,000) • silkeborgif.com
Major honours
Danish League (1) 1994; Danish Cup (1) 2001
Coach: Kim Poulsen;
(30/09/15) Peter Sørensen

AC Horsens

1994 • Casa Arena (10,495) • achorsens.dk
Coach: Bo Henriksen

Second level final table 2015/16

		Pld	W	D	L	F	A	Pts
1	Lyngby BK	33	19	7	7	59	37	64
2	Silkeborg IF	33	18	9	6	59	29	63
3	AC Horsens	33	18	6	9	52	34	60
4	Vendsyssel FF	33	16	8	9	41	33	56
5	Vejle BK	33	16	5	12	56	46	53
6	FC Fredericia	33	12	11	10	45	45	47
7	FC Helsingør	33	14	5	14	40	42	47
8	HB Køge	33	13	6	14	34	35	45
9	FC Roskilde	33	10	9	14	51	58	39
10	Næstved BK	33	10	4	19	37	48	34
11	Skive IK	33	8	7	18	37	50	31
12	FC Vestsjælland	33	2	7	24	19	73	7

NB FC Vestsjælland withdrew after round 19 – their
remaining matches were awarded as 0-3 defeats;
FC Vestsjælland – 6 pts deducted.

DOMESTIC CUP

Landspokalturneringen 2015/16

SECOND ROUND

(25/08/15)
Brabrand 1-2 Fredericia
Næstved 1-0 Nordsjælland

(01/09/15)
Fredensborg 1-0 B1908
Frederikssund 2-6 HB Køge
Herlufsholm 0-5 Brønshøj
Hillerød 1-2 Helsingør
Holbæk 4-2 B93
Lyseng 1-2 Kolding IF
Marienlyst 1-5 Viborg
Rishøj 2-0 Søllerød-Vedbæk
Svendborg 0-3 Silkeborg
Sædding/Guldager 1-5 Lystrup
Søhus Stige 0-9 Esbjerg fB
Thisted 1-2 SønderjyskE
Vejgaard 3-2 Sydvest

(02/09/15)
Aabyhøj 0-2 Sønderborg
Avedøre 0-3 Vestsjælland
Birkerød 1-4 KFUM Roskilde
Fremad Valby 2-2 Hvidovre *(aet; 4-5 on pens)*
Kjellerup 1-8 AGF
Ledøje-Smørum 0-5 Lyngby
Nyborg 0-5 Greve
Vejle 0-0 Hobro *(aet; 2-4 on pens)*

(08/09/15)
Aalborg Freja 0-6 Horsens
Odder 0-1 Skive

(09/09/15)
Tarup-Paarup 0-2 OB
Vendsyssel 0-2 AaB

(23/09/15)
Jægersborg 1-6 FC Roskilde

Byes – Brøndby, København, Midtjylland, Randers

THIRD ROUND

(22/09/15)
Fredericia 2-1 OB
Greve 2-1 Hvidovre
KFUM Roskilde 1-5 Viborg
Rishøj 3-1 Brønshøj
Silkeborg 0-1 AGF
Vejgaard 1-3 SønderjyskE

(23/09/15)
Fredensborg 0-1 Helsingør
HB Køge 2-0 Horsens
Holbæk 0-7 Brøndby
Kolding IF 1-3 Skive
Vestsjælland 0-2 København

(24/09/15)
Lyngby 1-0 Esbjerg fB
Næstved 0-3 Midtjylland
Sønderborg 0-6 Randers

(29/09/15)
Lystrup 0-4 AaB

(13/10/15)
FC Roskilde 0-0 Hobro *(aet; 7-6 on pens)*

FOURTH ROUND

(21/10/15)
Helsingør 0-2 Randers

(27/10/15)
Rishøj 0-3 AGF
Skive 3-2 Viborg

(28/10/15)
Greve 2-6 SønderjyskE
Lyngby 1-2 AaB
FC Roskilde 3-2 Midtjylland *(aet)*

(29/10/15)
Fredericia 1-2 København *(aet)*
HB Køge 0-1 Brøndby

QUARTER-FINALS

(01/03/16)
SønderjyskE 0-3 AGF *(M Rasmussen 8, Bjarnason 23, Lange 72)*

(02/03/16)
Skive 0-3 Brøndby *(Eriksson 48, Elmander 89, Kahlenberg 90)*

(16/03/16)
København 2-1 Randers *(Santander 60, M Jørgensen 116; Junker 90) (aet)*

(05/04/16)
FC Roskilde 0-4 AaB *(Thomsen 27p, Enevoldsen 32, 39, Børsting 54)*

SEMI-FINALS

(06/04/16 & 20/04/16)
København 1-1 Brøndby *(Delaney 83; Pukki 27)*
Brøndby 0-1 København *(N Jørgensen 78)*
(København 2-1)

(13/04/16 & 21/04/16)
AaB 0-2 AGF *(Bjarnason 22, M Rasmussen 62)*
AGF 2-2 AaB *(Petersen 56og, Bjarnason 90; Enevoldsen 26, Thomsen 52)*
(AGF 4-2)

FINAL

(05/05/16)
Telia Parken, Copenhagen
FC KØBENHAVN 2 *(N Jørgensen 29, Kvist 78)*
AGF AARHUS 1 *(M Rasmussen 45)*
Referee: *Kristoffersen*
KØBENHAVN: Kaminski, Ankersen, M Jørgensen, Antonsson (Johansson 46), Augustinsson, Kusk (Toutouh 32), Delaney, Kvist, Verbič, N Jørgensen, Cornelius
AGF: S Rasmussen, Andersen (Khodzhaniyazov 85), Elez, Backman, Christensen, Pedersen (Lange 85), Petersen, Jønsson, Olsen, Bjarnason (Aabech 63), M Rasmussen

FC København secured the first half of a domestic double with victory in the Danish Cup

TheFA

ENGLAND
The Football Association (FA)

Address   Wembley Stadium
PO Box 1966
GB-London SW1P 9EQ
Tel   +44 844 980 8200
Fax   +44 844 980 8201
E-mail   info@thefa.com
Website   thefa.com

Chairman   Greg Clarke
Chief executive   Martin Glenn
Media officer   Amanda Docherty
Year of formation   1863
National stadium   Wembley Stadium, London (90,000)

PREMIER LEAGUE CLUBS

 1 **Arsenal FC**

 2 **Aston Villa FC**

3 **AFC Bournemouth**

4 **Chelsea FC**

5 **Crystal Palace FC**

 6 **Everton FC**

 7 **Leicester City FC**

 8 **Liverpool FC**

 9 **Manchester City FC**

 10 **Manchester United FC**

 11 **Newcastle United FC**

 12 **Norwich City FC**

 13 **Southampton FC**

 14 **Stoke City FC**

 15 **Sunderland AFC**

 16 **Swansea City AFC**

 17 **Tottenham Hotspur FC**

 18 **Watford FC**

 19 **West Bromwich Albion FC**

 20 **West Ham United FC**

PROMOTED CLUBS

 21 **Burnley FC**

 22 **Middlesbrough FC**

 23 **Hull City AFC**

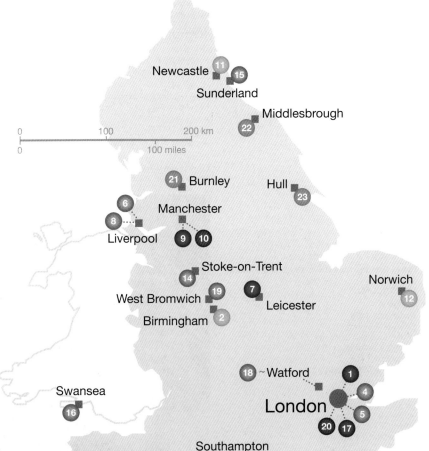

KEY

● UEFA Champions League
● UEFA Europa League
● Promoted
● Relegated

Magical Leicester live the dream

Against seemingly impossible odds Leicester City became the 2015/16 champions of England. It was a triumph of extraordinary spirit and resolve, one that captured the imagination of the whole country and far beyond, transforming Claudio Ranieri and his players into unlikely Premier League legends.

None of the big clubs could live with Leicester's remarkable consistency, leaving Manchester United and Manchester City to make do with domestic cup wins while London's finest ended up empty-handed. There was no joy either for Roy Hodgson's national team, eliminated early from UEFA EURO 2016 by Iceland.

Ranieri leads 5000/1 outsiders to title glory	Manchester clubs capture domestic cups	Hodgson quits after EURO defeat to Iceland

Domestic league

Promoted only in 2013/14, Leicester survived relegation by the skin of their teeth the following season, but despite a stunning late surge that kept them in the Premier League, the manager who supervised that great escape, Nigel Pearson, was dismissed by the club's Thai owners and replaced, to a generally unenthusiastic response, by experienced Italian coach Ranieri. Most pre-season predictions had Leicester down for another relegation battle. The thought of the club actually winning the league title for the first time in their history was so preposterous as to warrant widespread bookmakers' title odds of 5000/1.

However, with seven wins from their last nine games in 2014/15, Leicester had momentum. Furthermore, that run had forged an unbreakable team spirit, and although Pearson had gone, Ranieri, nicknamed the Tinkerman during his previous spell in England with Chelsea (2000-04), wisely decided to refrain from any major repair work. He also ensured continuity by retaining Pearson's back-up staff. In his first game, on a hot August afternoon at the King Power Stadium, Leicester played mesmerisingly well, going 3-0 up against Sunderland and eventually winning 4-2 to take up

position that Saturday evening on top of the Premier League table. None of the 32,242 spectators present could have imagined in their wildest dreams that Ranieri's team would still be there after another 37 matches. But that, incredibly, is what happened.

Manchester City would displace Leicester two days later and go on to win their opening five fixtures, but while Arsenal and Manchester United also moved into challenging positions, Leicester were the last team to be beaten. A 5-2 home defeat by the Gunners in late September provided Ranieri's men with their first major setback, but the manager responded by remodelling his team, giving the defence better protection while also encouraging his players to get the ball forward quickly and exploit the explosive pace of striker Jamie Vardy. It took Leicester ten games to post their first clean sheet, but in the meantime Vardy was on a seriously hot streak of form at the other end. The former non-league striker would go on to equal Ruud van Nistelrooy's record of scoring in ten successive Premier League games when he netted in a 3-0 win at Newcastle that put his team back on top of the table – and then break it a week later, to thunderous acclaim from the home fans, in a 1-1 draw against Manchester United.

Vardy's run ended next time out at Swansea, but his multi-talented Algerian accomplice, Riyad Mahrez, scored a hat-trick to return Leicester to the top with another 3-0 win. They would still be at the summit at Christmas, although a first away defeat, 1-0 at Liverpool, and two successive home goalless draws enabled Arsenal to replace them at the start of the New Year. However, just as Leicester's bubble seemed ready to burst, with their pre-season 40-point target safely reached, Ranieri rallied his troops again and they set off on another magical run, winning 1-0 at a resurgent Tottenham Hotspur before returning to the top with another 3-0 win – at home to Stoke City – and consolidating their position with magnificent victories against Liverpool (2-0 at home) and Manchester City (3-1 away).

A cruel stoppage-time winner conceded with ten men against Arsenal led to their third defeat. The manner of it might have shattered lesser sides, but Leicester's hunger for success was insatiable and they came back for more, winning five of their next six games, all by 1-0, to not just protect their position but effectively see off every potential challenger except Mauricio Pochettino's Tottenham. Over the closing weeks the fixture schedule always had Leicester playing before Spurs. There was pressure both ways,

but Ranieri's ruthlessly committed team, backed by feverish support, handled it better, refusing to crack. Even a red card for Vardy in a fractious 2-2 draw against West Ham United failed to rattle them. They simply would not be beaten, and when Tottenham stumbled to two successive Monday night draws, the second of them after being 2-0 up against Chelsea, Leicester, amazingly, were the Premier League champions.

Widely hailed as one of English sport's greatest tales of the unexpected, it was certainly an astonishing feat of endurance. Leicester lost just three of their 38 matches and won 23. It was helpful that the Premier League was the sole focus of their attention and, particularly, that Ranieri's first-choice XI barely changed from one week to the next. Goalkeeper Kasper Schmeichel played every minute and was outstanding in front of a superbly-drilled back four comprising right-back Danny Simpson, left-back Christian Fuchs and an old-school, no-nonsense central pairing of Robert Huth and ever-present captain Wes Morgan. Midfield terrier N'Golo Kanté was the signing of the season, an indefatigable ball-winner and the launch pad for many of the team's lethal counterattacks. Playmaker Danny Drinkwater also excelled alongside him, with Marc Albrighton a tireless worker on one flank and the dazzling Mahrez a left-footed artist on the other. The ever-willing Shinji Okazaki did not pose much of a goal threat – unlike 17-goal Mahrez – but he provided a useful attacking foil for the lightning-quick speed and finishing skills of 24-goal Vardy, while substitutes Leonardo Ulloa, Jeff Schlupp and Andy King also played important roles in a fantastic team effort. Masterminding everything with his sharp managerial brain was Ranieri, a model of avuncular charm and good humour all season and duly rewarded with the first domestic league title of his long and eventful career.

Ranieri and his players were feted in fabulous style on an unforgettable evening of heat, heavy rain and high emotion at the King Power Stadium, defeating Everton 3-1 before captain Morgan joined his manager in raising aloft the Premier League trophy. While Leicester's triumph of the underdog was applauded and enjoyed far and wide, their success nevertheless raised questions about the underachievement of the country's more powerful and established clubs, all of whom, for one reason or another, had a Premier League season to forget.

The fall of defending champions Chelsea was almost as mind-boggling as Leicester's rise. Never in the title hunt after an atrocious start, they were hovering nervously above the relegation zone when title-winning boss José Mourinho was sacked in mid-December. Guus Hiddink steadied the ship, taking the Blues on a 15-match unbeaten run, but with 2014/15 Player of the Year Eden Hazard totally out of sorts until he came to life with the wonderful goal against Spurs that sealed Leicester's title, Chelsea could only finish tenth. That was two places below Liverpool, who also changed their manager, getting rid of Brendan Rodgers in October and bringing in the charismatic Jürgen Klopp. The German would weave his magic elsewhere but not in the Premier League, where his team often flattered to deceive.

Manchester City and Manchester United finished level on points but it was Manuel Pellegrini's side, spearheaded by 24-goal Sergio Agüero, who took fourth place on goal difference, enabling new boss Pep Guardiola – whose arrival as Pellegrini's replacement for 2016/17, an open secret for many months, was confirmed in February – to launch his career in England in the UEFA Champions League. Not so Mourinho, who was appointed to replace Louis van Gaal after the Dutchman, roundly criticised for the team's unadventurous style of play, was given his marching orders in May.

Although a first league title for 55 years ultimately eluded them, Tottenham had an excellent campaign, their second under Pochettino, with young English guns Dele Alli, Eric Dier and 25-goal golden boot winner Harry Kane all firing effectively in unison alongside foreign stars Hugo Lloris, Christian Eriksen and Toby Alderweireld. However, a 5-1 defeat by Newcastle brought the season to an unworthy end, the pain of defeat aggravated by the fact that Arsenal overtook them to finish as runners-up – the 22nd successive season that the Gunners had finished above their north London rivals in the final Premier League standings.

While Arsenal fans rejoiced in retaining the local bragging rights, on sober reflection theirs was a season in which a big opportunity to claim a first league title in 12 years went begging. They beat

Jamie Vardy (bottom) is congratulated by team-mate Riyad Mahrez after scoring in a tenth successive Premier League game to help Leicester win 3-0 at Newcastle

Leicester twice but, as in previous seasons, were found wanting under pressure, a sticky spell from January to March all but ruling them out of contention. New signing Petr Čech did a fine job in goal, and Mesut Özil and Héctor Bellerín both repeatedly impressed, but the overall performances of Arsène Wenger's team drew increasing dissent from their frustrated supporters.

Fast-finishing Southampton and a Dimitri Payet-inspired West Ham both qualified for the UEFA Europa League, but gloom enveloped Aston Villa, who ended a 28-year run in the top flight by collecting just 17 points and finishing in a distant last place. The battle to avoid the other two relegation places was lost by newly-promoted Norwich City and, more surprisingly, Newcastle, whose appointment of Rafael Benítez as the replacement manager for Steve McClaren occurred too late to save them. Local rivals Sunderland gleefully sent them down while saving themselves when they beat Everton 3-0 after a strong finish under Sam Allardyce, who thus proudly protected his record of never having taken a team down. Burnley won the Championship (second division) to make an immediate return to the top flight, with Middlesbrough taking the second automatic promotion place before Hull, another team relegated 12 months earlier, bounced straight back thanks to a 1-0 play-off win at Wembley against Sheffield Wednesday.

Domestic cups

Pellegrini and Van Gaal both left Manchester with Wembley cup wins under their belt, City overcoming Liverpool on penalties in the League Cup final and United also needing extra time in the FA Cup final before overcoming Crystal Palace 2-1. City's victory was their second in the competition in three seasons, while United moved alongside Arsenal as the FA Cup's joint most successful club with their long-awaited 12th win. Palace looked on course for their first major trophy when Jason Puncheon blasted them into a 78th-minute lead, but shortly afterwards Juan Mata equalised, and although Chris Smalling was sent off in extra time, United's ten men grabbed the decisive goal shortly afterwards when Jesse Lingard lashed in a stunning shot to end Van Gaal's mercurial reign on a trophy-winning high.

Jesse Lingard celebrates his spectacular winning goal for Manchester United in the FA Cup final against Crystal Palace

Europe

Manchester United returned to the UEFA Champions League after a year's absence by overwhelming Club Brugge in the play-offs, but they could not get through a relatively straightforward group and thus became the competition's first English casualty in another disappointing season for the Premier League quartet. Manchester City fared better than ever before in reaching the last four, but they did not do themselves justice against Real Madrid in the semi-finals. City got to that stage by overcoming Paris Saint-Germain, who had eliminated Chelsea in the round of 16 for the second season running. Arsenal progressed beyond the group stage for the 16th successive season – thanks to a matchday six 3-0 win at Olympiacos – but prolonged a rather less enviable sequence by going out in the round of 16 for the sixth year running, after two defeats against bête noire Barcelona.

The most rousing European nights took place at Anfield, where Klopp's Liverpool beat Augsburg, Manchester United, Borussia Dortmund and

Villarreal in the knockout phase of the UEFA Europa League to reach the final in Basel, only to surrender a half-time lead provided by Daniel Sturridge's spectacular strike and lose 3-1 to holders Sevilla. Tottenham reached the last 16 before giving up the ghost against Dortmund, with West Ham and Southampton having gone out early in the preliminary rounds.

National team

England were the first team to qualify for UEFA EURO 2016 and the only one of the 23 to do so with a perfect record, yet when they got to the finals in France, as at so many previous tournaments, they failed to deliver and were eliminated earlier than expected. This time the scale of the disappointment reached a new level as the Three Lions were sent packing by Iceland after a harrowing 2-1 defeat by the North Atlantic debutants in Nice.

Manager Roy Hodgson wasted no time in announcing his resignation, jumping before the seemingly inevitable push. It was difficult for him or anyone else to explain how a team that had started the tournament so well, with a dominant (if goalless) first-half display against Russia, could have become so dysfunctional by the end of it. A late equalising goal conceded to Russia was offset by a stoppage-time Sturridge winner against Wales, but rather than use the momentum of that wildly-celebrated win, Hodgson made several changes against Slovakia, the match ending in a 0-0 stalemate and preventing England from winning the group. Further selection gambles against Iceland also had a negative effect, and with players such as Kane, Alli, Raheem Sterling and, ultimately, England's new all-time record goalscorer Wayne Rooney all submitting to big-match stage fright, the unthinkable happened and England were on their way home.

A few weeks later experienced Premier League campaigner Allardyce was appointed as Hodgson's replacement. The 61-year-old's first task will be to qualify the team for the 2018 FIFA World Cup in Russia. England are not in a difficult group and should make it through without undue concern, but that is to assume that the bitter experience of the summer of 2016, especially the nightmare of Nice, has not left any indelible scars.

DOMESTIC SEASON AT A GLANCE

Premier League 2015/16 final table

		Pld	Home					Away					Total					
			W	D	L	F	A	W	D	L	F	A	W	D	L	F	A	Pts
1	**Leicester City FC**	38	12	6	1	35	18	11	6	2	33	18	23	12	3	68	36	81
2	Arsenal FC	38	12	4	3	31	11	8	7	4	34	25	20	11	7	65	36	71
3	Tottenham Hotspur FC	38	10	6	3	35	15	9	7	3	34	20	19	13	6	69	35	70
4	Manchester City FC	38	12	2	5	47	21	7	7	5	24	20	19	9	10	71	41	66
5	Manchester United FC	38	12	5	2	27	9	7	4	8	22	26	19	9	10	49	35	66
6	Southampton FC	38	11	3	5	39	22	7	6	6	20	19	18	9	11	59	41	63
7	West Ham United FC	38	9	7	3	34	26	7	7	5	31	25	16	14	8	65	51	62
8	Liverpool FC	38	8	8	3	33	22	8	4	7	30	28	16	12	10	63	50	60
9	Stoke City FC	38	8	4	7	22	24	6	5	8	19	31	14	9	15	41	55	51
10	Chelsea FC	38	5	9	5	32	30	7	5	7	27	23	12	14	12	59	53	50
11	Everton FC	38	6	5	8	35	30	5	9	5	24	25	11	14	13	59	55	47
12	Swansea City AFC	38	8	6	5	20	20	4	5	10	22	32	12	11	15	42	52	47
13	Watford FC	38	6	6	7	20	19	6	3	10	20	31	12	9	17	40	50	45
14	West Bromwich Albion FC	38	6	5	8	20	26	4	8	7	14	22	10	13	15	34	48	43
15	Crystal Palace FC	38	6	3	10	19	23	5	6	8	20	28	11	9	18	39	51	42
16	AFC Bournemouth	38	5	5	9	23	34	6	4	9	22	33	11	9	18	45	67	42
17	Sunderland AFC	38	6	6	7	23	26	3	6	10	25	42	9	12	17	48	62	39
18	Newcastle United FC	38	7	7	5	32	24	2	3	14	12	41	9	10	19	44	65	37
19	Norwich City FC	38	6	5	8	26	30	3	2	14	13	37	9	7	22	39	67	34
20	Aston Villa FC	38	2	5	12	14	35	1	3	15	13	41	3	8	27	27	76	17

European qualification 2016/17

Champion: Leicester City FC (group stage)
Arsenal FC (group stage)
Tottenham Hotspur FC (group stage)
Manchester Ciy FC (play-offs)

Cup winner: Manchester United FC (group stage)
Southampton FC (group stage)
West Ham United FC (third qualifying round)

Top scorer	Harry Kane (Tottenham), 25 goals
Relegated clubs	Aston Villa FC, Norwich City FC, Newcastle United FC
Promoted clubs	Burnley FC, Middlesbrough FC, Hull City AFC
FA Cup final	Manchester United FC 2-1 Crystal Palace FC *(aet)*
League Cup final	Manchester City FC 1-1 Liverpool FC *(aet; 3-1 on pens)*

Team of the season
(4-4-2)

Manager: Ranieri *(Leicester)*

De Gea
(Man. United)

Bellerín *(Arsenal)* — Morgan *(Leicester)* — Alderweireld *(Tottenham)* — Rose *(Tottenham)*

Mahrez *(Leicester)* — Kanté *(Leicester)* — Alli *(Tottenham)* — Payet *(West Ham)*

Vardy *(Leicester)* — Kane *(Tottenham)*

Player of the season

Riyad Mahrez
(Leicester City FC)

While his team-mate Jamie Vardy claimed the vote of England's football writers, Mahrez topped the poll among his fellow professionals as the Premier League's Player of the Year. For sheer entertainment value there was no one else in the division to touch the brilliant Algerian, who acquired the nickname of 'Messi-lite' for the wonderful skills he displayed all season long, most of them with his magic wand of a left foot. He added substance to the style with 17 goals and was a huge contributor to the Foxes' fairytale success.

Newcomer of the season

Dele Alli
(Tottenham Hotspur FC)

The PFA Young Player of the Year award went to a Tottenham player for the fourth time in five years as 20-year-old Alli followed in the footsteps of previous recent winners Kyle Walker, Gareth Bale and Harry Kane. The young all-purpose midfielder's first season of top-flight football brought ten goals, including a breathtaking strike against Crystal Palace at Selhurst Park. He also forced his way into the England team, but alas, like many of his team-mates, was unable to rise to the occasion at UEFA EURO 2016.

NATIONAL TEAM

International honours
FIFA World Cup (1) 1966.

International tournament appearances
FIFA World Cup (14) 1950, 1954 (qtr-finals), 1958, 1962 (qtr-finals), 1966 (Winners), 1970 (qtr-finals), 1982 (2nd phase), 1986 (qtr-finals), 1990 (4th), 1998 (2nd round), 2002 (qtr-finals), 2006 (qtr-finals), 2010 (2nd round), 2014
UEFA European Championship (9) 1968 (3rd), 1980, 1988, 1992, 1996 (semi-finals), 2000, 2004 (qtr-finals), 2012 (qtr-finals), 2016 (round of 16)

Top five all-time caps
Peter Shilton (125); David Beckham & **Wayne Rooney** (115); Steven Gerrard (114); Bobby Moore (108)

Top five all-time goals
Wayne Rooney (53); Bobby Charlton (49); Gary Lineker (48); Jimmy Greaves (44); Michael Owen (40)

Results 2015/16

Date	Opponent		Venue		Score	Scorers
05/09/15	San Marino (ECQ)	A	Serravalle	W	6-0	Rooney (13p), Brolli (30og), Barkley (46), Walcott (68, 78), Kane (77)
08/09/15	Switzerland (ECQ)	H	London	W	2-0	Kane (67), Rooney (84p)
09/10/15	Estonia (ECQ)	H	London	W	2-0	Walcott (45), Sterling (85)
12/10/15	Lithuania (ECQ)	A	Vilnius	W	3-0	Barkley (29), Arlauskis (35og), Oxlade-Chamberlain (62)
13/11/15	Spain	A	Alicante	L	0-2	
17/11/15	France	H	London	W	2-0	Alli (39), Rooney (48)
26/03/16	Germany	A	Berlin	W	3-2	Kane (61), Vardy (75), Dier (90+1)
29/03/16	Netherlands	H	London	L	1-2	Vardy (41)
22/05/16	Turkey	H	Manchester	W	2-1	Kane (3), Vardy (83)
27/05/16	Australia	H	Sunderland	W	2-1	Rashford (3), Rooney (55)
02/06/16	Portugal	H	London	W	1-0	Smalling (86)
11/06/16	Russia (ECF)	N	Marseille (FRA)	D	1-1	Dier (73)
16/06/16	Wales (ECF)	N	Lille (FRA)	W	2-1	Vardy (56), Sturridge (90+2)
20/06/16	Slovakia (ECF)	N	Saint-Etienne (FRA)	D	0-0	
27/06/16	Iceland (ECF)	N	Nice (FRA)	L	1-2	Rooney (4p)

Appearances 2015/16

Coach: Roy Hodgson	09/08/47		SMR	SUI	EST	LTU	Esp	Fra	Ger	Ned	Tur	Aus	Por	RUS	WAL	SVK	ISL	Caps	Goals
Joe Hart	19/04/87	Man. City	G	G	G		G	G46		G		G	G	G	G	G	G	63	-
Nathaniel Clyne	05/04/91	Liverpool	D	D68	D			D	D	s57		D				D		13	-
John Stones	28/05/94	Everton	D	s68			D		D	D	D	D						10	-
Phil Jagielka	17/08/82	Everton	D			D				s70								39	3
Luke Shaw	12/07/95	Man. United	D	D														6	-
James Milner	04/01/86	Liverpool	M58	M	M				M81			s46	M66	s87				61	1
Jonjo Shelvey	27/02/92	Swansea	M	M58		M	s91	s79										6	-
Alex Oxlade-Chamberlain	15/08/93	Arsenal	M67	A	s73	M												24	5
Ross Barkley	05/12/93	Everton	M	s3	M88	M73	M73	M79	s71	M		s63						22	2
Jamie Vardy	11/01/87	Leicester	M		s82	M		s71	A	A		A66		s46	A	s60		11	4
Wayne Rooney	24/10/85	Man. United	A58	A			s73	A				s46	A78	M78	M	s55	M87	115	53
Fabian Delph	21/11/89	Man. City	s58	M3			M63											9	-
Harry Kane	28/07/93	Tottenham	s58	s58	A	A59	A	A80	A	s70	A		A78	A	A46	s75	A	16	5
Theo Walcott	16/03/89	Arsenal	s67		A82					s57								43	8
Gary Cahill	19/12/85	Chelsea		D	D		s84	D	D		D		D	D	D	D	D	47	3
Chris Smalling	22/11/89	Man. United		D	D		D84		D	D70		D73		D	D	D	D	29	1
Raheem Sterling	08/12/94	Man. City		A	A		M	M68			A73	A76	s66	A87	A46		A60	26	2
Ryan Bertrand	05/08/89	Southampton		D			D	s80				D			D			9	-
Adam Lallana	10/05/88	Liverpool			M73	M67	M63	s68	M71	M70		M46	s78	A	A73	A60		26	-
Dele Alli	11/04/96	Tottenham			s88	s67	s63	M88	M	s81	M		M90	M	M	s60	M	12	1
Jack Butland	10/03/93	Stoke				G		s46	G45									4	-
Kyle Walker	28/05/90	Tottenham				D	D			D	D		D	D	D		D	19	-
Phil Jones	21/02/92	Man. United				D	D	s88										20	-
Kieran Gibbs	26/09/89	Arsenal				D	D											10	-
Danny Ings	23/07/92	Liverpool					s59											1	-
Andros Townsend	16/07/91	Tottenham					s73					s76						11	3
Michael Carrick	28/07/81	Man. United				M91												34	-
Eric Dier	15/01/94	Tottenham					s63	M	M	s84	M	s73	M	M	M	M	M46	11	2
Danny Rose	02/07/90	Tottenham							D	D57	D		D	D	D		D	7	-
Jordan Henderson	17/06/90	Liverpool							M		s66	M	s90			M		27	-
Danny Welbeck	26/11/90	Arsenal							M71									34	14
Fraser Forster	17/03/88	Southampton							s45	G		G87						6	-
Danny Drinkwater	05/03/90	Leicester							M84	s73	M							3	-
Daniel Sturridge	01/09/89	Liverpool							A57			s78		s46	A75	A		21	6
Jack Wilshere	01/01/92	Arsenal								M66	M46	s66	s78		M55	s46		34	2
Marcus Rashford	31/10/97	Man. United								A63			s73		s87			3	1
Tom Heaton	15/04/86	Burnley								s87								1	-

EUROPE

Chelsea FC

Group G
Match 1 - Maccabi Tel-Aviv FC (ISR)
H 4-0 *Willian (15), Oscar (45+4p), Diego Costa (58), Fàbregas (78)*
Begović, Fàbregas, Zouma, Rahman, Oscar (Ramires 65), Hazard, Rémy, Willian (Diego Costa 23), Cahill, Azpilicueta, Loftus-Cheek (Traoré 77). Coach: José Mourinho (POR)
Match 2 - FC Porto (POR)
A 1-2 *Willian (45+2)*
Begović, Ivanović, Fàbregas, Zouma, Ramires (Matić 73), Mikel (Hazard 62), Pedro (Kenedy 73), Diego Costa, Willian, Cahill, Azpilicueta. Coach: José Mourinho (POR)
Match 3 - FC Dynamo Kyiv (UKR)
A 0-0
Begović, Fàbregas (Oscar 75), Zouma, Ramires, Hazard, Diego Costa, Matić, Willian, Cahill, Terry, Azpilicueta. Coach: José Mourinho (POR)
Match 4 - FC Dynamo Kyiv (UKR)
H 2-1 *Dragovic (34og), Willian (83)*
Begović, Fàbregas (Pedro 79), Zouma, Rahman, Ramires, Oscar (Hazard 79), Diego Costa, Matić, Willian (Cahill 90+2), Terry, Azpilicueta. Coach: José Mourinho (POR)
Match 5 - Maccabi Tel-Aviv FC (ISR)
A 4-0 *Cahill (20), Willian (73), Oscar (77), Zouma (90+1)*
Begović, Fàbregas, Rahman, Oscar, Hazard (Pedro 69), Diego Costa, Matić, Willian (Rémy 79), Cahill, Terry (Zouma 72), Azpilicueta. Coach: José Mourinho (POR)
Match 6 - FC Porto (POR)
H 2-0 *Marcano (12og), Willian (52)*
Courtois, Ivanović, Zouma, Ramires, Oscar (Pedro 81), Hazard (Rémy 90), Diego Costa (Mikel 86), Matić, Willian, Terry, Azpilicueta. Coach: José Mourinho (POR)

Round of 16 - Paris Saint-Germain (FRA)
A 1-2 *Mikel (45+1)*
Courtois, Ivanović, Fàbregas, Rahman, Hazard (Oscar 71), Mikel, Pedro, Diego Costa, Willian, Cahill, Azpilicueta. Coach: Guus Hiddink (NED)
H 1-2 *Diego Costa (27)*
Courtois, Ivanović, Fàbregas, Hazard (Oscar 77), Mikel, Kenedy, Pedro, Diego Costa (Traoré 60), Willian, Cahill, Azpilicueta. Coach: Guus Hiddink (NED)

Manchester City FC

Group D
Match 1 - Juventus FC (ITA)
H 1-2 *Chiellini (57og)*
Hart, Sagna, Kompany (Otamendi 75), Sterling (De Bruyne 71), Nasri (Agüero 84), Kolarov, Bony, Mangala, Silva, Fernandinho, Touré. Coach: Manuel Pellegrini (CHI)

Match 2 - VfL Borussia Mönchengladbach (GER)
A 2-1 *Demichelis (65), Agüero (90p)*
Hart, Sagna, Sterling (Zabaleta 90+4), Agüero, Kolarov, De Bruyne, Silva (Jesús Navas 65), Fernandinho, Demichelis, Otamendi, Touré (Fernando 46). Coach: Manuel Pellegrini (CHI)
Match 3 - Sevilla FC (ESP)
H 2-1 *Rami (36og), De Bruyne (90+1)*
Hart, Sagna, Zabaleta (Kolarov 60), Sterling, Bony (Fernando 76), Jesús Navas, De Bruyne (Kompany 90+3), Mangala, Fernandinho, Otamendi, Touré. Coach: Manuel Pellegrini (CHI)
Match 4 - Sevilla FC (ESP)
A 3-1 *Sterling (8), Fernandinho (11), Bony (36)*
Hart, Sagna, Kompany, Fernando, Sterling (De Bruyne 73), Kolarov, Bony (Delph 86), Jesús Navas, Fernandinho (Demichelis 90), Otamendi, Touré. Coach: Manuel Pellegrini (CHI)
Match 5 - Juventus FC (ITA)
A 0-1
Hart (Caballero 81), Sagna, Fernando, Agüero (Sterling 69), Jesús Navas, De Bruyne, Clichy, Fernandinho (Delph 60), Demichelis, Otamendi, Touré. Coach: Manuel Pellegrini (CHI)
Match 6 - VfL Borussia Mönchengladbach (GER)
H 4-2 *Sterling (16), Sterling (80, 81), Bony (85)*
Hart, Sterling, Kolarov, De Bruyne (Jesús Navas 65), Delph (Bony 65), Mangala, Silva, Clichy (Sagna 81), Fernandinho, Otamendi, Touré. Coach: Manuel Pellegrini (CHI)

Round of 16 - FC Dynamo Kyiv (UKR)
A 3-1 *Agüero (15), Silva (40), Touré (90)*
Hart, Sagna, Kompany, Fernando, Sterling, Agüero (Iheanacho 90), Silva, Clichy, Fernandinho, Otamendi, Touré. Coach: Manuel Pellegrini (CHI)
H 0-0
Hart, Kompany (Mangala 7), Zabaleta, Fernando, Agüero, Jesús Navas, Silva (Sterling 79), Clichy, Fernandinho, Otamendi (Demichelis 24), Touré. Coach: Manuel Pellegrini (CHI)

Quarter-finals - Paris Saint-Germain (FRA)
A 2-2 *De Bruyne (38), Fernandinho (72)*
Hart, Sagna, Fernando, Agüero (Kolarov 90+3), Jesús Navas, De Bruyne (Delph 77), Mangala, Silva (Bony 88), Clichy, Fernandinho, Otamendi. Coach: Manuel Pellegrini (CHI)
H 1-0 *De Bruyne (76)*
Hart, Sagna, Fernando, Agüero (Iheanacho 90+3), Jesús Navas, De Bruyne (Touré 84), Mangala, Silva (Delph 87), Clichy, Fernandinho, Otamendi. Coach: Manuel Pellegrini (CHI)

Semi-finals - Real Madrid CF (ESP)
H 0-0
Hart, Sagna, Kompany, Fernando, Agüero, Jesús Navas (Sterling 77), De Bruyne, Silva (Iheanacho 40), Clichy, Fernandinho, Otamendi. Coach: Manuel Pellegrini (CHI)
A 0-1
Hart, Sagna, Kompany (Mangala 10), Fernando, Agüero, Jesús Navas (Iheanacho 69), De Bruyne, Clichy, Fernandinho, Otamendi, Touré (Sterling 61). Coach: Manuel Pellegrini (CHI)

Arsenal FC

Group F
Match 1 - GNK Dinamo Zagreb (CRO)
A 1-2 *Walcott (79)*
Ospina, Debuchy, Gibbs (Campbell 65), Gabriel, Koscielny, Arteta (Coquelin 64), Özil, Giroud, Oxlade-Chamberlain (Walcott 65), Alexis Sánchez, Santi Cazorla. Coach: Arsène Wenger (FRA)
Red card: Giroud 40

Match 2 - Olympiacos FC (GRE)
H 2-3 *Walcott (35), Alexis Sánchez (65)*
Ospina, Gibbs, Gabriel, Koscielny (Mertesacker 57), Özil, Walcott, Oxlade-Chamberlain, Alexis Sánchez, Santi Cazorla, Bellerín (Campbell 86), Coquelin (Ramsey 60). Coach: Arsène Wenger (FRA)
Match 3 - FC Bayern München (GER)
H 2-0 *Giroud (77), Özil (90+4)*
Čech, Mertesacker, Koscielny, Özil, Walcott (Giroud 74), Ramsey (Oxlade-Chamberlain 57), Alexis Sánchez (Gibbs 82), Monreal, Santi Cazorla, Bellerín, Coquelin. Coach: Arsène Wenger (FRA)
Match 4 - FC Bayern München (GER)
A 1-5 *Giroud (69)*
Čech, Debuchy, Mertesacker, Gabriel, Özil, Giroud (Iwobi 85), Alexis Sánchez, Monreal, Santi Cazorla (Chambers 87), Campbell (Gibbs 59), Coquelin. Coach: Arsène Wenger (FRA)
Match 5 - GNK Dinamo Zagreb (CRO)
H 3-0 *Özil (29), Alexis Sánchez (33, 69)*
Čech, Mertesacker, Koscielny, Özil, Giroud (Ramsey 64), Alexis Sánchez, Monreal, Santi Cazorla (Chambers 82), Flamini, Bellerín (Debuchy 82), Campbell. Coach: Arsène Wenger (FRA)
Match 6 - Olympiacos FC (GRE)
A 3-0 *Giroud (29, 49, 67p)*
Čech, Mertesacker, Koscielny, Özil, Giroud (Chambers 90+2), Walcott (Gibbs 72), Ramsey, Monreal, Flamini, Bellerín, Campbell (Oxlade-Chamberlain 90+1). Coach: Arsène Wenger (FRA)

Round of 16 - FC Barcelona (ESP)
H 0-2
Čech, Mertesacker, Koscielny, Özil, Giroud (Welbeck 72), Oxlade-Chamberlain (Walcott 50), Ramsey, Alexis Sánchez, Monreal, Bellerín, Coquelin (Flamini 82). Coach: Arsène Wenger (FRA)
A 1-3 *Elneny (51)*
Ospina, Gabriel, Koscielny, Özil, Alexis Sánchez, Monreal, Flamini (Coquelin 45), Welbeck (Walcott 73), Bellerín, Elneny, Iwobi (Giroud 73). Coach: Arsène Wenger (FRA)

Manchester United FC

Play-offs - Club Brugge KV (BEL)
H 3-1 *Depay (13, 43), Fellaini (90+4)*
Romero, Depay, Mata, Rooney (Fellaini 84), Januzaj (Hernández 72), Smalling, Carrick (Schweinsteiger 46), Blind, Shaw, Schneiderlin, Darmian. Coach: Louis van Gaal (NED)
A 4-0 *Rooney (20, 49, 57), Ander Herrera (63)*
Romero, Depay, Mata (Young 62), Rooney, Januzaj (Schweinsteiger 46), Smalling, Carrick, Blind, Ander Herrera (Hernández 64), Shaw, Darmian. Coach: Louis van Gaal (NED)

Group B
Match 1 - PSV Eindhoven (NED)
A 1-2 *Depay (41)*
De Gea, Depay, Mata, Martial, Smalling, Blind, Young (Valencia 86), Ander Herrera (Fellaini 75), Shaw (Rojo 24), Schweinsteiger, Darmian. Coach: Louis van Gaal (NED)
Match 2 - VfL Wolfsburg (GER)
H 2-1 *Mata (34p), Smalling (53)*
De Gea, Depay (Andreas Pereira 62), Mata, Martial, Rooney, Smalling, Blind, Valencia (Young 46), Schneiderlin, Schweinsteiger (Jones 72), Darmian. Coach: Louis van Gaal (NED)

Match 3 - PFC CSKA Moskva (RUS)
A 1-1 *Martial (65)*
De Gea, Jones, Rojo (Blind 64), Martial, Rooney, Smalling, Ander Herrera, Valencia, Schneiderlin, Schweinsteiger (Fellaini 46), Lingard (Depay 80). Coach: Louis van Gaal (NED)

Match 4 - PFC CSKA Moskva (RUS)
H 1-0 *Rooney (79)*
De Gea, Rojo, Mata (Depay 74), Martial (Fellaini 66), Rooney, Smalling, Carrick, Blind, Young, Schweinsteiger (Ander Herrera 89), Lingard. Coach: Louis van Gaal (NED)

Match 5 - PSV Eindhoven (NED)
H 0-0
De Gea, Rojo, Depay (Young 59), Martial, Rooney, Smalling, Blind, Schneiderlin, Schweinsteiger (Fellaini 58), Lingard, Darmian (Mata 85). Coach: Louis van Gaal (NED)

Match 6 - VfL Wolfsburg (GER)
A 2-3 *Martial (10), Guilavogui (82og)*
De Gea, Depay, Mata (Powell 69), Martial, Smalling, Blind, Fellaini, Varela, Schweinsteiger (Carrick 69), Lingard, Darmian (Borthwick-Jackson 43). Coach: Louis van Gaal (NED)

Round of 32 - FC Midtjylland (DEN)
A 1-2 *Depay (37)*
Romero, Depay, Mata (Andreas Pereira 78), Martial, Smalling, Carrick, Blind, Ander Herrera (Schneiderlin 72), McNair, Lingard, Love. Coach: Louis van Gaal (NED)

H 5-1 *Bodurov (32og), Rashford (64, 75), Ander Herrera (88p), Depay (90)*
Romero, Depay, Mata, Carrick, Blind, Ander Herrera (Poole 90+1), Schneiderlin, Varela, Lingard (Andreas Pereira 86), Rashford, Riley (Rojo 79). Coach: Louis van Gaal (NED)

Round of 16 - Liverpool FC (ENG)
A 0-2
De Gea, Rojo, Depay, Mata (Ander Herrera 79), Martial, Smalling, Blind, Fellaini, Schneiderlin (Schweinsteiger 79), Varela, Rashford (Carrick 46). Coach: Louis van Gaal (NED)

H 1-1 *Martial (32p)*
De Gea, Rojo (Darmian 62), Mata, Martial, Smalling, Carrick (Schweinsteiger 70), Blind, Fellaini, Varela (Valencia 46), Lingard, Rashford. Coach: Louis van Gaal (NED)

Tottenham Hotspur FC

Group J
Match 1 - Qarabağ FK (AZE)
H 3-1 *Son (28, 30), Lamela (86)*
Lloris, Rose, Alderweireld, Son (Kane 68), Lamela, Dier (Winks 76), Trippier, Townsend (N'Jie 68), Alli, Wimmer, Carroll. Coach: Mauricio Pochettino (ARG)

Match 2 - AS Monaco FC (FRA)
A 1-1 *Lamela (35)*
Lloris, Rose, Alderweireld, Vertonghen, Kane, Lamela (N'Jie 65), Dier, Trippier, Alli, Chadli (Townsend 70), Eriksen (Carroll 90). Coach: Mauricio Pochettino (ARG)

Match 3 - RSC Anderlecht (BEL)
A 1-2 *Eriksen (4)*
Lloris, Alderweireld, Vertonghen, Lamela, N'Jie (Kane 59), Dier, Trippier, Townsend (Onomah 80), Dembélé (Alli 65), Eriksen, Davies. Coach: Mauricio Pochettino (ARG)

Match 4 - RSC Anderlecht (BEL)
H 2-1 *Kane (29), Dembélé (87)*
Lloris, Alderweireld, Vertonghen, Mason (Dembélé 73), Kane, Lamela, Dier, Trippier, Alli (Onomah 77), Eriksen (Son 59), Davies. Coach: Mauricio Pochettino (ARG)

Match 5 - Qarabağ FK (AZE)
A 1-0 *Kane (78)*
Lloris, Alderweireld, Vertonghen, Son (N'Jie 80), Mason (Carroll 73), Kane, Dier, Trippier, Alli (Eriksen (Onomah 90+1), Davies. Coach: Mauricio Pochettino (ARG)

Match 6 - AS Monaco FC (FRA)
H 4-1 *Lamela (2, 15, 38), Carroll (78)*
Lloris, Alderweireld, Son, Lamela (Chadli 62), N'Jie (Alli 79), Dier (Bentaleb 42), Trippier, Onomah, Wimmer, Carroll, Davies. Coach: Mauricio Pochettino (ARG)

Round of 32 - ACF Fiorentina (ITA)
A 1-1 *Chadli (37p)*
Vorm, Alderweireld, Son (Kane 69), Mason, Trippier, Alli, Chadli (Dier 79), Eriksen, Wimmer, Carroll (Dembélé 46), Davies. Coach: Mauricio Pochettino (ARG)

H 3-0 *Mason (25), Lamela (63), Gonzalo Rodríguez (81og)*
Lloris, Alderweireld, Mason (Winks 87), Lamela (Onomah 76), Dier, Trippier, Alli (Bentaleb 84), Chadli, Eriksen, Wimmer, Davies. Coach: Mauricio Pochettino (ARG)

Round of 16 - Borussia Dortmund (GER)
A 0-3
Lloris, Alderweireld, Son (Kane 76), Mason, Trippier, Chadli (Dembélé 58), Eriksen (Lamela 65), Onomah, Wimmer, Carroll, Davies. Coach: Mauricio Pochettino (ARG)

H 1-2 *Son (74)*
Lloris, Alderweireld, Son, Mason, Lamela (Onomah 74), Dier, Trippier, Alli (Carroll 70), Chadli, Wimmer, Davies (Rose 13). Coach: Mauricio Pochettino (ARG)

Liverpool FC

Group B
Match 1 - FC Girondins de Bordeaux (FRA)
A 1-1 *Lallana (65)*
Mignolet, Touré (Chirivella 28), Coutinho, Gomez, Sakho, Moreno, Lallana, Can, Origi (Ings 73), Ibe, Rossiter (Brannagan 80). Coach: Brendan Rodgers (NIR)

Match 2 - FC Sion (SUI)
H 1-1 *Lallana (4)*
Mignolet, Clyne (Moreno 46), Touré (Sakho 76), Gomez, Lallana, Can, Allen, Ings (Coutinho 61), Ibe, Rossiter. Coach: Brendan Rodgers (NIR)

Match 3 - FC Rubin (RUS)
H 1-1 *Can (37)*
Mignolet, Clyne, Milner, Coutinho (Benteke 63), Sakho, Moreno, Lallana, Can, Allen (Lucas 46), Origi (Roberto Firmino 74), Škrtel. Coach: Jürgen Klopp (GER)

Match 4 - FC Rubin (RUS)
A 1-0 *Ibe (52)*
Mignolet, Clyne, Lovren, Milner (Lallana 61), Benteke, Roberto Firmino (Lucas 81), Sakho, Moreno, Can (Škrtel 90+2), Allen, Ibe. Coach: Jürgen Klopp (GER)

Match 5 - FC Girondins de Bordeaux (FRA)
H 2-1 *Milner (38p), Benteke (45+1)*
Mignolet, Clyne, Touré, Lovren, Milner, Benteke, Roberto Firmino (Lallana 74), Moreno, Lucas, Allen (Can 67), Ibe (Origi 90+2). Coach: Jürgen Klopp (GER)

Match 6 - FC Sion (SUI)
A 0-0
Mignolet, Clyne, Touré, Lovren, Milner (Coutinho 61), Roberto Firmino (Brannagan 90), Henderson (Rossiter 77), Lallana, Can, Origi, Smith. Coach: Jürgen Klopp (GER)

Round of 32 - FC Augsburg (GER)
A 0-0
Mignolet, Clyne, Touré, Milner (Ibe 81), Coutinho, Roberto Firmino, Henderson, Sturridge (Origi 68), Sakho, Moreno, Can. Coach: Jürgen Klopp (GER)

H 1-0 *Milner (5p)*
Mignolet, Clyne, Milner, Coutinho (João Carlos 80), Roberto Firmino, Henderson, Sturridge (Origi 66), Sakho, Moreno, Lucas, Can. Coach: Jürgen Klopp (GER)

Round of 16 - Manchester United FC (ENG)
H 2-0 *Sturridge (20p), Roberto Firmino (73)*
Mignolet, Clyne, Lovren, Coutinho, Roberto Firmino (Origi 84), Henderson, Sturridge (Allen 64), Sakho, Moreno, Lallana, Can. Coach: Jürgen Klopp (GER)

A 1-1 *Coutinho (45)*
Mignolet, Clyne, Lovren, Milner, Coutinho, Firmino (Benteke 85), Henderson (Allen 71), Sturridge (Origi 68), Sakho, Lallana, Can. Coach: Jürgen Klopp (GER)

Quarter-finals - Borussia Dortmund (GER)
A 1-1 *Origi (36)*
Mignolet, Clyne, Lovren, Milner, Coutinho, Henderson (Allen 46), Sakho, Moreno, Lallana (Roberto Firmino 77), Can, Origi (Sturridge 84). Coach: Jürgen Klopp (GER)

H 4-3 *Origi (48), Coutinho (66), Sakho (78), Lovren (90+1)*
Mignolet, Clyne, Lovren, Milner, Coutinho, Roberto Firmino (Sturridge 62), Sakho, Moreno, Lallana (Allen 62), Can (Lucas 80), Origi. Coach: Jürgen Klopp (GER)

Semi-finals - Villarreal CF (ESP)
A 0-1
Mignolet, Clyne, Touré, Lovren, Milner, Coutinho (Ibe 46), Roberto Firmino (Benteke 90), Moreno, Lallana, Lucas, Allen. Coach: Jürgen Klopp (GER)

H 3-0 *Bruno Soriano (7og), Sturridge (63), Lallana (81)*
Mignolet, Clyne, Touré, Lovren, Milner, Coutinho (Allen 82), Roberto Firmino (Benteke 89), Sturridge (Lucas 90+2), Moreno, Lallana, Can. Coach: Jürgen Klopp (GER)

Final - Sevilla FC (ESP)
N 1-3 *Sturridge (35)*
Mignolet, Clyne, Touré (Benteke 82), Lovren, Milner, Coutinho, Roberto Firmino (Origi 69), Sturridge, Moreno, Lallana (Allen 73), Can. Coach: Jürgen Klopp (GER)

Southampton FC

Third qualifying round - Vitesse (NED)
H 3-0 *Pellè (36), Tadić (45+1p), Long (84)*
Stekelenburg, Cédric, Yoshida, Clasie (Juanmi 62), Fonte, S Davis, Mané (Reed 85), Tadić (Long 62), Wanyama, Pellè, Targett. Coach: Ronald Koeman (NED)

A 2-0 *Pellè (4), Mané (89)*
Stekelenburg, Yoshida, Fonte, S Davis (Reed 77), Mané, Tadić (Juanmi 65), Wanyama, Martina, Ward-Prowse, Pellè (Rodriguez 72), Caulker. Coach: Ronald Koeman (NED)

Play-offs - FC Midtjylland (DEN)
H 1-1 *Rodriguez (56p)*
Stekelenburg, Yoshida, Fonte, Rodriguez (Long 76), Mané, Wanyama, Romeu, Ward-Prowse (Juanmi 83), Pellè, Caulker, Targett. Coach: Ronald Koeman (NED)

A 0-1
Stekelenburg, Yoshida, Fonte, S Davis (Juanmi 82), Rodriguez (Long 75), Romeu, Martina, Ward-Prowse, Pellè, Caulker (Tadić 56), Targett. Coach: Ronald Koeman (NED)

West Ham United FC

First qualifying round - FC Lusitans (AND)
H 3-0 *Sakho (40, 45+2), Tomkins (58)*
Randolph, Tomkins, Jarvis, Zárate (Parfitt-Williams 74), Sakho (Lee 62), O'Brien (Cullen 60), Amalfitano, Poyet, Burke, Oxford, Page. Coach: Terry Westley (ENG)
A 1-0 *Lee (21)*
Randolph, Tomkins, Jarvis, Sakho, O'Brien (Burke 61), Amalfitano (Parfitt-Williams 76), Poyet, Oxford, Lee, Page, Cullen (Nasha 86). Coach: Slaven Bilić (CRO)
Red card: Sakho 14

Second qualifying round - Birkirkara FC (MLT)
H 1-0 *Tomkins (90)*
Adrián, Reid, Cresswell, Nolan (Poyet 79), Tomkins, Jarvis, Zárate, Noble, Maïga (Lee 70), Amalfitano (Samuelsen 59). Coach: Slaven Bilić (CRO)
A 0-1 (aet; 5-3 on pens)
Adrián, Cresswell, Nolan (Poyet 59), Tomkins, Jarvis (Samuelsen 120), Kouyaté, Zárate, Noble, O'Brien, Collins, Amalfitano (Maïga 59). Coach: Slaven Bilić (CRO)
Red card: Tomkins 45

Third qualifying round - FC Astra Giurgiu (ROU)
H 2-2 *Valencia (23), Zárate (51)*
Adrián, Cresswell, Kouyaté, Zárate (Jarvis 76), Noble, O'Brien (Burke 35), Collins, Ogbonna, Payet, Valencia (Maïga 37), Oxford. Coach: Slaven Bilić (CRO)
Red card: Collins 59
A 1-2 *Lanzini (4)*
Randolph, Nolan, Jenkinson, Maïga, Poyet, Henry, Lanzini, Lee (Brown 80), Page (Pike 90+2), Cullen, Knoyle. Coach: Julian Dicks (ENG)

Arsenal FC

1886 • Emirates Stadium (60,260) • arsenal.com
Major honours
UEFA Cup Winners' Cup (1) 1994; Inter Cities Fairs Cup (1) 1970; English League (13) 1931, 1933, 1934, 1935, 1938, 1948, 1953, 1971, 1989, 1991, 1998, 2002, 2004; FA Cup (12) 1930, 1936, 1950, 1971, 1979, 1993, 1998, 2002, 2003, 2005, 2014, 2015; League Cup (2) 1987, 1993
Manager: Arsène Wenger (FRA)

2015
09/08	h	West Ham	L	0-2	
16/08	a	Crystal Palace	W	2-1	Giroud, og (Delaney)
24/08	h	Liverpool	D	0-0	
29/08	a	Newcastle	W	1-0	og (Coloccini)
12/09	a	Stoke	W	2-0	Walcott, Giroud
19/09	a	Chelsea	L	0-2	
26/09	a	Leicester	W	5-2	Walcott, Alexis Sánchez 3, Giroud
04/10	h	Man. United	W	3-0	Alexis Sánchez 2, Özil
17/10	a	Watford	W	3-0	Alexis Sánchez, Giroud, Ramsey
24/10	h	Everton	W	2-1	Giroud, Koscielny
31/10	a	Swansea	W	3-0	Giroud, Koscielny, Campbell
08/11	h	Tottenham	D	1-1	Gibbs
21/11	a	West Brom	L	1-2	Giroud
29/11	h	Norwich	D	1-1	Özil
05/12	h	Sunderland	W	3-1	Campbell, Giroud, Ramsey
13/12	a	Aston Villa	W	2-0	Giroud (p), Ramsey
21/12	h	Man. City	W	2-1	Walcott, Giroud
26/12	a	Southampton	L	0-4	
28/12	h	Bournemouth	W	2-0	Gabriel, Özil
2016					
02/01	h	Newcastle	W	1-0	Koscielny
13/01	a	Liverpool	D	3-3	Ramsey, Giroud 2
17/01	h	Stoke	D	0-0	
24/01	h	Chelsea	L	0-1	
02/02	h	Southampton	D	0-0	
07/02	a	Bournemouth	W	2-0	Özil, Oxlade-Chamberlain
14/02	h	Leicester	W	2-1	Walcott, Welbeck
28/02	a	Man. United	L	2-3	Welbeck, Özil
02/03	h	Swansea	L	1-2	Campbell
05/03	a	Tottenham	D	2-2	Ramsey, Alexis Sánchez
19/03	a	Everton	W	2-0	Welbeck, Iwobi
02/04	h	Watford	W	4-0	Alexis Sánchez, Iwobi, Bellerín, Walcott
09/04	a	West Ham	D	3-3	Özil, Alexis Sánchez, Koscielny
17/04	h	Crystal Palace	D	1-1	Alexis Sánchez
21/04	h	West Brom	W	2-0	Alexis Sánchez 2
24/04	a	Sunderland	D	0-0	
30/04	h	Norwich	W	1-0	Welbeck
08/05	h	Man. City	D	2-2	Giroud, Alexis Sánchez
15/05	a	Aston Villa	W	4-0	Giroud 3, og (Bunn)

No	Name	Nat	DoB	Pos	Aps	(s)	Gls
17	Alexis Sánchez	CHI	19/12/88	A	28	(2)	13
8	Mikel Arteta	ESP	26/03/82	M		(9)	
24	Héctor Bellerín	ESP	19/03/95	D	36		1
28	Joel Campbell	CRC	26/06/92	A	11	(8)	3
33	Petr Čech	CZE	20/05/82	G	34		
21	Calum Chambers		20/01/95	D	2	(10)	
34	Francis Coquelin	FRA	13/05/91	M	21	(5)	
2	Mathieu Debuchy	FRA	28/07/85	D	2		
35	Mohamed Elneny	EGY	11/07/92	M	9	(2)	
20	Mathieu Flamini	FRA	07/03/84	M	12	(4)	
5	Gabriel	BRA	26/11/90	D	18	(3)	1
3	Kieran Gibbs		26/09/89	D	3	(12)	1
12	Olivier Giroud	FRA	30/09/86	A	26	(12)	16
45	Alex Iwobi	NGA	03/05/96	A	8	(5)	2
6	Laurent Koscielny	FRA	10/09/85	D	33		4
4	Per Mertesacker	GER	29/09/84	D	24		
18	Nacho Monreal	ESP	26/02/86	D	36	(1)	
13	David Ospina	COL	31/08/88	G	4		
15	Alex Oxlade-Chamberlain		15/08/93	M	9	(13)	1
11	Mesut Özil	GER	15/10/88	M	35		6
16	Aaron Ramsey	WAL	26/12/90	M	29	(2)	5
19	Santi Cazorla	ESP	13/12/84	M	15		
14	Theo Walcott		16/03/89	A	15	(13)	5
23	Danny Welbeck		26/11/90	A	7	(4)	4
10	Jack Wilshere		01/01/92	M	1	(2)	

Aston Villa FC

1874 • Villa Park (42,660) • avfc.co.uk
Major honours
European Champion Clubs' Cup (1) 1982; UEFA Super Cup (1) 1982; English League (7) 1894, 1896, 1897, 1899, 1900, 1910, 1981; FA Cup (7) 1887, 1895, 1897, 1905, 1913, 1920, 1957; League Cup (5) 1961, 1975, 1977, 1994, 1996

Manager: Tim Sherwood;
(25/10/15) (Kevin McDonald (SCO));
(02/11/15) Rémi Garde (FRA);
(29/03/16) (Eric Black (SCO))

2015
08/08	a	Bournemouth	W	1-0	Gestede
14/08	h	Man. United	L	0-1	
22/08	a	Crystal Palace	L	1-2	og (Souaré)
29/08	h	Sunderland	D	2-2	Sinclair 2 (1p)
13/09	a	Leicester	L	2-3	Grealish, Gil
19/09	h	West Brom	L	0-1	
26/09	a	Liverpool	L	2-3	Gestede 2
03/10	h	Stoke	L	0-1	
17/10	a	Chelsea	L	0-2	
24/10	h	Swansea	L	1-2	Ayew
02/11	a	Tottenham	L	1-3	Ayew
08/11	h	Man. City	D	0-0	
21/11	a	Everton	L	0-4	
28/11	h	Watford	L	2-3	Richards, Ayew
05/12	a	Southampton	D	1-1	Lescott
13/12	a	Arsenal	L	0-2	
19/12	a	Newcastle	D	1-1	Ayew
26/12	h	West Ham	D	1-1	Ayew (p)
28/12	a	Norwich	L	0-2	
2016					
02/01	a	Sunderland	L	1-3	Gil
12/01	h	Crystal Palace	W	1-0	og (Hennessey)
16/01	h	Leicester	L	1-1	Gestede
23/01	a	West Brom	D	0-0	
02/02	a	West Ham	D	0-2	
06/02	h	Norwich	W	2-0	og (Klose, Agbonlahor)
14/02	h	Liverpool	L	0-6	
27/02	a	Stoke	L	1-2	Bacuna
01/03	h	Everton	L	1-3	Gestede
05/03	a	Man. City	L	0-4	
13/03	h	Tottenham	L	0-2	
19/03	a	Swansea	L	0-1	
02/04	h	Chelsea	L	0-4	
09/04	a	Bournemouth	L	1-2	Ayew
16/04	a	Man. United	L	0-1	
23/04	h	Southampton	L	2-4	Westwood 2
30/04	a	Watford	L	2-3	Clark, Ayew
07/05	h	Newcastle	D	0-0	
15/05	a	Arsenal	L	0-4	

No	Name	Nat	DoB	Pos	Aps	(s)	Gls
11	Gabriel Agbonlahor		13/10/86	A	13	(2)	1
23	Jordan Amavi	FRA	09/03/94	D	9	(1)	
19	Jordan Ayew	GHA	11/09/91	A	27	(3)	7
7	Leandro Bacuna	NED	21/08/91	M	27	(4)	1
31	Mark Bunn		16/11/84	G	10		
43	Aly Cissokho	FRA	15/09/87	D	18		
6	Ciaran Clark	IRL	26/09/89	D	16	(2)	1
33	José Ángel Crespo	ESP	09/02/87	D	1		
39	Rudy Gestede	BEN	10/10/88	A	14	(18)	5
25	Carles Gil	ESP	22/11/92	M	17	(6)	2
40	Jack Grealish	IRL	10/09/95	M	9	(7)	1
30	André Green		26/07/98	M		(2)	
8	Idrissa Gueye	SEN	26/09/89	M	35		
1	Brad Guzan	USA	09/09/84	G	28		
29	Rushian Hepburn-Murphy		19/09/98	A		(1)	
21	Alan Hutton	SCO	30/11/84	D	26	(2)	
27	Libor Kozák	CZE	30/05/89	A	3	(1)	
16	Joleon Lescott		16/08/82	D	30		1
38	Jordan Lyden	AUS	30/01/96	M	2	(2)	
28	Charles N'Zogbia	FRA	28/05/86	M		(2)	
5	Jores Okore	DEN	11/08/92	D	12		
4	Micah Richards		24/06/88	D	23	(1)	1
18	Kieran Richardson		21/10/84	D	8	(3)	
24	Carlos Sánchez	COL	06/02/86	M	16	(4)	
9	Scott Sinclair		25/03/89	A	19	(8)	2
46	Kevin Toner	IRL	18/07/96	D	3	(1)	
20	Adama Traoré	ESP	25/01/96	A		(10)	
17	Jordan Veretout	FRA	01/03/93	M	21	(4)	
15	Ashley Westwood		01/04/90	M	31	(1)	2

AFC Bournemouth

1890 • Vitality Stadium (11,464) • afcb.co.uk
Manager: Eddie Howe

2015

08/08	h	Aston Villa	L	0-1	
17/08	a	Liverpool	L	0-1	
22/08	a	West Ham	W	4-3	Wilson 3 (1p), Pugh
29/08	h	Leicester	D	1-1	Wilson
12/09	a	Norwich	L	1-3	Cook
19/09	h	Sunderland	W	2-0	Wilson, Ritchie
26/09	a	Stoke	L	1-2	Gosling
03/10	a	Watford	D	1-1	Murray
17/10	a	Man. City	L	1-5	Murray
25/10	h	Tottenham	L	1-5	Ritchie
01/11	a	Southampton	L	0-2	
07/11	h	Newcastle	L	0-1	
21/11	a	Swansea	D	2-2	King, Gosling
28/11	h	Everton	D	3-3	Smith, Stanislas 2
05/12	a	Chelsea	W	1-0	Murray
12/12	h	Man. United	W	2-1	Stanislas, King
19/12	a	West Brom	W	2-1	Smith, Daniels (p)
26/12	h	Crystal Palace	D	0-0	
28/12	a	Arsenal	L	0-2	

2016

02/01	h	Leicester	D	0-0	
12/01	h	West Ham	L	1-3	Arter
16/01	a	Norwich	W	3-0	Gosling, Daniels (p), Afobe
23/01	a	Sunderland	D	1-1	Afobe
02/02	a	Crystal Palace	W	2-1	Pugh, Afobe
07/02	h	Arsenal	L	0-2	
13/02	h	Stoke	L	1-3	Ritchie
27/02	a	Watford	D	0-0	
01/03	h	Southampton	W	2-0	Cook, Afobe
05/03	a	Newcastle	W	3-1	og (Taylor), King, Daniels
12/03	h	Swansea	W	3-2	Gradel, King, Cook
20/03	a	Tottenham	L	0-3	
02/04	h	Man. City	L	0-4	
09/04	a	Aston Villa	W	2-1	Cook, King
17/04	h	Liverpool	L	1-2	King
23/04	h	Chelsea	L	1-4	Elphick
30/04	a	Everton	L	1-2	Pugh
07/05	h	West Brom	D	1-1	Ritchie
17/05	a	Man. United	L	1-3	og (Smalling)

No	Name	Nat	DoB	Pos	Aps	(s)	Gls
20	Benik Afobe		12/02/93	A	12	(2)	4
21	Ryan Allsop		17/06/92	G		(1)	
8	Harry Arter	IRL	28/12/89	M	22		1
1	Artur Boruc	POL	20/02/80	G	32		
3	Steve Cook		19/04/91	D	36		4
11	Charlie Daniels		07/09/86	D	37		3
25	Sylvain Distin	FRA	16/12/77	D	9	(3)	
5	Tommy Elphick		07/09/87	D	11	(1)	1
23	Adam Federici	AUS	31/01/85	G	6		
2	Simon Francis		16/02/85	D	38		
4	Dan Gosling		02/02/90	M	27	(6)	3
28	Lewis Grabban		12/01/88	A	4	(10)	
10	Max Gradel	CIV	30/11/87	A	11	(2)	1
12	Juan Manuel Iturbe	ARG	04/06/93	A		(2)	
18	Yann Kermorgant	FRA	08/11/81	M		(7)	
17	Joshua King	NOR	15/01/92	A	24	(7)	6
16	Shaun MacDonald	WAL	17/06/88	M		(3)	
14	Tyrone Mings		13/03/93	D		(1)	
27	Glenn Murray		25/09/83	A	6	(13)	3
32	Eunan O'Kane	IRL	10/07/90	M	6	(10)	
7	Marc Pugh		02/04/87	M	15	(11)	3
9	Tokelo Rantie	RSA	08/09/90	A		(3)	
30	Matt Ritchie	SCO	10/09/89	M	33	(4)	4
15	Adam Smith		29/04/91	D	22	(9)	2
19	Junior Stanislas		26/11/89	M	17	(4)	3
6	Andrew Surman		20/08/86	M	38		
24	Lee Tomlin		12/01/89	A	3	(3)	
13	Callum Wilson		27/02/92	A	9	(4)	5

Chelsea FC

1905 • Stamford Bridge (41,798) • chelseafc.co.uk

Major honours
UEFA Champions League (1) 2012; UEFA Cup Winners' Cup (2) 1971, 1998; UEFA Europa League (1) 2013; UEFA Super Cup (1) 1998; English League (5) 1955, 2005, 2006, 2010, 2015; FA Cup (7) 1970, 1997, 2000, 2007, 2009, 2010, 2012; League Cup (5) 1965, 1998, 2005, 2007, 2015

Manager: José Mourinho (POR);
(17/12/15) (Steve Holland);
(20/12/15) (Guus Hiddink (NED))

2015

08/08	h	Swansea	D	2-2	Oscar, og (Fernández)
16/08	a	Man. City	L	0-3	
23/08	a	West Brom	W	3-2	Pedro, Diego Costa, Azpilicueta
29/08	h	Crystal Palace	L	1-2	Falcao
12/09	a	Everton	L	1-3	Matić
19/09	h	Arsenal	W	2-0	Zouma, og (Chambers)
26/09	a	Newcastle	D	2-2	Ramires, Willian
03/10	a	Southampton	L	1-3	Willian
17/10	h	Aston Villa	W	2-0	Diego Costa, og (Hutton)
24/10	a	West Ham	L	1-2	Cahill
31/10	h	Liverpool	L	1-3	Ramires
07/11	a	Stoke	L	0-1	
21/11	h	Norwich	W	1-0	Diego Costa
29/11	a	Tottenham	D	0-0	
05/12	h	Bournemouth	L	0-1	
14/12	a	Leicester	L	1-2	Rémy
19/12	h	Sunderland	W	3-1	Ivanović, Pedro, Oscar (p)
26/12	h	Watford	D	2-2	Diego Costa 2
28/12	a	Man. United	D	0-0	

2016

03/01	a	Crystal Palace	W	3-0	Oscar, Willian, Diego Costa
13/01	h	West Brom	D	2-2	Azpilicueta, og (McAuley)
16/01	h	Everton	D	3-3	Diego Costa, Fàbregas, Terry
24/01	a	Arsenal	W	1-0	Diego Costa
03/02	a	Watford	D	0-0	
07/02	h	Man. United	W	1-0	Diego Costa
13/02	a	Newcastle	W	5-1	Diego Costa, Pedro 2, Willian, Traoré
27/02	a	Southampton	W	2-1	Fàbregas, Ivanović
01/03	a	Norwich	W	2-1	Kenedy, Diego Costa
05/03	h	Stoke	D	1-1	Traoré
19/03	h	West Ham	D	2-2	Fàbregas 2 (1p)
02/04	a	Aston Villa	W	4-0	Loftus-Cheek, Pato (p), Pedro 2
09/04	a	Swansea	L	0-1	
16/04	h	Man. City	L	0-3	
23/04	a	Bournemouth	W	4-1	Pedro, Hazard 2, Willian
02/05	h	Tottenham	D	2-2	Cahill, Hazard
07/05	a	Sunderland	L	2-3	Diego Costa, Matić
11/05	a	Liverpool	D	1-1	Hazard
15/05	h	Leicester	D	1-1	Fàbregas (p)

No	Name	Nat	DoB	Pos	Aps	(s)	Gls
42	Tammy Abraham		02/10/97	A		(2)	
28	César Azpilicueta	ESP	28/08/89	D	36	(1)	2
1	Asmir Begović	BIH	20/06/87	G	15	(2)	
24	Gary Cahill		19/12/85	D	21	(2)	2
37	Jake Clarke-Salter		22/09/97	D		(1)	
13	Thibaut Courtois	BEL	11/05/92	G	23		
23	Juan Cuadrado	COL	26/05/88	M		(1)	
19	Diego Costa	ESP	07/10/88	A	27	(1)	12
4	Cesc Fàbregas	ESP	04/05/87	M	33	(4)	5
9	Radamel Falcao	COL	10/02/86	A	1	(9)	1
10	Eden Hazard	BEL	07/01/91	M	25	(6)	4
4	Branislav Ivanović	SRB	22/02/84	D	33		2
16	Kenedy	BRA	08/02/96	M	4	(10)	1
36	Ruben Loftus-Cheek		23/01/96	M	4	(9)	1
21	Nemanja Matić	SRB	01/08/88	M	28	(5)	2
20	Matt Miazga	USA	19/07/95	D	2		
12	John Obi Mikel	NGA	22/04/87	M	19	(6)	
8	Oscar	BRA	09/09/91	M	20	(7)	3
11	Alexandre Pato	BRA	02/09/89	A	1	(1)	1
17	Pedro Rodríguez	ESP	28/07/87	A	24	(5)	7
6	Abdul Baba Rahman	GHA	02/07/94	D	11	(4)	
7	Ramires	BRA	24/03/87	M	7	(5)	2
18	Loïc Rémy	FRA	02/01/87	A	3	(10)	1
26	John Terry		07/12/80	D	24	(1)	1
43	Fikayo Tomori		19/12/97	D		(1)	
14	Bertrand Traoré	BFA	06/09/95	M	4	(6)	2
22	Willian	BRA	09/08/88	M	32	(3)	5
5	Kurt Zouma	FRA	27/10/94	D	21	(2)	1

Crystal Palace FC

1905 • Selhurst Park (25,073) • cpfc.co.uk
Manager: Alan Pardew

2015

08/08	a	Norwich	W	3-1	Zaha, Delaney, Cabaye
16/08	h	Arsenal	L	1-2	Ward
22/08	h	Aston Villa	W	2-1	Dann, Sako
29/08	h	Chelsea	W	2-1	Sako, Ward
12/09	h	Man. City	L	0-1	
20/09	a	Tottenham	L	0-1	
27/09	a	Watford	W	1-0	Cabaye (p)
03/10	a	West Brom	W	2-0	Bolasie, Cabaye (p)
17/10	h	West Ham	L	1-3	Cabaye (p)
24/10	a	Leicester	L	0-1	
31/10	h	Man. United	D	0-0	
08/11	a	Liverpool	W	2-1	Bolasie, Dann
23/11	a	Sunderland	L	0-1	
28/11	h	Newcastle	W	5-1	McArthur 2, Bolasie 2, Zaha
07/12	a	Everton	D	1-1	Dann
12/12	a	Southampton	W	1-0	Cabaye
19/12	a	Stoke	L	1-2	Wickham (p), Lee
26/12	a	Bournemouth	D	0-0	
28/12	h	Swansea	D	0-0	

2016

03/01	h	Chelsea	L	0-3	
12/01	a	Aston Villa	L	0-1	
16/01	a	Man. City	L	0-4	
23/01	h	Tottenham	L	1-3	og (Vertonghen)
02/02	h	Bournemouth	L	1-2	Dann
06/02	a	Swansea	D	1-1	Dann
13/02	h	Watford	L	1-2	Adebayor
27/02	a	West Brom	L	2-3	Wickham 2
01/03	a	Sunderland	D	2-2	Wickham 2
06/03	h	Liverpool	L	1-2	Ledley
19/03	a	Leicester	L	0-1	
02/04	a	West Ham	D	2-2	Delaney, Gayle
09/04	h	Norwich	W	1-0	Puncheon
13/04	h	Everton	D	0-0	
17/04	a	Arsenal	L	1-2	Bolasie
20/04	a	Man. United	L	0-2	
30/04	a	Newcastle	L	0-1	
07/05	h	Stoke	W	2-1	Gayle 2
15/05	a	Southampton	L	1-4	Puncheon

No	Name	Nat	DoB	Pos	Aps	(s)	Gls
25	Emmanuel Adebayor	TOG	26/02/84	A	7	(5)	1
8	Patrick Bamford		05/09/93	A		(6)	
38	Hiram Boateng		08/01/96	M		(1)	
10	Yannick Bolasie	COD	24/05/89	M	23	(3)	5
7	Yohan Cabaye	FRA	14/01/86	M	32	(1)	5
9	Fraizer Campbell		13/09/87	A	4	(7)	
29	Marouane Chamakh	MAR	10/01/84	A	1	(9)	
5	Scott Dann		14/02/87	D	35		5
27	Damien Delaney	IRL	29/07/81	D	32		2
16	Dwight Gayle		20/10/90	A	8	(8)	3
4	Brede Hangeland	NOR	20/06/81	D	7		
44	Wayne Hennessey	WAL	24/01/87	G	29		
15	Mile Jedinak	AUS	03/08/84	M	16	(11)	
43	Sullay Kaikai		26/08/95	M		(1)	
34	Martin Kelly		27/04/90	D	11	(2)	
28	Joe Ledley	WAL	23/01/87	M	11	(8)	1
14	Lee Chung-yong	KOR	02/07/88	M	4	(9)	1
3	Adrian Mariappa	JAM	03/10/86	D	3		
18	James McArthur	SCO	07/10/87	M	26	(2)	2
12	Alex McCarthy		03/12/89	G	7		
17	Glenn Murray		25/09/83	A	2		
22	Jordon Mutch		02/12/91	M	7	(13)	
42	Jason Puncheon		18/06/86	M	31		2
26	Bakary Sako	MLI	24/04/88	M	11	(9)	2
23	Pape Souaré	SEN	06/06/90	D	34		
1	Julián Speroni	ARG	18/05/79	G	2		
9	Joel Ward		29/10/89	D	30		2
21	Connor Wickham		31/03/93	A	15	(6)	5
20	Jonathan Williams	WAL	09/10/93	M		(1)	
11	Wilfried Zaha		10/11/92	M	30	(4)	2

Everton FC

1878 • Goodison Park (39,571) • evertonfc.com

Major honours

UEFA Cup Winners' Cup (1) 1985; English League (9) 1891, 1915, 1928, 1932, 1939, 1963, 1970, 1985, 1987; FA Cup (5) 1906, 1933, 1966, 1984, 1995

Manager: Roberto Martínez (ESP); (12/05/16) (David Unsworth)

2015

08/08	h	Watford	D	2-2	*Barkley, Koné*
15/08	a	Southampton	W	3-0	*Lukaku 2, Barkley*
23/08	h	Man. City	L	0-2	
29/08	h	Tottenham	D	0-0	
12/09	h	Chelsea	W	3-1	*Naismith 3*
19/09	a	Swansea	D	0-0	
28/09	a	West Brom	W	3-2	*Lukaku 2, Koné*
04/10	h	Liverpool	D	1-1	*Lukaku*
17/10	h	Man. United	L	0-3	
24/10	a	Arsenal	L	1-2	*Barkley*
01/11	h	Sunderland	W	6-2	*Deulofeu, Koné 3, og (Coates), Lukaku*
07/11	a	West Ham	D	1-1	*Lukaku*
21/11	h	Aston Villa	W	4-0	*Barkley 2, Lukaku 2*
28/11	a	Bournemouth	D	3-3	*Funes Mori, Lukaku, Barkley*
07/12	h	Crystal Palace	D	1-1	*Lukaku*
12/12	a	Norwich	D	1-1	*Lukaku*
19/12	h	Leicester	L	2-3	*Lukaku, Mirallas*
26/12	a	Newcastle	W	1-0	*Cleverley*
28/12	h	Stoke	L	3-4	*Lukaku 2, Deulofeu*

2016

03/01	h	Tottenham	D	1-1	*Lennon*
13/01	a	Man. City	D	0-0	
16/01	a	Chelsea	D	3-3	*og (Terry), Mirallas, Funes Mori*
24/01	h	Swansea	L	1-2	*og (Cork)*
03/02	h	Newcastle	W	3-0	*Lennon, Barkley 2 (2p)*
06/02	a	Stoke	W	3-0	*Lukaku (p), Coleman, Lennon*
13/02	h	West Brom	L	0-1	
01/03	a	Aston Villa	W	3-1	*Funes Mori, Lennon, Lukaku*
05/03	h	West Ham	L	2-3	*Lukaku, Lennon*
19/03	h	Arsenal	L	0-2	
03/04	a	Man. United	L	0-1	
09/04	a	Watford	D	1-1	*McCarthy*
13/04	a	Crystal Palace	D	0-0	
16/04	h	Southampton	D	1-1	*Funes Mori*
20/04	a	Liverpool	L	0-4	
30/04	h	Bournemouth	W	2-1	*Cleverley, Baines*
07/05	a	Leicester	L	1-3	*Mirallas*
11/05	a	Sunderland	L	0-3	
15/05	h	Norwich	W	3-0	*McCarthy, Baines (p), Mirallas*

No	Name	Nat	DoB	Pos	Aps	(s)	Gls
3	Leighton Baines		11/12/84	D	16	(2)	2
20	Ross Barkley		05/12/93	M	36	(2)	8
18	Gareth Barry		23/02/81	M	32	(1)	
17	Muhamed Bešić	BIH	10/09/92	M	7	(5)	
27	Tyias Browning		27/05/94	D	3	(2)	
15	Tom Cleverley		12/08/89	M	17	(5)	2
23	Séamus Coleman	IRL	11/10/88	D	27	(1)	1
33	Callum Connolly		23/09/97	D		(1)	
41	Tom Davies		30/06/98	M	1	(1)	
19	Gerard Deulofeu	ESP	13/03/94	A	16	(10)	2
51	Kieran Dowell		10/10/97	M	1	(1)	
25	Ramiro Funes Mori	ARG	05/03/91	D	24	(4)	4
32	Brendan Galloway		17/03/96	D	14	(1)	
4	Darron Gibson	IRL	25/10/87	M	2	(5)	
2	Tony Hibbert		20/02/81	D		(1)	
24	Tim Howard	USA	06/03/79	G	25		
6	Phil Jagielka		17/08/82	D	21		
1	Joel Robles	ESP	17/06/90	G	13		
43	Jonjoe Kenny		15/03/97	D		(1)	
9	Arouna Koné	CIV	11/11/83	A	16	(9)	5
12	Aaron Lennon		16/04/87	M	17	(8)	5
10	Romelu Lukaku	BEL	13/05/93	A	36	(1)	18
16	James McCarthy	IRL	12/11/90	M	29		2
11	Kevin Mirallas	BEL	05/10/87	M	10	(13)	4
14	Steven Naismith	SCO	14/09/86	A	4	(6)	3
14	Oumar Niasse	SEN	18/04/90	A	2	(3)	
21	Leon Osman		17/05/81	M	2	(7)	
8	Bryan Oviedo	CRC	18/02/90	D	12	(2)	
38	Matthew Pennington		06/10/94	D	4		
22	Steven Pienaar	RSA	17/03/82	M		(4)	
5	John Stones		28/05/94	D	31	(2)	

Leicester City FC

1884 • King Power Stadium (32,312) • lcfc.com

Major honours

English League (1) 2016; League Cup (3) 1964, 1997, 2000

Manager: Claudio Ranieri (ITA)

2015

08/08	h	Sunderland	W	4-2	*Vardy, Mahrez 2 (1p), Albrighton*
15/08	a	West Ham	W	2-1	*Okazaki, Mahrez*
22/08	h	Tottenham	D	1-1	*Mahrez*
29/08	a	Bournemouth	D	1-1	*Vardy (p)*
13/09	h	Aston Villa	W	3-2	*De Laet, Vardy, Dyer*
19/09	a	Stoke	D	2-2	*Mahrez (p), Vardy*
26/09	h	Arsenal	L	2-5	*Vardy 2*
03/10	a	Norwich	W	2-1	*Vardy (p), Schlupp*
17/10	a	Southampton	D	2-2	*Vardy 2*
24/10	h	Crystal Palace	W	1-0	*Vardy*
31/10	a	West Brom	W	3-2	*Mahrez 2, Vardy*
07/11	h	Watford	W	2-1	*Kanté, Vardy (p)*
21/11	a	Newcastle	W	3-0	*Vardy, Ulloa, Okazaki*
28/11	h	Man. United	D	1-1	*Vardy*
05/12	a	Swansea	W	3-0	*Mahrez 3*
14/12	h	Chelsea	W	2-1	*Vardy, Mahrez*
19/12	a	Everton	W	3-2	*Mahrez 2 (2p), Okazaki*
26/12	a	Liverpool	L	0-1	
29/12	h	Man. City	D	0-0	

2016

02/01	h	Bournemouth	D	0-0	
13/01	a	Tottenham	W	1-0	*Huth*
16/01	a	Aston Villa	D	1-1	*Okazaki*
23/01	h	Stoke	W	3-0	*Drinkwater, Vardy, Ulloa*
02/02	h	Liverpool	W	2-0	*Vardy 2*
06/02	a	Man. City	W	3-1	*Huth 2, Mahrez*
14/02	a	Arsenal	L	1-2	*Vardy (p)*
27/02	h	Norwich	W	1-0	*Ulloa*
01/03	h	West Brom	D	2-2	*og (Olsson), King*
05/03	a	Watford	W	1-0	*Mahrez*
14/03	h	Newcastle	W	1-0	*Okazaki*
19/03	a	Crystal Palace	W	1-0	*Mahrez*
03/04	h	Southampton	W	1-0	*Morgan*
10/04	a	Sunderland	W	2-0	*Vardy 2*
17/04	h	West Ham	D	2-2	*Vardy, Ulloa (p)*
24/04	h	Swansea	W	4-0	*Mahrez, Ulloa 2, Albrighton*
01/05	a	Man. United	D	1-1	*Morgan*
07/05	h	Everton	W	3-1	*Vardy 2 (1p), King*
15/05	a	Chelsea	D	1-1	*Drinkwater*

No	Name	Nat	DoB	Pos	Aps	(s)	Gls
11	Marc Albrighton		18/11/89	M	34	(4)	2
13	Daniel Amartey	GHA	21/12/94	D	1	(4)	
29	Yohan Benalouane	TUN	28/03/87	D		(4)	
2	Ritchie De Laet	BEL	28/11/88	D	7	(5)	1
36	Joe Dodoo		29/06/95	A		(1)	
4	Danny Drinkwater		05/03/90	M	35		2
24	Nathan Dyer		29/11/87	M		(12)	1
28	Christian Fuchs	AUT	07/04/86	D	30	(2)	
22	Demarai Gray		28/06/96	M	1	(11)	
6	Robert Huth	GER	18/08/84	D	35		3
33	Gökhan Inler	SUI	27/06/84	M	3	(2)	
14	N'Golo Kanté	FRA	29/03/91	M	33	(4)	1
10	Andy King	WAL	29/10/88	M	9	(16)	2
19	Andrej Kramarić	CRO	19/06/91	A		(2)	
26	Riyad Mahrez	ALG	21/02/91	M	36	(1)	17
5	Wes Morgan	JAM	21/01/84	D	38		2
20	Shinji Okazaki	JPN	16/04/86	A	28	(8)	5
15	Jeff Schlupp	GHA	23/12/92	M	14	(10)	1
1	Kasper Schmeichel	DEN	05/11/86	G	38		
17	Danny Simpson		04/01/87	D	30		
23	Leonardo Ulloa	ARG	26/07/86	A	7	(22)	6
9	Jamie Vardy		11/01/87	A	36		24
27	Marcin Wasilewski	POL	09/06/80	D	3	(1)	

Liverpool FC

1892 • Anfield (44,742) • liverpoolfc.com

Major honours

European Champion Clubs' Cup/UEFA Champions League (5) 1977, 1978, 1981, 1984, 2005; UEFA Cup (3) 1973, 1976, 2001; UEFA Super Cup (3) 1977, 2001, 2005; English League (18) 1901, 1906, 1922, 1923, 1947, 1964, 1966, 1973, 1976, 1977, 1979, 1980, 1982, 1983, 1984, 1986, 1988, 1990; FA Cup (7) 1965, 1974, 1986, 1989, 1992, 2001, 2006; League Cup (8) 1981, 1982, 1983, 1984, 1995, 2001, 2003, 2012

Manager: Brendan Rodgers (NIR); (08/10/15) Jürgen Klopp (GER)

2015

09/08	a	Stoke	W	1-0	*Coutinho*
17/08	h	Bournemouth	W	1-0	*Benteke*
24/08	a	Arsenal	D	0-0	
29/08	h	West Ham	L	0-3	
12/09	a	Man. United	L	1-3	*Benteke*
20/09	h	Norwich	D	1-1	*Ings*
26/09	h	Aston Villa	W	3-2	*Milner, Sturridge 2*
04/10	a	Everton	D	1-1	*Ings*
17/10	a	Tottenham	D	0-0	
25/10	h	Southampton	D	1-1	*Benteke*
31/10	a	Chelsea	W	3-1	*Coutinho 2, Benteke*
08/11	h	Crystal Palace	L	1-2	*Coutinho*
21/11	a	Man. City	W	4-1	*og (Mangala), Coutinho, Roberto Firmino, Škrtel*
29/11	h	Swansea	W	1-0	*Milner (p)*
06/12	a	Newcastle	L	0-2	
13/12	h	West Brom	D	2-2	*Henderson, Origi*
20/12	a	Watford	L	0-3	
26/12	h	Leicester	W	1-0	*Benteke*
30/12	a	Sunderland	W	1-0	*Benteke*

2016

02/01	a	West Ham	L	0-2	
13/01	h	Arsenal	D	3-3	*Roberto Firmino 2, Allen*
17/01	h	Man. United	L	0-1	
23/01	a	Norwich	W	5-4	*Roberto Firmino 2, Henderson, Milner, Lallana*
02/02	a	Leicester	L	0-2	
06/02	h	Sunderland	D	2-2	*Roberto Firmino, Lallana*
14/02	a	Aston Villa	W	6-0	*Sturridge, Milner, Can, Origi, Clyne, Touré*
02/03	h	Man. City	W	3-0	*Lallana, Milner, Roberto Firmino*
06/03	a	Crystal Palace	W	2-1	*Roberto Firmino, Benteke (p)*
20/03	a	Southampton	L	2-3	*Coutinho, Sturridge*
02/04	h	Tottenham	D	1-1	*Coutinho*
10/04	h	Stoke	W	4-1	*Moreno, Sturridge, Origi 2*
17/04	a	Bournemouth	W	2-1	*Roberto Firmino, Sturridge*
20/04	h	Everton	W	4-0	*Origi, Sakho, Sturridge, Coutinho*
23/04	h	Newcastle	D	2-2	*Sturridge, Lallana*
01/05	a	Swansea	L	1-3	*Benteke*
08/05	h	Watford	W	2-0	*Allen, Roberto Firmino*
11/05	h	Chelsea	D	1-1	*Benteke*
15/05	a	West Brom	D	1-1	*Ibe*

No	Name	Nat	DoB	Pos	Aps	(s)	Gls
24	Joe Allen	WAL	14/03/90	M	8	(11)	2
9	Christian Benteke	BEL	03/12/90	A	14	(15)	9
34	Ádám Bogdán	HUN	27/09/87	G	2		
32	Cameron Brannagan		09/05/96	M	1	(2)	
23	Emre Can	GER	12/01/94	M	28	(2)	1
19	Steven Caulker		29/12/91	D		(3)	
68	Pedro Chirivella	ESP	23/05/97	M	1		
2	Nathaniel Clyne		05/04/91	D	33		1
10	Philippe Coutinho	BRA	12/06/92	M	24	(2)	8
38	Jon Flanagan		01/01/93	D	5		
12	Joe Gomez		23/05/97	D	5		
14	Jordan Henderson		17/06/90	M	15	(2)	2
33	Jordon Ibe		08/12/95	M	12	(15)	1
28	Danny Ings		23/07/92	A	3	(3)	2
53	João Carlos Teixeira	POR	18/01/93	M		(1)	
20	Adam Lallana		10/05/88	M	23	(7)	4
6	Dejan Lovren	CRO	05/07/89	D	22	(2)	
21	Lucas Leiva	BRA	09/01/87	M	21	(6)	
22	Simon Mignolet	BEL	06/03/88	G	34		
7	James Milner		04/01/86	M	28		5
18	Alberto Moreno	ESP	05/07/92	D	28	(4)	1
54	Sheyi Ojo		19/06/97	M	5	(3)	
27	Divock Origi	BEL	18/04/95	A	7	(9)	5
56	Connor Randall		21/10/95	D	2	(1)	
11	Roberto Firmino	BRA	02/10/91	M	24	(7)	10
46	Jordan Rossiter		24/03/97	M		(1)	
17	Mamadou Sakho	FRA	13/02/90	D	21	(1)	1
64	Sergi Canós	ESP	02/02/97	M		(1)	
37	Martin Škrtel	SVK	15/12/84	D	21	(1)	1
44	Brad Smith	AUS	09/04/94	D	3	(1)	
35	Kevin Stewart		07/09/93	M	6	(1)	
15	Daniel Sturridge		01/09/89	A	11	(3)	8
4	Kolo Touré	CIV	19/03/81	D	9	(5)	1
52	Danny Ward	WAL	22/06/93	G	2		

Manchester City FC

1894 • Etihad Stadium (55,097) • mcfc.co.uk

Major honours
UEFA Cup Winners' Cup (1) 1970; English League (4) 1937, 1968, 2012, 2014; FA Cup (5) 1904, 1934, 1956, 1969, 2011; League Cup (4) 1970, 1976, 2014, 2016

Manager: Manuel Pellegrini (CHI)

2015					
10/08	a	West Brom	W	3-0	*Silva, Touré, Kompany*
16/08	h	Chelsea	W	3-0	*Agüero, Kompany, Fernandinho*
23/08	a	Everton	W	2-0	*Kolarov, Nasri*
29/08	h	Watford	W	2-0	*Sterling, Fernandinho*
12/09	a	Crystal Palace	W	1-0	*Iheanacho*
19/09	h	West Ham	L	1-2	*De Bruyne*
26/09	a	Tottenham	L	1-4	*De Bruyne*
03/10	h	Newcastle	W	6-1	*Agüero 5, De Bruyne*
17/10	h	Bournemouth	W	5-1	*Sterling 3, Bony 2*
25/10	a	Man. United	D	0-0	
31/10	h	Norwich	W	2-1	*Otamendi, Touré (p)*
08/11	a	Aston Villa	D	0-0	
21/11	h	Liverpool	L	1-4	*Agüero*
28/11	h	Southampton	W	3-1	*De Bruyne, Delph, Kolarov*
05/12	a	Stoke	L	0-2	
12/12	h	Swansea	W	2-1	*Bony, Iheanacho*
21/12	a	Arsenal	L	1-2	*Touré*
26/12	h	Sunderland	W	4-1	*Sterling, Touré, Bony, De Bruyne*
29/12	a	Leicester	D	0-0	
2016					
02/01	a	Watford	W	2-1	*Touré, Agüero*
13/01	h	Everton	D	0-0	
16/01	h	Crystal Palace	W	4-0	*Delph, Agüero 2, Silva*
23/01	a	West Ham	D	2-2	*Agüero 2 (1p)*
02/02	a	Sunderland	W	1-0	*Agüero*
06/02	h	Leicester	L	1-3	*Agüero*
14/02	h	Tottenham	L	1-2	*Iheanacho*
02/03	a	Liverpool	L	0-3	
05/03	h	Aston Villa	W	4-0	*Touré, Agüero 2, Sterling*
12/03	a	Norwich	D	0-0	
20/03	h	Man. United	L	0-1	
02/04	a	Bournemouth	W	4-0	*Fernando, De Bruyne, Agüero, Kolarov*
09/04	h	West Brom	W	2-1	*Agüero (p), Nasri*
16/04	a	Chelsea	W	3-0	*Agüero 3 (1p)*
19/04	a	Newcastle	D	1-1	*Agüero*
23/04	h	Stoke	W	4-0	*Fernando, Agüero (p), Iheanacho 2*
01/05	a	Southampton	L	2-4	*Iheanacho 2*
08/05	h	Arsenal	D	2-2	*Agüero, De Bruyne*
15/05	a	Swansea	D	1-1	*Iheanacho*

No	Name	Nat	DoB	Pos	Aps	(s)	Gls
10	Sergio Agüero	ARG	02/06/88	A	29	(1)	24
14	Wilfried Bony	CIV	10/12/88	A	13	(13)	4
13	Willy Caballero	ARG	28/09/81	G	3	(1)	
59	Bersant Celina	KOS	09/09/96	M		(1)	
22	Gaël Clichy	FRA	26/07/85	D	12	(2)	
17	Kevin De Bruyne	BEL	28/06/91	M	22	(3)	7
18	Fabian Delph		21/11/89	M	8	(9)	2
26	Martín Demichelis	ARG	20/12/80	D	10	(10)	
25	Fernandinho	BRA	04/05/85	M	31	(2)	2
6	Fernando	BRA	25/07/87	M	17	(7)	2
76	Manuel García	ESP	02/01/98	M		(1)	
1	Joe Hart		19/04/87	G	35		
72	Kelechi Iheanacho	NGA	03/10/96	A	7	(19)	8
15	Jesús Navas	ESP	21/11/85	M	24	(10)	
11	Aleksandar Kolarov	SRB	10/11/85	D	25	(4)	3
4	Vincent Kompany	BEL	10/04/86	D	13	(1)	2
20	Eliaquim Mangala	FRA	13/02/91	D	23		
8	Samir Nasri	FRA	26/06/87	M	4	(8)	2
30	Nicolás Otamendi	ARG	12/02/88	D	30		1
27	Patrick Roberts		05/02/97	M		(1)	
3	Bacary Sagna	FRA	14/02/83	D	27	(1)	
21	David Silva	ESP	08/01/86	M	22	(2)	2
7	Raheem Sterling		08/12/94	A	23	(8)	6
42	Yaya Touré	CIV	13/05/83	M	28	(4)	6
5	Pablo Zabaleta	ARG	16/01/85	D	12	(1)	

Manchester United FC

1878 • Old Trafford (75,653) • manutd.com

Major honours
European Champion Clubs' Cup/UEFA Champions League (3) 1968, 1999, 2008; UEFA Cup Winners' Cup (1) 1991; UEFA Super Cup (1) 1991; European/South American Cup (1) 1999; FIFA Club World Cup (1) 2008; English League (20) 1908, 1911, 1952, 1956, 1957, 1965, 1967, 1993, 1994, 1996, 1997, 1999, 2000, 2001, 2003, 2007, 2008, 2009, 2011, 2013; FA Cup (12) 1909, 1948, 1963, 1977, 1983, 1985, 1990, 1994, 1996, 1999, 2004, 2016; League Cup (4) 1992, 2006, 2009, 2010

Manager: Louis van Gaal (NED)

2015					
08/08	h	Tottenham	W	1-0	*og (Walker)*
14/08	a	Aston Villa	W	1-0	*Januzaj*
22/08	h	Newcastle	D	0-0	
30/08	a	Swansea	L	1-2	*Mata*
12/09	h	Liverpool	W	3-1	*Blind, Ander Herrera (p), Martial*
20/09	a	Southampton	W	3-2	*Martial 2, Mata*
26/09	h	Sunderland	W	3-0	*Depay, Rooney, Mata*
04/10	a	Arsenal	L	0-3	
17/10	a	Everton	W	3-0	*Schneiderlin, Ander Herrera, Rooney*
25/10	h	Man. City	D	0-0	
31/10	a	Crystal Palace	D	0-0	
07/11	h	West Brom	W	2-0	*Lingard, Mata (p)*
21/11	a	Watford	W	2-1	*Depay, og (Deeney)*
28/11	a	Leicester	D	1-1	*Schweinsteiger*
05/12	h	West Ham	D	0-0	
12/12	a	Bournemouth	L	1-2	*Fellaini*
19/12	h	Norwich	L	1-2	*Martial*
26/12	a	Stoke	L	0-2	
28/12	h	Chelsea	D	0-0	
2016					
02/01	h	Swansea	W	2-1	*Martial, Rooney*
12/01	a	Newcastle	D	3-3	*Rooney 2 (1p), Lingard*
17/01	a	Liverpool	W	1-0	*Rooney*
23/01	h	Southampton	L	0-1	
02/02	h	Stoke	W	3-0	*Lingard, Martial, Rooney*
07/02	a	Chelsea	D	1-1	*Lingard*
13/02	a	Sunderland	L	1-2	*Martial*
28/02	h	Arsenal	W	3-2	*Rashford 2, Ander Herrera*
02/03	h	Watford	W	1-0	*Mata*
06/03	a	West Brom	L	0-1	
20/03	a	Man. City	W	1-0	*Rashford*
03/04	h	Everton	W	1-0	*Martial*
10/04	a	Tottenham	L	0-3	
16/04	h	Aston Villa	W	1-0	*Rashford*
20/04	h	Crystal Palace	W	2-0	*og (Delaney), Darmian*
01/05	h	Leicester	D	1-1	*Martial*
07/05	a	Norwich	W	1-0	*Mata*
10/05	a	West Ham	L	2-3	*Martial 2*
17/05	h	Bournemouth	W	3-1	*Rooney, Rashford, Young*

No	Name	Nat	DoB	Pos	Aps	(s)	Gls
21	Ander Herrera	ESP	14/08/89	M	17	(9)	3
44	Andreas Pereira	BRA	01/01/96	M		(4)	
17	Daley Blind	NED	09/03/90	D	35		1
43	Cameron Borthwick-Jackson		02/02/97	D	6	(4)	
16	Michael Carrick		28/07/81	M	22	(6)	
36	Matteo Darmian	ITA	02/12/89	D	24	(4)	1
1	David de Gea	ESP	07/11/90	G	34		
7	Memphis Depay	NED	13/02/94	A	16	(12)	2
27	Marouane Fellaini	BEL	22/11/87	M	12	(6)	1
51	Timothy Fosu-Mensah	NED	02/01/98	D	2	(6)	
14	Javier Hernández	MEX	01/06/88	A		(1)	
11	Adnan Januzaj	BEL	05/02/95	M	2	(3)	1
4	Phil Jones		21/02/92	D	6	(4)	
48	Will Keane		11/01/93	A		(1)	
35	Jesse Lingard		15/12/92	M	19	(6)	4
37	Donald Love	SCO	02/12/94	D		(1)	
9	Anthony Martial	FRA	05/12/95	A	29	(2)	11
8	Juan Mata	ESP	28/04/88	M	34	(4)	6
33	Paddy McNair	NIR	27/04/95	D	3	(5)	
22	Nick Powell		23/03/94	M		(1)	
39	Marcus Rashford		31/10/97	A	11		5
5	Marcos Rojo	ARG	20/03/90	D	15	(1)	
20	Sergio Romero	ARG	22/02/87	G	4		
10	Wayne Rooney		24/10/85	A	27	(1)	8
28	Morgan Schneiderlin	FRA	08/11/89	M	25	(4)	1
31	Bastian Schweinsteiger	GER	01/08/84	M	13	(5)	1
23	Luke Shaw		12/07/95	D	5		
12	Chris Smalling		22/11/89	D	35		
25	Antonio Valencia	ECU	04/08/85	M	8	(6)	
30	Guillermo Varela	URU	24/03/93	D	3	(1)	
47	James Weir		04/08/95	M		(1)	
19	James Wilson		01/12/95	A		(1)	
18	Ashley Young		09/07/85	M	11	(6)	1

Newcastle United FC

1881 • St James' Park (52,338) • nufc.co.uk

Major honours
Inter Cities Fairs Cup (1) 1969; English League (4) 1905, 1907, 1909, 1927; FA Cup (6) 1910, 1924, 1932, 1951, 1952, 1955

Manager: Steve McClaren; (11/03/16) Rafael Benítez (ESP)

2015					
08/08	h	Southampton	D	2-2	*Cissé, Wijnaldum*
15/08	a	Swansea	L	0-2	
22/08	a	Man. United	D	0-0	
29/08	h	Arsenal	L	0-1	
14/09	a	West Ham	L	0-2	
19/09	h	Watford	L	1-2	*Janmaat*
26/09	h	Chelsea	D	2-2	*Ayoze, Wijnaldum*
03/10	a	Man. City	L	1-6	*Mitrović*
18/10	h	Norwich	W	6-2	*Wijnaldum 4, Ayoze, Mitrović*
25/10	a	Sunderland	L	0-3	
31/10	h	Stoke	D	0-0	
07/11	a	Bournemouth	W	1-0	*Ayoze*
21/11	h	Leicester	L	0-3	
28/11	a	Crystal Palace	L	1-5	*Cissé*
06/12	h	Liverpool	W	2-0	*og (Škrtel), Wijnaldum*
13/12	a	Tottenham	W	2-1	*Mitrović, Ayoze*
19/12	h	Aston Villa	D	1-1	*Coloccini*
26/12	h	Everton	L	0-1	
28/12	a	West Brom	L	0-1	
2016					
02/01	a	Arsenal	L	0-1	
12/01	h	Man. United	D	3-3	*Wijnaldum, Mitrović (p), Dummett*
16/01	h	West Ham	W	2-1	*Ayoze, Wijnaldum*
23/01	a	Watford	L	1-2	*Lascelles*
03/02	a	Everton	L	0-3	
06/02	h	West Brom	W	1-0	*Mitrović*
13/02	a	Chelsea	L	1-5	*Townsend*
02/03	a	Stoke	L	0-1	
05/03	h	Bournemouth	L	1-3	*Ayoze*
14/03	a	Leicester	L	0-1	
20/03	h	Sunderland	D	1-1	*Mitrović*
02/04	a	Norwich	L	2-3	*Mitrović 2 (1p)*
09/04	a	Southampton	L	1-3	*Townsend*
16/04	h	Swansea	W	3-0	*Lascelles, Sissoko, Townsend*
19/04	h	Man. City	D	1-1	*Anita*
23/04	a	Liverpool	D	2-2	*Cissé, Colback*
30/04	h	Crystal Palace	W	1-0	*Townsend*
07/05	a	Aston Villa	D	0-0	
15/05	h	Tottenham	W	5-1	*Wijnaldum 2 (1p), Mitrović, Aarons, Janmaat*

No	Name	Nat	DoB	Pos	Aps	(s)	Gls
16	Rolando Aarons		16/11/95	M	3	(7)	1
8	Vurnon Anita	NED	04/04/89	M	24	(4)	1
17	Ayoze Pérez	ESP	23/07/93	A	22	(12)	6
9	Papiss Cissé	SEN	03/06/85	A	14	(7)	3
4	Jack Colback		24/10/89	M	28	(1)	1
2	Fabricio Coloccini	ARG	22/01/82	D	26		1
26	Karl Darlow		08/10/90	G	9		
10	Siem de Jong	NED	28/01/89	M	3	(15)	
28	Seydou Doumbia	CIV	31/12/87	A		(3)	
3	Paul Dummett	WAL	26/09/91	D	23		1
21	Rob Elliot	IRL	30/04/86	G	21		
11	Yoan Gouffran	FRA	25/05/86	A	2	(6)	
19	Massadio Haïdara	FRA	02/12/92	D	6	(1)	
22	Daryl Janmaat	NED	22/07/89	D	32		2
1	Tim Krul	NED	03/04/88	G	8		
15	Jamaal Lascelles		11/11/93	D	10	(8)	2
43	Kevin Mbabu	SUI	19/04/95	D	2	(1)	
18	Chancel Mbemba	COD	08/08/94	D	33		
45	Aleksandar Mitrović	SRB	16/09/94	A	22	(12)	9
14	Gabriel Obertan	FRA	26/02/89	A	3	(2)	
29	Emmanuel Rivière	FRA	03/03/90	M	1	(2)	
23	Henri Saivet	SEN	26/10/90	M	2	(2)	
12	Jonjo Shelvey		27/02/92	M	11	(4)	
7	Moussa Sissoko	FRA	16/08/89	M	37		1
42	Jamie Sterry		21/11/95	D		(1)	
27	Steven Taylor		23/01/86	D	9	(1)	
20	Florian Thauvin	FRA	26/01/93	M	3	(10)	
24	Cheick Tioté	CIV	21/06/86	M	16	(4)	
36	Ivan Toney		16/03/96	A		(2)	
25	Andros Townsend		16/07/91	M	12	(1)	4
5	Georginio Wijnaldum	NED	11/11/90	M	36	(2)	11

Norwich City FC

1902 • Carrow Road (27,010) • canaries.co.uk
Major honours
League Cup (2) 1986, 1996
Manager: Alex Neil (SCO)

2015
08/08	h	Crystal Palace	L	1-3	Redmond
15/08	a	Sunderland	W	3-1	Martin, Whittaker, Redmond
22/08	h	Stoke	D	1-1	Martin
30/08	a	Southampton	L	0-3	
12/09	h	Bournemouth	W	3-1	Jerome, Hoolahan, Jarvis
20/09	a	Liverpool	D	1-1	Martin
26/09	h	West Ham	D	2-2	Brady, Redmond
03/10	a	Leicester	L	1-2	Mbokani
18/10	a	Newcastle	L	2-6	Mbokani, Redmond
24/10	h	West Brom	L	0-1	
31/10	a	Man. City	L	1-2	Jerome
07/11	h	Swansea	W	1-0	Howson
21/11	a	Chelsea	L	0-1	
29/11	h	Arsenal	D	1-1	Grabban
05/12	a	Watford	L	0-2	
12/12	h	Everton	D	1-1	Hoolahan
19/12	a	Man. United	W	2-1	Jerome, Tettey
26/12	a	Tottenham	L	0-3	
28/12	a	Aston Villa	W	2-0	Howson, Mbokani

2016
02/01	h	Southampton	W	1-0	Tettey
13/01	a	Stoke	L	1-3	Howson
16/01	a	Bournemouth	L	0-3	
23/01	h	Liverpool	L	4-5	Mbokani, Naismith, Hoolahan (p), Bassong
02/02	a	Tottenham	L	0-3	
06/02	a	Aston Villa	L	0-2	
13/02	h	West Ham	D	2-2	Brady, Hoolahan
27/02	a	Leicester	L	0-1	
01/03	h	Chelsea	L	1-2	Redmond
05/03	a	Swansea	L	0-1	
12/03	h	Man. City	D	0-0	
19/03	a	West Brom	W	1-0	Brady
02/04	h	Newcastle	W	3-2	Klose, Mbokani, Olsson
09/04	a	Crystal Palace	L	0-1	
16/04	a	Sunderland	L	0-3	
30/04	a	Arsenal	L	0-1	
07/05	h	Man. United	L	0-1	
11/05	h	Watford	W	4-2	Redmond, Mbokani 2, og (Cathcart)
15/05	a	Everton	L	0-3	

No	Name	Nat	DoB	Pos	Aps	(s)	Gls
11	Patrick Bamford		05/09/93	A	2	(5)	
6	Sebastian Bassong	CMR	09/07/86	D	30	(1)	1
24	Ryan Bennett		06/03/90	D	20	(2)	
12	Robbie Brady	IRL	14/01/92	D	34	(1)	3
18	Graham Dorrans	SCO	05/05/87	M	14	(7)	
7	Lewis Grabban		12/01/88	A	3	(3)	1
14	Wes Hoolahan	IRL	20/05/82	M	25	(4)	4
11	Gary Hooper		26/01/88	A		(2)	
8	Johnathan Howson		21/05/88	M	33	(3)	3
25	Ivo Pinto	POR	07/01/90	D	9	(1)	
16	Matt Jarvis		22/05/86	M	13	(6)	1
10	Cameron Jerome		14/08/86	A	19	(15)	3
4	Bradley Johnson		28/04/87	M	1	(3)	
1	Timm Klose	SUI	09/05/88	D	10		1
19	Kyle Lafferty	NIR	16/09/87	A		(1)	
5	Russell Martin	SCO	04/01/86	D	30		3
9	Dieumerci Mbokani	COD	22/11/85	A	15	(14)	7
21	Youssouf Mulumbu	COD	25/01/87	M	5	(2)	
7	Steven Naismith	SCO	14/09/86	A	11	(2)	1
28	Gary O'Neil		18/05/83	M	19	(8)	
32	Vadis Odjidja-Ofoe	BEL	21/02/89	M	3	(7)	
23	Martin Olsson	SWE	17/05/88	D	20	(4)	1
22	Nathan Redmond		06/03/94	A	24	(11)	6
13	Declan Rudd		16/01/91	G	11		
1	John Ruddy		24/10/86	G	27		
27	Alexander Tettey	NOR	04/04/86	M	23		2
2	Steven Whittaker	SCO	16/06/84	D	8		1
3	Andre Wisdom		09/05/93	D	9	(1)	

Southampton FC

1885 • St Mary's Stadium (32,505) •
saintsfc.co.uk
Major honours
FA Cup (1) 1976
Manager: Ronald Koeman (NED)

2015
09/08	a	Newcastle	D	2-2	Pellè, Long
15/08	h	Everton	L	0-3	
23/08	a	Watford	D	0-0	
30/08	h	Norwich	W	3-0	Pellè, Tadić 2
12/09	a	West Brom	D	0-0	
20/09	h	Man. United	L	2-3	Pellè 2
26/09	h	Swansea	W	3-1	Van Dijk, og (Ki), Mané
03/10	a	Chelsea	W	3-1	S Davis, Mané, Pellè
17/10	h	Leicester	D	2-2	José Fonte, Van Dijk
25/10	a	Liverpool	D	1-1	Mané
01/11	h	Bournemouth	W	2-0	S Davis, Pellè
07/11	a	Sunderland	W	1-0	Tadić (p)
21/11	h	Stoke	L	0-1	
28/11	a	Man. City	L	1-3	Long
05/12	a	Aston Villa	D	1-1	Romeu
12/12	h	Crystal Palace	L	0-1	
19/12	h	Tottenham	L	0-2	
26/12	h	Arsenal	W	4-0	Martina, Long 2, José Fonte
28/12	a	West Ham	L	1-2	og (Jenkinson)

2016
02/01	a	Norwich	L	0-1	
13/01	h	Watford	W	2-0	Long, Tadić
16/01	h	West Brom	W	3-0	Ward-Prowse 2 (1p), Tadić
23/01	a	Man. United	L	0-1	Austin
02/02	a	Arsenal	D	0-0	
06/02	h	West Ham	W	1-0	Yoshida
13/02	a	Swansea	L	1-2	Long
27/02	h	Chelsea	L	1-2	Long
01/03	a	Bournemouth	L	0-2	
05/03	h	Sunderland	D	1-1	Van Dijk
12/03	a	Stoke	W	2-1	Pellè 2
20/03	h	Liverpool	W	3-2	Mané 2, Pellè
03/04	a	Leicester	L	0-1	
09/04	h	Newcastle	W	3-1	Long, Pellè, Wanyama
16/04	a	Everton	D	1-1	Mané
23/04	a	Aston Villa	W	4-2	Long, Tadić 2, Mané
01/05	h	Man. City	W	4-2	Long, Mané 3
08/05	a	Tottenham	W	2-1	S Davis 2
15/05	h	Crystal Palace	W	4-1	Mané, Pellè, Bertrand (p), S Davis

No	Name	Nat	DoB	Pos	Aps	(s)	Gls
28	Charlie Austin		05/07/89	A	2	(5)	1
21	Ryan Bertrand		05/08/89	D	32		1
26	Steven Caulker		29/12/91	D	1	(2)	
2	Cédric	POR	31/08/91	D	23	(1)	
4	Jordy Clasie	NED	27/06/91	M	20	(2)	
1	Kelvin Davis		29/09/76	G	1		
8	Steven Davis	NIR	01/01/85	M	31	(3)	5
44	Fraser Forster		17/03/88	G	18		
25	Paulo Gazzaniga	ARG	02/01/92	G	2		
6	José Fonte	POR	22/12/83	D	37		2
20	Juanmi	ESP	20/05/93	A		(12)	
7	Shane Long	IRL	22/01/87	A	23	(5)	10
10	Sadio Mané	SEN	10/04/92	M	30	(1)	11
15	Cuco Martina	CUW	25/09/89	D	11	(4)	1
19	Graziano Pellè	ITA	15/07/85	A	23	(7)	11
23	Gastón Ramírez	URU	02/12/90	M		(3)	
18	Harrison Reed		27/01/95	M		(1)	
9	Jay Rodriguez		29/07/89	A	3	(9)	
14	Oriol Romeu	ESP	24/09/91	M	17	(12)	1
22	Maarten Stekelenburg	NED	22/09/82	G	17		
11	Dušan Tadić	SRB	20/11/88	M	27	(7)	7
33	Matt Targett		18/09/95	D	13	(1)	
17	Virgil van Dijk	NED	08/07/91	D	34		3
12	Victor Wanyama	KEN	25/06/91	M	29	(1)	1
16	James Ward-Prowse		01/11/94	M	14	(19)	2
3	Maya Yoshida	JPN	24/08/88	D	10	(10)	1

Stoke City FC

1868 • Britannia Stadium (27,740) •
stokecityfc.com
Major honours
League Cup (1) 1972
Manager: Mark Hughes (WAL)

2015
09/08	h	Liverpool	L	0-1	
15/08	a	Tottenham	D	2-2	Arnautovic (p), Diouf
22/08	a	Norwich	D	1-1	Diouf
29/08	h	West Brom	L	0-1	
12/09	a	Arsenal	L	0-2	
19/09	h	Leicester	D	2-2	Bojan, Walters
26/09	h	Bournemouth	W	2-1	Walters, Diouf
03/10	a	Aston Villa	W	1-0	Arnautovic
19/10	a	Swansea	W	1-0	Bojan (p)
24/10	h	Watford	L	0-2	
31/10	a	Newcastle	D	0-0	
07/11	h	Chelsea	W	1-0	Arnautovic
21/11	a	Southampton	W	1-0	Bojan
28/11	a	Sunderland	L	0-2	
05/12	h	Man. City	W	2-0	Arnautovic 2
12/12	h	West Ham	D	0-0	
19/12	h	Crystal Palace	L	1-2	Bojan (p)
26/12	h	Man. United	D	2-0	Bojan, Arnautovic
28/12	a	Everton	W	4-3	Shaqiri 2, Joselu, Arnautovic (p)

2016
02/01	h	West Brom	L	1-2	Walters
13/01	h	Norwich	W	3-1	Walters, Joselu, og (Bennett)
17/01	h	Arsenal	D	0-0	
23/01	a	Leicester	L	0-3	
02/02	a	Man. United	L	0-3	
06/02	h	Everton	L	0-3	
13/02	a	Bournemouth	W	3-1	Imbula, Afellay, Joselu
27/02	a	Aston Villa	W	2-1	Arnautovic 2 (1p)
02/03	h	Newcastle	W	1-0	Shaqiri
05/03	a	Chelsea	D	1-1	Diouf
12/03	h	Southampton	L	1-2	Arnautovic
19/03	a	Watford	W	2-1	Walters, Joselu
02/04	a	Swansea	D	2-2	Afellay, Bojan
10/04	a	Liverpool	L	1-4	Bojan
18/04	a	Tottenham	L	0-4	
23/04	a	Man. City	L	0-4	
30/04	a	Sunderland	D	1-1	Arnautovic
07/05	a	Crystal Palace	L	1-2	Adam
15/05	h	West Ham	W	2-1	Imbula, Diouf

No	Name	Nat	DoB	Pos	Aps	(s)	Gls
16	Charlie Adam	SCO	10/12/85	M	12	(10)	1
14	Ibrahim Afellay	NED	02/04/86	M	24	(7)	2
10	Marko Arnautovic	AUT	19/04/89	A	33	(1)	11
2	Phil Bardsley	SCO	28/06/85	D	9	(2)	
27	Bojan Krkić	ESP	28/08/90	A	22	(5)	7
1	Jack Butland		10/03/93	G	31		
20	Geoff Cameron	USA	11/07/85	D	27	(3)	
25	Peter Crouch		30/01/81	A	4	(7)	
18	Mame Biram Diouf	SEN	16/12/87	A	12	(14)	5
24	Shay Given	IRL	20/04/76	G	3		
29	Jakob Haugaard	DEN	01/05/92	G	4	(1)	
21	Giannelli Imbula	FRA	12/09/92	M	14		2
7	Stephen Ireland	IRL	22/08/86	M		(13)	
8	Glen Johnson		23/08/84	D	25		
11	Joselu	ESP	27/03/90	A	10	(12)	4
5	Marc Muniesa	ESP	27/03/92	D	12	(3)	
9	Peter Odemwingie	NGA	15/07/81	A		(5)	
3	Erik Pieters	NED	07/08/88	D	35		
22	Xherdan Shaqiri	SUI	10/10/91	A	27		3
17	Ryan Shawcross		04/10/87	D	20		
21	Steve Sidwell		14/12/82	M		(1)	
23	Dionatan Teixeira	SVK	24/07/92	D		(1)	
15	Marco van Ginkel	NED	01/12/92	M	8	(9)	
19	Jonathan Walters	IRL	20/09/83	A	18	(9)	5
6	Glenn Whelan	IRL	13/01/84	M	37		
12	Marc Wilson	IRL	17/08/87	D	1	(3)	
26	Philipp Wollscheid	GER	06/03/89	D	30	(1)	

Sunderland AFC

1879 • Stadium of Light (48,707) • safc.com

Major honours
English League (6) 1892, 1893, 1895, 1902, 1913, 1936; FA Cup (2) 1937, 1973

**Manager: Dick Advocaat (NED);
(09/10/15) Sam Allardyce**

2015

08/08	a	Leicester	L	2-4	Defoe, Fletcher
15/08	h	Norwich	L	1-3	Watmore
22/08	h	Swansea	D	1-1	Defoe
29/08	a	Aston Villa	D	2-2	M'Vila, Lens
13/09	h	Tottenham	L	0-1	
19/09	a	Bournemouth	L	0-2	
26/09	a	Man. United	L	0-3	
03/10	h	West Ham	D	2-2	Fletcher, Lens
17/10	a	West Brom	L	0-1	
25/10	h	Newcastle	W	3-0	Johnson (p), Jones, Fletcher
01/11	a	Everton	L	2-6	Defoe, Fletcher
07/11	h	Southampton	L	0-1	
23/11	a	Crystal Palace	W	1-0	Defoe
28/11	h	Stoke	W	2-0	Van Aanholt, Watmore
05/12	a	Arsenal	L	1-3	og (Giroud)
12/12	h	Watford	L	0-1	
19/12	a	Chelsea	L	1-3	Borini
26/12	a	Man. City	L	1-4	Borini
30/12	h	Liverpool	L	0-1	

2015

02/01	h	Aston Villa	W	3-1	og (Richards), Defoe 2
13/01	a	Swansea	W	4-2	Defoe 3, og (Fernández)
16/01	a	Tottenham	L	1-4	Van Aanholt
23/01	h	Bournemouth	D	1-1	Van Aanholt
02/02	h	Man. City	L	0-1	
06/02	a	Liverpool	D	2-2	Johnson, Defoe
13/02	h	Man. United	L	1-2	Khazri, og (De Gea)
27/02	a	West Ham	L	0-1	
01/03	h	Crystal Palace	D	2-2	N'Doye, Borini
05/03	a	Southampton	L	1-1	Defoe
20/03	a	Newcastle	D	1-1	Defoe
02/04	h	West Brom	D	0-0	
10/04	a	Leicester	L	0-2	
16/04	h	Norwich	W	3-0	Borini (p), Defoe, Watmore
24/04	a	Arsenal	D	0-0	
30/04	a	Stoke	D	1-1	Defoe (p)
07/05	h	Chelsea	W	3-2	Khazri, Borini, Defoe
11/05	h	Everton	W	3-0	Van Aanholt, Koné 2
15/05	a	Watford	D	2-2	Rodwell, Lens

No	Name	Nat	DoB	Pos	Aps	(s)	Gls
9	Fabio Borini	ITA	29/03/91	A	22	(4)	5
5	Wes Brown		13/10/79	D	6		
6	Lee Cattermole		21/03/88	M	27	(4)	
22	Sebastián Coates	URU	07/10/90	D	14	(2)	
18	Jermain Defoe		07/10/82	A	28	(5)	15
26	Steven Fletcher	SCO	26/03/87	A	11	(5)	4
19	Danny Graham		12/08/85	A	4	(6)	
37	Rees Greenwood		20/01/96	A	1		
39	George Honeyman		08/09/94	M		(1)	
11	Adam Johnson		14/07/87	M	11	(8)	2
2	Billy Jones		24/03/87	D	23	(1)	1
14	Jordi Goméz	ESP	24/05/85	M	5	(1)	
15	Younès Kaboul	FRA	04/01/86	D	22	(1)	
22	Wahbi Khazri	TUN	08/02/91	M	13	(1)	2
27	Jan Kirchhoff	GER	01/10/90	D	14	(1)	
23	Lamine Koné	CIV	01/02/89	D	15		2
7	Sebastian Larsson	SWE	06/06/85	M	6	(12)	
17	Jeremain Lens	NED	24/11/87	M	14	(6)	3
21	Yann M'Vila	FRA	29/06/90	M	36	(1)	1
25	Vito Mannone	ITA	02/03/88	G	19		
12	Adam Matthews	WAL	13/01/92	D		(1)	
10	Dame N'Doye	SEN	21/02/85	A	5	(6)	1
16	John O'Shea	IRL	30/04/81	D	23	(1)	
1	Costel Pantilimon	ROU	01/02/87	G	17		
13	Jordan Pickford		07/03/94	G	2		
34	Thomas Robson		11/09/95	M	1		
8	Jack Rodwell		11/03/91	M	9	(13)	1
20	Ola Toivonen	SWE	03/07/86	M	9	(3)	
3	Patrick van Aanholt	NED	29/08/90	D	33		4
41	Duncan Watmore		08/03/94	M	7	(16)	3
24	DeAndre Yedlin	USA	09/07/93	D	21	(2)	

Swansea City AFC

1912 • Liberty Stadium (20,909) • swanseacity.net

Major honours
League Cup (1) 2013; Welsh Cup (10) 1913, 1932, 1950, 1961, 1966, 1981, 1982, 1983, 1989, 1991

**Manager: Garry Monk;
(09/12/15) (Alan Curtis (WAL));
(18/01/16) Francesco Guidolin (ITA)**

2015

08/08	a	Chelsea	D	2-2	Ayew, Gomis (p)
15/08	h	Newcastle	W	2-0	Gomis, Ayew
22/08	a	Sunderland	D	1-1	Gomis
30/08	h	Man. United	W	2-1	Ayew, Gomis
12/09	a	Watford	L	0-1	
19/09	h	Everton	D	0-0	
26/09	a	Southampton	L	1-3	Sigurdsson (p)
04/10	h	Tottenham	D	2-2	Ayew, og (Kane)
19/10	a	Stoke	L	0-1	
24/10	h	Aston Villa	W	2-1	Sigurdsson, Ayew
31/10	a	Arsenal	L	0-3	
07/11	a	Norwich	L	0-1	
21/11	h	Bournemouth	D	2-2	Ayew, Shelvey (p)
29/11	a	Liverpool	L	0-1	
05/12	h	Leicester	L	0-3	
12/12	h	Man. City	L	1-2	Gomis
20/12	h	West Ham	D	0-0	
26/12	a	West Brom	W	1-0	Ki
28/12	a	Crystal Palace	D	0-0	

2016

02/01	h	Man. United	L	1-2	Sigurdsson
13/01	h	Sunderland	L	2-4	Sigurdsson (p), Ayew
18/01	h	Watford	W	1-0	Williams
24/01	a	Everton	W	2-1	Sigurdsson (p), Ayew
02/02	a	West Brom	D	1-1	Sigurdsson
06/02	h	Crystal Palace	D	1-1	Sigurdsson
13/02	a	Southampton	L	0-1	
28/02	a	Tottenham	L	1-2	Paloschi
02/03	h	Arsenal	W	2-1	Routledge, Williams
05/03	h	Norwich	W	1-0	Sigurdsson
12/03	a	Bournemouth	L	2-3	Barrow, Sigurdsson
19/03	a	Aston Villa	W	1-0	Fernández
02/04	a	Stoke	D	2-2	Sigurdsson, Paloschi
09/04	h	Chelsea	W	1-0	Sigurdsson
16/04	a	Newcastle	L	0-3	
24/04	a	Leicester	L	0-4	
01/05	h	Liverpool	W	3-1	Ayew 2, Cork
07/05	a	West Ham	W	4-1	Routledge, Ayew, Ki, Gomis
15/05	h	Man. City	D	1-1	Ayew

No	Name	Nat	DoB	Pos	Aps	(s)	Gls
10	André Ayew	GHA	17/12/89	A	34		12
58	Modou Barrow	GAM	13/10/92	A	6	(16)	1
27	Kyle Bartley		22/05/91	D	3	(2)	
7	Leon Britton		16/09/82	M	19	(6)	
24	Jack Cork		25/06/89	M	28	(7)	1
12	Nathan Dyer		29/11/87	M		(1)	
17	Éder	POR	22/12/87	A	2	(11)	
11	Marvin Emnes	NED	27/05/88	A	1	(1)	
1	Łukasz Fabiański	POL	18/04/85	G	37		
8	Leroy Fer	NED	05/01/90	M	9	(2)	
33	Federico Fernández	ARG	21/02/89	D	32		1
56	Jay Fulton	SCO	01/04/94	M		(2)	
18	Bafétimbi Gomis	FRA	06/08/85	A	18	(15)	6
21	Matt Grimes		15/07/95	M	1		
2	Jordi Amat	ESP	21/03/92	D	5	(3)	
4	Ki Sung-yueng	KOR	24/01/89	M	21	(7)	2
35	Stephen Kingsley	SCO	23/07/94	D	4		
20	Jefferson Montero	ECU	01/09/89	M	14	(9)	
26	Kyle Naughton		11/11/88	D	19	(8)	
13	Kristoffer Nordfeldt	SWE	23/06/89	G	1		
9	Alberto Paloschi	ITA	04/01/90	A	7	(3)	2
22	Àngel Rangel	ESP	28/10/82	D	20	(3)	
15	Wayne Routledge		07/01/85	M	22	(6)	2
15	Jonjo Shelvey		27/02/92	M	14	(2)	1
23	Gylfi Thór Sigurdsson	ISL	08/09/89	M	32	(4)	11
3	Neil Taylor	WAL	07/02/89	D	33	(1)	
6	Ashley Williams	WAL	23/08/84	D	36		2

Tottenham Hotspur FC

1882 • White Hart Lane (36,284) • tottenhamhotspur.com

Major honours
UEFA Cup Winners' Cup (1) 1963; UEFA Cup (2) 1972, 1984; English League (2) 1951, 1961; FA Cup (8) 1901, 1921, 1961, 1962, 1967, 1981, 1982, 1991; League Cup (4) 1971, 1973, 1999, 2008

Manager: Mauricio Pochettino (ARG)

2015

08/08	a	Man. United	L	0-1	
15/08	h	Stoke	D	2-2	Dier, Chadli
22/08	a	Leicester	D	1-1	Alli
29/08	a	Everton	D	0-0	
13/09	a	Sunderland	W	1-0	Mason
20/09	h	Crystal Palace	W	1-0	Son
26/09	h	Man. City	W	4-1	Dier, Alderweireld, Kane, Lamela
04/10	a	Swansea	D	2-2	Eriksen 2
17/10	h	Liverpool	D	0-0	
25/10	a	Bournemouth	W	5-1	Kane 3 (1p), Dembélé, Lamela
02/11	h	Aston Villa	W	3-1	Dembélé, Alli, Kane
08/11	a	Arsenal	D	1-1	Kane
22/11	h	West Ham	W	4-1	Kane 2, Alderweireld, Walker
29/11	a	Chelsea	D	0-0	
05/12	h	West Brom	D	1-1	Alli
13/12	h	Newcastle	L	1-2	Dier
19/12	a	Southampton	W	2-0	Kane, Alli
26/12	h	Norwich	W	3-0	Kane 2 (1p), Carroll
28/12	a	Watford	W	2-1	Lamela, Son

2016

03/01	a	Everton	D	1-1	Alli
13/01	h	Leicester	L	0-1	
16/01	h	Sunderland	W	4-1	Eriksen 2, Dembélé, Kane (p)
23/01	a	Crystal Palace	W	3-1	Kane, Alli, Chadli
02/02	a	Norwich	W	3-0	Alli, Kane 2 (1p)
06/02	h	Watford	W	1-0	Trippier
14/02	a	Man. City	W	2-1	Kane (p), Eriksen
28/02	h	Swansea	W	2-1	Chadli, Rose
02/03	a	West Ham	L	0-1	
05/03	a	Arsenal	D	2-2	Alderweireld, Kane
13/03	a	Aston Villa	W	2-0	Kane 2
20/03	h	Bournemouth	W	3-0	Kane 2, Eriksen
02/04	a	Liverpool	D	1-1	Kane
10/04	h	Man. United	W	3-0	Alli, Alderweireld, Lamela
18/04	a	Stoke	W	4-0	Kane 2, Alli 2
25/04	a	West Brom	D	1-1	og (Dawson)
02/05	a	Chelsea	D	2-2	Kane, Son
08/05	h	Southampton	L	1-2	Son
15/05	a	Newcastle	L	1-5	Lamela

No	Name	Nat	DoB	Pos	Aps	(s)	Gls
4	Toby Alderweireld	BEL	02/03/89	D	38		4
20	Dele Alli		11/04/96	M	28	(5)	10
6	Nabil Bentaleb	ALG	24/11/94	M	2	(3)	
28	Tom Carroll		28/05/92	M	4	(15)	1
22	Nacer Chadli	BEL	02/08/89	M	10	(19)	3
33	Ben Davies	WAL	24/04/93	D	14	(3)	
19	Mousa Dembélé	BEL	16/07/87	M	27	(2)	3
15	Eric Dier		15/01/94	M	37		3
23	Christian Eriksen	DEN	14/02/92	M	33	(2)	6
10	Harry Kane		28/07/93	A	38		25
11	Erik Lamela	ARG	04/03/92	M	28	(6)	5
1	Hugo Lloris	FRA	26/12/86	G	37		
7	Ryan Mason		13/06/91	M	8	(14)	1
14	Clinton N'Jie	CMR	15/08/93	A		(8)	
25	Josh Onomah		27/04/97	M		(8)	
24	Alex Pritchard		03/05/93	M		(1)	
2	Danny Rose		02/07/90	D	24		1
7	Son Heung-min	KOR	08/07/92	A	13	(15)	4
17	Andros Townsend		16/07/91	M		(3)	
16	Kieran Trippier		19/09/90	D	5	(1)	1
18	Jan Vertonghen	BEL	24/04/87	D	19		
13	Michel Vorm	NED	20/10/83	G	1		
2	Kyle Walker		28/05/90	D	33		1
27	Kevin Wimmer	AUT	15/11/92	D	9	(1)	

Watford FC

1881 • Vicarage Road (21,500) • watfordfc.com
Manager: Quique Sánchez Flores (ESP)

2015
08/08	a	Everton	D	2-2	Layún, Ighalo
15/08	h	West Brom	D	0-0	
23/08	h	Southampton	D	0-0	
29/08	a	Man. City	L	0-2	
12/09	h	Swansea	W	1-0	Ighalo
19/09	a	Newcastle	W	2-1	Ighalo 2
27/09	h	Crystal Palace	L	0-1	
03/10	a	Bournemouth	D	1-1	Ighalo
17/10	h	Arsenal	L	0-3	
24/10	a	Stoke	W	2-0	Deeney, Abdi
31/10	h	West Ham	W	2-0	Ighalo 2
07/11	h	Leicester	L	1-2	Deeney (p)
21/11	a	Man. United	L	1-2	Deeney (p)
28/11	a	Aston Villa	W	3-2	Ighalo, og (Hutton), Deeney
05/12	h	Norwich	W	2-0	Deeney (p), Ighalo
12/12	a	Sunderland	W	1-0	Ighalo 2
20/12	h	Liverpool	W	3-0	Aké, Ighalo 2
26/12	a	Chelsea	D	2-2	Deeney (p), og (Cahill)
28/12	h	Tottenham	L	1-2	Ighalo

2016
02/01	h	Man. City	L	1-2	Watson
13/01	a	Southampton	L	0-2	
18/01	a	Swansea	L	0-1	
23/01	h	Newcastle	W	2-1	Ighalo, Cathcart
02/02	h	Chelsea	D	0-0	
06/02	a	Tottenham	L	0-1	
13/02	a	Crystal Palace	W	2-1	Deeney 2 (1p)
27/02	h	Bournemouth	D	0-0	
02/03	a	Man. United	L	0-1	
05/03	a	Leicester	L	0-1	
19/03	h	Stoke	L	1-2	Deeney
02/04	a	Arsenal	L	0-4	
09/04	h	Everton	D	1-1	Holebas
16/04	a	West Brom	W	1-0	Watson
20/04	a	West Ham	L	1-3	Prödl
30/04	h	Aston Villa	W	3-2	Abdi, Deeney 2
08/05	a	Liverpool	L	0-2	
11/05	h	Norwich	L	2-4	Deeney, Ighalo
15/05	h	Sunderland	D	2-2	Prödl, Deeney (p)

No	Name	Nat	DoB	Pos	Aps	(s)	Gls
22	Almen Abdi	SUI	21/10/86	M	25	(7)	2
16	Nathan Aké	NED	18/02/95	D	20	(4)	1
11	Nordin Amrabat	MAR	31/03/87	M	4	(8)	
21	Ikechi Anya	SCO	03/01/88	M	17	(11)	
34	Giedrius Arlauskis	LTU	01/12/87	G		(1)	
8	Valon Behrami	SUI	19/04/85	M	14	(7)	
20	Steven Berghuis	NED	19/12/91	M		(9)	
3	Miguel Britos	URU	17/07/85	D	24		
29	Étienne Capoue	FRA	11/07/88	M	33		
15	Craig Cathcart	NIR	06/02/89	D	34	(1)	1
9	Troy Deeney		29/06/88	A	36	(2)	13
32	Alessandro Diamanti	ITA	02/05/83	A		(3)	
1	Heurelho Gomes	BRA	15/02/81	G	38		
17	Adlène Guedioura	ALG	12/11/85	M	3	(15)	
25	José Holebas	GRE	27/06/84	D	11		1
19	Víctor Ibarbo	COL	19/05/90	A		(4)	
24	Odion Ighalo	NGA	16/06/89	A	36	(1)	15
7	José Manuel Jurado	ESP	29/06/85	M	27		
19	Miguel Layún	MEX	25/06/88	D	2	(1)	1
4	Mario Suárez	ESP	24/02/87	M	8	(7)	
2	Allan Nyom	CMR	10/05/88	D	29	(3)	
10	Obbi Oularé	BEL	08/01/96	A		(2)	
14	Juan Carlos Paredes	ECU	08/07/87	D	7	(10)	
5	Sebastian Prödl	AUT	21/06/87	D	19	(2)	2
23	Ben Watson		09/07/85	M	31	(4)	2

West Bromwich Albion FC

1878 • The Hawthorns (26,850) • wba.co.uk
Major honours
English League (1) 1920; FA Cup (5) 1888, 1892, 1931, 1954, 1968; League Cup (1) 1966
Manager: Tony Pulis (WAL)

2015
10/08	h	Man. City	L	0-3	
15/08	a	Watford	D	0-0	
23/08	h	Chelsea	L	2-3	Morrison 2
29/08	a	Stoke	W	1-0	Rondón
12/09	h	Southampton	D	0-0	
19/09	a	Aston Villa	W	1-0	Berahino
28/09	h	Everton	L	2-3	Berahino, Dawson
03/10	a	Crystal Palace	L	0-2	
17/10	h	Sunderland	W	1-0	Berahino
24/10	h	Norwich	W	1-0	Rondón
31/10	h	Leicester	L	2-3	Rondón, Lambert (p)
07/11	a	Man. United	L	0-2	
21/11	h	Arsenal	W	2-1	Morrison, og (Arteta)
29/11	a	West Ham	D	1-1	og (Reid)
05/12	h	Tottenham	L	1-1	McClean
13/12	a	Liverpool	D	2-2	Dawson, Olsson
19/12	h	Bournemouth	L	1-2	McAuley
26/12	a	Swansea	L	0-1	
28/12	h	Newcastle	W	1-0	Fletcher

2016
02/01	h	Stoke	W	2-1	Sessègnon, Evans
13/01	h	Chelsea	D	2-2	Gardner, McClean
16/01	a	Southampton	L	0-3	
23/01	a	Aston Villa	W	1-0	
02/02	h	Swansea	D	1-1	Rondón
06/02	a	Newcastle	L	0-1	
13/02	a	Everton	W	1-0	Rondón
27/02	h	Crystal Palace	W	3-2	Gardner, Dawson, Berahino
01/03	a	Leicester	D	2-2	Rondón, Gardner
06/03	h	Man. United	W	1-0	Rondón
19/03	h	Norwich	L	0-1	
02/04	a	Sunderland	D	0-0	
09/04	a	Man. City	L	1-2	Sessègnon
16/04	h	Watford	L	0-1	
21/04	a	Arsenal	L	0-2	
25/04	a	Tottenham	D	1-1	Dawson
30/04	h	West Ham	L	0-3	
07/05	a	Bournemouth	L	1-2	Rondón
15/05	h	Liverpool	D	1-1	Rondón

No	Name	Nat	DoB	Pos	Aps	(s)	Gls
10	Victor Anichebe	NGA	23/04/88	A	3	(7)	
18	Saido Berahino		04/08/93	A	17	(14)	4
11	Chris Brunt	NIR	14/12/84	D	20	(2)	
4	James Chester	WAL	23/01/89	D	9	(4)	
25	Craig Dawson		06/05/90	D	38		4
6	Jonny Evans	NIR	03/01/88	D	30		1
47	Sam Field		08/05/98	M		(1)	
24	Darren Fletcher	SCO	01/02/84	M	38		1
1	Ben Foster		03/04/83	G	15		
16	Cristian Gamboa	CRC	24/10/89	D		(1)	
8	Craig Gardner		25/11/86	M	20	(14)	3
31	Serge Gnabry	GER	14/07/95	M		(1)	
17	Rickie Lambert		16/02/82	A	5	(14)	1
45	Jonathan Leko		24/04/99	A	3	(2)	
6	Joleon Lescott		16/08/82	D	2		
23	Gareth McAuley	NIR	05/12/79	D	34		1
14	James McClean	IRL	22/04/89	M	28	(7)	2
19	Callum McManaman		25/04/91	M	2	(10)	
7	James Morrison	SCO	25/05/86	M	17	(1)	3
13	Boaz Myhill	WAL	09/11/82	G	23		
3	Jonas Olsson	SWE	10/03/83	D	25	(3)	1
15	Sébastien Pocognoli	BEL	01/08/87	D		(1)	
20	Alex Pritchard		03/05/93	M		(2)	
44	Tyler Roberts	WAL	12/01/99	A		(1)	
33	José Salomón Rondón	VEN	16/09/89	A	30	(4)	9
30	Sandro	BRA	15/03/89	M	5	(7)	
29	Stéphane Sessègnon	BEN	01/06/84	M	21	(4)	2
5	Claudio Yacob	ARG	18/07/87	M	33	(1)	

West Ham United FC

1895 • Boleyn Ground (35,345) • whufc.com
Major honours
UEFA Cup Winners' Cup (1) 1965; FA Cup (3) 1964, 1975, 1980
Manager: Slaven Bilić (CRO)

2015
09/08	a	Arsenal	W	2-0	Kouyaté, Zárate
15/08	h	Leicester	L	1-2	Payet
22/08	h	Bournemouth	L	3-4	Noble (p), Kouyaté, Maïga
29/08	a	Liverpool	W	3-0	Lanzini, Noble, Sakho
14/09	h	Newcastle	W	2-0	Payet 2
19/09	a	Man. City	W	2-1	Moses, Sakho
26/09	h	Norwich	D	2-2	Sakho, Kouyaté
03/10	a	Sunderland	D	2-2	Jenkinson, Payet
17/10	a	Crystal Palace	W	3-1	Jenkinson, Lanzini, Payet
24/10	a	Chelsea	W	2-1	Zárate, Carroll
31/10	a	Watford	L	0-2	
07/11	h	Everton	D	1-1	Lanzini
22/11	a	Tottenham	L	1-4	Lanzini
29/11	a	West Brom	D	1-1	Zárate
05/12	a	Man. United	D	0-0	
12/12	h	Stoke	D	0-0	
20/12	a	Swansea	D	0-0	
26/12	a	Aston Villa	W	2-0	Cresswell
28/12	h	Southampton	W	2-1	Antonio, Carroll

2016
02/01	h	Liverpool	W	2-0	Antonio, Carroll
12/01	a	Bournemouth	W	3-1	Payet, Valencia 2
16/01	a	Newcastle	L	1-2	Jelavić
23/01	h	Man. City	D	2-2	Valencia 2
02/02	h	Aston Villa	W	2-0	Antonio, Kouyaté
06/02	a	Southampton	L	0-1	
13/02	h	Norwich	D	2-2	Payet, Noble
27/02	h	Sunderland	W	1-0	Antonio
02/03	h	Tottenham	W	1-0	Antonio
05/03	a	Everton	W	3-2	Antonio, Sakho, Payet
19/03	a	Chelsea	D	2-2	Lanzini, Carroll
02/04	h	Crystal Palace	D	2-2	Lanzini, Payet
09/04	a	Arsenal	D	3-3	Carroll 3
17/04	a	Leicester	D	2-2	Carroll (p), Cresswell
20/04	a	Watford	W	3-1	Carroll, Noble 2 (2p)
30/04	a	West Brom	W	3-0	Kouyaté, Noble 2
07/05	h	Swansea	L	1-4	og (Kingsley)
10/05	h	Man. United	W	3-2	Sakho, Antonio, Reid
15/05	a	Stoke	L	1-2	Antonio

No	Name	Nat	DoB	Pos	Aps	(s)	Gls
13	Adrián	ESP	03/01/87	G	32		
30	Michail Antonio		28/03/90	M	23	(3)	8
22	Sam Byram		16/09/93	D	2	(2)	
9	Andy Carroll		06/01/89	A	13	(14)	9
19	James Collins	WAL	23/08/83	D	16	(3)	
3	Aaron Cresswell		15/12/89	D	37		2
39	Josh Cullen	IRL	07/04/96	M		(1)	
29	Emmanuel Emenike	NGA	10/05/87	A	5	(8)	
7	Matt Jarvis		22/05/86	M		(3)	
26	Nikica Jelavić	CRO	27/03/85	A	1	(12)	1
12	Carl Jenkinson		08/02/92	D	13	(7)	2
8	Cheikhou Kouyaté	SEN	21/12/89	M	34		5
28	Manuel Lanzini	ARG	15/02/93	M	23	(3)	6
20	Modibo Maïga	MLI	03/09/87	A		(3)	1
20	Victor Moses	NGA	12/12/90	M	13	(8)	1
16	Mark Noble		08/05/87	M	37		7
4	Kevin Nolan		24/06/82	M	1	(1)	
21	Angelo Ogbonna	ITA	23/05/88	D	27	(1)	
35	Reece Oxford		16/12/98	M	3	(4)	
27	Dimitri Payet	FRA	29/03/87	M	29	(1)	9
14	Pedro Obiang	ESP	27/03/92	M	11	(13)	
1	Darren Randolph	IRL	12/05/87	G	6		
2	Winston Reid	NZL	03/07/88	D	24		1
15	Diafra Sakho	SEN	24/12/89	A	18	(3)	5
4	Alex Song	CMR	09/09/87	M	8	(4)	
5	James Tomkins		29/03/89	D	23	(2)	
11	Enner Valencia	ECU	04/11/89	A	10	(9)	4
10	Mauro Zárate	ARG	18/03/87	A	9	(6)	3

Top goalscorers

25	Harry Kane (Tottenham)
24	Jamie Vardy (Leicester)
	Sergio Agüero (Man. City)
18	Romelu Lukaku (Everton)
17	Riyad Mahrez (Leicester)
16	Olivier Giroud (Arsenal)
15	Jermain Defoe (Sunderland)
	Odion Ighalo (Watford)
13	Alexis Sánchez (Arsenal)
	Troy Deeney (Watford)

Promoted clubs

Burnley FC

1882 • Turf Moor (21,401) •
burnleyfootballclub.com
Major honours
English League (2) 1921, 1960; FA Cup (1) 1914
Manager: Sean Dyche

Middlesbrough FC

1876 • Riverside Stadium (34,742) • mfc.co.uk
Major honours
League Cup (1) 2004
Manager: Aitor Karanka (ESP)

Hull City AFC

1904 • KC Stadium (25,450) •
hullcitytigers.com
Manager: Steve Bruce

Second level final table 2015/16

		Pld	W	D	L	F	A	Pts
1	Burnley FC	46	26	15	5	72	35	93
2	Middlesbrough FC	46	26	11	9	63	31	89
3	Brighton & Hove Albion FC	46	24	17	5	72	42	89
4	Hull City AFC	46	24	11	11	69	35	83
5	Derby County FC	46	21	15	10	66	43	78
6	Sheffield Wednesday FC	46	19	17	10	66	45	74
7	Ipswich Town FC	46	18	15	13	53	51	69
8	Cardiff City FC	46	17	17	12	56	51	68
9	Brentford FC	46	19	8	19	72	67	65
10	Birmingham City FC	46	16	15	15	53	49	63
11	Preston North End FC	46	15	17	14	45	45	62
12	Queens Park Rangers FC	46	14	18	14	54	54	60
13	Leeds United AFC	46	14	17	15	50	58	59
14	Wolverhampton Wanderers FC	46	14	16	16	53	58	58
15	Blackburn Rovers FC	46	13	16	17	46	46	55
16	Nottingham Forest FC	46	13	16	17	43	47	55
17	Reading FC	46	13	13	20	52	59	52
18	Bristol City FC	46	13	13	20	54	71	52
19	Huddersfield Town FC	46	13	12	21	59	70	51
20	Fulham FC	46	12	15	19	66	79	51
21	Rotherham United FC	46	13	10	23	53	71	49
22	Charlton Athletic FC	46	9	13	24	40	80	40
23	Miton Keynes Dons FC	46	9	12	25	39	69	39
24	Bolton Wanderers FC	46	5	15	26	41	81	30

Promotion play-offs

(13/05/16 & 16/05/16)
Sheffield Wednesday 2-0 Brighton
Brighton 1-1 Sheffield Wednesday
(Sheffield Wednesday 3-1)

(14/05/16 & 17/05/16)
Derby 0-3 Hull
Hull 0-2 Derby
(Hull 3-2)

(28/05/16)
Hull 1-0 Sheffield Wednesday

DOMESTIC CUPS

FA Cup 2015/16

THIRD ROUND

(08/01/16)
Exeter 2-2 Liverpool

(09/01/16)
Arsenal 3-1 Sunderland
Birmingham 1-2 Bournemouth
Brentford 0-1 Walsall
Bury 0-0 Bradford
Colchester 2-1 Charlton
Doncaster 1-2 Stoke
Eastleigh 1-1 Bolton
Everton 2-0 Dagenham & Redbridge
Hartlepool 1-2 Derby
Huddersfield 2-2 Reading
Hull 1-0 Brighton
Ipswich 2-2 Portsmouth
Leeds 2-0 Rotherham
Man. United 1-0 Sheffield United
Middlesbrough 1-2 Burnley
Northampton 2-2 MK Dons
Norwich 0-3 Man. City
Nottingham Forest 1-0 QPR
Peterborough 2-0 Preston
Sheffield Wednesday 2-1 Fulham
Southampton 1-2 Crystal Palace
Watford 1-0 Newcastle
West Brom 2-2 Bristol City
West Ham 1-0 Wolves
Wycombe 1-1 Aston Villa

(10/01/16)
Cardiff 0-1 Shrewsbury
Carlisle 2-2 Yeovil
Chelsea 2-0 Scunthorpe
Oxford 3-2 Swansea
Tottenham 2-2 Leicester

(18/01/16)
Newport 1-2 Blackburn

Replays

(19/01/16)
Aston Villa 2-0 Wycombe
Bolton 3-2 Eastleigh
Bradford 0-0 Bury *(aet; 2-4 on pens)*
Bristol City 0-1 West Brom
MK Dons 3-0 Northampton
Portsmouth 2-1 Ipswich
Reading 5-2 Huddersfield
Yeovil 1-1 Carlisle *(aet; 4-5 on pens)*

(20/01/16)
Leicester 0-2 Tottenham
Liverpool 3-0 Exeter

FOURTH ROUND

(29/01/16)
Derby 1-3 Man. United

(30/01/16)
Arsenal 2-1 Burnley
Aston Villa 0-4 Man. City
Bolton 1-2 Leeds
Bury 1-3 Hull
Colchester 1-4 Tottenham
Crystal Palace 1-0 Stoke
Liverpool 0-0 West Ham
Nottingham Forest 0-1 Watford
Oxford 0-3 Blackburn

Continued over the page

The FA Cup is held aloft by Manchester United players for a record-equalling 12th time after the club's 2-1 extra-time win over Crystal Palace at Wembley

Portsmouth 1-2 Bournemouth
Reading 4-0 Walsall
Shrewsbury 3-2 Sheffield Wednesday
West Brom 2-2 Peterborough

(31/01/16)
Carlisle 0-3 Everton
MK Dons 1-5 Chelsea

Replays

(09/02/16)
West Ham 2-1 Liverpool *(aet)*

(10/02/16)
Peterborough 1-1 West Brom *(aet; 3-4 on pens)*

FIFTH ROUND

(20/02/16)
Arsenal 0-0 Hull
Bournemouth 0-2 Everton
Reading 3-1 West Brom
Watford 1-0 Leeds

(21/02/16)
Blackburn 1-5 West Ham
Chelsea 5-1 Man. City
Tottenham 0-1 Crystal Palace

(22/02/16)
Shrewsbury 0-3 Man. United

Replay

(08/03/16)
Hull 0-4 Arsenal

QUARTER-FINALS

(11/03/16)
Reading 0-2 Crystal Palace *(Cabaye 86p, Campbell 90)*

(12/03/16)
Everton 2-0 Chelsea *(Lukaku 77, 82)*

(13/03/16)
Arsenal 1-2 Watford *(Welbeck 88; Ighalo 50, Guedioura 63)*
Man. United 1-1 West Ham *(Martial 83; Payet 68)*

Replay

(13/04/16)
West Ham 1-2 Man. United *(Tomkins 79; Rashford 54, Fellaini 67)*

SEMI-FINALS

(23/04/16)
Man. United 2-1 Everton *(Fellaini 34, Martial 90+3; Smalling 75og)*

(24/04/16)
Crystal Palace 2-1 Watford *(Bolasie 6, Wickham 61; Deeney 55)*

FINAL

(21/05/16)
Wembley Stadium, London
MANCHESTER UNITED FC 2 *(Mata 81, Lingard 110)*
CRYSTAL PALACE FC 1 *(Puncheon 78)*
(aet)
Referee: *Clattenburg*
MAN. UNITED: *De Gea, Valencia, Smalling, Blind, Rojo (Darmian 66), Fellaini, Carrick, Rooney, Mata (Lingard 90), Martial, Rashford (Young 72)*
Red card: *Smalling (105)*
CRYSTAL PALACE: *Hennessey, Ward, Dann (Mariappa 90+4), Delaney, Souaré, Cabaye (Puncheon 72), McArthur, Jedinak, Zaha, Bolasie, Wickham (Gayle 86)*

League Cup 2015/16

QUARTER-FINALS

(01/12/15)
Middlesbrough 0-2 Everton *(Deulofeu 20, Lukaku 28)*

Stoke 2-0 Sheffield Wednesday *(Afellay 30, Bardsley 75)*

Man. City 4-1 Hull *(Bony 12, Iheanacho 80, De Bruyne 82, 87; Robertson 90)*

(02/12/15)
Southampton 1-6 Liverpool *(Mané 1; Sturridge 25, 29, Origi 45, 68, 86, Ibe 73)*

SEMI-FINALS

(05/01/16 & 26/01/16)
Stoke 0-1 Liverpool *(Ibe 37)*
Liverpool 0-1 Stoke *(Arnautovic 45+1) (aet)*
(1-1; Liverpool 6-5 on pens)

(06/01/16 & 27/01/16)
Everton 2-1 Man. City *(Funes Mori 45, Lukaku 78; Jesús Navas 76)*
Man. City 3-1 Everton *(Fernandinho 24, De Bruyne 70, Agüero 76; Barkley 18)*
(Man. City 4-3)

FINAL

(28/02/16)
Wembley Stadium, London
MANCHESTER CITY FC 1 *(Fernandinho 49)*
LIVERPOOL FC 1 *(Coutinho 83)*
(aet; 3-1 on pens)
Referee: *Oliver*
MAN. CITY: *Caballero, Sagna (Zabaleta 91), Kompany, Otamendi, Clichy, Touré, Fernando (Jesús Navas 91), Fernandinho, Silva (Bony 110), Sterling, Agüero*
LIVERPOOL: *Mignolet, Clyne, Lucas, Sakho (Touré 25), Moreno (Lallana 72), Milner, Henderson, Can, Coutinho, Roberto Firmino (Origi 80), Sturridge*

Manchester City skipper Vincent Kompany shows off the League Cup

ESTONIA
Eesti Jalgpalli Liit (EJL)

Address	A. Le Coq Arena, Asula 4c	**President**	Aivar Pohlak
	EE-11312 Tallinn	**General secretary**	Anne Rei
Tel	+372 627 9960	**Media officer**	Mihkel Uiboleht
Fax	+372 627 9969	**Year of formation**	1921
E-mail	efa@jalgpall.ee	**National stadium**	A. Le Coq Arena,
Website	jalgpall.ee		Tallinn (9,692)

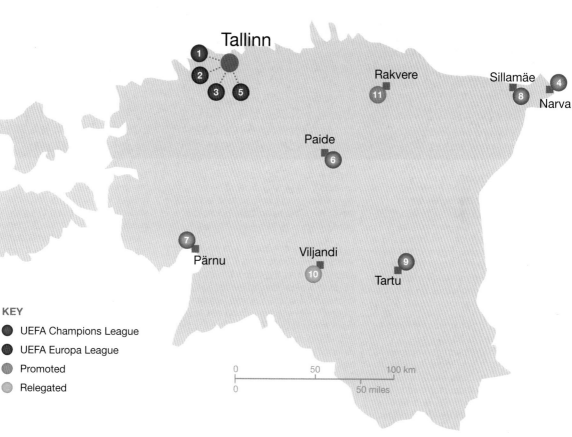

KEY
- ● UEFA Champions League
- ● UEFA Europa League
- ◍ Promoted
- ◯ Relegated

MEISTRILIIGA CLUBS

  ① FC Flora Tallinn

  ② FC Infonet Tallinn

  ③ FC Levadia Tallinn

  ④ JK Narva Trans

 ⑤ Nõmme Kalju FC

 ⑥ Paide Linnameeskond

  ⑦ Pärnu Linnameeskond

  ⑧ JK Sillamäe Kalev

  ⑨ JK Tammeka Tartu

 ⑩ JK Tulevik Viljandi

PROMOTED CLUB

  ⑪ Rakvere JK Tarvas

Flora win race to historic tenth title

There were significant bragging rights to be had in 2015 as Tallinn's two strongest clubs, FC Flora and FC Levadia, battled to become the first to claim ten Estonian Meistriliiga titles. It was a contest that went the way of Flora, in the year of their 25th anniversary, as 32-year-old Norbert Hurt's side produced a powerful late surge to stun their local rivals and early pacesetters Nõmme Kalju into submission.

There was more silverware for Flora the following spring as they triumphed in the Estonian Cup, collecting the trophy for the seventh time after they scored three extra-time goals to overcome gallant first-time finalists Sillamäe Kalev.

Runners-up Levadia beaten to landmark triumph

Late victory surge breaks back of rivals' challenge

Flora's extra-time flourish wins the cup final

Domestic league

Flora's quest to reach the ten-title milestone before Levadia, who had lifted the Meistriliiga trophy in each of the previous two campaigns, was thwarted by their two main challengers in the first half of the campaign as Kalju beat them 2-0 in their first two meetings and Levadia restricted them to a single point from back-to-back derbies in early May.

The first of Kalju's two wins over Flora came in the midst of an opening nine-match winning burst that suggested Sergei Terehhov's side might make both of their two Tallinn rivals wait at least another year for that coveted tenth crown. But five defeats in Kalju's next seven matches put a huge dent in their title aspirations, and it was at this point that Levadia rose to the challenge, Marko Kristal's side offsetting a disappointing, draw-ridden start to the campaign with eight successive victories.

Flora, however, were to provide the most timely winning sequence of all, racking up 12 three-pointers on the spin from mid-August through to the end of October, by which time their 2-0 win at Levadia – the first time they had come out on top against Kristal's men during the campaign – was purely decorative. The title had been clinched a week earlier with a 1-0 win at FC Infonet, enabling Hurt's in-form side to profit fully from Levadia's earlier 0-0 draw at home to lowly Pärnu and increase their lead at the top of the table to an insurmountable eight points with two games to go.

The star of Flora's surge was 19-year-old attacking midfielder Rauno Sappinen, who finished as the club's top scorer with 16 goals – eight behind the league's leading marksman, Levadia veteran Ingemar Teever – while Estonian national team stalwart Gert Kams proved to be a redoubtable captain and leader of a defence that conceded at a rate of only two goals every three games.

Flora's reserves also won the Esiliiga (second tier), pipping Levadia's equivalent by a point, though of course neither could earn promotion, which eventually went to a team 25 points off the summit, fourth-placed Rakvere JK Tarvas. They replaced Meistrilliga bottom club Tulevik Viljandi and were the only team to move up as Tallinna Kalev lost their play-off to Tammeka Tartu.

Domestic cup

Flora moved to within one of Levadia's record tally of eight Estonian Cup victories by reclaiming the trophy in 2016. A hazard-free path to the final was facilitated by their opponents Sillamäe, who eliminated Levadia and Kalju with 1-0 victories before seeing off new merger club Viimsi 2-0 in the semis to reach the final for the first time. The underdogs continued to keep their goal intact for the regulation 90 minutes against Flora before the champions ran riot in extra time, scoring three goals in five minutes after the ever-reliable Sappinen had broken the deadlock.

Europe

Once again, Estonian interest in continental club competition did not stretch beyond mid-summer. Indeed, only one of the four entrants survived the first qualifying round, with Kalju edging past Kazakhstan's FK Aktobe in the UEFA Europa League thanks to a single strike from Estonian international Ats Purje. The away goal rule proved fatal for Levadia in the UEFA Champions League, elimination by Crusaders proving especially galling as they were going so well domestically at the time.

National team

The international season began well, with a 1-0 home win over Baltic rivals Lithuania in the UEFA EURO 2016 qualifiers thanks to Konstantin Vassiljev's 20th international goal, but ended very badly as a Cristiano Ronaldo-led Portugal subjected Magnus Pehrsson's Estonia to a crushing 7-0 defeat in Lisbon.

DOMESTIC SEASON AT A GLANCE

Meistriliiga 2015 final table

		Pld	Home					Away					Total					Pts
			W	D	L	F	A	W	D	L	F	A	W	D	L	F	A	
1	**FC Flora Tallinn**	**36**	**12**	**2**	**4**	**35**	**13**	**15**	**1**	**2**	**37**	**11**	**27**	**3**	**6**	**72**	**24**	**84**
2	FC Levadia Tallinn	36	10	4	4	29	13	12	6	0	49	19	22	10	4	78	32	76
3	Nõmme Kalju FC	36	12	3	3	34	16	10	2	6	35	20	22	5	9	69	36	71
4	FC Infonet Tallinn	36	10	4	4	32	19	7	7	4	18	13	17	11	8	50	32	62
5	JK Sillamäe Kalev	36	9	5	4	32	22	8	3	7	31	21	17	8	11	63	43	59
6	JK Narva Trans	36	8	3	7	31	17	6	4	8	19	29	14	7	15	50	46	49
7	Paide Linnameeskond	36	6	3	9	33	40	3	3	12	17	33	9	6	21	50	73	33
8	Pärnu Linnameeskond	36	4	3	11	19	42	2	5	11	19	45	6	8	22	38	87	26
9	JK Tammeka Tartu	36	5	3	10	21	40	2	1	15	18	56	7	4	25	39	96	25
10	JK Tulevik Viljandi	36	5	3	10	23	33	1	1	16	12	42	6	4	26	35	75	22

European qualification 2016/17

 Champion/ Cup winner: FC Flora Tallinn (first qualifying round)

 FC Levadia Tallinn (first qualifying round)
Nõmme Kalju FC (first qualifying round)
FC Infonet Tallinn (first qualifying round)

Top scorer	Ingemar Teever (Levadia), 24 goals
Relegated club	JK Tulevik Viljandi
Promoted club	Rakvere JK Tarvas
Cup final	FC Flora Tallinn 3-0 JK Sillamäe Kalev (aet)

Team of the season
(4-2-3-1)

Coach: Hurt (Flora)

Toom (Flora)

Kams (Flora) — Baranov (Flora) — Cheminava (Sillamäe) — Pikk (Levadia)

Dmitrijev (Infonet) — Mbu Alidor (Kalju)

Purje (Kalju) — Sappinen (Flora) — Luts (Levadia)

Teever (Levadia)

Player of the season

Ingemar Teever
(FC Levadia Tallinn)

The 2015 season proved to be the last in the career of one of the Meistrilliga's most prolific goalscorers as Teever decided to call it quits at the age of 32. His swansong campaign was arguably his finest of all. Although he failed to collect a third successive league winner's medal with Levadia, he scored 24 goals to top the division's goal charts – for the second time, having done so with Nõmme Kalju in 2008 – and also earned official recognition as the Meistriliiga player of the year.

Newcomer of the season

Rauno Sappinen
(FC Flora Tallinn)

Having impressively captained the Estonia Under-19 side, Sappinen brought his talent thrillingly to the fore at club level in 2015 as his 16 goals propelled Flora to their historic tenth Meistriliiga title. Aged 19 throughout the league campaign, he won his first senior international cap in November and by the following spring, his teens consigned to history, he was not only an Estonia regular but had another medal of honour to cherish after inspiring Flora to victory in the domestic cup final against Sillamäe Kalev.

NATIONAL TEAM

Top five all-time caps
Martin Reim (157); Marko Kristal (143); Andres Oper (134); **Enar Jääger** (121); Mart Poom (120)

Top five all-time goals
Andres Oper (38); Indrek Zelinski (27); Eduard Ellmann-Eelma & **Konstantin Vassiljev** (21); Richard Kuremaa (19)

Results 2015/16

Date	Opponent	H/A/N	Venue	Res	Score	Scorers
05/09/15	Lithuania (ECQ)	H	Tallinn	W	1-0	*Vassiljev (71)*
08/09/15	Slovenia (ECQ)	A	Maribor	L	0-1	
09/10/15	England (ECQ)	A	London	L	0-2	
12/10/15	Switzerland (ECQ)	H	Tallinn	L	0-1	
11/11/15	Georgia	H	Tallinn	W	3-0	*Purje (61), Pikk (65), Gussev (88)*
17/11/15	St Kitts & Nevis	H	Tallinn	W	3-0	*Antonov (28), Vassiljev (50), Puri (57)*
06/01/16	Sweden	N	Abu Dhabi (UAE)	D	1-1	*Prosa (56)*
24/03/16	Norway	H	Tallinn	D	0-0	
29/03/16	Serbia	H	Tallinn	L	0-1	
29/05/16	Lithuania	A	Klaipeda	L	0-2	
01/06/16	Andorra	H	Tallinn	W	2-0	*Kruglov (24), Liivak (90+4)*
04/06/16	Latvia	H	Tallinn	D	0-0	
08/06/16	Portugal	A	Lisbon	L	0-7	

Appearances 2015/16

Coach: **Magnus Pehrsson (SWE)** 25/05/76

Player	DOB	Club	LTU	SVN	ENG	SUI	Geo	Skn	Swe	Nor	Srb	Ltu	And	Lva	Por	Caps	Goals
Mihkel Aksalu	07/11/84	SJK (FIN)	G	G	G	G	G			G	G			G		24	-
Taijo Teniste	31/01/88	Sogndal (NOR)	D	D	D	D			D46	D	D60			D	D	47	-
Enar Jääger	18/11/84	Vålerenga (NOR)	D	D	D	D	D	D		D	D					121	-
Ragnar Klavan	30/10/85	Augsburg (GER)	D	D	D	D	D		D86			D		D	D69	112	3
Artur Pikk	05/03/93	Levadia /BATE (BLR)	D	D	D	D	D66	D	D	D	D	D87	D73			15	1
Joel Lindpere	05/10/81	Kalju /unattached	M67	M84	s70	s67	s81	s70					M44			107	7
Karol Mets	16/05/93	Viking (NOR)	M	M	M	M	M	M18	D	M	M		M	M	M	29	-
Aleksandr Dmitrijev	18/02/82	Infonet	M		M70		M81	M70		M		M43			M63	99	-
Konstantin Vassiljev	16/08/84	Jagiellonia (POL)	M93	M	M	M	M89	M		M90	M				s70	88	21
Sergei Zenjov	20/04/89	Qäbälä (AZE)	A	M46	M	A61				A	M81					50	9
Ats Purje	03/08/85	Kalju	A86	A	A70	s61	A73	A46								56	8
Ken Kallaste	31/08/88	Kalju /Górnik Zabrze (POL)	s67	M88	M88	M80	M	M62		M74	M46	M	D	D		28	-
Sander Puri	07/05/88	Sligo (IRL) /Karviná (CZE)	s86	s46	s70	M67	s54	M81	M46	s74	s46	s73	s70	M87		69	4
Siim Luts	12/03/89	Levadia	s93	s88	s88	s80										24	1
Ingemar Teever	24/02/83	Levadia		s84												30	4
Ilja Antonov	05/12/92	Levadia						M	s18	M75	s90	M86	M	s46	M	28	1
Nikita Baranov	19/08/92	Flora					D	D	D	s86	D	M	D46	D	D	9	-
Gert Kams	25/05/85	Flora					M54	s81		s60						42	2
Maksim Gussev	20/07/94	Flora					s66	s62	M77		s81	s67	M73		s87	8	1
Rauno Sappinen	23/01/96	Flora					s73	s46	s46	s86		A79	s73	M90	s63	8	-
Andre Frolov	18/04/88	Flora					s89		s46			s43				4	-
Pavel Londak	14/05/80	Bodø/Glimt (NOR) /unattached /Rosenborg (NOR)						G46	G						G	27	-
Markus Jürgenson	09/09/87	Flora					D	s46				D79				8	-
Sergei Pareiko	31/01/77	Levadia						s46								65	-
Andreas Raudsepp	13/12/93	Levadia							M	M64		s79	D		s69	7	-
Igor Subbotin	26/06/90	Levadia							M46							5	-
Mattias Käit	29/06/98	Fulham (ENG)							A46							1	-
Albert Prosa	01/10/90	Flora							s46							5	1
Vladimir Avilov	10/03/95	Infonet							s75							2	-
Hindrek Ojamaa	12/06/95	Levadia							s77							1	-
Henri Anier	17/12/90	Dundee United (SCO)							s64	A	s67	A73	A	A70		29	6
Marko Meerits	26/04/92	Emmen (NED)										G				4	-
Joonas Tamm	02/02/92	Flora										D67				6	-
Pavel Marin	14/06/95	Levadia										M67	s73	M70	s66	4	-
Frank Liivak	07/07/86	Alcobendas (ESP)										s79	s44	s90	M66	6	1
Dmitri Kruglov	24/05/84	Infonet										s87	M	M	M66	103	4
Andreas Vaikla	19/02/97	Norrköping (SWE)										G				1	-
Jan Kokla	29/05/97	Flora										M				1	-

EUROPE

FC Levadia Tallinn

First qualifying round – Crusaders FC (NIR)
A 0-0
Pikker, Rakhmanov, Laitinen, El Hussieny, Teever (Saag 85), Luts, Kruglov, Marin (Antonov 61), Pikk, Rähn, Pecha. Coach: Marko Kristal (EST)
H 1-1 *Luts (22)*
Pikker, Rakhmanov, Laitinen, El Hussieny (Subbotin 88), Antonov, Teever, Luts, Kruglov, Pikk, Rähn, Pecha (Saag 72). Coach: Marko Kristal (EST)

Nõmme Kalju FC

First qualifying round - FC Aktobe (KAZ)
A 1-0 *Purje (72)*
Teleš, Bärengrub, Jorge Rodrigues, Dmitrijev, Purje, Kimbaloula (Listmann 90+2), Puri, Kallaste, Topić (Neemelo 82), Mööl, Wakui (Lindpere 58). Coach: Sergei Terehhov (EST)
H 0-0
Teleš, Bärengrub, Jorge Rodrigues, Dmitrijev (Neemelo 73), Purje, Kimbaloula, Puri, Kallaste, Topić (Mbu Alidor 57), Mööl, Wakui (Lindpere 61). Coach: Sergei Terehhov (EST)

Second qualifying round - FC Vaduz (LIE)
A 1-3 *Wakui (86)*
Teleš, Bärengrub, Jorge Rodrigues, Mbu Alidor, Dmitrijev (Lindpere 63), Purje (Neemelo 70), Kimbaloula, Kallaste, Topić (Puri 46), Mööl, Wakui. Coach: Sergei Terehhov (EST)
H 0-2
Teleš, Bärengrub, Jorge Rodrigues, Dmitrijev (Voskoboinikov 74), Purje, Kimbaloula, Puri (Neemelo 63), Kallaste, Lindpere (Topić 72), Mööl, Wakui. Coach: Sergei Terehhov (EST)

JK Sillamäe Kalev

First qualifying round - HNK Hajduk Split (CRO)
H 1-1 *Silich (40)*
Starodubtsev, Činikas, Cheminava, Kvasov, Vnukov (Ratnikov 65), Silich, Toomet, Tjapkin, Dudarev, Šišov, Russo. Coach: Algimantas Briaunys (LTU)
A 2-6 *Russo (36, 41)*
Usikov, Činikas (Aleksejev 78), Cheminava, Vnukov, Silich, Ratnikov, Toomet (Kvasov 70), Tjapkin, Dudarev, Šišov (Ivanjušin 61), Russo. Coach: Algimantas Briaunys (LTU)

FC Flora Tallinn

First qualifying round - FK Rabotnicki (MKD)
H 1-0 *Gussev (59)*
Toom, Jääger, Frolov, Logua (Tamm 73), Alliku, Sappinen (Beglarishvili 53), Jürgenson, Kams, Gussev, Baranov, Šlein (Luigend 80). Coach: Norbert Hurt (EST)
A 0-2
Toom, Jääger, Frolov, Logua (Gussev 55), Alliku, Sappinen, Jürgenson, Kams, Baranov (Aloe 68), Šlein, Tukiainen (Tamm 46). Coach: Norbert Hurt (EST)

DOMESTIC LEAGUE CLUB-BY-CLUB

FC Flora Tallinn

1990 • A. Le Coq Arena (9,692); Sportland Arena (540) • fcflora.ee
Major honours
Estonian League (10) 1994, 1995, 1998, 1998 (autumn), 2001, 2002, 2003, 2010, 2011, 2015; Estonian Cup (7) 1995, 1998, 2008, 2009, 2011, 2013, 2016
Coach: Norbert Hurt

2015

Date		Opp	Res	Scorers
07/03	h	Tulevik	W 3-0	Logua, Sappinen, Tukiainen
13/03	a	Infonet	W 2-0	Sappinen, Logua
21/03	h	Sillamäe	W 1-0	Sappinen
04/04	a	Trans	W 1-0	Tukiainen
11/04	h	Kalju	L 0-2	
14/04	a	Tammeka	W 3-1	Frolov, Tukiainen, Alliku
18/04	h	Pärnu	W 3-1	Ainsalu, Sappinen, Frolov
25/04	a	Paide	W 2-0	Tukiainen, Alliku
02/05	h	Levadia	L 0-1	
09/05	a	Levadia	D 1-1	Vihmann
16/05	h	Paide	W 2-1	Jürgenson (p), Sappinen
22/05	a	Pärnu	W 2-1	Jürgenson 2 (1p)
26/05	h	Tammeka	W 7-0	Gussev 2, Kase, Frolov 2, Õunap, Sappinen
02/06	a	Kalju	L 0-2	
05/06	h	Trans	L 0-1	
27/06	a	Sillamäe	W 2-1	Logua, Alliku
05/07	h	Infonet	W 1-0	Kams
13/07	h	Tulevik	W 4-0	Sappinen 2, Alliku, Prosa
20/07	h	Paide	W 1-0	Kams
27/07	a	Levadia	D 1-1	og (Kruglov)
31/07	h	Infonet	D 0-0	
03/08	a	Sillamäe	W 1-0	Gussev
08/08	h	Trans	L 2-3	Frolov, Prosa
14/08	a	Pärnu	W 5-1	Prosa 2, Jürgenson, Saliste, Sappinen
17/08	h	Tulevik	W 4-1	Saliste 2, Frolov, Ainsalu
21/08	a	Tammeka	W 4-1	Jürgenson (p), Prosa, Saliste, Sappinen
29/08	h	Kalju	W 1-0	Jürgenson (p)
12/09	h	Sillamäe	W 3-1	Baranov, og (Cheminava), Tamm
15/09	a	Kalju	W 2-0	Prosa, Saliste
18/09	a	Tammeka	W 2-1	Gussev, Kams
26/09	a	Tulevik	W 1-0	Sappinen
02/10	h	Pärnu	W 4-0	Sappinen 2, Frolov, Kams
17/10	a	Trans	W 3-1	Sappinen 2, Jürgenson
24/10	a	Infonet	W 1-0	Saliste
31/10	a	Levadia	W 2-0	Jürgenson (p), Lepistu
07/11	a	Paide	L 1-2	Sappinen

Name	Nat	DoB	Pos	Aps	(s)	Gls
Mihkel Ainsalu		08/03/96	M	5	(9)	2
Richard Aland		15/03/94	G	1		
Rauno Alliku		02/03/90	A	16	(5)	4
Kevin Aloe		07/05/95	D	7	(7)	
Nikita Baranov		19/08/92	D	30	(1)	1
Zakaria Beglarishvili	GEO	30/04/90	M	24	(7)	
Andre Frolov		18/04/88	M	21	(10)	7
Maksim Gussev		20/07/94	A	23	(10)	4
Enar Jääger		18/11/84	D	16		
Markus Jürgenson		09/09/87	D	31	(1)	8
Gert Kams		25/05/85	D	34	(1)	4
Magnus Karofeld		20/08/96	G	2	(1)	
Martin Kase		02/09/93	A	3	(1)	1
Jan Kokla		29/05/97	M	9		
Brent Lepistu		26/03/93	M	2	(5)	1
Irakli Logua	RUS	29/07/91	M	14	(5)	3
Karl-Eerik Luigend		15/01/93	M	13	(1)	
Janar Õunap		09/09/94	D	6		1
Tõnu Paavo		14/10/96	M	1		
Albert Prosa		01/10/90	A	8	(5)	6
Herol Riiberg		14/04/97	M	1	(3)	
Joseph Saliste		10/04/95	M	20	(8)	6
Rauno Sappinen		23/01/96	M	30	(2)	16
Juhan Jograf Siim		22/04/96	A		(1)	
German Šlein		28/03/96	M	14	(5)	
Joonas Tamm		02/02/92	D	6	(12)	1
Mait Toom		07/05/90	G	33		
Sakari Tukiainen	FIN	02/10/91	A	6	(8)	4
Madis Vihmann		05/10/95	D	20		1

ESTONIA

FC Infonet Tallinn

2002 • Lasnamäe KJH (500); Sportland Arena (540) • fcinfonet.ee
Coach: Aleksandr Puštov

2015

06/03	a	Levadia	D	0-0
13/03	h	Flora	L	0-2
20/03	a	Trans	D	0-0
04/04	h	Tammeka	D	2-2 Melts, Hajdari
11/04	a	Paide	W	4-2 Harin, Mashichev, Jevdokimov, Melts
14/04	h	Tulevik	W	2-0 Jevdokimov, Malov
17/04	h	Sillamäe	W	1-0 Malov
25/04	a	Kalju	L	0-1
30/04	a	Pärnu	W	2-0 Kozlovs, Volodin
08/05	a	Pärnu	W	2-0 Hajdari 2
16/05	h	Kalju	W	1-0 Kalimullin
23/05	a	Sillamäe	D	0-0
26/05	a	Tulevik	D	0-0
02/06	h	Paide	L	2-3 Harin, Melts (p)
05/06	a	Tammeka	W	2-1 Harin 2
26/06	h	Trans	W	3-0 Malov, Hajdari, Harin
05/07	a	Flora	L	0-1
10/07	a	Levadia	L	1-2 Dmitrijev
18/07	h	Levadia	D	2-2 Hajdari, Kozlovs
24/07	a	Trans	W	3-0 Kozlovs, og (Kilikevych), Harin
31/07	a	Flora	D	0-0
04/08	a	Paide	W	2-0 Kozlovs, Malov
07/08	h	Pärnu	W	1-1 Hajdari
14/08	a	Tulevik	W	1-0 Harin
18/08	h	Tammeka	W	4-2 Kozlovs 4
21/08	h	Kalju	D	2-2 Kozlovs, Elhi
29/08	a	Sillamäe	L	0-1
12/09	a	Paide	W	1-0 Tumasyan
15/09	h	Sillamäe	W	3-1 Mashichev, Harin, Kozlovs
19/09	a	Kalju	D	1-1 Avilov
25/09	a	Tammeka	D	1-1 og (Lorenz)
01/10	h	Tulevik	W	2-1 Mashichev, Tumasyan
17/10	a	Pärnu	W	4-0 Kozlovs 2, og (Tutk), Harin
24/10	h	Flora	L	0-1
30/10	a	Trans	W	1-0 Ivanov
07/11	a	Levadia	L	0-5

Name	Nat	DoB	Pos	Aps	(s)	Gls
Kassim Aidara	FRA	12/05/87	M	21	(3)	
Vadim Aksjonov		20/11/96	M		(1)	
Vladimir Avilov		10/03/95	D	25	(4)	1
Aleksandr Dmitrijev		18/02/82	M	33		1
Pavel Dõmov		31/12/93	M		(3)	
Trevor Elhi		11/04/93	D	33	(1)	1
Eduard Golovljov		25/01/97	A	1	(11)	
Jevgeni Gurtšioglujants		03/04/86	M	1	(3)	
Ermal Hajdari	SWE	04/12/92	A	14	(12)	6
Evgeni Harin	RUS	11/06/95	M	25	(5)	9
Matvei Igonen		02/10/96	G	7		
Vladislav Ivanov	RUS	24/01/86	A	6	(6)	1
Juri Jevdokimov		03/06/88	A	2	(4)	2
Andrei Kalimullin		06/10/77	D	34		1
Vladislavs Kozlovs	LVA	30/11/87	A	26	(1)	12
Aleksandr Kulinitš		24/05/92	D	8	(6)	
Mihhail Lavrentjev		22/02/90	G	29		
Deniss Malov		08/06/80	D	12	(14)	4
Nikolai Mashichev	RUS	05/12/88	M	31	(1)	3
Tanel Melts		20/11/88	M	30	(3)	3
Vladislav Ogorodnik		18/03/95	M	1	(11)	
Aleksandr Semakhin	RUS	10/01/95	D	16	(3)	
Sergei Tumasyan	RUS	31/01/90	M	10	(5)	2
Aleksandr Volodin		29/03/88	D	31		1

FC Levadia Tallinn

1998 • Kadriorg (5,000); Sportland Arena (540) • fclevadia.ee
Major honours
Estonian League (9) 1999, 2000, 2004, 2006, 2007, 2008, 2009, 2013, 2014; Estonian Cup (8) 1999, 2000, 2004, 2005, 2007, 2010, 2012, 2014
Coach: Marko Kristal

2015

06/03	h	Infonet	D	0-0
14/03	h	Trans	D	1-1 Luts
21/03	a	Tammeka	W	2-1 Antonov, Raudsepp
03/04	h	Paide	W	2-1 Teever 2
10/04	h	Tulevik	W	2-0 Teever, Rättel
13/04	a	Sillamäe	D	3-3 Kruglov 2, Teever
18/04	h	Kalju	L	0-2
25/04	a	Pärnu	D	2-2 Teever, Rättel
02/05	a	Flora	W	1-0 Teever
09/05	h	Flora	D	1-1 Teever
16/05	h	Pärnu	W	3-0 Teever 2, Rakhmanov
23/05	a	Kalju	W	2-1 Kruglov (p), Teever
26/05	h	Sillamäe	W	2-0 Rakhmanov, Laitinen
01/06	h	Tulevik	W	2-0 Luts, Saag
05/06	a	Paide	W	5-1 Teever 2, Pikk, Luts, Kruglov
26/06	a	Tammeka	W	3-2 Teever, Marin, Luts
05/07	a	Trans	W	3-1 Saag 3
10/07	a	Infonet	W	2-1 Luts 2
18/07	a	Infonet	D	2-2 Peetson, Luts
27/07	a	Flora	D	1-1 Rakhmanov
01/08	a	Pärnu	W	5-0 Subbotin 2, Kink 2, Marin
04/08	a	Trans	W	1-0 Teever
08/08	a	Tulevik	W	4-0 Teever 2, Kink, Rakhmanov
15/08	a	Tammeka	W	6-1 Teever, El Hussieny 2, Subbotin 2, Kink
18/08	a	Kalju	D	0-0
22/08	h	Sillamäe	W	2-1 Teever, Rakhmanov
28/08	a	Paide	W	4-2 Teever 3, Kink
12/09	h	Trans	L	0-1
15/09	h	Paide	W	5-1 Luts 2, Antonov, Subbotin 2
19/09	a	Sillamäe	D	2-2 Rähn, Luts
26/09	h	Kalju	L	1-2 Antonov
03/10	h	Tammeka	W	1-0 Mutso
17/10	a	Tulevik	W	3-0 Teever 2, Saag
24/10	h	Pärnu	D	0-0
31/10	h	Flora	L	0-2
07/11	h	Infonet	W	5-0 Teever, Luts, Marin, Kruglov, Peetson

Name	Nat	DoB	Pos	Aps	(s)	Gls
Ilja Antonov		05/12/92	M	18	(1)	3
Artjom Artjunin		24/01/90	D	13		
Omar El Hussieny	EGY	03/11/85	M	33	(2)	2
Tarmo Kink		06/10/85	A	12	(7)	5
Dmitri Kruglov		24/05/84	D	30	(1)	5
Juuso Laitinen	FIN	09/01/90	D	27	(2)	1
Maksim Lipin		17/03/92	M	4	(1)	
Siim Luts		12/03/89	M	26	(2)	11
Pavel Marin		14/06/95	M	10	(9)	3
Kaspar Mutso		01/08/98	M	7	(1)	1
Hindrek Ojamaa		12/06/95	D	8	(8)	
Sergei Pareiko		31/01/77	G	31		
Ivan Pecha	SVK	23/01/86	D	12	(1)	
Rasmus Peetson		03/05/95	M	22	(4)	2
Artur Pikk		05/03/93	D	29		1
Priit Pikker		15/03/86	G	4	(2)	
Taavi Rähn		16/05/81	D	19	(4)	1
Artem Rakhmanov	BLR	10/07/90	D	30	(1)	5
Artur Rättel		08/02/93	A	2	(8)	2
Andreas Raudsepp		13/12/93	M	4	(4)	1
Henry Rohtla		22/11/91	M	1	(1)	
Mark Oliver Roosnupp		12/05/97	M	2		
Kaimar Saag		05/08/88	A	8	(20)	5
Aleksei Shirokov	RUS	06/04/89	G	1		
Igor Subbotin		26/06/90	M	12	(7)	6
Ingemar Teever		24/02/83	A	33	(2)	24

JK Narva Trans

1979 • Kreenholm (1,080); Fama Kalev (1,200) • fctrans.ee
Major honours
Estonian Cup (1) 2001
Coach: Aleksei Yagudin (RUS); (20/05/15) (Nikolai Toštšev); (06/07/15) Adyam Kuzyaev (RUS)

2015

07/03	h	Pärnu	W	5-2 Andreev, Zijs 2, Škinjov, Kilikevych
14/03	a	Levadia	D	1-1 Zijs
20/03	h	Infonet	D	0-0
04/04	h	Flora	L	0-1
11/04	a	Tammeka	L	1-3 Nesterovski (p)
14/04	h	Paide	D	0-0
18/04	a	Tulevik	D	1-1 Kilikevych
25/04	h	Sillamäe	L	1-2 Kilikevych
02/05	a	Kalju	L	1-4 Andreev
08/05	h	Kalju	W	2-0 Barkov, Smirnov
15/05	a	Sillamäe	L	0-1
22/05	h	Tulevik	W	2-0 Barkov, Zijs
25/05	a	Paide	L	0-1
02/06	a	Tammeka	W	6-0 Nesterovski, Barkov (p), Avdeev, Zijs 3
05/06	a	Flora	W	1-0 Zijs
26/06	a	Infonet	L	0-3
05/07	a	Levadia	L	1-3 Jahhimovitš
11/07	a	Pärnu	W	1-0 Tamberg
17/07	h	Tammeka	W	4-2 Tamberg, Jakovlev, Zijs, Nesterovski
24/07	a	Infonet	L	0-3
31/07	a	Kalju	L	0-2
04/08	a	Levadia	L	0-1
08/08	a	Flora	W	3-2 Lipin, Tamberg, Zijs
15/08	a	Sillamäe	D	0-0
18/08	h	Pärnu	D	2-2 Sinyavskiy, Nesterovski (p)
22/08	h	Paide	W	2-0 Nesterovski (p), Škinjov
28/08	a	Tulevik	W	3-2 Zijs, Jahhimovitš, Škinjov
12/09	a	Levadia	W	1-0 Barkov
15/09	h	Tulevik	W	2-0 Sinyavskiy, og (Ilves)
19/09	a	Paide	W	2-1 Barkov, Nesterovski (p)
26/09	h	Pärnu	W	5-0 Nesterov, Barkov, Zijs, Mihhailov, Smirnov
03/10	a	Sillamäe	L	0-2
17/10	h	Flora	L	1-3 Zijs
24/10	a	Kalju	D	1-1 Barkov
30/10	h	Infonet	L	0-1
07/11	a	Tammeka	L	1-2 Barkov

Name	Nat	DoB	Pos	Aps	(s)	Gls
Vitali Andreev	RUS	22/02/86	M	9		2
Georgi Arkania	RUS	16/04/93	A	1	(5)	
Pavel Avdeev	RUS	26/09/90	D	25	(1)	1
Dmitri Barkov	RUS	19/06/92	A	24		8
Vladislav Fjodorov		31/07/92	D	9	(5)	
Akès Goore	CIV	31/12/84	D	1		
Bi Sehi Elysée Irié	CIV	13/09/89	M	1	(1)	
Aleksei Jahhimovitš		30/03/90	D	26	(1)	2
Svjatoslav Jakovlev		24/04/96	M	12	(3)	1
Andrei Jõgi		02/10/82	M	14	(12)	
Marek Kaljumäe		18/02/91	M	34	(1)	
Volodymyr Kilikevych	UKR	30/11/83	M	31	(1)	3
Deniss Kulikov		25/09/93	M		(1)	
Maksim Lipin		17/03/92	M	4	(1)	1
German-Guri Lvov		16/01/96	M	2	(9)	
Aleksei Matrossov		06/04/91	G	8	(2)	
Vadim Mihhailov		06/06/98	M	2	(12)	1
Kirill Nesterov	RUS	21/07/89	M	16		1
Roman Nesterovski		09/06/89	D	33		6
Roman Protasov	RUS	10/03/87	M	9	(5)	
Nikita Savenkov		28/07/98	D	1		
Vlasiy Sinyavskiy		27/11/96	M	14	(5)	2
Artjom Škinjov		30/01/96	A	23	(6)	3
Dmitri Smirnov		10/09/89	D	9	(13)	2
Roman Smishko	UKR	18/03/83	G	28		
Tanel Tamberg		06/06/92	D	26		3
Vitālijs Zijs	LVA	19/08/87	A	34		13

Nõmme Kalju FC

1923 • Hiiu (700) • jkkalju.ee

Major honours
Estonian League (1) 2012; Estonian Cup (1) 2015

Coach: Sergei Terehhov;
(12/09/15) Getúlio Fredo (BRA)

2015

07/03	h Tammeka	W	3-0	*Voskoboinikov, Kimbaloula, Neemelo*
14/03	a Paide	W	3-0	*Kimbaloula, Voskoboinikov, Neemelo*
21/03	h Tulevik	W	6-2	*Kimbaloula, Kallaste 2, Purje, Wakui 2 (1p)*
04/04	a Sillamäe	W	3-2	*Dmitrijev, Listmann, Purje*
11/04	a Flora	W	2-0	*Kimbaloula, Bärengrub*
14/04	h Pärnu	W	1-0	*Purje (p)*
18/04	a Levadia	W	2-0	*Lindpere, Neemelo*
25/04	h Infonet	W	1-0	*Wakui*
02/05	h Trans	W	4-1	*Kimbaloula, Wakui (p), Lindpere, Neemelo*
08/05	a Trans	L	0-2	
16/05	a Infonet	L	0-1	
23/05	h Levadia	L	1-2	*Wakui*
26/05	a Pärnu	W	3-0	*Kimbaloula, Järva, Jorge Rodrigues*
02/06	h Flora	W	2-0	*Purje, Neemelo*
06/06	h Sillamäe	L	0-2	
26/06	a Tulevik	L	0-1	
06/07	h Paide	W	2-1	*Voskoboinikov, Mbu Alidor*
13/07	a Tammeka	W	2-1	*Mööl, og (Anderson)*
20/07	h Tulevik	W	4-0	*Purje 3, Dmitrijev*
27/07	a Tammeka	W	3-0	*Neemelo, Purje 2*
31/07	a Trans	W	2-0	*Wakui (p), Purje*
04/08	h Pärnu	W	4-3	*Purje, Voskoboinikov, Kallaste, Neemelo*
07/08	h Sillamäe	W	2-1	*Wakui, Purje*
14/08	a Paide	L	4-5	*Purje, Wakui 2 (2p), Voskoboinikov*
18/08	h Levadia	D	0-0	
21/08	a Infonet	D	2-2	*Puri, Wakui (p)*
29/08	a Flora	L	0-1	
11/09	a Pärnu	L	1-2	*Bärengrub*
15/09	h Flora	L	0-2	
19/09	h Infonet	D	1-1	*Purje*
26/09	a Levadia	W	2-1	*Wakui (p), Neemelo*
03/10	h Paide	W	1-0	*Järva*
17/10	a Sillamäe	W	4-0	*Neemelo 2, Lindpere 2 (1p)*
24/10	h Trans	D	1-1	*Bärengrub*
01/11	h Tammeka	W	1-0	*Purje*
07/11	h Tulevik	D	2-2	*Purje (p), Neemelo*

Name	Nat	DoB	Pos	Aps	(s)	Gls
Alo Bärengrub		12/02/84	D	27	(1)	3
Artjom Dmitrijev		14/11/88	M	23	(3)	2
Nicolas Galpin	FRA	27/02/93	D	6		
Stanislav Goldberg		30/10/92	M	1	(4)	
Andre Järva		21/11/96	A	8	(12)	2
Jorge Rodrigues	POR	19/03/82	D	28		1
Erkki Junolainen		05/01/92	M	4	(2)	
Sören Kaldma		03/07/96	M	5	(1)	
Ken Kallaste		31/08/88	D	33	(2)	3
Allan Kimbaloula	CGO	01/01/92	M	18	(2)	6
Peeter Klein		28/01/97	A		(1)	
Joel Lindpere		05/10/81	M	25	(3)	4
Erik Listmann		09/02/95	M	21	(4)	1
Reginald Mbu Alidor	FRA	15/05/93	M	19	(8)	1
Karl Mööl		04/03/92	D	32		1
Tarmo Neemelo		10/02/82	A	10	(22)	11
Henrik Pürg		03/06/96	D	15	(5)	
Eino Puri		07/05/88	M	21	(10)	1
Ats Purje		03/08/85	M	24	(9)	16
Vitali Teleš		17/10/83	G	36		
Borislav Topić	SRB	22/05/84	D	8	(2)	
Vladimir Voskoboinikov		02/02/83	A	8	(4)	5
Hidetoshi Wakui	JPN	12/02/83	M	24	(4)	11

Paide Linnameeskond

1999 • Paide linnastaadion (450); Paide kunstmurustaadion (200) • paidelinnameeskond.ee

Coach: Meelis Rooba

2015

07/03	a Sillamäe	L	1-4	*Rõivassepp*
14/03	h Kalju	L	0-3	
21/03	a Pärnu	D	2-2	*Uwaegbulam, Zahovaiko*
03/04	a Levadia	L	1-2	*Zahovaiko*
11/04	h Infonet	L	2-4	*Zahovaiko 2*
14/04	a Trans	D	0-0	
18/04	a Tammeka	L	2-3	*Zahovaiko 2*
25/04	h Flora	L	0-2	
02/05	h Tulevik	L	0-3	
09/05	a Tulevik	L	0-2	
16/05	a Flora	L	1-2	*og (Luigend)*
22/05	a Tammeka	L	2-3	*Zahovaiko, Välja*
25/05	h Trans	W	1-0	*Sinilaid*
02/06	h Infonet	W	3-2	*Sillaste, Uwaegbulam, Veis*
05/06	h Levadia	L	1-5	*Rõivassepp*
27/06	h Pärnu	W	4-1	*Sillaste, Zahovaiko, Varendi, Uwaegbulam*
06/07	a Kalju	L	1-2	*Sillaste*
13/07	h Sillamäe	D	1-1	*Uwaegbulam*
20/07	a Flora	L	0-1	
25/07	a Pärnu	D	3-3	*Sillaste, Varendi, Rättel*
01/08	h Tulevik	W	4-1	*Varendi, Rättel, Uwaegbulam 2*
04/08	h Infonet	L	0-2	
08/08	a Tammeka	D	1-1	*Zahovaiko*
14/08	h Kalju	W	5-4	*Rättel, Uwaegbulam, Sinilaid, Varendi, Zahovaiko*
18/08	a Sillamäe	L	0-1	
22/08	a Trans	L	0-2	
28/08	h Levadia	L	2-4	*Varendi 2*
12/09	a Infonet	L	0-1	
15/09	a Levadia	L	1-5	*Zahovaiko*
19/09	h Trans	L	1-2	*Rättel (p)*
26/09	h Sillamäe	D	1-1	*Rättel*
03/10	a Kalju	L	0-1	
18/10	h Tammeka	W	4-0	*Zahovaiko 3 (2p), Varendi*
24/10	a Tulevik	W	3-2	*Zahovaiko 3*
31/10	a Pärnu	W	1-0	*Tomson*
07/11	h Flora	W	2-1	*Sillaste, Varendi*

Name	Nat	DoB	Pos	Aps	(s)	Gls
Marion Adusoo		13/10/84	M		(2)	
Edgars Butlers		27/08/94	D		(1)	
Hans-Kristjan Hansberg		06/05/96	D	8	(4)	
Joel Indermitte		27/12/92	D		(1)	
Joosep Juha		05/09/96	D	14	(2)	
Kaspar Kaldoja		01/01/90	D	2	(1)	
Viktor Klimeev	RUS	16/01/90	D	6	(1)	
Kennet Kukk		08/10/97	M		(4)	
Liivo Leetma		20/01/77	D	15	(12)	
Michael Lilander		10/06/97	D	26	(2)	
Timo Lomp		26/07/88	D	9	(4)	
Karl-Eerik Luigend		15/01/93	M	15		
Andre Mägi		14/01/88	D	13		
Mart-Mattis Niinepuu		23/07/92	G	36		
Märten Pajunurm		29/04/93	D	7		
Kaspar Paur		16/02/95	M	14	(3)	
Meelis Peitre		27/03/90	M	19	(4)	
Rene Puhke		16/08/94	D	1	(3)	
Artur Rättel		08/02/93	A	16	(1)	5
Sander Rõivassepp		23/08/90	A	11	(10)	2
Ats Sillaste		08/04/88	D	23	(8)	5
Sander Sinilaid		07/10/90	M	30		2
Rasmus Tomson		13/08/85	M	8	(16)	1
Martin Ustaal		09/09/96	M	33	(1)	
Jasper Uwaegbulam	NGA	12/12/94	A	29		7
Lauri Välja		25/05/95	M	7	(2)	1
Lauri Varendi		29/12/88	M	29	(1)	8
Aleksandr Vassiljev		24/06/88	A		(2)	
Andrei Veis		06/04/90	D	3	(3)	1
Vjatšeslav Zahovaiko		29/12/81	A	22	(5)	17

Pärnu Linnameeskond

2011 • Raeküla (450); Pärnu kunstmurustaadion (200) • no website

Coach: Marko Lelov

2015

07/03	a Trans	L	2-5	*Hanson, Laurits*
14/03	h Tammeka	W	4-2	*Saarts, Laurits 3*
21/03	h Paide	D	2-2	*Kirss, Tutk*
04/04	a Tulevik	L	2-5	*Issakov, Tutk*
10/04	h Sillamäe	L	1-6	*Kirss*
14/04	a Kalju	L	0-1	
18/04	a Flora	L	1-3	*Hanson*
25/04	h Levadia	D	2-2	*Kirss, Könninge*
30/04	h Infonet	L	0-2	
08/05	a Infonet	L	0-2	
16/05	a Levadia	L	0-3	
22/05	h Flora	L	1-2	*Kirss*
26/05	h Kalju	L	0-3	
02/06	a Sillamäe	D	0-0	
06/06	h Tulevik	W	2-1	*Kirss (p), Hanson*
27/06	a Paide	L	1-4	*Lauter*
04/07	a Tammeka	L	0-1	
11/07	h Trans	L	0-1	
20/07	a Sillamäe	D	3-3	*Vunk (p), Palatu, Kirss*
25/07	a Paide	D	3-3	*Laurits 2, Palatu*
01/08	h Levadia	L	0-5	
04/08	a Kalju	L	3-4	*Lauter 2, Laurits (p)*
07/08	a Infonet	D	1-1	*Laurits*
14/08	h Flora	L	1-5	*Laurits*
18/08	h Trans	D	2-2	*Tutk, Vunk (p)*
22/08	a Tulevik	W	2-1	*Laurits 2*
28/08	h Tammeka	L	0-1	
11/09	h Kalju	W	2-1	*Lenk, Issakov*
14/09	a Tammeka	W	1-0	*Lenk*
18/09	h Tulevik	W	1-0	*Vunk*
26/09	a Trans	L	0-5	
02/10	a Flora	L	0-4	
17/10	h Infonet	L	0-4	
24/10	a Levadia	D	0-0	
31/10	h Paide	L	0-1	
07/11	h Sillamäe	L	1-2	*Pärnat*

Name	Nat	DoB	Pos	Aps	(s)	Gls
Hevar Aas		27/10/92	D	5	(6)	
Chris Anderson		05/10/92	M	14	(1)	
Henri Hanson		18/04/95	M	31	(3)	3
Anton Issakov		26/09/94	M	15	(10)	2
Kaarel Kaarlimäe		13/10/91	M	13	(7)	
Jako Kanter		09/01/98	D		(1)	
Robert Kirss		03/09/94	A	32	(2)	6
Greger Könninge		23/01/91	M	20	(6)	1
Taavi Laurits		23/01/90	A	4	(24)	11
Envar Lauter		05/09/90	M	18	(5)	3
Kristian Lenk		20/05/97	A	8	(3)	2
Siim Mäeots		19/08/95	D	15	(1)	
Ander Paabut		28/09/90	M	4	(2)	
Karl Palatu		05/12/82	D	31		2
Risto Pärnat		11/10/92	M	11	(5)	1
Toomas Pent		28/09/90	M	6	(16)	
Ronek Saal		24/09/88	D	7		
Kristen Saarts		28/10/94	A	29	(3)	1
Joosep Sarapuu		30/07/94	D	31	(1)	
Kristjan Tamme		21/09/95	G	20		
Rauno Tutk		10/04/88	D	34		3
Joel Vabrit		09/09/87	G	14		
Hendrik Vainu		03/04/96	G	2		
Ivan Velikopolje		22/04/89	M		(1)	
Magnus Villota		11/02/98	D	21	(3)	
Martin Vunk		21/08/84	M	11	(4)	3

 **ESTONIA**

JK Sillamäe Kalev

1951 • Kalev (1,000); Sillamäe
kunstmurustaadion (490) • fcsillamae.ee
**Coach: Sergei Frantsev (RUS);
(28/05/15) Denis Ugarov (RUS)**

2015

07/03	h Paide	W	4-1	og (Mägi), Dubõkin, Kvasov 2
14/03	a Tulevik	W	2-0	og (Ilves), Sidorenkov (p)
21/03	a Flora	L	0-1	
04/04	h Kalju	L	2-3	Sidorenkov (p), Ratnikov
10/04	a Pärnu	W	6-1	Kvasov 3 (1p), og (Palatu), Ratnikov, Toomet
13/04	h Levadia	D	3-3	Sidorenkov 2 (2p), Ratnikov
17/04	a Infonet	L	0-1	
25/04	a Trans	W	2-1	Kvasov, Dubõkin
01/05	h Tammeka	W	4-0	Ratnikov 2, Kvasov, Silich
08/05	a Tammeka	W	5-0	Tjapkin, Kvasov 3, Sidorenkov (p)
15/05	h Trans	W	1-0	Ratnikov
23/05	h Infonet	D	0-0	
26/05	a Levadia	L	0-2	
02/06	h Pärnu	D	0-0	
06/06	a Kalju	W	2-0	Kvasov, Silich
27/06	h Flora	L	1-2	Dudarev
06/07	h Tulevik	W	2-1	Volkov, Silich
13/07	h Paide	D	1-1	Kvasov
20/07	h Pärnu	D	3-3	Ratnikov, Dudarev, Kvasov
27/07	a Tulevik	W	2-1	Vnukov, Volkov
31/07	h Tammeka	W	4-1	Volkov, Kvasov 2, Toomet
03/08	h Flora	L	0-1	
07/08	h Kalju	L	1-2	Cheminava
15/08	h Trans	D	0-0	
18/08	h Paide	W	1-0	Ratnikov
22/08	a Levadia	L	1-2	Sidorenkov (p)
29/08	h Infonet	W	1-0	Cheminava
12/09	a Flora	L	1-3	Cheminava
15/09	a Infonet	L	1-3	Cheminava
19/09	h Levadia	D	2-2	Silich, Ratnikov
26/09	a Paide	D	1-1	og (Juha)
03/10	h Trans	W	2-0	Kvasov 2 (1p)
17/10	h Kalju	L	0-4	
23/10	a Tammeka	W	4-1	Silich 2, Tjapkin, Sidorenkov (p)
01/11	h Tulevik	W	2-1	Kvasov 2
07/11	a Pärnu	W	2-1	Kabaev, Ratnikov

Name	Nat	DoB	Pos	Aps	(s)	Gls
Pavel Aleksejev		24/02/91	D	1	(2)	
Mindaugas Bagužis	LTU	10/04/83	D	7	(1)	
Igor Cheminava	RUS	23/03/91	D	31		4
Aleksei Cherkasov	RUS	01/09/94	D	2	(2)	
Marius Činikas	LTU	17/05/86	D	25	(4)	
Artjom Davõdov		04/03/99	D		(1)	
Aleksandr Dubõkin		06/05/83	M	13	(1)	2
Igor Dudarev	RUS	12/08/93	D	25	(2)	2
Aleksandr Ivanjušin		07/09/95	M	11	(8)	
Evgeni Kabaev	RUS	28/02/88	A	1	(1)	1
Yaroslav Kvasov	UKR	05/03/92	A	31	(2)	19
Rytis Leliuga	LTU	04/01/87	M	2	(1)	
Artem Levizi	RUS	02/03/93	G	2		
Darius Miceika	LTU	22/02/83	M	5		
Kirill Novikov		08/12/89	M	3	(11)	
Viktor Plotnikov		14/07/89	M	2	(10)	
Daniil Ratnikov		10/02/88	M	27	(5)	10
Giorgio Russo	ITA	03/02/89	M	13	(3)	
Andrei Sidorenkov		12/02/84	D	29		7
Kyrylo Silich	UKR	03/08/90	M	21	(2)	6
Tihhon Šišov		11/02/83	D	11	(5)	
Mihhail Starodubtsev		14/08/82	G	33		
Deniss Tjapkin		30/01/91	M	34	(1)	2
Janar Toomet		10/08/89	M	27	(8)	2
Eduard Usikov		06/12/89	G	1		
Denis Vnukov		01/11/91	M	21	(10)	1
Aleksandr Volkov		11/10/94	A	18	(6)	3

JK Tammeka Tartu

1989 • Tamme (1,645) • jktammeka.ee
Coach: Indrek Koser

2015

07/03	a Kalju	L	0-3	
14/03	a Pärnu	L	2-4	Tiirik (p), Hurt
21/03	a Levadia	L	1-2	Hurt
04/04	a Infonet	D	2-2	Tekko (p), Tamm
11/04	h Trans	W	3-1	Hurt 2, Tiirik
14/04	h Flora	L	1-3	Suurpere
18/04	a Paide	W	3-2	Suurpere, Tekko (p), Rääbis
24/04	h Tulevik	D	1-1	Suurpere
01/05	a Sillamäe	L	0-4	
08/05	h Sillamäe	L	0-5	
15/05	a Tulevik	L	1-3	Šabanov
22/05	h Paide	W	3-2	og (Mägi), Tiirik, Rääbis
26/05	a Flora	L	0-7	
02/06	a Trans	L	0-6	
05/06	h Infonet	L	1-2	Kiidron
26/06	h Levadia	L	2-3	Tauts, Hurt
04/07	h Pärnu	W	1-0	Tauts
13/07	h Kalju	L	1-2	Tiirik
17/07	a Trans	L	2-4	Tiirik, Rääbis
27/07	a Kalju	L	0-3	
31/07	a Sillamäe	L	1-4	Koskor
08/08	h Paide	D	1-1	Rääbis
15/08	h Levadia	L	1-6	Tiirik
18/08	a Infonet	L	2-4	Tiirik, Rääbis
21/08	h Flora	L	1-4	Hurt
28/08	a Pärnu	W	1-0	Rääbis
31/08	h Tulevik	W	1-0	Hurt
11/09	a Tulevik	L	2-3	Laabus, Tiirik
14/09	h Pärnu	L	0-1	
18/09	a Flora	L	1-2	Koskor
25/09	h Infonet	D	1-1	Lorenz
03/10	a Levadia	L	0-1	
18/10	a Paide	L	0-4	
23/10	h Sillamäe	L	1-4	Tiirik
01/11	a Kalju	L	0-1	
07/11	h Trans	W	2-1	Kiidron, Tiirik

Name	Nat	DoB	Pos	Aps	(s)	Gls
Kevin Anderson		10/11/93	D	20	(2)	
Ergo Eessaar		31/10/90	M		(2)	
Martin Hurt		27/06/84	A	26	(1)	7
Markus Jõgi		30/09/96	M	4	(4)	
Martin Jõgi		05/01/95	D	15	(5)	
Kaarel Kiidron		30/04/90	D	14	(1)	2
Johannes Theodor Kollist		13/06/97	M		(1)	
Tristan Koskor		28/11/95	M	12	(14)	2
Karli Kütt		17/02/93	G	27	(1)	
Reio Laabus		14/03/90	M	14	(1)	1
Jürgen Lorenz		11/05/93	D	33	(1)	1
Martin Miller		25/09/97	M	19	(5)	
Kristjan Moks		21/12/91	A		(4)	
Erki Mõttus		15/01/97	M		(1)	
Martin Naggel		22/05/90	D	20	(3)	
Temari Nuuma		09/04/96	M	2	(5)	
Andre Paju		05/01/95	D	30	(2)	
Eric Pärn		20/08/96	M		(1)	
Karl Johan Pechter		02/03/96	G	9	(1)	
Kevin Rääbis		02/01/94	A	20	(9)	6
Valeri Šabanov		19/04/95	D	1	(5)	1
Janno Saks		10/07/91	M	2	(4)	
Geir-Kristjan Suurpere		26/02/95	M	12	(8)	3
Heiko Tamm		18/03/87	M	8	(2)	1
Rasmus Tauts		07/01/97	M	26	(3)	2
Tauno Tekko		14/12/94	M	31		2
Siim Tenno		04/08/90	M	17		
Kristjan Tiirik		25/08/82	M	34		10
Marek Tšernjavski		15/05/92	A		(4)	

JK Tulevik Viljandi

1912 • Viljandi (1,084); Viljandi
kunstmurustaadion (250) •
jktulevik.ee
Coach: Aivar Lillevere

2015

07/03	a Flora	L	0-3	
14/03	h Sillamäe	L	0-2	
21/03	a Kalju	L	2-6	Ilves 2
04/04	h Pärnu	W	5-2	Post 2, Tamm, Juhkam, Maar
10/04	a Levadia	L	0-2	
14/04	a Infonet	L	0-2	
18/04	h Trans	D	1-1	Tamm (p)
24/04	a Tammeka	D	1-1	Tamm
02/05	a Paide	W	3-0	Tamm 3
09/05	h Paide	W	2-0	Tamm 2
15/05	h Tammeka	W	3-1	Post 2, Maar
22/05	a Trans	L	0-2	
26/05	h Infonet	D	0-0	
01/06	a Levadia	L	0-1	
06/06	a Pärnu	L	1-2	Tamm
26/06	h Kalju	W	1-0	Teor
06/07	a Sillamäe	L	1-2	Kübar
13/07	h Flora	L	0-4	
20/07	a Kalju	L	0-4	
27/07	a Sillamäe	L	1-2	Post
01/08	a Paide	L	1-4	Peips
08/08	h Levadia	L	0-4	
14/08	h Infonet	L	0-1	
17/08	a Flora	L	1-4	Juhkam
22/08	h Pärnu	L	1-2	Ilves
28/08	h Trans	L	2-3	Tukiainen 2 (1p)
31/08	a Tammeka	L	0-1	
11/09	h Tammeka	W	3-2	Lang, Tukiainen, Roman
15/09	a Trans	L	0-2	
18/09	a Pärnu	L	0-1	
26/09	h Flora	L	0-1	
01/10	a Infonet	L	1-2	Ilves
17/10	h Levadia	L	0-3	
24/10	h Paide	L	2-3	Tukiainen, Ilves
01/11	a Sillamäe	L	1-2	Tukiainen
07/11	h Kalju	D	2-2	Teor, Tukiainen

Name	Nat	DoB	Pos	Aps	(s)	Gls
Martin Allik		13/08/94	D	5	(4)	
Oskar Berggren		30/10/97	D	12	(1)	
Kaarel Henn		23/09/88	D	21	(1)	
Indrek Ilves		27/04/90	M	23	(3)	5
Gerdo Juhkam		19/06/94	D	31		2
Kristen Kähr		05/10/89	A	4	(2)	
Sander Kapper		08/12/94	M	20	(5)	
Martin Kase		02/09/93	A	14	(3)	
Karel Kübar		04/07/94	M	24	(2)	1
Erkki Kubber		30/04/94	M	8	(10)	
Maario Laansoo		03/05/94	D		(1)	
Tanel Lang		15/08/95	M	30	(1)	1
Sander Loigo		26/09/95	M	6	(8)	
Jaagup Luhakooder		29/07/90	M		(1)	
Rasmus Luhakooder		08/12/88	M	1	(6)	
Karl Ivar Maar		26/02/93	M	18	(6)	2
Raiko Mutle		07/07/84	M	3	(1)	
Karl-Romet Nõmm		04/01/98	G	24		
Rainer Peips		11/08/90	A	6	(19)	1
Ragnar Piir		17/10/94	D	29	(1)	
Sander Post		10/09/84	D	24	(2)	5
Martti Puolakainen		12/08/94	G	12		
Raido Roman		22/11/87	A	2	(5)	1
Siim Saar		09/07/95	D	28	(3)	
Robert Taar		24/03/94	M	6	(1)	
Joonas Tamm		02/02/92	A	15		9
Roger Teor		11/05/97	M	14	(11)	2
Sakari Tukiainen	FIN	02/10/91	A	16		6

Top goalscorers

24	Ingemar Teever (Levadia)
19	Yaroslav Kvasov (Sillamäe)
17	Vjatšeslav Zahovaiko (Paide)
16	Rauno Sappinen (Flora)
	Ats Purje (Kalju)
13	Vitālijs Ziļs (Trans)
12	Vladislavs Kozlovs (Infonet)
11	Siim Luts (Levadia)
	Tarmo Neemelo (Kalju)
	Hidetoshi Wakui (Kalju)
	Taavi Laurits (Pärnu)

Promoted club

Rakvere JK Tarvas

2004 • Rakvere (1,785); Rakvere
kunstmurustaadion (250) • jktarvas.ee
Coach: Valeri Bondarenko

Second level final table 2015

		Pld	W	D	L	F	A	Pts
1	FC Flora Tallinn II	36	22	6	8	76	40	72
2	FC Levadia Tallinn II	36	22	5	9	118	57	71
3	FC Infonet Tallinn II	36	20	6	10	108	48	66
4	Rakvere JK Tarvas	36	12	11	13	52	53	47
5	Nõmme Kalju FC II	36	14	4	18	50	56	46
6	JK Tallinna Kalev	36	13	7	16	47	59	46
7	FC Irbis Kiviõli	36	13	5	18	60	87	44
8	FC Santos Tartu	36	12	6	18	56	83	42
9	JK Vaprus Vändra	36	11	5	20	43	80	38
10	FC Kuressaare	36	10	7	19	48	95	37

NB FC Flora Tallinn II, FC Levadia Tallinn II, FC
Infonet Tallinn II and Nõmme Kalju FC II ineligible for
promotion; Rakvere JK Tarvas promoted directly; JK
Tallinna Kalev entered play-offs.

Promotion/Relegation play-offs

(18/11/15 & 21/11/15)
Tammeka 4-1 Kalev
Kalev 1-0 Tammeka
(Tammeka 4-2)

DOMESTIC CUP

Eesti Karikas 2015/16

FIRST ROUND

(08/06/15)
Kose 0-4 Tammeka
(10/06/15)
Ajax 1-4 Flora II
Castovanni Eagles 0-2 Piraaja
Elva 3-4 Tallinn CF
Harju Jalgpallikool 1-5 Infonet II
Jõgeva Wolves 1-2 Like & Share
Kuressaare 20-0 Lokomotiv
Rapla
(13/06/15)
Eestimaa Kasakad 0-14 Trans
Infonet 36-0 Virtsu
(14/06/15)
Tallinna Kalev 1-2 HÜJK
(20/06/15)
Forss 6-2 Twister
(22/06/15)
Kernu Kadakas 0-8 Levadia
(27/06/15)
Ganvix 3-1 Igiliikur
Navi 4-0 Warrior
Noorus-96 9-1 Jalgpallihaigla
TÜ Fauna 2-3 Kalju III
Tääksi 10-1 IceBears
(28/06/15)
Depoo 2-4 Tannem
Kaitseliit Kalev 12-1 Küsimärk
Lelle 1-0 Moe
Maardu United 4-3 Narva United
Olympic Olybet 2-0 Pedajamäe
Poseidon Nirvaana 3-2 Rumori
Calcio
Reliikvia 5-0 Helios Tartu
Reaal 1-2 Väätsa Vald
Roosad Pantrid 0-5 Bronx Wood
Raasiku Valla 1-7 Tõrva
Soccernet 2-1 Puhkus Mehhikos
(29/06/15)
Tulevik 2-1 Keila
(30/06/15)
Atli 2-6 Metropool
Paide 31-0 Raudteetöölised
(01/07/15)
Eston Villa 2-1 FC Tartu
Joker 3-4 Rada (aet)
(04/07/15)
Nõmme United 9-1 Kohtla-
Nõmme
RJK Märjamaa 2-1 TransferWise
Roosu 4-1 Charma
(05/07/15)
Retro7-5 Peedu
(07/07/15)
Forza w/o Laagri
(26/07/15)
Starbunker 3-0 Flora III

SECOND ROUND

(19/07/15)
Kalev III 1-0 Loo
(26/07/15)
Bronx Wood 1-3 MRJK Viimsi
Forza 7-2 Roosu
Merkuur 4-2 Rada (aet)
Väätsa Vald 3-0 Starbunker II

(28/07/15)
Fellin 1-5 EMÜ SK
(29/07/15)
Järve 0-0 Tõrva (aet; 3-4 on
pens)
Kalju III 4-1 Otepää
Lelle 0-2 Tannem
Maardu United 1-4 Infonet II
Noorus-96 1-4 Metropool
Pärnu 1-0 Haapsalu
Soccernet 4-2 Like & Share
Tallinna Jalgpalliselts 0-13 Paide
(02/08/15)
Ganvix 3-4 Nõmme United
HÜJK 6-0 Õismäe Torm
(04/08/15)
Santos 11-0 Poseidon Nirvaana
(05/08/15)
Dnipro 0-3 Welco
Järva-Jaani 1-2 Navi
Tabivere 0-0 Reliikvia (aet; 4-2
on pens)
Tammeka 5-1 Starbunker
(11/08/15)
Flora II 1-3 Flora
Infonet 8-0 Piraaja
Kalju 3-0 Tallinn CF
Levadia 14-0 Olympic Olybet
Lootos FCR 0-12 Retro
Tarvas 10-0 Ambla
Tulevik 7-0 Kaitseliit Kalev
(12/08/15)
Legion 1-5 Eston Villa
RJK Märjamaa 1-6 Sillamäe
(16/08/15)
Kuressaare 4-2 Tääksi
(25/08/15)
Trans 12-0 Forss

THIRD ROUND

(03/09/15)
Eston Villa 2-3 MRJK Viimsi
Nõmme United 8-0 Metropool
Retro 2-1 Kalju III
(04/09/15)
Santos 3-3 Kuressaare (aet; 4-2
on pens)
(06/09/15)
Navi 3-1 Tallinna Kalev III
Sillamäe 4-3 Paide
Tannem 5-0 Soccernet
Tarvas 0-4 Forza
(08/09/15)
EMÜ SK 1-1 Tõrva (aet; 2-4 on
pens)
Tabivere 4-7 Väätsa Vald
(29/09/15)
Infonet II 0-3 Pärnu
Levadia 13-1 Merkuur
Trans 1-2 Kalju (aet)
Welco 0-2 Flora
(30/09/15)
Tammeka 1-0 HÜJK
(04/10/15)
Tulevik 2-1 Infonet

FOURTH ROUND

(20/10/15)
Flora 17-0 Retro
Sillamäe 1-0 Levadia
(21/10/15)
Forza 6-2 Väätsa Vald
(27/10/15)
Tulevik 0-5 Kalju
(28/10/15)
Nõmme United 2-3 Santos
(01/11/15)
Navi 0-7 Tõrva
(08/11/15)
MRJK Viimsi 4-0 Tannem
(10/11/15)
Pärnu 1-2 Tammeka

QUARTER-FINALS

(12/04/16)
Sillamäe 1-0 Kalju (Lipin 18)
Tammeka 2-0 Tõrva
(Koskor 2, 12)
(13/04/16)
Flora 3-1 Santos (Sappinen 14,
Jürgenson 62p, Beglarishvili 90;
Aaviste 89)
Viimsi 6-1 Forza (Kane 16,
Kaljumäe 35, 64, Pajula 39,
Kesküla 77, 81; Tšigrinov 85)

NB MRJK Viimsi and HÜJK
Emmaste merged to become
Viimsi at winter break.

SEMI-FINALS

(03/05/16)
Flora 2-0 Tammeka (Jürgenson
50p, Gussev 63)
(04/05/16)
Sillamäe 2-0 Viimsi (Panov 43,
Volkov 77)

FINAL

(21/05/16)
A. Le Coq Arena, Tallinn
FC FLORA TALLINN 3
(Sappinen 102, Gussev 105+1,
Tukiainen 107)
JK SILLAMÄE KALEV 0
(aet)
Referee: Saar
FLORA: Toom, Kams, Baranov
(Vihmann 53), Tamm, Jürgenson,
Šlein, Ainsalu, Sappinen, Gussev,
Prosa (Tukiainen 84), Beglarishvili
(Alliku 108)
SILLAMÄE: Starodubtsev,
Semakhin, Malov (Panov 120),
Dudarev (Cherkasov 106),
Solovjovs, Tjapkin, Lipin,
Aidara, Savin, Kabaev, Volkov
(Davõdov 111)

FAROE ISLANDS

Fótbóltssamband Føroya (FSF)

Address	Gundadalur, PO Box 3028 FO-110 Tórshavn	**President**	Christian Andreasen
Tel	+298 351979	**General secretary**	Virgar Hvidbro
Fax	+298 319079	**Media officer**	Terji Nielsen
E-mail	fsf@football.fo	**Year of formation**	1979
Website	football.fo	**National stadium**	Tórsvøllur, Torshavn (4,132)

MEISTARADEILDIN CLUBS

 ① **AB Argir**

 ② **B36 Tórshavn**

 ③ **EB/Streymur**

 ④ **HB Tórshavn**

 ⑤ **ÍF Fuglafjørdur**

 ⑥ **KÍ Klaksvík**

 ⑦ **NSÍ Runavík**

 ⑧ **FC Suduroy**

 ⑨ **TB Tvøroyri**

 ⑩ **Víkingur**

PROMOTED CLUBS

 ⑪ **Skála ÍF**

 ⑫ **B68 Toftir**

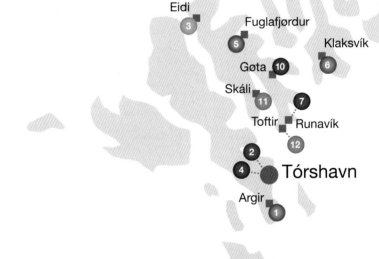

Eidi ③
Fuglafjørdur ⑤
Klaksvík ⑥
Gøta ⑩
Skáli ⑪
⑦
Toftir
Runavík
②
⑫
④
Tórshavn
Argir ①

0   20   40 km
0   20 miles

KEY
● UEFA Champions League
● UEFA Europa League
● Promoted
● Relegated

Tvøroyri ⑨

Vágur ⑧

Back-to-back titles for B36

B36 Tórshavn made club history in 2015 by successfully defending the Meistaradeildin title for the first time. They did so under a new head coach, Eydun Klakstein, but with largely the same group of players that had lifted the trophy 12 months previously.

There were encores too from NSÍ Runavík striker Klæmint Andrasson Olsen, who scored 21 goals to win the league's top scorer prize for the third year running, while Víkingur ensured that Olsen's club finished runners-up in both domestic competitions by defeating them 3-0 in the cup final to lift the trophy for the fourth successive year.

effo deildin
Meistarar 2015

| Torshavn club retain league trophy for first time | Golden boot hat-trick for Klæmint Olsen | Víkingur make it four cup wins in a row |

Domestic league

With their 2014 title-winning boss Sámal Erik Hentze having resigned at the end of that campaign, B36 brought in 42-year-old Klakstein, who had been dismissed by KÍ Klaksvík. The club also lost their star striker, Nigerian Adeshina Lawal, to ÍF Fuglafjørdur, but otherwise went with pretty much the same playing personnel. It took them a couple of games to shake off the winter cobwebs, but before long they were taking on NSÍ in what soon evolved into a private duel for the championship crown.

It actually took until round 17 before B36 ascended to the summit, but once they gained a foothold they were there to stay. Ten successive victories, including a pivotal 3-0 success at home to NSÍ in early August, catapulted them beyond the reach of their rivals and on to an 11th national title. It was after the last of those wins, 2-1 at home to TB Tvøroyri, that the club's first back-to-back triumph was confirmed, a ten-point cushion with three games to play sealing the deal.

The final winning margin was reduced to seven points, but B36 ended the campaign with the rare distinction of having scored in every game. NSÍ might have outgunned them by 73 goals to 60, but the Torshavn club's consistency of output, allied to a league-best tally of just 25 goals conceded, made them worthy champions. B36 only had one

goalscorer in double figures, Polish schemer Łukasz Cieślewicz, but 16 players found the net at least once, including veteran skipper Jákup á Borg with seven, and there were sterling defensive contributions from goalkeeper Tórdur Thomsen and centre-backs Odmar Færø and Høgni Eysturoy.

The league's top marksman, yet again, was NSÍ's ever-dependable Olsen, who struck 21 goals to become the first player to complete a hat-trick of Meistaradeildin golden boot successes outright. His club managed to hold on to second place despite losing all three games to the team one point below them, Víkingur, who, like B36, were unvanquished at home.

Record champions HB just scraped into the European places at the end of a lacklustre campaign, but there was far greater woe for EB/Streymur, the only club to have taken the championship trophy outside the capital in the previous seven years, who finished rock bottom with a paltry 11 points. Newly promoted FC Suduroy accompanied them down, while the two promotion places were taken by the clubs relegated a year earlier, Skála and B68 Toftir.

Domestic cup

Víkingur's love affair with the Faroe Islands Cup stretched to a fourth

successive year as they overcame a first-leg deficit in the semi-finals to eliminate B36 before maintaining their head-to-head superiority over NSÍ in the final at the Tórsvøllur, where a crowd of 3,367 gathered to see Sigfrídur Clementsen's men add another resounding win to the three they had handed out to Trygvi Mortensen's charges in the league (5-1, 4-2 and 3-1).

Europe

Víkingur had reached the third qualifying round of the UEFA Europa League in 2014 but there were no repeat heroics from any of the islands' representatives in 2015 as all four fell at the first hurdle.

The main curiosity of B36's UEFA Champions League tie with The New Saints was Cieślewicz's meeting with his brother Adrian, who helped the Welsh club to a 6-2 aggregate win.

National team

After the Faroe Islands' mighty double over Greece in the UEFA EURO 2016 qualifiers, the final four fixtures of the campaign were eagerly anticipated, but Lars Olsen's team were unable to provide the fans with any additional cheer, or indeed points – despite leading for almost an hour against Hungary in Budapest.

DOMESTIC SEASON AT A GLANCE

Meistaradeildin 2015 final table

		Pld	Home						Away						Total						Pts
			W	D	L	F	A	W	D	L	F	A	W	D	L	F	A		
1	B36 Tórshavn	27	9	4	0	27	9	9	3	2	33	16	18	7	2	60	25	61
2	NSÍ Runavík	27	10	3	1	45	13	6	3	4	28	24	16	6	5	73	37	54
3	Víkingur	27	10	4	0	45	17	5	4	4	23	18	15	8	4	68	35	53
4	HB Tórshavn	27	7	5	2	28	15	4	5	4	15	16	11	10	6	43	31	43
5	KÍ Klaksvík	27	9	2	2	29	14	2	6	6	21	27	11	8	8	50	41	41
6	ÍF Fuglafjørdur	27	4	5	4	26	25	1	7	6	18	31	5	12	10	44	56	27
7	TB Tvøroyri	27	2	8	3	20	21	2	6	6	16	26	4	14	9	36	47	26
8	AB Argir	27	2	5	6	12	18	2	7	5	22	24	4	12	11	34	42	24
9	FC Suduroy	27	4	2	7	22	28	2	2	10	17	40	6	4	17	39	68	22
10	EB/Streymur	27	1	5	9	15	45	1	0	11	12	47	2	5	20	27	92	11

European qualification 2016/17

 Champion: B36 Tórshavn (first qualifying round)

 Cup winner: Víkingur (first qualifying round)
NSÍ Runavík (first qualifying round)
HB Tórshavn (first qualifying round)

Top scorer   Klæmint Andrasson Olsen (NSÍ), 21 goals
Relegated clubs   EB/Streymur, FC Suduroy
Promoted clubs   Skála ÍF, B68 Toftir
Cup final   Víkingur 3-0 NSÍ Runavík

Team of the season
(3-5-2)

Coach: Klakstein (B36)

Thomsen (B36)

Eysturoy (B36)   Færø (B36)   Gregersen (Víkingur)

S Vatnhamar (Víkingur)   Cieślewicz (B36)   Samuelsen (B36)
Árni Frederiksberg (NSÍ)   Justinussen (NSÍ)

K Olsen (NSÍ)   Justinussen (Víkingur)

Player of the season

Łukasz Cieślewicz
(B36 Tórshavn)

As in 2011, his first season at B36, Cieślewicz ended the Meistaradeildin campaign not only as a champion of the Faroe Islands but also as the league's official player of the year. The 28-year-old Polish midfielder, who also contributed to the club's title triumph in 2014, was not only the main creative player in the side but also, ultimately, its leading scorer, finding the net ten times in ten different matches – and against eight of the other nine teams in the division, with only AB Argir managing to keep him at bay.

Newcomer of the season

Jóannes Bjartalíd
(KÍ Klaksvik)

Introduced to the KÍ first team at the start of the 2015 season, Bjartalíd ended the campaign with many locals enthusing about him as one of the hottest prospects the islands had ever produced. His superior technique was plain for all to see, and as the season developed and his experience grew, the 19-year-old attacking midfielder not only started to make and score a number of goals but also became a regular in the national Under-21 team, with senior recognition all but certain to follow.

FAROE ISLANDS

NATIONAL TEAM

Top five all-time caps
Fródi Benjaminsen (87); Óli Johannesen (83); Jákup Mikkelsen (73); Jens Martin Knudsen (65); Julian Johnsson (62)

Top five all-time goals
Rógvi Jacobsen (10); Todi Jónsson (9); Uni Arge (8); **Fródi Benjaminsen**, **Christian Lamhauge Holst** & John Petersen (6)

Results 2015/16

04/09/15	Northern Ireland (ECQ)	H	Torshavn	L	1-3	Edmundsson (36)	
07/09/15	Finland (ECQ)	A	Helsinki	L	0-1		
08/10/15	Hungary (ECQ)	A	Budapest	L	1-2	Jakobsen (11)	
11/10/15	Romania (ECQ)	H	Torshavn	L	0-3		
28/03/16	Liechtenstein	N	Marbella (ESP)	W	3-2	B Olsen (6), Edmundsson (43), Vatnhamar (58)	
03/06/16	Kosovo	N	Frankfurt am Main (GER)	L	0-2		

Appearances 2015/16

Coach: Lars Olsen (DEN)	02/02/61		NIR	FIN	HUN	ROU	Lie	Kos	Caps	Goals
Gunnar Nielsen	07/10/86	Stjarnan (ISL) /FH (ISL)	G	G	G	G	G15	G	33	-
Odmar Færø	01/11/89	B36 /Banks O'Dee (SCO)	D		s84	D		D	14	-
Sonni Nattestad	05/08/94	unattached /FH (ISL)	D	D	D84	D84	D		13	-
Jónas Tór Næs	27/12/86	B36	D	D	D	D	s68	s46	47	
Gilli Sørensen	11/08/92	AaB (DEN)	D	D	s78	D	D	D68	12	
Sølvi Vatnhamar	05/05/86	Víkingur	M	M	M	M69	M68	M79	11	1
Brandur H Olsen	19/12/95	København (DEN) /Vendsyssel (DEN)	M83	M		M	M87	M	10	2
Fródi Benjaminsen	14/12/77	HB	M87	M84					87	6
Hallur Hansson	08/07/92	Vendsyssel (DEN)	M	M		M	M	M	23	4
Christian Lamhauge Holst	25/12/81	Fremad Amager (DEN)	M76	M57		M69			51	6
Jóan Símun Edmundsson	26/07/91	Vejle (DEN) /OB (DEN)	A 65*		A	A	A79		37	5
Pól Jóhannus Justinussen	13/01/89	NSÍ	s76		s62		s87		24	-
Klæmint A Olsen	17/07/90	NSÍ	s83	A75			s79	A68	9	
Rógvi Baldvinsson	06/12/89	Fredericia (DEN) /Vidar (NOR)	s87	s84	M	s84		D85	25	2
Atli Gregersen	15/06/82	Víkingur		D	D 94*		D79		31	-
Kaj Leo í Bartalsstovu	23/06/91	Levanger (NOR) /Dinamo Bucureşti (ROU)		s57	M	M	M89	M	9	
Finnur Justinussen	30/03/89	Víkingur /Fremad Amager (DEN)		s75				s68	3	-
Viljormur Davidsen	19/07/91	Vejle (DEN)			D			D	15	-
René S Joensen	08/02/93	Vendsyssel (DEN)			M78			s85	6	-
Róaldur Jakobsen	23/01/91	B36			M62				3	1
Árni Frederiksberg	13/06/92	NSÍ				s69	s89		2	
Andreas Lava Olsen	09/10/87	Víkingur				s69			9	1
Bárdur J Hansen	13/03/92	Víkingur					D		2	
Tróndur Jensen	06/02/93	HB					M	M46	2	
Teitur M Gestsson	19/08/92	HB					s15		2	
Jóhan Troest Davidsen	31/01/88	HB					s79		32	
Páll A Klettskard	17/05/90	KÍ						s68	12	-
Bogi R Petersen	20/02/93	ÍF						s79 81*	1	-

EUROPE

B36 Tórshavn

First qualifying round - The New Saints FC (WAL)

H 1-2 *Samuelsen (7)*

Thomsen, Eriksen, Færø, E Nielsen, Samuelsen, Borg (Dam 62), Jakobsen (Mellemgaard 82), Cieślewicz, Heinesen, Eysturoy, Thorleifsson (P Petersen 90+1). Coach: Eydun Klakstein (FRO)

A 1-4 *Cieślewicz (90+1)*

Thomsen, Eriksen, Færø (Mellemgaard 37), E Nielsen, Samuelsen, Jakobsen (B Petersen 85), Cieślewicz, Dam (P Petersen 76), Heinesen, Eysturoy, Thorleifsson. Coach: Eydun Klakstein (FRO)

Víkingur

First qualifying round - Rosenborg BK (NOR)

H 0-2

Túri, A Olsen (G Hansen 87), H Jacobsen, Gregersen, Hedin Hansen (G Vatnhamar 80), Djordjević (Lervig 89), S Vatnhamar, B Hansen, E Jacobsen, Djurhuus, Justinussen. Coach: Sigfrídur Clementsen (FRO)

A 0-0

Túri, A Olsen (S Joensen 85), H Jacobsen, Gregersen, Hedin Hansen (G Hansen 75), Djordjević (G Vatnhamar 64), S Vatnhamar, B Hansen, E Jacobsen, Djurhuus, Justinussen. Coach: Sigfrídur Clementsen (FRO)

HB Tórshavn

First qualifying round - FK Trakai (LTU)

A 0-3

Gestsson, Jógvan Davidsen, Alex, Jóhan Davidsen (Haraldsen 65), Holm, Benjaminsen, Hansen (Jacobsen 79), Mouritsen (Wardum 74), Hanssen, R Joensen, Vatnsdal. Coach: Hedin Askham (FRO)

Red card: Alex 62

H 1-4 *Hanssen (90)*

Gestsson, Jógvan Davidsen, Holm, Benjaminsen, Hansen (Ingason 74), Hanssen, Haraldsen, Jacobsen (Justinussen 67), Wardum, R Joensen, Vatnsdal. Coach: Hedin Askham (FRO)

Red card: Holm 21

NSÍ Runavík

First qualifying round - Linfield FC (NIR)

A 0-2

Gángó, Langgaard, M Jacobsen, Joensen (Edmundsson 75), K Olsen, Árni Frederiksberg, Justinussen, J Jacobsen, J Fredriksberg (J Højgaard 69), Magnus Olsen, H Højgaard (Mortensen 63). Coach: Trygvi Mortensen (FRO)

H 4-3 *K Olsen (17), Justinussen (19, 85), Joensen (45+1)*

Gángó, Langgaard, M Jacobsen, Joensen, K Olsen, Árni Frederiksberg, Hansen, Justinussen, J Jacobsen, J Fredriksberg (Mortensen 68), Magnus Olsen (Meinhard Olsen 81), H Højgaard (Edmundsson 55). Coach: Trygvi Mortensen (FRO)

DOMESTIC LEAGUE CLUB-BY-CLUB

AB Argir

1973 • Blue Water Arena (2,000) • argjaboltfelag.com

Coach: Oddbjørn Joensen; (01/06/15) Sámal Erik Hentze

2015

01/03	a	HB	D	2-2	*Christiansen, Nolsøe*
08/03	h	TB	D	1-1	*Jóannesarson*
15/03	h	Víkingur	D	0-0	
21/03	a	EB/Streymur	D	0-0	
02/04	a	ÍF	D	1-1	*Poulsen*
11/04	a	Suduroy	L	1-3	*Nolsøe*
18/04	a	NSÍ	L	1-2	*Christiansen*
26/04	a	KÍ	L	1-2	*Nolsøe (p)*
03/05	a	B36	D	1-1	*Nolsøe (p)*
10/05	h	EB/Streymur	L	1-2	*Mouritsen*
14/05	a	Víkingur	L	1-3	*og (H Jacobsen)*
17/05	h	HB	L	0-1	
25/05	a	TB	D	1-1	*Christiansen*
31/05	h	KÍ	L	0-4	
06/06	a	Suduroy	D	1-1	*H Stenberg*
21/06	a	ÍF	D	3-3	*Nolsøe, Mouritsen, Mohr*
26/06	a	B36	L	1-3	*Nolsøe*
27/07	h	NSÍ	L	1-2	*Jensen*
02/08	a	EB/Streymur	W	4-0	*Splidt, Nolsøe, Mouritsen, Drangastein*
09/08	h	Víkingur	D	0-0	
16/08	h	HB	L	1-3	*Nolsøe*
23/08	h	TB	W	3-0	*Drangastein, Højgaard 2*
27/08	a	KÍ	W	3-1	*Poulsen, Mouritsen 2*
13/09	h	Suduroy	W	2-1	*Splidt 2 (1p)*
20/09	h	ÍF	D	2-2	*Poulsen, Eriksen*
27/09	a	B36	D	2-2	*Christiansen, Egilsson*
03/10	h	NSÍ	L	0-1	

No	Name	Nat	DoB	Pos	Aps	(s)	Gls
28	Sorin Vasile Anghel		16/07/79	D	2		
10	Álvur Fuglø Christiansen		29/05/89	M	21	(3)	4
3	Rói Danielsen		18/02/89	D	15	(1)	
7	Jobin Drangastein		01/11/90	D	12	(4)	2
20	Magnus Egilsson		19/03/94	M	16	(4)	1
22	Beinir Ellefsen		07/04/93	D	19	(2)	
9	Nicolaj Lindholm Eriksen	DEN	01/08/86	A	6	(11)	1
14	Mikkjal Theodor Hentze		08/12/86	M	11	(5)	
12	Karstin Højgaard		23/02/94	M		(9)	2
6	Dmitrije Janković	SRB	05/11/75	D	24	(1)	
24	Tróndur Jensen		06/02/93	M	10		1
4	Teitur Jóannesarson		18/03/89	D	2		1
18	Bjartur Kjærbo		26/11/88	A		(6)	
12	Tóki á Lofti		06/12/93	M		(3)	
15	Hørdur Mouritzarson Mohr		06/03/93	M		(8)	1
21	Kristin Restorff Mouritsen		23/04/91	A	23	(1)	5
8	Kári Nielsen		03/03/81	M	22	(1)	
23	Jógvan Andrias Nolsøe		20/05/92	A	22	(4)	8
11	Bárdur Olsen		05/12/85	M	8	(2)	
18	Rógvi Poulsen		31/10/89	M	12	(1)	3
19	Sørin Nygaard Samuelsen		29/04/92	D	9	(2)	
17	Dan í Soylu		09/07/96	M	1	(2)	
27	Dion Brynjolf Splidt		05/06/89	M	8		3
16	Hedin Stenberg		14/01/89	G	21		1
13	Jónas Stenberg		07/04/87	D	13	(2)	
1	Niklas Thomsen		23/06/95	G	6		
2	Andras Brixen Vágsheyg		01/01/92	D	14		

B36 Tórshavn

1936 • Gundadalur (5,000) • b36.fo

Major honours
Faroe Islands League (11) 1946, 1948, 1950, 1959, 1962, 1997, 2001, 2005, 2011, 2014, 2015; Faroe Islands Cup (5) 1965, 1991, 2001, 2003, 2006

Coach: Eydun Klakstein

2015

03/03	a	EB/Streymur	D	1-1	Camara
08/03	h	Víkingur	D	3-3	Thorleifsson, Borg, Camara
15/03	h	NSÍ	W	3-0	Camara, Jakobsen, Dam
21/03	a	Suduroy	W	3-1	Samuelsen, H Askham, Camara
02/04	h	KÍ	W	1-0	Borg
12/04	h	TB	W	3-0	Cieślewicz, Borg, Á Nielsen
19/04	a	ÍF	L	1-3	Borg
26/04	a	HB	W	3-1	Cieślewicz, Samuelsen 2
03/05	h	AB	D	1-1	Samuelsen
09/05	a	Suduroy	W	3-1	Cieślewicz, Samuelsen 2
14/05	a	NSÍ	D	2-2	Cieślewicz, Camara
17/05	a	EB/Streymur	W	2-0	Eriksen, Borg (p)
25/05	a	Víkingur	D	1-1	Dam
31/05	h	HB	D	1-1	Cieślewicz
07/06	a	TB	W	3-1	Cieślewicz, Eriksen, Samuelsen
21/06	h	KÍ	W	2-1	Borg (p), Cieślewicz
26/06	a	AB	W	3-1	Eysturoy 2, Jakobsen
28/07	h	ÍF	W	4-0	Jakobsen, Lund 2, Cieślewicz
02/08	h	Suduroy	W	1-0	Eysturoy
09/08	h	NSÍ	W	3-0	Færø, Mellemgaard, Samuelsen
16/08	a	EB/Streymur	W	5-0	Eysturoy, Heinesen, Samuelsen, og (Árni Olsen), Cieślewicz
23/08	h	Víkingur	W	1-0	Cieślewicz
27/08	a	HB	W	2-1	Eriksen, Eysturoy
13/09	h	TB	W	2-1	Eysturoy, Thorleifsson
20/09	a	KÍ	L	1-2	Lund
27/09	h	AB	D	2-2	Lund (p), Heinesen
03/10	a	ÍF	W	3-1	E Nielsen, Borg, Thorleifsson

No	Name	Nat	DoB	Pos	Aps	(s)	Gls
8	Hørdur Askham		22/09/94	D	12		1
25	Trygvi Askham		28/03/88	G	3	(1)	
9	Jákup á Borg		26/10/79	A	17	(2)	7
4	Robert Hedin Brockie		21/12/92	M	1	(1)	
29	Ibrahima Camara	SEN	30/07/91	A	14	(2)	5
11	Łukasz Cieślewicz	POL	15/11/87	A	23		10
13	Gestur Bogason Dam		17/09/94	D	15	(7)	2
4	Karl Martin Eivindsson Danielsen		20/04/95	D		(1)	
2	Andrias Høgnason Eriksen		22/02/94	D	16	(9)	3
20	Høgni Eysturoy		14/07/90	D	24		6
5	Odmar Færø		01/11/89	D	27		
18	Benjamin Heinesen		26/03/96	M	7	(11)	2
10	Róaldur Jakobsen		23/01/91	M	26		3
14	Philip Lund	DEN	05/09/89	A	6	(1)	4
17	Alex Mellemgaard		27/11/91	D	5	(5)	1
3	Jónas Tór Næs		27/02/86	D	10	(1)	
19	Árni Guldborg Nielsen		22/06/93	M	1	(11)	1
6	Eli Falkvard Nielsen		23/09/92	M	23	(1)	1
4	Bjarni Petersen		12/08/98	M		(1)	
16	Pætur Joensson Petersen		29/03/98	M		(3)	
7	Hans Pauli Samuelsen		18/10/84	M	26	(1)	9
23	Rasmus Dan Sørensen		27/05/95	A		(2)	
1	Tórdur Thomsen		11/06/86	G	24		
24	Hanus Thorleifsson		19/12/85	M	17	(3)	3

EB/Streymur

1993 • Vid Margáir (3,000) • eb-streymur.fo

Major honours
Faroe Islands League (2) 2008, 2012; Faroe Islands Cup (4) 2007, 2008, 2010, 2011

Coach: Eliesar Jónsson Olsen

2015

03/03	h	B36	D	1-1	Niclasen
07/03	a	NSÍ	L	1-5	Sørensen
14/03	h	ÍF	D	2-2	Andras Olsen, Niclasen
21/03	h	AB	D	0-0	
02/04	h	HB	L	2-4	R Danielsen, N Danielsen
12/04	h	Víkingur	L	1-2	og (S Olsen)
19/04	a	KÍ	L	0-4	
26/04	a	Suduroy	L	1-2	N Danielsen (p)
03/05	h	TB	L	0-3	
10/05	a	AB	W	2-1	B Olsen, Niclasen
14/05	h	ÍF	L	0-3	
17/05	h	B36	L	0-2	
25/05	h	NSÍ	L	0-8	
31/05	a	Suduroy	L	2-3	Djurhuus, Niclasen
07/06	a	Víkingur	L	0-3	
21/06	h	HB	L	0-3	
27/06	a	TB	L	2-3	N Danielsen, Andras Olsen
27/07	h	KÍ	D	4-4	Høgaryggi 2, B Olsen, Niclasen
02/08	h	AB	L	0-4	
09/08	a	ÍF	L	1-4	Andras Olsen
16/08	h	B36	L	0-5	
23/08	a	NSÍ	L	0-6	
30/08	h	Suduroy	L	3-5	B Olsen, Høgaryggi, R Danielsen
13/09	h	Víkingur	W	2-1	Dam, N Danielsen
20/09	a	HB	L	0-6	
27/09	h	TB	D	2-2	Andras Olsen, Nielsen
03/10	a	KÍ	L	1-6	Niclasen

No	Name	Nat	DoB	Pos	Aps	(s)	Gls
26	Egil á Bø		02/04/74	D	3		
19	Arnar Dam		19/10/91	A	20	(2)	1
17	Niels Pauli Bjartalid Danielsen		18/01/89	A	25		4
13	Ragnar Bjartalid Danielsen		24/04/92	D	22	(2)	2
5	Marni Djurhuus		06/09/85	M	5		1
6	Hans Høghamar Ejdesgaard		27/01/93	M		(1)	
21	Ólavur F Høghamar Ejdesgaard		11/05/90	M	5	(8)	
24	Jákup Andrias Hansen		15/12/93	G	11		
20	Jóhannes Hansen		31/12/95	D	18		
16	Jan á Høgaryggi		15/06/97	A	13	(7)	3
1	Jákup Højgaard		06/02/94	G	13		
28	Jens Michael Jensen		24/01/91	A	5	(2)	
28	Tóki Hammershaimb Johannesen		17/03/97	M	4	(3)	
9	Teitur Kruse Johansen		05/10/95	A		(1)	
5	Pól Sigurd Kristiansen		17/06/96	M		(3)	
5	Tonny Snogebæk Kruse		29/03/88	M	2	(4)	
7	Jónstein Magnussen		21/05/90	M	2	(9)	
23	Leif Niclasen		01/10/86	A	19	(5)	6
14	Rógvi Egilstoft Nielsen		07/12/92	D	27		1
12	Andras Olsen		24/10/95	D	24		4
3	Árni Grunnvøit Olsen		13/09/93	M	23		
18	Brian Olsen		22/08/85	M	25		3
15	Hanus Egil Olsen		15/02/90	M	6	(10)	
13	Rói Hedinsson Olsen		03/03/97	M	15	(9)	
6	Hans Poulsen		30/08/90	D	1	(4)	
22	Rasmus Dan Sørensen		27/05/95	A	6	(3)	1
1	Símun Jóhan Wolles		24/05/97	G	3		
28	Eydstein Zachariasen		14/05/98	D		(1)	
5	Petur Zachariassen		19/04/95	M		(1)	

HB Tórshavn

1904 • Gundadalur (5,000) • hb.fo

Major honours
Faroe Islands League (22) 1955, 1960, 1963, 1964, 1965, 1971, 1973, 1974, 1975, 1978, 1981, 1982, 1988, 1990, 1998, 2002, 2003, 2004, 2006, 2009, 2010, 2013; Faroe Islands Cup (26) 1955, 1957, 1959, 1962, 1963, 1964, 1968, 1969, 1971, 1972, 1973, 1975, 1976, 1978, 1979, 1980, 1981, 1982, 1984, 1987, 1988, 1989, 1992, 1995, 1998, 2004

Coach: Hedin Askham; (09/08/15) Milan Cimburović (SRB)

2015

01/03	h	AB	D	2-2	Hansen, Hanssen
08/03	a	ÍF	D	1-1	Pál Joensen
15/03	h	KÍ	W	2-0	Pál Joensen, Samuelsen
22/03	h	TB	D	0-0	
02/04	a	EB/Streymur	W	4-2	Hanssen (p), Hansen 3
12/04	a	NSÍ	L	0-2	
18/04	a	Suduroy	W	2-1	Hanssen (p), Benjaminsen
26/04	h	B36	L	1-3	Jógvan Davidsen
03/05	h	Víkingur	W	2-1	Hanssen, Alex
10/05	a	TB	D	1-1	Benjaminsen
14/05	h	KÍ	W	3-1	R Joensen, Hanssen, Alex
17/05	a	AB	W	1-0	Hanssen (p)
25/05	a	ÍF	W	1-0	Hansen
31/05	a	B36	D	1-1	Hansen
07/06	h	NSÍ	D	1-1	Hansen
21/06	a	EB/Streymur	W	3-0	Mouritsen, Hanssen, Fløtum
26/06	a	Víkingur	L	0-3	
29/07	h	Suduroy	D	0-0	
02/08	h	TB	D	2-2	Benjaminsen, og (Olsen)
07/08	a	KÍ	L	0-2	
16/08	a	AB	W	3-1	Benjaminsen, Mouritsen, Ingason
23/08	a	ÍF	D	2-2	Mouritsen, Fløtum
27/08	h	B36	L	1-2	Holm
13/09	a	NSÍ	D	0-0	
20/09	h	EB/Streymur	W	6-0	Jacobsen 2, Justinussen, Benjaminsen 2, Mouritsen
27/09	a	Víkingur	L	2-3	Ingason, Wardum
03/10	h	Suduroy	W	2-0	Ingason, Wardum

No	Name	Nat	DoB	Pos	Aps	(s)	Gls
4	Alex	BRA	28/03/81	D	27		2
7	Fródi Benjaminsen		14/12/77	M	23	(1)	6
3	Jógvan Rói Davidsen		09/10/91	M	21	(3)	1
5	Jóhan Troest Davidsen		31/01/88	D	20	(1)	
10	Andrew av Fløtum		13/06/79	A	7	(9)	2
1	Teitur Matras Gestsson		19/08/92	G	27		
8	Arnbjørn Theodor Hansen		27/02/86	A	9	(4)	7
12	Levi Hanssen		24/02/88	M	25	(1)	7
13	Gunnar Højgaard Haraldsen		21/11/87	D	18	(3)	
6	Rógvi Sjúrdarson Holm		24/01/90	D	18	(2)	1
20	Poul Ingason		28/09/95	A	9	(10)	3
14	Teit Jacobsen		16/03/98	M	5	(8)	2
19	Rókur av Fløtum Jespersen		16/03/85	M	6	(4)	
18	Pál Mohr Joensen		20/08/92	D	3		2
24	Páll Mohr Joensen		29/06/86	A		(2)	
23	René Shaki Joensen		08/02/93	M	16		1
26	Daniel Johansen		09/07/98	M		(3)	
21	Adrian Justinussen		21/07/98	M	11	(5)	1
15	Heri Hjalt Mohr		13/05/97	M		(3)	
11	Christian Restorff Mouritsen		03/12/88	M	21	(2)	4
9	Símun Samuelsen		21/05/85	M	4	(6)	1
27	Heini Vatnsdal		18/10/91	M	8		
17	Bartal Wardum		03/05/97	M	19	(4)	2

FAROE ISLANDS

ÍF Fuglafjørdur

1946 • Fløtugerdi (2,000) • if.fo

Major honours
Faroe Islands League (1) 1979

Coach: Aleksandar Jovević (SRB);
(08/09/15) Jákup Mikkelsen

2015

01/03	a	Víkingur	D	2-2	A Ellingsgaard 2
08/03	h	HB	D	1-1	Jakobsen
14/03	a	EB/Streymur	D	2-2	og (Nielsen), Andy Olsen
22/03	a	NSÍ	L	1-3	Løkin
02/04	a	AB	D	1-1	Á Petersen
12/04	h	KÍ	W	3-1	Eliasen, Lawal (p), Jakobsen
19/04	h	B36	W	3-1	Andy Olsen, Lakjuni, Joensen
26/04	a	TB	D	1-1	Joensen
03/05	h	Suduroy	L	2-3	Clayton, Lawal
08/05	h	NSÍ	L	0-3	
14/05	a	EB/Streymur	W	3-0	Andy Olsen, Clayton, Lawal
17/05	h	Víkingur	L	1-3	Clayton
25/05	a	HB	L	0-1	
31/05	h	TB	W	2-0	Lambanum, Lawal
07/06	a	KÍ	D	0-0	
21/06	h	AB	D	3-3	Sarić, Clayton, Eliasen
25/06	h	Suduroy	D	3-3	Lakjuni, Clayton, Lawal
28/07	a	B36	L	0-4	
03/08	a	NSÍ	L	1-5	Løkin
09/08	h	EB/Streymur	W	4-1	A Ellingsgaard, Sarić, Andy Olsen, J Ellingsgaard
16/08	a	Víkingur	L	2-4	J Ellingsgaard, Andy Olsen
23/08	h	HB	D	2-2	Andy Olsen, Eliasen
30/08	h	TB	D	1-1	Lawal
13/09	h	KÍ	D	1-1	Clayton
20/09	a	AB	D	2-2	Andy Olsen, Lakjuni
27/09	a	Suduroy	L	2-5	Joensen, Lawal
03/10	h	B36	L	1-3	og (Eriksen)

No	Name	Nat	DoB	Pos	Aps	(s)	Gls
18	Clayton	BRA	24/11/78	A	22	(2)	6
76	Bartal Eliasen		23/08/76	D	16	(2)	3
10	Ari Ólavsson Ellingsgaard		03/02/93	M	17	(5)	3
37	Jan Ólavsson Ellingsgaard		26/06/90	M	16		2
37	John Daniel Gudjónsson		17/09/96	D	3	(4)	
1	Hallgrím Gregersen Hansen		24/12/94	G	5	(1)	
24	Dánjal Pauli Højgaard		27/12/83	M		(2)	
4	Sjúrdur Jacobsen		29/08/76	D	8	(9)	
9	Kristoffur Jakobsen		07/11/88	M	9	(13)	2
20	Leivur Joensen		07/02/94	M	20	(3)	3
28	Arnold Kristiansen		24/03/95	A		(1)	
7	Dánjal á Lakjuni		22/09/90	A	10	(8)	3
5	Fritleif í Lambanum		13/04/86	D	16	(5)	1
30	Adeshina Lawal	NGA	17/10/84	A	16	(3)	7
16	Karl Abrahamson Løkin		19/04/91	M	21		2
38	Predrag Marković	SRB	01/02/77	G	18		
3	Poul Nolsøe Mikkelsen		19/04/95	D	24		
8	André Olsen		23/10/90	M	1	(2)	
23	Andy Ólavur Olsen		03/12/84	M	17	(6)	7
2	Áki Petersen		01/12/84	D	10	(1)	1
8	Bogi Reinert Petersen		20/02/93	M	8		
21	Andrias Poulsen		03/08/97	M		(3)	
11	Frank Højbjerg Poulsen		03/11/88	M	15	(7)	
22	Nenad Sarić	SRB	05/07/81	M	21	(4)	2
1	Fridi Sigurdsson		09/09/95	G	2		
1	Tóri Tórmódsson Tradará		16/07/96	G	2		

KÍ Klaksvík

1904 • Djúpumýra (3,000) • ki.fo

Major honours
Faroe Islands League (17) 1942, 1945, 1952, 1953, 1954, 1956, 1957, 1958, 1961, 1966, 1967, 1968, 1969, 1970, 1972, 1991, 1999; Faroe Islands Cup (5) 1966, 1967, 1990, 1994, 1999

Coach: Mikkjal Thomassen

2015

01/03	a	TB	D	1-1	A Danielsen
08/03	h	Suduroy	W	3-0	Hajdarević, J Andreasen, Gueye
15/03	h	HB	L	0-2	
22/03	a	Víkingur	D	3-3	Heinesen, Klettskard 2
02/04	a	B36	L	0-1	
12/04	a	ÍF	L	1-3	Klettskard
19/04	h	EB/Streymur	W	4-0	Bjartalíd, Kalsø, Klettskard, Klakstein
26/04	h	AB	W	2-1	Klettskard, Klakstein
03/05	a	NSÍ	L	0-3	
10/05	h	Víkingur	W	3-2	Bjartalíd, A Danielsen, Heinesen (p)
14/05	a	HB	L	1-3	Klettskard
17/05	h	TB	W	1-0	Klakstein
25/05	h	Suduroy	W	2-1	Hajdarević, Lakjuni
31/05	a	AB	W	4-0	Klakstein, Bjartalíd, Blé, Hajdarević
07/06	h	ÍF	D	0-0	
21/06	h	B36	L	1-2	Klakstein
26/06	h	NSÍ	D	3-3	Klakstein, Hajdarević, Heinesen (p)
27/07	a	EB/Streymur	D	4-4	Bjartalíd 2, Klakstein, Elttør
02/08	a	Víkingur	D	1-1	Heinesen
07/08	h	HB	W	2-0	Gueye, Klakstein
16/08	a	TB	D	1-1	Klakstein
23/08	a	Suduroy	W	2-0	Bjartalíd, Klakstein
27/08	h	AB	L	1-3	Hajdarević
13/09	a	ÍF	D	1-1	A Danielsen
20/09	h	B36	W	2-1	Hajdarević, Gueye
27/09	a	NSÍ	L	1-4	Elttør
03/10	h	EB/Streymur	W	6-1	Klettskard 2, Bjartalíd 2 (1p), Elttør, Klakstein

No	Name	Nat	DoB	Pos	Aps	(s)	Gls
20	Mayowa Oladele Alli	USA	21/03/92	D	15	(5)	
19	Jákup Biskopstø Andreasen		31/05/98	M	10	(7)	1
13	Petur Andreasen		19/02/94	A	1	(2)	
8	Jóannes Bjartalíd		10/07/96	A	23	(4)	8
17	Evrard Blé	CIV	02/01/82	M	10	(1)	1
22	Gunnar Christiansen		08/08/92	D		(1)	
11	Atli Danielsen		15/08/83	D	23	(1)	3
23	Jóannes Kalsø Danielsen		10/09/97	M		(11)	
10	Hjalgrím Elttør		03/03/83	M	24		3
15	Ndende Adama Gueye	SEN	05/01/83	M	27		3
25	Kenan Hajdarević	BIH	29/01/90	A	16	(5)	6
12	Henry Heinesen		01/06/88	M	18	(2)	4
7	Ivan Joensen		20/02/92	M	1		
16	Meinhard Joensen		27/11/79	G	26		
14	Tórur Justesen		04/01/95	D	3	(9)	
6	Sørmundur Árni Kalsø		20/01/92	D	17	(1)	1
21	Hedin Klakstein		30/04/92	M	20	(3)	11
9	Páll Andrasson Klettskard		17/05/90	A	15	(3)	8
18	Hedin á Lakjuni		19/02/78	D	3	(11)	1
2	Dávid Langgaard		30/03/95	M		(1)	
4	Jonas Flindt Rasmussen	DEN	07/11/88	D	25		
1	Frídi Sigurdsson		09/09/95	G	1		
3	Ísak Simonsen		12/10/93	D	15	(4)	
24	Sani Tahir	NGA	28/08/92	M	4	(1)	

NSÍ Runavík

1957 • Vid Løkin (2,000) • nsi.fo

Major honours
Faroe Islands League (1) 2007; Faroe Islands Cup (2) 1986, 2002

Coach: Trygvi Mortensen

2015

01/03	h	Suduroy	W	6-1	J Frederiksberg 2, K Olsen 3, Árni Frederiksberg
07/03	h	EB/Streymur	W	5-1	og (Nielsen), Árni Frederiksberg, K Olsen 2, Meinhard Olsen
15/03	a	B36	L	0-3	
22/03	h	ÍF	W	3-1	K Olsen 2, J Frederiksberg
02/04	a	TB	W	3-2	J Højgaard, K Olsen 2
12/04	h	HB	W	2-0	og (R Joensen), K Olsen
18/04	h	AB	W	2-1	K Olsen, J Frederiksberg
26/04	a	Víkingur	L	1-5	Magnus Olsen
03/05	a	KÍ	W	3-0	Edmundsson, J Frederiksberg, K Olsen
08/05	a	ÍF	W	3-0	Justinussen 2, K Olsen
14/05	h	B36	D	2-2	Árni Frederiksberg, Justinussen
17/05	h	Suduroy	W	3-1	Magnus Olsen, Justinussen, H Højgaard
25/05	a	EB/Streymur	W	8-0	Justinussen, H Højgaard, K Olsen 3, Árni Frederiksberg, Hansen 2
31/05	h	Víkingur	L	2-4	Magnus Olsen, Árni Frederiksberg
07/06	a	HB	D	1-1	Magnus Olsen
20/06	h	TB	W	2-0	
26/06	a	KÍ	D	3-3	K Olsen, Magnus Olsen, J Frederiksberg
27/07	a	AB	W	2-1	Mortensen 2
03/08	a	ÍF	W	5-1	Justinussen 3, K Olsen, Joensen
09/08	a	B36	L	0-3	
12/08	a	Víkingur	L	1-3	K Olsen
16/08	h	Suduroy	W	5-1	K Olsen, Árni Frederiksberg 3, C Jacobsen
23/08	h	EB/Streymur	W	6-0	Árni Frederiksberg, H Højgaard, C Jacobsen 2, K Olsen, Justinussen
13/09	h	HB	D	0-0	
20/09	a	TB	D	2-2	Magnus Olsen, J Jacobsen
27/09	h	KÍ	W	4-1	Justinussen 3, Mortensen
03/10	a	AB	W	1-0	Árni Frederiksberg

No	Name	Nat	DoB	Pos	Aps	(s)	Gls
20	Hákun Edmundsson		21/03/96	M	15	(5)	1
6	Andras Frederiksberg		02/12/92	M	2	(7)	
11	Árni Frederiksberg		13/06/92	M	21		10
17	Jónhard Frederiksberg		27/08/80	D	16	(7)	6
5	Jákup Andrias Gaardbo		22/09/95	D		(1)	
1	András Gángó	HUN	02/03/84	G	27		
12	Einar Tróndargjógv Hansen		02/04/88	D	19	(2)	2
19	Haraldur Reinert Højgaard		21/03/95	M	13	(9)	3
9	Jonleif Højgaard		26/10/88	M	4	(12)	1
23	Christian Høgni Jacobsen		12/05/80	A	1	(5)	3
15	Johan Jacobsen		02/07/92	D	26		1
3	Monrad Holm Jacobsen		23/04/91	D	21		
4	Jens Joensen		17/05/89	D	14	(1)	
13	Pól Jóhannus Justinussen		13/01/89	M	24		12
16	Petur Knudsen		24/04/98	M		(6)	
2	Per Langgaard		30/05/91	D	23	(1)	
7	Jann Martin Mortensen		18/07/89	M	20	(7)	3
10	Klæmint Andrasson Olsen		17/07/90	A	27		21
18	Magnus Hendriksson Olsen		26/10/86	M	22	(2)	6
14	Meinhard Egilsson Olsen		10/04/97	M		(12)	1
8	Michal Przybylski		29/12/97	M	2	(2)	

FC Suduroy

2010 • Vesturi á Eidinum (3,000) •
fcsuduroy.com

Major honours
*Faroe Islands League (1) 2000 (as VB Vágur);
Faroe Islands Cup (1) 1974 (as VB Vágur)*

Coach: Jón Pauli Olsen

2015

01/03	a	NSÍ	L	1-6	S Bech
08/03	a	KÍ	L	0-3	
14/03	h	TB	L	1-3	Jón Poulsen
21/03	h	B36	L	1-3	Augustinussen
02/04	a	Víkingur	L	0-4	
11/04	h	AB	W	3-1	Iobashvili, Toronjadze 2
18/04	h	HB	L	1-2	Toronjadze
26/04	h	EB/Streymur	W	2-1	Egilsson, John Poulsen
03/05	a	ÍF	W	3-2	Jón Poulsen, John Poulsen, Toronjadze
09/05	h	B36	L	1-3	Egilsson
14/05	a	TB	L	1-4	Iobashvili
17/05	h	NSÍ	L	1-3	Jón Poulsen
25/05	a	KÍ	L	1-2	Iobashvili
31/05	h	EB/Streymur	W	3-2	Jón Poulsen, og (R Danielsen), Toronjadze
06/06	h	AB	D	1-1	Jón Poulsen
21/06	h	Víkingur	L	1-3	Ibeagha
25/06	a	ÍF	D	3-3	Iobashvili, Jón Poulsen, Toronjadze
29/07	a	HB	D	0-0	
02/08	a	B36	L	0-1	
09/08	h	TB	D	2-2	Jón Poulsen, Augustinussen
16/08	a	NSÍ	L	1-5	S Bech
23/08	h	KÍ	L	0-2	
30/08	a	EB/Streymur	W	5-3	Madsen 3, S Bech, Toronjadze
13/09	a	AB	L	1-2	Augustinussen
20/09	a	Víkingur	L	1-3	Jón Poulsen
27/09	h	ÍF	W	5-2	Toronjadze, Iobashvili, Jón Poulsen 3 (1p)
03/10	a	HB	L	0-2	

No	Name	Nat	DoB	Pos	Aps	(s)	Gls
9	Palli Augustinussen		16/12/80	M	26		3
6	Heini Bech		21/06/90	D	6	(9)	
5	Salmundur Bech		16/01/96	M	14	(1)	3
17	Eiler Brattalíd		13/10/96	M		(5)	
14	Dan Djurhuus		15/08/78	D	1		
3	Búi Egilsson		04/01/96	A	23	(2)	2
5	Dánjal Godtfred		07/03/96	D	20	(1)	
2	Christian Ibeagha	NGA	10/01/90	D	23	(1)	1
4	Valerian Iobashvili	GEO	18/12/88	D	22		5
13	Jón Áki Jacobsen		02/11/95	D	1		
1	Kári Jacobsen		28/08/95	G	7		
6	Reidar Dahl Joensen		27/03/91	A		(2)	
16	Rani Nolsøe Johannessen		25/02/90	G	20		
6	Rani Johansen		30/06/97	M	1	(3)	
8	Heri Eydunsson Kjærbo		01/06/95	D	23	(1)	
18	Gutti Kristiansen		22/10/97	M		(1)	
19	John Villi Leo		13/08/97	M	4	(9)	
4	Høgni Madsen		04/02/85	M	21	(1)	3
12	Teitur Krosslá Mortensen		01/01/96	M		(9)	
18	Tóki Krosslá Mortensen		01/01/96	D	17	(5)	
11	Ari Krosslá Poulsen		27/07/97	M	4	(6)	
20	John Tordar Poulsen		17/09/85	M	12	(3)	2
10	Jón Krosslá Poulsen		17/02/88	A	20	(3)	11
17	Símun Samuelsen		21/05/85	M	8		
21	Teitur Tausen		27/03/91	D		(3)	
7	Mamuka Toronjadze	GEO	13/05/86	M	24		8

TB Tvøroyri

1892 • Vid Stórá (3,000) • tb.fo

Major honours
*Faroe Islands League (7) 1943, 1949, 1951, 1976,
1977, 1980, 1987; Faroe Islands Cup (5) 1956, 1958,
1960, 1961, 1977*

Coach: Páll Gudlaugsson (ISL)

2015

01/03	h	KÍ	D	1-1	og (M Joensen)
08/03	a	AB	D	1-1	Heini Mortensen
14/03	a	Suduroy	W	3-1	Able, Johannesen 2
22/03	a	HB	D	0-0	
02/04	h	NSÍ	L	2-3	Adu 2
12/04	a	B36	L	0-3	
19/04	h	Víkingur	D	2-2	Justinussen 2
26/04	h	ÍF	D	1-1	Adu
03/05	a	EB/Streymur	W	3-0	Ellendersen, Adu, Able
10/05	h	HB	D	1-1	Adu
14/05	h	Suduroy	W	4-1	Adu 3, Able
17/05	a	KÍ	L	0-1	
25/05	h	AB	D	1-1	Ellendersen
31/05	a	ÍF	L	0-2	
07/06	h	B36	L	1-3	Justinussen
20/06	a	NSÍ	D	0-0	
27/06	h	EB/Streymur	W	3-2	Bech, Adu, Justinussen
26/07	a	Víkingur	L	2-7	Johannesen, R Tausen
02/08	a	HB	D	2-2	og (Benjaminsen), Justinussen
09/08	a	Suduroy	D	2-2	Rógvi Joensen, Adu (p)
16/08	h	KÍ	D	1-1	og (Kalsø)
23/08	a	AB	L	0-3	
30/08	h	ÍF	D	1-1	Johannesen
13/09	a	B36	L	1-2	Johannesen
20/09	h	NSÍ	D	2-2	Johannesen, Justinussen
27/09	a	EB/Streymur	D	2-2	Ellendersen, Hansen
03/10	h	Víkingur	L	0-2	

No	Name	Nat	DoB	Pos	Aps	(s)	Gls
27	Franck Odje Able	CIV	09/12/91	M	7	(5)	3
10	Albert Adu	NED	08/08/88	A	20	(1)	10
12	Hávar Albinus		19/02/98	M		(2)	
19	Kofi Appiah	GHA	24/12/88	A	2		
24	Carl Mikkjal Bech		15/01/89	D	8	(4)	1
23	Andri Freyr Björnsson	ISL	12/08/86	D	26		
11	Eirikur Magnusarson Ellendersen		05/03/94	D	17	(7)	3
2	Jónhard Ferjá		30/04/93	M		(2)	
18	Jonas Gejel Hansen		07/08/95	M	10		1
5	Ragnar Joensen		14/07/93	D	5	(6)	
6	Rógvi Joensen		14/07/93	M	24		1
9	Patrik Johannesen		07/09/95	M	21	(4)	6
1	Patrik Johannesen		07/09/95	G	1		
7	Teitur Wiberg Justinussen		08/04/93	M	24		6
4	Regin í Lágabø		08/08/98	M		(1)	
3	Reynir Magnússon	ISL	20/10/92	D	15	(1)	
19	Hanus Mortensen		26/02/91	A	1	(1)	
20	Heine Mortensen		26/02/91	D	21	(1)	
18	Heini Mikal Mortensen		20/09/94	D	13	(2)	1
19	Petur Mortensen		20/04/90	M	1	(4)	
15	Teitur Jespersen Olsen		10/05/95	D	26	(1)	
69	Arthur Djurhuus Poulsen		29/12/92	M	8	(7)	
13	Ivan Stojković	SRB	30/01/77	G	26		
12	Martin Tausen		04/05/90	M	21	(1)	
11	Ragnar Tausen		06/09/94	A		(1)	1
4	Jákup Brimstrond Thomasen		10/01/93	M		(5)	

Víkingur

2008 • Sarpugerdi (2,000) • vikingur.fo

Major honours
*Faroe Islands League (6) 1983, 1986, 1993, 1994,
1995, 1996 (as GÍ Gøta); Faroe Islands Cup (11)
1983, 1985, 1996, 1997, 2000, 2005 (as GÍ Gøta),
2009, 2012, 2013, 2014, 2015*

Coach: Sigfrídur Clementsen

2015

01/03	h	ÍF	D	2-2	Justinussen, S Olsen
08/03	a	B36	D	3-3	A Olsen 3
15/03	a	AB	D	0-0	
22/03	h	KÍ	D	3-3	A Olsen, S Olsen, og (Alli)
02/04	h	Suduroy	W	4-0	Justinussen 4
12/04	a	EB/Streymur	W	2-1	G Vatnhamar 2
19/04	a	TB	D	2-2	A Olsen, Justinussen
26/04	h	NSÍ	W	5-1	B Hansen, E Jacobsen 2, Justinussen, G Vatnhamar
03/05	a	HB	L	1-2	Justinussen
10/05	a	KÍ	L	2-3	Justinussen, H Jacobsen
14/05	h	AB	W	3-1	Hedin Hansen, H Jacobsen, A Olsen
17/05	a	ÍF	W	3-1	Gregersen, Justinussen, A Olsen
25/05	h	B36	D	1-1	Hedin Hansen
31/05	a	NSÍ	W	4-2	Hedin Hansen, A Olsen 3
07/06	h	EB/Streymur	W	3-0	Gregersen, Justinussen, H Jacobsen
21/06	a	Suduroy	W	3-1	Djordjević, A Olsen, Hjartvard Hansen
26/06	h	HB	W	3-0	G Vatnhamar, Hedin Hansen, Gregersen
26/07	h	TB	W	7-2	Hedin Hansen, Justinussen 2, H Jacobsen, Jarnskor, S Vatnhamar 2
02/08	a	KÍ	D	1-1	H Jacobsen
09/08	a	AB	D	0-0	
12/08	h	NSÍ	W	3-1	Justinussen, A Olsen, S Vatnhamar
16/08	h	ÍF	W	4-2	Djordjević, Justinussen, S Olsen, H Jacobsen
23/08	a	B36	L	0-1	
13/09	a	EB/Streymur	L	1-2	Jarnskor
20/09	h	Suduroy	W	3-1	G Hansen, Hedin Hansen, G Vatnhamar
27/09	h	HB	W	3-2	P Joensen, Hedin Hansen, S Vatnhamar
03/10	a	TB	W	2-0	og (Ellendersen), J Olsen

No	Name	Nat	DoB	Pos	Aps	(s)	Gls
9	Filip Djordjević	SRB	07/03/94	M	22		2
16	Hans Jørgin Djurhuus		29/11/78	M	11	(2)	
4	Atli Gregersen		15/06/82	D	25		3
12	Bárdur Jógvansson Hansen		13/03/92	D	17	(1)	1
21	Gert Åge Hansen		25/07/84	M	17	(6)	1
8	Hedin Hansen		30/07/93	M	18	(6)	7
25	Hjartvard Hansen		17/09/88	M		(4)	1
19	Tróndur Jóannesarson á Høvdanum		19/08/95	D		(1)	
13	Erling Dávidsson Jacobsen		13/02/90	D	26		2
3	Hanus Jacobsen		25/05/85	D	22	(1)	6
14	Magnus Jarnskor		14/12/95	M	2	(9)	2
23	Páll Mohr Joensen		29/06/86	A	1	(7)	1
6	Sámal Jákup Joensen		07/04/93	M	6	(6)	
17	Finnur Justinussen		30/03/89	A	23		15
5	Dánjal Pauli Lervig		26/04/91	D	6	(5)	
2	Andreas Lava Olsen		09/10/87	A	20	(3)	12
15	Jákup Vatnhamar Olsen		30/05/96	M	1	(4)	1
7	Súni Olsen		07/03/81	M	13	(3)	3
27	Elias Rasmussen		13/05/96	G	2	(2)	
18	Fannhard Antonson Skoradal		23/08/98	M		(1)	
20	Hjalti Strømsten		21/01/97	M		(3)	
1	Géza Tamás Túri	HUN	11/03/74	G	25		
24	Gunnar Vatnhamar		29/03/95	D	14	(6)	5
10	Sølvi Vatnhamar		05/05/86	M	26		4

Top goalscorers

21	Klæmint Andrasson Olsen (NSÍ)
15	Finnur Justinussen (Víkingur)
12	Pól Jóhannus Justinussen (NSÍ)
	Andreas Lava Olsen (Víkingur)
11	Hedin Klakstein (KÍ)
	Jón Krosslá Poulsen (Suduroy)
10	Łukasz Cieślewicz (B36)
	Árni Frederiksberg (NSÍ)
	Albert Adu (TB)
9	Hans Pauli Samuelsen (B36)

Promoted clubs

Skála ÍF

1965 • Undir Mýruhjalla (2,000) • skalaif.fo
Coach: Pauli Poulsen

B68 Toftir

1962 • Svangarskard (5,000) • b68.fo
Major honours
Faroe Islands League (3) 1984, 1985, 1992
Coach: Súni Frídi Barbá

Second level final table 2015

		Pld	W	D	L	F	A	Pts
1	Skála ÍF	27	22	4	1	96	17	70
2	B68 Toftir	27	17	5	5	61	27	56
3	07 Vestur	27	14	6	7	66	36	48
4	AB Argir II	27	13	7	7	50	41	46
5	KÍ Klaksvík II	27	12	2	13	65	50	38
6	Víkingur II	27	9	6	12	39	43	33
7	B71 Sandoy	27	9	6	12	47	56	33
8	NSÍ Runavík II	27	9	4	14	54	54	31
9	B36 Tórshavn II	27	4	8	15	32	71	20
10	MB Midvágur	27	1	2	24	18	133	5

DOMESTIC CUP

Løgmanssteypid 2015

SECOND ROUND

(06/04/15)
07 Vestur 1-2 AB
B36 2-1 TB
EB/Streymur 3-2 KÍ
HB 1-0 Skála
ÍF 5-0 B71
MB 0-3 Giza/Hoyvík
NSÍ 2-1 Suduroy
Víkingur 4-0 B68

QUARTER-FINALS

(21/04/15)
Giza/Hoyvík 1-4 HB *(Keita 9; Hansen 61, Haraldsen 66, Benjaminsen 82, Holm 90)*

(22/04/15)
B36 4-0 EB/Streymur *(Cieślewicz 4, 15, Borg 32p, Færø 85)*

ÍF 3-3 Víkingur *(Sarić 61, Eliasen 90, A Ellingsgaard 94; G Vatnhamar 18, Gregersen 34, Hedin Hansen 120) (aet; 8-9 on pens)*

NSÍ 2-2 AB *(K Olsen 105p, H Højgaard 115; H Stenberg 110, Nolsøe 111) (aet; 5-4 on pens)*

SEMI-FINALS

(21/05/15 & 03/06/15)
Víkingur 0-1 B36 *(Dam 18)*
B36 0-2 Víkingur *(B Hansen 4, Djordjević 86).*
(Víkingur 2-1)

(21/05/15 & 04/06/15)
NSÍ 1-0 HB *(K Olsen 79p)*
HB 0-1 NSÍ *(Árni Frederiksberg 80)*
(NSÍ 2-0)

FINAL

(29/08/15)
Tórsvøllur, Torshavn
VÍKINGUR 3 *(S Olsen 10, G Hansen 32, Hedin Hansen 58)*
NSÍ RUNAVIK 0
Referee: Rasmussen
VÍKINGUR: *Túri, G Vatnhamar (Djordjević 83), Gregersen, E Jacobsen, H Jacobsen, G Hansen, S Olsen (P Joensen 75), S Vatnhamar, Hedin Hansen (Lervig 85), S Joensen, Justinussen*
NSÍ: *Gángó, J Jacobsen (C Jacobsen 46), Joensen, M Jacobsen, Hansen, Justinussen, Edmundsson (H Højgaard 51), Magnus Olsen, Mortensen (J Frederiksberg 64), Árni Frederiksberg, K Olsen*
Red card: *Árni Frederiksberg (38)*

Víkingur players celebrate the club's fourth successive domestic cup triumph

FINLAND

Suomen Palloliitto – Finlands Bollförbund (SPL-FBF)

Address	Urheilukatu 5, PO Box 191
	FI-00251 Helsinki
Tel	+358 9 742 151
Fax	+358 9 454 3352
E-mail	sami.terava@palloliitto.fi
Website	palloliitto.fi

President	Pertti Alaja
General secretary	Marco Casagrande
Media officer	Sami Terävä
Year of formation	1907
National stadium	Olympic Stadium, Helsinki (40,682)

VEIKKAUSLIIGA CLUBS

 1 **HIFK Helsinki**

 2 **HJK Helsinki**

 3 **Ilves Tampere**

 4 **FC Inter Turku**

 5 **FF Jaro**

 6 **FC KTP Kotka**

 7 **KuPS Kuopio**

 8 **FC Lahti**

 9 **IFK Mariehamn**

 10 **RoPS Rovaniemi**

 11 **SJK Seinäjoki**

 12 **VPS Vaasa**

PROMOTED CLUBS

 13 **PS Kemi**

 14 **PK-35 Vantaa**

KEY

● UEFA Champions League

● UEFA Europa League

● Promoted

● Relegated

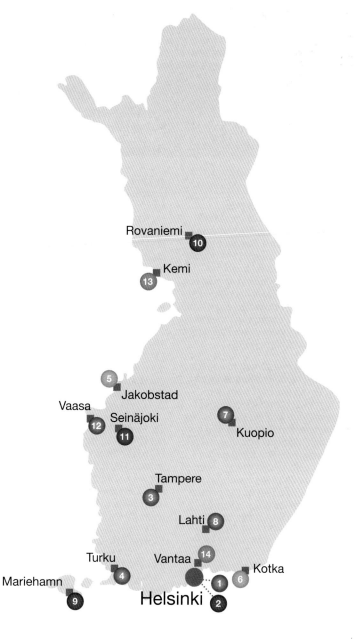

Second-season success for SJK

After six years of unbroken Veikkausliiga dominance by the country's most decorated club, HJK Helsinki, the 2015 season brought about a shake-up in the established order as SJK Seinäjoki, runners-up in their debut top-flight campaign a year earlier, upset the odds again to become the champions of Finland.

There was a first major trophy success too in the Finnish Cup, with the islanders of IFK Mariehamn beating FC Inter Turku in the final, while unfancied northerners RoPS Roveniemi completed a trio of upsets by edging HJK to the league runners-up spot.

Domestic league

HJK were fully expected to extend the longest title-winning sequence in their history when the Veikkausliiga season kicked off in mid-April. For most of the campaign Mika Lehkosuo's 2014 double winners looked on course for further glory, reaching the midpoint with just one defeat on a balance sheet strengthened by victories in all three games against the two sides that had emerged as their most threatening challengers – Simo Valakari's SJK and Juha Malinen's RoPS.

However, as summer turned to autumn, the perennial champions suddenly lost their way. Seven matches from mid-August to late September yielded just three points, transforming the landscape of the title race. RoPS and SJK had both been through tricky periods themselves, but the two provincial sides were not found wanting when it mattered, each of them claiming comprehensive wins over HJK in the run-in so that as the contest entered its final showdown, all three teams were still in title contention.

Crucially, SJK were on top of the table going into the final game. They held a one-point advantage over RoPS, with HJK a further point back, and their closing fixture was at home to an FF Jaro side propping up the table. Jaro, who needed a long-awaited win to have any chance of staying up, proved doughtier opponents than expected but ultimately succumbed 2-0, with Mehmet Hemetaj scoring early and Roope Riski late to give SJK the title. RoPS and HJK also won, leaving the positions at the start of the day unaltered, which meant that both the champions and runners-up finished higher than ever before.

SJK's was a team well stocked with foreigners, but it was their Finnish contingent, headed by attacking midfielder Akseli Pelvas, that supplied most of the goals – 37 out of the 50 that gave them the most productive attack in the league (albeit with 15 fewer than HJK's championship-winning class of 2014) as well as the best defence.

Jaro were duly relegated, later to be accompanied down by newly promoted FC KTP Kotka, whose efforts were eclipsed by the two teams that had come up with them, HIFK Helsinki and Ilves Tampere, the former particularly impressing in their three sell-out derbies against HJK, all of which ended 1-1.

Domestic cup

Mariehamn were another team that saved their best for HJK, hammering the holders 5-1 in the Finnish Cup semi-finals to book a date with FC Inter, the team that had lost the 2014 final on penalties. There would be more final torment for the team from Turku, however, as a double from Mariehamn's Brazilian midfielder Diego Assis steered Pekka Lyyski's unheralded side to a famous 2-1 win in the club's first ever final.

Europe

HJK were unable to reach the UEFA Europa League group stage for the second season running but they did make it to the play-offs, which was much further than Finland's other three representatives – SJK, FC Lahti and VPS Vaasa – who all exited in the first qualifying round.

National team

With Mixu Paatelainen relived of his duties, his assistant Markku Kanerva took charge for Finland's final four UEFA EURO 2016 qualifiers, and he proved a more than capable stand-in, leading the team to two wins and two draws. Young striker Joel Pohjanpalo, in particular, thrived under Kanerva's command, scoring vital goals in successive games against Greece, the Faroe Islands and Romania. The team fared considerably less well in friendlies following the permanent appointment of Hans Backe, a Swede with three Danish league titles on his CV, whose one saving grace would be a 1-1 draw with Belgium in Brussels.

DOMESTIC SEASON AT A GLANCE

Veikkausliiga 2015 final table

		Pld	Home W	D	L	F	A	Away W	D	L	F	A	Total W	D	L	F	A	Pts
1	**SJK Seinäjoki**	**33**	**13**	**1**	**3**	**34**	**8**	**5**	**5**	**6**	**16**	**14**	**18**	**6**	**9**	**50**	**22**	**60**
2	RoPS Rovaniemi	33	9	4	3	24	15	8	4	5	20	14	17	8	8	44	29	59
3	HJK Helsinki	33	11	4	2	28	11	5	6	5	17	19	16	10	7	45	30	58
4	FC Inter Turku	33	9	4	3	29	14	4	6	7	16	21	13	10	10	45	35	49
5	FC Lahti	33	7	6	4	19	19	5	6	5	19	17	12	12	9	38	36	48
6	IFK Mariehamn	33	7	4	6	18	20	4	8	4	12	16	11	12	10	30	36	45
7	HIFK Helsinki	33	5	9	2	22	19	5	4	8	20	23	10	13	10	42	42	43
8	Ilves Tampere	33	7	4	5	15	15	4	3	10	17	33	11	7	15	32	48	40
9	KuPS Kuopio	33	6	6	4	16	13	3	5	9	16	27	9	11	13	32	40	38
10	VPS Vaasa	33	6	5	6	23	21	2	4	10	13	22	8	9	16	36	43	33
11	FC KTP Kotka	33	5	5	6	16	19	2	6	9	11	25	7	11	15	27	44	32
12	FF Jaro	33	4	8	5	15	15	2	3	11	12	28	6	11	16	27	43	29

European qualification 2016/17

 Champion: SJK Seinäjoki (second qualifying round)

 Cup winner: IFK Mariehamn (first qualifying round)
RoPS Rovaniemi (first qualifying round)
HJK Helsinki (first qualifying round)

Top scorers	Aleksandr Kokko (RoPS), 17 goals
Relegated clubs	FF Jaro, FC KTP Kotka
Promoted clubs	PS Kemi, PK-35 Vantaa
Cup final	IFK Mariehamn 2-1 FC Inter Turku

Team of the season
(4-2-3-1)

Coach: Malinen (RoPS)

Bahne (Inter)

Saksela (RoPS) — Obilor (RoPS) — Gogoua (SJK) — Tahvanainen (SJK)

Yaghoubi (RoPS) — Okkonen (RoPS)

Soiri (VPS) — Tanaka (HJK) — Pelvas (SJK)

Kokko (RoPS)

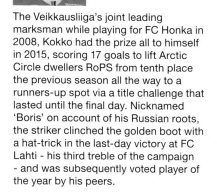

Player of the season

Aleksandr Kokko
(RoPS Rovaniemi)

The Veikkausliiga's joint leading marksman while playing for FC Honka in 2008, Kokko had the prize all to himself in 2015, scoring 17 goals to lift Arctic Circle dwellers RoPS from tenth place the previous season all the way to a runners-up spot via a title challenge that lasted until the final day. Nicknamed 'Boris' on account of his Russian roots, the striker clinched the golden boot with a hat-trick in the last-day victory at FC Lahti - his third treble of the campaign - and was subsequently voted player of the year by his peers.

Newcomer of the season

Kaan Kairinen
(FC Inter Turku)

The revelation of the 2015 Veikkausliiga was a player who did not turn 17 years of age until two months after it had drawn to a close. Kairinen had been given his league debut on the final day of the 2014 season and despite his tender years he became a regular in the FC Inter midfield, his ability to dictate the play with his exceptional left foot leading many local observers to predict a great future for him. A cup finalist with Inter, he was to leave the club in the winter, joining reigning Danish champions FC Midtjylland.

NATIONAL TEAM

Top five all-time caps
Jari Litmanen (137); Sami Hyypiä &
Jonatan Johansson (105); Ari Hjelm (100);
Joonas Kolkka (98)

Top five all-time goals
Jari Litmanen (32); Mikael Forssell (29);
Jonatan Johansson (22); Ari Hjelm (20);
Mixu Paatelainen (18)

Results 2015/16

Date	Opponent		Venue	Res	Score	Scorers
04/09/15	Greece (ECQ)	A	Piraeus	W	1-0	Pohjanpalo (75)
07/09/15	Faroe Islands (ECQ)	H	Helsinki	W	1-0	Pohjanpalo (23)
08/10/15	Romania (ECQ)	A	Bucharest	D	1-1	Pohjanpalo (67)
11/10/15	Northern Ireland (ECQ)	H	Helsinki	D	1-1	Arajuuri (87)
10/01/16	Sweden	N	Abu Dhabi (UAE)	L	0-3	
13/01/16	Iceland	N	Abu Dhabi (UAE)	L	0-1	
26/03/16	Poland	A	Wroclaw	L	0-5	
29/03/16	Norway	A	Oslo	L	0-2	
01/06/16	Belgium	A	Brussels	D	1-1	Hämäläinen (53)
06/06/16	Italy	A	Verona	L	0-2	

Appearances 2015/16

Coach: (Markku Kanerva) 24/05/64 / (01/01/16) Hans Backe (SWE) 14/02/52

Name	DOB	Club	GRE	FRO	ROU	NIR	Swe	Isl	Pol	Nor	Bel	Ita	Caps	Goals
Lukas Hradecky	24/11/89	Eintracht Frankfurt (GER)	G	G	G	G			G		G	G	29	-
Kari Arkivuo	23/06/83	Häcken (SWE)	D	D	D64			D76	D	D38	D71	D	46	1
Joona Toivio	10/03/88	Molde (NOR)	D		s62				D	D	D	D	38	2
Paulus Arajuuri	15/06/88	Lech (POL)	D	D	D62	D			D	D	D	D	15	1
Jere Uronen	13/07/94	Helsingborg (SWE) /Genk (BEL)	D	D	D	D				D	s79	D72	19	-
Alexander Ring	09/04/91	Kaiserslautern (GER)	M	M	M	M44			M83		M54	M72	37	1
Tim Sparv	20/02/87	Midtjylland (DEN)	M	M		M				M	M	M	54	1
Markus Halsti	19/03/84	DC United (USA) /unattached	M	D	M						D	D	28	-
Perparim Hetemaj	12/12/86	Chievo (ITA)	M	M	M				M46	M	M83	M	43	4
Kasper Hämäläinen	08/08/86	Lech (POL) /Legia (POL)	A46	s93	s77	s79			A46	s63	A68		52	8
Teemu Pukki	29/03/90	Brondby (DEN)	A67		A	s66	A63	A	s62	A63		A46	49	8
Berat Sadik	14/09/86	Krylya Sovetov (RUS)	s46/81			A66							11	1
Joel Pohjanpalo	13/09/94	Düsseldorf (GER)	s67	A93	A77	A			A62		s68		20	4
Sakari Mattila	14/07/89	Fulham (ENG)	s81	s84		M							9	-
Thomas Lam	18/12/93	Zwolle (NED)			M84				s78		s83	s72	5	-
Riku Riski	16/08/89	Göteborg (SWE)			A74								26	4
Tim Väyrynen	30/03/93	Dynamo Dresden (GER)		s74						s86			6	-
Niklas Moisander	29/09/85	Sampdoria (ITA)			D								51	2
Rasmus Schüller	18/06/91	HJK /Häcken (SWE)			M	M79	M72	M61	s46	s46			17	-
Ville Jalasto	19/04/86	Stabæk (NOR) /HJK			s64	D	D86			D79			8	-
Juhani Ojala	19/06/89	HJK				D							15	-
Robin Lod	17/04/93	Panathinaikos (GRE)				s44			s46	A46		s46	7	-
Mika Hilander	17/08/83	Ilves					G						1	-
Jukka Raitala	15/09/88	AaB (DEN) /Sogndal (NOR)					D	D46		s38	D	s72	31	-
Tapio Heikkilä	08/04/90	SJK					D	D61					3	-
Hannu Patronen	23/05/84	Sogndal (NOR)					D46	s61					6	-
Petteri Forsell	16/10/90	Mariehamn					M46	s76					6	1
Mehmet Hetemaj	08/12/87	SJK					M46	M46					5	-
Akseli Pelvas	08/02/89	Falkenberg (SWE)					M46	A46					3	-
Roope Riski	16/08/91	Haugesund (NOR)					A72	s46					4	1
Jarkko Hurme	04/06/86	SJK					s46						12	1
Juha Pirinen	22/10/91	RoPS					s46	M					2	-
Johannes Laaksonen	13/12/90	SJK					s46	s46					3	-
Janne Saksela	14/03/93	RoPS					s46	M	s83		s71		4	-
Aleksandr Kokko	04/06/87	RoPS					s63						1	-
Timo Tahvanainen	26/06/86	SJK					s72	s46					2	-
Simon Skrabb	19/01/95	Gefle (SWE)					s72						1	-
Daniel O'Shaughnessy	14/09/94	Brentford (ENG)					s86	D					2	-
Henrik Moisander	29/09/85	Lahti						G					2	-
Matej Hradecky	17/04/95	unattached						s61					1	-
Roman Eremenko	19/03/87	CSKA Moskva (RUS)							M78	M	M	M	72	5
Niki Mäenpää	23/01/85	Brighton (ENG)								G46			26	-
Valtteri Moren	15/06/91	Waasland-Beveren (BEL)								D86			4	1
Jesse Joronen	21/03/93	Fulham (ENG)								s46			2	-
Joni Kauko	12/07/90	Cottbus (GER)									s54		7	-

EUROPE

HJK Helsinki

CHAMPIONS LEAGUE

Second qualifying round - FK Ventspils (LVA)
A 3-1 Zeneli (75p), Jallow (86), Tanaka (90+2)
Örlund, Baah, Heikkilä, Heikkinen, Savage, Tanaka, Havenaar (Jallow 84), Sorsa, Schüller, Zeneli, Moussi. Coach: Mika Lehkosuo (FIN)

H 1-0 Havenaar (83)
Örlund, Baah, Heikkilä, Heikkinen, Savage, Tanaka (Klinga 67), Havenaar, Sorsa (Peiponen 87), Schüller, Zeneli (Jallow 85), Moussi. Coach: Mika Lehkosuo (FIN)

Third qualifying round - FC Astana (KAZ)
H 0-0
Örlund, Baah, Heikkinen, Savage, Tanaka, Havenaar (Jallow 90+2), Moren, Sorsa, Schüller, Zeneli, Moussi. Coach: Mika Lehkosuo (FIN)

A 3-4 Jallow (4), Baah (42), Zeneli (86p)
Örlund, Baah, Heikkinen, Tanaka (Heikkilä 90), Havenaar, Moren, Jallow (Mendy 78), Sorsa, Schüller, Zeneli, Moussi. Coach: Mika Lehkosuo (FIN)

EUROPA LEAGUE

Play-offs - FC Krasnodar (RUS)
A 1-5 Jallow (18)
Örlund, Baah (Heikkilä 60), Ojala, Heikkinen, Tanaka (Kolehmainen 22), Peiponen, Jallow, Mendy (Malolo 84), Schüller, Zeneli, Moussi. Coach: Mika Lehkosuo (FIN)

H 0-0
Dähne, Lehtinen, Ojala (Heikkinen 64), Heikkilä, Peiponen, Jallow (Tanaka 68), Klinga (Lingman 77), Mendy, Schüller, Zeneli, Moussi. Coach: Mika Lehkosuo (FIN)

SJK Seinäjoki

EUROPA LEAGUE

First qualifying round - FH Hafnarfjördur (ISL)
H 0-1
Aksalu, Dorman, Milosavljević, Laaksonen, Vasara (Atajić 64), Brown (Tahvanainen 81), Lehtinen (Ngueukam 67), Savić, Pelvas, Gogoua, Hetemaj. Coach: Simo Valakari (FIN)

A 0-1
Aksalu, Milosavljević, Tahvanainen, Laaksonen, Brown (Vasara 65), Ngueukam, Lehtinen (Atajić 45), Pelvas (Lidman 89), Aalto, Gogoua, Hetemaj. Coach: Simo Valakari (FIN)

FC Lahti

EUROPA LEAGUE

First qualifying round - IF Elfsborg (SWE)
H 2-2 Lagerblom (25), Matheus Alves (61)
Moisander, Hauhia, Gela, Kärkkäinen, Shala (Ristola 78), Lagerblom (Sesay 41), Joenmäki, Paananen, Matheus Alves (Rafael 72), Pasanen, Länsitalo. Coach: Toni Korkeakunnas (FIN)

A 0-5
H Moisander, Hauhia, Gela, Kärkkäinen, Shala (M'Boma 46), Joenmäki, Toivomäki, Paananen, Sesay (Rafael 55), Matheus Alves (Ristola 85), Pasanen. Coach: Toni Korkeakunnas (FIN)

VPS Vaasa

EUROPA LEAGUE

First qualifying round - AIK Solna (SWE)
H 2-2 Catovic (45+3), Seabrook (65)
Sillanpää, Lahti, Koskimaa, Engström, Abdulahi, Catovic, Björk (Kula 84), Soiri, Seabrook (Tamminen 68), Mäkelä, Niemi. Coach: Petri Vuorinen (FIN)

A 0-4
Sillanpää, Lahti, Koskimaa, Engström, Viitikko, Abdulahi (Alanko 77), Catovic, Björk (Hertsi 63), Soiri, Kula, Seabrook (Tamminen 46). Coach: Petri Vuorinen (FIN)

DOMESTIC LEAGUE CLUB-BY-CLUB

HIFK Helsinki

1897 • Sonera Stadium (10,800) •
hifkfotboll.fi
Major honours
Finnish League (7) 1930, 1931, 1933, 1937, 1947, 1959, 1961
Coach: Jani Honkavaara

2015

19/04	a	Mariehamn	D	1-1	Terävä
23/04	h	HJK	D	1-1	Korhonen (p)
29/04	a	RoPS	L	0-2	
03/05	a	SJK	L	0-2	
08/05	h	Inter	W	2-1	Peltonen, Kuusijärvi
14/05	a	Ilves	D	1-1	Halme
17/05	h	Jaro	W	3-2	Sihvola 2, Jurvainen
21/05	a	KTP	W	2-1	Salmikivi, Bäckman
25/05	h	KuPS	D	1-1	Sihvola
03/06	a	Lahti	L	0-2	
06/06	h	Jaro	D	0-0	
16/06	h	RoPS	D	1-1	Lassas
22/06	a	Inter	L	1-3	Rahimi
25/06	a	VPS	W	2-0	Korhonen (p), Kastrati
28/06	h	Mariehamn	D	1-1	Kastrati
06/07	a	HJK	D	1-1	Vesala
19/07	h	SJK	L	1-4	Halme
25/07	a	Jaro	W	2-0	Terävä, Sihvola
01/08	h	Ilves	D	2-2	Peltonen, Sihvola
09/08	a	KuPS	L	1-2	
17/08	h	RoPS	D	1-1	Salmikivi
23/08	a	HJK	D	1-1	Sinisalo
30/08	h	VPS	W	3-0	Sihvola 2, Anyamele
10/09	a	Mariehamn	L	0-1	
14/09	h	KuPS	L	1-3	Salmikivi
17/09	h	VPS	L	0-3	
20/09	a	Lahti	W	5-0	Peltonen, Salmikivi, Terävä, Jurvainen, Sihvola
23/09	h	KTP	D	0-0	
28/09	h	SJK	W	1-0	Korhonen
04/10	a	KTP	L	0-1	
15/10	h	Lahti	D	3-3	Jurvainen 2, Aho
18/10	a	Ilves	W	3-1	Ahonen, Salmikivi 2
25/10	h	Inter	W	2-0	Väisänen, Sihvola

No	Name	Nat	DoB	Pos	Aps	(s)	Gls
2	Tuomas Aho		27/05/81	D	21	(2)	1
23	Jesse Ahonen		22/06/92	D	6	(5)	
27	Nnaemeka Anyamele		16/05/94	M	15	(6)	1
17	Jani Bäckman		20/03/88	A	19	(3)	1
71	Carljohan Eriksson		25/04/95	G	20		
8	Jukka Halme		29/05/85	M	25	(3)	2
18	Matias Hänninen		15/03/91	D	13	(3)	
6	Keaton Isaksson		21/04/94	M		(2)	
1	Mika Johansson		13/03/84	G	13		
12	Otto-Pekka Jurvainen		01/02/85	D	14	(1)	4
99	Kastriot Kastrati		02/10/93	M	3	(11)	2
31	Joni Korhonen		08/02/87	A	28	(3)	3
3	Pauli Kuusijärvi		21/03/86	D	24	(2)	1
10	Fredrik Lassas		01/10/96	A	18	(7)	1
16	Tuomas Mustonen		04/06/85	A	1		
11	Eero Peltonen		22/12/86	A	22	(8)	3
14	Youness Rahimi		13/02/95	A	16	(9)	1
26	Ville Salmikivi		20/05/92	A	14	(11)	6
9	Pekka Sihvola		22/04/84	A	22	(7)	9
5	Jukka Sinisalo		21/05/82	D	18	(4)	1
7	Kalle Sotka		04/10/91	D	2	(1)	
21	Ville Taulo		14/08/85	M	8	(4)	
13	Esa Terävä		08/11/87	A	12	(4)	3
4	Tommi Vesala		12/01/86	D	23		1
15	Sauli Väisänen		05/06/94	D	6		1

HJK Helsinki

1907 • Sonera Stadium (10,800) • hjk.fi

Major honours
Finnish League (27) 1911, 1912, 1917, 1918, 1919, 1923, 1925, 1936, 1938, 1964, 1973, 1978, 1981, 1985, 1987, 1988, 1990, 1992, 1997, 2002, 2003, 2009, 2010, 2011, 2012, 2013, 2014; Finnish Cup (12) 1966, 1981, 1984, 1993, 1996, 1998, 2000, 2003, 2006, 2008, 2011, 2014

Coach: Mika Lehkosuo

2015

12/04	a	RoPS	W	3-1	Heikkilä, Zeneli, Tanaka
19/04	h	Lahti	D	1-1	Klinga
23/04	a	HIFK	D	1-1	Havenaar
29/04	h	KTP	W	1-0	Savage
03/05	h	Jaro	W	3-0	Zeneli, Savage 2
08/05	a	KuPS	L	0-1	
11/05	h	VPS	W	1-0	Lod
14/05	h	Mariehamn	W	1-0	Mendy
17/05	h	VPS	D	2-2	og (Koskimaa), Tanaka
21/05	h	Inter	W	2-0	Havenaar 2
24/05	a	SJK	W	2-1	Savage, Tanaka
29/05	a	KuPS	D	1-1	Savage
03/06	h	Ilves	W	2-1	Savage, Sorsa
06/06	a	Lahti	D	0-0	
17/06	h	SJK	W	3-1	Zeneli, Havenaar, Tanaka
22/06	a	Jaro	W	4-0	Tanaka, Zeneli 2 (1p), Jallow
26/06	a	Ilves	D	1-1	Tanaka
29/06	a	Inter	L	0-3	
06/07	h	HIFK	D	1-1	Tanaka
10/07	a	RoPS	L	1-2	Zeneli (p)
25/07	a	KTP	W	2-1	Zeneli, Jallow (p)
12/08	h	Lahti	W	1-0	Jallow
23/08	h	HIFK	D	1-1	Mendy
30/08	a	Ilves	L	0-1	
10/09	h	Inter	L	0-2	
13/09	a	Jaro	D	1-1	Tanaka
20/09	h	RoPS	L	0-2	
23/09	a	SJK	L	0-3	
27/09	h	KTP	D	1-1	Jallow
01/10	a	Mariehamn	W	2-0	Peiponen, Kolehmainen
04/10	a	VPS	W	2-1	Heikkilä, og (Koskimaa)
18/10	h	Mariehamn	W	4-0	Zeneli (p), Jallow, Savage 2
25/10	a	KuPS	W	1-0	Jallow

No	Name	Nat	DoB	Pos	Aps	(s)	Gls
95	Ademir	BRA	30/01/95	A		(2)	
17	Nikolai Alho		12/03/93	A		(2)	
3	Gideon Baah	GHA	01/10/91	D	14	(2)	
25	Joachim Böckerman		24/07/97	D		(2)	
21	Thomas Dähne	GER	04/01/94	G	6		
24	Aapo Halme		22/05/98	D	2		
14	Mike Havenaar	JPN	20/05/87	A	15	(5)	4
5	Tapio Heikkilä		08/04/90	D	25	(2)	2
6	Markus Heikkinen		13/10/78	D	17	(2)	
18	Ousman Jallow	GAM	21/10/88	A	11	(9)	6
99	Macoumba Kandji	SEN	02/08/85	A	5		
20	Matti Klinga		10/12/94	M	11	(8)	1
13	Toni Kolehmainen		20/07/88	M	14	(7)	1
11	Veli Lampi		18/07/84	D	13	(1)	
2	Alex Lehtinen		09/04/96	D	3	(2)	
7	Lucas Lingman		25/01/98	M	2	(2)	
31	Robin Lod		17/04/93	M	9	(1)	1
26	Obed Malolo		18/04/97	M	6	(9)	
22	Formose Mendy	GNB	23/03/89	A	5	(8)	2
16	Valtteri Moren		15/06/91	D	12		
91	Guy Moussi	FRA	23/01/85	M	15	(7)	
4	Juhani Ojala		19/06/89	D	4		
15	Roni Peiponen		09/04/97	D	14	(3)	1
35	Saku-Pekka Sahlgren		08/04/92	G	7		
8	Demba Savage	GAM	17/06/88	A	18	(7)	8
28	Rasmus Schüller		18/06/91	M	27	(2)	
27	Sebastian Sorsa		25/01/84	D	20	(4)	1
33	Taye Taiwo	NGA	16/04/85	D	11		
10	Atomu Tanaka	JPN	04/10/87	M	30	(1)	8
80	Erfan Zeneli		28/12/86	M	27		8
1	Daniel Örlund	SWE	23/06/80	G	20		

Ilves Tampere

1931 • Tammelan stadion (5,000) • ilvesedustus.com

Major honours
Finnish League (1) 1983; Finnish Cup (2) 1979, 1990

Coach: Keith Armstrong (ENG);
(07/10/15) Marco Baruffato (ITA)

2015

19/04	a	Inter	L	1-3	Petrescu
23/04	h	KTP	D	0-0	
29/04	a	Jaro	L	1-3	Mäkijärvi
03/05	h	RoPS	L	0-1	
08/05	a	VPS	W	3-2	Kujala, Lahtinen, Hjelm
14/05	h	HIFK	D	1-1	Nieminen
17/05	a	Mariehamn	L	0-2	
20/05	a	SJK	L	0-3	
23/05	h	Lahti	W	2-1	Emenike, og (Ristola)
03/06	a	HJK	L	1-2	Kdouh
06/06	h	Inter	W	1-0	Petrescu
16/06	a	Jaro	L	0-3	
22/06	a	RoPS	L	1-4	Lahtinen
26/06	h	HJK	D	1-1	Hjelm
05/07	a	Mariehamn	D	0-0	
12/07	h	KuPS	W	1-0	Petrescu (p)
19/07	a	Lahti	L	1-3	Korte
26/07	h	SJK	D	0-0	
01/08	a	HIFK	D	2-2	Lahtinen 2
09/08	h	KTP	W	2-0	Korte, Ala-Myllymäki
12/08	a	Inter	W	2-1	Lahtinen 2
16/08	a	Jaro	W	1-0	Aho
22/08	a	RoPS	D	0-0	
30/08	h	HJK	W	1-0	Petrescu
10/09	a	VPS	L	0-1	
13/09	a	Mariehamn	L	1-3	Lahtinen
17/09	h	KuPS	W	1-0	Aho
20/09	a	VPS	W	2-1	Aho, Hjelm
27/09	h	Lahti	L	1-2	Hynynen
04/10	a	SJK	L	1-2	Ugwunna
15/10	h	VPS	L	1-3	Petrescu (p)
18/10	h	HIFK	L	1-3	Lahtinen
25/10	a	KTP	W	2-1	Lahtinen 2 (1p)

No	Name	Nat	DoB	Pos	Aps	(s)	Gls
3	Heikki Aho		16/03/83	D	18	(1)	3
15	Lauri Ala-Myllymäki		04/06/97	M	15	(12)	1
24	Mamadou Diouf	SEN	15/09/90	A	4	(4)	
20	Mbachu Emenike	NGA	21/05/89	M	10	(17)	1
1	Mika Hilander		17/08/83	G	33		
9	Jonne Hjelm		14/01/88	A	26	(3)	3
24	Antti Hynynen		30/05/84	D	31		1
19	Jaakko Juuti		13/08/87	M	15	(9)	
93	Mohammad Kdouh	LIB	04/05/93	A	3	(4)	1
18	Omar Khary		12/05/95	M	7	(7)	
25	Eero Korte		20/09/87	M	20	(3)	2
28	Antti Koskinen		19/07/88	D	5	(1)	
28	Roope Kostiainen		22/05/95	A		(1)	
7	Jussi Kujala		04/04/83	M	29		1
23	Ibrahim Köse		04/03/92	M	3	(4)	
23	Mika Lahtinen		30/04/85	A	24	(5)	10
26	Mikko-Jussi Laine		08/09/96	M		(1)	
16	Tatu Miettunen		24/04/95	M	19	(2)	
21	Antti Mäkijärvi		08/12/93	M	10	(7)	1
6	Samu Nieminen		14/01/92	D	24		1
5	Antti Ojanperä		06/04/83	M	29	(2)	
27	Tomi Petrescu		24/07/86	M	28	(2)	5
27	Jaakko Rantanen		10/09/92	D	5	(2)	
28	Matti Saari		03/11/94	D	2	(1)	
31	Diogo Tomas		31/07/97	D	1		
14	Henry Ugwunna	NGA	09/05/89	A	2	(2)	1
4	Olli Vakkala		27/06/82	D		(4)	
22	Gullit Zolameso		02/06/95	M		(1)	

FC Inter Turku

1990 • Veritas Stadion (9,300) • fcinter.fi

Major honours
Finnish League (1) 2008; Finnish Cup (1) 2009

Coach: Job Dragtsma (NED)

2015

12/04	h	SJK	D	1-1	Njoku
19/04	h	Ilves	W	3-1	Gnabouyou, Hambo 2
23/04	a	RoPS	W	4-0	og (Lahdenmäki), Kauppi, Hambo 2
03/05	a	Lahti	D	1-1	Gnabouyou
08/05	h	HIFK	L	1-2	Ojala (p)
11/05	h	Jaro	W	2-0	Gnabouyou, Ojala
14/05	h	KTP	W	4-1	Gnabouyou, Njoku, Duah, Aho (p)
17/05	a	KuPS	D	1-1	Aho (p)
21/05	a	HJK	L	0-2	
25/05	h	Mariehamn	L	1-1	Aho
03/06	a	VPS	L	0-3	
06/06	a	Ilves	L	0-1	
17/06	h	KTP	W	3-0	Ojala 2, Gnabouyou
22/06	h	HIFK	W	3-1	Lehtonen, Duah, Njoku
25/06	a	RoPS	D	1-1	Onovo
29/06	h	HJK	W	3-0	Onovo 3
05/07	a	VPS	D	0-0	
13/07	h	Mariehamn	D	1-1	Hämäläinen
19/07	a	KuPS	D	1-1	Duah
26/07	h	Lahti	L	0-2	
02/08	a	SJK	W	1-0	Aho (p)
12/08	h	Ilves	L	1-2	Salminen
19/08	a	KTP	L	1-4	Ferati
23/08	a	Jaro	D	0-0	
29/08	h	RoPS	W	2-0	Aho (p), Lehtonen
10/09	a	HJK	W	2-0	Gnabouyou (p), Mannström
14/09	h	VPS	D	1-1	Njoku
21/09	a	Mariehamn	W	1-0	N'Gal 2
30/09	h	KuPS	W	3-1	Duah 2, Aho (p)
04/10	a	Lahti	L	1-3	Kauppi
15/10	h	Jaro	W	1-0	Lehtonen
18/10	h	SJK	L	0-2	
25/10	a	HIFK	L	0-2	

No	Name	Nat	DoB	Pos	Aps	(s)	Gls
14	Joni Aho		12/04/86	D	21	(5)	6
1	Magnus Bahne		15/03/79	G	28		
2	Egzon Belica	MKD	03/09/90	D	23	(4)	
26	Demba Camara	GUI	11/08/95	A		(6)	
19	Diogo	BRA	14/01/88	M	6	(7)	
21	Solomon Duah		07/01/93	A	21	(6)	5
20	Alban Ferati		01/11/91	M	3	(11)	1
10	Guy Gnabouyou	FRA	01/12/89	A	27	(1)	6
9	Vahid Hambo		03/02/95	M	6		4
3	Juuso Hämäläinen		28/12/93	D	25	(2)	1
22	Kaan Kairinen		22/12/98	M	17	(9)	
6	Petros Kanakoudis	GRE	16/04/84	D	24		
16	Kalle Kauppi		06/05/92	M	4	(5)	2
27	Aleksi Laiho		17/06/93	M		(2)	
29	Henri Lehtonen		28/07/80	M	31	(1)	3
12	Jukka Lehtovaara		15/03/88	G	3		
8	Sebastian Mannström		29/10/88	M	10		1
5	Eric Matoukou	CMR	08/07/83	D	24	(1)	
23	Serge N'Gal	CMR	13/01/86	A	6	(5)	2
25	Philip Njoku	NGA	03/06/96	A	14	(10)	4
7	Ari Nyman		07/02/84	M	28	(3)	
17	Mika Ojala		21/06/88	M	14		4
4	Vincent Onovo	NGA	10/12/95	M	18	(3)	4
28	Oskari Qvick		15/12/97	M	2	(3)	
13	Eemeli Reponen		06/06/90	G	2	(1)	
24	Juho Salminen		08/08/95	D	6	(6)	1

FF Jaro

1965 • Centralplan (5,000) • ffjaro.fi
Coach: Alexei Eremenko Sr

2015

12/04	h	Mariehamn	D	1-1	Brunell
23/04	h	SJK	L	0-1	
29/04	h	Ilves	W	3-1	Moore, Kadio 2
03/05	a	HJK	L	0-3	
08/05	h	RoPS	L	1-2	Denis
11/05	a	Inter	L	0-2	
14/05	h	Lahti	D	1-1	Brunell
17/05	h	HIFK	L	2-3	Dixon, Atakayi
21/05	a	VPS	W	2-1	Vaganov, Atakayi
24/05	h	KTP	L	0-2	
06/06	h	HIFK	D	0-0	
16/06	h	Ilves	W	3-0	Rivera, Kadio, Virtanen
22/06	a	HJK	L	0-4	
25/06	h	KTP	L	0-2	
28/06	h	RoPS	L	0-1	
05/07	a	KuPS	W	3-1	Dixon, Rivera, S Eremenko
12/07	h	VPS	W	2-1	Virtanen, Kadio
19/07	a	Mariehamn	L	3-4	Rivera, Vaganov, Moore
25/07	h	HIFK	L	0-1	
02/08	a	Lahti	D	1-1	Rivera
09/08	h	SJK	W	1-0	Moore
16/08	a	Ilves	L	0-1	
23/08	h	Inter	D	0-0	
29/08	a	KTP	L	0-1	
10/09	a	RoPS	D	0-0	
13/09	h	HJK	D	1-1	Kadio
17/09	h	Mariehamn	D	0-0	
20/09	a	VPS	L	1-2	S Eremenko
23/09	h	KuPS	D	1-1	Denis
04/10	a	KuPS	L	0-2	
15/10	a	Inter	L	0-1	
18/10	h	Lahti	D	1-1	Dixon
25/10	a	SJK	L	0-2	

No	Name	Nat	DoB	Pos	Aps	(s)	Gls
24	Alibek Aliev	SWE	16/08/96	A	5	(5)	
19	Serge Atakayi		30/01/99	A	3	(13)	2
6	Johan Brunell		29/05/91	D	15		2
9	David Carlsson	SWE	07/03/83	A		(2)	
13	David Silva	CPV	11/10/86	A	9	(1)	
11	Denis	BRA	29/12/89	A	23	(3)	2
22	Jamar Dixon	CAN	05/06/89	D	19	(8)	3
10	Jonas Emet		13/02/88	M	5	(1)	
14	Alexei Eremenko		24/03/83	M	11		
23	Sergei Eremenko		06/01/99	M	3	(16)	2
7	Didier Kadio	CIV	05/04/90	D	31		5
4	Mathias Kullström		02/01/87	D	19	(1)	
17	Kevin Larsson		31/01/96	A		(3)	
15	Walter Moore	GUY	01/09/84	D	29		3
18	Peter Opiyo	KEN	01/08/92	M	22	(1)	
30	Seth Paintsil	GHA	20/04/95	A	10	(8)	
5	Reginaldo	BRA	08/07/92	D	16	(6)	
21	José Manuel Rivera	MEX	16/06/86	A	26	(2)	4
20	Oskar Sandström		16/04/98	D	1	(3)	
8	Jari Sara		25/04/89	D	20		
27	Ilya Vaganov	RUS	15/01/89	D	29	(2)	2
7	Joona Veteli		31/04/95	M	18	(9)	
16	Adam Vidjeskog		07/07/98	M		(1)	
26	Jani Virtanen		06/05/88	M	16	(10)	2
25	Emil Öhberg		20/06/93	G	5	(1)	
1	Jesse Öst		20/10/90	G	28		

FC KTP Kotka

1927 • Arto Tolsa Areena (4,200) • fcktp.fi
Major honours
*Finnish League (2) 1951, 1952; Finnish Cup (4)
1958, 1961, 1967, 1980*
Coach: Sami Ristilä

2015

12/04	a	Lahti	D	1-1	Äijälä
19/04	h	KuPS	L	0-1	
23/04	a	Ilves	D	0-0	
29/04	h	HJK	L	0-1	
03/05	h	VPS	W	3-2	Gruborovics, Minkenen, Äijälä
08/05	a	Mariehamn	L	1-2	Kaivonurmi
14/05	a	Inter	L	1-4	Salonen
17/05	h	SJK	D	0-0	
21/05	h	HIFK	L	1-2	Lehtonen
24/05	a	Jaro	W	2-0	Gruborovics, Äijälä
28/05	h	Lahti	D	0-0	
03/06	a	RoPS	L	0-4	
08/06	h	Mariehamn	L	0-2	
17/06	a	Inter	L	0-3	
22/06	h	KuPS	W	3-1	Lehtonen 2, Gruborovics
25/06	a	Jaro	D	0-0	
06/07	h	RoPS	D	0-0	
12/07	a	SJK	L	0-1	
25/07	a	HJK	L	1-2	Gruborovics
03/08	h	VPS	D	0-0	
09/08	h	Ilves	L	0-2	
12/08	a	Mariehamn	L	0-1	Äijälä (p)
19/08	h	Inter	W	4-1	Anttilainen 2, Gruborovics, Ikävalko
23/08	a	KuPS	D	1-1	Ikävalko
29/08	h	Jaro	W	1-0	Oksanen
10/09	a	Lahti	L	2-3	Ikävalko, Wusu
14/09	h	RoPS	L	0-4	
20/09	h	SJK	L	1-3	Ikävalko
23/09	a	HIFK	D	0-0	
27/09	h	HJK	D	1-1	A Lody
04/10	h	HIFK	W	1-0	Äijälä
18/10	a	VPS	D	1-1	Äijälä (p)
25/10	h	Ilves	L	1-2	Wusu

No	Name	Nat	DoB	Pos	Aps	(s)	Gls
21	Nosh A Lody		17/07/89	D	29	(1)	1
30	Sasha Anttilainen		19/12/86	A	8	(2)	2
15	Felipe Aspegren		12/02/94	D	29	(1)	
10	Tamás Gruborovics	HUN	03/07/84	A	25	(4)	5
17	Emerik Grönroos		06/07/94	M		(3)	
33	Marcus Heimonen		11/10/93	M	7	(9)	
33	Craig Hill	USA	27/12/87	G	6		
99	Niko Ikävalko		24/04/88	A	15	(8)	4
4	Henri Järviniemi		18/08/89	D	10	(9)	
31	Samuli Kaivonurmi		03/03/88	A	8	(3)	1
31	Sauli Kilpeläinen		12/08/96	G	1	(1)	
9	Juho Lehtonen		03/08/92	A	14	(9)	3
22	Drew Lewis	ENG	09/04/95	A		(1)	
5	Shane McFaul	IRL	23/05/86	M	24	(2)	
6	Joel Mero		07/02/95	D	1	(3)	
20	Valeri Minkenen		09/04/89	M	20	(7)	1
25	Eetu Muinonen		11/06/96	M	7	(1)	
7	Josh Mulvany	ENG	26/12/88	M	8	(5)	
8	Ville Oksanen		25/02/87	M	26	(4)	1
13	Giorgi Ositashvili	GEO	13/03/85	D	12	(9)	
2	Topi Pasi		23/05/96	D		(2)	
1	Jere Pyhäranta		06/07/92	G	22		
12	Saku-Pekka Sahlgren		08/04/92	G	4		
3	Juuso Salonen		28/07/91	D	13	(4)	1
18	Aleksi Tarvonen		19/07/94	A	10	(6)	
23	Jordi van Gelderen	NED	26/04/90	D	31		
24	Babatunde Wusu	NGA	18/04/84	A	3	(4)	2
11	Ilari Äijälä		30/09/86	M	30	(1)	6

KuPS Kuopio

1923 • Savon Sanomat Areena (3,700) • kups.fi
Major honours
*Finnish League (5) 1956, 1958, 1966, 1974, 1976;
Finnish Cup (2) 1968, 1989*
Coach: Marko Rajamäki

2015

19/04	a	KTP	W	1-0	og (Gruborovics)
23/04	h	VPS	W	1-0	Savolainen
03/05	a	Mariehamn	D	1-1	Vartiainen
08/05	h	HJK	W	1-0	Trafford
11/05	h	SJK	L	0-5	
14/05	a	RoPS	L	0-1	
17/05	h	Inter	D	1-1	Pennanen (p)
20/05	h	Lahti	L	0-3	
25/05	a	HIFK	D	1-1	Diallo
29/05	a	HJK	D	1-1	Trafford
06/06	h	VPS	D	0-0	
17/06	a	Mariehamn	W	3-2	Markić, Trafford 2
22/06	a	KTP	L	1-3	Poutiainen
25/06	h	Lahti	W	1-0	Trafford
05/07	h	Jaro	L	1-3	Ilo
12/07	a	Ilves	L	0-1	
19/07	h	Inter	D	1-1	Ilo
02/08	h	RoPS	W	3-0	Markić, Savolainen 2
09/08	h	HIFK	W	2-0	Niskanen, Savolainen
12/08	a	VPS	D	2-2	Sirbiladze, Bowen
19/08	h	Mariehamn	D	0-0	
23/08	h	KTP	D	1-1	Sirbiladze
26/08	a	SJK	L	0-1	
30/08	a	Lahti	L	0-1	
10/09	h	SJK	D	1-1	Nissilä
14/09	a	HIFK	W	3-1	Rannankari, Bowen, Ilo
17/09	a	Ilves	L	0-1	
20/09	h	Ilves	L	1-2	Nissilä
23/09	a	Jaro	D	1-1	Sirbiladze
30/09	a	Inter	L	1-3	Hakola
04/10	h	Jaro	W	2-0	Hakola, Nissilä
18/10	a	RoPS	L	1-2	Nissilä
25/10	h	HJK	L	0-1	

No	Name	Nat	DoB	Pos	Aps	(s)	Gls
11	Freddy Adu	USA	02/06/89	A	3	(2)	
31	Ali Al-Musawi		12/09/96	A		(1)	
11	Tristan Bowen	USA	30/01/91	A	11	(1)	2
9	Francis Chibuike	NGA	06/06/93	A	5	(5)	
3	Hamed Coulibaly	CIV	16/12/96	D	14	(3)	
29	Babacar Diallo	SEN	25/03/89	D	32		1
7	Juha Hakola		27/10/87	A	5	(4)	2
26	Dani Hatakka		12/03/94	D	23	(6)	
20	Miikka Ilo		09/05/82	A	19	(7)	3
28	Aatu Laatikainen		03/01/97	M		(4)	
14	Tomi Maanoja		21/05/91	G	31		
14	Toni Markić	BIH	25/10/90	D	27		2
17	Stephen McCarthy	USA	21/06/88	D	7	(3)	
15	Ilmari Niskanen		27/10/97	A	9	(11)	1
30	Urho Nissilä		04/04/96	M	16	(7)	4
30	Joonas Nissinen		24/04/97	M		(1)	
30	Joachim Osvold	NOR	23/09/94	A	6	(4)	
8	Petteri Pennanen		19/09/90	M	9		1
21	Patrick Poutiainen		14/06/91	M	26	(2)	1
16	Joonas Pöntinen		19/03/90	G	2		
32	Tuomas Rannankari		21/05/91	D	29		1
31	Antti-Ville Räisänen		04/04/98	M		(2)	
6	Saku Savolainen		13/08/96	A	16	(11)	4
10	Irakli Sirbiladze	GEO	27/09/82	A	25	(4)	3
23	Ebrima Sohna	GAM	14/12/88	M	25	(4)	
19	Charlie Trafford	CAN	24/05/92	M	23	(5)	5
22	Joel Vartiainen		14/03/94	M		(2)	1

FC Lahti

1996 • Kisapuisto (3,000) • fclahti.fi
Coach: Toni Korkeakunnas

2015

12/04	h	KTP	D	1-1	Matheus Alves
19/04	a	HJK	D	1-1	Leandro Motta
23/04	h	Mariehamn	L	0-1	
03/05	h	Inter	D	1-1	Länsitalo
08/05	h	SJK	W	1-0	Ristola
14/05	a	Jaro	D	1-1	Ristola
17/05	h	RoPS	L	1-2	Matheus Alves
20/05	a	KuPS	W	3-0	Toivomäki, Matheus Alves (p), Gela
23/05	a	Ilves	L	1-2	Shala
28/05	a	KTP	D	0-0	
03/06	h	HIFK	W	2-0	Matheus Alves (p), Länsitalo
06/06	h	HJK	D	0-0	
17/06	a	VPS	L	0-2	
22/06	h	Mariehamn	D	0-0	
25/06	h	KuPS	L	0-1	
06/07	h	SJK	W	1-0	M'Boma
19/07	h	Ilves	W	3-1	Shala, Kuningas, Rafael (p)
26/07	a	Inter	W	2-0	Matheus Alves, M'Boma
02/08	h	Jaro	D	1-1	Shala
09/08	a	RoPS	W	2-1	Matheus Alves (p), Rafael
12/08	a	HJK	L	0-1	
16/08	h	VPS	D	0-0	
23/08	a	Mariehamn	W	2-0	Matheus Alves, Kärkkäinen
26/08	a	VPS	L	1-3	Ääritalo
30/08	h	KuPS	W	1-0	Matheus Alves
10/09	h	KTP	W	3-2	Matheus Alves (p), Ääritalo, Lagerblom
13/09	a	SJK	D	0-0	
20/09	h	HIFK	L	0-5	
27/09	a	Ilves	W	2-1	Ääritalo, Ristola
04/10	h	Inter	W	3-1	Gela 2, Matheus Alves
15/10	a	HIFK	D	3-3	Tanska, Matheus Alves, Ääritalo
18/10	a	Jaro	D	1-1	Tanska
25/10	h	RoPS	L	1-4	Matheus Alves

No	Name	Nat	DoB	Pos	Aps	(s)	Gls
4	Xhevdet Gela		14/11/89	M	26	(1)	3
3	Mikko Hauhia		03/09/84	D	33		
13	Markus Joenmäki		11/02/88	D	26		
18	Justus Kauppinen		28/04/97	M		(2)	
25	Mikko Kuningas		30/07/97	M	8	(2)	1
6	Pyry Kärkkäinen		10/11/86	D	29		1
10	Pekka Lagerblom		19/10/82	M	9	(11)	1
92	Leandro Motta	BRA	14/01/92	M	5	(1)	1
31	Jussi Länsitalo		30/06/90	A	15	(3)	2
15	Aristote M'Boma		30/06/94	A	5	(11)	2
23	Matheus Alves	BRA	19/05/93	A	26	(5)	12
12	Joonas Meronen		11/06/93	G	3		
1	Henrik Moisander		29/09/85	G	28		
30	Miikka Mujunen		14/08/96	G	2		
19	Aleksi Paananen		25/01/93	M	26	(1)	
24	Petri Pasanen		24/09/80	D	13	(6)	
9	Rafael	BRA	01/08/78	A	12	(13)	2
17	Aleksi Ristola		06/11/89	A	10	(15)	3
20	Hassan Sesay	SLE	22/10/87	M	21	(4)	
7	Drilon Shala		20/03/87	A	18	(7)	3
2	Jani Tanska		29/07/88	D	8		2
16	Henri Toivomäki		21/02/91	D	20		1
14	Jasse Tuominen		12/11/95	M	6		
11	Mika Ääritalo		25/07/88	A	14	(10)	4

IFK Mariehamn

1919 • Wiklöf Holding Arena (4,000) • ifkmariehamn.com
Major honours
Finnish Cup (1) 2015
Coach: Pekka Lyyski

2015

12/04	a	Jaro	D	1-1	Tammilehto
19/04	h	HIFK	D	1-1	Orgill
23/04	a	Lahti	W	1-0	Orgill
29/04	h	VPS	W	1-0	Diego Assis
03/05	h	KuPS	D	1-1	Lyyski
08/05	h	KTP	W	2-1	Wirtanen, Tammilehto (p)
14/05	a	HJK	L	0-1	
17/05	h	Ilves	W	2-0	Diego Assis 2
20/05	h	RoPS	W	1-0	Lyyski
25/05	a	Inter	D	1-1	Orgill
03/06	h	SJK	L	0-3	
08/06	a	KTP	W	2-0	Span, Ibrahim
17/06	h	KuPS	L	2-3	Lyyski, Kojola
22/06	a	Lahti	D	0-0	
25/06	h	SJK	D	1-1	Tammilehto
28/06	a	HIFK	D	1-1	Span
05/07	h	Ilves	D	0-0	
13/07	a	Inter	D	1-1	Ibrahim
19/07	h	Jaro	W	4-3	Orgill 2, Sparrdal Mantilla, Span
26/07	a	RoPS	D	1-1	Forsell (p)
09/08	a	VPS	L	0-1	
12/08	h	KTP	L	0-1	
19/08	a	KuPS	D	0-0	
23/08	h	Lahti	L	0-2	
30/08	a	SJK	L	0-4	
10/09	h	HIFK	W	1-0	Forsell (p)
13/09	a	Ilves	W	3-1	Forsell, Orgill 2
17/09	a	Jaro	D	0-0	
21/09	h	Inter	L	0-2	
01/10	h	HJK	L	0-2	
05/10	h	RoPS	W	1-0	Kangaskolkka
18/10	a	HJK	L	0-4	
25/10	h	VPS	W	2-0	Orgill, Kangaskolkka

No	Name	Nat	DoB	Pos	Aps	(s)	Gls
20	Anthony Dafaa	KEN	26/06/88	M	22	(4)	
25	Diego Assis	BRA	14/09/87	M	26	(2)	3
15	Amos Ekhalie	KEN	08/07/88	M	21	(7)	
14	Elias Eriksson		31/12/96	M		(2)	
10	Petteri Forsell		16/10/90	M	17		3
55	Bobbie Friberg da Cruz	SWE	16/02/82	D	22	(2)	
2	Albin Granlund		01/09/89	D	20	(2)	
11	Josef Ibrahim	SWE	13/03/91	M	5	(11)	2
33	Aleksei Kangaskolkka		29/10/88	A	3	(7)	2
3	Kristian Kojola		12/09/86	D	29	(1)	1
8	Jani Lyyski		16/03/83	D	30		3
26	Joel Mattsson		17/03/99	M		(2)	
18	Thomas Mäkinen		30/01/97	M	11	(8)	
5	Dever Orgill	JAM	08/03/90	A	25	(2)	8
17	Robin Sid		21/09/94	M	10	(8)	
9	Brian Span	USA	23/02/92	A	32	(1)	3
4	Philip Sparrdal Mantilla	SWE	11/08/93	D	24	(3)	1
6	Duarte Tammilehto		15/02/90	M	29		3
92	Walter Viitala		09/01/92	G	7	(1)	
1	Otso Virtanen		03/04/94	G	26		
7	Tommy Wirtanen		19/01/83	D	4	(4)	1

RoPS Rovaniemi

1950 • Keskuskenttä (3,400) • rops.fi
Major honours
Finnish Cup (2) 1986, 2013
Coach: Juha Malinen

2015

12/04	h	HJK	L	1-3	Ibiyomi
19/04	a	SJK	L	0-1	
23/04	h	Inter	L	0-4	
29/04	h	HIFK	W	2-0	Saksela, Pirinen
03/05	a	Ilves	W	1-0	Kokko
08/05	a	Jaro	W	2-1	Kokko, Mäkitalo
14/05	a	KuPS	W	1-0	Obilor
17/05	a	Lahti	W	2-1	Kokko, Posinković
20/05	a	Mariehamn	L	0-1	
29/05	h	VPS	W	1-0	Roiha
03/06	h	KTP	W	4-0	Pirinen, Kokko 3 (1p)
06/06	a	SJK	W	1-0	Mäkitalo
16/06	h	HIFK	D	1-1	Pirinen
22/06	h	Ilves	W	4-1	Kokko 3 (1p), Pirinen
25/06	h	Inter	D	1-1	Yaghoubi
28/06	a	Jaro	W	1-0	Kokko (p)
06/07	h	KTP	D	0-0	
10/07	h	HJK	W	2-1	Pirinen, Kokko
19/07	a	VPS	W	2-1	Yaghoubi
26/07	h	Mariehamn	D	1-1	Kokko
02/08	a	KuPS	L	0-3	
09/08	h	Lahti	L	1-2	Pöyliö
12/08	h	SJK	W	2-0	Roiha 2
17/08	a	HIFK	D	1-1	Hradecky
22/08	h	Ilves	D	0-0	
29/08	a	Inter	L	0-2	
10/09	h	Jaro	D	0-0	
14/09	a	KTP	W	4-0	John 2, Saxman, Kokko (p)
20/09	a	HJK	W	2-0	Kokko, Markkanen
27/09	h	VPS	W	3-0	John, Obilor
05/10	a	Mariehamn	L	0-1	
18/10	h	KuPS	W	2-1	Yaghoubi, Mäkitalo
25/10	a	Lahti	W	4-1	Yaghoubi, Kokko 3 (2p)

No	Name	Nat	DoB	Pos	Aps	(s)	Gls
14	Tomer Chencinski	CAN	01/12/84	G	12		
21	Tommi Haanpää		21/04/90	M	2	(5)	
8	Tomas Hradecky		13/10/92	M	19	(2)	1
35	Michael Ibiyomi	NGA	20/10/93	A	7	(16)	1
1	Ville Iiskola		26/04/85	G	4		
86	Abdou Jammeh	GAM	13/02/86	D	30		
19	Will John	USA	13/06/85	M	10	(1)	3
11	Aleksandr Kokko		04/06/87	A	28	(1)	17
3	Jarkko Lahdenmäki		16/04/91	D	16	(5)	
26	Eero Markkanen		03/07/91	A		(6)	1
7	Mika Mäkitalo		12/06/85	M	32		3
1	Jean Fridolin Ngbane Ngbane	CMR	11/05/88	A		(3)	
12	Harri Nykänen		04/02/94	G		(2)	
80	Faith Obilor	NGA	05/03/91	D	30		2
4	Antti Okkonen		06/06/82	M	30		
6	Juha Pirinen		22/10/91	D	31		5
91	Vilim Posinković	CRO	10/01/90	A	4	(9)	1
17	Olli Pöyliö		11/08/95	M	1	(11)	1
32	David Ramadingaye		14/09/89	M		(4)	
22	Ricardo	BRA	18/02/93	G	17		
20	Simo Roiha		27/12/91	A	6	(15)	3
5	Janne Saksela		14/03/93	D	27		1
16	Ville Saxman		15/11/89	D	31	(2)	1
9	Tremaine Stewart	JAM	05/01/88	A		(4)	
77	Moshtagh Yaghoubi		08/11/94	M	26	(4)	4

SJK Seinäjoki

2007 • Seinäjoen keskuskenttä (3,500) •
sjk2007.fi
Major honours
Finnish League (1) 2015
Coach: Simo Valakari

2015

12/04	a	Inter	D	1-1	*Atajić*
19/04	h	RoPS	W	1-0	*Vasara*
23/04	a	Jaro	W	1-0	*Pelvas*
03/05	h	HIFK	W	2-0	*Ngueukam, Lehtinen*
08/05	a	Lahti	L	0-1	
11/05	h	KuPS	W	5-0	*Brown, Dorman, Laaksonen, Ngueukam, Lähde*
14/05	h	VPS	W	2-0	*Hetemaj, Brown (p)*
17/05	a	KTP	D	0-0	
20/05	h	Ilves	W	3-0	*Lehtinen, Vasara, Dorman*
24/05	h	HJK	L	1-2	*Pelvas*
03/06	a	Mariehamn	W	3-0	*Ngueukam, Pelvas 2 (1p)*
06/06	h	RoPS	L	0-1	
17/06	a	HJK	L	1-3	*Lehtinen*
22/06	h	VPS	W	3-2	*Gogoua, Lehtinen (p), Pelvas*
25/06	a	Mariehamn	D	1-1	*Lehtinen (p)*
06/07	a	Lahti	L	0-1	
12/07	h	KTP	W	1-0	*Lidman*
19/07	h	HIFK	W	4-1	*Pelvas 4*
26/07	a	Ilves	D	0-0	
02/08	h	Inter	L	0-1	
09/08	a	Jaro	L	0-1	
12/08	a	RoPS	L	0-2	
23/08	a	VPS	W	3-1	*Ngueukam, Riski 2*
26/08	h	KuPS	W	1-0	*Riski*
30/08	h	Mariehamn	W	4-0	*Gogoua, Pelvas 2, Laaksonen*
10/09	a	KuPS	D	1-1	*Allan*
13/09	h	Lahti	W	0-0	
20/09	a	KTP	W	3-1	*Riski 2 (1p), Lehtinen*
23/09	h	HJK	W	3-0	*Tahvanainen, Riski, Ngueukam*
28/09	a	HIFK	L	0-1	
04/10	h	Ilves	W	2-1	*Pelvas 2 (1p)*
18/10	a	Inter	W	2-0	*Pelvas, Riski*
25/10	a	Jaro	W	2-0	*Hetemaj, Riski*

No	Name	Nat	DoB	Pos	Aps	(s)	Gls
24	Henri Aalto		20/04/89	D	19	(2)	
33	Mihkel Aksalu	EST	07/11/84	G	32		
28	Allan	BRA	03/03/97	M	7	(1)	1
21	Bahrudin Atajić	BIH	16/11/93	A	13	(6)	1
10	Wayne Brown	ENG	06/08/88	M	19	(6)	2
4	Richard Dorman	WAL	14/06/88	D	20	(3)	2
27	Cédric Gogoua	CIV	10/07/94	D	28	(1)	2
58	Mehmet Hetemaj		08/12/87	M	30	(1)	2
1	Jere Koponen		23/05/92	G	1		
8	Johannes Laaksonen		13/12/90	M	19	(13)	2
14	Toni Lehtinen		05/05/84	A	13	(11)	6
19	Emil Lidman		20/09/97	M		(4)	1
6	Juho Lähde		11/02/91	M	3	(5)	1
20	Marco Matrone			M		(1)	
5	Pavle Milosavljević	SRB	21/06/87	D	17	(1)	
11	Ariel Ngueukam	CMR	15/11/88	A	23	(9)	5
16	Akseli Pelvas		08/02/89	M	28	(5)	14
17	Teemu Penninkangas		24/07/92	A		(6)	
18	Roope Riski		16/08/91	A	13		8
26	Jesse Sarajärvi		20/05/95	M		(1)	
15	Željko Savić	SRB	18/03/88	D	30		
7	Timo Tahvanainen		26/06/86	D	26		1
9	Jussi Vasara		14/05/87	M	22	(7)	2

VPS Vaasa

1924 • Hietalahden jalkapallostadion (4,600) •
vepsu.fi
Major honours
Finnish League (2) 1945, 1948
**Coach: Olli Huttunen;
(29/06/15) Petri Vuorinen**

2015

23/04	a	KuPS	L	0-1	
29/04	h	Mariehamn	L	0-1	
03/05	a	KTP	L	2-3	*Seabrook, Mäkelä (p)*
08/05	h	Ilves	L	2-3	*Catovic, Mäkelä*
11/05	a	HJK	L	0-1	
14/05	a	SJK	L	0-2	
17/05	h	HJK	D	2-2	*Seabrook, Mäkelä*
21/05	h	Jaro	L	1-2	*Mäkelä*
29/05	a	RoPS	L	0-1	
03/06	h	Inter	W	3-0	*Mäkelä, Lahti, Tamminen*
06/06	h	KuPS	D	0-0	
17/06	h	Lahti	W	2-0	*Mäkelä 2*
22/06	a	SJK	L	2-3	*Mäkelä 2 (1p)*
25/06	h	HIFK	L	0-2	
05/07	h	Inter	D	0-0	
12/07	a	Jaro	L	1-2	*Soiri*
19/07	h	RoPS	D	1-1	*Lahti*
03/08	a	KTP	D	0-0	
09/08	h	Mariehamn	W	1-0	*og (Kojola)*
12/08	h	KuPS	D	2-2	*Kula, Soiri*
16/08	a	Lahti	D	0-0	
23/08	h	SJK	L	1-3	*Mäkelä*
26/08	h	Lahti	W	3-1	*Voutilainen 2, Lähde*
30/08	a	HIFK	L	0-3	
10/09	h	Ilves	W	1-0	*Broekhuizen*
14/09	a	Inter	D	1-1	*Soiri*
17/09	a	HIFK	W	3-0	*Mäkelä 2, Clennon*
20/09	h	Jaro	L	1-2	*Clennon, Lahti*
27/09	a	RoPS	L	1-2	*Soiri*
04/10	h	HJK	L	1-2	*Mäkelä*
15/10	a	Ilves	W	3-1	*Clennon, Mäkelä 2*
18/10	h	KTP	D	1-1	*Mäkelä*
25/10	a	Mariehamn	L	0-2	

No	Name	Nat	DoB	Pos	Aps	(s)	Gls
8	Denis Abdulahi		22/05/90	M	13	(3)	
13	Samu Alanko		16/05/98	A		(1)	
14	Charles Bantanga	CIV	10/02/94	M	4	(1)	
10	Tony Björk		25/10/83	M	15	(4)	
27	Nikko Boxall	NZL	24/02/92	M	12		
24	Joe Broekhuizen	USA	08/07/91	A	1	(3)	1
9	Admir Catovic	SWE	05/09/87	A	9	(2)	1
28	Andre Clennon	JAM	15/08/89	A	7	(1)	3
4	Jesper Engström		24/04/92	M	28	(1)	
17	Hughan Gray	JAM	25/03/87	D	1		
22	Loorents Hertsi		13/11/92	M	10	(12)	
16	Teemu Honkaniemi		20/01/91	D	15	(5)	
3	Ville Koskimaa		21/05/83	D	31		
15	Thomas Kula		24/05/91	M	18	(5)	1
12	Timi Lahti		28/06/90	D	25	(2)	3
9	Juho Lähde		11/02/91	M	12	(1)	1
18	Clifton Miheso	KEN	05/02/93	M	7	(3)	
26	Steven Morrissey	JAM	25/07/86	A	1	(3)	
20	Juho Mäkelä		23/06/83	A	28	(3)	16
23	Miika Niemi		04/03/94	D	1	(5)	
25	Isaiah Schafer	USA	07/06/90	D	11	(1)	
19	Jordan Seabrook	USA	27/06/87	A	11	(11)	2
32	Henri Sillanpää		04/06/79	G	33		
11	Pyry Soiri		22/09/94	M	28	(4)	4
7	Eero Tamminen		19/05/95	M	15	(9)	1
5	Mikko Viitikko		18/04/95	D	12	(2)	
6	Jerry Voutilainen		29/03/95	M	15	(3)	2

Top goalscorers

17	Aleksandr Kokko	(RoPS)
16	Juho Mäkelä	(VPS)
14	Akseli Pelvas	(SJK)
12	Matheus Alves	(Lahti)
10	Mika Lahtinen	(Ilves)
9	Pekka Sihvola	(HIFK)
8	Demba Savage	(HJK)
	Atomu Tanaka	(HJK)
	Erfan Zeneli	(HJK)
	Dever Orgill	(Mariehamn)
	Roope Riski	(SJK)

Promoted clubs

PS Kemi

1999 • Sauvosaaren urheilupuisto (4,500) •
pskemi.fi
Coach: Jari Åhman

PK-35 Vantaa

1935 • Myyrmäen jalkapallostadion (4,600) •
pk35vantaa.fi
Coach: Shefki Kuqi

Second level final table 2015

		Pld	W	D	L	F	A	Pts
1	PS Kemi	27	16	5	6	50	30	53
2	PK-35 Vantaa	27	15	4	8	53	25	49
3	TPS Turku	27	14	7	6	40	18	49
4	JJK Jyväskylä	27	13	7	7	43	27	46
5	AC Oulu	27	12	8	7	31	28	44
6	Valkeakosken Haka	27	11	8	8	48	41	41
7	FC Jazz Pori	27	9	5	13	37	48	32
8	EIF Ekenäs	27	8	7	12	36	49	31
9	MP Mikkeli	27	5	2	20	31	56	17
10	VIFK Vaasa	27	3	5	19	27	74	14

Promotion/Relegation play-offs

(28/10/15 & 31/10/15)
PK-35 0-0 KTP
KTP 2-3 PK-35
(PK-35 3-2)

DOMESTIC CUP

Suomen Cup 2015

FOURTH ROUND

(13/03/15)
KajHa 2-0 SiPS
Töölön Taisto 0-1 Haka

(14/03/15)
Atlantis 1-4 EIF
KäPa 1-1 PK-35 *(aet; 2-4 on pens)*
KPV 3-0 Jaro
FC Myllypuro 0-1 PK Keski-Uusimaa *(aet)*
PaiHa 0-4 Honka
TPS 2-0 FC Jazz

(15/03/15)
GBK 1-4 PS Kemi
PEPO 0-6 KuPS
Sexypöxyt 1-2 Gnistan

(16/03/15)
Legirus Inter 0-4 BK-46
OTP 0-2 AC Oulu

(17/03/15)
EsPa 3-0 HPS
MP 2-2 KTP *(aet; 4-2 on pens)*

(18/03/15)
TuPS 2-2 Viikingit *(aet; 6-7 on pens)*

(19/03/15)
TamU-K 0-12 Mariehamn

(20/03/15)
SAPA 0-1 MuSa

(21/03/15)
JIPPO 0-3 JJK

(22/03/15)
JanPa 0-5 MPS/Atletico Malmi

FIFTH ROUND

(27/03/15)
Viikingit 1-7 PK-35

(28/03/15)
KajHa 0-5 KPV
MPS/Atletico Malmi 0-2 Lahti
MuSa 1-1 EIF *(aet; 3-0 on pens)*

(29/03/15)
EsPa 0-5 Mariehamn
MP 1-2 PK Keski-Uusimaa *(aet)*

(01/04/15)
Gnistan 1-2 BK-46
JJK 0-1 PS Kemi

(02/04/15)
AC Oulu 2-1 VPS
Haka 3-2 Honka
TPS 1-3 Inter

(04/04/15)
SJK 1-2 KuPS

SIXTH ROUND

(15/04/15)
KuPS 2-1 Lahti
PK-35 1-2 HJK *(aet)*

(16/04/15)
Haka 2-2 MuSa *(aet; 4-3 on pens)*
Ilves 0-2 Mariehamn
Inter 7-3 RoPS
PK Keski-Uusimaa 4-1 BK-46 *(aet)*
KPV 0-2 HIFK *(aet)*
AC Oulu 3-3 PS Kemi *(aet; 4-3 on pens)*

QUARTER-FINALS

(26/04/15)
Haka 1-3 HJK *(Lähdesmäki 49; Savage 18, 52, Tanaka 90+1)*
HIFK 0-2 Inter *(Hambo 43, 84)*
KuPS 4-0 PK Keski-Uusimaa *(Sirbiladze 18, 21, 58, Pennanen 42p)*
Mariehamn 4-1 AC Oulu *(Orgill 45, 64, Lyyski 76, Span 90+1; Tahvanainen 20)*

SEMI-FINALS

(15/08/15)
Inter 1-1 KuPS *(Gnabouyou 55; Bowen 34) (aet; 3-2 on pens)*
Mariehamn 5-1 HJK *(Diego Assis 3, Orgill 33, 67, Tammilehto 50, Forsell 52; Tanaka 47)*

FINAL

(26/09/15)
Tehtaan kenttä, Valkeakoski
IFK MARIEHAMN 2 *(Diego Assis 45, 58)*
FC INTER TURKU 1 *(Gnabouyou 88)*
Referee: *Antamo*
MARIEHAMN: *Viitala, Friberg da Cruz, Kojola, Lyyski, Granlund, Tammilehto, Sparrdal Mantilla, Forsell, Diego Assis (Dafaa 90+3), Orgill, Span (Ekhalie 71)*
Red card: *Tammilehto (39)*
INTER: *Bahne, Hämäläinen, Matoukou, Kanakoudis, Aho, Nyman (Duah 65), Kairinen (Belica 83), Lehtonen, Mannström, Gnabouyou, Njoku (N'Gal 65)*

Hats on for Mariehamn, Finnish Cup winners for the first time

FRANCE

Fédération Française de Football (FFF)

Address 87 boulevard de Grenelle
FR-75738 Paris, Cedex 15
Tel +33 1 4431 7300
Fax +33 1 4431 7373
E-mail competitions.
internationales@fff.fr
Website fff.fr

President Noël Le Graët
Chief executive Florence Hardouin
Media officer Yann Perrin
Year of formation 1919
National stadium Stade de France,
Saint-Denis (81,338)

LIGUE 1 CLUBS

 1 **Angers SCO**

 2 **SC Bastia**

 3 **FC Girondins de Bordeaux**

 4 **SM Caen**

 5 **Gazélec FC Ajaccio**

 6 **EA Guingamp**

 7 **LOSC Lille**

 8 **FC Lorient**

 9 **Olympique Lyonnais**

 10 **Olympique de Marseille**

 11 **AS Monaco FC**

 12 **Montpellier Hérault SC**

 13 **FC Nantes**

 14 **OGC Nice**

 15 **Paris Saint-Germain**

 16 **Stade de Reims**

 17 **Stade Rennais FC**

 18 **AS Saint-Étienne**

 19 **Toulouse FC**

 20 **ES Troyes AC**

PROMOTED CLUBS

 21 **AS Nancy-Lorraine**

 22 **Dijon FCO**

 23 **FC Metz**

0   150   300 km
0   150 miles

Lille 7
Reims 16
Metz 23
Caen 4
Paris 15
Nancy 21
Guingamp 6
Rennes 17
Troyes 20
Lorient 8
Angers 1
Dijon 22
Nantes 13
Lyon 9
Saint-Étienne 18
Bordeaux 3
Toulouse 19
Montpellier 12
Monaco 11
Marseille 10
Nice 14
Bastia 2
Ajaccio 5

KEY

 UEFA Champions League

 UEFA Europa League

 Promoted

Relegated

Another clean sweep for Paris Saint-Germain

There was a distinct sense of déjà vu for Paris Saint-Germain in 2015/16 as they won all four domestic pieces of silverware for the second season in a row but failed once again to get beyond the quarter-finals of the UEFA Champions League – as a result of which coach Laurent Blanc, for all his team's dominance on the home front, lost his job.

Paris romped to their fourth successive Ligue 1 crown with unprecedented, record-breaking ease, but there would be no trophy-lifting jubilation in the French capital for Didier Deschamps' national side as they reached the final of UEFA EURO 2016 but lost the Stade de France showdown against Portugal.

Capital giants retain all four domestic trophies

European quarter-final jinx again strikes Blanc's team

UEFA EURO 2016 hosts lose to Portugal in final

Domestic league

There was no race for the Ligue 1 title in 2015/16. It was a one-club procession practically from start to early finish as PSG strode unhindered to victory, wrapping things up in mid-March with eight matches in reserve thanks to a 9-0 win away to bottom club Troyes. Zlatan Ibrahimović, the club's Swedish superstar, scored four goals in that match and would end the season with a grand total in the league of 38 – the most scored by an individual in a single French top-flight season since 1970/71.

Paris scored 102 goals and conceded just 19, giving them the biggest goal difference ever recorded by a French championship-winning side. Their final tally of 96 points was also a league record – as was the 31-point distance that separated them from runners-up Lyon. Indeed, the gap between second place and the relegation zone was considerably smaller (26 points). No team had ever previously run up as many wins, either, with PSG registering number 30 on the final day with a celebratory 4-0 jaunt against Nantes, in which Ibrahimović, on his last league appearance for the club, scored twice, his late second breaking the club's previous record tally for a season – the 37 set by Carlos Bianchi in 1977/78.

Having won the last nine games of the 2014/15 Ligue 1 campaign, PSG went unbeaten through another 27 in 2015/16 before Lyon defeated them 2-1 at the end of February. Three weeks later they lost again, 2-0 to Monaco, this time at the Parc des Princes, where they had gone 34 league games without defeat, but by then the title had already been secured with that thumping 9-0 win at Troyes – the biggest margin of victory ever recorded away from home in France's top division.

In addition to the remarkable Ibrahimović, who would leave the club at the end of the season as the club's all-time top scorer, PSG possessed an impressive roster of talent. It barely mattered that two of their 2014/15 stalwarts, Marco Verratti and Javier Pastore, were largely inactive because of injury. The squad's formidable strength in depth ensured adequate cover for every eventuality, and while Brazilian duo Thiago Silva and David Luiz continued to excel as a central-defensive pairing and Uruguayan Edinson Cavani maintained a decent strike rate in front of goal (albeit with only half as many goals as partner Ibrahimović), there were impressive contributions from new arrivals such as German goalkeeper Kevin Trapp, right-back Serge Aurier (despite a club

suspension imposed after some inadvisable social media utterings) and, especially, club record signing Ángel Di María, who supplied a league-best haul of 18 assists.

Paris certainly gave their fans plenty to shout about, but evidently the league as a whole suffered from the lack of a credible challenge from elsewhere. With the leaders boasting a 19-point advantage already at the halfway stage, the main focus of interest switched to the battle for the European qualifying positions and the fight to escape relegation.

Plus, somewhere in between, there were the trials and tribulations at Marseille. PSG's traditional rivals lost coach Marcelo Bielsa after just one match of the season and struggled for form under his successor, ex-Spain midfielder Míchel, before he too made way. Astonishingly, the team went 16 successive matches without a win at Stade Vélodrome and but for the consistently excellent performances of goalkeeper Steve Mandanda, resurgent defensive midfielder Lassana Diarra and 17-goal striker Michy Batshuayi, they would have been in serious trouble at the wrong end of the table. It was quite a comedown for a club that had challenged PSG at the top for much of the 2014/15

season but perhaps not such a surprise given that they had sold off key players such as Dimitri Payet, André Ayew, Giannelli Imbula and André-Pierrre Gignac during the summer.

While Marseille dropped from fourth in 2014/15 to 13th, Lyon and Monaco remained in second and third place, respectively – albeit with significantly reduced points tallies. Lyon, who lost young midfield star Nabil Fekir to a serious knee injury in early September, endured a wretched autumn and were down in ninth place at the winter break. Their season, however, was revived both by a change of coach – Bruno Génésio taking over from Hubert Fournier – and a change of stadium – with the brand new UEFA EURO 2016-ready Parc OL replacing the Stade de Gerland. Under Génésio the team won 12 of their next 18 games, posting eight wins and two draws in the ten fixtures at their new home, to seize second place and the UEFA Champions League group stage spot.

It was with a 6-1 defeat in the Parc OL on the penultimate matchday – in which Lyon's top scorer Alexandre Lacazette struck a hat-trick to make it 11 in the stadium and 21 for the season – that

Monaco ceded second place. Like Lyon, they started poorly, winning just three of their opening ten games, but although, like Marseille, draws remained something of a speciality, they did just enough to edge Cote d'Azur rivals Nice out of third place and clinch a UEFA Champions League qualifying berth. Monaco, led again by Leonardo Jardim, had no standout individual performers – exciting wingers Anthony Martial and Yannick Carrasco had both been sold, to Manchester United and Atlético Madrid, respectively – but Nice did, with the mercurial Hatem Ben Arfa returning to the blistering form of his youth and scoring 17 goals, many of them majestic solo efforts, to lift Claude Puel's team up from 11th in 2014/15 to fourth.

Joining Nice in the 2016/17 UEFA Europa League were Lille – who thundered up the table in the closing weeks under Frédéric Antonetti after a terrible start under new boss Hervé Renard – and Saint-Étienne, whose sixth-place finish ensured European qualification for the fourth season in a row, all of them under Christophe Galtier, the longest-serving coach in Ligue 1. Two clubs that spent much of the campaign occupying places in the top three before fading in the

spring were Caen and newly-promoted Angers. Neither team scored many goals but, given their relatively small budgets, they overachieved spectacularly in finishing above heavyweights such as Marseille and Bordeaux in the top half of the table.

Troyes, who came up with Angers, failed to register a win until January and were always doomed to the drop, but Gazélec Ajaccio, the third of the newly promoted teams, hit a purple patch in the run-up to Christmas that suggested they might survive. Alas, a finish almost as bad as their start eventually condemned them on the final day, when Reims, despite a 4-1 victory over Lyon, also went down after Toulouse completed a dramatic escape with a 3-2 win at Angers, late goals from Martin Braithwaite and youngster Yann Bodiger ensuring that Pascal Dupraz's outstanding short spell in charge ended on a joyful note. When he replaced Dominique Arribagé in early March, Toulouse's hopes of staying up seemed forlorn, but 18 points from Dupraz's ten matches at the helm, with top scorer Wissam Ben Yedder scoring freely, finally lifted them out of the bottom three for the first time since October. The three promoted teams were all from the east – Nancy winning Ligue 2 ahead of Dijon and Metz, who pipped Le Havre only on number of goals scored to return to the top flight after just a year's absence.

Domestic cups

With the Champions Trophy (French Super Cup) safely retained after a 2-0 victory over Lyon in Montreal, PSG duly completed the domestic quadruple for the second season in a row thanks to Stade de France victories in April and May against, respectively, Lille in the Coupe de la Ligue and Marseille in the Coupe de France.

The first of those finals was won the hard way against in-form Lille as Ángel Di María exploited a defensive error to score the winner four minutes after his team-mate Adrien Rabiot had been red-carded. The 2-1 win gave Blanc's side the trophy for the third year in a row, making it a record six victories for the club overall.

Four weeks later, in the final domestic fixture of the season, Ibrahimović was the inevitable star of the show on his farewell appearance, scoring two goals

Ángel Di María gestures in celebration after scoring Paris Saint-Germain's winning goal in the League Cup final against Lille

and setting up another for Cavani in a 4-2 victory over Marseille that enabled PSG to match their opponents' all-time record of ten French Cup wins. The Swede was substituted in the final minute to rapturous acclaim at the end of a sensational four-year sojourn in the French capital during which he picked up 12 winner's medals.

Europe

With the domestic league title a foregone conclusion from early on, PSG had the opportunity to devote much of their time and energy to the UEFA Champions League. They sailed through the group stage, conceding just one goal – in their only defeat, a game at Real Madrid that they largely dominated – before knocking out Chelsea for the second successive year in the round of 16. Impressive home and away wins over the Londoners, with Ibrahimović scoring in both, suggested that Blanc's team were ready to break through the quarter-final barrier at last after three successive exits at that stage, but the curse struck again as they fell to another English club, Manchester City, after an uncharacteristically disjointed display in the second leg. That would be Blanc's last tilt at the UEFA Champions League, with the club's Qatari owners dismissing him in June and bringing in Sevilla's three-time UEFA Europa League-winning boss Unai Emery as his replacement.

There were no European fireworks from any of the other Ligue 1 representatives. Lyon were eliminated from their UEFA Champions League group before they won a game, with Monaco having earlier lost their play-off to Valencia and joined three other French teams – Marseille, Saint-Étienne and Bordeaux – in the UEFA Europa League group stage. Only two of them – Marseille and Saint-Étienne – made it through, as runners-up, and France's poor record in the competition continued as both crashed out in the round of 32.

National team

France put on a fine show at UEFA EURO 2016 – both off the field, where a party atmosphere prevailed despite heightened security following the terrorist atrocities that had struck Paris the previous November, and on it, where Didier Deschamps' team came extremely close to emulating home-turf heroes of EURO '84 and the 1998 FIFA

Antoine Griezmann (right) scores his second goal as France defeat Germany 2-0 in the UEFA EURO 2016 semi-final

World Cup. Partly because of their excellent record in previous tournaments that they had hosted, and partly because of their positive results going into UEFA EURO 2016, France were widely regarded as favourites to lift the Henri Delaunay Cup. They gave it their best shot, bringing the country together as they worked their way diligently through six matches to the Stade de France final, but on this occasion there would be no *jour de gloire* as Portugal pooped their party with a 1-0 extra-time win.

The tournament ended in frustration and defeat, but it also provided many joyous moments for the French fans – Dimitri Payet's brilliant last-minute winner in the opening match against Romania, Antoine Griezmann's doubles against the Republic of Ireland and Germany, and a scintillating four-goal first-half display in the rain against Iceland.

Griezmann, with six goals, was the Golden Boot winner and also the official Player of the Tournament, while Payet was another to excel alongside captain Hugo Lloris, right-back Bacary Sagna

and debutant Samuel Umtiti, who belatedly solved a problem in central defence that had left France short in that area following the unavailability of Raphaël Varane, Jérémy Mathieu (both injured) and Mamadou Sakho (suspended). Deschamps also had to make do without France's No1 striker Karim Benzema, who was barred from playing in the tournament by the French Football Federation.

Deschamps demonstrated plenty of flexibility throughout the tournament, shuffling his pack from game to game and invariably coming up trumps with both his tactics and selection. France will forever look back on UEFA EURO 2016 as a missed opportunity, a case of what might have been, but the foundations would appear to be in place for Les Bleus to build on what they achieved in the summer of 2016 and make tracks for Russia, where, assuming they can negotiate a qualifying group containing the Netherlands, Sweden, Bulgaria, Belarus and Luxembourg, they should once again be one of the strongest teams on show.

DOMESTIC SEASON AT A GLANCE

Ligue 1 2015/16 final table

		Pld	Home					Away					Total					Pts
			W	D	L	F	A	W	D	L	F	A	W	D	L	F	A	
1	**Paris Saint-Germain**	38	15	3	1	59	12	15	3	1	43	7	30	6	2	102	19	96
2	Olympique Lyonnais	38	12	4	3	42	16	7	4	8	25	27	19	8	11	67	43	65
3	AS Monaco FC	38	10	6	3	30	19	7	8	4	27	31	17	14	7	57	50	65
4	OGC Nice	38	12	2	5	32	16	6	7	6	26	25	18	9	11	58	41	63
5	LOSC Lille	38	9	6	4	21	11	6	9	4	18	16	15	15	8	39	27	60
6	AS Saint-Étienne	38	10	4	5	25	15	7	3	9	17	22	17	7	14	42	37	58
7	SM Caen	38	9	3	7	19	23	7	3	9	20	29	16	6	16	39	52	54
8	Stade Rennais FC	38	6	7	8	25	25	7	6	6	27	29	13	13	12	52	54	52
9	Angers SCO	38	6	8	5	20	15	7	3	9	20	23	13	11	14	40	38	50
10	SC Bastia	38	11	2	6	23	14	3	6	10	13	28	14	8	16	36	42	50
11	FC Girondins de Bordeaux	38	8	7	4	27	20	4	7	8	23	37	12	14	12	50	57	50
12	Montpellier Hérault FC	38	9	0	10	26	23	5	7	7	23	24	14	7	17	49	47	49
13	Olympique de Marseille	38	3	11	5	27	24	7	7	5	21	18	10	18	10	48	42	48
14	FC Nantes	38	8	5	6	20	20	4	7	8	13	24	12	12	14	33	44	48
15	FC Lorient	38	7	7	5	26	21	4	6	9	21	37	11	13	14	47	58	46
16	EA Guingamp	38	6	7	6	31	28	5	4	10	16	28	11	11	16	47	56	44
17	Toulouse FC	38	6	7	6	29	21	3	6	10	16	34	9	13	16	45	55	40
18	Stade de Reims	38	7	5	7	28	23	3	4	12	16	34	10	9	19	44	57	39
19	Gazélec FC Ajaccio	38	5	7	7	23	32	3	6	10	14	26	8	13	17	37	58	37
20	ES Troyes AC	38	1	7	11	13	36	2	2	15	15	47	3	9	26	28	83	18

European qualification 2016/17

Champion/Cup winner: Paris Saint-Germain (group stage)
Olympique Lyonnais (group stage)
AS Monaco FC (third qualifying round)

OGC Nice (group stage)
LOSC Lille (third qualifying round)
AS Saint-Étienne (third qualifying round)

Top scorer	Zlatan Ibrahimović (Paris), 38 goals
Relegated clubs	ES Troyes AC, Gazélec FC Ajaccio, Stade de Reims
Promoted clubs	AS Nancy-Lorraine, Dijon FCO, FC Metz
French Cup final	Paris Saint-Germain 4-2 Olympique de Marseille
League Cup final	Paris Saint-Germain 2-1 LOSC Lille

Player of the season

Zlatan Ibrahimović
(Paris Saint-Germain)

Ibrahimović's fourth and final season at Paris Saint-Germain could scarcely have turned out better if he had written the script himself. The tall, technically gifted Swede had never spent more than three seasons at any previous club, but his beloved admirers in the French capital were treated to an extra-special supplementary campaign. He racked up 50 goals in all competitions, including 38 in Ligue 1, and spearheaded the team to a second successive domestic clean sweep before departing for a new challenge at Manchester United.

Newcomer of the season

Ousmane Dembélé
(Stade Rennais FC)

A star of the future surfaced in France during the course of the 2015/16 campaign as Dembélé emerged from nowhere to take Ligue 1 by storm, score 12 goals and earn himself a lucrative end-of-season move from Rennes to German Bundesliga giants Borussia Dortmund. Handed his first-team debut in November by Rennes boss Philippe Montanier, the 18-year-old was quickly into his stride, and before long the French youth international's glorious two-footed talent and eye for a goal had attracted scouts from far and wide.

Team of the season
(4-3-3)

Coach: Blanc *(Paris)*

Mandanda *(Marseille)*

Aurier *(Paris)* — Thiago Silva *(Paris)* — David Luiz *(Paris)* — Maxwell *(Paris)*

Verratti *(Paris)* — Diarra *(Marseille)* — Matuidi *(Paris)*

Ben Arfa *(Nice)* — Ibrahimović *(Paris)* — Di María *(Paris)*

NATIONAL TEAM

International honours
FIFA World Cup (1) 1998
UEFA European Championship (2) 1984, 2000
FIFA Confederations Cup (2) 2001, 2003

International tournament appearances
FIFA World Cup (13) 1930, 1938 (2nd round), 1954, 1958 (3rd), 1966, 1978, 1982 (4th), 1986 (3rd), 1998 (Winners), 2002, 2006 (runners-up), 2010, 2014 (qtr-finals)
UEFA European Championship (9) 1960 (4th), 1984 (Winners), 1992, 1996 (semi-finals), 2000 (Winners), 2004 (qtr-finals), 2008, 2012 (qtr-finals), 2016 (runners-up)

Top five all-time caps
Lilian Thuram (142); Thierry Henry (123); Marcel Desailly (116); Zinédine Zidane (108); Patrick Vieira (107)

Top five all-time goals
Thierry Henry (51); Michel Platini (41); David Trezeguet (34); Zinédine Zidane (31); Just Fontaine & Jean-Pierre Papin (30)

Results 2015/16

Date	Opponent		Venue		Result	Scorers
04/09/15	Portugal	A	Lisbon	W	1-0	Valbuena (85)
07/09/15	Serbia	H	Bordeaux	W	2-1	Matuidi (9, 25)
08/10/15	Armenia	H	Nice	W	4-0	Griezmann (35), Cabaye (55), Benzema (77, 79)
11/10/15	Denmark	A	Copenhagen	W	2-1	Giroud (4, 6)
13/11/15	Germany	H	Saint-Denis	W	2-0	Giroud (45+1), Gignac (86)
17/11/15	England	A	London	L	0-2	
25/03/16	Netherlands	A	Amsterdam	W	3-2	Griezmann (6), Giroud (13), Matuidi (88)
29/03/16	Russia	H	Saint-Denis	W	4-2	Kanté (9), Gignac (38), Payet (64), Coman (76)
30/05/16	Cameroon	H	Nantes	W	3-2	Matuidi (20), Giroud (41), Payet (90)
04/06/16	Scotland	H	Metz	W	3-0	Giroud (8, 35), Koscielny (39)
10/06/16	Romania (ECF)	H	Saint-Denis	W	2-1	Giroud (57), Payet (90)
15/06/16	Albania (ECF)	H	Marseille	W	2-0	Griezmann (90), Payet (90+6)
19/06/16	Switzerland (ECF)	H	Lille	D	0-0	
26/06/16	Republic of Ireland (ECF)	H	Lyon	W	2-1	Griezmann (58, 61)
03/07/16	Iceland (ECF)	H	Saint-Denis	W	5-2	Giroud (12, 59), Pogba (20), Payet (43), Griezmann (45)
07/07/16	Germany (ECF)	H	Marseille	W	2-0	Griezmann (45+2p, 72)
10/07/16	Portugal (ECF)	H	Saint-Denis	L	0-1	(aet)

Appearances 2015/16

Coach: Didier Deschamps	15/10/68		Por	Srb	Arm	Den	Ger	Eng	Ned	Rus	Cmr	Sco	ROU	ALB	SUI	IRL	ISL	GER	POR	Caps	Goals
Hugo Lloris	26/12/86	Tottenham (ENG)	G	G	G		G	G		G	G	G	G	G	G	G	G	G	G	82	-
Bacary Sagna	14/02/83	Man. City (ENG)	D	D46	D		D	D		D	D	D	D	D	D	D	D	D	D	64	-
Raphaël Varane	25/04/93	Real Madrid (ESP)	D	D	D	D46	D	D	D	D										29	2
Laurent Koscielny	10/09/85	Arsenal (ENG)	D				D	D	D	D		D	D	D	D	D72	D	D	D	36	1
Patrice Evra	15/05/81	Juventus (ITA)	D		D		D		D46	D46	D	D83	D	D	D	D	D	D	D	80	-
Moussa Sissoko	16/08/89	Newcastle (ENG)	M80	s90	s77	M		s82	s87	s69	s65	s88	s92		M	s93	M	M	M110	44	1
Yohan Cabaye	14/01/86	Crystal Palace (ENG)	M46		M77	s88	s86	M57			s76	s69			M			s92		48	4
Blaise Matuidi	09/04/87	Paris	M	M46	M63	M	M86	M46	M		M	M69	M	M	s77	M	M	M	M	51	8
Paul Pogba	15/03/93	Juventus (ITA)	M	M			M	s46	M87	M69	M65	M	M77	s46	M	M	M	M	M	38	6
Karim Benzema	19/12/87	Real Madrid (ESP)	A74	s62	A81															81	27
Nabil Fekir	18/07/93	Lyon	A14																	5	1
Antoine Griezmann	21/03/91	Atlético (ESP)	s14 /88	A90	A87	A78	A80	s67	A46	A63		s46	A66	s68	A77	A	M	M92	M	34	13
Morgan Schneiderlin	08/11/89	Man. United (ENG)	s46	M	s63	M	s80	M82												15	-
Anthony Martial	05/12/95	Man. United (ENG)	s74	s76	s63	A88	A69	A67	s46	A46		s46	s77	A46				s110		12	-
Mathieu Valbuena	28/09/84	Lyon	s80	A76	A63	s78														52	8
Olivier Giroud	30/09/86	Arsenal (ENG)	s88	A62	s81	A73	A68	A57	A73	s79	A65	A63	A	A77		A73	A60	A78	A78	55	20
Eliaquim Mangala	13/02/91	Man. City (ENG)	D		D											s72				8	-
Benoît Trémoulinas	28/12/85	Sevilla (ESP)	D																	5	-
Mathieu Debuchy	28/07/85	Arsenal (ENG)	s46																	27	2
Geoffrey Kondogbia	15/02/93	Internazionale (ITA)	s46																	5	-
Mamadou Sakho	13/02/90	Liverpool (ENG)		D					D											28	2
Lassana Diarra	10/03/85	Marseille		M		M80	s57	M46	M	M46										34	-
Alexandre Lacazette	28/05/91	Lyon		s87	s73															10	1
Steve Mandanda	28/03/88	Marseille				G		G												22	-
Christophe Jallet	31/10/83	Lyon				D		D												11	1
Lucas Digne	20/07/93	Roma (ITA)				D		D	s46	s54		s83								13	-
Kurt Zouma	27/10/94	Chelsea (ENG)				s46														2	-
André-Pierre Gignac	05/12/85	Tigres (MEX)					s68	A57	s73	A79	s65	s63		s77	A	s73	s60	s78	s78	33	7
Kingsley Coman	13/06/96	Bayern (GER)					s69	s46		s46	A76	A46	s66	A68	A63	s46 /93	s80		s58	11	1
Hatem Ben Arfa	07/03/87	Nice					s80	A46												15	2
Dimitri Payet	29/03/87	West Ham (ENG)							A	s63	A	A46	A92	M	s63	A	M80	M71	M58	26	6
N'Golo Kanté	29/03/91	Leicester (ENG)							s46	M	s46	M88	M	M		M46		s71		8	1
Jérémy Mathieu	29/10/83	Barcelona (ESP)								s46 /54										5	-
Adil Rami	27/12/85	Sevilla (ESP)								D	D	D	D	D	D					32	1
Samuel Umtiti	14/11/93	Lyon															D	D	D	3	-

EUROPE

Paris Saint-Germain

CHAMPIONS LEAGUE

Group A
Match 1 - Malmö FF (SWE)
H **2-0** *Di María (4), Cavani (61)*
Trapp, Thiago Silva, Verratti, Thiago Motta, Cavani, Ibrahimović (Pastore 75), Di María (Lavezzi 85), Matuidi, Maxwell, Van der Wiel, David Luiz. Coach: Laurent Blanc (FRA)
Match 2 - FC Shakhtar Donetsk (UKR)
A **3-0** *Aurier (7), David Luiz (23), Srna (90og)*
Trapp, Thiago Silva, Verratti, Thiago Motta, Cavani (Lucas 80), Ibrahimović (Lavezzi 90+2), Di María (Pastore 82), Matuidi, Maxwell, Aurier, David Luiz. Coach: Laurent Blanc (FRA)
Match 3 - Real Madrid CF (ESP)
H **0-0**
Trapp, Thiago Silva, Marquinhos, Verratti (Lavezzi 80), Thiago Motta, Cavani (Lucas 67), Ibrahimović, Di María (Pastore 67), Matuidi, Maxwell, Aurier. Coach: Laurent Blanc (FRA)
Match 4 - Real Madrid CF (ESP)
A **0-1**
Trapp, Thiago Silva, Verratti (Rabiot 17), Thiago Motta, Cavani, Ibrahimović, Di María, Matuidi (Lucas 75), Maxwell, Aurier, David Luiz. Coach: Laurent Blanc (FRA)
Match 5 - Malmö FF (SWE)
A **5-0** *Rabiot (3), Di María (14, 68), Ibrahimović (50), Lucas (82)*
Trapp, Thiago Silva, Marquinhos, Thiago Motta (Stambouli 69), Cavani, Ibrahimović (Augustin 85), Di María (Lucas 69), Matuidi, Maxwell, Van der Wiel, Rabiot. Coach: Laurent Blanc (FRA)
Match 6 - FC Shakhtar Donetsk (UKR)
H **2-0** *Lucas (57), Ibrahimović (86)*
Trapp, Stambouli, Marquinhos, Lucas (Nkunku 87), Ibrahimović, Matuidi (Di María 68), Kurzawa, Lavezzi (Cavani 69), Van der Wiel, Rabiot, David Luiz. Coach: Laurent Blanc (FRA)

Round of 16 - Chelsea FC (ENG)
H **2-1** *Ibrahimović (39), Cavani (78)*
Trapp, Thiago Silva, Marquinhos, Verratti (Rabiot 81), Lucas (Cavani 74), Thiago Motta, Ibrahimović, Di María, Matuidi (Pastore 81), Maxwell, David Luiz. Coach: Laurent Blanc (FRA)
A **2-1** *Rabiot (16), Ibrahimović (67)*
Trapp, Thiago Silva, Marquinhos, Lucas (Pastore 77), Thiago Motta, Ibrahimović, Di María (Cavani 82), Matuidi (Van der Wiel 87), Maxwell, Rabiot, David Luiz. Coach: Laurent Blanc (FRA)

Quarter-finals - Manchester City FC (ENG)
H **2-2** *Ibrahimović (41), Rabiot (59)*
Trapp, Thiago Silva, Marquinhos, Cavani, Ibrahimović, Di María, Matuidi, Maxwell, Aurier (Van der Wiel 78), Rabiot (Lucas 78), David Luiz. Coach: Laurent Blanc (FRA)
A **0-1**
Trapp, Thiago Silva, Marquinhos, Thiago Motta (Lucas 44), Cavani, Ibrahimović, Di María, Maxwell, Aurier (Pastore 61), Van der Wiel, Rabiot. Coach: Laurent Blanc (FRA)

Olympique Lyonnais

CHAMPIONS LEAGUE

Group H
Match 1 - KAA Gent (BEL)
A **1-1** *Jallet (58)*
Anthony Lopes, Yanga-Mbiwa, Tolisso, Beauvue (Kalulu 69), Lacazette, Ferri (Malbranque 81), Morel, Valbuena, Rafael (Jallet 46), Gonalons, Umtiti. Coach: Hubert Fournier (FRA)
Match 2 - Valencia CF (ESP)
H **0-1**
Anthony Lopes, Biševac, Tolisso, Lacazette (Beauvue 74), Jallet, Darder (Ferri 43), Morel (Ghezzal 78), Valbuena, Gonalons, Umtiti, Kalulu. Coach: Hubert Fournier (FRA)
Match 3 - FC Zenit (RUS)
A **1-3** *Lacazette (49)*
Anthony Lopes, Yanga-Mbiwa, Tolisso, Lacazette (Beauvue 80), Ferri (Ghezzal 71), Jallet, Morel, Valbuena, Rafael (Cornet 83), Gonalons, Umtiti. Coach: Hubert Fournier (FRA)
Match 4 - FC Zenit (RUS)
H **0-2**
Anthony Lopes, Yanga-Mbiwa, Bedimo, Tolisso, Beauvue (Cornet 69), Lacazette, Rafael (Rafael 61), Darder (Ferri 77), Valbuena, Gonalons, Umtiti. Coach: Hubert Fournier (FRA)
Red card: Gonalons 72
Match 5 - KAA Gent (BEL)
H **1-2** *Ferri (7)*
Anthony Lopes, Yanga-Mbiwa, Bedimo, Biševac, Tolisso, Lacazette, Ghezzal (Beauvue 74), Ferri (Cornet 85), Malbranque (Darder 64), Valbuena, Rafael. Coach: Hubert Fournier (FRA)
Match 6 - Valencia CF (ESP)
A **2-0** *Cornet (37), Lacazette (76)*
Anthony Lopes, Yanga-Mbiwa, Bedimo, Grenier (Ghezzal 70), Tolisso, Lacazette (Beauvue 77), Darder (Koné 77), Morel, Rafael, Gonalons, Cornet. Coach: Hubert Fournier (FRA)

AS Monaco FC

CHAMPIONS LEAGUE

Third qualifying round - BSC Young Boys (SUI)
A **3-1** *Kurzawa (64), Carrillo (72), Pašalić (75)*
Subašić, Fabinho, Kurzawa, Ricardo Carvalho, Dirar (Bahlouli 90+3), João Moutinho, Martial (El Shaarawy 83), Ivan Cavaleiro (Carrillo 70), Pašalić, Raggi, Toulalan. Coach: Leonardo Jardim (POR)
H **4-0** *Ivan Cavaleiro (54), Kurzawa (64), Martial (70), El Shaarawy (77)*
Subašić, Fabinho, Kurzawa, Ricardo Carvalho, Dirar, João Moutinho, Martial (Carrillo 70), Ivan Cavaleiro (El Shaarawy 74), Pašalić (A Traoré 80), Raggi, Toulalan. Coach: Leonardo Jardim (POR)

Play-offs - Valencia CF (ESP)

A **1-3** *Pašalić (49)*
Subašić, Fabinho, Ricardo Carvalho, Martial, Bernardo Silva (El Shaarawy 78), Wallace, Ivan Cavaleiro (Dirar 63), Pašalić (Bahlouli 76), Echiéjilé, Raggi, Toulalan. Coach: Leonardo Jardim (POR)
H **2-1** *Raggi (17), Echiéjilé (75)*
Subašić, Fabinho, Kurzawa (Echiéjilé 62), Ricardo Carvalho, Dirar, Martial, Bernardo Silva, Ivan Cavaleiro (Carrillo 64), Pašalić (Lemar 52), Raggi, Toulalan. Coach: Leonardo Jardim (POR)

EUROPA LEAGUE

Group J
Match 1 - RSC Anderlecht (BEL)
A **1-1** *L Traoré (85)*
Subašić, Fabinho, Fábio Coentrão, João Moutinho, Bernardo Silva, Wallace, Ivan Cavaleiro (Lemar 76), Pašalić (L Traoré 46), Echiéjilé (El Shaarawy 61), Raggi, Touré. Coach: Leonardo Jardim (POR)
Match 2 - Tottenham Hotspur FC (ENG)
H **1-1** *El Shaarawy (81)*
Subašić, Fabinho, Fábio Coentrão, Ricardo Carvalho (Dirar 76), João Moutinho, Bernardo Silva, L Traoré (Carrillo 68), A Traoré, Raggi, Lemar (El Shaarawy 60), Toulalan. Coach: Leonardo Jardim (POR)
Match 3 - Qarabağ FK (AZE)
H **1-0** *L Traoré (70)*
Subašić, Fabinho, Ricardo Carvalho, João Moutinho, Bernardo Silva (Pašalić 57), Wallace, L Traoré (Carrillo 90+1), El Shaarawy, Raggi, Lemar (Dirar 79), Toulalan. Coach: Leonardo Jardim (POR)
Match 4 - Qarabağ FK (AZE)
A **1-1** *Ivan Cavaleiro (72)*
Subašić, Fabinho, Ricardo Carvalho, João Moutinho, Bernardo Silva, Wallace, L Traoré (Echiéjilé 78), Pašalić (Ivan Cavaleiro 61), El Shaarawy (Carrillo 70), Raggi, Toulalan. Coach: Leonardo Jardim (POR)
Match 5 - RSC Anderlecht (BEL)
H **0-2**
Subašić, Fabinho, Fábio Coentrão, Ricardo Carvalho, João Moutinho, Bernardo Silva, L Traoré (Echiéjilé 84), Pašalić (Carrillo 62), El Shaarawy, Raggi, Toulalan (Touré 29). Coach: Leonardo Jardim (POR)
Match 6 - Tottenham Hotspur FC (ENG)
A **1-4** *El Shaarawy (61)*
Subašić, Dirar, João Moutinho (Lemar 46), Bernardo Silva (Diarra 65), Wallace, Bakayoko, L Traoré (Mbappé Lottin 56), Pašalić, Echiéjilé, El Shaarawy, Toulalan. Coach: Leonardo Jardim (POR)

Olympique de Marseille

DROIT AU BUT

EUROPA LEAGUE

Group F
Match 1 - FC Groningen (NED)
A **3-0** *N'Koudou (25), Ocampos (40), Alessandrini (61)*
Mandanda, Rekik, Ocampos, Lucas Silva (Rolando 82), Alessandrini (Sarr 75), N'Koudou, Sparagna, Isla, Romao, Mendy (De Ceglie 66), Zambo Anguissa. Coach: Míchel (ESP)

Match 2 - FC Slovan Liberec (CZE)
H 0-1
Mandanda, Rekik, Rolando, Ocampos, Lucas Silva, Alessandrini (Sarr 82), Cabella (Barrada 71), Isla (Dja Djédjé 67), Romao, Batshuayi, Mendy. Coach: Míchel (ESP)
Match 3 - SC Braga (POR)
A 2-3 *Alessandrini (84), Batshuayi (87)*
Mandanda, Rekik, Lucas Silva, Diarra (Ocampos 83), Alessandrini, Sparagna, Isla, Barrada (N'Koudou 75), Batshuayi, Mendy, Dja Djédjé (Cabella 65). Coach: Míchel (ESP)
Match 4 - SC Braga (POR)
H 1-0 *N'Koudou (39)*
Mandanda, N'Koulou, Rekik, Ocampos, Lucas Silva (Sparagna 70), Cabella, N'Koudou (Barrada 83), Isla, Romao, Batshuayi (Javi Manquillo 90+1), Mendy. Coach: Míchel (ESP)
Match 5 - FC Groningen (NED)
H 2-1 *N'Koudou (28), Batshuayi (88)*
Mandanda, N'Koulou, Rolando (Barrada 87), Ocampos (Alessandrini 57), Diarra, Cabella, N'Koudou, Isla (Lucas Silva 65), Batshuayi, Mendy, Dja Djédjé. Coach: Míchel (ESP)
Match 6 - FC Slovan Liberec (CZE)
A 4-2 *Batshuayi (14), N'Koudou (43), Barrada (48), Ocampos (90+4)*
Mandanda, Javi Manquillo, N'Koulou, Rolando, Cabella (Lucas Silva 54), N'Koudou (Sparagna 66), Isla, Barrada, Romao, Batshuayi (Ocampos 73), Mendy. Coach: Míchel (ESP)

Round of 32 - Athletic Club (ESP)
H 0-1
Mandanda, Javi Manquillo, N'Koulou, Rolando, Fletcher, Diarra, Alessandrini (Batshuayi 59), N'Koudou (Sarr 82), Isla, Barrada (Thauvin 59), Romao. Coach: Míchel (ESP)
A 1-1 *Batshuayi (40)*
Mandanda, Javi Manquillo (Thauvin 85), N'Koulou, Rekik (Alessandrini 86), Fletcher, Diarra, Cabella, N'Koudou, Isla, Batshuayi, Mendy. Coach: Míchel (ESP)

AS Saint-Étienne

Third qualifying round - ASA Tîrgu Mureș (ROU)
A 3-0 *Diomandé (24), Hamouma (75, 83)*
Ruffier, Théophile-Catherine, Clément, Gradel, Roux (Mollo 74), Pogba, Hamouma (Monnet-Paquet 83), Perrin, Bayal Sall, Diomandé, Assou-Ekotto (Brison 61). Coach: Christophe Galtier (FRA)
H 1-2 *Iván González (72og)*
Ruffier, Clément, Roux, Mollo, Pogba, Brison, Monnet-Paquet (Hamouma 56), Perrin, Bayal Sall, Diomandé (Lemoine 67), Clerc (Théophile-Catherine 78). Coach: Christophe Galtier (FRA)

Play-offs - FC Milsami Orhei (MDA)
A 1-1 *Hamouma (40)*
Ruffier, Théophile-Catherine, Bahebeck (Monnet-Paquet 62), Corgnet (Bamba 80), Roux (Brison 87), Lemoine, Pogba, Hamouma, Bayal Sall, Diomandé, Assou-Ekotto. Coach: Christophe Galtier (FRA)
Red card: Hamouma 55
H 1-0 *Corgnet (15)*
Ruffier, Théophile-Catherine, Clément, Corgnet (Bamba 63), Roux (Maupay 75), Lemoine, Monnet-Paquet (Polomat 89), Perrin, Eysseric, Bayal Sall, Assou-Ekotto. Coach: Christophe Galtier (FRA)

Group G
Match 1 - Rosenborg BK (NOR)
H 2-2 *Berič (4), Roux (87p)*
Ruffier, Clément, Roux, Eysseric (Corgnet 64), Lemoine (Pajot 76), Monnet-Paquet (Bamba 71), Perrin, Bayal Sall, Berič, Clerc, Assou-Ekotto. Coach: Christophe Galtier (FRA)
Match 2 - SS Lazio (ITA)
A 2-3 *Bayal Sall (6), Monnet-Paquet (84)*
Ruffier, Polomat, Pajot, Corgnet (Diomandé 64), Roux (Monnet-Paquet 74), Lemoine, Hamouma (Bahebeck 64), Perrin, Bayal Sall, Berič, Clerc. Coach: Christophe Galtier (FRA)
Red cards: Berič 33, Bayal Sall 77
Match 3 - FC Dnipro Dnipropetrovsk (UKR)
A 1-0 *Hamouma (44)*
Ruffier, Pajot, Roux, Eysseric (Diomandé 80), Lemoine, Pogba, Hamouma (Bahebeck 82), Monnet-Paquet (Polomat 87), Perrin, Clerc, Assou-Ekotto. Coach: Christophe Galtier (FRA)
Match 4 - FC Dnipro Dnipropetrovsk (UKR)
H 3-0 *Monnet-Paquet (38), Berič (52), Hamouma (65)*
Ruffier, Pajot (Clément 70), Roux, Eysseric (Corgnet 80), Lemoine, Pogba, Monnet-Paquet (Hamouma 61), Perrin, Berič, Clerc, Assou-Ekotto. Coach: Christophe Galtier (FRA)
Match 5 - Rosenborg BK (NOR)
A 1-1 *Roux (80p)*
Ruffier, Polomat, Pajot, Clément, Roux (Diomandé 87), Cohade (Maupay 71), Hamouma, Monnet-Paquet, Perrin, Clerc, Assou-Ekotto. Coach: Christophe Galtier (FRA)
Match 6 - SS Lazio (ITA)
H 1-1 *Eysseric (76)*
Moulin, Polomat, Clément, Bahebeck, Corgnet (Bamba 64), Eysseric, Maupay, Pogba, Brison, Diomandé (Erin Pinheiro 57), Karamoko (Bayal Sall 27). Coach: Christophe Galtier (FRA)

Round of 32 - FC Basel 1893 (SUI)
H 3-2 *Bayal Sall (9), Monnet-Paquet (39), Bahebeck (77)*
Ruffier, Théophile-Catherine, Tannane (Pajot 67), Roux (Bahebeck 72), Cohade, Tabanou, Lemoine, Pogba, Monnet-Paquet (Hamouma 75), Bayal Sall. Coach: Christophe Galtier (FRA)
A 1-2 *Bayal Sall (90)*
Ruffier, Théophile-Catherine, Tannane (Hamouma 60), Clément, Bahebeck (Roux 55), Cohade, Tabanou, Lemoine (Eysseric 75), Pogba, Monnet-Paquet, Bayal Sall. Coach: Christophe Galtier (FRA)
Red card: Eysseric 82

FC Girondins de Bordeaux

Third qualifying round - AEK Larnaca FC (CYP)
H 3-0 *Biyogo Poko (53), Diabaté (74p), Maurice-Belay (80)*
Carrasso, Pallois, Sertic, Saivet, Chantôme, Touré (Maulun 84), Diabaté (Kiese Thelin 89), Biyogo Poko, Khazri (Maurice-Belay 66), Guilbert, Poundjé. Coach: Willy Sagnol (FRA)
A 1-0 *Kiese Thelin (29)*
Carrasso, Gajić, Contento, Pallois, Traoré (Biyogo Poko 79), Chantôme, Kiese Thelin, Maurice-Belay, Yambéré, Khazri (Touré 54), Maulun (Sertic 64). Coach: Willy Sagnol (FRA)
Red card: Chantôme 45

Play-offs - FC Kairat Almaty (KAZ)
H 1-0 *Khazri (27)*
Prior, Contento (Poundjé 14), Pallois, Traoré (Maurice-Belay 71), Rolán (Crivelli 85), Saivet, Kiese Thelin, Biyogo Poko, Yambéré, Khazri, Guilbert. Coach: Willy Sagnol (FRA)
A 1-2 *Crivelli (76)*
Prior, Pallois, Traoré (Maurice-Belay 69), Rolán (Crivelli 69), Saivet, Kiese Thelin, Biyogo Poko, Yambéré, Khazri (Gajić 86), Guilbert, Poundjé. Coach: Willy Sagnol (FRA)

Group B
Match 1 - Liverpool FC (ENG)
H 1-1 *Jussiê (81)*
Carrasso, Gajić (Guilbert 86), Pablo, Pallois, Rolán, Saivet (Biyogo Poko 76), Chantôme, Maurice-Belay, Khazri (Jussiê 69), Crivelli, Poundjé. Coach: Willy Sagnol (FRA)
Match 2 - FC Rubin (RUS)
A 0-0
Carrasso, Contento, Pallois, Saivet, Chantôme, Biyogo Poko (Khazri 58), Maurice-Belay, Jussiê (Plašil 58), Yambéré (Sané 88), Guilbert, Crivelli. Coach: Willy Sagnol (FRA)
Match 3 - FC Sion (SUI)
H 0-1
Carrasso, Pallois, Sané, Rolán, Saivet, Chantôme, Touré (Ounas 77), Diabaté (Khazri 65), Biyogo Poko, Plašil (Crivelli 64), Poundjé. Coach: Willy Sagnol (FRA)
Red card: Khazri 86
Match 4 - FC Sion (SUI)
A 1-1 *Touré (67)*
Carrasso, Contento, Pallois, Sané, Chantôme, Touré (Saivet 90+1), Diabaté (Crivelli 80), Biyogo Poko, Plašil, Jussiê (Maurice-Belay 65), Yambéré. Coach: Willy Sagnol (FRA)
Match 5 - Liverpool FC (ENG)
A 1-2 *Saivet (33)*
Carrasso, Contento, Sané, Rolán, Saivet, Chantôme, Biyogo Poko, Plašil (Ounas 84), Jussiê (Maurice-Belay 76), Yambéré, Crivelli (Diabaté 67). Coach: Willy Sagnol (FRA)
Match 6 - FC Rubin (RUS)
H 2-2 *Laborde (58), Rolán (63)*
Prior, Traoré (Soni 64), Rolán (Crivelli 83), Kiese Thelin, Laborde (Khazri 72), Biyogo Poko, Yambéré, Vada, Guilbert, Poundjé, Maulun. Coach: Willy Sagnol (FRA)
Red card: Guilbert 86

DOMESTIC LEAGUE CLUB-BY-CLUB

Angers SCO

1919 • Jean Bouin (15,603) • angers-sco.fr
Coach: Stéphane Moulin

2015

08/08	a	Montpellier	W	2-0	Camara, Sunu
15/08	a	Nantes	D	0-0	
22/08	a	GFC Ajaccio	W	2-0	N'Doye 2
29/08	h	Nice	D	1-1	Mangani
12/09	a	Lorient	L	1-3	Saïss
19/09	h	Troyes	W	1-0	Mangani (p)
22/09	h	Reims	D	0-0	
27/09	a	Marseille	W	2-1	Mangani (p), Thomas
03/10	h	Bastia	W	1-0	Ketkeophomphone
17/10	a	Toulouse	W	2-0	N'Doye, Camara
24/10	h	Guingamp	D	0-0	
01/11	a	Monaco	L	0-1	
06/11	h	Rennes	L	0-2	
22/11	a	Caen	D	0-0	
28/11	h	LOSC	W	2-0	Sunu, Traoré
01/12	h	Paris	D	0-0	
05/12	a	Lyon	W	2-0	N'Doye 2
13/12	h	Bordeaux	D	1-1	Thomas
20/12	a	St-Étienne	L	0-1	

2016

09/01	h	Caen	W	2-0	Capelle, Ketkeophomphone
15/01	a	Nice	L	1-2	Capelle
23/01	a	Paris	L	1-5	Capelle
30/01	h	Monaco	W	3-0	N'Doye 2, Yattara
03/02	a	Reims	L	1-2	Bouka Moutou
06/02	h	Lyon	L	0-3	
12/02	a	Rennes	L	0-1	
20/02	h	Montpellier	L	2-3	Bouka Moutou, Karanovic
27/02	a	Guingamp	D	2-2	Capelle, Ketkeophomphone (p)
05/03	a	St-Étienne	D	0-0	
13/03	a	Nantes	L	0-2	
19/03	h	Lorient	W	5-1	Ketkeophomphone, Mangani 2 (1p), Saïss, N'Doye
02/04	a	Troyes	W	1-0	Diers
09/04	h	GFC Ajaccio	D	0-0	
16/04	a	Bordeaux	W	3-1	N'Doye, Yattara, Bourillon
27/04	a	LOSC	D	0-0	
01/05	h	Marseille	L	0-1	
07/05	a	Bastia	L	0-1	
14/05	h	Toulouse	L	2-3	Ketkeophomphone, Benrahma

No	Name	Nat	DoB	Pos	Aps	(s)	Gls
21	Yoann Andreu		03/05/89	D	31		
2	Gaël Angoula		18/07/82	D	10	(3)	
7	Olivier Auriac		14/09/83	M	3	(12)	
25	Saïd Benrahma	ALG	10/08/95	A	1	(11)	1
3	Arnold Bouka Moutou	CGO	28/11/88	D	12	(10)	2
6	Grégory Bourillon		01/07/84	M	6	(2)	1
1	Ludovic Butelle		03/04/83	G	19		
9	Abdoul Camara	GUI	20/02/90	M	17		2
15	Pierrick Capelle		15/04/87	M	15	(13)	4
20	Charles Diers		06/06/81	M	5	(10)	1
27	Férébory Doré	CGO	21/01/89	A	7	(2)	
13	Diego Gómez	ARG	05/01/84	A		(1)	
22	Goran Karanovic	SUI	13/10/87	A	2	(10)	1
14	Billy Ketkeophomphone		24/03/90	A	31	(4)	5
33	Aïssa Laidouni		13/12/96	M	1		
30	Alexandre Letellier		11/12/90	G	17		
29	Vincent Manceau		10/07/89	D	27		
5	Thomas Mangani		29/04/87	M	31	(2)	5
17	Cheikh N'Doye	SEN	29/03/86	M	32		9
26	Guy N'Gosso	CMR	11/11/85	M	1	(2)	
12	Jean-Pierre N'Same	CMR	01/05/93	A		(5)	
1	Denis Petrič	SVN	24/05/88	G	2		
28	Romain Saïss	MAR	26/03/90	M	35		2
19	Mathias Serin		01/08/91	M		(1)	
11	Slimane Sissoko		20/03/91	A	2	(10)	
10	Gilles Sunu		30/03/91	A	32		2
24	Romain Thomas		12/06/88	D	36		2
8	Ismaël Traoré	CIV	18/08/86	D	34		1
9	Mohamed Yattara	GUI	28/07/93	A	9	(9)	2

SC Bastia

1905 • Armand-Cesari (16,078) • sc-bastia.net
Major honours
French Cup (1) 1981
Coach: Ghislain Printant;
(29/01/16) François Ciccolini

2015

08/08	h	Rennes	W	2-1	Ayité, Kamano
16/08	a	Lorient	D	1-1	Ayité
22/08	h	Guingamp	W	3-0	Palmieri, og (Baca), Coulibaly
30/08	a	St-Étienne	L	1-2	Danic
13/09	a	Marseille	L	1-4	Brandão
19/09	h	Nice	L	1-3	Danic
23/09	a	Lyon	L	0-2	
26/09	a	Toulouse	W	3-0	Palmieri, Squillaci 2
03/10	a	Angers	L	0-1	
17/10	h	Paris	L	0-2	
24/10	a	Montpellier	L	0-2	
31/10	h	Caen	W	1-0	Diallo
07/11	a	LOSC	D	1-1	Danic
22/11	h	GFC Ajaccio	L	1-2	Brandão
28/11	a	Nantes	D	0-0	
02/12	h	Bordeaux	W	1-0	Raspentino
05/12	h	Monaco	L	1-2	Romain
12/12	a	Troyes	D	1-1	Fofana
19/12	h	Reims	W	2-0	Ayité, Romain

2016

08/01	a	Paris	L	0-2	
16/01	h	Montpellier	W	1-0	Ayité
23/01	a	Guingamp	L	0-1	
30/01	h	Lyon	W	1-0	Brandão
02/02	a	Monaco	L	0-2	
06/02	h	Troyes	W	2-0	Ayité 2 (1p)
13/02	a	Reims	W	1-0	og (Traoré)
26/02	a	Nice	W	2-0	Diallo, Ayité
05/03	h	Lorient	D	0-0	
09/03	h	Nantes	D	0-0	
12/03	h	LOSC	L	1-2	Danic
20/03	a	Bordeaux	D	1-1	Ngando
03/04	a	Marseille	W	2-1	og (Rekik), Danic (p)
09/04	a	Toulouse	L	0-4	
16/04	h	St-Étienne	L	0-1	
24/04	a	GFC Ajaccio	L	2-3	Ngando, Cahuzac
30/04	a	Caen	D	0-0	
07/05	h	Angers	W	1-0	Cahuzac
14/05	a	Rennes	W	2-1	Kamano 2

No	Name	Nat	DoB	Pos	Aps	(s)	Gls
7	Floyd Ayité	TOG	15/12/88	M	30	(2)	7
11	Brandão	BRA	16/06/80	A	19	(8)	3
29	Yannick Cahuzac		18/01/85	M	29	(2)	2
29	Gilles Cioni		14/06/84	D	17	(3)	
33	Lassana Coulibaly	MLI	10/04/96	A	7	(8)	1
2	Gaël Danic		19/11/81	M	32	(5)	5
2	Sadio Diallo	GUI	28/12/90	A	9	(6)	2
23	Alexander Djiku		09/08/94	D	19	(1)	
6	Seko Fofana		07/05/95	M	25	(7)	1
1	Jesper Hansen	DEN	31/03/85	G	3	(1)	
10	Lyes Houri	MAR	19/01/96	M		(1)	
24	Yassine Jebbour	MAR	24/01/91	D	2	(2)	
24	François Kamano	GUI	01/05/96	A	17	(6)	3
12	Abdoulaye Keïta	MLI	05/01/94	M		(4)	
16	Jean-Louis Leca		21/09/85	G	34		
22	Christopher Maboulou		19/03/90	M	2	(7)	
28	Florian Marange		03/03/86	D	19	(5)	
9	François Modesto		19/08/78	D	27	(2)	
14	Mehdi Mostefa	ALG	30/08/83	M	20	(5)	
19	Axel Ngando		13/07/93	M	15	(8)	2
15	Julian Palmieri		17/12/86	D	33	(1)	2
21	Mathieu Peybernes		21/10/90	D	23	(2)	
9	Florian Raspentino		06/06/89	A	5	(6)	1
34	Julien Romain		23/02/96	M	1	(4)	2
5	Sébastien Squillaci		11/08/80	D	29	(2)	2
30	Thomas Vincensini		12/09/93	M		(1)	

FC Girondins de Bordeaux

1881 • Matmut Atlantique (41,908) • girondins.com
Major honours
French League (6) 1950, 1984, 1985, 1987, 1999, 2009; French Cup (4) 1941, 1986, 1987, 2013; League Cup (3) 2002, 2007, 2009
Coach: Willy Sagnol;
(14/03/16) Ulrich Ramé

2015

09/08	h	Reims	L	1-2	Khazri
15/08	a	St-Étienne	D	1-1	Saivet
23/08	a	LOSC	D	0-0	
30/08	h	Nantes	W	2-0	Khazri, Gajić
11/09	a	Paris	D	2-2	og (Trapp), Khazri
20/09	h	Toulouse	D	1-1	Crivelli
23/09	a	Nice	L	1-6	Plašil
26/09	h	Lyon	W	3-1	Khazri, Plašil, Pablo
04/10	a	Lorient	L	2-3	Rolán, Ounas
18/10	h	Montpellier	D	0-0	
25/10	h	Troyes	W	1-0	Ounas
31/10	a	GFC Ajaccio	L	0-2	
08/11	h	Monaco	W	3-1	Maurice-Belay, Yambéré, Plašil
22/11	a	Rennes	D	2-2	Crivelli, Contento
29/11	h	Caen	L	1-4	Crivelli
02/12	a	Bastia	L	0-1	
06/12	h	Guingamp	D	1-1	Yambéré
13/12	a	Angers	D	1-1	Rolán
20/12	h	Marseille	D	1-1	Khazri

2016

09/01	a	Montpellier	W	1-0	Diabaté
16/01	h	LOSC	W	1-0	Diabaté
23/01	a	Nantes	D	2-2	Diabaté, og (Cana)
31/01	h	Rennes	W	4-0	Diabaté 2, Rolán, Touré
03/02	a	Lyon	L	0-3	
07/02	h	St-Étienne	L	1-4	Yambéré
13/02	a	Guingamp	W	4-2	Ounas, Rolán, Chantôme, Diabaté
19/02	h	Nice	D	0-0	
27/02	a	Reims	L	1-4	Ounas
05/03	h	GFC Ajaccio	D	1-1	Diabaté (p)
12/03	a	Toulouse	D	0-0	
20/03	h	Bastia	D	1-1	Contento
01/04	a	Monaco	W	2-1	Touré, Ounas
10/04	a	Marseille	D	0-0	
16/04	h	Angers	L	1-3	Rolán
30/04	a	Troyes	W	4-2	Rolán 2, og (Mavinga), Diabaté
07/05	h	Lorient	W	3-0	Malcom, Diabaté 2
11/05	h	Paris	D	1-1	Pallois
14/05	a	Caen	L	0-1	

No	Name	Nat	DoB	Pos	Aps	(s)	Gls
34	Jean Ambrose		27/09/93	D		(1)	
10	Mauro Arambarri	URU	30/09/95	M	2	(3)	
1	Paul Bernardoni		18/04/97	G	7		
17	André Biyogo Poko	GAB	01/01/93	M	19	(6)	
16	Cédric Carrasso		30/12/81	G	20		
11	Clément Chantôme		11/09/87	M	25	(1)	1
27	Diego Contento	GER	01/05/90	D	24	(1)	2
24	Enzo Crivelli		06/02/95	A	15	(14)	3
14	Mathieu Debuchy		28/07/85	D	9		
14	Cheick Diabaté	MLI	25/04/88	A	17	(5)	10
2	Milan Gajić	SRB	28/01/96	D	7	(2)	1
26	Frédéric Guilbert		24/12/94	D	29	(1)	
34	Ilias Hassani		08/11/95	D		(1)	
20	Jussiê	BRA	19/03/83	A	5	(9)	
24	Wahbi Khazri	TUN	08/02/91	M	20		5
12	Isaac Kiese Thelin	SWE	24/06/92	A	3	(4)	
15	Gaëtan Laborde		03/05/94	A		(1)	
25	Malcom	BRA	26/02/97	A	5	(7)	1
33	Robin Maulun		23/11/96	M		(1)	
19	Nicolas Maurice-Belay		19/04/85	M	15	(3)	1
33	Adam Ounas		11/11/96	M	15	(8)	5
4	Pablo	BRA	21/06/91	D	16		1
5	Nicolas Pallois		19/09/87	D	17		1
18	Jaroslav Plašil	CZE	05/01/82	M	25	(2)	3
29	Maxime Poundjé		16/08/92	D	14		
30	Jérôme Prior		08/08/95	G	11	(2)	
9	Diego Rolán	URU	23/03/93	A	22	(9)	7
10	Henri Saivet	SEN	26/10/90	M	18		1
7	Lamine Sané	SEN	22/03/87	D	11	(2)	
8	Grégory Sertic		05/08/89	M	1		
28	Kévin Soni	CMR	17/04/98	M	1	(1)	
7	Thomas Touré	CIV	27/12/93	A	7	(15)	2
7	Abdou Traoré	MLI	17/01/88	M	4	(6)	
23	Valentin Vada	ARG	06/03/96	M	10	(6)	
21	Cédric Yambéré		06/11/90	D	24	(3)	3

FRANCE

SM Caen

1913 • Stade Michel d'Ornano (21,068) • smcaen.fr
Coach: Patrice Garande

2015
08/08	a	Marseille	W	1-0	Delort
15/08	h	Toulouse	W	1-0	Da Silva
22/08	a	Nice	L	1-2	Delort
29/08	h	Lyon	L	0-4	
12/09	a	Troyes	W	3-1	Féret, Yahia, Bessat
19/09	h	Montpellier	W	2-1	Rodelin, Louis
23/09	a	Lorient	L	0-2	
26/09	h	GFC Ajaccio	W	2-0	Rodelin, Imorou
04/10	h	St-Étienne	W	1-0	Delort
17/10	h	Reims	W	1-0	Féret
23/10	h	Nantes	L	0-2	
31/10	h	Bastia	L	0-1	
07/11	h	Guingamp	W	2-1	Féret, Delort
22/11	h	Angers	D	0-0	
29/11	a	Bordeaux	W	4-1	Ben Youssef, Da Silva, og (Carrasso), Delort
02/12	a	Monaco	D	1-1	Rodelin
05/12	h	LOSC	L	1-2	Delort (p)
11/12	h	Rennes	D	1-1	Ben Youssef
19/12	h	Paris	L	0-3	

2016
09/01	a	Angers	L	0-2	
17/01	h	Marseille	L	1-3	Rodelin
23/01	a	Montpellier	W	2-1	Rodelin, Delort
31/01	h	Nice	W	2-0	Rodelin, Delort (p)
03/02	a	LOSC	L	0-1	
06/02	h	Reims	L	0-2	
14/02	a	Lyon	L	1-4	Delort
21/02	a	Rennes	W	1-0	Ntibazonkiza
28/02	a	St-Étienne	W	2-1	Delort, Rodelin
04/03	h	Monaco	D	2-2	Féret (p), Kouakou
12/03	a	GFC Ajaccio	W	1-0	
19/03	h	Troyes	W	2-1	Yahia, Rodelin
02/04	a	Toulouse	L	0-2	
09/04	h	Lorient	L	1-2	Appiah
16/04	a	Paris	L	0-6	
24/04	h	Guingamp	D	1-1	Rodelin
30/04	a	Bastia	D	0-0	
07/05	h	Nantes	W	2-1	Rodelin, Delort (p)
14/05	a	Bordeaux	W	1-0	Delort (p)

No	Name	Nat	DoB	Pos	Aps	(s)	Gls
18	Jordan Adéoti	BEN	12/03/89	M	16	(15)	
21	Chaker Alhadhur	COM	04/12/91	D	8	(2)	
12	Dennis Appiah		09/06/92	D	38		1
20	Hervé Bazile	HAI	18/03/90	A	11	(14)	
13	Syam Ben Youssef	TUN	31/03/89	D	16	(2)	2
11	Vincent Bessat		08/11/85	M	32	(3)	1
28	Damien Da Silva		17/05/88	D	28		2
6	Jonathan Delaplace		20/03/86	M	21	(1)	
9	Andy Delort		09/10/91	A	34	(2)	12
4	Ismaël Diomandé	CIV	28/09/92	M	5	(1)	
25	Julien Féret		05/07/82	M	37	(1)	4
15	Emmanuel Imorou	BEN	16/09/88	D	15		1
24	Christian Kouakou	CIV	01/05/91	A		(6)	1
19	Jordan Leborgne		29/09/95	A	7	(6)	
14	Jeff Louis	HAI	08/08/92	M	7	(12)	1
17	Jean Makengo		12/06/98	M	5	(5)	
8	Jordan N'Kololo	COD	09/11/92	M	5	(10)	
10	Lenny Nangis		24/03/94	M	3		
10	Saidi Ntibazonkiza	BUR	01/05/87	M	6	(8)	1
22	Alexandre Raineau		21/06/86	D	3	(4)	
23	Ronny Rodelin		18/11/89	A	33	(1)	10
2	Nicolas Seube		11/08/79	M	24	(8)	
1	Rémy Vercoutre		26/06/80	G	38		
5	Alaeddine Yahia	TUN	26/09/81	D	26		2

Gazélec FC Ajaccio

1910 • Ange Casanova (4,158) • gfca-foot.com
Coach: Thierry Laurey

2015
08/08	a	Troyes	D	0-0	
16/08	a	Paris	L	0-2	
22/08	h	Angers	L	0-2	
29/08	a	LOSC	L	0-1	
13/09	h	Monaco	L	0-1	
19/09	a	Guingamp	L	1-2	Mangane
23/09	h	Rennes	D	1-1	Larbi
26/09	a	Caen	L	0-2	
03/10	h	Toulouse	D	2-2	Mayi, Pujol
17/10	a	St-Étienne	L	0-2	
24/10	h	Nice	W	3-1	Pujol, Filippi, Djoković
31/10	h	Bordeaux	W	2-0	Larbi 2
07/11	a	Reims	W	2-0	Boutaïb, Zoua
22/11	a	Bastia	W	2-1	Zoua (p), Boutaïb
28/11	h	Lorient	W	2-1	Larbi
02/12	a	Montpellier	W	2-0	Zoua, Tshibumbu
05/12	h	Nantes	D	1-1	Tshibumbu
13/12	a	Marseille	D	1-1	Zoua (p)
20/12	h	Lyon	W	2-1	Larbi 2

2016
09/01	a	Monaco	D	2-2	Boutaïb, Tshibumbu
16/01	h	Reims	D	2-2	Boutaïb, Djoković
22/01	a	Rennes	L	0-1	
30/01	h	Montpellier	L	0-4	
03/02	a	Nantes	L	1-3	Mayi
06/02	h	Guingamp	D	0-0	
13/02	h	Troyes	L	2-3	Zoua, Filippi
20/02	a	Toulouse	D	1-1	Mayi
05/03	a	Bordeaux	D	1-1	Larbi
09/03	h	Marseille	D	1-1	og (Rekik)
12/03	h	Caen	W	1-0	Boutaïb
20/03	a	Nice	L	0-3	
02/04	h	St-Étienne	L	0-2	
09/04	a	Angers	D	0-0	
16/04	h	LOSC	L	2-4	Pujol, Touré
24/04	h	Bastia	W	3-2	Boutaïb, Pujol, Larbi (p)
30/04	a	Lyon	L	1-2	Pujol
07/05	h	Paris	L	0-4	
14/05	a	Lorient	L	0-1	

No	Name	Nat	DoB	Pos	Aps	(s)	Gls
9	Khalid Boutaïb		24/04/87	A	22	(9)	6
5	Jérémie Bréchet		14/08/79	D	23		
27	Amine Chermiti	TUN	26/12/87	A	4	(5)	
29	Alexandre Coeff		20/02/92	D	22	(2)	
22	Issiar Dia	SEN	08/06/87	M	5	(6)	
23	Damjan Djoković	CRO	18/04/90	M	26	(9)	2
6	David Ducourtioux		11/04/78	M	29	(4)	
4	Rodéric Filippi		25/02/89	D	21	(5)	2
30	Jules Goda	CMR	30/05/89	G	3		
40	Paul André Guerin		26/09/97	G	1	(1)	
10	Mohammed Larbi	TUN	02/09/87	M	26	(4)	8
8	Jérôme Le Moigne		15/02/83	M	27	(4)	
15	Kader Mangane		13/03/83	D	28	(3)	1
21	Pablo Martinez		21/02/89	D	26	(2)	
1	Clément Maury		20/11/85	G	34		
7	Kévin Mayi		14/01/93	A	8	(15)	3
20	Louis Poggi		18/06/84	M	9	(6)	
28	Grégory Pujol		25/01/80	A	12	(7)	5
3	Issiaga Sylla	GUI	01/01/94	D	29	(5)	
13	Alassane Touré		09/02/89	D	11	(2)	1
24	John Tshibumbu	COD	06/01/89	A	12	(11)	3
18	Amos Youga	CTA	08/12/92	M	14	(4)	
19	Jacques Zoua	CMR	06/09/91	A	26	(5)	5

EA Guingamp

1912 • Roudourou (18,197) • eaguingamp.com
Major honours
French Cup (2) 2009, 2014
Coach: Jocelyn Gourvennec

2015
08/08	a	Nantes	L	0-1	
15/08	h	Lyon	L	0-1	
22/08	a	Bastia	L	0-3	
28/08	h	Marseille	W	2-0	Privat, Benezet
12/09	a	Nice	W	1-0	Sankharé
19/09	h	GFC Ajaccio	W	2-1	Privat, Briand
22/09	a	Paris	L	0-3	
27/09	h	Monaco	D	3-3	Privat, Benezet 2
03/10	a	Troyes	W	1-0	Sankharé
17/10	h	LOSC	D	1-1	Briand
24/10	a	Angers	D	0-0	
31/10	a	Lorient	D	2-2	Briand, Salibur
07/11	a	Caen	L	1-2	Lévêque
21/11	h	Toulouse	W	2-0	Privat, Salibur
29/11	a	St-Étienne	L	0-3	
02/12	h	Reims	L	1-2	Salibur
06/12	a	Bordeaux	L	0-1	
12/12	a	Montpellier	L	1-2	Privat
19/12	h	Rennes	L	0-2	

2016
10/01	a	Marseille	D	0-0	
16/01	h	Nantes	D	2-2	Benezet, Salibur
23/01	h	Bastia	W	1-0	Giresse (p)
30/01	a	Toulouse	W	2-1	Sankharé, Briand
03/02	a	Troyes	W	4-0	Mevlüt, Sankharé, Giresse, Blas
06/02	a	GFC Ajaccio	D	0-0	
13/02	h	Bordeaux	L	2-4	Giresse, Coco
20/02	a	Lorient	L	3-4	Salibur 2, Briand
27/02	a	Angers	D	2-2	Privat, Giresse (p)
06/03	a	Lyon	L	1-5	Mevlüt
12/03	h	St-Étienne	W	2-0	Briand, Privat
19/03	h	Reims	W	1-0	Sankharé
02/04	h	Montpellier	D	2-2	Salibur, Sorbon
09/04	a	Paris	L	0-2	
17/04	a	Rennes	W	3-0	Diallo, Briand, Sankharé
24/04	a	Caen	D	1-1	Sorbon
30/04	a	Monaco	L	2-3	Mevlüt, Angoua
07/05	a	LOSC	D	0-0	
14/05	h	Nice	L	2-3	Mevlüt, og (Genevois)

No	Name	Nat	DoB	Pos	Aps	(s)	Gls
4	Benjamin Angoua	CIV	28/11/86	D	13	(5)	1
6	Maxime Baca		02/06/83	D	2		
17	Julien Bègue		08/08/93	M		(3)	
10	Nicolas Benezet		24/02/91	M	14	(5)	4
3	Ludovic Blas		31/12/97	M	6	(8)	1
23	Jimmy Briand		02/08/85	A	33	(2)	7
8	Julien Cardy		29/09/81	M	4	(10)	
24	Marcus Coco		24/06/96	M	20	(10)	1
12	Nill De Pauw	BEL	06/01/90	A	3	(10)	
9	Mana Dembélé		29/11/88	A	4	(9)	
5	Moustapha Diallo	SEN	14/05/86	M	21	(9)	1
20	Laurent Dos Santos		21/03/93	M	6	(3)	
26	Thibault Giresse		25/05/81	M	20	(5)	4
27	Franck Héry		26/04/93	D	3		
2	Lars Jacobsen	DEN	20/09/79	D	31	(1)	
29	Christophe Kerbrat		02/08/86	D	29		
25	Reynald Lemaître		28/06/83	D	4	(1)	
7	Dorian Lévêque		22/11/89	D	14	(1)	1
33	Jeremy Livolant		09/01/98	M		(1)	
1	Jonas Lössl	DEN	01/02/89	G	37		
22	Jonathan Martins Pereira		30/01/86	D	16		
18	Lionel Mathis		04/10/81	M	17	(3)	
28	Mevlüt Erdinç	TUR	25/02/87	A	11	(4)	4
11	Sloan Privat		24/07/89	A	14	(13)	7
19	Yannis Salibur		21/01/91	M	28	(2)	7
30	Mamadou Samassa	MLI	16/02/90	G	1		
13	Younousse Sankharé	SEN	10/09/89	M	33		6
15	Jérémy Sorbon		05/08/83	D	34		2

LOSC Lille

1944 • Pierre-Mauroy (50,157) • losc.fr

Major honours
*French League (3) 1946, 1954, 2011; French Cup (6)
1946, 1947, 1948, 1953, 1955, 2011*
**Coach: Hervé Renard;
(11/11/15) (Patrick Collot);
(22/11/15) Frédéric Antonetti**

2015
07/08	h	Paris	L	0-1	
14/08	a	Monaco	D	0-0	
23/08	h	Bordeaux	D	0-0	
29/08	h	GFC Ajaccio	W	1-0	*Boufal*
12/09	a	Lyon	D	0-0	
18/09	a	Rennes	D	1-1	*Boufal*
25/09	a	Reims	L	0-1	
29/09	h	Nantes	L	0-1	
02/10	h	Montpellier	W	2-0	*Boufal (p), Sidibé*
17/10	a	Guingamp	D	1-1	*Boufal*
25/10	h	Marseille	L	1-2	*Corchia*
01/11	h	Nice	D	0-0	
07/11	h	Bastia	D	1-1	*Sidibé*
21/11	a	Troyes	D	1-1	*Benzia*
28/11	a	Angers	L	0-2	
02/12	h	St-Étienne	W	1-0	*Benzia*
05/12	a	Caen	W	2-1	*Benzia 2*
12/12	h	Lorient	W	3-0	*Bauthéac 2, Sidibé*
19/12	a	Toulouse	D	1-1	*Boufal*

2016
10/01	h	Nice	D	1-1	*Benzia*
16/01	a	Bordeaux	L	0-1	
23/01	h	Troyes	L	1-3	*Boufal (p)*
29/01	a	Marseille	D	1-1	*Corchia*
03/02	h	Caen	W	1-0	*Soumaoro*
07/02	a	Rennes	D	1-1	*Éder*
13/02	a	Paris	D	0-0	
21/02	h	Lyon	W	1-0	*Boufal*
27/02	a	Montpellier	L	0-3	
05/03	h	Reims	W	2-0	*Rony Lopes, Éder*
12/03	a	Bastia	W	2-1	*Boufal, Amadou*
19/03	h	Toulouse	W	1-0	*Amalfitano*
03/04	a	Nantes	W	3-0	*Éder 2, Sunzu*
10/04	h	Monaco	W	4-1	*Amalfitano, Éder, Obbadi, Sidibé*
16/04	a	GFC Ajaccio	W	4-2	*Boufal 3, og (Martinez)*
27/04	a	Angers	D	0-0	
30/04	a	Lorient	W	1-0	*Rony Lopes*
07/05	h	Guingamp	D	0-0	
14/05	a	St-Étienne	W	1-0	*Éder (p)*

No	Name	Nat	DoB	Pos	Aps	(s)	Gls
6	Ibrahim Amadou	CMR	06/04/93	M	18	(4)	1
31	Morgan Amalfitano		20/03/85	M	10	(5)	2
35	Alexis Araujo		07/12/96	M		(1)	
4	Florent Balmont		02/02/80	M	25	(1)	
25	Marko Baša	MNE	29/12/82	D	15		
11	Éric Bauthéac		24/08/87	M	25	(3)	2
9	Yassine Benzia	ALG	08/09/94	A	17	(8)	5
18	Franck Béria		23/05/83	D	1	(1)	
7	Sofiane Boufal	MAR	17/09/93	M	27	(2)	11
5	Renato Civelli	ARG	14/10/83	D	32		
2	Sébastien Corchia		01/11/90	D	30	(3)	2
39	Éder	POR	22/12/87	A	12	(1)	6
1	Vincent Enyeama	NGA	29/08/82	G	35		
27	Baptiste Guillaume	BEL	16/06/95	A	5	(5)	
12	Sehrou Guirassy		12/03/96	A	3	(5)	
33	Youssouf Koné	MLI	05/07/95	D		(1)	
40	Mike Maignan		03/07/95	G	3	(1)	
10	Marvin Martin		10/01/88	M	4	(8)	
24	Rio Mavuba		08/03/84	M	31	(4)	
33	Nolan Mbemba		19/02/95	M	1		
17	Soualiho Meïté		17/03/94	M		(3)	
15	Lenny Nangis		24/03/94	M	3	(8)	
8	Mounir Obbadi	MAR	04/04/83	M	25	(5)	1
28	Benjamin Pavard		28/03/96	D	6	(7)	
21	Ronny Rodelin		18/11/89	A	1		
32	Rony Lopes	POR	28/12/95	M	5	(7)	2
20	Ryan Mendes	CPV	08/01/90	A		(3)	
19	Djibril Sidibé		29/07/92	D	36	(1)	4
23	Adama Soumaoro		18/06/92	D	25	(3)	1
13	Stoppila Sunzu	ZAM	22/06/89	D	10	(2)	1
22	Junior Tallo	CIV	21/12/92	A	12	(11)	
14	Yaw Yeboah	GHA	28/03/97	A	1	(2)	

FC Lorient

1926 • Le Moustoir-Yves-Allainmat (17,755) • fclweb.fr

Major honours
French Cup (1) 2002
Coach: Sylvain Ripoll

2015
09/08	a	Lyon	D	0-0	
16/08	h	Bastia	D	1-1	*Moukandjo (p)*
23/08	h	St-Étienne	L	0-1	
29/08	a	Reims	L	1-4	*Bouanga*
12/09	h	Angers	W	3-1	*Jouffre, Waris, Jeannot*
20/09	a	Monaco	W	3-2	*N'Dong, Jeannot, Moukandjo*
23/09	h	Caen	W	2-0	*Moukandjo, Waris*
27/09	a	Montpellier	L	1-2	*Abdullah*
04/10	h	Bordeaux	W	3-2	*Moukandjo, Waris (p), Touré*
18/10	a	Marseille	D	1-1	*Moukandjo*
24/10	h	Rennes	D	1-1	*Raphael Guerreiro*
31/10	a	Guingamp	D	2-2	*Moukandjo 2 (1p)*
07/11	h	Troyes	W	4-1	*Jeannot, Moukandjo 2 (1p), N'Dong*
21/11	h	Paris	L	1-2	*Moukandjo (p)*
28/11	a	GFC Ajaccio	D	1-1	*Moukandjo (p)*
01/12	h	Nice	D	0-0	
05/12	a	Toulouse	W	3-2	*Jeannot 2, Mesloub*
12/12	a	LOSC	L	0-3	
19/12	h	Nantes	D	0-0	

2016
09/01	h	Rennes	D	2-2	*og (Diagné), Waris*
17/01	h	Monaco	L	0-2	
23/01	a	Nice	L	1-2	*Jouffre*
30/01	h	Reims	W	2-0	*Touré 2*
03/02	a	Paris	L	1-3	*Raphael Guerreiro*
06/02	h	Montpellier	D	1-1	*Cabot*
13/02	a	Nantes	L	1-2	*Moukandjo (p)*
20/02	h	Guingamp	W	4-3	*Waris 2, Jeannot, Raphael Guerreiro*
27/02	a	Troyes	W	1-0	*Waris*
05/03	a	Bastia	D	0-0	
12/03	h	Marseille	D	1-1	*Waris*
19/03	a	Angers	L	1-5	*Waris*
03/04	h	Lyon	L	1-3	*Waris*
09/04	a	Caen	W	2-1	*Jeannot, Waris (p)*
16/04	h	Toulouse	D	1-1	*Touré*
24/04	a	St-Étienne	L	0-2	
30/04	h	LOSC	L	0-1	
07/05	a	Bordeaux	L	0-3	
14/05	h	GFC Ajaccio	W	1-0	*Moukandjo*

No	Name	Nat	DoB	Pos	Aps	(s)	Gls
13	Raffidine Abdullah		15/01/94	M	6	(6)	1
28	Maxime Barthelmé		08/09/88	M	16	(8)	
6	François Bellugou		25/04/87	M	27	(6)	
35	Issam Ben Khemis		10/01/96	M		(1)	
20	Denis Bouanga		11/11/94	M	3	(1)	1
27	Jimmy Cabot		18/04/94	M	8	(5)	1
30	Florent Chaigneau		21/03/84	G	1	(1)	
23	Moryké Fofana	CIV	23/11/91	A		(6)	
11	Marvin Gakpa		01/11/93	A		(3)	
25	Lamine Gassama	SEN	20/10/89	D	31		
22	Benjamin Jeannot		22/01/92	A	19	(11)	7
8	Yann Jouffre		23/07/84	M	21	(5)	2
18	Hamadou Karamoko		31/10/95	D	3		
34	Erwin Koffi		10/01/95	M	1		
2	Lamine Koné		01/02/89	D	17	(1)	
24	Wesley Lautoa		25/08/87	D	11	(2)	
31	Valentin Lavigne		04/06/94	A	1	(5)	
4	Vincent Le Goff		15/09/89	D	19	(8)	
1	Benjamin Lecomte		26/04/91	G	37		
17	Walid Mesloub	ALG	04/09/85	M	23	(6)	1
5	Mehdi Mostefa	ALG	30/08/83	M	1		
12	Benjamin Moukandjo	CMR	12/11/88	A	26	(5)	13
15	Rémi Mulumba	COD	02/11/92	M	1	(5)	
3	Yrondu Musavu-King	GAB	08/01/92	D	2	(1)	
7	Didier N'Dong	GAB	17/06/94	M	34		2
29	Pape Abdou Paye	SEN	31/05/90	D	8	(2)	
19	Romain Philippoteaux		02/03/88	M	16	(15)	
14	Raphael Guerreiro	POR	22/12/93	D	27	(7)	3
26	Lindsay Rose		08/02/92	D	10		
5	Zargo Touré	SEN	11/10/89	D	29		4
21	Alain Traoré	BFA	31/12/88	M		(3)	
9	Majeed Waris	GHA	19/09/91	A	20	(1)	11

Olympique Lyonnais

1950 • Gerland (39,490); Parc OL (59,186) • olweb.fr

Major honours
French League (7) 2002, 2003, 2004, 2005, 2006, 2007, 2008; French Cup (5) 1964, 1967, 1973, 2008, 2012; League Cup (1) 2001
**Coach: Hubert Fournier;
(24/12/15) Bruno Génésio**

2015
09/08	h	Lorient	D	0-0	
15/08	a	Guingamp	W	1-0	*Beauvue*
22/08	h	Rennes	L	1-2	*Fekir*
29/08	a	Caen	W	4-0	*Fekir 3, Beauvue*
12/09	h	LOSC	D	0-0	
20/09	a	Marseille	D	1-1	*Lacazette (p)*
23/09	h	Bastia	W	2-0	*Kalulu, Tolisso*
26/09	a	Bordeaux	L	1-3	*Beauvue*
03/10	h	Reims	W	1-0	*Lacazette*
16/10	a	Monaco	D	1-1	*Rafael*
23/10	h	Toulouse	W	3-0	*Darder, Valbuena, Cornet*
31/10	a	Troyes	W	1-0	*Beauvue (p)*
08/11	h	St-Étienne	W	3-0	*Lacazette 3*
20/11	a	Nice	L	0-3	
27/11	h	Montpellier	L	2-4	*Lacazette, Ghezzal*
01/12	a	Nantes	L	0-2	
05/12	a	Angers	L	0-2	
13/12	a	Paris	L	1-5	*Ferri*
20/12	h	GFC Ajaccio	L	1-2	*Grenier*

2016
09/01	h	Troyes	W	4-1	*Lacazette, Ghezzal, Ferri, Beauvue*
17/01	h	St-Étienne	L	0-1	
24/01	h	Marseille	D	1-1	*Tolisso*
30/01	h	Bastia	L	0-1	
03/02	a	Bordeaux	W	3-0	*Lacazette 2, Kalulu*
06/02	a	Angers	W	3-0	*Jallet, Ghezzal, Tolisso*
14/02	h	Caen	W	4-1	*Umtiti, Lacazette, Cornet, Tolisso*
21/02	a	LOSC	L	0-1	
28/02	h	Paris	W	2-1	*Cornet, Darder*
06/03	h	Guingamp	W	5-1	*Ghezzal, Lacazette 2, Cornet, og (Lemaître)*
13/03	a	Rennes	D	2-2	*Ghezzal, Lacazette*
19/03	h	Nantes	W	2-0	*Perrin, Lacazette (p)*
03/04	a	Lorient	W	3-1	*Lacazette 2, Ghezzal*
08/04	a	Montpellier	W	2-0	*Cornet 2*
15/04	a	Nice	D	1-1	*Lacazette*
23/04	a	Toulouse	W	3-2	*Grenier, Lacazette, Tolisso*
30/04	a	GFC Ajaccio	W	2-1	*Ghezzal, Cornet*
07/05	a	Monaco	W	6-1	*Ghezzal, Lacazette 3, Yanga-Mbiwa 2*
14/05	a	Reims	L	1-4	*Cornet*

No	Name	Nat	DoB	Pos	Aps	(s)	Gls
1	Anthony Lopes	POR	01/10/90	G	37		
9	Claudio Beauvue		16/04/88	A	15	(4)	5
3	Henri Bedimo	CMR	04/06/84	D	14	(4)	
33	Milan Biševac	SRB	31/08/83	D	6		
27	Maxwel Cornet		27/09/96	A	16	(15)	8
14	Sergi Darder	ESP	22/12/93	M	18	(8)	2
33	Romain Del Castillo		29/03/96	M		(2)	
18	Nabil Fekir		18/07/93	M	5	(4)	4
12	Jordan Ferri		12/03/92	M	26	(8)	2
11	Rachid Ghezzal	ALG	09/05/92	M	16	(13)	8
21	Maxime Gonalons		10/03/89	M	33		
30	Mathieu Gorgelin		05/08/90	G	1		
7	Clément Grenier		07/01/91	M	10	(8)	2
13	Christophe Jallet		31/10/83	D	20	(3)	1
26	Aldo Kalulu		21/01/96	A	1	(9)	2
24	Olivier Kemen		20/07/96	M	1	(1)	
4	Bakary Koné	BFA	27/04/88	D	4	(2)	
32	Zakarie Labidi		08/02/95	A		(3)	
10	Alexandre Lacazette		28/05/91	A	34		21
17	Steed Malbranque		06/01/80	M	5	(6)	
15	Jérémy Morel		02/04/84	D	27	(4)	
28	Arnold Mvuemba		28/01/85	M	3	(3)	
33	Gaëtan Perrin		07/06/96	M		(2)	1
20	Rafael	POR	09/07/90	D	18	(3)	1
22	Lindsay Rose		03/02/92	D	1		
8	Corentin Tolisso		03/08/94	M	28	(5)	5
23	Lucas Tousart		29/04/97	M	1		
23	Samuel Umtiti		14/11/93	D	30		1
19	Mathieu Valbuena		28/09/84	M	21	(5)	1
2	Mapou Yanga-Mbiwa		15/05/89	D	27		2

FRANCE

Olympique de Marseille

1899 • Vélodrome (65,960) • om.net
Major honours
*UEFA Champions League (1) 1993; French League
(9) 1937, 1948, 1971, 1972, 1989, 1990, 1991, 1992,
2010; French Cup (10) 1924, 1926, 1927, 1935,
1938, 1943, 1969, 1972, 1976, 1989; League Cup
(3) 2010, 2011, 2012*
**Coach: Marcelo Bielsa (ARG);
(09/08/15) (Franck Passi);
(19/08/15) Míchel (ESP);
(19/04/16) (Franck Passi)**

2015
08/08	h	Caen	L	0-1
16/08	a	Reims	L	0-1
23/08	h	Troyes	W	6-0	Barrada, Diarra, Batshuayi 2, Ocampos, Alessandrini
28/08	a	Guingamp	L	0-2
13/09	h	Bastia	W	4-1	Mendy, Alessandrini 2, Batshuayi
20/09	a	Lyon	D	1-1	Rekik
23/09	a	Toulouse	D	1-1	Batshuayi
27/09	h	Angers	L	1-2	Batshuayi (p)
04/10	a	Paris	L	1-2	Batshuayi
18/10	h	Lorient	D	1-1	Batshuayi (p)
25/10	a	LOSC	W	2-1	Batshuayi, Alessandrini
01/11	a	Nantes	W	1-0	N'Koudou
08/11	h	Nice	L	0-1
22/11	a	St-Étienne	W	2-0	Batshuayi, N'Koudou
29/11	h	Monaco	D	3-3	Alessandrini, Batshuayi, N'Koudou
03/12	a	Rennes	W	1-0	Cabella
06/12	h	Montpellier	D	2-2	Cabella, Sarr
13/12	h	GFC Ajaccio	D	1-1	Batshuayi
20/12	a	Bordeaux	D	1-1	Romao

2016
10/01	h	Guingamp	D	0-0
17/01	a	Caen	W	3-1	Batshuayi, N'Koudou, Sarr
24/01	a	Lyon	D	1-1	Cabella
29/01	h	LOSC	D	1-1	Rabillard
02/02	a	Montpellier	W	1-0	N'Koudou
07/02	h	Paris	L	1-2	Cabella
14/02	a	Nice	D	1-1	Isla
21/02	h	St-Étienne	D	1-1	Batshuayi
06/03	h	Toulouse	D	1-1	Fletcher
09/03	a	GFC Ajaccio	D	1-1	Cabella
12/03	a	Lorient	D	1-1	Isla
18/03	h	Rennes	L	2-5	Thauvin, Rolando
03/04	a	Bastia	W	1-0	Batshuayi
10/04	h	Bordeaux	D	0-0
17/04	a	Monaco	L	1-2	Batshuayi
24/04	h	Nantes	D	1-1	Thauvin
01/05	a	Angers	W	1-0	Batshuayi
07/05	h	Reims	W	1-0	Batshuayi
14/05	a	Troyes	D	1-1	Fletcher

No	Name	Nat	DoB	Pos	Aps	(s)	Gls
11	Romain Alessandrini		03/04/89	M	16	(6)	5
19	Abdelaziz Barrada	MAR	19/06/89	M	17	(7)	1
22	Michy Batshuayi	BEL	02/10/93	A	32	(4)	17
13	Rémy Cabella		08/03/90	M	30	(4)	5
25	Paolo De Ceglie	ITA	17/09/86	D	3	(4)	
5	Abou Diaby		11/03/86	M	2	(1)	
6	Lassana Diarra		10/03/85	M	25	(1)	1
26	Brice Dja Djédjé	CIV	23/12/90	D	17	(2)	
9	Steven Fletcher	SCO	26/03/87	A	9	(3)	2
18	Mauricio Isla	CHI	12/06/88	M	21	(3)	2
2	Javi Manquillo	ESP	05/05/94	D	30		
8	Mario Lemina	GAB	01/09/93	M	4		
8	Lucas Silva	BRA	16/02/93	M	11	(11)	
30	Steve Mandanda		28/03/85	G	36		
23	Benjamin Mendy		17/07/94	D	22	(2)	1
14	Georges-Kévin N'Koudou		13/02/95	M	22	(6)	5
3	Nicolas N'Koulou	CMR	27/03/90	D	33		
7	Lucas Ocampos	ARG	11/07/94	M	7	(10)	1
16	Yohann Pelé		04/11/82	G	2		
34	Jérémie Porsan-Clemente		16/12/97	A		(1)	
28	Antoine Rabillard		22/09/95	A	1	(2)	1
4	Karim Rekik	NED	02/12/94	D	23	(1)	1
6	Rolando	POR	31/08/85	D	18	(1)	1
20	Alaixys Romao	TOG	18/01/84	M	13	(10)	1
17	Bouna Sarr		31/01/92	M	9	(16)	2
15	Stéphane Sparagna		17/02/95	D	2	(1)	
10	Florian Thauvin		26/01/93	M	11	(5)	2
29	André Zambo Anguissa	CMR	16/11/95	M	2	(7)	

AS Monaco FC

1919 • Louis-II (18,174) • asmonaco.com
Major honours
*French League (7) 1961, 1963, 1978, 1982, 1988,
1997, 2000; French Cup (5) 1960, 1963, 1980, 1985,
1991; League Cup (1) 2003*
Coach: Leonardo Jardim (POR)

2015
08/08	a	Nice	W	2-1	Bernardo Silva, Kurzawa
14/08	h	LOSC	D	0-0
22/08	h	Toulouse	D	1-1	Lemar
30/08	h	Paris	L	0-3
13/09	a	GFC Ajaccio	W	1-0	Fabinho (p)
20/09	h	Lorient	L	2-3	Touré, Lemar
24/09	a	Montpellier	W	3-2	Fábio Coentrão, Lemar, Fabinho (p)
27/09	a	Guingamp	D	3-3	Bernardo Silva, Raggi, Dirar
04/10	h	Rennes	D	1-1	Wallace
16/10	h	Lyon	D	1-1	Pašalić
25/10	a	Reims	W	1-0	Bernardo Silva
01/11	h	Angers	W	1-0	Pašalić
08/11	a	Bordeaux	L	1-3	Hélder Costa
21/11	h	Nantes	W	1-0	Pašalić
29/11	a	Marseille	D	3-3	Touré 2, Fábio Coentrão
02/12	h	Caen	D	1-1	Carrillo
05/12	a	Bastia	W	2-1	L Traoré 2
13/12	h	St-Étienne	W	1-0	Fabinho (p)
19/12	a	Troyes	D	0-0

2016
09/01	h	GFC Ajaccio	D	2-2	Fabinho (p), Ricardo Carvalho
17/01	a	Lorient	W	2-0	Lemar, João Moutinho
24/01	h	Toulouse	W	4-0	Bernardo Silva, Fábio Coentrão, Carrillo, Hélder Costa
30/01	a	Angers	L	0-3
02/02	h	Bastia	W	2-0	og (Modesto), Bernardo Silva
06/02	h	Nice	W	1-0	Bakayoko
14/02	a	St-Étienne	D	1-1	Vágner Love
20/02	h	Troyes	W	3-1	Carrillo 2, Mbappé Lottin
28/02	a	Nantes	D	0-0
04/03	a	Caen	D	2-2	Lemar, og (Yahia)
11/03	h	Reims	W	2-2	Vágner Love 2
20/03	a	Paris	W	2-0	Vágner Love, Fabinho (p)
01/04	h	Bordeaux	L	1-2	og (Guilbert)
10/04	a	LOSC	L	1-4	Bahlouli
17/04	h	Marseille	W	2-1	Bernardo Silva, Raggi
24/04	a	Rennes	D	1-1	Hélder Costa
30/04	h	Guingamp	W	3-2	L Traoré, Dirar, Bernardo Silva
07/05	h	Lyon	L	1-6	Ricardo Carvalho
14/05	h	Montpellier	W	2-0	Ivan Cavaleiro, Fabinho (p)

No	Name	Nat	DoB	Pos	Aps	(s)	Gls
12	Farès Bahlouli		08/04/95	M	2	(6)	1
14	Tiémoué Bakayoko		17/08/94	M	14	(5)	1
10	Bernardo Silva	POR	10/08/94	M	22	(10)	7
29	Boschilia	BRA	05/03/96	M	1	(4)	
11	Guido Carrillo	ARG	25/05/91	A	15	(16)	4
35	Nabil Chaïbi		12/10/96	A		(1)	
7	Nabil Dirar	MAR	25/02/86	M	20		2
21	Elderson Echiéjilé	NGA	20/01/88	D	18	(2)	
22	Stephan El Shaarawy	ITA	27/10/92	A	7	(8)	
2	Fabinho	BRA	23/10/93	D	34		6
4	Fábio Coentrão	POR	11/03/88	D	13	(2)	3
18	Hélder Costa	POR	12/01/94	A	15	(10)	3
17	Ivan Cavaleiro	POR	18/10/93	A	6	(6)	1
5	Jemerson	BRA	24/08/92	D	3	(1)	
8	João Moutinho	POR	08/09/86	M	24	(2)	1
3	Layvin Kurzawa		04/09/92	D	3		1
27	Thomas Lemar		12/11/95	M	20	(6)	5
9	Anthony Martial		05/12/95	A	2	(1)	
33	Kylian Mbappé Lottin		20/12/98	A	2	(9)	1
16	Paul Nardi		18/05/94	G	2		
20	Mario Pašalić	CRO	09/02/95	M	12	(4)	3
24	Andrea Raggi	ITA	24/06/84	D	29	(2)	2
6	Ricardo Carvalho	POR	18/05/78	D	33		2
25	Rony Lopes	POR	28/09/95	M	2		
1	Danijel Subašić	CRO	27/10/84	G	36		
28	Jérémy Toulalan		10/09/83	M	25		
38	Almamy Touré	MLI	28/04/96	D	10	(1)	3
23	Adama Traoré	MLI	28/06/95	M	3	(2)	
19	Lacina Traoré	CIV	20/08/90	A	11	(8)	3
9	Vágner Love	BRA	11/06/84	A	9	(3)	4
13	Wallace	BRA	14/10/94	D	25	(1)	1

Montpellier Hérault SC

1974 • La Mosson (28,500) • mhscfoot.com
Major honours
French League (1) 2012; French Cup (1) 1990
**Coach: Rolland Courbis;
(27/12/15) Frédéric Hantz**

2015
08/08	h	Angers	L	0-2
15/08	a	Rennes	L	0-1
21/08	h	Paris	L	0-1
29/08	a	Troyes	D	0-0
12/09	h	St-Étienne	L	1-2	Marveaux
19/09	a	Caen	D	1-1	Martin
24/09	h	Monaco	L	2-3	Congré, og (Carrillo)
27/09	h	Lorient	W	2-1	Bensebaini, Martin
02/10	a	LOSC	L	0-2
18/10	a	Bordeaux	D	0-0
24/10	h	Bastia	W	2-0	Boudebouz, Ninga
31/10	a	Toulouse	D	1-1	Roussillon
07/11	h	Nantes	W	2-1	Roussillon, Hilton
21/11	h	Reims	W	3-1	Yatabaré, Camara, Dabo
27/11	a	Lyon	W	4-2	og (Gonalons), Ninga 2, Camara
02/12	h	GFC Ajaccio	L	0-2
06/12	a	Marseille	D	2-2	Ninga 2
12/12	h	Guingamp	W	2-1	Camara, Ninga
18/12	a	Nice	L	0-1

2016
09/01	h	Bordeaux	L	0-1
16/01	a	Bastia	L	0-1
23/01	h	Caen	L	1-2	Bensebaini
30/01	a	GFC Ajaccio	W	4-0	Yatabaré, Martin (p), Dabo 2
02/02	h	Marseille	L	0-1
06/02	a	Lorient	D	1-1	Bérigaud
13/02	h	Toulouse	W	2-0	Yatabaré, Camara
20/02	a	Angers	W	3-2	Bérigaud, Yatabaré, Camara
27/02	h	LOSC	W	3-0	Bérigaud, Dabo, Skhiri
05/03	a	Paris	D	0-0
12/03	h	Nice	L	0-2
19/03	a	St-Étienne	L	0-3
02/04	a	Guingamp	D	2-2	Sanson 2
08/04	h	Lyon	L	0-2
17/04	a	Nantes	W	2-0	Dabo, Skhiri
24/04	h	Troyes	W	4-1	Roussillon, og (Saunier), Martin, Camara
30/04	a	Reims	W	3-2	Camara, Congré, Sanson
07/05	h	Rennes	W	2-0	Ninga, Boudebouz
14/05	a	Monaco	L	0-2

No	Name	Nat	DoB	Pos	Aps	(s)	Gls
19	Djamel Bakar		06/04/89	A	2	(4)	
15	Ramy Bensebaini	ALG	16/04/95	D	15	(7)	2
26	Kévin Bérigaud		09/05/88	A	10	(9)	3
10	Ryad Boudebouz	ALG	19/02/90	M	37	(2)	2
19	Souleymane Camara	SEN	22/12/82	A	22	(10)	7
3	Daniel Congré		05/04/85	D	35		2
31	Quentin Cornette		17/01/94	A	1	(1)	
14	Bryan Dabo		18/02/92	M	32	(4)	5
25	Mathieu Deplagne		01/10/91	D	21	(4)	
32	Jean Deza	PER	09/06/93	M	2	(4)	
4	Hilton	BRA	13/09/77	D	36		1
16	Geoffrey Jourdren		04/02/86	G	7		
17	Paul Lasne		16/01/89	M	6	(3)	
30	Jonathan Ligali		28/05/91	G	6		
8	Jonas Martin		09/04/90	M	35	(1)	4
6	Joris Marveaux		15/08/82	D	5	(4)	1
27	Steve Mounié	BEN	29/09/94	A		(2)	
7	Anthony Mounier		27/09/87	M	3		
2	Mamadou N'Diaye	SEN	28/05/95	D	1	(7)	
29	Casimir Ninga	CHA	17/05/93	A	20	(6)	7
1	Laurent Pionnier		24/05/82	G	25		
5	William Rémy		04/04/91	D	27	(1)	
33	Anthony Ribelin		08/04/96	M	1		
24	Jérôme Roussillon		06/01/93	D	31	(2)	3
23	Jamel Saihi	TUN	27/01/87	M	8	(5)	
20	Morgan Sanson		18/08/94	M	30	(4)	3
13	Ellyes Skhiri		10/05/95	M	9	(3)	2
12	Florian Sotoca		25/10/90	A		(1)	
22	Sébastien Wüthrich	SUI	29/05/90	M	1	(1)	
9	Mustapha Yatabaré	MLI	26/01/86	A	15	(13)	4

FC Nantes

1943 • La Beaujoire (37,555) • fcnantes.com

Major honours
French League (8) 1965, 1966, 1973, 1977, 1980, 1983, 1995, 2001; French Cup (3) 1979, 1999, 2000

Coach: Michel Der Zakarian (ARM)

2015					
08/08	h	Guingamp	W	1-0	*og (Sorbon)*
15/08	a	Angers	D	0-0	
22/08	h	Reims	W	1-0	*Lenjani*
30/08	a	Bordeaux	L	0-2	
13/09	h	Rennes	L	0-2	
20/09	a	St-Étienne	L	0-2	
26/09	h	Paris	L	1-4	*Bammou*
29/09	a	LOSC	W	1-0	*Iloki*
17/10	h	Troyes	W	3-0	*Rongier, Sabaly, Bammou*
23/10	a	Caen	W	2-0	*Bammou, Thomasson*
01/11	h	Marseille	L	0-1	
04/11	a	Nice	W	2-1	*Alegue, Sigthórsson*
07/11	a	Montpellier	L	1-2	*Bammou*
21/11	a	Monaco	L	0-1	
28/11	h	Bastia	D	0-0	
01/12	h	Lyon	D	0-0	
05/12	a	GFC Ajaccio	D	1-1	*Sala*
12/12	h	Toulouse	D	1-1	*Sala*
19/12	a	Lorient	D	0-0	
2016					
10/01	h	St-Étienne	W	2-1	*Audel, Sigthórsson*
16/01	a	Guingamp	D	2-2	*og (Kerbrat), Sabaly*
23/01	h	Bordeaux	D	2-2	*Sigthórsson, Bedoya*
30/01	a	Troyes	W	1-0	*Gillet*
03/02	h	GFC Ajaccio	W	3-1	*Sala, Bedoya, Adryan*
06/02	a	Toulouse	D	0-0	
13/02	h	Lorient	W	2-1	*Adryan, Sala*
28/02	h	Monaco	D	0-0	
06/03	a	Rennes	L	1-4	*Adryan*
09/03	a	Bastia	D	0-0	
13/03	h	Angers	W	2-0	*Sala 2*
19/03	a	Lyon	L	0-2	
03/04	h	LOSC	L	0-3	
09/04	a	Reims	L	1-2	*Audel*
17/04	h	Montpellier	L	0-2	
24/04	a	Marseille	D	1-1	*og (N'Koulou)*
30/04	h	Nice	W	1-0	*Thomasson*
07/05	h	Caen	L	1-2	*Bedoya*
14/05	a	Paris	L	0-4	

No	Name	Nat	DoB	Pos	Aps	(s)	Gls
23	Adryan	BRA	10/08/94	M	19	(7)	3
24	Alexis Alegue	CMR	23/12/96	A	1	(2)	1
21	Johan Audel		12/12/83	A	11	(18)	2
10	Yacine Bammou		11/09/91	A	17	(15)	4
7	Alejandro Bedoya	USA	29/04/87	M	22	(6)	3
5	Lorik Cana	ALB	27/07/83	D	20	(1)	
18	Lucas Déaux		26/12/88	M	13	(3)	
26	Koffi Djidji		30/11/92	D	20	(2)	
15	Léo Dubois		14/09/94	D	22	(2)	
30	Maxime Dupé		04/03/93	G	7		
27	Guillaume Gillet	BEL	09/03/84	M	19		1
6	Rémi Gomis	SEN	14/02/84	M	13	(4)	
34	Thomas Henry		20/09/94	A		(2)	
20	Jules Iloki		14/01/92	M	10	(11)	1
36	Enock Kwateng		09/04/97	D		(2)	
5	Ermir Lenjani	ALB	05/08/89	D	15	(5)	1
33	Hicham Mlaab		27/02/90	M		(2)	
13	Wilfried Moimbé		18/10/88	D	15		
1	Rémy Riou		06/08/87	G	31		
28	Valentin Rongier		07/12/94	M	9	(2)	1
14	Youssouf Sabaly		05/03/93	D	28		2
22	Emiliano Sala	ARG	31/10/90	A	22	(9)	6
9	Kolbeinn Sigthórsson	ISL	14/03/90	A	19	(7)	3
8	Adrien Thomasson		10/12/93	M	30	(4)	2
19	Abdoulaye Touré		03/03/94	M	2	(2)	
12	Birama Touré	MLI	06/06/92	M	21	(2)	
5	Olivier Veigneau		16/07/85	D	2		
4	Oswaldo Vizcarrondo	VEN	31/05/84	D	29	(1)	
17	Anthony Walongwa	COD	15/10/93	D	1		

OGC Nice

1904 • Allianz Riviera (27,478) • ogcnice.com

Major honours
French League (4) 1951, 1952, 1956, 1959; French Cup (3) 1952, 1954, 1997

Coach: Claude Puel

2015					
08/08	h	Monaco	L	1-2	*Germain*
15/08	a	Troyes	D	3-3	*Ben Arfa (p), Pléa, Le Marchand*
22/08	h	Caen	W	2-1	*Ben Arfa, Pléa*
29/08	a	Angers	D	1-1	*Germain*
12/09	h	Guingamp	L	0-1	
19/09	a	Bastia	W	3-1	*N Mendy, Germain, Benrahma*
23/09	h	Bordeaux	W	6-1	*Germain, Le Bihan, og (Pallois), Ben Arfa 2, A Mendy*
27/09	a	St-Étienne	W	4-1	*Koziello, Ben Arfa 2, Seri*
18/10	a	Rennes	W	4-1	*Bodmer, Ben Arfa, Traoré, Benrahma*
24/10	a	GFC Ajaccio	L	1-3	*og (Filippi)*
01/11	h	LOSC	D	0-0	
04/11	h	Nantes	L	1-2	*Genevois*
08/11	a	Marseille	W	1-0	*Germain*
20/11	h	Lyon	W	3-0	*Germain, og (Yanga-Mbiwa), Koziello*
28/11	a	Toulouse	L	0-2	
01/12	a	Lorient	D	0-0	
04/12	h	Paris	L	0-3	
12/12	a	Reims	D	1-1	*Germain*
18/12	h	Montpellier	W	1-0	*Boscagli*
2016					
10/01	a	LOSC	D	1-1	*Hult*
15/01	h	Angers	W	2-1	*Ben Arfa 2 (2p)*
23/01	h	Lorient	W	2-1	*Ben Arfa, Koziello*
31/01	a	Caen	L	0-2	
03/02	h	Toulouse	W	1-0	*Ben Arfa*
06/02	a	Monaco	L	0-1	
14/02	h	Marseille	D	1-1	*Germain*
19/02	a	Bordeaux	D	0-0	
26/02	h	Bastia	L	0-2	
05/03	h	Troyes	W	2-1	*Germain, Traoré*
12/03	a	Montpellier	W	2-0	*Germain, Pléa*
20/03	h	GFC Ajaccio	W	3-0	*Ben Arfa, Pléa, Seri*
02/04	a	Paris	L	1-4	*Ben Arfa*
10/04	h	Rennes	W	3-0	*Ben Arfa 3 (1p)*
15/04	a	Lyon	D	1-1	*Germain*
22/04	h	Reims	W	2-0	*Germain, Ben Arfa (p)*
30/04	a	Nantes	L	0-1	
07/05	h	St-Étienne	W	2-0	*Germain 2*
14/05	a	Guingamp	W	3-2	*Pléa 2, Seri*

No	Name	Nat	DoB	Pos	Aps	(s)	Gls
4	Paul Baysse		18/05/88	D	29	(1)	
9	Hatem Ben Arfa		07/03/87	M	33	(1)	17
11	Saïd Benrahma	ALG	10/08/95	A		(9)	2
24	Mathieu Bodmer		22/11/82	D	16	(3)	1
33	Olivier Boscagli		18/11/97	D	8	(3)	1
36	Dorian Caddy		20/03/95	A	3	(4)	
30	Yoan Cardinale		27/03/94	G	25	(1)	
34	Jonathan Correia		13/02/94	D	2	(2)	
10	Valentin Eysseric		25/03/92	M		(1)	
25	Romain Genevois	HAI	28/10/87	D	10	(4)	1
28	Valère Germain		17/04/90	A	36	(2)	14
5	Kévin Gomis		20/01/89	D	1	(2)	
1	Mouez Hassen		05/03/95	G	12	(2)	
34	Franck Honorat		11/08/96	A		(6)	
13	Niklas Hult	SWE	13/02/90	M	9	(6)	1
26	Vincent Koziello		28/10/95	M	32	(3)	3
10	Mickaêl Le Bihan		16/05/90	M	1	(2)	1
20	Maxime Le Marchand		11/10/89	D	26		1
3	Gauthier Lloris		18/07/95	D	1	(1)	
15	Alexandre Mendy		14/12/83	A	3	(15)	1
22	Nampalys Mendy		23/06/92	M	38		1
29	Jérémy Pied		23/02/89	D	33		
14	Alassane Pléa		10/03/93	A	17	(2)	6
16	Simon Pouplin		28/05/85	G	1		
34	Paulin Puel		09/05/97	A	2	(9)	
12	Albert Rafetraniaina	MAD	09/09/96	M		(1)	
21	Stéphan Raheriharimanana	MAD	16/08/93	M	1	(3)	
35	Antony Ranieri		21/06/97	A		(2)	
23	Ricardo	POR	06/10/93	D	26		
6	Jean Michaël Seri	CIV	19/07/91	M	35	(3)	3
8	Mahamane Traoré	MLI	31/08/88	M	4	(8)	2
19	Wallyson Mallmann	BRA	16/02/94	M	8	(9)	
18	Rémi Walter		26/04/95	M	6	(6)	

Paris Saint-Germain

1970 • Parc des Princes (47,929) • psg.fr

Major honours
UEFA Cup Winners' Cup (1) 1996; French League (6) 1986, 1994, 2013, 2014, 2015, 2016; French Cup (10) 1982, 1983, 1993, 1995, 1998, 2004, 2006, 2010, 2015, 2016; League Cup (6) 1995, 1998, 2008, 2014, 2015, 2016

Coach: Laurent Blanc

2015					
07/08	a	LOSC	W	1-0	*Lucas*
16/08	h	GFC Ajaccio	W	2-0	*Matuidi, Thiago Silva*
21/08	a	Montpellier	W	1-0	*Matuidi*
30/08	a	Monaco	W	3-0	*Cavani 2, Lavezzi*
11/09	h	Bordeaux	D	2-2	*Cavani 2*
19/09	a	Reims	D	1-1	*Cavani*
22/09	h	Guingamp	W	3-0	*Pastore, Di María, Ibrahimović*
26/09	a	Nantes	W	4-1	*Ibrahimović, Cavani, Di María, Aurier*
04/10	h	Marseille	W	2-1	*Ibrahimović 2 (2p)*
17/10	a	Bastia	W	2-0	*Ibrahimović 2*
25/10	h	St-Étienne	W	4-1	*Kurzawa, Cavani, Ibrahimović, Lucas*
30/10	a	Rennes	W	1-0	*Di María*
07/11	h	Toulouse	W	5-0	*Di María, Ibrahimović 2, Lucas, Lavezzi*
21/11	a	Lorient	W	2-1	*Ongenda, Matuidi*
28/11	h	Troyes	W	4-1	*Cavani, Ibrahimović (p), Kurzawa, Augustin*
01/12	a	Angers	D	0-0	
04/12	a	Nice	W	3-0	*Cavani, Ibrahimović 2 (1p)*
13/12	h	Lyon	W	5-1	*Ibrahimović 2 (1p), Aurier, Cavani, Lucas*
19/12	a	Caen	W	3-0	*Di María 2, Ibrahimović*
2016					
08/01	h	Bastia	W	2-0	*Thiago Motta, Maxwell*
16/01	a	Toulouse	W	1-0	*Ibrahimović*
23/01	h	Angers	W	5-1	*Ibrahimović, Lucas, Van der Wiel, Di María 2*
31/01	a	St-Étienne	W	2-0	*Ibrahimović 2*
03/02	h	Lorient	W	3-1	*Cavani, Ibrahimović, Kurzawa*
07/02	a	Marseille	W	2-1	*Ibrahimović, Di María*
13/02	h	LOSC	D	0-0	
20/02	h	Reims	W	4-1	*Van der Wiel, Ibrahimović 2, Cavani*
28/02	a	Lyon	L	1-2	*Lucas*
05/03	h	Montpellier	D	0-0	
13/03	a	Troyes	W	9-0	*Cavani 2, Pastore, Rabiot, Ibrahimović 4, og (Saunier)*
20/03	h	Monaco	L	0-2	
02/04	h	Nice	W	4-1	*Ibrahimović 3, David Luiz*
09/04	a	Guingamp	W	2-0	*Lucas 2 (1p)*
16/04	h	Caen	W	6-0	*Ibrahimović 2, Matuidi, Cavani, Di María, Maxwell*
29/04	h	Rennes	W	4-0	*Maxwell, Ibrahimović 2, Cavani*
07/05	a	GFC Ajaccio	W	4-0	*Cavani 3, Ibrahimović*
11/05	a	Bordeaux	D	1-1	*Ibrahimović*
14/05	h	Nantes	W	4-0	*Ibrahimović 2, Lucas, Marquinhos*

No	Name	Nat	DoB	Pos	Aps	(s)	Gls
29	Jean-Kévin Augustin		16/06/97	A	4	(9)	1
19	Serge Aurier	CIV	24/12/92	D	21		2
9	Edinson Cavani	URU	14/02/87	A	24	(8)	19
32	David Luiz	BRA	22/04/87	D	23	(2)	1
11	Ángel Di María	ARG	14/02/88	M	26	(3)	10
1	Nicolas Douchez		22/04/80	G	1		
10	Zlatan Ibrahimović	SWE	03/10/81	A	29	(2)	38
3	Presnel Kimpembe		13/08/95	D	5	(1)	
20	Layvin Kurzawa		04/09/92	D	14	(2)	3
22	Ezequiel Lavezzi	ARG	03/05/85	A	3	(12)	2
7	Lucas	BRA	13/08/92	M	26	(9)	9
5	Marquinhos	BRA	14/05/94	D	20	(9)	1
14	Blaise Matuidi		09/04/87	M	23	(7)	4
17	Maxwell	BRA	27/08/81	D	24	(4)	3
36	Yakou Meïté	CIV	11/02/96	M		(1)	
33	Christopher Nkunku		14/11/97	M	4	(1)	
35	Hervin Ongenda		24/06/95	A	4	(1)	1
27	Javier Pastore	ARG	20/06/89	M	11	(5)	2
25	Adrien Rabiot		03/04/95	M	19	(5)	1
34	Kévin Rimane		23/02/91	D		(1)	
30	Salvatore Sirigu	ITA	12/01/87	G	2	(1)	
4	Benjamin Stambouli		13/08/90	M	18	(9)	
36	Timothée Taufflieb		01/12/92	A		(1)	
8	Thiago Motta	ITA	28/08/82	M	26	(6)	1
2	Thiago Silva	BRA	22/09/84	D	29	(1)	1
16	Kevin Trapp	GER	08/07/90	G	35		
23	Gregory van der Wiel	NED	03/02/88	D	16	(1)	2
6	Marco Verratti	ITA	05/11/92	M	11	(7)	

Stade de Reims

1911 • Auguste-Delaune (21,100) •
stade-de-reims.com
Major honours
French League (6) 1949, 1953, 1955, 1958, 1960,
1962; French Cup (2) 1950, 1958
Coach: Olivier Guégan;
(23/04/16) (David Guion)

2015
09/08	a	Bordeaux	W	2-1	*De Préville, Siebatcheu*
16/08	h	Marseille	W	1-0	*Traoré*
22/08	a	Nantes	L	0-1	
29/08	h	Lorient	W	4-1	*Charbonnier, De Préville, Kyei, Turan*
12/09	a	Toulouse	D	2-2	*Siebatcheu, Bulot*
19/09	h	Paris	D	1-1	*Siebatcheu*
22/09	a	Angers	D	0-0	
25/09	h	LOSC	W	1-0	*N'Gog*
03/10	a	Lyon	L	0-1	
17/10	h	Caen	L	0-1	
25/10	h	Monaco	L	0-1	
31/10	a	St-Étienne	L	0-3	
07/11	h	GFC Ajaccio	L	1-2	*Kyei*
21/11	a	Montpellier	L	0-1	*Weber*
28/11	h	Rennes	D	2-2	*Mandi, De Préville*
02/12	h	Guingamp	W	2-1	*N'Gog 2*
05/12	h	Troyes	D	1-1	*De Préville*
12/12	h	Nice	D	1-1	*Diego (p)*
19/12	a	Bastia	L	0-2	

2016
09/01	h	Toulouse	L	1-3	*Devaux*
16/01	a	GFC Ajaccio	D	2-2	*De Préville 2*
24/01	h	St-Étienne	D	1-1	*Mandi*
30/01	a	Lorient	L	0-2	
03/02	h	Angers	W	2-1	*Traoré, Charbonnier*
06/02	h	Caen	W	2-0	*Thievy, Oniangué*
13/02	a	Bastia	L	0-1	
20/02	a	Paris	L	0-1	
27/02	h	Bordeaux	W	4-1	*Mandi, Thievy, Charbonnier, Bangoura*
05/03	a	LOSC	L	0-2	
11/03	a	Monaco	D	2-2	*Charbonnier, Diego*
19/03	h	Guingamp	L	0-1	
02/04	a	Rennes	L	1-3	*Mandi*
09/04	h	Nantes	W	2-1	*Oniangué, og (Sabaly)*
16/04	a	Troyes	L	1-2	*Thievy*
22/04	a	Nice	L	0-2	
30/04	h	Montpellier	L	2-3	*Oniangué, Thievy*
07/05	a	Marseille	L	0-1	
14/05	h	Lyon	W	4-1	*Mandi, Diego, Turan, Kyei (p)*

No	Name	Nat	DoB	Pos	Aps	(s)	Gls
16	Kossi Agassa	TOG	07/07/78	G	11		
14	Alhassane "Lass" Bangoura	GUI	30/03/92	M	3	(7)	1
18	Frédéric Bulot	GAB	27/09/90	M	11	(5)	1
1	Johann Carrasso		07/05/88	G	10		
10	Gaëtan Charbonnier		27/12/88	A	16	(6)	4
28	Antoine Conte		29/01/94	D	11		
12	Nicolas De Préville		08/01/91	A	34	(2)	6
6	Antoine Devaux		21/02/85	M	33		1
11	Diego	BRA	09/03/88	A	15	(8)	3
5	Abdelhamid El Kaoutari	MAR	17/03/90	D	7	(1)	
2	Mohamed Fofana	MLI	07/03/85	D	12	(1)	
13	Hassane Kamara	GAM	05/03/94	M		(2)	
4	Jaba Kankava	GEO	18/03/86	M	27		
29	Grejohn Kyei		12/08/95	A	7	(9)	3
30	Omenuke M'Fulu	COD	20/03/94	M	2	(11)	
33	Eddy Maanane		03/02/95	A		(1)	
23	Aïssa Mandi	ALG	22/10/91	D	32		5
21	Aly N'Dom		30/05/96	A	4	(4)	
24	David N'Gog		01/04/89	A	11	(5)	3
7	Odair Fortes	CPV	31/03/87	A	4	(12)	
8	Prince Oniangué	CGO	04/11/88	M	23	(4)	4
19	Alexi Peuget		18/12/90	M	8	(4)	
30	Johnny Placide	HAI	29/01/88	G	17	(2)	
21	Hugo Rodríguez		02/04/91	M	2	(1)	
20	Theoson Siebatcheu		26/04/96	A	6	(19)	3
3	Franck Signorino		19/09/81	D	29		
22	Mickaël Tacalfred		13/08/81	D	14	(1)	
9	Thievy Bifouma	CGO	13/05/92	A	10	(4)	4
27	Hamari Traoré	MLI	27/01/92	D	32	(1)	2
15	Atila Turan		10/04/92	D	8	(3)	2
25	Anthony Weber		11/06/87	D	19		1

Stade Rennais FC

1901 • Roazhon Park (29,269) •
staderennais.com
Major honours
French Cup (2) 1965, 1971
Coach: Philippe Montanier;
(21/01/16) Rolland Courbis

2015
08/08	a	Bastia	L	1-2	*Sio*
15/08	h	Montpellier	W	1-0	*Grosicki*
22/08	a	Lyon	W	2-1	*Pedro Henrique, Zeffane*
29/08	h	Toulouse	W	3-1	*og (Yago), Armand, Sio*
13/09	a	Nantes	W	2-0	*Ntep, Sio*
18/09	h	LOSC	D	1-1	*Ntep*
23/09	a	GFC Ajaccio	D	1-1	*Sio*
26/09	h	Troyes	D	1-1	*Diagné*
04/10	a	Monaco	D	1-1	*Doucouré*
18/10	h	Nice	L	1-4	*Grosicki*
24/10	a	Lorient	D	1-1	*Grosicki*
30/10	h	Paris	L	0-1	
06/11	a	Angers	W	2-0	*Doucouré, Fernandes*
22/11	h	Bordeaux	D	2-2	*Dembélé, Grosicki*
28/11	a	Reims	D	2-2	*Boga, Grosicki*
03/12	h	Marseille	L	0-1	
06/12	h	St-Étienne	D	1-1	*Pedro Henrique*
11/12	h	Caen	D	1-1	*Quintero*
19/12	a	Guingamp	W	2-0	*Dembélé, Sio*

2016
09/01	h	Lorient	D	2-2	*Dembélé, Boga*
16/01	a	Troyes	W	4-2	*Diagné 2 (2p), Dembélé, Grosicki*
22/01	h	GFC Ajaccio	W	1-0	*og (Filippi)*
31/01	a	Bordeaux	L	0-4	
04/02	a	St-Étienne	L	0-1	
07/02	h	LOSC	D	1-1	*Dembélé (p)*
12/02	h	Angers	W	1-0	*og (Bouka Moutou)*
21/02	a	Caen	L	0-1	
27/02	a	Toulouse	W	2-1	*Dembélé, Grosicki*
06/03	h	Nantes	W	4-1	*Dembélé 3, Grosicki*
13/03	a	Lyon	D	2-2	*Diagné, og (Rafael)*
18/03	h	Marseille	W	5-2	*Gourcuff 2, Diagné, Dembélé, Sio*
02/04	h	Reims	W	3-1	*Grosicki, Dembélé 2*
10/04	a	Nice	L	0-3	
17/04	h	Guingamp	L	0-3	
24/04	a	Monaco	D	1-1	*Sio*
29/04	a	Paris	L	0-4	
07/05	a	Montpellier	L	0-2	
14/05	h	Bastia	L	1-2	*Pedro Henrique*

No	Name	Nat	DoB	Pos	Aps	(s)	Gls
21	Benjamin André		03/08/90	M	30	(2)	
22	Sylvain Armand		01/08/80	D	33	(1)	1
24	Ludovic Baal		24/05/86	D	18	(4)	
17	Jeremie Boga		03/01/91	M	6	(20)	2
1	Benoît Costil		03/07/87	G	31		
29	Romain Danzé		03/07/86	M	19	(2)	
23	Ousmane Dembélé		15/05/97	M	22	(4)	12
14	Fallou Diagné	SEN	14/08/89	D	21	(1)	5
40	Abdoulaye Diallo	SEN	30/03/92	G	7		
8	Abdoulaye Doucouré		01/01/93	M	11	(5)	2
9	Kermit Erasmus	RSA	08/07/90	A		(2)	
6	Gelson Fernandes	SUI	02/09/86	M	33		1
33	Joris Sasportas		13/01/97	D	2	(4)	
28	Yoann Gourcuff		11/07/86	M	8	(4)	2
10	Kamil Grosicki	POL	08/06/88	M	14	(19)	9
27	Habib Habibou	CTA	16/04/87	A		(1)	
35	Nicolas Janvier		11/08/98	M		(1)	
19	Ermir Lenjani	ALB	05/08/89	D		(1)	
3	Cheikh M'Bengue	SEN	23/07/88	D	21	(1)	
4	Mexer	MOZ	08/12/88	D	17		
12	Steven Moreira		13/08/94	D	14	(2)	
7	Paul-Georges Ntep		29/07/92	A	11	(3)	2
18	Pedro Henrique	BRA	16/06/90	A	15	(8)	3
5	Pedro Mendes	POR	01/10/90	D	20	(1)	
11	Juan Quintero	COL	18/01/93	M	9	(3)	1
31	Wesley Saïd		19/04/95	A		(1)	
34	Sébastien Salles-Lamonge		28/01/96	M	1	(2)	
13	Giovanni Sio	CIV	31/03/89	A	28	(6)	7
20	Yacouba Sylla	MLI	29/11/90	M	18	(2)	
9	Ola Toivonen	SWE	03/07/86	A		(1)	
2	Mehdi Zeffane	ALG	19/05/92	D	9	(7)	1

AS Saint-Étienne

1933 • Geoffroy-Guichard (42,000) • asse.fr
Major honours
French League (10) 1957, 1964, 1967, 1968, 1969,
1970, 1974, 1975, 1976, 1981; French Cup (6) 1962,
1968, 1970, 1974, 1975, 1977; League Cup (1) 2013
Coach: Christophe Galtier

2015
09/08	a	Toulouse	L	1-2	*Perrin*
15/08	h	Bordeaux	D	1-1	*Hamouma*
23/08	a	Lorient	W	1-0	*Hamouma*
30/08	h	Bastia	W	2-1	*Perrin, Eysseric*
12/09	a	Montpellier	W	2-1	*Bayal Sall, Roux*
20/09	h	Nantes	W	2-0	*Bamba, Berič*
23/09	a	Troyes	W	1-0	*og (Ayasse)*
27/09	h	Nice	L	1-4	*Perrin*
04/10	a	Caen	L	0-1	
17/10	h	GFC Ajaccio	W	2-0	*Berič, Monnet-Paquet*
25/10	a	Paris	L	1-4	*og (Verratti)*
31/10	h	Reims	W	3-0	*Berič, og (Oniangué), Eysseric*
08/11	a	Lyon	L	0-3	
22/11	a	Marseille	L	0-2	
29/11	h	Guingamp	W	3-0	*Hamouma, Eysseric (p), Roux*
02/12	a	LOSC	L	0-1	
06/12	h	Rennes	D	1-1	*Eysseric (p)*
13/12	a	Monaco	L	0-1	
20/12	h	Angers	W	1-0	*Corgnet*

2016
10/01	a	Nantes	L	1-2	*Roux (p)*
17/01	h	Lyon	W	1-0	*Søderlund*
24/01	a	Reims	D	1-1	*Bahebeck*
31/01	h	Paris	L	0-2	
04/02	a	Rennes	W	1-0	*Bayal Sall*
07/02	a	Bordeaux	W	4-1	*Pajot, Tannane, Søderlund, Roux*
14/02	h	Monaco	D	1-1	*Bayal Sall*
21/02	h	Marseille	D	1-1	*Monnet-Paquet*
28/02	h	Caen	L	1-2	*Eysseric*
05/03	a	Angers	D	0-0	
12/03	a	Guingamp	L	0-2	
19/03	h	Montpellier	W	3-0	*Roux, Tannane, Eysseric*
02/04	a	GFC Ajaccio	W	2-0	*Roux, Théophile-Catherine*
09/04	h	Troyes	W	1-0	*Maupay*
16/04	a	Bastia	W	1-0	*Roux*
24/04	h	Lorient	W	2-0	*Roux 2*
30/04	a	Toulouse	D	0-0	
07/05	a	Nice	L	0-2	
14/05	h	LOSC	L	0-1	

No	Name	Nat	DoB	Pos	Aps	(s)	Gls
32	Benoît Assou-Ekotto	CMR	24/03/84	D	19	(1)	
7	Jean-Christophe Bahebeck		01/05/93	M	11	(4)	1
17	Jonathan Bamba		26/03/96	M	4	(1)	1
26	Moustapha Bayal Sall	SEN	30/11/85	D	27	(1)	3
27	Robert Berič	SVN	17/06/91	A	7	(3)	5
20	Jonathan Brison		07/02/83	D	4	(3)	
6	Jérémy Clément		26/08/84	M	25	(2)	
29	François Clerc		18/04/83	D	10		
10	Renaud Cohade		29/09/84	M	14	(5)	
8	Benjamin Corgnet		06/04/87	M	5	(10)	1
28	Ismaël Diomandé	CIV	28/08/92	M	3	(4)	
15	Erin Pinheiro	CPV	15/07/97	M		(2)	
11	Valentin Eysseric		25/03/92	M	19	(10)	6
21	Romain Hamouma		29/03/87	M	17	(7)	3
18	Fabien Lemoine		16/03/87	M	29	(4)	
25	Kévin Malcuit		31/07/91	D	9		
14	Neal Maupay		14/08/96	M	5	(9)	1
9	Yohan Mollo		18/07/89	A		(1)	
22	Kévin Monnet-Paquet		19/08/88	A	25	(6)	2
5	Vincent Pajot		19/08/90	M	19	(9)	1
15	Loïc Perrin		07/08/85	D	24		3
33	Ronaël Pierre-Gabriel		13/06/98	D	4	(1)	
19	Florentin Pogba	GUI	19/08/90	D	21	(2)	
3	Pierre-Yves Polomat		27/12/93	D	9	(6)	
9	Nolan Roux		01/03/88	A	21	(8)	9
16	Stéphane Ruffier		27/09/86	G	38		
17	Ole Kristian Selnæs	NOR	07/07/94	M	2	(1)	
23	Alexander Søderlund	NOR	03/08/87	A	10	(4)	2
12	Franck Tabanou		30/01/89	D	8	(3)	
4	Oussama Tannane	MAR	23/03/94	A	7	(3)	2
2	Kévin Théophile-Catherine		28/10/89	D	22		1

Toulouse FC

1937 • Stadium Municipal (20,907) • tfc.info
Major honours
French Cup (1) 1957
Coach: Dominique Arribagé;
(01/03/16) Pascal Dupraz

2015

09/08	h	St-Étienne	W 2-1	Braithwaite, Ben Yedder
15/08	a	Caen	L 0-1	
22/08	h	Monaco	D 1-1	Doumbia
29/08	a	Rennes	L 1-3	Braithwaite
12/09	h	Reims	D 2-2	Kana-Biyik, Braithwaite
20/09	a	Bordeaux	D 1-1	Regattin
23/09	h	Marseille	D 1-1	Braithwaite
26/09	a	Bastia	L 0-3	
03/10	a	GFC Ajaccio	D 2-2	Braithwaite, og (Sylla)
17/10	h	Angers	L 1-2	Trejo
23/10	a	Lyon	L 0-1	
31/10	h	Montpellier	D 1-1	Machach
07/11	a	Paris	L 0-5	
21/11	a	Guingamp	L 0-2	
28/11	h	Nice	W 2-0	Braithwaite (p), Ben Yedder
02/12	a	Troyes	W 3-0	Diop, Akpa-Akpro, Pešić
05/12	h	Lorient	L 2-3	Kana-Biyik, Ben Yedder
12/12	a	Nantes	D 1-1	Pešić
19/12	h	LOSC	D 1-1	Ben Yedder

2016

09/01	a	Reims	W 3-1	Ben Yedder 3
16/01	h	Paris	L 0-1	
24/01	a	Monaco	L 0-4	
30/01	h	Guingamp	L 1-2	Ben Yedder (p)
03/02	a	Nice	L 0-1	
06/02	h	Nantes	D 0-0	
13/02	a	Montpellier	L 0-2	
20/02	h	GFC Ajaccio	D 1-1	Braithwaite
27/02	a	Rennes	L 0-1	Ben Yedder
06/03	a	Marseille	D 1-1	Ben Yedder
12/03	h	Bordeaux	W 4-0	Ben Yedder 2 (1p), Braithwaite (p), Trejo
19/03	a	LOSC	L 0-1	
02/04	h	Caen	W 2-0	og (Rodelin), Braithwaite
09/04	h	Bastia	W 4-0	Ben Yedder 2, Braithwaite, Trejo
16/04	a	Lorient	D 1-1	Ben Yedder
23/04	h	Lyon	L 2-3	Tisserand, Ben Yedder
30/04	a	St-Étienne	D 0-0	
07/05	h	Troyes	W 1-0	Trejo
14/05	a	Angers	W 3-2	Ben Yedder, Braithwaite, Bodiger

No	Name	Nat	DoB	Pos	Aps	(s)	Gls
30	Ali Ahamada		14/07/90	G	6		
7	Jean-Daniel Akpa-Akpro	CIV	11/10/92	M	29	(4)	1
10	Wissam Ben Yedder		12/08/90	A	34	(2)	17
12	Youssef Benali		04/02/95	M		(1)	
27	Alexis Blin		16/09/96	M	15	(9)	
23	Yann Bodiger		09/02/95	M	12	(9)	1
9	Martin Braithwaite	DEN	05/06/91	A	33	(3)	11
8	Étienne Didot		24/07/83	M	21	(2)	
33	Issa Diop		09/01/97	D	21		1
4	Tongo Doumbia	MLI	06/08/89	M	22	(3)	1
1	Mauro Goicoechea	URU	27/03/88	G	8	(1)	
3	Jean-Armel Kana-Biyik	CMR	03/07/89	D	17	(1)	2
40	Alban Lafont		23/01/99	G	24		
13	Zinédine Machach		05/01/96	M	10	(6)	1
29	François Moubandje	SUI	21/06/90	D	20	(3)	
24	Pavle Ninkov	SRB	20/04/85	D	5	(4)	
11	Aleksandar Pešić	SRB	21/04/92	A	5	(18)	2
17	Adrien Regattin	MAR	22/08/91	M	16	(17)	1
14	François Sireix		07/10/80	M		(5)	
19	Somália	BRA	28/09/86	M	24	(5)	
15	Uroš Spajić	SRB	13/02/93	D	11	(3)	
26	Marcel Tisserand		10/01/93	D	32	(1)	1
18	Óscar Trejo	ARG	26/04/88	M	23	(10)	4
6	William Matheus	BRA	02/04/90	D	14		
20	Steeve Yago	BFA	16/12/92	D	16	(3)	

ES Troyes AC

1986 • L'Aube (19,208) • estac.fr
Coach: Jean-Marc Furlan;
(03/12/15) (Mohamed Bradja (ALG));
(08/12/15) Claude Robin;
(05/02/16) Olivier Tingry

2015

08/08	h	GFC Ajaccio	D 0-0	
15/08	h	Nice	D 3-3	Jean, Camus, Thiago Xavier
23/08	a	Marseille	L 0-6	
29/08	h	Montpellier	D 0-0	
12/09	h	Caen	L 1-3	Othon
19/09	a	Angers	L 0-1	
23/09	h	St-Étienne	L 0-1	
26/09	a	Rennes	D 1-1	Pi
03/10	h	Guingamp	L 0-1	
17/10	a	Nantes	L 0-3	
25/10	a	Bordeaux	L 0-1	
31/10	h	Lyon	L 0-1	
07/11	a	Lorient	L 1-4	Nivet (p)
21/11	h	LOSC	D 1-1	Jean
28/11	a	Paris	L 1-4	Ayasse
02/12	h	Toulouse	L 0-3	
05/12	a	Reims	D 1-1	Pi
12/12	h	Bastia	D 1-1	Cabot
19/12	h	Monaco	D 0-0	

2016

09/01	a	Lyon	L 1-4	Camus
16/01	h	Rennes	L 2-4	Camus, Jean
23/01	a	LOSC	W 3-1	Cabot 2, Pi
30/01	h	Nantes	L 0-1	
03/02	a	Guingamp	L 0-4	
06/02	a	Bastia	L 0-2	
13/02	a	GFC Ajaccio	W 3-2	Ben Saada, Azamoum 2
20/02	a	Monaco	L 1-3	Gueye
27/02	h	Lorient	L 0-1	
05/03	a	Nice	L 1-2	og (Cardinale)
13/03	h	Paris	L 0-9	
19/03	a	Caen	L 1-2	Thiago Xavier
02/04	h	Angers	L 0-1	
09/04	a	St-Étienne	L 0-1	
16/04	h	Reims	W 2-1	Camus, Nivet (p)
24/04	a	Montpellier	L 1-4	Darbion
30/04	h	Bordeaux	L 2-4	Nivet (p), Jean
07/05	a	Toulouse	L 0-1	
14/05	h	Marseille	D 1-1	Camus

No	Name	Nat	DoB	Pos	Aps	(s)	Gls
4	Thomas Ayasse		17/02/87	M	12	(2)	1
19	Karim Azamoum		17/01/90	M	9	(5)	2
18	Chaouki Ben Saada	TUN	01/07/84	M	8	(10)	1
40	Paul Bernardoni		18/04/97	G	14		
12	Henri Bienvenu	CMR	05/07/88	A		(6)	
21	Jimmy Cabot		18/04/94	A	7	(8)	3
23	Fabien Camus	TUN	28/02/85	M	28	(7)	5
33	Alois Confais		07/09/96	M	13	(2)	
7	Yoann Court		14/01/90	M	11	(15)	
35	Mouhamadou Dabo	SEN	28/11/96	D	14	(2)	
8	Stéphane Darbion		22/03/84	M	18	(8)	1
26	Deniz Hümmet	TUR	13/09/96	A	2	(4)	
1	Matthieu Dreyer		20/03/89	G	15		
34	Samuel Grandsir		14/08/96	A		(1)	
9	Babacar Gueye	SEN	02/03/86	A	6	(5)	1
27	Corentin Jean		15/07/95	A	31	(4)	4
24	Lossémy Karaboué	CIV	18/03/88	M	23	(8)	
22	Mory Koné		21/04/94	D	3		
2	Johan Martial		30/05/91	D	7	(1)	
6	Jonathan Martins Pereira		30/01/86	D	11		
3	Chris Mavinga	COD	26/05/91	D	19	(1)	
20	Mahamadou N'Diaye	MLI	21/06/90	D		(1)	
31	Anele Ngcongca	RSA	21/10/87	D	18	(2)	
10	Benjamin Nivet		02/01/77	M	27	(7)	3
29	Quentin Othon		27/03/88	M	6	(2)	1
13	Brayan Perea	COL	25/03/94	A	6	(6)	
30	Denis Petrič	SVN	24/05/88	G	9		
25	Jessy Pi		24/09/93	M	35	(2)	3
11	Rincón	BRA	31/05/87	D	8		
5	Matthieu Saunier		07/02/90	D	28		
14	Thiago Xavier	BRA	27/12/83	M	13	(3)	2
28	Charles Traoré		01/01/92	D	5		
32	Dušan Veškovac	SRB	16/03/86	D	11	(2)	

Top goalscorers

38 Zlatan Ibrahimović (Paris)

21 Alexandre Lacazette (Lyon)

19 Edinson Cavani (Paris)

17 Michy Batshuayi (Marseille)
Hatem Ben Arfa (Nice)
Wissam Ben Yedder (Toulouse)

14 Valère Germain (Nice)

13 Benjamin Moukandjo (Lorient)

12 Andy Delort (Caen)
Ousmane Dembélé (Rennes)

Promoted clubs

AS Nancy-Lorraine

1967 • Marcel Picot (19,823) • asnl.net
Major honours
French Cup (1) 1978; League Cup (1) 2006
Coach: Pablo Correa (URU)

Dijon FCO

1998 • Gaston Gérard (10,578) • dfco.fr
Coach: Olivier Dall'Oglio

FC Metz

1932 • Saint-Symphorien (25,636) • fcmetz.com
Major honours
French Cup (2) 1984, 1988; League Cup (1) 1996
Coach: José Riga (BEL):
(24/12/15) Philippe Hinschberger

Second level final table 2015/16

		Pld	W	D	L	F	A	Pts
1	AS Nancy-Lorraine	38	21	11	6	60	32	74
2	Dijon FCO	38	20	10	8	62	36	70
3	FC Metz	38	19	8	11	54	39	65
4	Le Havre AC	38	19	8	11	52	37	65
5	Red Star FC	38	18	10	10	43	38	64
6	RC Lens	38	15	13	10	39	35	58
7	Clermont Foot Auvergne	38	16	10	12	56	53	58
8	AJ Auxerre	38	15	10	13	47	46	55
9	Tours FC	38	11	14	13	36	41	47
10	Stade Brestois 29	38	12	11	15	34	41	47
11	Football Bourg-en-Bresse Péronnas 01	38	13	8	17	47	59	47
12	Valenciennes FC	38	10	14	14	39	43	44
13	Stade Lavallois MFC	38	9	17	12	35	42	44
14	Nîmes Olympique	38	13	12	13	50	52	43
15	FC Sochaux-Montbéliard	38	11	14	13	34	36	42
16	Chamois Niortais FC	38	8	18	12	38	45	42
17	AC Ajaccio	38	9	15	14	34	42	42
18	Évian Thonon Gaillard FC	38	9	12	17	41	41	39
19	US Créteil	38	8	10	20	42	66	34
20	Paris FC	38	4	18	16	32	51	30

NB Nîmes Olympique – 8 pts deducted.

DOMESTIC CUPS

Coupe de France 2015/16

1/32 FINALS

(02/01/16)
Avranches 1-1 St Malo *(aet; 1-3 on pens)*
Blanc Mesnil 0-2 Nantes
Chambly 4-1 Reims
Concarneau 3-0 TA Rennes
Dunkerque 3-4 Troyes *(aet)*
Entente SSG 0-5 Toulouse
GFC Ajaccio 2-0 Sainte-Marienne
Granville 2-1 Laval
Mantes 78 2-0 Stade Briochin
Moulins 1-2 Niort
Pagny Sur Moselle 0-2 Sochaux
Racing Besançon 1-3 Angers
Rodéo 0-1 Mt de Marsan Stade
Sedan 0-2 SC Bastia
Villafranche 1-2 Sarre Union

(03/01/16)
Amiens 0-1 LOSC
Annecy 1-4 Évian *(aet)*
Caen 0-0 Marseille *(aet; 1-3 on pens)*
Chantilly 0-4 Guingamp
Épernay 0-1 Montpellier
Fréjus-St-Raphaël 2-3 Bordeaux
Limoges 0-7 Lyon
Lorient 3-2 Tours *(aet)*
Monaco 10-2 St-Jean Boulieu
Mulhouse 1-3 Bourg-en-Bresse
Muret 0-2 Trélissac
Raôn l'Etape 1-1 St-Étienne *(aet; 3-4 on pens)*
St-Omer 2-2 Boulogne *(aet; 3-4 on pens)*
Sarreguemines 1-0 Valenciennes
Volvic 0-1 AC Ajaccio
Wasquehal 0-1 Paris SG

(04/01/16)
Nice 2-2 Rennes *(aet; 6-7 on pens)*

1/16 FINALS

(16/01/16)
St Malo 1-0 Mt de Marsan Stade

(19/01/16)
Angers 1-2 Bordeaux
SC Bastia 1-2 Sochaux
GFC Ajaccio 3-0 Guingamp
Paris SG 2-1 Toulouse
Rennes 1-3 Bourg-en-Bresse
Sarre Union 1-0 Niort

(20/01/16)
Boulogne 1-3 Lorient *(aet)*
Chambly 0-2 Lyon
Concarneau 1-3 Troyes
Évian 1-3 Monaco *(aet)*
Mantes 78 0-1 Nantes *(aet)*
Marseille 2-0 Montpellier
Trélissac 1-1 LOSC *(aet; 4-2 on pens)*

(21/01/16)
St-Étienne 2-1 AC Ajaccio *(aet)*

(23/01/16)
Granville 3-1 Sarreguemines

1/8 FINALS

(09/02/16)
Granville 1-0 Bourg-en-Bresse *(aet)*
Sochaux 2-1 Monaco
St Malo 1-2 GFC Ajaccio

(10/02/16)
Bordeaux 3-4 Nantes *(aet)*
Paris SG 3-0 Lyon
Sarre Union 0-4 Lorient
Troyes 1-2 St-Étienne *(aet)*

(11/02/16)
Trélissac 0-2 Marseille

QUARTER-FINALS

(02/03/16)
Lorient 3-0 GFC Ajaccio *(Philippoteaux 9, Bathelmé 43, Paye 90)*
Sochaux 3-2 Nantes *(Sao 87, 106, Cissé 98; Gillet 5, Adryan 116) (aet)*
St-Étienne 1-3 Paris SG *(Eysseric 43p; Cavani 12, Marquinhos 35, Lucas 90+2)*

(03/03/16)
Granville 0-1 Marseille *(Batshuayi 50)*

SEMI-FINALS

(19/04/16)
Lorient 0-1 Paris SG *(Ibrahimović 75)*

(20/04/16)
Sochaux 0-1 Marseille *(Thauvin 49)*

FINAL

(21/05/16)
Stade de France, Saint-Denis
PARIS SAINT-GERMAIN 4 *(Matuidi 3, Ibrahimović 47p, 82, Cavani 57)*
OLYMPIQUE DE MARSEILLE 2 *(Thauvin 12, Batshuayi 87)*
Referee: *Turpin*
PARIS: *Sirigu, Maxwell, Thiago Silva, Marquinhos, Aurier, Stambouli (David Luiz 75), Rabiot, Matuidi, Di María, Ibrahimović (Kurzawa 90), Cavani (Lucas 75)*
MARSEILLE: *Mandanda, Javi Manquillo, N'Koulou, Rekik, Mendy, Diarra, Isla, Thauvin (N'Koudou 81), Barrada (Dja Djédjé 70), Fletcher (Cabella 60), Batshuayi*

Coupe de la Ligue 2015/16

QUARTER-FINALS

(12/01/16)
Bordeaux 2-0 Lorient *(Plašil 44, Chaigneau 56og)*

(13/01/16)
Guingamp 0-0 LOSC *(aet; 2-4 on pens)*
Paris SG 2-1 Lyon *(Rabiot 17, Lucas 73; Tolisso 42)*
Toulouse 2-1 Marseille *(Ben Yedder 25, Braithwaite 99; N'Koudou 27) (aet)*

SEMI-FINALS

(26/01/16)
LOSC 5-1 Bordeaux *(Benzia 7, Sané 41og, Soumaoro 45, Bauthéac 56, Boufal 90+3; Chantôme 33)*

(27/01/16)
Paris SG 2-0 Toulouse *(Lavezzi 65, Di María 72)*

FINAL

(23/04/16)
Stade de France, Saint-Denis
PARIS SAINT-GERMAIN 2 *(Pastore 40, Di María 74)*
LOSC LILLE 1 *(Sidibé 49)*
Referee: *Buquet*
PARIS: *Sirigu, Aurier, Marquinhos, Thiago Silva, Kurzawa, Rabiot, Pastore (David Luiz 79), Matuidi, Lucas (Verratti 75), Di María (Cavani 90), Ibrahimović*
Red card: *Rabiot (70)*
LOSC: *Enyeama, Corchia, Soumaoro, Baša, Sidibé, Amadou, Obbadi, Mavuba (Rony Lopes 77), Amalfitano, Boufal, Éder*

Thiago Silva lifts the Coupe de France as Paris Saint-Germain complete back-to-back domestic trebles

GEORGIA
Georgian Football Federation (GFF)

Address	76a Chavchavadze Ave. GE-0179 Tbilisi	**President**	Levan Kobiashvili
Tel	+995 32 291 2670	**General secretary**	David Mujiri
Fax	+995 32 291 5995	**Media officer**	Otar Giorgadze
E-mail	gff@gff.ge	**Year of formation**	1990
Website	gff.ge	**National stadium**	Boris Paichadze Dinamo Arena, Tbilisi (53,233)

KEY

● UEFA Champions League
◐ UEFA Europa League
○ Relegated

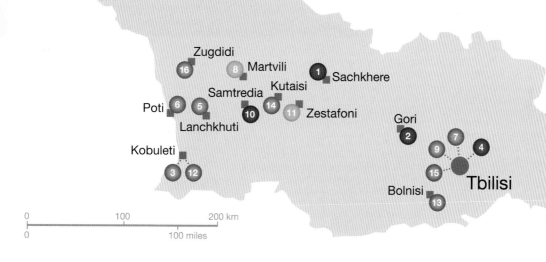

0 ___ 100 ___ 200 km
0 ___ 100 miles

UMAGLESI LIGA CLUBS

  **1** FC Chikhura Sachkhere

  2 FC Dila Gori

  **3** FC Dinamo Batumi

 4 FC Dinamo Tbilisi

 5 FC Guria Lanchkhuti

 6 FC Kolkheti Poti

  **7** FC Lokomotivi Tbilisi

  **8** FC Merani Martvili

  **9** FC Saburtalo Tbilisi

  10 FC Samtredia

  **11** FC Sapovnela Terjola

 12 FC Shukura Kobuleti

  **13** FC Sioni Bolnisi

  **14** FC Torpedo Kutaisi

  15 FC Tskhinvali

 16 FC Zugdidi

Easy pickings for Dinamo Tbilisi

Dinamo Tbilisi were back to their usual dominant self in 2015/16, running away with another Umaglesi Liga title – their 16th in the 27 years since Georgian independence – and completing a tenth domestic double in that time with a 13th cup triumph.

Reigning champions Dila Gori had another decent season, finishing third, a point behind runners-up Samtredia. It was fifth-placed Sioni Bolnisi who reached the Georgian Cup final, but they were unable to stop Dinamo from getting their hands on the trophy for the fourth year in a row.

Capital club claim tenth domestic double	**Records extend to 16th league and 13th cup wins**	**Defending champions Dila finish third**

Domestic league

Dinamo began their bid to dethrone Dila under the man who had arrived just in time to lead the club to victory in the 2015 Georgian Cup final, Gia Geguchadze. There was no doubting the resolve of both the coach and his players as Dinamo won their opening five matches, scoring 19 goals in the process. Dila, still led by the youthful Ucha Sosiashvili, halted their charge with a 2-0 win that put them top, but a 5-0 thrashing by Samtredia in the title holders' next match meant their stay at the summit was short-lived.

From then on Dinamo became irrepressible frontrunners. Seven successive victories carried them into the winter break, their lead over Dila up to five points, with third-placed FC Tskhinvali, buoyed by the 13 goals of Nika Kacharava, a further three points adrift. Tskhinvali's token challenge would collapse after Kacharava was sold, but Dinamo's form would be unaffected by the departure of Geguchadze, who quit to take charge of the Georgia Under-21 side.

Dinamo appointed Juraj Jarábek, formerly with Spartak Trnava, in Geguchadze's stead, and the transition was seamless, with the team winning their first five games under the Slovakian until once again Dila halted them in their tracks, completing the double with a 1-0 win at the Boris Paichadze Dinamo Arena, where

the league leaders had won every previous game. As in the autumn, however, losing to Dila proved inconsequential, Dinamo eventually wrapping up their 16th Georgian title with a 3-1 win at Kolkheti Poti four rounds before the season's end.

Jarábek's tally of 36 points was four fewer than Geguchadze had amassed in his 15 games, but it was more than enough to see Dinamo home in comfort. Dila would be pipped to second place by Samtredia, who, skilfully marshalled by coach Gia Tsetsadze, amassed just one point less than Dinamo in the spring, their 11 wins including the biggest of the season, 8-2 against Saburtalo Tbilisi. Dinamo were the highest-scoring team, with 76 goals, and also boasted the leading individual marksman in 22-year-old ex-Dila striker Giorgi Kvilitaia, who registered 24 times.

Newly-promoted Sapovnela Terjola finished bottom of the table and were relegated with Merani Martvili, but there were no teams promoted after 14th-placed Zugdidi won their play-off against Kolkheti Kobi and the top two clubs in the second tier, Liakhvi Tskhinvali and WIT Georgia, were both denied Umaglesi Liga licences.

Domestic cup

Dinamo's fourth successive Georgian Cup win was obtained in flawless

fashion as they won all seven matches, the last of them 1-0 against Sioni in a repeat of the 2003 final – the Bolnisi club's only previous appearance. Midfielder Vakhtang Chanturishvili scored the goal that wrapped up Dinamo's double and kept the club on course to emulate the six successive cup wins they achieved in the 1990s.

Europe

Dinamo preceded their season of domestic dominance with immediate elimination from Europe, and that was the unhappy narrative across the board for Georgia's four entries in one of the country's worst ever collective performances.

National team

Not long after Dinamo appointed a Slovakian coach, the Georgian national team followed suit, with Vladimír Weiss, who led his country to a famous victory over Italy at the 2010 World Cup, returning to international football after a spell in Kazakhstan. He replaced Kakhaber Tskhadadze, whose 12 months in charge would be most fondly remembered for a 1-0 win in their UEFA EURO 2016 qualifier against Scotland in Tbilisi. Weiss also had a 1-0 win to treasure when, after an inauspicious start, he led Georgia to a remarkable victory away to Spain in what would be their hosts' last friendly as European champions.

DOMESTIC SEASON AT A GLANCE

Umaglesi Liga 2015/16 final table

		Pld	Home					Away					Total					Pts
			W	D	L	F	A	W	D	L	F	A	W	D	L	F	A	
1	**FC Dinamo Tbilisi**	30	14	0	1	39	12	11	1	3	35	17	25	1	4	74	29	76
2	FC Samtredia	30	13	0	2	41	11	7	3	5	25	21	20	3	7	66	32	63
3	FC Dila Gori	30	10	2	3	29	11	9	3	3	22	14	19	5	6	51	25	62
4	FC Chikhura Sachkhere	30	11	2	2	32	7	6	4	5	21	19	17	6	7	53	26	57
5	FC Sioni Bolnisi	30	9	2	4	30	14	5	6	4	20	20	14	8	8	50	34	50
6	FC Torpedo Kutaisi	30	10	2	3	26	11	4	4	7	24	31	14	6	10	50	42	48
7	FC Tskhinvali	30	7	6	2	30	13	5	4	6	21	23	12	10	8	51	36	46
8	FC Dinamo Batumi	30	7	5	3	26	16	5	3	7	15	16	12	8	10	41	32	44
9	FC Saburtalo Tbilisi	30	8	3	4	33	27	3	3	9	14	34	11	6	13	47	61	39
10	FC Shukura Kobuleti	30	7	4	4	19	15	2	4	9	9	24	9	8	13	28	39	35
11	FC Guria Lanchkhuti	30	3	7	5	13	15	3	2	10	15	34	6	9	15	28	49	27
12	FC Kolkheti Poti	30	6	3	6	13	11	1	3	11	8	30	7	6	17	21	41	27
13	FC Lokomotivi Tbilisi	30	4	6	5	16	16	1	4	10	10	21	5	10	15	26	37	25
14	FC Zugdidi	30	5	5	5	24	23	0	3	12	6	37	5	8	17	30	60	23
15	FC Merani Martvili	30	5	3	7	22	31	0	5	10	6	31	5	8	17	28	62	23
16	FC Sapovnela Terjola	30	5	4	6	17	25	0	2	13	7	38	5	6	19	24	63	21

European qualification 2016/17

Champion/Cup winner: FC Dinamo Tbilisi (second qualifying round)

FC Samtredia (first qualifying round)
FC Dila Gori (first qualifying round)
FC Chikhura Sachkhere (first qualifying round)

Top scorer	Giorgi Kvilitaia (Dinamo Tbilisi), 24 goals
Relegated clubs	FC Sapovnela Terjola, FC Merani Martvili
Promoted clubs	none
Cup final	FC Dinamo Tbilisi 1-0 FC Sioni Bolnisi

Player of the season

Aleksandre Iashvili
(FC Dinamo Tbilisi)

Back at his first club Dinamo after an 18-year gap, during which he became a star of German football, notably with Freiburg, Iashvili's last season before hanging up his boots was everything the 38-year-old would have wanted. Not only did he win the Georgian domestic double with Dinamo for the fifth time – the previous four having come during the mid-1990s – but he also made a significant contribution. Once a prolific striker, he operated as a midfielder in 2015/16, his vast experience proving invaluable in a youthful team.

Newcomer of the season

Giorgi Kharaishvili
(FC Saburtalo Tbilisi)

A scorer of 21 goals in Saburtalo's 2014/15 promotion-winning campaign, 19-year-old Kharaishvili maintained an impressive goal ratio in the Georgian top flight, scoring 12 times in 24 starts to help his team to a respectable ninth-place finish. A busy, technically accomplished attacking midfielder with an eagerness to get involved and make goals as well as score them, he progressed from Georgia's Under-19 to Under-21 team during the season and is expected to graduate to senior recognition before too long.

Team of the season
(4-4-2)

Coach: Tsetsadze *(Samtredia)*

Hrdlička
(Dinamo Tbilisi)

Gongadze *(Dila)*   Rene *(Dinamo Tbilisi)*   Amisulashvili *(Dinamo Tbilisi)*   Shergelashvili *(Samtredia)*

Iashvili *(Dinamo Tbilisi)*   Chanturishvili *(Dinamo Tbilisi)*   Jigauri *(Dinamo Tbilisi)*   Kharaishvili *(Saburtalo)*

Modebadze *(Dila)*   Kvilitaia *(Dinamo Tbilisi)*

NATIONAL TEAM

Top five all-time caps

Levan Kobiashvili (100); **Zurab Khizanishvili** (93); Kakha Kaladze (83); Giorgi Nemsadze (69); Aleksandre Iashvili (67)

Top five all-time goals

Shota Arveladze (26); Temur Ketsbaia (17); Aleksandre Iashvili (15); Giorgi Demetradze & Levan Kobiashvili (12)

Results 2015/16

04/09/15	Scotland (ECQ)	H	Tbilisi	W	1-0	*Kazaishvili (38)*
07/09/15	Republic of Ireland (ECQ)	A	Dublin	L	0-1	
08/10/15	Gibraltar (ECQ)	H	Tbilisi	W	4-0	*Vatsadze (30, 45), Okriashvili (35p), Kazaishvili (87)*
11/10/15	Germany (ECQ)	A	Leipzig	L	1-2	*Kankava (53)*
11/11/15	Estonia	A	Tallinn	L	0-3	
16/11/15	Albania	A	Tirana	D	2-2	*Amisulashvili (2), Chanturia (51)*
29/03/16	Kazakhstan	H	Tbilisi	D	1-1	*Okriashvili (38)*
27/05/16	Slovakia	N	Wels (AUT)	L	1-3	*Kenia (71)*
03/06/16	Romania	A	Bucharest	L	1-5	*Mchedlidze (68)*
07/06/16	Spain	A	Getafe	W	1-0	*Okriashvili (40)*

Appearances 2015/16

Coach: Kakhaber Tskhadadze 07/09/68 /(14/03/16) Vladimir Weiss (SVK) 22/09/64			SCO	IRL	GIB	GER	Est	Alb	Kaz	Svk	Rou	Esp	Caps	Goals
Nukri Revishvili	02/03/87	Mordovia (RUS)	G	G	G	G		G	G	G		G55	32	-
Ucha Lobjanidze	23/02/87	Omonia (CYP) /Dinamo Tbilisi	D	D		D		D	D90		D	D	49	1
Solomon Kverkvelia	06/02/92	Rubin (RUS)	D	D		D			s46	D	D	D	16	-
Aleksandre Amisulashvili	20/08/82	Karşıyaka (TUR) /Dinamo Tbilisi	D	D	D	D	D	D	D46	s46	D	D	49	4
Giorgi Navalovski	28/06/86	Dila /SKA-Energia (RUS)	D	D		D	D68	D	D	D66	D64	D84	15	-
Jaba Kankava	18/03/86	Reims (FRA)	M	M	M58	M	M	M	M				62	7
Guram Kashia	04/07/87	Vitesse (NED)	M	M76	M	M	M	M	D	D	M	M	47	1
Jano Ananidze	10/10/92	Spartak Moskva (RUS)	M82						M77				31	3
Tornike Okriashvili	12/02/92	Genk (BEL) /Eskişehirspor (TUR)	M71	M	M58	M			M	M	M	M	30	7
Valeri Kazaishvili	29/01/93	Vitesse (NED)	M	M64	M	M90	M78	M81	M	M78	M	M72	17	3
Levan Mchedlidze	24/03/90	Empoli (ITA)	A93	A					A46	s34			29	3
Giorgi Merebashvili	15/08/86	Veria (GRE)	s71										18	-
Murtaz Daushvili	01/05/89	Karpaty (UKR)	s82			s72	M						28	-
Mate Vatsadze	17/12/88	AGF (DEN)	s93		A73	s46	A46		s90				15	4
Zurab Khizanishvili	06/10/81	İnter Bakı (AZE)		D81		s78							93	1
Giorgi Papunashvili	02/09/95	Bremen (GER)		s64									3	-
Mate Tsintsadze	07/01/95	Dinamo Tbilisi		s76			M72						2	-
Levan Kenia	18/10/90	Slavia Praha (CZE)		s81					s77	s46			29	4
Otar Kakabadze	27/06/95	Dinamo Tbilisi			D		D	s90		D			4	-
Gia Grigalava	05/08/89	Pafos (CYP)			D		D68	D					23	-
Nika Kvekveskiri	29/05/92	İnter Bakı (AZE)			M	M78			s77	M	s65		5	-
Aleksandre Kobakhidze	11/02/87	Volyn (UKR) /Dnipro (UKR)			M	s90	M46	s81	M46			s84	33	3
Nika Dzalamidze	06/01/92	Rizespor (TUR)			s58								7	-
Guga Palavandishvili	14/08/93	Dila			s58								1	-
Bachana Tskhadadze	23/10/87	Flamurtari (ALB)			s73		s46	s75					8	-
Nikoloz Gelashvili	05/08/85	Pafos (CYP)				A46		A75					25	1
Giorgi Loria	27/01/86	Krylya Sovetov (RUS)					G						34	-
Giorgi Chanturia	11/04/93	Duisburg (GER)				s46	M90	A46				s72	12	2
Lucas Hufnagel	29/01/94	Freiburg (GER)				s68							1	-
Giorgi Popkhadze	25/09/86	Flamurtari (ALB)				s68							12	-
Zakaria Beglarishvili	30/04/90	Flora (EST)				s78							1	-
Giorgi Aburjania	02/01/95	Gimnàstic (ESP)							M77		M65	M78	3	-
Nika Kacharava	13/07/94	Rostov (RUS)							s46				1	-
Vakhtang Chanturishvili	05/08/93	Dinamo Tbilisi							M46				1	-
Giorgi Kvilitaia	01/10/93	Dinamo Tbilisi							s46	s78	s72		3	-
Lasha Dvali	14/05/95	Śląsk (POL)							s66	D34			5	-
Jambul Jigauri	08/07/92	Dinamo Tbilisi							s78		M		2	-
Roin Kvaskhvadze	31/05/89	Torpedo Kutaisi								G	s55		5	-
Vladimer Dvalishvili	20/04/86	Pogoń (POL)								A78	A72		34	5
Zurab Tsiskaridze	08/09/86	Teplice (CZE)								s64	s78		2	-

EUROPE

DOMESTIC LEAGUE CLUB-BY-CLUB

FC Dila Gori

CHAMPIONS
LEAGUE

Second qualifying round - FK Partizan (SRB)
A 0-1
Shevchenko, Khurtsilava, Papava, Palavandishvili, Razmadze, Iluridze (Gongadze 90+1), Kvirkvelia, Kvakhadze, Gvalia, Navalovski, Martsvaladze (Dzaria 83). Coach: Ucha Sosiashvili (GEO)
Red card: Palavandishvili 82
H 0-2
Shevchenko, Khurtsilava, Papava (Kvirkvia 46), Iluridze (Mashukov 46), Bagaev, Modebadze, Dzaria, Kvakhadze, Gvalia, Navalovski, Martsvaladze (Eristavi 82). Coach: Ucha Sosiashvili (GEO)

FC Dinamo Tbilisi

DINAMO TBILISI
1925

EUROPA
LEAGUE

First qualifying round - Qäbälä FK (AZE)
H 2-1 Jigauri (65), Papunashvili (84)
Hrdlička, Totadze, Tvildiani, Tsintsadze, Papunashvili, Kvilitaia (Iashvili 62), Kiteishvili (Rene 54), Gvelesiani, Jigauri, Chelidze, Chanturishvili (Parunashvili 79). Coach: Gia Geguchadze (GEO)
Red card: Gvelesiani 51
A 0-2
Hrdlička, Totadze, Tvildiani (Janelidze 84), Tsintsadze, Iashvili (Kiteishvili 61), Papunashvili, Kvilitaia (Guruli 74), Rene, Jigauri, Chelidze, Chanturishvili. Coach: Gia Geguchadze (GEO)
Red card: Totadze 71

FC Dinamo Batumi

EUROPA
LEAGUE

First qualifying round - AC Omonia (CYP)
H 1-0 Gabedava (40)
Alavidze, Tetunashvili, Kavtaradze (Chirikashvili 83), Gogitidze, Shonia, Beriashvili (Varshanidze 87), Gabedava, Tatanashvili (Tevdoradze 75), Poniava, Makharadze, Sukhiashvili. Coach: Shota Cheishvili (GEO)
A 0-2
Alavidze, Tetunashvili, Kavtaradze (Chirikashvili 79), Gogitidze, Shonia, Beriashvili, Gabedava, Tatanashvili (Koridze 58), Poniava (Varshanidze 52), Makharadze, Sukhiashvili. Coach: Shota Cheishvili (GEO)
Red card: Tetunashvili 54

FC Tskhinvali

EUROPA
LEAGUE

First qualifying round - FC Botoşani (ROU)
A 1-1 Kacharava (46)
Nadiradze, Bachiashvili, Tsertsvadze, Lekvtadze (Shulaia 63), Gigauri (Burdzenadze 77), Kacharava, Ivanishvili (Kachkachishvili 89), Kakubava, Tsatskrialashvili, Kardava, Kilasonia. Coach: Kakhi Kacharava (GEO)
H 1-3 Kilasonia (65p)
Nadiradze, Bachiashvili, Tsertsvadze, Gigauri (Shulaia 63), Makharoblidze, Kacharava, Ivanishvili, Kakubava, Tsatskrialashvili (Burdzenadze 78), Kardava (Lobjanidze 71), Kilasonia. Coach: Kakhi Kacharava (GEO)
Red card: Kacharava 37

FC Chikhura Sachkhere

1938 • Central (750) • fcchikhura.ge
Coach: Soso Pruidze

2015

13/08	h	Lokomotivi	W 1-0	Chankotadze
22/08	a	Saburtalo	L 0-1	
30/08	h	Merani	W 3-0	Mumladze, Chikvaidze, Jokhadze
12/09	a	Zugdidi	W 4-1	Mumladze 2, Kuchukhidze 2
20/09	h	Dila	L 0-1	
26/09	a	Dinamo Batumi	D 1-1	Mumladze
04/10	h	Torpedo	W 3-0	Kuchukhidze, Chikvaidze, Sardalishvili
18/10	a	Tskhinvali	D 1-1	Koripadze
23/10	h	Kolkheti	L 0-1	
01/11	a	Dinamo Tbilisi	L 0-2	
08/11	h	Samtredia	W 1-0	Dobrovolski
21/11	h	Guria	W 5-0	Sardalishvili 2, Mumladze 2, Chankotadze (p)
28/11	a	Sioni	L 0-4	
06/12	h	Shukura	W 1-0	Mumladze
12/12	a	Sapovnela	W 2-0	Mumladze, Koripadze

2016

19/02	a	Lokomotivi	D 2-2	T Kirkitadze, Chikvaidze
23/02	h	Saburtalo	W 5-0	Chankotadze, T Kirkitadze, Sardalishvili (p), Ganugrava
27/02	a	Merani	L 2-3	Chankotadze, Chikvaidze
06/03	h	Zugdidi	W 4-0	Sardalishvili 2, Kuchukhidze, Enukidze
12/03	a	Dila	D 1-1	Sardalishvili
18/03	a	Dinamo Batumi	W 2-0	Volkovi, Sardalishvili
02/04	a	Torpedo	W 2-0	Volkovi 2
06/04	h	Tskhinvali	W 2-1	Ganugrava, Chikvaidze
11/04	a	Kolkheti	L 0-2	
16/04	h	Dinamo Tbilisi	W 1-0	Sardalishvili
24/04	h	Samtredia	D 1-1	Chankotadze (p)
30/04	a	Guria	W 3-1	Volkovi, Rekhviashvili, Kuchukhidze
09/05	h	Sioni	D 1-1	Mumladze
14/05	a	Shukura	W 2-0	T Kirkitadze, Mumladze
22/05	h	Sapovnela	W 3-2	T Kirkitadze, Chikvaidze, Mumladze

Name	Nat	DoB	Pos	Aps	(s)	Gls
Giorgi Chankotadze		06/05/91	M	7	(12)	6
Chiaber Chechelashvili		10/10/95	M	20		
Lasha Chikvaidze		04/10/89	D	29		6
Besik Dekanoidze		01/03/92	M	12	(7)	
Denis Dobrovolski		10/10/85	M	28		1
Guram Enukidze		09/01/93	M	4	(3)	1
Nikoloz Gabadze		29/05/96	D	5		
Giorgi Ganugrava		21/02/88	M	27		2
Tornike Grigalashvili		28/01/93	D	11		
Dino Hamzić	BIH	22/01/88	G	10		
Giorgi Jokhadze		24/03/90	A	3	(8)	1
Teimuraz Kakaladze		06/05/88	G	1		
Kakhaber Kakashvili		26/06/93	M	4	(6)	
Shota Kashia		22/10/84	D	30		
David Kirkitadze		03/09/92	A		(4)	
Tornike Kirkitadze		23/07/96	M	12		4
Giorgi Koripadze		13/10/89	M	20	(5)	2
Lasha Kuchukhidze		14/03/92	A	17	(5)	5
David Kupatadze		06/06/91	G	19		
Omar Kurtanidze		09/01/95	M	3		
Otar Kusiani		16/03/95	D	11		
Anej Lovrečič	SVN	10/05/87	M	2	(2)	
David Megrelishvili		25/09/91	D	15	(4)	
Tornike Mumladze		23/07/92	A	8	(13)	11
Giorgi Rekhviashvili		22/02/88	D	8	(1)	1
Nika Samkharadze		24/10/95	M	1		
Mikheil Sardalishvili		17/02/92	A	11	(14)	9
David Volkovi		03/06/95	A	8		4
Marko Vukasović	SRB	10/09/90	M	4	(2)	

GEORGIA

FC Dila Gori

1936 • Tengiz Burjanadze (4,483) • no website
Major honours
Georgian League (1) 2015; Georgian Cup (1) 2012
Coach: Ucha Sosiashvili

2015
14/08	h	Kolkheti Poti	W 2-0	Navalovski, Martsvaladze
21/08	h	Dinamo Batumi	D 1-1	Martsvaladze
30/08	a	Torpedo	W 2-0	Modebadze 2
12/09	h	Tskhinvali	W 3-0	Martsvaladze 2, Nonikashvili
20/09	a	Chikhura	W 1-0	Modebadze
26/09	h	Dinamo Tbilisi	W 2-0	Modebadze 2 (1p)
03/10	a	Samtredia	L 0-5	
18/10	h	Guria	W 5-0	Eristavi (p), Samkharadze, Martsvaladze 3
23/10	a	Sioni	W 1-0	Martsvaladze
01/11	h	Shukura	L 1-3	Martsvaladze
07/11	a	Sapovnela	W 5-1	Modebadze (p), Martsvaladze, Eristavi, Iluridze, Mashukov
21/11	h	Lokomotivi	W 1-0	Mashukov
29/11	h	Saburtalo	W 3-1	Mashukov, Gogua, Navalovski
07/12	h	Merani	W 2-0	Modebadze, Martsvaladze
12/12	h	Zugdidi	D 1-1	Modebadze (p)

2016
19/02	h	Kolkheti	W 1-0	Kvirkvia
23/02	a	Dinamo Batumi	D 2-2	Martsvaladze 2
27/02	h	Torpedo	L 0-1	
06/03	a	Tskhinvali	D 0-0	
12/03	h	Chikhura	D 1-1	Modebadze
17/03	a	Dinamo Tbilisi	W 1-0	Gongadze
02/04	h	Samtredia	L 1-2	Martsvaladze
06/04	a	Guria	W 1-0	Mashukov
10/04	h	Sioni	W 2-1	Martsvaladze, Nonikashvili
17/04	h	Shukura	L 0-1	
23/04	h	Sapovnela	W 3-1	Gongadze, Nonikashvili, Modebadze
30/04	a	Lokomotivi	W 2-0	Martsvaladze, Dzaria
08/05	h	Saburtalo	W 2-1	Mashukov, Martsvaladze
14/05	a	Merani	L 2-3	Dzaria, Palavandishvili
22/05	h	Zugdidi	W 3-0	Modebadze (p), Martsvaladze 2

Name	Nat	DoB	Pos	Aps	(s)	Gls
Roman Akhalkatsi		20/02/81	M		(5)	
Alan Bagaev	RUS	07/04/91	D	10	(1)	
Giorgi Chelebadze		01/01/92	M	7	(3)	
Irakli Dzaria		01/12/87	M	15	(6)	2
Nika Eliauri		13/02/97	M		(1)	
Giorgi Eristavi		04/02/94	M	9	(2)	2
Aleksandre Gamtsemlidze		24/10/97	M		(1)	
Gogita Gogua		04/09/83	M	7	(3)	1
Teimuraz Gongadze		08/09/85	D	17	(3)	2
Lasha Gvalia		06/10/91	M	6	(6)	
Giorgi Iluridze		20/02/92	A	1	(8)	1
Givi Karkuzashvili		20/09/86	D	14	(1)	
David Khurtsilava		09/03/88	D	19	(4)	
Aleksandre Kvakhadze		17/08/84	D	18		
David Kvirkvelia		27/06/80	D	19		
Mate Kvirkvia		14/06/96	M	9		1
David Legashvili		09/02/93	G	6	(1)	
Ilia Lomidze		04/11/89	D		(3)	
Otar Martsvaladze		14/07/84	A	24	(3)	19
Islam Mashukov	RUS	22/02/95	A	10	(10)	5
Irakli Modebadze		04/10/84	A	17	(10)	11
Mikheil Mujrishvili		30/04/84	G	14		
Giorgi Navalovski		28/06/86	D	13		2
Levan Nonikashvili		05/04/95	M	15	(6)	3
Guga Palavandishvili		14/08/93	M	27		1
Giorgi Papava		16/02/93	M	6		
Levan Sabadze		17/03/92	D	2	(5)	
Giga Samkharadze		28/04/95	M	20		1
Olexiy Shevchenko	UKR	24/02/92	G	10		
Giorgi Tekturmanidze		17/09/90	M	7	(1)	
Gulverd Tomashvili		13/10/88	D	1	(3)	
Tengiz Tsikaridze		21/12/95	M	7	(3)	

FC Dinamo Batumi

1923 • Chele Arena, Kobuleti (3,800) • dinamobatumi.com
Major honours
Georgian Cup (1) 1998
**Coach: Shota Cheishvili;
(13/04/16) Levan Khomeriki**

2015
14/08	h	Zugdidi	W 5-0	Beriashvili 3 (1p), Gabedava, Luís Alberto
21/08	a	Dila	D 1-1	Beriashvili
30/08	h	Kolkheti	W 2-0	Gabedava, Beriashvili
12/09	h	Torpedo	D 1-1	Gogitidze
20/09	a	Tskhinvali	L 2-3	og (Kakubava), Beriashvili
26/09	h	Chikhura	D 1-1	Luís Alberto
03/10	a	Dinamo Tbilisi	L 0-1	
17/10	h	Samtredia	W 2-0	Beriashvili 2
23/10	a	Guria	D 1-1	Abuselidze
01/11	h	Sioni	L 3-5	Luís Alberto, Tetunashvili, Kavtaradze
07/11	a	Shukura	W 1-0	Makatsaria
21/11	h	Sapovnela	W 1-0	Tevdoradze
27/11	a	Lokomotivi	D 1-1	Gogitidze
06/12	h	Saburtalo	W 2-1	Diasamidze, Beriashvili
12/12	a	Merani	W 4-0	Koridze, Poniava, Gogitidze, Beriashvili

2016
19/02	a	Zugdidi	W 1-0	Mihajlović
23/02	h	Dila	D 2-2	Komazec (p), Shonia
27/02	a	Kolkheti	W 1-0	Shonia
06/03	a	Torpedo	L 0-1	
13/03	h	Tskhinvali	W 2-0	Komazec, Gabedava
18/03	a	Chikhura	L 0-2	
02/04	h	Dinamo Tbilisi	L 1-2	Tvildiani
06/04	a	Samtredia	L 0-2	
10/04	h	Guria	L 1-2	Komazec
16/04	a	Sioni	L 0-1	
23/04	h	Shukura	D 2-2	Komazec, Shonia
30/04	a	Sapovnela	L 1-2	Chkuaseli
08/05	h	Lokomotivi	W 1-0	Shonia
14/05	a	Saburtalo	W 2-1	Makatsaria, Shonia
22/05	h	Merani	D 0-0	

Name	Nat	DoB	Pos	Aps	(s)	Gls
Amiran Abuselidze		16/03/93	M	2	(5)	1
Mikheil Alavidze		05/11/87	G	19		
Giorgi Beriashvili		10/09/86	A	13	(4)	10
Irakli Chirikashvili		10/01/87	M	1	(7)	
Beka Chkuaseli		12/10/96	M	9	(6)	1
Nika Diasamidze		02/09/94	M	12	(1)	1
Giorgi Gabedava		03/10/89	A	7	(4)	3
Gela Gogitidze		25/11/90	M	27		3
Giorgi Kashia		23/07/90	M	5	(8)	
Zurab Katamadze		18/01/96	D	5		
Giorgi Kavtaradze		01/01/89	M	22	(1)	1
Nikola Komazec	SRB	15/11/87	A	12	(1)	4
Vaja Koridze		05/01/87	D	10	(1)	1
Nika Kvantaliani		06/02/98	M	4	(4)	
Luís Alberto	POR	12/10/91	A	7	(4)	3
Tamaz Makatsaria		03/10/95	M	5	(7)	2
Boris Makharadze		08/11/90	M	10	(2)	
Shota Maminashvili		30/08/86	G	8		
Nika Mgeladze		20/12/85	D	11	(1)	
Marko Mihajlović	BIH	04/08/87	D	9	(1)	1
Papuna Poniava		10/03/94	M	20		1
Teimuraz Shonia		28/05/90	M	23		5
Guram Sirabidze		29/06/95	M		(2)	
Anzor Sukhiashvili		27/10/88	D	29		
Roman Takidze		30/01/94	G	3		
Badri Tetunashvili		09/02/90	D	12	(8)	1
Valerian Tevdoradze		11/10/93	M	14	(9)	1
Archil Tvildiani		31/01/93	D	12		1
Beka Varshanidze		01/12/93	M	19	(6)	

FC Dinamo Tbilisi

1925 • Boris Paichadze Dinamo Arena (53,233) • fcdinamo.ge
Major honours
UEFA Cup Winners Cup (1) 1981; USSR League (2) 1964, 1978; Georgian League (16) 1990, 1991, 1992, 1993, 1994, 1995, 1996, 1997, 1998, 1999, 2003, 2005, 2008, 2013, 2014, 2016; USSR Cup (2) 1976, 1979; Georgian Cup (13) 1992, 1993, 1994, 1995, 1996, 1997, 2003, 2004, 2009, 2013, 2014, 2015, 2016
**Coach: Gia Geguchadze;
(27/01/16) Juraj Jarábek (SVK)**

2015
14/08	h	Sapovnela	W 4-0	Jigauri 2, Iashvili, og (Endeladze)
21/08	a	Lokomotivi	W 4-1	Tevzadze, Tsintsadze (p), Jigauri, Chelidze
29/08	h	Saburtalo	W 4-0	Tsintsadze (p), Kvilitaia, Chanturishvili, Iashvili
11/09	a	Merani	W 4-1	Kvilitaia 2, Tsintsadze, Jigauri
20/09	h	Zugdidi	W 3-1	Gvelesiani, Kvilitaia 2
26/09	a	Dila	L 0-2	
03/10	h	Dinamo Batumi	W 1-0	Kiteishvili
17/10	a	Torpedo	D 1-1	Kvilitaia
23/10	h	Tskhinvali	W 2-1	Kvilitaia, Kakabadze
01/11	a	Chikhura	W 2-0	Kiteishvili 2
08/11	h	Kolkheti	W 5-2	Jigauri 2, Kvilitaia 3
21/11	h	Samtredia	W 3-1	Jigauri 2, Guruli
28/11	a	Guria	W 2-0	Kvilitaia, og (Khizaneishvili)
06/12	h	Sioni	W 5-2	Guruli 2, Kvilitaia, Rene, S Lobjanidze
12/12	a	Shukura	W 3-1	Kvilitaia, Guruli, Jigauri

2016
19/02	a	Sapovnela	W 2-1	Kvilitaia, Iashvili (p)
23/02	h	Lokomotivi	W 2-1	Iashvili (p), Kiteishvili
27/02	a	Saburtalo	W 4-0	Jigauri, Kvilitaia 2, Gvelesiani
06/03	h	Merani	W 2-0	Kvilitaia, Amisulashvili
12/03	a	Zugdidi	W 3-2	Chelidze, Arabuli, Jigauri
17/03	h	Dila	L 0-1	
02/04	a	Dinamo Batumi	W 2-1	Jigauri, Guruli
06/04	h	Torpedo	W 2-1	Gelashvili, Kvilitaia (p)
10/04	a	Tskhinvali	W 4-2	Chanturishvili, Iashvili, Kvilitaia 2 (1p)
16/04	a	Chikhura	L 0-1	
24/04	h	Kolkheti	W 3-1	Kvilitaia (p), Jigauri, Rene
30/04	a	Samtredia	L 1-2	Chanturishvili
08/05	h	Guria	W 3-2	Kvilitaia 3 (1p)
14/05	a	Sioni	W 2-1	S Lobjanidze, Kvilitaia
22/05	h	Shukura	W 1-0	Chanturishvili

Name	Nat	DoB	Pos	Aps	(s)	Gls
Aleksandre Amisulashvili		20/08/82	D	12		1
Bachana Arabuli		05/01/94	A	3	(17)	2
Giorgi Begashvili		12/02/91	G	10	(1)	
Vakhtang Chanturishvili		05/08/93	M	19	(5)	4
Zaza Chelidze		12/01/87	D	13	(6)	2
Nikoloz Gelashvili		05/08/85	A	6	(3)	1
Giorgi Guruli		31/07/88	D	10	(4)	5
Giorgi Gvelesiani		05/05/91	D	19	(2)	2
Libor Hrdlička	SVK	02/01/86	G	20	(1)	
Aleksandre Iashvili		23/10/77	M	22	(2)	5
Giorgi Janelidze		25/09/89	M	2	(11)	
Jambul Jigauri		08/07/92	M	23	(5)	13
Otar Kakabadze		27/06/96	D	17		1
Otar Kiteishvili		26/03/96	M	24	(3)	4
David Kobouri		24/01/98	M	1		
Giorgi Kvilitaia		01/10/93	A	25	(4)	24
Enver Liluashvili		04/11/97	M		(1)	
Saba Lobjanidze		18/12/94	M	6	(9)	2
Ucha Lobjanidze		23/02/87	D	13		
Mikel Álvaro	ESP	20/12/82	M	2	(5)	
Beka Mikeltadze		26/11/97	M	1		
Lasha Parunashvili		14/02/93	M	25		
Rene	BRA	21/04/92	D	20		2
Giorgi Tevzadze		25/08/96	D	2	(3)	1
Mate Tsintsadze		07/01/95	M	16	(1)	3
Archil Tvildiani		31/01/93	D	3	(1)	
David Volkovi		03/06/95	A		(3)	

FC Guria Lanchkhuti

1924 • Evgrapi Shevardnadze (4,500) •
no website
Major honours
Georgian Cup (1) 1990
Coach: Kakhi Gogichaishvili;
(23/09/15) (Badri Kvaratskhelia);
(28/09/15) Gia Chkhaidze;
(20/01/16) Viktor Demidov (RUS);
(05/04/16) Gia Gogua

2015
14/08	h	Sioni	D	1-1	Chapidze
22/08	a	Shukura	L	1-2	Maisuradze
30/08	h	Sapovnela	W	3-0	Jikia, Mosiashvili, V Tsilosani
11/09	a	Lokomotivi	L	0-3	
20/09	h	Saburtalo	D	0-0	
26/09	a	Merani	L	0-2	
10/10	h	Zugdidi	W	2-0	Bakhia, Rekhviashvili
18/10	a	Dila	L	0-5	
23/10	h	Dinamo Batumi	D	1-1	V Tsilosani
01/11	a	Torpedo	L	1-2	Bakhia
08/11	h	Tskhinvali	L	1-2	V Tsilosani (p)
21/11	a	Chikhura	L	0-5	
28/11	h	Dinamo Tbilisi	L	0-2	
06/12	a	Samtredia	L	1-3	Tsereteli
11/12	a	Kolkheti	D	1-1	V Tsilosani

2016
19/02	a	Sioni	D	1-1	Morozenko
23/02	h	Shukura	D	0-0	
27/02	a	Sapovnela	W	2-0	Panebeng-Fodoup, Shtander
06/03	h	Lokomotivi	D	0-0	
13/03	h	Saburtalo	L	2-4	Zozulya, Morozenko
19/03	h	Merani	D	0-0	
02/04	a	Zugdidi	L	2-3	Gamkrelidze, Kakhelishvili (p)
06/04	h	Dila	L	0-1	
10/04	a	Dinamo Batumi	W	2-1	Small 2
17/04	h	Torpedo	W	3-2	Morozenko 2, Small
23/04	a	Tskhinvali	D	0-0	
30/04	h	Chikhura	L	1-3	Kvekveskiri
09/05	a	Dinamo Tbilisi	L	2-3	Kakhelishvili, Alaverdashvili
14/05	h	Samtredia	L	0-2	
22/05	a	Kolkheti	W	1-0	Gamkrelidze

Name	Nat	DoB	Pos	Aps	(s)	Gls
Giorgi Alaverdashvili		21/11/87	A	13	(1)	1
Sandro Bakhia		08/01/93	M	9	(3)	2
Alvin Bennett	CRC	12/11/94	D	7	(2)	
Gia Chaduneli		15/05/94	D	25		
Lasha Chapidze		08/07/92	A	3	(1)	1
Nika Daushvili		16/10/89	G	7		
Boti Demel	CIV	03/03/89	A	3	(2)	
Georgi Gamkrelidze	UKR	30/09/87	M	11	(4)	2
Zurab Gelashvili		09/04/96	D	18	(2)	
Solomon Gujabidze		24/02/97	M		(4)	
Robert Imerlishvili		24/07/93	G	14	(2)	
Shota Jikia		30/12/84	M	10	(2)	1
Aleksandar Jovanović	SRB	25/07/92	G	7		
Paterson Kaboré	BFA	05/05/90	D	8	(1)	
Giorgi Kakhelishvili		22/05/87	M	7	(2)	2
Konstantine Khizaneishvili		30/04/93	D	13		
Erekle Kiladze		11/01/90	M	19	(2)	
Luka Koberidze		09/09/94	M	4	(9)	
Levan Kurdadze		03/09/90	D	9	(2)	
Irakli Kvekveskiri		12/03/90	M	12		1
Lasha Labadze		19/10/94	M	1	(1)	
Nika Maisuradze		29/05/89	M	11	(1)	1
Lasha Mchedlishvili		07/02/93	D	5	(2)	
Yevhen Morozenko	UKR	16/12/91	A	15		4
Tornike Mosiashvili		09/10/91	M	12	(1)	1
Luka Nozadze		25/12/96	D	26	(1)	
Mauricio Núñez Bong	CRC	28/10/93	D	9		
Panebeng-Fodoup	FRA	01/01/93	A	7	(4)	1
Andriy Poltavtsev	UKR	01/01/91	G	2		
Aleksandre Rekhviashvili		23/03/93	A		(9)	1
Jhamal Rodríguez	PAN	28/01/95	M		(4)	
Vasyl Shtander	UKR	02/06/96	M	3	(7)	1
Carlos Small	PAN	13/03/95	A	2	(1)	3
Teimuraz Toboev	RUS	09/03/95	M		(3)	
Nika Tsereteli		17/04/94	D	1	(4)	1
Revaz Tsilosani		18/01/95	M		(1)	
Vano Tsilosani		14/02/94	M	14		4
Beka Zakradze		30/05/90	M	4	(5)	
Dmytro Zozulya	UKR	09/06/88	M	19		1

FC Kolkheti Poti

1913 • Evgrapi Shevardnadze, Lanchkhuti
(4,500); Erosi Manjgaladze, Samtredia (3,000);
Park Arena (2,800) • no website
Coach: Zaza Inashvili;
(04/10/15) Gela Sanaia

2015
14/08	a	Dila	L	0-2	
22/08	h	Sioni	L	0-1	
30/08	a	Dinamo Batumi	L	0-2	
12/09	h	Shukura	W	1-0	Keburia
20/09	a	Torpedo	L	0-1	
26/09	h	Sapovnela	L	0-1	
03/10	a	Tskhinvali	L	1-5	Gogonaia (p)
17/10	h	Lokomotivi	W	4-0	Koshkadze, N Sichinava, Gigauri 2
23/10	a	Chikhura	W	1-0	Gogonaia
31/10	h	Saburtalo	W	1-0	Gigauri
08/11	a	Dinamo Tbilisi	L	2-5	Tevzadze, Jishkariani
21/11	h	Merani	W	2-1	N Sichinava, Kukhaleishvili
28/11	a	Samtredia	L	0-1	
06/12	h	Zugdidi	D	0-0	
11/12	a	Guria	D	1-1	Kvaratskhelia

2016
19/02	h	Dila	L	0-1	
23/02	a	Sioni	L	1-3	Nikabadze
27/02	h	Dinamo Batumi	L	0-1	
06/03	a	Shukura	L	0-1	
13/03	h	Torpedo	W	2-0	Nikabadze, D Sichinava
19/03	a	Sapovnela	D	0-0	
02/04	a	Tskhinvali	D	0-0	
04/04	a	Lokomotivi	L	0-1	
11/04	h	Chikhura	W	2-0	Kvaratskhelia 2
17/04	a	Saburtalo	L	0-5	
24/04	h	Dinamo Tbilisi	L	1-3	Gogonaia (p)
30/04	a	Merani	D	1-1	og (Tsimakuridze)
08/05	h	Samtredia	L	0-3	
14/05	a	Zugdidi	L	1-2	Korobka
22/05	h	Guria	L	0-1	

Name	Nat	DoB	Pos	Aps	(s)	Gls
Konstantine Baramidze		12/01/91	M	1		
Temur Bechekhia		16/04/94	M		(1)	
Aliko Chakvetadze		26/03/95	D	28		
Lasha Dzagania		14/01/88	G	5		
Merab Gigauri		05/06/93	M	21	(3)	3
Omar Gogonaia		24/01/89	M	22	(4)	3
Mamuka Gongadze		25/11/85	A		(2)	
Tengiz Gorozia		21/01/96	M		(1)	
Amiran Gugushvili		02/06/95	M	1		
Guram Gureshidze		08/10/89	M	23	(2)	
Amberki Injibashvili	UKR	28/10/91	M		(1)	
Tamaz Jishkariani		13/03/93	A	22	(3)	1
Levan Kakulia		28/07/92	M	14	(6)	
Tedo Kakulia		26/09/92	D	10	(8)	
Iona Kalajishvili		22/07/96	M	1		
Tsotne Keburia		24/02/95	D	14	(5)	1
Giorgi Kilasonia		21/05/86	D	11	(1)	
Volodymyr Korobka	UKR	22/07/89	A	5		1
Aleksandre Koshkadze		04/12/81	M	11		1
Levan Kukhaleishvili		24/02/92	A	3	(5)	1
Gocha Kvaratskhelia		14/11/95	M	7	(12)	3
Giorgi Lemonjava		20/11/90	D	21	(1)	
Tsotne Meskhi		31/05/96	M		(1)	
Giorgi Nikabadze		10/01/91	A	10	(2)	2
Mykyta Polyulyakh	UKR	15/03/93	M	12	(11)	
Konstantine Sepiashvili		19/03/86	G	25		
Tornike Shalikashvili		24/10/90	D	3	(1)	
Aleksandre Shengelia		27/06/89	M	1	(3)	
Data Sichinava		21/03/89	M	9	(5)	1
Nika Sichinava		17/07/94	M	12	(2)	2
Zurab Tevzadze		28/08/94	D	21		1
Nika Tugushi		08/09/96	A	5	(7)	
Tornike Tukhareli		09/11/91	M	12	(2)	

FC Lokomotivi Tbilisi

1936 • Mikheil Meskhi (24,939) • fcloco.ge
Coach: Vasil Maisuradze;
(12/10/15) Gerard Zaragoza (ESP)

2015
13/08	a	Chikhura	L	0-1	
21/08	h	Dinamo Tbilisi	L	1-4	Diasamidze
30/08	a	Samtredia	L	2-3	Gavashelishvili, Kantaria
11/09	h	Guria	W	3-0	Chikhladze, Gavashelishvili, Kantaria
20/09	a	Sioni	L	0-1	
25/09	h	Shukura	D	0-0	
03/10	a	Sapovnela	L	1-2	Khidesheli
17/10	a	Kolkheti	L	0-4	
25/10	h	Saburtalo	W	3-2	Ubilava, Artmeladze, Benashvili
01/11	a	Merani	W	3-0	Kantaria 2, Artmeladze
06/11	h	Zugdidi	W	3-0	Kantaria, Khidesheli, Gavashelishvili
21/11	a	Dila	L	0-1	
27/11	h	Dinamo Batumi	D	1-1	Chikhladze
06/12	a	Torpedo	L	0-2	
11/12	h	Tskhinvali	L	0-1	

2016
19/02	h	Chikhura	D	2-2	Gavashelishvili, Kiknadze
23/02	a	Dinamo Tbilisi	L	1-2	Chiteishvili
27/02	h	Samtredia	L	0-1	
06/03	a	Guria	D	0-0	
11/03	h	Sioni	D	0-0	
18/03	a	Shukura	L	1-2	Chagelishvili
02/04	a	Sapovnela	D	0-0	
06/04	h	Kolkheti	W	1-0	Chagelishvili
11/04	a	Saburtalo	D	0-0	
15/04	h	Merani	D	1-1	Ubilava
23/04	a	Zugdidi	D	1-1	Diasamidze
30/04	h	Dila	L	0-2	
08/05	a	Dinamo Batumi	L	0-1	
13/05	h	Torpedo	L	1-2	Popkhadze
22/05	a	Tskhinvali	D	1-1	Gavashelishvili

Name	Nat	DoB	Pos	Aps	(s)	Gls
Rati Ardazishvili		27/01/98	M	6	(6)	
Shermadin Artmeladze		01/01/97	M	6	(2)	2
Vato Arveladze		04/03/98	M	1	(2)	
Aleksi Benashvili		20/03/89	M	14	(1)	1
David Chagelishvili		10/01/87	A	11		2
Nika Chanturia		19/01/95	D	7	(1)	
Demur Chikhladze		23/09/96	M	11	(7)	2
Revaz Chiteishvili		30/01/94	D	17	(1)	1
David Dartcimelia		28/01/95	A	2	(1)	
Giorgi Diasamidze		20/02/92	M	17	(4)	2
Giorgi Dumbadze		08/01/96	M	2	(1)	
Giorgi Gabadze		02/03/95	M	11	(2)	
Konstantine Gaganidze		03/02/94	D	8		
Mamia Gavashelishvili		08/01/95	A	12	(13)	5
Guram Getiashvili		07/03/90	D	26		
Giorgi Gvinashvili		02/08/97	M		(3)	
Zviad Kantaria		03/06/90	A	14	(7)	5
Giorgi Khidesheli		23/01/88	D	12		2
Luka Kikabidze		21/01/95	M	2	(4)	
Vaja Kikava		28/12/90	M	24	(1)	
Giorgi Kiknadze		27/09/97	A	5	(10)	1
Lazare Kupatadze		08/02/96	G	12		
Boris Makharadze		08/11/90	M	12		
Bacho Mikava		12/01/94	G	8		
Aleko Mzevashvili		10/03/95	M	9	(3)	
Giorgi Papuashvili		21/02/97	M	1	(1)	
Omar Patarkatsishvili		05/02/96	M		(2)	
Giorgi Popkhadze		25/09/86	D	13		1
David Samurkasovi		05/02/98	M	13	(3)	
Luka Sherozia		11/08/97	D		(1)	
Erekle Sultanishvili		11/07/94	M	13	(5)	
Giorgi Tekturmanidze		17/09/90	M	4	(5)	
Revaz Tevdoradze		14/02/88	G	10		
Bachana Tskhadadze		23/10/87	A	6	(1)	
David Ubilava		27/01/94	D	21		2

FC Merani Martvili

1936 • Murtaz Khurtsilava (3,000) • fcmerani.ge
Coach: Volodymyr Lobas (UKR); (21/09/15) (Galaktion Chubabria); (05/10/15) Badri Kvaratskhelia

2015
14/08	a	Torpedo	L	0-4
22/08	h	Tskhinvali	L	2-3 *Pachkoria, Gogolidze*
30/08	a	Chikhura	L	0-3
11/09	h	Dinamo Tbilisi	L	1-4 *Jgamaia*
20/09	a	Samtredia	L	0-4
26/09	h	Guria	W	2-0 *og (Kiladze), Ashortia*
04/10	a	Sioni	L	0-3
17/10	h	Shukura	L	1-2 *og (Bagaev)*
24/10	a	Sapovnela	L	1-2 *Jgamaia*
01/11	h	Lokomotivi	L	0-3
07/11	a	Saburtalo	L	2-4 *Broladze, Jgamaia*
21/11	h	Kolkheti	L	1-2 *Gogolidze*
28/11	h	Zugdidi	D	0-0
07/12	a	Dila	L	0-2
12/12	h	Dinamo Batumi	L	0-4

2016
19/02	h	Torpedo	W	2-1 *Khabelashvili 2*
23/02	a	Tskhinvali	D	1-1 *Khabelashvili*
27/02	h	Chikhura	W	3-2 *Sabanadze 2, Goguadze*
06/03	a	Dinamo Tbilisi	L	0-2
13/03	h	Samtredia	L	2-3 *Jikia, og (Shergelashvili)*
19/03	a	Guria	D	0-0
02/04	a	Sioni	D	1-1 *Giorgadze*
06/04	a	Shukura	D	0-0
10/04	h	Sapovnela	W	2-0 *Sabanadze 2*
15/04	a	Lokomotivi	D	1-1 *Sabanadze*
23/04	a	Saburtalo	L	2-5 *Chimakadze 2*
30/04	h	Kolkheti	D	1-1 *Tsimakuridze*
08/05	a	Zugdidi	L	0-3
14/05	h	Dila	W	3-2 *Ugulava, Khabelashvili (p), Jikia*
22/05	a	Dinamo Batumi	D	0-0

Name	Nat	DoB	Pos	Aps	(s)	Gls
Imeda Ashortia		01/01/96	A	7	(14)	1
Konstantine Broladze		22/01/89	M	4	(2)	1
Besik Chimakadze		24/06/88	A	8	(1)	2
Teimuraz Chkhetia		26/05/97	D	3	(1)	
Gaga Gazdeliani		13/10/97	M	6	(3)	
Giorgi Gegia		25/08/95	M	21	(3)	
Andro Giorgadze		03/05/96	D	15		1
Vasil Gogolidze		25/01/95	M	4	(6)	2
Zaur Goguadze		12/08/96	M	6	(5)	1
Shota Gvazava		26/10/92	M	7	(2)	
Lasha Jgamaia		03/10/95	M	17	(4)	3
Shota Jikia		30/12/84	M	14		2
Evgeni Kajaia		20/04/96	M		(1)	
Ivane Khabelashvili		04/09/93	M	12	(1)	4
Pavle Khorguashvili		13/08/87	M	6	(1)	
Giorgi Khubua		19/04/93	M	5		
Nodar Kiknavelidze		25/04/93	M	6	(8)	
Levan Kutalia		19/07/89	M	9		
Zurab Mamaladze		10/02/82	G	15		
Piruz Marakvelidze		21/01/95	D	5		
Kichi Meliava		14/04/92	D	13		
Sergi Orbeladze		01/05/82	D	10		
Giorgi Pachkoria		29/05/89	D	4		1
Tornike Pailodze		05/03/94	M	4	(4)	
Alexandros Papadopoulos	GRE	07/09/84	M	9	(3)	
Mikheil Rukhaia		23/08/96	M	8	(3)	
Nikoloz Sabanadze		02/05/91	A	13	(1)	5
Petr Sevostyanenko	RUS	08/02/92	G	8		
Givi Shalamberidze		25/11/95	M	4		
Tornike Shalikashvili		24/10/90	D	8	(1)	
Aleksandre Shengelia		27/06/89	M	1	(3)	
Benjamin Teidi	NGA	05/05/94	M	14		
Tengiz Tolordava		19/10/99	M		(1)	
Beka Tsikolia		28/02/94	M	1	(5)	
Giorgi Tsimakuridze		10/11/83	D	11		1
David Tsitskhvaia		30/11/83	A	13		
Irakli Tsitskhvaia		28/01/95	D	13	(3)	
Akaki Tskarozia		02/08/88	M	6	(1)	
Levan Tsotsonava		12/02/97	M	4	(2)	
Giga Tsursumia		14/04/97	M	4	(2)	
Jaba Ugulava		08/04/92	A	5	(1)	1
Tornike Zarkua		01/09/90	G	7		

FC Saburtalo Tbilisi

1999 • Bendela (650); Mikheil Meskhi reserve pitch (2,000) • fcsaburtalo.ge
Coach: Giorgi Chiabrishvili; (10/03/16) Pablo Franco (ESP)

2015
13/08	a	Tskhinvali	W	2-1 *Goshteliani, Kharaishvili (p)*
22/08	h	Chikhura	W	1-0 *Goshteliani*
29/08	a	Dinamo Tbilisi	L	0-4
12/09	h	Samtredia	W	3-2 *Kharaishvili, Margvelashvili, og (Tebidze)*
20/09	a	Guria	D	0-0
25/09	h	Sioni	L	2-3 *Sabanadze, Dvali*
04/10	a	Shukura	L	0-1
16/10	h	Sapovnela	W	2-1 *Iashvili, Goshteliani*
25/10	a	Lokomotivi	L	2-3 *Altunashvili, Goshteliani*
31/10	a	Kolkheti	L	0-1
07/11	h	Merani	W	4-2 *Sabanadze, Goshteliani, Pantsulaia 2*
22/11	h	Zugdidi	W	1-0 *Kokhreidze*
29/11	h	Dila	L	1-3 *Dvali*
06/12	a	Dinamo Batumi	L	1-2 *Kharaishvili*
12/12	h	Torpedo	D	4-4 *Kharaishvili, Kokhreidze 2, Gvaradze*

2016
19/02	h	Tskhinvali	D	2-2 *Kharaishvili, Pantsulaia*
23/02	a	Chikhura	L	0-5
27/02	h	Dinamo Tbilisi	L	0-4
07/03	a	Samtredia	L	2-8 *Tsatskrialashvili, Kharaishvili*
13/03	h	Guria	W	4-2 *Kharaishvili 3 (1p), Khorkheli*
18/03	a	Sioni	D	0-0
02/04	h	Shukura	W	3-2 *Pantsulaia 2, Tsatskrialashvili*
06/04	a	Sapovnela	D	0-0
11/04	h	Lokomotivi	D	0-0
17/04	h	Kolkheti	W	5-0 *Goshteliani 2, Pantsulaia, Kharaishvili (p), Tsatskrialashvili*
23/04	a	Merani	W	5-2 *Rukhadze, Goshteliani 2, Kharaishvili, Tsatskrialashvili*
30/04	a	Zugdidi	W	1-0 *Kharaishvili*
08/05	a	Dila	L	1-2 *Pantsulaia*
14/05	h	Dinamo Batumi	L	1-2 *Tsatskrialashvili*
22/05	a	Torpedo	L	0-5

Name	Nat	DoB	Pos	Aps	(s)	Gls
Sandro Altunashvili		14/01/97	M	18	(6)	1
Tera Alwyn	KEN	18/01/97	M	12	(3)	
Irakli Bidzinashvili		27/02/87	M	15	(10)	
Omar Bulukhadze		04/03/98	D	1	(1)	
Grigol Chabradze		20/04/96	D	15	(1)	
Temur Chogadze		05/05/98	M		(2)	
Jaba Dvali		08/02/85	A	7	(1)	2
Otar Goshadze		13/01/97	G	10		
Guram Goshteliani		05/01/97	M	26	(3)	9
Beka Gvaradze		11/08/97	M	8	(10)	1
Nodar Iashvili		24/01/93	D	20	(2)	1
Giorgi Kharaishvili		29/07/96	M	24	(1)	12
Giorgi Khorkheli		05/01/96	M	4	(4)	1
Giorgi Kokhreidze		18/11/98	M	9	(13)	3
Beka Kurdadze		24/01/97	G	16	(1)	
Luka Lakvekheliani		20/10/98	M	1		
Vladimer Mamuchashvili		28/08/97	M	16	(6)	
Gagi Margvelashvili		30/10/96	D	24		1
Tornike Muzashvili		25/07/98	M		(1)	
Tsotne Nadaraia		21/02/97	D	6	(3)	
Beka Nikolashvili		09/06/98	D	1		
Giorgi Pantsulaia		06/01/94	A	22	(5)	7
Irakli Rukhadze		28/10/96	M	6	(7)	1
Nikoloz Sabanadze		02/05/91	A	10		2
Luka Sanikidze		19/11/98	G	4	(1)	
Andro Sopromadze		25/03/93	M	20	(2)	
Lasha Totadze		24/08/88	D	26		
Rati Tsatskrialashvili		11/10/93	M	9	(5)	5
Mikheil Vacharadze		09/11/97	D		(1)	

FC Samtredia

1936 • Erosi Manjgaladze (3,000) • fcsamtredia.com
Coach: Gia Tsetsadze

2015
14/08	h	Shukura	W	2-0 *Sikharulidze 2*
22/08	a	Sapovnela	W	3-2 *Sikharulidze 2, Jikia*
30/08	h	Lokomotivi	W	3-2 *Zivzivadze, Endeladze, Rajamashvili*
12/09	a	Saburtalo	L	2-3 *Tsnobiladze, Tsintsadze*
20/09	h	Merani	W	4-0 *Zivzivadze 2, Markozashvili, Jikia*
26/09	a	Zugdidi	D	3-3 *Datunaishvili, Endeladze, Sikharulidze*
03/10	h	Dila	W	5-0 *Zivzivadze, Sandokhadze, Endeladze 2, Sikharulidze*
17/10	a	Dinamo Batumi	L	0-2
23/10	h	Torpedo	W	3-1 *Endeladze, Zivzivadze, Jikia*
01/11	a	Tskhinvali	L	0-1
08/11	h	Chikhura	L	0-1
21/11	a	Dinamo Tbilisi	L	1-3 *Zivzivadze*
28/11	h	Kolkheti	W	1-0 *Jikia*
06/12	h	Guria	W	3-1 *Sikharulidze 3*
12/12	a	Sioni	W	2-0 *Sikharulidze, Zivzivadze*

2016
19/02	a	Shukura	D	1-1 *Zivzivadze*
23/02	h	Sapovnela	W	3-0 *Zivzivadze, Markozashvili, Jikia*
27/02	a	Lokomotivi	W	1-0 *Zivzivadze*
07/03	h	Saburtalo	W	8-2 *Shergelashvili 2, Tsnobiladze, Jikia, Ioseliani, Zivzivadze 2, Datunaishvili*
13/03	a	Merani	W	3-2 *Rajamashvili, Sikharulidze 2*
18/03	h	Zugdidi	W	2-0 *Shergelashvili 2*
02/04	a	Dila	W	2-1 *Jikia, Rajamashvili*
06/04	h	Dinamo Batumi	W	2-0 *Zivzivadze, Jikia*
10/04	a	Torpedo	L	1-2 *Zivzivadze*
17/04	h	Tskhinvali	W	2-1 *Sikharulidze, Zivzivadze*
24/04	a	Chikhura	D	1-1 *Ioseliani*
30/04	a	Dinamo Tbilisi	W	2-1 *Ioseliani, Jikia*
08/05	a	Kolkheti	W	3-0 *Datunaishvili 2, Zivzivadze*
14/05	a	Guria	W	2-0 *Sandokhadze, Datunaishvili*
22/05	h	Sioni	L	1-2 *Endeladze*

Name	Nat	DoB	Pos	Aps	(s)	Gls
Giorgi Akhaladze		26/07/97	M		(7)	
Giorgi Cheishvili		16/01/96	M		(1)	
Giorgi Datunaishvili		09/02/85	M	25	(1)	5
Avtandil Endeladze		17/09/94	M	24	(4)	6
Jemal Gogiashvili		06/05/88	D	28	(1)	
Givi Ioseliani		25/10/90	D	7	(10)	3
David Jikia		10/01/95	A	15	(13)	9
Shota Kerdzevadze		10/03/93	M	2	(2)	
Aleksandre Kvaratskhelia		21/02/94	M		(2)	
Teimuraz Markozashvili		09/08/94	M	19	(8)	2
Giorgi Mchedlishvili		18/01/92	D	20	(5)	
Kakhaber Meshveliani		14/04/92	G	10	(1)	
Omar Migineishvili		02/06/84	G	13		
David Mtivlishvili		26/10/94	D	12	(5)	
David Rajamashvili		28/10/88	M	25	(3)	3
Nika Sandokhadze		20/02/94	D	19	(3)	2
Lasha Shergelashvili		17/01/92	D	29		4
Irakli Sikharulidze		18/07/92	A	19	(10)	13
Gabriel Tebidze		10/11/94	G	7		
Bidzina Tsintsadze		04/06/89	D	5	(1)	1
Dachi Tsnobiladze		28/01/94	D	24	(2)	2
Budu Zivzivadze		10/03/94	A	27	(2)	16

FC Sapovnela Terjola

1936 • Ramaz Shengelia, Kutaisi (11,800);
David Abashidze, Zestafoni (5,000) • no website
Coach: Mamuka Khundadze;
(15/01/16) Zviad Jeladze;
(04/03/16) Mamuka Khundadze

2015

14/08	a	Dinamo Tbilisi	L	0-4	
22/08	h	Samtredia	L	2-3	Shugladze, Bukhaidze (p)
30/08	a	Guria	L	0-3	
12/09	h	Sioni	D	0-0	
20/09	a	Shukura	L	0-4	
26/09	a	Kolkheti	L	0-3	
03/10	h	Lokomotivi	W	2-1	Bukhaidze, Tkeshelashvili
16/10	a	Saburtalo	L	1-2	Bukhaidze
24/10	h	Merani	W	2-1	Tkeshelashvili, Bukhaidze
01/11	a	Zugdidi	L	1-2	Jimsheleishvili
07/11	h	Dila	L	1-5	Ambroladze
21/11	a	Dinamo Batumi	L	0-1	
28/11	h	Torpedo	L	1-5	Bukhaidze
06/12	a	Tskhinvali	L	0-3	
12/12	h	Chikhura	L	0-2	

2016

19/02	h	Dinamo Tbilisi	L	1-2	Chikviladze
23/02	a	Samtredia	L	0-3	
27/02	h	Guria	L	0-2	
06/03	a	Sioni	L	1-4	Bukhaidze
13/03	h	Shukura	W	2-0	Narimanidze, Bukhaidze
19/03	h	Kolkheti	D	0-0	
02/04	a	Lokomotivi	D	0-0	
06/04	h	Saburtalo	D	0-0	
10/04	a	Merani	L	0-2	
17/04	h	Zugdidi	D	2-2	Bukhaidze 2
23/04	a	Dila	L	1-3	Bukhaidze
30/04	h	Dinamo Batumi	W	2-1	Bukhaidze (p), Tkeshelashvili
08/05	a	Torpedo	L	1-4	Bukhaidze
14/05	h	Tskhinvali	W	2-1	Bibileishvili, Bukhaidze (p)
22/05	a	Chikhura	L	2-3	Bukhaidze 2 (1p)

Name	Nat	DoB	Pos	Aps	(s)	Gls
Zurab Abesadze		30/06/94	M	3	(6)	
Zurab Abuladze		20/03/94	A		(1)	
Giorgi Alavidze		01/07/94	M	2	(6)	
Giga Ambroladze		28/12/90	A	14		1
Ushangi Bandzeladze		09/02/93	D	16	(11)	
David Beruashvili		21/09/89	D	18	(2)	
Giorgi Bibileishvili		29/05/89	M	1	(5)	
David Bolkvadze		05/06/80	M	10	(1)	
Giorgi Bukhaidze		09/12/91	A	21	(9)	15
Anzor Butskhrikidze		20/05/88	D	2		
Lasha Chelidze		13/03/85	D	5	(2)	
Tengiz Chikviladze		12/08/83	D	10	(2)	1
Jaba Dvali		08/02/85	A	9		
Zurab Endeladze		23/04/91	D	26	(1)	
Aleksandre Giorgadze		02/03/92	G	17		
Bakur Gulua		27/04/95	M	5		
Avtandil Jikhvadze		30/08/95	M	2		
Tornike Jimsheleishvili		04/10/92	M	15		1
Irakli Katamadze		25/02/93	M	12		
Aleksandre Koshkadze		04/12/81	M	2		
Revaz Machavariani		12/02/93	D	1	(1)	
Giorgi Makaridze		15/07/95	M	24	(4)	
Giorgi Mikaberidze		14/09/88	M	3	(4)	
Vepkhvia Muradashvili		10/03/92	M	4	(7)	
Giorgi Narimanidze		25/11/93	D	12		1
David Odikadze		14/04/81	D	15		
Mirian Robakidze		14/03/95	D	13		
Nikoloz Shalamberidze		25/06/94	D	7	(4)	
Levan Sharikadze		16/07/89	M	5	(3)	
Sandro Shugladze	UKR	24/10/90	A	4	(4)	1
Giorgi Somkhishvili		27/10/80	G	13		
Saba Tavadze	UKR	14/02/93	D		(4)	
Giorgi Tkeshelashvili		24/01/90	A	22	(4)	3
Shalva Tskipurishvili		15/01/92	M	9	(3)	
Mikheil Vacharadze		09/11/97	D	8		
Vladimer Zeinklishvili		18/11/93	M		(2)	

FC Shukura Kobuleti

1936 • Chele Arena (3,800) • no website
Coach: Gela Sanaia;
(27/08/15) (Avtandil Namgaladze);
(01/09/15) Teimuraz Shalamberidze

2015

14/08	a	Samtredia	L	0-2	
22/08	h	Guria	W	2-1	Tsikaridze 2
30/08	a	Sioni	L	0-2	
12/09	a	Kolkheti	L	0-1	
20/09	h	Sapovnela	W	4-0	Guguchia, Tsikaridze, Chelebadze, Gegechkori
25/09	a	Lokomotivi	D	0-0	
04/10	h	Saburtalo	W	1-0	Chelebadze
17/10	a	Merani	W	2-1	Chelebadze, Lobjanidze
23/10	h	Zugdidi	W	2-1	Chelebadze (p), Lobjanidze
01/11	a	Dila	W	3-1	Chelebadze (p), Uridia 2
07/11	h	Dinamo Batumi	L	0-1	
21/11	a	Torpedo	D	0-0	
28/11	h	Tskhinvali	D	2-2	Lobjanidze 2
06/12	a	Chikhura	L	0-1	
12/12	h	Dinamo Tbilisi	L	1-3	Chelebadze

2016

19/02	h	Samtredia	D	1-1	Dolidze
23/02	a	Guria	D	0-0	
27/02	h	Sioni	D	0-0	
06/03	h	Kolkheti	W	1-0	Lobjanidze
13/03	a	Sapovnela	L	0-2	
17/03	h	Lokomotivi	W	2-1	Mosiashvili, Lobjanidze
02/04	a	Saburtalo	L	2-3	Uridia, Apakidze
06/04	h	Merani	D	0-0	
10/04	a	Zugdidi	L	0-3	
17/04	h	Dila	W	1-0	Lobjanidze
23/04	a	Dinamo Batumi	D	2-2	Tarkhnishvili (p), og (Shonia)
30/04	h	Torpedo	L	2-3	Malania, Mosiashvili
08/05	a	Tskhinvali	L	0-5	
14/05	h	Chikhura	L	0-2	
22/05	a	Dinamo Tbilisi	L	0-1	

Name	Nat	DoB	Pos	Aps	(s)	Gls
Nika Apakidze		04/04/92	D	12		1
Alan Bagaev	RUS	07/04/91	D	12		
Archil Bajelidze		07/04/86	D	5		
Avtandil Brachuli		02/04/92	D	6	(5)	
Roman Chachua		01/01/97	M	2	(2)	
Lasha Chaladze		05/11/87	D	23	(1)	
Giorgi Chanukvadze		07/03/95	M	1	(5)	
Giga Cheishvili		17/09/93	D	9		
Giorgi Chelebadze		01/01/92	M	14		6
Grigol Dolidze		25/10/82	M	17	(8)	1
Azamat Dzhioev	RUS	06/01/91	G	24		
Levan Gegechkori		05/06/94	M	26		1
Revaz Getsadze		11/01/85	M	13	(7)	
Luka Guguchia		10/12/91	M	3		1
Levan Ingorokva		08/07/94	M	4	(6)	
Mikheil Kakaladze		06/06/82	A	1	(6)	
Teimuraz Kakaladze		06/05/88	G	5		
Giorgi Kalandadze		02/07/85	M	2	(1)	
Ilia Kerdzevadze		19/01/96	A	8	(4)	
Irakli Komakhidze		26/03/97	M	16	(1)	
Merab Kopaliani		31/03/92	A		(3)	
Elguja Lobjanidze		17/09/92	A	21	(7)	7
Zurab Malania		07/10/96	D	13		1
Tornike Mosiashvili		07/10/96	M	11	(2)	2
Adrian Pukanych	UKR	22/06/83	M	21		
Levan Sharikadze		16/07/89	M	6	(3)	
Ilia Sturua		09/12/95	G	1	(1)	
Irakli Takidze		01/02/96	M	1	(3)	
Tornike Tarkhnishvili		30/06/90	D	27		1
Tengiz Tsikaridze		21/12/95	M	8	(1)	3
Albert Tskhovrebov	RUS	01/05/93	D	7		
Merab Uridia		07/04/93	A	11	(12)	3

FC Sioni Bolnisi

1936 • Teimuraz Stepania (3,500) •
fcsionibolnisi.com
Major honours
Georgian League (1) 2006
Coach: Varlam Kilasonia;
(14/04/16) Armaz Jeladze

2015

14/08	a	Guria	D	1-1	Tatanashvili
22/08	a	Kolkheti	W	1-0	Shalamberidze (p)
30/08	h	Shukura	W	2-0	Tatanashvili, og (Bajelidze)
12/09	a	Sapovnela	D	0-0	
20/09	h	Lokomotivi	W	1-0	Svanidze
25/09	a	Saburtalo	W	3-2	Svanidze, Isiani 2
04/10	h	Merani	W	3-0	Tatanashvili 2, Ugulava
23/10	h	Dila	L	0-1	
01/11	a	Dinamo Batumi	W	5-3	Tatanashvili 3, Isiani, Svanidze
08/11	h	Torpedo	W	6-2	Isiani 2, Manjgaladze, Tatanashvili, Ugulava (p), Vasadze
14/11	a	Zugdidi	W	3-1	Shalamberidze, Vasadze, Isiani
22/11	a	Tskhinvali	L	0-2	
28/11	h	Chikhura	W	4-0	Isiani (p), V Kilasonia, Razmadze, Kobakhidze
06/12	a	Dinamo Tbilisi	L	2-5	Vasadze, V Kilasonia (p)
12/12	h	Samtredia	L	0-2	

2016

19/02	h	Guria	D	1-1	V Kilasonia (p)
23/02	h	Kolkheti	W	3-1	Tatanashvili 2 (1p), Goginashvili
27/02	a	Shukura	D	0-0	
06/03	h	Sapovnela	W	4-1	Razmadze, Tatanashvili 2, Kobakhidze
11/03	a	Lokomotivi	D	0-0	
18/03	h	Saburtalo	D	0-0	
02/04	a	Merani	D	1-1	Manjgaladze
06/04	h	Zugdidi	W	3-1	Kobakhidze 2, Luís Alberto
10/04	a	Dila	L	1-2	Kobakhidze
16/04	h	Dinamo Batumi	W	1-0	Kobakhidze
24/04	a	Torpedo	L	0-1	
30/04	h	Tskhinvali	L	1-3	Tatanashvili (p)
09/05	a	Chikhura	D	1-1	Vasadze
14/05	h	Dinamo Tbilisi	L	1-2	Skubuliani
22/05	a	Samtredia	W	2-1	Tatanashvili, og (Gogiashvili)

Name	Nat	DoB	Pos	Aps	(s)	Gls
Soso Chikaidze		22/07/87	A		(1)	
Giorgi Gaprindashvili		06/05/95	M	28	(1)	
Guram Giorbelidze		25/02/96	D	7	(2)	
Irakli Goginashvili		29/03/94	M	6	(3)	1
Aleksandre Gogoberishvili		22/07/77	M	19	(4)	
Aleksandre Gureshidze		23/04/95	D	7		
Lasha Gvalia		06/10/91	M	10	(3)	
Vili Isiani		22/03/91	A	12	(2)	7
Zurab Japiashvili		26/05/96	D	16		
Lasha Jincharashvili		19/02/96	M	1	(1)	
Giorgi Kilasonia		04/05/96	M		(1)	
Varlam Kilasonia		04/05/96	D	16	(2)	3
Otar Kobakhidze		29/02/96	A	10	(11)	6
Luís Alberto	POR	12/10/91	A	6	(5)	1
Lasha Managadze		11/11/94	D	1	(3)	
Giuly Manjgaladze	UKR	09/09/92	M	24	(1)	2
Mirza Merlani		05/10/80	G	23		
Archil Meskhi		02/11/95	M		(1)	
Giorgi Mikaberidze		14/09/88	M	2	(7)	
Papuna Mosemgvdlishvili		27/04/94	D	1		
Soslan Naniev	RUS	08/12/89	G	7		
Giorgi Otarishvili		12/12/90	D		(1)	
Dachi Popkhadze		27/01/84	D	24		
Luka Razmadze		30/12/83	M	23	(1)	2
David Sajaia		23/08/93	D	15	(7)	
Koba Shalamberidze		15/10/84	M	9	(9)	2
Akaki Shulaia		06/09/96	M	3	(1)	
Mindia Skubuliani		23/07/96	A		(1)	1
David Svanidze		14/10/79	D	23	(1)	3
Dimitri Tatanashvili		19/10/83	A	25	(2)	14
Jaba Ugulava		08/04/92	A	2	(10)	2
Giorgi Vasadze		14/06/89	M	10	(7)	4

FC Torpedo Kutaisi

1946 • Ramaz Shengelia (11,880) •
fctorpedo.ge
Major honours
*Georgian League (3) 2000, 2001, 2002; Georgian
Cup (2) 1999, 2001*
**Coach: Giorgi Daraselia;
(05/10/15) Olexandr Shtelin (UKR)**

2015
14/08	h	Merani	W	4-0	*Odikadze (p), Klimiashvili, Kvernadze, Kapanadze*
22/08	a	Zugdidi	D	1-1	*Sichinava*
30/08	h	Dila	L	0-2	
12/09	a	Dinamo Batumi	D	1-1	*Kimadze*
20/09	h	Kolkheti	W	1-0	*Kukhianidze*
26/09	a	Tskhinvali	L	1-3	*Sichinava*
04/10	a	Chikhura	L	0-3	
17/10	h	Dinamo Tbilisi	D	1-1	*Sichinava*
23/10	a	Samtredia	L	1-3	*Klimiashvili*
01/11	h	Guria	W	2-1	*Klimiashvili, Kapanadze*
08/11	a	Sioni	L	2-6	*Kapanadze, Shindagoridze*
21/11	h	Shukura	D	0-0	
28/11	h	Sapovnela	W	5-1	*Kukhianidze, Bregvadze, Shindagoridze 2 (1p), Sichinava*
06/12	h	Lokomotivi	W	2-0	*Shindagoridze, Kvernadze*
12/12	a	Saburtalo	D	4-4	*Shindagoridze 2, Kukhianidze, Sichinava*

2016
19/02	a	Merani	L	1-2	*Mamasakhlisi*
23/02	h	Zugdidi	W	2-0	*Kimadze, Kapanadze*
27/02	a	Dila	W	1-0	*Kapanadze*
06/03	h	Dinamo Batumi	W	1-0	*Kapanadze*
13/03	a	Kolkheti	L	1-2	
18/03	h	Tskhinvali	D	0-0	
02/04	h	Chikhura	L	0-2	
06/04	a	Dinamo Tbilisi	L	1-2	*Kukhianidze (p)*
10/04	h	Samtredia	W	2-1	*Kapanadze, Tabatadze*
17/04	a	Guria	L	2-3	*Kapanadze, Adamadze*
24/04	h	Sioni	W	1-0	*Kukhianidze*
30/04	a	Shukura	W	3-2	*Kukhianidze (p), Tabatadze, Kvernadze*
08/05	a	Sapovnela	W	4-1	*Mirtskhulava, Nergadze, Kvaratskhelia, Shindagoridze*
13/05	a	Lokomotivi	W	2-1	*Tugushi, Kukhianidze*
22/05	h	Saburtalo	W	5-0	*Mamasakhlisi, Babunashvili, Klimiashvili, Kapanadze, Purtskhvanidze*

Name	Nat	DoB	Pos	Aps	(s)	Gls
Guram Adamadze		31/08/88	D	11		1
Shota Babunashvili		17/11/80	M	12	(9)	1
Tengiz Bregvadze		15/03/95	M	11	(4)	1
Anri Chichinadze		26/08/97	D	19	(2)	
Zaur Goguadze		12/08/96	M	4		
Giorgi Kakhelishvili		22/05/87	M	5	(1)	
Tornike Kapanadze		04/06/92	A	20	(5)	9
Tariel Khaindrava		12/04/95	G	1	(1)	
Giorgi Kimadze		11/02/92	D	25	(3)	2
David Kirkitadze		03/09/92	M	8	(2)	
Irakli Klimiashvili		30/05/88	M	26	(2)	4
Giorgi Kukhianidze		01/07/92	M	24	(1)	7
Vakhtang Kvaratskhelia		30/03/88	A		(5)	1
Roin Kvaskhvadze		31/05/89	G	11		
Otar Kvernadze		10/09/93	M	11	(3)	3
Maksime Kvilitaia		17/09/85	G	4		
Oleg Mamasakhlisi		25/11/95	D	21	(4)	2
Bakar Mirtskhulava		24/05/92	D	12	(1)	1
Giorgi Nergadze		20/08/82	M	19	(3)	1
Andrei Nikonov	RUS	12/12/94	D	1	(2)	
David Odikadze		14/04/81	D	6	(2)	1
Zurab Pantskhava		10/12/96	D	2	(1)	
Shalva Purtskhvanidze		22/09/97	M	1	(10)	1
Gabriel Sagrishvili		17/06/98	M	7	(2)	
Lasha Shindagoridze		30/01/93	A	12	(12)	7
Data Sichinava		21/03/89	M	9	(5)	5
Giorgi Somkhishvili		27/10/80	G	2		
Vaja Tabatadze		01/02/91	D	22	(1)	2
Revaz Tevdoradze		14/02/88	G	12	(1)	
Vano Tsilosani		09/11/95	A	4	(2)	
Beka Tugushi		24/01/89	A	8	(6)	1

FC Tskhinvali

2007 • Mikheil Meskhi reserve pitch,
Tbilisi (2,000) • fcspartak.ge
Coach: Kakhi Kacharava

2015
13/08	h	Saburtalo	L	1-2	*Tsatskrialashvili*
22/08	a	Merani	W	3-2	*Kacharava 2, Maisashvili*
30/08	h	Zugdidi	W	5-1	*Kacharava 2, Lekvtadze, Tsertsvadze, Makharoblidze*
12/09	a	Dila	L	0-3	
20/09	h	Dinamo Batumi	W	3-2	*Bachiashvili, Kakubava, Lekvtadze*
26/09	a	Torpedo	W	3-1	*Lekvtadze, Kacharava 2*
03/10	h	Kolkheti	W	5-1	*Maisashvili, Lobjanidze, Makharoblidze, Kacharava 2*
18/10	h	Chikhura	D	1-1	*Bachiashvili*
23/10	a	Dinamo Tbilisi	L	1-2	*Ivanishvili*
01/11	h	Samtredia	W	1-0	*Lekvtadze*
08/11	a	Guria	W	2-1	*Kakubava, Kacharava*
22/11	h	Sioni	W	2-0	*Gorgiashvili, Ivanishvili*
28/11	a	Shukura	D	2-2	*Kacharava, Ivanishvili*
06/12	h	Sapovnela	W	3-0	*Kacharava 3*
11/12	a	Lokomotivi	W	1-0	*Maisashvili*

2016
19/02	a	Saburtalo	D	2-2	*Ivanishvili, Gorgiashvili (p)*
23/02	h	Merani	D	1-1	*Kochladze*
27/02	a	Zugdidi	D	1-1	*Lekvtadze*
06/03	h	Dila	D	0-0	
13/03	a	Dinamo Batumi	L	0-2	
18/03	h	Torpedo	D	0-0	
02/04	a	Kolkheti	D	0-0	
06/04	a	Chikhura	L	1-2	*Kochladze*
10/04	h	Dinamo Tbilisi	L	2-4	*Gorgiashvili (p), Bechvaia*
17/04	a	Samtredia	L	1-2	*Gabrichidze*
23/04	h	Guria	D	0-0	
30/04	a	Sioni	W	3-1	*Isiani, Kochladze, Lobjanidze*
08/05	h	Shukura	W	5-0	*Isiani, Kakubava, Ivanishvili 2 (1p), Gabrichidze*
14/05	a	Sapovnela	L	1-2	*Isiani*
22/05	h	Lokomotivi	D	1-1	*Lekvtadze*

Name	Nat	DoB	Pos	Aps	(s)	Gls
Vasiko Bachiashvili		04/11/92	D	13	(3)	2
Giga Bechvaia		29/08/86	M	13	(10)	1
David Bolkvadze		05/06/80	M		(1)	
Ucha Burdzenadze		23/04/93	D		(10)	
Marat Butuev	KAZ	08/05/92	D	2	(1)	
Levan Chapodze		21/10/88	D	2	(1)	
Soslanbek Dzagoev	RUS	12/02/98	M		(1)	
Nikoloz Gabrichidze		16/09/97	M	1	(3)	2
Merab Gigauri		05/06/93	M		(2)	
Tornike Gorgiashvili		27/04/88	M	21	(1)	3
Vili Isiani		22/03/91	A	7	(5)	3
Giorgi Ivanishvili		18/10/89	A	29		6
Lasha Japaridze		16/04/85	D	20	(3)	
Nikoloz Jishkariani		04/06/90	D		(7)	
Nika Kacharava		13/01/94	A	15	(2)	13
Levan Kakubava		15/10/90	D	27		3
Bakar Kardava		04/10/94	M	27		
Lasha Kochladze		22/08/95	M	23	(1)	3
Irakli Lekvtadze		30/08/91	M	24	(4)	6
Zviad Lobjanidze		19/04/90	M	7	(12)	2
David Maisashvili		18/02/89	D	26		3
Bidzina Makharoblidze		10/10/92	M	15	(5)	2
Giorgi Nadiradze		14/03/92	G	30		
Nika Nozadze		01/10/94	D	4		
Ilia Shengelia		06/06/96	M		(1)	
Akaki Shulaia		06/09/96	M		(10)	
Rati Tsatskrialashvili		11/10/93	M	6	(1)	1
Giorgi Tsertsvadze		15/11/89	D	18	(1)	1

FC Zugdidi

2005 • Baia (1,000); Central, Zeda Etseri (1,800)
• fczugdidi.ge
**Coach: Besik Sherozia;
(15/11/15) Levan Mikadze;
(12/01/16) Yuriy Bakalov (UKR);
(26/04/16) Levan Mikadze**

2015
14/08	a	Dinamo Batumi	L	0-5	
22/08	h	Torpedo	D	1-1	*G Samushia (p)*
30/08	a	Tskhinvali	L	1-5	*Tsurtsumia*
12/09	h	Chikhura	L	1-4	*G Samushia (p)*
20/09	a	Dinamo Tbilisi	L	1-3	*T Samushia*
26/09	h	Samtredia	D	3-3	*Bulia 2, Tsurtsumia (p)*
10/10	a	Guria	L	0-2	
23/10	a	Shukura	L	1-2	*Narmania*
01/11	h	Sapovnela	W	2-1	*Tutberidze, Tsurtsumia (p)*
06/11	a	Lokomotivi	L	0-3	
14/11	h	Sioni	L	1-3	*Tskarozia*
22/11	a	Saburtalo	L	0-1	
28/11	a	Merani	D	0-0	
06/12	a	Kolkheti	D	0-0	
12/12	h	Dila	D	1-1	*Narmania*

2016
19/02	h	Dinamo Batumi	L	0-1	
23/02	a	Torpedo	L	0-2	
27/02	h	Tskhinvali	D	1-1	*Kovalenko*
06/03	a	Chikhura	L	0-4	
12/03	h	Dinamo Tbilisi	L	2-3	*S Malania, Shevel*
18/03	a	Samtredia	L	0-2	
02/04	h	Guria	W	3-2	*Gagoshidze, Tsurtsumia, Chanturia*
06/04	a	Sioni	L	1-3	*Chukwurah*
10/04	h	Shukura	W	3-0	*og (Kalandadze), G Samushia (p), og (Pukanych)*
17/04	a	Sapovnela	D	2-2	*Tsurtsumia 2 (1p)*
23/04	h	Lokomotivi	D	1-1	*Tkemaladze*
30/04	a	Saburtalo	L	0-1	
08/05	h	Merani	W	3-0	*G Samushia 3 (1p)*
14/05	a	Kolkheti	W	2-1	*G Samushia 2 (1p)*
22/05	a	Dila	L	0-3	

Name	Nat	DoB	Pos	Aps	(s)	Gls
Giorgi Bulia		06/05/94	M	9	(4)	2
Giorgi Chanadiri		01/07/95	M	11	(3)	
Murtaz Changelia		26/06/92	M		(3)	
Paata Chanturia		13/02/94	D		(1)	1
Serhiy Chebotarev	UKR	26/03/91	M	5	(3)	
Raphael Chukwurah	NGA	17/05/92	D	14		1
Zaal Eliava		02/01/85	D	2	(1)	
Malkhaz Gagoshidze		20/02/93	D	16		1
Giorgi Gavashelishvili		31/10/89	D	3		
Otar Javashvili		17/08/93	D	22		
Vakhtang Jomidava		25/04/91	G	10	(1)	
Irakli Jvania		18/08/97	D		(3)	
Beka Kakachia		31/05/97	M		(1)	
Giorgi Kantaria		27/04/97	D	18	(1)	
Nika Kiria		04/01/94	M	12	(6)	
Irakli Kobalia		13/03/92	A	4	(6)	
Yevheniy Kovalenko	UKR	11/08/90	M	8	(2)	1
Vakhtang Kvaratskhelia		30/03/88	A	2	(2)	
Nika Lashkhia		28/01/97	M	9	(4)	
Goderdzi Machaidze		17/07/92	D	11	(1)	
Giorgi Malania		27/06/98	D	2		
Soso Malania		09/02/95	M	10	(5)	1
Zurab Malania		07/10/96	D	8		
Zurab Mamaladze		10/02/82	G	6		
Giorgi Mikadze		12/08/94	M		(1)	
Nika Narmania		15/08/94	D	8	(1)	2
Akaki Parjikia		25/09/93	A		(1)	
Gogi Pipia		04/02/85	A	6	(2)	
Saba Pipia		08/06/96	D	3	(2)	
Guram Samushia		05/09/94	M	20	(2)	8
Tsotne Samushia		24/10/94	A	9	(6)	1
Yuriy Shevel	UKR	29/01/88	A	3	(5)	1
Zviad Sikharulia		01/08/92	M	6		
Gaga Tibilashvili		01/10/84	M	11	(4)	
Valiko Tkemaladze		14/11/87	M	27		1
Akaki Tskarozia		02/08/88	M	12		1
Levan Tsurtsumia		28/01/89	M	19	(1)	6
Tornike Tukhareli		09/11/91	M		(4)	
Dimitri Tutberidze		22/03/97	M	6	(13)	1
Tornike Zarkua		01/09/90	G	14		

Top goalscorers

24	Giorgi Kvilitaia (Dinamo Tbilisi)
19	Otar Martsvaladze (Dila)
16	Budu Zivzivadze (Samtredia)
15	Giorgi Bukhaidze (Sapovnela)
14	Dimitri Tatanashvili (Sioni)
13	Jambul Jigauri (Dinamo Tbilisi)
	Irakli Sikharulidze (Samtredia)
	Nika Kacharava (Tskhinvali)
12	Giorgi Kharaishvili (Saburtalo)
11	Tornike Mumladze (Chikhura)
	Irakli Modebadze (Dila)

Second level

Second level final table 2015/16

		Pld	W	D	L	F	A	Pts
1	FC Liakhvi Tskhinvali	34	20	9	5	82	36	69
2	FC WIT Georgia	34	18	10	6	61	26	64
3	FC Kolkheti Khobi	34	18	10	6	58	29	64
4	FC Borjomi	34	17	10	7	45	29	61
5	FC Gagra	34	16	4	14	54	38	52
6	FC Samgurali Tskhaltubo	34	16	3	15	60	46	51
7	FC Odishi 1919 Zugdidi	34	14	6	14	52	58	48
8	FC Chkherimela Kharagauli	34	12	7	15	39	50	43
9	FC Rustavi	34	10	13	11	33	33	43
10	FC Skuri Tsalenjikha	34	11	10	13	32	36	43
11	FC Meshakhte Tkibuli	34	10	12	12	28	31	42
12	FC Chiatura	34	9	15	10	41	48	42
13	FC Imereti Khoni	34	10	11	13	34	53	41
14	FC Betlemi Keda	34	12	4	18	41	65	40
15	FC Samegrelo Chkhorotsku	34	10	8	16	32	50	38
16	FC Machakhela Khelvachauri	34	8	13	13	30	43	37
17	FC Algeti Marneuli	34	9	7	18	34	50	34
18	FC Mertskhali Ozurgeti	34	6	8	20	42	77	26

Promotion/Relegation play-offs

(29/05/16)
Zugdidi 2-1 Kolkheti

NB No clubs subsequently obtained licence for 2016/17 Umaglesi Liga.

DOMESTIC CUP

Sakartvelos Tasi 2015/16

FIRST ROUND

(17/08/15 & 25/08/15)
Saburtalo 0-2, 1-1 WIT Georgia *(1-3)*

(17/08/15 & 26/08/15)
Chikhura 1-0, 4-0 Mertskhali *(5-0)*
Liakhvi Tskhinvali 1-0, 2-0 Lokomotivi Tbilisi *(3-0)*

(18/08/15 & 26/08/15)
Betlemi 1-2, 3-4 Shukura *(4-6)*
Chkherimela 1-2, 0-4 Torpedo *(1-6)*
Guria 7-0, 1-1 Samegrelo *(8-1)*
Kolkheti Khobi 1-2, 1-6 Sapovnela *(2-8)*
Kolkheti Poti 2-0, 2-0 Meshakhte *(4-0)*
Merani Martvili 0-1, 1-1 Chiatura *(1-2)*
Samtredia 2-0, 3-0 Machakhela *(5-0)*
Sioni 0-0, 1-1 Rustavi *(1-1; Sioni on away goal)*
Zugdidi 2-1, 0-0 Imereti *(2-1)*

Byes – Dila, Dinamo Batumi, Dinamo Tbilisi, Tskhinvali

SECOND ROUND

(16/09/15 & 27/10/15)
Chiatura 0-1, 1-6 Torpedo *(1-7)*
Dila 1-2, 1-0 Zugdidi *(2-2; Zugdidi on away goals)*
Dinamo Tbilisi 1-0, 1-0 Kolkheti Poti *(2-0)*
Guria 0-2, 1-1 Sioni *(1-3)*
Samtredia 3-0, 4-1 Liakhvi Tskhinvali *(7-1)*
Shukura 3-1, 1-1 Tskhinvali *(4-2)*
WIT Georgia 3-2, 1-0 Dinamo Batumi *(4-2)*

(16/09/15 & 28/10/15)
Sapovnela 0-2, 0-0 Chikhura *(0-2)*

QUARTER-FINALS

(02/12/15 & 16/12/15)
Chikhura 2-0 Shukura *(Sardalishvili 11, Chechelashvili 29)*
Shukura 1-1 Chikhura *(Lobjanidze 84; Dekanoidze 72)*
(Chikhura 3-1)

Samtredia 0-0 Sioni
Sioni 0-0 Samtredia *(aet)*
(0-0; Sioni 2-0 on pens)

Torpedo 0-1 Dinamo Tbilisi *(Kvilitaia 78)*
Dinamo Tbilisi 2-1 Torpedo *(Kvilitaia 18, Tsintsadze 71p; Sagrishvili 49)*
(Dinamo Tbilisi 3-1)

Zugdidi 1-0 WIT Georgia *(Lashkhia 36)*
WIT Georgia 1-0 Zugdidi *(Kurdgelashvili 43) (aet)*
(1-1; WIT Georgia 5-3 on pens)

SEMI-FINALS

(20/04/16 & 05/05/16)
Dinamo Tbilisi 3-0 Chikhura *(Chanturishvili 16, Jigauri 58, Kvilitaia 62)*
Chikhura 1-2 Dinamo Tbilisi *(Dekanoidze 31; Kvilitaia 67, Guruli 90)*
(Dinamo Tbilisi 5-1)

WIT Georgia 2-2 Sioni *(Vazagashvili 45, Girdaladze 47; Luís Alberto 21, Tatanashvili 72)*
Sioni 3-1 WIT Georgia *(Tatanashvili 18p, 30, 81; Kurdgelashvili 71p)*
(Sioni 5-3)

FINAL

(18/05/16)
Ramaz Shengelia, Kutaisi
FC DINAMO TBILISI 1 *(Chanturishvili 29)*
FC SIONI BOLNISI 0
Referee: *Kruashvili*
DINAMO TBILISI: *Hrdlička, Kakabadze, Amisulashvili, Rene, U Lobjanidze, Mikel Álvaro (Chelidze 82), Kiteishvili, Jigauri, Chanturishvili, Iashvili (Parunashvili 70), Kvilitaia (Gelashvili 67)*
SIONI: *Merlani, Popkhadze (Shalamberidze 86), Svanidze, V Kilasonia, Giorbelidze, Manjgaladze (Managadze 82), Razmadze, Vasadze, Gvalia (Luís Alberto 73), Gaprindashvili, Tatanashvili*
Red card: *Giorbelidze (90+2)*

The triumphant Dinamo Tbilisi squad after their cup final victory against Sioni

GERMANY
Deutscher Fussball-Bund (DFB)

Address   Otto-Fleck-Schneise 6
Postfach 710265
DE-60492 Frankfurt
am Main
Tel   +49 69 67 880
Fax   +49 69 67 88266
E-mail   info@dfb.de
Website   dfb.de

President   Reinhard Grindel
General secretary   Friedrich Curtius
Media officer   Ralf Köttker
Year of formation   1900

BUNDESLIGA CLUBS

1. FC Augsburg
2. Bayer 04 Leverkusen
3. FC Bayern München
4. Borussia Dortmund
5. VfL Borussia Mönchengladbach
6. SV Darmstadt 98
7. Eintracht Frankfurt
8. Hamburger SV
9. Hannover 96
10. Hertha BSC Berlin
11. TSG 1899 Hoffenheim
12. FC Ingolstadt 04
13. 1. FC Köln
14. 1. FSV Mainz 05
15. FC Schalke 04
16. VfB Stuttgart
17. SV Werder Bremen
18. VfL Wolfsburg

PROMOTED CLUBS

19. SC Freiburg
20. RB Leipzig

Hamburg

Bremen

Hannover (Hanover)

Wolfsburg

Berlin

Gelsenkirchen

Mönchengladbach

Dortmund

Köln (Cologne)

Leverkusen

Leipzig

Frankfurt~

~Mainz

Darmstadt~

Sinsheim-Hoffenheim

Ingolstadt

Stuttgart

Augsburg

Freiburg

München (Munich)

| 0 | 100 | 200 km |
| 0 | 100 miles | |

KEY

● UEFA Champions League
● UEFA Europa League
● Promoted
● Relegated

Double delight for ruthless Bayern

FC Bayern München made history in 2015/16 by becoming the first club to win the Bundesliga four years running. It was a successful third, and last, season in Germany for coach Pep Guardiola as he bowed out with a DFB-Pokal final victory in Berlin, where Bayern defeated league runners-up Borussia Dortmund on penalties.

There would be no European glory, however, for Guardiola as Bayern lost a third successive UEFA Champions League semi-final. Joachim Löw's national team also suffered last-four disappointment as their bid to add the European title to their world crown ended in Marseille with a 2-0 defeat by hosts France.

| **Bundesliga title hat-trick for departing Guardiola** | **Dortmund finish runners-up in league and cup** | **World champions reach EURO semi-finals** |

Domestic league

Bayern had completed Bundesliga hat-tricks in the 1970s and '80s but neither they nor any other club had strung together four successive title-winning campaigns, so it was with a particular sense of purpose that Guardiola and his players embarked on the 2015/16 season. The team's determination was self-evident from the off as they beat Hamburg 5-0 on the opening day and proceeded to win all of their next nine fixtures as well, setting a new Bundesliga record in the process.

The eighth of those opening ten victories – a 5-1 home win over Dortmund – was the most telling as in many spectators' eyes it ended the title race with more than three quarters of it still to run. Dortmund, under new coach Thomas Tuchel, the replacement for long-serving Jürgen Klopp, had opened the campaign almost as impressively as Bayern, scoring 18 goals in their first five matches, all of which yielded maximum points. Pierre-Emerick Aubameyang was in red-hot form and would score for the eighth successive game in the Munich defeat, but so too were Bayern's Robert Lewandowski and Thomas Müller, each of whom would find the net twice as the defending champions ruthlessly overpowered their rivals in the Allianz Arena.

Lewandowski, indeed, made it 12 goals in four games (in all competitions) with his double, having sensationally struck all five in just nine minutes after coming on as a half-time substitute to turn Bayern's previous home game, against Wolfsburg, into another 5-1 win. They were heady times for the Pole and his team, and although Bayern dropped their first points at the end of October in a goalless draw at Eintracht Frankfurt and then lost for the first time in early December at Borussia Mönchengladbach, 3-1, their advantage over Dortmund was still a comfortable eight points going into the winter break.

To Dortmund's enormous credit, they refused to back off and let Bayern freewheel to the title. As the competition resumed, Tuchel's charges continued to pile up the points on a weekly basis, and when Mainz sprung a big surprise by ending Bayern's 100% home record with a 2-1 win in early March – Colombian striker Jhon Córdoba scored the winner four minutes from time – suddenly Bayern's 26th German title was not quite the foregone conclusion it seemed. Dortmund were now just five points behind and had an immediate chance to reduce the gap further as they hosted the leaders at the Signal-Iduna-Park just three days later.

It was an opportunity they were unable to seize, however. An intense game of high quality had everything but goals, and that was fine for Bayern, who retained their five-point buffer with nine games to go. Six wins later they were seven points ahead, but with 75,000 fans anticipating a celebration party in the penultimate home game of the season, against Mönchengladbach, the visitors scored a 72nd-minute equaliser through André Hahn that, combined with Dortmund's 5-1 win at Wolfsburg, put the champagne on ice for another week, when another Lewandowski double got the job done in a 2-1 win at Ingolstadt.

Lewandowski scored again a week later, as Bayern toasted their historic achievement with a 3-1 victory at home to Hannover, to end up with 30 Bundesliga goals for the season. With Müller having also scored 20, the club's lethal twin strike force had a half-century to celebrate. No other Bayern player managed more than four goals, but with Arjen Robben and Franck Ribéry suffering from injuries for much of the campaign, new wingers Douglas Costa and Kingsley Coman came excitingly to the fore, both entertaining the crowds with their speed and skill and setting up countless chances from the flanks. Bayern also defended brilliantly, conceding only 17 goals – one fewer than the previous season and a new Bundesliga record. Manuel Neuer was as dependable as ever in goal, captain Philipp Lahm equally so at right-back, and although an injury to Jérôme Boateng caused disruption in the centre of defence, Guardiola plugged the gap with diligence and dexterity.

Indeed, the Spaniard displayed extraordinary versatility and tactical sophistication throughout his three-year spell in Munich, the possession-based football he made famous at Barcelona being supplemented by an aggressive pressing game and a variety of ad hoc tweaks and touch-ups that almost always paid off. His departure at the end of the season was made public just before Christmas, with the identity of his next club, Manchester City, confirmed a couple of months later, but the team continued to play their socks off for him. His successor, Carlo Ancelotti, has all the pedigree necessary to bring further success to Bayern, but Guardiola will still be a hard act to follow.

Tuchel did a fine job of following in Klopp's formidable footsteps in his debut season at Dortmund. A self-confessed Guardiola disciple, he lived up to all the forecasts for success that had followed him during a progressive five-year spell at Mainz. There was a case for labelling Dortmund as the Bundesliga's best ever runners-up, not just in terms of their final figures – 24 wins in 34 games, no defeats at home, 78 points and 82 goals (two more than Bayern) – but also because of the style and swagger inherent in their play. Aubameyang was their star performer with 25 goals, though not far behind was Armenian playmaker Henrikh Mkhitaryan, the team's main creative force and a scorer of 11 goals himself. Young Julian Weigl enjoyed a magnificent first season at the club in the midfield anchor role, while Mats Hummels reinforced his reputation as the Bundesliga's most accomplished and elegant central defender – albeit in his final season in yellow and black before returning to former club Bayern.

Bayer Leverkusen, led again by Roger Schmidt, won eight of their last nine games to grab third place and qualify alongside Bayern and Dortmund for the UEFA Champions League group stage. Inspired by the goals of Manchester United cast-off Javier Hernández and – during that successful run-in – up-and-coming attacking midfielder Julian Brandt, they forged ahead of Mönchengladbach, who finished fourth.

Such a lofty final placing looked highly unlikely when Gladbach lost their first five games and coach Lucien Favre resigned, but his stand-in successor André Schubert promptly supervised a complete transformation in the team's fortunes and was subsequently given the job full time.

The three UEFA Europa League spots were filled by Schalke, Mainz and Hertha Berlin, with Wolfsburg, the previous season's runners-up, rolling home a disappointing eighth. Schalke, despite the emergence of the exciting Leroy Sané, generally flattered to deceive, and they parted company with coach André Breitenreiter after just one season, with Augsburg's highly-regarded Markus Weinzierl coming in as his replacement. Mainz and Hertha, on the other hand, exceeded expectations, although the Berliners were riding high in third place for much of the spring campaign until their form nosedived towards the finish following a 5-0 hammering at Gladbach.

There were surprise goings-on at the foot of the table, with newly-promoted Ingolstadt and Darmstadt both doing enough, against all odds, to survive, while Hoffenheim scrambled to safety thanks to a timely improvement in form following the appointment in February of 28-year-old Julian Nagelsmann – the youngest ever Bundesliga coach. Relegation, however, befell established clubs Hannover 96 and VfB Stuttgart, the latter dropping out of the Bundesliga for the first time in 39 years after losing all of their last six fixtures. Werder Bremen escaped the play-offs only with an 88th-minute winner at Frankfurt, who therefore took on the second division's third-placed team, Nürnberg, and beat them, 2-1 on aggregate, to retain their top-flight status. Freiburg won the 2. Bundesliga to rejoin the elite after a year away and were accompanied by big-spending runners-up RB Leipzig.

Domestic cup

The Bundesliga's top two met in the final of the German Cup and it was to end in the fixture's first penalty shoot-out for 17 years after Bayern and Dortmund cancelled each other out in another 0-0 draw. Aubameyang and Lewandowski both missed good chances to win an evenly-balanced contest before Douglas Costa became Bayern's hero with the winning penalty after Sven Bender and Sokratis Papastathopoulos had both

Pierre-Emerick Aubameyang (in yellow) scores for Dortmund in the Ruhr derby against Schalke

missed for Dortmund. It was Bayern's record 18th victory in the competition (three times as many as any other club) and ensured that Guardiola – unlike Klopp 12 months earlier – got the victorious big-stage farewell he craved and deserved. For Dortmund, however, defeat saddled them with the unwanted record of being the first team to lose the DFB-Pokal final three years running.

Europe

Bayern reached the UEFA Champions League semi-finals for a club-record fifth season in a row, but that was not an achievement Guardiola wished to dwell upon. Defeat on away goals by Atlético Madrid meant that his Bayern side went out at the last-four stage to a third different Spanish club in as many years, having done so in the coach's two previous seasons at the helm against Real Madrid and Barcelona. While Bayern won all of their games in Munich, including an epic last-16 encounter against Juventus in extra time, they were not so clever on their travels, failing to win any of their three away fixtures in the knockout phase for the second season in a row.

Whereas Bayern's European ambition was not met, Wolfsburg were happy to reach the quarter-finals of the same competition – although after beating Real Madrid 2-0 at home, Dieter Hecking and his players were left to reflect on what might have been when a Cristiano Ronaldo hat-trick rescued the eventual champions in the Bernabéu return. Neither Leverkusen nor Mönchengladbach made it to the knockout phase, although the Werkself did go on to reach the last 16 of the UEFA Europa League. The only Bundesliga side to outlast Leverkusen were Dortmund, who, having started out in the third qualifying round, raced through to the quarter-finals, convincingly eliminating FC Porto and Tottenham Hotspur before falling victim to an astonishing comeback by ex-boss Klopp's Liverpool at Anfield.

National team

Germany travelled to France for UEFA EURO 2016 as the world champions and therefore one of the favourites to win the Henri Delaunay Cup – a trophy no German captain had lifted since Jürgen Klinsmann did the honours at Wembley Stadium in 1996. The wait would have to continue as

Jonas Hector performed impressively at left-back for Germany at UEFA EURO 2016 – his first international tournament

Löw's team lost in the semi-finals for the second EURO in succession, going down 2-0 to the hosts in an enthralling encounter at Marseille's Stade Vélodrome.

While Germany could take satisfaction from the enviable achievement of reaching a sixth successive major tournament semi-final, especially as it came after they had finally won for the first time in a tournament against Italy – albeit with a victory on penalties – there were also reasons for regret. While world champions such as Neuer, Boateng, Höwedes, Mesut Özil and, especially, midfield ringmaster Toni Kroos all distinguished themselves in France, with newcomers Jonas Hector and Joshua Kimmich also performing well, it was not a good tournament for World Cup final match-winner Mario Götze nor his Bayern team-mate Müller, who failed to score for the second successive EURO and also missed his penalty in the shoot-out against Italy.

The lack of punch in the Germany attack restricted the team to just seven goals in their six games, which was a poor return

for the amount of possession they commanded and the number of chances they created. Indeed, Mario Gomez, the only orthodox striker in the squad, was the sole player to score more than once. Against that, Germany were outstanding in defence, keeping their goal intact until they conceded a penalty against Italy, which Leonardo Bonucci converted. The only goal Neuer conceded from open play was Antoine Griezmann's second in the semi-final.

Coach Löw, who completed a decade in charge in France, has extended his contract until the summer of 2018, which is when – on the safe assumption that Germany maintain their 100% qualifying record in FIFA World Cups in a group comprising the Czech Republic, Northern Ireland, Norway, Azerbaijan and San Marino – they will be defending their trophy in Russia. No country has won back-to-back World Cups since Brazil in 1962. On the evidence of UEFA EURO 2016, it will be quite a challenge but one that Germany, the perennial tournament specialists, will be ready, willing and able to meet head on.

DOMESTIC SEASON AT A GLANCE

Bundesliga 2015/16 final table

		Pld	Home					Away					Total					Pts
			W	D	L	F	A	W	D	L	F	A	W	D	L	F	A	
1	**FC Bayern München**	34	15	1	1	51	8	13	3	1	29	9	28	4	2	80	17	88
2	Borussia Dortmund	34	14	3	0	49	14	10	3	4	33	20	24	6	4	82	34	78
3	Bayer 04 Leverkusen	34	10	3	4	31	17	8	3	6	25	23	18	6	10	56	40	60
4	VfL Borussia Mönchengladbach	34	13	1	3	42	18	4	3	10	25	32	17	4	13	67	50	55
5	FC Schalke 04	34	8	5	4	28	24	7	2	8	23	25	15	7	12	51	49	52
6	1. FSV Mainz 05	34	8	4	5	23	18	6	4	7	23	24	14	8	12	46	42	50
7	Hertha BSC Berlin	34	9	5	3	24	15	5	3	9	18	27	14	8	12	42	42	50
8	VfL Wolfsburg	34	9	5	3	32	17	3	4	10	15	32	12	9	13	47	49	45
9	1. FC Köln	34	5	5	7	16	18	5	8	4	22	24	10	13	11	38	42	43
10	Hamburger SV	34	5	4	8	20	23	6	4	7	20	23	11	8	15	40	46	41
11	FC Ingolstadt 04	34	7	5	5	22	18	3	5	9	11	24	10	10	14	33	42	40
12	FC Augsburg	34	3	6	8	18	27	6	5	6	24	25	9	11	14	42	52	38
13	SV Werder Bremen	34	5	5	7	27	30	5	3	9	23	35	10	8	16	50	65	38
14	SV Darmstadt 98	34	2	6	9	15	29	7	5	5	23	24	9	11	14	38	53	38
15	TSG 1899 Hoffenheim	34	6	6	5	22	25	3	4	10	17	29	9	10	15	39	54	37
16	Eintracht Frankfurt	34	6	6	5	22	24	3	3	11	12	28	9	9	16	34	52	36
17	VfB Stuttgart	34	6	1	10	22	32	3	5	9	28	43	9	6	19	50	75	33
18	Hannover 96	34	4	0	13	15	30	3	4	10	16	32	7	4	23	31	62	25

European qualification 2016/17

Champion/Cup winner: FC Bayern München (group stage)
Borussia Dortmund (group stage)
Bayer 04 Leverkusen (group stage)
VfL Borussia Mönchengladbach (play-offs)

FC Schalke 04 (group stage)
1. FSV Mainz 05 (group stage)
Hertha BSC Berlin (third qualifying round)

Top scorer	Robert Lewandowski (Bayern), 30 goals
Relegated clubs	Hannover 96, VfB Stuttgart
Promoted clubs	SC Freiburg, RB Leipzig
Cup final	FC Bayern München 0-0 Borussia Dortmund *(aet; 4-3 on pens)*

Player of the season

Robert Lewandowski
(FC Bayern München)

There was no second-season syndrome for Lewandowski at Bayern. Quite the opposite. The Polish No9 powered the Munich giants to another Bundesliga title with a succession of goals, including five in nine minutes against Wolfsburg, the last of them a brilliant flying volley from distance that was many observers' choice as Germany's goal of the season. His final figure of 30 was the highest goal tally for a Bundesliga *Torschützenkönig* in 39 years, and he added another nine in the UEFA Champions League.

Newcomer of the season

Julian Weigl
(Borussia Dortmund)

Recruited from 1860 München, where he was the captain at just 18, Weigl enjoyed a magnificent debut season in Thomas Tuchel's team. Demonstrating composure and authority beyond his years, the 20-year-old became Dortmund's distribution hub in central midfield and made 50 appearances in all competitions, breaking a Bundesliga record for the number of touches in a game when he chalked up 214 in the final league encounter against Köln. He was included in Germany's UEFA EURO 2016 squad but did not get a game.

Team of the season
(4-1-3-2)

Coach: Tuchel *(Dortmund)*

Neuer *(Bayern)*
Lahm *(Bayern)* — Tah *(Leverkusen)* — Hummels *(Dortmund)* — Alaba *(Bayern)*
Dahoud *(Mönchengladbach)*
Douglas Costa *(Bayern)* — Mkhitaryan *(Dortmund)* — Müller *(Bayern)*
Lewandowski *(Bayern)* — Aubameyang *(Dortmund)*

NATIONAL TEAM

International honours*
FIFA World Cup (4) 1954, 1974, 1990, 2014
UEFA European Championship (3) 1972, 1980, 1996

International tournament appearances*
FIFA World Cup (18) 1934 (3rd), 1938, 1954 (Winners), 1958 (4th), 1962 (qtr-finals), 1966 (runners-up), 1970 (3rd), 1974 (Winners), 1978 (2nd phase), 1982 (runners-up), 1986 (runners-up), 1990 (Winners), 1994 (qtr-finals), 1998 (qtr-finals), 2002 (runners-up), 2006 (3rd), 2010 (3rd), 2014 (Winners)
UEFA European Championship (12) 1972 (Winners), 1976 (runners-up), 1980 (Winners), 1984, 1988 (semi-finals), 1992 (runners-up), 1996 (Winners), 2000, 2004, 2008 (runners-up), 2012 (semi-finals), 2016 (semi-finals)

Top five all-time caps
Lothar Matthäus (150); Miroslav Klose (137); **Lukas Podolski** (129); **Bastian Schweinsteiger** (120); Philipp Lahm (113)

Top five all-time goals
Miroslav Klose (71); Gerd Müller (68); **Lukas Podolski** (48); Jürgen Klinsmann & Rudi Völler (47)

(* before 1992 as West Germany)

Results 2015/16

04/09/15	Poland (ECQ)	H	Frankfurt am Main	W	3-1	Müller (12), Götze (19, 82)
07/09/15	Scotland (ECQ)	A	Glasgow	W	3-2	Müller (18, 34), Gündoğan (54)
08/10/15	Republic of Ireland (ECQ)	A	Dublin	L	0-1	
11/10/15	Georgia (ECQ)	H	Leipzig	W	2-1	Müller (50p), Kruse (79)
13/11/15	France	A	Saint-Denis	L	0-2	
26/03/16	England	H	Berlin	L	2-3	Kroos (43), Gomez (57)
29/03/16	Italy	H	Munich	W	4-1	Kroos (24), Götze (45), Hector (59), Özil (75p)
29/05/16	Slovakia	H	Augsburg	L	1-3	Gomez (13p)
04/06/16	Hungary	H	Gelsenkirchen	W	2-0	Lang (39og), Müller (63)
12/06/16	Ukraine (ECF)	N	Lille (FRA)	W	2-0	Mustafi (19), Schweinsteiger (90+2)
16/06/16	Poland (ECF)	N	Saint-Denis (FRA)	D	0-0	
21/06/16	Northern Ireland (ECF)	N	Paris (FRA)	W	1-0	Gomez (30)
26/06/16	Slovakia (ECF)	N	Lille (FRA)	W	3-0	Boateng (8), Gomez (43), Draxler (63)
02/07/16	Italy (ECF)	N	Bordeaux (FRA)	D	1-1	Özil (65) (aet; 6-5 on pens)
07/07/16	France (ECF)	A	Marseille	L	0-2	

Appearances 2015/16

Coach: Joachim Löw 03/02/60

			POL	SCO	IRL	GEO	Fra	Eng	Ita	Svk	Hun	UKR	POL	NIR	SVK	ITA	FRA	Caps	Goals
Manuel Neuer	27/03/86	Bayern	G	G	G	G	G	G			G	G	G	G	G	G	G	71	-
Emre Can	12/01/94	Liverpool (ENG)	D	D			s34	D	s69		s46						M67	7	-
Jérôme Boateng	03/09/88	Bayern	D	D	D	D	D46			D64	D	D	D	D76	D72	D	D61	65	1
Mats Hummels	16/12/88	Dortmund	D	D	D	D	D	D46	D				D	D	D	D		50	4
Jonas Hector	27/05/90	Köln	D	D	D	D	M34	D	D85	M	D46	D	D	D	D	M	D	20	1
Bastian Schweinsteiger	01/08/84	Man. United (ENG)	M	M			M			s68	s90		s69	s76	s16	M79		120	24
Toni Kroos	04/01/90	Real Madrid (ESP)	M	M	M	M		M	M90		M68	M	M	M	M	M	M	71	11
Thomas Müller	13/09/89	Bayern	M	M	A	M	M	M75	M69		M69	M	M	M	M	M	M	77	32
Mesut Özil	15/10/88	Arsenal (ENG)	M	M92	M	M		M	M		M	M	M	M	M	M	M	79	20
Karim Bellarabi	08/04/90	Leverkusen	M53		s77	s90												10	1
Mario Götze	03/06/92	Bayern	A91	A86	A35			s80	A61	M	A79	A90	A66	M55			s67	56	17
İlkay Gündoğan	24/10/90	Dortmund	s53	M	M85	M	s61											16	4
Lukas Podolski	04/06/85	Galatasaray (TUR)	s91					s75			s79				s72			129	48
André Schürrle	06/11/90	Wolfsburg		s86	s35	A76		s64		s75	s60	s78	s66	s55				55	20
Christoph Kramer	19/02/91	Leverkusen		s92					s90									12	-
Matthias Ginter	19/01/94	Dortmund			D77	D	D79		s85									9	-
Marco Reus	31/05/89	Dortmund			M	M90		M64	s61									29	9
Kevin Volland	30/07/92	Hoffenheim			s85		s79		s85									6	-
Max Kruse	19/03/88	Wolfsburg				s76												14	4
Antonio Rüdiger	03/03/93	Roma (ITA)					D	D	D	D	D							11	-
Sami Khedira	04/04/87	Juventus (ITA)					M61	M		M46	M46	M	M	M69	M76	M16		65	5
Julian Draxler	20/09/93	Wolfsburg					M61		M85	M	M60	M78	M71		M72	s72	M	24	2
Mario Gomez	10/07/85	Beşiktaş (TUR)					A	A80		A46	s46		s71	A	A	A72		68	29
Shkodran Mustafi	17/04/92	Valencia (ESP)					s46	D			D					s61		12	1
Leroy Sané	11/01/96	Schalke					s61			A	s69					s79		4	-
Jonathan Tah	11/02/96	Leverkusen					s46											1	-
Marc-André ter Stegen	30/04/92	Barcelona (ESP)							G	s46								6	-
Sebastian Rudy	28/02/90	Hoffenheim							D	M								11	-
Bernd Leno	04/03/92	Leverkusen							G46									1	-
Joshua Kimmich	08/02/95	Bayern							D75				D	D	M	D		5	-
Julian Brandt	02/05/96	Leverkusen							s46									1	-
Julian Weigl	08/09/95	Dortmund							s46									1	-
Benedikt Höwedes	29/02/88	Schalke							s64	D	D	D	s76	s72	D	D		40	2

FC Bayern München

Group F
Match 1 - Olympiacos FC (GRE)
A 3-0 Müller (52, 90+2p), Götze (89)
Neuer, Thiago, Lewandowski (Coman 59), Douglas Costa, Xabi Alonso (Kimmich 76), Boateng, Bernat, Lahm, Vidal (Götze 79), Müller, Alaba. Coach: Josep Guardiola (ESP)
Match 2 - GNK Dinamo Zagreb (CRO)
H 5-0 Douglas Costa (13), Lewandowski (21, 28, 55), Götze (25)
Neuer, Thiago, Lewandowski, Douglas Costa (Müller 58), Boateng (Rafinha 64), Bernat (Javi Martínez 46), Götze, Lahm, Alaba, Coman, Kimmich. Coach: Josep Guardiola (ESP)
Match 3 - Arsenal FC (ENG)
A 0-2
Neuer, Thiago, Lewandowski, Douglas Costa, Xabi Alonso (Kimmich 71), Boateng, Bernat, Lahm, Vidal (Rafinha 71), Müller, Alaba. Coach: Josep Guardiola (ESP)
Match 4 - Arsenal FC (ENG)
H 5-1 Lewandowski (10), Müller (29, 89), Alaba (44), Robben (55)
Neuer, Thiago, Javi Martínez, Lewandowski (Vidal 71), Douglas Costa, Xabi Alonso, Boateng (Benatia 68), Lahm, Müller, Alaba, Coman (Robben 54). Coach: Josep Guardiola (ESP)
Match 5 - Olympiacos FC (GRE)
H 4-0 Douglas Costa (8), Lewandowski (16), Müller (20), Coman (69)
Neuer, Lewandowski (Benatia 56), Robben (Kimmich 33), Douglas Costa (Javi Martínez 72), Rafinha, Boateng, Lahm, Vidal, Müller, Badstuber, Coman. Coach: Josep Guardiola (ESP)
Red card: Badstuber 52
Match 6 - GNK Dinamo Zagreb (CRO)
A 2-0 Lewandowski (61, 64)
Ulreich, Benatia (Boateng 46), Ribéry (Müller 46), Javi Martínez, Lewandowski, Rafinha, Xabi Alonso, Rode, Lahm, Kimmich, Green (Vidal 62). Coach: Josep Guardiola (ESP)

Round of 16 – Juventus FC (ITA)
A 2-2 Müller (43), Robben (55)
Neuer, Thiago, Lewandowski, Robben, Douglas Costa (Ribéry 84), Bernat (Benatia 74), Lahm, Vidal, Müller, Alaba, Kimmich. Coach: Josep Guardiola (ESP)
H 4-2 (aet) Lewandowski (73), Müller (90+1), Thiago (108), Coman (110)
Neuer, Benatia (Bernat 46), Ribéry (Thiago 101), Lewandowski, Douglas Costa, Xabi Alonso (Coman 60), Lahm, Vidal, Müller, Alaba, Kimmich. Coach: Josep Guardiola (ESP)

Quarter-finals - SL Benfica (POR)
H 1-0 Vidal (2)
Neuer, Thiago, Ribéry, Lewandowski, Douglas Costa (Coman 70), Bernat, Lahm, Vidal, Müller (Götze 85), Alaba, Kimmich (Javi Martínez 60). Coach: Josep Guardiola (ESP)
A 2-2 Vidal (38), Müller (52)
Neuer, Thiago, Ribéry (Götze 90+2), Javi Martínez, Douglas Costa, Xabi Alonso (Bernat 90), Lahm, Vidal, Müller (Lewandowski 84), Alaba, Kimmich. Coach: Josep Guardiola (ESP)

Semi-finals - Club Atlético de Madrid (ESP)
A 0-1
Neuer, Thiago (Müller 70), Javi Martínez, Lewandowski, Douglas Costa, Xabi Alonso, Bernat (Benatia 77), Lahm, Vidal, Alaba, Coman (Ribéry 64). Coach: Josep Guardiola (ESP)
H 2-1 Xabi Alonso (31), Lewandowski (74)
Neuer, Ribéry, Javi Martínez, Lewandowski, Douglas Costa (Coman 73), Xabi Alonso, Boateng, Lahm, Vidal, Müller, Alaba. Coach: Josep Guardiola (ESP)

VfL Wolfsburg

Group B
Match 1 - PFC CSKA Moskva (RUS)
H 1-0 Draxler (40)
Benaglio, Caligiuri (Guilavogui 85), Draxler, Kruse, Dost (Bendtner 46), Träsch, Schürrle (Arnold 76), Dante, Luiz Gustavo, Naldo, R Rodriguez. Coach: Dieter Hecking (GER)
Match 2 - Manchester United FC (ENG)
A 1-2 Caligiuri (4)
Benaglio, Caligiuri, Draxler, Kruse, Dost (Bendtner 70), Träsch (Jung 77), Dante, Guilavogui, Naldo, Arnold (Schürrle 70), R Rodriguez. Coach: Dieter Hecking (GER)
Match 3 - PSV Eindhoven (NED)
H 2-0 Dost (46), Kruse (57)
Benaglio, Caligiuri (Vieirinha 73), Draxler (Schürrle 80), Kruse, Dost, Träsch, Dante, Luiz Gustavo, Guilavogui (Arnold 85), Naldo, R Rodriguez. Coach: Dieter Hecking (GER)
Match 4 - PSV Eindhoven (NED)
A 0-2
Benaglio, Klose, Caligiuri, Dost (Bendtner 69), Schürrle (Vieirinha 65), Luiz Gustavo, Guilavogui (Draxler 69), Jung, Naldo, Arnold, R Rodriguez. Coach: Dieter Hecking (GER)
Match 5 - PFC CSKA Moskva (RUS)
A 2-0 Akinfeev (67og), Schürrle (88)
Benaglio, Schäfer, Caligiuri (Schürrle 61), Vieirinha, Kruse (Jung 81), Dost (Bendtner 86), Träsch, Dante, Guilavogui, Naldo, Arnold. Coach: Dieter Hecking (GER)
Match 6 - Manchester United FC (ENG)
H 3-2 Naldo (13, 84), Vieirinha (29)
Benaglio, Vieirinha (Klose 78), Draxler (Caligiuri 85), Kruse, Träsch, Schürrle, Dante, Guilavogui, Naldo, Arnold, R Rodriguez. Coach: Dieter Hecking (GER)

Round of 16 - KAA Gent (BEL)
A 3-2 Draxler (44, 54), Kruse (60)
Casteels, Vieirinha (Schäfer 80), Draxler, Kruse (Putaro 90+2), Träsch, Dante, Luiz Gustavo, Jung (Schürrle 45+1), Arnold, Knoche, R Rodriguez. Coach: Dieter Hecking (GER)
H 1-0 Schürrle (74)
Casteels, Draxler (Caligiuri 78), Kruse, Träsch, Schürrle (Schäfer 89), Dante, Luiz Gustavo, Guilavogui, Arnold (Vieirinha 83), Knoche, R Rodriguez. Coach: Dieter Hecking (GER)

Quarter-finals - Real Madrid CF (ESP)
H 2-0 R Rodriguez (18p), Arnold (25)
Benaglio, Vieirinha, Draxler (Schäfer 90+3), Bruno Henrique (Träsch 80), Schürrle (Kruse 85), Dante, Luiz Gustavo, Guilavogui, Naldo, Arnold, R Rodriguez. Coach: Dieter Hecking (GER)

A 0-3
Benaglio, Vieirinha, Draxler (Kruse 32), Bruno Henrique (Caligiuri 73), Schürrle, Dante, Luiz Gustavo, Guilavogui (Dost 80), Naldo, Arnold, R Rodriguez. Coach: Dieter Hecking (GER)

VfL Borussia Mönchengladbach

Group D
Match 1 - Sevilla FC (ESP)
A 0-3
Sommer, Brouwers, Nordtveit, Hazard, Raffael (Drmic 83), Stindl (Dahoud 67), Traoré, Wendt, Jantschke, Korb, Hahn (N Schulz 73). Coach: Lucien Favre (SUI)
Match 2 - Manchester City FC (ENG)
H 1-2 Stindl (54)
Sommer, Christensen, Herrmann (Hahn 72), Dahoud (Nordtveit 84), Raffael, Stindl, Álvaro Domínguez, Wendt, Johnson, Korb (Traoré 78), Xhaka. Coach: André Schubert (GER)
Match 3 – Juventus FC (ITA)
A 0-0
Sommer, Christensen, Dahoud (Nordtveit 87), Raffael (Hazard 74), Stindl, Álvaro Domínguez, Traoré (Hahn 82), Wendt, Johnson, Korb, Xhaka. Coach: André Schubert (GER)
Match 4 – Juventus FC (ITA)
H 1-1 Johnson (18)
Sommer, Christensen, Nordtveit, Dahoud, Raffael, Stindl, Álvaro Domínguez, Traoré, Wendt, Johnson (Hazard 85), Xhaka. Coach: André Schubert (GER)
Match 5 - Sevilla FC (ESP)
H 4-2 Stindl (29, 83), Johnson (68), Raffael (78)
Sommer, Christensen, Nordtveit, Dahoud (M Schulz 79), Raffael, Stindl, Traoré (Drmic 13), Wendt, Johnson (Elvedi 87), Korb, Xhaka. Coach: André Schubert (GER)
Match 6 - Manchester City FC (ENG)
A 2-4 Korb (19), Raffael (42)
Sommer, Christensen, Nordtveit, Dahoud (M Schulz 66), Raffael, Stindl, Wendt (Hazard 84), Johnson (Drmic 72), Korb, Elvedi, Xhaka. Coach: André Schubert (GER)

Bayer 04 Leverkusen

Play-offs - SS Lazio (ITA)
A 0-1
Leno, Tah, Papadopoulos, Son (Mehmedi 46), Bender, Hakan Çalhanoğlu (Brandt 84), Kiessling (Kruse 90+4), Hilbert, Wendell, Kramer, Bellarabi. Coach: Roger Schmidt (GER)
H 3-0 Hakan Çalhanoğlu (40), Mehmedi (48), Bellarabi (88)
Leno, Tah, Papadopoulos, Bender, Hakan Çalhanoğlu (Kruse 80), Kiessling, Hilbert, Mehmedi (Brandt 76), Wendell, Kramer, Bellarabi (André Ramalho 89). Coach: Roger Schmidt (GER)

Group E
Match 1 - FC BATE Borisov (BLR)
H 4-1 Mehmedi (4), Hakan Çalhanoğlu (47, 76p),
Hernández (59)
Leno, Tah, Papadopoulos, Hernández (Kiessling 72), Bender
(Kramer 44), Hakan Çalhanoğlu (Brandt 77), Hilbert, Mehmedi,
Wendell, Bellarabi, Kampl. Coach: Roger Schmidt (GER)
Match 2 - FC Barcelona (ESP)
A 1-2 Papadopoulos (22)
Leno, Tah, Papadopoulos, Hernández (Kiessling 55), Bender,
Hakan Çalhanoğlu, Wendell, Kramer, Donati (Hilbert 76),
Bellarabi (Brandt 66), Kampl. Coach: Roger Schmidt (GER)
Match 3 - AS Roma (ITA)
H 4-4 Hernández (4p, 19), Kampl (84), Mehmedi (86)
Leno, Tah, Papadopoulos, Hernández, Hakan Çalhanoğlu,
Wendell, Ömer Toprak (Yurchenko 79), Kramer (Brandt
66), Donati, Bellarabi (Mehmedi 56), Kampl. Coach: Roger
Schmidt (GER)
Match 4 - AS Roma (ITA)
A 2-3 Mehmedi (46), Hernández (51)
Leno, Tah, Papadopoulos, Hernández, Hakan Çalhanoğlu,
Kiessling (Bellarabi 46; Kramer 73), Mehmedi (Brandt
88), Wendell, Ömer Toprak, Donati, Kampl. Coach: Roger
Schmidt (GER)
Red card: Ömer Toprak 79
Match 5 - FC BATE Borisov (BLR)
A 1-1 Mehmedi (68)
Leno, André Ramalho, Tah, Hernández, Hakan Çalhanoğlu
(Brandt 78), Mehmedi (Yurchenko 89), Wendell, Kramer,
Donati, Bellarabi, Kampl. Coach: Roger Schmidt (GER)
Match 6 - FC Barcelona (ESP)
H 1-1 Hernández (23)
Leno, Tah, Hernández, Hakan Çalhanoğlu (Brandt 79),
Hilbert, Mehmedi (Kiessling 70), Wendell, Ömer Toprak,
Kramer (Papadopoulos 90), Bellarabi, Kampl. Coach: Roger
Schmidt (GER)

Round of 32 - Sporting Clube de Portugal (POR)
A 1-0 Bellarabi (26)
Leno, Tah, Hakan Çalhanoğlu, Kiessling, Mehmedi (Henrichs
79), Jedvaj (Hilbert 85), Wendell, Brandt (Papadopoulos 66),
Ömer Toprak, Kramer, Bellarabi. Coach: Roger Schmidt (GER)
H 3-1 Bellarabi (30, 67), Hakan Çalhanoğlu (87)
Leno, Tah, Papadopoulos (Kruse 88), Hernández, Hakan
Çalhanoğlu, Kiessling (André Ramalho 63), Jedvaj, Wendell,
Brandt (Mehmedi 46), Kramer, Bellarabi. Coach: Roger
Schmidt (GER)

Round of 16 - Villarreal CF (ESP)
A 0-2
Leno, Tah, Papadopoulos, Hernández, Hakan Çalhanoğlu,
Kiessling (Kruse 67), Jedvaj, Wendell, Brandt, Kramer (Frey
65), Bellarabi (Mehmedi 86). Coach: Roger Schmidt (GER)
Red card: Jedvaj 90+5
H 0-0
Leno, Tah, Papadopoulos (André Ramalho 79), Hernández,
Hakan Çalhanoğlu, Mehmedi (Kruse 59), Wendell, Brandt,
Kramer (Yurchenko 68), Frey, Bellarabi. Coach: Roger
Schmidt (GER)

FC Augsburg

Group L
Match 1 - Athletic Club (ESP)
A 1-3 Halil Altıntop (15)
Hitz, Verhaegh, Klavan, Halil Altıntop (Koo 59), Feulner, Baier,
Esswein, Callsen-Bracker, Kohr (Trochowski 72), Ji, Matavž
(Werner 66). Coach: Markus Weinzierl (GER)
Match 2 - FK Partizan (SRB)
H 1-3 Bobadilla (58)
Hitz, Verhaegh, Halil Altıntop, Feulner (Max 46), Baier,
Callsen-Bracker (Trochowski 75), Koo, Hong, Ji, Matavž
(Esswein 46), Bobadilla. Coach: Markus Weinzierl (GER)
Match 3 - AZ Alkmaar (NED)
A 1-0 Trochowski (43)
Hitz, Verhaegh, Klavan, Baier (Kohr 58), Werner, Trochowski
(Feulner 70), Callsen-Bracker, Koo, Bobadilla (Esswein 79),
Caiuby, Max. Coach: Markus Weinzierl (GER)
Match 4 - AZ Alkmaar (NED)
H 4-1 Bobadilla (24, 33, 74), Ji (66)
Hitz, Verhaegh, Klavan, Baier (Feulner 65), Janker, Kohr, Ji,
Matavž (Koo 55), Bobadilla (Werner 78), Caiuby, Max. Coach:
Markus Weinzierl (GER)
Match 5 - Athletic Club (ESP)
H 2-3 Trochowski (41), Bobadilla (59)
Hitz, Verhaegh, Stafylidis, Klavan, Halil Altıntop (Bobadilla
56), Baier, Esswein (Koo 76), Trochowski (Caiuby 56), Janker,
Kohr, Ji. Coach: Markus Weinzierl (GER)
Match 6 - FK Partizan (SRB)
A 3-1 Hong (45+2), Verhaegh (51), Bobadilla (89)
Hitz, Verhaegh, Stafylidis (Max 80), Baier, Trochowski, Janker,
Callsen-Bracker (Hong 40), Koo (Caiuby 60), Ji, Matavž,
Bobadilla. Coach: Markus Weinzierl (GER)

Round of 32 - Liverpool FC (ENG)
H 0-0
Hitz, Verhaegh, Stafylidis, Klavan, Halil Altıntop (Koo 87),
Feulner, Esswein, Werner (Ji 81), Janker, Kohr, Bobadilla
(Caiuby 23). Coach: Markus Weinzierl (GER)
A 0-1
Hitz, Verhaegh, Stafylidis, Klavan, Halil Altıntop, Esswein,
Werner (Bobadilla 72), Janker (Parker 90), Koo (Morávek 80),
Kohr, Caiuby. Coach: Markus Weinzierl (GER)

FC Schalke 04

Group K
Match 1 - APOEL FC (CYP)
A 3-0 Matip (28), Huntelaar (35, 71)
Fährmann, Júnior Caiçara, Geis, Höger 61), Meyer, Goretzka,
Di Santo, Aogo, Sané (Sam 80), Huntelaar (Højbjerg 75),
Matip, Neustädter. Coach: André Breitenreiter (GER)

Match 2 - Asteras Tripolis FC (GRE)
H 4-0 Di Santo (28, 37, 44p), Huntelaar (84)
Fährmann, Höwedes, Geis (Kaan Ayhan 46), Kolašinac,
Goretzka (Meyer 73), Di Santo (Choupo-Moting 63),
Sané, Højbjerg, Huntelaar, Riether, Matip. Coach: André
Breitenreiter (GER)
Match 3 - AC Sparta Praha (CZE)
H 2-2 Di Santo (6), Sané (73)
Fährmann, Júnior Caiçara, Höwedes, Kolašinac (Aogo
83), Meyer, Goretzka, Di Santo, Choupo-Moting, Højbjerg
(Sané 61), Kaan Ayhan (Geis 61), Neustädter. Coach: André
Breitenreiter (GER)
Match 4 - AC Sparta Praha (CZE)
A 1-1 Geis (20p)
Fährmann, Júnior Caiçara, Geis, Goretzka (Kolašinac 87),
Choupo-Moting, Aogo, Sané (Meyer 82), Højbjerg, Kaan
Ayhan, Huntelaar (Di Santo 77), Neustädter. Coach: André
Breitenreiter (GER)
Match 5 - APOEL FC (CYP)
H 1-0 Choupo-Moting (86)
Fährmann, Júnior Caiçara (Riether 83), Geis (Højbjerg 79),
Goretzka, Di Santo (Meyer 62), Choupo-Moting, Aogo,
Sané, Huntelaar, Matip, Neustädter. Coach: André
Breitenreiter (GER)
Match 6 - Asteras Tripolis FC (GRE)
A 4-0 Di Santo (29), Choupo-Moting (37, 78), Meyer (86)
Fährmann, Júnior Caiçara, Höwedes (Friedrich 79), Geis
(Kaan Ayhan 65), Kolašinac, Di Santo, Choupo-Moting, Sam,
Højbjerg, Huntelaar (Meyer 79), Neustädter. Coach: André
Breitenreiter (GER)

Round of 32 - FC Shakhtar Donetsk (UKR)
A 0-0
Fährmann, Júnior Caiçara, Geis, Kolašinac, Meyer (Schöpf
81), Goretzka, Belhanda (Huntelaar 88), Choupo-Moting,
Sané (Sam 87), Matip, Neustädter. Coach: André
Breitenreiter (GER)
H 0-3
Fährmann, Júnior Caiçara, Geis, Kolašinac (Aogo 46),
Goretzka (Di Santo 45+2), Belhanda, Sané, Schöpf (Sam 58),
Huntelaar, Matip, Neustädter. Coach: André
Breitenreiter (GER)

Borussia Dortmund

Third qualifying round - Wolfsberger AC (AUT)
A 1-0 Hofmann (16)
Bürki, Hofmann (Kagawa 66), Gündoğan, Mkhitaryan, Reus
(Kampl 80), Hummels, Aubameyang, Papastathopoulos,
Piszczek, Schmelzer, Weigl (Castro 66). Coach: Thomas
Tuchel (GER)
H 5-0 Reus (48), Aubameyang (64), Mkhitaryan (73, 82, 86)
Weidenfeller, Gündoğan (Bender 77), Mkhitaryan, Reus
(Hofmann 77), Hummels, Aubameyang, Kagawa (Castro
65), Papastathopoulos, Piszczek, Schmelzer, Weigl. Coach:
Thomas Tuchel (GER)

Play-offs - Odds BK (NOR)
A 4-3 Aubameyang (34, 76), Kagawa (47), Mkhitaryan (85)
Weidenfeller, Bender (Weigl 68), Gündoğan, Mkhitaryan,
Hummels, Aubameyang, Kagawa, Castro (Papastathopoulos
46), Ginter, Schmelzer, Kampl (Ramos 63). Coach: Thomas
Tuchel (GER)

DOMESTIC LEAGUE CLUB-BY-CLUB

H 7-2 *Mkhitaryan (25), Reus (27, 32, 57), Kagawa (40, 90), Gündoğan (51)*
Weidenfeller, Hofmann, Gündoğan (Bender 66), Mkhitaryan (Aubameyang 64), Reus, Hummels, Kagawa, Papastathopoulos (Piszczek 64), Ginter, Schmelzer, Weigl. Coach: Thomas Tuchel (GER)

Group C
Match 1 - FC Krasnodar (RUS)
H 2-1 *Ginter (45+1), Park (90+3)*
Weidenfeller, Park, Gündoğan, Januzaj, Mkhitaryan, Hummels, Aubameyang (Ramos 72), Papastathopoulos, Castro (Weigl 61), Ginter, Schmelzer (Kagawa 46). Coach: Thomas Tuchel (GER)
Match 2 - PAOK FC (GRE)
A 1-1 *Castro (72)*
Weidenfeller, Park, Subotić, Bender, Hofmann, Januzaj (Leitner 84), Mkhitaryan (Ramos 65), Reus, Piszczek, Castro, Weigl (Schmelzer 66). Coach: Thomas Tuchel (GER)
Match 3 - Qäbälä FK (AZE)
A 3-1 *Aubameyang (31, 38, 72)*
Weidenfeller, Park (Schmelzer 69), Hofmann, Gündoğan (Bender 63), Reus, Hummels (Piszczek 63), Aubameyang, Kagawa, Papastathopoulos, Ginter, Weigl. Coach: Thomas Tuchel (GER)
Match 4 - Qäbälä FK (AZE)
H 4-0 *Reus (28), Aubameyang (45), Zenjov (67og), Mkhitaryan (70)*
Weidenfeller, Bender, Mkhitaryan, Reus (Januzaj 46), Hummels, Aubameyang (Ramos 68), Piszczek, Castro, Ginter (Gündoğan 62), Schmelzer, Weigl. Coach: Thomas Tuchel (GER)
Match 5 - FC Krasnodar (RUS)
A 0-1
Weidenfeller, Bender, Hofmann (Januzaj 68), Gündoğan, Mkhitaryan, Hummels, Ramos, Piszczek (Ginter 80), Castro, Schmelzer, Weigl (Leitner 86). Coach: Thomas Tuchel (GER)
Match 6 - PAOK FC (GRE)
H 0-1
Weidenfeller, Park, Subotić, Bender (Weigl 46), Januzaj, Reus (Mkhitaryan 46), Hummels, Ramos, Kagawa (Aubameyang 66), Ginter, Stenzel. Coach: Thomas Tuchel (GER)

Round of 32 - FC Porto (POR)
H 2-0 *Piszczek (6), Reus (71)*
Bürki, Mkhitaryan, Reus (Pulisic 87), Hummels, Aubameyang, Nuri Şahin (Leitner 57), Kagawa (Ginter 87), Papastathopoulos, Piszczek, Schmelzer, Weigl. Coach: Thomas Tuchel (GER)
A 1-0 *Casillas (23og)*
Bürki, Bender, Gündoğan (Nuri Şahin 46), Mkhitaryan, Reus (Ramos 70), Hummels (Subotić 46), Aubameyang, Kagawa, Ginter, Schmelzer, Weigl. Coach: Thomas Tuchel (GER)

Round of 16 - Tottenham Hotspur FC (ENG)
H 3-0 *Aubameyang (30), Reus (61, 70)*
Weidenfeller, Bender (Subotić 58), Mkhitaryan, Reus (Ramos 82), Hummels, Aubameyang (Kagawa 82), Piszczek, Castro, Schmelzer, Durm. Coach: Thomas Tuchel (GER)
A 2-1 *Aubameyang (24, 71)*
Weidenfeller, Subotić, Mkhitaryan (Kagawa 72), Reus (Pulisic 60), Aubameyang, Papastathopoulos (Durm 54), Piszczek, Castro, Ginter, Schmelzer, Weigl. Coach: Thomas Tuchel (GER)

Quarter-finals - Liverpool FC (ENG)
H 1-1 *Hummels (48)*
Weidenfeller, Bender (Papastathopoulos 76), Mkhitaryan, Reus, Hummels, Aubameyang (Pulisic 76), Piszczek, Castro, Schmelzer, Weigl, Durm (Nuri Şahin 46). Coach: Thomas Tuchel (GER)
A 3-4 *Mkhitaryan (5), Aubameyang (9), Reus (57)*
Weidenfeller, Mkhitaryan, Reus (Ramos 83), Hummels, Aubameyang, Kagawa (Ginter 77), Papastathopoulos, Piszczek, Castro (Gündoğan 82), Schmelzer, Weigl. Coach: Thomas Tuchel (GER)

FC Augsburg

1907 • SGL-Arena (30,660) • fcaugsburg.de
Coach: Markus Weinzierl

2015

15/08	h Hertha	L	0-1	
22/08	a Frankfurt	D	1-1	Caiuby
29/08	h Ingolstadt	L	0-1	
12/09	a Bayern	L	1-2	Esswein
20/09	h Hannover	W	2-0	Esswein, Verhaegh (p)
23/09	a Mönchengladbach	L	2-4	Verhaegh 2 (2p)
26/09	h Hoffenheim	L	1-3	Koo
04/10	a Leverkusen	D	1-1	og (Leno)
17/10	h Darmstadt	L	0-2	
25/10	a Dortmund	L	1-5	Bobadilla
31/10	h Mainz	D	3-3	Verhaegh (p), Koo, Bobadilla
08/11	h Bremen	L	1-2	Verhaegh (p)
21/11	a Stuttgart	W	4-0	Esswein, og (Baumgartl), Callsen-Bracker, Koo
29/11	h Wolfsburg	D	0-0	
05/12	a Köln	W	1-0	Bobadilla
13/12	h Schalke	W	2-1	Hong, Caiuby
19/12	a Hamburg	W	1-0	Morávek

2016

23/01	a Hertha	D	0-0	
30/01	h Frankfurt	D	0-0	
06/02	a Ingolstadt	L	1-2	Stafylidis
14/02	h Bayern	L	1-3	Bobadilla
21/02	a Hannover	W	1-0	Koo
28/02	h Mönchengladbach	D	2-2	Finnbogason, Caiuby
02/03	a Hoffenheim	L	1-2	Verhaegh (p)
05/03	h Leverkusen	D	3-3	Koo 3
12/03	a Darmstadt	D	2-2	Feulner, Finnbogason (p)
20/03	h Dortmund	L	1-3	Finnbogason
02/04	a Mainz	L	2-4	Caiuby, Koo
09/04	a Bremen	W	2-1	Finnbogason, Hong
16/04	h Stuttgart	W	1-0	Finnbogason
23/04	a Wolfsburg	W	2-0	Finnbogason, Halil
29/04	h Köln	D	0-0	
07/05	a Schalke	D	1-1	Baier
14/05	h Hamburg	L	1-3	Finnbogason

No	Name	Nat	DoB	Pos	Aps	(s)	Gls
17	Albian Ajeti	SUI	26/02/97	A		(1)	
10	Daniel Baier		18/05/84	M	28		1
25	Raúl Bobadilla	PAR	18/06/87	A	19	(8)	4
30	Caiuby	BRA	14/07/88	M	25	(1)	4
18	Jan-Ingwer Callsen-Bracker		23/09/84	D	8	(2)	1
11	Alexander Esswein		25/03/90	M	22	(7)	3
8	Markus Feulner		12/02/82	M	10	(9)	1
27	Alfred Finnbogason	ISL	01/02/89	A	13	(1)	7
6	Jeffrey Gouweleeuw	NED	10/07/91	D	11		
7	Halil Altıntop	TUR	08/12/82	M	15	(4)	1
35	Marwin Hitz	SUI	18/09/87	G	33		
20	Hong Jeong-ho	KOR	12/08/89	D	19	(4)	2
16	Christoph Janker		14/02/85	D	3	(9)	
24	Ji Dong-won	KOR	28/05/91	A	7	(14)	
5	Ragnar Klavan	EST	30/10/85	D	31		
21	Dominik Kohr		31/01/94	M	30	(1)	
19	Koo Ja-cheol	KOR	27/02/89	M	24	(3)	8
1	Alexander Manninger	AUT	04/06/77	G	1	(1)	
23	Tim Matavž	SVN	13/01/89	A	3	(8)	
31	Philipp Max		30/09/93	D	23	(3)	
33	Sascha Mölders		22/03/85	A		(3)	
14	Jan Morávek	CZE	01/11/89	M	3	(8)	1
4	Daniel Opare	GHA	18/10/90	D	4		
3	Kostas Stafylidis	GRE	02/12/93	D	8	(3)	1
15	Piotr Trochowski		22/03/84	M	2	(4)	
2	Paul Verhaegh	NED	01/09/83	D	25		6
13	Tobias Werner		19/07/85	M	7	(6)	

Bayer 04 Leverkusen

1904 • BayArena (30,210) • bayer04.de
Major honours
German Cup (1) 1993; UEFA Cup (1) 1988
Coach: Roger Schmidt

2015

15/08	h Hoffenheim	W	2-1	Kiessling, Brandt
22/08	a Hannover	W	1-0	Hakan
29/08	a Bayern	L	0-3	
12/09	h Darmstadt	L	0-1	
20/09	a Dortmund	L	0-3	
23/09	h Mainz	W	1-0	Hernández
26/09	a Bremen	W	3-0	Mehmedi, Brandt, Kampl
04/10	h Augsburg	D	1-1	Bellarabi
17/10	a Hamburg	D	0-0	
24/10	h Stuttgart	W	4-3	Bellarabi, Boenisch, Hernández, Mehmedi
31/10	a Wolfsburg	L	1-2	Hernández
07/11	h Köln	L	1-2	Hernández
21/11	a Frankfurt	W	3-1	Hernández 2, Hakan
29/11	h Schalke	D	1-1	og (Riether)
05/12	a Hertha	L	1-2	Hernández
12/12	h Mönchengladbach	W	5-0	Kiessling 2, Hernández 3
19/12	a Ingolstadt	W	1-0	Hernández

2016

23/01	a Hoffenheim	D	1-1	Ömer
30/01	h Hannover	W	3-0	Kiessling, Hernández 2 (1p)
06/02	h Bayern	D	0-0	
13/02	a Darmstadt	W	2-1	og (Aytaç), Brandt
21/02	h Dortmund	L	0-1	
28/02	h Mainz	L	1-3	Hernández
02/03	h Bremen	L	1-4	og (Djilobodji)
05/03	a Augsburg	D	3-3	Bellarabi, og (Verhaegh), Hakan (p)
13/03	a Hamburg	W	1-0	og (Ekdal)
20/03	a Stuttgart	W	2-0	Brandt, Bellarabi
01/04	h Wolfsburg	W	3-0	Brandt, Hernández, Yurchenko
10/04	a Köln	W	2-0	Brandt, Hernández
16/04	h Frankfurt	W	3-0	Kampl, Brandt, Bellarabi
23/04	a Schalke	W	3-2	Brandt, Bellarabi, Hernández
30/04	h Hertha	W	2-1	Brandt, Bender
07/05	a Mönchengladbach	L	1-2	Aránguiz
14/05	h Ingolstadt	W	3-2	Aránguiz, Kampl, Kiessling

No	Name	Nat	DoB	Pos	Aps	(s)	Gls
20	Charles Aránguiz	CHI	17/04/89	M	5	(2)	2
2	André Ramalho	BRA	16/02/92	D	11	(8)	
38	Karim Bellarabi		08/04/90	M	31	(2)	6
8	Lars Bender		27/04/89	M	11		1
17	Sebastian Boenisch	POL	01/02/87	D	7	(1)	1
19	Julian Brandt		02/05/96	M	18	(11)	9
26	Giulio Donati	ITA	05/02/90	D	10	(2)	
37	Marlon Frey		24/03/96	M	2	(7)	
10	Hakan Çalhanoğlu	TUR	08/02/94	M	27	(8)	3
39	Benjamin Henrichs		23/02/97	M	5	(4)	
7	Javier Hernández	MEX	01/06/88	A	25	(3)	17
13	Roberto Hilbert		16/10/84	D	3	(2)	
16	Tin Jedvaj	CRO	28/11/95	D	11	(4)	
44	Kevin Kampl	SVN	09/10/90	M	19	(3)	3
11	Stefan Kiessling		25/01/84	A	19	(11)	5
23	Christoph Kramer		19/02/91	M	28		
25	Dario Kresic	CRO	10/01/84	G	1		
27	Robbie Kruse	AUS	05/10/88	A	2	(7)	
1	Bernd Leno		04/03/92	G	33		
14	Admir Mehmedi	SUI	16/03/91	A	14	(14)	2
21	Ömer Toprak	TUR	21/07/89	D	17	(2)	1
14	Kyriakos Papadopoulos	GRE	23/02/92	D	10	(6)	
24	Son Heung-min	KOR	08/07/92	A	1		
4	Jonathan Tah		11/02/96	D	29		
18	Wendell	BRA	20/07/93	D	26	(2)	
22	David Yelldell	USA	01/10/81	G		(1)	
35	Vladlen Yurchenko	UKR	22/01/94	M	3	(4)	1

FC Bayern München

1900 • Allianz-Arena (75,024) • fcbayern.de

Major honours
European Champion Clubs' Cup/UEFA Champions League (5) 1974, 1975, 1976, 2001, 2013; UEFA Cup Winners' Cup (1) 1967; UEFA Cup (1) 1996; UEFA Super Cup (1) 2013; European/South American Cup (2) 1976, 2001; FIFA Club World Cup (1) 2013; German League (26) 1932, 1969, 1972, 1973, 1974, 1980, 1981, 1985, 1986, 1987, 1989, 1990, 1994, 1997, 1999, 2000, 2001, 2003, 2005, 2006, 2008, 2010, 2013, 2014, 2015, 2016; German Cup (18) 1957, 1966, 1967, 1969, 1971, 1982, 1984, 1986, 1998, 2000, 2003, 2005, 2006, 2008, 2010, 2013, 2014, 2016

Coach: Josep Guardiola (ESP)

2015

Date		Opponent	Result	Scorers
14/08	h	Hamburg	W 5-0	Benatia, Lewandowski, Müller 2, Douglas Costa
22/08	a	Hoffenheim	W 2-1	Müller, Lewandowski
29/08	h	Leverkusen	W 3-0	Müller 2 (1p), Robben (p)
12/09	h	Augsburg	W 2-1	Lewandowski, Müller (p)
19/09	a	Darmstadt	W 3-0	Vidal, Coman, Rode
22/09	h	Wolfsburg	W 5-1	Lewandowski 5
26/09	a	Mainz	W 3-0	Lewandowski 2, Coman
04/10	h	Dortmund	W 5-1	Müller 2 (1p), Lewandowski 2, Götze
17/10	a	Bremen	W 1-0	Müller
24/10	h	Köln	W 4-0	Robben, Vidal, Lewandowski, Müller (p)
30/10	a	Frankfurt	D 0-0	
07/11	h	Stuttgart	W 4-0	Robben, Douglas Costa, Lewandowski, Müller
21/11	a	Schalke	W 3-1	og (Goretzka), Javi Martínez, Müller
28/11	h	Hertha	W 2-0	Müller, Coman
05/12	a	Mönchengladbach	L 1-3	Ribéry
12/12	h	Ingolstadt	W 2-0	Lewandowski, Lahm
19/12	a	Hannover	W 1-0	Müller (p)

2016

Date		Opponent	Result	Scorers
22/01	h	Hamburg	W 2-1	Lewandowski 2 (1p)
31/01	h	Hoffenheim	W 2-0	Lewandowski 2
06/02	a	Leverkusen	D 0-0	
14/02	a	Augsburg	W 3-1	Lewandowski 2, Müller
20/02	h	Darmstadt	W 3-1	Müller 2, Lewandowski
27/02	a	Wolfsburg	W 2-0	Coman, Lewandowski
02/03	h	Mainz	L 1-2	Robben
05/03	a	Dortmund	D 0-0	
12/03	h	Bremen	W 5-0	Thiago 2, Müller 2, Lewandowski
19/03	a	Köln	W 1-0	Lewandowski
02/04	h	Frankfurt	W 1-0	Ribéry
09/04	a	Stuttgart	W 3-1	og (Niedermeier), Alaba, Douglas Costa
16/04	h	Schalke	W 3-0	Lewandowski 2, Vidal
23/04	a	Hertha	W 2-0	Vidal, Douglas Costa
30/04	h	Mönchengladbach	D 1-1	Müller
07/05	a	Ingolstadt	W 2-1	Lewandowski 2 (1p)
14/05	h	Hannover	W 3-1	Lewandowski, Götze 2

No	Name	Nat	DoB	Pos	Aps	(s)	Gls
27	David Alaba	AUT	24/06/92	D	27	(3)	1
28	Holger Badstuber		13/03/89	D	5	(2)	
5	Medhi Benatia	MAR	17/04/87	D	11	(3)	1
18	Juan Bernat	ESP	01/03/93	D	13	(3)	
17	Jérôme Boateng		03/09/88	D	17	(2)	
29	Kingsley Coman	FRA	13/06/96	M	20	(3)	4
4	Dante	BRA	18/10/83	D		(1)	
11	Douglas Costa	BRA	14/09/90	M	23	(4)	4
19	Mario Götze		03/06/92	M	11	(3)	3
8	Javi Martínez	ESP	02/09/88	M	11	(5)	1
32	Joshua Kimmich		08/02/95	M	15	(8)	
21	Philipp Lahm		11/11/83	D	25	(1)	1
9	Robert Lewandowski	POL	21/08/88	A	29	(3)	30
25	Thomas Müller		13/09/89	A	26	(5)	20
1	Manuel Neuer		27/03/86	G	34		
20	Miloš Pantović	SRB	07/07/96	A		(1)	
13	Rafinha	BRA	07/09/85	D	18	(7)	
7	Franck Ribéry	FRA	07/04/83	M	6	(7)	2
10	Arjen Robben	NED	23/01/84	A	14	(1)	4
20	Sebastian Rode		11/10/90	M	3	(12)	1
4	Serdar Taşçı		24/04/87	D	3		
6	Thiago Alcántara	ESP	11/04/91	M	16	(11)	2
26	Sven Ullreich		03/08/88	G		(1)	
23	Arturo Vidal	CHI	22/05/87	M	24	(6)	4
14	Xabi Alonso	ESP	25/11/81	M	23	(3)	

Borussia Dortmund

1909 • Signal-Iduna-Park (81,359) • bvb.de

Major honours
UEFA Champions League (1) 1997; UEFA Cup Winners' Cup (1) 1966; European/South American Cup (1) 1997; German League (8) 1956, 1957, 1963, 1995, 1996, 2002, 2011, 2012; German Cup (3) 1965, 1989, 2012

Coach: Thomas Tuchel

2015

Date		Opponent	Result	Scorers
15/08	h	Mönchengladbach	W 4-0	Reus, Aubameyang, Mkhitaryan 2
23/08	a	Ingolstadt	W 4-0	Ginter, Reus (p), Kagawa, Aubameyang
30/08	h	Hertha	W 3-1	Hummels, Aubameyang, Ramos
12/09	a	Hannover	W 4-2	Aubameyang 2 (2p), Mkhitaryan, og (Felipe)
20/09	h	Leverkusen	W 3-0	Hofmann, Kagawa, Aubameyang (p)
23/09	a	Hoffenheim	D 1-1	Aubameyang
27/09	h	Darmstadt	D 2-2	Aubameyang 2
04/10	a	Bayern	L 1-5	Aubameyang
16/10	a	Mainz	W 2-0	Reus, Mkhitaryan
25/10	h	Augsburg	W 5-1	Aubameyang 3, Reus 2
31/10	a	Bremen	W 3-1	Reus 2, Mkhitaryan
08/11	h	Schalke	W 3-2	Kagawa, Ginter, Aubameyang
20/11	a	Hamburg	L 1-3	Aubameyang
29/11	h	Stuttgart	W 4-1	Castro, Aubameyang 2, og (Niedermeier)
05/12	a	Wolfsburg	W 2-1	Reus, Kagawa
13/12	h	Frankfurt	W 4-1	Mkhitaryan, Aubameyang, Hummels, Ramos
19/12	a	Köln	L 1-2	Papastathopoulos

2016

Date		Opponent	Result	Scorers
23/01	a	Mönchengladbach	W 3-1	Reus, Mkhitaryan, Gündoğan
30/01	h	Ingolstadt	W 2-0	Aubameyang 2
06/02	a	Hertha	D 0-0	
13/02	h	Hannover	W 1-0	Mkhitaryan
21/02	a	Leverkusen	W 1-0	Aubameyang
28/02	h	Hoffenheim	W 3-1	Mkhitaryan, Ramos, Aubameyang
02/03	a	Darmstadt	W 2-0	Ramos, Durm
05/03	h	Bayern	D 0-0	
13/03	h	Mainz	W 2-0	Reus, Kagawa
20/03	a	Augsburg	W 3-1	Mkhitaryan, Castro, Ramos
02/04	h	Bremen	W 3-2	Aubameyang, Kagawa, Ramos
10/04	a	Schalke	D 2-2	Kagawa, Ginter
17/04	h	Hamburg	W 3-0	Pulisic, Ramos 2
23/04	a	Stuttgart	W 3-0	Kagawa, Pulisic, Mkhitaryan
30/04	h	Wolfsburg	W 5-1	Kagawa, Ramos, Reus, Aubameyang 2
07/05	a	Frankfurt	L 0-1	
14/05	h	Köln	D 2-2	Castro, Reus

No	Name	Nat	DoB	Pos	Aps	(s)	Gls
17	Pierre-Emerick Aubameyang	GAB	18/06/89	A	28	(3)	25
6	Sven Bender		27/04/89	M	14	(5)	
38	Roman Bürki	SUI	14/11/90	G	33		
27	Gonzalo Castro		11/06/87	M	16	(9)	3
37	Erik Durm		12/05/92	D	10	(4)	1
28	Matthias Ginter		19/01/94	D	21	(3)	3
8	İlkay Gündoğan		24/10/90	M	22	(3)	1
7	Jonas Hofmann		14/07/92	M	4	(3)	1
15	Mats Hummels		16/12/88	D	29	(1)	2
9	Adnan Januzaj	BEL	05/02/95	M		(6)	
7	Shinji Kagawa	JPN	17/03/89	M	26	(3)	9
23	Kevin Kampl	SVN	09/10/90	M		(1)	
14	Moritz Leitner		08/12/92	M	2	(7)	
10	Henrikh Mkhitaryan	ARM	21/01/89	M	28	(3)	11
18	Nuri Şahin	TUR	05/09/88	M	6	(3)	
25	Sokratis Papastathopoulos	GRE	09/06/88	D	23	(2)	1
3	Park Joo-ho	KOR	16/01/87	D	4	(1)	
30	Felix Passlack		29/05/98	M	2	(1)	
26	Łukasz Piszczek	POL	03/06/85	D	16	(4)	
22	Christian Pulisic	USA	18/09/98	M	4	(5)	2
20	Adrián Ramos	COL	22/01/86	A	9	(18)	9
11	Marco Reus		31/05/89	M	24	(2)	12
29	Marcel Schmelzer		22/01/88	D	22	(4)	
4	Neven Subotić	SRB	10/12/88	D	5	(1)	
1	Roman Weidenfeller		06/08/80	G	1		
33	Julian Weigl		08/09/95	M	25	(4)	

GERMANY

VfL Borussia Mönchengladbach

1900 • Borussia-Park (54,010) • borussia.de

Major honours
UEFA Cup (2) 1975, 1979; German League (5) 1970, 1971, 1975, 1976, 1977; German Cup (3) 1960, 1973, 1995
Coach: Lucien Favre (SUI);
(21/09/15) André Schubert

2015
15/08	a	Dortmund	L	0-4	
23/08	h	Mainz	L	1-2	Herrmann
30/08	a	Bremen	L	1-2	Stindl
11/09	h	Hamburg	L	0-3	
19/09	a	Köln	L	0-1	
23/09	h	Augsburg	W	4-2	Johnson, Xhaka, Stindl, Dahoud
26/09	a	Stuttgart	W	3-1	Xhaka, og (Gentner), Raffael
03/10	h	Wolfsburg	W	2-0	Nordtveit, Traoré
17/10	a	Frankfurt	W	5-1	Raffael 2, Dahoud, Hahn 2 (1p)
25/10	h	Schalke	W	3-1	Stindl, Raffael, Korb
31/10	a	Hertha	W	4-1	Wendt, Raffael, Xhaka (p), Nordtveit
07/11	h	Ingolstadt	D	0-0	
21/11	h	Hannover	W	2-1	Traoré, Raffael
28/11	a	Hoffenheim	D	3-3	Johnson 2, Drmic
05/12	h	Bayern	W	3-1	Wendt, Stindl, Johnson
12/12	a	Leverkusen	L	0-5	
20/12	h	Darmstadt	W	3-2	Stindl, Nordtveit, Wendt
2016					
23/01	h	Dortmund	L	1-3	Raffael
29/01	a	Mainz	L	0-1	
05/02	h	Bremen	W	5-1	Stindl, Christensen 2, Raffael (p), Nordtveit
14/02	a	Hamburg	L	2-3	Johnson, Raffael
20/02	h	Köln	W	1-0	Dahoud
28/02	a	Augsburg	D	2-2	Raffael, Johnson
02/03	h	Stuttgart	W	4-0	Hazard, Raffael, Herrmann, og (Grosskreutz)
05/03	a	Wolfsburg	L	1-2	Raffael
12/03	h	Frankfurt	W	3-0	Stindl, Raffael, Dahoud
18/03	a	Schalke	L	1-2	Christensen
03/04	h	Hertha	W	5-0	Hazard 2, Hahn, Herrmann, Traoré
09/04	a	Ingolstadt	L	0-1	
15/04	a	Hannover	L	0-2	
24/04	h	Hoffenheim	W	3-1	og (Toljan), Dahoud, Hahn
30/04	a	Bayern	D	1-1	Hahn
07/05	h	Leverkusen	W	2-1	Hahn 2
14/05	a	Darmstadt	W	2-0	Hazard, Hahn

No	Name	Nat	DoB	Pos	Aps	(s)	Gls
15	Álvaro Domínguez	ESP	16/05/89	D	5	(1)	
4	Roel Brouwers	NED	28/11/81	D	3	(5)	
3	Andreas Christensen	DEN	10/04/96	D	31		3
6	Mahmoud Dahoud		01/01/96	M	27	(5)	5
9	Josip Drmic	SUI	08/08/92	A	4	(9)	1
30	Nico Elvedi	SUI	30/09/96	D	17	(4)	
28	André Hahn		13/08/90	M	7	(8)	8
26	Thorgan Hazard	BEL	29/03/93	M	19	(10)	4
7	Patrick Herrmann		12/02/91	M	5	(13)	3
5	Martin Hinteregger	AUT	07/09/92	D	6	(4)	
23	Jonas Hofmann		14/07/92	M	2	(6)	
31	Branimir Hrgota	SWE	12/01/93	A		(9)	
24	Tony Jantschke		07/04/90	D	8	(4)	
19	Fabian Johnson	USA	11/12/87	M	25	(1)	6
27	Julian Korb		21/03/92	D	14	(3)	1
16	Håvard Nordtveit	NOR	21/06/90	M	27	(4)	4
11	Raffael	BRA	28/03/85	A	30	(1)	13
18	Marvin Schulz		15/01/95	D	4	(4)	
14	Nico Schulz		01/04/93	M		(1)	
21	Tobias Sippel		22/03/88	G	2		
1	Yann Sommer	SUI	17/12/88	G	32		
13	Lars Stindl		26/08/88	A	29	(1)	7
39	Martin Stranzl	AUT	16/06/80	D	2	(2)	
8	Ibrahima Traoré	GUI	21/04/88	M	17	(7)	3
17	Oscar Wendt	SWE	24/10/85	D	30		3
34	Granit Xhaka	SUI	27/09/92	M	28		3

SV Darmstadt 98

1898 • Merck-Stadion (16,250) • sv98.de
Coach: Dirk Schuster

2015
15/08	h	Hannover	D	2-2	Heller 2
22/08	a	Schalke	D	1-1	Rausch
29/08	h	Hoffenheim	D	0-0	
12/09	a	Leverkusen	W	1-0	Aytaç
19/09	h	Bayern	L	0-3	
22/09	h	Bremen	W	2-1	Wagner 2 (1p)
27/09	a	Dortmund	D	2-2	Heller, Aytaç
02/10	h	Mainz	L	2-3	Heller, Sailer
17/10	a	Augsburg	W	2-0	Wagner, Niemeyer
24/10	h	Wolfsburg	L	0-1	
01/11	a	Stuttgart	L	0-2	
07/11	h	Hamburg	D	1-1	Heller
22/11	a	Ingolstadt	L	1-3	Aytaç
27/11	h	Köln	D	0-0	
06/12	a	Frankfurt	W	1-0	Aytaç
12/12	h	Hertha	L	0-4	
20/12	a	Mönchengladbach	L	2-3	Heller, Wagner
2016					
23/01	a	Hannover	W	2-1	Wagner 2
30/01	h	Schalke	L	0-2	
07/02	a	Hoffenheim	W	2-0	Aytaç, Rajković
13/02	h	Leverkusen	L	1-2	Wagner
20/02	a	Bayern	L	1-3	Wagner
27/02	a	Bremen	D	2-2	Wagner (p), Aytaç
02/03	h	Dortmund	L	0-2	
06/03	a	Mainz	D	0-0	
12/03	h	Augsburg	D	2-2	Vrančić, Wagner
19/03	a	Wolfsburg	D	1-1	Wagner
02/04	h	Stuttgart	D	2-2	Wagner, Niemeyer
09/04	a	Hamburg	W	2-1	Aytaç, Gondorf
16/04	h	Ingolstadt	W	2-0	Rausch, Wagner
23/04	a	Köln	L	1-4	Gondorf
30/04	h	Frankfurt	L	1-2	Vrančić
07/05	a	Hertha	W	2-1	Gondorf, Wagner
14/05	h	Mönchengladbach	L	0-2	

No	Name	Nat	DoB	Pos	Aps	(s)	Gls
4	Aytaç Sulu	TUR	11/12/85	D	33		7
33	Luca Caldirola	ITA	01/02/91	D	34		
13	György Garics	AUT	08/03/84	D	20	(1)	
8	Jérôme Gondorf		26/06/88	M	33		3
6	Benjamin Gorka		15/04/84	D		(4)	
20	Marcel Heller		12/02/86	M	33		6
32	Fabian Holland		11/07/90	D	16	(2)	
27	Milan Ivana	SVK	26/11/83	M		(1)	
23	Florian Jungwirth		27/01/89	M	16	(3)	
15	Júnior Díaz	CRC	12/09/83	D	9	(3)	
11	Tobias Kempe		27/06/89	M	9	(22)	
31	Christian Mathenia		31/03/92	G	33		
31	Peter Niemeyer		22/11/83	M	31		2
19	Felix Platte		11/02/96	A	1	(10)	
35	Slobodan Rajković	SRB	03/02/89	D	12	(3)	1
34	Konstantin Rausch		15/03/90	M	27	(4)	2
10	Jan Rosenthal		07/04/86	M	17	(6)	
8	Marco Sailer		16/11/85	A	3	(11)	1
17	Sandro Sirigu		07/10/88	D	1	(5)	
9	Dominik Stroh-Engel		27/11/85	A	6	(9)	
7	Mario Vrančić	BIH	23/05/89	M	12	(10)	2
14	Sandro Wagner		29/11/87	A	27	(5)	14
40	Łukasz Załuska	POL	16/06/82	G	1		

Eintracht Frankfurt

1899 • Commerzbank-Arena (51,500) • eintracht.de

Major honours
UEFA Cup (1) 1980; German League (1) 1959; German Cup (4) 1974, 1975, 1981, 1988
Coach: Armin Veh;
(08/03/16) Niko Kovač (CRO)

2015
16/08	a	Wolfsburg	L	1-2	Reinartz
22/08	h	Augsburg	D	1-1	Russ
29/08	a	Stuttgart	W	4-1	og (Hloušek), Castaignos 2, Seferovic (p)
12/09	h	Köln	W	6-2	Meier 3, Castaignos 2, Seferovic
19/09	a	Hamburg	D	0-0	
23/09	a	Schalke	L	0-2	
27/09	h	Hertha	D	1-1	Meier
03/10	a	Ingolstadt	L	0-2	
17/10	h	Mönchengladbach	L	1-5	Meier (p)
24/10	a	Hannover	W	2-1	Stendera 2
30/10	h	Bayern	D	0-0	
07/11	a	Hoffenheim	D	0-0	
21/11	h	Leverkusen	L	1-3	Medojević
28/11	a	Mainz	L	1-2	Seferovic
06/12	h	Darmstadt	L	0-1	
13/12	a	Dortmund	L	1-4	Meier
19/12	h	Bremen	W	2-1	Meier, Aigner
2016					
24/01	h	Wolfsburg	W	3-2	Meier 3
30/01	a	Augsburg	D	0-0	
06/02	h	Stuttgart	L	2-4	Meier, Huszti
13/02	h	Köln	L	1-3	Meier
19/02	h	Hamburg	D	0-0	
28/02	h	Schalke	D	0-0	
02/03	a	Hertha	L	0-2	
05/03	h	Ingolstadt	D	1-1	Russ
12/03	a	Mönchengladbach	L	0-3	
19/03	a	Hannover	W	1-0	Ben-Hatira
02/04	a	Bayern	L	0-1	
09/04	h	Hoffenheim	L	0-1	
16/04	a	Leverkusen	L	0-3	
24/04	h	Mainz	W	2-1	Russ, og (Bell)
30/04	a	Darmstadt	W	2-1	Hasebe, Aigner
07/05	a	Dortmund	W	1-0	Aigner
14/05	a	Bremen	L	0-1	

No	Name	Nat	DoB	Pos	Aps	(s)	Gls
19	David Abraham	ARG	15/07/86	D	28	(3)	
16	Stefan Aigner		20/08/87	M	27	(4)	3
32	Änis Ben-Hatira	TUN	18/07/88	M	7	(2)	1
30	Luc Castaignos	NED	27/09/92	A	12	(7)	4
22	Timothy Chandler	USA	29/03/90	D	5	(7)	
15	Constant Djakpa	CIV	17/10/86	D	8	(4)	
10	Marco Fabián	MEX	21/07/89	M	9	(2)	
18	Johannes Flum		14/12/87	M	1	(4)	
11	Mijat Gaćinović	SRB	08/02/95	M	4	(3)	
32	Joel Gerezgiher		09/10/95	M	1	(2)	
20	Makoto Hasebe	JPN	18/01/84	M	31	(1)	1
1	Lukas Hradecky	FIN	24/11/89	G	34		
8	Szabolcs Huszti	HUN	18/04/83	M	14	(1)	1
27	Aleksandar Ignjovski	SRB	27/01/91	D	13	(5)	
8	Takashi Inui	JPN	02/06/88	M	1		
3	Kaan Ayhan	TUR	10/11/94	D	1	(1)	
10	Václav Kadlec	CZE	20/05/92	A	2	(3)	
31	David Kinsombi		12/12/95	D	1	(1)	
28	Sony Kittel		06/01/93	M	1	(7)	
25	Slobodan Medojević	SRB	20/11/90	M	6	(8)	1
14	Alexander Meier		17/01/83	M	19		12
6	Bastian Oczipka		12/01/89	D	30		
2	Yanni Regäsel		13/01/96	D	9	(1)	
8	Stefan Reinartz		01/01/89	M	14	(1)	1
35	Nico Rinderknecht		11/10/97	M		(1)	
4	Marco Russ		04/08/85	D	26	(2)	3
9	Haris Seferovic	SUI	22/02/92	A	25	(4)	3
21	Marc Stendera		10/11/95	M	24	(2)	2
24	Luca Waldschmidt		19/05/96	A		(12)	
5	Carlos Zambrano	PER	10/07/89	D	21	(3)	

Hamburger SV

1887 • Imtech-Arena (57,000) • hsv.de

Major honours
European Champion Clubs' Cup (1) 1983;
UEFA Cup Winners' Cup (1) 1977; German League (6)
1923, 1928, 1960, 1979, 1982, 1983; German
Cup (3) 1963, 1976, 1987

Coach: Bruno Labbadia

2015

14/08	a	Bayern	L	0-5
22/08	h	Stuttgart	W	3-2 *Ilićević, Lasogga, Djourou*
29/08	a	Köln	L	1-2 *Holtby*
11/09	a	Mönchengladbach	W	3-0 *Lasogga 2, Müller*
19/09	h	Frankfurt	D	0-0
22/09	a	Ingolstadt	W	1-0 *Gregoritsch*
26/09	h	Schalke	L	0-1
03/10	a	Hertha	L	0-3
17/10	a	Leverkusen	D	0-0
23/10	h	Hoffenheim	W	1-0 *Lasogga*
01/11	h	Hannover	L	1-2 *Gregoritsch*
07/11	a	Darmstadt	D	1-1 *Lasogga (p)*
20/11	h	Dortmund	W	3-1 *Lasogga (p), Holtby, og (Hummels)*
28/11	a	Bremen	W	3-1 *Lasogga, Gregoritsch, Müller*
05/12	h	Mainz	L	1-3 *Djourou*
12/12	h	Wolfsburg	D	1-1 *Müller*
19/12	h	Augsburg	L	0-1

2016

22/01	h	Bayern	L	1-2 *Hunt*
30/01	a	Stuttgart	L	1-2 *Rudņevs*
07/02	h	Köln	D	1-1 *Müller*
14/02	h	Mönchengladbach	W	3-2 *og (Hinteregger), Rudņevs, Ilićević*
19/02	a	Frankfurt	D	0-0
27/02	h	Ingolstadt	D	1-1 *Drmic*
02/03	a	Schalke	L	2-3 *Müller, Kačar*
06/03	h	Hertha	W	2-0 *Müller 2*
13/03	a	Leverkusen	L	0-1
19/03	h	Hoffenheim	L	1-3 *Hunt (p)*
02/04	h	Hannover	W	3-0 *Cléber, Ilićević, Müller*
09/04	a	Darmstadt	L	1-2 *Holtby*
17/04	a	Dortmund	L	0-3
22/04	h	Bremen	W	2-1 *Lasogga 2*
30/04	a	Mainz	D	0-0
07/05	h	Wolfsburg	L	0-1
14/05	a	Augsburg	W	3-1 *Gregoritsch 2, Müller*

No	Name	Nat	DoB	Pos	Aps	(s)	Gls
15	René Adler		15/01/85	G	24		
12	Ahmet Arslan		23/03/94	M		(1)	
21	Nabil Bahoui	SWE	05/02/91	M	2	(4)	
33	Batuhan Altıntas	TUR	14/03/86	M		(1)	
3	Cléber	BRA	05/12/90	D	15	(8)	1
20	Marcelo Díaz	CHI	30/12/86	M	4	(7)	
2	Dennis Diekmeier		20/10/89	D	15	(7)	
5	Johan Djourou	SUI	18/01/87	D	26		2
18	Josip Drmic	SUI	08/08/92	A	5	(1)	1
1	Jaroslav Drobný	CZE	18/10/79	G	9	(1)	
20	Albin Ekdal	SWE	28/07/89	M	14		
23	Michael Gregoritsch	AUT	18/04/94	A	15	(10)	5
30	Andreas Hirzel	SUI	25/03/93	G		(1)	
18	Lewis Holtby		18/09/90	M	34		3
14	Aaron Hunt		04/09/86	M	19	(2)	2
11	Ivo Ilićević	CRO	14/11/86	M	24	(7)	4
28	Gideon Jung		12/09/94	D	13	(6)	
40	Gojko Kačar	SRB	26/01/87	M	12	(7)	1
20	Pierre-Michel Lasogga		15/12/91	A	21	(9)	8
12	Tom Mickel		19/04/89	G	1		
27	Nicolai Müller		25/09/87	M	27	(2)	9
8	Ivica Olić	CRO	14/09/79	A		(9)	
22	Matthias Ostrzolek		05/06/90	D	32		
10	Artjoms Rudņevs	LVA	13/01/88	A	6	(5)	2
24	Gotoku Sakai	JPN	14/03/91	D	21	(1)	
9	Sven Schipplock		08/11/88	A	9	(11)	
4	Emir Spahić	BIH	18/08/80	D	26		
17	Zoltán Stieber	HUN	16/10/88	M		(2)	

Hannover 96

1896 • HDI-Arena (49,000) • hannover96.de

Major honours
German League (2) 1938, 1954; German Cup (1)
1992

Coach: Michael Frontzeck;
(28/12/15) Thomas Schaaf;
(03/04/16) Daniel Stendel

2015

15/08	a	Darmstadt	D	2-2 *Benschop, og (Aytaç)*
22/08	h	Leverkusen	L	0-1
29/08	a	Mainz	L	0-3
12/09	h	Dortmund	L	2-4 *Sobiech 2*
20/09	a	Augsburg	L	0-2
23/09	h	Stuttgart	L	1-3 *Kenan*
26/09	a	Wolfsburg	D	1-1 *Kiyotake*
03/10	h	Bremen	W	1-0 *Sané*
18/10	a	Köln	W	1-0 *Andreasen*
24/10	h	Frankfurt	L	1-2 *Klaus*
01/11	a	Hamburg	W	2-1 *Kiyotake (p), Sané*
06/11	h	Hertha	L	1-3 *Kiyotake (p)*
21/11	a	Mönchengladbach	L	1-2 *Sobiech*
28/11	h	Ingolstadt	W	4-0 *Marcelo, Andreasen, Kenan, Bech*
04/12	a	Schalke	L	1-3 *Saint-Maximin*
12/12	h	Hoffenheim	L	0-1
19/12	h	Bayern	L	0-1

2016

23/01	h	Darmstadt	L	1-2 *Hugo Almeida*
30/01	a	Leverkusen	L	0-3
06/02	h	Mainz	L	0-1
13/02	a	Dortmund	L	0-1
21/02	h	Augsburg	L	0-1
27/02	a	Stuttgart	W	2-1 *Schulz 2*
01/03	h	Wolfsburg	L	0-4
05/03	a	Bremen	L	1-4 *Kenan*
12/03	h	Köln	L	0-2
19/03	a	Frankfurt	L	0-1
02/04	h	Hamburg	L	0-3
08/04	a	Hertha	D	2-2 *Sobiech, Schmiedebach*
15/04	h	Mönchengladbach	W	2-0 *Anton, Sobiech*
23/04	a	Ingolstadt	D	2-2 *Sakai, Kiyotake*
30/04	h	Schalke	L	1-3 *Sobiech*
07/05	h	Hoffenheim	W	1-0 *Kiyotake*
14/05	a	Bayern	L	1-3 *Sobiech*

No	Name	Nat	DoB	Pos	Aps	(s)	Gls
3	Miiko Albornoz	CHI	30/11/90	D	23		
2	Leon Andreasen	DEN	23/04/83	M	13	(2)	2
4	Waldemar Anton		20/07/96	D	6	(2)	1
19	Fynn Arkenberg		04/03/96	D	2		
33	Mike-Steven Bähre		10/08/95	M		(1)	
17	Uffe Bech	DEN	13/01/93	M	8	(3)	1
35	Charlison Benschop	NED	21/08/89	A	2	(7)	1
6	Ceyhun Gülselam	TUR	25/12/87	M	9	(4)	
34	Tim Dierssen		15/01/96	M		(1)	
3	Felipe	BRA	15/05/87	D	1	(7)	
18	Iver Fossum	NOR	15/07/96	M	8	(1)	
15	André Hoffmann		28/02/93	D	7	(1)	
22	Hugo Almeida	POR	23/05/84	A	5	(2)	1
26	Kenan Karaman	TUR	05/03/94	A	19	(4)	3
28	Hiroshi Kiyotake	JPN	12/11/89	M	20	(1)	5
16	Felix Klaus		13/09/92	M	9	(9)	1
25	Marcelo	BRA	20/05/87	D	19		1
39	Mevlüt Erdinç	TUR	25/02/87	A	3	(8)	
24	Alexander Milosevic	SWE	30/01/92	D	10		
7	Edgar Prib		15/12/89	M	16	(4)	
14	Allan Saint-Maximin	FRA	12/03/97	A	1	(15)	1
5	Hiroki Sakai	JPN	12/04/90	D	25	(1)	1
5	Salif Sané	SEN	25/08/90	D	30	(1)	2
37	Noah-Joel Sarenren-Bazee		21/08/96	M	5		
8	Manuel Schmiedebach		05/12/88	M	22		1
15	Christian Schulz		01/04/83	D	24	(1)	2
9	Artur Sobiech	POL	12/06/90	A	19	(6)	7
29	Oliver Sorg		29/05/90	D	19	(1)	
38	Valmir Sulejmani	KOS	01/02/96	M	1	(3)	
28	Ádám Szalai	HUN	09/12/87	A	6	(6)	
21	Marius Wolf		27/05/95	A	2		
16	Hotaru Yamaguchi	JPN	06/10/90	M	6		
1	Ron-Robert Zieler		12/02/89	G	34		

Hertha BSC Berlin

1892 • Olympiastadion (74,649) •
herthabsc.de

Major honours
German League (2) 1930, 1931

Coach: Pál Dárdai (HUN)

2015

15/08	a	Augsburg	W	1-0 *Kalou (p)*
21/08	h	Bremen	D	1-1 *Stocker*
30/08	a	Dortmund	L	1-3 *Kalou*
12/09	h	Stuttgart	W	2-1 *Haraguchi, Lustenberger*
19/09	a	Wolfsburg	L	0-2
22/09	h	Köln	W	2-0 *Ibišević 2*
27/09	a	Frankfurt	D	1-1 *Darida*
03/10	a	Hamburg	W	3-0 *Kalou, Ibišević 2*
17/10	a	Schalke	L	1-2 *Kalou*
24/10	a	Ingolstadt	W	1-0 *Weiser*
31/10	h	Mönchengladbach	L	1-4 *Baumjohann (p)*
06/11	a	Hannover	W	3-1 *Kalou 3 (1p)*
22/11	h	Hoffenheim	W	1-0 *og (Polanski)*
28/11	a	Bayern	L	0-2
05/12	h	Leverkusen	W	2-1 *Darida, Brooks*
12/12	h	Darmstadt	W	4-0 *Ibišević 2, Plattenhardt, Kalou*
20/12	h	Mainz	W	2-0 *Darida, Kalou*

2016

23/01	h	Augsburg	D	0-0
30/01	a	Bremen	D	3-3 *Darida, Plattenhardt, Kalou*
06/02	h	Dortmund	D	0-0
13/02	a	Stuttgart	L	0-2
20/02	h	Wolfsburg	D	1-1 *Kalou*
26/02	a	Köln	W	1-0 *Ibišević*
02/03	h	Frankfurt	W	2-0 *Weiser, Kalou*
06/03	a	Hamburg	L	0-2
11/03	h	Schalke	W	2-0 *Ibišević, Stark*
19/03	h	Ingolstadt	W	2-1 *Haraguchi, Kalou*
03/04	a	Mönchengladbach	L	0-5
08/04	h	Hannover	W	2-0 *Ibišević, Kalou*
16/04	h	Hoffenheim	L	1-2 *Stark*
23/04	h	Bayern	L	0-2
30/04	a	Leverkusen	L	1-2 *Ibišević*
07/05	a	Darmstadt	L	1-2 *Darida*
14/05	a	Mainz	D	0-0

No	Name	Nat	DoB	Pos	Aps	(s)	Gls
9	Alexander Baumjohann		23/01/87	M	1	(23)	1
27	Roy Beerens	NED	22/12/87	M	2		
25	John Brooks	USA	28/01/93	D	20	(3)	1
6	Vladimír Darida	CZE	08/08/90	M	30	(1)	5
24	Genki Haraguchi	JPN	09/05/91	M	28	(4)	2
13	Jens Hegeler		22/01/88	M	3	(13)	
22	Vedad Ibišević	BIH	06/08/84	A	25	(1)	10
22	Rune Almenning Jarstein	NOR	29/09/84	G	28	(1)	
11	Salomon Kalou	CIV	05/08/85	A	30	(2)	14
31	Florian Kohls		03/04/95	M		(1)	
1	Thomas Kraft		22/07/88	G	6		
15	Sebastian Langkamp		15/01/88	D	22		
28	Fabian Lustenberger	SUI	02/05/88	M	30		1
34	Maximilian Mittelstädt		18/03/97	D	2	(1)	
2	Peter Pekarík	SVK	30/10/86	D	12		
39	Marvin Plattenhardt		26/01/92	D	33		2
39	Yanni Regäsel		13/01/96	D	5	(1)	
12	Ronny	BRA	11/05/86	M		(1)	
16	Julian Schieber		13/02/89	A		(6)	
26	Nico Schulz		01/04/93	D		(1)	
13	Per Ciljan Skjelbred	NOR	16/06/87	M	31		
5	Niklas Stark		14/04/95	D	15	(6)	2
14	Valentin Stocker	SUI	12/04/89	M	10	(12)	1
17	Tolga Ciğerci	TUR	23/03/92	M	13	(5)	
23	Johannes van den Bergh		21/11/86	D	1	(12)	
20	Mitchell Weiser		21/04/94	D	27	(2)	2

GERMANY

TSG 1899 Hoffenheim

1899 • Rhein-Neckar-Arena (30,150) • achtzehn99.de
**Coach: Markus Gisdol;
(27/10/15) Huub Stevens (NED);
(11/02/16) Julian Nagelsmann**

2015
15/08	a	Leverkusen	L	1-2	Zuber
22/08	h	Bayern	L	1-2	Volland
29/08	a	Darmstadt	D	0-0	
13/09	h	Bremen	L	1-3	Vargas
18/09	a	Mainz	L	1-3	Schmid
23/09	h	Dortmund	D	1-1	Rudy
26/09	a	Augsburg	W	3-1	Volland 2 (1p), Schmid
03/10	h	Stuttgart	D	2-2	Volland 2 (1p)
17/10	a	Wolfsburg	L	2-4	Toljan, Schmid
23/10	h	Hamburg	L	0-1	
31/10	a	Köln	D	0-0	
07/11	h	Frankfurt	D	0-0	
22/11	a	Hertha	D	0-0	
28/11	h	Mönchengladbach	D	3-3	Zuber, Polanski, Amiri
05/12	a	Ingolstadt	D	1-1	Uth
12/12	h	Hannover	W	1-0	Schmid
18/12	a	Schalke	L	0-1	

2016
23/01	h	Leverkusen	D	1-1	Hamad
31/01	a	Bayern	L	0-2	
07/02	h	Darmstadt	L	0-2	
13/02	a	Bremen	D	1-1	Kramarić
20/02	h	Mainz	W	3-2	Amiri, Uth 2
28/02	a	Dortmund	L	1-3	Rudy
02/03	h	Augsburg	W	2-1	Volland, Uth
05/03	a	Stuttgart	L	1-5	Kramarić
12/03	h	Wolfsburg	W	1-0	Kramarić
19/03	a	Hamburg	W	3-1	Kramarić (p), Volland, Vargas
03/04	a	Köln	D	1-1	Volland
09/04	a	Frankfurt	W	2-0	Amiri, Uth
16/04	h	Hertha	W	2-1	Schär, Uth
24/04	a	Mönchengladbach	L	1-3	Kramarić
30/04	h	Ingolstadt	W	2-1	Uth, Amiri
07/04	a	Hannover	L	0-1	
14/05	h	Schalke	L	1-4	Uth

No	Name	Nat	DoB	Pos	Aps	(s)	Gls
34	Nadiem Amiri		27/10/96	M	16	(9)	4
1	Oliver Baumann		02/06/90	G	33		
4	Ermin Bičakčić	BIH	24/01/90	D	18	(3)	
16	Russell Canouse	USA	11/06/95	M		(1)	
14	Tarik Elyounoussi	NOR	23/02/88	M	5	(1)	
13	Jens Grahl		22/09/88	G	1		
11	Jiloan Hamad	SWE	06/11/90	M	4	(3)	1
40	Joelinton	BRA	14/08/96	A		(1)	
3	Pavel Kadeřábek	CZE	25/04/92	D	25	(3)	
20	Kim Jin-su	KOR	13/06/92	D	14	(1)	
27	Andrej Kramarić	CRO	19/06/91	A	12	(3)	5
22	Kevin Kuranyi		02/03/82	A	5	(9)	
30	Philipp Ochs		17/04/97	A	6	(7)	
8	Eugen Polanski	POL	17/03/86	M	20	(7)	1
5	Sebastian Rudy		28/02/90	M	22	(2)	2
5	Fabian Schär	SUI	20/12/91	D	20	(4)	1
10	Jonathan Schmid	FRA	22/06/90	M	16	(7)	4
16	Pirmin Schwegler	SUI	09/03/87	M	16	(5)	
12	Tobias Strobl		12/05/90	M	22	(4)	
25	Niklas Süle		03/09/95	D	33		
28	Ádám Szalai	HUN	09/12/87	A	1	(3)	
36	Jeremy Toljan		08/08/94	D	16	(2)	1
19	Mark Uth		24/08/91	A	16	(9)	8
9	Eduardo Vargas	CHI	20/11/89	A	16	(8)	2
31	Kevin Volland		30/07/92	A	31	(2)	8
17	Steven Zuber	SUI	17/08/91	M	6	(6)	2

FC Ingolstadt 04

2004 • Audi-Sportpark (15,800) • fcingolstadt.de
Coach: Ralph Hasenhüttl (AUT)

2015
15/08	a	Mainz	W	1-0	Hinterseer
23/08	h	Dortmund	L	0-4	
29/08	a	Augsburg	W	1-0	Leckie
12/09	h	Wolfsburg	D	0-0	
19/09	a	Bremen	W	1-0	Hartmann (p)
22/09	h	Hamburg	L	0-1	
25/09	a	Köln	D	1-1	Matip
03/10	h	Frankfurt	W	2-0	Gross, Lex
18/10	a	Stuttgart	L	0-1	
24/10	h	Hertha	L	0-1	
31/10	a	Schalke	D	1-1	Levels
07/11	a	Mönchengladbach	D	0-0	
22/11	h	Darmstadt	W	3-1	Bauer, Hartmann 2 (1p)
28/11	a	Hannover	L	0-4	
05/12	h	Hoffenheim	D	1-1	Roger
12/12	a	Bayern	L	0-2	
19/12	h	Leverkusen	L	0-1	

2016
23/01	h	Mainz	W	1-0	Hartmann (p)
30/01	a	Dortmund	L	0-2	
06/02	h	Augsburg	W	2-1	Matip, Hartmann (p)
13/02	a	Wolfsburg	L	0-2	
20/02	h	Bremen	W	2-0	Hübner, Hinterseer (p)
27/02	a	Hamburg	D	1-1	Hinterseer
01/03	h	Köln	D	1-1	Hinterseer
05/03	a	Frankfurt	D	1-1	Hartmann (p)
12/03	h	Stuttgart	D	3-3	Hartmann, Leckie, Lezcano
19/03	a	Hertha	L	1-2	Hinterseer
02/04	h	Schalke	W	3-0	Hartmann (p), Hinterseer, Lezcano
09/04	h	Mönchengladbach	W	1-0	Hartmann
16/04	a	Darmstadt	L	0-2	
23/04	h	Hannover	D	2-2	Morales, Hartmann
30/04	a	Hoffenheim	L	1-2	Lex
07/05	h	Bayern	L	1-2	Hartmann (p)
14/05	a	Leverkusen	L	2-3	Leckie, Hartmann (p)

No	Name	Nat	DoB	Pos	Aps	(s)	Gls
23	Robert Bauer		09/04/95	M	18	(6)	1
18	Romain Brégerie	FRA	09/08/86	D	12	(10)	
19	Max Christansen		25/09/96	M	12	(7)	
36	Almog Cohen	ISR	01/09/88	M	8	(12)	
21	Danny Da Costa		13/07/93	D	17	(3)	
15	Danilo	BRA	29/10/91	D	1		
20	Konstantin Engel	KAZ	27/07/88	D	2	(2)	
10	Pascal Gross		15/06/91	M	32		1
9	Moritz Hartmann		06/08/86	A	24	(6)	12
16	Lukas Hinterseer	AUT	28/03/91	A	19	(9)	6
5	Benjamin Hübner		04/07/89	D	30		1
25	Elias Kachunga		22/04/92	A	3	(7)	
7	Matthew Leckie	AUS	04/02/91	A	28	(4)	3
28	Tobias Levels		22/11/86	D	16		1
14	Stefan Lex		27/11/89	A	9	(12)	2
37	Darío Lezcano	PAR	30/06/90	A	15	(2)	2
34	Marvin Matip	CMR	25/09/85	D	32	(1)	2
6	Alfredo Morales	USA	12/05/90	M	18	(6)	1
31	Maurice Multhaup		15/12/96	M		(4)	
26	Ørjan Håskjold Nyland	NOR	10/09/90	G	6		
1	Ramazan Özcan	AUT	28/06/84	G	28		
11	Tomáš Pekhart	CZE	26/05/89	A	1	(3)	
8	Roger	BRA	10/08/85	M	28	(1)	1
29	Markus Suttner	AUT	16/04/87	D	15	(1)	
22	Stefan Wannenwetsch		19/01/92	M		(1)	

1. FC Köln

1948 • Rhein-Energie-Stadion (50,000) • fc-koeln.de
Major honours
German League (3) 1962, 1964, 1978; German Cup (4) 1968, 1977, 1978, 1983
Coach: Peter Stöger (AUT)

2015
16/08	a	Stuttgart	W	3-1	Modeste (p), Zoller, Osako
22/08	h	Wolfsburg	D	1-1	Zoller
29/08	h	Hamburg	W	2-1	Hosiner, Modeste (p)
12/09	a	Frankfurt	L	2-6	Modeste, Heintz
19/09	h	Mönchengladbach	W	1-0	Modeste
22/09	a	Hertha	L	0-2	
25/09	h	Ingolstadt	D	1-1	Modeste
04/10	a	Schalke	W	3-0	Modeste, Gerhardt, Zoller
18/10	h	Hannover	L	0-1	
24/10	a	Bayern	L	0-4	
31/10	h	Hoffenheim	D	0-0	
07/11	a	Leverkusen	W	2-1	Maroh 2
21/11	h	Mainz	D	0-0	
27/11	a	Darmstadt	D	0-0	
05/12	h	Augsburg	L	0-1	
12/12	a	Bremen	D	1-1	Švento
19/12	h	Dortmund	W	2-1	Zoller, Modeste

2016
23/01	h	Stuttgart	L	1-3	Modeste (p)
31/01	a	Wolfsburg	D	1-1	Modeste
07/02	h	Hamburg	D	1-1	Zoller
13/02	h	Frankfurt	W	3-1	Gerhardt, Heintz, Modeste
20/02	a	Mönchengladbach	L	0-1	
26/02	h	Hertha	L	0-1	
01/03	a	Ingolstadt	D	1-1	Modeste
05/03	h	Schalke	L	1-3	Bittencourt
12/03	a	Hannover	W	2-0	Bittencourt 2
19/03	h	Bayern	L	0-1	
03/04	h	Hoffenheim	D	1-1	Zoller
10/04	a	Leverkusen	L	0-2	
17/04	a	Mainz	W	3-2	Risse, Jojić, Modeste
23/04	h	Darmstadt	W	4-1	Modeste 2, Risse 2
29/04	a	Augsburg	D	0-0	
07/05	h	Bremen	D	0-0	
14/05	a	Dortmund	D	2-2	Modeste, Jojić

No	Name	Nat	DoB	Pos	Aps	(s)	Gls
21	Leonardo Bittencourt		19/12/93	M	27	(2)	3
31	Yannick Gerhardt		13/03/94	M	22	(7)	2
16	Marcel Hartel		19/01/96	M		(6)	
14	Jonas Hector		27/05/90	D	32		
3	Dominique Heintz		15/08/93	D	32	(1)	2
1	Timo Horn		12/05/93	G	33		
15	Philipp Hosiner	AUT	15/05/89	A	4	(11)	1
8	Miloš Jojić	SRB	19/03/92	M	2	(13)	2
18	Thomas Kessler		20/01/86	G	1		
33	Lukas Klünter		26/05/96	D		(1)	
33	Matthias Lehmann		28/05/83	M	31	(1)	
5	Dominic Maroh	SVN	04/03/87	D	23	(2)	2
19	Mērgim Mavraj	ALB	09/06/86	D	11	(1)	
25	Filip Mladenović	SRB	15/08/91	D	10	(4)	
27	Anthony Modeste	FRA	14/04/88	A	33	(1)	15
25	Kazuki Nagasawa	JPN	16/12/91	M	1		
16	Paweł Olkowski	POL	13/02/90	D	13	(6)	
13	Yuya Osako	JPN	18/05/90	A	14	(11)	1
7	Marcel Risse		17/12/89	M	33		5
29	Dušan Švento	SVK	01/08/85	M	2	(5)	1
4	Frederik Sørensen	DEN	14/04/92	D	19	(3)	
6	Kevin Vogt		23/09/91	M	17	(6)	
23	Simon Zoller		26/06/91	A	14	(10)	6

1. FSV Mainz 05

1905 • Coface-Arena (34,000) • mainz05.de
Coach: Martin Schmidt (SUI)

2015

15/08	h	Ingolstadt	L	0-1	
23/08	a	Mönchengladbach	W	2-1	Jairo Samperio, Clemens
29/08	h	Hannover	W	3-0	Muto 2, Yunus
13/09	a	Schalke	L	1-2	Yunus
18/09	h	Hoffenheim	W	3-1	Yunus 3
23/09	a	Leverkusen	L	0-1	
26/09	h	Bayern	L	0-3	
02/10	a	Darmstadt	W	3-2	Bell, Yunus, De Blasis
16/10	a	Dortmund	L	0-2	
24/10	h	Bremen	L	1-3	Muto
31/10	a	Augsburg	D	3-3	Muto 3
07/11	h	Wolfsburg	W	2-0	De Blasis, Yunus
21/11	a	Köln	D	0-0	
28/11	h	Frankfurt	W	2-1	Muto, Yunus
05/12	h	Hamburg	W	3-1	Jairo Samperio 2, Clemens
11/12	h	Stuttgart	D	0-0	
20/12	a	Hertha	L	0-2	

2016

23/01	a	Ingolstadt	L	0-1	
29/01	h	Mönchengladbach	W	1-0	Clemens
06/02	a	Hannover	W	1-0	Jairo Samperio
12/02	h	Schalke	W	2-1	Bussmann, Baumgartlinger
20/02	a	Hoffenheim	L	2-3	Córdoba, Jairo Samperio
28/02	a	Leverkusen	W	3-1	Yunus 2 (1p), Córdoba
02/03	a	Bayern	W	2-1	Jairo Samperio, Córdoba
06/03	h	Darmstadt	D	0-0	
13/03	a	Dortmund	L	0-2	
19/03	a	Bremen	D	1-1	Baumgartlinger
02/04	h	Augsburg	W	4-2	Clemens 2, De Blasis 2
09/04	a	Wolfsburg	D	1-1	Jairo Samperio
17/04	h	Köln	L	2-3	Córdoba, Balogun
24/04	a	Frankfurt	L	1-2	Brosinski
30/04	h	Hamburg	D	0-0	
07/05	a	Stuttgart	W	3-1	Yunus, Córdoba, Onisiwo
14/05	h	Hertha	D	0-0	

No	Name	Nat	DoB	Pos	Aps	(s)	Gls
3	Leon Balogun	NGA	28/06/88	D	17	(4)	1
14	Julian Baumgartlinger	AUT	02/01/88	M	30	(1)	2
11	Maximilian Beister		06/09/90	A		(1)	
16	Stefan Bell		24/08/91	D	29	(1)	1
7	Pierre Bengtsson	SWE	12/04/88	D	14	(2)	
18	Daniel Brosinski		17/07/88	D	24	(6)	1
26	Niko Bungert		24/10/86	D	20	(1)	
24	Gaëtan Bussmann	FRA	02/02/91	D	13		1
27	Christian Clemens		04/08/91	M	20	(8)	5
15	Jhon Córdoba	COL	11/05/93	A	14	(8)	5
15	Pablo De Blasis	ARG	04/02/88	M	18	(8)	4
2	Giulio Donati	ITA	05/02/90	D	11		
20	Fabian Frei	SUI	08/01/89	M	11	(7)	
42	Alexander Hack		08/09/93	D	7		
17	Jairo Samperio	ESP	11/07/93	M	26	(5)	7
2	Gonzalo Jara	CHI	29/08/85	D	5	(1)	
21	Loris Karius		22/06/93	G	34		
47	Philipp Klement		09/09/92	M		(2)	
13	Koo Ja-cheol	KOR	27/02/89	M		(2)	
6	Danny Latza		07/12/89	M	20	(7)	
8	Christoph Moritz		27/01/90	M	3	(5)	
9	Yoshinori Muto	JPN	15/07/92	A	18	(2)	7
31	Florian Niederlechner		24/10/90	A	1	(11)	
21	Karim Onisiwo	AUT	17/03/92	A	3	(6)	1
24	Park Joo-ho	KOR	16/01/87	D	1		
29	Devante Parker		16/03/96	A		(1)	
45	Suat Serdar			M	2	(10	
19	Elkin Soto	COL	04/08/80	M		(1)	
11	Yunus Mallı	TUR	24/02/92	M	33	(1)	11

FC Schalke 04

1904 • Veltins-Arena (62,271) • schalke04.de
Major honours
UEFA Cup (1) 1997; German League (7) 1934, 1935, 1937, 1939, 1940, 1942, 1958; German Cup (5) 1937, 1972, 2001, 2002, 2011
Coach: André Breitenreiter

2015

15/08	a	Bremen	W	3-0	og (Gebre Selassie), Choupo-Moting, Huntelaar
22/08	h	Darmstadt	D	1-1	Draxler
28/08	h	Wolfsburg	L	0-3	
13/09	a	Mainz	W	2-1	Matip, Huntelaar
20/09	a	Stuttgart	W	1-0	Sané
23/09	h	Frankfurt	W	2-0	Matip, Sané
26/09	a	Hamburg	W	1-0	Sané
04/10	h	Köln	L	0-3	
17/10	h	Hertha	W	2-1	Höwedes, Meyer
25/10	a	Mönchengladbach	L	1-3	og (Christensen)
31/10	h	Ingolstadt	D	1-1	Sané
08/11	h	Dortmund	L	2-3	Huntelaar 2
21/11	h	Bayern	L	1-3	Meyer
29/11	a	Leverkusen	D	1-1	Choupo-Moting
04/12	h	Hannover	W	3-1	Geis (p), Huntelaar, Di Santo
13/12	a	Augsburg	L	1-2	Kolašinac
18/12	h	Hoffenheim	W	1-0	Choupo-Moting

2016

24/01	h	Bremen	L	1-3	Matip
30/01	a	Darmstadt	W	2-0	Meyer, Sané
06/02	h	Wolfsburg	W	3-0	Huntelaar, Geis, Schöpf
12/02	a	Mainz	L	1-2	Belhanda
21/02	h	Stuttgart	D	1-1	Belhanda
28/02	a	Frankfurt	D	0-0	
02/03	h	Hamburg	W	3-2	Meyer, Huntelaar, Schöpf
05/03	a	Köln	W	3-1	Huntelaar (p), Meyer, Di Santo
11/03	a	Hertha	L	0-2	
18/03	h	Mönchengladbach	W	2-1	og (Hinteregger), Goretzka
02/04	a	Ingolstadt	L	0-3	
10/04	h	Dortmund	D	2-2	Sané, Huntelaar (p)
16/04	a	Bayern	L	0-3	
23/04	h	Leverkusen	L	2-3	Choupo-Moting, Sané
30/04	a	Hannover	W	3-1	Choupo-Moting, Huntelaar, Schöpf
07/05	h	Augsburg	D	1-1	Huntelaar
14/05	a	Hoffenheim	W	4-1	Huntelaar, Choupo-Moting, Sané, og (Schär)

No	Name	Nat	DoB	Pos	Aps	(s)	Gls
15	Dennis Aogo		14/01/87	D	20	(3)	
11	Younes Belhanda	MAR	25/02/90	M	8	(7)	2
13	Eric Maxim Choupo-Moting	CMR	23/03/89	A	21	(7)	6
9	Franco Di Santo	ARG	07/04/89	A	13	(12)	2
10	Julian Draxler		20/09/93	M	3		1
1	Ralf Fährmann		27/09/88	G	34		
2	Marvin Friedrich		13/12/95	D		(2)	
5	Johannes Geis		17/08/93	M	27	(1)	2
8	Leon Goretzka		06/02/95	M	23	(2)	1
12	Marco Höger		16/09/89	M	3	(2)	
23	Pierre Højbjerg	DEN	05/08/95	M	13	(10)	
4	Benedikt Höwedes		29/02/88	D	10	(5)	1
25	Klaas-Jan Huntelaar	NED	12/08/83	A	29	(2)	12
3	Júnior Caiçara	BRA	27/03/89	D	22	(1)	
24	Kaan Ayhan	TUR	10/11/94	D		(1)	
20	Thilo Kehrer		21/09/96	D		(1)	
6	Sead Kolašinac	BIH	20/06/93	D	18	(5)	1
32	Joël Matip	CMR	08/08/91	D	34		3
7	Max Meyer		18/09/95	M	27	(5)	5
31	Matija Nastasić	SRB	28/03/93	D	1		
33	Roman Neustädter	RUS	18/02/88	D	26	(4)	
35	Alexander Nübel		30/09/96	G		(1)	
36	Felix Platte		11/02/96	A		(1)	
16	Fabian Reese		29/11/97	A		(1)	
27	Sascha Riether		23/03/83	D	14	(1)	
18	Sidney Sam		31/01/88	M		(2)	
13	Leroy Sané		11/01/96	M	23	(10)	8
21	Alessandro Schöpf	AUT	07/02/94	M	5	(8)	3

VfB Stuttgart

1893 • Mercedes-Benz-Arena (60,441) • vfb.de
Major honours
German League (5) 1950, 1952, 1984, 1992, 2007; German Cup (3) 1954, 1958, 1997
Coach: Alexander Zorniger; (24/11/15) Jürgen Kramny

2015

16/08	h	Köln	L	1-3	Didavi (p)
22/08	a	Hamburg	L	2-3	Ginczek 2
29/08	h	Frankfurt	L	1-4	Didavi
12/09	a	Hertha	L	1-2	Šunjić
20/09	h	Schalke	L	0-1	
23/09	a	Hannover	W	3-1	Gentner, Werner, Maxim
26/09	h	Mönchengladbach	L	1-3	Ginczek 2
03/10	a	Hoffenheim	D	2-2	Kliment, Werner
18/10	h	Ingolstadt	W	1-0	Didavi
24/10	a	Leverkusen	L	3-4	Harnik, Didavi, Rupp
01/11	h	Darmstadt	W	2-0	og (Garics), Werner
07/11	a	Bayern	L	0-4	
21/11	h	Augsburg	L	0-4	
29/11	a	Dortmund	L	1-4	Didavi
06/12	h	Bremen	D	1-1	Rupp
11/12	a	Mainz	D	0-0	
19/12	h	Wolfsburg	W	3-1	Didavi 2, Kostić

2016

23/01	a	Köln	W	3-1	Didavi, Werner, Gentner
30/01	h	Hamburg	W	2-1	og (Hunt), Kravets
06/02	a	Frankfurt	W	4-2	Gentner, Didavi, Niedermeier, Kostić (p)
13/02	h	Hertha	W	2-0	Serey Dié, Kostić
21/02	a	Schalke	D	1-1	Harnik
27/02	h	Hannover	L	1-2	Werner
02/03	a	Mönchengladbach	L	0-4	
05/03	h	Hoffenheim	W	5-1	Niedermeier 2, Rupp, Kostić, Werner
12/03	a	Ingolstadt	D	3-3	Kostić, Rupp, Didavi (p)
20/03	h	Leverkusen	L	0-2	
02/04	a	Darmstadt	D	2-2	Gentner, Rupp
09/04	h	Bayern	L	1-3	Didavi
16/04	a	Augsburg	L	0-1	
23/04	h	Dortmund	L	0-3	
02/05	h	Bremen	L	2-6	Didavi, Barba
07/05	h	Mainz	L	1-3	Gentner
14/05	a	Wolfsburg	L	1-3	Didavi

No	Name	Nat	DoB	Pos	Aps	(s)	Gls
24	Federico Barba	ITA	01/09/93	D	2		1
32	Timo Baumgartl		04/03/96	D	17	(2)	
10	Daniel Didavi		21/02/90	M	30	(1)	13
31	Arianit Ferati		07/09/97	M		(3)	
20	Christian Gentner		14/08/85	M	29		5
33	Daniel Ginczek		13/04/91	A	7		3
15	Kevin Grosskreutz		19/07/88	D	10		
11	Carlos Gruezo	ECU	19/04/95	M	1	(1)	
7	Martin Harnik	AUT	10/06/87	A	11	(8)	2
14	Philip Heise		20/06/91	D	4	(3)	
21	Adam Hloušek	CZE	20/12/88	M	4	(3)	
2	Emiliano Insúa	ARG	07/01/89	D	33		
16	Florian Klein	AUT	17/11/86	D	17	(5)	
39	Jan Kliment	CZE	01/09/93	A		(8)	1
18	Filip Kostić	SRB	01/11/92	M	30		5
23	Artem Kravets	UKR	03/06/89	A	5	(10)	1
9	Robbie Kruse	AUS	05/10/88	A		(3)	
1	Mitchell Langerak	AUS	22/08/88	G	2		
44	Alexandru Maxim	ROU	08/07/90	M	9	(16)	1
6	Georg Niedermeier		26/02/86	D	16	(2)	3
27	Mart Ristl		07/07/96	M		(3)	
8	Lukas Rupp		08/01/91	M	24	(5)	5
3	Daniel Schwaab		23/08/88	D	26	(3)	
26	Serey Dié	CIV	07/11/84	M	23		1
4	Toni Šunjić	BIH	15/12/88	D	17	(2)	1
34	Borys Tashchy	UKR	26/07/93	A		(9)	
22	Przemysław Tytoń	POL	04/01/87	G	30		
17	Odisseas Vlachodimos	GRE	26/04/94	G	2	(1)	
28	Marvin Wanitzek		07/05/93	M		(1)	
19	Timo Werner		06/03/96	A	26	(7)	6
25	Matthias Zimmermann		16/06/92	D	2		

 # GERMANY

SV Werder Bremen

1899 • Weserstadion (42,100) • werder.de

Major honours
UEFA Cup Winners' Cup (1) 1992; German League (4) 1965, 1988, 1993, 2004; German Cup (6) 1961, 1991, 1994, 1999, 2004, 2009

Coach: Viktor Skrypnyk (UKR)

2015
15/08	h	Schalke	L 0-3	
21/08	a	Hertha	D 1-1	Ujah
30/08	h	Mönchengladbach	W 2-1	Jóhannsson (p), Vestergaard
13/09	a	Hoffenheim	W 3-1	Junuzovic 2, Ujah
19/09	a	Ingolstadt	L 0-1	
22/09	a	Darmstadt	L 1-2	Jóhannsson
26/09	h	Leverkusen	L 0-3	
03/10	a	Hannover	L 0-1	
17/10	h	Bayern	L 0-1	
24/10	a	Mainz	W 3-1	Ujah 2, Bartels
31/10	h	Dortmund	L 1-3	Ujah
08/11	a	Augsburg	W 2-1	Pizarro, Bartels
21/11	a	Wolfsburg	L 0-6	
28/11	h	Hamburg	L 1-3	Ujah
06/12	a	Stuttgart	D 1-1	Ujah
12/12	h	Köln	D 1-1	Vestergaard
19/12	a	Frankfurt	L 1-2	Pizarro

2016
24/01	h	Schalke	W 3-1	Fritz, Pizarro, Ujah
30/01	h	Hertha	D 3-3	Bartels, Pizarro 2 (1p)
05/02	a	Mönchengladbach	L 1-5	Pizarro (p)
13/02	h	Hoffenheim	D 1-1	Djilobodji
20/02	a	Ingolstadt	L 0-2	
27/02	h	Darmstadt	D 2-2	Ujah, Pizarro
02/03	a	Leverkusen	W 4-1	Bartels, Pizarro 3 (1p)
05/03	h	Hannover	W 4-1	Bartels, Pizarro, Gebre Selassie, Junuzovic
12/03	a	Bayern	L 0-5	
19/03	h	Mainz	D 1-1	Pizarro (p)
02/04	a	Dortmund	L 2-3	Gálvez, Junuzovic
09/04	h	Augsburg	L 1-2	Grillitsch
16/04	h	Wolfsburg	W 3-2	Pizarro (p), Bartels, Yatabaré
22/04	a	Hamburg	L 1-2	Ujah
02/05	h	Stuttgart	W 6-2	Bartels 2, og (Barba), Öztunali, Pizarro, Ujah
07/05	a	Köln	D 0-0	
14/05	h	Frankfurt	W 1-0	Djilobodji

No	Name	Nat	DoB	Pos	Aps	(s)	Gls
44	Philipp Bargfrede		03/03/89	M	14		
22	Fin Bartels		07/02/87	M	22	(8)	8
3	Papy Djilobodji	SEN	01/12/88	D	14		2
35	Maximilian Eggestein		08/12/96	M	2	(5)	
8	Clemens Fritz		07/12/80	M	29		1
39	Lukas Fröde		23/01/95	M	1	(7)	
4	Alejandro Gálvez	ESP	06/06/89	D	15	(6)	1
20	Ulisses Garcia	SUI	11/01/96	D	7	(4)	
2	Santiago García	ARG	08/07/88	D	29		
23	Theodor Gebre Selassie	CZE	24/12/86	D	33		1
27	Florian Grillitsch	AUT	07/08/95	M	23	(2)	1
29	Leon Guwara		28/06/96	D	1		
33	Marcel Hilssner		30/01/95	M		(1)	
25	Oliver Hüsing		17/02/93	D		(1)	
9	Aron Jóhannsson	USA	10/11/90	A	5	(1)	2
16	Zlatko Junuzovic	AUT	26/09/87	M	26	(4)	4
6	László Kleinheisler	HUN	08/04/94	M	1	(5)	
18	Felix Kroos		12/03/91	M	2	(6)	
22	Melvyn Lorenzen		26/11/94	A	1	(8)	
5	Assani Lukimya	COD	25/01/86	D	10	(2)	
11	Levin Öztunali		15/03/96	M	17	(8)	1
14	Claudio Pizarro	PER	03/10/78	A	17	(11)	14
37	Janek Sternberg		19/10/92	D	4	(5)	
21	Anthony Ujah	NGA	14/10/90	A	26	(6)	11
13	Miloš Veljković	SRB	26/09/95	D	1	(2)	
7	Jannik Vestergaard	DEN	03/08/92	D	33		2
42	Felix Wiedwald		15/03/90	G	34		
5	Sambou Yatabaré	MLI	02/03/89	M	6	(2)	1
17	Özkan Yıldırım		10/04/93	M		(1)	
19	Luca-Milan Zander		09/08/95	D	1	(1)	

VfL Wolfsburg

1945 • Volkswagen-Arena (30,000) • vfl-wolfsburg.de

Major honours
German League (1) 2009; German Cup (1) 2015

Coach: Dieter Hecking

2015
16/08	h	Frankfurt	W 2-1	Perišić, Dost
22/08	a	Köln	D 1-1	Bendtner
28/08	h	Schalke	W 3-0	Dost, R Rodriguez (p), Klose
12/09	a	Ingolstadt	D 0-0	
19/09	h	Hertha	W 2-0	Dost 2 (1p)
22/09	a	Bayern	L 1-5	Caligiuri
26/09	h	Hannover	D 1-1	Dost
03/10	a	Mönchengladbach	L 0-2	
17/10	h	Hoffenheim	W 4-2	Kruse 3, Dost
24/10	a	Darmstadt	W 1-0	Caligiuri
31/10	h	Leverkusen	W 2-1	Bendtner, Draxler
07/11	a	Mainz	L 0-2	
21/11	h	Bremen	W 6-0	og (Gálvez), Kruse 2, Vieirinha, Guilavogui, Dost
29/11	a	Augsburg	D 0-0	
05/12	h	Dortmund	L 1-2	R Rodriguez (p)
12/12	h	Hamburg	D 1-1	Arnold
19/12	a	Stuttgart	L 1-3	Arnold

2016
24/01	a	Frankfurt	L 2-3	Dante, Schürrle
31/01	h	Köln	D 1-1	Draxler
06/02	a	Schalke	L 0-3	
13/02	h	Ingolstadt	W 2-0	Draxler, Knoche
20/02	a	Hertha	D 1-1	Schäfer
27/02	h	Bayern	L 0-2	
01/03	a	Hannover	W 4-0	Schürrle 3, Draxler
05/03	h	Mönchengladbach	W 2-1	Draxler, Kruse
12/03	a	Hoffenheim	L 0-1	
19/03	h	Darmstadt	D 1-1	Schürrle
01/04	a	Leverkusen	L 0-3	
09/04	h	Mainz	D 1-1	Schürrle
16/04	a	Bremen	L 2-3	Guilavogui, Dost
23/04	h	Augsburg	L 0-2	
30/04	a	Dortmund	L 1-5	Schürrle
07/05	h	Hamburg	W 1-0	Luiz Gustavo
14/05	h	Stuttgart	W 3-1	Arnold, Schürrle 2

No	Name	Nat	DoB	Pos	Aps	(s)	Gls
27	Maximilian Arnold		27/05/94	M	22	(9)	3
6	Carlos Ascues	PER	19/06/92	M		(1)	
38	Ismail Azzaoui	BEL	06/01/98	M		(2)	
1	Diego Benaglio	SUI	08/09/83	G	21		
3	Nicklas Bendtner	DEN	16/01/88	A	4	(9)	2
16	Bruno Henrique	BRA	30/12/90	A	2	(5)	
7	Daniel Caligiuri	ITA	15/01/88	M	20	(9)	2
28	Koen Casteels	BEL	25/06/92	G	13		
18	Dante	BRA	18/10/83	D	23		1
14	Kevin De Bruyne	BEL	28/06/91	M	2		
12	Bas Dost	NED	31/05/89	A	14	(8)	8
10	Julian Draxler		20/09/93	M	19	(2)	5
23	Josuha Guilavogui	FRA	19/09/90	M	26	(4)	2
10	Aaron Hunt		04/09/86	M	1	(1)	
24	Sebastian Jung		22/06/90	D	5	(6)	
5	Timm Klose	SUI	09/05/88	D	7	(1)	1
31	Robin Knoche		22/05/92	D	9	(2)	1
11	Max Kruse		19/03/88	A	28	(4)	6
22	Luiz Gustavo	BRA	23/07/87	M	22		1
25	Naldo	BRA	10/09/82	D	29		
9	Ivan Perišić	CRO	02/02/89	M	2		1
32	Leandro Putaro		07/01/97	A		(4)	
35	Francisco Rodriguez	SUI	14/09/95	M		(1)	
34	Ricardo Rodriguez	SUI	25/08/92	D	23	(1)	2
4	Marcel Schäfer		07/06/84	D	14	(7)	1
17	André Schürrle		06/11/90	M	21	(8)	9
30	Paul Seguin		29/03/95	M	2	(2)	
15	Christian Träsch		01/09/87	D	23	(6)	
8	Vieirinha	POR	24/01/86	M	22	(4)	1

Top goalscorers

30	Robert Lewandowski (Bayern)
25	Pierre-Emerick Aubameyang (Dortmund)
20	Thomas Müller (Bayern)
17	Javier Hernández (Leverkusen)
15	Anthony Modeste (Köln)
14	Sandro Wagner (Darmstadt) Salomon Kalou (Hertha) Claudio Pizarro (Bremen)
13	Raffael (Mönchengladbach) Daniel Didavi (Stuttgart)

Promoted clubs

SC Freiburg

1904 • Schwarzwald-Stadion (24,000) • scfreiburg.com

Coach: Christian Streich

RB Leipzig

2009 • Red-Bull-Arena (43,348) • dierotenbullen.com

Coach: Ralf Rangnick

Second level final table 2015/16

		Pld	W	D	L	F	A	Pts
1	SC Freiburg	34	22	6	6	75	39	72
2	RB Leipzig	34	20	7	7	54	32	67
3	1. FC Nürnberg	34	19	8	7	68	41	65
4	FC St Pauli	34	15	8	11	45	39	53
5	VfL Bochum	34	13	12	9	56	40	51
6	1. FC Union Berlin	34	13	10	11	56	50	49
7	Karlsruher SC	34	12	11	11	35	37	47
8	TSV Eintracht Braunschweig	34	12	10	12	44	38	46
9	SpVgg Greuther Fürth	34	13	7	14	49	55	46
10	1. FC Kaiserslautern	34	12	9	13	49	47	45
11	1. FC Heidenheim	34	11	12	11	42	40	45
12	DSC Arminia Bielefeld	34	8	18	8	38	39	42
13	SV Sandhausen	34	12	7	15	40	50	40
14	Fortuna Düsseldorf	34	9	8	17	32	47	35
15	TSV 1860 München	34	8	10	16	32	46	34
16	MSV Duisburg	34	7	11	16	32	54	32
17	FSV Frankfurt	34	8	8	18	33	59	32
18	SC Paderborn 07	34	6	10	18	28	55	28

NB SV Sandhausen – 3pts deducted.

Promotion/Relegation play-offs

(19/05/16 & 23/05/16)
Eintracht Frankfurt 1-1 Nürnberg
Nürnberg 0-1 Eintracht Frankfurt
(Eintracht Frankfurt 2-1)

DOMESTIC CUP

DFB-Pokal 2015/16

FIRST ROUND

(07/08/15)
Dynamo Berlin 0-2 FSV Frankfurt
Elversberg 1-3 Augsburg *(aet)*
Erndtebrück 0-5 Darmstadt

(08/08/15)
1860 München 2-0 Hoffenheim
Aue 1-0 Greuther Fürth
Bremer SV 0-3 Eintracht Frankfurt
Duisburg 0-5 Schalke
Halle 0-1 Eintracht Braunschweig
Kiel 1-2 Stuttgart
Lotte 0-3 Leverkusen
Meppen 0-4 1. FC Köln
Reutlingen 3-1 Karlsruhe
Stuttgarter Kickers 1-4 Wolfsburg
Viktoria Köln 2-1 Union Berlin
Würzburg 0-2 Werder Bremen *(aet)*

(09/08/15)
Bahlingen 0-0 Sandhausen *(aet; 3-5 on pens)*
Barmbek-Uhlenhorst 0-5 Freiburg
Chemnitz 0-2 Dortmund
Cottbus 0-3 Mainz
Jena 3-2 Hamburger SV *(aet)*
Kassel 0-2 Hannover
Lübeck 1-2 Paderborn
Nöttingen 1-3 Bayern
Pirmasens 1-4 Heidenheim
Rostock 0-0 Kaiserslautern *(aet; 4-5 on pens)*
Rot-Weiss Essen 0-0 Düsseldorf *(aet; 1-3 on pens)*
Salmrohr 0-5 Bochum
Unterhaching 2-1 Ingolstadt

(10/08/15)
Aalen 0-0 Nürnberg *(aet; 1-2 on pens)*
Bielefeld 0-2 Hertha BSC
Osnabrück 0-2 Leipzig *(abandoned; awarded to Leipzig)*
St Pauli 1-4 Mönchengladbach

SECOND ROUND

(27/10/15)
Aue 1-0 Eintracht Frankfurt
Bochum 1-0 Kaiserslautern
Darmstadt 2-1 Hannover
FSV Frankfurt 1-2 Hertha BSC *(aet)*
Mainz 1-2 1860 München
Nürnberg 5-1 Düsseldorf
Unterhaching 3-0 Leipzig
Wolfsburg 1-3 Bayern

(28/10/15)
Dortmund 7-1 Paderborn
Freiburg 0-3 Augsburg
Jena 0-2 Stuttgart
Reutlingen 0-4 Eintracht Braunschweig
Sandhausen 0-0 Heidenheim *(aet; 3-4 on pens)*
Schalke 0-2 Mönchengladbach
Viktoria Köln 0-6 Leverkusen
Werder Bremen 1-0 Köln

THIRD ROUND

(15/12/15)
Aue 0-2 Heidenheim
Bayern 1-0 Darmstadt
Mönchengladbach 3-4 Werder Bremen
Unterhaching 1-3 Leverkusen

(16/12/15)
1860 München 0-2 Bochum
Augsburg 0-2 Dortmund
Nürnberg 0-2 Hertha BSC
Stuttgart 3-2 Braunschweig *(aet)*

QUARTER-FINALS

(09/02/16)
Leverkusen 1-3 Werder Bremen *(Hernández 22p; S García 31, Pizarro 42p, Grillitsch 82)*
Stuttgart 1-3 Dortmund *(Rupp 21; Reus 5, Aubameyang 31, Mkhitaryan 89)*

(10/02/16)
Bochum 0-3 Bayern *(Lewandowski 39, 90, Thiago 61)*
Heidenheim 2-3 Hertha BSC *(Feick 10, Schnatterer 82p; Ibišević 14, 21, Haraguchi 58)*

SEMI-FINALS

(19/04/16)
Bayern 2-0 Werder Bremen *(Müller 30, 71p)*

(20/04/16)
Hertha BSC 0-3 Dortmund *(Castro 21, Reus 75, Mkhitaryan 83)*

FINAL

(21/05/16)
Olympiastadion, Berlin
FC BAYERN MÜNCHEN 0
BORUSSIA DORTMUND 0
(aet; 4-3 on pens)
Referee: *Fritz*
BAYERN: *Neuer, Lahm, Kimmich, Boateng, Alaba, Vidal, Douglas Costa, Müller, Thiago, Ribéry (Coman 108), Lewandowski*
DORTMUND: *Bürki, Bender, Papastathopoulos, Hummels (Ginter 78), Piszczek, Weigl, Castro (Kagawa 106), Schmelzer (Durm 70), Mkhitaryan, Aubameyang, Reus*

Pep Guardiola lifts the DFB-Pokal after his final game as Bayern boss, departing with a German domestic double

GIBRALTAR
Gibraltar Football Association (GFA)

Address	PO Box 513 2nd Floor, 62/64 Irish town GX11 1AA Gibraltar	**President**	Michael Llamas
		General secretary	Richard Manning
		Media officer	Steven Gonzalez
Tel	+350 200 42 941	**Year of formation**	1895
Fax	+350 200 42 211	**National stadium**	Victoria Stadium
E-mail	info@gibraltarfa.com		(5,000)
Website	gibraltarfa.com		

PREMIER DIVISION CLUBS

 ① **Angels FC**

 ② **FC Britannia XI**

 ③ **Europa FC**

 ④ **Gibraltar United FC**

 ⑤ **Glacis United FC**

 ⑥ **Lincoln FC**

 ⑦ **Lions Gibraltar FC**

 ⑧ **Lynx FC**

 ⑨ **Manchester 62 FC**

 ⑩ **St Joseph's FC**

PROMOTED CLUBS

 ⑪ **Europa Point FC**

 ⑫ **Mons Calpe SC**

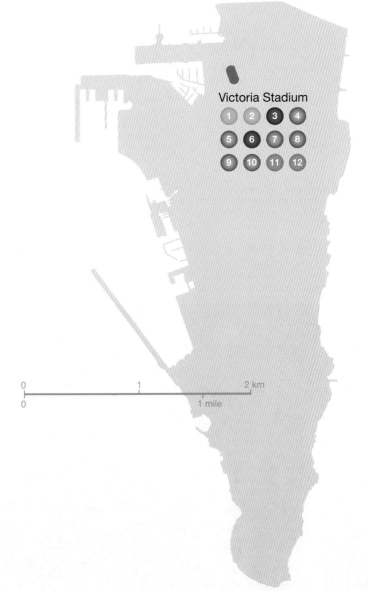

Victoria Stadium

KEY

● UEFA Champions League

● UEFA Europa League

● Promoted

● Relegated

Two more trophies for Lincoln

The long reign of Lincoln FC as champions of Gibraltar extended to a 14th successive season as the Red Imps powered their way to yet another straightforward Premier Division title triumph, scoring prolifically along the way.

The only team to take points off the champions were the newly-named Europa FC, who finished 11 points behind them and a whopping 20 ahead of third-placed St Joseph's. Europa also met Lincoln in the Rock Cup final but were unable to prevent their opponents from completing a third successive domestic double.

| Red Imps claim hat-trick of domestic doubles | Europa take runners-up spot in league and cup | EURO qualifying campaign ends point-less |

Domestic league

For the second successive season Lincoln failed to win their opening game, drawing 1-1 against Europa, but after that it was the familiar tale of one-sided victories and abundant goalscoring as the men in the red and black stripes stormed to a record-extending 22nd championship triumph. No matter that the Premier Division had been increased in size to incorporate two additional teams and six extra fixtures. Raúl Procopio's side simply did as they had done the previous season, steamrollering their way from one big win to the next and ending up just five points short of the maximum.

The champions' 27 games yielded 130 goals, with four of their 25 wins in double digits, including 13-0 and 13-1 against Angels FC, a newly promoted club who finished bottom and were relegated with just nine points. FC Britannia XI also went down, after a play-off, into which they went with confidence shredded after their last two regular league encounters had ended 16-1 (to Europa) and 10-0 (to Lincoln). In the first of those, Europa's Spanish striker Pedro Carrión helped himself to an incredible personal haul of 11 goals, which increased his season's aggregate to 29, making him the Premier Division's top scorer.

Not surprisingly, Lincoln had four players among the top six in the final golden boot listing, George Cabrera leading the way on 24 goals with Guido Abaylan (20) and the Casciaro brothers, Kyle and Lee (both 17), not far behind. Two other Gibraltar internationals, Joseph Chipolina and Liam Walker, also reached double figures, while there were favourable statistics for the team's generally underworked 38-year-old goalkeeper Raúl Navas, who played every minute of the 27 fixtures and kept clean sheets in 20 of them, conceding just nine goals.

Europa, who actually dared to beat Lincoln, 2-0 on 29 February, a day for unusual occurrences, and therefore matched them head-to-head over the season, would have been a closer rival had they not lost unexpectedly to St Joseph's and Glacis United – results that ultimately led to a change of coach. New man Juan José Gallardo could hardly have imagined a better start as his first game was that 16-1 thrashing of Britannia XI.

Domestic cup

Two weeks later Gallardo faced the rather tougher task of trying to deny Lincoln – now also under a new coach, Julio César Ribas – a 17th victory in the Rock Cup final while steering Europa to their first major trophy. The underdogs gave it their best shot and were still level at 0-0 on 70 minutes when injured referee Tim Reoch had to be replaced by the fourth official, but late goals from Joseph Chipolina and Walker eventually won the day as the Red Imps celebrated another domestic one-two.

Europe

Lincoln became the first team from Gibraltar to win a European tie, overcoming fellow minnows FC Santa Coloma from Andorra 2-1 on aggregate with a winning goal from Lee Casciaro before going out in the next round to Danish champions FC Midtjylland.

National team

As expected, Gibraltar did not collect a point from their inaugural UEFA European Championship campaign, conceding 56 goals in their ten defeats. Bristol Rovers' Jake Gosling did become the first Gibraltar international to score more than one goal with his consolation effort in an 8-1 defeat by Poland, and there was an end to a 12-game losing sequence when Gibraltar drew a friendly at home to Liechtenstein, but having been belatedly admitted to the 2018 FIFA World Cup qualifying competition, coach Jeff Wood and his players will hope to add a few more positives when they face Belgium, Bosnia & Herzegovina, Cyprus, Estonia and Greece on the road to Russia.

DOMESTIC SEASON AT A GLANCE

DOMESTIC CUP

Premier Division 2015/16 final table

		Pld	W	D	L	F	A	Pts
1	**Lincoln FC**	**27**	**25**	**1**	**1**	**130**	**9**	**76**
2	Europa FC	27	21	2	4	82	18	65
3	St Joseph's FC	27	14	3	10	50	37	45
4	Lions Gibraltar FC	27	14	3	10	49	44	45
5	Lynx FC	27	11	2	14	37	40	35
6	Manchester 62 FC	27	9	5	13	41	49	32
7	Glacis United FC	27	10	2	15	40	67	32
8	Gibraltar United FC	27	9	2	16	28	57	29
9	FC Britannia XI	27	8	2	17	35	84	26
10	Angels FC	27	3	0	24	20	107	9

European qualification 2016/17

Champion/Cup winner: Lincoln FC (first qualifying round)

Europa FC (first qualifying round)

Top scorer	Pedro Carrión (Europa), 29 goals
Relegated clubs	Angels FC, FC Britannia XI
Promoted clubs	Europa Point FC, Mons Calpe SC
Cup final	Lincoln FC 2-0 Europa FC

Player of the season

Kyle Casciaro
(Lincoln FC)

The youngest of the three Casciaro brothers, the 28-year-old attacking midfielder was a reassuring presence for club and country in 2015/16, missing just one game in Lincoln's league title triumph, to which he contributed 17 goals.

Newcomer of the season

Javier Martínez
(Europa FC)

A former Sevilla FC apprentice, Martínez was the standout figure among the plethora of Spanish imports in the Europa side – and not just because of his dyed blond hair. With his pace and trickery the ever-present winger posed a constant threat.

Team of the season
(4-2-3-1)

Coach: Núñez *(Gibraltar United)*

Muñoz
(Europa)

Garcia   **R Chipolina**   **Power**   **J Chipolina**
(Lincoln)   *(Lincoln)*   *(Gibraltar United)*   *(Lincoln)*

Moya   **Walker**
(Europa)   *(Lincoln)*

Martínez   **Cabrera**   **K Casciaro**
(Europa)   *(Lincoln)*   *(Lincoln)*

Pereira
(Lynx/Glacis)

Rock Cup 2015/16

SECOND ROUND

(10/02/16)
Gibraltar United 2-1 Red Imps

(11/02/16)
Manchester 62 1-0 Lynx

(12/02/16)
St Joseph's 0-1 Europa

(13/02/16)
Lincoln 5-1 Britannia XI
Mons Calpe 1-4 Lions Gibraltar

(14/02/16)
Gibraltar Phoenix 0-4 Angels
Leo 0-1 College 1975

(15/02/16)
Glacis 7-0 Bruno's Magpies

QUARTER-FINALS

(16/03/16)
College 1975 0-7 Manchester 62 *(JP Duarte 13, 17, 54, Navarro 41, Toncheff 80, 86, Rovegno 87)*

(18/03/16)
Lincoln 4-0 Glacis *(Calderón 67p, Cabrera 68, Livramento 72, 78)*

(19/03/16)
Angels 1-4 Europa *(Mena 68; Rodríguez 23, Martínez 34, Roldán 52, Pavón 90)*

Lions Gibraltar 1-0 Gibraltar United *(García 55p)*

SEMI-FINALS

(23/04/16)
Lincoln 6-2 Manchester 62 *(Walker 13, 19, K Casciaro 28, 63, Sergeant 36og, Abayian 90; Mejías 27, Toncheff 31)*

Europa 1-0 Lions Gibraltar *(Roldán 70)*

FINAL

(22/05/16)
Victoria Stadium, Gibraltar
LINCOLN FC 2 *(J Chipolina 75, Walker 85)*
EUROPA FC 0
Referee: *Reoch (Borg 70)*
LINCOLN: Navas, Garcia, J Chipolina, R Casciaro, L Casciaro (Abayian 86), K Casciaro, R Chipolina, Calderón, Patiño, Livramento (Bernardo Lopes 72), Walker
EUROPA: Cafer, Moya, Toscano, Belfortti, Merino, García, Pavón, Rodríguez (Burdujan 86), González (Vásquez 78), Carrión (Martínez 65), Roldán

NATIONAL TEAM

Top five all-time caps
Joseph Chipolina (18); **Roy Chipolina** & **Liam Walker** (17); **Kyle Casciaro** & **Ryan Casciaro** (16)

Top five all-time goals
Jake Gosling (2); **Kyle Casciaro**, **Lee Casciaro** & **Roy Chipolina** (1)

Results 2015/16

04/09/15	Republic of Ireland (ECQ)	H	Faro (POR)	L	0-4	
07/09/15	Poland (ECQ)	A	Warsaw	L	1-8	*Gosling (87)*
08/10/15	Georgia (ECQ)	A	Tbilisi	L	0-4	
11/10/15	Scotland (ECQ)	H	Faro (POR)	L	0-6	
23/03/16	Liechtenstein	H	Gibraltar	D	0-0	
29/03/16	Latvia	H	Gibraltar	L	0-5	

Appearances 2015/16

Coach: Jeff Wood (ENG)	04/02/54		IRL	POL	GEO	SCO	Lie	Lva	Caps	Goals
Jordan Perez	13/11/86	St Joseph's	G	G	G		G	G	14	-
Jean-Carlos Garcia	05/07/92	Lincoln	D	D	D	D	D	D70	13	-
Joseph Chipolina	14/12/87	Lincoln	D	D	D	D	M	M53	18	-
Roy Chipolina	20/01/83	Lincoln	D	D	D	D	D87	D	17	1
Erin Barnett	02/09/96	Lions Gibraltar	D	D		D	s87	s53	5	-
Jack Sergeant	27/02/95	Manchester 62	M85				s52	M60	11	-
Anthony Bardon	19/01/93	Lincoln	M	M	M	M	M52		9	-
Liam Walker	13/04/88	Lincoln	M	M	M	M	M	M	17	-
Kyle Casciaro	02/12/87	Lincoln	M61	s46	M85	A89	A81	A	16	1
Lee Casciaro	29/09/81	Lincoln	M	M79	M76	M82			10	1
John Paul Duarte	13/12/86	Manchester 62	A73	A68	s76	s82			9	-
Jake Gosling	11/08/93	Bristol Rovers (ENG)	s61	M	M				11	2
Michael Yome	29/08/94	Lincoln /Manchester 62	s73		s85	s89		s70	4	-
Robert Guiling	14/10/80	Lynx	s85				s81	s53	9	-
Jamie Coombes	27/05/96	Manchester 62		A46					3	-
Jamie Bosio	24/09/91	Canterbury (ENG)		s68			s70	D60	5	-
Jeremy Lopez	09/07/89	Manchester 62		s79			s70		6	-
Ryan Casciaro	11/05/84	Lincoln			D	D	D	D70	16	-
George Cabrera	14/12/88	Lincoln			A46		A81	A53	5	-
Brian Perez	16/09/86	Manchester 62			s46	s57			6	-
Jamie Robba	26/10/91	Le Pontet (FRA)					G		7	-
Daniel Duarte	25/10/79	Manchester 62				M57			5	-
Jayce Mascarenhas-Olivero	02/07/98	Lions Gibraltar					D70	s70	2	-
Aaron Payas	24/05/85	Manchester 62					M70	M	8	-
Robert Montovio	03/08/84	Gibraltar United					s81	s60	2	-
Anthony Hernandez	03/02/95	Manchester 62						s60	3	-

EUROPE

DOMESTIC LEAGUE CLUB-BY-CLUB

Lincoln FC

First qualifying round - FC Santa Coloma (AND)
H 0-0
Navas, Chietino, J Chipolina, R Casciaro, L Casciaro, K Casciaro, R Chipolina, Pegalajar (Yome 75), Sambruno (Bardon 82), Garcia, Walker. Coach: Raúl Procopio (ESP)
A 2-1 *Bardon (48), L Casciaro (64)*
Navas, Chietino, J Chipolina, R Casciaro, L Casciaro (Chrayeh 90+2), K Casciaro (Garcia 78), R Chipolina, Bardon, Pegalajar (Calderón 46), Sambruno, Walker. Coach: Raúl Procopio (ESP)

Second qualifying round - FC Midtjylland (DEN)
A 0-1
Navas, Chietino, J Chipolina, R Casciaro, L Casciaro (Bosio 90+1), K Casciaro, Bardon, Pegalajar (Yome 78), Sambruno, Garcia, Walker. Coach: Raúl Procopio (ESP)
H 0-2
Navas, Chietino, J Chipolina (Jolley 82), R Casciaro, L Casciaro, K Casciaro, R Chipolina, Bardon, Pegalajar (Parker 86), Sambruno (Yome 72), Walker. Coach: Raúl Procopio (ESP)

Europa FC

First qualifying round - ŠK Slovan Bratislava (SVK)
H 0-6
Cafer, Vargas, Sánchez, Jukić (Mouelhi 45), Piñero, Lopez, Ledesma (Luque 51), Toncheff, Sokol (Ortega 72), Plazanić, Akrapovic. Coach: Juan Fernández (ESP)
A 0-3
Bellido, Sánchez, Pacheco, Jukić (Ortega 64), Piñero, Luque, Lopez, Toncheff (Morgan 86), Moreno (Sokol 71), Plazanić, Akrapovic. Coach: Juan Fernández (ESP)

Stadium

Victoria Stadium (5,000)

Angels FC

2014 • no website
Coach: Albert Ferri (ESP);
(22/01/16) José Morales (ESP)

2015

26/09	Lynx	L	1-2	*Mena (p)*
01/10	St Joseph's	L	0-4	
17/10	Lions Gibraltar	L	0-3	
25/10	Manchester 62	L	1-5	*Mena*
31/10	Britannia XI	L	1-3	*Palomino*
09/11	Europa	L	2-3	*Touré, Paredes*
14/11	Lincoln	L	0-5	
23/11	Gibraltar United	L	1-2	*Palomino*
28/11	Glacis	W	2-0	*Alegre, Mena*
06/12	Lynx	L	0-6	
13/12	St Joseph's	L	0-3	
18/12	Lions Gibraltar	L	0-2	

2016

03/01	Manchester 62	L	1-4	*Alegre (p)*
09/01	Britannia XI	L	0-3	
15/01	Europa	L	0-3	
22/01	Lincoln	L	0-13	
06/02	Gibraltar United	W	2-1	*Sánchez 2*
20/02	Glacis	L	0-3	
27/02	Lynx	L	1-2	*og (Villegas)*
06/03	St Joseph's	W	1-0	*Mena*
13/03	Lions Gibraltar	L	0-1	
03/04	Manchester 62	L	1-6	*Rojas*
08/04	Britannia XI	L	3-4	*Mena, Sánchez, Del Real*
18/04	Europa	L	0-3	
30/04	Lincoln	L	1-13	*Casorla*
09/05	Gibraltar United	L	1-7	*Mena*
16/05	Glacis	L	1-6	*García*

No	Name	Nat	DoB	Pos	Aps	(s)	Gls
6	Salvador Alegre	ESP	04/05/91	M	5		2
2	David Casorla	ESP	07/02/97	D	10		1
14	Javier Crespo	ESP	23/03/97	M	2		
15	Guillermo Cuevas	ESP	12/08/96	M	1		
23	Daniel Del Real	ESP	30/08/93	D	9		1
17	Miko Di Pierro	ITA	17/03/95	M	4	(1)	
18	Ismael Espejo	ESP	28/08/97	M	7		
13	Cristian Fernández	ESP	20/02/97	G	3	(1)	
4	José Carlos Fernández	ESP	24/05/90	D	5		
3	Guillermo García	ESP	08/08/93	D	11		1
15	Bruno Gómez	ESP	22/02/97	M	4	(1)	
25	Edmund Hosken		15/08/90	M	1	(5)	
10	Ndiaga Kane	SEN	10/01/86	M	2	(3)	
9	Fernando Lara	ESP	06/01/89	G	1		
9	Fernando Lara	ESP	06/01/89	M	8	(6)	
17	Toufik Larouia		27/08/90	A	12	(3)	
18	Fernando Learde		09/12/93	A	1		
7	Adrián López	ESP	15/08/93	M	1		
6	Jorge Manrique	ESP	25/12/85	D	2	(1)	
1	Juan Antonio Mateo	ESP	24/12/80	G	15		
10	Christian Mena	ESP	21/03/89	A	11	(7)	6
22	Manuel Morales	ESP	21/09/85	A		(3)	
18	Álvaro Moreno	ESP	28/07/87	M	1	(1)	
8	David Moreno	ESP	19/07/88	M	12	(2)	
3	Fernando Moya	ESP	25/08/84	D	13		
4	José Luis Muñoz	ESP	07/11/83	D	12	(2)	
7	Francisco Nieto	ESP	19/03/91	M	12	(1)	
19	Michel Núñez	ESP	10/08/96	D	1		
9	Juan Antonio Palomino	ESP	16/02/87	A	9		2
14	Alberto Paredes	ESP	26/04/86	M	9		1
13	Benjamin Parody	ESP	25/03/72	G		(1)	
6	Álvaro Pino	ESP	30/07/89	D	2	(6)	
2	José Manuel Pino	ESP	10/07/90	D	12	(1)	
8	Daniel Rodríguez	ESP	26/11/92	D	7	(1)	
20	Jonathan Rojas	ESP	13/12/85	D	23		1
11	Boris Sánchez	ESP	16/01/91	A	11		3
14	Fernando Silveira	ESP	29/02/88	M	10		
16	Omar Touré	ESP	22/02/96	A	17	(5)	1
5	Juan Villada	ESP	08/06/82	M	23	(1)	
1	Welerson Ribeiro	BRA	31/01/96	G	8		

FC Britannia XI

1907• fcbritanniaxi.com
Major honours
Gibraltar League (14) 1908, 1912, 1913, 1918, 1920, 1937, 1940, 1955, 1956, 1957, 1958, 1959, 1961, 1963; Gibraltar Cup (3) 1937, 1940, 1948
Coach: Alan Arruda (BRA);
(27/01/16) (Adam Golt);
(25/04/16) Garry Lowe (ENG)

2015

27/09	Gibraltar United	D	1-1	*Pishvaie (p)*
14/10	Glacis	W	3-0	*Funes (p), Mancilla, Jiménez*
18/10	Lynx	L	0-1	
24/10	St Joseph's	D	1-1	*Jiménez*
31/10	Angels	W	3-1	*Otero, Renan Bernardes, Warren*
07/11	Manchester 62	W	2-0	*Kägo, Renan Bernardes*
16/11	Lions Gibraltar	L	0-4	
21/11	Europa	L	1-4	*Grimmer*
27/11	Lincoln	L	2-3	*Grimmer, Guerra*
05/12	Gibraltar United	W	3-1	*Grimmer, Otero, Funes*
12/12	Glacis	L	2-3	*Grimmer (p), Camacho*
19/12	Lynx	W	3-0	*Jiménez, Camacho, Kägo*

2016

03/01	St Joseph's	W	4-3	*Guerra, Camacho 3*
09/01	Angels	W	3-0	*Camacho 2, Renan Bernardes*
16/01	Manchester 62	L	0-2	
25/01	Lions Gibraltar	L	0-1	
30/01	Europa	L	1-10	*Roche*
22/02	Lincoln	L	0-1	
29/02	Gibraltar United	L	0-2	
04/03	Glacis	L	0-1	
15/03	Lynx	L	0-2	
02/04	St Joseph's	L	0-4	
08/04	Angels	W	4-3	*Pizarro 2, Camacho 2 (1p)*
16/04	Manchester 62	L	0-6	
27/04	Lions Gibraltar	L	1-4	*Graham*
07/05	Europa	L	1-16	*Del Rio*
13/05	Lincoln	L	0-10	

No	Name	Nat	DoB	Pos	Aps	(s)	Gls
81	Alan Arruda	BRA	12/09/81	D	7		
2	André Santos	BRA	19/02/92	D	14		
1	Louie Barnfather Marfe		07/10/92	G	23		
16	Shea Breakspear		22/11/91	D	10	(4)	
15	Dario Buitrago	ESP	26/01/85	A	3	(1)	
21	Daniel Camacho	ARG	07/02/93	M	19	(1)	9
15	Loubière Clément	FRA	09/03/86	M	2	(2)	
7	Alberto Del Rio	ESP	13/09/90	M	10		1
10	Sacha Funes	ITA	15/08/84	M	7		2
20	Jesús María García	ESP	11/01/95	D	5	(5)	
32	Samuel Gilroy	ESP	27/06/93	M	24	(3)	
29	Óscar González	ESP	20/05/79	M	9	(2)	
5	Lee Graham		09/06/83	D	1		1
34	Peter Grimmer	ESP	18/06/87	A	21		4
16	José Manuel Guerra	ESP	03/11/93	M	7	(5)	2
33	Steven Hall		12/03/98	M		(4)	
34	Thomas Hastings		23/09/92	D	5	(2)	
16	Stefan Jarv	EST	07/07/91	D	8		
18	Yeray Jiménez	ESP	14/07/91	D	14	(3)	3
13	Risto Kägo	EST	04/08/89	M	19		2
24	Salvador Mancilla	ESP	18/11/91	M	3	(6)	1
22	Sergio Méndez	ESP	14/12/85	M		(2)	
17	Chris Mousdell	ENG	23/04/86	G	1		
17	Chris Mousdell	ENG	23/04/86	M	4		
16	Luke Nixon	IRL	14/09/86	D	1		
28	Óscar Orozco	ESP	07/02/93	D	1		
4	José Luis Otero	ESP	03/02/96	D	26		2
7	Saam Pishvaie	FRA	11/02/96	M	1		1
10	Theo Pizarro		10/07/98	A	11	(1)	2
4	Renan Bernardes	BRA	21/03/92	M	15		3
19	Phillip Reyes		28/09/92	G	3	(2)	
8	Liam Roche		11/12/85	M	1	(9)	1
2	Juan Sánchez	ESP	06/03/89	D		(1)	
31	Emilio Sansolini	ITA	04/08/84	M	15	(4)	
35	Robin Sheppard-Capurro		14/05/90	D		(3)	
23	Peter Warren	ENG	11/06/89	A		(3)	1
14	James Watson		30/04/83	D	6		
25	Kamil Zaragoza	ESP	06/11/97	D	1	(3)	

Europa FC

1925 • europafc.gi

Coach: Dimas Carrasco (ESP);
(06/05/16) Juan José Gallardo (ESP)

2015

28/09	Lincoln	D	1-1	Trujillo
03/10	Gibraltar United	W	2-0	Carrión, Martínez
19/10	Glacis	W	6-0	Trujillo 3, og (Quiñones), Carrión 2
23/10	Lynx	W	2-1	González, Pavón
29/10	St Joseph's	W	2-0	Trujillo, Carrión
09/11	Angels	W	3-2	Roldán 2, Martínez
14/11	Manchester 62	W	4-0	Carrión, González, Roldán (p), Yared
21/11	Britannia XI	W	4-1	Trujillo, Merino, Carrión 2
29/11	Lions Gibraltar	W	2-0	Carrión (p), Yared
05/12	Lincoln	L	0-2	
11/12	Gibraltar United	W	2-0	Sánchez, Trujillo
20/12	Glacis	W	2-0	Carrión 2

2016

04/01	Lynx	W	2-1	Martínez, González
10/01	St Joseph's	L	1-3	Roldán
15/01	Angels	W	3-0	González 2, Roldán (p)
23/01	Manchester 62	D	1-1	Rodríguez
30/01	Britannia XI	W	10-1	Belfortti, Carrión 2 (1p), González 5, Martínez (p), Pavón
19/02	Lions Gibraltar	W	3-0	Rodríguez 2, Pavón
29/02	Lincoln	W	2-0	Roldán, Pavón
05/03	Gibraltar United	W	3-1	Carrión 2, Rodríguez
12/03	Glacis	L	0-1	
02/04	Lynx	W	1-0	Carrión
09/04	St Joseph's	W	2-0	og (Cortijo), Carrión
18/04	Angels	W	3-0	Pavón 2, Carrión
30/04	Manchester 62	W	5-0	Martínez, García 2, Rodríguez, Carrión
07/05	Britannia XI	W	16-1	Carrión 11, Martínez, Pavón, Burdujan, Trofimenko, González
15/05	Lions Gibraltar	L	0-1	

No	Name	Nat	DoB	Pos	Aps	(s)	Gls
22	Martin Belfortti	ARG	07/04/81	D	11	(1)	1
24	Juan José Bezares	ESP	17/05/81	D	8	(3)	
23	Lucian Burdujan	ROU	18/12/94	A	2	(3)	1
3	Lance Cabezutto		03/03/93	D		(2)	
13	Matthew Cafer	ENG	27/09/94	G	3	(1)	
9	Pedro Carrión	ESP	25/01/78	A	19	(8)	29
11	Francisco Fernández	ESP	22/02/88	M		(2)	
7	Antonio García	ESP	07/08/91	D	11		2
19	José Miguel González	ESP	10/05/92	A	18	(5)	11
10	Javier Martínez	ESP	01/07/88	M	27		6
40	Alberto Merino	ESP	02/05/75	D	22	(1)	1
15	José Manuel Morales	ESP	19/02/91	D	17	(1)	
6	Iván Moya	ESP	16/09/87	M	23		
1	Javier Muñoz	ESP	27/01/82	G	24		
2	Jesús Negrillo	ESP	03/02/90	D	14	(2)	
8	Adrián Pavón	ESP	16/03/89	M	19	(3)	7
7	Manuel Picon	ESP	05/10/94	M		(3)	
18	Alejandro Rodríguez	ESP	17/04/92	M	12	(1)	5
17	Guillermo Roldán	ESP	23/06/81	A	22		6
4	Francisco Sánchez	ESP	18/02/87	D	11	(4)	1
14	Jesús Toscano	ESP	13/12/90	D	19	(5)	
5	Kirill Trofimenko	RUS	19/12/96	A	1	(9)	1
22	Antonio Trujillo	ESP	11/10/87	A	9	(4)	7
21	Alejandro Vásquez	ESP	16/03/83	D	5	(6)	
21	José Yared	ESP	27/07/92	D		(9)	2

Gibraltar United FC

1943 • no website

Major honours
Gibraltar League (11) 1947, 1948, 1949, 1950, 1951, 1954, 1960, 1962, 1964, 1965, 2002; Gibraltar Cup (3) 1947, 2000, 2001

Coach: Manolo Sánchez Núñez (ESP)

2015

27/09	Britannia XI	D	1-1	Montovio
03/10	Europa	L	0-2	
16/10	Lincoln	L	0-7	
07/11	Lynx	L	0-3	
13/11	St Joseph's	L	0-2	
21/11	Angels	W	2-1	Montovio (p), Anes
28/11	Manchester 62	W	1-0	Montovio
02/12	Lions Gibraltar	L	0-3	
05/12	Britannia XI	L	1-3	Montovio (p)
11/12	Europa	L	0-2	
21/12	Lincoln	L	0-6	

2016

02/01	Lions Gibraltar	W	1-0	Montovio
11/01	Glacis	W	2-1	Montovio, Power
17/01	Lynx	L	1-3	Montovio
23/01	St Joseph's	L	0-4	
31/01	Glacis	W	1-0	Montovio (p)
06/02	Angels	L	1-2	Green
21/02	Manchester 62	L	0-1	
28/02	Britannia XI	W	2-0	L Buhagiar, Green
05/03	Europa	L	1-3	Green
12/03	Lincoln	L	0-4	
04/04	Lions Gibraltar	W	3-1	Montovio 2, Perez
10/04	Glacis	L	0-2	
16/04	Lynx	W	1-0	Montovio
27/04	St Joseph's	L	1-3	Marquez
09/05	Angels	W	7-1	Power, Montovio 4 (1p), Currer, Rumbo
14/05	Manchester 62	D	2-2	Perez, Marquez

No	Name	Nat	DoB	Pos	Aps	(s)	Gls
20	Aziz Aitlahcen		19/04/89	M		(1)	
24	Adolfo Anes		28/03/84	M	8	(8)	1
23	Derek Asquez		20/08/85	D	1	(1)	
20	Abderkahman Bakkari	MAR	22/02/88	M	3	(3)	
99	Jamie Bosio		27/03/91	M	6		
3	Jared Buhagiar		20/10/92	D	1		
11	Lee Buhagiar		03/07/87	D	27		1
15	Steffan Cardona		03/03/92	D	6	(1)	
25	Mark Casciaro		11/07/84	M	1		
26	Jaydan Catania		06/03/93	D	3		
23	Kenneth Chipolina		08/04/94	D	4	(1)	
2	Aaron Collado		11/12/86	D	3		
7	Justin Collado		03/11/88	M	1	(1)	
90	James Currer		29/06/92	A	12	(4)	1
22	Naoufal El Andaloussi		07/03/91	M	3	(3)	
89	Carl Ellul		20/03/85	A	3	(2)	
5	Jamie Ellul		09/04/94	M		(1)	
18	Byron Espinosa		15/03/99	A	10	(3)	
30	David Gallardo		04/05/91	D	16	(1)	
14	Sean Gilbert		14/11/92	M	6	(9)	
16	Steven Gilbert		05/06/89	M	2	(7)	
1	Kyle Goldwin		24/04/85	G	25		
8	Evan Green		13/03/93	M	6	(3)	3
93	Adrian Lopez		20/04/88	D	1	(1)	
10	Andrew Lopez		15/04/84	M	17	(1)	
9	Lython Marquez		06/02/95	A	2	(3)	2
26	Sean Mascarenhas		26/11/84	D	1	(1)	
4	Neil Medina		15/04/87	D		(1)	
8	Robert Montovio		03/08/84	A	24		15
21	Liam Neale		01/12/96	G	1	(1)	
6	Dexter Panzavechia		30/12/90	M	9		
33	Alan Parker		15/05/96	M	5	(2)	
3	Ashley Perez		22/02/89	D	11	(2)	2
19	Brad Power		29/10/92	D	17	(1)	2
21	Duane Robba		19/06/75	M	17	(1)	
77	Kaylan Rumbo		12/12/90	D	13	(4)	1
88	Carl Thomas		06/07/88	D	24	(1)	
31	Ayden Viñales		13/02/98	G	1	(1)	

Glacis United FC

1965 • no website

Major honours
Gibraltar League (17) 1966, 1967, 1968, 1969, 1970, 1971, 1972, 1973, 1974, 1976, 1981, 1982, 1983, 1985, 1989, 1997, 2000; Gibraltar Cup (4) 1975, 1981, 1982, 1996

Coach: Javier Sánchez Alfaro (ESP);
(01/12/15) Daniel Rodríguez Amaya (ESP)

2015

26/09	Manchester 62	L	0-1	
14/10	Britannia XI	L	0-3	
19/10	Europa	L	0-6	
24/10	Lincoln	L	1-6	Jiménez
06/11	Lions Gibraltar	L	0-5	
15/11	Lynx	L	0-3	
20/11	St Joseph's	L	0-3	
28/11	Angels	L	0-2	
04/12	Manchester 62	D	1-1	C Méndez
12/12	Britannia XI	W	3-2	Bado, Cortes 2
20/12	Europa	L	0-2	

2016

02/01	Lincoln	L	0-11	
11/01	Gibraltar United	L	1-2	Barletta
18/01	Lions Gibraltar	W	6-0	Alonso, Funes, Cortes 2, Carrasco 2
24/01	Lynx	W	1-0	Carrasco
31/01	Gibraltar United	L	0-1	
05/02	St Joseph's	L	3-5	Pereira 2, Carrasco
20/02	Angels	W	3-0	Pereira 2 (1p), Alonso
27/02	Manchester 62	W	3-1	Pereira 3
04/03	Britannia XI	W	1-0	Cortes
12/03	Europa	W	1-0	Alonso
01/04	Lincoln	L	1-4	Carrasco
10/04	Gibraltar United	W	2-0	og (Perez), Pereira
15/04	Lions Gibraltar	L	3-6	Funes, Pereira (p), Carrasco
01/05	Lynx	W	2-1	Pereira 2 (1p)
07/05	St Joseph's	D	2-2	og (Lobato), Pereira
16/05	Angels	W	6-1	Thorne 2, Carrasco 3, Lavagna

No	Name	Nat	DoB	Pos	Aps	(s)	Gls
34	Mariano Abeleira	ARG	31/12/92	D	5	(8)	
22	Antonio Alonso	ESP	15/07/92	M	6	(5)	3
3	José Álvarez	ESP	25/11/86	D	15	(2)	
5	Pedro Ardanaz	ESP	07/04/95	D	3	(1)	
20	Julio Bado		03/06/83	M	18	(4)	1
32	Tomas Barletta	ARG	01/01/92	A	16	(2)	1
30	Ichor Borg		13/06/78	A		(1)	
1	Jamie Carlin		27/08/92	G	10		
24	Salvador Carrasco	ESP	24/03/86	M	10	(1)	9
14	Manuel Carrillo	ESP	11/05/85	D		(3)	
19	German Cortes	ARG	03/02/94	A	13	(7)	5
15	Alberto Del Rio	ESP	13/09/90	M	11	(2)	
7	Jaylan Desoiza		12/01/92	D		(1)	
16	Haitam Fakir Sellam	MAR	09/04/94	A	1		
26	Juan José Fernández	ESP	29/11/88	M	1		
33	Sacha Funes	ARG	15/08/84	M	13		2
37	Ismael Garcia		06/05/99	D		(1)	
25	Alonso García	ESP	18/06/88	G	2		
33	Javi García	ESP	16/08/86	M	2		
14	Francisco González	ESP	04/05/86	D	1		
28	Ivan Jiménez	ESP	25/08/91	M	4	(1)	1
21	Julian Lavagna		30/10/91	A		(3)	1
35	Kevin Martínez	ESP	21/10/93	D	7	(1)	
18	Carlos Méndez	ESP	23/06/87	D	21		1
10	Sergio Méndez	ESP	14/12/85	M	2	(3)	
29	Francisco Moreno	ESP	18/09/90	M	10	(2)	
6	Kyle Moreno		27/08/92	D		(3)	
22	Manuel Muinos	ESP	12/11/93	D	1		
12	Dexter Panzavechia		30/12/90	M	8	(3)	
12	Juan Pablo Pereira	ARG	02/07/87	A	7	(1)	12
27	Leandro Pereyra	ARG	27/02/85	M	26		
14	Daniel Pratts		06/06/98	M		(1)	
11	Daniel Quiñones	ESP	10/04/84	D	5	(3)	
13	José Antonio Rico	ESP	21/10/86	G	6		
28	Jesús Romero	ESP	25/06/89	A	1	(4)	
13	Francisco Rosales	ESP	09/12/85	M	9		
8	Álex Ruesca	ESP	01/11/85	M	7	(6)	
2	Juan José Ruesca	ESP	24/11/90	D	24	(2)	
2	Amael Sempere	ESP	08/08/87	M	5	(3)	2
36	Liam Thorne		13/01/98	A	2	(2)	2
23	Miguel Ángel Tirado	ESP	01/10/84	D	14		
24	Israel Ubeda	ESP	14/11/94	M	1		
11	Adrián Vera	ESP	21/02/90	M	10	(2)	

GIBRALTAR

Lincoln FC

1975 • lincolnredimpsfc.com

Major honours
Gibraltar League (22) 1985 (shared), 1986, 1990, 1991, 1992, 1993, 1994, 2001, 2003, 2004, 2005, 2006, 2007, 2008, 2009, 2010, 2011, 2012, 2013, 2014, 2015, 2016; Gibraltar Cup (17) 1986, 1989, 1990, 1993, 1994, 2002, 2004, 2005, 2006, 2007, 2008, 2009, 2010, 2011, 2014, 2015, 2016

Coach: Raúl Procopio (ESP);
(10/04/16) Julio César Ribas (URU)

2015
28/09	Europa	D 1-1	*Bernardo Lopes*
03/10	Lions Gibraltar	W 2-0	*J Chipolina, Abayian*
16/10	Gibraltar United	W 7-0	*L Casciaro, Abayian 2, Livramento, Cabrera 2, K Casciaro*
24/10	Glacis	W 6-1	*R Chipolina, K Casciaro (p), L Casciaro, Cabrera, Abayian, Patiño*
02/11	Lynx	W 4-0	*L Casciaro, Walker, K Casciaro, Abayian*
08/11	St Joseph's	W 2-0	*R Chipolina, K Casciaro*
14/11	Angels	W 5-0	*L Casciaro 2, Livramento 2, Abayian*
22/11	Manchester 62	W 4-0	*Yome, Abayian, L Casciaro, Walker*
27/11	Britannia XI	W 3-2	*J Chipolina, Walker 2*
05/12	Europa	W 2-0	*K Casciaro, J Chipolina (p)*
13/12	Lions Gibraltar	W 4-0	*Abayian 2, J Chipolina 2*
21/12	Gibraltar United	W 6-0	*J Chipolina, Walker 2, L Casciaro, Livramento, R Chipolina*

2016
02/01	Glacis	W 11-0	*K Casciaro 3, L Casciaro 4, Patiño, Walker, J Chipolina, Soussi*
09/01	Lynx	W 2-0	*J Chipolina, Cabrera*
16/01	St Joseph's	W 4-0	*J Chipolina 2, K Casciaro 2*
22/01	Angels	W 13-0	*K Casciaro 2, Cabrera 4, Abayian 5, Calderón, J Chipolina*
29/01	Manchester 62	W 4-0	*K Casciaro, Abayian, Cabrera, J Chipolina*
22/02	Britannia XI	W 1-0	*Cabrera*
29/02	Europa	L 0-2	
07/03	Lions Gibraltar	W 7-1	*Patiño, Abayian, Cabrera 2, Walker, Rúben Freitas, Garcia*
12/03	Gibraltar United	W 4-0	*K Casciaro, Cabrera, Walker, Livramento*
01/04	Glacis	W 4-1	*Livramento, Cabrera 2, L Casciaro*
11/04	Lynx	W 4-0	*L Casciaro 2, R Chipolina, Cabrera*
17/04	St Joseph's	W 3-0	*Cabrera 2, J Chipolina (p)*
30/04	Angels	W 13-1	*Cabrera 4, L Casciaro, R Chipolina, K Casciaro 2, Walker, Abayian 3, Clinton*
06/05	Manchester 62	W 4-0	*Cabrera 2 (1p), K Casciaro, L Casciaro*
13/05	Britannia XI	W 10-0	*L Casciaro, Walker 3, J Chipolina 3 (1p), Abayian, Garcia, R Chipolina*

No	Name	Nat	DoB	Pos	Aps	(s)	Gls
9	Guido Abayian	ESP	26/04/89	A	9	(13)	20
8	Anthony Bardon		19/01/93	M	10		
6	Bernardo Lopes	POR	30/07/93	D	11	(5)	1
24	Ethan Britto		30/11/00	M		(3)	
11	George Cabrera		14/12/88	A	17	(2)	24
19	Antonio Calderón	ESP	31/03/84	M	11	(2)	1
10	Kyle Casciaro		02/12/87	M	25	(1)	17
7	Lee Casciaro		29/09/81	A	16	(4)	17
5	Ryan Casciaro		11/05/84	D	22		
82	Nicholas Chietino	ESP	17/04/82	M	7	(1)	
3	Joseph Chipolina		14/12/87	D	23	(1)	16
14	Roy Chipolina		20/01/83	D	26		6
15	Daniel Cifuentes	ESP	13/07/80	D	8	(1)	
17	Leon Clinton		19/07/98	A	1	(6)	1
2	Jean-Carlos Garcia		05/07/92	D	19	(3)	2
86	Antonio Livramento	POR	03/03/92	M	19	(3)	6
1	Raúl Navas	ESP	03/05/78	G	27		
20	Yeray Patiño	ESP	19/05/91	M	20	(6)	3
26	Leon Payas		26/02/98	M		(2)	
15	Rúben Freitas	POR	02/01/93	D		(5)	1
21	Steven Soussi		30/07/92	A		(5)	1
12	Dean Torrilla		30/07/94	M	2	(6)	
88	Liam Walker		13/04/88	M	23	(1)	13
18	Michael Yome		29/08/94	A	1	(3)	1

Lions Gibraltar FC

1966 • lionsgibraltarfc.com

Coach: Juan Luis Pérez Herrera (ESP);
(06/04/16) (Adrian Parral);
(15/04/16) Rafael Bado (ESP)

2015
25/09	St Joseph's	D 1-1	*Gines*
03/10	Lincoln	L 0-2	
17/10	Angels	W 3-0	*Salas, Narvaez, Cantizano*
31/10	Manchester 62	W 3-2	*Gines, López, Salas*
06/11	Glacis	W 5-0	*Gines 3, Fernández, Garro*
16/11	Britannia XI	W 4-0	*Gines, Moreno, Narvaez 2*
21/11	Lynx	D 1-1	*Gines*
29/11	Europa	L 0-2	
02/12	Gibraltar United	W 3-0	*Rodriguez, Gines 2 (1p)*
07/12	St Joseph's	W 3-1	*Gines, Santos, Narvaez*
13/12	Lincoln	L 0-4	
18/12	Angels	W 2-0	*Santos, Narvaez*

2016
02/01	Gibraltar United	L 0-1	
08/01	Manchester 62	L 0-1	
18/01	Glacis	L 0-6	
25/01	Britannia XI	W 1-0	*Romero*
30/01	Lynx	W 2-1	*Gines, García*
19/02	Europa	L 0-3	
26/02	St Joseph's	L 1-2	*García*
07/03	Lincoln	L 1-7	*Gines*
13/03	Angels	W 1-0	*García*
04/04	Gibraltar United	L 1-3	*Mouelhi*
09/04	Manchester 62	D 2-2	*Romero, Guerrero*
15/04	Glacis	W 6-3	*Narvaez, Rodriguez, Gines 3, Segura*
27/04	Britannia XI	W 4-1	*García 2, Gines 2*
08/05	Lynx	W 4-1	*Narvaez 2, Gines 2*
15/05	Europa	W 1-0	*García (p)*

Name	Nat	DoB	Pos	Aps	(s)	Gls
11 Rafael Bado		30/12/84	M	8	(2)	
3 Jesús Cantizano	ESP	01/01/89	D	18	(5)	1
5 Jaydan Catania		06/03/93	D		(1)	
8 Ismael Fernández	ESP	13/10/86	D	16		1
43 Salvador García	ESP	17/02/87	A	5	(4)	6
10 Sykes Garro		26/02/93	M	12	(5)	1
19 Sergio Gines	ESP	27/12/78	M	25	(2)	19
41 Alberto González	ESP	11/02/85	M	8	(2)	
7 Evan Green		13/03/93	M	5	(4)	
38 Albi Guerrero	ESP	16/07/83	D	10		1
21 Jonay López	ESP	17/01/91	M	7	(8)	1
9 Lython Marquez		06/02/95	A		(1)	
18 Jayce Mascarenhas-Olivero		02/07/98	D	14	(3)	
24 Luis McCoy		02/09/94	M		(4)	
17 Enrique Moreno	ESP	09/01/92	M	9	(5)	1
45 Aymen Mouelhi	TUN	14/09/86	D	17	(1)	1
28 David Narvaez	ESP	11/07/85	M	21	(4)	8
33 Liam Neale		01/12/96	G	4		
2 Diego Pacheco	ESP	06/09/96	D	9	(2)	
12 Kailan Perez		22/08/88	D	10	(1)	
20 Pedro Pinazo	ESP	18/01/85	M	4	(1)	
6 Ashley Rodriguez		13/11/89	M	21	(3)	2
45 José Luis Romero	ESP	19/07/92	A	7	(7)	2
4 Andrés Salas	ESP	12/05/85	D	25		2
14 Nathan Santos		11/10/88	A	9	(9)	2
23 Raúl Segura	ESP	11/04/91	M	10	(4)	1
1 Adam Szpilczynski	ESP	19/11/84	G	23		

Lynx FC

2007 • lynxfc.com

Coach: Albert Parody

2015
26/09	Angels	W 2-1	*Pereira, Sánchez*
02/10	Manchester 62	D 2-2	*A González, Sánchez*
18/10	Britannia XI	W 1-0	*Pereira (p)*
23/10	Europa	L 1-2	*Cuby*
02/11	Lincoln	L 0-4	
07/11	Gibraltar United	W 3-0	*Gutiérrez, A González, Doxagarat*
15/11	Glacis	W 2-0	*Hassan, Doxagarat*
21/11	Lions Gibraltar	D 1-1	*Guiling*
30/11	St Joseph's	W 1-0	*Doxagarat*
07/12	Angels	W 6-0	*Sánchez 2, Doxagarat, Pereira, A González, Hassan*
14/12	Manchester 62	W 2-1	*Chacón, Pereira*
19/12	Britannia XI	L 0-3	

2016
04/01	Europa	L 1-2	*Doxagarat*
09/01	Lincoln	L 0-2	
17/01	Gibraltar United	W 3-1	*Gómez 3*
24/01	Glacis	L 0-1	
30/01	Lions Gibraltar	L 1-2	*Sánchez*
20/02	St Joseph's	L 0-1	
27/02	Angels	W 2-1	*Gómez, Doxagarat*
05/03	Manchester 62	W 3-0	*Vidić 3*
15/03	Britannia XI	W 2-0	*Vidić, Doxagarat*
02/04	Europa	L 0-1	
11/04	Lincoln	L 0-4	
16/04	Gibraltar United	L 0-1	
01/05	Glacis	L 1-2	*Sánchez*
08/05	Lions Gibraltar	L 1-4	*Hassan*
14/05	St Joseph's	L 2-4	*Montenegro, og (Lobato)*

No	Name	Nat	DoB	Pos	Aps	(s)	Gls
6	Aaron Akrapovic	ITA	02/03/94	M	21	(1)	
30	Tyronne Avellano		01/05/00	M		(3)	
15	Tobias Campoy	ESP	01/11/89	D	15	(8)	
4	Francisco Chacón	ESP	29/03/94	D	19	(6)	1
88	Mark Chichon		24/12/94	M		(2)	
11	Joshua Cuby		25/05/92	M	10	(8)	1
2	Karim Dechraoui		30/04/92	D	2		
22	Agustin Doxagarat	ARG	14/05/91	A	18	(6)	7
1	Christian Fraiz	ESP	22/02/88	G	7		
10	Francisco Gómez	ESP	13/03/83	M	13		4
10	Alberto González	ESP	11/02/85	M	7	(1)	3
14	Borja González	ESP	30/06/88	M		(8)	
1	Francisco González	ESP	22/05/84	G	1		
9	Robert Guiling		14/10/80	M	21	(2)	1
77	Unai Gutiérrez	ESP	15/02/91	M	7	(11)	1
7	Mohamed Hassan	EGY	25/11/89	M	12	(9)	3
5	Ethan Jolley		29/03/97	D	19	(2)	
23	Javier López	ESP	21/04/90	M	19	(1)	
2	Jesus López	ESP	22/01/96	D	4		
30	Julian Montenegro	ARG	23/03/89	M	12		1
8	Javan Parody		06/04/88	D		(1)	
20	Juan Pablo Pereira	ESP	02/07/87	A	11	(3)	4
20	Ethan Perez		14/10/98	M		(1)	
12	Robert Rae	ENG	30/05/99	G	2		
1	Jamie Robba		26/10/91	G	17		
30	Ian Rodriguez		20/07/88	M		(2)	
8	Carlos Sánchez	ESP	28/12/87	M	21	(4)	6
19	Leonardo Vela	ITA	05/07/82	D	20	(1)	
20	Lazar Vidić	SRB	10/07/89	A	5		4
2	Eden Villegas	ESP	12/08/92	D	14		

Manchester 62 FC

1962 • man62fc.com
Major honours
Gibraltar League (7) 1975, 1977, 1979, 1980, 1984, 1995, 1999; Gibraltar Cup (3) 1977, 1980, 2003
Coach: David Ochello;
(01/01/16) José Manuel Prieto (ESP)

2015
26/09	Glacis	W	1-0	og (Martínez)
02/10	Lynx	D	2-2	Toncheff 2
17/10	St Joseph's	L	0-1	
25/10	Angels	W	5-1	Toncheff 4 (1p), og (Muñoz)
31/10	Lions Gibraltar	L	2-3	Hoefkens, Toncheff
07/11	Britannia XI	L	0-2	
14/11	Europa	L	0-4	
22/11	Lincoln	L	0-4	
28/11	Gibraltar United	L	0-1	
04/12	Glacis	D	1-1	Victory
14/12	Lynx	L	1-2	Hoefkens
19/12	St Joseph's	L	0-2	

2016
03/01	Angels	W	4-1	Anthony Hernandez, Payas, Toncheff, Gonzalez
08/01	Lions Gibraltar	W	1-0	J Lopez
16/01	Britannia XI	W	2-0	Durán, Toncheff
23/01	Europa	D	1-1	Rovegno
29/01	Lincoln	L	0-4	
21/02	Gibraltar United	W	1-0	Yome
28/02	Glacis	L	1-3	I Ruiz
05/03	Lynx	L	0-3	
11/03	St Joseph's	W	3-0	(w/o; original result 1-2 Toncheff (p))
03/04	Angels	W	6-1	Toncheff 3, Anthony Hernandez, Payas, J Lopez
09/04	Lions Gibraltar	D	2-2	Toncheff, JP Duarte
16/04	Britannia XI	W	6-0	Andrew Hernandez, og (Hastings), Toncheff 2, Isola, J Lopez
30/04	Europa	L	0-5	
06/05	Lincoln	L	0-4	
14/05	Gibraltar United	D	2-2	Yome, Sergeant

No	Name	Nat	DoB	Pos	Aps	(s)	Gls
19	Liam Clarke		04/12/87	M	4	(1)	
26	Dayle Coleing		23/10/96	G	2		
63	Jamie Coombes		27/05/96	A	1	(1)	
33	Lee Coombes		20/06/96	D	1	(2)	
27	Max Cottrell		15/09/99	M	1	(4)	
46	Liam Crisp		23/09/99	D		(1)	
88	Shaun De Los Santos		26/01/98	M	14	(7)	
25	Hafed Droubi	ENG	30/03/95	G	3		
21	Daniel Duarte		25/10/79	M	3	(6)	
9	John Paul Duarte		13/12/86	A	8	(4)	1
12	Aaron Durán	ESP	26/01/94	D	21	(4)	1
31	Kieron Gallardo		14/10/98	M		(1)	
74	Kieron Garcia		04/08/98	M	1	(2)	
22	Philip Gillingwater Pedersen		16/01/99	D	2	(1)	
20	Gabriel Gonzalez		16/07/91	A	16	(1)	1
44	Andrew Hernandez		10/01/99	M	6	(2)	1
40	Anthony Hernandez		03/02/95	M	8		2
36	Carl Hoefkens	BEL	06/10/78	D	19		2
14	Thomas Isola		17/01/96	M	2	(2)	1
14	Gareth Lopez		18/02/86	M	9	(1)	
7	Jeremy Lopez		09/07/89	M	10	(7)	3
1	Kaaron Macedo		27/03/84	G	14		
80	Juan Mateo	ESP	24/12/80	G	8		
15	Francisco Mejías	ESP	05/05/87	M	10		
37	Javier Moreno	ESP	11/01/94	M		(1)	
11	Estiven Morente		16/02/91	M		(3)	
17	Álvaro Navarro	ESP	14/04/91	A	11	(2)	
8	Aaron Payas		24/05/85	M	21	(3)	2
23	Brian Perez		16/09/86	M	5	(2)	
15	Theo Pizarro		10/07/98	A	3	(3)	
55	Jason Pusey		18/02/89	D	1		
47	Stefan Ramirez		18/11/98	D		(1)	
4	Matthew Reoch		25/02/83	D	1	(1)	
3	Justin Rovegno		17/07/89	D	15	(3)	1
34	Iván Ruiz	ESP	16/09/90	M	1	(2)	1
6	Tyson Ruiz		10/03/88	M	9	(1)	
2	Yogen Santos		15/01/85	D	2	(1)	
5	Jack Sergeant		27/02/95	D	17		1
10	Cristian Toncheff	ARG	25/03/82	A	25		16
66	Jesse Victory		02/04/96	M	15	(3)	1
29	Michael Yome		29/08/94	A	8	(4)	2

St Joseph's FC

1912 • stjosephsfcgib.com
Major honours
Gibraltar League (1) 1996; Gibraltar Cup (9) 1979, 1983, 1984, 1985, 1987, 1991, 1995, 2012, 2013
Coach: Alfonso Cortijo Cabrera (ESP)

2015
25/09	Lions Gibraltar	D	1-1	Lobato
01/10	Angels	W	4-0	Corpas, Verdejo 2, Merchán
17/10	Manchester 62	W	1-0	Corpas
24/10	Britannia XI	D	1-1	Corpas
29/10	Europa	L	0-2	
08/11	Lincoln	L	0-2	
13/11	Gibraltar United	W	2-0	Merchán 2 (1p)
20/11	Glacis	W	3-0	Merchán 2, Verdejo
30/11	Lynx	L	0-1	
07/12	Lions Gibraltar	L	1-3	Samaniego
12/12	Angels	W	3-0	Garrido, Contreras, Gómez
19/12	Manchester 62	W	2-0	Merchán, Garrido

2016
03/01	Britannia XI	L	3-4	Merchán, Lobato, Samaniego (p)
10/01	Europa	W	3-1	Verdejo, López, Castle
16/01	Lincoln	L	0-4	
23/01	Gibraltar United	W	4-0	og (Currer), Samaniego, Verdejo 2
05/02	Glacis	W	5-3	López, Montes, Morlán 2, Gómez
20/02	Lynx	W	1-0	López
26/02	Lions Gibraltar	W	2-1	Cortijo, Gómez
06/03	Angels	L	0-1	
11/03	Manchester 62	L	0-3	(w/o; original result 2-1 López, Gómez)
02/04	Britannia XI	W	4-0	Morlán 3, Verdejo
09/04	Europa	L	1-2	D Pérez
17/04	Lincoln	L	0-3	
29/04	Gibraltar United	W	3-1	López 2, Corpas
07/05	Glacis	D	2-2	López, Verdejo
14/05	Lynx	W	4-2	Morlán, Verdejo, Ferrer, López

No	Name	Nat	DoB	Pos	Aps	(s)	Gls
22	Abderkahman Bakkari	MAR	22/02/88	M	2		
10	Kevin Bonilla	ESP	05/10/87	M	2	(2)	
14	Carlos Briones	GUI	18/02/90	M	5	(2)	
27	Juan Pedro Caretero	ESP	11/07/89	A	15	(2)	
7	Kivan Castle		21/02/90	A		(5)	1
25	Jamie Contreras	ESP	23/04/93	D	14		1
24	Jorge Corpas	ESP	11/05/96	D	23	(1)	4
4	Alejandro Cortijo	ESP	13/11/96	M	25		1
3	Riki Duarte		08/10/92	D	7		
14	José Durán	ESP	17/02/96	M	10	(1)	
14	Emerson	BRA	06/11/90	M	4	(1)	
26	Francisco Fernández	ESP	11/01/86	M	4	(2)	
10	Juan Carlos Fernández	ESP	21/11/95	A	5	(6)	
25	José Antonio Ferrer	ESP	16/10/95	M	1	(4)	1
18	José Garrido	ESP	23/06/88	M	10	(4)	2
18	Aidan Ghio		22/09/98	D		(1)	
28	Borja Gómez	ESP	13/08/92	A	13	(3)	4
6	Iván Lobato	ESP	28/05/91	D	26		2
15	Javier López	ESP	13/11/87	A	24	(2)	8
13	Albano Marín	ESP	11/10/92	G	5		
9	Diego Merchán	ESP	05/01/95	A	7	(5)	7
5	Esteban Montes	ESP	03/04/88	D	13	(3)	1
11	Manuel Morlán	ESP	27/08/93	A	8		6
16	Michael Negrette		14/09/98	M	1	(11)	
1	Jordan Perez		13/11/86	G	22		
20	David Pérez	ESP	19/09/90	A	2	(6)	1
17	Cecil Prescott		10/05/99	A	1	(11)	
21	Christopher Remorino		24/10/92	D	1		
20	Daniel Rodríguez	ESP	26/11/92	D	1		
12	Alejandro Samaniego	ESP	30/06/93	M	9		3
2	Thyago Catharino	BRA	05/10/87	D	7		
4	Carlos Trujillo	ESP	24/01/87	D	9	(2)	
7	José Luis Verdejo	ESP	05/10/81	A	21	(3)	9

Top goalscorers

29	Pedro Carrión (Europa)
24	George Cabrera (Lincoln)
20	Guido Abayian (Lincoln)
19	Sergio Gines (Lions Gibraltar)
17	Kyle Casciaro (Lincoln)
	Lee Casciaro (Lincoln)
16	Joseph Chipolina (Lincoln)
	Juan Pablo Pereira (Lynx/Glacis)
	Cristian Toncheff (Manchester 62)
15	Robert Montovio (Gibraltar United)

Promoted clubs

Europa Point FC

2014 • europapointfc.com
Coach: Miguel Ángel Pérez Redondo (ESP)

Mons Calpe SC

2013 • monscalpesc.com
Coach: Kailan Prescott;
(16/10/15) (Jansen Dalli);
(01/11/15) Juan José Exposito Jiménez (ESP)

Second level final table 2015/16

		Pld	W	D	L	F	A	Pts
1	Europa Point FC	22	17	5	0	75	19	56
2	Mons Calpe SC	22	17	2	3	82	12	53
3	Gibraltar Phoenix FC	22	14	5	3	67	17	47
4	FC Bruno's Magpies	22	14	2	6	54	24	44
5	FC Olympique Gibraltar 13	22	12	2	8	38	42	38
6	Red Imps FC	22	11	1	10	45	37	34
7	Leo FC	22	10	3	9	44	36	33
8	FC Boca Juniors Gibraltar	22	6	2	14	30	55	20
9	Europa Pegasus	22	6	2	14	24	54	20
10	FC Hound Dogs	22	5	3	14	21	54	18
11	Cannons FC	22	4	1	17	23	60	13
12	College 1975 FC	22	2	0	20	20	113	6

Promotion/Relegation play-off

(31/05/16)
Britannia XI 1-2 Mons Calpe

GREECE
Ellinikos Podosfairikos Omospondia (EPO)

Address	Goudi Park
	PO Box 14161
	GR-11510 Athens
Tel	+30 210 930 6000
Fax	+30 210 935 9666
E-mail	epo@epo.gr
Website	epo.gr

President	Georgios Girtzikis
General secretary	Pafsanias
	Papanikolaou
Media officer	Michalis Tsapidis
Year of formation	1926
National stadium	Georgios Karaiskakis,
	Piraeus (32,130)

SUPERLEAGUE CLUBS

 1 **AEK Athens FC**

 2 **Asteras Tripolis FC**

3 **Atromitos FC**

 4 **Iraklis FC**

 5 **Kalloni FC**

 6 **Levadiakos FC**

 7 **Olympiacos FC**

 8 **Panathinaikos FC**

 9 **Panetolikos GFS**

 10 **Panionios GSS**

 11 **Panthrakikos FC**

 12 **PAOK FC**

 13 **PAS Giannina FC**

 14 **Platanias FC**

 15 **Veria FC**

 16 **Xanthi FC**

PROMOTED CLUBS

 17 **AE Larissa FC**

 18 **Kerkyra FC**

KEY

- ● UEFA Champions League
- ◑ UEFA Europa League
- ◍ Promoted
- ◌ Relegated

Olympiacos in overdrive

Olympiacos's ownership of the Greek Superleague was more pronounced than ever in 2015/16 as the Piraeus club raced to their sixth straight title in double-quick time, concluding proceedings as early as February after winning all of their first 17 matches.

New coach Marco Silva enjoyed a record-breaking debut season in the league but he could not lead Olympiacos to the double, with back-from-the-dead AEK Athens beating them in the Greek Cup final, nor to success in Europe, where a couple of rare home defeats proved costly.

Piraeus giants romp to sixth successive title

AEK Athens shock champions in cup final

PAOK pip Panathinaikos in play-offs

Domestic league

Olympiacos's 43rd league title was a foregone conclusion almost from the outset. A hyperactive summer had resulted in the arrival of not just a new coach – with ex-Sporting Clube de Portugal boss Silva replacing his compatriot Vítor Pereira – but a whole phalanx of new players, among them experienced Argentinian international Esteban Cambiasso, Nigerian striker Brown Ideye and Serbian midfielder Luka Milivojević.

The new mix proved irresistible, with 14 of their 15 Superleague opponents bowing to Olympiacos's omnipotence in the first half of the season and the other, arch-rivals Panathinaikos, presenting them with another three points by forfeit following violent incidents that caused the big derby to be abandoned without a ball being kicked.

Olympiacos stretched their winning sequence to a club-record 17 matches before Platanias made it in mid-January with a 1-1 draw in Crete. The perennial champions' first defeat came closer to home when they lost 1-0 at AEK, a 78th-minute winner from Venezuelan midfielder Ronald Vargas coming only after Olympiacos had been reduced to nine men. Two weeks later, however, with a 3-0 home win over Veria, the men in red and white stripes were celebrating yet another Superleague triumph.

Never before had Olympiacos – or any other club – sealed the Greek title in February, and that was not the only record-breaking feat. They won their last six matches, the first of them 3-1 against Panathinaikos, to end with 28 victories out of a possible 30 and a 28-point gap between themselves and second-placed AEK. Flawless in Piraeus, they also set a new club record of 25 consecutive home wins, and in 18-goal midfielder Kostas Fortounis they possessed the Superleague's leading marksman – with three more than Panathinaikos's Marcus Berg, who boosted his total with five goals against relegated Panthrakikos on the final day.

While Olympiacos's league campaign ended in mid-April, the four teams placed second to fifth ventured into the UEFA Champions League qualifying play-offs, and it was not until the last day of May, with a 1-1 home draw against Panathinaikos, that PAOK emerged triumphant from that particular contest.

Domestic cup

With Olympiacos receiving a Greek Cup semi-final walkover over PAOK because of crowd violence that forced the abandonment of the first leg in Salonika, the champions had a month-long wait before they took the field for the final, against AEK. Perhaps it was rustiness that allowed their opponents – promoted back to the Superleague only the previous summer after recovering from financial collapse – to take a two-goal lead. Olympiacos pulled one back late on, but AEK, under the temporary stewardship of former defender Stelios Manolas following the sacking of coach Gus Poyet a month earlier, held on to lift the trophy for the 15th time.

Europe

The path travelled by Greece's European taskforce in 2015/16 was very similar to that of the previous campaign, with Olympiacos dropping from the UEFA Champions League to the UEFA Europa League after the group stage and the other clubs reaching journey's end before Christmas. The main difference to the script was that Olympiacos beat Arsenal away – their first win in England – but then lost the crunch return fixture in Piraeus 3-0. It was also in the Karaiskakis stadium that they surrendered arms in the UEFA Europa League, losing to Anderlecht in extra time.

National team

A best forgotten UEFA EURO 2016 qualifying campaign that left Greece propping up their group with just one victory – 4-3 at home to Hungary on the final matchday – led to the appointment of a new coach, with the much-travelled German, Michael Skibbe, signing a deal to take the team through the 2018 FIFA World Cup qualifiers.

DOMESTIC SEASON AT A GLANCE

Superleague 2015/16 final table

		Pld	Home					Away					Total					Pts
			W	D	L	F	A	W	D	L	F	A	W	D	L	F	A	
1	**Olympiacos FC**	**30**	**15**	**0**	**0**	**45**	**5**	**13**	**1**	**1**	**36**	**11**	**28**	**1**	**1**	**81**	**16**	**85**
2	Panathinaikos FC	30	10	3	2	34	12	8	1	6	18	14	18	4	8	52	26	55
3	AEK Athens FC	30	13	0	2	31	6	4	6	5	12	15	17	6	7	43	21	54
4	PAOK FC	30	9	4	2	24	12	4	5	6	21	20	13	9	8	45	32	45
5	Panionios GSS	30	8	3	4	19	11	4	5	6	14	16	12	8	10	33	27	44
6	PAS Giannina FC	30	7	3	5	19	17	5	3	7	17	23	12	6	12	36	40	42
7	Asteras Tripolis FC	30	7	5	3	20	12	4	3	8	11	18	11	8	11	31	30	41
8	Atromitos FC	30	7	2	6	12	12	5	4	6	14	19	12	6	12	26	31	39
9	Platanias FC	30	5	6	4	18	14	5	3	7	14	16	10	9	11	32	30	39
10	Levadiakos FC	30	4	7	4	14	17	5	3	7	13	19	9	10	11	27	36	37
11	Panetolikos GFS	30	7	3	5	20	23	2	5	8	10	23	9	8	13	30	46	35
12	Iraklis FC	30	4	7	4	13	11	4	4	7	11	21	8	11	11	24	32	35
13	Xanthi FC	30	4	7	4	15	14	2	8	5	12	18	6	15	9	27	32	33
14	Veria FC	30	2	6	7	7	14	3	6	6	12	19	5	12	13	19	33	27
15	Panthrakikos FC	30	2	3	10	10	25	1	5	9	8	33	3	8	19	18	58	17
16	Kalloni FC	30	3	5	7	16	21	0	2	13	3	32	3	7	20	19	53	16

NB AEK Athens FC, Atromitos FC, Panathinaikos FC & PAOK FC – 3 pts deducted.

European qualification 2016/17

 Champion: Olympiacos FC (third qualifying round)
PAOK FC (third qualifying round)

 Cup winner: AEK Athens FC (third qualifying round)
Panathinaikos FC (third qualifying round)
PAS Giannina FC (second qualifying round)

Top scorer Kostas Fortounis (Olympiacos), 18 goals
Relegated clubs Kalloni FC, Panthrakikos FC
Promoted clubs AE Larissa FC, Kerkyra FC
Cup final AEK Athens FC 2-1 Olympiacos FC

Team of the season
(4-3-3)

Coach: Marco Silva (Olympiacos)

Roberto (Olympiacos)

Elabdellaoui (Olympiacos) · Lazaridis (Atromitos) · Siovas (Olympiacos) · Masuaku (Olympiacos)

Milivojević (Olympiacos) · Fortounis (Olympiacos) · Durmaz (Olympiacos)

Vellios (Iraklis) · Ideye (Olympiacos) · Bakasetas (Panionios)

Player of the season

Kostas Fortounis
(Olympiacos FC)

In his second season at Olympiacos, 23-year-old Fortounis became the serial champions' new star. Brought back to his original club in July 2014, after a spell in the German second division with Kaiserslautern, the pacy, creative attacking midfielder illuminated the Superleague as he inspired the Piraeus giants to a record run of victories and ultimately to yet another emphatic title triumph. He topped the league's golden boot listing with 18 goals and was also credited with the largest number of assists – 12.

Newcomer of the season

Dimitrios Giannoulis
(Veria FC)

Unable to make the breakthrough at his parent club PAOK, Giannoulis, the younger brother of Asteras Tripolis's Konstantinos, was sent out on loan for the whole of the 2015/16 season to Veria. It proved to be a smart move for all concerned as the 20-year-old left-back produced a string of eye-catching performances, helping Veria to ward off relegation from the Superleague and earning himself graduation to the Greek Under-21 team. PAOK were more than happy to bring him back to Salonika in the summer.

NATIONAL TEAM

International honours
UEFA European Championship (1) 2004

International tournament appearances
FIFA World Cup (3) 1994, 2010, 2014 (2nd round)
UEFA European Championship (4) 1980, 2004 (Winners), 2008, 2012 (qtr-finals)

Top five all-time caps
Georgios Karagounis (139); Theodoros Zagorakis (120); Kostas Katsouranis (116); Angelos Basinas (100); Efstratios Apostolakis (96)

Top five all-time goals
Nikolaos Anastopoulos (29); Angelos Charisteas (25); Theofanis Gekas (24); Dimitrios Saravakos (22); Dimitrios "Mimis" Papaioannou (20)

Results 2015/16

Date	Opponent		Venue		Score	Scorers
04/09/15	Finland (ECQ)	H	Piraeus	L	0-1	
07/09/15	Romania (ECQ)	A	Bucharest	D	0-0	
08/10/15	Northern Ireland (ECQ)	A	Belfast	L	1-3	*Aravidis (87)*
11/10/15	Hungary (ECQ)	H	Piraeus	W	4-3	*Stafylidis (5), Tachtsidis (57), Mitroglou (79), Kone (86)*
13/11/15	Luxembourg	A	Differdange	L	0-1	
17/11/15	Turkey	A	Istanbul	D	0-0	
24/03/16	Montenegro	H	Piraeus	W	2-1	*Tzavellas (54), Karelis (63)*
29/03/16	Iceland	H	Piraeus	L	2-3	*Fortounis (19p, 31)*
04/06/16	Australia	A	Sydney	L	0-1	
07/06/16	Australia	A	Melbourne	W	2-1	*Mantalos (8), Maniatis (20)*

Appearances 2015/16

Coach: (Kostas Tsanas) 22/08/67 /(29/10/15) Michael Skibbe (GER) 04/08/65

Player	DOB	Club	FIN	ROU	NIR	HUN	Lux	Tur	Mne	Isl	Aus	Aus	Caps	Goals
Orestis Karnezis	11/07/85	Udinese (ITA)	G	G	G	G		G	G	G15			36	-
Loukas Vyntra	05/02/81	H. Tel-Aviv (ISR)	D	s46		D							57	-
Kyriakos Papadopoulos	23/02/92	Leverkusen (GER)	D				D	D					20	4
Sokratis Papastathopoulos	09/06/88	Dortmund (GER)	D	D	D	D64		D	D		D	D	65	2
José Holebas	27/06/84	Watford (ENG)	D	D	D	s35	M69	M92		M	s46	D65	36	1
Alexandros Tziolis	13/02/85	PAOK	M	M	M		s46	M	s85	M		s70	59	1
Andreas Samaris	13/06/89	Benfica (POR)	M86	M	M	M	M	M	M		M56	M	23	1
Kostas Fortounis	16/10/92	Olympiacos	M	M54		M	A90	A		M77			19	2
Christos Aravidis	13/03/87	AEK Athens	A68	M	A		s69				s74		5	1
Kostas Mitroglou	12/03/88	Benfica (POR)	A	A87	A76	A	A	A70	A93				47	9
Nikolaos Karelis	24/02/92	Panathinaikos /Genk (BEL)	A77	s87	A65		A	s90		s46	A46		12	2
Panagiotis Kone	26/07/87	Udinese (ITA)	s68	s54	M71	s72							28	2
Taxiarhis Fountas	04/09/95	Asteras	s77										3	-
Panagiotis Tachtsidis	15/02/91	Genoa (ITA)	s86			M	M	M46	s93	s77	s56		17	1
Stilianos Kitsiou	28/09/93	PAOK		D	D								2	-
Kostas Manolas	14/06/91	Roma (ITA)		D					D79	D66			23	-
Ioannis Fetfatzidis	21/12/90	Al-Ahli (KSA)		M46									25	3
Vasilios Torosidis	10/06/85	Roma (ITA)			D		M	M85	M77	D	D		83	7
Vangelis Moras	26/08/81	Verona (ITA)		D	D	s78				D			27	-
Petros Mantalos	31/08/91	AEK Athens		s65		M72			M46			M	7	1
Dimitrios Pelkas	26/10/93	PAOK		s71	M	M46							3	-
Stefanos Athanasiadis	24/12/88	PAOK			s76								12	-
Kostas Stafylidis	02/12/93	Augsburg (GER)				D35			M85	M	M	M	10	1
Adam Tzanetopoulos	10/02/95	AEK Athens				s64							1	-
Stefanos Kapino	18/03/94	Olympiacos					G			G	s15	G	7	-
Georgios Tzavellas	26/11/87	PAOK					D	s92	D	s81		D	18	1
Dimitrios Siovas	16/09/88	Olympiacos					D78	s79	s85	D81			12	-
Thanos Petsos	05/06/91	Rapid Wien (AUT)						s46	M	s77			4	-
Apostolos Giannou	25/01/90	Asteras						s70					1	-
Marios Oikonomou	06/10/92	Bologna (ITA)							s66	D	D		3	-
Sakis Papazoglou	30/03/88	Kortrijk (BEL)								A46	s90	s79	3	-
Dimitrios Diamantakos	05/03/93	Karlsruhe (GER)								s46	A46		3	-
Apostolos Vellios	08/01/92	Iraklis								s46	A90	A79	3	-
Ioannis Maniatis	12/10/86	Olympiacos									M	M70	40	1
Lazaros Christodoulopoulos	19/12/86	Sampdoria (ITA)									M46	s65	28	1
Ioannis Gianniotas	29/04/93	APOEL (CYP)									A74		2	-
Anastasios Bakasetas	28/06/93	Panionios									s46	A	2	-

EUROPE

Olympiacos FC

Group F

Match 1 - FC Bayern München (GER)
H 0-3
Roberto, Manuel da Costa, Domínguez (Hernâni 61), Kasami, Elabdellaoui, Siovas, Masuaku, Leandro Salino, Pardo (Sebá 81), Cambiasso (Fortounis 66), Ideye. Coach: Marco Silva (POR)

Match 2 - Arsenal FC (ENG)
A 3-2 *Pardo (33), Ospina (40og), Finnbogason (66)*
Roberto, Botía, Fortounis (Vouros 87), Kasami, Elabdellaoui, Siovas, Leandro Salino, Pardo, Cambiasso, Sebá (Hernâni 73), Ideye (Finnbogason 46). Coach: Marco Silva (POR)

Match 3 - GNK Dinamo Zagreb (CRO)
A 1-0 *Ideye (79)*
Roberto, Botía, Milivojević, Fortounis (Domínguez 72), Kasami, Elabdellaoui, Siovas, Masuaku, Pardo (Leandro Salino 83), Sebá (Manuel da Costa 90), Ideye. Coach: Marco Silva (POR)

Match 4 - GNK Dinamo Zagreb (CRO)
H 2-1 *Pardo (65, 90)*
Roberto, Botía (Manuel da Costa 51), Milivojević, Fortounis, Kasami (Finnbogason 80), Elabdellaoui, Siovas, Masuaku, Hernâni (Pardo 64), Sebá, Ideye. Coach: Marco Silva (POR)

Match 5 - FC Bayern München (GER)
A 0-4
Roberto, Milivojević, Manuel da Costa, Kasami (Fortounis 67), Elabdellaoui (Leandro Salino 78), Siovas, Masuaku, Pardo (Hernâni 67), Cambiasso, Sebá, Ideye. Coach: Marco Silva (POR)

Match 6 - Arsenal FC (ENG)
H 0-3
Roberto, Milivojević, Manuel da Costa, Fortounis, Kasami (Domínguez 72), Elabdellaoui, Siovas, Masuaku, Pardo (Finnbogason 86), Sebá (Hernâni 77), Ideye. Coach: Marco Silva (POR)

Round of 32 - RSC Anderlecht (BEL)
A 0-1
Roberto, Botía, Milivojević, Manuel da Costa, Fortounis, Durmaz (Domínguez 84), Masuaku, Leandro Salino, Zdjelar (Kasami 69), Sebá (Pulido 81), Ideye. Coach: Marco Silva (POR)

H 1-2 (aet) *Fortounis (29p)*
Roberto, Botía, Milivojević, Manuel da Costa, Fortounis, Elabdellaoui, Pulido (Sebá 83), Durmaz (Domínguez 51), Masuaku, Cambiasso (Zdjelar 67), Ideye. Coach: Marco Silva (POR)

Panathinaikos FC

Third qualifying round - Club Brugge KV (BEL)
H 2-1 *Berg (37), Karelis (65p)*
Kotsolis, Koutroumbis, Berg, Zeca, Wemmer, Ajagun (Lagos 46), Karelis (Lod 74), Tavlaridis, Sergio Sánchez, Ninis (Triantafyllopoulos 46), Pranjić. Coach: Ioannis Anastasiou (GRE)
Red card: Sergio Sánchez 44

A 0-3
Kotsolis, Koutroumbis (Petrić 60), Triantafyllopoulos, Lagos, Berg, Zeca, Wemmer, Karelis (Klonaridis 73), Tavlaridis, Ninis (Lod 73), Pranjić. Coach: Ioannis Anastasiou (GRE)

Play-offs - Qäbälä FK (AZE)
A 0-0
Steele, Koutroumbis, Zeca, Wemmer, Lod (Ajagun 67), Karelis (Berg 58), Tavlaridis, Nano, Kaltsas (Lagos 76), Pranjić, Petrić. Coach: Ioannis Anastasiou (GRE)

H 2-2 *Berg (34), Nano (78)*
Steele, Koutroumbis, Berg, Zeca, Karelis (Klonaridis 67), Tavlaridis, Nano, Sergio Sánchez, Bourbos (Lagos 77), Ninis, Pranjić (Petrić 67). Coach: Ioannis Anastasiou (GRE)

Asteras Tripolis FC

Group K

Match 1 - AC Sparta Praha (CZE)
H 1-1 *Mazza (2)*
Košický, Alloco, Mazza, Giannoulis, Fountas (Dimoutsos 66), Bertoglio (Fernández 71), Lluy, Goian, Iglesias, Ederson (Hamdani 77), Giannou. Coach: Staikos Vergetis (GRE)

Match 2 - FC Schalke 04 (GER)
A 0-4
Theodoropoulos, Mazza (Tsokanis 59), Zisopoulos, Sankaré, Giannoulis, Lluy, Goian (Fountas 70), Hamdani, Iglesias, Ederson (Kourbelis 79), Giannou. Coach: Staikos Vergetis (GRE)

Match 3 - APOEL FC (CYP)
A 1-2 *Lluy (8)*
Theodoropoulos, Alloco, Mazza (Shkurtaj 88), Dimoutsos (Fernández 62), Sankaré, Giannoulis, Bertoglio, Kourbelis (Lanzarote 74), Lluy, Iglesias, Giannou. Coach: Staikos Vergetis (GRE)

Match 4 - APOEL FC (CYP)
H 2-0 *Bertoglio (2), Giannou (45+1)*
Theodoropoulos, Panteliadis, Mazza, Lanzarote (Fountas 63), Zisopoulos, Sankaré, Bertoglio (Hamdani 64), Kourbelis, Lluy, Iglesias, Giannou (Alloco 90+1). Coach: Staikos Vergetis (GRE)

Match 5 - AC Sparta Praha (CZE)
A 0-1
Theodoropoulos, Mazza, Fernández, Zisopoulos, Sankaré, Giannoulis, Fountas (Lanzarote 78), Kourbelis (Dimoutsos 66), Lluy, Iglesias (Panteliadis 81), Giannou. Coach: Staikos Vergetis (GRE)

Match 6 - FC Schalke 04 (GER)
H 0-4
Theodoropoulos, Panteliadis, Lanzarote (Bertoglio 65), Fernández, Sankaré, Tsokanis, Lluy, Goian (Zisopoulos 63), Hamdani, Iglesias (Dimoutsos 69), Giannou. Coach: Staikos Vergetis (GRE)

Atromitos FC

Third qualifying round - AIK Solna (SWE)
A 3-1 *Napoleoni (3), Marcelinho (15), Umbides (80p)*
Gorbunov, Fitanidis, Usero, Napoleoni (Ballas 90+3), Umbides, Marcelinho (Eduardo Brito 86), Godoy, Kyvrakidis, Bíttolo, Lazaridis, Pitu (M'Bow 75). Coach: Mihail-Rizos Grigoriou (GRE)

H 1-0 *Marcelinho (67)*
Gorbunov, Fitanidis, Usero, Napoleoni (Le Tallec 85), Umbides (Limnios 90), Marcelinho, Godoy, Kyvrakidis, Bíttolo, Lazaridis, Pitu (Eduardo Brito 75). Coach: Mihail-Rizos Grigoriou (GRE)

Play-offs - Fenerbahçe SK (TUR)
H 0-1
Gorbunov, Fitanidis, Usero (M'Bow 90+2), Napoleoni, Umbides, Marcelinho (Eduardo Brito 76), Godoy, Kyvrakidis, Bíttolo, Lazaridis, Pitu (Le Tallec 85). Coach: Mihail-Rizos Grigoriou (GRE)

A 0-3
Gorbunov, Fitanidis, Usero, Napoleoni, Umbides, Marcelinho, Godoy (Ballas 62), Kyvrakidis, Bíttolo (Kouros 82), Lazaridis, Pitu (Le Tallec 62). Coach: Mihail-Rizos Grigoriou (GRE)

DOMESTIC LEAGUE CLUB-BY-CLUB

PAOK FC

Second qualifying round - NK Lokomotiva Zagreb (CRO)
A 1-2 *Mak (90+2)*
Olsen, Skondras (Raţ 79), Tziolis (Maduro 61), Mak, Salpingidis (Mystakidis 68), Miguel Vítor, Ricardo Costa, Kaçe, Tzavellas, Kitsiou, Pelkas. Coach: Igor Tudor (CRO)
H 6-0 *Lucas Pérez (3), Mak (7, 84), Pelkas (14), Kitsiou (34), Andrijašević (59og)*
Olsen, Tziolis (Maduro 46), Lucas Pérez (Mystakidis 82), Mak, Miguel Vítor, Koulouris (Raţ 60), Ricardo Costa, Kaçe, Tzavellas, Kitsiou, Pelkas. Coach: Igor Tudor (CRO)

Third qualifying round - FC Spartak Trnava (SVK)
H 1-0 *Lucas Pérez (82)*
Olsen, Tziolis (Savvidis 73), Lucas Pérez, Mak (Mystakidis 78), Miguel Vítor, Koulouris (Skondras 5), Ricardo Costa, Kaçe, Tzavellas, Kitsiou, Pelkas. Coach: Igor Tudor (CRO)
Red card: Miguel Vítor 2
A 1-1 *Konstantinidis (48)*
Olsen, Skondras, Tziolis, Mak, Ricardo Costa, Konstantinidis, Kaçe (Savvidis 81), Mystakidis (Koulouris 57; Pougouras 69), Tzavellas, Korovesis, Pelkas. Coach: Igor Tudor (CRO)
Red card: Skondras 67

Play-offs - Brøndby IF (DEN)
H 5-0 *Mak (17, 80, 82), Pelkas (36), Mendes Rodrigues (51)*
Olsen, Tziolis, Mak, Malezas, Miguel Vítor, Ricardo Costa, Konstantinidis (Korovesis 83), Mendes Rodrigues (Mystakidis 71), Kaçe, Kitsiou, Pelkas (Savvidis 66). Coach: Igor Tudor (CRO)
A 1-1 *Ricardo Costa (21)*
Glykos, Tziolis (Mak 64), Miguel Vítor, Koulouris (Deligiannidis 76), Ricardo Costa, Konstantinidis (Savvidis 64), Mendes Rodrigues, Kaçe, Mystakidis, Tzavellas, Kitsiou. Coach: Igor Tudor (CRO)

Group C
Match 1 - Qäbälä FK (AZE)
A 0-0
Olsen, Tziolis, Mak, Miguel Vítor, Ricardo Costa, Mendes Rodrigues, Tzavellas, Athanasiadis (Berbatov 59), Sabo (Jairo 84), Kitsiou, Pelkas (Golasa 75). Coach: Igor Tudor (CRO)
Match 2 - Borussia Dortmund (GER)
H 1-1 *Mak (34)*
Olsen, Tziolis, Berbatov (Pelkas 89), Mak (Jairo 73), Miguel Vítor, Ricardo Costa, Konstantinidis, Mendes Rodrigues, Kaçe (Charisis 85), Tzavellas, Sabo. Coach: Igor Tudor (CRO)
Match 3 - FC Krasnodar (RUS)
H 0-0
Glykos, Skondras, Jairo, Malezas, Miguel Vítor (Leovac 46), Ricardo Costa, Mendes Rodrigues, Kaçe, Athanasiadis (Berbatov 57), Sabo, Pelkas (Mak 72). Coach: Igor Tudor (CRO)
Red card: Jairo 89
Match 4 - FC Krasnodar (RUS)
A 1-2 *Mak (90+1)*
Glykos, Skondras, Tziolis, Golasa (Athanasiadis 68), Mak, Malezas, Ricardo Costa, Charisis, Mendes Rodrigues, Tzavellas (Kitsiou 81), Sabo (Pelkas 58). Coach: Igor Tudor (CRO)
Match 5 - Qäbälä FK (AZE)
H 0-0
Glykos, Skondras, Tziolis, Berbatov (Mystakidis 71), Mak, Malezas, Mendes Rodrigues, Kaçe, Tzavellas, Kitsiou (Athanasiadis 78), Pelkas (Sabo 46). Coach: Igor Tudor (CRO)
Match 6 - Borussia Dortmund (GER)
A 1-0 *Mak (33)*
Glykos, Skondras, Tziolis, Berbatov (Sabo 71), Mak (Leovac 66), Malezas, Cimirot, Konstantinidis, Kaçe, Mystakidis (Mendes Rodrigues 77), Tzavellas. Coach: Igor Tudor (CRO)

AEK Athens FC

1924 • OACA Spyro Louis (74,767) • aekfc.gr
Major honours
Greek League (11) 1939, 1940, 1963, 1968, 1971, 1978, 1979, 1989, 1992, 1993, 1994; Greek Cup (15) 1932, 1939, 1949, 1950, 1956, 1964, 1966, 1978, 1983, 1996, 1997, 2000, 2002, 2011, 2016
Coach: Traianos Dellas;
(20/10/15) (Stelios Manolas);
(29/10/15) Gustavo Poyet (URU);
(20/04/16) (Stelios Manolas)

2015
22/08	h	Platanias	W	3-0	*Vargas, Rodrigo Galo, Aravidis*
29/08	a	Xanthi	D	0-0	
13/09	h	Giannina	W	3-1	*Buonanotte 2 (1p), Vargas*
23/09	a	PAOK	L	1-2	*Aravidis*
28/09	a	Veria	W	2-1	*Buonanotte, Hélder Barbosa*
04/10	h	Atromitos	W	1-0	*Chrisantus*
17/10	a	Olympiacos	L	0-4	
24/10	h	Iraklis	W	5-1	*Vargas 2, Aravidis, Hélder Barbosa, Buonanotte*
01/11	a	Panathinaikos	D	0-0	
08/11	h	Asteras	L	0-1	
22/11	h	Panthrakikos	W	2-1	*Johansson, Buonanotte (p)*
29/11	h	Panetolikos	W	2-0	*Johansson, Platellas*
06/12	h	Kalloni	W	3-0	*Djebbour, Aravidis 2*
12/12	a	Panionios	D	1-1	*Hélder Barbosa*
21/12	h	Levadiakos	L	1-2	*Johansson*

2016
03/01	a	Platanias	W	3-0	*Hélder Barbosa 2, Djebbour*
09/01	h	Xanthi	W	2-1	*Aravidis, Hélder Barbosa*
17/01	a	Giannina	W	2-0	*Vargas, Hélder Barbosa*
24/01	h	PAOK	W	1-0	*Vargas*
31/01	h	Veria	W	3-0	*Vargas, Aravidis, Mantalos*
07/02	a	Atromitos	L	0-1	
13/02	h	Olympiacos	W	1-0	*Vargas*
20/02	a	Iraklis	D	1-1	*Pekhart*
28/02	h	Panathinaikos	W	1-0	*Vargas*
07/03	a	Asteras	D	0-0	
14/03	h	Panthrakikos	W	3-0	*Buonanotte, Aravidis 2*
20/03	a	Panetolikos	L	0-1	
03/04	a	Kalloni	D	0-0	
10/04	h	Panionios	W	2-0	*Pekhart 2*
17/04	a	Levadiakos	L	0-3	

No	Name	Nat	DoB	Pos	Aps	(s)	Gls
10	Dimitrios Anakoglou		06/09/91	M	1	(2)	
8	André Simões	POR	16/12/89	M	26		
22	Ioannis Anestis		09/03/91	G	7		
13	Christos Aravidis		13/03/87	A	24	(4)	9
7	Mihail Bakakis		18/03/91	M	3		
1	Alain Baroja	VEN	23/10/89	G	23		
30	Diego Buonanotte	ARG	19/04/88	M	11	(13)	6
4	César Arzo	ESP	21/01/86	D	19		
99	Macauley Chrisantus	NGA	20/08/90	A	2	(6)	1
23	Dídac Vilà	ESP	09/06/89	D	21		
10	Rafik Djebbour	ALG	08/03/84	A	7	(11)	2
7	Hélder Barbosa	POR	25/05/87	A	22	(4)	7
18	Jakob Johansson	SWE	21/06/90	M	27	(2)	3
26	Dimitrios Kolovetsios		16/10/91	D	23	(1)	
5	Vasilios Lambropoulos		31/03/90	D	11	(8)	
20	Petros Mantalos		31/08/91	M	22	(3)	1
6	Miguel Cordero	ESP	10/09/87	M	4	(9)	
14	Tomáš Pekhart	CZE	26/05/89	A	4	(5)	3
7	Evangelos Platellas		01/12/88	M	7	(7)	1
12	Rodrigo Galo	BRA	19/09/86	D	27		
2	Aristidis Soiledis		08/02/91	D	9	(3)	
55	Adam Tzanetopoulos		10/02/95	D	8	(2)	
9	Ronald Vargas	VEN	02/12/86	M	20	(5)	9
77	Stavros Vasilantonopoulos		28/01/92	A		(1)	
36	Bruno Zuculini	ARG	02/04/93	M	2		

Asteras Tripolis FC

1931 • Theodoros Kolokotronis (7,493) • asterastripolis.gr
Coach: Staikos Vergetis;
(29/01/16) (Dimitrios Terezopoulos);
(28/02/16) Ioakim Havos

2015
22/08	a	Panthrakikos	W	2-0	*Bertoglio, Giannou*
30/08	h	Panetolikos	L	0-2	
12/09	a	Kalloni	D	1-1	*Giannou (p)*
23/09	h	Panionios	W	2-1	*Giannou, Dimoutsos*
27/09	a	Levadiakos	L	1-2	*Giannou*
05/10	h	Platanias	D	1-1	*Giannou*
18/10	h	Xanthi	D	1-1	*Shkurtaj*
25/10	a	Giannina	W	2-1	*Giannou 2 (1p)*
01/11	h	PAOK	W	2-1	*Bertoglio, Sankaré*
08/11	a	AEK	W	1-0	*Papadopoulos*
21/11	h	Atromitos	L	0-1	*Fernández*
29/11	a	Olympiacos	L	1-3	*Giannou*
05/12	h	Iraklis	L	1-2	*Giannou (p)*
13/12	a	Panathinaikos	L	0-2	
19/12	a	Veria	L	0-1	

2016
02/01	h	Panthrakikos	W	4-0	*Giannou 2, Iglesias, Fountas*
10/01	a	Panetolikos	L	1-2	*Giannou*
17/01	h	Kalloni	W	3-1	*Iglesias 2, Giannou*
23/01	a	Panionios	D	0-0	
31/01	h	Levadiakos	W	2-0	*Bertoglio, Mazza*
06/02	a	Platanias	L	0-2	
15/02	a	Xanthi	D	0-0	
20/02	h	Giannina	D	0-0	
27/02	a	PAOK	L	0-5	
07/03	h	AEK	D	0-0	
13/03	a	Atromitos	L	1-2	*Dimoutsos*
20/03	h	Olympiacos	L	1-2	*Dimoutsos*
03/04	a	Iraklis	W	1-0	*Fernández*
10/04	h	Panathinaikos	D	0-0	
17/04	h	Veria	W	2-1	*Ioannidis 2*

No	Name	Nat	DoB	Pos	Aps	(s)	Gls
6	Fernando Alloco	ARG	30/04/86	D	8	(3)	
37	Georgios Bantis		30/04/85	G	23		
23	Facundo Bertoglio	ARG	30/06/90	M	19	(1)	3
9	Cristian Chávez	ARG	16/06/86	M	1	(5)	
8	Elini Dimoutsos		18/06/88	M	11	(8)	3
2	Dudú	BRA	14/03/89	M	6	(1)	
86	Ederson	BRA	14/03/86	M	2	(2)	
11	Nicolás Fernández	ARG	17/11/86	M	12	(7)	2
20	Taxiarhis Fountas		04/09/95	M	7	(9)	1
99	Apostolos Giannou	AUS	25/01/90	A	18	(3)	13
18	Konstantinos Giannoulis		09/12/87	D	19		
30	Dorin Goian	ROU	12/12/80	D	13		
54	Rachid Hamdani	MAR	08/04/85	M	16	(6)	
62	Walter Iglesias	ARG	18/05/85	M	20	(1)	3
10	Nikolaos Ioannidis		26/04/94	A	3	(7)	2
17	Ritchie Kitoko	BEL	11/06/88	D	7		
25	Tomáš Košický	SVK	11/03/86	G	4		
25	Dimitrios Kourbelis		02/11/93	M	16	(4)	
10	Manuel Lanzarote	ESP	20/01/84	M	9	(2)	
7	Braian Lluy	ARG	25/04/93	D	22	(1)	
7	Pablo Mazza	ARG	21/12/87	A	22	(3)	1
94	Hervaine Moukam	FRA	24/05/94	M	2	(6)	
8	Athanasios Panteliadis		06/09/87	M	11	(2)	
9	Dimitrios Papadopoulos		20/10/81	A	7	(5)	1
15	Khalifa Sankaré	SEN	15/08/84	D	18	(2)	1
12	Vasil Shkurtaj	ALB	27/02/92	A	4	(1)	1
31	Aleksandar Stanisavljević	SRB	11/06/89	M	5	(4)	
21	Konstantinos Theodoropoulos		27/03/90	G	3		
5	Konstantinos Triantafyllopoulos		03/04/93	D	1		
19	Anastasios Tsokanis		02/05/91	M		(5)	
13	Georgios Zisopoulos		23/05/84	M	21	(2)	

Atromitos FC

1923 • Dimotiko Peristeriou (9,000) •
atromitosfc.gr
Coach: Mihail-Rizos Grigoriou;
(04/11/15) Traianos Dellas

2015

23/08	h	Levadiakos	W	1-0	Eduardo Brito
31/08	a	Platanias	W	2-1	Le Tallec, Napoleoni
13/09	h	Xanthi	L	0-1	
23/09	a	Giannina	L	1-2	
27/09	h	PAOK	L	1-2	Umbides
04/10	a	AEK	L	0-1	
18/10	h	Veria	W	1-0	Le Tallec
25/10	a	Olympiacos	L	1-2	Stojčev
02/11	h	Iraklis	L	0-2	
07/11	h	Panathinaikos	L	1-2	Napoleoni
21/11	a	Asteras	L	0-1	
28/11	h	Panthrakikos	L	1-2	Napoleoni
07/12	a	Panetolikos	D	1-1	Eduardo Brito
13/12	h	Kalloni	W	1-0	Usero
19/12	a	Panionios	W	1-0	Lazaridis

2016

09/01	h	Platanias	D	0-0	
16/01	h	Xanthi	D	2-2	Umbides, Lazaridis
24/01	h	Giannina	L	0-2	
30/01	a	PAOK	D	1-1	Lazaridis
07/02	h	AEK	W	1-0	Eduardo Brito
13/02	h	Veria	D	0-0	
17/02	a	Levadiakos	D	1-1	Fitanidis
21/02	a	Olympiacos	L	0-4	
29/02	h	Iraklis	W	1-0	Le Tallec
05/03	a	Panathinaikos	L	0-2	
13/03	h	Asteras	W	2-1	Lazaridis, Le Tallec
20/03	a	Panthrakikos	W	1-0	Le Tallec
03/04	a	Panetolikos	W	1-0	Le Tallec
10/04	h	Kalloni	W	4-2	Matei, Usero, Eduardo Brito, Le Tallec
17/04	a	Panionios	W	1-0	Stojčev

No	Name	Nat	DoB	Pos	Aps	(s)	Gls
16	Panagiotis Ballas		06/09/93	M	1	(5)	
1	Vasileios Barkas		30/05/94	G	12		
25	Mihail Bastakos		27/07/96	M	2	(4)	
20	Mariano Bittolo	ARG	24/04/90	D	26		
86	Chumbinho	BRA	21/09/86	M	7	(1)	
7	Eduardo Brito	BRA	21/09/82	M	25	(5)	4
6	Sokratis Fitanidis		25/05/84	D	23		1
15	Fernando Godoy	ARG	01/05/90	M	13	(2)	
30	Andrei Gorbunov	BLR	25/05/83	G	18		
80	Dimitrios Grontis		21/08/94	M	3	(6)	
34	Paul Keita	SEN	26/06/92	M	8	(1)	
2	Ioannis Kontoes		24/05/86	D	13	(4)	
3	Alexandros Kouros		21/07/92	D	6	(4)	
19	Kyriakos Kyvrakidis		21/07/92	D	21		
24	Nikolaos Lazaridis		12/07/79	D	28	(1)	4
14	Anthony Le Tallec	FRA	03/10/84	A	19	(8)	7
17	Dimitrios Limnios		27/05/98	A	3	(5)	
21	Pape M'Bow	SEN	22/05/88	D	1		
18	Marcelinho	BRA	22/06/87	M	7	(4)	
9	Cosmin Matei	ROU	30/09/91	M	8	(3)	1
9	Stefano Napoleoni	ITA	26/06/86	A	15	(2)	3
33	Dimitrios Papadopoulos		20/10/81	A	4	(6)	
26	Pitu	ARG	27/01/84	M	11	(5)	
18	Miloš Stojčev	MNE	19/01/87	M	9	(15)	2
5	Borislav Stoychev	BUL	26/11/86	D	2	(1)	
22	Pantelis Theologou		07/05/91	D		(1)	
10	Javier Umbides	ARG	09/02/82	M	24	(1)	2
8	Fernando Usero	ESP	27/03/84	M	21	(5)	2

Iraklis FC

1908 • Kaftanzoglio (29,080) • fciraklis.gr
Major honours
Greek Cup (1) 1976
Coach: Nikos Papadopoulos

2015

22/08	h	Kalloni	W	1-0	Perrone
30/08	h	Panionios	L	0-1	
14/09	h	Levadiakos	L	0-1	
22/09	a	Platanias	D	0-0	
26/09	h	Xanthi	D	1-1	Vellios
04/10	a	Giannina	D	2-2	Vellios, Kyriakidis
18/10	h	PAOK	D	3-3	Makris, Vellios, Bartolini
24/10	a	AEK	L	1-5	Vellios
02/11	h	Atromitos	W	2-0	Romano 2
08/11	a	Olympiacos	L	0-2	
23/11	a	Veria	D	0-0	
28/11	h	Panthrakikos	W	1-0	Vellios
05/12	a	Asteras	W	2-1	Vellios, Bulut
12/12	h	Panthrakikos	D	0-0	
20/12	a	Panetolikos	L	0-2	

2016

02/01	h	Kalloni	W	3-0	Vellios 3 (1p)
10/01	a	Panionios	L	0-1	
16/01	a	Levadiakos	D	1-1	Tsilianidis
25/01	h	Platanias	D	0-0	
31/01	a	Xanthi	L	0-2	
07/02	h	Giannina	W	1-0	Vellios (p)
14/02	a	PAOK	W	1-0	Leozinho
20/02	h	AEK	D	1-1	Ziabaris
29/02	a	Atromitos	L	0-1	
13/03	h	Veria	D	1-1	Vellios
19/03	a	Panathinaikos	L	0-4	
03/04	h	Asteras	L	0-1	
06/04	h	Olympiacos	L	0-2	
10/04	a	Panthrakikos	W	3-0	Leozinho, Romano, Perrone
17/04	h	Panetolikos	D	0-0	

No	Name	Nat	DoB	Pos	Aps	(s)	Gls
21	Angelos Abdelchadi		07/09/89	A	1	(6)	
90	Vasilios Amarantidis		02/04/97	A		(1)	
22	Sebastián Bartolini	ARG	01/02/82	D	20	(1)	1
2	Mihail Boukouvalas		14/01/88	D	27		
99	Kerem Bulut	AUS	03/02/92	A	11	(6)	1
23	Carlitos	CPV	23/04/85	D	4	(1)	
40	Serafeim Giannikoglou		25/03/93	G	2		
1	Huanderson	BRA	03/08/83	G	17		
8	Eleftherios Intzoglou		03/03/87	M	20	(3)	
32	Vasilios Karagounis		18/01/94	D	2	(1)	
4	Aristotelis Karasalidis		03/05/91	D	19		
6	Paschalis Kassos		05/12/92	A		(2)	
19	Pavlos Kyriakidis		03/09/91	M	25	(3)	1
15	Costin Lazăr	ROU	24/04/81	M	6		
85	Leozinho	BRA	12/12/85	M	8	(2)	2
17	Ioannis Loukinas		20/09/91	A	2	(11)	
54	Georgios Makris		15/11/84	M	7	(1)	1
27	Monteiro	POR	15/08/88	M	7		
11	Ioannis Passas		07/10/90	M	18	(4)	
30	Dušan Perniš	SVK	28/11/84	G	11		
9	Emanuel Perrone	ARG	14/06/83	A	6	(11)	2
11	Nikolaos Pourtoulidis		07/10/83	M	6	(7)	
10	Diego Romano	ARG	02/03/80	M	13	(7)	3
3	Georgios Saramantas		29/01/92	D	22	(1)	
5	Dimitrios Stamou		27/04/91	D	12	(2)	
7	Kosmas Tsilianidis		09/05/94	A	15	(3)	1
77	Ioannis Tsotras		30/04/96	D	3	(4)	
39	Apostolos Vellios		08/01/92	A	25	(2)	11
20	Emmanouil Zabazis		24/04/97	A	2	(7)	
33	Nikolaos Ziabaris		18/02/91	D	19	(2)	1

Kalloni FC

1994 • Dimotiko Stadio Mytilinis "Tarlas" (3,000)
• kallonifc.gr
Coach: Thalis Theodoridis;
(26/12/15) Nikolaos Karageorgiou

2015

22/08	h	Iraklis	L	0-1	
30/08	a	Panathinaikos	L	0-4	
12/09	h	Asteras	D	1-1	Anastasiadis
23/09	a	Panthrakikos	D	0-0	
26/09	h	Panetolikos	W	5-1	Ellacopulos, Georgiou 2, Adejo, Manousos
04/10	h	Veria	L	0-1	
17/10	a	Panionios	L	0-2	
24/10	h	Levadiakos	D	0-0	
31/10	a	Platanias	L	1-2	Bargan
07/11	h	Xanthi	D	2-2	Manousos 2 (1p)
21/11	a	Giannina	L	1-2	Bargan
30/11	h	PAOK	L	1-3	Manousos (p)
06/12	a	AEK	L	0-3	
13/12	a	Atromitos	L	0-1	
19/12	a	Olympiacos	L	0-2	

2016

02/01	a	Iraklis	L	0-3	
11/01	h	Panathinaikos	L	0-2	
17/01	a	Asteras	L	1-3	Manousos (p)
23/01	h	Panthrakikos	W	2-0	Favali, Anastasiadis
30/01	a	Panetolikos	L	0-1	
07/02	a	Veria	L	0-1	
14/02	h	Panionios	D	1-1	Anastasiadis
20/02	a	Levadiakos	L	0-1	
27/02	h	Platanias	W	2-1	Marković, Ellacopulos
06/03	a	Xanthi	D	0-0	
12/03	h	Giannina	D	0-2	
20/03	a	PAOK	L	0-3	
03/04	h	AEK	D	0-0	
10/04	a	Atromitos	L	2-4	Manousos (p), Anastasiadis
17/04	a	Olympiacos	L	0-5	

No	Name	Nat	DoB	Pos	Aps	(s)	Gls
4	Daniel Adejo	NGA	07/08/89	D	9	(2)	1
14	Anestis Anastasiadis		21/01/83	D	28		4
99	Kenan Bargan		25/10/88	A	7	(6)	2
32	Marko Blažić	SRB	02/08/85	M	9		
23	Dimitrios Bourous		23/02/93	A		(6)	
85	Braulio	ESP	18/09/85	A		(5)	
90	Alexandros Chidasheli		16/02/94	M	1	(1)	
1	Konstantinos Dafkos		10/06/88	G	16	(1)	
18	Emiliano Ellacopulos	ARG	14/01/92	M	9	(6)	2
16	Kyriakos Evangelidakis		02/01/94	M		(3)	
25	Lucas Favalli	ARG	16/07/85	M	8		1
5	Alexandros Fioretos		27/01/95	M		(1)	
30	Efthimios Gamagas		26/09/95	A		(2)	
11	Fotios Georgiou		19/07/85	M	25	(3)	2
26	Rafael Gioukaris		27/02/95	D	3	(4)	
3	Vasilios Golias		01/06/85	D	12		
21	Mihail Hatzidimitriou		19/05/95	M		(1)	
17	Andrew Hogg	MLT	02/03/85	G	14		
27	Nikolaos V Kaltsas		28/06/89	M	25	(1)	
77	Sonny Karlsson	SWE	14/06/88	A	2	(6)	
24	Paul Keita	SEN	26/06/92	M	13		
33	Jiří Kladrubský	CZE	19/11/85	M	4	(5)	
23	Krzysztof Król	POL	06/02/87	D	10	(1)	
40	Nikolaos Mallis		01/03/96	G	1		
9	Georgios Manousos		03/12/87	A	29		6
10	Miroslav Marković	SRB	04/11/89	A	11	(3)	1
33	Nikola Mikić	SRB	13/09/85	D	11		
69	Raúl Llorente	ESP	02/04/86	D	9	(5)	
2	Panagiotis Spyropoulos		21/08/92	D	6	(5)	
31	Savvas Tsabouris		16/07/86	M	25		
19	Ugo Ukah	NGA	18/01/84	D	16	(4)	
55	Efstratios Valios		09/01/89	D	8	(1)	
2	Vitor Saba	BRA	11/07/90	M	10	(2)	
29	Paul Were	KEN	08/01/91	A	7	(3)	
28	Georgios Xydas		14/04/97	A	3	(4)	

Levadiakos FC

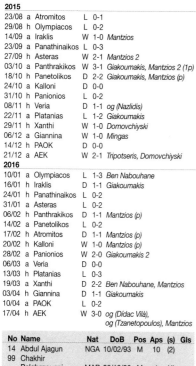

1961 • Dimotiko Livadias (6,200) •
levadiakosfc.gr
**Coach: Apostolos Mantzios;
(08/04/16) Dimitrios Farantos**

2015

23/08	a	Atromitos	L	0-1
29/08	h	Olympiacos	L	0-2
14/09	a	Iraklis	W	1-0 *Mantzios*
23/09	a	Panathinaikos	L	0-3
27/09	h	Asteras	W	2-1 *Mantzios 2*
03/10	a	Panthrakikos	W	3-1 *Giakoumakis, Mantzios 2 (1p)*
18/10	h	Panetolikos	D	2-2 *Giakoumakis, Mantzios (p)*
24/10	a	Kalloni	D	0-0
31/10	h	Panionios	L	0-2
08/11	h	Veria	D	1-1 *og (Nazlidis)*
22/11	a	Platanias	L	1-2 *Giakoumakis*
29/11	h	Xanthi	W	1-0 *Domovchiyski*
06/12	a	Giannina	W	1-0 *Mingas*
14/12	h	PAOK	D	0-0
21/12	a	AEK	W	2-1 *Tripotseris, Domovchiyski*

2016

10/01	a	Olympiacos	L	1-3 *Ben Nabouhane*
16/01	h	Iraklis	D	1-1 *Giakoumakis*
24/01	h	Panathinaikos	L	0-2
31/01	a	Asteras	L	0-2
06/02	h	Panthrakikos	D	1-1 *Mantzios (p)*
14/02	h	Panetolikos	L	0-2
17/02	h	Atromitos	D	1-1 *Mantzios (p)*
20/02	h	Kalloni	W	1-0 *Mantzios (p)*
28/02	a	Panionios	W	2-0 *Giakoumakis 2*
06/03	a	Veria	D	0-0
13/03	h	Platanias	L	0-3
19/03	a	Xanthi	D	2-2 *Ben Nabouhane, Mantzios*
03/04	h	Giannina	D	1-1 *Giakoumakis*
10/04	a	PAOK	L	0-2
17/04	h	AEK	W	3-0 *og (Dídac Vilà), og (Tzanetopoulos), Mantzios*

No	Name	Nat	DoB	Pos	Aps	(s)	Gls
14	Abdul Ajagun	NGA	10/02/93	M	10	(2)	
99	Chakhir Belghazouani	MAR	06/10/86	M	1	(4)	
31	El Fardou Ben Nabouhane	COM	10/06/89	M	11	(1)	2
55	Carlos Milhazes	POR	17/03/81	D	8	(1)	
19	Valeri Domovchiyski	BUL	05/10/86	A	7	(4)	2
5	Lucas Favalli	ARG	16/07/85	M	7	(2)	
20	Petros Giakoumakis		03/07/92	M	21	(4)	7
12	Sanel Jahić	BIH	10/12/81	D	13	(6)	
17	Mattheos Kapsaskis		12/08/96	M	1	(6)	
16	Antonios Magas		28/02/94	D	4	(3)	
8	Azrack-Yassine Mahamat	CHA	24/03/88	M	10	(1)	
6	Dimitrios Maheras		16/08/90	M	17	(2)	
3	Kostas S Manolas		26/03/93	D	13	(3)	
9	Evangelos Mantzios		22/04/83	A	28		11
23	Ivan Marković	SRB	20/06/94	M	1	(3)	
76	Jackson Mendy	SEN	25/05/87	D	12	(1)	
20	Giorgi Merebashvili	GEO	15/08/86	M	7	(5)	
27	Vladan Milosavljev	SRB	01/02/87			(1)	
11	Christos Mingas		15/04/84	M	12	(10)	1
28	Theodoros Moshonas		03/12/90	G	5		
2	Athanasios Moulopoulos		09/06/85	D	19	(2)	
83	Marios Nikolaou	CYP	04/10/83	M	13	(2)	
29	Edwin Ouon	RWA	26/01/81	D	16	(1)	
33	Konstantinos Pappas		30/11/91	A		(5)	
21	Romeu	BRA	13/02/85	M	6	(2)	
25	Ioannis Stathis		20/05/87	D	21	(2)	
22	Georgios Theos		22/08/91	A	1	(2)	
12	Marius Topi		19/10/95	D	2	(6)	
2	Theodoros Tripotseris		04/03/86	D	25		1
1	Panagiotis Tsintotas		04/07/93	G	16	(1)	
27	Andriy Tsurikov	UKR	05/10/92	D	7	(2)	
32	Sergei Veremko	BLR	16/10/82	G	9		
23	Ximo Navarro	ESP	12/09/88	D	7	(4)	

Olympiacos FC

1925 • Georgios Karaiskakis (32,130) • olympiacos.org
Major honours
Greek League (43) 1931, 1933, 1934, 1936, 1937, 1938, 1947, 1948, 1951, 1954, 1955, 1956, 1957, 1958, 1959, 1966, 1967, 1973, 1974, 1975, 1980, 1981, 1982, 1983, 1987, 1997, 1998, 1999, 2000, 2001, 2002, 2003, 2005, 2006, 2007, 2008, 2009, 2011, 2012, 2013, 2014, 2015, 2016;
Greek Cup (27) 1947, 1951, 1952, 1953, 1954, 1957, 1958, 1959, 1960, 1961, 1963, 1965, 1968, 1971, 1973, 1975, 1981, 1990, 1992, 1999, 2005, 2006, 2008, 2009, 2012, 2013, 2015
Coach: Marco Silva (POR)

2015

23/08	h	Panionios	W	3-0 *Fortounis, Bouhalakis, Dossevi*
29/08	a	Levadiakos	W	2-0 *Milivojević, Fortounis*
12/09	h	Platanias	W	3-1 *Durmaz, Domínguez, Masuaku*
22/09	h	Xanthi	W	3-1 *Durmaz, Fortounis 2 (1p)*
26/09	h	Giannina	W	5-1 *Kasami, Fortounis, Botía, og (Tzimopoulos), Durmaz (p)*
04/10	a	PAOK	W	2-0 *Ideye, Milivojević*
17/10	h	AEK	W	4-0 *Botía, Ideye, Fortounis 2 (1p)*
25/10	a	Atromitos	W	2-1 *Botía 2*
31/10	a	Veria	W	2-0 *Ideye, Durmaz*
08/11	h	Iraklis	W	2-0 *Milivojević, Ideye*
21/11	a	Panathinaikos	W	3-0 *(w/o)*
29/11	h	Asteras	W	3-1 *Fortounis 2 (1p), Ideye*
05/12	a	Panthrakikos	W	4-3 *Durmaz, Fortounis (p), Finnbogason (p), Sebá*
13/12	h	Panetolikos	W	1-0 *Domínguez*
19/12	a	Kalloni	W	2-0 *Fortounis 2 (2p)*

2016

03/01	a	Panionios	W	3-1 *Domínguez, Pardo, Ideye*
10/01	h	Levadiakos	W	3-1 *Ideye, Pardo, Domínguez*
18/01	a	Platanias	D	1-1 *Fortounis*
23/01	h	Xanthi	W	1-0 *Pulido*
31/01	a	Giannina	W	3-0 *Fortounis 2 (1p), Durmaz*
07/02	h	PAOK	W	1-0 *Elabdellaoui*
13/02	a	AEK	L	0-1
21/02	h	Atromitos	W	4-0 *Domínguez, Pulido, Cambiasso, Fortounis*
28/02	h	Veria	W	3-0 *David Fuster 2, Pulido*
13/03	h	Panathinaikos	W	3-1 *Cambiasso, Manuel da Costa, Ideye*
20/03	a	Asteras	W	2-1 *Hernâni 2*
03/04	h	Panthrakikos	W	4-0 *Pulido, Pardo, Hernâni 2*
06/04	a	Iraklis	W	2-0 *Durmaz, Ideye*
10/04	a	Panetolikos	W	5-2 *Fortounis, Manuel da Costa, Sebá, Pulido, Pardo*
17/04	h	Kalloni	W	5-0 *Fortounis, David Fuster, Kasami, Elabdellaoui, Ideye*

No	Name	Nat	DoB	Pos	Aps	(s)	Gls
3	Alberto Botía	ESP	27/01/89	D	15	(2)	4
8	Andreas Bouhalakis		05/04/93	M	1	(4)	
91	Esteban Cambiasso	ARG	18/08/80	M	11	(3)	2
19	David Fuster	ESP	03/02/82	M	5	(5)	3
10	Alejandro Domínguez	ARG	10/06/81	M	11	(7)	5
77	Mathieu Dossevi	TOG	12/02/88	M		(2)	
21	Jimmy Durmaz	SWE	22/03/89	M	20	(3)	7
14	Omar Elabdellaoui	NOR	05/12/91	D	20		2
9	Alfred Finnbogason	ISL	01/02/89	A	2	(5)	1
7	Kostas Fortounis		16/10/92	A	22	(5)	18
77	Hernâni	POR	20/08/91	A	5	(11)	4
33	Lefteris Houtesiotis		20/07/94	G		(1)	
99	Brown Ideye	NGA	10/10/88	A	21	(2)	10
12	Franco Jara	ARG	15/07/88	A	1	(1)	
37	Stefanos Kapino		18/03/94	G	3		
11	Pajtim Kasami	SUI	02/06/92	M	16	(3)	2
20	Dimitrios Kolovos		27/04/93	M	2	(3)	
30	Leandro Salino	BRA	22/04/85	D	13	(1)	
2	Ioannis Maniatis		12/10/86	M		(2)	
6	Manuel da Costa	MAR	06/05/86	D	20	(2)	2
26	Arthur Masuaku	FRA	07/11/93	D	23		1
5	Luka Milivojević	SRB	07/04/91	M	22		3
90	Felipe Pardo	COL	17/08/90	A	15	(6)	4
71	Alan Pulido	MEX	08/03/91	A	5	(3)	5
16	Roberto	ESP	10/02/86	G	26		
92	Sebá	BRA	08/06/92	A	7	(12)	2
23	Dimitrios Siovas		16/09/88	D	21	(1)	
41	Konstantinos Tsimikas		12/05/96	D	2	(1)	
29	Praxitelis Vouros		05/05/95	D	2		
44	Saša Zdjelar	SRB	20/03/95	M	8		

Panathinaikos FC

1908 • Apostolos Nikolaidis (16,003) • pao.gr

Major honours
Greek League (20) 1930, 1949, 1953, 1960, 1961, 1962, 1964, 1965, 1969, 1970, 1972, 1977, 1984, 1986, 1990, 1991, 1995, 1996, 2004, 2010; Greek Cup (18) 1940, 1948, 1955, 1967, 1969, 1977, 1982, 1984, 1986, 1988, 1989, 1991, 1993, 1994, 1995, 2004, 2010, 2014

Coach: Ioannis Anastasiou; (02/11/15) Steve Rutter) (ENG); (08/11/15) Andrea Stramaccioni (ITA)

2015
24/08	a	Panetolikos	W	2-1	*Karelis, Berg*
30/08	h	Kalloni	W	4-0	*Karelis, Berg, Tavlaridis, Petrić*
13/09	a	Panionios	L	0-1	
23/09	h	Levadiakos	W	3-0	*Nano, Karelis, Ajagun*
27/09	h	Platanias	W	1-0	*Ajagun*
03/10	a	Xanthi	W	1-0	*Thelander*
19/10	a	Giannina	W	3-1	*Karelis, Petrić (p), Abeid*
25/10	a	PAOK	L	1-3	*Karelis (p)*
01/11	h	AEK	D	0-0	
07/11	a	Atromitos	W	2-1	*Karelis, Berg*
21/11	h	Olympiacos	L	0-3	*(w/o)*
28/11	a	Iraklis	L	0-1	
06/12	a	Veria	W	1-0	*Karelis*
13/12	h	Asteras	W	2-0	*Karelis, Kaltsas*
20/12	a	Panthrakikos	L	0-1	

2016
04/01	h	Panetolikos	W	4-2	*Abeid 2, Petrić 2*
11/01	a	Kalloni	W	2-0	*Kaltsas, Boumale*
17/01	h	Panionios	D	0-0	
24/01	a	Levadiakos	W	2-0	*Berg, Essien*
31/01	a	Platanias	W	3-2	*Kaltsas 2, Klonaridis*
06/02	h	Xanthi	L	0-1	
14/02	a	Giannina	W	3-0	*P Vlahodimos, Berg 2*
21/02	h	PAOK	D	2-2	*Berg, Kaltsas*
28/02	a	AEK	L	0-1	
05/03	h	Atromitos	W	2-0	*Lucas Evangelista, Villáfáñez*
13/03	a	Olympiacos	L	1-3	*Berg*
19/03	h	Iraklis	W	4-0	*Berg 2, Rodrigo Moledo 2*
03/04	h	Veria	W	3-2	*og (Pougouras), Leto 2*
10/04	a	Asteras	D	0-0	
17/04	h	Panthrakikos	W	6-1	*Berg 5, Villáfáñez*

No	Name	Nat	DoB	Pos	Aps	(s)	Gls
6	Mehdi Abeid	ALG	06/08/92	M	18	(5)	3
14	Abdul Ajagun	NGA	10/02/93	M	6	(5)	2
9	Marcus Berg	SWE	17/08/86	A	19	(3)	15
30	Olivier Boumale	CMR	17/09/89	M	4	(4)	1
28	Christos Bourbos		01/06/83	D	1		
3	Diamantis Chouchoumis		17/07/94	D	1		
2	Michael Essien	GHA	03/12/82	M	10	(2)	1
45	Nikolaos Giannakopoulos		19/02/93	G	1		
23	Nikolaos A Kaltsas		03/05/90	M	10	(9)	5
19	Nikolaos Karelis		24/02/92	A	14	(1)	8
7	Viktor Klonaridis	BEL	28/07/92	A	6	(6)	1
4	Georgios Koutroumbis		10/02/91	D	15	(3)	
8	Anastasios Lagos		12/04/92	M	9	(6)	
5	Sebastián Leto	ARG	30/08/86	M	4	(2)	2
17	Robin Lod	FIN	17/04/93	M	4	(4)	
95	Lucas Evangelista	BRA	06/02/95	M	4	(4)	1
12	Nikolaos Marinakis		12/09/93	D	10	(3)	
27	Giandomenico Mesto	ITA	25/05/82	D	12		
21	Nano	ESP	27/10/84	D	15	(3)	1
29	Sotirios Ninis		03/04/90	M	4	(3)	
33	Mladen Petrić	CRO	01/01/81	A	9	(9)	4
32	Danijel Pranjić	CRO	02/12/81	M	21	(2)	
31	Rodrigo Moledo	BRA	27/10/87	D	7		2
24	Sergio Sánchez	ESP	03/04/86	D	8	(2)	
5	Luke Steele	ENG	24/09/84	G	27		
20	Efstathios Tavlaridis		25/01/80	D	14	(2)	1
25	Rasmus Thelander	DEN	09/07/91	D	18		1
5	Konstantinos Triantafyllopoulos		03/04/93	D	2	(1)	
19	Lucas Villáfáñez	ARG	04/10/91	M	6	(1)	2
99	Odysseas Vlahodimos		26/04/94	G	1		
71	Panagiotis Vlahodimos		11/10/91	A	4	(1)	1
11	Jens Wemmer	GER	31/10/85	D	4		
77	Yuri Mamute	BRA	07/05/95	A	1	(5)	
10	Zeca	POR	31/08/88	M	26		

Panetolikos GFS

1926 • Panetolikou (6,000) • panetolikos.gr

Coach: Leonel Pontes (POR); (30/09/15) Ioannis Dalakouras); (07/10/15) Ioannis Matzourakis

2015
24/08	h	Panathinaikos	L	1-2	*Kappel*
30/08	a	Asteras	W	2-0	*Warda, Villáfáñez*
13/09	h	Panthrakikos	W	1-0	*Markovski*
22/09	h	Veria	D	1-1	*Romero*
26/09	a	Kalloni	L	1-5	*Marcos Paulo*
03/10	h	Panionios	L	1-5	*Villáfáñez (p)*
18/10	a	Levadiakos	D	2-2	*Markovski 2*
24/10	h	Platanias	L	1-2	*Kappel*
01/11	a	Xanthi	L	1-3	*Markovski*
09/11	h	Giannina	W	2-1	*og (Tsoukalas), Markovski*
22/11	a	PAOK	D	0-0	
29/11	a	AEK	L	0-1	
07/12	h	Atromitos	D	1-1	*Villáfáñez*
13/12	a	Olympiacos	L	0-1	
20/12	h	Iraklis	W	2-0	*Warda (p), Markovski*

2016
04/01	a	Panathinaikos	L	2-4	*Villáfáñez, Markovski*
10/01	h	Asteras	W	2-1	*Rusculleda, Papazoglou*
16/01	a	Panthrakikos	D	0-0	
24/01	a	Veria	W	1-0	*Villáfáñez*
30/01	h	Kalloni	W	1-0	*Kappel*
08/02	a	Panionios	L	0-2	
14/02	h	Levadiakos	W	2-0	*Muñoz 2*
21/02	a	Platanias	D	1-1	*Markovski*
27/02	h	Xanthi	D	2-2	*Warda 2 (1p)*
05/03	a	Giannina	L	0-2	
12/03	h	PAOK	L	0-3	
20/03	h	AEK	W	1-0	*Marcos Paulo*
03/04	a	Atromitos	L	0-1	
10/04	h	Olympiacos	L	2-5	*Warda, Kappel*
17/04	a	Iraklis	D	0-0	

No	Name	Nat	DoB	Pos	Aps	(s)	Gls
8	Ilya Aleksiyevich	BLR	10/02/91	M	1	(2)	
16	Danny Bejarano	BOL	03/01/94	M	8	(1)	
8	Diego Bejarano	BOL	24/08/91	D	3		
1	Henri Camara	SEN	10/05/77	A		(5)	
10	Clésio	MOZ	11/10/94	A	2	(5)	
99	Cristiano	POR	29/11/90	G	1		
18	Osmar Ferreyra	ARG	09/01/83	M	5	(4)	
44	Dimitrios Hantakias		04/01/95	M	5	(5)	
11	Leandro Kappel	NED	14/11/89	A	21	(4)	4
3	Kevin	ESP	08/09/89	D	23	(1)	
27	Panagiotis Konstantinopoulos		05/09/95	M		(2)	
5	Georgios Kousas		12/08/82	D	28		
2	Dimitrios Koutromanos		25/02/87	D	12	(8)	
82	Dimitrios Kyriakidis		24/06/86	G	24		
14	Grigorios Makos		25/01/85	D	28		
17	Marcos Paulo	BRA	13/07/88	M	26	(2)	2
15	Marko Markovski	SRB	26/05/86	A	28		8
22	Georgios Migas		07/04/94	M	19		
9	Fabián Muñoz	ARG	03/11/91	A	7	(2)	2
12	Anastasios Papazoglou		24/09/88	D	22		1
28	Stefanos Papoutsogiannopoulos		10/08/94	M	3	(3)	
18	Emiliano Romero	ARG	11/09/85	M		(3)	1
20	Simos Rouboulakou		30/12/91	D	5	(2)	
7	Sebastián Rusculleda	ARG	28/04/85	M	13	(8)	1
21	Emmanouil Stefanakos		17/08/89	G	5	(1)	
29	Stilianos Vasiliou		29/04/91	A	1	(11)	
96	Efstathios Vasiloudis		23/02/96	A	2	(7)	
10	Lucas Villáfáñez	ARG	04/10/91	M	16	(3)	5
74	Amr Warda	EGY	17/09/93	M	22	(5)	5
30	Anastasios Zarkadas		04/11/94	M		(1)	

Panionios GSS

1890 • Panionios GSS (16,800) • panionios.gr

Major honours
Greek Cup (2) 1979, 1998

Coach: Marinos Ouzounidis

2015
23/08	a	Olympiacos	L	0-3	
30/08	a	Iraklis	W	1-0	*Bakasetas*
13/09	h	Panathinaikos	W	1-0	*Bakasetas*
23/09	a	Asteras	L	1-2	*og (Goian)*
27/09	h	Panthrakikos	D	1-1	*Karamanos*
03/10	a	Panetolikos	W	5-1	*Villalba, Boumale 2 (1p), Bakasetas, Ansarifard*
17/10	a	Kalloni	W	2-0	*Bakasetas 2*
25/10	h	Veria	L	0-1	
31/10	a	Levadiakos	W	2-0	*Karamanos, Boumale*
07/11	h	Platanias	W	2-1	*Karamanos, Ansarifard*
22/11	a	Xanthi	L	0-2	
28/11	h	Giannina	W	2-0	*Ansarifard 2*
06/12	a	PAOK	L	1-2	*Ikonomou*
12/12	h	AEK	D	1-1	*Boumale*
19/12	a	Atromitos	L	0-1	

2016
03/01	h	Olympiacos	L	1-3	*Risvanis*
10/01	h	Iraklis	W	1-0	*Ansarifard*
17/01	h	Panathinaikos	D	0-0	
23/01	a	Asteras	D	0-0	
30/01	a	Panthrakikos	W	1-0	*Ikonomou (p)*
08/02	h	Panetolikos	W	2-0	*Ansarifard, Karamanos*
14/02	a	Kalloni	D	1-1	*Ansarifard*
22/02	a	Veria	D	1-1	*Bakasetas*
28/02	h	Levadiakos	L	0-2	
05/03	a	Platanias	D	0-0	
12/03	h	Xanthi	W	3-0	*Bakasetas 3*
21/03	a	Giannina	D	1-1	*Karamanos*
03/04	h	PAOK	W	3-1	*Bakasetas 2, Ansarifard*
10/04	a	AEK	L	0-2	
17/04	h	Atromitos	L	0-1	

No	Name	Nat	DoB	Pos	Aps	(s)	Gls
11	Karim Ansarifard	IRN	03/04/90	A	16	11	8
20	Leonidas Argiropoulos		29/05/90	D	9	(2)	
14	Anastasios Bakasetas		28/06/93	A	27	(1)	11
10	Kenan Bargan		25/10/88	A	3	(5)	
10	Olivier Boumale	CMR	17/09/89	M	15		4
13	Sokratis Dioudis		03/02/93	G	18		
17	Fiorin Durmishaj	ALB	14/11/96	A	1	(1)	
22	Andreas Gianniotis		18/12/92	G	1		
21	Bruno Halkiadakis		07/04/93	M	2	(18)	
4	Dimitrios Hatziisaias		21/09/92	D	19		
6	Evangelos Ikonomou		18/07/87	D	27		2
9	Anastasios Karamanos		21/09/90	A	21	(6)	5
64	Nikolaos Katharios		07/10/94	M	8	(8)	
30	Panagiotis Korbos		11/09/86	M	27		
19	Georgios Masouras		01/01/94	M	19	(7)	
82	Pavlos Mitropoulos		04/09/90	M	2	(8)	
1	Nikolaos G Papadopoulos		11/04/90	G	11		
5	Vasileios Patsatzoglou		14/04/94	D	3	(3)	
25	Angelos Piniotis		22/04/96	M		(1)	
44	Spiridon Risvanis		03/01/94	D	25		1
11	Emmanouil Siopis		14/05/94	M	28	(1)	
3	Christos Tasoulis		03/05/91	D	14	(2)	
33	Theofanis Tzandaris		13/06/93	M	4	(5)	
26	Leonardo Villalba	ARG	29/11/94	A	9	(8)	1
37	Valentinos Vlahos		14/01/92	D	21	(1)	

Panthrakikos FC

1963 • Dimotiko Komotinis (3,000) •
panthrakikos.com
Coach: José Manuel Roca Cases (ESP);
(19/09/15) Dimitrios Eleftheropoulos;
(26/01/16) Ioannis Hatzinikolaou;
(17/03/16) Zoran Stojnović (SRB)

2015

22/08	h	Asteras	L	0-2	
29/08	h	Veria	L	0-2	
13/09	a	Panetolikos	L	0-1	
23/09	h	Kalloni	D	0-0	
27/09	a	Panionios	D	1-1	Diguiny
03/10	a	Levadiakos	L	1-3	Rogério Martins (p)
17/10	a	Platanias	L	0-4	
25/10	h	Xanthi	D	0-0	
01/11	a	Giannina	L	0-2	
08/11	a	PAOK	D	3-3	Papageorgiou, Deniz 2
22/11	h	AEK	L	1-2	Rogério Martins
28/11	a	Atromitos	W	2-1	Melissis, Iliadis
05/12	h	Olympiacos	L	3-4	Diguiny 2, Iliadis
12/12	a	Iraklis	L	0-2	
20/12	h	Panathinaikos	W	1-0	Rogério Martins

2016

02/01	a	Asteras	L	0-4	
09/01	a	Veria	D	0-0	
16/01	h	Panetolikos	D	0-0	
23/01	h	Kalloni	L	0-2	
30/01	h	Panionios	L	0-1	
06/02	a	Levadiakos	D	1-1	Iliadis
13/02	h	Platanias	L	0-2	
21/02	h	Xanthi	L	0-1	
28/02	h	Giannina	L	2-4	Igor, Diguiny (p)
06/03	a	PAOK	W	2-1	Igor, Papageorgiou
14/03	a	AEK	L	0-3	
20/03	h	Atromitos	L	0-1	
03/04	a	Olympiacos	L	0-3	
10/04	h	Iraklis	L	0-3	
17/04	a	Panathinaikos	L	1-6	Moudouroglou

No	Name	Nat	DoB	Pos	Aps	(s)	Gls
30	Georgios Athanasiadis		07/04/93	G	24		
24	Mavroudis Bougaidis		01/06/93	D	13	(1)	
13	Sofyane Cherfa	ALG	13/08/84	D	15		
21	Ioannis Christou		05/03/81	D	8	(3)	
34	Deniz Baykara	TUR	13/03/84	M	21	(2)	2
9	Nicolas Diguiny	FRA	31/05/88	M	25		4
32	Georgios Fotakis		29/10/81	M		(1)	
14	Vasileios Gavriilidis		20/10/92	D	2	(3)	
18	Trifon Gioudas		18/02/93	G	1		
11	Dimitrios Hasomeris		23/06/89	A	22	(4)	
99	Igor	BRA	19/02/80	A	12	(7)	2
22	Stilianos Iliadis		03/06/86	M	13	(5)	3
20	Javito	ESP	04/11/83	A	17	(4)	
84	Antonios Ladakis		25/01/82	M	13	(4)	
79	Konstantinos Markopoulos		08/02/92	A	1	(3)	
6	Alfredo Mejía	HON	03/04/90	M	18	(2)	
4	Christos Melissis		01/12/82	D	27		1
89	Savvas Moudouroglou		15/12/91	A	3	(6)	1
39	Georgios Nikoltsis		06/04/92	A	2	(11)	
3	Anastasios Papachristos		05/03/93	D	2	(1)	
2	Athanasios Papageorgiou		09/05/87	A	24	(1)	2
1	Alexandros Pashalakis		28/07/89	G	4		
3	Stavros Petavrakis		09/11/92	D	1	(3)	
92	Ioannis Potouridis		27/02/92	D	27		
25	Theoharis Psaltis		27/04/96	M	1	(2)	
8	Rogério Martins	BRA	19/11/84	M	14	(5)	3
22	Albert Roussos		22/02/96	M	2	(1)	
15	Sebastián Setti	ARG	09/02/84	D	3	(4)	
88	Antonios Tsiaras		07/09/93	M	8	(1)	
7	Christos Tzanis		22/04/85	A	2		
77	Georgios Tzelepis		12/11/99	G	1	(1)	
20	Walter Fernández	ESP	14/08/89	M	4	(8)	
19	Konstantinos Zdravos-Rizos		16/08/93	M		(2)	

PAOK FC

Major honours
Greek League (2) 1976, 1985; Greek Cup (4) 1972,
1974, 2001, 2003
Coach: Igor Tudor (CRO);
(09/03/16) Vladimir Ivić (SRB)

1926 • Toumbas (31,060) • paokfc.gr

2015

23/08	h	Xanthi	D	0-0	
30/08	a	Giannina	L	1-3	Miguel Vítor
12/09	a	Veria	W	3-0	Athanasiadis, Mak, Tziolis
23/09	h	AEK	W	2-1	Mendes Rodrigues, Athanasiadis (p)
27/09	a	Atromitos	W	2-1	Berbatov, Mak
04/10	h	Olympiacos	L	0-2	
18/10	a	Iraklis	D	3-3	Pelkas, Berbatov, Tzavellas
25/10	h	Panathinaikos	W	3-1	Berbatov (p), Mendes Rodrigues, Miguel Vítor
01/11	a	Asteras	L	1-2	Pelkas
08/11	h	Panthrakikos	D	3-3	Mendes Rodrigues 2, Athanasiadis
22/11	h	Panetolikos	D	0-0	
30/11	a	Kalloni	W	3-1	Athanasiadis 2, Mystakidis
06/12	h	Panionios	W	2-1	Mak, Tzavellas
14/12	a	Levadiakos	D	0-0	
20/12	h	Platanias	W	1-0	Athanasiadis (p)

2016

10/01	h	Giannina	W	3-1	Athanasiadis, Charisis, Jairo
17/01	h	Veria	W	2-1	Berbatov (p), Athanasiadis
20/01	a	Xanthi	D	1-1	Mystakidis
24/01	a	AEK	L	0-1	
30/01	h	Atromitos	D	1-1	Mak
07/02	a	Olympiacos	L	0-1	
14/02	h	Iraklis	L	0-1	
21/02	a	Panathinaikos	D	2-2	Cimirot, Pelkas
27/02	a	Asteras	W	2-0	Pelkas, Mak
06/03	h	Panthrakikos	L	1-2	Hatziisaias
12/03	a	Panetolikos	W	3-0	Athanasiadis 2, Korovesis
20/03	h	Kalloni	W	3-0	Mystakidis, Athanasiadis, Korovesis
03/04	a	Panionios	L	1-3	Tziolis
10/04	h	Levadiakos	W	2-0	Leovac, Mak
17/04	a	Platanias	D	0-0	

No	Name	Nat	DoB	Pos	Aps	(s)	Gls
93	Terry Antonis	AUS	15/11/92	M	2	(2)	
33	Stefanos Athanasiadis		24/12/88	A	17	(5)	11
10	Dimitar Berbatov	BUL	30/01/81	A	6	(8)	4
21	Charilaos Charisis		12/01/95	M	10	(4)	1
16	Gojko Cimirot	BIH	19/12/92	M	12	(1)	1
80	Anastasios Dimitriadis		27/02/97	M		(1)	
71	Panagiotis Glykos		10/10/86	G	7		
7	Eyal Golasa	ISR	07/10/91	M	4	(7)	
5	Dimitrios Hatziisaias		21/09/92	D	6		1
3	Jairo	BRA	06/05/92	A	8	(5)	1
26	Ergys Kaçe	ALB	08/07/93	M	14	(5)	
60	Georgios Kakko		18/05/97	M		(1)	
70	Stilianos Kitsiou		28/09/93	D	16	(1)	
22	Dimitrios Konstantinidis		02/06/94	D	5	(4)	
33	Nikolaos Korovesis		10/08/91	M	6	(6)	2
66	Kristjan Kushta	ALB	16/12/97	A		(1)	
4	Marin Leovac	CRO	07/08/88	D	19		1
13	Róbert Mak	SVK	08/03/91	A	24		6
30	Nikolaos Melissas		24/02/93	G	1	(1)	
24	Garry Mendes Rodrigues	CPV	27/11/90	M	16	(4)	4
15	Miguel Vítor	POR	30/06/89	D	22	(1)	2
27	Ioannis Mystakidis		07/12/94	M	7	(9)	3
25	Robin Olsen	SWE	08/01/90	G	11		
77	Dimitrios Pelkas		26/10/93	M	23	(5)	4
20	Ricardo Costa	POR	16/05/81	D	10	(1)	
52	Erik Sabo	SVK	22/11/91	M	8	(6)	
88	Kyriakos Savvidis		20/06/95	M		(1)	
2	Ioannis Skondras		21/02/90	D	5	(2)	
31	Georgios Tzavellas		26/11/87	D	25	(1)	2
8	Alexandros Tziolis		13/02/85	M	26	(1)	2
1	Markos Vellidis		04/04/87	G	11		

PAS Giannina FC

1966 • Oi Zosimades (7,652) • pasgiannina.gr
Coach: Ioannis Petrakis

2015

23/08	a	Veria	D	1-1	Noé Acosta
30/08	h	PAOK	W	3-1	Manias, og (Sabo), Chávez
13/09	a	AEK	L	1-3	Noé Acosta
23/09	h	Atromitos	W	1-0	Tsoukalas
26/09	a	Olympiacos	L	1-5	Lila
04/10	h	Iraklis	D	2-2	Ilić, Kozoronis
19/10	a	Panathinaikos	L	1-3	Chávez (p)
25/10	h	Asteras	L	1-2	Manias
01/11	h	Panthrakikos	W	2-0	Mihail, Ilić
09/11	a	Panetolikos	L	1-2	Iliadis
21/11	h	Kalloni	W	2-1	Manias 2
28/11	a	Panionios	L	0-2	
06/12	h	Levadiakos	L	0-1	
12/12	a	Platanias	W	1-0	Giakos
20/12	h	Xanthi	D	1-1	Tsoukalas (p)

2016

02/01	h	Veria	W	2-0	Manias, Tzimopoulos
10/01	a	PAOK	L	1-3	Kozoronis
17/01	h	AEK	L	0-2	
24/01	a	Atromitos	W	2-0	Manias, Tsoukalas
31/01	h	Olympiacos	L	0-3	
07/02	a	Iraklis	L	0-1	
14/02	h	Panathinaikos	L	0-3	
20/02	a	Asteras	D	0-0	
28/02	a	Panthrakikos	W	4-2	og (Christou), Skondras, Manias, Ilić
05/03	h	Panetolikos	W	2-0	Lila, Noé Acosta
12/03	a	Kalloni	W	2-0	Tzimopoulos, Manias
21/03	h	Panionios	D	1-1	Ilić
03/04	a	Levadiakos	D	1-1	Giakos
10/04	h	Platanias	W	2-0	Manias 2
17/04	a	Xanthi	W	1-0	Tsoukalas

No	Name	Nat	DoB	Pos	Aps	(s)	Gls
4	Theodoros Berios		21/03/89	D	15	(2)	
10	Cristian Chávez	ARG	04/06/87	M	12		2
77	Dimitrios Ferfelis		05/04/93	A	1	(11)	
17	Fonsi	ESP	22/01/86	D	24	(2)	
5	Iraklis Garoufalias		01/05/93	D	11	(1)	
19	Evripidis Giakos		09/04/91	A	12	(13)	2
19	Antonios Iliadis		27/07/93	A	4	(12)	1
9	Brana Ilić	SRB	16/02/85	A	27		4
20	Nikolaos Karanikas		04/03/92	D	11	(8)	
27	Leonardo Koutris		23/07/95	M	1		
22	Chrisovalantis Kozoronis		03/08/92	M	10	(13)	2
3	Andi Lila	ALB	12/02/86	D	12	(7)	2
33	Mihail Manias		20/02/90	A	24	(4)	10
6	Alexios Mihail		18/08/86	D	25		1
66	Alexandros Nikolias		23/07/94	M		(2)	
11	Noé Acosta	ESP	10/12/83	M	27	(2)	3
12	Konstantinos Peristeridis		24/01/91	G	12		
14	Stamatis Sapalidis		05/07/90	A		(1)	
44	Apostolos Skondras		29/12/88	D	10	(4)	1
23	Andraž Struna	SVN	23/04/89	D	22		
21	Stavros Tsoukalas		23/05/88	M	27	(1)	4
8	Themistoklis Tzimopoulos		20/11/85	M	25		2
1	Markos Vellidis		04/04/87	G	18		

 # GREECE

Platanias FC

1931 • Dimotiko Perivolion (3,700) • fcplatanias.gr
Coach: Georgios Parashos

2015
22/08	a	AEK	L	0-3	
31/08	h	Atromitos	L	1-2	og (Kyvrakidis)
12/09	a	Olympiacos	L	1-3	Banana
22/09	h	Iraklis	D	0-0	
27/09	a	Panathinaikos	L	0-1	
05/10	a	Asteras	D	1-1	Milunović
17/10	h	Panthrakikos	W	4-0	Tsourakis, Milunović 2, Ramos
24/10	a	Panetolikos	W	2-1	Milunović, Coulibaly
31/10	h	Kalloni	W	2-1	Angulo, Giakoumakis
07/11	a	Panionios	L	1-2	Onanga Itoua
22/11	h	Levadiakos	W	2-1	Ramos, Giakoumakis
29/11	h	Veria	D	0-0	
05/12	a	Xanthi	W	2-0	Milunović, Angulo
12/12	h	Giannina	L	0-1	
20/12	h	PAOK	L	0-1	

2016
03/01	h	AEK	L	0-3	
09/01	a	Atromitos	D	0-0	
18/01	h	Olympiacos	D	1-1	Ramos
25/01	a	Iraklis	D	0-0	
31/01	h	Panathinaikos	L	2-3	Goundoulakis, Ramos
06/02	h	Asteras	W	2-0	Goundoulakis, Angulo
13/02	a	Panthrakikos	W	2-0	Selin, Angulo
21/02	h	Panetolikos	D	1-1	Goundoulakis
27/02	a	Kalloni	L	1-2	Angulo
05/03	h	Panionios	D	0-0	
13/03	a	Levadiakos	W	3-0	Coulibaly, Apostolopoulos, Angulo
19/03	a	Veria	W	1-0	Mendrinos
03/04	h	Xanthi	W	3-1	Angulo 2, Milunović
10/04	a	Giannina	L	0-2	
17/04	h	PAOK	D	0-0	

No	Name	Nat	DoB	Pos	Aps	(s)	Gls
19	Igor Angulo	ESP	26/01/84	A	19	(6)	8
77	Alexandros Apostolopoulos		07/11/91	D	14	(4)	1
3	Yaya Banana	CMR	29/07/91	D	28		1
18	Tawonga Chimodzi	MWI	26/06/88	M		(1)	
23	Ousmane Coulibaly	MLI	09/07/89	D	26		2
5	Alkiviadis Dimitris		23/07/80	D	2	(4)	
26	Athanasios Dinas		12/11/89	M	12	(11)	
99	Georgios Giakoumakis		09/12/94	A	9	(1)	2
14	Gilvan Gomes	BRA	09/04/84	A	1	(5)	
6	Ognjen Gnjatić	BIH	16/10/91	M	25	(1)	
20	Fanourios Goundoulakis		13/07/83	M	13	(5)	3
92	Antonios Kokkalas		16/02/92	G	1	(1)	
8	Azrack-Yassine Mahamat	CHA	24/03/88	M	2	(2)	
7	Konstantinos Mendrinos		28/05/85	M	21	(4)	1
10	Luka Milunović	SRB	21/12/92	A	18	(6)	6
24	Juan Munafo	ARG	20/03/83	M	20	(3)	
1	Kévin Olimpa	FRA	10/03/88	G	6		
22	Bernard Onanga Itoua	FRA	07/09/88	D	5	(4)	1
28	Konstantinos Pangalos		03/07/87	A	2	(4)	
9	Leonardo Ramos	ARG	21/08/89	A	12	(9)	4
33	Yevhen Selin	UKR	09/05/88	D	27		1
32	Dimitrios Sotiriou		13/09/87	G	23		
4	Filip Stanisavljević	SRB	20/05/87	M	14	(7)	
11	Athanasios Tsourakis		12/05/90	A	1	(9)	1
25	Georgios Valerianos		13/02/92	D		(2)	
27	Vanderson	BRA	27/09/84	D	29		

Veria FC

1960 • Dimotikon Verias (7,000) • veriafc.gr
**Coach: Georgios H Georgiadis;
(19/01/16) (Nikolaos Karabiberis);
(26/01/16) Dimitrios Eleftheropoulos**

2015
23/08	h	Giannina	D	1-1	Nazlidis
29/08	a	Panthrakikos	W	2-0	Abdoun 2 (1p)
12/09	h	PAOK	L	0-3	
22/09	a	Panetolikos	D	1-1	Nazlidis
28/09	h	AEK	L	1-2	Neto
04/10	a	Kalloni	W	1-0	Abdoun (p)
18/10	h	Atromitos	L	0-1	
25/10	a	Panionios	W	1-0	Nazlidis
31/10	h	Olympiacos	L	0-2	
08/11	a	Levadiakos	D	1-1	Merebashvili
23/11	h	Iraklis	D	0-0	
29/11	a	Platanias	D	0-0	
06/12	h	Panathinaikos	L	0-1	
13/12	a	Xanthi	D	1-1	Nazlidis (p)
19/12	h	Asteras	W	1-0	Kola

2016
02/01	a	Giannina	L	0-2	
09/01	h	Panthrakikos	D	0-0	
17/01	a	PAOK	L	1-2	Majewski
24/01	h	Panetolikos	D	1-1	
31/01	a	AEK	L	0-3	
07/02	h	Kalloni	W	2-0	Majewski, Anakoglou
13/02	a	Atromitos	D	0-0	
22/02	h	Panionios	D	1-1	Iván Malón
28/02	a	Olympiacos	L	0-3	
06/03	h	Levadiakos	D	0-0	
13/03	a	Iraklis	D	1-1	Anakoglou
19/03	h	Platanias	L	0-1	
03/04	a	Panathinaikos	L	2-3	Nazlidis, Melikiotis
10/04	h	Xanthi	D	1-1	Youssouf
17/04	a	Asteras	L	1-2	Balafas

No	Name	Nat	DoB	Pos	Aps	(s)	Gls
93	Djamel Abdoun	ALG	14/02/86	M	10	(5)	3
10	Dimitrios Anakoglou		06/09/91	M	8	(2)	2
15	Pedro Arce	MEX	25/11/91	M	22		
25	Sotirios Balafas		19/08/86	M	3		1
6	Roberto Battión	ARG	02/03/82	M	6	(1)	
23	William Edjenguélé	FRA	07/05/87	D	10	(2)	
77	Georgios K Georgiadis		14/11/87	A	10	(4)	
31	Dimitrios Giannoulis		17/10/95	D	24		
25	Abdisalam Ibrahim	NOR	01/05/91	M	5	(2)	
18	Iván Malón	ESP	26/08/86	D	24		1
55	Jonathan López	ESP	16/04/81	G	15		
77	Saša Kajkut	BIH	07/07/84	A	8	(12)	
1	Georgios Kantimiris		19/09/82	G	15	(1)	
9	Anestis Karakostas		15/06/91	D		(1)	
14	Rodgers Kola	ZAM	04/07/89	A	9	(9)	1
86	Radosław Majewski	POL	15/12/86	M	26	(3)	2
33	Dimitrios Manos		16/09/94	A		(4)	
5	Stilianos Marangos		04/05/89	D	17	(3)	
20	Dimitrios Melikiotis		10/07/96	A	3	(2)	1
11	Giorgi Merebashvili	GEO	15/08/86	M	4	(5)	1
28	Evangelos Nastos		13/09/80	D	4	(3)	
9	Thomas Nazlidis		23/10/87	A	26	(3)	5
16	Neto	BRA	07/02/81	D	11	(8)	1
8	Branko Ostojić	SRB	03/01/84	M	11	(1)	
44	Achilleas Pougouras		13/12/95	D	17	(2)	
2	Raúl Bravo	ESP	14/04/81	D	6		
22	Stefanos Siondis		04/09/87	M	17	(4)	
10	Andreas Tatos		11/05/89	M		(2)	
21	Nicolaos Tsoumanis		08/06/90	M	1		
21	Alexandros Vergonis		01/12/85	M	8		
80	Panagiotis Xoblios		27/02/96	A		(2)	
13	Mohamed Youssouf	COM	26/03/88	M	10	(7)	1

Xanthi FC

1967 • Škoda Xanthi Arena (7,500) • skodaxanthifc.gr
Coach: Răzvan Lucescu (ROU)

2014
23/08	a	PAOK	D	0-0	
29/08	h	AEK	D	0-0	
13/09	a	Atromitos	W	1-0	Soltani
22/09	h	Olympiacos	L	1-3	Dimitrov
26/09	a	Iraklis	D	1-1	Lucero
03/10	a	Panathinaikos	L	0-1	
18/10	a	Asteras	D	1-1	Nieto
25/10	a	Panthrakikos	D	0-0	
01/11	h	Panetolikos	W	3-1	Dimitrov, Papasterianos, Herea (p)
07/11	a	Kalloni	D	2-2	Soltani, Herea
22/11	h	Panionios	W	2-0	Nieto, Ranos
29/11	a	Levadiakos	L	0-1	
05/12	h	Platanias	L	0-2	
13/12	a	Veria	D	1-1	Nieto (p)
20/12	a	Giannina	D	1-1	Herea

2015
09/01	a	AEK	L	1-2	Soltani
16/01	h	Atromitos	D	2-2	Kapetanos, Nieto
20/01	h	PAOK	D	1-1	Soltani
23/01	a	Olympiacos	L	0-1	
31/01	h	Iraklis	W	2-0	Nieto 2
06/02	a	Panathinaikos	W	1-0	Soltani
15/02	h	Asteras	D	0-0	
21/02	h	Panthrakikos	W	1-0	Papasterianos
27/02	a	Panetolikos	D	2-2	Kapetanos, Papasterianos
06/03	h	Kalloni	D	0-0	
12/03	a	Panionios	L	0-3	
19/03	h	Levadiakos	D	2-2	Karipidis, Lucero (p)
03/04	a	Platanias	L	1-3	Lisgaras
10/04	a	Veria	D	1-1	og (Nazlidis)
17/04	h	Giannina	L	0-1	

No	Name	Nat	DoB	Pos	Aps	(s)	Gls
5	Dimosthenis Baxevanidis		14/04/88	D	15	(6)	
4	Emmanouil Bertos		13/05/89	D	23		
66	Khassa Camara	MTN	22/10/92	D	2	(1)	
1	Luigi Cennamo	ITA	07/02/80	G	22		
37	Christopher	BRA	22/01/95	A		(2)	
87	Nikolay Dimitrov	BUL	15/10/87	A	17	(6)	2
10	Elton	BRA	12/02/86	D	3		
26	Pavol Farkaš	SVK	27/03/85	D	5	(1)	
77	Vasilios Fasidis		22/06/96	A		(1)	
21	Konstantinos Fliskas		22/12/80	M	22		
28	Dimitrios Goutas		04/04/94	D	7		
2	Ovidiu Herea	ROU	26/03/85	M	11	(8)	3
30	Pantelis Kapetanos		08/06/83	A	16	(11)	2
55	Christos Karipidis		02/12/82	D	18	(1)	1
3	Christos Lisgaras		12/02/86	D	18	(1)	1
11	Adrián Lucero	ARG	16/08/84	M	28		2
23	Daniel Nieto	ESP	04/05/91	M	17	(8)	6
24	Petros Orfanidis		23/03/96	M	11	(4)	
17	Emmanouil Papasterianos		15/08/87	M	10	(9)	3
99	Antonios Ranos		15/06/93	A	6	(4)	1
19	Vasil Shkurtaj	ALB	27/02/92	A	4	(8)	
9	Karim Soltani	ALG	29/08/84	A	23	(1)	5
7	Panagiotis Triadis		09/09/92	A	1	(9)	
16	Theodoros Vasilakakis		20/07/88	M	19	(3)	
8	Wallace	BRA	29/10/86	D	20	(1)	
33	Ioannis Zaradoukas		12/12/85	D	4		
91	Mihail Zaropoulos		12/07/91	G	8		

Top goalscorers

18	Kostas Fortounis (Olympiacos)
15	Marcus Berg (Panathinaikos)
13	Apostolos Giannou (Asteras)
11	Apostolos Vellios (Iraklis)
	Evangelos Mantzios (Levadiakos)
	Anastasios Bakasetas (Panionios)
	Stefanos Athanasiadis (PAOK)
10	Brown Ideye (Olympiacos)
	Mihail Manias (Giannina)
9	Christos Aravidis (AEK)
	Ronald Vargas (AEK)

Promoted clubs

AE Larissa FC

1964 • AEL FC Arena (16,118) • aelfc.gr
Major honours
Greek League (1) 1988; Greek Cup (2) 1985, 2007
Coach: Ratko Dostanić (SRB);
(23/02/16) Sakis Tsiolis

Kerkyra FC

1968 • Ethniko Athlitiko Kentro (EAK)
Kerkyras (2,685) • kerkyrafc.gr
Coach: Angelos Digozis;
(24/11/15) Alekos Vosniadis

Second level final table 2015/16

		Pld	W	D	L	F	A	Pts
1	AE Larissa FC	34	24	6	4	49	15	78
2	Kerkyra FC	34	23	6	5	57	24	75
3	AO Trikala FC	34	19	10	5	53	22	67
4	Apollon Smyrnis FC	34	18	10	6	46	19	61
5	PAS Lamia FC	34	16	11	7	41	24	59
6	PGS Kissamikos FC	34	13	12	9	29	19	51
7	Kallithea FC	34	15	7	12	41	31	46
8	Anagennisis Karditsas FC	34	13	6	15	30	34	45
9	Agrotikos Asteras FC	34	11	10	13	27	24	43
10	Panserraikos FC	34	12	7	15	39	43	43
11	Acharnaikos FC	34	12	9	13	30	29	42
12	AO Chania FC	34	10	11	13	34	37	41
13	Panegialios FC	34	11	8	15	34	40	41
14	Panelefsiniakos FC	34	10	5	19	34	53	35
15	Zakynthos FC	34	10	7	17	31	32	31
16	Panachaiki FC	34	8	7	19	26	47	25
17	Olympiacos Volou FC	34	5	4	25	16	72	-6
18	Ergotelis FC	34	5	4	25	18	76	-6

NB Ergotelis FC withdrew after round 15; Olympiacos Volou FC withdrew after round 16 – both clubs' remaining matches were awarded as 0-3 defeats; Ergotelis FC & Olympiacos Volou FC – 25 pts deducted; Kallithea FC, Panachaiki FC & Zakynthos FC – 6 pts deducted; Acharnaikos FC & Apollon Smyrnis FC – 3 pts deducted.

UEFA Champions League qualification play-offs 2015/16

(11/05/16)
Panionios 1-1 Panathinaikos *(Ansarifard 52; Leto 23)*

PAOK 2-1 AEK *(Mendes Rodrigues 7, Mystakidis; Johansson 44)*

(15/05/16)
Panathinaikos 1-1 PAOK *(Berg 46; Charisis 49)*

(20/05/16)
AEK 1-0 Panionios *(Mantalos 57)*

(23/05/16)
Panathinaikos 3-0 AEK *(Lod 11, Berg 30, Klonaridis 90)*

Panionios 0-2 PAOK *(Athanasiadis 23, Mak 77)*

(26/05/16)
AEK 3-1 Panathinaikos *(Johansson 5, Hélder Barbosa 40, 69; Leto 54)*

PAOK 2-0 Panionios *(Athanasiadis 14, 25)*

(29/05/16)
AEK 0-0 PAOK

Panathinaikos 1-0 Panionios *(Leto 78)*

(31/05/16)
Panionios 1-0 AEK *(Masouras 41)*

PAOK 1-1 Panathinaikos *(Mendes Rodrigues 17; Lod 26)*

			Home					Away					Total					
		Pld	W	D	L	F	A	W	D	L	F	A	W	D	L	F	A	Pts
2	PAOK FC	6	2	1	0	5	2	1	2	0	3	1	3	3	0	8	3	12
3	Panathinaikos FC	6	2	1	0	5	1	0	2	1	3	5	2	3	1	8	6	11
4	AEK Athens FC	6	2	1	0	4	1	0	0	3	1	6	2	1	3	5	7	9
5	Panionios GSS	6	1	1	1	2	3	0	0	3	0	4	1	1	4	2	7	4

NB Points carried forward from Superleague – AEK & Panathinaikos 2 pts, Panionios & PAOK 0 pts.

DOMESTIC CUP

Kypello Ellados 2015/16

SECOND ROUND

Group 1

(27/10/15)
Anagennisis Karditsas 0-1 Acharnaikos

(29/10/15)
Giannina 1-1 Iraklis

(01/12/15)
Acharnaikos 1-2 Giannina
Iraklis 4-0 Anagennisis Karditsas

(15/12/15)
Acharnaikos 0-2 Iraklis
Anagennisis Karditsas 0-0 Giannina

Final standings
1 Iraklis 7 pts; 2 Giannina 5 pts *(qualified);*
3 Acharnaikos 3 pts; 4 Anagennisis Karditsas 1 pt
(eliminated)

Group 2

(27/10/15)
Zakynthos 2-2 Ergotelis

(28/10/15)
Panetolikos 1-2 Panionios

(01/12/15)
Panionios 1-0 Zakynthos

(03/12/15)
Ergotelis 3-2 Panetolikos

(16/12/15)
Ergotelis 1-2 Panionios
Zakynthos 1-0 Panetolikos

Final standings
1 Panionios 9 pts; 2 Ergotelis 4 pts *(qualified);*
3 Zakynthos 4 pts; 4 Panetolikos 0 pts *(eliminated)*

Group 3

(28/10/15)
PAOK 2-0 Panthrakikos

(29/10/15)
Olympiacos Volou 1-2 AO Chania

(01/12/15)
Panthrakikos 1-0 Olympiacos Volou

(03/12/15)
AO Chania 2-6 PAOK Xanthi

(17/12/15)
AO Chania 2-2 Panthrakikos
Olympiacos Volou 1-1 PAOK

Final standings
1 PAOK 7 pts; 2 AO Chania 4 pts *(qualified);*
3 Panthrakikos 4 pts; 4 Olympiacos Volou 1 pt
(eliminated)

Group 4

(27/10/15)
Kerkyra 1-1 Panachaiki

(28/10/15)
Panathinaikos 3-0 Levadiakos

(02/12/15)
Levadiakos 2-0 Kerkyra

(03/12/15)
Panachaiki 1-2 Panathinaikos

(17/12/15)
Kerkyra 1-1 Panathinaikos
Panachaiki 1-4 Levadiakos

Final standings
1 Panathinaikos 7 pts; 2 Levadiakos 6 pts *(qualified);*
3 Kerkyra 2 pts; 4 Panachaiki 1 pt *(eliminated)*

Group 5

(27/10/15)
Apollon Smyrnis 0-1 Panegialios

(28/10/15)
Olympiacos 2-2 Platanias

(02/12/15)
Panegialios 0-4 Olympiacos
Platanias 3-1 Apollon Smyrnis

(16/12/15)
Apollon Smyrnis 1-2 Olympiacos
Panegialios 1-0 Platanias

Final standings
1 Olympiacos 7 pts; 2 Platanias 4 pts *(qualified)*;
3 Apollon Smyrnis 3 pts; 4 Panegialios 3 pts
(eliminated)

Group 6

(27/10/15)
Kallithea 2-1 Lamia

(28/10/15)
Atromitos 2-2 Veria

(01/12/15)
Lamia 0-2 Atromitos

(03/12/15)
Veria 1-0 Kallithea

(16/12/15)
Kallithea 2-4 Atromitos
Lamia 0-1 Veria

Final standings
1 Atromitos 7 pts; 2 Veria 7 pts *(qualified)*;
3 Kallithea 3 pts; 4 Lamia 0 pts *(eliminated)*

Group 7

(28/10/15)
Xanthi 0-1 AEK

(29/10/15)
Panelefsiniakos 1-4 Larissa

(02/12/15)
AEK 6-0 Panelefsiniakos
Larissa 1-0 Xanthi

(17/12/15)
Larissa 0-5 AEK
Panelefsiniakos 0-5 Xanthi

Final standings
1 AEK 9 pts; 2 Larissa 6 pts *(qualified)*;
3 Xanthi 3 pts; 4 Panelefsiniakos 0 pts *(eliminated)*

Group 8

(27/10/15)
Panserraikos 0-0 Kissamikos

(28/10/15)
Asteras Tripolis 4-0 Kalloni

(02/12/15)
Kissamikos 1-3 Asteras Tripolis

(03/12/15)
Kalloni 2-1 Panserraikos

(16/12/15)
Kissamikos 1-2 Kalloni
Panserraikos 0-1 Asteras Tripolis

Final standings
1 Asteras Tripolis 9 pts; 2 Kalloni 6 pts *(qualified)*;
3 Panserraikos 1 pt; 4 Kissamikos 1 pt *(eliminated)*

THIRD ROUND

(05/01/16 & 13/01/16)
Larissa 0-3, 0-3 Asteras Tripolis *(0-6)*
Veria 0-1, 0-1 Iraklis *(0-2)*

(06/01/16 & 12/01/16)
Platanias 0-0, 1-2 Atromitos *(1-2)*

(06/01/16 & 13/01/16)
Levadiakos 0-1, 0-2 AEK *(0-3)*

(06/01/16 & 14/01/16)
Ergotelis 0-1, 0-1 Panionios *(0-2)*
Kalloni 2-1, 0-3 PAOK *(2-4)*

(07/01/16 & 13/01/16)
AO Chania 1-4, 0-6 Olympiacos *(1-10)*

(07/01/16 & 14/01/16)
Giannina 1-2, 1-0 Panathinaikos *(2-2;
Panathinaikos on away goals)*

QUARTER-FINALS

(27/01/16 & 03/02/16)
Olympiacos 5-0 Asteras Tripolis *(Ideye 13, 41,
Fortounis 50, 64, Pardo 79)*
Asteras Tripolis 1-1 Olympiacos *(Iglesias 20;
Manuel da Costa 53)*
(Olympiacos 6-1)

(27/01/16 & 10/02/16)
Panathinaikos 0-0 Atromitos
Atromitos 1-0 Panathinaikos *(Stojčev 65)*
(Atromitos 1-0)

(27/01/16 & 11/02/16)
Panionios 1-1 PAOK *(Masouras 34; Pelkas 11)*
PAOK 0-0 Panionios
(1-1; PAOK on away goal)

(28/01/16 & 04/02/16)
AEK 4-1 Iraklis *(Ziabaris 7og, Kolovetsios 44,
Platellas 72, Aravidis 85p; Vellios 90)*
Iraklis 0-1 AEK *(Mantalos 50)*
(AEK 5-1)

SEMI-FINALS

(02/03/16 & 27/04/16)
PAOK 0-3 Olympiacos *(w/o; original match
abandoned after 90 mins at 1-2 Mak 9; Cambiasso
27, David Fuster 57)*
Olympiacos 3-0 PAOK *(w/o)*
(Olympiacos 6-0)

(20/04/16 & 26/04/16)
AEK 1-0 Atromitos *(Mantalos 73)*
Atromitos 1-1 AEK *(Eduardo Brito 68p;
Djebbour 88)*
(AEK 2-1)

FINAL

(17/05/16)
OACA Spyro Louis, Athens
AEK ATHENS FC 2 *(Mantalos 38, Djebbour 51)*
OLYMPIACOS FC 1 *(Domínguez 85)*
Referee: *Sidiropoulos*
AEK: *Anestis, Rodrigo Galo, César Arzo,
Kolovetsios, Dídac Vilà, André Simões, Johansson,
Mantalos (Tzanetopoulos 81), Vargas (Bakakis 58),
Aravidis (Pekhart 90), Djebbour*
OLYMPIACOS: *Roberto, Leandro Salino, Botía,
Manuel da Costa, Masuaku, Milivojević, Kasami
(Pardo 53), Fortounis, David Fuster (Domínguez
65), Pulido, Hernâni (Ideye 53)*

AEK players bathe in the glory of their Greek Cup final victory over league champions Olympiacos

HUNGARY

Magyar Labdarúgó Szövetség (MLSZ)

Address	Kánai út 2.D
	HU-1112 Budapest
Tel	+36 1 577 9500
Fax	+36 1 577 9503
E-mail	mlsz@mlsz.hu
Website	mlsz.hu

President	Sándor Csányi
General secretary	Márton Vági
Media officer	Márton Dinnyés
Year of formation	1901

NB I CLUBS

 ① **Békéscsaba 1912 Előre**

 ② **Budapest Honvéd FC**

 ③ **Debreceni VSC**

 ④ **Diósgyőri VTK**

 ⑤ **Ferencvárosi TC**

 ⑥ **MTK Budapest**

 ⑦ **Paksi FC**

 ⑧ **Puskás Akadémia FC**

 ⑨ **Szombathelyi Haladás**

 ⑩ **Újpest FC**

 ⑪ **Vasas FC**

 ⑫ **Videoton FC**

PROMOTED CLUBS

 ⑬ **Gyirmót FC Győr**

 ⑭ **Mezőkövesd-Zsóry SE**

KEY

● UEFA Champions League

● UEFA Europa League

● Promoted

● Relegated

Ferencváros double up under Doll

The 2015/16 season brought about the restoration of former glories to Hungarian football as the national side finally reached a major tournament after 30 years in the wilderness and Ferencváros, the country's record champions, won their first league title since 2004. Both feats were achieved under a German coach.

The Budapest giants of yesteryear confirmed their resurgence by successfully defending the Hungarian Cup with a 1-0 win over traditional rivals Újpest to complete a seventh domestic double.

Resurgent Fradi victorious in league and cup

Runaway NB I triumph for Budapest club

National team finally back in the big time

Domestic league

An end to Ferencváros's 12-year wait for a 29th Hungarian title looked promising when they won the pre-season Super Cup with a 3-0 win over reigning champions Videoton – the same team they had trounced 4-0 in the 2015 cup final. Thomas Doll's first full season as Fradi coach had ended with the side on an unbeaten 20-match run in the league, and that would be extended to 34 games as a team largely unaltered from the previous campaign, captained still by veteran midfielder Zoltán Gera, stormed to the top of the NB I standings, dropping just two points out of a possible 42.

Although there were 19 games left to play in the new 12-team, 33-game division, Ferencváros were effectively home and dry. A first league defeat in over a year, 1-0 at MTK, was followed by three further victories, and although another sequence ended when they lost for the first time at their new Groupama Aréna home, 1-0 to in-form Újpest, their winter-break advantage was a whopping 18 points, with the team that had just defeated them heading a distant and forlorn chasing pack.

Újpest would fall back to sixth after a disappointing spring, with MTK also finishing poorly to drop from second to fourth, allowing the champions of the previous two seasons, Debrecen and Videoton, to climb up to third and second place, respectively. Videoton thus recovered from a dreadful start, which cost new French coach Bernard Casoni – the replacement for title-winning Spaniard Joan Carrillo – his job, but despite a revival under Ferenc Horváth they still ended up 21 points adrift of Ferencváros. The champions also scored 21 goals more than Debrecen, the team with the second best attack, and in 17-goal striker Dániel Böde supplied the league's most proficient marksman – the first Ferencváros player to top the scoring charts for 26 years.

Békéscsaba finished bottom and were joined through the trapdoor by Puskás Akademia after Vasas won their last two games, the first of them against the team they leapfrogged to safety. There were two unfamiliar clubs promoted, Gyirmót Győr gaining access to the top flight for the first time alongside Mezőkövesd-Zsóry, led up by ex-Hungary boss Attila Pintér.

Domestic cup

As in their 2003/04 double success, Ferencváros completed the feat by making a successful defence of the Hungarian Cup. Although the final took place in the Groupama Aréna, the fact that their opponents were Újpest, the only visiting team to have won a league game there, made a Fradi victory less certain. Sure enough, it proved to be a tight, even contest, with Gera, a double scorer in the semi-final against Debrecen, not striking the winner until 11 minutes from time.

Europe

For the third season in a row there were no Hungarian clubs in European action after August, interest ending when Videoton, already eliminated from the UEFA Champions League by BATE Borisov on Casoni's brief watch, fell heavily to Lech Poznań in the UEFA Europa League play-offs under his temporary replacement, Tamás Pető.

National team

The bells finally rang out for Hungarian football when, after agonisingly missing out on an automatic place at UEFA EURO 2016 via the best runners-up spot, the national team ended a 30-year major tournament absence by overcoming Norway in the play-offs. It had taken new German coach Bernd Storck just six games to deliver Hungary to the promised land, and there was to be more for the team's long-suffering fans to enjoy at the finals in France as they unexpectedly topped their group, playing with panache and scoring six goals, before going out in the round of 16 to Belgium.

DOMESTIC SEASON AT A GLANCE

NB I 2015/16 final table

		Pld	Home					Away					Total					Pts
			W	D	L	F	A	W	D	L	F	A	W	D	L	F	A	
1	**Ferencvárosi TC**	**33**	**13**	**3**	**1**	**41**	**14**	**11**	**1**	**4**	**28**	**9**	**24**	**4**	**5**	**69**	**23**	**76**
2	Videoton FC	33	12	3	2	30	12	5	1	10	12	17	17	4	12	42	29	55
3	Debreceni VSC	33	10	3	4	31	16	4	8	4	17	18	14	11	8	48	34	53
4	MTK Budapest	33	12	2	3	23	8	2	7	7	16	29	14	9	10	39	37	51
5	Szombathelyi Haladás	33	6	7	3	18	18	7	4	6	15	19	13	11	9	33	37	50
6	Újpest FC	33	6	9	2	21	16	5	4	7	21	21	11	13	9	42	37	46
7	Paksi FC	33	9	3	5	29	18	3	4	9	12	22	12	7	14	41	40	43
8	Budapest Honvéd FC	33	8	4	4	20	15	4	3	10	20	24	12	7	14	40	39	43
9	Diósgyőri VTK	33	8	3	5	23	20	2	5	10	14	27	10	8	15	37	47	38
10	Vasas FC	33	6	1	9	19	25	3	4	10	13	29	9	5	19	32	54	32
11	Puskás Akadémia FC	33	5	6	5	14	16	2	4	11	21	35	7	10	16	35	51	31
12	Békéscsaba 1912 Előre	33	3	5	8	14	22	3	4	10	11	33	6	9	18	25	55	27

European qualification 2016/17

 Champion/Cup winner: Ferencvárosi TC (second qualifying round)

 Videoton FC (first qualifying round)
Debreceni VSC (first qualifying round)
MTK Budapest (first qualifying round)

Top scorer	Dániel Böde (Ferencváros), 17 goals
Relegated clubs	Békéscsaba 1912 Előre, Puskás Akadémia FC
Promoted clubs	Gyirmót FC Győr, Mezőkövesd-Zsóry SE
Cup final	Ferencvárosi TC 1-0 Újpest FC

Team of the season
(3-5-2)

Coach: Doll (Ferencváros)

Player of the season

Zoltán Gera
(Ferencvárosi TC)

Twice a champion of Hungary with Ferencváros in the early years of his career, prior to a decade spent in England, Gera completed a hat-trick of NB I triumphs in 2015/16, skippering Fradi to a comprehensive triumph. He also won the double for the second time, 12 years after the first, thanks to his winning goal in the cup final against Újpest, then went on to scale a career peak with the Hungarian national side by appearing in his first major tournament – and scoring a great goal against Portugal – at UEFA EURO 2016.

Newcomer of the season

Ádám Nagy
(Ferencvárosi TC)

Introduced to the Ferencváros first team only at the back-end of the 2014/15 season, Nagy would not only be a Hungarian league and cup winner 12 months later but also an important member of the Hungarian national team that reached the last 16 of UEFA EURO 2016, during which he celebrated his 21st birthday. An elegant, athletic midfielder with a deft touch and excellent tactical awareness, his outstanding breakthrough season for club and country inevitably led to transfer interest from abroad.

NATIONAL TEAM

International tournament appearances

FIFA World Cup (9) 1934 (2nd round), 1938 (runners-up), 1954 (runners-up), 1958, 1962 (qtr-finals), 1966 (qtr finals), 1978, 1982, 1986 UEFA European Championship (3) 1964 (3rd), 1972 (4th), 2016 (round of 16)

Top five all-time caps

Gábor Király (107); József Bozsik (101); **Roland Juhász** (94); **Zoltán Gera** (93); László Fazekas (92)

Top five all-time goals

Ferenc Puskás (84); Sándor Kocsis (75); Imre Schlosser (59); Lajos Tichy (51); György Sárosi (42)

Results 2015/16

Date	Opponent		Venue		Result	Scorers
04/09/15	Romania (ECQ)	H	Budapest	D	0-0	
07/09/15	Northern Ireland (ECQ)	A	Belfast	D	1-1	Guzmics (74)
08/10/15	Faroe Islands (ECQ)	H	Budapest	W	2-1	Böde (63, 71)
11/10/15	Greece (ECQ)	A	Piraeus	L	3-4	Lovrencsics (26), Németh (55, 75)
12/11/15	Norway (ECQ)	A	Oslo	W	1-0	Kleinheisler (26)
15/11/15	Norway (ECQ)	H	Budapest	W	2-1	Priskin (14), Henriksen (83og)
26/03/16	Croatia	H	Budapest	D	1-1	Dzsudzsák (79)
20/05/16	Ivory Coast	H	Budapest	D	0-0	
04/06/16	Germany	A	Gelsenkirchen	L	0-2	
14/06/16	Austria (ECF)	N	Bordeaux (FRA)	W	2-0	Szalai (62), Stieber (87)
18/06/16	Iceland (ECF)	N	Marseille (FRA)	D	1-1	Sævarsson (88og)
22/06/16	Portugal (ECF)	N	Lyon (FRA)	D	3-3	Gera (19), Dzsudzsák (47, 55)
26/06/16	Belgium (ECF)	N	Toulouse (FRA)	L	0-4	

Appearances 2015/16

Coach: Bernd Storck (GER)	25/01/63		ROU	NIR	FRO	GRE	NOR	NOR	Cro	Civ	Ger	AUT	ISL	POR	BEL	Caps	Goals
Gábor Király	01/04/76	Haladás	G	G	G	G	G	G		G46	G	G	G	G	G	107	-
Attila Fiola	17/02/90	Puskás Akadémia	D	D	D	D	D	D	D	D	D82	D				16	-
Roland Juhász	01/07/83	Videoton	D24		D	D				D			D84	D	D79	94	6
Tamás Kádár	14/03/90	Lech (POL)	D	D	D	D	D	D		D	D	D	D		D	33	-
Leandro	19/03/82	Ferencváros	D	D		D										16	-
Zoltán Stieber	16/10/88	Hamburg (GER) /Nürnberg (GER)	M88							s82		s82	s80	M66	s83	15	3
Dániel Tőzsér	12/05/85	QPR (ENG)	M		M46											31	1
Ákos Elek	21/07/88	Changchun Yatai (CHN) /Diósgyőr	M	M22		M	M	M46	s67					M	s46	40	1
Balázs Dzsudzsák	23/12/86	Bursaspor (TUR)	M	M	M	M71	M76	M	M82	M89	M	M	M	M	M	82	20
Ádám Szalai	09/12/87	Hoffenheim (GER) /Hannover (GER)	A	A68			A92		s46	A79	A64	A69	s84	A71	A	36	9
Nemanja Nikolić	31/12/87	Legia (POL)	A70		A75	s62			s46	s64			s66		s75	20	3
Richárd Guzmics	16/04/87	Wisła Kraków (POL)	s24	D	D		D	D	D		D	D	D	D	D	18	1
Krisztián Németh	05/01/89	Kansas City (USA) /Al-Gharafa (QAT)	s70	M89	s46	M	M	s75	M67		M89		s71			26	3
Tamás Priskin	27/09/86	Slovan Bratislava (SVK)	s88	s68	s75		s92	A62	A46		s64	s69	A66			58	17
Zsolt Kalmár	09/06/95	RB Leipzig (GER)		M		s71										7	-
Zoltán Gera	22/04/79	Ferencváros		M	M	M71	M		M	s46	s59	M	M	M46	M46	93	25
Ádám Nagy	17/06/95	Ferencváros		s22	M	s71	s72	M	M46	M70	M		M	M	M	11	-
Vilmos Vanczák	20/06/83	Sion (SUI)		s89												79	4
Ádám Bódi	18/10/90	Debrecen			M46											1	-
Dániel Böde	24/10/86	Ferencváros			s46	A		s62	s79	s70			s66		s79	14	4
Gergő Lovrencsics	01/09/88	Lech (POL)				M62	s76	M			M			M83	M	14	1
Ádám Lang	17/01/93	Videoton					D	D	D	D	D	D	D	D	D	15	-
László Kleinheisler	08/04/94	Videoton /Bremen (GER)					M72	M75	M79	M46	M82	M80	M			7	1
Ádám Pintér	12/06/88	Ferencváros						s46		M	M59	s89		M	M75	24	-
Dénes Dibusz	16/11/90	Ferencváros							G46							4	-
Mihály Korhut	01/12/88	Debrecen							D					D		6	-
Ádám Bogdán	27/09/87	Liverpool (ENG)							s46							20	-
Ádám Gyurcsó	06/03/91	Pogoń (POL)								M64						13	1
Péter Gulácsi	06/05/90	RB Leipzig (GER)								s46						3	-
Roland Sallai	22/05/97	Puskás Akadémia								s79						1	-
Máté Vida	08/03/96	Vasas								s89						1	-
Barnabás Bese	06/05/94	MTK										s82		s46		2	-

EUROPE

Videoton FC

CHAMPIONS LEAGUE

Second qualifying round - The New Saints FC (WAL)
A 1-0 Gyurcsó (77)
Gábor, Paulo Vinícius, Fejes, Gyurcsó, Kovács, Koltai (Pajač 66), Filipe Oliveira (Luijckx 83), Pátkai (Trebotić 70), Juhász, Szolnoki, Simon. Coach: Bernard Casoni (FRA)
H 1-1 (aet) Gyurcsó (107)
Danilović, Luijckx (Simon 86), Fejes, Gyurcsó, Filipe Oliveira, Pátkai, Lang, Ivanovski (Kovács 56), Juhász (Paulo Vinícius 67), Szolnoki, Trebotić. Coach: Bernard Casoni (FRA)

Third qualifying round - FC BATE Borisov (BLR)
H 1-1 Paulo Vinícius (89)
Danilović, Paulo Vinícius, Luijckx, Gyurcsó, Kovács (Soumah 59), Filipe Oliveira, Ivanovski, Juhász (Lang 29), Szolnoki, Maréval (Fejes 73), Trebotić. Coach: Bernard Casoni (FRA)
A 0-1
Danilović, Paulo Vinícius, Luijckx, Gyurcsó (Pátkai 61), Kovács (Soumah 74), Filipe Oliveira, Lang, Ivanovski, Szolnoki, Maréval (Fejes 50), Trebotić. Coach: Bernard Casoni (FRA)
Red card: Luijckx 60

EUROPA LEAGUE

Play-offs - KKS Lech Poznań (POL)
A 0-3
Danilović, Paulo Vinícius, Fejes, Gyurcsó (Sejben 89), Filipe Oliveira, Pátkai (Trebotić 71), Lang, Ivanovski, Soumah (Kovács 57), Szolnoki, Simon. Coach: Tamás Pető (HUN)
H 0-1
Danilović, Paulo Vinícius, Luijckx (Simon 57), Fejes, Feczesin (Rudolf 70), Kovács, Koltai (Gyurcsó 58), Ivanovski, Juhász, Szolnoki, Trebotić. Coach: Tamás Pető (HUN)

Ferencvárosi TC

EUROPA LEAGUE

First qualifying round - Go Ahead Eagles (NED)
A 1-1 Gera (3)
Dibusz, Böde, Leandro, Gyömbér, Gera, Lamah (Ugrai 79), Nalepa, Mateos, Ramírez, Somália (Busai 86), Varga (D Nagy 79). Coach: Thomas Doll (GER)
H 4-1 Gera (4), Böde (20), Busai (45), Haraszti (89)
Dibusz, Böde, Leandro, Gera, Busai (Hajnal 72), Lamah, Nalepa, Dilaver (Gyömbér 28), Ramírez, Somália, Varga (Haraszti 79). Coach: Thomas Doll (GER)

Second qualifying round - FK Željezničar (BIH)
H 0-1
Dibusz, Böde, Leandro, Gera, Busai (Hajnal 46), Lamah (Gyömbér 68), Nalepa, Dilaver, Ramírez (Šesták 46), Somália, Varga. Coach: Thomas Doll (GER)

A 0-2
Dibusz, Böde (Busai 58), Hajnal (Šesták 46), Leandro, Gyömbér, Gera, Lamah, Nalepa, Dilaver, Somália, Varga (Radó 41). Coach: Thomas Doll (GER)

MTK Budapest

EUROPA LEAGUE

First qualifying round - FK Vojvodina (SRB)
H 0-0
Hegedűs, Grgić, Thiam, Varga (L Szatmári 59), Torghelle (Schrammel 90+3), Střeštík (Myke 46), Bese, Kanta, Vukmir, Vadnai, Vass. Coach: Csaba László (HUN)
A 1-3 Střeštík (3)
Hegedűs, Grgić, Thiam, Varga (Myke 53), Torghelle, Střeštík (L Szatmári 63), Bese, Kanta, Vukmir, Vadnai, Vass (Gera 90+2). Coach: Csaba László (HUN)

Debreceni VSC

EUROPA LEAGUE

First qualifying round - FK Sutjeska (MNE)
H 3-0 Mihelič (16), Brković (71), Sidibé (74)
Verpecz, Mihelič, Balogh (Sidibé 46), Mészáros, Brković, Bódi (Zsidai 85), Varga, Szakály, Korhut, Kulcsár (Horváth 66), Jovanović. Coach: Elemér Kondás (HUN)
A 0-2
Verpecz, Mészáros, Brković, Sidibé, Bódi, Varga, Szakály (Morozov 90+1), Korhut, Kulcsár (Balogh 73), Jovanović, Horváth (Szécsi 46). Coach: Elemér Kondás (HUN)

Second qualifying round - Skonto FC (LVA)
A 2-2 Tisza (9), Castillion (72)
Verpecz, Balogh (Horváth 90+3), Mészáros, Brković, Sidibé (Castillion 71), Bódi, Varga, Tisza (Szécsi 80), Szakály, Korhut, Jovanović. Coach: Elemér Kondás (HUN)
H 9-2 Tisza (7, 45+2), Balogh (12), Sidibé (29, 31), Brković (51), Szakály (54p), Bódi (58), Castillion (70)
Verpecz, Balogh (Castillion 56), Mészáros, Brković, Sidibé, Bódi (Horváth 62), Varga (Zsidai 46), Tisza, Szakály, Korhut, Jovanović. Coach: Elemér Kondás (HUN)

Third qualifying round - Rosenborg BK (NOR)
H 2-3 Balogh (33), Bódi (90)
Verpecz, Balogh, Máté, Brković, Sidibé (Castillion 64), Bódi, Varga, Tisza (Mihelič 84), Szakály (Zsidai 84), Korhut, Jovanović. Coach: Elemér Kondás (HUN)
A 1-3 Castillion (43)
Verpecz, Balogh (Zsidai 62), Mészáros, Máté, Sidibé (Mihelič 77), Bódi, Varga, Tisza (Morozov 52), Korhut, Jovanović, Castillion. Coach: Elemér Kondás (HUN)
Red card: Máté 48

DOMESTIC LEAGUE CLUB-BY-CLUB

Békéscsaba 1912 Előre

1912 • Kórház utcai (13,000) • 1912elore.hu
Major honours
Hungarian Cup (1) 1988
Coach: Zoran Spisljak (SRB)

2015

19/07	h	Debrecen	L	2-3	Laczkó, Viczián
25/07	a	Paks	L	0-4	
01/08	a	Újpest	L	0-2	
08/08	h	Vasas	L	0-2	
15/08	a	Puskás Akadémia	W	2-1	Szilágyi, Bényei
22/08	h	Honvéd	L	1-4	Ezequiel
29/08	h	Haladás	L	0-1	
12/09	h	Diósgyőr	D	1-1	Birtalan
19/09	a	Ferencváros	L	0-1	
26/09	h	Videoton	W	2-0	Viczián, Ezequiel
03/10	h	MTK	D	1-1	Punoševac
17/10	a	Debrecen	L	0-7	
24/10	h	Paks	L	1-3	Birtalan 2
31/10	h	Újpest	L	1-3	Birtalan
21/11	a	Puskás Akadémia	W	2-1	Laczkó, Damjanović
28/11	a	Honvéd	L	2-3	Vaskó, Birtalan
02/12	a	Vasas	L	0-4	
05/12	a	Haladás	D	1-1	Ezequiel
12/12	a	Diósgyőr	L	0-2	

2016

13/02	h	Ferencváros	L	0-1	
20/02	a	Videoton	D	1-1	Laczkó
27/02	a	MTK	D	0-0	
05/03	h	Paks	W	2-0	Eccleston, Punoševac
09/03	h	Ferencváros	L	0-1	
12/03	a	Videoton	D	1-1	Laczkó
19/03	h	Újpest	W	1-0	Paukner
02/04	a	Diósgyőr	D	0-0	
06/04	a	MTK	L	0-3	
09/04	a	Haladás	D	1-1	
16/04	a	Puskás Akadémia	W	1-0	Vaskó
19/04	h	Vasas	D	1-1	Vaskó
23/04	a	Honvéd	L	1-2	Laczkó
30/04	h	Debrecen	D	0-0	

No	Name	Nat	DoB	Pos	Aps	(s)	Gls
8	István Bagi		23/03/89	M	3	(2)	
11	Zsolt Balog		10/11/78	D	8	(1)	
4	Balázs Bényei		10/01/90	D	28		1
6	Botond Birtalan		08/04/89	A	18	(10)	5
14	Bálint Borbély		30/11/89	M	11	(3)	
23	Slavko Damjanović	MNE	02/11/92	D	18	(2)	1
8	Nathan Eccleston	ENG	30/12/90	A	3	(2)	1
24	Ezequiel	ESP	12/01/91	M	25	(1)	3
2	Fábio Guarú	BRA	03/09/87	D	29	(1)	
15	Zsolt Fehér		13/09/85	D	12	(5)	
67	Martin Hudák		22/02/94	M	4	(4)	
12	Ľuboš Ilizi	SVK	13/10/82	G	7		
21	György Juhász		21/06/87	D	2	(4)	
9	Tamás Kertész		30/05/90	A		(6)	
88	Georgi Korudzhiev	BUL	02/03/88	M	6	(3)	
5	Balázs Koszó		20/03/88	D	6		
86	Zsolt Laczkó		18/12/86	M	29		5
1	Roland Mursits		14/03/91	G	13		
17	László Oláh		16/12/95	A		(1)	
20	Matúš Paukner	SVK	20/06/91	A	2	(7)	1
25	Thomas Piermayr	AUT	02/08/89	M	23		
27	Márkó Pilán		17/06/98	M	2		
44	Vukašin Poleksić	MNE	30/08/82	G	13		
13	Bratislav Punoševac	SRB	09/07/87	A	21	(6)	2
10	István Spitzmüller		14/05/86	M	30	(2)	
30	Alex Pál Svedyuk		11/07/96	M		(2)	
7	Dániel Szalai		05/09/96	A	1	(6)	
42	Norbert Szélpál		03/03/96	M		(1)	
20	Péter Szilágyi		26/01/88	A	4	(8)	1
9	Péter Takács		25/01/90	M	7	(4)	
18	Viktor Vadász		15/08/86	D	4	(3)	
28	Tamás Vaskó		20/02/84	D	22		3
22	Ádám Viczián		24/11/95	A	16	(4)	2

HUNGARY

Budapest Honvéd FC

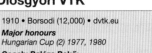

1909 • Bozsik József (13,500) • honvedfc.hu
Major honours
Hungarian League (13) 1950, 1950 (autumn), 1952,
1954, 1955, 1980, 1984, 1985, 1986, 1988, 1989,
1991, 1993; Hungarian Cup (7) 1926, 1964, 1985,
1989, 1996, 2007, 2009
Coach: Marco Rossi (ITA)

2015
18/07	h	Videoton	W	1-0	Youla
25/07	h	MTK	W	2-1	Kamber, Vernes
02/08	a	Debrecen	D	3-3	og (Zsidai), Botka, Holender
08/08	a	Paks	L	1-3	Ignjatović
15/08	a	Újpest	D	1-1	Youla
22/08	a	Békéscsaba	W	4-1	Kamber 2, Youla, og (Koszó)
29/08	h	Puskás Akadémia	D	0-0	
12/09	h	Vasas	L	0-1	
19/09	a	Haladás	D	0-0	
26/09	h	Diósgyőr	W	2-1	Vernes, Kamber
03/10	a	Ferencváros	L	1-2	Youla
17/10	a	Videoton	L	0-3	
24/10	h	MTK	L	1-2	Kamber
31/10	a	Debrecen	D	0-0	
21/11	h	Újpest	L	1-2	Bobál
28/11	h	Békéscsaba	W	3-2	G Nagy 2, Baráth
02/12	h	Paks	D	0-0	
05/12	a	Puskás Akadémia	W	3-0	Prosser, Youla, Kamber
12/12	h	Vasas	L	1-2	Kamber

2016
13/02	h	Haladás	L	0-1	
20/02	a	Diósgyőr	L	1-2	Kamber
27/02	h	Ferencváros	W	2-1	Baráth, Vasiljević
05/03	h	Vasas	D	0-0	
09/03	a	MTK	L	0-1	
12/03	h	Debrecen	W	3-0	Eppel 2, Hidi
19/03	h	Paks	W	2-0	Eppel 2
02/04	h	Videoton	W	2-1	Eppel, Vernes
06/04	a	Újpest	L	0-2	
10/04	a	Ferencváros	L	1-2	og (Busai)
16/04	h	Haladás	L	0-1	
20/04	a	Diósgyőr	W	2-1	Holender, Kamber
23/04	h	Békéscsaba	W	2-1	Baráth, Vasiljević
30/04	a	Puskás Akadémia	L	1-2	Bobál

No	Name	Nat	DoB	Pos	Aps	(s)	Gls
36	Botond Baráth		21/04/92	D	30		3
2	Dávid Bobál		31/08/95	D	31		2
21	Endre Botka		25/04/94	D	29	(2)	1
96	Dan Constantinescu	ROU	25/04/96	A		(5)	
16	Mihály Csábi		25/05/95	M		(4)	
87	Gergely Délczeg		09/08/87	A		(10)	
9	Márton Eppel		26/10/91	M	11		5
63	László Erdélyi		10/07/93	A		(1)	
6	Dániel Gazdag		02/03/96	M	12	(12)	
26	Patrik Hidi		27/11/90	A	24	(5)	1
57	Filip Holender	SRB	27/07/94	A	20	(8)	2
18	András Horváth		03/02/88	G	15		
5	Aleksandar Ignjatović	SRB	11/04/88	D	12	(2)	1
94	Sebestyén Ihrig Farkas		28/04/94	A		(2)	
6	George Ikenne	NGA	29/10/92	M	8	(3)	
70	Richárd Jelena		08/01/98	A		(2)	
24	Djordje Kamber	SRB	20/11/83	M	31		9
71	Szabolcs Kemenes		18/05/86	G	17		
2	Dániel Kovács		14/06/96	A		(1)	
25	Ivan Lovrić	CRO	11/07/85	D	21		
50	Dániel Lukács		03/04/96	A		(2)	
27	András Márton		09/07/96	D		(1)	
77	Gergő Nagy		07/01/93	M	31	(1)	2
1	Sándor Nagy	UKR	02/09/85	G	1		
30	Raul Palmes	ROU	18/06/96	D		(1)	
7	Dániel Prosser		15/06/94	M	11	(8)	1
14	Loránd Szilágyi	ROU	21/09/85	D	4		
66	Dušan Vasiljević	SRB	07/05/82	M	14	(8)	2
30	Bálint Vécsei		13/07/93	A		(1)	
7	Richárd Vernes		24/02/92	M	9	(18)	3
99	Souleymane Youla	GUI	29/11/81	A	27	(2)	5

Debreceni VSC

1902 • Nagyerdei (20,000) • dvsc.hu
Major honours
Hungarian League (7) 2005, 2006, 2007, 2009,
2010, 2012, 2014; Hungarian Cup (6) 1999, 2001,
2008, 2010, 2012, 2013
Coach: Elemér Kondás

2015
19/07	a	Békéscsaba	W	3-2	Nagy, Tisza, og (Bényei)
26/07	h	Puskás Akadémia	D	1-1	Castillion
02/08	a	Honvéd	D	3-3	Castillion, Balogh, Tisza
09/08	a	Haladás	L	0-1	
15/08	a	Diósgyőr	W	2-0	Máté, Balogh
22/08	h	Ferencváros	L	0-3	
30/08	a	Videoton	L	0-1	
12/09	h	MTK	W	1-0	Sidibé
19/09	a	Vasas	W	1-0	Kulcsár
26/09	a	Paks	D	1-1	Tisza
03/10	h	Újpest	D	1-1	Tisza
17/10	h	Békéscsaba	W	7-0	Kulcsár 2, Sidibé, Balogh, Tisza, Zsidai, Jovanović
24/10	a	Puskás Akadémia	D	1-1	Korhut
31/10	h	Honvéd	D	0-0	
21/11	h	Diósgyőr	W	1-0	Sidibé
28/11	a	Ferencváros	L	0-3	
02/12	a	Haladás	D	2-2	Brković, og (Gaál)
05/12	h	Videoton	L	1-2	Korhut
12/12	h	MTK	W	3-1	Horváth 3

2016
13/02	h	Vasas	W	4-0	Bódi, Horváth, Holman, Sidibé
20/02	h	Paks	W	2-0	Sidibé (p), Holman
27/02	a	Újpest	D	1-1	Szakály (p)
05/03	h	Puskás Akadémia	W	4-2	Takács, Szakály, Horváth 2
08/03	a	Vasas	D	0-0	
12/03	h	Honvéd	L	0-3	
19/03	a	MTK	L	0-1	
02/04	a	Ferencváros	W	2-1	Takács 2
05/04	a	Videoton	L	0-1	
09/04	a	Paks	W	1-0	og (Szabó)
16/04	h	Újpest	W	1-0	Tisza
20/04	a	Haladás	D	2-2	Jovanović, Takács
23/04	h	Diósgyőr	W	3-1	Jovanović, Takács, Bódi
30/04	a	Békéscsaba	D	0-0	

No	Name	Nat	DoB	Pos	Aps	(s)	Gls
16	Norbert Balogh		21/02/96	A	16	(2)	3
53	Péter Berdó		14/01/93	M		(1)	
23	Dániel Bereczki		02/06/95	A	1	(4)	
27	Ádám Bódi		18/10/90	M	23	(4)	2
25	Dušan Brković	SRB	20/01/89	D	28		1
91	Geoffrey Castillion	NED	25/05/91	A	8	(7)	2
39	Adamo Coulibaly	FRA	14/08/81	A	2	(5)	
16	Ognjen Djelmić	BIH	18/08/88	M	3	(4)	
11	János Ferenczi		03/04/91	M	6	(8)	
8	Dávid Holman		17/03/93	M	13		2
88	Zsolt Horváth		19/05/88	A	15	(3)	6
77	Aleksandar Jovanović	BIH	26/10/84	M	26	(3)	3
69	Mihály Korhut		01/12/88	D	31		2
70	Tamás Kulcsár		13/10/82	A	7	(11)	3
70	Pál Lázár		11/03/88	D	13	(3)	
18	Péter Máté		02/12/84	D	14	(1)	1
17	Norbert Mészáros		19/08/80	D	29		
10	René Mihelič	SVN	05/07/88	M	3		
24	Igor Morozov	EST	27/05/89	D	2		
28	Zoltán Nagy		25/10/85	D	4		1
22	Božidar Radošević	CRO	04/04/89	G	23		
26	Ibrahima Sidibé	SEN	10/08/80	A	13	(9)	5
15	Bence Sós		10/05/94	M	1	(2)	
55	Péter Szakály		17/08/86	M	16	(3)	2
3	Csaba Szatmári		14/06/94	D	1	(1)	
66	Márk Szécsi		22/05/94	A	4	(3)	
20	Tamás Takács		20/02/91	A	9	(1)	5
44	Tibor Tisza		10/11/84	A	10	(14)	6
33	József Varga		06/06/88	M	21	(4)	
87	István Verpecz		04/02/87	G	10		
6	László Zsidai		16/07/86	M	11	(2)	1

Diósgyőri VTK

1910 • Borsodi (12,000) • dvtk.eu
Major honours
Hungarian Cup (2) 1977, 1980
**Coach: Balázs Bekő;
(29/12/15) Sándor Egervári**

2015
18/07	h	Vasas	W	2-1	Grumić, og (Grúz)
26/07	a	Ferencváros	L	1-3	Barczi
01/08	h	Videoton	L	1-2	Koman (p)
08/08	a	MTK	L	0-5	
15/08	h	Debrecen	L	0-2	
22/08	a	Paks	D	1-1	Nikházi (p)
29/08	h	Újpest	W	2-1	Bognár, Tamás
12/09	a	Békéscsaba	D	1-1	Okuka
19/09	h	Puskás Akadémia	W	3-2	Okuka, Novothny, Egerszegi
26/09	a	Honvéd	L	1-2	Barczi
03/10	h	Haladás	L	1-2	Novothny
17/10	a	Vasas	W	1-0	Bacsa
24/10	h	Ferencváros	L	0-2	
31/10	a	Videoton	L	1-2	Grumić
21/11	a	Debrecen	L	0-1	
28/11	h	Paks	D	1-1	Griffiths
02/12	h	MTK	D	1-1	Bacsa
05/12	a	Újpest	L	1-2	Novothny
12/12	h	Békéscsaba	W	2-0	Novothny, Koman

2016
13/02	a	Puskás Akadémia	L	0-1	
20/02	h	Honvéd	W	2-1	Bacsa 2
27/02	a	Haladás	L	1-2	Barczi (p)
05/03	a	Ferencváros	D	2-2	Bognár, Novothny
09/03	h	Videoton	W	2-1	Barczi (p), Novothny
12/03	a	Újpest	L	0-1	
19/03	h	Haladás	W	3-0	Elek 2, Novothny
02/04	a	Békéscsaba	D	0-0	
06/04	h	Puskás Akadémia	W	2-1	Koman (p), Elek
09/04	a	MTK	D	0-0	
16/04	a	Vasas	W	3-1	Egerszegi 2, Elek
20/04	h	Honvéd	L	1-2	Novothny
23/04	a	Debrecen	L	1-3	Egerszegi
30/04	h	Paks	L	0-2	

No	Name	Nat	DoB	Pos	Aps	(s)	Gls
99	Botond Antal		22/08/91	G	4	(1)	
9	Patrik Bacsa		03/06/92	A	20	(8)	4
31	Dávid Barczi		01/02/89	M	27	(5)	4
10	István Bognár		06/05/91	M	20	(7)	2
72	Gábriel Boros		26/09/97	M		(2)	
11	Tamás Egerszegi		02/08/91	M	23	(6)	4
25	Ákos Elek		21/07/88	M	11		4
94	Gábor Eperjesi		12/01/94	D	10	(1)	
50	Georges Griffiths	CIV	24/02/90	A		(7)	1
19	Miroslav Grumić	SRB	28/06/84	A	9	(7)	2
68	Ramon Halmai		18/04/94	M		(3)	
3	Senad Husić	BIH	12/04/90	D	4		
18	Miklós Kitl		01/06/97	M	14	(1)	
78	Vladimir Koman		16/03/89	M	25	(1)	3
6	Gábor Kovács		04/09/87	D	14	(4)	
16	Zoltán Lipták		10/12/84	D	32		
5	James Manjrekar	CAN	05/08/93	M	11	(6)	
33	Milán Imre Nemes		27/09/96	D	23		
29	Milán Németh		29/05/88	D	5	(3)	
20	Márk Nikházi		02/02/89	M	7	(9)	1
86	Soma Novothny		16/06/94	A	23	(4)	8
7	Dražen Okuka	SRB	05/03/86	D	29	(1)	2
22	Ivan Radoš	CRO	21/02/84	G	29		
11	Balázs Szabó		16/04/98	A		(1)	
1	Tamás Takács		20/02/91	A	1	(11)	
26	Márk Tamás		28/10/93	D	22	(1)	1
74	Patrik Ternován		10/06/97	A		(4)	

Ferencvárosi TC

1899 • Groupama Aréna (22,000) • fradi.hu

Major honours
Inter Cities Fairs Cup (1) 1965; Hungarian League (29)
1903, 1905, 1907, 1909, 1910, 1911, 1912, 1913,
1926, 1927, 1928, 1932, 1934, 1938, 1940, 1941,
1949, 1963, 1964, 1967, 1968, 1976, 1981, 1992,
1995, 1996, 2001, 2004, 2016; Hungarian Cup (22)
1913, 1922, 1927, 1928, 1933, 1935, 1942, 1943,
1944, 1958, 1972, 1974, 1976, 1978, 1991, 1993,
1994, 1995, 2003, 2004, 2015, 2016

Coach: Thomas Doll (GER)

2015

19/07	a	Haladás	W 2-0	Lamah, Šesták
26/07	h	Diósgyőr	W 3-1	Nalepa, Leandro, Böde
01/08	a	Vasas	W 2-0	Böde 2
08/08	a	Videoton	W 3-1	og (Heffler), Böde 2
15/08	h	MTK	W 2-0	Gera, Böde
22/08	a	Debrecen	W 3-0	Böde, Šesták, Radó
29/08	a	Paks	W 2-0	Böde, Lamah
12/09	a	Újpest	W 2-1	Böde 2
19/09	h	Békéscsaba	W 1-0	Böde
26/09	a	Puskás Akadémia	D 0-0	
03/10	h	Honvéd	W 2-1	Hajnal, Varga
17/10	h	Haladás	W 3-1	Šesták, Varga, Ramírez
24/10	a	Diósgyőr	W 2-0	Šesták, Lamah
31/10	a	Vasas	W 5-1	Varga 2, Šesták, Leandro, Ramírez
21/11	a	MTK	L 0-1	
28/11	h	Debrecen	W 3-0	Ramírez, Gera (p), Radó
02/12	h	Videoton	W 1-0	Radó
05/12	a	Paks	W 5-0	Lamah, Šesták, Böde, Busai, Varga
12/12	h	Újpest	L 0-1	

2016

13/02	a	Békéscsaba	W 1-0	Pintér
20/02	a	Puskás Akadémia	W 2-0	Ramírez, Böde
27/02	a	Honvéd	L 1-2	Lamah
05/03	h	Diósgyőr	D 2-2	Gera (p), Pintér
09/03	a	Békéscsaba	W 1-0	Radó
12/03	h	Puskás Akadémia	W 4-0	Lamah (p), Böde 2 (1p), Radó
19/03	a	Vasas	W 4-1	Šesták, Böde 2 (1p)
02/04	a	Debrecen	L 1-2	Šesták
06/04	h	Paks	W 5-2	Radó, Hajnal, Gyömbér, og (Gévay), Lamah
10/04	h	Honvéd	W 2-1	Trinks, Busai
16/04	h	MTK	D 2-2	Gera, Varga
20/04	a	Videoton	L 0-1	
23/04	h	Újpest	D 2-2	Varga, og (Litauszki)
30/04	h	Haladás	W 1-0	og (Kovács)

No	Name	Nat	DoB	Pos	Aps	(s)	Gls
13	Dániel Böde		24/10/86	A	28	(3)	17
22	Attila Busai		21/01/89	M	6	(13)	2
30	Vladan Čukić	SRB	27/06/80	M	6	(6)	
90	Dénes Dibusz		19/11/90	G	31		
66	Emir Dilaver	AUT	07/05/91	D	27		
20	Zoltán Gera		22/04/79	M	29	(1)	4
19	Gábor Gyömbér		27/02/88	M	5	(6)	1
15	Tamás Hajnal		15/03/81	M	18	(3)	2
8	Zsolt Haraszti		04/11/91	A		(5)	
55	Levente Jova		30/01/92	G	2		
67	István Lakatos		04/04/99	A		(1)	
24	Roland Lamah	BEL	31/12/87	A	27	(6)	7
16	Leandro		19/03/82	D	30		2
99	Ádám Nagy		17/06/95	M	22	(3)	
14	Dominik Nagy		08/05/95	M	6	(9)	
27	Michał Nalepa	POL	22/01/93	D	29		1
17	Ádám Pintér		12/06/88	D	12	(6)	2
10	András Radó		09/09/93	A	9	(16)	6
77	Cristian Ramírez	ECU	08/12/94	D	27	(1)	4
11	Stanislav Šesták	SVK	16/12/82	A	17	(7)	9
88	Somália	BRA	28/09/88	A	3		
35	Florian Trinks	GER	11/03/92	M	8	(4)	1
97	Roland Varga		23/01/90	A	21	(9)	7

MTK Budapest

1888 • Illovszky Rudolf (18,000); Dunaújváros
(10,046) • mtk.hu

Major honours
Hungarian League (23) 1904, 1908, 1914, 1917, 1918,
1919, 1920, 1921, 1922, 1923, 1924, 1925, 1929, 1936,
1937, 1951, 1953, 1958, 1987, 1997, 1999, 2003,
2008; Hungarian Cup (12) 1910, 1911, 1912, 1914,
1923, 1925, 1932, 1952, 1968, 1997, 1998, 2000

Coach: Csaba László;
(03/02/16) Vaszilisz Teodoru

2015

18/07	h	Puskás Akadémia	W 1-0	Torghelle
25/07	a	Honvéd	L 1-2	Střeštík
01/08	a	Haladás	D 2-2	Hrepka, Thiam
08/08	h	Diósgyőr	W 5-0	Kanta 2 (1p), Vadnai, Hrepka, Myke
15/08	a	Ferencváros	L 0-2	
23/08	h	Videoton	W 1-0	Kanta (p)
29/08	a	Vasas	W 1-0	L Szatmári
12/09	a	Debrecen	L 0-1	
19/09	a	Paks	D 0-0	
26/09	a	Újpest	D 2-2	Torghelle, Kanta
03/10	a	Békéscsaba	D 1-1	Torghelle
17/10	a	Puskás Akadémia	W 3-2	Kanta 2 (1p), Bese
24/10	h	Honvéd	W 2-1	Torghelle 2
31/10	h	Haladás	L 0-1	
21/11	h	Ferencváros	W 1-0	Torghelle
28/11	a	Videoton	L 0-1	
02/12	a	Diósgyőr	D 1-1	Torghelle
05/12	h	Vasas	W 2-1	Torghelle 2
12/12	a	Debrecen	L 1-3	Myke

2016

20/02	a	Újpest	D 1-1	Torghelle
27/02	h	Békéscsaba	D 0-0	
05/03	h	Újpest	W 2-1	Střeštík, Hrepka
09/03	h	Honvéd	W 1-0	Hrepka
12/03	h	Haladás	W 3-1	Thiam, Střeštík 2 (1p)
19/03	h	Debrecen	W 1-0	Nikač
02/04	a	Paks	L 1-4	Střeštík
06/04	h	Békéscsaba	W 3-0	Nikač, Gera, Hajdú
09/04	h	Diósgyőr	D 0-0	
12/04	h	Paks	W 1-0	Baki
16/04	a	Ferencváros	D 2-2	Kanta, Torghelle
20/04	h	Puskás Akadémia	L 0-1	
23/04	a	Videoton	L 0-5	
30/04	h	Vasas	L 0-2	

No	Name	Nat	DoB	Pos	Aps	(s)	Gls
4	Ákos Baki		24/08/94	D	6	(12)	1
18	Barnabás Bese		06/05/94	D	33		1
3	Bence Deutsch		04/08/92	D		(9)	
56	Dániel Gera		29/08/95	A	22	(5)	1
3	Mato Grgić	CRO	27/09/87	D	30		
8	Ádám Hajdú		16/01/93	M	6	(7)	1
1	Lajos Hegedűs		19/12/87	G	33		
13	Adam Hrepka		15/04/87	A	10	(8)	4
59	Tamás Hujber		19/07/95	M		(5)	
19	József Kanta		24/03/84	M	27		7
7	Myke	BRA	30/10/92	A	11	(8)	2
9	Darko Nikač	MNE	15/09/90	A	8	(4)	2
24	Patrik Poór		15/11/93	D	25	(3)	
15	Marek Střeštík	CZE	01/02/87	M	20	(2)	5
58	István Szatmári		27/05/97	A		(1)	
10	Lóránd Szatmári		03/10/88	M	3	(7)	1
6	Khaly Thiam	SEN	07/01/94	M	27	(4)	2
14	Sándor Torghelle		05/05/82	A	24	(2)	11
23	Dániel Vadnai		19/02/88	D	32		1
13	Szabolcs Varga		17/03/95	A	9	(9)	
38	Ádám Vass		09/08/88	M	27	(1)	
55	Bálint Vogyicska		27/02/98	M	2	(4)	
21	Dragan Vukmir	SRB	02/08/78	D	8		

Paksi FC

1952 • Városi (5,000) • paksifc.hu

Coach: Aurél Csertői

2015

18/07	a	Újpest	D 0-0	
25/07	h	Békéscsaba	W 4-0	Gévay 2, Balázs, Szakály (p)
01/08	a	Puskás Akadémia	L 0-1	
08/08	h	Honvéd	W 3-1	Szabó, Balázs 2
15/08	a	Haladás	L 0-1	
22/08	h	Diósgyőr	D 1-1	Hahn
29/08	h	Ferencváros	L 0-2	
12/09	h	Videoton	W 2-0	Szakály (p), og (Paulo Vinícius)
19/09	h	MTK	D 0-0	
26/09	h	Debrecen	D 1-1	Bartha
03/10	a	Vasas	W 2-1	Koltai, Bartha
17/10	h	Újpest	W 1-0	Bertus
24/10	a	Békéscsaba	W 3-2	Papp, Szakály, Bartha
31/10	h	Puskás Akadémia	W 4-2	Papp 2, Hahn, og (Bačelić-Grgić)
21/11	h	Haladás	W 2-0	Lenzsér, Bajner
28/11	a	Diósgyőr	D 1-1	Balázs
02/12	h	Honvéd	D 0-0	
05/12	h	Ferencváros	L 0-5	
12/12	h	Videoton	L 0-1	

2016

20/02	a	Debrecen	L 0-2	
27/02	h	Vasas	W 3-0	Lenzsér, Bartha, Kulcsár
05/03	h	Békéscsaba	L 0-2	
09/03	a	Puskás Akadémia	L 1-2	Hahn
12/03	h	Vasas	W 2-0	Bertus, Hahn
19/03	a	Honvéd	L 0-2	
02/04	h	MTK	W 4-1	Bertus, Szakály, og (Střeštík), Hahn
06/04	a	Ferencváros	L 2-5	Szakály, Hahn
09/04	a	Debrecen	L 0-1	
12/04	a	MTK	L 0-1	
16/04	h	Videoton	L 0-1	
20/04	a	Újpest	D 1-1	Hahn
23/04	h	Haladás	L 2-3	Gévay, Papp
30/04	a	Diósgyőr	W 2-0	Bartha, Kecskés

No	Name	Nat	DoB	Pos	Aps	(s)	Gls
28	Dávid Asztalos		09/03/95	D	3	(1)	
44	Bálint Bajner		18/11/90	A	3	(11)	1
92	Zsolt Balázs		11/08/88	A	20	(11)	4
7	Tamás Báló		12/01/84	D	2	(2)	
39	László Bartha		09/02/87	M	30	(1)	5
26	Lajos Bertus		26/09/90	M	33		3
14	Dávid Bor		10/12/94	A		(1)	
24	Norbert Csernyánszki		01/02/76	G	1		
3	Roland Fröhlich		08/08/88	A	1	(5)	
5	Zsolt Gévay		19/11/87	D	31		3
9	János Hahn		15/05/95	A	16	(13)	7
8	Tamás Kecskés		15/01/86	M	17	(6)	1
32	Dávid Kelemen		24/05/92	D	1		
19	Barna Kesztyűs		04/09/93	M	11	(8)	
10	Tamás Kiss		27/09/79	A		(1)	
29	Tamás Koltai		30/04/87	M	22	(3)	1
42	Norbert Könyves	SRB	10/06/89	A	2	(1)	
77	Róbert Kővári		23/11/95	A	3	(7)	
77	Dávid Kulcsár		25/02/88	M	32		1
96	Bence Lenzsér		09/06/96	D	27		2
12	Péter Molnár	SVK	14/12/83	G	26		
12	Richárd Nagy		15/08/95	M		(1)	
6	Kristóf Papp		04/05/93	M	25	(2)	4
20	István Rodenbücher		22/02/84	D	4	(1)	
30	János Szabó		11/07/89	D	30		1
17	Dénes Szakály		15/03/88	M	15	(10)	5
25	György Székely		02/06/95	G	6		
22	András Vági		25/12/88	D	2	(4)	

Puskás Akadémia FC

2012 • Pancho (3,500) • puskasakademia.hu
Coach: Robert Jarni (CRO);
(17/04/16) István Szijjártó

2015
18/07	a MTK	L 0-1	
26/07	a Debrecen	D 1-1	Pekár
01/08	h Paks	W 1-0	Pekár
08/08	a Újpest	D 2-2	Sallai, og (Heris)
15/08	h Békéscsaba	L 1-2	Márkvárt
22/08	h Vasas	W 1-0	Pekár
29/08	a Honvéd	D 0-0	
12/09	h Haladás	D 1-1	Pekár
19/09	a Diósgyőr	L 2-3	Pekár, Zsótér
26/09	h Ferencváros	D 0-0	
03/10	a Videoton	L 2-3	Pekár, Lencse
17/10	h MTK	L 2-3	Lencse (p), Fodor
24/10	h Debrecen	D 1-1	Lencse
31/10	h Paks	L 2-4	Márkvárt, Tischler
21/11	a Békéscsaba	L 1-2	Pauljević
28/11	h Vasas	W 4-2	Tischler 2, og (Debreceni), Bačelić-Grgić
01/12	h Újpest	D 1-1	Nagy
05/12	h Honvéd	L 0-3	
12/12	a Haladás	L 1-2	Lencse

2016
13/02	h Diósgyőr	W 1-0	Pekár (p)
20/02	a Ferencváros	L 0-2	
27/02	h Videoton	L 0-1	
05/03	a Debrecen	L 2-4	Churko, Mészáros
09/03	h Paks	W 2-1	Churko, Mészáros
12/03	a Ferencváros	L 0-4	
19/03	h Videoton	D 0-0	
02/04	h Haladás	D 1-1	Márkvárt
06/04	a Diósgyőr	L 1-2	Mészáros
09/04	a Újpest	D 2-2	Fiola, Churko
16/04	h Békéscsaba	L 0-1	
20/04	a MTK	W 1-0	Zsótér
23/04	a Vasas	L 0-1	
30/04	h Honvéd	W 2-1	Bačelić-Grgić, Tar

No	Name	Nat	DoB	Pos	Aps	(s)	Gls
8	Stipe Bačelić-Grgić	CRO	16/02/88	M	18	(6)	2
91	Geoffrey Castillion	NED	25/05/91	A	2	(6)	
20	Vyacheslav Churko	UKR	10/05/93	M	11	(1)	3
23	Marko Dinjar	CRO	21/05/86	D	14	(2)	
24	Attila Fiola		17/02/90	D	25		1
5	Ferenc Fodor		22/03/91	D	19	(1)	1
14	Gyula Forró		06/06/88	D	11		
39	Ivan Herceg	CRO	10/02/90	D	3	(3)	
31	Tamás Horváth		18/06/87	G	1		
7	Martin Hudák		22/02/94	M		(8)	
3	Renato Kelić	CRO	31/03/91	D	25		
64	Gergő Kocsis		07/03/94	D	2	(1)	
29	László Lencse		02/07/88	A	15	(2)	4
4	Ádám Lipcsei		22/05/97	D	2	(2)	
42	Márton Lorentz		01/02/95	M		(1)	
7	Dmytro Lyopa	UKR	23/11/88	M	6		
88	Dávid Márkvárt		20/09/94	M	26	(5)	3
11	Karol Mészáros	SVK	25/07/93	M	9	(5)	3
25	Zsolt Nagy		25/05/93	D	9	(9)	1
15	Filip Pajović	SRB	30/07/93	G	5		
49	Branko Pauljević	SRB	12/06/89	M	31		1
77	László Pekár		20/01/93	M	30	(1)	7
50	Bence Péter		18/08/97	A		(1)	
6	Bence Pintér		02/04/96	M	1	(8)	
1	Krisztián Pogacsics		17/10/85	G	27		
18	Attila Polonkai		12/06/79	M	9	(3)	
5	Roland Sallai		22/05/97	M	29	(2)	1
22	Zsolt Tar		13/02/93	D	7	(2)	1
9	Patrik Tischler		30/07/91	A	9	(9)	3
17	László Zsidai		16/07/86	M	12		
27	Donát Zsótér		06/01/96	A	5	(12)	2

Szombathelyi Haladás

1919 • Rohonci úti (12,500); Sopron (6,000) •
haladasfc.nyugat.hu
Coach: Géza Mészöly

2015
19/07	h Ferencváros	L 0-2	
25/07	a Videoton	W 1-0	og (Juhász)
01/08	h MTK	D 2-2	Ugrai, Jagodics
09/08	a Debrecen	W 1-0	Halmosi
15/08	h Paks	W 1-0	Németh
22/08	a Újpest	D 0-0	
29/08	a Békéscsaba	W 1-0	Németh
12/09	a Puskás Akadémia	D 1-1	Németh
19/09	h Honvéd	D 0-0	
26/09	h Vasas	D 1-1	Gaál
03/10	a Diósgyőr	D 1-1	Németh
17/10	a Ferencváros	L 1-3	Nagy
24/10	h Videoton	W 1-0	Gaál
31/10	a MTK	W 1-0	Gaál
21/11	a Paks	L 0-2	
28/11	h Újpest	L 0-3	
02/12	h Debrecen	D 2-2	Martínez, Németh
05/12	h Békéscsaba	D 1-1	Iszlai
12/12	h Puskás Akadémia	W 2-1	Németh, Halmosi

2016
13/02	a Honvéd	W 1-0	S Wils
20/02	a Vasas	L 0-1	
27/02	h Diósgyőr	W 2-1	S Wils, Ugrai
05/03	a Videoton	L 1-2	Popin
09/03	h Újpest	D 1-1	Williams
12/03	a MTK	L 1-3	Ugrai
19/03	a Diósgyőr	L 0-3	
02/04	a Puskás Akadémia	D 1-1	Gaál
06/04	a Vasas	W 2-1	Németh, Gaál
09/04	a Békéscsaba	W 1-0	Williams
16/04	a Honvéd	W 1-0	Iszlai (p)
20/04	h Debrecen	D 2-2	Gaál, Halmosi
23/04	a Paks	W 3-2	T Wils, og (Rodenbücher), Gaál
30/04	h Ferencváros	L 0-1	

No	Name	Nat	DoB	Pos	Aps	(s)	Gls
24	Zsolt Angyal		24/03/94	D	22	(3)	
25	Ante Batarelo	CRO	21/11/84	M	2	(4)	
35	Predrag Bošnjak		13/11/85	D	31		
3	Zoltán Fehér		12/06/81	D	3	(3)	
14	Bálint Gaál		14/07/91	A	23	(3)	7
18	András Gosztonyi		07/11/90	A	9	(6)	
7	Gergő Gyürki		03/10/93	A		(3)	
79	Péter Halmosi		25/09/79	M	27	(2)	3
15	Bence Iszlai		29/05/90	M	28		2
26	Márk Jagodics		12/04/92	D	22	(1)	1
4	Gábor Jánvári		25/04/90	D	9	(3)	
1	Gábor Király		01/04/76	G	33		
27	Lóránt Kovács	ROU	06/06/93	M	12		
10	Leandro Martínez	ITA	15/10/89	A	10	(7)	1
77	Zoltán Medgyes		23/07/95	A	7	(20)	
31	Patrik Nagy		16/02/91	M	6	(11)	1
31	Márió Németh		01/05/95	A	26	(5)	7
80	Balázs Petró		01/07/97	M		(1)	
89	Saša Popin	SRB	28/10/89	A	5	(9)	1
23	Szabolcs Schimmer		24/02/84	M	11	(2)	
70	Roland Ugrai		13/11/92	A	10	(7)	3
11	David Williams	AUS	26/02/88	A	13	(1)	2
6	Stef Wils	BEL	08/02/82	D	28		2
20	Thomas Wils	BEL	24/04/90	M	26	(2)	1

Újpest FC

1885 • Szusza Ferenc (13,500) • ujpestfc.hu
Major honours
Hungarian League (20) 1930, 1931, 1933, 1935, 1939, 1945, 1946, 1947, 1960, 1969, 1970, 1971, 1972, 1973, 1974, 1975, 1978, 1979, 1990, 1998; Hungarian Cup (9) 1969, 1970, 1975, 1982, 1983, 1987, 1992, 2002, 2014
Coach: Nebojša Vignjević (SRB)

2015
18/07	h Paks	D 0-0	
25/07	a Vasas	W 3-1	Mohl, Sallói, Sanković
01/08	h Békéscsaba	W 2-0	Kálnoki Kis, Perović
08/08	h Puskás Akadémia	D 2-2	Perović, Bardi
15/08	h Honvéd	D 1-1	Tóth
22/08	h Haladás	D 0-0	
29/08	a Diósgyőr	L 1-2	Balogh (p)
12/09	h Ferencváros	L 1-2	Diagne
19/09	a Videoton	L 0-3	
26/09	h MTK	D 2-2	Diagne, Bardi
03/10	a Debrecen	D 1-1	Diagne
17/10	a Paks	L 0-1	
24/10	h Vasas	W 2-0	Diagne 2 (1p)
31/10	a Békéscsaba	W 3-1	Diagne, Perović, Balogh
21/11	a Honvéd	W 2-1	Diagne, Hazard
28/11	a Haladás	W 3-0	Hazard, Litauszki, Diagne
01/12	a Puskás Akadémia	D 1-1	Diagne
05/12	h Diósgyőr	D 2-2	Bardi, Diagne
12/12	h Ferencváros	W 1-0	Diagne

2016
13/02	h Videoton	W 1-0	Hazard
20/02	h MTK	D 1-1	Andrić
27/02	h Debrecen	D 1-1	Lencse (p)
05/03	a MTK	L 1-2	Bardi
09/03	a Haladás	D 1-1	Lencse
12/03	h Diósgyőr	W 1-0	Andrić
19/03	a Békéscsaba	L 0-1	
02/04	a Vasas	L 2-3	Andrić, Bardi
06/04	h Honvéd	W 2-0	Balogh, Bardi
09/04	h Puskás Akadémia	D 2-2	Balogh, Kabát
16/04	a Debrecen	L 0-1	
20/04	h Paks	D 1-1	Windecker
23/04	a Ferencváros	D 2-2	Andrić, Lencse
30/04	h Videoton	L 0-3	

No	Name	Nat	DoB	Pos	Aps	(s)	Gls
19	Nemanja Andrić	SRB	13/06/87	M	19	(6)	4
17	Viktor Angelov	MKD	27/03/94	M	5	(5)	
1	Szabolcs Balajcza		14/07/79	G	31		
21	Benjámin Balázs		26/04/90	M	11	(2)	
8	Balázs Balogh		11/06/90	M	29	(1)	4
23	Dávid Banai		09/05/94	G		(1)	
29	Enis Bardi	MKD	02/07/95	M	23	(6)	6
26	Benjámin Cseke		22/07/94	M	4	(12)	
9	Mbaye Diagne	SEN	28/10/91	A	13	(1)	11
9	Souleymane Diarra	MLI	30/01/95	M	8	(3)	
88	Attila Filkor		12/07/88	M	3	(4)	
17	Gyula Forró		06/06/88	D	3	(1)	
7	Kylian Hazard	BEL	05/08/95	M	26	(3)	3
3	Jonathan Heris	BEL	03/09/90	D	24		
22	Péter Kabát		25/09/77	A	1	(13)	1
4	Dávid Kálnoki Kis		06/08/91	D	22		
15	Ákos Kecskés		04/01/96	D	7	(2)	
32	Zoltán Kovács		29/10/84	G	2		
9	László Lencse		02/07/88	A	12	(1)	3
5	Róbert Litauszki		15/03/90	D	29	(1)	1
13	Dávid Mohl		28/04/85	D	27	(3)	1
14	Gábor Nagy		16/10/85	M	9	(2)	
2	Tibor Nagy		14/08/91	D	8	(1)	
11	Mihailo Perović	MNE	23/01/97	A	3	(5)	3
30	Dániel Sallói		19/07/96	A	7	(5)	1
18	Bojan Sanković	MNE	21/11/93	M	21	(2)	1
99	Asmir Suljić	BIH	11/09/91	A	5		
24	Patrik Tóth		31/07/96	A	1	(5)	1
25	Viktor Vadász		15/08/86	D	1	(2)	
6	József Windecker		02/12/92	M	9	(3)	1

Vasas FC

1911 • Illovszky Rudolf (18,000) • vasasfutballclub.hu

Major honours
Hungarian League (6) 1957, 1961, 1962, 1965, 1966, 1977; Hungarian Cup (4) 1955, 1973, 1981, 1986

Coach: Károly Szanyó;
(19/10/15) Antal Simon;
(02/01/16) Michael Oenning (GER)

2015

18/07	a	Diósgyőr	L 1-2	Lázok
25/07	h	Újpest	L 1-3	Remili
01/08	h	Ferencváros	L 0-2	
08/08	a	Békéscsaba	W 2-0	Remili, Novák
15/08	a	Videoton	W 2-1	Novák, Remili
22/08	a	Puskás Akadémia	L 0-1	
29/08	h	MTK	L 0-1	
12/09	a	Honvéd	W 1-0	Osváth
19/09	h	Debrecen	L 0-1	
26/09	a	Haladás	D 1-1	Kenesei (p)
03/10	a	Paks	L 1-2	Remili
17/10	h	Diósgyőr	L 0-1	
24/10	a	Újpest	L 0-2	
31/10	a	Ferencváros	L 1-5	Ubiparip
21/11	a	Videoton	L 0-2	
28/11	h	Puskás Akadémia	L 2-4	Ádám, Czvitkovics
02/12	h	Békéscsaba	W 4-0	Könyves 2, Pavlov, Kenesei (p)
05/12	a	MTK	L 1-2	Pavlov
12/12	h	Honvéd	W 2-1	Kenesei (p), Debreceni

2016

13/02	a	Debrecen	L 0-4	
20/02	h	Haladás	W 1-0	Ferenczi (p)
27/02	a	Paks	L 0-3	
05/03	h	Honvéd	D 0-0	
08/03	h	Debrecen	D 0-0	
12/03	a	Paks	L 0-2	
19/03	h	Ferencváros	L 1-4	Pavlov
02/04	h	Újpest	W 3-2	Ádám, Könyves, Hangya
06/04	a	Haladás	L 1-2	Müller
09/04	a	Videoton	D 2-2	Remili 2
16/04	h	Diósgyőr	L 1-3	Ferenczi
19/04	a	Békéscsaba	D 1-1	og (Laczkó)
23/04	h	Puskás Akadémia	L 0-2	Korcsmár
30/04	a	MTK	W 2-0	Vida, Pavlov

No	Name	Nat	DoB	Pos	Aps	(s)	Gls
8	Martin Ádám		06/11/94	A	17	(4)	2
12	Miloš Adamović	SRB	19/06/88	M	11	(5)	
13	Zsombor Berecz		13/12/95	M	23	(6)	
21	Gábor Bori		16/01/84	M		(2)	
77	Péter Czvitkovics		10/02/83	M	11	(3)	1
89	András Debreceni		21/04/89	D	25	(1)	1
39	István Ferenczi		14/09/77	A		(5)	2
15	Mátyás Gál		18/03/92	M		(1)	
17	Dávid Görgényi		16/08/90	D		(1)	
26	Tamás Grúz		08/11/85	D	17		
7	Szilveszter Hangya		02/01/94	M	26		1
31	Bence Hermány		27/04/90	G	10	(1)	
9	Ilias Ignatidis	GRE	11/11/96	A	1	(2)	
20	Krisztián Kenesei		07/01/77	A	2	(7)	3
15	Norbert Könyves	SRB	10/06/89	A	12	(7)	3
21	Zsolt Korcsmár		09/01/89	D	14		1
19	János Lázok		04/10/84	A	9	(4)	1
37	Christian Müller	GER	28/02/84	M	12		1
29	Benedek Murka		10/09/97	A		(2)	
1	Gergely Nagy		27/05/94	G	23		
99	Csanád Novák		24/09/94	A	13	(10)	2
2	Attila Osváth		10/12/95	D	10	(1)	1
33	Tomislav Pajović	SRB	15/03/86	D	17		
16	Yevhen Pavlov	UKR	23/12/91	A	9	(12)	4
14	Csaba Preklet		25/01/91	D	11	(3)	
10	Mohamed Remili		31/05/85	A	26	(1)	6
4	Kire Ristevski	MKD	22/10/90	D	11	(1)	
93	Danijel Romić	CRO	19/03/93	D	2	(1)	
6	Donát Szivacski		18/01/97	M	6	(2)	
22	Vojo Ubiparip	SRB	10/05/88	A	5	(4)	1
23	Máté Vida		08/03/96	M	26	(5)	1
5	Marko Vukasović	MNE	10/09/90	M	13	(2)	

Videoton FC

1941 • Sóstói (15,000); Pancho, Felcsút (3,500) • vidi.hu

Major honours
Hungarian League (2) 2011, 2015; Hungarian Cup (1) 2006

Coach: Bernard Casoni (FRA);
(19/08/15) (Tamás Pető);
(06/10/15) Ferenc Horváth

2015

18/07	a	Honvéd	L 0-1	
25/07	h	Haladás	L 0-1	
01/08	a	Diósgyőr	W 2-1	Filipe Oliveira, Pátkai
08/08	h	Ferencváros	L 1-3	Ivanovski
15/08	h	Vasas	L 1-2	Kovács
23/08	a	MTK	L 0-1	
30/08	h	Debrecen	W 1-0	Filipe Oliveira
12/09	a	Paks	L 0-2	
19/09	h	Újpest	W 3-0	Gyurcsó 2 (1p), Kovács
26/09	a	Békéscsaba	L 0-2	
03/10	h	Puskás Akadémia	W 3-2	Gyurcsó 2, Suljić
17/10	h	Honvéd	W 3-0	Feczesin, Gyurcsó, Juhász
24/10	a	Haladás	L 0-2	
31/10	h	Diósgyőr	W 2-1	Sejben, Nego
21/11	h	Vasas	W 2-0	Kovács, Gyurcsó
28/11	h	MTK	W 1-0	Filipe Oliveira
02/12	a	Ferencváros	L 0-1	
05/12	a	Debrecen	W 2-1	Gyurcsó, Kovács
12/12	h	Paks	W 1-0	Géresi

2016

13/02	a	Újpest	L 0-1	
20/02	h	Békéscsaba	D 1-1	og (Vaskó)
27/02	a	Puskás Akadémia	W 1-0	Feczesin
05/03	h	Haladás	W 2-1	Filipe Oliveira, Feczesin (p)
09/03	h	Diósgyőr	L 1-2	Nego
12/03	h	Békéscsaba	D 1-1	Stopira
19/03	a	Puskás Akadémia	D 0-0	
02/04	a	Honvéd	L 0-1	Feczesin
05/04	h	Debrecen	W 1-0	Feczesin
09/04	h	Vasas	D 2-2	Géresi, Nego
16/04	a	Paks	W 1-0	og (Papp)
20/04	h	Ferencváros	W 1-0	Stopira
23/04	h	MTK	W 5-0	Nego 2, og (Grgić), Tischler, Suljić
30/04	a	Újpest	W 3-0	Nego, Tischler, Juhász

No	Name	Nat	DoB	Pos	Aps	(s)	Gls
44	Branislav Danilović	SRB	24/06/88	G	25		
9	Róbert Feczesin		22/02/86	A	21	(5)	5
6	András Fejes		26/08/88	D	9	(2)	
16	Filipe Oliveira	POR	27/05/84	M	24	(6)	4
49	Krisztián Géresi		14/06/94	M	5	(8)	2
7	Ádám Gyurcsó		06/03/91	A	15	(2)	7
88	Zsolt Haraszti		04/11/91	A	8	(4)	
5	Tibor Heffler		17/05/87	D	6	(4)	
19	Mirko Ivanovski	MKD	31/10/89	A	4	(4)	1
23	Roland Juhász		01/07/83	D	24		2
11	Tamás Koltai		30/04/87	M	1	(1)	
10	István Kovács		27/03/92	M	20	(6)	4
74	Ádám Kovácsik		04/04/91	G	7		
18	Ádám Lang		17/01/93	D	16		
4	Kees Luijckx	NED	11/02/86	D	3	(2)	
31	Rémi Maréval	FRA	24/02/83	D	2		
2	Loïc Nego	FRA	15/01/91	D	23	(3)	6
77	Filip Pajović	SRB	30/07/93	G	1		
17	Máté Pátkai		06/03/88	M	28	(1)	1
3	Paulo Vinícius	BRA	21/02/90	D	25	(2)	
8	Zsolt Pölöskei		19/02/91	A	13	(7)	
15	Viktor Sejben		04/06/96	M		(9)	1
46	Ádám Simon		30/03/90	M	18	(2)	
27	Alhassane Soumah	GUI	02/03/96	A	2	(9)	
22	Stopira	CPV	20/05/88	D	14	(2)	2
99	Asmir Suljić	BIH	11/09/91	A	22	(2)	2
30	Roland Szolnoki		21/01/92	D	18	(3)	
19	Patrik Tischler		30/07/91	A	5	(6)	2
33	Dinko Trebotić	CRO	30/07/90	M	2	(2)	

Top goalscorers

17	Dániel Böde (Ferencváros)
11	Sándor Torghelle (MTK)
	Mbaye Diagne (Újpest)
9	Djordje Kamber (Honvéd)
	Stanislav Šesták (Ferencváros)
8	Soma Novothny (Diósgyőr)
7	Roland Lamah (Ferencváros)
	Roland Varga (Ferencváros)
	József Kanta (MTK)
	János Hahn (Paks)
	László Lencse (Puskás Akadémia/Újpest)
	László Pekár (Puskás Akadémia)
	Bálint Gaál (Haladás)
	Márió Németh (Haladás)
	Ádám Gyurcsó (Videoton)

Promoted clubs

Gyirmót FC Győr

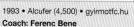

1993 • Alcufer (4,500) • gyirmotfc.hu
Coach: Ferenc Bene

Mezőkövesd-Zsóry SE

1975 • Városi (5,200) • mezokovesdzsory.hu
Coach: Miklós Benczés;
(10/11/15) (László Tóth);
(30/12/15) Attila Pintér

Second level final table 2015/16

		Pld	W	D	L	F	A	Pts
1	Gyirmót FC Győr	30	20	5	5	58	28	65
2	Mezőkövesd-Zsóry SE	30	17	6	7	45	25	57
3	Zalaegerszegi TE	30	17	4	9	55	30	55
4	Várda SE	30	15	7	8	63	36	52
5	Balmazújvárosi FC	30	15	6	9	46	39	51
6	Csákvári TK	30	15	3	12	55	55	48
7	Soroksár SC	30	13	8	9	45	29	47
8	Budaörsi SC	30	13	4	13	45	43	43
9	BFC Siófok	30	12	5	13	36	47	41
10	Szeged 2011	30	11	7	12	42	40	40
11	Vác FC	30	8	3	17	32	51	33
12	Soproni VSE	30	9	6	15	38	42	33
13	Szolnoki MÁV FC	30	7	10	13	34	41	31
14	Szigetszentmiklósi TK	30	9	15	31	61	27	
15	Dunaújváros PASE	30	6	9	15	32	63	27
16	FC Ajka	30	4	8	18	24	51	20

DOMESTIC CUP

Magyar Kupa 2015/16

FIRST ROUND

(05/08/15)
Babócsa 0-2 Mátészalka
Nagyecsed 4-3 REAC
Tiszakanyár 1-1 Nyírbátor *(aet; 5-4 on pens)*

(09/08/15)
Vép 2-0 Nagyréde

(11/08/15)
Bajai LSE 0-5 Zalaegerszeg

(12/08/15)
Ásotthalom 4-0 Szerencs
Bácsalmás 5-1 MTE 1904
Balatonalmádi 0-5 Velence
BKV Előre 3-1 Kazincbarcika
Bölcske 2-4 Balmazújváros
Bonyhád 3-2 Hatvan *(aet)*
Celldömölk 2-1 Iváncsa
Ceredvölgye 0-4 Csákvár
Cigánd 3-1 Szentlőrinc
Csepel 0-1 Békéscsaba
Csorna 0-2 Diósgyőr
Dabas 0-3 Vác
DAC 0-5 Szekszárd
Dudar 0-2 Újbuda
Érd 0-2 Tállya
ETO Futsal 0-2 Honvéd
Felsőtárkány 2-3 Dorog *(aet)*
Füzesgyarmat 1-4 Budaörs
Gyöngyös 1-0 Dunaújváros *(aet)*
Hajdúböszörmény 1-0 SZEOL
Hajdúszoboszló 1-4 Rákosmente
Hévíz 0-1 Szolnok
Hidasnémeti 0-12 Vasas
Hódmezővásárhely 1-2 Gyula
Jászberény 0-2 Ajka
Komló 3-2 Szigetszentmiklós
Kozármisleny 4-2 Siófok *(aet)*
Lenti 0-2 Pénzügyőr
Maglód 1-6 Paks
Mezőhegyes 3-2 Szajol
Monor 1-3 Szeged 2011
Nagyatád 0-8 Cegléd
Nagykáta 0-12 Várda
Nyúl 1-3 Haladás
Salgótarjáni BTC 1-4 DTC-Select
Sárisáp 0-7 Soroksár
Sárrétudvari 0-5 Puskás Akadémia
Siklós 4-3 Sárvár
Somogyvár 2-6 Dunaharaszti
Tatabánya 0-2 Soproni VSE
Tiszaújváros 4-1 ESMTK
Tököl 1-2 Gyirmót
Veresegyház 0-2 Mezőkövesd-Zsóry
Vértessomló 1-14 Újpest
Viadukt SE 2-2 III. Kerületi TVE *(aet; 4-5 on pens)*

(13/08/15)
Nyíregyháza 2-0 Putnok *(aet)*

Byes – Andráshida, Balatonfüred, Debrecen, Ferencváros, Géderlaki KSE, Inter CGF, MTK, Somos, Videoton

SECOND ROUND

(22/09/15)
Kozármisleny 2-0 Puskás Akadémia
Szolnok 1-2 Vasas

(23/09/15)
Andráshida 4-2 DTC-Select *(aet)*
Ásotthalom 1-2 Nagyecsed
Bácsalmás 3-5 Zalaegerszeg
Balatonfüred 0-7 Diósgyőr
BKV Előre 0-3 Soproni VSE
Bonyhád 0-2 Honvéd
Cegléd 1-3 Várda
Celldömölk 0-9 Újpest
Cigánd 2-4 Soroksár
Dorog 1-1 Gyirmót *(aet; 5-4 on pens)*
Géderlaki KSE 2-1 Tiszakanyár
Gyöngyös 0-2 Paks *(aet)*
Gyula 1-2 Szeged 2011 *(aet)*
III. Kerületi TVE 2-0 Budaörs
Inter CGF 5-1 Hajdúböszörmény
Mátészalka 0-5 Balmazújváros
Mezőkövesd-Zsóry 0-2 Békéscsaba *(aet)*
Nyíregyháza 4-0 Vác
Pénzügyőr 1-3 Haladás
Rákosmente 2-3 Ajka
Siklós 1-4 Velence *(aet)*
Szekszárd 0-3 Dunaharaszti
Tállya 0-3 Csákvár
Tiszaújváros 2-1 Komló
Újbuda 0-1 Somos
Vép 0-2 Mezőhegyes

Byes – Debrecen, Ferencváros, MTK, Videoton

THIRD ROUND

(13/10/15)
Balmazújváros 2-3 Soproni VSE
Dunaharaszti 0-1 Zalaegerszeg

(14/10/15)
Andráshida 0-2 Videoton
Dorog 1-3 Csákvár
Géderlaki KSE 0-3 Debrecen
Inter CGF 2-1 III. Kerületi TVE
Kozármisleny 1-0 Diósgyőr
Mezőhegyes 0-6 MTK
Nagyecsed 0-10 Ferencváros
Somos 1-3 Haladás
Soroksár 3-5 Honvéd *(aet)*
Tiszaújváros 4-3 Paks
Várda 1-2 Békéscsaba
Velence 1-2 Újpest

(15/10/15)
Szeged 2011 1-0 Ajka

(21/10/15)
Nyíregyháza 1-1 Vasas *(aet; 5-3 on pens)*

FOURTH ROUND

(27/10/15 & 17/11/15)
Békéscsaba 0-0, 1-0 MTK *(1-0)*

(28/10/15 & 18/11/15)
Ferencváros 4-1, 3-4 Csákvár *(7-5)*
Haladás 0-1, 1-1 Videoton *(1-2)*
Honvéd 1-2, 1-2 Kozármisleny *(2-4)*
Nyíregyháza 4-1, 0-0 Soproni VSE *(4-1)*
Szeged 2011 0-0, 0-3 Debrecen *(0-3)*
Tiszaújváros 3-0, 1-0 Inter CGF *(4-0)*
Zalaegerszeg 0-5, 1-1 Újpest *(1-6)*

QUARTER-FINALS

(09/02/16 & 01/03/16)
Nyíregyháza 1-2 Debrecen *(Rezes 25; Brković 37, Ferenczi 90+4)*
Debrecen 5-0 Nyíregyháza *(Takács 16, 37, 52, Tisza 71, Djelmić 85)*
(Debrecen 7-1)

(10/02/16 & 02/03/16)
Békéscsaba 2-1 Kozármisleny *(Birtalan 6, Kovács 27og; Beke 16)*
Kozármisleny 1-1 Békéscsaba *(Kocsis 12; Punoševac53)*
(Békéscsaba 3-2)

Ferencváros 0-1 Videoton *(Feczesin 42)*
Videoton 1-2 Ferencváros *(Stopira 22; Böde 52, Kovácsik 82og)*
(2-2; Ferencváros on away goals)

Újpest 8-1 Tiszaújváros *(Andrić 42, 48, Balogh 45, 57, Katona 60og, Bardi 62, Hazard 65, Mohl 73; Katona 11)*
Tiszaújváros 0-2 Újpest *(Cseke 61, Kabát 79)*
(Újpest 10-1)

SEMI-FINALS

(16/03/16 & 12/04/16)
Újpest 2-0 Békéscsaba *(Lencse 53, 87)*
Békéscsaba 1-1 Újpest *(Birtalan 36; Andrić 65)*
(Újpest 3-1)

(16/03/16 & 13/04/16)
Debrecen 0-0 Ferencváros
Ferencváros 3-0 Debrecen *(Gera 22p, 79, D Nagy 90)*
(Ferencváros 3-0)

FINAL

(07/05/16)
Groupama Aréna, Budapest
FERENCVÁROSI TC 1 *(Gera 79)*
ÚJPEST FC 0
Referee: Iványi
FERENCVÁROS: Dibusz, Dilaver, Nalepa *(Radó 46)*, Leandro, Ramírez, Pintér, Gera, Varga *(Čukić 88)*, Hajnal, Lamah *(Gyömbér 56)*, Böde
ÚJPEST: Balajcza, Heris, Litauszki, Kecskés, Balogh, Cseke, Sanković, Hazard *(Mohl 33)*, Bardi *(Kabát 85)*, Andrić *(Diarra 73)*, Lencse

ICELAND
Knattspyrnusamband Íslands (KSÍ)

Address	Laugardal	**President**	Geir Thorsteinsson
	IS-104 Reykjavík	**Media officer**	Oskar Örn
Tel	+354 510 2900		Gudbrandsson
Fax	+354 568 9793	**Year of formation**	1947
E-mail	ksi@ksi.is	**National stadium**	Laugardalsvöllur,
Website	ksi.is		Reykjavik (15,182)

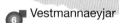

Ólafsvík
13

~Kópavogur
1
5 Akranes
2 ~Hafnarfjördur
Reykjavík~ 3 4 8 9 11 12 14
Keflavík
7
Gardabær~ 10

6 Vestmannaeyjar

KEY

● UEFA Champions League
● UEFA Europa League
● Promoted
● Relegated

ÚRVALSDEILD CLUBS

 1 **Breidablik**

 2 **FH Hafnarfjördur**

 3 **Fjölnir**

 4 **Fylkir**

 5 **ÍA Akranes**

 6 **ÍBV Vestmannaeyjar**

 7 **Keflavík**

 8 **KR Reykjavík**

 9 **Leiknir Reykjavík**

 10 **Stjarnan**

 11 **Valur Reykjavík**

 12 **Víkingur Reykjavík**

PROMOTED CLUBS

 13 **Víkingur Ólafsvík**

 14 **Thróttur Reykjavík**

FH enter seventh heaven

In the year that Icelandic football broke new ground with the national team's first ever qualification for a major tournament, there was a familiar outcome to the domestic title race as FH, denied at the last in 2014, recovered to claim their seventh national crown in 12 years. Valur, meanwhile, ended a ten-year wait to capture their tenth Icelandic Cup.

The big story, however, was the fairytale written by the Icelandic national side, who, expertly led by joint coaches Lars Lagerbäck and Heimir Hallgrímsson, defied logic and reason by going all the way to the quarter-finals of UEFA EURO 2016.

Hafnarfjordur club end three-year wait for title

Valur defeat holders KR to win cup final

National team heroes make history in France

Domestic league

The traumatic conclusion to the 2014 Úrvalsdeild, when FH lost the title with the season's final kick, left no visible scars on coach Heimir Gudjónsson and his players. Time appeared to be the healer as the seven-month gap between the end of the old campaign and the start of the new one eroded the unhappy memories of Stjarnan's last-minute winning penalty at their Kaplakriki stadium. Although FH suffered an early defeat to Valur – it had taken them until that fateful final round to lose a game in 2014 – their reaction was positive, and by the midpoint of the campaign they led the way, with Breidablik and KR in close pursuit.

KR actually leapfrogged their way to the top of the standings when they inflicted a second defeat of the campaign on FH in round 12, but the record champions from Reykjavik drew their next game 0-0 with Breidablik and then suffered a surprise loss at Fjölnir, enabling FH to retake the lead and then extend it with a stunning seven-win sequence that effectively ended the title race as a contest. Breidablik delayed FH's celebrations by beating them 2-1 in round 20, but the gap at the top was still five points in FH's favour – with KR now out for the count after three games without a win – and six days later Gudjónsson and his players

were able to pop the champagne corks after a 2-1 home win against Fjölnir, the 79th-minute winner having been scored, perhaps inevitably, by midfielder Emil Pálsson, who had returned from a loan spell at Fjölnir only a few weeks earlier.

Breidablik reduced FH's final margin of victory to two points, with their last seven games yielding five wins and two draws. While the champions won more games and scored considerably more goals than the runners-up, Arnar Grétarsson's side were the toughest team in the league to beat. They lost just twice, with their resilient defence, underpinned by ever-present 40-year-old goalkeeper Gunnleifur Gunnleifsson, the league's oldest participant, conceding a mere 13 goals and keeping clean sheets in exactly half of their fixtures.

Domestic cup

KR's fade-out in the title race was preceded, perhaps triggered, by defeat in the final of the Icelandic Cup. Bidding to win the trophy for the fourth time in five years, they were found wanting against a Valur outfit who had already beaten them 3-0 in the league. Two goals in the final quarter at the Laugardalsvöllur, from defender Bjarni Eiríksson and midfielder Kristinn Halldórsson (rather than Danish No9 Patrick Pedersen, who would scoop

the Úrvalsdeild golden boot), brought the Reykjavik Reds a first cup win in a decade and tenth in all, putting them second alone to their vanquished city rivals (14 wins) in the competition's roll of honour.

Europe

Stjarnan, who finished a disappointing fourth in defence of their league title, were also unable to reprise their European heroics of the previous season, with a tough draw against Scottish champions Celtic predictably strangling their UEFA Champions League campaign at birth.

National team

Iceland not only made history by qualifying for UEFA EURO 2016, but the smallest country (in population terms) ever to participate in the final tournament had immense fun when they got there, finishing second in their group thanks to draws against Portugal and Hungary and a last-gasp winner against Austria before sensationally beating England 2-1 in the round of 16. It was estimated that around ten percent of the country's 350,000 inhabitants travelled to support their team in France. Even though the hosts brought their magical journey to a brusque end in the quarter-finals, they certainly got their money's worth.

DOMESTIC SEASON AT A GLANCE

Úrvalsdeild 2015 final table

		Pld	Home					Away					Total					Pts
			W	D	L	F	A	W	D	L	F	A	W	D	L	F	A	
1	FH Hafnarfjördur	22	8	2	1	26	12	7	1	3	21	14	15	3	4	47	26	48
2	Breidablik	22	8	2	1	22	6	5	5	1	12	7	13	7	2	34	13	46
3	KR Reykjavík	22	6	3	2	19	11	6	3	2	17	10	12	6	4	36	21	42
4	Stjarnan	22	3	4	4	17	11	6	2	3	15	13	9	6	7	32	24	33
5	Valur Reykjavík	22	5	2	4	21	17	4	4	3	17	14	9	6	7	38	31	33
6	Fjölnir	22	6	3	2	17	12	3	3	5	19	23	9	6	7	36	35	33
7	ÍA Akranes	22	4	4	3	17	14	3	4	4	14	17	7	8	7	31	31	29
8	Fylkir	22	4	3	4	15	19	3	5	3	11	12	7	8	7	26	31	29
9	Víkingur Reykjavík	22	3	6	2	18	13	2	2	7	14	23	5	8	9	32	36	23
10	ÍBV Vestmannaeyjar	22	4	3	4	20	17	1	1	9	6	20	5	4	13	26	37	19
11	Leiknir Reykjavík	22	2	2	7	7	14	1	4	6	13	20	3	6	13	20	34	15
12	Keflavík	22	2	2	7	13	22	0	2	9	9	39	2	4	16	22	61	10

European qualification 2016/17

Champion: FH Hafnarfjördur (second qualifying round)

Cup winner: Valur Reykjavík (first qualifying round)
Breidablik (first qualifying round)
KR Reykjavík (first qualifying round)

Top scorer Patrick Pedersen (Valur), 13 goals
Relegated clubs Keflavík, Leiknir Reykjavík
Promoted clubs Víkingur Ólafsvík, Thróttur Reykjavík
Cup final Valur Reykjavík 2-0 KR Reykjavík

Team of the season
(4-3-3)

Coach: Gudjónsson *(FH)*

Player of the season

Emil Pálsson
(Fjölnir/FH Hafnarfjördur)

A champion of Iceland with FH in 2012 and a frustrated runner-up in 2014, Pálsson was sent out on loan to Fjölnir at the start of the 2015 season. Halfway through it, however, he was back at his parent club, and the 22-year-old midfielder was to have a profound influence on FH's surge to the title, scoring six goals in his 12 matches, including the winner in the game that clinched their triumph – against, of all clubs, Fjölnir. Voted Úrvalsdeild player of the season, he won his first senior cap for Iceland in January.

Newcomer of the season

Oliver Sigurjónsson
(Breidablik)

Breidablik's prolonged challenge for the 2015 Icelandic league title was constructed on the foundations of a rock-solid defence, with Damir Muminovic, Kristinn Jónsson and veteran 'keeper Gunnleifur Gunnleifsson its key components. Further up field, the man who most frequently caught the eye was midfield schemer Sigurjónsson, a long-time Icelandic youth international, whose reward for a season of unerring consistency was a first full cap for his country – in a November friendly against Slovakia – at the age of 20.

NATIONAL TEAM

International tournament appearances

UEFA European Championship (1) 2016 (qtr-finals)

Top five all-time caps

Rúnar Kristinsson (104); Hermann Hreidarsson (89); **Eidur Smári Gudjohnsen** (88); Gudni Bergsson (80); Brynjar Björn Gunnarsson & Birkir Kristinsson (74)

Top five all-time goals

Eidur Smári Gudjohnsen (26); Kolbeinn **Sigthórsson (22)**; Ríkhardur Jónsson (17); Ríkhardur Dadason, Arnór Gudjohnsen & **Gylfi Thór Sigurdsson (14)**

Results 2015/16

03/09/15	Netherlands (ECQ)	A	Amsterdam	W	1-0	G Sigurdsson (51p)
06/09/15	Kazakhstan (ECQ)	H	Reykjavik	D	0-0	
10/10/15	Latvia (ECQ)	H	Reykjavik	D	2-2	Sigthórsson (5), G Sigurdsson (27)
13/10/15	Turkey (ECQ)	A	Konya	L	0-1	
13/11/15	Poland	A	Warsaw	L	2-4	G Sigurdsson (4p), A Finnbogason (69)
17/11/15	Slovakia	A	Zilina	L	1-3	A Finnbogason (8)
13/01/16	Finland	N	Abu Dhabi (UAE)	W	1-0	Traustason (16)
16/01/16	United Arab Emirates	A	Dubai	L	1-2	Kjartansson (14)
31/01/16	United States	A	Carson	L	2-3	Steindórsson (12), Sigurdarson (48)
24/03/16	Denmark	A	Herning	L	1-2	Traustason (90)
29/03/16	Greece	A	Piraeus	W	3-2	Traustason (34), Ingason (70), Sigthórsson (82)
01/06/16	Norway	A	Oslo	L	2-3	Ingason (36), G Sigurdsson (81p)
06/06/16	Liechtenstein	H	Reykjavik	W	4-0	Sigthórsson (10), Sævarsson (20), A Finnbogason (42), Gudjohnsen (82)
14/06/16	Portugal (ECF)	N	Saint-Etienne (FRA)	D	1-1	B Bjarnason (50)
18/06/16	Hungary (ECF)	N	Marseille (FRA)	D	1-1	G Sigurdsson (40p)
22/06/16	Austria (ECF)	N	Saint-Denis (FRA)	W	2-1	Bödvarsson (18), Traustason (90+4)
27/06/16	England (ECF)	N	Nice (FRA)	W	2-1	R Sigurdsson (6), Sigthórsson (18)
03/07/16	France (ECF)	A	Saint-Denis	L	2-5	Sigthórsson (56), B Bjarnason (84)

Appearances 2015/16

Coach: Lars Lagerbäck (SWE) 16/07/48
& Heimir Hallgrímsson 10/06/67

Player	DoB	Club	NED	KAZ	LVA	TUR	Pol	Svk	Fin	Uae	Usa	Den	Gre	Nor	Lie	POR	HUN	AUT	ENG	FRA	Caps	Goals
Hannes Thór Halldórsson	27/04/84	NEC (NED)/Bodø/Glimt (NOR)	G	G	G							s46		G	G	G	G	G	G	38	-
Birkir Már Sævarsson	11/11/84	Hammarby (SWE)	D	D	D	D	D	s55		D		D		D	D	D	D	D	D	62	1
Kári Árnason	13/10/82	Malmö (SWE)	D	D	D18	D		D76	D		D				D	D	D	D	D46	52	2
Ragnar Sigurdsson	19/06/86	Krasnodar (RUS)	D	D	D	D	D	s76	D46	D	D		D	D54	D	D	D	D	D	61	2
Ari Freyr Skúlason	14/05/87	OB (DEN)	D	D	D	D	D	D55		D84		D		D87	D	D	D	D	D	43	-
Jóhann Berg Gudmundsson	27/10/90	Charlton (ENG)	M	M	M	M	s76	M81			s46	M	M	M46	M90	M	M86	M	M	52	5
Aron Einar Gunnarsson	22/04/89	Cardiff (ENG)	M86	M89*		M	M46				M	M46	M82	M	M	M65	M	M	M	64	3
Gylfi Thór Sigurdsson	08/09/89	Swansea (ENG)	M	M	M	M					M81	s46	M	M	M	M	M	M	M	44	14
Birkir Bjarnason	27/05/88	Basel (SUI)	M	M	M	M	M46	M10			M71	s46	s46		M	M	M	M	M	52	8
Jón Dadi Bödvarsson	25/05/92	Viking (NOR)/Kaiserslautern (GER)	A78	A85		A82	A76	s19			s71	A83	A46	A	A69	A71	A89	A46		26	2
Kolbeinn Sigthórsson	14/03/90	Nantes (FRA)	A64	A	A	A88	A16	A			A71	s61	s62	A79	A81	A84	A80	A76	A83	44	22
Eidur Smári Gudjohnsen	15/09/78	Shijiazhuang (CHN)/unattached/Molde (NOR)	s64		s65				M	A60	A71			s46	s46		s84		s83	88	26
Alfred Finnbogason	01/02/89	Olympiacos (GRE)/Augsburg (GER)	s78	A65	s88	s16	A90					A	s83	A62	A46	s81	s69		s46	37	8
Ólafur Ingi Skúlason	01/04/83	Gençlerbirliği (TUR)	s86																	26	1
Vidar Örn Kjartansson	11/03/90	Jiangsu Sainty (CHN)/Malmö (SWE)		s85		s82			A46	A71			A61							9	1
Emil Hallfredsson	29/06/84	Verona (ITA)/Udinese (ITA)			M							M46	M46	M46	s69		s65			55	1
Sölvi Geir Ottesen	18/02/84	Jiangsu Sainty (CHN)		s18				D												28	-
Ögmundur Kristinsson	19/06/89	Hammarby (SWE)			G	G	G			G	G	G46	G46							11	-
Hólmar Örn Eyjólfsson	06/08/90	Rosenborg (NOR)			D		s46													4	-
Arnór Ingvi Traustason	30/04/93	Norrköping (SWE)				M	M19	M46	M60		s71	M46		M69		s80	s89			9	4
Theódór Elmar Bjarnason	04/03/87	AGF (DEN)				s46	s10	M	s78		s81	s46	s62	s46	s90		s71	s76		30	-
Rúnar Már Sigurjónsson	18/06/90	Sundsvall (SWE)				s46	M	M70	M	M		s82	s79							11	1
Haukur Heidar Hauksson	01/09/91	AIK (SWE)					D	D	s71		D62									7	-
Sverrir Ingi Ingason	05/08/93	Lokeren (BEL)					D					D	D	D		s86		s46		8	2
Oliver Sigurjónsson	03/03/95	Breidablik					s81													1	-
Elías Már Ómarsson	18/01/95	Vålerenga (NOR)					s90	s70	M78											5	-
Ingvar Jónsson	18/10/89	Start (NOR)/Sandefjord (NOR)					G46	G						s46						5	-
Hjörtur Logi Valgardsson	27/09/88	Örebro (SWE)					D													10	-
Gardar Gunnlaugsson	25/04/83	ÍA					A76													1	-
Haraldur Björnsson	11/01/89	Östersund (SWE)					s46													1	-
Björn Daníel Sverrisson	29/05/90	Viking (NOR)					s46	s46												6	-
Matthías Vilhjálmsson	30/01/87	Rosenborg (NOR)					s46	s60												15	2
Kjartan Henry Finnbogason	09/07/86	Horsens (DEN)					s76	s71	s71											4	-
Andrés Már Jóhannesson	21/12/88	Fylkir						D71												1	-
Kristinn Jónsson	04/08/90	Sarpsborg (NOR)						D												5	-
Emil Pálsson	10/06/93	FH						M46												1	-
Thórarinn Ingi Valdimarsson	23/04/90	FH						s60												4	-
Hallgrimur Jónasson	04/05/86	OB (DEN)									D46									15	3
Jón Gudni Fjóluson	10/04/89	Norrköping (SWE)									D									8	-
Kristinn Steindórsson	29/04/90	Sundsvall (SWE)									M46									2	2
Gudmundur Thórarinsson	15/04/92	Nordsjælland (DEN)									M46									3	-
Aron Sigurdarson	08/10/93	Fjölnir									M									1	1
Arnór Smárason	07/09/88	Hammarby (SWE)									A									18	2
Diego Jóhannesson	03/10/93	Oviedo (ESP)									s46									1	-
Hjörtur Hermannsson	08/02/95	PSV (NED)/Göteborg (SWE)									s46		D		s54					3	-
Aron Elís Thrándarson	10/11/94	Aalesund (NOR)									s46									1	-
Ævar Ingi Jóhannesson	31/01/95	KA									s84									1	-
Hördur Björgvin Magnússon	11/02/93	Cesena (ITA)										D		D	s87					5	-

EUROPE

Stjarnan

CHAMPIONS
LEAGUE

Second qualifying round - Celtic FC (SCO)
A 0-2
Nielsen, Gudjónsson, Præst, A Jóhannsson (Rúnarsson 74), D Laxdal, Björgvinsson (Ottesen 86), Ægisson, Árnason, Finsen, Hansen, H Björnsson (Gunnarsson 81). Coach: Rúnar Páll Sigmundsson (ISL)
H 1-4 Finsen (7)
Nielsen, Gudjónsson, Præst, Rúnarsson (Gunnarsson 59), Punyed, D Laxdal, Björgvinsson (H Björnsson 46), Ægisson, Árnason, Finsen, Hansen (Barddal 80). Coach: Rúnar Páll Sigmundsson (ISL)

KR Reykjavík

EUROPA
LEAGUE

First qualifying round - Cork City FC (IRL)
A 1-1 Hauksson (28)
S Magnússon, Christiansen, Balbi (Jósepsson 31), Fridgeirsson, Gunnarsson, Sævarsson, Pálmason, Ormarsson (Ragnarsson 74), Frederiksen, Schoop, Hauksson (Martin 68). Coach: Bjarni Gudjónsson (ISL)
H 2-1 (aet) Pálmason (75), Schoop (99)
S Magnússon, Christiansen, Fridgeirsson, Gunnarsson (Ragnarsson 71), Martin (G Sigurdarson 104), Sævarsson (Ormarsson 53), Pálmason, Jósepsson, Frederiksen, Schoop, Hauksson. Coach: Bjarni Gudjónsson (ISL)
Red card: Fridgeirsson 44

Second qualifying round - Rosenborg BK (NOR)
H 0-1
S Magnússon, G Sigurdarson, Christiansen, Gunnarsson, Sævarsson, Ragnarsson (Martin 29), Pálmason, Jósepsson, Frederiksen (Fridjónsson 66), Schoop, Hauksson (Ormarsson 80). Coach: Bjarni Gudjónsson (ISL)
A 0-3
S Magnússon, Christiansen, Fridgeirsson, Gunnarsson, Martin, Sævarsson (G Sigurdarson 46), Pálmason, Ormarsson, Fridjónsson (M Magnússon 46), Jósepsson, Hauksson (Balbi 61). Coach: Bjarni Gudjónsson (ISL)

FH Hafnarfjördur

EUROPA
LEAGUE

First qualifying round - SJK Seinäjoki (FIN)
A 1-0 Lennon (56)
Óskarsson, P Vidarsson, Lennon (K F Finnbogason 81), Pálsson, Valdimarsson, D Vidarsson, Gudnason (B Vidarsson 76), Thórisson, Doumbia, Bödvarsson, Gudmundsson. Coach: Heimir Gudjónsson (ISL)
H 1-0 K F Finnbogason (90+1)
Óskarsson, P Vidarsson, Lennon (B Vidarsson 73), Pálsson, Valdimarsson (K F Finnbogason 81), D Vidarsson, Gudnason, Thórisson, Doumbia, Bödvarsson, Hendrickx. Coach: Heimir Gudjónsson (ISL)

Second qualifying round - İnter Bakı PİK (AZE)
H 1-2 Gudnason (39p)
Óskarsson, P Vidarsson, Pálsson (K Finnbogason 52), Valdimarsson (Björnsson 83), D Vidarsson, Gudnason, B Vidarsson (K F Finnbogason 70), Thórisson, Doumbia, Bödvarsson, Hendrickx. Coach: Heimir Gudjónsson (ISL)
Red card: Óskarsson 50
A 2-2 (aet) Valdimarsson (47), K F Finnbogason (52)
K Finnbogason, Tillen (Bödvarsson 78), P Vidarsson, Pálsson, Valdimarsson, D Vidarsson, Gudnason (Gudmundsson 97), B Vidarsson (K F Finnbogason 38), Doumbia, Serwy, Hendrickx. Coach: Heimir Gudjónsson (ISL)
Red card: K F Finnbogason 55

Víkingur Reykjavík

EUROPA
LEAGUE

First qualifying round - FC Koper (SVN)
H 0-1
Nielsen, Í Jónsson, Tasković, Baldvinsson, Toft (Kristinsson 64), Snorrason (Steingrímsson 52), Bjarnason (Arnarsson 86), Živković, Lowing, Ólafsson, Atlason. Coach: Ólafur Thórdarson (ISL) & Milos Milojevic (ISL)
A 2-2 Kristinsson (51, 76)
Nielsen, Í Jónsson, Tasković, Gudmundsson, Baldvinsson, Snorrason, Kristinsson, Bjarnason (Steingrímsson 73), Živković, Ólafsson (Sigurdsson 77), Atlason (Toft 57). Coach: Ólafur Thórdarson (ISL) & Milos Milojevic (ISL)

Breidablik

1950 • Kópavogsvöllur (3,009); Stjörnuvöllur (1,400) • breidablik.is
Major honours
Icelandic League (1) 2010; Icelandic Cup (1) 2009
Coach: Arnar Grétarsson

2015

07/05	a	Fylkir	D 1-1	Lýdsson (p)
11/05	h	KR	D 2-2	Gunnlaugsson, Lýdsson
17/05	a	Keflavík	D 1-1	Lýdsson
20/05	h	Valur	W 1-0	Gunnlaugsson
26/05	a	ÍA	W 1-0	Atlason
31/05	h	Stjarnan	W 3-0	Lýdsson (p), Atlason, Helgason
07/06	a	Leiknir	W 2-0	Hreinsson, A Sigurjónsson
14/06	h	Víkingur	W 4-1	Jónsson 2, Gunnlaugsson, Hreinsson
21/06	a	FH	D 1-1	Atlason
28/06	a	ÍBV	L 0-2	
13/07	h	Fjölnir	W 2-0	O Sigurjónsson, Adalsteinsson
20/07	h	Fylkir	L 0-1	
27/07	a	KR	D 0-0	
05/08	a	Keflavík	W 4-0	Glenn, Gunnlaugsson 2, Atlason
10/08	a	Valur	W 1-0	Glenn
17/08	h	ÍA	W 3-1	Glenn 3
24/08	a	Stjarnan	W 1-0	Glenn
30/08	h	Leiknir	D 0-0	
13/09	a	Víkingur	D 2-2	O Sigurjónsson, Gunnlaugsson
20/09	h	FH	W 2-1	Glenn, Muminovic
26/09	h	ÍBV	W 1-0	A Sigurjónsson
03/10	a	Fjölnir	W 2-0	Glenn, Yeoman

No	Name	Nat	DoB	Pos	Aps	(s)	Gls
29	Arnór Sveinn Adalsteinsson		26/01/86	D	19		1
6	Kári Ársælsson		02/07/85	D		(3)	
8	Arnthór Ari Atlason		12/10/93	M	19	(2)	4
19	Gunnlaugur Birgisson		04/06/95	M	2		
33	Gísli Eyjólfsson		31/05/94	M	1	(4)	
31	Gudmundur Fridriksson		06/02/94	D	3	(4)	
17	Jonathan Glenn	TRI	27/08/87	A	8	(1)	8
7	Höskuldur Gunnlaugsson		26/09/94	A	19	(1)	6
1	Gunnleifur Gunnleifsson		14/07/75	G	22		
5	Elfar Freyr Helgason		27/07/89	D	21		1
22	Ellert Hreinsson		12/10/86	A	18	(2)	2
23	Kristinn Jónsson		04/08/90	D	22		2
13	Sólon Breki Leifsson		20/06/98	A		(4)	
10	Gudjón Pétur Lýdsson		28/12/87	M	17	(3)	4
21	Viktor Örn Margeirsson		22/07/94	D	2		
4	Damir Muminovic		13/05/90	D	21		1
28	David Kristján Ólafsson		15/05/95	A	4	(5)	
27	Arnór Gauti Ragnarsson		04/02/97	A		(2)	
11	Olgeir Sigurgeirsson		22/10/82	M		(10)	
20	Atli Sigurjónsson		01/07/91	M	8	(11)	2
3	Oliver Sigurjónsson		03/03/95	M	19		2
9	Ismar Tandir	USA	19/08/95	A		(2)	
30	Andri Rafn Yeoman		18/04/92	M	17	(5)	1

FH Hafnarfjördur

1929 • Kaplakriki (6,450) • fh.is
Major honours
Icelandic League (7) 2004, 2005, 2006, 2008, 2009,
2012, 2015; Icelandic Cup (2) 2007, 2010
Coach: Heimir Gudjónsson

2015

Date		Opp	Res		Scorers
04/05	a	KR	W	3-1	Finnbogason, Gudnason 2
10/05	h	Keflavík	W	2-0	Björnsson, Lennon
17/05	a	Valur	L	0-2	
20/05	h	ÍA	W	4-1	Björnsson, Gudmundsson, og (Gudmundsson), Serwy
26/05	a	Stjarnan	D	1-1	Doumbia
31/05	h	Leiknir	W	4-2	Lennon 3 (1p), Gudnason
07/06	a	Víkingur	W	1-0	B Vidarsson
14/06	a	ÍBV	W	4-1	Finnbogason 3, Lennon
21/06	h	Breidablik	D	1-1	
28/06	a	Fjölnir	W	3-1	Valdimarsson, Serwy, Gudnason
12/07	h	Fylkir	D	2-2	Bödvarsson, Gudmundsson
19/07	h	KR	L	1-3	Pálsson
28/07	a	Keflavík	W	2-1	Pálsson, Björnsson
05/08	a	Valur	W	2-1	Björnsson, B Vidarsson
10/08	a	ÍA	W	3-2	Björnsson 2, Pálsson
17/08	h	Stjarnan	W	4-0	Björnsson, B Vidarsson, Gudnason, Pálsson
24/08	a	Leiknir	W	1-0	Lennon
30/08	h	Víkingur	W	1-0	Lennon (p)
13/09	h	ÍBV	W	3-1	Lennon 2 (1p), Gudnason
20/09	a	Breidablik	L	1-2	Gudnason
26/09	h	Fjölnir	W	2-1	Gudnason, Pálsson
03/10	a	Fylkir	L	2-3	Björnsson, Pálsson

No	Name	Nat	DoB	Pos	Aps	(s)	Gls
17	Atli Vidar Björnsson		04/01/80	A	7	(11)	8
21	Bödvar Bödvarsson		09/04/95	D	19		1
20	Kassim Doumbia	MLI	18/06/90	D	14	(1)	2
18	Kristján Flóki Finnbogason		12/01/95	A	8	(12)	4
23	Brynjar Ásgeir Gudmundsson		22/06/92	D	7	(5)	2
11	Atli Gudnason		28/09/84	A	20	(1)	8
26	Jonathan Hendrickx	BEL	25/12/93	D	11		
6	Sam Hewson	ENG	28/11/88	M	7		
16	Jón Ragnar Jónsson		30/10/85	D	9	(4)	
7	Steven Lennon	SCO	20/01/88	A	14	(4)	9
1	Róbert Örn Óskarsson		27/03/87	G	22		
8	Emil Pálsson		10/06/93	M	12		6
22	Jérémy Serwy	BEL	04/06/91	A	18	(3)	2
28	Sigurdur Gísli Snorrason		17/03/95	A		(2)	
15	Gudmann Thórisson		30/01/87	D	6	(1)	
4	Samuel Tillen	ENG	16/04/85	D	3	(5)	
9	Thórarinn Ingi Valdimarsson		23/04/90	M	10	(8)	1
13	Bjarni Thór Vidarsson		05/03/88	M	15	(4)	3
10	Davíd Thór Vidarsson		24/04/84	M	21		
5	Pétur Vidarsson		25/11/87	D	19		

Fjölnir

1988 • Fjölnisvöllur (1,300) • fjolnir.is
Coach: Ágúst Thór Gylfason

2015

Date		Opp	Res		Scorers
03/05	h	ÍBV	W	1-0	T Gudjónsson
11/05	h	Fylkir	D	1-1	Gudmundur Gudmundsson
17/05	a	KR	L	0-2	
20/05	h	Keflavík	W	1-0	T Gudjónsson (p)
25/05	a	Valur	D	3-3	Sigurdarson, T Gudjónsson, Pálsson
31/05	h	ÍA	W	2-0	B Ólafsson, T Gudjónsson
07/06	a	Stjarnan	W	3-1	Magee 2, og (Gudjónsson)
15/06	h	Leiknir	W	3-0	Sigurdarson 2, T Gudjónsson
22/06	a	Víkingur	L	0-2	
28/06	h	FH	L	1-3	Gudmundur Gudmundsson
13/07	a	Breidablik	L	0-2	
19/07	a	ÍBV	L	0-4	
26/07	a	Fylkir	W	4-0	T Gudjónsson 2, Chopart, Magee
05/08	h	KR	W	2-1	Gudmundur Gudmundsson, Magee
10/08	a	Keflavík	D	1-1	Chopart
20/08	h	Valur	D	1-1	Sigurdarson
24/08	a	ÍA	D	4-4	Magee 2, Sigurdarson, Chopart
30/08	h	Stjarnan	D	1-1	Gunnar Gudmundsson
13/09	h	Leiknir	W	3-2	Gudmundur Gudmundsson 2, Chopart
20/09	h	Víkingur	W	4-3	Chopart, B Ólafsson, Sigurdarson, G Gudjónsson
26/09	a	FH	L	1-2	Chopart
03/10	h	Breidablik	L	0-2	

No	Name	Nat	DoB	Pos	Aps	(s)	Gls
27	Anton Freyr Ársælsson		11/05/96	M		(2)	
17	Magnús Pétur Bjarnason		26/01/96	A		(1)	
30	Jökull Blængsson		09/01/97	G		(1)	
13	Kennie Chopart	DEN	01/06/90	A	11		6
16	Gudmundur Gudjónsson		03/08/89	M	15	(4)	1
9	Thórir Gudjónsson		07/04/91	A	16		7
29	Gudmundur Karl Gudmundsson		30/03/91	M	20	(1)	5
4	Gunnar Már Gudmundsson		15/12/83	A	16	(4)	1
28	Hans Viktor Gudmundsson		09/09/96	M	2	(2)	
3	Illugi Thór Gunnarsson		22/06/88	M	5	(7)	
1	Steinar Örn Gunnarsson		11/02/91	G	6		
20	Birnir Snær Ingason		04/12/96	A		(5)	
12	Thórdur Ingason		03/03/88	M	16		
3	Daniel Ivanovski	MKD	27/06/83	D	8		
11	Ægir Jarl Jónasson		08/03/98	M		(3)	
7	Vidar Ari Jónsson		10/03/94	D	22		
15	Haukur Lárusson		01/07/87	D	1		
8	Ragnar Leósson		20/03/91	M	10	(11)	
18	Mark Magee	ENG	03/10/89	A	5	(13)	4
26	Jonatan Neftalí	ESP	26/08/84	D	11		
19	Arnór Eyvar Ólafsson		27/11/89	D	11	(4)	
5	Bergsveinn Ólafsson		09/09/92	D	20		2
23	Emil Pálsson		10/06/93	M	9		1
10	Aron Sigurdarson		08/10/93	A	18	(4)	6
22	Ólafur Páll Snorrason		22/04/82	M	13		
6	Atli Már Thorbergsson		13/03/92	D	7	(1)	

Fylkir

1967 • Fylkisvöllur (1,892) • fylkir.com
Major honours
Icelandic Cup (2) 2001, 2002
Coach: Ásmundur Arnarsson;
(06/07/15) Hermann Hreidarsson

2015

Date		Opp	Res		Scorers
07/05	h	Breidablik	D	1-1	Ingason
11/05	a	Fjölnir	D	1-1	Radovnikovic
17/05	h	ÍBV	W	3-0	Gudmundsson 2, Radovnikovic
20/05	h	KR	L	1-3	Ingason
25/05	a	Keflavík	W	3-1	Jóhannesson, Ingason, Gudmundsson
31/05	h	Valur	L	0-3	
07/06	a	ÍA	D	0-0	
15/06	h	Stjarnan	L	0-2	
22/06	a	Leiknir	D	1-1	Ingason
26/06	h	Víkingur	W	1-0	Arnthórsson
12/07	h	FH	D	2-2	Arnthórsson, Breiddal
20/07	a	Breidablik	W	1-0	Ingason
26/07	h	Fjölnir	L	0-4	
05/08	a	ÍBV	W	1-0	Gudjónsson
10/08	a	KR	L	0-2	
17/08	h	Keflavík	D	3-3	Óskarsson, Ingason 2
24/08	a	Valur	L	2-4	Eythórsson 2
30/08	h	ÍA	D	0-0	
14/09	a	Stjarnan	L	0-1	
20/09	h	Leiknir	W	3-1	Sveinsson 2 (1p), Gudjónsson
26/09	a	Víkingur	D	0-0	
03/10	h	FH	W	3-2	Jóhannesson, Óskarsson, Radovnikovic

No	Name	Nat	DoB	Pos	Aps	(s)	Gls
29	Axel Andri Antonsson		29/09/98	M	1	(2)	
17	Ásgeir Örn Arnthórsson		02/05/90	M	9	(11)	2
3	Ásgeir Börkur Ásgeirsson		16/04/87	M	20		
24	Elís Rafn Björnsson		13/10/92	M	4	(3)	
11	Kjartan Ágúst Breiddal		20/03/86	M	1	(8)	1
22	Davíd Einarsson		24/08/92	A	2	(1)	
5	Ásgeir Eythórsson		29/04/93	D	21		2
13	Kolbeinn Finnsson		25/08/99	M	3	(6)	
8	Jóhannes Karl Gudjónsson		25/05/80	M	15	(1)	2
20	Stefán Ragnar Gudlaugsson		19/03/91	D	8	(1)	
6	Oddur Ingi Gudmundsson		28/01/89	M	12	(3)	3
1	Bjarni Halldórsson		26/07/83	G	8		
2	Kristján Hauksson		03/02/86	D	5	(2)	
14	Albert Brynjar Ingason		16/01/86	A	21		7
10	Andrés Már Jóhannesson		21/12/88	M	19	(3)	2
23	Andri Thór Jónsson		24/02/91	D	3	(2)	
15	Hákon Ingi Jónsson		10/11/95	A	6	(7)	
26	Ari Leifsson		19/04/98	D		(2)	
21	Dadi Ólafsson		05/01/94	D	6	(2)	
12	Ólafur Íshólm Ólafsson		08/05/95	G	14		
7	Ingimundur Níels Óskarsson		04/02/86	A	13	(7)	2
4	Tonči Radovnikovic	CRO	27/10/88	D	21		3
9	Ragnar Bragi Sveinsson		18/12/94	A	15	(4)	2
16	Tómas Thorsteinsson		08/12/88	D	15		

ÍA Akranes

1946 • Nordurálsvöllur (5,550) • ia.is

Major honours
Icelandic League (18) 1951, 1953, 1954, 1957, 1958, 1960, 1970, 1974, 1975, 1977, 1983, 1984, 1992, 1993, 1994, 1995, 1996, 2001; Icelandic Cup (9) 1978, 1982, 1983, 1984, 1986, 1993, 1996, 2000, 2003

Coach: Gunnlaugur Jónsson

2015

Date		Opp	Res		Scorers
03/05	h	Stjarnan	L	0-1	
11/05	a	Leiknir	W	1-0	Gunnlaugsson
17/05	h	Víkingur	D	1-1	Gunnlaugsson
20/05	a	FH	L	1-4	Buinickij
26/05	h	Breidablik	L	0-1	
31/05	a	Fjölnir	L	0-2	
07/06	h	Fylkir	D	0-0	
15/06	a	KR	D	1-1	Marteinsson
22/06	h	Keflavík	W	4-2	Buinickij, og (Einarsson), Hafsteinsson, Marteinsson
28/06	a	Valur	L	2-4	Ákason, Buinickij
12/07	h	ÍBV	W	3-1	Gudjónsson, Buinickij, Flosason
18/07	a	Stjarnan	D	1-1	Gunnlaugsson
26/07	h	Leiknir	W	2-1	Karlsson, Andjelković
05/08	a	Víkingur	D	1-1	Gunnlaugsson
10/08	h	FH	L	2-3	Gudjónsson, Gunnlaugsson
17/08	a	Breidablik	L	1-3	Hafsteinsson
24/08	h	Fjölnir	D	4-4	Ákason 2, Gudjónsson, Gunnlaugsson
30/08	a	Fylkir	D	0-0	
13/09	h	KR	D	0-0	
20/09	a	Keflavík	W	4-0	Gunnlaugsson 2, Thórdarson, Flosason
26/09	a	Valur	W	1-0	Gudjónsson
03/10	a	ÍBV	W	2-1	Gunnlaugsson, Lough

No	Name	Nat	DoB	Pos	Aps	(s)	Gls
10	Jón Vilhelm Ákason		20/11/86	M	18	(3)	3
31	Marko Andjelković	SRB	12/10/84	M	7	(9)	1
5	Ármann Smári Björnsson		07/01/81	D	22		
13	Arsenij Buinickij	LTU	10/10/85	A	11	(3)	4
8	Hallur Flosason		01/05/93	M	8	(7)	2
11	Arnar Már Gudjónsson		20/02/87	M	16	(3)	4
4	Arnór Snær Gudmundsson		20/04/93	D	16		
9	Gardar Gunnlaugsson		25/04/83	A	15	(2)	9
20	Gylfi Veigar Gylfason		12/04/93	D	8	(4)	
18	Albert Hafsteinsson		05/06/96	M	20	(1)	2
17	Tryggvi Hrafn Haraldsson		30/09/96	A	1	(3)	
6	Ingimar Elí Hlynsson		10/09/92	M	7	(4)	
1	Páll Gísli Jónsson		26/03/83	G	1		
19	Eggert Kári Karlsson		14/05/91	M	2	(8)	1
3	Ragnar Már Lárusson		09/06/97	M		(1)	
27	Darren Lough	ENG	23/09/89	D	18	(1)	1
23	Ásgeir Marteinsson		07/07/94	M	16	(6)	2
12	Árni Snær Ólafsson		16/08/91	G	21		
15	Teitur Pétursson		07/07/93	D	4	(1)	
21	Arnór Sigurdsson		15/05/99	A		(1)	
16	Thórdur Thorsteinn Thórdarson		22/02/95	D	22		1
22	Steinar Thorsteinsson		06/12/97	A		(1)	
14	Ólafur Valur Valdimarsson		13/12/90	M	9	(3)	

ÍBV Vestmannaeyjar

1945 • Hásteinsvöllur (3,000) • ibv.is

Major honours
Icelandic League (3) 1979, 1997, 1998; Icelandic Cup (4) 1968, 1972, 1981, 1998

Coach: Jóhannes Hardarson; (22/07/15) Ásmundur Arnarsson

2015

Date		Opp	Res		Scorers
03/05	a	Fjölnir	L	0-1	
10/05	h	Stjarnan	L	0-2	
17/05	a	Fylkir	L	0-3	
20/05	h	Leiknir	D	2-2	V Thorvardarson, Jeffs
25/05	a	KR	L	0-1	
31/05	h	Víkingur	W	3-2	Briem, A Bjarnason, Glenn
07/06	a	Keflavík	L	1-3	Glenn (p)
14/06	h	FH	L	1-4	A Bjarnason
21/06	a	Valur	L	1-1	Glenn (p)
28/06	h	Breidablik	W	2-0	Glenn, V Thorvardarson
12/07	a	ÍA	L	1-3	V Thorvardarson
19/07	h	Fjölnir	W	4-0	Seoane 2, Briem, Thorvaldsson (p)
26/07	a	Stjarnan	L	0-3	
05/08	h	Fylkir	L	0-1	
09/08	a	Leiknir	W	2-0	Seoane 2
21/08	h	KR	D	1-1	Seoane
25/08	a	Víkingur	L	0-1	
30/08	h	Keflavík	W	3-0	Jeffs, Thorvaldsson (p), Briem
13/09	a	FH	L	1-3	Jeffs
20/09	h	Valur	D	3-3	Seoane, Thorvaldsson, Jeffs
26/09	a	Breidablik	L	0-1	
03/10	h	ÍA	L	1-2	Thorvaldsson

No	Name	Nat	DoB	Pos	Aps	(s)	Gls
21	Dominic Adams	TRI	10/02/88	M		(5)	
14	Jonathan Barden	ENG	09/11/92	D	15	(1)	
7	Aron Bjarnason		14/10/95	M	12	(5)	2
23	Benedikt Októ Bjarnason		03/04/95	D	3	(6)	
4	Hafsteinn Briem		28/02/91	D	18	(1)	3
19	Mario Brlečić	CRO	10/01/89	M	8	(1)	
1	Abel Dhaira	UGA	09/09/87	G	9		
13	Ásgeir Elíasson		29/04/98	A		(1)	
28	Sead Gavranovic	DEN	01/07/91	A		(1)	
17	Jonathan Glenn	TRI	27/08/87	A	8	(3)	4
17	Devon Már Griffin		23/04/97	D	3	(1)	
17	Stefán Ragnar Gudlaugsson		19/03/91	D	3	(2)	
10	Bjarni Gunnarsson		29/01/93	M	13	(5)	
8	Jón Ingason		21/09/95	D	16	(2)	
30	Ian Jeffs	ENG	12/10/82	M	15	(4)	4
32	Andri Ólafsson		26/06/85	M	3		
5	Avni Pepa	KOS	14/11/88	D	19		
9	José Seoane	ESP	16/03/89	A	10	(1)	6
16	Mees Siers	NED	06/10/87	M	20		
25	Gudjón Orri Sigurjónsson		01/12/92	G	13		
2	Tom Even Skogsrud	NOR	14/04/93	D	13	(2)	
6	Gunnar Thorsteinsson		01/02/94	M	9	(8)	
34	Gunnar Heidar Thorvaldsson		01/04/82	A	11		4
22	Gauti Thorvardarson		19/02/89	A	3	(8)	
11	Vídir Thorvardarson		07/07/92	M	18	(3)	3

Keflavík

1929 • Nettóvöllurinn (2,554) • keflavik.is

Major honours
Icelandic League (4) 1964, 1969, 1971, 1973; Icelandic Cup (4) 1975, 1997, 2004, 2006

Coach: Kristján Gudmundsson; (05/06/15) Haukur Ingi Gudnason & Jóhann Birnir Gudmundsson

2015

Date		Opp	Res		Scorers
03/05	a	Víkingur	L	1-3	Sveinsson
10/05	a	FH	L	0-2	
17/05	h	Breidablik	D	1-1	Elísson
20/05	a	Fjölnir	L	0-1	
25/05	h	Fylkir	L	1-3	M Thorsteinsson
31/05	a	KR	L	0-4	
07/06	h	ÍBV	W	3-1	Sveinsson, Einarsson, Sigurdsson
14/06	h	Valur	L	1-2	Rúnarsson
22/06	a	ÍA	L	2-4	S Magnússon 2
29/06	h	Stjarnan	L	1-2	Elísson
13/07	a	Leiknir	D	1-1	Matthíasson
19/07	a	Víkingur	L	1-7	Matthíasson
28/07	h	FH	L	1-2	og (D Vidarsson)
05/08	a	Breidablik	L	0-4	
10/08	h	Fjölnir	D	1-1	Hummervoll
17/08	a	Fylkir	D	3-3	Rúnarsson, Hummervoll, Matthíasson (p)
25/08	h	KR	L	0-1	
30/08	a	ÍBV	L	0-3	
13/09	a	Valur	L	2-3	Matthíasson (p), Hummervoll
20/09	h	ÍA	L	0-4	
26/09	a	Stjarnan	L	0-7	
03/10	h	Leiknir	W	3-2	Sveinsson 2, Elísson

No	Name	Nat	DoB	Pos	Aps	(s)	Gls
20	Gudjón Árni Antoniusson		03/09/83	D	15		
1	Richard Arends	NED	05/09/90	G	7		
5	Paul Bignot	ENG	14/02/86	D	9		
27	Sigurbergur Bjarnason		28/02/99	M		(1)	
32	Chukwudi Chijindu	USA	20/02/86	A	7	(1)	
6	Einar Orri Einarsson		28/10/89	M	16		1
9	Sigurbergur Elísson		10/06/92	M	13	(2)	3
25	Frans Elvarsson		14/08/90	M	14	(4)	
28	Arnór Smári Fridriksson		11/06/96	D	1		
27	Patrekur Örn Fridriksson		11/06/96	M		(1)	
4	Haraldur Freyr Gudmundsson		14/12/81	D	12		
7	Jóhann Birnir Gudmundsson		05/12/77	M	4	(4)	
24	Daniel Gylfason		30/07/93	A	4	(6)	
33	Martin Hummervoll	NOR	13/03/96	M	7	(2)	3
5	Kiko Insa	ESP	25/01/88	D	7		
18	Einar Thór Kjartansson		13/02/96	M		(1)	
8	Bojan Stefán Ljubicic		22/06/92	M	6	(6)	
26	Stefan Alexander Ljubicic		05/10/99	M		(3)	
14	Alexander Magnússon		10/11/89	D		(1)	
23	Sindri Snær Magnússon		18/02/92	M	16	(1)	2
3	Magnús Thórir Matthíasson		22/01/90	M	13	(4)	4
21	Sindri Kristinn Ólafsson		19/01/97	G	14		
17	Hólmar Örn Rúnarsson		10/12/81	M	19	(1)	2
2	Samu Jiménez	ESP	20/02/88	D	14	(2)	
1	Sigmar Ingi Sigurdarson		25/06/83	G	1		
19	Leonard Sigurdsson		30/04/96	M	6	(6)	1
10	Hördur Sveinsson		24/03/83	A	8	(3)	4
29	Fannar Orri Sævarsson		28/10/97	M	4	(1)	
22	Indridi Áki Thorláksson		02/08/95	A	3	(3)	
11	Magnús Sverrir Thorsteinsson		22/09/82	M	5	(5)	1
16	Páll Olgeir Thorsteinsson		30/10/95	M		(4)	
30	Samúel Thór Traustason		12/04/98	D	1		
13	Unnar Már Unnarsson		25/09/94	D	7		
22	Farid Zato-Arouna	TOG	23/04/92	M	5	(3)	

KR Reykjavík

1899 • Alvogenvöllurinn (2,801) • kr.is

Major honours
Icelandic League (26) 1912, 1919, 1926, 1927, 1928, 1929, 1931, 1932, 1934, 1941, 1948, 1949, 1950, 1952, 1955, 1959, 1961, 1963, 1965, 1968, 1999, 2000, 2002, 2003, 2011, 2013; Icelandic Cup (14) 1960, 1961, 1962, 1963, 1964, 1966, 1967, 1994, 1995, 1999, 2008, 2011, 2012, 2014

Coach: Bjarni Gudjónsson

2015

04/05	h	FH	L	1-3	Schoop
11/05	a	Breidablik	D	2-2	Hauksson, Frederiksen
17/05	h	Fjölnir	W	2-0	Martin (p), Pálmason
20/05	a	Fylkir	W	3-1	Frederiksen, Fridgeirsson, Ragnarsson
25/05	h	ÍBV	W	1-0	Hauksson
31/05	h	Keflavík	W	4-0	Ragnarsson, Hauksson 2 (1p), Fridgeirsson
07/06	a	Valur	L	0-3	
15/06	h	ÍA	D	1-1	Ormarsson
22/06	a	Stjarnan	W	1-0	Ormarsson
28/06	h	Leiknir	W	1-0	Ragnarsson
12/07	a	Víkingur	W	3-0	Ragnarsson, Frederiksen 2
19/07	a	FH	W	3-1	Fridjónsson (p), Martin, Hauksson
27/07	h	Breidablik	D	0-0	
05/08	a	Fjölnir	L	1-2	Fridjónsson
10/08	h	Fylkir	W	2-0	Ragnarsson, Pálmason
21/08	a	ÍBV	D	1-1	Gunnarsson
25/08	a	Keflavík	W	1-0	Pálmason
30/08	h	Valur	D	2-2	og (K Sigurdsson), Ormarsson
13/09	a	ÍA	D	0-0	
20/09	h	Stjarnan	L	0-3	
26/09	a	Leiknir	W	2-0	Hauksson, Martin
03/10	h	Víkingur	W	5-2	Hauksson 2, Fridjónsson, Martin 2

No	Name	Nat	DoB	Pos	Aps	(s)	Gls
28	Atli Hrafn Andrason		04/01/99	A		(2)	
4	Gonzalo Balbi	URU	05/06/92	D	10	(5)	
3	Rasmus Christiansen	DEN	06/10/89	D	17		
19	Søren Frederiksen	DEN	08/07/89	A	18	(1)	4
5	Skúli Jón Fridgeirsson		30/07/88	D	22		2
17	Hólmbert Aron Fridjónsson		19/04/93	A	7	(3)	3
6	Gunnar Thór Gunnarsson		04/10/85	D	20		1
22	Óskar Örn Hauksson		22/08/84	A	19	(2)	8
13	Sindri Snær Jensson		12/08/86	G	3	(1)	
18	Aron Bjarki Jósepsson		21/11/89	D	9	(3)	
16	Kristinn Magnússon		29/04/84	M	3	(7)	
1	Stefán Logi Magnússon		05/09/80	G	19		
7	Gary Martin	ENG	10/10/90	A	8	(7)	5
11	Almarr Ormarsson		25/02/88	A	10	(12)	3
10	Pálmi Rafn Pálmason		09/11/84	M	21		3
9	Thorsteinn Már Ragnarsson		19/04/90	A	9	(10)	5
20	Jacob Schoop	DEN	23/12/88	M	21		1
30	Axel Sigurdarson		18/04/98	M		(2)	
2	Grétar Sigurdarson		09/10/82	D	6	(5)	
8	Jónas Gudni Sævarsson		28/11/83	M	20		
27	Gudmundur Andri Tryggvason		04/11/99	A		(1)	

Leiknir Reykjavík

1973 • Leiknisvöllur (1,215) • leiknir.com

Coach: Freyr Alexandersson & David Snorri Jónasson

2015

03/05	a	Valur	W	3-0	Kárason, Björnsson, Hilmar Halldórsson
11/05	h	ÍA	L	0-1	
17/05	a	Stjarnan	D	1-1	Hilmar Halldórsson (p)
20/05	a	ÍBV	D	2-2	Halldór Halldórsson, Kristjánsson
26/05	h	Víkingur	W	2-0	Björnsson, Fomen
31/05	a	FH	L	2-4	Kristjánsson, Hilmar Halldórsson
07/06	h	Breidablik	L	0-2	
15/06	a	Fjölnir	L	0-3	
22/06	h	Fylkir	D	1-1	Kristjánsson
28/06	a	KR	L	0-1	
13/07	a	Keflavík	D	1-1	Jónsson
20/07	h	Valur	L	0-1	
26/07	a	ÍA	L	1-2	Halldór Halldórsson
05/08	a	Stjarnan	W	1-0	Halldór Halldórsson
09/08	h	ÍBV	L	0-2	
17/08	a	Víkingur R.	D	1-1	og (Sigurdsson)
24/08	h	FH	L	0-1	
30/08	a	Breidablik	D	0-0	
13/09	h	Fjölnir	L	2-3	Hilmar Halldórsson, Jónsson
20/09	a	Fylkir	L	1-3	Björnsson
26/09	h	KR	L	0-2	
03/10	a	Keflavík	L	2-3	Kárason, Kristjánsson

No	Name	Nat	DoB	Pos	Aps	(s)	Gls
7	Atli Arnarson		29/11/93	M	11	(5)	
10	Fannar Thór Arnarsson		14/05/89	M	10	(1)	
26	Dadi Bergsson		11/03/95	M		(5)	
8	Sindri Björnsson		29/03/95	M	18	(2)	3
19	Amath Diedhiou	SEN	19/11/89	A	3	(3)	
27	Magnús Már Einarsson		13/02/89	A		(2)	
30	Charley Fomen	CMR	09/07/89	D	16	(1)	1
20	Óttar Bjarni Gudmundsson		15/04/90	D	17		
25	Dadi Bærings Halldórsson		08/04/97	M		(4)	
4	Halldór Kristin Halldórsson		13/04/88	D	22		3
21	Hilmar Árni Halldórsson		14/02/92	M	22		4
23	Gestur Ingi Hardarson		11/05/87	D	13	(1)	
11	Brynjar Hlödversson		03/04/89	M	13	(2)	
15	Kristján Páll Jónsson		14/09/88	A	12	(7)	2
9	Kolbeinn Kárason		02/04/91	A	11	(6)	2
6	Ólafur Hrannar Kristjánsson		05/02/90	A	14	(6)	4
3	Eiríkur Ingi Magnússon		08/08/91	D	20		
19	Sævar Atli Magnússon		16/06/00	A		(1)	
1	Arnar Freyr Ólafsson		06/03/93	G	1		
5	Edvard Börkur Óttharsson		23/04/92	D	1	(2)	
16	Danny Schreurs	NED	28/08/87	A	5	(2)	
18	Elvar Páll Sigurdsson		30/07/91	A	12	(8)	
22	Eyjólfur Tómasson		04/01/89	G	21		
16	Frymezin Veselaj		28/10/95	A		(4)	

Stjarnan

1960 • Samsungvöllurinn (1,400) • stjarnan.is

Major honours
Icelandic League (1) 2014

Coach: Rúnar Páll Sigmundsson

2015

03/05	a	ÍA	W	1-0	Finsen
10/05	a	ÍBV	W	2-0	Hansen, Rúnarsson
17/05	h	Leiknir	D	1-1	Hansen
20/05	a	Víkingur	D	2-2	og (Lowing), Hansen
26/05	h	FH	D	1-1	Finsen
31/05	a	Breidablik	L	0-3	
07/06	h	Fjölnir	L	1-3	H Björnsson (p)
15/06	a	Fylkir	W	2-0	Barddal, H Björnsson
22/06	h	KR	W	3-0	
29/06	a	Keflavík	W	2-1	Hansen, og (Rúnarsson)
10/07	h	Valur	L	1-2	H Björnsson
18/07	h	ÍA	D	0-0	
26/07	h	ÍBV	W	3-0	Hansen 2, Knútsson
05/08	a	Leiknir	L	0-1	
09/08	h	Víkingur	D	1-1	Knútsson
17/08	a	FH	L	0-4	
24/08	h	Breidablik	L	0-1	
30/08	h	Fjölnir	D	1-1	Baldvinsson
14/09	h	Fylkir	W	1-0	Punyed
20/09	a	KR	W	3-0	Gunnarsson (p), Baldvinsson, Punyed
26/09	h	Keflavík	W	7-0	Baldvinsson 3, H Björnsson, Knútsson, Hansen, Ægisson
03/10	a	Valur	W	2-1	Hansen, Björvinsson

No	Name	Nat	DoB	Pos	Aps	(s)	Gls
14	Hördur Árnason		19/05/89	D	18	(1)	
16	Gudjón Baldvinsson		15/02/86	A	11		5
18	Jón Arnar Barddal		07/10/95	M	1	(4)	1
11	Arnar Már Björgvinsson		10/02/90	A	17	(4)	1
24	Brynjar Már Björnsson		13/01/95	D		(1)	
23	Halldór Orri Björnsson		02/03/87	M	13	(5)	4
17	Ólafur Karl Finsen		30/03/92	A	15	(1)	3
2	Brynjar Gauti Gudjónsson		27/02/92	D	21		
10	Veigar Páll Gunnarsson		21/03/80	A	6	(11)	1
19	Jeppe Hansen	DEN	10/02/89	A	16	(5)	8
25	Sveinn Jóhannesson		22/01/95	G	2	(1)	
7	Atli Jóhannsson		05/10/82	M	1	(2)	
27	Gardar Jóhannsson		01/04/80	A	1	(6)	
22	Thórhallur Kári Knútsson		16/05/95	M	5	(7)	3
26	Kristófer Konrádsson		31/03/98	A		(1)	
9	Daniel Laxdal		22/09/86	D	21		
33	Jóhann Laxdal		27/01/90	D	1	(6)	
1	Gunnar Nielsen	FRO	07/10/86	G	20		
20	Atli Freyr Ottesen		22/04/95	M		(2)	
30	Kári Pétursson		01/10/96	A		(2)	
8	Michael Præst	DEN	25/07/86	M	16		
8	Pablo Punyed	SLV	18/04/90	M	18	(1)	2
6	Thorri Geir Rúnarsson		24/04/95	M	17	(2)	1
12	Heidar Ægisson		10/08/95	D	22		

Valur Reykjavík

1911 • Valsvöllur (2,465) • valur.is

Major honours
Icelandic League (20) 1930, 1933, 1935, 1936, 1937, 1938, 1940, 1942, 1943, 1944, 1945, 1956, 1966, 1967, 1976, 1978, 1980, 1985, 1987, 2007; Icelandic Cup (10) 1965, 1974, 1976, 1977, 1988, 1990, 1991, 1992, 2005, 2015

Coach: Ólafur Jóhannesson

2015

03/05	h	Leiknir	L	0-3
10/05	a	Víkingur	D	2-2 K Sigurdsson, Pedersen
17/05	h	FH	W	2-0 Lárusson 2
20/05	a	Breidablik	L	0-1
25/05	h	Fjölnir	D	3-3 Eiríksson, Sturluson, Pedersen
31/05	a	Fylkir	W	3-0 Pedersen, Halldórsson, Lárusson
07/06	h	KR	W	3-0 Pedersen 2 (1p), Hilmarsson
14/06	a	Keflavík	W	2-1 Pedersen (p), og (Kiko Insa)
21/06	h	ÍBV	D	1-1 K Sigurdsson
28/06	h	ÍA	W	4-2 Stefánsson, Pedersen 2, Halldórsson
10/07	a	Stjarnan	W	2-1 og (Árnason), K Sigurdsson
20/07	a	Leiknir	W	1-0 Halldórsson
25/07	h	Víkingur	L	0-1
05/08	a	FH	L	1-2 Lárusson
10/08	h	Breidablik	L	0-1
20/08	a	Fjölnir	D	1-1 Ingvarsson
24/08	h	Fylkir	W	4-2 Pedersen 2 (1p), Halldórsson, Ingvarsson
30/08	a	KR	D	2-2 Halldórsson, Lárusson
13/09	h	Keflavík	W	3-2 Pedersen 2 (1p), Atlason
20/09	a	ÍBV	D	3-3 Pedersen, Lárusson, K Sigurdsson
26/09	a	ÍA	L	0-1
03/10	h	Stjarnan	L	1-2 Atlason

No	Name	Nat	DoB	Pos	Aps	(s)	Gls
17	Andri Adolphsson		01/12/92	M	6	(4)	
19	Emil Atlason		22/07/93	A	5	(3)	2
6	Dadi Bergsson		11/03/95	M	1	(6)	
2	Thomas Christensen	DEN	20/01/84	D	13		
12	Anton Ari Einarsson		25/08/94	G	3	(1)	
21	Bjarni Ólafur Eiríksson		28/03/82	D	19		1
16	Tómas Óli Gardarsson		25/10/93	M	1	(9)	
14	Gunnar Gunnarsson		22/09/93	D	8		
8	Kristinn Ingi Halldórsson		08/04/89	M	14	(2)	5
18	Haukur Ásberg Hilmarsson		18/05/95	A		(8)	1
15	Thórdur Steinar Hreidarsson		13/12/86	D	1	(1)	
4	Einar Karl Ingvarsson		08/10/93	M	7	(6)	2
1	Ingvar Thór Kale		08/12/83	G	19		
11	Sigurdur Egill Lárusson		22/01/92	M	20		6
20	Orri Sigurdur Ómarsson		18/02/95	D	22		
9	Patrick Pedersen	DEN	25/11/91	A	19	(1)	13
22	Mathias Schlie	DEN	31/01/88	M	8		
7	Haukur Páll Sigurdsson		05/08/87	M	17		
10	Kristinn Freyr Sigurdsson		25/12/91	M	21		4
23	Andri Fannar Stefánsson		22/04/91	D	19		1
5	Baldvin Sturluson		09/04/89	M	11	(4)	1
3	Iain Williamson	SCO	12/01/88	M	8	(8)	

Víkingur Reykjavík

1908 • Víkingsvöllur (1,449); Thróttarvöllur (2,000) • vikingur.is

Major honours
Icelandic League (5) 1920, 1924, 1981, 1982, 1991; Icelandic Cup (1) 1971

Coach: Ólafur Thórdarson & Milos Milojevic; (15/07/15) Milos Milojevic

2015

03/05	a	Keflavík	W	3-1 Atlason, Tasković, Í Jónsson
10/05	h	Valur	D	2-2 Faye, Sverrisson
17/05	a	ÍA	D	1-1 og (Thórdarson)
20/05	h	Stjarnan	D	2-2 Toft, Bjarnason
26/05	a	Leiknir	L	0-2
31/05	a	ÍBV	L	2-3 Tasković 2 (1p)
07/06	h	FH	L	0-1
14/06	a	Breidablik	L	1-4 Toft
22/06	h	Fjölnir	W	2-0 Toft, Atlason
26/06	a	Fylkir	L	0-1
12/07	h	KR	L	0-3
19/07	a	Keflavík	W	7-1 Steingrímsson 2, og (Unnarsson), Tufegdžić, Toft, Sverrisson 2
25/07	a	Valur	W	1-0 Í Jónsson (p)
05/08	a	ÍA	D	1-1 Steingrímsson
09/08	a	Stjarnan	D	1-1 Tufegdžić
17/08	a	Leiknir	D	1-1 Í Jónsson (p)
25/08	h	ÍBV	W	1-0 Bjarnason
30/08	a	FH	L	0-1
13/09	h	Breidablik	D	2-2 Tufegdžić, Í Jónsson (p)
20/09	a	Fjölnir	L	3-4 Í Jónsson, Steingrímsson, Atlason
26/09	h	Fylkir	D	0-0
03/10	a	KR	L	2-5 Agnarsson, Baldvinsson

No	Name	Nat	DoB	Pos	Aps	(s)	Gls
19	Erlingur Agnarsson		05/03/98	M	2		1
8	Viktor Bjarki Arnarsson		22/01/83	M	13	(6)	
27	Davíd Örn Atlason		18/08/94	D	20	(2)	3
9	Haukur Baldvinsson		05/05/90	M	11	(3)	1
15	Andri Rúnar Bjarnason		12/11/90	A	8	(9)	2
12	Denis Cardaklija		11/10/88	G	5		
20	Pape Mamadou Faye		06/03/91	A	3	(1)	1
5	Tómas Gudmundsson		10/02/92	D	5	(3)	
14	Atli Fannar Jónsson		31/08/95	M		(1)	
3	Ívar Örn Jónsson		02/02/94	M	17	(3)	5
13	Arnthór Ingi Kristinsson		15/03/90	M	10	(4)	
22	Alan Lowing	SCO	07/01/88	D	13		
1	Thomas Nielsen	DEN	23/07/92	G	17		
23	Finnur Ólafsson		30/01/84	M	10	(5)	
18	Stefán Thór Pálsson		31/05/95	M	2	(7)	
21	Bjarni Páll Runólfsson		10/09/96	D		(3)	
6	Halldór Smári Sigurdsson		04/10/88	M	15		
11	Dofri Snorrason		21/07/90	M	18		
7	Hallgrímur Mar Steingrímsson		02/10/90	M	11	(3)	4
29	Agnar Darri Sverrisson		24/11/94	M		(9)	3
4	Igor Tasković	SRB	04/01/82	M	19		3
10	Rolf Toft	DEN	04/08/92	A	19	(3)	4
25	Vladimir Tufegdžić	SRB	12/06/91	A	7	(2)	3
17	Tómas Ingi Urbancic		13/11/96	M		(1)	
16	Miloš Živković	SRB	01/12/84	D	17		

Top goalscorers

13 Patrick Pedersen (Valur)

12 Jonathan Glenn (ÍBV/Breidablik)

9 Steven Lennon (FH)
Gardar Gunnlaugsson (ÍA)

8 Atli Vidar Björnsson (FH)
Atli Gudnason (FH)
Óskar Örn Hauksson (KR)
Jeppe Hansen (Stjarnan)

7 Thórir Gudjónsson (Fjölnir)
Emil Pálsson (Fjölnir/FH)
Albert Brynjar Ingason (Fylkir)

Promoted clubs

Víkingur Ólafsvík

1928 • Ólafsvíkurvöllur (1,300) • no website
Coach: Ejub Purisevic

Thróttur Reykjavík

1949 • Thróttarvöllur (2,500) • trottur.is
Coach: Gregg Ryder (ENG)

Second level final table 2015

		Pld	W	D	L	F	A	Pts
1	Víkingur Ólafsvík	22	17	3	2	53	14	54
2	Thróttur Reykjavík	22	14	2	6	45	21	44
3	KA Akureyri	22	12	5	5	42	22	41
4	Thór Akureyri	22	12	2	8	40	34	38
5	Grindavík	22	11	3	8	41	30	36
6	Haukar	22	10	4	8	32	28	34
7	Fjardabyggd	22	9	4	9	35	37	31
8	HK Kópavogur	22	10	1	11	26	33	31
9	Fram Reykjavík	22	5	6	11	34	45	21
10	Selfoss	22	5	5	12	20	38	20
11	Grótta	22	4	3	15	10	39	15
12	BÍ/Bolungarvík	22	2	4	16	22	59	10

DOMESTIC CUP

Bikarkeppnin 2015

THIRD ROUND

(02/06/15)
Fjardabyggd 4-0 Kári
KA 4-0 Álftanes
KV 2-1 Fram
Thróttur R. 4-1 Bí/Bolungarvík
Vatnaliljur 0-3 Afturelding
Völsungur 3-4 Grindavík

(03/06/15)
FH 2-1 HK
Fylkir 3-2 Njardvík
ÍA 0-3 Fjölnir
Keflavík 0-5 KR
Léttir 0-6 ÍBV
Stjarnan 1-1 Leiknir R. *(aet; 6-5 on pens)*
Thór 2-3 Víkingur Ó.
Valur 4-0 Selfoss
Víkingur R. 2-0 Höttur *(aet)*

(04/06/15)
KFG 1-3 Breidablik

FOURTH ROUND

(18/06/15)
Breidablik 0-1 KA *(aet)*
FH 2-1 Grindavík
Fjardabyggd 0-4 Valur
Fjölnir 4-0 Víkingur Ó.
KV 1-7 KR
Stjarnan 0-3 Fylkir
Thróttur R. 0-2 ÍBV
Víkingur R. 1-0 Afturelding

QUARTER-FINALS

(04/07/15)
ÍBV 4-0 Fylkir *(Gunnarsson 34, 70, Jeffs 54, A Bjarnason 60)*

(05/07/15)
KR 2-1 FH *(Hauksson 15, Martin 61; Doumbia 17)*
Víkingur R. 1-2 Valur *(Bjarnason 34; Nielsen 47og, Williamson 80)*

(06/07/15)
KA 2-1 Fjölnir *(Bjarnason 6, Jóhannesson 7; Magee 53)*

SEMI-FINALS

(29/07/15)
KA 1-1 Valur *(Adalsteinsson 6p; Ómarsson 23) (aet; 4-5 on pens)*

(30/07/15)
KR 4-1 ÍBV *(Fridjónsson 23, 41, Hauksson 54, Ragnarsson 67; Gunnarsson 70)*

FINAL

(15/08/15)
Laugardalsvöllur, Reykjavik
VALUR REYKJAVÍK 2 *(Eiríksson 72, Halldórsson 87)*
KR REYKJAVÍK 0
Referee: *Eiríksson*
VALUR: *Kale, Stefánsson, Christensen, Ómarsson, Eiríksson, Schlie, H Sigurdsson, Halldórsson, K Sigurdsson (Williamson 88), Pedersen (Adolphsson 80), Lárusson (Ingvarsson 85)*
KR: *S Magnússon, Jósepsson, Fridgeirsson, Christiansen, Gunnarsson, Pálmason, Schoop, Sævarsson (Ragnarsson 74), Ormarsson, Fridjónsson (Martin 55), Hauksson (Frederiksen 70)*

Valur captured the Icelandic Cup for the tenth time with a 2-0 win over Reykjavik rivals KR

ISRAEL
Israel Football Association (IFA)

Address Ramat Gan Stadium
299 Aba Hillel Street
PO Box 3591
Il-52134 Ramat Gan
Tel +972 3 617 1500
Fax +972 3 570 2044
E-Mail info@football.org.il
Website football.org.il

President Ofer Eini
Chief executive Rotem Kamer
Media officer Shlomi Barzel
Year of formation 1928

LIGAT HA'AL CLUBS

 1 Beitar Jerusalem FC

 2 Bnei Sakhnin FC

 3 Bnei Yehuda Tel-Aviv FC

 4 Hapoel Akko FC

 5 Hapoel Beer Sheva FC

 6 Hapoel Haifa FC

 7 Hapoel Kfar-Saba FC

 8 Hapoel Kiryat Shmona FC

 9 Hapoel Ra'anana FC

 10 Hapoel Tel-Aviv FC

 11 Maccabi Haifa FC

 12 Maccabi Netanya FC

 13 Maccabi Petach-Tikva FC

 14 Maccabi Tel-Aviv FC

PROMOTED CLUBS

 15 FC Ashdod

16 Hapoel Ashkelon FC

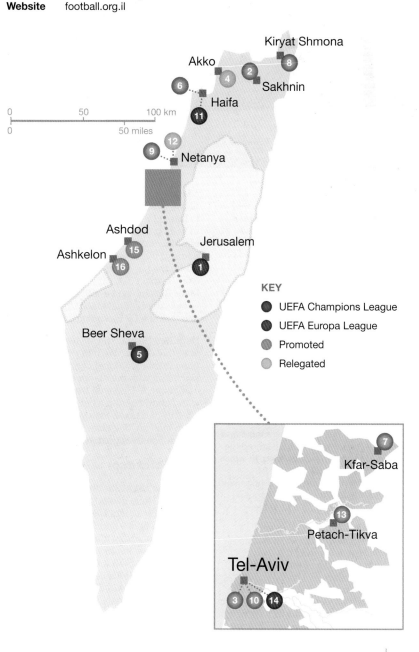

KEY
- UEFA Champions League
- UEFA Europa League
- Promoted
- Relegated

Hapoel Beer Sheva end 40-year wait

For the first time in 40 years the Israeli title went south, with the Crazy Reds of Hapoel Beer Sheva emerging victorious at the end of an exciting season-long dogfight with defending champions Maccabi Tel-Aviv.

Despite the phenomenal goalscoring exploits of the prolific Eran Zahavi, the Yellows not only missed out on a fourth successive Ligat Ha'al title but also failed to retain the State Cup, losing 1-0 in the final to arch-rivals Maccabi Haifa.

| Maccabi Tel-Aviv edged out in thrilling title duel | Maccabi Haifa win State Cup for sixth time | Golden boot hat-trick for ever-prolific Eran Zahavi |

Domestic league

Beer Sheva, who had finished third in the 2014/15 championship, replaced the experienced Elisha Levi with the youthful coach of the team that had finished one place above them, Hapoel Kiryat Shmona, and it would prove an inspired choice as the charismatic Barak Bakhar, who turned 36 a month into the campaign, led the club to a success that the Negev desert locals had not enjoyed since before he was born.

Beer Sheva did not get off to the best of starts under their new boss, losing their opening home game 1-0 to Maccabi Tel-Aviv and also going down by the same scoreline to relegation favourites Hapoel Akko. From October onwards, however, Bakhar worked his magic and the team responded with an incredible surge of form that would bring 18 wins and three draws in their next 21 matches, giving them a three-point lead over the title holders as the league reached the end of its first stage.

Maccabi Tel-Aviv had replaced double-winning coach Pako Ayestarán with Slaviša Jokanović, but the ex-Watford boss was relieved of his duties in January and succeeded by ex-Netherlands midfielder Peter Bosz. The Dutchman would not lose any of his 19 league games, but it was not enough to keep the yellow ribbons on the

championship trophy. Four successive draws in the run-in enabled Beer Sheva to return to the summit, and although their long unbeaten run finally ended, after 29 matches, in the penultimate game of the season, away to Maccabi Haifa, Bakhar's men recovered to beat Bnei Sakhnin 3-1, with two goals from Maor Buzaglo and another from fellow Israeli international Maor Melikson, and take the title by two points.

Had Beer Sheva not claimed that final-day victory, the title would have gone to the defending champions, who signed off with their biggest win of the campaign, 6-0 against Maccabi Haifa, with Zahavi scoring a hat-trick to boost his end-of-season tally to 35 goals – 21 more than anyone else– and claim a third successive golden boot.

Domestic cup

Just three days after that heavy defeat, Maccabi Haifa gained ample revenge by defeating Maccabi Tel-Aviv 1-0 in the State Cup final – and finally getting their hands on a trophy that had escaped their clutches for 18 years, four final defeats having left a trail of frustration. The match in Jerusalem was decided by a 36th-minute free-kick from Haifa's Polish international Ludovic Obraniak, giving coach Ronny Levi a trophy in his first season back at the club he had led

to three successive league titles during his first spell. As for his opposite number, Bosz, the Dutchman's first defeat would come in his final game as he left Tel-Aviv to take over at Ajax.

Europe

It was Bosz's predecessor Jokanović who took the credit for leading Maccabi Tel-Aviv into the group stage of the UEFA Champions League thanks to Zahavi-inspired wins over Viktoria Plzeň and FC Basel. However, the Serb was also in charge – and would later pay the price – for the team's subsequent whitewash in the competition proper, in which they lost home and away to Chelsea, Dynamo Kyiv and FC Porto and scored just one goal, a Zahavi penalty.

National team

The Israeli national team did not get out much in 2015/16. Just two friendlies followed the completion of the UEFA EURO 2016 qualifying campaign, which ended badly with two defeats, prompting coach Eli Gutman to announce his immediate resignation. Ex-Beer Sheva boss Elisha Levi was appointed as his successor six months later, albeit with little or no expectation of taking Israel to the 2018 FIFA World Cup from a qualifying group containing both Italy and Spain.

DOMESTIC SEASON AT A GLANCE

Ligat Ha'al 2015/16 final table

		Pld	Home W	D	L	F	A	Away W	D	L	F	A	Total W	D	L	F	A	Pts
1	**Hapoel Beer Sheva FC**	36	12	5	1	34	11	13	3	2	32	13	25	8	3	66	24	83
2	Maccabi Tel-Aviv FC	36	13	2	3	49	17	11	7	0	27	7	24	9	3	76	24	81
3	Beitar Jerusalem FC	36	11	3	4	23	16	7	3	8	23	21	18	6	12	46	37	58
4	Maccabi Haifa FC	36	8	6	4	24	16	6	5	7	21	26	14	11	11	45	42	53
5	Bnei Sakhnin FC	36	6	5	7	19	19	7	4	7	27	21	13	9	14	46	40	48
6	Hapoel Ra'anana FC	36	5	4	9	21	28	6	5	7	17	20	11	9	16	38	48	42
7	Maccabi Petach-Tikva FC	33	7	4	6	19	15	6	3	7	15	20	13	7	13	34	35	46
8	Bnei Yehuda Tel-Aviv FC	33	5	4	8	18	25	8	3	5	19	18	13	7	13	37	43	46
9	Hapoel Tel-Aviv FC	33	3	5	8	10	22	7	7	3	20	15	10	12	11	30	37	42
10	Hapoel Kfar-Saba FC	33	5	6	6	11	14	4	5	7	12	23	9	11	13	23	37	38
11	Hapoel Kiryat Shmona FC	33	5	6	5	17	15	3	6	8	15	24	8	12	13	32	39	36
12	Hapoel Haifa FC	33	4	5	7	17	24	3	8	6	21	24	7	13	13	38	48	34
13	Hapoel Akko FC	33	5	4	8	17	22	4	3	9	10	26	9	7	17	27	48	34
14	Maccabi Netanya FC	33	0	6	10	6	23	1	3	13	8	27	1	9	23	14	50	12

NB League splits into top six and bottom eight after 26 games, after which the clubs play exclusively against teams in their group;
Beitar Jerusalem FC – 2 pts deducted.

European qualification 2016/17

CHAMPIONS LEAGUE

Champion: Hapoel Beer Sheva FC (second qualifying round)

EUROPA LEAGUE

Cup winner: Maccabi Haifa FC (second qualifying round)
Maccabi Tel-Aviv FC (first qualifying round)
Beitar Jerusalem FC (first qualifying round)

Top scorer	Eran Zahavi (M. Tel-Aviv), 35 goals
Relegated clubs	Maccabi Netanya FC, Hapoel Akko FC
Promoted clubs	FC Ashdod, Hapoel Ashkelon FC
Cup final	Maccabi Haifa FC 1-0 Maccabi Tel-Aviv FC

Team of the season
(4-3-3)

Coach: Bakhar (H. Beer Sheva)

Stojković (M. Haifa)

Dasa (M. Tel-Aviv) — Tzedek (H. Beer Sheva) — Tibi (M. Tel-Aviv) — Davidzada (H. Beer Sheva)

Mugrabi (Bnei Sakhnin) — Ogu (H. Beer Sheva) — Melikson (H. Beer Sheva)

Rukavytsya (Beitar) — Zahavi (M. Tel-Aviv) — Barda (H. Beer Sheva)

Player of the season

Elyaniv Barda
(Hapoel Beer Sheva FC)

Although Barda had previously won two league titles with Maccabi Haifa – plus another in Belgium with Genk – nothing that had gone before could match the thrill of skippering his hometown and boyhood club to Ligat Ha'al glory in 2015/16. The 34-year-old Israeli international striker might not have found the back of the net with the fluency of Maccabi Tel-Aviv's Eran Zahavi, but he was Beer Sheba's leading marksman with 14 goals and a thoroughly deserved winner of the Israeli footballer of the year award.

Newcomer of the season

Neta Lavi
(Maccabi Haifa FC)

Born in the United States, Lavi moved to Israel aged 14 and worked his way through the youth ranks at Maccabi Haifa before making his first-team debut in the Haifa derby against Hapoel on 7 December 2015. The 19-year-old holding midfielder would become a regular in Ronny Levi's side thereafter, performing with discipline and authority and closing the season with an excellent display in the club's State Cup final victory over Maccabi Tel-Aviv. A week later he won his first senior cap for Israel in a friendly against Serbia.

ISRAEL

NATIONAL TEAM

International tournament appearances
FIFA World Cup (1) 1970

Top five all-time caps
Yossi Benayoun (97); Arik Benado (94); **Tal Ben Haim I** (91); Alon Harazi (88); Amir Shelach (85)

Top five all-time goals
Mordechay Shpiegler (33); **Yossi Benayoun** & Yehushua Feigenboim (24); Ronen Harazi (23); Nahum Stelmach (22)

Results 2015/16

03/09/15	Andorra (ECQ)	H	Haifa	W	4-0	*Zahavi (3), N Biton (22), Hemed (26p), Dabbur (38)*
06/09/15	Wales (ECQ)	A	Cardiff	D	0-0	
10/10/15	Cyprus (ECQ)	H	Jerusalem	L	1-2	*N Biton (76)*
13/10/15	Belgium (ECQ)	A	Brussels	L	1-3	*Hemed (88)*
23/03/16	Croatia	A	Osijek	L	0-2	
31/05/16	Serbia	A	Novi Sad	L	1-3	*Zahavi (50p)*

Appearances 2015/16

Coach: Eli Gutman /(12/02/16) (Alon Hazan) /(20/04/16) Elisha Levi	24/02/58 14/09/67 18/11/57		AND	WAL	CYP	BEL	Cro	Srb	Caps	Goals
Ofir Marciano	07/10/89	Mouscron-Péruwelz (BEL)	G	G	G	G			10	-
Eli Dasa	03/12/92	M. Tel-Aviv	D	D	D54				3	-
Tal Ben Haim I	31/03/82	M. Tel-Aviv	D46	D	D	D			91	1
Eitan Tibi	16/11/87	M. Tel-Aviv	D	D	D	D	D	D	26	-
Avi Rikan	10/09/88	M. Tel-Aviv	D		s59				5	-
Nir Biton	30/10/91	Celtic (SCO)	M	M	M		M	M85	18	2
Eran Zahavi	25/07/87	M. Tel-Aviv	M46	M93	M	M		A	31	5
Bebras Natcho	18/02/88	CSKA Moskva (RUS)	M	M				M71	42	1
Munas Dabbur	14/05/92	Grasshoppers (SUI)	A	A46	A		A	A46	6	1
Tomer Hemed	02/05/87	Brighton (ENG)	A75	s46	s65	A	A76		22	12
Tal Ben Haim II	05/08/89	M. Tel-Aviv	A	s46	M	M59	M76	A58	19	3
Maor Buzaglo	14/01/88	H. Beer Sheva	s46				M46	s58	20	1
Maor Melikson	30/10/84	H. Beer Sheva	s46		s71			M60	21	3
Beram Kayal	02/05/88	Brighton (ENG)	s75	M46	M	M66	s83		31	1
Orel Dgani	08/01/89	M. Haifa		D	s54	D			8	-
Omri Ben Harush	07/03/90	M. Tel-Aviv		D	D71	D			14	-
Ben Sahar	10/08/89	H. Beer Sheva		s93				s46	38	6
Gil Vermouth	05/08/85	M. Tel-Aviv			M65	s77			28	2
Sheran Yeini	08/12/86	Vitesse (NED)			M77		D		17	-
Dor Peretz	17/05/95	M. Tel-Aviv				M	s85		2	-
Omer Damari	24/03/89	Salzburg (AUT)				s66			20	9
Boris Kleiman	26/10/90	Beitar Jerusalem					G		1	-
Ben Biton	03/01/91	H. Beer Sheva					D46		1	-
Rami Gershon	12/08/88	Gent (BEL)					D		22	2
Taleb Tawatha	21/06/92	M. Haifa					D67		5	-
Roi Kehat	12/05/92	Austria Wien (AUT)					M83	s60	3	-
Almog Cohen	01/09/88	Ingolstadt (GER)					s46		14	-
Shir Tzedek	22/08/89	H. Beer Sheva					s46	D	5	-
Kenny Saief	17/12/93	Gent (BEL)					s67	s80	2	-
Yossi Benayoun	05/05/80	M. Haifa					s76		97	24
Elyaniv Barda	15/12/81	H. Beer Sheva					s76		38	12
Dudu Goresh	01/02/80	H. Beer Sheva						G	1	-
Ofir Davidzada	05/05/91	H. Beer Sheva						D80	5	-
Neta Lavi	25/08/96	M. Haifa						s71	1	-

EUROPE

Maccabi Tel-Aviv FC

Second qualifying round - Hibernians FC (MLT)
A 1-2 *Igiebor (22)*
Juan Pablo, Alberman, Ben Haim (II), Micha, Tibi, Mitrović (Ben Harush 46), Ben Haim (I), Vermouth (Itzhaki 59), Carlos García, Igiebor, Ben Basat. Coach: Slaviša Jokanović (SRB)
H 5-1 *Jorginho (32og), Zahavi (58p, 90), Ben Haim (II) (61), Igiebor (82)*
Juan Pablo, Shpungin, Alberman, Zahavi, Ben Haim (II) (Itzhaki 81), Micha (Ben Basat 86), Ben Harush (Ziv 62), Mitrović, Ben Haim (I), Carlos García, Igiebor. Coach: Slaviša Jokanović (SRB)

Third qualifying round - FC Viktoria Plzeň (CZE)
H 1-2 *Itzhaki (79)*
Juan Pablo, Shpungin, Alberman, Zahavi, Ben Basat (Rikan 46), Ben Haim (II) (Itzhaki 64), Ziv, Micha (Vermouth 46), Ben Haim (I), Carlos García, Igiebor. Coach: Slaviša Jokanović (SRB)
A 2-0 *Zahavi (76p, 83)*
Juan Pablo, Shpungin, Alberman, Zahavi, Itzhaki (Micha 73), Ben Haim (II) (Mitrović 59), Tibi, Ben Harush, Rikan (Vermouth 65), Ben Haim (I), Igiebor. Coach: Slaviša Jokanović (SRB)

Play-offs - FC Basel 1893 (SUI)
A 2-2 *Zahavi (31, 90+6)*
Juan Pablo, Shpungin, Alberman, Zahavi, Ben Basat (Mitrović 51), Ben Haim (II), Tibi, Ben Harush, Rikan (Micha 89), Ben Haim (I), Igiebor (D Peretz 71). Coach: Slaviša Jokanović (SRB)
H 1-1 *Zahavi (24)*
Juan Pablo, Shpungin, Alberman, Zahavi, Ben Haim (II) (Micha 83), Tibi, Ben Harush, Rikan, Mitrović (Itzhaki 90+1), Ben Haim (I), Igiebor (D Peretz 70). Coach: Slaviša Jokanović (SRB)

Group G
Match 1 - Chelsea FC (ENG)
A 0-4
Rajković, Shpungin (D Peretz 71), Alberman, Zahavi, Ben Haim (II) (Micha 64), Tibi, Ben Harush, Rikan (Radonjić 64), Mitrović, Ben Haim (I), Igiebor. Coach: Slaviša Jokanović (SRB)
Match 2 - FC Dynamo Kyiv (UKR)
H 0-2
Rajković, Dasa, Alberman, Zahavi, Ben Basat (Ben Haim (II) 46), Tibi, Rikan, Mitrović (Itzhaki 61), Ben Haim (I), Vermouth (Micha 79), D Peretz. Coach: Slaviša Jokanović (SRB)
Match 3 - FC Porto (POR)
A 0-2
Rajković, Alberman, Zahavi, Ben Haim (II) (Itzhaki 84), Micha (Vermouth 73), Tibi, Ben Harush, Mitrović (Rikan 56), Ben Haim (I), Carlos García, D Peretz. Coach: Slaviša Jokanović (SRB)
Match 4 - FC Porto (POR)
H 1-3 *Zahavi (75p)*
Rajković, Alberman, Zahavi, Ben Haim (II), Tibi, Ben Harush (Ben Basat 46), Rikan, Ben Haim (I), Vermouth (Mitrović 46), Carlos García, D Peretz (Igiebor 82). Coach: Slaviša Jokanović (SRB)

Match 5 - Chelsea FC (ENG)
H 0-4
Rajković, Dasa, Alberman (Azulay 85), Zahavi (Itzhaki 89), Ben Haim (II) (Ben Basat 80), Ben Harush, Rikan, Ben Haim (I), Carlos García, Igiebor, D Peretz. Coach: Slaviša Jokanović (SRB)
Red card: Ben Haim (I) 41
Match 6 - FC Dynamo Kyiv (UKR)
A 0-1
Rajković, Dasa, Alberman, Zahavi, Ben Haim (II) (Itzhaki 83), Micha (Vermouth 72), Tibi, Ben Harush, Rikan, Carlos García, Igiebor (D Peretz 72). Coach: Slaviša Jokanović (SRB)

Hapoel Kiryat Shmona FC

Third qualifying round - FC Slovan Liberec (CZE)
A 1-2 *Abed (89)*
Haimov, Borhel, Kassio, Gutiérrez, Abed, Ostvind (Mizrahi 75), Elkayam, Broun, Shukrani (Rochet 51), Bruno, Exbrad (Chukwuma 46). Coach: Saleh Hasarma (ISR)
H 0-3
Haimov, Borhel, Kassio, Gutiérrez, Abed, Chukwuma, Ostvind (Mizrahi 54), Elkayam, Broun (Shamir 61), Rochet (Shukrani 78), Bruno. Coach: Saleh Hasarma (ISR)

Hapoel Beer Sheva FC

Second qualifying round - FC Thun (SUI)
H 1-1 *Hoban (26)*
Goresh, B Biton, Tzedek, Radi (Gordana 88), Barda (Sahar 61), Buzaglo, Hoban, Davidzada, Melikson (Nwakaeme 77), William, Ogu. Coach: Barak Bakhar (ISR)
A 1-2 *Ogu (6)*
Goresh, B Biton, Tzedek, Radi, Barda (Taha 39), Buzaglo, Hoban (Sahar 75), Davidzada, Melikson (Nwakaeme 83), William, Ogu. Coach: Barak Bakhar (ISR)
Red card: Tzedek 20

Beitar Jerusalem FC

First qualifying round - FC Ordabasy Shymkent (KAZ)
A 0-0
Kleiman, Kachila, Atzili (Nachmani 64), Claudemir, Gabay, L Cohen (Zamir 54), Yerouham, Magbo (I Cohen 73), Zhairi, Matović, Askling. Coach: Slobodan Drapich (ISR)
H 2-1 *Atzili (17), Gabay (60)*
Kleiman, Dasa (Yerouham 67), Kachila, Atzili, Claudemir, Prada (L Cohen 53), Gabay, Zhairi, Nachmani (Magbo 74), Matović, Askling. Coach: Slobodan Drapich (ISR)

Second qualifying round - R. Charleroi SC (BEL)
A 1-5 *Gabay (35)*
Kleiman, Dasa, Kachila, Atzili (L Cohen 75), Claudemir, Prada (De Lucas 55), Gabay, Zhairi, Nachmani (Zamir 30), Matović, Askling. Coach: Slobodan Drapich (ISR)
Red cards: Dasa 45+2, De Lucas 76
H 1-4 *Atzili (16)*
Kleiman, Kapiloto, Kachila, Atzili, A Cohen (L Cohen 61), Claudemir, Prada (Zamir 61), Gabay, Zhairi (I Cohen 46), Magbo, Matović. Coach: Slobodan Drapich (ISR)

DOMESTIC LEAGUE CLUB-BY-CLUB

Beitar Jerusalem FC

1939 • Teddy (34,000) • beitarfc.co.il

Major honours
Israeli League (6) 1987, 1993, 1997, 1998, 2007, 2008;
Israeli Cup (7) 1976, 1979, 1985, 1986, 1989, 2008,
2009

Coach: Slobodan Drapich

2015

24/08	h	H. Tel-Aviv	D	0-0
30/08	a	M. Netanya	D	0-0
12/09	h	H. Haifa	D	1-1	*Atzili*
19/09	a	Bnei Yehuda	L	1-2	*L Cohen*
28/09	h	H. Kfar-Saba	W	3-1	*Zhairi, Jesús Rueda, Rukavytsya*
05/10	a	Bnei Sakhnin	W	3-1	*Gabay, Atzili 2*
19/10	h	H. Beer Sheva	L	1-3	*Rukavytsya*
26/10	a	M. Tel-Aviv	W	4-2	*Rukavytsya 3, L Cohen*
02/11	h	H. Ra'anana	W	1-0	*L Cohen*
08/11	a	M. Haifa	W	2-0	*Gabay, Atzili*
22/11	h	H. Akko	W	1-0	*Gabai*
28/11	a	H. Petach-Tikva	L	0-2	
06/12	h	H. Kiryat Shmona	W	2-0	*L Cohen, Atzili (p)*
12/12	a	H. Tel-Aviv	D	0-0	
19/12	h	M. Netanya	W	1-0	*Matović*
26/12	a	H. Haifa	D	1-1	*Rukavytsya*

2016

02/01	h	Bnei Yehuda	W	1-0	*Atzili (p)*
10/01	a	H. Kfar-Saba	L	0-1	
18/01	h	Bnei Sakhnin	W	1-0	*L Cohen*
24/01	a	H. Beer Sheva	L	1-2	*Matović*
01/02	h	M. Tel-Aviv	D	2-2	*Atzili, Keltjens*
08/02	a	H. Ra'anana	W	2-0	*Rukavytsya, Shechter*
15/02	h	M. Haifa	W	3-0	*Shechter, Rukavytsya, Einbinder*
21/02	h	H. Akko	W	3-1	*og (Mishaelov), Rukavytsya, Gabay*
27/02	h	M. Petach-Tikva	W	2-0	*Claudemir, Rukavytsya*
05/03	a	H. Kiryat Shmona	W	2-0	*Claudemir, Rukavytsya*
14/03	h	M. Haifa	W	3-2	*Rukavytsya, Einbinder, Valpoort*
19/03	a	Bnei Sakhnin	L	0-2	
04/04	h	H. Beer Sheva	L	0-2	
11/04	a	M. Tel-Aviv	L	2-3	*Rukavytsya 2 (1p)*
18/04	h	H. Ra'anana	W	1-0	*Gabay*
24/04	a	M. Haifa	L	0-1	
01/05	h	Bnei Sakhnin	L	0-3	
09/05	a	H. Beer Sheva	L	0-2	
14/05	h	M. Tel-Aviv	L	0-2	
21/05	a	H. Ra'anana	W	2-1	*Valpoort, Shechter*

No	Name	Nat	DoB	Pos	Aps	(s)	Gls
90	Joakim Askling		04/01/90	A	4	(2)	
7	Omer Atzili		27/07/93	M	26	(3)	7
14	Claudemir	BRA	17/08/84	M	35	(1)	2
12	Avishay Cohen		19/06/95	A	9	(3)	
9	Itzhak Cohen		01/01/90	A		(7)	
17	Lidor Cohen		16/12/92	M	20	(16)	5
91	Pablo De Lucas	ESP	20/09/86	M	8	(1)	
11	Dan Einbinder		16/02/89	M	26	(2)	2
26	El'ad Gabai		15/11/85	D	27	(3)	1
16	Dovev Gabay		01/04/87	A	13	(18)	4
4	Jesús Rueda	ESP	19/02/87	D	29		1
6	Tal Kachila		26/06/92	D	22		
1	Nissim Kapiloto		01/10/89	D	15		
3	David Keltjens		11/06/95	D	23	(2)	1
1	Boris Kleiman		26/10/90	G	34		
77	Ori Magbo		12/09/87	D	6	(6)	
81	Dušan Matović	SRB	08/07/83	D	31	(2)	2
28	Snir Mishan		13/11/88	D	3		
22	Omer Nachmani		29/10/83	A	1	(2)	
10	Dani Prada		01/04/87	M		(5)	
13	Nikita Rukavytsya	AUS	22/06/87	A	29	(1)	14
9	Etay Shechter		22/02/87	A	16		3
22	Stav Shushan		14/05/95	G	2		
19	Arsenio Valpoort	NED	05/08/92	A	3	(5)	2
23	Tomer Yeruham		06/04/93	D	2		
15	Nes Zamir		31/10/90	M	2	(5)	
18	Liroy Zhairi		02/03/89	M	10	(15)	1
18	Roi Zickry		13/10/92	A		(3)	

Bnei Sakhnin FC

1993 • Doha (8,500) • no website

Major honours
Israeli Cup (1) 2004

Coach: Eli Cohen;
(19/12/15) Yossi Abuksis

2015

22/08	a	M. Tel-Aviv	L	2-3	*Georginho, Amasha*
29/08	h	H. Ra'anana	L	2-3	*Amasha, Georginho*
12/09	a	M. Haifa	D	0-0	
19/09	h	H. Akko	W	2-0	*Mugrabi, Georginho*
26/09	a	H. Petach-Tikva	W	1-0	*Amasha*
05/10	h	Beitar	L	1-3	*Azulay*
17/10	a	H. Tel-Aviv	W	4-0	*Amasha (p), Azulay, Osman, Elihen*
24/10	h	M. Netanya	D	0-0	
31/10	a	H. Haifa	L	0-2	
07/11	h	Bnei Yehuda	D	2-2	*Amasha, Osman*
21/11	a	H. Kfar-Saba	L	0-1	
28/11	a	H. Kiryat Shmona	W	2-0	*Amasha, Azulay*
05/12	h	H. Beer Sheva	L	0-1	
14/12	h	M. Tel-Aviv	L	0-2	
19/12	a	H. Ra'anana	L	0-1	
26/12	h	M. Haifa	L	1-2	*Azulay*

2016

02/01	a	H. Akko	D	2-2	*Georginho, Amasha*
09/01	h	M. Petach-Tikva	W	1-0	*Osman*
18/01	a	Beitar	L	0-1	
23/01	h	H. Tel-Aviv	W	1-0	*Mugrabi*
30/01	h	M. Netanya	W	2-0	*Mugrabi 2 (1p)*
06/02	h	H. Haifa	D	0-0	
13/02	a	Bnei Yehuda	W	2-0	*og (Azoz), Amasha*
20/02	h	M. Kfar-Saba	W	2-0	*Mugrabi, Mousa*
27/02	h	H. Kiryat Shmona	W	3-0	*Mugrabi, Azulay (p), Amasha*
07/03	h	H. Beer Sheva	D	2-2	*Osman, Azulay*
12/03	a	M. Tel-Aviv	L	0-1	
19/03	h	Beitar	W	2-0	*Amasha, Azulay*
02/04	h	M. Haifa	D	3-3	*Azulay 2, Georginho*
09/04	a	H. Ra'anana	W	3-2	*Georginho 2, Azulay*
16/04	h	H. Beer Sheva	L	1-4	*Mugrabi*
25/04	a	M. Tel-Aviv	D	0-0	
01/05	a	Beitar	W	3-0	*Azulay 3*
07/05	h	M. Haifa	L	0-1	
14/05	h	H. Ra'anana	D	1-1	*Mugrabi (p)*
21/05	a	H. Beer Sheva	L	1-3	*Mugrabi*

No	Name	Nat	DoB	Pos	Aps	(s)	Gls
5	Abraham Paz	ESP	29/06/79	D	31		
8	Ala'a Abu Saleh		25/06/87	D	20	(1)	
20	Muamen Agbaria		24/08/93	D		(3)	
14	Wiyam Amasha		08/08/85	A	21	(7)	9
11	Yuval Avidor		19/10/86	A	8	(1)	
9	Shlomi Azulay		18/10/89	A	34	(2)	14
23	Muhamad Badarna		15/11/95	A	1	(1)	
3	Itzhak Cohen		22/04/83	D	23		
88	Diogo Kachuba	BRA	16/02/90	M	23	(5)	
77	Tzachi Elihen		03/04/91	M	3	(15)	1
52	Georginho	BRA	28/05/89	M	28	(3)	7
17	Hamed Ghanayim		08/07/87	M	9	(9)	
29,10	Amir Halaila		21/03/97	A	1	(6)	
15	Haled Halaula		16/12/82	M	25	(2)	
44	Eldar Hasanović	BIH	12/01/90	M	9	(9)	
68	Igor Jovanovic	GER	03/05/89	D	3		
1	Ran Kadosh		04/10/85	G	17	(1)	
22	Mahmoud Kandil		11/08/88	G	19		
99,3	Obeida Khatab		14/07/92	M	3		
23	Hilal Mousa	PLE	31/05/90	M	4	(16)	1
10	Firas Mugrabi		24/07/91	M	31	(2)	9
18	Ali Osman		08/02/87	M	34		4
6	Tambi Sages		21/10/94	M	14	(6)	
27	Ihab Shami		18/09/93	D	17	(5)	
25	Wanderson	BRA	13/09/91	D	14		
24	Ali Zbedat		08/03/94	M	2		
7	Mohamed Zbedat		15/11/91	D	2	(2)	
21	Safwan Zoabi		08/06/92	M	4		

Bnei Yehuda Tel-Aviv FC

1936 • Bloomfield (14,413) • bneiyehuda.com

Major honours
Israeli League (1) 1990; Israeli Cup (2) 1968, 1981

Coach: Yossi Abuksis;
(09/12/15) Yossi Mizrahi

2015

22/08	a	M. Haifa	W	3-0	*Doubai, Buzaglo, Galván*
31/08	h	H. Akko	L	0-2	
12/09	a	M. Petach-Tikva	L	1-3	*Falach*
19/09	h	Beitar	W	2-1	*Galván, Agaiev*
28/09	a	H. Tel-Aviv	L	1-3	*Hadad*
03/10	h	M. Netanya	L	1-2	*Agaiev*
17/10	a	H. Haifa	W	1-0	*Galván*
24/10	h	H. Kiryat Shmona	D	2-2	*Kadusi, Galván (p)*
01/11	h	H. Kfar-Saba	W	2-1	*Nworuh, Galván*
07/11	a	Bnei Sakhnin	D	2-2	*Nworuh 2*
21/11	h	H. Beer Sheva	D	0-0	
29/11	a	M. Tel-Aviv	L	0-4	
05/12	h	H. Ra'anana	L	1-3	*Nworuh*
12/12	h	M. Haifa	D	0-0	
19/12	a	H. Akko	W	1-0	*Galván*
26/12	h	M. Petach-Tikva	D	1-1	*Galván*

2016

02/01	a	Beitar	L	0-1	
09/01	h	H. Tel-Aviv	L	1-3	*Buzaglo*
16/01	a	M. Netanya	W	2-0	*Nworuh, Galván (p)*
23/01	h	H. Haifa	W	1-0	*Agaiev*
30/01	a	H. Kiryat Shmona	D	1-1	*Agaiev*
06/02	h	H. Kfar-Saba	W	2-1	*Agaiev, Mori*
13/02	h	Bnei Sakhnin	L	0-2	
22/02	a	H. Beer Sheva	L	0-2	
27/02	h	M. Tel-Aviv	L	0-1	
05/03	a	H. Ra'anana	W	2-0	*Galván, Agaiev*
19/03	h	H. Kiryat Shmona	W	1-0	*Galván*
02/04	h	M. Petach-Tikva	L	1-2	*Buzaglo*
09/04	a	H. Kfar-Saba	W	1-0	*Haziza*
17/04	h	H. Akko	W	3-1	*Galván (p), Agaiev, Mršić*
01/05	a	M. Netanya	W	1-0	*Nworuh*
07/05	h	H. Tel-Aviv	L	2-4	*Galván, Nworuh*
16/05	a	H. Haifa	D	1-1	*Agaiev*

No	Name	Nat	DoB	Pos	Aps	(s)	Gls
10	Hasan Abu Zaid		04/02/91	M	10	(1)	
9	Amir Agaiev		10/02/92	M	25	(7)	8
1	Bamidele Aiyenugba	NGA	20/11/83	G	31		
17	Itzhak Azoz		30/11/85	D	26		
8	Asi Baldut		21/10/81	M	14	(11)	
18	Aviad Bourla		13/12/93	M	5	(4)	
5	Tal Bublil		19/09/88	D	2	(1)	
4	Almog Buzaglo		08/12/92	A	17	(9)	3
6	Thierry Doubai	CIV	01/07/88	M	16	(2)	1
15	Sari Falach		22/11/91	D	18	(1)	1
30	Stav Finish		26/03/92	M	22	(6)	
20	Pedro Galván	ARG	18/08/85	M	32	(1)	12
24	Sean Goldberg		13/06/92	D	17	(3)	
16	Ben Grabli		08/04/94	M	3		
21	Aviv Hadad		04/02/84	D	13	(1)	1
7	Dolev Haziza		05/07/95	A	4	(12)	1
22	Itamar Israeli		22/03/92	G	2	(1)	
10	Gil Itzhak		29/06/93	A		(1)	
31	Ohad Kadusi		24/09/85	A	3	(9)	1
27	Maor Kandil		27/11/93	M	6	(2)	
23	Shay Konstantini		27/06/96	A	10	(1)	
11	Raz Meir		30/11/96	M	7	(14)	
4	Dan Mori		29/07/90	D	20		1
5	Antonio Mršić	CRO	05/06/87	M	12	(1)	1
19	Jude Nworuh	NGA	09/06/89	A	18	(4)	7
3	Ben Zairi		17/05/92	D	21	(1)	
14	Gal Zruya		23/10/89	A	9	(5)	

Hapoel Akko FC

1946 • Akko Municipal (5,000) •
hapoelakko.co.il
**Coach: Yaron Hochenboim
(03/05/16) Momi Zaafran**

2015
22/08	h	H. Haifa	L	0-1
31/08	a	Bnei Yehuda	W	2-0 Kochav, Seider
12/09	h	H. Kfar-Saba	W	1-0 Seider
19/09	a	Bnei Sakhnin	L	0-2
26/09	h	H. Beer Sheva	W	1-0 Gilmore
03/10	a	M. Tel-Aviv	L	0-5
17/10	a	H. Ra'anana	L	0-1
24/10	a	M. Haifa	L	0-4
31/10	a	H. Kiryat Shmona	D	0-0
07/11	h	M. Petach-Tikva	W	1-0 Tzemach
22/11	a	Beitar	L	0-1
30/11	a	M. Tel-Aviv	L	0-1
05/12	a	M. Netanya	D	0-0
12/12	a	H. Haifa	L	1-3 Mishaelov (p)
19/12	h	Bnei Yehuda	L	0-1
26/12	a	H. Kfar-Saba	W	1-0 Kasum

2016
02/01	h	Bnei Sakhnin	D	2-2 Mishaelov, Tzemach (p)
09/01	a	H. Beer Sheva	L	0-3
18/01	h	M. Tel-Aviv	L	0-3
23/01	h	H. Ra'anana	L	1-3 Dayan
31/01	h	M. Haifa	D	1-1 Kopitović
06/02	h	H. Kiryat Shmona	W	1-0 Kopitović
13/02	a	M. Petach-Tikva	W	2-1 Dayan, Tzemach
21/02	h	Beitar	L	1-3 Jovanović
29/02	a	M. Tel-Aviv	W	2-0 Kehinde 2
05/03	a	M. Netanya	D	1-1 Kopitović
20/03	h	M. Netanya	W	4-1 Seys 2, Peretz, Gilmore
02/04	a	M. Tel-Aviv	L	0-1
09/04	h	H. Haifa	L	2-3 Kehinde 2
17/04	a	Bnei Yehuda	L	1-3 Kasum
30/04	h	M. Petach-Tikva	L	1-3 Seys
07/05	a	H. Kfar-Saba	D	0-0
16/05	h	H. Kiryat Shmona	D	1-1 Seider

No	Name	Nat	DoB	Pos	Aps	(s)	Gls
1	Dani Amos		02/02/87	G	33		
12	Bar Avitan		28/01/93	M		(1)	
20	Yaniv Brik		28/05/95	M	10		
10	Guy Dayan		20/08/86	M	11	(5)	2
45	Samuel Gilmore	NGA	20/07/96	A	23	(6)	2
9	Azat Halaila		27/03/94	A	1	(5)	
51	Rom Iluz		05/10/94	G		(1)	
2	A'la Jaffer		16/03/95	D	5	(8)	
24	Dor Jan		16/12/94	A		(9)	
21	Branislav Jovanović	SRB	21/09/85	M	31		1
7	Ahmed Kasum		25/01/85	A	32		3
99	Olanrewaju Kehinde	NGA	07/05/94	M	10		4
77	Obeida Khattab		14/07/92	D	7	(2)	
15	Dor Kochav		06/05/93	M	12	(12)	1
77	Adi Konstantinos		09/11/94	D	5	(7)	
55	Boris Kopitović	MNE	17/09/94	D	31		3
22	Lior Levi		26/10/87	D	13		
14	Shmuel Malul		03/04/93	M	30	(1)	
5	Moshe Mishaelov		14/09/83	D	30		2
9	Oz Peretz		19/04/94	A	8	(3)	1
16	Elior Seider		17/11/97	M	19	(12)	3
17	Dylan Seys	BEL	26/09/96	A	12	(1)	3
10	Shadi Sha'aban	PLE	04/03/92	M		(2)	
8	Zion Tzemach		19/01/90	M	13	(10)	3
13	Shon Weissman		14/02/96	A	8	(10)	
6	Adnan Zahirović	BIH	23/03/90	M	19	(1)	

Hapoel Beer Sheva FC

1949 • Turner (16,100) • hapoelb7.co.il
Major honours
Israeli League (3) 1975, 1976, 2016; Israeli Cup (1) 1997
Coach: Barak Bakhar

2015
23/08	a	H. Kiryat Shmona	W	3-1 Melikson, Sahar, Radi
30/08	h	M. Tel-Aviv	L	0-1
12/09	a	H. Ra'anana	W	3-2 Radi (p), Hoban, Sahar
21/09	h	M. Haifa	D	0-0
26/09	a	H. Akko	L	0-1
03/10	h	M. Petach-Tikva	W	5-2 Nwakaeme 2, Barda 2, Radi
19/10	a	Beitar	W	3-1 Melikson, Nwakaeme, Barda
25/10	h	H. Tel-Aviv	W	3-1 Nwakaeme, William, Barda
01/11	a	M. Netanya	W	2-0 Barda 2
09/11	h	H. Haifa	W	1-0 Arbeitman
21/11	a	Bnei Yehuda	D	0-0
28/11	h	H. Kfar-Saba	W	3-0 Radi, Tzedek, Barda
05/12	a	Bnei Sakhnin	W	1-0 Radi
13/12	h	H. Kiryat Shmona	W	2-1 Hoban, Ogu
21/12	a	M. Tel-Aviv	W	2-1 Barda, Melikson
28/12	h	H. Ra'anana	W	2-0 Barda, Nwakaeme

2016
04/01	a	M. Haifa	D	1-1 Buzaglo
09/01	h	H. Akko	W	3-0 Barda, Melikson, Nwakaeme
16/01	a	M. Petach-Tikva	W	1-0 Buzaglo (p)
24/01	h	Beitar	W	2-1 Buzaglo, Nwakaeme
30/01	a	M. Tel-Aviv	W	1-0 og (Yadin)
06/02	h	M. Netanya	W	2-0 Barda, Ogu
13/02	a	H. Haifa	W	2-1 Barda, Sahar
22/02	h	Bnei Yehuda	W	2-0 Barda, Broun
28/02	a	H. Kfar-Saba	W	2-1 Nwakaeme, Ogu
07/03	h	Bnei Sakhnin	D	2-2 Sahar, Buzaglo
12/03	h	H. Ra'anana	D	0-0
20/03	h	M. Tel-Aviv	D	1-1 Hoban
04/04	a	Beitar	W	2-0 Sahar 2
09/04	a	M. Haifa	D	1-1 Sahar (p)
16/04	a	Bnei Sakhnin	W	4-1 Ogu, Nwakaeme 2, Buzaglo
25/04	a	H. Ra'anana	W	4-1 Radi, Melikson, Sahar (p), Nwakaeme
02/05	a	M. Tel-Aviv	D	0-0
09/05	h	Beitar	W	2-0 Barda, Hoban
14/05	a	M. Haifa	L	1-2 Melikson
21/05	h	Bnei Sakhnin	W	3-1 Buzaglo 2, Melikson

No	Name	Nat	DoB	Pos	Aps	(s)	Gls
18	Shlomi Arbeitman		14/05/85	A	2	(12)	1
10	Elyaniv Barda		15/12/82	A	27	(8)	14
2	Ben Biton		03/01/91	D	26	(3)	
19	Dan Biton		20/07/95	M	1	(9)	
6	Vladimir Broun		06/05/89	M	2	(10)	1
11	Maor Buzaglo		14/01/88	M	20	(5)	7
13	Ofir Davidzada		05/05/91	D	29		
16	Muhammad Ghadir		21/01/91	A	1	(8)	
15	Roy Gordana		06/04/90	M	5	(11)	
1	Dudu Goresh		01/02/80	G	36		
28	Or Havivyan		27/12/94	M		(1)	
12	Ovidiu Hoban	ROU	27/12/82	M	33	(1)	4
24	Maor Melikson		30/10/84	A	24	(6)	7
9	Anthony Nwakaeme	NGA	21/03/89	A	29	(5)	11
30	John Ogu	NGA	20/04/88	M	34		4
7	Matan Ohayon		25/02/86	D	3	(3)	
7	Mahran Radi		01/07/82	M	27	(7)	6
14	Ben Sahar		10/08/89	A	11	(13)	8
20	Loai Taha		26/11/89	D	13	(2)	
7	Ben Turgeman		09/01/89	D	7	(1)	
5	Shir Tzedek		22/08/89	D	36		1
25	William	BRA	07/02/85	D	22	(2)	1

Hapoel Haifa FC

1924 • Sammy Ofer (30,820) •
hapoel-haifa.org.il
Major honours
Israeli League (1) 1999; Israeli Cup (3) 1963, 1966, 1974
**Coach: Tal Banin;
(21/12/15) (Meir Ben-Margi);
(15/02/16) Eli Cohen**

2015
22/08	a	H. Akko	W	1-0 Kijanskas
29/08	h	M. Petach-Tikva	L	0-3
12/09	a	Beitar	D	1-1 Suissa
19/09	h	M. Tel-Aviv	L	0-1
26/09	a	M. Netanya	W	2-1 Al Lala 2
03/10	h	H. Kiryat Shmona	L	1-4 Al Lala
17/10	h	Bnei Yehuda	L	0-1
24/10	a	H. Kfar-Saba	D	2-2 Al Lala, Abu-El-Nir
31/10	h	Bnei Sakhnin	W	2-0 Suissa, Kijanskas
09/11	a	H. Beer Sheva	L	0-1
21/11	h	M. Tel-Aviv	L	0-1
28/11	a	H. Ra'anana	D	2-2 Al Lala 2
07/12	h	M. Haifa	L	2-4 og (Stojković), Suissa
12/12	h	H. Akko	W	3-1 Suissa, Kijanskas, Korać
19/12	a	M. Petach-Tikva	D	1-1 Al Lala
26/12	h	Beitar	D	1-1 Al Lala

2016
03/01	h	M. Tel-Aviv	D	0-0
09/01	a	M. Netanya	W	2-0 Elbaz, Al Lala
16/01	a	H. Kiryat Shmona	D	1-1 Korać
23/01	a	Bnei Yehuda	L	0-1
30/01	h	H. Kfar-Saba	D	1-1 og (Badash)
06/02	a	Bnei Sakhnin	D	0-0
13/02	h	H. Beer Sheva	L	1-2 Elbaz
20/02	a	M. Tel-Aviv	L	1-2 Korać
27/02	h	H. Ra'anana	D	1-1 Korać
06/03	a	M. Haifa	L	2-3 Kiwan, og (Tawatha)
19/03	a	M. Petach-Tikva	L	1-2 og (Allyson)
03/04	h	H. Kfar-Saba	D	0-0
09/04	a	H. Akko	W	3-2 Al Lala 2, Falkoschenko
16/04	h	M. Netanya	W	2-1 Arbeitman, Falkoschenko
30/04	a	H. Tel-Aviv	D	3-3 Arbeitman 2, Falkoschenko
07/05	a	H. Kiryat Shmona	L	1-2 Al Lala
16/05	h	Bnei Yehuda	D	1-1 Arbeitman

No	Name	Nat	DoB	Pos	Aps	(s)	Gls
12	Amir Abu-El-Nir		27/02/89	A	7	(4)	1
11	Maaran Al Lala		07/03/82	A	23	(6)	12
17	Dabur Anes		29/04/91	D	2	(9)	
1	Niv Antman		02/08/92	G	12		
30	Marijan Antolović	CRO	07/05/89	G	10		
35	Shlomi Arbeitman		14/05/85	A	10	(2)	4
55	Dmitri Baga	BLR	04/01/90	M	13	(1)	
16	Bruno Pinheiro	POR	21/08/87	D	27	(3)	
26	Yossi Dora		25/08/91	M	26	(1)	
7	Eli Elbaz		21/01/92	A	5	(12)	2
28	Maxim Falkoschenko		04/01/96	A	5		3
9	Ofek Fishler		24/08/96	D	4	(1)	
19	Idan Golan		29/02/96	M		(1)	
18	Ali Khatib		18/03/89	M	4	(6)	
2	Tadas Kijanskas	LTU	06/09/85	D	29	(1)	3
8	Hiasham Kiwan		17/05/87	M	3	(12)	1
25	Žarko Korać	MNE	11/06/87	A	13	(12)	4
13	Přemysl Kovář	CZE	14/10/85	G	11		
4	Dor Malul		30/04/89	D	20	(1)	
5	Hanan Maman		28/08/89	M	21	(8)	
3	Haim Megrelashvili		04/07/82	D	28	(1)	
21	Oshri Roash		25/07/88	D	18	(1)	
23	Adrian Rochet		26/05/87	M	21	(5)	
24	Liran Sardal		02/07/94	M	4	(4)	
9	Tomer Suissa		21/12/88	A	23	(6)	4
6	Miki Yazao		01/01/91	M	6	(4)	

ISRAEL

Hapoel Kfar-Saba FC

1928 • Levita (5,800) • hapoel-kfs.org.il
Major honours
Israeli League (1) 1982; Israeli Cup (3) 1975, 1980, 1990
Coach: Felix Naim;
(11/01/16) Sharon Mimer

2015

22/08	a	H. Ra'anana	D	2-2	Mesika 2
29/08	h	M. Haifa	W	1-0	Tchibota
12/09	a	H. Akko	L	0-1	
19/09	h	M. Petach-Tikva	L	0-1	
28/09	a	Beitar	L	1-3	R Cohen
03/10	h	H. Tel-Aviv	D	1-1	Hugo López
17/10	a	M. Netanya	W	1-0	Itzhak
24/10	h	H. Haifa	D	2-2	Kehinde, Mesika
01/11	a	Bnei Yehuda	L	1-2	Hugo López (p)
07/11	h	H. Kiryat Shmona	D	0-0	
21/11	h	Bnei Sakhnin	W	1-0	Itzhak
28/11	a	H. Beer Sheva	L	0-3	
05/12	a	M. Tel-Aviv	D	0-0	
12/12	h	H. Ra'anana	D	0-0	
20/12	a	M. Haifa	D	1-1	Papadopoulos
26/12	h	H. Akko	L	0-1	

2016

02/01	a	M. Petach-Tikva	L	0-2	
10/01	h	Beitar	W	1-0	Itzhak
16/01	a	H. Tel-Aviv	W	1-0	Tchibota
23/01	h	M. Netanya	W	1-0	Itzhak (p)
30/01	a	H. Haifa	D	1-1	Itzhak
06/02	h	Bnei Yehuda	L	1-2	Biton
13/02	a	H. Kiryat Shmona	W	2-0	Tchibota, Biton
20/02	a	Bnei Sakhnin	L	0-2	
28/02	h	H. Beer Sheva	L	1-2	Fadida
05/03	a	M. Tel-Aviv	L	0-5	
19/03	h	H. Tel-Aviv	L	0-3	
03/04	a	H. Haifa	D	0-0	
09/04	h	Bnei Yehuda	L	0-1	
16/04	a	M. Petach-Tikva	W	1-0	Itzhak (p)
30/04	h	H. Kiryat Shmona	W	2-1	Papadopoulos, Fadida
07/05	h	H. Akko	D	0-0	
14/05	a	M. Netanya	L	1-2	Benesh

No	Name	Nat	DoB	Pos	Aps	(s)	Gls
10	Tal Ayele		25/05/89	A	5	(5)	
11	Guy Badash		24/05/94	A		(5)	
16	Tal Benesh		26/10/89	D	24	(1)	1
9	Dudu Biton		01/03/88	A	4	(6)	2
41	Sahar Braun		06/10/94	M		(2)	
22	Ohad Cohen		10/06/75	G	29		
15	Raz Cohen		11/11/94	M	26	(3)	1
1	Idan David		21/05/87	A	1	(7)	
26	Hezi Dilmoni		07/05/89	D	7	(1)	
20	Semi Elyakim		30/03/87	M	16	(3)	
28	Amar Fadida		17/07/90	M	18	(9)	2
7	Hugo López	ESP	15/05/88	M	29	(1)	2
21	Ran Itzhak		09/10/87	M	20	(8)	6
23	Liran Jan		11/03/93	D	9	(8)	
9	Olanrewaju Kehinde	NGA	07/05/94	M	8	(8)	1
4	Ben Khawaz		19/07/91	D	11	(4)	
7	Reef Mesika		15/06/89	M	19	(7)	3
77	Nevo Mizrahi		26/07/87	M	1	(3)	
6	Amir Nussbaum		09/10/80	D	31		
19	Ioannis Papadopoulos	GRE	09/03/89	M	14	(7)	2
1	Ben Rahav		29/04/89	G	4	(2)	
3	Ori Shitrit		21/01/86	D	11	(1)	
5	Eliran Simon		02/09/88	D	22		
25	Dino Škvorc	CRO	02/02/90	D	29		
8	Mavis Tchibota	CGO	07/05/96	A	25	(4)	3

Hapoel Kiryat Shmona FC

2000 • Kiryat Shmona Municipal (5,300) •
iturank8.co.il
Major honours
Israeli League (1) 2012; Israeli Cup (1) 2014
Coach: Salah Hasarma;
(14/02/16) Shlomi Dora

2015

23/08	h	H. Beer Sheva	L	1-3	Bruno
29/08	a	H. Tel-Aviv	W	3-0	Mizrahi 2 (1p), Abed
12/09	h	M. Tel-Aviv	D	1-1	Kassio
19/09	a	M. Netanya	D	1-1	Abed
26/09	h	H. Ra'anana	D	0-0	
03/10	a	M. Haifa	W	4-1	Shamir 2, Abed, Mizrahi
18/10	h	M. Haifa	W	2-0	Shamir, Mizrahi
24/10	a	Bnei Yehuda	D	2-2	Abed 2
31/10	h	H. Akko	D	0-0	
07/11	a	H. Kfar-Saba	D	0-0	
21/11	h	M. Petach-Tikva	L	0-1	
28/11	h	Bnei Sakhnin	L	0-2	
06/12	a	Beitar	L	0-2	
13/12	a	H. Beer Sheva	L	1-2	Mizrahi
19/12	h	H. Tel-Aviv	W	3-0	Mizrahi, Bruno, Ostvind
27/12	a	M. Tel-Aviv	L	0-5	

2016

02/01	h	M. Netanya	W	3-0	Bruno, Mizrahi 2
09/01	a	H. Ra'anana	D	1-1	Mizrahi
16/01	h	H. Haifa	D	1-1	Amutu
24/01	a	M. Haifa	W	1-0	Amutu
30/01	h	Bnei Yehuda	D	1-1	Bruno
06/02	h	H. Akko	L	0-1	
13/02	h	H. Kfar-Saba	L	0-2	
20/02	a	M. Petach-Tikva	D	0-0	
27/02	a	Bnei Sakhnin	L	0-3	
05/03	a	Beitar	L	0-2	
19/03	a	Bnei Yehuda	L	0-1	
02/04	h	M. Netanya	W	2-0	Ostvind, Tchalisher
10/04	a	M. Petach-Tikva	L	0-2	
16/04	h	H. Tel-Aviv	D	1-1	Amutu
30/04	a	H. Kfar-Saba	L	1-2	Mizrahi
07/05	h	H. Haifa	W	2-1	Abed, Amutu
16/05	a	H. Akko	D	1-1	Amutu

No	Name	Nat	DoB	Pos	Aps	(s)	Gls
7	Ahmed Abed		30/03/90	M	27	(2)	6
20	Naor Aboudi		17/07/93	M		(13)	
29	Austin Amutu	NGA	20/02/93	D	12	(2)	5
16	Eli Baliliti		23/02/94	M	3	(1)	
2	Daniel Borhel		14/06/91	D	19	(3)	
15	Vladimir Broun		06/05/89	M	18		
37	Bruno	BRA	22/07/93	A	24	(3)	4
9	Ugwu Chukwuma	NGA	20/06/96	A	3	(8)	
6	Hen Dilmoni		07/05/89	D	7	(4)	
27	Oded Elkayam		09/02/88	D	27		
77	Ido Exbard		16/12/88	A	3	(3)	
5	Luis Gutiérrez	BOL	15/01/85	D	26	(2)	
55	Guy Haimov		09/03/86	G	23		
3	Kassio	BRA	11/02/87	D	26		1
26	Dean Maimoni		04/05/90	D	18	(4)	
9	David Manga	CTA	03/02/89	A	3	(4)	
22	Mauricio	BRA	31/12/92	A	1		
8	Ofir Mizrahi		04/12/93	M	28	(4)	10
10	Or Ostvind		18/12/87	M	15	(14)	2
21	Oz Rali		22/12/87	M	9	(6)	
21	Adrian Rochet		26/05/87	M	2		
18	Eden Shamir		25/06/95	M	29	(3)	3
28	Roei Shukrani		26/06/90	M	20	(7)	
11	Rokas Stanulevičius	LTU	02/10/94	M	3	(3)	
16	Omer Tchalisher		22/01/93	D	9	(3)	1
45	Mahdi Zoabi		15/07/95	G	10	(1)	

Hapoel Ra'anana FC

1972 • Municipal, Netanya (14,300) •
hapoel-raanana.co.il
Coach: Haim Silvas

2015

22/08	h	H. Kfar-Saba	D	2-2	Thiam (p), Nimni
29/08	a	Bnei Sakhnin	W	3-2	Kangwa 2, Eiloz
12/09	h	H. Beer Sheva	L	2-3	Mihelič, Arshid
20/09	a	M. Tel-Aviv	W	2-1	Kangwa, Shoker
26/09	a	H. Kiryat Shmona	D	0-0	
03/10	h	M. Haifa	L	0-2	
17/10	a	H. Akko	W	1-0	Badash
24/10	a	M. Petach-Tikva	W	2-0	Badash (p), Shoker
02/11	a	Beitar	L	0-1	
07/11	h	H. Tel-Aviv	L	0-1	
21/11	a	M. Netanya	W	3-1	Vahaba, Badash, Babayev
28/11	h	H. Haifa	D	2-2	Shoker, Mihelič
05/12	a	Bnei Yehuda	W	3-1	Shabtai, Kangwa 2
12/12	a	H. Kfar-Saba	D	0-0	
19/12	h	Bnei Sakhnin	W	1-0	Kangwa
28/12	a	H. Beer Sheva	L	0-2	

2016

02/01	h	M. Tel-Aviv	L	0-2	
09/01	h	H. Kiryat Shmona	D	1-1	Thiam
17/01	a	M. Haifa	L	0-2	
23/01	h	H. Akko	W	3-1	Vahaba, Badash, Kangwa
30/01	h	M. Petach-Tikva	W	1-0	Kangwa
08/02	h	Beitar	L	0-2	
13/02	a	H. Tel-Aviv	L	1-2	Shabtai
20/02	h	M. Netanya	W	1-0	Kangwa
27/02	a	H. Haifa	D	1-1	Kangwa
05/03	h	Bnei Yehuda	L	0-1	
12/03	a	H. Beer Sheva	D	0-0	
20/03	h	M. Haifa	W	3-0	Mihelič (p), Shabtai, Badash
03/04	a	M. Tel-Aviv	L	0-3	
09/04	h	Bnei Sakhnin	L	2-3	Kangwa, Radonjić
18/04	a	Beitar	L	0-1	
25/04	h	H. Beer Sheva	L	1-4	Radonjić
30/04	a	M. Haifa	L	0-2	
09/05	h	M. Tel-Aviv	D	1-1	Badash
14/05	a	Bnei Sakhnin	D	1-1	Shabtai
21/05	h	Beitar	L	1-2	Shaker

No	Name	Nat	DoB	Pos	Aps	(s)	Gls
12	Yosef Abu Laben		26/05/92	A		(2)	
28	Karem Arshid		24/01/95	A	3	(13)	1
7	Eli Babayev		01/11/90	M	29	(1)	1
99,10	Barak Badash		30/08/92	A	15	(11)	6
80	Elis Bakaj	ALB	25/06/87	A	1		
10	Sahar Benbenisti		26/11/91	M	1	(6)	
19	Ben Binyamin		17/12/85	M	35		
14	Sagi Dror		07/08/96	M		(1)	
9	Ori Or Eiloz		12/01/96	M	2	(9)	1
55	Omri Glazer		11/03/96	G	5	(1)	
11	Evans Kangwa	ZAM	09/10/92	A	32	(1)	11
21	Ido Levy		31/07/90	D	31		
26	Lior Levy		26/10/87	D	11	(2)	
24	Guy Lipka		03/04/91	D	8	(4)	
23	Emmanuel Mbola	ZAM	10/05/93	D	31		
82	Rene Mihelič	SVN	05/07/88	M	30		3
5	Adi Nimni		27/08/91	D	26	(2)	1
15	Dejan Radonjić	CRO	23/07/90	A	9	(4)	2
17	Eran Rozenbaum		26/08/92	M		(3)	
2	Yuval Shabtai		18/12/86	M	30	(2)	4
3	Ahmed Shacban		14/04/93	D	4	(1)	
16	Mohammad Shaker		14/11/96	M	4	(4)	1
8	Snir Shoker		08/05/89	M	7	(15)	3
18	Mamadou Thiam	SEN	22/10/92	A	7	(18)	2
4	Dudi Tiram		16/09/93	D	8	(6)	
32	Ben Vahaba		27/03/92	D	36		2
22	Arie Yanko		21/12/91	G	31		

ISRAEL ✡

Hapoel Tel-Aviv FC

1927 • Bloomfield (14,413) • hapoelta-fc.co.il

Major honours
Israeli League (13) 1934, 1935, 1938, 1940, 1944, 1957, 1966, 1969, 1981, 1986, 1988, 2000, 2010; Israeli Cup (15) 1928 (shared), 1934, 1937, 1938, 1939, 1961, 1972, 1983, 1999, 2000, 2006, 2007, 2010, 2011, 2012

Coach: César Mendiondo (ESP); (03/09/15) (Walid Badir); (05/11/15) Guy Levi; (19/01/16) Eli Gutman

2015
24/08	a	Beitar	D	0-0
29/08	h	Kiryat Shmona	L	0-3
12/09	h	M. Netanya	D	1-1	Antal
19/09	a	H. Haifa	W	1-0	Safuri
28/09	h	Bnei Yehuda	W	3-1	Antal, Bumba 2
03/10	a	H. Kfar-Saba	D	1-1	Biton
17/10	h	Bnei Sakhnin	L	0-4	
25/10	a	H. Beer Sheva	L	1-3	Nasser
31/10	h	M. Tel-Aviv	L	0-1	
07/11	a	H. Ra'anana	W	1-0	Gutliv
23/11	h	M. Haifa	L	0-3	
30/11	a	H. Akko	W	1-0	Gutliv
05/12	h	M. Petach-Tikva	L	0-1	
12/12	h	Beitar	D	0-0	
19/12	a	H. Kiryat Shmona	L	0-3	
26/12	a	M. Netanya	D	1-1	Nasser

2016
03/01	h	H. Haifa	D	0-0	
09/01	a	Bnei Yehuda	W	3-1	Altman, Gutliv, Yehezkel
16/01	h	H. Kfar-Saba	L	0-1	
23/01	a	Bnei Sakhnin	L	0-1	
30/01	h	H. Beer Sheva	L	0-1	
07/02	a	M. Tel-Aviv	D	1-1	Schoenfeld
13/02	h	H. Ra'anana	W	2-1	Turgeman, Schoenfeld
20/02	a	M. Haifa	D	0-0	
29/02	h	H. Akko	L	0-2	
05/03	a	M. Petach-Tikva	D	1-1	Schoenfeld
19/03	a	H. Kfar-Saba	W	3-0	Nikolić 2, Scheimann
02/04	h	H. Akko	W	1-0	Nikolić
10/04	a	M. Netanya	W	1-0	Yehezkel
16/04	a	H. Kiryat Shmona	D	1-1	Schoenfeld
30/04	h	H. Haifa	D	3-3	Schoenfeld, Yehezkel 2
07/05	a	Bnei Yehuda	W	4-2	Schoenfeld 3 (1p), Safuri
15/05	h	M. Petach-Tikva	D	0-0	

No	Name	Nat	DoB	Pos	Aps	(s)	Gls
5	Iyad Abu Abaid		31/12/94	D	28		
33	David Alon		30/01/97	G		(1)	
10	Omri Altman		23/03/94	M	16	(7)	1
28	Liviu Antal	ROU	02/06/89	M	14	(2)	2
29	Guy Asulin		09/04/91	M		(7)	
20	Hamza Barry	GAM	15/10/94	M	12		
20	Dudu Biton		01/03/88	A	4	(6)	1
7	Claudiu Bumba	ROU	05/01/94	M	20	(7)	2
19	Cauê	BRA	24/05/89	A	4	(3)	
23	Mohammed El Hija		11/01/95	A		(1)	
4	Ben Grabli		08/04/94	M	2		
6	Edi Gutliv		16/08/92	D	29		3
1	Ariel Harush		08/02/88	G	16		
22	Tzlil Hatuka		06/02/89	G	16		
15	Nir Lax		10/08/94	M	6	(2)	
14	Issoumaila Lingane	CIV	15/03/91	M	11	(5)	
21	Anas Mahamid		26/04/98	M	2	(10)	
77	Siraj Nasser		02/09/90	M	6	(7)	2
23	Nemanja Nikolić	MNE	01/01/88	M	10		3
99	Moshe Ohayon		24/05/83	M	4	(3)	
8	Mihai Pintilii	ROU	09/11/84	M	13	(1)	
9	Ben Reichert		04/03/94	M	16	(1)	
11	Ramzi Safuri		21/10/95	A	8	(7)	2
18	Shmuel Scheimann		03/11/87	D	22	(3)	1
12	Aaron Schoenfeld	USA	17/04/90	A	10	(2)	8
15	Omri Shekel		03/01/93	M	2	(1)	
4	Gal Shish		28/01/89	D	1		
13	Ram Strauss		28/04/92	G	1		
17	Alon Turgeman		09/06/91	A	10	(4)	1
24	Loukas Vyntra	GRE	05/02/81	D	25		
2	Ofer Werta		23/05/90	D	25	(4)	
26	Avihai Yadin		26/10/86	M	14		
16	Sagiv Yehezkel		31/03/95	A	15	(4)	4
8	Lotem Zino		16/03/92	M	1	(1)	

Maccabi Haifa FC

1913 • Sammy Ofer (30,820) • mhaifafc.com

Major honours
Israeli League (12) 1984, 1985, 1989, 1991, 1994, 2001, 2002, 2004, 2005, 2006, 2009, 2011; Israeli Cup (6) 1962, 1991, 1993, 1995, 1998, 2016

Coach: Ronny Levi

2015
22/08	h	Bnei Yehuda	L	0-3	
29/08	a	H. Kfar-Saba	L	0-1	
12/09	h	Bnei Sakhnin	D	0-0	
21/09	h	Beer Sheva	D	0-0	
26/09	h	M. Tel-Aviv	L	0-2	
03/10	a	H. Ra'anana	W	2-0	Atar (p), Ezra
18/10	a	H. Kiryat Shmona	L	0-2	
24/10	h	H. Akko	W	4-0	Plet, Valiente, Atar, Obraniak
31/10	a	M. Petach-Tikva	D	1-1	Atar (p)
08/11	h	Beitar	L	0-2	
23/11	h	H. Tel-Aviv	W	3-0	Keinan 2, Plet
28/11	h	M. Netanya	W	1-0	Benayoun
07/12	h	Haifa	W	4-2	Atar, Raiyan, Keinan, Plet
12/12	a	Bnei Yehuda	D	0-0	
20/12	h	H. Kfar-Saba	D	1-1	Obraniak
26/12	a	Bnei Sakhnin	W	2-1	Benayoun, Atar

2016
04/01	h	H. Beer Sheva	D	1-1	Plet
10/01	a	M. Tel-Aviv	L	1-2	Benayoun
17/01	h	H. Ra'anana	W	2-0	Benayoun, Plet
24/01	h	H. Kiryat Shmona	L	0-1	
31/01	h	H. Akko	D	1-1	Plet (p)
06/02	a	M. Petach-Tikva	W	4-0	Benayoun, Atar 2, Vermouth
15/02	a	Beitar	L	0-3	
20/02	h	H. Tel-Aviv	D	0-0	
27/02	a	M. Netanya	W	3-0	Keinan, Atar (p), Plet
06/03	h	H. Haifa	W	3-2	Plet, Jaber, og (Fishler)
14/03	a	Beitar	L	2-3	Benayoun, Keinan
20/03	h	H. Ra'anana	L	0-3	
02/04	h	Bnei Sakhnin	D	3-3	og (Abraham Paz), Plet, Atar
09/04	h	H. Beer Sheva	D	1-1	Atar
17/04	h	M. Tel-Aviv	D	0-0	
24/04	h	Beitar	W	1-0	Obraniak
30/04	h	H. Ra'anana	W	2-0	Ezra 2
07/05	a	Bnei Sakhnin	W	1-0	Hirsh
14/05	h	H. Beer Sheva	W	2-0	Ezra, Meshumar
21/05	a	M. Tel-Aviv	L	0-6	

No	Name	Nat	DoB	Pos	Aps	(s)	Gls
16	Eliran Atar		17/02/87	A	22	(4)	10
5	Shay Ben David		19/07/97	D	1		
5	Yossi Benayoun		05/05/80	M	20	(9)	6
30	Eran Biton		16/01/96	M		(1)	
12	Orel Dgani		08/01/89	D	21	(2)	
18	Nikola Drinčić	MNE	07/09/84	M	11	(2)	
8	Hen Ezra		19/01/89	M	12	(14)	4
32	Shoval Gozlan		25/04/94	A	6	(10)	
2	Ayad Habashi		05/05/95	D	8	(7)	
14,19	Shahar Hirsh		13/02/93	M		(14)	1
23	Ataa Jaber		03/10/94	M	18	(1)	1
21	Dekel Keinan		15/09/84	D	30	(1)	5
7	Ofir Kriaf		17/03/91	M	10	(5)	
31	Neta Lavi		25/08/96	M	22		
1	Ohad Levita		17/02/86	G	5		
27	Sun Menachem		07/09/93	M	8	(2)	
27	Eyal Meshumar		10/08/83	D	18	(2)	1
32	Kobi Moyal		12/06/87	M	2	(2)	
24	Ludovic Obraniak	POL	10/11/84	M	25	(1)	3
24	Glynor Plet	NED	30/01/87	A	23	(2)	9
11	Ismail Raiyan		24/04/94	A	15	(9)	1
23	Romário	BRA	16/01/89	M	8	(5)	
9	Etay Shechter		22/02/87	A	6	(4)	
13	Vladimir Stojković	SRB	28/07/83	G	31		
13	Taleb Tawatha		21/06/92	D	27		
17	Alon Turgeman		09/06/91	A	4	(3)	
14	Marc Valiente	ESP	29/03/87	D	30		1
14	Gil Vermouth		05/08/85	M	10	(4)	1
26	Avihai Yadin		26/10/86	M	3		
28	Yuval Yossipovich		22/02/94	D		(2)	

Maccabi Netanya FC

1934 • Municipal (14,300) • fcmn.co.il

Major honours
Israeli League (5) 1971, 1974, 1978, 1980, 1983; Israeli Cup (1) 1978

Coach: Shlomi Dora; (06/11/15) Reuven Atar; (20/01/16) Menahem Koretzki (27/03/16) Omer Peretz

2015
22/08	a	M. Petach-Tikva	L	0-1	
30/08	h	Beitar	D	0-0	
12/09	a	H. Tel-Aviv	D	1-1	Barry
19/09	h	H. Kiryat Shmona	D	1-1	Românio (p)
26/09	h	H. Haifa	L	1-2	Margoulis
03/10	a	Bnei Yehuda	W	2-1	Margoulis, Barry
17/10	h	H. Kfar-Saba	D	0-0	
24/10	a	Bnei Sakhnin	D	0-0	
01/11	h	H. Beer Sheva	L	0-2	
09/11	a	M. Tel-Aviv	L	1-2	Mishchenko
21/11	h	H. Ra'anana	L	1-3	Ceesay
28/11	a	M. Haifa	L	0-1	
05/12	h	H. Akko	D	0-0	
12/12	h	M. Petach-Tikva	D	0-0	
19/12	a	Beitar	L	0-1	
26/12	h	H. Tel-Aviv	D	1-1	Românio (p)

2016
02/01	a	H. Kiryat Shmona	L	0-3	
09/01	a	H. Haifa	L	0-2	
16/01	h	Bnei Yehuda	L	0-2	
23/01	a	H. Kfar-Saba	L	0-1	
30/01	h	Bnei Sakhnin	L	0-2	
06/02	a	H. Beer Sheva	L	0-2	
14/02	h	M. Tel-Aviv	L	1-3	Benbenisti
20/02	a	H. Ra'anana	L	0-1	
27/02	h	M. Haifa	L	0-3	
05/03	h	H. Akko	D	1-1	Malka
20/03	a	H. Akko	L	1-4	Benbenisti
02/04	a	H. Kiryat Shmona	L	0-2	
10/04	h	H. Tel-Aviv	L	0-1	
16/04	a	H. Haifa	L	1-2	Mishchenko
01/05	h	Bnei Yehuda	L	0-1	
08/05	a	M. Petach-Tikva	L	1-2	Mareev
14/05	h	H. Kfar-Saba	D	1-1	Taga

No	Name	Nat	DoB	Pos	Aps	(s)	Gls
27	Yuval Avidor		19/10/86	A	12	(4)	
21	Aviv Avraham		30/03/96	M		(2)	
14	Mircea Axente	ROU	14/03/87	A	8	(1)	
8	Tal Ayele		25/05/89	A	8	(9)	
5	Hamza Barry	GAM	15/10/94	M	21		2
52	Sahar Benbenisti		26/11/91	M	11	(7)	2
28	Noor Bisan		17/01/95	M		(1)	
7	Elad Boaron		29/12/96	M		(1)	
9	Omer Boaron		27/06/92	A		(3)	
8	Aviad Bourla		13/12/93	M	4	(2)	
29	Momoudou Ceesay	GAM	24/12/88	A	8	(3)	1
4	Itzhak Cohen		01/01/90	A	13	(9)	
25	Seif Fadul		07/01/96	M	4		
13	Dean Gal		13/02/95	G	10		
2,28	Zeev Haimovich		07/04/83	D	7		
16	Shimon Harush		20/02/87	D	15	(2)	
12	Yarin Hassan		22/03/94	D	27		
77	Abed Jabarin		19/12/98	A	1	(5)	
1	Barak Levi		07/01/93	A	23		
5	Issoumaila Lingane	CIV	15/03/91	M	6	(1)	
29	Moshe Lugasi		04/02/91	D	16	(6)	
52	Moti Malka		13/12/90	A	8	(2)	1
52	Sameh Mareev		08/01/91	A	2	(6)	1
15	Gael Margoulis		03/04/94	M	16	(7)	2
26	Amer Masarwa		26/03/95	D		(1)	
22	Andriy Mishchenko	UKR	07/07/87	D	28		2
7	Nevo Mizrachi		26/07/87	M	1	(8)	
27,39	Nemanja Petrović	SRB	17/04/92	D	10	(2)	
23	Românio	BRA	16/01/89	M	19	(1)	2
8	Aaron Schoenfeld	USA	17/04/90	A	1	(1)	
10	Dia Seba		18/11/92	M		(3)	
3	Milan Smiljanić	SRB	19/11/86	M	30	(1)	
18	Amaya Taga		04/02/85	M	14	(3)	1
70	Thiago	BRA	12/07/87	A	1	(1)	
4	Dudi Tiram		16/09/93	D	1		
4	Omer Vered		25/01/92	D	26		
33	Eylon Yerushalmi		10/03/97	M		(4)	
20	Israel Zaguri		29/01/90	M	2	(2)	
20	Yair Ziv		27/04/94	D	10	(1)	

ISRAEL

Maccabi Petach-Tikva FC

1912 • HaMoshava (11,500) • m-pt.co.il
Major honours
Israeli Cup (2) 1935, 1952
Coach: Ran Ben-Shimon;
(01/03/16) Dani Golan

2015
22/08	h	M. Netanya	W 1-0	*Kanuk*
29/08	a	H. Haifa	W 3-0	*Kanuk, Twitto, Melamed*
12/09	h	Bnei Yehuda	W 3-1	*Mununga (p), Shemesh, Kalibat*
19/09	a	H. Kfar-Saba	W 1-0	*Panka*
26/09	h	Bnei Sakhnin	L 0-1	
03/10	a	H. Beer Sheva	L 2-5	*Tomas, Hugy*
17/10	h	M. Tel-Aviv	L 1-2	*Melamed*
24/10	h	H. Ra'anana	L 0-2	
31/10	a	M. Haifa	D 1-1	*Melamed*
07/11	a	H. Akko	L 0-1	
21/11	a	H. Kiryat Shmona	W 1-0	*Peretz*
28/11	h	Beitar	W 2-0	*Shemesh, Tomas*
05/12	a	H. Tel-Aviv	W 1-0	*Mununga (p)*
12/12	a	M. Netanya	D 0-0	
19/12	h	H. Haifa	D 1-1	*Tomas*
26/12	h	Bnei Yehuda	D 1-1	*Melamed*

2016
02/01	h	H. Kfar-Saba	W 2-0	*Melamed, Kalibat*
09/01	a	Bnei Sakhnin	L 0-1	
16/01	h	H. Beer Sheva	L 0-1	
23/01	a	M. Tel-Aviv	L 1-3	*Hugy*
30/01	h	H. Ra'anana	L 0-1	
06/02	a	M. Haifa	L 0-4	
13/02	h	H. Akko	L 1-2	*Prica*
20/02	h	H. Kiryat Shmona	D 0-0	
27/02	a	Beitar	L 0-2	
05/03	h	H. Tel-Aviv	D 1-1	*Kanuk*
19/03	h	H. Haifa	W 2-1	*Gordana, Goldenberg*
02/04	a	Bnei Yehuda	W 2-1	*Kalibat, Prica*
10/04	h	H. Kiryat Shmona	W 2-0	*Prica, Hugy*
16/04	h	H. Kfar-Saba	L 0-1	
30/04	a	H. Akko	W 3-1	*Kalibat, Melamed, Kanuk*
08/05	h	M. Netanya	W 2-1	*Tomas, Elo*
15/05	a	H. Tel-Aviv	D 0-0	

No	Name	Nat	DoB	Pos	Aps	(s)	Gls
62	Aitor Monroy	ESP	08/10/87	M	27	(1)	
2	Allyson	BRA	23/10/90	M	26	(2)	
3	Omer Danino		17/02/95	D	24		
18	Dor Elo		26/09/93	D	29	(1)	1
23	Oded Gavish		23/06/89	D	9	(4)	
16	Itzhak Gigi		01/12/88	G	15		
7	Hagai Goldenberg		15/09/90	D	7	(9)	1
9	Roy Gordana		06/07/90	M	9	(3)	1
20	Dor Hugy		10/07/95	A	14	(12)	3
8	Yuval Jakobovich		09/11/92	M	10	(10)	
99	Mohammed Kalibat		15/06/90	A	21	(10)	4
26	Gidi Kanuk		11/02/93	M	25	(4)	4
10	Guy Melamed		21/12/92	A	9	(14)	6
39	Joachim Mununga	BEL	30/06/88	M	25	(3)	2
1	Itamar Nitzan		23/06/87	G	18		
17	Mindaugas Panka	LTU	01/05/84	M	6	(2)	1
11	Naor Paser		18/10/85	D	17	(1)	
9	Oz Peretz		19/04/94	A	3	(7)	1
28	Rade Prica	SWE	30/06/80	A	6	(4)	3
77	Omer Retman		25/02/98	D		(1)	
77	Liran Rotman		07/06/96	M	4	(1)	
22	Mor Shaked		23/12/86	M		(1)	
80	Idan Shemesh		06/08/90	A	16	(5)	2
5	Xavier Tomas	FRA	04/01/86	D	32		4
6	Dudi Twitto		06/02/94	D	11	(4)	1

Maccabi Tel-Aviv FC

1906 • Bloomfield (14,413) • maccabi-tlv.co.il
Major honours
Israeli League (21) 1936, 1937, 1942, 1947, 1950, 1952, 1954, 1956, 1958, 1968, 1970, 1972, 1977, 1979, 1992, 1995, 1996, 2003, 2013, 2014, 2015; Israeli Cup (23) 1929, 1930, 1933, 1941, 1946, 1947, 1954, 1955, 1958, 1959, 1964, 1965, 1967, 1970, 1977, 1987, 1988, 1994, 1996, 2001, 2002, 2005, 2015
Coach: Slaviša Jokanović (SRB);
(04/01/16) Peter Bosz (NED)

2015
22/08	h	Bnei Sakhnin	W 3-2	*Zahavi 2, Ben Haim (II)*
30/08	a	H. Beer Sheva	W 1-0	*Zahavi*
12/09	a	H. Kiryat Shmona	D 1-1	*Alberman*
20/09	h	H. Ra'anana	L 1-2	*Itzhaki*
26/09	a	M. Haifa	W 2-0	*Ben Basat, D Peretz*
03/10	h	H. Akko	W 5-0	*og (Kopitović), Itzhaki, Zahavi 2, Ben Haim (I)*
17/10	a	M. Petach-Tikva	W 2-1	*Carlos García, Zahavi (p)*
26/10	h	Beitar	L 2-4	*Zahavi 2*
31/10	a	H. Tel-Aviv	W 1-0	*Carlos García*
07/11	h	M. Netanya	W 2-1	*Zahavi (p), Ben Haim (II)*
21/11	a	H. Haifa	W 3-0	*Zahavi (p), Igiebor, Rikan*
29/11	h	Bnei Yehuda	W 4-0	*Azulay, Zahavi 2, Ben Haim (II)*
05/12	a	H. Kfar-Saba	D 0-0	
14/12	a	Bnei Sakhnin	W 2-0	*Zahavi 2*
21/12	h	H. Beer Sheva	L 1-2	*Dasa*
27/12	h	H. Kiryat Shmona	W 5-0	*Zahavi 4, Ben Harush*

2016
02/01	a	H. Ra'anana	W 2-0	*Zahavi, Rikan*
10/01	a	M. Haifa	W 2-1	*Zahavi, Ben Haim (II)*
18/01	a	H. Akko	W 3-0	*Ben Haim (II), Igiebor, Azulay*
23/01	h	M. Petach-Tikva	W 3-1	*Zahavi 2, Igiebor*
01/02	a	Beitar	D 2-2	*Zahavi 2*
07/02	h	H. Tel-Aviv	D 1-1	*Micha*
14/02	a	M. Netanya	W 3-1	*Ben Basat, Zahavi, Ben Haim (II)*
20/02	h	H. Haifa	W 2-1	*Zahavi (p), Ben Haim (II)*
27/02	a	Bnei Yehuda	W 1-0	*Dasa*
05/03	h	H. Kfar-Saba	W 5-0	*Micha, Orlando Sá 2, Zahavi (p), Itzhaki*
12/03	h	Bnei Sakhnin	W 1-0	*Zahavi*
20/03	a	H. Beer Sheva	D 1-1	*Carlos García*
03/04	h	H. Ra'anana	W 3-0	*Zahavi (p), Ben Haim (I), Medunjanin*
11/04	h	Beitar	W 3-2	*Micha, Zahavi 2*
17/04	a	M. Haifa	D 0-0	
25/04	a	Bnei Sakhnin	D 0-0	
02/05	h	H. Beer Sheva	D 0-0	
09/05	a	H. Ra'anana	D 1-1	*Igiebor*
14/05	a	Beitar	W 2-0	*Zahavi (p), Medunjanin*
21/05	h	M. Haifa	W 6-0	*Zahavi 3 (1p), Ben Haim (II), Carlos García, Medunjanin*

No	Name	Nat	DoB	Pos	Aps	(s)	Gls
6	Gal Alberman		17/04/83	M	33	(1)	1
16	Shlomi Azulay		30/03/90	M	8	(8)	2
9	Eden Ben Basat		08/09/86	A	9	(13)	2
26	Tal Ben Haim (I)		31/03/82	D	13		2
11	Tal Ben Haim (II)		05/08/89	A	20	(11)	8
20	Omri Ben Harush		07/03/90	D	16	(3)	1
31	Carlos García	ESP	29/04/84	D	31		4
2	Eli Dasa		03/12/92	D	26	(2)	2
40	Emmanuel Nosa Igiebor	NGA	09/11/90	M	14	(4)	4
10	Barak Itzhaki		25/09/84	A	9	(18)	3
25	Juan Pablo	ESP	02/09/78	G	1		
1	Daniel Lifshitz		24/04/88	G	1		
4	Haris Medunjanin	BIH	08/03/85	M	13	(2)	3
15	Dor Micha		02/03/92	M	23	(7)	3
24	Nikola Mitrović	SRB	02/01/87	M	9	(5)	
70	Orlando Sá	POR	26/05/88	A	7	(3)	2
42	Dor Peretz		17/05/95	M	16	(8)	1
45	Eliel Peretz		18/11/96	M	2	(1)	
99	Dejan Radonjić	CRO	23/07/90	A	2	(1)	
95	Predrag Rajković	SRB	31/10/95	G	34		
27	Oz Rali		22/12/87	M	2		
22	Avi Rikan		10/09/88	D	19	(4)	2
3	Yuval Shpungin		03/04/87	D	10	(2)	
18	Eitan Tibi		16/11/87	D	31		
28	Gil Vermouth		05/08/85	M	10	(5)	
7	Eran Zahavi		25/07/87	M	36		35
14	Yoav Ziv		16/03/81	D	1	(3)	

Top goalscorers

35	Eran Zahavi (M. Tel-Aviv)
14	Nikita Rukavytsya (Beitar)
	Shlomi Azulay (Bnei Sakhnin)
	Elyaniv Barda (H. Beer Sheva)
12	Pedro Galván (Bnei Yehuda)
	Maaran Al Lala (H. Haifa)
11	Anthony Nwakaeme (H. Beer Sheva)
	Evans Kangwa (H. Ra'anana)
10	Ofir Mizrahi (H. Kiryat Shmona)
	Eliran Atar (M. Haifa)

Promoted clubs

FC Ashdod

1999 • Yud Alef (8,200) • no website
**Coach: Eyal Lahman;
(18/12/15) Ronny Awat**

Hapoel Ashkelon FC

1955 • Sala (10,000) • no website
Coach: Yuval Naim

Second level final table 2015/16

		Pld	W	D	L	F	A	Pts
1	FC Ashdod	37	19	13	5	66	38	70
2	Hapoel Ashkelon FC	37	16	14	7	62	40	62
3	Hapoel Ramat Gan FC	37	14	14	9	56	38	56
4	Hapoel Katamon Jerusalem FC	37	15	11	11	44	49	56
5	Maccabi Herzliya FC	37	14	13	10	50	43	55
6	Hapoel Petach-Tikva FC	37	13	13	11	54	55	52
7	Maccabi Ahi Nazareth FC	37	15	6	16	40	49	51
8	Hapoel Bnei Lod FC	37	11	11	15	36	42	44
9	Beitar Tel-Aviv Ramla FC	37	19	4	14	60	50	61
10	Hapoel Ironi Nir Ramat HaSharon FC	37	13	11	13	57	49	50
11	Hapoel Afula FC	37	13	11	13	53	53	50
12	Hapoel Ironi Rishon-LeZion FC	37	13	9	15	51	53	48
13	Hapoel Nazareth Illit FC	37	11	11	15	44	47	44
14	Hapoel Jerusalem FC	37	9	13	15	39	50	40
15	Maccabi Yavne FC	37	9	9	19	44	58	36
16	Maccabi Kiryat Gat FC	37	5	11	21	28	70	26

NB League splits into top and bottom halves after 30 games, after which the clubs play exclusively against teams in their group.

DOMESTIC CUP

G'Viaa Hamedina (State Cup) 2015/16

EIGHTH ROUND

(12/01/16)
Ashdod 2-0 M. Ahi Nazareth
Beitar Kfar-Saba 1-2 Bnei Sakhnin *(aet)*
Bnei Yehuda 2-1 H. Akko
H. Haifa 3-1 M. Kabilio Jaffa
H. Katamon Jerusalem 0-2 H. Rishon LeZion
Ironi Baqa al-Gharbiyye 0-3 H. Ashkelon
M. Kiryat Gat 0-1 H. Beer Sheva
M. Netanya 0-1 Sektzia Nes Tziona
M. Petach-Tikva 2-0 H. Kiryat Shmona
M. Yavne 2-2 H. Ramat Gan *(aet; 4-5 on pens)*

(13/01/16)
H. Kfar-Saba 2-0 H. Afula
H. Nazareth Illit 3-3 H. Tel-Aviv *(aet; 2-4 on pens)*
H. Ra'anana 3-0 Hakoah Ramat Gan
M. Haifa 2-1 Beitar Jerusalem
M. Herzliya 1-2 Beitar Tel-Aviv Ramla

(14/01/16)
H. Ramat HaSharon 1-3 M. Tel-Aviv

NINTH ROUND

(26/01/16)
Ashdod 1-2 Bnei Yehuda
H. Ashkelon 2-0 H. Ramat Gan
H. Kfar-Saba 2-1 H. Tel-Aviv
H. Ra'anana 0-0 Beitar Tel-Aviv Ramla *(aet; 4-5 on pens)*
Sektzia Nes Tziona 0-0 Bnei Sakhnin *(aet; 4-5 on pens)*

(27/01/16)
M. Haifa 1-0 H. Haifa
M. Petach-Tikva 1-2 H. Beer Sheva

(28/01/16)
H. Rishon LeZion 1-2 M. Tel-Aviv *(aet)*

QUARTER-FINALS

(09/02/16 & 02/03/16)
H. Beer Sheva 2-0 Beitar Tel-Aviv Ramla *(Sahar 59, Barda 90)*
Beitar Tel-Aviv Ramla 0-2 H. Beer Sheva *(D Biton 31, Tarabin 80)*
(H. Beer Sheva 4-0)

(09/02/16 & 01/03/16)
Bnei Yehuda 2-2 M. Haifa *(Zruya 69, Galván 74; Atar 55p, Plet 83)*
M. Haifa 4-1 Bnei Yehuda *(Vermouth 33, Grabli 42og, Benayoun 56, Plet 71; Galván 31)*
(M. Haifa 6-3)

(10/02/16 & 01/03/16)
Bnei Sakhnin 3-0 H. Ashkelon *(Mugrabi 4, Georginho 42, Sages 62)*
H. Ashkelon 2-0 Bnei Sakhnin *(Mahfud 22, Shriki 68)*
(Bnei Sakhnin 3-2)

(10/02/16 & 02/03/16)
H. Kfar-Saba 0-3 M. Tel-Aviv *(Medunjanin 33, Ben Basat 54, Micha 88)*
M. Tel-Aviv 2-0 H. Kfar-Saba *(Azulay 22, Ben Basat 45)*
(M. Tel-Aviv 5-0)

SEMI-FINALS

(20/04/16)
H. Beer Sheva 1-3 M. Haifa *(Nwakaeme 87; Plet 29, 31, Atar 80)*

(21/04/16)
Bnei Sakhnin 2-3 M. Tel-Aviv *(Mugrabi 22, Azulay 52; Itzhaki 27, Zahavi 66p, Ben Haim (II) 85)*

FINAL

(24/05/16)
Teddy, Jerusalem
MACCABI HAIFA FC 1 *(Obraniak 36)*
MACCABI TEL-AVIV FC 0
Referee: *Reinshreiber*
M. HAIFA: *Stojković, Meshumar, Keinan, Valiente, Tawatha, Lavi, Romário, Obraniak, Ezra (Kriaf 85), Benayoun (Raiyan 79), Gozlan (Hirsh 67)*
M. TEL-AVIV: *Rajković, Dasa, Carlos García (Ben Basat 83), Tibi, Rikan, Medunjanin, Alberman (E Peretz 71), Zahavi, Igiebor (Itzhaki 76), Micha, Ben Haim (II)*

Maccabi Haifa players savour the club's first State Cup win for 18 years

ITALY

Federazione Italiana Giuoco Calcio (FIGC)

Address Via Gregorio Allegri 14
CP 2450
IT-00198 Roma
Tel +39 0684 912 553
Fax +39 0625 496 455
E-mail figc.segreteria@figc.it
Website figc.it

President Carlo Tavecchio
General secretary Michele Uva
Media officer Paolo Corbi
Year of formation 1898

SERIE A CLUBS

 1 Atalanta BC

 2 Bologna FC

 3 Carpi FC 1909

 4 AC Chievo Verona

 5 Empoli FC

 6 ACF Fiorentina

 7 Frosinone Calcio

 8 Genoa CFC

 9 FC Internazionale Milano

 10 Juventus FC

 11 SS Lazio

 12 AC Milan

 13 SSC Napoli

 14 US Città di Palermo

 15 AS Roma

 16 UC Sampdoria

 17 US Sassuolo Calcio

18 Torino FC

19 Udinese Calcio

20 Hellas Verona FC

PROMOTED CLUBS

 21 Cagliari Calcio

 22 FC Crotone

 23 Pescara Calcio

KEY

● UEFA Champions League
● UEFA Europa League
● Promoted
● Relegated

Double double for Juventus

There was no stopping Juventus once again in 2015/16 as the Turin giants shrugged off the handicap of a false start to steamroller their way to a fifth successive Serie A title. They also retained the Coppa Italia, making it two domestic doubles in as many seasons for coach Massimiliano Allegri.

Napoli, one of several teams to lead the league until Juve assumed command in February, finished runners-up, just ahead of Roma, thanks to a Serie A record haul of 36 goals from striker Gonzalo Higuaín. At UEFA EURO 2016 ex-Juve boss Antonio Conte led Italy to the quarter-finals in his first and last major tournament as Azzurri coach.

Bianconeri storm to fifth straight scudetto	**Higuaín breaks Serie A goalscoring record**	**Conte's Azzurri reach EURO quarter-finals**

Domestic league

The final Serie A table, showing Juventus nine points clear at the top with 29 wins from their 38 games, might suggest that the 2015/16 campaign was another straightforward scudetto triumph for Italy's record champions. In fact, it was anything but. In the early autumn grave misgivings were widely expressed about the sale of star players Andrea Pirlo, Carlos Tévez and Arturo Vidal as the Bianconeri lost their opening two Serie A games for the first time, won only one of their first six, and were still floundering in the bottom half of the table after matchday ten.

The turning point came on the last day of October when Juan Cuadrado, one of several new additions to the club's double-winning roster, bundled home a 93rd-minute winner to give Juventus three precious points at home to city rivals Torino. That would be the first of 15 successive victories – a club record – which enabled the team to climb their way stealthily up the Serie A standings and reach the summit for the first time on 13 February with a crucial 1-0 victory over table-topping Napoli.

A deflected 88th-minute strike from Simone Zaza, another new recruit, allowed Juve to leapfrog their rivals – who were on an impressive eight-match winning run of their own, also setting a club record – and see their way clear to a fifth successive Italian championship, a feat the club had not achieved since the early 1930s. Although newly-promoted Bologna surprisingly ended Juve's winning run next time out, holding them to a 0-0 draw, Napoli failed to capitalise, drawing 1-1 at home to AC Milan the following day. Allegri's men responded with another long winning streak, eclipsing two further Serie A records in the process as they went ten games without conceding and inspirational skipper Gianluigi Buffon kept his goal intact for 974 minutes, beating the previous mark of 929 set by Milan's Sebastiano Rossi 22 years earlier.

So relentless were Juve in pursuit of their 32nd scudetto that they accumulated enough points to be crowned champions with three games to spare, a 2-1 win at Fiorentina and Napoli's 1-0 defeat at Roma combining to make their victory a mathematical certainty. They rounded off the season in fitting style with their biggest win of the campaign – 5-0 at home to Sampdoria – although not before they had lost for the first time in six months, 2-1 at relegated Verona, to halt an astonishing unbeaten run of 26 matches, 25 of them victories.

Despite having given their rivals a head start, Juve were convincing champions once again. Buffon and his fellow stalwarts in the three-man defensive line – Andrea Barzagli, Leonardo Bonucci and, when fit, Giorgio Chiellini – had all performed with customary class, conceding as a unit just 20 goals, while the statuesque Paul Pogba was the standout operator in midfield. The pick of the new signings was 22-year-old Argentinian striker Paulo Dybala, who maintained the excellent form he had shown for Palermo the previous season and scored 19 goals – nine more than Juve's next highest scorer Mario Mandžukić, another newcomer.

In terms of individual scoring feats, there was no one to touch Napoli sharpshooter Higuaín. The prolific Argentinian international tore Serie A defences apart all season, and even a three-match ban in April could not prevent him from breaking the record for the number of goals scored in a single Serie A campaign as he struck a brilliant hat-trick against Frosinone on the final day – his first of the season after nine doubles – to lift his final total to a staggering 36 in 35 appearances. Napoli's 4-0 win that day was also crucial from the team's perspective as the three points enabled them to finish two points ahead of Roma and qualify for the UEFA Champions League group stage – a splendid achievement for native Neapolitan coach Maurizio Sarri at the end of his first season.

Another coach with good reason to be proud of his accomplishments in 2015/16 was Luciano Spalletti, who returned to Roma to replace Rudi Garcia in mid-season and led the Giallorossi to 14 wins and three draws in their last 17 matches, the only blemish on his watch coming at the start with a 1-0 defeat at Juventus. The 57-year-old Tuscan, who had led the club to back-to-back Coppa Italia successes during his first spell (2005-09), showed that his magic touch was still intact, transforming Roma into a cohesive and entertaining team. At its core were foreign stars such as Miralem Pjanić, Radja Nainggolan, Kostas Manolas and Mohamed Salah, while opportunities still knocked for 39-year-old Francesco Totti to come off the bench and make an impact – as he did in particularly dramatic circumstances with a late double in a 3-2 home win over Torino. Totti set new club Serie A records of 300 goals and 600 appearances during a campaign in which his long-standing team-mate Daniel De Rossi also played his 500th game for the club.

While Totti signed a new one-year contract extension, other illustrious veteran strikers decided to make the 2015/16 season their last, with Luca Toni bowing out at Verona, Miroslav Klose signing off at Lazio and Antonio Di Natale ending a 12-year career at Udinese. Curiously, all three players scored penalties on their farewell home appearance, with Toni perhaps stealing the show courtesy of his 'Panenka' finish against Juventus.

While Verona, Toni's final club, went down – they did not record a win until their 23rd fixture – one of his former teams, Fiorentina, enjoyed a productive first season under Portuguese coach Paulo Sousa, eventually finishing fifth to qualify for the UEFA Europa League. Inspired by their Balkan duo Josip Iličić and Nikola Kalinić, the Viola topped the Serie A table for a number of weeks in the autumn – as did Roberto Mancini's Internazionale, who equalled a club record by winning their first five fixtures and then came on strong again to lead the standings again at Christmas before struggling to string two wins together thereafter. Mauro Icardi scored 16 goals, but Italian international Éder, a mid-

Roma striker Francesco Totti continued to prove his worth at 39, scoring this winning goal against Torino

season signing from Sampdoria, managed just one as the Nerazzurri returned to European competition in fourth place.

Inter's stadium-sharing local rivals Milan missed out on Europe for the third successive season, however, as the recruitment of Sampdoria boss Siniša Mihajlović failed to pay off. After a brief spell under youth trainer Cristian Brocchi, Milan went back to Sampdoria for their next coach, appointing Vincenzo Montella, who had only been with the Genoa club for six months. There was stability, however, at Sassuolo, where Eusebio Di Francesco was rewarded with a new contract after prolonging the small-town club's fairytale ride from the fourth tier of Italian football all the way into Europe via a best-ever Serie A finish of sixth. The team's most talked-about player was ex-Italy Under-21 goalkeeper Andrea Consigli, who made the save of the season, in a 1-0 win at Inter, but then provided the campaign's most bizarre own goal, in a 3-1 defeat against Fiorentina.

Frosinone and Carpi, the two low-budget clubs promoted to Serie A for the first time in 2015, were unable to extend their stay beyond one season as they dropped down with Verona. Carpi's fate was not decided until the final day, and although they won at Udinese, relegation rivals Palermo, whose president Maurizio Zamparini changed his coach no fewer than eight times during the campaign, also claimed three points at home to Verona to retain their top-flight status. Cagliari won Serie B to restore top-flight football to the island of Sardinia in 2016/17, while Crotone, from Calabria in Italy's deep south, won a place in the elite division for the first time. Pescara, defeated by Bologna in the 2014/15 promotion play-offs, made amends by winning the same event 12 months on to book in for a seventh Serie A campaign.

Domestic cup

Milan would have denied Sassuolo their European spot had they managed to win the Coppa Italia for the first time in 13 years. But having comfortably seen off third-tier Alessandria in the semi-finals – while Juventus survived a second-leg comeback by Internazionale to prevail on penalties – the Rossoneri were unable to deny former boss Allegri a historic second successive domestic double. They tried their best, taking the game into extra time, but a close-range strike by Álvaro Morata from a Cuadrado cross decided the contest with 110 minutes on the clock, enabling Juve to lift the trophy for a record-extending 11th time.

Europe

Juventus reached the UEFA Champions League final in Allegri's first season but they lasted only as far as the round of 16 in his second. Runners-up in their group despite beating Manchester City, the team that finished above them, home and away, they were drawn to face Bayern München in the first knockout round, and the German champions just got the better of them, in extra time, after Juve had taken a 4-2 aggregate lead with a brilliant first-half display in Munich. Roma also dropped out at the same stage, a mere six points in the group having proved sufficient to earn them a last-16 date with Real Madrid, who scored four times without reply to end their interest.

Lazio, having been denied access to the UEFA Champions League proper with a play-off defeat by Bayer Leverkusen, were Italy's last team standing in the UEFA Europa League. But as they only got as far as the round of 16, where they were humbled 3-0 at home by Sparta Praha, it was a sub-standard season all round for Serie A's European contingent. Napoli and Fiorentina had both reached the previous season's UEFA Europa League semi-finals, but they fell by the wayside in the round of 32, Napoli to Villarreal after powering through their group with maximum points and a competition-record tally of 22 goals, scoring five in each of their matches at the Stadio San Paolo.

National team

Undefeated qualifiers for UEFA EURO 2016, Italy got off to a terrific start at the finals when they opened up with a 2-0 win over much-fancied Belgium – who had defeated them 3-1 in a November 2015 friendly – and then scored a late winner against Sweden to qualify for the knockout phase with a game in hand. Although Conte's unbeaten run in

competitive matches ended in the third group game, against the Republic of Ireland. It was a dead rubber from Italy's perspective, and the benefit of resting several first-teamers was reaped five days later when the Azzurri staged a near-replica of their victory over Belgium to end Spain's eight-year reign as European champions with a marvellous 2-0 win at the Stade de France.

By now Italy had grand designs on returning to Saint-Denis for the final, but they would last just one round longer, going down 6-5 on penalties to world champions Germany after a lengthy shoot-out in Bordeaux. Although technically it was not a defeat, with the scores ending 1-1 after extra time, it was still the first time Italy had ever been eliminated from a major tournament by Germany. It was also Conte's last game in charge after just two years in office. He had already announced prior to the tournament that he would be standing down and resuming his club career in England with Chelsea. He did his

reputation no harm at all with his performances in France. The common consensus was that Italy's squad was one of the weakest to have represented the country at a tournament, but Conte's tactical expertise and powers of motivation were plain for all to see.

The Azzurri attack, as expected, was the team's weakest link, with just six goals scored in five games and two of those from defenders. By contrast, the Italian back line was one of the sturdiest at the tournament, with the first XI conceding just once, against Germany, and although none of the all-Juventus rearguard of Buffon, Barzagli, Bonucci and Chiellini made it into the official Team of the Tournament, all four could look back with satisfaction on their three weeks' work. The likelihood is that they will again be called upon en bloc on the road to Russia 2018 by 68-year-old Giampiero Ventura, the man appointed to follow in Conte's footsteps after completing a fifth successive season with Torino.

Italian defenders Andrea Barzagli, Leonardo Bonucci and Giorgio Chiellini (left to right) get themselves organised in their victory against Spain at UEFA EURO 2016

DOMESTIC SEASON AT A GLANCE

Serie A 2015/16 final table

		Pld		Home					Away					Total				Pts
			W	D	L	F	A	W	D	L	F	A	W	D	L	F	A	
1	**Juventus FC**	38	16	2	1	37	6	13	2	4	38	14	29	4	5	75	20	91
2	SSC Napoli	38	16	3	0	49	12	9	4	6	31	20	25	7	6	80	32	82
3	AS Roma	38	13	5	1	44	17	10	6	3	39	24	23	11	4	83	41	80
4	FC Internazionale Milano	38	13	2	4	29	15	7	5	7	21	23	20	7	11	50	38	67
5	ACF Fiorentina	38	11	5	3	34	16	7	5	7	26	26	18	10	10	60	42	64
6	US Sassuolo Calcio	38	8	8	3	25	20	8	5	6	24	20	16	13	9	49	40	61
7	AC Milan	38	9	6	4	28	22	6	6	7	21	21	15	12	11	49	43	57
8	SS Lazio	38	10	3	6	32	23	5	6	8	20	29	15	9	14	52	52	54
9	AC Chievo Verona	38	7	8	4	25	18	6	3	10	18	27	13	11	14	43	45	50
10	Empoli FC	38	7	6	6	22	20	5	4	10	18	29	12	10	16	40	49	46
11	Genoa CFC	38	10	3	6	29	19	3	4	12	16	29	13	7	18	45	48	46
12	Torino FC	38	6	6	7	25	25	6	3	10	27	30	12	9	17	52	55	45
13	Atalanta BC	38	8	6	5	27	21	3	6	10	14	26	11	12	15	41	47	45
14	Bologna FC	38	5	5	9	20	21	6	4	9	13	24	11	9	18	33	45	42
15	UC Sampdoria	38	8	4	7	29	25	2	6	11	19	36	10	10	18	48	61	40
16	US Città di Palermo	38	6	4	9	24	30	4	5	10	14	35	10	9	19	38	65	39
17	Udinese Calcio	38	6	4	9	18	28	4	5	10	17	32	10	9	19	35	60	39
18	Carpi FC 1909	38	6	5	8	23	26	3	6	10	14	31	9	11	18	37	57	38
19	Frosinone Calcio	38	6	4	9	18	26	2	3	14	17	50	8	7	23	35	76	31
20	Hellas Verona FC	38	4	6	9	21	30	1	7	11	13	33	5	13	20	34	63	28

European qualification 2016/17

 Champion/Cup winner: Juventus FC (group stage)
SSC Napoli (group stage)
AS Roma (play-offs)

 FC Internazionale Milano (group stage)
ACF Fiorentina (group stage)
US Sassuolo Calcio (third qualifying round)

Top scorer	Gonzalo Higuaín (Napoli), 36 goals
Relegated clubs	Hellas Verona FC, Frosinone Calcio, Carpi FC 1909
Promoted clubs	Cagliari Calcio, FC Crotone, Pescara Calcio
Cup final	Juventus FC 1-0 AC Milan (aet)

Team of the season
(3-4-3)

Coach: Allegri (Juventus)

Player of the season

Gonzalo Higuaín
(SSC Napoli)

A record that had stood for 66 years was broken on the final day of the 2015/16 Serie A season as Higuaín completed a hat-trick against Frosinone with an acrobatic overhead kick to increase his goal tally for the season to 36 goals. That was one more than the mark set by Milan's legendary Swedish forward Gunnar Nordahl in the 1949/50 campaign and ensured the Argentinian striker a place in history at the end of what proved to be the last of his three seasons in Naples, a €90m transfer taking him north to Juventus in July.

Newcomer of the season

Gianluigi Donnarumma
(AC Milan)

If, as it is often claimed, goalkeepers do not reach their peak until their 30s, Donnarumma looks set for a remarkably long career. He was just 16 years and eight months old when he made his Serie A debut, against Sassuolo on 25 October 2015. Furthermore, he played so well in that game and others afterwards that before long he was the Rossoneri's undisputed first choice, keeping 34-year-old Diego López and 38-year-old Christian Abbiati on the bench and ending the season with an appearance in the Coppa Italia final.

NATIONAL TEAM

International honours
FIFA World Cup (4) 1934, 1938, 1982, 2006
UEFA European Championship (1) 1968

International tournament appearances
FIFA World Cup (18) 1934 (Winners), 1938 (Winners), 1950, 1954, 1962, 1966, 1970 (runners-up), 1974, 1978 (4th), 1982 (Winners), 1986 (2nd round), 1990 (3rd), 1994 (runners-up), 1998 (qtr-finals), 2002 (2nd round), 2006 (Winners), 2010, 2014
UEFA European Championship (9) 1968 (Winners), 1980 (4th), 1988 (semi-finals), 1996, 2000 (runners-up), 2004, 2008 (qtr-finals), 2012 (runners-up), 2016 (qtr-finals)

Top five all-time caps
Gianluigi Buffon (161); Fabio Cannavaro (136); Paolo Maldini (126); **Andrea Pirlo** (116); Dino Zoff (112)

Top five all-time goals
Luigi Riva (35); Giuseppe Meazza (33); Silvio Piola (30); Roberto Baggio & Alessandro Del Piero (27)

Results 2015/16

Date	Opponent		Venue		Score	Scorers
03/09/15	Malta (ECQ)	H	Florence	W	1-0	Pellè (69)
06/09/15	Bulgaria (ECQ)	H	Palermo	W	1-0	De Rossi (6p)
10/10/15	Azerbaijan (ECQ)	A	Baku	W	3-1	Éder (11), El Shaarawy (43), Darmian (65)
13/10/15	Norway (ECQ)	H	Rome	W	2-1	Florenzi (73), Pellè (82)
13/11/15	Belgium	A	Brussels	L	1-3	Candreva (3)
17/11/15	Romania	H	Bologna	D	2-2	Marchisio (56p), Gabbiadini (66)
24/03/16	Spain	H	Udine	D	1-1	Insigne (68)
29/03/16	Germany	A	Munich	L	1-4	El Shaarawy (83)
29/05/16	Scotland	N	Ta' Qali (MLT)	W	1-0	Pellè (57)
06/06/16	Finland	H	Verona	W	2-0	Candreva (27p), De Rossi (71)
13/06/16	Belgium (ECF)	N	Lyon (FRA)	W	2-0	Giaccherini (32), Pellè (90+3)
17/06/16	Sweden (ECF)	N	Toulouse (FRA)	W	1-0	Éder (88)
22/06/16	Republic of Ireland (ECF)	N	Lille (FRA)	L	0-1	
27/06/16	Spain (ECF)	N	Saint-Denis (FRA)	W	2-0	Chiellini (33), Pellè (90+1)
02/07/16	Germany (ECF)	N	Bordeaux (FRA)	D	1-1	Bonucci (78p) (aet; 5-6 on pens)

Appearances 2015/16

Coach: Antonio Conte 31/07/69

Player	DOB	Club	MLT	BUL	AZE	NOR	Bel	Rou	Esp	Ger	Sco	Fin	BEL	SWE	IRL	ESP	GER	Caps	Goals
Gianluigi Buffon	28/01/78	Juventus	G	G	G	G	G	G69	G	G	G		G	G		G	G	161	-
Matteo Darmian	02/12/89	Man. United (ENG)	D	D	D	M	D	D	D	D	M60		M58		s60	s84	s86	26	1
Leonardo Bonucci	01/05/87	Juventus	D	D	D	D	D90	D	D	D62	D	D85	D	D	D	D	D	62	4
Giorgio Chiellini	14/08/84	Juventus	D	D	D	D	D	D			D	D	D	D		D	D121	88	7
Manuel Pasqual	13/03/82	Fiorentina	D															11	-
Marco Verratti	05/11/92	Paris (FRA)	M77	M	M													15	1
Andrea Pirlo	19/05/79	New York City (USA)	M															116	13
Andrea Bertolacci	11/01/91	Milan	M55			s68												5	-
Manolo Gabbiadini	26/11/91	Napoli	A64					s60										6	1
Graziano Pellè	15/07/85	Southampton (ENG)	A	A73	A	A	A80	A60	A60		A67	s81	A	A60		A	A	17	7
Éder	15/11/86	Sampdoria /Internazionale	A	s86	A79	A62	A80	A60		A51		A59		A75	A	A82	A108	14	3
Marco Parolo	25/01/85	Lazio	s55	M	M		M60	s77	M89	s68	s62	M	M	M		M	M	24	-
Antonio Candreva	28/02/87	Lazio	s64	A86	M88	s72	M	s81	A60		M62	M76	M	M		M	M	40	4
Roberto Soriano	08/02/91	Sampdoria	s77			M	s60	M60										8	-
Mattia De Sciglio	20/10/92	Milan		D	D	M	D89					s58			M81	M	M	26	-
Daniele De Rossi	24/07/83	Roma	M 55*							M67	s63	M78	M74			M54		106	18
Stephan El Shaarawy	27/10/92	Monaco (FRA) /Roma		A72	M74		s80	M81		s68		M69			s81			20	3
Alessandro Florenzi	11/03/91	Roma		s72	s74	M	M80	M	M89	M61	M	s69		M85	M	M84	M86	21	2
Simone Zaza	25/06/91	Juventus		s73		s80		s60	A78	s67	A81		s60	A			s121	14	1
Sebastian Giovinco	26/01/87	Toronto (USA)			s79	s62												23	1
Riccardo Montolivo	18/01/85	Milan		s88	M68		s60		M									62	2
Andrea Barzagli	08/05/81	Juventus				D72	s90	D		D		D	D	D	D	D	D	61	-
Claudio Marchisio	19/01/86	Juventus					M	M77										54	5
Stefano Okaka	09/08/89	Anderlecht (BEL)					s80	s60		s68								4	1
Luca Antonelli	11/02/87	Milan					s89		s79	s78								12	-
Salvatore Sirigu	12/01/87	Paris (FRA)					s69				G				G			17	-
Davide Astori	07/01/87	Fiorentina					D											11	1
Thiago Motta	28/08/82	Paris (FRA)					M			M68	M63	s78	s74		M	s54		30	1
Emanuele Giaccherini	05/05/85	Bologna					M79	M68	M80	M64	M	M			M	M	M	29	4
Lorenzo Insigne	04/06/91	Napoli					s51	A68	s59						s74	s82	s108	12	2
Federico Bernardeschi	16/02/94	Fiorentina					s60	A	s60	s76					M60			5	-
Lorenzo De Silvestri	23/05/88	Sampdoria					s89		s61									6	-
Jorginho	20/12/91	Napoli					s89				s67							2	-
Francesco Acerbi	10/02/88	Sassuolo							D									2	-
Andrea Ranocchia	16/02/88	Sampdoria								s62								21	-
Giacomo Bonaventura	22/08/89	Milan									s80							3	-
Ciro Immobile	20/02/90	Torino										A		s75		A74		15	1
Stefano Sturaro	09/03/93	Juventus										s64		s85		M	M	4	-
Angelo Ogbonna	23/05/88	West Ham (ENG)										s85			D			12	-

EUROPE

Juventus FC

Group D

Match 1 - Manchester City FC (ENG)
A 2-1 *Mandžukić (70), Morata (81)*
Buffon, Chiellini, Morata (Barzagli 85), Pogba, Hernanes, Cuadrado, Mandžukić (Dybala 78), Bonucci, Lichtsteiner, Sturaro, Evra. Coach: Massimiliano Allegri (ITA)

Match 2 - Sevilla FC (ESP)
H 2-0 *Morata (41), Zaza (87)*
Buffon, Chiellini, Khedira (Alex Sandro 76), Morata (Zaza 80), Pogba, Hernanes, Barzagli, Cuadrado, Dybala (Rugani 88), Evra. Coach: Massimiliano Allegri (ITA)

Match 3 - VfL Borussia Mönchengladbach (GER)
H 0-0
Buffon, Chiellini, Khedira, Marchisio, Morata (Dybala 81), Pogba, Alex Sandro, Barzagli, Cuadrado (Pereyra 60), Mandžukić (Zaza 70), Bonucci. Coach: Massimiliano Allegri (ITA)

Match 4 - VfL Borussia Mönchengladbach (GER)
A 1-1 *Lichtsteiner (44)*
Buffon, Chiellini, Marchisio, Morata (Barzagli 75), Pogba, Hernanes, Bonucci, Dybala (Cuadrado 63), Lichtsteiner, Sturaro (Lemina 87), Evra. Coach: Massimiliano Allegri (ITA)
Red card: Hernanes 53

Match 5 - Manchester City FC (ENG)
H 1-0 *Mandžukić (18)*
Buffon, Chiellini, Marchisio, Pogba, Alex Sandro (Evra 78), Barzagli, Mandžukić (Morata 55), Bonucci, Dybala (Cuadrado 82), Lichtsteiner, Sturaro. Coach: Massimiliano Allegri (ITA)

Match 6 - Sevilla FC (ESP)
A 0-1
Buffon, Chiellini, Marchisio, Morata, Pogba, Alex Sandro, Barzagli, Bonucci, Dybala, Lichtsteiner (Cuadrado 77), Sturaro. Coach: Massimiliano Allegri (ITA)

Round of 16 - FC Bayern München (GER)
H 2-2 *Dybala (63), Sturaro (76)*
Buffon, Khedira (Sturaro 69), Marchisio (Hernanes 46), Pogba, Barzagli, Cuadrado, Mandžukić, Bonucci, Dybala (Morata 75), Lichtsteiner, Evra. Coach: Massimiliano Allegri (ITA)
A 2-4 (aet) *Pogba (5), Cuadrado (28)*
Buffon, Khedira (Sturaro 68), Morata (Mandžukić 72), Pogba, Hernanes, Alex Sandro, Barzagli, Cuadrado (Pereyra 89), Bonucci, Lichtsteiner, Evra. Coach: Massimiliano Allegri (ITA)

AS Roma

Group E

Match 1 - FC Barcelona (ESP)
H 1-1 *Florenzi (31)*
Szczęsny (De Sanctis 50), Rüdiger, Digne, Nainggolan, Džeko, Salah, Iago Falqué (Iturbe 81), De Rossi, Keita, Florenzi (Torosidis 85), Manolas. Coach: Rudi Garcia (FRA)

Match 2 - FC BATE Borisov (BLR)
A 2-3 *Gervinho (66), Torosidis (82)*
Szczęsny, Digne, Nainggolan, Iturbe (Torosidis 46), Salah, Pjanić, De Rossi, Vainqueur (Iago Falqué 39), Florenzi (Soleri 90+2), Gervinho, Manolas. Coach: Rudi Garcia (FRA)

Match 3 - Bayer 04 Leverkusen (GER)
A 4-4 *De Rossi (29, 38), Pjanić (54), Iago Falqué (73)*
Szczęsny, Rüdiger, Digne, Nainggolan, Salah (Iago Falqué 62), Pjanić, De Rossi, Florenzi (Iturbe 90), Gervinho (Džeko 85), Torosidis, Manolas. Coach: Rudi Garcia (FRA)

Match 4 - Bayer 04 Leverkusen (GER)
H 3-2 *Salah (2), Džeko (29), Pjanić (80p)*
Szczęsny, Digne, Nainggolan, Džeko, Salah, Pjanić, De Rossi, Florenzi (Maicon 56; Torosidis 76), Gervinho (Iturbe 68), Manolas. Coach: Rudi Garcia (FRA)

Match 5 - FC Barcelona (ESP)
A 1-6 *Džeko (90+1)*
Szczęsny, Rüdiger, Digne, Nainggolan (Iturbe 46), Džeko, Maicon, Iago Falqué, Pjanić (Salih Uçan 75), Keita, Florenzi (Vainqueur 58), Manolas. Coach: Rudi Garcia (FRA)

Match 6 - FC BATE Borisov (BLR)
H 0-0
Szczęsny, Rüdiger, Digne, Nainggolan, Iturbe (Salah 59), Džeko, Iago Falqué (Salih Uçan 83), Pjanić, De Rossi, Florenzi, Manolas. Coach: Rudi Garcia (FRA)

Round of 16 - Real Madrid CF (ESP)
H 0-2
Szczęsny, Rüdiger, Digne, Nainggolan, Perotti, Salah, Pjanić, Vainqueur (De Rossi 77), El Shaarawy (Džeko 64), Florenzi (Totti 87), Manolas. Coach: Luciano Spalletti (ITA)
A 0-2
Szczęsny, Digne, Perotti, Džeko, Salah, Pjanić (Vainqueur 46), Keita (Maicon 86), El Shaarawy (Totti 74), Florenzi, Manolas, Zukanovic. Coach: Luciano Spalletti (ITA)

SS Lazio

Play-offs - Bayer 04 Leverkusen (GER)
H 1-0 *Baldé (77)*
Berisha, De Vrij (Gentiletti 89), Basta, Felipe Anderson, Klose (Baldé 46), Parolo, Lulić, Biglia, Onazi (Milinković-Savić 53), Maurício, Candreva. Coach: Stefano Pioli (ITA)
A 0-3
Berisha, De Vrij, Basta, Felipe Anderson (Gentiletti 70), Baldé, Parolo, Lulić, Onazi (Morrison 82), Radu (Kishna 56), Maurício, Candreva. Coach: Stefano Pioli (ITA)
Red card: Maurício 68

Group G

Match 1 - FC Dnipro Dnipropetrovsk (UKR)
A 1-1 *Milinković-Savić (34)*
Marchetti, Klose, Felipe Anderson, Parolo, Matri (Baldé 76), Gentiletti, Milinković-Savić (Mauri 89), Onazi, Radu, Konko, Kishna (Candreva 76). Coach: Stefano Pioli (ITA)

Match 2 - AS Saint-Étienne (FRA)
H 3-2 *Onazi (22), Hoedt (48), Biglia (80)*
Berisha, Hoedt, Mauri (Matri 64), Basta, Felipe Anderson, Baldé, Biglia, Milinković-Savić, Onazi (Cataldi 74), Radu, Maurício (Gentiletti 46). Coach: Stefano Pioli (ITA)

Match 3 - Rosenborg BK (NOR)
H 3-1 *Matri (28), Felipe Anderson (54), Candreva (79)*
Berisha, Hoedt, Mauri (Milinković-Savić 75), Felipe Anderson (Lulić 70), Matri, Onazi (Gentiletti 11), Radu, Konko, Cataldi, Maurício, Candreva. Coach: Stefano Pioli (ITA)
Red card: Maurício 6

Match 4 - Rosenborg BK (NOR)
A 2-0 *Djordjević (9, 29)*
Berisha, Hoedt, Morrison (Mauri 76), Djordjević (Matri 66), Gentiletti, Onazi, Radu, Konko, Cataldi, Candreva (Baldé 46), Kishna. Coach: Stefano Pioli (ITA)
Red card: Baldé 83

Match 5 - FC Dnipro Dnipropetrovsk (UKR)
H 3-1 *Candreva (4), Parolo (68), Djordjević (90+3)*
Berisha, Klose (Milinković-Savić 65), Parolo, Matri (Djordjević 70), Gentiletti, Radu, Konko, Cataldi, Maurício, Candreva, Kishna (Lulić 81). Coach: Stefano Pioli (ITA)

Match 6 - AS Saint-Étienne (FRA)
A 1-1 *Matri (52)*
Berisha, Hoedt, Basta, Djordjević, Felipe Anderson, Parolo, Matri (Morrison 74), Konko, Cataldi, Maurício, Ikonomidis (Candreva 84). Coach: Stefano Pioli (ITA)

Round of 32 - Galatasaray AŞ (TUR)
A 1-1 *Milinković-Savić (21)*
Marchetti, Hoedt, Felipe Anderson (Candreva 58), Parolo, Matri (Klose 69), Lulić (Mauri 90), Biglia, Milinković-Savić, Radu, Konko, Maurício. Coach: Stefano Pioli (ITA)
H 3-1 *Parolo (59), Felipe Anderson (61), Klose (72)*
Marchetti, Felipe Anderson, Biševac, Parolo, Matri (Klose 70), Lulić (Candreva 57), Biglia, Milinković-Savić, Radu, Konko, Maurício. Coach: Stefano Pioli (ITA)

Round of 16 - AC Sparta Praha (CZE)
A 1-1 *Parolo (38)*
Marchetti, Hoedt, Biševac, Baldé, Parolo, Matri (Lulić 55),
Biglia, Milinković-Savić, Radu, Konko (Basta 46; Maurício
66), Candreva. Coach: Stefano Pioli (ITA)
H 0-3
Marchetti, Hoedt, Mauri (Felipe Anderson 58), Klose (Matri
58), Biševac, Baldé, Parolo, Lulić, Biglia, Konko (Maurício 67),
Candreva. Coach: Stefano Pioli (ITA)

ACF Fiorentina

Group I
Match 1 - FC Basel 1893 (SUI)
H 1-2 *Kalinić (4)*
Sepe, Gonzalo Rodríguez, Badelj, Kalinić, Astori (Tomović 68),
Fernández (Pasqual 68), Błaszczykowski, Borja Valero, Alonso,
Roncaglia, Iličić (Babacar 46). Coach: Paulo Sousa (POR)
Red card: Gonzalo Rodríguez 66
Match 2 - Os Belenenses (POR)
A 4-0 *Bernardeschi (18), Babacar (45+1), Tonel (83og),
Rossi (90)*
Sepe, Tomović, Vecino, Bernardeschi (Badelj 60), Rebić
(Błaszczykowski 81), Astori, Fernández, Mario Suárez, Rossi,
Alonso, Babacar (Joan Verdú 78). Coach: Paulo Sousa (POR)
Match 3 - KKS Lech Poznań (POL)
H 1-2 *Rossi (90)*
Sepe, Tomović, Rebić, Astori, Fernández, Mario Suárez (Iličić
73), Joan Verdú (Vecino 65), Rossi, Pasqual (Bernardeschi 68),
Babacar, Roncaglia. Coach: Paulo Sousa (POR)
Red card: Rebić 90+2
Match 4 - KKS Lech Poznań (POL)
A 2-0 *Iličić (42, 83)*
Sepe, Gonzalo Rodríguez, Tomović, Vecino, Bernardeschi,
Astori, Fernández, Błaszczykowski (Alonso 72), Mario Suárez
(Badelj 79), Rossi (Kalinić 63), Iličić. Coach: Paulo Sousa (POR)
Match 5 - FC Basel 1893 (SUI)
A 2-2 *Bernardeschi (23, 36)*
Sepe, Gonzalo Rodríguez, Badelj (Gilberto 85), Vecino, Kalinić,
Bernardeschi (Babacar 85), Astori, Borja Valero, Alonso,
Roncaglia, Iličić (Tomović 33). Coach: Paulo Sousa (POR)
Red card: Roncaglia 26
Match 6 - Os Belenenses (POR)
H 1-0 *Babacar (67)*
Sepe, Gilberto (Bernardeschi 57), Tomović, Badelj (Mario
Suárez 79), Astori, Borja Valero (Vecino 62), Joan Verdú, Rossi,
Pasqual, Alonso, Babacar. Coach: Paulo Sousa (POR)

Round of 32 - Tottenham Hotspur FC (ENG)
H 1-1 *Bernardeschi (59)*
Tătărușanu, Gonzalo Rodríguez, Tomović, Tino Costa (Vecino
67), Zárate, Bernardeschi, Astori, Błaszczykowski (Kalinić 62),
Borja Valero, Alonso, Iličić (Badelj 61). Coach: Paulo Sousa (POR)
A 0-3
Tătărușanu, Gonzalo Rodríguez, Tomović, Badelj (Fernández
82), Vecino, Kalinić, Bernardeschi, Astori, Borja Valero
(Błaszczykowski 74), Alonso, Iličić (Zárate 61). Coach: Paulo
Sousa (POR)

SSC Napoli

Group D
Match 1 - Club Brugge KV (BEL)
H 5-0 *Callejón (5, 77), Mertens (19, 25), Hamšík (53)*
Reina, Hysaj, Callejón, Jorginho, Higuaín (Gabbiadini 72),
Mertens (Insigne 75), Hamšík (Allan 62), David López,
Koulibaly, Ghoulam, Albiol. Coach: Maurizio Sarri (ITA)
Match 2 - Legia Warszawa (POL)
A 2-0 *Mertens (53), Higuaín (84)*
Gabriel, Allan (Chalobah 83), Valdifiori, Callejón (Higuaín 76),
Maggio, Mertens (El Kaddouri 72), David López, Chiricheș,
Gabbiadini, Koulibaly, Ghoulam. Coach: Maurizio Sarri (ITA)
Match 3 - FC Midtjylland (DEN)
A 4-1 *Callejón (19), Gabbiadini (31, 40), Higuaín (90+4)*
Reina, Allan (Hamšík 60), Valdifiori, Callejón (Higuaín 64),
Maggio, David López, Chiricheș, Gabbiadini, Koulibaly,
Ghoulam (Strinić 81), El Kaddouri. Coach: Maurizio Sarri (ITA)
Match 4 - FC Midtjylland (DEN)
H 5-0 *El Kaddouri (13), Gabbiadini (23, 38), Maggio (54),
Callejón (77)*
Reina, Strinić (Hysaj 69), Valdifiori, Maggio, Hamšík (Allan 53),
David López, Chiricheș, Gabbiadini, Insigne (Callejón 57),
Koulibaly, El Kaddouri. Coach: Maurizio Sarri (ITA)
Match 5 - Club Brugge KV (BEL)
A 1-0 *Chiricheș (41)*
Gabriel, Strinić, Valdifiori, Callejón (Ghoulam 77), Maggio,
Hamšík (Hysaj 69), David López, Chiricheș, Koulibaly, El
Kaddouri, Chalobah (Allan 81). Coach: Maurizio Sarri (ITA)
Match 6 - Legia Warszawa (POL)
H 5-2 *Chalobah (32), Insigne (39), Callejón (57),
Mertens (65, 90+1)*
Gabriel, Strinić, Valdifiori, Maggio, Mertens, David López,
Chiricheș (Luperto 79), Insigne (Callejón 55), Koulibaly (Albiol
68), El Kaddouri, Chalobah. Coach: Maurizio Sarri (ITA)

Round of 32 - Villarreal CF (ESP)
A 0-1
Reina, Hysaj, Strinić, Valdifiori, Callejón (Insigne 73), Mertens,
Hamšík, David López (Allan 83), Chiricheș, Gabbiadini
(Higuaín 67), Koulibaly. Coach: Maurizio Sarri (ITA)
H 1-1 *Hamšík (17)*
Reina, Hysaj, Strinić (Maggio 64), Valdifiori (Jorginho 75),
Higuaín, Mertens, Hamšík, David López (Gabbiadini 78),
Chiricheș, Insigne, Albiol. Coach: Maurizio Sarri (ITA)

UC Sampdoria

Third qualifying round - FK Vojvodina (SRB)
H 0-4
Viviano, Cassani, Fernando, Barreto, Palombo (Regini 59),
Krstičić (Wszołek 59), Soriano, Éder, Muriel (Bonazzoli 73),
Silvestre, Zukanović. Coach: Walter Zenga (ITA)
A 2-0 *Éder (15), Muriel (70)*
Viviano, Cassani, Coda, Fernando, Barreto, Krstičić (Ivan 79),
Soriano (Wszołek 85), Éder, Muriel (Bonazzoli 75), Silvestre,
Zukanović. Coach: Walter Zenga (ITA)

DOMESTIC LEAGUE CLUB-BY-CLUB

Atalanta BC

1907 • Atleti Azzurri d'Italia (26,542) • atalanta.it
Major honours
Italian Cup (1) 1963
Coach: Edoardo Reja

2015
23/08	a	Internazionale	L	0-1	
30/08	h	Frosinone	W	2-0	Stendardo, Gómez
13/09	a	Sassuolo	D	2-2	Pinilla 2
20/09	h	Verona	D	1-1	Moralez
24/09	a	Empoli	W	1-0	Rafael Tolói
28/09	h	Sampdoria	W	2-1	og (Moisander), Denis
04/10	a	Fiorentina	L	0-3	
18/10	h	Carpi	W	3-0	Pinilla, Gómez, Cigarini (p)
25/10	a	Juventus	L	0-2	
28/10	h	Lazio	W	2-1	og (Basta), Gómez
01/11	a	Bologna	L	0-3	
07/11	h	Milan	D	0-0	
22/11	h	Torino	L	0-1	
29/11	a	Roma	W	2-0	Gómez, Denis (p)
06/12	h	Palermo	W	3-0	Denis, Cherubin, De Roon
13/12	a	Chievo	L	0-1	
20/12	h	Napoli	L	1-3	Gómez

2016
06/01	a	Udinese	L	1-2	D'Alessandro
10/01	h	Genoa	L	0-2	
16/01	h	Internazionale	D	1-1	og (Murillo)
23/01	a	Frosinone	D	0-0	
30/01	h	Sassuolo	D	1-1	Denis
03/02	a	Verona	L	1-2	Conti
07/02	h	Empoli	D	0-0	
14/02	a	Sampdoria	D	0-0	
21/02	h	Fiorentina	L	2-3	Conti, Pinilla
28/02	a	Carpi	D	1-1	Kurtić
06/03	h	Juventus	L	0-2	
13/03	a	Lazio	L	0-2	
20/03	h	Bologna	W	2-0	Gómez, Diamanti
03/04	h	Milan	W	2-1	Pinilla, Gómez
10/04	a	Torino	L	1-2	Cigarini
17/04	h	Roma	D	3-3	D'Alessandro, Borriello 2
20/04	a	Palermo	W	2-1	Borriello (p), Paletta
24/04	h	Chievo	W	1-0	Borriello
02/05	a	Napoli	L	1-2	og (Albiol)
08/05	h	Udinese	D	1-1	Bellini (p)
15/05	a	Genoa	W	2-1	D'Alessandro, Kurtić

No	Name	Nat	DoB	Pos	Aps	(s)	Gls
30	Davide Bassi		12/04/85	G	1		
6	Gianpaolo Bellini		27/03/80	D	11	(4)	1
22	Marco Borriello		18/06/82	A	8	(7)	4
28	Davide Brivio		17/03/88	D	10	(4)	
17	Carlos Carmona	CHI	21/02/87	M	5	(3)	
33	Nicolò Cherubin		02/12/86	D	10	(4)	1
21	Luca Cigarini		20/06/86	M	21	(4)	2
24	Andrea Conti		02/03/94	D	10	(4)	2
7	Marco D'Alessandro		17/02/91	M	11	(12)	3
15	Marten de Roon	NED	29/03/91	M	35	(1)	1
19	Germán Denis	ARG	10/09/81	A	12	(3)	4
23	Alessandro Diamanti		05/05/83	M	9	(7)	1
55	Berat Djimsiti	ALB	19/02/93	D	3		
93	Boukary Dramé	SEN	22/07/85	D	25		
8	Marcelo Estigarribia	PAR	21/09/87	M		(4)	
11	Remo Freuler	SUI	15/04/92	M	5	(1)	
4	Roberto Gagliardini		07/04/94	M	1		
13	Serge Gakpé	TOG	07/05/87	A		(5)	
4	Luigi Giorgi		19/04/87	M		(1)	
10	Alejandro Gómez	ARG	15/02/88	M	33	(1)	7
88	Alberto Grassi		07/03/95	M	13		
27	Jasmin Kurtić	SVN	10/01/89	M	30	(2)	2
5	Andrea Masiello		05/02/86	D	27	(2)	
8	Giulio Migliaccio		23/06/81	M	3	(15)	
45	Gaetano Monachello		03/03/94	A	3	(7)	
7	Maximiliano Moralez	ARG	27/02/87	M	16	(1)	1
29	Gabriel Paletta		15/02/86	D	24		1
51	Mauricio Pinilla	CHI	04/02/84	A	16	(4)	5
1	Boris Radunović	SRB	26/05/96	G	1		
3	Rafael Tolói	BRA	10/10/90	D	21	(3)	1
77	Cristian Raimondi		30/04/81	M	6	(12)	
57	Marco Sportiello		10/05/92	G	36		
2	Guglielmo Stendardo		06/05/81	D	12	(3)	1

Bologna FC

1909 • Renato Dall'Ara (39,444) • bolognafc.it
Major honours
Italian League (7) 1925, 1929, 1936, 1937, 1939, 1941, 1964; Italian Cup (2) 1970, 1974
Coach: Delio Rossi;
(28/10/15) Roberto Donadoni

2015
22/08	a	Lazio	L	1-2	Mancosu
29/08	h	Sassuolo	L	0-1	
14/09	a	Sampdoria	L	0-2	
20/09	h	Frosinone	W	1-0	Mounier
23/09	a	Fiorentina	L	0-2	
27/09	h	Udinese	L	1-2	Mounier
04/10	a	Juventus	L	1-3	Mounier
18/10	h	Palermo	L	0-1	
24/10	a	Carpi	W	2-1	Gastaldello, Masina
27/10	h	Internazionale	L	0-1	
01/11	a	Atalanta	W	3-0	Giaccherini, Destro, Brienza
07/11	h	Verona	W	2-0	Giaccherini, Donsah
21/11	h	Napoli	D	2-2	Masina, Destro (p)
28/11	a	Torino	L	0-2	
06/12	h	Napoli	W	3-2	Destro 2, Rossettini
12/12	a	Genoa	W	1-0	Rossettini
19/12	h	Empoli	L	2-3	Brienza, Destro

2016
06/01	h	Milan	W	1-0	Giaccherini
10/01	a	Chievo	L	0-1	
17/01	h	Lazio	D	2-2	Giaccherini, Destro
24/01	a	Sassuolo	W	2-1	Giaccherini, Floccari
31/01	h	Sampdoria	W	3-2	Mounier, Donsah, Destro (p)
03/02	a	Frosinone	L	0-1	
06/02	h	Fiorentina	D	1-1	Giaccherini
14/02	a	Udinese	W	1-0	Destro
19/02	h	Juventus	D	0-0	
28/02	a	Palermo	D	0-0	
06/03	h	Carpi	D	0-0	
12/03	a	Internazionale	L	1-2	Brienza
20/03	h	Atalanta	L	0-2	
04/04	h	Verona	D	0-0	
11/04	a	Roma	D	1-1	Rossettini
16/04	h	Torino	L	0-1	
19/04	a	Napoli	L	0-6	
24/04	a	Genoa	W	2-0	Giaccherini, Floccari
01/05	a	Empoli	D	0-0	
07/05	h	Milan	D	0-0	
15/05	a	Chievo	D	0-0	

No	Name	Nat	DoB	Pos	Aps	(s)	Gls
18	Robert Acquafresca		11/09/87	A	2	(4)	
23	Franco Brienza		19/03/79	M	16	(13)	3
33	Matteo Brighi		14/02/81	M	14	(9)	
19	Kévin Constant	GUI	10/05/87	D	3	(4)	
90	Marco Crimi		17/03/90	M	1		
6	Lorenzo Crisetig		20/01/93	M	4	(1)	
10	Mattia Destro		20/03/91	A	25	(2)	8
21	Amadou Diawara	GUI	17/07/97	M	31	(3)	
30	Godfred Donsah	GHA	07/06/96	M	18	(2)	2
7	Filippo Falco		11/02/92	A	1	(8)	
4	Alex Ferrari		01/07/94	D	13	(8)	
99	Sergio Floccari		12/11/81	A	10	(8)	2
28	Daniele Gastaldello		25/06/83	D	26		1
17	Emanuele Giaccherini		05/05/85	M	27	(1)	7
1	Júnior Costa	BRA	12/11/83	G	5		
4	Emil Krafth	SWE	02/08/94	D	2	(2)	
20	Domenico Maietta		03/08/82	D	18	(1)	
11	Matteo Mancosu		22/12/84	A	3	(6)	1
25	Adam Masina		02/01/94	D	30	(3)	2
15	Ibrahima Mbaye	SEN	19/11/94	D	11	(4)	
83	Antonio Mirante		08/07/83	G	33		
3	Archimede Morleo		26/09/83	D	5		
26	Anthony Mounier	FRA	27/09/87	M	24	(6)	4
2	Marios Oikonomou	GRE	06/10/92	D	17	(3)	
5	Erick Pulgar	CHI	15/01/94	M	6	(7)	
22	Luca Rizzo		24/04/92	M	17	(6)	
13	Luca Rossettini		09/05/85	D	28	(1)	3
98	Aaron Tabacchi		26/06/98	D		(1)	
8	Saphir Taïder	ALG	29/02/92	M	25	(4)	
11	Franco Zuculini	ARG	09/09/90	M		(1)	
11	Juan Camilo Zúñiga	COL	14/12/85	D	3	(6)	

Carpi FC 1909

1909 • Alberto Braglia, Modena (21,092) • carpifc.com
Coach: Fabrizio Castori;
(29/09/15) Giuseppe Sannino;
(03/11/15) Fabrizio Castori

2015
23/08	a	Sampdoria	L	2-5	Lazzari, Ryder Matos
30/08	h	Internazionale	L	1-2	Di Gaudio
13/09	a	Palermo	D	2-2	og (Vitiello), Borriello
20/09	h	Fiorentina	D	0-0	
23/09	h	Napoli	D	0-0	
26/09	a	Roma	L	1-5	Borriello
03/10	h	Torino	W	2-1	og (Padelli), Ryder Matos
18/10	a	Atalanta	L	0-3	
24/10	h	Bologna	L	1-2	Letizia
28/10	h	Frosinone	L	1-2	Marrone
01/11	h	Verona	D	0-0	
08/11	a	Sassuolo	L	0-1	
22/11	h	Chievo	L	1-2	og (Gamberini)
29/11	a	Genoa	W	2-1	Borriello, Zaccardo
06/12	h	Milan	D	0-0	
13/12	a	Empoli	L	0-3	
20/12	h	Juventus	L	2-3	Borriello, og (Bonucci)

2016
06/01	a	Lazio	D	0-0	
09/01	h	Udinese	W	2-1	Pasciuti, Lollo
17/01	h	Sampdoria	W	2-1	Lollo, Mbakogu (p)
24/01	a	Internazionale	D	1-1	Lasagna
30/01	h	Palermo	D	1-1	Mancosu (p)
03/02	a	Fiorentina	W	2-1	Lasagna
07/02	h	Napoli	L	0-1	
12/02	h	Roma	L	1-3	Lasagna
21/02	a	Torino	D	0-0	
28/02	h	Atalanta	D	1-1	Verdi (p)
06/03	a	Bologna	D	0-0	
13/03	h	Frosinone	W	2-1	Bianco, De Guzmán (p)
20/03	a	Verona	W	2-1	Di Gaudio, Lasagna
02/04	h	Sassuolo	L	1-3	Gagliolo
09/04	a	Chievo	L	0-1	
16/04	h	Genoa	W	4-1	Di Gaudio, Lollo, Pasciuti, Sabelli
21/04	a	Milan	D	0-0	
25/04	h	Empoli	W	1-0	Lasagna
01/05	a	Juventus	L	0-2	
08/05	h	Lazio	L	1-3	Mbakogu
15/05	a	Udinese	W	2-1	Verdi 2 (1p)

No	Name	Nat	DoB	Pos	Aps	(s)	Gls
27	Vid Belec	SVN	06/06/90	G	30		
22	Francesco Benussi		15/10/81	G	4		
8	Raffaele Bianco		25/08/87	M	21	(5)	1
12	Marco Borriello		18/06/82	A	8	(4)	4
1	Željko Brkić	SRB	09/07/86	G	3	(1)	
18	Igor Bubnjić	CRO	17/07/92	D	8	(1)	
4	Isaac Cofie	GHA	20/09/91	M	26	(3)	
91	Simone Colombi		01/07/91	G	1		
17	Marco Crimi		17/03/90	M	10	(9)	
36	Fabio Daprelà	SUI	19/02/91	D		(2)	
16	Jonathan de Guzmán	NED	13/09/87	M	1	(4)	1
11	Antonio Di Gaudio		16/08/89	M	16	(13)	3
58	Matteo Fedele	SUI	20/07/92	M	8		
34	Gabriel Silva	BRA	13/05/91	M	14	(2)	
6	Riccardo Gagliolo		28/04/90	D	29	(2)	1
15	Kevin Lasagna		10/08/92	A	8	(28)	5
10	Andrea Lazzari		03/12/84	M	3	(5)	1
3	Gaetano Letizia		29/06/90	D	33	(2)	1
20	Lorenzo Lollo		08/12/90	M	25	(2)	3
25	Matteo Mancosu		22/12/84	A	7	(5)	1
39	Luca Marrone		28/03/90	M	9		1
99	Jerry Mbakogu	NGA	01/10/92	A	20	(4)	2
17	Lorenzo Pasciuti		24/09/89	M	19	(2)	2
13	Fabrizio Poli		26/05/89	D	10		
28	Filippo Porcari		28/04/84	M	2	(2)	
29	Raphael Martinho	BRA	15/04/88	M	10	(1)	
21	Simone Romagnoli		09/02/90	D	30		
7	Ryder Matos	BRA	22/02/93	A	14	(1)	2
2	Stefano Sabelli		13/01/93	D	6	(1)	1
33	Nicolás Spolli	ARG	20/02/83	D	4		
2	Emanuele Suagher		26/11/92	D	8	(1)	
10	Simone Verdi		12/07/92	A	3	(5)	3
2	Wallace	BRA	01/05/94	D	1	(5)	
9	Kamil Wilczek	POL	14/01/88	A	1	(2)	
5	Cristian Zaccardo		21/12/81	D	26	(1)	1

AC Chievo Verona

1929 • Marc'Antonio Bentegodi (38,402) • chievoverona.it

Coach: Rolando Maran

2015

23/08	a	Empoli	W	3-1	Meggiorini, Birsa, Paloschi
30/08	h	Lazio	W	4-0	Meggiorini, Paloschi 2, Birsa
12/09	a	Juventus	D	1-1	Hetemaj
20/09	h	Internazionale	L	0-1	
23/09	h	Torino	W	1-0	Castro
27/09	a	Sassuolo	D	1-1	Pepe
03/10	h	Verona	D	1-1	Castro
18/10	a	Genoa	L	2-3	Paloschi, Pellissier
25/10	h	Napoli	L	0-1	
28/10	a	Milan	L	0-1	
02/11	a	Sampdoria	D	1-1	Inglese
08/11	h	Palermo	L	0-1	
22/11	a	Carpi	W	2-1	Inglese, Meggiorini
29/11	h	Udinese	L	2-3	Paloschi, Inglese
06/12	a	Frosinone	W	2-0	Paloschi (p), Meggiorini
13/12	h	Atalanta	W	1-0	Birsa
20/12	a	Fiorentina	L	0-2	

2016

06/01	h	Roma	D	3-3	Paloschi, Dainelli, Pepe
10/01	a	Bologna	W	1-0	Pepe
17/01	h	Empoli	D	1-1	Paloschi
24/01	a	Lazio	L	1-4	Cesar
31/01	h	Juventus	L	0-4	
03/02	a	Internazionale	L	0-1	
07/02	a	Torino	W	2-1	og (Bruno Peres), Birsa (p)
13/02	h	Sassuolo	D	1-1	Birsa (p)
20/02	a	Verona	L	1-3	Pellissier (p)
28/02	h	Genoa	W	1-0	Castro
05/03	a	Napoli	L	1-3	Rigoni
13/03	h	Milan	D	0-0	
20/03	a	Sampdoria	W	1-0	Meggiorini
03/04	h	Palermo	W	3-1	Cacciatore, Rigoni, Birsa
09/04	a	Carpi	W	1-0	Pellissier
17/04	h	Udinese	D	0-0	
20/04	h	Frosinone	W	5-1	Floro Flores, Pellissier 2 (1p), Rigoni, Sardo
24/04	a	Atalanta	L	0-1	
30/04	h	Fiorentina	D	0-0	
08/05	a	Roma	L	0-3	
15/05	h	Bologna	D	0-0	

No	Name	Nat	DoB	Pos	Aps	(s)	Gls
23	Valter Birsa	SVN	07/08/86	M	32	(3)	6
1	Albano Bizzarri	ARG	09/11/77	G	35		
29	Fabrizio Cacciatore		08/10/86	D	25	(4)	1
19	Lucas Castro	ARG	09/04/89	M	32	(2)	3
12	Boštjan Cesar	SVN	09/07/82	D	30	(1)	1
36	Filippo Costa		21/05/95	D		(6)	
3	Dario Dainelli		09/06/79	D	15	(3)	1
83	Antonio Floro Flores		18/06/83	A	8	(6)	1
21	Nicolas Frey	FRA	06/03/84	D	17	(2)	
5	Alessandro Gamberini		27/08/81	D	22		
18	Massimo Gobbi		31/10/80	D	31	(3)	
56	Perparim Hetemaj	FIN	12/12/86	M	26	(2)	1
45	Roberto Inglese		12/11/91	A	14	(12)	3
40	Paul-José M'Poku	COD	19/04/92	A	6	(14)	
11	Federico Mattiello		14/07/95	D	1		
69	Riccardo Meggiorini		04/09/85	A	19	(7)	5
10	Nikola Ninković	SRB	19/12/94	M		(1)	
43	Alberto Paloschi		04/01/90	A	19	(2)	8
31	Sergio Pellissier		12/04/79	A	10	(9)	5
7	Simone Pepe		30/08/83	M	6	(16)	3
6	Giampiero Pinzi		11/03/81	M	9	(9)	
8	Ivan Radovanović	SRB	29/08/88	M	25	(1)	
4	Nicola Rigoni		12/11/90	M	22	(6)	3
20	Gennaro Sardo		08/05/79	D	3	(3)	1
90	Andrea Seculin		14/07/90	G	3		
2	Nicolás Spolli	ARG	20/02/83	D	8	(2)	

Empoli FC

1920 • Carlo Castellani (21,113) • empolicalcio.it

Coach: Marco Giampaolo

2015

23/08	h	Chievo	L	1-3	Saponara
29/08	a	Milan	L	1-2	Saponara
13/09	h	Napoli	D	2-2	Saponara, Pucciarelli
19/09	a	Udinese	W	2-1	Paredes, Maccarone
24/09	h	Atalanta	L	0-1	
28/09	a	Frosinone	L	0-2	
04/10	h	Sassuolo	W	1-0	Maccarone
17/10	a	Roma	L	1-3	Büchel
24/10	h	Genoa	W	2-0	Krunić, Zieliński
29/10	a	Sampdoria	D	1-1	Pucciarelli
02/11	a	Palermo	W	1-0	Saponara
08/11	h	Juventus	L	1-3	Maccarone
22/11	a	Fiorentina	D	2-2	Livaja, Büchel
29/11	h	Lazio	W	1-0	Tonelli
06/12	a	Verona	W	1-0	Costa
13/12	h	Carpi	W	3-0	Maccarone 2, Saponara
19/12	a	Bologna	W	3-2	Pucciarelli, Maccarone 2

2016

06/01	h	Internazionale	L	0-1	
10/01	a	Torino	W	1-0	Maccarone
17/01	a	Chievo	D	1-1	Tonelli
23/01	h	Milan	D	2-2	Zieliński, Maccarone
31/01	a	Napoli	L	1-5	Paredes
03/02	h	Udinese	W	1-0	Pucciarelli
07/02	a	Atalanta	D	0-0	
13/02	h	Frosinone	L	1-2	Maccarone
21/02	a	Sassuolo	L	2-3	Zieliński, Maccarone (p)
27/02	h	Roma	L	1-3	og (Zukanović)
06/03	a	Genoa	L	0-1	
12/03	h	Sampdoria	D	1-1	Laurini
19/03	h	Palermo	D	0-0	
02/04	a	Juventus	L	0-1	
10/04	h	Fiorentina	W	2-0	Pucciarelli, Zieliński
17/04	a	Lazio	L	0-2	
24/04	h	Verona	W	1-0	Maccarone
25/04	a	Carpi	L	0-1	
01/05	h	Bologna	D	0-0	
07/05	a	Internazionale	L	1-2	Pucciarelli
15/05	h	Torino	W	2-1	Maccarone, Zieliński

No	Name	Nat	DoB	Pos	Aps	(s)	Gls
37	Lorenzo Ariaudo		11/06/89	D	5		
19	Federico Barba		01/09/93	D	10		
6	Luca Bittante		14/08/93	D	3	(13)	
77	Marcel Büchel	LIE	18/03/91	M	18	(10)	2
31	Michele Camporese		19/05/92	D	2		
24	Uroš Ćosić	SRB	24/10/92	D	9		
15	Andrea Costa		01/02/86	D	23	(1)	1
11	Daniele Croce		09/09/82	M	19	(9)	
14	Assane Dioussé	SEN	20/09/97	M	9	(6)	
33	Rade Krunić	BIH	07/10/93	M	5	(10)	1
2	Vincent Laurini	FRA	10/06/89	D	24	(1)	1
39	Marko Livaja	CRO	26/08/93	A	4	(14)	1
7	Massimo Maccarone		06/09/79	A	35	(2)	13
13	Raffaele Maiello		10/07/91	M	4	(8)	
21	Mário Rui	POR	27/05/91	D	36		
55	Luca Martinelli		21/12/88	D	1		
9	Levan Mchedlidze	GEO	24/03/90	A	2	(11)	
32	Leandro Paredes	ARG	29/06/94	M	29	(4)	2
23	Alberto Pelagotti		03/09/89	G	6		
23	Alessandro Piu		30/07/94	A	2	(8)	
20	Manuel Pucciarelli		17/06/91	A	33	(5)	6
1	Maurizio Pugliesi		27/12/76	G	1		
12	Ronaldo	BRA	18/04/90	M	1	(2)	
5	Riccardo Saponara		21/12/91	M	32	(1)	5
18	Franco Signorelli	VEN	01/01/91	M		(1)	
28	Łukasz Skorupski	POL	05/05/91	G	31		
26	Lorenzo Tonelli		17/01/90	D	26		2
3	Marco Zambelli		22/08/85	D	13	(6)	
17	Piotr Zieliński	POL	20/05/94	M	35		5

ACF Fiorentina

1926 • Artemio Franchi (43,147) • violachannel.tv

Major honours
UEFA Cup Winners' Cup (1) 1961; Italian League (2) 1956, 1969; Italian Cup (6) 1940, 1961, 1966, 1975, 1996, 2001

Coach: Paulo Sousa (POR)

2015

23/08	h	Milan	W	2-0	Alonso, Iličić (p)
30/08	a	Torino	L	1-3	Alonso
12/09	h	Genoa	W	1-0	Babacar
20/09	a	Carpi	W	1-0	Babacar
23/09	h	Bologna	W	2-0	Błaszczykowski, Kalinić
27/09	a	Internazionale	W	4-1	Iličić (p), Kalinić 3
04/10	h	Atalanta	W	3-0	Iličić (p), Borja Valero, Joan Verdú
18/10	a	Napoli	L	1-2	Kalinić
25/10	h	Roma	L	1-2	Babacar
28/10	a	Verona	W	2-0	og (Márquez), Kalinić
01/11	h	Frosinone	W	4-1	Rebić, Gonzalo Rodríguez, Babacar (p), Mario Suárez
08/11	a	Sampdoria	W	2-0	Iličić (p), Kalinić
22/11	h	Empoli	D	2-2	Kalinić 2
30/11	a	Sassuolo	D	1-1	Borja Valero
06/12	h	Udinese	W	3-0	Badelj, Iličić (p), Gonzalo Rodríguez
13/12	a	Juventus	L	1-3	Iličić (p)
20/12	h	Chievo	W	2-0	Kalinić, Iličić

2016

06/01	h	Palermo	W	3-1	Iličić 2, Błaszczykowski
09/01	h	Lazio	L	1-3	Roncaglia
17/01	a	Milan	L	0-2	
24/01	h	Torino	W	2-0	Iličić, Gonzalo Rodríguez
31/01	a	Genoa	D	0-0	
03/02	h	Carpi	W	2-0	Borja Valero, Zárate
06/02	a	Bologna	D	1-1	Bernardeschi
14/02	h	Internazionale	W	2-1	Borja Valero, Babacar
21/02	a	Atalanta	L	3-2	Fernández, Tello, Kalinić
29/02	h	Napoli	D	1-1	Alonso
04/03	a	Roma	L	1-4	Iličić (p)
13/03	h	Verona	D	1-1	Zárate
20/03	h	Frosinone	D	0-0	
03/04	a	Sampdoria	D	1-1	Iličić
10/04	a	Empoli	L	0-2	
17/04	h	Sassuolo	W	3-1	Gonzalo Rodríguez, Iličić, og (Consigli)
20/04	a	Udinese	L	1-2	Zárate
24/04	a	Juventus	L	1-2	Kalinić
30/04	a	Chievo	D	0-0	
08/05	h	Palermo	D	0-0	
15/05	a	Lazio	W	4-2	Vecino 2, Bernardeschi, Tello

No	Name	Nat	DoB	Pos	Aps	(s)	Gls
28	Marcos Alonso	ESP	28/12/90	D	26	(5)	3
13	Davide Astori		07/01/87	D	32	(1)	
30	Khouma Babacar	SEN	17/03/93	A	11	(7)	5
5	Milan Badelj	CRO	25/02/89	M	25	(2)	1
10	Federico Bernardeschi		16/02/94	A	25	(8)	2
16	Jakub Błaszczykowski	POL	14/12/85	M	9	(6)	2
20	Borja Valero	ESP	12/01/85	M	35	(2)	4
14	Matías Fernández	CHI	15/05/86	M	11	(11)	1
3	Gilberto	BRA	07/03/93	D	3		
2	Gonzalo Rodríguez	ARG	10/04/84	D	35		4
72	Josip Iličić	SVN	29/01/88	M	24	(6)	13
21	Joan Verdú	ESP	05/05/83	M	1	(4)	1
9	Nikola Kalinić	CRO	05/01/88	A	25	(11)	12
26	Panagiotis Kone	GRE	26/07/87	M		(1)	
24	Luca Lezzerini		24/03/95	G	1	(1)	
18	Mario Suárez	ESP	24/02/87	M	5	(4)	1
23	Manuel Pasqual		13/03/82	D	12	(5)	
11	Ante Rebić	CRO	21/09/93	A	3	(1)	1
32	Facundo Roncaglia	ARG	07/01/87	D	26	(4)	1
22	Giuseppe Rossi		01/02/87	A	4	(7)	
12	Ciprian Tătărușanu	ROU	09/02/86	G	37		
27	Cristian Tello	ESP	11/08/91	A	13	(2)	2
6	Tino Costa	ARG	09/01/85	M	3	(4)	
4	Nenad Tomović	SRB	30/08/87	D	19	(5)	
8	Matías Vecino	URU	24/08/91	M	27	(3)	2
7	Mauro Zárate	ARG	18/03/87	A	6	(9)	3

Frosinone Calcio

1928 • Matusa (9,680) • frosinonecalcio.com
Coach: Roberto Stellone

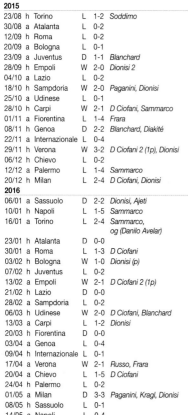

2015
23/08	h	Torino	L	1-2	Soddimo
30/08	a	Atalanta	L	0-2	
12/09	h	Roma	L	0-2	
20/09	a	Bologna	L	0-1	
23/09	h	Juventus	D	1-1	Blanchard
28/09	h	Empoli	W	2-0	Dionisi 2
04/10	a	Lazio	L	0-2	
18/10	h	Sampdoria	W	2-0	Paganini, Dionisi
25/10	a	Udinese	L	0-1	
28/10	h	Carpi	W	2-1	D Ciofani, Sammarco
01/11	a	Fiorentina	L	1-4	Frara
08/11	h	Genoa	D	2-2	Blanchard, Diakité
22/11	a	Internazionale	L	0-4	
29/11	h	Verona	W	3-2	D Ciofani 2 (1p), Dionisi
06/12	a	Chievo	L	0-1	
12/12	h	Palermo	L	1-4	Sammarco
20/12	a	Milan	L	2-4	D Ciofani, Dionisi

2016
06/01	a	Sassuolo	D	2-2	Dionisi, Ajeti
10/01	a	Napoli	L	1-5	Sammarco
16/01	a	Torino	L	2-4	Sammarco, og (Danilo Avelar)
23/01	h	Atalanta	D	0-0	
30/01	a	Roma	L	1-3	D Ciofani
03/02	h	Bologna	W	1-0	Dionisi (p)
07/02	a	Juventus	L	0-2	
13/02	h	Empoli	W	2-1	D Ciofani 2 (1p)
21/02	a	Lazio	D	0-0	
28/02	a	Sampdoria	L	0-2	
06/03	h	Udinese	W	2-0	D Ciofani, Blanchard
13/03	a	Carpi	L	1-2	Dionisi
20/03	h	Fiorentina	D	0-0	
03/04	a	Genoa	L	0-4	
09/04	h	Internazionale	L	0-1	
17/04	a	Verona	W	2-1	Russo, Frara
20/04	a	Chievo	L	1-5	D Ciofani
24/04	h	Palermo	L	0-2	
01/05	h	Milan	D	3-3	Paganini, Kragl, Dionisi
08/05	h	Sassuolo	L	0-1	
14/05	a	Napoli	L	0-4	

No	Name	Nat	DoB	Pos	Aps	(s)	Gls
93	Arlind Ajeti	ALB	25/09/93	D	15	(1)	1
25	Francesco Bardi		18/11/92	G	2		
69	Davide Bertoncini		09/05/91	D	4	(1)	
6	Leonardo Blanchard		06/05/88	D	27	(1)	3
29	Massimiliano Carlini		20/08/86	A	2	(12)	
30	Nicolás Castillo	CHI	14/02/93	A	3	(3)	
22	Raman Chibsah	GHA	10/03/93	M	14	(8)	
9	Daniel Ciofani		31/07/85	A	33	(4)	9
13	Matteo Ciofani		26/02/88	D	14	(4)	
3	Roberto Crivello		14/09/91	D	16	(1)	
24	Modibo Diakité	FRA	02/03/87	D	18		1
18	Federico Dionisi		16/06/87	A	28	(4)	9
7	Alessandro Frara		07/11/82	M	14	(6)	2
5	Mirko Gori		04/02/93	M	26	(2)	
8	Robert Gucher	AUT	20/02/91	M	15	(9)	
11	Oliver Kragl	GER	12/05/90	M	12	(3)	1
33	Nicola Leali		17/02/93	G	33		
12	Samuele Longo		12/01/92	A	3	(15)	
17	Luca Paganini		08/06/93	A	21	(6)	2
20	Daniel Pavlovic	SUI	22/04/88	D	22		
44	Vasyl Pryima	UKR	10/06/91	D	3	(2)	
28	Aleandro Rosi		17/05/87	D	24	(3)	
4	Adriano Russo		06/06/87	D	9	(1)	1
21	Paolo Sammarco		17/03/83	M	25	(3)	4
10	Danilo Soddimo		27/09/87	M	20	(8)	1
19	Aleksandar Tonev	BUL	03/02/90	M	11	(11)	
11	Daniele Verde		20/06/96	A	1	(5)	
1	Massimo Zappino		12/06/81	G	3	(1)	

Genoa CFC

1893 • Luigi Ferraris (36,599) • genoacfc.it
Major honours
Italian League (9) 1898, 1899, 1900, 1902, 1903, 1904, 1915, 1923, 1924; Italian Cup (1) 1937
Coach: Gian Piero Gasperini

2015
23/08	a	Palermo	L	0-1	
30/08	h	Verona	W	2-0	Pavoletti, Gakpé
12/09	a	Fiorentina	L	0-1	
20/09	h	Juventus	L	0-2	
23/09	a	Lazio	L	0-2	
27/09	h	Milan	W	1-0	Dzemaili
04/10	a	Udinese	D	1-1	Perotti (p)
18/10	h	Chievo	W	3-2	Pavoletti, Gakpé, Tachtsidis
24/10	a	Empoli	L	0-2	
28/10	a	Torino	D	3-3	Laxalt 2, Pavoletti
01/11	a	Napoli	D	0-0	
08/11	a	Frosinone	D	2-2	Pavoletti, Gakpé
22/11	h	Sassuolo	W	2-1	Rincón, Pavoletti
29/11	h	Carpi	L	1-2	Diogo Figueiras
05/12	a	Internazionale	L	0-1	
12/12	h	Bologna	L	0-1	
20/12	a	Roma	L	0-2	

2016
05/01	h	Sampdoria	L	2-3	Pavoletti 2
10/01	a	Atalanta	W	2-0	Dzemaili, Pavoletti
17/01	h	Palermo	W	4-0	Suso, Pavoletti 2, Rincón
24/01	a	Verona	D	1-1	og (Coppola)
31/01	h	Fiorentina	D	0-0	
03/02	a	Juventus	L	0-1	
06/02	h	Lazio	D	0-0	
14/02	a	Milan	L	1-2	Cerci
21/02	h	Udinese	W	2-1	Cerci (p), Laxalt
28/02	a	Chievo	L	0-1	
06/03	h	Empoli	W	1-0	Rigoni
13/03	h	Torino	W	3-2	Cerci 2 (2p), Rigoni
20/03	a	Napoli	L	1-3	Rincón
03/04	h	Frosinone	W	4-0	Suso 3, Rigoni
09/04	a	Sassuolo	W	1-0	Dzemaili
16/04	a	Carpi	L	1-2	Pavoletti
20/04	h	Internazionale	W	1-0	De Maio
24/04	a	Bologna	L	0-2	
02/05	h	Roma	L	2-3	Tachtsidis, Pavoletti
08/05	a	Sampdoria	W	3-0	Pavoletti, Suso 2
15/05	h	Atalanta	L	1-2	Pavoletti

No	Name	Nat	DoB	Pos	Aps	(s)	Gls
3	Cristian Ansaldi	ARG	20/09/86	D	23	(1)	
8	Nicolás Burdisso	ARG	12/04/81	D	28		
11	Alessio Cerci		23/07/87	M	6	(5)	4
90	Issa Cissokho	SEN	23/02/85	D	6	(7)	
4	Sebastian De Maio	FRA	05/03/87	D	25	(3)	1
16	Diego Capel	ESP	16/02/88	M	5	(16)	
11	Diogo Figueiras	POR	01/07/91	D	7	(2)	1
31	Blerim Dzemaili	SUI	12/04/86	M	22	(5)	3
29	Riccardo Fiamozzi		18/05/93	D	4	(4)	
34	Gabriel Silva	BRA	13/05/91	M	8	(3)	
13	Serge Gakpé	TOG	07/05/87	A	8	(5)	3
5	Armando Izzo		02/03/92	D	30	(3)	
27	Juraj Kucka	SVK	26/02/87	M	1		
23	Eugenio Lamanna		07/08/89	G	13		
93	Diego Laxalt	URU	07/02/93	M	35		3
24	Darko Lazović	SRB	12/09/90	M	6	(9)	
15	Giovanni Marchese		17/10/84	D	7	(4)	
42	Tim Matavž	SVN	13/01/89	A	5	(2)	
24	Ezequiel Muñoz	ARG	08/10/90	D	17	(1)	
18	Olivier Ntcham	FRA	09/02/96	M	11	(6)	
21	Goran Pandev	MKD	27/07/83	A	9	(6)	
37	Giuseppe Panico		10/05/97	A		(1)	
9	Leonardo Pavoletti		26/11/88	A	22	(3)	14
1	Mattia Perin		10/11/92	G	25		
10	Diego Perotti	ARG	26/07/88	M	14	(2)	1
30	Luca Rigoni		07/12/84	M	14	(4)	3
88	Tomás Rincón	COL	13/01/88	M	33		3
17	Suso	ESP	19/11/93	M	15	(4)	6
77	Panagiotis Tachtsidis	GRE	15/02/91	M	7	(17)	2
20	Tino Costa	ARG	09/01/85	M	12		

FC Internazionale Milano

1908 • Giuseppe Meazza (80,018) • inter.it
Major honours
European Champion Clubs' Cup/UEFA Champions League (3) 1964, 1965, 2010; UEFA Cup (3) 1991, 1994, 1998; European/South American Cup (2) 1964, 1965; FIFA Club World Cup (1) 2010; Italian League (18) 1910, 1920, 1930, 1938, 1940, 1953, 1954, 1963, 1965, 1966, 1971, 1980, 1989, 2006, 2007, 2008, 2009, 2010; Italian Cup (7) 1939, 1978, 1982, 2005, 2006, 2010, 2011
Coach: Roberto Mancini

2015
23/08	h	Atalanta	W	1-0	Jovetić
30/08	a	Carpi	W	2-1	Jovetić 2 (1p)
13/09	h	Milan	W	1-0	Guarín
20/09	a	Chievo	W	1-0	Icardi
23/09	h	Verona	W	1-0	Felipe Melo
27/09	h	Fiorentina	L	1-4	Icardi
04/10	a	Sampdoria	D	1-1	Perišić
18/10	h	Juventus	D	0-0	
24/10	a	Palermo	D	1-1	Perišić
27/10	a	Bologna	W	1-0	Icardi
31/10	h	Roma	W	1-0	Medel
08/11	a	Torino	W	1-0	Kondogbia
22/11	h	Frosinone	W	4-0	Biabiany, Icardi, Murillo, Brozović
30/11	a	Napoli	L	1-2	Ljajić
05/12	h	Genoa	W	1-0	Ljajić
12/12	a	Udinese	W	4-0	Icardi 2, Jovetić, Brozović
20/12	h	Lazio	L	1-2	Icardi

2016
06/01	a	Empoli	W	1-0	Icardi
10/01	h	Sassuolo	L	0-1	
16/01	a	Atalanta	D	1-1	og (Rafael Tolói)
24/01	h	Carpi	D	1-1	Palacio
31/01	a	Milan	L	0-3	
03/02	h	Chievo	W	1-0	Icardi
07/02	a	Verona	D	3-3	Murillo, Icardi, Perišić
14/02	a	Fiorentina	L	1-2	Brozović
20/02	h	Sampdoria	W	3-1	D'Ambrosio, Miranda, Icardi
28/02	a	Juventus	L	0-2	
06/03	h	Palermo	W	3-1	Ljajić, Icardi, Perišić
12/03	h	Bologna	W	2-1	Perišić, D'Ambrosio
19/03	a	Roma	D	1-1	Perišić
03/04	h	Torino	L	1-2	Icardi (p)
09/04	a	Frosinone	W	1-0	Icardi
16/04	h	Napoli	W	2-0	Icardi, Brozović
20/04	a	Genoa	L	0-1	
23/04	h	Udinese	W	3-1	Jovetić 2, Éder
01/05	a	Lazio	L	0-2	
07/05	h	Empoli	W	2-1	Icardi, Perišić
14/05	a	Sassuolo	L	1-3	Palacio

No	Name	Nat	DoB	Pos	Aps	(s)	Gls
12	Alex Telles	BRA	15/12/92	D	18	(3)	
11	Jonathan Biabiany	FRA	28/04/88	A	7	(13)	1
77	Marcelo Brozović	CRO	16/11/92	M	25	(7)	4
30	Juan Pablo Carrizo	ARG	06/05/84	G	2		
33	Danilo D'Ambrosio		09/09/88	D	18	(2)	2
28	Fabio Della Giovanna		21/03/97	D		(1)	
23	Éder		15/11/86	A	8	(6)	
83	Felipe Melo	BRA	26/06/83	M	21	(5)	1
27	Assane Gnoukouri	CIV	28/09/96	M	1	(1)	
13	Fredy Guarín	COL	30/06/86	M	11	(5)	1
1	Samir Handanovič	SVN	14/07/84	G	36		
88	Hernanes	BRA	29/05/85	M		(2)	
9	Mauro Icardi	ARG	19/02/93	A	32	(1)	16
10	Stevan Jovetić	MNE	02/11/89	A	18	(8)	6
5	Juan	BRA	10/06/91	D	16	(3)	
7	Geoffrey Kondogbia	FRA	15/02/93	M	23	(3)	1
22	Adem Ljajić	SRB	29/09/91	M	16	(9)	3
97	Rey Manaj	ALB	24/02/97	A		(4)	
17	Gary Medel	CHI	03/08/87	M	28	(2)	1
25	Miranda	BRA	07/09/84	D	31	(1)	1
14	Martín Montoya	ESP	14/04/91	D	3		
24	Jeison Murillo	COL	27/05/92	D	32	(2)	2
55	Yuto Nagatomo	JPN	12/09/86	D	19	(3)	
8	Rodrigo Palacio	ARG	05/02/82	A	15	(12)	2
44	Ivan Perišić	CRO	02/02/89	M	26	(8)	7
98	Ionuţ Radu	ROU	28/05/97	G		(1)	
23	Andrea Ranocchia		16/02/88	D	1	(9)	
21	Davide Santon		02/01/91	D	11	(1)	

Juventus FC

1897 • Juventus Stadium (41,254) • juventus.com

Major honours

European Champion Clubs' Cup/UEFA Champions League (2) 1985, 1996; UEFA Cup Winners' Cup (1) 1984; UEFA Cup (3) 1977, 1990, 1993; UEFA Super Cup (2) 1984, 1997; European/South American Cup (2) 1985, 1996; Italian League (32) 1905, 1926, 1931, 1932, 1933, 1934, 1935, 1950, 1952, 1958, 1960, 1961, 1967, 1972, 1973, 1975, 1977, 1978, 1981, 1982, 1984, 1986, 1995, 1997, 1998, 2002, 2003, 2012, 2013, 2014, 2015, 2016; Italian Cup (11) 1938, 1942, 1959, 1960, 1965, 1979, 1983, 1990, 1995, 2015, 2016

Coach: Massimiliano Allegri

2015

23/08	h	Udinese	L	0-1	
30/08	a	Roma	L	1-2	*Dybala*
12/09	h	Chievo	D	1-1	*Dybala (p)*
20/09	a	Genoa	W	2-0	*og (Lamanna), Pogba (p)*
23/09	h	Frosinone	D	1-1	*Zaza*
26/09	a	Napoli	L	1-2	*Lemina*
04/10	h	Bologna	W	3-1	*Morata, Dybala (p), Khedira*
18/10	a	Internazionale	D	0-0	
25/10	h	Atalanta	W	2-0	*Dybala, Mandžukić*
28/10	a	Sassuolo	L	0-1	
31/10	h	Torino	W	2-1	*Pogba, Cuadrado*
08/11	a	Empoli	W	3-1	*Mandžukić, Evra, Dybala*
21/11	h	Milan	W	1-0	*Dybala*
29/11	a	Palermo	W	3-0	*Mandžukić, Sturaro, Zaza*
04/12	a	Lazio	W	2-0	*og (Gentiletti), Dybala*
13/12	h	Fiorentina	W	3-1	*Cuadrado, Mandžukić, Dybala*
20/12	a	Carpi	W	3-2	*Mandžukić 2, Pogba*

2016

06/01	h	Verona	W	3-0	*Dybala, Bonucci, Zaza*
10/01	a	Sampdoria	W	2-1	*Pogba, Khedira*
17/01	a	Udinese	W	4-0	*Dybala 2 (1p), Khedira, Alex Sandro*
24/01	h	Roma	W	1-0	*Dybala*
31/01	a	Chievo	W	4-0	*Morata 2, Alex Sandro, Pogba*
03/02	h	Genoa	W	1-0	*og (De Maio)*
07/02	a	Frosinone	W	2-0	*Cuadrado, Dybala*
13/02	h	Napoli	W	1-0	*Zaza*
19/02	a	Bologna	D	0-0	
28/02	h	Internazionale	W	2-0	*Bonucci, Morata (p)*
06/03	a	Atalanta	W	2-0	*Barzagli, Lemina*
11/03	h	Sassuolo	W	1-0	*Dybala*
20/03	a	Torino	W	4-1	*Pogba, Khedira, Morata 2*
02/04	h	Empoli	W	1-0	*Mandžukić*
09/04	a	Milan	W	2-1	*Mandžukić, Pogba*
17/04	h	Palermo	W	4-0	*Khedira, Pogba, Cuadrado, Padoin*
20/04	h	Lazio	W	3-0	*Mandžukić, Dybala 2 (1p)*
24/04	a	Fiorentina	W	2-1	*Mandžukić, Morata*
01/05	h	Carpi	W	2-0	*Hernanes, Zaza*
08/05	a	Verona	L	1-2	*Dybala (p)*
14/05	h	Sampdoria	W	5-0	*Evra, Dybala 2 (1p), Chiellini, Bonucci*

No	Name	Nat	DoB	Pos	Aps	(s)	Gls
12	Alex Sandro	BRA	26/01/91	D	15	(7)	2
22	Kwadwo Asamoah	GHA	09/12/88	M	6	(5)	
15	Andrea Barzagli		08/05/81	D	31		1
19	Leonardo Bonucci		01/05/87	D	35	(1)	3
1	Gianluigi Buffon		28/01/78	G	35		
4	Martín Cáceres	URU	07/04/87	D	5	(1)	
3	Giorgio Chiellini		14/08/84	D	21	(3)	1
11	Kingsley Coman	FRA	13/06/96	A	1		
16	Juan Cuadrado	COL	26/05/88	M	16	(12)	4
21	Paulo Dybala	ARG	15/11/93	A	29	(5)	19
33	Patrice Evra	FRA	15/05/81	D	24	(2)	2
39	Andrea Favilli		17/05/97	A		(1)	
11	Hernanes	BRA	29/05/85	M	10	(4)	1
18	Mauricio Isla	CHI	12/06/88	M		(1)	
6	Sami Khedira	GER	04/04/87	M	20		5
18	Mario Lemina	GAB	01/09/93	M	7	(3)	2
26	Stephan Lichtsteiner	SUI	16/01/84	D	22	(4)	
24	Fernando Llorente	ESP	26/02/85	A		(1)	
17	Mario Mandžukić	CRO	21/05/86	A	24	(3)	10
8	Claudio Marchisio		19/01/86	M	23		
9	Álvaro Morata	ESP	23/10/92	A	16	(18)	7
25	Neto	BRA	19/07/89	G	3		
20	Simone Padoin		18/03/84	M	6	(6)	1
37	Roberto Pereyra	ARG	07/01/91	M	9	(4)	
10	Paul Pogba	FRA	15/03/93	M	33	(2)	8
24	Daniele Rugani		29/07/94	D	11	(6)	
27	Stefano Sturaro		09/03/93	M	11	(8)	1
7	Simone Zaza		25/06/91	A	5	(14)	5

SS Lazio

1900 • Olimpico (70,634) • sslazio.it

Major honours

UEFA Cup Winners' Cup (1) 1999; UEFA Super Cup (1) 1999; Italian League (2) 1974, 2000; Italian Cup (6) 1958, 1998, 2000, 2004, 2009, 2013

Coach: Stefano Pioli; (03/04/16) Simone Inzaghi

2015

22/08	h	Bologna	W	2-1	*Biglia, Kishna*
30/08	a	Chievo	L	0-4	
13/09	h	Udinese	W	2-0	*Matri 2*
20/09	a	Napoli	L	0-5	
23/09	h	Genoa	W	2-0	*Djordjević, Felipe Anderson*
27/09	a	Verona	W	2-1	*Biglia (p), Parolo*
04/10	h	Frosinone	W	2-0	*Baldé, Djordjević*
18/10	a	Sassuolo	L	1-2	*Felipe Anderson*
25/10	h	Torino	W	3-0	*Lulić, Felipe Anderson 2*
28/10	a	Atalanta	L	1-2	*Biglia*
01/11	h	Milan	L	1-3	*Kishna*
08/11	a	Roma	L	0-2	
22/11	h	Palermo	D	1-1	*Candreva (p)*
29/11	a	Empoli	L	0-1	
04/12	h	Juventus	L	0-2	
14/12	h	Sampdoria	D	1-1	*Matri*
20/12	a	Internazionale	W	2-1	*Candreva 2*

2016

06/01	h	Carpi	D	0-0	
09/01	a	Fiorentina	W	3-1	*Baldé, Milinković-Savić, Felipe Anderson*
17/01	a	Bologna	D	2-2	*Candreva (p), Lulić*
24/01	h	Chievo	W	4-1	*Candreva 2 (1p), Cataldi, Baldé*
31/01	a	Udinese	D	0-0	
03/02	h	Napoli	L	0-2	
06/02	a	Genoa	D	0-0	
11/02	h	Verona	W	5-2	*Matri, Mauri, Felipe Anderson, Baldé, Candreva (p)*
21/02	a	Frosinone	D	0-0	
29/02	h	Sassuolo	L	0-2	
06/03	a	Torino	D	1-1	*Biglia (p)*
13/03	h	Atalanta	W	2-0	*Klose 2*
20/03	a	Milan	D	1-1	*Parolo*
03/04	h	Roma	L	1-4	*Parolo*
10/04	a	Palermo	W	3-0	*Klose 2, Felipe Anderson*
17/04	h	Empoli	W	2-0	*Candreva (p), Onazi*
20/04	a	Juventus	L	0-3	
24/04	a	Sampdoria	L	1-2	*Djordjević*
01/05	h	Internazionale	W	2-0	*Klose, Candreva (p)*
08/05	a	Carpi	W	3-1	*Biševac, Candreva, Klose*
15/05	h	Fiorentina	L	2-4	*Lulić, Klose (p)*

No	Name	Nat	DoB	Pos	Aps	(s)	Gls
14	Keita Baldé	SEN	08/03/95	A	15	(16)	4
8	Dušan Basta	SRB	18/08/84	D	21	(2)	
99	Etrit Berisha	ALB	10/03/89	G	9	(2)	
20	Lucas Biglia	ARG	30/01/86	M	26	(1)	4
13	Milan Biševac	SRB	31/08/83	D	11		1
5	Edson Braafheid	NED	08/04/83	D	3	(2)	
87	Antonio Candreva		28/02/87	M	28	(2)	10
32	Danilo Cataldi		06/08/94	M	16	(4)	1
3	Stefan de Vrij	NED	05/02/92	D	2		
9	Filip Djordjević	SRB	28/09/87	A	16	(11)	3
10	Felipe Anderson	BRA	15/04/93	M	21	(14)	7
18	Santiago Gentiletti	ARG	09/01/85	D	19		
2	Wesley Hoedt	NED	06/03/94	D	24	(1)	
88	Ricardo Kishna	NED	04/01/95	A	7	(4)	2
11	Miroslav Klose	GER	09/06/78	A	14	(10)	7
29	Abdoulay Konko	FRA	09/03/84	D	17	(1)	
19	Senad Lulić	BIH	18/01/86	M	28	(2)	3
22	Federico Marchetti		07/02/83	G	29		
17	Alessandro Matri		19/08/84	A	7	(12)	4
6	Stefano Mauri		08/01/80	M	6	(6)	1
33	Maurício	BRA	20/09/88	D	19	(5)	
21	Sergej Milinković-Savić	SRB	27/02/95	M	17	(8)	1
7	Ravel Morrison	ENG	02/02/93	M		(4)	
23	Ogenyi Onazi	NGA	25/12/92	M	14	(1)	1
16	Marco Parolo		25/01/85	M	30	(1)	3
4	Patric	ESP	17/04/93	M	6	(3)	
26	Ştefan Radu	ROU	22/10/86	D	13		

AC Milan

1899 • Giuseppe Meazza (80,018) • acmilan.com

Major honours

European Champion Clubs' Cup/UEFA Champions League (7) 1963, 1969, 1989, 1990, 1994, 2003, 2007; UEFA Cup Winners' Cup (2) 1968, 1973; UEFA Super Cup (5) 1989, 1990, 1995, 2003, 2007; European/ South American Cup (3) 1969, 1989, 1990; FIFA Club World Cup (1) 2007; Italian League (18) 1901, 1906, 1907, 1951, 1955, 1957, 1959, 1962, 1968, 1979, 1988, 1992, 1993, 1994, 1996, 1999, 2004, 2011; Italian Cup (5) 1967, 1972, 1973, 1977, 2003

Coach: Siniša Mihajlović (SRB); (12/04/16) Cristian Brocchi

2015

23/08	a	Fiorentina	L	0-2	
29/08	h	Empoli	W	2-1	*Bacca, Luiz Adriano*
13/09	a	Internazionale	L	0-1	
19/09	h	Palermo	W	3-2	*Bacca 2, Bonaventura*
22/09	a	Udinese	W	3-2	*Balotelli, Bonaventura, Zapata*
27/09	a	Genoa	L	0-1	
04/10	h	Napoli	L	0-4	
17/10	a	Torino	D	1-1	*Bacca*
25/10	h	Sassuolo	W	2-1	*Bacca (p), Luiz Adriano*
28/10	h	Chievo	W	1-0	*Antonelli*
01/11	a	Lazio	W	3-1	*Bertolacci, Mexès, Bacca*
07/11	h	Atalanta	D	0-0	
21/11	a	Juventus	L	0-1	
28/11	h	Sampdoria	W	4-1	*Bonaventura, Niang 2 (1p), Luiz Adriano*
06/12	a	Carpi	D	0-0	
13/12	h	Verona	D	1-1	*Bacca*
20/12	a	Frosinone	W	4-2	*Abate, Bacca, Alex, Bonaventura*

2016

06/01	h	Bologna	L	0-1	
09/01	a	Roma	D	1-1	*Kucka*
17/01	h	Fiorentina	W	2-0	*Bacca, Boateng*
23/01	a	Empoli	D	2-2	*Bacca, Bonaventura*
31/01	h	Internazionale	W	3-0	*Alex, Bacca, Niang*
03/02	a	Palermo	W	2-0	*Bacca, Niang (p)*
07/02	h	Udinese	D	1-1	*Niang*
14/02	h	Genoa	W	2-1	*Bacca, Honda*
22/02	a	Napoli	D	1-1	*Bonaventura*
27/02	h	Torino	W	1-0	*Antonelli*
06/03	a	Sassuolo	L	0-2	
13/03	a	Chievo	D	0-0	
20/03	h	Lazio	D	1-1	*Bacca*
03/04	a	Atalanta	L	1-2	*Luiz Adriano (p)*
09/04	h	Juventus	L	1-2	*Alex*
17/04	a	Sampdoria	W	1-0	*Bacca*
21/04	h	Carpi	D	0-0	
25/04	a	Verona	L	1-2	*Ménez*
01/05	h	Frosinone	D	3-3	*Bacca, Antonelli, Ménez (p)*
07/05	a	Bologna	W	1-0	*Bacca (p)*
14/05	h	Roma	L	1-3	*Bacca*

No	Name	Nat	DoB	Pos	Aps	(s)	Gls
20	Ignazio Abate		12/11/86	D	27		1
32	Christian Abbiati		08/07/77	G		(1)	
33	Alex	BRA	17/06/82	D	24	(1)	3
31	Luca Antonelli		11/02/87	D	25	(3)	3
70	Carlos Bacca	COL	08/09/86	A	36	(2)	18
45	Mario Balotelli		12/08/90	A	8	(12)	1
91	Andrea Bertolacci		11/01/91	M	21	(6)	1
72	Kevin-Prince Boateng	GHA	06/03/87	M	1	(10)	1
28	Giacomo Bonaventura		22/08/89	M	31	(2)	6
96	Davide Calabria		06/12/96	D	3	(3)	
11	Alessio Cerci		23/07/87	M	8	(5)	
34	Nigel de Jong	NED	30/11/84	M	5		
2	Mattia De Sciglio		20/10/92	D	21	(1)	
1	Diego López	ESP	03/11/81	G	8		
99	Gianluigi Donnarumma		25/02/99	G	30		
10	Keisuke Honda	JPN	13/06/86	M	23	(7)	1
27	Juraj Kucka	SVK	26/02/87	M	24	(5)	1
73	Manuel Locatelli		08/01/98	M	1	(1)	
9	Luiz Adriano	BRA	12/04/87	A	12	(14)	4
4	José Mauri		16/05/96	M	3	(2)	
7	Jérémy Ménez	FRA	07/05/87	A	2	(8)	2
5	Philippe Mexès	FRA	30/03/82	D	4	(1)	1
18	Riccardo Montolivo		18/01/85	M	31		
19	M'Baye Niang	FRA	19/12/94	A	15	(1)	5
23	Antonio Nocerino		09/04/85	M	1	(1)	
16	Andrea Poli		29/09/89	M	4	(14)	
15	Rodrigo Ely	BRA	03/11/93	D	2	(1)	
13	Alessio Romagnoli		12/01/95	D	33	(1)	
8	Suso	ESP	19/11/93	M	1		
17	Cristián Zapata	COL	30/09/86	D	14	(2)	1

ITALY

SSC Napoli

1926 • San Paolo (60,240) • sscnapoli.it

Major honours
UEFA Cup (1) 1989; Italian League (2) 1987, 1990; Italian Cup (5) 1962, 1976, 1987, 2012, 2014

Coach: Maurizio Sarri

2015					
23/08	a	Sassuolo	L	1-2	*Hamšík*
30/08	h	Sampdoria	D	2-2	*Higuaín 2*
13/09	a	Empoli	D	2-2	*Insigne, Allan*
20/09	h	Lazio	W	5-0	*Higuaín 2, Allan, Insigne, Gabbiadini*
23/09	a	Carpi	D	0-0	
26/09	h	Juventus	W	2-1	*Insigne, Higuaín*
04/10	a	Milan	W	4-0	*Allan, Insigne 2, og (Rodrigo Ely)*
18/10	h	Fiorentina	W	2-1	*Insigne, Higuaín*
25/10	a	Chievo	W	1-0	*Higuaín*
28/10	h	Palermo	W	2-0	*Higuaín, Mertens*
01/11	a	Genoa	D	0-0	
08/11	h	Udinese	W	1-0	*Higuaín*
22/11	a	Verona	W	2-0	*Insigne, Higuaín*
30/11	h	Internazionale	W	2-1	*Higuaín 2*
06/12	a	Bologna	L	2-3	*Higuaín 2*
13/12	h	Roma	D	0-0	
20/12	a	Atalanta	W	3-1	*Hamšík (p), Higuaín 2*
2016					
06/01	h	Torino	W	2-1	*Insigne, Hamšík*
10/01	a	Frosinone	W	5-1	*Albiol, Higuaín 2 (1p), Hamšík, Gabbiadini*
16/01	h	Sassuolo	W	3-1	*Callejón, Higuaín 2*
24/01	a	Sampdoria	W	4-2	*Higuaín, Insigne (p), Hamšík, Mertens*
31/01	h	Empoli	W	5-1	*Higuaín, Insigne, og (Camporese), Callejón 2*
03/02	a	Lazio	W	2-0	*Higuaín, Callejón*
07/02	h	Carpi	W	1-0	*Higuaín (p)*
13/02	a	Juventus	L	0-1	
22/02	h	Milan	D	1-1	*Insigne*
29/02	a	Fiorentina	D	1-1	*Higuaín*
05/03	h	Chievo	W	3-1	*Higuaín, Chiricheş, Callejón*
13/03	a	Palermo	W	1-0	*Higuaín (p)*
20/03	h	Genoa	W	3-1	*Higuaín 2, El Kaddouri*
03/04	a	Udinese	L	1-3	*Higuaín*
10/04	h	Verona	W	3-0	*Gabbiadini, Insigne (p), Callejón*
16/04	a	Internazionale	L	0-2	
19/04	h	Bologna	W	6-0	*Gabbiadini 2 (1p), Mertens 3, David López*
25/04	a	Roma	L	0-1	
02/05	h	Atalanta	W	2-1	*Higuaín 2*
08/05	a	Torino	W	2-1	*Higuaín, Callejón*
14/05	h	Frosinone	W	4-0	*Hamšík, Higuaín 3*

No	Name	Nat	DoB	Pos	Aps	(s)	Gls
33	Raúl Albiol	ESP	04/09/85	D	36		1
5	Allan	BRA	08/01/91	M	32	(3)	3
7	José Callejón	ESP	11/02/87	M	35	(3)	7
94	Nathaniel Chalobah	ENG	12/12/94	M		(5)	
21	Vlad Chiricheş	ROU	14/11/89	D	8		1
19	David López	ESP	09/10/89	M	6	(19)	1
77	Omar El Kaddouri	MAR	21/08/90	M		(20)	1
23	Manolo Gabbiadini		26/11/91	A	4	(19)	5
22	Gabriel	BRA	27/09/92	G	1		
31	Faouzi Ghoulam	ALG	01/02/91	D	32	(2)	
17	Marek Hamšík	SVK	27/07/87	M	38		6
9	Gonzalo Higuaín	ARG	10/12/87	A	35		36
2	Elseid Hysaj	ALB	20/02/94	D	37		
24	Lorenzo Insigne		04/06/91	A	34	(3)	12
8	Jorginho		20/12/91	M	32	(3)	
26	Kalidou Koulibaly	SEN	20/06/91	D	32	(1)	
11	Christian Maggio		11/02/82	D	4	(4)	
14	Dries Mertens	BEL	06/05/87	M	6	(27)	5
18	Vasco Regini		09/09/90	D		(1)	
25	Pepe Reina	ESP	31/08/82	G	37		
3	Ivan Strinić	CRO	17/07/87	D	3	(2)	
6	Mirko Valdifiori		21/04/86	M	6		

US Città di Palermo

1900 • Renzo Barbera (36,349) • palermocalcio.it

Coach: Giuseppe Iachini;
(10/11/15) Davide Ballardini;
(11/01/16) (Fabio Viviani);
(18/01/16) (Giovanni Bosi);
(26/01/16) (Giovanni Tedesco);
(10/02/16) (Giovanni Bosi);
(15/02/16) Giuseppe Iachini:
(10/03/16) Walter Novellino;
(12/04/16) Davide Ballardini

2015					
23/08	h	Genoa	W	1-0	*El Kaoutari*
30/08	a	Udinese	W	1-0	*Rigoni*
13/09	h	Carpi	D	2-2	*Hiljemark, Djurdjević*
19/09	a	Milan	L	2-3	*Hiljemark 2*
23/09	h	Sassuolo	L	0-1	
27/09	a	Torino	L	1-2	*González*
04/10	h	Roma	L	2-4	*Gilardino, González*
18/10	a	Bologna	W	1-0	*Vázquez*
24/10	h	Internazionale	D	1-1	*Gilardino*
28/10	a	Napoli	L	0-2	
02/11	h	Empoli	L	0-1	
08/11	h	Chievo	W	1-0	*Gilardino*
22/11	a	Lazio	D	1-1	*Goldaniga*
29/11	h	Juventus	L	0-3	
06/12	a	Atalanta	L	0-3	
12/12	h	Frosinone	W	4-1	*Goldaniga, Vázquez, Trajkovski, Gilardino*
20/12	a	Sampdoria	L	0-2	
2016					
06/01	h	Fiorentina	L	1-3	*Gilardino*
10/01	a	Verona	W	1-0	*Vázquez*
17/01	a	Genoa	L	0-4	
24/01	h	Udinese	W	4-1	*Quaison, Hiljemark, Lazaar, Trajkovski*
30/01	a	Carpi	D	1-1	*Gilardino*
03/02	h	Milan	L	0-2	
07/02	a	Sassuolo	D	2-2	*Vázquez, Djurdjević*
14/02	h	Torino	L	1-3	*Gilardino*
21/02	a	Roma	L	0-5	
28/02	h	Bologna	D	0-0	
06/03	a	Internazionale	L	1-3	*Vázquez*
13/03	h	Napoli	L	0-1	
19/03	a	Empoli	D	0-0	
03/04	a	Chievo	L	1-3	*Gilardino*
10/04	h	Lazio	L	0-3	
17/04	a	Juventus	L	0-4	
20/04	h	Atalanta	D	2-2	*Vázquez (p), Struna*
24/04	a	Frosinone	W	2-0	*Gilardino, Trajkovski*
01/05	h	Sampdoria	W	2-0	*Vázquez, og (Krstičić)*
08/05	a	Fiorentina	D	0-0	
15/05	h	Verona	W	3-2	*Vázquez, Maresca, Gilardino*

No	Name	Nat	DoB	Pos	Aps	(s)	Gls
53	Fabrizio Alastra		01/10/97	G	1	(1)	
4	Siniša Andjelkovič	SVN	13/02/86	D	21	(2)	
22	Norbert Balogh	HUN	21/02/96	A		(4)	
9	Accursio Bentivegna		21/06/96	A		(1)	
16	Gastón Brugman	URU	07/09/92	M	10	(4)	
18	Ivaylo Chochev	BUL	18/02/93	M	21	(6)	
15	Thiago Cionek	POL	21/04/86	D	5		
91	Simone Colombi		01/07/91	G	1		
24	Bryan Cristante		03/03/95	M	1	(3)	
33	Fabio Daprelà	SUI	19/02/91	D	1	(4)	
99	Uroš Djurdjević	SRB	02/03/94	A	5	(9)	2
34	Abdelhamid El Kaoutari	MAR	17/03/90	D	7		1
11	Alberto Gilardino		05/07/82	A	26	(7)	10
6	Edoardo Goldaniga		02/11/93	D	14	(3)	2
12	Giancarlo González	CRC	08/02/88	D	35		2
10	Oscar Hiljemark	SWE	28/06/92	M	36	(2)	4
28	Mato Jajalo	CRO	25/05/88	M	24	(4)	
54	Antonino La Gumina		06/03/96	A		(3)	
7	Achraf Lazaar	MAR	22/01/92	D	26	(4)	1
25	Enzo Maresca		10/02/80	M	10	(5)	1
77	Michel Morganella	SUI	17/05/89	D	11	(3)	
97	Giuseppe Pezzella		29/11/97	D	7	(2)	
1	Josip Posavec	CRO	10/03/96	G	1		
21	Robin Quaison	SWE	09/10/93	M	14	(16)	1
27	Luca Rigoni		07/12/84	M	8	(2)	1
3	Andrea Rispoli		29/09/88	D	16	(6)	
70	Stefano Sorrentino		28/03/79	G	35		
23	Aljaž Struna	SVN	04/08/90	D	22		1
8	Aleksandar Trajkovski	MKD	05/09/92	A	16	(16)	3
20	Franco Vázquez		22/02/89	M	36		8
2	Roberto Vitiello		08/05/83	D	8	(2)	

AS Roma

1927 • Olimpico (70,634) • asroma.com

Major honours
Inter Cities Fairs Cup (1) 1961; Italian League (3) 1942, 1983, 2001; Italian Cup (9) 1964, 1969, 1980, 1981, 1984, 1986, 1991, 2007, 2008

Coach: Rudi Garcia (FRA);
(13/01/16) Luciano Spalletti

2015					
22/08	a	Verona	D	1-1	*Florenzi*
30/08	h	Juventus	W	2-1	*Pjanić, Džeko*
12/09	a	Frosinone	W	2-0	*Iago Falqué, Iturbe*
20/09	h	Sassuolo	D	2-2	*Totti, Salah*
23/09	a	Sampdoria	L	1-2	*Salah*
26/09	h	Carpi	W	5-1	*Manolas, Pjanić, Gervinho, Salah, Digne*
04/10	a	Palermo	W	4-2	*Pjanić, Florenzi, Gervinho 2*
17/10	h	Empoli	W	3-1	*Pjanić, De Rossi, Salah*
25/10	a	Fiorentina	W	2-1	*Salah, Gervinho*
28/10	h	Udinese	W	3-1	*Pjanić, Maicon, Gervinho*
31/10	a	Internazionale	L	0-1	
08/11	h	Lazio	W	2-0	*Džeko (p), Gervinho*
21/11	a	Bologna	D	2-2	*Pjanić (p), Džeko (p)*
29/11	h	Atalanta	L	0-2	
05/12	a	Torino	D	1-1	*Pjanić*
13/12	a	Napoli	D	0-0	
20/12	h	Genoa	W	2-0	*Florenzi, Umar*
2016					
06/01	a	Chievo	D	3-3	*Umar, Florenzi, Iago Falqué*
09/01	h	Milan	D	1-1	*Rüdiger*
17/01	h	Verona	D	1-1	*Nainggolan*
24/01	a	Juventus	L	0-1	
30/01	h	Frosinone	W	3-1	*Nainggolan, El Shaarawy, Pjanić*
02/02	a	Sassuolo	W	2-0	*Salah, El Shaarawy*
07/02	h	Sampdoria	W	2-1	*Florenzi, Perotti*
12/02	a	Carpi	W	3-1	*Digne, Džeko, Salah*
21/02	h	Palermo	W	5-0	*Džeko 2, Keita, Salah 2*
27/02	a	Empoli	W	3-1	*El Shaarawy 2, Pjanić*
04/03	h	Fiorentina	W	4-1	*El Shaarawy, Salah 2, Perotti*
13/03	a	Udinese	W	2-1	*Džeko, Florenzi*
19/03	h	Internazionale	D	1-1	*Nainggolan*
03/04	a	Lazio	W	4-1	*El Shaarawy, Džeko, Florenzi, Perotti*
11/04	h	Bologna	D	1-1	*Salah*
17/04	a	Atalanta	D	3-3	*Digne, Nainggolan, Totti*
20/04	h	Torino	W	3-2	*Manolas, Totti 2 (1p)*
25/04	h	Napoli	W	1-0	*Nainggolan*
02/05	a	Genoa	W	3-2	*Salah, Totti, El Shaarawy*
08/05	h	Chievo	W	3-0	*Nainggolan, Rüdiger, Pjanić*
14/05	a	Milan	W	3-1	*Salah, El Shaarawy, Emerson*

No	Name	Nat	DoB	Pos	Aps	(s)	Gls
16	Daniele De Rossi		24/07/83	M	23	(1)	1
26	Morgan De Sanctis		26/03/77	G	4		
52	Lorenzo Di Livio		11/01/97	M		(1)	
3	Lucas Digne	FRA	20/07/93	D	32	(1)	3
9	Edin Džeko	BIH	17/03/86	A	21	(10)	8
22	Stephan El Shaarawy		27/10/92	A	15	(1)	8
33	Emerson	BRA	13/03/94	D	1	(7)	1
24	Alessandro Florenzi		11/03/91	D	31	(2)	7
27	Gervinho	CIV	27/05/87	A	13	(1)	6
23	Norbert Gyömbér	SVK	03/07/92	D		(6)	
14	Iago Falqué	ESP	04/01/90	M	13	(9)	2
19	Víctor Ibarbo	COL	19/05/90	A		(2)	
7	Juan Manuel Iturbe	ARG	04/06/93	A	3	(9)	1
20	Seydou Keita	MLI	16/01/80	M	16	(4)	1
5	Leandro Castán	BRA	05/11/86	D	4	(1)	
8	Adem Ljajić	SRB	29/09/91	M		(1)	
13	Maicon	BRA	26/07/81	D	12	(3)	1
44	Kostas Manolas	GRE	14/06/91	D	36	(1)	2
4	Radja Nainggolan	BEL	04/05/88	M	33	(2)	6
8	Diego Perotti	ARG	26/07/88	M	14	(1)	3
15	Miralem Pjanić	BIH	02/04/90	M	30	(3)	10
2	Antonio Rüdiger	GER	03/03/93	D	29	(1)	2
11	Mohamed Salah	EGY	15/06/92	A	32	(2)	14
48	Salih Uçan	TUR	06/01/94	M		(3)	
6	Kevin Strootman	NED	13/02/90	M	2	(3)	
25	Wojciech Szczęsny	POL	18/04/90	G	34		
35	Vasilios Torosidis	GRE	10/06/85	D	6	(5)	
10	Francesco Totti		27/09/76	A	2	(11)	5
93	Marco Tumminello		06/11/98	A		(1)	
97	Sadiq Umar	NGA	02/02/97	A	2	(4)	2
21	William Vainqueur	FRA	19/11/88	M	4	(12)	
87	Ervin Zukanović	BIH	11/02/87	D	6	(3)	

UC Sampdoria

1946 • Luigi Ferraris (36,599) • sampdoria.it
Major honours
UEFA Cup Winners' Cup (1) 1990; Italian League (1)
1991; Italian Cup (4) 1985, 1988, 1989, 1994
Coach: Walter Zenga;
(15/11/15) Vincenzo Montella

2015
23/08	h	Carpi	W	5-2	Éder 2 (1p), Muriel 2, Fernando
30/08	a	Napoli	D	2-2	Éder 2 (1p)
14/09	h	Bologna	W	2-0	Éder, Soriano
20/09	a	Torino	L	0-2	
23/09	h	Roma	W	2-1	Éder, og (Manolas)
28/09	a	Atalanta	L	1-2	Soriano
04/10	a	Internazionale	D	1-1	Muriel
18/10	a	Frosinone	L	0-2	
25/10	h	Verona	W	4-1	Muriel, Zukanović, Soriano, Éder
29/10	h	Empoli	D	1-1	Éder
02/11	a	Chievo	D	1-1	Éder
08/11	h	Fiorentina	L	0-2	
22/11	a	Udinese	L	0-1	
28/11	h	Milan	L	1-4	Éder (p)
06/12	h	Sassuolo	L	1-3	Zukanović
14/12	a	Lazio	D	1-1	Zukanović
20/12	a	Palermo	W	2-0	Soriano, Ivan

2016
05/01	a	Genoa	W	3-2	Soriano 2, Éder
10/01	h	Juventus	L	1-2	Cassano
17/01	a	Carpi	L	1-2	Correa
24/01	h	Napoli	L	2-4	Correa, Éder
31/01	a	Bologna	L	2-3	Muriel, Correa
03/02	h	Torino	D	2-2	Muriel, Soriano
07/02	a	Roma	L	1-2	og (Pjanić)
14/02	h	Atalanta	D	0-0	
20/02	a	Internazionale	L	1-3	Quagliarella
28/02	h	Frosinone	W	2-0	Fernando, Quagliarella
05/03	a	Verona	W	3-0	Soriano, Cassano, Christodoulopoulos
12/03	a	Empoli	D	1-1	Quagliarella
20/03	h	Chievo	L	0-1	
03/04	h	Fiorentina	D	1-1	Álvarez
10/04	h	Udinese	W	2-0	og (Armero), Fernando
17/04	h	Milan	L	0-1	
20/04	a	Sassuolo	D	0-0	
24/04	h	Lazio	W	2-1	Fernando, De Silvestri
01/05	a	Palermo	L	0-2	
08/05	h	Genoa	L	0-3	
14/05	a	Juventus	L	0-5	

No	Name	Nat	DoB	Pos	Aps	(s)	Gls
25	Ricardo Álvarez	ARG	12/04/88	M	9	(4)	1
8	Édgar Barreto	PAR	15/07/84	M	26	(4)	
11	Federico Bonazzoli		21/05/97	A		(4)	
57	Alberto Brignoli		19/08/91	G	1		
77	Carlos Carbonero	COL	25/07/90	M	11	(3)	
5	Mattia Cassani		26/08/83	D	23	(2)	
99	Antonio Cassano		12/07/82	A	14	(10)	2
18	Lazaros Christodoulopoulos	GRE	19/12/86	M	3	(7)	1
6	Andrea Coda		25/04/85	D	2	(2)	
10	Joaquín Correa	ARG	13/08/94	M	14	(11)	3
29	Lorenzo De Silvestri		23/05/88	D	17	(1)	1
23	Modibo Diakité	FRA	02/03/87	D	7	(1)	
11	Dodô	BRA	06/02/92	D	16	(1)	
23	Éder		15/11/86	A	19		12
7	Fernando	BRA	03/03/92	M	34	(1)	4
95	Dávid Ivan	SVK	26/02/95	M	12	(9)	1
20	Nenad Krstičić	SRB	03/07/90	M	6	(4)	
3	Djamel Mesbah	ALG	09/10/84	D	6	(1)	
4	Niklas Moisander	FIN	29/09/85	D	19	(3)	
24	Luis Muriel	COL	16/04/91	A	19	(13)	6
17	Angelo Palombo		25/09/81	M	3	(4)	
13	Pedro Pereira	POR	22/01/98	D	7	(2)	
30	Andrés Ponce	VEN	11/11/96	A		(1)	
27	Fabio Quagliarella		31/01/83	A	13	(3)	3
16	Andrea Ranocchia		16/02/88	D	13	(1)	
19	Vasco Regini		09/09/90	D	14		
92	Michele Rocca		06/02/96	M		(1)	
9	Alejandro Rodríguez	ESP	30/07/91	A		(6)	
22	Jacopo Sala		05/12/91	M	3	(2)	
26	Matías Silvestre	ARG	25/09/84	D	21	(4)	
37	Milan Škriniar	SVK	11/02/95	D	2	(1)	
21	Roberto Soriano		08/02/91	M	33	(4)	8
2	Emiliano Viviano		01/12/85	G	37		
13	Paweł Wszołek	POL	30/04/92	M		(2)	
87	Ervin Zukanović	BIH	11/02/87	D	14	(2)	3

US Sassuolo Calcio

1922 • Città del Tricolore, Reggio
Emilia (21,584) • sassuolocalcio.it
Coach: Eusebio Di Francesco

2015
23/08	h	Napoli	W	2-1	Floro Flores, Sansone
29/08	a	Bologna	W	1-0	Floro Flores
13/09	h	Atalanta	D	2-2	Magnanelli, Floro Flores
20/09	a	Roma	D	2-2	Defrel, Politano
23/09	a	Palermo	W	1-0	Floccari
27/09	h	Chievo	D	1-1	Defrel
04/10	a	Empoli	L	0-1	
18/10	h	Lazio	W	2-1	Berardi (p), Missiroli
25/10	a	Milan	L	1-2	Berardi
28/10	h	Juventus	W	1-0	Sansone
01/11	a	Udinese	D	0-0	
08/11	h	Carpi	W	1-0	Sansone
22/11	a	Genoa	L	1-2	Acerbi
30/11	h	Fiorentina	D	1-1	Floccari
06/12	a	Sampdoria	W	3-1	Acerbi, Floccari, Pellegrini
20/12	a	Verona	D	1-1	Floccari

2016
06/01	h	Frosinone	D	2-2	og (Ajeti), Falcinelli
10/01	a	Internazionale	W	1-0	Berardi (p)
16/01	a	Napoli	L	1-3	Falcinelli (p)
20/01	h	Torino	D	1-1	Berardi (p)
24/01	a	Bologna	L	0-2	
30/01	a	Atalanta	D	1-1	Berardi
02/02	h	Roma	L	0-2	
07/02	h	Palermo	D	2-2	Defrel, Missiroli
13/02	a	Chievo	D	1-1	Sansone
21/02	h	Empoli	W	3-2	Berardi, Defrel 2
29/02	a	Lazio	W	2-0	Berardi (p), Defrel
06/03	a	Milan	W	2-0	Duncan, Sansone
11/03	h	Juventus	L	0-1	
20/03	h	Udinese	D	1-1	Politano
02/04	a	Carpi	W	3-1	Sansone, Defrel, Acerbi
09/04	a	Genoa	L	0-1	
17/04	a	Fiorentina	L	1-3	Berardi
20/04	h	Sampdoria	D	0-0	
24/04	a	Torino	W	3-1	Sansone, Peluso, Trotta
01/05	h	Verona	W	1-0	Pellegrini
08/05	a	Frosinone	W	1-0	Politano
14/05	h	Internazionale	W	3-1	Politano 2, Pellegrini

No	Name	Nat	DoB	Pos	Aps	(s)	Gls
15	Francesco Acerbi		10/02/88	D	36		4
98	Claud Adjapong	GHA	06/05/98	D		(2)	
5	Luca Antei		19/04/92	D	4	(1)	
20	Lorenzo Ariaudo		11/06/89	D	2	(2)	
25	Domenico Berardi		01/08/94	A	26	(3)	7
8	Davide Biondini		24/01/83	M	12	(10)	
28	Paolo Cannavaro		26/06/81	D	30	(1)	
47	Andrea Consigli		27/01/87	G	37		
92	Grégoire Defrel	FRA	17/06/91	A	24	(9)	7
32	Alfred Duncan	GHA	10/03/93	M	27	(6)	1
9	Diego Falcinelli		26/06/91	A	11	(15)	2
99	Sergio Floccari		12/11/81	A	5	(2)	4
83	Antonio Floro Flores		18/06/83	A	8	(6)	3
23	Marcello Gazzola		03/04/85	D	4	(5)	
10	Karim Laribi		20/04/91	M	6	(5)	
3	Alessandro Longhi		25/06/89	D	4	(2)	
4	Francesco Magnanelli		12/11/84	M	34		1
7	Simone Missiroli		23/05/86	M	22	(2)	2
79	Gianluca Pegolo		25/03/81	G	1	(1)	
6	Lorenzo Pellegrini		19/06/96	M	13	(6)	3
13	Federico Peluso		20/01/84	D	34		1
14	Matteo Politano		03/08/93	A	11	(17)	5
17	Nicola Sansone		10/09/91	A	28	(9)	7
26	Emanuele Terranova		14/04/87	D	3	(5)	
29	Marcello Trotta		29/09/92	A	1	(7)	1
11	Šime Vrsaljko	CRO	10/01/92	D	35		

Torino FC

1906 • Olimpico (27,958) • torinofc.it
Major honours
Italian League (7) 1928, 1943, 1946, 1947, 1948, 1949,
1976; Italian Cup (5) 1936, 1943, 1968, 1971, 1993
Coach: Giampiero Ventura

2015
23/08	a	Frosinone	W	2-1	Quagliarella, Baselli
30/08	h	Fiorentina	W	3-1	Moretti, Quagliarella, Baselli
13/09	a	Verona	D	2-2	Baselli, Acquah
20/09	h	Sampdoria	W	2-0	Quagliarella 2
23/09	a	Chievo	L	0-1	
27/09	h	Palermo	W	2-1	og (González), Benassi
03/10	a	Carpi	L	1-2	Maxi López (p)
17/10	h	Milan	D	1-1	Baselli
25/10	a	Lazio	L	0-3	
28/10	h	Genoa	D	3-3	Maxi López, Zappacosta, og (Tachtsidis)
31/10	a	Juventus	L	1-2	Bovo
08/11	h	Internazionale	L	0-1	
22/11	a	Atalanta	W	1-0	Bovo
28/11	h	Bologna	W	2-0	Belotti, Vives
05/12	h	Roma	D	1-1	Maxi López (p)
20/12	a	Udinese	L	0-1	

2016
06/01	a	Napoli	L	1-2	Quagliarella (p)
10/01	h	Empoli	L	0-1	
16/01	h	Frosinone	W	4-2	Immobile (p), Belotti 2, Benassi
20/01	a	Sassuolo	D	1-1	Belotti
24/01	a	Fiorentina	L	0-2	
31/01	h	Verona	D	0-0	
03/02	a	Sampdoria	D	2-2	Belotti 2
07/02	h	Chievo	L	1-2	Benassi
14/02	a	Palermo	W	3-1	Immobile 2 (1p), og (González)
21/02	h	Carpi	D	0-0	
27/02	a	Milan	L	0-1	
06/03	h	Lazio	D	1-1	Belotti
13/03	a	Genoa	L	2-3	Immobile 2
20/03	h	Juventus	L	1-4	Belotti (p)
03/04	a	Internazionale	W	2-1	Molinaro, Belotti (p)
10/04	h	Atalanta	W	2-1	Bruno Peres, Maxi López
16/04	a	Bologna	W	1-0	Belotti (p)
20/04	a	Roma	L	1-3	Belotti (p), Martínez
24/04	h	Sassuolo	L	1-3	Bruno Peres
30/04	a	Udinese	W	5-1	Jansson, Acquah, Martínez 2, Belotti
08/05	h	Napoli	L	1-2	Bruno Peres
15/05	a	Empoli	L	1-2	Obi

No	Name	Nat	DoB	Pos	Aps	(s)	Gls
6	Afriyie Acquah	GHA	05/01/92	M	22	(7)	2
22	Amauri		03/06/80	A		(1)	
16	Daniele Baselli		12/03/92	M	25	(10)	4
9	Andrea Belotti		20/12/93	A	31	(4)	12
15	Marco Benassi		08/09/94	M	21	(11)	3
5	Cesare Bovo		14/01/83	D	20	(1)	2
33	Bruno Peres	BRA	01/03/90	D	30	(1)	3
26	Danilo Avelar	BRA	09/06/89	D	4	(2)	
90	Simone Edera		09/01/97	A		(2)	
8	Alexander Farnerud	SWE	01/05/84	M		(5)	
14	Alessandro Gazzi		28/01/83	M	11	(4)	
25	Kamil Glik	POL	03/02/88	D	33		
28	Salvador Ichazo	URU	26/01/92	G	3		
10	Ciro Immobile		20/02/90	A	11	(3)	5
18	Pontus Jansson	SWE	13/02/91	D	6	(1)	1
91	Nikola Maksimović	SRB	25/11/91	D	16		
17	Josef Martínez	VEN	19/05/93	A	10	(11)	3
11	Maxi López	ARG	03/04/84	A	8	(18)	4
24	Cristian Molinaro		30/07/83	D	23	(4)	1
94	Emiliano Moretti		11/06/81	D	35		1
4	Joel Obi	NGA	22/05/91	M	7	(3)	1
1	Daniele Padelli		25/10/85	G	35		
13	Sanjin Prcić	BIH	20/11/93	M		(2)	
27	Fabio Quagliarella		31/01/83	A	16		5
21	Gastón Silva	URU	05/03/94	D	10	(2)	
20	Giuseppe Vives		14/07/80	M	28	(5)	1
7	Davide Zappacosta		11/06/92	D	13	(12)	1

Udinese Calcio

1896 • Dacia Arena (25,144) • udinese.it
**Coach: Stefano Colantuono;
(15/03/16) Luigi De Canio**

2015

23/08	a	Juventus	W	1-0	Théréau
30/08	h	Palermo	L	0-1	
13/09	a	Lazio	L	0-2	
19/09	h	Empoli	L	1-2	Zapata
22/09	h	Milan	L	2-3	Agyemang-Badu, Zapata
27/09	a	Bologna	W	2-1	Agyemang-Badu, Zapata
04/10	h	Genoa	D	1-1	Di Natale
18/10	a	Verona	D	1-1	Théréau
25/10	h	Frosinone	W	1-0	Lodi
28/10	h	Roma	L	1-3	Théréau
01/11	h	Sassuolo	D	0-0	
08/11	h	Napoli	L	0-1	
22/11	h	Sampdoria	W	1-0	Agyemang-Badu
29/11	a	Chievo	W	3-2	og (Frey), Théréau 2
06/12	a	Fiorentina	L	0-3	
12/12	h	Internazionale	L	0-4	
20/12	a	Torino	W	1-0	Perica

2016

06/01	h	Atalanta	W	2-1	Théréau, Perica
09/01	a	Carpi	L	1-2	Zapata
17/01	a	Juventus	L	0-4	
24/01	a	Palermo	L	1-4	Théréau
31/01	h	Lazio	D	0-0	
03/02	a	Empoli	D	1-1	Zapata
07/02	h	Milan	D	1-1	Armero
14/02	h	Bologna	L	0-1	
21/02	a	Genoa	L	1-2	Adnan
28/02	h	Verona	W	2-0	Agyemang-Badu, Théréau
06/03	h	Frosinone	L	0-2	
13/03	h	Roma	L	1-2	Bruno Fernandes
20/03	a	Sassuolo	D	1-1	Zapata
03/04	a	Napoli	W	3-1	Bruno Fernandes 2 (1p), Théréau
10/04	a	Sampdoria	L	0-2	
17/04	h	Chievo	D	0-0	
20/04	h	Fiorentina	W	2-1	Zapata, Théréau
23/04	a	Internazionale	L	1-3	Théréau
30/04	h	Torino	L	1-5	Felipe
08/05	a	Atalanta	D	1-1	Zapata
15/05	h	Carpi	L	1-2	Di Natale (p)

No	Name	Nat	DoB	Pos	Aps	(s)	Gls
53	Ali Adnan	IRQ	19/12/93	D	21	(7)	1
74	Rodrigo Aguirre	URU	01/10/94	A	3	(7)	
7	Emmanuel Agyemang-Badu	GHA	02/12/90	M	30	(3)	4
17	Pablo Armero	COL	02/11/86	D	5		1
8	Bruno Fernandes	POR	08/09/94	M	24	(7)	3
5	Danilo	BRA	10/05/84	D	34		
10	Antonio Di Natale		13/10/77	A	12	(11)	2
11	Maurizio Domizzi		28/06/80	D	3	(2)	
21	Edenílson	BRA	18/12/89	D	26	(3)	
30	Felipe	BRA	31/07/84	D	26		1
19	Guilherme	BRA	05/04/91	M	4	(1)	
55	Emil Hallfredsson	ISL	29/06/84	M	7	(4)	
75	Thomas Heurtaux	FRA	03/07/88	D	10	(5)	
16	Manuel Iturra	CHI	23/06/84	M	14	(3)	
31	Orestis Karnezis	GRE	11/07/85	G	38		
33	Panagiotis Kone	GRE	26/07/87	M	2	(3)	
22	Zdravko Kuzmanović	SRB	22/09/87	M	13	(3)	
20	Francesco Lodi		23/03/84	M	20	(4)	1
23	Marquinho	BRA	03/07/86	M	4	(7)	
52	Aleksandr Merkel	KAZ	22/02/92	M	1		
26	Giovanni Pasquale		05/01/82	D	2	(4)	
18	Stipe Perica	CRO	07/07/95	A	5	(6)	2
89	Iván Piris	PAR	10/03/89	D	20	(7)	
88	Ryder Matos	BRA	27/02/93	A	4	(7)	
77	Cyril Théréau	FRA	24/04/83	A	34	(2)	11
2	Molla Wagué	MLI	21/02/91	D	20	(1)	
27	Silvan Widmer	SUI	05/03/93	D	21	(6)	
9	Duván Zapata	COL	01/04/91	A	15	(10)	8

Hellas Verona FC

1903 • Marc'Antonio Bentegodi (38,402) • hellasverona.it
Major honours
Italian League (1) 1985
**Coach: Andrea Mandorlini;
(01/12/15) Luigi Delneri**

2015

22/08	h	Roma	D	1-1	Janković
30/08	a	Genoa	L	0-2	
13/09	h	Torino	D	2-2	Toni (p), Gómez Taleb
20/09	a	Atalanta	D	1-1	Pisano
23/09	a	Internazionale	L	0-1	
27/09	h	Lazio	L	1-2	Helander
03/10	h	Chievo	D	1-1	Pisano
18/10	h	Udinese	L	1-2	Pazzini (p)
25/10	a	Sampdoria	L	1-4	Ionita
28/10	h	Fiorentina	L	0-2	
01/11	a	Carpi	D	0-0	
07/11	h	Bologna	L	0-1	
22/11	h	Napoli	L	0-2	
29/11	a	Frosinone	L	2-3	Viviani, Moras
06/12	h	Empoli	L	0-1	
13/12	a	Milan	D	1-1	Toni (p)
20/12	h	Sassuolo	D	1-1	Toni

2016

06/01	h	Juventus	L	0-3	
10/01	h	Palermo	L	0-1	
17/01	a	Roma	D	1-1	Pazzini (p)
24/01	a	Genoa	D	1-1	Pazzini
31/01	h	Torino	D	0-0	
03/02	h	Atalanta	W	2-1	Siligardi, Pazzini
07/02	h	Internazionale	D	3-3	Helander, Pisano, Ionita
11/02	a	Lazio	L	2-5	Greco, Toni
20/02	h	Chievo	W	3-1	Toni, Pazzini, Ionita
28/02	a	Udinese	L	0-2	
05/03	h	Sampdoria	L	0-3	
13/03	a	Fiorentina	D	1-1	Pisano
20/03	h	Carpi	L	1-2	Ionita
04/04	a	Bologna	W	1-0	Samir
10/04	a	Napoli	L	0-3	
17/04	h	Frosinone	L	1-2	Bianchetti
20/04	a	Empoli	L	0-1	
25/04	h	Milan	W	2-1	Pazzini (p), Siligardi
01/05	a	Sassuolo	L	0-1	
08/05	h	Juventus	W	2-1	Toni (p), Viviani
15/05	a	Palermo	L	2-3	Viviani, Pisano

No	Name	Nat	DoB	Pos	Aps	(s)	Gls
6	Michelangelo Albertazzi		07/01/91	D	9	(1)	
22	Matteo Bianchetti		17/03/93	D	17	(6)	1
97	Luca Checchin		03/05/97	M	1	(3)	
37	Ferdinando Coppola		10/06/78	G	1		
28	Urby Emanuelson	NED	16/06/86	M	6	(5)	
93	Mohamed Fares	FRA	15/02/96	A	7	(4)	
14	Dominik Furman	POL	06/07/92	M		(1)	
12	Gilberto	BRA	07/03/93	D		(1)	
95	Pierluigi Gollini		18/03/95	G	25	(1)	
21	Juanito Gómez Taleb	ARG	20/05/85	A	19	(14)	1
19	Leandro Greco		19/07/86	M	22	(4)	1
10	Emil Hallfredsson	ISL	29/06/84	M	15	(1)	
5	Filip Helander	SWE	22/04/93	D	21	(3)	2
23	Artur Ionita	MDA	17/08/90	M	27	(4)	4
7	Boško Janković	SRB	01/03/84	M	11	(4)	1
4	Rafael Márquez	MEX	13/02/79	D	9		
8	Luca Marrone		28/03/90	M	10	(2)	
27	Matuzalém	BRA	10/06/80	M	2	(5)	
18	Vangelis Moras	GRE	26/08/81	D	30	(1)	1
11	Giampaolo Pazzini		02/08/84	A	20	(10)	6
3	Eros Pisano		31/03/87	D	33	(1)	5
1	Rafael	BRA	03/03/82	G	12		
27	Ante Rebić	CRO	21/09/93	A	6	(4)	
2	Rômulo		22/05/87	M		(9)	
26	Jacopo Sala		05/12/91	M	17	(1)	
4	Samir	BRA	05/12/94	D	3		1
16	Luca Siligardi		26/01/88	A	17	(11)	2
69	Samuel Souprayen	FRA	18/02/89	D	18	(2)	
9	Luca Toni		26/05/77	A	20	(3)	6
24	Federico Viviani		24/03/92	M	17	(2)	3
13	Paweł Wszołek	POL	30/04/92	M	23	(3)	
20	Mattia Zaccagni		16/06/95	M		(3)	

Top goalscorers

36	Gonzalo Higuaín (Napoli)
19	Paulo Dybala (Juventus)
18	Carlos Bacca (Milan)
16	Mauro Icardi (Internazionale)
14	Leonardo Pavoletti (Genoa)
	Mohamed Salah (Roma)
13	Massimo Maccarone (Empoli)
	Josip Iličič (Fiorentina)
	Éder (Sampdoria/Internazionale)
12	Nikola Kalinić (Fiorentina)
	Lorenzo Insigne (Napoli)
	Andrea Belotti (Torino)

Promoted clubs

Cagliari Calcio

1920 • Sant'Elia (16,000) • cagliaricalcio.com
Major honours
Italian League (1) 1970
Coach: Massimo Rastelli

FC Crotone

1923 • Ezio Scida (9,631) • fccrotone.it
Coach: Ivan Jurić (CRO)

Pescara Calcio

1936 • Adriatico (20,476) • pescaracalcio.com
Coach: Massimo Oddo

Second level final table 2015/16

		Pld	W	D	L	F	A	Pts
1	Cagliari Calcio	42	25	8	9	78	41	83
2	FC Crotone	42	23	13	6	61	36	82
3	Trapani Calcio	42	20	13	9	64	49	73
4	Pescara Calcio	42	21	9	12	69	52	72
5	FC Bari 1908	42	19	11	12	58	48	68
6	AC Cesena	42	19	11	12	57	37	68
7	Spezia Calcio	42	17	15	10	47	45	66
8	Novara Calcio	42	19	10	13	57	35	65
9	Virtus Entella	42	17	13	12	51	40	64
10	AC Perugia	42	14	13	15	40	40	55
11	Brescia Calcio	42	14	12	16	55	64	54
12	Ternana Calcio	42	15	8	19	50	56	53
13	Vicenza Calcio	42	11	16	15	41	53	49
14	AS Avellino	42	13	10	19	52	66	49
15	Ascoli FC	42	13	8	21	45	64	47
16	Latina Calcio	42	10	16	16	44	51	46
17	FC Pro Vercelli 1892	42	11	13	18	43	53	46
18	US Salernitana 1919	42	9	18	15	48	62	45
19	Virtus Lanciano	42	12	12	18	43	56	44
20	AS Livorno Calcio	42	10	12	20	45	57	42
21	Modena FC	42	11	9	22	37	55	42
22	Calcio Como	42	5	18	19	39	64	33

NB Virtus Lanciano – 4 pts deducted;
Novara Calcio – 2 pts deducted.

Promotion play-offs

(24/05/16)
Cesena 1-2 Spezia

(25/05/16)
Bari 3-4 Novara *(aet)*

(28/05/16 & 31/05/16)
Spezia 0-1 Trapani
Trapani 2-0 Spezia
(Trapani 3-0)

(29/05/16 & 01/06/16)
Novara 0-2 Pescara
Pescara 4-2 Novara
(Pescara 6-2)

(05/06/16 & 09/06/16)
Pescara 2-0 Trapani
Trapani 1-1 Pescara
(Pescara 3-1)

DOMESTIC CUP

Coppa Italia 2015/16

THIRD ROUND

(14/08/15)
Bologna 0-1 Pavia
Crotone 1-0 Ternana

(15/08/15)
Alessandria 1-0 Juve Stabia
Atalanta 3-0 Cittadella
Empoli 0-1 Vicenza
Frosinone 0-0 Spezia *(aet; 5-6 on pens)*
Palermo 2-1 Avellino
Sassuolo 2-0 Modena
Trapani 1-1 Cagliari *(aet; 2-4 on pens)*
Verona 3-1 Foggia

(16/08/15)
Carpi 2-0 Livorno *(aet)*
Torino 4-1 Pescara
Udinese 3-1 Novara

(17/08/15)
Chievo 0-1 Salernitana *(aet)*
Milan 2-0 Perugia

(20/08/15)
Catania 1-4 Cesena

FOURTH ROUND

(01/12/15)
Milan 3-1 Crotone *(aet)*
Spezia 2-0 Salernitana
Torino 4-1 Cesena

(02/12/15)
Palermo 2-3 Alessandria
Udinese 3-1 Atalanta
Verona 1-0 Pavia

(03/12/15)
Carpi 2-1 Vicenza
Sassuolo 0-1 Cagliari

FIFTH ROUND

(15/12/15)
Genoa 1-2 Alessandria *(aet)*
Internazionale 3-0 Cagliari

(16/12/15)
Fiorentina 0-1 Carpi
Juventus 4-0 Torino
Napoli 3-0 Verona
Roma 0-0 Spezia *(aet; 2-4 on pens)*

(17/12/15)
Lazio 2-1 Udinese
Sampdoria 0-2 Milan

QUARTER-FINALS

(13/01/16)
Milan 2-1 Carpi *(Bacca 14, Niang 28; Mancosu 50)*

(18/01/16)
Spezia 1-2 Alessandria *(Calaiò 20p;*
Bocalon 83, 90)

(19/01/16)
Napoli 0-2 Internazionale *(Jovetić 74, Ljajić 90+2)*

(20/01/16)
Lazio 0-1 Juventus *(Lichtsteiner 66)*

SEMI-FINALS

(26/01/16 & 01/03/16)
Alessandria 0-1 Milan *(Balotelli 43p)*
Milan 5-0 Alessandria *(Ménez 20, 39, Romagnoli
24, Sabato 80og, Balotelli 89)*
(Milan 6-0)

(27/01/16 & 02/03/16)
Juventus 3-0 Internazionale *(Morata 36p, 63,
Dybala 83)*
Internazionale 3-0 Juventus *(Brozović 17, 82p,
Perišić 49) (aet)*
(3-3; Juventus 5-3 on pens)

FINAL

(21/05/16)
Stadio Olimpico, Rome
JUVENTUS FC 1 *(Morata 110)*
AC MILAN 0
(aet)
Referee: Rocchi
JUVENTUS: Neto, Rugani, Barzagli, Chiellini,
Lichtsteiner *(Cuadrado 75)*, Lemina, Hernanes
(Morata 108), Pogba, Evra *(Alex Sandro 62)*,
Mandžukić, Dybala
MILAN: Donnarumma, Calabria, Zapata, Romagnoli,
De Sciglio, Kucka *(Balotelli 112)*, Montolivo
(Mauri 109), Poli *(Niang 85)*, Honda,
Bonaventura, Bacca

Juventus successfully defended the Coppa Italia after edging to an extra-time win over Milan in Rome

KAZAKHSTAN
Kazakhstanning Futbol Federatsiyasi (KFF)

Address	8 Sakarya ave. 4th floor KZ-010000 Astana	**President**	Yerlan Kozhagapanov
Tel	+7 7172 790780	**General secretary**	Azamat Aitkhozhin
Fax	+7 7172 790788	**Media officer**	Izmail Bzarov
E-mail	info@kff.kz	**Year of formation**	1992
Website	kff.kz	**National stadium**	Astana Arena, Astana (30,200)

Uralsk
13

Kostanay
11

Kokshetau
7

Astana
2

Atyrau
3

Aktobe
1

Pavlodar
4

Karagandy
9

Kyzylorda
6

Taldykorgan
12

Taraz
10

Shymkent
8

Almaty
5

KEY
- ● UEFA Champions League
- ● UEFA Europa League
- ● Promoted
- ● Relegated

0   500   1000 km
0   500 miles

PREMIER LEAGUE CLUBS

 1 FC Aktobe

 2 FC Astana

 3 FC Atyrau

 4 FC Irtysh Pavlodar

 5 FC Kairat Almaty

6 FC Kaysar Kyzylorda

 7 FC Okzhetpes Kokshetau

 8 FC Ordabasy Shymkent

 9 FC Shakhter Karagandy

 10 FC Taraz

 11 FC Tobol Kostanay

 12 FC Zhetysu Taldykorgan

PROMOTED CLUB

13 FC Akzhayik Uralsk

Last-gasp Astana retain their crown

A hotly contested race for the Kazakh Premier League title remained unresolved until three minutes from time in the final round of matches when defending champions FC Astana snatched a late winner against FC Aktobe to edge out previous frontrunners Kairat Almaty.

The roles of the country's two dominant clubs were reversed, however, in the domestic cup final, with Kairat coming from behind to defeat their rivals 2-1 and thus retain the trophy. It was a busy autumn all round for Astana, who became the first team from Kazakhstan to reach the group stage of the UEFA Champions League.

Final-day drama as Kabananga strikes late winner

Kairat gain revenge on champions in cup final

Stoilov's charges rub shoulders with Europe's elite

Domestic league

In their first full season under ex-Bulgaria coach Stanimir Stoilov, Astana made it two titles in a row. Their early form was patchy, with a repeated failure to turn draws into victories, but, just as they had done 12 months earlier, they came into their own during the run-in, taking maximum points from their last six matches.

There was a certain irony that Astana should find their most consistent form at a time when they were under the pressure of playing regular top-level European football, but Stoilov pooled his resources with skill and care and his last decisive act of the domestic season paid huge dividends as his introduction from the bench of Junior Kabananga midway through the second half of the title-deciding fixture at home to Aktobe led to the 87th-minute goal that decided the outcome of the championship.

At the 22-match split, Astana, Aktobe and Kairat were dead level at the top. Aktobe, the 2013 champions, soon fell off the pace, the arrival of new coach Ioan Andone in place of Vladimir Gazzaev failing to have the desired effect, but the other two contenders rose to the challenge. Indeed, it was Kairat, led by ex-Slovakia boss Vladimír Weiss, who looked set for their first league title in 11 years when they held a seven-point lead with four games remaining. But Astana crucially defeated them 1-0 in Almaty, with their leading scorer Tanat Nuserbayev striking on the stroke of half-time, and three wins later the title was theirs.

Had Astana's half-point not been rounded up at the split, the two title contenders would have had the same totals. In fact, although both teams won 20 and lost five of their matches, Kairat had the superior goal difference courtesy of the best attack and defence in the division. In that respect the final outcome was rough justice on Weiss's men – though they did boast the league's top scorer in 22-goal Gerard Gohou.

Domestic cup

Two weeks after the conclusion of the Premier League, Astana and Kairat met for the fifth time in the season to dispute the final of the Kazakh Cup. With two wins apiece there was no obvious favourite, and the match proved to be as tight as predicted. Astana, playing in their home stadium, went ahead, through Patrick Twumasi, but the hero of the day this time was not one of Astana's Africans but Kairat's Serbian forward Djordje Despotović, who, having scored twice in his team's final league game – and been denied glory then by

Kabananga – repeated the trick with a second-half double to give Kairat back-to-back cup triumphs.

Europe

Astana's accession to the UEFA Champions League group stage – thanks to a late play-off goal in Cyprus – enabled Kazakhstan to become the 32nd European nation represented at that stage of the competition. Stoilov's men failed to post a victory but they drew all three home fixtures against Galatasaray, Atlético Madrid and Benfica and bowed out with another draw in Istanbul. That was seen as a respectable showing – as was Kairat's progress to the UEFA Europa League play-offs via the elimination of continental trophy winners FK Crvena zvezda and Aberdeen.

National team

While Kazakhstan's clubs make their mark in Europe, the national team continues to tread water. Their only victory in the UEFA EURO 2016 qualifiers came right at the end, when, in what proved to be coach Yuri Krasnozhan's swansong, they defeated Latvia in Riga – a win that actually proved more crucial to Group A rivals Turkey as they beat Hungary to the best third place automatic qualifying slot.

KAZAKHSTAN

DOMESTIC SEASON AT A GLANCE

Premier League 2015 final table

		Pld	Home					Away					Total					Pts
			W	D	L	F	A	W	D	L	F	A	W	D	L	F	A	
1	**FC Astana**	**32**	**11**	**4**	**1**	**31**	**12**	**9**	**3**	**4**	**24**	**14**	**20**	**7**	**5**	**55**	**26**	**46**
2	FC Kairat Almaty	32	12	1	3	32	8	8	6	2	28	11	20	7	5	60	19	45
3	FC Aktobe	32	8	5	3	19	13	7	4	5	16	12	15	9	8	35	25	32
4	FC Ordabasy Shymkent	32	6	6	4	16	13	6	4	6	16	18	12	10	10	32	31	29
5	FC Atyrau	32	6	5	5	17	16	5	7	4	14	17	11	12	9	31	33	27
6	FC Irtysh Pavlodar	32	9	2	5	23	17	1	8	7	14	22	10	10	12	37	39	25
7	FC Tobol Kostanay	32	7	4	5	21	19	5	2	9	11	23	12	6	14	32	42	30
8	FC Okzhetpes Kokshetau	32	7	3	6	18	16	5	3	8	18	25	12	6	14	36	41	29
9	FC Taraz	32	8	5	3	18	8	2	3	11	7	25	10	8	14	25	33	26
10	FC Shakhter Karagandy	32	6	4	6	20	21	3	1	12	7	26	9	5	18	27	47	23
11	FC Zhetysu Taldykorgan	32	7	3	6	19	18	1	3	12	9	28	8	6	18	28	46	22
12	FC Kaysar Kyzylorda	32	3	7	6	10	13	1	5	10	10	23	4	12	16	20	36	16

NB League splits into top and bottom halves after 22 games, after which the clubs play exclusively against teams in their group.
Points obtained during the regular season are halved (and rounded upwards).

European qualification 2016/17

Champion: FC Astana (second qualifying round)

Cup winner: FC Kairat Almaty (first qualifying round)
FC Aktobe (first qualifying round)
FC Ordabasy Shymkent (first qualifying round)

Top scorer	Gerard Gohou (Kairat), 22 goals
Relegated club	FC Kaysar Kyzylorda
Promoted club	FC Akzhayik Uralsk
Cup final	FC Kairat Almaty 2-1 FC Astana

Team of the season
(4-3-3)

Coach: Stoilov (Astana)

Pokatilov (Aktobe)
Kuantayev (Kairat) — Smakov (Irtysh) — Maliy (Ordabasy) — Shomko (Astana)
Maksimović (Astana) — Cañas (Astana) — Kéthévoama (Astana)
Nuserbayev (Astana) — Gohou (Kairat) — Tunggyshbayev (Ordabasy)

Player of the season

Gerard Gohou
(FC Kairat Almaty)

After experiencing varying degrees of success in Switzerland, Turkey and Russia, Gohou appears to have found the perfect stage for his goalscoring talents in Kazakhstan. A prolific start to his career with Kairat in the second half of the 2014 season – 12 games in 13 games and a double in the cup final – was followed up by a golden boot-winning haul of 22 goals in 2015 as he played a starring role in the club's title challenge, driving Premier League defences to distraction with his power and pace.

Newcomer of the season

Georgi Zhukov
(FC Astana)

Born in Kazakhstan but brought up in Belgium, Zhukov was a Standard Liège player when he returned to his country of birth in 2014 to play on loan for Astana. He made little impact at first but in 2015, at the age of 20, the midfielder had the locals chanting his name repeatedly in admiration of his energetic and productive displays – both on the domestic front and in the UEFA Champions League. He returned to Standard in the winter and spent the first half of 2016 on loan to Dutch Eredivise club Roda JC.

NATIONAL TEAM

Top five all-time caps
Samat Smakov (74); Ruslan Baltiyev (73); Nurbol Zhumaskaliyev (58); Andrei Karpovich (55); Sergei Ostapenko (42)

Top five all-time goals
Ruslan Baltiyev (13); Viktor Zubarev (12); Dmitri Byakov (8); Nurbol Zhumaskaliyev (7); Igor Avdeev, **Sergei Khizhnichenko,** Oleg Litvinenko & Sergei Ostapenko (6)

Results 2015/16

03/09/15	Czech Republic (ECQ)	A	Plzen	L	1-2	Logvinenko (21)
06/09/15	Iceland (ECQ)	A	Reykjavik	D	0-0	
10/10/15	Netherlands (ECQ)	H	Astana	L	1-2	Kuat (90+6)
13/10/15	Latvia (ECQ)	A	Riga	W	1-0	Kuat (65)
26/03/16	Azerbaijan	N	Antalya (TUR)	W	1-0	Bayzhanov (8)
29/03/16	Georgia	A	Tbilisi	D	1-1	Nurgaliyev (36)
07/06/16	China	A	Dalian	W	1-0	Nurgaliyev (67)

Appearances 2015/16

Coach: Yuri Krasnozhan (RUS) 07/06/63 /(11/03/16) (Talgat Baysufinov) 04/09/68			CZE	ISL	NED	LVA	Aze	Geo	Chn	Caps	Goals
Stas Pokatilov	08/12/92	Aktobe /Rostov (RUS)	G	G	G	G	G			8	-
Mark Gurman	09/02/89	Kairat	D	D		s82				25	-
Yuri Logvinenko	22/07/88	Aktobe /Astana	D	D	D	D	D	D	D	37	4
Sergei Maliy	05/06/90	Ordabasy /Irtysh	D	D	D	D	D	D	D	15	-
Dmitri Shomko	19/03/90	Astana	D			D	D	D	D	24	2
Samat Smakov	08/12/78	Irtysh /Aktobe	M	M	M	M	M88	M74	M88	74	2
Ulan Konysbayev	28/05/89	Astana /Atyrau	M88	M	M	s68	M67	s64	M46	32	3
Baurzhan Islamkhan	23/02/93	Kairat	M78	M	M16		M64	s80		21	2
Baurzhan Dzholchiev	08/05/90	Astana	M	M46						14	3
Islambek Kuat	12/01/93	Kairat	M	M	M	M	s59	M82		6	2
Tanat Nuserbayev	01/01/87	Astana	A72	A76		A82		A76		25	2
Sergei Khizhnichenko	17/07/91	Aktobe /Tobol	s72		s63	A90	A71	s46	A60	37	6
Gafurzhan Suyumbayev	19/08/90	Ordabasy	s78	D	D	M	s76	M	s46	12	-
Zhambyl Kukeyev	20/09/88	Kairat	s88							29	2
Alexandr Merkel	22/02/92	Udinese (ITA)		s46						1	-
Aleksei Shchetkin	21/05/91	Astana		s76	A63	s90	s71	A46		18	1
Konstantin Engel	27/07/88	Ingolstadt (GER)			D	D				11	-
Timur Dosmagambetov	01/05/89	Taraz /Tobol			M81	M68	s67		s90	5	-
Kazbek Geteriev	30/06/85	Irtysh			s16					7	-
Azat Nurgaliyev	30/06/86	Ordabasy			s81		s64	M80	s60	29	3
Eldos Akhmetov	01/06/90	Irtysh					D		D 82*	3	-
Maksat Bayzhanov	06/08/84	Shakhter					M59	s74	M66	23	1
Serikzhan Muzhikov	17/06/89	Astana					M76	M64	M90	8	-
Askhat Tagybergen	09/08/90	Astana					s88	s82	s88	8	-
David Loria	31/10/81	Irtysh						G46	G	40	-
Abzal Beysebekov	30/11/92	Astana						D		5	-
Vladimir Plotnikov	03/04/86	Kairat						s46		1	-
Almir Mukhutdinov	09/06/85	Tobol							s66	1	-
Roman Murtazayev	10/09/93	Irtysh							s76	1	-

FC Astana

Second qualifying round - NK Maribor (SVN)
A 0-1
Loginovski, Aničić, Maksimović, Zhukov (Dedechko 82), Nuserbayev (Kabananga 72), Dzholchiev (Kéthévoama 90), Twumasi, Ilič, Postnikov, Shomko, Cañas. Coach: Stanimir Stoilov (BUL)
H 3-1 *Dzholchiev (12), Cañas (43), Twumasi (58)*
Loginovski, Aničić, Maksimović (Kéthévoama 46), Zhukov, Nuserbayev (Dedechko 71), Dzholchiev, Twumasi (Beysebekov 83), Ilič, Postnikov, Shomko, Cañas. Coach: Stanimir Stoilov (BUL)
Red card: Cañas 67

Third qualifying round - HJK Helsinki (FIN)
A 0-0
Eric, Aničić, Maksimović, Zhukov, Kéthévoama (Muzhikov 80), Nuserbayev (Shchetkin 88), Dzholchiev, Twumasi (Beysebekov 90+3), Ilič, Postnikov, Shomko. Coach: Stanimir Stoilov (BUL)
H 4-3 *Twumasi (44), Cañas (47p), Shomko (56), Postnikov (90+3)*
Eric, Aničić, Maksimović, Zhukov (Kéthévoama 88), Nuserbayev (Beysebekov 60), Dzholchiev, Twumasi, Ilič (Kabananga 46), Postnikov, Shomko, Cañas. Coach: Stanimir Stoilov (BUL)
Red card: Twumasi 71

Play-offs - APOEL FC (CYP)
H 1-0 *Dzholchiev (14)*
Eric, Aničić, Maksimović, Zhukov (Beysebekov 85), Kéthévoama (Muzhikov 90+2), Nuserbayev (Kabananga 68), Dzholchiev, Ilič, Postnikov, Shomko, Cañas. Coach: Stanimir Stoilov (BUL)
A 1-1 *Maksimović (84)*
Eric, Aničić, Maksimović, Zhukov (Beysebekov 89), Kéthévoama (Shchetkin 90+2), Nuserbayev (Kabananga 68), Dzholchiev, Ilič, Postnikov, Shomko, Cañas. Coach: Stanimir Stoilov (BUL)

Group C
Match 1 - SL Benfica (POR)
A 0-2
Eric, Aničić, Maksimović, Zhukov, Kéthévoama, Dzholchiev (Beysebekov 81), Ilič (Dedechko 90+2), Postnikov, Shomko, Cañas, Kabananga (Shchetkin 46). Coach: Stanimir Stoilov (BUL)
Match 2 - Galatasaray AŞ (TUR)
H 2-2 *Hakan Balta (77og), Carole (89og)*
Eric, Aničić, Maksimović, Zhukov (Shchetkin 89), Kéthévoama (Muzhikov 82), Dzholchiev (Nuserbayev 78), Ilič, Postnikov, Shomko, Cañas, Kabananga. Coach: Stanimir Stoilov (BUL)
Match 3 - Club Atlético de Madrid (ESP)
A 0-4
Eric, Y Akhmetov, Zhukov (Pikalkin 64), Shchetkin (Kulbekov 80), Kéthévoama, Muzhikov (Kozhamberdy 83), Beysebekov, Dedechko, Ilič, Postnikov, Kabananga. Coach: Stanimir Stoilov (BUL)

Match 4 - Club Atlético de Madrid (ESP)
H 0-0
Eric, Aničić, Maksimović, Kéthévoama, Muzhikov (Zhukov 78), Dzholchiev (Beysebekov 90), Ilič, Postnikov, Shomko, Cañas, Kabananga (Shchetkin 80). Coach: Stanimir Stoilov (BUL)
Match 5 - SL Benfica (POR)
H 2-2 *Twumasi (19), Aničić (31)*
Eric, Aničić, Maksimović, Kéthévoama (Zhukov 87), Muzhikov, Twumasi (Dedechko 90+1), Ilič, Postnikov, Shomko, Cañas, Kabananga (Shchetkin 84). Coach: Stanimir Stoilov (BUL)
Match 6 - Galatasaray AŞ (TUR)
A 1-1 *Twumasi (62)*
Eric, Aničić, Maksimović, Kéthévoama (Nuserbayev 74), Muzhikov (Zhukov 88), Twumasi, Ilič, Postnikov, Shomko, Cañas, Kabananga (Dzholchiev 74). Coach: Stanimir Stoilov (BUL)

FC Kairat Almaty

First qualifying round - FK Crvena zvezda (SRB)
A 2-0 *Gohou (45), Kuantayev (64)*
Plotnikov, Bruno Soares, Gurman, Marković, Islamkhan (Serginho 62), Isael (Darabayev 81), Gohou, Kuantayev, Sito Riera, Lunin, Kuat (Kukeyev 85). Coach: Vladimír Weiss (SVK)
H 2-1 *Islamkhan (29), Kuat (47)*
Plotnikov, Bruno Soares, Gurman, Marković, Islamkhan (Serginho 66), Isael, Gohou (Kukeyev 90+3), Kuantayev, Sito Riera, Lunin, Kuat (Darabayev 84). Coach: Vladimír Weiss (SVK)

Second qualifying round - Alashkert FC (ARM)
H 3-0 *Islamkhan (14p), Gohou (55), Despotović (69)*
Plotnikov, Bruno Soares, Marković, Islamkhan (Kukeyev 90), Isael, Gohou (Gurman 87), Kuantayev, Sito Riera, Lunin, Kuat (Despotović 64), Tymoshchuk. Coach: Vladimír Weiss (SVK)
A 1-2 *Gohou (45+2)*
Plotnikov, Bruno Soares, Marković (Gurman 85), Islamkhan, Isael, Gohou, Kuantayev, Sito Riera (Despotović 71), Lunin, Kuat (Konysbayev 67), Tymoshchuk. Coach: Vladimír Weiss (SVK)

Third qualifying round - Aberdeen FC (SCO)
H 2-1 *Bakaev (13), Islamkhan (22)*
Plotnikov, Bruno Soares, Gurman (Serginho 79), Marković, Bakaev, Islamkhan, Isael, Kuantayev, Lunin, Despotović (Konysbayev 68), Tymoshchuk. Coach: Vladimír Weiss (SVK)
A 1-1 *Gohou (59)*
Plotnikov, Bruno Soares, Gurman, Marković, Bakaev, Islamkhan, Isael (Serginho 82), Gohou (Despotović 74), Kuantayev, Lunin (Kuat 90+3), Tymoshchuk. Coach: Vladimír Weiss (SVK)

Play-offs - FC Girondins de Bordeaux (FRA)
A 0-1
Plotnikov, Bruno Soares, Gurman, Bakaev, Islamkhan (Serginho 68), Isael, Gohou, Kuantayev, Sito Riera (Despotović 83), Kuat, Tymoshchuk (Rudoselskiy 90+3). Coach: Vladimír Weiss (SVK)
H 2-1 *Guilbert (1og), Kuat (66)*
Plotnikov, Bruno Soares, Marković, Bakaev, Islamkhan (Despotović 83), Isael, Gohou, Kuantayev (Kukeyev 87), Sito Riera, Kuat, Tymoshchuk. Coach: Vladimír Weiss (SVK)

FC Aktobe

First qualifying round - Nõmme Kalju FC (EST)
H 0-1
Pokatilov, Adeleye, Žulpa, Miroshnichenko, Dmitrenko, Khairullin, Danilo Neco (Zhalmukan 87), Deac, Logvinenko, Pizzelli (Bekbaev 78), Danilo (Khizhnichenko 81). Coach: Vladimir Gazzaev (RUS)
Red card: Pokatilov 77
A 0-0
Bekbaev, Adeleye, Korobkin, Žulpa, Miroshnichenko, Danilo Neco, Deac, Logvinenko, Pizzelli (Khairullin 79), Khizhnichenko, Danilo (Zhalmukan 62). Coach: Vladimir Gazzaev (RUS)

FC Ordabasy Shymkent

First qualifying round - Beitar Jerusalem FC (ISR)
H 0-0
Sidelnikov, Suyumbayev, Nurgaliyev, Ashirbekov (Tolebek 75), Kasyanov, Abdulin, Maliy, Božić, Geynrikh (Petrov 90+3), Adyrbekov, Simčević. Coach: Viktor Kumykov (RUS)
A 1-2 *Petrov (66)*
Sidelnikov, Suyumbayev, Nurgaliyev, Ashirbekov (Tunggyshbayev 62), Kasyanov, Tazhimbetov, Abdulin, Maliy, Geynrikh, Adyrbekov (Petrov 58), Simčević. Coach: Viktor Kumykov (RUS)
Red card: Kasyanov 90+3

DOMESTIC LEAGUE CLUB-BY-CLUB

FC Aktobe

1967 • Koblandy Batyr (12,729) •
fc-aktobe.kz
Major honours
*Kazakhstan League (5) 2005, 2007, 2008, 2009,
2013; Kazakhstan Cup (1) 2008*
**Coach: Vladimir Gazzaev (RUS);
(20/07/15) Ioan Andone (ROU)**

2015

07/03	h	Atyrau	D	1-1	*Zhalmukan*
11/03	h	Kairat	D	0-0	
15/03	a	Taraz	W	1-0	*Khizhnichenko*
21/03	a	Ordabasy	D	0-0	
05/04	a	Astana	D	0-0	
11/04	h	Kaysar	D	0-0	
15/04	a	Tobol	W	2-0	*Danilo, Khizhnichenko*
19/04	a	Zhetysu	W	2-0	*Khizhnichenko, Zhalmukan*
25/04	a	Okzhetpes	W	3-2	*Khairullin, Pizzelli, Danilo Neco*
03/05	a	Irtysh	W	2-0	*Adeleye, Pizzelli (p)*
07/05	a	Shakhter	W	1-0	*Danilo*
16/05	a	Kairat	W	2-1	*Khizhnichenko, Antonov*
24/05	h	Taraz	W	3-1	*Aimbetov, Tagybergen, Dmitrenko*
29/05	a	Ordabasy	W	1-0	*Zhalmukan*
06/06	h	Astana	D	0-0	
20/06	a	Kaysar	D	0-0	
24/06	h	Tobol	W	2-1	*Pizzelli, Danilo Neco*
27/06	a	Zhetysu	D	1-1	*Zhalmukan*
05/07	h	Okzhetpes	W	4-2	*Korobkin, Khizhnichenko 3*
12/07	h	Irtysh	L	0-1	
19/07	a	Shakhter	L	0-1	
26/07	a	Atyrau	W	2-0	*Khizhnichenko, Pizzelli*
13/08	a	Kairat	L	0-1	
23/08	h	Ordabasy	W	1-0	*Deac (p)*
12/09	a	Irtysh	L	0-1	
20/09	a	Atyrau	W	1-0	*Danilo*
27/09	a	Kairat	L	1-2	*Danilo*
03/10	a	Ordabasy	L	1-2	*Khizhnichenko*
17/10	h	Irtysh	W	3-2	*Pizzelli, Danilo 2*
24/10	a	Atyrau	D	1-1	*Dmitrenko*
31/10	h	Kairat	L	0-3	
08/11	a	Astana	L	1-4	

No	Name	Nat	DoB	Pos	Aps	(s)	Gls
2	Dele Adeleye	NGA	25/12/88	D	29		1
95	Abat Aimbetov		07/08/95	A	12	(11)	1
55	Anderson Mineiro	BRA	24/04/86	D	23		
69	Olexiy Antonov	UKR	08/05/86	A		(3)	1
99	Danilo	BRA	12/11/86	A	14	(9)	6
11	Danilo Neco	BRA	27/01/86	A	18	(6)	2
20	Ciprian Deac	ROU	16/02/86	M	13	(2)	1
8	Viktor Dmitrenko		04/04/91	D	12	(4)	2
10	Marat Khairullin		26/04/84	M	13	(7)	1
91	Sergei Khizhnichenko		17/07/91	A	18	(9)	9
3	Valeri Korobkin		02/07/84	M	25	(2)	1
4	Evgeni Levin		12/07/92	D	12	(2)	
23	Yuri Logvinenko		22/07/88	D	27		
7	Dmitri Miroshnichenko		26/02/92	D	15	(2)	
35	Stanislav Pavlov		30/05/94	G	1		
34	Marcos Pizzelli	ARM	03/10/84	M	17	(10)	5
1	Stas Pokatilov		08/12/92	G	31		
33	Rustam Sakhibov		28/04/96	M		(2)	
29	Pavel Shabalin		23/10/88	M	1	(3)	
17	Askhat Tagybergen		09/08/90	M	21	(5)	1
88	Aleksandr Wolf		16/03/93	M		(2)	
73	Didar Zhalmukan		22/05/96	M	20	(9)	4
25	Sayat Zhumagali		25/04/95	M	1		
5	Artūras Žulpa	LTU	10/06/90	M	29	(1)	

FC Astana

2009 • Astana Arena (30,200) • fca.kz
Major honours
*Kazakhstan League (2) 2014, 2015; Kazakhstan
Cup (2) 2010, 2012*
Coach: Stanimir Stoilov (BUL)

2015

07/03	h	Okzhetpes	W	2-0	*Cañas, Twumasi*
11/03	a	Irtysh	W	3-0	*Cañas (p), Twumasi, Maksimović*
15/03	h	Shakhter	W	2-1	*Maksimović, Cañas*
21/03	a	Atyrau	D	1-1	*og (Grigoryev)*
05/04	h	Aktobe	D	0-0	
11/04	a	Taraz	L	0-2	
15/04	h	Ordabasy	D	1-1	*Cañas*
19/04	h	Kairat	W	4-3	*Zhukov, Maksimović, Dzholchiev, Nuserbayev*
25/04	a	Kaysar	L	1-2	*Maksimović*
03/05	h	Tobol	W	4-0	*Shomko, Nuserbayev, Kéthévoama, Dzholchiev*
07/05	a	Zhetysu	W	3-1	*Cañas, Twumasi, Shchetkin*
16/05	h	Irtysh	D	2-2	*Kéthévoama, Nuserbayev*
24/05	a	Shakhter	W	4-0	*Nuserbayev, Twumasi, Dzholchiev, Shchetkin*
29/05	h	Atyrau	D	0-0	
06/06	a	Aktobe	D	0-0	
20/06	h	Taraz	W	4-1	*Nuserbayev, Shchetkin, Zhukov, Kéthévoama*
24/06	a	Ordabasy	W	2-0	*Twumasi 2*
28/06	a	Kairat	L	0-2	
04/07	h	Kaysar	W	2-0	*og (Rozybakiev), Nuserbayev*
10/07	a	Tobol	D	1-1	*Kéthévoama*
18/07	h	Zhetysu	W	2-1	*Dedechko, Maksimović*
25/07	a	Okzhetpes	W	2-1	*Kabananga 2*
13/08	a	Aktobe	W	1-0	*Cañas*
11/09	a	Ordabasy	W	3-2	*Muzhikov, Kabananga, Nuserbayev*
20/09	h	Kairat	L	0-1	
26/09	a	Irtysh	L	1-2	*Maksimović*
04/10	a	Atyrau	W	1-0	*Nuserbayev*
17/10	h	Ordabasy	W	2-1	*og (Maliy), Cañas*
25/10	a	Kairat	W	1-0	*Nuserbayev*
28/10	h	Atyrau	W	4-1	*Cañas, Beysebekov, Nuserbayev, Kabananga*
31/10	h	Irtysh	W	1-0	*Nuserbayev*
08/11	h	Aktobe	W	1-0	*Kabananga*

No	Name	Nat	DoB	Pos	Aps	(s)	Gls
2	Eldos Akhmetov		01/06/90	D	14	(2)	
5	Marin Aničić	BIH	17/08/89	D	28	(1)	
15	Abzal Beysebekov		30/11/92	D	26	(3)	1
88	Roger Cañas	COL	27/03/90	M	30		8
24	Denys Dedechko	UKR	02/07/87	M	5	(5)	1
22	Baurzhan Dzholchiev		08/05/90	A	19	(6)	3
1	Nenad Erić		26/05/82	G	25		
40	Mikhail Golubnichi		31/01/95	G	6		
33	Branko Ilič	SVN	06/02/83	D	8	(1)	
89	Junior Kabananga	COD	04/04/89	A	6	(7)	5
10	Foxi Kéthévoama	CTA	30/05/86	M	28	(3)	4
7	Ulan Konysbayev		28/05/89	M	3	(9)	
28	Birzhan Kulbekov		22/04/94	D		(5)	
85	Vladimir Loginovski		08/10/85	G	1	(1)	
6	Nemanja Maksimović	SRB	26/01/95	M	18	(5)	6
16	Vladislav Mendybayev		01/05/96	M	1		
11	Serikzhan Muzhikov		17/06/89	M	6	(3)	1
17	Tanat Nuserbayev		01/01/87	A	17	(8)	11
12	Igor Pikalkin		19/03/92	D	4		
44	Evgeni Postnikov		16/04/86	D	28		
19	Aleksei Rodionov		29/03/94	M		(1)	
13	Berik Shaikhov		20/02/94	M		(1)	
9	Aleksei Shchetkin		21/05/91	A	6	(14)	3
77	Dmitri Shomko		19/03/90	D	25	(1)	1
23	Patrick Twumasi	GHA	09/05/94	A	23	(5)	6
25	Tokhtar Zhangylyshbay		25/05/93	A		(5)	
8	Georgi Zhukov		19/11/94	M	25	(2)	2

FC Atyrau

1980 • Munayshi (8,700) • rfcatyrau.kz
Major honours
Kazakhstan Cup (1) 2009
Coach: Vladimir Nikitenko

2015

07/03	a	Aktobe	D	1-1	*Bayzhanov*
11/03	h	Taraz	W	2-1	*Trifunović, Bayzhanov*
15/03	a	Ordabasy	L	0-2	
21/03	h	Astana	D	1-1	*Bayzhanov*
05/04	a	Kaysar	D	0-0	
11/04	h	Tobol	L	1-2	*Arzhanov*
15/04	a	Zhetysu	W	2-1	*Arzhanov, Bayzhanov*
19/04	h	Okzhetpes	W	2-1	*Aytbaev, Diakhate*
25/04	a	Irtysh	W	2-1	*Essame, Tleshev (p)*
03/05	h	Shakhter	W	1-0	*Essame (p)*
07/05	a	Kairat	W	1-0	*Parkhachev*
16/05	a	Taraz	W	1-0	*Aytbaev*
24/05	h	Ordabasy	D	1-1	*og (Simčević)*
29/05	a	Astana	D	0-0	
06/06	h	Kaysar	W	2-1	*Ivanović, Grigoryev*
20/06	a	Tobol	D	2-2	*Grigoryev, Zarechny*
24/06	h	Zhetysu	W	3-0	*(w/o; original result 1-2 Grigoryev)*
28/06	a	Okzhetpes	D	2-2	*Grigoryev, og (Tuliev)*
04/07	h	Irtysh	D	0-0	
11/07	a	Shakhter	D	1-1	*Essame*
19/07	h	Kairat	D	0-0	
26/07	h	Aktobe	L	0-2	
15/08	a	Irtysh	L	0-2	
12/09	h	Kairat	L	1-2	*Essame*
20/09	a	Astana	L	0-1	
26/09	h	Ordabasy	L	1-3	*Arzhanov*
04/10	a	Astana	L	0-1	
17/10	a	Kairat	D	0-0	
24/10	h	Aktobe	D	1-1	*Diakhate*
28/10	a	Astana	L	1-4	*Arzhanov*
31/10	a	Ordabasy	W	1-0	*Arzhanov*
08/11	h	Irtysh	W	1-0	*Bayzhanov*

No	Name	Nat	DoB	Pos	Aps	(s)	Gls
9	Volodymyr Arzhanov	UKR	29/11/85	M	30	(2)	5
14	Berik Aytbaev		26/06/91	D	18	(2)	2
1	Ilya Bayteryakov		13/08/84	G	4		
11	Maksat Bayzhanov		06/08/84	M	24	(2)	5
66	Anton Chichulin		27/10/84	D	25	(4)	
8	Valentin Chureev		29/08/86	D	5		
22	Abdoulaye Diakhate	SEN	16/01/88	M	23	(1)	2
12	Ruslan Esatov		31/10/84	D	19	(4)	
7	Guy Stéphane Essame	CMR	25/11/84	A	31		4
24	Ruslan Fomin	UKR	02/03/86	A	6	(6)	
23	Anton Grigoryev	RUS	13/12/85	D	31		4
99	Ivan Ivanović	MNE	14/09/89	M	12	(12)	1
18	Kuanysh Kalmuratov		27/08/96	D	18	(2)	
17	Bauyrzhan Kasymov		01/03/96	A		(3)	
28	Vladislav Kuzmin		03/07/87	D	18	(6)	
12	Aleksei Marov		02/10/95	M	8	(3)	
77	Zhasur Narzikulov		13/04/84	G	28		
13	Aybar Nuribekov		29/08/92	A	3	(3)	
20	Mike Odibe	NGA	23/07/88	D	16	(4)	
85	Dmitri Parkhachev	BLR	02/01/85	M	14	(5)	1
6	Altynbek Sarapov		26/04/95	M	6	(1)	
39	Murat Tleshev		12/04/80	A	3	(16)	1
14	Miloš Trifunović	SRB	15/10/84	A	4	(5)	1
10	Konstantin Zarechny		14/02/84	M	6	(13)	1

KAZAKHSTAN

FC Irtysh Pavlodar

1965 • Tsentralny (11,828) • fcirtysh.kz

Major honours
Kazakhstan League (5) 1993, 1997, 1999, 2002, 2003; Kazakhstan Cup (1) 1998

Coach: Dmitri Cheryshev (RUS);
(08/05/15) (Sergei Klimov);
(01/06/15) Dimitar Dimitrov (BUL)

2015

07/03	a	Ordabasy	D	1-1	Gatagov
11/03	h	Astana	L	0-3	
15/03	a	Kaysar	D	0-0	
21/03	h	Tobol	D	1-1	Sartakov
05/04	a	Zhetysu	D	2-2	Azuka, Aliyev
08/04	a	Kairat	L	0-1	
11/04	h	Okzhetpes	W	3-1	Smakov, Azuka, Bancé
20/04	a	Shakhter	D	2-2	Azuka, og (David)
25/04	h	Atyrau	L	1-2	Smakov
03/05	a	Aktobe	L	1-2	Bancé
07/05	h	Taraz	L	0-1	
16/05	a	Astana	D	2-2	Dudchenko, Ersalimov
24/05	h	Kaysar	W	4-2	Dudchenko 3, Kislitsyn
29/05	a	Tobol	L	0-1	
06/06	h	Zhetysu	W	1-0	Dudchenko
20/06	a	Okzhetpes	W	1-0	N'Diaye
24/06	a	Kairat	L	1-1	Dudchenko
28/06	h	Shakhter	W	3-1	N'Diaye 2, Chernyshov
04/07	a	Atyrau	D	0-0	
12/07	h	Aktobe	W	1-0	Carlos Fonseca
18/07	a	Taraz	D	0-0	
26/07	h	Ordabasy	W	2-0	Dudchenko, Evandro Roncatto (p)
15/08	h	Atyrau	W	2-0	Kassaï, Evandro Roncatto
24/08	a	Kairat	L	2-5	Evandro Roncatto, N'Diaye
12/09	h	Aktobe	W	1-0	Geteriev
20/09	a	Ordabasy	D	1-1	Evandro Roncatto (p)
26/09	h	Astana	W	2-1	N'Diaye, Carlos Fonseca
03/10	h	Kairat	L	0-2	
17/10	a	Aktobe	L	2-3	Smakov (p), Dudchenko
25/10	h	Ordabasy	L	1-2	Evandro Roncatto (p)
31/10	a	Astana	L	0-1	
08/11	a	Atyrau	L	0-1	

No	Name	Nat	DoB	Pos	Aps	(s)	Gls
5	Pirali Aliyev		13/01/84	D	18	(6)	1
90	António Ferreira	BRA	24/10/84	D	2	(3)	
13	Alibek Ayaganov		13/01/92	M	1	(6)	
89	Izu Azuka	NGA	24/05/89	A	14	(3)	3
15	Aristide Bancé	BFA	19/09/84	A	9	(2)	2
9	Kuanysh Begalyn		05/09/92	A		(3)	
40	Carlos Fonseca	POR	23/08/87	A	14		2
3	Vladislav Chernyshov		16/03/81	D	26		1
30	Kostyantyn Dudchenko	UKR	08/07/86	A	16	(5)	8
14	Azat Ersalimov		19/07/88	M	9	(7)	1
25	Ruslan Esimov		28/04/90	A	8	(5)	
60	Evandro Roncatto	BRA	24/05/86	A	7	(4)	5
7	Alan Gatagov	RUS	23/01/91	M	15	(2)	1
33	Kazbek Geteriev		30/06/85	M	23		1
55	Ivan Graf	CRO	17/06/87	D	9	(3)	
27	Sergei Ignatyev		09/02/86	D	2	(3)	
20	Tomáš Jirsák	CZE	29/06/84	M	17		
21	Nikita Kalmykov		24/08/89	G	3		
50	Fernander Kassaï	CTA	01/07/87	D	14		1
4	Aleksandr Kislitsyn		08/03/86	D	25		1
23	Zakhar Korobov		18/05/88	D	1		
1	David Loria		31/10/80	G	29		
80	Alassane N'Diaye	FRA	25/02/90	M	16		5
11	Yerkebulan Nurgaliyev		12/09/93	D	4	(4)	
57	Artem Popov		17/01/98	M		(1)	
22	Artem Samsonov	RUS	06/02/89	D	9		
19	Grigori Sartakov		19/08/94	D	28	(3)	1
2	Vladimir Sedelnikov		15/10/91	M		(1)	
8	Samat Smakov		08/12/78	D	26		3
10	Alisher Suley		01/11/95	A	3	(5)	
17	Abylaykhan Totay		16/02/92	M		(3)	
77	Vladimir Vomenko		22/05/95	M	4	(4)	

FC Kairat Almaty

1954 • Tsentralny (26,242) • fckairat.kz

Major honours
Kazakhstan League (2) 1992, 2004; Kazakhstan Cup (7) 1992, 1996, 2000, 2001 (autumn), 2003, 2014, 2015

Coach: Vladimír Weiss (SVK)

2015

07/03	h	Tobol	W	4-0	Gohou 3 (1p), Islamkhan (p)
11/03	a	Aktobe	D	0-0	
15/03	h	Zhetysu	W	2-0	Kuantayev, Gohou (p)
21/03	a	Taraz	L	0-1	
05/04	h	Okzhetpes	W	4-0	Gohou, Isael 2, Sito Riera
08/04	h	Irtysh	W	1-0	Gohou
11/04	a	Ordabasy	D	2-2	Gohou (p), Marković
19/04	a	Astana	L	3-4	Gohou 2, Islamkhan
25/04	h	Shakhter	W	4-0	Marković, Isael, Islamkhan, Gohou
03/05	a	Kaysar	D	0-0	
07/05	a	Atyrau	L	0-1	
16/05	h	Aktobe	L	1-2	Gohou
24/05	a	Zhetysu	W	3-0	Islamkhan, Gohou, Kukeyev
29/05	h	Taraz	W	2-0	Gohou 2
06/06	a	Okzhetpes	W	3-1	Gohou 3
20/06	h	Ordabasy	W	2-1	Pliev, Islamkhan (p)
24/06	a	Irtysh	D	1-1	Gohou
28/06	h	Astana	W	2-0	Isael, Islamkhan (p)
05/07	a	Shakhter	W	5-0	Serginho, Sito Riera 2, Ceesay, Kukeyev
12/07	h	Kaysar	W	1-0	Despotović
19/07	a	Atyrau	D	0-0	
26/07	a	Tobol	W	3-1	Despotović 2, Darabayev
14/08	a	Ordabasy	D	0-0	
24/08	h	Irtysh	W	5-2	Kuat, Gohou 2, Kuantayev, Despotović
12/09	a	Atyrau	W	2-1	Islamkhan, Gohou
20/09	a	Astana	W	1-0	Isael
27/09	h	Aktobe	W	2-1	Isael, Gohou
03/10	a	Irtysh	W	2-0	Despotović, Bruno Soares
17/10	a	Atyrau	D	0-0	
25/10	a	Astana	L	0-1	
31/10	a	Aktobe	W	3-0	Serginho 2 (1p), Despotović
08/11	h	Ordabasy	W	2-0	Despotović 2

No	Name	Nat	DoB	Pos	Aps	(s)	Gls
8	Mikhail Bakaev		05/08/87	M	26		
14	Baurzhan Baytana		06/06/92	M	2	(1)	
4	Bruno Soares	BRA	21/08/88	D	11	(3)	1
21	Momodou Ceesay	GAM	24/12/88	A		(5)	1
17	Aslan Darabayev		21/01/89	M	7	(10)	1
28	Djordje Despotović	SRB	04/03/92	A	5	(4)	8
11	Gerard Gohou	CIV	29/12/88	A	23	(5)	22
5	Mark Gurman		09/02/89	D	24	(4)	
19	Isael	BRA	13/05/88	M	26	(1)	6
9	Baurzhan Islamkhan		23/02/93	M	22	(7)	7
23	Ilya Kalinin		03/02/92	M		(1)	
27	Ulan Konysbayev		28/05/89	M	5	(1)	
13	Yermek Kuantayev		13/10/90	D	23	(2)	2
20	Islambek Kuat		12/01/93	M	17	(2)	1
7	Zhambyl Kukeyev		20/09/88	A	4	(4)	2
18	Vitali Li		13/03/94	A	8	(8)	
19	Stanislav Lunin		02/05/93	A	8	(8)	
6	Žarko Marković	SRB	28/01/87	D	26	(3)	2
3	Zaurbek Pliev		27/09/91	D	20	(2)	1
1	Vladimir Plotnikov		03/04/86	G	29		
2	Timur Rudoselskiy		21/12/94	D	23	(7)	
22	Serginho	BRA	03/12/90	A	7	(7)	3
15	Sito Riera	ESP	05/01/87	A	21	(6)	3
51	Kuanysh Sovetov		11/05/95	M	1		
24	Sergei Tkachuk		15/02/92	G	3		
44	Anatoliy Tymoshchuk	UKR	30/03/79	M	10		
29	Tokhtar Zhangylyshbay		25/05/93	A	1	(1)	

FC Kaysar Kyzylorda

1968 • Ghani Muratbayev (7,000) • fckaysar.kz

Major honours
Kazakhstan Cup (1) 1999

Coach: Dmitriy Ogay;
(23/07/15) (Sultan Abildayev);
(06/08/15) Fyodor Shcherbachenko (RUS)

2015

07/03	h	Zhetysu	D	0-0	
11/03	a	Okzhetpes	L	0-1	
15/03	h	Irtysh	D	0-0	
21/03	a	Shakhter	W	2-1	Dimov, Junuzović
05/04	h	Atyrau	D	0-0	
11/04	a	Aktobe	D	0-0	
15/04	h	Taraz	L	1-3	Muldarov
19/04	a	Ordabasy	D	0-0	
25/04	h	Astana	W	2-1	Muldarov, Moldakaraev
03/05	h	Kairat	D	0-0	
07/05	a	Tobol	L	0-1	
16/05	h	Okzhetpes	L	0-2	
24/05	a	Irtysh	L	2-4	Junuzović, Hunt
29/05	h	Shakhter	L	1-2	Strukov, Junuzović
06/06	a	Atyrau	L	1-2	Vorogovskiy
20/06	h	Aktobe	D	0-0	
24/06	a	Taraz	L	0-3	
27/06	h	Ordabasy	D	1-1	Moldakaraev
04/07	a	Astana	L	0-2	
12/07	a	Kairat	L	0-1	
18/07	h	Tobol	L	0-1	
26/07	a	Zhetysu	L	1-2	Shestakov
15/08	h	Taraz	D	0-0	
23/08	a	Okzhetpes	L	1-2	Moldakaraev
13/09	h	Tobol	L	1-2	Knežević
19/09	a	Shakhter	D	1-1	Moldakaraev
27/09	h	Zhetysu	W	3-1	Klein, Moldakaraev, Kalinin
03/10	a	Okzhetpes	L	0-1	
18/10	a	Tobol	D	0-0	
24/10	h	Shakhter	L	0-1	
31/10	a	Zhetysu	L	1-2	Baltaev
08/11	a	Taraz	D	1-1	Moldakaraev

No	Name	Nat	DoB	Pos	Aps	(s)	Gls
23	Olzhas Altaev		15/07/89	D	5	(1)	
11	Elzhas Altynbekov		22/11/93	A	2	(11)	
3	Aldan Baltaev		15/01/89	D	28		1
37	Samat Balymbetov		10/04/94	M		(1)	
25	Plamen Dimov	BUL	29/10/90	D	2		1
28	Rimo Hunt	EST	05/11/85	A	9	(14)	1
14	Farhadbek Irismetov		10/08/81	D	20	(3)	
29	Edin Junuzović	CRO	28/04/86	A	11	(5)	3
77	Ilya Kalinin		03/02/92	M	8		1
15	Georgi Karaneychev	BUL	09/06/88	A	2	(3)	
30	Sergei Keiler		08/11/94	D	14		
44	Martin Klein	CZE	02/07/84	D	30		1
18	Josip Knežević	CRO	03/10/88	M	8	(3)	1
27	Anton Matveenko	BLR	28/04/89	D	10	(2)	
25	Vuk Mitošević	SRB	12/02/91	M	22	(1)	
7	Zhasulan Moldakaraev		07/05/87	A	17	(7)	6
31	Aleksei Muldarov		24/04/84	D	9		2
6	Serikzhan Muzhikov		17/06/89	M	13	(4)	
8	Duman Narzildaev		06/09/93	A	5	(3)	
20	Vladislav Nekhty		19/12/91	M	8	(2)	
21	Kairat Nurdauletov		06/11/82	D	15	(2)	
35	Ramil Nurmukhametov		21/12/87	G	4		
33	Juraj Piroska	SVK	27/02/87	A	5		
13	Kirill Pryadkin	KGZ	06/07/77	G	27		
6	Rakhimzhan Rozybakiev		02/01/91	M	22	(1)	
1	Maksat Seydakhmet		17/11/89	G	1		
22	Kirill Shestakov		14/11/85	M	15	(6)	1
10	Sergei Skorykh		25/05/84	D	4	(3)	
9	Sergei Strukov	RUS	17/09/82	A	14	(8)	1
18	Danil Tsoy		25/06/95	D	10	(4)	
24	Yan Vorogovskiy		07/08/96	M	12	(12)	1

FC Okzhetpes Kokshetau

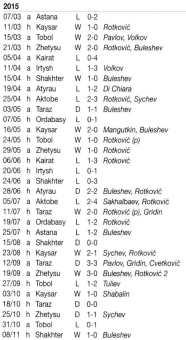

1957 • Torpedo (10,000) • okzhetpes.kz
Coach: Vladimir Mukhanov (RUS)

2015

07/03	a	Astana	L	0-2	
11/03	h	Kaysar	W	1-0	Rotković
15/03	a	Tobol	W	2-0	Pavlov, Volkov
21/03	h	Zhetysu	W	2-0	Rotković, Buleshev
05/04	a	Kairat	L	0-4	
11/04	a	Irtysh	L	1-3	Volkov
15/04	h	Shakhter	W	1-0	Buleshev
19/04	a	Atyrau	L	1-2	Di Chiara
25/04	h	Aktobe	L	2-3	Rotković, Sychev
03/05	a	Taraz	L	0-1	
07/05	h	Ordabasy	L	0-1	
16/05	a	Kaysar	W	2-0	Mangutkin, Buleshev
24/05	h	Tobol	W	1-0	Rotković (p)
29/05	a	Zhetysu	W	1-0	Rotković
06/06	h	Kairat	L	1-3	Rotković
20/06	h	Irtysh	L	0-1	
24/06	a	Shakhter	L	0-3	
28/06	h	Atyrau	D	2-2	Buleshev, Rotković
05/07	a	Aktobe	L	2-4	Sakhalbaev, Rotković
11/07	h	Taraz	W	2-0	Rotković (p), Gridin
19/07	a	Ordabasy	L	1-2	Rotković
25/07	h	Astana	L	1-2	Buleshev
15/08	a	Shakhter	D	0-0	
23/08	h	Kaysar	W	2-1	Sychev, Rotković
12/09	a	Taraz	D	3-3	Pavlov, Gridin, Cvetković
19/09	a	Zhetysu	W	2-0	Buleshev, Rotković 2
27/09	h	Tobol	L	1-2	Tuliev
03/10	a	Kaysar	W	1-0	Shabalin
18/10	h	Taraz	D	0-0	
25/10	h	Zhetysu	D	1-1	Sychev
31/10	a	Tobol	L	0-1	
08/11	h	Shakhter	W	1-0	Buleshev

No	Name	Nat	DoB	Pos	Aps	(s)	Gls
25	Ruslan Abzhanov		28/04/90	G	10		
3	Egor Azovskiy		10/01/85	D	13	(3)	
1	Yaroslav Baginski		03/10/87	G	1		
10	Alibek Buleshev		09/04/81	A	27	(2)	8
88	Daniil Chertov	RUS	15/11/90	M	24	(3)	
77	Olexander Chizhov	UKR	10/08/86	D	30		
29	Ivan Cvetković	SRB	12/02/81	M	12	(1)	1
92	Joseph Di Chiara	CAN	30/01/92	M	7	(5)	1
28	Sergei Gridin		20/05/87	A	9	(4)	2
9	Nikita Khokhlov		27/10/83	M	15	(6)	
14	Viktor Kryukov		30/06/90	D	8	(1)	
15	Anton Kuksin		03/07/95	M	8		
36	Oleg Lebedev		27/03/95	M	1		
6	Ilnur Mangutkin		16/09/86	D	13	(4)	1
24	Aleksandr Marochkin		14/07/90	D	7	(2)	
17	Daniyar Nukebay		01/10/95	M		(5)	
8	Yerkin Nurzhanov			M	5	(11)	
19	Aleksandr Pavlov	BLR	18/08/84	M	24	(4)	2
45	Luka Rotković	MNE	05/07/88	A	14	(17)	13
7	Ruslan Sakhalbaev		27/06/84	M	15	(7)	1
27	Pavel Shabalin		23/10/88	M	11	(1)	1
22	Michal Smejkal	CZE	21/02/86	D	9	(5)	
26	Dmitri Sychev	RUS	26/10/83	A	8	(11)	3
20	Anton Tsirin		10/08/87	G	21		
23	Miras Tuliev		30/08/94	M	29	(1)	1
11	Vitali Volkov	RUS	22/03/81	M	31	(1)	2

FC Ordabasy Shymkent

1998 • Kazhimukan (20,000) • fcordabasy.kz
Major honours
Kazakhstan Cup (1) 2011
Coach: Viktor Kumykov (RUS)

2015

07/03	h	Irtysh	D	1-1	Božić
11/03	a	Shakhter	W	1-0	Tunggyshbayev
15/03	h	Atyrau	W	2-0	Nurgaliyev, Tazhimbetov
21/03	a	Aktobe	D	0-0	
05/04	h	Taraz	W	1-0	Tunggyshbayev
11/04	h	Kairat	D	2-2	Maliy, Tazhimbetov
15/04	a	Astana	D	1-1	Geynrikh
19/04	h	Kaysar	D	0-0	
25/04	a	Tobol	W	3-1	Geynrikh, Simčević, Božić
03/05	a	Zhetysu	D	0-0	
07/05	a	Okzhetpes	W	1-0	Geynrikh
16/05	h	Shakhter	W	1-0	Trajković
24/05	h	Atyrau	D	1-1	Trajković
29/05	a	Aktobe	L	0-1	
06/06	a	Taraz	W	1-0	Tunggyshbayev
20/06	a	Kairat	L	1-2	Nurgaliyev
24/06	h	Astana	L	0-2	
27/06	a	Kaysar	D	1-1	Nurgaliyev
05/07	h	Tobol	W	2-0	Maliy, Nurgaliyev
12/07	a	Zhetysu	L	0-3	
19/07	h	Okzhetpes	W	2-1	Tunggyshbayev, Kasyanov
26/07	a	Irtysh	L	0-2	
14/08	h	Kairat	D	0-0	
23/08	a	Aktobe	L	0-1	
11/09	h	Astana	L	2-3	Tunggyshbayev, Junuzović
20/09	h	Irtysh	D	1-1	Junuzović
26/09	a	Atyrau	W	3-1	Simčević, Junuzović 2
03/10	a	Aktobe	W	2-1	Junuzović, Simčević
17/10	a	Astana	L	1-2	Tunggyshbayev
25/10	a	Irtysh	W	2-1	Simčević, Tunggyshbayev
31/10	h	Atyrau	L	0-1	
08/11	a	Kairat	L	0-2	

No	Name	Nat	DoB	Pos	Aps	(s)	Gls
23	Renat Abdulin		14/04/82	D	12	(5)	
77	Talgat Adyrbekov		26/01/89	D	4	(4)	
10	Kairat Ashirbekov		21/10/82	M	9	(17)	
8	Bekzat Beysenov		18/02/87	M	15	(3)	
29	Sergei Boychenko		27/09/77	G	21		
40	Ivan Božić	BIH	19/11/83	A	13	(11)	2
50	Aleksandr Geynrikh	UZB	06/10/84	A	17	(5)	3
86	Edin Junuzović	CRO	28/04/86	A	13		5
12	Artem Kasyanov	UKR	20/04/83	M	21	(2)	1
11	Dauren Kaykibasov		10/06/95	A		(1)	
2	Bakdaulet Kozhabayev		19/06/92	D	4	(7)	
25	Sergei Maliy		05/06/90	D	21	(1)	2
4	Mukhtar Mukhtarov		01/01/86	D	16	(1)	
7	Azat Nurgaliyev		30/06/86	M	29	(1)	4
26	Kyrylo Petrov	UKR	22/06/90	M	22	(5)	
22	Rauan Sariyev		22/01/94	A	2	(9)	
55	Andrei Sidelnikov		08/03/80	G	11		
87	Aleksandar Simčević	SRB	15/02/87	D	29	(2)	4
5	Gafurzhan Suyumbayev		19/08/90	D	28	(1)	
18	Daurenbek Tazhimbetov		02/07/85	A	8	(11)	2
17	Mardan Tolebek		18/12/90	M	1	(2)	
15	Branislav Trajković	SRB	29/08/89	M	26	(1)	2
21	Yerkebulan Tunggyshbayev		14/01/95	A	30	(1)	7

FC Shakhter Karagandy

1958 • Shakhter (19,500) • shahter.kz
Major honours
Kazakhstan League (2) 2011, 2012; Kazakhstan Cup (1) 2013

Coach: Vladimir Cheburin;
(08/05/15) (Evgeni Sveshnikov);
(05/06/15) Ihor Zaharyak (UKR)

2015

07/03	a	Taraz	D	0-0	
11/03	h	Ordabasy	L	0-1	
15/03	a	Astana	L	1-2	Topčagić
21/03	h	Kaysar	L	1-2	Topčagić
05/04	a	Tobol	L	1-4	Najaryan
11/04	h	Zhetysu	W	2-1	Karpovich, Murtazayev
15/04	a	Okzhetpes	L	0-1	
20/04	h	Irtysh	D	2-2	Topčagić, Murtazayev
25/04	a	Kairat	L	0-4	
03/05	h	Atyrau	L	0-1	
07/05	h	Aktobe	L	0-1	
16/05	a	Ordabasy	L	0-1	
24/05	h	Astana	L	0-4	
29/05	a	Kaysar	L	0-2	
06/06	h	Tobol	W	1-0	Yermekov
20/06	a	Zhetysu	L	0-3	
24/06	h	Okzhetpes	W	3-0	Topčagić, og (Pavlov), Vetrov
28/06	a	Irtysh	L	1-3	Murtazayev
05/07	h	Kairat	L	0-5	
11/07	h	Atyrau	D	1-1	Vasiljević
19/07	a	Aktobe	W	1-0	Vetrov
26/07	a	Taraz	W	2-0	Feshchuk, Murtazayev
15/08	h	Okzhetpes	D	0-0	
23/08	a	Tobol	L	1-2	Dimov
13/09	h	Zhetysu	W	3-1	Džidić, Topčagić (p), Feshchuk
19/09	h	Kaysar	D	1-1	Feshchuk
27/09	a	Taraz	L	0-2	
03/10	h	Tobol	L	1-2	Muldarov
18/10	a	Zhetysu	W	1-0	Karpovich
24/10	a	Kaysar	W	1-0	Dimov
31/10	h	Taraz	W	3-0	Topčagić, Karpovich, Vassiljev
08/11	a	Okzhetpes	L	0-1	

No	Name	Nat	DoB	Pos	Aps	(s)	Gls
25	Evgeni Azamatov		21/03/90	D	9	(2)	
52	Aubrey David	TRI	11/10/90	D	17	(2)	
70	Plamen Dimov	BUL	29/10/90	D	10		2
21	Grigori Dubkov		22/11/90	M	2	(1)	
20	Aldin Džidić	BIH	30/08/83	D	27		1
10	Maxym Feshchuk	UKR	25/11/85	A	9	(2)	3
14	Andrei Finonchenko		21/06/82	M	7	(5)	
22	Mikhail Gabyshev		02/01/90	D	15		
6	Andrei Karpovich		18/01/81	M	15	(6)	3
23	Evgeni Kostrub		27/08/82	M	22	(3)	
35	Aleksandr Mokin		19/06/81	G	12		
3	Aleksei Muldarov		24/04/84	D	7	(1)	1
45	Roman Murtazayev		10/09/93	A	21	(7)	4
7	Gevorg Najaryan		06/01/98	M	5	(3)	1
15	Aybar Nuribekov		29/08/92	A	6	(3)	
8	Oralkhan Omirtayev		16/07/98	A		(7)	
5	Pedro Petrazzi	BRA	15/09/90	M	15	(8)	
10	Nikola Pokrivač	CRO	26/11/85	M	13		
17	Andrei Poryvaev	BLR	03/01/82	D	22	(1)	
1	Igor Shatskiy		11/05/89	G	11		
84	Sergei Skorykh		25/05/84	D	1		
19	Evgeni Tarasov		16/04/85	D	13	(1)	
9	Mihret Topčagić	BIH	21/06/88	A	24	(2)	6
77	Desley Ubbink	NED	15/06/93	M	6	(4)	
4	Nikola Vasiljević	BIH	19/12/83	D	6	(2)	1
4	Vladislav Vassiljev		10/04/97	A	8	(7)	1
16	Sergei Vetrov		11/11/94	A	9	(4)	2
24	Jan Vošahlík	CZE	08/03/89	A	19	(7)	
44	Kuanysh Yermekov		14/04/94	M	12	(5)	1
13	Aleksandr Zarutskiy		26/08/93	G	9		

KAZAKHSTAN

FC Taraz

1960 • Tsentralny (12,527) • fctaraz.kz

Major honours
Kazakhstan League (1) 1996; Kazakhstan Cup (1) 2004
Coach: Yevhen Yarovenko (UKR)

2015

07/03	h	Shakhter	D	0-0	
11/03	a	Atyrau	L	1-2	Golić
15/03	a	Aktobe	L	0-1	
21/03	h	Kairat	W	1-0	Pishchur
05/04	a	Ordabasy	L	0-1	
11/04	a	Astana	W	2-0	Pishchur, Sergienko
15/04	a	Kaysar	W	3-1	Mera, Pishchur 2 (1p)
19/04	h	Tobol	W	1-0	Mukhutdinov
25/04	a	Zhetysu	L	0-1	
03/05	h	Okzhetpes	D	1-1	Taubay
07/05	a	Irtysh	L	1-2	Yarovenko
16/05	a	Atyrau	L	0-1	
24/05	a	Aktobe	L	1-3	D Yevstigneev
29/05	a	Kairat	L	0-2	
06/06	h	Ordabasy	L	0-2	
20/06	h	Astana	L	1-4	Dosmagambetov (p)
24/06	a	Kaysar	W	3-0	Pishchur, Zhumakhanov, Golić
28/06	a	Tobol	L	0-3	
04/07	h	Zhetysu	W	2-0	Suley, Pishchur
11/07	a	Okzhetpes	L	0-2	
18/07	h	Irtysh	D	0-0	
26/07	a	Shakhter	L	0-2	
15/08	a	Kaysar	D	0-0	
23/08	a	Zhetysu	L	0-1	
12/09	h	Okzhetpes	D	3-3	Suley, Dosmagambetov, Zhumakhanov
19/09	a	Tobol	D	0-0	
27/09	h	Shakhter	W	2-0	Azuka, Pishchur (p)
03/10	h	Zhetysu	W	1-0	Mukhutdinov
18/10	a	Okzhetpes	D	0-0	
24/10	h	Tobol	W	1-0	Pishchur
31/10	a	Shakhter	L	0-3	
08/11	h	Kaysar	D	1-1	Pishchur (p)

No	Name	Nat	DoB	Pos	Aps	(s)	Gls
44	Adylet Abdenabi		04/02/96	M	2	(2)	
21	Maksat Amirkhanov		10/02/92	D	14	(1)	
30	Evgeni Averchenko		06/04/82	M	18	(2)	
13	Izu Azuka	NGA	24/05/89	A	7		1
24	Dzhurakhon Babakhanov		31/10/91	G	8		
3	Dmytro Bashlay	UKR	25/04/90	M	23	(1)	
11	Sherkhan Bauyrzhan		28/08/92	M	1	(3)	
2	Daniyar Bayaliev		30/01/93	D	4		
16	Azat Bitabarov		14/01/90	G	2	(2)	
23	Timur Dosmagambetov		01/05/89	M	21	(8)	2
71	Alan Gatagov	RUS	23/01/91	M		(6)	
5	Jovan Golić	SRB	18/09/86	M	16	(2)	2
1	Aleksandr Grigorenko		06/02/85	G	22		
39	Adylet Kenesbek		05/01/96	D		(1)	
10	Zhakyp Kozhamberdy		26/02/92	M	6	(6)	
12	Ioan Mera	ROU	05/01/87	D	30		1
77	Almir Mukhutdinov		09/06/85	M	25		2
22	Madiyar Nuraly		20/01/95	D	4		
17	Olexandr Pishchur	UKR	26/01/81	A	23	(9)	9
36	Bakhytzhan Rymtaev		01/02/95	M		(1)	
35	Alibek Satybaldy		28/06/95	M	1		
7	Eduard Sergienko		18/02/83	M	12	(11)	1
18	Alisher Suley		01/11/95	A	14		2
6	Abzal Taubay		18/02/95	M	8	(6)	1
32	Marat Togyzbay		18/11/95	D	3		
20	Desley Ubbink	NED	15/06/93	M	1	(7)	
14	Denys Vasilyev	UKR	08/05/87	D	15	(1)	
4	Ilya Vorotnikov		01/02/86	D	23	(1)	
27	Olexandr Yarovenko	UKR	19/12/87	A	8	(13)	1
19	Dmitri Yevstigneev		27/11/86	D	25		1
8	Vitali Yevstigneev		08/05/85	M		(1)	
9	Sanat Zhumakhanov		30/01/88	M	16	(11)	2

FC Tobol Kostanay

1967 • Tsentralny (8,050) • fc-tobol.kz

Major honours
Kazakhstan League (1) 2010; Kazakhstan Cup (1) 2007
Coach: Vardan Minasyan (ARM); (16/04/15) Sergei Maslenov

2015

07/03	a	Kairat	L	0-4	
11/03	a	Zhetysu	D	0-0	
15/03	h	Okzhetpes	L	0-2	
21/03	a	Irtysh	D	1-1	Mošnikov
05/04	h	Shakhter	W	4-1	Zhumaskaliyev 3, Simkovic
11/04	a	Atyrau	W	2-1	Kalu, Bugaiov (p)
15/04	h	Aktobe	L	0-2	
19/04	a	Taraz	L	0-1	
25/04	h	Ordabasy	L	1-3	Bugaiov
03/05	a	Astana	L	0-4	
07/05	h	Kaysar	W	1-0	Sadovnichi
16/05	h	Zhetysu	W	3-1	Kalu 3
24/05	a	Okzhetpes	L	0-1	
29/05	h	Irtysh	W	1-0	Kalu (p)
06/06	a	Shakhter	L	0-1	
20/06	h	Atyrau	D	2-2	Sadovnichi, Yavorskiy
24/06	a	Aktobe	L	1-2	Yurin
28/06	h	Taraz	W	3-0	Yurin 2, Zenkovich
05/07	a	Ordabasy	L	0-2	
10/07	a	Astana	D	1-1	Bugaiov
18/07	a	Kaysar	W	1-0	Zhumaskaliyev
26/07	h	Kairat	L	1-3	Zhumaskaliyev
16/08	h	Zhetysu	L	1-3	Zenkovich (p)
23/08	h	Shakhter	W	2-1	Simkovic 2
13/09	a	Kaysar	W	2-1	Krasić, Zenkovich
19/09	h	Taraz	D	0-0	
27/09	a	Okzhetpes	W	2-1	Simkovic 2
03/10	a	Shakhter	W	2-1	Zenkovich, Bogdanov
18/10	h	Kaysar	D	0-0	
24/10	a	Taraz	L	0-1	
31/10	h	Okzhetpes	W	1-0	Yurin
08/11	a	Zhetysu	L	0-2	

No	Name	Nat	DoB	Pos	Aps	(s)	Gls
28	Anuar Agaysin		26/10/94	D	18	(2)	
2	Rafkat Aslan		02/02/94	D	12	(4)	
96	Bolat Aulabaev		21/12/96	D		(1)	
5	Anatoli Bogdanov		07/08/81	M	27		1
10	Igor Bugaiov	MDA	26/06/84	A	14	(8)	3
30	Sultan Busurmanov		10/05/96	G	4		
7	Artem Deli		02/03/89	M	7	(6)	
50	Temirlan Elmurzayev		03/01/96	A	4	(6)	
15	Uche Kalu	NGA	14/11/87	A	10	(12)	5
80	Evgeni Kaptel		05/01/95	A		(1)	
24	Arūnas Klimavičius	LTU	05/10/82	D	21	(1)	
11	Ognjen Krasić	SRB	09/04/88	M	19	(6)	1
25	Štěpán Kučera	CZE	11/06/84	D	5		
19	Nurtas Kurgulin		20/09/86	D	17	(4)	
99	Deivydas Matulevičius	LTU	08/04/89	A	10	(3)	
6	Karlen Mkrtchyan	ARM	25/11/88	M	2	(2)	
16	Sergei Mošnikov	EST	07/01/88	M	2	(3)	1
88	Ramiz Mukanov		15/09/90	M		(1)	
17	Oleg Nedashkovsky		09/09/87	M	17	(2)	
12	Yermek Nurgaliyev		08/08/86	M	1	(6)	
35	Aleksandr Petukhov		11/01/85	G	28		
20	Ivan Sadovnichi	BLR	05/10/82	D	27	(1)	2
13	Islam Shadukayev		09/03/95	D		(1)	
81	Tomas Simkovic	AUT	16/04/87	M	24	(3)	5
8	Nenad Šljivić	SRB	08/06/85	M	17	(4)	
23	Serhiy Yavorskiy	UKR	05/07/89	D	16		1
14	Igor Yurin		03/07/82	M	20	(8)	4
78	Igor Zenkovich	BLR	17/09/87	A	13	(2)	4
70	Timur Zhakupov		06/09/95	D		(1)	
9	Nurbol Zhumaskaliyev		11/05/81	M	17	(2)	5

FC Zhetysu Taldykorgan

1981 • Zhetysu (5,550) • fc-zhetisu.kz

Coach: Askar Kozhabergenov; (20/04/15) Ivan Azovskiy

2015

07/03	a	Kaysar	D	0-0	
11/03	h	Tobol	D	0-0	
15/03	a	Kairat	L	0-2	
21/03	a	Okzhetpes	L	0-2	
05/04	h	Irtysh	D	2-2	Despotović, Savic
11/04	a	Shakhter	L	1-2	Despotović
15/04	h	Atyrau	L	1-2	Savic
19/04	a	Aktobe	L	0-2	
25/04	h	Taraz	W	1-0	Despotović
03/05	a	Ordabasy	D	0-0	
07/05	h	Astana	L	1-3	Despotović
16/05	a	Tobol	L	1-3	Savic
24/05	h	Kairat	L	0-3	
29/05	h	Okzhetpes	L	0-1	
06/06	a	Irtysh	L	0-1	
20/06	h	Shakhter	W	3-0	Turysbek, Savic 2 (w/o; original result 2-1 Savic 2)
24/06	a	Atyrau	L	0-3	
27/06	h	Aktobe	D	1-1	Despotović
04/07	a	Taraz	L	0-2	
12/07	h	Ordabasy	W	3-0	Savic (p), Galiakberov, Turysbek
18/07	a	Astana	L	1-2	Galiakberov
26/07	h	Kaysar	W	2-1	Galiakberov 2
16/08	a	Tobol	W	3-1	Galiakberov 2, Turysbek
23/08	h	Taraz	W	1-0	Savic
13/09	a	Shakhter	L	1-3	Savic
19/09	h	Okzhetpes	L	0-3	
27/09	a	Kaysar	L	1-3	Turysbek
03/10	a	Taraz	L	0-1	
18/10	h	Shakhter	L	0-1	
25/10	a	Okzhetpes	D	1-1	Savic
31/10	h	Kaysar	W	2-1	Quliyev, Savic
08/11	h	Tobol	W	2-0	Savic 2

No	Name	Nat	DoB	Pos	Aps	(s)	Gls
2	Timerlan Adilkhanov		28/03/94	D	21	(6)	
13	Ilyas Amirseitov		22/10/89	D	13	(5)	
18	Maksim Azovskiy		04/06/86	M	23	(6)	
15	Ruslan Barzukayev		05/12/87	M	1	(2)	
31	Ivan Cvetković	SRB	12/02/81	M	14		
19	Bobir Davlyatov	UZB	01/03/96	M	7	(2)	
89	Djordje Despotović	SRB	04/03/92	A	17	(1)	5
4	Davron Erghashev	TJK	19/03/88	D	18		
23	Ruslan Galiakberov	RUS	20/11/89	A	13		6
88	Aleksei Gerasimov	RUS	15/04/93	D	8	(1)	
14	Evgeni Goriachiy		02/02/91	D	10	(1)	
19	Rinat Khairullin		19/02/94	M	8	(5)	
14	Aleksandr Kirov		04/06/84	D	13	(1)	
21	Miloš Mihajlov	SRB	15/11/82	D	19		
11	Marlan Muzhikov		01/12/86	M	2	(6)	
23	Askhat Muybaev		21/02/91	D		(1)	
17	Dias Mynbaev		06/12/95	M	2	(2)	
20	Andrei Pasechenko		09/08/87	G	13	(1)	
6	Mikhail Petrolay	RUS	19/08/94	M	5	(3)	
21	Elbeyi Quliyev	AZE	14/10/95	A	1	(6)	1
6	Denis Rodionov		26/07/85	M	3		
8	Serik Sagyndykov		09/01/84	D	23	(3)	
91	Ilsur Samigulin	RUS	06/02/91	M	10		
46	Sanzhar Sapiyanov		07/09/95	A		(3)	
7	Sauyat Sariyev		15/10/92	M	12	(8)	
10	Dusan Savic	MKD	01/01/85	A	32		14
25	Zhaksylyk Seydakhmetov		25/12/95	M	1	(4)	
1	Andrei Shabanov		17/11/86	G	19		
5	Marat Shakhmetov		06/02/89	M	21	(9)	
9	Baurzhan Turysbek		15/10/91	A	19	(7)	4
3	Gediminas Vičius	LTU	05/07/85	M	4	(4)	

Top goalscorers

22	Gerard Gohou (Kairat)
14	Dusan Savic (Zhetysu)
13	Luka Rotković (Okzhetpes)
	Djordje Despotović (Zhetysu/Kairat)
11	Tanat Nuserbayev (Astana)
9	Sergei Khizhnichenko (Aktobe)
	Olexandr Pishchur (Taraz)
8	Roger Cañas (Astana)
	Kostyantyn Dudchenko (Irtysh)
	Edin Junuzović (Kaysar/Ordabasy)
	Alibek Buleshev (Okzhetpes)

Promoted club

FC Akzhayik Uralsk

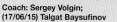

1968 • Puyotr Atoyan (8,320) • fc-akzhayik.kz
**Coach: Sergey Volgin;
(17/06/15) Talgat Baysufinov**

Second level final table 2015

		Pld	W	D	L	F	A	Pts
1	FC Akzhayik Uralsk	24	17	2	5	60	21	53
2	FC Vostok Oskemen	24	15	5	4	37	22	50
3	FC Bolat	24	15	3	6	40	23	48
4	FC Kyzylzhar Petropavlovsk SK	24	14	4	6	41	19	46
5	FC Kaspiy Aktau	24	12	7	5	35	18	43
6	FC Spartak Semey	24	11	6	7	34	19	39
7	FC Kyran Shymkent	24	10	6	8	38	28	36
8	FC Makhtaaral Zhetysay	24	7	11	6	22	17	32
9	CSKA Almaty	24	8	3	13	29	46	27
10	FC Ekibastuz	24	7	5	12	21	31	26
11	FC Baykonur	24	6	4	14	19	38	22
12	FC Bayterek Astana	24	2	4	18	13	52	10
13	FC Lashyn Karatau	24	2	0	22	4	59	6

Promotion/Relegation play-off

(14/11/15)
Zhetysu 1-0 Vostok

DOMESTIC CUP

Kubok Kazakhstana 2015

THIRD ROUND

(28/04/15)
Kaysar 1-0 Spartak Semey
(29/04/15)
Akzhayik 0-5 Aktobe
Atyrau 0-1 Zhetysu
Ekibastuz 2-3 Astana
Kairat 0-0 Irtysh *(aet; 4-1 on pens)*
Ordabasy 0-1 Taraz
Shakhter 1-2 Okzhetpes *(aet)*
Tobol 2-1 CSKA Almaty

QUARTER-FINALS

(20/05/15)
Kairat 4-1 Taraz *(Gohou 6, 58, Islamkhan 13, Kukeyev 87; Mukhutdinov 62p)*

Kaysar 1-2 Astana *(Junuzović 45; Twumasi 69, 110) (aet)*

Okzhetpes 2-3 Aktobe *(Rotković 25, Azovskiy 90; Pizzelli 20, Žulpa 41, Danilo 45+1)*

Tobol 2-0 Zhetysu *(Simkovic 6, Deli 83)*

SEMI-FINALS

(02/06/15 & 23/09/15)
Aktobe 0-2 Astana *(Dzholchiev 19, Kulbekov 38)*
Astana 1-1 Aktobe *(Twumasi 67; Khizhnichenko 40)*
(Astana 3-1)

Tobol 0-3 Kairat *(Gohou 18, Islamkhan 59, Isael 76)*
Kairat 2-1 Tobol *(Sito Riera 8, Gurman 20; Zhumaskaliyev 89)*
(Kairat 5-1)

FINAL

(21/11/15)
Astana Arena, Astana
FC KAIRAT ALMATY 2 *(Despotović 48, 70)*
FC ASTANA 1 *(Twumasi 28)*
Referee: Cüneyt Çakır (TUR)
KAIRAT: Plotnikov, Rudoselskiy (Nurmugamet 83), Marković, Bruno Soares, Pliev, Tymoshchuk, Bakaev, Islamkhan, Kuat (Gurman 89), Sito Riera, Despotović (Gohou 90+3)
ASTANA: Erić, Beysebekov (Kéthévoama 76), Aničić, Postnikov, Shomko, Muzhikov, Zhukov, Maksimović, Dzholchiev (Kabananga 76), Nuserbayev (Shchetkin 86), Twumasi

Kairat turned the tables on league conquerors Astana to retain the domestic cup

LATVIA
Latvijas Futbola Federācija (LFF)

Address	Olympic Sports Centre	**President**	Guntis Indriksons
	Grostonas Street 6b	**General secretary**	Jānis Mežeckis
	LV-1013 Rīga	**Media officer**	Rūdolfs Petrovs
Tel	+371 67 292988	**Year of formation**	1921
Fax	+371 67 315604	**National stadium**	Skonto, Riga (9,500)
E-mail	futbols@lff.lv		
Website	lff.lv		

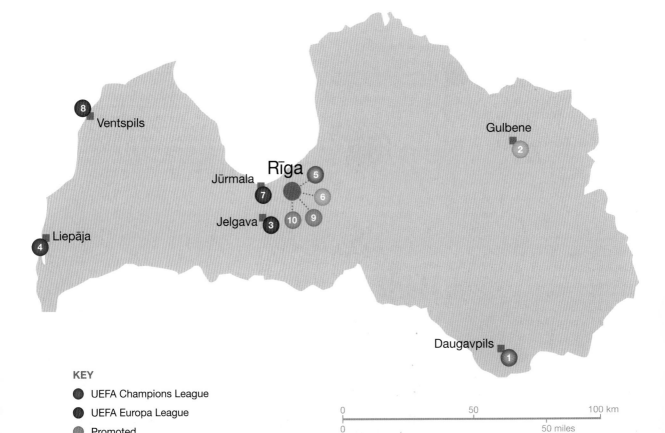

KEY
- ● UEFA Champions League
- ◑ UEFA Europa League
- ◔ Promoted
- ◯ Relegated

VIRSLĪGA CLUBS

  ① **BFC Daugavpils**

  ② **FB Gulbene**

  ③ **FK Jelgava**

 ④ **FK Liepāja**

 ⑤ **FS METTA/LU**

  ⑥ **Skonto FC**

  ⑦ **FK Spartaks Jūrmala**

 ⑧ **FK Ventspils**

PROMOTED CLUBS

  ⑨ **FC Caramba/Dinamo**
NB Renamed Riga FC for 2016 season

  ⑩ **Rīgas Futbola skola**

Liepāja leave rivals standing

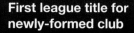

A 2015 Virslīga distorted and weakened by financial troubles and exclusions was won, less than two years after their formation, by FK Liepāja. Fourth in their debut campaign, Viktors Dobrecovs' side became comprehensive champions in their second, losing just twice and finishing seven points clear of record champions Skonto FC.

There would be post-season trauma for Skonto as they were refused a licence to compete in the top division in 2016, but the new year brought gladder tidings for FK Jelgava as they won the Latvian Cup for the third year in a row, defeating local rivals FK Spartaks Jūrmala 1-0 in the final.

| First league title for newly-formed club | Runners-up Skonto denied top-flight licence | Jelgava complete Latvian Cup hat-trick |

Domestic league

With FC Daugava Rīga denied permission to compete and FC Daugava Daugavpils having gone out of business, the number of participants in the 2015 Virslīga dropped from ten to eight teams. Before long the cast list had been pruned further when newly-promoted FB Gulbene, who lost their first eight matches, were expelled with immediate effect and their results declared null and void.

That left a reduced programme of 24 matches – 12 fewer than the previous season – and the team that most benefited from the weekends off and extra training sessions were Liepāja, a club presided over by Latvia's all-time leading scorer Māris Verpakovskis. An opening 3-2 home win over Skonto set them on the right path, and there was a confidence and consistency about their performances over the course of the campaign that their chief rivals – Skonto and defending champions FK Ventspils – found difficult to match. After a 1-0 defeat by Skonto in late May, Dobrecovs' side went 15 matches unbeaten – a run concluding with a 4-0 win at FS METTA/LU on 19 October that sealed the club's first title with two matches to spare.

Many of the Virslīga's outstanding performers wore Liepāja's white, green and red – from Argentinian duo Cristián Torres and Leonel Strumia to veteran midfielder Valērijs Afanasjevs and the league's top scorer, 21-year-old Dāvis Ikaunieks, whose 16 goals helped the champions boast the league's most productive attack – an average of two goals a game – as well as an unbeaten home record.

Ventspils' hopes of a third successive league title foundered on a calamitous mid-campaign stutter that yielded just one win from nine games. That prompted the dismissal of the man who had led them in the previous two title-winning campaigns, Jurģis Pučinskis. Englishman Paul Ashworth, the ex-Skonto coach, took over and promptly oversaw five straight victories, which enabled Ventspils to ensure a return to Europe with a third-place finish – although Skonto's subsequent off-the-field woes would lead to their exclusion from the 2016/17 UEFA Europa League as well as the Virslīga.

With Gulbene and Skonto out of the picture, the top division required two additional participants in 2016. The first of them, merger club FC Caramba/Dinamo (later to be renamed Riga FC), arrived by conventional means, with a runaway success in the 1. līga (second tier), but a special invitation was needed to bring in a second promoted club, Rīgas Futbola skola accepting it after 1. līga runners-up Valmiera, who had already lost a play-off to METTA/LU, turned it down.

Domestic cup

Despite the distraction of losing their coach, legendary ex-Latvia international midfielder Vitālijs Astafjevs, on the eve of the final after a poor run of form in the league, Jelgava kept their focus to defeat Spartaks Jūrmala and lift the Latvian Cup for the third year running. New signing Kyrylo Silich, a Ukrainian midfielder drafted in from Estonian side Sillamäe Kalev, scored the only goal after 20 minutes, enabling Jelgava to match the previous hat-trick exploits of Skonto (2000-02) and Ventspils (2003-05).

Europe

There were exits in the second qualifying round of their respective European competitions for all four Latvian clubs, with Skonto left to lick some particularly painful wounds after losing 9-2 away to the Hungarians of Debrecen following an encouraging first-leg 2-2 draw in Riga.

National team

A home defeat by Kazakhstan in Latvia's final UEFA EURO 2016 qualifier left Marians Pahars' side bottom of the Group A table without a win – a frustrating end to the campaign, especially as the team had preceded it with two unexpected score draws in Turkey and Iceland, in which emerging young striker Valērijs Šabala enhanced his growing reputation with a couple of valuable goals.

LATVIA

DOMESTIC SEASON AT A GLANCE

Virslīga 2015 final table

		Pld	Home					Away					Total					Pts
			W	D	L	F	A	W	D	L	F	A	W	D	L	F	A	
1	**FK Liepāja**	**24**	**8**	**4**	**0**	**22**	**10**	**7**	**3**	**2**	**26**	**13**	**15**	**7**	**2**	**48**	**23**	**52**
2	Skonto FC	24	7	2	3	21	12	6	4	2	22	11	13	6	5	43	23	45
3	FK Ventspils	24	7	3	2	25	10	4	7	1	14	6	11	10	3	39	16	43
4	FK Jelgava	24	5	5	2	11	8	6	3	3	15	10	11	8	5	26	18	41
5	FK Spartaks Jūrmala	24	2	4	6	8	17	3	2	7	12	19	5	6	13	20	36	21
6	BFC Daugavpils	24	1	5	6	7	16	1	3	8	7	21	2	8	14	14	37	14
7	FS METTA/LU	24	2	1	9	11	31	1	2	9	8	25	3	3	18	19	56	12
8	FB Gulbene	0	0	0	0	0	0	0	0	0	0	0	0	0	0	0	0	0

NB FB Gulbene excluded from the league after round 8; all of their matches were annulled.

European qualification 2016/17

Champion: FK Liepāja (second qualifying round)

Cup winner: FK Jelgava (first qualifying round)
FK Ventspils (first qualifying round)
FK Spartaks Jūrmala (first qualifying round)

Top scorer	Dāvis Ikaunieks (Liepāja), 16 goals
Relegated clubs	FB Gulbene (excluded), Skonto FC (excluded)
Promoted clubs	FC Caramba/Dinamo, Rīgas Futbola skola
Cup final	FK Jelgava 1-0 FK Spartaks Jūrmala

Team of the season
(4-3-3)

Coach: Dobrecovs *(Liepāja)*

Player of the season

Cristián Torres
(FK Liepāja)

Signed by Liepāja in early 2014 after he had met club president Māris Verpakovskis on holiday, Argentinian midfielder Torres returned to Latvia, where he had once played for Daugava Rīga, following a five-year sojourn in Azerbaijan. After a promising first season, the 30-year-old schemer became the heartbeat of Viktors Dobrecovs' championship-winning side, making the play from deep and providing the platform for many potent attacks. The only thing missing from his tick-list was a goal.

Newcomer of the season

Ņikita Juhņevičs
(FS METTA/LU)

The 2015 Virslīga campaign may have been a struggle for his club, METTA/LU, as they won just three of their 24 matches and only stayed up after a play-off, but in precocious 18-year-old midfielder Juhņevičs it looked as if Latvian football had discovered a star-in-the-making. Already a captain of the Latvian Under-17 side, the youngster was promoted into the national U21 squad on the strength of his consistent and inventive club displays and in the winter transferred to newly-promoted Riga FC.

NATIONAL TEAM

International tournament appearances
UEFA European Championship (1) 2004

Top five all-time caps
Vitālijs Astafjevs (167); Andrejs Rubins (117); Juris Laizāns (108); Imants Bleidelis (106); Mihails Zemļinskis (105)

Top five all-time goals
Māris Verpakovskis (29); Ēriks Pētersons (21); Vitālijs Astafjevs (16); Juris Laizāns & Marians Pahars (15)

Results 2015/16

03/09/15	Turkey (ECQ)	A	Konya	D	1-1	*Šabala (90+1)*
06/09/15	Czech Republic (ECQ)	H	Riga	L	1-2	*Zjuzins (73)*
10/10/15	Iceland (ECQ)	A	Reykjavik	D	2-2	*Cauņa (49), Šabala (68)*
13/10/15	Kazakhstan (ECQ)	H	Riga	L	0-1	
13/11/15	Northern Ireland	A	Belfast	L	0-1	
25/03/16	Slovakia	A	Trnava	D	0-0	
29/03/16	Gibraltar	A	Gibraltar	W	5-0	*J Ikaunieks (46, 84), Dubra (53), Šabala (57), A Višņakovs (82)*
01/06/16	Lithuania	H	Liepaja	W	2-1	*Zjuzins (50), Rudņevs (70)*
04/06/16	Estonia	A	Tallinn	D	0-0	

Appearances 2015/16

Coach: Marians Pahars	05/08/76		TUR	CZE	ISL	KAZ	Nir	Svk	Gib	Ltu	Est	Caps	Goals
Andris Vaņins	30/04/80	Sion (SUI)	G	G	G	G	G73	G	G	G	G	74	-
Vladislavs Gabovs	13/07/87	Korona (POL)	D	s33	D	D	D	D	D	D	D	25	-
Vitālijs Jagodinskis	28/02/92	Hoverla (UKR)	D				D	s90	s76		D	8	-
Kaspars Dubra	20/12/90	BATE (BLR)	D	D	D	D		D	D	D		14	1
Vitālijs Maksimenko	08/12/90	Mattersburg (AUT)	D	D	D	D		D	D72	D	D	23	1
Oļegs Laizāns	28/03/87	Ventspils /Rīga	M82		s77	M	M78	s76	M46	s88	M46	33	-
Aleksandrs Cauņa	19/01/88	CSKA Moskva (RUS)	M60	s66	M	M72						45	12
Igors Tarasovs	16/10/88	Jagiellonia (POL)	M	M	M77		M	M90	M46	M46	s70	15	-
Aleksejs Višņakovs	03/02/84	Skonto /Rīgas Fs	M	s29	M65	M57	M59	s57	s12	s46	s46	68	9
Deniss Rakels	20/08/92	Cracovia (POL)	M	M	M	M	M85					14	-
Artūrs Karašausks	29/01/92	Skonto /Piast (POL)	A85	A66	s65	s57		s81	s81			10	-
Artūrs Zjuzins	18/06/91	Gazovik (RUS)	s60	M	M85	M83	M	M66	s46	s46	s46	31	4
Eduards Višņakovs	10/05/90	Westerlo (BEL)	s82			s72	A71					14	-
Valērijs Šabala	12/10/94	Miedź Legnica (POL) /Příbram (CZE)	s85		A	A	s71	s66	A81	A88	A70	26	9
Gints Freimanis	09/05/85	Jelgava	D33									6	-
Kaspars Gorkšs	06/11/81	unattached /Dukla Praha (CZE)	D		D	D	D	D	D76	D	D	77	5
Aleksandrs Fertovs	16/06/87	Korona (POL)	M									35	-
Vladimirs Kamešs	28/10/88	Liepāja	M29			s85						13	1
Jānis Ikaunieks	16/02/95	Metz (FRA)		s85	s83	s78		M57	M	M65	M79	11	2
Antons Kurakins	01/01/90	Hamilton (SCO)						D	s72			8	-
Artjoms Rudņevs	13/01/88	Hamburg (GER)					s59	A81	A	A77	A90	36	2
Pāvels Šteinbors	21/09/85	Nea Salamis (CYP)					s73					1	-
Roberts Savaļnieks	04/02/93	Rīga						M76	M12	M46	M46	4	-
Artis Lazdiņš	03/05/86	Jelgava						M	s46	M	M	25	-
Dāvis Ikaunieks	07/01/94	Liepāja								s65	s79	2	-
Sergejs Vorobjovs	09/10/95	Rīga								s77	s90	2	-

LATVIA

EUROPE

DOMESTIC LEAGUE CLUB-BY-CLUB

FK Ventspils

Second qualifying round - HJK Helsinki (FIN)
H 1-3 *Jemeļins (63)*
Meļņičenko, Žuļevs, Krjauklis, Barinovs, Siņeļņikovs, Mujeci (Turkovs 82), Žigajevs (Dorić 71), Karlsons, Paulius, Rugins (Mordatenko 86), Jemeļins. Coach: Jurģis Pučinskis (LVA)
A 0-1
Meļņičenko, Žuļevs (Tidenbergs 90+1), Krjauklis, Barinovs, Turkovs (Karlsons 81), Siņeļņikovs, Mujeci (Mordatenko 77), Paulius, Rugins, Jemeļins, Dorić. Coach: Jurģis Pučinskis (LVA)

FK Jelgava

First qualifying round - PFC Litex Lovech (BUL)
H 1-1 *Malašenoks (83)*
Ikstens, Freimanis, Sosranov, Łatka, Bogdaškins, Diallo, Gubins, Eriba (Kiriļins 69), Ošs, Kļuškins (Jaudzems 83), Sushkin (Malašenoks 70). Coach: Vitālijs Astafjevs (LVA)
A 2-2 *Ošs (11), Diallo (60)*
Ikstens, Freimanis, Redjko (Sushkin 59), Sosranov, Łatka, Bogdaškins (Eriba 90+1), Malašenoks (Kiriļins 74), Diallo, Gubins, Ošs, Kļuškins. Coach: Vitālijs Astafjevs (LVA)

Second qualifying round - FK Rabotnicki (MKD)
H 1-0 *Kļuškins (87)*
Ikstens, Freimanis (Redjko 86), Sosranov, Łatka, Bogdaškins, Diallo, Gubins, Eriba (Kiriļins 56), Ošs, Kļuškins, Sushkin (Malašenoks 63). Coach: Vitālijs Astafjevs (LVA)
A 0-2
Ikstens, Freimanis, Redjko, Sosranov, Łatka, Bogdaškins, Diallo, Gubins (Kiriļins 60), Ošs, Kļuškins (Jaudzems 84), Sushkin (Malašenoks 79). Coach: Vitālijs Astafjevs (LVA)

Skonto FC

First qualifying round - Saint Patrick's Athletic FC (IRL)
H 2-1 *Karašausks (38), Gutkovskis (65)*
Pavlovs, Timofejevs, Rode, Smirnovs, Murillo (Tatiefang 90+1), Višņakovs (Isajevs 72), Kozlovs, Jermolajevs, Gutkovskis (Lukanyuk 83), Kovaļovs, Karašausks. Coach: Tamaz Pertia (GEO)
A 2-0 *Sorokins (37), Karašausks (59p)*
Pavlovs, Timofejevs, Rode, Smirnovs, Murillo (Isajevs 77), Kozlovs, Jermolajevs, Gutkovskis (Višņakovs 64), Kovaļovs, Karašausks (Ivanovs 83), Sorokins. Coach: Tamaz Pertia (GEO)

Second qualifying round - Debreceni VSC (HUN)
H 2-2 *Karašausks (27, 47)*
Pavlovs, Timofejevs, Rode, Murillo, Višņakovs (Lukanyuk 71), Kozlovs, Jermolajevs, Gutkovskis (Isajevs 57), Kovaļovs, Karašausks, Sorokins. Coach: Tamaz Pertia (GEO)
A 2-9 *Gutkovskis (59), Rode (65)*
Pavlovs, Timofejevs, Rode, Murillo (Indrāns 54), Višņakovs (Bērenfelds 46), Kozlovs, Jermolajevs, Gutkovskis, Kovaļovs, Karašausks (Lukanyuk 61), Sorokins. Coach: Tamaz Pertia (GEO)
Red card: Kovaļovs 80

FK Spartaks Jūrmala

First qualifying round - FK Budućnost Podgorica (MNE)
A 3-1 *Bulvītis (22, 74p), Mickēvičs (42)*
Koļinko, Maksymenko, Nazarenko, Mežs, Ulimbaševs (Bespalovs 90+1), Kazačoks, Mickēvičs, Vivacqua (Mena 81), Takyi, Bulvītis, Šlampe (Stuglis 90+3). Coach: Roman Pylypchuk (UKR)
H 0-0
Koļinko, Maksymenko, Nazarenko, Mežs, Ulimbaševs, Kazačoks, Mickēvičs, Vivacqua (Abdultaofik 90+1), Takyi (Stuglis 82), Bulvītis, Šlampe. Coach: Roman Pylypchuk (UKR)

Second qualifying round - FK Vojvodina (SRB)
A 0-3
Koļinko, Maksymenko, Nazarenko, Ulimbaševs, Kazačoks (Mežs 46), Stuglis (Takyi 21), Mickēvičs, Vivacqua, Bulvītis, Abdultaofik (Punculs 75), Šlampe. Coach: Roman Pylypchuk (UKR)
H 1-1 *Vivacqua (90+3)*
Davidovs, Maksymenko, Nazarenko, Mežs, Ulimbaševs, Bespalovs (Punculs 54), Vivacqua, Takyi (Stuglis 71), Bulvītis, Abdultaofik (Mickēvičs 46), Šlampe. Coach: Aleksandrs Koļinko (LVA)

BFC Daugavpils

2009 • Celtnieks (1,980) • bfcdaugava.lv
Coach: Kirils Kurbatovs;
(06/07/15) Sergejs Pogodins

2015

Date		Opp		Result	Scorers
14/03	h	Jelgava	L	0-1	
21/03	h	METTA/LU	W	2-0	Kokins, Ryzhevski
12/04	h	Gulbene	W	2-0	Kokins, Ryotaro (match annulled)
18/04	h	Ventspils	D	1-1	Kokins
04/05	a	Spartaks	D	1-1	Vērdiņš
11/05	a	Skonto	L	1-4	Ly
17/05	h	Liepāja	D	1-1	Miguel Cid
24/05	a	Jelgava	L	0-2	
31/05	a	METTA/LU	L	1-2	Sokolovs
21/06	a	Ventspils	L	0-3	
26/06	h	Spartaks	L	0-1	
11/07	a	Liepāja	D	1-1	Vērdiņš
27/07	a	Jelgava	L	0-1	
03/08	h	METTA/LU	D	0-0	
15/08	h	Ventspils	D	1-1	Ryzhevski
19/08	h	Skonto	D	0-0	
23/08	a	Spartaks	L	1-2	Ryzhevski
28/08	a	Skonto	D	0-0	
13/09	h	Liepāja	L	0-4	
19/09	h	Jelgava	L	0-2	
25/09	a	METTA/LU	W	2-0	Ryotaro (p), Ryzhevski
17/10	a	Ventspils	L	0-4	
24/10	a	Spartaks	L	0-2	
31/10	h	Skonto	L	2-3	Sokolovs, Ryzhevski
07/11	a	Liepāja	L	0-1	

Name	Nat	DoB	Pos	Aps	(s)	Gls
Marks Deružinskis		23/10/97	M	10	(4)	
Nikita Dobratuļins		20/07/95	M	4	(3)	
Vitālijs Dubrovskis		21/06/96	A	5	(4)	
Vladislavs Fjodorovs		27/09/96	M	2	(5)	
Tomoki Fujikawa	JPN	15/06/86	M	6	(7)	
Deniss Ivanovs		11/01/84	D	2		
Daniels Jakovļevs		06/08/97	D	2	(7)	
Ņikita Kaļiņins		26/11/95	M	14		
Dmitrijs Klimaševičs		16/04/95	D	25		
Ēriks Kokins		11/01/91	D	11	(1)	3
Vladislavs Kurakins		09/07/96	G	10		
Pāvels Liholetovs		04/07/97	M		(1)	
Viktors Litvinskis		07/02/96	D	22		
Ivan Lukanyuk	UKR	05/02/93	A	9		
Yoro Lamien Ly	SEN	27/08/88	M	3	(1)	1
Dmytro Makhniev	UKR	02/03/96	D	8		
Miguel Cid	POR	21/05/92	M	10		1
Artjoms Murdasovs		24/08/91	D	8	(10)	
Jevģēņijs Nerugals		22/02/89	G	15		
Dieu Nzembani-Biaka	FRA	28/03/94	M	2	(2)	
Pāvels Ostrovskis		24/05/94	D	4	(4)	
Jans Radevičs		14/03/89	M	11		
Nakano Ryotaro	JPN	13/06/88	M	22		2
Pavel Ryzhevski	BLR	03/03/81	A	20	(1)	5
Jurijs Sokolovs		12/09/83	M	22	(1)	2
Pāvels Tarasovs		16/01/88	M	1	(4)	
Ričards Tupits		05/06/99	M		(1)	
Aivars Ugarenko		05/06/97	D		(2)	
Edgars Vērdiņš		29/03/93	M	22	(1)	2
Verners Zalaks		05/04/97	A	5	(10)	

FB Gulbene

2005 • Gulbenes Sporta Centrs (1,500) • no website
Coach: Vladimirs Pačko

2015

Date		Opponent	Res	Scorers
15/03	h	Spartaks	L 0-3	
21/03	a	Ventspils	L 1-2	Solovjovs
14/04	a	Daugavpils	L 0-2	
18/04	a	Skonto	L 0-5	
01/05	h	Liepāja	L 0-2	
10/05	a	Jelgava	L 1-3	Volkovs
17/05	h	METTA/LU	L 0-2	
25/05	a	Spartaks	L 0-6	

NB Gulbene excluded from the league after round 8; all of their matches were annulled.

Name	Nat	DoB	Pos	Aps	(s)	Gls
Marks Bogdanovs		02/12/86	G	1		
Konstantīns Budilovs		21/03/91	M	3	(1)	
Viktors Čebotarjovs		08/04/99	A		(1)	
Aleksandrs Ivanovs		16/11/85	D	7		
Kirils Jeļkins		01/09/87	D	1		
Daniils Jevdakimovs		18/06/97	D		(1)	
Ruslans Ķeirāns		13/03/96	A	1	(3)	
Aleksandrs Kļimovs		16/11/91	M	6	(1)	
Igors Korabļovs		23/11/74	D	7	(1)	
Viktors Kurma		04/07/91	A	5		
Jānis Lapss		16/09/86	A	8		
Sergejs Mišins		02/06/87	M	1	(2)	
Alberts Nikoļskis		08/12/80	G	7		
Ņikita Pačko		05/04/99	M	4	(2)	
Vladislavs Pavļučenko		14/03/92	D	7		
Ernests Pilats		15/03/93	M	2	(3)	
Otto Šeļegovičs		27/05/97	D	1		
Aleksandrs Solovjovs		25/02/88	D	3		1
Gatis Štrauss		21/01/97	D	1	(1)	
Kirils Telegins		23/12/93	D	2	(2)	
Dmitrijs Telešs		19/07/92	D	8		
Vladimirs Volkovs		10/08/84	M	8		1
Jaroslavs Zoricovs		01/04/90	M	5	(2)	

FK Jelgava

2004 • Zemgales Olimpiskā centra (1,560); Olaine (2,500) • fkjelgava.lv
Major honours
Latvian Cup (4) 2010, 2014, 2015, 2016
Coach: Vitālijs Astafjevs

2015

Date		Opponent	Res	Scorers
14/03	a	Daugavpils	W 1-0	Bogdaškins
21/03	h	Skonto	D 0-0	
10/04	h	Liepāja	L 1-2	Kārkliņš
19/04	a	Spartaks	D 0-0	
01/05	a	METTA/LU	D 1-1	Kļuškins
10/05	h	Gulbene	W 3-1	Ošs, Eriba 2 (match annulled)
16/05	a	Ventspils	D 0-0	
24/05	h	Daugavpils	W 2-0	Malašenoks, Redjko
29/05	a	Skonto	L 0-1	
06/06	a	Liepāja	L 1-2	og (Savaļnieks)
19/06	h	Spartaks	D 1-1	Malašenoks
26/06	h	METTA/LU	W 1-0	Kļuškins
27/07	h	Daugavpils	W 1-0	Malašenoks
02/08	a	Skonto	W 3-2	Ošs, Bogdaškins, Sushkin
09/08	h	Liepāja	D 1-1	Bogdaškins (p)
15/08	h	Spartaks	W 1-0	Eriba
19/08	h	Ventspils	D 0-0	
24/08	a	METTA/LU	W 4-2	Malašenoks, Eriba, Kirijins, Sushkin
11/09	a	Ventspils	W 2-1	Bogdaškins 2
19/09	a	Daugavpils	W 2-0	Sushkin, Musa
26/09	h	Skonto	L 0-3	(w/o; original result 0-2)
02/10	a	Liepāja	L 0-1	
18/10	a	Spartaks	W 1-0	Ošs
25/10	h	METTA/LU	W 3-1	Malašenoks 3
07/11	h	Ventspils	D 0-0	

Name	Nat	DoB	Pos	Aps	(s)	Gls
Boriss Bogdaškins		21/02/90	M	23	(1)	5
Abdoulaye Diallo	SEN	21/10/92	D	22		
Antons Dresmanis		02/08/86	A		(1)	
Kennedy Eriba	NGA	21/12/90	M	19	(5)	4
Gints Freimanis		09/05/85	D	19		
Aleksandrs Gubins		16/05/88	D	18		
Kaspars Ikstens		05/06/88	G	25		
Artis Jaudzems		04/04/95	M	2	(9)	
Edgars Kārkliņš		21/07/91	D	3	(6)	1
Andrejs Kirijins		01/11/95	M	2	(10)	1
Gļebs Kļuškins		01/10/92	A	17	(3)	2
Dariusz Łatka	POL	14/09/78	M	16	(1)	
Artis Lazdiņš		03/05/86	M	6	(1)	
Oļegs Malašenoks		27/04/86	A	16	(5)	7
Ismaila Musa	SEN	26/02/96	A	2	(11)	1
Mārcis Ošs		25/07/91	D	24	(1)	3
Artūrs Pallo		27/02/89	M	7	(1)	
Valerijs Redjko		10/03/83	D	18	(2)	1
Igors Savčenkovs		03/11/82	D	4	(1)	
Rustam Sosranov	RUS	23/07/94	M	18	(3)	
Vyacheslav Sushkin	RUS	11/03/91	A	10	(1)	3
Andreas Themistocleous	CYP	01/03/94	D	4	(1)	

FK Liepāja

2014 • Daugava (5,083); Daugava Artificial (2,000) • fkliepaja.lv
Major honours
Latvian League (1) 2015
Coach: Viktors Dobrecovs

2015

Date		Opponent	Res	Scorers
13/03	h	Skonto	W 3-2	Gucs, Ikaunieks, Afanasjevs
20/03	h	Spartaks	D 0-0	
10/04	a	Jelgava	W 2-1	Ikaunieks, og (Freimanis)
17/04	a	METTA/LU	W 4-1	Hmizs, Mihadjuks, Jurkovskis, Ikaunieks
01/05	a	Gulbene	W 2-0	Afanasjevs, Ikaunieks (match annulled)
10/05	h	Ventspils	D 0-0	
17/05	a	Daugavpils	D 1-1	Hmizs
24/05	a	Skonto	L 0-1	
30/05	a	Spartaks	W 2-1	Afanasjevs, Grebis
06/06	h	Jelgava	W 2-1	Grebis, Hmizs
20/06	h	METTA/LU	W 3-1	Ikaunieks 2, Savaļnieks
04/07	a	Ventspils	D 3-3	Mihadjuks, Kamešs, Grebis
11/07	h	Daugavpils	D 1-1	Ikaunieks
27/07	h	Skonto	D 2-2	Ikaunieks, Strumia
01/08	h	Spartaks	W 4-1	Ikaunieks 2, Hmizs, Jurkovskis
09/08	a	Jelgava	D 1-1	Šadčins
15/08	h	METTA/LU	W 2-0	Šadčins, Maksimenko
28/08	h	Ventspils	W 3-2	Ivanovs, Ikaunieks, Kamešs
13/09	a	Daugavpils	W 4-0	Ikaunieks, Grebis, Hmizs, Afanasjevs
18/09	a	Skonto	W 2-1	Afanasjevs 2
27/09	a	Spartaks	W 2-0	Ikaunieks, Grebis
02/10	a	Jelgava	W 1-0	Ikaunieks
19/10	a	METTA/LU	W 4-0	Ikaunieks, Hmizs (p), Grebis, og (Stuglis)
31/10	a	Ventspils	L 1-3	Šadčins
07/11	h	Daugavpils	W 1-0	Ikaunieks

Name	Nat	DoB	Pos	Aps	(s)	Gls
Valerijs Afanasjevs		20/09/82	M	20	(2)	6
Alexis Carrasco	BOL	11/02/95	A	1	(1)	
Devids Dobrecovs		26/02/97	M	1	(2)	
Pāvels Doroševs		09/10/80	G	8		
Reinis Flaksis		03/04/94	D	5	(4)	
Kristaps Grebis		31/12/80	A	14	(5)	6
Toms Gucs		28/04/92	A	7	(8)	1
Dmitrijs Hmizs		31/07/92	M	24		6
Dāvis Ikaunieks		07/01/94	A	25		16
Deniss Ivanovs		31/08/97	D	14		1
Raivis Jurkovskis		09/12/96	M	2	(12)	2
Vladimirs Kamešs		28/10/88	D	10	(1)	2
Krišs Kārkliņš		31/01/96	M	9	(2)	
Oskars Kļava		08/08/83	D	13		
Andris Krušatins		01/09/96	M	1	(5)	
Vitālijs Maksimenko		08/12/90	D	2		1
Martín Mercau	ARG	09/08/95	A		(3)	
Pāvels Mihadjuks		27/05/80	D	20		2
Ilja Šadčins		02/07/94	M	7	(13)	3
Roberts Savaļnieks		04/02/93	M	9	(7)	1
Endijs Šlampe		24/07/94	D	21	(1)	
Gļebs Sopots		18/08/96	G	1		
Leonel Strumia	ARG	29/09/92	M	18	(3)	1
Cristián Torres	ARG	18/06/85	A	19	(1)	
Antons Tumanovs		16/04/97	D	8	(2)	
Artūrs Vaičulis		26/02/90	G		(1)	
Raivo Varažinskis		07/03/93	G	16		
Māris Verpakovskis		15/10/79	A		(1)	

FS METTA/LU

2006 • Hanzas Vidusskolas (460) • fsmetta.lv
Coach: Andris Riherts

2015

14/03	h	Ventspils	L	0-3	
21/03	a	Daugavpils	L	0-2	
12/04	h	Skonto	L	0-1	
17/04	h	Liepāja	L	1-4	Pētersons
01/05	h	Jelgava	D	1-1	Ševeļovs
08/05	h	Spartaks	L	1-2	Stuglis
17/05	a	Gulbene	W	2-0	Kalniņš, Juhnevičs (match annulled)
25/05	a	Ventspils	L	0-2	
31/05	h	Daugavpils	W	2-1	Vardanjans (p), Kalniņš
05/06	a	Skonto	L	0-4	
20/06	a	Liepāja	L	1-3	Vardanjans
26/06	a	Jelgava	L	0-1	
26/07	h	Ventspils	L	0-2	
03/08	a	Daugavpils	D	0-0	
10/08	h	Skonto	L	1-5	Pētersons
15/08	a	Liepāja	L	0-2	
19/08	a	Spartaks	D	2-2	N'Dekre, Pētersons
24/08	h	Jelgava	L	2-4	N'Dekre, Vardanjans
29/08	h	Spartaks	W	3-2	Ševeļovs, N'Dekre 2
19/09	a	Ventspils	L	0-3	
25/09	a	Daugavpils	L	0-2	
02/10	a	Skonto	L	1-3	Juhnevičs
19/10	h	Liepāja	L	0-4	
25/10	a	Jelgava	L	1-3	Pētersons
31/10	h	Spartaks	W	3-0	Ostrovskis, Uldriķis, Vardanjans

Name	Nat	DoB	Pos	Aps	(s)	Gls
Klāvs Bāliņš		09/02/96	M	1		
Maksims Daņilovs		02/08/86	A	4	(5)	
Oskars Darģis		03/06/93	G	8		
Dāvis Daugavietis		22/08/96	D	3		
Eduards Emsis		23/03/96	M	4	(3)	
Konstantīns Fjodorovs		28/04/96	A	4	(10)	
Aleksejs Giļņičs		29/05/93	D	22	(1)	
Ismael Guiti	FRA	24/07/91	D	11		
Edijs Joksts		21/07/92	D	4	(1)	
Ņikita Juhnevičs		28/05/97	M	11	(4)	2
Gatis Kalniņš		12/08/81	A	16	(3)	2
Mareks Labanovskis		09/09/97	M		(5)	
Artjoms Loginovs		20/07/93	A	1		
Elie N'Dekre	CIV	01/01/92	A	12		4
Dāvis Ošs		03/12/94	G	15		
Artis Ostrovskis		31/01/93	D	13		1
Armands Pētersons		15/12/90	M	23	(1)	4
Deniss Petrenko		14/03/88	D	8	(1)	
Kristaps Priedēns		12/01/90	M	6	(6)	
Rūdolfs Puķītis		14/02/91	D	12	(1)	
Kristers Putniņš		16/07/93	G	2		
Māris Riherts		11/02/92	D	2		
Romans Rožkovskis		03/12/90	D	5	(2)	
Kirils Ševeļovs		02/06/90	D	24		2
Rendijs Šibass		01/05/97	A		(1)	
Andrejs Siņicins		30/01/91	M	10		
Ingars Stuglis		12/02/96	M	18	(3)	1
Artūrs Švalbe		27/03/95	A		(1)	
Deniss Tarasovs		14/10/90	M		(1)	
Roberts Uldriķis		03/04/98	M	6	(9)	1
Edgars Vardanjans		09/05/93	M	23		4
Sergejs Vasiļjevs		13/06/96	A		(5)	

Skonto FC

1991 • Skonto (9,500) • skontofc.com
Major honours
Latvian League (15) 1991, 1992, 1993, 1994, 1995, 1996, 1997, 1998, 1999, 2000, 2001, 2002, 2003, 2004, 2010; Latvian Cup (8) 1992, 1995, 1997, 1998, 2000, 2001, 2002, 2012
Coach: Tamaz Pertia (GEO)

2015

13/03	a	Liepāja	L	2-3	Višņakovs, Ivanovs
21/03	a	Jelgava	D	0-0	
12/04	a	METTA/LU	W	1-0	Karašausks
18/04	h	Gulbene	W	5-0	Karašausks, Jiménez 2, Krivošeja, Bērenfelds (match annulled)
04/05	a	Ventspils	D	0-0	
11/05	h	Daugavpils	W	4-1	Gutkovskis 3, Kalonas
16/05	a	Spartaks	L	0-1	
24/05	h	Liepāja	W	1-0	Rode
29/05	h	Jelgava	W	1-0	Karašausks
05/06	h	METTA/LU	W	4-0	Karašausks (p), Gutkovskis 2, Ivanovs
28/06	h	Ventspils	D	1-1	Kovaļovs
12/07	h	Spartaks	W	2-1	Jermolajevs, Lukanyuk
27/07	a	Liepāja	D	2-2	Jermolajevs, Timofejevs
02/08	h	Jelgava	L	2-3	Gutkovskis, Bērenfelds
10/08	a	METTA/LU	W	5-1	Kovaļovs 3 (1p), Jermolajevs, Višņakovs
19/08	a	Daugavpils	D	0-0	
23/08	a	Ventspils	W	3-1	Kovaļovs, Karašausks, Gutkovskis
28/08	h	Daugavpils	D	0-0	
13/09	a	Spartaks	W	3-1	Ofosu-Appiah, Gutkovskis, Timofejevs
18/09	h	Liepāja	L	1-2	Gutkovskis
26/09	a	Jelgava	W	3-0	(w/o; original result 2-0 Kovaļovs (p), og (Redjko))
02/10	h	METTA/LU	W	3-1	Kovaļovs (p), Osipovs, Bērenfelds
25/10	h	Ventspils	L	0-2	
31/10	a	Daugavpils	W	3-2	Kovaļovs, Ofosu-Appiah, Karašausks
07/11	h	Spartaks	W	2-1	Gutkovskis, Sorokins

Name	Nat	DoB	Pos	Aps	(s)	Gls
Ņikita Bērenfelds		07/06/95	D	14	(6)	3
Vladislavs Gutkovskis		02/04/95	A	20	(3)	10
Dāvis Indrāns		06/06/95	M		(3)	
Vjačeslavs Isajevs		27/08/93	M	5	(2)	
Ņikita Ivanovs		25/03/96	A		(8)	2
Edgars Jermolajevs		16/06/92	M	19	(2)	3
Santiago Jiménez	COL	16/04/95	M		(3)	2
Mindaugas Kalonas	LTU	28/02/84	M	4	(2)	1
Artūrs Karašausks		29/01/92	A	16		6
Garry Kenneth	SCO	21/06/87	D	5	(2)	
Andrejs Kovaļovs		23/03/89	M	14	(1)	8
Igors Kozlovs		26/06/87	M	22		
Jurijs Krivošeja		14/01/97	A	2	(1)	1
Ivan Lukanyuk	UKR	05/02/93	A	3	(9)	1
Levan Makharadze	GEO	14/08/93	D	7		
Germans Māliņš		12/10/87	G	7		
Mārtiņš Milaševičs		12/02/92	M	2	(8)	
Yarleison Mosquera	COL	22/12/96	A		(1)	
Iván Murillo	COL	10/03/93	D	11	(4)	
Mike Ofosu-Appiah	GHA	29/12/89	D	6		2
Artjoms Osipovs		08/01/89	D	12	1	1
Artūrs Pallo		27/02/89	M	6		
Andrejs Pavlovs		22/02/79	G	18		
Renārs Rode		06/04/89	D	22	(1)	1
Vitālijs Smirnovs		28/06/86	D	8	(2)	
Vladislavs Sorokins		10/05/97	M	11	(2)	1
Dāvis Strods		24/04/96	D		(1)	
Oļegs Timofejevs		28/11/88	D	21	(1)	2
Maksim Usanov	RUS	05/03/85	D	2	(2)	
Aleksejs Višņakovs		03/02/84	M	18	(2)	2

FK Spartaks Jūrmala

2007 • Sloka (2,500); Kauguru Vidusskola (2,000) • spartaksjurmala.com
Coach: Roman Pylypchuk (UKR); (24/07/15) Aleksandrs Koļinko

2015

15/03	h	Gulbene	W	3-0	Mena, Gridin, Abdultaofik (match annulled)
20/03	a	Liepāja	D	0-0	
12/04	h	Ventspils	L	0-2	
19/04	h	Jelgava	D	0-0	
04/05	h	Daugavpils	D	1-1	Gridin
08/05	a	METTA/LU	W	2-1	Punculs, Mickēvičs
16/05	h	Skonto	W	1-0	Punculs
25/05	h	Gulbene	W	6-0	Abdultaofik, Silyuk, Stuglis 3, Ulimbaševs (match annulled)
30/05	h	Liepāja	L	1-2	Stuglis
06/06	a	Ventspils	L	0-2	
19/06	a	Jelgava	D	1-1	Bespalovs
26/06	a	Daugavpils	W	1-0	Šlampe
12/07	a	Skonto	L	1-2	Bulvītis (p)
01/08	a	Liepāja	L	1-4	Kazačoks
09/08	h	Ventspils	D	0-0	
15/08	a	Jelgava	L	0-1	
19/08	h	METTA/LU	D	2-2	Mežs, Mickēvičs
23/08	h	Daugavpils	W	2-1	Mickēvičs, Gauračs
29/08	a	METTA/LU	L	2-3	Mežs, Bulvītis
13/09	h	Skonto	L	1-3	Vivacqua
27/09	h	Liepāja	L	0-2	
03/10	a	Ventspils	L	1-3	Ulimbaševs
18/10	h	Jelgava	L	0-1	
24/10	a	Daugavpils	W	2-0	Gauračs 2
31/10	h	METTA/LU	L	0-3	
07/11	a	Skonto	L	1-2	Gauračs

Name	Nat	DoB	Pos	Aps	(s)	Gls
Ahmed Abdultaofik	NGA	25/04/92	A	11	(1)	2
Tyrone Aboagye	GHA	16/01/94	M	8	(1)	
Romāns Bespalovs		18/10/88	M	16	(4)	1
Nauris Bulvītis		15/03/87	D	26		2
Pavels Davidovs		30/12/80	G	13		
Edgars Gauračs		10/03/88	A	5	(1)	4
Sergei Gridin	KAZ	20/05/87	A	5	(1)	2
Dmitrijs Grigorjevs		13/05/92	G	12		
Jevgeņijs Kazačoks		12/08/95	M	12	(1)	1
Aleksandrs Koļinko		18/06/75	G	1		
Ričards Korzāns		03/05/97	A	2	(9)	
Maxym Maksymenko	UKR	28/05/90	D	22		
Kevin Mena	COL	19/02/93	A	9	(5)	1
Toms Mežs		07/09/89	D	20	(2)	2
Romāns Mickēvičs		23/03/93	M	23	(2)	4
Dmytro Nazarenko	UKR	14/09/87	D	10	(1)	
Pāvels Pilāts		04/02/97	M		(1)	
Ēriks Punculs		18/01/94	A	5	(14)	2
Serhiy Silyuk	UKR	05/06/85	D	6	(4)	1
Ingus Šlampe		31/01/89	D	23		1
Elvis Stuglis		04/07/93	A	7	(7)	4
Ferdinand Takyi	GER	28/08/94	A	3	(3)	
Eric Tuffor	GHA	25/10/95	M	4	(3)	
Deniss Ulimbaševs		12/03/92	M	23		2
Raivis Vitolnieks		29/07/95	M	1		
Francesco Vivacqua	ITA	19/06/94	M	19	(4)	1

FK Ventspils

1997 • OSC Ventspils (3,200) • fkventspils.lv

Major honours
Latvian League (6) 2006, 2007, 2008, 2011, 2013, 2014;
Latvian Cup (6) 2003, 2004, 2005, 2007, 2011, 2013
Coach: Jurģis Pučinskis;
(16/09/15) Paul Ashworth (ENG)

2015

Date		Opp	Res	Scorers
14/03	a	METTA/LU	W 3-0	Žigajevs, Diagne, og (Giļņičs)
21/03	h	Gulbene	W 2-1	Karlsons, Diagne (match annulled)
12/04	a	Spartaks	W 2-0	Jemeļins, Žigajevs
18/04	a	Daugavpils	D 1-1	Karlsons
04/05	h	Skonto	D 0-0	
10/05	a	Liepāja	D 0-0	
16/05	h	Jelgava	D 0-0	
25/05	h	METTA/LU	W 2-0	Diagne, Karlsons
06/06	h	Spartaks	W 2-0	Karlsons, Turkovs
21/06	h	Daugavpils	W 3-0	Siņeļņikovs, Turkovs, Mordatenko
28/06	a	Skonto	D 1-1	Turkovs
04/07	h	Liepāja	D 3-3	Mujeci 2 (1p), Krjauklis
26/07	a	METTA/LU	W 2-0	Mujeci 2
09/08	a	Spartaks	D 0-0	
15/08	a	Daugavpils	D 1-1	og (Nerugals)
19/08	a	Jelgava	D 0-0	
23/08	h	Skonto	L 1-3	Karlsons
28/08	a	Liepāja	L 2-3	Laizāns, Mujeci
11/09	h	Jelgava	L 1-2	Mordatenko
19/09	h	METTA/LU	W 3-0	Mujeci 3
03/10	a	Spartaks	W 3-1	Rugins, Karlsons 2
17/10	h	Daugavpils	W 4-0	Karlsons 2, Rugins, Rečickis
25/10	a	Skonto	W 2-0	Mujeci 2
31/10	h	Liepāja	W 3-1	Jemeļins, Tīdenbergs 2
07/11	a	Jelgava	D 0-0	

Name	Nat	DoB	Pos	Aps	(s)	Gls
Vitālijs Barinovs		04/05/93	D	9	(4)	
Nikola Boranijašević	SRB	31/05/89	D	4	(1)	
Cheikh Diagne	MTN	20/09/90	A	1	(2)	3
Ivan Dorić	SRB	07/07/95	M	4	(3)	
Visvaldis Ignatāns		03/08/91	M		(3)	
Antons Jemeļins		19/02/84	D	24		2
Ģirts Karlsons		07/06/81	A	22	(3)	9
Ņikita Koļesovs		25/09/96	D	4		
Ritus Krjauklis		23/04/86	D	20		1
Antons Kurakins		01/01/90	D	11		
Oļegs Laizāns		28/03/87	M	11	(1)	1
Vitālijs Meļņičenko		11/11/87	G	25		
Anastasijs Mordatenko		24/08/96	M	2	(11)	2
Ndue Mujeci	ALB	24/02/93	A	15	(6)	10
Simonas Paulius	LTU	12/05/91	M	25		
Vitālijs Rečickis		08/09/86	M	8	(5)	1
Ritvars Rugins		17/10/89	M	23		2
Alans Siņeļņikovs		14/05/90	M	22		1
Eduards Tīdenbergs		18/12/94	M	3	(8)	2
Daniils Turkovs		17/02/88	A	12	(7)	3
Jurijs Žigajevs		14/11/85	M	21	(1)	2
Vadims Žuļevs		01/03/88	M	9		

Top goalscorers

16	Dāvis Ikaunieks (Liepāja)
10	Vladislavs Gutkovskis (Skonto)
	Ndue Mujeci (Ventspils)
9	Ģirts Karlsons (Ventspils)
8	Andrejs Kovaļovs (Skonto)
7	Oļegs Malašenoks (Jelgava)
6	Valerijs Afanasjevs (Liepāja)
	Kristaps Grebis (Liepāja)
	Dmitrijs Hmizs (Liepāja)
	Artūrs Karašausks (Skonto)

Promoted clubs

FC Caramba/Dinamo

2015 • Arkādija artificial (650) • no website
Coach: Mihails Koņevs

Rīgas Futbola skola

1962 • Arkādija (1,000); Arkādija artificial (650)
• rigasfutbolaskola.lv
Coach: Jurijs Popkovs

Second level final table 2015

		Pld	W	D	L	F	A	Pts
1	FC Caramba/Dinamo	30	27	3	0	142	14	84
2	Valmiera Glass FK/BSS	30	24	3	3	89	33	75
3	Rīgas Futbola skola	30	24	2	4	94	25	74
4	FK 1625 Liepāja	30	18	7	5	91	39	61
5	FK Auda	30	13	9	8	62	43	48
6	Rēzeknes FA	30	14	3	13	56	66	45
7	FK Tukums 2000 TSS	30	13	3	14	65	70	42
8	AFA Olaine	30	9	9	12	41	49	36
9	JDFS Alberts	30	11	2	17	35	55	35
10	FK Ogre	30	9	6	15	52	70	33
11	Salaspils	30	8	6	16	31	57	30
12	FK Jēkabpils/JSC	30	9	3	18	46	99	30
13	FK Staiceles Bebri	30	8	3	19	42	84	27
14	JFK Saldus/Brocēnu NBJSS	30	7	3	20	22	59	24
15	FK Smiltene/BJSS	30	6	4	20	52	97	22
16	Preiļu BJSS	30	4	6	20	40	100	18

NB Rīgas Futbola skola were subsequently invited to Virslīga 2016.

Promotion/Relegation play-offs

(21/11/15 & 25/11/15)
Valmiera 1-3 METTA/LU
METTA/LU 6-2 Valmiera
(METTA/LU 9-3)

DOMESTIC CUP

Latvijas Kauss 2015/16

FIFTH ROUND

(18/07/15)
Rēzekne 0-4 METTA/LU
Valmiera 0-2 BFC Daugavpils
Salaspils 0-4 Liepāja
(19/07/15)
JDFS Alberts 0-4 Skonto
(29/07/15)
Auda 0-7 Ventspils
(05/08/15)
Preiļu 1-6 Spartaks
(16/09/15)
Caramba/Dinamo 0-1 Jelgava
Bye – Babīte

QUARTER-FINALS

(09/04/16)
Spartaks 3-1 Skonto *(Bespalovs 38, Bulvītis 46, Platonov 79p; Morozs 7)*
Ventspils 1-0 Liepāja *(Karlsons 3)*
(10/04/16)
METTA/LU 0-2 BFC Daugavpils *(Qurbanlı 27, Deružinskis 78)*
(13/04/16)
Babīte 2-3 Jelgava *(Kuzmins 28, Savaļnieks 80; Kauber 20, Turkovs 52, 73)*

SEMI-FINALS

(27/04/16 & 04/05/16)
BFC Daugavpils 0-1 Spartaks *(Klimaševičs 69og)*
Spartaks 1-0 BFC Daugavpils *(Kazačoks 70)*
(Spartaks 2-0)
Jelgava 0-1 Ventspils *(Diallo 38og)*
Ventspils 0-2 Jelgava *(Žuļevs 48og, Kļuškins 60)*
(Jelgava 2-1)

FINAL

(22/05/16)
Sloka, Jurmala
FK JELGAVA 1 *(Silich 20)*
FK SPARTAKS JŪRMALA 0
Referee: *Anufrijevs*
JELGAVA: *Ikstens, Freimanis, Redjko, Savčenkovs, Smirnovs, Bogdaškins (Malašenoks 90), Ryotaro, Kovaļovs, Silich (Klimovich 63), Kļuškins (Litvinskis 80), Lazdiņš*
SPARTAKS: *Kurakins, Kožans, Bulvītis, Šlampe, Kazačoks, Kiriļins (Stuglis 64), Kozeka, Pushnyakov, Felipe (Ulimbaševs 56), Kozlovs, Kozlov*

Jelgava lift the Latvian Cup for the third season in a row

LIECHTENSTEIN

Liechtensteiner Fussballverband (FLV)

Address	Landstrasse 149
	FL-9494 Schaan
Tel	+423 237 4747
Fax	+423 237 4748
E-mail	info@lfv.li
Website	lfv.li

President	Hugo Quaderer
General secretary	Roland Ospelt
Media officer	Anton Banzer
Year of formation	1934
National stadium	Rheinpark, Vaduz
	(7,838)

CLUBS

 1 FC Balzers

 2 USV Eschen/Mauren

 3 FC Ruggell

 4 FC Schaan

 5 FC Triesen

 6 FC Triesenberg

 7 FC Vaduz

0 — 5 — 10 km

0 — 10 miles

KEY:

⬤ – UEFA Europa League

Ruggell
3

Mauren
2
Eschen

Schaan
4

7 ······ ⬤ Vaduz

Triesenberg
6

Triesen
5

Balzers
1

Vaduz make history on three fronts

FC Vaduz's 2015/16 season was more memorable than most, bringing Giorgio Contini's team history-making satisfaction in every competition they entered.

A 44th domestic cup was claimed with a record winning scoreline, while there was also unprecedented success both in Europe, where Vaduz reached the third qualifying round of the UEFA Europa League, and in the Swiss Super League, where they finished higher than ever before in eighth place.

Record-breaking cup win for Contini's men	European ties won back-to-back for first time	Highest position reached in Swiss Super League

Retaining their place in Switzerland's top flight was Vaduz's primary concern, and they accomplished their mission with a game to spare thanks in no small part to the mid-season arrival of Albanian international striker Armando Sadiku, who struck seven goals in his 16 games and would go on to play – and score – for his country at UEFA EURO 2016.

Sadiku also netted the two goals that enabled Vaduz to defeat USV Eschen/Mauren 2-1 in the Liechtenstein Cup semi-final, but he was scarcely needed a month later in the final, where a crowd of 1,298 gathered in the Rheinpark to watch the perennial winners take apart FC Schaan. Seven different players got on the scoresheet, Paraguayan striker Mauro Caballero on four occasions, as Vaduz ran up a record 11-0 scoreline, eclipsing their previous highest winning margin of 9-0 against FC Ruggell in 2001.

On the international front, Vaduz won two successive European ties for the first time – in their 20th season of continental participation – but Liechtenstein's national side lost their last four UEFA EURO 2016 qualifiers without scoring, at which point Mario Frick, the country's record cap-holder and scorer, finally decided to bring his 22-year international career to an end at the age of 41.

EUROPE

FC Vaduz

First qualifying round - SP La Fiorita (SMR)
A 5-0 *Schürpf (5), Sutter (26), Pergl (41), Abegglen (78), Ciccone (90+2)*
Jehle, Pergl, Lang, Ciccone, Sutter (Kuzmanovic 72), Schürpf, Von Niederhäusern (Abegglen 46), Hasler (Kamber 66), Stahel, Neumayr, Aliji. Coach: Giorgio Contini (SUI)
H 5-1 *Kamber (25, 33), Schürpf (41), Muntwiler (71), Lang (84)*
Hirzel, Grippo, Lang, Ciccone (Kuzmanovic 57), Cecchini, Schürpf (Sutter 46), Von Niederhäusern, Neumayr, Muntwiler, Bühler, Kamber (Hasler 58). Coach: Giorgio Contini (SUI)

Second qualifying round - Nõmme Kalju FC (EST)
H 3-1 *Ciccone (20), Neumayr (53, 90+2)*
Jehle, Grippo, Pergl, Lang (Schürpf 84), Ciccone, Messaoud (Caballero 66), Stahel, Neumayr, Kukuruzović (Kamber 75), Muntwiler, Aliji. Coach: Giorgio Contini (SUI)
A 2-0 *Caballero (59), Aliji (74)*
Klaus, Grippo, Sutter, Cecchini, Von Niederhäusern (Aliji 62), Stahel, Neumayr (Kukuruzovic 71), Muntwiler, Bühler, Caballero, Kamber (Ciccone 62). Coach: Giorgio Contini (SUI)

Third qualifying round - FC Thun (SUI)
A 0-0
Klaus, Grippo, Pergl, Ciccone, Cecchini (Messaoud 72), Costanzo (Kamber 78), Von Niederhäusern, Kukuruzović, Muntwiler, Aliji, Caballero (Neumayr 66). Coach: Giorgio Contini (SUI)
H 2-2 *Costanzo (32), Neumayr (45+1)*
Klaus, Grippo, Pergl, Ciccone, Messaoud (Cecchini 77), Costanzo, Neumayr, Kukuruzović, Bühler, Aliji, Kamber (Hasler 69). Coach: Giorgio Contini (SUI)

European qualification 2016/17

Cup winner: FC Vaduz
(first qualifying round)

NATIONAL TEAM

Top five all-time caps
Mario Frick (125); **Peter Jehle** (119); Martin Stocklasa (113); **Franz Burgmeier** (99); Thomas Beck (92)

Top five all-time goals
Mario Frick (16); **Franz Burgmeier** (9); Thomas Beck, **Michele Polverino** & Martin Stocklasa (5)

Results 2015/16

05/09/15	Montenegro (ECQ)	A	Podgorica	L	0-2	
08/09/15	Russia (ECQ)	H	Vaduz	L	0-7	
09/10/15	Sweden (ECQ)	H	Vaduz	L	0-2	
12/10/15	Austria (ECQ)	A	Vienna	L	0-3	
23/03/16	Gibraltar	A	Gibraltar	D	0-0	
28/03/16	Faroe Islands	N	Marbella (ESP)	L	2-3	Gubser (73), Wolfinger (90+3)
06/06/16	Iceland	A	Reykjavik	L	0-4	

Appearances 2015/16

René Pauritsch (AUT)	04/02/64		MNE	RUS	SWE	AUT	Gib	Fro	Isl	Caps	Goals
Peter Jehle	22/01/82	Vaduz	G	G	G	G	G	G	G46	119	-
Seyhan Yildiz	30/04/89	Balzers	D	M	s72	s62	D61	D87	D80	22	-
Mario Frick	07/09/74	Balzers	D	D	D	D90				125	16
Daniel Kaufmann	22/12/90	Vaduz	D	D 40*	D	D	D	D	D	36	1
Martin Rechsteiner	15/02/89	Balzers	D	D	D	D	D	D	D	26	-
Michele Polverino	26/09/84	Ried (AUT)	M	M	M59	M	M	M		54	5
Andreas Christen	29/08/89	Balzers	M	s88	M83					24	-
Martin Büchel	19/02/87	Unterföhring (GER)	M86	M84	M	M	M	M	M	60	2
Sandro Wieser	03/02/93	Thun (SUI)	M66		D	M	M	M90		33	1
Franz Burgmeier	07/04/82	Vaduz	M76	D	M	M	D	D71		99	9
Nicolas Hasler	04/05/91	Vaduz	A	M					M90	39	1
Dennis Salanovic	26/02/96	Istra 1961 (CRO) /Balzers	s66	A88			M	M86	M	13	-
Niklas Kieber	04/03/93	Eschen/Mauren	s76	M77	s83	M62				9	-
Robin Gubser	17/04/91	Balzers	s86	s84	s59		s88	s69	A87	20	1
Mathias Sele	28/05/92	Eschen/Mauren		s77				s87	s84	3	-
Yves Oehri	15/03/87	YF Juventus (SUI)				D	D46			50	-
Marcel Büchel	18/03/91	Empoli (ITA)			M	A	A88	A69		4	-
Simon Kühne	30/04/94	St Gallen (SUI)			A72	s90	M46	s86		13	-
Daniel Brändle	23/01/92	Münsingen (SUI)				s46	s61	s71	M84	11	-
Sandro Wolfinger	24/08/91	Heimstetten (GER)					s46	M	M72	11	1
Philipp Ospelt	07/10/92	Wattens (AUT)						s90	s87	3	-
Maximilian Göppel	31/08/97	Balzers							D	1	-
Benjamin Büchel	04/07/89	Oxford (ENG)							s46	10	-
Aron Sele	02/09/96	Balzers							s72	1	-
Andreas Malin	31/01/94	Eschen/Mauren							s80	1	-
Pascal Foser	16/10/92	Balzers							s90	1	-

DOMESTIC CUP

FL1 Aktiv Cup 2015/16

FIRST ROUND

(25/08/15)
Balzers III 0-6 Schaan
Triesen II 1-3 Balzers II
Triesenberg II 0-5 Eschen/Mauren II

(26/08/15)
Schaan Azzurri 0-3 Ruggell
Triesen 1-4 Balzers

SECOND ROUND

(15/09/15)
Ruggell II 3-0 Eschen/Mauren II

(16/09/15)
Schaan 4-2 Balzers *(aet)*

(30/09/15)
Eschen/Mauren III 1-4 Balzers II
Schaan II 0-3 Ruggell

QUARTER-FINALS

(27/10/15)
Ruggell II 0-6 Eschen/Mauren

(03/11/15)
Ruggell 0-4 Vaduz

(04/11/15)
Balzers II 1-0 Vaduz U23
Schaan 3-2 Triesenberg *(aet)*

SEMI-FINALS

(05/04/16)
Eschen/Mauren 1-2 Vaduz *(Bärtsch 54; Sadiku 37, 45)*

(06/04/16)
Balzers II 2-2 Schaan *(Bürgler 78, Ferreira 85; D Nikolic 45+3, Zeciri 76) (aet; 3-5 on pens)*

FINAL

(04/05/16)
Rheinpark, Vaduz
FC VADUZ 11 *(Caballero 11, 13, 45, 77, Avdijaj 20, Borgmann 30, Messaoud 43, Sutter 68, 85, Schürpf 81, Hasler 90)*
FC SCHAAN 0
Referee: *Hänni*
VADUZ: *Klaus, Von Niederhäusern, Bühler, Gülen, Borgmann (Sutter 46), Hasler, Ciccone (Schürpf 46), Kamber, Caballero, Messaoud, Avdijaj (Sadiku 76)*
SCHAAN: *Thomann, M Nikolic (Walser 83), Hagmann, M Quaderer (Ismaili 46), F Quaderer, Rui Almeida, L Eberle, Mohammed, F Eberle (Schweiger 61), Eris, Zeciri*

LITHUANIA
Lietuvos futbolo federacija (LFF)

Address	Stadiono g. 2	**President**	Edvinas Eimontas
	LT-02106 Vilnius	**General secretary**	Nerijus Dunauskas
Tel	+370 5 2638741	**Media officer**	Vaiva Zizaitė
Fax	+370 5 2638740	**Year of formation**	1922
E-mail	v.zizaite@lff.lt	**National stadium**	LFF Stadium, Vilnius
Website	lff.lt		(5,067)

KEY

- ● UEFA Champions League
- ● UEFA Europa League
- ● Promoted
- ● Relegated

A LYGA CLUBS

  ① **FK Atlantas**

 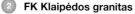 ② **FK Klaipėdos granitas**

  ③ **FK Kruoja**

 ④ **FK Spyris**
NB Renamed FK Kauno Žalgiris for 2016 season

 ⑤ **FC Stumbras**

 ⑥ **FK Sūduva**

  ⑦ **FC Šiauliai**

  ⑧ **FK Trakai**

  ⑨ **FK Utenis**

  ⑩ **FK Žalgiris**

PROMOTED CLUB

  ⑪ **FK Lietava**

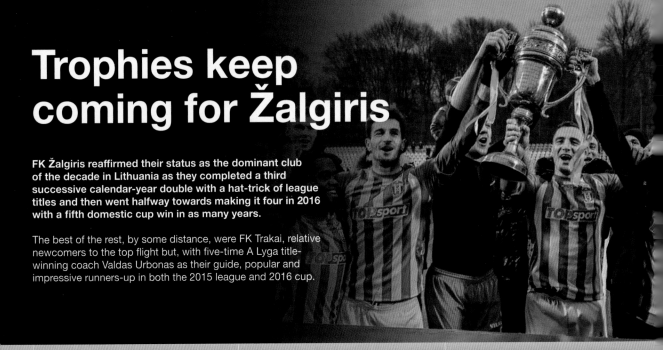

Trophies keep coming for Žalgiris

FK Žalgiris reaffirmed their status as the dominant club of the decade in Lithuania as they completed a third successive calendar-year double with a hat-trick of league titles and then went halfway towards making it four in 2016 with a fifth domestic cup win in as many years.

The best of the rest, by some distance, were FK Trakai, relative newcomers to the top flight but, with five-time A Lyga title-winning coach Valdas Urbonas as their guide, popular and impressive runners-up in both the 2015 league and 2016 cup.

A Lyga title hat-trick for Green Machine

Vilnius club claim fifth successive cup win

Trakai finish runners-up in league and cup

Domestic league

Žalgiris began the league campaign with a new coach in 38-year-old Valdas Dambrauskas, whose only top-flight experience had been a brief spell in charge of FK Ekranas, the club from Panevezys where Urbonas had won all of his championship titles before they folded at the end of 2014. Any doubts that the new man would be able to carry on the good work of his predecessor, Marek Zub, were quelled as Žalgiris won their first seven matches and 13 of their first 14.

Although Trakai put together a tidy winning streak of their own, and went on to maintain a high level of performance throughout the season, the chances of Žalgiris's title hat-trick bid ever coming unstuck remained remote. Victories were routine and frequent, and although FK Atlantas emulated Trakai by defeating them twice, the only other points dropped by the Green Machine were in an incongruous mid-season 2-2 draw at lowly FK Kruoja – a team that two months later would drop out of the division amidst claims that they had breached fair play regulations.

The league would be further put out of joint when another team, FK Klaipėdos granitas, were excluded two rounds before the end. By then, though, Žalgiris had the title in the bag, mathematical certainty having been provided on the penultimate day of October when Dambrauskas's men travelled to face bogey side Atlantas in the seaside town of Klaipeda and beat them 1-0 with a goal from leading scorer Linas Pilibaitis. By the end of term he had been usurped as the club's top marksman by another Lithuanian international, mid-season signing Darvydas Šernas, who shrugged off the disappointment of an ill-starred spell in Scotland with Ross County by scoring 17 times in 16 games to help his new team smash the 100-goal barrier.

Žalgiris's final points tally of 94 was ten more than they had managed in cruising to the previous season's title. Their 84-point mark of 2014 was emulated 12 months on by Trakai thanks to victories in three quarters of their matches and a sharp-shooting attack led by 25-goal Russian newcomer David Arshakyan. Trakai finished 14 points clear of third-placed Atlantas, but the biggest gap was the 22 points that separated fourth-placed FK Sūduva from fifth-placed FK Spyris, one of the three newly promoted clubs who all retained their top-flight status.

Domestic cup

Dambrauskas became the first Žalgiris coach to retain the Lithuanian Cup as the club captured the trophy for the fifth year in succession, defeating Trakai 1-0 thanks to a 99th-minute strike from, of all people, defender Linas Klimavičius, who had left Trakai for Žalgiris in the winter and was playing against his older brother Arūnas, newly recruited by Trakai. The final took place in Telsiai – the fifth different venue in five years at which Žalgiris had lifted the trophy. Trakai, furthermore, were the fifth different losing finalists in that sequence.

Europe

Trakai were the only one of the A Lyga's four European entrants to win a tie, indeed a match, in 2015, with Žalgiris's bid to make hay on foreign as well as domestic fields frustratingly halted by a 1-0 aggregate loss to a Malmö FF side that went on to compete in the group stage.

National team

The Lithuanian national side were placed under the command of a former star player in January 2016 as ex-FC Porto forward Edgaras Jankauskas, a coach of relatively limited experience, was sworn in as the replacement for Igoris Pankratjevas. The change came about after an uninspiring UEFA EURO 2016 qualifying series in which the team won just three of their ten games and finished fifth in their group.

DOMESTIC SEASON AT A GLANCE

A Lyga 2015 final table

		Pld	Home					Away					Total					Pts
			W	D	L	F	A	W	D	L	F	A	W	D	L	F	A	
1	**FK Žalgiris**	**36**	**16**	**0**	**2**	**54**	**9**	**15**	**1**	**2**	**50**	**16**	**31**	**1**	**4**	**104**	**25**	**94**
2	FK Trakai	36	15	2	1	52	10	12	1	5	40	23	27	3	6	92	33	84
3	FK Atlantas	36	13	2	3	40	13	8	5	5	25	21	21	7	8	65	34	70
4	FK Sūduva	36	11	2	5	44	14	10	2	6	32	20	21	4	11	76	34	67
5	FK Spyris	36	7	4	7	24	31	6	2	10	23	43	13	6	17	47	74	45
6	FK Utenis	36	6	7	5	22	20	5	2	11	19	30	11	9	16	41	50	42
7	FC Stumbras	36	6	3	9	24	40	5	5	8	27	34	11	8	17	51	74	41
8	FK Klaipėdos granitas	36	3	3	12	23	49	3	6	9	14	34	6	9	21	37	83	27
9	FC Šiauliai	36	4	3	11	18	33	1	2	15	19	61	5	5	26	37	94	20
10	FK Kruoja	36	2	4	12	15	38	2	4	12	8	34	4	8	24	23	72	20

NB FK Kruoja withdrew after round 24; FK Klaipėdos granitas excluded after round 34 – both clubs' remaining matches were awarded as 0-3 defeats.

European qualification 2016/17

 Champion/Cup winner: FK Žalgiris (second qualifying round)

 FK Trakai (first qualifying round)
FK Atlantas (first qualifying round)
FK Sūduva (first qualifying round)

Top scorer	Tomas Radzinevičius (Sūduva), 28 goals
Relegated clubs	FK Kruoja (withdrew), FC Šiauliai (withdrew), FK Klaipėdos granitas (excluded)
Promoted club	FK Lietava
Cup final	FK Žalgiris 1-0 FK Trakai (aet)

Team of the season
(4-4-2)

Coach: Urbonas *(Trakai)*

Vitkauskas *(Žalgiris)*

Česnauskis *(Trakai)* Kerla *(Žalgiris)* Klimavičius *(Trakai)* Švrljuga *(Žalgiris)*

Pilibaitis *(Žalgiris)* Šemberas *(Žalgiris)* Kuklys *(Žalgiris)* Mamaev *(Trakai)*

Radzinevičius *(Sūduva)* Arshakyan *(Trakai)*

Player of the season

Tomas Radzinevičius
(FK Sūduva)

Although he celebrated his 34th birthday in mid-season, former Lithuania forward Radzinevičius showed no sign of wear and tear as he racked up goal after goal to claim the A Lyga golden boot with a final tally of 28 and help the club from his home town of Marijampole qualify for the UEFA Europa League. The evergreen striker, who started his career with Sūduva before playing abroad in the Czech Republic and Poland, bagged two hat-tricks, the second of them in the A Lyga's biggest win of the season, 8-1 at Klaipėdos granitas.

Newcomer of the season

David Arshakyan
(FK Trakai)

Arshakyan was twiddling his thumbs as an unemployed free agent when Trakai coach Valdas Urbonas decided to take a gamble on the Russian striker, 20 years old at the time, in February 2015. Pre-season training went so well that the St Petersburg native was handed the team's prestigious No10 shirt, and before long he was taking the A Lyga by storm as not only one of its most prolific goalscorers – he ended up with 25 for the season – but also one of its biggest crowd pleasers as he spearheaded Trakai to second place.

NATIONAL TEAM

Top five all-time caps
Andrius Skerla (84); Deividas Šemberas (82); **Saulius Mikoliūnas** (75); Tomas Danilevičius (71); Žydrūnas Karčemarskas (66)

Top five all-time goals
Tomas Danilevičius (19); Antanas Lingis (12); Edgaras Jankauskas & Robertas Poškus (10); Virginijus Baltušnikas (9)

Results 2015/16

05/09/15	Estonia (ECQ)	A	Tallinn	L	0-1
08/09/15	San Marino (ECQ)	H	Vilnius	W	2-1	Černych (7), Spalvis (90+2)
09/10/15	Slovenia (ECQ)	A	Ljubljana	D	1-1	Novikovas (79p)
12/10/15	England (ECQ)	H	Vilnius	L	0-3
23/03/16	Romania	A	Giurgiu	L	0-1
26/03/16	Russia	A	Moscow	L	0-3
29/05/16	Estonia	H	Klaipeda	W	2-0	Valskis (30), Černych (45)
01/06/16	Latvia	A	Liepaja	L	1-2	Černych (84)
06/06/16	Poland	A	Krakow	D	0-0

Appearances 2015/16

Coach: Igoris Pankratjevas /(12/01/16) Edgaras Jankauskas	09/08/64 12/03/75		EST	SMR	SVN	ENG	Rou	Rus	Est	Lva	Pol	Caps	Goals
Giedrius Arlauskis	01/12/87	Watford (ENG)	G	G 50*		G						23	-
Deividas Česnauskis	30/06/81	Trakai	D79		s63			D60	D74			64	4
Marius Žaliūkas	10/11/83	unattached	D	D	D90							29	1
Linas Klimavičius	10/04/89	Trakai /Žalgiris	D	D	D	D		D		D		9	-
Egidijus Vaitkūnas	08/08/88	Žalgiris	D			s82	D	s46	s74	D	D	26	-
Fedor Černych	21/05/91	Jagiellonia (POL)	M	M	M63	M	M83	M80	M53	M	M50	26	5
Mindaugas Panka	01/05/84	M. Petach-Tikva (ISR) /H. Petach-Tikva (ISR)	M78		M	M		s83				40	-
Vykintas Slivka	29/04/95	Den Bosch (NED)	M	M53	M69	M	M68	M86	s53	M57	M69	12	-
Artūras Žulpa	10/06/90	Aktobe (KAZ) /Tobol (KAZ)	M	M	M	M	M	M			M90	17	-
Arvydas Novikovas	18/12/90	Bochum (GER)	M	M	M	M63			M	M	M	30	3
Deivydas Matulevičius	08/04/89	Tobol (KAZ) /Botoşani (ROU)	A63	s73		s86	s68	s60				28	5
Lukas Spalvis	27/07/94	AaB (DEN)	s63	A	A	A86	A68	A60	A82	A	AaB	15	2
Deimantas Petravičius	02/09/95	Nottingham Forest (ENG)	s78		s69	s63	M83	s46				7	-
Georgas Freidgeimas	10/08/87	Žalgiris /Irtysh (KAZ)	s79	D	D	D	D				D	24	-
Vaidas Slavickas	26/02/86	Sūduva	D73	D					D74	D	s60	10	-
Linas Pilibaitis	05/04/85	Žalgiris		M82								30	-
Vytautas Černiauskas	12/03/89	Dinamo Bucureşti (ROU)		s53				G				4	-
Karolis Chvedukas	21/04/91	Sūduva		s82								14	-
Emilijus Zubas	10/07/90	Podbeskidzie (POL)			G		G		G		G	9	-
Tomas Mikuckis	13/01/83	SKA-Energia (RUS)			s90	D		D				16	-
Vytautas Andriuškevičius	08/10/90	Cambuur (NED)				D82	D	D46				23	-
Edvinas Girdvainis	17/01/93	Marbella (ESP)					D		D	D	D	4	-
Vytautas Lukša	14/08/84	Žalgiris					M58	s80	s74	s79		26	-
Saulius Mikoliūnas	02/05/84	Žalgiris					s58	M46				75	5
Mantas Kuklys	10/06/87	Žalgiris					s68	s86	M	M	M46	15	-
Ernestas Veliulis	22/08/92	Sūduva					s83					1	-
Ovidijus Verbickas	04/07/93	Atlantas						M				1	-
Markas Beneta	08/07/93	Atlantas						s60				1	-
Arūnas Klimavičius	05/10/82	Trakai							D			42	3
Dovydas Norvilas	05/04/93	Atlantas							M82	M79	s69	3	-
Nerijus Valskis	04/08/87	Trakai							M74	s57	s50	7	1
Rolandas Baravykas	23/08/95	Atlantas							s74		D60	3	-
Simonas Paulius	12/05/91	Ventspils (LVA)							s82		s46	2	-
Donatas Kazlauskas	31/03/94	Atlantas							s82		s90	6	-
Ernestas Šetkus	25/05/85	Sivasspor (TUR)								G		8	-

EUROPE

FK Žalgiris

CHAMPIONS LEAGUE

Second qualifying round - Malmö FF (SWE)
A 0-0
Vitkauskas, Šemberas, Kendysh, Vaitkūnas, Jorge Chula (Nyuiadzi 58), Švrljuga, Kerla, Lukša (Janušauskas 78), Šernas (Lucas Gaúcho 86), Pilibaitis, Kuklys. Coach: Valdas Dambrauskas (LTU)
H 0-1
Vitkauskas, Šemberas, Kendysh, Vaitkūnas, Švrljuga, Kerla, Lukša (Lucas Gaúcho 64), Šernas (Jorge Chula 77), Nyuiadzi, Pilibaitis, Kuklys (Janušauskas 34). Coach: Valdas Dambrauskas (LTU)
Red card: Kerla 79

FK Kruoja

EUROPA LEAGUE

First qualifying round - Jagiellonia Białystok (POL)
H 0-1
Matuzas, Crisan, Pocevičius, Beniušis (Birškys 80), Salamanavičius (Diarra 85), Tautvydas Eliošius, Navikas, Bagočius (Tadas Eliošius 75), Jankauskas, Strockis, Skroblas. Coach: Mykola Trubachov (UKR)
A 0-8
Matuzas, Pocevičius, Beniušis (Barba 59), Salamanavičius (Tadas Eliošius 46), Tautvydas Eliošius, Navikas, Bagočius (Birškys 57), Tarasenko, Jankauskas, Strockis, Skroblas. Coach: Mykola Trubachov (UKR)

FK Atlantas

EUROPA LEAGUE

First qualifying round - PFC Beroe Stara Zagora (BUL)
H 0-2
Malinauskas, Bartkus (Žukauskas 46), Maksimov, Panyukov, Jokšas, Virkšas, Norvilas (Beneta 65), Baravykas (Baranauskas 69), Epifanov, Gnedojus, Vēževičius. Coach: Konstantin Sarsania (RUS)
A 1-3 Vēževičius (65)
Malinauskas, Maksimov, Panyukov (Baranauskas 77), Jokšas, Virkšas (Beneta 57), Norvilas (Šveikauskas 55), Baravykas, Gnedojus, Vēževičius, Žarskis, Verbickas. Coach: Konstantin Sarsania (RUS)

FK Trakai

EUROPA LEAGUE

First qualifying round - HB Tórshavn (FRO)
H 3-0 Bychenok (20), Arshakyan (61), Solomin (86)
Rapalis, Klimavičius, Česnauskis, Arshakyan, Solomin, Januševskij, Kochanauskas (Šēgžda 40), Šilēnas, Zasavitschi, Bychenok, Mamaev. Coach: Valdas Urbonas (LTU)
A 4-1 Arshakyan (30, 90+3p), Solomin (38), Bychenok (83p)
Rapalis, Klimavičius (Apakidze 55), Česnauskis, Arshakyan, Solomin, Januševskij, Šilēnas, Zasavitschi (Stanulevičius 70), Bychenok, Mamaev (Masenzovas 63), Šēgžda. Coach: Valdas Urbonas (LTU)

Second qualifying round - Apollon Limassol FC (CYP)
A 0-4
Rapalis, Klimavičius, Česnauskis, Arshakyan, Solomin, Stanulevičius (Šēgžda 68), Januševskij, Šilēnas, Zasavitschi (Apakidze 88), Bychenok, Mamaev. Coach: Valdas Urbonas (LTU)
H 0-0
Rapalis, Klimavičius, Česnauskis, Arshakyan, Solomin (Gaurilovas 75), Januševskij, Šilēnas, Zasavitschi (Stanulevičius 78), Bychenok, Mamaev, Šēgžda (Apakidze 59). Coach: Valdas Urbonas (LTU)

DOMESTIC LEAGUE CLUB-BY-CLUB

FK Atlantas

1962 • Centrinis (4,428); Centrinis Artificial (1,500) • atlantas.lt
Major honours
Lithuanian Cup (2) 2001, 2003
Coach: Konstantin Sarsania (RUS)

2015

Date		Opponent		Result	Scorers
28/03	h	Trakai	W	5-1	Panyukov 4, Maksimov
08/03	a	Utenis	W	2-1	Panyukov 2
14/03	h	Klaipēdos granitas	L	0-1	
17/03	h	Šiauliai	W	5-0	Maksimov, Panyukov 4 (1p)
02/04	a	Žalgiris	L	0-2	
07/04	h	Stumbras	W	2-0	Maksimov, Norvilas
11/04	h	Kruoja	W	3-1	Vēževičius 2, Panyukov
17/04	a	Sūduva	D	1-1	Norvilas
25/04	a	Trakai	L	0-2	
02/05	h	Utenis	D	1-1	Panyukov
11/05	a	Klaipēdos granitas	W	2-1	Maksimov 2 (1p)
16/05	a	Šiauliai	D	0-0	
19/05	h	Spyris	L	0-1	
28/05	h	Spyris	W	2-0	Panyukov 2 (1p)
01/06	h	Žalgiris	W	4-2	Panyukov 3, Maksimov
21/06	a	Kruoja	W	2-1	Virkšas, Jokšas
27/07	a	Utenis	D	0-0	
01/08	h	Klaipēdos granitas	D	1-1	Verbickas
05/08	a	Stumbras	D	2-2	Vēževičius 2
08/08	a	Šiauliai	W	2-0	Vēževičius, Verbickas
12/08	h	Trakai	W	1-0	Verbickas
16/08	h	Spyris	W	2-1	Panyukov 2 (1p)
24/08	a	Žalgiris	W	1-0	Panyukov
28/08	h	Stumbras	W	4-1	Rakauskas 2, Bartkus, Norvilas (p)
12/09	h	Kruoja	W	3-0	(w/o)
15/09	a	Sūduva	L	1-3	Verbickas
19/09	a	Trakai	L	1-5	Maksimov
22/09	h	Sūduva	L	0-1	
26/09	a	Utenis	W	1-0	Norvilas
04/10	a	Klaipēdos granitas	W	5-1	Maksimov, Norvilas (p), Vēževičius, Verbickas, Baranauskas
17/10	h	Šiauliai	W	4-1	Beneta, Baranauskas, Verbickas, og (Rapalavičius)
24/10	a	Spyris	D	1-1	Malinauskas
30/10	h	Žalgiris	L	0-1	
08/11	a	Stumbras	W	2-0	Maksimov, Norvilas
21/11	a	Kruoja	W	3-0	(w/o)
28/11	h	Sūduva	W	2-1	Bartkus, Maksimov

No	Name	Nat	DoB	Pos	Aps	(s)	Gls
31	Mantas Adamonis		13/05/99	G	2		
4	Lukas Artimavičius		12/08/94	D	4		
21	Lukas Baranauskas		26/11/93	A	7	(13)	2
23	Rolandas Baravykas		23/08/95	D	31		
6	Andrius Bartkus		21/01/86	M	32		2
17	Markas Beneta		08/07/97	A	3	(5)	1
99	Oleg Dmitriev	RUS	18/11/95	M	3	(4)	
25	Aleksei Epifanov	RUS	21/07/83	D	26		
88	Dominykas Galkevičius		16/10/86	M	1	(6)	
12	Edvinas Gertmonas		01/06/96	G	15		
30	Kazimieras Gnedojus		28/02/86	D	10		
18	Andrius Jokšas		12/01/79	D	20	(1)	1
10	Aurimas Jurgelevičius		09/01/97	M	3	(7)	
15	Erlandas Juška		05/03/97	D	1		
95	Julius Kasparavičius		03/04/94	A	1	(3)	
33	Marius Kazlauskas		01/05/84	D	5		
9	Rokas Krušnauskas		04/11/95	A	2	(1)	
7	Maksim Maksimov	RUS	04/11/95	A	23	(6)	10
1	Mindaugas Malinauskas		11/08/83	G	17		1
13	Donatas Navikas		30/06/83	M	1	(5)	
20	Dovydas Norvilas		05/04/93	M	29	(1)	6
11	Andrei Panyukov	RUS	25/09/94	A	16	(4)	20
8	Rokas Petrikas		30/06/98	M		(1)	
14	Skirmantas Rakauskas		07/01/96	M	8	(11)	2
28	Justas Raziūnas		23/01/95	M	13	(1)	
29	Artur Skuratovič		15/01/96	A	1	(3)	
5	Ričardas Šveikauskas		09/04/97	D	3		
22	Simonas Urbys		07/11/95	M	2	(5)	
74	Ovidijus Verbickas		04/07/93	M	16		6
32	Robertas Vēževičius		05/01/86	M	23	(7)	6
19	Dovydas Virkšas		01/07/97	A	4	(5)	1
35	Edgaras Žarskis		04/05/94	D	19		
77	Gerardas Žukauskas		07/07/94	M	15	(7)	

FK Klaipėdos granitas

2012 • Centrinis (4,428); Centrinis Artificial (1,500) • klaipedos-granitas.lt
Coach: Gediminas Jarmalavičius

2015

01/03	a Spyris	L	1-2	D Lukošius
08/03	h Žalgiris	L	0-2	
14/03	a Atlantas	W	1-0	Vitukynas
19/03	h Kruoja	L	0-3	
23/03	a Sūduva	L	1-3	D Lukošius
04/04	h Trakai	L	2-4	Papšys, Laukžemis
07/04	a Utenis	W	3-1	Vitukynas, Gnedojus, Laukžemis
11/04	a Stumbras	D	1-1	Potapov
19/04	a Šiauliai	D	2-2	Laukžemis, Vitukynas
26/04	h Spyris	D	1-1	Laukžemis
01/05	a Žalgiris	L	0-6	
11/05	h Atlantas	L	1-2	Laukžemis
17/05	a Kruoja	D	1-1	og (Matuzas)
26/05	h Sūduva	L	1-2	Laukžemis
31/05	a Trakai	L	0-5	
06/06	h Utenis	W	2-1	Papšys, Laukžemis
21/06	h Stumbras	L	1-5	og (Elza)
25/06	a Šiauliai	D	0-0	
30/06	a Spyris	L	1-4	Papšys
25/07	h Žalgiris	L	1-2	Papšys
01/08	a Atlantas	D	1-1	Pejić
06/08	h Kruoja	W	2-0	Sušić, Papšys
15/08	a Sūduva	L	0-1	
20/08	h Trakai	L	1-4	Vitukynas
27/08	a Utenis	D	0-0	
11/09	a Stumbras	D	1-1	D Lukošius
17/09	h Šiauliai	W	4-1	Vitukynas 2, Papšys 2
20/09	h Spyris	D	2-2	Pejić, Papšys
27/09	a Žalgiris	L	0-2	
04/10	h Atlantas	L	1-5	Duminika
17/10	a Kruoja	W	3-0	(w/o)
25/10	h Sūduva	L	1-8	Papšys
30/10	a Trakai	L	0-3	
10/11	h Utenis	L	1-2	Peretiatko
22/11	h Stumbras	L	0-3	(w/o)
28/11	h Šiauliai	L	0-3	(w/o)

No	Name	Nat	DoB	Pos	Aps	(s)	Gls
17	Alison Silva	BRA	01/06/88	M	3		
13	Rokas Borusas		03/01/90	D	23	(4)	
70	Dragomir Duminika	RUS	28/03/89	M	10		1
77	Almantas Eidėjus		04/02/98	A	1		
20	Kazimieras Gnedojus		28/02/86	D	15		1
97	Vili Grigaitis		28/09/97	M	4	(7)	
70	Artioma Jerošenko		06/04/94	D	1	(8)	
77	Zigmantas Jesipovas		08/11/94	M	10	(5)	
4	Laurynas Kielaitis		16/09/96	D		(1)	
2	Tamirlan Kozubaev	KGZ	01/07/94	D	11		
90	Gediminas Kruša		31/10/90	M	9		
29	Artūras Kurbangalijevas		29/06/90	M	5	(1)	
23	Franko Lalić	CRO	05/02/91	G	4		
92	Karolis Laukžemis		11/03/92	M	16	(2)	7
25	Aivaras Lukošius		16/04/88	D	3	(5)	
99	Deividas Lukošius		24/01/91	A	25	(5)	3
92	Rokas Mickūnas		13/11/98	M		(1)	
88	Tadas Norbutas		25/02/94	G	11		
10	Marius Papšys		13/05/89	M	30		9
6	Juro Pejić	CRO	25/11/91	A	13		2
17	Nikita Peretiatko		25/10/98	D	2	(1)	1
5	Egor Potapov	RUS	21/09/93	D	32		1
8	Liutauras Rimkus		16/08/97	M	9	(16)	
92	Andrew Samuels	CAN	20/08/93	M		(2)	
23	Tadas Simaitis		29/12/90	G	18		
19	Levas Sonas		02/08/97	M	5	(8)	
34	Alen Stepanjan	EST	23/07/91	M	3	(3)	
14	Mindaugas Strauka		29/06/90	M	7	(1)	
50	Pavle Sušić	SRB	15/04/88	A	12		1
15	Dmitrij Šiškin		17/07/87	D	23		
7	Rokas Urbelis		27/01/90	A	25	(5)	
9	Justas Vilavičius		20/12/92	M	2	(2)	
11	Titas Vitukynas		23/10/94	M	31		6

FK Kruoja

2001 • Pakruojis (2,000); PFA, Panevezys (1,089) • fkkruoja.lt
Coach: Aidas Dambrauskas; (08/04/15) Divaldo Alves (ANG); (26/07/15) Mykola Trubachov (UKR)

2015

01/03	h Sūduva	L	1-3	Birškys
09/03	a Trakai	D	1-1	Beniušis
15/03	h Utenis	W	1-0	Bagočius
19/03	a Klaipėdos granitas	W	3-0	Strockis, Beniušis (p), Birškys
22/03	h Šiauliai	D	2-2	Birškys, Tautvydas Eliošius
02/04	a Spyris	W	2-0	Bagočius, Tautvydas Eliošius
08/04	h Žalgiris	L	0-2	
11/04	a Atlantas	L	1-3	Birškys
19/04	a Stumbras	L	0-2	
28/04	a Sūduva	L	0-3	
02/05	h Trakai	L	0-2	
12/05	a Utenis	D	0-0	
17/05	h Klaipėdos granitas	D	1-1	Beniušis
27/05	a Šiauliai	L	0-1	
02/06	h Spyris	L	1-2	Crisan
17/06	h Žalgiris	D	2-2	Beniušis 2 (1p)
21/06	h Atlantas	L	1-2	Beniušis (p)
25/06	h Stumbras	D	1-1	Edelino Ié
26/07	a Trakai	D	0-0	
01/08	h Utenis	W	2-1	Birškys, Salamanavičius
06/08	a Klaipėdos granitas	L	0-2	
11/08	h Sūduva	L	1-2	Pocevičius
16/08	h Šiauliai	L	2-3	Barba, Beniušis
23/08	a Spyris	D	1-1	Beniušis
29/08	a Žalgiris	L	0-3	(w/o)
12/09	a Atlantas	L	0-3	(w/o)
16/09	h Stumbras	L	0-3	(w/o)
19/09	a Sūduva	L	0-3	(w/o)
27/09	a Trakai	L	0-3	(w/o)
03/10	a Utenis	L	0-3	(w/o)
17/10	h Klaipėdos granitas	L	0-3	(w/o)
24/10	h Šiauliai	L	0-3	(w/o)
30/10	h Spyris	L	0-3	(w/o)
09/11	a Žalgiris	L	0-3	(w/o)
21/11	h Atlantas	L	0-3	(w/o)
28/11	h Stumbras	L	0-3	(w/o)

No	Name	Nat	DoB	Pos	Aps	(s)	Gls
22	Maxym Adamenko	UKR	19/01/91	D	5	(3)	
18	Aivaras Bagočius		10/10/87	A	22		2
7	Vadym Barba	UKR	07/09/86	M	4	(1)	1
8	Ričardas Beniušis		23/04/80	A	23	(1)	8
21	Tomas Birškys		05/11/92	M	16	(1)	5
12	Aivaras Bražinskas		01/11/90	G	1		
23	Horia Crisan	ROU	27/06/91	D	15		1
36	Boubakary Diarra	MLI	30/08/93	M	9	(4)	
66	Diogo Gouveia	POR	25/01/95	M	11	(4)	
25	Prince Eboagwu	NGA	01/06/86	D	1		
45	Edelino Ié	POR	01/05/94	M	9	(8)	1
19	Eldon Maquemba	POR	08/06/84	A	1	(1)	
11	Tadas Barčius		01/03/90	M	1	(2)	
10	Tautvydas Eliošius		03/11/91	M	17	(1)	2
15	Felipe	BRA	16/12/88	G	3		
88	Dominykas Galkevičius		16/10/86	M	5		
27	Darius Jankauskas		27/04/92	M	6	(5)	
1	Martynas Matuzas		28/08/89	G	20		
7	Arnas Mikaitis		21/07/92	D	8	(3)	
80	Taras Mikhailyuk	UKR	26/08/84	D	5		
13	Donatas Navikas		30/06/83	M	5		
50	Sigitas Olberkis		19/04/97	M	1	(6)	
4	Valdas Pocevičius		16/05/86	D	21		1
9	Tomas Salamanavičius		31/03/93	A	10	(9)	1
84	Alfredas Skroblas		11/03/84	D	23		
77	Donatas Strockis		23/03/87	D	18	(2)	1
23	Olexandr Tarasenko	UKR	11/12/78	D	4		
26	Robertas Visockas		17/09/96	D		(1)	

FK Spyris

2005 • S.Dariaus ir S.Girėno (9,180); NFA (1,500) • no website
Coach: Laimis Bičkauskas

2015

01/03	h Klaipėdos granitas	W	2-1	Olencevičius, Velička
07/03	a Šiauliai	W	2-1	Velička, Rekish
14/03	h Stumbras	L	1-4	Sikorskis
18/03	h Žalgiris	L	0-1	
02/04	h Kruoja	L	0-2	
09/04	a Sūduva	L	1-5	Miškinis
12/04	a Trakai	L	0-2	
18/04	h Utenis	W	2-1	Velička, Rekish
26/04	a Klaipėdos granitas	D	1-1	Rekish
01/05	h Šiauliai	W	2-1	Velička (p), Palma
10/05	h Stumbras	W	4-2	Sendžikas, Bučma, Velička, Rekish
15/05	a Žalgiris	L	0-4	
19/05	h Atlantas	W	1-0	Bučma
28/05	a Atlantas	L	0-2	
02/06	a Kruoja	W	2-1	Velička, Moroz
07/06	h Sūduva	W	2-1	Velička 2 (1p)
18/06	h Trakai	L	0-3	
23/06	a Utenis	W	3-2	Sendžikas 2 (1p), Velička (p)
30/06	h Klaipėdos granitas	W	4-1	Rekish 2, Bučma, Velička (p)
24/07	a Šiauliai	W	2-1	og (Petrauskas), Rekish
30/07	h Stumbras	D	1-1	Moroz
10/08	a Žalgiris	L	0-3	
16/08	a Atlantas	L	1-2	Velička
23/08	h Kruoja	D	1-1	Daukša
30/08	h Sūduva	L	0-1	
12/09	a Trakai	L	0-5	
15/09	h Utenis	D	1-1	Krušnauskas
20/09	a Klaipėdos granitas	D	2-2	Rekish, Krušnauskas
26/09	h Šiauliai	W	3-2	Rekish 2, Sendžikas
03/10	a Stumbras	L	0-1	
17/10	h Žalgiris	L	2-4	Velička, Moroz
24/10	h Atlantas	D	1-1	Sendžikas
30/10	a Kruoja	W	3-0	(w/o)
07/11	a Sūduva	L	1-5	Rekish (p)
21/11	h Trakai	L	1-5	Krušnauskas
28/11	a Utenis	L	1-5	Krušnauskas

No	Name	Nat	DoB	Pos	Aps	(s)	Gls
8	Tomas Bučma		27/01/94	M	29	(2)	3
77	Paulius Daukša		09/09/93	D	30		1
2	Rytis Daunys		03/07/95	D		(2)	
20	Ignas Dedura		01/06/78	D	26		
6	Matas Gavrilovas		22/11/95	M	7	(13)	
4	Klimas Gusočenko		09/03/89	M	17		
7	Karolis Gvildys		13/05/94	M	12	(2)	
18	Edvinas Kloniūnas		28/06/98	M	1	(4)	
99	Rokas Krušnauskas		04/11/95	A	8	(3)	4
29	Audrius Kšanavičius		14/01/77	M		(8)	
5	Ernestas Mickevičius		11/11/96	M	2	(5)	
1	Deividas Mikelionis		08/05/95	G	29		
3	Marius Miškinis		19/02/92	D	23	(2)	1
22	Jevgenij Moroz		20/01/90	M	28	(2)	3
14	Benas Olencevičius		07/08/95	M	8	(11)	1
23	Giuseppe Palma	ITA	20/01/94	M	18		1
9	Dmitri Rekish	BLR	14/09/88	M	34	(1)	11
11	Lukas Sendžikas		28/11/92	M	20	(7)	5
13	Rokas Sikorskis		13/04/95	A	12	(19)	1
33	Modestas Stonys		17/01/80	G	6		
10	Donatas Stulga		22/08/95	M	8	(10)	
15	Karolis Šilkaitis		02/06/96	D	18	(3)	
21	Darius Šinkūnas		13/10/92	D	24	(6)	
17	Andrius Velička		05/04/79	A	25	(3)	12

FC Stumbras

2010 • S.Dariaus ir S.Girėno (9,180);
NFA (1,500) • fcstumbras.lt
Coach: Darius Gvildys

2015

28/02	h	Šiauliai	W 3-1	Skripnikas, Račkus, Rimkevičius
07/03	h	Sūduva	L 0-2	
14/03	a	Spyris	W 4-1	Rimkevičius 2 (2p), Račkus, Mačiulis
17/03	a	Trakai	L 1-3	Rimkevičius
03/04	h	Utenis	L 0-1	
07/04	a	Atlantas	L 0-2	
11/04	h	Klaipėdos granitas	D 1-1	Dapkus
19/04	h	Kruoja	W 2-0	Stradalovas 2
24/04	a	Šiauliai	D 1-1	Djabrailov
03/05	a	Sūduva	D 1-1	Djabrailov
10/05	h	Spyris	L 2-4	Rimkevičius 2
14/05	h	Trakai	L 2-3	Rimkevičius 2
19/05	a	Žalgiris	L 1-4	Rimkevičius
28/05	h	Žalgiris	L 0-4	
01/06	a	Utenis	D 1-1	Rimkevičius
21/06	a	Klaipėdos granitas	W 5-1	Račkus, Mačiulis, Stradalovas, Dapkus, Rimkevičius
25/06	a	Kruoja	D 1-1	Rimkevičius
30/06	a	Šiauliai	W 2-1	Rimkevičius 2 (1p)
22/07	h	Sūduva	L 0-4	
30/07	a	Spyris	D 1-1	Upstas
05/08	h	Atlantas	D 2-2	Grigaravičius, Sadauskas
09/08	h	Trakai	L 0-5	
13/08	h	Žalgiris	L 1-7	Rimkevičius
20/08	h	Utenis	W 3-1	Snapkauskas, Rimkevičius, Janonis
28/08	a	Atlantas	L 1-4	Stradalovas
11/09	h	Klaipėdos granitas	D 1-1	Mačiulis
16/09	a	Kruoja	W 3-0	(w/o)
23/09	h	Šiauliai	W 3-2	Rimkevičius 2, Račkus
27/09	a	Sūduva	L 0-3	
03/10	h	Spyris	W 1-0	Rimkevičius (p)
18/10	a	Trakai	L 1-3	Stradalovas
26/10	a	Žalgiris	L 0-4	
31/10	a	Utenis	L 1-3	Rimkevičius
08/11	h	Atlantas	L 0-2	
22/11	a	Klaipėdos granitas	W 3-0	(w/o)
28/11	h	Kruoja	W 3-0	(w/o)

No	Name	Nat	DoB	Pos	Aps	(s)	Gls
8	Vilius Armanavičius		08/05/95	M	17	(5)	
29	Ainas Bareikis		30/09/96	M	14	(12)	
27	Aleksandr Belov	RUS	24/05/96	A	1	(1)	
22	Romualdas Blaževičius		06/04/97	M	2	(10)	
55	Lukas Čerkauskas		12/03/94	D	28	(2)	
21	Martynas Dapkus		16/02/93	M	27	(2)	2
95	Mohamed Eli Djabrailov	RUS	24/03/93	M	17	(10)	2
15	Mantvydas Eiza		15/05/93	M	12	(2)	
27	Mindaugas Grigaravičius		15/07/92	M	14	(1)	1
10	Klaidas Janonis		13/05/97	M	2	(8)	1
17	Laimonas Jurevičius		07/01/96	D	4		
1	Giedrius Kvedaras		09/07/91	G	32		
23	Nerijus Mačiulis		01/04/85	M	27	(2)	3
19	Lukas Pangonis		25/08/95	D	6	(2)	
30	Ignas Prieskenis		11/04/96	M	2	(7)	
16	Lukas Pupšys		19/07/96	D	1	(3)	
5	Audrius Račkus		27/12/88	D	29		4
11	Artūras Rimkevičius		14/04/83	A	26	(1)	20
18	Rimvydas Sadauskas		21/07/96	D	28		1
12	Aleksandr Sikorski	RUS	01/06/95	G	1	(1)	
7	Erikas Skripnikas		07/01/95	M	15	(8)	1
20	Tomas Snapkauskas		12/06/92	D	24		1
25	Deividas Stradalovas		15/04/87	A	6	(13)	5
9	Klaudijus Upstas		30/10/94	A	21	1	
13	Mantas Varanauskas		14/01/86	A	1	(4)	
99	Martynas Zaleckis		30/01/96	D	6	(1)	

FK Sūduva

1968 • ARVI (6,250); ARVI Arena (2,500) •
fksuduva.lt
Major honours
Lithuanian Cup (2) 2006, 2009
Coach: Aleksandar Veselinović (SRB)

2015

01/03	a	Kruoja	W 3-1	Radzinevičius 2, Uggė (p)
07/03	a	Stumbras	W 2-0	Radzinevičius 2
14/03	h	Trakai	L 0-1	
18/03	a	Utenis	D 1-1	Veliulis
23/03	h	Klaipėdos granitas	W 3-1	Radzinevičius 2, Chvedukas
04/04	a	Šiauliai	W 3-0	Chvedukas, Kiselevskis, Radzinevičius
09/04	h	Spyris	W 5-1	Radzinevičius 2, Uggė (p), Šilėnas, Chvedukas
13/04	a	Žalgiris	L 0-2	
17/04	h	Atlantas	D 1-1	Chvedukas
28/04	h	Kruoja	W 3-0	Chvedukas, Šilėnas, Radzinevičius
03/05	h	Stumbras	D 1-1	Radzinevičius
09/05	a	Trakai	L 1-4	Radzinevičius
16/05	h	Utenis	L 0-1	
26/05	a	Klaipėdos granitas	W 2-1	Baranovskij, Veliulis
31/05	h	Šiauliai	W 6-0	Živković, Chvedukas, Radzinevičius 3, Tamulevičius
07/06	a	Spyris	L 1-2	Tamulevičius
23/06	h	Žalgiris	L 1-2	Šoblinskas
22/07	a	Stumbras	W 4-0	Radzinevičius 2, Jamak 2
02/08	h	Trakai	L 0-1	
06/08	a	Utenis	D 0-0	
11/08	a	Kruoja	W 2-1	Chvedukas, Radzinevičius
15/08	h	Klaipėdos granitas	W 1-0	Kecap
19/08	a	Šiauliai	W 2-0	Kecap, Uggė
30/08	a	Spyris	W 1-0	Slavickas
12/09	a	Žalgiris	L 0-3	
15/09	a	Atlantas	W 3-1	Veliulis, Radzinevičius 2
19/09	h	Kruoja	W 3-0	(w/o)
22/09	a	Atlantas	W 1-0	Uggė
27/09	h	Stumbras	W 3-0	Jamak, Radzinevičius (p), Veliulis
03/10	a	Trakai	L 0-2	
18/10	h	Utenis	W 3-0	Radzinevičius 2, Slavickas
25/10	a	Klaipėdos granitas	W 8-1	Veliulis 4, Radzinevičius 3, Baranovskij
31/10	h	Šiauliai	W 5-0	Jamak, Šoblinskas, Radzinevičius 2 (1p), Slavickas
07/11	h	Spyris	W 5-1	Kecap, og (Dedura), Laukžemis, Veliulis, Uggė
22/11	a	Žalgiris	L 1-3	Veliulis
28/11	a	Atlantas	L 1-2	Jamak (p)

No	Name	Nat	DoB	Pos	Aps	(s)	Gls
40	Domantas Antanavičius		18/11/98	M		(5)	
8	Vilmantas Bagdanavičius		01/10/92	M	12	(2)	
2	Valentin Baranovskij		15/10/86	M	18	(13)	2
31	Džiugas Bartkus		07/11/89	G	31		
16	Audrius Brokas		20/08/90	A		(11)	
13	Karolis Chvedukas		21/04/91	M	29		7
12	Paulius Grybauskas		02/06/84	G	4		
5	Darius Isoda		27/07/94	D	8	(2)	
24	Nermin Jamak	BIH	30/08/86	M	17	(2)	5
45	Markas Kardokas		19/09/97	M	2	(2)	
14	Admir Kecap	SRB	25/11/87	A	17	(2)	3
94	Povilas Kiselevskis		05/07/94	M	19	(3)	1
33	Miloš Kovačević	SRB	31/03/91	D	7	(2)	
32	Karolis Laukžemis		11/03/92	M	4	(12)	1
3	Nikola Prebiraček	SRB	23/03/87	D	18	(2)	
10	Tomas Radzinevičius		05/06/81	A	33		28
19	Vaidas Slavickas		26/02/86	D	16		3
20	Vaidotas Šilėnas		16/07/85	M	13		2
88	Marius Šoblinskas		23/08/87	M	21	(11)	2
9	Edvardas Tamulevičius		04/01/94	A		(5)	2
17	Ilya Tsyvilko	BLR	27/07/92	D	12	(3)	
91	Maximiliano Uggė	ITA	24/09/91	D	33		5
21	Arminas Vaskela		12/08/90	M	14	(3)	
7	Ernestas Veliulis		22/08/92	M	24	(10)	10
22	Marko Živković	SRB	17/05/94	D	35		1

FC Šiauliai

1995 • Savivaldybės (3,000); Gytariai (1,500) •
fcsiauliai.lt
**Coach: Tomas Ražanauskas;
(24/07/15) Deivis Kančelskis**

2015

28/02	a	Stumbras	L 1-3	Radavičius (p)
07/03	h	Spyris	L 1-2	Jasaitis
13/03	a	Žalgiris	L 2-3	Leščius, og (Kendysh)
17/03	a	Atlantas	L 0-5	
22/03	a	Kruoja	D 2-2	Shevchuk, Gedminas
04/04	h	Sūduva	L 0-3	
09/04	a	Trakai	L 0-4	
12/04	h	Utenis	L 0-2	
19/04	a	Klaipėdos granitas	D 2-2	Shevchuk, Nesterenko
24/04	h	Stumbras	D 1-1	Radavičius (p)
01/05	a	Spyris	L 1-2	Radavičius
11/05	h	Žalgiris	L 1-6	Fomenka
16/05	h	Atlantas	D 0-0	
27/05	h	Kruoja	W 1-0	Fomenka
31/05	a	Sūduva	L 0-6	
19/06	a	Utenis	L 0-1	
25/06	h	Klaipėdos granitas	D 0-0	
30/06	h	Stumbras	L 1-2	Jasaitis
22/07	h	Spyris	L 1-2	Šešplaukis
01/08	a	Žalgiris	L 0-5	
05/08	h	Trakai	W 3-1	Gedminas 2, Radavičius (p)
08/08	h	Atlantas	L 0-2	
16/08	a	Kruoja	W 3-2	Rapalavičius, Radavičius (p), Jasaitis
19/08	h	Sūduva	L 0-2	
27/08	h	Trakai	L 2-4	Šešplaukis, Tamulevičius
11/09	a	Utenis	L 0-2	
17/09	a	Klaipėdos granitas	L 1-4	Šešplaukis
23/09	a	Stumbras	L 2-3	Medžiaušis, Godin
26/09	a	Spyris	L 2-3	Godin (p), Mika
07/10	h	Žalgiris	L 1-4	Godin
17/10	a	Atlantas	L 1-4	Birškys
24/10	h	Kruoja	W 3-0	(w/o)
31/10	a	Sūduva	L 0-5	
08/11	a	Trakai	L 0-4	
22/11	a	Utenis	L 2-3	Tamulevičius 2
28/11	h	Klaipėdos granitas	W 3-0	(w/o)

No	Name	Nat	DoB	Pos	Aps	(s)	Gls
18	Rimvydas Balčiūnas		05/04/97	M			
20	Tomas Birškys		05/11/92	M	4	(1)	1
11	Tamaz Chargeishvili	GEO	12/01/89	M	9	(2)	
20	Tadas Eliošius		01/03/90	A	13	(1)	
28	Yuriy Fomenka	UKR	31/12/86	A	6		2
3	Vytas Gašpuitis		04/03/94	D	28	(1)	
9	Rokas Gedminas		13/04/90	M	13	(5)	3
18	Olexiy Godin	UKR	02/02/83	M	9		3
67	Luka Hadžić	CRO	28/02/93	M	4	(1)	
8	Maksim Ivanov	RUS	27/03/96	M	15	(4)	
8	Eligijus Jankauskas		22/06/98	A	3	(12)	
7	Edvinas Jasaitis		11/04/90	M	21	(2)	3
32	Simonas Jurgilas		14/10/98	D	11	(2)	
67	Donatas Konikas		21/04/98	A		(8)	
27	Sergejs Kožans	LVA	16/02/86	D	7		
44	Rokas Lekiatas		07/11/98	D		(6)	
18	Rolandas Leščius		05/09/94	M	7	(5)	1
9	Lucas Moraes	BRA	15/02/90	A	4	(1)	
17	Dovydas Medžiaušis		23/01/95	A	21	(6)	1
22	Adomas Mika		25/07/96	M	9	(4)	1
12	Edgaras Mikšėnas		25/10/97	G	2	(1)	
88	Kyrylo Nesterenko	UKR	01/03/92	D	8	(1)	1
70	Sigitas Olberkis		19/04/97	M	2	(1)	
6	Donatas Petrauskas		16/03/84	M	21		
34	Justas Petravičius		10/01/96	M	4	(5)	
12	Ernestas Pilypas		17/05/90	D	17	(1)	
77	Ramūnas Radavičius		20/01/81	D	23	(1)	5
5	Tomas Rapalavičius		14/04/94	D	26	(2)	1
14	Serhiy Semenyuk	UKR	27/01/91	D	9		
19	Serhiy Shevchuk	UKR	21/09/90	M	10	(2)	2
02	Deividas Šešplaukis		02/02/98	M	5	(7)	3
88	Edvardas Tamulevičius		04/01/94	A	14		3
1	Milvydas Tupikas		01/01/98	G		(1)	
38	Jonas Ulberkis		12/06/98	A		(3)	
95	Bekhan Usmanov	RUS	16/07/93	M	4		
30	Povilas Valinčius		16/05/89	G	32		
57	Modestas Vorobjovas		30/12/95	M	13	(4)	

FK Trakai

2005 • LFF, Vilnius (5,067); Trakai (2,500) • fkt.lt
Coach: Valdas Urbonas

2015

Date		Opponent	Res		Scorers
28/02	a	Atlantas	L	1-5	Kochanauskas
09/03	h	Kruoja	D	1-1	Kochanauskas
14/03	a	Sūduva	W	1-0	og (Radzinevičius)
17/03	h	Stumbras	W	3-1	Arshakyan, Mamaev 2 (1p)
21/03	h	Utenis	W	5-1	Solomin, Arshakyan 3, Mamaev
04/04	a	Klaipėdos granitas	W	4-2	Arshakyan, Česnauskis, Januševskij, Kochanauskas
09/04	h	Šiauliai	W	4-0	Gurenko, Kochanauskas 2, Bychenok
12/04	h	Spyris	W	2-0	Klimavičius, Mamaev
17/04	h	Žalgiris	W	2-1	Gurenko, Bychenok
25/04	h	Atlantas	W	2-0	Januševskij, Šėgžda
02/05	a	Kruoja	W	2-0	Bychenok, Kochanauskas
09/05	h	Sūduva	W	4-1	Bychenok, Januševskij, Kochanauskas, Zasavitschi
14/05	a	Stumbras	W	3-2	Kochanauskas, Mamaev (p), Arshakyan
27/05	a	Utenis	L	0-1	
31/05	h	Klaipėdos granitas	W	5-0	Arshakyan 3, Kochanauskas, Gurenko
18/06	h	Spyris	W	3-0	Arshakyan 2, Kochanauskas
27/07	h	Kruoja	D	0-0	
02/08	a	Sūduva	W	1-0	Arshakyan
05/08	a	Šiauliai	L	1-3	Šilėnas
09/08	a	Stumbras	W	5-0	og (Snapkauskas), og (Račkus), Šėgžda, Stanulevičius, Šilėnas
12/08	a	Atlantas	L	0-1	
16/08	h	Utenis	W	2-1	Šilėnas, Arshakyan
20/08	a	Klaipėdos granitas	W	4-1	Valskis 2, Bychenok (p), Šilėnas
27/08	a	Šiauliai	W	4-2	Arshakyan 3 (1p), Šilėnas
12/09	h	Spyris	W	5-0	Gurenko, Bychenok, Arshakyan, Stanulevičius, Valskis
16/09	h	Žalgiris	L	0-2	
19/09	h	Atlantas	W	5-1	Šilėnas, Valskis, Arshakyan, Mamaev, Shevchuk
23/09	a	Žalgiris	W	2-1	Klimavičius, Arshakyan
27/09	a	Kruoja	W	3-0	(w/o)
03/10	a	Sūduva	W	2-0	Valskis, Arshakyan
18/10	h	Stumbras	W	3-1	Česnauskis, Valskis, Klimavičius
25/10	a	Utenis	D	1-1	Arshakyan (p)
30/10	h	Klaipėdos granitas	W	3-0	Valskis, Arshakyan 2
08/11	h	Šiauliai	W	4-0	Šilėnas, Shevchuk, og (Mika), Gurenko
21/11	a	Spyris	W	5-1	Arshakyan 2 (1p), Gurenko 2, Mamaev
28/11	a	Žalgiris	L	0-3	

No	Name	Nat	DoB	Pos	Aps	(s)	Gls
4	Nikoloz Apakidze	GEO	04/04/92	D	4	(11)	
10	David Arshakyan	RUS	16/08/94	A	33	(1)	25
77	Aleksandr Bychenok	BLR	30/05/85	M	24	(2)	6
7	Deividas Česnauskis		30/06/81	D	31		2
22	Edvardas Gaurilovas		18/06/94	D	28		
41	Artem Gurenko	BLR	18/06/94	M	23	(4)	7
1	Justinas Januševskij		26/03/94	D	25	(1)	3
5	Andrius Kazakevičius		28/03/91	D		(1)	
2	Linas Klimavičius		10/04/89	D	33		3
18	Lukas Kochanauskas		27/02/90	A	16		10
19	Mantas Leonavičius		19/01/94	D		(3)	
33	Andrius Lipskis		16/02/88	M	2	(6)	
17	Povilas Malinauskas		20/10/94	M	4	(9)	
79	Yuri Mamaev	RUS	03/02/84	M	32	(2)	7
30	Rokas Masenzovas		02/08/94	M		(6)	
1	Marius Rapalis		22/03/83	G	33		
29	Serhiy Shevchuk	UKR	21/09/90	M	2	(7)	2
11	Ronald Solomin		23/03/91	A	11	(13)	1
14	Rokas Stanulevičius		10/02/94	M	10	(15)	2
96	Donatas Šėgžda		16/01/96	A	8	(18)	2
27	Nerijus Valskis		04/08/87	M	14		7
24	Evgheny Zasavitschi	MDA	24/11/92	M	32		1
16	Lukas Žukauskas		18/06/93	G	2		

FK Utenis

1933 • Utenis (3,000); Visaginas Artificial (1,000) • utenosutenis.lt
Coach: Mindaugas Čepas

2015

Date		Opponent	Res		Scorers
02/03	a	Žalgiris	L	0-2	
08/03	h	Atlantas	L	1-2	Jeriomenko
15/03	a	Kruoja	L	0-1	
18/03	h	Sūduva	D	1-1	Kavaliauskas
21/03	a	Trakai	L	1-5	M Krasnovskis
03/04	a	Stumbras	W	1-0	Grigaravičius
07/04	h	Klaipėdos granitas	L	1-3	Kazubovičius
12/04	a	Šiauliai	W	2-0	Kazubovičius, og (Hadžić)
18/04	a	Spyris	L	1-2	M Krasnovskis
26/04	h	Žalgiris	L	0-2	
02/05	a	Atlantas	D	1-1	Freidgeimas
12/05	h	Kruoja	D	0-0	
16/05	a	Sūduva	W	1-0	P Krasnovskis
27/05	h	Trakai	W	1-0	P Krasnovskis
01/06	h	Stumbras	D	1-1	Freidgeimas
06/06	a	Klaipėdos granitas	L	1-2	Vereshchak
19/06	h	Šiauliai	W	1-0	Trachinski
23/06	h	Spyris	L	2-3	P Krasnovskis 2 (2p)
27/06	h	Žalgiris	L	0-3	
27/07	a	Atlantas	D	0-0	
30/07	a	Kruoja	L	1-2	Mastianica
06/08	h	Sūduva	D	0-0	
16/08	a	Trakai	L	1-2	Mastianica
20/08	a	Stumbras	L	1-3	Mastianica
27/08	h	Klaipėdos granitas	D	0-0	
11/09	h	Šiauliai	W	2-0	P Krasnovskis 2 (1p)
15/09	a	Spyris	D	1-1	Savastas
19/09	a	Žalgiris	L	3-4	Mastianica 2, Aleksandravičius
26/09	a	Atlantas	L	0-1	
03/10	h	Kruoja	W	3-0	(w/o)
18/10	a	Sūduva	L	0-3	
25/10	h	Trakai	D	1-1	Freidgeimas (p)
31/10	h	Stumbras	W	3-1	Kazubovičius, Trachinski, Fridrikas
10/11	a	Klaipėdos granitas	W	2-1	Mastianica, P Krasnovskis
22/11	h	Šiauliai	W	3-2	Mastianica, Kazubovičius 2
28/11	h	Spyris	W	4-1	Kazubovičius, Vereshchak, og (Šinkūnas), Savastas

No	Name	Nat	DoB	Pos	Aps	(s)	Gls
5	Julius Aleksandravičius		13/01/95	D	29	(1)	1
17	Andrius Arlauskas		16/01/86	M	2	(5)	
4	Lukas Artimavičius		12/08/94	D	9	(2)	
10	Žilvinas Banys		25/02/86	M	6	(2)	
23	Mademba Cisse	MLI	04/05/95	A		(1)	
23	Tomas Dombrauskis		24/09/96	M	13	(3)	
4	Martynas Dūda		23/01/93	D	6	(3)	
20	Yuriy Flyak	UKR	24/04/94	M	5		
3	Robertas Freidgeimas		21/02/89	D	25	(1)	3
25	Mantas Fridrikas		13/09/88	D	31		1
1	Mindaugas Grigaravičius		04/05/93	M	11	(2)	1
22	Daniel Gunevič		20/02/92	D	9		
24	Valentin Jeriomenko		19/02/89	M	27	(3)	1
77	Vitalijus Kavaliauskas		02/07/83	A	4	(3)	1
21	Darius Kazubovičius		19/02/95	A	14	(11)	6
8	Mykolas Krasnovskis		08/07/94	M	16	(6)	2
29	Povilas Krasnovskis		29/04/89	M	21	(2)	7
12	Pavel Leus		15/09/78	G	25		
9	Edgaras Mastianica		26/10/88	A	34		7
1	Ignas Plūkas		08/12/93	G	10		
11	Volodymyr Sadocha	UKR	19/02/94	M		(1)	
7	Linas Savastas		24/01/86	M	23	(4)	2
40	Ilya Trachinski	BLR	29/05/89	M	13	(13)	2
2	Aurimas Tručinskas		25/10/94	M	23		
88	Erikas Vainoras		26/04/96	M	3	(8)	
27	Yuriy Vereshchak	UKR	04/04/94	A	7	(15)	2
13	Gabrielius Zagurskas		13/05/92	D	19	(2)	

FK Žalgiris

1947 • LFF (5,067) • fkzalgiris.lt
Major honours
Lithuanian League (6) 1991, 1992, 1999, 2013, 2014, 2015; Lithuanian Cup (10) 1991, 1993, 1994, 1997, 2003 (autumn), 2012, 2013, 2014, 2015, 2016
Coach: Valdas Dambrauskas

2015

Date		Opponent	Res		Scorers
02/03	h	Utenis	W	2-0	Elivelto 2
08/03	a	Klaipėdos granitas	W	2-0	Lukša, Wilk
13/03	h	Šiauliai	W	3-2	Kendysh, Elivelto 2
18/03	a	Spyris	W	1-0	Nyuiadzi
03/04	h	Atlantas	W	2-0	Pilibaitis, Kuklys
08/04	a	Kruoja	W	2-0	Šemberas (p), Janušauskas
13/04	a	Sūduva	W	2-0	Janušauskas, Elivelto
18/04	a	Trakai	L	1-2	Šemberas (p)
26/04	a	Utenis	W	2-0	Švrljuga, Lukša
01/05	h	Klaipėdos granitas	W	6-0	Pilibaitis, Wilk, Elivelto, Janušauskas 2, Švrljuga
11/05	a	Šiauliai	W	6-1	Pilibaitis, Wilk, Kuklys, Pilibaitis, Janušauskas
15/05	h	Spyris	W	4-0	Švrljuga 2, Pilibaitis, Elivelto
19/05	h	Stumbras	W	4-1	Kuklys, Kendysh, Andreou, Švrljuga
28/05	a	Stumbras	W	4-0	Pilibaitis 2, Andreou 2
01/06	a	Atlantas	L	2-4	Pilibaitis
17/06	a	Kruoja	D	2-2	Kuklys, Pilibaitis
23/06	a	Sūduva	W	2-1	Jorge Chula, Kerla
27/06	a	Utenis	W	3-0	Elivelto, Kuklys, Janušauskas
25/07	a	Klaipėdos granitas	W	2-1	Janušauskas, Kendysh
31/07	h	Šiauliai	W	5-0	Šernas 2, Kendysh, og (Jurgilas), Pilibaitis
10/08	h	Spyris	W	3-0	Nyuiadzi 2, Pilibaitis
13/08	a	Stumbras	W	7-1	Šernas 2, Pilibaitis (p), Eliandro 3, Jankauskas
24/08	h	Atlantas	L	0-1	
29/08	h	Kruoja	W	3-0	(w/o)
12/09	h	Sūduva	W	3-0	Šernas 2, Nyuiadzi
16/09	a	Trakai	W	2-0	Kuklys, Kendysh
19/09	h	Utenis	W	4-3	Švrljuga, Šernas 2, Lucas Gaúcho
23/09	h	Trakai	L	1-2	Švrljuga
27/09	a	Klaipėdos granitas	W	2-0	Kuklys, Pilibaitis
04/10	a	Šiauliai	W	4-1	Šernas 2, Šemberas, Kendysh
17/10	a	Spyris	W	4-2	Kerla, Šernas 2, og (Gvildys)
26/10	h	Stumbras	W	4-0	Šernas (p), Pilibaitis 2, Lukša
30/10	a	Atlantas	W	1-0	Pilibaitis
07/11	h	Kruoja	W	3-0	(w/o)
22/11	a	Sūduva	W	3-1	Šernas 3
28/11	h	Trakai	W	3-0	Šernas, Elivelto, Kuklys

No	Name	Nat	DoB	Pos	Aps	(s)	Gls
14	Kristis Andreou	CYP	12/09/94	A	2	(13)	3
45	Edvinas Baniulis		03/01/97	A	1	(1)	
38	Dominykas Barauskas		28/04/97	D		(1)	
12	Eliandro	BRA	23/04/90	A	2	(9)	3
17	Tautvydas Eliošius		03/11/91	M		(2)	
80	Elivelto	BRA	02/01/92	A	20	(4)	11
3	Georgas Freidgeimas		10/08/87	D	20	(5)	
5	Algis Jankauskas		27/09/82	D	12	(4)	3
16	Paulius Janušauskas		28/02/89	M	3	(15)	5
9	Jorge Chula	POR	13/02/90	M	2	(1)	1
7	Yuri Kendysh	BLR	10/06/90	M	31		6
5	Samir Kerla	BIH	26/09/87	D	25		2
55	Saulius Klevinskas		04/08/84	G	12	(1)	
88	Mantas Kuklys		10/06/87	M	25	(2)	8
23	Justas Lasickas		26/10/97	M	2	(2)	
19	Lucas Gaúcho	BRA	13/06/91	A	5	(5)	1
21	Vytautas Lukša		14/08/84	M	22	(8)	3
24	Serge Nyuiadzi	FRA	15/11/94	A	13	(10)	4
77	Linas Pilibaitis		05/04/85	M	27	(2)	16
13	Daniel Romanovskij		19/06/96	M	2	(4)	
20	Donovan Slijngard	NED	28/08/87	D	15		
2	Deividas Šemberas		02/08/78	M	24	(1)	3
23	Darvydas Šernas		22/07/85	A	16		17
11	Andro Švrljuga	CRO	24/10/85	D	30	(1)	7
8	Egidijus Vaitkūnas		08/08/88	D	23	(5)	
1	Armantas Vitkauskas		23/03/89	G	22		
10	Jakub Wilk	POL	11/07/85	M	13	(1)	3
17	Artak Yedigaryan	ARM	18/03/90	D	5	(4)	

Top goalscorers

28	Tomas Radzinevičius (Sūduva)
25	David Arshakyan (Trakai)
20	Andrei Panyukov (Atlantas)
	Artūras Rimkevičius (Stumbras)
17	Darvydas Šernas (Žalgiris)
16	Linas Pilibaitis (Žalgiris)
12	Andrius Velička (Spyris)
11	Dmitri Rekish (Spyris)
	Elivelto (Žalgiris)
10	Maksim Maksimov (Atlantas)
	Ernestas Veliulis (Sūduva)
	Lukas Kochanauskas (Trakai)

Promoted club

FK Lietava

1991 • Centrinis (1,000) • fklietava.lt
Coach: Marius Bezykornovas

Second level final table 2015

		Pld	W	D	L	F	A	Pts
1	FK Lietava	34	25	5	4	103	24	80
2	FK Žalgiris B	34	24	4	6	112	37	76
3	FK Banga	34	24	5	5	77	28	74
4	FK Šilas	34	22	4	8	82	45	70
5	FK Palanga	34	19	7	8	84	38	64
6	FK Nevėžis	34	20	3	11	75	59	63
7	FK Trakai-2	34	19	3	12	81	52	60
8	FK Panevėžys	34	18	7	9	78	48	55
9	FK Silute	34	14	5	15	61	50	47
10	FK Džiugas	34	12	5	17	43	51	41
11	FK Lokomotyvas	34	12	3	19	57	74	39
12	FBK Kaunas	34	10	7	17	44	64	37
13	FK Kražantė	34	10	5	19	52	101	35
14	FK MRU	34	9	7	18	46	65	34
15	FK Auska	34	10	6	18	41	66	33
16	FK Minija	34	6	7	21	46	74	25
17	FK Tauras	34	7	1	26	41	150	22
18	FK Kruoja-2	34	3	0	31	17	114	9

NB FK Panevėžys – 6 pts deducted; FK Auska &
FK Banga – 3 pts deducted; FK Kruoja-2 withdrew after
round 23 – their remaining matches were awarded as
0-3 defeats.

DOMESTIC CUP

LFF Taurė 2015/16

THIRD ROUND

(22/09/15)
Druskininkai 0-3 Banga
Džiugas 7-1 Nevėžis *(aet)*
FBK Kaunas 0-3 Spyris
Lokomotyvas 2-3 Utenis
Pramogos-SC 3-1 Visaginas
Prelegentai 3-1 Panevezys
Šilas 0-4 Lietava
Tauras 5-4 MRU *(aet)*

FOURTH ROUND

(29/09/15)
Atlantas 4-0 Šiauliai
Pramogos-SC 1-4 Spyris
Prelegentai 0-8 Utenis
Trakai 3-0 Kruoja *(w/o)*

(30/09/15)
Banga 1-4 Žalgiris
Džiugas 0-2 Sūduva
Lietava 2-1 Klaipėdos granitas *(aet)*
Tauras 2-12 Stumbras

QUARTER-FINALS

(20/10/15 & 03/11/15)
Žalgiris 5-0 Spyris *(Nyuiadzi 15, Kuklys 29, Švrljuga 59, Lucas Gaúcho 59, 69)*
Spyris 2-7 Žalgiris *(Rekish 30, Krušnauskas 53; Romanovskij 4, Jankauskas 13, Nyuiadzi 18, Elivelto 48, Lucas Gaúcho 54, 58, 71)*
(Žalgiris 12-2)

(21/10/15 & 03/11/15)
Atlantas 1-2 Trakai *(Baranauskas 90; Valskis 18, Arshakyan 90+3)*
Trakai 2-0 Atlantas *(Shevchuk 82, Bychenok 90+3)*
(Trakai 4-1)

(21/10/15 & 04/11/15)
Stumbras 2-1 Utenis *(Grigaravičius 51, Rimkevičius 81; P Krasnovskis 65)*
Utenis 2-3 Stumbras *(Mastianica 19, Kazubovičius 22; Račkus 12, 53, Grigaravičius 67)*
(Stumbras 5-3)

Sūduva 3-0 Lietava *(Laukžemis 74, Mockus 80og, Šoblinskas 84)*
Lietava 0-3 Sūduva *(Živković 17, Šoblinskas 34, Laukžemis 88)*
(Sūduva 6-0)

SEMI-FINALS

(12/04/16 & 24/04/16)
Žalgiris 1-1 Stumbras *(Pilibaitis 90+2; Russo 66)*
Stumbras 0-2 Žalgiris *(Lukša 32, 83)*
(Žalgiris 3-1)

(13/04/16 & 23/04/16)
Trakai 2-0 Sūduva *(Česnauskis 71, Valskis 90+4)*
Sūduva 0-1 Trakai *(Arshakyan 73)*
(Trakai 3-0)

FINAL

(15/05/16)
Telšių miesto stadionas, Telsiai
FK ŽALGIRIS 1 *(Klimavičius 99)*
FK TRAKAI 0
(aet)
Referee: Gaigalas
ŽALGIRIS: Vitkauskas, Vaitkūnas, Klimavičius, Mbodj, Slijngard, Matoš (Žaliūkas 105), Kuklys, Lukša, Mikoliūnas (Lasickas 91), Pilibaitis, Elivelto (Stankevičius 91)
TRAKAI: Rapalis, Česnauskis, Klimavičius, Januševskij, Šilėnas, Gurenko, Zasavitschi, Rekish, Bychenok (Vorobjovas 69), Valskis (Vitukynas 80), Arshakyan

Žalgiris players celebrate the club's fifth successive Lithuanian Cup win and tenth in all

LUXEMBOURG
Fédération Luxembourgeoise de Football (FLF)

Address	BP5, Rue de Limpach LU-3901 Mondercange	**President**	Paul Philipp
Tel	+352 488 665 1	**General secretary**	Joël Wolff
Fax	+352 488 665 82	**Media officer**	Marc Diederich
E-mail	flf@football.lu	**Year of formation**	1908
Website	football.lu	**National stadium**	Josy Barthel, Luxembourg (8,022)

NATIONAL DIVISION CLUBS

 1 FC Differdange 03

 2 F91 Dudelange

 3 FC Etzella Ettelbruck

 4 CS Fola Esch

 5 CS Grevenmacher

 6 FC RM Hamm Benfica

 7 AS Jeunesse Esch

 8 US Mondorf-les-Bains

 9 FC Progrès Niederkorn

 10 Racing FC Union Lëtzebuerg

 11 US Rumelange

 12 FC UNA Strassen

 13 FC Victoria Rosport

 14 FC Wiltz 71

PROMOTED CLUBS

 15 UN Käerjéng 97

 16 FC Union Titus Pétange

 17 FC Jeunesse Canach

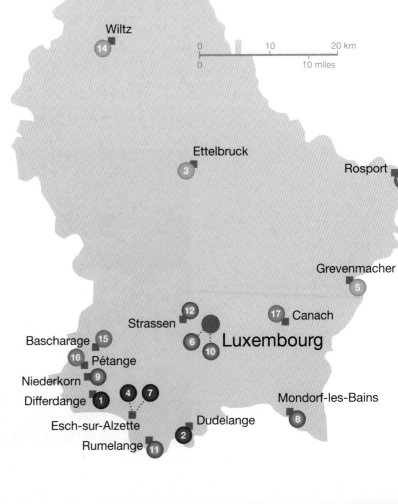

KEY
- UEFA Champions League
- UEFA Europa League
- Promoted
- Relegated

Dudelange do it the hard way

Reunited with Michel Leflochmoan, the coach who had led them to five successive National Division titles during his first spell at the club, from 2004-09, F91 Dudelange made it 12 championship wins in all in 2015/16 but only after surviving a nerve-racking finale.

Eight points clear of defending champions Fola Esch with four games left, Dudelange's form suddenly deserted them and they eventually had to rely on their superior goal difference to take the first prize. A week later they completed a fourth double by lifting the Luxembourg Cup.

| Club's 12th title won on goal difference | Late-season lapse almost lets in Fola | Leflochmoan's side complete double with cup win |

Domestic league

Dudelange succeeded in coaxing club legend Leflochmoan out of retirement to help them wrest the title back from Fola, and for most of the campaign the 64-year-old Frenchman looked set to maintain his 100% success rate. Victories were commonplace, and although Fola, led again by their double title-winning boss Jeff Strasser, did their best to keep pace, trailing the leaders by just two points at the mid-season shutdown, that deficit had quadrupled by late March.

Dudelange won their next four matches and so did Fola, which meant that if the leaders stretched their winning streak to 11 matches at their rivals' Stade Émile Mayrisch on the last day of April, the title would be theirs. Instead it was the home side who triumphed, 3-1, inflicting a first defeat of the season on the visitors. Eight days later, perhaps feeling the effects of a midweek cup semi-final that had gone to extra time, Leflochmoan's side lost again, 1-0 at home to third-placed Differdange. With Fola winning once more, the gap was down to two points.

Both challengers drew their penultimate fixture, but thanks to their significant goal difference buffer, Dudelange could afford another one-pointer at home to relegation-threatened Wiltz even if Fola simultaneously won at home to

Differdange. Although they were in the box seat at kick-off, Dudelange trailed at half-time, and with Fola then going 4-1 up, it looked as if the long-time leaders' season was about to unravel completely. But with 19 minutes left they found the vital equaliser, midfielder Rodrigue Dikaba firing home from long range to put his team back in the driving seat.

Much to the home fans' relief, the scoreline stayed unchanged until the final whistle, enabling Dudelange to reclaim the title and their opponents to avoid automatic relegation, with Etzella Ettelbruck, defeated 5-1 by Victoria Rosport, finishing 13th and going down alongside bottom club Grevenmacher. Wiltz's reprieve was only temporary, though, as five days later they lost to a 120th-minute goal in their play-off against Jeunesse Canach, who thus won promotion alongside the second division's top two, UN Käerjéng 97 and Union Titus Pétange.

Domestic cup

Pétange were the team that took Dudelange to extra time in the cup semi-final – before conceding four times in the additional 30 minutes. In the other last-four encounter an upset did materialise as Fola were beaten 1-0 by mid-table Mondorf-les-Bains, but the underdogs were unable to stage an encore in the final, going down to a first-half goal from

Dudelange's Luxembourg international midfielder Daniel Da Mota.

Europe

European football is an annual struggle for National Division clubs, but one player who evidently enjoys the experience is Differdange striker Omar Er Rafik, whose three goals in the 2015/16 UEFA Europa League qualifiers increased his tally to 12 in four consecutive European campaigns. Differdange were the only one of Luxembourg's four teams to win a tie, a 95th-minute Er Rafik strike taking them past Bala Town in the first qualifying round.

National team

The brothers Thill were the talk of the Luxembourg national team in 2015/16. Sébastien scored on his debut, in the 92nd minute of a UEFA EURO 2016 qualifier at home to FYR Macedonia, to give his country their first competitive win for two years. Six months later, his younger sibling Vincent made history by becoming the first player born in the new millennium to appear in a senior international for a European team. At the age of 16 years and 51 days, he became Luxembourg's youngest ever international, and a little over two months later the multi-talented teenager also became his country's youngest scorer with a late consolation goal against Nigeria.

DOMESTIC SEASON AT A GLANCE

National Division 2015/16 final table

		Pld	Home					Away					Total					Pts
			W	D	L	F	A	W	D	L	F	A	W	D	L	F	A	
1	F91 Dudelange	26	11	1	1	35	10	8	4	1	30	11	19	5	2	65	21	62
2	CS Fola Esch	26	12	1	0	37	10	7	4	2	24	13	19	5	2	61	23	62
3	FC Differdange 03	26	11	1	1	35	8	6	3	4	28	24	17	4	5	63	32	55
4	AS Jeunesse Esch	26	7	4	2	29	14	6	3	4	19	16	13	7	6	48	30	46
5	FC UNA Strassen	26	8	3	2	31	21	3	2	8	19	29	11	5	10	50	50	38
6	FC Progrès Niederkorn	26	7	0	6	21	15	3	6	4	20	15	10	6	10	41	30	36
7	US Mondorf-les-Bains	26	5	5	3	22	19	5	1	7	14	15	10	6	10	36	34	36
8	Racing FC Union Lëtzebuerg	26	4	4	5	19	23	6	1	6	26	31	10	5	11	45	54	35
9	FC RM Hamm Benfica	26	4	6	3	28	22	5	1	7	24	27	9	7	10	52	49	34
10	US Rumelange	26	3	7	3	18	29	5	1	7	20	23	8	4	14	38	52	28
11	FC Victoria Rosport	26	2	3	8	18	24	5	2	6	28	25	7	5	14	46	49	26
12	FC Wiltz 71	26	4	1	8	13	30	1	5	7	9	30	5	6	15	22	60	21
13	FC Etzella Ettelbruck	26	2	2	9	13	38	2	3	8	12	32	4	5	17	25	70	17
14	CS Grevenmacher	26	1	3	9	4	21	2	1	10	11	32	3	4	19	15	53	13

European qualification 2016/17

Champion/Cup winner: F91 Dudelange (second qualifying round)

CS Fola Esch (first qualifying round)
FC Differdange 03 (first qualifying round)
AS Jeunesse Esch (first qualifying round)

Top scorer	Julien Jahier (Racing Union), 25 goals
Relegated clubs	CS Grevenmacher, FC Etzella Ettelbruck, FC Wiltz 71
Promoted clubs	UN Käerjéng 97, FC Union Titus Pétange, FC Jeunesse Canach
Cup final	F91 Dudelange 1-0 US Mondorf-les-Bains

Team of the season
(4-4-2)

Coach: Leflochmoan (Dudelange)

Joubert
(Dudelange)

Franzoni (Differdange) — Bouzid (Progrès) — Dikaba (Dudelange) — Klein (Fola)

Er Rafik (Differdange) — Pedro (Dudelange) — Dallevedove (Fola) — O Thill (Progrès)

Jahier (Racing Union) — N'Diaye (Jeunesse)

Player of the season

Jonathan Joubert
(F91 Dudelange)

Still going strong for club and country at the age of 36, Joubert added to his copious collection of winner's medals by starring in Dudelange's 2015/16 double triumph. It was his 12th successive season at the club and his ninth league title during that time, making it a personal ten in all following his 2002/03 triumph with former club Grevenmacher. The veteran 'keeper played all 26 league games during the season, keeping clean sheets in half of them, and also completed a decade of service for the Luxembourg national team.

Newcomer of the season

Momar N'Diaye
(AS Jeunesse Esch)

While Dudelange and Fola slugged it out for the National Division title on the final day, another battle was being waged for the golden boot. Although Senegalese striker N'Diaye narrowly missed out on the prize to Racing Union's Julien Jahier, his 24-goal tally, which included ten in his last three games, still represented an impressive return for his debut season in Luxembourg's top flight following spells in France, Germany and China. Dudelange's cup win also meant that his goals helped Jeunesse qualify for Europe.

NATIONAL TEAM

Top five all-time caps
Jeff Strasser (98); René Peters (92); Eric Hoffmann & Carlo Weis (88); **Mario Mutsch** (87)

Top five all-time goals
Léon Mart (16); Gusty Kemp (15); Camille Libar (14); Nicolas Kettel (13); François Müller (12)

Results 2015/16

05/09/15	FYR Macedonia (ECQ)	H	Luxembourg	W	1-0	S Thill (90+2)
08/09/15	Belarus (ECQ)	A	Borisov	L	0-2	
09/10/15	Spain (ECQ)	A	Logrono	L	0-4	
12/10/15	Slovakia (ECQ)	H	Luxembourg	L	2-4	Mutsch (61), Gerson (65p)
13/11/15	Greece	H	Differdange	W	1-0	Joachim (90+1)
17/11/15	Portugal	H	Luxembourg	L	0-2	
25/03/16	Bosnia & Herzegovina	H	Luxembourg	L	0-3	
29/03/16	Albania	H	Luxembourg	L	0-2	
31/05/16	Nigeria	H	Luxembourg	L	1-3	V Thill (90)

Appearances 2015/16

Coach: Luc Holtz	14/06/69		MKD	BLR	ESP	SVK	Gre	Por	Bih	Alb	Nga	Caps	Goals
Jonathan Joubert	12/09/79	Dudelange	G	G	G	G	G	G		G 44*		84	-
Laurent Jans	05/08/92	Waasland-Beveren (BEL)	D	M	D	D	D	D	D	D	D	31	-
Maxime Chanot	21/11/89	Kortrijk (BEL)	D	D	D	D	D	D	D	D	D	21	1
Chris Philipps	08/03/94	Preussen Münster (GER)	D	D		D	M66	M46	M84	M	M78	32	-
Ricardo Delgado	22/02/94	Jeunesse Esch	D		D	D81	D	D	D53	D85		7	-
Lars Gerson	05/02/90	Sundsvall (SWE)	M	M	M	M	M76	M90	M	M71	M78	54	4
Ben Payal	08/09/88	Fola	M	M46	M	M57	s66	s46	s84	s71		73	-
Christopher Martins	19/02/97	Lyon (FRA)	M72		M79	M	M64	M46	M60	s61	D	13	-
Daniel Da Mota	11/09/85	Dudelange	M	s46	s79		s64	s46	s60	M45		70	4
Maurice Deville	31/07/92	Kaiserslautern (GER)	A64	A69	s64		s66	s60	M61	s46		29	3
Aurélien Joachim	10/08/86	Burton (ENG) /White Star (BEL)	A	A46	A90	A	A	A73	A84	A	A	62	8
Stefano Bensi	11/08/88	Fola	s64	s46	A64	A66	A93	A66	A60	A90	A55	37	4
Sébastien Thill	29/12/93	Progrès	s72			s66	s76	s46		s90	s78	6	1
Tom Schnell	08/10/85	Dudelange	D			s93		s53				48	-
Mathias Jänisch	27/08/90	Differdange	M							D66		43	1
Mario Mutsch	03/09/84	St Gallen (SUI)	M	M	M	M85	M	M68		M		87	4
David Turpel	19/10/92	Dudelange		s69	s90	s81		s73	s84			20	1
Kevin Malget	15/01/91	Dudelange			D	s57	D	D46	D	D		12	-
Dwayn Holter	15/06/95	Aalen (GER)					s85	s90				11	-
Anthony Moris	29/04/90	Mechelen (BEL)							G	s45	G	5	-
Vincent Thill	04/02/00	Metz (FRA)							s68		s55	2	1
Cédric Sacras	28/09/96	Metz (FRA)								s85	s78	2	-
Florian Bohnert	09/11/97	Saarbrücken (GER)									M46	1	-
Tom Laterza	09/05/92	Fola									s66	33	-

EUROPE

CS Fola Esch

Second qualifying round - GNK Dinamo Zagreb (CRO)
A 1-1 *Hadji (25)*
Hym, Martino, Martin, Payal, Dallevedove, Françoise (Rani 78), Hadji (Camerling 82), Kirch, Ronny, Bensi (Hornuss 25), Klein. Coach: Jeff Strasser (LUX)
Red card: Ronny 64
H 0-3
Hym, Martino, Martin, Payal, Hornuss (Camerling 57), Dallevedove, Françoise (Rachid 79), Hadji, Rani (Klapp 68), Kirch, Klein. Coach: Jeff Strasser (LUX)

FC Differdange 03

First qualifying round - Bala Town FC (WAL)
H 3-1 *Er Rafik (4), Caron (7), Sinani (26)*
Weber, Rodrigues, Siebenaler (Caillet 78), Pedro Ribeiro, Er Rafik, Sinani (Almeida 69), Caron, Bukvic, Lebresne (May 46), Franzoni, Luisi. Coach: Marc Thomé (LUX)
A 1-2 *Er Rafik (90+5)*
Weber, Rodrigues, Siebenaler, Pedro Ribeiro (Sinani 72), Er Rafik, Caron, Bukvic, Yéyé (Almeida 63), Jänisch, Lebresne (Luisi 85), Franzoni. Coach: Marc Thomé (LUX)

Second qualifying round - Trabzonspor AŞ (TUR)
A 0-1
Weber, Rodrigues, Siebenaler, Pedro Ribeiro (May 90+3), Er Rafik, Sinani (Lebresne 64), Caron (Méligner 76), Bukvic, Yéyé, Jänisch, Franzoni. Coach: Denis Pfeiffer (LUX)
H 1-2 *Er Rafik (81)*
Weber, Rodrigues (Lebresne 70), Siebenaler, Pedro Ribeiro (Bettmer 79), Er Rafik, Sinani (Luisi 57), Caron, Bukvic, Yéyé, Jänisch, Franzoni. Coach: Marc Thomé (LUX)

F91 Dudelange

First qualifying round - University College Dublin AFC (IRL)
A 0-1
Joubert, Moreira, Ney, Schnell, Ibrahimović (Teixeira Pinto 83), Da Mota (Laurentié 74), Benzouien, Pedro, Nakache, Prempeh, Adler (Turpel 58). Coach: Michel Leflochmoan (FRA)
H 2-1 *Pedro (43), Nakache (45+3)*
Joubert, Moreira (Ibrahimović 65), Ney, Schnell, Da Mota (Laurentié 76), Benzouien (Adler 71), Pedro, Stélvio, Nakache, Prempeh, Turpel. Coach: Michel Leflochmoan (FRA)

FC Progrès Niederkorn

First qualifying round - Shamrock Rovers FC (IRL)
H 0-0
Flauss, Dog, Bouzid, Poinsignon (Fiorani 80), Menaï (Rougeaux 68), Cassan, Rigo (Ferino 40), David Soares, Rossini, Garos, S Thill. Coach: Olivier Ciancanelli (LUX)
A 0-3
Flauss, Dog, Bouzid, Menaï, Cassan, Fiorani (Bossi 75), Ferino, Rossini, Garos, S Thill (O Thill 77), Rougeaux (Poinsignon 67). Coach: Olivier Ciancanelli (LUX)

DOMESTIC LEAGUE CLUB-BY-CLUB

FC Differdange 03

2003 • Parc des Sports (1,800) • fcd03.lu
Major honours
Luxembourg Cup (4) 2010, 2011, 2014, 2015
Coach: Marc Thomé

2015
01/08	h	Fola	L 0-3	
09/08	a	Racing Union	D 1-1	Er Rafik
16/08	a	Mondorf-les-Bains	D 2-2	Er Rafik, Sinani
23/08	h	Wiltz	W 5-0	Almeida, Er Rafik, Luisi 2, Martin
30/08	a	Rosport	W 3-2	Er Rafik 2, Almeida
13/09	h	UNA Strassen	W 2-0	Er Rafik, Luisi
21/09	a	Jeunesse	D 1-1	Er Rafik
27/09	h	Hamm Benfica	W 4-1	Er Rafik 2, Luisi, Caron
16/10	h	Progrès	W 1-0	Yéyé
25/10	h	Grevenmacher	W 4-0	Rodrigues, Pedro Ribeiro, Luisi, Bastos
31/10	a	Etzella	W 3-2	Martin, Er Rafik, Franzoni (p)
08/11	h	Dudelange	D 2-2	Er Rafik, Sinani (p)
29/11	a	Rumelange	L 1-4	Franzoni (p)

2016
21/02	h	Racing Union	W 6-0	Jänisch 2, Sinani, Er Rafik, Bettmer, Luisi
28/02	h	Mondorf-les-Bains	W 1-0	Vandenbroeck
06/03	a	Wiltz	L 2-3	Vandenbroeck, Bastos
13/03	h	Rosport	W 2-1	Pedro Ribeiro, Yéyé
20/03	a	UNA Strassen	W 4-1	Vandenbroeck, Er Rafik 2, Bettmer
03/04	a	Jeunesse	W 3-0	Er Rafik 2, Bastos
09/04	a	Hamm Benfica	L 1-2	Pedro Ribeiro, Rodrigues (p)
15/04	h	Progrès	W 1-0	Vandenbroeck
24/04	a	Grevenmacher	W 5-0	Bastos 2, Sinani 2 (2p), Yéyé
30/04	h	Etzella	W 2-1	Vandenbroeck, Er Rafik
08/05	a	Dudelange	W 1-0	Yéyé
14/05	h	Rumelange	W 3-0	Pedro Ribeiro, Bastos, Méligner
22/05	a	Fola	L 2-4	Rodrigues, Sinani

Name	Nat	DoB	Pos	Aps	(s)	Gls
Gonçalo Almeida		26/11/90	A	8	(4)	2
Yannick Bastos		30/05/93	M	10	(7)	6
Gilles Bettmer		31/03/89	M	14	(6)	2
Ante Bukvic		14/11/87	D	10	(2)	
Gauthier Caron	FRA	27/12/89	A	9	(9)	1
Omar Er Rafik	FRA	07/01/86	M	23	(2)	18
Geoffrey Franzoni	FRA	18/02/91	D	25		2
Mathias Jänisch		27/08/90	D	14	(1)	2
Jorge Ribeiro	POR	24/10/92	M		(3)	
Philippe Lebresne	FRA	09/07/78	M	1	(2)	
Antonio Luisi		07/10/94	A	10	(7)	6
Mehdi Martin	FRA	11/01/90	D	11	(2)	2
Andy May		02/09/89	M	19	(3)	
Jérémy Méligner	FRA	11/06/91	M	2	(8)	1
Arthur Michaux	FRA	06/06/94	M	1	(4)	
Pedro Ribeiro	POR	07/01/89	M	18	(5)	3
Pierre Piskor	FRA	02/05/84	A		(1)	
André Rodrigues		06/12/87	D	21		3
Arnaud Schaab	FRA	03/09/90	G	1		
Tom Siebenaler		28/09/90	D	20	(1)	
Dejvid Sinani	ALB	02/04/93	M	12	(4)	6
David Vandenbroeck	BEL	12/07/85	D	13		5
Julien Weber	FRA	12/10/85	G	25		
Jordan Yéyé	FRA	02/11/88	A	19	(2)	4

F91 Dudelange

1991 • Jos Nosbaum (4,500) • f91.lu
Major honours
Luxembourg League (12) 2000, 2001, 2002, 2005, 2006, 2007, 2008, 2009, 2011, 2012, 2014, 2016; Luxembourg Cup (6) 2004, 2006, 2007, 2009, 2012, 2016
Coach: Michel Leflochmoan (FRA)

2015

02/08	a	Wiltz	W 6-0	*Ibrahimović 2, Pedro, Da Mota, Turpel 2*
09/08	h	Rosport	W 7-1	*Ibrahimović 2, Benzouien, Laurentié, Schnell (p), Adler, Da Mota*
16/08	a	UNA Strassen	D 2-2	*Da Mota, Turpel*
23/08	h	Jeunesse	W 1-0	*Nakache*
28/08	a	Hamm Benfica	D 0-0	
13/09	h	Progrès	W 2-1	*Pedro 2*
20/09	a	Grevenmacher	W 1-0	*Da Mota*
27/09	h	Etzella	W 6-0	*Nakache 2, Ibrahimović, Turpel 2, Marques*
18/10	h	Racing Union	W 4-2	*Turpel 3 (1p), Marques*
25/10	a	Rumelange	W 4-2	*Turpel, Da Mota 3*
31/10	h	Fola	W 2-0	*Turpel, Moreira*
08/11	a	Differdange	D 2-2	*Ibrahimović 2*
29/11	h	Mondorf-les-Bains	W 3-0	*Turpel 2 (1p), Stélvio*

2016

21/02	a	Rosport	W 2-1	*Dikaba, Da Mota*
28/02	h	UNA Strassen	W 1-0	*Turpel*
04/03	a	Jeunesse	W 2-1	*Ibrahimović, Pedro*
13/03	h	Hamm Benfica	W 2-1	*Ibrahimović, Malget*
19/03	h	Progrès	W 3-0	*Turpel 2, Benzouien*
03/04	a	Grevenmacher	W 2-0	*Turpel 2 (1p)*
10/04	a	Etzella	W 5-0	*Ney, Benzouien, Ibrahimović, Prempeh, Turpel*
17/04	a	Racing Union	W 2-0	*Pedro, Malget*
24/04	h	Rumelange	W 4-3	*Ibrahimović, Turpel 3 (1p)*
30/04	a	Fola	L 1-3	*Humbert*
08/05	h	Differdange	D 0-1	
13/05	a	Mondorf-les-Bains	D 0-0	
22/05	h	Wiltz	D 1-1	*Dikaba*

Name	Nat	DoB	Pos	Aps	(s)	Gls
Grégory Adler	FRA	27/04/89	M	5	(7)	1
Yassine Ben Ajiba	MAR	01/11/84	M	4	(5)	
Sofian Benzouien	BEL	11/08/86	M	5	(3)	3
Daniel Da Mota		11/09/85	M	22	(1)	8
Raphaël De Sousa		05/06/93	M		(1)	
Dylan Deligny	FRA	05/08/93	M		(3)	
Rodrigue Dikaba	COD	28/10/85	M	24		2
Julien Humbert	FRA	23/06/84	M	11	(10)	1
Sanel Ibrahimović	BIH	24/11/87	A	20	(6)	12
Jonathan Joubert		12/09/79	G	26		
Alexandre Laurentié	FRA	19/11/89	M	19	(1)	1
Kevin Malget		15/01/91	D	14	(4)	2
Frédéric Marques	FRA	05/06/85	A	2	(14)	2
Clayton de Sousa Moreira		24/02/88	D	18	(4)	1
Kevin Nakache	FRA	05/04/89	M	19	(2)	3
Romain Ney	FRA	06/01/92	D	6	(1)	
Joël Pedro		10/04/92	M	23	(1)	5
Jerry Prempeh	FRA	29/12/88	D	18	(1)	1
Tom Schnell		08/10/85	D	21		1
Stélvio	ANG	24/01/89	M	9	(6)	1
David Turpel		19/10/92	A	20	(6)	20

FC Etzella Ettelbruck

1917 • Stade du Centre Sportif Deich (2,024) • fc-etzella.lu
Major honours
Luxembourg Cup (1) 2001
Coach: Niki Wagner (GER); (25/09/15) (Frank Thömmes (GER)); (02/10/15) Claude Ottelé

2015

02/08	a	Rosport	W 2-1	*Holtz, Augusto*
09/08	h	UNA Strassen	L 2-6	*Augusto 2*
16/08	a	Jeunesse	L 0-6	
22/08	h	Hamm Benfica	L 0-4	
28/08	a	Progrès	L 0-4	
12/09	h	Grevenmacher	D 2-2	*Kühne, Novic*
20/09	h	Racing Union	L 2-4	*Novic, Magalhaes*
27/09	a	Dudelange	L 0-6	
18/10	h	Rumelange	W 1-0	*Augusto*
25/10	a	Fola	L 1-3	*Novic*
31/10	h	Differdange	L 2-3	*Kühne, Augusto*
08/11	a	Mondorf-les-Bains	D 1-1	*og (Kuduzović)*
29/11	h	Wiltz	D 1-1	*og (Cheriak)*

2016

21/02	a	UNA Strassen	L 0-2	
28/02	h	Jeunesse	L 0-1	
06/03	h	Hamm Benfica	D 2-2	*Ingrao, Novic*
13/03	h	Progrès	L 0-2	
20/03	a	Grevenmacher	W 2-0	*Augusto 2*
03/04	a	Racing Union	L 1-2	*Novic*
10/04	h	Dudelange	L 0-5	
17/04	h	Rumelange	L 0-1	
24/04	h	Fola	L 0-4	
30/04	a	Differdange	L 1-2	*Mesec*
08/05	h	Mondorf-les-Bains	W 2-1	*Catic, Augusto*
13/05	a	Wiltz	D 2-2	*Novic 2*
22/05	h	Rosport	L 1-5	*Agovic*

Name	Nat	DoB	Pos	Aps	(s)	Gls
Ernest Agovic		09/02/97	A	7	(9)	1
André Gonçalves	POR	26/09/88	M	14	(2)	
François Augusto		02/06/88	A	21	(2)	8
André Bastos		18/03/91	M	12	(1)	
Tom Bintner		12/03/98	D	1	(1)	
Felix Börner		14/03/96	M	1	(5)	
Kader Camara	GUI	18/03/82	M	9		
Amar Catic		07/08/95	A	18	(6)	1
Léo Clement		29/11/88	G	16		
Cataldo Cozza	GER	13/04/85	M	16		
Ugur Dündar	GER	01/11/92	D	9		
Shahin Farindonpur	GER	30/12/92	D	4	(4)	
Jeff Fernandes		20/05/97	M		(2)	
Frederico	POR	28/12/92	M	7	(2)	
Kevin Holtz		06/03/93	M	8	(5)	1
Marco Ingrao	BEL	28/07/82	M	1		1
João Freitas	POR	06/07/96	M		(1)	
Jorge Silva	POR	24/07/88	G	1		
Gaël Kipeya	BEL	01/10/86	D	10	(4)	
Johannes Kühne	GER	02/05/88	D	22		2
Luka Lazitch	BEL	08/02/93	G	9		
Kevin Liu		06/05/97	A		(4)	
Joël Magalhaes		22/04/91	D	22	(1)	1
Vedran Mesec	CRO	20/02/88	A	13		1
Yanis N'Gbin		22/10/99	M		(1)	
Killien Neves		01/04/96	A		(1)	
Lex Nicolay		27/03/97	D	22	(3)	
Xavier Novic	FRA	18/04/88	A	22	(7)	7
Bartłomiej Pietrasik	POL	25/05/84	D		(4)	
Jader Soares		19/08/96	D	16	(1)	
Frédéric Thill		15/01/96	M	5	(9)	

CS Fola Esch

1906 • Emile Mayrisch (6,000) • csfola.lu
Major honours
Luxembourg League (7) 1918, 1920, 1922, 1924, 1930, 2013, 2015; Luxembourg Cup (3) 1923, 1924, 1955
Coach: Jeff Strasser

2015

01/08	a	Differdange	W 3-0	*Hadji, Françoise, Bensi*
09/08	h	Mondorf-les-Bains	W 2-1	*Hadji, Bensi*
16/08	a	Wiltz	W 2-0	*Dallevedove, Bensi*
23/08	h	Rosport	W 3-1	*Dallevedove, Bensi*
28/08	a	UNA Strassen	L 2-4	*Bensi (p), Françoise (p)*
13/09	h	Jeunesse	W 4-1	*Bensi 2, Hadji, Hornuss*
20/09	a	Hamm Benfica	W 3-2	*Françoise 2 (1p), Bensi*
26/09	h	Progrès	D 1-1	*Hadji*
18/10	a	Grevenmacher	W 2-0	*Dallevedove, Bensi*
25/10	h	Etzella	W 3-1	*Klapp 2, Hadji (p)*
31/10	a	Dudelange	L 0-2	
08/11	h	Rumelange	W 3-1	*Hadji, Klapp, Bensi*
29/11	a	Racing Union	W 1-0	*Françoise*

2016

21/02	a	Mondorf-les-Bains	D 0-0	
28/02	h	Wiltz	W 5-0	*Ronny, Hadji, Bensi, Dallevedove 2*
06/03	a	Rosport	D 1-1	*Hadji*
13/03	h	UNA Strassen	W 3-1	*Ronny, Laterza, Hadji*
20/03	a	Jeunesse	D 1-1	*Dallevedove*
03/04	h	Hamm Benfica	W 3-1	*Laterza, Dallevedove, Hadji*
09/04	a	Progrès	W 1-0	*Bernard*
15/04	h	Grevenmacher	W 3-0	*Bensi, Hadji, Rani*
24/04	a	Etzella	W 4-0	*Bensi 2, Ronny, Françoise*
30/04	a	Dudelange	W 3-1	*Hadji, Bensi, Klapp*
08/05	a	Rumelange	W 3-1	*Bensi, Dallevedove, Klapp*
13/05	a	Racing Union	D 2-2	*Bensi 2 (1p)*
22/05	h	Differdange	W 4-2	*Klapp, Bensi, Hadji, Laterza*

Name	Nat	DoB	Pos	Aps	(s)	Gls
Stefano Bensi		11/08/88	A	23	(3)	18
Billy Bernard		09/04/91	D	15	(1)	1
Emanuel Cabral		02/08/96	G	1		
Basile Camerling	FRA	19/04/87	A	2	(4)	
Jakob Dallevedove	GER	21/11/87	M	22	(4)	7
Emmanuel Françoise	FRA	07/06/82	M	20	(3)	7
Samir Hadji	FRA	12/09/89	D	24	(2)	13
Dwayn Holter		15/06/95	M	5	(5)	
Julien Hornuss	FRA	01/08/87	A	5	(12)	1
Thomas Hym	FRA	29/08/87	G	25		
Losseni Keita	FRA	01/04/84	D	7	(3)	
Mehdi Kirch	FRA	27/01/90	D	24		
Ryan Klapp		10/01/93	M	12	(8)	6
Julien Klein	FRA	07/04/87	D	26		
Tom Laterza		09/05/92	D	21	(4)	4
Zarko Lukic		22/05/83	A		(3)	
Enes Mahmutovic		22/05/97	D		(2)	
Erwan Martin	FRA	06/01/93	D	4		
Massimo Martino		18/09/90	D	8	(2)	
Gérard Mersch		08/09/96	M		(7)	
Ben Payal		08/09/88	M	10	(3)	
Fouad Rachid	COM	15/11/91	A	4		
Ahmed Rani	FRA	20/08/87	A	4	(10)	1
Ronny	CPV	07/12/78	A	24	(1)	3

LUXEMBOURG

CS Grevenmacher

1909 • Op Flohr (4,000) • csg.lu
Major honours
*Luxembourg League (1) 2003; Luxembourg Cup (4)
1995, 1998, 2003, 2008*
**Coach: Roland Schaack;
(18/04/16) Markus Weis & Christoph Schesnia**

2015
02/08	a	UNA Strassen	L	1-4	*Kitenge*
10/08	h	Jeunesse	L	0-2	
16/08	a	Hamm Benfica	L	0-3	
23/08	h	Progrès	D	0-0	
28/08	h	Racing Union	L	0-3	
12/09	a	Etzella	D	2-2	*Bechtold, Peters*
20/09	h	Dudelange	L	0-1	
27/09	a	Rumelange	L	1-2	*Gaspar*
18/10	h	Fola	L	0-2	
25/10	a	Differdange	L	0-4	
31/10	h	Mondorf-les-Bains	D	0-0	
08/11	h	Wiltz	L	2-3	*Heinz, Steinmetz*
29/11	a	Rosport	L	0-2	
2016					
21/02	a	Jeunesse	L	0-1	
28/02	h	Hamm Benfica	L	0-1	
06/03	a	Progrès	W	2-1	*Feltes, Makiadi*
13/03	a	Racing Union	L	1-2	*Gaspar*
20/03	h	Etzella	L	0-2	
03/04	h	Dudelange	L	0-2	
09/04	h	Rumelange	D	1-1	*Ontiveros*
15/04	a	Fola	L	0-3	
24/04	h	Differdange	L	0-5	
30/04	a	Mondorf-les-Bains	L	1-5	*og (Mutuale)*
07/05	h	Wiltz	L	0-2	
14/05	a	Rosport	W	1-0	*Steinmetz*
22/05	h	UNA Strassen	W	3-0	*Dervisevic, Bechtold, Schott*

Name	Nat	DoB	Pos	Aps	(s)	Gls
Michał Augustyn	POL	13/04/91	G	23		
Michel Bechtold		01/07/95	M	16	(2)	2
Dariusz Brzyski	POL	06/09/86	D	6	(1)	
Bob Dahlke		09/09/96	D	7		
Esteban Delaporte		07/08/93	G	1		
Din Dervisevic		19/05/91	M	15	(9)	1
Jeffrey Eshun	GER	21/08/89	A	4	(4)	
Gilles Feltes		06/12/95	D	25	(1)	1
Giuseppe Ferretti		25/05/97	A	1	(5)	
Florian Gaspar	GER	07/07/87	A	16	(3)	2
Keiven Goncalves	CPV	26/08/86	M	3	(1)	
Ben Guettai		11/05/96	M	12	(3)	
Tim Heinz		05/02/84	D	11		1
Bobby Jiang		08/05/99	G	1	(1)	
Joël Kitenge		12/11/87	A	3	(1)	1
Matondo Makiadi	GER	24/07/88	M	11	(6)	1
Kevin Marques		16/01/98	M	2	(1)	
André Mota		02/08/92	M	8		
Janik Müller	GER	05/02/98	G	1		
Omar Ontiveros	USA	15/05/95	D	20	(1)	1
Yanis Papassarantis	BEL	12/03/88	M	6	(1)	
Christophe Pazos	ESP	19/05/90	M	13	(2)	
René Peters		15/06/81	M	25		1
Mensur Reckovic		24/05/97	M	5	(10)	
Giuseppe Schipani	FRA	11/03/95	A	3	(4)	
Maxime Schott		02/02/98	M		(4)	1
Inas Sehovic		18/07/94	D	10	(2)	
Vic Speller		03/07/92	D	12	(2)	
Damian Steinmetz		04/02/95	A	11	(10)	2
Mathieu Trierweiler		15/05/96	D	15	(2)	

FC RM Hamm Benfica

2004 • Hans Sowa (2,800) • rmhb.lu
Coach: Dino Toppmöller (GER)

2015
02/08	a	Racing Union	W	4-1	*Zinram 2, Pinna (p), Da Mata*
08/08	a	Progrès	L	0-2	
16/08	h	Grevenmacher	W	3-0	*Eurico Gomes, Toppmöller, Rizzi*
22/08	a	Etzella	W	4-0	*Stumpf 2 (1p), Ontiveros, Zinram*
28/08	h	Dudelange	D	0-0	
13/09	a	Rumelange	W	5-2	*Stumpf, Filipe Ribeiro 2, Ontiveros, Mertinitz*
20/09	h	Fola	L	2-3	*Filipe Ribeiro, Stumpf*
27/09	a	Differdange	L	1-4	*Pinna (p)*
18/10	h	Mondorf-les-Bains	W	3-1	*Stumpf 3*
25/10	a	Wiltz	W	1-0	*Pinna*
31/10	h	Rosport	L	2-3	*Ontiveros 2*
08/11	a	UNA Strassen	D	0-0	
29/11	h	Jeunesse	D	2-2	*Paulo Arantes, Pinna*
2016					
21/02	h	Progrès	D	2-2	*Lapierre, Zinram*
28/02	a	Grevenmacher	W	1-0	*Zinram*
06/03	h	Etzella	D	2-2	*Stumpf, Ontiveros*
13/03	a	Dudelange	L	1-2	*Toppmöller*
20/03	h	Rumelange	L	1-4	*Veiga*
03/04	a	Fola	L	1-3	*Da Mata*
09/04	h	Differdange	W	4-2	*Stumpf, Paulo Arantes 2, Toppmöller*
16/04	a	Mondorf-les-Bains	L	1-2	*Zinram*
24/04	h	Wiltz	D	0-0	
30/04	a	Rosport	L	1-5	*Mertinitz*
08/05	h	UNA Strassen	W	4-0	*Paulo Arantes 2, Stumpf 2*
13/05	a	Jeunesse	L	4-6	*Paulo Arantes, Zinram, Stumpf 2*
22/05	h	Racing Union	D	3-3	*Paulo Arantes 3*

Name	Nat	DoB	Pos	Aps	(s)	Gls
Chris Clement		29/12/91	G	13		
Joël Da Mata		04/09/95	D	10	(6)	2
Nicolas Desgranges		19/06/96	D	1	(7)	
Dany Gomes	POR	17/02/96	D		(2)	
Eurico Gomes	POR	26/08/87	M	18	(1)	1
Filipe Ribeiro	POR	27/04/86	M	13	(6)	3
Emmanuel Lapierre	FRA	05/08/93	D	10	(3)	1
Tony Mastrangelo		01/09/94	D	19	(5)	
Robin Mertinitz	GER	19/04/90	M	18	(2)	2
Martin Ontiveros	USA	06/12/91	M	23	(1)	5
Paulo Arantes	POR	15/11/86	D	25		9
Giancarlo Pinna	ITA	31/03/89	D	17	(1)	4
Piero Rizzi		18/05/96	M	6	(10)	1
Mike Schneider		01/02/95	A	15	(7)	
Fabio Sebastiani		10/12/97	G	1		
Patrick Stumpf	GER	11/04/88	A	22	(4)	13
Pit Theis		25/01/79	G	12	(2)	
Dino Toppmöller	GER	23/11/80	A	4	(12)	3
Jan Umlauf	GER	12/10/94	D	13	(3)	
David Veiga		12/06/91	D	22	(1)	1
Jonathan Zinram	GER	01/12/91	M	24		7

AS Jeunesse Esch

1907 • Stade de la Frontière (7,000) •
jeunesse-esch.lu
Major honours
*Luxembourg League (28) 1921, 1937, 1951, 1954,
1958, 1959, 1960, 1963, 1967, 1968, 1970, 1973,
1974, 1975, 1976, 1977, 1980, 1983, 1985, 1987,
1988, 1995, 1996, 1997, 1998, 1999, 2004, 2010;
Luxembourg Cup (13) 1935, 1937, 1946, 1954, 1973,
1974, 1976, 1981, 1988, 1997, 1999, 2000, 2013*
Coach: Carlo Weis

2015
03/08	h	Progrès	D	0-0	
10/08	a	Grevenmacher	W	2-0	*Menèssou, N'Diaye*
16/08	h	Etzella	W	6-0	*N'Diaye 3, De Sousa, Do Rosario, A Deidda*
23/08	a	Dudelange	L	0-1	
28/08	h	Rumelange	W	1-0	*Kintziger*
13/09	a	Fola	L	1-4	*Corral*
21/09	h	Differdange	D	1-1	*N'Diaye (p)*
27/09	a	Mondorf-les-Bains	W	2-1	*N'Diaye (p) (Mutuale)*
18/10	h	Wiltz	W	2-1	*Molnar, N'Diaye (p)*
25/10	a	Rosport	W	2-1	*N'Diaye, Kintziger*
31/10	h	UNA Strassen	W	4-3	*De Sousa, N'Diaye 2 (1p), Delgado*
08/11	a	Racing Union	D	0-0	
29/11	h	Hamm Benfica	D	2-2	*Corral, N'Diaye*
2016					
21/02	h	Grevenmacher	W	1-0	*Corral*
28/02	a	Etzella	W	1-0	*Hugo Fernandes*
04/03	h	Dudelange	L	1-2	*Corral*
13/03	a	Rumelange	D	1-1	*N'Diaye*
20/03	h	Fola	D	1-1	*N'Diaye*
03/04	a	Differdange	L	0-3	
10/04	h	Mondorf-les-Bains	L	0-2	
17/04	a	Wiltz	W	5-1	*De Sousa, Menèssou, Molnar, Mélisse, Corral*
24/04	h	Rosport	D	1-1	*N'Diaye*
30/04	a	UNA Strassen	L	1-2	*Mélisse*
08/05	h	Racing Union	W	5-0	*N'Diaye 4, Sardaryan*
13/05	h	Hamm Benfica	W	6-4	*N'Diaye 4 (1p), og (Veiga), Mélisse*
22/05	a	Progrès	W	2-0	*N'Diaye 2*

Name	Nat	DoB	Pos	Aps	(s)	Gls
Yannick Breckler		01/07/98	A		(1)	
Ken Corral		08/05/92	A	24		5
David De Sousa		15/07/95	M	14	(2)	3
Andrea Deidda		15/12/93	A	6	(12)	1
Illario Deidda		18/12/89	A		(1)	
Ricardo Delgado		22/02/94	D	26		1
Frank Devas		06/03/94	G		(1)	
Sébastien Do Rosario	FRA	12/01/84	D	14		1
Eric Hoffmann		21/06/84	D	24		
Hugo Fernandes	POR	01/01/90	M	5	(1)	1
Kim Kintziger		02/04/87	D	19		2
Marvin Martins		17/02/95	D	2	(3)	
Bryan Mélisse	FRA	25/03/89	D	19		3
Arsène Menèssou	BEN	15/12/87	M	25		2
Grégory Molnar	FRA	10/07/83	A	9	(3)	2
Momar N'Diaye	SEN	13/07/87	A	25		24
Marc Oberweis		06/11/82	G	26		
Adrien Portier	FRA	02/02/88	D	5	(3)	
Dylan Proietti		28/09/95	A		(2)	
Ashot Sardaryan	ARM	23/03/92	A	14	(4)	1
Brandon Soares Rosa		15/08/98	D	1	(2)	
Milos Todorovic		18/08/95	M	10	(4)	
Fabio Tonini	BEL	30/05/93	A		(4)	
Alexandre Vitali	FRA	17/01/89	D	9	(7)	
Thibault Westermann	FRA	27/10/97	M		(1)	
Jonathan Zydko	FRA	12/01/84	M	9	(3)	

US Mondorf-les-Bains

1915 • John Grün (3,500) • usmondorf.lu
Coach: Arno Bonvini

2015

02/08	h	Rumelange	L 0-3	
09/08	a	Fola	L 1-2	Soares
16/08	h	Differdange	D 2-2	Ramiro Valente, Nabli
23/08	a	Racing Union	L 1-2	Guerra
30/08	a	Wiltz	W 1-0	Ramiro Valente
13/09	h	Rosport	W 3-2	Nabli 2, og (Werdel)
20/09	a	UNA Strassen	L 1-2	Mutuale
27/09	a	Jeunesse	L 1-2	Pjanić
18/10	a	Hamm Benfica	L 1-3	Mutuale
25/10	h	Progrès	W 2-1	Nabli, Kuduzović
31/10	a	Grevenmacher	D 0-0	
08/11	h	Etzella	D 1-1	Pjanić
29/11	a	Dudelange	L 0-3	

2016

21/02	h	Fola	D 0-0	
28/02	a	Differdange	L 0-1	
06/03	h	Racing Union	L 1-3	Nabli
13/03	h	Wiltz	W 4-2	Teixeira Pinto 2, Haddadji, Mutuale
20/03	a	Rosport	W 3-0	Teixeira Pinto, Yao 2 (1p)
03/04	h	UNA Strassen	D 1-1	Yao
10/04	a	Jeunesse	W 2-0	Yao, Pjanić
16/04	h	Hamm Benfica	W 2-1	Mutuale, Pjanić
24/04	a	Progrès	W 1-0	Thonon
30/04	h	Grevenmacher	W 5-1	Nabli, Thonon, og (Sehovic), Hégué, Yao
08/05	a	Etzella	L 1-2	Pjanić
13/05	h	Dudelange	D 0-0	
22/05	h	Rumelange	W 2-0	og (Johnny Santos), Yao

Name	Nat	DoB	Pos	Aps	(s)	Gls
Besart Aliu	GER	27/08/92	A	1	(2)	
Almin Babacic		16/01/84	M	5	(7)	
Ahmed Benhemine	FRA	15/01/87	D	16	(3)	
Papa Aye Dione	SEN	08/03/86	D	5	(4)	
Filipe Macedo	POR	10/06/95	M	3	(2)	
Anthony Guerra	FRA	20/01/90	M	4	(3)	1
Ilies Haddadji	FRA	09/04/90	M	17	(4)	1
Benjamin Hégué	FRA	16/03/89	A	2	(4)	1
Fahrudin Kuduzović	BIH	10/10/84	M	16	(4)	1
Romario Lima		30/01/95	D	1		
Olivier Marques		21/03/92	M	13	(6)	
Glenn Marques da Costa		10/06/94	G	11		
Anthony Medri	FRA	20/04/89	A	8	(7)	
Michael Monteiro		11/12/91	D	22	(1)	
Edis Muhić	BIH	10/08/93	D	13		
Yamukile Mutuale	FRA	25/08/87	A	22	(1)	4
Mohamed Nabli	TUN	27/05/85	M	24	(2)	6
Anel Pjanić	BIH	26/12/83	A	10	(4)	5
Rick Risch		30/06/95	M	3	(1)	
Alex Semedo		22/08/89	D	25		
Cédric Soares		19/10/95	M	11	(7)	1
Patrik Teixeira Pinto		10/05/96	M	8	(1)	3
Thibaut Thonon	FRA	05/02/87	M	14	(2)	2
Rafael Valente		27/04/87	A		(4)	
Ramiro Valente		26/01/89	A	9	(3)	2
Patrick Worré		01/10/84	G	15		
Fabrice Yao	FRA	29/12/95	A	8	(2)	6

FC Progrès Niederkorn

1919 • Jos Haupert (4,000) • progres.lu
Major honours
Luxembourg League (3) 1953, 1978, 1981;
Luxembourg Cup (4) 1933, 1945, 1977, 1978
Coach: Olivier Ciancanelli;
(20/10/15) Pascal Carzaniga (BEL)

2015

03/08	a	Jeunesse	D 0-0	
08/08	h	Hamm Benfica	W 2-0	Bouzid, Poinsignon
16/08	h	Racing Union	W 2-1	og (Dragovic), Poinsignon
23/08	a	Grevenmacher	D 0-0	
28/08	h	Etzella	W 4-0	Rossini 2, Bouzid, Menaï
13/09	a	Dudelange	L 1-2	Rossini (p)
19/09	h	Rumelange	W 2-0	Rougeaux, Bouzid (p)
26/09	a	Fola	D 1-1	S Thill
16/10	h	Differdange	L 0-1	
25/10	a	Mondorf-les-Bains	L 1-2	Rossini
31/10	h	Wiltz	W 4-1	Bossi, Rossini, Poinsignon, Cassan
08/11	a	Rosport	W 4-1	Rossini, Menaï, Cassan, Garos
29/11	h	UNA Strassen	W 4-2	Garos, Cassan, Menaï 2

2016

21/02	a	Hamm Benfica	D 2-2	Rossini, Fiorani
27/02	a	Racing Union	D 2-2	Rigo (p), Cassan
06/03	h	Grevenmacher	L 1-2	Bouzid
13/03	a	Etzella	W 2-0	O Thill, og (Magalhaes)
19/03	h	Dudelange	L 0-3	
03/04	a	Rumelange	W 4-0	S Thill 2, Poinsignon, O Thill
09/04	h	Fola	L 0-1	
15/04	a	Differdange	L 0-1	
24/04	h	Mondorf-les-Bains	L 0-1	
30/04	a	Wiltz	L 2-3	Bouzid 2 (1p)
08/05	h	Rosport	W 2-1	S Thill, Menaï
13/05	a	UNA Strassen	D 1-1	S Thill
22/05	h	Jeunesse	L 0-2	

Name	Nat	DoB	Pos	Aps	(s)	Gls
Valerio Barbaro		16/02/98	M	1	(1)	
Paul Bossi		22/07/91	M	8	(7)	1
Ismaël Bouzid	ALG	21/07/83	D	24		6
Olivier Cassan	FRA	01/06/84	M	17	(7)	4
Fabiano Castellani Christophe		11/05/89	G	1	(2)	
Cunha da Fonseca		08/01/95	A		(4)	
David Soares	POR	20/02/91	D	16	(4)	
Samuel Dog	FRA	13/02/85	D	17	(1)	
Adrien Ferino	FRA	19/06/92	D	25		
Alessandro Fiorani		16/02/89	D	19	(6)	1
Sébastien Flauss	FRA	29/12/92	G	25		
Mickaël Garos	FRA	10/05/88	M	24		2
Tim Lehnen		17/06/86	D	2	(6)	
Hakim Menaï	FRA	27/03/86	A	18	(4)	5
Valentin Poinsignon	FRA	23/03/94	M	20	(5)	4
Dzenid Ramdedović	MNE	25/02/92	M	14	(4)	
Jonathan Rigo	FRA	16/09/87	D	10	(1)	1
Giuseppe Rossini	BEL	23/08/86	A	11	(4)	7
Lévy Rougeaux	FRA	05/05/85	M	2	(3)	1
Olivier Thill		17/12/96	M	14	(9)	2
Sébastien Thill		29/12/93	M	18	(4)	5

Racing FC Union Lëtzebuerg

2005 • Achille Hammerel (5,864) • racing-fc.lu
Coach: Fabien Matagne (FRA);
(18/03/16) Philippe Ciancanelli & Mickaël Ménétier (FRA)

2015

02/08	h	Hamm Benfica	L 1-4	Bop (p)
09/08	a	Differdange	D 1-1	Bop
16/08	a	Progrès	L 1-2	Jahier
23/08	h	Mondorf-les-Bains	W 2-1	Jahier 2
28/08	a	Grevenmacher	W 3-0	Jahier 2, Lahoussine
13/09	h	Wiltz	W 4-0	Bop 2, Jahier 2
20/09	a	Etzella	W 4-2	Sinani, Jahier 2, Bop
27/09	h	Rosport	L 0-4	
18/10	a	Dudelange	L 2-4	Jahier (p), Sinani
25/10	h	UNA Strassen	L 1-2	Rodrigues
31/10	a	Rumelange	W 4-2	Bellini, Jahier 2 (1p), Sinani
08/11	h	Jeunesse	D 0-0	
29/11	a	Fola	L 0-1	

2016

21/02	a	Differdange	L 0-6	
27/02	h	Progrès	D 2-2	Bernardelli 2 (1p)
06/03	a	Mondorf-les-Bains	W 3-1	Bop, Lacroix, Jahier
13/03	h	Grevenmacher	W 2-1	Bernardelli, Jahier
20/03	a	Wiltz	W 2-0	Bernardelli, Jahier
03/04	h	Etzella	W 2-1	Jahier, og (Magalhaes)
10/04	a	Rosport	L 2-4	Jahier 2 (1p)
17/04	h	Dudelange	L 0-2	
24/04	a	UNA Strassen	W 2-1	Rodrigues, Jahier
30/04	h	Rumelange	L 2-3	Rodrigues, Jahier
08/05	a	Jeunesse	L 0-5	
13/05	h	Fola	D 2-2	Jahier 2
22/05	h	Hamm Benfica	D 3-3	Jahier 3 (1p)

Name	Nat	DoB	Pos	Aps	(s)	Gls
Ismaël Assekour	FRA	08/11/87	A	1	(4)	
Johan Bellini	FRA	02/06/83	M	15		1
Gauthier Bernardelli	FRA	28/08/91	D	9	(3)	4
Fine Bop	SEN	12/10/89	M	19	(4)	6
Dirk Carlson		01/04/98	D		(1)	
Yannick Dias da Graca		13/07/96	D	14	(3)	
Ricardo Diomisio		23/01/98	A	1	(4)	
Nenad Dragovic		04/06/94	D	15	(8)	
Jason Goncalves		01/11/95	G	8	(2)	
Philippe Hahm		13/01/90	G	5		
Jonathan Hennetier	FRA	06/11/91	D	17	(1)	
Giuliano Jackson		23/09/94	D	1	(4)	
Julien Jahier	FRA	28/11/80	A	22	(1)	25
Fodé Kébé	FRA	21/10/77	D	15		
Kevin Lacroix	FRA	13/10/84	D	22		1
Kamel Lahoussine	FRA	10/01/91	M	15	(4)	1
Pape M'Boup	SEN	13/08/87	M	21		
Mickaël Ménétrier	FRA	23/09/78	G	13		
Idir Mokrani	ALG	23/01/91	A	5	(8)	
Gerson Rodrigues		20/06/95	M	20	(3)	3
Nikola Schreiner		01/09/95	M	2	(6)	
Florik Shala		19/07/97	M		(4)	
Danel Sinani		05/04/97	M	16	(7)	3
Admir Skrijelj		03/06/92	M	24	(2)	
Dylan Tavares		17/07/96	D		(1)	
Jérémy Vilmain	FRA	28/08/90	A	6	(4)	

LUXEMBOURG

US Rumelange

1908 • Stade Municipal (2,950) • usrumelange.lu
Major honours
Luxembourg Cup (2) 1968, 1975
Coach: Marc Birsens;
(05/01/16) Christian Joachim

2015
02/08 a	Mondorf-les-Bains	W 3-0	Thior, Tino Barbosa, Inácio Cabral
09/08 h	Wiltz	D 1-1	Bryan Gomes
16/08 a	Rosport	W 1-0	Pupovac
23/08 h	UNA Strassen	L 1-2	Inácio Cabral
28/08 a	Jeunesse	L 0-1	
13/09 h	Hamm Benfica	L 2-5	Bryan Gomes, Inácio Cabral
19/09 a	Progrès	L 0-2	
27/09 h	Grevenmacher	W 2-1	Cabral, Inácio Cabral
18/10 a	Etzella	L 0-1	
25/10 h	Dudelange	L 2-4	Cabral 2
31/10 a	Racing Union	L 2-4	Cabral, Tino Barbosa
08/11 a	Fola	L 1-3	Cabral
29/11 h	Differdange	W 4-1	Cabral 2, Diallo, Tino Barbosa

2016
21/02 a	Wiltz	W 1-0	Bryan Gomes
28/02 h	Rosport	D 1-1	Inácio Cabral
06/03 a	UNA Strassen	L 3-5	Diallo, Tino Barbosa, Cabral
13/03 h	Jeunesse	D 1-1	Diallo
20/03 a	Hamm Benfica	W 4-1	Diallo (p), Pupovac, Thior, Lopes
03/04 h	Progrès	L 0-4	
09/04 a	Grevenmacher	D 1-1	Lopes
17/04 h	Etzella	W 1-0	Diallo
24/04 a	Dudelange	L 3-4	Cabral (p), Lopes, Bryan Gomes
30/04 a	Racing Union	W 3-2	Diallo, Sahin 2
08/05 h	Fola	L 1-3	Cabral
14/05 a	Differdange	L 0-3	
22/05 h	Mondorf-les-Bains	L 0-2	

Name	Nat	DoB	Pos	Aps	(s)	Gls
André Rodrigues Vaz	POR	16/10/87	M	2	(5)	
Bryan Gomes	POR	05/12/93	M	17	(7)	4
Cabral	POR	30/09/87	A	22	(1)	10
Samuel Correia		29/09/97	M	14	(8)	
Quentin Depré	FRA	19/11/91	D	8	(2)	
Jules Diallo	FRA	08/03/93	A	15	(3)	6
Etienne Donval	FRA	04/04/95	D	10	(3)	
Igor Pereira	POR	06/07/87	M	7	(1)	
Inácio Cabral	POR	15/11/83	D	18		5
Johnny Santos	POR	06/06/94	M	1	(3)	
Kim Kleber		24/12/87	D	8	(3)	
Tony Lopes	FRA	04/11/81	A	15	(4)	3
Kevin Majerus		30/09/85	M	1	(2)	
Merlin Muhovic		22/09/94	M	7	(8)	
Jeff Pauly		01/03/93	G	1	(1)	
Nikola Pupovac	FRA	16/02/84	M	19	(1)	2
Raphaël Rodrigues		16/02/89	D	9	(1)	
Fatih Sahin	FRA	18/01/85	A	16	(4)	2
Charly Schinker		05/11/87	G	25		
Mateusz Siebert	POL	04/04/89	D	22		
Kerim Skenderović	MNE	26/06/97	A	1	(4)	
François Thior	FRA	11/02/85	M	17	(2)	2
Tino Barbosa	POR	06/05/92	M	12	(4)	4
Glodi Zingha		04/11/93	D	19	(2)	

FC UNA Strassen

1922 • Complexe Sportif Jean Wirtz (2,000) • fcuna-strassen.lu
Coach: Patrick Grettnich

2015
02/08 h	Grevenmacher	W 4-1	Jager 3, Dragolovcanin
09/08 a	Etzella	W 6-2	Gilson Delgado 2, D Agovic, Dragolovcanin, Lourenco, Collette
16/08 h	Dudelange	D 2-2	Mondon-Konan, Alomerovic
23/08 a	Rumelange	W 2-1	Gilson Delgado, Rondel
28/08 h	Fola	W 4-2	Dragolovcanin, Jager 2, Kettenmeyer
13/09 a	Differdange	L 0-2	
20/09 h	Mondorf-les-Bains	W 2-1	Jager 2 (1p)
27/09 a	Wiltz	L 0-1	
18/10 h	Rosport	W 4-3	Jager 2, E Agovic 2
25/10 a	Racing Union	W 2-1	Gilson Delgado, Jager
31/10 a	Jeunesse	L 3-4	Jager 2, Rondel
08/11 h	Hamm Benfica	D 0-0	
29/11 a	Progrès	L 2-4	E Agovic, Kerger

2016
21/02 h	Etzella	W 2-0	Gilson Delgado, Lourenco
28/02 a	Dudelange	L 0-1	
06/03 h	Rumelange	W 5-3	E Agovic, Jager 2, Rondel, Lourenco
13/03 a	Fola	L 1-3	E Agovic
20/03 h	Differdange	L 1-4	Gilson Delgado
03/04 a	Mondorf-les-Bains	D 1-1	E Agovic
10/04 h	Wiltz	W 3-1	Jager, og (Dennis Souza), Lourenco
16/04 a	Rosport	D 2-2	Jager, Gilson Delgado
24/04 h	Racing Union	L 1-2	Jager (p)
30/04 h	Jeunesse	W 2-1	Ruppert 2
08/05 a	Hamm Benfica	L 0-4	
13/05 h	Progrès	D 1-1	Collette
22/05 a	Grevenmacher	L 0-3	

Name	Nat	DoB	Pos	Aps	(s)	Gls
Denis Agovic		12/07/93	M	24	(1)	1
Edis Agovic		12/07/93	A	24		6
Assim Alomerovic		25/01/83	M	13	(8)	1
Emanuele Chioato		26/12/79	G	23		
Dan Collette		02/04/85	M	11	(12)	2
David Da Mota		05/12/89	M	6	(3)	
Denis Dragolovcanin		17/12/90	A	7	(3)	3
Gilson Delgado	CPV	19/10/92	D	24	(1)	7
Emmanuel Hannachi	FRA	11/05/89	M	4	(3)	
Edvin Humerovic		15/10/92	M	2	(2)	
Mickaël Jager	FRA	13/01/89	A	24	(1)	17
Jocelino Silva	POR	29/08/89	D	20	(1)	
Kevin Kerger		17/11/94	D	22		1
Michel Kettenmeyer		07/02/89	M	6	(12)	1
Kevin Lourenco		12/05/92	M	21	(1)	4
Luís Oliveira	POR	26/07/92	D	2		
Lex Menster		13/10/91	G	3		
Patrice Mondon-Konan	CIV	17/03/83	D	24		1
Nélson Morgado	POR	30/04/87	M	3	(2)	
Christophe Quiring		18/03/90	D	1		
Christopher Rondel	FRA	15/01/90	M	12	(13)	3
Kevin Ruppert		16/08/91	A	1	(3)	2
Taimo Vaz Djassi	POR	09/03/88	M	9	(5)	

FC Victoria Rosport

1928 • Stade du Camping (1,500) • fcvictoriarosport.lu
Coach: Dan Theis;
(21/03/16) Claude Osweiler

2015
02/08 h	Etzella	L 1-2	Schulz
09/08 a	Dudelange	L 1-7	Gaspar
16/08 h	Rumelange	L 0-1	
23/08 a	Fola	L 0-2	
28/08 h	Differdange	L 2-3	Förg, Lascak
13/09 a	Mondorf-les-Bains	L 2-3	Weirich, Lascak
19/09 h	Wiltz	D 0-0	
27/09 a	Racing Union	W 4-0	Pott, Schulz, Pedro dos Santos, Weirich
18/10 a	UNA Strassen	L 3-4	Förg, Poloshenko, Steinbach (p)
25/10 h	Jeunesse	L 1-2	Förg
31/10 a	Hamm Benfica	W 3-2	Pedro dos Santos 2, Lascak
08/11 h	Progrès	L 1-4	Lascak
29/11 a	Grevenmacher	W 2-0	Steinbach, Lascak

2016
21/02 h	Dudelange	L 1-2	Isaías Cardoso
28/02 a	Rumelange	D 1-1	Pedro dos Santos
06/03 h	Fola	D 1-1	Lascak
13/03 a	Differdange	D 1-1	Weirich
20/03 h	Mondorf-les-Bains	L 0-3	
03/04 a	Wiltz	W 4-0	Weirich, Dücker, Pedro dos Santos, Lascak
10/04 h	Racing Union	W 4-2	Karapetyan, Weirich, Lascak 2
16/04 a	UNA Strassen	D 2-2	Weirich 2
24/04 a	Jeunesse	D 1-1	Lascak
30/04 h	Hamm Benfica	W 5-1	Lascak 2, Karapetyan 2, Weirich
08/05 a	Progrès	L 1-2	Karapetyan
14/05 h	Grevenmacher	L 0-1	
22/05 a	Etzella	W 5-1	Poloshenko, Karapetyan 2, Lascak 2

Name	Nat	DoB	Pos	Aps	(s)	Gls
Christian Adams	GER	22/08/88	M	16	(3)	
Niklas Bürger	GER	07/10/92	G	25		
Raphaël De Sousa		05/06/93	M	11	(1)	
Julian Dücker	GER	05/02/90	D		(1)	
Nicolas Dücker	GER	05/02/90	D	14	(8)	1
Raphael Duhr		04/08/93	M	3	(4)	
Sebastian Förg	GER	26/04/88	M	10	(7)	3
Gabriel Gaspar		20/07/90	M	20	(2)	1
Isaías Cardoso	POR	15/12/88	A	1	(5)	1
Nicolas Jakob	GER	12/03/93	M		(2)	
Alexander Karapetyan	ARM	23/12/87	A	10	(1)	6
Jeff Lascak		13/02/94	A	18	(4)	14
Olivier Lickes		27/06/88	D	5	(2)	
Tim Lieser	GER	03/02/95	G		(1)	
Pedro dos Santos	POR	21/11/90	M	23	(2)	5
Lars Peifer	GER	03/07/93	M		(1)	
Daniel Petersch	GER	28/01/91	D	2	(1)	
Artur Poloshenko	GER	06/01/87	M	7	(7)	2
Alex Pott		21/10/88	A	2	(9)	1
Théo Ramsden		23/04/98	M	2	(1)	
Gustav Schulz	GER	27/06/85	M	19	(4)	2
Flavio Schuster	GER	13/02/92	D	6		
Johannes Steinbach	GER	02/07/92	D	25		2
Ben Vogel		22/12/94	D	25		
Dylan Vogel		29/10/98	G	1	(1)	
Florian Weirich	GER	23/09/90	M	25	(1)	8
Philippe Werdel		12/05/90	D	16	(3)	

FC Wiltz 71

1971 • Stade Géitzt (2,000); Stade am Pëtz (2,000) • fcwiltz.com
Coach: Henri Bossi; (23/03/16) Pascal Lebrun (BEL)

2015

02/08	h	Dudelange	L	0-6
09/08	a	Rumelange	D	1-1 Osmanović
16/08	h	Fola	L	0-2
23/08	a	Differdange	L	0-5
30/08	h	Mondorf-les-Bains	L	0-1
13/09	a	Racing Union	L	0-4
19/09	a	Rosport	D	0-0
27/09	h	UNA Strassen	W	1-0 Keïta
18/10	a	Jeunesse	L	0-2
25/10	h	Hamm Benfica	L	0-1
31/10	a	Progrès	L	1-4 Osmanović
08/11	h	Grevenmacher	W	3-2 Dennis Souza, Verbist 2
29/11	h	Etzella	D	1-1 Osmanović (p)

2016

21/02	h	Rumelange	L	0-1
28/02	a	Fola	L	0-5
06/03	h	Differdange	W	3-2 Burkič, Civic, Keïta
13/03	a	Mondorf-les-Bains	L	2-4 Keïta, Osmanović
20/03	h	Racing Union	L	0-2
03/04	a	Rosport	L	0-4
10/04	a	UNA Strassen	L	1-3 Joachim
17/04	a	Jeunesse	L	1-5 Dennis Souza
24/04	a	Hamm Benfica	D	0-0
30/04	h	Progrès	W	3-2 Conrad, Joachim, Keïta
07/05	a	Grevenmacher	W	2-0 Osmanović, Joachim
13/05	h	Etzella	D	2-2 Osmanović (p), Keïta
22/05	a	Dudelange	D	1-1 Osmanović (p)

Name	Nat	DoB	Pos	Aps	(s)	Gls
Mirko Albanese		04/09/89	A	8	(13)	
Ivan Bilus	CRO	09/06/93	M	3	(1)	
Emir Burkič	SVN	27/07/93	M	10		1
Mustafa Cheriak	ALG	09/05/93	M	21		
Adis Civic		26/11/94	M	8	(10)	1
Jason Conrad	BEL	03/01/90	D	17	(1)	1
Amel Cosic		19/11/89	A	1	(4)	
Dany Fernandes	POR	09/05/94	D	10	(7)	
Dennis Souza	BRA	09/01/80	D	23		2
Thomas Doyennel	FRA	14/12/89	D	4		
Haris Faljic		01/06/91	D	10	(2)	
Ben Gasper		14/03/95	M		(2)	
Jean-Michel Joachim	FRA	13/05/92	A	9	(1)	3
Emko Kalabic		30/03/89	M	8	(7)	
Mory Keïta	GUI	13/12/92	M	12	(5)	5
Rodrigue Kouayep	CMR	07/12/86	D	24	(1)	
Mehmet Mujkic		26/09/83	M	6	(4)	
Matías Navarrete	ARG		M	1	(3)	
Eldin Nurkovic		17/10/91	D	5	(1)	
Edis Osmanović	BIH	30/06/88	A	22	(2)	7
Romain Ruffier	FRA	04/10/89	G	26		
Babacar Sené	SEN	01/01/83	D	19		
Sérgio Oliveira	POR	17/01/94	D	18	(1)	
Christopher Verbist	BEL	08/10/91	M	21	(1)	2

Top goalscorers

25	Julien Jahier (Racing Union)
24	Momar N'Diaye (Jeunesse)
20	David Turpel (Dudelange)
18	Omar Er Rafik (Differdange) Stefano Bensi (Fola)
17	Mickaël Jager (UNA Strassen)
14	Jeff Lascak (Rosport)
13	Samir Hadji (Fola) Patrick Stumpf (Hamm Benfica)
12	Sanel Ibrahimović (Dudelange)

Promoted clubs

UN Käerjéng 97

1997 • Um Dribbel (2,000) • un-kaerjeng.lu
Coach: Angelo Fiorucci (ITA)

FC Union Titus Pétange

2015 • Stade Municipal (2,400) • uniontituspetange.lu
Coach: Paolo Amodio

FC Jeunesse Canach

1957 • Stade rue de Lenningen (1,500) • fccanach.lu
Coach: Patrick Maurer; (06/01/16) Oséias Ferreira (POR)

Second level final table 2015/16

		Pld	W	D	L	F	A	Pts
1	UN Käerjéng 97	26	18	5	3	58	26	59
2	FC Union Titus Pétange	26	18	4	4	60	28	58
3	FC Jeunesse Canach	26	15	5	6	52	29	50
4	US Hostert	26	12	7	7	47	29	43
5	FC Rodange 91	26	13	3	10	39	37	42
6	FF Norden 02	26	12	4	10	41	46	40
7	FC Mondercange	26	10	6	10	48	52	36
8	FC Mamer 32	26	8	9	9	34	38	33
9	FC Swift Hesperange	26	8	8	10	37	37	32
10	US Sandweiler	26	8	3	14	39	49	30
11	FC Avenir Beggen	26	8	4	14	39	49	28
12	FC 72 Erpeldange	26	7	5	14	32	50	26
13	FC Union 05 Kayl-Tétange	26	6	5	15	37	47	23
14	FC Union Remich-Bous	26	3	2	21	20	66	11

Promotion/Relegation play-off

(27/05/16)
Jeunesse Canach 1-0 Wiltz *(aet)*

DOMESTIC CUP

Coupe de Luxembourg 2015/16

FIFTH ROUND

(20/11/15)
Bissen 1-2 Etzella

(21/11/15)
Rodange 3-4 Titus Pétange
Schieren 1-4 Wiltz

(22/11/15)
Bastendorf 0-5 Progrès
Beggen 1-4 Differdange
Erpeldange 0-2 Dudelange
Hostert 1-2 Mondorf-les-Bains
Jeunesse Canach 1-4 Jeunesse Esch *(aet)*
Käerjéng 1-0 Grevenmacher
Lintgen 1-3 Fola
Mamer 0-2 Rumelange *(aet)*
Mersch 0-6 UNA Strassen
Muhlenbach 0-3 Rosport
Norden 0-3 US Esch
Swift 2-3 Racing Union *(aet)*

(25/11/15)
Bertrange 0-4 Hamm Benfica

SIXTH ROUND

(05/12/15)
Racing Union 2-0 Rosport

(06/12/15)
Jeunesse Esch 0-5 Dudelange
Käerjéng 3-2 Differdange
Mondorf-les-Bains 2-0 Hamm Benfica
Progrès 0-4 Fola
Rumelange 1-0 Wiltz
UNA Strassen 3-1 Etzella
US Esch 0-1 Titus Pétange

QUARTER-FINALS

(20/04/16)
Fola 4-0 UNA Strassen *(Hadji 49, Laterza 81, Bensi 85, Keita 89)*

Käerjéng 2-4 Dudelange *(Terzic 1, Khemici 62; Turpel 6p, 42, 92, Marques 118) (aet)*

Mondorf-les-Bains 2-0 Racing Union *(Soares 78, Thonon 90+2)*

Titus Pétange 3-2 Rumelange *(Baier 17, De Sousa 66, 76; Zingha 48, Diallo 60)*

SEMI-FINALS

(05/05/16)
Dudelange 4-0 Titus Pétange *(Turpel 93, Ben Ajiba 108, Nakache 109, 117) (aet)*

Mondorf-les-Bains 1-0 Fola *(Yao 11)*

FINAL

(29/05/16)
Stade Josy Barthel, Luxembourg
F91 DUDELANGE 1 *(Da Mota 32)*
US MONDORF-LES-BAINS 0
Referee: *Krüger*
DUDELANGE: Joubert, Malget, Prempeh, Schnell, Ney, Dikaba, Pedro (Stélvio 67), Moreira, Nakache (Humbert 75), Da Mota (Turpel 88), Ibrahimović
MONDORF-LES-BAINS: Worré, Semedo, Dione (Kuduzović 83), Benhemine, Monteiro, Nabli, Thonon, Haddadji (Pjanić 72), Marques, Soares, Yao

Former Yugoslav Republic of
MACEDONIA
Fudbalska Federacija na Makedonija (FFM)

Address	Bul. ASNOM bb MK-1000 Skopje	**President**	Ilco Gjorgioski
Tel	+389 23 129 291	**General secretary**	Filip Popovski
Fax	+389 23 165 448	**Media officer**	Zoran Nikolovski
E-mail	biljana.velkovska @ffm.com.mk	**Year of formation**	1948
Website	ffm.com.mk	**National stadium**	Filip II Arena, Skopje (33,000)

PRVA LIGA CLUBS

 1 FK Bregalnica Stip

 2 FK Metalurg Skopje

 3 FK Mladost Carev Dvor

 4 FK Rabotnicki

 5 KF Renova

 6 KF Shkëndija

 7 FK Shkupi

 8 FK Sileks

 9 FK Turnovo

 10 FK Vardar

PROMOTED CLUBS

 11 FK Pobeda

 12 FK Makedonija

 13 FK Pelister

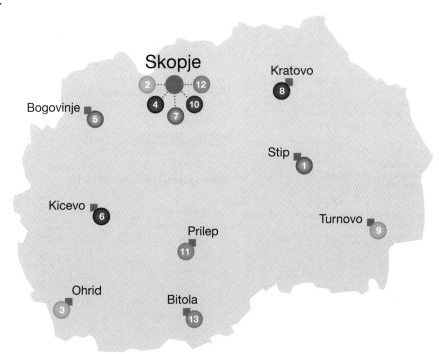

KEY

● UEFA Champions League

◗ UEFA Europa League

● Promoted

● Relegated

Vardar remain on victory trail

FK Vardar retained the Macedonian Prva Liga title in 2015/16, winning 25 of their 32 matches and losing just twice. It was an impressive return under new head coach Goce Sedloski, but while they led throughout, tenacious challengers KF Shkëndija were never far from their coat-tails.

Although edged out in the league, Shkëndija, who finished 31 points ahead of third-placed FK Sileks, consoled themselves by winning the Macedonian Cup for the first time and in the process denying beaten finalists Rabotnicki a competition hat-trick.

Fourth title in five years for Skopje club

Shkëndija go close in league and win the cup

Another change of coach for national team

Domestic league

Vardar's 2014/15 title-winning coach Sergei Andreev did not get the opportunity to defend the trophy. He was sacked on the eve of the league campaign after the team's early exit from Europe, with the reins being passed on to the club's director of football, Goce Sedloski – the only man to have won 100 caps for the FYR Macedonia national team. After drawing their opening fixture, at home to newly-promoted Shkupi, Vardar won 3-1 away at Shkëndija and then 6-0 at home to the other top-flight newcomers, Mladost Carev Dvor, and suddenly they were top of the table.

The season was 15 rounds old before Sedloski's side suffered their first defeat, 2-1 away to Turnovo, but although Shkëndija – led by Albanian coach Shpëtim Duro and fired by the goals of Besart Ibraimi and Ferhan Hasani – got off to a brilliant start, taking maximum points from eight of their opening nine games, they lost that winning habit in the late autumn – following a serious injury to skipper Hasani – and by the winter break, with 18 of the 32 matches played, Vardar held a five-point lead.

Duro paid for that pre-Christmas slump with his job, with ex-Bosnia & Herzegovina international Bruno Akrapović, who had been working in

Gibraltar, summoned to reignite Shkëndija's title challenge. He did just that, with Ibraimi continuing to score prolifically in an eight-game winning sequence that closed the gap on Vardar to two points before the rivals met in the 27th and final round of the first phase. A 1-1 draw left the status quo unaltered, but in the re-match, at the same Filip II Arena just seven days later, Vardar scored early, through midfielder Jasir Asani, and held on for the win that effectively secured the club's ninth Macedonian title.

Unsurprisingly, both clubs won their last three matches, leaving Vardar on a remarkable 80 points – 11 more than their 2014/15 winning total – and Shkëndija on 75, up 16 on the previous campaign. It was a contest neither team deserved to lose, with Vardar having the better defence (17 goals conceded) and Shkëndija the superior attack, golden boot winner Ibraimi contributing 26 of the team's 74 goals. The deciding factor in the title race was the outcome of the four head-to-head fixtures, from which Vardar collected eight points and Shkëndija just two.

Domestic cup

Vardar may have had the upper hand in the league, but Shkëndija defeated them home and away in the quarter-finals of the Macedonian Cup en route to lifting

the trophy for the first time. Their victims in the final were Rabotnicki, victorious in each of the previous two seasons but unable to complete the hat-trick as a result of Marjan Radeski's early strike and a stoppage-time second from Brazilian striker Sténio Júnior.

Europe

Rabotnicki ended the season in disappointment, but they began it with an impressive run from the first qualifying round of the UEFA Europa League to the play-offs, claiming the notable scalp of Turkish club Trabzonspor before narrowly going out to Russian competition specialists Rubin. Vardar and Shkëndija, meanwhile, both fell at the first hurdle on the away goals rule.

National team

Igor Angelovski was the man who oversaw Rabotnicki's European adventure – although it was his assistant Tomislav Franc who was officially named as coach for licensing reasons – and the two-time domestic cup winner was to be named as the new man in charge of the FYR Macedonia national side following a poor finish to the UEFA EURO 2016 qualifying campaign that left them bottom of their group with just four points. Ljubinko Drulović, the man Angelovski replaced, had been in the job for a mere six months.

DOMESTIC SEASON AT A GLANCE

Prva Liga 2015/16 final table

			Home					Away					Total					
		Pld	W	D	L	F	A	W	D	L	F	A	W	D	L	F	A	Pts
1	**FK Vardar**	**32**	**14**	**3**	**0**	**42**	**9**	**11**	**2**	**2**	**25**	**8**	**25**	**5**	**2**	**67**	**17**	**80**
2	KF Shkëndija	32	14	2	1	46	15	9	4	2	28	9	23	6	3	74	24	75
3	FK Sileks	32	10	5	2	25	13	2	3	10	10	27	12	8	12	35	40	44
4	FK Rabotnicki	32	7	6	3	22	13	3	7	6	14	17	10	13	9	36	30	43
5	FK Shkupi	32	5	6	5	16	14	4	5	7	13	20	9	11	12	29	34	38
6	FK Bregalnica Stip	32	7	2	6	21	19	3	6	8	21	30	10	8	14	42	49	38
7	KF Renova	33	11	5	0	34	11	2	3	12	15	31	13	8	12	49	42	47
8	FK Turnovo	33	9	5	2	25	10	3	5	9	20	33	12	10	11	45	43	46
9	FK Metalurg Skopje	33	3	2	11	14	30	2	2	13	13	36	5	4	24	27	66	19
10	FK Mladost Carev Dvor	33	4	1	11	12	35	2	0	15	10	46	6	1	26	22	81	19

NB League splits into top six and bottom four after 27 games, after which the clubs play exclusively against teams in their group.

European qualification 2016/17

Champion: FK Vardar (second qualifying round)

Cup winner: KF Shkëndija (first qualifying round)
FK Sileks (first qualifying round)
FK Rabotnicki (first qualifying round)

Top scorer	Besart Ibraimi (Shkëndija), 26 goals
Relegated clubs	FK Mladost Carev Dvor, FK Metalurg Skopje, FK Turnovo
Promoted clubs	FK Pobeda, FK Makedonija, FK Pelister
Cup final	KF Shkëndija 2-0 FK Rabotnicki

Team of the season
(4-3-1-2)

Coach: Sedloski *(Vardar)*

Pacovski *(Vardar)*

Hambardzumyan *(Vardar)* — Ilievski *(Rabotnicki)* — Grncarov *(Vardar)* — Popov *(Vardar)*

Najdenov *(Turnovo/Rabotnicki)* — Alimi *(Shkëndija)* — Radeski *(Shkëndija)*

Juan Felipe *(Vardar)*

Ibraimi *(Shkëndija)* — Nedeljković *(Sileks)*

Player of the season

Juan Felipe
(FK Vardar)

A newcomer to the Vardar ranks for 2015/16, Juan Felipe made the short trip across the border from Sofia, where he had spent a season with Bulgarian giants CSKA before their enforced relegation. The 28-year-old added some classical Brazilian flair to the Skopje club's play in his advanced midfield role, scoring eight goals and setting up countless opportunities for his team-mates. He started more games than any other Vardar player – 30 – and was a major contributor to most of the 25 wins that propelled them to the title.

Newcomer of the season

Marjan Radeski
(KF Shkëndija)

Radeski broke the Macedonian Prva Liga transfer record when he left Metalurg Skopje for Shkëndija in 2015, and although already billed as a rising star, the 21-year-old went on to fulfil his potential with a brilliant breakthrough season, scoring ten goals and catching the eye with a succession of energetic and creative displays as Shkëndija launched a season-long assault on the league title. He missed out on that prize but got his hands on the Macedonian Cup after scoring the all-important opening goal in the final against Rabotnicki.

NATIONAL TEAM

Top five all-time caps
Goce Sedloski (100); Velice Sumulikoski (84); **Goran Pandev** (79); Artim Sakiri (72); Igor Mitreski (70)

Top five all-time goals
Goran Pandev (27); Georgi Hristov (16); Artim Sakiri (15); Goran Maznov (10); Ilco Naumoski (9)

Results 2015/16

05/09/15	Luxembourg (ECQ)	A	Luxembourg	L	0-1	
08/09/15	Spain (ECQ)	H	Skopje	L	0-1	
09/10/15	Ukraine (ECQ)	H	Skopje	L	0-2	
12/10/15	Belarus (ECQ)	A	Borisov	D	0-0	
12/11/15	Montenegro	H	Skopje	W	4-1	*Sikov (35), Trajkovski (38p, 40, 64)*
17/11/15	Lebanon	H	Skopje	L	0-1	
23/03/16	Slovenia	A	Koper	L	0-1	
29/03/16	Bulgaria	H	Skopje	L	0-2	
29/05/16	Azerbaijan	N	Bad Erlach (AUT)	W	3-1	*Radeski (20), Pandev (33), Nestorovski (90+2)*
02/06/16	Iran	H	Skopje	L	1-3	*Trajkovski (10)*

Appearances 2015/16

Coach: Ljubinko Drulović (SRB) 11/09/68 /(16/10/15) Igor Angelovski 02/06/76			LUX	ESP	UKR	BLR	Mne	Lib	Svn	Bul	Aze	Irn	Caps	Goals
Tomislav Pacovski	28/06/82	Vardar	G	G	G								46	-
Stefan Ristovski	12/02/92	Rijeka (CRO)	D			D	D	D69	D82	D75	D	D	25	
Daniel Mojsov	25/12/87	Adana Demirspor (TUR)	D37			D	D	D					32	-
Vance Sikov	19/07/85	Austria Wien (AUT)	D	D	D	D	D	D	D	D	D	D	49	4
Leonard Zhuta	09/08/92	Rijeka (CRO)	D	D	D	D	D	D	D82	D	D	s46	11	-
Nikola Gligorov	15/08/83	Vardar	M	M			M	M63	M73	M			25	-
Milovan Petrovic	23/01/90	Rabotnicki	M	M	M	M	s57	s63					6	-
Agim Ibraimi	29/08/88	Maribor (SVN)	M80	s84	M	M86			M55	M76			39	7
Besart Abdurahimi	31/07/90	Lokeren (BEL)	M		s22	s73							12	1
Aleksandar Trajkovski	05/09/92	Palermo (ITA)	M74	s68	A		M83	M	M		A60	A	31	8
Mirko Ivanovski	31/10/89	Videoton (HUN)	A	A68	s64								27	1
Kire Ristevski	22/10/90	Rabotnicki /Vasas (HUN)	s37	D	D				D	D75	D	D	11	-
Blaze Ilijoski	09/07/84	Rabotnicki	s74		A64		s83	s46					14	1
Stefan Askovski	24/02/92	Novi Pazar (SRB)	s80	M76	M78								3	-
Vladica Brdarovski	07/02/90	Vardar		D	D	M73	s72	s69					7	-
Ferhan Hasani	18/06/90	Shkëndija		M	M22								23	1
Marjan Radeski	10/02/95	Shkëndija		M84							M46	M62	7	1
Enis Bardi	02/07/95	Újpest (HUN)		s76				s46			M30		5	-
Armend Alimi	11/12/87	Shkëndija			M	s84			s46	s60			13	-
Ilija Nestorovski	12/03/90	Inter Zaprešić (CRO)			s78	s86	s58	A46	s46	s76	s74	s62	8	1
David Mitov Nilsson	12/01/91	Norrköping (SWE)				G							1	-
Ostoja Stjepanovic	17/01/85	OFK Beograd (SRB) /AEL (CYP)				M84	M72	M46	M	M60			14	-
Ivan Trickovski	18/04/87	Legia (POL) /AEK Larnaca (CYP)				M	M57	M	M46	M	M60	M63	41	4
Stole Dimitrievski	25/12/93	Granada (ESP)					G	G	G	G	G	G	6	-
Krste Velkoski	20/02/88	Sarajevo (BIH)					A58	A77					10	-
Viktor Angelov	27/03/94	Metalurg Skopje						s77					1	-
Goran Pandev	27/07/83	Genoa (ITA)							A46	A	A74	A46	79	27
Adis Jahovic	18/03/87	Krylya Sovetov (RUS)							s55	A60			14	3
Mite Cikarski	06/01/93	Rabotnicki							s73	s75			3	-
Jovan Kostovski	19/04/87	Leuven (BEL)							s82	s60			13	2
Goran Siljanovski	01/07/90	Rabotnicki							s82	s75			4	-
Bojan Najdenov	27/08/91	Rabotnicki									M83	M63	4	-
Boban Nikolov	28/07/94	Vardar									s30	M46	2	-
Dejan Pesevski	05/08/93	Podbrezová (SVK)									s46	s63	2	-
Nikola Gjorgjev	22/08/97	Grasshoppers (SUI)									s60	s63	2	-
David Babunski	01/03/94	Crvena zvezda (SRB)									s60	s46	8	-
Besir Demiri	01/08/94	Shkëndija									s83	s46	2	-
Gjoko Zajkov	10/02/95	Charleroi (BEL)										D46	1	-

EUROPE

FK Vardar

Second qualifying round - APOEL FC (CYP)
A 0-0
Pacovski, Popov, Mijušković, Grncarov, Blazevski (Asani 88), Velkovski, Gligorov, Hambardzumyan, Nikolov, Ivanovski (Stojkov 75), Juan Felipe (Dashyan 64). Coach: Sergei Andreev (RUS)
H 1-1 *Ljamčevski (90+4)*
Pacovski, Popov, Mijušković, Grncarov, Blazevski, Dashyan (Ivanovski 79), Velkoski (Stojkov 64), Gligorov, Hambardzumyan, Juan Felipe, Grozdanoski (Ljamcevski 71). Coach: Sergei Andreev (RUS)

FK Rabotnicki

First qualifying round - FC Flora Tallinn (EST)
A 0-1
Efremov, S Sahiti (Markoski 63), Vujcic, Ilijoski, Siljanovski, Petrovic, Mitrov (Anene 46), Altiparmakovski, Trajcevski (Jovanovski 73), Cikarski, Ilievski. Coach: Tomislav Franc (MKD)
H 2-0 *Anene (48), Altiparmakovski (54)*
Bozinovski, S Sahiti (Jovanovski 85), Vujcic, Anene, Ilijoski (Mitrov 75), Siljanovski, Ristevski, Petrovic, Altiparmakovski (Trajcevski 80), Cikarski, Ilievski. Coach: Tomislav Franc (MKD)

Second qualifying round - FK Jelgava (LVA)
A 0-1
Bozinovski, Vujcic, Anene, Ilijoski (S Sahiti 65), Siljanovski, Ristevski, Petrovic, Altiparmakovski (Jovanovski 79), Trajcevski, Cikarski (Mitrov 88), Ilievski. Coach: Tomislav Franc (MKD)
H 2-0 *Ilijoski (6), S Sahiti (17)*
Bozinovski, S Sahiti, Vujcic, Anene (Trajcevski 68), Ilijoski (Markoski 90+1), Siljanovski, Ristevski, Petrovic, Altiparmakovski (Jovanovski 86), Cikarski, Ilievski. Coach: Tomislav Franc (MKD)

Third qualifying round - Trabzonspor AŞ (TUR)
H 1-0 *Ilijoski (23)*
Bozinovski, S Sahiti (Mitrov 85), Vujcic, Anene, Ilijoski (Trajcevski 64), Siljanovski, Ristevski, Petrovic, Altiparmakovski (Markoski 82), Cikarski, Ilievski. Coach: Tomislav Franc (MKD)
A 1-1 (aet) *Markoski (112)*
Bozinovski, S Sahiti (Altiparmakovski 61), Vujcic, Anene (Markoski 89), Ilijoski (Mitrov 74), Siljanovski, Ristevski, Petrovic, Trajcevski, Cikarski, Ilievski. Coach: Tomislav Franc (MKD)
Red card: Trajcevski 65

Play-offs - FC Rubin (RUS)
H 1-1 *Ristevski (85)*
Bozinovski (Siskovski 90+5), Vujcic, Anene (Najdovski 86), Siljanovski, Ristevski, Markoski, Petrovic, Jovanovski (Ristovski 70), Altiparmakovski, Cikarski, Ilievski. Coach: Tomislav Franc (MKD)
Red card: Petrovic 54
A 0-1
Bozinovski, S Sahiti (Markoski 46), Vujcic, Anene, Ilijoski, Siljanovski, Ristevski, Altiparmakovski, Trajcevski (Jovanovski 87), Cikarski, Ilievski. Coach: Tomislav Franc (MKD)

KF Shkëndija

First qualifying round - Aberdeen FC (SCO)
H 1-1 *Kirovski (84)*
Jovanovski, Abdula (Kirovski 84), Alimi, Cuculi, Polozani, Vručina (Ibraimi 46), Demiri, Todorovski, Stênio Júnior, Victor Juffo (Bejtulai 80), Hasani. Coach: Shpëtim Duro (ALB)
A 0-0
Jovanovski, Abdula (Kirovski 80), Alimi, Cuculi, Polozani, Demiri, Todorovski, Stênio Júnior (Vručina 85), Victor Juffo (Bejtulai 72), Hasani, Ibraimi. Coach: Shpëtim Duro (ALB)

KF Renova

First qualifying round - FC Dacia Chisinau (MDA)
H 0-1
Mustafi, Memedi, Musliu, Emini, Nuhiu, Ramadani (R Selmani 80), Gafuri, Velija (M Neziri 46), Miskovski, Mojsov, Mecinovic (Skenderi 70). Coach: Catip Osmani (MKD)
A 1-4 *Emini (32)*
Mustafi, M Neziri, Memedi, Musliu, Sadiki, Emini, Ramadani (Redzepi 80), Gafuri, Miskovski, Mojsov (Jusufi 71), Mecinovic (Skenderi 71). Coach: Catip Osmani (MKD)

FK Bregalnica Stip

1921 • City, Stip (6,000); Nikola Mantov, Kocani (5,000)• no website
Coach: Vlatko Kostov;
(15/09/15) Dragan Hristovski;
(14/01/16) Igor Stojanov

2015
10/08	h	Rabotnicki	W	1-0	*Mitrev*
16/08	a	Sileks	L	0-1	
23/08	h	Shkupi	L	1-2	*Tonev*
26/08	a	Shkëndija	L	1-5	*Nacev*
29/08	a	Vardar	L	0-2	
13/09	h	Metalurg	W	3-0	*Stojanov, Nacev, Mitrev*
19/09	h	Mladost	L	2-3	*Kocev, Nacev*
27/09	h	Turnovo	W	3-0	*Nacev, Velkovski, Zdravkov (p)*
04/10	a	Renova	D	1-1	*Zdravkov*
17/10	a	Rabotnicki	D	0-0	
25/10	h	Sileks	D	1-1	*Velkovski*
28/10	a	Shkupi	D	0-0	
01/11	h	Shkëndija	L	0-2	
08/11	a	Vardar	L	1-3	*Nacev*
22/11	h	Metalurg	L	0-2	
29/11	a	Mladost	W	4-1	*Zdravkov 2, Stojanov 2*
06/12	a	Turnovo	L	0-2	
10/12	h	Renova	W	3-2	*Hristov, Zdravkov, Nacev*

2016
21/02	h	Sileks	D	2-2	*Zdravkov, Temelkov*
28/02	h	Shkëndija	L	0-3	
08/03	a	Vardar	L	0-4	
13/03	h	Turnovo	W	2-0	*Naumov, Velinov*
19/03	a	Renova	L	0-3	
03/04	a	Mladost	W	5-0	*Mitrev, Stojanov, Tanushev 2, Nacev*
06/04	h	Metalurg	W	4-1	*Mitrev, Velinov, Zdravkov, Nacev*
10/04	a	Shkupi	D	2-2	*Tanushev, Velinov*
17/04	h	Rabotnicki	W	2-1	*Tanushev, Kostov*
20/04	a	Vardar	L	1-2	*Tanushev*
24/04	a	Shkupi	W	2-0	*Tanushev, Ristovski*
30/04	a	Shkëndija	L	0-3	
08/05	h	Renova	D	0-0	
19/05	a	Sileks	D	1-1	*Kostov*

Name	Nat	DoB	Pos	Aps	(s)	Gls
Tomislav Blazevski		30/08/89	D	18	(3)	
Pepi Davitkov		31/07/93	G	2	(1)	
Mario Filipovski		08/08/96	M	2	(1)	
Boban Georgiev		26/01/97	M	1	(1)	
Nikolay Hristov	BUL	01/08/89	M	28		1
Lazar Iliev		23/05/87	A	4	(19)	
Stefan Kocev		23/02/94	D	22	(6)	1
Ljupco Kolev		06/12/78	G	3		
Stefan Kostov		31/10/96	M	18	(4)	2
Mihajlo Mihailov		29/05/91	M		(5)	
Stefan Misev		11/03/96	M	10		
Dejan Mitrev		20/07/88	D	27	(1)	3
Ivan Mitrov		24/10/88	M	12		1
Angel Nacev		10/10/89	A	24	(6)	8
Riste Naumov		14/04/81	A	2	(7)	1
Georgi Nikovski		27/08/92	M	13	(9)	
Dusan Pavlov		12/01/91	G	14		
Stefan Ristovski		22/12/92	M	19	(6)	1
Zvonimir Stanković	SRB	22/11/83	D	16	(7)	
Darko Stojanov		11/02/90	D	20		4
Gjorgi Tanushev		07/01/91	M	12	(1)	6
Aleksandar Temelkov		06/10/87	M	5	(4)	1
Nikola Tonev		12/11/85	D	16		1
Stojanco Velinov		03/09/89	A	7	(2)	3
Slavce Velkovski		05/07/87	M	15	(3)	2
Kostadin Zahov		08/11/87	G	13		
Goran Zdravkov		11/11/80	A	28	(3)	7
Miki Zezov		05/03/97	M	1		

FK Metalurg Skopje

1964 • Boris Trajkovski (2,500);
Železarnica (4,000) • no website
Major honours
Macedonian Cup (1) 2011
Coach: Marjan Gerasimovski;
(02/09/15) Alekso Mackov

2015
09/08	h	Sileks	L 1-3	*Mitrevski*
16/08	a	Shkupi	D 0-0	
23/08	h	Shkëndija	L 0-3	
26/08	a	Vardar	L 0-1	
29/08	h	Mladost	L 1-2	*Stojanovski*
13/09	h	Bregalnica	L 0-3	
20/09	a	Turnovo	D 1-1	*Danoski*
27/09	h	Renova	W 1-0	*Danoski*
04/10	a	Rabotnicki	L 0-2	
18/10	a	Sileks	L 1-3	*Bakracheski*
25/10	h	Shkupi	L 0-1	
28/10	a	Shkëndija	L 0-2	
01/11	h	Vardar	L 0-1	
08/11	h	Mladost	W 5-1	*Naumovski, Tanturovski, Danoski, Stojanovski, Angelov*
22/11	a	Bregalnica	W 2-0	*Naumovski, Mitrevski*
29/11	h	Turnovo	D 2-2	*Stojanovski 2 (1p)*
07/12	a	Renova	L 0-2	
10/12	h	Rabotnicki	D 0-0	

2016
21/02	a	Shkupi	L 0-1	
28/02	h	Rabotnicki	L 1-2	*Stojanovski*
06/03	a	Sileks	L 0-2	
13/03	h	Shkëndija	L 0-4	
19/03	a	Vardar	L 1-2	*Asani*
03/04	h	Turnovo	L 0-1	
06/04	a	Bregalnica	L 1-4	*Naumovski (p)*
10/04	h	Mladost	W 2-0	*Stojanovski, Naumovski*
17/04	a	Renova	L 1-4	*Jakimoski*
20/04	a	Renova	L 1-3	*Naumovski*
24/04	a	Mladost	L 0-2	
30/04	h	Turnovo	L 0-4	
04/05	h	Renova	L 2-4	*Stojcevski, Dodev*
08/05	h	Mladost	W 4-0	*Naumovski, Stojanovski, Dodev, Shoposki*
15/05	a	Turnovo	L 0-5	

Name	Nat	DoB	Pos	Aps	(s)	Gls
Viktor Angelov		27/03/94	M	12	(1)	1
Dzelil Asani		12/09/95	M	10	(4)	1
Naumce Bakracheski		15/11/96	M	9	(1)	1
Antonio Bujcevski		24/01/90	A	2	(6)	
Nikola Camdzic		21/04/98	M		(1)	
Zoran Danoski		20/10/90	M	10	(2)	3
Darko Digalovski		19/01/97	D	6	(1)	
Stojan Dimovski		19/09/82	G	6		
Aladin Djakovac	BIH	22/05/91	M	8	(1)	
Darko Dodev		16/01/98	A	3	(5)	2
Bojan Gjorgjievski		25/01/92	D	12	(2)	
Nikola Gjurcinovski		03/08/96	M	4	(4)	
Filip Ilic		26/01/97	G	16		
Darko Ilieski		14/10/95	D	7	(2)	
Mihajlo Jakimoski		16/04/96	M	11	(8)	1
Stefan Jevtoski		02/09/97	M	13		
Petar Kanzurov		29/07/99	A	3	(12)	
Hristijan Karanfilovski		31/03/97	D	14	(2)	
Meriton Korenica	ALB	15/12/97	M	6	(2)	
Besart Krivanjeva		28/02/92	D	29	(1)	
Mile Krstev		13/05/79	M	5	(5)	
Filip Lazarevski		13/04/97	G	2		
Martin Lekoski		03/05/96	D	5	(2)	
Dejan Leskaroski		17/10/85	D	19	(1)	
Edin Mersovski		11/07/94	M	7	(2)	
Antonio Mitrev		21/01/99	D	14	(2)	
Risto Mitrevski		05/10/91	D	12		2
Mihailo Mitrov		05/03/95	M	1	(2)	
Jordanco Naumoski		15/02/95	M	4	(5)	
Blagoja Naumovski		24/11/93	M	29	(1)	6
Filip Ristovski		03/01/95	D	12	(1)	
Ognen Sazdovski		07/05/97	M		(1)	
Saso Shoposki		18/06/97	M	11	(5)	1
Perica Stanceski		29/01/85	M	5	(1)	
Vlatko Stojanovski		23/04/97	A	25	(4)	7
Filip Stojcevski		04/02/99	M	8	(4)	1
Viktor Stojkovski		03/07/98	D	9	(2)	
Davor Taleski		19/05/95	G	9		
Dejan Tanturovski		12/08/92	M	4		1
Todor Todoroski		26/02/99	D	1	(2)	

FK Mladost Carev Dvor

1930 • City, Ohrid (7,000) • no website
Coach: Zdravko Cvetanovski;
(14/03/16) Kire Sterjov

2015
09/08	a	Shkëndija	L 1-3	*Cvetanovski*
16/08	h	Renova	W 2-1	*Kalanoski, Markovski*
23/08	a	Vardar	L 0-6	
29/08	a	Metalurg	W 2-1	*Dalceski, Konjarski*
13/09	h	Sileks	W 3-1	*Markovski, Kalanoski, Simjanovski*
19/09	a	Bregalnica	W 3-2	*Markovski 2, N Veljanovski*
27/09	h	Shkupi	L 0-1	
04/10	a	Turnovo	L 0-1	
18/10	h	Shkëndija	D 1-1	*Sali*
25/10	a	Renova	L 0-1	
28/10	h	Vardar	L 0-1	
01/11	a	Rabotnicki	L 0-2	
04/11	h	Rabotnicki	L 0-3	
08/11	h	Metalurg	L 1-5	*Kalanoski*
22/11	a	Sileks	L 0-3	
29/11	h	Bregalnica	L 1-4	*Kalanoski*
06/12	a	Shkupi	L 0-5	
10/12	h	Turnovo	W 2-1	*Cvetanovski, Dalceski*

2016
20/02	a	Rabotnicki	L 1-2	*Sakiri*
28/02	h	Sileks	L 0-1	
09/03	a	Shkëndija	L 0-2	
13/03	h	Vardar	L 0-3	
19/03	a	Turnovo	L 1-3	*Saliu*
03/04	h	Bregalnica	L 0-5	
06/04	a	Renova	L 0-3	
10/04	a	Metalurg	L 0-2	
17/04	h	Shkupi	L 0-1	
20/04	a	Turnovo	L 0-2	
24/04	h	Metalurg	W 2-0	*Celeski, Saliu*
28/04	a	Renova	L 2-4	*Celeski, Saliu*
04/05	h	Turnovo	L 0-2	
08/05	a	Metalurg	L 0-4	
15/05	h	Renova	L 0-4	

Name	Nat	DoB	Pos	Aps	(s)	Gls
Saso Aluposki		16/07/97	M		(1)	
Dejan Apostolovski		06/08/90	G	14	(1)	
Nasir Azizi		31/05/92	D		(7)	
Caminata	POR	04/01/95	M	9	(2)	
Aleksandar Celeski		24/08/96	M	9	(3)	2
Dejan Cvetanovski		15/05/90	A	11	(1)	2
Aleksandar Dalceski		18/04/91	M	23		2
Hristijan Dimovski		29/06/85	M	11	(3)	
Naum Dzaleski		18/07/88	M	10	(3)	
Ilir Elmazovski		18/11/79	D	12	(4)	
Saso Gjoreski		18/09/82	D	22		
Valentin Gjorgjieski		16/02/90	D		(1)	
Nikola Gonoski		03/02/93	G	1		
Hristijan Grozdanovski		05/06/93	D	22	(3)	
Zudi Hajredini		28/05/98	M	2	(3)	
Agon Hani		06/04/98	M	8	(2)	
Veton Hani		31/05/94	D	9	(2)	
Riste Ilijovski		27/09/94	M	4	(4)	
Antonio Kalanoski		25/04/94	A	30		4
Ivica Kelesoski		17/06/90	D	11		
Moussa Konaté	FRA	12/02/94	D	6		
Blagojce Konjarski		18/02/89	M	17		1
Koken Kuroki	JPN	22/08/96	M	1		
Dani Ladeira	RSA	28/05/96	M	4	(1)	
Petar Markoski		11/03/98	M	3	(2)	
Blagojce Markovski		13/10/87	A	8	(7)	4
Meriton Merko		03/01/96	M	8	(2)	
Hristijan Nikolovski		05/10/93	M	5	(5)	
Ilce Petrovski		22/07/89	G	18		
Aleksandar Ristevski		21/08/89	D	7		
Dimce Ristevski		06/11/82	M	1	(1)	
Ardit Sakiri		04/05/85	M	8	(5)	1
Ersen Sali		05/10/87	A	7	(4)	1
Pajazit Saliu		27/04/93	A	11	(1)	3
Rondi Selimi		17/04/97	M		(3)	
Ramadan Sherifi		10/11/96	M	7	(1)	
Mirko Simjanovski		01/01/94	D	15	(3)	1
Andjelko Stevanović	SRB	26/07/91	A	2	(3)	
Ljupco Trpeski		24/07/94	M	3		
Dejan Velevski		22/10/93	M		(11)	
Naum Veljanovski		21/12/92	D	13	(1)	1
Toni Veljanovski		12/04/84	M	17		

FK Rabotnicki

1937 • Filip II Arena (33,000); Boris Trajkovski
(2,500); Gjorce Petrov (2,500); City, Veles (6,000) •
fkrabotnicki.com
Major honours
Macedonian League (4) 2005, 2006, 2008, 2014;
Macedonian Cup (4) 2008, 2009, 2014, 2015
Coach: Igor Angelovski;
(17/12/15) Tomislav Franc

2015
10/08	a	Bregalnica	L 0-1	
16/08	h	Turnovo	W 4-2	*Anene 2, Ilijoski, Jovanovski*
30/08	h	Sileks	W 2-0	*Ilijoski 2*
13/09	a	Shkupi	D 1-1	*Ilijoski*
17/09	a	Renóva	L 1-3	*Ilijoski*
20/09	h	Shkëndija	L 2-4	*Ilijoski, Trajcevski*
27/09	a	Vardar	L 1-2	*Ilijoski*
04/10	h	Metalurg	W 2-0	*Cikarski (p), Ilijoski (p)*
17/10	h	Bregalnica	D 0-0	
25/10	h	Turnovo	D 2-2	*Cikarski (p), Ilijoski*
28/10	h	Renova	D 1-1	*Ilijoski*
01/11	h	Mladost	D 1-1	*Ilijoski, Vujcic*
04/11	a	Mladost	W 3-0	*Ilijoski 2 (1p), Markoski*
08/11	a	Sileks	D 0-0	
21/11	h	Shkupi	D 1-1	*Altiparmakovski*
29/11	a	Shkëndija	D 1-1	*Petrovic*
05/12	h	Vardar	D 1-1	*Vujcic (p)*
10/12	a	Metalurg	D 0-0	

2016
20/02	h	Mladost	W 2-1	*Altiparmakovski (p), Herrera*
28/02	a	Metalurg	W 2-1	*Ristovski, Najdenov*
06/03	h	Shkupi	D 1-1	*Trajcevski*
12/03	h	Renova	D 0-0	
19/03	a	Sileks	D 0-0	
02/04	h	Shkëndija	L 0-1	
06/04	a	Vardar	L 0-1	
10/04	h	Turnovo	W 2-0	*Elmas, Altiparmakovski*
17/04	a	Bregalnica	L 1-2	*Altiparmakovski*
20/04	a	Shkëndija	L 1-3	*Najdenov*
24/04	h	Sileks	W 2-0	*Manevski, Jovanovski*
30/04	a	Shkupi	W 1-0	*Altiparmakovski*
08/05	a	Bregalnica	D 0-0	
19/05	h	Vardar	L 0-1	

Name	Nat	DoB	Pos	Aps	(s)	Gls
Kristijan Ackovski		15/02/98	M		(2)	
Marjan Altiparmakovski		18/07/91	M	30	(1)	5
Chuma Anene	NOR	14/05/93	A	1	(1)	2
Slobodan Bocevski		05/05/97	D		(2)	
Daniel Bozinovski		09/07/89	G	18		
Mite Cikarski		06/01/93	D	27	(2)	2
Eljif Elmas		24/09/99	M	7	(4)	1
Ivan Galić	CRO	09/01/95	A	7	(3)	
Sebastián Herrera	COL	23/01/95	D	10	(5)	1
Milan Ilievski		21/07/82	D	29		
Blaze Ilijoski		09/07/84	A	17	(1)	13
Miroslav Jovanovski		13/05/91	M	12	(17)	2
Andrej Kudijan		04/09/97	A		(2)	
Borce Manevski		05/07/85	A	1	(1)	1
Kire Markoski		20/05/95	M	14	(5)	1
Bojan Markovski		08/08/83	D	7		
Ivan Mitrov		24/10/88	M	3	(6)	
Bojan Najdenov		27/08/91	M	12		2
Leon Najdovski		17/10/94	D	11	(4)	
Milovan Petrovic		23/01/90	M	32		1
Marko Puškarić	CRO	07/04/97	A	2	(2)	
Kire Ristevski		22/10/90	D	17		
Milan Ristovski		08/04/98	M	2	(16)	1
Emir Sahiti		29/11/98	M	2	(5)	
Suad Sahiti	ALB	06/02/95	M	15	(4)	
Goran Siljanovski		01/07/90	D	20		
Damjan Siskovski		18/03/95	G	14	(1)	
Dusko Trajcevski		01/11/90	D	26	(2)	2
Stephan Vujcic	GER	03/01/86	M	16	(1)	2

KF Renova

2003 • Bogovinje (3,500);
City, Kicevo (5,000) • kfrenova.com
Major honours
*Macedonian League (1) 2010; Macedonian Cup (1)
2012*
Coach: Catip Osmani

2015

09/08	a	Turnovo	L	0-4
16/08	a	Mladost	L	1-2 *Gafuri*
26/08	a	Sileks	L	0-1
29/08	h	Shkupi	D	1-1 *Jusufi*
14/09	a	Shkëndija	L	1-3 *Emini (p)*
17/09	h	Rabotnicki	W	3-1 *Miskovski, Emini, Shabani*
20/09	h	Vardar	D	0-0
27/09	a	Metalurg	L	0-1
04/10	a	Bregalnica	D	1-1 *Emini*
18/10	h	Turnovo	W	5-2 *Memedi, Emini, Jusufi, Gafuri, Nuhiu*
25/10	h	Mladost	W	1-0 *Gafuri*
28/10	a	Rabotnicki	D	1-1 *Emini*
01/11	h	Sileks	W	2-1 *Mojsov, Emini*
08/11	a	Shkupi	L	0-3
23/11	h	Shkëndija	D	0-0
29/11	a	Vardar	L	0-2
07/12	h	Metalurg	W	2-0 *Ramadani, Gafuri*
10/12	a	Bregalnica	L	2-3 *Skenderi 2*

2016

21/02	a	Vardar	L	1-4 *Gafuri*
28/02	a	Shkupi	L	0-1
06/03	h	Turnovo	D	1-1 *Miskovski*
12/03	h	Rabotnicki	D	0-0
19/03	h	Bregalnica	W	3-0 *Gafuri, Musliu, R Selmani*
03/04	a	Sileks	L	0-1
06/04	h	Mladost	W	3-0 *Musliu 2, Skenderi*
10/04	a	Shkëndija	L	1-3 *Skenderi*
17/04	h	Metalurg	W	4-1 *Nuhiu, Gafuri 2, R Selmani*
20/04	a	Metalurg	W	3-1 *Skenderi, Gafuri, D Imeri*
24/04	a	Turnovo	D	0-0
28/04	h	Mladost	W	4-2 *Shabani, Abdula, Memedi (p), R Selmani*
04/05	a	Metalurg	W	4-2 *D Imeri 2, Ramadani 2*
08/05	h	Turnovo	W	1-0 *Ramadani*
15/05	a	Mladost	W	4-0 *D Imeri, R Selmani, Jusufi 2*

Name	Nat	DoB	Pos	Aps	(s)	Gls
Dzhelil Abdula		25/09/91	D	12	(1)	1
Arlind Bajrami		05/11/95	D	1	(3)	
Andreja Efremov		02/09/92	G	29		
Izair Emini		04/10/85	A	14		6
Saimir Fetai		04/04/89	D	18		
Ardjen Gafuri		01/02/89	M	32		9
Demir Imeri		27/10/95	A	8	(4)	4
Platin Imeri		27/09/94	M		(5)	
Fatjon Jusufi		06/03/97	M	2	(17)	4
Jasmin Mecinovic		22/10/90	D	11	(1)	
Agron Memedi		05/12/80	D	22		2
Nenad Miskovski		19/12/86	D	30		2
Gjorgi Mojsov		27/05/85	M	14	(2)	1
Visar Musliu		13/11/94	D	29	(1)	3
Valon Neziri		22/10/93	G	4		
Fisnik Nuhiu		26/01/83	M	30		2
Emran Ramadani		29/01/92	M	15	(8)	4
Elmedin Redzepi		30/09/88	M	1	(6)	
Burim Sadiki		05/08/89	M	9	(9)	
Jasir Selmani		21/01/91	M	12	(5)	
Remzi Selmani		05/05/97	A	9	(10)	4
Bunjamin Shabani		30/01/91	M	25	(3)	2
Erblin Shakiri		21/04/96	A	1	(2)	
Ljavdrim Skenderi		17/01/94	A	11	(13)	5
Alban Sulejmani		14/04/98	M	4	(4)	
Darko Trajcev		19/03/88	M	1	(1)	
Muhamed Useini		21/11/88	M	11		
Bashkim Velija		01/08/93	D	8	(2)	

KF Shkëndija

1979 • City, Kumanovo (2,000); City, Kicevo
(5,000); Cair, Skopje (6,000); City, Veles (6,000) •
kfshkendija.com
Major honours
*Macedonian League (1) 2011; Macedonian Cup (1)
2016*
**Coach: Shpëtim Duro (ALB);
(22/12/15) Bruno Akrapović (BIH)**

2015

09/08	h	Mladost	W	3-1 *Hasani, Ibraimi, Vrućina*
16/08	h	Vardar	L	1-3 *Radeski*
23/08	a	Metalurg	W	3-0 *Ibraimi, Demiri, Stênio Júnior*
26/08	h	Bregalnica	W	5-1 *Ibraimi 2, Hasani, og (Hristov), Alimi*
29/08	a	Turnovo	W	3-0 *Hasani 2, Todorovski*
14/09	h	Renova	W	3-1 *Alimi, Hasani (p), Stênio Júnior*
20/09	a	Rabotnicki	W	4-2 *Hasani 3, Vrućina*
27/09	h	Sileks	W	3-1 *Ibraimi, Hasani 2*
04/10	a	Shkupi	W	2-0 *Hasani, Ibraimi*
18/10	h	Mladost	D	1-1 *Ibraimi (p)*
25/10	a	Vardar	D	0-0
28/10	h	Metalurg	W	2-0 *Radeski, Ibraimi*
01/11	a	Bregalnica	W	2-0 *Alimi, Radeski*
08/11	h	Turnovo	D	2-2 *Ibraimi (p), Stênio Júnior*
23/11	a	Renova	D	0-0
29/11	h	Rabotnicki	L	1-3 *Ibraimi*
06/12	a	Sileks	L	1-3 *Ibraimi*
10/12	h	Shkupi	W	4-1 *Ibraimi 2, Alimi, Asani*

2016

21/02	h	Turnovo	W	2-0 *Radeski 2*
28/02	a	Bregalnica	W	3-0 *Ibraimi 2 (1p), Alimi*
09/03	h	Mladost	W	2-0 *Ibraimi, Stênio Júnior*
13/03	a	Metalurg	W	4-0 *Radeski 2, Totre, Alimi*
19/03	h	Shkupi	W	3-1 *Ibraimi, Radeski, Todorovski*
02/04	a	Rabotnicki	W	1-0 *Ibraimi*
06/04	h	Sileks	W	3-1 *Ibraimi 3*
10/04	h	Renova	W	3-1 *Ibraimi, Radeski, Asani*
17/04	a	Vardar	D	1-1 *Alimi*
20/04	h	Rabotnicki	W	3-1 *Stênio Júnior, Ibraimi (p), Alimi*
24/04	a	Vardar	L	0-1
30/04	h	Bregalnica	W	3-0 *Victor Juffo 2, Ibraimi*
08/05	h	Sileks	W	3-0 *Victor Juffo, Radeski, Hasani*
19/05	a	Shkupi	W	3-1 *Ibraimi 2, Alimi*

Name	Nat	DoB	Pos	Aps	(s)	Gls
Dzhelil Abdula		25/09/91	D	1	(1)	
Armend Alimi		11/12/87	M	29	(1)	9
Shpend Asani		14/11/96	M		(7)	2
Enes Azizi		09/02/94	G		(1)	
Egzon Bejtulai		07/01/94	D	22	(4)	
Sedat Berisha		23/09/89	D	3	(1)	
Besmir Bojku		03/01/95	A		(1)	
Carlinho Rech	BRA	05/06/87	D	10	(2)	
Ardian Cuculi		19/07/87	D	30		
Besir Demiri		01/08/94	M	26	(3)	1
Ferhan Hasani		18/06/90	M	9	(2)	12
Besart Ibraimi		20/12/86	A	32		26
Marko Jovanovski		24/07/88	G	20		
Ervin Jusufovic	BIH	07/05/95	D	2	(1)	
Hristijan Kirovski		12/10/85	A	2	(13)	
Meriton Korenica	ALB	15/12/97	M		(1)	
Alem Merajić	BIH	04/02/94	D	10	(1)	
Nderim Nedzipi		22/05/84	M	3	(2)	
Artim Polozani		25/06/82	M	19	(8)	
Marjan Radeski		10/02/95	M	26	(2)	10
Besnik Rexha		20/06/98	M		(1)	
Shefit Shefiti		19/02/98	M		(2)	
Stênio Júnior	BRA	10/06/91	A	29	(1)	5
Blagoja Todorovski		11/06/85	D	31		2
Ennur Totre		29/10/96	M	13	(13)	1
Muhamed Useini		21/11/88	M	4	(6)	
Victor Juffo	BRA	24/02/93	M	3	(5)	3
Bojan Vrućina	CRO	08/11/84	A	2	(9)	2
Stephan Vujcic	GER	03/01/86	M	14		
Kostadin Zahov		08/11/87	G	12		
Arbin Zejnulai		15/02/99	M		(2)	

FK Shkupi

2012 • Cair (6,000); City, Kicevo (5,000) •
fcshkupi.com
**Coach: Zekirija Ramadani;
(05/01/16) Visar Ganiu**

2015

09/08	a	Vardar	D	2-2 *Nuhiu, Osmani*
16/08	h	Metalurg	D	0-0
23/08	a	Bregalnica	W	2-1 *Adili, Nuhiu*
26/08	h	Turnovo	D	1-1 *Arif*
29/08	a	Renova	D	1-1 *Demiri*
13/09	h	Rabotnicki	D	1-1 *M Bajrami (p)*
20/09	a	Sileks	L	0-1
27/09	a	Mladost	W	2-0 *Adem, Demiri*
04/10	h	Shkëndija	L	0-2
18/10	h	Vardar	L	0-3
25/10	a	Metalurg	W	1-0 *Bae*
28/10	h	Bregalnica	D	0-0
01/11	a	Turnovo	D	0-0
08/11	h	Renova	W	3-0 *Osmani 2, Nuhiu*
21/11	a	Rabotnicki	D	1-1 *Iseni*
29/11	h	Sileks	D	0-0
06/12	h	Mladost	W	5-0 *M Bajrami, Maksuti, Osmani 2, Demiri*
10/12	a	Shkëndija	L	1-4 *M Bajrami*

2016

21/02	h	Metalurg	W	1-0 *M Bajrami*
28/02	h	Renova	W	1-0 *Enes*
06/03	a	Rabotnicki	D	1-1 *Nuhiu*
13/03	h	Sileks	W	1-0 *Petkovski*
19/03	a	Shkëndija	L	1-3 *M Bajrami*
03/04	h	Vardar	L	0-1
06/04	a	Turnovo	L	0-1
10/04	h	Bregalnica	D	2-2 *M Bajrami, Osmani*
17/04	a	Mladost	W	1-0 *Berisha*
20/04	a	Sileks	L	0-1
24/04	a	Bregalnica	L	0-2
30/04	h	Rabotnicki	L	0-1
08/05	a	Vardar	L	0-2
19/05	h	Shkëndija	L	1-3 *Demiri*

Name	Nat	DoB	Pos	Aps	(s)	Gls
Ermadin Adem		07/07/90	M	19	(5)	1
Mevlan Adili		30/03/94	D	26	(2)	1
Fljakron Ajdari		20/08/93	A		(1)	
Fatmir Arif		17/06/93	D	7	(13)	1
Bujamin Asani		10/08/88	D	27	(4)	
Ersen Asani		28/05/93	D	12		
Bae Beom-geun	KOR	04/03/93	M	5	(3)	1
Jasir Bajrami		19/01/94	G	1		
Muharem Bajrami		29/11/85	M	30	(1)	6
Sedat Berisha		03/09/89	D	10		1
Besmir Bojku		03/01/95	M	3	(5)	
Husein Demiri		06/09/95	A	16	(8)	4
Enes Akgün	TUR	20/09/95	M	3	(9)	1
Flakron Hajdari		20/08/93	A		(1)	
Besar Iseni		18/01/97	M	25	(2)	1
Filip Janevski		08/03/94	M	15	(5)	
Dimitrija Lazarevski		23/09/82	D	27		
Marjan Madzarovski		30/07/86	G	4		
Miran Maksuti		15/07/93	A	5	(11)	1
Edis Maliqi		04/03/95	D	5	(4)	
Mevlan Murati		05/03/94	D	24	(1)	
Ardijan Nuhiu		12/07/78	A	20	(2)	4
Florent Osmani		28/05/88	M	22	(8)	6
Filip Petkovski		24/05/90	M	6	(1)	1
Xhinan Seferi		19/11/91	A		(2)	
Suat Zendeli		24/02/81	G	27		
Fisnik Zuka		03/09/95	M	13	(6)	

FK Sileks

1965 • Sileks (5,000) • no website
Major honours
Macedonian League (3) 1996, 1997, 1998;
Macedonian Cup (2) 1994, 1997
Coach: Momcilo Mitevski

2015

09/08	a	Metalurg	W 3-1	*Georgiev, Ivanov, Nedeljković*
16/08	h	Bregalnica	W 1-0	*Georgiev*
23/08	a	Turnovo	D 0-0	
26/08	h	Renova	W 1-0	*Nedeljković (p)*
30/08	a	Rabotnicki	L 0-2	
13/09	a	Mladost	L 1-3	*Nedeljković (p)*
20/09	h	Shkupi	W 1-0	*Nedeljković*
27/09	a	Shkëndija	L 1-3	*Nedeljković*
04/10	h	Vardar	L 0-3	
18/10	h	Metalurg	W 3-1	*Nedeljković (p), Gligorov, Georgiev*
25/10	a	Bregalnica	D 1-1	*Duranski*
28/10	a	Turnovo	D 1-1	*Georgiev*
01/11	a	Renova	L 1-2	*Maric*
08/11	h	Rabotnicki	D 0-0	
22/11	h	Mladost	W 3-0	*Georgiev (p), Gligorov, Gucev*
29/11	a	Shkupi	D 0-0	
06/12	h	Shkëndija	W 3-1	*Georgiev, Nedeljković 2*
10/12	a	Vardar	L 0-4	

2016

21/02	h	Bregalnica	D 2-2	*Dzonov, Nedeljković*
28/02	h	Mladost	W 1-0	*Panovski*
06/03	h	Metalurg	W 3-0	*Panovski, Gligorov, Mickov*
13/03	a	Shkupi	L 0-1	
19/03	h	Rabotnicki	D 0-0	
03/04	h	Renova	W 1-0	*Nedeljković (p)*
06/04	a	Shkëndija	L 1-3	*Nedeljković*
10/04	a	Vardar	W 3-2	*Panovski, Nedeljković, Duranski*
17/04	a	Turnovo	L 1-2	*Panovski (p)*
20/04	h	Shkupi	W 1-0	*Duranski*
24/04	a	Rabotnicki	L 0-2	
30/04	h	Vardar	L 1-2	*Panovski*
08/05	a	Shkëndija	L 0-3	
19/05	h	Bregalnica	D 1-1	*Panovski*

Name	Nat	DoB	Pos	Aps	(s)	Gls
Andrej Acevski		05/06/91	M	17	(13)	
Aleksandar Bagasovski		15/11/93	D	1		
Lutfi Biljali	SVN	14/04/92	A	3	(3)	
Filip Duranski		17/07/91	M	23	(3)	3
Gjorgje Dzonov		20/09/91	D	21	(1)	1
Kristijan Filipovski		02/10/96	M	9	(11)	
Nikola Georgiev		18/12/83	A	19	(7)	6
Darko Gjurcinovski		20/10/93	M	1	(3)	
Gligor Gligorov		15/03/87	A	20	(3)	3
Blagoj Gucev		22/03/90	M	27	(1)	1
Nemanja Ivanov	SRB	06/10/94	D	30	(1)	1
Igor Kleckarovski		04/03/87	A	1	(2)	
Boban Maric		24/11/88	A		(8)	1
Marjan Mickov		10/02/87	M	26	(1)	1
Slagjan Mitevski		04/05/91	M	4	(7)	
Milan Mitrović	SRB	27/02/91	G	32		
Igor Nedeljković	SRB	24/09/91	A	29	(1)	12
Aleksandar Panovski		30/06/88	M	19	(8)	6
Vasko Raspashkovski		10/07/95	A	3	(1)	
Kirce Ristevski		12/06/93	M		(3)	
Momčilo Rudan	SRB	09/01/90	D	3	(2)	
Stefan Rudan	SRB	09/01/90	D	25	(1)	
Angel Timovski		13/11/94	D	30	(1)	
Krste Todorov		24/12/87	M	9	(10)	

FK Turnovo

1950 • Kukus (3,000) • no website
Coach: Sefki Arifovski;
(16/09/15) Jane Nikoloski

2015

09/08	h	Renova	W 4-0	*Pandev 2, Imeri 2*
16/08	a	Rabotnicki	L 2-4	*Matute, Pandev*
23/08	h	Sileks	D 0-0	
26/08	a	Shkupi	D 1-1	*Pandev (p)*
29/08	h	Shkëndija	L 0-3	
13/09	a	Vardar	L 1-5	*K Ivanov*
20/09	a	Metalurg	D 1-1	*Pandev (p)*
27/09	a	Bregalnica	L 0-3	
04/10	h	Mladost	W 1-0	*Kocoski*
18/10	a	Renova	L 2-5	*Imeri (p), Pandev (p)*
25/10	h	Rabotnicki	D 2-2	*Milusev 2*
28/10	a	Sileks	D 1-1	*og (Mickov)*
01/11	h	Shkupi	D 0-0	
08/11	a	Shkëndija	D 2-2	*Pandev, Najdenov*
22/11	h	Vardar	W 2-1	*Pandev, Najdenov*
29/11	a	Metalurg	D 2-2	*Kocoski, Krstovski*
06/12	h	Bregalnica	W 2-0	*Tanushev, Milusev*
10/12	a	Mladost	L 1-2	*og (Gjoreski)*

2016

21/02	a	Shkëndija	L 0-2	
28/02	h	Vardar	L 0-1	
06/03	a	Renova	D 1-1	*Pandev*
13/03	a	Bregalnica	L 0-2	
19/03	h	Mladost	W 3-1	*Stoilov, Pandev, Gjorgjievski*
03/04	a	Metalurg	W 1-0	*Pandev*
06/04	h	Shkupi	W 1-0	*Timov*
10/04	a	Rabotnicki	L 0-2	
17/04	h	Sileks	W 2-1	*Stoilov, Mitev*
20/04	a	Mladost	W 2-0	*Pandev 2*
24/04	h	Renova	D 0-0	
30/04	a	Metalurg	W 4-0	*Pandev 3, Timov*
04/05	a	Mladost	W 2-0	*Stoilov, Timov*
08/05	a	Renova	L 0-1	
15/05	h	Metalurg	W 5-0	*Krstovski 2, Timov, Vasilev, Mavrov*

Name	Nat	DoB	Pos	Aps	(s)	Gls
Nikola Bozinov		15/03/96	M	13	(13)	
Dime Dimov		25/07/94	D	12	(2)	
Bojan Gjorgjievski		25/01/92	D	8		1
Aleksandar Igeski		12/05/92	G	14		
Tome Iliev		02/12/93	D	30	(2)	
Demir Imeri		27/10/95	A	16		3
Kristijan Ivanov		21/05/95	M	23	(8)	1
Trajce Ivanov		13/07/96	A		(3)	
Hristijan Jakimov		07/10/97	D		(1)	
Atanas Jovanov		06/04/96	G	1	(1)	
Valentin Kocoski		01/03/97	A	11	(5)	2
Martin Krstev		09/03/98	G	1		
Mario Krstovski		03/04/98	A	3	(14)	3
David Matute	ECU	23/12/93	M	7	(4)	1
Mitko Mavrov		08/04/91	D	30	(1)	1
Aleksandar Milusev		05/04/88	D	18		3
Petar Mitev		07/05/95	D	7	(3)	1
Bojan Najdenov		27/08/91	M	12	(3)	2
Sasko Pandev		01/05/87	A	29		16
Darko Ristevski		30/04/91	G	1		
Kiril Stanojkov		29/05/97	M		(1)	
Andjelko Stevanović	SRB	26/07/95	M		(1)	
Kristijan Stoilkov		24/06/96	A	16		
Gjorgji Stoilov		25/08/95	M	17	(7)	3
Arben Tafe		06/04/92	D	20	(3)	
Shqiprim Taipi	ALB	19/02/97	M	6	(15)	
Gjorgi Tanushev		07/01/91	M	11	(5)	1
Marjan Tasev		02/05/85	M	29	(3)	
Filip Timov		22/05/92	A	14		4
Aleksandar Vasilev		03/07/85	D	14	(1)	1

FK Vardar

1947 • Filip II Arena (33,000); Gjorce Petrov (2,500); City, Probistip (2,000) • fkvardar.mk
Major honours
Macedonian League (9) 1993, 1994, 1995, 2002, 2003, 2012, 2013, 2015, 2016; Yugoslav Cup (1) 1961; Macedonian Cup (5) 1993, 1995, 1998, 1999, 2007
Coach: Sergei Andreev (RUS);
(27/07/15) Goce Sedloski

2015

09/08	h	Shkupi	D 2-2	*Blazevski (p), Ivanovski*
16/08	a	Shkëndija	W 3-1	*Ivanovski, Juan Felipe, Romero*
23/08	h	Mladost	W 6-0	*Blazevski 2, Dashyan 2, Hambardzumyan, Ljamcevski*
26/08	h	Metalurg	W 1-0	*Blazevski (p)*
29/08	a	Bregalnica	W 2-0	*Blazevski, Juan Felipe*
13/09	h	Turnovo	W 5-1	*Ivanovski, Blazevski 2, Romero 2*
20/09	a	Renova	D 0-0	
27/09	h	Rabotnicki	W 2-1	*Ivanovski, Popov*
04/10	a	Sileks	W 3-0	*Mijušković, Hambardzumyan, Asani*
18/10	a	Shkupi	W 3-0	*Ivanovski, Blazevski, Ljamcevski*
25/10	a	Shkëndija	D 0-0	
28/10	a	Mladost	W 1-0	*Juan Felipe (p)*
01/11	a	Metalurg	W 1-0	*Romero*
08/11	h	Bregalnica	W 3-1	*Ivanovski, Hambardzumyan, Spirovski*
22/11	a	Turnovo	L 1-2	*Stojkov*
29/11	a	Renova	W 2-0	*Dashyan, P Petkovski*
05/12	a	Rabotnicki	D 1-1	*P Petkovski*
10/12	a	Sileks	W 4-0	*Grncarov, Ivanovski, Stojkov 2*

2016

21/02	h	Renova	W 4-1	*Ćeran 2, Juan Felipe, Blazevski*
28/02	a	Turnovo	W 1-0	*Hambardzumyan*
08/03	h	Bregalnica	W 4-0	*Grncarov 2, Juan Felipe (p), Hambardzumyan*
13/03	a	Mladost	W 3-0	*Ćeran, Nikolov, Hambardzumyan*
19/03	h	Metalurg	W 2-1	*Kojašević (p), Ćeran*
03/04	a	Shkupi	W 1-0	*Juan Felipe*
06/04	h	Rabotnicki	W 1-0	*Kojašević*
10/04	a	Sileks	L 2-3	*Grncarov, Kojašević (p)*
17/04	h	Shkëndija	D 1-1	*Juan Felipe*
20/04	h	Bregalnica	W 2-1	*Asani, Stojkov*
24/04	a	Shkëndija	W 1-0	*Asani*
30/04	a	Sileks	W 2-1	*Juan Felipe, Ćeran*
08/05	h	Shkupi	W 2-0	*Grncarov, Hambardzumyan*
19/05	a	Rabotnicki	W 1-0	*Tanevski*

Name	Nat	DoB	Pos	Aps	(s)	Gls
Jasir Asani		19/05/95	M	12	(3)	3
Dejan Blazevski		06/12/85	M	17	(2)	9
Vladica Brdarovski		07/02/90	D	8	(4)	
Dragan Ćeran	SRB	06/10/87	A	9	(3)	5
Artak Dashyan	ARM	20/11/89	M	12	(6)	3
Hristijan Denkovski		15/04/94	M	1		
Filip Gacevski		17/08/90	G	6		
Nikola Gligorov		15/08/83	M	28		
Darko Glishic		23/09/91	D	4	(5)	
Boban Grncarov		12/08/82	D	26		5
Vlatko Grozdanoski		30/01/83	M		(5)	
Hovhannes Hambardzumyan	ARM	04/10/90	D	24	(2)	7
Filip Ivanovski		01/05/85	A	20	(7)	7
Juan Felipe	BRA	05/12/87	M	30	(1)	8
Damir Kojašević	MNE	03/06/87	M	10	(3)	3
Blagojce Ljamcevski		07/04/87	M	10	(10)	2
Nemanja Mijušković	MNE	04/03/92	D	22		1
Boban Nikolov		28/07/94	M	14	(6)	1
Yevheniy Novak	UKR	01/02/89	D	10	(2)	
Tomislav Pacovski		28/06/82	G	26		
Filip Petkovski		24/05/90	A		(2)	
Petar Petkovski		03/01/97	M	5	(9)	2
Goran Popov		02/10/84	D	24		1
Cesar Romero	USA	02/08/89	A	5	(3)	4
Stefan Spirovski		23/08/90	M	9	(7)	1
Aco Stojkov		29/04/83	A	8	(11)	4
Zlatko Tanevski		03/08/83	D	1		1
Aleksandar Temelkov		06/10/87	M		(1)	
Darko Velkovski		21/06/95	M	11	(3)	

Top goalscorers

26	Besart Ibraimi (Shkëndija)
16	Sasko Pandev (Turnovo)
13	Blaze Ilijoski (Rabotnicki)
12	Ferhan Hasani (Shkëndija)
	Igor Nedeljković (Sileks)
10	Marjan Radeski (Shkëndija)
9	Ardjen Gafuri (Renova)
	Armend Alimi (Shkëndija)
	Dejan Blazevski (Vardar)
8	Angel Nacev (Bregalnica)
	Juan Felipe (Vardar)

Promoted clubs

FK Pobeda

2010 • Goce Delcev (15,000) • no website
Coach: Darko Krsteski

FK Makedonija

1932 • Gjorce Petrov (2,500) • no website
Major honours
Macedonian League (1) 2009; Macedonian Cup (1) 2006
Coach: Jovica Knežević (SRB)
(08/04/16) Bobi Stojkovski

FK Pelister

1945 • Tumbe Kafe (8,000); Goce Delcev, Prilep (15,000); Biljanini Izvori, Ohrid (3,000); Novaci Stadium (500) • no website
Major honours
Macedonian Cup (1) 2001
Coach: Naum Ljamcevski

Second level final table 2015/16

		Pld	W	D	L	F	A	Pts
1	FK Pobeda	27	13	8	6	40	23	47
2	FK Makedonija	27	13	7	7	34	33	46
3	FK Pelister	27	9	12	6	33	31	39
4	FK Teteks	27	10	9	8	27	25	39
5	KF Vëllazërimi	27	10	8	9	30	30	38
6	FK Skopje	27	9	9	9	27	23	36
7	FK Gorno Lisice	27	9	9	9	26	29	36
8	FK Ljubanci	27	9	7	11	32	31	34
9	FK Gostivar	27	9	6	12	29	34	33
10	FK Kozuf	27	4	5	20	17	36	17

Promotion/Relegation play-offs
(25/05/16 & 29/05/16)
Turnovo 1-2 Pelister
Pelister 1-0 Turnovo
(Pelister 3-1)

DOMESTIC CUP

Kup na Makedonija 2015/16

FIRST ROUND

(12/08/15)
Belasica 0-2 Skopje
Gorno Lisice 1-2 Renova
Kozuv 0-1 Vardar
Lirija 0-11 Turnovo
Ljubanci 1-1 Teteks *(4-3 on pens)*
Ljuboten 1-5 Shkupi
Males 1-9 Metalurg
Pobeda 1-1 Mladost Carev Dvor *(6-7 on pens)*
Poesevo 0-0 Gostivar *(3-5 on pens)*
Prevalec 0-4 Sileks
Vulkan 0-3 Makedonija *(w/o)*
Zajas 0-4 Shkëndija

(13/08/15)
11 Oktomvri 0-8 Pelister
Fortuna 0-11 Rabotnicki
Plackovica 0-2 Bregalnica

Bye – Vëllazërimi

SECOND ROUND

(30/09/15 & 21/10/15)
Bregalnica 2-0, 0-1 Shkupi *(2-1)*
Gostivar 0-4, 0-4 Rabotnicki *(0-8)*
Makedonija 3-2, 0-0 Ljubanci *(3-2)*
Renova 1-2, 1-3 Sileks *(2-5)*
Shkëndija 2-0, 5-0 Metalurg *(7-0)*
Turnovo 3-1, 2-2 Skopje *(5-3)*
Vardar 4-1, 2-0 Pelister *(6-1)*
Vëllazërimi 2-4, 3-3 Mladost Carev Dvor *(5-7)*

QUARTER-FINALS

(25/11/15 & 02/12/15)
Makedonija 2-4 Turnovo *(Sajnoski 62, Misovski 90; Stoilov 17, Imeri 67, 72, Bozinov 83)*
Turnovo 0-1 Makedonija *(Kostovski 26)*
(Turnovo 4-3)

Mladost Carev Dvor 1-1 Bregalnica *(Cvetanovski 45; Ristovski 80)*
Bregalnica 4-1 Mladost Carev Dvor *(Misev 27, Zdravkov 36p, Stojanov 57, Nikovski 75; Merko 85)*
(Bregalnica 5-2)

Rabotnicki 3-0 Sileks *(Altiparmakovski 55, Ilijoski 68, Vujcic 83p)*
Sileks 1-2 Rabotnicki *(Maric 59p; Altiparmakovski 13, Markoski 59p)*
(Rabotnicki 5-1)

(26/11/15 & 02/12/15)
Shkëndija 3-0 Vardar *(Stênio Júnior 22, Cuculi 41, Radeski 90)*
Vardar 1-2 Shkëndija *(Mijušković 59; Stênio Júnior 43, Kirovski 82)*
(Shkëndija 5-1)

SEMI-FINALS

(02/03/16 & 13/04/16)
Bregalnica 1-1 Rabotnicki *(Nacev 63; Altiparmakovski 73p)*
Rabotnicki 3-0 Bregalnica *(Altiparmakovski 21, 59, Elmas 85)*
(Rabotnicki 4-1)

Turnovo 0-2 Shkëndija *(Ibraimi 11, Radeski 51)*
Shkëndija 2-1 Turnovo *(Victor Juffo 44p, Nedzipi 57; Timov 56)*
(Shkëndija 4-1)

FINAL

(16/05/16)
Filip II Arena, Skopje
KF SHKËNDIJA 2 *(Radeski 8, Stênio Júnior 90+5)*
FK RABOTNICKI 0
Referee: *Spirkoski*
SHKËNDIJA: *Jovanovski, Todorovski, Bejtulai, Cuculi, Demiri, Vujcic, Alimi (Hasani 85), Victor Juffo (Polozani 75), Stênio Júnior, Radeski, Ibraimi (Carlinho Rech 90)*
RABOTNICKI: *Siskovski, Siljanovski, Ilievski, Herrera, Trajcevski, Petrovic, Elmas (Manevski 86), Najdenov, S Sahiti (E Sahiti 90), Altiparmakovski, Galić (Markoski 75)*

Shkëndija players savour the club's maiden Macedonian Cup triumph

MALTA
Malta Football Association (MFA)

Address	Millennium Stand, Floor 2 National Stadium MT-Ta' Qali ATD 4000	**President**	Norman Darmanin Demajo
Tel	+356 21 232 581	**General secretary**	Bjorn Vassallo
Fax	+356 21 245 136	**Media officer**	Mark Attard
E-mail	info@mfa.com.mt	**Year of formation**	1900
Website	mfa.com.mt	**National stadium**	Ta' Qali National Stadium, Ta' Qali (15,914)

KEY
- ● UEFA Champions League
- ● UEFA Europa League
- ● Promoted
- ● Relegated

PREMIER LEAGUE CLUBS

- 1 **Balzan FC**
- 2 **Birkirkara FC**
- 3 **Floriana FC**
- 4 **Hibernians FC**
- 5 **Mosta FC**
- 6 **Naxxar Lions FC**
- 7 **Pembroke Athleta FC**
- 8 **Qormi FC**
- 9 **St Andrews FC**
- 10 **Sliema Wanderers FC**
- 11 **Tarxien Rainbows FC**
- 12 **Valletta FC**

PROMOTED CLUBS

- 13 **Gzira United FC**
- 14 **Hamrun Spartans FC**

St Andrews · 7 Pembroke · 9 · 10 Gzira ~ 13 · Naxxar 6 · Sliema · Mosta 5 · 1 Birkirkara · 12 · Balzan 2 · Valletta · 14 ~Hamrun · Floriana ~ 3 · Qormi 8 · 4 Paola · Tarxien 11

Valletta return to the summit

Valletta FC made it four titles in six years after edging out defending champions Hibernians at the end of an exciting season-long struggle for supremacy at the top of the Premier League table.

Pre-season favourites Birkirkara and surprise package Balzan also threatened to join in the race but were repelled by the top two's impressive consistency. Balzan were foiled in their bid to claim a first major trophy when they lost the FA Trophy final to Sliema Wanderers on penalties.

Citizens capture 23rd league title

Hibernians come up just short

Sliema win FA Trophy on penalties

Domestic league

Valletta began the 2015/16 campaign buoyed by the return of coach Paul Zammit, who had led the Lilywhites to the title in 2007/08 before moving on to Birkirkara, where he landed another couple of Premier League crowns as well as the 2014/15 FA Trophy. Birkirkara replaced him with Floriana's Italian coach Giovanni Tedesco - and also staged quite a coup by signing 36-year-old ex-Juventus and Italy striker Fabrizio Miccoli. Hibernians, meanwhile, stuck with their 2014/15 title-winning boss Branko Nišević while supplementing their stock of Brazilian players.

With each of the main contenders suitably reinforced, an open and interesting title race ensued, with Oliver Spiteri's Balzan leading early on before a run of five defeats in seven games cut them adrift. By the turn of the year Valletta had their noses in front, leading Hibernians by three points and Birkirkara by five, and when the league reached its 22-game cut-off, where all points were halved/rounded up, the bunching at the top was even tighter.

Valletta were on a roll, however, having won ten of their 11 games in the middle third of the campaign. Their next seven fixtures would all end in victory too, giving Zammit's team a seemingly impregnable six-point advantage with four games to go. But as closest pursuers Hibernians

won their next two games, Valletta dropped five points and suddenly the race was on again. Or at least it was for a week. On the penultimate matchday Valletta rediscovered their winning habit as an 81st-minute goal from Malta's record scorer Michael Mifsud, who had returned in mid-campaign from Sliema for a third spell at the club, gave them a 2-1 victory over Balzan at the Ta' Qali. The following day Birkirkara beat Hibernians by the same scoreline at the same stadium with an 89th-minute winner and that was that. Valletta were the champions with a game to spare.

Valletta's triumph was very much a team effort, with South American imports Federico Falcone and Jhonnattann their standout attackers and Maltese internationals Ryan Camilleri and Jonathan Caruana their most prominent defenders. Veteran midfielder Roderick Briffa also enjoyed an excellent campaign, as did goalkeeper Henry Bonello, a Hibernians player the previous season and therefore a champion two years in a row.

Domestic cup

Valletta and Hibernians both exited the FA Trophy in January, and there was disappointment too for holders Birkirkara as they lost in the semi-finals, 1-0 to Sliema. Balzan, meanwhile, reached their first final with a 3-1 win over eighth-placed

Premier League debutants Pembroke Athleta, but a first major trophy eluded them as Sliema, the competition's most successful club, survived 35 minutes with ten men to win the match on penalties after a goalless draw, Balzan skipper Dylan Grima missing from the spot as all five Sliema kickers converted.

Europe

Another penalty shoot-out the previous summer had brought Maltese fans to the edge of their seats as Birkirkara threatened to eliminate English Premier League side West Ham from the second qualifying round of the UEFA Europa League. Unfortunately, they ended up second best to the east Londoners from the spot but still took enormous credit from their 1-0 win at Ta' Qali. The goalscorer, new boy Miccoli, would not see out the season with the Stripes, retiring from the game a few months later.

National team

There were no wins in eight matches for Malta and their Italian coach Pietro Ghedin in 2015/16, although they proved resolute opponents in the UEFA EURO 2016 qualifying campaign, conceding just 16 goals in their ten matches. Two of the three goals they scored came in a home draw against Azerbaijan, in which Mifsud increased his astonishing international haul to 40.

DOMESTIC SEASON AT A GLANCE

Premier League 2015/16 final tables

First Phase

		Pld	W	D	L	F	A	Pts	
1	Valletta FC	22	17	2	3	49	21	53	(27)
2	Hibernians FC	22	15	5	2	53	25	50	(25)
3	Balzan FC	22	14	3	5	42	21	45	(23)
4	Birkirkara FC	22	12	6	4	41	20	42	(21)
5	Floriana FC	22	12	3	7	36	25	39	(20)
6	Tarxien Rainbows FC	22	10	7	5	37	17	37	(19)
7	Mosta FC	22	8	6	8	29	33	30	(15)
8	Pembroke Athleta FC	22	7	4	11	33	39	25	(13)
9	Sliema Wanderers FC	22	7	3	12	31	36	24	(12)
10	Naxxar Lions FC	22	4	2	16	22	54	14	(7)
11	Qormi FC	22	2	3	17	19	49	9	(5)
12	St Andrews FC	22	1	2	19	14	66	5	(3)

Second Phase

		Pld	W	D	L	F	A	Pts
1	**Valletta FC**	33	25	4	4	69	27	53
2	Hibernians FC	33	22	8	3	85	33	49
3	Birkirkara FC	33	20	8	5	64	29	47
4	Balzan FC	33	20	6	7	69	33	44
5	Floriana FC	33	18	4	11	60	42	39
6	Tarxien Rainbows FC	33	15	8	10	59	31	35
7	Sliema Wanderers FC	33	12	6	15	49	51	30
8	Pembroke Athleta FC	33	10	6	17	48	61	24
9	Mosta FC	33	10	7	16	42	60	22
10	St Andrews FC	33	4	3	26	32	90	13
11	Naxxar Lions FC	33	5	4	24	29	95	12
12	Qormi FC	33	3	4	26	26	80	9

NB Figures in brackets indicate points carried forward to the Second Phase.

European qualification 2016/17

Champion: Valletta FC (first qualifying round)

Hibernians FC (first qualifying round)
Birkirkara FC (first qualifying round)
Balzan FC (first qualifying round)
NB Cup winner Sliema Wanderers FC did not receive a licence.

Top scorer	Mario Fontanella (Floriana), 20 goals
Relegated clubs	Qormi FC, Naxxar Lions FC
Promoted clubs	Gzira United FC, Hamrun Spartans FC
Cup final	Sliema Wanderers FC 0-0 Balzan FC *(aet; 5-4 on pens)*

Team of the season
(4-3-3)

Coach: Zammit *(Valletta)*

Player of the season

Gilmar
(Hibernians FC)

After an excellent debut season in the Maltese Premier League with Naxxar Lions, Brazilian playmaker Gilmar was recruited on a season-long loan by Hibernians, where he settled quickly among his fellow countrymen and went on to dazzle throughout a campaign in which the Paola club narrowly lost the title to Valletta. He scored 15 goals from midfield – just five fewer than golden boot-winning Floriana striker Mario Fontanella – and set up chances galore for his team-mates, notably 19-goal compatriot Jorginho.

Newcomer of the season

Lydon Micallef
(Balzan FC)

Micallef enjoyed an outstanding breakthrough season in 2015/16, repeatedly promoting himself with a succession of important goals, 16 in total, to help Balzan finish fourth in the Premier League. The young striker also helped his club reach their first FA Trophy final, not least with a quarter-final extra-time winner against Tarxien Rainbows, and although they lost it on penalties to Sliema, their opponents' failure to receive a UEFA licence enabled Balzan to enter the UEFA Europa League for the second year in a row.

NATIONAL TEAM

Top five all-time caps
David Carabott (121); Gilbert Agius (120); **Michael Mifsud** (117); Carmel Busuttil (111); Joe Brincat (103)

Top five all-time goals
Michael Mifsud (40); Carmel Busuttil (23); David Carabott (12); Gilbert Agius & Hubert Suda (8)

Results 2015/16

Date	Opponent		Venue	Result	Score	Scorers
03/09/15	Italy (ECQ)	A	Florence	L	0-1	
06/09/15	Azerbaijan (ECQ)	H	Ta' Qali	D	2-2	*Mifsud (55), Effiong (71)*
10/10/15	Norway (ECQ)	A	Oslo	L	0-2	
13/10/15	Croatia (ECQ)	H	Ta' Qali	L	0-1	
11/11/15	Jordan	N	Istanbul (TUR)	L	0-2	
24/03/16	Moldova	H	Ta' Qali	D	0-0	
27/05/16	Czech Republic	N	Kufstein (AUT)	L	0-6	
31/05/16	Austria	A	Klagenfurt	L	1-2	*Alaba (87og)*

Appearances 2015/16

Coach: Pietro Ghedin (ITA)	21/11/52		ITA	AZE	NOR	CRO	Jor	Mda	Cze	Aus	Caps	Goals
Andrew Hogg	02/03/85	Kalloni (GRE)	G	G	G	G	G				45	-
Alex Muscat	14/12/84	Sliema	D	D	D56						32	-
Steve Borg	15/05/88	Aris Limassol (CYP)	D	D	D83	D	D	s56			19	-
Zach Muscat	22/08/93	Birkirkara /Akragas (ITA)	D		D	D		D56	D	D	15	-
Andrei Agius	12/08/86	Hibernians	D	D	D	D	D	D	D	D	58	1
Clayton Failla	08/01/86	Hibernians	D	M85	D	D	D58	D80	D75	D	49	2
Paul Fenech	20/12/86	Birkirkara /Balzan	M		M	s79	M64	M87	s46		34	1
Rowen Muscat	05/06/91	Birkirkara /Pavia (ITA)	M	M	M	M		M	s62	s77	25	-
Roderick Briffa	24/08/81	Valletta	M91	M	M	M79	M54		M62	M	91	1
André Schembri	27/05/86	Omonia (CYP)	M73	M	M81	M92	s71	M84			72	3
Alfred Effiong	29/11/84	Balzan	A93	A	A	A75	A		A46		11	2
Bjorn Kristensen	05/04/93	Hibernians	s73		s81	M	M71	M52	M46	M77	14	-
Gareth Sciberras	29/03/83	Birkirkara	s91				M87	s52	M90	M83	45	-
Michael Mifsud	17/04/81	Sliema /Valletta	s93	A62		s75	s54	s84	s46	s67	117	40
Ryan Camilleri	22/05/88	Valletta		D80	s83			s80	s46	D79	27	-
Andrew Cohen	13/05/81	Hibernians			s62	s92					66	1
Joseph Zerafa	31/05/88	Birkirkara			s80	s56	D	D81	D		8	-
Steve Pisani	07/08/92	Floriana			s85				s90	s79	4	-
Owen Bugeja	20/02/90	Pembroke					D				1	-
Ryan Camenzuli	08/09/94	Birkirkara						s58	s75		3	-
Llywelyn Cremona	07/05/95	Valletta						s64	s74	s83	3	-
Manuel Briffa	13/02/94	Floriana						s81			1	-
Clyde Borg	20/03/92	Floriana						s87			1	-
Henry Bonello	13/10/88	Valletta						G	G87	G90	4	-
Jonathan Caruana	24/07/86	Valletta						D87			36	2
Ryan Scicluna	30/07/93	Birkirkara							s87		4	-
Justin Grioli	20/09/87	Balzan							s87		2	-
Cain Attard	10/09/94	Birkirkara							D46		1	-
Clifford Gatt Baldacchino	09/02/88	Sliema							D	D	4	-
Luke Gambin	16/03/93	Barnet (ENG)							M74	M	2	-
Justin Haber	09/06/81	Hibernians							s87	s90	56	-
Jean-Paul Farrugia	21/03/92	Hibernians								A67	4	-

EUROPE

Hibernians FC

Second qualifying round - Maccabi Tel-Aviv FC (ISR)
H 2-1 *Jorginho (74), Jackson (85)*
Borg, Rui da Gracia, Jackson, Rodolfo Soares, Marcelo Dias, Cohen (Bezzina 90+2), Kristensen, Failla, Agius, Jorginho (Mbong 90+4), Gilmar (Jorge Santos 64). Coach: Branko Nišević (SRB)
A 1-5 *Rodolfo Soares (52)*
Borg, Rui da Gracia, Jackson, Rodolfo Soares, Marcelo Dias (Mbong 88), Cohen, Kristensen (Bezzina 83), Failla, Agius, Jorginho, Gilmar (Jorge Santos 63). Coach: Branko Nišević (SRB)

Birkirkara FC

First qualifying round - Ulisses FC (ARM)
H 0-0
Haber (Akpan 37), Mazzetti, Fenech, Camenzuli, Agius (Miccoli 72), Plut (Murga 65), Vukanac, Liliu, Zerafa, Z Muscat, R Muscat. Coach: Giovanni Tedesco (ITA)
A 3-1 *Miccoli (21), Mazzetti (44), Fenech (80p)*
Akpan, Mazzetti, Fenech, Camenzuli, Miccoli (Agius 65), Vukanac, Murga (Vella 71), Liliu (Plut 68), Zerafa, Z Muscat, R Muscat. Coach: Giovanni Tedesco (ITA)
Red card: Vella 76

Second qualifying round - West Ham United FC (ENG)
A 0-1
Haber, Mazzetti, Fenech (Zammit 49), Camenzuli, Miccoli, Vukanac, Murga (Agius 46), Liliu (Plut 66), Zerafa, Z Muscat, R Muscat. Coach: Giovanni Tedesco (ITA)
H 1-0 (aet; 3-5 on pens) *Miccoli (15)*
Haber, Emerson (Zammit 96), Mazzetti, Fenech, Camenzuli, Miccoli (Plut 77), Vukanac, Liliu, Zerafa, Z Muscat, R Muscat (Agius 70). Coach: Giovanni Tedesco (ITA)
Red card: Mazzetti 107

Valletta FC

First qualifying round - Newtown AFC (WAL)
A 1-2 *Jhonnattann (73)*
Vella, Azzopardi, R Camilleri, Falzon, Umeh (Jhonnattann 62), Montebello (Mifsud Triganza 54), Pani, Gill, Cremona, Focsa, Nafti (D Camilleri 87). Coach: Paul Zammit (MLT)
Red card: Azzopardi 85
H 1-2 *Fidjeu (46)*
Vella, Caruana, R Camilleri, Falzon, Fidjeu (Mifsud Triganza 63), Briffa, Pani, Jhonnattann, Gill, Cremona, Nafti (Umeh 87). Coach: Paul Zammit (MLT)
Red card: R Camilleri 74

Balzan FC

First qualifying round - FK Željezničar (BIH)
H 0-2
Cassar, Grioli, Micallef (Cipriott 90+1), Zárate, Grima (Darmanin 84), Bezzina, Sciberras (Arab 78), Brincat, Agius, Serrano, Guobadia. Coach: Oliver Spiteri (MLT)
A 0-1
Senatore, Grioli, Arab, R Fenech, Zárate, Grima (Darmanin 79), Bezzina, Brincat, Agius (Micallef 73), Serrano, Guobadia (Borg 90). Coach: Oliver Spiteri (MLT)

DOMESTIC LEAGUE CLUB-BY-CLUB

Stadiums
Ta' Qali National Stadium (15,914)
Hibernians Ground (2,000)
Victor Tedesco Stadium (2,000)
MFA Centenary Stadium (2,000)

Balzan FC
1937 • balzanfc.com
Coach: Oliver Spiteri

2015
22/08	Hibernians	D	1-1	Vujačić
28/08	Naxxar	W	2-0	Mensha, Zárate
13/09	Tarxien	D	0-0	
19/09	Valletta	W	1-0	Micallef
22/09	Pembroke	W	5-1	Effiong, Micallef, Grioli, Mensha, Darmanin
27/09	Mosta	W	3-1	Effiong 3
03/10	Qormi	W	1-0	Vujačić
17/10	St Andrews	W	2-0	Vujačić 2
25/10	Floriana	L	0-2	
02/11	Birkirkara	L	1-4	Focsa
07/11	Sliema	W	1-0	Micallef
22/11	Hibernians	L	2-3	Effiong, Serrano
01/12	Naxxar	W	4-2	Mensha, Effiong 2, Micallef
06/12	Tarxien	L	0-3	
13/12	Valletta	L	1-2	Effiong
19/12	Pembroke	D	0-0	

2016
09/01	Mosta	W	4-1	Micallef, Effiong, R Fenech, Alan
24/01	St Andrews	W	5-1	Alan, Micallef 2, Effiong, Pedrinho
27/01	Qormi	W	5-0	Effiong, Micallef, Alan (p), Pedrinho, Vujačić
31/01	Sliema	W	2-0	Pedrinho, Effiong
06/02	Birkirkara	W	1-0	Micallef
14/02	Floriana	W	1-0	Kaljević
20/02	Pembroke	W	2-1	Micallef, og (Tanti)
27/02	Mosta	W	3-0	Micallef, Vujačić, P Fenech
01/03	Tarxien	D	2-2	Effiong, P Fenech
05/03	Floriana	W	2-0	Effiong, Serrano
12/03	Naxxar	W	8-0	Effiong 2, Pedrinho (p), Micallef 3, Vujačić 2
19/03	Sliema	D	3-3	og (Dimech), Vujačić, Micallef
02/04	St Andrews	W	1-0	Vujačić
09/04	Qormi	W	3-0	P Fenech, Vujačić, Micallef
16/04	Hibernians	L	1-3	Grioli
23/04	Valletta	L	1-2	Kaljević
29/04	Birkirkara	D	1-1	og (Attard)

Name	Nat	DoB	Pos	Aps	(s)	Gls
Terence Agius		15/01/94	M	5	(8)	
Alan	BRA	09/12/87	M	10	(5)	3
Samir Arab		25/03/94	D	21	(4)	
Steve Bezzina		05/01/87	D	26	(1)	
Clive Brincat		31/05/83	M	22	(4)	
Christian Cassar		22/03/92	G	16	(1)	
Sean Cipriott		10/09/97	D		(5)	
Juan Corbolan		03/03/97	M		(1)	
Ryan Darmanin		12/12/85	A		(12)	1
Alfred Effiong		29/11/84	A	32		16
Paul Fenech		20/12/86	M	16		3
Ryan Fenech		20/04/86	M	3	(4)	1
Maxim Focsa	MDA	21/04/92	D	9	(11)	1
Dylan Grima		18/07/90	M	28	(2)	
Justin Grioli		20/09/87	D	30		2
Ivan Janjušević	MNE	11/07/86	G	11		
Bojan Kaljević	MNE	25/01/86	A	3	(5)	2
Paul Lapira		05/02/98	A		(1)	
Godwin Mensha	NGA	02/09/89	A	13	(2)	3
Lydon Micallef		16/05/92	A	26	(6)	16
Pedrinho	BRA	04/08/86	A	15		4
Luke Sciberras		15/09/89	A	15	(8)	
Valerio Senatore	ITA	15/11/87	G	6		
Elkin Serrano	COL	17/03/84	D	30		2
Aleksandar Vujačić	MNE	19/03/90	A	11	(11)	11
Edison Zárate	CHI	03/06/87	M	15		1
James Zerafa		02/03/98	M		(3)	

Birkirkara FC

1950 • birkirkarafc.com
Major honours
*Maltese League (4) 2000, 2006, 2010, 2013;
Maltese Cup (5) 2002, 2003, 2005, 2008, 2015*
**Coach: Giovanni Tedesco (ITA);
(29/12/15) Dražen Besek (CRO)**

2015

21/08	Naxxar	W	4-0	*Miccoli, Plut, Sciberras, Fenech*
28/08	Tarxien	D	2-2	*Vukanac, Miccoli*
13/09	Valletta	L	1-2	*Liliu*
19/09	Pembroke	W	4-1	*Mazzetti, Plut 2, Z Muscat*
22/09	Mosta	D	1-1	*Plut*
27/09	Qormi	W	2-1	*Plut, Miccoli*
04/10	St Andrews	W	4-0	*Miccoli 2 (1p), Plut, Liliu*
18/10	Sliema	W	3-1	*Miccoli, Liliu, Camenzuli*
25/10	Hibernians	D	1-1	*Camenzuli*
02/11	Balzan	W	4-1	*Z Muscat 2, Fenech, Scicluna*
07/11	Floriana	D	0-0	
21/11	Naxxar	D	2-2	*Scicluna, Liliu*
02/12	Tarxien	W	1-0	*Camenzuli*
05/12	Valletta	L	0-4	
13/12	Pembroke	W	3-0	*Camenzuli, Plut, Agius*
19/12	Mosta	W	3-0	*Agius, Juan Quero, Camenzuli*

2016

10/01	Qormi	W	1-0	*og (Sidibé)*
23/01	Sliema	W	2-0	*Camenzuli, Temile*
27/01	St Andrews	W	3-1	*Mujanović, Plut, Temile*
31/01	Floriana	D	0-0	
06/02	Balzan	L	0-1	
14/02	Hibernians	L	0-2	
21/02	Mosta	W	6-3	*Seydi 3, Smrekar 2, Camenzuli*
28/02	Pembroke	W	1-0	*Smrekar*
02/03	Floriana	L	0-1	
05/03	Tarxien	W	2-1	*Temile, Mujanović*
12/03	Sliema	W	2-1	*Temile, Smrekar*
20/03	Naxxar	W	4-0	*Smrekar, Camenzuli, Agius, Zárate*
03/04	Qormi	W	2-0	*Mazzetti, Temile (p)*
10/04	St Andrews	W	3-1	*Zammit, Bubalović, Plut*
17/04	Valletta	D	0-0	
24/04	Hibernians	W	2-1	*Plut, Agius*
29/04	Balzan	D	1-1	*Camenzuli*

Name	Nat	DoB	Pos	Aps	(s)	Gls
Edmond Agius		23/02/87	M	7	(16)	4
Ini Etim Akpan	NGA	03/08/84	G	5	(1)	
Mislav Andjelković	CRO	22/04/88	M	12		
Cain Attard		10/09/94	M	21	(1)	
Christian Bubalović	CRO	09/08/91	D	14		1
Ryan Camenzuli		08/09/94	D	24	(4)	9
Andrea Curmi		10/04/96	M		(1)	
Ryan Darmanin		12/12/85	A		(6)	
Emerson	BRA	24/02/91	M	9	(5)	
Paul Fenech		20/12/86	M	11		2
Matthew Guillaumier		30/11/96	M	4	(8)	
Justin Haber		09/06/81	G	13		
Edward Herrera		14/11/86	D	3	(1)	
Juan Quero	ESP	17/10/84	M	2	(6)	1
Miroslav Koprić	CRO	23/12/84	G	15		
Liliu	BRA	30/03/90	A	13	(3)	4
Mauricio Mazzetti	ARG	18/06/86	D	23		2
Fabrizio Miccoli	ITA	27/06/79	A	10	(1)	6
Goran Mujanović	CRO	29/09/83	A	14		2
Rowen Muscat		05/06/91	M	10	(1)	
Zach Muscat		22/08/93	D	13	(2)	3
Vito Plut	SVN	08/07/88	A	21	(3)	10
Gareth Sciberras		29/03/82	M	26	(3)	1
Ryan Scicluna		30/07/93	M	13	(5)	2
L'Imam Seydi	SEN	31/08/85	A	7		3
Matia Smrekar	CRO	08/04/89	A	8		5
Franc Temile	NGA	15/07/90	M	14	(6)	5
Nikola Vukanac	SRB	14/01/86	D	17		1
Kurt Zammit		21/01/93	A	2	(13)	1
Edison Zárate	CHI	06/03/87	M	12		1
Joseph Zerafa		31/05/88	D	20	(2)	

Floriana FC

1894 • florianafc.com
Major honours
*Maltese League (25) 1910, 1912, 1913, 1921, 1922,
1925, 1927, 1928, 1929, 1931, 1935, 1937, 1950, 1951,
1952, 1953, 1955, 1958, 1962, 1968, 1970, 1973, 1975,
1977, 1993; Maltese Cup (19) 1938, 1945, 1947, 1949,
1950, 1953, 1954, 1955, 1957, 1958, 1961, 1966, 1967,
1972, 1976, 1981, 1993, 1994, 2011*
Coach: Luis Oliveira (BEL)

2015

22/08	Mosta	L	1-2	*Bonnici*
28/08	Hibernians	L	1-2	*Villa (p)*
12/09	Qormi	W	3-0	*Fontanella (p), Bonnici, Scozzese*
20/09	Naxxar	W	1-0	*Fontanella*
23/09	St Andrews	W	3-2	*Scozzeze, Piciollo, Chiesa*
26/09	Tarxien	D	1-1	*Fontanella*
03/10	Sliema	W	3-0	*Piciollo 2, S Pisani*
18/10	Valletta	L	1-3	*Fontanella*
25/10	Balzan	W	2-0	*Fontanella, Juninho*
31/10	Pembroke	W	2-1	*Villa, Fontanella*
07/11	Birkirkara	D	0-0	
22/11	Mosta	W	1-0	*Monticelli*
02/12	Hibernians	L	2-4	*Piciollo, Fontanella*
06/12	Qormi	W	1-0	*Fontanella*
12/12	Naxxar	W	2-1	*Fontanella (p), Villa*
19/12	St Andrews	W	5-0	*Villa 2, og (Uzeh), Piciollo, Fontanella (p)*

2016

10/01	Tarxien	L	0-3	
17/01	Sliema	W	2-1	*Villa 2*
23/01	Valletta	L	1-2	*Villa (p)*
31/01	Birkirkara	D	0-0	
05/02	Pembroke	W	4-2	*Piciollo, Emerson, Juninho 2 (1p)*
14/02	Balzan	L	0-1	
20/02	Naxxar	W	4-0	*Chiesa, S Pisani, Fontanella, Piciollo*
27/02	Sliema	D	2-2	*Piciollo, Fontanella (p)*
02/03	Birkirkara	W	1-0	*Juninho*
05/03	Balzan	L	0-2	
12/03	St Andrews	W	3-1	*Chiesa, Fontanella, Villa*
19/03	Qormi	W	3-1	*Fontanella, Scozzese, Villa*
03/04	Hibernians	L	1-3	*S Pisani*
09/04	Valletta	W	2-0	*Fontanella, Villa*
16/04	Pembroke	L	2-3	*Fontanella 2 (2p)*
24/04	Mosta	W	4-2	*Juninho, Fontanella 2, Villa*
29/04	Tarxien	L	2-3	*Fontanella, Clyde Borg*

Name	Nat	DoB	Pos	Aps	(s)	Gls
Firas Aboulezz		25/07/86	A	1	(14)	
Daniel Agius		15/11/96	D		(6)	
Darrell Baldacchino		28/02/96	D		(2)	
Steve Bonnici		02/02/89	D	24	(2)	2
Clyde Borg		20/03/92	M	25	(3)	1
Conor Borg		13/02/94	M	6	(13)	
Manuel Briffa		13/02/94	M	29	(1)	
Matthew Calleja Cremona		14/09/94	G	25		
Nicolás Chiesa	ARG	26/05/80	A	31		3
Jake Davies		17/07/97	M		(1)	
Emerson	BRA	24/02/91	M	11		1
Simeon Ezeadi	NGA	12/10/87	M	2		
Mario Fontanella	ITA	09/04/95	A	27	(4)	20
Luca Gatt		21/12/99	M		(1)	
Tyrone Gauci		08/11/97	G	3	(1)	
Matthew Grech		16/05/92	G	5	(1)	
Juninho	BRA	10/03/92	A	10	(14)	5
Antonio Monticelli	ITA	25/05/89	M	28		1
Enrico Pepe	ITA	12/11/89	D	26		
Matteo Piciollo	ITA	15/10/82	A	24	(5)	8
Jurgen Pisani		03/09/92	D	14		
Steve Pisani		07/08/92	M	25	(4)	3
Andre Scicluna		22/09/98	D	13	(3)	
Filippo Scozzese	ITA	09/12/88	D	16	(1)	3
Neil Spiteri		03/06/97	D	1	(2)	
Mauricio Villa	ARG	20/08/85	A	17	(8)	12
Mattia Zarb		15/03/00	M		(1)	

Hibernians FC

1922 • hiberniansfc.org
Major honours
*Maltese League (11) 1961, 1967, 1969, 1979, 1981,
1982, 1994, 1995, 2002, 2009, 2015; Maltese Cup
(10) 1962, 1970, 1971, 1980, 1982, 1998, 2006,
2007, 2012, 2013*
Coach: Branko Nišević (SRB)

2015

22/08	Balzan	D	1-1	*Jorginho*
28/08	Floriana	W	2-1	*Failla, Marcelo Dias*
12/09	Naxxar	W	4-1	*Jorge Santos, Denni, Jorginho, Failla*
20/09	Tarxien	W	1-0	*Cohen*
23/09	Valletta	W	1-0	*Jorge Santos*
26/09	Pembroke	D	1-1	*Jorginho*
04/10	Mosta	L	1-4	*Jorginho*
17/10	Qormi	W	2-1	*Cohen, Agius*
25/10	Birkirkara	D	1-1	*Jorginho*
02/11	Sliema	D	2-2	*Agius, Kristensen*
06/11	St Andrews	W	3-0	*Jorge Santos 2, Gilmar*
22/11	Balzan	W	3-2	*Kristensen 2, Pearson*
02/12	Floriana	W	4-2	*Cohen 2, Jorginho, Gilmar*
06/12	Naxxar	W	7-0	*Jackson, Jorginho 2, Gilmar, Degabriele 2, Cohen*
12/12	Tarxien	W	2-0	*og (Zerafa), Agius*
20/12	Valletta	L	2-3	*Jorginho, og (Caruana)*

2016

09/01	Pembroke	W	2-1	*Jorginho, Gilmar*
17/01	Mosta	W	4-0	*Failla (p), Jorginho, Gilmar 2*
24/01	Qormi	W	4-2	*Degabriele, Jorginho, Gilmar, Failla (p)*
30/01	St Andrews	D	2-2	*Failla (p), Gilmar*
06/02	Sliema	W	2-1	*Agius, Kristensen*
14/02	Birkirkara	W	2-0	*Gilmar, Kristensen*
20/02	Qormi	W	6-0	*Agius, Jorginho, Cohen, Edison 2 (2p), Gilmar*
28/02	St Andrews	W	4-1	*Gilmar 2, Edison, Jorginho*
02/03	Sliema	D	1-1	*Jorginho*
06/03	Naxxar	W	8-0	*og (Scicluna), Degabriele 3, Jorginho 2, Gilmar (p), Cohen*
13/03	Mosta	W	3-0	*Kristensen, Gilmar, Jorginho*
19/03	Pembroke	D	1-1	*Kristensen*
03/04	Floriana	W	3-1	*Jackson, Degabriele, Gilmar*
10/04	Tarxien	W	1-0	*Jackson*
16/04	Balzan	W	3-1	*Jorginho, Jorge Santos 2*
24/04	Birkirkara	L	1-2	*Cohen*
30/04	Valletta	D	1-1	*Marcelo Dias*

Name	Nat	DoB	Pos	Aps	(s)	Gls
Andrei Agius		12/08/86	D	29		5
Johann Bezzina		30/05/94	A		(1)	
Jurgen Borg		08/08/94	G	11		
Rudi Briffa		21/08/96	G	10	(1)	
Daniel Buckle		29/07/97	D		(1)	
Andrew Cohen		13/05/81	M	27	(2)	8
Jurgen Degabriele		10/10/96	A	11	(16)	7
Denni	BRA	21/08/82	A	3	(9)	1
Edison	BRA	09/12/85	A	5	(1)	3
Clayton Failla		08/01/86	M	26	(3)	5
Jean-Paul Farrugia		21/03/92	D		(6)	
Gilmar	BRA	26/03/90	M	23	(7)	15
Justin Haber		09/06/81	G	12		
Jackson	BRA	09/07/82	M	30		3
Jorge Santos	BRA	23/04/87	A	23		6
Jorginho	BRA	04/12/85	A	22	(4)	19
Bjorn Kristensen		05/04/93	M	31		7
Marcelo Dias	BRA	29/09/85	A	28	(1)	2
Diosdado Mbele	EQG	08/04/97	D	2	(7)	
Joseph Essien Mbong		15/07/97	A	9	(11)	
Jonathan Pearson		13/01/87	D	19	(6)	1
Rodolfo Soares	BRA	25/05/85	D	25	(1)	
Rui da Gracia	EQG	28/05/85	D	16	(1)	
Zachary Scerri		06/11/86	M	1	(3)	
Dunstan Vella		27/04/96	M		(3)	
David Xuereb		30/03/98	M		(1)	

Mosta FC

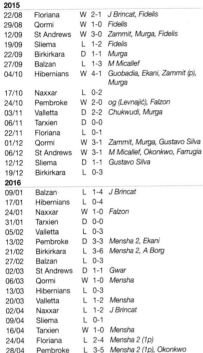

1935 • no website
Coach: Ivan Zammit

2015

22/08	Floriana	W	2-1	J Brincat, Fidelis
29/08	Qormi	W	1-0	Fidelis
12/09	St Andrews	W	3-0	Zammit, Murga, Fidelis
19/09	Sliema	L	1-2	Fidelis
22/09	Birkirkara	D	1-1	Murga
27/09	Balzan	L	1-3	M Micallef
04/10	Hibernians	W	4-1	Guobadia, Ekani, Zammit (p), Murga
17/10	Naxxar	L	0-2	
24/10	Pembroke	W	2-0	og (Levnajić), Falzon
03/11	Valletta	D	2-2	Chukwudi, Murga
06/11	Tarxien	D	0-0	
22/11	Floriana	L	0-1	
01/12	Qormi	W	3-1	Zammit, Murga, Gustavo Silva
06/12	St Andrews	W	3-1	M Micallef, Okonkwo, Farrugia
12/12	Sliema	D	1-1	Gustavo Silva
19/12	Birkirkara	L	0-3	

2016

09/01	Balzan	L	1-4	J Brincat
17/01	Hibernians	L	0-4	
24/01	Naxxar	W	1-0	Falzon
31/01	Tarxien	D	0-0	
05/02	Valletta	L	0-3	
13/02	Pembroke	D	3-3	Mensha 2, Ekani
21/02	Birkirkara	L	3-6	Mensha 2, A Borg
27/02	Balzan	L	0-3	
02/03	St Andrews	D	1-1	Gwar
06/03	Qormi	W	1-0	Mensha
13/03	Hibernians	L	0-3	
20/03	Valletta	L	1-2	Mensha
02/04	Naxxar	L	1-2	J Brincat
09/04	Sliema	L	0-1	
16/04	Tarxien	W	1-0	Mensha
24/04	Floriana	L	2-4	Mensha 2 (1p)
28/04	Pembroke	L	3-5	Mensha 2 (1p), Okonkwo

Name	Nat	DoB	Pos	Aps	(s)	Gls
Fredrick Abel	NGA	10/10/95	A	5	(6)	
Fatai Alabi	USA	15/06/89	M	13		
Godwin Aouaduna	NGA	26/12/95	A		(1)	
Adrian Borg		20/05/89	D	14	(7)	1
Omar Borg		12/02/81	G	23		
James Brincat		03/12/96	M	17	(14)	3
Mark Brincat		15/06/86	D	2	(3)	
Zachary Brincat		24/06/98	A	4	(7)	
Calvin Camilleri		02/01/00	M		(1)	
Francis Chijioke	NGA	18/09/89	A	2		
Samuel Chukwudi	NGA	14/11/93	A	10	(2)	1
Yenz Cini		04/01/94	G	10		
Jonas Ekani	CMR	13/10/92	D	27		2
Dyson Falzon		09/03/86	M	17	(6)	2
Tyrone Farrugia		22/02/89	D	31	(1)	1
Saviour Fidelis	NGA	18/04/88	A	10	(5)	4
Kyle Frendo		30/06/95	M	16	(5)	
Neil Frendo		04/01/99	M		(1)	
Kyle Gatt		18/04/99	A		(1)	
Jurgen Grech		28/04/99	D		(1)	
Ryan Grech		03/04/85	M	6	(3)	
Osa Guobadia	NGA	01/06/87	A	30	(1)	1
Gustavo Silva	BRA	23/11/90	A	3	(4)	2
Sibi Gwar	NGA	09/09/87	A	3	(5)	1
Yau Hassan	NGA	15/03/92	A	14		
Godwin Mensha	NGA	02/09/89	A	16		11
Lyden Micallef		27/03/91	A	5	(11)	
Manolito Micallef		16/11/83	D	16		2
Edil Micheletti	ITA	02/10/92	M	20	(1)	
Abdulmalik Mohammed	NGA	12/07/90	A	1	(2)	
Carlos Montes	USA	31/12/91	A		(2)	
Edin Murga	ITA	21/12/94	A	12		5
Leonard Njoussou	CMR	20/09/87	D	6		
Onyekachi Okonkwo	NGA	13/05/82	M	17		2
Dexter Xuereb		21/09/97	D	3	(5)	
Ian Zammit		09/12/86	A	10	(2)	3

Naxxar Lions FC

1920 • no website
**Coach: Stefano Grima;
(08/10/15) Clive Mizzi**

2015

21/08	Birkirkara	L	0-4	
28/08	Balzan	L	0-2	
12/09	Hibernians	L	1-4	Oussou
19/09	Floriana	L	0-1	
23/09	Tarxien	L	0-5	
27/09	Valletta	L	1-3	Falzon
03/10	Pembroke	L	1-5	Cardozo
17/10	Mosta	W	2-0	Lattes 2
24/10	Sliema	L	1-3	Falzon
31/10	St Andrews	W	2-1	Debono, Rajović
06/11	Qormi	D	1-1	Buhagiar
21/11	Birkirkara	D	2-2	Touré, Cardozo
01/12	Balzan	L	2-4	Touré, og (Bezzina)
06/12	Hibernians	L	0-7	
12/12	Floriana	L	1-2	Scicluna
19/12	Tarxien	L	0-4	

2016

10/01	Valletta	L	1-2	Bonnici
16/01	Pembroke	L	0-2	
24/01	Mosta	L	0-1	
30/01	Qormi	W	5-0	Touré 3 (1p), og (Sidibé), Cekaj
05/02	St Andrews	L	0-1	
13/02	Sliema	W	2-1	Touré, Bonnici
20/02	Floriana	L	0-4	
27/02	Tarxien	L	0-3	
01/03	Valletta	L	0-4	
06/03	Hibernians	L	0-8	
12/03	Balzan	L	0-8	
20/03	Birkirkara	L	0-1	
02/04	Mosta	W	2-1	Vellacillo, D Fenech
08/04	Pembroke	D	1-1	Hamutenya
17/04	Qormi	D	1-1	Falzon
23/04	St Andrews	L	1-3	Vellacillo (p)
29/04	Sliema	L	2-4	Vellacillo 2 (1p)

Name	Nat	DoB	Pos	Aps	(s)	Gls
Ayrton Azzopardi		10/09/96	A		(1)	
Julian Azzopardi		09/10/87	G	15	(1)	
Duane Bonnici		10/10/95	D	7	(20)	2
Angus Buhagiar		29/04/87	A	23	(2)	1
Richard Cardozo	AUS	28/03/86	A	11	(2)	2
Gilmour Ryan Cassar		20/11/95	D	3	(2)	
Xhoeijan Cekaj	ALB	07/10/87	A	3		1
Jurgen Debono		13/12/95	M	20	(10)	1
Mattia Del Negro		07/09/92	M	2	(4)	
Joel Ellul		14/11/97	M	1	(4)	
Darren Falzon		08/05/92	A	20	(7)	3
David Fenech		17/06/88	M	24	(4)	1
Mark Fenech		06/06/90	M	6	(6)	
Alberto Gallinetta	ITA	16/04/92	G	11	(1)	
Zady Gnenegbe	FRA	08/02/90	D	8	(1)	
Ishmael Grech		26/09/91	D	18	(3)	
Ryan Grech		03/04/85	M	9		
Gianluca Grima		25/04/99	D	1	(2)	
Sead Hadzibulić	SRB	30/01/83	A	3	(1)	
Ennio Hamutenya	NAM	21/05/89	A	14		1
Javier Hungría	COL	24/03/92	D	7	(4)	
José Ángel	ESP	03/06/90	D	16	(1)	
Emiliano Lattes	ARG	28/01/85	A	13		2
Luca Lodetti	ITA	18/11/89	D	7		
Mandinho	BRA	28/01/84	M	14	(1)	
Sidoine Oussou	BEN	14/11/92	A	8	(2)	1
Adam Pace		14/07/97	D		(2)	
Luke Pecorella		04/01/95	G	7	(1)	
Blažo Rajović	MNE	26/03/86	D	12	(1)	1
Yaron Sammut		16/11/95	M		(1)	
Thomas Sarina	ITA	23/04/87	A	4	(2)	
Andrew Scicluna		17/06/90	D	31		1
Nikola Tasić	SRB	22/03/88	D	14		
Demba Touré	SEN	31/12/84	A	17	(2)	6
Eduardo Vellacillo	ESP	21/03/91	A	14		4

Pembroke Athleta FC

1962 • no website
Coach: Winston Muscat

2015

21/08	Qormi	W	2-1	Villalobos 2
29/08	St Andrews	W	4-3	Martz 2, Bardsley, O'Brien
12/09	Sliema	L	0-1	
19/09	Birkirkara	L	1-4	Martz
22/09	Balzan	L	1-5	Togbah
26/09	Hibernians	D	1-1	Martz
03/10	Naxxar	W	5-1	O'Brien, Grech, Villalobos 2 (1p), L Micallef
17/10	Tarxien	L	1-2	Laudisi
24/10	Mosta	L	0-2	
31/10	Floriana	L	1-2	og (Bonnici)
06/11	Valletta	W	2-0	Laudisi, Martz
21/11	Qormi	D	0-0	
01/12	St Andrews	W	4-0	Villalobos, og (Cumbo), Laudisi, O'Brien
05/12	Sliema	L	0-2	
13/12	Birkirkara	L	0-3	
19/12	Balzan	D	0-0	

2016

09/01	Hibernians	L	1-2	Arab
16/01	Naxxar	W	2-0	M Micallef, Villalobos
24/01	Tarxien	W	1-0	Arab
31/01	Valletta	L	2-3	Arab, Villalobos
05/02	Floriana	L	2-4	Villalobos 2
13/02	Mosta	D	3-3	Villalobos (p), O'Brien, Laudisi
20/02	Balzan	L	1-2	Laudisi
28/02	Birkirkara	L	0-1	
02/03	Qormi	W	3-1	Villalobos, Obiefule 2 (1p)
06/03	St Andrews	L	1-3	Laudisi (p)
13/03	Valletta	L	0-2	
19/03	Hibernians	D	1-1	Villalobos
02/04	Sliema	L	0-2	
08/04	Naxxar	D	1-1	Villalobos
16/04	Floriana	W	3-2	Villalobos, M Micallef, Gustavo Silva
23/04	Tarxien	L	0-4	
28/04	Mosta	W	5-3	Gustavo Silva 3, O'Brien, M Micallef

Name	Nat	DoB	Pos	Aps	(s)	Gls
Terence Agius		15/01/94	M	5	(7)	
Siraj Arab		25/03/94	A	17	(14)	3
Miguel Attard		10/03/95	M	17	(2)	
Paltemio Barbetti	ITA	25/10/89	M	29		
Gibson Bardsley	USA	23/07/89	A	7	(2)	1
Owen Bugeja		20/02/90	D	31	(2)	
Alex Cini		28/10/91	D	32		
Louis John Cutajar		05/08/92	D	6		
Sunday Eboh	NGA	30/09/81	M		(4)	
Matthew Farrugia		17/04/81	G	10		
Tyron Fenech		20/10/95	M	1	(3)	
Giacomo Ferri	ITA	28/07/91	A	1		
Leighton Grech		23/03/90	A	3	(5)	1
Gustavo Silva	BRA	23/11/90	A	3	(10)	4
Ariel Laudisi	ARG	03/10/91	M	31	(1)	6
Zoran Levnajić	CRO	04/04/87	M	30		
Austin Martz	USA	31/05/92	M	14	(2)	5
Lyden Micallef		27/03/91	A		(6)	1
Manolito Micallef		16/11/83	M	14	(1)	3
Mario Muscat		18/08/76	G	23	(1)	
Kyle O'Brien	USA	27/05/90	M	30		5
Obinna Obiefule	NGA	07/01/88	A	3	(10)	2
Peter Paul Sammut		28/12/91	A	1	(7)	
Patmore Shereni	ZIM	14/09/84	D	10	(1)	
Geoffrey Spiteri		30/10/88	M	1	(1)	
Rennie Tanti		19/09/92	D	9	(1)	
James Togbah	USA	27/10/95	A	4	(1)	1
Gustavo Villalobos	USA	19/10/91	A	31		14

MALTA

Qormi FC

1961 • no website

Coach: Jesmond Zerafa;
(23/10/15) Johann Scicluna

2015

21/08	Pembroke	L	1-2	Gauci
29/08	Mosta	L	0-1	
12/09	Floriana	L	0-3	
19/09	St Andrews	W	3-0	Cassar, Nilsson 2 (1p)
23/09	Sliema	D	0-0	
27/09	Birkirkara	L	1-2	Nilsson
03/10	Balzan	L	0-1	
17/10	Hibernians	L	1-2	Sidibé
24/10	Valletta	L	1-2	T Vella
03/11	Tarxien	L	1-4	T Vella
06/11	Naxxar	D	1-1	Nilsson
21/11	Pembroke	D	0-0	
01/12	Mosta	L	1-3	Leeflang
06/12	Floriana	L	0-1	
12/12	St Andrews	W	4-0	Ojuola, Nilsson, Leeflang, R Micallef
20/12	Sliema	L	3-6	Nilsson, Ojuola, R Micallef

2016

10/01	Birkirkara	L	0-1	
24/01	Hibernians	L	2-4	Leeflang 2 (1p)
27/01	Balzan	L	0-5	
30/01	Naxxar	L	0-5	
05/02	Tarxien	L	0-4	
13/02	Valletta	L	0-2	
20/02	Hibernians	L	0-6	
27/02	Valletta	L	0-2	
02/03	Pembroke	L	1-3	Ojuola
06/03	Mosta	L	0-1	
12/03	Tarxien	L	1-6	T Vella
19/03	Floriana	L	1-3	Leeflang (p)
03/04	Birkirkara	L	0-2	
09/04	Balzan	L	0-3	
17/04	Naxxar	D	1-1	Ojuola
23/04	Sliema	W	1-0	Ojuola
29/04	St Andrews	L	2-4	R Micallef, T Vella

Name	Nat	DoB	Pos	Aps	(s)	Gls
Steve Agius		15/05/93	D	8	(3)	
Gilmore Azzopardi		09/11/96	M	4	(6)	
Clint Barbara		31/12/95	M		(5)	
Joshua Barbara		27/12/95	A	2	(4)	
Billy Berntsson	SWE	06/01/84	D	14		
Jonathan Bondin		11/10/82	D	1		
Aidan Bonnici		19/08/99	D		(1)	
Alessio Cassar		27/02/92	M	31		1
Joseph Chetcuti		16/08/82	M	4	(1)	
Edward Falzon		03/05/89	M		(1)	
Luke Farrugia		12/11/98	M		(4)	
Matthew Farrugia		17/04/81	G	1		
Clifford Gauci		08/04/92	A	26	(1)	1
Leighton Grech		23/03/90	A	1		
Tensior Gusman		24/01/97	M	7	(4)	
Djamel Leeflang	NED	25/03/92	M	20	(2)	5
Kurt Magro		04/06/86	D	29	(1)	
Immy Micallef		31/08/98	D	20	(4)	
Ryan Micallef		13/10/95	M	6	(3)	3
Carlo Monti	SCO	10/07/90	A	14		
Go Nagaoka	JPN	23/05/84	M	5	(1)	
Alexander Nilsson	SWE	23/10/92	A	15		6
Noah Ojuola	NGA	12/05/93	D	32		5
Sorin Oproiescu	ROU	12/09/87	M		(2)	
Peixoto	BRA	02/06/94	A		(11)	
Ousmane Sidibé	GUI	23/04/85	D	29		1
Kyle Spiteri		14/07/97	A	3	(1)	
Andreas Vella		14/10/98	G	16		
Emerson Vella		09/09/91	D	16	(7)	
Jean Matthias Vella		01/09/92	M	16	(1)	
Terence Vella		20/04/90	A	15	(6)	4
Pietro Viggiani	ITA	29/10/91	A	5	(10)	
Yannick Yankam		12/12/97	M	17	(4)	
Iven Zammit		17/05/97	M	5	(1)	
Shamison Zammit		02/05/97	M	1	(6)	

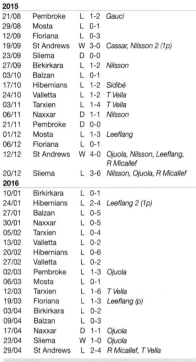

St Andrews FC

1968 • luxolsportsclub.com/fc

Coach: Jose Borg

2015

21/08	Valletta	L	0-3	
29/08	Pembroke	L	3-4	Sehitaj, De Nguidjol, Desira Buttigieg
12/09	Mosta	L	0-3	
19/09	Qormi	L	0-3	
23/09	Floriana	L	2-3	Nwoko, De Nguidjol
27/09	Sliema	L	0-1	
04/10	Birkirkara	L	0-4	
17/10	Balzan	L	0-2	
24/10	Tarxien	L	0-1	
31/10	Naxxar	L	1-2	Desira Buttigieg
06/11	Hibernians	L	0-3	
20/11	Valletta	L	0-4	
01/12	Pembroke	L	0-4	
06/12	Mosta	L	1-3	Johnson
12/12	Qormi	L	0-4	
19/12	Floriana	L	0-5	

2016

10/01	Sliema	L	1-6	Farrugia
24/01	Balzan	L	1-5	Farrugia (p)
27/01	Birkirkara	L	1-3	Farrugia (p)
30/01	Hibernians	D	2-2	Farrugia 2 (1p)
05/02	Naxxar	W	1-0	Salomon
13/02	Tarxien	D	1-1	Nwoko
21/02	Valletta	L	1-2	Enmy Peña
28/02	Hibernians	L	1-4	Oseghale
02/03	Mosta	D	1-1	Oseghale
06/03	Pembroke	W	3-1	Jonathan Pérez, Nwoko, Desira Buttigieg
12/03	Floriana	L	1-3	Farrugia (p)
19/03	Tarxien	L	2-3	Johnson, Farrugia (p)
02/04	Balzan	L	0-1	
10/04	Birkirkara	L	1-3	Salomon
16/04	Sliema	L	1-3	Oseghale
23/04	Naxxar	W	3-1	Nwoko 2, Oseghale
29/04	Qormi	W	4-2	Choi, Eloy, Salomon, Jonathan Pérez

Name	Nat	DoB	Pos	Aps	(s)	Gls
Nicola Andreis	ITA	11/01/95	D	7		
Dorian Bugeja		24/01/98	G	2		
Kris Calleja		13/04/83	G	10		
Dale Camilleri		17/10/92	M	29	(1)	
Choi Bong-won	KOR	16/05/94	D	16		1
Luca Cosmai	ITA	19/02/94	A	7		
Clyde Cumbo		20/12/95	D	12	(1)	
Chris De Nguidjol	ITA	01/05/94	A	8	(3)	2
Matteo Desira Buttigieg		17/06/94	D	13	(11)	3
Eloy	EQG	16/03/85	D	17	(2)	1
Enmy Peña	ESP	17/09/92	M	16		1
Joseph Farrugia		26/07/81	M	31		7
Jake Galea		15/04/96	G	16		
Nick Ghio		18/06/98	D	6	(1)	
Liam Grech		03/02/97	M	5	(9)	
Michael Grima		07/03/91	M	7	(5)	
Matthew Guillaumier		09/04/98	M	15	(1)	
Michael Johnson		11/05/94	D	23	(4)	2
Jonathan Pérez	ESP	01/12/90	A	15		2
Jamie Magri Overand		07/02/98	M		(1)	
Wade Moodley	RSA	26/09/96	M	3	(1)	
Kyrian Nwoko		09/07/97	M	18	(9)	5
Chenato Onwudinjo	NGA	28/08/92	D	16		
Sorin Oproiescu	ROU	12/09/87	M	5	(1)	
Victor Oseghale	NGA	12/08/95	D	11	(3)	4
Josh Parry	WAL	02/07/93	M	1	(2)	
Diego Rossetto	ITA	19/01/96	G	5	(1)	
Michel Salomon	BEN	01/10/88	A	15	(1)	3
Ryan Sammut		06/04/92	M		(6)	
Marigen Sehitaj	ALB	15/09/95	D	7	(2)	1
Manuel Stefanoni	ITA	13/03/98	A		(1)	
Edafe Uzeh	NGA	22/03/88	M	4		
Nicki Vella Petroni		10/09/91	M	5	(1)	
Jacob Walker		31/07/97	A	3	(16)	
Jordan Williams	ENG	28/07/97	D	15	(1)	

Sliema Wanderers FC

1909 • no website

Major honours
Maltese League (26) 1920, 1923, 1924, 1926, 1930,
1933, 1934, 1936, 1938, 1939, 1940, 1949, 1954,
1956, 1957, 1964, 1965, 1966, 1971, 1972, 1976,
1989, 1996, 2003, 2004, 2005; Maltese Cup (21)
1935, 1936, 1937, 1940, 1946, 1948, 1951, 1952,
1956, 1959, 1963, 1965, 1968, 1969, 1974, 1979,
1990, 2000, 2004, 2009, 2016

Coach: Stephen Azzopardi;
(23/02/16) Alfonso Greco (ITA)

2015

21/08	Tarxien	L	0-2	
28/08	Valletta	L	0-1	
12/09	Pembroke	W	1-0	Pedrinho
19/09	Mosta	W	2-1	Mifsud, Kerlon
23/09	Qormi	D	0-0	
27/09	St Andrews	W	1-0	og (Andreis)
03/10	Floriana	L	1-3	
18/10	Birkirkara	L	1-3	Muscat
24/10	Naxxar	W	2-1	Friggieri, Rafael Ledesma
02/11	Hibernians	D	2-2	Scerri, Rafael Ledesma
07/11	Balzan	L	0-1	
20/11	Tarxien	L	2-3	Muir, Muscat (p)
01/12	Valletta	L	2-4	Potezica, Kerlon (p)
05/12	Pembroke	W	2-0	Mifsud 2
12/12	Mosta	D	1-1	Scerri
20/12	Qormi	W	6-3	Friggieri, Rafael Ledesma, Muscat, og (Berntsson), Mifsud 2

2016

10/01	St Andrews	W	6-1	Mifsud 4 (1p), Bianciardi, Hendry
17/01	Floriana	L	1-2	Scerri
23/01	Birkirkara	L	0-2	
31/01	Balzan	L	0-2	
06/02	Hibernians	L	1-2	Farrugia
13/02	Naxxar	L	1-2	Shodiya
20/02	Tarxien	W	1-0	Bezzina
27/02	Floriana	D	2-2	Potezica 2
02/03	Hibernians	D	1-1	Denni
06/03	Valletta	L	0-3	
12/03	Birkirkara	L	1-2	Priso
19/03	Balzan	D	3-3	Farrugia 2, Denni
02/04	Pembroke	W	2-0	Farrugia, Denni
09/04	Mosta	W	1-0	Farrugia
16/04	St Andrews	W	3-1	Farrugia, Perdomo, Priso
23/04	Qormi	L	0-1	
29/04	Naxxar	W	4-2	Denni, Farrugia 2, Bezzina

Name	Nat	DoB	Pos	Aps	(s)	Gls
Timothy Aquilina		12/06/98	G	6		
Johann Bezzina		30/05/94	M	27	(2)	2
Stefano Bianciardi	ITA	15/03/85	D	26	(1)	1
Ryan Dalli		18/03/93	M	1	(2)	
Denni	BRA	21/08/82	A	10	(1)	4
Luke Dimech		11/01/77	D	23	(1)	
Antonjo Elezaj	ALB	14/07/96	M	7	(1)	
Omar Elouni		16/03/99	A		(1)	
Benjamin Essel	GHA	16/02/95	D	11	(3)	
Jean-Paul Farrugia		21/03/92	M	12	(1)	8
Saviour Fidelis	NGA	18/04/88	A	2	(1)	
Aldan Jake Friggieri Clifford		28/04/94	A	16	(10)	1
Gatt Baldacchino		02/09/88	D	26	(2)	
Kyle Hendry		28/07/91	M	2	(7)	1
Kerlon	BRA	27/01/88	A	7	(1)	2
Mandinho	BRA	28/01/84	M	3	(1)	
Michael Mifsud		17/04/81	A	13	(2)	9
John Mintoff		23/08/88	M	1	(5)	
Gary Muir	SCO	15/12/85	M	30	(1)	1
Alex Muscat		14/12/84	D	30	(1)	3
Pedrinho	BRA	04/08/86	A	9	(1)	1
Sebastián Perdomo	COL	03/06/94	M	2	(2)	1
Marko Potezica	SRB	05/12/85	M	21	(9)	3
Njongo Priso	CMR	24/12/88	A	9		2
Rafael Ledesma	BRA	31/12/82	M	17	(3)	3
Michele Sansone		02/07/98	M	3	(2)	
Mark Scerri		16/01/90	M	20	(3)	3
Shola Shodiya	NGA	17/06/91	A		(4)	1
Justin Vella		02/03/98	D		(1)	
Axl Xuereb		02/01/96	A		(1)	
Peter Xuereb		07/05/92	M	9	(14)	
Glenn Zammit		08/05/87	G	20	(2)	

Tarxien Rainbows FC

1944 • no website
Coach: Jacques Scerri

2015
21/08	Sliema	W	2-0	Azzopardi (p), Carlinos
28/08	Birkirkara	D	2-2	Pedrinho (p), Baker
13/09	Balzan	D	0-0	
20/09	Hibernians	L	0-1	
23/09	Naxxar	W	5-0	Pedrinho, Omerou, T Caruana, Danilo Santos, Montebello
26/09	Floriana	D	1-1	Pedrinho
03/10	Valletta	L	1-3	Montebello
17/10	Pembroke	W	2-1	Montebello, Zerafa
24/10	St Andrews	W	1-0	Azzopardi
03/11	Qormi	W	4-1	T Caruana, Pedrinho, Baker, Danilo Santos
06/11	Mosta	D	0-0	
20/11	Sliema	W	3-2	og (Scerri), Pedrinho, Azzopardi
02/12	Birkirkara	L	0-1	
06/12	Balzan	W	3-0	Zerafa, Montebello, Lecão (p)
12/12	Hibernians	L	0-2	
19/12	Naxxar	W	4-0	Pedrinho, Azzopardi, Lecão, Montebello

2016
10/01	Floriana	W	3-0	Azzopardi, Lecão, Pedrinho
16/01	Valletta	D	1-1	Lecão
24/01	Pembroke	L	0-1	
31/01	Mosta	D	0-0	
05/02	Qormi	W	4-0	Pedrinho, Azzopardi, Carlinos, Montebello (p)
13/02	St Andrews	D	1-1	Montebello
20/02	Sliema	L	0-1	
27/02	Naxxar	W	3-0	Azzopardi, Lecão, Nilsson
01/03	Balzan	D	2-2	Pedrinho, Nilsson
05/03	Birkirkara	L	1-2	Nilsson
12/03	Qormi	W	6-1	Montebello 2, Azzopardi, Zerafa 2, Francés
19/03	St Andrews	W	3-2	Montebello 2, T Caruana
02/04	Valletta	L	0-2	
10/04	Hibernians	L	0-1	
16/04	Mosta	L	0-1	
23/04	Pembroke	W	4-0	Francés 2, Pedrinho, Azzopardi
29/04	Floriana	W	3-2	Nilsson, Francés, Montebello

Name	Nat	DoB	Pos	Aps	(s)	Gls
Anderson	BRA	26/09/86	M	6	(4)	
Ayrton Azzopardi		12/09/93	M	27	(6)	9
Roderick Bajada		04/01/83	M	1	(11)	
Ebiabowei Baker	NGA	30/01/94	D	26	(1)	2
Bruno Oliveira	BRA	20/08/85	D	24	(3)	
Carlinos	ESP	17/02/87	A	22	(1)	2
Manuel Caruana		17/02/85	D	10	(6)	
Triston Caruana		15/09/91	M	30		3
Andrea Cassar		19/12/92	G	31		
Danilo Santos	BRA	12/11/83	A	3	(8)	2
Claudio Francés	ARG	26/06/92	M	8	(3)	4
Gaetano Gesualdi		15/02/92	D		(1)	
Lecão	BRA	17/01/93	A	27	(1)	5
John Mintoff		23/08/88	M	4	(4)	
Sean Mintoff		30/10/85	G	2		
Ren Mizugashira	JPN	17/12/91	A		(1)	
Luke Montebello		13/08/95	M	24	(7)	12
Brandon Muscat		03/11/94	M	16	(8)	
Alexander Nilsson	SWE	23/10/92	A	7	(5)	4
Lucky Omerou	NGA	15/09/95	A	8	(6)	1
Pedrinho	BRA	18/06/93	M	28		10
Nicolás Rios	ARG	29/03/95	M	1		
Sergio Prendes	ESP	15/07/86	A	9		
Ryan Spiteri		02/02/95	M	2	(3)	
Matthew Tabone		29/04/92	D	8	(9)	
Timothy Tabone Desira		15/07/95	M	19	(2)	
Daniel Zerafa		08/04/94	D	20	(3)	4

Valletta FC

1943 • vallettafc.net
Major honours
Maltese League (23) 1915, 1932, 1945, 1946, 1948, 1959, 1960, 1963, 1974, 1978, 1980, 1984, 1990, 1992, 1997, 1998, 1999, 2001, 2008, 2011, 2012, 2014, 2016; Maltese Cup (13) 1960, 1964, 1975, 1977, 1978, 1991, 1995, 1996, 1997, 1999, 2001, 2010, 2014

Coach: Paul Zammit

2015
21/08	St Andrews	W	3-0	Priso 2 (2p), Falcone
28/08	Sliema	W	1-0	Falcone
13/09	Birkirkara	W	2-1	Falcone, Priso
19/09	Balzan	L	0-1	
23/09	Hibernians	L	0-1	
27/09	Naxxar	W	3-1	Nafti 2, Umeh
03/10	Tarxien	W	3-1	Nafti, og (Bruno Oliveira), Mifsud Triganza
18/10	Floriana	W	3-1	Falcone, Azzopardi, Jhonnattann
24/10	Qormi	W	2-1	Falcone, Nafti
03/11	Mosta	D	2-2	Cremona, Priso (p)
06/11	Pembroke	L	0-1	
20/11	St Andrews	W	4-0	Priso 2, Umeh, Mifsud Triganza
01/12	Sliema	W	4-2	Priso, Falcone 2, Nafti
05/12	Birkirkara	W	4-0	Falcone, Briffa, Priso (p), Borg
13/12	Balzan	W	2-1	Pani, Nafti
20/12	Hibernians	W	3-2	Jhonnattann, Borg, Nafti

2016
10/01	Naxxar	W	2-1	Falcone, Suda
16/01	Tarxien	D	1-1	Falcone
23/01	Floriana	W	2-1	Jhonnattann, Umeh
31/01	Pembroke	W	3-2	Romeu, Briffa, Mifsud
05/02	Mosta	W	3-0	Falcone, Jhonnattann, Cremona
13/02	Qormi	W	2-0	Gill, Falcone
21/02	St Andrews	W	2-1	Nafti 2
27/02	Qormi	W	2-0	Cremona, Mifsud
01/03	Naxxar	W	4-0	Umeh, Rafael Ledesma (p), Falcone, Mifsud
06/03	Sliema	W	3-0	Umeh, Jhonnattann, Nafti
13/03	Pembroke	W	2-0	Jhonnattann, Nafti
20/03	Mosta	W	2-1	Jhonnattann, Borg
02/04	Tarxien	W	2-0	Falcone, Nafti
09/04	Floriana	L	0-2	
17/04	Birkirkara	D	0-0	
23/04	Balzan	W	2-1	Falcone, Mifsud
30/04	Hibernians	D	1-1	Falcone

Name	Nat	DoB	Pos	Aps	(s)	Gls
Ian Azzopardi		12/08/82	D	19	(6)	1
Shaun Bajada		19/10/83	M		(1)	
Henry Bonello		13/10/88	G	25		
Jean Pierre Borg		08/01/98	D	3	(13)	3
Roderick Briffa		24/08/81	M	27	(1)	2
Albert Bruce	GHA	30/12/93	M	6	(3)	
Daniel Camilleri		13/05/95	D		(3)	
Ryan Camilleri		22/05/88	D	29	(1)	
Jonathan Caruana		24/07/86	D	25		
Llywelyn Cremona		07/05/95	A	19	(9)	3
Diego Balbinot	BRA	07/01/84	D	2		
Federico Falcone	ARG	21/12/90	A	28	(2)	16
Russell Fenech		07/02/98	A		(5)	
Juan Cruz Gill	ARG	18/07/83	D	31		1
Jhonnattann	BRA	27/07/89	A	23		7
Michael Mifsud		17/04/81	A	6	(8)	4
Jean Pierre Mifsud Triganza		20/11/81	A	4	(12)	2
Abdelkarim Nafti	TUN	03/08/81	M	24	(4)	12
Claudio Pani	ITA	11/03/86	M	27		1
Njongo Priso	CMR	24/12/88	A	11	(2)	8
Nicholas Pulis		28/01/98	D		(4)	
Rafael Ledesma	BRA	31/12/82	A	8	(2)	1
Romeu	BRA	10/04/90	M	21	(3)	1
Jurgen Suda		24/09/96	A	1	(13)	1
Uchenna Umeh	NGA	10/10/91	A	16	(7)	5
Nicholas Vella		27/08/89	G	8		

Top goalscorers

20 Mario Fontanella (Floriana)

19 Jorginho (Hibernians)

16 Alfred Effiong (Balzan)
Lydon Micallef (Balzan)
Federico Falcone (Valletta)

15 Gilmar (Hibernians)

14 Godwin Mensha (Balzan/Mosta)
Gustavo Villalobos (Pembroke)

13 Michael Mifsud (Sliema/Valletta)

12 Mauricio Villa (Floriana)
Luke Montebello (Tarxien)
Abdelkarim Nafti (Valletta)

MALTA

Promoted clubs

Gzira United FC

1947 • no website
Major honours
Maltese Cup (1) 1973
Coach: Darren Abdilla

Hamrun Spartans FC

1907 • hamrunspartans.com
Major honours
Maltese League (7) 1914, 1918, 1947, 1983, 1987, 1988, 1991; Maltese Cup (6) 1983, 1984, 1987, 1988, 1989, 1992
Coach: Steve D'Amato

Second level final table 2015/16

		Pld	W	D	L	F	A	Pts
1	Gzira United FC	26	19	7	0	58	13	64
2	Hamrun Spartans FC	26	18	7	1	57	17	61
3	Senglea Athletic FC	26	16	4	6	47	21	52
4	Pietà Hotspurs FC	26	13	5	8	32	27	44
5	Lija Athletic FC	26	12	5	9	40	27	41
6	Vittoriosa Stars FC	26	10	7	9	39	31	37
7	Mqabba FC	26	10	5	11	44	33	35
8	Żebbuġ Rangers FC	26	9	5	12	30	32	32
9	Rabat Ajax FC	26	9	3	14	27	37	30
10	Fgura United FC	26	8	6	12	24	35	30
11	Melita FC	26	8	4	14	23	48	28
12	San Gwann FC	26	7	6	13	30	50	27
13	St George's FC	26	4	7	15	20	46	19
14	Gudja United FC	26	2	3	21	22	76	9

Promotion/Relegation play-off

(06/05/16)
St Andrews 2-1 Senglea

DOMESTIC CUP

FA Trophy 2015/16

THIRD ROUND

(01/12/15)
St George's 1-0 Mqabba

(02/12/15)
Pietà 4-1 Zejtun
Rabat 1-4 Melita
St Venera 0-2 Gharghur
Zabbar 0-3 Gzira

(09/12/15)
Balzan 2-1 Fgura
Birkirkara 6-0 Kirkop
Floriana 3-0 St Laurence
Pembroke 3-0 San Gwann

(15/12/15)
Mosta 1-2 Hibernians
Swieqi 2-4 St. Andrews

(16/12/15)
Naxxar 0-1 Lija
Qormi 1-0 Ghajnsielem
Vittoriosa 0-1 Sliema
Zebbug 1-4 Tarxien

(06/01/16)
Xewkija 3-0 Valletta

FOURTH ROUND

(19/01/16)
Balzan 2-0 Melita
Qormi 1-4 Tarxien *(aet)*

(20/01/16)
Birkirkara 1-0 Valletta
Floriana 2-1 Lija
Gharghur 1-2 Sliema
Hibernians 1-2 Pembroke
Pietà 3-2 St George's
St Andrews 1-1 Gzira *(aet; 4-2 on pens)*

QUARTER-FINALS

(19/04/16)
Balzan 1-0 Tarxien *(Micallef 106) (aet)*
Sliema 2-1 St Andrews *(Bezzina 32, Friggieri 86; Farrugia 67p)*

(20/04/16)
Birkirkara 2-0 Floriana *(Briffa 7og, Mazzetti 23)*
Pembroke 3-1 Pietà *(Laudisi 43, M Micallef 110, Agius 117; John 53) (aet)*

SEMI-FINALS

(07/05/16)
Sliema 1-0 Birkirkara *(Denni 45)*

(08/05/16)
Balzan 3-1 Pembroke *(Alan 80, Kaljević 97, Pedrinho 120p; Laudisi 34) (aet)*

FINAL

(14/05/16)
National Stadium, Ta' Qali
SLIEMA WANDERERS FC 0
BALZAN FC 0
(aet; 5-4 on pens)
Referee: *Borg*
SLIEMA: *Elezaj, Muscat, Gatt Baldacchino, Bianciardi, Bezzina (Friggieri 116), Potezica, Scerri, P Xuereb, Farrugia, Priso, Denni (Mandinho 74)*
Sent off: *Priso (85)*
BALZAN: *Janjušević, Bezzina, Serrano, Grioli, Brincat (Focsa 95), P Fenech, Grima, Kaljević (Alan 57), Micallef (Sciberras 112), Pedrinho, Effiong*

Jubilation for Sliema Wanderers as players and associates pose with the FA Trophy

MOLDOVA
Federatia Moldoveneasca de Fotbal (FMF)

Address	Str. Tricolorului 39 MD-2012 Chisinau	**President**	Pavel Cebanu
Tel	+373 22 210 413	**General secretary**	Nicolai Cebotari
Fax	+373 22 210 432	**Media officer**	Victor Daghi
E-mail	fmf@fmf.md	**Year of formation**	1990
Website	fmf.md	**National stadium**	Zimbru, Chisinau (10,400)

DIVIZIA NATIONALA CLUBS

 1 **FC Academia Chisinau**

 2 **FC Dacia Chisinau**

 3 **FC Dinamo-Auto**

 4 **FC Milsami Orhei**

 5 **CS Petrocub**

 6 **FC Saxan**

 7 **FC Sheriff**

 8 **CSF Speranta**

 9 **FC Zaria Balti**

 10 **FC Zimbru Chisinau**

KEY

● UEFA Champions League

● UEFA Europa League

● Promoted

PROMOTED CLUB

 11 **FC Ungheni**

Sheriff strike gold

MECIUL DE AUR
DIVIZIA NAȚIONALĂ
EDIȚIA 2015-2016

For the second season running the Divizia Nationala did not have a clear winner at the end of its regular season. Unlike in 2014/15, however, when three teams finished level and Milsami Orhei took the title on the head-to-head rule at the expense of Dacia Chisinau and FC Sheriff, there were just two teams tied at the top – and that meant a championship play-off.

Sheriff and Dacia could not be separated again, and it was the former who went on to win the Golden Match and claim a 14th league title in 16 years. There was a first-time winner in the cup, though, as Zaria Balti overcame Milsami in the final.

| Dacia defeated in championship play-off | Regular season ends with two teams tied at top | Zaria Balti claim first trophy in cup triumph |

Domestic league

Ten teams started and finished the 2015/16 Moldovan championship – unlike its disrupted predecessor, which began with 11 and ended with nine – but there were only ever two in contention to win it. Four early defeats put Milsami out of the equation, and although Zimbru Chisinau got off to a bright start, they were unable to sustain it. That left Sheriff and Dacia to duel for a title they were both desperate to win after the near-miss of the previous campaign.

Dacia removed coach Igor Dobrovolski after just one game – a 3-0 forfeit loss to Zimbru. His successor, Oleg Bejenari, then steered the team through 23 matches undefeated, 19 of them victories. Sheriff, though, were equally proficient at picking up points – though they too opted to change their coach, replacing Lilian Popescu with Croatian Zoran Vulić in early October after a trio of draws, the third of them 0-0 at home to Dacia.

Neck and neck at the winter break, with 37 points apiece, the two teams met again in the second game after the restart at the Buiucani stadium in Chisinau. A 79th-minute goal from Dacia's Ukrainian striker Maxym Feshchuk won the game, sending his team three points clear. It was an advantage they would protect throughout the months of March and April, but in

early May Dacia's long unbeaten run was brought to a halt with a 2-0 defeat at Milsami. Sheriff won the next day to join them at the top and after both teams won the following week the Divizia Nationala had the last-day showdown it wanted – a winner-takes-all head-to-head at the Stadionul Moldova in Speia. Feshchuk put Dacia ahead once again but 15 minutes from time Sheriff equalised through Croatian striker Josip Ivančić and at the final whistle, with both teams locked on 65 points, the title remained up for grabs.

Nine days later the two teams faced off again, this time in the Zimbru stadium in Chisinau. A crowd of around 6,500 gathered to watch the first Golden Match in Divizia Nationala history, and for 88 minutes the two teams continued to cancel each other out before Sheriff substitute Goran Galešić's deflected shot from the corner of the penalty area decided the game and the championship.

Domestic cup

Four days before the league title climax the Zimbru stadium also hosted the Moldovan Cup final. That too was settled by a single goal – scored nine minutes into extra time by Zaria's top scorer Gheorghe Boghiu to defeat 2012 winners Milsami and give his club their first significant silverware. Zaria had

eliminated Sheriff after extra time in the semi-finals while Milsami did the same to Dacia.

Europe

Milsami made a superb start to life in the UEFA Champions League when they won both legs of their second qualifying round tie against Bulgarian title holders Ludogorets, who had competed in the group stage the previous season, but they could not follow that up against Albania's Skënderbeu and switched over to the UEFA Europa League play-offs, where they valiantly lost 2-1 on aggregate to Saint-Étienne.

National team

Four and a half months after his dismissal by Dacia, Dobrovolski resurfaced for a second spell as head coach of the Moldovan national side. The ex-USSR midfielder who had led the team from 2007-09, was under little pressure on his return as Moldova had gone 17 games without a win under his three predecessors – Ion Caras, Alexandru Curteian and caretaker boss Ștefan Stoica – and ended their UEFA EURO 2016 qualifying campaign with a mere two points. Only San Marino, Gibraltar and Andorra – against whom Dobrovolski stopped the rot, with a 1-0 win in Malta – fared worse.

DOMESTIC SEASON AT A GLANCE

Divizia Nationala 2015/16 final table

		Pld	Home					Away					Total					Pts
			W	D	L	F	A	W	D	L	F	A	W	D	L	F	A	
1=	FC Dacia Chisinau	27	10	4	0	25	5	10	1	2	19	7	20	5	2	44	12	65
	FC Sheriff	27	12	2	0	31	4	8	3	2	19	7	20	5	2	50	11	65
3	FC Zimbru Chisinau	27	9	1	4	22	9	6	3	4	20	17	15	4	8	42	26	49
4	FC Zaria Balti	27	6	3	5	21	15	6	3	4	15	14	12	6	9	36	29	42
5	FC Dinamo-Auto	27	6	3	4	13	12	6	2	6	20	22	12	5	10	33	34	41
6	FC Milsami Orhei	27	6	4	3	23	10	4	2	8	10	13	10	6	11	33	23	36
7	CSF Speranta	27	4	4	5	10	16	4	3	7	14	20	8	7	12	24	36	31
8	CS Petrocub	27	5	1	8	13	23	1	2	10	8	30	6	3	18	21	53	21
9	FC Academia Chisinau	27	2	2	9	7	26	3	4	7	11	16	5	6	16	18	42	21
10	FC Saxan	27	1	2	10	6	20	0	3	11	4	25	1	5	21	10	45	8

Championship play-off

(29/05/16)
Zimbru, Chisinau
FC SHERIFF 1 *(Galešić 88)*
FC DACIA CHISINAU 0
Referee: *Andó-Szabó (HUN)*
SHERIFF: *Coselev, Sušić, Savic, Dupovac, Aliti, Ginsari, Jabbie, Patras, Ivančić (Golec 90+2), Rebenja (Urvantev 85), Subotic (Galešić 62)*
DACIA: *Gaiducevici, Bordian, Bulgaru, Posmac, Mamah, Neziri (Cemirtan 89), Lozoviy, Bejan (Cojocaru 84), Mani (Gavrilenko 71), Cociuc, Feshchuk*

European qualification 2016/17

Champion: FC Sheriff (second qualifying round)

Cup winner: FC Zaria Balti (first qualifying round)
FC Dacia Chisinau (first qualifying round)
FC Zimbru Chisinau (first qualifying round)

Top scorer	Danijel Subotic (Sheriff), 12 goals
Relegated clubs	None
Promoted club	FC Ungheni
Cup final	FC Zaria Balti 1-0 FC Milsami Orhei (aet)

Team of the season
(4-4-1-1)

Coach: Vulić *(Sheriff)*

Player of the season

Danijel Subotic
(FC Sheriff)

A much-travelled former Swiss youth international, Subotic arrived at Sheriff from Kuwaiti side Qadsia – following earlier spells in Romania, Ukraine and Azerbaijan – and enjoyed the most fruitful season of his career. It ended with the 27-year-old striker not just picking up a Moldovan championship winner's medal but also the Divizia Nationala's golden boot, his 12 goals proving sufficient to top the charts and succeed his Brazilian team-mate Ricardinho, who had found the net 21 times the season before.

Newcomer of the season

Alexandru Bejan
(FC Dacia Chisinau)

Born in the Moldovan capital and a Dacia player from a very early age, Bejan emerged as one of the club's most important players during the 2015/16 season, knitting things together with his tidy midfield play, setting up attacking opportunities, scoring four goals and generally doing what was expected of a No10 to help Dacia challenge Sheriff for the Divizia Nationala title. A Moldovan Under-21 international, he can expect to be involved for the senior team in the 2018 FIFA World Cup qualifiers.

MOLDOVA

NATIONAL TEAM

Top five all-time caps
Radu Rebeja (74); **Alexandru Epureanu** & **Victor Golovatenco** (73); Serghey Clescenco (69); Ivan Testimitanu (56)

Top five all-time goals
Serghey Clescenco (11); Serghey Rogaciov (9); Serghey Dadu & Iurie Miterev (8); Igor Bugaiov, **Alexandru Epureanu**, Viorel Frunza & **Eugen Sidorenco** (7)

Results 2015/16

Date	Opponent		Venue		Result	Scorers
05/09/15	Austria (ECQ)	A	Vienna	L	0-1	
08/09/15	Montenegro (ECQ)	H	Chisinau	L	0-2	
09/10/15	Russia (ECQ)	H	Chisinau	L	1-2	*Cebotari (85)*
12/10/15	Sweden (ECQ)	A	Solna	L	0-2	
17/11/15	Azerbaijan	A	Baku	L	1-2	*Antoniuc (44)*
24/03/16	Malta	A	Ta' Qali	D	0-0	
28/03/16	Andorra	N	Paola (MLT)	W	1-0	*Armas (45+2)*
27/05/16	Croatia	A	Koprivnica	L	0-1	
03/06/16	Switzerland	A	Lugano	L	1-2	*Ginsari (69)*

Appearances 2015/16

Coach: Alexandru Curteian 11/02/74
/(21/09/15) (Ştefan Stoica (ROU)) 23/06/67
/(23/12/15) Igor Dobrovolski (RUS) 27/08/67

Player	DOB	Club	AUT	MNE	RUS	SWE	Aze	Mlt	And	Cro	Sui	Caps	Goals
Ilie Cebanu	29/12/86	Mordovia (RUS)	G	G		G	G			G	G	21	-
Ion Jardan	10/01/90	Zimbru	D	D	D	D80	D			D	D92	13	-
Victor Golovatenco	28/04/84	Sibir (RUS)	D	D		D	D		D90	D	D79	73	3
Igor Armas	14/07/87	Kuban (RUS)	D	D	D	s63	D	D	D			49	4
Iulian Erhan	01/07/86	Milsami	D	D		D63						10	-
Andrei Cojocari	21/01/87	Milsami	M	M			M68	M		s60	M	23	1
Evgheny Cebotari	16/10/84	Sibir (RUS)	M79	M36	M	M				M87	M87	46	1
Artur Patras	01/10/88	Milsami	M	M71		M61						27	-
Gheorghe Andronic	25/09/91	Milsami	M55									6	1
Alexandr Dedov	26/07/89	Tirgu Mureş (ROU)	M	M			A	s62	M			33	2
Nicolae Milinceanu	01/08/92	Petrolul (ROU)/Speranta	A87	A	A88					s53	s89	7	-
Petru Racu	17/07/87	Milsami	s55	s36				s46				37	-
Radu Ginsari	10/12/91	Sheriff	s79	s71				s77	s76		A	10	1
Catalin Carp	20/10/93	Steaua (ROU)	s87		M70		M	M	M60		s92	10	1
Alexandru Gatcan	27/03/84	Rostov (RUS)		M				M	M			49	3
Alexei Coselev	19/11/93	Sheriff			G							1	-
Vitalie Bordian	11/08/84	Helios (UKR)/Dacia			D	M	D	D				40	1
Stefan Burghiu	28/03/91	Zimbru			D	D						7	-
Alexandru Antoniuc	23/05/89	Milsami			M	s61	M73	M72	M87			23	3
Alexandru Onica	29/07/84	Zaria			M79		M					22	-
Dan Spataru	24/05/94	Zimbru			M	s80				M76	s58	5	-
Alexandru Vremea	03/11/91	Zimbru			s70	M						4	-
Vladimir Ambros	30/12/93	Petrocub			s79						s87	2	-
Sergiu Istrati	07/08/88	Saxan			s88	A	s68					3	-
Maxim Potiriche	13/06/89	Sheriff				M	M87					6	-
Alexandru Maxim	19/01/86	Speranta				s73						1	-
Eugen Cociuc	11/05/93	Dacia				s87						2	-
Artiom Gaiducevici	22/04/87	Dacia						G				8	-
Alexandru Epureanu	27/09/86	İstanbul Başakşehir (TUR)						D46	D	D	D	73	7
Andrian Cascaval	10/06/87	Dinamo-Auto						D	s57	D	D	7	-
Artur Ionita	17/08/90	Verona (ITA)						M	M	M75	M89	23	2
Eugen Sidorenco	19/03/89	Milsami						M62		s60	M60	28	7
Vadim Cemirtan	21/07/87	Dacia						A77	A76			2	-
Maxim Mihaliov	22/08/86	Dacia						s72	s87	s75	s87	4	-
Denis Ilescu	20/01/87	Dinamo-Auto							D57		s79	4	-
Valeriu Andronic	21/12/82	Petrocub								M60	s90	36	4
Andrei Bugneac	30/03/88	Dinamo-Auto								A53	s60	3	-
Vladislav Ivanov	07/05/90	Dinamo-Auto								s76	M58	5	-
Stanislav Namasco	10/11/86	Olimpik-Şüvälän (AZE)									G	42	-

EUROPE

FC Milsami Orhei

Second qualifying round - PFC Ludogorets Razgrad (BUL)
A 1-0 *Antoniuc (41)*
Mitu, Rhaili, Erhan, Monday, Patras, Surdu (Bud 59), Belak (Bolohan 69), Rassulov, Antoniuc, G Andronic (Zarichnyuk 90), Cojocari. Coach: Iurie Osipenco (MDA)
H 2-1 *G Andronic (26), Racu (89)*
Mitu, Rhaili, Erhan, Monday, Patras, Belak, Rassulov, Antoniuc (Zarichnyuk 77), G Andronic (Bolohan 76), Bud (Racu 87), Cojocari. Coach: Iurie Osipenco (MDA)
Red card: Cojocari 73

Third qualifying round - KF Skënderbeu (ALB)
H 0-2
Mitu, Rhaili, Erhan, Monday, Zarichnyuk (Antoniuc 51), Patras (Suvorov 56), G Andronic, Belak, Rassulov, Bolohan (Banović 73), Bud. Coach: Iurie Osipenco (MDA)
A 0-2
Mitu, Erhan (Gheți 57), Racu, Monday, Patras, G Andronic, Belak (Bud 46), Rassulov, Antoniuc (Zarichnyuk 67), Banović, Cojocari. Coach: Iurie Osipenco (MDA)
Red card: G Andronic 14

Play-offs - AS Saint-Étienne (FRA)
H 1-1 *Bud (56)*
Mitu, Rhaili, Erhan (Gheți 64), Racu, Monday, Patras, Belak (Zarichnyuk 69), Rassulov (Bolohan 73), Banović, Bud, Cojocari. Coach: Iurie Osipenco (MDA)
A 0-1
Mitu, Rhaili, Gheți, Erhan, Racu, Patras, Belak (Zarichnyuk 62), Antoniuc, Banović (Slivca 78), Bud (Bolohan 70), Cojocari. Coach: Iurie Osipenco (MDA)

FC Sheriff

First qualifying round - Odds BK (NOR)
H 0-3
Mitrev, Jugović (Sharpar 63), Juninho Potiguar (Crnov 33), Ricardinho, Metoua, Cadú, Potirniche, Dupovac (Novicov 19), Ernandes, Yahaya, Sušić. Coach: Lilian Popescu (MDA)
A 0-0
Mitrev, Cakić, Sharpar, Juninho Potiguar (Balima 72), Ricardinho, Novicov, Potirniche, Ernandes, Yahaya, V Macritschi (Ginsari 67), Sušić (A Macritschi 71). Coach: Lilian Popescu (MDA)

FC Dacia Chisinau

First qualifying round - KF Renova (MKD)
A 1-0 *Rosca (12)*
Gaiducevichi, Rosca, Cojocari (Gavrilenko 46), Posmac, Lozoviy, Mani, Cociuc, Pidnebennoy (Zaginaylov 46), Zastavniy, Pavlov (Mihaliov 64), Mamah. Coach: Igor Dobrovolski (RUS)
H 4-1 *Cociuc (9), Jardan (55), Pavlov (60), Lozoviy (88)*
Gaiducevichi, Rosca, Posmac, Frunza (Jardan 52), Mihaliov, Mani (Lozoviy 52), Cociuc, Gavrilenko, Zastavniy, Pavlov (Bejan 75), Mamah. Coach: Igor Dobrovolski (RUS)

Second qualifying round - MŠK Žilina (SVK)
H 1-2 *Mihaliov (80)*
Gaiducevichi, Rosca, Jardan (Frunza 68), Posmac, Lozoviy, Mani (Mihaliov 46), Cociuc, Gavrilenko, Zastavniy, Pavlov (Stjepanović 57), Mamah. Coach: Igor Dobrovolski (RUS)
A 2-4 *Cociuc (64), Leuca (87)*
Gaiducevichi, Rosca, Posmac, Frunza (Gavrilenko 55), Lozoviy, Mihaliov, Mani (Pavlov 55), Cociuc, Pidnebennoy (Leuca 55), Zastavniy, Mamah. Coach: Igor Dobrovolski (RUS)
Red card: Lozoviy 30

FC Saxan

First qualifying round - Apollon Limassol FC (CYP)
H 0-2
Chirinciuc, Kouadja, Popovici, Puntus (Bogdanov 64), Bamba, Dao, Arabadji, Koné, Catan, Truhanov (Fofana 80), Né (Doumbia 89). Coach: Vlad Goian (MDA)
A 0-2
Chirinciuc, Kouadja, Popovici, Bamba (Fofana 80), Dao, Arabadji, Sebai (Puntus 62), Koné, Catan (Bogdanov 58), Truhanov, Né. Coach: Vlad Goian (MDA)

DOMESTIC LEAGUE CLUB-BY-CLUB

FC Academia Chisinau

2006 • Buiucani (1,200); Satesc, Ghidighici (1,500) • academia.md
Coach: Yury Groshev; (22/09/15) Vladimir Vusatii; (26/10/15) Vlad Goian

2015
25/07	a	Dinamo-Auto	L	0-1	
01/08	h	Speranta	L	2-3	Matei (p), Popovici
08/08	h	Zaria	W	1-0	Shauhvalov
15/08	h	Sheriff	L	0-1	
23/08	h	Dacia	L	0-1	
30/08	h	Milsami	L	0-2	
12/09	a	Saxan	W	3-0	Pascenco (p), Prodan, Stoleru
18/09	h	Zimbru	L	1-5	Pascenco
27/09	a	Petrocub	D	0-0	
02/10	a	Dinamo-Auto	L	1-3	Pascenco (p)
17/10	a	Speranta	L	0-2	
23/10	h	Zaria	L	0-2	
31/10	h	Sheriff	L	1-3	Tiron
08/11	h	Dacia	L	0-2	
21/11	a	Milsami	D	0-0	
28/11	a	Saxan	D	1-1	Dragovozov

2016
05/03	h	Zimbru	D	0-0	
13/03	h	Petrocub	W	1-0	Jardan
18/03	a	Sheriff	L	0-2	
02/04	h	Dacia	L	0-3	
10/04	h	Saxan	W	3-0	Matei, Cricimari, Istrati
15/04	a	Zaria	L	0-2	
24/04	a	Dinamo-Auto	L	1-3	Istrati
30/04	h	Milsami	L	0-1	Suvorov
07/05	a	Petrocub	L	2-4	Picusceac 2
15/05	a	Speranta	D	0-0	
20/05	h	Zimbru	D	0-0	

No	Name	Nat	DoB	Pos	Aps	(s)	Gls
18	Maxim Antoniuc		15/01/91	A	7	(1)	
28	Andrian Apostol		19/01/92	M	3	(3)	
15	Jairo Aquino	USA	18/07/90	M	1	(1)	
27	Cristian Avram		27/07/94	G	19		
28	Valentin Birdan		13/05/95	M	3		
5	Dumitru Bogdan		04/03/89	D	7	(2)	
26	Maxim Boghiu		24/05/91	D	6	(2)	
13	Eugen Celeadnic		09/10/90	D	17	(1)	
3	Alexandru Chiciuc		07/11/88	D	2		
2	Sergiu Cojocari		15/05/88	D	19	(1)	
23	Maxim Copeliciuc		08/08/88	G	8		
8	Vadim Cricimari	RUS	22/08/88	D	5	(6)	1
20	Vladimir Dragovozov		01/01/84	A	10	(2)	1
24	Iulian Erhan		01/07/86	D	11		
14	Igor Gritco		22/05/96	M	2	(1)	
20	Sergiu Istrati		07/08/88	A	3	(6)	2
4	Vasile Jardan		20/07/93	D	20		1
14	Ben Adama Koné	CIV	16/05/92	D	4	(5)	
21	Victor Lisa		10/03/91	A	1	(6)	
10	Sergiu Matei		23/04/92	A	13	(8)	2
21	Farkhat Musabekov	KGZ	03/01/94	M	2	(1)	
19	Alexandr Pascenco		28/05/89	M	9	(4)	3
27	Viktor Patrashko	RUS	26/09/98	D	5		
9	Igor Picusceac		27/03/83	A	4	(2)	2
31	Dumitru Popescu		11/04/95	A	7	(5)	
9	Alexandru Popovici		09/04/77	M	12	(1)	1
32	Ion Prodan		21/03/92	D	7	(4)	1
3	Mihai Rosca		26/03/95	D	10	(2)	
6	Ion Sandu		09/03/93	D	12	(1)	
18	Ruslan Shauhvalov	RUS	31/12/96	M	3	(11)	1
8	Veaceslav Sofroni		30/04/84	A	2	(1)	
6	Vasile Soltan		09/12/92	M	21	(3)	
8	Marian Stoieru		20/11/88	M	1	(1)	1
16	Alexandru Suvorov		02/02/87	M	6	(2)	1
7	Valeriu Tiron		08/04/93	M	15	(10)	1
26	Alexandru Vremea		03/11/91	M	10		

MOLDOVA

FC Dacia Chisinau

1999 • Moldova, Speia (8,550); Buiucani (1,200) • fcdacia.md
Major honours
Moldovan League (1) 2011
Coach: Igor Dobrovolski (RUS);
(03/08/15) Oleg Bejenari

2015

02/08	a	Zimbru	L	0-3	*(w/o; original result 0-2)*
09/08	h	Dinamo-Auto	W	4-0	*Leuca, Pidnebennoy, Zastavniy, Stjepanović*
15/08	a	Zaria	W	2-0	*Stjepanović, Bejan*
23/08	h	Academia	W	1-0	*Pidnebennoy*
29/08	h	Saxan	W	2-1	*Stjepanović, Cociuc*
12/09	a	Petrocub	W	2-1	*Coicuc (p), Stjepanović*
16/09	h	Milsami	W	1-0	*Gavrilenko*
19/09	h	Speranta	D	1-1	*Gavrilenko*
26/09	a	Sheriff	D	0-0	
03/10	a	Milsami	W	1-0	*Bejan*
17/10	h	Zimbru	D	0-0	
24/10	a	Dinamo-Auto	W	2-0	*Onofrei, Zaginaylov*
01/11	h	Zaria	D	1-1	*Zaginaylov*
08/11	a	Academia	W	2-0	*Zaginaylov 2*
22/11	h	Saxan	W	3-1	*Cociuc 2 (1p), Mihaliov*
29/11	h	Petrocub	W	2-0	*Zaginaylov, Onofrei*

2016

05/03	a	Speranta	W	1-0	*Zastavniy*
12/03	h	Sheriff	W	1-0	*Feshchuk*
18/03	h	Saxan	W	2-0	*Cemirtan 2*
02/04	a	Academia	W	3-0	*Zaginaylov 3*
09/04	h	Petrocub	W	3-0	*(w/o; match abandoned after 57 mins, at 1-0 Feshchuk)*
15/04	h	Speranta	W	2-0	*Posmac, Bejan*
23/04	a	Zaria	W	1-0	*Cemirtan*
29/04	h	Dinamo-Auto	W	4-1	*Zaginaylov, Feshchuk 2 (1p), Onofrei*
06/05	a	Milsami	L	0-2	
15/05	a	Zimbru	W	2-0	*Bejan, Zaginaylov*
20/05	h	Sheriff	D	1-1	*Feshchuk*

No	Name	Nat	DoB	Pos	Aps	(s)	Gls
10	Alexandru Bejan		07/05/96	M	24	(1)	4
18	Vitalie Bordian		11/08/84	D	7	(1)	
4	Simeon Bulgaru		26/05/85	D	23		
14	Andrei Bursuc		23/05/97	M	2	(10)	
26	Vadim Cemirtan		21/07/87	A	6	(1)	3
17	Eugen Cociuc		11/05/93	M	26		4
20	Maxim Cojocaru		13/01/98	D	3	(8)	
3	Petru Costin		08/07/97	D		(1)	
28	Maxym Feshchuk	UKR	25/11/85	A	9	(1)	5
7	Viorel Frunza		06/12/79	A		(1)	
8	Valentin Furdui		01/09/87	M	3	(9)	
1	Artiom Gaiducevici		22/04/87	G	24		
19	Maxym Gavrilenko	UKR	18/08/91	M	18	(7)	2
3	Vasile Jardan		20/07/93	D	2		
23	Vasko Kalezić	MNE	14/03/94	M	1	(3)	
29	Petru Leuca		19/07/97	A	4	(5)	1
9	Evgeniy Lozoviy	UKR	25/03/88	M	4	(2)	
24	Abdul-Gafar Mamah	TOG	24/08/85	D	26		
15	Sapol Mani	TOG	05/06/91	M	14	(4)	
11	Maxim Mihaliov		28/08/86	M	10	(12)	1
6	Mexhit Neziri	MKD	02/09/90	M	11	(2)	
7	Octavian Onofrei		16/05/91	A	8	(3)	3
23	Vasili Pavlov	RUS	24/07/90	A	4	(7)	
20	Vyacheslav Pidnebennoy	UKR	03/05/88	M	1	(6)	2
5	Veaceslav Posmac		07/11/90	D	26		1
16	Dorian Railean		13/10/93	G	3		
2	Mihai Rosca		26/03/95	D	2	(1)	
13	Ruslan Shauhvalov	RUS	31/12/96	M		(2)	
25	Slaven Stjepanović	MNE	02/11/87	A	9	(8)	4
22	Serhiy Zaginaylov	UKR	03/01/91	M	10	(10)	10
21	Volodymyr Zastavniy	UKR	02/09/90	D	17	(1)	2

FC Dinamo-Auto

2009 • Dinamo-Auto, Tirnauca (1,300) • dinamo-auto.com
Coach: Nicolai Mandricenco

2015

25/07	h	Academia	W	1-0	*Pisla*
02/08	h	Zaria	D	0-0	
09/08	a	Dacia	L	0-4	
16/08	h	Saxan	D	0-0	
22/08	a	Petrocub	L	1-2	*Mudrac*
28/08	h	Speranta	W	3-1	*Volosin, Ivanov, Cemirtan*
13/09	a	Sheriff	D	1-1	*Bugneac*
19/09	h	Milsami	L	1-2	*Cemirtan*
26/09	a	Zimbru	W	2-1	*Tofan, Pisla*
02/10	a	Academia	W	3-1	*D Mandricenco, Bugneac 2*
17/10	a	Zaria	L	1-3	*Volosin*
24/10	h	Dacia	L	0-2	
01/11	a	Saxan	W	1-0	*Cemirtan*
07/11	h	Petrocub	W	2-0	*Cemirtan, Bugneac*
21/11	a	Speranta	L	2-3	*Pisla, Bugneac*
28/11	h	Sheriff	D	0-0	

2016

06/03	a	Milsami	D	0-0	
13/03	h	Zimbru	D	0-4	
18/03	a	Zaria	W	2-0	*Bugneac, Ivanov*
03/04	h	Speranta	W	2-1	*Ivanov, Bugneac*
09/04	a	Zimbru	W	1-0	*Pascenco*
16/04	a	Petrocub	W	4-1	*Bugneac 2, Ivanov, Mudrac*
24/04	h	Academia	W	3-1	*Bugneac 2, Ivanov*
29/04	a	Dacia	L	1-4	*og (Cociuc)*
06/05	h	Sheriff	L	0-1	
15/05	h	Milsami	W	1-0	*Cascaval*
20/05	a	Saxan	W	1-0	*Mudrac*

No	Name	Nat	DoB	Pos	Aps	(s)	Gls
11	Serghei Alexeev		31/05/86	A	4	(2)	
22	Serghei Bobrov		07/09/91	A	3	(13)	
18	Alexandr Bolsacov		19/11/94	D	1	(2)	
25	Andrei Bugneac		30/03/88	A	19	(7)	11
15	Andrian Cascaval		10/06/87	D	10		1
5	Alexei Casian		01/10/87	D	24		
14	Alexandr Ceh		18/06/97	D	2		
12	Dumitru Celeadnic		23/04/92	G	15	(1)	
11	Vadim Cemirtan		21/07/87	A	12		4
24	Anatol Cheptine		20/05/90	M	3	(1)	
20	Igor Costrov		03/08/87	M	13	(2)	
23	Serghei Diulgher		21/03/91	D	22		
3	Denis Ilescu		20/01/87	D	21	(1)	
21	Alexei Iularji		03/12/92	M	1	(6)	
2	Vladislav Ivanov		07/05/90	A	24	(1)	5
19	Constantin Mandricenco		19/02/91	A	14	(4)	
7	Dmitrii Mandricenco		13/05/97	M	3	(2)	1
4	Victor Mudrac		03/03/94	M	23		3
7	Alexandr Pascenco		28/05/89	M	5	(4)	1
17	Mihail Paseciniuc		09/03/91	M	2	(4)	
10	Daniel Pisla		14/06/86	M	9	(8)	3
16	Daniil Popov		13/06/96	G		(1)	
6	Alexandr Scripcenco		13/01/91	D	21	(4)	
24	Stanislav Sinkovskii		16/04/94	M	3	(3)	
19	Alexandr Tofan		19/08/87	M	19	(3)	1
18	Victor Truhanov		30/01/91	M	4	(5)	
17	Andrei Turculet		14/07/96	D		(1)	
8	Dmitrii Volosin		26/07/94	M	8	(6)	2
1	Alexandr Zveagintsev		26/07/87	G	12		

FC Milsami Orhei

2005 • Municipal (3,000) • milsami.md
Major honours
Moldovan League (1) 2015; Moldovan Cup (1) 2012
Coach: Iurie Osipenco;
(03/11/15) Vladimir Veber;
(16/11/15) Iurie Osipenco;
(03/02/16) Andrian Sosnovschi

2015

01/08	h	Saxan	W	4-1	*G Andronic 2, Antoniuc, Zarichnyuk*
09/08	a	Petrocub	L	0-1	
15/08	h	Speranta	W	5-0	*Patras, G Andronic, Antoniuc, Gheți, Bud*
23/08	h	Sheriff	L	0-3	
30/08	a	Academia	W	2-0	*Antoniuc, Slivca*
12/09	h	Zimbru	L	0-2	
16/09	a	Dacia	L	0-1	
19/09	a	Dinamo-Auto	W	2-1	*Diulghier, Bud*
27/09	h	Zaria	W	3-0	*Surdu, Bud, Diulghier*
03/10	h	Dacia	L	0-1	
18/10	a	Saxan	D	0-0	
23/10	h	Petrocub	D	2-2	*Diulghier, Banović*
01/11	a	Speranta	L	0-1	
08/11	a	Sheriff	L	0-1	
21/11	h	Academia	D	0-0	
29/11	a	Zimbru	L	1-2	*Gheți*

2016

06/03	h	Dinamo-Auto	D	0-0	
13/03	a	Zaria	D	0-0	
18/03	a	Speranta	W	4-0	*Rakhmanov, Racu, Sidorenco, Bolohan*
02/04	h	Zimbru	W	4-1	*Rhaili, Banović, Surdu, Bolohan (p)*
09/04	h	Sheriff	L	0-2	
15/04	a	Saxan	W	1-0	*Rakhmanov*
24/04	h	Petrocub	W	2-1	*Surdu (p), Banović*
30/04	a	Academia	L	0-1	
06/05	h	Dacia	W	2-0	*Belak, Surdu*
15/05	a	Dinamo-Auto	L	0-1	
20/05	h	Zaria	D	1-1	*Ciuntu*

No	Name	Nat	DoB	Pos	Aps	(s)	Gls
22	Gheorghe Andronic		25/09/91	M	11	(5)	3
20	Valeriu Andronic		21/12/82	M	8		
9	Alexandru Antoniuc		23/05/89	M	20	(3)	3
24	Igor Banović	CRO	28/03/93	M	23	(3)	3
21	Gheorghe Bantis		19/06/89	G	9		
14	Karlo Belak	CRO	22/04/91	D	5	(3)	1
8	Radu Beseti		22/01/97	M	1	(1)	
95	Valentin Birdan		13/05/95	M	3	(2)	
23	Vadim Bolohan		15/08/86	D	22	(2)	2
26	Cristian Bud	ROU	26/06/86	A	7	(7)	3
11	Octavian Ciuntu		14/06/95	M	3	(4)	1
27	Andrei Cojocari		21/01/87	M	18	(4)	
18	Adrian Costin		10/08/97	M		(1)	
9	Alexandru Diulghier		03/01/95	D	8	(9)	3
4	Iulian Erhan		01/07/86	D	7	(3)	
3	Cornel Gheți	ROU	23/06/86	D	14	(5)	2
30	Jô	BRA	19/09/88	A	1	(1)	
99	Juninho	BRA	18/07/85	A	3	(2)	
4	Serhiy Melnyk	UKR	04/09/88	D	7	(1)	
1	Radu Mitu		04/11/94	G	17		
6	Ovye Monday	NGA	14/08/92	D	8	(3)	
11	Bohdan Myshenko	UKR	29/12/94	M	1	(7)	
22	Sergiu Nazar		02/07/97	A		(1)	
12	Andrian Negai		28/01/85	G	1		
8	Artur Patras		01/10/88	M	13	(2)	1
5	Petru Racu		17/07/87	D	12		1
20	Artem Rakhmanov	BLR	10/07/90	D	10		2
15	Denis Rassulov		02/01/90	A	10	(3)	
2	Adil Rhaili	MAR	25/04/91	D	22		1
32	Eugen Sidorenco		19/03/89	M	11		1
17	Eugen Slivca		13/07/89	M	3	(6)	1
19	Romeo Surdu	ROU	12/01/84	A	11	(4)	4
87	Alexandru Suvorov		02/02/87	M	1	(4)	
7	Yevhen Zarichnyuk	UKR	03/02/89	M	12	(8)	1

CS Petrocub

1994 • Municipal (2,672) • no website
Coach: Eduard Blanuta

2015

26/07	h	Speranta	L	0-4	
01/08	a	Sheriff	L	0-4	
09/08	h	Milsami	W	1-0	Sumchin
15/08	a	Zimbru	L	0-3	
22/08	h	Dinamo-Auto	W	2-1	Sumchin 2
28/08	a	Zaria	L	1-5	Sandu
12/09	h	Dacia	L	1-2	Sumchin
19/09	a	Saxan	W	1-0	D Taras
27/09	h	Academia	D	0-0	
03/10	a	Speranta	D	1-1	Slivca
18/10	h	Sheriff	L	0-3	
23/10	a	Milsami	D	2-2	Barcari, V Rusu
31/10	h	Zimbru	L	1-2	Ambros (p)
07/11	a	Dinamo-Auto	L	0-2	
21/11	h	Zaria	L	0-2	
29/11	a	Dacia	L	0-2	

2016

06/03	h	Saxan	W	1-0	Sumchin
13/03	a	Academia	L	0-1	
18/03	a	Zimbru	L	0-1	
02/04	h	Sheriff	L	0-1	
09/04	a	Dacia	L	0-3	(w/o; match abandoned after 57 mins, at 0-1)
16/04	h	Dinamo-Auto	L	1-4	Ambros
24/04	a	Milsami	L	1-2	Andronic
30/04	h	Saxan	W	2-0	Talmazan, Sumchin
07/05	h	Academia	W	4-2	Sumchin, Ambros 2, V Rusu
15/05	a	Zaria	L	2-4	Ambros 2
20/05	h	Speranta	L	0-2	

No	Name	Nat	DoB	Pos	Aps	(s)	Gls
9	Vladimir Ambros		30/12/93	A	26		6
18	Valeriu Andronic		21/12/82	M	11		1
24	Dumitru Bacal		28/11/85	D	8	(5)	
7	Dinu Barcari		27/05/93	M	15		1
94	Victor Buga		26/06/94	G	26		
3	Vedat Cazacu		23/06/95	M		(2)	
16	David Chemschi		12/05/95	D	9	(1)	
3	Alexandru Chiciuc		07/11/88	D	1	(1)	
4	Emil Ciornii		27/03/97	D	9	(2)	
13	Vladimir Cojocaru		18/04/88	M		(3)	
18	Victor Lisa		10/03/91	A	1	(4)	
13	Mihail Lobco		27/07/92	M		(7)	
20	Valeriu Osipenco		27/07/96	M	22	(2)	
8	Alexandru Panas		06/03/96	M	5	(6)	
22	Corneliu Pavalachi		15/05/94	M		(7)	
16	Iulian Petrache	ROU	14/03/91	M	12		
22	Dorin Popovici		01/07/96	M	10	(1)	
24	Ion Prodan		21/03/92	D	3		
7	Cristian Prozorovschi		21/04/94	M	11	(12)	
12	Ion Rimbu		03/10/87	G	1		
5	Arcadie Rusu		28/06/93	D	21	(4)	
14	Vasile Rusu		28/06/85	D	13	(6)	2
17	Constantin Sandu		15/09/93	M	1	(8)	1
17	Cornel Schiopu		31/07/94	D	7	(2)	
6	Vladislva Slivca		10/09/98	D	22	(5)	1
11	Roman Sumchin		11/03/93	M	21	(4)	7
23	Ion Talmazan		02/06/88	M	15	(8)	1
21	Cristian Taras		26/09/98	M		(3)	
10	Dan Taras		13/02/94	M	27		1

FC Saxan

2010 • Ceadir-Lunga municipal (2,000) • fc-saxan.com
Coach: Vlad Goian;
(16/09/15) Nicolai Panu;
(08/02/16) Oleg Fistican

2015

25/07	a	Sheriff	L	0-2	
01/08	a	Milsami	L	1-4	Istrati
09/08	h	Zimbru	L	1-2	Istrati
16/08	a	Dinamo-Auto	D	0-0	
22/08	h	Zaria	L	1-3	Istrati
29/08	a	Dacia	L	1-2	Bulat
12/09	h	Academia	L	0-3	
19/09	h	Petrocub	L	0-1	
27/09	a	Speranta	D	0-0	
02/10	h	Sheriff	L	1-2	Istrati
18/10	h	Milsami	D	0-0	
24/10	a	Zimbru	L	0-4	
01/11	h	Dinamo-Auto	L	0-1	
07/11	a	Zaria	L	1-2	Truhanov
22/11	h	Dacia	L	1-3	Istrati
28/11	a	Academia	D	1-1	Erman

2016

06/03	a	Petrocub	L	0-1	
12/03	h	Speranta	D	0-0	
18/03	a	Zaria	L	0-2	
03/04	a	Zaria	L	0-2	
10/04	h	Academia	L	0-3	
15/04	h	Milsami	L	0-1	
24/04	a	Zimbru	L	0-1	
30/04	a	Petrocub	L	0-2	
07/05	h	Speranta	W	2-0	Ursu, Maghaldadze
15/05	a	Sheriff	L	0-2	
20/05	h	Dinamo-Auto	L	0-1	

No	Name	Nat	DoB	Pos	Aps	(s)	Gls
21	Ağaç Çağrıhan	TUR	07/06/96	M	15	(3)	
77	Yao Konan Allou	CIV	10/11/95	D	15		
15	Ion Arabadji		31/07/84	D	15		
4	Anatolie Boestean		26/03/85	D	6		
24	Victor Bulat		05/01/85	M	12	(4)	1
12	Vasilii Buza		01/03/92	G	13		
14	Constantin Calmis		19/08/95	D	12	(3)	
7	Ivan Carandasov		21/01/91	D	6	(4)	
30	Radu Catan		30/05/89	A	3	(3)	
17	Cengizhan Gündüz	TUR	13/02/95	A	14	(6)	
89	Anatol Chirinciuc		04/02/89	G	5		
22	Evgheny Cimpoes		29/06/98	A		(2)	
5	Cristian Cirlan		09/01/95	M	1	(4)	
28	Oleg Clonin		04/02/88	M	4		
8	Nicolai Copusciu		06/11/97	M		(1)	
15	Samuel Duah	GHA	13/10/96	M	10		
22	Erman Taşkın	TUR	01/01/95	D	11		1
25	Vladimir Ghenaitis		30/03/95	D	9	(2)	
10	Irakli Goginashvili	GEO	29/03/94	M	10	(2)	
19	Vladimir Haritov		05/01/95	M	1		
5	Salif Inoua	CMR	11/04/95	D	12		
7	Sergiu Istrati		07/08/88	A	11	(4)	5
22	Mohamed Koné	CIV	12/12/93	M		(1)	
8	Nikita Lorne	CIV	09/06/95	A		(3)	
88	Guram Maghaldadze	GEO	02/02/84	M	9	(2)	1
77	Andrei Mincev		30/09/98	M	1	(4)	
11	Oleg Molla		22/02/86	A	4	(2)	
93	Eric Né	CIV	22/01/96	M	12	(4)	
30	Vitalie Negru		15/01/87	M	8		
23	Ion Pislaru		02/02/95	M	6	(4)	
17	Dumitru Popovici		05/08/83	D	7	(1)	
9	Artiom Puntus		31/05/95	A	7	(4)	
1	Dmitri Radu		03/03/88	G	9		
10	Vladimir Rassulov		11/11/92	M	7	(1)	
11	Constantin Sandu		15/09/95	M	6	(5)	
23	Giorgi Sarjveladze	GEO	24/06/94	M	4	(3)	
20	Dmitri Semirov		27/12/95	M	6	(8)	
88	Victor Truhanov		30/01/91	M	14		1
23	Ion Ursu		19/08/94	A	10	(8)	1
8	Artiom Zabun		23/04/96	A	2	(5)	

FC Sheriff

1997 • Sheriff Main (13,300); Sheriff Small (8,000) • fc-sheriff.com
Major honours
Moldovan League (14) 2001, 2002, 2003, 2004, 2005, 2006, 2007, 2008, 2009, 2010, 2012, 2013, 2014, 2016; Moldovan Cup (8) 1999, 2001, 2002, 2006, 2008, 2009, 2010, 2015
Coach: Lilian Popescu;
(07/10/15) Zoran Vulić (CRO)

2015

25/07	h	Saxan	W	2-0	Cakić, Ricardinho
01/08	h	Petrocub	W	4-0	Picusceac, Novicov, Ricardinho, Iurcu
09/08	a	Speranta	L	0-1	
15/08	a	Academia	W	3-0	og (Cojocari) 2, Cadú
23/08	h	Milsami	W	3-0	Ricardinho 2, Subotic
29/08	a	Zimbru	W	2-1	Ricardinho, Subotic
13/09	h	Dinamo-Auto	D	1-1	Iurcu
19/09	a	Zaria	D	1-1	Savic
26/09	h	Dacia	D	0-0	
02/10	a	Saxan	W	2-1	Subotic, og (Ağaç)
18/10	a	Petrocub	W	3-0	Sušić, Subotic, Ricardinho
23/10	h	Speranta	W	2-1	Subotic 2
31/10	h	Academia	W	3-1	Subotic (p), Juninho Potiguar, Ginsari
08/11	a	Milsami	W	1-0	Juninho Potiguar
22/11	h	Zimbru	W	4-1	Novicov, Juninho Potiguar, Subotic, og (Jardan)
28/11	a	Dinamo-Auto	D	0-0	

2016

05/03	h	Zaria	W	1-0	Patras
12/03	a	Dacia	L	0-1	
18/03	a	Academia	W	2-0	Balima, Ivančić
02/04	a	Petrocub	W	1-0	Subotic (p)
09/04	h	Milsami	W	2-0	og (Rakhmanov), Balima
15/04	h	Zimbru	W	2-0	Jóalísson, Ivančić
23/04	a	Speranta	W	4-1	Ginsari, Subotic, Ivančić, Rebenja
29/04	h	Zaria	W	3-0	Subotic, Balima, Ginsari
07/05	a	Dinamo-Auto	W	1-0	Subotic
15/05	h	Saxan	W	2-0	Rebenja, Ginsari
20/05	a	Dacia	D	1-1	Ivančić

No	Name	Nat	DoB	Pos	Aps	(s)	Gls
3	Fidan Aliti	ALB	03/10/93	D	3	(5)	
14	Wilfried Balima	BFA	20/03/85	M	15	(7)	3
9	Bruno Pelissari	BRA	03/01/93	M		(3)	
20	Cadú	BRA	31/08/86	M	17	(1)	1
4	Mihajlo Cakić	SRB	27/05/90	M	8		1
28	Alexei Coselev		19/11/93	G	24		
22	Amer Dupovac	BIH	30/11/90	D	3	(3)	
23	Ernandes	BRA	11/11/87	D	1		
77	Goran Galešić	BIH	11/03/89	D	9		
8	Radu Ginsari		10/12/91	M	24	(1)	4
6	Anthony Golec	AUS	29/05/90	D	10		
89	Maxim Iurcu		01/02/93	A	3	(12)	2
11	Josip Ivančić	CRO	29/03/91	A	4	(7)	4
13	Khalifa Jabbie	SLE	22/01/96	M	5	(4)	
7	Jóalísson	BRA	31/03/91	A	3	(1)	
6	Igor Jugović	CRO	23/01/89	M		(5)	
9	Juninho Potiguar	BRA	22/02/90	A	4	(3)	3
25	Denis Macogonenco		20/02/96	G		(1)	
33	Valeriu Macritschi		13/02/96	M	2		
15	Marcel Metoua	CIV	15/11/88	D	3	(2)	
1	Bozhidar Mitrev	BUL	31/03/87	G	3		
18	Andrei Novicov		24/04/86	A	16		2
16	Vadim Paireli		08/11/95	A	1	(4)	
35	Artur Patras		01/10/88	M	2	(8)	1
32	Igor Picusceac		27/03/83	A	2	(4)	1
21	Maxim Potirniche		13/06/89	D	10	(2)	
88	Artiom Razgoniuc		01/10/95	M	15	(4)	
88	Eugeniu Rebenja		05/03/95	A	3	(5)	2
11	Ricardinho	BRA	04/09/89	M	13		6
90	Vujadin Savic	FRA	01/07/90	D	16	(1)	1
7	Vyacheslav Sharpar	UKR	02/06/87	M	1		
31	Danijel Subotic	SUI	31/01/89	A	23	(2)	12
55	Mateo Sušić	BIH	18/11/90	D	24	(1)	
19	Serghei Svinarenco		18/09/96	D	8	(7)	
34	Ivan Urvantev		02/05/97	A		(3)	
24	Seidu Yahaya	GHA	31/12/89	M	22	(1)	

CSF Speranta

1991 • Nisporeni municipal (2,000) •
fcsperanta.com
Coach: Cristian Efros

2015

26/07	a	Petrocub	W	4-0	Grosu 2 (1p), Maxim, Efros
01/08	a	Academia	W	3-2	Pavlov 2, Şeroni
09/08	h	Sheriff	W	1-0	Onicaş
15/08	a	Milsami	L	0-5	
23/08	h	Zimbru	D	0-0	
28/08	a	Dinamo-Auto	L	1-3	Secrier
12/09	h	Zaria	L	0-2	
19/09	a	Dacia	D	1-1	Dragan
27/09	a	Saxan	D	0-0	
03/10	h	Petrocub	L	1-2	Secrier
17/10	h	Academia	W	2-0	Cravcescu, Maxim
23/10	a	Sheriff	L	1-2	Maxim
01/11	h	Milsami	W	1-0	Ocinca
07/11	a	Zimbru	W	1-0	Reindorf
21/11	h	Dinamo-Auto	W	3-2	Şeroni, Dragan, Plamadeala
28/11	a	Zaria	D	0-0	

2016

05/03	h	Dacia	L	0-1	
12/03	a	Saxan	D	0-0	
18/03	h	Milsami	L	0-4	
03/04	a	Dinamo-Auto	L	1-2	Platica
10/04	a	Zaria	L	1-2	Platica
15/04	a	Dacia	L	0-2	
23/04	h	Sheriff	L	1-4	Milinceanu
29/04	h	Zimbru	L	0-1	
07/05	a	Saxan	L	0-2	
15/05	h	Academia	L	0-1	
20/05	a	Petrocub	W	2-0	Milinceanu, Ciofu

No	Name	Nat	DoB	Pos	Aps	(s)	Gls
18	David Andronic		09/07/95	M	12	(3)	
20	Igor Andronic		11/03/88	D	4	(3)	
5	Mihail Bolun		16/05/89	D	23	(2)	
9	Denis Calincov		15/09/85	M		(1)	
10	Vadim Calugher		07/09/95	M		(1)	
1	Anatol Chirinciuc		04/02/89	G	1		
27	Andrei Ciofu		31/05/84	M	7	(3)	1
2	Vadim Costandachi		22/09/91	D	8	(2)	
9	Vadim Cravcescu		07/03/85	M	16	(2)	1
13	Igor Dima		11/02/93	A	7	(10)	
23	Ion Dragan		14/06/94	A	14	(8)	2
22	Stefan Efros		08/05/90	D	24	(1)	1
21	Alexandru A Grosu		18/04/88	M	7	(4)	2
12	Andrei Gubanov	RUS	15/01/94	M	4	(1)	
4	Cristain Jalba		02/02/97	M	2	(2)	
11	Alexandru Maxim		19/01/86	M	7	(8)	3
7	Serghei Maximov		06/07/89	M		(1)	
14	Nicolae Milinceanu		01/08/92	A	7	(4)	2
24	Victor Negara		14/07/91	D	10	(2)	
3	Ghenadie Ocinca		01/03/84	D	17	(1)	1
10	Mihai Onicaş	ROU	27/01/90	M	6	(3)	1
9	Ghenadie Orbu		08/07/82	A	1	(2)	
8	Ion Pavlov		29/08/91	M	7	(1)	2
7	Vitalie Plamadeala		21/05/85	M	18	(2)	1
21	Sergiu Platica		05/06/91	A	7	(4)	2
4	Vadim Rata		05/05/93	M	7		
14	Jessy Reindorf	RWA	19/07/91	A	4	(8)	1
17	Pavel Secrier		11/01/91	M	8	(15)	2
16	Alin Şeroni	ROU	26/03/87	D	23		2
6	Corneliu Tibuleac		23/08/96	M	3	(2)	
24	Nicolai Tiverenco		30/03/96	D	2	(4)	
33	Nicolae Turcan		09/12/89	G	26		
15	Sergiu Viţu	ROU	04/06/92	D	15	(4)	

FC Zaria Balti

1984 • Municipal (5,953) • no website
Major honours
Moldovan Cup (1) 2016
Coach: Viktor Dogodailo (UKR)
(12/01/16) Ihor Rakhaev (UKR)

2015

25/07	h	Zimbru	L	0-1	
02/08	a	Dinamo-Auto	D	0-0	
08/08	h	Academia	L	0-1	
15/08	h	Dacia	L	0-2	
22/08	a	Saxan	W	3-1	Onica, Koné, Rassulov
28/08	h	Petrocub	W	5-1	Josan, Dao, Rata, Boghiu 2
12/09	a	Speranta	W	2-0	Dao, Koné
19/09	h	Sheriff	D	1-1	Boghiu (p)
27/09	a	Milsami	L	0-3	
03/10	a	Zimbru	L	0-3	
17/10	h	Dinamo-Auto	W	3-1	Boghiu 2, Rata
23/10	a	Academia	W	2-1	Vasilache 2
01/11	a	Dacia	D	1-1	Pisotskiy
07/11	h	Saxan	W	2-1	Yakovlev 2
21/11	a	Petrocub	W	2-0	Pisotskiy, Yakovlev
28/11	h	Speranta	D	0-0	

2016

05/03	a	Sheriff	L	0-1	
13/03	h	Milsami	D	0-0	
18/03	h	Dinamo.Auto	L	0-2	
03/04	a	Saxan	W	2-0	Boghiu, Bamba (p)
10/04	a	Speranta	W	2-1	Onica, Slinkin
15/04	a	Academia	W	2-0	Bamba, Boychuk
23/04	h	Dacia	L	0-1	
29/04	a	Sheriff	L	0-2	
06/05	h	Zimbru	W	4-2	Slinkin, Dao, Boghiu 2
15/05	h	Petrocub	W	4-2	Dao, Onica, Boghiu 2 (1p)
20/05	a	Milsami	D	1-1	Bamba (p)

No	Name	Nat	DoB	Pos	Aps	(s)	Gls
8	Yacouba Bamba	CIV	30/11/91	M	7	(1)	3
11	Gheorghe Boghiu		26/10/81	A	23	(3)	10
16	Bohdan Boychuk	UKR	30/05/96	A	3	(3)	1
3	Ion Burlacu		03/02/92	D	14		
20	Vladimir Cheptenari		26/09/89	D	2	(2)	
19	Lassina Dao	CIV	20/12/96	A	12	(10)	4
27	Aziz Deen-Conteh	SLE	14/01/03	D	6		
18	Sékou Doumbia	CIV	11/02/94	M	3	(7)	
23	Artem Dovbyk	UKR	21/06/97	A		(3)	
4	Cristian Dros		15/04/98	M		(1)	
77	Olexandr Ermachenko	UKR	29/01/93	A	4	(7)	
9	Mamadou Fofana	CIV	21/05/95	M		(1)	
22	Rubén Gómez	ARG	26/01/84	M	13	(4)	
7	Alexandru S Grosu		16/05/86	A	6	(15)	
28	Vadim Gulceac		06/08/98	M	2		
9	Nicolae Josan		18/09/83	M	5	(1)	1
26	Artem Khachaturov	ARM	18/06/92	D	4	(1)	
23	Mohamed Koné	CIV	12/12/93	D	25		2
99	Ivan Lacusta		24/01/95	A		(9)	
1	Vladimir Livsit		23/03/84	G	19		
12	Andrei Marina		21/02/90	M		(2)	
5	Andriy Nesterov	UKR	02/07/90	D	16		
4	Alexandru Onica		29/07/84	M	22		3
22	Octavian Onofrei		16/05/91	A		(2)	
18	Ihor Oshchypko	UKR	25/10/85	D	8	(2)	
9	Gheorghe Ovsiannicov		12/10/85	A		(6)	
33	Serghei Pascenco		18/12/82	G	8		
1	Yevhen Pisotskiy	UKR	22/04/87	M	7		2
5	Dmitry Popovici		05/08/82	D	4	(1)	
15	Vladimir Rassulov		11/11/92	M	5	(7)	1
8	Vadim Rata		05/05/93	M	15		2
14	Radu Rogac		07/06/95	D	15	(1)	
2	Andriy Slinkin	UKR	19/02/91	D	10		2
10	Igor Tigirlas		24/02/84	M	20	(4)	
16	Ciprian Vasilache	ROU	14/09/83	M	4	(5)	2
24	Andriy Yakovlev	UKR	20/02/89	M	15	(4)	3

FC Zimbru Chisinau

1947 • Zimbru (10,400); Baza Zimbru (2,142) •
zimbru.md
Major honours
Moldovan League (8) 1992, 1993, 1994, 1995, 1996,
1998, 1999, 2000; Moldovan Cup (6) 1997, 1998,
2003, 2004, 2007, 2014
Coach: Ştefan Stoica (ROU);
(24/11/15) (Veaceslav Rusnac);
(23/12/15) Simão Freitas (POR);
(11/05/16) Flavius Stoican (ROU)

2015

25/07	a	Zaria	W	1-0	Edivândio
02/08	h	Dacia	W	3-0	(w/o; original result 2-0 Calú, Vremea)
09/08	a	Saxan	W	2-1	Amani, Calú
15/08	h	Petrocub	W	3-0	Rui Miguel 2 (1p), Burghiu
23/08	a	Speranta	D	0-0	
29/08	h	Sheriff	L	1-2	Rui Miguel (p)
12/09	a	Milsami	W	2-0	Joálisson, Hélio Baptista
18/09	a	Academia	W	5-1	Amani, Rui Miguel 3, og (Prodan)
26/09	h	Dinamo-Auto	L	1-2	Joálisson
03/10	h	Zaria	W	3-0	Spataru, Hélio Baptista, Joálisson
17/10	a	Dacia	D	0-0	
23/10	h	Saxan	W	4-0	Vremea, Joálisson, Spataru, Alex Bruno (p)
31/10	a	Petrocub	W	2-1	Staris, Calú
07/11	h	Speranta	L	0-1	
22/11	a	Sheriff	L	1-4	Amani
29/11	h	Milsami	W	2-1	Calú, Spataru

2016

05/03	h	Academia	D	0-0	
13/03	a	Dinamo-Auto	W	4-0	Rui Miguel, og (Mudrac), Talles Cunha 2
18/03	h	Petrocub	W	1-0	Rui Miguel
02/04	a	Milsami	L	1-4	Alex Bruno
09/04	a	Dinamo-Auto	W	2-1	Alex Bruno, Rui Miguel
15/04	a	Sheriff	L	0-2	
24/04	h	Saxan	W	1-0	Ludovic
29/04	h	Speranta	W	1-0	Talles Cunha
06/05	a	Zaria	L	2-4	Edivândio 2
15/05	h	Dacia	L	0-2	
20/05	a	Academia			

No	Name	Nat	DoB	Pos	Aps	(s)	Gls
30	Alex Bruno	BRA	07/10/93	M	20	(4)	3
77	Álvaro Jaló	POR	13/03/92	A	3	(4)	
77	Amâncio Fortes	POR	18/04/90	M	3	(2)	
25	Jean-Marie Amani	FRA	15/04/89	A	18	(5)	3
8	Gheorghe Anton		27/01/93	M	15	(8)	
18	Vadim Bejenari		16/05/97	M		(2)	
15	Alexandru Belevschi		21/03/95	D	7	(4)	
18	Nicolai Borta		19/06/97	D		(2)	
3	Stefan Burghiu		28/03/91	D	26	(1)	1
21	Calú	CPV	20/09/83	D	23		4
18	Vadim Calugher		07/09/95	M	1	(9)	
95	Ilie Damascan		12/10/95	A		(10)	
11	Vitalie Domascan		24/01/99	M	3	(1)	
55	Edivândio	CPV	01/01/91	A	2	(5)	3
20	Artur Focsa		29/06/98	D		(1)	
44	Dinu Graur		27/01/94	D	5	(11)	
18	Hélio Baptista	BRA	28/03/91	D	21		2
90	Ion Jardan		10/01/90	D	25		
7	Joálisson	BRA	31/03/91	A	12		4
7	Ludovic	POR	18/06/90	A	4	(3)	1
11	Ion Nicolaescu		07/09/98	M		(1)	
33	Anatolie Prepelita		06/08/97	D	2	(2)	
10	Rui Miguel	POR	15/11/83	M	21		9
7	Andrei Rusnac		22/09/96	A	2		
23	Denis Rusu		02/08/90	G	1		
94	Dan Spataru		24/05/94	M	23	(1)	3
5	Alexandru Staris		04/01/95	D	11	(8)	1
29	Victor Stina		03/03/98	M		(1)	
11	Talles Cunha	BRA	13/03/89	A	10		3
4	Daniel Vlas		09/06/95	D		(2)	
89	Vozinha	CPV	03/06/86	G	26		
26	Alexandru Vremea		03/11/91	M	14	(2)	2
25	Veaceslav Zagaevschi		04/04/96	M	1	(2)	

Top goalscorers

12	Danijel Subotic (Sheriff)
11	Andrei Bugneac (Dinamo-Auto)
10	Serhiy Zaginaylov (Dacia)
	Gheorghe Boghiu (Zaria)
9	Rui Miguel (Zimbru)
7	Sergiu Istrati (Saxan/Academia)
	Vadim Cemirtan (Dinamo-Auto/Dacia)
	Roman Sumchin (Petrocub)
6	Vladimir Ambros (Petrocub)
	Ricardinho (Sheriff)

Promoted club

FC Ungheni

2013 • Municipal (1,000) • fcungheni.cf
Coach: Dorin Bambuleac

Second level final table 2015/16

		Pld	W	D	L	F	A	Pts
1	FC Spicul Chiscareni	26	22	2	2	85	19	68
2	FC Sheriff-2	26	19	2	5	64	25	59
3	FC Zimbru-2 Chisinau	26	15	6	5	53	23	51
4	FC Ungheni	26	14	4	8	49	38	46
5	FC Dacia-2 Buiucani	26	12	5	9	40	41	41
6	CF Gagauziya-Oguzsport	26	11	4	11	43	44	37
7	FC Victoria Bardar	26	11	3	12	38	34	36
8	FC Codru Lozova	26	8	8	10	44	51	32
9	FC Iskra	26	8	5	13	47	63	29
10	FC Edinet	26	7	6	13	42	47	27
11	CF Intersport-Aroma	26	6	8	12	31	48	26
12	FC Sfintul Gheorghe	26	6	6	14	43	60	24
13	Real Succes Lilcora FC	26	7	2	17	29	56	23
14	FC Prut Leova	26	4	3	19	30	89	15

*NB FC Spicul Chiscareni declined promotion;
FC Sheriff-2 & FC Zimbru-2 Chisinau ineligible for
promotion.*

DOMESTIC CUP

Cupa Moldovei 2015/16

1/16 FINALS

(22/09/15)
Petrocub 4-0 Victoria
Sireti 2-3 Gagauziya-Oguzsport
Ungheni 1-0 Edinet *(aet)*

(23/09/15)
Politeh 0-6 Intersport-Aroma
Speranta 5-0 Cahul-2005

1/8 ROUND

(27/10/15)
Intersport 1-6 Milsami
Sheriff 8-1 Intersport-Aroma
Spicul 2-2 Academia *(aet; 3-5 on pens)*
Zaria 3-0 Gagauziya-Oguzsport

(28/10/15)
Zimbru 3-0 Petrocub
Saxan 0-0 Speranta *(aet; 7-6 on pens)*
Ungheni 0-3 Dacia
Dinamo-Auto 5-1 Codru

QUARTER-FINALS

(19/04/16)
Dacia 1-0 Zimbru *(Onofrei 23)*
Sheriff 1-0 Academia *(Ivančić 5)*
Zaria 5-1 Saxan *(Boychuk 2, Onica 27, Boghiu 73,
Yakovlev 77, Boghiu 79; Sandu 85)*

(20/04/16)
Dinamo-Auto 0-3 Milsami *(Cojocari 12, Antoniuc
64, Diulghier 69)*

SEMI-FINALS

(10/05/16)
Milsami 1-0 Dacia *(Sidorenco 92) (aet)*
Sheriff 1-2 Zaria *(Ginsari 90; Slinkin 63,
Boghiu 108) (aet)*

FINAL

(25/05/16)
Zimbru, Chisinau
FC ZARIA BALTI 1 *(Boghiu 99)*
FC MILSAMI ORHEI 0
(aet)
Referee: *Raczkowski (POL)*
ZARIA: *Pascenco, Nesterov, Koné, Slinkin, Onica,
Bamba, Tigirlas, Gómez, Grosu (Boghiu 84) Boychuk
(Deen-Conteh 77), Dao*
MILSAMI: *Bantis, Melnyk, Rakhmanov, Bolohan,
Diulghier (Ciuntu 91), Belak, Zarichnyuk, Banović,
Cojocari (Slivca 102), Sidorenco, Antoniuc
(Surdu 75)*

Zaria picked up their first major trophy by defeating Milsami 1-0 in the Moldovan Cup final

MONTENEGRO
Futbalski savez Crne Gore (FSCG)

Address	Ulica "19. decembra" 13 ME-81000 Podgorica	**President**	Dejan Savićević
		General secretary	Momir Djurdjevac
Tel	+382 20 445 600	**Media officer**	Ivan Radović
Fax	+382 20 445 660	**Year of formation**	1931
E-mail	info@fscg.me	**National stadium**	Pod Goricom,
Website	fscg.me		Podgorica (12,508)

PRVA LIGA CLUBS

 1 FK Bokelj

 2 FK Budućnost Podgorica

 3 FK Dečić

 4 OFK Grbalj

 5 FK Iskra

 6 FK Lovćen

 7 FK Mladost Podgorica

 8 FK Mornar

 9 OFK Petrovac

 10 FK Rudar Pljevlja

 11 FK Sutjeska

 12 FK Zeta

KEY

- ● UEFA Champions League
- ● UEFA Europa League
- ● Promoted
- ● Relegated

Pljevlja **10**

Bijelo Polje **13**

Nikšić **11**

5

Danilovgrad

7 Podgorica

Kotor **1**

2

4 Cetinje **12** **3** Tuzi

Radanovići **6** Golubovci

9

Petrovac Bar

8

PROMOTED CLUB

 13 FK Jedinstvo Bijelo Polje

0	40	80 km

0	40 miles

Maiden title for Mladost

Montenegrin football witnessed a trophy swap in 2015/16 as the previous season's domestic cup winners Mladost Podgorica picked up their first league title while Rudar Pljevla, the champions of 2014/15, raised the cup for a record fourth time.

Mladost's capital city rivals Budućnost were the runners-up in both competitions as they strove in vain to avoid a third successive season without silverware, while Bokelj, fourth in the league, upset the odds to claim a European berth for the first time.

| Underdogs from the capital power to victory | Local rivals Budućnost edged into second place | Rudar taste cup glory for record fourth time |

Domestic league

Mladost reappointed the man many fans felt had been harshly jettisoned a couple of summers earlier following a heavy European defeat by Sevilla, and Nikola Rakojević, one of Montenegro's most experienced coaches, responded by steering the club to unprecedented heights. Fancied by few at the outset, and by even fewer after a couple of early defeats, Mladost eventually found their rhythm and transformed themselves into an unstoppable force. Powered by the goals of Marko Šćepanović, they racked up nine successive victories during October, November and December, the last of them 2-0 at home to Budućnost, and by the winter break they had opened up a nine-point gap at the top of the table, with defending champions Rudar a distant second.

The two-and-a-half-month rest did not do the leaders any favours, and after losing two of their first three games back, concerns grew that Rakojević and his players might not have the stamina to see the job through. Fortunately for them, though, no other clubs were in a position to take advantage of those slip-ups. Miodrag Vukotić's Budućnost made a late bid for glory, stringing together seven successive victories, but after moving to within a point of their city rivals with four games to go, they lost two in succession,

the second of them at home to Mladost, who, with their first back-to-back wins of the spring campaign, were home and dry with two matches to spare.

Mladost lost those final two fixtures and Budućnost won theirs, which made the final table with its one-point differential somewhat misleading. Rudar, with their fourth different coach, rolled home in third place, two points above Bokelj, whose settled side under Slobodan Drašković secured the club's highest ever placing and, with Rudar facing Budućnost in the cup final, a first appearance in Europe. Only one of the Prva Liga's dozen participants suffered relegation, bottom club Mornar dropping down alone after Iskra and Petrovac both won their play-off ties, which left second division champions Jedinstvo as the sole newcomers for 2016/17.

Domestic cup

The Montenegrin Cup was the last of Europe's domestic trophies to be decided in 2015/16, and it was late in the evening of 2 June before the final concluded, Rudar and Budućnost failing to find a way to goal in both the regular 90 minutes and the additional 30 before Rudar's 35-year-old 'keeper Miloš Radanović became the hero of the night, saving two penalties in the shoot-out before converting the deciding spot kick

himself. Rudar's fourth cup win meant they were still the only club to have won the trophy more than once.

Europe

Rakojević's Mladost threatened to reach the third qualifying round of the UEFA Europa League for the second time in three seasons when they followed up an away goals success against Azerbaijan's Neftçi by winning the first leg of their next tie away to Albania's Kukës. However, a surprise 4-2 defeat in Podgorica not only stopped Mladost in their tracks but also ended Montenegro's interest in Europe for another season.

National team

Montenegro concluded an unsatisfactory UEFA EURO 2016 qualifying series with defeats by Austria and Russia, leaving them well adrift of a play-off spot with just three wins in their ten group games. Consequently, coach Branko Brnović's contract was not renewed and in the spring he was replaced by 63-year-old Serbian Ljubiša Tumbaković, a man with six Yugoslavian titles (all with Partizan) on his CV but no previous experience of the international game. After three friendlies, all of them admittedly without key players Stefan Savić, Stevan Jovetić and Mirko Vučinić, he was still looking for his first win.

DOMESTIC SEASON AT A GLANCE

Prva Liga 2015/16 final table

		Pld	Home					Away					Total					
			W	D	L	F	A	W	D	L	F	A	W	D	L	F	A	Pts
1	**FK Mladost Podgorica**	**33**	**14**	**0**	**3**	**35**	**11**	**7**	**4**	**5**	**18**	**17**	**21**	**4**	**8**	**53**	**28**	**64**
2	FK Budućnost Podgorica	33	10	3	4	26	11	9	3	4	22	10	19	6	8	48	21	63
3	FK Rudar Pljevlja	33	8	7	2	23	13	8	3	5	16	13	16	10	7	39	26	58
4	FK Bokelj	33	10	2	5	26	13	7	3	6	17	15	17	5	11	43	28	56
5	FK Sutjeska	33	7	5	5	20	15	8	4	4	26	16	15	9	9	46	31	54
6	FK Dečić	33	9	2	6	27	20	2	4	10	11	29	11	6	16	38	49	39
7	OFK Grbalj	33	7	3	6	22	16	4	2	11	16	33	11	5	17	38	49	38
8	FK Zeta	33	6	3	7	17	15	4	5	8	20	27	10	8	15	37	42	38
9	FK Lovćen	33	6	5	5	23	18	3	4	10	9	24	9	9	15	32	42	36
10	FK Iskra	33	2	7	7	10	23	5	6	6	19	28	7	13	13	29	51	34
11	OFK Petrovac	33	5	3	8	18	27	3	6	8	15	24	8	9	16	33	51	33
12	FK Mornar	33	5	5	6	18	19	4	1	12	12	29	9	6	18	30	48	33

NB FK Mladost Podgorica – 3 pts deducted.

European qualification 2016/17

Champion: FK Mladost Podgorica (second qualifying round)

Cup winner: FK Rudar Pljevlja (first qualifying round)
FK Budućnost Podgorica (first qualifying round)
FK Bokelj (first qualifying round)

Top scorer	Marko Šćepanović (Mladost), 19 goals
Relegated club	FK Mornar
Promoted club	FK Jedinstvo Bijelo Polje
Cup final	FK Rudar Pljevlja 0-0 FK Budućnost Podgorica *(aet; 4-3 on pens)*

Team of the season
(4-3-3)

Coach: Drašković *(Bokelj)*

Player of the season

Marko Šćepanović
(FK Mladost Podgorica)

A tall, versatile forward with something of a scattergun career that has taken him from his home town of Podgorica to Hungary and Iran and back again, Šćepanović discovered the form of his life at the age of 33 to spearhead Mladost's drive to the Montenegrin Prva Liga title. On fire in the autumn, when he scored eight goals in as many games, all victories, he continued to find the mark in the spring and ended up as the league's top marksman, his final tally of 19 leaving him one clear of Zeta's Darko Bjedov.

Newcomer of the season

Aleksandar Šćekić
(FK Bokelj)

Only three home-based players were considered worthy of inclusion in the Montenegro national team during the 2015/16 season, and none of them had ever been capped before. The youngest of the trio was Šćekić, who made his debut in new national team coach Ljubiša Tumbaković's first game, a friendly in Greece. It was the 24-year-old's reward for an outstanding campaign in a Bokelj side that defied all pre-season predictions by winning over half of their Prva Liga fixtures and finishing up in fourth place.

Radanović
(Rudar)

Radunović *(Budućnost)* — Šofranac *(Sutjeska)* — Radišić *(Rudar)* — Novović *(Mladost)*

Šćekić *(Bokelj)* — P Vukčević *(Grbalj)* — M Burzanović *(Budućnost)*

Šćepanović *(Mladost)* — Djenić *(Bokelj)* — Bjedov *(Zeta)*

NATIONAL TEAM

Top five all-time caps
Elsad Zverotić (58); **Simon Vukčević** (45);
Mirko Vučinić (44); **Vladimir Božović** (42);
Fatos Bećiraj & **Stevan Jovetić** (40)

Top five all-time goals
Mirko Vučinić (17); **Stevan Jovetić** (16);
Dejan Damjanović (8); **Radomir Djalović** (7);
Andrija Delibašić (6)

Results 2015/16

Date	Opponent	H/A	Venue	Res	Score	Scorers
05/09/15	Liechtenstein (ECQ)	H	Podgorica	W	2-0	Bećiraj (38), Jovetić (56)
08/09/15	Moldova (ECQ)	A	Chisinau	W	2-0	Savić (9), Racu (65og)
09/10/15	Austria (ECQ)	H	Podgorica	L	2-3	Vučinić (32), Bećiraj (68)
12/10/15	Russia (ECQ)	A	Moscow	L	0-2	
12/11/15	FYR Macedonia	A	Skopje	L	1-4	Jovetić (89)
24/03/16	Greece	A	Piraeus	L	1-2	Tomašević (56)
29/03/16	Belarus	H	Podgorica	D	0-0	
29/05/16	Turkey	A	Antalya	L	0-1	

Appearances 2015/16

Coach: Branko Brnović — 08/08/67
/(Radislav Dragićević) — 13/09/71
/(19/01/16) Ljubiša Tumbaković (SRB) — 02/09/52

Player	Born	Club	LIE	MDA	AUT	RUS	Mkd	Gre	Blr	Tur	Caps	Goals
Vukašin Poleksić	30/08/82	Sutjeska /Békéscsaba (HUN)	G	G	G		G		G	G	38	-
Stefan Savić	08/01/91	Atlético (ESP)	D	D	D	D	D		D46		36	3
Marko Baša	29/12/82	LOSC (FRA)	D	D			D		D		37	2
Žarko Tomašević	22/02/90	Kortrijk (BEL)	D	D	D74		D81	D75	D	D	17	2
Vladimir Volkov	06/06/86	Mechelen (BEL)	D								17	-
Vladimir Boljević	17/01/88	AEK Larnaca (CYP)	M	M	M56	s85	M46	s85			8	-
Nikola Vukčević	13/12/91	Braga (POR)	M	M	M	M85	M68	M	M	M	16	-
Adam Marušić	17/10/92	Kortrijk (BEL)	M69	M69	M	s67	M46	D	D		9	-
Fatos Bećiraj	05/05/88	Dinamo Minsk (BLR) /Dinamo Moskva (RUS)	M	M	M	A	A68	A	A	A	40	5
Mirko Vučinić	01/10/83	Al-Jazira (UAE)	A59		A 87*		s46				44	17
Stevan Jovetić	02/11/89	Internazionale (ITA)	A69	A88			A				40	16
Dejan Damjanović	27/07/81	Beijing Guoan (CHN)	s59	A46							30	8
Stefan Mugoša	26/02/92	1860 München (GER)	s69	s46	A64	s46	s68	A69	A56	A64	10	-
Elsad Zverotić	31/10/86	Sion (SUI)	s69		s56		s46	s75		s78	58	5
Marko Simić	16/06/87	Kayserispor (TUR)		D	D	D	D	D	D	D22	17	-
Staniša Mandić	27/01/95	Čukarički (SRB)		s69	s64	M	s46				4	-
Mladen Kašćelan	13/02/83	Arsenal Tula (RUS) /Tosno (RUS)			s88		M			M12	25	-
Vladimir Rodić	07/09/93	Malmö (SWE)				D	M67	M46	M88	M70	5	-
Saša Balić	29/01/90	Tirgu Mureş (ROU)			s74	D	s81				12	-
Milan Mijatović	26/07/87	Bokelj				G		G			2	-
Esteban Saveljić	20/05/91	Defenca y Justicia (ARG) /Almería (ESP)				D		D			4	-
Nemanja Nikolić	01/01/88	BATE (BLR) /H. Tel-Aviv (ISR)				M46				M	10	-
Aleksandar Šćekić	12/12/91	Bokelj						M85		s12/83	2	-
Marko Bakić	01/11/93	Belenenses (POR)						M75	M70		9	-
Filip Raičević	02/07/93	Vicenza (ITA)						s69	s56		2	-
Petar Grbić	07/08/88	Akhisar (TUR)						s75	s70		7	-
Darko Zorić	12/09/93	Borac Čačak (SRB)						s88	s70		3	-
Aleksandar Šofranac	21/10/90	Sutjeska								s46	2	-
Filip Stojković	22/01/93	Čukarički (SRB)								D	1	-
Marko Vešović	28/08/91	Rijeka (CRO)								M78	7	-
Vladimir Jovović	26/10/94	OFK Beograd (SRB)								M75	6	-
Nemanja Mijušković	04/03/92	Vardar (MKD)								s22	1	-
Marko Janković	09/07/95	Maribor (SVN)								s64	1	-
Emrah Klimenta	13/02/91	Sacramento (USA)								s75	1	-
Nebojša Kosović	24/02/95	Partizan (SRB)								s83	1	-

EUROPE

FK Rudar Pljevlja

Second qualifying round - Qarabağ FK (AZE)
A 0-0
Radanović, Djurić, Vuković, Knežević (Soppo 86), Ivanović, Nestorović, Brnović, Živković (Tomašević 66), Jovanović (Reljić 60), Radišić, Vlahović. Coach: Mirko Marić (MNE)
H 0-1
Radanović, Djurić, Vuković (Reljić 78), Knežević, Ivanović, Nestorović, Brnović, Živković, Jovanović (Soppo 81), Radišić, Vlahović. Coach: Mirko Marić (MNE)

FK Mladost Podgorica

First qualifying round - Neftçi PFK (AZE)
A 2-2 Lagator (34), Mirković (87)
Mileta Radulović, Pejović, Lagator (Mirković 63), Raičević, Igumanović, Djurišić (Šćepanović 61), Novović, Miloš S Radulović (Adžović 90+1), Lakić, Vuković, Miloš B Radulović. Coach: Nikola Rakojević (MNE)
H 1-1 Vuković (90+1)
Mileta Radulović, Pejović, Igumanović, Djurišić, Mirković (Novović 31), Miloš S Radulović (Muhović 80), Lakić, Vuković, Miloš B Radulović (Adžović 69). Coach: Nikola Rakojević (MNE)
Red card: Miloš S Radulović 90+9

Second qualifying round - FK Kukësi (ALB)
A 1-0 Lakić (52)
Mileta Radulović, Pejović, Igumanović, Muhović 77), Djurišić, Novović, Lakić, Vuković, Miloš M Radulović, Miloš B Radulović, Šćepanović (Mirković 74). Coach: Nikola Rakojević (MNE)
H 2-4 Šćepanović (62), Adžović (87)
Mileta Radulović, Pejović, Lagator (Mirković 70), Raičević, Djurišić, Novović, Lakić, Vuković, Miloš M Radulović (Muhović 57), Miloš B Radulović (Adžović 80), Šćepanović. Coach: Nikola Rakojević (MNE)

FK Sutjeska

First qualifying round - Debreceni VSC (HUN)
A 0-3
Radović, Ognjanović, D Božović, Kovačević, J Nikolić, Stijepović, Miloš Vučić (Marko Vučić 59), Šofranac, Vujović, Lukić, Fukui. Coach: Dragoslav Albijanić (MNE)
H 2-0 Fukui (53), D Božović (81p)
Radović, Ognjanović, D Božović, Kovačević, J Nikolić, Stijepović (Marko Vučić 84), Miloš Vučić (V Karadžić 71), Šofranac, Vujović (Vorotović 90+2), Lukić, Fukui. Coach: Dragoslav Albijanić (MNE)

FK Budućnost Podgorica

First qualifying round - FK Spartaks Jūrmala (LVA)
H 1-3 Raičević (6)
Agović, Tomković, Ilinčić (Gazivoda 60), Nikač, A Vukčević (Milošević 71), Pavićević, Raspopović, Milivoje Raičević, Hočko (Raičković 77), Simović, Flávio Beck. Coach: Miodrag Vukotić (MNE)
A 0-0
Agović, Tomković, Ilinčić, Nikač, A Vukčević (Milošević 74), Pavićević (Gazivoda 65), Milivoje Raičević (M Burzanović 56), Raspopović, Raičević, Simović, Flávio Beck. Coach: Miodrag Vukotić (MNE)
Red card: Raspopović 82

DOMESTIC LEAGUE CLUB-BY-CLUB

FK Bokelj

1922 • pod Vrmcem (5,000) • no website
Coach: Slobodan Drašković

2015

08/08	a	Lovćen	W	2-1	Šćekić, Nikezić
15/08	h	Zeta	D	1-1	Nikezić
22/08	a	Petrovac	W	3-0	Nikezić, Pržica 2
26/08	a	Budućnost	D	0-0	
29/08	h	Mladost	L	0-1	
12/09	a	Mornar	W	1-0	Nikezić
19/09	h	Dečić	W	4-1	Macanović, Došljak, Pajović, Kotorac
26/09	a	Grbalj	D	1-1	Nikezić (p)
01/10	h	Iskra	L	1-2	Došljak
06/10	a	Rudar	L	0-1	
18/10	h	Sutjeska	W	3-1	Macanović 2, og (Stijepović)
26/10	a	Lovćen	W	1-0	M Todorović
31/10	a	Zeta	L	0-1	
07/11	h	Petrovac	W	2-1	Pepić, Macanović
20/11	h	Budućnost	L	0-1	
28/11	a	Mladost	L	0-1	
06/12	h	Mornar	W	2-0	Nikezić, Kotorac

2016

23/02	a	Dečić	W	1-0	Nikezić
27/02	h	Grbalj	W	3-0	Djenić, Bogdanović, Kotorac
05/03	a	Iskra	D	0-0	
09/03	h	Rudar	D	1-1	Petrović
12/03	a	Sutjeska	L	0-1	
19/03	a	Lovćen	W	2-1	Djenić 2
02/04	h	Grbalj	W	3-0	Šćekić, Djenić, Pepić
09/04	a	Dečić	W	2-1	Ognjanović, Nikezić (p)
16/04	h	Sutjeska	L	0-2	
23/04	h	Mornar	W	2-0	Macanović, Kotorac
30/04	a	Budućnost	L	2-4	Šćekić, Djenić
07/05	h	Rudar	W	1-0	Djenić
11/05	a	Mladost	L	0-1	
14/05	h	Petrovac	W	2-1	Pepić, Djenić
21/05	a	Zeta	W	3-2	Djenić, M Todorović 2
29/05	h	Iskra	L	0-1	

Name	Nat	DoB	Pos	Aps	(s)	Gls
Ilija Bogdanović		14/03/92	D	8	(6)	1
Nikola Braunović		21/07/97	D		(1)	
Nikola Čelebić		04/07/89	D	30		
Dejan Djenić	SRB	02/06/86	A	12	(2)	8
Boris Došljak		04/06/89	M	11	(5)	2
Dejan Kotorac		31/05/96	M	9	(15)	4
Aleksandar Macanović		16/04/93	M	28	(2)	5
Luka Maraš		24/05/96	G	20	(9)	
Milan Mijatović		26/07/87	G	31		
Siniša Mladenović	SRB	05/01/91	D	30		
Milenko Nerić		11/03/88	A		(3)	
Miloš Nikezić		02/03/87	A	25	(6)	8
Dejan Ognjanović		21/06/78	M	26		1
Lazar Pajović		10/11/95	M	11	(11)	1
Dejan Pepić		27/07/93	M	18	(9)	3
Mihailo Petrović		12/12/89	D	10	(5)	1
Dejan Pržica		19/01/91	M	3	(15)	2
Miloš Spalević		19/06/91	D		(1)	
Aleksandar Šćekić		12/12/91	M	31		3
Ilija Todorović		22/02/92	G	2		
Mirko Todorović	SRB	22/08/85	D	30		3
Marko Vujović		23/07/85	M	2	(7)	
Miroslav Zlatičanin	SRB	26/05/85	M	26	(1)	

FK Budućnost Podgorica

1925 • Pod Goricom (12,508) • no website
Major honours
Montenegrin League (2) 2008, 2012; Montenegrin Cup (1) 2013
Coach: Miodrag Vukotić

2015
08/08	a	Grbalj	W	2-0	*Milivoje Raičević 2*
16/08	h	Petrovac	L	1-2	*Milivoje Raičević*
22/08	a	Iskra	W	4-0	*Nikač 2, Hočko, og (D Vuković)*
26/08	h	Bokelj	D	0-0	
29/08	a	Rudar	L	0-1	
12/09	h	Mladost	L	1-3	*Nikač*
19/09	a	Sutjeska	D	0-0	
26/09	h	Mornar	W	3-0	*Nikač 2, Vušurović*
01/10	a	Lovćen	D	2-2	*Nikač, Simović*
06/10	h	Dečić	W	2-0	*Pejaković, Nikač*
18/10	a	Zeta	D	0-0	
26/10	h	Grbalj	W	3-0	*Tomković, Nikač 2*
31/10	a	Petrovac	W	2-0	*og (Jovović), M Burzanović*
07/11	h	Iskra	W	1-0	*Vušurović*
20/11	a	Bokelj	W	1-0	*Pejaković*
29/11	h	Rudar	W	2-1	*Nikač, M Burzanović*
06/12	a	Mladost	L	0-2	

2016
23/02	h	Sutjeska	D	0-0	
27/02	h	Mornar	L	0-1	
05/03	h	Lovćen	D	0-0	
09/03	a	Dečić	W	2-1	*I Burzanović (p), Djalović*
12/03	h	Zeta	D	0-1	
19/03	a	Iskra	W	3-1	*M Burzanović, Vušurović, Djalović*
02/04	h	Lovćen	W	4-0	*M Burzanović, Hočko, Djalović, Mirković*
09/04	a	Grbalj	W	1-0	*Djalović*
16/04	h	Dečić	W	2-0	*Djalović, Vušurović*
23/04	a	Sutjeska	W	4-0	*Raspopović, Pajović, Vušurović, M Burzanović*
30/04	h	Bokelj	W	4-2	*Raičković 2, N Vukčević, Pejaković*
07/05	h	Mornar	W	1-0	*Djalović*
11/05	a	Rudar	L	0-2	
14/05	h	Mladost	L	1-2	*Raspopović*
21/05	a	Petrovac	W	1-0	*Mirković*
29/05	h	Zeta	W	1-0	*Vušurović*

Name	Nat	DoB	Pos	Aps	(s)	Gls
Jasmin Agović		13/02/91	G	3	(1)	
Igor Burzanović		25/08/85	M	4	(1)	1
Marko Burzanović		13/01/98	M	12	(12)	5
Radomir Djalović		29/10/82	A	12	(3)	6
Andjeo Drobnjak		31/07/95	A		(1)	
Savo Gazivoda		18/07/94	M		(4)	
Deni Hočko		22/04/94	M	27	(4)	2
Marko Ilinčić		06/11/95	M	10	(12)	
Velizar Janketić		15/11/96	M	2	(4)	
Marko Kažić		16/11/95	M		(3)	
Damir Ljujanović		23/02/92	G	30		
Luka Malešević		01/08/98	D	1		
Vladimir Mandić	SVN	05/07/87	M	3	(2)	
Danilo Marković		15/07/98	M	1	(2)	
Luka Mirković		01/11/90	D	23	(5)	2
Milan Mirosavljev	SRB	24/04/95	A	1	(4)	
Filip Mitrović		17/11/93	M	8		
Darko Nikač		15/09/90	A	14	(1)	10
Tomislav Pajović	SRB	15/03/86	D	10		1
Miloš Pavićević		09/02/94	M		(1)	
Ivan Pejaković		22/08/92	M	24	(5)	3
Risto Radunović		04/05/92	D	31		
Marko Raičević		31/05/88	M	4	(3)	
Milivoje Raičević		21/07/93	M	4		3
Miloš Raičević		02/12/93	M	20	(3)	2
Momčilo Raspopović		18/03/94	D	27	(1)	2
Marko Roganović		21/06/96	D		(2)	
Ermin Seratlić		21/08/90	A	3	(4)	
Janko Simović		02/04/87	D	16		1
Vasilije Terzić		12/05/99	M		(1)	
Mihailo Tomković		10/06/91	D	20	(1)	1
Vule Vujačić		20/03/88	A	4	(7)	
Andrija Vukčević		11/10/96	D	5	(10)	
Nikola Vukčević		22/03/84	D	13		1
Milan Vušurović		18/04/95	M	31		6

FK Dečić

1926 • Tuško polje (3,000) • no website
**Coach: Viktor Trenevski
(28/10/16) Fuad Krkanović**

2015
08/08	a	Iskra	W	2-1	*Gardašević, Lazarević*
15/08	h	Rudar	L	0-2	
22/08	a	Sutjeska	W	2-0	*Gardašević, A Krnić*
26/08	h	Lovćen	W	3-2	*Gardašević, Ljuljdjuraj 2*
29/08	a	Zeta	D	1-1	*Lakićević*
12/09	h	Petrovac	W	3-1	*Lakićević (p), Ljuljdjuraj 2*
19/09	a	Bokelj	L	1-4	*Ljuljdjuraj*
26/09	h	Mladost	D	2-2	*Lazarević, Ljuljdjuraj*
01/10	a	Mornar	D	2-2	*Gardašević, Lakićević (p)*
06/10	a	Budućnost	L	0-2	
18/10	h	Grbalj	W	3-1	*Ljuljdjuraj, I Camaj, Adžović*
26/10	h	Iskra	D	1-1	*Lazarević*
31/10	a	Rudar	L	0-2	
07/11	h	Sutjeska	W	1-0	*Djukić*
20/11	a	Lovćen	D	0-0	
28/11	h	Zeta	W	3-1	*Dedić 2, Djukić*
05/12	a	Petrovac	L	0-1	

2016
23/02	h	Bokelj	L	0-1	
27/02	a	Mladost	L	0-4	
05/03	h	Mornar	W	1-0	*S Krnić*
09/03	h	Budućnost	L	1-2	*Andjušić*
12/03	a	Grbalj	L	1-2	*I Camaj*
19/03	h	Mornar	W	2-0	*I Camaj, Lazarević*
02/04	a	Sutjeska	D	1-1	*I Camaj*
09/04	h	Bokelj	L	1-2	*Lazarević*
16/04	a	Budućnost	L	0-2	
23/04	h	Rudar	L	0-1	
30/04	a	Mladost	L	0-2	
07/05	h	Petrovac	W	1-0	*Ljuljdjuraj*
11/05	a	Zeta	L	0-3	
14/05	h	Iskra	W	2-1	*I Camaj, Djukić (p)*
21/05	a	Lovćen	L	1-2	*Djukić*
29/05	h	Grbalj	W	3-1	*Ljuljdjuraj, I Camaj, Djukić*

Name	Nat	DoB	Pos	Aps	(s)	Gls
Aldin Adžović		18/06/94	A	17		1
Dražen Andjušić		19/01/93	M	4	(7)	1
Sulejman Bibezić		02/07/96	D		(1)	
Matija Božanović		13/04/94	M	27	(3)	
Driton Camaj		07/03/97	A	3	(7)	
Ilir Camaj		24/06/96	M	19	(8)	6
Radoš Dedić		17/05/93	D	26	(2)	2
Demir Djoković		12/02/97	M		(2)	
Dalibor Djukić		19/09/86	M	17	(7)	5
Nikola Djurković		03/01/94	M	1	(4)	
Sava Gardašević		27/01/93	A	16	(7)	4
Nikola Jovićević		04/01/96	M	1		
Demir Krkanović		19/07/96	M	8	(2)	
Alija Krnić		02/01/98	A	12	(12)	1
Sead Krnić		25/08/86	A	2	(1)	1
Stefan Kruščić		20/11/93	A		(4)	
Slobodan Lakićević		12/01/88	D	13		3
Bojan Lazarević		09/09/93	M	29	(2)	5
Pjeter Ljuljdjuraj		29/06/92	M	28		9
Nikola Mihailović		15/09/84	D	30		
Ivan Mijušković		17/02/88	M	2		
Nijazim Padović		19/11/87	D	30		
Rijad Pepić		12/07/90	M	17	(7)	
Demir Ramović		03/01/82	M	5	(2)	
Jovan Perović		28/12/89	G	31		
Momčilo Rašo		08/02/97	D	4	(1)	
Filip Rosandić		27/03/97	G	2		
Nikola Sekulović		27/03/97	M		(1)	
Kabir Šabotić		31/08/95	M		(1)	
Mario Toskić		14/12/96	M		(1)	
Amel Tuzović		31/03/95	M	15	(6)	
Kristijan Vulaj		25/06/98	M	4	(9)	

OFK Grbalj

1970 • Donja Sutvara (1,500) • no website
**Coach: Bogdan Korak;
(01/09/15) (Dušan Vlaisavljević);
(01/01/16) Dragoljub Djuretić**

2015
08/08	h	Budućnost	L	0-2	
15/08	h	Iskra	L	1-2	*Tučević*
22/08	a	Rudar	L	1-2	*P Vukčević*
26/08	h	Sutjeska	D	1-1	*Kopitović*
29/08	a	Lovćen	L	1-3	*Glavan*
12/09	h	Zeta	W	4-1	*P Vukčević, Tučević 2, Kopitović*
19/09	a	Petrovac	W	1-0	*P Vukčević (p)*
26/09	h	Bokelj	D	1-1	*P Vukčević (p)*
01/10	a	Mladost	L	1-3	*Kopitović*
06/10	h	Mornar	W	2-1	*Milojko, Grivić*
18/10	a	Dečić	L	1-3	*Zorica*
26/10	a	Budućnost	L	0-3	
31/10	a	Iskra	W	2-0	*Kopitović 2*
07/11	h	Rudar	L	0-1	
20/11	a	Sutjeska	L	0-2	
28/11	h	Lovćen	D	0-0	
06/12	a	Zeta	W	2-1	*Raičević, P Vukčević*

2016
23/02	h	Petrovac	W	4-1	*Jablan 2, Zorica, P Vukčević*
27/02	a	Bokelj	L	0-3	
05/03	h	Mladost	W	1-0	*Grivić*
09/03	a	Mornar	L	0-1	
12/03	h	Dečić	W	2-1	*Zorica, P Vukčević*
19/03	a	Sutjeska	L	1-2	*P Vukčević*
02/04	a	Bokelj	L	0-3	
09/04	h	Budućnost	L	0-1	
16/04	a	Rudar	D	1-1	*M Carević*
23/04	h	Mladost	W	2-0	*Zorica, Jablan*
30/04	a	Petrovac	D	1-1	*Tučević*
07/05	h	Zeta	L	1-2	*Dragićević*
11/05	a	Iskra	W	3-1	*Zorica, Pavlović, Kopitović*
14/05	h	Lovćen	W	2-0	*Tučević, Jablan*
21/05	a	Mornar	L	1-3	*Zorica*
29/05	a	Dečić	L	1-3	*Dragićević (p)*

Name	Nat	DoB	Pos	Aps	(s)	Gls
Ilija Bogdanović		14/03/92	M	4		
Lazar Carević		16/03/99	G	27		
Milan Carević		05/10/93	D	25	(2)	1
Petar Čavor		05/12/97	A	1		
Petar Čolaković		13/09/93	M	7	(4)	
Vuk Damjanović		20/04/96	A	1	(4)	
Zdravko Dragićević		17/06/86	A	13	(1)	2
Ilija Glavan	BIH	03/07/90	D	15		1
Dragan Grivić		12/02/96	D	27	(1)	2
Ivan Jablan		18/07/79	A	14		4
Kim Lea-kyun	KOR	19/01/94	M	6	(1)	
Bojan Kopitović		12/10/93	A	17	(8)	6
Vladan Kordić		22/06/98	M	2	(7)	
Bojan Magud		10/12/97	M	2	(4)	
Ćetko Manojlović		03/01/91	D	25		
Milenko Malović	SRB	23/08/94	D	12	(2)	
Goran Milojko		05/01/94	D	15	(1)	1
Marko Mugoša		04/04/84	M	2	(7)	
Nemanja Nedić		06/04/95	M	7	(4)	
Marko Nikolić	SRB	09/06/89	M	15		
Vojin Pavlović		09/11/93	M	30	(1)	1
Marko Raičević		31/05/88	M	14	(1)	1
Milan Simonović		11/03/93	M		(2)	
Kristijan Soldatović		27/05/96	M	1	(1)	
Stefan Spasojević		23/08/93	G	6		
Stefan Stevanović	SRB	23/11/90	M	1	(2)	
Gorčin Todorović		28/05/94	A	2	(5)	
Ilija Tučević		18/10/95	D	19	(5)	5
Jovan Vujović		20/01/96	M	2	(7)	
Djordje Vukčević		18/08/96	D	2	(1)	
Petar Vukčević		15/08/87	M	29		8
Saša Vukčević		01/04/94	M	1	(4)	
Ilija Vukotić		07/01/99	M		(5)	
Milan Zorica	SRB	07/01/92	M	19	(6)	6
Miloš Zvicer		23/02/97	M		(1)	

MONTENEGRO

FK Iskra

1919 • Braće Velašević (2,000) • no website
Coach: Goran Jovanović;
(01/01/16) Ratko Stevović

2015

08/08	h	Dečić	L	1-2	D Kovačević
15/08	a	Grbalj	W	2-1	D Kovačević (p), Djuranović
22/08	h	Budućnost	L	0-4	
26/08	h	Rudar	D	0-0	
29/08	a	Sutjeska	L	0-3	
12/09	h	Lovćen	D	0-0	
19/09	a	Zeta	W	2-0	Vučić, D Kovačević
26/09	h	Petrovac	D	0-0	
01/10	h	Bokelj	W	2-1	Djuranović, Obagbemiro
06/10	h	Mladost	L	2-3	Vučić, D Kovačević
17/10	a	Mornar	D	0-0	
26/10	a	Dečić	D	1-1	Novović
31/10	h	Grbalj	L	0-2	
07/11	a	Budućnost	L	0-1	
20/11	h	Rudar	D	2-2	D Kovačević, Šahman
28/11	h	Sutjeska	L	0-4	
06/12	a	Lovćen	L	1-4	Pavićević

2016

23/02	h	Zeta	W	1-0	Burzanović
27/02	a	Petrovac	W	4-2	Djuranović, Vučić, Obagbemiro, Kalezić
05/03	h	Bokelj	D	0-0	
09/03	a	Mladost	L	0-5	
12/03	h	Mornar	W	2-0	Vučić, Novović
19/03	a	Budućnost	L	1-3	D Kovačević
02/04	a	Rudar	D	0-0	
09/04	a	Mladost	D	0-0	
16/04	a	Petrovac	D	1-1	Jerkovic
23/04	a	Zeta	D	1-1	Kalezić
30/04	a	Mornar	L	0-3	
07/05	a	Lovćen	D	2-2	Djuranović, Vučić
11/05	h	Grbalj	L	1-3	Burzanović
14/05	h	Dečić	L	1-2	Burzanović (p)
21/05	h	Sutjeska	D	1-1	D Kovačević
29/05	h	Bokelj	W	1-0	Kalezić

Name	Nat	DoB	Pos	Aps	(s)	Gls
Bojan Begović		01/04/83	D	4	(4)	
Goran Burzanović		04/08/84	M	15		3
Uroš Djuranović		01/02/94	A	26	(5)	4
Dragan Djurović		11/09/92	D		(3)	
Radivoje Golubović		24/02/90	D	7	(1)	
Kyosuke Goto	JPN	29/07/92	M	6	(2)	
Goran Jerkovic	FRA	10/11/86	A	6	(2)	1
Miloš Kalezić		09/08/93	M	30	(1)	3
Andrija Kaludjerović		14/06/90	M	7	(2)	
Marko Kasalica		13/10/86	A	5	(9)	
Nemanja Kosović		15/05/93	D	16	(3)	
Srđa Kosović		02/05/92	M	9	(4)	
Danko Kovačević		10/07/91	A	21	(7)	7
Miroslav Kovačević		03/05/94	M	1		
Željko Krstović		15/10/89	M	24	(2)	
Boris Lakićević		24/10/88	G	18		
Nikola Marčelja		27/11/86	D	15		
Anton Memčević		23/08/98	M		(3)	
Dušan Mladenović	SRB	13/10/90	D	13		
Igor Mrvaljević		02/05/98	M		(1)	
Milivoje Novović		29/02/84	D	28		2
Samson Obagbemiro	NGA	18/03/93	M	12	(11)	2
Stevan Pavićević		07/11/86	A	4	(8)	1
Miloš Petošević	SRB	28/07/91	A	3		
Davor Popović		18/07/85	D	2	(1)	
Argzim Redžoviž		26/02/92	D	11	(1)	
Vladimir Savićević		27/11/89	M	10	(13)	
Marko Stanovčić	SRB	09/05/90	D	5	(4)	
Irfan Šahman		05/10/93	M	5	(1)	1
Darko Vučić		28/08/91	A	19	(1)	5
Nikola Vukčević		23/06/93	D	11	(2)	
Danilo Vuković		01/04/89	D	15		
Pavle Vuković		11/02/84	D	15	(8)	

FK Lovćen

1913 • Obilića Poljana (5,000) • fklovcen.me
Major honours
Montenegrin Cup (1) 2014
Coach: Slobodan Halilović;
(24/10/15) (Dragan Djukanović);
(04/04/16) Milorad Malovrazić

2015

08/08	h	Bokelj	L	1-2	Tatar
15/08	a	Mladost	L	0-2	
22/08	a	Mornar	W	3-1	N Draganić, Vujanović, Djalac
26/08	a	Dečić	L	2-3	Djalac 2
29/08	h	Grbalj	W	3-1	N Draganić, Vujanović, Perutović
12/09	a	Iskra	D	0-0	
19/09	h	Rudar	D	1-1	Radović
26/09	a	Sutjeska	L	0-2	
01/10	h	Budućnost	D	2-2	Djalac, N Vujović
06/10	h	Zeta	L	1-2	N Draganić
18/10	a	Petrovac	L	1-2	Djalac
26/10	h	Bokelj	L	0-1	
31/10	h	Mladost	L	1-2	Perutović
07/11	a	Mornar	W	1-0	Jablan
20/11	h	Dečić	D	0-0	
28/11	h	Grbalj	D	0-0	
06/12	h	Iskra	W	4-1	Perutović, Martinović, Djalac, Radović

2016

23/02	a	Rudar	D	1-1	Tatar (p)
28/02	h	Sutjeska	D	0-0	
05/03	a	Budućnost	D	0-0	
09/03	a	Zeta	W	2-0	Rogošić, Tatar (p)
12/03	h	Petrovac	W	1-0	Tatar (p)
19/03	h	Bokelj	L	1-2	Došljak
02/04	a	Budućnost	L	0-4	
09/04	h	Rudar	L	0-1	
16/04	a	Mladost	L	0-1	
23/04	a	Petrovac	W	1-0	Perutović
30/04	a	Zeta	L	0-2	
07/05	h	Iskra	D	2-2	Ibrić, Perutović
11/05	a	Mornar	W	1-0	Tatar (p)
14/05	a	Grbalj	L	0-2	
21/05	h	Dečić	W	2-1	Perutović 2
29/05	a	Sutjeska	L	1-4	Perutović

Name	Nat	DoB	Pos	Aps	(s)	Gls
Draško Adžić		22/08/96	M	2		
Dejan Bogdanović		08/08/90	M	1		
Ivan Buturović		23/11/93	G	1		
Mitar Čuković		06/04/95	D	3	(6)	
Miloš Djalac		17/10/82	A	17		6
Boris Došljak		04/06/89	M	13	(3)	1
Marko Draganić		19/09/94	M	6	(4)	
Nikola Draganić		19/09/94	M	11	(3)	3
Flávio Beck	BRA	14/03/87	M	22		
Damir Ibrić	BIH	30/03/84	A	2	(11)	1
Ivan Jablan		18/07/79	A	8	(7)	1
Željko Marković		25/02/96	M	5	(3)	
Ilija Martinović		31/07/94	D	24		1
Stefan Milošević		23/06/96	D	1	(6)	
Miloš Pejaković		16/08/95	M	8	(12)	
Mićo Perović		04/07/93	G	1		
Blažo Perutović		08/12/83	M	13	(1)	8
Danijel Petković		25/05/93	G	31		
Bojan Petrić	BIH	29/11/84	D	14		
Balša Radović		04/01/91	M	27	(1)	2
Miloš Radunović		07/07/90	D	25	(2)	
Vladislav Rogošić		21/09/94	D	19	(5)	1
Vladimir Sjekloća		11/02/95	A	3	(2)	
Vladan Tatar		28/01/84	D	28		5
Luka Tiodorović		21/01/86	M	17	(8)	
Danilo Tomić		23/06/86	M	28		
Luka Vujanović		17/07/94	M	32		2
Filip Vujović		18/10/97	M		(1)	
Nikola Vujović		23/06/81	M	1	(12)	1

FK Mladost Podgorica

1950 • Stari Aerodrom (1,000) •
fkmladost.me
Major honours
Montenegrin League (1) 2016 ; Montenegrin Cup (1) 2015
Coach: Nikola Rakojević

2015

09/08	a	Sutjeska	W	1-0	Šćepanović
15/08	h	Lovćen	W	2-0	Rudović, Djurišić
22/08	a	Zeta	L	0-1	
26/08	h	Petrovac	L	1-2	Kojašević
29/08	a	Bokelj	W	1-0	Kojašević
12/09	a	Budućnost	W	3-1	Šćepanović, Raičević, Novović
19/09	h	Mornar	W	2-1	Djurišić, Šćepanović
26/09	a	Dečić	D	2-2	Novović, Kojašević
01/10	h	Grbalj	W	3-1	Šćepanović, Djurišić, Kojašević
06/10	a	Iskra	W	3-2	Šćepanović 2, Kojašević
18/10	h	Rudar	W	1-0	Šćepanović
26/10	a	Sutjeska	W	4-3	Raičević, Muhović 2, Kojašević
31/10	a	Lovćen	W	2-1	Šćepanović, Kojašević
07/11	h	Zeta	W	2-0	Muhović, Šćepanović
20/11	a	Petrovac	W	2-1	Rudović, Šćepanović
28/11	h	Bokelj	W	1-0	Šćepanović
06/12	h	Budućnost	W	2-0	Lagator, Djurišić

2016

23/02	a	Mornar	L	0-2	
27/02	a	Dečić	W	4-0	Vuković, Kokot, Šćepanović 2 (1p)
05/03	a	Grbalj	L	0-2	
09/03	h	Iskra	W	5-0	Vuković 2, Šćepanović (p), Muhović, Petrović
12/03	a	Rudar	D	0-0	
19/03	a	Petrovac	D	1-1	Šćepanović
02/04	h	Zeta	W	2-0	Šćepanović, Vuković (p)
09/04	a	Iskra	D	0-0	
16/04	h	Lovćen	W	1-0	Raičević
23/04	a	Grbalj	L	0-2	
30/04	h	Dečić	W	2-0	Lakić, Raičević
07/05	a	Sutjeska	L	1-2	Raičević
11/05	h	Bokelj	W	1-0	Šćepanović
14/05	a	Budućnost	W	2-1	Djurišić, Kokot
21/05	h	Rudar	L	2-3	Šćepanović 2
29/05	h	Mornar	L	0-1	

Name	Nat	DoB	Pos	Aps	(s)	Gls
Balša Boričić		07/01/97	M		(2)	
Nenad Djukanović		08/12/92	M		(2)	
Milan Djurišić		11/04/87	M	30	(1)	5
Ilija Glavan		03/07/90	D	3	(4)	
Radivoje Golubović		22/04/90	D		(1)	
Ryo Kato	JPN	20/08/91	D	1	(1)	
Damir Kojašević		03/06/87	M	13	(1)	7
Zoran Kokot	BIH	28/06/85	D	6	(8)	2
Edvin Kuč		27/10/93	A	1	(11)	
Dušan Lagator		29/03/94	D	15		1
Miloš Lakić		21/12/85	D	32		1
Vojin Manojlović		14/09/98	M			
Jasmin Muhović		02/04/89	A	22	(3)	4
Ivan Novović		26/04/89	D	30	(1)	2
Božo Osmajlić		01/02/94	M	1		
Luka Pejović		31/07/85	D	30		
Luka Petričević		06/07/92	M	7	(5)	
Zoran Petrović		14/07/97	A	2	(16)	1
Dragoljub Radišević		17/12/96	M		(2)	
Vuk Radović		28/02/93	G	2		
Mileta Radulović		29/01/91	G	31		
Miloš B Radulović		06/08/90	D	24	(3)	
Miloš M Radulović		19/10/92	M	5	(1)	
Miloš S Radulović		23/02/90	D	5	(5)	
Igor Radusinović		15/03/84	D	8	(1)	
Mirko Raičević		22/03/82	M	32		5
Andjelo Radulović		03/05/96	M	8	(17)	1
Boško Stupić	BIH	27/06/84	A	1	(3)	
Marko Šćepanović		08/08/82	A	29		19
Saša Tomanović		20/09/89	M	9	(4)	
Nemanja Vlahović		04/01/91	M		(2)	
Ivan Vuković		09/02/87	A	16		4

FK Mornar

1923 • Topolica (2,500) • no website
Coach: Rudolf Marčić;
(25/03/16) Zoran Mijović

2015
08/08	a	Rudar	D 2-2	Vujačić 2
15/08	h	Sutjeska	L 1-3	Leverda
22/08	a	Lovćen	L 1-3	Kacić
26/08	h	Zeta	L 1-5	Leverda
30/08	a	Petrovac	L 1-2	Vučinić
12/09	h	Bokelj	L 0-1	
19/09	a	Mladost	L 1-2	Bogdanović
26/09	a	Budućnost	L 0-3	
01/10	h	Dečić	D 2-2	Vujačić, Vučinić
06/10	a	Grbalj	L 1-2	Kacić (p)
17/10	h	Iskra	D 0-0	
26/10	h	Rudar	L 1-2	Novaković
31/10	a	Sutjeska	L 1-4	Kacić (p)
07/11	h	Lovćen	L 0-1	
20/11	a	Zeta	W 2-1	Shimura, Kalezić
28/11	h	Petrovac	D 1-1	Vojvodić
06/12	h	Bokelj	L 0-2	

2016
23/02	h	Mladost	W 2-0	Marković, Vučinić (p)
27/02	h	Budućnost	W 1-0	Vučinić
05/03	a	Dečić	L 0-1	
09/03	h	Grbalj	W 1-0	Leverda
12/03	a	Iskra	L 0-2	
19/03	a	Dečić	L 0-2	
02/04	h	Petrovac	D 0-0	
09/04	a	Sutjeska	W 1-0	Nikolić
16/04	h	Zeta	D 2-2	Vučinić, Kacić
23/04	a	Bokelj	L 0-2	
30/04	h	Iskra	W 3-0	Djurović 2, Leverda (p)
07/05	a	Budućnost	L 0-1	
11/05	h	Lovćen	L 0-1	
14/05	a	Rudar	W 1-0	Vučinić
21/05	h	Grbalj	W 3-1	Leverda 2, og (Nedić)
29/05	a	Mladost	W 1-0	Djurović

Name	Nat	DoB	Pos	Aps	(s)	Gls
Bogdan Bogdanović		05/03/89	A	8	(14)	1
Francis Bossman	GHA	24/06/84	M	2		
Danko Bubanja		12/09/88	D	3	(4)	
Nemanja Ćosović		07/05/92	M		(1)	
Marko Djurović		08/05/88	A	5	(9)	3
Denis Džanović		03/06/93	M	2	(5)	
Igor Gajević	SRB	16/07/95	D	15		
Siniša Graovac	BIH	01/09/84	D	9		
Bojan Ivanović		03/12/81	D	11		
Saša Ivanović		26/06/84	G	7		
Benjamin Kacić		28/06/91	M	31		4
Bojan Kalezić		11/03/88	M	11	(4)	1
Marko Kažić		16/11/95	A	1	(8)	
Kim Young-seop	KOR	10/08/91	M	24	(1)	
Lazar Lalošević		07/05/95	A	1	(4)	
Marko Leković		07/05/96	M		(1)	
Nemanja Leverda		07/06/92	M	15	(14)	6
Stevan Marković		31/01/88	D	25		1
Dragan Masoničić		01/11/88	G	10		
Luka Merdović		06/10/97	M	1	(4)	
Daisuke Miyata	JPN	07/06/91	M	3	(2)	
Baćo Nikolić		19/01/86	M	16		1
Mitar Novaković		27/09/81	M	1	(3)	1
Vuk Orlandić		01/09/97	M	7	(3)	
Aleksandar Petrović	SRB	08/02/85	D	10		
Nemanja Popović		20/05/84	G	16		
Dženan Radončić		02/08/83	A	2	(3)	
Kenan Ragipović	SRB	16/09/82	M	15		
Blažo Rajović		26/03/86	D	7	(2)	
Noboru Shimura	JPN	11/03/93	M	30		1
Željko Tomašević		05/04/88	D	15		
Djordje Vojvodić		31/05/86	D	7	(2)	1
Jovan Vučinić		20/01/92	A	27	(1)	6
Vule Vujačić		20/03/88	A	12	(3)	3
Nino Vukmarković		17/12/94	M	14	(10)	

OFK Petrovac

1969 • Pod Malim brdom (1,630) • no website
Major honours
Montenegrin Cup (1) 2009
Coach: Milorad Malovrazić;
(14/03/16) Ivan Brnović

2015
08/08	a	Zeta	L 0-2	
16/08	a	Budućnost	W 2-1	Vujović, Kapisoda
22/08	h	Bokelj	L 0-3	
26/08	a	Mladost	W 2-1	Joboshi, Kopitović
30/08	h	Mornar	W 2-1	Kopitović 2
12/09	a	Dečić	L 1-3	Kapisoda
19/09	h	Grbalj	L 0-1	
26/09	a	Iskra	D 0-0	
01/10	h	Rudar	W 2-0	Stevović, Andjelković
06/10	a	Sutjeska	D 0-0	
18/10	h	Lovćen	W 2-1	Kopitović 2 (1p)
26/10	h	Zeta	W 5-3	Kopitović 2, Božović, Andjelković, Mijušković
31/10	h	Budućnost	L 0-2	
07/11	h	Bokelj	L 1-2	Andjelković
20/11	h	Mladost	L 1-2	Kopitović
28/11	a	Mornar	D 1-1	Joboshi
05/12	h	Dečić	W 1-0	Kopitović

2016
23/02	a	Grbalj	L 1-4	Kopitović
27/02	h	Iskra	L 2-4	Kopitović, Joboshi
05/03	a	Rudar	L 2-3	Kopitović, Mikijelj
09/03	h	Sutjeska	L 0-4	
12/03	a	Lovćen	L 0-1	
19/03	h	Mladost	D 1-1	Kalačević
02/04	a	Mornar	D 0-0	
09/04	a	Zeta	D 1-1	Vujović
16/04	h	Iskra	D 1-1	Čolaković
23/04	a	Lovćen	L 0-1	
30/04	h	Grbalj	D 1-1	Marković
07/05	a	Dečić	W 2-1	Kopitović (p), Joboshi
11/05	h	Sutjeska	L 0-2	
14/05	a	Bokelj	L 1-2	Marković
21/05	h	Budućnost	L 0-1	
29/05	a	Rudar	D 1-1	Bulatović

Name	Nat	DoB	Pos	Aps	(s)	Gls
Dragoljub Andjelković	SRB	14/04/93	A	5	(5)	3
Danilo Bakić		28/10/95	M	1	(2)	
Balša Božović		01/05/87	M	6	(3)	1
Nikola Bulatović		19/05/96	M	2	(8)	1
Goran Burzanović		04/08/84	M	2	(9)	
Petar Čolaković		13/09/93	M	9	(2)	1
Mitar Čuković		06/04/95	D	4	(3)	
Miloš Dragojević		03/02/89	G	13		
Bojan Golubović		28/11/85	M	31		
Boris Grbović		31/01/80	D	15	(4)	
Shuta Joboshi	JPN	02/03/92	M	15	(11)	4
Petar Jovović		31/01/91	A	6	(2)	
Demir Kajević		20/04/89	M	27		
Filip Kalačević		12/03/94	M	19	(10)	1
Aleksandar Kapisoda		17/09/89	D	12		2
Boris Kopitović		27/04/95	A	28	(2)	13
Rajko Leković		21/06/94	D		(2)	
Marko Marković		05/09/87	M	27	(1)	2
Ivan Mijušković		17/02/88	M	3	(6)	1
Zoran Mikijelj		13/12/91	D	12		1
Marko Milosavljević		14/06/93	M	3	(3)	
Stefan Popović		11/01/93	G	5		
Ivan Racković		13/09/94	M	3	(5)	
Ilija Radović		09/05/95	D	15		
Argzim Redžović		26/02/92	M	10		
Nikola Savović		30/09/94	M	12	(5)	
Miloš Stevović		14/09/89	M	4	(3)	1
Boris Stijepović		22/05/96	M	1	(4)	
Stefan Trajkovic	MKD	22/07/95	D	5	(2)	
Nenad Vujović		02/01/89	M	26		2
Goran Vukliš	BIH	24/09/89	G	15		
Woo Sang-hoon	KOR	07/12/92	M	29		

FK Rudar Pljevlja

1920 • Pod Golubinjom (8,500) • no website
Major honours
Montenegrin League (2) 2010, 2015; Montenegrin Cup (4) 2007, 2010, 2011, 2016
Coach: Mirko Marić;
(14/03/16) (Srdjan Bajić);
(16/05/16) (Vuko Bogavac);
(23/05/16) Dragan Radojičić

2015
08/08	h	Mornar	D 2-2	Radanović (p), Soppo
15/08	a	Dečić	W 2-0	Knežević, Reljić
22/08	h	Grbalj	W 2-1	Knežević, Marković
26/08	a	Iskra	D 0-0	
29/08	h	Budućnost	W 1-0	Djurić
12/09	h	Sutjeska	W 4-1	Živković, Radanović (p), Marković 2
19/09	a	Lovćen	D 1-1	Marković
26/09	a	Zeta	W 1-0	Božović
01/10	a	Petrovac	L 0-2	
06/10	h	Bokelj	W 1-0	Marković
18/10	a	Mladost	L 0-1	
26/10	a	Mornar	W 2-1	Brnović, Radanović (p)
31/10	h	Dečić	W 2-0	Božović, Živković
07/11	h	Grbalj	W 1-0	Radanović (p)
20/11	h	Iskra	D 2-2	Djurić, Marković
29/11	a	Budućnost	L 1-2	Božović
05/12	a	Sutjeska	W 2-0	Marković, Knežević

2016
23/02	h	Lovćen	D 1-1	Noma
27/02	a	Zeta	L 0-2	
05/03	h	Petrovac	W 3-2	Brnović 2, Reljić
09/03	h	Bokelj	D 1-1	Radanović (p)
12/03	h	Mladost	D 0-0	
19/03	a	Zeta	W 1-0	Radanović (p)
02/04	a	Iskra	D 0-0	
09/04	a	Lovćen	W 1-0	Živković
16/04	h	Grbalj	W 1-0	Marković
23/04	a	Dečić	W 1-0	Jovanović
30/04	h	Sutjeska	L 0-1	
07/05	a	Bokelj	L 0-1	
11/05	h	Budućnost	W 2-0	Brnović, Knežević
14/05	h	Mornar	L 0-1	
21/05	a	Mladost	W 3-2	Knežević, Ivanović, Jovanović
29/05	h	Petrovac	D 1-1	Ivanović

Name	Nat	DoB	Pos	Aps	(s)	Gls
Ermin Alić		23/02/92	D	14	(1)	
Draško Božović		30/06/88	M	22	(3)	3
Predrag Brnović		22/10/86	M	25	(3)	4
Dejan Damjanović		08/07/86	D	16		2
Djordje Djurić	SRB	10/08/91	D	16		2
Nikola Gačević		14/05/87	M	3	(8)	
Milija Golubović		25/04/96	D		(1)	
Vladan Gordić		27/07/90	D		(2)	
Ivan Ivanović		14/09/89	A	13	(2)	2
Miroje Jovanović		10/03/87	M	14	(17)	2
Andrija Kaludjerović		29/10/93	M	9	(1)	
Ivan Knežević		22/02/86	A	11	(13)	5
Ivan Marković	SRB	23/12/91	A	21	(7)	4
Stefan Milošević		23/06/96	M		(4)	
Dušan Nestorović	SRB	26/06/86	D	28		
Ryota Noma	JPN	15/11/92	M	14	(1)	1
Balša Pelićić		05/08/96	M	2	(3)	
Miloš Radanović		05/11/80	G	33		6
Mirko Radišić		01/09/90	D	24	(1)	
Stevan Reljić		31/03/86	D	17	(2)	2
Alphonse Soppo	CMR	15/05/85	D	28	(1)	1
Željko Tomašević		05/04/88	D	1	(1)	
Nedjeljko Vlahović		15/01/84	M	26	(2)	
Marko Vuković		20/03/96	A	10	(9)	
Radule Živković		22/10/90	D	30	(1)	3

MONTENEGRO

FK Sutjeska

1927 • Kraj Bistrice (10,800) • fksutjeska.me
Major honours
Montenegrin League (2) 2013, 2014
Coach: Aleksandar Nedović

2015

09/08	h	Mladost	L	0-1	
15/08	a	Mornar	W	3-1	D Karadžić, Kordić, Zarubica
22/08	h	Dečić	L	0-2	
26/08	a	Grbalj	D	1-1	Lončar
29/08	h	Iskra	W	3-0	Inuma 3
12/09	a	Rudar	L	1-4	D Karadžić
19/09	h	Budućnost	D	0-0	
26/09	h	Lovćen	W	2-0	Kordić 2
01/10	a	Zeta	W	1-0	Grbović
06/10	h	Petrovac	D	0-0	
18/10	a	Bokelj	L	1-3	Zarubica
26/10	a	Mladost	L	3-4	D Karadžić, og (Miloš B Radulović), Kordić
31/10	h	Mornar	W	4-1	Kordić 2, Zarubica, og (Petrović)
07/11	a	Dečić	L	0-1	
20/11	h	Grbalj	W	2-0	Miloš Vučić, Zarubica
28/11	a	Iskra	W	4-0	Stefanović, Zarubica 2, Marko Vučić
05/12	h	Rudar	L	0-2	

2016

23/02	a	Budućnost	D	0-0	
28/02	a	Lovćen	D	0-0	
05/03	h	Zeta	D	1-1	og (Šofranac)
09/03	a	Petrovac	W	4-0	Kordić, Vukovic, Zarubica, Milovac
12/03	h	Bokelj	W	1-0	Zarubica
19/03	a	Grbalj	W	2-1	Zarubica, Kordić
02/04	h	Dečić	D	1-1	Ćuković
09/04	h	Mornar	L	0-1	
16/04	a	Bokelj	W	2-0	Zarubica 2
23/04	h	Budućnost	L	0-4	
30/04	a	Rudar	W	1-0	Milovac
07/05	h	Mladost	W	2-1	Kordić, Zarubica
11/05	a	Petrovac	W	2-0	Kordić, Zarubica
14/05	h	Zeta	D	0-0	
21/05	a	Iskra	D	1-1	Kordić
29/05	h	Lovćen	W	4-1	Milovac, Zarubica 3

Name	Nat	DoB	Pos	Aps	(s)	Gls
Boris Bulajić		27/04/88	M		(3)	
Igor Ćuković		06/06/93	D	30		1
Žarko Grbović		20/05/95	M	21	(3)	1
Masaki Inuma	JPN	27/11/92	M	4	(2)	3
Darko Karadžić		17/04/89	M	10	(7)	3
Vladan Karadžić		04/02/95	A	1	(11)	
Šaleta Kordić		19/04/93	A	29	(1)	11
Srdja Kosović		02/05/92	M	6	(1)	
Stevan Kovačević	SRB	09/01/88	M	3	(6)	
Suad Ličina		08/02/95	G	20		
Stefan Lončar		19/02/96	M	18	(8)	1
Lazar Martinović		03/07/89	D	12	(3)	
Ivan Mićunović		22/02/00	D	1	(1)	
Zoran Milovac	SRB	29/10/98	M	11	(2)	3
Jovan Nikolić		21/07/91	M	15		
Nemanja Nikolić		18/05/97	M	2	(1)	
Vukašin Poleksić		30/08/82	G	13		
Nikola Popović		13/09/97	D	2		
Miloš Radulović		23/02/90	D	14		
Stefan Stefanović	SRB	22/08/91	M	30		1
Nikola Stijepović		02/11/93	D	30		
Aleksandar Šofranac		21/10/90	D	28		
Filip Vorotović		08/03/98	A		(4)	
Marko Vučić		30/12/96	M	4	(13)	1
Miloš Vučić		26/08/95	M	12	(9)	1
Matija Vujović		09/06/96	M	7	(8)	
Bojan Vukćević		29/05/97	M		(1)	
Veljko Vuković	SRB	14/07/89	A	9	(3)	1
Dejan Zarubica		11/04/93	A	31		16

FK Zeta

1927 • Trešnjica (5,000) • no website
Major honours
Montenegrin League (1) 2007
Coach: Miodrag Martać;
(03/10/15) (Nenad Brnović);
(08/11/15) Dejan Vukićević

2015

08/08	h	Petrovac	W	2-0	Trišović, Bjedov
15/08	a	Bokelj	D	1-1	Kukuličić
22/08	h	Mladost	W	1-0	Bjedov
26/08	a	Mornar	W	5-1	Bjedov 2, Klikovac 2, Vlaisavljević (p)
29/08	h	Dečić	D	1-1	Šofranac
12/09	a	Grbalj	L	1-4	Bjedov
19/09	h	Iskra	L	0-2	
26/09	a	Rudar	L	0-1	
01/10	h	Sutjeska	L	0-1	
06/10	a	Lovćen	W	2-1	Vlaisavljević 2
18/10	h	Budućnost	D	0-0	
26/10	a	Petrovac	L	3-5	Bjedov 3 (1p)
31/10	h	Bokelj	W	1-0	Vlaisavljević (p)
07/11	a	Mladost	L	0-2	
20/11	h	Mornar	L	1-2	Klikovac
28/11	a	Dečić	L	1-3	Bjedov
06/12	h	Grbalj	L	1-2	Bjedov

2016

23/02	a	Iskra	L	0-1	
27/02	h	Rudar	W	2-0	Bjedov, Vlaisavljević
05/03	a	Sutjeska	D	1-1	Bjedov
09/03	h	Lovćen	L	0-2	
12/03	a	Budućnost	W	1-0	Bjedov
19/03	h	Rudar	L	0-1	
02/04	h	Mladost	L	0-2	
09/04	h	Petrovac	D	1-1	Bjedov
16/04	a	Mornar	D	2-2	Klikovac, Šofranac
23/04	a	Iskra	D	1-1	Živković
30/04	h	Lovćen	W	2-0	Bjedov, Kukuličić
07/05	a	Grbalj	W	2-1	Živković 2
11/05	h	Dečić	W	3-0	Klikovac, Kukuličić, Bjedov
14/05	a	Sutjeska	D	0-0	
21/05	h	Bokelj	L	2-3	Bjedov 2 (1p)
29/05	a	Budućnost	L	0-1	

Name	Nat	DoB	Pos	Aps	(s)	Gls
Bojan Aligrudić		08/02/95	D	16	(9)	
Mladen Božović		01/08/84	G	16		
Darko Bjedov	SRB	28/03/89	A	33		18
Izzet Bylyalov	UKR	13/01/95	A		(3)	
Nemanja Cavnić		05/09/95	D	24	(1)	
Stefan Cvetanović	SRB	03/08/96	D	1		
Božidar Djukić		25/09/97	D	1	(4)	
Nemanja Jakšić	SRB	11/07/95	D	16	(1)	
Luka Klikovac		01/06/93	M	16	(8)	5
Stefan Knežević		07/05/97	M	3		
Koča Krstović		27/03/95	A		(4)	
Nikola Krstović		05/04/00	A		(4)	
Filip Kukuličić		13/02/96	M	23	(9)	3
Darko Marković		15/05/87	M	31		
Goran Milojko		05/01/94	M	14		
Marko Novović		24/11/96	G	4		
Periša Pešukić		07/12/97	M	2	(7)	
Predrag Petošević	SRB	18/10/94	M	3		
Jovan Popović		08/02/96	M		(6)	
Miloš Popović		05/12/96	M	4	(6)	
Filip Radonjić		20/05/96	M		(1)	
Onimisi Segun	NGA	29/11/93	M	4	(7)	
Marko Sekulić		03/02/96	M	4	(1)	
Nemanja Sekulić		29/03/94	D	15		
Radisav Sekulić		27/09/85	A	3	(1)	
Demir Škrijelj		10/07/97	M	3	(9)	
Nenad Šofranac		20/04/83	M	25	(3)	2
Ivan Tomašević		29/10/89	M	1	(2)	
Aleksandar Trišović	SRB	25/11/83	D	16		1
Pavle Velimirović		11/04/90	G	13		
Miljan Vlaisavljević		16/04/91	A	19	(1)	5
Igor Vujačić		08/08/94	D	26		
Stefan Vukčević		11/04/97	M	12	(4)	
Velimir Vukčević		17/05/95	M		(1)	
Stevan Živković	SRB	18/10/89	M	15		3

Top goalscorers

19	Marko Šćepanović (Mladost)
18	Darko Bjedov (Zeta)
16	Dejan Zarubica (Sutjeska)
13	Boris Kopitović (Petrovac)
11	Šaleta Kordić (Sutjeska)
10	Darko Nikač (Budućnost)
9	Pjeter Ljuljdjuraj (Dečić)
8	Darko Djenić (Bokelj)
	Miloš Nikezić (Bokelj)
	Petar Vukčević (Grbalj)
	Blažo Perutović (Lovćen)
	Ivan Marković (Rudar)

Promoted club

FK Jedinstvo Bijelo Polje

1922 • Gradski (5,000) • no website
**Coach: Sead Babača;
(16/01/16) Radislav Dragićević**

Second level final table 2015/16

		Pld	W	D	L	F	A	Pts
1	FK Jedinstvo Bijelo Polje	30	20	5	5	53	15	65
2	FK Cetinje	30	14	8	8	42	31	50
3	FK Bratstvo	30	13	9	8	37	32	48
4	FK Berane	30	11	8	11	45	52	41
5	FK Kom	30	10	10	10	27	31	40
6	FK Radnički	30	9	11	10	39	37	38
7	FK Ibar	30	10	9	11	39	47	35
8	FK Grafičar	30	10	4	16	37	41	34
9	OFK Igalo	30	8	9	13	34	38	33
10	FK Jezero	30	8	7	15	29	46	31
11	FK Brskovo	30	5	14	11	23	35	29

NB FK Ibar – 4 pts deducted.

Promotion/Relegation play-offs

(02/06/16 & 06/06/16)
Bratstvo 2-2 Iskra
Iskra 6-0 Bratstvo
(Iskra 8-2)

Cetinje 0-0 Petrovac
Petrovac 1-0 Cetinje
(Petrovac 1-0)

DOMESTIC CUP

Kup Crne Gore 2015/16

FIRST ROUND

(16/09/15)
Bratstvo 0-3 Sutjeska
Brskovo 2-1 Jezero
Budućnost 5-0 Berane
Cetinje 1-2 Lovćen
Fair Play 0-7 Mornar
Grafičar 1-4 Grbalj
Hajduk 1-2 Jedinstvo
Kom 1-2 Iskra
Petnjica 0-3 Bokelj
Rudar 1-0 Radnički
Sloga 1-2 Mladost Lješkopolje
Zeta 3-1 Igalo
Zora 0-1 Dečić

Byes – Mladost Podgorica, Ibar, Petrovac

SECOND ROUND

(23/09/15 & 21/10/15)
Bokelj 3-0, 1-2 Iskra *(4-2)*
Grbalj 1-2, 0-4 Budućnost *(1-6)*
Ibar 0-2, 1-5 Dečić *(1-7)*
Lovćen 3-0, 2-3 Mladost Lješkopolje *(5-3)*
Mladost Podgorica 2-0, 0-0 Jedinstvo *(2-0)*
Petrovac 0-1, 1-1 Mornar *(1-2)*
Rudar 1-0, 3-0 Sutjeska *(4-0)*
Zeta 3-0, 1-2 Brskovo *(4-2)*

QUARTER-FINALS

(04/11/15 & 25/11/15)
Budućnost 2-0 Zeta *(M Burzanović 61, Hočko 82)*
Zeta 0-0 Budućnost
(Budućnost 2-0)

Dečić 2-2 Rudar *(Pepić 89, Ljuljdjuraj 90; Vlahović 51, Knežević 78)*
Rudar 2-1 Dečić *(Knežević 59, 72; Ramović 69)*
(Rudar 4-3)

Lovćen 3-1 Mornar *(Vojvodić 4og, Djalac 24, Flávio Beck 35; Kim 21)*
Mornar 0-3 Lovćen *(Djalac 20, Jablan 29, Rogošić 77)*
(Lovćen 6-1)

(04/11/15 & 02/12/15)
Mladost Podgorica 0-2 Bokelj *(Mladenović 31, Pepić 90)*
Bokelj 2-1 Mladost Podgorica *(Nikezić 7, Pepić 40; Golubović 90)*
(Bokelj 4-1)

SEMI-FINALS

(13/04/16 & 27/04/16)
Bokelj 0-1 Rudar *(Božović 38)*
Rudar 2-0 Bokelj *(Marković 21, 25)*
(Rudar 3-0)

Budućnost 2-0 Lovćen *(Pejaković 64, Mirković 86)*
Lovćen 1-1 Budućnost *(Marković 5; Djalović 58p)*
(Budućnost 3-1)

FINAL

(02/06/16)
Pod Goricom, Podgorica
FK RUDAR PLJEVLJA 0
FK BUDUĆNOST PODGORICA 0
(aet; 4-3 on pens)
Referee: Novović
RUDAR: Radanović, Nestorović, Reljić, Živković, Alić, Soppo, Vlahović, Brnović, Jovanović (Božović 60), Noma (Knežević 105; Marković 118), Ivanović
BUDUĆNOST: Ljuljanović, N Vukčević, Pajović (Mitrović 6), Mirković, Raspopović, Tomković, Pejaković, Hočko (Vušurović 66), Raičković, M Burzanović (Vujačić 108), Djalović

A penalty shoot-out win against Budućnost brought Rudar a record fourth Montenegrin Cup triumph

NETHERLANDS
Koninklijke Nederlandse Voetbalbond (KNVB)

Address	Woudenbergseweg 56-58	**President**	Michael van Praag
	Postbus 515	**General secretary**	Bert van Oostveen
	NL-3700 AM Zeist	**Media officer**	Bas Ticheler
Tel	+31 343 499 201	**Year of formation**	1889
Fax	+31 343 499 189		
E-mail	concern@knvb.nl		
Website	knvb.nl		

EREDIVISIE CLUBS

 1 **ADO Den Haag**

 2 **AFC Ajax**

 3 **AZ Alkmaar**

 4 **SC Cambuur**

 5 **SBV Excelsior**

 6 **Feyenoord**

 7 **De Graafschap**

 8 **FC Groningen**

 9 **sc Heerenveen**

 10 **Heracles Almelo**

 11 **NEC Nijmegen**

 12 **PEC Zwolle**

 13 **PSV Eindhoven**

 14 **Roda JC**

 15 **FC Twente**

 16 **FC Utrecht**

 17 **Vitesse**

 18 **Willem II**

PROMOTED CLUBS

 19 **Sparta Rotterdam**

 20 **Go Ahead Eagles**

KEY

● UEFA Champions League

● UEFA Europa League

● Promoted

● Relegated

PSV prevail in gripping finale

Runaway Dutch champions the previous season, PSV Eindhoven retained the Eredivisie title against the odds on the final day in 2015/16, winning 3-1 at PEC Zwolle as their rivals Ajax, ahead at kick-off on goal difference, were dramatically held 1-1 at lowly De Graafschap.

The Netherlands was plunged into mourning in March with the death of the country's most iconic footballer, Johan Cruyff. His passing intensified the gloom surrounding Dutch football following the national team's failure to qualify for UEFA EURO 2016.

Eredivisie title eludes Ajax after last-day draw

Feyenoord overcome Utrecht to win Dutch Cup

Dutch legend Johan Cruyff passes away at 68

Domestic league

Never shy of passing an opinion or two, the incomparable Cruyff would undoubtedly have had some harsh words to say about his beloved Ajax for the way in which they allowed the Dutch title to slip through their fingers on a sunny Sunday afternoon of high drama in early May.

Having defeated PSV 2-0 in Eindhoven on 20 March – just four days before Cruyff's death – Ajax looked firmly in control of the race for a title they had surrendered to their southern rivals the previous season after winning it for a record-equalling four years in a row. They now had a two-point advantage with six games to go, and although that lead would be erased with a 2-2 home draw against FC Utrecht, the Amsterdammers' goal difference was sufficiently advantageous to leave them comfortable in the knowledge that any win on the final day in Doetinchem – where PSV had won 6-3 earlier in the season – would secure a record-extending 34th national title.

PSV, meanwhile, travelled to Zwolle on a wing and a prayer. Phillip Cocu's title holders had won all five fixtures since the home defeat by Ajax – the first time in 55 league games that they had failed

to score – and they had also significantly increased their goal tally, but not enough to give themselves a realistic chance of taking the title on goal difference. For that to happen they had to beat Zwolle by a margin of six goals more than Ajax managed against De Graafschap.

At half-time the expected scenario was being played out, with PSV 2-0 up at Zwolle – through Jürgen Locadia and leading marksman Luuk de Jong – and Ajax a goal to the good in De Vijverberg thanks to Amin Younes's 16th-minute curler. But ten minutes into the second half things got very interesting when Bryan Smeets, without a goal all season, drove in from the edge of the area and equalised for De Graafschap. Zwolle also pulled a goal back against PSV, but that was immediately wiped out by De Jong's second, putting three points safely in PSV's pocket. The spotlight was now fully focused on Ajax's efforts to restore their lead, but their hosts, already consigned to the promotion/relegation play-offs, repelled everything Ajax could throw at them, heroically holding out until the final whistle.

Ajax's agony spelt ecstasy for PSV as they celebrated their 23rd Dutch title. There had been concern that the club would struggle to fill the void left by their

two Dutch international stars Georginio Wijnaldum and Memphis Depay, both departed for the English Premier League, but newcomers Davy Pröpper and Gastón Pereiro – who scored both goals in the 2-1 win at Ajax in October – both performed well, as did 2014/15 stalwarts De Jong, Andrés Guardado, Jeffrey Bruma and Jeroen Zoet, who together formed a solid backbone on which Cocu could always depend. The final tallies of 84 points and 88 goals were both just four short of the previous season's totals, but the decisive figure was the 13 away wins, one more than Ajax, who otherwise had an identical breakdown of results.

Ajax boasted as many quality performers as PSV, with skipper Davy Klaassen and full-backs Joël Veltman and Mitchell Dijks the cream of the local crop alongside 21-goal Polish international Arkadiusz 'Arek' Milik and Serbian midfielder Nebojša Gudelj, a shrewd buy from AZ Alkmaar. As he had done since he took over in November 2010, Frank de Boer did a fine job of putting all the pieces together and making Ajax both successful and entertaining to watch – as average home gates of 46,853 in 2015/16 testified – but a failure to clinch a fifth title in six seasons resulted in his resignation just three days after the season's climax.

Former Vitesse coach Peter Bosz – a man with strong Feyenoord connections – was the surprise appointment to replace him.

Feyenoord, with Giovanni van Bronckhorst in charge, were actually rubbing shoulders at the top with PSV and Ajax until December, when their form suddenly evaporated and they succumbed to a club-record seven successive league defeats. They did, however, recover to finish third, with veteran striker Dirk Kuyt, back at the club after nine years away, showing few signs of wear and tear at 35 by scoring 19 goals. Fourth-placed AZ possessed the Eredivisie's top marksman in 21-year-old Vincent Janssen, whose debut top-flight campaign produced a remarkable yield of 27 goals – one more than PSV's De Jong.

The post-season action delivered a couple of interesting outcomes. De Graafschap, for all their efforts against Ajax, could not avoid relegation, going down with bottom-placed SC Cambuur after a two-legged 5-2 play-off defeat against Go Ahead Eagles, who thus joined Eerste Divisie champions Sparta Rotterdam in promotion. In the UEFA Europa League qualification play-offs Heracles Almelo beat FC Groningen and Utrecht to qualify for a first tilt at European football and bring a happy ending to the campaign for John

Stegeman's side, who began it like a house on fire with eight wins in 11 games, including a first victory over PSV (2-1) for over half a century.

Domestic cup

Ajax and holders Groningen were both early fallers in the KNVB-Beker. Both of their respective conquerors, Feyenoord and Utrecht, would go on to contest the Rotterdam final, the latter after winning 3-1 at PSV in the quarter-finals and then ending the fairytale run of seaside club VVSB – the first amateur side to reach the semi-finals for 41 years. Feyenoord, whose 1-0 victory over Ajax came courtesy of a Veltman own goal, were also indebted to a member of the opposition for their winner in the final – Utrecht goalkeeper Filip Bednarek, who diverted Eljero Elia's effort into his own net 15 minutes from time. The 2-1 victory gave Van Bronckhorst his first trophy as a coach and the club their first silverware for eight years – since their 2008 cup final win over Roda JC, also played on home turf at De Kuip.

Europe

In addition to defending their Eredivisie crown, PSV made 2015/16 a season to remember by reaching the knockout phase of the UEFA Champions League – the first Dutch club to so since they

advanced to the quarter-finals in 2006/07. Another last-eight appearance only eluded them because of a penalty shoot-out defeat by Atlético Madrid – the team that would eliminate Barcelona and Bayern München before succumbing to penalties themselves in the final. PSV progressed through the group stage thanks to nine points out of nine in Eindhoven plus a goalless draw away to Manchester United.

There was no such joy for the Netherlands' three operatives in the UEFA Europa League group stage as Ajax – unexpectedly eliminated from the UEFA Champions League preliminaries by Rapid Wien – joined AZ and Groningen as pre-Christmas casualties, the three teams managing just two victories between them. Ajax's only defeat was at Fenerbahçe but four draws meant that the UEFA Europa League knockout phase took place without them for the first time.

National team

New Bondscoach Danny Blind got his reign off to a rotten start as the Netherlands lost a crucial UEFA EURO 2016 qualifier at home to Iceland, who thus did the double over them, but things would get even worse for Guus Hiddink's successor as the Oranje lost two of their next three qualifiers as well, conceding three goals both away to Turkey and at home to the Czech Republic, to suffer premature elimination from a competition whose final tournament they had attended on each of the past seven occasions, winning the first of them in 1988. Even with room for 24 nations in the expanded tournament, the team that finished third at the 2014 FIFA World Cup could not qualify – nor indeed make it to the play-offs.

A renaissance in the spring, when a new-look Oranje took on four UEFA EURO 2016 participants away from home and beat three of them (England, Poland and Austria) while drawing with the other (Republic of Ireland), hinted at better times ahead. Preceding those matches was a friendly against France in Amsterdam that was halted in the 14th minute in order to allow everyone present to pay due respect and tribute to the one and only Johan Cruyff – not only the greatest Dutch footballer of them all but also one of the best players and coaches the world has ever seen, a true and unforgettable legend of the game.

Joy for PSV's Davy Pröpper as he scores the winning goal against CSKA Moskva that puts his team into the UEFA Champions League knockout phase

DOMESTIC SEASON AT A GLANCE

Eredivisie 2015/16 final table

		Pld	Home					Away					Total					Pts
			W	D	L	F	A	W	D	L	F	A	W	D	L	F	A	
1	**PSV Eindhoven**	34	13	3	1	41	16	13	3	1	47	16	26	6	2	88	32	84
2	AFC Ajax	34	13	3	1	49	12	12	4	1	32	9	25	7	2	81	21	82
3	Feyenoord	34	11	3	3	33	14	8	3	6	29	26	19	6	9	62	40	63
4	AZ Alkmaar	34	10	2	5	38	24	8	3	6	32	29	18	5	11	70	53	59
5	FC Utrecht	34	9	4	4	30	24	6	4	7	27	24	15	8	11	57	48	53
6	Heracles Almelo	34	9	5	3	28	23	5	4	8	19	26	14	9	11	47	49	51
7	FC Groningen	34	10	3	4	25	19	4	5	8	16	29	14	8	12	41	48	50
8	PEC Zwolle	34	10	2	5	35	27	4	4	9	21	27	14	6	14	56	54	48
9	Vitesse	34	7	4	6	30	18	5	6	6	25	20	12	10	12	55	38	46
10	NEC Nijmegen	34	11	2	4	25	17	2	5	10	12	25	13	7	14	37	42	46
11	ADO Den Haag	34	4	8	5	20	22	6	5	6	28	27	10	13	11	48	49	43
12	sc Heerenveen	34	6	4	7	24	29	5	5	7	22	32	11	9	14	46	61	42
13	FC Twente	34	9	3	5	31	25	3	4	10	18	39	12	7	15	49	64	40
14	Roda JC	34	3	6	8	15	25	5	4	8	19	30	8	10	16	34	55	34
15	SBV Excelsior	34	4	5	8	21	31	3	4	10	13	29	7	9	18	34	60	30
16	Willem II	34	3	6	8	19	26	3	5	9	16	27	6	11	17	35	53	29
17	De Graafschap	34	3	6	8	23	29	2	2	13	16	37	5	8	21	39	66	23
18	SC Cambuur	34	2	5	10	12	32	1	4	12	21	47	3	9	22	33	79	18

NB FC Twente – 3 pts deducted.

European qualification 2016/17

Champion: PSV Eindhoven (group stage)
AFC Ajax (third qualifying round)

Cup winner: Feyenoord (group stage)
AZ Alkmaar (third qualifying round)
Heracles Almelo (third qualifying round)

Top scorer	Vincent Janssen (AZ), 27 goals
Relegated clubs	SC Cambuur, De Graafschap
Promoted clubs	Sparta Rotterdam, Go Ahead Eagles
Cup final	Feyenoord 2-1 FC Utrecht

Team of the season
(4-4-2)

Coach: Stegeman (Heracles)

Vermeer (Feyenoord)

Veltman (Ajax) — Letschert (Utrecht) — Moreno (PSV) — Dijks (Ajax)

Klaassen (Ajax) — Guardado (PSV) — Bel Hassani (Heracles) — Younes (Ajax)

Janssen (AZ) — De Jong (PSV)

Player of the season

Davy Klaassen
(AFC Ajax)

Named as the new Ajax captain for 2015/16, Klaassen did everything he could to bring the Dutch title back to Amsterdam, only to fall frustratingly short at the finish. The armband brought out the best in the blond schemer – as did the acquisition of the more defensively-minded Nebojša Gudelj – and he more than doubled his tally of Eredivisie goals from the previous campaign, scoring 13 times. The 23-year-old may not have lifted the league trophy but he did win the Golden Shoe awarded to the Eredivisie player of the season.

Newcomer of the season

Vincent Janssen
(AZ Alkmaar)

Released as a youngster by Feyenoord, Janssen went on to score for fun in the Dutch second division with Almere City, but the impact he had on his debut Eredivisie campaign with AZ was none the less remarkable. By the turn of the year the 21-year-old had scored only six goals, but thereafter he became unstoppable, adding another 21 to his tally, including a hat-trick against Feyenoord, to win the golden boot. He also turned on the style for the Netherlands and joined Tottenham Hotspur in the summer for a €20 million fee.

NETHERLANDS

NATIONAL TEAM

International honours
UEFA European Championship (1) 1988

International tournament appearances
FIFA World Cup (10) 1934, 1938, 1974 (runners-up), 1978 (runners-up), 1990 (2nd round), 1994 (qtr-finals), 1998 (4th), 2006 (2nd round), 2010 (runners-up), 2014 (3rd)
UEFA European Championship (9) 1976 (3rd), 1980, 1988 (Winners), 1992 (semi-finals), 1996 (qtr-finals), 2000 (semi-finals), 2004 (semi-finals), 2008 (qtr-finals), 2012

Top five all-time caps
Edwin van der Sar (130); **Wesley Sneijder** (121); Frank de Boer (112); Rafael van der Vaart (109); Giovanni van Bronckhorst (106)

Top five all-time goals
Robin van Persie (50); **Klaas-Jan Huntelaar** (42); Patrick Kluivert (40); Dennis Bergkamp (37); Ruud van Nistelrooy & Faas Wilkes (35)

Results 2015/16

Date	Opponent	H/A	Venue	Res	Score	Scorers
03/09/15	Iceland (ECQ)	H	Amsterdam	L	0-1	
06/09/15	Turkey (ECQ)	A	Konya	L	0-3	
10/10/15	Kazakhstan (ECQ)	A	Astana	W	2-1	Wijnaldum (33), Sneijder (50)
13/10/15	Czech Republic (ECQ)	H	Amsterdam	L	2-3	Huntelaar (70), Van Persie (83)
13/11/15	Wales	A	Cardiff	W	3-2	Dost (32), Robben (54, 81)
25/03/16	France	H	Amsterdam	L	2-3	De Jong (47), Afellay (86)
29/03/16	England	A	London	W	2-1	Janssen (50p), Narsingh (77)
27/05/16	Republic of Ireland	A	Dublin	D	1-1	De Jong (85)
01/06/16	Poland	A	Gdansk	W	2-1	Janssen (33), Wijnaldum (76)
04/06/16	Austria	A	Vienna	W	2-0	Janssen (9), Wijnaldum (66)

Appearances 2015/16

Coach: Danny Blind 01/08/61

Name	DOB	Club	ISL	TUR	KAZ	CZE	Wal	Fra	Eng	Irl	Pol	Aut	Caps	Goals
Jasper Cillessen	22/04/89	Ajax	G	G			G	G		G	G	s74	30	-
Gregory van der Wiel	03/02/88	Paris (FRA)	D	D									46	-
Stefan de Vrij	05/02/92	Lazio (ITA)	D	D46									30	3
Bruno Martins Indi	08/02/92	Porto (POR)	D33*										31	2
Daley Blind	09/03/90	Man. United (ENG)	D	M74	M	M	D	D	D				36	2
Georginio Wijnaldum	11/11/90	Newcastle (ENG)	M80	s46	M	M	s90	s76	M	M82	M	M	30	6
Davy Klaassen	21/02/93	Ajax	M	M				M76					5	1
Wesley Sneijder	09/06/84	Galatasaray (TUR)	M	M	M80	M	M	M37					121	29
Arjen Robben	23/01/84	Bayern (GER)	A31					A					88	30
Klaas-Jan Huntelaar	12/08/83	Schalke (GER)	A40		A87	A							76	42
Memphis Depay	13/02/94	Man. United (ENG)	A	A	A	A		s46	A		A61		24	3
Luciano Narsingh	13/09/90	PSV	s31	A69				s37			s67	s61	18	4
Jeffrey Bruma	13/11/91	PSV	s40	D	D	D	D	D	D	D	D	D	19	1
Quincy Promes	04/01/92	Spartak Moskva (RUS)	s80	s69			A90	A	A37	A	A	A	12	-
Jaïro Riedewald	09/09/96	Ajax			D	D39							3	-
Robin van Persie	06/08/83	Fenerbahçe (TUR)				A	s87	s39					101	50
Luuk de Jong	27/08/90	PSV		s74									12	3
Tim Krul	03/04/88	Newcastle (ENG)					G81						8	-
Kenny Tete	09/10/95	Ajax			D	D							4	-
Virgil van Dijk	08/07/91	Southampton (ENG)			D	D64	M46	D46		D	D	D	7	-
Anwar El Ghazi	03/05/95	Ajax			A	A69							2	-
Ibrahim Afellay	02/04/86	Stoke (ENG)					s80	s46	M				53	7
Jeroen Zoet	06/01/91	PSV				G			G			G74	4	-
Bas Dost	31/05/89	Wolfsburg (GER)					A	s64					6	1
Jeremain Lens	24/11/87	Sunderland (ENG)					s69	A					31	8
Daryl Janmaat	22/07/89	Newcastle (ENG)								D			27	-
Terence Kongolo	14/02/94	Feyenoord								D			3	-
Jordy Clasie	27/06/91	Southampton (ENG)					M87	M46	s90				15	-
Joël Veltman	15/01/92	Ajax						s46	D	D		s86	12	-
Riechedly Bazoer	12/10/96	Ajax					s87	s37	M78	M	M	M79	6	-
Jetro Willems	30/03/94	PSV						D78	D82	D	D46		20	-
Patrick van Aanholt	29/08/90	Sunderland (ENG)						s78	s82		s46		6	-
Vincent Janssen	15/06/94	AZ						s81	A90	A75	A74	A65	5	3
Marco van Ginkel	01/12/92	PSV							s78	s70	M71	s71	6	-
Kevin Strootman	13/02/90	Roma (ITA)								M70	s71	M71	28	3
Steven Berghuis	19/12/91	Watford (ENG)								s61	A67	A61	3	-
Tonny Trindade de Vilhena	03/01/95	Feyenoord										s79	1	-

EUROPE

AFC Ajax

Third qualifying round - SK Rapid Wien (AUT)
A 2-2 *Klaassen (25, 43)*
Cillessen, Veltman, Bazoer, Sinkgraven, Milik (Sanogo 84), Klaassen, El Ghazi (Fischer 74), Riedewald, Tete, Gudelj, Dijks. Coach: Frank de Boer (NED)
H 2-3 *Milik (52), Gudelj (75)*
Cillessen, Veltman (Sanogo 71), Bazoer, Fischer (Gudelj 59), Sinkgraven (Schöne 87), Milik, Klaassen, El Ghazi, Riedewald, Tete, Dijks. Coach: Frank de Boer (NED)

Play-offs - FK Jablonec (CZE)
H 1-0 *Milik (54p)*
Cillessen, Veltman, Bazoer, Sinkgraven (Schöne 71), Milik, Klaassen, El Ghazi (Černý 85), Riedewald, Tete, Gudelj, Dijks. Coach: Frank de Boer (NED)
A 0-0
Cillessen, Veltman, Bazoer, Sinkgraven (Fischer 46), Milik (Van Rhijn 69), Klaassen, El Ghazi, Riedewald, Tete, Dijks. Coach: Frank de Boer (NED)
Red card: Bazoer 59

Group A
Match 1 - Celtic FC (SCO)
H 2-2 *Fischer (25), Schöne (84)*
Cillessen, Veltman, Fischer (Schöne 75), Sinkgraven (Serero 62), Klaassen, Younes (Milik 62), El Ghazi, Riedewald, Tete, Gudelj, Dijks. Coach: Frank de Boer (NED)
Match 2 - Molde FK (NOR)
A 1-1 *Fischer (19)*
Cillessen, Veltman, Bazoer (Serero 89), Fischer, Milik (Younes 81), Klaassen, El Ghazi, Riedewald, Tete, Gudelj, Dijks. Coach: Frank de Boer (NED)
Match 3 - Fenerbahçe SK (TUR)
A 0-1
Cillessen, Van Rhijn (Tete 63), Veltman, Bazoer, Fischer (Younes 63), Klaassen, Schöne, El Ghazi (Sinkgraven 77), Riedewald, Gudelj, Dijks. Coach: Frank de Boer (NED)
Match 4 - Fenerbahçe SK (TUR)
H 0-0
Cillessen, Veltman, Bazoer, Fischer (Younes 52), Milik, Klaassen, El Ghazi (Schöne 33), Riedewald, Tete, Viergever, Gudelj (Serero 76). Coach: Frank de Boer (NED)
Match 5 - Celtic FC (SCO)
A 2-1 *Milik (22), Černý (88)*
Cillessen, Van der Hoorn (Sanogo 80), Fischer (Černý 69), Milik, Klaassen, Younes, Schöne (Van de Beek 72), Riedewald, Tete, Gudelj, Dijks. Coach: Frank de Boer (NED)
Match 6 - Molde FK (NOR)
H 1-1 *Van de Beek (14)*
Cillessen, Van Rhijn, Veltman, Fischer (Schöne 78), Milik, Klaassen, Younes (El Ghazi 62), Riedewald, Gudelj, Van de Beek (Bazoer 64), Dijks. Coach: Frank de Boer (NED)
Red card: Gudelj 90

PSV Eindhoven

Group B
Match 1 - Manchester United FC (ENG)
H 2-1 *Moreno (45+2), Narsingh (57)*
Zoet, Moreno, Arias, Bruma, Pröpper, De Jong, Narsingh, Lestienne (Locadia 86), Guardado (Schaars 72), Brenet, Hendrix. Coach: Phillip Cocu (NED)
Match 2 - PFC CSKA Moskva (RUS)
A 2-3 *Lestienne (60, 68)*
Zoet, Moreno, Arias, Bruma, Pröpper, Maher (Vloet 89), Narsingh, Lestienne (Pereiro 77), Locadia, Brenet (Poulsen 77), Hendrix. Coach: Phillip Cocu (NED)
Red card: Arias 80
Match 3 - VfL Wolfsburg (GER)
A 0-2
Zoet, Moreno, Bruma, Pröpper, De Jong (Pereiro 81), Maher, Narsingh, Poulsen (De Wijs 74), Guardado, Brenet, Hendrix (Locadia 73). Coach: Phillip Cocu (NED)
Match 4 - VfL Wolfsburg (GER)
H 2-0 *Locadia (55), De Jong (86)*
Zoet, Moreno, Arias, Bruma, Pröpper, De Jong, Maher (Hendrix 74), Narsingh (Pereiro 83), Guardado, Locadia (Isimat-Mirin 75), Brenet. Coach: Phillip Cocu (NED)
Match 5 - Manchester United FC (ENG)
A 0-0
Zoet, Moreno, Arias, Bruma, Pröpper, De Jong, Narsingh (Pereiro 18), Guardado, Locadia, Brenet, Hendrix (Isimat-Mirin 60). Coach: Phillip Cocu (NED)
Match 6 - PFC CSKA Moskva (RUS)
H 2-1 *De Jong (78), Pröpper (86)*
Zoet, Isimat-Mirin, Moreno, Bruma, Pröpper, Pereiro (Bergwijn 85), De Jong, Guardado, Locadia, Brenet, Hendrix. Coach: Phillip Cocu (NED)

Round of 16 - Club Atlético de Madrid (ESP)
H 0-0
Zoet, Moreno, Arias, Bruma, Pröpper, Pereiro, Narsingh (Isimat-Mirin 65), Willems, Guardado (Hendrix 75), Locadia (Lestienne 86), Van Ginkel. Coach: Phillip Cocu (NED)
Red card: Pereiro 68
A 0-0 (aet; 7-8 on pens)
Zoet, Isimat-Mirin, Moreno, Arias, Bruma, Pröpper, De Jong (Narsingh 118), Willems (Brenet 75), Guardado, Locadia (Lestienne 87), Van Ginkel. Coach: Phillip Cocu (NED)

FC Groningen

Group F
Match 1 - Olympique de Marseille (FRA)
H 0-3
Padt, Kappelhof, De Leeuw, Hoesen (Mahi 66), Rusnák (Drost 70), Linssen, Lindgren, Tibbling, Maduro, Tamata, Hateboer. Coach: Erwin van de Looi (NED)
Match 2 - SC Braga (POR)
A 0-1
Padt, Kappelhof, Reijnen, De Leeuw (Hoesen 83), Rusnák (Larsen 32), Linssen, Mahi (Antonia 82), Tibbling, Maduro, Tamata, Hateboer. Coach: Erwin van de Looi (NED)
Match 3 - FC Slovan Liberec (CZE)
A 1-1 *Hoesen (90+6)*
Padt, Kappelhof, Larsen (Antonia 88), Reijnen, Rusnák, Linssen (Hoesen 69), Mahi, Tibbling, Maduro (De Leeuw 78), Tamata, Hateboer. Coach: Erwin van de Looi (NED)
Red card: De Leeuw 83
Match 4 - FC Slovan Liberec (CZE)
H 0-1
Padt, Kappelhof, Larsen, Burnet, Reijnen, Antonia, Hoesen (Bacuna 67), Rusnák, Linssen, Tibbling (Hateboer 83), Maduro (Drost 78). Coach: Erwin van de Looi (NED)
Match 5 - Olympique de Marseille (FRA)
A 1-2 *Maduro (50)*
Padt, Kappelhof, Larsen, Reijnen, Antonia (Drost 84), Hoesen, Rusnák, Linssen (Tibbling 71), Maduro, Tamata, Hateboer. Coach: Erwin van de Looi (NED)
Match 6 - SC Braga (POR)
H 0-0
Padt, Kappelhof, Larsen, Reijnen, Hoesen (De Leeuw 74), Rusnák, Linssen (Antonia 74), Tibbling, Maduro, Tamata, Hateboer. Coach: Erwin van de Looi (NED)

AZ Alkmaar

Third qualifying round - İstanbul Başakşehir (TUR)
H 2-0 *Van der Linden (18p), Janssen (63)*
Rochet, Johansson, Gouweleeuw, Ortíz, Van Overeem (Jóhannsson 46), Henriksen, Van der Linden, Janssen (Tankovic 74), Dos Santos (Mühren 86), Haye, Haps. Coach: John van den Brom (NED)
A 2-1 *Henriksen (21), Van Overeem (75)*
Rochet, Johansson, Gouweleeuw, Ortíz, Van Overeem (Hupperts 86), Henriksen, Van der Linden, Janssen (Mühren 68), Dos Santos (Vaarnold 78), Haye, Haps. Coach: John van den Brom (NED)

Play-offs - FC Astra Giurgiu (ROU)
A 2-3 *Henriksen (11), Janssen (13)*
Rochet, Johansson, Gouweleeuw, Ortíz (Haye 65), Hupperts (Lewis 46), Van Overeem, Henriksen, Van der Linden, Janssen (Mühren 78), Luckassen, Haps. Coach: John van den Brom (NED)
H 2-0 *Van der Linden (80), Mühren (85)*
Rochet, Johansson, Gouweleeuw, Hupperts, Henriksen, Van der Linden, Janssen (Mühren 78), Dos Santos (Wuytens 89), Haye, Luckassen (Tankovic 78), Haps. Coach: John van den Brom (NED)

Group L
Match 1 - FK Partizan (SRB)
A 2-3 *Van der Linden (34), Henriksen (90+3)*
Rochet, Johansson, Gouweleeuw, Brežančić, Hupperts, Van Overeem (Dos Santos 63), Henriksen, Van der Linden, Rienstra, Janssen (Mühren 73), Haye (Tankovic 73). Coach: John van den Brom (NED)
Red card: Hupperts 77
Match 2 - Athletic Club (ESP)
H 2-1 *Henriksen (55), Bóveda (65og)*
Coutinho, Johansson, Gouweleeuw, Van Overeem, Henriksen, Tankovic (Luckassen 76), Van der Linden, Rienstra, Janssen (Jahanbakhsh 78), Dos Santos (Haye 87), Haps. Coach: John van den Brom (NED)
Match 3 - FC Augsburg (GER)
H 0-1
Coutinho, Johansson (Hupperts 77), Gouweleeuw, Van Overeem, Henriksen, Van der Linden, Rienstra (Haye 61), Janssen, Dos Santos (Tankovic 70), Luckassen, Haps. Coach: John van den Brom (NED)
Match 4 - FC Augsburg (GER)
A 1-4 *Janssen (45+1)*
Coutinho, Johansson, Gouweleeuw, Van Overeem, Jahanbakhsh (Hupperts 76), Henriksen (Haye 37), Van der Linden, Rienstra (Ortíz 52), Janssen, Luckassen, Haps. Coach: John van den Brom (NED)
Match 5 - FK Partizan (SRB)
H 1-2 *Dos Santos (48)*
Coutinho, Johansson, Gouweleeuw, Brežančić, Ortíz (Hupperts 88), Van Overeem (Tankovic 75), Jahanbakhsh (Mühren 80), Henriksen, Janssen, Dos Santos, Luckassen. Coach: John van den Brom (NED)
Match 6 - Athletic Club (ESP)
A 2-2 *Van Overeem (26), Enric Saborit (88og)*
Coutinho, Johansson, Gouweleeuw, Ortíz, Hupperts (Tankovic 64), Van Overeem (Mühren 80), Rienstra, Janssen, Haye, Luckassen, Ouwejan (Hatzidiakos 74). Coach: John van den Brom (NED)

Vitesse

Third qualifying round - Southampton FC (ENG)
A 0-3
Room, Leerdam, Brown, Djurdjević (Rashica 60), Kazaishvili (Pantić 67), Oliynyk, Diks (Lelieveld 90+2), Nakamba, Baker, Achenteh, Kashia. Coach: Peter Bosz (NED)
H 0-2
Room, van der Werff (Achenteh 72), Leerdam, Brown (Nathan 69), Kazaishvili, Oliynyk, Diks, Nakamba, Rashica, Baker (Pantić 81), Kashia. Coach: Peter Bosz (NED)

Go Ahead Eagles

First qualifying round - Ferencvárosi TC (HUN)
H 1-1 *Vriends (45+2)*
Cummins, Vriends, Schenk, Teijsse, Duits (Lambooij 74), Van Overbeek, Türüc, Wolters, Van Ewijk (Rijsdijk 63), Nieuwpoort, Ten Den (Schalk 83). Coach: Dennis Demmers (NED)
A 1-4 *Türüc (90+3)*
Cummins, Vriends, Schenk, Teijsse, Duits (Van Ewijk 73), Van Overbeek, Türüc, Schalk (Ten Den 59), Rijsdijk, Wolters, Nieuwpoort (Lambooij 76). Coach: Dennis Demmers (NED)

DOMESTIC LEAGUE CLUB-BY-CLUB

ADO Den Haag

1971 • ADO Den Haag (15,000) • adodenhaag.nl
Major honours
Dutch Cup (2) 1968, 1975
Coach: Henk Fräser

2015

11/08	h	PSV	D	2-2	Alberg (p), Hansen
15/08	a	Twente	W	4-1	Havenaar, Schaken, Wormgoor, Duplan
23/08	h	Utrecht	D	1-1	Havenaar
30/08	a	Ajax	L	0-4	
13/09	h	Heracles	L	0-1	
19/09	a	Zwolle	L	1-2	Havenaar
27/09	h	Excelsior	D	3-3	Havenaar 2, Zuiverloon
03/10	a	NEC	L	1-4	Wormgoor
18/10	h	De Graafschap	D	1-1	Havenaar
25/10	a	Cambuur	D	1-1	Havenaar
01/11	h	Feyenoord	W	1-0	og (Van Beek)
06/11	a	Roda	D	1-1	Havenaar
22/11	a	Vitesse	D	2-2	Schaken, Derijck (p)
29/11	h	Groningen	L	1-2	Duplan
04/12	a	AZ	W	1-0	Bakker
12/12	h	Willem II	D	1-1	Jansen
20/12	h	Heerenveen	W	4-0	Meijers, Bakker, Beugelsdijk, Jansen

2016

17/01	h	Ajax	L	0-1	
24/01	h	Cambuur	W	2-1	Havenaar 2
27/01	a	De Graafschap	L	1-3	Havenaar
31/01	a	Feyenoord	W	2-0	Jansen, Zuiverloon
06/02	h	Roda	D	2-2	Jansen, Derijck
14/02	a	Excelsior	W	4-2	Jansen, Van der Heijden 2, Havenaar
19/02	h	Zwolle	L	0-2	
27/02	a	PSV	L	0-2	
04/03	h	Twente	W	2-1	Kristensen, Derijck (p)
13/03	a	Utrecht	D	2-2	Bakker, Havenaar
20/03	h	NEC	W	1-0	Malone
03/04	h	Groningen	L	0-1	
09/04	a	Vitesse	D	2-2	Havenaar, og (Van der Werff)
17/04	a	Willem II	W	2-0	Havenaar, og (Van der Struijk)
21/04	h	AZ	L	1-2	Beugelsdijk
01/05	a	Heracles	D	1-1	Duplan
08/05	h	Heerenveen	D	1-1	Havenaar (p)

No	Name	Nat	DoB	Pos	Aps	(s)	Gls
23	Roland Alberg		06/08/90	M	8	(5)	1
17	Danny Bakker		16/01/95	M	32	(1)	3
15	Tom Beugelsdijk		07/08/90	D	21	(3)	2
4	Timothy Derijck	BEL	25/05/87	M	23	(4)	3
21	Édouard Duplan	FRA	13/05/83	A	31		3
15	Kyle Ebecilio		17/04/94	M	1	(5)	
28	Tyronne Ebuehi		16/12/95	D	14		
12	Kenji Gorré		29/09/94	A	1	(4)	
1	Martin Hansen	DEN	15/06/90	G	33		1
9	Mike Havenaar	JPN	20/05/87	A	31		16
31	Hector Hevel		15/05/96	M	1	(2)	
7	Kevin Jansen		08/04/92	M	24	(4)	5
5	Wilfried Kanon	CIV	06/07/93	D	12	(2)	
33	Gervane Kastaneer		09/06/96	A		(5)	
14	Giovanni Korte		01/08/93	A	4	(13)	
6	Thomas Kristensen	DEN	17/04/83	M	14	(4)	1
2	Dion Malone		13/02/89	D	21	(4)	1
11	Ludcinio Marengo		14/09/91	A	3	(18)	
8	Aaron Meijers		28/10/87	D	30		1
20	Ruben Schaken		03/04/82	A	27	(2)	2
19	Dennis van der Heijden		17/02/97	A	1	(8)	2
3	Vito Wormgoor		16/11/88	D	23		2
51	Gianni Zuiverloon		30/12/86	D	18	(4)	2
22	Robert Zwinkels		04/05/83	G	1		

NETHERLANDS

AFC Ajax

1900 • Amsterdam ArenA (51,638) • ajax.nl
Major honours
*European Champion Clubs' Cup/UEFA Champions
League (4) 1971, 1972, 1973, 1995; UEFA Cup
Winners' Cup (1) 1987; UEFA Cup (1) 1992;
UEFA Super Cup (3) 1972, 1974, 1995; European/
South American Cup (2) 1972, 1995; Dutch League
(33) 1918, 1919, 1931, 1932, 1934, 1937, 1939,
1947, 1957, 1960, 1966, 1967, 1968, 1970, 1972,
1973, 1977, 1979, 1980, 1982, 1983, 1985, 1990,
1994, 1995, 1996, 1998, 2002, 2004, 2011, 2012,
2013, 2014; Dutch Cup (18) 1917, 1943, 1961, 1967,
1970, 1971, 1972, 1979, 1983, 1986, 1987, 1993,
1998, 1999, 2002, 2006, 2007, 2010*

Coach: Frank de Boer

2015

09/08	a	AZ	W	3-0	El Ghazi 2, Gudelj
15/08	h	Willem II	W	3-0	Milik, El Ghazi 2
23/08	a	NEC	W	2-0	Milik, og (Van Eijden)
30/08	h	Den Haag	W	4-0	El Ghazi 2, Klaassen, Veltman
12/09	a	Twente	D	2-2	Fischer, Gudelj (p)
20/09	a	Excelsior	W	2-0	El Ghazi, Milik
26/09	h	Groningen	W	2-0	Gudelj, Fischer
04/10	h	PSV	L	1-2	Younes
17/10	a	Heracles	W	2-0	El Ghazi, Gudelj
25/10	a	Vitesse	W	3-1	Fischer, Bazoer, Schöne
31/10	h	Roda	W	6-0	Fischer 2, Milik 2, Klaassen 2
08/11	a	Feyenoord	D	1-1	Klaassen
21/11	h	Cambuur	W	5-1	Veltman, Milik, Klaassen 2, Younes
29/11	a	Zwolle	W	2-0	Younes, Serero
05/12	h	Heerenveen	W	5-2	Fischer 2, Milik, Younes, Klaassen
13/12	a	Utrecht	L	0-1	
20/12	h	De Graafschap	W	2-1	Milik, Bazoer
2016					
17/01	h	Den Haag	W	1-0	Younes
23/01	a	Vitesse	W	1-0	Bazoer
26/01	h	Heracles	D	0-0	
31/01	h	Roda	D	2-2	Milik, El Ghazi
07/02	h	Feyenoord	W	2-1	Younes, Bazoer
14/02	a	Groningen	W	2-1	El Ghazi, Schöne (p)
21/02	h	Excelsior	W	3-0	Milik 2, Klaassen
28/02	a	AZ	W	4-1	Milik 2, Klaassen 2
06/03	a	Willem II	W	4-0	Milik, Bazoer, Schöne, Klaassen
13/03	h	NEC	D	2-2	Milik, og (Van Eijden)
20/03	a	PSV	W	2-0	Milik, El Ghazi
03/04	h	Zwolle	W	3-0	Schöne, Milik 2
09/04	a	Cambuur	W	1-0	Klaassen
17/04	a	Utrecht	D	2-2	Klaassen, Milik (p)
20/04	h	Heerenveen	W	2-0	Milik 2 (1p)
01/05	h	Twente	W	4-0	Černý, Van der Hoorn, Fischer, Younes
08/05	a	De Graafschap	D	1-1	Younes

No	Name	Nat	DoB	Pos	Aps	(s)	Gls
6	Riechedly Bazoer		12/10/96	M	27	(2)	5
33	Diederik Boer		24/09/80	G	1		
32	Václav Černý	CZE	17/10/97	A	2	(5)	1
1	Jasper Cillessen		22/04/89	G	33		
35	Mitchell Dijks		09/02/93	D	29		
21	Anwar El Ghazi		03/05/95	A	20	(7)	11
7	Viktor Fischer	DEN	09/06/94	A	10	(18)	8
	Nemanja Gudelj	SRB	16/11/91	M	34		4
5	John Heitinga		15/11/83	D		(2)	
29	Sam Hendriks		25/01/95	A		(1)	
10	Davy Klaassen		21/02/93	M	30	(1)	13
9	Arkadiusz Milik	POL	28/02/94	A	28	(3)	21
18	Robert Murić	CRO	12/03/96	M		(2)	
22	Jaïro Riedewald		09/09/96	D	21	(2)	
19	Yaya Sanogo	FRA	27/01/93	A		(3)	
20	Lasse Schöne	DEN	27/05/86	M	12	(12)	4
25	Thulani Serero	RSA	11/04/90	M	6	(8)	1
8	Daley Sinkgraven		04/07/95	M	10	(6)	
23	Kenny Tete		09/10/95	D	19	(2)	
30	Donny van de Beek		18/04/97	M	4	(4)	
4	Mike van der Hoorn		15/10/92	D	13	(2)	1
2	Ricardo van Rhijn		13/06/91	D	2	(10)	
	Joël Veltman		15/01/92	D	34		2
26	Nick Viergever		03/08/89	D	14	(3)	
11	Amin Younes	GER	06/08/93	M	25	(2)	8

AZ Alkmaar

1967 • DSB (17,150) • az.nl
Major honours
*Dutch League (2) 1981, 2009; Dutch Cup (4) 1978,
1981, 1982, 2013*

Coach: John van den Brom

2015

09/08	h	Ajax	L	0-3	
15/08	a	Excelsior	D	2-2	Henriksen, Mühren
23/08	h	Willem II	D	0-0	
30/08	h	Roda	L	0-1	
12/09	a	De Graafschap	W	3-1	Brežančić, Henriksen 2
20/09	a	Groningen	L	0-2	
26/09	h	Heracles	W	3-1	Henriksen, Gouweleeuw, Tankovic
04/10	h	Twente	W	3-1	Janssen 2, Hupperts
17/10	a	Cambuur	D	1-1	Janssen
25/10	a	Feyenoord	L	1-3	Van Overeem
01/11	h	NEC	L	2-4	Henriksen 2
08/11	a	Vitesse	W	2-0	Janssen, Henriksen
21/11	h	Heerenveen	W	3-1	Janssen 2, El Hamdaoui
29/11	a	PSV	L	0-3	
04/12	h	Den Haag	L	0-1	
13/12	a	Zwolle	L	1-2	Tankovic
19/12	h	Utrecht	D	2-2	Johansson, Gouweleeuw (p)
2016					
16/01	h	Roda	W	1-0	Janssen
24/01	h	Feyenoord	W	4-2	Henriksen, Janssen 3
27/01	h	Cambuur	W	3-1	Janssen 2, Van Overeem
30/01	a	NEC	W	3-0	Henriksen, Jahanbakhsh, Garcia
06/02	h	Vitesse	W	1-0	Janssen
13/02	a	Heracles	W	6-3	Janssen, Henriksen (p), Van Overeem, Jahanbakhsh, og (Bruns), Rienstra
20/02	h	Groningen	W	4-1	Janssen, Vlaar, Haps, Henriksen
28/02	a	Ajax	L	1-4	Janssen
06/03	h	Excelsior	W	2-0	Luckassen, Janssen (p)
12/03	h	Willem II	W	2-0	Janssen 2 (1p)
20/03	a	Twente	D	2-2	Janssen, Haye
02/04	h	PSV	L	2-4	Van der Linden, Tankovic
10/04	a	Heerenveen	L	2-4	Dos Santos, Janssen
16/04	a	Zwolle	W	5-1	Janssen 4 (2p), Dos Santos
21/04	a	Den Haag	W	2-1	Dos Santos, Henriksen
01/05	h	De Graafschap	W	4-1	Janssen (p), Haps, Jahanbakhsh, Van Overeem
08/05	a	Utrecht	W	3-1	Haps, Dos Santos, Janssen

No	Name	Nat	DoB	Pos	Aps	(s)	Gls
5	Rajko Brežančić	SRB	21/08/89	D	7	(1)	1
7	Gino Coutinho		05/08/82	G	11		
19	Dabney dos Santos		31/07/96	M	25	(5)	4
15	Mounir El Hamdaoui	MAR	14/07/84	A	7		1
28	Levi Garcia	TRI	20/11/97	A	4	(4)	1
3	Jeffrey Gouweleeuw		10/07/91	D	16		2
24	Ridgeciano Haps		12/06/93	D	26	(1)	4
33	Pantelis Hatzidiakos	GRE	18/01/97	D	1	(3)	
20	Thom Haye		09/02/95	M	10	(15)	1
10	Markus Henriksen	NOR	25/07/92	M	28		12
7	Guus Hupperts		25/04/92	A	4	(9)	1
9	Alireza Jahanbakhsh	IRN	11/08/93	A	21	(2)	3
18	Vincent Janssen		15/06/94	A	32	(2)	27
2	Mattias Johansson	SWE	16/02/92	D	26		1
29	Fernando Lewis		31/01/93	D	1		
23	Derrick Luckassen		21/07/95	D	13	(8)	1
21	Robert Mühren		18/05/89	M	1	(17)	1
32	Levi Opdam		03/05/96	D	1		
38	Celso Ortíz	PAR	26/01/89	M	6	(12)	
38	Thomas Ouwejan		24/06/96	M	2	(1)	
17	Ben Rienstra		13/05/90	M	26	(2)	1
1	Sergio Rochet	URU	23/03/93	G	23		
11	Muamer Tankovic	SWE	22/02/95	A	6	(13)	3
22	Achille Vaarnold		26/01/96	A	1		
14	Jop van der Linden		17/07/90	D	13	(1)	1
8	Joris van Overeem		01/06/94	M	31	(2)	4
12	Ron Vlaar		16/02/85	D	17		1
30	Stijn Wuytens	BEL	08/10/89	M	15		

SC Cambuur

1964 • Cambuurstadion (10,000) • cambuur.nl
**Coach: Henk de Jong;
(13/02/16) Marcel Keizer**

2015

12/08	h	Zwolle	D	2-2	Bakker, Overgoor
16/08	h	Feyenoord	L	0-2	
22/08	h	Heracles	L	1-6	Ogbeche
30/08	a	Vitesse	L	1-4	Van de Streek
12/09	h	PSV	L	0-6	
19/09	h	Twente	D	0-0	
26/09	a	Utrecht	D	3-3	Ogbeche 2, Van de Streek
03/10	a	Roda	D	1-1	Ogbeche
17/10	h	AZ	D	1-1	Ogbeche
25/10	h	Den Haag	D	1-1	Narsingh
01/11	a	Heerenveen	L	0-2	
08/11	h	Groningen	D	2-2	Barto 2
21/11	a	Ajax	L	1-5	Van de Streek
27/11	h	De Graafschap	L	2-3	Overgoor, og (Will)
06/12	a	Willem II	L	0-2	
12/12	h	NEC	W	3-1	Ogbeche 2, og (Santos)
20/12	a	Excelsior	W	4-1	Ogbeche 2, Byrne, Monteiro
2016					
16/01	h	Vitesse	L	0-2	
24/01	a	Den Haag	L	1-2	Van de Streek
27/01	a	AZ	L	1-3	Barto
31/01	h	Heerenveen	L	0-1	
07/02	a	Groningen	L	0-2	
12/02	h	Utrecht	L	0-2	
20/02	a	Twente	L	0-3	
27/02	h	Zwolle	W	1-0	Byrne
06/03	a	Feyenoord	L	1-3	Barto
13/03	h	Heracles	L	1-3	Byrne
19/03	h	Roda	L	0-1	
02/04	a	De Graafschap	D	2-2	Mac-Intosch, Van Veen
09/04	a	Ajax	L	1-1	
17/04	a	NEC	L	1-2	Hoefdraad
21/04	h	Willem II	D	1-1	Monteiro
01/05	h	PSV	L	2-6	Mac-Intosch, Byrne
08/05	h	Excelsior	L	0-2	

No	Name	Nat	DoB	Pos	Aps	(s)	Gls
16	Djavan Anderson		21/04/95	D	8	(1)	
4	Vytautas Andriuškevičius	LTU	08/10/90	D	25		
6	Erik Bakker		21/03/90	M	22	(3)	1
8	Martijn Barto		23/08/84	A	20	(8)	4
19	Valmir Berisha	SWE	06/06/96	A	1	(5)	
39	Noureddine Boutzamar		09/04/94	M		(1)	
10	Jack Byrne	IRL	24/04/96	M	25	(2)	4
3	Wessel Dammers		01/03/95	D	14	(5)	
41	Omar El Baad		01/02/96	D	1		
2	Kai Heerings		12/01/90	D	3	(2)	
24	Tom Hiariej		25/07/88	M	5	(5)	
15	Jergé Hoefdraad		17/07/96	M	4	(4)	1
12	Xander Houtkoop		26/03/89	A	8	(12)	
45	Ron Janzen		05/01/94	D		(1)	
29	Darryl Lachman	CUW	11/11/89	D	15		
30	Calvin Mac-Intosch		09/08/90	D	12	(2)	2
11	Dominik Mašek	CZE	10/07/95	A	1	(1)	
35	Jamiro Monteiro		28/11/93	M	17	(3)	2
7	Furdjel Narsingh		13/03/88	A	19	(7)	1
22	Leonard Nienhuis		16/03/90	G	28	(1)	
18	Bartholomew Ogbeche	NGA	01/10/84	A	15	(1)	9
8	Sjoerd Overgoor		06/09/88	M	21	(1)	2
23	Marvin Peersman	BEL	10/02/91	D	31	(1)	
5	Marlon Pereira		26/03/87	D	5		
3	Etiënne Reijnen		05/04/87	D	1		
14	Mikhail Rosheuvel		02/04/90	A	12	(8)	
24	Sebastian Steblecki	POL	16/01/92	M		(2)	
20	Sander van de Streek		24/03/93	M	29	(3)	4
21	Martijn van der Laan		29/07/87	D	18	(3)	
18	Kevin van Veen		01/06/91	A	5	(7)	1
17	Rai Vloet		08/05/95	M	3	(5)	
26	Harm Zeinstra		21/07/89	G	6	(2)	

SBV Excelsior

1902 • Stadion Woudestein (3,531) •
sbvexcelsior.nl

Coach: Alfons Groenendijk

2015

12/08	a	NEC	L	0-1	
15/08	h	AZ	D	2-2	Stans, Van Weert
21/08	a	Groningen	L	0-2	
29/08	h	De Graafschap	W	3-0	Fischer, Kuwas, Van Mieghem
12/09	a	Zwolle	L	0-3	
20/09	h	Ajax	L	0-2	
27/09	a	Den Haag	D	3-3	Auassar 2, Kuwas
03/10	h	Utrecht	W	1-0	Stans (p)
17/10	a	PSV	D	1-1	Hasselbaink
24/10	a	Roda	W	2-1	Fischer, Stans
31/10	h	Vitesse	L	0-3	
07/11	a	Willem II	W	3-2	Van Weert, Stans (p), Van Mieghem
22/11	a	Heracles	D	0-0	
28/11	h	Feyenoord	L	2-4	Van Mieghem, Van Weert
05/12	h	Twente	D	1-1	Van Weert
11/12	a	Heerenveen	L	1-2	Stans (p)
20/12	h	Cambuur	L	1-4	Vermeulen

2016

16/01	a	De Graafschap	L	0-2	
23/01	h	Roda	L	0-1	
27/01	h	PSV	L	1-3	og (Bruma)
30/01	a	Vitesse	D	0-0	
05/02	h	Willem II	D	0-0	
14/02	h	Den Haag	L	2-4	Van Weert 2
21/02	a	Ajax	L	0-3	
26/02	h	NEC	W	2-0	Van Weert 2
06/03	a	AZ	L	0-2	
12/03	h	Groningen	W	2-1	Van Weert, Stans (p)
18/03	a	Utrecht	L	1-2	Kruys
02/04	a	Feyenoord	L	0-3	
09/04	h	Heracles	L	1-3	Kuwas
17/04	h	Heerenveen	D	1-1	Kuwas
20/04	a	Twente	L	0-2	
01/05	h	Zwolle	D	2-2	Van Weert, Bovenberg
08/05	a	Cambuur	W	2-0	Van Weert, Vermeulen

No	Name	Nat	DoB	Pos	Aps	(s)	Gls
8	Adil Auassar		06/10/86	M	33	(1)	2
14	Cedric Badjeck	CMR	25/01/95	A		(1)	
20	Jordan Botaka	COD	24/06/93	A	2	(2)	
24	Daan Bovenberg		25/10/88	D	13	(3)	1
23	Luigi Bruins		09/03/87	M	17	(1)	
3	Danilho Doekhi		30/06/98	D		(1)	
21	Henrico Drost		21/01/87	D	11	(2)	
27	Stanley Elbers		14/05/92	A	8	(10)	
15	Sander Fischer		03/09/88	D	32		2
15	Nigel Hasselbaink		21/11/90	A	6	(11)	1
25	Michiel Hemmen		28/06/87	A		(4)	
2	Khalid Karami		29/12/89	D	29		
4	Rick Kruys		09/05/85	M	31	(1)	1
5	Bas Kuipers		17/08/94	D	25		
1	Filip Kurto	POL	14/06/91	G	11		
17	Brandley Kuwas		19/09/92	A	29	(5)	4
12	Jurgen Mattheij		01/04/93	D	21		
22	Tom Muyters	BEL	05/12/84	G	23	(2)	
19	Tom Overtoom		20/11/90	M		(2)	
10	Jeff Stans		20/03/90	M	28	(4)	6
3	Kevin van Diermen		03/07/89	D	4		
11	Daryl van Mieghem		05/12/89	A	14	(15)	3
7	Yoëll van Nieff		17/06/93	M	3	(2)	
7	Tom van Weert		07/06/90	A	31	(1)	11
18	Kevin Vermeulen		20/11/94	A	3	(20)	2

Feyenoord

1908 • De Kuip (51,137) • feyenoord.nl

Major honours
European Champion Clubs' Cup (1) 1970; UEFA Cup (2) 1974, 2002; European/South American Cup (1) 1970; Dutch League (14) 1924, 1928, 1936, 1938, 1940, 1961, 1962, 1965, 1969, 1971, 1974, 1984, 1993, 1999; Dutch Cup (12) 1930, 1935, 1965, 1969, 1980, 1984, 1991, 1992, 1994, 1995, 2008, 2016

Coach: Giovanni van Bronckhorst

2015

08/08	h	Utrecht	W	3-2	Kazim-Richards, Trindade de Vilhena, Kuyt (p)
16/08	a	Cambuur	W	2-0	Kramer, Kuyt (p)
23/08	h	Vitesse	W	2-0	Kuyt (p), Bilal
30/08	h	PSV	L	1-3	og (Bruma)
13/09	h	Willem II	W	1-0	Elia
20/09	a	Roda	D	1-1	Kramer
27/09	h	Zwolle	W	2-0	Kuyt, Elia
04/10	a	De Graafschap	W	2-1	Kramer, Elia
18/10	a	Heerenveen	W	5-2	Kuyt 3, Kramer, Gustafsson
25/10	h	AZ	W	3-1	Kuyt 3 (1p)
01/11	a	Den Haag	L	0-1	
08/11	h	Ajax	D	1-1	Van Beek
22/11	h	Twente	W	5-0	Gustafsson 2, Kramer, El Ahmadi, Bilal
28/11	a	Excelsior	W	4-2	Kuyt, Kramer 3
06/12	h	Heracles	W	3-0	Elia, Kuyt, Kramer
13/12	a	Groningen	D	1-1	Kuyt
20/12	h	NEC	L	1-3	Trindade de Vilhena

2016

17/01	h	PSV	L	0-2	
24/01	a	AZ	L	2-4	Kramer, Trindade de Vilhena
28/01	h	Heerenveen	L	1-2	Achahbar
31/01	h	Den Haag	L	0-2	
07/02	a	Ajax	L	1-2	Toornstra
14/02	a	Zwolle	L	1-3	Van Beek
21/02	h	Roda	D	1-1	Kuyt
28/02	a	Utrecht	W	2-1	Trindade de Vilhena, Kuyt
06/03	h	Cambuur	W	3-1	Toornstra, Kuyt, Elia
13/03	a	Vitesse	W	2-0	Kramer, Bilal
19/03	a	De Graafschap	W	3-1	Kramer, Elia, og (Bouma)
02/04	h	Excelsior	W	3-0	Kuyt 2, Elia
10/04	a	Twente	W	1-0	Kramer
16/04	h	Groningen	D	1-1	Trindade de Vilhena
20/04	a	Heracles	D	2-2	Kramer, Elia
01/05	a	Willem II	W	1-0	Achahbar
08/05	h	NEC	W	1-0	Kuyt

No	Name	Nat	DoB	Pos	Aps	(s)	Gls
29	Anass Achahbar		13/01/94	A	1	(6)	2
14	Bilal Başaçıkoğlu	TUR	26/03/95	A	12	(15)	1
33	Eric Botteghin	BRA	31/08/87	D	18	(4)	
8	Karim El Ahmadi	MAR	27/01/85	M	32		1
11	Eljero Elia		13/02/87	A	27	(4)	8
27	Simon Gustafsson	SWE	11/01/95	M	12	(3)	3
10	Lex Immers		08/06/86	M	2	(4)	
2	Karl Karsdorp		11/02/95	D	28	(1)	
9	Colin Kazim-Richards	TUR	26/08/86	A	4	(7)	1
4	Terence Kongolo		14/02/94	D	29		
31	Michiel Kramer		03/12/88	A	25	(5)	14
7	Dirk Kuyt		22/07/80	M	31	(1)	19
17	Elvis Manu		13/08/93	A		(1)	
18	Miguel Nelom		22/09/90	D	12	(4)	
26	Bart Nieuwkoop		07/03/96	M	5		
39	Nigel Robertha		13/02/98	A		(1)	
30	Jari Schuurman		22/02/97	M		(1)	
20	Renato Tapia	PER	28/07/95	M	2	(1)	
28	Jens Toornstra		04/04/89	M	16	(1)	2
21	Tonny Trindade de Vilhena		03/01/95	M	19	(8)	5
3	Sven van Beek		28/07/94	D	30	(2)	2
6	Jan-Arie van der Heijden		03/03/88	D	14	(5)	
5	Marko Vejinovic		03/02/90	M	21	(2)	
1	Kenneth Vermeer		10/01/86	G	34		

De Graafschap

1954 • De Vijverberg (12,600) •
degraafschap.nl

Coach: Jan Vreman

2015

11/08	a	Heerenveen	L	1-3	Vermeij
15/08	h	Zwolle	L	0-3	
22/08	a	Roda	L	0-1	
29/08	a	Excelsior	L	0-3	
12/09	h	AZ	L	1-3	Will
20/09	a	Vitesse	L	0-3	
27/09	h	Willem II	D	2-2	Peters (p), Vermeij
04/10	h	Feyenoord	L	1-2	og (Van Beek)
18/10	a	Den Haag	D	1-1	og (Zuiverloon)
24/10	h	Heracles	L	0-1	
31/10	h	PSV	L	3-6	Driver, Bannink, Kabasele
07/11	a	NEC	L	0-2	
21/11	h	Groningen	L	1-2	Kabasele (p)
27/11	a	Cambuur	W	3-2	Peters, Straalman, Tarfi
05/12	h	Utrecht	L	0-1	
12/12	a	Twente	L	1-2	Driver
20/12	a	Ajax	L	1-2	Vida

2016

16/01	h	Excelsior	W	2-0	Peters, Vermeij
23/01	a	Heracles	L	1-2	Driver
27/01	h	Den Haag	W	3-1	Vermeij, Tarfi, Peters
30/01	a	PSV	L	2-4	Van de Pavert, Straalman
07/02	h	NEC	D	1-1	Driver
13/02	a	Willem II	D	0-0	
21/02	h	Vitesse	D	2-2	Vermeij 2
28/02	h	Heerenveen	L	0-1	
05/03	h	Zwolle	L	1-2	Kabasele
11/03	h	Roda	W	3-0	El Jebli, Pröpper, Parzyszek
19/03	a	Feyenoord	L	1-3	Pröpper
02/04	h	Cambuur	D	2-2	Vermeij, Van de Pavert
10/04	a	Groningen	L	1-3	Peters
15/04	h	Twente	D	1-1	Parzyszek
20/04	a	Utrecht	W	2-0	Vermeij 2
01/05	a	AZ	L	1-4	Diemers
08/05	h	Ajax	D	1-1	Smeets

No	Name	Nat	DoB	Pos	Aps	(s)	Gls
7	Alexander Bannink		20/02/90	M	11	(1)	1
2	Thijs Bouma		02/04/92	D	4	(2)	
25	Tolgahan Cicek		19/06/95	D	13	(1)	
22	Mark Diemers		11/10/93	M	11	(2)	1
15	Andrew Driver	ENG	20/11/87	M	25	(2)	4
20	Youssef El Jebli		27/12/92	M	18	(13)	1
1	Hidde Jurjus		09/02/94	G	34		
6	Lion Kaak		26/06/91	M	9	(5)	
17	Nathan Kabasele	BEL	14/01/94	A	10	(11)	3
10	Dean Koolhof		15/12/94	M	5	(8)	
24	Jan Lammers		10/05/95	D	4	(1)	
18	Tim Linthorst		03/07/94	D	5		
29	Tom Menting		29/11/94	M		(6)	
43	Piotr Parzyszek	POL	08/06/93	A		(9)	2
13	Cas Peters		13/05/93	A	28	(1)	5
3	Robin Pröpper		23/09/93	D	28	(3)	2
11	Erik Quekel		16/04/87	A	7	(1)	
14	Bryan Smeets		22/11/92	M	27	(1)	1
12	Bart Straalman		22/08/96	D	17	(2)	2
8	Karim Tarfi	BEL	05/12/92	M	13	(4)	2
5	Jeroen Tesselaar		16/01/89	D	18	(3)	
4	Ted van de Pavert		06/01/92	D	28		2
9	Vincent Vermeij		09/08/94	A	21	(12)	9
23	Kristopher Vida	HUN	26/06/95	A	12	(9)	1
19	Nathaniel Will		16/02/89	M	26	(2)	1

FC Groningen

1926 • Euroborg (22,329) • fcgroningen.nl

Major honours
Dutch Cup (1) 2015

Coach: Erwin van de Looi

2015

12/08	h	Twente	D	1-1	De Leeuw
16/08	a	PSV	L	0-2	
21/08	h	Excelsior	W	2-0	Mahi 2
29/08	a	Utrecht	L	0-2	
13/09	h	Heerenveen	W	3-1	Hoesen, Linssen, Mahi
20/09	a	AZ	W	2-0	Linssen, Mahi
26/09	a	Ajax	L	0-2	
04/10	a	Vitesse	L	0-5	
17/10	h	Willem II	W	2-1	Mahi, Hoesen
25/10	a	NEC	D	1-1	Rusnák
31/10	h	Zwolle	W	2-0	De Leeuw, Burnet
08/11	a	Cambuur	D	2-2	Kappelhof, Drost
21/11	a	De Graafschap	W	2-1	Rusnák, De Leeuw
29/11	h	Den Haag	W	2-1	og (Beugelsdijk), Hoesen
06/12	a	Roda	D	0-0	
13/12	h	Feyenoord	D	1-1	De Leeuw
19/12	a	Heracles	L	1-2	Linssen

2016

17/01	h	Utrecht	L	1-4	Sørloth
22/01	h	NEC	D	0-0	
26/01	a	Willem II	D	1-1	Maduro
30/01	h	Zwolle	W	3-1	Sørloth, De Leeuw, Hoesen
07/02	h	Cambuur	W	2-0	De Leeuw, Idrissi
14/02	h	Ajax	L	1-2	Hoesen
20/02	a	AZ	L	1-4	De Leeuw (p)
27/02	a	Twente	L	0-2	
05/03	h	PSV	L	0-3	
12/03	h	Excelsior	L	1-2	De Leeuw
20/03	a	Vitesse	L	0-3	
03/04	a	Den Haag	W	1-0	Lindgren
10/04	h	De Graafschap	W	3-1	Lindgren, og (Jurjus), Idrissi
16/04	h	Feyenoord	D	1-1	De Leeuw
19/04	h	Roda	W	1-0	Rusnák
01/05	a	Heerenveen	W	2-1	Idrissi, Rusnák
08/05	h	Heracles	W	2-1	Lindgren 2

No	Name	Nat	DoB	Pos	Aps	(s)	Gls
7	Jarchinio Antonia		27/12/90	A	9	(8)	
38	Juninho Bacuna		07/08/97	M	9	(5)	
3	Eric Botteghin	BRA	31/08/87	D	1		
5	Lorenzo Burnet		11/01/91	D	20		1
8	Michael de Leeuw		07/10/86	A	28	(1)	9
17	Jesper Drost		11/01/93	M	22	(7)	1
33	Hans Hateboer		09/01/94	D	31		
24	Tom Hiariej		25/07/88	M	4		
9	Danny Hoesen		15/01/91	A	9	(16)	5
45	Oussama Idrissi		26/02/96	M	7	(9)	3
2	Johan Kappelhof		05/08/90	D	18		1
21	Kasper Larsen	DEN	04/05/93	D	6	(7)	
21	Rasmus Lindgren	SWE	29/11/84	D	20	(1)	4
11	Bryan Linssen		08/10/90	A	19	(9)	3
23	Hedwiges Maduro		13/02/85	M	25	(3)	1
14	Mimoun Mahi		13/03/94	M	4	(9)	5
1	Sergio Padt		06/06/90	G	34		
37	Desevio Payne	USA	30/11/95	D	5	(4)	
6	Etiënne Reijnen		05/04/87	D	31	(2)	
10	Albert Rusnák	SVK	07/07/94	M	27	(3)	4
13	Alexander Sørloth	NOR	05/12/95	A	6	(7)	2
28	Abel Tamata	COD	05/12/90	D	9	(5)	
22	Simon Tibbling	SWE	07/09/94	M	30	(1)	
50	Keziah Veendorp		17/02/97	D		(1)	

sc Heerenveen

1920 • Abe Lenstra (26,100) • sc-heerenveen.nl

Major honours
Dutch Cup (1) 2009

Coach: Dwight Lodeweges;
(21/10/15) Foppe de Haan

2015

11/08	h	De Graafschap	W	3-1	Thern 2, Te Vrede
16/08	a	Utrecht	D	1-1	Slagveer
22/08	h	PSV	D	1-1	Cavlan (p)
29/08	h	Zwolle	D	1-1	Larsson
13/09	a	Groningen	L	1-3	Thern
18/09	a	NEC	L	0-2	
26/09	h	Vitesse	D	0-0	
02/10	a	Heracles	L	0-2	
18/10	h	Feyenoord	L	2-5	Veerman 2
24/10	a	Willem II	D	2-2	Veerman, Slagveer
01/11	h	Cambuur	W	2-0	og (Dammers), Te Vrede (p)
07/11	a	Twente	W	4-1	Slagveer, Otigba, og (Andersen), Larsson
21/11	a	AZ	L	1-3	Te Vrede
28/11	h	Roda	W	3-0	Te Vrede 2 (1p), Slagveer
05/12	a	Ajax	L	2-5	Te Vrede
11/12	h	Excelsior	W	2-1	Otigba, Larsson
20/12	h	Den Haag	L	0-4	

2016

16/01	h	Zwolle	L	2-5	Te Vrede, St Juste
23/01	h	Willem II	W	3-1	Zeneli, Otigba, Larsson
28/01	a	Feyenoord	W	2-1	Veerman, Van den Berg
31/01	a	Cambuur	W	1-0	Zeneli
06/02	h	Twente	L	1-3	Veerman
13/02	a	Vitesse	L	0-3	
20/02	h	NEC	D	1-1	Veerman
28/02	a	De Graafschap	W	1-0	Thorsby
05/03	a	Utrecht	L	0-4	
12/03	h	PSV	D	1-1	Te Vrede
19/03	h	Heracles	L	0-1	
03/04	a	Roda	W	3-1	Zeneli, Van den Boomen, og (Vlaar)
10/04	h	AZ	W	4-2	Van den Berg, Zeneli, Slagveer
17/04	a	Excelsior	D	1-1	Larsson
20/04	h	Ajax	L	0-2	
01/05	h	Groningen	L	1-2	Larsson
08/05	a	Den Haag	D	1-1	Te Vrede

No	Name	Nat	DoB	Pos	Aps	(s)	Gls
5	Lucas Bijker		04/03/93	D	21	(7)	
23	Jordy Buijs		28/12/88	M	2	(1)	
22	Caner Cavlan		05/02/92	D	27	(4)	1
25	Willem Huizing		01/02/95	D		(2)	
36	Tarik Kada		26/05/96	A		(2)	
11	Sam Larsson	SWE	10/04/93	A	34		6
6	Stefano Marzo	BEL	22/03/91	D	21	(8)	
1	Erwin Mulder		03/03/89	G	34		
24	Younes Namli	DEN	20/06/94	M		(3)	
3	Kenny Otigba	HUN	29/08/92	D	23	(8)	3
7	Luciano Slagveer		05/10/93	A	21	(9)	5
16	Jerry St Juste		19/10/96	M	27	(1)	1
9	Mitchell te Vrede		07/08/91	A	20	(7)	10
10	Simon Thern	SWE	18/09/92	M	9	(5)	3
8	Morten Thorsby	NOR	05/05/96	M	20	(5)	1
4	Joost van Aken		13/05/94	D	19	(1)	
2	Pele van Anholt		23/04/91	D	22		
21	Joey van den Berg		13/02/86	M	26		2
17	Branco van den Boomen		21/07/95	M	16	(7)	1
20	Henk Veerman		30/06/93	A	15	(12)	6
15	Luka Zahovič	SVN	15/11/95	A		(6)	
13	Arber Zeneli	SWE	25/02/95	A	17		4

Heracles Almelo

1903 • Polman (8,500) • heracles.nl

Major honours
Dutch League (2) 1927, 1941

Coach: John Stegeman

2015

08/08	a	Roda	L	1-3	Bel Hassani
16/08	h	NEC	W	3-0	Tannane, Bruns, Weghorst
22/08	a	Cambuur	W	6-1	Tannane 4 (1p), Weghorst, Bruns
29/08	h	Twente	W	2-0	Bel Hassani, Weghorst
13/09	a	Den Haag	W	1-0	Weghorst
19/09	h	PSV	W	2-1	Fledderus, Bruns
26/09	a	AZ	L	1-3	Navrátil
02/10	a	Heerenveen	W	2-0	Bel Hassani, Weghorst
17/10	a	Ajax	L	0-2	
24/10	a	De Graafschap	W	1-0	Bel Hassani
30/10	h	Willem II	W	2-1	Navrátil, Zomer
07/11	a	Zwolle	D	1-1	Weghorst
22/11	h	Excelsior	D	0-0	
29/11	a	Utrecht	L	2-4	Bel Hassani, Tannane
06/12	a	Feyenoord	L	0-3	
13/12	h	Vitesse	D	1-1	Tannane
19/12	h	Groningen	W	2-1	Gladon, Bosz

2016

15/01	h	Twente	L	0-4	
23/01	h	De Graafschap	W	2-1	Darri, Bruns
26/01	a	Ajax	D	0-0	
29/01	a	Willem II	D	0-0	
06/02	h	Zwolle	W	2-0	Bel Hassani, Navrátil
13/02	a	AZ	L	3-6	Bruns, Fledderus, Weghorst
20/02	a	PSV	L	0-2	
28/02	h	Roda	L	0-5	
06/03	a	NEC	L	0-1	
13/03	h	Cambuur	W	3-1	Weghorst, Gosens, Bel Hassani
19/03	h	Heerenveen	W	1-0	Navrátil
02/04	h	Utrecht	D	1-1	Navrátil
09/04	a	Excelsior	W	3-1	Weghorst 2, Zomer
16/04	a	Vitesse	D	1-1	Weghorst (p)
20/04	h	Feyenoord	D	2-2	Gosens, Weghorst
01/05	h	Den Haag	D	1-1	Gladon
08/05	a	Groningen	L	1-2	Bel Hassani

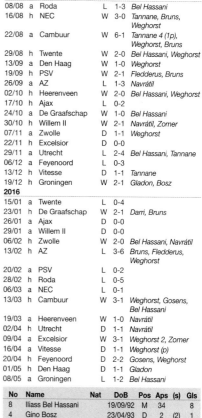

No	Name	Nat	DoB	Pos	Aps	(s)	Gls
8	Iliass Bel Hassani		19/09/92	M	34		8
4	Gino Bosz		23/04/93	D	2	(2)	1
2	Tim Breukers		04/11/87	D	1	(4)	
10	Thomas Bruns		07/01/92	M	33		5
1	Bram Castro	BEL	30/09/82	G	34		
7	Brahim Darri		14/09/94	A	19	(11)	1
12	Wout Droste		20/05/89	D	29		
23	Mark-Jan Fledderus		14/12/82	D	30		2
9	Paul Gladon		18/03/92	A	3	(18)	2
22	Gonzalo García	ESP	13/10/83	M	3	(5)	
21	Robin Gosens	GER	05/07/94	M	20	(12)	2
24	Menno Heerkes		22/07/93	M	1	(2)	
27	Justin Hoogma		11/06/98	D	1	(1)	
11	Tarik Kada		26/05/96	A	2	(2)	
15	Jaroslav Navrátil	CZE	30/12/91	A	17	(7)	5
14	Joey Pelupessy		15/05/93	M	34		
11	Oussama Tannane	MAR	23/03/94	A	9	(2)	7
3	Mike te Wierik		08/06/92	D	32		
20	Peter van Ooijen		30/09/82	M	5	(18)	
17	Dario Vujičević	CRO	01/04/90	M	2	(3)	
19	Wout Weghorst		07/08/92	A	32	(1)	12
18	Ramon Zomer		13/04/83	D	31		2

NEC Nijmegen

1900 • Goffert (12,500) • nec-nijmegen.nl
Coach: Ernest Faber

2015

12/08	h	Excelsior	W	1-0	Foor
16/08	a	Heracles	L	0-3	
23/08	h	Ajax	L	0-2	
28/08	a	Willem II	W	1-0	Foor
12/09	a	Roda	D	0-0	
18/09	h	Heerenveen	W	2-0	Santos 2
26/09	h	PSV	L	1-2	Santos (p)
03/10	a	Den Haag	W	4-1	og (Meijers), Santos 2, Limbombe
18/10	a	Twente	L	0-1	
25/10	h	Groningen	D	1-1	Santos (p)
01/11	a	AZ	W	4-2	Limbombe 2, Santos, Woudenberg
07/11	h	De Graafschap	W	2-0	Santos 2 (1p)
22/11	h	Utrecht	W	1-0	Santos (p)
29/11	a	Vitesse	L	0-1	
06/12	h	Zwolle	D	2-2	Janio Bikel, Limbombe
12/12	a	Cambuur	L	1-3	og (Houtkoop)
20/12	h	Feyenoord	W	3-1	Janio Bikel, Limbombe, Santos

2016

17/01	h	Willem II	W	1-0	Santos (p)
22/01	a	Groningen	D	0-0	
27/01	h	Twente	W	2-0	Limbombe, Santos
30/01	h	AZ	L	0-3	
07/02	a	De Graafschap	D	1-1	Ritzmaier
14/02	h	PSV	L	0-3	
20/02	a	Heerenveen	D	1-1	og (St Juste)
26/02	a	Excelsior	L	0-2	
06/03	h	Heracles	W	1-0	Santos
13/03	a	Ajax	D	2-2	Foor, Santos
20/03	a	Den Haag	L	0-1	
03/04	h	Vitesse	W	2-1	Limbombe, Dumic
10/04	h	Utrecht	L	1-3	Kane
17/04	h	Cambuur	W	2-1	Santos, Roman
20/04	a	Zwolle	L	0-2	
01/05	h	Roda	L	1-2	Foor
08/05	a	Feyenoord	L	0-1	

No	Name	Nat	DoB	Pos	Aps	(s)	Gls
2	Marcel Appiah	GER	26/03/88	D	17	(6)	
9	Sjoerd Ars		15/04/84	A	2		
8	Gregor Breinburg	ARU	16/09/91	M	29	(1)	
5	Bart Buysse	BEL	16/10/86	D	4		
23	Cihat Celik		02/01/96	A		(4)	
3	Dario Dumic	DEN	30/01/92	D	16		1
6	Mikael Dyrestam	SWE	10/12/91	D		(2)	
14	Kristján Gauti Emilsson	ISL	26/04/93	M	1	(2)	
25	Navarone Foor		04/02/92	M	34		4
19	Wojciech Golla	POL	12/01/92	D	29		
31	Jay-Roy Grot		13/03/98	A	2	(8)	
1	Hannes Thór Halldórsson	ISL	27/04/84	G	8		
19	Janio Bikel	POR	28/06/95	M	32		2
13	Brad Jones	AUS	19/03/82	G	17		
16	Todd Kane	ENG	17/09/93	D	29	(2)	1
13	Benjamin Kirsten	GER	02/06/87	G	6		
37	Jeffrey Leiwakabessy		23/02/81	D	1	(4)	
7	Anthony Limbombe	BEL	15/07/94	M	32		7
7	Sam Lundholm	SWE	01/07/94	A		(9)	
20	Mohammed Rayhi		01/07/94	M	4	(12)	
24	Marcel Ritzmaier	AUT	22/04/93	M	13	(7)	1
11	Mihai Roman	ROU	31/05/92	A	2	(11)	1
11	Christian Santos	VEN	24/03/88	A	29	(1)	16
9	Joey Sleegers		20/07/94	M	10	(8)	
26	Marco van Duin		11/02/87	G	3		
8	Rens van Eijden		03/03/88	D	25		
15	Lucas Woudenberg		25/04/94	D	29	(1)	1

PEC Zwolle

1990 • FC Zwolle Stadion (12,500) • peczwolle.nl
Major honours
Dutch Cup (1) 2014
Coach: Ron Jans

2015

12/08	h	Cambuur	D	2-2	Marcellis, Becker
15/08	a	De Graafschap	W	3-0	Marinus, Van Hintum, Becker
23/08	h	Twente	W	2-1	Veldwijk (p), Rienstra
29/08	a	Heerenveen	D	1-1	Veldwijk
12/09	h	Excelsior	W	3-0	Veldwijk 3
19/09	h	Den Haag	W	2-1	Becker, Veldwijk
27/09	a	Feyenoord	L	0-2	
03/10	a	Willem II	W	1-0	Bouy
18/10	h	Vitesse	L	1-5	Lam
23/10	h	Utrecht	L	1-2	Marinus
31/10	a	Groningen	L	0-2	
07/11	h	Heracles	D	1-1	Nijland
21/11	a	Roda	W	5-0	Marinus, R Thomas 2 (1p), Veldwijk, Nijland
29/11	h	Ajax	L	0-2	
06/12	a	NEC	D	2-2	Sainsbury, Veldwijk
13/12	a	AZ	W	2-1	Menig, Ehizibue
19/12	h	PSV	L	2-3	Van Polen (p), Veldwijk

2016

16/01	h	Heerenveen	W	5-2	Marcellis, Van Polen 2 (1p), Brama, Nijland
24/01	a	Utrecht	L	0-1	
27/01	a	Vitesse	D	1-1	Marcellis
30/01	h	Groningen	L	1-3	Lam
06/02	a	Heracles	L	0-2	
14/02	h	Feyenoord	W	3-1	Veldwijk 2, Ehizibue
19/02	h	Den Haag	W	2-0	Dekker, Veldwijk
27/02	a	Cambuur	L	0-2	
05/03	a	De Graafschap	W	2-1	Nijland 2
12/03	a	Twente	L	1-2	Ehizibue
19/03	a	Willem II	W	4-1	Marcellis, Menig, Veldwijk, Nijland
03/04	a	Ajax	L	0-3	
08/04	a	Roda	W	3-1	Menig, Bouy 2
16/04	a	AZ	L	1-5	Ehizibue
20/04	h	NEC	W	2-0	Becker, Menig
01/05	a	Excelsior	D	2-2	Veldwijk, Menig
08/05	h	PSV	L	1-3	Bouy

No	Name	Nat	DoB	Pos	Aps	(s)	Gls
7	Sheraldo Becker		09/02/95	A	14	(9)	4
16	Kevin Begois	BEL	13/05/82	G	16		
8	Ouasim Bouy		11/06/93	M	25	(1)	4
14	Wout Brama		21/08/86	M	23	(2)	1
45	Mark Bruintjes		26/06/96	D		(1)	
25	Boy de Jong		10/04/94	G		(1)	
19	Rick Dekker		15/03/95	D	20	(5)	1
20	Kingsley Ehizibue		25/05/95	M	17	(9)	4
21	Abdelmalek El Hasnaoui		09/02/94	M	5	(8)	
48	Tarik Evre		29/05/96	D		(1)	
38	Gustavo	BRA	05/04/96	M	2	(5)	
28	Thomas Lam	FIN	18/12/93	D	33		2
24	Boban Lazic		29/01/94	A		(5)	
4	Dirk Marcellis		13/04/88	D	29		4
18	Wouter Marinus		18/02/95	M	22	(9)	3
11	Queensy Menig		19/08/95	A	27	(6)	5
10	Stefan Nijland		10/08/88	A	11	(15)	6
26	Boris Rašević	BIH	26/01/95	M		(1)	
23	Ben Rienstra		05/06/90	D	3		1
3	Trent Sainsbury	AUS	05/01/92	D	8	(1)	1
15	Samet Bulut	TUR	26/02/96	A		(1)	
22	Bart Schenkeveld		28/08/91	D	8	(4)	
23	Dario Tanda		02/01/95	M		(3)	
30	Ryan Thomas	NZL	20/11/94	M	10	(2)	2
42	Sander Thomas		26/06/97	M		(3)	
1	Mickey van der Hart		13/06/94	G	18		
5	Bart van Hintum		16/01/87	D	23	(1)	1
2	Bram van Polen		11/10/85	D	27	(2)	3
9	Lars Veldwijk		21/08/91	A	33		14

PSV Eindhoven

1913 • Philips (35,000) • psv.nl
Major honours
*European Champion Clubs' Cup (1) 1988;
UEFA Cup (1) 1978; Dutch League (23) 1929, 1935,
1951, 1963, 1975, 1976, 1978, 1986, 1987, 1988,
1989, 1991, 1992, 2000, 2001, 2003, 2005,
2006, 2007, 2008, 2015, 2016; Dutch Cup (9) 1950,
1974, 1976, 1988, 1989, 1990, 1996, 2005, 2012*
Coach: Phillip Cocu

2015

11/08	a	Den Haag	D	2-2	Maher, De Jong
16/08	h	Groningen	W	2-0	Narsingh 2
22/08	a	Heerenveen	D	1-1	De Jong
30/08	h	Feyenoord	W	3-1	Lestienne, Arias, Locadia (p)
12/09	a	Cambuur	W	6-0	De Jong 3 (1p), Pröpper, Locadia 2
19/09	a	Heracles	L	1-2	De Jong
26/09	h	NEC	W	2-1	De Jong, Locadia
04/10	a	Ajax	W	2-1	Pereiro 2
17/10	h	Excelsior	D	1-1	Pröpper
24/10	a	Twente	W	3-1	De Jong, Locadia, Pereiro
31/10	a	De Graafschap	W	6-3	Pröpper 2, Guardado, De Jong, Narsingh, Pereiro
08/11	h	Utrecht	W	3-1	Moreno, Arias, De Jong
21/11	a	Willem II	D	2-2	Pereiro, De Jong
29/11	h	AZ	W	3-0	og (Luckassen), De Jong 2
05/12	a	Vitesse	W	1-0	Hendrix
12/12	h	Roda	D	1-1	Pröpper
19/12	h	Zwolle	W	3-2	Pereiro 2, De Jong

2016

17/01	a	Feyenoord	W	2-0	Moreno, Narsingh
24/01	h	Twente	W	4-2	Moreno 2, Narsingh, Jozefzoon
27/01	a	Excelsior	W	3-1	De Jong, Hendrix, Narsingh
30/01	h	De Graafschap	W	4-2	De Jong, Pröpper, Narsingh, Pereiro
07/02	a	Utrecht	W	2-0	Arias, Van Ginkel
14/02	a	NEC	W	3-0	De Jong, Locadia, Van Ginkel
20/02	h	Heracles	W	2-0	Pröpper, Pereiro (p)
27/02	h	Den Haag	W	2-0	Van Ginkel, De Jong
05/03	a	Groningen	W	3-0	Willems, Pröpper, Locadia
12/03	h	Heerenveen	D	1-1	De Jong
20/03	h	Ajax	L	0-2	
02/04	a	AZ	W	4-2	Pereiro, Van Ginkel 2, Narsingh
09/04	h	Willem II	W	2-0	Van Ginkel, De Jong (p)
16/04	a	Roda	W	2-0	De Jong 2, Pröpper
19/04	h	Vitesse	W	2-0	Pröpper, De Jong (p)
01/05	h	Cambuur	W	6-2	Van Ginkel 2, De Jong, Pereiro, Maher, Willems
08/05	a	Zwolle	W	3-1	Locadia, De Jong 2

No	Name	Nat	DoB	Pos	Aps	(s)	Gls
4	Santiago Arias	COL	13/01/92	D	32		3
27	Steven Bergwijn		08/10/97	A		(5)	
20	Joshua Brenet		20/03/94	D	21	(6)	
5	Jeffrey Bruma		13/11/91	D	30	(2)	
9	Luuk de Jong		27/08/90	A	32	(1)	26
30	Jordy de Wijs		08/01/95	D		(1)	
18	Andrés Guardado	MEX	28/09/86	M	25		1
29	Jorrit Hendrix		06/02/95	M	21	(5)	2
2	Nicolas Isimat-Mirin	FRA	15/11/91	D	12	(5)	
17	Florian Jozefzoon		09/02/91	A	1	(8)	1
16	Maxime Lestienne	BEL	17/06/92	A	6	(8)	1
19	Jürgen Locadia		07/11/93	A	23	(6)	8
10	Adam Maher		20/07/93	M	8	(6)	2
3	Héctor Moreno	MEX	17/01/88	D	29		4
11	Luciano Narsingh		13/09/90	A	25	(5)	8
7	Gastón Pereiro	URU	11/06/95	M	15	(14)	11
14	Simon Busk Poulsen	DEN	07/10/84	D	1	(1)	
6	Davy Pröpper		02/09/91	M	33		10
8	Stijn Schaars		11/01/84	M	2	(10)	
28	Marco van Ginkel		01/12/92	M	13		8
23	Rai Vloet			M		(1)	
15	Jetro Willems		30/03/94	D	11	(4)	2
1	Jeroen Zoet		06/01/91	G	34		

Roda JC

1962 • Parkstad Limburg (18,936) • rodajc.nl

Major honours
Dutch Cup (2) 1997, 2000
Coach: Darije Kalezić (BIH)

2015

08/08	h	Heracles	W	3-1	Gyasi, Van Hyfte, Faik
14/08	a	Vitesse	L	0-3	
22/08	h	De Graafschap	W	1-0	Van Hyfte
30/08	a	AZ	W	1-0	Griffiths
12/09	h	NEC	D	0-0	
20/09	h	Feyenoord	D	1-1	Faik
27/09	a	Twente	L	1-2	Juric
03/10	h	Cambuur	D	1-1	Van Hyfte
17/10	a	Utrecht	D	1-1	Juric
24/10	h	Excelsior	L	1-2	Juric
31/10	a	Ajax	L	0-6	
06/11	h	Den Haag	D	1-1	Van Hyfte
21/11	a	Zwolle	L	0-5	
28/11	a	Heerenveen	L	0-3	
06/12	h	Groningen	D	0-0	
12/12	h	PSV	D	1-1	og (Brenet)
20/12	a	Willem II	L	2-3	Juric (p), Griffiths

2016

16/01	h	AZ	L	0-1	
23/01	a	Excelsior	W	1-0	Faik
28/01	h	Utrecht	W	1-0	Ngombo
31/01	h	Ajax	D	2-2	Poepon, Ngombo
06/02	a	Den Haag	D	2-2	Van Hyfte, Peterson
13/02	h	Twente	D	1-1	Ngombo
21/02	a	Feyenoord	D	1-1	Ngombo
28/02	a	Heracles	W	5-0	Zhukov, Van Duinen, Poepon 2, Ngombo
06/03	h	Vitesse	L	1-2	Van Duinen
11/03	a	De Graafschap	L	0-3	
19/03	a	Cambuur	W	1-0	Van Hyfte
03/04	h	Heerenveen	L	1-2	Van Hyfte
08/04	a	Zwolle	L	1-3	Marcos Gullón
16/04	h	PSV	L	0-3	
19/04	a	Groningen	L	0-1	
01/05	a	NEC	W	2-1	Van Hyfte, Poepon
08/05	h	Willem II	L	2-3	Buijs, Uğur

No	Name	Nat	DoB	Pos	Aps	(s)	Gls
3	Bart Biemans	BEL	14/03/98	D	1		
29	Tim Blättler		04/09/94	A		(2)	
11	Richmond Boakye	GHA	28/01/93	A	7	(2)	
3	Jordy Buijs		28/12/88	D	17		1
9	Rigino Cicilia	CUW	23/09/94	A		(2)	
10	Daniel De Silva	AUS	06/03/97	M	1	(7)	
17	Henk Dijkhuizen		09/06/92	D	23		
8	Hicham Faik		19/03/92	M	21	(6)	3
4	Rostyn Griffiths	AUS	10/03/88	M	17	(1)	2
27	Edwin Gyasi		01/07/91	A	14	(4)	1
10	Marc Höcher		09/09/84	A		(1)	
16	Brian Jacobs		30/03/95	M		(1)	
11	Anco Jansen		09/03/89	A	3		
9	Tomi Juric	AUS	22/07/91	A	12	(5)	4
16	Marcos Gullón	ESP	20/02/89	M	11	(4)	1
2	Martin Milec	SVN	20/09/91	D	12		
28	Martijn Monteyne	BEL	12/11/84	D	2	(1)	
15	Maecky Ngombo	BEL	13/08/93	A		(17)	4
24	Farshad Noor		02/10/94	M	11	(1)	
19	Mitchel Paulissen		21/04/93	M	7	(8)	
11	Kristoffer Peterson	SWE	28/11/94	A	9	(5)	1
14	Rydell Poepon		28/08/87	A	16	(1)	4
6	Nathan Rutjes		01/12/83	M	3	(11)	
3	Gibril Sankoh	SLE	15/05/83	D	17		
23	Arjan Swinkels		15/10/84	D	31		
31	Uğur İnceman	TUR	25/05/81	M	16		1
19	Mike van Duinen		06/11/91	A	11	(2)	2
7	Tom Van Hyfte	BEL	28/04/86	M	33		8
1	Benjamin van Leer		09/04/92	G	34		
5	Ard van Peppen		26/06/85	D	26	(2)	
18	Jens van Son		19/08/87	M	2	(9)	
20	Daryl Werker		27/06/94	D	2	(3)	
30	Georgi Zhukov	KAZ	19/11/94	M	15	(1)	1

FC Twente

1965 • De Grolsch Veste (24,244) • fctwente.nl

Major honours
Dutch League (1) 2010; Dutch Cup (3) 1977, 2001, 2011
Coach: Alfred Schreuder; (30/08/15) René Hake

2015

12/08	a	Groningen	D	1-1	Tapia
15/08	h	Den Haag	L	1-4	Ziyech
23/08	a	Zwolle	L	1-2	Ziyech
29/08	a	Heracles	L	0-2	
12/09	h	Ajax	D	2-2	Gutiérrez, Ziyech (p)
19/09	a	Cambuur	D	0-0	
27/09	h	Roda	W	2-1	Oosterwijk, Mokotjo
04/10	a	AZ	L	1-3	Ziyech
18/10	h	NEC	W	1-0	Bijen
24/10	h	PSV	L	1-3	Ziyech
01/11	a	Utrecht	L	2-4	Agyepong, Ziyech
07/11	a	Heerenveen	L	1-4	Ziyech
22/11	a	Feyenoord	L	0-5	
28/11	h	Willem II	L	1-3	Oosterwijk
05/12	a	Excelsior	D	1-1	Ziyech
12/12	h	De Graafschap	W	2-1	Andersen, Ziyech
18/12	a	Vitesse	L	1-5	Ziyech

2016

15/01	h	Heracles	W	4-0	Ede 2, Ziyech, Ter Avest
24/01	a	PSV	L	2-4	Oosterwijk, Ede
27/01	a	NEC	L	0-2	
31/01	h	Utrecht	W	3-1	Bruno Uvini, El Azzouzi, Gutiérrez
06/02	a	Heerenveen	W	3-1	Bruno Uvini, Cabral, Ziyech
13/02	a	Roda	W	1-0	Ede
20/02	h	Cambuur	W	3-0	og (Peersman), Cabral, Ziyech (p)
27/02	a	Groningen	W	2-0	El Azzouzi, Cabral
04/03	h	Den Haag	L	1-2	Ziyech
12/03	h	Zwolle	W	2-1	Ziyech, Cabral
20/03	a	AZ	D	2-2	Thesker 2
02/04	a	Willem II	W	3-2	Ziyech 2, Ede
10/04	h	Feyenoord	L	0-1	
15/04	a	De Graafschap	D	1-1	Cabral
20/04	h	Excelsior	W	2-0	Cabral, El Azzouzi
01/05	a	Ajax	L	0-4	
08/05	h	Vitesse	D	2-2	El Azzouzi, Ede

No	Name	Nat	DoB	Pos	Aps	(s)	Gls
11	Thomas Agyepong	GHA	10/10/96	M	6	(8)	1
23	Joachim Andersen	DEN	31/05/96	D	18		1
25	Peet Bijen		28/01/95	D	16	(2)	1
3	Bruno Uvini	BRA	03/06/91	D	32	(1)	2
9	Torgeir Børven	NOR	03/12/91	A		(4)	
26	Jerson Cabral		03/01/91	A	21	(3)	6
9	Jesús Corona	MEX	06/01/93	M	2	(2)	
27	Alessio Da Cruz		18/01/97	M	1	(2)	
16	Joël Drommel		16/11/96	G	11	(1)	
7	Chinedu Ede	GER	05/02/87	M	25	(2)	6
19	Shadrach Eghan	GHA	04/07/94	M	1	(3)	
18	Zakaria El Azzouzi		07/05/96	A	12	(1)	4
6	Felipe Gutiérrez	CHI	08/10/90	M	26	(3)	2
12	Tim Hölscher	GER	21/01/95	M	5	(12)	
4	Georgios Katsikas	GRE	14/06/90	D	3		
1	Nick Marsman		01/10/90	G	23		
22	Kamohelo Mokotjo	RSA	11/03/91	M	31		1
99	Michael Olaitan	NGA	01/01/93	A	11	(4)	
24	Jari Oosterwijk		03/03/95	A	11	(3)	3
5	Robbert Schilder		18/04/86	D	21	(2)	
33	Vincent Schmidt		10/01/96	M		(1)	
14	Renato Tapia	PER	28/07/95	M	10	(4)	1
17	Hidde ter Avest		20/05/97	D	28	(1)	1
2	Stefan Thesker	GER	11/04/91	D	6	(2)	2
23	Jelle van der Heyden		31/08/95	M	5	(6)	
28	Jeroen van der Lely		22/03/96	D	12	(9)	
8	Oskar Zawada	POL	01/02/96	A	4	(7)	
10	Hakim Ziyech	MAR	19/03/93	M	33		17

FC Utrecht

1970 • Galgenwaard (24,500) • fcutrecht.nl

Major honours
Dutch Cup (3) 1985, 2003, 2004
Coach: Erik ten Hag

2015

08/08	a	Feyenoord	L	2-3	Haller 2 (1p)
16/08	h	Heerenveen	D	1-1	Haller (p)
23/08	a	Den Haag	D	1-1	Haller (p)
29/08	h	Groningen	W	2-0	Ramselaar, Letschert
13/09	a	Vitesse	W	2-1	Janssen, Ramselaar
19/09	a	Willem II	L	1-3	Barazite
26/09	h	Cambuur	D	3-3	Janssen 2 (1p), Barazite
03/10	h	Excelsior	L	0-1	
17/10	h	Roda	D	1-1	Haller
23/10	a	Zwolle	W	2-1	Haller 2 (1p)
01/11	h	Twente	W	4-2	Letschert, og (Drommel), Barazite, Haller (p)
08/11	h	PSV	L	1-3	Ramselaar
22/11	a	NEC	L	0-1	
29/11	h	Heracles	W	4-2	Barazite 2, Haller 2
05/12	a	De Graafschap	W	1-0	Strieder
13/12	h	Ajax	W	1-0	Ayoub
19/12	a	AZ	D	2-2	Boymans, Haller

2016

17/01	a	Groningen	W	4-1	Ramselaar, Letschert, Kum, Ludwig
24/01	h	Zwolle	W	1-0	Boymans
28/01	a	Roda	L	0-1	
31/01	a	Twente	L	1-3	Boymans
07/02	h	PSV	L	0-2	
12/02	a	Cambuur	W	2-0	Van der Maarel, Haller
21/02	h	Willem II	W	2-1	Boymans 2
28/02	a	Feyenoord	L	1-2	Haller
05/03	a	Heerenveen	W	4-0	Ludwig, Boymans 2, Kum
13/03	h	Den Haag	D	2-2	Haller, Boymans
18/03	a	Excelsior	W	2-1	Haller 2 (1p)
02/04	a	Heracles	D	1-1	Ludwig
10/04	h	NEC	W	3-1	Boymans, Barazite, Haller
17/04	a	Ajax	D	2-2	Barazite, Joosten
20/04	a	De Graafschap	L	0-2	
01/05	a	Vitesse	W	3-1	Barazite, Boymans, Leeuwin
08/05	h	AZ	L	1-3	Strieder

No	Name	Nat	DoB	Pos	Aps	(s)	Gls
25	Sofyan Amrabat	MAR	21/08/96	M	2	(5)	
6	Yassine Ayoub		06/03/94	M	22	(2)	1
10	Nacer Barazite		27/05/90	A	28	(4)	8
16	Filip Bednarek	POL	26/09/92	G	5		
9	Ruud Boymans		28/04/89	A	7	(8)	10
24	Kevin Conboy	DEN	15/10/87	D	6	(2)	
15	Yannick Cortie		07/05/93	D		(2)	
15	Mark Diemers		11/10/93	M	2	(4)	
22	Sébastien Haller	FRA	22/06/94	A	33		17
8	Willem Janssen		04/07/86	M	16	(3)	3
37	Patrick Joosten		14/04/96	M	13	(6)	1
28	Issa Kallon		03/01/96	A		(1)	
17	Sean Klaiber		31/07/94	M	16	(1)	
5	Christian Kum		13/09/85	D	18	(4)	2
3	Ramon Leeuwin		01/09/87	D	19	(8)	1
14	Timo Letschert		25/05/93	D	34		3
19	Ruben Ligeon		24/05/92	D	4	(3)	
11	Andreas Ludwig	GER	11/09/90	M	14	(11)	3
20	Louis Nganioni	FRA	03/06/95	D	8	(3)	
21	Kristoffer Peterson	SWE	28/11/94	A	1	(6)	
23	Bart Ramselaar		29/06/96	M	32	(2)	4
38	Darren Rosheuvel		15/05/94	M	1		
18	Rubio Rubin	USA	01/03/96	A	1	(6)	
1	Robbin Ruiter		25/03/87	G	29		
7	Rico Strieder	GER	06/07/92	M	31	(1)	2
47	Giovanni Troupée		20/03/98	D		(3)	
2	Mark van der Maarel		12/08/89	D	32		1

NETHERLANDS

Vitesse

1892 • Gelredome (26,600) • vitesse.nl

Coach: Peter Bosz;
(04/01/16) Rob Maas

2015

09/08	a	Willem II	D	1-1	Oliynyk
14/08	h	Roda	W	3-0	Baker (p), Dauda, Nathan
23/08	a	Feyenoord	L	0-2	
30/08	h	Cambuur	W	4-1	Baker (p), Dauda, Kashia, Solanke
13/09	a	Utrecht	L	1-2	Kashia
20/09	h	De Graafschap	W	3-0	Kashia, Kazaishvili, Rashica
26/09	a	Heerenveen	D	0-0	
04/10	h	Groningen	W	5-0	Solanke, Diks, Kazaishvili, Nathan, Dauda
18/10	a	Zwolle	W	5-1	Baker, Solanke (p), Kazaishvili, Oliynyk (p), Rashica
25/10	h	Ajax	L	1-3	Kazaishvili
31/10	a	Excelsior	W	3-0	Solanke (p), Diks, Rashica
08/11	h	AZ	L	0-2	
22/11	a	Den Haag	D	2-2	Yeini, Leerdam
29/11	h	NEC	W	1-0	Kazaishvili
05/12	a	PSV	L	0-1	
13/12	a	Heracles	D	1-1	Rashica
18/12	h	Twente	W	5-1	Kazaishvili, Rashica 2, Solanke, Oliynyk

2016

16/01	a	Cambuur	W	2-0	Rashica, Kazaishvili
23/01	a	Ajax	L	0-1	
27/01	h	Zwolle	D	1-1	og (Van Polen)
30/01	h	Excelsior	D	0-0	
06/02	a	AZ	L	0-1	
13/02	h	Heerenveen	W	3-0	Oliynyk, Kazaishvili 2 (1p)
21/02	a	De Graafschap	D	2-2	Nakamba, Baker
27/02	h	Willem II	L	0-1	
06/03	a	Roda	W	2-1	Brown, Zhang
13/03	h	Feyenoord	L	0-2	
20/03	a	Groningen	W	3-0	Solanke 2, Kazaishvili
03/04	a	NEC	L	1-2	Baker
09/04	h	Den Haag	D	2-2	Kashia, Oliynyk
16/04	h	Heracles	D	1-1	Rashica
19/04	a	PSV	L	0-2	
01/05	h	Utrecht	L	1-3	Kashia
08/05	a	Twente	D	2-2	og (Bruno Uvini), Zhang

No	Name	Nat	DoB	Pos	Aps	(s)	Gls
35	Rochdi Achenteh	MAR	07/03/88	D	5		
34	Lewis Baker	ENG	25/04/95	M	23	(8)	5
7	Isaiah Brown	ENG	07/01/97	M	12	(10)	1
14	Abiola Dauda	NGA	03/02/88	A	4	(7)	3
17	Kevin Diks		06/10/96	D	29	(1)	2
9	Uroš Djurdjević	SRB	02/03/94	A		(1)	
30	Renato Ibarra	ECU	20/01/91	A	8	(8)	
37	Guram Kashia	GEO	04/07/87	D	26	(1)	5
10	Valeri Kazaishvili	GEO	29/01/93	A	31	(2)	10
6	Arnold Kruisweg		02/11/84	D	20	(2)	
5	Kelvin Leerdam		24/06/90	D	14	(1)	1
49	Julian Lelieveld		24/11/97	D	1		
18	Marvelous Nakamba	ZIM	19/01/94	M	30		1
13	Nathan	BRA	13/03/96	M	4	(14)	2
11	Denys Oliynyk	UKR	16/06/87	M	18	(7)	5
41	Mohammed Osman		01/01/94	M		(1)	
8	Kosuke Ota	JPN	23/07/87	D	15	(1)	
44	Thomas Oude Kotte		20/03/96	D	1	(1)	
20	Danilo Pantić	SRB	26/10/96	M		(6)	
26	Milot Rashica	ALB	28/06/96	M	29	(2)	8
1	Eloy Room	CUW	06/02/89	G	34		
9	Dominic Solanke	ENG	14/09/97	A	21	(4)	7
42	Mitchell van Bergen		27/08/99	M		(1)	
3	Maikel van der Werff		22/04/89	D	25	(1)	
21	Sheran Yeini	ISR	08/12/86	M	23	(3)	1
43	Zhang Yuning	CHN	05/01/97	A	1	(7)	2

Willem II

1896 • Koning Willem II stadion (14,700) • willem-ii.nl

Major honours
Dutch League (3) 1916, 1952, 1955; Dutch Cup (2) 1944, 1963

Coach: Jürgen Streppel

2015

09/08	h	Vitesse	D	1-1	Falkenburg
15/08	a	Ajax	L	0-3	
23/08	a	AZ	D	0-0	
28/08	h	NEC	L	0-1	
13/09	a	Feyenoord	L	0-1	
19/09	h	Utrecht	W	3-1	Falkenburg, og (Nganioni), Haemhouts
27/09	a	De Graafschap	D	2-2	Falkenburg 2
03/10	h	Zwolle	L	0-1	
17/10	a	Groningen	L	1-2	og (Reijnen)
24/10	h	Heerenveen	D	2-2	Zivkovic, Andersen
30/10	a	Heracles	L	1-2	Falkenburg
07/11	a	Excelsior	L	2-3	Zivkovic, D Wuytens
21/11	h	PSV	D	2-2	Falkenburg 2
28/11	a	Twente	W	3-1	Andersen 3
06/12	h	Cambuur	W	3-0	Joppen, Falkenburg, S Wuytens
12/12	a	Den Haag	D	1-1	Van der Velden (p)
20/12	h	Roda	W	3-2	D Wuytens 2, Van der Velden

2016

17/01	a	NEC	L	0-1	
23/01	a	Heerenveen	L	1-3	Van der Velden (p)
26/01	h	Groningen	D	1-1	D Wuytens
29/01	h	Heracles	D	0-0	
05/02	a	Excelsior	D	0-0	
13/02	h	De Graafschap	D	0-0	
21/02	a	Utrecht	L	1-2	Ogbeche (p)
27/02	a	Vitesse	W	1-0	Ondaan
06/03	h	Ajax	L	0-4	
12/03	h	AZ	L	0-2	
19/03	a	Zwolle	L	1-4	Falkenburg
02/04	h	Twente	L	2-3	Falkenburg, Andersen
09/04	a	PSV	L	0-2	
17/04	a	Den Haag	L	0-2	
21/04	a	Cambuur	D	1-1	Peters
01/05	a	Feyenoord	L	0-1	
08/05	a	Roda	W	3-2	Falkenburg, Bruno Andrade, Andersen

No	Name	Nat	DoB	Pos	Aps	(s)	Gls
28	Asumah Abubakar	POR	10/05/97	A		(1)	
35	Rochdi Achenteh	MAR	07/03/88	D	13		
18	Lucas Andersen	DEN	13/09/94	M	27	(3)	6
17	Robert Braber		09/11/82	M	2	(23)	
11	Bruno Andrade	BRA	02/03/89	A	6	(5)	1
27	Frenkie de Jong		12/05/97	M		(1)	
19	Lesley de Sa		02/04/93	A	6	(12)	
10	Erik Falkenburg		05/05/88	M	34		11
8	Robbie Haemhouts	BEL	09/12/83	M	12	(4)	1
3	Freek Heerkens		13/09/89	D	8	(2)	
14	Guus Huppperts		25/04/92	A	9	(4)	
24	Guus Joppen		14/11/89	D	11	(4)	1
2	Anouar Kali	MAR	03/06/91	M	1	(1)	
14	Andy Kawaya	BEL	23/08/96	A	1	(1)	
5	Dico Koppers		31/01/92	D	18	(5)	
1	Kostas Lamprou	GRE	18/09/91	G	34		
22	Justin Mathieu		12/04/96	A		(4)	
37	Adam Nemec	SVK	02/09/85	A	3	(7)	
16	Bartholomew Ogbeche	NGA	01/10/84	A	4		1
6	Funso Ojo	BEL	28/08/91	M	32		
7	Terell Ondaan		09/09/93	A	7	(4)	1
4	Jordens Peters		03/05/87	D	29		1
20	Frank van der Struijk		28/03/85	D	30		
23	Nick van der Velden		16/12/81	M	21	(4)	3
30	Jordy Vleugels	BEL	17/05/96	M		(1)	
15	Dries Wuytens	BEL	18/03/91	D	33		4
29	Stijn Wuytens	BEL	08/10/89	M	18		1
9	Richairo Zivkovic		05/09/96	A	13	(3)	2

Top goalscorers

27	Vincent Janssen (AZ)
26	Luuk de Jong (PSV)
21	Arkadiusz Milik (Ajax)
19	Dirk Kuyt (Feyenoord)
17	Hakim Ziyech (Twente)
	Sébastien Haller (Utrecht)
16	Mike Havenaar (Den Haag)
	Christian Santos (NEC)
14	Michiel Kramer (Feyenoord)
	Lars Veldwijk (Zwolle)

UEFA Europa League qualification play-offs

FIRST ROUND

(12/05/16 & 15/05/16)
Groningen 2-1 Heracles (Hateboer 11, Lindgren 50; Weghorst 45)
Heracles 5-1 Groningen (Zomer 83, Gladon 90, Weghorst 111, Darri 115, Pelupessy 119; Rusnák 63) (aet)
(Heracles 6-3)

Zwolle 0-0 Utrecht
Utrecht 5-2 Zwolle (Haller 5, 73p, Ramselaar 23, Kum 28, Troupée 62; Menig 53, Brama 65)
(Utrecht 5-2)

SECOND ROUND

(19/05/16 & 22/05/16)
Heracles 1-1 Utrecht (Bruns 40; Strieder 51)
Utrecht 0-2 Heracles (Bruns 68, Gladon 85)
(Heracles 3-1)

Promoted clubs

Sparta Rotterdam

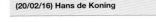

1888 • Kasteel (11,000) • sparta-rotterdam.nl
Major honours
Dutch League (6) 1909, 1911, 1912, 1913, 1915, 1959;
Dutch Cup (3) 1958, 1962, 1966
Coach: Alex Pastoor

Go Ahead Eagles

1902 • Adelaarshorst (6,750) • ga-eagles.nl
Major honours
Dutch League (4) 1917, 1922, 1930, 1933
Coach: Dennis Demmers;
(20/02/16) Hans de Koning

Second level final table 2015/16

		Pld	W	D	L	F	A	Pts
1	Sparta Rotterdam (*2)	36	24	7	5	83	40	79
2	VVV-Venlo	36	23	6	7	85	39	75
3	NAC Breda	36	20	7	9	84	42	67
4	FC Eindhoven (*3)	36	19	6	11	55	44	63
5	Go Ahead Eagles	36	18	7	11	61	41	61
6	FC Volendam (*1)	36	14	10	12	54	40	52
7	FC Emmen	36	15	6	15	58	57	51
8	Almere City FC (*4)	36	14	8	14	68	66	50
9	Jong Ajax	36	13	11	12	59	57	50
10	MVV Maastricht	36	14	8	14	52	60	50
11	Jong PSV	36	13	9	14	51	71	48
12	Telstar	36	12	8	16	57	64	44
13	Helmond Sport	36	11	9	16	52	59	42
14	FC Dordrecht	36	11	7	18	47	67	40
15	Achilles '29	36	10	9	17	43	61	39
16	Fortuna Sittard	36	11	6	19	41	74	39
17	FC Den Bosch	36	9	11	16	47	53	38
18	RKC Waalwijk	36	7	11	18	41	66	32
19	FC Oss	36	7	8	21	43	80	29

N.B. (*) period champions

Promotion/Relegation play-offs

FIRST ROUND

(02/05/16 & 06/05/16)
Almere City 4-1 Emmen
Emmen 1-4 Almere City
(Almere City 8-2)

MVV 2-1 Volendam
Volendam 1-2 MVV
(MVV 4-2)

SECOND ROUND

(13/05/16 & 16/05/16)
Almere City 0-1 Willem II
Willem II 5-2 Almere City
(Willem II 6-2)

Eindhoven 1-0 NAC
NAC 2-0 Eindhoven
(NAC 2-1)

Go Ahead Eagles 1-0 VVV
VVV 2-2 Go Ahead Eagles
(Go Ahead Eagles 3-2)

MVV 0-1 De Graafschap
De Graafschap 2-1 MVV
(De Graafschap 3-1)

THIRD ROUND

(19/05/16 & 22/05/16)
Go Ahead Eagles 4-1 De Graafschap
De Graafschap 1-1 Go Ahead Eagles
(Go Ahead Eagles 5-2)

NAC 2-1 Willem II
Willem II 3-1 NAC
(Willem II 4-3)

DOMESTIC CUP

KNVB-Beker 2015/16

SECOND ROUND

(22/09/15)
ACV 1-2 Excelsior 31
AFC 2-3 Emmen
Capelle 1-1 MVV *(aet; 5-4 on pens)*
DOVO 0-3 Willem II
EVV 0-3 Almere City
Feyenoord (amateurs) 0-2 Dordrecht
Genemuiden 3-3 Den Haag *(aet; 3-1 on pens)*
Kozakken Boys 4-2 Staphorst
Lienden 1-0 Volendam
Lisse 0-4 HHC
NAC 0-1 Heerenveen
Noordwijk 0-3 NEC
OJC 3-4 Sparta *(aet)*
ONS 0-2 Utrecht
PSV 3-2 Cambuur
Scheveningen 0-0 Telstar *(aet; 5-6 on pens)*
Spakenburg 3-0 Ter Leede

(23/09/15)
Ajax 2-0 Graafschap
AZ 6-1 VVV
Barendrecht 0-2 Excelsior
Berkum 4-4 JVC *(aet; 5-3 on pens)*
De Treffers 0-3 Roda
Fortuna Sittard 1-3 Achilles 29 *(aet)*
Groningen 2-1 Twente
HBS 4-1 Oss
Heracles 4-1 Vitesse *(aet)*
HFC 3-2 Eindhoven
HSC 21 2-2 Go Ahead Eagles *(aet; 9-10 on pens)*
Rijnsburgse Boys 3-3 VVSB *(aet; 5-6 on pens)*
WKE 2-5 Den Bosch *(aet)*

(24/09/15)
Feyenoord 3-0 Zwolle
RKC 1-2 Helmond Sport

THIRD ROUND

(27/10/15)
Achilles 29 2-1 Spakenburg
Almere City 0-3 Den Bosch
Berkum 0-3 HHC
Dordrecht 0-1 Capelle *(aet)*
Go Ahead Eagles 0-2 Willem II
Heracles 3-1 HFC
PSV 6-0 Genemuiden
VVSB 3-1 Emmen

(28/10/15)
Excelsior 31 4-3 Excelsior
Feyenoord 1-0 Ajax
HBS 1-2 Kozakken Boys
Lienden 1-1 Roda *(aet; 5-6 on pens)*
Utrecht 5-3 Groningen *(aet)*

(29/10/15)
Heerenveen 1-0 Helmond Sport
NEC 4-0 Sparta
Telstar 0-1 AZ

FOURTH ROUND

(15/12/15)
Excelsior 31 1-3 Den Bosch
HHC 2-0 NEC
Roda 3-1 Heerenveen

(16/12/15)
Achilles 29 0-5 Utrecht
Capelle 2-3 VVSB
Heracles 2-3 PSV
Kozakken Boys 1-3 AZ

(17/12/15)
Feyenoord 2-1 Willem II *(aet)*

QUARTER-FINALS

(02/02/16)
AZ 1-0 HHC *(Janssen 9)*

(03/02/16)
Den Bosch 2-3 VVSB *(Carlone 21, Khalouta 31; Bekooij 82, P van der Slot 83, Parami 87)*

Roda 0-1 Feyenoord *(Botteghin 105) (aet)*

(04/02/16)
PSV 1-3 Utrecht *(Leeuwin 74og; Ramselaar 32, 58, Haller 41)*

SEMI-FINALS

(02/03/16)
Utrecht 3-0 VVSB *(P van der Slot 73og, Haller 75, Joosten 90+1)*

(03/03/16)
Feyenoord 3-1 AZ *(Henriksen 15og, Kramer 78, Kuyt 85p; Henriksen 46)*

FINAL

(24/04/16)
De Kuip, Rotterdam
FEYENOORD 2 *(Kramer 42, Bednarek 75og)*
FC UTRECHT 1 *(Leeuwin 51)*
Referee: Kuipers
FEYENOORD: *Vermeer, Van Beek, Botteghin, Kongolo, Karsdorp, El Ahmadi, Kuyt (Nelom 89), Trindade de Vilhena, Toornstra, Kramer (Bilal 80), Elia*
UTRECHT: *Bednarek, Van der Maarel, Leeuwin, Letschert, Kum (Joosten 86), Ramselaar, Strieder, Janssen (Ligeon 86), Ludwig (Boymans 76), Barazite, Haller*

Feyenoord overcame Utrecht 2-1 in their home stadium to win the Dutch Cup

NORTHERN IRELAND

Irish Football Association (IFA)

Address	National Football Stadium Donegal Avenue GB-Belfast BT12 5LW	**President**	Jim Shaw
		Chief executive	Patrick Nelson
		Media officer	Neil Brittain
Tel	+44 2890 669 458	**Year of formation**	1880
Fax	+44 2890 667 620	**National stadium**	Windsor Park, Belfast
E-mail	info@irishfa.com		(18,000)
Website	irishfa.com		

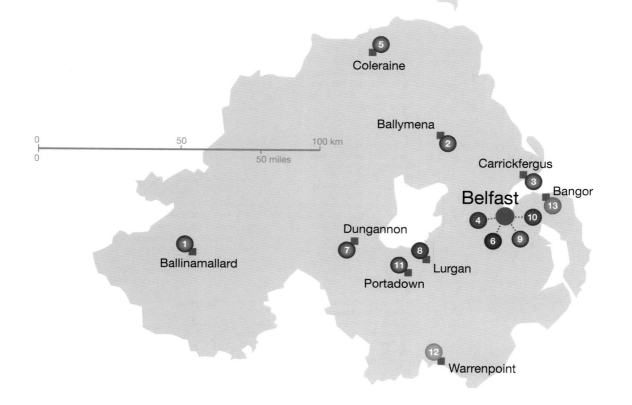

PREMIERSHIP CLUBS

 1 **Ballinamallard United FC**

 2 **Ballymena United FC**

 3 **Carrick Rangers FC**

 4 **Cliftonville FC**

 5 **Coleraine FC**

 6 **Crusaders FC**

 7 **Dungannon Swifts FC**

 8 **Glenavon FC**

 9 **Glentoran FC**

 10 **Linfield FC**

11 **Portadown FC**

 12 **Warrenpoint Town FC**

PROMOTED CLUB

 13 **Ards FC**

KEY

● UEFA Champions League

● UEFA Europa League

● Promoted

● Relegated

Crusaders go back-to-back

Northern Irish football followers will remember the 2015/16 season with fondness for the national team's first appearance at the UEFA European Championship finals, and it was also one to treasure for fans of Crusaders as the club made a successful defence of the Irish League title for the first time in their 118-year history.

Stephen Baxter's side were comprehensive champions, losing just three games and ending up eight points clear of Linfield, who also finished runners-up in the Irish Cup, defeated 2-0 in the final by Glenavon.

| **North Belfast outfit retain title for the first time** | **Glenavon beat Linfield to win Irish Cup** | **National team reach last 16 on EURO debut** |

Domestic league

Crusaders' bid for unprecedented back-to-back league titles got off to a false start when they lost their opening game at home to Portadown, but that would be no indicator of the season to come – one in which Ronnie McFall, Europe's longest serving manager/head coach, stepped down as Portadown boss after over 29 years' service. The Crues, whose own manager, Baxter, had led the team for over a decade, would not lose again until New Year's Day, by which time they had assumed a commanding position at the Premiership summit.

Although it was Linfield who defeated them, the country's record champions still had a lot of catching-up to do following a horrible run of defeats in November – the month after they appointed Northern Ireland's record goalscorer David Healy as manager in place of Warren Feeney. Healy duly turned things around, but Crusaders had built up a protective buffer, and after claiming their third win of the season over Linfield, 2-0 at Seaview, they found themselves eight points clear with four games to go.

Baxter's boys duly freewheeled to the title, a 3-1 win at Cliftonville featuring a brace of goals from Paul Heatley clinching the club's sixth league title. Heatley, who formed a prolific attacking alliance with Jordan Owens, would end

the season as the division's joint top marksman alongside Linfield's Andrew Waterworth on 22 goals. Linfield were the top-scoring team, with 91 goals, but the more significant figure was Crusaders' tally of 91 points – nine more than they had amassed the previous season.

A tense battle to avoid relegation dragged into overtime as a dispute over a touchline ban for Carrick Rangers manager Gary Haveron led to a disciplinary hearing that called into question the final placings of the bottom three clubs and postponed the second leg of the play-off between Ballinamallard and Institute. Eventually, the matter was resolved as Carrick stayed up, Ballinamallard won the play-off and Warrenpoint Town went down, with First Division champions Ards coming up.

Domestic cup

Glenavon won the Irish Cup for the second time in three seasons, goals either side of half-time from Kevin Braniff and Andy Hall accounting for Linfield in the final. Braniff had scored all four goals as Glenavon came from behind three times to defeat Crusaders 4-3 in an exhilarating semi-final, while a hat-trick from Linfield's Aaron Burns saw off Lurgan Celtic, the team responsible for ending McFall's long reign at Portadown with a shock 3-2 victory in the previous round.

Europe

Crusaders and Linfield both passed the first qualifying round of their respective European competitions before falling at the next hurdle, the Crues snatching a farewell victory from the jaws of defeat as they beat Skënderbeu 3-2 at home thanks to two added-time goals.

National team

Michael O'Neill did what no other Northern Ireland manager had previously managed and led the country to the UEFA European Championship finals, thus ending a 30-year wait for major tournament football. Furthermore, the team qualified as group winners, and they travelled to France, backed by thousands of fans, undefeated in 12 matches.

That run ended in a subdued opening 1-0 loss to Poland, but a rousing 2-0 win against Ukraine opened the gates to the round of 16, and although they were then beaten by Germany, the 1-0 scoreline, made possible by a brilliant performance from goalkeeper Michael McGovern, enabled them to progress on goal difference as the fourth best third-placed team. That was as far as they went, however, with Wales edging a dour Parc des Princes encounter 1-0 with an own goal from the man who had put them ahead against Ukraine, centre-back Gareth McAuley.

DOMESTIC SEASON AT A GLANCE

Premiership 2015/16 final table

		Pld	Home					Away					Total					Pts
			W	D	L	F	A	W	D	L	F	A	W	D	L	F	A	
1	**Crusaders FC**	38	14	3	1	42	10	14	4	2	37	18	28	7	3	79	28	91
2	Linfield FC	38	13	4	2	49	13	13	1	5	42	22	26	5	7	91	35	83
3	Glenavon FC	38	10	4	5	35	19	10	5	4	37	21	20	9	9	72	40	69
4	Cliftonville FC	38	11	4	5	35	24	7	6	5	23	29	18	10	10	58	53	64
5	Coleraine FC	38	9	3	6	23	17	9	1	10	24	29	18	4	16	47	46	58
6	Glentoran FC	38	8	3	8	20	25	7	4	8	26	30	15	7	16	46	55	52
7	Dungannon Swifts FC	38	8	1	10	32	31	4	6	9	19	35	12	7	19	51	66	43
8	Ballymena United FC	38	5	4	10	27	40	6	3	10	30	41	11	7	20	57	81	40
9	Portadown FC	38	6	4	9	29	34	5	1	13	14	33	11	5	22	43	67	38
10	Carrick Rangers FC	38	4	5	11	23	39	4	6	8	20	29	8	11	19	43	68	35
11	Ballinamallard United FC	38	5	3	10	19	23	4	4	12	20	36	9	7	22	39	59	34
12	Warrenpoint Town FC	38	5	5	10	25	37	4	2	12	20	36	9	7	22	45	73	34

NB League splits into top and bottom halves after 33 games, after which the clubs play exclusively against teams in their group.

European qualification 2016/17

CHAMPIONS LEAGUE

Champion: Crusaders FC (second qualifying round)

EUROPA LEAGUE

Cup winner: Glenavon FC (first qualifying round)
Linfield FC (first qualifying round)
Cliftonville FC (first qualifying round)

Top scorer	Paul Heatley (Crusaders) & Andrew Waterworth (Linfield), 22 goals
Relegated club	Warrenpoint Town FC
Promoted club	Ards FC
Cup final	Glenavon FC 2-0 Linfield FC

Team of the season
(4-4-2)

Coach: Baxter *(Crusaders)*

Player of the season

Billy Joe Burns
(Crusaders FC)

A right-back who loves to get forward, Burns was awarded the Ulster Footballer of the Year award at the end of a season in which he starred repeatedly for Crusaders, both as a defender and attacker. He started all but two of the Premiership champions' 38 games and scored all of his six goals in a heady eight-match period around the turn of the year. Recruited from Linfield in 2014, where he won three league titles, the 27-year-old is now on five, having also been a standout performer for Stuart Baxter's side in his debut season.

Newcomer of the season

Joel Cooper
(Glenavon FC)

The Ulster Young Player of the Year prize was picked up by Glenavon's 20-year-old winger, who adapted supremely well to life in Northern Irish football's elite division following a summer transfer from second-tier Ballyclare Comrades. Cooper scored six goals in the Premiership, where the Lurgan side finished third, and he also played a leading role in helping the team to win the Irish Cup for the seventh time, not least in the final, which Glenavon won 2-0 in the Windsor Park home of their defeated opponents Linfield.

Tuffey *(Glenavon)*

Burns *(Crusaders)* **Coates** *(Crusaders)* **Callacher** *(Linfield)* **McClean** *(Crusaders)*

Hall *(Glenavon)* **Snoddy** *(Crusaders)* **Burns** *(Linfield)* **Heatley** *(Crusaders)*

Waterworth *(Linfield)* **Bradley** *(Glenavon)*

NATIONAL TEAM

International tournament appearances
FIFA World Cup (3) 1958 (qtr-finals), 1982 (2nd phase), 1986
UEFA European Championship (1) 2016 (round of 16)

Top five all-time caps
Pat Jennings (119); **Aaron Hughes** (103); David Healy (95); Mal Donaghy (91); Sammy McIlroy & Maik Taylor (88)

Top five all-time goals
David Healy (36); **Kyle Lafferty** (17); Colin Clarke & Billy Gillespie (13); Gerry Armstrong, Joe Bambrick, Iain Dowie & Jimmy Quinn (12)

Results 2015/16

04/09/15	Faroe Islands (ECQ)	A	Torshavn	W	3-1	McAuley (12, 71), K Lafferty (75)
07/09/15	Hungary (ECQ)	H	Belfast	D	1-1	K Lafferty (90+3)
08/10/15	Greece (ECQ)	H	Belfast	W	3-1	Davis (35, 58), Magennis (49)
11/10/15	Finland (ECQ)	A	Helsinki	D	1-1	Cathcart (31)
13/11/15	Latvia	H	Belfast	W	1-0	Davis (55)
24/03/16	Wales	A	Cardiff	D	1-1	Cathcart (60)
28/03/16	Slovenia	H	Belfast	W	1-0	Washington (41)
27/05/16	Belarus	H	Belfast	W	3-0	K Lafferty (6), Washington (44), Grigg (88)
04/06/16	Slovakia	A	Trnava	D	0-0	
12/06/16	Poland (ECF)	N	Nice (FRA)	L	0-1	
16/06/16	Ukraine (ECF)	N	Lyon (FRA)	W	2-0	McAuley (49), McGinn (90+6)
21/06/16	Germany (ECF)	N	Paris (FRA)	L	0-1	
25/06/16	Wales (ECF)	N	Paris (FRA)	L	0-1	

Appearances 2015/16

Coach: Michael O'Neill	05/07/69		FRO	HUN	GRE	FIN	Lva	Wal	Svn	Blr	Svk	POL	UKR	GER	WAL	Caps	Goals
Michael McGovern	12/07/84	Hamilton (SCO)	G	G	G	G	G46	G			G	G	G	G	G	15	-
Conor McLaughlin	26/07/91	Fleetwood (ENG)	D70	D		s51	M	M81	s71	D	s90	M				19	-
Gareth McAuley	05/12/79	West Brom (ENG)	D	D	D	D	D	D	D46		D	D	D	D	D84	65	8
Jonny Evans	03/01/88	West Brom (ENG)	D	D			D	D73	D	D	D	D	D	D	D	53	1
Chris Brunt	14/12/84	West Brom (ENG)	D83	D	D	D										54	1
Chris Baird	25/02/82	Derby (ENG)	M	M 81*		M	M			M	M	M76				79	-
Niall McGinn	20/07/87	Aberdeen (SCO)	M	s56	s81	M71			s79	s74			s69	s84	s79	45	3
Steven Davis	01/01/85	Southampton (ENG)	M	M	M	M	M84	M	M	M46	M	M	M	M	M	87	8
Oliver Norwood	12/04/91	Reading (ENG)	M	M75	M	M	M46	M	M	s46	M83	M	M	M	M79	38	-
Stuart Dallas	19/04/91	Leeds (ENG)	M	M84	M	M	M69	M91	s60	M74		s46	M	M	M	17	1
Kyle Lafferty	16/09/87	Norwich (ENG) /Birmingham (ENG)	A78	A		A79	A54	A81	s60	A61	A55	A		s59	A	54	17
Josh Magennis	15/08/90	Kilmarnock (SCO)	s70	s75	A78	s79	s54		s70		s46		s84	s70	s84	22	1
Paddy McNair	27/04/95	Man. United (ENG)	s78		D85	D51		M74	M79	M	M90	M46	s93			11	-
Shane Ferguson	12/07/91	Millwall (ENG)	s83	s84		s71	s69	s91	M60		M86	M66				26	1
Corry Evans	30/07/90	Blackburn (ENG)		M56	M		s46			M74	s83		M93	M84	M	37	1
Craig Cathcart	06/02/89	Watford (ENG)			D	D	D	D	D	D	D30	D	D	D	D	32	2
Jamie Ward	12/05/86	Nottingham Forest (ENG)			M81		A69	s46	A60	s60	M46	s76	M69	M70	M69	26	2
Liam Boyce	08/04/91	Ross County (SCO)			s78		s69									7	-
Luke McCullough	15/02/94	Doncaster (ENG)			s85											5	-
Roy Carroll	30/09/77	Notts County (ENG)					s46		G	G46						44	-
Paddy McCourt	16/12/83	Luton (ENG)					s84									18	2
Conor Washington	18/05/92	QPR (ENG)						A46	A70	A60	s55	s66	A84	A59	s69	8	2
Daniel Lafferty	18/05/89	Burnley (ENG)						s73								13	-
Paul Paton	18/04/87	Dundee United (SCO)						s74								2	-
Aaron Hughes	08/11/79	Melbourne City (AUS)						s81	s46	s74	s30		D	D	D	103	1
Billy McKay	22/10/88	Dundee United (SCO)						s81								11	-
Michael Smith	04/09/88	Peterborough (ENG)							M71							1	-
Alan Mannus	19/05/82	St Johnstone (SCO)								s46						8	-
Will Grigg	03/07/91	Wigan (ENG)								s61						8	1
Lee Hodson	02/10/91	MK Dons (ENG)									s86					16	-

EUROPE

Crusaders FC

First qualifying round - FC Levadia Tallinn (EST)
H 0-0
O'Neill, Burns, Coates, Robinson, Caddell (Forsythe 76), McClean, Owens (O'Flynn 85), Clarke, Heatley, Carvill, Mitchell. Coach: Stephen Baxter (NIR)
A 1-1 *Carvill (4)*
O'Neill, Burns, Magowan, Robinson, Caddell (Clarke 79), Forsythe, McClean, Owens (O'Flynn 70), Heatley, Carvill (O'Carroll 90+3), Mitchell. Coach: Stephen Baxter (NIR)

Second qualifying round - KF Skënderbeu (ALB)
A 1-4 *Owens (48)*
O'Neill, Burns, Magowan, Robinson, Caddell, McClean, Owens, Clarke (O'Carroll 88), Heatley, Carvill (Forsythe 58; Snoddy 71), Mitchell. Coach: Stephen Baxter (NIR)
H 3-2 *O'Flynn (50), Snoddy (90+2), Mitchell (90+3)*
O'Neill, Burns, Coates, Robinson, Caddell (Clarke 73), O'Flynn (O'Carroll 67), McClean, Owens, Snoddy, Carvill, Mitchell. Coach: Stephen Baxter (NIR)

Glentoran FC

First qualifying round - MŠK Žilina (SVK)
H 1-4 *McMenamin (66)*
Morris, Kane, Holland, Birney, Magee, McCaffrey (McAlorum 82), Stewart (Addis 63), Gibson, Gordon, McMenamin, McCullough. Coach: Eddie Patterson (NIR)
A 0-3
Morris, Kane, Holland, Birney, Magee (Garrett 79), McCaffrey (Addis 76), McAlorum (Nelson 67), Gibson, Gordon, McMenamin, McCullough. Coach: Eddie Patterson (NIR)

Linfield FC

First qualifying round - NSÍ Runavík (FRO)
H 2-0 *Waterworth (57), Bates (73)*
Ross Glendinning, Hegarty (Reece Glendinning 65), Haughey, Waterworth, Lowry, Bates (Millar 90), Burns, Ward, M Clarke, Kee, Sproule. Coach: Warren Feeney (NIR)
A 3-4 *Reece Glendinning (13), Bates (33), Waterworth (69)*
Ross Glendinning, Hegarty, Waterworth, Lowry, Bates (R Clarke 71), Burns (Murray 83), Ward, M Clarke, Kee, Reece Glendinning, Sproule. Coach: Warren Feeney (NIR)

Second qualifying round - FC Spartak Trnava (SVK)
A 1-2 *Kee (21)*
Ross Glendinning, Hegarty, Haughey, Waterworth, Lowry, Bates, Burns (R Clarke 57), M Clarke, Kee, Reece Glendinning, Sproule. Coach: Warren Feeney (NIR)
H 1-3 *Lowry (34)*
Ross Glendinning, Hegarty, Haughey (Ward 76), Waterworth, Lowry, Bates, Burns, M Clarke, Kee, Reece Glendinning, Sproule (R Clarke 63). Coach: Warren Feeney (NIR)

Glenavon FC

First qualifying round - FC Shakhtyor Soligorsk (BLR)
H 1-2 *Patton (86)*
McGrath, Kelly, Kilmartin (Patton 67), Marshall, Bradley, Hall (Hamilton 83), Dillon, Braniff, Martyn, Elebert (Lindsay 64), Singleton. Coach: Gary Hamilton (NIR)
A 0-3
Tuffey, Kelly, Lindsay (Caldwell 69), Kilmartin (Hamilton 62), Marshall, Bradley, Hall (Patton 35), Dillon, Braniff, Martyn, Singleton. Coach: Gary Hamilton (NIR)

DOMESTIC LEAGUE CLUB-BY-CLUB

Ballinamallard United FC

1975 • Ferney Park (2,000) • no website
Manager: Whitey Anderson

2015
08/08	a	Warrenpoint	W	3-0	*(w/o; original result 1-0 Currie)*
12/08	h	Dungannon	D	0-0	
15/08	a	Crusaders	L	0-5	
22/08	h	Portadown	L	1-2	*Martin*
28/08	a	Coleraine	L	1-2	*Martin*
05/09	h	Linfield	L	0-1	
12/09	h	Carrick	L	1-3	*McCartney (p)*
19/09	a	Ballymena	D	1-1	*McCrudden*
26/09	h	Cliftonville	L	0-2	
03/10	a	Glentoran	W	2-0	*Courtney, Beacom*
07/10	h	Glenavon	L	0-1	
17/10	h	Crusaders	D	1-1	*Feeney*
24/10	a	Portadown	W	3-0	*Martin 2, Campbell*
30/10	h	Warrenpoint	W	3-0	*McCrudden, Martin, Campbell*
07/11	a	Glenavon	L	1-5	*McCartney (p)*
14/11	h	Ballymena	L	0-1	
21/11	a	Cliftonville	L	1-3	*McKenna*
27/11	h	Coleraine	L	1-2	*Lecky*
05/12	h	Glentoran	L	2-4	*Lecky, McCartney (p)*
12/12	a	Linfield	D	1-1	*McCrudden*
19/12	h	Carrick	L	1-4	*McKenna*
26/12	h	Dungannon	D	1-1	*McKenna*

2016
01/01	a	Coleraine	L	0-1	
23/01	a	Cliftonville	L	0-2	
30/01	h	Ballymena	W	4-2	*McKenna, O'Flynn, Campbell, McCartney (p)*
12/02	a	Warrenpoint	L	0-3	
15/02	h	Portadown	W	1-0	*McKenna*
20/02	a	Dungannon	L	0-2	
27/02	h	Glentoran	W	1-0	*Lecky*
12/03	a	Carrick	D	1-1	*O'Flynn*
19/03	a	Glenavon	L	0-1	
24/03	a	Linfield	L	1-2	*Lecky*
29/03	h	Crusaders	L	0-1	
09/04	a	Dungannon	D	0-0	
16/04	h	Warrenpoint	W	2-0	*McCabe, Campbell*
19/04	a	Dungannon	L	2-4	*Campbell, Lecky*
23/04	a	Ballymena	W	2-1	*Friars, O'Flynn (p)*
30/04	a	Carrick	L	1-2	*Sproule*

No	Name	Nat	DoB	Pos	Aps	(s)	Gls
16	Cathal Beacom		01/08/88	M	14	(3)	1
20	Ryan Campbell		08/07/81	A	25	(13)	5
4	Leon Carters		23/07/84	D	5	(1)	
22	Jonathan Courtney		09/03/95	A	2	(12)	1
14	Christopher Crilly		03/03/84	D	7		
12	John Currie		10/09/93	M	12	(6)	1
30	Jake Dykes		30/06/95	D	9	(2)	
25	David Elliott		08/09/95	D	16		
4	Gareth Falconer		28/04/90	M	3	(1)	
5	Steve Feeney	IRL	16/05/84	D	17	(3)	1
21	Emmett Friars		14/09/85	D	33	(1)	1
19	Robbie Hume		02/02/92	M		(3)	
23	Jakub Klobusek	POL	11/08/95	A		(5)	
10	Johnny Lafferty		02/01/87	M	20	(9)	
17	Adam Lecky		03/05/91	A	25	(9)	5
7	Liam Martin	IRL	23/01/94	M	17	(4)	5
19	Ryan Mayse		07/12/93	A	4	(5)	
6	Shane McCabe		21/12/81	M	23	(2)	1
11	Jason McCartney	IRL	06/09/86	M	28	(8)	4
18	Michael McCrudden		31/07/91	A	18	(2)	3
13	Stefan McCusker		01/12/89	G	13		
9	Joshua McIlwaine		13/11/94	A		(1)	
8	James McKenna		20/07/84	M	22	(2)	5
3	Colm McLaughlin		01/08/93	D	23		
2	Liam McMenamin		10/04/89	D	24	(1)	
18	Ryan Morris		04/09/97	A	8		
27	Stephen O'Flynn	IRL	27/04/82	A	8	(3)	3
9	Aaron Patterson		26/04/95	A	3	(3)	
18	Gary Phair		24/01/94	D	1	(1)	
1	Alvin Rouse	BRB	17/01/80	G	25		
15	Ciaran Smith		16/01/97	A		(1)	
9	Ivan Sproule		18/02/81	A	13		1

Ballymena United FC

1928 • The Showgrounds (4,390) •
ballymenaunitedfc.com
Major honours
Irish Cup (6) 1929, 1940, 1958, 1981, 1984, 1989
**Manager: Glenn Ferguson;
(08/03/16) David Jeffrey**

2015

08/08	a	Linfield	L	0-4	
12/08	h	Glenavon	L	1-7	*Shevlin*
15/08	h	Coleraine	L	0-2	
22/08	a	Dungannon	L	0-2	
28/08	a	Carrick	D	1-1	*Jenkins*
05/09	a	Glentoran	W	3-1	*Shevlin, Tipton, Faulkner*
12/09	h	Cliftonville	W	6-1	*Tipton 3 (3p), Cushley, Ruddy, Ervin*
19/09	h	Ballinamallard	D	1-1	*Rodger*
26/09	a	Warrenpoint	W	2-1	*Tipton, Cushley*
03/10	h	Crusaders	L	2-4	*Jenkins, Thompson*
10/10	a	Portadown	L	2-3	*Gawley, Tipton*
17/10	a	Glenavon	L	1-3	*Cushley*
24/10	h	Dungannon	W	1-0	*Cushley*
31/10	a	Carrick	D	2-2	*Cushley 2*
07/11	h	Glentoran	L	0-1	
14/11	a	Ballinamallard	W	1-0	*Jenkins (p)*
21/11	h	Portadown	D	1-1	*Jenkins*
28/11	a	Crusaders	L	2-3	*Tipton 2*
05/12	h	Cliftonville	L	2-4	*Faulkner, Thompson*
12/12	h	Warrenpoint	W	4-2	*Jenkins 3 (1p), McVey*
19/12	h	Linfield	L	1-3	*Cushley*
26/12	a	Coleraine	L	1-2	*Cushley*

2016

01/01	a	Portadown	W	4-3	*Jenkins 2, McBride, Cushley*
19/01	h	Carrick	W	1-0	*Hanley*
23/01	h	Linfield	L	0-4	
30/01	a	Ballinamallard	L	2-4	*Tipton, Millar*
12/02	h	Coleraine	L	0-2	
20/02	a	Glentoran	L	0-2	
27/02	h	Dungannon	L	2-4	*Cushley, Jenkins*
12/03	a	Crusaders	D	0-0	
19/03	h	Warrenpoint	W	3-1	*Jenkins, Faulkner 2*
02/04	h	Cliftonville	D	2-2	*McVey, T Kane (p)*
05/04	a	Glenavon	D	1-1	*Taylor*
09/04	a	Dungannon	W	4-2	*Henderson 2, McVey, Frazer*
16/04	a	Carrick	W	2-0	*Cushley, Ruddy*
19/04	a	Warrenpoint	L	1-4	*Faulkner*
23/04	h	Ballinamallard	L	1-2	*T Kane*
30/04	h	Portadown	L	0-2	

No	Name	Nat	DoB	Pos	Aps	(s)	Gls
18	Alan Blayney		09/10/81	G	21		
31	Kyle Crawford		29/06/97	D	1		
11	David Cushley		22/07/89	M	33	(1)	11
14	Chandler Douglas		20/06/96	M		(1)	
21	Jim Ervin		05/06/85	D	36		1
12	Willie Faulkner		18/01/90	A	23	(3)	5
19	Matthew Ferguson		21/11/95	M	5	(7)	
30	Jonathan Frazer		30/05/96	A	10	(2)	1
27	Neal Gawley		20/02/86	M	4	(4)	1
24	Nathan Hanley		18/07/90	M	7	(5)	1
8	Darren Henderson		25/01/86	A	8	(18)	2
10	Allan Jenkins	SCO	07/10/81	M	37	(1)	11
15	Eoin Kane		10/01/96	M	14	(8)	
2	Tony Kane		29/08/87	D	30		2
6	Mark Magennis		15/03/83	M	2	(5)	
3	Stephen McBride		06/04/83	D	20	(1)	1
3	Paddy McNally		20/08/94	D	11	(1)	
22	Kyle McVey		07/07/86	D	22	(3)	3
23	Leroy Millar		01/09/95	M	5	(9)	1
1	Dwayne Nelson		05/09/84	G	17		
32	Stewart Nixon		08/05/97	A	1	(1)	
25	Gareth Rodger	SCO	22/02/94	D	12		1
17	Michael Ruddy		05/08/93	D	13	(4)	2
16	Matthew Shevlin		07/12/98	A	13	(5)	2
28	Michael Smyth		01/07/92	M	1	(1)	
9	Gavin Taggart		15/11/84	M	8	(4)	
5	Johnny Taylor		30/06/88	D	24	(3)	1
7	Gary Thompson		26/05/90	A	24	(8)	2
14	Matthew Tipton	WAL	29/06/80	A	16	(4)	9

Carrick Rangers FC

1939 • Taylors Avenue (6,000) •
carrickrangers.co.uk
Manager: Gary Haveron

2015

08/08	a	Dungannon	W	2-1	*Miguel Chines 2 (1p)*
12/08	h	Linfield	L	0-3	
15/08	h	Glentoran	D	1-1	*Roy*
22/08	a	Cliftonville	L	0-1	
28/08	h	Ballymena	D	1-1	*Miguel Chines (p)*
05/09	h	Warrenpoint	L	1-2	*Miguel Chines (p)*
12/09	a	Ballinamallard	W	3-1	*Cherry, Miguel Chines, Surgenor*
19/09	h	Glenavon	D	2-2	*Kelly, Miguel Chines*
26/09	a	Crusaders	L	0-5	
03/10	h	Portadown	L	0-2	
10/10	h	Coleraine	L	1-2	*Roy*
17/10	a	Glentoran	L	0-2	
24/10	a	Linfield	D	1-1	*Miguel Chines (p)*
31/10	h	Ballymena	D	2-2	*Kane, Roy*
14/11	a	Portadown	L	2-3	*Miguel Chines, McCloskey*
21/11	a	Coleraine	L	1-2	*Harmon*
04/12	a	Glenavon	L	0-2	
19/12	a	Ballinamallard	W	2-1	*og (Lafferty), Traynor*
26/12	a	Warrenpoint	D	1-1	*Kelly*

2016

12/01	a	Cliftonville	D	3-3	*Harmon, McCaul, Cherry*
19/01	h	Ballymena	L	0-1	
23/01	h	Coleraine	W	2-1	*McCloskey 2*
30/01	h	Linfield	L	0-2	
02/02	h	Glenavon	L	1-5	*Miguel Chines*
11/02	h	Dungannon	D	2-2	*Miguel Chines, McCloskey*
19/02	h	Warrenpoint	L	0-1	
27/02	a	Portadown	D	0-0	
02/03	a	Dungannon	W	1-0	*Cherry*
12/03	h	Ballinamallard	D	1-1	*Miguel Chines*
19/03	h	Crusaders	L	0-4	
22/03	h	Crusaders	W	4-3	*Kelly, Salley, Harmon, Roy*
26/03	h	Glentoran	L	1-2	*Wright*
05/04	h	Cliftonville	L	1-2	*Doyle*
09/04	a	Warrenpoint	D	1-1	*Salley*
16/04	h	Ballymena	L	0-2	
19/04	h	Portadown	L	1-2	*Surgenor*
23/04	a	Dungannon	W	3-1	*Salley, Harmon, Miguel Chines*
30/04	h	Ballinamallard	W	2-1	*Surgenor, Miguel Chines*

No	Name	Nat	DoB	Pos	Aps	(s)	Gls
15	Ryan Arthur		06/09/95	D	1		
24	Gary Browne		17/01/83	A	10	(9)	
22	Josh Cash		20/07/92	M	1	(2)	
8	Kyle Cherry		13/05/93	M	23	(4)	3
25	Adam Dick		24/03/88	A	2	(3)	
19	Andrew Doyle		28/10/90	D	26	(4)	1
6	Aaron Harmon		05/11/89	A	30		4
14	Barry Johnston		28/10/80	M	22		
12	Ryan Kane		02/09/87	D	5	(7)	1
5	Daniel Kelly		06/01/93	D	21	(10)	3
23	Kyle Mackie		28/10/94	M	1	(5)	
39	Brian McCaul		06/08/90	M	12	(9)	1
11	Conor McCloskey		29/01/92	M	30		4
21	Michael McKenna		21/02/97	M		(1)	
30	Gareth McKeown		14/07/93	D	4		
7	Joseph McNeill		23/08/88	M	18	(8)	
9	Miguel Chines	POR	04/09/79	A	25	(9)	13
99	Mark Miskimmin		11/06/88	A	1	(8)	
1	Brian Neeson		28/06/89	G	35		
24	Francis Rice		09/06/96	A		(2)	
10	Ben Roy		10/02/89	A	21	(10)	4
32	Adam Salley		07/02/97	A	16	(1)	3
2	Aaron Smyth		25/08/87	D	19	(1)	
4	Mark Surgenor		19/12/85	D	34		3
88	Glenn Taggart		02/11/80	M	18		
18	James Taylor		12/05/84	G	3		
3	Aaron Traynor		24/07/90	M	33		1
25	Daniel Wallace		21/10/94	D	3	(2)	
33	James Wright		17/12/88	A	4	(2)	1

Cliftonville FC

1879 • Solitude (5,442) • cliftonvillefc.net
Major honours
Irish League (5) 1906 (shared), 1910, 1998, 2013, 2014; Irish Cup (8) 1883, 1888, 1897, 1900, 1901, 1907, 1909, 1979
**Manager: Tommy Breslin;
(15/10/15) Gerard Lyttle**

2014

08/08	a	Glenavon	W	1-0	*McDaid*
12/08	h	Coleraine	W	4-0	*McDaid (p), J Donnelly 2, Garrett*
15/08	a	Portadown	W	1-0	*J Donnelly*
22/08	h	Carrick	W	1-0	*McMullan*
30/08	a	Warrenpoint	D	2-2	*og (Dane), Bonner*
05/09	h	Crusaders	L	0-1	
12/09	h	Ballymena	L	1-6	*Curran*
19/09	h	Glentoran	W	1-0	*McDaid*
26/09	a	Ballinamallard	W	2-0	*Garrett, McDaid (p)*
03/10	h	Linfield	D	3-3	*M Donnelly, Bonner, McMullan*
10/10	a	Dungannon	W	1-0	*Curran*
17/10	h	Portadown	W	3-0	*Garrett 2 (1p), J Donnelly*
24/10	a	Coleraine	D	0-0	
31/10	h	Glenavon	D	1-1	*Curran*
06/11	h	Warrenpoint	W	2-1	*Winchester 2*
14/11	a	Linfield	W	2-1	*McDaid (p), J Donnelly*
21/11	h	Ballinamallard	W	3-1	*Curran, McDaid 2*
05/12	h	Ballymena	W	4-2	*Curran, McDaid 2 (2p), Knowles*
12/12	h	Dungannon	W	1-0	*M Donnelly*
19/12	a	Glentoran	L	0-2	
26/12	a	Crusaders	D	2-2	*McDaid, J Donnelly*

2015

01/01	h	Warrenpoint	D	1-1	*McDaid*
12/01	h	Carrick	D	3-3	*Flynn, Garrett, Knowles (p)*
16/01	a	Glenavon	D	3-3	*Knowles 2, McGovern*
23/01	h	Ballinamallard	W	2-0	*D Murray, Curran*
30/01	h	Portadown	W	1-0	*J Donnelly*
20/02	a	Crusaders	L	0-1	
27/02	a	Coleraine	W	1-0	*McDaid*
01/03	a	Glentoran	W	2-0	*J Donnelly, Garrett*
12/03	a	Dungannon	W	2-0	*D Murray 2*
19/03	h	Linfield	L	0-2	
02/04	a	Ballymena	D	2-2	*J Donnelly, Hughes*
05/04	a	Carrick	W	2-1	*J Donnelly, Hughes*
09/04	a	Glenavon	W	3-1	*D Murray, Winchester, J Donnelly*
16/04	h	Glentoran	L	0-2	
19/04	h	Crusaders	L	1-3	*McMullan*
23/04	a	Linfield	L	0-4	
30/04	a	Coleraine	L	0-3	

No	Name	Nat	DoB	Pos	Aps	(s)	Gls
4	Caoimhin Bonner		15/01/93	D	17	(2)	2
14	Francis Brennan		11/08/91	M	7	(1)	
12	Peter Burke	IRL	03/03/96	G	18		
17	Ryan Catney		17/02/87	M	27	(3)	
23	Tomas Cosgrove		11/12/92	D	22		
7	Chris Curran		05/01/91	M	32	(4)	6
1	Conor Devlin		23/09/91	G	20		
21	Jay Donnelly		10/04/95	A	25	(8)	11
11	Martin Donnelly		28/08/88	M	28	(3)	2
5	Johnny Flynn		18/11/89	D	32		1
10	Stephen Garrett		13/04/87	A	22	(12)	6
24	Paul George	IRL	27/01/94	M	1	(5)	
29	Daniel Hughes		03/05/92	A	8	(5)	2
3	Levi Ives		28/06/97	D	25	(1)	
6	James Knowles		06/04/93	M	25	(5)	4
30	Ross Lavery		29/07/96	M		(3)	
9	David McDaid		03/12/90	A	25	(5)	12
2	Jamie McGovern		29/05/89	D	22	(2)	1
8	George McMullan		04/08/81	D	18	(5)	3
25	Jonathan McMurray		19/09/94	A		(2)	
13	Tiarnan McNicholl		26/05/95	A		(3)	
26	Andrew Mooney		08/02/97	A		(3)	
19	Ciaran Murray		29/04/98	A		(7)	
13	Darren Murray		24/10/91	A	8	(3)	4
20	Martin Murray		18/08/93	M		(14)	
15	Eamon Seydak		25/02/86	D	11	(1)	
16	Marc Smyth	SCO	27/12/82	D	14	(1)	
18	Jude Winchester		13/04/93	M	11	(4)	3

Coleraine FC

1927 • The Showgrounds (3,960) •
colerainefc.com
Major honours
*Irish League (1) 1974; Irish Cup (5) 1965, 1972,
1975, 1977, 2003*
Manager: Oran Kearney

2015
08/08	h	Glentoran	W	1-0	McLaughlin
12/08	a	Cliftonville	L	0-4	
15/08	a	Ballymena	W	2-0	Morrow, Canning
22/08	h	Linfield	L	1-3	Brown
28/08	a	Ballinamallard	W	2-1	McLaughlin, McGonigle
05/09	a	Dungannon	W	3-0	Brown, McGonigle 2
12/09	a	Glenavon	L	0-3	
19/09	h	Crusaders	D	1-1	McLaughlin
26/09	a	Portadown	W	2-1	McLaughlin, Morrow
03/10	h	Warrenpoint	W	2-0	McCauley, McLaughlin
10/10	a	Carrick	W	2-1	Lyons, McLaughlin
17/10	a	Dungannon	W	1-0	McLaughlin
24/10	h	Cliftonville	D	0-0	
31/10	a	Glentoran	D	1-1	Brown
07/11	h	Portadown	W	4-0	McCauley 3, McLaughlin
14/11	a	Warrenpoint	W	4-0	McLaughlin, Parkhill 2, McCauley
21/11	h	Carrick	W	2-1	Kane, McGonigle
27/11	a	Ballinamallard	W	2-1	Parkhill, Brown
05/12	a	Linfield	L	0-1	
12/12	h	Glenavon	L	0-2	
18/12	a	Crusaders	L	1-3	Harkin
26/12	h	Ballymena	W	2-1	McGonigle 2

2016
01/01	h	Ballinamallard	W	1-0	Brown
16/01	a	Warrenpoint	L	0-3	
23/01	h	Carrick	L	1-2	McCauley
30/01	h	Crusaders	L	0-2	
12/02	a	Ballymena	W	2-0	McCauley, McLaughlin
20/02	h	Linfield	L	2-3	Parkhill, Lyons
27/02	a	Cliftonville	W	3-1	Brown, McLaughlin, Lyons
12/03	a	Portadown	W	1-0	Brown
19/03	h	Dungannon	L	0-1	
26/03	a	Glenavon	L	0-1	
29/03	a	Glentoran	L	0-1	
09/04	h	Glentoran	D	1-1	McLaughlin
16/04	a	Linfield	L	0-3	
19/04	a	Glenavon	L	0-3	
23/04	a	Crusaders	L	0-1	
30/04	h	Cliftonville	W	3-0	Lyons, McCafferty 2 (2p)

No	Name	Nat	DoB	Pos	Aps	(s)	Gls
2	Howard Beverland		30/03/90	D	36	(1)	
11	Rodney Brown		13/08/95	M	31	(6)	7
12	Aaron Canning		07/03/92	D	6	(1)	1
1	Michael Doherty		19/10/83	G	23		
5	Stephen Douglas		27/09/77	D	26		
23	Mark Edgar		17/02/97	D	4		
3	Gareth Falconer		28/04/90	M	10	(2)	
20	Andy Findlay		01/02/95	G	2		
10	Ruairi Harkin	IRL	11/10/89	M	33		1
4	Ruaidhri Higgins		23/10/84	M	19	(5)	
1	Chris Johns		13/05/95	G	13		
18	Lyndon Kane		15/02/97	D	25		1
27	Colin Kanwischer	GER	02/06/91	M		(2)	
18	Glenn Law		25/03/87	M		(3)	
17	Bradley Lyons		26/05/97	A	20	(10)	4
8	Neil McCafferty	IRL	19/07/84	M	18	(1)	2
7	Darren McCauley		21/02/91	M	24	(6)	7
19	Jamie McGonigle		05/03/96	M	20	(16)	6
17	Conor McGuinness		14/01/98	M		(1)	
15	James McLaughlin		06/03/80	A	25	(8)	12
9	Sammy Morrow		03/03/85	A	12	(9)	2
3	Adam Mullan		24/10/95	A	28	(2)	
6	David Ogilby		02/06/84	D	15	(1)	
16	Ian Parkhill		07/04/90	A	21	(11)	4
14	John Watt		20/03/86	D	7	(3)	

Crusaders FC

1898 • Seaview (3,330) • crusadersfc.com
Major honours
*Irish League (6) 1973, 1976, 1995, 1997, 2015, 2016;
Irish Cup (3) 1967, 1968, 2009*
Manager: Stephen Baxter

2015
08/08	h	Portadown	L	1-2	Heatley
12/08	a	Glentoran	D	2-2	Robinson, Owens
15/08	h	Ballinamallard	W	5-0	O'Carroll, Heatley 2, Owens 2
22/08	h	Glenavon	W	2-1	Snoddy, og (Neill)
29/08	h	Dungannon	W	4-0	Robinson, Owens 2, Snoddy
05/09	a	Cliftonville	W	1-0	Owens
12/09	h	Linfield	W	3-0	Owens 2, Heatley
19/09	a	Coleraine	D	1-1	O'Flynn
26/09	h	Carrick	W	5-0	Heatley 4 (1p), Mitchell
03/10	h	Ballymena	W	4-2	Heatley (p), Owens, Whyte, Forsythe
10/10	h	Warrenpoint	W	1-0	O'Carroll
17/10	a	Ballinamallard	D	1-1	O'Carroll
24/10	h	Glenavon	W	1-0	Heatley
31/10	a	Portadown	W	3-1	Coates, Owens, Heatley
07/11	a	Linfield	W	1-0	Owens
14/11	h	Glentoran	W	3-0	Heatley, Forsythe, O'Flynn
21/11	a	Warrenpoint	W	3-1	Heatley (p), Forsythe 2
28/11	h	Ballymena	W	3-2	Owens, og (Nelson), Burns (p)
05/12	a	Dungannon	W	2-1	Heatley, O'Flynn
18/12	h	Coleraine	W	3-1	Robinson, Burns (p), Owens
26/12	a	Cliftonville	D	2-2	Forsythe, Burns (p)

2016
01/01	a	Linfield	L	0-2	
16/01	h	Glentoran	W	4-2	Forsythe, Snoddy, Burns, Owens
23/01	a	Portadown	W	1-0	Robinson
30/01	a	Coleraine	W	2-0	Burns 2 (2p)
12/02	h	Glenavon	D	1-1	Owens
20/02	h	Cliftonville	W	1-0	Heatley
27/02	a	Warrenpoint	D	1-1	O'Carroll (p)
12/03	h	Ballymena	D	0-0	
19/03	a	Carrick	W	4-0	Forsythe, Heatley 2, Owens
22/03	a	Carrick	L	3-4	Carvill, Heatley, og (Smyth)
26/03	h	Dungannon	W	2-0	Heatley 2
29/03	a	Ballinamallard	W	1-0	Coates
09/04	h	Linfield	W	2-0	Whyte, Forsythe
16/04	a	Glenavon	W	1-0	Owens
19/04	h	Cliftonville	W	3-1	Whyte, Heatley 2
23/04	h	Coleraine	W	1-0	Owens
30/04	a	Glentoran	W	1-0	Holden

No	Name	Nat	DoB	Pos	Aps	(s)	Gls
2	Billy Joe Burns		28/04/89	D	36		6
12	Declan Caddell		13/04/88	M	17	(3)	
25	Michael Carvill		03/04/88	M	16	(9)	1
20	Richard Clarke		28/11/85	M	20	(6)	
14	Colin Coates		26/10/85	D	35		2
14	Jordan Forsythe		11/02/91	M	28	(9)	8
22	Paul Heatley		30/06/87	M	35		22
28	Ross Holden		27/11/97	A	1		1
5	David Magowan		04/10/83	D	15	(2)	
17	Craig McClean		06/07/85	D	36		
24	Graeme McKibben		23/11/90	G	1		
27	Andrew Mitchell		06/04/92	M	13	(9)	1
16	Barry Molloy		28/11/83	M		(4)	
10	Diarmuid O'Carroll	IRL	16/03/97	A	9	(13)	4
27	Stephen O'Flynn	IRL	27/04/82	A		(6)	3
1	Sean O'Neill		11/04/88	G	37		
11	Jordan Owens		09/07/89	A	37		18
11	Joshua Robinson		30/06/93	D	27	(3)	4
19	Matthew Snoddy		02/06/93	M	32	(5)	4
3	Cameron Stewart		11/03/97	D	2	(1)	
26	Richard Vauls		08/09/85	D	1		
23	Gavin Whyte		31/01/96	A	20	(7)	4

Dungannon Swifts FC

1949 • Stangmore Park (2,154) •
dungannonswifts.co.uk
**Manager: Darren Murphy;
(27/10/15) Rodney McAree**

2015
08/08	h	Carrick	L	1-2	Teggart
12/08	a	Ballinamallard	D	0-0	
15/08	a	Linfield	L	1-5	Armstrong
22/08	h	Ballymena	W	2-0	Harpur, McElroy
29/08	a	Crusaders	L	0-4	
05/09	h	Coleraine	L	0-3	
12/09	a	Warrenpoint	W	2-0	Mitchell, Harpur
19/09	a	Portadown	D	3-3	Hazley, Harpur, Mitchell
26/09	h	Glentoran	L	2-4	Armstrong, Mitchell
03/10	a	Glenavon	L	1-3	Harpur
10/10	h	Cliftonville	L	0-1	
17/10	a	Coleraine	L	0-1	
24/10	a	Ballymena	L	0-1	
31/10	h	Linfield	L	0-1	
14/11	h	Glenavon	L	1-2	Burns
21/11	a	Glentoran	D	1-1	Mitchell
28/11	h	Warrenpoint	W	5-1	McElroy 2, og (Shanahan), Mitchell, Burke
05/12	h	Crusaders	L	1-2	Mitchell
12/12	a	Cliftonville	L	0-1	
19/12	h	Portadown	W	3-1	Burns, Harpur, Mitchell
26/12	a	Ballinamallard	D	1-1	Liggett

2016
01/01	h	Glentoran	W	3-1	McElroy 2, Teggart
23/01	h	Glenavon	L	0-1	
02/02	a	Linfield	L	0-6	
11/02	a	Carrick	D	2-2	Fitzpatrick, Wilson
15/02	h	Warrenpoint	W	1-0	Mitchell
20/02	h	Ballinamallard	W	2-0	Teggart, Harpur
27/02	a	Ballymena	W	4-2	Mitchell, Harpur 3 (1p)
02/03	a	Carrick	L	0-1	
12/03	h	Cliftonville	D	2-2	Mitchell 2
19/03	a	Coleraine	W	1-0	Hazley
26/03	a	Crusaders	L	0-2	
29/03	h	Portadown	W	2-1	Liggett, Mitchell
09/04	h	Ballymena	L	2-4	Glackin, Mitchell
16/04	a	Portadown	W	2-1	Mitchell 2
19/04	h	Ballinamallard	W	4-2	Teggart, Burke 2, Liggett
23/04	h	Carrick	L	1-3	Burke
30/04	a	Warrenpoint	L	0-1	

No	Name	Nat	DoB	Pos	Aps	(s)	Gls
18	Stuart Addis		05/07/79	G	2	(1)	
5	David Armstrong		23/01/87	D	29		2
19	Cormac Burke		11/11/93	M	26	(5)	4
14	Andrew Burns		29/05/92	D	24		2
1	Andy Coleman		13/06/85	G	36		
17	Jamie Douglas		04/07/92	A	1	(9)	
6	Terry Fitzpatrick		23/03/82	M	18	(10)	1
7	Jamie Glackin		16/02/95	M	21	(7)	1
3	Cameron Grieve		22/12/81	A	1		
10	Ryan Harpur		01/12/88	M	32	(1)	9
8	Matt Hazley		25/02/87	M	15	(13)	2
3	Chris Hegarty		13/08/92	D	13		
9	Gary Liggett		28/09/87	A	3	(18)	3
15	Kris Lowe		06/01/96	M	16	(10)	
22	Dermot McCaffrey		29/03/86	D	31		
21	Marc McConnell		08/03/96	M		(1)	
2	David McCullough		24/04/87	D	2	(4)	
25	Ruairi McDonald		11/03/97	M		(1)	
20	Paul McElroy		07/07/94	A	22		5
16	Andrew Mitchell		25/01/94	A	30	(5)	16
23	Dale Montgomery		19/04/91	D	24	(3)	
24	Ryan Mullan		11/11/98	D	3		
24	Conor Mullen		19/10/96	A		(5)	
12	Jarlath O'Rourke		13/02/95	D	15	(2)	
11	Alan Teggart		24/11/86	M	27	(8)	4
4	Douglas Wilson		03/03/93	A	27		1

Glenavon FC

1889 • Mourneview Park (4,160) • glenavonfc.com

Major honours
Irish League (3) 1952, 1957, 1960; Irish Cup (7) 1957, 1959, 1961, 1992, 1997, 2014, 2016

Manager: Gary Hamilton

2015

08/08	h	Cliftonville	L	0-1	
12/08	a	Ballymena	W	7-1	*Marshall, Elebert, Braniff, Bradley 3, Hall*
15/08	a	Warrenpoint	W	3-0	*og (Clarke), Bradley, Cooper*
22/08	h	Crusaders	L	1-2	*Singleton*
28/08	h	Glentoran	D	0-0	
12/09	h	Coleraine	W	3-0	*Hall, Marshall, McGrory*
19/09	a	Carrick	D	2-2	*Marshall, Hamilton*
22/09	a	Portadown	D	2-2	*Bradley, Singleton*
26/09	a	Linfield	L	3-4	*Neill, Lindsay, Bradley*
03/10	h	Dungannon	W	3-1	*Braniff (p), Lindsay, Singleton*
07/10	a	Ballinamallard	W	1-0	*Cooper*
17/10	h	Ballymena	W	3-1	*Bradley 3*
24/10	a	Crusaders	L	0-1	
31/10	a	Cliftonville	D	1-1	*O'Brien*
07/11	h	Ballinamallard	W	5-1	*Kearns, O'Brien 3, Hamilton (p)*
14/11	a	Dungannon	W	2-1	*Kearns, Bradley*
21/11	h	Linfield	W	3-2	*Kearns, Cooper 2*
28/11	a	Glentoran	L	0-2	
04/12	h	Carrick	W	2-0	*Kearns 2 (1p)*
12/12	a	Coleraine	W	2-0	*Marshall, og (Morrow)*
19/12	h	Warrenpoint	D	1-1	*Hall*
26/12	h	Portadown	W	1-0	*Marshall*

2016

16/01	h	Cliftonville	D	3-3	*Bradley 3*
23/01	a	Dungannon	W	1-0	*Cooper*
02/02	a	Carrick	W	5-1	*Cooper, Bradley, Dillon, Braniff, Martyn*
12/02	a	Crusaders	D	1-1	*Bradley*
15/02	h	Glentoran	L	1-3	*Braniff*
20/02	h	Portadown	W	4-1	*Braniff, Bradley 2, Kilmartin*
27/02	a	Linfield	D	1-1	*McGrory (p)*
12/03	a	Warrenpoint	W	3-1	*O'Brien 2, Sykes*
19/03	h	Ballinamallard	W	1-0	*Hamilton*
26/03	a	Coleraine	W	1-0	*Braniff*
05/04	h	Ballymena	D	1-1	*Martyn*
09/04	a	Cliftonville	L	1-3	*Kelly*
16/04	h	Crusaders	L	0-1	
19/04	h	Coleraine	W	3-0	*og (McCafferty), Kelly, Braniff*
23/04	a	Glentoran	W	1-0	*Braniff*
30/04	h	Linfield	L	0-1	

No	Name	Nat	DoB	Pos	Aps	(s)	Gls
10	Eoin Bradley		30/12/83	A	28	(1)	17
22	Kevin Braniff		04/03/83	A	26	(1)	8
18	Kyle Buckley		23/11/90	D	4	(1)	
35	Bobby Burns		07/09/99	D	1		
16	Ciaran Caldwell		10/10/89	M	1		
9	Joel Cooper		29/02/96	M	29	(2)	6
32	Conall Delaney		08/02/98	A	1		
15	Conor Dillon	IRL	07/12/88	D	29	(3)	1
25	David Elebert	IRL	21/03/96	D	5	(2)	1
11	Andy Hall		19/09/89	M	33	(1)	3
20	Gary Hamilton		06/10/80	A	2	(29)	3
23	Daniel Kearns	IRL	26/08/91	M	16	(2)	5
4	Simon Kelly		04/07/84	D	24	(2)	2
7	Andy Kilmartin		08/01/83	M	31	(2)	1
6	Kris Lindsay		05/02/84	D	27	(2)	2
28	Josh Lynch		06/04/97	M		(1)	
35	Caolan Marron		04/07/98	D		(1)	
8	Rhys Marshall	IRL	16/01/95	D	36		5
24	Ciaran Martyn		25/03/80	M	11	(1)	2
33	James McGrath		19/04/88	G	1		
17	Andrew McGrory		15/12/91	M	11	(10)	2
32	Alex McIlmail		07/12/00	M	1	(1)	
39	Daniel McKeown		03/04/00	D		(1)	
2	Gareth McKeown		14/07/83	D	1		
38	Ruairi Morgan		22/04/98	M	1		
2	Ian Morris	IRL	27/02/87	D	1	(1)	
3	Kyle Neill		30/03/78	D	18	(2)	1
37	Robbie Norton		16/04/98	A		(1)	
19	Declan O'Brien		16/06/79	A	7	(9)	6
12	Mark Patton		21/06/89	D	7	(18)	
40	Harry Robinson		26/09/00	A		(1)	
36	Carter Savage		30/09/88	D	1		
27	James Singleton		22/08/95	D	8		3
14	Mark Sykes		04/08/97	M	20	(5)	1
1	Jonathan Tuffey		20/01/87	G	37		

Glentoran FC

1882 • The Oval (9,400) • glentoran.com

Major honours
Irish League (23) 1894, 1897, 1905, 1912, 1913, 1921, 1925, 1931, 1951, 1953, 1964, 1967, 1968, 1970, 1972, 1977, 1981, 1988, 1992, 1999, 2003, 2005, 2009; Irish Cup (22) 1914, 1917, 1921, 1932, 1933, 1935, 1951, 1966, 1973, 1983, 1985, 1986, 1987, 1988, 1990, 1996, 1998, 2000, 2001, 2004, 2013, 2015

Manager: Eddie Patterson; (18/10/15) (Roy Coyle); (09/11/15) Alan Kernaghan (IRL)

2015

08/08	a	Coleraine	L	0-1	
12/08	h	Crusaders	D	2-2	*Stewart 2 (1p)*
15/08	a	Carrick	D	1-1	*Kane*
22/08	h	Warrenpoint	W	2-1	*Allen 2*
28/08	a	Glenavon	D	0-0	
05/09	h	Ballymena	L	1-3	*Allen*
12/09	h	Portadown	W	1-0	*Kane*
19/09	a	Cliftonville	L	0-1	
26/09	h	Dungannon	W	4-2	*Birney 2, Addis, Allen*
03/10	h	Ballinamallard	L	0-2	
10/10	a	Linfield	D	1-1	*Allen*
17/10	h	Carrick	W	2-0	*McAlorum, McMenamin*
24/10	a	Warrenpoint	W	1-0	*O'Hanlon*
31/10	h	Coleraine	D	1-1	*Allen (p)*
07/11	a	Ballymena	W	1-0	*Caldwell*
14/11	a	Crusaders	L	0-3	
21/11	h	Dungannon	D	1-1	*J Smith*
28/11	h	Glenavon	W	2-0	*J Smith, Gordon*
05/12	a	Ballinamallard	W	4-2	*McCaffrey 2, J Smith, Allen*
14/12	a	Portadown	L	3-5	*Kane, Allen 2*
19/12	h	Cliftonville	W	2-0	*J Smith, McCaffrey*
26/12	h	Linfield	L	1-2	*J Smith*

2016

01/01	a	Dungannon	L	1-3	*Addis*
16/01	a	Crusaders	L	2-4	*Allen 2*
23/01	h	Warrenpoint	L	0-4	
15/02	a	Glenavon	W	3-1	*Allen 2, J Smith*
20/02	h	Ballymena	W	2-0	*J Smith (p), Caldwell*
27/02	a	Ballinamallard	L	0-1	
01/03	h	Cliftonville	L	0-2	
12/03	a	Linfield	L	0-3	
19/03	h	Portadown	W	2-1	*Allen 2*
26/03	a	Carrick	W	2-1	*Allen 2*
29/03	h	Coleraine	W	1-0	*Scullion*
09/04	a	Coleraine	D	1-1	*J Smith*
16/04	a	Cliftonville	W	2-0	*Kane, Allen*
19/04	h	Linfield	L	0-4	
23/04	h	Glenavon	L	0-1	
30/04	h	Crusaders	L	0-1	

No	Name	Nat	DoB	Pos	Aps	(s)	Gls
19	Jonny Addis		27/09/92	M	31	(2)	2
9	Curtis Allen		22/02/88	A	37		18
5	Calum Birney		19/04/93	D	15		2
14	Caolan Boyd-Munce		26/01/00	A		(1)	
32	Patrick Cafolla		06/03/98	M	1	(4)	
23	Ciaran Caldwell		10/10/89	M	19	(4)	2
15	Cieran Clougherty		15/09/96	A		(1)	
2	William Garrett		31/08/91	D	10		
17	Kristian Gibson		21/03/95	M	2	(7)	
22	Steven Gordon		27/07/93	D	24	(4)	1
27	George Gray		20/03/96	D	1	(1)	
31	Karl Hamill		06/08/98	D	1	(3)	
14	Niall Henderson		07/02/88	M	7	(2)	
18	Aaron Hogg		14/01/88	G	12	(1)	
4	Barry Holland		10/05/84	D	33		
8	David Howland		17/09/86	M	1		
3	Marcus Kane		08/12/91	M	34		4
11	Chris Lavery		20/01/91	M	9	(1)	
6	Jay Magee		04/05/88	D	25		
16	Stephen McAlorum		11/06/86	M	19		1
10	Francis McCaffrey		22/04/93	M	17	(10)	3
26	Stephen McCullough		30/08/94	D	20	(6)	
12	Danny McKee		10/06/95	A	3	(1)	
24	Conor McMenamin		24/08/95	M	9	(8)	1
1	Elliott Morris		04/05/81	G	26	(1)	
8	Chris Morrow		20/09/85	M	6	(5)	
21	Kym Nelson		18/07/95	M	7	(1)	
20	Jim O'Hanlon		14/03/93	M	2	(3)	1
36	Dale Patton		21/09/96	A		(3)	
27	Stephen Rice	IRL	06/10/84	M	4		
7	David Scullion		27/04/84	A	19	(8)	1
12	Colin Smith		02/05/94	D	1		
25	Jonathan Smith		12/07/97	A	20	(6)	8
11	Jordan Stewart		31/03/95	A	3		2

Linfield FC

1886 • Windsor Park (18,000) • linfieldfc.com

Major honours
Irish League (51) 1891, 1892, 1893, 1895, 1898, 1902, 1904, 1907, 1908, 1909, 1911, 1914, 1922, 1923, 1930, 1932, 1934, 1935, 1949, 1950, 1954, 1955, 1956, 1959, 1961, 1962, 1966, 1969, 1971, 1975, 1978, 1979, 1980, 1982, 1983, 1984, 1985, 1986, 1987, 1989, 1993, 1994, 2000, 2001, 2004, 2006, 2007, 2008, 2010, 2011, 2012; Irish Cup (42) 1891, 1892, 1893, 1895, 1898, 1899, 1902, 1904, 1912, 1913, 1915, 1916, 1919, 1922, 1923, 1930, 1931, 1934, 1936, 1939, 1942, 1945, 1946, 1948, 1950, 1953, 1960, 1962, 1963, 1970, 1978, 1980, 1982, 1994, 1995, 2002, 2006, 2007, 2008, 2010, 2011, 2012

Manager: Warren Feeney; (14/10/15) David Healy

2015

08/08	h	Ballymena	W	4-0	*Burns 2, Waterworth, Reece Glendinning*
12/08	a	Carrick	W	3-0	*Lowry, Burns, Millar*
15/08	h	Dungannon	W	5-1	*Burns, Waterworth 3, Salley*
22/08	a	Coleraine	W	3-1	*Burns, M Clarke, Mulgrew*
29/08	h	Portadown	W	3-0	*Waterworth 2, Bates*
05/09	a	Ballinamallard	W	1-0	*Ward*
12/09	a	Crusaders	L	0-3	
19/09	h	Warrenpoint	W	5-1	*Waterworth 4, Haughey*
26/09	h	Glenavon	W	4-3	*Waterworth 2, Millar, Haughey*
03/10	a	Cliftonville	D	3-3	*Kee, Haughey, Burns*
10/10	h	Glentoran	D	1-1	*Kee*
17/10	a	Warrenpoint	W	3-0	*Burns 2 (1p), Bates*
24/10	h	Carrick	D	1-1	*Burns*
31/10	a	Dungannon	W	1-0	*Sproule*
07/11	h	Crusaders	L	0-1	
14/11	h	Cliftonville	L	1-2	*Waterworth*
21/11	a	Glenavon	L	2-3	*Mulgrew, Millar*
28/11	a	Portadown	L	0-2	
05/12	h	Coleraine	W	1-0	*Callacher*
12/12	h	Ballinamallard	D	1-1	*Waterworth*
19/12	a	Ballymena	W	3-1	*Ward, Waterworth, Bates*
26/12	a	Glentoran	W	2-1	*Quinn, Smyth*

2016

01/01	h	Crusaders	W	2-0	*Waterworth, Callacher*
23/01	a	Ballymena	W	4-0	*Ward, Gaynor (p), Smyth, Waterworth*
30/01	h	Carrick	W	2-0	*Stafford, Waterworth*
02/02	h	Dungannon	W	6-0	*Waterworth, Smyth, Stafford 2, Burns, McLellan*
12/02	a	Portadown	L	1-2	*M Clarke*
20/02	a	Coleraine	W	3-2	*Burns, Haughey 2*
27/02	h	Glenavon	D	1-1	*Burns (p)*
12/03	h	Glentoran	W	3-0	*Gaynor 2 (1p), Burns*
19/03	a	Cliftonville	W	2-0	*Callacher, Smyth*
24/03	h	Ballinamallard	W	2-1	*Waterworth, og (Morris)*
29/03	a	Warrenpoint	W	6-2	*Burns 2 (1p), Millar 2, Gaynor, Kee*
09/04	a	Crusaders	L	0-2	
16/04	h	Coleraine	W	3-0	*Millar 2, Callacher*
19/04	a	Glentoran	W	4-0	*Waterworth 2, Burns 2*
23/04	h	Cliftonville	W	4-0	*Burns 2, Smyth, Gaynor*
30/04	a	Glenavon	W	1-0	*Croskery*

No	Name	Nat	DoB	Pos	Aps	(s)	Gls
9	Guy Bates	ENG	31/10/85	A	20	(10)	3
14	Aaron Burns		29/05/92	M	22	(9)	19
6	Jimmy Callacher		11/06/91	D	23	(2)	4
16	Matthew Clarke		03/03/94	D	33		2
32	Ross Clarke		17/05/93	A	1	(1)	
18	Rauiri Croskery		10/12/96	A	1		1
35	Gareth Deane		14/06/94	G	3		
21	Stephen Fallon		03/03/97	M	2	(5)	
3	Seanna Foster		29/01/97	D	1		
27	Jonathan Frazer		30/05/96	A		(3)	
34	Ross Gaynor	IRL	09/09/87	D	13		5
23	Reece Glendinning		09/06/95	D	22	(2)	1
19	Ross Glendinning		18/05/93	G	35		
5	Mark Haughey		23/01/91	D	29		5
4	Chris Hegarty		13/08/92	D	3		
17	David Kee		09/08/88	M	12	(10)	3
24	Gary Lavery		04/05/97	A	1	(1)	
8	Stephen Lowry		14/10/86	M	18	(4)	1
40	Adam McCallum		18/07/97	D	1		
10	Michael McLellan		22/01/93	A	3	(9)	1
12	Kirk Millar		07/07/92	M	30	(4)	7
43	Jake Moore		18/07/97	A		(1)	
22	Jamie Mulgrew		05/06/86	M	33	(2)	2
20	Thomas Murray		23/03/95	M		(3)	
42	Reece Neale		14/05/98	D		(1)	
31	Niall Quinn		02/08/93	D	9	(12)	1
27	Adam Salley		07/02/97	A	1	(8)	1
44	Eamon Scannell		10/01/99	A		(1)	
38	Paul Smyth		10/09/97	A	17	(2)	5
26	Ivan Sproule		18/02/81	A	2	(10)	1
2	Mark Stafford		20/08/87	D	17		3
15	Sean Ward		12/01/84	D	31	(1)	3
7	Andrew Waterworth		11/04/86	A	35		22

NORTHERN IRELAND

Portadown FC

1924 • Shamrock Park (15,800) •
portadownfc.co.uk
Major honours
*Irish League (4) 1990, 1991, 1996, 2002; Irish Cup (3)
1991, 1999, 2005*
**Manager: Ronnie McFall;
(08/03/16) Pat McGibbon**

2015
08/08	a	Crusaders	W	2-1	Murray 2 (1p)
12/08	h	Warrenpoint	W	2-1	Twigg, O'Hara
15/08	h	Cliftonville	L	0-1	
22/08	a	Ballinamallard	W	2-1	Murray, Oman
29/08	a	Linfield	L	0-3	
12/09	a	Glentoran	L	0-1	
19/09	h	Dungannon	D	3-3	Breen, Twigg, Márcio Soares
22/09	h	Glenavon	D	2-2	Murray (p), Twigg
26/09	h	Coleraine	L	1-2	McMahon
03/10	a	Carrick	W	1-0	Twigg (p)
10/10	h	Ballymena	W	3-2	Oman, Mackle, McMahon
17/10	a	Cliftonville	L	0-3	
24/10	h	Ballinamallard	L	0-3	
31/10	h	Crusaders	L	1-3	Murray
07/11	a	Coleraine	L	0-4	
14/11	h	Carrick	W	3-2	Twigg, Oman 2
21/11	h	Ballymena	D	1-1	Mackle
28/11	h	Linfield	W	2-0	Casement, Márcio Soares
14/12	h	Glentoran	W	5-3	Twigg 2, Murray 2, Garrett
19/12	a	Dungannon	L	1-3	Casement
26/12	a	Glenavon	L	0-1	

2016
01/01	h	Ballymena	L	3-4	Márcio Soares, Breen, Mackle
19/01	a	Warrenpoint	L	0-2	
23/01	a	Crusaders	L	0-1	
30/01	a	Cliftonville	L	0-1	
12/02	h	Linfield	W	2-1	McAllister (p), Lowry
15/02	a	Ballinamallard	L	0-1	
20/02	a	Glenavon	L	1-4	Casement
27/02	a	Carrick	D	0-0	
12/03	h	Coleraine	L	0-1	
19/03	a	Glentoran	L	1-2	Márcio Soares
26/03	h	Warrenpoint	L	1-3	Márcio Soares
29/03	a	Dungannon	L	1-2	Ferris
09/04	h	Ballinamallard	D	0-0	
16/04	h	Dungannon	L	1-2	Ferris
19/04	a	Carrick	W	2-1	Casement (p), Breen
23/04	a	Warrenpoint	L	0-2	
30/04	a	Ballymena	W	2-0	Oman, Parker

No	Name	Nat	DoB	Pos	Aps	(s)	Gls
6	Gary Breen	IRL	17/03/89	D	21	(4)	3
13	Billy Brennan	IRL	06/03/85	G	8	(1)	
19	Adam Brown		16/01/98	D	1		
21	Mark Carson		09/11/92	M		(1)	
2	Chris Casement		12/01/88	D	36		4
19	Shea Conaty		19/01/98	A	1		
23	Nathaniel Ferris		03/12/98	A	4	(5)	2
20	Robert Garrett		05/05/88	M	32		1
16	Michael Gault		15/04/83	M	29		
22	Padraig Judge		13/03/96	M		(2)	
15	Philip Lowry		15/07/89	M	7		1
23	Jordan Lyttle		14/05/96	D		(1)	
8	Sean Mackle	SCO	10/04/88	M	31	(2)	3
26	Márcio Soares	POR	07/04/96	A	10	(13)	5
13	Martin Marron		24/01/96	G		(1)	
10	Mark McAllister		26/04/84	A	12	(12)	1
7	Pete McMahon	IRL	20/04/89	M	11	(2)	2
1	David Miskelly		03/09/79	G	30		
11	Tim Mouncey		27/04/82	M	13	(5)	
9	Darren Murray		24/10/91	A	18	(2)	7
4	Keith O'Hara		03/02/81	D	23		1
12	Ken Oman	IRL	29/07/82	D	29	(2)	5
17	Matthew Parker		24/05/95	D	12		1
5	Chris Ramsey		24/05/90	D	20	(3)	
3	Ross Redman		23/11/89	D	34	(1)	
24	Jake Richardson		18/08/96	D	5	(5)	
25	Christian Stewart		13/02/96	D	2	(7)	
18	Gary Twigg	SCO	19/03/84	A	27	(2)	7
30	Mikey Withers		23/05/94	A	2	(4)	

Warrenpoint Town FC

1987 • Milltown (1,280) •
warrenpointtownfc.co.uk
Manager: Barry Gray

2015
08/08	h	Ballinamallard	L	0-3	(w/o; original result 0-1)
12/08	a	Portadown	L	1-2	D Hughes
15/08	h	Glenavon	L	0-3	
22/08	a	Glentoran	L	1-2	S Hughes
30/08	h	Cliftonville	D	2-2	S Hughes, M Hughes
05/09	a	Carrick	W	2-1	McDonald, Clarke
12/09	h	Dungannon	L	0-2	
19/09	a	Linfield	L	1-5	M Hughes
26/09	h	Ballymena	L	1-2	S Hughes
03/10	a	Coleraine	L	0-2	
10/10	a	Crusaders	L	0-1	
17/10	h	Linfield	L	0-3	
24/10	h	Glentoran	L	0-1	
30/10	a	Ballinamallard	L	0-3	
06/11	a	Cliftonville	L	1-2	D Hughes
14/11	h	Coleraine	L	0-4	
21/11	h	Crusaders	L	1-3	D Hughes
28/11	a	Dungannon	L	1-5	D Hughes
12/12	h	Ballymena	L	2-4	S Murray 2
19/12	a	Glenavon	D	1-1	S Murray
26/12	h	Carrick	D	1-1	Donnelly

2016
01/01	a	Cliftonville	D	1-1	S Murray
16/01	h	Coleraine	W	3-0	S Murray 2, M Murray
19/01	h	Portadown	W	2-0	M Murray, McMurray
23/01	a	Glentoran	W	4-0	M Murray 2, McGuigan, McMurray
12/02	h	Ballinamallard	W	3-0	Mulvenna, S Murray, McMurray
15/02	a	Dungannon	L	0-1	
19/02	a	Carrick	W	1-0	McDonald
27/02	h	Crusaders	D	1-1	M Hughes
12/03	h	Glenavon	L	1-3	Bagnall
19/03	a	Ballymena	L	1-3	McMurray
26/03	a	Portadown	W	3-1	McDonald, S Murray 2
29/03	h	Linfield	L	2-6	Bagnall, S Murray
09/04	a	Carrick	D	1-1	S Murray (p)
16/04	a	Ballinamallard	L	0-2	
19/04	h	Ballymena	W	4-1	S Murray 3 (1p), McMurray
23/04	h	Portadown	W	2-0	McDonald, S Murray
30/04	h	Dungannon	D	1-1	S Hughes

No	Name	Nat	DoB	Pos	Aps	(s)	Gls
16	Liam Bagnall		17/05/92	D	34		2
21	John Boyle		01/03/96	D	27	(2)	
4	Mark Clarke		23/08/89	D	21	(5)	1
14	Jordan Dane		21/04/95	M	28	(3)	
20	Shane Dolan	IRL	06/02/88	M	2	(1)	
25	Sean Donnelly		02/03/95	M	9	(8)	1
24	Stefan Graham		18/03/98	G	1		
9	Daniel Hughes		03/05/92	A	19		4
17	Mark Hughes		23/03/85	M	37	(1)	3
10	Stephen Hughes		18/11/86	A	17	(10)	4
19	Roy Kierans	IRL	10/02/95	D	6	(5)	
2	Darren King		16/10/85	D	12		
12	Mark McCabe		27/05/97	A	6	(7)	
7	Conor McDonald	IRL	14/06/95	M	29	(2)	4
6	John McGuigan		26/08/93	M	7	(8)	1
22	Jonathan McMurray		19/09/94	A	7	(8)	5
5	Dermot McVeigh		24/07/90	D	33	(2)	
18	Stephen Moan		04/09/90	D	29	(2)	
28	Tiarnan Mulvenna	IRL	10/12/88	A	4	(8)	1
3	Nathan Murphy	IRL	25/02/95	M	7	(7)	
23	Martin Murray		18/08/93	A	15		4
11	Stephen Murray		29/12/88	A	25	(6)	15
1	Jonny Parr		26/11/85	G	24		
15	Matthew Rooney		18/02/90	A		(3)	
30	Aaron Shanahan	IRL	20/04/84	G	13		
8	Padraig Smith		30/09/82	M	6	(3)	

Top goalscorers

Paul Heatley

Andrew Waterworth

22	Paul Heatley (Crusaders)
	Andrew Waterworth (Linfield)
19	Aaron Burns (Linfield)
18	Jordan Owens (Crusaders)
	Curtis Allen (Glentoran)
17	Eoin Bradley (Glenavon)
16	Andrew Mitchell (Dungannon)
15	Stephen Murray (Warrenpoint)
13	Miguel Chines (Carrick)
12	David McDaid (Cliftonville)
	James McLaughlin (Coleraine)

UEFA Europa League qualification play-offs

SEMI-FINAL

(06/05/16)
Coleraine 1-2 Glentoran *(McGonigle 85; Birney 33, Allen 58)*

FINAL

(10/05/16)
Cliftonville 3-2 Glentoran *(J Donnelly 11, Knowles 61p, McDaid 79; Allen 17, Magee 28)*

Promoted club

Ards FC

1900 • Clandeboye Park, Bangor (1,895) •
ardsfc.co.uk
Major honours
*Irish League (1) 1958; Irish Cup (4) 1927, 1952,
1969, 1974*
Manager: Niall Currie

Second level final table 2015/16

		Pld	W	D	L	F	A	Pts
1	Ards FC	26	17	3	6	59	35	54
2	Harland & Wolff Welders FC	26	15	6	5	54	28	51
3	Armagh City FC	26	13	5	8	64	36	44
4	Knockbreda FC	26	12	7	7	48	32	43
5	Institute FC	26	12	6	8	40	20	42
6	Larne FC	26	12	6	8	64	45	42
7	Lurgan Celtic FC	26	11	6	9	40	40	39
8	Ballyclare Comrades FC	26	9	10	7	44	40	37
9	Loughgall FC	26	10	6	10	45	54	36
10	Bangor FC	26	10	5	11	44	40	35
11	Dergview FC	26	9	8	9	41	40	35
12	Annagh United FC	26	7	6	13	37	57	27
13	Donegal Celtic FC	26	2	4	20	34	80	10
14	Lisburn Distillery FC	26	2	4	20	18	85	10

*NB Institute enter play-off as highest-ranked team with
promotion licence.*

Promotion/Relegation play-offs

(06/05/16 & 22/06/16)
Institute 1-2 Ballinamallard
Ballinamallard 3-3 Institute
(Ballinamallard 5-4)

DOMESTIC CUP

Irish Cup 2015/16

FIFTH ROUND

(09/01/16)
Armagh City 2-2 Portstewart *(aet; 4-1 on pens)*
Banbridge Town 0-2 Carrick
Cliftonville 2-0 Immaculata
Coleraine 2-2 Ballinamallard *(aet; 4-2 on pens)*
Crumlin Star 3-2 Oxford United Stars
Crusaders 3-0 Rathfriland Rangers
Dungannon 4-3 Warrenpoint
Harland & Wolff Welders 1-4 Glenavon
Linfield 2-1 Ballymena *(aet)*
Loughgall 5-2 Larne
Lurgan Celtic 2-1 Bangor
Portadown 6-1 Wakehurst
Sport & Leisure Swifts 3-2 Institute *(aet)*
Tobermore United 0-2 PSNI

(19/01/16)
Annagh United 1-5 Knockbreda
Glentoran 4-1 Ards

SIXTH ROUND

(06/02/16)
Cliftonville 4-0 Sport & Leisure Swifts
Dungannon 1-3 Crusaders
Glentoran 1-4 Glenavon
Linfield 7-0 Armagh City
Loughgall 2-0 PSNI
Lurgan Celtic 1-0 Knockbreda
Portadown 3-1 Coleraine

(15/02/16)
Carrick 1-0 Crumlin Star

QUARTER-FINALS

(05/03/16)
Carrick 0-3 Crusaders *(Heatley 16, 52,
O'Carroll 33)*
Cliftonville 0-3 Linfield *(Gaynor 56, 90p,
Waterworth 76)*
Glenavon 2-1 Loughgall *(O'Brien 40, McGrory 66p;
Mallen 67)*
Portadown 2-3 Lurgan Celtic *(Márcio Soares 58,
Mackle 70; Haire 13, Conaty 54, Fitzpatrick 90p)*

SEMI-FINALS

(01/04/16)
Glenavon 4-3 Crusaders *(Braniff 27, 43, 53, 72;
Snoddy 24, 28, Heatley 47)*

(02/04/16)
Linfield 3-0 Lurgan Celtic *(Burns 61, 71, 90p)*

FINAL

(07/05/16)
Windsor Park, Belfast
GLENAVON FC 2 *(Braniff 45, Hall 48)*
LINFIELD FC 0
Referee: Heatherington
GLENAVON: *Tuffey, Marshall, Patton, Kelly,
Dillon, Martyn (Sykes 68), Cooper (Kearns 90+1),
Kilmartin, Hall, Braniff, Bradley (Hamilton 84)*
LINFIELD: *Deane, Ward, Haughey, Callacher
(Quinn 77), Gaynor, Mulgrew, Burns, Lowry, M
Clarke (Millar 56), Waterworth, Smyth*

Mark Patton shows off the Irish Cup after Glenavon's 2-0 victory in the final against Linfield

NORWAY
Norges Fotballforbund (NFF)

Address	Serviceboks 1	**President**	Terje Svendsen
	Ullevaal stadion	**General secretary**	Kjetil P Siem
	NO-0840 Oslo	**Media officer**	Yngve Haavik
Tel	+47 210 29300	**Year of formation**	1902
Fax	+47 210 29301	**National stadium**	Ullevaal, Oslo
E-mail	nff@fotball.no		(27,182)
Website	fotball.no		

TIPPELIGAEN CLUBS

1. Aalesunds FK
2. FK Bodø/Glimt
3. FK Haugesund
4. Lillestrøm SK
5. Mjøndalen IF
6. Molde FK
7. Odds BK
8. Rosenborg BK
9. Sandefjord Fotball
10. Sarpsborg 08 FF
11. Stabæk Fotball
12. IK Start
13. Strømsgodset IF
14. Tromsø IL
15. Viking FK
16. Vålerenga Fotball

PROMOTED CLUBS

17. Sogndal Fotball
18. SK Brann

KEY
- UEFA Champions League
- UEFA Europa League
- Promoted
- Relegated

Rosenborg rewind the clock

Without a trophy for five years, Rosenborg BK ended the drought in style by racing virtually unopposed towards a record 23rd Norwegian title and doubling up with a tenth victory in the Norwegian Cup. It was a triumphant first full season in charge for coach Kåre Ingebrigtsen, a winner of eight league titles with the Trondheim club during his playing days.

2014 double winners Molde fared better in Europe than they did domestically, enabling Strømsgodset and Stabæk to take the other two places on the Tippeligaen podium, while Sarpsborg were surprise first-time finalists in the cup.

| Trondheim club end five-year wait for title | Cup win completes first double for 12 years | Molde make headlines in Europe |

Domestic league

Runners-up to Molde in 2014 thanks to a strong finish of nine wins in ten games following the appointment of former Norwegian international midfielder Ingebrigtsen, Rosenborg carried that fine form into the new season with a pair of crushing opening wins, and that set the tone for what was to be a comprehensive return to power for the club that had won the championship 13 years in a row from 1992 to 2004.

Leaders from start to finish, Rosenborg would not be knocked out of their stride. Every time they failed to win – an infrequent occurrence – the response was positive. In fact, they dropped points in successive games only twice, the first time in mid-season, to which they reacted by winning six games in a row, the second time at the end, when a second successive draw, 3-3 at Strømsgodset, confirmed them as champions.

It was like a return to the glory days for the Rosenborg fans, who regularly flocked to the Lerkendal, where the team remained unbeaten all season, providing an average attendance of 17,846, by far the biggest in the league. The style of football was also reminiscent of times gone by, with Ingebrigtsen encouraging a pacy and direct attacking style that reaped its reward in the 'goals for' column of the

table, 22 of the team's handsome final total of 73 coming from the division's top marksman, Alexander Søderlund.

Rosenborg also posted the best defensive figures, conceding just 27 times, but it was in midfield where arguably the team's finest assets lay, with Danish schemer Mike Jensen, 21-year-old Ole Kristian Selnæs and, a bit further forward, 13-goal Norwegian international Pål André Helland all having seasons to remember.

Strømsgodset, the 2013 champions, put together an 11-match unbeaten run at the close to claim the runners-up spot, while Stabæk, second for so long, had to settle for third after losing three of their last four matches, their autumn struggles largely attributable to the early-September departure of 17-goal striker Adama Diomandé to Hull City. Fourth place went to Odds BK, who, thanks to Rosenborg's double, qualified for the UEFA Europa League for the second year running, rendering fruitless Molde's fast finish under their restored double title-winning coach Ole Gunnar Solskjær. There were happier fans down the coast at Bergen, where Brann returned to the top flight just a year after their shock relegation – as runners-up to Sogndal.

Domestic cup

After a semi-final thriller against Stabæk, which they won 3-2 after extra

time, Rosenborg had things pretty much all their own way in the Norwegian Cup final against Sarpsborg, first-half goals from Helland and Jensen putting the champions in total control at a sold-out Ullevaal and ultimately ending the club's 12-year wait for a tenth cup triumph.

Europe

Rosenborg supplemented a successful domestic season by playing 16 matches in the UEFA Europa League, but despite their impressive run from the first qualifying round to the group stage it was Molde, originally in the UEFA Champions League, who outlasted them. While Ingebrigtsen's men were unable to claim a group win, Solskjær led Molde to a double over Celtic and into a round of 32 tie with holders Sevilla that brought a memorable 1-0 home win after a 3-0 first-leg loss in Andalusia.

National team

The second half of the UEFA EURO 2016 qualifying campaign proved to be a bittersweet experience for Per-Mathias Høgmo and his players. Three successive wins over Bulgaria, Croatia and Malta revived hopes of automatic qualification for France, but a closing 2-1 defeat in Italy sent them into the play-offs, where, despite controlling much of the play, they lost home and away to Hungary.

DOMESTIC SEASON AT A GLANCE

Tippeligaen 2015 final table

		Pld	Home					Away					Total					Pts
			W	D	L	F	A	W	D	L	F	A	W	D	L	F	A	
1	**Rosenborg BK**	30	11	4	0	36	12	10	2	3	37	15	21	6	3	73	27	69
2	Strømsgodset IF	30	10	4	1	34	17	7	2	6	33	27	17	6	7	67	44	57
3	Stabæk Fotball	30	10	2	3	28	19	7	3	5	26	24	17	5	8	54	43	56
4	Odds BK	30	7	6	2	30	19	8	4	3	31	22	15	10	5	61	41	55
5	Viking FK	30	10	2	3	29	18	7	0	8	24	21	17	2	11	53	39	53
6	Molde FK	30	8	4	3	37	15	7	3	5	25	16	15	7	8	62	31	52
7	Vålerenga Fotball	30	7	2	6	25	20	7	5	3	24	21	14	7	9	49	41	49
8	Lillestrøm SK	30	9	3	3	26	18	3	6	6	19	25	12	9	9	45	43	44
9	FK Bodø/Glimt	30	8	1	6	32	26	4	3	8	21	30	12	4	14	53	56	40
10	Aalesunds FK	30	7	3	5	22	21	4	2	9	20	36	11	5	14	42	57	38
11	Sarpsborg 08 FF	30	6	3	6	22	26	2	7	6	15	23	8	10	12	37	49	34
12	FK Haugesund	30	3	5	7	19	27	5	2	8	14	25	8	7	15	33	52	31
13	Tromsø IL	30	5	6	4	22	23	2	2	11	14	27	7	8	15	36	50	29
14	IK Start	30	4	3	8	18	29	1	4	10	17	35	5	7	18	35	64	22
15	Mjøndalen IF	30	4	3	8	23	36	0	6	9	15	33	4	9	17	38	69	21
16	Sandefjord Fotball	30	4	2	9	19	26	0	2	13	17	42	4	4	22	36	68	16

NB Lillestrøm SK – 1 pt deducted.

European qualification 2016/17

 Champion/Cup winner: Rosenborg BK (second qualifying round)

 Strømsgodset IF (second qualifying round)
Stabæk Fotball (first qualifying round)
Odds BK (first qualifying round)

Top scorer	Alexander Søderlund (Rosenborg), 22 goals
Relegated clubs	Sandefjord Fotball, Mjøndalen IF
Promoted clubs	Sogndal Fotball, SK Brann
Cup final	Rosenborg BK 2-0 Sarpsborg 08 FF

Team of the season
(4-4-2)

Coach: Bradley (Stabæk)

Player of the season

Mike Jensen
(Rosenborg BK)

A former Danish youth international at every age group with three senior caps, Jensen left his homeland in 2013 – after a long spell at formative club Brøndby – to try his luck further north at Rosenborg, and in his third season at the Lerkendal, aged 27, the crafty midfielder enjoyed the most consistently productive form of his career. He topped the Tippeligaen table for assists with 12 and scored the second goal in the Norwegian Cup final against Sarpsborg to help the Trondheim club to the double.

Newcomer of the season

Iver Fossum
(Strømsgodset IF)

Aged only 18 at the start of the 2015 Tippeligaen campaign, Fossum went on to start all 30 of Strømsgodset's matches, scoring a total of 11 goals to end up as the club's joint leading scorer alongside prolific mid-season recruit Marcus Pedersen. It was a season of startling progress for the gifted young attacking midfielder, and his fortunes would improve still further in 2016 as he signed a contract with German club Hannover and was handed his first senior caps for the Norwegian national side.

NATIONAL TEAM

International tournament appearances

FIFA World Cup (3) 1938, 1994, 1998 (2nd round)
UEFA European Championship (1) 2000

Top five all-time caps

John Arne Riise (110); Thorbjørn Svenssen (104); Henning Berg (100); Erik Thorstvedt (97); John Carew & Brede Hangeland (91)

Top five all-time goals

Jørgen Juve (33); Einar Gundersen (26); Harald Hennum (25); John Carew (24); Tore André Flo & Ole Gunnar Solskjær (23)

Results 2015/16

03/09/15	Bulgaria (ECQ)	A	Sofia	W	1-0	Forren (57)
06/09/15	Croatia (ECQ)	H	Oslo	W	2-0	Berget (51), Ćorluka (69og)
10/10/15	Malta (ECQ)	H	Oslo	W	2-0	Tettey (19), Søderlund (52)
13/10/15	Italy (ECQ)	A	Rome	L	1-2	Tettey (23)
12/11/15	Hungary (ECQ)	H	Oslo	L	0-1	
15/11/15	Hungary (ECQ)	A	Budapest	L	1-2	Henriksen (87)
24/03/16	Estonia	A	Tallinn	D	0-0	
29/03/16	Finland	H	Oslo	W	2-0	Berget (57), Johansen (83)
29/05/16	Portugal	A	Porto	L	0-3	
01/06/16	Iceland	H	Oslo	W	3-2	Johansen (1), Helland (41), Sørloth (67)
05/06/16	Belgium	A	Brussels	L	2-3	King (21), Veton Berisha (48)

Appearances 2015/16

Coach: Per-Mathias Høgmo	01/12/59		BUL	CRO	MLT	ITA	HUN	HUN	Est	Fin	Por	Isl	Bel	Caps	Goals
Ørjan Håskjold Nyland	10/09/90	Ingolstadt (GER)	G	G	G	G	G	G		G46		G	G	22	-
Omar Elabdellaoui	05/12/91	Olympiacos (GRE)	D	D	D	D	D	D		D				22	-
Even Hovland	14/02/89	Nürnberg (GER)	D	D	D	D	D	D	D	D	D	D	D	17	-
Vegard Forren	16/02/88	Molde	D75	D	D	D	D	D	D			D	D	32	1
Tom Høgli	24/02/84	København (DEN)	D	D			D							49	2
Alexander Tettey	04/04/86	Norwich (ENG)	M	M	M	M	M	M						30	3
Stefan Johansen	08/01/91	Celtic (SCO)	M87	M92	M	M	M	M	M	s61	M	M82	M75	29	3
Jone Samuelsen	06/07/84	Odd	M64			s51								10	-
Markus Henriksen	25/07/92	AZ (NED)	M	M	M	M	M	A			A	M	M	27	2
Jo Inge Berget	11/09/90	Malmö (SWE)	M	M	M84	M78	M74	s80	M	s46				12	2
Alexander Søderlund	03/08/87	Rosenborg /St-Étienne (FRA)	A	A94	A77	A60	A61			s64	s46			26	1
Per Ciljan Skjelbred	16/06/87	Hertha (GER)	s64	M91	M53	M51	M86	M80	M86	M79				40	1
Håvard Nordtveit	21/06/90	Mönchengladbach (GER)	s75	s92					M64	M61				28	2
Stefan Strandberg	25/07/90	Krasnodar (RUS)	s87						D	D		s73		7	-
Håvard Nielsen	15/07/93	Salzburg (AUT)		s91										14	2
Valon Berisha	07/02/93	Salzburg (AUT)		s94	s84	s78			M	M	M75		s66	20	-
Haitam Aleesami	31/07/91	Göteborg (SWE)			D	D		D	D	D		D	D	7	-
Martin Ødegaard	17/12/98	Real Madrid (ESP)			s53		A46		M46					9	-
Joshua King	15/01/92	Bournemouth (ENG)			s77	s60					A86	A53	A81	22	5
Marcus Pedersen	08/06/90	Strømsgodset					s61	s46						9	1
Mohamed Elyounoussi	04/08/94	Molde					s74	M46						5	-
Pål André Helland	04/01/90	Rosenborg					s86	s46				A53		5	1
Rune Almenning Jarstein	29/09/84	Hertha (GER)							G	G				40	-
Martin Linnes	20/09/91	Galatasaray (TUR)							D		D86			14	-
Adama Diomandé	14/02/90	Hull (ENG)							A64	A46		A72	M66	5	-
Ole Kristian Selnæs	07/07/94	St-Étienne (FRA)							s64	s79	s73	M	M73	5	-
Fredrik Midtsjø	11/08/93	Rosenborg							s86					1	-
Fredrik Gulbrandsen	10/09/92	Molde								M46				3	-
André Hansen	17/12/89	Rosenborg								s46				3	-
Ruben Yttergård Jenssen	04/05/88	Kaiserslautern (GER)								s46	M73	s82	s75	38	-
Anders Trondsen	30/03/95	Sarpsborg									D			1	-
Veton Berisha	13/04/94	Greuther Fürth (GER)									M		M73	2	1
Iver Fossum	15/07/96	Hannover (GER)									s75	s72	s73	3	-
Niklas Gunnarsson	27/04/91	Hibernian (SCO)									s86			1	-
Alexander Sørloth	05/12/95	Groningen (NED)									s86	s53	s81	3	1
Jonas Svensson	06/03/93	Rosenborg										D	D	2	-
Martin Samuelsen	17/04/97	West Ham (ENG)											s53	1	-

NORWAY

EUROPE

Molde FK

Second qualifying round - FC Pyunik (ARM)
H 5-0 *Elyounoussi (35, 44), Kamara (84, 90+2), Moström (90+5)*
Horvath, Gabrielsen, Toivio, Singh (Berg Hestad 81), Kamara, Linnes (Moström 66), Hussain, Rindarøy, Elyounoussi, Forren, Svendsen (Høiland 68). Coach: Tor Ole Skullerud (NOR)
A 0-1
Linde, Gabrielsen, Toivio, Moström (Agnaldo 73), Kamara (Høiland 61), Flo, Hussain (Bendiksen 67), Hestad, Elyounoussi, Forren, Svendsen. Coach: Tor Ole Skullerud (NOR)

Third qualifying round - GNK Dinamo Zagreb (CRO)
A 1-1 *Kamara (21)*
Horvath, Toivio, Singh, Moström (Flo 72), Kamara, Linnes, Hussain (Berg Hestad 67), Hestad, Rindarøy (Gabrielsen 80), Elyounoussi, Forren. Coach: Tor Ole Skullerud (NOR)
H 3-3 *Hussain (43), Elyounoussi (52p), Kamara (75)*
Horvath, Toivio, Singh, Moström (Svendsen 75), Kamara, Linnes, Hussain (Berg Hestad 87), Hestad (Gabrielsen 77), Rindarøy, Elyounoussi, Forren. Coach: Tor Ole Skullerud (NOR)
Red card: Forren 72

Play-offs - R. Standard de Liège (BEL)
H 2-0 *Høiland (24), Elyounoussi (28)*
Horvath, Gabrielsen, Toivio, Berg Hestad, Singh, Moström, Linnes, Flo, Hestad (Svendsen 80), Høiland (Simonsen 90), Elyounoussi. Coach: Erling Moe (NOR)
A 1-3 *Hussain (42)*
Horvath, Gabrielsen, Berg Hestad, Singh, Moström (Toivio 70), Kamara (Høiland 77), Linnes, Flo, Hussain, Elyounoussi, Forren. Coach: Erling Moe (NOR)

Group A
Match 1 - Fenerbahçe SK (TUR)
A 3-1 *Høiland (36p), Elyounoussi (53), Linnes (65)*
Horvath, Gabrielsen, Berg Hestad, Singh, Moström (Toivio 87), Linnes, Hestad (Hussain 79), Høiland (Kamara 66), Rindarøy, Elyounoussi, Forren. Coach: Erling Moe (NOR)
Red card: Elyounoussi 84
Match 2 - AFC Ajax (NED)
H 1-1 *Hestad (8)*
Horvath, Gabrielsen, Berg Hestad, Singh, Moström, Linnes (Toivio 61), Hussain, Hestad (Svendsen 59), Høiland (Kamara 80), Rindarøy, Forren. Coach: Erling Moe (NOR)
Match 3 - Celtic FC (SCO)
H 3-1 *Kamara (11), Forren (18), Elyounoussi (56)*
Horvath, Toivio, Berg Hestad, Singh, Kamara (Hestad 74), Linnes, Hussain, Rindarøy (Flo 53), Elyounoussi (Bakenga 84), Forren. Coach: Ole Gunnar Solskjær (NOR)
Match 4 - Celtic FC (SCO)
A 2-1 *Elyounoussi (21), Berg Hestad (37)*
Horvath, Toivio, Berg Hestad, Singh, Moström (Hestad 62), Linnes, Hussain (Gabrielsen 90+5), Høiland (Kamara 46), Rindarøy, Elyounoussi, Forren. Coach: Ole Gunnar Solskjær (NOR)

Match 5 - Fenerbahçe SK (TUR)
H 0-2
Horvath, Toivio, Berg Hestad (Hestad 76), Singh, Gulbrandsen (Kamara 46), Linnes, Hussain, Rindarøy, Elyounoussi, Forren, Svendsen (Gabrielsen 86). Coach: Ole Gunnar Solskjær (NOR)
Red card: Rindarøy 90+1
Match 6 - AFC Ajax (NED)
A 1-1 *Singh (29)*
Horvath, Gabrielsen, Toivio (Berg Hestad 19), Singh, Moström (Hestad 76), Kamara (Gulbrandsen 52), Linnes, Flo, Hussain, Elyounoussi, Forren. Coach: Ole Gunnar Solskjær (NOR)

Round of 32 - Sevilla FC (ESP)
A 0-3
Horvath, Gabrielsen, Toivio, Berg Hestad, Gulbrandsen (Agnaldo 73), Moström, Flo, Aursnes (Svendsen 80), Elyounoussi (Hestad 63), Forren, Diouf. Coach: Ole Gunnar Solskjær (NOR)
H 1-0 *Hestad (43)*
Horvath, Gabrielsen, Toivio, Berg Hestad (Strande 90+4), Moström (Strand 80), Flo, Aursnes, Hestad, Elyounoussi, Forren, Svendsen (Diop 67). Coach: Ole Gunnar Solskjær (NOR)

Rosenborg BK

First qualifying round - Víkingur (FRO)
A 2-0 *Søderlund (82, 90+2)*
Hansen, Dorsin, Eyjólfsson, Jensen, Riski (Helmersen 80), Malec (Søderlund 64), Mikkelsen, Skjelvik, Selnæs, Midtsjø, Svensson. Coach: Erik Hoftun (NOR)
H 0-0
Lund Hansen, Dorsin, Eyjólfsson, Riski (Søderlund 74), Malec, Skjelvik, Nielsen, Selnæs (Jensen 66), Midtsjø (Helmersen 84), Svensson, Saeter. Coach: Kåre Ingebrigtsen (NOR)

Second qualifying round - KR Reykjavík (ISL)
A 1-0 *Helland (56p)*
Hansen, Dorsin, Eyjólfsson, Jensen, Mikkelsen, Søderlund, Skjelvik, Selnæs, Midtsjø, Svensson, Helland (Riski 78). Coach: Kåre Ingebrigtsen (NOR)
H 3-0 *Midtsjø (4), Helland (7), Søderlund (18)*
Hansen, Dorsin, Eyjólfsson, Jensen, Mikkelsen, Søderlund (Helmersen 79), Skjelvik, Selnæs (Riski 37), Midtsjø, Svensson, Helland (Nielsen 72). Coach: Kåre Ingebrigtsen (NOR)

Third qualifying round - Debreceni VSC (HUN)
A 3-2 *Mikkelsen (52, 87), Helland (58)*
Hansen, Dorsin, Eyjólfsson, Jensen, Mikkelsen (Riski 90+1), Søderlund (Vilhjálmsson 89), Skjelvik, Selnæs, Midtsjø, Svensson, Helland (De Lanlay 73). Coach: Kåre Ingebrigtsen (NOR)
H 3-1 *Søderlund (27), Jensen (40), Vilhjálmsson (86)*
Hansen, Eyjólfsson, Jensen (Solli 90), Mikkelsen, Bjørdal, Søderlund (Vilhjálmsson 77), Skjelvik, Selnæs, Midtsjø (Saeter 82), Svensson, Helland. Coach: Kåre Ingebrigtsen (NOR)

Play-offs - FC Steaua Bucureşti (ROU)
A 3-0 *Mikkelsen (61), Helland (67), Jensen (90+3)*
Hansen, Eyjólfsson, Jensen, Mikkelsen, Bjørdal, Søderlund (Vilhjálmsson 89), Skjelvik, Selnæs, Midtsjø (Konradsen 66), Svensson, Helland (De Lanlay 76). Coach: Kåre Ingebrigtsen (NOR)

H 0-1
Hansen, Eyjólfsson, Jensen, Mikkelsen, Bjørdal, Søderlund, Selnæs (Vilhjálmsson 29), Midtsjø, Svensson, Helland, Konradsen. Coach: Kåre Ingebrigtsen (NOR)

Group G
Match 1 - AS Saint-Étienne (FRA)
A 2-2 *Mikkelsen (16), Svensson (78)*
Hansen, Eyjólfsson, Jensen, Mikkelsen, Søderlund, Skjelvik, Selnæs, Midtsjø, Svensson, Helland (De Lanlay 76), Konradsen. Coach: Kåre Ingebrigtsen (NOR)
Match 2 - FC Dnipro Dnipropetrovsk (UKR)
H 0-1
Hansen, Eyjólfsson, Mikkelsen, Bjørdal, Søderlund, Skjelvik, Selnæs, Midtsjø (Jensen 71), Svensson, Helland (De Lanlay 46), Konradsen. Coach: Kåre Ingebrigtsen (NOR)
Match 3 - SS Lazio (ITA)
A 1-3 *Søderlund (69)*
Hansen, Dorsin (Mikkelsen 62), Eyjólfsson, Jensen, Bjørdal, Søderlund, Skjelvik, De Lanlay, Selnæs (Vilhjálmsson 89), Midtsjø, Svensson (Konradsen 76). Coach: Kåre Ingebrigtsen (NOR)
Match 4 - SS Lazio (ITA)
H 0-2
Hansen, Reginiussen (Bjørdal 33), Eyjólfsson, Jensen, Mikkelsen, Søderlund (Vilhjálmsson 65), Skjelvik, Selnæs, Midtsjø (Konradsen 61), Svensson, Helland. Coach: Kåre Ingebrigtsen (NOR)
Match 5 - AS Saint-Étienne (FRA)
H 1-1 *Søderlund (40)*
Lund Hansen, Eyjólfsson, Jensen, Mikkelsen, Bjørdal, Søderlund, Skjelvik, Selnæs, Svensson, Helland (De Lanlay 81), Konradsen (Vilhjálmsson 82). Coach: Kåre Ingebrigtsen (NOR)
Match 6 - FC Dnipro Dnipropetrovsk (UKR)
A 0-3
Hansen, Dorsin (Sæter 84), Jensen, Vilhjálmsson, Søderlund, Skjelvik, De Lanlay (Konradsen 68), Selnæs, Midtsjø, Svensson, Helland (Mikkelsen 69). Coach: Kåre Ingebrigtsen (NOR)

Odds BK

First qualifying round - FC Sheriff (MDA)
A 3-0 *Akabueze (2), Johnsen (11), Hagen (28)*
Rossbach, Ruud, Gashi, Berg, Halvorsen, Samuelsen, Johnsen (Océan 18), Jonassen (Grøgaard 52), Hagen, Eriksen, Akabueze (Harvard 73). Coach: Dag-Eilev Fagermo (NOR)
H 0-0
Rossbach, Ruud, Gashi, Grøgaard, Berg, Halvorsen, Samuelsen (Zekhnini 83), Océan (Bergan 73), Hagen, Eriksen, Akabueze (Harvard 66). Coach: Dag-Eilev Fagermo (NOR)

Second qualifying round - Shamrock Rovers FC (IRL)
A 2-0 *Océan (53p, 67)*
Rossbach, Ruud, Gashi (Jensen 46), Halvorsen, Samuelsen, Océan (Bergan 85), Nordkvelle, Jonassen, Hagen, Eriksen, Akabueze (Harvard 82). Coach: Dag-Eilev Fagermo (NOR)
H 2-1 *Halvorsen (72), Hagen (90)*
Rossbach, Ruud, Gashi, Berg, Halvorsen, Nordkvelle (Samuelsen 62), Zekhnini, Jonassen, Hagen, Eriksen (Bergan 78), Akabueze (Océan 46). Coach: Dag-Eilev Fagermo (NOR)

DOMESTIC LEAGUE CLUB-BY-CLUB

Third qualifying round - IF Elfsborg (SWE)

A 1-2 Occéan (21p)
Rossbach, Ruud, Grøgaard, Halvorsen, Samuelsen, Diouf (Akabueze 68), Occéan, Nordkvelle (Berg 43), Jensen, Hagen, Eriksen. Coach: Dag-Eilev Fagermo (NOR)
H 2-0 Occéan (27), Akabueze (71)
Rossbach, Ruud, Grøgaard, Samuelsen (Gashi 82), Diouf (Halvorsen 46), Occéan, Nordkvelle (Berg 84), Jensen, Hagen, Eriksen, Akabueze. Coach: Dag-Eilev Fagermo (NOR)

Play-offs - Borussia Dortmund (GER)

H 3-4 Samuelsen (1), Nordkvelle (20), Ruud (22)
Rossbach, Ruud, Bergan, Grøgaard, Samuelsen (Berg 57), Occéan (Flo 77), Nordkvelle, Zekhnini, Jensen, Hagen, Akabueze (Halvorsen 65). Coach: Dag-Eilev Fagermo (NOR)
A 2-7 Halvorsen (19), Berg (64)
Rossbach, Bergan, Grøgaard, Berg, Halvorsen, Occéan (Flo 46), Nordkvelle (Gashi 64), Zekhnini (Akabueze 76), Hurme, Jensen, Hagen. Coach: Dag-Eilev Fagermo (NOR)

Strømsgodset IF

First qualifying round - FK Partizani (ALB)

H 3-1 Vilsvik (21, 73), Ogunjimi (66)
Bugge Pettersen, Madsen, Hanin, Storflor, Fossum, Wikheim (Kastrati 79), Abu, Adjei-Boateng, Vilsvik, Høibråten, Ogunjimi (Kovács 84). Coach: Bjørn Petter Ingebretsen (NOR)
A 1-0 Vaagan Moen (90+5)
Bugge Pettersen, Hamoud, Madsen, Rønning, Fossum, Kastrati (Vaagan Moen 58), Wikheim, Abu (Jradi 84), Vilsvik, Valsvik, Ogunjimi (Sørum 87). Coach: Bjørn Petter Ingebretsen (NOR)

Second qualifying round - FK Mladá Boleslav (CZE)

A 2-1 Sørum (44), Jradi (85)
Bugge Pettersen, Hamoud, Vaagan Moen (Jradi 61), Storflor (Kastrati 85), Fossum, Wikheim, Abu, Sørum (Olsen 53), Vilsvik, Høibråten, Valsvik. Coach: Bjørn Petter Ingebretsen (NOR)
H 0-1
Bugge Pettersen, Madsen, Hanin, Vaagan Moen (Rønning 70), Storflor (Kastrati 86), Fossum, Wikheim, Abu, Sørum (Olsen 69), Vilsvik, Valsvik. Coach: Bjørn Petter Ingebretsen (NOR)

Third qualifying round - HNK Hajduk Split (CRO)

A 0-2
Bugge Pettersen, Hamoud, Madsen, Rønning (Vaagan Moen 82), Fossum, Kastrati (Jradi 72), Olsen (Sørum 66), Wikheim, Abu, Vilsvik, Valsvik. Coach: Bjørn Petter Ingebretsen (NOR)
H 0-2
Bugge Pettersen, Hanin (Hamoud 30), Jradi (Storflor 60), Fossum, Kastrati (Sørum 72), Olsen, Wikheim, Abu, Vilsvik, Høibråten, Valsvik. Coach: Bjørn Petter Ingebretsen (NOR)

Aalesunds FK

1914 • Color Line (10,778) • aafk.no
Major honours
Norwegian Cup (2) 2009, 2011
**Coach: Harald Aabrekk;
(28/04/15) (Trond Fredriksen);
(30/10/15) Trond Fredriksen**

2015

06/04	a	Rosenborg	L	0-5	
12/04	h	Lillestrøm	D	1-1	Larsen
19/04	a	Molde	L	1-5	Barrantes
26/04	h	Tromsø	L	0-2	
30/04	a	Vålerenga	W	2-1	James, Mattila
03/05	h	Bodø/Glimt	W	2-0	James, Abdellaoue
10/05	a	Sandefjord	W	3-1	Abdellaoue, Barrantes, Mattila (p)
13/05	h	Sarpsborg	D	2-2	James, Larsen
16/05	a	Strømsgodset	L	1-3	Latifu
25/05	h	Viking	L	0-4	
29/05	a	Odd	D	1-1	Björk
07/06	h	Haugesund	W	2-1	Larsen, Barrantes
21/06	h	Stabæk	D	1-1	Abdellaoue
27/06	a	Start	L	1-3	Thrándarson
05/07	h	Mjøndalen	W	4-2	James 2, Thrándarson, Björk
11/07	a	Viking	L	1-4	Abdellaoue
26/07	a	Bodø/Glimt	L	0-1	
02/08	h	Start	W	2-0	Thrándarson, Matland
09/08	a	Haugesund	L	1-3	James (p)
14/08	h	Strømsgodset	W	2-1	Bjørdal, Abdellaoue
23/08	a	Sarpsborg	L	1-3	James (p)
28/08	h	Vålerenga	W	2-0	James, Larsen
13/09	a	Lillestrøm	L	1-3	James (p)
20/09	h	Odd	L	1-3	James
27/09	a	Tromsø	D	1-1	og (R Johansen)
04/10	h	Sandefjord	W	2-1	Abdellaoue, Thrándarson
17/10	a	Stabæk	W	4-1	Hoseth 2, Matland, James
25/10	h	Molde	L	1-2	James
01/11	a	Mjøndalen	W	2-1	James, Thrándarson
08/11	h	Rosenborg	L	0-1	

No	Name	Nat	DoB	Pos	Aps	(s)	Gls
30	Mustafa Abdellaoue		01/08/88	A	19	(7)	6
31	Michael Barrantes	CRC	04/10/83	M	12		3
17	Henrik Bjørdal		04/02/97	M	28	(2)	1
9	Carl Björk	SWE	04/02/92	A		(14)	2
8	Fredrik Carlsen		01/12/89	M	2	(2)	
33	Elias Dahlberg		29/07/96	M		(1)	
6	Mikael Dyrestam	SWE	10/12/91	D	27		
40	Sondre Fet		17/01/97	M		(3)	
3	Daniel Leo Grétarsson	ISL	02/10/95	D	3	(5)	
13	Sten Grytebust		25/10/89	G	27		
37	Torbjørn Grytten		06/04/95	A	2	(7)	
39	Vebjørn Hoff		13/02/96	M	14	(11)	
16	Magne Hoseth		13/10/80	M	8	(2)	2
14	Leke James	NGA	01/11/92	A	29		13
10	Peter Orry Larsen		25/02/89	M	23	(2)	4
2	Akeem Latifu	NGA	16/11/89	D	28	(1)	1
1	Andreas Lie		31/08/87	G	3		
5	Oddbjørn Lie		31/08/87	D	19	(2)	
15	Marlinho	BRA	24/03/94	A	1	(3)	
20	Thomas Martinussen		05/02/95	M	2	(3)	
22	Jo Nymo Matland		21/04/87	D	15	(6)	2
7	Sakari Mattila	FIN	14/07/89	M	12		2
4	Tero Mäntylä	FIN	18/04/91	D	12	(4)	
21	Bjørn Helge Riise		21/06/83	M	13		
24	Helge Sandvik		05/02/90	G		(1)	
23	Edvard Skagestad		06/07/88	D	18	(5)	
11	Aron Elís Thrándarson	ISL	10/11/94	M	13	(5)	5

FK Bodø/Glimt

1916 • Aspmyra (7,354) • glimt.no
Major honours
Norwegian Cup (2) 1975, 1993
Coach: Jan Halvor Halvorsen

2015

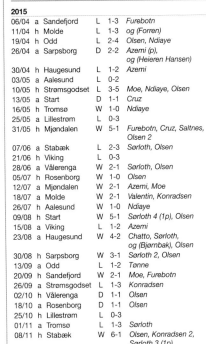

06/04	a	Sandefjord	L	1-3	Furebotn
11/04	h	Molde	L	1-3	og (Forren)
19/04	h	Odd	L	2-4	Olsen, Ndiaye
26/04	a	Sarpsborg	D	2-2	Azemi (p), og (Heieren Hansen)
30/04	h	Haugesund	L	1-2	Azemi
03/05	a	Aalesund	L	0-2	
10/05	h	Strømsgodset	L	3-5	Moe, Ndiaye, Olsen
13/05	a	Start	D	1-1	Cruz
16/05	h	Tromsø	W	1-0	Ndiaye
25/05	a	Lillestrøm	L	0-3	
31/05	h	Mjøndalen	W	5-1	Furebotn, Cruz, Saltnes, Olsen 2
07/06	a	Stabæk	L	2-3	Sørloth, Olsen
21/06	h	Viking	L	0-3	
28/06	a	Vålerenga	W	2-1	Sørloth, Olsen
05/07	h	Rosenborg	W	1-0	Olsen
12/07	a	Mjøndalen	W	2-1	Azemi, Moe
18/07	a	Molde	W	2-1	Valentin, Konradsen
26/07	h	Aalesund	W	1-0	Ndiaye
09/08	h	Start	W	5-1	Sørloth 4 (1p), Olsen
15/08	a	Viking	L	1-2	Azemi
23/08	a	Haugesund	W	4-2	Chatto, Sørloth, og (Bjørnbak), Olsen
30/08	h	Sarpsborg	W	3-1	Sørloth 2, Olsen
13/09	a	Odd	L	1-2	Tønne
20/09	h	Sandefjord	W	2-1	Moe, Furebotn
26/09	a	Strømsgodset	L	1-3	Konradsen
02/10	a	Vålerenga	D	1-1	Olsen
18/10	a	Rosenborg	D	1-1	Olsen
25/10	h	Lillestrøm	L	0-3	
01/11	a	Tromsø	L	1-3	Sørloth
08/11	h	Stabæk	W	6-1	Olsen, Konradsen 2, Sørloth 3 (1p)

No	Name	Nat	DoB	Pos	Aps	(s)	Gls
10	Fitim Azemi		25/06/92	A	27	(3)	4
27	Patrick Berg		24/11/97	M		(4)	
20	Ulrik Berglann		31/05/92	A	1	(3)	
24	Kristian Brix		13/06/90	D	13	(6)	
15	Dominic Chatto	NGA	12/07/85	M	16	(3)	1
26	Danny Cruz	USA	03/01/90	A	8	(7)	2
21	Daniel Edvardsen		31/08/91	M	7	(10)	
8	Henrik Furebotn		11/02/86	M	26		4
2	Ruben Imingen		04/12/86	D	2		
5	Thomas Jacobsen		16/09/83	D	27	(1)	
16	Anders Karlsen		15/02/90	M	3	(16)	
16	Morten Konradsen		03/05/96	M	15	(12)	4
1	Pavel Londak	EST	14/05/80	G	22		
18	Brede Moe		15/12/91	D	27		3
7	Papa Alioune Ndiaye	SEN	27/10/90	M	15	(1)	4
30	Trond Olsen		05/02/84	A	28	(1)	13
14	Ulrik Saltnes		10/11/92	M	16	(1)	1
23	Vieux Sané	SEN	04/08/89	D	25		
25	Lasse Staw		01/01/88	G	8	(1)	
11	Alexander Sørloth		05/12/95	A	19	(7)	13
19	Erik Tønne		03/07/91	M	2	(7)	1
3	Zarek Valentin	USA	06/08/91	D	23	(1)	1
29	Vebjørn Vinje		07/04/95	D		(1)	

NORWAY

FK Haugesund

1993 • Haugesund (8,993) • fkh.no
Coach: Jostein Grindhaug

2015

06/04	a	Stabæk	D	1-1	Diedhiou
12/04	h	Rosenborg	L	0-6	
17/04	a	Vålerenga	L	0-2	
26/04	h	Molde	D	0-0	
30/04	a	Bodø/Glimt	W	2-1	Nilsen, Skjerve
03/05	h	Sandefjord	W	2-1	Diedhiou, Gytkjær
10/05	a	Sarpsborg	L	0-3	
13/05	h	Viking	L	0-2	
16/05	a	Odd	D	0-0	
24/05	h	Strømsgodset	W	4-0	Bjørnbak, Diedhiou 2, Daniel Bamberg
30/05	h	Start	L	0-2	
07/06	a	Aalesund	L	1-2	Diedhiou
21/06	h	Mjøndalen	D	1-1	Gytkjær
28/06	a	Tromsø	L	0-2	
04/07	a	Lillestrøm	D	3-3	Gytkjær 3 (1p)
10/07	a	Molde	W	1-0	Diedhiou
25/07	h	Stabæk	D	2-2	Haukås, Skjerve
31/07	a	Viking	W	1-0	og (Mets)
09/08	h	Aalesund	W	3-1	Gytkjær 3
16/08	a	Mjøndalen	L	1-2	og (Hurtado)
23/08	h	Bodø/Glimt	L	2-4	Andreassen, Skjerve
30/08	a	Start	W	3-1	Haraldseid, Diedhiou, Gytkjær
11/09	a	Strømsgodset	L	0-5	
20/09	h	Sarpsborg	D	1-1	Stølås
27/09	a	Sandefjord	W	1-0	Diedhiou
04/10	h	Odd	L	1-2	Diedhiou
18/10	a	Lillestrøm	L	0-2	
24/10	h	Vålerenga	L	0-1	
01/11	a	Rosenborg	L	3-4	Gytkjær (p), Andreassen, Haukås
08/11	h	Tromsø	L	0-1	

No	Name	Nat	DoB	Pos	Aps	(s)	Gls
27	Tor André Aasheim		06/03/96	A		(1)	
14	Torbjørn Agdestein		18/09/91	A	2	(7)	
11	Tor Arne Andreassen		16/03/83	M	10	(6)	2
26	Sverre Bjørkkjær		12/07/96	D	6	(6)	
15	Martin Bjørnbak		22/03/92	D	18		
12	Per Kristian Bråtveit		15/02/96	G	27		
7	Søren Christensen	DEN	29/06/86	M	27	(1)	
50	Dušan Cvetinović	SRB	24/12/88	D	14		
23	Daniel Bamberg	BRA	23/04/84	M	21	(4)	1
20	Simon Diedhiou	SEN	10/09/90	A	22	(7)	9
7	Christian Gytkjær	DEN	06/05/90	A	29	(1)	10
19	Kristoffer Haraldseid		17/01/94	M	27	(1)	1
28	Arent-Emil Hauge		09/10/97	M		(3)	
8	Michael Haukås		21/11/86	M	16	(9)	2
6	Filip Kiss	SVK	13/10/90	M	9		
29	Robert Kling		01/05/97	M		(1)	
1	Per Morten Kristiansen		14/07/81	G	3		
30	Erling Myklebust		28/05/96	A		(2)	
3	David Myrestam	SWE	04/04/87	D	22		
13	Eirik Mæland		15/02/89	M	7	(1)	
10	Joakim Våge Nilsen		24/04/91	M	7	(3)	1
6	Patrick Olsen	DEN	23/04/94	M	10	(1)	
21	Roope Riski	FIN	16/08/91	A	2	(8)	
18	Vegard Skjerve		22/05/88	D	25		3
22	Alexander Stølås		30/04/89	A	8	(12)	1
5	William Troost-Ekong	NGA	01/09/93	D	13		
16	Sad'eeq Yusuf	NGA	23/07/96	M	5	(2)	

Lillestrøm SK

1917 • Åråsen (11,637) • lsk.no
Major honours
Norwegian League (5) 1959, 1976, 1977, 1986, 1989;
Norwegian Cup (5) 1977, 1978, 1981, 1985, 2007
Coach: Rúnar Kristinsson (ISL)

2015

07/04	h	Start	D	1-1	Mikalsen
12/04	a	Aalesund	D	1-1	Knudtzon
19/04	a	Tromsø	D	1-1	Knudtzon
26/04	h	Stabæk	L	0-2	
30/04	a	Mjøndalen	W	4-1	Friday 3, Fofana
03/05	a	Vålerenga	L	1-1	Andersson (p)
09/05	a	Rosenborg	L	0-3	
13/05	h	Molde	W	2-1	Knudtzon 2
16/05	a	Sarpsborg	W	3-1	og (Ernemann), Andersson, Krogstad
25/05	h	Bodø/Glimt	W	3-0	Knudtzon, Kolstad, Fofana
31/05	a	Strømsgodset	L	0-2	
07/06	h	Viking	W	2-1	Fofana, Knudtzon
20/06	a	Sandefjord	D	0-0	
28/06	h	Odd	D	1-1	Fofana (p)
04/07	a	Haugesund	D	3-3	Knudtzon, Fofana 2
12/07	h	Strømsgodset	L	1-2	Fofana (p)
27/07	a	Vålerenga	L	0-2	
02/08	h	Sandefjord	W	3-2	Kippe, Knudtzon, Friday
09/08	h	Rosenborg	L	0-5	
16/08	a	Stabæk	L	2-3	Friday, Koistad
21/08	h	Tromsø	W	1-0	Martin
30/08	a	Molde	D	2-2	Martin, Friday
13/09	h	Aalesund	W	3-1	Lundemo, Kolstad, Friday
19/09	a	Start	D	0-0	
26/09	h	Mjøndalen	W	3-0	Friday, Knudtzon, Martin
04/10	a	Viking	L	0-1	
18/10	h	Haugesund	W	2-0	og (Skjerve), Vilhjálmsson
25/10	h	Bodø/Glimt	W	3-0	Vilhjálmsson, Friday 2
01/11	h	Sarpsborg	W	3-1	Friday, Mikalsen, Knudtzon
08/11	a	Odd	L	0-5	

No	Name	Nat	DoB	Pos	Aps	(s)	Gls
4	Marius Amundsen		30/11/91	D	30		
7	Johan Andersson	SWE	22/08/83	M	12		2
27	Markus Brændsrød		06/09/95	M		(5)	
21	Moryké Fofana	CIV	23/11/91	M	15		7
23	Fred Friday	NGA	22/05/95	A	18	(8)	11
18	Bonke Innocent	NGA	20/01/96	M	16	(4)	
13	Frode Kippe		17/01/78	D	24		1
11	Erling Knudtzon		15/12/88	A	29		10
17	Jørgen Kolstad		31/08/95	M	16	(9)	3
35	Henrik Kristiansen		04/01/99	M		(1)	
14	Fredrik Krogstad		06/06/95	M	2	(9)	1
10	Marius Lundemo		11/04/94	M	14	(1)	1
6	Finnur Orri Margeirsson	ISL	08/03/91	M	21	(6)	
8	Malaury Martin	FRA	25/08/88	M	11		3
3	Simen Kind Mikalsen		04/05/93	D	20	(7)	2
30	Mohamed Ofkir		04/08/96	M	11	(1)	
37	Petter Mathias Olsen		13/01/98	A		(1)	
77	Arnold Origi	KEN	15/11/83	G	30		
19	Joachim Osvold		23/09/94	A		(1)	
90	Amahl Pellegrino		18/06/90	A	4	(9)	
8	Bjørn Helge Riise		21/06/83	M	15		
20	Stian Ringstad		29/08/91	D	18	(2)	
16	Håkon Skogseid		14/01/88	D	6	(1)	
2	Michael Timisela	NED	05/05/86	D	10	(1)	
9	Árni Vilhjálmsson	ISL	09/05/94	M	8	(6)	2

Mjøndalen IF

1910 • Isachsen (4,350) • mif.no
Coach: Vegard Hansen

2015

06/04	h	Viking	W	1-0	Kapidzic
11/04	a	Strømsgodset	D	1-1	Midtgarden
18/04	h	Start	D	1-1	Gundersen
25/04	a	Odd	D	2-2	Aasmundsen, Kapidzic
30/04	h	Lillestrøm	L	1-4	Sylling Olsen
03/05	a	Stabæk	L	0-1	
09/05	h	Tromsø	W	4-3	Gauseth 2 (1p), Bernstein 2
12/05	h	Rosenborg	W	3-2	Hansen, Bernstein 2
16/05	a	Vålerenga	L	2-4	Gundersen, Sylling Olsen
22/05	h	Molde	L	0-3	
31/05	a	Bodø/Glimt	L	1-5	Sundli
07/06	h	Sarpsborg	D	1-1	Gauseth (p)
21/06	a	Haugesund	D	1-1	Sundli
28/06	h	Sandefjord	D	2-2	Nilsen, Arneberg
05/07	a	Aalesund	L	2-4	Gauseth, Olsen Solberg
12/07	h	Bodø/Glimt	L	1-2	Aasmundsen
26/07	a	Sarpsborg	D	2-2	Sosseh, Sundli
02/08	h	Odd	L	3-6	Midtgarden, Kapidzic 2
07/08	a	Sandefjord	L	1-2	Midtgarden
16/08	h	Haugesund	W	2-1	Bernstein, Henderson
23/08	a	Rosenborg	L	0-1	
30/08	h	Strømsgodset	L	2-4	Aasmundsen, Pellegrino
13/09	a	Tromsø	D	0-0	
20/09	h	Vålerenga	L	0-1	
26/09	a	Lillestrøm	L	0-3	
03/10	h	Stabæk	L	1-4	Hurtado
18/10	a	Molde	L	1-3	Nguen
23/10	a	Start	D	1-1	Sundli
01/11	h	Aalesund	L	1-2	Nguen
08/11	a	Viking	L	1-3	Midtgarden

No	Name	Nat	DoB	Pos	Aps	(s)	Gls
15	Stian Aasmundsen		02/11/89	M	24		3
2	Ulrik Arneberg		22/07/87	D	29		1
18	Rhett Bernstein	USA	10/09/87	D	13	(7)	5
20	Ousseynou Boye	SEN	07/09/92	A	1	(2)	
14	Vamouti Diomande	CIV	20/01/91	M	3		
24	Amidou Diop	SEN	25/02/92	M	8	(2)	
1	Ivar Andreas Forn		24/06/83	G	20	(1)	
11	Christian Gauseth		26/06/84	A	28		4
5	Karanveer Grewal		23/04/93	D	4	(2)	
24	Henrik Gulden		29/12/95	M	2	(2)	
16	Mads Gundersen		31/03/93	M	13	(5)	2
9	Mads Hansen		02/02/84	M	30		1
6	Craig Henderson	NZL	24/06/87	M	5	(2)	1
23	Erik Hurtado	USA	15/11/90	A	6	(5)	1
30	Marco Priis Jørgensen	DEN	02/06/91	G	10		
7	Sanel Kapidzic	DEN	14/04/90	A	19	(9)	4
10	Erik Midtgarden		18/11/87	M	23	(1)	4
19	Tokmac Nguen		20/10/93	A	2	(4)	2
23	Tim André Nilsen		07/10/92	A	1	(9)	1
3	Joachim Olsen Solberg		11/04/89	D	28		1
17	Amahl Pellegrino		18/06/90	A	8	(3)	1
8	Stian Rasch		10/03/87	M	3	(4)	
20	Alagie Sosseh	GAM	21/07/86	A	7	(7)	1
6	Michael Stilson		04/07/87	M	1	(4)	
4	Martin Strange		16/01/91	D	4	(5)	
22	Morten Sundli		31/03/90	D	23		4
21	Magnus Sylling Olsen		02/07/83	M	15	(7)	2

Molde FK

1911 • Aker (11,249) • moldefk.no

Major honours
Norwegian League (3) 2011, 2012, 2014;
Norwegian Cup (4) 1994, 2005, 2013, 2014

Coach: Tor Ole Skullerud;
(06/08/15) (Erling Moe);
(21/10/15) Ole Gunnar Solskjær

2015

07/04	h	Odd	L	1-2	Elyounoussi
11/04	a	Bodø/Glimt	W	3-1	Kamara 2, Elyounoussi
19/04	a	Aalesund	W	5-1	Svendsen 2, Kamara 2, Høiland
26/04	a	Haugesund	D	0-0	
29/04	h	Strømsgodset	W	3-1	Kamara, Elyounoussi 2
04/05	a	Viking	L	1-2	Høiland
10/05	h	Start	W	4-0	Høiland 3, Agnaldo
13/05	a	Lillestrøm	L	1-2	Toivio
16/05	h	Stabæk	D	3-3	Svendsen 2, Kamara
22/05	a	Mjøndalen	W	3-0	Elyounoussi, Forren, Svendsen
30/05	h	Sandefjord	W	6-1	Linnes, Elyounoussi 3, Høiland 2
05/06	a	Tromsø	L	0-2	
20/06	h	Vålerenga	D	0-0	
27/06	a	Rosenborg	D	1-1	og (Hansen)
03/07	a	Sarpsborg	W	4-1	Kamara 3, Svendsen
10/07	h	Haugesund	L	0-1	
18/07	a	Bodø/Glimt	L	1-2	Linnes
09/08	a	Odd	D	2-2	Elyounoussi, Toivio
15/08	h	Sarpsborg	D	0-0	
23/08	a	Vålerenga	W	1-0	Flo
30/08	a	Lillestrøm	D	2-2	Høiland, Moström
12/09	a	Sandefjord	W	4-2	Kamara 2, Hussain, Elyounoussi
20/09	h	Rosenborg	W	1-0	Kamara
23/09	a	Strømsgodset	L	0-1	
27/09	h	Stabæk	L	0-1	
04/10	h	Tromsø	W	4-0	Hestad, Simonsen, Flo, Kamara (p)
18/10	h	Mjøndalen	W	3-1	Kamara, Svendsen, Singh
25/10	a	Aalesund	W	2-1	Høiland, Elyounoussi
01/11	h	Viking	W	4-1	Moström, Semb Berge, Elyounoussi, Bakenga
08/11	a	Start	W	3-0	Svendsen, Gabrielsen, Flo

No	Name	Nat	DoB	Pos	Aps	(s)	Gls
21	Agnaldo	BRA	11/03/94	A	5	(9)	1
27	Mushaga Bakenga		08/08/92	A	2	(4)	1
10	Thomas Kind Bendiksen		08/08/89	M	2	(4)	
6	Daniel Berg Hestad		30/07/75	M	3	(19)	
30	Pape Paté Diouf	SEN	04/04/86	A	1	(6)	
24	Mohamed Elyounoussi		04/08/94	A	25	(3)	12
15	Per-Egil Flo		18/01/89	D	21	(4)	3
25	Vegard Forren		16/02/88	D	27		1
4	Ruben Gabrielsen		10/03/92	D	11	(4)	1
22	Joshua Gatt	USA	29/08/91	A		(1)	
19	Eirik Hestad		26/06/95	M	11	(2)	1
1	Ethan Horvath	USA	09/06/95	G	15	(2)	
16	Etzaz Hussain		27/01/93	M	23	(4)	1
20	Tommy Høiland		11/04/89	A	12	(11)	9
11	Ola Kamara		15/10/89	A	27	(2)	14
26	Andreas Linde	SWE	24/07/93	G	2		
14	Martin Linnes		20/09/91	D	27	(1)	2
9	Mattias Moström	SWE	25/02/83	M	17	(2)	2
34	Neydson	BRA	28/10/96	G		(1)	
12	Ørjan Håskjold Nyland		10/09/90	G	13		
23	Knut Olav Rindarøy		17/07/85	D	9	(2)	
2	Fredrik Semb Berge		06/02/90	D	10		1
18	Magne Simonsen		13/07/88	D	3		1
7	Harmeet Singh		12/11/90	M	25		1
32	Sander Svendsen		06/08/97	A	20	(6)	8
5	Joona Toivio	FIN	10/03/88	D	19	(3)	2

Odds BK

1894 • Skagerak Arena (12,590) • odd.no

Major honours
Norwegian Cup (12) 1903, 1904, 1905, 1906, 1913,
1915, 1919, 1922, 1924, 1926, 1931, 2000

Coach: Dag-Eilev Fagermo

2015

07/04	a	Molde	W	2-1	Johnsen, Halvorsen
12/04	h	Stabæk	W	2-0	Ruud (p), og (Næss)
19/04	a	Bodø/Glimt	W	4-2	Johnsen, Hagen, Nordkvelle, Halvorsen
25/04	h	Mjøndalen	D	2-2	Ruud 2
29/04	a	Sarpsborg	L	0-2	
03/05	h	Rosenborg	L	1-2	Akabueze
10/05	a	Viking	D	1-1	Occéan
13/05	h	Strømsgodset	W	2-0	Samuelsen, Akabueze
16/05	h	Haugesund	D	0-0	
25/05	a	Tromsø	D	2-2	Akabueze, Ruud
29/05	a	Aalesund	D	1-1	Occéan
06/06	h	Sandefjord	W	1-0	Occéan
19/06	h	Start	D	3-3	Occéan (p), Eriksen, Samuelsen
28/06	a	Lillestrøm	D	1-1	Occéan
05/07	h	Vålerenga	L	1-2	Occéan
12/07	a	Rosenborg	L	0-3	
26/07	a	Tromsø	W	3-0	Nordkvelle, Occéan, Zekhnini
02/08	a	Mjøndalen	W	6-3	Jensen, og (Arneberg), Occéan, Akabueze, Halvorsen 2
09/08	a	Molde	D	2-2	Akabueze, Occéan (p)
16/08	a	Start	W	4-0	Zekhnini, Akabueze, Occéan (p), Halvorsen
23/08	a	Viking	W	1-0	Nordkvelle
30/08	a	Stabæk	W	2-1	Akabueze, Occéan (p)
13/09	h	Bodø/Glimt	W	2-1	Occéan (p), Nordkvelle
20/09	a	Aalesund	W	3-1	Diouf 2, Jensen
27/09	h	Sarpsborg	D	1-1	Diouf
04/10	a	Haugesund	W	2-1	Nordkvelle, Occéan
16/10	a	Strømsgodset	L	1-2	Diouf
25/10	h	Sandefjord	W	4-3	Samuelsen 2, Diouf, Occéan
01/11	a	Vålerenga	D	2-2	Nordkvelle, Storbæk
08/11	h	Lillestrøm	W	5-0	Occéan, Akabueze, Nordkvelle 3

No	Name	Nat	DoB	Pos	Aps	(s)	Gls
26	Chukwuma Akabueze	NGA	06/05/89	A	29	(1)	8
6	Oliver Berg		28/08/89	M	8	(11)	
4	Vegard Bergan		20/02/95	D	4	(2)	
9	Pape Paté Diouf	SEN	04/04/86	A	9	(1)	5
23	Lars-Kristian Eriksen		28/06/83	D	26		1
12	Ulrik Flo		06/10/88	A		(3)	
25	Mathias Fredriksen		28/04/94	M		(8)	
3	Ardian Gashi		20/06/81	M	8	(8)	
5	Thomas Grøgaard		08/02/94	D	25	(2)	
21	Steffen Hagen		08/03/86	D	29		1
7	Ole Jørgen Halvorsen		02/10/87	A	16	(8)	5
18	Jarkko Hurme	FIN	04/06/86	D	2		
20	Fredrik Oldrup Jensen		18/05/93	M	21	(2)	2
11	Frode Johnsen		17/03/74	A	3	(6)	2
19	Emil Jonassen		17/02/93	D	6	(2)	
14	Fredrik Nordkvelle		13/09/85	M	23	(1)	9
10	Olivier Occéan	CAN	23/10/81	A	25	(2)	15
1	Sondre Rossbach		07/02/96	G	30		
2	Espen Ruud		26/02/84	D	28		4
8	Jone Samuelsen		06/07/84	M	26	(1)	4
22	Håvard Storbæk		25/05/86	A	7	(19)	1
15	Rafik Zekhnini		12/01/98	A	5	(6)	2

Rosenborg BK

1917 • Lerkendal (21,405) • rbk.no

Major honours
Norwegian League (23) 1967, 1969, 1971, 1985,
1988, 1990, 1992, 1993, 1994, 1995, 1996, 1997,
1998, 1999, 2000, 2001, 2002, 2003, 2004, 2006,
2009, 2010, 2015; Norwegian Cup (10) 1960, 1964,
1971, 1988, 1990, 1992, 1995, 1999, 2003, 2015

Coach: Kåre Ingebrigtsen

2015

06/04	h	Aalesund	W	5-0	Helland 2, Søderlund 2, Malec
12/04	a	Haugesund	W	6-0	Søderlund 2, Mikkelsen, Midtsjø, Malec, Skjelvik
18/04	h	Strømsgodset	D	1-1	Mikkelsen
25/04	a	Viking	W	4-1	Søderlund, Mikkelsen, Henderson 2
30/04	h	Start	W	3-2	Søderlund 2, Henderson
03/05	h	Odd	W	2-1	Helland, Riski (p)
09/05	h	Lillestrøm	W	3-0	Søderlund 2, Helland
12/05	a	Mjøndalen	L	2-3	Helland, Mikkelsen
16/05	h	Sandefjord	W	5-1	Søderlund, Mikkelsen 2, Midtsjø, Helland
25/05	a	Stabæk	W	3-2	Helland (p), Søderlund 2
31/05	h	Tromsø	D	1-1	Jensen
06/06	a	Vålerenga	W	2-1	Helland 2
21/06	a	Sarpsborg	W	2-0	Helland, Jensen
27/06	h	Molde	D	1-1	Søderlund
05/07	a	Bodø/Glimt	L	0-1	
12/07	h	Odd	W	3-0	Selnæs, Helland, Søderlund
26/07	a	Sandefjord	W	2-1	Mikkelsen, Søderlund
02/08	a	Sarpsborg	W	3-2	Midtsjø, Helland, Søderlund
09/08	a	Lillestrøm	W	5-0	Helland, Bjørdal 2, Søderlund 2 (2p)
16/08	h	Vålerenga	W	2-0	Søderlund, Eyjólfsson
23/08	h	Mjøndalen	W	1-0	Vilhjálmsson
30/08	a	Tromsø	D	1-1	Søderlund
13/09	h	Stabæk	W	1-0	Konradsen
20/09	a	Molde	L	0-1	
27/09	h	Viking	W	2-0	De Lanlay, Søderlund
04/10	a	Start	W	4-0	Konradsen, Helland (p), Midtsjø, Skjelvik
18/10	h	Bodø/Glimt	D	1-1	Søderlund
25/10	a	Strømsgodset	D	3-3	Konradsen 2, De Lanlay
01/11	h	Haugesund	W	4-3	De Lanlay, Mikkelsen, Selnæs, Vilhjálmsson
08/11	a	Aalesund	W	1-0	Jensen (p)

No	Name	Nat	DoB	Pos	Aps	(s)	Gls
14	Johan Lædre Bjørdal		05/05/86	D	13		2
19	Yann-Erik de Lanlay		14/05/92	A	10	(2)	3
3	Mikael Dorsin	SWE	06/10/81	D	18	(2)	1
5	Hólmar Örn Eyjólfsson	ISL	06/08/90	D	25	(3)	1
8	Morten Gamst Pedersen		08/09/81	M	1	(3)	
1	André Hansen		17/12/89	G	28		
23	Pål André Helland		04/01/90	A	18	(3)	13
18	Liam Henderson	SCO	25/04/96	M		(9)	3
7	Mike Jensen	DEN	19/02/88	M	27	(2)	3
24	Anders Konradsen		18/07/90	M	8	(1)	4
12	Alexander Lund Hansen		06/10/82	G	2	(1)	
10	Tomáš Malec	SVK	05/01/93	A		(10)	2
21	Fredrik Midtsjø		11/08/93	M	28	(1)	4
11	Tobias Mikkelsen	DEN	18/09/86	A	22	(5)	8
17	Emil Nielsen	DEN	18/11/93	A		(5)	
4	Tore Reginiussen		10/04/86	D	2	(2)	
9	Riku Riski	FIN	16/08/89	A	8	(8)	1
20	Ole Kristian Selnæs		07/07/94	M	22	(3)	2
16	Jørgen Skjelvik		05/07/91	D	19	(6)	2
18	Magnus Stamnestrø		18/04/92	M	4		
24	Stefan Strandberg		25/07/90	D	13		
22	Jonas Svensson		06/03/93	D	29		
32	John Hou Sæter		13/01/98	M		(3)	
15	Alexander Søderlund		03/08/87	A	26	(1)	22
10	Matthías Vilhjálmsson	ISL	30/01/87	A	7	(5)	2

Sandefjord Fotball

1998 • Komplett Arena (6,000) •
sandefjordfotball.no
Coach: Lars Bohinen

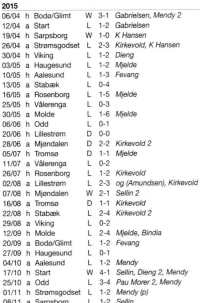

2015

06/04	h	Bodø/Glimt	W	3-1	Gabrielsen, Mendy 2
12/04	a	Start	L	1-2	Gabrielsen
19/04	h	Sarpsborg	W	1-0	K Hansen
26/04	a	Strømsgodset	L	2-3	Kirkevold, K Hansen
30/04	h	Viking	L	1-2	Dieng
03/05	a	Haugesund	L	1-2	Mjelde
10/05	h	Aalesund	L	1-3	Fevang
13/05	a	Stabæk	L	0-4	
16/05	a	Rosenborg	L	1-5	Mjelde
25/05	h	Vålerenga	L	0-3	
30/05	h	Molde	L	1-6	Mjelde
06/06	h	Odd	L	0-1	
20/06	h	Lillestrøm	D	0-0	
28/06	a	Mjøndalen	D	2-2	Kirkevold 2
05/07	a	Tromsø	D	1-1	Mjelde
11/07	a	Vålerenga	L	0-2	
26/07	h	Rosenborg	L	1-2	Kirkevold
02/08	a	Lillestrøm	L	2-3	og (Amundsen), Kirkevold
07/08	h	Mjøndalen	W	2-1	Sellin 2
16/08	a	Tromsø	D	1-1	Kirkevold
22/08	h	Stabæk	L	2-4	Kirkevold 2
29/08	a	Viking	L	0-2	
12/09	h	Molde	L	2-4	Mjelde, Bindia
20/09	a	Bodø/Glimt	L	1-2	Fevang
27/09	a	Haugesund	L	0-1	
04/10	a	Aalesund	L	1-2	Mendy
17/10	h	Start	W	4-1	Sellin, Dieng 2, Mendy
25/10	a	Odd	L	3-4	Pau Morer 2, Mendy
01/11	h	Strømsgodset	L	1-2	Mendy (p)
08/11	a	Sarpsborg	L	1-2	Sellin

No	Name	Nat	DoB	Pos	Aps	(s)	Gls
3	Yaw-Ihle Amankwah		07/07/88	D	5		
15	Martin Andresen		02/02/77	M	3		
13	Vegard Bakker		15/05/96	M		(1)	
4	Victor Demba Bindia	SEN	06/08/89	D	29		1
1	Jakob Busk	DEN	12/09/93	G	14		
18	Cheikhou Dieng	SEN	23/11/93	A	25	(2)	3
7	Geir Ludvig Fevang		17/11/80	M	25	(1)	2
5	Alexander Gabrielsen		18/11/85	D	11		2
2	Lars Grorud		02/07/83	D	8		
12	Anders Gundersen		10/04/94	G	6		
23	Mats Haakenstad		14/11/93	A	3	(2)	
27	Christer Reppesgård Hansen		29/03/93	D	18		
21	Kristoffer Normann Hansen		12/08/94	M	17	(9)	2
12	Lars Herlofsen		18/09/94	G	1		
40	Gary Hogan	IRL	05/01/83	G	1		
17	Thomas Juel-Nielsen	DEN	18/06/90	D	11	(9)	
16	Pål Alexander Kirkevold		10/11/90	A	21		8
25	William Kurtovic	SWE	22/06/96	M	8	(5)	
10	Eirik Lamøy		07/11/84	M	16		
14	Kevin Larsen		10/05/86	D	14	(4)	
20	Jean Alassane Mendy		02/02/90	A	13	(10)	6
8	Erik Mjelde		06/03/84	M	24	(2)	5
29	Eirik Offenberg		06/06/96	D	6	(1)	
6	Pau Morer	ESP	10/10/95	A	4	(2)	2
9	Mads Pedersen	DEN	17/01/93	M	7	(11)	
6	Roger Risholt		10/04/79	M	11	(2)	
19	Kjell Rune Sellin		01/06/89	A	18	(5)	4
28	Varg Støvland		23/01/96	M		(3)	
26	André Sødlund		22/12/96	M		(4)	
11	Martin Torp		03/03/92	M	3	(6)	
40	Michael Tørnes	DEN	08/01/86	G	8	(1)	

Sarpsborg 08 FF

2000 • Sarpsborg (5,137) • sarpsborg08.no
Coach: Geir Bakke

2015

06/04	a	Tromsø	W	1-0	Heieren Hansen
10/04	h	Vålerenga	D	1-1	Nordvik
19/04	a	Sandefjord	L	0-1	
26/04	h	Bodø/Glimt	D	2-2	Heieren Hansen, Ernemann
29/04	h	Odd	W	2-0	Jensen, Askar
02/05	a	Strømsgodset	D	1-1	Tokstad
10/05	h	Haugesund	W	3-0	Heieren Hansen, Nordvik, Zajić
13/05	a	Aalesund	D	2-2	og (Grytebust), Kalludra
16/05	h	Lillestrøm	W	1-0	Trondsen
25/05	a	Start	W	2-1	Tokstad, Wiig
31/05	h	Stabæk	L	0-1	
07/06	h	Mjøndalen	D	1-1	Zajić
21/06	h	Rosenborg	L	0-1	
28/06	a	Viking	L	1-3	Nordvik
03/07	h	Molde	L	1-4	Zajić
12/07	a	Stabæk	D	0-0	
26/07	a	Mjøndalen	D	2-2	Kovács, Mortensen
02/08	a	Rosenborg	L	2-3	Mortensen, Ernemann
08/08	h	Viking	L	0-2	
15/08	h	Molde	D	0-0	
23/08	h	Aalesund	W	3-1	Zajić, Wiig 2
30/08	a	Bodø/Glimt	L	1-3	Zajić
13/09	h	Start	W	3-1	Mortensen, Tokstad, Wiig
20/09	a	Haugesund	D	1-1	Maguire
27/09	a	Odd	D	1-1	Ugwuadu
03/10	h	Strømsgodset	L	1-6	Askar
18/10	a	Vålerenga	L	1-3	Groven
24/10	h	Tromsø	W	1-0	Wiig
01/11	a	Lillestrøm	L	1-3	Zajić (p)
08/11	h	Sandefjord	W	2-1	Ugwuadu, Ernemann (p)

No	Name	Nat	DoB	Pos	Aps	(s)	Gls
77	Amin Askar		01/10/85	M	27		2
19	Habib Bellaïd	ALG	28/03/86	D	5	(2)	
4	Kjetil Berge		05/06/81	D	13	(2)	
23	Tom Erik Breive		18/04/80	M	5	(2)	
20	Simen Brenne		17/03/81	M	5	(4)	
17	Steffen Ernemann	DEN	26/04/82	M	28		3
21	Oliver Feldballe	DEN	03/04/90	A	1	(6)	
29	Alexander Groven		02/01/92	D	11		1
42	Magnus Hart		20/04/96	M		(2)	
13	Ole Heieren Hansen		26/02/87	D	24	(2)	3
1	Lasse Heinze	DEN	03/04/86	G	3		
26	Martin Thømt Jensen		08/07/90	D	14	(3)	1
10	Liridon Kalludra	SWE	05/11/91	M	6	(8)	1
27	Duwayne Kerr	JAM	16/01/87	G	23		
28	Péter Kovács	HUN	07/02/78	A	5	(5)	1
22	Claes Kronberg	DEN	19/04/87	D	24	(1)	
10	Barry Maguire	NED	27/10/89	M	1	(2)	1
24	Amani Mbedule		19/09/96	A		(2)	
69	Patrick Mortensen	DEN	13/07/89	A	10		3
3	Andreas Nordvik		18/03/87	D	21	(5)	3
8	Henrik Ojamaa	EST	20/05/91	A	8	(2)	
92	Kamer Qaka		11/04/95	M	4	(8)	
15	Sigurd Rosted		22/07/94	D		(1)	
16	Joachim Thomassen		04/05/88	D	5		
11	Kristoffer Tokstad		05/07/91	M	23	(3)	3
6	Anders Trondsen		30/03/95	M	24		1
8	Onyekachi Hope Ugwuadu	NGA	05/05/97	A	2	(5)	2
45	Quentin Westberg	USA	25/04/86	G	4		
7	Martin Wiig		22/08/83	A	14	(6)	5
36	Bojan Zajić	SRB	17/06/80	M	18	(10)	6
5	Olav Øby		13/10/94	M	2	(3)	

Stabæk Fotball

1912 • Nadderud (7,000) • stabak.no
Major honours
Norwegian League (1) 2008; Norwegian Cup (1) 1998
Coach: Bob Bradley (USA)

2015

06/04	h	Haugesund	D	1-1	Diomandé
12/04	a	Odd	L	0-2	
19/04	h	Viking	W	1-0	Grossman
26/04	a	Lillestrøm	W	2-0	Asante, Issah
30/04	a	Tromsø	W	2-0	Asante, Grossman
03/05	h	Mjøndalen	W	1-0	Asante
09/05	a	Vålerenga	W	2-0	Diomandé (p), Asante
13/05	h	Sandefjord	W	4-0	Diomandé 3, Asante
16/05	a	Molde	D	3-3	Diomandé 2, Issah
25/05	h	Rosenborg	L	2-3	Diomandé, og (Dorsin)
31/05	a	Sarpsborg	W	1-0	Diomandé
07/06	h	Bodø/Glimt	W	3-2	Jalasto, Asante, Gorozia
21/06	a	Aalesund	D	1-1	Grossman
27/06	h	Strømsgodset	W	3-2	Meling, Asante, El Ghanassy
04/07	a	Start	L	1-4	Diomandé
12/07	a	Sarpsborg	D	0-0	
25/07	a	Haugesund	D	2-2	Jalasto, Diomandé
01/08	h	Vålerenga	W	2-0	Asante, Kassi
09/08	a	Strømsgodset	W	2-0	Diomandé 2
16/08	a	Lillestrøm	W	3-2	Diomandé 2, Næss
22/08	a	Sandefjord	W	4-2	Diomandé 2 (1p), Grossman, Kassi
30/08	h	Odd	L	1-2	Kassi
13/09	a	Rosenborg	L	0-1	
19/09	h	Tromsø	W	2-1	Kassi, Keita
27/09	h	Molde	W	1-0	Keita
03/10	a	Mjøndalen	W	4-1	Asante, Kassi 2, El Ghanassy (p)
17/10	a	Aalesund	L	1-4	Asante
25/10	a	Viking	L	0-2	Kassi
01/11	h	Start	W	3-2	Kassi, Issah, Jalasto
08/11	a	Bodø/Glimt	L	1-6	El Ghanassy

No	Name	Nat	DoB	Pos	Aps	(s)	Gls
6	Anthony Annan	GHA	21/07/86	M	7		
7	Ernest Asante	GHA	06/11/88	A	30		10
30	Cornelius Bencsik		22/10/97	M		(2)	
10	Adama Diomandé		14/02/90	A	21		17
14	Emil Ekblom		29/01/94	A		(5)	
11	Yassine El Ghanassy	BEL	12/07/90	M	24	(2)	3
9	Giorgi Gorozia	GEO	26/03/95	M	15	(11)	1
21	Daniel Granli		01/05/94	D	8	(14)	
8	Cole Grossman	USA	10/04/89	M	28		4
5	Jørgen Hammer		02/04/91	D		(1)	
13	Eirik Haugstad		17/01/94	M		(23)	
20	Kamal Issah	GHA	29/08/92	M	21	(5)	3
15	Ville Jalasto	FIN	19/04/86	D	29		3
28	Luc Kassi	CIV	20/08/94	A	23	(5)	8
77	Muhamed Keita		02/09/90	A	9	(2)	2
1	Sayouba Mandé	CIV	15/06/93	G	30		
25	Birger Meling		17/12/94	D	26	(1)	1
4	Nicolai Næss		18/01/93	D	29		1
60	Edvard Race		22/05/97	D		(1)	
3	Morten Morisbak Skjønsberg		12/02/83	D	30		

IK Start

1905 • Sparebanken Sør Arena (14,300) • ikstart.no
Major honours
Norwegian League (2) 1978, 1980
Coach: Mons Ivar Mjelde;
(07/09/15) (Bård Borgersen)

2015

07/04	a	Lillestrøm	D	1-1	Børufsen	
12/04	h	Sandefjord	W	2-1	Hoff 2	
18/04	a	Mjøndalen	D	1-1	Vilhjálmsson	
24/04	a	Vålerenga	L	2-3	Børufsen, Vilhjálmsson	
30/04	a	Rosenborg	L	2-3	Børufsen, Ajer	
03/05	h	Tromsø	W	3-1	Hollingen, Vilhjálmsson, Ajer	
10/05	a	Molde	L	0-4		
13/05	h	Bodø/Glimt	D	1-1	Vikstøl	
16/05	a	Viking	L	0-1		
25/05	h	Sarpsborg	L	1-2	Vilhjálmsson	
30/05	a	Haugesund	W	2-0	Ajer 2	
07/06	h	Strømsgodset	L	0-1		
19/06	a	Odd	D	3-3	Børufsen, Vilhjálmsson, Salvesen (p)	
27/06	h	Aalesund	W	3-1	Vilhjálmsson, Børufsen, Ajer (p)	
04/07	h	Stabæk	W	4-1	Vilhjálmsson, Hoff, Ajer 2	
12/07	a	Tromsø	L	1-2	Ajer	
24/07	h	Viking	L	0-3		
02/08	a	Aalesund	L	0-2		
09/08	a	Bodø/Glimt	L	1-5	Salvesen	
16/08	h	Odd	L	0-4		
23/08	a	Strømsgodset	L	1-2	Vikstøl	
30/08	h	Haugesund	L	1-3	Kristjánsson	
13/09	a	Sarpsborg	L	1-3	Børufsen	
19/09	h	Lillestrøm	D	0-0		
25/09	a	Vålerenga	D	1-1	Opdal	
04/10	h	Rosenborg	L	0-4		
17/10	a	Sandefjord	L	1-4	og (Bindia)	
23/10	h	Mjøndalen	D	1-1	Aase	
01/11	a	Stabæk	L	2-3	Stokkelien, Vikstøl	
08/11	h	Molde	L	0-3		

No	Name	Nat	DoB	Pos	Aps	(s)	Gls
9	Daniel Aase		22/06/89	A	5	(5)	1
6	Kristoffer Ajer		17/04/98	M	29	(1)	8
21	Henrik Breimyr		20/07/93	M	12		
14	Espen Børufsen		04/03/88	M	25		6
15	Michael Christensen	DEN	06/02/83	D	27		
9	Emil Dahle		30/10/90	A	8	(4)	
4	Alex De John	USA	10/05/91	D	17	(5)	
33	Jørgen Hammer		02/04/91	D	10		
2	Jon Hodnemyr		04/12/95	D	7	(5)	
8	Espen Hoff		20/11/81	A	21	(5)	3
16	Andreas Hollingen		03/10/94	M	15	(4)	1
36	Markus Håbestad		15/03/99			(1)	
19	Austin Ikenna	NGA	15/08/93	A		(5)	
25	Ingvar Jónsson	ISL	18/10/89	G	1		
17	Gudmundur Kristjánsson	ISL	01/03/89	M	23		1
20	John Olav Norheim		05/04/95	D		(4)	
1	Håkon André Opdal		11/06/82	G	29		1
10	Solomon Owello	NGA	25/12/88	M	14	(5)	
32	Mathias Rasmussen		25/11/97	M	4	(7)	
3	Ole Martin Rindarøy		16/05/95	D	15	(1)	
22	Lars-Jørgen Salvesen		19/02/96	A	7	(15)	2
5	Robert Sandnes		29/12/91	D	10	(10)	
23	Erlend Segberg		12/04/97	M	1	(9)	
18	Mads Stokkelien		15/03/90	A	9	(1)	1
28	Rolf Daniel Vikstøl		22/02/89	D	26		3
18	Matthías Vilhjálmsson	ISL	30/01/87	A	15		7

Strømsgodset IF

1907 • Marienlyst (8,935) • godset.no
Major honours
Norwegian League (2) 1970, 2013; Norwegian Cup (5) 1969, 1970, 1973, 1991, 2010
Coach: David Nielsen (DEN);
(26/05/15) Bjørn Petter Ingebretsen

2015

06/04	a	Vålerenga	L	1-3	og (Wæhler)	
11/04	h	Mjøndalen	D	1-1	Hamoud	
18/04	a	Rosenborg	D	1-1	Kovács	
26/04	a	Sandefjord	W	3-2	Olsen, Storflor 2	
29/04	a	Molde	L	1-3	Kovács	
02/05	h	Sarpsborg	D	1-1	Fossum	
10/05	a	Bodø/Glimt	W	5-3	Adjei-Boateng, Sørum, Storflor, Wikheim, Kastrati	
13/05	a	Odd	L	0-2		
16/05	h	Aalesund	W	3-1	Fossum 2, Sørum	
24/05	a	Haugesund	L	0-4		
31/05	a	Lillestrøm	W	2-0	Wikheim, Fossum	
07/06	a	Start	W	1-0	Fossum	
21/06	h	Tromsø	W	2-1	Ogunjimi, Vilsvik	
27/06	a	Stabæk	L	2-3	Ogunjimi, Wikheim	
05/07	h	Viking	W	4-1	Ogunjimi 2, Wikheim, Vilsvik	
12/07	a	Lillestrøm	W	2-1	Kastrati, Wikheim	
02/08	a	Tromsø	W	6-0	Wikheim 2, Vilsvik, Hanin, Fossum 2	
09/08	h	Stabæk	L	0-2		
14/08	a	Aalesund	L	1-2	Jradi	
23/08	h	Start	W	2-1	og (Hammer), Pedersen (p)	
30/08	a	Mjøndalen	W	4-2	Pedersen 3, Fossum	
11/09	h	Haugesund	W	5-0	Vilsvik, Tagbajumi 2, Adjei-Boateng, Abu	
18/09	a	Viking	D	1-1	Fossum	
23/09	h	Molde	W	1-0	Pedersen	
26/09	h	Bodø/Glimt	W	3-1	og (Londak), Pedersen, Tagbajumi	
03/10	a	Sarpsborg	W	6-1	Wikheim 2, Storflor, Fossum, Jradi, Sørum	
16/10	h	Odd	W	2-1	Pedersen, Fossum	
25/10	h	Rosenborg	D	3-3	Pedersen 2, Adjei-Boateng	
01/11	a	Sandefjord	W	2-1	Tagbajumi, Adjei-Boateng	
08/11	h	Vålerenga	D	2-2	Pedersen 2	

No	Name	Nat	DoB	Pos	Aps	(s)	Gls
20	Mohammed Abu	GHA	14/11/91	M	27		1
22	Bismark Adjei-Boateng	GHA	10/05/94	M	16	(5)	4
1	Espen Bugge Pettersen		10/05/80	G	30		
14	Iver Fossum		15/07/96	M	30		11
21	Mathias Gjerstrøm		30/06/97	M		(1)	
2	Mounir Hamoud		01/02/85	D	7	(5)	1
6	Florent Hanin	FRA	04/02/90	D	26		1
5	Jørgen Horn		07/06/87	D	14		
28	Marius Høibråten		23/01/95	D	15		
7	Bassel Jradi	DEN	06/07/93	M	2	(10)	2
15	Flamur Kastrati	KOS	14/11/91	A	7	(14)	2
10	Petr Kovács	HUN	07/02/78	A	2	(8)	2
4	Kim André Madsen		12/03/89	D	6	(1)	
93	Tokmac Nguen		20/10/93	A		(1)	
75	Marvin Ogunjimi	BEL	12/10/87	A	2	(2)	4
17	Thomas Lehne Olsen		29/06/91	A	4	(3)	1
11	Martin Rønning Ovenstad		18/04/94	M	15	(12)	
10	Marcus Pedersen		08/06/90	A	10		11
9	Øyvind Storflor		18/12/79	A	24	(3)	4
23	Thomas Sørum		17/11/82	A	6	(6)	3
33	Marco Tagbajumi	NGA	01/07/88	A	2	(8)	4
8	Petter Vaagan Moen		05/02/84	M	2	(4)	
71	Gustav Valsvik		26/05/93	D	28	(1)	
26	Lars Christopher Vilsvik		18/10/88	D	24		4
19	Gustav Wikheim		18/03/93	A	27	(1)	9

Tromsø IL

1920 • Alfheim (6,859) • til.no
Major honours
Norwegian Cup (2) 1986, 1996
Coach: Steinar Nilsen;
(18/08/15) (Bård Flovik);
(02/09/15) Bård Flovik

2015

06/04	h	Sarpsborg	L	0-1		
12/04	a	Viking	L	1-3	Åsen	
19/04	h	Lillestrøm	D	1-1	Åsen	
26/04	a	Aalesund	W	2-0	Ingebrigtsen, Ondrášek	
30/04	h	Stabæk	L	0-2		
03/05	a	Start	L	1-3	Ondrášek	
09/05	a	Mjøndalen	L	3-4	Åsen, Ondrášek 2	
12/05	h	Vålerenga	L	4-5	Ingebrigtsen, Ondrášek, Andersen 2	
16/05	a	Bodø/Glimt	L	0-1		
25/05	h	Odd	D	2-2	R Johansen, Andersen	
31/05	a	Rosenborg	D	1-1	Andersen	
05/06	h	Molde	W	2-0	Antonsen, Hansson	
21/06	a	Strømsgodset	L	1-2	Ondrášek	
28/06	h	Haugesund	W	2-0	Ondrášek, R Johansen	
05/07	a	Sandefjord	D	1-1	J Johansen	
12/07	h	Start	W	2-1	Andersen, og (Sandnes)	
26/07	a	Odd	L	2-3	Andersen, Moldskred	
02/08	h	Strømsgodset	L	0-6		
07/08	a	Vålerenga	L	0-1		
16/08	h	Sandefjord	D	1-1	Antonsen	
21/08	a	Lillestrøm	L	0-1		
30/08	h	Rosenborg	D	1-1	Andersen	
13/09	h	Mjøndalen	D	0-0		
19/09	a	Stabæk	L	1-2	R Johansen	
27/09	a	Aalesund	D	1-1	Espejord	
04/10	a	Molde	L	0-1		
18/10	h	Viking	W	3-1	Espejord 2, og (Sigurdsson)	
24/10	a	Sarpsborg	L	0-1		
01/11	h	Bodø/Glimt	W	3-1	Ondrášek 2, Ingebrigtsen	
08/11	a	Haugesund	W	1-0	Antonsen	

No	Name	Nat	DoB	Pos	Aps	(s)	Gls
15	Magnus Andersen		28/05/86	M	30		7
3	Kent-Are Antonsen		12/02/95	D	27	(1)	3
21	Thomas Kind Bendiksen		08/08/89	M	9	(2)	
10	Thomas Drage		20/02/92	M	2	(7)	
30	Runar Espejord		26/02/96	A	5	(7)	3
4	Henrik Gjesdal		19/07/93	D	2	(4)	
27	Jostein Gundersen		02/04/96	D	3		
7	Marcus Hansson	SWE	12/02/90	M	19	(6)	1
23	Pål Vestly Heigre		15/03/95	G	18	(2)	
24	Mikael Ingebrigtsen		21/07/96	M	10	(10)	3
11	Jonas Johansen		22/03/85	M	7	(11)	1
17	Remi Johansen		04/09/90	M	19	(7)	3
16	Lars-Gunnar Johnsen		02/07/91	M	1		
12	Gudmund Kongshavn		23/01/91	G	3		
6	Christian Landu Landu		25/01/92	M	20		
1	Benny Lekström	SWE	19/02/81	G	9		
5	Morten Moldskred		13/06/80	A	17	(8)	1
25	Lasse Nilsen		21/02/92	D	5	(6)	
14	Hans Nordbye		16/01/87	D	19	(2)	
13	Zdeněk Ondrášek	CZE	22/12/88	A	27		9
48	Marin Oršulić	CRO	25/08/87	D	3	(4)	
22	Simen Wangberg		06/05/91	D	29		
2	Magnar Ødegaard		11/05/93	D	29	(1)	
8	Gjermund Åsen		22/05/91	M	20	(1)	3

Viking FK

1899 • Viking (16,300) • viking-fk.no
Major honours
Norwegian League (8) 1958, 1972, 1973, 1974, 1975, 1979, 1982, 1991; Norwegian Cup (5) 1953, 1959, 1979, 1989, 2001
Coach: Kjell Jonevret (SWE)

2015

06/04	a	Mjøndalen	L	0-1	
12/04	h	Tromsø	W	3-1	og (Ødegaard), Berisha, Bytyqi
19/04	a	Stabæk	L	0-1	
25/04	h	Rosenborg	L	1-4	Abdullahi
30/04	a	Sandefjord	W	2-1	Abdullahi, Berisha (p)
04/05	h	Molde	W	2-1	Adegbenro, Berisha
10/05	h	Odd	D	1-1	De Lanlay
13/05	a	Haugesund	W	2-0	De Lanlay, Bödvarsson
16/05	h	Start	W	1-0	Bytyqi
25/05	a	Aalesund	W	4-0	Abdullahi, Berisha 2, Bödvarsson
31/05	h	Vålerenga	L	3-4	Berisha 2, Bödvarsson
07/06	a	Lillestrøm	L	1-2	Berisha
21/06	h	Bodø/Glimt	W	3-0	Berisha, De Lanlay, Adegbenro
28/06	h	Sarpsborg	W	3-1	Berisha 2, Bödvarsson
05/07	a	Strømsgodset	L	1-4	Abdullahi
11/07	h	Aalesund	W	4-1	Abdullahi, Bödvarsson 2, Sigurdsson
24/07	a	Start	W	3-0	Nisja, Danielsen (p), Bödvarsson
31/07	h	Haugesund	L	0-1	
08/08	a	Sarpsborg	W	2-0	Danielsen (p), Bödvarsson
15/08	h	Bodø/Glimt	W	2-1	Danielsen (p), Nisja
23/08	a	Odd	L	0-1	
29/08	h	Sandefjord	W	2-0	Bytyqi, Bödvarsson
13/09	a	Vålerenga	W	4-2	Abdullahi, Adegbenro, Jørgensen, Danielsen (p)
18/09	h	Strømsgodset	D	1-1	Adegbenro
27/09	a	Rosenborg	L	0-2	
04/10	h	Lillestrøm	W	1-0	Thorsteinsson
18/10	a	Tromsø	L	1-3	Abdullahi
25/10	h	Stabæk	W	2-1	Danielsen, Abdullahi
01/11	a	Molde	L	1-4	Sverrisson
08/11	h	Mjøndalen	W	3-1	Bytyqi, Haugen, Adegbenro

No	Name	Nat	DoB	Pos	Aps	(s)	Gls
19	Suleiman Abdullahi	NGA	10/12/96	A	24	(3)	8
26	Samuel Adegbenro	NGA	03/12/95	A	23	(1)	5
30	Iven Austbø		22/02/85	G	30		
10	Veton Berisha		13/04/94	A	14		11
27	Zymer Bytyqi		14/09/96	M	12	(9)	4
17	Jón Dadi Bödvarsson	ISL	25/05/92	A	22	(7)	9
18	Osita Chikere	NGA	03/02/91	A		(5)	
14	André Danielsen		20/01/85	D	30		5
16	Yann-Erik de Lanlay		14/05/92	A	16		3
28	Kristoffer Haugen		21/02/94	D	30		1
9	Magne Hoseth		13/10/80	M	1	(8)	
4	Joachim Jørgensen		20/09/88	M	21	(2)	1
50	Herman Kleppa		17/09/96	M		(1)	
25	Rasmus Martinsen		14/04/96			(1)	
6	Karol Mets	EST	16/05/93	D	27	(1)	
10	Kieffer Moore	ENG	08/08/92	A	1	(8)	
8	Vidar Nisja		21/08/86	M	8	(11)	2
51	Julian Ryerson		17/11/97	D		(2)	
20	Indridi Sigurdsson	ISL	12/10/81	D	25	(1)	1
5	Anthony Soares	USA	28/11/88	D	19	(1)	
24	Aleksander Solli		16/03/90	D		(2)	
7	Björn Daniel Sverrisson	ISL	29/05/90	M	3	(5)	1
11	El Hadji Makhtar Thioune	SEN	05/08/84	M	17	(6)	
23	Steinthór Thorsteinsson	ISL	29/07/85	M	7	(13)	1
21	Julian Veen Uldal		11/06/97	A		(1)	
1	Arild Østbø		19/04/91	G		(1)	

Vålerenga Fotball

1913 • Ullevaal (27,200) • vif-fotball.no
Major honours
Norwegian League (5) 1965, 1981, 1983, 1984, 2005; Norwegian Cup (4) 1980, 1997, 2002, 2008
Coach: Kjetil Rekdal

2015

06/04	h	Strømsgodset	W	3-1	Grindheim, Holm (p), Gunnarsson
10/04	a	Sarpsborg	D	1-1	Zahid
17/04	h	Haugesund	W	2-0	Brown 2
24/04	a	Start	W	3-2	Zahid, Brown, Stengel
30/04	h	Aalesund	L	1-2	Gunnarsson
03/05	a	Lillestrøm	D	1-1	Holm
09/05	h	Stabæk	L	0-2	
12/05	a	Tromsø	W	5-4	Stengel, Larsen, Grindheim, Lindkvist, Holm
16/05	h	Mjøndalen	W	4-2	Lindkvist 2, Grindheim, Berre
25/05	a	Sandefjord	W	3-0	Braaten, Wæhler, Holm (p)
31/05	a	Viking	W	4-3	Zahid 2, Brown, Grindheim
06/06	h	Rosenborg	L	1-2	Brown
20/06	a	Molde	D	0-0	
28/06	h	Bodø/Glimt	L	1-2	Holm
05/07	a	Odd	W	2-1	Ómarsson 2
11/07	h	Sandefjord	W	2-0	Ómarsson, Wæhler
27/07	h	Lillestrøm	W	2-0	Mathisen (p), og (Amundsen)
01/08	a	Stabæk	L	0-2	
07/08	h	Tromsø	W	1-0	Zahid
16/08	a	Rosenborg	L	0-2	
23/08	h	Molde	L	0-1	
28/08	a	Aalesund	L	0-2	
13/09	h	Viking	L	2-4	Abdellaoue, Jääger
20/09	a	Mjøndalen	W	1-0	Jääger
25/09	h	Start	D	1-1	Holm
02/10	a	Bodø/Glimt	D	1-1	Brown
18/10	h	Sarpsborg	W	3-1	Ómarsson, Zahid, Holm
24/10	a	Haugesund	W	1-0	Grindheim
01/11	h	Odd	D	2-2	Hallberg, Brown
08/11	h	Strømsgodset	D	2-2	Hallberg, Zahid

No	Name	Nat	DoB	Pos	Aps	(s)	Gls
18	Mohammed Abdellaoue		23/10/85	A	3	(1)	1
23	Sander Berge		14/02/98	M	6	(5)	
11	Morten Berre		10/08/75	A		(8)	1
17	Daniel Braaten		25/05/82	A	11	(11)	1
26	Deshorn Brown	JAM	22/12/90	A	16	(7)	7
38	Sascha Burchert	GER	30/10/89	G	14		
38	Otto Fredrikson	FIN	30/11/81	G	2		
19	Christian Grindheim		17/07/83	M	30		5
2	Niklas Gunnarsson		27/04/91	D	8	(4)	2
8	Melker Hallberg	SWE	20/10/95	M	6	(4)	2
7	Daniel Fredheim Holm		30/07/85	A	23	(1)	7
3	Enar Jääger	EST	18/11/84	D	9		2
3	Ruben Kristiansen		20/02/88	D	15	(1)	
30	Michael Langer	AUT	06/01/85	G	14		
6	Simon Larsen		01/06/88	D	20	(5)	1
9	Rasmus Lindkvist	SWE	16/05/90	M	18	(5)	3
5	Robert Lundström	SWE	01/11/89	D	9		
21	Alexander Mathisen		24/11/86	M	13	(7)	1
25	Markus Nakkim		21/07/96	D	2	(6)	
8	Sivert Heltne Nilsen		02/10/91	M	7	(6)	
37	Ivan Näsberg		22/04/96	D	6	(3)	
22	Elias Már Ómarsson	ISL	09/09/95	A	8	(7)	4
14	Herman Stengel		26/08/95	M	16	(7)	2
4	Jonatan Tollås		01/07/90	D	21		
24	Kjetil Wæhler		16/03/76	D	25		2
10	Ghayas Zahid		18/11/94	M	28	(1)	7

Top goalscorers

22	Alexander Søderlund (Rosenborg)
17	Adama Diomandé (Stabæk)
15	Olivier Occéan (Odd)
14	Ola Kamara (Molde)
13	Leke James (Aalesund)
	Trond Olsen (Bodø/Glimt)
	Alexander Sørloth (Bodø/Glimt)
	Pål André Helland (Rosenborg)
12	Mohamed Elyounoussi (Molde)
11	Fred Friday (Lillestrøm)
	Iver Fossum (Strømsgodset)
	Marcus Pedersen (Strømsgodset)
	Veton Berisha (Viking)

Promoted clubs

Sogndal Fotball

1926 • Fosshaugane Campus (5,539) • sogndalfotball.no
Coach: Eirik Bakke

SK Brann

1908 • Brann (17,686) • brann.no
Major honours
Norwegian League (3) 1962, 1963, 2007; Norwegian Cup (6) 1923, 1925, 1972, 1976, 1982, 2004
Coach: Rikard Norling (SWE); (27/05/15) (Robert Hauge); (29/05/15) Lars Arne Nilsen

Second level final table 2015

		Pld	W	D	L	F	A	Pts
1	Sogndal Fotball	30	18	8	4	59	31	62
2	SK Brann	30	14	11	5	46	35	53
3	Kristiansund BK	30	14	7	9	37	30	49
4	IL Hødd Fotball	30	14	6	10	43	40	48
5	FK Jerv	30	12	11	7	47	28	47
6	Ranheim IL	30	13	8	9	48	36	47
7	Sandnes Ulf	30	13	8	9	49	40	47
8	Strømmen IF	30	10	7	13	33	39	37
9	Levanger FK	30	10	6	14	48	53	36
10	Bryne FK	30	10	6	14	43	50	36
11	Åsane Fotball	30	8	11	11	46	46	35
12	Fredrikstad FK	30	8	11	11	41	61	35
13	Follo FK	30	8	9	13	42	43	33
14	IL Nest-Sotra	30	8	7	15	41	51	31
15	Bærum SK	30	7	15	44	67	31	
16	Hønefoss BK	30	7	7	16	35	52	28

Promotion/Relegation play-offs

(08/11/15)
Hødd 1-1 Jerv *(aet; 5-6 on pens)*
Kristiansund 1-0 Ranheim

(15/11/15)
Kristiansund 0-2 Jerv

(21/11/15 & 25/11/15)
Jerv 1-1 Start
Start 3-1 Jerv
(Start 4-2)

DOMESTIC CUP

Norgesmesterskapet 2015

FIRST ROUND

(21/04/15)
Lokomotiv Oslo 0-8 Vålerenga
Vigør 0-5 Start

(22/04/15)
Arendal 3-1 Donn
Asker 1-2 Sandefjord
Bossekop 0-1 Mjølner
Brattvåg 0-2 Molde
Brodd 0-2 Bryne
Byåsen 3-1 Sverresborg
Finnsnes 3-0 Harstad
Fløy 1-1 Vindbjart *(aet; 4-5 on pens)*
Fløya 1-0 Alta
Fram Larvik 3-2 Lyn *(aet)*
Funnefoss/Vormsund 1-3 Kongsvinger
Førde 0-5 Fyllingsdalen
Hallingdal 1-4 Hønefoss
HamKam 2-1 Lørenskog
Hauerseter 2-4 KFUM Oslo
Holmen 0-1 Notodden
Kirkenes 0-6 Bodø/Glimt
Kjelsås 3-1 Sprint-Jeløy
Kråkerøy 0-4 Sarpsborg 08
Lillehammer 3-4 Elverum
Lyskloster 1-5 Sogndal
Mo 1-2 Tromsø
Moss 1-2 Grorud *(aet)*
Nardo 0-1 Stjørdals-Blink
Nybergsund 1-3 Ullensaker/Kisa
Odda 0-1 Fana
Oppsal 5-5 Kvik Halden *(aet; 4-5 on pens)*
Pors Grenland 2-4 Jerv
Randaberg 0-4 Haugesund
Rilindja 0-2 Bærum
Riska 1-2 Sandnes Ulf
Runar 0-6 Stabæk
Rælingen 3-9 Lillestrøm
Rødde 1-0 NTNUI
Sander 1-6 Strømmen
Sandnessjøen 0-13 Ranheim
Skedsmo 0-2 Raufoss
Skotfoss 0-13 Odd
Sortland 2-3 Tromsdalen
Spjelkavik 0-1 Træff
Stord 0-2 Nest-Sotra
Stryn 1-3 Aalesund
Surnadal 0-5 Kristiansund
Trosvik 2-3 Follo
Tynset 0-3 Strindheim
Tønsberg 0-5 Strømsgodset
Valdres 1-3 Gjøvik-Lyn
Vard Haugesund 2-0 Vidar
Varegg 4-2 Florø
Vestfossen 0-7 Mjøndalen
Vuku 0-3 Rosenborg
Øystese 0-2 Åsane
Ålgård 0-7 Viking

(23/04/15)
Egersund 0-2 Sola *(aet)*
Eidsvold 2-0 Brumunddal
Herd 0-4 Hødd
Neset 0-5 Levanger
Os 1-6 Brann
Salangen 1-3 Senja
Skeid 5-1 Drammen
Ørn-Horten 3-2 Ullern
Ås 1-5 Fredrikstad

SECOND ROUND

(06/05/15)
Arendal 3-2 Sandnes Ulf *(aet)*
Byåsen 2-3 Ranheim *(aet)*
Eidsvold 0-3 Lillestrøm
Fana 1-3 Hødd
Fløya 0-6 Rosenborg
Fram Larvik 0-1 Sandefjord
Fyllingsdalen 4-1 Haugesund
Gjøvik-Lyn 1-0 Vålerenga
HamKam 0-2 Sogndal
KFUM Oslo 1-3 Stabæk
Kjelsås 0-4 Strømsgodset
Kongsvinger 3-1 Follo
Kvik Halden 2-2 Fredrikstad *(aet; 4-3 on pens)*
Mjølner 0-1 Bodø/Glimt
Notodden 3-1 Jerv
Raufoss 0-1 Hønefoss
Rødde 1-4 Levanger *(aet)*
Senja 2-1 Tromsø
Skeid 1-4 Odd
Sola 1-2 Bryne
Stjørdals-Blink 1-2 Kristiansund
Strindheim 2-5 Aalesund
Tromsdalen 3-1 Finnsnes *(aet)*
Ullensaker/Kisa 1-3 Strømmen *(aet)*
Vard Haugesund 1-1 Brann *(aet; 3-4 on pens)*
Vindbjart 4-0 Start
Ørn-Horten 2-2 Mjøndalen *(aet; 3-4 on pens)*
Åsane 2-0 Nest-Sotra

(07/05/15)
Elverum 1-2 Bærum *(aet)*
Grorud 0-3 Sarpsborg 08
Træff 0-2 Molde
Varegg 0-9 Viking

THIRD ROUND

(02/06/15)
Fyllingsdalen 0-4 Molde

(03/06/15)
Arendal 3-5 Viking
Bærum 0-1 Kristiansund
Gjøvik-Lyn 0-2 Sarpsborg 08
Hødd 1-0 Aalesund
Kongsvinger 3-3 Sandefjord *(aet; 5-6 on pens)*
Kvik Halden 0-0 Strømsgodset *(aet; 4-2 on pens)*
Levanger 0-7 Rosenborg
Notodden 1-4 Mjøndalen
Ranheim 0-2 Åsane
Senja 1-3 Stabæk
Sogndal 1-2 Hønefoss

Strømmen 2-1 Lillestrøm *(aet)*
Vindbjart 2-4 Odd

(04/06/15)
Bryne 1-4 Brann
Tromsdalen 6-2 Bodø/Glimt

FOURTH ROUND

(24/06/15)
Brann 0-0 Sarpsborg 08 *(aet; 1-4 on pens)*
Hønefoss 2-3 Sandefjord
Kristiansund 2-2 Viking *(aet; 0-3 on pens)*
Mjøndalen 4-0 Hødd
Molde 3-0 Kvik Halden
Odd 4-0 Åsane
Rosenborg 7-1 Tromsdalen
Stabæk 5-1 Strømmen

QUARTER-FINALS

(12/08/15)
Sarpsborg 08 2-1 Odd *(Mortensen 14, 47; Trondsen 6og)*

Viking 3-0 Molde *(Adegbenro 22, Bödvarsson 37, Sigurdsson 83)*

(13/08/15)
Rosenborg 4-0 Mjøndalen *(Søderlund 16, De Lanlay 28, Vilhjálmsson 34, Helland 59)*

Sandefjord 0-1 Stabæk *(Diomandé 64)*

SEMI-FINALS

(23/09/15)
Rosenborg 3-2 Stabæk *(Helland 7, Søderlund 78p, Vilhjálmsson 95; Keita 52, Næss 70p) (aet)*

(24/09/15)
Viking 0-1 Sarpsborg 08 *(Mortensen 98) (aet)*

FINAL

(22/11/15)
Ullevaal stadion, Oslo
ROSENBORG BK 2 *(Helland 22, Jensen 40)*
SARPSBORG 08 FF 0
Referee: *Johnsen*
ROSENBORG: Hansen, Svensson, Eyjólfsson, Skjelvik, Dorsin (Reginiussen 88), Jensen, Selnæs, Midtsjø (Konradsen 71), Helland, Søderlund, De Lanlay (Stamnestrø 90)
SARPSBORG: Kerr, Kronberg, Berge, Heieren Hansen (Kovács 89), Jensen (Brønne 85), Tokstad, Ernemann, Zajić, Askar, Wiig, Mortensen (Ugwuadu 83)

Rosenborg won the Norwegian Cup for the tenth time to complete the domestic double

POLAND

Polski Związek Piłki Nożnej (PZPN)

Address	Bitwy Warszawskiej 1920 r.7 PL-02 366 Warszawa
Tel	+48 22 551 2300
Fax	+48 22 551 2240
E-mail	pzpn@pzpn.pl
Website	pzpn.pl

President	Zbigniew Boniek
General secretary	Maciej Sawicki
Media officer	Janusz Basałaj
Year of formation	1919
National stadium	Stadion Narodowy, Warsaw (53,224)

EKSTRAKLASA CLUBS

 1 MKS Cracovia Kraków

 2 GKS Górnik Łęczna

 3 Górnik Zabrze

 4 Jagiellonia Białystok

 5 Korona Kielce

 6 KKS Lech Poznań

 7 KS Lechia Gdańsk

 8 Legia Warszawa

 9 KS Nieciecza

 10 GKS Piast Gliwice

 11 TS Podbeskidzie Bielsko-Biała

 12 MKS Pogoń Szczecin

 13 Ruch Chorzów

 14 WKS Śląsk Wrocław

 15 Wisła Kraków

16 Zagłębie Lubin

PROMOTED CLUBS

 17 Arka Gdynia

 18 Wisła Płock

KEY

- UEFA Champions League
- UEFA Europa League
- Promoted
- Relegated

Centenary joy for Legia

Legia Warszawa celebrated their centenary in the best way possible by winning a Polish league and cup double. A third Ekstraklasa triumph in four years was not sealed until the final day following a strong challenge from unheralded Piast Gliwice, while Lech Poznań were Legia's victims in the Polish Cup final for the second year in a row.

Poland's national team enjoyed their finest ever UEFA European Championship. Unbeaten in five matches at the finals, they were eliminated only on penalties by eventual champions Portugal.

Domestic double for 100-year-old Warsaw club

League runners-up spot for Piast Gliwice

National team reach EURO quarter-finals

Domestic league

Having surrendered their league crown on the last day to Lech in 2014/15, Legia were eager to atone in a season that concluded in the year of the club's 100th anniversary. They began strongly, but then came a shaky spell of just one win in seven matches that dropped the team down to fourth place and cost coach Henning Berg his job. He was replaced by the experienced Russian, Stanislav Cherchesov.

At the time of Cherchesov's arrival, it was Piast, a club from the footballing hot bed of Upper Silesia with no major honours, just five previous seasons of Ekstraklasa experience and a lowly 12th-place finish in 2014/15, who topped the table. Nine wins in their first 11 games under Czech boss Radoslav Látal, including 2-1 at home to Legia, had put them there, and surprisingly they still led, by five points from a resurgent Legia and nine from Cracovia Kraków, at the winter break.

The two-month rest did Piast no favours, however. Legia, in contrast, found form, reeling off six wins in the next seven matches to displace the leaders and enter the second phase with a one-point lead. It was nip-and-tuck from there on in, but crucially Legia won the head-to-head fixture, defeating Piast 4-0 in front of almost 30,000 fans

to move three points clear with two games to go. Legia, because of their higher position at the end of the first phase, now needed just one more win, but a defeat at Lechia Gdańsk and a 3-0 win for Piast at Ruch Chorzów ensured a nervous last-day fixture at home to Pogoń Szczecin. Another big crowd assembled in Warsaw, and they were not disappointed as Legia led through an early own goal and scored twice late on, with the prolific Nemanja Nikolić grabbing his 28th of the campaign, to wrap up the championship in style.

Piast lost anyway, 1-0 at home to fast-finishing, freshly-promoted Zagłębie Lubin, who took third place, with Cracovia also springing a surprise by grabbing fourth spot and joining the two teams above them in the UEFA Europa League. There was another tale of the unexpected at the foot of the table as joint record champions Górnik Zabrze were relegated.

Domestic cup

Polish Cup specialists Legia lifted the trophy for the fifth time in six years thanks to a repeat triumph over Lech, now under ex-Legia coach Jan Urban. Swiss striker Aleksandar Prijovic scored the only goal of the game for a team featuring five prospective UEFA EURO 2016 participants – Polish internationals Michał Pazdan, Artur Jędrzejczyk and

Tomasz Jodłowiec, Slovakian midfield schemer Ondrej Duda, and Hungarian striker Nikolić.

Europe

Legia and Lech both had extensive European campaigns in 2015/16, playing a dozen games each, but neither could progress beyond the group stage of the UEFA Europa League, claiming just one win apiece. For Lech, that occurred in Urban's first European game in charge, a memorable 2-1 victory away to Fiorentina.

National team

Impressive qualifiers for UEFA EURO 2016, with the most goals scored (33) and the top individual marksman in 13-goal Robert Lewandowski, Poland performed admirably if unspectacularly in France. They scored just four goals in five games but conceded only two and were never behind at any stage. Having recorded their first ever UEFA EURO finals win in their opening fixture against Northern Ireland, they finished second in their group behind Germany on goal difference, then overcame Switzerland on penalties in Saint-Etienne before succumbing by the same method to Portugal in Marseille, with the experienced Jakub Błaszczykowski, one of the team's standout performers, the unfortunate man to miss from the spot.

DOMESTIC SEASON AT A GLANCE

Ekstraklasa 2015/16 final table

		Home					Away					Total					
	Pld	W	D	L	F	A	W	D	L	F	A	W	D	L	F	A	Pts
1 Legia Warszawa	37	12	5	2	40	12	9	5	4	30	20	21	10	6	70	32	43
2 GKS Piast Gliwice	37	14	3	2	33	12	6	6	6	27	33	20	9	8	60	45	40
3 Zagłębie Lubin	37	9	4	6	33	24	8	5	5	22	18	17	9	11	55	42	38
4 MKS Cracovia Kraków	37	10	4	4	39	19	6	6	7	27	31	16	10	11	66	50	36
5 KS Lechia Gdańsk	37	11	4	3	34	13	3	6	10	19	31	14	10	13	53	44	32
6 MKS Pogoń Szczecin	37	7	9	3	25	21	5	8	5	18	22	12	17	8	43	43	30
7 KKS Lech Poznań	37	7	5	6	25	19	7	1	11	17	28	14	6	17	42	47	27
8 Ruch Chorzów	37	6	3	9	20	30	5	5	9	20	30	11	8	18	40	60	21
9 Wisła Kraków	37	5	10	4	27	21	7	5	6	34	24	12	15	10	61	45	32
10 WKS Śląsk Wrocław	37	8	6	4	22	18	4	6	9	19	28	12	12	13	41	46	31
11 Jagiellonia Białystok	37	8	4	7	21	25	5	2	11	25	37	13	6	18	46	62	28
12 Korona Kielce	37	4	7	8	22	31	6	8	4	17	14	10	15	12	39	45	27
13 KS Niecieza	37	5	6	7	22	22	5	6	8	17	28	10	12	15	39	50	26
14 GKS Górnik Łęczna	37	7	2	9	24	28	3	7	9	16	25	10	9	18	40	53	24
15 Górnik Zabrze	37	4	9	5	20	22	2	9	8	18	29	6	18	13	38	51	23
16 TS Podbeskidzie Bielsko-Biała	37	3	8	8	24	30	6	4	8	21	33	9	12	16	45	63	20

NB League splits into top and bottom halves after 30 games, after which the clubs play exclusively against teams in their group. Points obtained during the regular season are halved (and rounded upwards); KS Lechia Gdańsk, Górnik Zabrze, Ruch Chorzów & Wisła Kraków – 1 pt deducted.

European qualification 2016/17

Champion/Cup winner: Legia Warszawa (second qualifying round)

GKS Piast Gliwice (second qualifying round)
Zagłębie Lubin (first qualifying round)
MKS Cracovia Kraków (first qualifying round)

Top scorer Nemanja Nikolić (Legia), 28 goals
Relegated clubs TS Podbeskidzie Bielsko-Biała, Górnik Zabrze
Promoted clubs Arka Gdynia, Wisła Płock
Cup final Legia Warszawa 1-0 KKS Lech Poznań

Team of the season
(4-2-3-1)

Coach: Látal (Piast)

Szmatuła (Piast)

Mráz (Piast) — Pazdan (Legia) — Dąbrowski (Zagłębie) — Jędrzejczyk (Legia)

R Murawski (Pogoń) — Jodłowiec (Legia)

Kapustka (Cracovia) — Cetnarski (Cracovia) — Bonin (Górnik Łęczna)

Nikolić (Legia)

Player of the season

Nemanja Nikolić
(Legia Warszawa)

Signed up after winning the 2014/15 Hungarian NB I golden boot with champions Videoton, Nikolić repeated the trick with Legia, starting all 37 games and scoring an Ekstraklasa-best tally of 28 goals as the Warsaw club won the Polish title. The 28-year-old Serbia-born Hungarian international displayed an astonishing consistency of performance, enabling him to score at least one goal against every one of the other 15 teams in the division. He completed the set against Pogoń Szczecin in the title-clinching final game.

Newcomer of the season

Bartosz Kapustka
(MKS Cracovia Kraków)

Polish football discovered a new star during the 2015/16 season as Kapustka, a technically gifted left-footer, blossomed for club and country. Just 18 at the start of the campaign, when he made a goalscoring international debut in a UEFA EURO 2016 qualifier against Gibraltar, the winger won selection into Adam Nawałka's 23-man squad for the finals with a series of sparkling Ekstraklasa displays for Cracovia and rewarded the Poland coach's faith with a stunning opening performance against Northern Ireland.

NATIONAL TEAM

International tournament appearances

FIFA World Cup (7) 1938, 1974 (3rd), 1978 (2nd phase), 1982 (3rd), 1986 (2nd round), 2002, 2006
UEFA European Championship (3) 2008, 2012, 2016 (qtr-finals)

Top five all-time caps

Michał Żewłakow (102); Grzegorz Lato (100); Kazimierz Deyna (97); Jacek Bąk & Jacek Krzynówek (96)

Top five all-time goals

Włodzimierz Lubański (48); Grzegorz Lato (45); Kazimierz Deyna (41); Ernest Pol (39); **Robert Lewandowski** (35)

Results 2015/16

04/09/15	Germany (ECQ)	A	Frankfurt am Main	L	1-3	Lewandowski (37)
07/09/15	Gibraltar (ECQ)	H	Warsaw	W	8-1	Grosicki (8, 15), Lewandowski (18, 29), Milik (56, 72), Błaszczykowski (59p), Kapustka (73)
08/10/15	Scotland (ECQ)	A	Glasgow	D	2-2	Lewandowski (3, 90+4)
11/10/15	Republic of Ireland (ECQ)	H	Warsaw	W	2-1	Krychowiak (13), Lewandowski (42)
13/11/15	Iceland	H	Warsaw	W	4-2	Grosicki (52), Kapustka (66), Lewandowski (76, 79)
17/11/15	Czech Republic	H	Wroclaw	W	3-1	Milik (3), Jodłowiec (12), Grosicki (70)
23/03/16	Serbia	H	Poznan	W	1-0	Błaszczykowski (28)
26/03/16	Finland	H	Wroclaw	W	5-0	Grosicki (18, 85), Wszołek (20, 66), Starzyński (32)
01/06/16	Netherlands	H	Gdansk	L	1-2	Jędrzejczyk (60)
06/06/16	Lithuania	H	Krakow	D	0-0	
12/06/16	Northern Ireland (ECF)	N	Nice (FRA)	W	1-0	Milik (51)
16/06/16	Germany (ECF)	N	Saint-Denis (FRA)	D	0-0	
21/06/16	Ukraine (ECF)	N	Marseille (FRA)	W	1-0	Błaszczykowski (54)
25/06/16	Switzerland (ECF)	N	Saint-Etienne (FRA)	D	1-1	Błaszczykowski (39) (aet; 5-4 on pens)
30/06/16	Portugal (ECF)	N	Marseille (FRA)	D	1-1	Lewandowski (2) (aet; 3-5 on pens)

Appearances 2015/16

Coach: Adam Nawałka 23/10/57		GER	GIB	SCO	IRL	Isl	Cze	Srb	Fin	Ned	Ltu	NIR	GER	UKR	SUI	POR	Caps	Goals
Łukasz Fabiański	18/04/85 Swansea (ENG)	G	G	G	G			G46			G46		G	G	G	G	34	-
Łukasz Piszczek	03/06/85 Dortmund (GER)	D43		D	D	D		D		D46		D	D		D	D	50	2
Kamil Glik	03/02/88 Torino (ITA)	D	D	D	D	D	D46	D	D	D	D46	D	D	D	D	D	46	3
Łukasz Szukała	26/05/84 Osmanlıspor (TUR)	D	D		s78	D		D									17	1
Maciej Rybus	19/08/89 Terek (RUS)	D	D	D71		s12	D	D									41	2
Kamil Grosicki	08/06/88 Rennes (FRA)	M83	M		M85	M86	M73	M75	M	M77	M77	s80	M87	s71	M104	M82	44	8
Tomasz Jodłowiec	08/09/85 Legia	M		s63			M78	s76	s46	s80	s46	s78	s76	M	s101	s98	49	1
Grzegorz Krychowiak	29/01/90 Sevilla (ESP)	M	M	M	M	M		M76	M46		M85	M	M	M	M	M	39	2
Krzysztof Mączyński	23/05/87 Wisła Kraków	M63	M	M	M78	s65	M			M80	M46	M78	M76		M101	M98	20	1
Arkadiusz Milik	28/02/94 Ajax (NED)	M	M	M63		M86	A	M	A63	M87	A	M	M	M93	M	M	31	11
Robert Lewandowski	21/08/88 Bayern (GER)	A	A66	A	A	A90		A73	s63	A67	A	A	A	A	A	A	81	35
Paweł Olkowski	13/02/90 Köln (GER)	s43	D87	s83	M63												13	-
Jakub Błaszczykowski	14/12/85 Fiorentina (ITA)	s63	M62	M83	s63	M12		M	s86	M46	M74	M80	M80	s46	M	M	84	18
Sławomir Peszko	19/02/85 Lechia	s83			s85		s73		s77	s77	s88	s87		s104			40	2
Bartosz Kapustka	23/12/96 Cracovia		s62			s65	M83	s75	M79	s46	D	M88	s80	M71		s82	11	2
Piotr Zieliński	20/05/94 Empoli (ITA)		s66			M65		M83	s67	M	s85			M46			16	3
Sebastian Mila	10/07/82 Lechia		s87				s77										38	8
Michał Pazdan	21/09/87 Legia			D	D		D87	s87	D	D		D	D	D	D	D	22	-
Jakub Wawrzyniak	07/07/83 Lechia			s71	D	D65			D		D						49	1
Karol Linetty	02/02/95 Lech				M	s86	M77			s67							10	1
Wojciech Szczęsny	18/04/90 Roma (ITA)					G		s46		G		G					27	-
Mariusz Stępiński	12/05/95 Ruch					s86			s87								3	-
Artur Sobiech	12/06/90 Hannover (GER)					s90	s83										13	2
Artur Boruc	20/02/80 Bournemouth (ENG)					G		G46		s46							63	-
Artur Jędrzejczyk	04/11/87 Krasnodar (RUS) /Legia					D			D	D	s74	D	D	D	D	D	24	3
Thiago Cionek	21/04/86 Modena (ITA) /Palermo (ITA)					s46			s46	D				D			7	-
Ariel Borysiuk	29/07/91 Lechia /Legia					s78		s83									12	-
Paweł Dawidowicz	20/05/95 Benfica (POR)					s87											1	-
Bartosz Salamon	01/05/91 Cagliari (ITA)						D87	s79	s46								8	-
Łukasz Teodorczyk	03/06/91 Dynamo Kyiv (UKR)						s73										8	3
Paweł Wszołek	30/04/92 Verona (ITA)								M86								8	2
Filip Starzyński	27/05/91 Zagłębie								M67		M			s93			4	1
Przemysław Tytoń	04/01/87 Stuttgart (GER)								s46								14	-

POLAND

EUROPE

KKS Lech Poznań

Second qualifying round - FK Sarajevo (BIH)
A 2-0 *Hämäläinen (40), Thomalla (62)*
Burić, Douglas, Kędziora, Kádár, Trałka, Linetty (Dudka 8), Pawłowski (Jevtic 78), Thomalla, Hämäläinen, Kownacki (Formella 38), Kamiński. Coach: Maciej Skorża (POL)
H 1-0 *Douglas (6)*
Burić, Douglas, Kędziora, Kádár, Trałka, Pawłowski (Lovrencsics 78), Dudka (Tetteh 72), Thomalla, Hämäläinen (Jevtic 69), Formella, Kamiński. Coach: Maciej Skorża (POL)

Third qualifying round - FC Basel 1893 (SUI)
H 1-3 *Thomalla (36)*
Burić, Douglas, Kędziora, Kádár, Trałka, Linetty, Pawłowski, Thomalla (Robak 55), Hämäläinen (Lovrencsics 75), Formella (Ceesay 69), Kamiński. Coach: Maciej Skorża (POL)
Red card: Kędziora 66
A 0-1
Burić, Douglas, Trałka, Linetty, Pawłowski, Jevtic (Thomalla 73), Dudka, Hämäläinen (Robak 84), Ceesay, Formella (Lovrencsics 69), Kamiński. Coach: Maciej Skorża (POL)

Play-offs - Videoton FC (HUN)
H 3-0 *Linetty (11), Thomalla (57), Trałka (68)*
Burić, Douglas, Kędziora, Trałka, Linetty, Pawłowski, Lovrencsics (Robak 79; Holman 89), Dudka, Thomalla, Hämäläinen (Formella 83), Kamiński. Coach: Maciej Skorża (POL)
A 1-0 *Kędziora (57)*
Burić, Douglas, Kędziora, Kádár, Trałka, Pawłowski (Lovrencsics 74), Dudka, Thomalla (Kurbiel 81), Hämäläinen (Holman 72), Formella, Kamiński. Coach: Maciej Skorża (POL)

Group I
Match 1 - Os Belenenses (POR)
H 0-0
Burić, Kádár, Trałka (Linetty 46), Lovrencsics (Pawłowski 68), Dudka, Thomalla, Ceesay, Arajuuri, Kownacki (Hämäläinen 60), Formella, Kamiński. Coach: Maciej Skorża (POL)
Match 2 - FC Basel 1893 (SUI)
A 0-2
Gostomski, Kádár, Linetty, Jevtic (Trałka 54), Gajos (Lovrencsics 69), Ceesay, Arajuuri, Kownacki (Hämäläinen 46), Formella, Kamiński, Tetteh. Coach: Maciej Skorża (POL)
Red card: Linetty 49
Match 3 - ACF Fiorentina (ITA)
A 2-1 *Kownacki (65), Gajos (82)*
Burić, Kędziora, Kádár, Trałka, Lovrencsics, Dudka, Thomalla (Kownacki 63; Gajos 78), Holman (Hämäläinen 68), Formella, Kamiński, Tetteh. Coach: Jan Urban (POL)
Match 4 - ACF Fiorentina (ITA)
H 0-2
Burić, Kędziora, Kádár, Trałka, Linetty, Pawłowski, Dudka, Hämäläinen (Gajos 77), Formella (Lovrencsics 60), Kamiński, Tetteh (Thomalla 72). Coach: Jan Urban (POL)

Match 5 - Os Belenenses (POR)
A 0-0
Burić, Douglas, Kędziora, Kádár, Trałka (Tetteh 46), Linetty, Lovrencsics, Gajos, Dudka, Thomalla (Hämäläinen 74), Formella (Pawłowski 65). Coach: Jan Urban (POL)
Match 6 - FC Basel 1893 (SUI)
H 0-1
Burić, Kędziora, Kádár, Trałka (Tetteh 46), Linetty (Formella 61), Pawłowski, Jevtic (Hämäläinen 73), Gajos, Arajuuri, Kownacki, Kamiński. Coach: Jan Urban (POL)

Legia Warszawa

Second qualifying round - FC Botoşani (ROU)
H 1-0 *Duda (78)*
Kuciak, Pazdan, Jodłowiec, Guilherme (Żyro 68), Duda (Masłowski 90+3), Nikolić (Prijovic 68), Brzyski, Kucharczyk, Rzeźniczak, Broź, Furman. Coach: Henning Berg (NOR)
A 3-0 *Guilherme (7), Nikolić (38p), Prijovic (84)*
Kuciak, Pazdan, Jodłowiec (Masłowski 80), Guilherme, Duda, Nikolić (Prijovic 70), Brzyski (Żyro 46), Kucharczyk, Rzeźniczak, Broź, Furman. Coach: Henning Berg (NOR)

Third qualifying round - FK Kukësi (ALB)
A 2-1 *Nikolić (29), Rzeźniczak (51)* **(awarded as 3-0)**
Kuciak, Pazdan, Jodłowiec (Masłowski 42), Guilherme, Duda, Nikolić, Brzyski, Kucharczyk, Rzeźniczak, Broź, Furman. Coach: Henning Berg (NOR)
H 1-0 *Kucharczyk (47)*
Kuciak, Pazdan (Makowski 61), Lewczuk, Duda, Brzyski, Kucharczyk (Bartczak 68), Bereszyński, Rzeźniczak, Żyro (Guilherme 45+2), Furman, Prijovic. Coach: Henning Berg (NOR)

Play-offs - FC Zorya Luhansk (UKR)
A 1-0 *Kucharczyk (48)*
Kuciak, Pazdan, Jodłowiec, Guilherme, Nikolić (Saganowski 88), Brzyski, Kucharczyk, Bereszyński, Rzeźniczak, Furman, Prijovic (Duda 75). Coach: Henning Berg (NOR)
H 3-2 *Brzyski (16), Guilherme (62), Duda (90+5p)*
Kuciak, Pazdan (Lewczuk 7), Jodłowiec, Guilherme, Nikolić (Duda 67), Brzyski, Kucharczyk, Bereszyński, Rzeźniczak, Furman, Prijovic (Saganowski 90+3). Coach: Henning Berg (NOR)

Group D
Match 1 - FC Midtjylland (DEN)
A 0-1
Kuciak, Lewczuk, Guilherme, Nikolić, Brzyski, Kucharczyk (Trickovski 74), Bereszyński, Vranješ (Makowski 82), Rzeźniczak, Furman, Prijovic. Coach: Henning Berg (NOR)
Red card: Furman 88
Match 2 - SSC Napoli (ITA)
H 0-2
Kuciak, Pazdan (Makowski 89), Jodłowiec, Lewczuk, Guilherme, Brzyski, Kucharczyk (Nikolić 62), Bereszyński, Trickovski (Duda 62), Rzeźniczak, Prijovic. Coach: Henning Berg (NOR)

Match 3 - Club Brugge KV (BEL)
H 1-1 *Kucharczyk (51)*
Kuciak, Pazdan, Jodłowiec, Lewczuk, Guilherme (Duda 46), Nikolić (Prijovic 76), Brzyski, Kucharczyk, Rzeźniczak, Broź, Furman (Trickovski 46). Coach: Stanislav Cherchesov (RUS)
Match 4 - Club Brugge KV (BEL)
A 0-1
Kuciak, Pazdan, Jodłowiec (Guilherme 62), Lewczuk, Duda, Saganowski (Prijovic 59), Brzyski, Bereszyński (Kucharczyk 67), Trickovski, Vranješ, Rzeźniczak. Coach: Stanislav Cherchesov (RUS)
Match 5 - FC Midtjylland (DEN)
H 1-0 *Prijovic (35)*
Malarz, Jodłowiec, Lewczuk, Duda, Nikolić (Saganowski 90+1), Kucharczyk, Bereszyński, Trickovski (Żyro 82), Vranješ, Broź, Prijovic (Guilherme 64). Coach: Stanislav Cherchesov (RUS)
Match 6 - SSC Napoli (ITA)
A 2-5 *Vranješ (62), Prijovic (90+2)*
Kuciak, Pazdan, Jodłowiec, Lewczuk, Guilherme, Duda (Trickovski 71), Nikolić (Prijovic 60), Kucharczyk (Pablo Dyego 79), Bereszyński, Vranješ, Broź. Coach: Stanislav Cherchesov (RUS)

Jagiellonia Białystok

First qualifying round - FK Kruoja (LTU)
A 1-0 *Swiderski (90+3)*
Drągowski, Modelski, Vassiljev (Romanchuk 64), Madera, Tuszyński (Sekulski 63), Dzalamidze (Swiderski 80), Mackiewicz, Tarasovs, Gajos, Grzyb, Tomasik. Coach: Michał Probierz (POL)
Red card: Grzyb 82
H 8-0 *Gajos (3), Swiderski (8), Tuszyński (18, 45+1, 49), Frankowski (64, 75, 80)*
Drągowski, Modelski, Romanchuk, Madera, Tuszyński (Sekulski 74), Dzalamidze, Grzelczak (Frankowski 62), Tarasovs, Gajos, Swiderski (Vassiljev 55), Tomasik. Coach: Michał Probierz (POL)

Second qualifying round - AC Omonia (CYP)
H 0-0
Drągowski, Modelski, Romanchuk (Vassiljev 23; Sekulski 85), Madera, Tuszyński, Dzalamidze, Tarasovs, Gajos, Frankowski (Swiderski 78), Grzyb, Tomasik. Coach: Michał Probierz (POL)
A 0-1
Drągowski, Modelski, Romanchuk (Swiderski 75), Madera, Tuszyński, Dzalamidze (Grzelczak 46), Tarasovs, Gajos, Frankowski (Sekulski 62), Grzyb, Tomasik. Coach: Michał Probierz (POL)

DOMESTIC LEAGUE CLUB-BY-CLUB

WKS Śląsk Wrocław

First qualifying round - NK Celje (SVN)
A 1-0 *Pich (32)*
Pawełek, Celeban, Hateley, Hołota, Kiełb, Pich (Dankowski 90), Dudu, Pawelec, Zieliński, Flávio Paixão (Ostrowski 78), Grajciar (Machaj 69). Coach: Tadeusz Pawłowski (POL)
H 3-1 *Ostrowski (46), Kiełb (56, 90)*
Pawełek, Celeban, Hateley, Hołota, Kiełb (Dankowski 90+1), Pich, Dudu, Pawelec, Zieliński, Flávio Paixão (Ostrowski 11), Grajciar (Bartkowiak 76). Coach: Tadeusz Pawłowski (POL)

Second qualifying round - IFK Göteborg (SWE)
H 0-0
Pawełek, Celeban, Hateley (Biliński 67), Hołota, Kiełb (Flávio Paixão 77), Pich, Dudu, Pawelec, Kokoszka (Gecov 59), Zieliński, Grajciar. Coach: Tadeusz Pawłowski (POL)
A 0-2
Pawełek, Celeban, Hateley, Hołota, Kiełb, Pich, Dudu, Kokoszka, Zieliński (Machaj 87), Flávio Paixão (Gecov 76), Grajciar (Biliński 68). Coach: Tadeusz Pawłowski (POL)

MKS Cracovia Kraków

1906 • im. Józefa Piłsudskiego (15,016) • cracovia.pl
Major honours
Polish League (5) 1921, 1930, 1932, 1937, 1948
Coach: Jacek Zieliński

2015
17/07	a	Lechia	W	1-0	Polczak
24/07	h	Wisła	D	1-1	Cetnarski
01/08	a	Podbeskidzie	W	1-0	Čovilo
07/08	h	Piast	L	1-2	Diabang
14/08	a	Korona	W	3-0	Rakels, Cetnarski, Kapustka
22/08	h	Jagiellonia	D	1-1	Budziński
30/08	a	Górnik Zabrze	D	1-1	Zjawiński
12/09	h	Nieciecza	L	2-3	Čovilo, Zjawiński
18/09	a	Zagłębie	L	2-4	Cetnarski (p), Jendrišek
26/09	h	Ruch	W	2-1	Rakels 2
04/10	h	Lech	W	5-2	Kapustka, Rakels, Cetnarski (p), Jendrišek, Wójcicki
18/10	a	Legia	L	1-3	Jendrišek
24/10	h	Pogoń	W	4-1	Cetnarski, Rakels 2, Budziński
30/10	a	Górnik Łęczna	L	0-1	
06/11	h	Śląsk	W	4-1	Jendrišek 2, Rakels, Cetnarski
23/11	h	Lechia	W	3-0	Rakels, Cetnarski, Jendrišek
29/11	a	Wisła	W	2-1	Rakels, Deleu
02/12	h	Podbeskidzie	W	3-1	Rakels 2, Jendrišek, Budziński
05/12	a	Piast	D	2-2	Rakels, Jaroszyński
14/12	h	Korona	D	2-2	Rakels 2
19/12	a	Jagiellonia	D	2-2	Jendrišek, Rakels

2016
13/02	h	Górnik Zabrze	W	3-0	Kapustka, Jendrišek, Cetnarski
20/02	a	Nieciecza	D	1-1	Jendrišek
26/02	h	Zagłębie	L	1-2	Diabang
02/03	a	Ruch	W	3-2	Jendrišek, Cetnarski, Dąbrowski
06/03	a	Lech	L	1-2	Kapustka
12/03	h	Legia	L	1-2	Jendrišek
20/03	a	Pogoń	D	2-2	Vestenický, Wdowiak
02/04	h	Górnik Łęczna	D	0-0	
09/04	a	Śląsk	L	1-2	Cetnarski
16/04	a	Piast	D	1-1	Čovilo
19/04	h	Zagłębie	W	1-0	Cetnarski (p)
22/04	a	Legia	L	0-4	
29/04	a	Ruch	W	1-0	Čovilo
08/05	h	Lech	W	2-0	Jendrišek, Budziński
11/05	a	Pogoń	L	2-3	og (Fojut), Cetnarski
15/05	h	Lechia	W	2-0	Cetnarski, og (Janicki)

No	Name	Nat	DoB	Pos	Aps	(s)	Gls
18	Hubert Adamczyk		23/02/98	M		(1)	
6	Florin Bejan	ROU	28/03/91	D	10	(1)	
27	Marcin Budziński		06/07/90	M	27	(7)	4
10	Mateusz Cetnarski		06/07/88	M	35	(1)	13
5	Miroslav Čovilo	SRB	06/05/86	M	26	(3)	4
14	Damian Dąbrowski		27/08/92	M	25		1
26	Deleu	BRA	01/03/84	D	26	(3)	1
7	Boubacar Diabang	SEN	13/07/88	A	3	(14)	2
44	Paweł Jaroszyński		02/10/94	D	22		1
62	Erik Jendrišek	SVK	26/10/86	A	31	(4)	13
67	Bartosz Kapustka		23/12/96	M	29	(4)	4
71	Anton Karachanakov	BUL	17/01/92	M		(5)	
80	Krzysztof Pilarz		09/11/80	G	9		
24	Piotr Polczak		25/08/86	D	29	(2)	1
74	Przemysław Pyrdek		12/07/96	M		(1)	
92	Deniss Rakels	LVA	20/08/92	A	20		15
25	Bartosz Rymaniak		13/11/89	D	6	(5)	
29	Grzegorz Sandomierski		05/09/89	G	28		
3	Sreten Sretenović	SRB	12/01/85	D	14		
32	Krzysztof Szewczyk		06/03/96	A		(3)	
99	Tomáš Vestenický	SVK	06/04/96	A	4	(9)	1
96	Mateusz Wdowiak		28/08/96	A	3	(13)	1
21	Hubert Wołąkiewicz		21/10/85	D	28	(1)	
22	Jakub Wójcicki		09/07/88	D	25	(5)	1
23	Łukasz Zejdler		22/03/92	M	2	(11)	
9	Dariusz Zjawiński		19/08/86	A	5	(18)	2

GKS Górnik Łęczna

1979 • GKS Górnik Łęczna (7,496) • gornik.leczna.pl
Coach: Yuriy Shatalov (UKR);
(06/05/16) (Andrzej Rybarski)

2015
18/07	a	Ruch	W	2-0	Černych, Śpiączka
27/07	h	Górnik Zabrze	W	2-1	Poźniak, Śpiączka
02/08	h	Legia	L	0-2	
08/08	h	Pogoń	D	0-0	
15/08	h	Śląsk	L	2-3	Pitry, Bonin
21/08	a	Lechia	L	1-3	Piesio
29/08	a	Piast	L	0-3	
14/09	h	Wisła	W	1-0	Bonin
21/09	a	Korona	W	2-0	Bonin, Piesio
26/09	h	Podbeskidzie	L	1-2	Nowak (p)
03/10	a	Nieciecza	D	1-1	Świerczok
17/10	h	Jagiellonia	W	3-2	Śpiączka, Piesio, Bonin
24/10	a	Zagłębie	D	0-0	
30/10	h	Cracovia	W	1-0	Bonin
08/11	a	Lech	L	1-3	Leandro
21/11	h	Ruch	W	1-0	
28/11	a	Górnik Zabrze	D	1-1	Mierzejewski
02/12	a	Legia	L	1-2	Bonin
07/12	h	Pogoń	L	2-3	Świerczok, Śpiączka
11/12	a	Śląsk	L	1-2	Świerczok
19/12	h	Lechia	W	3-1	Piesio 2, Śpiączka

2016
13/02	h	Piast	D	0-0	
22/02	a	Wisła	D	1-1	Danielewicz
27/02	h	Korona	W	3-2	Świerczok 3 (2p)
01/03	a	Podbeskidzie	L	1-2	Śpiączka
05/03	h	Nieciecza	L	1-2	Śpiączka
12/03	a	Jagiellonia	L	0-1	
20/03	h	Zagłębie	L	0-1	
02/04	a	Cracovia	D	0-0	
09/04	h	Lech	L	0-1	
17/04	a	Jagiellonia	L	0-1	
20/04	h	Wisła	L	0-3	
23/04	a	Korona	D	1-1	Śpiączka (p)
30/04	a	Nieciecza	W	2-0	Pitry, Świerczok
07/05	h	Górnik Zabrze	D	0-0	
10/05	h	Podbeskidzie	W	5-1	Pitry, Piesio, Bonin 2, Śpiączka
14/05	a	Śląsk	L	2-3	Pitry, Śpiączka

No	Name	Nat	DoB	Pos	Aps	(s)	Gls
12	Džiugas Bartkus	LTU	07/11/89	G	7		
27	Adrian Basta		01/12/88	D	3		
14	Jan Bednarek		12/04/96	D	12	(5)	
20	Lukáš Bielák	SVK	14/12/86	D	11	(4)	
93	Łukasz Bogusławski		11/02/93	D	8	(2)	
15	Grzegorz Bonin		02/12/83	M	33	(2)	8
24	Tomislav Božić	CRO	01/11/87	D	31		
11	Fedor Černych	LTU	21/05/91	A	5	(1)	1
77	Krzysztof Danielewicz		26/07/91	M	6	(3)	1
26	Damian Jakubik		25/03/90	D	7		
18	Wojciech Kalinowski		09/09/93	M		(2)	
2	Leandro	BRA	29/12/83	D	31		1
21	Marquitos	ESP	21/03/87	M	2	(3)	
22	Łukasz Mierzejewski		31/08/82	D	25	(3)	1
4	Veljko Nikitović	SRB	03/10/80	M	11		
7	Tomasz Nowak		30/10/85	M	26	(5)	1
8	Grzegorz Piesio		17/07/88	M	32	(3)	6
45	Przemysław Pitry		11/09/81	A	16	(11)	4
19	Kamil Poźniak		11/12/89	M	5	(1)	1
17	Radosław Pruchnik		11/10/86	M	25	(3)	
79	Sergiusz Prusak		01/05/79	G	20		
1	Silvio Rodić	CRO	25/07/87	G	10	(2)	
6	Paweł Sasin		02/10/83	D	10	(14)	
23	Maciej Szmatiuk		09/05/80	D	19	(1)	
18	Bartosz Śpiączka		19/08/91	A	20	(15)	9
10	Jakub Świerczok		28/12/92	A	17	(14)	7
5	Łukasz Tymiński		08/11/90	M	15	(9)	

POLAND

Górnik Zabrze

1948 • Arena Zabrze (31,871) • gornikzabrze.pl

Major honours
Polish League (14) 1957, 1959, 1961, 1963, 1964, 1965, 1966, 1967, 1971, 1972, 1985, 1986, 1987, 1988; Polish Cup (6) 1965, 1968, 1969, 1970, 1971, 1972

Coach: Robert Warzycha; (13/08/15) Leszek Ojrzyński; (03/03/16) Jan Żurek

2015

17/07	a	Wisła	D	1-1	*Gergel*
27/07	a	Górnik Łęczna	L	1-2	*Gergel*
31/07	a	Piast	L	2-3	*Danch, Magiera (p)*
08/08	h	Jagiellonia	L	1-3	*Madej*
15/08	a	Nieciecza	L	0-3	
24/08	h	Zagłębie	D	2-2	*Sobolewski, Grendel (p)*
30/08	h	Cracovia	D	1-1	*Danch*
13/09	a	Ruch	L	0-1	
18/09	h	Śląsk	W	2-0	*Kwiek, Korzym*
26/09	a	Lech	D	1-1	*Gergel (p)*
04/10	h	Legia	D	2-2	*Shevelyukhin, Sobolewski*
16/10	a	Lechia	D	1-1	*Korzym*
26/10	h	Podbeskidzie	L	0-2	
30/10	a	Pogoń	D	1-1	*Kwiek*
08/11	h	Korona	L	0-1	
20/11	h	Wisła	D	1-1	*Kopacz*
28/11	h	Górnik Łęczna	D	1-1	*Skrzypczak*
01/12	h	Piast	W	5-2	*Gergel 4 (1p), Kwiek*
04/12	a	Jagiellonia	W	3-2	*Skrzypczak, Madej, Gergel*
12/12	h	Nieciecza	D	0-0	
18/12	a	Zagłębie	W	4-2	*Gergel, Kopacz, Sobolewski, Shevelyukhin*

2016

13/02	a	Cracovia	L	0-3	
21/02	h	Ruch	L	0-2	
26/02	a	Śląsk	D	0-0	
02/03	h	Lech	L	0-2	
05/03	a	Legia	L	1-3	*Steblecki*
13/03	h	Lechia	D	1-1	*Kopacz*
19/03	a	Podbeskidzie	D	0-0	
01/04	h	Pogoń	D	1-1	*Kopacz*
09/04	a	Korona	L	1-2	*Przybylski*
17/04	a	Wisła	L	1-3	*Gergel*
20/04	h	Podbeskidzie	W	1-0	*og (Mójta)*
24/04	a	Jagiellonia	D	0-0	
29/04	h	Śląsk	W	2-1	*Ćerimagić, Steblecki*
07/05	a	Górnik Łęczna	D	0-0	
10/05	h	Korona	D	0-0	
14/05	a	Nieciecza	D	1-1	*Kurzawa*

No	Name	Nat	DoB	Pos	Aps	(s)	Gls
22	Kamil Cupriak		11/11/94	A		(2)	
14	Armin Ćerimagić	BIH	14/01/94	M	7	(11)	1
26	Adam Danch		15/12/87	D	36		2
29	Adam Dźwigała		25/09/95	D	4	(4)	
11	Roman Gergel	SVK	22/02/88	M	35	(1)	10
44	Paweł Golański		12/10/82	D	5	(1)	
8	Erik Grendel	SVK	13/10/88	M	11		1
25	Dzikamai Gwaze	ZIM	22/04/89	M	1		
38	Bartosz Iwan		18/04/84	M		(4)	
16	Michał Janota		29/07/90	A	2	(9)	
84	Radosław Janukiewicz		05/05/84	G	12		
81	Róbert Jež	SVK	10/07/81	M	7	(6)	
15	Ken Kallaste	EST	31/08/88	D	13	(2)	
29	José Kanté	ESP	27/09/90	A	14	(2)	
99	Grzegorz Kasprzik		20/09/83	G	20		
2	Bartosz Kopacz		21/05/92	D	28		4
24	Maciej Korzym		02/05/88	A	10	(6)	2
4	Rafał Kosznik		17/12/83	D	16	(1)	
6	Rafał Kurzawa		29/01/93	M	13	(10)	1
9	Aleksander Kwiek		13/01/83	M	20	(6)	3
18	Łukasz Madej		14/04/82	M	27	(2)	2
21	Mariusz Magiera		25/08/84	D	8	(3)	1
23	Szymon Matuszek		07/01/89	M	10	(1)	
10	Konrad Nowak		07/11/94	M		(2)	
25	Mārcis Ošs	LVA	25/07/91	D	8	(1)	
15	Fabian Piasecki		04/05/95	A		(2)	
19	Mariusz Przybylski		19/01/82	M	15	(5)	1
33	Sebastian Przyrowski		30/11/81	G	5		
17	Dominik Sadzawicki		19/04/94	D	4	(5)	
5	Olexandr Shevelyukhin	UKR	27/08/82	D	17	(1)	2
23	Szymon Skrzypczak		14/03/90	A	9	(13)	2
3	Mateusz Słodowy		08/08/91	D	11	(3)	
7	Radosław Sobolewski		13/12/76	M	17		3
71	Sebastian Steblecki		16/01/92	M	7	(6)	2
20	Marcin Urynowicz		16/03/96	A	2	(1)	
31	Pavel Vidanov	BUL	08/01/88	D	13		

Jagiellonia Białystok

1932 • Miejski (22,432) • jagiellonia.pl

Major honours
Polish Cup (1) 2010

Coach: Michał Probierz

2015

19/07	a	Korona	L	2-3	*Sekulski, Grzelczak*
26/07	h	Nieciecza	W	2-0	*Gajos, Tuszyński*
02/08	h	Zagłębie	L	1-2	*Gajos*
08/08	a	Górnik Zabrze	W	3-1	*Vassiljev, Grzelczak, Gajos*
16/08	h	Ruch	W	2-1	*Madera, Vassiljev*
22/08	a	Cracovia	D	1-1	*Vassiljev*
30/08	h	Legia	D	1-1	*Gajos*
12/09	a	Śląsk	L	1-3	*Grzelczak*
20/09	h	Lech	W	1-0	*Frankowski*
28/09	a	Pogoń	L	1-2	*Černych*
02/10	h	Lechia	L	0-3	
17/10	a	Górnik Łęczna	L	2-3	*Frankowski, Grzelczak*
23/10	h	Wisła	L	1-4	*Tarasovs*
02/11	a	Podbeskidzie	D	1-1	*Świderski*
07/11	h	Piast	L	0-2	
21/11	h	Korona	W	1-0	*Černych*
01/12	a	Zagłębie	W	2-0	*og (Jach), Świderski*
04/12	h	Górnik Zabrze	L	2-3	*Frankowski, Grzelczak*
11/12	a	Ruch	W	4-0	*Romanchuk (p), Mackiewicz, Frankowski, Tomasik (p)*
16/12	a	Nieciecza	L	0-2	
19/12	h	Cracovia	D	2-2	*Frankowski, Grzelczak*

2016

14/02	a	Legia	L	0-4	
19/02	h	Śląsk	W	2-1	*Grzyb, Świderski*
28/02	a	Lech	W	2-0	*Tarasovs, Tomasik (p)*
02/03	h	Pogoń	D	0-0	
06/03	a	Lechia	L	1-5	*Černych*
12/03	h	Górnik Łęczna	W	1-0	*Vassiljev*
18/03	a	Wisła	L	1-5	*Świderski*
04/04	h	Podbeskidzie	L	0-3	
09/04	a	Piast	L	0-2	
17/04	h	Górnik Łęczna	W	2-0	*Tomasik (p), Vassiljev*
20/04	a	Śląsk	L	1-3	*Vassiljev*
24/04	h	Górnik Zabrze	D	0-0	
01/05	h	Podbeskidzie	W	3-2	*Szymonowicz, Vassiljev, Romanchuk*
06/05	a	Wisła	L	0-1	
10/05	h	Nieciecza	L	0-1	
14/05	a	Korona	W	3-1	*Mystkowski, Frankowski, Romanchuk (p)*

No	Name	Nat	DoB	Pos	Aps	(s)	Gls
10	Alvarinho	POR	03/09/90	A	4	(6)	
25	Rafał Augustyniak		14/10/93	D	3	(1)	
33	Krzysztof Baran		12/02/90	G	3		
18	Martin Baran	SVK	03/01/88	D	7	(1)	
8	Łukasz Burliga		10/05/88	D	12	(1)	
15	Fedor Černych	LTU	21/05/91	A	25	(2)	3
69	Bartłomiej Drągowski		19/08/97	G	34		
10	Nika Dzalamidze	GEO	06/01/92	M	1		
21	Przemysław Frankowski		12/04/95	M	25	(6)	6
26	Emil Gajko		10/05/96	A		(1)	
14	Maciej Gajos		19/03/91	M	6		4
27	Bartosz Giełażyn		13/10/94	A		(2)	
4	Jacek Góralski		21/09/92	M	24	(4)	
12	Piotr Grzelczak		02/03/88	A	17	(14)	6
22	Rafał Grzyb		16/01/83	M	29	(4)	1
25	Guti	BRA	29/06/91	D	12		
44	Emil Łupiński		13/01/96	D		(1)	
11	Karol Mackiewicz		01/06/92	A	17	(8)	1
7	Sebastian Madera		30/05/85	D	22	(1)	1
2	Filip Modelski		28/09/92	D	12		
13	Przemysław Mystkowski		25/04/98	A	3	(12)	1
52	Paweł Olszewski		07/06/99	D	1		
23	Michał Pawlik		08/05/95	M	1		
6	Taras Romanchuk	UKR	14/11/91	M	24	(9)	3
17	Łukasz Sekulski		03/11/90	A	4	(5)	1
24	Matija Širok	SVN	31/05/91	D	3		
3	Jonatan Straus		30/06/94	D	5	(3)	
20	Dawid Szymonowicz		07/07/95	M	6	(2)	1
28	Karol Świderski		23/01/97	A	14	(17)	4
19	Igors Tarasovs	LVA	16/10/88	M	25	(1)	2
77	Piotr Tomasik		31/10/87	D	29		3
8	Patryk Tuszyński		13/12/89	A	1		1
5	Konstantin Vassiljev	EST	16/08/84	M	29	(6)	7
14	Marek Wasiluk		03/06/87	D	9	(1)	

Korona Kielce

1973 • Miejski Arena Kielc (15,550) • korona-kielce.pl

Coach: Ryszard Tarasiewicz

2015

19/07	h	Jagiellonia	W	3-2	*Przybyła 2, Sylwestrzak*
25/07	a	Zagłębie	W	2-0	*Pylypchuk, Przybyła*
03/08	h	Ruch	L	1-2	*Sobolewski*
08/08	a	Lech	D	0-0	
14/08	h	Cracovia	L	0-3	
23/08	a	Legia	W	2-1	*Trytko, Przybyła*
29/08	h	Pogoń	D	1-1	*Trytko (p)*
11/09	a	Lechia	D	0-0	
21/09	h	Górnik Łęczna	L	0-2	
25/09	a	Wisła	D	0-0	
03/10	h	Podbeskidzie	D	0-0	
16/10	a	Śląsk	W	1-0	*Cabrera (p)*
24/10	a	Piast	W	1-0	*Pawłowski*
02/11	h	Nieciecza	L	0-1	
08/11	a	Górnik Zabrze	W	1-0	*Cabrera*
21/11	a	Jagiellonia	L	0-1	
27/11	h	Zagłębie	L	0-2	
01/12	a	Ruch	L	1-2	*Pawłowski*
05/12	h	Lech	L	0-1	
14/12	a	Cracovia	D	2-2	*Cabrera 2*
20/12	h	Legia	L	1-3	*Sierpina*

2016

15/02	a	Pogoń	L	2-3	*Pawłowski, Cabrera*
20/02	h	Lechia	W	4-2	*Cabrera 3 (2p), Sierpina*
27/02	a	Górnik Łęczna	L	2-3	*Pawłowski, Cabrera*
04/03	a	Podbeskidzie	D	1-1	*Przybyła*
08/03	h	Wisła	D	1-1	*Cabrera*
11/03	h	Śląsk	D	2-2	*Cabrera 2 (1p)*
18/03	h	Piast	D	1-1	*Cabrera*
02/04	a	Nieciecza	W	1-0	*Sylwestrzak*
09/04	h	Górnik Zabrze	W	2-1	*Jovanović, Pylypchuk*
16/04	h	Śląsk	D	1-1	*Cabrera*
20/04	a	Nieciecza	D	0-0	
23/04	h	Górnik Łęczna	D	1-1	*Cabrera*
30/04	h	Wisła	W	3-2	*Cabrera, Verkhovtsov, Pylypchuk*
06/05	a	Podbeskidzie	D	1-1	*Sylwestrzak*
10/05	a	Górnik Zabrze	D	0-0	
14/05	h	Jagiellonia	L	1-3	*Pawłowski*

No	Name	Nat	DoB	Pos	Aps	(s)	Gls
19	Nabil Aankour	MAR	09/08/93	M	18	(9)	
18	Airam Cabrera	ESP	21/10/87	A	25	(3)	16
7	Marcin Cebula		06/12/95	M	13	(13)	
32	Radek Dejmek	CZE	02/02/88	D	33	(1)	
23	El Hadji Diaw	SEN	31/12/94	D	12		
87	Aleksandrs Fertovs	LVA	16/06/87	M	21	(8)	
28	Vladislavs Gabovs	LVA	13/07/87	D	26	(7)	
27	Rafał Grzelak		07/08/88	D	24	(1)	
8	Vlastimir Jovanović	BIH	03/04/85	M	36		1
13	Krzysztof Kiercz		16/02/89	D	3	(1)	
56	Hubert Laskowski		22/03/95	A		(1)	
4	Piotr Malarczyk		01/08/91	D	5		
1	Zbigniew Małkowski		19/01/78	G	19		
23	Vanja Marković	SRB	20/06/94	M	1	(4)	
10	Bartłomiej Pawłowski		13/11/92	M	23	(4)	5
77	Michał Przybyła		01/07/94	A	7	(15)	5
5	Serhiy Pylypchuk	UKR	26/11/84	M	14	(5)	3
26	Bartosz Rymaniak		13/11/89	D	11	(1)	
44	Łukasz Sekulski		03/11/90	A	3	(6)	
15	Łukasz Sierpina		27/03/88	M	24	(5)	2
29	Paweł Sobolewski		20/06/79	M	5	(6)	1
2	Kamil Sylwestrzak		16/07/88	D	34		3
4	Charlie Trafford	CAN	24/05/92	M	2	(1)	
12	Dariusz Trela		05/12/89	G	18	(1)	
9	Przemysław Trytko		26/08/87	A	5	(7)	2
13	Dmitri Verkhovtsov	BLR	10/10/86	D	6		1
23	Maciej Wilusz		25/09/88	D	13		
11	Tomasz Zając		14/07/95	M	6	(12)	

KKS Lech Poznań

1922 • INEA (42,837) • lechpoznan.pl

Major honours
Polish League (7) 1983, 1984, 1990, 1992, 1993, 2010, 2015; Polish Cup (5) 1982, 1984, 1988, 2004, 2009

Coach: Maciej Skorża;
(12/10/15) Jan Urban

2015					
18/07	h	Pogoń	L	1-2	*Jevtic*
25/07	h	Lechia	W	2-1	*Hämäläinen, Robak*
01/08	a	Wisła	L	0-2	
08/08	h	Korona	D	0-0	
14/08	a	Zagłębie	L	1-2	*Robak*
23/08	h	Piast	L	0-1	
30/08	a	Nieciecza	L	1-3	*Formella*
12/09	h	Podbeskidzie	L	0-1	
20/09	a	Jagiellonia	L	0-1	
26/09	h	Górnik Zabrze	D	1-1	*Kownacki*
04/10	a	Cracovia	L	2-5	*Hämäläinen 2*
17/10	h	Ruch	D	2-2	*Pawłowski, Kamiński*
25/10	a	Legia	W	1-0	*Hämäläinen*
31/10	a	Śląsk	D	1-1	*Gajos*
08/11	h	Górnik Łęczna	W	3-1	*Gajos 2, Linetty*
22/11	a	Pogoń	W	2-0	*Hämäläinen, Trałka*
29/11	a	Lechia	W	1-0	*Hämäläinen*
02/12	h	Wisła	W	2-0	*Kownacki (p), Pawłowski*
05/12	a	Korona	W	1-0	*Hämäläinen*
13/12	h	Zagłębie	W	2-0	*Hämäläinen, Pawłowski*
20/12	a	Piast	L	0-2	
2016					
14/02	h	Nieciecza	W	5-2	*Pawłowski 2, Bille Nielsen, Kownacki 2 (1p)*
20/02	a	Podbeskidzie	L	1-4	*Kownacki*
28/02	h	Jagiellonia	L	0-2	
02/03	a	Górnik Zabrze	W	2-0	*Kownacki, Pawłowski*
06/03	h	Cracovia	W	2-1	*Jevtic, Gajos*
12/03	a	Ruch	W	3-1	*Gajos, Jevtic 2*
19/03	h	Legia	L	0-2	
01/04	h	Śląsk	L	0-1	
09/04	a	Górnik Łęczna	W	1-0	*Bille Nielsen*
15/04	a	Legia	L	0-1	
19/04	h	Piast	D	2-2	*Linetty, Bille Nielsen*
23/04	a	Pogoń	L	0-1	
28/04	h	Lechia	D	0-0	
08/05	a	Cracovia	L	0-2	
11/05	a	Zagłębie	L	0-3	
15/05	h	Ruch	W	3-0	*Jóźwiak, Linetty, Gajos*

No	Name	Nat	DoB	Pos	Aps	(s)	Gls
23	Paulus Arajuuri	FIN	15/06/88	D	27	(1)	
19	Nicki Bille Nielsen	DEN	07/02/88	A	9	(1)	3
1	Jasmin Burić	BIH	18/02/87	G	35		
21	Kebba Ceesay	GAM	14/11/87	D	14	(4)	
3	Barry Douglas	SCO	04/09/89	D	13		
15	Dariusz Dudka		09/12/83	D	7	(2)	
28	Dariusz Formella		21/10/95	A	1	(18)	1
14	Maciej Gajos		19/03/91	M	21	(7)	6
33	Maciej Gostomski		27/09/88	G	2		
2	Robert Gumny		04/06/98	D	2	(2)	
19	Kasper Hämäläinen	FIN	08/08/86	M	15		8
20	Dávid Holman	HUN	17/03/93	M	2	(1)	
10	Darko Jevtic	SUI	08/02/93	M	15	(11)	4
29	Kamil Jóźwiak		22/04/98	M	3	(7)	1
5	Tamás Kádár	HUN	14/03/90	D	27	(2)	
35	Marcin Kamiński		15/01/92	D	31	(4)	1
4	Tomasz Kędziora		11/06/94	D	23	(1)	
27	Krzysztof Kotorowski		12/09/76	G		(1)	
24	Dawid Kownacki		14/03/97	M	11	(13)	6
34	Piotr Kurbiel		07/02/96	A		(3)	
7	Karol Linetty		02/02/95	M	26	(2)	3
11	Gergő Lovrencsics	HUN	01/09/88	A	20	(3)	
8	Szymon Pawłowski		04/11/86	M	29	(2)	6
22	Marcin Robak		29/11/82	A	5	(3)	2
25	Sisi	ESP	22/04/86	M	3	(1)	
55	Abdul Aziz Tetteh	GHA	25/05/90	M	25	(3)	
18	Denis Thomalla	GER	16/08/92	A	3	(10)	
6	Łukasz Trałka		11/05/84	M	28	(2)	1
3	Vladimir Volkov	MNE	06/06/86	D	5	(2)	
26	Maciej Wilusz		25/09/88	D	5	(1)	

KS Lechia Gdańsk

1945 • PGE Arena Gdańsk (43,165) • lechia.pl

Major honours
Polish Cup (1) 1983

Coach: Jerzy Brzęczek;
(01/09/15) Thomas von Heesen (GER);
(03/12/15) (Dawid Banaczek);
(13/01/16) Piotr Nowak

2015					
17/07	h	Cracovia	L	0-1	
25/07	a	Lech	L	1-2	*Janicki*
31/07	h	Pogoń	D	1-1	*Buksa*
09/08	a	Śląsk	D	0-0	
16/08	a	Wisła	D	3-3	*Łukasik, Haraslín, Maloča*
21/08	h	Górnik Łęczna	W	3-1	*Haraslín 2, Vranješ (p)*
28/08	a	Podbeskidzie	D	1-1	*Borysiuk*
11/09	h	Korona	D	0-0	
19/09	a	Piast	L	1-2	*Borysiuk*
27/09	h	Zagłębie	W	3-1	*Kuświk 2 (1p), Mak*
02/10	a	Jagiellonia	W	3-0	*Mak, Makuszewski, Kuświk*
16/10	h	Górnik Zabrze	D	1-1	*Makuszewski*
25/10	a	Nieciecza	W	1-0	*Kuświk (p)*
31/10	h	Legia	L	1-3	*Kovačević*
07/11	a	Ruch	L	2-3	*Mak 2*
23/11	a	Cracovia	L	0-3	
29/11	h	Lech	L	0-1	
02/12	a	Pogoń	L	0-1	
06/12	h	Śląsk	W	1-0	*Gérson*
12/12	h	Wisła	W	2-0	*Mak, Makuszewski*
19/12	a	Górnik Łęczna	L	1-3	*Janicki*
2016					
13/02	h	Podbeskidzie	W	5-0	*Mila (p), Maloča, Kuświk, Krasić, Peszko*
20/02	a	Korona	L	2-4	*Wojtkowiak, Kuświk*
27/02	h	Piast	W	3-1	*Kuświk, Mak, Stolarski*
01/03	a	Zagłębie	L	0-1	
06/03	h	Jagiellonia	W	5-1	*Flávio Paixão 3, Kuświk, Krasić (p)*
13/03	a	Górnik Zabrze	D	1-1	*Kovačević*
20/03	h	Nieciecza	D	1-1	*Chrapek*
02/04	a	Legia	D	1-1	*Kuświk*
09/04	h	Ruch	W	2-0	*Mila (p), Flávio Paixão*
16/04	a	Zagłębie	W	2-1	*Kuświk, Flávio Paixão*
19/04	h	Pogoń	W	2-0	*Krasić, Wojtkowiak*
24/04	a	Piast	L	0-3	
28/04	a	Lech	D	0-0	
07/05	h	Ruch	W	2-1	*Kuświk, Flávio Paixão*
11/05	h	Legia	W	2-0	*Peszko, Krasić*
15/05	a	Cracovia	L	0-2	

No	Name	Nat	DoB	Pos	Aps	(s)	Gls
16	Ariel Borysiuk		29/07/91	M	20		2
10	Bruno Nazário	BRA	09/02/95	M	6	(3)	
1	Łukasz Budziłek		19/03/91	G	2		
18	Adam Buksa		12/07/96	A	4	(4)	1
20	Michał Chrapek		03/04/92	M	12	(2)	1
25	Adam Chrzanowski		31/03/99	D		(1)	
28	Flávio Paixão	POR	19/09/84	A	16		6
35	Gérson	BRA	07/01/92	D	12	(3)	1
17	Lukáš Haraslín	SVK	26/05/96	M	10	(10)	3
2	Rafał Janicki		05/07/92	D	33	(2)	2
11	Martin Kobylański		08/03/94	M		(3)	
4	Aleksandar Kovačević	SRB	09/01/92	M	18	(7)	2
7	Miloš Krasić	SRB	01/11/84	M	18	(5)	4
30	Grzegorz Kuświk		23/05/87	A	28	(5)	11
33	Nikola Leković	SRB	19/12/89	D		(2)	
8	Daniel Łukasik		28/04/91	M	14	(6)	1
9	Michał Mak		14/11/91	M	15	(8)	6
11	Maciej Makuszewski		29/09/89	M	19	(1)	3
22	Mario Maloča	CRO	04/05/89	D	24	(4)	2
50	Marko Marić	CRO	03/01/96	G	24		
10	Marco Paixão	POR	19/09/84	A	2	(1)	
29	Neven Marković	SRB	20/02/87	D	5		
6	Sebastian Mila		10/07/82	M	24	(5)	2
32	Vanja Milinković-Savić	SRB	20/02/97	G	11		
21	Sławomir Peszko		19/02/85	M	21	(6)	2
5	Rudinilson	POR	20/08/94	D		(1)	
41	Paweł Stolarski		28/01/96	D	10	(11)	1
21	Stojan Vranješ	BIH	11/10/86	M	3	(2)	1
3	Jakub Wawrzyniak		07/07/83	D	31	(1)	
14	Piotr Wiśniewski		11/08/82	M	3	(6)	
23	Grzegorz Wojtkowiak		26/01/84	D	22	(6)	2
44	Michał Żebrakowski		07/01/97	A		(3)	

Legia Warszawa

1916 • Wojska Polskiego im. Marszałka Józefa Piłsudskiego (31,284) • legia.com

Major honours
Polish League (11) 1955, 1956, 1969, 1970, 1994, 1995, 2002, 2006, 2013, 2014, 2016; Polish Cup (18) 1955, 1956, 1964, 1966, 1973, 1980, 1981, 1989, 1990, 1994, 1995, 1997, 2008, 2011, 2012, 2013, 2015, 2016

Coach: Henning Berg (NOR);
(06/10/15) Stanislav Cherchesov (RUS)

2015					
19/07	a	Śląsk	W	4-1	*Furman, Jodłowiec, Nikolić 2*
26/07	h	Podbeskidzie	W	5-0	*og (Jaroch), Nikolić, Kucharczyk, Żyro, Duda*
02/08	a	Górnik Łęczna	W	2-0	*Nikolić 2*
09/08	h	Wisła	D	1-1	*Furman*
15/08	a	Piast	L	1-2	*Nikolić*
23/08	h	Korona	L	1-2	*Nikolić (p)*
30/08	a	Jagiellonia	D	1-1	*Guilherme*
11/09	h	Zagłębie	D	2-2	*Trickovski, Nikolić*
20/09	a	Ruch	W	4-1	*Nikolić, Vranješ, Kucharczyk, Prijovic*
27/09	h	Nieciecza	D	1-1	*Nikolić*
04/10	a	Górnik Zabrze	D	2-2	*Nikolić 2 (1p)*
18/10	h	Cracovia	W	3-1	*Nikolić 3*
25/10	h	Lech	L	0-1	
31/10	a	Lechia	W	3-1	*Guilherme, Nikolić, Jodłowiec*
08/11	h	Pogoń	W	1-0	*Jodłowiec*
21/11	h	Śląsk	W	1-0	*Prijovic*
29/11	a	Podbeskidzie	D	2-2	*Nikolić, Vranješ*
02/12	h	Górnik Łęczna	W	2-1	*Nikolić 2*
06/12	a	Wisła	W	2-0	*Nikolić, Prijovic*
13/12	h	Piast	D	1-1	*og (Hebert)*
20/12	a	Korona	W	3-1	*Guilherme, Kucharczyk, Nikolić*
2016					
14/02	h	Jagiellonia	W	4-0	*Nikolić 2, Kucharczyk, Jodłowiec*
21/02	a	Zagłębie	W	2-1	*Prijovic, Kucharczyk*
28/02	h	Ruch	W	2-0	*og (Oleksy), Hloušek*
02/03	a	Nieciecza	L	0-3	
05/03	h	Górnik Zabrze	W	3-1	*Hloušek, Jędrzejczyk, Prijovic*
12/03	a	Cracovia	W	2-1	*Guilherme, Prijovic*
19/03	a	Lech	W	2-0	*Nikolić 2 (1p)*
02/04	h	Lechia	D	1-1	*Duda*
09/04	a	Pogoń	D	0-0	
15/04	h	Lech	W	1-0	*Prijovic*
19/04	a	Ruch	D	0-0	
22/04	h	Cracovia	W	4-0	*Prijovic, Kucharczyk, Nikolić, Hämäläinen*
28/04	a	Zagłębie	L	0-2	
08/05	h	Piast	W	4-0	*Lewczuk, Guilherme, Hämäläinen, Nikolić (p)*
11/05	a	Lechia	L	0-2	
15/05	h	Pogoń	W	3-0	*og (Czerwiński), Nikolić, Hämäläinen*

No	Name	Nat	DoB	Pos	Aps	(s)	Gls
77	Mihail Alexandrov	BUL	11/06/89	M	5	(6)	
19	Bartosz Bereszyński		12/07/92	D	8	(8)	
7	Ariel Borysiuk		29/07/91	M	12	(1)	
28	Łukasz Broź		17/12/85	D	16	(4)	
17	Tomasz Brzyski		10/01/82	D	22	(1)	
8	Ondrej Duda	SVK	05/12/94	M	22	(5)	2
37	Dominik Furman		06/07/92	M	11	(3)	2
6	Guilherme	BRA	21/05/91	M	29	(6)	5
22	Kasper Hämäläinen	FIN	08/08/86	M	3	(8)	3
14	Adam Hloušek	CZE	20/12/88	D	16		2
5	Artur Jędrzejczyk		04/11/87	D	16		1
3	Tomasz Jodłowiec		08/09/85	M	25	(2)	4
15	Michał Kopczyński		15/06/92	M		(2)	
18	Michał Kucharczyk		20/03/91	A	29	(3)	6
12	Dušan Kuciak	SVK	21/05/85	G	18		
4	Igor Lewczuk		30/05/85	D	29		1
47	Rafał Makowski		05/08/96	M	3	(4)	
1	Arkadiusz Malarz		19/06/80	G	19		
16	Michał Masłowski		19/12/89	M	4	(6)	
11	Nemanja Nikolić	HUN	31/12/87	A	37		28
2	Michał Pazdan		21/09/87	D	23	(1)	
13	Arkadiusz Piech		07/06/85	A		(6)	
99	Aleksandar Prijovic	SUI	21/04/90	A	20	(10)	8
45	Adam Ryczkowski		30/04/97	A	1		
25	Jakub Rzeźniczak		26/10/86	D	20		
9	Marek Saganowski		31/10/78	A	1	(6)	
20	Ivan Trickovski	MKD	18/04/87	M	3	(8)	1
23	Stojan Vranješ	BIH	11/10/86	M	14	(5)	2
33	Michał Żyro		20/09/92	M	1	(4)	1

 **POLAND**

KS Nieciecza

1922 • MOSiR, Mielec (6,864);
Bruk-Bet (4,666) • termalica.brukbet.com
Coach: Piotr Mandrysz

2015
20/07	a	Piast	L	0-1
26/07	a	Jagiellonia	L	0-2
02/08	a	Śląsk	L	0-2
07/08	h	Zagłębie	W	1-0 Staňo
15/08	h	Górnik Zabrze	W	3-0 Drozdowicz, Plizga 2 (1p)
22/08	a	Ruch	L	1-4 Kędziora
30/08	h	Lech	W	3-1 Kędziora, Pleva, Babiarz
12/09	a	Cracovia	W	3-2 Biskup 2 (1p), Babiarz
19/09	h	Pogoń	D	1-1 Juhar
27/09	a	Legia	D	1-1 Juhar
03/10	h	Górnik Łęczna	D	1-1 og (Rodić)
18/10	h	Wisła	D	0-0
25/10	h	Lechia	L	0-1
02/11	a	Korona	W	1-0 Jarecki
07/11	h	Podbeskidzie	L	0-2
20/11	h	Piast	L	3-5 Sołdecki, Foszmańczyk 2
01/12	h	Śląsk	D	1-1 Plizga
04/12	a	Zagłębie	D	0-0
12/12	a	Górnik Zabrze	D	0-0
16/12	h	Jagiellonia	W	2-0 Sołdecki (p), og (Tarasovs)
19/12	h	Ruch	L	0-1

2016
14/02	a	Lech	L	2-5 Kędziora 2
20/02	h	Cracovia	D	1-1 Jarecki
28/02	h	Pogoń	D	1-1 Kędziora
02/03	h	Legia	W	3-0 Kędziora, Mišák, Plizga
05/03	a	Górnik Łęczna	W	2-1 Sołdecki, Kędziora
14/03	h	Wisła	L	2-4 Babiarz, Sołdecki (p)
20/03	a	Lechia	D	1-1 Smuczyński
02/04	h	Korona	L	0-1
09/04	a	Podbeskidzie	L	0-2
17/04	h	Podbeskidzie	W	1-0 Kupczak
20/04	h	Korona	D	0-0
25/04	a	Wisła	D	2-2 Kędziora, Nowak
30/04	h	Górnik Łęczna	L	0-2
07/05	a	Śląsk	L	1-2 og (Dvali)
10/05	a	Jagiellonia	W	1-0 og (Tarasovs)
14/05	h	Górnik Zabrze	D	1-1 Kędziora

No	Name	Nat	DoB	Pos	Aps	(s)	Gls
6	Bartłomiej Babiarz		03/02/89	M	30	(2)	3
20	Jakub Biskup		08/05/83	M	20	(8)	2
92	Elvis Bratanovič	SVN	21/08/92	A	1	(3)	
25	Adrian Chomiuk		23/06/88	M	1		
21	Emil Drozdowicz		05/07/86	A	8	(8)	1
7	Tomasz Foszmańczyk		07/02/86	M	20	(6)	2
8	Patryk Fryc		24/02/93	D	19	(2)	
21	Vladislavs Gutkovskis	LVA	02/04/95	A	3	(1)	
27	Dariusz Jarecki		23/03/81	D	23	(3)	2
99	Martin Juhar	SVK	09/03/88	A	14	(10)	2
19	Krzysztof Kaczmarczyk		29/06/80	M	3		
10	Wojciech Kędziora		20/12/80	A	27	(9)	9
88	Volodymyr Koval	UKR	06/03/92	A	2	(9)	
25	Mateusz Kupczak		20/02/92	M	30	(3)	1
77	Mario Lička	CZE	30/04/82	M	4	(7)	
4	Michał Markowski		14/03/90	D	9	(3)	
11	Patrik Mišák	SVK	29/03/91	M	7	(5)	1
90	Stefan Nikolić	MNE	16/04/90	A	3		
82	Sebastian Nowak		13/01/82	G	24		1
16	Adrian Paluchowski		19/08/87	A	1	(2)	
80	Krzysztof Pilarz		09/11/80	G	8		
17	Dalibor Pleva	SVK	02/04/84	D	25	(2)	1
77	Dawid Plizga		17/11/85	M	26	(7)	4
77	Artem Putivtsev	UKR	29/08/88	D	15		
9	Bartłomiej Smuczyński		25/08/95	M	2	(12)	1
2	Dawid Sołdecki		29/04/87	D	31	(1)	4
18	Pavol Staňo	SVK	29/09/77	D	23		1
22	Andrzej Witan		22/02/90	G	5		
14	Jakub Wróbel		30/07/93	A	1	(2)	
5	Sebastian Ziajka		15/12/82	D	22	(1)	

GKS Piast Gliwice

1945 • Miejski (10,037) • piast-gliwice.eu
Coach: Radoslav Látal (CZE)

2015
20/07	h	Nieciecza	W	1-0 Mráz
24/07	a	Ruch	L	0-2
31/07	h	Górnik Zabrze	W	3-2 Živec, Nešpor 2
07/08	a	Cracovia	W	2-1 Mráz, Nešpor
15/08	h	Legia	W	2-1 Nešpor, Živec
23/08	a	Lech	W	1-0 Vacek
29/08	h	Górnik Łęczna	W	3-0 Murawski, Osyra, Barišić
13/09	a	Pogoń	L	1-3 Živec
19/09	h	Lechia	W	2-1 Nešpor, og (Janicki)
25/09	a	Śląsk	W	2-1 Hebert, Korun
03/10	h	Wisła	W	1-0 Nešpor
17/10	h	Podbeskidzie	D	2-2 Vacek 2 (2p)
24/10	h	Korona	L	0-1
31/10	h	Zagłębie	W	2-0 Barišić 2
07/11	a	Jagiellonia	W	2-0 Mak, Osyra
20/11	a	Nieciecza	W	5-3 Osyra, Vacek, Barišić, Nešpor, Mokwa
27/11	h	Ruch	W	3-0 og (Cichocki), Barišić, Gerard Badía
01/12	a	Górnik Zabrze	L	2-5 og (Słodowy), Mak
05/12	h	Cracovia	D	2-2 og (Rymaniak), Nešpor
13/12	a	Legia	D	1-1 Gerard Badía
20/12	h	Lech	W	2-0 Szeliga, Barišić

2016
13/02	a	Górnik Łęczna	D	0-0
19/02	h	Pogoń	D	0-0
27/02	a	Lechia	L	1-3 Mak
04/03	h	Wisła	D	1-1 Barišić
08/03	h	Śląsk	W	1-0 Barišić
11/03	h	Podbeskidzie	W	3-2 og (Baranowski), Barišić, Vacek
18/03	a	Zagłębie	D	1-1 Mak
03/04	a	Zagłębie	L	1-4 Mak
09/04	h	Jagiellonia	W	2-0 Szeliga, Nešpor
16/04	h	Cracovia	D	1-1 Mak
19/04	a	Lech	D	2-2 Živec, Mráz
24/04	h	Lechia	W	3-0 Korun, Mak (p), Barišić
01/05	h	Pogoń	W	2-1 Živec, Nešpor
08/05	a	Legia	L	0-4
11/05	a	Ruch	W	3-0 Barišić, Nešpor, Szeliga
15/05	h	Zagłębie	L	0-1

No	Name	Nat	DoB	Pos	Aps	(s)	Gls
10	Karol Angielski		20/03/96	A		(4)	
90	Josip Barišić	CRO	14/11/86	A	24	(10)	11
82	Martin Bukata	SVK	02/10/93	M	8	(6)	
21	Gerard Badía	ESP	18/10/89	M	10	(20)	2
91	Hebert	BRA	23/05/91	D	35		1
4	Kristijan Ipša	CRO	04/04/86	D	2	(2)	
20	Maciej Jankowski		04/01/90	M	2	(4)	
29	Artūrs Karašausks	LVA	29/01/92	A		(2)	
14	Adrian Klepczyński		04/01/81	D	3	(1)	
88	Uroš Korun	SVN	25/05/87	D	33	(1)	2
55	Jakub Kuzdra		08/12/97	M		(1)	
19	Mateusz Mak		14/11/91	M	17	(9)	7
22	Tomasz Mokwa		10/02/93	M	7	(13)	1
11	Paweł Moskwik		08/06/92	D	5	(13)	
2	Patrik Mráz	SVK	01/02/87	D	34		3
9	Radosław Murawski		22/04/94	M	35		1
96	Sebastian Musiolik		19/05/96	A		(5)	
16	Martin Nešpor	CZE	05/06/90	A	31	(2)	11
28	Kornel Osyra		07/02/93	D	19	(2)	3
5	Marcin Pietrowski		01/03/88	D	32	(2)	
77	Igor Sapała		11/10/95	M		(2)	
26	Bartosz Szeliga		10/01/93	M	18	(7)	3
1	Jakub Szmatuła		22/03/81	G	37		
12	Kamil Vacek	CZE	18/05/87	M	33		5
12	Saša Živec	SVN	02/04/91	M	22	(4)	5

TS Podbeskidzie Bielsko-Biała

1995 • Miejski (6,962) • tspodbeskidzie.pl
Coach: Dariusz Kubicki;
(20/09/15) Robert Podoliński

2015
18/07	a	Zagłębie	D	1-1 Demjan
26/07	a	Legia	L	0-5
01/08	h	Cracovia	L	0-1
10/08	a	Ruch	D	1-1 Szczepaniak
17/08	h	Pogoń	L	2-3 Chmiel, Szczepaniak
22/08	a	Śląsk	D	1-1 Sokołowski (p)
28/08	h	Lechia	D	1-1 Adu Kwame
12/09	a	Lech	W	1-0 Szczepaniak
19/09	h	Wisła	L	0-6
26/09	a	Górnik Łęczn	W	2-1 Mójta (p), Szczepaniak
03/10	a	Korona	D	0-0
17/10	h	Piast	D	2-2 Szczepaniak, Możdżeń
26/10	a	Górnik Zabrze	W	2-0 Demjan, Mójta
02/11	a	Jagiellonia	D	1-1 Mójta
07/11	a	Nieciecza	W	2-0 Możdżeń, Demjan
22/11	h	Zagłębie	L	1-2 Demjan
29/11	h	Legia	D	2-2 Demjan, og (Lewczuk)
02/12	a	Cracovia	L	1-4 Szczepaniak
05/12	h	Ruch	D	1-1 Kołodziej (p)
12/12	a	Pogoń	L	0-2
21/12	h	Śląsk	L	0-1

2016
13/02	a	Lechia	L	0-5
20/02	h	Lech	W	4-1 Demjan, Sokołowski, Szczepaniak, Kowalski
27/02	a	Wisła	W	2-1 Możdżeń (p), Štefánik
01/03	h	Górnik Łęczna	W	2-0 Szczepaniak, og (Bartkus)
04/03	h	Korona	D	1-1 Szczepaniak
11/03	a	Piast	L	2-3 Kato, Piaček
19/03	h	Górnik Zabrze	D	0-0
04/04	a	Jagiellonia	W	3-0 og (Wasiluk), og (Gutì), Mójta (p)
09/04	h	Nieciecza	W	2-0 Mójta, Możdżeń
17/04	a	Nieciecza	L	0-1
20/04	a	Górnik Zabrze	L	0-1
23/04	a	Śląsk	L	1-2 Mójta (p)
01/05	a	Jagiellonia	L	2-3 Mójta (p), Szczepaniak
06/05	h	Korona	D	1-1 Baranowski
10/05	a	Górnik Łęczna	L	1-5 Deja
14/05	h	Wisła	L	3-4 Demjan, Štefánik 2

No	Name	Nat	DoB	Pos	Aps	(s)	Gls
5	Frank Adu Kwame	GHA	16/05/85	D	9	(4)	1
2	Paweł Baranowski		11/10/90	D	14		1
94	Sebastian Bartlewski		13/06/94	A		(1)	
14	Damian Chmiel		06/05/87	M	19	(4)	1
27	Adam Deja		24/06/93	M	19	(6)	1
23	Róbert Demjan	SVK	26/10/82	A	28	(5)	7
93	Fabian Hiszpański		26/10/93	M	1	(4)	
4	Grzegorz Horoszkiewicz		18/03/95	D	3		
22	Mateusz Janeczko		30/11/94	M		(1)	
28	Lukáš Jakl	SVK	30/12/86	M	2	(5)	
25	Bartosz Jaroch		25/01/95	D	5	(1)	
6	Kamil Jonkisz		29/08/95	A		(12)	
83	Wojciech Kaczmarek		29/03/83	G	4		
6	Kohei Kato	JPN	14/06/89	M	32	(3)	1
90	Kristián Kolčák	SVK	30/01/90	D	17	(4)	
9	Dariusz Kołodziej		17/04/82	M	3	(10)	1
77	Maciej Korzym		02/05/88	A		(2)	
8	Jakub Kowalski		09/10/87	M	24	(8)	1
92	Celestine Lazarus	NGA	13/11/92	D	4		
7	Mateusz Możdżeń		14/03/91	M	31	(2)	4
15	Adam Mójta		30/06/86	D	31		7
3	Krystian Nowak		01/04/94	D	21		
32	Adam Pazio		27/09/92	D	13	(2)	
24	Jozef Piaček	SVK	20/06/83	D	14		1
11	Anton Sloboda	SVK	10/07/87	M	8	(3)	
10	Marek Sokołowski		11/03/78	D	27	(1)	2
13	Samuel Štefánik	SVK	16/11/91	M	5	(9)	3
20	Mateusz Szczepaniak		23/01/91	A	30	(3)	10
31	Paweł Tarnowski		26/06/90	M	3	(9)	
4	Oleg Veretilo	BLR	10/07/88	D	7	(3)	
1	Emilijus Zubas	LTU	10/07/90	G	33	(1)	

MKS Pogoń Szczecin

1948 • im. Floriana Krygiera (15,717) • pogonszczecin.pl
Coach: Czesław Michniewicz

2015

18/07	a	Lech	W 2-1	Zwoliński, Lewandowski
26/07	h	Śląsk	D 1-1	Zwoliński
31/07	a	Lechia	D 1-1	Zwoliński
08/08	h	Górnik Łęczna	D 0-0	
17/08	a	Podbeskidzie	W 3-2	Fojut, R Murawski, Małecki
21/08	h	Wisła	D 1-1	Frączczak (p)
29/08	a	Korona	D 1-1	Matras
13/09	h	Piast	W 3-1	Zwoliński 2, Fojut
19/09	a	Niecieca	D 1-1	Frączczak
28/09	h	Jagiellonia	W 2-1	Czerwiński, Akahoshi
02/10	a	Ruch	W 2-0	Akahoshi 2
19/10	h	Zagłębie	D 0-0	
24/10	a	Cracovia	L 1-4	Zwoliński
30/10	h	Górnik Zabrze	D 1-1	Matras
08/11	a	Legia	L 0-1	
22/11	h	Lech	L 0-2	
28/11	a	Śląsk	D 0-0	
02/12	h	Lechia	W 1-0	R Murawski
07/12	a	Górnik Łęczna	W 3-2	Lewandowski, Frączczak 2 (1p)
12/12	h	Podbeskidzie	W 2-0	Dvalishvili 2
18/12	a	Wisła	W 1-0	R Murawski

2016

15/02	h	Korona	W 3-2	R Murawski, Frączczak, Gyurcsó
19/02	a	Piast	D 0-0	
28/02	h	Niecieca	D 1-1	Przybecki
02/03	a	Jagiellonia	D 0-0	
07/03	h	Ruch	L 2-3	Akahoshi 2
13/03	a	Zagłębie	D 1-1	R Murawski
20/03	h	Cracovia	D 2-2	Gyurcsó, Kort
01/04	a	Górnik Zabrze	D 1-1	R Murawski
09/04	h	Legia	D 0-0	
15/04	h	Ruch	D 1-1	R Murawski
19/04	a	Lechia	L 0-2	
23/04	h	Lech	W 1-0	Zwoliński
01/05	a	Piast	L 1-2	Dvalishvili
08/05	h	Zagłębie	L 1-3	Ricardo Nunes
11/05	h	Cracovia	W 3-2	Kort, Frączczak (p), Zwoliński
15/05	a	Legia	L 0-3	

No	Name	Nat	DoB	Pos	Aps	(s)	Gls
27	Takafumi Akahoshi	JPN	27/05/86	M	29	(3)	5
4	Jarosław Czerwiński		06/08/91	D	33		1
20	Karol Danielak		29/09/91	M	6	(5)	
11	Vladimer Dvalishvili	GEO	20/04/86	A	16	(12)	3
3	Jarosław Fojut		17/10/87	D	30		2
9	Adam Frączczak		07/08/87	M	35		6
7	Ádám Gyurcsó	HUN	06/03/91	M	13	(1)	2
10	Dawid Kort		29/04/95	M	3	(7)	2
66	Dawid Kudła		21/03/92	G	20	(1)	
1	Dominik Kun		22/06/93	M		(1)	
33	Mateusz Lewandowski		18/03/93	D	27	(3)	2
29	Marcin Listkowski		10/02/98	A	12	(12)	
10	Patryk Małecki		01/08/88	M	12	(6)	1
23	Mateusz Matras		23/01/91	M	35		2
6	Rafał Murawski		09/10/81	M	36		7
26	Sebastian Murawski		01/03/94	D	4		
13	Takuya Murayama	JPN	08/08/89	A	4	(9)	
32	Robert Obst		06/07/95	M		(4)	
22	Jakub Okuszko		03/03/95	A		(1)	
19	Jakub Piotrowski		04/10/97	M	2	(2)	
14	Miłosz Przybecki		02/01/91	M	8	(22)	1
77	Ricardo Nunes	RSA	18/06/86	D	21	(1)	1
21	Sebastian Rudol		21/02/95	D	21	(1)	
1	Jakub Słowik		31/08/91	G	17		
16	Michał Walski		27/02/97	M	1	(6)	
93	Łukasz Zwoliński		24/02/93	A	22	(8)	8

Ruch Chorzów

1920 • Miejski (9,300) • ruchchorzow.com.pl
Major honours
Polish League (14) 1933, 1934, 1935, 1936, 1938, 1951, 1952, 1953, 1960, 1968, 1974, 1975, 1979, 1989; Polish Cup (3) 1951, 1974, 1996
Coach: Waldemar Fornalik

2015

18/07	h	Górnik Łęczna	L 0-2	
24/07	h	Piast	W 2-0	Višňakovs, Efir
03/08	a	Korona	W 2-1	Višňakovs, Stępiński
10/08	h	Podbeskidzie	D 1-1	Lipski
16/08	a	Jagiellonia	L 1-2	Stępiński
22/08	h	Niecieca	W 4-1	Višňakovs, Lipski, Gigolaev, Lenartowski
29/08	a	Zagłębie	L 1-3	Surma
13/09	h	Górnik Zabrze	W 1-0	Oleksy
20/09	h	Legia	L 1-4	Stępiński
26/09	a	Cracovia	L 1-2	Stępiński
02/10	h	Pogoń	L 0-2	
17/10	a	Lech	D 2-2	Stępiński 2
23/10	h	Śląsk	W 1-0	Stępiński
30/10	a	Wisła	D 0-0	
07/11	h	Lechia	W 3-2	Stępiński, Zieńczuk, Koj
21/11	a	Górnik Łęczna	W 3-0	Koj, Stępiński, Zieńczuk
27/11	a	Piast	L 0-3	
01/12	h	Korona	W 2-1	Iwański, Stępiński
05/12	a	Podbeskidzie	D 1-1	Stępiński (p)
11/12	h	Jagiellonia	L 0-4	
19/12	a	Niecieca	W 1-0	Mazek

2016

12/02	h	Zagłębie	D 0-0	
21/02	a	Górnik Zabrze	W 2-0	Oleksy, Mazek
28/02	a	Legia	L 0-2	
02/03	h	Cracovia	L 2-3	Mazek, Stępiński
07/03	a	Pogoń	W 3-2	og (Słowik), Lipski 2 (1p)
12/03	h	Lech	L 1-3	Stępiński
19/03	a	Śląsk	D 0-0	
03/04	h	Wisła	L 2-3	Stępiński, Koj
09/04	a	Lechia	L 0-2	
15/04	a	Pogoń	D 1-1	Stępiński
19/04	h	Legia	D 0-0	
22/04	a	Zagłębie	L 1-4	Koj
29/04	h	Cracovia	L 0-1	
07/05	a	Lechia	L 1-2	Podgórski
11/05	h	Piast	L 0-3	
15/05	a	Lech	L 0-3	

No	Name	Nat	DoB	Pos	Aps	(s)	Gls
72	Przemysław Bargiel		26/03/00	M		(4)	
2	Mateusz Cichocki		31/01/92	D	20		
8	Michał Efir		14/04/92	A	1	(23)	1
13	Roland Gigolaev	RUS	04/01/90	M	6	(3)	1
51	Rafał Grodzicki		28/10/83	D	33		
22	Łukasz Hanzel		16/09/86	M	9	(7)	
7	Maciej Iwański		07/05/81	M	19	(6)	1
14	Michał Koj		28/07/93	D	26		4
15	Martin Konczkowski		14/09/93	M	35		
17	Artur Lenartowski		17/03/88	M	1	(7)	1
10	Patryk Lipski		12/06/94	M	35	(1)	4
27	Kamil Mazek		22/07/94	M	25	(3)	3
13	Łukasz Moneta		13/05/94	M	8	(5)	
19	Paweł Oleksy		01/04/91	D	21	(1)	2
19	Tomasz Podgórski		30/12/85	M	13	(13)	1
30	Matúš Putnocký	SVK	01/11/84	G	34		
9	Adam Setla		26/10/92	A		(1)	
97	Łukasz Siedlik		06/05/97	A		(2)	
84	Wojciech Skaba		09/04/84	G	3	(1)	
18	Mariusz Stępiński		12/05/95	A	30	(4)	15
4	Łukasz Surma		28/06/77	M	37		1
6	Michał Szewczyk		17/10/92	M		(3)	
20	Marek Szyndrowski		30/10/80	D	11	(4)	
17	Maciej Urbańczyk		21/04/95	M	10		
90	Eduards Višňakovs	LVA	10/05/90	A	6		3
29	Kamil Włodyka		11/10/94	M		(1)	
5	Marek Zieńczuk		24/09/78	M	24	(8)	2

WKS Śląsk Wrocław

1947 • Miejski (42,771) • slaskwroclaw.pl
Major honours
Polish League (2) 1977, 2012; Polish Cup (2) 1976, 1987
Coach: Tadeusz Pawłowski;
(02/12/15) (Grzegorz Kowalski);
(07/12/15) Romuald Szukiełowicz;
(09/03/16) Mariusz Rumak

2015

19/07	h	Legia	L 1-4	Flávio Paixão
26/07	a	Pogoń	D 1-1	Pich
02/08	h	Niecieca	W 2-0	Biliński, Flávio Paixão
09/08	h	Lechia	D 0-0	
15/08	a	Górnik Łęczna	W 3-2	Pich, Biliński, Flávio Paixão
22/08	h	Podbeskidzie	D 1-1	Pich
28/08	a	Wisła	L 2-4	og (Cierzniak), Kiełb
12/09	h	Jagiellonia	W 3-1	Celeban, og (Tomasik), Hateley
18/09	a	Górnik Zabrze	L 0-2	
25/09	h	Piast	L 0-1	Biliński
04/10	a	Zagłębie	D 1-1	Flávio Paixão
16/10	h	Korona	L 0-1	
23/10	a	Ruch	L 0-1	
31/10	h	Lech	D 1-1	Flávio Paixão
06/11	a	Cracovia	L 1-4	Bartkowiak
21/11	a	Legia	L 0-1	
28/11	h	Pogoń	D 0-0	
01/12	a	Niecieca	D 1-1	Kiełb (p)
06/12	h	Lechia	L 0-1	
11/12	h	Górnik Łęczna	W 2-1	Dudu Paraíba, Biliński
21/12	a	Podbeskidzie	W 1-0	Grajciar

2016

12/02	h	Wisła	W 1-0	Hołota
19/02	a	Jagiellonia	L 1-2	Hołota (p)
26/02	h	Górnik Zabrze	D 0-0	
05/03	a	Zagłębie	L 0-2	
08/03	a	Piast	L 0-1	
11/03	h	Korona	D 2-2	Hołota, Dvali
19/03	h	Ruch	D 0-0	
01/04	a	Lech	W 1-0	Marioka
09/04	h	Cracovia	W 2-1	Mervó, Marioka
16/04	h	Korona	D 1-1	Celeban
20/04	h	Jagiellonia	W 3-1	Mervó 2, Marioka
23/04	a	Podbeskidzie	W 2-1	Mervó, Marioka
29/04	a	Górnik Zabrze	L 1-2	Biliński
07/05	h	Niecieca	W 2-1	Marioka, og (Fryc)
10/05	a	Wisła	D 1-1	Grajciar
14/05	h	Górnik Łęczna	W 3-2	Marioka 2, Hołota

No	Name	Nat	DoB	Pos	Aps	(s)	Gls
1	Mateusz Abramowicz		08/11/92	G	10		
25	Michał Bartkowiak		03/02/97	M	1	(9)	1
19	Kamil Biliński		23/01/88	A	19	(12)	5
3	Piotr Celeban		25/06/85	D	36		2
5	Krzysztof Danielewicz		26/07/91	M	9	(2)	
30	Kamil Dankowski		22/07/96	M	12	(9)	
12	Dudu Paraíba	BRA	11/03/85	D	21	(3)	1
21	Lasha Dvali	GEO	14/05/95	D	14	(1)	1
28	Flávio Paixão	POR	19/09/84	A	21		5
15	Marcel Gecov	CZE	01/01/88	M	19	(4)	
8	András Gosztonyi	HUN	07/11/90	M	3	(4)	
29	Peter Grajciar	SVK	17/09/83	M	12	(16)	2
8	Tom Hateley	ENG	12/09/89	M	27	(2)	1
6	Tomasz Hołota		27/01/91	M	33	(2)	4
27	Mariusz Idzik		01/04/97	A		(1)	
18	Konrad Kaczmarek		01/03/91	M		(8)	
9	Jacek Kiełb		10/01/88	M	14	(11)	2
20	Adam Kokoszka		06/10/86	D	24	(3)	
8	Mateusz Machaj		26/09/89	M	3		
11	Ryota Marioka	JPN	12/04/91	M	14	(1)	7
24	Maciej Matusik		12/01/95	M		(1)	
11	Bence Mervó	HUN	05/03/95	A	9	(1)	4
7	Krzysztof Ostrowski		03/05/82	D	7	(12)	
17	Mariusz Pawelec		14/04/86	D	26	(1)	
33	Mariusz Pawełek		17/03/81	G	24		
10	Róbert Pich	SVK	12/11/88	M	21	(2)	3
15	Ihor Tyshchenko	UKR	11/05/89	M	2		
22	Jakub Wrąbel		08/06/96	G	3	(1)	
23	Paweł Zieliński		17/07/90	D	23	(3)	

Wisła Kraków

1906 • im. Henryka Reymana (33,326) •
wisla.krakow.pl
Major honours
Polish League (13) 1927, 1928, 1949, 1950, 1978,
1999, 2001, 2003, 2004, 2005, 2008, 2009, 2011;
Polish Cup (4) 1926, 1967, 2002, 2003
Coach: Kazimierz Moskal;
(30/11/15) (Marcin Broniszewski);
(22/12/15) Tadeusz Pawłowski;
(29/02/16) (Marcin Broniszewski);
(13/03/16) Dariusz Wdowczyk

2015
17/07	h	Górnik Zabrze	D	1-1	Rafael Crivellaro
24/07	a	Cracovia	D	1-1	Mączyński
01/08	h	Lech	W	2-0	Boguski 2
09/08	a	Legia	D	1-1	Guerrier
16/08	h	Lechia	D	3-3	Guerrier, Jankowski 2
21/08	a	Pogoń	D	1-1	Rafael Crivellaro (p)
28/08	h	Śląsk	W	4-2	Brożek 2, Boguski, Guerrier
14/09	a	Górnik Łęczna	L	0-1	
19/09	h	Podbeskidzie	W	6-0	Brożek 2, Popović, Burliga, Boguski, Rafael Crivellaro
25/09	h	Korona	D	0-0	
03/10	a	Piast	L	0-1	
18/10	h	Niecieca	D	0-0	
23/10	a	Jagiellonia	W	4-1	Brożek (p), Jankowski 2, Guerrier
30/10	h	Ruch	D	0-0	
06/11	a	Zagłębie	W	3-1	Boguski, og (Todorovski), Guerrier
20/11	a	Górnik Zabrze	D	1-1	Brożek
29/11	h	Cracovia	L	1-2	Brożek
02/12	a	Lech	L	0-2	
06/12	h	Legia	L	0-2	
12/12	a	Lechia	L	0-2	
18/12	h	Pogoń	L	0-1	

2016
12/02	a	Śląsk	L	0-1	
22/02	h	Górnik Łęczna	D	1-1	Guerrier
27/02	h	Podbeskidzie	L	1-2	Ondrášek
04/03	a	Piast	D	1-1	Jović
08/03	a	Korona	D	1-1	Popović (p)
14/03	a	Niecieca	W	4-2	Małecki, Brożek, Wolski, Boguski
18/03	h	Jagiellonia	W	5-1	Sadlok, Brożek 2, Wolski, Boguski
03/04	a	Ruch	W	3-2	Głowacki, Ondrášek, Wolski
09/04	h	Zagłębie	W	2-1	Boguski
17/04	h	Górnik Zabrze	W	3-1	Małecki, Wolski, Ondrášek
20/04	a	Górnik Łęczna	W	3-0	Popović (p), og (Bogusławski), Ondrášek
25/04	h	Niecieca	D	2-2	Popović (p), Guerrier
30/04	a	Korona	L	2-3	Brożek 2
06/05	h	Jagiellonia	W	1-0	Brożek
10/05	h	Śląsk	D	1-1	Ondrášek
14/05	a	Podbeskidzie	W	4-3	Brożek, Boguski, Ondrášek, Mączyński

No	Name	Nat	DoB	Pos	Aps	(s)	Gls
7	Vitaliy Balashov	UKR	15/01/91	M	4	(4)	
38	Jakub Bartosz		13/08/96	D	4	(1)	
9	Rafał Boguski		09/06/84	A	31	(5)	9
21	Peter Brlek	CRO	29/01/94	M	3	(4)	
23	Paweł Brożek		21/04/83	A	25	(4)	14
21	Łukasz Burliga		10/05/88	D	19	(1)	1
33	Radosław Cierzniak		24/04/83	G	21		
7	Tomasz Cywka		27/06/88	M	10	(17)	
13	Krzysztof Drzazga		20/06/95	A	2	(5)	
6	Arkadiusz Głowacki		13/03/79	D	32		1
77	Wilde-Donald Guerrier	HAI	31/03/89	M	16	(6)	7
26	Richárd Guzmics	HUN	16/04/87	D	32	(1)	
23	Konrad Handzlik		13/02/98	M		(1)	
7	Maciej Jankowski		04/01/90	M	14	(5)	4
5	Boban Jović	SVN	25/06/91	D	32		1
27	Kamil Kuczak		02/03/96	M	1	(3)	
42	Krystian Kujawa		22/03/96	D	1	(1)	
88	Patryk Małecki		01/08/88	M	12	(2)	2
40	Grzegorz Marszalik		17/03/96	M		(4)	
29	Krzysztof Mączyński		23/05/87	M	22	(2)	2
1	Michał Miśkiewicz		20/01/89	G	16		
30	Jakub Mordec		27/03/96	M		(1)	
14	Zdeněk Ondrášek	CZE	22/12/88	A	16	(4)	6
2	Rafał Pietrzak		30/01/92	D	6		
10	Denis Popović	SVN	15/10/89	M	19	(11)	4
50	Rafael Crivellaro	BRA	18/02/89	M	7	(13)	3
27	Maciej Sadlok		29/06/89	D	27		1
8	Alan Uryga		19/02/94	M	21	(3)	
24	Szymon Witek		03/10/94	D		(1)	
27	Rafał Wolski		10/11/92	M	13	(1)	4
43	Piotr Żemło		10/07/95	D	1		

Zagłębie Lubin

1945 • Zagłębia (16,100) • zaglebie.com
Major honours
Polish League (2) 1991, 2007
Coach: Piotr Stokowiec

2014
18/07	h	Podbeskidzie	D	1-1	Papadopulos (p)
25/07	h	Korona	L	0-2	
02/08	a	Jagiellonia	W	2-1	Papadopulos, Rakowski
07/08	a	Niecieca	L	0-1	
14/08	h	Lech	W	2-1	Janus, K Piątek
24/08	a	Górnik Zabrze	D	2-2	Tosik, Čotra
29/08	h	Ruch	W	3-1	Rakowski, Janus, Papadopulos
11/09	a	Legia	D	2-2	K Piątek, Papadopulos
18/09	h	Cracovia	W	4-2	og (Sretenović), Kubicki, Janus, Dąbrowski
27/09	a	Lechia	L	1-2	Papadopulos
04/10	h	Śląsk	D	1-1	Papadopulos
19/10	a	Pogoń	D	0-0	
24/10	h	Górnik Łęczna	D	0-0	
31/10	a	Piast	L	0-2	
06/11	h	Wisła	D	1-3	Woźniak
22/11	a	Podbeskidzie	W	2-1	Jach, Janoszka
27/11	h	Korona	W	2-0	Janoszka, Jach
01/12	a	Jagiellonia	L	0-2	
04/12	h	Niecieca	W	2-0	Tosik, Woźniak
13/12	a	Lech	L	0-2	
18/12	h	Górnik Zabrze	L	2-4	Janoszka, Zbozień

2015
12/02	a	Ruch	D	0-0	
21/02	h	Legia	L	1-2	K Piątek
26/02	a	Cracovia	W	2-1	Starzyński (p), Janoszka
01/03	h	Lechia	W	1-0	Starzyński
05/03	a	Śląsk	W	2-0	Ł Piątek, Kubicki
13/03	a	Pogoń	D	1-1	Ł Piątek
20/03	a	Górnik Łęczna	W	2-0	K Piątek, Kubicki
03/04	h	Piast	W	4-1	Janoszka 2, Starzyński (p), Jagiełło
09/04	a	Wisła	D	1-1	Papadopulos
16/04	h	Lechia	L	1-2	Janoszka
19/04	a	Cracovia	L	0-1	
22/04	h	Ruch	W	4-1	K Piątek, Woźniak, og (Oleksy), Ł Piątek
28/04	h	Legia	W	2-0	Tosik, K Piątek
08/05	a	Pogoń	W	3-1	Kubicki, Woźniak, Ł Piątek
11/05	h	Lech	W	3-0	Dąbrowski 2, Woźniak
15/05	a	Piast	W	1-0	Papadopulos

No	Name	Nat	DoB	Pos	Aps	(s)	Gls
15	Adrian Błąd		16/04/91	M		(5)	
8	Sebastian Bonecki		13/02/95	M	2		
3	Djordje Čotra	SRB	13/09/84	D	32		1
2	Maciej Dąbrowski		20/04/87	D	28	(2)	3
12	Konrad Forenc		17/07/92	G	15		
33	Ľubomír Guldan	SVK	30/01/83	D	32		
1	Jarosław Jach		17/02/94	D	11	(2)	2
19	Filip Jagiełło		08/08/97	M		(4)	1
14	Łukasz Janoszka		18/03/87	M	34	(2)	7
7	Krzysztof Janus		25/03/86	M	20	(10)	3
20	Jarosław Kubicki		07/08/95	M	28		4
25	Luís Carlos	BRA	15/06/87	M		(3)	
27	Michal Papadopulos	CZE	14/04/85	A	24	(11)	8
26	Krzysztof Piątek		01/07/95	A	24	(9)	6
28	Łukasz Piątek		21/09/85	M	21	(4)	4
1	Martin Polaček	SVK	02/04/90	G	22	(1)	
17	Adrian Rakowski		07/10/90	M	15	(12)	2
22	Eryk Sobków		12/02/97	A		(9)	
18	Filip Starzyński		27/05/91	M	16		3
4	Aleksandar Todorovski	MKD	26/02/84	D	32	(1)	
24	Jakub Tosik		21/05/87	M	22	(2)	3
90	Ján Vlasko	SVK	11/01/90	M	3	(9)	
9	Arkadiusz Woźniak		01/06/90	M	18	(12)	5
55	Damian Zbozień		25/04/89	D	7	(8)	1
13	Karol Żmijewski		16/04/97	M		(2)	
16	Paweł Żyra		07/04/98	M		(3)	

Top goalscorers

28	Nemanja Nikolić (Legia)
16	Airam Cabrera (Korona)
15	Deniss Rakels (Cracovia)
	Mariusz Stępiński (Ruch)
14	Paweł Brożek (Wisła)
13	Mateusz Cetnarski (Cracovia)
	Erik Jendrišek (Cracovia)
11	Kasper Hämäläinen (Lech/Legia)
	Grzegorz Kuświk (Lechia)
	Josip Barišić (Piast)
	Martin Nešpor (Piast)
	Flávio Paixão (Śląsk/Lechia)

Promoted clubs

Arka Gdynia

1929 • Miejski (15,139) • arka.gdynia.pl
Major honours
Polish Cup (1) 1979
Coach: Grzegorz Niciński

Wisła Płock

1947 • im. Kazimierza Górskiego (12,800) •
wisla.plock.pl
Major honours
Polish Cup (1) 2006
Coach: Marcin Kaczmarek

Second level final table 2015/16

		Pld	W	D	L	F	A	Pts
1	Arka Gdynia	34	19	12	3	60	29	69
2	Wisła Płock	34	19	6	9	51	28	63
3	Zagłębie Sosnowiec	34	16	4	14	53	53	52
4	GKS Katowice	34	15	7	12	42	36	52
5	Zawisza Bydgoszcz	34	15	7	12	57	51	52
6	Chrobry Głogów	34	14	9	11	47	33	51
7	Miedź Legnica	34	13	12	9	41	34	51
8	MKS Bytovia Bytów	34	11	15	8	46	44	48
9	MKS Sandecja Nowy Sącz	34	13	8	13	51	49	47
10	Wigry Suwałki	34	12	9	13	41	35	45
11	Stomil Olsztyn	34	11	11	12	34	42	44
12	Chojniczanka Chojnice	34	12	7	15	40	45	43
13	GKS Olimpia Grudziądz	34	11	9	14	39	43	42
14	MKP Pogoń Siedlce	34	11	8	15	31	46	41
15	MKS Kluczbork	34	11	8	15	40	55	41
16	GKS Bełchatów	34	10	8	16	35	40	38
17	Rozwój Katowice	34	11	2	21	35	56	35
18	MKS Dolcan Ząbki	34	8	6	20	37	67	30

*NB MKS Dolcan Ząbki withdrew after round 19; their
remaining matches were awarded as 0-3 defeats.*

DOMESTIC CUP

Puchar Polski 2015/16

FIRST ROUND

(25/07/15)
Arka Gdynia 4-1 Pogoń Siedlce
Boruta Zgierz 0-3 Puszcza Niepołomice
Górnik Wałbrzych 0-2 Wigry Suwałki
Rodło Kwidzyn 2-4 Olimpia Grudziądz *(aet)*
ROW 1964 Rybnik 0-4 Dolcan Ząbki
Siarka Tarnobrzeg 1-4 Chojniczanka Chojnice
Stilon Gorzów 0-1 Stal Stalowa Wola
Stomil Olsztyn 2-0 Sandecja Nowy Sącz
Wda Świecie 1-0 Legionovia Legionowo
Wisła Puławy 2-2 Zagłębie Sosnowiec *(aet; 2-4 on pens)*

(26/07/15)
Garbarnia Kraków 0-2 Miedź Legnica
GKS Katowice 2-0 Rozwój Katowice
ŁKS 1926 Łomża 0-0 Chrobry Głogów *(aet; 6-7 on pens)*
Wisła Płock 1-2 Bytovia Bytów

(28/07/15)
Nadwiślan Góra 0-3 Zagłębie Lubin

(29/07/15)
Błękitni Stargard Szczeciński 2-1 Nieciecza

SECOND ROUND

(11/08/15)
Błękitni Stargard Szczeciński 2-4 Zagłębie Lubin
Dolcan Ząbki 2-3 Cracovia Kraków
Olimpia Grudziądz 0-2 Lech Poznań
Wda Świecie 3-0 Korona Kielce *(w/o)*

(12/08/15)
Arka Gdynia 1-1 Chojniczanka Chojnice *(aet; 2-3 on pens)*
GKS Bełchatów 1-0 Bytovia Bytów
Górnik Łęczna 0-2 Legia Warszawa
Jagiellonia Białystok 2-1 Pogoń Szczecin
Puszcza Niepołomice 1-5 Lechia Gdańsk
Stal Stalowa Wola 2-2 Piast Gliwice *(aet; 3-0 on pens)*
Stomil Olsztyn 1-5 Śląsk Wrocław
Wigry Suwałki 0-2 GKS Katowice
Zagłębie Sosnowiec 3-1 Górnik Zabrze
Zawisza Bydgoszcz 4-1 Chrobry Głogów

(13/08/15)
Miedź Legnica 1-2 Podbeskidzie Bielsko-Biała *(aet)*
Ruch Chorzów 2-1 Wisła Kraków

THIRD ROUND

(15/09/15)
Wda Świecie 1-4 Zagłębie Sosnowiec

(16/09/15)
Stal Stalowa Wola 1-2 Zawisza Bydgoszcz

(22/09/15)
GKS Katowice 1-3 Cracovia Kraków
Podbeskidzie Bielsko-Biała 0-1 Śląsk Wrocław

(23/09/15)
Jagiellonia Białystok 0-2 Zagłębie Lubin
Lech Poznań 1-0 Ruch Chorzów

(24/09/15)
Chojniczanka Chojnice 2-1 GKS Bełchatów *(aet)*
Legia Warszawa 4-1 Lechia Gdańsk

QUARTER-FINALS

(27/10/15 & 19/11/15)
Zagłębie Sosnowiec 1-2 Cracovia Kraków
(Fidziukiewicz 43; Čovilo 22, Rakels 90)
Cracovia Kraków 0-2 Zagłębie Sosnowiec
(Pribula 26, Dudek 40p)
(Zagłębie Sosnowiec 3-2)

(27/10/15 & 16/12/15)
Zawisza Bydgoszcz 0-0 Śląsk Wrocław
Śląsk Wrocław 1-2 Zawisza Bydgoszcz *(Biliński 74; Lewicki 69, Drygas 78)*
(Zawisza Bydgoszcz 2-1)

(28/10/15 & 18/11/15)
Chojniczanka Chojnice 1-2 Legia Warszawa
(Mikita 48; Vranješ 23, Duda 78)
Legia Warszawa 4-1 Chojniczanka Chojnice
(Vranješ 29, Prijovic 33, Brzyski 38, Nikolić 63; Rybski 5)
(Legia Warszawa 6-2)

(28/10/15 & 19/11/15)
Zagłębie Lubin 0-1 Lech Poznań *(Arajuuri 81)*
Lech Poznań 1-0 Zagłębie Lubin *(Pawłowski 90)*
(Lech Poznań 2-0)

SEMI-FINALS

(15/03/16 & 05/04/16)
Lech Poznań 1-0 Zagłębie Sosnowiec *(Volkov 38)*
Zagłębie Sosnowiec 1-1 Lech Poznań
(Paluchowski 82; Gajos 70)
(Lech Poznań 2-1)

(16/03/16 & 06/04/16)
Legia Warszawa 4-0 Zawisza Bydgoszcz
(Nikolić 6, 63, 79, Broź 50)
Zawisza Bydgoszcz 1-2 Legia Warszawa *(Danielak 60; Nikolić 16, Guilherme 79)*
(Legia Warszawa 6-1)

FINAL

(02/05/16)
Stadion Narodowy, Warsaw
LEGIA WARSZAWA 1 *(Prijovic 69)*
KKS LECH POZNAŃ 0
Referee: Marciniak
LEGIA: Malarz, Jędrzejczyk, Lewczuk, Pazdan, Hloušek, Duda (Guilherme 67), Jodłowiec, Borysiuk, Kucharczyk, Nikolić (Aleksandrov 83), Prijovic (Hämäläinen 90)
LECH: Burić, Kędziora, Arajuuri, Kamiński, Kádár, Trałka (Gajos 79), Tetteh, Linetty, Pawłowski, Lovrencsics (Jóźwiak 90), Kownacki (Jevtic 87)

Polish Cup specialists Legia lift the trophy for the fifth time in six years

PORTUGAL
Federação Portuguesa de Futebol (FPF)

Address	Avenida das Seleções	**President**	Fernando Gomes
	PT-1495-433 Cruz Quebrada	**General secretary**	Paulo Manuel
	– Dafundo		Lourenço
Tel	+351 21 325 2700	**Media officer**	Onofre Costa
Fax	+351 21 325 2780	**Year of formation**	1914
E-mail	ceo@fpf.pt		
Website	fpf.pt		

PRIMEIRA LIGA CLUBS

 1 A. Académica de Coimbra

 2 FC Arouca

 3 Os Belenenses

 4 SL Benfica

 5 Boavista FC

 6 SC Braga

 7 Estoril Praia

 8 CS Marítimo

 9 Moreirense FC

 10 CD Nacional

 11 FC Paços de Ferreira

 12 FC Porto

 13 Rio Ave FC

 14 Sporting Clube de Portugal

 15 CD Tondela

 16 CF União da Madeira

 17 Vitória FC

 18 Vitória SC

PROMOTED CLUBS

 19 GD Chaves

 20 CD Feirense

Chaves **19**

Braga **6**

Guimarães~ **18**

Vila do Conde **13**

Moreira de Cónegos~ **9**

5

Paços de Ferreira~ **11**

12

Porto

Santa Maria da Feira **20**

2

Arouca

Tondela

15

1

Coimbra

Atlantic
Ocean

4 **14**

7

Lisboa
(Lisbon)

Estoril

3 **17**

Setúbal

MADEIRA

Ribeira
Brava

Funchal

16

8 **10**

0		100		200 km

0   100 miles

KEY

● UEFA Champions League

● UEFA Europa League

● Promoted

● Relegated

Benfica stay strong to see off Sporting

Benfica made it three Primeira Liga titles in a row for the first time since the mid-1970s, new coach Rui Vitória prolonging the run started by Jorge Jesus, who, having switched to local rivals Sporting, ran his former club close in an all-Lisbon battle for supremacy that lasted until the final day.

Braga prevailed on penalties against FC Porto to win the Portuguese Cup for the first time in 50 years, but the season's big history-makers were Fernando Santos's heroic UEFA EURO 2016-winning national side, who captured the first major international trophy in Portugal's history.

All-Lisbon Liga title race goes to the wire	**Braga end 50-year wait for domestic cup**	**Portugal make history with EURO triumph**

Domestic league

As ever, the race for the Portuguese title was restricted to three runners and riders – Benfica, Porto and Sporting. It would be engaging from start to finish, with each of the trio setting the pace at one stage or another before the defending champions took over with a crucial 1-0 win at Sporting in early March and impressively held their ground on the long run for home, winning every remaining game to end up with 88 points – the most ever recorded in a 34-game Portuguese top flight.

When Benfica were beaten 3-0 at home by Sporting in October – a dream return to the Estádio da Luz for Jorge Jesus – it looked as if Rui Vitória's days might be numbered. It was his third defeat in seven league games, following 1-0 reverses at Arouca and Porto in the first two away fixtures, and already they were eight and six points, respectively, behind Sporting and Porto, albeit with a game in hand. But the club would retain faith in the man they had prised from Vitória Guimarães and be rewarded with an astonishing response as the Eagles won 25 of their next 27 matches.

It was not until early February that Benfica finally reached the Primeira Liga summit, with a thumping 5-0 win at

Belenenses. Just a week later, though, they were unseated as Porto, who had effectively dropped out of the race with just three wins in their first seven matches since the turn of the year, surprised them with a brilliant comeback 2-1 win in a Friday-night classic at the Luz. Sporting were one point ahead of Benfica before they hosted them in a huge derby on 5 March. Jorge Jesus had gone a full four years without overseeing a home league defeat, but that run came to an end as Benfica took an early lead through Greek international Kostas Mitroglou and subsequently held on to it, surviving extensive Sporting pressure and an open-goal miss from Mitroglou's former Fulham team-mate Bryan Ruiz.

Two months of the season remained, but that was the title decided there and then. Neither Benfica nor Sporting would put a foot wrong from there on in. Sporting even kept up the pressure by completing the double over Porto, with a 3-1 win at the Dragão, but Benfica would not be moved. Because of Sporting's superior head-to-head record, the defending champions' two-point lead was always precarious, but they kept on winning and on the final day defeated Nacional 4-1 in front of 64,235 joyous supporters to complete their first title hat-trick for 39 years and

35th championship overall. Benfica were well served in all areas, with Jardel a tower of strength in central defence, his fellow Brazilian Jonas a 32-goal scoring machine up front, Argentinian schemer Nicolás Gaitan the king of assists, and all-action 18-year-old midfielder Renato Sanches not just the revelation of the season but arguably Portuguese football's find of the century.

Sporting could not have done much more to end their 14-year wait for the title. Their final tally of 86 points was one more than Benfica had accrued in 2014/15 and 11 more than their own winning total in 2001/02. For the second successive season they ended up with fewer defeats than the champions, again losing just twice. Their style of play was always pleasing on the eye, with ever-present goalkeeper Rui Patrício keeping a clean sheet every other game, fellow Portuguese internationals João Mário and skipper Adrien Silva brimming with quality and endeavour in midfield, and Islam Slimani consistently delivering the goods in attack. Indeed, the Algerian's 27-goal haul would have earned him the league's top scorer prize in any of the previous 13 seasons,

Porto were top and unbeaten at Christmas under Julen Lopetegui, but a first defeat, at Sporting, followed by a

home draw against Rio Ave, led to his dismissal – a move that looked hasty when his successor, ex-Sporting boss José Peseiro, oversaw four further defeats as Porto slipped to a final position 15 points below Benfica. Porto had fine performers in Mexican left-back Miguel Layún and midfield powerhouse Danilo Pereira – one of the few Portuguese players in the team – but they missed the goals of Jackson Martínez, sold to Atlético Madrid, and ended the season parting company with Peseiro and replacing him ex-Valencia boss Nuno Espírito Santo.

Peseiro would return to former club Braga, fourth-place finishers ahead of surprise packages Arouca and Rio Ave, who both qualified alongside them for the UEFA Europa League, the former claiming entry to Europe for the first time. A shock pre-Christmas win over Sporting could not keep newly-promoted União Madeira in the Primeira Liga as they allowed the team that accompanied them up, Tondela, to overtake them on the final day and send them down with Académica Coimbra. Chaves and Feirense came up, although both finished behind Porto's B side in the second-level LigaPro.

Domestic cup

Defeated on penalties by Sporting in the 2015 Portuguese Cup final after surrendering a two-goal lead, Braga looked set for an agonising repeat when yet again they allowed the opposition – in this case Porto – to come from behind and make it 2-2 in added time. On this occasion, though, the hand of fate smiled on them as they won the shoot-out 4-2, giving coach Paulo Fonseca a satisfying victory over the club that had sacked him two years previously and Braga their second cup triumph 50 years to the day since the first. Having previously eliminated Sporting – fourth-round conquerors of Benfica – then Arouca and Rio Ave, it was an impressive campaign, enhancing the CV of their coach to such a degree that he left a few days after the final to become the new boss at Shakhtar Donetsk.

Europe

Not content with eclipsing Sporting and Porto at home, Benfica also outlasted them in the UEFA Champions League, where they won away to Atlético Madrid and Zenit en route to the quarter-finals. As on their previous three last-eight appearances, however, they were beaten, 3-2 on aggregate by Bayern München. Porto looked likely to join them in the knockout phase after taking ten points from their first four matches, but back-to-back defeats relegated them to the UEFA Europa League, where they were eliminated on entry by Borussia Dortmund. Sporting's European campaign also ended in the UEFA Europa League round of 32, leaving Braga to fly the Portuguese flag alone in that competition until they were defeated with ease in the quarter-finals by Paulo Fonseca's future employers Shakhtar.

National team

The date of 10 July, 2016 will be treasured forever by Portuguese football fans. That was the day their national team became champions of Europe for the first time, with captain Cristiano Ronaldo lifting the Henri Delaunay Cup after a dramatic 1-0 extra-time victory over the host nation at the Stade de France. It was a remarkable triumph for Fernando Santos and his players, not least because it did not conform to convention. Portugal were unbeaten in all seven of their matches in France, but they won only one of them in 90 minutes. All three group games – against Iceland, Austria and Hungary – were drawn, and extra-time was required in three of their four knockout fixtures, with one of them, against Poland in the quarter-final, going to penalties.

There was a suggestion that Portugal got lucky when Iceland's late win over Austria in the final group fixture despatched them to the 'easy' side of the draw, but three of the four teams they went on to eliminate – Croatia, Wales and France – were by common consent among the best in the competition. Although Portugal possessed, in Ronaldo, the tournament's No1 attraction, they did not rely on his individual talent. Instead, they succeeded because of their powers of endurance and togetherness as a team, the prime example coming in the final when their talismanic skipper was forced off early through injury. Santos's pragmatic tactics and shrewd man-management worked a treat, and while Rui Patrício, Pepe, Nani, Raphael Guerreiro, Renato Sanches and final match-winner Éder will all have particularly happy memories of what they achieved during that historic month, every one of the 23 players on duty in France returned home as a national hero for life.

Portugal players celebrate a goal in their UEFA EURO 2016 semi-final win against Wales

DOMESTIC SEASON AT A GLANCE

Primeira Liga 2015/16 final table

		Pld	Home					Away					Total					Pts
			W	D	L	F	A	W	D	L	F	A	W	D	L	F	A	
1	SL Benfica	34	15	0	2	52	13	14	1	2	36	9	29	1	4	88	22	88
2	Sporting Clube de Portugal	34	13	3	1	39	12	14	2	1	40	9	27	5	2	79	21	86
3	FC Porto	34	12	2	3	35	13	11	2	4	32	17	23	4	7	67	30	73
4	SC Braga	34	11	4	2	41	17	5	6	6	13	18	16	10	8	54	35	58
5	FC Arouca	34	8	6	3	28	18	5	9	3	19	20	13	15	6	47	38	54
6	Rio Ave FC	34	9	1	7	20	18	5	7	5	24	26	14	8	12	44	44	50
7	FC Paços de Ferreira	34	7	4	6	24	22	6	6	5	19	20	13	10	11	43	42	49
8	Estoril Praia	34	9	4	4	24	16	4	4	9	16	25	13	8	13	40	41	47
9	Os Belenenses	34	6	5	6	24	31	4	6	7	20	35	10	11	13	44	66	41
10	Vitória SC	34	5	7	5	23	19	4	6	7	22	34	9	13	12	45	53	40
11	CD Nacional	34	8	4	5	29	24	2	4	11	11	32	10	8	16	40	56	38
12	Moreirense FC	34	3	5	9	19	28	6	4	7	19	26	9	9	16	38	54	36
13	CS Marítimo	34	7	2	8	25	23	3	3	11	20	40	10	5	19	45	63	35
14	Boavista FC	34	4	5	8	10	17	4	4	9	14	24	8	9	17	24	41	33
15	Vitória FC	34	2	9	6	16	26	4	3	10	24	35	6	12	16	40	61	30
16	CD Tondela	34	3	4	10	15	26	5	2	10	19	28	8	6	20	34	54	30
17	CF União da Madeira	34	6	6	5	19	17	1	2	14	8	33	7	8	19	27	50	29
18	A. Académica de Coimbra	34	5	5	7	20	28	0	5	12	12	32	5	10	19	32	60	25

European qualification 2016/17

Champion: SL Benfica (group stage)
Sporting Clube de Portugal (group stage)
FC Porto (play-offs)

Cup winner: SC Braga (group stage)
FC Arouca (third qualifying round)
Rio Ave FC (third qualifying round)

Top scorer   Jonas (Benfica), 32 goals
Relegated clubs   A. Académica de Coimbra, CF União da Madeira
Promoted clubs   GD Chaves, CD Feirense
Cup final   SC Braga 2-2 FC Porto (aet; 4-2 on pens)

Team of the season
(4-3-1-2)

Coach: Rui Vitória (Benfica)

Player of the season

Jonas
(SL Benfica)

Voted Primeira Liga player of the year for the second season in a row – a feat achieved only once before, by his Brazilian compatriot Hulk – Jonas was even more deserving of the prize than he had been in 2014/15. The 32-year-old striker racked up as many goals as his age – compared to just 20 the season before – to win the Bola de Prata as the league's top scorer and help fire Benfica to their third successive league title. His prolific form also earned him a belated recall to the Brazil squad for the 2016 Copa América.

Newcomer of the season

Renato Sanches
(SL Benfica)

Renato Sanches began the 2015/16 season playing in the UEFA Youth League for Benfica. The dreadlocked 18-year-old ended it not only as a regular starter for the first team but as a key contributor to the Lisbon club's Primeira Liga title success with his swaggering brilliance in midfield. There was more to come, too – a move to Bayern München and a starring role in Portugal's UEFA EURO 2016 triumph with the additional recognition of the Young Player of the Tournament award. All in all, quite a debut season.

PORTUGAL

NATIONAL TEAM

International honours
UEFA European Championship (1) 2016

International tournament appearances
FIFA World Cup (6) 1966 (3rd), 1986, 2002, 2006 (4th), 2010 (2nd round), 2014
UEFA European Championship (7) 1984 (semi-finals), 1996 (qtr-finals), 2000 (semi-finals), 2004 (runners-up), 2008 (qtr-finals), 2012 (semi-finals), 2016 (Winners)

Top five all-time caps
Cristiano Ronaldo (133); Luís Figo (127); Fernando Couto (110); **Nani** (103); Rui Costa (94)

Top five all-time goals
Cristiano Ronaldo (61); Pauleta (47); Eusébio (41); Luís Figo (32); Nuno Gomes (29)

Results 2015/16

04/09/15	France	H	Lisbon	L	0-1	
07/09/15	Albania (ECQ)	A	Elbasan	W	1-0	Miguel Veloso (90+2)
08/10/15	Denmark (ECQ)	H	Braga	W	1-0	João Moutinho (66)
11/10/15	Serbia (ECQ)	A	Belgrade	W	2-1	Nani (5), João Moutinho (78)
14/11/15	Russia	A	Krasnodar	L	0-1	
17/11/15	Luxembourg	A	Luxembourg	W	2-0	André André (31), Nani (88)
25/03/16	Bulgaria	H	Leiria	L	0-1	
29/03/16	Belgium	H	Leiria	W	2-1	Nani (20), Cristiano Ronaldo (40)
29/05/16	Norway	H	Porto	W	3-0	Ricardo Quaresma (13), Raphael Guerreiro (65), Éder (71)
02/06/16	England	A	London	L	0-1	
08/06/16	Estonia	H	Lisbon	W	7-0	Cristiano Ronaldo (36, 45), Ricardo Quaresma (39, 77), Danilo Pereira (55), Mets (61og), Éder (80)
14/06/16	Iceland (ECF)	N	Saint-Etienne (FRA)	D	1-1	Nani (31)
18/06/16	Austria (ECF)	N	Paris (FRA)	D	0-0	
22/06/16	Hungary (ECF)	N	Lyon (FRA)	D	3-3	Nani (42), Cristiano Ronaldo (50, 62)
25/06/16	Croatia (ECF)	N	Lens (FRA)	W	1-0	Ricardo Quaresma (117) (aet)
30/06/16	Poland (ECF)	N	Marseille (FRA)	D	1-1	Renato Sanches (33) (aet; 5-3 on pens)
06/07/16	Wales (ECF)	N	Lyon (FRA)	W	2-0	Cristiano Ronaldo (50), Nani (53)
10/07/16	France (ECF)	A	Saint-Denis	W	1-0	Éder (109) (aet)

Appearances 2015/16

Coach: Fernando Santos 10/10/54			Fra	ALB	DEN	SRB	Rus	Lux	Bul	Bel	Nor	Eng	Est	ISL	AUT	HUN	CRO	POL	WAL	FRA	Caps	Goals
Rui Patrício	15/02/88	Sporting	G	G	G	G	G			G		G	G	G	G	G	G	G	G	G	52	-
Vieirinha	24/01/86	Wolfsburg (GER)	D60	D54			D		D		s79	D	s46	D	D	D					25	1
Pepe	26/02/83	Real Madrid (ESP)	D	D			D		D	D			D58	D	D	D	D	D		D	77	3
Ricardo Carvalho	18/05/78	Monaco (FRA)	D27	D	D					D60	D89	s58	D	D	D						89	5
Eliseu	01/10/83	Benfica	D	D		D	D		D81		s79	D			D		D	D			18	1
Danilo Pereira	09/09/91	Porto	M86	M	M	M		M90	s75	M87	s60	M	M69	M		s81	s108	s96	M		17	1
João Mário	19/01/93	Sporting	M79			M90	s70		M65	M46	M72	M46	M59	M76	s71	M					18	-
Adrien Silva	15/03/89	Sporting	M60						M65	M46	s55	M71					M108	M73	M79	M66	13	-
Nani	17/11/86	Fenerbahçe (TUR)	A	A	A82	A	A	s63	A81	A60		A60	s46	A	A89	A81	A	A	A86	A	103	21
Éder	22/12/87	Swansea (ENG) /LOSC (FRA)	A	s76		s57			s81	s60	A	s89	s59	s84	s83					s79	29	4
Cristiano Ronaldo	05/02/85	Real Madrid (ESP)	A68	A	A				A	A60		A46	A	A	A	A	A	A	A25		133	61
José Fonte	22/12/83	Southampton (ENG)	s27		s91	D		D		D	D	s38	D			D	D	D	D		16	-
Miguel Veloso	11/05/86	Dynamo Kyiv (UKR)	s60	M		M70															56	3
Cédric	31/08/91	Southampton (ENG)	s60	s54	D		D			D	D		D46			D	D	D	D		15	-
Ricardo Quaresma	26/09/83	Beşiktaş (TUR)	s68	s68	s82	A			s65	s60	A60	s60	A	s76	A71	s61	s87	s80	s86	s25	57	8
Danny	07/08/83	Zenit (RUS)	s79	A76	s76	A57			s65	s87											38	4
Bernardo Silva	10/08/94	Monaco (FRA)	s86	M65	A76			A63		s46											6	-
Bruno Alves	27/11/81	Fenerbahçe (TUR)			D	D46	D		D			D 35*						D			86	10
Fábio Coentrão	11/03/88	Monaco (FRA)			D																51	5
Tiago	02/05/81	Atlético (ESP)			M																66	3
João Moutinho	08/09/86	Monaco (FRA)			M91	s70				M55	M72	M58	M71	M	M46		s73	s79	s66		90	4
Nélson Semedo	16/11/93	Benfica			D																1	-
André André	26/08/89	Porto				M	M72	M70													4	1
Luís Neto	26/05/88	Zenit (RUS)				s46		D													11	-
William Carvalho	07/04/92	Sporting				M	s80	M75	s74	M	s72	s69			M	M	M	M96		M	25	-
Nélson Oliveira	08/08/91	Nottingham Forest (ENG)				A72	s80														16	1
Gonçalo Guedes	29/11/96	Benfica				A82	s63														2	-
Rúben Neves	13/03/97	Porto				s72	M80														2	-
Lucas João	04/09/93	Sheffield Wednesday (ENG)				s72	A80														2	-
Ricardo	06/10/93	Nice (FRA)				s82	s90														2	-
Rafa Silva	17/05/93	Braga				s90	A63	A65		s60	A38			s89							9	-
Anthony Lopes	01/10/90	Lyon (FRA)					G	G		G											4	-
Raphael Guerreiro	22/12/93	Lorient (FRA)					D	s81	D	D79		D	D	D		D		D	D		12	2
Renato Sanches	18/08/97	Benfica						s75	s46	s72	s71	s58	s71		s46	s50	M	M74	M79		11	1
André Gomes	30/07/93	Valencia (ESP)							M74	M79	s46	M	M84	M83	M61	M50		s74			13	-

EUROPE

SL Benfica

Group C

Match 1 - FC Astana (KAZ)
H 2-0 *Gaitán (51), Mitroglou (62)*
Júlio César, Luisão, Samaris (Fejsa 85), Gaitán, Mitroglou, Jonas (Pizzi 72), Eliseu, Gonçalo Guedes, Talisca (Jiménez 77), Jardel, Nélson Semedo. Coach: Rui Vitória (POR)

Match 2 - Club Atlético de Madrid (ESP)
A 2-1 *Gaitán (36), Gonçalo Guedes (51)*
Júlio César, Luisão, Samaris (Fejsa 73), Jiménez (Mitroglou 72), Gaitán, Jonas (Pizzi 80), Eliseu, Gonçalo Guedes, Jardel, André Almeida, Nélson Semedo. Coach: Rui Vitória (POR)

Match 3 - Galatasaray AŞ (TUR)
A 1-2 *Gaitán (2)*
Júlio César, Luisão, Samaris, Jiménez, Gaitán, Jonas, Eliseu (Pizzi 66), Gonçalo Guedes (Victor Andrade 75), Sílvio (Mitroglou 82), Jardel, André Almeida. Coach: Rui Vitória (POR)

Match 4 - Galatasaray AŞ (TUR)
H 2-1 *Jonas (52), Luisão (67)*
Júlio César, Luisão, Jiménez, Gaitán, Jonas (Pizzi 81), Eliseu, Gonçalo Guedes (Carcela-González 73), Sílvio, Talisca (Cristante 90+3), Jardel, André Almeida. Coach: Rui Vitória (POR)
Red card: Gaitán 85

Match 5 - FC Astana (KAZ)
A 2-2 *Jiménez (40, 72)*
Júlio César, Lisandro López, Samaris (Talisca 65), Jiménez, Jonas (Cristante 80), Eliseu, Gonçalo Guedes, Pizzi, Sílvio (André Almeida 65), Jardel, Renato Sanches. Coach: Rui Vitória (POR)

Match 6 - Club Atlético de Madrid (ESP)
H 1-2 *Mitroglou (75)*
Júlio César, Lisandro López, Fejsa, Gaitán (Carcela-González 76), Jonas (Jiménez 61), Eliseu, Gonçalo Guedes (Mitroglou 46), Pizzi, Jardel, André Almeida, Renato Sanches. Coach: Rui Vitória (POR)

Round of 16 - FC Zenit (RUS)
H 1-0 *Jonas (90+1)*
Júlio César, Samaris, Gaitán, Mitroglou (Jiménez 63), Nilsson-Lindelöf, Jonas, Eliseu, Pizzi (Carcela-González 71), Jardel, André Almeida, Renato Sanches. Coach: Rui Vitória (POR)
A 2-1 *Gaitán (85), Talisca (90+6)*
Ederson, Fejsa, Samaris, Gaitán, Mitroglou (Jiménez 67), Nilsson-Lindelöf, Jonas (Talisca 90+2), Eliseu, Pizzi (Salvio 73), Semedo, Renato Sanches. Coach: Rui Vitória (POR)

Quarter-finals - FC Bayern München (GER)
A 0-1
Ederson, Fejsa, Gaitán, Mitroglou (Jiménez 70), Nilsson-Lindelöf, Jonas (Salvio 83), Eliseu, Pizzi (Samaris 90+1), Jardel, André Almeida, Renato Sanches. Coach: Rui Vitória (POR)
H 2-2 *Jiménez (27), Talisca (76)*
Ederson, Fejsa, Jiménez, Nilsson-Lindelöf, Salvio (Talisca 68), Eliseu (Jović 88), Pizzi (Gonçalo Guedes 58), Jardel, André Almeida, Carcela-González, Renato Sanches. Coach: Rui Vitória (POR)

FC Porto

Group G

Match 1 - FC Dynamo Kyiv (UKR)
A 2-2 *Aboubakar (23, 81)*
Casillas, Maxi Pereira, Martins Indi, Maicon, Rúben Neves, Brahimi (Corona 78), Aboubakar (Osvaldo 90+2), Herrera (Tello 65), André André, Layún, Danilo Pereira. Coach: Rui Gil Soares Barros (POR)

Match 2 - Chelsea FC (ENG)
H 2-1 *André André (39), Maicon (52)*
Casillas, Maxi Pereira, Martins Indi, Maicon, Marcano, Rúben Neves (Evandro 78), Brahimi (Osvaldo 86), Aboubakar, André André (Layún 80), Danilo Pereira, Imbula. Coach: Julen Lopetegui (ESP)

Match 3 - Maccabi Tel-Aviv FC (ISR)
H 2-0 *Aboubakar (37), Brahimi (41)*
Casillas, Maxi Pereira, Martins Indi, Marcano, Rúben Neves, Brahimi (Herrera 84), Aboubakar, Corona (Tello 54), André André, Layún, Imbula (Danilo Pereira 54). Coach: Julen Lopetegui (ESP)

Match 4 - Maccabi Tel-Aviv FC (ISR)
A 3-1 *Tello (19), André André (49), Layún (72)*
Casillas, Maxi Pereira, Martins Indi, Marcano, Rúben Neves, Aboubakar, Tello (Varela 76), Evandro (Herrera 62), André André (Imbula 89), Layún, Danilo Pereira. Coach: Julen Lopetegui (ESP)

Match 5 - FC Dynamo Kyiv (UKR)
H 0-2
Casillas, Maxi Pereira (André André 46), Martins Indi, Marcano, Rúben Neves, Brahimi (Osvaldo 67), Aboubakar, Tello, Layún, Danilo Pereira, Imbula (Corona 67). Coach: Julen Lopetegui (ESP)

Match 6 - Chelsea FC (ENG)
A 0-2
Casillas, Maxi Pereira (Rúben Neves 57), Martins Indi, Maicon, Marcano, Brahimi, Herrera (Tello 71), Corona, Layún, Danilo Pereira, Imbula (Aboubakar 56). Coach: Julen Lopetegui (ESP)

Round of 32 - Borussia Dortmund (GER)
A 0-2
Casillas, Martins Indi, Rúben Neves, Varela, Brahimi (André André 59), Aboubakar (Suk 87), Marega, Sérgio Oliveira (Evandro 76), José Ángel, Herrera, Layún. Coach: José Peseiro (POR)
H 0-1
Casillas, Maxi Pereira, Marcano, Rúben Neves, Varela (Brahimi 66), Aboubakar (Suk 56), Marega, José Ángel, Evandro (Herrera 71), Layún, Danilo Pereira. Coach: José Peseiro (POR)

Sporting Clube de Portugal

Play-offs - PFC CSKA Moskva (RUS)
H 2-1 *Gutiérrez (12), Slimani (82)*
Rui Patrício, Jefferson, Slimani, Paulo Oliveira, João Mário (Carlos Mané 76), Carrillo, Gutiérrez (Gelson Martins 76), Ruiz (Aquilani 65), João Pereira, Adrien Silva, Naldo. Coach: Jorge Jesus (POR)
A 1-3 *Gutiérrez (36)*
Rui Patrício, Silva, Aquilani (Montero 89), Paulo Oliveira, João Mário, Carrillo, Gutiérrez (Slimani 68), Ruiz (Carlos Mané 89), João Pereira, Adrien Silva, Naldo. Coach: Jorge Jesus (POR)
Red card: João Mário 90+2

Group H

Match 1 - FC Lokomotiv Moskva (RUS)
H 1-3 *Montero (50)*
Rui Patrício, Jefferson, Aquilani (André Martins 71), Montero (Slimani 63), Paulo Oliveira, Gutiérrez, João Pereira, Adrien Silva, Carlos Mané (Ruiz 63), Tobias Figueiredo, Gelson Martins. Coach: Jorge Jesus (POR)

Match 2 - Beşiktaş JK (TUR)
A 1-1 *Ruiz (16)*
Rui Patrício, Silva, Aquilani (Gelson Martins 78), William Carvalho, Gutiérrez (Slimani 69), Ruiz, João Pereira, Carlos Mané, Naldo, Tobias Figueiredo, Matheus Pereira (Adrien Silva 55). Coach: Jorge Jesus (POR)

Match 3 - KF Skënderbeu (ALB)
H 5-1 *Aquilani (38p), Montero (41p), Matheus Pereira (64, 77), Tobias Figueiredo (69)*
Rui Patrício, Silva, Ewerton, Aquilani (William Carvalho 72), Montero, André Martins (Slimani 59), Bruno Paulista, Carlos Mané (Gelson Martins 65), Ricardo Esgaio, Tobias Figueiredo, Matheus Pereira. Coach: Jorge Jesus (POR)

Match 4 - KF Skënderbeu (ALB)
A 0-3
Rui Patrício, Silva, Ewerton (Paulo Oliveira 71), Tanaka (Marcelo 19), Montero, Adrien Silva (João Mário 59), Bruno Paulista, Carlos Mané, Ricardo Esgaio, Tobias Figueiredo, Matheus Pereira. Coach: Jorge Jesus (POR)
Red card: Rui Patrício 17

Match 5 - FC Lokomotiv Moskva (RUS)
A 4-2 *Montero (20), Ruiz (38), Gelson Martins (43), Matheus Pereira (60)*
Marcelo, Silva, Ewerton, Montero (Slimani 71), João Mário (Aquilani 79), Ruiz, Adrien Silva, Naldo, Ricardo Esgaio, Gelson Martins, Matheus Pereira (André Martins 67). Coach: Jorge Jesus (POR)

Match 6 - Beşiktaş JK (TUR)
H 3-1 *Slimani (67), Ruiz (72), Gutiérrez (78)*
Rui Patrício, Jefferson, Slimani (Matheus Pereira 88), Montero (Gelson Martins 46), William Carvalho, Paulo Oliveira, João Mário, Ruiz, João Pereira, Adrien Silva (Gutiérrez 64), Naldo. Coach: Jorge Jesus (POR)

Round of 32 - Bayer 04 Leverkusen (GER)
H 0-1
Rui Patrício, Jefferson, Aquilani (Adrien Silva 61), Coates (Ewerton 73), William Carvalho, João Mário, Gutiérrez (Slimani 61), Ruiz, João Pereira, Rúben Semedo, Carlos Mané. Coach: Jorge Jesus (POR)
Red card: Ruben Semedo 74
A 1-3 *João Mário (38)*
Rui Patrício, Jefferson, Ewerton, Aquilani, Bruno César (Gelson Martins 78), William Carvalho, João Mário, Gutiérrez (Slimani 67), João Pereira, Carlos Mané (Ruiz 62), Naldo. Coach: Jorge Jesus (POR)

SC Braga

Group F
Match 1 - FC Slovan Liberec (CZE)
A 1-0 *Rafa Silva (60)*
Matheus, Boly, André Pinto, Crislan (Wilson Eduardo 62), Baiano, Djavan, Rui Fonte (Ricardo Ferreira 86), Rafa Silva, Alan (Filipe Augusto 75), Vukčević, Mauro. Coach: Paulo Fonseca (POR)
Match 2 - FC Groningen (NED)
H 1-0 *Hassan (5)*
Matheus, Boly, Luíz Carlos, Djavan (Pedro Santos 83), Rui Fonte (Wilson Eduardo 71), Rafa Silva, Hassan, Alan, Arghus (Mauro 40), Vukčević, Marcelo Goiano. Coach: Paulo Fonseca (POR)
Match 3 - Olympique de Marseille (FRA)
H 3-2 *Hassan (61), Wilson Eduardo (77), Alan (88)*
Matheus, Boly, Djavan, Rui Fonte (Wilson Eduardo 65), Rafa Silva (Luíz Carlos 85), Hassan (Crislan 75), Ricardo Ferreira, Alan, Vukčević, Mauro, Marcelo Goiano. Coach: Paulo Fonseca (POR)
Match 4 - Olympique de Marseille (FRA)
A 0-1
Matheus, Boly, Baiano, Rui Fonte, Rafa Silva, Hassan (Crislan 67), Ricardo Ferreira, Alan (Wilson Eduardo 78), Vukčević, Mauro (Luíz Carlos 53), Marcelo Goiano. Coach: Paulo Fonseca (POR)
Match 5 - FC Slovan Liberec (CZE)
H 2-1 *Ricardo Ferreira (42), Crislan (90+2)*
Matheus, Boly, Luíz Carlos, Djavan, Rui Fonte (Crislan 59), Rafa Silva, Hassan (Wilson Eduardo 90+4), Ricardo Ferreira, Alan (Pedro Santos 86), Vukčević, Marcelo Goiano. Coach: Paulo Fonseca (POR)
Match 6 - FC Groningen (NED)
A 0-0
Matheus, Boly, André Pinto, Wilson Eduardo (Rui Fonte 90+3), Luíz Carlos, Baiano, Rafa Silva, Hassan, Alan (Pedro Santos 80), Vukčević, Marcelo Goiano. Coach: Paulo Fonseca (POR)

Round of 32 - FC Sion (SUI)
A 2-1 *Stoiljković (13), Rafa Silva (61)*
Matheus, Boly, André Pinto, Wilson Eduardo, Luíz Carlos, Baiano, Rafa Silva, Stoiljković (Ricardo Ferreira 90+2), Hassan (Josué 84), Alan (Pedro Santos 66), Vukčević. Coach: Paulo Fonseca (POR)
Red card: Vukčević 90

H 2-2 *Josué (27p), Stoiljković (48)*
Matheus, Boly, Luíz Carlos, Baiano, Rafa Silva, Stoiljković (Rui Fonte 81), Hassan (André Pinto 90+2), Ricardo Ferreira, Josué (Pedro Santos 62), Mauro, Marcelo Goiano. Coach: Paulo Fonseca (POR)

Round of 16 - Fenerbahçe SK (TUR)
A 0-1
Matheus, André Pinto, Wilson Eduardo (Stoiljković 72), Luíz Carlos, Baiano, Rafa Silva (Pedro Santos 85), Hassan, Ricardo Ferreira (Boly 15), Josué, Vukčević, Marcelo Goiano. Coach: Paulo Fonseca (POR)
H 4-1 *Hassan (11), Josué (69p), Stoiljković (74), Rafa Silva (83)*
Matheus, Boly, André Pinto, Baiano, Rafa Silva, Stoiljković (Filipe Augusto 90), Hassan, Josué, Vukčević (Pedro Santos 73), Mauro, Marcelo Goiano. Coach: Paulo Fonseca (POR)

Quarter-finals - FC Shakhtar Donetsk (UKR)
H 1-2 *Wilson Eduardo (89)*
Matheus, Boly, Luíz Carlos, Baiano, Rafa Silva, Stoiljković (Wilson Eduardo 75), Hassan, Pedro Santos, Ricardo Ferreira, Vukčević (Filipe Augusto 87), Marcelo Goiano. Coach: Paulo Fonseca (POR)
A 0-4
Matheus, Boly (André Pinto 78), Wilson Eduardo (Stoiljković 57), Luíz Carlos (Mauro 78), Djavan, Rafa Silva, Hassan, Ricardo Ferreira, Josué, Vukčević, Marcelo Goiano. Coach: Paulo Fonseca (POR)

Vitória SC

Third qualifying round - SCR Altach (AUT)
A 1-2 *Tozé (71)*
Douglas, Luís Rocha, Moreno, Ricardo Valente (Henrique Dourado 70), Tomané , Montoya (Tozé 52), Alex (Licá 90+3), João Afonso, Cafú, Arrondel, Bruno Alves. Coach: Armando Evangelista (POR)
H 1-4 *Tomané (67)*
Douglas, Luís Rocha (Tomané 59), Moreno, Licá (Ricardo Valente 69), Alex, João Afonso, Pedro Correia, Cafú, Bruno Alves (Otávio 46), Tozé, Henrique Dourado. Coach: Armando Evangelista (POR)
Red card: Pedro Correia 74

Os Belenenses

Third qualifying round - IFK Göteborg (SWE)
H 2-1 *Carlos Martins (23, 41)*
Ventura, João Amorim, Tonel, Rúben Pinto, Miguel Rosa, André Sousa (Ricardo Dias 67), Fábio Sturgeon, André Geraldes, Carlos Martins (Tiago Silva 87), Gonçalo Brandão, Abel Camará (Fábio Nunes 67). Coach: Ricardo Sá Pinto (POR)
A 0-0
Ventura, João Amorim, Tonel, Rúben Pinto, Miguel Rosa (Dálcio 68), André Sousa, Fábio Sturgeon, André Geraldes, Carlos Martins (Tiago Silva 78), Gonçalo Brandão, Abel Camará (João Afonso 89). Coach: Ricardo Sá Pinto (POR)

Play-offs - SCR Altach (AUT)
A 1-0 *Tiago Caeiro (13)*
Ventura, João Amorim, Tonel, Rúben Pinto, Miguel Rosa, André Sousa (Ricardo Dias 64), Tiago Caeiro (Abel Camará 66), Tiago Silva (Fábio Nunes 77), Fábio Sturgeon, André Geraldes, Gonçalo Brandão. Coach: Ricardo Sá Pinto (POR)
H 0-0
Ventura, João Amorim, Tonel, Rúben Pinto (Ricardo Dias 90+3), Miguel Rosa, André Sousa, Tiago Caeiro (João Afonso 87), Fábio Sturgeon, André Geraldes, Gonçalo Brandão, Abel Camará (Tiago Silva 69). Coach: Ricardo Sá Pinto (POR)

Group I
Match 1 - KKS Lech Poznań (POL)
A 0-0
Ventura, João Amorim, Tonel, Rúben Pinto, Miguel Rosa, André Sousa (Ricardo Dias 80), Fábio Sturgeon (Kuca 63), André Geraldes, Carlos Martins (Dálcio 89), Gonçalo Brandão, Luís Leal. Coach: Ricardo Sá Pinto (POR)
Match 2 - ACF Fiorentina (ITA)
H 0-4
Ventura, Tonel, Rúben Pinto, André Sousa, Kuca (Fábio Nunes 63), Fábio Sturgeon (Dálcio 40), André Geraldes, Filipe Ferreira, Carlos Martins (Tiago Caeiro 78), Gonçalo Brandão, Luís Leal. Coach: Ricardo Sá Pinto (POR)
Match 3 - FC Basel 1893 (SUI)
A 2-1 *Leal (27), Kuca (45+1)*
Ventura, João Amorim, Rúben Pinto, André Sousa (Ricardo Dias 84), Tiago Silva (Gonçalo Silva 90+3), Kuca, João Afonso, Fábio Sturgeon, Filipe Ferreira, Gonçalo Brandão, Luís Leal (Tiago Caeiro 87). Coach: Ricardo Sá Pinto (POR)
Match 4 - FC Basel 1893 (SUI)
H 0-2
Ventura, João Amorim, Rúben Pinto, André Sousa (Tiago Caeiro 66), Tiago Silva, Kuca (Fábio Nunes 83), Fábio Sturgeon, Filipe Ferreira, Gonçalo Brandão (Tonel 28), Gonçalo Silva, Luís Leal. Coach: Ricardo Sá Pinto (POR)
Match 5 - KKS Lech Poznań (POL)
H 0-0
Ventura, Tonel, Rúben Pinto, Tiago Caeiro (Luís Leal 76), Tiago Silva (Carlos Martins 67), Kuca, Fábio Sturgeon (Dálcio 79), Ricardo Dias, André Geraldes, Filipe Ferreira, Gonçalo Brandão. Coach: Ricardo Sá Pinto (POR)
Match 6 - ACF Fiorentina (ITA)
A 0-1
Ventura, João Amorim, Rúben Pinto (Fábio Nunes 79), André Sousa (Kuca 56), João Afonso, Fábio Sturgeon (Tiago Caeiro 83), Ricardo Dias, Filipe Ferreira, Carlos Martins, Gonçalo Silva, Luís Leal. Coach: Ricardo Sá Pinto (POR)

DOMESTIC LEAGUE CLUB-BY-CLUB

A. Académica de Coimbra

1876 • Cidade de Coimbra (30,075) • academica-oaf.pt
Major honours
Portuguese Cup (2) 1939, 2012
Coach: José Viterbo;
(24/09/15) Filipe Gouveia

2015

17/08	a	Paços Ferreira	L	0-1	
24/08	h	Setúbal	L	0-4	
30/08	h	Sporting	L	1-3	*Rabiola (p)*
13/09	a	Nacional	L	0-2	
20/09	h	Boavista	L	0-2	
28/09	a	Rio Ave	L	0-1	
03/10	h	Marítimo	W	1-0	*Rui Pedro (p)*
24/10	a	Guimarães	D	1-1	*Rafael Lopes*
01/11	h	Moreirense	D	1-1	*Obiora*
06/11	h	Estoril	D	1-1	*Rabiola*
29/11	a	Arouca	D	1-1	*Gonçalo Paciência*
04/12	a	Benfica	L	0-3	
14/12	h	Belenenses	W	4-3	*Gonçalo Paciência (p), Pedro Nuno, Ivanildo, Fernando Alexandre*
20/12	a	Porto	L	1-3	*Rui Pedro*

2016

02/01	h	União	W	3-1	*Ricardo Nascimento, Fernando Alexandre, João Real*
06/01	a	Braga	L	0-3	
10/01	h	Tondela	W	2-1	*Rafael Lopes, Hugo Seco*
16/01	a	Paços Ferreira	D	1-1	*João Real*
22/01	a	Setúbal	L	1-2	*Nuno Piloto*
30/01	h	Sporting	L	1-2	*Rafa Soares, og (Ewerton)*
07/02	h	Nacional	D	2-2	*Plange, João Real*
14/02	a	Boavista	D	0-0	
20/02	h	Rio Ave	L	0-2	
28/02	a	Marítimo	L	0-1	
06/03	h	Guimarães	W	2-0	*Marinho 2*
13/03	a	Moreirense	D	2-2	*Plange, Leandro Silva*
20/03	h	Estoril	L	0-3	
02/04	a	Arouca	L	2-3	*Pedro Nuno, Gonçalo Paciência*
09/04	h	Benfica	L	1-2	*Pedro Nuno*
17/04	a	Belenenses	D	1-1	*Rafael Lopes (p)*
23/04	h	Porto	L	1-2	*Pedro Nuno*
01/05	a	União	L	1-3	*Fernando Alexandre*
07/05	h	Braga	D	0-0	
14/05	a	Tondela	L	0-2	

No	Name	Nat	DoB	Pos	Aps	(s)	Gls
2	Aderlan	BRA	18/08/90	D	23	(2)	
8	Selim Bouadla	FRA	26/08/88	M	5	(2)	
3	Emídio Rafael		24/01/86	D	9		
65	Fernando Alexandre		02/08/85	M	27		3
19	Gonçalo Paciência		01/08/94	A	17	(10)	3
17	Inters Gui	CIV	08/08/93	A	1	(5)	
77	Hugo Seco		17/06/88	M	7	(20)	1
14	Iago Santos	BRA	22/05/92	D	17		
10	Ivanildo	GNB	09/01/86	M	18	(2)	1
18	João Real		13/05/83	D	24	(2)	3
24	Ki Hwang-mun	KOR	08/12/96	M		(1)	
21	Leandro Silva		04/05/94	M	23	(4)	1
32	Lee	BRA	09/03/88	G	1	(1)	
6	Tripy Makonda	FRA	24/01/90	M		(1)	
7	Marinho		26/04/83	A	10	(8)	2
28	Nuno Piloto		19/02/82	M	13	(5)	1
4	Nwankwo Obiora	NGA	12/07/91	M	10	(1)	
37	Richard Ofori	GHA	24/04/93	D	4	(1)	
22	Christopher Oualembo	COD	31/01/87	D	12	(1)	
27	Pedro Nuno		13/01/95	M	12		4
88	Pedro Trigueira		04/01/88	G	33		
43	Nii Plange	BFA	26/06/89	M	28		2
9	Rabiola		25/07/89	A	9	(14)	2
55	Rafa Soares		28/07/91	D	15		1
30	Rafael Lopes		28/07/91	A	13	(13)	3
5	Ricardo Nascimento	BRA	07/02/87	D	24	(1)	1
20	Rui Pedro		07/07/88	M	16	(5)	2
23	William Gustavo	BRA	09/01/92	D	3	(3)	

FC Arouca

1951 • Municipal de Arouca (5,100) • fcarouca.eu
Coach: Lito Vidigal (ANG)

2015

16/08	a	Moreirense	W	2-0	*Nuno Coelho, Maurides*
23/08	h	Benfica	W	1-0	*Roberto*
30/08	a	Paços Ferreira	D	1-1	*Nuno Valente*
12/09	h	Porto	L	1-3	*Maurides*
20/09	h	União	D	0-0	
27/09	h	Belenenses	D	2-2	*Nuno Valente, Hugo Basto*
04/10	a	Braga	D	0-0	
25/10	h	Tondela	D	1-1	*Ivo Rodrigues*
01/11	a	Setúbal	D	0-0	
08/11	h	Sporting	L	0-1	
29/11	a	Académica	D	1-1	*Maurides*
06/12	h	Boavista	W	3-2	*Maurides, Ivo Rodrigues, Nuno Coelho*
12/12	a	Rio Ave	L	1-3	*Velázquez*
19/12	h	Marítimo	W	4-1	*Nuno Valente, Ivo Rodrigues, Velázquez, Maurides*

2016

02/01	a	Nacional	D	2-2	*Zequinha, David Simão (p)*
06/01	h	Estoril	W	1-0	*David Simão (p)*
09/01	a	Guimarães	D	2-2	*Roberto, González*
17/01	h	Moreirense	L	1-2	*David Simão (p)*
23/01	a	Benfica	L	1-3	*Velázquez*
31/01	h	Paços Ferreira	D	2-2	*Lucas Lima, og (Fábio Cardoso)*
07/02	a	Porto	W	2-1	*González 2*
14/02	h	União	W	3-0	*Lucas Lima, Mateus, Adilson Goiano*
21/02	a	Belenenses	W	2-0	*González, Lucas Lima*
27/02	h	Braga	D	0-0	
06/03	a	Tondela	W	1-0	*Mateus*
13/03	h	Setúbal	W	1-0	*Mateus*
19/03	a	Sporting	L	1-5	*Gegé*
02/04	h	Académica	W	3-2	*Jubal, Lucas Lima, Artur*
08/04	a	Boavista	D	0-0	
16/04	h	Rio Ave	D	0-0	
24/04	a	Marítimo	W	2-1	*Jubal, David Simão (p)*
01/05	h	Nacional	W	3-0	*González 2, Mateus (p)*
09/05	a	Estoril	D	1-1	*og (Anderson Luís)*
14/05	h	Guimarães	D	2-2	*González, Adilson Goiano*

No	Name	Nat	DoB	Pos	Aps	(s)	Gls
22	Adilson Goiano	BRA	09/02/88	M	13	(13)	2
24	Emiliano Albín	URU	24/01/89	M	2	(5)	
28	Alex Azevedo		28/01/97	M	1		
7	Artur		18/02/84	M	27	(1)	1
5	Borja López	ESP	02/02/94	D		(1)	
19	Caio Rangel	BRA	16/01/96	A		(1)	
8	David Simão		15/05/90	M	16	(2)	4
14	Gegé	CPV	24/02/88	D	18	(3)	1
95	Walter González	PAR	21/06/95	A	11	(5)	7
3	Hugo Basto		14/05/93	D	32		1
11	Ivo Rodrigues		30/03/95	A	26	(4)	3
13	Jaílson	BRA	21/01/91	D	13		
21	Jorginho		20/01/95	A	1	(3)	
33	Jubal	BRA	29/08/93	D	9	(2)	2
77	Leandro	BRA	13/01/95	M	1	(4)	
6	Lucas Lima	BRA	10/04/91	D	31		4
12	Mateus	ANG	19/06/84	A	13	(1)	4
99	Maurides	BRA	10/03/94	A	13	(19)	5
55	Nelsinho	BRA	01/01/88	D	3	(2)	
30	Nildo	BRA	01/05/86	A	2	(5)	
66	Nuno Coelho		23/11/87	D	31	(1)	2
50	Nuno Valente		22/11/91	M	22	(2)	3
10	Pintassilgo		30/06/85	M	1	(4)	
1	Rafael Bracalli	BRA	05/05/81	G	33		
17	Roberto		28/11/84	A	10	(1)	2
85	Rui Sacramento		31/01/85	G	1		
16	Tomás Dabó		20/10/93	D	7	(1)	
4	José Manuel Velázquez	VEN	08/09/90	D	21	(2)	3
9	Agustín Vuletich	ARG	03/11/91	A		(1)	
88	Rodney Wallace	CRC	17/06/88	M		(2)	
87	Zequinha		07/01/87	A	16	(9)	1

Os Belenenses

1919 • Restelo (19,856) • osbelenenses.com
Major honours
Portuguese League (1) 1946; Portuguese Cup (3) 1942, 1960, 1989
Coach: Ricardo Sá Pinto;
(16/12/15) Julio Velázquez (ESP)

2015

15/08	h	Rio Ave	D	3-3	*Gonçalo Brandão, Rúben Pinto, Carlos Martins (p)*
23/08	a	Guimarães	D	1-1	*Fábio Sturgeon*
31/08	h	Marítimo	D	1-1	*Miguel Rosa*
11/09	a	Benfica	L	0-6	
21/09	h	Moreirense	W	2-0	*Luís Leal, Miguel Rosa*
27/09	a	Arouca	D	2-2	*André Sousa, Luís Leal*
04/10	a	Porto	L	0-4	
26/10	h	União	W	1-0	*Tiago Caeiro*
31/10	a	Braga	L	0-4	
09/11	h	Tondela	W	2-1	*Tiago Silva, Tiago Caeiro*
30/11	a	Sporting	L	0-1	
05/12	h	Setúbal	L	0-3	
14/12	a	Académica	L	3-4	*og (Ricardo Nascimento), Tiago Caeiro, Rúben Pinto*
21/12	h	Boavista	W	1-0	*Filipe Ferreira*

2016

02/01	a	Paços Ferreira	D	2-2	*Tiago Caeiro, André Sousa*
06/01	h	Nacional	D	2-2	*Kuca, Tiago Caeiro*
10/01	a	Estoril	L	0-2	
17/01	h	Rio Ave	W	2-1	*Filipe Ferreira, Fábio Sturgeon*
24/01	h	Guimarães	D	3-3	*Miguel Rosa, Bakić, Juanto*
01/02	a	Marítimo	W	2-1	*Fábio Sturgeon, Miguel Rosa*
05/02	h	Benfica	L	0-5	
13/02	a	Moreirense	W	3-2	*Aguilar, Fábio Sturgeon, Bakić*
21/02	h	Arouca	L	0-2	
28/02	h	Porto	L	1-2	*Juanto*
06/03	a	União	D	0-0	
13/03	h	Braga	W	3-0	*Gonçalo Silva, Miguel Rosa, Tiago Caeiro*
20/03	a	Tondela	D	2-2	*Gonçalo Silva, Carlos Martins*
03/04	h	Sporting	L	2-5	*Bakić, Tiago Silva*
10/04	a	Setúbal	W	1-0	*Juanto*
17/04	h	Académica	D	1-1	*Juanto*
22/04	a	Boavista	L	0-1	
30/04	h	Paços Ferreira	D	2-2	*Tiago Caeiro, Filipe Ferreira*
08/05	a	Nacional	D	2-2	*Tiago Caeiro, Filipe Ferreira*
14/05	h	Estoril	W	2-1	*Miguel Rosa, Bakić (p)*

No	Name	Nat	DoB	Pos	Aps	(s)	Gls
30	Abel Camará	GNB	06/01/90	A	2	(2)	
26	Abel Aguilar	COL	06/11/85	M	9		1
19	André Geraldes		02/05/91	D	28		
8	André Sousa		09/07/90	M	24	(3)	2
88	Marko Bakić	MNE	01/11/93	M	12	(2)	4
11	Betinho		21/07/93	A		(3)	
22	Carlos Martins		29/04/82	M	21	(3)	2
14	Dálcio		22/05/96	A	2	(1)	
92	Fábio Nunes		24/07/92	A	9	(7)	
17	Fábio Sturgeon		04/02/94	A	31	(3)	4
20	Filipe Ferreira		27/09/90	D	22	(3)	3
28	Gonçalo Brandão		09/10/86	D	29		1
37	Gonçalo Silva		04/06/91	D	15	(4)	2
13	João Afonso		11/02/82	D	8		
2	João Amorim		26/07/92	D	7	(1)	
5	João Vilela		09/09/85	M		(1)	
23	Juanto	ESP	11/02/92	A	9	(3)	4
12	Kuca	CPV	02/08/89	A	14		1
99	Luís Leal		29/05/87	A	9	(1)	2
7	Miguel Rosa		13/01/89	M	16	(9)	6
44	Rafael Amorim	BRA	30/07/87	D	6	(1)	
18	Ricardo Dias		25/02/91	M	11	(12)	
1	Ricardo Ribeiro		27/01/90	G	6		
6	Rúben Pinto		24/04/92	M	25	(6)	2
21	Tiago Almeida	CPV	13/09/90	A	2	(3)	
9	Tiago Caeiro		29/03/84	A	9	(17)	7
10	Tiago Silva		02/06/93	M	9	(8)	2
4	Tonel		13/04/80	D	11	(1)	
27	Traquina		29/08/88	A		(6)	
24	Ventura		14/01/88	G	28		

PORTUGAL

SL Benfica

1904 • Sport Lisboa e Benfica (65,647) • slbenfica.pt

Major honours
European Champion Clubs' Cup (2) 1961, 1962;
Portuguese League (35) 1936, 1937, 1938, 1942,
1943, 1945, 1950, 1955, 1957, 1960, 1961, 1963,
1964, 1965, 1967, 1968, 1969, 1971, 1972, 1973,
1975, 1976, 1977, 1981, 1983, 1984, 1987, 1989,
1991, 1994, 2005, 2010, 2014, 2015, 2016;
Portuguese Cup (25) 1940, 1943, 1944, 1949, 1951,
1952, 1953, 1955, 1957, 1959, 1962, 1964, 1969,
1970, 1972, 1980, 1981, 1983, 1985, 1986, 1987,
1993, 1996, 2004, 2014

Coach: Rui Vitória

2015
16/08	h	Estoril	W 4-0	Mitroglou, Jonas 2 (1p), Nélson Semedo
23/08	a	Arouca	L 0-1	
29/08	h	Moreirense	W 3-2	Jiménez, Samaris, Jonas
11/09	h	Belenenses	W 6-0	Mitroglou 2, Jonas 2, Gaitán, Talisca
20/09	a	Porto	L 0-1	
26/09	a	Paços Ferreira	W 3-0	Jonas 2, Gonçalo Guedes
25/10	h	Sporting	L 0-3	
30/10	a	Tondela	W 4-0	Jonas, og (Berger), Gonçalo Guedes, Carcela-González
08/11	h	Boavista	W 2-0	Gonçalo Guedes, Carcela-González
30/11	a	Braga	W 2-0	Pizzi, López
04/12	h	Académica	W 3-0	Jonas 2 (2p), Renato Sanches
12/12	a	Setúbal	W 4-2	Pizzi. Jonas, Mitroglou, og (Ricardo)
15/12	h	União	D 0-0	
20/12	h	Rio Ave	W 3-1	Jonas 2, Jiménez

2016
02/01	a	Guimarães	W 1-0	Renato Sanches
06/01	h	Marítimo	W 6-0	Pizzi 2, Jiménez, Jonas 2 (1p), Talisca
11/01	a	Nacional	W 4-1	Jonas 3, Mitroglou
16/01	a	Estoril	W 2-1	Mitroglou, Pizzi
23/01	h	Arouca	W 3-1	Pizzi, Mitroglou, Jonas
31/01	a	Moreirense	W 4-1	Jonas 2, Mitroglou, Gaitán
05/02	a	Belenenses	W 5-0	Mitroglou 3, Jonas 2
12/02	h	Porto	L 1-2	Mitroglou
20/02	a	Paços Ferreira	W 3-0	Mitroglou, Jonas (p), Nilsson-Lindelöf
29/02	h	União	W 2-0	Jonas 2
05/03	a	Sporting	W 1-0	Mitroglou
14/03	h	Tondela	W 4-1	Jardel, Jonas 2, Mitroglou
20/03	a	Boavista	W 1-0	Jonas
01/04	h	Braga	W 5-1	Mitroglou 2, Jonas (p), Pizzi, Samaris
09/04	a	Académica	W 2-1	Mitroglou, Jiménez
18/04	h	Setúbal	W 2-1	Jonas, Jardel
24/04	a	Rio Ave	W 1-0	Jiménez
29/04	h	Guimarães	W 1-0	Jardel
08/05	a	Marítimo	W 2-0	Mitroglou, Talisca
15/05	h	Nacional	W 4-1	Gaitán 2, Jonas, Pizzi

No	Name	Nat	DoB	Pos	Aps	(s)	Gls
3	Álex Grimaldo	ESP	20/09/95	D	2		
34	André Almeida		10/09/90	M	25	(1)	
39	Mehdi Carcela-González	MAR	01/07/89	M	6	(14)	2
61	Clésio	MOZ	11/10/94	A	1		
24	Bryan Cristante	ITA	03/03/95	M		(2)	
22	Filip Djuričić	SRB	30/01/92	M		(1)	
1	Ederson	BRA	17/08/93	G	10		
1	Eliseu		01/10/83	D	31		
5	Ljubomir Fejsa	SRB	14/08/88	M	16	(4)	
10	Nicolás Gaitán	ARG	23/02/88	M	23	(1)	4
20	Gonçalo Guedes		29/11/96	M	10	(8)	3
33	Jardel	BRA	29/03/86	D	30		3
9	Raúl Jiménez	MEX	05/05/91	A	8	(20)	5
15	Ola John	NED	19/05/92	A	2		
17	Jonas	BRA	01/04/84	A	33	(1)	32
35	Luka Jović	SRB	23/12/97	M		(1)	
12	Júlio César	BRA	03/09/79	G	24		
2	Lisandro López	ARG	01/09/89	D	14		1
11	Luisão	BRA	13/02/81	D	9		
11	Kostas Mitroglou	GRE	12/03/88	A	26	(6)	19
50	Nélson Semedo		16/11/93	D	10	(2)	1
14	Victor Nilsson-Lindelöf	SWE	17/07/94	D	14	(1)	1
38	Nuno Santos		13/02/95	M		(1)	
13	Paulo Lopes		29/06/78	G		(1)	
21	Pizzi		06/10/89	M	28	(3)	8
85	Renato Sanches		18/08/97	M	22	(2)	2
7	Eduardo Salvio	ARG	13/07/90	M	1	(7)	
7	Andreas Samaris	GRE	13/06/89	M	19	(7)	2
28	Sílvio		28/09/87	D	3	(2)	
30	Talisca	BRA	01/02/94	M	6	(15)	3
31	Victor Andrade	BRA	30/09/95	A	1	(2)	

Boavista FC

1903 • Bessa (30,000) • boavistafc.pt

Major honours
Portuguese League (1) 2001; Portuguese Cup (5)
1975, 1976, 1979, 1992, 1997

Coach: Petit;
(01/12/15) Erwin Sánchez (BOL)

2015
16/08	a	Setúbal	D 2-2	Afonso Figueiredo, Luisinho
23/08	h	Tondela	W 1-0	Luisinho
30/08	a	Braga	L 0-4	
14/09	h	Paços Ferreira	L 0-1	
20/09	a	Académica	W 2-0	José Manuel, Anderson Carvalho
26/09	h	Sporting	D 0-0	
03/10	a	Rio Ave	L 0-1	
23/10	a	Nacional	D 0-0	
01/11	h	Marítimo	L 0-1	
08/11	a	Benfica	L 0-2	
28/11	h	Guimarães	L 1-2	Douglas Abner
06/12	a	Arouca	L 2-3	Tengarrinha (p), Nuno Henrique
11/12	h	Estoril	D 1-1	Nwofor
21/12	a	Belenenses	L 0-1	

2016
02/01	h	Moreirense	L 0-3	
06/01	a	União	L 0-1	
10/01	h	Porto	L 0-5	
18/01	a	Setúbal	W 4-0	Renato Santos, Gabriel, José Manuel, Paulo Vinícius
25/01	a	Tondela	W 2-1	Iriberri, Mandiang
31/01	h	Braga	D 0-0	
07/02	a	Paços Ferreira	W 1-0	Mario Martínez
14/02	h	Académica	D 0-0	
22/02	a	Sporting	L 0-2	
27/02	h	Rio Ave	L 1-2	Renato Santos
06/03	h	Nacional	L 0-1	
11/03	a	Marítimo	W 3-0	Anderson Carvalho, José Manuel 2
20/03	h	Benfica	L 0-1	
02/04	a	Guimarães	D 1-1	Paulo Vinícius
08/04	h	Arouca	D 0-0	
16/04	a	Estoril	L 0-1	
22/04	h	Belenenses	W 1-0	José Manuel
01/05	a	Moreirense	D 1-1	Nuno Henrique
08/05	h	União	W 1-0	José Manuel
14/05	a	Porto	L 0-4	

No	Name	Nat	DoB	Pos	Aps	(s)	Gls
25	Afonso Figueiredo		06/01/93	D	24	(1)	1
80	Ancelmo Júnior	BRA	03/04/90	A	1	(1)	
27	Anderson Carvalho	BRA	20/05/90	M	19	(11)	2
6	Anderson Correia	BRA	06/05/91	D	9	(6)	
95	André Bukia	COD	03/03/95	M	3	(3)	
99	Cristian Cangá	COL	23/02/91	A		(2)	
22	Carlos Santos		31/03/89	D	2		
20	Diego Lima	BRA	30/09/88	M	5	(2)	
15	Douglas Abner	BRA	30/01/96	M	5	(2)	1
4	Reuben Gabriel	NGA	05/06/90	M	17	(2)	1
12	Gideão	BRA	19/12/87	G	8		
14	Emmanuel Hackman	GHA	14/05/95	D	8	(4)	
2	Samuel Inkoom	GHA	01/06/89	D	8		
79	Imanol Iriberri	ARG	04/03/87	A	10	(5)	1
19	José Manuel		23/10/90	A	20	(11)	6
8	Leozinho	BRA	07/06/88	A	2	(1)	
77	Luisinho		27/03/90	A	21	(9)	2
42	Idrissa Mandiang	SEN	27/12/84	M	29	(1)	1
11	Mario Martínez	ESP	25/03/85	M	5	(8)	1
1	Mika		08/03/91	G	26		
23	Nuno Henrique		19/10/86	D	22		2
9	Uche Nwofor	NGA	03/02/90	A	1	(4)	1
9	Paulo Vinícius	BRA	12/08/84	D	32		2
94	Philipe Sampaio	BRA	11/11/94	D	12		
11	Christian Pouga	CMR	19/06/86	A		(1)	
17	Renato Santos		05/10/91	M	15	(10)	2
99	Rivaldinho	BRA	29/04/95	A		(1)	
7	Rúben Ribeiro		01/08/87	M	17		
3	Samu		21/04/86	M	1	(3)	
21	Aymen Tahar	ALG	02/10/89	M	9	(2)	
8	Tengarrinha		17/02/89	M	13	(2)	1
28	Tiago Mesquita		23/11/90	D	23		
75	Michael Uchebo	NGA	03/02/90	A	7	(9)	

SC Braga

1921 • Municipal de Braga (30,286) • scbraga.pt

Major honours
Portuguese Cup (2) 1966, 2016

Coach: Paulo Fonseca

2015
16/08	h	Nacional	W 2-1	Pedro Santos (p), Joan Román
21/08	a	Rio Ave	L 0-1	
30/08	h	Boavista	W 4-0	Vukčević 2, Crislan, Alan (p)
12/09	a	Estoril	L 0-1	
21/09	h	Marítimo	W 5-1	Stojiljković 2, Rafa Silva, Alan (p), Rui Fonte
27/09	a	Guimarães	W 1-0	Rafa Silva
04/10	h	Arouca	D 0-0	
25/10	a	Porto	D 0-0	
31/10	h	Belenenses	W 4-0	Hassan, Ricardo Ferreira, Stojiljković, Rafa Silva
09/11	a	União	W 1-0	Stojiljković
30/11	h	Benfica	L 0-2	
06/12	a	Moreirense	D 0-0	
13/12	a	Tondela	W 1-0	Stojiljković
21/12	h	Paços Ferreira	D 1-1	Stojiljković

2016
02/01	a	Setúbal	D 1-1	Marcelo Goiano
06/01	h	Académica	W 3-0	Hassan 2, Stojiljković
10/01	a	Sporting	L 2-3	Wilson Eduardo, Rafa Silva
17/01	a	Nacional	W 3-2	Boly, Pedro Santos, Stojiljković
24/01	h	Rio Ave	W 5-1	Hassan 2, Pedro Santos, Rafa Silva, Rui Fonte
31/01	a	Boavista	D 0-0	
08/02	h	Estoril	W 2-0	Rui Fonte, Hassan
14/02	a	Marítimo	W 3-1	Pedro Santos 2 (1p), Hassan
21/02	h	Guimarães	D 3-3	Pedro Santos, Rui Fonte, Hassan
27/02	a	Arouca	D 0-0	
06/03	a	Porto	W 3-1	Hassan, Rafa Silva, Alan
13/03	h	Belenenses	L 0-3	
20/03	h	União	W 2-0	Josué, Stojiljković
01/04	a	Benfica	L 1-5	Pedro Santos (p)
10/04	h	Moreirense	D 1-1	Boly
18/04	h	Tondela	W 3-0	Hassan, Stojiljković, Crislan
23/04	a	Paços Ferreira	L 0-1	
29/04	h	Setúbal	W 3-2	Rafa Silva 2, Josué (p)
07/05	a	Académica	D 0-0	
15/05	h	Sporting	L 0-2	

No	Name	Nat	DoB	Pos	Aps	(s)	Gls
14	Aarón Ñíguez	ESP	26/04/89	M	4	(8)	
75	Aderlan Santos	BRA	09/04/89	D	2		
30	Alan	BRA	19/09/79	M	13	(12)	3
4	Alef	BRA	28/01/95	M	1		
6	André Pinto		05/10/89	D	20	(2)	
32	Arghus	BRA	19/01/88	D	4	(4)	
15	Baiano	BRA	23/02/87	D	26		
5	Willy Boly	FRA	03/02/91	D	21	(1)	2
99	Carlos Fortes		09/11/94	A	1		
9	Crislan	BRA	13/03/92	A	6	(7)	2
16	Djavan	BRA	31/12/87	D	15		
21	Filipe Augusto	BRA	12/08/93	M	12	(3)	
20	Ahmed Hassan	EGY	05/03/93	A	16	(7)	10
10	Joan Román	ESP	18/05/93	A	2	(4)	1
27	Josué	BRA	19/09/90	M	10	(2)	2
1	Stanislav Kritsyuk	RUS	01/12/90	G	18		
8	Luíz Carlos	BRA	05/07/85	M	22	(5)	
28	Marafona		08/05/87	G	13		
87	Marcelo Goiano	BRA	13/10/87	D	22	(4)	1
92	Matheus	BRA	29/03/92	G	3		
63	Mauro	BRA	30/10/90	M	19	(2)	
4	Pedro Monteiro		30/01/94	D	1		
23	Pedro Santos	BRA	22/04/88	M	16	(7)	7
18	Rafa Silva		17/05/93	M	22	(8)	8
24	Ricardo Ferreira		25/11/92	D	21	(2)	1
25	Stian Ringstad	NOR	29/08/91	D	4	(3)	
11	Rodrigo Pinho	BRA	30/05/91	A	3		
17	Rui Fonte		23/04/90	A	11	(4)	4
19	Nikola Stojiljković	SRB	17/08/92	A	23	(8)	10
35	Nikola Vukčević	MNE	13/12/91	M	15	(3)	2
7	Wilson Eduardo		08/07/90	A	8	(5)	1

Estoril Praia

1939 • António Coimbra da Mota (5,015) •
estorilpraia.pt
Coach: Fabiano Soares (BRA)

2015
16/08	a	Benfica	L	0-4	
23/08	h	Moreirense	W	2-0	Gerso, Léo Bonatini
28/08	a	Porto	L	0-2	
12/09	h	Braga	W	1-0	Léo Bonatini
19/09	a	Tondela	W	1-0	Léo Bonatini
27/09	h	União	W	2-1	Léo Bonatini, Bruno César
02/10	a	Setúbal	L	0-1	
24/10	h	Rio Ave	D	2-2	Diego Carlos, Afonso Taira
31/10	a	Sporting	L	0-1	
06/11	a	Académica	D	1-1	Léo Bonatini
29/11	a	Paços Ferreira	L	0-2	
06/12	h	Nacional	D	1-1	Léo Bonatini
11/12	a	Boavista	D	1-1	Léo Bonatini
19/12	a	Guimarães	L	0-1	

2016
02/01	a	Marítimo	D	1-1	Léo Bonatini (p)
06/01	a	Arouca	L	0-1	
10/01	h	Belenenses	W	2-0	Anderson Luís, Léo Bonatini
16/01	h	Benfica	L	1-2	Léo Bonatini
23/01	a	Moreirense	W	3-1	Anderson Luís, Diogo Amado, Felipe Augusto
30/01	h	Porto	L	1-3	Diego Carlos
08/02	a	Braga	L	0-2	
14/02	h	Tondela	W	2-1	Mendy, og (Thicot)
19/02	a	União	D	1-1	Mendy
27/02	h	Setúbal	W	3-0	Léo Bonatini 3
07/03	a	Rio Ave	W	3-1	Mattheus 2, Léo Bonatini (p)
12/03	h	Sporting	L	1-2	Léo Bonatini
20/03	a	Académica	W	3-0	Mattheus 2, Gerso
02/04	a	Paços Ferreira	W	1-0	Diogo Amado
10/04	a	Nacional	L	1-4	Marion
16/04	h	Boavista	W	1-0	og (Paulo Vinícius)
24/04	a	Guimarães	D	1-1	Felipe Augusto
01/05	a	Marítimo	W	2-1	Léo Bonatini (p), Mendy
09/05	a	Arouca	D	1-1	Diakhité
14/05	a	Belenenses	L	1-2	Léo Bonatini

No	Name	Nat	DoB	Pos	Aps	(s)	Gls
6	Afonso Taira		17/06/92	M	28	(3)	1
5	Anderson Luís	BRA	31/07/88	D	33		2
55	Babanco	CPV	27/07/85	M	16	(3)	
20	Bruno César	BRA	03/11/88	M	9	(1)	1
4	Bruno Miguel		24/09/82	D		(1)	
91	Leandro Chaparro	ARG	07/01/91	M	13	(2)	
15	Oumar Diakhité	SEN	09/12/93	M	8	(3)	1
34	Diego Carlos	BRA	15/03/93	D	31		2
30	Dieguinho	BRA	07/06/92	M	6	(15)	
25	Diogo Amado		21/01/90	M	15	(1)	2
15	Anderson Esiti	NGA	24/05/94	M	14	(11)	
92	Felipe Augusto	BRA	06/03/92	A	4	(5)	2
12	Georgemy	BRA	15/08/95	G	3		
10	Gerso		23/02/91	M	30		2
1	Paweł Kieszek	POL	16/04/84	G	31		
3	Alex Kukuba	UGA	12/06/91	D		(1)	
9	Léo Bonatini	BRA	28/03/94	A	33		17
28	Luiz Phellype	BRA	27/09/93	A		(9)	
7	Mano		09/04/87	D	23		
22	Marion	BRA	07/09/91	A	6	(5)	1
93	Matheuzinho	BRA	21/02/93	M	2	(6)	
27	Mattheus	BRA	07/06/84	M	17	(4)	4
21	Fréderic Mendy	FRA	18/09/88	A	14	(1)	3
14	Michael	BRA	19/04/93	M		(14)	
26	Pedro Botelho	BRA	14/12/89	D	7	(4)	
19	Sebá	BRA	08/06/92	A	1		
8	Billal Sebaihi	FRA	31/05/92	M		(7)	
2	Yohan Tavares		02/03/88	D	30		

CS Marítimo

1910 • Barreiros (9,117) • csmaritimo.org.pt
**Coach: Ivo Vieira;
(19/01/16) Nelo Vingada**

2015
16/08	a	União	L	1-2	Dyego Sousa
22/08	h	Porto	D	1-1	Edgar Costa
31/08	a	Belenenses	D	1-1	Fransérgio
13/09	h	Setúbal	W	5-2	Rúben Ferreira, Dyego Sousa 2, Ghazaryan 2
21/09	a	Braga	L	1-5	Dyego Sousa
27/09	h	Tondela	W	1-0	Marega
03/10	a	Académica	L	0-1	
24/10	h	Paços Ferreira	L	0-2	
01/11	h	Boavista	W	1-0	Dyego Sousa
08/11	h	Rio Ave	W	3-2	Dyego Sousa, Raúl Silva, António Xavier
27/11	a	Nacional	L	1-3	Dirceu
05/12	h	Sporting	L	0-1	
12/12	a	Guimarães	W	4-3	Alex Soares, Marega, Edgar Costa, Fransérgio
19/12	a	Arouca	L	1-4	Dyego Sousa

2016
02/01	h	Estoril	D	1-1	Marega
06/01	a	Benfica	L	0-6	
10/01	h	Moreirense	W	5-1	Rúben Ferreira, Marega 2 (1p), Tiago Rodrigues, Baba Diawara
16/01	h	União	L	0-1	
24/01	a	Porto	L	0-1	
01/02	h	Belenenses	D	1-2	Dyego Sousa
06/02	a	Setúbal	D	1-1	Fransérgio (p)
14/02	h	Braga	L	1-3	Dyego Sousa
21/02	a	Tondela	W	4-3	Edgar Costa, Dyego Sousa, Dirceu, Baba Diawara
28/02	h	Académica	W	1-0	Baba Diawara
04/03	a	Paços Ferreira	D	2-2	João Diogo, Dyego Sousa
11/03	h	Boavista	L	0-3	
18/03	a	Rio Ave	L	0-1	
02/04	a	Nacional	W	2-0	Edgar Costa, Éber Bessa
09/04	a	Sporting	L	1-3	Ghazaryan
17/04	h	Guimarães	W	3-0	Fransérgio 2 (1p), Djoussé
24/04	a	Arouca	L	1-2	Dyego Sousa
01/05	a	Estoril	L	1-2	Plessis
08/05	h	Benfica	L	0-2	
15/05	a	Moreirense	L	1-2	Baba Diawara

No	Name	Nat	DoB	Pos	Aps	(s)	Gls
7	Alex Soares	BRA	01/03/91	M	21	(5)	1
50	António Xavier		06/07/92	A	3	(14)	1
90	Baba Diawara	SEN	05/01/88	A	4	(12)	4
21	Briguel		08/03/79	D	9	(1)	
4	Deyvison	BRA	18/10/88	D	12	(6)	
22	Ulysse Diallo	MLI	26/10/92	A	1	(5)	
3	Diney	BRA	17/01/95	D	1		
5	Dirceu	BRA	05/01/88	D	25	(1)	2
60	Donald Djoussé	CMR	18/03/90	A	7	(3)	1
9	Dyego Sousa	BRA	14/09/89	A	21	(7)	12
11	Éber Bessa	BRA	23/03/92	M	26	(4)	1
12	Edgar Costa		14/04/87	A	28	(1)	4
37	Fábio Abreu	ANG	29/01/93	M		(1)	
45	Fábio China		07/07/92	D	1		
14	Fernando Ferreira		20/11/86	M	3	(2)	
35	Fransérgio	BRA	18/10/90	M	30	(1)	5
10	Gevorg Ghazaryan	ARM	05/04/88	M	14	(8)	3
80	Alireza Haghighi	IRN	02/05/88	G	3	(1)	
2	João Diogo		28/02/88	D	26		1
91	José Sá		17/01/93	G	3	(2)	
99	Lynneeker	BRA	11/01/94	M	1	(2)	
42	Marcos Barbeiro	STP	29/07/95	A		(4)	
32	Moussa Marega	MLI	14/04/91	A	14	(1)	5
62	Maurício	BRA	06/02/92	D	12		
17	Gevaro Nepomuceno	CUW	10/11/92	A	3	(4)	
91	Patrick	BRA	22/01/91	D	27	(2)	
23	Damien Plessis	FRA	05/03/88	M	8	(1)	1
34	Raúl Silva	BRA	04/11/89	D	11	(1)	1
26	Romário Leiria	BRA	28/06/92	D	6	(3)	
41	Rúben Ferreira		17/02/90	D	14	(3)	2
78	Romain Salin	FRA	29/07/84	G	28		
29	Tiago Rodrigues		29/01/92	M	11	(7)	1
15	Lassina Touré	BFA	18/02/92	D	1		

Moreirense FC

1938 • Comendador Joaquim Almeida
Freitas (6,151) • moreirensefc.pt
Coach: Miguel Leal

2015
16/08	h	Arouca	L	0-2	
23/08	a	Estoril	L	0-2	
29/08	a	Benfica	L	2-3	Rafael Martins, Cardozo
13/09	h	União	D	0-0	
21/09	a	Belenenses	L	0-2	
25/09	h	Porto	D	2-2	Iuri Medeiros, André Fontes
03/10	a	Tondela	D	1-1	Rafael Martins
25/10	h	Setúbal	L	0-2	
01/11	a	Académica	L	1-1	Ença Fati
08/11	h	Paços Ferreira	W	2-0	Iuri Medeiros, Battaglia
29/11	h	Rio Ave	W	1-0	Iuri Medeiros
06/12	h	Braga	D	0-0	
13/12	a	Sporting	L	1-3	Rafael Martins (p)
20/12	h	Nacional	W	2-0	Rafael Martins 2

2016
02/01	a	Boavista	W	3-0	Iuri Medeiros, Rafael Martins, Vítor Gomes (p)
06/01	h	Guimarães	L	3-4	Rafael Martins (p), Boateng, Iuri Medeiros
10/01	a	Marítimo	L	1-5	Rafael Martins
17/01	a	Arouca	W	2-1	Sagna, Vítor Gomes
23/01	h	Estoril	L	1-3	Rafael Martins
31/01	h	Benfica	L	1-4	Iuri Medeiros
07/02	a	União	W	1-0	Rafael Martins
13/02	a	Belenenses	L	2-3	Rafael Martins 2
21/02	a	Porto	L	2-3	Iuri Medeiros, Fábio Espinho
28/02	h	Tondela	L	1-2	Rafael Martins
06/03	a	Setúbal	W	1-0	Nildo
13/03	h	Académica	D	2-2	Boateng, Rafael Martins (p)
20/03	a	Paços Ferreira	D	0-0	
02/04	h	Rio Ave	L	0-1	
10/04	a	Braga	D	1-1	Evaldo
16/04	h	Sporting	L	0-1	
24/04	a	Nacional	W	1-0	Vítor Gomes
01/05	h	Boavista	D	1-1	Iuri Medeiros
08/05	a	Guimarães	L	1-4	Fábio Espinho
15/05	h	Marítimo	W	2-1	Rafael Martins 2

No	Name	Nat	DoB	Pos	Aps	(s)	Gls
7	Alan Schons	BRA	24/05/93	M	5	(8)	
8	André Fontes		27/05/85	A	1	(5)	1
3	André Micael		04/02/89	D	19		
16	Rodrigo Battaglia	ARG	12/07/91	M	10		1
29	Emmanuel Boateng	GHA	23/05/96	A	5	(22)	2
9	Ramón Cardozo	PAR	21/04/86	A	2	(3)	1
2	Danielson	BRA	09/01/81	D	20		
17	Ença Fati		11/08/93	M	10	(8)	1
6	Evaldo	BRA	18/03/82	D	34		1
10	Fábio Espinho		18/08/85	M	13	(2)	2
66	Filipe Gonçalves		12/08/84	D	16	(9)	
14	Caleb Gomina	GHA	24/09/96	A		(1)	
4	Iuri Medeiros		10/07/94	A	29		8
60	João Palhinha		09/07/95	M	26	(3)	
13	João Sousa		16/05/94	D	1	(1)	
25	Luís Carlos	BRA	15/06/87	A	3	(12)	
26	Marcelo Oliveira	BRA	05/09/81	D	28	(1)	
1	Nildo	BRA	01/05/86	A	11	(1)	1
1	Nilson	BRA	26/12/75	G	2		
11	Ernest Ohemeng	GHA	17/01/96	A	10	(9)	
27	Patrick	CPV	09/02/93	M	2	(2)	
12	Pedro Coronas		19/09/90	M	12	(6)	
30	Rafa Sousa		26/06/88	M	2	(4)	
99	Rafael Martins	BRA	17/03/89	A	27		16
72	Ricardo Almeida		09/05/97	A		(1)	
95	Pierre Sagna	FRA	21/08/90	D	23	(3)	1
51	Igor Stefanović	SRB	17/07/87	G	31		
92	Victor Braga	BRA	17/02/92	G	1		
23	Vítor Gomes		25/12/87	M	31		3

 **PORTUGAL**

CD Nacional

1910 • Madeira (5,132) • cdnacional.pt
Coach: Manuel Machado

2015
16/08	a	Braga	L	1-2 *Francisco Soares*
23/08	h	União	W	1-0 *Francisco Soares*
30/08	a	Tondela	L	0-1
13/09	h	Académica	W	2-0 *Francisco Soares, Salvador Agra*
21/09	a	Sporting	L	0-1
27/09	h	Setúbal	D	1-1 *Rui Correia*
03/10	a	Paços Ferreira	L	1-3 *og (Bruno Moreira)*
23/10	h	Boavista	D	0-0
01/11	a	Rio Ave	L	0-1
07/11	a	Guimarães	W	1-0 *Francisco Soares*
27/11	h	Marítimo	W	3-1 *Nuno Sequeira, Rui Correia, Willyan*
06/12	a	Estoril	D	1-1 *Salvador Agra*
14/12	h	Porto	L	1-2 *Willyan*
20/12	a	Moreirense	L	0-2

2016
02/01	h	Arouca	D	2-2 *Salvador Agra, Luís Aurélio*
06/01	a	Belenenses	D	2-2 *Luís Aurélio, Fofana*
11/01	h	Benfica	L	1-4 *Francisco Soares*
17/01	h	Braga	L	2-3 *Willyan (p), Salvador Agra*
23/01	a	União	L	0-3
31/01	h	Tondela	W	3-1 *Rodrigo Pinho, Salvador Agra 2*
07/02	a	Académica	D	2-2 *og (Oualembo), og (Ricardo Nascimento)*
13/02	h	Sporting	L	0-4
21/02	a	Setúbal	D	1-1 *Francisco Soares*
26/02	h	Paços Ferreira	W	3-0 *og (Marco Baixinho), Rui Correia, Luís Aurélio*
06/03	a	Boavista	W	1-0 *Salvador Agra*
13/03	h	Rio Ave	W	1-0 *Ricardo Gomes*
20/03	a	Guimarães	W	3-2 *Rui Correia, Francisco Soares 2*
02/04	a	Marítimo	L	0-2
10/04	h	Estoril	W	4-1 *Francisco Soares, Salvador Agra, Nenê Bonilha, Witi*
17/04	a	Porto	L	0-4
24/04	h	Moreirense	L	0-2
01/05	a	Arouca	L	0-3
08/05	h	Belenenses	D	2-2 *Francisco Soares, Rui Correia*
15/05	a	Benfica	L	1-4 *Salvador Agra*

No	Name	Nat	DoB	Pos	Aps	(s)	Gls
4	Alan Henrique	BRA	19/06/91	D	5		
31	Hicham Belkaroui	ALG	24/08/90	D	10		
11	Camacho		23/06/94	M	4	(2)	
68	Edgar Abreu		16/02/94	M	2	(2)	
7	Boubacar Fofana	GUI	06/11/89	M	7	(8)	1
18	Francisco Soares	BRA	17/01/91	A	28	(2)	10
6	Ali Ghazal	EGY	01/02/92	M	27		
1	Gottardi	BRA	18/10/85	G	14		
8	Gustavo Henrique	BRA	29/03/94	A	2	(11)	
19	Joan Román	ESP	18/05/93	M		(6)	
2	João Aurélio		17/08/88	D	31		
20	Jota		07/03/93	M		(6)	
30	Luís Aurélio		17/08/88	M	11	(16)	3
55	Mauro Cerqueira		20/08/92	D	2		
3	Miguel Rodrigues		16/03/93	D	1	(1)	
8	Nenê Bonilha	BRA	17/02/92	A	17	(7)	1
22	Nuno Campos		13/06/93	D	9	(3)	
55	Nuno Sequeira		08/04/92	D	31		1
27	Ricardo Gomes	CPV	18/12/91	A	6	(9)	1
91	Rodrigo Pinho	BRA	30/05/91	A	2	(9)	1
33	Rui Correia		23/08/90	D	32		5
12	Rui Silva		07/02/94	G	20	(2)	
7	Salvador Agra		11/11/91	A	33	(1)	9
11	Wanderson	BRA	31/05/92	A	1		
89	Washington	BRA	20/01/89	M	29	(3)	
28	Willyan	BRA	17/02/94	M	16	(6)	3
81	Witi	MOZ	26/08/96	M	13	(5)	1
3	Zainadine Júnior	MOZ	24/06/88	D	20		
10	Zezinho	BRA	14/03/92	M	1		

FC Paços de Ferreira
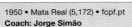

1950 • Mata Real (5,172) • fcpf.pt
Coach: Jorge Simão

2015
17/08	h	Académica	W	1-0 *Roniel*
23/08	h	Sporting	D	1-1 *Pelé (p)*
30/08	h	Arouca	D	1-1 *Bruno Moreira*
14/09	a	Boavista	W	1-0 *Diogo Jota*
19/09	h	Rio Ave	L	0-3
26/09	h	Benfica	L	0-3
03/10	h	Nacional	W	3-1 *Bruno Moreira 2, Pelé (p)*
24/10	a	Marítimo	W	2-0 *Osei, Diogo Jota*
02/11	a	Guimarães	L	0-1
08/11	a	Moreirense	L	0-2
29/11	h	Estoril	W	2-0 *Diogo Jota, Bruno Moreira*
05/12	a	Porto	L	1-2 *Bruno Moreira*
12/12	h	União	W	6-0 *Romeu, Bruno Moreira 2 (1p), Andrézinho, Christian, Diogo Jota*
21/12	a	Braga	D	1-1 *Pelé (p)*

2016
02/01	h	Belenenses	D	2-2 *Bruno Moreira (p), Andrézinho*
06/01	a	Tondela	W	2-0 *Bruno Moreira, Diogo Jota*
11/01	h	Setúbal	W	2-1 *Bruno Moreira 2 (1p)*
16/01	a	Académica	D	1-1 *Diogo Jota*
23/01	h	Sporting	L	1-3 *Bruno Moreira*
31/01	a	Arouca	D	2-2 *Bruno Moreira, Roniel*
07/02	h	Boavista	L	0-1
15/02	a	Rio Ave	D	1-1 *Bruno Moreira (p)*
20/02	h	Benfica	L	1-3 *Diogo Jota*
26/02	a	Nacional	L	0-3
04/03	h	Marítimo	D	2-2 *Diogo Jota 2*
13/03	a	Guimarães	W	1-0 *Fábio Cardoso*
20/03	h	Moreirense	D	0-0
02/04	a	Estoril	L	0-1
10/04	h	Porto	W	1-0 *Diogo Jota*
17/04	a	União	W	4-3 *Minhoca, Cícero, Paulo Henrique, Diogo Jota*
23/04	h	Braga	W	1-0 *Diogo Jota*
30/04	a	Belenenses	W	2-0 *Osei, Pelé*
06/05	h	Tondela	L	1-4 *Minhoca*
14/05	a	Setúbal	D	0-0

No	Name	Nat	DoB	Pos	Aps	(s)	Gls
20	Andrézinho		06/08/95	M	24	(4)	2
11	Bruno Moreira		06/09/87	A	26	(3)	14
94	Bruno Santos		07/02/93	D	15		
14	Carlos Ponck	CPV	13/01/95	M	3	(5)	
8	Christian	BRA	14/06/89	M	11	(6)	1
9	Cícero	GNB	08/05/86	A	5	(10)	1
18	Diogo Jota		04/12/96	M	31		12
12	Edson Farias	BRA	12/01/92	A	11	(14)	
37	Edu Pinheiro		08/01/97	M	1		
6	Fábio Cardoso		19/04/94	D	21	(2)	1
47	Fábio Martins		24/07/93	A	6	(11)	
33	Francisco Afonso		24/04/97	D	2		
5	Hélder Lopes		04/01/89	D	31		
13	João Gois		05/05/90	D	18		
21	João Silva		21/05/90	A	3	(9)	
81	Manuel José		04/02/81	M	4	(7)	
28	Marafona		08/05/87	G	19		
2	Marco Baixinho		11/07/89	D	21		
22	Miguel Vieira		08/10/90	D	8	(1)	
10	Minhoca		29/04/89	A	6	(5)	2
16	Barnes Osei	GHA	08/05/91	A	11	(8)	2
23	Paulo Henrique		23/10/96	D	2		1
25	Pelé		29/09/91	M	26	(3)	4
1	Rafael Defendi	BRA	22/12/83	G	15		
19	Ricardo	CPV	19/08/80	D	23		
27	Rodrigo Antônio	BRA	07/07/87	M	8	(2)	
4	Romeu		17/02/86	M	15		1
7	Roniel	BRA	02/06/84	A	8	(11)	2

FC Porto

1893 • Dragão (50,476) • fcporto.pt
Major honours
European Champion Clubs' Cup/UEFA Champions League (2) 1987, 2004; UEFA Cup (1) 2003; UEFA Europa League (1) 2011; UEFA Super Cup (1) 1987; European/South American Cup (2) 1987, 2004; Portuguese League (27) 1935, 1939, 1940, 1956, 1959, 1978, 1979, 1985, 1986, 1988, 1990, 1992, 1993, 1995, 1996, 1997, 1998, 1999, 2003, 2004, 2006, 2007, 2008, 2009, 2011, 2012, 2013; Portuguese Cup (16) 1956, 1958, 1968, 1977, 1984, 1988, 1991, 1994, 1998, 2000, 2001, 2003, 2006, 2009, 2010, 2011

Coach: Julen Lopetegui (ESP); (08/01/16) (Rui Barros); (21/01/16) José Peseiro

2015
15/08	h	Guimarães	W	3-0 *Aboubakar 2, Varela*
22/08	a	Marítimo	D	1-1 *Herrera*
29/08	h	Estoril	W	2-0 *Aboubakar, Maicon*
12/09	a	Arouca	W	3-1 *Corona 2, Aboubakar*
20/09	h	Benfica	W	1-0 *André André*
25/09	h	Moreirense	D	2-2 *Maicon, Corona*
04/10	h	Belenenses	W	4-0 *Corona, Brahimi, Osvaldo, Marcano*
25/10	h	Braga	D	0-0
08/11	h	Setúbal	W	2-0 *Aboubakar, Layún*
28/11	h	Tondela	W	1-0 *Brahimi*
02/12	a	União	W	4-0 *Herrera, Brahimi, Corona, Danilo Pereira*
05/12	h	Paços Ferreira	W	2-1 *Corona, Layún*
14/12	a	Nacional	W	2-1 *Marcano, Brahimi*
20/12	a	Académica	W	3-1 *Danilo Pereira, Herrera, Aboubakar*

2016
02/01	a	Sporting	L	0-2
06/01	h	Rio Ave	D	1-1 *Herrera*
10/01	a	Boavista	W	5-0 *Herrera, Corona, Aboubakar 2, Danilo Pereira*
17/01	a	Guimarães	L	0-1
24/01	h	Marítimo	W	1-0 *og (Salin)*
30/01	a	Estoril	W	3-1 *Aboubakar, Danilo Pereira, André André*
07/02	h	Arouca	D	1-2 *Aboubakar*
12/02	a	Benfica	W	2-1 *Herrera, Aboubakar*
21/02	a	Moreirense	W	3-2 *Layún (p), Suk, Evandro*
28/02	a	Belenenses	W	2-1 *Brahimi, og (Tonel)*
06/03	a	Braga	L	1-3 *Maxi Pereira*
12/03	h	União	W	3-2 *Aboubakar, Herrera, Corona*
19/03	a	Setúbal	W	1-0 *Sérgio Oliveira*
03/04	h	Tondela	L	0-1
10/04	a	Paços Ferreira	L	0-1
17/04	h	Nacional	W	4-0 *Varela, Herrera, Danilo Pereira, Aboubakar*
23/04	a	Académica	W	2-1 *Rúben Neves, Brahimi*
30/04	a	Sporting	L	1-3 *Herrera (p)*
07/05	a	Rio Ave	W	3-1 *Layún (p), Sérgio Oliveira, Varela*
14/05	h	Boavista	W	4-0 *Danilo Pereira, Layún, Brahimi (p), André Silva*

No	Name	Nat	DoB	Pos	Aps	(s)	Gls
9	Vincent Aboubakar	CMR	22/01/92	A	24	(4)	13
26	Alex Sandro	BRA	26/01/91	D	1		
20	André André		26/08/89	M	20	(7)	2
19	André Silva		06/11/95	A	4	(5)	1
63	Chidozie Awaziem	NGA	01/01/97	D	10		
8	Yacine Brahimi	ALG	08/02/90	M	29	(4)	7
23	Alberto Bueno	ESP	20/03/88	A	1	(3)	
12	Iker Casillas	ESP	20/05/81	G	32		
28	Aly Cissokho	FRA	15/09/87	D	2		
17	Jesús Corona	MEX	06/01/93	A	26	(2)	8
22	Danilo Pereira		09/09/91	M	28	(5)	6
15	Evandro	BRA	23/08/86	M	1	(10)	1
48	Francisco Ramos		10/04/95	M		(3)	
1	Helton	BRA	18/05/78	G	2		
16	Héctor Herrera	MEX	19/04/90	M	27	(2)	9
25	Giannelli Imbula	FRA	12/09/92	M	7	(3)	
14	José Angel	ESP	05/09/89	D	6	(1)	
7	Miguel Layún	MEX	25/06/88	D	27		5
4	Maicon	BRA	14/09/88	D	11	(3)	2
5	Iván Marcano	ESP	23/06/87	D	22		2
9	Moussa Marega	MLI	14/04/91	A		(9)	
3	Bruno Martins Indi	NED	08/02/92	D	23		
2	Maxi Pereira	URU	08/06/84	D	32		1
10	Pablo Osvaldo	ITA	12/01/86	A	2	(5)	1
6	Rúben Neves		13/03/97	M	13	(9)	1
13	Sérgio Oliveira		02/06/92	M	8	(1)	2
39	Suk Hyun-jun	KOR	29/06/91	A	4	(5)	1
11	Cristian Tello	ESP	11/08/91	A	4	(7)	
7	Silvestre Varela		02/02/85	A	8	(14)	3

Rio Ave FC

1939 • Rio Ave (12,815) • rioavefc.pt
Coach: Pedro Martins

2015

15/08	a	Belenenses	D	3-3	Renan Bressan, og (Gonçalo Brandão), Guedes
21/08	h	Braga	W	1-0	Hassan
29/08	a	Setúbal	D	2-2	Yazalde, André Vilas Boas
13/09	h	Sporting	L	1-2	Yazalde
19/09	a	Paços Ferreira	W	3-0	Héldon 2, Edimar
28/09	h	Académica	W	1-0	Renan Bressan
03/10	a	Boavista	W	1-0	Renan Bressan
24/10	a	Estoril	D	2-2	Zeegelaar, Guedes
01/11	h	Nacional	W	1-0	Zeegelaar
08/11	a	Marítimo	L	2-3	Zeegelaar, Guedes
29/11	h	Moreirense	L	0-1	
07/12	a	Guimarães	L	1-3	Renan Bressan
12/12	h	Arouca	W	3-1	og (Gegé), Marcelo, João Novais
20/12	a	Benfica	L	1-3	Renan Bressan

2016

03/01	h	Tondela	L	2-3	Tarantini, Héldon
06/01	a	Porto	D	1-1	João Novais
10/01	h	União	W	1-0	Guedes
17/01	h	Belenenses	L	1-2	Ukra
24/01	a	Braga	L	1-5	Kayembe
31/01	h	Setúbal	W	2-1	Marcelo, Tarantini
08/02	a	Sporting	D	0-0	
15/02	h	Paços Ferreira	D	1-1	Kuca
20/02	a	Académica	W	2-0	Kuca, Yazalde
27/02	a	Boavista	W	2-1	Hélder Postiga, Kayembe
07/03	h	Estoril	L	1-3	Hélder Postiga
13/03	a	Nacional	L	0-1	
18/03	h	Marítimo	W	1-0	Roderick
02/04	a	Moreirense	W	1-0	Guedes
11/04	h	Guimarães	W	2-0	Guedes, Héldon (p)
16/04	a	Arouca	D	0-0	
24/04	h	Benfica	L	0-1	
30/04	a	Tondela	D	1-1	Hélder Postiga
07/05	h	Porto	L	1-3	Hélder Postiga
14/05	a	União	W	2-1	Renan Bressan, Hélder Postiga

No	Name	Nat	DoB	Pos	Aps	(s)	Gls
14	André Vilas Boas		04/06/83	D	4	(5)	1
3	Aníbal Capela		08/05/91	D	11		
1	Cássio	BRA	12/08/90	G	32		
16	Edimar	BRA	21/05/86	D	26		1
5	Filipe Augusto	BRA	12/08/93	M	1	(1)	
7	Guedes		07/05/87	A	16	(10)	6
9	Ahmed Hassan	EGY	05/03/93	A	2		1
9	Hélder Postiga		02/08/82	A	4	(6)	5
24	Héldon	CPV	14/11/88	A	17	(7)	4
70	Jaime Pinto		28/08/97	M		(2)	
27	João Novais		10/07/93	M	7	(9)	2
89	José Pedro		08/07/92	A		(1)	
77	Joris Kayembe	BEL	08/08/94	M	11	(15)	2
19	William Kizito	UGA	20/12/93	A	1	(1)	
23	Filip Krovinović	CRO	29/08/95	M	4	(5)	
10	Kuca	CPV	02/08/89	A	11	(1)	2
12	Lionn	BRA	29/01/89	D	27	(1)	
46	Marcelo	BRA	27/07/89	D	25		2
44	Nélson Monte		30/07/95	D	10	(2)	
26	Pedrinho		06/03/85	D	10	(2)	
20	Pedro Moreira		15/03/89	M	15	(2)	
11	Renan Bressan	BLR	03/11/88	M	21	(3)	6
25	Roderick		30/03/91	D	18		1
99	Ronan	BRA	22/04/95	A		(2)	
71	Rui Vieira		13/11/91	G	2	(1)	
8	Tarantini		07/10/83	M	25		2
17	Ukra		16/03/88	A	19	(7)	1
30	Alhassan Wakaso	GHA	07/01/92	M	29	(1)	
88	Yazalde		10/09/88	A	14	(13)	3
29	Zé Paulo	BRA	26/03/94	M		(3)	
21	Marvin Zeegelaar	NED	12/08/90	D	12		3

Sporting Clube de Portugal

1906 • José Alvalade (50,466) • sporting.pt

Major honours
UEFA Cup Winners' Cup (1) 1964; Portuguese League (18) 1941, 1944, 1947, 1948, 1949, 1951, 1952, 1953, 1954, 1958, 1962, 1966, 1970, 1974, 1980, 1982, 2000, 2002; Portuguese Cup (16) 1941, 1945, 1946, 1948, 1954, 1963, 1971, 1973, 1974, 1978, 1982, 1995, 2002, 2007, 2008, 2015
Coach: Jorge Jesus

2015

14/08	a	Tondela	W	2-1	João Mário, Adrien Silva (p)
22/08	h	Paços Ferreira	D	1-1	Carrillo
30/08	a	Académica	W	3-1	Carlos Mané, Slimani, Aquilani (p)
13/09	a	Rio Ave	W	2-1	Adrien Silva (p), Slimani
21/09	h	Nacional	W	1-0	Montero
26/09	a	Boavista	D	0-0	
04/10	h	Guimarães	W	5-1	Slimani 3, Gutiérrez, Adrien Silva
25/10	a	Benfica	W	3-0	Gutiérrez, Slimani, Ruiz
31/10	h	Estoril	W	1-0	Gutiérrez (p)
08/11	a	Arouca	W	1-0	Slimani
30/11	h	Belenenses	W	1-0	William Carvalho (p)
05/12	a	Marítimo	W	1-0	Adrien Silva
13/12	h	Moreirense	W	3-1	Gelson Martins, Aquilani, Slimani
20/12	a	União	L	0-1	

2016

02/01	h	Porto	W	2-0	Slimani 2
06/01	a	Setúbal	W	6-0	Slimani 2, Bruno César 2, João Mário, Aquilani
10/01	h	Braga	W	3-2	Adrien Silva (p), Montero, Slimani
15/01	h	Tondela	D	2-2	Slimani, Gelson Martins
23/01	a	Paços Ferreira	W	3-1	Bruno César, Slimani 2
30/01	a	Académica	W	3-2	Adrien Silva, Ruiz, Montero
08/02	h	Rio Ave	D	0-0	
13/02	a	Nacional	W	4-0	Slimani 2 (1p), Adrien Silva (p), João Mário
22/02	h	Boavista	W	2-0	Ewerton, Ruiz
29/02	a	Guimarães	D	0-0	
05/03	h	Benfica	L	0-1	
12/03	a	Estoril	W	2-1	Slimani 2
19/03	h	Arouca	W	5-1	Gutiérrez 2, João Mário 2, Ruiz
03/04	a	Belenenses	W	5-2	Slimani 2 (1p), Gutiérrez 2, Adrien Silva
09/04	h	Marítimo	W	3-1	Gutiérrez, Slimani, William Carvalho
16/04	a	Moreirense	W	1-0	Slimani
23/04	h	União	W	2-0	Gutiérrez, João Mário
30/04	a	Porto	W	3-1	Slimani 2, Bruno César
07/05	h	Setúbal	W	5-0	Gelson Martins 2, Gutiérrez, Ruiz 2
15/05	a	Braga	W	4-0	Gutiérrez, Slimani, Ruiz 2

No	Name	Nat	DoB	Pos	Aps	(s)	Gls
23	Adrien Silva		15/03/89	M	28	(1)	8
28	André Martins		21/01/90	M	1		
6	Alberto Aquilani	ITA	07/07/84	M	5	(14)	3
29	Hernán Barcos	ARG	11/04/84	A		(8)	
11	Bruno César	BRA	03/11/88	M	13	(3)	4
30	Bruno Paulista	BRA	21/08/95	M		(1)	
36	Carlos Mané		11/03/94	M	2	(9)	1
18	André Carrillo	PER	14/06/91	A	4		1
13	Sebastián Coates	URU	07/10/90	D	13		
5	Ewerton	BRA	23/03/89	D	7	(1)	1
60	Gelson Martins		11/05/95	M	10	(19)	4
10	Teófilo Gutiérrez	COL	17/05/85	A	20	(3)	11
4	Jefferson	BRA	05/07/88	D	18		
17	João Mário		19/01/93	M	31	(2)	6
21	João Pereira		25/02/84	D	17	(2)	
22	Marcelo	BRA	28/11/84	G		(1)	
73	Matheus Pereira	BRA	05/05/96	A	1	(7)	
10	Fredy Montero	COL	26/07/87	A	5	(7)	3
44	Naldo	BRA	25/08/88	D	17	(1)	
15	Paulo Oliveira		08/01/92	D	17	(2)	
47	Ricardo Esgaio		16/05/93	D	6	(2)	
35	Rúben Semedo		04/04/94	D	13	(1)	
1	Rui Patrício		15/02/88	G	34		
20	Bryan Ruiz	CRC	18/08/85	A	32	(2)	8
77	Ezequiel Schelotto	ITA	23/05/89	M	11	(3)	
3	Jonathan Silva	ARG	29/06/94	D	2	(2)	
9	Islam Slimani	ALG	18/06/88	A	33		27
8	Junya Tanaka	JPN	15/07/87	A		(3)	
55	Tobias Figueiredo		02/02/94	D	1		
14	William Carvalho		07/04/92	M	25	(1)	2
31	Marvin Zeegelaar	NED	12/08/90	D	9	(1)	

CD Tondela

1933 • João Cardoso (2,674); Municipal, Aveiro (30,498) • cdtondela.pt

Coach: Vítor Paneira; (06/10/15) Rui Bento; (09/12/15) Petit

2015

14/08	h	Sporting	L	1-2	Luís Alberto
23/08	a	Boavista	L	0-1	
30/08	h	Nacional	W	1-0	Kaká
13/09	a	Guimarães	L	0-1	
19/09	h	Estoril	L	0-1	
27/09	a	Marítimo	L	0-1	
03/10	h	Moreirense	D	1-1	Romário Baldé
25/10	a	Arouca	D	1-1	Romário Baldé
30/10	h	Benfica	L	0-4	
09/11	a	Belenenses	L	1-2	Piojo
28/11	h	Porto	L	0-2	
06/12	a	União	L	0-1	
13/12	h	Braga	L	0-1	
20/12	a	Setúbal	L	1-3	Nathan Júnior

2016

03/01	a	Rio Ave	W	3-2	Murillo, Wagner, Nathan Júnior
06/01	h	Paços Ferreira	L	0-2	
10/01	a	Académica	L	1-2	Murillo
15/01	a	Sporting	D	2-2	Nathan Júnior (p), Salva Chamorro
25/01	h	Boavista	L	1-2	Nathan Júnior (p)
31/01	a	Nacional	L	0-1	Murillo
06/02	h	Guimarães	D	1-1	Nathan Júnior
14/02	a	Estoril	L	1-2	Nathan Júnior (p)
21/02	h	Marítimo	L	3-4	Nathan Júnior 2, Moreno
28/02	a	Moreirense	W	2-1	Nathan Júnior, og (Rafael Martins)
06/03	a	Arouca	L	0-1	
14/03	h	Benfica	L	1-4	Nathan Júnior
20/03	h	Belenenses	D	2-2	Nathan Júnior (p), Pica
03/04	a	Porto	W	1-0	Luís Alberto
10/04	h	União	W	1-0	Pica
18/04	a	Braga	L	0-3	
24/04	a	Setúbal	W	1-0	Pica
30/04	h	Rio Ave	D	1-1	Wagner
06/05	a	Paços Ferreira	W	4-1	Nathan Júnior 2, Lucas Souza 2
14/05	h	Académica	W	2-0	Pica, Luís Alberto

No	Name	Nat	DoB	Pos	Aps	(s)	Gls
5	Markus Berger	AUT	21/01/85	D	2	(1)	
27	Bruno Monteiro		05/10/84	M	17	(7)	
14	Bruno Nascimento	BRA	30/05/91	D	24		
1	Cláudio Ramos		16/11/91	G	19	(1)	
70	Dolly Menga	ANG	02/05/93	A	10	(15)	
21	Edu Machado		26/04/90	D	11		
41	Hélder Tavares		26/12/89	M	27	(3)	
8	João Jaquité	GNB	22/02/86	M	1		
12	Matt Jones	ENG	11/05/86	G	10		
4	Kaká	BRA	16/05/81	D	20		1
77	Karl	BRA	07/04/93	M	5	(2)	
6	Lucas Souza	BRA	04/06/90	M	26		2
20	Luís Alberto	BRA	17/11/83	M	17	(5)	3
7	Luís Machado		04/11/92	M	5	(1)	
24	Luís Tinoco		17/10/86	D	11		
16	Erick Moreno	COL	24/11/91	A	4	(7)	1
77	Jhon Murillo	VEN	04/06/95	A	15	(7)	3
11	Nathan Júnior	BRA	10/03/89	A	32	(2)	13
17	Nuno Santos		19/06/80	D	20	(5)	
42	Junior Oto'o	GAB	23/05/94	D	18	(1)	
3	Pica		08/09/86	D	9	(1)	4
9	Cristian Amado "Piojo"	ARG	07/06/85	A	3	(11)	1
86	Raphael Guzzo	BRA	06/01/95	A	11	5	
14	Romário Baldé		25/12/96	A	16	(8)	2
89	Salva Chamorro	ESP	08/05/90	A	1	(6)	1
14	Steven Thicot	FRA	14/02/87	D	13	(3)	
28	Wagner	BRA	03/04/87	M	15	(8)	2
48	Wanderson	BRA	09/02/95	M	7		
13	Eñaut Zubikarai	ESP	26/02/84	G	5		

CF União da Madeira

1913 • Centro Desportivo da Madeira (2,500);
Madeira (5,132) • uniaodamadeira.com
Coach: Luís Norton de Matos

2015

16/08	h	Marítimo	W	2-1	Breitner, Élio Martins
23/08	a	Nacional	L	0-1	
31/08	h	Guimarães	D	0-0	
13/09	a	Moreirense	D	0-0	
20/09	h	Arouca	D	0-0	
27/09	a	Estoril	L	1-2	Farías
26/10	a	Belenenses	L	0-1	
09/11	h	Braga	L	0-1	
28/11	h	Setúbal	D	2-2	Danilo Dias, Amílton
02/12	h	Porto	L	0-4	
06/12	a	Tondela	W	2-0	Danilo Dias, Cádiz
12/12	a	Paços Ferreira	L	0-6	
15/12	h	Benfica	D	0-0	
20/12	h	Sporting	W	1-0	Danilo Dias

2016

02/01	a	Académica	L	1-3	Paulo Monteiro (p)
06/01	h	Boavista	W	1-0	Toni Silva
10/01	a	Rio Ave	L	0-1	
16/01	h	Marítimo	W	1-0	Cádiz
23/01	h	Nacional	W	3-0	Shehu, Toni Silva 2
29/01	a	Guimarães	L	1-3	Danilo Dias
07/02	h	Moreirense	L	0-1	
14/02	a	Arouca	L	0-3	
19/02	h	Estoril	D	1-1	Danilo Dias
29/02	a	Benfica	L	0-2	
06/03	h	Belenenses	D	0-0	
12/03	a	Porto	L	2-3	Danilo Dias 2
20/03	a	Braga	L	0-1	
03/04	h	Setúbal	D	2-2	Amílton 2
10/04	a	Tondela	L	0-1	
17/04	h	Paços Ferreira	L	3-4	Élio Martins, Breitner, Amílton
23/04	a	Sporting	L	0-2	
01/05	h	Académica	W	3-1	Élio Martins 2, Gian Martins
08/05	a	Boavista	L	0-1	
14/05	h	Rio Ave	L	1-2	Amílton

No	Name	Nat	DoB	Pos	Aps	(s)	Gls
23	Amílton	BRA	12/08/89	M	30	(1)	5
95	André Moreira		02/12/95	G	19		
10	Breitner	BRA	09/09/89	M	17	(10)	2
11	Gonzalo Bueno	URU	16/01/93	A		(1)	
18	Jhonder Cádiz	VEN	29/07/95	A	12	(11)	2
1	Carlos Manuel		24/11/85	D	1	(2)	
5	Danilo Dias	BRA	06/11/85	M	21	(9)	7
44	Diego Galo	BRA	14/01/84	D	34		
17	Diogo Firmino		14/03/96	A		(1)	
29	Élio Martins		26/03/85	M	14	(6)	4
27	Edder Farías	VEN	12/04/88	A	7	(5)	1
88	Gian Martins	BRA	02/04/93	M	23	(2)	1
71	Raúlm Gudiño	MEX	22/04/96	G	11		
5	Joãozinho		02/07/88	D	29		
90	Kisley	CPV	22/11/90	A	2	(2)	
21	Kusunga	ANG	12/03/88	D	1	(3)	
28	Marco Túlio	BRA	30/03/92	M		(1)	
25	Miguel Cardoso		19/06/94	M	2	(7)	
9	Miguel Fidalgo		19/03/82	A	1	(14)	
1	Nilson	CPV	05/08/87	D	1		
2	Paulinho		13/07/91	D	33		
37	Paulo Monteiro		21/01/85	D	33		1
21	Rafael Alves		04/01/94	G	2		
1	Ricardo Campos	MOZ	14/07/85	G	1		
7	Rúben Andrade		07/06/82	M	6	(9)	
19	Rúben Lima		03/10/89	D	2		
14	Abdullahi Shehu	NGA	12/03/93	M	26	(2)	1
7	Tiago Ferreira		10/07/93	D	4	(3)	
20	Toni Silva		15/09/93	M	12	(2)	3
1	Renny Vega	VEN	04/07/79	G	1		
3	William Soares	BRA	30/12/88	M	29		
30	Kheireddine Zarabi	ALG	08/07/84	D		(3)	

Vitória FC (Setúbal)

1910 • Bonfim (18,694) • vfc.pt
Major honours
Portuguese Cup (3) 1965, 1967, 2005
Coach: Quim Machado

2015

16/08	h	Boavista	D	2-2	André Claro, Ruca
24/08	a	Académica	W	4-0	Suk 2, André Claro, Costinha
29/08	h	Rio Ave	D	2-2	André Claro (p), Suk
13/09	a	Marítimo	L	2-5	Costinha, Suk
18/09	h	Guimarães	D	2-2	Issoko 2
27/09	a	Nacional	D	1-1	Suk
02/10	h	Estoril	W	1-0	André Claro
25/10	a	Moreirense	W	2-0	André Claro, Fábio Pacheco
01/11	h	Arouca	D	0-0	
08/11	a	Porto	L	0-2	
28/11	a	União	D	2-2	Issoko 2
05/12	h	Belenenses	W	3-0	Suk 2, André Horta
12/12	h	Benfica	L	2-4	Vasco Costa, Suk
20/12	a	Tondela	W	3-1	André Claro 2 (1p), André Horta

2016

02/01	h	Braga	D	1-1	Suk
06/01	h	Sporting	L	0-6	
11/01	a	Paços Ferreira	L	1-2	André Claro
18/01	h	Boavista	L	0-4	
22/01	h	Académica	W	2-1	Mohcine Hassan, Issoko
31/01	a	Rio Ave	L	1-2	Costinha
06/02	h	Marítimo	D	1-1	André Claro
13/02	a	Guimarães	D	2-2	André Claro, Cissé
21/02	h	Nacional	D	1-1	André Claro
27/02	a	Estoril	L	0-3	
06/03	h	Moreirense	L	0-1	
13/03	a	Arouca	L	0-1	
19/03	h	Porto	L	0-1	
03/04	h	União	D	2-2	Cissé, Vasco Costa
10/04	h	Belenenses	L	0-1	
18/04	a	Benfica	L	1-2	André Claro
24/04	h	Tondela	L	0-1	
29/04	a	Braga	L	2-3	Vasco Costa, Costinha
07/05	a	Sporting	L	0-5	
14/05	h	Paços Ferreira	D	0-0	

No	Name	Nat	DoB	Pos	Aps	(s)	Gls
18	André Claro		31/03/91	A	32	(2)	12
90	André Horta		07/11/96	M	21	(11)	2
92	Salim Cissé	GUI	24/12/92	A	8	(1)	2
11	Costinha		28/05/92	M	21	(7)	4
66	Dani		30/01/82	M	15	(10)	
14	Ulises Dávila	MEX	13/04/91	A		(3)	
6	Fábio Pacheco		26/05/88	M	28	(1)	1
20	Toni Gorupec	CRO	04/07/93	D	10	(3)	
19	Arnold Issoko	COD	06/04/92	A	21	(9)	5
17	Maciej Makuszewski	POL	29/09/89	M	8	(6)	
14	Shaher Mansour	KSA	29/04/92	M		(1)	
30	Albert Meyong	CMR	19/10/80	A	7	(7)	
44	Miguel Lourenço		27/05/92	D	7	(6)	
9	Mohcine Hassan		30/09/94	A	4	(8)	1
21	Nuno Pinto		06/08/86	D	28		
8	Paulo Tavares		09/12/85	M	12	(8)	
1	Lukas Raeder	GER	30/12/93	G	10		
82	Ricardo		06/12/86	G	24		
35	Rúben Semedo		04/04/94	D	13	(2)	
90	Ruca		11/09/90	D	20	(3)	1
40	François Sene	SEN	30/11/89	D	1		
39	Suk Hyun-jun	KOR	29/06/91	A	16		9
2	Tiago Valente		24/04/85	D	7		
23	Vasco Costa		08/08/91	M	9	(7)	3
3	Venâncio		04/02/93	D	31		
22	William Alves	BRA	29/04/87	D	28	(1)	
87	Zéquinha		07/01/87	A		(1)	

Vitória SC (Guimarães)

1922 • D. Afonso Henriques (30,146) • vitoriasc.pt
Major honours
Portuguese Cup (1) 2013
**Coach: Armando Evangelista;
(23/09/15) Sérgio Conceição**

2015

15/08	a	Porto	L	0-3	
23/08	h	Belenenses	D	1-1	Ricardo Valente
31/08	a	União	D	0-0	
13/09	h	Tondela	W	1-0	og (Edu Machado)
18/09	a	Setúbal	D	2-2	Henrique Dourado (p), og (Rúben Semedo)
27/09	h	Braga	L	0-1	
04/10	a	Sporting	L	1-5	Josué Sá
24/10	a	Académica	D	1-1	Tómané
02/11	a	Paços Ferreira	W	1-0	Ricardo Valente
07/11	h	Nacional	L	0-1	
28/11	h	Boavista	W	2-1	Henrique Dourado, Cafú
07/12	h	Rio Ave	W	3-1	Henrique Dourado 2, Alex Silva
12/12	h	Marítimo	L	3-4	Ricardo Valente, Cafú, Otávio (p)
19/12	a	Estoril	W	1-0	Otávio

2016

02/01	h	Benfica	L	0-1	
06/01	h	Moreirense	W	4-3	Ricardo Valente, Henrique Dourado 2, Luís Rocha
09/01	h	Arouca	D	2-2	Saré, Otávio
17/01	h	Porto	W	1-0	Saré
24/01	a	Belenenses	D	3-3	Saré, og (Filipe Ferreira), Henrique Dourado
29/01	h	União	W	3-1	Licá, Henrique Dourado, Otávio
06/02	a	Tondela	D	1-1	Licá
13/02	h	Setúbal	D	2-2	Josué Sá, Otávio
21/02	a	Braga	D	3-3	Licá, Henrique Dourado, Otávio (p)
29/02	h	Sporting	D	0-0	
06/03	a	Académica	L	0-2	
13/03	a	Paços Ferreira	L	0-1	
20/03	a	Nacional	L	2-3	Licá, Henrique Dourado (p)
02/04	h	Boavista	D	1-1	Ricardo Valente
11/04	a	Rio Ave	L	0-2	
17/04	a	Marítimo	L	0-3	
24/04	a	Estoril	D	1-1	Licá
29/04	a	Benfica	L	0-1	
08/05	h	Moreirense	W	4-1	Henrique Dourado 2, João Teixeira, og (Stefanović)
14/05	a	Arouca	D	2-2	Cafú, Hurtado

No	Name	Nat	DoB	Pos	Aps	(s)	Gls
14	Alex		27/08/91	A	2	(1)	
45	Alex Silva		16/03/97	A	6	(14)	1
29	Alvin Arrondel	FRA	11/11/93	D		(3)	
32	Tyler Boyd	NZL	30/12/94	M	1	(1)	
66	Breno	BRA	06/03/95	D	2		
48	Bruno Alves		09/06/90	M	3	(1)	
76	Bruno Gaspar		21/04/93	D	28		
38	Bruno Mendes	BRA	02/08/94	A	1	(1)	
26	Cafú		26/02/93	M	31	(1)	3
93	Dalbert	BRA	08/09/93	D	23	(2)	
1	Douglas	BRA	03/08/83	G	10		
89	Henrique Dourado	BRA	15/09/89	A	24	(4)	12
88	Francis	BRA	16/04/90	A		(7)	
16	Paolo Hurtado	PER	27/07/90	A	5	(2)	1
15	João Afonso		28/05/90	D	21	(3)	
58	João Pedro		03/04/93	M	1	(1)	
24	João Teixeira		06/02/94	M	2	(3)	1
33	João Vigário		20/11/95	A		(6)	
3	Josué Sá		17/06/92	D	30	(1)	2
11	Licá		08/09/88	A	24	(5)	5
5	Luís Rocha		27/06/93	D	8	(1)	1
56	Miguel Silva		07/04/95	G	24		
77	Santiago Montoya	COL	15/09/91	M	4	(3)	
6	Moreno		19/08/81	D	1	(3)	
25	Oriol Rosell	ESP	07/07/92	M	3	(1)	
52	Otávio	BRA	09/02/95	M	21	(4)	6
2	Pedrão	BRA	18/12/92	D	19		
23	Pedro Correia		27/03/87	D	2		
94	Thibang Phete	RSA	04/04/94	M	6	(5)	
81	Rafinha	BRA	14/02/96	A		(1)	
18	Ricardo Gomes	CPV	18/12/91	M	3	(3)	
7	Ricardo Valente		03/04/91	A	23	(8)	5
49	Rui Areias		22/11/93	A		(1)	
99	Bakary Saré	CIV	05/04/90	M	23		3
9	Tómané		23/10/92	A	12	(5)	1
70	Tozé		14/01/93	M	10	(2)	
28	Victor Andrade	BRA	30/09/95	A	1	(6)	

Top goalscorers

32	Jonas (Benfica)
27	Islam Slimani (Sporting)
19	Kostas Mitroglou (Benfica)
17	Léo Bonatini (Estoril)
16	Rafael Martins (Moreirense)
14	Bruno Moreira (Paços Ferreira)
13	Vincent Aboubakar (Porto)
	Nathan Júnior (Tondela)
12	Dyego Sousa (Marítimo)
	Diogo Jota (Paços Ferreira)
	André Claro (Setúbal)
	Henrique Dourado (Guimarães)

Promoted clubs

GD Chaves

1949 • Municipal Eng Manuel Branco Teixeira (8,000) • gdchaves.pt
Coach: Vítor Oliveira

CD Feirense

1918 • Estádio Marcolino Castro (5,401) • cdfeirense.pt
Coach: Pepa;
(25/03/16) José Mota

Second level final table 2015/16

		Pld	W	D	L	F	A	Pts
1	FC Porto B	46	26	8	12	84	52	86
2	GD Chaves	46	21	18	7	60	39	81
3	CD Feirense	46	21	15	10	55	38	78
4	Portimonense SC	46	20	18	8	57	45	78
5	SC Freamunde	46	20	14	12	52	36	74
6	FC Famalicão	46	18	18	10	64	51	72
7	SC Olhanense	46	19	12	15	42	39	69
8	CD Aves	46	19	10	17	58	48	67
9	Varzim SC	46	17	14	15	51	48	65
10	Sporting Clube de Portugal B	46	18	11	17	61	59	65
11	Gil Vicente FC	46	16	14	16	58	56	62
12	Penafiel FC	46	13	22	11	49	46	61
13	Vitória SC B	46	16	12	18	60	67	60
14	SC Covilhã	46	13	19	14	45	48	58
15	SC Braga B	46	15	12	19	47	54	57
16	CD Santa Clara	46	15	12	19	49	52	57
17	Académico de Viseu FC	46	13	17	16	46	60	56
18	Leixões SC	46	14	13	19	45	56	55
19	SL Benfica B	46	15	10	21	59	64	55
20	SC Farense	46	15	11	20	49	56	54
21	CD Mafra	46	12	18	16	37	40	54
22	Atlético CP	46	12	15	19	49	56	51
23	Clube Oriental de Lisboa	46	9	14	23	47	67	41
24	UD Oliveirense	46	6	11	29	42	89	29

NB FC Porto B ineligible for promotion;
SC Farense – 2 pts deducted.

DOMESTIC CUP

Taça de Portugal 2015/16

THIRD ROUND

(16/10/15)
Vianense 1-2 Benfica

(17/10/15)
Académico Viseu 0-3 Braga
Aves 3-2 Moreirense *(aet)*
Casa Pia 3-1 Oriental
Coruchense 0-2 Setúbal
Famalicão 1-1 Feirense *(aet; 4-5 on pens)*
Louletano 0-5 Chaves
Olhanense 0-1 Belenenses
Trofense 1-0 Santa Clara
Varzim 0-2 Porto
Vilafranquense 0-4 Sporting

(18/10/15)
Amarante 2-2 Bragança *(aet; 3-2 on pens)*
Angrense 4-1 Torre Moncorvo
Coimbrões 2-3 Fafe
Cova Piedade 4-3 Alcanenense
Farense 1-0 Rio Tinto
Gil Vicente 2-1 Tondela
Gondomar 0-1 Estoril *(aet)*
Leiria Marrazes 1-5 Benfica Castelo Branco
Leixões 1-2 Arouca *(aet)*
Loures 1-2 Boavista *(aet)*
Lourosa 0-2 Marítimo *(aet)*
Malveira 3-0 Praiense
Mosteirão 0-6 Nacional
Naval 1-7 Paços Ferreira
Operário 1-0 Salgueiros 08
Pampilhosa 0-5 Portimonense
Penafiel 2-0 Guimarães
Sanjoanense 1-5 Académica
Sertanense 1-5 União Madeira
União Montemor 0-3 Rio Ave
Valdevez 0-3 Caldas

FOURTH ROUND

(20/11/15)
Portimonense 3-2 Belenenses

(21/11/15)
Angrense 0-2 Porto
Arouca 0-0 Chaves *(aet; 6-5 on pens)*
Benfica Castelo Branco 1-3 Gil Vicente
Malveira 0-1 Feirense
Sporting 2-1 Benfica *(aet)*
Trofense 0-0 Académica *(aet; 1-4 on pens)*

(22/11/15)
Amarante 1-0 Marítimo
Aves 3-3 União Madeira *(aet; 5-4 on pens)*
Boavista 1-0 Operário
Caldas 0-1 Estoril
Casa Pia 0-1 Setúbal
Fafe 1-1 Penafiel *(aet; 1-3 on pens)*

Farense 0-1 Braga *(aet)*
Nacional 5-0 Cova Piedade
Paços Ferreira 1-2 Rio Ave

FIFTH ROUND

(15/12/15)
Setúbal 1-1 Rio Ave *(aet; 1-3 on pens)*

(16/12/15)
Amarante 1-2 Arouca
Aves 2-2 Nacional *(aet; 2-4 on pens)*
Braga 4-3 Sporting *(aet)*
Estoril 1-0 Penafiel
Feirense 0-1 Porto
Gil Vicente 1-1 Portimonense *(aet; 4-3 on pens)*

(17/12/15)
Boavista 1-0 Académica

QUARTER-FINALS

(13/01/16)
Boavista 0-1 Porto *(Brahimi 24)*

Braga 2-0 Arouca *(Hugo Basto 57og, Stojiljković 60)*

Gil Vicente 1-0 Nacional *(Pecks 31)*

Rio Ave 3-0 Estoril *(Tarantini 7, Krovinović 53, Edimar 77)*

SEMI-FINALS

(03/02/16 & 02/03/16)
Gil Vicente 0-3 Porto *(Rúben Neves 45, Suk 59, Sérgio Oliveira 70)*
Porto 2-0 Gil Vicente *(Awaziem 11, Marega 80)*
(Porto 5-0)

(04/02/16 & 02/03/16)
Braga 1-0 Rio Ave *(Pedro Santos 7p)*
Rio Ave 0-0 Braga
(Braga 1-0)

FINAL

(22/05/16)
Estádio Nacional, Lisbon
SC BRAGA 2 *(Rui Fonte 12, Josué 58)*
FC PORTO 2 *(André Silva 61, 90+1)*
(aet; 4-2 on pens)
Referee: Artur Soares
BRAGA: Marafona, Baiano, André Pinto, Ricardo Ferreira (Boly 77), Marcelo Goiano, Mauro, Luíz Carlos, Josué (Pedro Santos 84), Rafa Silva, Rui Fonte (Stojiljković 60), Hassan
PORTO: Helton, Maxi Pereira, Awaziem (Rúben Neves 46), Marcano, Layún, Herrera, Danilo Pereira, Sérgio Oliveira (André André 74), Varela (Aboubakar 79), André Silva, Brahimi

Braga ended a 50-year wait by winning the Portuguese Cup

REPUBLIC OF IRELAND
Cumann Peile na héireann/Football Association of Ireland (FAI)

Address	National Sports Campus	**President**	Tony Fitzgerald
	Abbotstown	**Chief executive**	John Delaney
	IE-Dublin 15	**Media officer**	Ian Mallon
Tel	+353 1 8999500	**Year of formation**	1921
Fax	+353 1 8999502	**National stadium**	Dublin Arena, Dublin
E-mail	info@fai.ie		(51,700)
Website	fai.ie		

PREMIER DIVISION CLUBS

 1 **Bohemian FC**

 2 **Bray Wanderers FC**

 3 **Cork City FC**

 4 **Derry City FC**

 5 **Drogheda United FC**

 6 **Dundalk FC**

 7 **Galway United FC**

 8 **Limerick FC**

 9 **Longford Town FC**

 10 **Saint Patrick's Athletic FC**

 11 **Shamrock Rovers FC**

 12 **Sligo Rovers FC**

PROMOTED CLUBS

 13 **Wexford Youths FC**

 14 **Finn Harps FC**

KEY

● UEFA Champions League

● UEFA Europa League

● Promoted

● Relegated

Dominant Dundalk do the double

Dundalk retained the League of Ireland title for the first time in their history as Stephen Kenny's dominant side lost only once en route to a comprehensive triumph. They also completed a first domestic double in 27 years – and third in all – by defeating Premier Division runners-up Cork City in the FAI Cup final with an extra-time winner from leading scorer Richie Towell.

Martin O'Neill succeeded in qualifying the Republic of Ireland for UEFA EURO 2016, where one win – over a second-string Italy – sufficed to satisfy the team's legion of fans before hosts France eliminated them in the round of 16.

Historic title defence for County Louth club	**Top scorer Towell seals cup final win over Cork**	**National team reach knockout phase of EURO 2016**

Domestic league

In comparison to the 2014 title win, secured only after a last-day 2-0 victory over Cork at Oriel Park, Dundalk's re-acquisition of the Premier Division trophy was tension-free. Kenny's team, shorn of goalkeeper Peter Cherrie and 20-goal striker Patrick Hoban but otherwise virtually unchanged, got off to an excellent start – five successive wins without conceding a goal – and it soon became clear that they would once again be the team to beat.

The clean sheets, goals, wins and points continued to accumulate, but with two thirds of the campaign complete, Dundalk were not out of sight. Although they had lost just once in 22 matches, so, too, had John Caulfield's Cork, and their lead was just four points with a trip to Turner's Cross still to come. But while Dundalk were to add another six points to their total in the next two games, Cork suffered back-to-back defeats and suddenly Kenny's men were in the clear.

The County Louth club's 11th national title was duly wrapped up in early October thanks to a late equalising penalty from prolific midfielder Towell at Shamrock Rovers, the 1-1 draw putting Dundalk 13 points ahead of Cork, who had four matches remaining. Towell would end the campaign with a remarkable tally of 25 goals, one that

helped Dundalk to a record haul of 78 in their 33 matches.

Cork posted just four wins in their last 11 games but managed to hold off a late charge from Pat Fenlon's Shamrock Rovers and claim a second successive runners-up spot. Rovers were the best of the three Dublin sides, with St Patrick's Athletic and Bohemians filling the next two places beneath them and Longford Town completing the top half. Dundalk's local rivals Drogheda finished bottom and were relegated, with Limerick joining them after a play-off defeat to the north-westerners of Finn Harps – runners-up in the First Division to the south-easterners of Wexford Youths, promoted to the top flight for the first time.

Domestic cup

Dundalk got the better of Cork once again in the final of the FAI Cup to lift the trophy for the tenth time. A tight encounter was settled by the inevitable Towell, who struck on 107 minutes after a fine assist from Daryl Horgan to complete a perfect domestic season for the club.

Europe

Dundalk's only away defeat of 2015 came in Borisov, Belarus where FC BATE defeated them 2-1 in the second

qualifying round of the UEFA Champions League. One goal without reply in the Oriel Park return would have sent Ireland's finest through, but they could manage only a gutsy goalless draw. There was precious little excitement elsewhere, with the only opposition defeated by an Irish club coming from Luxembourg.

National team

The Republic of Ireland reached the UEFA European Championship finals for the second tournament running, a memorable home win over Germany preceding an impressive play-off success over Bosnia & Herzegovina.

The objective in France was to reach the round of 16, which they achieved despite surrendering the lead in a 1-1 draw against Sweden and losing heavily to Belgium. Luckily for them, Italy, their last group opponents, had already won the section so rested virtually all of their first XI, and a late Robbie Brady header made them pay while sending Irish fans and players into a state of delirium as the team won 1-0 to progress in third place.

Brady struck again, with an early penalty, to give O'Neill's men a lead against France in Lyon, but a second-half onslaught from the hosts, punctuated by two Antoine Griezmann goals and a red card for Shane Duffy, brought the Irish party to an end.

DOMESTIC SEASON AT A GLANCE

Premier Division 2015 final table

		Pld	Home					Away					Total					Pts
			W	D	L	F	A	W	D	L	F	A	W	D	L	F	A	
1	**Dundalk FC**	33	12	4	1	46	9	11	5	0	32	14	23	9	1	78	23	78
2	Cork City FC	33	10	3	3	35	14	9	7	1	22	11	19	10	4	57	25	67
3	Shamrock Rovers FC	33	11	5	1	36	14	7	6	3	20	13	18	11	4	56	27	65
4	Saint Patrick's Athletic FC	33	9	3	4	26	13	9	1	7	26	21	18	4	11	52	34	58
5	Bohemian FC	33	8	4	4	23	14	7	4	6	26	28	15	8	10	49	42	53
6	Longford Town FC	33	5	5	6	17	23	5	4	8	24	30	10	9	14	41	53	39
7	Derry City FC	33	4	4	8	14	19	5	4	8	18	23	9	8	16	32	42	35
8	Bray Wanderers FC	33	6	4	7	16	19	3	2	11	11	32	9	6	18	27	51	33
9	Sligo Rovers FC	33	4	6	7	19	26	3	4	9	20	29	7	10	16	39	55	31
10	Galway United FC	33	5	1	11	24	36	4	3	9	15	25	9	4	20	39	61	31
11	Limerick FC	33	3	4	10	22	35	4	4	8	24	38	7	8	18	46	73	29
12	Drogheda United FC	33	3	4	9	17	31	4	3	10	15	31	7	7	19	32	62	28

European qualification 2016/17

CHAMPIONS LEAGUE

Champion/Cup winner: Dundalk FC (second qualifying round)

EUROPA LEAGUE

Cork City FC (first qualifying round)
Shamrock Rovers FC (first qualifying round)
Saint Patrick's Athletic FC (first qualifying round)

Top scorer   Richie Towell (Dundalk), 25 goals
Relegated clubs   Drogheda United FC, Limerick FC
Promoted clubs   Wexford Youths FC, Finn Harps FC
Cup final   Dundalk FC 1-0 Cork City FC *(aet)*

Team of the season
(4-5-1)

Coach: Kenny *(Dundalk)*

Schlingermann *(Drogheda)*

Gannon *(Dundalk)*   Gartland *(Dundalk)*   Boyle *(Dundalk)*   Massey *(Dundalk)*

Miele *(Shamrock Rovers)*   O'Donnell *(Dundalk)*   Chambers *(St Patrick's)*

Horgan *(Dundalk)*   Towell *(Dundalk)*

O'Sullivan *(Cork)*

Player of the season

Richie Towell
(Dundalk FC)

A major factor in Dundalk's 2015 domestic double was the phenomenally consistent goalscoring of attacking midfielder Towell, whose final Premier Division tally of 25 was more than twice as many as any other player in the division could muster. The ex-Celtic and Hibernian player would cross the Irish Sea once again at the end of the year to join English Championship challengers Brighton, but before then he was to sign off triumphantly for Dundalk by scoring the extra-time winner in the FAI Cup final.

Newcomer of the season

Brandon Miele
(Shamrock Rovers FC)

The 2015 PFAI Young Player of the Season prize went to midfield starlet Miele, who thus became the fourth Shamrock Rover to claim the award – after Liam O'Brien, Vinny Arkins and 2011 winner Enda Stevens. New to the Premier Division at the start of term, the ex-Newcastle United trainee enjoyed a fabulous debut campaign, scoring 11 goals and contributing to several others as the famous club from his native Tallaght in the south Dublin suburbs amassed 65 points from 33 games to finish in third place.

NATIONAL TEAM

International tournament appearances

FIFA World Cup (3) 1990 (qtr-finals), 1994 (2nd round), 2002 (2nd round)
UEFA European Championship (3) 1988, 2012, 2016 (round of 16)

Top five all-time caps

Robbie Keane (145); **Shay Given** (134); **John O'Shea** (114); Kevin Kilbane (110); Stephen Staunton (102)

Top five all-time goals

Robbie Keane (67); Niall Quinn (21); Frank Stapleton (20); John Aldridge, Tony Cascarino & Don Givens (19)

Results 2015/16

04/09/15	Gibraltar (ECQ)	A	Faro (POR)	W	4-0	Christie (26), Keane (49, 51p), Long (79)
07/09/15	Georgia (ECQ)	H	Dublin	W	1-0	Walters (69)
08/10/15	Germany (ECQ)	H	Dublin	W	1-0	Long (70)
11/10/15	Poland (ECQ)	A	Warsaw	L	1-2	Walters (16p)
13/11/15	Bosnia & Herzegovina (ECQ)	A	Zenica	D	1-1	Brady (82)
16/11/15	Bosnia & Herzegovina (ECQ)	H	Dublin	W	2-0	Walters (24p, 70)
25/03/16	Switzerland	H	Dublin	W	1-0	Clark (2)
29/03/16	Slovakia	H	Dublin	D	2-2	Long (22p), McClean (24p)
27/05/16	Netherlands	H	Dublin	D	1-1	Long (31)
31/05/16	Belarus	H	Cork	L	1-2	Ward (71)
13/06/16	Sweden (ECF)	N	Saint-Denis (FRA)	D	1-1	Hoolahan (48)
18/06/16	Belgium (ECF)	N	Bordeaux (FRA)	L	0-3	
22/06/16	Italy (ECF)	N	Lille (FRA)	W	1-0	Brady (85)
26/06/16	France (ECF)	A	Lyon	L	1-2	Brady (2p)

Appearances 2015/16

Coach: Martin O'Neill (NIR) 01/03/52			GIB	GEO	GER	POL	BIH	BIH	Sui	Svk	Ned	Blr	SWE	BEL	ITA	FRA	Caps	Goals
Shay Given	20/04/76	Stoke (ENG)	G	G	G43							G69					134	-
Cyrus Christie	30/09/92	Derby (ENG)	D		D					D		D					5	1
John O'Shea	30/04/81	Sunderland (ENG)	D	D	D	D 92*		s90		D46	D		D	D		s68	114	3
Ciaran Clark	26/09/89	Aston Villa (ENG)	D	D			D	D	D			D	D	D			19	2
Robbie Brady	14/01/92	Norwich (ENG)	D	D	M	D	M86	D	D	s46	D		D	M	M	M	27	6
Glenn Whelan	13/01/84	Stoke (ENG)	M	M		M58	M	M90		M	M67		M	M			73	2
James McCarthy	12/11/90	Everton (ENG)	M70	M	M	M	M	M	s62	M			M85	M62	M77	M71	39	-
Wes Hoolahan	20/05/82	Norwich (ENG)	M77	M75	M	s73	M60	M55	s79	M73	s76	s68	M78	M71	s77	s71	34	3
Jeff Hendrick	31/01/92	Derby (ENG)	M	M	M	M	M	M		s67	M		M	M	M	M	25	-
Jonathan Walters	20/09/83	Stoke (ENG)	M	M	M	M	M	M			M		M64			s65	41	10
Robbie Keane	08/07/80	LA Galaxy (USA)	A71	A46		s55							s78	s79			145	67
Stephen Quinn	01/04/86	Reading (ENG)	s70						M62		M67				s90		16	-
Shane Long	22/01/87	Southampton (ENG)	s71	s46	s65	A55		s55	A84	A46	A67	s68	A	A79	A90	A	67	16
Aiden McGeady	04/04/86	Everton (ENG) /Sheffield Wednesday (ENG)	s77			s58	s86				M61	s73	M75	s85	s71	s70	85	5
Séamus Coleman	11/10/88	Everton (ENG)		D		D	D	D	D		D		D	D	D	D	38	-
James McClean	22/04/89	West Brom (ENG)		s75		M73	s60	s55	s84	M	s67	M79	s64	s62	M	M68	42	5
Richard Keogh	11/08/86	Derby (ENG)			D	D	D	D				D			D	D	14	1
Stephen Ward	20/08/85	Burnley (ENG)			D69		D67			D79		D		D	D	D	36	3
Daryl Murphy	15/03/83	Ipswich (ENG)			A65		A	A55	s26 /79		A68			A70	A65		22	-
Darren Randolph	12/05/87	West Ham (ENG)			s43	G	G	G	G	s16	G		G	G	G	G	13	-
David Meyler	29/05/89	Hull (ENG)			s69				M61		M75						16	-
Marc Wilson	17/08/87	Stoke (ENG)				s67											24	1
Shane Duffy	01/01/92	Blackburn (ENG)							D		D				D	D 66*	5	-
Alan Judge	11/11/88	Brentford (ENG)							M								1	-
Kevin Doyle	18/09/83	Colorado Rapids (USA)							A26								62	14
Eunan O'Kane	10/07/90	Bournemouth (ENG)							s61	M66	s82	s75					4	-
Jonny Hayes	09/07/87	Aberdeen (SCO)							s61	s79							2	-
Rob Elliot	30/04/86	Newcastle (ENG)							G16								4	-
Paul McShane	06/01/86	Reading (ENG)							D								33	-
Alex Pearce	09/11/88	Bristol City (ENG)								s46							7	2
Anthony Pilkington	06/06/88	Cardiff (ENG)								s66							9	1
Harry Arter	28/12/89	Bournemouth (ENG)										M82					2	-
David McGoldrick	29/11/87	Ipswich (ENG)										A76	s79				4	-
Darron Gibson	25/10/87	Everton (ENG)										s67	M68				27	1
David Forde	20/12/79	Millwall (ENG)												s69			24	-
Callum O'Dowda	23/04/95	Oxford (ENG)												s75			1	-

EUROPE

Dundalk FC

CHAMPIONS LEAGUE

Second qualifying round - FC BATE Borisov (BLR)
A 1-2 *McMillan (32)*
Rogers, Gannon, Gartland, Boyle, Shields, O'Donnell, Horgan (Byrne 88), Mountney (Meenan 70), McMillan (Finn 77), Massey, Towell. Coach: Stephen Kenny (IRL)
H 0-0
Rogers, Gannon, Gartland, Boyle, O'Donnell, Horgan (Byrne 82), McMillan, Finn (Mountney 76), Massey, Towell, Meenan (Shields 56). Coach: Stephen Kenny (IRL)

Saint Patrick's Athletic FC

EUROPA LEAGUE

First qualifying round - Skonto FC (LVA)
A 1-2 *Greene (21)*
Clarke, O'Brien (Desmond 46), Bermingham, Hoare (McGuinness 67), Bolger, Fagan (McGrath 73), Brennan, Chambers, Browne, Forrester, Greene. Coach: Liam Buckley (IRL)
H 0-2
Clarke, O'Brien, Bermingham, Bolger, Byrne, Fagan (McGrath 65), Brennan, Desmond, Browne, Forrester, Greene (Langley 65). Coach: Liam Buckley (IRL)

Cork City FC

EUROPA LEAGUE

First qualifying round - KR Reykjavík (ISL)
H 1-1 *Bennett (19)*
McNulty, Bennett, D Dennehy, Healy (Murray 66), O'Flynn (O'Sullivan 59), Gaynor (Dunleavy 46), O'Connor, Sheppard, B Dennehy, Miller, Buckley. Coach: John Caulfield (IRL)
A 1-2 (aet) *O'Sullivan (13)*
McNulty, Bennett, Dunleavy, Murray, Healy, Gaynor, O'Connor, Sheppard (O'Flynn 80), Miller (Kearney 65), O'Sullivan (Morrissey 107), Buckley. Coach: John Caulfield (IRL)

Shamrock Rovers FC

EUROPA LEAGUE

First qualifying round - FC Progrès Niederkorn (LUX)
A 0-0
Hyland, Byrne, McCabe, Waters (D Kavanagh 75), Webster, G Brennan, Cregg, Madden, Clancy, Miele (C Kavanagh 81), Drennan. Coach: Pat Fenlon (IRL)
H 3-0 *Webster (21), Waters (41, 57)*
Hyland, Byrne, McCabe, Waters (R Brennan 74), Webster, G Brennan, Cregg, Madden, Clancy, Miele, Drennan (North 87). Coach: Pat Fenlon (IRL)

Second qualifying round - Odds BK (NOR)
H 0-2
Hyland, Byrne, Kenna, McCabe, R Brennan (C Kavanagh 86), Waters (Miele 67), Webster, G Brennan (North 80), Cregg, Madden, Drennan. Coach: Pat Fenlon (IRL)
A 1-2 *G Brennan (90)*
Hyland, Byrne, Kenna, McCabe, R Brennan, Webster, G Brennan, Cregg (C Kavanagh 67), Madden, Miele (North 79), Drennan. Coach: Pat Fenlon (IRL)

University College Dublin AFC

EUROPA LEAGUE

First qualifying round - F91 Dudelange (LUX)
H 1-0 *Swan (45+1)*
Corbet, Langtry, Leahy, O'Neill, Benson, Mulhall, McLaughlin, Swan, Doyle, Boyle, Watts (Watson 90+2). Coach: Colin O'Neill (IRL)
A 1-2 *Swan (17)*
Corbet, Coyne, Langtry, Leahy (Harney 79), O'Neill, Benson, Mulhall, Swan (Belhout 67), Doyle, Boyle, Watts (Kouogun 31). Coach: Colin O'Neill (IRL)
Red card: Coyne 28

Second qualifying round - ŠK Slovan Bratislava (SVK)
A 0-1
Corbet, Langtry, Leahy, O'Neill, Benson, Mulhall, Swan, Doyle, Boyle, Kouogun, Watts (Cannon 85). Coach: Colin O'Neill (IRL)
H 1-5 *Swan (57)*
Corbet, Langtry, Leahy, O'Neill, Benson, Mulhall (Belhout 88), Swan, Doyle (Kirwan 76), Boyle, Kouogun, Watts (Cannon 56). Coach: Colin O'Neill (IRL)

DOMESTIC LEAGUE CLUB-BY-CLUB

Bohemian FC

1890 • Dalymount Park (4,500) • bohemianfc.com
Major honours
League of Ireland (11) 1924, 1928, 1930, 1934, 1936, 1975, 1978, 2001, 2003 (spring), 2008, 2009; Irish Cup (1) 1908; FAI Cup (7) 1928, 1935, 1970, 1976, 1992, 2001, 2008
Manager: Keith Long

2015

07/03	a Limerick	W	3-0	Evans, D Kelly, Fitzgerald
13/03	h Galway	W	2-0	Murphy 2
21/03	a Bray	W	1-0	Evans
24/03	h Dundalk	L	0-3	
27/03	a Shamrock Rovers	D	0-0	
03/04	a Drogheda	W	1-0	Griffin
10/04	a Longford	W	2-0	D Kelly, Evans
17/04	h St Patrick's	L	0-1	
20/04	a Sligo	D	0-0	
24/04	a Derry	W	2-1	Dillon, Griffin
04/05	h Cork	D	1-1	Evans
08/05	h Limerick	W	2-1	Prendergast, J Byrne
15/05	a Galway	L	3-5	Kavanagh, D Kelly (p), Evans
22/05	h Bray	D	0-0	
05/06	a Dundalk	W	2-1	og (Rogers), Mulcahy
09/06	a St Patrick's	L	0-1	
12/06	h Shamrock Rovers	W	3-1	Prendergast, D Kelly 2
26/06	h Drogheda	L	0-1	
04/07	a Longford	L	1-2	Buckley
17/07	h Sligo	W	1-0	Akinade
24/07	a Derry	W	4-2	Prendergast, Buckley, Akinade, Creevy
31/07	a Cork	L	0-4	
08/08	a Limerick	L	3-4	Akinade, J Kelly 2 (1p)
14/08	h Galway	W	3-0	Akinade, J Kelly 2 (1p)
17/08	a Bray	L	1-3	Creevy
28/08	h Dundalk	D	2-2	Buckley, Akinade
05/09	a Shamrock Rovers	D	1-1	Akinade
18/09	h Longford	D	1-1	Kavanagh
25/09	a Drogheda	D	2-2	Akinade, Kavanagh
09/10	h St Patrick's	W	2-0	Murphy, Moore
17/10	a Sligo	W	2-0	Akinade, Murphy
23/10	a Derry	W	3-2	Akinade 2, J Kelly
30/10	h Cork	L	0-1	

No	Name	Nat	DoB	Pos	Aps	(s)	Gls
24	Ismahil Akinade	NGA	17/06/92	A	18	(1)	10
12	Aaron Ashe		07/05/96	A		(1)	
22	Stephen Best		15/03/97	D	12	(1)	
8	Keith Buckley		17/06/92	M	28	(1)	3
6	Dan Byrne		07/05/93	D		(2)	
10	Jason Byrne		23/02/78	A	2	(18)	1
29	Jason Caffrey		26/06/96	M	3	(1)	
21	Robbie Creevy		24/08/89	M	14	(7)	2
1	Dean Delany		15/09/80	G	32		
16	Kealan Dillon		21/02/94	M	12	(9)	1
18	Adam Evans		03/05/94	A	18	(8)	5
3	Lorcan Fitzgerald		03/01/89	D	27		1
11	Mark Griffin		16/06/91	A	2	(8)	2
15	Dylan Hayes		09/04/95	D	11	(1)	
12	Jake Hyland		10/08/95	M	1	(1)	
14	Patrick Kavanagh		29/12/85	M	25	(3)	3
9	Dean Kelly		18/09/85	A	13	(3)	5
9	Jake Kelly		18/06/90	M	9	(1)	5
4	Roberto Lopes		17/06/92	D	31		
7	Karl Moore		09/11/88	M	14	(7)	1
26	Dave Mulcahy		28/01/78	M	18	(5)	1
17	Anthony Murphy		01/08/82	M	22	(1)	4
19	James O'Brien		08/06/90	M	2	(6)	
2	Derek Pender		02/10/84	D	13		
5	Derek Prendergast		17/10/84	D	27	(1)	4
25	Lee Steacy		18/01/93	G	1		
20	Eoin Wearen		02/10/92	M	8	(3)	

Bray Wanderers FC

1942 • Carlisle Grounds (3,000) • bwfc.ie

Major honours
FAI Cup (2) 1990, 1999

Manager: Alan Mathews;
(02/04/15) (Maciej Tarnogrodzki (POL));
(07/05/15) (David Cassidy);
(11/05/15) Trevor Croly;
(07/07/15) Mick Cooke

2015

07/03 h Drogheda	L	0-1		
13/03 a St Patrick's	L	0-3		
21/03 h Bohemians	L	0-1		
24/03 a Longford	L	0-2		
28/03 h Cork	L	0-1		
03/04 a Sligo	W	3-1	Cassidy 3 (2p)	
11/04 h Limerick	W	4-0	Hanlon, Onwubiko, Cassidy, Kelly	
17/04 a Derry	D	0-0		
20/04 h Shamrock Rovers	L	0-3		
25/04 h Galway	L	0-5		
04/05 a Dundalk	L	1-8	Cassidy (p)	
08/05 h Drogheda	L	2-4	Lyons, McGlynn	
16/05 h St Patrick's	W	1-0	McGlynn	
22/05 a Bohemians	D	0-0		
05/06 h Longford	L	0-1		
12/06 a Cork	L	0-1		
27/06 h Sligo	W	1-0	McNally	
04/07 a Limerick	W	1-0	Scully	
11/07 h Derry	W	1-0	Hanlon	
24/07 a Galway	W	1-0	og (Oji)	
01/08 h Dundalk	L	0-1		
08/08 h Drogheda	W	1-0	Douglas	
14/08 a St Patrick's	L	0-1		
17/08 h Bohemians	W	3-1	Lyons (p), McGlynn, Scully	
29/08 a Longford	L	0-1		
05/09 h Cork	D	0-0		
19/09 h Limerick	D	2-2	McEvoy 2	
22/09 a Shamrock Rovers	L	0-1		
26/09 a Sligo	L	2-3	Lyons, Scully	
09/10 a Derry	L	1-3	Kelly	
17/10 h Shamrock Rovers	D	2-2	Douglas, Sullivan	
24/10 h Galway	D	1-1	Sullivan	
30/10 a Dundalk	L	0-4		

No	Name	Nat	DoB	Pos	Aps	(s)	Gls
2	Michael Barker		16/08/93	D	32		
25	Daniel Blackbyrne		13/07/96	D		(1)	
8	David Cassidy		23/05/85	M	26	(1)	5
50	Peter Cherrie	SCO	01/10/83	G	16		
12	Niall Cooney		21/08/92	D	19	(1)	
20	Hugh Douglas		22/06/93	D	29	(1)	2
17	Peter Durrad		16/12/94	A	1	(3)	
22	Luke Fitzpatrick		23/01/86	D	1	(2)	
14	Luke Gallagher		29/07/94	M	7	(6)	
11	Adam Hanlon		03/06/92	M	14	(5)	2
1	Brian Kane		06/07/90	G		(1)	
24	Graham Kelly		31/10/91	M	29		2
18	Chris Lyons		08/05/93	A	23	(7)	3
23	Gareth McDonagh		27/02/96	M	7	(8)	
10	Ryan McEvoy		19/07/90	M	33		2
13	Peter McGlynn		02/05/89	M	21	(2)	3
32	Stephen McGuinness		10/03/95	G	17		
5	Alan McNally		15/09/82	D	30		1
3	Jack Memery		05/03/93	D	4	(1)	
6	Adam Mitchell		02/10/84	D	7	(1)	
4	Daniel O'Reilly		11/04/95	D	13	(1)	
19	Emeka Onwubiko		20/12/89	A	5	(17)	1
7	Dave Scully		20/01/85	A	9	(14)	3
15	John Sullivan		06/01/91	D	17	(1)	2
9	Adam Wixted		03/08/95	A	3	(4)	

Cork City FC

1984 • Turner's Cross (7,365) • corkcityfc.ie

Major honours
League of Ireland (2) 1993, 2005; FAI Cup (2) 1998, 2007

Manager: John Caulfield

2015

07/03 a Sligo	D	1-1	Gaynor	
13/03 h Limerick	W	5-0	D Dennehy 2, B Dennehy 2 (1p), Holohan	
20/03 a Shamrock Rovers	D	0-0		
24/03 h Galway	W	2-0	Sheppard, Bennett	
28/03 h Bray	W	1-0	Djilali	
03/04 h Derry	W	3-0	O'Flynn, Sheppard 2	
10/04 a St Patrick's	D	0-0		
17/04 a Drogheda	W	2-1	B Dennehy, Djilali	
20/04 h Longford	W	2-0	Buckley, Healy	
24/04 a Dundalk	L	1-2	og (Boyle)	
04/05 a Bohemians	D	1-1	O'Sullivan	
08/05 h Sligo	W	3-2	Sheppard 2, O'Sullivan	
11/05 h Drogheda	W	4-1	B Dennehy 3 (1p), Sheppard	
16/05 a Limerick	W	1-0	Sheppard	
22/05 h Shamrock Rovers	D	0-0		
05/06 a Galway	W	3-1	Murray, B Dennehy, Buckley	
12/06 h Bray	W	1-0	O'Sullivan	
26/06 a Derry	W	2-0	Sheppard, B Dennehy (p)	
18/07 a Longford	W	4-1	Beattie, og (Tyrell), O'Sullivan, Sheppard	
26/07 a Dundalk	D	1-1	O'Sullivan	
31/07 h Bohemians	W	4-0	O'Sullivan 2, Healy (p), Morrissey	
08/08 a Sligo	W	2-0	O'Sullivan, Gaynor	
14/08 h Limerick	L	2-3	Gaynor, O'Flynn	
17/08 a Shamrock Rovers	L	0-3		
28/08 a Galway	W	1-0	B Dennehy	
31/08 h St Patrick's	W	3-1	Bennett, O'Connor, D Dennehy	
05/09 a Bray	D	0-0		
25/09 h Derry	D	0-0		
09/10 a Drogheda	D	1-1	Sheppard	
16/10 h Longford	L	2-3	Sheppard, Beattie	
19/10 a St Patrick's	W	2-1	Beattie, Morrissey	
23/10 a Dundalk	D	2-2	O'Sullivan, Sheppard	
30/10 a Bohemians	W	1-0	B Dennehy (p)	

No	Name	Nat	DoB	Pos	Aps	(s)	Gls
21	Steven Beattie		20/08/88	M	13	(1)	3
3	Alan Bennett		04/10/81	D	22	(1)	2
26	Garry Buckley		19/08/93	M	23	(4)	2
25	Cian Coleman		01/01/97	M		(1)	
20	Billy Dennehy		17/02/87	M	21	(4)	10
5	Darren Dennehy		21/09/88	D	22	(2)	3
10	Kieran Djilali	ENG	01/01/91	A	4	(6)	2
4	John Dunleavy		03/07/91	D	19	(1)	
17	Connor Ellis		12/05/97	A		(1)	
32	Stephen Folan		14/01/92	D		(2)	
11	Ross Gaynor		09/09/87	D	21	(6)	3
7	Colin Healy		14/03/80	M	17	(3)	2
8	Gavan Holohan		15/12/91	M	9	(9)	1
2	John Kavanagh		22/11/87	D	15	(1)	
30	Liam Kearney		10/01/83	M	2	(9)	
24	Robert Lehane		19/02/94	A		(6)	
1	Mark McNulty		13/10/80	G	33		
18	Michael McSweeney		17/06/88	D	9	(4)	
22	Liam Miller		13/02/81	M	29		
15	Danny Morrissey		13/12/93	A	2	(15)	2
6	Dan Murray	ENG	16/05/82	D	23	(2)	1
27	Danny O'Connell		30/11/94	M		(1)	
14	Kevin O'Connor		07/05/95	M	20	(1)	1
9	John O'Flynn		11/07/82	A	5	(9)	2
23	Mark O'Sullivan		01/02/83	A	24	(4)	9
31	Chiedozie Ogbene		01/05/97	M		(1)	
19	Karl Sheppard		14/02/91	A	30	(1)	12

Derry City FC

1928 • The Brandywell (7,700) • derrycityfc.net

Major honours
Irish League (1) 1965; League of Ireland (2) 1989, 1997; Irish Cup (3) 1949, 1954, 1964; FAI Cup (5) 1989, 1995, 2002 (autumn), 2006, 2012

Manager: Peter Hutton (NIR);
(15/09/15) (Paul Hegarty)

2015

06/03 a Galway	W	2-1	Houston, Curran	
13/03 h Dundalk	L	0-1		
21/03 a Sligo	D	1-1	Lowry	
24/03 a St Patrick's	L	0-2		
27/03 h Drogheda	W	3-0	Elding 2 (1p), McNamee	
03/04 a Cork	L	0-3		
10/04 h Shamrock Rovers	D	0-0		
17/04 h Bray	D	0-0		
20/04 a Limerick	W	2-0	McNamee (p), Timlin	
24/04 h Bohemians	L	1-2	Lowry	
02/05 a Longford	D	0-0		
08/05 h Galway	L	0-2		
15/05 a Dundalk	L	0-1		
22/05 h Sligo	D	1-1	Clucas	
05/06 h St Patrick's	L	0-3		
08/06 h Shamrock Rovers	L	1-4	Curran	
12/06 a Drogheda	D	1-1	Timlin	
26/06 h Cork	L	0-2		
11/07 a Bray	L	0-1		
17/07 h Limerick	D	0-0		
24/07 a Bohemians	L	2-4	Timlin 2	
31/07 h Longford	W	3-0	og (Sullivan), Timlin 2	
07/08 a Galway	W	4-0	O'Connor, Timlin 2 (1p), Dooley	
14/08 h Dundalk	L	0-2		
17/08 a Sligo	L	0-1		
28/08 h St Patrick's	W	1-0	O'Connor	
05/09 h Drogheda	L	0-2		
18/09 h Shamrock Rovers	W	1-0	Jarvis	
25/09 a Cork	D	0-0		
09/10 h Bray	W	3-1	Timlin, Jarvis, P McEleney	
17/10 a Limerick	W	2-0	Dooley, Timlin	
23/10 h Bohemians	L	2-3	O'Connor, McNamee	
30/10 a Longford	L	2-4	Curtis, Cornwall	

No	Name	Nat	DoB	Pos	Aps	(s)	Gls
30	Aaron Barry		24/11/94	D	30		
4	Seanan Clucas	NIR	22/11/92	M	9	(3)	1
18	Robert Cornwall		16/10/94	D	12		1
23	Ryan Curran		13/10/93	A	7	(13)	2
27	Ronan Curtis	NIR	29/03/96	A	2	(11)	1
12	Joshua Daniels	NIR	22/02/96	M	6	(3)	
1	Gerard Doherty		24/08/81	G	29		
11	Stephen Dooley		19/10/91	M	14	(1)	2
9	Anthony Elding	ENG	16/04/82	A	7	(2)	2
32	Ciaron Harkin	NIR	15/01/96	M		(1)	
16	Sean Houston		29/10/89	M	6	(5)	1
3	Dean Jarvis	NIR	01/06/92	D	25	(1)	2
26	Georgie Kelly		12/11/96	A		(3)	
2	Shaun Kelly		15/10/89	D	10		
8	Philip Lowry	NIR	15/07/89	M	24	(1)	2
5	Ryan McBride		15/12/89	D	23		
36	Patrick McClean		22/11/96	D	1	(1)	
6	Conor McCormack		18/05/90	M	9		
10	Patrick McEleney		26/09/92	A	26	(2)	1
6	Shane McEleney		31/01/91	D	21		
4	Aaron McEneff	NIR	09/07/95	M	5	(4)	
7	Ben McLaughlin		15/04/96	D	4	(1)	
7	Barry McNamee		17/02/92	M	32	(1)	3
15	Cillian Morrison		25/07/91	A	9	(11)	
14	Ciaran O'Connor		04/07/96	A	8	(2)	3
20	Shaun Patton		22/08/95	G	4	(2)	
9	Mark Quigley		27/10/85	A	2	(11)	
25	Seamus Sharkey	ENG	11/05/90	D	10	(1)	
19	Mark Timlin		07/11/94	M	28		10

Drogheda United FC

1919 • Hunky Dorys Park (2,500) • droghedaunited.ie
Major honours
League of Ireland (1) 2007; FAI Cup (1) 2005
Manager: John McDonnell;
(30/08/15) Mark Kinsella;
(28/10/15) (Pete Mahon)

2015
07/03	a	Bray	W	1-0	Kavanagh
13/03	h	Sligo	W	3-2	Kavanagh, Brady, Yadolahi
20/03	a	Galway	L	0-1	
24/03	h	Limerick	D	1-1	Thornton
27/03	h	Derry	L	0-3	
03/04	h	Bohemians	L	0-1	
10/04	a	Dundalk	L	0-1	
17/04	h	Cork	L	1-2	Buckley
20/04	a	St Patrick's	D	2-2	Buckley, Duffy (p)
24/04	h	Longford	L	0-3	
01/05	a	Shamrock Rovers	L	0-1	
08/05	h	Bray	W	4-2	Brennan, M Daly, Kavanagh, Mulvenna
11/05	a	Cork	L	1-4	Duffy
16/05	a	Sligo	L	0-2	
22/05	h	Galway	W	2-0	Duffy, Thornton
05/06	a	Limerick	W	2-1	M Daly, Duffy
12/06	h	Derry	D	1-1	Whelan
26/06	a	Bohemians	W	1-0	Mulvenna
03/07	h	Dundalk	L	1-2	Duffy
17/07	h	St Patrick's	L	0-2	
25/07	a	Longford	D	1-1	Duffy
31/07	h	Shamrock Rovers	L	0-1	
08/08	a	Bray	L	0-1	
14/08	h	Sligo	L	0-4	
17/08	a	Galway	D	1-1	M Daly
28/08	h	Limerick	L	1-4	Mulvenna
05/09	a	Derry	W	2-0	Thornton, Marks
18/09	a	Dundalk	L	0-6	
25/09	h	Bohemians	D	2-2	Treacy, Thornton
09/10	h	Cork	D	1-1	Treacy
16/10	a	St Patrick's	L	1-2	Byrne
23/10	h	Longford	L	0-3	
30/10	a	Shamrock Rovers	L	3-5	M Daly, Mulvenna, Duffy

No	Name	Nat	DoB	Pos	Aps	(s)	Gls
45	Robert Bayly		22/02/88	M	4	(5)	
7	Cathal Brady		24/03/85	M	12	(4)	1
9	Seán Brennan		01/01/86	M	22	(4)	1
21	Lloyd Buckley		02/09/96	D	13		2
5	Alan Byrne		21/07/83	D	29		1
19	James Daly		09/01/95	M		(1)	
6	Michael Daly		10/01/89	M	32		4
2	Liam Donnelly		03/08/90	M		(2)	
12	Lee Duffy		07/10/91	A	17	(9)	7
15	Shane Dunne		04/10/91	M	1	(3)	
3	Joe Gorman		01/09/94	D	30		
4	Mark Hughes		28/04/93	M	18	(7)	
22	Daryl Kavanagh		11/08/86	A	11	(1)	3
20	Stephen Maher		03/03/88	M	17	(6)	
23	Jason Marks		02/05/89	M	28	(2)	1
18	Sam McGowan		29/12/96	D	2	(2)	
22	Bob McKenna		16/05/94	A		(8)	
10	Tiarnán Mulvenna		10/12/88	A	13	(12)	4
15	Mark O'Brien		30/10/97	M	1		
14	Robert O'Reilly		26/12/95	D	19	(2)	
11	Ger Pender		22/05/94	A	6	(4)	
26	Fionn Reilly		06/07/96	D		(2)	
24	Matthew Rooney		18/02/90	M		(2)	
16	Michael Schlingermann		23/06/91	G	33		
17	Michael Scott		23/04/94	A	1	(5)	
8	Sean Thornton		18/05/83	M	25	(1)	4
17	Keith Treacy		13/09/88	M	7	(1)	2
11	Carl Walshe		07/10/92	M	6	(8)	
13	Adam Whelan		02/06/95	A	12	(2)	1
45	Neil Yadolahi		19/06/93	D	4		1

Dundalk FC

1903 • Oriel Park (4,500) • dundalkfc.com
Major honours
League of Ireland (11) 1933, 1963, 1967, 1976, 1979, 1982, 1988, 1991, 1995, 2014, 2015; FAI Cup (10) 1942, 1949, 1952, 1958, 1977, 1979, 1981, 1988, 2002 (spring), 2015
Manager: Stephen Kenny

2015
06/03	h	Longford	W	1-0	Horgan
13/03	a	Derry	W	1-0	Massey
20/03	h	St Patrick's	W	3-0	Gartland, McMillan 2
24/03	a	Bohemians	W	3-0	McMillan, Kelly, Meenan
27/03	h	Sligo	W	3-0	McMillan, Towell 2
04/04	a	Limerick	D	1-1	Towell
10/04	h	Drogheda	W	1-0	Towell
17/04	a	Shamrock Rovers	D	2-2	McMillan, Finn
20/04	h	Galway	W	3-0	Towell 3 (1p)
24/04	a	Cork	W	2-1	Towell 2 (1p)
04/05	h	Bray	W	8-1	Towell, Gartland 2, Boyle, Horgan 2, Massey, Finn
09/05	a	Longford	W	2-0	Horgan, Mountney
15/05	h	Derry	W	1-0	Mountney
22/05	a	St Patrick's	W	2-0	Horgan 2
05/06	h	Bohemians	L	1-2	Massey
12/06	a	Sligo	W	2-1	og (Ledwith), Towell (p)
26/06	h	Limerick	W	6-2	O'Donnell, Gartland 2, McMillan 2, og (Whitehead)
03/07	a	Drogheda	W	2-1	Meenan 2
07/07	a	Galway	W	4-2	Towell 2, Massey, Mountney
26/07	h	Cork	D	1-1	Towell (p)
01/08	a	Bray	W	1-0	Kilduff
07/08	h	Longford	D	0-0	
14/08	a	Derry	W	2-0	Kilduff, McMillan
17/08	h	St Patrick's	W	4-1	Gartland, McMillan 2, Horgan
28/08	a	Bohemians	D	2-2	O'Donnell, Towell
01/09	h	Shamrock Rovers	W	2-0	Finn, Gannon
05/09	h	Sligo	D	2-2	Finn 2
18/09	h	Drogheda	W	6-0	Horgan, Towell 4 (1p), McMillan
26/09	a	Limerick	W	3-1	Towell 2, Kilduff
09/10	a	Shamrock Rovers	D	1-1	Towell (p)
16/10	h	Galway	D	0-0	
23/10	a	Cork	D	2-2	McMillan, Towell
30/10	h	Bray	W	4-0	Kilduff, Horgan, Towell 2

No	Name	Nat	DoB	Pos	Aps	(s)	Gls
15	Paddy Barrett		22/07/93	D	6	(5)	
4	Andy Boyle		07/03/91	D	33		1
11	Kurtis Byrne		09/04/90	A		(14)	
10	Ronan Finn		21/12/87	M	33		5
2	Sean Gannon		11/07/91	D	31	(1)	1
3	Brian Gartland		04/11/86	D	27		6
12	Shane Grimes		09/03/87	D	1	(3)	
7	Daryl Horgan		10/08/92	M	32	(1)	9
19	Jake Kelly		18/06/90	M		(6)	1
16	Ciaran Kilduff		29/09/88	A	4	(8)	4
19	Sean Maguire		01/05/94	A	1	(5)	
14	Dane Massey		17/04/88	D	32		4
9	David McMillan		14/12/88	A	29	(4)	12
21	Darren Meenan	NIR	16/11/86	M	21	(7)	3
8	John Mountney		22/02/93	M	13	(20)	3
6	Stephen O'Donnell		15/01/86	M	12	(12)	2
24	Georgie Poynton		08/09/97	M		(2)	
1	Gary Rogers		25/09/81	G	31		
22	Gabriel Sava	ITA	15/10/86	G	2	(1)	
5	Chris Shields		27/12/90	M	23	(7)	
17	Richie Towell		17/07/91	M	32		25

Galway United FC

2013 • Eamonn Deacy Park (5,000) • galwayunitedfc.ie
Manager: Tommy Dunne

2015
06/03	h	Derry	L	1-2	Oji
13/03	a	Bohemians	L	0-2	
20/03	a	Drogheda	W	1-0	Curran
24/03	a	Cork	L	0-2	
27/03	h	Longford	L	1-2	Keegan
03/04	a	Shamrock Rovers	L	0-3	
10/04	a	Sligo	L	0-1	
17/04	h	Limerick	W	3-2	Curran 2 (1p), Shanahan
20/04	a	Dundalk	L	0-3	
25/04	a	Bray	W	5-0	Curran 3, Connolly, Cunningham
01/05	h	St Patrick's	L	1-4	O'Leary
08/05	a	Derry	W	2-0	Cunningham, Keegan
15/05	h	Bohemians	W	5-3	Keegan, Curran 2 (2p), Cunningham, Connolly
22/05	a	Drogheda	L	0-2	
05/06	h	Cork	L	1-3	Molloy
12/06	a	Longford	W	1-0	Keegan
26/06	h	Shamrock Rovers	L	1-2	Curran
04/07	a	Sligo	D	1-1	Connolly
07/07	h	Dundalk	L	2-4	Curran, Cunningham
11/07	a	Limerick	W	4-2	Keegan 3, Shanahan
24/07	h	Bray	L	0-1	
31/07	a	St Patrick's	L	1-3	Keegan
07/08	h	Derry	L	0-4	
14/08	a	Bohemians	L	0-3	
17/08	h	Drogheda	D	1-1	Keegan
28/08	a	Cork	L	0-1	
05/09	h	Longford	W	4-2	Keegan 3, Shanahan
25/09	a	Shamrock Rovers	L	0-2	
02/10	h	Sligo	W	2-1	Curran 2
09/10	h	Limerick	L	1-3	Oji
16/10	a	Dundalk	D	0-0	
24/10	a	Bray	D	1-1	Shanahan
30/10	h	St Patrick's	L	0-1	

No	Name	Nat	DoB	Pos	Aps	(s)	Gls
21	Conor Barry		02/09/95	M	1	(2)	
4	Alex Byrne		08/03/95	M	18	(4)	
5	Kilian Cantwell		24/05/95	D	7	(2)	
10	Ryan Connolly		13/01/92	M	25	(1)	3
18	Padraic Cunningham		13/11/96	A	9	(12)	4
9	Enda Curran		11/06/92	A	22	(3)	12
20	Kevin Garcia	USA	21/08/90	D	8	(3)	
16	Connor Gleeson		13/06/93	G	7		
1	Ger Hanley		04/01/91	G	8	(1)	
2	Colm Horgan		02/07/94	D	31		
16	Kevin Horgan		26/04/97	G		(1)	
12	Jake Keegan	USA	21/04/91	A	32	(1)	12
3	Marc Ludden		28/02/90	D	18	(2)	
14	Aran McConnell		18/07/96	D	1	(1)	
22	Conor Melody		15/03/97	M	4	(5)	
11	Jason Molloy		22/09/88	M	11	(4)	1
19	Andy O'Connell		09/03/93	D	4	(6)	
22	Colm O'Donovan		22/08/90	A	1		
15	Antaine O'Laoi		03/02/97	M	1	(3)	
8	David O'Leary		17/07/92	M	23	(6)	1
24	Sam Oji	ENG	09/10/85	D	21	(2)	2
13	Cormac Raftery		27/04/95	D	10	(3)	
28	Tomi Saarelma	FIN	30/11/88	M	1	(4)	
17	Gary Shanahan		15/02/93	A	30	(3)	4
6	Paul Sinnott		24/07/86	M	26	(2)	
7	Stephen Walsh		29/08/90	M	26	(2)	
25	Conor Winn		26/02/92	G	18		

Limerick FC

1937 • Jackman Park (2,500);
Market's Field (3,000) • limerickfc.ie
Major honours
League of Ireland (2) 1960, 1980; FAI Cup (2) 1971, 1982
Manager: Martin Russell

2015

Date		Opponent	Res	Scorers
07/03	h	Bohemians	L	0-3	
13/03	a	Cork	L	0-5	
21/03	h	Longford	D	2-2	Russell 2
24/03	a	Drogheda	D	1-1	Turner (p)
28/03	a	St Patrick's	L	1-2	Turner
04/04	h	Dundalk	D	1-1	O'Conor
11/04	a	Bray	L	0-4	
17/04	a	Galway	L	2-3	og (Garcia), Faherty
20/04	h	Derry	L	0-2	
25/04	h	Shamrock Rovers	D	1-1	Duggan
02/05	a	Sligo	D	1-1	O'Conor
08/05	h	Bohemians	L	1-2	Clarke
16/05	h	Cork	L	0-1	
23/05	a	Longford	L	0-1	
05/06	h	Drogheda	L	1-2	O'Conor
12/06	a	St Patrick's	L	1-3	Clarke
26/06	a	Dundalk	L	2-6	Harding, Duggan
04/07	h	Bray	L	0-1	
11/07	h	Galway	L	2-4	Faherty, Turner (p)
17/07	a	Derry	D	0-0	
26/07	a	Shamrock Rovers	L	1-4	Turner
01/08	h	Sligo	W	3-2	Faherty 2, Clarke
08/08	h	Bohemians	W	4-3	Faherty, Russell, Lynch, Tracy (p)
14/08	a	Cork	W	3-2	Faherty, Clarke, O'Connor
17/08	h	Longford	D	3-3	Turner, Tracy, Williams
28/08	a	Drogheda	W	4-1	Faherty, Turner (p), Rainsford, Williams
05/09	h	St Patrick's	W	3-1	Turner 2, Faherty
19/09	a	Bray	D	2-2	Clarke, Faherty
26/09	h	Dundalk	L	1-3	Clarke
09/10	a	Galway	W	3-1	Faherty 2, Turner
17/10	h	Derry	L	0-2	
24/10	h	Shamrock Rovers	L	0-2	
30/10	a	Sligo	W	3-2	Duggan, O'Conor, Faherty

No	Name	Nat	DoB	Pos	Aps	(s)	Gls
16	Prince Agyemang	GHA	25/12/94	M	1	(5)	
9	Dean Clarke		29/03/93	A	32		6
17	Shane Costelloe		03/08/95	D	1	(2)	
8	Shane Duggan		11/03/89	M	29	(1)	3
10	Vinny Faherty		13/06/87	A	19	(9)	12
18	Val Feeney		12/01/96	M		(2)	
33	Cyril Guedjé	TOG	19/06/92	A		(3)	
34	Freddy Hall	BER	08/03/85	G	14		
22	Kieran Hanlon		11/04/95	A	1	(5)	
2	Sean Harding		17/09/88	D	13		1
30	Tommy Holland		01/04/98	G	2		
29	Jason Hughes		09/04/91	M	11	(5)	
32	Patrick Kanyuka	COD	19/07/87	D	10		
2	Shaun Kelly		15/10/89	D	9	(1)	
28	Lee Lynch		27/11/91	M	14	(1)	1
19	Ross Mann		09/01/96	A	2	(8)	
25	Sean McSweeney		08/10/97	A		(2)	
24	Paudie O'Connor		14/07/97	D	15	(1)	1
6	Paul O'Conor		10/08/87	M	32		4
1	Conor O'Donnell		17/01/94	G	17		
5	Aidan Price		08/12/81	D	14		
12	Daragh Rainsford		15/11/94	A	13	(12)	1
14	Seán Russell		10/12/93	M	25	(5)	3
11	Shane Tracy		14/09/88	M	23	(2)	2
7	Ian Turner		19/04/89	M	29	(3)	9
15	Tony Whitehead		22/12/94	M	7	(6)	
3	Robbie Williams	ENG	02/10/84	D	30		

Longford Town FC

1924 • City Calling Stadium (4,500) • ltfc.ie
Major honours
FAI Cup (2) 2003, 2004
Manager: Tony Cousins

2015

Date		Opponent	Res	Scorers
06/03	a	Dundalk	L	0-1	
14/03	h	Shamrock Rovers	L	0-2	
21/03	a	Limerick	D	2-2	O'Sullivan 2
24/03	h	Bray	W	2-0	Flynn, Shaw
27/03	a	Galway	W	2-1	Shaw, Cowan
04/04	h	St Patrick's	D	2-2	O'Connor, Salmon (p)
10/04	a	Bohemians	L	0-2	
17/04	h	Sligo	D	1-1	O'Connor
20/04	a	Cork	L	0-2	
24/04	a	Drogheda	W	3-0	O'Sullivan, Salmon 2
02/05	h	Derry	D	0-0	
09/05	h	Dundalk	L	0-2	
15/05	a	Shamrock Rovers	L	2-3	Flynn, Simon
23/05	h	Limerick	W	1-0	Salmon
05/06	a	Bray	W	1-0	Ben Mohamed
12/06	h	Galway	L	0-1	
26/06	a	St Patrick's	L	0-3	
04/07	h	Bohemians	W	2-1	O'Sullivan, Ben Mohamed
11/07	a	Sligo	L	2-3	Salmon (p), Kelly
18/07	h	Cork	L	1-4	Kelly
25/07	h	Drogheda	D	1-1	Simon
31/07	a	Derry	L	0-3	
07/08	a	Dundalk	D	0-0	
14/08	h	Shamrock Rovers	L	1-3	Shannon
17/08	a	Limerick	D	3-3	Gorman, Salmon, Rice
29/08	h	Bray	W	1-0	O'Sullivan
05/09	a	Galway	L	2-4	Kelly 2 (1p)
18/09	a	Bohemians	D	1-1	Haverty
26/09	h	St Patrick's	L	0-3	
10/10	h	Sligo	D	1-1	Simon
16/10	a	Cork	W	3-2	O'Sullivan, Rice, O'Connor
23/10	a	Drogheda	W	3-0	Shaw 2, Rice
30/10	h	Derry	W	4-2	O'Sullivan (p), Rossiter, Shaw, Sullivan (p)

No	Name	Nat	DoB	Pos	Aps	(s)	Gls
16	Ayman Ben Mohamed	TUN	08/12/94	M	19	(8)	2
9	Don Cowan		16/11/89	A	4	(6)	1
3	Martin Deady		07/09/89	M	13	(2)	
26	Jack Doherty		03/08/94	M	4		
20	Pat Flynn		13/01/85	D	11		2
21	Philip Gannon		11/10/96	M	6	(2)	
24	Rhys Gorman		24/01/94	M	21	(5)	1
4	Noel Haverty		24/02/89	D	3		1
1	Paul Hunt	ENG	06/04/90	G	17		
25	Dean Kelly		18/09/85	A	7	(5)	4
2	Jamie Mulhall		29/01/96	D	12	(6)	
11	Kevin O'Connor		19/10/85	M	32		3
15	David O'Sullivan		04/10/87	A	19	(11)	7
12	Conor Powell		26/08/87	D	28	(1)	
6	Stephen Rice		06/10/84	M	29	(1)	3
22	Mark Rossiter		27/05/83	D	17	(1)	1
8	Mark Salmon		31/10/88	M	21	(6)	6
7	Lorcan Shannon		10/11/93	M	10	(11)	1
10	Gary Shaw		10/05/92	A	32		5
19	Kaleem Simon		08/07/96	M	7	(18)	3
18	Paul Skinner		03/02/89	G	16	(1)	
14	Pat Sullivan		30/10/82	D	27		1
5	Willie Tyrell		19/08/84	D	8	(3)	

Saint Patrick's Athletic FC

1929 • Richmond Park (4,000) • stpatsfc.com
Major honours
League of Ireland (8) 1952, 1955, 1956, 1990, 1996, 1998, 1999, 2013; FAI Cup (3) 1959, 1961, 2014
Manager: Liam Buckley

2015

Date		Opponent	Res	Scorers
06/03	a	Shamrock Rovers	L	0-1	
13/03	h	Bray	W	3-0	Brennan (p), Forrester, Fagan
20/03	a	Dundalk	L	0-3	
24/03	h	Derry	W	2-0	Bolger, Langley
28/03	h	Limerick	W	2-1	Greene 2
04/04	a	Longford	D	2-2	Forrester, Byrne
10/04	h	Cork	D	0-0	
17/04	a	Bohemians	W	1-0	Kilduff
20/04	h	Drogheda	D	2-2	Byrne, Kilduff
24/04	h	Sligo	W	3-0	Greene 2, Forrester
01/05	a	Galway	W	4-1	Brennan (p), Byrne 2, Kilduff
11/05	h	Shamrock Rovers	D	0-0	
16/05	a	Bray	L	0-1	
22/05	h	Dundalk	L	0-2	
05/06	a	Derry	W	3-0	Greene, Chambers, Forrester
09/06	h	Bohemians	W	3-1	Fagan 2, Brennan
12/06	a	Limerick	W	3-1	Forrester, Greene, Fagan
26/06	a	Longford	W	3-0	Forrester 2 (1p), Chambers
17/07	a	Drogheda	W	2-0	Brennan, McGrath
25/07	a	Sligo	W	3-0	Forrester 2, McGrath
31/07	h	Galway	W	3-1	Forrester, Byrne 2 (1p)
07/08	a	Shamrock Rovers	W	2-0	Forrester, Langley
14/08	h	Bray	W	1-0	Bolger
17/08	a	Dundalk	L	1-4	Chambers
28/08	h	Derry	L	0-1	
31/08	a	Cork	L	1-3	Langley
05/09	a	Limerick	L	1-3	Chambers
26/09	h	Longford	W	3-0	Fagan, Chambers, Greene
09/10	a	Bohemians	L	0-2	
16/10	h	Drogheda	W	2-1	Byrne (p), Fagan
19/10	h	Cork	L	1-2	Greene
23/10	a	Sligo	L	0-2	
30/10	h	Galway	W	1-0	Greene

No	Name	Nat	DoB	Pos	Aps	(s)	Gls
26	Jack Bayly		18/06/96	M		(5)	
3	Ian Bermingham		16/06/89	D	30		
6	Greg Bolger		09/09/88	M	21	(2)	2
11	Killian Brennan		31/01/84	M	24	(1)	4
15	Kenny Browne		07/08/86	D	18		
7	Conán Byrne		10/07/85	M	29		7
14	James Chambers		14/02/87	M	29	(3)	5
1	Brendan Clarke		17/09/85	G	16		
12	Lee Desmond		22/01/95	D	16	(8)	
9	Christy Fagan		11/05/89	A	16		6
17	Chris Forrester		17/12/92	M	24		11
20	Aaron Greene		02/01/90	M	29	(2)	8
23	Cyril Guedjé	TOG	19/06/92	A		(1)	
5	Sean Hoare		15/03/94	D	20	(2)	
10	Ciaran Kilduff		29/09/88	A	9	(4)	3
8	Morgan Langley	USA	09/06/89	M	3	(15)	3
21	Darren Markey		23/05/97	M		(4)	
22	Conor McCormack		18/05/90	M	5	(10)	
22	Shane McEleney		31/01/91	D	8		
19	Jamie McGrath		30/09/96	M	14	(9)	2
4	Jason McGuinness		08/08/82	D	9	(3)	
27	Ian Morris		27/02/87	M	2	(5)	
2	Ger O'Brien		02/07/84	D	21		
16	Conor O'Malley		01/08/94	G	17		
18	Sam Verdon		03/09/95	A	3	(6)	

 # REPUBLIC OF IRELAND

Shamrock Rovers FC

1901 • Tallaght Stadium (6,500) •
shamrockrovers.ie

Major honours
*League of Ireland (17) 1923, 1925, 1927, 1932, 1938,
1939, 1954, 1957, 1959, 1964, 1984, 1985, 1986,
1987, 1994, 2010, 2011; FAI Cup (24) 1925, 1929,
1930, 1931, 1932, 1933, 1936, 1940, 1944, 1945,
1948, 1955, 1956, 1962, 1964, 1965, 1966, 1967,
1968, 1969, 1978, 1985, 1986, 1987*

Manager: Pat Fenlon

2015

06/03	h	St Patrick's	W	1-0	*North*	
14/03	a	Longford	W	2-0	*S O'Connor, Waters*	
20/03	h	Cork	D	0-0		
24/03	a	Sligo	W	2-1	*S O'Connor, Drennan*	
27/03	h	Bohemians	D	0-0		
03/04	h	Galway	W	3-0	*Drennan 2, Miele*	
10/04	a	Derry	D	0-0		
17/04	h	Dundalk	D	2-2	*Drennan 2 (1p)*	
20/04	a	Bray	W	3-0	*Drennan, R Brennan, Blanchard*	
25/04	a	Limerick	D	1-1	*Miele*	
01/05	h	Drogheda	W	1-0	*Drennan*	
11/05	a	St Patrick's	D	0-0		
15/05	h	Longford	W	3-2	*G Brennan, Blanchard 2*	
22/05	a	Cork	D	0-0		
05/06	h	Sligo	W	5-1	*Miele 2, Waters, Drennan 2 (1p)*	
08/06	h	Derry	W	4-1	*Drennan, McCabe, Waters, Miele*	
12/06	a	Bohemians	L	1-3	*Waters*	
26/06	a	Galway	W	2-1	*Byrne, Waters*	
26/07	h	Limerick	W	4-1	*Miele 2, Kenna, Cregg*	
31/07	a	Drogheda	W	1-0	*Miele*	
07/08	h	St Patrick's	L	0-2		
14/08	a	Longford	W	3-1	*Drennan, North 2*	
17/08	h	Cork	W	3-0	*G Brennan, North, Miele*	
29/08	a	Sligo	D	1-1	*McCabe*	
01/09	a	Dundalk	L	0-2		
05/09	h	Bohemians	D	1-1	*McCaffrey*	
18/09	a	Derry	L	0-1		
22/09	h	Bray	W	1-0	*Miele*	
25/09	a	Galway	W	2-0	*G Brennan, North*	
09/10	h	Dundalk	D	1-1	*North*	
17/10	a	Bray	D	2-2	*Drennan, Blanchard*	
24/10	a	Limerick	W	2-0	*Miele, McPhail*	
30/10	h	Drogheda	W	5-3	*og (O'Reilly), North 3 (2p), Waters*	

No	Name	Nat	DoB	Pos	Aps	(s)	Gls
6	Maxime Blanchard	FRA	27/09/86	D	17		4
15	Gavin Brennan		23/01/88	M	21	(6)	3
8	Ryan Brennan		11/11/91	M	13	(12)	1
3	Luke Byrne		08/07/93	D	21		1
19	Tim Clancy		08/06/84	D	1	(2)	
16	Patrick Cregg		21/02/86	M	26	(3)	1
21	Michael Drennan		02/02/94	A	23	(6)	12
32	Damien Duff		02/03/79	M	4	(5)	
18	Keith Fahey		15/01/83	M	12		
25	Craig Hyland		08/09/90	G	20		
22	Cian Kavanagh		16/09/96	M	1	(1)	
28	Dylan Kavanagh		13/04/96	M		(1)	
4	Conor Kenna		21/11/84	D	27	(1)	1
17	Simon Madden		01/05/88	D	33		
7	Gary McCabe		01/08/88	M	22	(4)	2
27	Gareth McCaffrey		16/01/96	A	3	(12)	1
37	Stephen McPhail		09/12/79	M	13	(5)	1
20	Brandon Miele		28/08/94	M	24	(4)	11
1	Barry Murphy		08/06/85	G	13		
9	Danny North		07/09/87	A	15	(5)	9
5	David O'Connor		24/08/91	D	15	(1)	
10	Sean O'Connor		21/10/83	M	7	(3)	2
11	Kieran Waters		05/05/90	M	9	(12)	6
14	David Webster		08/09/89	D	23	(1)	

Sligo Rovers FC

1928 • The Showgrounds (5,500) •
sligorovers.com

Major honours
*League of Ireland (3) 1937, 1977, 2012; FAI Cup (5)
1983, 1994, 2010, 2011, 2013*

**Manager: Owen Heary;
(29/06/15) (Gavin Dykes & Joseph Ndo (CMR));
(04/08/15) Micky Adams (ENG)**

2015

07/03	h	Cork	D	1-1	*Beattie*
13/03	a	Drogheda	L	2-3	*Corcoran, Peers*
21/03	a	Derry	D	1-1	*Wearen*
24/03	h	Shamrock Rovers	L	1-2	*Ledwith*
27/03	a	Dundalk	L	0-3	
03/04	h	Bray	L	1-3	*Beattie*
10/04	a	Galway	W	1-0	*Corcoran (p)*
17/04	a	Longford	D	1-1	*Cawley*
20/04	h	Bohemians	D	0-0	
24/04	a	St Patrick's	L	0-3	
02/05	h	Limerick	D	1-1	*Corcoran*
08/05	a	Cork	L	2-3	*Russell, Devaney*
16/05	h	Drogheda	W	2-0	*Corcoran 2*
22/05	a	Derry	D	1-1	*Puri*
05/06	a	Shamrock Rovers	L	1-5	*Corcoran*
12/06	h	Dundalk	L	1-2	*Nielsen*
27/06	a	Bray	L	0-1	
04/07	h	Galway	D	1-1	*Corcoran*
11/07	h	Longford	W	3-2	*Cawley, Ward, Corcoran*
17/07	a	Bohemians	L	0-1	
25/07	h	St Patrick's	L	0-3	
01/08	a	Limerick	L	2-3	*Lehane, Armstrong*
08/08	h	Cork	L	0-2	
14/08	a	Drogheda	W	4-0	*Nielsen 2, Hughes, Elding (p)*
17/08	h	Derry	W	1-0	*Clancy*
29/08	h	Shamrock Rovers	D	1-1	*Puri*
05/09	a	Dundalk	D	2-2	*Corcoran, Keane*
26/09	h	Bray	W	3-2	*Corcoran, Puri, Nielsen*
02/10	a	Galway	L	1-2	*Nielsen*
10/10	a	Longford	D	1-1	*Elding*
17/10	h	Bohemians	L	0-2	
23/10	a	St Patrick's	W	2-0	*Corcoran 2 (1p)*
30/10	h	Limerick	L	2-3	*Puri, Keating*

No	Name	Nat	DoB	Pos	Aps	(s)	Gls
20	Gary Armstrong		28/01/96	M	5	(7)	1
22	Steven Beattie		20/08/88	M	14		2
14	Gary Boylan		24/04/96	D	21		
42	Richard Brush	ENG	26/11/84	G	27		
8	David Cawley		17/09/91	M	30		2
5	Tim Clancy		08/06/84	D	8		1
9	Daniel Corcoran		13/02/89	A	23	(5)	12
1	Ryan Coulter		08/02/93	G	6	(1)	
10	Raffaele Cretaro		15/10/81	M	18	(9)	
7	Kevin Devaney		26/09/90	M	7	(8)	1
19	Regan Donelon		17/04/96	D	12	(1)	
15	Jake Dykes		30/06/95	D	10	(2)	
99	Anthony Elding	ENG	16/04/82	A		(8)	2
24	Liam Flatley		21/11/96	M	2	(1)	
5	Stephen Folan		14/01/92	D	16		
11	Jason Hughes		09/04/91	M	8	(1)	1
2	Alan Keane		23/09/84	D	31	(1)	1
16	Ruairi Keating		16/07/95	A		(7)	1
3	Danny Ledwith		17/08/91	M	15	(5)	1
22	Robert Lehane		19/02/94	A	1	(1)	1
26	Ryan McManus		15/06/96	M	3	(1)	
31	Jennison Myrie-Williams	ENG	17/05/88	M	7		
21	Morten Nielsen	DEN	24/02/90	A	19	(8)	5
29	Patrick Nzuzi	COD	24/10/92	D	1		
4	Gavin Peers		10/11/85	D	24		1
12	Sander Puri	EST	07/05/88	M	23	(4)	4
18	John Russell		18/05/85	M	13		1
17	Keith Ward		12/10/90	M	9	(8)	1
11	Eoin Wearen		02/10/92	M	10	(1)	1

Top goalscorers

25	Richie Towell (Dundalk)
12	Karl Sheppard (Cork)
	David McMillan (Dundalk)
	Enda Curran (Galway)
	Jake Keegan (Galway)
	Vinny Faherty (Limerick)
	Michael Drennan (Shamrock Rovers)
	Daniel Corcoran (Sligo)
11	Chris Forrester (St Patrick's)
	Brandon Miele (Shamrock Rovers)

Promoted clubs

Wexford Youths FC

2007 • Ferrycarrig Park (3,000) •
wexfordyouthsfc.ie
Manager: Shane Keegan

Finn Harps FC

1954 • Finn Park (4,000) • finnharps.com

Major honours
FAI Cup (1) 1974
Manager: Ollie Horgan

Second level final table 2015

		Pld	W	D	L	F	A	Pts
1	Wexford Youths FC	28	20	1	7	63	32	61
2	Finn Harps FC	28	16	7	5	42	23	55
3	University College Dublin AFC	28	14	7	7	51	26	49
4	Shelbourne FC	28	13	6	9	37	34	45
5	Athlone Town FC	28	9	6	13	36	42	33
6	Cobh Ramblers FC	28	8	6	14	27	45	30
7	Waterford United FC	28	5	6	17	25	51	21
8	Cabinteely FC	28	5	5	18	22	50	20

Promotion/Relegation play-offs

(23/10/15 & 30/10/15)
UCD 0-1 Finn Harps
Finn Harps 2-1 UCD
(Finn Harps 3-1)

(02/11/15 & 06/11/15)
Limerick 1-0 Finn Harps
Finn Harps 2-0 Limerick *(aet)*
(Finn Harps 2-1)

DOMESTIC CUP

FAI Cup 2015

SECOND ROUND

(29/05/15)
Bohemians 4-1 Firhouse
Bray 3-1 Limerick
Drogheda 3-1 Cabinteely
Dundalk 5-0 Shelbourne
Galway 1-0 North End
Longford 1-1 Finn Harps
St Patrick's 2-1 Shamrock Rovers
Tolka 2-1 Waterford
Wexford 0-2 Cork

(30/05/15)
Athlone 3-2 Liffey
Killester 3-0 Cobh Ramblers

(31/05/15)
Cobh Wanderers 3-3 Avondale
Cockhill 3-0 St Mochta's
Edenderry 0-3 Derry
Sligo 2-0 Crumlin
UCD 1-3 Sheriff

Replays

(01/06/15)
Finn Harps 0-0 Longford *(aet; 3-4 on pens)*

(03/06/15)
Avondale 0-3 Cobh Wanderers

THIRD ROUND

(21/08/15)
Bohemians 0-1 Bray
Cork 4-0 St Patrick's
Derry 3-0 Drogheda
Galway 1-4 Dundalk
Sheriff 2-2 Athlone
Tolka 0-4 Killester

(22/08/15)
Cockhill 0-2 Longford
Cobh Wanderers 0-4 Sligo

Replay

(24/08/15)
Athlone 0-0 Sheriff *(aet; 3-4 on pens)*

QUARTER-FINALS

(11/09/15)
Bray 2-0 Killester *(Douglas 7, Scully 57)*
Derry 1-1 Cork *(McBride 5; O'Sullivan 50)*
Dundalk 4-0 Sligo *(Horgan 55, Kilduff 63, Finn 75, Maguire 88)*
Longford 3-1 Sheriff *(O'Sullivan 25, Ben Mohamed 46, Shannon 48; Flood 45+1)*

Replay

(14/09/15)
Cork 3-0 Derry *(Gaynor 75, Buckley 77, O'Flynn 86)*

SEMI-FINALS

(02/10/15)
Dundalk 2-0 Longford *(Barrett 36, Finn 49)*

(04/10/15)
Bray 0-1 Cork *(Morrissey 60)*

FINAL

(08/11/15)
Aviva Stadium, Dublin
DUNDALK FC 1 *(Towell 107)*
CORK CITY FC 0
(aet)
Referee: *McKeon*
DUNDALK: *Rogers, Gannon (O'Donnell 43), Boyle, Gartland, Massey, Meenan (Mountney 77), Shields, Towell, Finn, Horgan, McMillan (Kilduff 71)*
CORK: *McNulty, Dunleavy, Bennett, D Dennehy, Gaynor, B Dennehy, O'Connor, Miller (Healy 59), Buckley, Sheppard (Murray 101), O'Sullivan (Morrissey 79)*

Dundalk completed the double with an extra-time victory over Cork in the FAI Cup final

ROMANIA
Federaţia Română de Fotbal (FRF)

Address   Casa Fotbalului
Str. Serg. Serbanica
Vasile 12
RO-022186 Bucureşti
Tel   +40 21 325 0678
Fax   +40 21 325 0679
E-mail   frf@frf.ro
Website   frf.ro

President   Răzvan Burleanu
General secretary   Radu Traian Visan
Media officer   Gabriel Berceanu
Year of formation   1909
National stadium   Arena Naţională,
Bucharest (54,600)

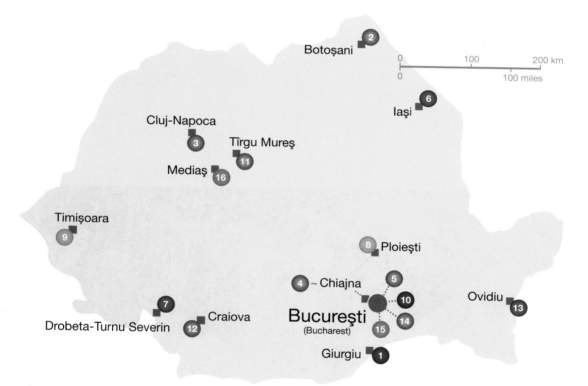

LIGA I CLUBS

 1 FC Astra Giurgiu

 2 FC Botoşani

 3 CFR 1907 Cluj

 4 CS Concordia Chiajna

 5 FC Dinamo Bucureşti

 6 CSMS Iaşi

 7 CS Pandurii Târgu Jiu

 8 FC Petrolul Ploieşti

 9 ACS Poli Timişoara

 10 FC Steaua Bucureşti

 11 ASA Tîrgu Mureş

 12 CS Universitatea Craiova

 13 FC Viitorul

 14 FC Voluntari

PROMOTED CLUBS

 15 FC Rapid Bucureşti

 16 CS Gaz Metan Mediaş

KEY

● UEFA Champions League

● UEFA Europa League

● Promoted

● Relegated

Astra reach for the stars

A revised format to the Romanian Liga I produced a new champion as Astra Giurgiu impressively stood up to the challenge of a strenuous two-tiered, 36-match campaign, leading the way from August to May and landing their first league title ahead of deposed champions Steaua Bucureşti.

There was a fourth Romanian Cup win for CFR 1907 Cluj, although neither they nor defeated finalists Dinamo Bucureşti were able to obtain a licence to compete in Europe. Anghel Iordănescu's national side did make it to the UEFA EURO 2016 finals but returned home early after finishing bottom of their group.

Resilient frontrunners claim first league title	Cluj beat Dinamo on penalties to win cup	Albania defeat brings early EURO exit

Domestic league

Second in 2013/14 and third in 2014/15, Astra, who relocated themselves from Ploiesti to Giurgiu in 2012, had already established themselves as a coming force in the Romanian game, so it was no great surprise that they emerged as credible Liga I title challengers again in 2015/16. They got off to a tentative start but a 2-0 home win over Steaua, the champions of the past three seasons, rekindled their ambitions and by the end of August they were sitting pretty at the top of the table.

It was a position from which Marius Şumudica's disciplined and determined unit would never be shifted. By the winter break, with 23 matches played, Astra were three points ahead of Gheorghe Hagi's FC Viitorul, with Dinamo and Steaua third and fourth, respectively. Steaua had gambled by appointing 34-year-old playing legend Mirel Rădoi as coach following the departure of double-winning Constantin Gâlcă, but it backfired and he quit after a home defeat by Astra, to be replaced a few days later by Laurenţiu Reghecampf, the club's title-winning coach in 2012/13 and 2013/14.

Revived by Reghecampf and with young playmaker Nicolae Stanciu back to his best, Steaua came hard at Astra in the spring as the other prospective challengers, notably a free-falling Viitorul, faded away, but the leaders would not be budged. Despite a 2-0 defeat by Steaua, which ended a 12-game unbeaten run, they carried a two-point lead into the second phase and proceeded to increase it. A revenge 2-0 win over Steaua, in which Romanian internationals Valeriu Găman and top-scoring striker Denis Alibec both scored penalties, effectively sealed the club's first title – although mathematical confirmation was suspended until Steaua's May Day 1-1 draw at home to third-placed Pandurii Târgu Jiu, the visitors' goal coming from Liga I golden boot winner Ioan Hora.

By finishing second, Steaua claimed the same UEFA Champions League prize as Astra – a spot in the third qualifying round – while licensing issues meant that Pandurii were accompanied into the UEFA Europa League by fifth-placed Vittorul and relegation pool winners CSMS Iaşi.

Domestic cup

CFR Cluj regained the trophy they had won three years running from 2008-10, defeating Dinamo the hard way in the Arena Naţionala after clawing back a 2-0 half-time deficit, scoring an 89th-minute equaliser and prevailing 5-4 on penalties. It was tough to take for Dinamo and their coach Mircea Rednic, who had reached the final after eliminating all three clubs that finished above them in the league – Pandurii, Astra and, on away goals in the semi-final, arch-rivals Steaua.

Europe

All Romanian interest in 2015/16 European club competition was extinguished early as the last two remaining teams, Astra and Steaua, both lost their UEFA Europa League play-offs. Astra departed with a feather in their cap, however, having knocked out West Ham United in the third qualifying round thanks to two goals in the second leg from Romanian international Constantin Budescu.

National team

There were nine Liga I players selected for Romania's UEFA EURO 2016 squad, but Budescu, who also scored twice in the 3-0 win over the Faroe Islands that booked the team's place at the finals, was not among them. Although Iordănescu went 12 games unbeaten on his return to the job – until a 4-3 friendly defeat by Ukraine – the 'General' was unable to rekindle the glory and excitement of the 1994 FIFA World Cup, when he led a Hagi-inspired Romania to the quarter-finals. Instead, there was a rather subdued look to the class of 2016 as they exited early after a shock 1-0 defeat by Albania in Lyon, departing with just one point and two goals – both Bogdan Stancu penalties.

DOMESTIC SEASON AT A GLANCE

Liga I 2015/16 final table

		Pld	Home					Away					Total					Pts
			W	D	L	F	A	W	D	L	F	A	W	D	L	F	A	
1	**FC Astra Giurgiu**	36	9	7	2	32	21	12	3	3	30	17	21	10	5	62	38	48
2	FC Steaua Bucureşti	36	9	8	1	30	14	9	3	6	23	19	18	11	7	53	33	43
3	CS Pandurii Târgu Jiu	36	8	7	3	27	20	8	7	3	20	13	16	14	6	47	33	39
4	FC Dinamo Bucureşti	36	10	4	4	28	21	5	11	2	20	18	15	15	6	48	39	36
5	FC Viitorul	36	8	2	8	34	24	6	8	4	29	27	14	10	12	63	51	29
6	ASA Tîrgu Mureş	36	4	10	4	15	19	5	4	9	20	26	9	14	13	35	45	22
7	CSMS Iaşi	40	8	6	6	18	15	6	9	5	21	25	14	15	11	39	40	39
8	CS Universitatea Craiova	40	10	5	5	29	15	5	4	11	16	29	15	9	16	45	44	39
9	FC Botoşani	40	10	6	4	37	23	3	6	11	22	31	13	12	15	59	54	38
10	CFR 1907 Cluj	40	11	6	3	34	11	4	8	8	22	27	15	14	11	56	38	36
11	CS Concordia Chiajna	40	4	9	7	21	26	6	4	10	20	33	10	13	17	41	59	35
12	FC Voluntari	40	5	7	8	25	25	5	4	11	22	37	10	11	19	47	62	29
13	ACS Poli Timişoara	40	6	4	10	23	30	0	10	10	15	41	6	14	20	38	71	20
14	FC Petrolul Ploieşti	40	5	5	10	17	25	1	5	14	9	27	6	10	24	26	52	18

NB League splits into top six and bottom eight after 26 games, after which the clubs play exclusively against teams in their group. Points obtained during the regular season are halved (and rounded upwards).

European qualification 2016/17

Champion: FC Astra Giurgiu (third qualifying round)
FC Steaua Bucureşti (third qualifying round)

CS Pandurii Târgu Jiu (third qualifying round)
FC Viitorul (third qualifying round)
CSMS Iaşi (second qualifying round)
NB Cup winner CFR 1907 Cluj did not receive a licence.

Top scorer	Ioan Hora (Pandurii), 19 goals
Relegated clubs	FC Petrolul Ploieşti, ACS Poli Timişoara
Promoted clubs	FC Rapid Bucureşti, CS Gaz Metan Mediaş
Cup final	CFR 1907 Cluj 2-2 FC Dinamo Bucureşti *(aet; 5-4 on pens)*

Team of the season
(4-4-2)

Coach: Şumudică *(Astra)*

Niță *(Steaua)*

Benzar *(Viitorul)* — Săpunaru *(Pandurii)* — Găman *(Astra)* — Vătăjelu *(U Craiova)*

Tănase *(Viitorul)* — Stanciu *(Steaua)* — Rotariu *(Dinamo)* — Hamroun *(Steaua)*

Hora *(Pandurii)* — Alibec *(Astra)*

Player of the season

Denis Alibec
(FC Astra Giurgiu)

A strapping centre-forward of the old school with a booming left-foot shot, Alibec was the attacking spearhead of Astra's 2015/16 Liga I title-winning side, scoring 16 goals in 26 starts, all of them in singles with the exception of a brilliant hat-trick away to Dinamo Bucureşti. Once on the books of Italian giants Internazionale, for whom he made two Serie A appearances, the 25-year-old's coming of age in 2015/16 earned him a first call-up for Romania and a place in his country's UEFA EURO 2016 finals squad.

Newcomer of the season

Florin Tănase
(FC Viitorul)

Playing for a club owned and coached by the legendary Gheorghe Hagi is the dream of most, perhaps all, Romanian footballers, and Tănase has been able to live it at Viitorul. The 21-year-old midfielder-cum-winger was the revelation of the 2015/16 Liga I season, dazzling spectators and opponents alike with his nimble, on-the-ball trickery and also topping the team's scoring charts by a distance with 15 goals – despite having reluctantly ceded the club's precious No10 shirt to returning veteran Florin Cernat.

NATIONAL TEAM

International tournament appearances

FIFA World Cup (7) 1930, 1934, 1938, 1970, 1990 (2nd round), 1994 (qtr-finals), 1998 (2nd round)
UEFA European Championship (5) 1984, 1996, 2000 (qtr-finals), 2008, 2016

Top five all-time caps

Dorinel Munteanu (134); Gheorghe Hagi (124); Gheorghe Popescu (115); **Răzvan Raţ** (113); László Bölöni (102)

Top five all-time goals

Gheorghe Hagi & Adrian Mutu (35); Iuliu Bodola (30); Ciprian Marica & Viorel Moldovan (25)

Results 2015/16

04/09/15	Hungary (ECQ)	A	Budapest	D	0-0
07/09/15	Greece (ECQ)	H	Bucharest	D	0-0
08/10/15	Finland (ECQ)	H	Bucharest	D	1-1	*Hoban (90+1)*
11/10/15	Faroe Islands (ECQ)	A	Torshavn	W	3-0	*Budescu (4, 45+1), Maxim (83)*
17/11/15	Italy	A	Bologna	D	2-2	*Stancu (8), Andone (89)*
23/03/16	Lithuania	H	Giurgiu	W	1-0	*Stanciu (65)*
27/03/16	Spain	H	Cluj-Napoca	D	0-0	
25/05/16	Congo DR	N	Como (ITA)	D	1-1	*Stanciu (27)*
29/05/16	Ukraine	N	Turin (ITA)	L	3-4	*Torje (23), Alibec (75), Stanciu (85)*
03/06/16	Georgia	H	Bucharest	W	5-1	*Popa (2), Amisulashvili (3og), Stanciu (48), Torje (80), Keşerü (86)*
10/06/16	France (ECF)	A	Saint-Denis	L	1-2	*Stancu (65p)*
15/06/16	Switzerland (ECF)	N	Paris (FRA)	D	1-1	*Stancu (18p)*
19/06/16	Albania (ECF)	N	Lyon (FRA)	L	0-1	

Appearances 2015/16

Coach: Anghel Iordănescu 04/05/50

			HUN	GRE	FIN	FRO	Ita	Ltu	Esp	Cod	Ukr	Geo	FRA	SUI	ALB	Caps	Goals
Ciprian Tătăruşanu	09/02/86	Fiorentina (ITA)	G	G	G	G	G		G		G	G	G	G	G	40	-
Paul Papp	11/11/89	Steaua	D	D	D											18	3
Vlad Chircheş	14/11/89	Napoli (ITA)	D	D	D	D	D	D	D	D	D			D	D	D	44	-
Dragoş Grigore	07/09/86	Al-Sailiya (QAT)	D	D	D	D	D			D		D	D	D	D	23	-
Răzvan Raţ	26/05/81	Rayo Vallecano (ESP)	D	D	D	D	D83			D88	s46	D	D	D62		113	2
Andrei Prepeliţă	08/12/85	Ludogorets (BUL)	M			s88	s68			s46	M60	s63		M	M46	12	-
Ovidiu Hoban	27/12/82	H. Beer Sheva (ISR)	M	M80	M	M	M	s59	M		s60	M63	M	s46	M	23	1
Adrian Popa	24/07/88	Steaua	M68	s64	s87	M			M61	M59	s70	M71	M82		M68	16	1
Lucian Sânmărtean	13/03/80	Al-Ittihad (KSA)	M78	s64	M		s46	M59	s85		M58	s84			s46	21	-
Gabriel Torje	22/11/89	Osmanlıspor (TUR)	M90	M	M87	M78	M69	M59	s61	s59	M70	s73	s82	M	s57	54	12
Claudiu Keşerü	02/12/86	Ludogorets (BUL)	A	A	A		A46	s46		s78	A58	s71		A		14	5
Alexandru Chipciu	18/05/89	Steaua	s68		M60					M59		s63	s72	M		24	3
Constantin Budescu	19/02/89	Astra	s78	M64		M88	M46									4	2
Alexandru Maxim	08/07/90	Stuttgart (GER)	s90	M64	s60	s78	s46			s59	s58					28	3
Mihai Pintilii	09/11/84	H. Tel-Aviv (ISR) /Steaua		M		M	M68	M	M90	M	M	M84	M	M46		34	1
Florin Andone	11/04/93	Córdoba (ESP)		s80	s69		s69		A74		A63	A61	s84		s68	9	1
Bogdan Stancu	28/06/87	Gençlerbirliği (TUR)			A69	A90	M85	M77	M66		M79	M73	M	M84	M	44	11
Alexandru Măţel	17/10/89	Dinamo Zagreb (CRO)				D		D		D					D	17	-
Denis Alibec	05/01/91	Astra				s90				A68	s58	s83	s61		A57	6	1
Cristian Săpunaru	05/04/84	Pandurii					D		D	D		D	D	D		16	-
Steliano Filip	15/05/94	Dinamo Bucureşti					s83	D87	D		D46			s62		5	-
Andrei Ivan	04/01/97	U Craiova						s85	s59	s66						3	-
Costel Pantilimon	01/02/87	Watford (ENG)						G		G						22	-
Cosmin Moţi	03/12/84	Ludogorets (BUL)						D				D				8	-
Florin Tănase	30/12/94	Viitorul						M46								2	-
Raul Rusescu	09/07/88	Osmanlıspor (TUR)						A46	s74							10	1
Nicolae Stanciu	07/05/93	Steaua						s46	M85	M78	s79	M83	M72		M	7	4
Ioan Hora	21/08/88	Pandurii						s77		s68						2	-
Alin Toşca	14/03/92	Steaua						s87		s88						2	-
Adrian Ropotan	08/05/86	Pandurii							s90	M46						7	-
Valerică Găman	25/02/89	Astra								D						14	1

EUROPE

FC Steaua Bucureşti

Second qualifying round - FK AS Trenčín (SVK)

A 2-0 *Stanciu (63), Hamroun (70)*
Cojocaru, Papp, Chipciu (Hamroun 59), Stanciu, Muniru,
Tadé (Tudorie 87), Guilherme, Breeveld (Tahar 81), Tamaş,
Varela, Popa. Coach: Massimo Pedrazzini (ITA)

H 2-3 *Muniru (57), Tadé (60p)*
Cojocaru, Papp, Chipciu, Stanciu (Hamroun 19), Muniru,
Toşca, Tadé (Tahar 82), Guilherme, Breeveld, Varela (Râpă
35), Popa. Coach: Massimo Pedrazzini (ITA)

Third qualifying round - FK Partizan (SRB)

H 1-1 *Varela (81)*
Cojocaru, Papp, Chipciu, Muniru, Toşca, Hamroun (Mihalcea
90+2), Tadé, Breeveld (Tahar 75), Alcénat, Varela, Popa
(Tudorie 65). Coach: Massimo Pedrazzini (ITA)

A 2-4 *Muniru (11), Hamroun (33)*
Cojocaru, Papp, Chipciu (Guilherme 50), Muniru, Toşca,
Hamroun (Iancu 70), Tadé, Breeveld (Tudorie 72), Alcénat,
Varela, Popa. Coach: Massimo Pedrazzini (ITA)
Red card: Varela 47

Play-offs - Rosenborg BK (NOR)

H 0-3
Cojocaru, Hamroun (Stanciu 46), Papp, Chipciu, Filip, Muniru
(Tahar 68), Toşca, Tadé, Guilherme, Alcénat (Iancu 75), Popa.
Coach: Massimo Pedrazzini (ITA)

A 1-0 *Popa (54)*
Niţă, Chipciu, Filip (Enceanu 75), Stanciu, Muniru, Toşca,
Guilherme, Alcénat (Papp 46), Varela, Popa, Iancu (Tadé 46).
Coach: Massimo Pedrazzini (ITA)

ASA Tîrgu Mureş

Third qualifying round - AS Saint-Étienne (FRA)

H 0-3
Stăncioiu, Balić, Iván González, Bejan, Mureşan (Costa 67),
Golański, Jazvić, Brandán (Pedro 61), Axente (Manolov 79),
Gorobsov, N'Doye. Coach: Vasile Miriuţă (HUN)

A 2-1 *Pedro (39), Iván González (62)*
Stăncioiu, Velayos, Balić, Iván González, Mureşan, Golański,
Jurado (Brandán 46), Axente, Pedro (Costa 71), Gorobsov,
Hanca (Jazvić 60). Coach: Vasile Miriuţă (HUN)

FC Astra Giurgiu

**Second qualifying round - Inverness Caledonian
Thistle FC (SCO)**

A 1-0 *Budescu (24)*
Lung, Geraldo Alves, Seto, Enache (Stan 71), Budescu
(Florea 82), Júnior Morais, Fernando Boldrin, Găman (Oroş
47), Filipe Teixeira, Pedro Queirós, William. Coach: Marius
Şumudică (ROU)

H 0-0
Lung, Geraldo Alves, Seto, Enache (Florea 80), Budescu
(Lovin 89), Júnior Morais, Fernando Boldrin (Dandea 84),
Găman, Filipe Teixeira, Pedro Queirós, William. Coach:
Marius Şumudică (ROU)

Third qualifying round - West Ham United FC (ENG)

A 2-2 *Fernando Boldrin (71), Ogbonna (82og)*
Lung, Geraldo Alves, Seto, Enache, Budescu (Lovin 90+1),
Júnior Morais, Fernando Boldrin (Dandea 86), Găman, Filipe
Teixeira, Pedro Queirós, William (Florea 76). Coach: Marius
Şumudică (ROU)

H 2-1 *Budescu (32, 36)*
Lung, Geraldo Alves (Oroş 19), Seto, Enache, Budescu
(Lovin 83), Júnior Morais, Fernando Boldrin, Găman, Filipe
Teixeira (Alibec 67), Pedro Queirós, William. Coach: Marius
Şumudică (ROU)

Play-offs - AZ Alkmaar (NED)

H 3-2 *Fernando Boldrin (25), Alibec (41), Dandea (45+3)*
Lung, Alibec (Florea 67), Enache, Budescu, Júnior Morais,
Oroş, Lovin, Fernando Boldrin (Dandea 35), Găman, Pedro
Queirós, William (Stan 83). Coach: Marius Şumudică (ROU)

A 0-2
Lung, Alibec (Fernando Boldrin 62), Enache (Ioniţă 83), Budescu,
Júnior Morais, Oroş, Lovin (Florea 84), Găman, Dandea, Pedro
Queirós, William. Coach: Marius Şumudică (ROU)

FC Botoşani

First qualifying round - FC Tskhinvali (GEO)

H 1-1 *Ivanovici (21)*
Iliev, Cordoş, Plămadă, Croitoru (Brata 74), Ivanovici (Batin
86), Vaşvari, Martinus, Browne, Costin, Hadnagy (Roman 46),
Dimitrov. Coach: Leontin Grozavu (ROU)

A 3-1 *Roman (6, 59), Batin (68)*
Iliev, Cordoş, Plămadă, Ivanovici (Batin 46), Vaşvari, Martinus
(Croitoru 53), Cucu, Patache, Roman (Hadnagy 74), Browne,
Costin. Coach: Leontin Grozavu (ROU)
Red card: Plămadă 49

Second qualifying round - Legia Warszawa (POL)

A 0-1
Iliev, Cordoş, Miron, Brata (Ivanovici 69), Vaşvari (Robertson
64), Cucu, Acsinte, Roman, Batin, Costin (Croitoru 84),
Dimitrov. Coach: Leontin Grozavu (ROU)

H 0-3
Iliev, Cordoş (Vaşvari 46), Plămadă, Brata, Croitoru, Cucu,
Patache (Martinus 33), Acsinte, Costin (Robertson 73),
Hadnagy, Dimitrov. Coach: Leontin Grozavu (ROU)

DOMESTIC LEAGUE CLUB-BY-CLUB

FC Astra Giurgiu

1937 • Marin Anastasovici (8,057) • afcastragiurgiu.ro

Major honours
Romanian League (1) 2016; Romanian Cup (1) 2014

Coach: Marius Şumudică

2015					
10/07	h	Concordia	D	2-2	*Budescu, Oroş*
19/07	h	Tîrgu Mureş	L	1-5	*Budescu*
26/07	a	U Craiova	W	2-1	*Fernando Boldrin, Dandea*
02/08	h	Viitorul	D	2-2	*Găman, Budescu*
09/08	a	Poli Timişoara	W	3-1	*Enache (p), Fernando Boldrin, Roşu*
12/08	h	Steaua	W	2-0	*Alibec, Budescu (p)*
16/08	a	Voluntari	W	2-1	*Alibec, William*
23/08	h	Iaşi	W	4-1	*Budescu 2, Florea, William*
30/08	a	Petrolul	W	1-0	*Dandea*
13/09	h	Pandurii	L	1-2	*Alibec*
19/09	a	CFR Cluj	D	1-1	*Alibec*
27/09	h	Botoşani	W	1-0	*Alibec (p)*
03/10	a	Dinamo	W	1-0	*Filipe Teixeira*
18/10	a	Concordia	W	2-0	*Stan, Ioniţă*
24/10	a	Tîrgu Mureş	L	1-3	*og (Velayos)*
30/10	h	U Craiova	W	1-0	*Florea*
06/11	a	Viitorul	W	2-1	*Niculae, William*
21/11	h	Poli Timişoara	D	2-2	*William, Budescu (p)*
29/11	a	Steaua	W	1-0	*Găman*
03/12	h	Voluntari	D	1-1	*Alibec (p)*
06/12	a	Iaşi	D	1-1	*Alibec*
12/12	h	Petrolul	W	3-1	*Alibec, Budescu, Niculae*
19/12	a	Pandurii	D	1-1	*Fernando Boldrin*
2016					
13/02	h	CFR Cluj	D	2-2	*Fernando Boldrin 2*
19/02	a	Botoşani	W	1-0	*Filipe Teixeira*
28/02	h	Dinamo	D	1-1	*William*
05/03	h	Viitorul	W	2-0	*Găman, Alibec*
13/03	a	Steaua	L	0-2	
18/03	h	Tîrgu Mureş	W	1-0	*Filipe Teixeira*
01/04	a	Dinamo	W	4-1	*Boudjemaa, Alibec 3*
05/04	h	Pandurii	D	0-0	
09/04	a	Viitorul	W	3-1	*og (Ganea), Găman (p), Alibec*
16/04	h	Steaua	W	2-0	*Găman (p), Alibec (p)*
25/04	a	Tîrgu Mureş	W	4-1	*Găman (p), Filipe Teixeira, Alibec, Florea*
02/05	h	Dinamo	W	4-2	*Júnior Morais, Alibec, Ioniţă 2*
09/05	a	Pandurii	L	0-2	

No	Name	Nat	DoB	Pos	Aps	(s)	Gls
7	Denis Alibec		05/01/91	A	26		16
33	Ionuţ Boşneag		15/02/82	G		(1)	
24	Damien Boudjemaa	FRA	07/06/85	M	10	(1)	1
10	Constantin Budescu		19/02/89	M	16	(2)	8
30	Alexandru Dandea		23/01/88	D	10	(9)	2
9	Gabriel Enache		18/08/90	M	22		1
23	Fernando Boldrin	BRA	23/02/89	M	30	(2)	5
80	Filipe Teixeira	POR	02/10/80	M	23	(3)	4
11	Daniel Florea		17/04/88	A	5	(24)	3
12	George Gavrilaş		15/12/90	G	9		
25	Valerică Găman		25/02/89	D	28		6
2	Geraldo Alves	POR	08/12/80	D	23		
8	Ninos Gouriye	NED	14/01/91	A		(4)	
31	Alexandru Ioniţă		14/12/94	M	3	(16)	3
13	Júnior Morais	BRA	22/07/86	D	29		1
20	Florin Lovin		11/02/82	M	19	(6)	
1	Silviu Lung		04/06/89	G	27		
19	Boubacar Mansaly	SEN	04/02/88	M	9	(4)	
18	Romario Moise		21/09/96	M		(1)	
21	Daniel Niculae		06/10/82	A	5	(14)	2
15	Cristian Oroş		15/08/84	D	16	(3)	1
84	Pedro Queirós	POR	08/08/84	D	31	(1)	
6	Mădălin Răileanu		06/05/97	A		(1)	
34	Ricardo Alves	POR	09/05/91	D	4		
24	Iulian Roşu		30/05/94	M		(4)	1
27	Manuel Scarlatache		05/12/86	D	1		
8	Takayuki Seto	JPN	05/02/86	M	14	(1)	
77	Constantin Stan		07/02/89	M	7	(5)	1
30	Fwayo Tembo	ZAM	02/05/89	M	1	(2)	
91	William	BRA	15/12/91	M	28	(2)	5

FC Botoşani

2001 • Municipal (7,782) • fcbotosani.ro

Coach: Leontin Grozavu;
(14/09/15) (Mugurel Cornăţeanu);
(01/10/15) Cristian Pustai;
(01/04/16) (Alin Bordeianu);
(05/04/16) Leontin Grozavu

2015					
12/07	a	U Craiova	D	0-0	
20/07	h	Viitorul	D	2-2	*Croitoru 2*
27/07	a	Poli Timişoara	L	0-1	
01/08	h	Steaua	L	0-1	
07/08	a	Voluntari	D	1-1	*Cabrera*
11/08	h	Iaşi	W	1-0	*Vaşvari (p)*
14/08	a	Petrolul	L	1-2	*Dimitrov*
22/08	h	Pandurii	L	0-2	
31/08	a	CFR Cluj	L	1-3	*Vaşvari (p)*
12/09	a	Concordia	D	0-0	
20/09	h	Dinamo	D	1-1	*Cabrera*
27/09	a	Astra	L	0-1	
04/10	h	Tîrgu Mureş	D	1-1	*Hadnagy*
16/10	h	U Craiova	W	3-2	*Hadnagy 2, Martinus*
26/10	a	Viitorul	L	1-3	*Roman*
02/11	h	Poli Timişoara	D	1-1	*Ivanovici*
08/11	a	Steaua	L	3-5	*Roman, Martinus, Cabrera*
23/11	h	Voluntari	D	2-2	*Hadnagy, Ivanovici*
29/11	a	Iaşi	L	0-1	
02/12	h	Petrolul	W	2-1	*Hadnagy, Fülöp (p)*
05/12	a	Pandurii	W	3-0	*Ngadeu, Popovici, Cucu*
13/12	h	CFR Cluj	W	2-1	*Ngadeu, Fülöp*
18/12	h	Concordia	W	5-1	*Ngadeu, Vaşvari, Martinus 2, Ivanovici*
2016					
14/02	a	Dinamo	L	0-1	
19/02	h	Astra	L	0-1	
27/02	a	Tîrgu Mureş	L	0-1	
04/03	h	Petrolul	W	1-0	*Vaşvari (p)*
12/03	a	Voluntari	D	1-1	*Roman*
19/03	h	Concordia	L	0-3	
31/03	a	U Craiova	L	1-2	*Ngadeu*
04/04	h	Poli Timişoara	W	6-1	*Vaşvari (p), Ngadeu, Matulevičius 2, Bujor, Cabrera*
11/04	h	Iaşi	D	0-0	
16/04	a	CFR Cluj	L	0-6	
22/04	a	Petrolul	W	4-0	*Cabrera 2, Fülöp, Ivanovici*
29/04	h	Voluntari	W	4-2	*Vaşvari (p), Cabrera 2, Matulevičius*
10/05	a	Concordia	D	1-1	*Muşat*
16/05	h	U Craiova	W	2-1	*Fülöp, Cabrera*
22/05	a	Poli Timişoara	W	4-1	*Bordeianu, Fülöp, Cabrera, Ivanovici*
26/05	a	Iaşi	D	1-1	*Ngadeu*
29/05	h	CFR Cluj	W	4-0	*Ivanovici, Cabrera, Hadnagy, Popovici*

No	Name	Nat	DoB	Pos	Aps	(s)	Gls
20	Florin Acsinte		10/04/87	D	16		
29	Paul Batin		29/06/87	A	9	(3)	
37	Cătălin Bordeianu		18/11/91	M	18	(5)	1
7	Ciprian Brata		24/03/91	M	4	(6)	
23	Rashid Browne	NED	28/09/93	A	1	(2)	
7	Vlad Bujor		03/02/89	A		(5)	1
15	Gonzalo Cabrera	ARG	15/01/89	M	34	(3)	11
20	Fernando Carralero	ESP	16/05/86	M	3	(7)	
8	José David Casado	ESP	14/01/88	M	2	(7)	
3	Andrei Cordoş		06/06/88	D	9	(2)	
30	Raul Costin		29/01/85	M	8	(3)	
8	Marius Croitoru		02/10/80	M	3	(1)	2
17	Stelian Cucu		15/09/89	M	28	(3)	1
28	Flavius Cuedan		08/01/93	M	1		
88	Radoslav Dimitrov	BUL	12/08/88	M	29	(4)	1
24	Istvan Fülöp		18/05/90	A	20	(8)	5
80	Attila Hadnagy		08/09/80	A	21	(6)	6
16	Alexandru Ichim		21/08/89	D	2		
1	Plamen Iliev	BUL	30/11/91	G	24		
9	Petre Ivanovici		02/03/90	M	13	(10)	6
11	Quenten Martinus	CUW	07/03/91	A	18	(3)	4
77	Deivydas Matulevičius	LTU	08/04/89	A	10	(3)	3
4	George Miron		28/05/94	D	22	(4)	
30	Nicolae Muşat		04/12/86	D	14		1
77	Mergim Neziri	GER	30/04/93	A	2	(3)	
13	Michael Ngadeu	CMR	23/11/90	D	25		6
19	Andrei Patache		29/10/87	D	12	(9)	
5	Florin Plămadă		30/04/92	D	20	(3)	
12	Răzvan Pleşca		25/11/82	G	16	(1)	
93	Cristian Popovici		23/03/93	M	8	(6)	2
16	Scott Robertson	SCO	07/04/85	M		(1)	
21	Dan Roman		22/12/85	A	13	(9)	3
28	Constantin Roşu		26/05/90	M	1	(1)	
29	Marius Tomozei		09/09/90	D	2		
10	Gabriel Vaşvari		13/11/86	M	32	(1)	6

CFR 1907 Cluj

1907 • Dr Constantin Rădulescu (23,500) • cfr1907.ro

Major honours
Romanian League (3) 2008, 2010, 2012; Romanian Cup (4) 2008, 2009, 2010, 2016

Coach: Francisc Dican;
(07/12/15) Toni Conceição (POR)

2015					
11/07	a	Viitorul	D	2-2	*Tadé, Guima*
19/07	h	Poli Timişoara	W	1-0	*Jakoliš*
25/07	a	Steaua	D	1-1	*Tiago Lopes*
31/07	h	Voluntari	W	2-0	*Petrucci, Păun-Alexandru (p)*
07/08	a	Iaşi	L	1-2	*Larie (p)*
11/08	h	Petrolul	W	1-0	*Cristian López*
17/08	a	Pandurii	D	1-1	*og (Şandru)*
24/08	a	Concordia	L	1-2	*Beleck*
31/08	h	Botoşani	W	3-1	*Cristian López 3*
14/09	a	Dinamo	W	2-0	*Cristian López (p), Voiculeţ*
19/09	h	Astra	D	1-1	*Jakoliš*
25/09	a	Tîrgu Mureş	D	0-0	
04/10	h	U Craiova	L	1-2	*Beleck*
19/10	h	Viitorul	L	1-2	*Cristian López*
23/10	a	Poli Timişoara	W	2-1	*Filipe Nascimento, Cristian López*
01/11	h	Steaua	W	2-0	*Vítor Bruno, Păun-Alexandru*
07/11	a	Voluntari	D	2-2	*Cristian López 2 (1p)*
21/11	h	Iaşi	D	0-0	
27/11	a	Petrolul	L	0-1	
01/12	h	Pandurii	L	1-2	*Jakoliš*
04/12	h	Concordia	D	0-0	
13/12	a	Botoşani	L	1-2	*Cristian López*
20/12	h	Dinamo	D	1-1	*Jakoliš*
2016					
13/02	a	Astra	D	2-2	*Juan Carlos, Vítor Bruno*
21/02	h	Tîrgu Mureş	W	1-0	*Nouvier*
27/02	a	U Craiova	W	1-0	*Bud*
05/03	a	Iaşi	W	2-0	*Bud, Dani*
13/03	a	Poli Timişoara	D	2-2	*Camora, Petrucci*
21/03	h	Petrolul	D	0-0	
30/03	a	Voluntari	L	0-1	
02/04	h	Concordia	W	2-0	*Juan Carlos 2*
09/04	a	U Craiova	D	1-1	*Păun-Alexandru*
16/04	h	FC Botoşani	W	6-0	*Bud 2 (1p), Juan Carlos 2, Nouvier, Cristian López*
24/04	h	Iaşi	D	0-0	
30/04	h	Poli Timişoara	W	5-1	*Nouvier, Juan Carlos, Bud, Beleck, Cristian López*
06/05	a	Petrolul	L	0-1	
13/05	h	Voluntari	W	2-1	*Nouvier, Petrucci*
21/05	a	Concordia	L	1-2	*Beleck*
26/05	h	U Craiova	W	4-0	*Camora, Jakoliš 2, Petrucci*
29/05	a	FC Botoşani	L	0-4	

No	Name	Nat	DoB	Pos	Aps	(s)	Gls
19	Steve Beleck	CMR	10/02/93	A	14	(11)	4
26	Cristian Bud		26/06/85	A	8	(5)	5
45	Camora	POR	21/09/86	D	37		2
31	Anthony Carter	AUS	31/08/94	A		(2)	
11	Cristian López	ESP	24/07/89	A	29	(9)	12
20	Dani	POR	17/01/90	D	17	(1)	1
28	Cornel Ene		21/07/93	D	1		
8	Filipe Nascimento	POR	07/01/95	M	11	(5)	1
18	Lucian Goian		10/02/83	D	21	(3)	
15	Tomislav Gomelt	CRO	07/01/95	M	25		
9	Guima	POR	11/03/86	A	3	(1)	1
17	Antonio Jakoliš	CRO	28/02/92	M	27	(7)	6
25	Juan Carlos	ESP	15/03/91	M	13	(2)	6
6	Ionuţ Larie		16/01/87	D	33	(1)	1
28	Traian Marc		16/01/83	G	30	(1)	
1	Mihai Mincă		08/10/84	G	6		
30	Andrei Mureşan		01/08/85	D	24	(3)	
21	Sergiu Negruţ		01/04/93	A	2	(9)	
57	Bryan Nouvier	FRA	21/06/95	M	15	(14)	4
7	Adrian Păun-Alexandru		01/04/95	M	13	(19)	3
10	Davide Petrucci	ITA	05/10/91	M	38		4
93	Neluţ Roşu		05/07/93	M	6	(1)	
15	Grégory Tadé	FRA	02/09/86	A	1		1
23	Andrei Tânc		03/10/85	D	10	(3)	
22	Tiago Lopes	POR	04/01/89	D	30	(1)	1
12	Cosmin Vâtcă		12/05/82	G	4	(1)	
16	Szilard Vereş		27/01/96	M	1		
90	Vítor Bruno	POR	13/01/90	M	18	(11)	2
29	Claudiu Voiculeţ		08/08/85	M	3	(6)	1

ROMANIA

CS Concordia Chiajna

1957 • Concordia (4,600) • csconcordia.ro

Coach: Marius Baciu; (01/09/15) Cornel Ţălnar; (25/11/15) Adrian Falub

2015					
10/07	a	Astra	D	2-2	*Purece, og (Oroş)*
17/07	h	Iaşi	L	0-1	
24/07	a	Tîrgu Mureş	L	0-1	
31/07	h	Petrolul	D	2-2	*og (Benga), Serediuc*
08/08	a	U Craiova	L	0-2	
13/08	h	Pandurii	W	3-0	*Constantinescu, Purece, Pena*
17/08	a	Viitorul	L	1-3	*Serediuc*
24/08	h	CFR Cluj	W	2-1	*Cristescu 2*
29/08	a	Poli Timişoara	L	0-1	
12/09	h	Botoşani	D	0-0	
21/09	a	Steaua	L	1-3	*Lazăr*
28/09	h	Dinamo	L	1-3	*Pena*
02/10	a	Voluntari	D	1-1	*Giurgiu (p)*
18/10	h	Astra	L	0-2	
23/10	a	Iaşi	W	1-0	*Bruno Madeira*
31/10	h	Tîrgu Mureş	L	1-2	*Serediuc*
09/11	a	Petrolul	D	1-1	*Serediuc*
20/11	h	U Craiova	L	0-2	
27/11	a	Pandurii	L	0-2	
01/12	h	Viitorul	D	2-2	*Giurgiu (p), Pena*
04/12	a	CFR Cluj	D	0-0	
11/12	h	Poli Timişoara	D	2-2	*Răducanu, Lazăr*
18/12	a	Botoşani	L	1-5	*Cristescu*
2016					
15/02	h	Steaua	L	0-2	
20/02	a	Dinamo	L	0-4	
28/02	h	Voluntari	L	1-2	*Milevskiy (p)*
07/03	h	Poli Timişoara	D	0-0	
14/03	h	U Craiova	W	1-0	*Giurgiu*
19/03	a	FC Botoşani	W	3-0	*Milevskiy 2 (1p), Obodo*
30/03	h	Iaşi	D	1-1	*Obodo (p)*
02/04	a	CFR Cluj	L	0-2	
08/04	h	Petrolul	D	1-1	*Obodo (p)*
17/04	a	Voluntari	W	2-1	*Milevskiy, Cristescu*
23/04	a	Poli Timişoara	W	3-1	*Milevskiy (p), Obodo, Odibe*
01/05	a	U Craiova	L	0-2	
10/05	h	FC Botoşani	D	1-1	*Pena*
15/05	a	Iaşi	W	3-2	*Cristescu, Giurgiu, Roşu*
21/05	h	CFR Cluj	W	2-1	*Pena, Purece*
24/05	a	Petrolul	W	1-0	*Odibe*
29/05	h	Voluntari	D	1-1	*Odibe*

No	Name	Nat	DoB	Pos	Aps	(s)	Gls
34	Cristian Bălgrădean		12/09/91	G	15		
2	Ştefan Bărboianu		24/01/88	D	19	(6)	
6	Bruno Madeira	POR	17/09/84	M	9	(2)	1
21	Bogdan Bucurică		11/02/86	D	35		
91	Florian Buleică		12/09/91	M	1	(1)	
11	Cristian Ciobanu		03/07/94	M		(3)	
20	Marian Constantinescu		08/08/81	A	11	(7)	1
33	Adrian Cristea		30/11/83	M	1	(4)	
18	Marian Cristescu		17/03/85	M	25	(7)	5
9	Mihai Dina		15/09/85	A	4	(6)	
26	Patrice Feussi	CMR	03/10/86	D	12	(1)	
80	Cristian García	ARG	29/04/88	A	5	(6)	
29	Gabriel Giurgiu		03/09/82	M	32	(4)	4
95	Toni Grădinaru		23/08/95	M	8	(6)	
93	Florin Iacob		16/08/93	G	6		
94	Lucian Ion		10/03/94	D	3	(1)	
8	Valentin Lazăr		21/08/89	D	13	(1)	2
15	Iulian Mamele		17/02/85	D	21	(3)	
3	Marian Marin		11/09/87	D	2	(1)	
1	Florin Matache		03/08/92	G	19		
9	Artem Milevskiy	UKR	12/01/85	A	11	(2)	5
5	Ibrahima Niasse	SEN	18/04/88	D	13		
99	Christian Obodo	NGA	11/05/84	M	17		4
6	Michael Odibe	NGA	23/07/88	D	14		3
24	Silviu Pană		24/09/91	M	7	(2)	
30	Marius Pena		02/05/85	A	24	(11)	5
10	Florin Purece		06/11/91	M	30	(6)	3
96	Robert Răducanu		05/09/96	A	6	(12)	1
17	Florin Răsdan		13/04/95	A	2	(1)	
93	Neluţ Roşu		05/07/93	M	4	(5)	1
77	Tiberiu Serediuc		02/07/92	M	18	(11)	4
16	Cristian Sîrghi		23/11/86	D	13	(1)	
4	Răzvan Tincu		15/07/87	D	32		
99	Ştefan Ţîră		18/06/94	A	3	(4)	
22	Alexandru Vagner		19/08/89	M	4	(1)	
19	Andrei Voineag		12/11/93	D	1		
22	Gabriele Zerbo	ITA	16/05/94	A		(3)	

FC Dinamo Bucureşti

1948 • Dinamo (15,400) • fcdinamo.ro

Major honours

Romanian League (18) 1955, 1962, 1963, 1964, 1965, 1971, 1973, 1975, 1977, 1982, 1983, 1984, 1990, 1992, 2000 ,2002, 2004, 2007; Romanian Cup (13) 1959, 1964, 1968, 1982, 1984, 1986, 1990, 2000, 2001, 2003, 2004, 2005, 2012

Coach: Mircea Rednic

2015					
12/07	a	Tîrgu Mureş	D	0-0	
17/07	h	U Craiova	W	1-0	*Rotariu*
25/07	a	Viitorul	D	1-1	*Petre*
03/08	h	Poli Timişoara	W	2-1	*Matei (p), Gnohéré*
09/08	a	Steaua	D	0-0	
13/08	h	Voluntari	W	3-0	*Filip, Matei, Rotariu*
16/08	a	Iaşi	D	0-0	
22/08	h	Petrolul	W	2-0	*Essombé, Gnohéré*
29/08	a	Pandurii	D	2-2	*Essombé, Gnohéré*
14/09	h	CFR Cluj	L	0-2	
20/09	a	Botoşani	D	1-1	*Essombé*
28/09	a	Concordia	W	3-1	*Rotariu, Gnohéré 2*
03/10	h	Astra	L	0-1	
17/10	h	Tîrgu Mureş	W	2-1	*Marc 2*
25/10	a	U Craiova	L	0-3	
02/11	h	Viitorul	L	1-5	*Gnohéré*
07/11	a	Poli Timişoara	W	1-0	*Essombé*
22/11	h	Steaua	W	3-1	*og (Varela), Palić, Gnohéré*
30/11	a	Voluntari	W	3-1	*Gnohéré, Filip, Anton*
03/12	h	Iaşi	D	0-0	
07/12	a	Petrolul	W	2-1	*og (Tudose), Rotariu*
12/12	h	Pandurii	W	2-1	*og (Filippetto), Puljić*
20/12	a	CFR Cluj	D	1-1	*Palić*
2016					
14/02	h	Botoşani	W	1-0	*Costache*
20/02	h	Concordia	W	4-0	*Rotariu (p), Essombé 2, Gnohéré*
28/02	a	Astra	D	1-1	*Rotariu*
06/03	h	Steaua	D	1-1	*Bicfalvi*
14/03	a	Tîrgu Mureş	D	0-0	
20/03	h	Pandurii	D	1-1	*Palić*
01/04	h	Astra	L	1-4	*Anton*
04/04	a	Viitorul	W	2-1	*Kortzorg, Lazăr*
10/04	a	Steaua	D	1-1	*Gnohéré*
17/04	h	Tîrgu Mureş	W	1-0	*Rotariu*
24/04	a	Pandurii	D	0-0	
02/05	a	Astra	L	2-4	*Palić, Lazăr*
06/05	h	Viitorul	D	3-3	*Gnohéré 2, Rotariu*

No	Name	Nat	DoB	Pos	Aps	(s)	Gls
55	Marius Alexe		22/02/90	A	1		
28	Paul Anton		10/05/91	M	22	(1)	2
21	Kaj Leo í Bartalsstovu	FRO	23/06/91	M	1	(5)	
29	Paul Batin		29/06/87	A	1	(2)	
8	Eric Bicfalvi		05/02/88	M	6	(1)	1
1	Vytautas Černiauskas	LTU	12/03/89	G	34		
94	Laurenţiu Corbu		10/05/94	D	2		
24	Ionuţ Costache		02/08/98	M	1	(3)	1
14	Patrick Ekeng	CMR	26/03/90	M	6	(4)	
18	Marcel Essombé	CMR	06/05/88	A	15	(8)	6
14	Collins Fai	CMR	13/08/92	D	19	(2)	
26	Patrice Feussi	CMR	03/10/86	D	9	(2)	
7	Steliano Filip		15/05/94	D	26		2
77	Bogdan Gavrilă		06/02/92	M	11	(5)	
3	Antonio Ghomsi	CMR	22/04/86	D	2	(2)	
31	Harlem Gnohéré	FRA	21/02/88	A	18	(13)	12
44	Sergiu Hanca		04/04/92	D	11		
19	Fabian Himcinschi		21/05/94	A		(1)	
22	Romario Kortzorg	NED	25/08/89	M	8	(1)	1
93	Valentin Lazăr		21/08/89	M	11	(5)	2
73	Andrei Marc		29/04/93	D	22	(4)	2
10	Cosmin Matei		30/09/91	M	18	(1)	2
17	Miha Mevlja	SVN	12/06/90	D	34	(1)	
99	Robert Moldoveanu		08/03/99	A		(2)	
41	Vlad Muţiu		02/02/95	G	1		
5	Ionuţ Nedelcearu		25/04/96	D	14	(7)	
96	Vlad Olteanu		21/03/96	M	6	(3)	
20	Antun Palić	CRO	25/06/88	M	23	(5)	4
13	Patrick Petre		09/05/97	A		(3)	1
41	Iustin Popescu		01/09/93	G	1		
6	Ante Puljić	CRO	05/11/87	D	14	(7)	1
9	Dorin Rotariu		29/07/95	M	28	(4)	8
90	Gezim Shalaj	SUI	28/07/90	M	1	(6)	
6	Orlin Starokin	BUL	08/01/87	D	1		
23	Ionuţ Şerban		07/08/95	D	6	(2)	
30	Andrei Tîrcoveanu		22/05/97	M	1	(2)	
8	Ricky van Haaren	NED	21/06/91	M	4	(4)	
80	Aljoša Vojnović	CRO	24/10/85	A	18	(1)	

CSMS Iaşi

2010 • Emil Alexandrescu (11,310) • csmsiasi.ro

Coach: Nicolò Napoli (ITA)

2015					
10/07	a	Voluntari	D	1-1	*Grigorie*
17/07	a	Concordia	W	1-0	*Bőle*
26/07	h	Petrolul	W	1-0	*Golubović*
01/08	a	Pandurii	L	0-3	
07/08	h	CFR Cluj	W	2-1	*Golubović (p), Enescu*
11/08	a	Botoşani	L	0-1	
16/08	h	Dinamo	D	0-0	
23/08	a	Astra	L	1-4	*Gheorghe*
28/08	h	Tîrgu Mureş	L	0-1	
13/09	a	U Craiova	L	0-2	
19/09	h	Viitorul	D	0-0	
25/09	a	Poli Timişoara	D	2-2	*Golubović, Ciucă*
03/10	h	Steaua	L	1-2	*Gheorghe*
17/10	h	Voluntari	W	2-1	*Golubović, Nuno Viveiros*
23/10	h	Concordia	L	0-1	
31/10	a	Petrolul	W	2-1	*Gheorghe, Frăsinescu*
06/11	h	Pandurii	W	1-0	*Golubović (p)*
21/11	a	CFR Cluj	D	0-0	
29/11	h	Botoşani	W	1-0	*Gheorghe*
03/12	a	Dinamo	D	0-0	
06/12	h	Astra	D	1-1	*Gheorghe*
11/12	a	Tîrgu Mureş	D	1-1	*Golubović*
19/12	h	U Craiova	W	1-0	*Ciucă*
2016					
13/02	a	Viitorul	W	2-1	*Golubović, Nuno Viveiros*
20/02	h	Poli Timişoara	D	1-1	*Cristea*
27/02	a	Steaua	D	1-1	*Golubović*
05/03	h	CFR Cluj	L	0-2	
11/03	a	Petrolul	W	2-1	*Bőle, Cristea*
18/03	h	Voluntari	L	0-1	
30/03	a	Concordia	D	1-1	*Cristea*
03/04	h	U Craiova	W	3-0	*Gheorghe, Golubović, Ţigănaşu*
11/04	a	FC Botoşani	D	0-0	
18/04	h	Poli Timişoara	D	0-0	
24/04	a	CFR Cluj	D	0-0	
30/04	h	Petrolul	W	1-0	*Piccioni*
09/05	a	Voluntari	W	2-1	*Cristea (p), og (Maftei)*
15/05	h	Concordia	L	2-3	*Cristea, Piccioni*
22/05	a	U Craiova	L	2-3	*Golubović, Cristea*
26/05	h	FC Botoşani	D	1-1	*Golubović*
29/05	a	Poli Timişoara	W	3-2	*Golubović, Cristea, Piccioni*

No	Name	Nat	DoB	Pos	Aps	(s)	Gls
5	Narcis Bădic		15/07/91	M	8	(6)	
9	Alexandru Boiciuc	MDA	21/08/97	A		(4)	
21	Lukács Bőle	HUN	27/03/90	M	32	(1)	2
8	Gabriel Boşoi		11/08/87	M	6	(7)	
1	Alessandro Caparco	ITA	07/09/83	G	5	(1)	
16	Mădălin Ciucă		04/11/82	D	29	(2)	2
6	Alexandru Creţu		24/04/92	M	16	(18)	
10	Andrei Cristea		10/05/84	A	17		7
13	Andrei Enescu		12/10/87	M	18	(12)	1
23	Cosmin Frăsinescu		10/02/85	D	31	(1)	1
88	Liviu Ganea		23/02/88	A		(3)	
7	Vasile Gheorghe		05/09/85	M	28	(7)	6
14	Bojan Golubović	SRB	22/08/83	A	39	(1)	12
12	Branko Grahovac	BIH	08/07/93	G	35		
10	Ştefan Grigorie		31/01/82	M	13	(5)	1
27	Azdren Llullaku	ALB	15/02/88	A	9	(5)	
4	Marius Mihalache		14/12/84	D	28		
22	Milan Mitić	SRB	22/01/84	M	31		
28	Nuno Viveiros	POR	22/06/83	M	19	(7)	2
16	Gomo Onduku	NGA	17/11/93	A	5	(8)	
11	Gianmarco Piccioni	ITA	18/07/91	A	5	(15)	3
44	Ante Sarić	CRO	17/06/92	D	1	(2)	
30	Alexandru Ţigănaşu		12/06/90	D	27		1
20	Ionuţ Voicu		02/08/84	D	38		

CS Pandurii Târgu Jiu

1962 • Municipal, Drobeta Turnu Severin (19,128) • panduriics.ro

Coach: Edward Iordănescu

2015

13/07	a	Poli Timişoara	W	1-0	*Răduţ*
18/07	h	Steaua	L	0-3	
24/07	a	Voluntari	D	0-0	
01/08	h	Iaşi	W	3-0	*Roman 2, Hora*
08/08	a	Petrolul	D	1-1	*Roman (p)*
13/08	a	Concordia	L	0-3	
17/08	h	CFR Cluj	D	1-1	*Momčilović*
22/08	a	Botoşani	W	2-0	*Hora, Roman*
29/08	h	Dinamo	D	2-2	*Filippetto, Hora*
13/09	a	Astra	W	2-1	*Hora 2 (1p)*
18/09	h	Tîrgu Mureş	W	2-0	*Nicoară, Hora*
26/09	a	U Craiova	D	0-0	
02/10	h	Viitorul	W	1-0	*og (Achim)*
19/10	h	Poli Timişoara	W	3-1	*Săpunaru, Hora 2*
25/10	a	Steaua	D	1-1	*Răduţ*
01/11	h	Voluntari	W	2-1	*Răduţ, Hora*
06/11	a	Iaşi	L	0-1	
23/11	h	Petrolul	W	3-2	*Săpunaru (p), Filippetto, Hora*
27/11	h	Concordia	W	2-0	*Răduţ, Hora (p)*
01/12	a	CFR Cluj	W	2-1	*Săpunaru, Hora*
05/12	h	Botoşani	L	0-3	
12/12	a	Dinamo	L	1-2	*Munteanu*
19/12	h	Astra	D	1-1	*Săpunaru*

2016

12/02	a	Tîrgu Mureş	W	1-0	*Săpunaru (p)*
22/02	h	U Craiova	D	1-1	*Wellington*
29/02	a	Viitorul	W	3-1	*Hora, Ropotan, Mrzljak*
07/03	a	Tîrgu Mureş	W	2-0	*Vasiljević, Hora*
12/03	h	Viitorul	D	1-1	*Nicoară*
20/03	a	Dinamo	D	1-1	*Hora*
30/03	h	Steaua	L	0-1	
05/04	a	Astra	D	0-0	
11/04	h	Tîrgu Mureş	D	3-3	*Hora, Antal 2*
18/04	a	Viitorul	W	2-0	*Hora, Nistor*
24/04	h	Dinamo	D	0-0	
01/05	a	Steaua	D	1-1	*Hora*
09/05	h	Astra	W	2-0	*Antal, Hora*

No	Name	Nat	DoB	Pos	Aps	(s)	Gls
20	Florin Acsinte		10/04/87	D	8	(1)	
89	Liviu Antal		02/06/89	M	11		3
19	Paul Anton		10/05/91	D	3	(1)	
3	Gordan Bunoza	BIH	05/02/88	D	4		
11	Alexandru Ciucur		01/03/90	M	14	(18)	
16	Alexandru Dan		30/01/94	A		(1)	
7	Lukaš Droppa	CZE	22/04/89	M	20	(3)	
21	Erico	BRA	20/07/89	D	2	(1)	
29	Ezequiel Filippetto	ARG	09/12/87	D	14	(2)	2
23	Constantin Grecu		08/06/88	D	6	(5)	
9	Ioan Hora		21/08/88	A	33	(2)	19
27	Abdelaziz Khalouta	MAR	08/08/89	A		(4)	
1	David Lazar		08/08/91	G	1		
3	Daniel Mărgărit		30/08/96	A		(1)	
4	Marko Momčilović	SRB	11/06/87	D	22		1
24	Filip Mrzljak	CRO	16/04/93	D	22	(3)	1
5	Valentin Munteanu		24/10/89	M	1	(14)	1
26	Viorel Nicoară		27/09/87	M	14	(13)	2
88	Dan Nistor		05/06/88	M	34	(1)	1
80	Pedro Mingote	POR	02/08/80	G	21		
17	Andrei Piţian		16/11/95	M	4	(7)	
25	Marian Pleaşcă		06/02/90	D	1	(1)	
8	Mihai Răduţ		18/03/90	M	30	(1)	4
52	Alexandru Răuţă		17/06/92	M	4	(4)	
10	Mihai Roman		31/05/92	A	7	(2)	4
4	Adrian Ropotan		08/05/86	M	10		1
19	Cristian Săpunaru		05/04/84	D	22		5
33	Răzvan Stanca		18/01/80	G	14		
20	Bogdan Şandru		25/07/90	D	8	(1)	
77	Rodemis Trifu		08/10/95	M		(4)	
18	Bogdan Unguruşan		20/02/83	D	32		
2	Vasco Fernandes	POR	12/11/86	D	28		
6	Nikola Vasiljević	SRB	30/06/91	D	5	(5)	1
99	Wellington	BRA	05/10/87	A	1	(13)	1

FC Petrolul Ploieşti

1952 • Ilie Oană (15,073) • fcpetrolul.ro

Major honours
Romanian League (3) 1958, 1959, 1966; Romanian Cup (3) 1963, 1995, 2013

Coach: Tibor Selymes;
(25/08/15) Eusebiu Tudor;
(28/10/15) Mihai Stoichiţă;
(05/01/16) Constantin Schumacher;
(15/03/16) Ionel Gane

2015

11/07	a	Steaua	D	0-0	
18/07	h	Voluntari	D	1-1	*og (Maftei)*
26/07	a	Iaşi	L	0-1	
31/07	a	Concordia	D	2-2	*Moussa, Marinescu*
08/08	h	Pandurii	D	1-1	*Moussa*
11/08	a	CFR Cluj	L	0-1	
14/08	h	Botoşani	W	2-1	*Rusu, Varga*
22/08	a	Dinamo	L	0-2	
30/08	h	Astra	L	0-1	
12/09	a	Tîrgu Mureş	D	1-1	*Ropotan (p)*
20/09	h	U Craiova	L	0-1	
26/09	a	Viitorul	L	0-1	
05/10	h	Poli Timişoara	D	1-1	*Velasco*
18/10	h	Steaua	D	0-0	
24/10	a	Voluntari	L	0-1	
31/10	h	Iaşi	L	1-2	*Benga*
09/11	h	Concordia	D	1-1	*Zoubir*
23/11	a	Pandurii	L	2-3	*Marinescu, Lemnaru*
27/11	h	CFR Cluj	W	1-0	*Zoubir*
02/12	a	Botoşani	L	1-2	*Zoubir*
07/12	h	Dinamo	L	1-2	*Moussa*
12/12	a	Astra	L	1-3	*Ropotan*
20/12	h	Tîrgu Mureş	L	0-1	

2016

14/02	a	U Craiova	L	0-2	
21/02	h	Viitorul	L	1-2	*Paolucci (p)*
26/02	a	Poli Timişoara	L	0-1	
04/03	a	FC Botoşani	L	0-1	
11/03	h	Iaşi	L	1-2	*Begeorgi*
21/03	a	CFR Cluj	D	0-0	
29/03	a	Poli Timişoara	W	1-0	*Astafei*
02/04	h	Voluntari	L	1-2	*Gavrilă*
08/04	a	Concordia	D	1-1	*Astafei*
15/04	h	U Craiova	W	1-0	*Astafei*
22/04	h	FC Botoşani	L	0-4	
30/04	a	Iaşi	L	0-1	
06/05	h	CFR Cluj	W	1-0	*Zoubir*
16/05	h	Poli Timişoara	W	3-2	*Astafei (p), Zoubir (p), Pacar*
21/05	a	Voluntari	L	0-2	
24/05	h	Concordia	L	0-1	
29/05	a	U Craiova	L	0-2	

No	Name	Nat	DoB	Pos	Aps	(s)	Gls
40	Roberto Alecsandru		13/09/96	D	2	(2)	
14	Sanaa Altama	FRA	23/07/90	M	2	(1)	
41	Victoraş Astafei		06/07/87	A	11		4
13	Fabrice Begeorgi	FRA	20/04/87	D	11		1
16	Alexandru Benga		15/06/89	D	33	(1)	1
22	Dean Beţa		11/05/91	D	17	(2)	
5	Mihai Bucşa		23/06/88	M	31	(4)	
93	Alexandru Chiriţă		24/06/96	M		(7)	
12	Alberto Cobrea		01/11/90	G	16		
87	Constantin Costache		05/06/97	D		(2)	
37	Alexandru David		15/06/91	D	9	(1)	
23	Nicolas Farina	FRA	09/08/86	M	7	(1)	
37	Jérémy Faug-Porret	FRA	04/02/87	D	19		
77	Bogdan Gavrilă		06/02/92	M	10	(3)	1
3	Viktor Genev	BUL	27/10/88	D	12		
21	Ludovic Guerriero	FRA	05/01/85	M	7	(5)	
87	Ahmed Hassan	FRA	23/05/87	M		(1)	
3	Romain Inez	FRA	30/04/88	D	3	(1)	
14	Cosmin Lambru		26/11/98	A		(1)	
78	Valentin Lemnaru		24/06/84	A	2	(5)	1
11	George Mareş		16/05/96	A	5	(7)	
10	Laurenţiu Marinescu		25/08/84	M	17	(8)	2
11	Markos Michail	CYP	13/06/91	A	2	(9)	
15	Nicolae Milinceanu	MDA	01/08/92	A		(5)	
25	Constantin Mişelăricu		25/09/89	D	15		
9	Sofien Moussa	TUN	06/02/88	A	16	(1)	3
7	Gevaro Nepomuceno	CUW	10/11/92	M	15	(7)	
15	Janko Pacar	SUI	18/08/90	A	8	(6)	1
9	Michele Paolucci	ITA	06/02/86	A	10	(2)	1
1	Peçanha	BRA	11/01/80	G	22		
77	Andrei Peteleu		20/08/92	D	12	(2)	
12	Iustin Popescu		01/09/93	G	2		
6	Giuseppe Prestia	ITA	13/11/93	D	5		
14	Cristian Pulhac		17/08/84	D	4	(3)	
3	Guillaume Rippert	FRA	30/04/85	D	6	(1)	
8	Adrian Ropotan		08/05/86	M	18		2
90	Vlad Rusu		22/06/90	A	2	(3)	1
23	Daniel Stana		02/12/82	M	8		
99	Toto Tamuz	ISR	01/04/88	A	4	(10)	
6	Alexandru Tudose		03/04/87	D	12		
30	Dacian Varga		15/10/84	M	16	(1)	1
11	Fernando Velasco	ESP	08/01/85	M	3	(2)	1
11	Petrişor Voinea		28/05/90	A		(3)	
8	Karim Ziani	ALG	17/08/82	M	12	(2)	
17	Abdellah Zoubir	FRA	05/12/91	A	34	(4)	5

ACS Poli Timişoara

2012 • Dan Păltinişanu (32,972) • acspoli.ro

Coach: Dan Alexa;
(25/08/15) Florin Marin;
(25/03/16) Petre Grigoraş;
(24/05/16) Ionuţ Popa

2015

13/07	h	Pandurii	L	0-1	
19/07	a	CFR Cluj	L	0-1	
27/07	h	Botoşani	W	1-0	*Elek*
03/08	a	Dinamo	L	1-2	*Elek*
09/08	h	Astra	L	1-3	*Segovia*
12/08	a	Tîrgu Mureş	D	0-0	
15/08	h	U Craiova	D	1-1	*Elek*
21/08	a	Viitorul	L	0-4	
29/08	h	Concordia	W	1-0	*Goga*
13/09	h	Steaua	W	1-0	*Javi Hernández*
18/09	a	Voluntari	D	0-0	
25/09	h	Iaşi	D	2-2	*Luchin, Goga (p)*
05/10	a	Petrolul	D	1-1	*Llorente*
19/10	a	Pandurii	L	1-3	*Goga*
23/10	h	CFR Cluj	L	1-2	*Javi Hernández*
02/11	a	Botoşani	D	1-1	*Javi Hernández*
07/11	h	Dinamo	L	0-1	
21/11	a	Astra	D	2-2	*Zicu, Curtean*
28/11	h	Tîrgu Mureş	W	2-0	*Luchin, Segovia*
01/12	a	U Craiova	D	1-1	*Javi Hernández (p)*
05/12	h	Viitorul	L	1-2	*Zicu*
11/12	a	Concordia	D	2-2	*Elek, Luchin*
21/12	a	Steaua	L	1-3	*D Popescu*

2016

14/02	h	Voluntari	L	1-2	*Zicu*
20/02	a	Iaşi	D	1-1	*O Popescu*
26/02	h	Petrolul	W	1-0	*Bărbuţ*
07/03	a	Concordia	D	0-0	
13/03	h	CFR Cluj	D	2-2	*O Popescu, Zicu*
20/03	a	U Craiova	L	0-1	
29/03	h	Petrolul	L	0-1	
04/04	a	FC Botoşani	L	1-6	*Goga (p)*
10/04	h	Voluntari	W	2-1	*Goga (p), Javi Hernández*
18/04	a	Iaşi	D	0-0	
23/04	h	Concordia	L	1-3	*Nimely*
30/04	a	CFR Cluj	L	1-5	*Goga*
11/05	h	U Craiova	D	2-2	*Goga (p), D Popescu*
16/05	a	Petrolul	L	2-3	*Nimely, Jenkins*
22/05	h	FC Botoşani	L	1-4	*Doman*
25/05	a	Voluntari	L	0-5	
29/05	h	Iaşi	L	2-3	*Mailat, Nimely*

No	Name	Nat	DoB	Pos	Aps	(s)	Gls
6	Abel Suárez	ESP	11/04/91	M	3	(4)	
18	Andrei Artean		14/08/93	M	4	(3)	
77	Cristian Bărbuţ		22/04/95	M	19	(11)	1
7	Claudiu Belu-Iordache		07/11/93	D	28	(4)	
18	Cosmin Bîrnoi		17/08/97	M		(1)	
15	Cristian Bocşan		31/01/95	D	8	(2)	
12	Cristian Boldea		12/12/85	M	1		
23	Gabriel Cânu		18/01/81	D	20	(2)	
88	Marius Croitoru		02/10/80	M	6	(7)	
8	Alexandru Curtean		27/03/87	M	13	(3)	1
55	Cătălin Doman		30/01/88	M	1	(9)	1
19	Robert Elek		13/06/88	A	28	(6)	4
30	Harald Fridrich		20/02/98	D	1		
10	Dorin Goga		02/07/84	A	20	(3)	7
22	Lys Gomis	SEN	06/10/89	G	1		
11	Javi Hernández	ESP	06/06/89	M	32	(2)	5
18	Ross Jenkins	ENG	09/11/90	M	6	(3)	1
35	Sascha Kirschstein	GER	09/06/80	G	20		
25	Fernando Llorente	ESP	18/09/90	M	31		1
4	Srdjan Luchin		04/03/86	D	17		3
12	Sebastian Mailat		12/12/97	M	1		1
4	Manu Torres	ESP	14/08/89	D	12	(1)	
26	Cristian Melinte		09/05/88	D	29	(3)	
3	George Neagu		24/04/85	M	1		
8	Alex Nimely	LBR	11/05/91	A	8	(2)	3
15	Lucian Oprea		31/03/98	M		(1)	
29	Eduard Pap		01/07/94	G	3		
91	Pedro Henrique	BRA	28/03/91	A		(1)	
17	Everon Pisas	NED	13/10/94	A	2	(5)	
5	Adrian Poparadu		13/10/87	M		(1)	
24	Daniel Popescu		20/02/88	D	37		2
99	Ovidiu Popescu		27/02/94	M	20	(5)	2
81	Alexandru Popovici		06/09/88	A		(4)	
9	Prince Rajcomar	CUW	25/04/85	A	2	(3)	
16	Georgi Sarmov	BUL	07/09/85	M	8	(7)	
13	Cristian Scutaru		13/04/87	D	20	(3)	
17	Rufino Segovia	ESP	01/03/85	M	5	(11)	2
1	Mădălin Smaranda		05/09/84	G	7		
42	Deian Sorescu		29/08/97	M	1	(1)	
28	Ram Strauss	ISR	28/04/92	G	9	(1)	
17	Sebastian Velcotă		20/03/98	A		(1)	
27	Ianis Zicu		23/10/83	M	16	(10)	4

ROMANIA

FC Steaua Bucureşti

1947 • Steaua (27,557); Arena Naţională (54,600); Nicolae Dobrin, Pitesti (16,500) • steauafc.com

Major honours
European Champion Clubs' Cup (1) 1986; UEFA Super Cup (1) 1986; Romanian League (26) 1951, 1952, 1953, 1956, 1960, 1961, 1968, 1976, 1978, 1985, 1986, 1987, 1988, 1989, 1993, 1994, 1995, 1996, 1997, 1998, 2001, 2005, 2006, 2013, 2014, 2015; Romanian Cup (23) 1949, 1950, 1951, 1952, 1955, 1962, 1966, 1967, 1969, 1970, 1971, 1976, 1979, 1985, 1987, 1988, 1989, 1992, 1996, 1997, 1999, 2011, 2015

Coach: Mirel Rădoi;
(03/12/15) Laurenţiu Reghecampf

2015					
11/07	h	Petrolul	D	0-0	
18/07	a	Pandurii	W	3-0	*Chipciu 2, Hamroun*
25/07	h	CFR Cluj	D	1-1	*Tudorie*
01/08	a	Botoşani	W	1-0	*Iancu*
09/08	h	Dinamo	D	0-0	
12/08	a	Astra	L	0-2	
15/08	h	Tîrgu Mureş	D	1-1	*Popa*
23/08	a	U Craiova	W	2-1	*Stanciu, Tadé (p)*
30/08	h	Viitorul	W	1-0	*Stanciu*
13/09	a	Poli Timişoara	L	0-1	
21/09	h	Concordia	W	3-1	*Varela, Stanciu (p), Chipciu*
27/09	h	Voluntari	W	3-1	*Hamroun, Chipciu, Stanciu (p)*
03/10	a	Iaşi	W	2-1	*Chipciu, Tahar*
18/10	a	Petrolul	D	0-0	
25/10	h	Pandurii	D	1-1	*Muniru*
01/11	a	CFR Cluj	L	0-2	
08/11	h	Botoşani	W	5-3	*Breeveld, Stanciu 2, Tadé, Râpă*
22/11	a	Dinamo	L	1-3	*Stanciu*
29/11	h	Astra	L	0-1	
02/12	a	Tîrgu Mureş	D	1-1	*Filip*
06/12	h	U Craiova	W	2-0	*Papp, Tadé*
14/12	a	Viitorul	W	1-0	*Hamroun*
21/12	h	Poli Timişoara	W	3-1	*og (Bocşan), Stanciu, Hamroun*
2016					
15/02	a	Concordia	W	2-0	*Varela, Hamroun*
22/02	a	Voluntari	L	1-3	*Popa*
27/02	h	Iaşi	D	1-1	*Stanciu*
06/03	a	Dinamo	D	1-1	*Hamroun*
13/03	h	Astra	W	2-0	*Momčilović, Stanciu*
19/03	a	Viitorul	W	3-1	*Hamroun (p), Popa, Stanciu*
30/03	a	Pandurii	W	1-0	*Stanciu (p)*
03/04	h	Tîrgu Mureş	W	2-1	*Popa, og (Iván González)*
10/04	h	Dinamo	D	1-1	*og (Filip)*
16/04	a	Astra	L	0-2	
23/04	h	Viitorul	W	3-0	*Varela, Chipciu, Tadé*
01/05	h	Pandurii	D	1-1	*Enache*
10/05	a	Tîrgu Mureş	W	4-1	*Bawab, Chipciu, Popadiuc, Onţel*

No	Name	Nat	DoB	Pos	Aps	(s)	Gls
22	Jean Sony Alcénat	HAI	23/01/86	D	3	(4)	
20	Thaer Bawab	JOR	01/03/85	A	2	(6)	1
6	Alexandru Bourceanu		24/04/85	M	8	(1)	
21	Nicandro Breeveld	SUR	07/10/86	M	10	(4)	1
4	Catalin Carp	MDA	20/10/93	D	5	(4)	
7	Alexandru Chipciu		18/05/89	M	27		7
12	Valentin Cojocaru		01/10/95	G	7		
44	Gabriel Enache		18/08/90	M	9	(2)	1
94	Rareş Enceanu		05/08/94	M	5	(6)	
8	Lucian Filip		25/09/90	D	18	(4)	1
18	Timo Gebhart	GER	12/04/89	M	1	(4)	
27	Toni Grădinaru		23/08/95	M	1	(1)	
16	Guilherme	BRA	01/04/90	D	20		
14	Jugurtha Hamroun	ALG	27/01/89	M	23	(3)	7
80	Gabriel Iancu		15/04/94	A	3	(2)	1
14	Houssine Kharja	MAR	09/11/82	M	6	(2)	
9	Ciprian Marica		02/10/85	A	5	(2)	
19	Vlad Mihalcea		28/10/98	M		(5)	
15	Marko Momčilović	SRB	11/06/87	D	8		1
11	Sulley Muniru	GHA	25/10/92	M	9	(8)	1
26	Ionuţ Neagu		26/10/89	M	2		
1	Florin Niţă		03/07/87	G	29		
27	Cristian Onţel		05/04/98	M		(4)	1
6	Paul Papp		11/11/89	D	13	(4)	1
25	Mihai Pintilii		09/11/84	M	11		
77	Adrian Popa		24/07/88	M	29	(3)	4
95	Doru Popadiuc		18/02/95	M		(2)	1
2	Cornel Râpă		16/01/90	D	16	(2)	1
10	Nicolae Stanciu		07/05/93	M	28		12
15	Grégory Tadé	FRA	02/09/86	A	12	(12)	4
23	Aymen Tahar	ALG	02/10/89	M	7	(8)	1
30	Gabriel Tamaş		09/11/83	D	11	(1)	
28	Alexandru Tărnovan		27/07/95	A		(1)	
13	Alin Toşca		14/03/92	D	34		
17	Alexandru Tudorie		19/03/96	A	5	(11)	1
33	Fernando Varela	CPV	26/11/87	D	29		3

ASA Tîrgu Mureş

2008 • Trans-Sil (8,200) • asatirgumures.ro

Coach: Vasile Miriuţă (HUN);
(22/09/15) Cristiano Bergodi (ITA);
(17/12/15) (Carol Fekete);
(04/01/16) Petre Grigoraş;
(22/02/16) (Carol Fekete);
(07/03/16) (Adrian Pop);
(08/03/16) George Ciorceri

2015					
12/07	h	Dinamo	D	0-0	
19/07	a	Astra	W	5-1	*Mureşan, Jazvić 2, Axente, Manolov*
24/07	h	Concordia	W	1-0	*Axente*
02/08	h	U Craiova	D	0-0	
09/08	a	Viitorul	L	0-1	
12/08	h	Poli Timişoara	D	0-0	
15/08	a	Steaua	D	1-1	*Jazvić*
21/08	h	Voluntari	W	2-1	*Costa 2*
28/08	a	Iaşi	W	1-0	*Costa*
12/09	h	Petrolul	D	1-1	*Balaur*
18/09	a	Pandurii	L	0-2	
25/09	h	CFR Cluj	D	0-0	
04/10	a	Botoşani	D	1-1	*Iván González*
17/10	a	Dinamo	L	1-2	*N'Doye*
24/10	h	Astra	W	3-1	*Brandán (p), Mureşan, Pedro*
31/10	a	Concordia	W	2-1	*og (Mamele), N'Doye*
08/11	a	U Craiova	D	1-1	*Jazvić*
22/11	h	Viitorul	D	2-2	*Brandán, Balaur*
28/11	a	Poli Timişoara	L	0-2	
02/12	h	Steaua	D	1-1	*Costa*
07/12	a	Voluntari	W	2-0	*Jazvić, Axente*
11/12	h	Iaşi	D	1-1	*Balaur*
20/12	a	Petrolul	W	1-0	*Gorobsov*
2016					
12/02	h	Pandurii	L	0-1	
21/02	a	CFR Cluj	L	0-1	
27/02	h	Botoşani	W	1-0	*Ţucudean*
07/03	h	Pandurii	L	0-2	
14/03	h	Dinamo	D	0-0	
18/03	a	Astra	L	0-1	
31/03	h	Viitorul	D	1-1	*Ţucudean*
03/04	a	Steaua	L	1-2	*Brandán (p)*
11/04	a	Pandurii	D	3-3	*Voiculeţ, Gorobsov, Balaur*
17/04	a	Dinamo	L	0-1	
25/04	h	Astra	L	1-4	*Gorobsov*
02/05	a	Viitorul	L	1-6	*Dedov*
10/05	h	Steaua	L	1-4	*Gorobsov (p)*

No	Name	Nat	DoB	Pos	Aps	(s)	Gls
20	Mircea Axente		14/03/87	A	12	(6)	3
27	Ionuţ Balaur		06/06/89	D	19	(1)	4
3	Saša Balić	MNE	29/01/90	D	18	(1)	
5	Florin Bejan		28/03/91	D	15		
30	Adrian Borza		18/02/85	M	4	(2)	
19	Pablo Brandán	ARG	05/03/83	M	31	(3)	3
77	Bruno Martins	BRA	21/07/86	M		(1)	
17	Laurenţiu Buş		27/08/87	M	8	(4)	
13	Robert Candrea		03/02/95	D	2		
11	Andrei Ciolacu		09/08/92	A	5	(4)	
23	Marius Constantin		25/10/84	D	8	(1)	
16	Ramiro Costa	ARG	21/08/92	A	14	(6)	4
26	Alexandr Dedov	MDA	26/07/89	A	10	(7)	1
96	Norbert Feketics		13/06/96	A	1	(2)	
93	Lucian German		18/08/96	M		(3)	
8	Paweł Golański	POL	12/10/82	D	13		
25	Nicolás Gorobsov	ARG	25/11/89	M	26	(3)	4
44	Sergiu Hanca		04/04/92	M	6	(11)	
4	Iván González	ESP	15/02/88	D	26	(2)	1
9	Filip Jazvić	BIH	22/10/90	A	24	(2)	5
11	Rubén Jurado	ESP	25/04/86	A		(4)	
7	Romario Kortzorg	NED	25/08/89	M	9	(5)	
31	Miroslav Manolov	BUL	20/05/85	A	6	(6)	1
14	Gabriel Matei		26/02/90	D	11		
6	Gabriel Mureşan		13/02/82	M	27		2
67	Sergiu Muth		24/06/90	D	1	(1)	
10	Adrian Nalaţi		08/01/79	A	3	(1)	
78	Ousmane N'Doye	SEN	21/03/78	M	8	(5)	2
7	Paul Pârvulescu		11/08/88	D	9		
21	Luis Pedro	NED	27/04/90	A	11	(6)	1
33	Eduard Stăncioiu		03/03/81	G	34		
18	Răzvan Stoica		19/01/95	A		(1)	
24	Adrian Şut		30/04/99	D		(2)	
29	Marius Ţucudean		30/04/91	A	8	(1)	2
2	Javier Velayos	ESP	06/04/87	D	14	(4)	
1	Adrian Viciu		14/01/91	G	2		
10	Claudiu Voiculeţ		08/08/85	M	11	(5)	1

CS Universitatea Craiova

2013 • Extensiv (6,071) • csuc.ro

Coach: Emil Săndoi;
(08/01/16) Daniel Mogoşanu

2015					
12/07	h	Botoşani	D	0-0	
17/07	a	Dinamo	L	0-1	
26/07	h	Astra	L	1-2	*Mateiu*
02/08	a	Tîrgu Mureş	D	0-0	
08/08	h	Concordia	W	2-0	*Băluţă, Zlatinski*
12/08	h	Viitorul	L	1-2	*Vătăjelu (p)*
15/08	a	Poli Timişoara	D	1-1	*Nunu Rocha*
23/08	h	Steaua	L	1-2	*Vătăjelu (p)*
28/08	a	Voluntari	W	2-1	*Băluţă, Vătăjelu*
13/09	h	Iaşi	W	2-0	*Ivan, Bawab*
20/09	a	Petrolul	W	1-0	*Ivan*
26/09	h	Pandurii	D	0-0	
04/10	a	CFR Cluj	W	2-1	*Nuno Rocha, Dumitraş*
16/10	a	Botoşani	L	2-3	*Nuno Rocha, Ivan*
25/10	h	Dinamo	W	3-0	*Bawab 2, Bancu*
30/10	a	Astra	L	0-1	
08/11	h	Tîrgu Mureş	D	1-1	*og (Costa)*
20/11	a	Concordia	W	2-0	*Kay, Ivan*
28/11	a	Viitorul	L	0-4	
01/12	h	Poli Timişoara	D	1-1	*Nuno Rocha*
06/12	a	Steaua	L	0-2	
13/12	h	Voluntari	L	1-2	*Bancu*
19/12	a	Iaşi	L	0-1	
2016					
14/02	h	Petrolul	W	2-0	*Vătăjelu, Nuno Rocha*
22/02	a	Pandurii	D	1-1	*Mazarache*
27/02	h	CFR Cluj	L	0-1	
06/03	h	Voluntari	W	3-0	*Ivan 2, Nuno Rocha*
14/03	a	Concordia	L	0-1	
20/03	h	Poli Timişoara	W	1-0	*Nuno Rocha*
31/03	h	FC Botoşani	W	2-1	*Acka, Herghelegiu*
03/04	a	Iaşi	L	0-3	
09/04	h	CFR Cluj	D	1-1	*Zlatinski*
15/04	a	Petrolul	L	0-1	
25/04	a	Voluntari	W	2-0	*Nuno Rocha, Bancu*
01/05	h	Concordia	W	2-0	*Băluţă, Ivan*
11/05	a	Poli Timişoara	D	2-2	*Nuno Rocha, Băluţă*
16/05	a	FC Botoşani	L	1-2	*Popov*
22/05	h	Iaşi	W	3-2	*Vătăjelu (p), Herghelegiu, Iliev*
26/05	a	CFR Cluj	L	0-4	
29/05	h	Petrolul	W	2-0	*Herghelegiu 2*

No	Name	Nat	DoB	Pos	Aps	(s)	Gls
2	Sebastian Achim		02/06/86	D	22	(4)	
3	Stephane Acka	CIV	11/10/93	D	23	(1)	1
11	Nicuşor Bancu		18/09/92	D	24	(8)	3
10	Thaer Bawab	JOR	01/03/85	A	17	(2)	3
34	Cristian Bălgrădean		21/03/88	G	23		
22	Alexandru Băluţă		13/09/93	M	18	(15)	4
36	Andrei Burlacu		12/01/97	A		(1)	
38	Cosmin Ciocoteală		21/07/97	D		(1)	
9	Costin Curelea		11/07/84	A	5	(9)	
19	Andrei Dumitraş		23/01/88	D	19	(5)	1
14	Viorel Ferfelea		26/04/85	A	5	(2)	
17	Andrei Herghelegiu		21/03/92	A	8	(16)	4
43	Paul Hodea		29/06/98	M		(1)	
33	Valentin Iliev	BUL	11/08/80	D	16	(4)	1
16	Andrei Ivan		04/01/97	A	30	(2)	7
30	Silviu Izvoranu		03/12/83	D	4	(5)	
4	Kay	CPV	05/01/88	D	16	(5)	1
28	Mádson	BRA	09/05/91	M	18	(7)	
46	Alin Manea		09/01/97	M		(1)	
8	Alexandru Mateiu		10/12/89	M	26	(4)	1
27	Simon Mazarache		10/01/93	A	12	(11)	1
15	Nuno Rocha	CPV	25/03/92	M	38		9
20	Robert Petre		27/04/97	M	1	(5)	
49	Laurenţiu Popescu		18/01/97	G	7		
18	Apostol Popov	BUL	22/12/82	D	28		1
12	Cătălin Straton		09/10/89	G	10	(1)	
36	Olivian Surugiu		23/06/90	M	1		
24	Ionuţ Târnăcop		22/04/87	M	2	(1)	
5	Bogdan Vătăjelu		24/04/93	D	36		5
23	Hristo Zlatinski	BUL	22/01/85	M	31	(2)	2

FC Viitorul

2009 • Orăşenesc, Ovidiu (4,500) • academiahagi.tv

Coach: Gheorghe Hagi; (18/04/16) Cătălin Anghel; (01/05/16) Gheorghe Hagi

2015

11/07	h	CFR Cluj	D	2-2	Cernat 2 (2p)
20/07	a	Botoşani	D	2-2	Mitrea, Filip
25/07	a	Dinamo	D	1-1	Marin
02/08	a	Astra	D	2-2	Cernat 2
09/08	h	Tirgu Mureş	W	1-0	Tănase
12/08	a	U Craiova	W	2-1	Tănase (p), Aganović
17/08	h	Concordia	W	3-1	Tănase (p), Nedelcu, Chiţu
21/08	h	Poli Timişoara	W	4-0	Aganović, Hagi, Tănase, Nicoliţă
30/08	a	Steaua	L	0-1	
14/09	h	Voluntari	W	3-0	Aganović, Nicoliţă, Mitrea
19/09	a	Iaşi	D	0-0	
26/09	h	Petrolul	W	1-0	Marin
03/10	a	Pandurii	L	0-1	
19/10	a	CFR Cluj	W	2-1	Chiţu, Benzar
26/10	h	Botoşani	W	3-1	Benzar, Chiţu, Cernat
02/11	a	Dinamo	W	5-1	Tănase (p), Achim 2, Aganović 2
06/11	h	Astra	L	1-2	Tănase
22/11	a	Tirgu Mureş	D	2-2	og (Balaur), Aganović
28/11	h	U Craiova	W	4-0	Nicoliţă, Tănase 2, Aganović
01/12	a	Concordia	D	2-2	Chiţu, Nicoliţă
05/12	a	Poli Timişoara	W	2-1	Cernat 2 (1p)
14/12	a	Steaua	L	0-1	
21/12	a	Voluntari	W	3-2	Cernat, Ganea 2

2016

13/02	h	Iaşi	L	1-2	Tănase (p)
21/02	a	Petrolul	W	2-1	De Lucas, Ganea
29/02	a	Pandurii	L	1-3	Tănase
05/03	a	Astra	L	0-2	
12/03	a	Pandurii	D	1-1	Rusu
19/03	a	Steaua	L	1-3	Tănase
31/03	a	Tirgu Mureş	D	1-1	De Lucas
04/04	h	Dinamo	L	1-2	Tănase
09/04	h	Astra	L	1-3	Ciobanu
18/04	h	Pandurii	L	0-2	
23/04	a	Steaua	L	0-3	
02/05	a	Tirgu Mureş	W	6-1	og (Buş), Hagi, Boli, Casap, Tănase 2
06/05	a	Dinamo	D	3-3	Marin, Tănase (p), Măţan (p)

No	Name	Nat	DoB	Pos	Aps	(s)	Gls
17	Vlad Achim		07/04/89	M	13	(4)	2
19	Adnan Aganović	CRO	03/10/87	M	23		7
99	Tudor Băluţă		27/03/99	D		(2)	
30	Romario Benzar		26/03/92	D	29	(2)	2
21	Kevin Boli	FRA	21/06/91	D	25	(3)	1
31	Alexandru Buzbuchi		31/10/93	G	10		
8	Carlo Casap		29/12/98	M		(2)	1
23	Alin Cârstocea		16/01/92	M		(1)	
10	Florin Cernat		10/03/80	M	12	(5)	8
25	Aurelian Chiţu		25/03/91	A	17	(16)	4
15	Alexandru Cicâldău		08/07/97	M		(2)	
28	Andrei Ciobanu		18/01/98	A		(2)	1
13	Raul Ciupe		24/11/83	D	4	(2)	
98	Florinel Coman		10/04/98	A		(10)	
11	Pablo De Lucas	ESP	20/09/86	M	13		2
4	Ioan Filip		20/05/89	M	33	(1)	1
22	Cristian Ganea		24/05/92	A	33	(1)	3
9	Cristian Gavra		03/04/93	A	1	(5)	
3	Hérold Goulon	FRA	12/06/88	D	4		
20	Ianis Hagi		22/10/98	M	27	(4)	2
29	Robert Hodorogea		24/03/95	D	24	(2)	
18	Răzvan Marin		23/05/96	M	19	(9)	3
28	Alexandru Măţan		29/08/99	M		(1)	1
23	Constantin Mişelăricu		25/09/89	D		(1)	
14	Bogdan Mitache		01/01/94	D		(1)	
3	Bogdan Mitrea		29/09/87	D	21	(1)	2
28	Alexandru Mitriţă		08/02/95	M		(1)	
6	Cristian Munteanu		17/10/80	M	2		
16	Dragoş Nedelcu		16/02/97	D	15	(7)	1
24	Bănel Nicoliţă		07/01/84	M	11	(11)	4
1	Peçanha	BRA	11/01/80	G	6		
21	Ciprian Perju		18/03/96	M	1	(1)	
12	Victor Râmniceanu		30/11/89	G	16		
9	Vlad Rusu		22/06/90	A	2	(6)	1
7	Florin Tănase		30/12/94	M	31	(1)	15
97	Arpad Tordai		11/03/97	G	4		
15	Bogdan Ţiru		15/03/94	D		(3)	

FC Voluntari

2010 • Dinamo, Bucharest (15,400); Anghel Iordănescu (4,600) • voluntarifc.ro

Coach: Bogdan Vintilă; (15/08/15) Flavius Stoican; (02/09/15) (Daniel Pancu); (06/10/15) Gheorghe Mulţescu; (24/01/16) Ionel Ganea; (27/04/16) Sorin Popescu; (21/05/16) Florin Marin

2015

10/07	h	Iaşi	D	1-1	Pârvulescu (p)
18/07	a	Petrolul	D	1-1	Vâlceanu
24/07	a	Pandurii	D	0-0	
31/07	a	CFR Cluj	L	0-2	
07/08	h	Botoşani	D	1-1	A Bălan
13/08	a	Dinamo	W	0-3	
16/08	h	Astra	L	1-2	Koné
21/08	a	Tirgu Mureş	L	1-2	Pancu
28/08	a	U Craiova	L	1-2	Voduţ
12/09	a	Viitorul	L	0-3	
18/09	h	Poli Timişoara	D	0-0	
27/09	a	Steaua	L	1-3	Goossens (p)
02/10	h	Concordia	D	1-1	Maftei
17/10	a	Iaşi	L	1-2	A Bălan
24/10	h	Petrolul	W	1-0	Koné
01/11	a	Pandurii	L	1-2	Todoran
07/11	h	CFR Cluj	D	2-2	Voduţ, Novac
23/11	a	Botoşani	D	2-2	Koné, Spahija
30/11	h	Dinamo	L	1-3	Spahija
03/12	a	Astra	D	1-1	Pancu (p)
07/12	h	Tirgu Mureş	L	0-2	
13/12	a	U Craiova	W	2-1	A Bălan, Pancu (p)
21/12	h	Viitorul	L	2-3	A Bălan 2

2016

14/02	a	Poli Timişoara	W	2-1	Rus, Tudorie
22/02	h	Steaua	W	3-1	V Achim, Koné 2
28/02	a	Concordia	W	2-1	Ţîru, V Achim
06/03	a	U Craiova	L	0-3	
12/03	h	FC Botoşani	D	1-1	A Bălan
18/03	a	Iaşi	W	1-0	A Bălan
30/03	h	CFR Cluj	W	1-0	Rus
02/04	a	Petrolul	W	2-1	A Bălan (p), Pancu
10/04	a	Poli Timişoara	L	1-2	Tudorie
17/04	h	Concordia	L	1-2	Voduţ
25/04	a	Iaşi	L	1-2	A Bălan
29/04	a	FC Botoşani	L	2-4	Ştefănescu, Pancu (p)
09/05	h	Iaşi	L	1-2	A Bălan
13/05	a	CFR Cluj	L	1-2	Novaković
21/05	h	Petrolul	W	2-0	A Bălan 2 (1p)
25/05	a	Poli Timişoara	W	5-0	Enceanu, Rus (p), Tudorie 2, Voduţ
29/05	a	Concordia	D	1-1	Voduţ

No	Name	Nat	DoB	Pos	Aps	(s)	Gls
2	Cosmin Achim		19/09/95	D	11	(5)	
5	Vlad Achim		07/04/89	M	14	(1)	2
28	Jean Sony Alcénat	HAI	23/01/86	D	5		
33	Dragoş Balauru		11/11/89	G	22	(1)	
12	Daniel Barna		22/09/86	D	11		
90	Adrian Bălan		14/03/90	A	28	(2)	11
90	Tiberiu Bălan		17/02/81	M		(2)	
23	Mircea Bornescu		03/05/80	G	8		
1	Paul Botaş		10/02/90	G	1	(1)	
3	Marius Briceag		06/04/92	D	14		
22	Nicolae Calancea	MDA	29/08/86	G	7		
11	George Călinţaru		26/02/89	M	3	(2)	
3	Mihai Căpăţână		16/12/95	M	2	(1)	
12	Alin Cârstocea		16/01/92	M	3	(2)	
92	Sebastian Chitoşcă		02/10/92	M		(4)	
29	Mihai Costea		29/05/88	A	5	(2)	
26	Gabriel Deac		26/04/95	M	1	(4)	
94	Rareş Enceanu		05/08/94	M	2	(5)	1
45	Venelin Filipov	BUL	10/10/89	D	13	(1)	
27	John Goossens	NED	25/07/88	M	13	(1)	1
18	Nicolae Grigore		19/07/83	M	9	(4)	
11	Alexandru Ioniţă		05/08/89	A		(4)	
17	Cătălin Iorga		17/03/88	M	10	(7)	
10	Hamed Koné	CIV	02/11/87	A	28	(2)	5
72	Ihor Lytovka	UKR	05/06/88	G	2		
24	Vasile Maftei		01/01/81	D	29		1
99	Marius Matei		01/02/84	A		(2)	
5	Florin Maxim		02/03/81	D	2	(1)	
15	Vasile Mihai		29/11/95	M		(1)	
14	Bogdan Mitache		01/01/94	D	4	(2)	
21	Wilfred Moke	COD	12/02/88	M	15		
77	Jeffrey Monakana	ENG	05/11/93	M		(3)	
8	Daniel Novac		26/09/87	M	25	(2)	1
47	Saša Novaković	CRO	27/05/91	D	18	(6)	1
19	Daniel Pancu		17/08/77	A	9	(15)	5
22	Paul Pârvulescu		11/08/88	D	12		1
4	Andrei Poverlovici		17/10/85	D	1		
6	Sorin Rădoi		30/06/85	D	12	(2)	
4	Laurenţiu Rus		07/05/85	D	31		3
44	Hrvoje Spahija	CRO	23/03/88	D	14		2
40	Cătălin Ştefănescu		30/10/94	M	1	(3)	1
43	Franck Tchoutou	CMR	15/05/95	M	1	(3)	
7	Dinu Todoran		08/09/78	M	9	(7)	1
96	Alexandru Tudorie		19/03/96	A	4	(8)	4
15	Bogdan Ţîru		15/03/94	M	14		1
97	Alexandru Vâlceanu		29/03/97	A	9	(3)	1
9	Mihai Voduţ		28/07/94	A	14	(9)	5
30	Radu Zaharia		25/01/89	D	4		

Top goalscorers

19	Ioan Hora (Pandurii)
16	Denis Alibec (Astra)
15	Florin Tănase (Viitorul)
12	Cristian López (CFR Cluj)
	Harlem Gnohéré (Dinamo)
	Bojan Golubović (Iaşi)
	Nicolae Stanciu (Steaua)
11	Gonzalo Cabrera (Botoşani)
	Adrian Bălan (Voluntari)
9	Nuno Rocha (U Craiova)

Promoted clubs

FC Rapid Bucureşti

1923 • Valentin Stănescu (18,000) • fcrapid.ro
Major honours
Romanian League (3) 1967, 1999, 2003; Romanian
Cup (13) 1935, 1937, 1938, 1939, 1940, 1941, 1942,
1972, 1975, 1998, 2002, 2006, 2007
Coach: Dan Alexa

CS Gaz Metan Mediaş

1945 • Gaz Metan (7,814) •
gaz-metan-medias.ro
**Coach: Ion Balaur;
(09/10/15) (Flavius Şomfălean);
(12/10/15) Leontin Grozavu
(05/04/16) Cristian Pustai**

Second level final tables 2015/16

Seria 1
Regular season

		Pld	W	D	L	F	A	Pts
1	FC Rapid Bucureşti	24	16	6	2	43	10	54
2	FC Dunărea 2005 Călăraşi	24	15	7	2	50	13	52
3	FC Farul Constanţa	24	13	5	6	46	30	44
4	ACS Dacia Unirea Brăila	24	13	5	6	30	19	44
5	FC Academica Clinceni	24	13	4	7	45	23	43
6	SC Bacău	24	11	3	10	28	28	36
7	ACS Berceni	24	9	7	8	32	35	34
8	FC Gloria Buzău	24	9	4	11	23	39	31
9	CS Baloteşti	24	6	8	10	23	30	26
10	ACS Rapid CFR Suceava	24	6	7	11	22	36	25
11	ACS Bucovina Pojorâta	24	3	8	13	28	50	17
12	FC Ceahlăul Piatra Neamţ	24	3	5	16	14	40	14
13	FC Oţelul Galaţi	24	3	3	18	12	43	12

NB FCM Dorohoi withdrew pre-season.

Promotion play-offs

		Pld	W	D	L	F	A	Pts
1	FC Rapid Bucureşti	10	6	1	3	12	11	44
2	FC Dunărea 2005 Călăraşi	10	5	3	2	22	8	41
3	ACS Dacia Unirea Brăila	10	4	2	4	16	13	35
4	SC Bacău	10	4	3	3	16	16	30
5	FC Farul Constanţa	10	3	1	6	17	23	29
6	FC Academica Clinceni	10	2	2	6	15	27	27

Seria 2
Regular season

		Pld	W	D	L	F	A	Pts
1	CS Gaz Metan Mediaş	26	16	5	5	37	18	53
2	FC Chindia Târgovişte	26	16	4	6	48	18	52
3	UTA Bătrâna Doamnă Arad	26	15	6	5	48	28	51
4	FCM Baia Mare	26	13	7	6	33	15	46
5	FC Braşov	26	12	9	5	48	24	45
6	CS Mioveni	26	13	6	7	40	18	45
7	CSM Râmnicu Vâlcea	26	12	8	6	39	23	44
8	FC Universitatea Cluj	26	13	5	8	30	15	44
9	CS Şoimii Pâncota	26	9	8	9	30	29	35
10	FC Olimpia 2010 Satu Mare	26	9	6	11	35	36	33
11	CS Unirea Târlungeni	26	5	9	12	26	34	24
12	FC Bihor Oradea	25	4	1	20	10	58	13
13	CSM Metalul Reşiţa	26	3	1	22	18	74	-5
14	FC Caransebeş	25	3	1	21	11	63	-86

*NB FC Bihor Oradea & FC Caransebeş withdrew after
round 18 – their matches from round 14 onwards
were awarded as 0-3 defeats; FC Caransebeş – 96 pts
deducted; CSM Metalul Reşiţa – 15 pts deducted.*

Promotion play-offs

		Pld	W	D	L	F	A	Pts
1	CS Gaz Metan Mediaş	10	6	2	2	17	9	41
2	UTA Bătrâna Doamnă Arad	10	6	3	1	18	14	41
3	FC Chindia Târgovişte	10	6	2	2	18	12	40
4	CS Mioveni	10	2	4	4	15	17	27
5	FC Braşov	10	1	1	8	14	26	23
6	FCM Baia Mare	10	2	2	6	16	20	13

NB FCM Baia Mare – 12 pts deducted.

*NB After 24 and 26 rounds, respectively, the top six clubs enter a promotion play-off, carrying forward half of their
points total gained against the top 12 teams (half points rounded upwards).*

Promotion play-offs

(01/06/16 & 04/06/16)
Dunărea 3-1 Bătrâna Doamnă
Bătrâna Doamnă 4-1 Dunărea *(aet)*
(Bătrâna Doamnă 5-4)

(08/06/16 & 12/06/16)
Voluntari 3-0 Bătrâna Doamnă
Bătrâna Doamnă 1-0 Voluntari
(Voluntari 3-1)

DOMESTIC CUP

Cupa României 2015/16

FIRST ROUND

(22/09/15)
Baloteşti 0-1 CFR Cluj *(aet)*
Berceni 1-1 Iaşi *(aet; 1-3 on pens)*
Bucovina Pojorâta 1-4 Tîrgu Mureş
Râmnicu Vâlcea 0-2 Poli Timişoara
UTA Bătrâna Doamnă 1-1 Pandurii *(aet; 1-3 on pens)*
Viitorul II 2-1 Academica

(23/09/15)
Bacău 1-1 U Craiova *(aet; 5-3 on pens)*
Baia Mare 1-0 Voluntari
Mioveni 1-2 Botoşani
Rapid CFR Suceava 0-2 Braşov
Ripensia 0-2 Viitorul
Unirea Brânceni 0-5 Astra
Unirea Târlungeni 0-6 Petrolul

(24/09/15)
Dacia Unirea 2-3 Dinamo
Tîrgu Mureş II 0-4 Concordia
U Cluj 0-1 Steaua

SECOND ROUND

(27/10/15)
Braşov 3-4 Astra *(aet)*
Concordia 1-2 Iaşi
Poli Timişoara 2-1 Petrolul

(28/10/15)
Bacău 0-1 Tîrgu Mureş
Pandurii 2-3 Dinamo
Viitorul II 0-1 CFR Cluj

(29/10/15)
Baia Mare 1-1 Steaua *(aet; 1-4 on pens)*
Viitorul 1-0 Botoşani

QUARTER-FINALS

(15/12/15)
Dinamo 2-1 Astra *(Gnohéré 16, Palić 90+4;
Enache 90+1)*

Poli Timişoara 1-1 Tîrgu Mureş *(Elek 24; Balić 80)
(aet; 6-7 on pens)*

(16/12/15)
Iaşi 1-2 CFR Cluj *(Gheorghe 77;
Păun-Alexandru 55, Beleck 82)*

(17/12/15)
Viitorul 0-1 Steaua *(Stanciu 48)*

SEMI-FINALS

(02/03/16 & 21/04/16)
Tîrgu Mureş 0-0 CFR Cluj
CFR Cluj 2-0 Tîrgu Mureş *(Bud 17, 70)*
(CFR Cluj 2-0)

(03/03/16 & 20/04/16)
Dinamo 0-0 Steaua
Steaua 2-2 Dinamo *(Enache 17, Chipciu 51; Ekeng
51, Puljić 75)*
(2-2; Dinamo on away goals)

FINAL

(17/05/16)
Arena Naţională, Bucharest
CFR 1907 CLUJ 2 *(Juan Carlos 47, Cristian López 89)*
FC DINAMO BUCUREŞTI 2 *(Gnohéré 23p,
Bicfalvi 35)*
Referee: Haţegan
(aet; 5-4 on pens)
CFR CLUJ: *Marc, Tiago Lopes, Larie, Mureşan,
Camora, Juan Carlos, Petrucci, Gomelt (Cristian
López 46), Jakoliš, Bud (Beleck 59), Nouvier (Vítor
Bruno 80)*
DINAMO: *Černiauskas, Hanca (Marc 73), Puljić,
Mevlja, Filip, Anton, Rotariu, Bicfalvi, Palić
(Nedelcearu 83), Kortzorg (Lazăr 75), Gnohéré*

RUSSIA
Russian Football Union (RFS)

Address Ulitsa Narodnaya 7
RU-115172 Moskva
Tel +7 495 926 1300
Fax +7 495 201 1303
E-mail info@rfs.ru
Website rfs.ru

President Vitali Mutko
General secretary Anatoli Vorobyev
Media officer Igor Vladimirov
Year of formation 1912

St Peterburg (St Petersburg)

Moskva (Moscow)

Tula

Saransk

Kazan

Perm

Rostov-na-Donu

Samara

Ufa

Yekaterinburg

Orenburg

Tomsk

Grozny

Makhachkala

KEY
● UEFA Champions League
● UEFA Europa League
● Promoted
● Relegated

0 1000 2000 km
0 1000 miles

PREMIER-LIGA CLUBS

  1 FC Amkar Perm

  2 FC Anji

  3 PFC CSKA Moskva

  4 FC Dinamo Moskva

  5 FC Krasnodar

 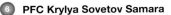 6 PFC Krylya Sovetov Samara

  7 FC Kuban Krasnodar

 8 FC Lokomotiv Moskva

  9 FC Mordovia Saransk

  10 FC Rostov

  11 FC Rubin

  12 FC Spartak Moskva

  13 FC Terek Grozny

  14 FC Ufa

  15 FC Ural Sverdlovsk Oblast

 16 FC Zenit

PROMOTED CLUBS

  17 FC Gazovik Orenburg
NB Renamed FC Orenburg for 2016/17 season

  18 PFC Arsenal Tula

 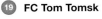 19 FC Tom Tomsk

CSKA hold firm in final-day drama

CSKA Moskva came on strong at the finish to collect their sixth Russian Premier-Liga title, but the story of the 2015/16 season was the astonishing challenge presented to them by previously unheralded FC Rostov.

It was only thanks to an edgy last-day 1-0 win at FC Rubin, the former club of Rostov coach Kurban Berdyev, that CSKA kept the underdogs at bay. Leonid Slutski's delight at leading his club to a third championship win in four years was tempered by the subsequent misadventure of his Russia side at UEFA EURO 2016.

| Surprise challengers Rostov denied at the last | Zenit win cup as Dinamo drop down | Slutski's national team misfire in France |

Domestic league

Second-best to André Villas-Boas's FC Zenit in 2014/15, Slutski and his players demonstrated their eagerness to reclaim the Premier-Liga crown by picking up maximum points from their opening seven matches. Their perfect record ended in September when they surrendered a 2-0 lead at home to Zenit, who equalised two minutes from time, but they bounced back in extraordinary fashion when they recovered from the shock of going three down to Mordovia Saransk after 15 minutes to run out 6-4 winners.

Unbeaten after 14 matches and seemingly on an unstoppable course towards the title, CSKA suddenly hit the buffers in the final month before the winter break, taking just one point from four matches. They still carried a three-point lead into the three-month shutdown, but when Rostov, their closest pursuers, beat them 2-0 at home in the second game after the resumption, the long-time frontrunners were replaced at the summit by their conquerors on the head-to-head rule.

The lead changed hands repeatedly over the next few weeks as neither club could string two wins together. But when Rostov did just that with a magnificent 3-0 home success against

in-form Zenit, there was no longer any doubt that Berdyev's team of unknowns were capable of tranforming fantasy into reality. After all, they were now a point in front of CSKA with just five games to go, all of which seemed eminently winnable.

Disaster, however, struck in Rostov's very next match. Under pressure following an easy midweek win for their title rivals at Ural (a match brought forward because of CSKA's involvement in the Russian Cup final), Berdyev's men fluffed their lines at relegation strugglers Mordovia, losing 2-1 to a late penalty. Now CSKA were back in control, and as both they and Rostov won their next three games, the title came down to the wire. The mathematics were simple. If CSKA made it six wins in a row by beating Rubin in Kazan, the title would be theirs, but if they drew or lost and Rostov won, away at Terek Grozny, the team that had never previously finished higher than sixth (back in 1998) would create the biggest upset Russian football had ever known.

An extra ingredient in an already spicy mix was Berdyev's association with Rubin – a club he coached for 13 years, winning back-to-back titles in 2008 and 2009. In the event, though, his former club could not help him out. Alan Dzagoev rifled CSKA into an early lead,

and although goalkeeper Igor Akinfeev was forced into a dramatic late double save, the Army Men dug in for a 1-0 victory, rendering Rostov's 2-0 win at Terek insufficient to supply a happy ending to their season-long adventure.

CSKA's 20th win of the season had just nudged them over the line. Their key contributors were Akinfeev, who kept clean sheets in half of his 30 appearances, outfield ever-present Ahmed Musa, who supplied incredible pace as well as 13 goals, and midfield maestro Dzagoev, who returned to the kind of form that had marked him out as the most talented Russian footballer of his generation. As for Rostov, no one played better than 36-year-old Spanish centre-back César Navas, a former associate of Berdyev's at Rubin – as was Iranian striker Sardar Azmoun, whose hot form in the run-in (six goals in five games) so nearly transported the team from the River Don to Premier-Liga paradise.

Zenit, who trailed CSKA by seven points at the winter break, would have needed victories in all 12 of their spring fixtures to recover that ground and retain their title. They gave it a good try, winning nine of them and losing only once – to Rostov – but third place, their lowest final position since 2009, was ultimately a disappointing outcome, even if they were the only team in the league to average more than two goals a game and possessed the deadliest strike force in mercurial Brazilian Hulk and newly-acquired Russian international target man Artem Dzyuba. Villas-Boas had announced as early as September that the 2015/16 season would be his last in charge, and he was replaced at the end of term by Shakhtar Donetsk's long-serving Romanian, Mircea Lucescu.

Fourth place went to FC Krasnodar, greatly assisted by the 20 goals of golden boot winner Fedor Smolov – the first Russian to top the Premier-Liga goal charts for eight seasons – and the 13 assists of his creator-in-chief Pavel Mamaev. Spartak Moskva, the country's best-supported club, made a welcome return to Europe following an encouraging first season under ex-player Dmitri Alenichev, their fifth-place finish facilitated by the brilliance of Dutch winger Quincy Promes, who scored 18 goals. Spartak edged city rivals Lokomotiv into sixth by virtue of their greater number of victories, having trailed them by eight points with five games to go.

Another Moscow club, Dinamo, managed only half as many points as Spartak and Lokomotiv and as a consequence were relegated for the first time in their 93-year history. Only Mordovia finished beneath them, while

Krasnodar's city rivals Kuban also went down after a play-off defeat to Tom Tomsk, who thus moved in the opposite direction alongside the second division's top two, Gazovik Orenburg and Arsenal Tula.

Domestic cup

Victorious on their last seven visits to the Russian Cup final, and therefore the competition's most successful club, CSKA were denied a prospective double as Zenit defeated them 4-1 with a resounding second-half display in the same Kazan-Arena where Slutski's team would claim the league title 19 days later. Hulk scored two penalties, with Aleksanadr Kokorin and Artur Yusupov also finding the net as Zenit ensured that Villas-Boas would leave St Petersburg with both of Russia's domestic trophies on his list of achievements. Zenit had needed extra time and a penalty shoot-out to come through the previous two rounds, but they were clearly superior to a CSKA side whose minds were perhaps distracted by the bigger prize of the Premier-Liga title.

Europe

Zenit also gave Villas-Boas a decent send-off in Europe, striding through their UEFA Champions League group with an ease and confidence never previously

witnessed as they qualified for the knockout phase with two games to spare. Indeed, they were only denied a clean sweep of victories when they lost on matchday six at Gent. Unfortunately, they were beaten twice more in the round of 16 by Benfica – a team they had defeated home and away in the previous season's group stage – and, with their exit, Russian involvement in Europe ended for another year.

CSKA had Musa's timely goals to thank for taking them past Sparta Praha and Sporting Clube de Portugal and back into the UEFA Champions League group stage for the third year in a row, but as in the previous two seasons they advanced no further. Rubin and Krasnodar both joined Lokomotiv in the UEFA Europa League group stage, but while the latter two progressed into the round of 32, both clubs got no further.

National team

Hired as a replacement for the sacked Fabio Capello with four games to go in the UEFA EURO 2016 qualifying campaign, Slutski worked wonders in leading Russia to victories in every one of them and qualifying the team for the finals without recourse to the play-offs. However, the feelgood factor instilled by the CSKA boss in the autumn was gone the following summer as Russia, missing key midfielders Dzagoev and Igor Denisov through injury, suffered a nightmare tournament in France.

As at the 2014 FIFA World Cup under Capello, Russia seemed gripped by stage fright – a worrying portent for the 2018 World Cup, which of course takes place on Russian soil. A fortunate 1-1 draw against England in Marseille was overshadowed by rioting fans at the Stade Vélodrome, which led to a formal UEFA warning of expulsion from the tournament for any repeat offence. A week or so later Russia were out anyway, eliminated on the field of play after defeats against Slovakia and Wales, the second of them by a 3-0 scoreline. Ten days later Slutski announced that his time as national team boss was over and that he would be returning to work solely for CSKA, leaving his successor with the challenging task of rebuilding a team that will be sufficiently competitive to do the nation proud in front of a global audience in 2018.

Artem Dzyuba points the way forward for Zenit in the UEFA Champions League after scoring against Lyon

DOMESTIC SEASON AT A GLANCE

Premier-Liga 2015/16 final table

		Pld	Home					Away					Total					
			W	D	L	F	A	W	D	L	F	A	W	D	L	F	A	Pts
1	**PFC CSKA Moskva**	30	12	2	1	28	9	8	3	4	23	16	20	5	5	51	25	65
2	FC Rostov	30	11	4	0	22	7	8	2	5	19	13	19	6	5	41	20	63
3	FC Zenit	30	9	4	2	35	15	8	4	3	26	17	17	8	5	61	32	59
4	FC Krasnodar	30	9	4	2	30	8	7	4	4	24	17	16	8	6	54	25	56
5	FC Spartak Moskva	30	7	4	4	25	18	8	1	6	23	21	15	5	10	48	39	50
6	FC Lokomotiv Moskva	30	7	4	4	19	12	7	4	4	24	21	14	8	8	43	33	50
7	FC Terek Grozny	30	7	5	3	22	14	4	6	5	13	16	11	11	8	35	30	44
8	FC Ural Sverdlovsk Oblast	30	6	3	6	24	24	4	6	5	15	22	10	9	11	39	46	39
9	PFC Krylya Sovetov Samara	30	3	6	6	7	15	6	2	7	12	16	9	8	13	19	31	35
10	FC Rubin	30	5	3	7	20	21	4	3	8	13	18	9	6	15	33	39	33
11	FC Amkar Perm	30	5	5	5	13	14	2	5	8	9	19	7	10	13	22	33	31
12	FC Ufa	30	5	4	6	16	18	1	5	9	9	26	6	9	15	25	44	27
13	FC Anji	30	2	5	8	13	22	4	3	8	15	28	6	8	16	28	50	26
14	FC Kuban Krasnodar	30	4	5	6	22	19	1	6	8	12	25	5	11	14	34	44	26
15	FC Dinamo Moskva	30	3	4	8	14	24	2	6	7	11	23	5	10	15	25	47	25
16	FC Mordovia Saransk	30	3	5	7	17	21	1	7	7	13	29	4	12	14	30	50	24

European qualification 2016/17

Champion: PFC CSKA Moskva (group stage)
FC Rostov (third qualifying round)

Cup winner: FC Zenit (group stage)
FC Krasnodar (third qualifying round)
FC Spartak Moskva (third qualifying round)

Top scorer	Fedor Smolov (Krasnodar), 20 goals
Relegated clubs	FC Mordovia Saransk, FC Dinamo Moskva, FC Kuban Krasnodar
Promoted clubs	FC Gazovik Orenburg, PFC Arsenal Tula, FC Tom Tomsk
Cup final	FC Zenit 4-1 PFC CSKA Moskva

Team of the season
(4-4-2)

Coach: Slutski (CSKA)

Akinfeev (CSKA)

Mário Fernandes (CSKA) — César Navas (Rostov) — V Berezutski (CSKA) — Kudryashov (Terek/Rostov)

Promes (Spartak) — Dzagoev (CSKA) — Mamaev (Krasnodar) — Shatov (Zenit)

Hulk (Zenit) — Smolov (Krasnodar)

Player of the season

Quincy Promes
(FC Spartak Moskva)

Spartak Moskva won no prizes in 2015/16 other than a place in the UEFA Europa League for finishing fifth in the Russian Premier-Liga, but they did possess arguably the most consistently entertaining individual in the division. Promes finished as the club's top scorer for the second successive season, increasing his 2014/15 tally of 13 to 18 as he repeatedly bewitched defenders with his skill, speed and finishing power. The winger's sustained excellence was rewarded with regular selection in Danny Blind's new-look Netherlands side.

Newcomer of the season

Aleksandr Golovin
(PFC CSKA Moskva)

Golovin turned 20 shortly after helping CSKA win the Russian Premier-Liga title and, although his 17 appearances contained just six starts, he was given the additional birthday present of a place in Russia's UEFA EURO 2016 squad, having scored on his debut in a March friendly against Lithuania. The all-purpose midfielder, who made his name as the No10 in the Russia side that won the 2013 UEFA European Under-17 Championship, has the talent to become a key player for his country at the 2018 FIFA World Cup.

NATIONAL TEAM

International honours*
UEFA European Championship (1) 1960

International tournament appearances*
FIFA World Cup (10) 1958 (qtr-finals), 1962 (qtr-finals), 1966 (4th), 1970 (qtr-finals), 1982 (2nd phase), 1986 (2nd round), 1990, 1994, 2002, 2014
UEFA European Championship (11) 1960 (Winners), 1964 (runners-up), 1968 (4th), 1972 (runners-up), 1988 (runners-up), 1992, 1996, 2004, 2008 (semi-finals), 2012, 2016

Top five all-time caps
Sergei Ignashevich (120); Viktor Onopko (113); Oleh Blokhin (112); **Vasili Berezutski** (98); Rinat Dasaev & **Aleksandr Kerzhakov** (91)

Top five all-time goals
Oleh Blokhin (42); **Aleksandr Kerzhakov** (30); Oleh Protasov (29); Vladimir Beschastnykh & Valentin Ivanov (26)

(before 1992 as USSR; 1992 as CIS)*

Results 2015/16

05/09/15	Sweden (ECQ)	H	Moscow	W	1-0	Dzyuba (38)	
08/09/15	Liechtenstein (ECQ)	A	Vaduz	W	7-0	Dzyuba (21, 45, 73, 90), Kokorin (40p), Smolov (77), Dzagoev (85)	
09/10/15	Moldova (ECQ)	A	Chisinau	W	2-1	Ignashevich (58), Dzyuba (78)	
12/10/15	Montenegro (ECQ)	H	Moscow	W	2-0	Kuzmin (33), Kokorin (37p)	
14/11/15	Portugal	H	Krasnodar	W	1-0	Shirokov (89)	
17/11/15	Croatia	H	Rostov-na-Donu	L	1-3	Smolov (14)	
26/03/16	Lithuania	H	Moscow	W	3-0	Smolov (41), Golovin (61), Glushakov (72)	
29/03/16	France	A	Saint-Denis	L	2-4	Kokorin (56), Zhirkov (68)	
01/06/16	Czech Republic	N	Innsbruck (AUT)	L	1-2	Kokorin (6)	
05/06/16	Serbia	N	Monaco (FRA)	D	1-1	Dzyuba (85)	
11/06/16	England (ECF)	N	Marseille (FRA)	D	1-1	V Berezutski (90+2)	
15/06/16	Slovakia (ECF)	N	Lille (FRA)	L	1-2	Glushakov (80)	
20/06/16	Wales (ECF)	N	Toulouse (FRA)	L	0-3		

Appearances 2015/16

Coach: Leonid Slutski 04/05/71			SWE	LIE	MDA	MNE	Por	Cro	Ltu	Fra	Cze	Srb	ENG	SVK	WAL	Caps	Goals
Igor Akinfeev	08/04/86	CSKA Moskva	G	G	G	G	G			G46		G	G	G	G	90	-
Igor Smolnikov	08/08/88	Zenit	D	D	D27				D	s69	D	D62	D	D	D	17	-
Vasili Berezutski	20/06/82	CSKA Moskva	D	D						D	D64	D	D	D	D46	98	5
Sergei Ignashevich	14/07/79	CSKA Moskva	D	D	D	D	D	s89	D		D	D	D	D	D	120	8
Yuri Zhirkov	20/08/83	Dinamo Moskva /Zenit	D71				D			D69						68	2
Igor Denisov	17/05/84	Dinamo Moskva	M	M46	M	M	M					M	M51			54	-
Roman Shirokov	06/07/81	Spartak Moskva /CSKA Moskva	M83	M75	M76	M	M	M		M69		s75	s77	s75	M52	57	13
Aleksandr Kokorin	19/03/91	Dinamo Moskva /Zenit	M	M	M	M				M79	M64	M	M	M75	M	42	12
Alan Dzagoev	17/06/90	CSKA Moskva	M	M		M86	M			M						49	9
Oleg Shatov	29/07/90	Zenit	M	M65	M	M69				M88	M	M75	M	M		25	2
Artem Dzyuba	22/08/88	Zenit	A79	A	A88	A84	A	s70		A	A46	A	A	A	A	21	9
Oleg Kuzmin	09/05/81	Rubin	s71		s27	D	D45			D						5	1
Aleksei Ionov	18/02/89	Dinamo Moskva	s79					M65	s46							11	-
Aleksei Berezutski	20/06/82	CSKA Moskva	s83		D	D	D			D46	D				s46	58	-
Dmitri Kombarov	22/01/87	Spartak Moskva		D	D	D		D65	D		s64				D	40	2
Denis Glushakov	27/01/87	Spartak Moskva		s46	s76			M71	M	s79		s51	s80	s46	M	46	5
Pavel Mamaev	17/09/88	Krasnodar		s65	M	s69	M77	s71	M46	s69	s46	s46	s85	s46	M	15	-
Fedor Smolov	09/02/90	Krasnodar		s75	s88	s84	s66	A	A46	s79	M	M46	M85	M	M70	17	5
Denis Cheryshev	26/12/90	Real Madrid (ESP)				s86		M70								9	-
Aleksandr Samedov	19/07/84	Lokomotiv Moskva					M66		M46	s88	s64				s70	30	3
Roman Shishkin	27/01/87	Lokomotiv Moskva					s45	D				s62				11	-
Vladislav Ignatyev	20/01/87	Kuban					s77	s65								2	-
Yuri Lodygin	26/05/90	Zenit						G46		s46	G46					11	-
Andrei Semyonov	24/03/89	Terek						D								3	-
Viktor Vasin	06/10/88	CSKA Moskva						D89								2	-
Artur Yusupov	01/09/89	Zenit						M	s46							2	-
Artem Rebrov	04/03/84	Spartak Moskva						s46								1	-
Ivan Novoseltsev	25/08/91	Rostov						s65								3	-
Stanislav Kritsyuk	01/12/90	Krasnodar						G46								1	-
Dmitri Tarasov	18/03/87	Lokomotiv Moskva						M								3	1
Oleg Ivanov	04/08/86	Terek							M69		M64	s60				5	-
Guilherme	12/12/85	Lokomotiv Moskva							s46		s46					2	-
Aleksandr Golovin	30/05/96	CSKA Moskva							s46	M79	s64	M60	M77	M46	s52	8	2
Aleksandr Kerzhakov	27/11/82	Zürich (SUI)							s46							91	30
Ilya Maksimov	02/02/87	Anji							s69							1	-
Dmitri Torbinski	28/04/84	Krasnodar									D64	s76				30	2
Roman Neustädter	18/02/88	Schalke (GER)									s64		M80	M46		3	-
Georgi Schennikov	27/04/91	CSKA Moskva										D76	D	D		10	-

FC Zenit

Group H
Match 1 - Valencia CF (ESP)
A 3-2 *Hulk (9, 44), Witsel (76)*
Lodygin, Anyukov (Luís Neto 77), Criscito, Lombaerts, Hulk, Danny, Smolnikov (Shatov 69), Javi García, Dzyuba (Fayzulin 59), Garay, Witsel. Coach: André Villas-Boas (POR)
Match 2 - KAA Gent (BEL)
H 2-1 *Dzyuba (35), Shatov (67)*
Kerzhakov, Anyukov, Lombaerts (Luís Neto 62), Hulk, Danny, Shatov (Ryazantsev 88), Smolnikov, Javi García, Dzyuba (Yusupov 72), Garay, Witsel. Coach: André Villas-Boas (POR)
Match 3 - Olympique Lyonnais (FRA)
H 3-1 *Dzyuba (3), Hulk (56), Danny (82)*
Kerzhakov, Anyukov, Criscito, Lombaerts, Hulk, Danny (Ryazantsev 89), Shatov, Javi García (Luís Neto 84), Dzyuba (Yusupov 75), Garay, Witsel. Coach: André Villas-Boas (POR)
Match 4 - Olympique Lyonnais (FRA)
A 2-0 *Dzyuba (25, 57)*
Lodygin, Anyukov, Criscito (Smolnikov 73), Lombaerts, Hulk, Danny, Luís Neto, Shatov, Javi García (Yusupov 80), Dzyuba (Ryazantsev 83), Witsel. Coach: André Villas-Boas (POR)
Red card: Anyukov 88
Match 5 - Valencia CF (ESP)
H 2-0 *Shatov (15), Dzyuba (74)*
Lodygin, Criscito, Lombaerts, Hulk, Danny, Luís Neto (Evseev 86), Shatov (Ryazantsev 84), Smolnikov (Yusupov 65), Dzyuba, Garay, Witsel. Coach: André Villas-Boas (POR)
Match 6 - KAA Gent (BEL)
A 1-2 *Dzyuba (65)*
Lodygin, Anyukov (Bogaev 82), Criscito, Ryazantsev (Dolgov 61), Lombaerts, Danny, Luís Neto, Yusupov, Javi García (Troyanov 86), Dzyuba, Garay. Coach: André Villas-Boas (POR)

Round of 16 - SL Benfica (POR)
A 0-1
Lodygin, Anyukov, Criscito, Lombaerts, Hulk, Danny (Maurício 87), Shatov (Zhirkov 81), Javi García, Dzyuba (Kokorin 74), Garay, Witsel. Coach: André Villas-Boas (POR)
Red card: Criscito 90
H 1-2 *Hulk (69)*
Lodygin, Anyukov (Smolnikov 58), Lombaerts, Hulk, Maurício (Yusupov 82), Kokorin (Shatov 58), Danny, Luís Neto, Dzyuba, Witsel, Zhirkov. Coach: André Villas-Boas (POR)

PFC CSKA Moskva

Third qualifying round - AC Sparta Praha (CZE)
H 2-2 *Dzagoev (14), Tošić (53)*
Akinfeev, Mário Fernandes, Wernbloom, Ignashevich, A Berezutski, Tošić (Strandberg 86), Dzagoev (Milanov 72), Nababkin (Schennikov 46), Musa, Eremenko, Natcho. Coach: Leonid Slutski (RUS)
A 3-2 *Musa (34, 51), Dzagoev (76)*
Akinfeev, Mário Fernandes, Wernbloom, A Berezutski, Tošić (Milanov 83), Dzagoev (Golovin 90+4), Nababkin, Musa, V Berezutski, Eremenko, Natcho. Coach: Leonid Slutski (RUS)

Play-offs - Sporting Clube de Portugal (POR)
A 1-2 *Doumbia (40)*
Akinfeev, Mário Fernandes, Wernbloom, Ignashevich, Tošić (Milanov 79), Dzagoev, Nababkin (A Berezutski 90+2), Musa, V Berezutski, Eremenko, Doumbia (Natcho 89). Coach: Leonid Slutski (RUS)
H 3-1 *Doumbia (49, 72), Musa (85)*
Akinfeev, Mário Fernandes (Nababkin 34), Wernbloom, Ignashevich, Tošić, Dzagoev, Musa (Milanov 90+4), V Berezutski, Eremenko, Schennikov, Doumbia (A Berezutski 89). Coach: Leonid Slutski (RUS)

Group B
Match 1 - VfL Wolfsburg (GER)
A 0-1
Akinfeev, Mário Fernandes, Wernbloom, Ignashevich, Tošić (Milanov 78), Dzagoev, Musa, V Berezutski, Eremenko, Schennikov, Natcho (Doumbia 65). Coach: Leonid Slutski (RUS)
Match 2 - PSV Eindhoven (NED)
H 3-2 *Musa (7), Doumbia (21, 36p)*
Akinfeev, Mário Fernandes, Wernbloom, Ignashevich, A Berezutski, Tošić (Milanov 67), Dzagoev, Musa, Schennikov, Natcho (Eremenko 67), Doumbia (Panchenko 90+3). Coach: Leonid Slutski (RUS)
Match 3 - Manchester United FC (ENG)
H 1-1 *Doumbia (15)*
Akinfeev, Mário Fernandes, Wernbloom, Ignashevich, Tošić, Dzagoev (Cauņa 87), Musa, V Berezutski (A Berezutski 41), Eremenko (Panchenko 84), Schennikov, Doumbia. Coach: Leonid Slutski (RUS)
Match 4 - Manchester United FC (ENG)
A 0-1
Akinfeev, Mário Fernandes, Wernbloom, Ignashevich, A Berezutski, Tošić (Golovin 76), Dzagoev (Panchenko 85), Musa, Milanov, Schennikov, Natcho (Doumbia 55). Coach: Leonid Slutski (RUS)
Match 5 - VfL Wolfsburg (GER)
H 0-2
Akinfeev, Mário Fernandes, Wernbloom, Ignashevich (Vasin 46), A Berezutski, Tošić, Dzagoev (Panchenko 90), Nababkin (Natcho 75), Musa, Milanov, Doumbia. Coach: Leonid Slutski (RUS)
Match 6 - PSV Eindhoven (NED)
A 1-2 *Ignashevich (76p)*
Akinfeev, Wernbloom, Ignashevich, A Berezutski, Tošić, Dzagoev, Nababkin, Musa, Cauņa, Natcho, Doumbia. Coach: Leonid Slutski (RUS)

FC Lokomotiv Moskva

Group H
Match 1 - Sporting Clube de Portugal (POR)
A 3-1 *Samedov (12, 56), Niasse (65)*
Guilherme, Manuel Fernandes (Kolomeytsev 81), Pejčinović, Maicon (Grigoryev 82), Ćorluka, Samedov, Niasse, Tarasov (Mikhalik 86), Denisov, Shishkin, N'Dinga. Coach: Igor Cherevchenko (RUS)
Match 2 - KF Skënderbeu (ALB)
H 2-0 *Niasse (35), Samedov (73)*
Guilherme, Manuel Fernandes (Miranchuk 46), Pejčinović, Maicon, Ćorluka, Logashov, Kolomeytsev (N'Dinga 66), Samedov, Niasse (Škuletić 81), Tarasov, Yanbaev. Coach: Igor Cherevchenko (RUS)
Match 3 - Beşiktaş JK (TUR)
H 1-1 *Maicon (54)*
Guilherme, Manuel Fernandes (Ďurica 73), Maicon (Kasaev 79), Ćorluka, Mikhalik, Kolomeytsev, Samedov, Niasse (Grigoryev 88), Denisov, Shishkin, N'Dinga. Coach: Igor Cherevchenko (RUS)
Red card: Ćorluka 69
Match 4 - Beşiktaş JK (TUR)
A 1-1 *Niasse (76)*
Guilherme, Manuel Fernandes (Miranchuk 74), Maicon (Grigoryev 90+3), Kolomeytsev, Samedov, Niasse (Škuletić 90), Ďurica, Denisov, Shishkin, Yanbaev, N'Dinga. Coach: Igor Cherevchenko (RUS)
Match 5 - Sporting Clube de Portugal (POR)
H 2-4 *Maicon (5), Miranchuk (86)*
Guilherme, Manuel Fernandes (Miranchuk 78), Maicon (Kasaev 81), Mikhalik, Samedov, Niasse, Tarasov (Kolomeytsev 65), Ďurica, Denisov, Shishkin, N'Dinga. Coach: Igor Cherevchenko (RUS)
Match 6 - KF Skënderbeu (ALB)
A 3-0 *Tarasov (18), Niasse (89), Samedov (90)*
Guilherme, Kasaev (Maicon 75), Pejčinović, Mikhalik (Ďurica 82), Kolomeytsev, Samedov, Niasse (Miranchuk 90+1), Tarasov, Denisov, Shishkin, N'Dinga. Coach: Igor Cherevchenko (RUS)

Round of 32 - Fenerbahçe SK (TUR)
A 0-2
Guilherme, Kasaev (Maicon 62; Mikhalik 76), Manuel Fernandes, Pejčinović, Samedov, Tarasov, Ďurica, Denisov, Škuletić (Miranchuk 80), Yanbaev, N'Dinga. Coach: Igor Cherevchenko (RUS)
H 1-1 *Samedov (45)*
Guilherme, Kasaev (Zhemaletdinov 81), Manuel Fernandes (Škuletić 73), Pejčinović, Ćorluka, Kolomeytsev, Samedov, Ďurica, Denisov, Miranchuk, N'Dinga (Mikhalik 13). Coach: Igor Cherevchenko (RUS)

FC Krasnodar

Third qualifying round - ŠK Slovan Bratislava (SVK)
H 2-0 *Granqvist (45), Mamaev (59p)*
Dykan, Jędrzejczyk, Granqvist, Mamaev (Akhmedov 68), Gazinski (Strandberg 81), Ari, Wanderson, Kaleshin, Sigurdsson, Pereyra, Smolov (Laborde 62). Coach: Oleg Kononov (BLR)
A 3-3 *Mamaev (8p, 11), Smolov (90+3p)*
Dykan, Jędrzejczyk, Granqvist, Mamaev (Torbinski 46), Gazinski (Strandberg 64), Ari, Akhmedov, Laborde (Wanderson 78), Sigurdsson, Smolov, Petrov. Coach: Oleg Kononov (BLR)

Play-offs - HJK Helsinki (FIN)
H 5-1 *Ojala (80g), Mamaev (10p), Smolov (57p), Wanderson (62), Gazinski (64)*
Dykan, Strandberg, Granqvist, Mamaev, Gazinski, Akhmedov (Ari 58), Kaleshin, Bystrov (Wanderson 58), Sigurdsson, Smolov (Torbinski 74), Petrov. Coach: Oleg Kononov (BLR)
A 0-0
Dykan, Strandberg, Torbinski, Granqvist, Ari (Smolov 75), Akhmedov, Wanderson (Laborde 67), Markov, Kaleshin (Jędrzejczyk 70), Sigurdsson, Petrov. Coach: Oleg Kononov (BLR)

Group C
Match 1 - Borussia Dortmund (GER)
A 1-2 *Mamaev (12)*
Dykan, Strandberg, Jędrzejczyk, Granqvist, Mamaev (Ari 81), Akhmedov, Sigurdsson, Pereyra (Laborde 60), Kaboré (Gazinski 70), Smolov, Petrov. Coach: Oleg Kononov (BLR)
Match 2 - Qäbälä FK (AZE)
H 2-1 *Wanderson (8), Smolov (84)*
Sinitsin, Strandberg, Jędrzejczyk, Granqvist, Mamaev (Laborde 66), Gazinski (Joãozinho 76), Ari (Smolov 60), Akhmedov, Wanderson, Kaleshin, Kaboré. Coach: Oleg Kononov (BLR)
Match 3 - PAOK FC (GRE)
A 0-0
Dykan, Strandberg, Torbinski (Gazinski 82), Jędrzejczyk, Granqvist, Akhmedov (Mamaev 65), Kaleshin, Laborde, Joãozinho, Kaboré, Smolov (Ari 63). Coach: Oleg Kononov (BLR)
Red card: Jędrzejczyk 88
Match 4 - PAOK FC (GRE)
H 2-1 *Ari (33), Joãozinho (67p)*
Dykan, Torbinski, Granqvist, Ari, Akhmedov (Gazinski 77), Kaleshin (Mamaev 69), Laborde (Smolov 62), Joãozinho, Sigurdsson, Kaboré, Petrov. Coach: Oleg Kononov (BLR)
Match 5 - Borussia Dortmund (GER)
H 1-0 *Mamaev (2p)*
Dykan, Jędrzejczyk, Granqvist, Mamaev (Laborde 84), Ari, Akhmedov (Torbinski 85), Kaleshin, Sigurdsson, Pereyra (Gazinski 74), Kaboré, Smolov. Coach: Oleg Kononov (BLR)
Match 6 - Qäbälä FK (AZE)
A 3-0 *Sigurdsson (26), Pereyra (41), Wanderson (76)*
Dykan, Granqvist, Akhmedov, Wanderson (Smolov 76), Kaleshin (Laborde 65), Joãozinho, Sigurdsson, Pereyra (Gazinski 69), Kaboré, Petrov. Coach: Oleg Kononov (BLR)

Round of 32 - AC Sparta Praha (CZE)
A 0-1
Dykan, Granqvist, Mamaev, Ari, Akhmedov, Kaleshin, Joãozinho (Bystrov 82), Sigurdsson, Pereyra (Gazinski 66), Smolov (Wanderson 68), Petrov. Coach: Oleg Kononov (BLR)

H 0-3
Dykan, Strandberg, Granqvist, Mamaev (Joãozinho 62), Ari, Akhmedov , Kaleshin, Pereyra (Wanderson 62), Kaboré, Smolov (Torbinski 75), Petrov. Coach: Oleg Kononov (BLR)
Red card: Kaboré 68

FC Rubin

Third qualifying round - SK Sturm Graz (AUT)
A 3-2 *Kanunnikov (14), Gökdeniz Karadeniz (25p), Portnyagin (61)*
Ryzhikov, Kuzmin, Nabiullin, Kverkvelia, Carlos Eduardo, Bilyaletdinov (Kislyak 66), Cotugno, Ozdoev, Gökdeniz Karadeniz, Kambolov (Georgiev 46), Kanunnikov (Portnyagin 46). Coach: Rinat Bilyaletdinov (RUS)
H 1-1 *Kuzmin (85)*
Ryzhikov, Kuzmin, Nabiullin (Batov 79), Lemos, Kverkvelia, Portnyagin, Dyadyun (Kanunnikov 60), Ozdoev, Gökdeniz Karadeniz (Cotugno 88), Georgiev, Kambolov. Coach: Rinat Bilyaletdinov (RUS)

Play-offs - FK Rabotnicki (MKD)
A 1-1 *Gökdeniz Karadeniz (68)*
Ryzhikov, Kuzmin, Kverkvelia, Carlos Eduardo (Kislyak 81), Bilyaletdinov (Portnyagin 58), Cotugno, Ozdoev, Gökdeniz Karadeniz (Batov 71), Georgiev, Kambolov, Kanunnikov. Coach: Rinat Bilyaletdinov (RUS)
H 1-0 *Carlos Eduardo (35)*
Ryzhikov, Kuzmin, Lemos, Kverkvelia, Carlos Eduardo (Portnyagin 79), Bilyaletdinov, Cotugno, Dyadyun (Batov 90+3), Ozdoev, Georgiev, Kanunnikov. Coach: Rinat Bilyaletdinov (RUS)

Group B
Match 1 - FC Sion (SUI)
A 1-2 *Kanunnikov (65)*
Ryzhikov, Kuzmin, Nabiullin, Kverkvelia, Portnyagin, Carlos Eduardo (Dyadyun 90), Bilyaletdinov (Ozdoev 46), Gökdeniz Karadeniz (Dević 86), Georgiev, Kambolov, Kanunnikov. Coach: Valeri Chaly (RUS)
Match 2 - FC Girondins de Bordeaux (FRA)
H 0-0
Ryzhikov, Kuzmin, Nabiullin, Kverkvelia, Portnyagin (Dyadyun 74), Carlos Eduardo, Dević (Bilyaletdinov 46), Kislyak, Ozdoev, Kambolov, Kanunnikov. Coach: Valeri Chaly (RUS)
Red card: Kislyak 80
Match 3 - Liverpool FC (ENG)
A 1-1 *Dević (15)*
Ryzhikov, Kuzmin, Nabiullin, Kverkvelia, Carlos Eduardo (Portnyagin 63), Dević (Cotugno 46), Ozdoev, Gökdeniz Karadeniz (Dyadyun 81), Georgiev, Kambolov, Kanunnikov. Coach: Valeri Chaly (RUS)
Red card: Kuzmin 36
Match 4 - Liverpool FC (ENG)
H 0-1
Ryzhikov, Nabiullin, Kverkvelia, Carlos Eduardo (Ozdoev 46), Dević, Kislyak (Akhmetov 70), Cotugno (Ustinov 81), Gökdeniz Karadeniz, Georgiev, Kanunnikov. Coach: Valeri Chaly (RUS)
Match 5 - FC Sion (SUI)
H 2-0 *Georgiev (72), Dević (90)*
Ryzhikov, Nabiullin, Kverkvelia, Carlos Eduardo (Bilyaletdinov 70), Dević (Akhmetov 90+2), Kislyak (Dyadyun 46), Ozdoev, Ustinov, Georgiev, Kambolov, Kanunnikov. Coach: Valeri Chaly (RUS)
Match 6 - FC Girondins de Bordeaux (FRA)
A 2-2 *Kanunnikov (31), Ustinov (76)*
Ryzhikov, Kuzmin (Ustinov 75), Nabiullin, Kverkvelia, Carlos Eduardo, Dević, Kislyak (Bilyaletdinov 46; Dyadyun 77), Ozdoev, Georgiev, Kambolov, Kanunnikov. Coach: Valeri Chaly (RUS)

FC Amkar Perm

1994 • Zvezda (19,500) • fc-amkar.org
Coach: Gadzhi Gadzhiev

2015

20/07	h	Krasnodar	L 0-1	
26/07	a	Rubin	W 2-0	og (Kverkvelia), Peev (p)
01/08	h	Krylya Sovetov	W 1-0	Belorukov
09/08	a	CSKA	L 0-2	
14/08	h	Anji	D 1-1	Gol
22/08	h	Spartak	L 1-3	Gol
28/08	a	Rostov	L 0-1	
12/09	h	Kuban	D 1-1	Shavaev
20/09	a	Zenit	D 1-1	Anene
28/09	h	Mordovia	W 2-1	Shavaev, Peev (p)
04/10	a	Lokomotiv	L 0-3	
17/10	h	Dinamo	D 1-1	Prudnikov
24/10	a	Ural	L 1-3	Salugin
02/11	h	Terek	W 1-0	og (Utsiyev)
07/11	a	Ufa	L 1-2	Salugin
21/11	h	Rubin	L 1-2	Shavaev
28/11	a	Krylya Sovetov	D 0-0	
03/12	h	CSKA	W 2-0	Shavaev, Salugin

2016

07/03	h	Anji	W 1-0	Peev
12/03	a	Spartak	L 1-2	Komolov
18/03	h	Rostov	D 0-0	
02/04	a	Kuban	D 1-1	Prudnikov (p)
09/04	h	Zenit	L 0-2	
15/04	a	Mordovia	D 1-1	Dzhikia
24/04	h	Lokomotiv	L 0-1	
29/04	a	Dinamo	D 0-0	
08/05	h	Ural	D 1-1	Gol
12/05	a	Terek	L 0-2	
16/05	h	Ufa	W 1-0	Dzhikia
21/05	a	Krasnodar	L 0-1	

No	Name	Nat	DoB	Pos	Aps	(s)	Gls
11	Chuma Anene	NOR	14/05/93	A	5	(9)	1
50	Robert Arzumanyan	ARM	24/07/85	D	5		
13	Sergei Balanovich	BLR	29/08/87	M	25	(1)	
21	Dmitri Belorukov		24/03/83	D	17	(1)	1
91	Bohdan Butko	UKR	13/01/91	D	26		
23	Ivan Cherenchikov		25/08/84	D	11	(1)	
	Chinedu Dike	NGA	02/02/87	A	2	(2)	
17	David Dzakhov		06/10/88	M	2	(2)	
14	Georgi Dzhikia		21/11/93	D	16	(6)	2
1	Roman Gerus		14/09/80	G	7		
24	Roland Gigolaev		04/01/90	M	6	(2)	
5	Janusz Gol	POL	11/11/85	M	27		3
19	Brian Oladapo Idowu		18/05/92	D	15	(7)	
33	Branko Jovičić	SRB	18/03/93	M	10	(6)	
20	Pavel Komolov		10/03/89	M	12	(5)	1
18	Aleksei Kurzenyov		09/01/95	A		(3)	
99	Oleh Mishchenko	UKR	10/10/89	A	1		
36	Fegor Ogude	NGA	29/07/87	M	22		
36	Aleksandr Pantsyrev		08/12/93	M		(2)	
7	Georgi Peev	BUL	11/03/79	M	15	(5)	3
20	Aleksandr Prudnikov		26/02/89	A	20	(9)	2
77	Aleksandr Salugin		23/10/88	A	8	(12)	3
57	Aleksandr Selikhov		07/04/94	G	23		
22	Alikhan Shavaev		05/01/93	M	9	(8)	4
43	Izunna Uzochukwu	NGA	11/04/90	M	6	(3)	
4	Nikolai Zaitsev		01/06/89	D	17	(5)	
3	Petar Zanev	BUL	18/10/85	D	23		

FC Anji

1991 • Anji-Arena (30,000) • fc-anji.ru
Coach: Yuri Semin;
(29/09/15) Ruslan Agalarov

2015

19/07	h	Krylya Sovetov	L	0-1	
27/07	h	Lokomotiv	L	1-3	Haruna
01/08	a	CSKA	L	0-1	
08/08	h	Dinamo	L	2-3	Maksimov, Boli (p)
14/08	a	Amkar	D	1-1	Boli
22/08	h	Ural	D	1-1	Leonardo (p)
29/08	a	Spartak	W	2-1	Ebecilio, Zhirov
13/09	h	Terek	L	0-2	
18/09	a	Rostov	L	0-1	
26/09	h	Ufa	D	1-1	Hugo Almeida
03/10	a	Kuban	D	1-1	Boli
18/10	h	Krasnodar	D	2-2	Hugo Almeida, Boli
24/10	a	Zenit	L	1-5	Maksimov
01/11	h	Rubin	L	1-2	Maksimov
06/11	a	Mordovia	L	0-4	
21/11	a	Lokomotiv	W	2-0	Abdulavov, Boli
29/11	h	CSKA	D	1-1	Nababkin
04/12	h	Dinamo	W	2-1	Ebecilio, Maksimov

2016

07/03	h	Amkar	L	0-1	
12/03	a	Ural	L	2-4	Berisha, Maksimov
18/03	h	Spartak	L	0-4	
02/04	a	Terek	L	2-3	Lazić, Boli
08/04	h	Rostov	D	0-0	
17/04	a	Ufa	L	0-2	
24/04	h	Kuban	W	1-0	Boli (p)
01/05	a	Krasnodar	L	0-3	
07/05	h	Zenit	L	0-1	
11/05	h	Rubin	W	2-1	Boli, Lazić
15/05	h	Mordovia	W	3-0	Boli, Mkrtchyan, Musalov
21/05	a	Krylya Sovetov	D	0-0	

No	Name	Nat	DoB	Pos	Aps	(s)	Gls
99	Islamnur Abdulavov		07/03/94	A	8	(11)	1
7	Kamil Agalarov		11/06/88	M	8	(2)	
14	Bernard Berisha	KOS	24/10/91	A	8	(3)	1
94	Yannick Boli	FRA	13/01/88	A	21	(7)	9
8	Lorenzo Ebecilio	NED	24/09/91	M	19	(6)	2
2	Andrei Eschenko		09/02/84	D	15	(1)	
3	Ali Gadzhibekov		06/08/89	D	19		
30	Shamil Gasanov		30/07/93	D	5	(6)	
33	Anvar Gazimagomedov		11/05/88	M	3	(2)	
10	Lukman Haruna	NGA	12/04/90	M	10	(2)	1
22	Hugo Almeida	POR	23/05/84	A	7	(5)	2
37	Batraz Khadartsev		23/05/93	M	10	(5)	
1	Aleksandr Krivoruchko		23/09/84	G		(1)	
4	Darko Lazić	SRB	19/07/94	D	21	(4)	2
12	Leonardo	BRA	18/03/92	M	7	(3)	1
87	Ilya Maksimov		02/02/87	M	22		6
18	Ivan Mayevski	BLR	05/05/88	M	17	(1)	
25	Jonathan Mensah	GHA	13/07/90	D	6		
6	Karlen Mkrtchyan	ARM	25/11/88	M	15	(5)	1
20	Amadou Moutari	NIG	19/01/94	M	13	(4)	
57	Magomed Musalov		09/02/94	D	9		1
33	Sergei Pesyakov		16/12/88	G	11		
55	Evgeni Pomazan		31/01/89	G	9		
28	Serder Serderov		10/03/94	A		(1)	
13	Rasim Tagirbekov		04/05/84	D	9		
77	Georgi Tigiev		20/06/95	D	16	(3)	
1	David Yurchenko		27/03/86	G	10		
5	Aleksandr Zhirov		24/01/91	D	30		1
15	Georgi Zotov		12/01/90	D	2	(2)	

PFC CSKA Moskva

1911 • Arena Khimki (18,636); Eduard Streltsov (13,450) • pfc-cska.com
Major honours
UEFA Cup (1) 2005; USSR League (7) 1946, 1947, 1948, 1950, 1951, 1970, 1991; Russian League (6) 2003, 2005, 2006, 2013, 2014, 2016; USSR Cup (5) 1945, 1948, 1951, 1955, 1991; Russian Cup (7) 2002, 2005, 2006, 2008, 2009, 2011, 2013

Coach: Leonid Slutski

2015

18/07	h	Rubin	W	1-0	Musa
24/07	a	Krylya Sovetov	W	2-0	Tošić, Natcho (p)
01/08	h	Anji	W	1-0	Mário Fernandes
09/08	h	Amkar	W	2-0	Natcho (p), Tošić
14/08	a	Spartak	W	2-1	Ignashevich, Musa
22/08	h	Rostov	W	2-1	Musa, Dzagoev
30/08	a	Kuban	W	1-0	Nababkin
12/09	h	Zenit	D	2-2	og (Lombaerts), Doumbia
20/09	a	Mordovia	W	6-4	Panchenko, Tošić, Doumbia 2, Musa 2
26/09	h	Lokomotiv	D	1-1	Doumbia (p)
04/10	a	Dinamo	W	2-0	Wernbloom, Musa
17/10	h	Ural	W	3-2	Panchenko, Doumbia, Wernbloom
25/10	a	Terek	D	0-0	
31/10	h	Ufa	W	2-0	Ignashevich (p), Tošić
08/11	a	Krasnodar	L	1-2	Dzagoev
21/11	h	Krylya Sovetov	L	0-2	
29/11	a	Anji	D	1-1	Nababkin
03/12	a	Amkar	L	0-2	

2016

06/03	h	Spartak	W	1-0	Musa
11/03	a	Rostov	L	0-2	
19/03	h	Kuban	W	2-0	Musa 2
03/04	a	Zenit	L	0-2	
09/04	h	Mordovia	W	7-1	og (Shitov), Eremenko 2, Golovin, Musa, Ignashevich, Dzagoev
16/04	a	Lokomotiv	D	1-1	Olanare
24/04	h	Dinamo	W	1-0	A Berezutski
28/04	a	Ural	W	3-0	Olanare, Musa, Dzagoev
07/05	h	Terek	W	1-0	Wernbloom
11/05	a	Ufa	W	3-1	Dzagoev, Wernbloom, Musa
16/05	h	Krasnodar	W	2-0	Musa, Eremenko
21/05	a	Rubin	W	1-0	Dzagoev

No	Name	Nat	DoB	Pos	Aps	(s)	Gls
35	Igor Akinfeev		08/04/86	G	30		
6	Aleksei Berezutski		20/06/82	D	16	(5)	1
24	Vasili Berezutski		20/06/82	D	18		
19	Aleksandrs Cauņa	LVA	19/01/88	M	2	(7)	
88	Seydou Doumbia	CIV	31/12/87	A	11	(2)	5
10	Alan Dzagoev		17/06/90	M	29		6
25	Roman Eremenko	FIN	19/03/87	M	23	(2)	3
60	Aleksandr Golovin		30/05/96	M	6	(11)	1
4	Sergei Ignashevich		14/07/79	D	24	(1)	3
2	Mário Fernandes	BRA	19/09/90	D	27		1
23	Georgi Milanov	BUL	19/02/92	M	4	(14)	
18	Ahmed Musa	NGA	14/10/92	A	30		13
14	Kirill Nababkin		08/09/86	D	11	(2)	2
66	Bebras Natcho	ISR	18/02/88	M	15	(5)	2
99	Aaron Olanare	NGA	04/06/94	A	3	(4)	2
8	Kirill Panchenko		16/10/89	A	3	(11)	2
42	Georgi Schennikov		27/04/91	D	18	(1)	
15	Roman Shirokov		06/07/81	M	2	(6)	
11	Carlos Strandberg	SWE	14/04/96	A		(1)	
17	Sergei Tkachyov		19/05/89	M	2	(6)	
7	Zoran Tošić	SRB	28/04/87	M	27	(1)	4
5	Viktor Vasin		06/10/88	D	3		
3	Pontus Wernbloom	SWE	25/06/86	M	26	(1)	4
15	Dmitri Yefremov		01/04/95	M		(1)	

FC Dinamo Moskva

1923 • Arena Khimki (18,636) • fcdynamo.ru
Major honours
USSR League (11) 1936 (spring), 1937, 1940, 1945, 1949, 1954, 1955, 1957, 1959, 1963, 1976 (spring); USSR Cup (6) 1937, 1953, 1967, 1970, 1977, 1984; Russian Cup (1) 1995

Coach: Andrei Kobelev;
(10/05/16) (Sergei Chikishev)

2015

19/07	a	Zenit	L	1-2	Kokorin
25/07	h	Mordovia	D	2-2	Ionov, Valbuena (p)
02/08	a	Lokomotiv	D	1-1	Morozov
09/08	a	Anji	W	3-2	Kozlov, Hubočan, Valbuena (p)
16/08	h	Ural	W	1-0	Morozov
21/08	a	Terek	W	1-0	Kokorin
29/08	h	Ufa	W	2-0	Kozlov, Dyakov (p)
13/09	h	Krasnodar	L	0-4	
21/09	h	Rubin	D	0-0	
27/09	a	Krylya Sovetov	D	0-0	
04/10	h	CSKA	L	0-2	
17/10	a	Amkar	D	1-1	Kokorin
25/10	h	Spartak	L	2-3	Kokorin, Pogrebnyak
02/11	a	Rostov	L	0-1	
07/11	h	Kuban	W	2-1	Kozlov, Zobnin
22/11	a	Mordovia	D	1-1	Tashaev
30/11	h	Lokomotiv	D	2-2	Dyakov 2 (1p)
01/12	h	Anji	L	1-2	Kozlov

2016

07/03	a	Ural	D	1-1	Ionov
14/03	a	Terek	L	0-1	
19/03	a	Ufa	W	1-0	Bećiraj
04/04	h	Krasnodar	L	1-4	Ionov (p)
09/04	a	Rubin	L	1-4	Ionov (p)
17/04	h	Krylya Sovetov	L	0-1	
24/04	a	CSKA	L	0-1	
29/04	h	Amkar	D	0-0	
08/05	a	Spartak	L	0-3	
12/05	h	Rostov	L	1-3	Bećiraj
16/05	a	Kuban	L	0-2	
21/05	h	Zenit	L	0-3	

No	Name	Nat	DoB	Pos	Aps	(s)	Gls
21	Fatos Bećiraj	MNE	05/05/88	A	12		2
3	Alexander Büttner	NED	11/02/89	D		(1)	
12	Egor Danilkin		01/08/95	D	2		
27	Igor Denisov		17/05/84	M	22	(1)	
5	Douglas	BRA	12/01/88	D		(2)	
7	Stanislav Dragun	BLR	04/06/88	M	8	(1)	
20	Vitali Dyakov		31/01/89	D	19	(1)	3
7	Balázs Dzsudzsák	HUN	23/12/86	M	1		
38	Andrei Eschenko		09/02/84	D	9		
30	Vladimir Gabulov		19/10/83	G	23		
3	Sebastian Holmén	SWE	29/04/92	D	9	(1)	
11	Tomáš Hubočan	SVK	17/09/85	D	22		1
11	Aleksei Ionov		18/02/89	M	28	(1)	4
72	Aleksandr Kalyashin		24/01/95	D		(1)	
77	Anatoli Katrich		09/07/94	M	4	(2)	
9	Aleksandr Kokorin		19/03/91	A	8		4
25	Aleksei Kozlov		25/12/86	D	21	(1)	4
13	Maksim Kuzmin		01/09/96	M	1	(5)	
80	Vladislav Levin		28/03/95	M	1	(2)	
2	Grigori Morozov		06/06/94	D	20	(1)	2
90	Nikolai Obolski		14/01/97	A		(7)	
8	Pavel Pogrebnyak		08/11/83	A	14	(2)	1
4	Christopher Samba	CGO	28/03/84	D	3	(1)	
87	Valeri Saramutin		17/05/95	M		(1)	
1	Anton Shunin		27/01/87	G	7		
22	Pavel Solomatin		04/04/93	A		(2)	
23	Anton Sosnin		27/01/90	M	18	(4)	
88	Aleksandr Tashaev		23/06/94	M	21	(4)	1
98	Anton Terekhov		30/01/98	M	1	(3)	
6	William Vainqueur	FRA	19/11/88	M		(1)	
14	Mathieu Valbuena	FRA	28/09/84	M	4		2
18	Yuri Zhirkov		20/08/83	M	16		
17	Dmitri Zhivoglyadov		29/05/94	D	11	(10)	
47	Roman Zobnin		11/02/94	M	25	(4)	1

FC Krasnodar

2008 • Kuban (35,200) • fckrasnodar.ru
Coach: Oleg Kononov (BLR)

2015

20/07	a	Amkar	W	1-0	Petrov
26/07	h	Spartak	L	0-1	
02/08	a	Rostov	D	0-0	
10/08	h	Kuban	D	1-1	Smolov
15/08	a	Zenit	W	2-0	Sigurdsson, Laborde
23/08	h	Mordovia	D	0-0	
30/08	a	Lokomotiv	L	1-2	Smolov
13/09	h	Dinamo	W	4-0	Laborde, Mamaev 2, Akhmedov
21/09	a	Ural	L	1-3	Akhmedov
27/09	h	Terek	D	1-1	Petrov
04/10	a	Ufa	D	1-1	Mamaev
18/10	a	Anji	D	2-2	Laborde, Ari
25/10	h	Rubin	W	2-1	Ari 2
01/11	a	Krylya Sovetov	W	4-0	Mamaev 2, Smolov, Ari
08/11	h	CSKA	W	2-1	Smolov 2
22/11	a	Spartak	L	2-3	Ari, Granqvist
30/11	h	Rostov	W	2-1	Mamaev (p), Wanderson
04/12	a	Kuban	W	3-2	Wanderson, Mamaev (p), Smolov

2016

05/03	h	Zenit	D	0-0	
13/03	a	Mordovia	W	1-0	Smolov
20/03	a	Lokomotiv	L	1-2	Pereyra
04/04	h	Dinamo	W	4-1	Mamaev (p), Podberyozkin, Smolov, Akhmedov
10/04	h	Ural	W	6-0	Smolov 4, og (Manucharyan), Wanderson
16/04	a	Terek	W	1-0	Smolov
24/04	h	Ufa	W	4-0	Wanderson 2, Smolov, Petrov
01/05	h	Anji	W	3-0	Smolov 2, Mamaev
07/05	a	Rubin	D	1-1	Smolov
11/05	h	Krylya Sovetov	W	3-0	Smolov 3
16/05	a	CSKA	L	0-2	
21/05	h	Amkar	W	1-0	Mamaev

No	Name	Nat	DoB	Pos	Aps	(s)	Gls
10	Odil Akhmedov	UZB	25/11/87	M	24	(3)	3
9	Ari	BRA	11/12/85	A	15	(6)	5
18	Vladimir Bystrov		31/01/84	M	4	(9)	
31	Andriy Dykan	UKR	16/07/77	G	14		
38	Kouassi Eboue	CIV	13/12/97	M	1		
8	Yuri Gazinski		20/07/89	M	14	(7)	
6	Andreas Granqvist	SWE	16/04/85	D	29		1
5	Artur Jędrzejczyk	POL	04/11/87	D	5	(1)	
22	Joãozinho	BRA	25/12/88	M	3	(11)	
77	Charles Kaboré	BFA	09/02/88	M	20	(1)	
17	Vitali Kaleshin		03/10/80	D	24	(1)	
1	Stanislav Kritsyuk		01/12/90	G	12		
21	Ricardo Laborde	COL	16/02/88	M	5	(14)	3
7	Pavel Mamaev		17/09/88	M	28	(1)	10
15	Nikolai Markov		20/04/85	D	2	(5)	
33	Mauricio Pereyra	URU	15/03/90	M	16	(4)	1
98	Sergei Petrov		02/01/91	D	23	(1)	3
14	Vyacheslav Podberyozkin		21/06/92	M	4	(4)	1
27	Ragnar Sigurdsson	ISL	19/06/86	D	23	(1)	1
88	Andrei Sinitsin		23/06/88	G	4		
90	Fedor Smolov		09/02/90	A	29		20
3	Stefan Strandberg	NOR	25/07/90	D	13	(2)	
4	Dmitri Torbinski		28/04/84	M	8	(7)	
14	Wanderson	BRA	18/02/86	A	10	(12)	5

PFC Krylya Sovetov Samara

1942 • Metallurg (33,001) • kc-camapa.ru
Coach: Frank Vercauteren (BEL)

2015

19/07	a	Anji	W	1-0	Gabulov
24/07	h	CSKA	L	0-2	
01/08	a	Amkar	L	0-1	
09/08	h	Spartak	L	0-1	
16/08	a	Rostov	D	1-1	Gabulov
24/08	h	Kuban	W	3-0	Dragun 2, Kornilenko
29/08	a	Zenit	W	3-1	Gabulov, Kornilenko 2
14/09	h	Mordovia	W	1-0	Gabulov
20/09	a	Lokomotiv	L	0-2	
27/09	h	Dinamo	D	0-0	
02/10	a	Ural	D	1-1	Tsallagov
18/10	h	Terek	L	0-1	
23/10	a	Ufa	L	0-1	
01/11	h	Krasnodar	L	0-4	
08/11	h	Rubin	L	0-1	
21/11	a	CSKA	W	2-0	Jahovic 2
28/11	h	Amkar	D	0-0	
04/12	a	Spartak	L	0-1	

2016

05/03	h	Rostov	L	0-1	
11/03	a	Kuban	L	0-2	
20/03	h	Zenit	L	0-2	
04/04	a	Mordovia	W	2-1	Taranov, Kornilenko
11/04	h	Lokomotiv	D	0-0	
17/04	a	Dinamo	W	1-0	Bruno
23/04	h	Ural	D	1-1	Rodić
01/05	a	Terek	W	1-0	Jahovic
06/05	h	Ufa	W	1-0	Yakovlev
11/05	a	Krasnodar	L	0-3	
15/05	h	Rubin	D	1-1	Bruno
21/05	h	Anji	D	0-0	

No	Name	Nat	DoB	Pos	Aps	(s)	Gls
19	Sheldon Bateau	TRI	21/01/91	D	9	(9)	
29	Gianni Bruno	BEL	19/08/91	A	8	(3)	2
90	Taras Burlak		22/02/90	D	28		
10	Alan Chochiyev		07/09/91	M	12	(7)	
2	Stanislav Dragun	BLR	04/06/88	M	12	(2)	2
5	Georgi Gabulov		04/09/88	M	21	(1)	4
77	Igor Gorbatenko		13/02/89	M	1	(7)	
45	Adis Jahovic	MKD	18/03/87	A	12	(4)	3
13	Evgeni Konyukhov		21/11/86	G	16		
8	Sergei Kornilenko	BLR	14/06/83	A	12	(4)	4
1	Miroslav Lobantsev		27/05/95	G		(1)	
17	Giorgi Loria	GEO	27/01/86	G	14		
11	Emin Makhmudov		27/04/92	M		(1)	
7	Yohan Mollo	FRA	18/07/89	M	22	(1)	
6	Nadson	BRA	18/10/84	D	24	(1)	
20	Aleksei Pomerko		03/05/90	M	27		
33	Milan Rodić	SRB	02/04/91	D	10	(6)	1
9	Berat Sadik	FIN	14/09/86	A	4	(7)	
16	Jeroen Simaeys	BEL	12/05/85	D	13	(10)	
4	Ivan Taranov		22/06/86	D	26		1
15	Ibragim Tsallagov		12/12/90	M	30		1
98	Ilya Viznovich		10/02/98	A		(1)	
91	Pavel Yakovlev		07/04/91	A	6	(6)	1
3	Dmitri Yatchenko		25/08/86	D	12	(6)	

FC Kuban Krasnodar

1928 • Kuban (35,200) • fckuban.ru
Coach: Dmitri Khokhlov;
(17/09/15) Sergei Tashuev;
(26/04/16)(Arsen Papikyan)
(04/05/16) Igor Osinkin

2015

20/07	h	Ural	L	0-2	
25/07	a	Terek	D	1-1	Melgarejo
31/07	h	Ufa	D	1-1	Ignatyev
10/08	a	Krasnodar	D	1-1	Melgarejo
15/08	h	Rubin	L	0-1	
24/08	a	Krylya Sovetov	L	0-3	
30/08	h	CSKA	L	0-1	
12/09	a	Amkar	D	1-1	Melgarejo
19/09	h	Spartak	W	3-0	Khubulov, Melgarejo, Ignatyev
28/09	a	Rostov	L	1-2	Tkachyov
03/10	h	Anji	D	1-1	Melgarejo
17/10	h	Zenit	D	2-2	Xandão, Melgarejo
24/10	a	Mordovia	D	1-1	Baldé
01/11	a	Lokomotiv	W	6-2	Ignatyev 2, Melgarejo 2, Armas, Tkachyov
07/11	h	Dinamo	L	1-2	Ignatyev
22/11	h	Terek	D	2-2	Baldé 2
28/11	h	Ufa	D	2-2	Ignatyev, Khubulov
04/12	a	Krasnodar	L	2-3	Tkachyov, Ignatyev

2016

05/03	h	Rubin	L	0-1	
11/03	h	Krylya Sovetov	W	2-0	Karetnik, Seleznyov
19/03	a	CSKA	L	0-2	
02/04	h	Amkar	D	1-1	Seleznyov (p)
10/04	a	Spartak	D	2-2	Apodí, Mairovich
17/04	h	Rostov	L	0-1	
24/04	a	Anji	L	0-1	
28/04	a	Zenit	L	1-4	Seleznyov
07/05	h	Mordovia	L	1-2	Baldé
11/05	a	Lokomotiv	W	1-0	Pavlyuchenko (p)
16/05	h	Dinamo	W	1-0	Pavlyuchenko
21/05	a	Ural	L	0-2	

No	Name	Nat	DoB	Pos	Aps	(s)	Gls
22	Apodí	BRA	13/12/86	D	12		1
2	Igor Armas	MDA	14/07/87	D	24	(1)	1
19	Andrei Arshavin		29/05/81	M	4	(4)	
99	Ibrahima Baldé	SEN	04/04/89	A	10	(11)	4
11	Gheorghe Bucur	ROU	08/04/80	A	8	(5)	
43	Roman Bugaev		11/02/89	D	21		
9	Felipe Santana	BRA	17/03/86	D	9		
17	Svyatoslav Georgievski		26/08/95	M	3	(2)	
20	Vladislav Ignatyev		20/01/87	M	17		7
20	Sergei Karetnik		14/02/95	M	6	(6)	1
78	Arsen Khubulov		13/12/90	M	18	(8)	2
84	Aleksandr Kleshchenko		02/11/95	M	2	(3)	
72	Igor Konovalov		08/07/96	M		(3)	
14	Roman Kontsedalov		11/05/86	M	2	(5)	
7	Vladislav Kulik		27/02/85	M	14	(2)	
21	Vladimir Lobkarev		17/09/93	D	4	(6)	
83	Aleksandr Mairovich		06/02/96	A	6	(6)	1
16	Stanislav Manolev	BUL	16/12/85	D	12	(3)	
25	Lorenzo Melgarejo	PAR	10/08/90	M	14	(2)	8
9	Roman Pavlyuchenko		15/12/81	A	4	(6)	2
5	Mohammed Rabiu	GHA	31/12/89	M	20		
10	Yevhen Seleznyov	UKR	20/07/85	A	9		3
1	Dmitri Stajila	MDA	02/08/91	G	1	(1)	
14	Toni Šunjić	BIH	15/12/88	D	9		
77	Sergei Tkachyov		19/05/89	M	15	(1)	3
8	Artur Tlisov		10/06/82	M	9	(5)	
4	Xandão	BRA	23/02/88	D	27		1
73	Denis Yakuba		26/05/96	D	12	(1)	
30	Ihor Zhurakhovskiy	UKR	19/09/94	M		(2)	
15	Georgi Zotov		12/01/90	D	12		

RUSSIA

FC Lokomotiv Moskva

1923 • Lokomotiv (28,800) • fclm.ru
Major honours
Russian League (2) 2002, 2004; USSR Cup (2) 1936, 1957; Russian Cup (6) 1996, 1997, 2000, 2001, 2007, 2015
Coach: Igor Cherevchenko

2015
19/07	a	Mordovia	W 1-0	*Škuletić*
27/07	a	Anji	W 3-1	*Škuletić, Maicon, Kasaev*
02/08	h	Dinamo	D 1-1	*Čorluka*
08/08	a	Ural	W 3-1	*Samedov, Niasse, Maicon*
16/08	h	Terek	D 0-0	
23/08	a	Ufa	W 3-0	*Niasse, Kasaev, Pejčinović*
30/08	h	Krasnodar	W 2-1	*Niasse, Kasaev*
12/09	a	Rubin	L 1-3	*Samedov*
20/09	h	Krylya Sovetov	W 2-0	*Čorluka, Niasse*
26/09	a	CSKA	D 1-1	*Niasse (p)*
04/10	h	Amkar	W 3-0	*Kolomeytsev, Samedov, Miranchuk*
18/10	a	Spartak	W 2-1	*Kolomeytsev, Niasse*
26/10	h	Rostov	L 0-2	
01/11	a	Kuban	L 2-6	*Niasse, Kolomeytsev*
08/11	h	Zenit	W 2-0	*og (Lombaerts), Samedov*
21/11	a	Anji	L 0-2	
30/11	a	Dinamo	D 2-2	*Samedov, Maicon*
04/12	a	Ural	D 2-2	*Miranchuk, Niasse*

2016
06/03	a	Terek	L 1-2	*Samedov*
13/03	h	Ufa	W 2-0	*Ignatyev (p), Samedov*
20/03	a	Krasnodar	W 2-1	*Ðurica, Samedov*
03/04	h	Rubin	W 1-0	*Škuletić*
11/04	a	Krylya Sovetov	D 0-0	
16/04	h	CSKA	D 1-1	*Čorluka*
24/04	a	Amkar	W 1-0	*Škuletić*
30/04	h	Spartak	L 0-2	
06/05	a	Rostov	L 1-2	*Škuletić*
11/05	h	Kuban	L 0-1	
15/05	a	Zenit	D 1-1	*Samedov (p)*
21/05	h	Mordovia	W 3-0	*Zhemaletdinov 2, Škuletić*

No	Name	Nat	DoB	Pos	Aps	(s)	Gls
36	Dmitri Barinov		11/09/96	M	2		
11	Mbark Boussoufa	MAR	15/08/84	M	1		
14	Vedran Čorluka	CRO	05/02/86	D	23	(1)	3
29	Vitali Denisov	UZB	23/02/87	D	29		
28	Ján Ďurica	SVK	10/12/81	D	13		1
9	Maksim Grigoryev		06/07/90	M	1	(4)	
1	Guilherme		12/12/85	G	30		
45	Ezekiel Henty	NGA	13/05/93	A	5	(5)	
20	Vladislav Ignatyev		20/01/87	M	2	(5)	1
3	Alan Kasaev		08/04/86	M	21	(3)	3
18	Aleksandr Kolomeytsev		21/02/89	M	25	(3)	3
15	Arseni Logashov		20/08/91	D	4	(4)	
7	Maicon	BRA	18/02/90	A	3	(11)	3
70	Georgi Makhatadze		26/03/98	M		(1)	
4	Manuel Fernandes	POR	05/02/86	M	2	(2)	
17	Taras Mikhalik	UKR	28/10/83	D	16	(5)	
59	Aleksei Miranchuk		17/10/95	M	16	(11)	2
88	Delvin N'Dinga	CGO	14/03/88	M	15	(9)	
21	Oumar Niasse	SEN	18/04/90	A	13	(3)	8
5	Nemanja Pejčinović	SRB	04/11/87	D	21		1
19	Aleksandr Samedov		19/07/84	M	28		9
49	Roman Shishkin		27/01/87	D	19		
32	Petar Škuletić	SRB	29/06/90	A	12	(6)	6
23	Dmitri Tarasov		18/03/87	M	20	(3)	
55	Renat Yanbaev		07/04/84	D	6	(4)	
96	Rifat Zhemaletdinov		20/09/96	A	3	(2)	2

FC Mordovia Saransk

1961 • Start (11,613) • fc-mordovia.ru
Coach: Andrei Gordeev;
(07/04/16) (Marat Mustafin)

2015
19/07	h	Lokomotiv	L 0-1	
25/07	a	Dinamo	D 2-2	*Lutsenko, Donald (p)*
02/08	h	Ural	D 1-1	*Lutsenko*
07/08	a	Terek	D 0-0	
17/08	h	Ufa	L 0-1	
23/08	a	Krasnodar	D 0-0	
30/08	h	Rubin	W 2-1	*Stevanović (p), Mukhametshin*
14/09	a	Krylya Sovetov	L 0-1	
20/09	h	CSKA	L 4-6	*Lutsenko 2, Rykov, Mukhametshin*
28/09	a	Amkar	L 1-2	*Mukhametshin*
03/10	h	Spartak	L 0-1	
19/10	a	Rostov	L 2-3	*Rykov, Mukhametshin*
24/10	h	Kuban	D 1-1	*Lutsenko*
31/10	a	Zenit	D 0-0	
06/11	h	Anji	W 4-0	*Vlasov, Lutsenko 2, Yannick Djaló*
22/11	h	Dinamo	D 1-1	*Le Tallec*
27/11	a	Ural	L 1-3	*Phibel*
03/12	h	Terek	D 0-0	

2016
06/03	a	Ufa	D 1-1	*Lomić (p)*
13/03	h	Krasnodar	L 0-1	
20/03	a	Rubin	D 1-1	*Mukhametshin*
04/04	h	Krylya Sovetov	L 1-2	*Lutsenko*
09/04	a	CSKA	L 1-7	*Samodin*
15/04	h	Amkar	D 1-1	*Mukhametshin*
23/04	a	Spartak	D 2-2	*Samodin, Lutsenko*
01/05	h	Rostov	W 2-1	*Samodin, Stevanović (p)*
07/05	a	Kuban	W 2-1	*Lutsenko, Perendija*
11/05	h	Zenit	L 0-3	
15/05	a	Anji	L 0-3	
21/05	a	Lokomotiv	L 0-3	

No	Name	Nat	DoB	Pos	Aps	(s)	Gls
8	Anton Bober		28/09/82	M	5	(5)	
1	Ilie Cebanu	MDA	29/12/86	G	8	(1)	
6	Mitchell Donald	NED	10/12/88	M	1	(1)	1
17	Aslan Dudiev		15/06/90	D	24	(2)	
9	Evgeni Gapon		20/04/90	D	10	(1)	
10	Pavel Ignatovich		24/05/89	M	2	(16)	
88	Aleksei Ivanov		01/09/81	M	7	(6)	
5	Mamuka Kobakhidze	GEO	23/08/92	D		(1)	
7	Damien Le Tallec	FRA	19/04/90	A	13	(2)	1
32	Marko Lomić	SRB	13/09/83	D	7		1
48	Evgeni Lutsenko		25/02/87	A	20	(7)	10
15	Emin Makhmudov		27/04/92	M	16	(2)	
13	Mikhail Markin		21/11/93	A		(1)	
23	Ruslan Mukhametshin		29/10/81	A	26	(2)	6
55	Ruslan Nakhushev		05/09/84	D	16		
57	Ruslan Navletov		10/12/93	A		(2)	
40	Milan Perendija	SRB	05/01/86	D	7	(3)	1
97	Thomas Phibel	FRA	31/05/86	D	17		1
77	Nukri Revishvili	GEO	02/03/87	G	22		
33	Vladimir Rykov		13/11/87	D	27		2
22	Sergei Samodin		14/02/85	A	12	(5)	3
25	Evgeni Shipitsin		16/07/86	M	4	(9)	
4	Igor Shitov	BLR	24/10/86	D	16	(1)	
16	Dalibor Stevanović	SVN	27/09/84	M	26	(1)	2
11	Dmitri Sysuev		13/01/88	M	1	(8)	
71	Maksim Tishkin		11/11/89	D	15	(3)	
84	Oleg Vlasov		10/12/84	M	26	(4)	1
20	Yannick Djaló	POR	05/05/86	M	2	(5)	1

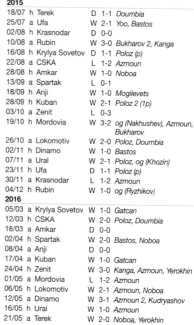

FC Rostov

1930 • Olimp 2 (17,023) • fc-rostov.ru
Major honours
Russian Cup (1) 2014
Coach: Kurban Berdyev

2015
18/07	h	Terek	D 1-1	*Doumbia*
25/07	a	Ufa	W 2-1	*Yoo, Bastos*
02/08	h	Krasnodar	D 0-0	
10/08	a	Rubin	W 3-0	*Bukharov 2, Kanga*
16/08	h	Krylya Sovetov	D 1-1	*Poloz (p)*
22/08	a	CSKA	L 1-2	*Azmoun*
28/08	h	Amkar	W 1-0	*Noboa*
13/09	a	Spartak	L 0-1	
18/09	h	Anji	W 1-0	*Mogilevets*
28/09	h	Kuban	W 2-1	*Poloz 2 (1p)*
03/10	a	Zenit	L 0-3	
19/10	h	Mordovia	W 3-2	*og (Nakhushev), Azmoun, Bukharov*
26/10	a	Lokomotiv	W 2-0	*Poloz, Doumbia*
02/11	a	Dinamo	W 1-0	*Bastos*
07/11	a	Ural	W 2-1	*Poloz, og (Khozin)*
23/11	h	Ufa	D 1-1	*Poloz (p)*
30/11	a	Krasnodar	L 1-2	*Azmoun*
04/12	h	Rubin	W 1-0	*og (Ryzhikov)*

2016
05/03	a	Krylya Sovetov	W 1-0	*Gatcan*
12/03	h	CSKA	W 2-0	*Poloz, Doumbia*
18/03	a	Amkar	D 0-0	
02/04	h	Spartak	W 2-0	*Bastos, Noboa*
08/04	a	Anji	D 0-0	
17/04	a	Kuban	W 1-0	*Gatcan*
24/04	h	Zenit	W 3-0	*Kanga, Azmoun, Yerokhin*
01/05	a	Mordovia	L 1-2	*Azmoun*
06/05	h	Lokomotiv	W 2-1	*Azmoun, Noboa*
12/05	a	Dinamo	W 3-1	*Azmoun 2, Kudryashov*
16/05	h	Ural	W 1-0	*Azmoun*
21/05	a	Terek	W 2-0	*Noboa, Yerokhin*

No	Name	Nat	DoB	Pos	Aps	(s)	Gls
20	Sardar Azmoun	IRN	01/01/95	A	15	(9)	9
15	Bastos	ANG	27/03/91	D	26		3
19	Khoren Bayramyan		07/01/92	M	2	(5)	
11	Aleksandr Bukharov		12/03/85	A	13	(12)	3
44	César Navas	ESP	14/02/80	D	28		
8	Moussa Doumbia	MLI	15/08/94	A	3	(9)	3
35	Soslan Dzhanaev		13/03/87	G	30		
6	Saeid Ezatolahi	IRN	01/10/96	M		(1)	
84	Alexandru Gatcan	MDA	27/03/84	M	23		2
2	Timofei Kalachev	BLR	01/05/81	M	18	(4)	
9	Guélor Kanga	GAB	01/09/90	M	14	(3)	2
	Igor Kireev		17/02/92	M		(1)	
30	Fedor Kudryashov		05/04/87	D	10	(1)	1
34	Timofei Margasov		12/06/92	D	23	(2)	
18	Pavel Mogilevets		25/01/93	M	19	(7)	1
19	Christian Noboa	ECU	08/04/85	M	24		4
25	Ivan Novoseltsev		25/08/91	D	28		
7	Dmitri Poloz		12/07/91	A	27	(3)	7
28	Boris Rotenberg	FIN	19/05/86	D	13	(2)	
4	Denis Terentev		13/08/92	D	6	(8)	
23	Aleksandr Troshechkin		23/04/96	M		(1)	
89	Aleksandr Yerokhin		13/10/89	M	5	(6)	2
86	Yoo Byung-soo	KOR	26/03/88	A	3	(4)	1

FC Rubin

1958 • Kazan-Arena (45,105); Central (27,756) • rubin-kazan.ru

Major honours
Russian League (2) 2008, 2009; Russian Cup (1) 2012

**Coach: Rinat Bilyaletdinov;
(10/09/15) Valeri Chaly**

2015
18/07	a	CSKA	L	0-1
26/07	h	Amkar	L	0-2
03/08	a	Spartak	L	0-1
10/08	h	Rostov	L	0-3
15/08	a	Kuban	W	1-0 *Gökdeniz*
24/08	h	Zenit	L	1-3 *Bilyaletdinov*
30/08	a	Mordovia	L	1-2 *Portnyagin*
12/09	h	Lokomotiv	W	3-1 *Carlos Eduardo, Kanunnikov, Bilyaletdinov*
21/09	a	Dinamo	D	0-0
27/09	h	Ural	L	1-2 *Nabiullin*
04/10	a	Terek	L	1-2 *Ozdoev*
17/10	h	Ufa	W	3-1 *Kuzmin 2, Kislyak*
25/10	a	Krasnodar	L	1-2 *Kanunnikov*
01/11	a	Anji	W	2-1 *Dević 2*
08/11	h	Krylya Sovetov	W	2-0 *Gökdeniz 2*
21/11	a	Amkar	W	2-1 *Dević 2 (1p)*
30/11	h	Spartak	D	2-2 *Dević, Kverkvelia*
04/12	a	Rostov	L	0-1

2016
05/03	h	Kuban	W	1-0 *Tkachuk*
13/03	a	Zenit	L	2-4 *Dević, Portnyagin*
20/03	h	Mordovia	D	1-1 *Gökdeniz*
03/04	h	Lokomotiv	L	0-1
09/04	h	Dinamo	W	4-1 *Gökdeniz, Kanunnikov, Portnyagin, Dević (p)*
18/04	a	Ural	W	1-0 *Bergström*
23/04	h	Terek	L	0-1
01/05	a	Ufa	D	1-1 *Ozdoev*
07/05	h	Krasnodar	D	1-1 *Kanunnikov*
11/05	h	Anji	L	1-2 *Portnyagin*
15/05	a	Krylya Sovetov	D	1-1 *Caktaš*
21/05	h	CSKA	L	0-1

No	Name	Nat	DoB	Pos	Aps	(s)	Gls
85	Ilzat Akhmetov		31/12/97	M		(3)	
8	Maksim Batov		05/06/92	D	2	(1)	
13	Emil Bergström	SWE	19/05/93	D	12		1
14	Diniyar Bilyaletdinov		27/02/85	M	8	(6)	2
20	Mijo Caktaš	CRO	08/05/92	M	8	(3)	1
10	Carlos Eduardo	BRA	18/07/87	M	10	(6)	1
21	Guillermo Cotugno	URU	12/03/95	D	20	(3)	
11	Marko Dević	UKR	27/10/83	A	11	(8)	7
22	Vladimir Dyadyun		12/07/88	A	3	(11)	
63	Alisher Dzhalilov		29/08/93	M	1	(3)	
77	Blagoy Georgiev	BUL	21/12/81	M	14	(1)	
61	Gökdeniz Karadeniz	TUR	11/01/80	M	17	(5)	5
88	Ruslan Kambolov		01/01/90	D	24	(3)	
99	Maksim Kanunnikov		14/07/91	A	30		4
15	Sergei Kislyak	BLR	06/08/87	M	14	(3)	1
2	Oleg Kuzmin		09/05/81	D	21		2
5	Solomon Kverkvelia	GEO	06/02/92	D	29		1
7	Mauricio Lemos	URU	28/12/95	D	4		
3	Elmir Nabiullin		08/03/95	D	15	(1)	1
91	Yuri Nesterenko		12/06/91	G		(1)	
27	Magomed Ozdoev		05/11/92	M	28	(1)	2
79	Andriy Pylyavskiy	UKR	04/12/88	D	2	(1)	
7	Igor Portnyagin		07/01/89	A	15	(9)	4
1	Sergei Ryzhikov		19/09/80	G	30		
93	Albert Sharipov		11/04/93	M		(1)	
9	Ramil Sheydaev		15/03/96	A	1		
31	Denis Tkachuk		02/07/89	M	7	(3)	1
49	Vitali Ustinov		03/05/91	D	4	(4)	

FC Spartak Moskva

1922 • Otkrytie-Arena (44,929) • spartak.com

Major honours
USSR League (12) 1936 (autumn), 1938, 1939, 1952, 1953, 1956, 1958, 1962, 1969, 1979, 1987, 1989; Russian League (9) 1992, 1993, 1994, 1996, 1997, 1998, 1999, 2000, 2001; USSR Cup (10) 1938, 1939, 1946, 1947, 1950, 1958, 1963, 1965, 1971, 1992; Russian Cup (3) 1994, 1998, 2003

Coach: Dmitri Alenichev

2015
17/07	h	Ufa	D	2-2 *Taşçı, Zé Luís*
26/07	a	Krasnodar	W	1-0 *Movsisyan*
03/08	h	Rubin	W	1-0 *Movsisyan*
09/08	h	Krylya Sovetov	W	2-0 *Promes 2*
14/08	h	CSKA	L	1-2 *D Kombarov (p)*
22/08	a	Amkar	W	3-1 *Movsisyan, Promes 2*
29/08	h	Anji	W	1-2 *D Kombarov (p)*
13/09	h	Rostov	W	1-0 *Promes*
19/09	a	Kuban	L	0-3
26/09	h	Zenit	D	2-2 *Zé Luís, Popov*
03/10	a	Mordovia	W	1-0 *Popov*
18/10	h	Lokomotiv	L	1-2 *Bocchetti*
25/10	a	Dinamo	W	3-2 *Promes 2, Davydov*
01/11	h	Ural	D	0-1
07/11	a	Terek	L	1-2 *og (Semyonov)*
22/11	h	Krasnodar	W	3-2 *Glushakov, Promes*
30/11	a	Rubin	D	2-2 *Zé Luís, Promes (p)*
04/12	h	Krylya Sovetov	W	1-0 *Promes*

2016
06/03	a	CSKA	L	0-1
12/03	h	Amkar	W	2-1 *Zé Luís, Promes (p)*
18/03	a	Anji	W	4-0 *Zé Luís 2, Glushakov, Promes*
02/04	a	Rostov	L	0-2
10/04	h	Kuban	D	2-2 *Popov, Promes*
16/04	a	Zenit	L	2-5 *Popov, Glushakov*
23/04	a	Mordovia	D	2-2 *Bocchetti, Promes*
30/04	a	Lokomotiv	W	2-0 *og (Đurica), Zé Luís*
08/05	h	Dinamo	W	3-0 *Promes 2, Zé Luís*
12/05	a	Ural	W	1-0 *Promes*
16/05	h	Terek	W	3-0 *Bocchetti, Melgarejo, Promes*
21/05	a	Ufa	L	1-3 *Melgarejo*

No	Name	Nat	DoB	Pos	Aps	(s)	Gls
49	Jano Ananidze	GEO	10/10/92	M	6	(5)	
16	Salvatore Bocchetti	ITA	30/11/86	D	28		3
3	Sergei Bryzgalov		15/11/92	D	6		
9	Denis Davydov		22/03/95	A	1	(7)	1
55	Nikolai Fadeev		09/05/93	D		(1)	
8	Denis Glushakov		27/01/87	M	27		4
13	Vladimir Granat		22/05/87	D	10	(4)	
19	José Manuel Jurado	ESP	29/06/86	M	1		
3	Dmitri Kombarov		22/01/87	D	24	(1)	2
7	Kirill Kombarov		22/01/87	D	9	(3)	
70	Aleksandr Kozlov		19/03/93	A		(1)	
18	Ilya Kutepov		29/07/93	D	9	(1)	
64	Denis Kutin		05/10/93	D		(1)	
52	Igor Leontiev		18/03/94	M		(3)	
34	Evgeni Makeev		24/07/89	D	13	(2)	
25	Lorenzo Melgarejo	PAR	10/08/90	M	6	(5)	2
37	Georgi Melkadze		04/04/97	M		(4)	
10	Yura Movsisyan	ARM	02/08/87	A	10	(1)	3
1	Aras Özbiliz	ARM	09/03/90	M	1	(6)	
4	Sergei Parshivlyuk		18/03/89	D	11	(5)	
30	Sergei Pesyakov		16/12/88	G	6		
71	Ivelin Popov	BUL	26/10/87	M	28	(1)	4
24	Quincy Promes	NED	04/01/92	A	29	(1)	18
45	Aleksandr Putsko		24/02/93	D	2		
32	Artem Rebrov		04/03/84	G	24		
5	Rômulo	BRA	19/09/90	M	18	(3)	
15	Roman Shirokov		06/07/81	M	14		
35	Serdar Taşçı	GER	24/04/87	D	16		1
40	Artem Timofeev		12/01/94	M		(3)	
20	Zé Luís	CPV	24/01/91	A	17	(7)	8
27	Aleksandr Zotov		27/08/90	A	12	(8)	
17	Aleksandr Zuev		26/06/96	M	2	(12)	

FC Terek Grozny

1946 • Ahmat-Arena (30,597) • fc-terek.ru

Major honours
Russian Cup (1) 2004

Coach: Rashid Rakhimov

2015
18/07	a	Rostov	D	1-1 *Lebedenko*
25/07	h	Kuban	D	1-1 *Píriz*
01/08	a	Zenit	L	0-3
07/08	h	Mordovia	D	0-0
16/08	a	Lokomotiv	D	0-0
21/08	h	Dinamo	D	1-1 *Maurício*
28/08	a	Ural	D	3-3 *Rybus, Sadaev, Aissati*
13/09	a	Anji	W	2-0 *og (Lazić), Lebedenko*
19/09	h	Ufa	W	4-1 *Maurício 2 (1p), Sadaev, Rybus*
27/09	a	Krasnodar	D	1-1 *Sadaev*
04/10	h	Rubin	W	2-1 *Sadaev 2*
18/10	a	Krylya Sovetov	W	2-0 *Adilson, Mitrishev*
25/10	h	CSKA	D	0-0
02/11	a	Amkar	L	0-1
07/11	h	Spartak	W	2-1 *Adilson, Mbengue*
22/11	h	Kuban	D	2-2 *Utsiyev, Rybus*
28/11	a	Zenit	W	4-1 *Mitrishev 2, Rybus 2*
03/12	a	Mordovia	D	0-0

2016
06/03	h	Lokomotiv	W	2-1 *Rybus 2 (1p)*
14/03	a	Dinamo	W	1-0 *Mitrishev*
19/03	h	Ural	D	1-1 *Ivanov*
02/04	h	Anji	W	3-2 *Grozav 2, Mbengue*
10/04	a	Ufa	L	0-1
16/04	h	Krasnodar	L	0-1
23/04	a	Rubin	W	1-0 *Rybus*
01/05	h	Krylya Sovetov	L	0-1
07/05	a	CSKA	L	0-1
12/05	h	Amkar	W	2-0 *Rybus, Mbengue*
16/05	a	Spartak	L	0-3
21/05	h	Rostov	L	0-2

No	Name	Nat	DoB	Pos	Aps	(s)	Gls
6	Adilson	BRA	16/01/87	M	24	(2)	2
14	Ismail Aissati	MAR	16/08/88	M	27	(1)	1
93	Apti Akhyadov		24/08/93	A		(1)	
16	Evgeni Gorodov		13/12/85	G	22		
30	Gheorghe Grozav	ROU	29/09/90	M	9	(9)	2
1	Yaroslav Hodzyur	UKR	06/03/85	G	8	(1)	
19	Oleg Ivanov		04/08/86	M	28		1
7	Khalid Kadyrov		19/04/94	A	1	(3)	
20	Kanu	BRA	23/09/87	M		(5)	
13	Fedor Kudryashov		05/04/87	D	13		
21	Daler Kuzyaev		15/01/93	M	17	(4)	
55	Igor Lebedenko		27/05/83	A	16	(9)	2
8	Maurício	BRA	21/10/88	M	15	(2)	3
17	Ablaye Mbengue	SEN	19/05/92	A	6	(15)	3
22	Reziuan Mirzov		22/06/93	M	1	(4)	
95	Magomed Mitrishev		10/09/92	A	15	(7)	4
13	Milad Mohammadi	IRN	29/09/93	D	1	(2)	
14	Pedro Ken	BRA	20/03/87	M	15	(2)	
23	Facundo Píriz	URU	27/03/90	M	8	(3)	1
5	Zaurbek Pliev		27/09/91	D	7	(2)	
2	Rodolfo	BRA	23/10/82	D	25	(1)	
31	Maciej Rybus	POL	19/08/89	M	22	(6)	9
9	Zaur Sadaev		06/11/89	A	8	(7)	5
15	Andrei Semyonov		24/03/89	D	29		
40	Rizvan Utsiyev		07/02/88	D	19		1
29	Luke Wilkshire	AUS	02/10/81	D	6		

RUSSIA

FC Ufa

2010 • Dinamo (6,000); Neftyanik (16,000) • fcufa.pro

Coach: Igor Kolyvanov;
(21/10/15) Evgeni Perevertailo;
(18/05/16) (Sergei Tomarov)

2015
17/07	a Spartak	D	2-2	Handžić, Stotski
25/07	h Rostov	L	1-2	Zinchenko
31/07	a Kuban	D	1-1	Igboun
09/08	h Zenit	L	0-1	
17/08	a Mordovia	W	1-0	Stotski
23/08	h Lokomotiv	L	0-3	
29/08	a Dinamo	L	0-2	
14/09	h Ural	L	0-1	
19/09	a Terek	L	1-4	Igboun (p)
26/09	a Anji	D	1-1	og (Eschenko)
04/10	h Krasnodar	D	1-1	Fomin
17/10	a Rubin	L	1-3	Pourie
23/10	h Krylya Sovetov	W	1-0	Alikin
31/10	a CSKA	L	0-2	
07/11	h Amkar	W	2-1	Igboun, Krotov
23/11	a Rostov	D	1-1	Marcinho
28/11	h Kuban	D	2-2	Krotov, Paurević
03/12	a Zenit	D	1-1	Zinchenko
2016				
06/03	h Mordovia	D	1-1	Nikitin
13/03	a Lokomotiv	L	0-2	
19/03	h Dinamo	L	0-1	
02/04	a Ural	L	0-1	
10/04	h Terek	W	1-0	Safronidi
17/04	h Anji	W	2-0	Tumasyan, Zubarev
24/04	a Krasnodar	L	0-4	
01/05	h Rubin	D	1-1	Sysuev
06/05	a Krylya Sovetov	L	0-1	
11/05	h CSKA	L	1-3	Sysuev
16/05	a Amkar	L	0-1	
21/05	h Spartak	W	3-1	Paurević 2, Igboun (p)

No	Name	Nat	DoB	Pos	Aps	(s)	Gls
3	Pavel Alikin		06/03/84	D	16	(1)	1
87	Igor Bezdenezhnykh		08/08/96	M		(5)	
11	Diego Carlos	BRA	15/05/88	A	12	(6)	
2	Olexandr Filin	UKR	25/06/96	D	1		
5	Semyon Fomin		10/01/89	M	4	(9)	1
5	Emmanuel Frimpong	GHA	10/01/92	M	5	(3)	
22	Vagiz Galiulin	UZB	10/10/87	M	1	(8)	
9	Haris Handžić	BIH	20/06/90	A	9	(10)	1
44	Sylvester Igboun	NGA	08/09/90	A	24	(1)	4
34	Aleksandr Katsalapov		05/04/86	D	13	(3)	
93	Vyacheslav Krotov		14/02/93	A	15	(5)	2
10	Marcinho	BRA	14/05/86	M	13	(4)	1
42	Sergei Narubin		05/12/81	G	6	(1)	
4	Aleksei Nikitin		27/01/92	D	19	(2)	1
7	Evgeni Osipov		29/10/86	D	8	(5)	
19	Ivan Paurević	CRO	01/07/91	M	28		3
6	Marvin Pourie	GER	08/01/91	A	5	(6)	1
70	Nikolai Safronidi		10/09/83	D	12	(3)	1
14	Maksim Semakin		26/10/83	M	1	(2)	
88	Georgi Sheliya		11/12/88	G	12		
39	Dmitri Stotski		01/12/89	M	30		2
33	Aleksandr Sukhov		03/01/86	D	16	(1)	
31	Dmitri Sysuev		13/01/88	M	7	(4)	2
20	Denis Tumasyan		24/04/85	D	15	(1)	1
81	Dmitri Verkhovtsov	BLR	10/10/86	D	6	(3)	
1	David Yurchenko		27/03/86	G	12		
13	Azamat Zaseev		29/04/88	M	10		
17	Olexandr Zinchenko	UKR	15/12/96	M	19	(5)	2
60	Vladimir Zubarev		05/01/93	M	11		1

FC Ural Sverdlovsk Oblast

1930 • SKB Bank Arena (10,500) • fc-ural.ru

Coach: Viktor Goncharenko (BLR);
(03/09/15) Vadim Skripchenko (BLR)

2015
20/07	a Kuban	W	2-0	Manucharyan, Acevedo (p)
26/07	h Zenit	L	1-4	Yerokhin
02/08	a Mordovia	D	1-1	Manucharyan
08/08	h Lokomotiv	L	1-3	Yerokhin
16/08	a Dinamo	L	0-1	
22/08	a Anji	D	1-1	Yerokhin
28/08	h Terek	D	3-3	Manucharyan, Fontanello, Yerokhin
14/09	a Ufa	W	1-0	Acevedo
21/09	h Krasnodar	W	3-1	Podberyozkin, Acevedo, Fontanello
27/09	a Rubin	W	2-1	Podberyozkin, og (Kverkvelia)
02/10	h Krylya Sovetov	D	1-1	Lungu
17/10	a CSKA	L	2-3	Acevedo, Gogniev
24/10	h Amkar	W	3-1	Fontanello, Sapeta, Manucharyan (p)
01/11	a Spartak	W	1-0	Acevedo
07/11	a Rostov	L	1-2	Manucharyan
21/11	a Zenit	L	0-3	
27/11	h Mordovia	W	3-1	Sapeta 2, Gogniev
04/12	a Lokomotiv	D	2-2	Sapeta, Manucharyan
2016				
07/03	h Dinamo	D	1-1	Acevedo
12/03	h Anji	W	4-2	Gogniev 3, Sapeta
19/03	a Terek	D	1-1	Dorozhkin
02/04	h Ufa	W	1-0	Gogniev
10/04	a Krasnodar	L	0-6	
18/04	a Rubin	L	0-1	
23/04	a Krylya Sovetov	D	1-1	Sapeta
28/04	h CSKA	L	0-3	
08/05	a Amkar	D	1-1	Gogniev
15/05	h Spartak	L	0-1	
16/05	a Rostov	L	0-1	
21/05	h Kuban	W	2-0	Gogniev, Sapeta

No	Name	Nat	DoB	Pos	Aps	(s)	Gls
21	Gerson Acevedo	CHI	05/04/88	M	20	(2)	6
35	Dmitri Arapov		09/06/93	G	9		
77	Dmytro Bilonog	UKR	26/11/95	D		(2)	
18	Nikita Burmistrov		06/07/89	M	6	(6)	
7	Aleksandr Dantsev		14/10/84	D	22	(1)	
34	Denis Dorozhkin		08/06/87	A	3	(6)	1
57	Artem Fidler		14/07/83	M	19	(2)	
29	Pablo Fontanello	ARG	26/09/84	D	27		3
62	Rezo Gavtadze		11/07/95	M		(1)	
9	Spartak Gogniev		19/01/81	A	13	(4)	8
71	Albeyi Guliev		14/10/95	M		(1)	
2	Vladimir Khozin		03/07/89	D	9	(5)	
88	Dmitri Korobov		10/06/94	M	9	(2)	
15	Denis Kulakov	UKR	01/05/86	D	26		
3	Chisamba Lungu	ZAM	02/10/91	A	15	(3)	1
10	Edgar Manucharyan	ARM	19/01/87	A	13	(9)	6
4	Aleksandr Martynovich	BLR	26/08/87	D	24		
33	Mikhail Merkulov		26/01/94	D	2	(2)	
12	Andrei Novikov		12/10/84	D	6	(1)	
14	Vyacheslav Podberyozkin		21/06/92	M	10	(3)	2
54	Aleksandr Ryazantsev		05/09/86	M	6	(5)	
41	Aleksandr Sapeta		28/06/89	M	27	(2)	7
75	Sergei Serchenkov		01/01/97	M	1	(3)	
90	Aleksand Shcherbakov		26/06/98	M	1	(3)	
25	Aleksandr Stavpets		04/07/89	A	5	(14)	
98	Carlos Strandberg	SWE	14/04/96	A		(2)	
8	Kostyantyn Yaroshenko	UKR	12/09/86	M	3	(6)	
92	Roman Yemelianov		08/05/92	M	21	(3)	
89	Aleksandr Yerokhin		13/10/89	M	12		4
28	Nikolai Zabolotnyi		16/04/90	G	10		
30	Yuri Zhevnov	BLR	17/04/81	G	11		

FC Zenit

1925 • Petrovski (21,405) • fc-zenit.ru

Major honours
UEFA Cup (1) 2008; UEFA Super Cup (1) 2008; USSR League (1) 1984; Russian League (4) 2007, 2010, 2012, 2015; USSR Cup (1) 1944; Russian Cup (3) 1999, 2010, 2016

Coach: André Villas-Boas (POR)

2015
19/07	h Dinamo	W	2-1	Hulk (p), Shatov
26/07	a Ural	W	4-1	Dzyuba, Hulk 2 (1p), Danny
01/08	h Terek	W	3-0	Smolnikov, Shatov, Danny
09/08	a Ufa	W	1-0	Danny
15/08	h Krasnodar	L	0-2	
24/08	a Rubin	W	3-1	Shatov 2, Hulk
29/08	h Krylya Sovetov	L	1-3	og (Nadson)
12/09	a CSKA	D	2-2	Hulk (p), Smolnikov
20/09	h Amkar	D	1-1	Dzyuba
26/09	a Spartak	D	2-2	Hulk, Dzyuba
03/10	h Rostov	W	3-0	Smolnikov, Dzyuba, Danny
17/10	a Kuban	D	2-2	Dzyuba, Shatov
24/10	a Anji	W	5-1	Dzyuba 2, Witsel, Shatov, Hulk
31/10	h Mordovia	D	0-0	
08/11	a Lokomotiv	L	0-2	
21/11	a Ural	W	3-0	Garay, Dzyuba, Javi García
28/11	a Terek	L	1-4	Hulk
03/12	a Ufa	D	1-1	Garay (p)
2016				
05/03	h Krasnodar	D	0-0	
13/03	h Rubin	W	4-2	Danny 2, Dzyuba, Hulk
20/03	a Krylya Sovetov	W	2-0	Dzyuba, Hulk (p)
03/04	h CSKA	W	2-0	Hulk 2
09/04	a Amkar	W	2-0	Dzyuba, Kokorin
16/04	h Spartak	W	5-2	Witsel, Hulk, Dzyuba, Maurício, Javi García
24/04	a Rostov	L	0-3	
28/04	h Kuban	W	4-1	Shatov 2, Dzyuba, Hulk
07/05	a Anji	W	1-0	Dzyuba
11/05	a Mordovia	W	3-0	Witsel, Hulk 2 (2p)
15/05	h Lokomotiv	D	1-1	Hulk (p)
21/05	a Dinamo	W	3-0	Dzyuba, Kokorin, Criscito (p)

No	Name	Nat	DoB	Pos	Aps	(s)	Gls
2	Aleksandr Anyukov		28/09/82	D	12	(3)	
71	Egor Baburin		09/08/90	G		(1)	
40	Yuri Baron		05/02/94	M		(1)	
70	Dmitri Bogaev		24/01/94	A	2	(3)	
4	Domenico Criscito	ITA	30/12/86	D	17	(6)	1
10	Danny	POR	07/08/83	M	18	(5)	6
77	Luka Djordjević	MNE	09/07/94	A		(1)	
92	Pavel Dolgov		16/08/96	A		(8)	
22	Artem Dzyuba		22/08/88	A	30		15
94	Aleksei Evseev		30/03/94	M		(5)	
20	Viktor Fayzulin		22/04/86	M	1	(4)	
24	Ezequiel Garay	ARG	10/10/86	D	19	(1)	2
7	Hulk	BRA	25/07/86	A	26	(1)	17
52	Andrei Ivanov		02/09/94	D	1		
21	Javi García	ESP	08/02/87	M	21	(5)	2
41	Mikhail Kerzhakov		28/01/87	G	3		
9	Aleksandr Kokorin		19/03/91	A	3	(7)	2
1	Yuri Lodygin		26/05/90	G	27		
6	Nicolas Lombaerts	BEL	20/03/85	D	18		
13	Luís Neto	POR	26/05/88	D	22		
8	Maurício	BRA	21/10/88	M	8	(3)	1
60	Maksim Palienko		18/10/94	M		(2)	
23	José Salomón Rondón	VEN	16/09/89	A		(1)	
5	Aleksandr Ryazantsev		05/09/86	M	1	(10)	
17	Oleg Shatov		29/07/90	M	25	(2)	8
19	Igor Smolnikov		08/08/88	D	23	(3)	3
31	Denis Tkachuk		02/07/97	M		(7)	
28	Axel Witsel	BEL	12/01/89	M	28	(1)	3
14	Artur Yusupov		01/09/89	M	19	(4)	
81	Yuri Zhirkov		20/08/83	M	7	(2)	

Top goalscorers

20	Fedor Smolov (Krasnodar)
18	Quincy Promes (Spartak)
17	Hulk (Zenit)
15	Artem Dzyuba (Zenit)
13	Ahmed Musa (CSKA)
10	Pavel Mamaev (Krasnodar)
	Lorenzo Melgarejo (Kuban/Spartak)
	Evgeni Lutsenko (Mordovia)
9	Yannick Boli (Anji)
	Aleksandr Samedov (Lokomotiv)
	Sardar Azmoun (Rostov)
	Maciej Rybus (Terek)

Promoted clubs

FC Gazovik Orenburg

1976 • Gazovik (10,500) • fcgazovik.ru
Coach: Robert Yevdokimov

PFC Arsenal Tula

1946 • Arsenal (20,074) • arsenaltula.ru
Coach: Viktor Bulatov;
(24/02/16) Sergei Pavlov

FC Tom Tomsk

1957 • Trud (15,000) • fctomtomsk.ru
Coach: Valeri Nepomnyashchy;
(13/04/16) Valeri Petrakov

Second level final table 2015/16

		Pld	W	D	L	F	A	Pts
1	FC Gazovik Orenburg	38	26	8	4	61	20	86
2	PFC Arsenal Tula	38	25	7	6	64	36	82
3	FC Tom Tomsk	38	22	8	8	58	35	74
4	FC Volgar Astrakhan	38	17	12	9	57	37	63
5	FC Spartak Moskva-2	38	17	8	13	52	49	59
6	FC Fakel Voronezh	38	17	5	16	51	42	56
7	FC Tosno	38	17	4	17	57	53	55
8	FC Tyumen	38	15	9	14	44	45	54
9	PFC Sokol Saratov	38	14	11	13	43	38	53
10	FC Volga Nizhny Novgorod	38	14	9	15	39	37	51
11	FC Sibir Novosibirsk	38	14	9	15	47	50	51
12	FC Shinnik Yaroslavl	38	13	11	14	50	49	50
13	FC Zenit-2	38	13	11	14	61	56	50
14	FC SKA-Energia Khabarovsk	38	13	10	15	36	35	49
15	FC Luch-Energia Vladivostok	38	12	9	17	31	46	45
16	FC Yenisey Krasnoyarsk	38	12	8	18	36	49	44
17	FC Baltika Kaliningrad	38	11	11	16	37	47	44
18	FC Torpedo Armavir	38	10	10	18	28	44	40
19	FC Baikal Irkutsk	38	8	2	28	29	73	26
20	FC KAMAZ Naberezhnye Chelny	38	6	6	26	20	60	24

Promotion/Relegation play-offs

(24/05/16 & 27/05/16)
Kuban 1-0 Tom
Tom 2-0 Kuban
(Tom 2-1)

Volgar 0-1 Anji
Anji 2-0 Volgar
(Anji 3-0)

DOMESTIC CUP

Kubok Rossii 2015/16

1/16 FINALS

(23/09/15)
Baikal 1-2 CSKA Moskva *(aet)*
Nosta 0-2 Terek
Sakhalin 0-4 Ufa
Shinnik Yaroslavl 1-2 Kuban
Sokol Saratov 2-4 Anji
Tambov 2-3 Krylya Sovetov
Torpedo Armavir 0-1 Lokomotiv Moskva
Volga Nizhny Novgorod 0-7 Spartak Moskva
Volga Tver 0-3 Zenit *(aet)*

(24/09/15)
Khimki 1-0 Mordovia
Lokomotiv Liski 0-2 Dinamo Moskva
SKA-Energia 2-0 Rubin
Spartak Nalchik 0-2 Amkar
Tosno 1-0 Rostov *(aet)*
Yenisey Krasnoyarsk 1-2 Ural
Zenit Izhevsk 0-1 Krasnodar

1/8 FINALS

(28/10/15)
CSKA Moskva 2-1 Ural
Kuban 1-0 Spartak Moskva
Terek 2-1 Khimki *(aet)*
Ufa 1-0 SKA-Energia
Zenit 5-0 Tosno

(29/10/15)
Krasnodar 3-1 Anji
Krylya Sovetov 0-1 Dinamo Moskva
Lokomotiv Moskva 0-1 Amkar

QUARTER-FINALS

(28/02/16)
Zenit 1-0 Kuban *(Maurício 104) (aet)*

(01/03/16)
Krasnodar 1-0 Terek *(Granqvist 116) (aet)*

Ufa 0-2 CSKA Moskva *(Shirokov 57, Musa 75)*

(02/03/16)
Amkar 3-1 Dinamo Moskva *(Prudnikov 27, Zaitsev 41, Shavaev 90p; Dragun 87)*

SEMI-FINALS

(20/04/16)
Amkar 1-1 Zenit *(Idowu 19; Javi García 41)*
(aet; 3-4 on pens)

CSKA Moskva 3-1 Krasnodar *(Golovin 35, 40, Dzagoev 46; Sigurdsson 73)*

FINAL

(02/05/16)
Kazan-Arena, Kazan
FC ZENIT 4 *(Hulk 34p, 63p, Kokorin 55, Yusupov 69)*
PFC CSKA MOSKVA 1 *(Olanare 36)*
Referee: Yegorov
ZENIT: Kerzhakov, Smolnikov, Luís Neto, Garay, Criscito, Javi García, Yusupov, Hulk (Zhirkov 83), Witsel (Maurício 82), Shatov, Kokorin (Dzyuba 74)
CSKA MOSKVA: Akinfeev, Mário Fernandes, V Berezutski, Ignashevich, A Berezutski (Tkachyov 60), Dzagoev, Natcho, Golovin, Eremenko (Vasin 66), Musa, Olanare (Panchenko 39)
Red card: *V Berezutski (62)*

SAN MARINO

Federazione Sammarinese Giuoco Calcio (FSGC)

Address	Strada di Montecchio 17 SM-47890 San Marino	**President**	Giorgio Crescentini
		General secretary	Luciano Casadei
Tel	+378 0549 990 515	**Media officer**	Matteo Rossi
Fax	+378 0549 992 348	**Year of formation**	1931
E-mail	fsgc@omniway.sm	**National stadium**	San Marino Stadium,
Website	fsgc.sm		Serravalle (4,801)

CAMPIONATO SAMMARINESE CLUBS

 1 **SP Cailungo**

 2 **SS Cosmos**

 3 **FC Domagnano**

 4 **SC Faetano**

 5 **FC Fiorentino**

 6 **SS Folgore**

 7 **AC Juvenes/Dogana**

 8 **SP La Fiorita**

 9 **AC Libertas**

 10 **SS Murata**

 11 **SS Pennarossa**

 12 **SS San Giovanni**

 13 **SP Tre Fiori**

 14 **SP Tre Penne**

 15 **Virtus FC**

KEY

● UEFA Champions League

● UEFA Europa League

0   5   10 km

0   5 miles

Three titles for Tre Penne

The 2015/16 season was a reprise of the 2011/12 and 2012/13 campaigns, with Tre Penne winning the Campionato Sammarinese and La Fiorita lifting the Coppa Titano. The latter also finished as runners-up in the league, losing 3-1 in the play-off final to Marco Protti's irrepressible champions.

The San Marino national team managed to restrict their UEFA EURO 2016 qualifying opponents to 36 goals, even scoring one themselves, but a subsequent 10-0 defeat to Croatia was their heaviest in an international friendly.

| Convincing triumph for Marco Protti's men | La Fiorita lift Coppa Titano for fourth time | One point and one goal in EURO qualifiers |

Domestic league

Rather like 2014/15 champions Folgore, Tre Penne were on top of their game from start to finish of the two-tier championship, losing just two of their 20 fixtures in the regular season and winning all three – one after a penalty shoot-out – in the play-offs. They kicked off their Group B campaign by defeating Folgore 1-0 with a goal from the man who would become their leading goalscorer, Nicola Gai, then started 2016 with a comprehensive 3-0 victory over Group A leaders La Fiorita. By mid-April, as the first phase ended, Protti's team boasted an eight-point winning margin at the top of their section.

Tre Penne were escorted into the play-offs from Group B by record seven-time winners Tre Fiori and defending champions Folgore, who, led again by double-winning boss Nicola Berardi, made it through with a game to spare thanks to a 3-0 win over closest rivals Fiorentino. In Group A, La Fiorita were emphatic winners, striker Marco Martini's 19 goals helping them to finish six points ahead of Pennarossa, who in turn were four points clear of the third qualifier, 2014/15 runners-up Juvenes/Dogana.

Pennarossa were the first team eliminated in the labyrinthine play-off series, and they were followed successively out of the competition by Tre Fiori, Juvenes/Dogana and – after a 2-1 semi-final defeat by La Fiorita – Folgore. Tre Penne had ended Folgore's five-match winning streak in the play-offs by defeating them on penalties in the previous round, which guaranteed them an early booking for the final in the San Marino Stadium ten days later.

Having already defeated La Fiorita 2-1 in the third round of the play-offs – as well as in the regular season – Protti's men were not short of confidence going into the competition's 30th play-off final. However, they had Martini to thank for missing a third-minute penalty before they scored from the spot themselves five minutes later and went on to win the game 3-1, Gai wrapping up proceedings with Tre Penne's third goal in the fourth minute of added time.

Domestic cup

The 2016 Coppa Titano final, staged in advance of the championship play-offs, was a re-run of the 2012 fixture, and it had the same outcome as La Fiorita got the better of Pennarossa, beating them 2-0 with second-half goals from San Marino internationals Andy Selva – from the penalty spot – and Danilo Rinaldi, to lift the trophy for the fourth time. La Fiorita had claimed a welcome semi-final win over Tre Penne five days earlier thanks to a late Marco Gasperoni goal, their opponents having earlier ousted holders Folgore in a quarter-final penalty shoot-out.

Europe

There were no surprises in Europe as San Marino's trio endured their perennial early exits, with Juvenes/Dogana finding the going particularly tough as they lost 9-0 away to Brøndby en route to an 11-0 aggregate defeat in the first qualifying round of the UEFA Europa League.

National team

Thanks to their 0-0 draw at home to Estonia, San Marino enjoyed their most successful UEFA European Championship qualifying campaign yet. The last four fixtures yielded no more points but they did enable midfielder Matteo Vitaioli to become the 13th Sammarinese player to score an international goal. Indeed, his 55th-minute equaliser against Lithuania in Vilnius came within seconds of delivering another precious point, only for the home side to grab a second goal in stoppage time. That heartbreaking last-gasp defeat was probably more difficult to digest for the team's fans than the 10-0 trouncing at the hands of Croatia in Rijeka nine months later – the sixth time San Marino had lost to their opponents with a goal tally stretching into double figures.

DOMESTIC SEASON AT A GLANCE

Campionato Sammarinese 2015/16 final tables

FIRST PHASE

Group A

		Pld	W	D	L	F	A	Pts
1	SP La Fiorita	21	13	2	6	56	25	41
2	SS Pennarossa	21	9	8	4	32	20	35
3	AC Juvenes/Dogana	21	9	4	8	34	27	31
4	AC Libertas	21	7	6	8	23	26	27
5	SS Cosmos	21	3	8	10	25	37	17
6	SP Cailungo	21	4	4	13	19	50	16
7	SC Faetano	21	3	6	12	18	35	15
8	SS San Giovanni	21	1	3	17	13	63	6

Group B

		Pld	W	D	L	F	A	Pts
1	SP Tre Penne	20	15	3	2	50	14	48
2	SP Tre Fiori	20	13	1	6	37	27	40
3	SS Folgore	20	12	3	5	44	25	39
4	FC Fiorentino	20	11	2	7	30	24	35
5	FC Domagnano	20	9	3	8	33	32	30
6	Virtus FC	20	8	4	8	37	36	28
7	SS Murata	20	7	3	10	35	45	24

CHAMPIONSHIP PLAY-OFFS

FIRST ROUND

(04/05/16)
Pennarossa 0-3 Folgore *(Rossi 13, Genestreti 30, Valeriani 90+1)*
Tre Fiori 1-0 Juvenes/Dogana *(Ferri 74)*

SECOND ROUND

(07/05/16)
Tre Fiori 2-3 Folgore *(Ferri 24, 90; Rossi 20, Perrotta 42, Genestreti 90+3)*

(09/05/16)
Juvenes/Dogana 2-2 Pennarossa *(Santini 49, Villa 118; Giunchi 27, Gualtieri 104) (aet; 7-6 on pens)*
(Pennarossa eliminated)

THIRD ROUND

(10/05/16)
La Fiorita 1-2 Tre Penne *(Guidi 85; Fraternali 24og; Rispoli 39)*

(13/05/16)
Juvenes/Dogana 1-0 Tre Fiori *(Santini 76)*
(Tre Fiori eliminated)

FOURTH ROUND

(16/05/16)
Folgore 1-1 Tre Penne *(Rossi 8; Gai 71) (aet; 0-3 on pens)*

(17/05/16)
Juvenes/Dogana 0-3 La Fiorita *(T Zafferani 37, M Martini 60, Rinaldi 85)*
(Juvenes/Dogana eliminated)

SEMI-FINAL

(21/05/16)
La Fiorita 2-1 Folgore *(Selva 7, T Zafferani 69; Valeriani 10)*
(Folgore eliminated)

FINAL

(26/05/16)
San Marino Stadium, Serravalle
SP TRE PENNE 3 *(Rispoli 8p, Palazzi 34, Gai 90+4)*
SP LA FIORITA 1 *(T Zafferani 13)*
Referee: *Barbeno*
TRE PENNE: *Migani, Cesarini, A Rossi (Chiaruzzi 86), Fattori (Capicchioni 72), Palazzi (Calzolari 62), Merendino, Gasperoni, Patregnani, Gai, Valli, Rispoli*
LA FIORITA: *Vivan, Gasperoni, Bugli, A Martini, Fraternali, Pensalfini, Cavalli (Selva 62; Guidi 65), Cangini, T Zafferani, M Martini, Rinaldi*

European qualification 2016/17

Champion: SP Tre Penne (first qualifying round)

Cup winner: SP La Fiorita (first qualifying round)
SS Folgore (first qualifying round)

Top scorer	Marco Martini (La Fiorita), 19 goals
Cup final	SP La Fiorita 2-0 SS Pennarossa

Team of the season
(3-4-3)

Coach: Bizzotto *(La Fiorita)*

Migani *(Tre Penne)*

Gasperoni *(La Fiorita)* — Mantovani *(Juvenes/Dogana)* — Merendino *(Tre Penne)*

Gai *(Tre Penne)* — Cangini *(La Fiorita)* — Domeniconi *(Folgore)* — T Zafferani *(La Fiorita)*

Selva *(La Fiorita)* — M Martini *(La Fiorita)* — Hirsch *(Folgore)*

Player of the season

Nicola Gai
(SP Tre Penne)

The Pallone di Cristallo (Crystal Ball) – the prize awarded to the best player in the Campionate Sammarinese – was won in 2015/16 by Tre Penne's Italian winger Gai, who, in his debut season for the club, had a decisive say in the outcome of the title. The 28-year-old top-scored for the team in the first phase, registering 11 times in 19 matches, before maintaining his fine form in the play-offs with a crucial equaliser against Folgore and a championship-clinching strike in the 3-1 final win against La Fiorita.

Newcomer of the season

Tommaso Zafferani
(SP La Fiorita)

An influential member of the La Fiorita side that won the Coppa Titano and reached the final of the championship play-offs, Zafferini was voted San Marino's Young Player of the Year for 2015/16. Cleverly tutored by Coach of the Year Luigi Bizzotto, the 20-year-old midfielder improved as the season went along, and after winning the cup, he scored in three successive matches during the play-offs. His first cap for San Marino followed, although the 10-0 defeat by Croatia probably served to spoil his big day.

NATIONAL TEAM

Top five all-time caps
Andy Selva (72); Damiano Vannucci (68); Simone Bacciocchi (60); **Alessandro Della Valle** (59); Mirco Gennari & **Aldo Simoncini** (48)

Top five all-time goals
Andy Selva (8); Manuel Marani (2)

NB No other player has scored more than one goal.

Results 2015/16

05/09/15	England (ECQ)	H	Serravalle	L	0-6	
08/09/15	Lithuania (ECQ)	A	Vilnius	L	1-2	*M Vitaioli (55)*
09/10/15	Switzerland (ECQ)	A	St Gallen	L	0-7	
12/10/15	Slovenia (ECQ)	H	Serravalle	L	0-2	
04/06/16	Croatia	A	Rijeka	L	0-10	

Appearances 2015/16

Coach: Pierangelo Manzaroli	25/03/69		ENG	LTU	SUI	SVN	Cro	Caps	Goals
Aldo Simoncini	30/08/86	Libertas	G		G	G	G53	48	-
Giovanni Bonini	05/09/86	Tre Penne & Pietracuta (ITA)	D72					23	-
Cristian Brolli	28/02/92	Sammaurese (ITA)	D	D		D	D	14	-
Davide Simoncini	30/08/86	Libertas	D81		D	D	D	41	-
Mirko Palazzi	24/03/87	Tre Penne & Gualdo Casacastalda (ITA)	D	D	D	D	D84	26	-
Marco Berardi	12/02/93	Folgore	D		D			2	-
Adolfo Hirsch	31/01/86	Folgore	M	s73	s83	M	s53	13	-
Manuel Battistini	22/07/94	Juvenes/Dogana	M	D		D		13	-
Nicola Chiaruzzi	25/12/87	Tre Penne	M	M 88*		M		8	-
Matteo Vitaioli	27/10/89	Tropical Coriano (ITA)	M	M80	M	M90		42	1
Andy Selva	23/05/76	La Fiorita	A75	s80		A71		72	8
Luca Tosi	04/11/92	Sant'Ermete (ITA)	s72		M			9	-
Danilo Rinaldi	18/04/86	La Fiorita	s75	M		s71	M	24	1
Alessandro Della Valle	08/06/82	Sant'Ermete (ITA)	s81	D	D	s73	D	59	1
Elia Benedettini	22/06/95	Pianese (ITA)		G		s53		3	-
Fabio Vitaioli	05/04/84	Tropical Coriano (ITA)		D	s78			41	-
Lorenzo Gasperoni	03/01/90	Juvenes/Dogana		M68	M64	M78		9	-
Mattia Stefanelli	12/03/93	San Marino Calcio (ITA)		A73	A	A53		7	-
Maicol Berretti	01/05/89	Murata		s68		M53		24	-
Davide Cesarini	16/02/95	Tre Penne			D78	s84		3	-
Enrico Golinucci	16/07/91	Libertas			M83			3	-
Matteo Coppini	05/05/89	Amerina (ITA)			s64			13	-
Carlo Valentini	15/03/82	Murata & Pietracuta (ITA)				D73		43	-
Alex Gasperoni	30/06/84	Tre Penne				M		36	1
Pier Filippo Mazza	20/08/88	Sant'Ermete (ITA)				s90	s78	13	-
Juri Biordi	01/01/95	Fiorentino					D	2	-
Tommaso Zafferani	19/02/96	La Fiorita					M78	1	-
Eugenio Colombini	16/01/92	Juvenes/Dogana					s53	2	-
Michele Cervellini	14/04/88	Pennarossa					s78	28	-

NB The San Marino amateur players are permitted to appear for more than one club at the same time.

EUROPE

SS Folgore

CHAMPIONS LEAGUE

First qualifying round - FC Pyunik (ARM)
A 1-2 *Hirsch (71)*
Bicchiarelli, Muccini, Traini, Pacini (Casadei 72), Ceschi, Perrotta (Della Valle 80), G Bollini, Berardi, Hirsch (Amici 90+5), F Bollini, Mazzola. Coach: Nicola Berardi (SMR)
Red card: Ceschi 71
H 1-2 *Traini (65)*
Bicchiarelli, Nucci (Della Valle 59), Muccini, Traini, Pacini, G Bollini (Casadei 83), Genestreti, Berardi, Hirsch, F Bollini (Rossi 71), Mazzola. Coach: Nicola Berardi (SMR)

AC Juvenes/Dogana

EUROPA LEAGUE

First qualifying round - Brøndby IF (DEN)
A 0-9
Manzaroli, T Cavalli (Canini 53), Bagli (Ugolini 76), Villa, Maccagno, Santini, Mariotti (Bernardi 59), Merlini, Gasperoni, Mantovani, Battistini. Coach: Fabrizio Costantini (SMR)
H 0-2
Manzaroli, Villa, Ugolini, Maccagno, Santini (N Zafferani 65), Mariotti (Zonzini 77), Merlini, Canini (Bagli 85), Gasperoni, Mantovani, Battistini. Coach: Fabrizio Costantini (SMR)

SP La Fiorita

EUROPA LEAGUE

First qualifying round - FC Vaduz (LIE)
H 0-5
Pazzini, A Martini, Bugli, Macerata, Ricchiuti (Cavalli 70), Rinaldi, Tommasi, Gasperoni, Cangini (Righi 78), Selva, T Zafferani (Casadei 88). Coach: Luigi Bizzotto (ITA)
A 1-5 *Tommasi (74)*
Pazzini, A Martini, Macerata, Cavalli (Guidi 70), Ricchiuti, Rinaldi (De Biagi 82), Tommasi, Gasperoni, Cangini, T Zafferani, Righi (Casadei 60). Coach: Luigi Bizzotto (ITA)

DOMESTIC LEAGUE CLUB-BY-CLUB

Stadiums

Stadio di Domagnano, Domagnano (200)
Serravalle B, Serravalle (350)
Stadio Federico Crescentini, Fiorentino (1,500)
Montecchio, Città di San Marino (500)
Stadio Ezio Conti, Dogana (350)
San Marino Stadium, Serravalle (4,801)

SP Cailungo

1974 • spcailungo.com
Coach: Sereno Uraldi (ITA)

2015

13/09	Cosmos	W	2-1	Fabbri, Casali
19/09	Libertas	D	1-1	Bartoli
27/09	Faetano	L	1-2	Renzi
03/10	La Fiorita	L	0-5	
17/10	San Giovanni	L	0-1	
25/10	Pennarossa	D	0-0	
31/10	Juvenes/Dogana	L	0-3	
07/11	Fiorentino	L	0-2	
21/11	Tre Fiori	W	4-1	Bartoli 2 (1p), Iuzzolino, Polidori
29/11	Domagnano	L	0-3	
05/12	Tre Penne	L	1-2	Ciavatta
12/12	Murata	W	5-3	Semprini, Iuzzolino, Polidori, Bartoli, Renzi

2016

07/02	Folgore	L	1-5	Bartoli
14/02	Virtus	L	1-4	Bartoli
27/02	Cosmos	W	2-1	Semeraro, Manzari
06/03	Libertas	L	0-4	
12/03	Faetano	D	1-1	Casali
20/03	La Fiorita	L	0-6	
03/04	San Giovanni	D	0-0	
09/04	Pennarossa	L	0-3	
16/04	Juvenes/Dogana	L	0-2	

Name	Nat	DoB	Pos	Aps	(s)	Gls
Michele Andreini		15/04/90	D	2	(6)	
Andrea Bartoli	ITA	20/09/76	A	20	(1)	6
Lorenzo Boschi		30/04/86	A	9	(4)	
Michele Boschi		19/08/90	D	3	(8)	
Ivan Brighi	ITA	20/12/82	M	4		
Enrico Casadei		18/02/96	M	2	(1)	
Massimiliano Casali		02/02/96	M	15	(5)	2
Simone Ciavatta		18/09/91	M	19	(2)	1
Stefano Fabbri	ITA	27/11/82	M	9		1
Massimo Francioni		17/06/93	G	11	(1)	
Eridon Gega	ALB	13/09/90	M	4	(1)	
Manuel Iuzzolino	ITA	05/05/90	D	19		2
Jacopo Manzari		01/06/88	A	3	(5)	1
Gianluca Micheloni		21/03/90	M	13	(4)	
Daniele Palanghi	ITA	24/12/81	A	3	(5)	
Nicola Polidori		12/03/91	M	14		2
Andrea Renzi	ITA	13/01/84	A	8	(2)	2
Andrea Sammaritani		14/05/79	D	3	(4)	
Alessio Sammartino	ITA	30/03/92	M	2		
Simone Santarini		17/10/91	M	15	(4)	
Paolo Semeraro	ITA	03/02/88	M	4		1
Stefano Semprini		12/09/85	M	19		1
Nicolò Tamagnini		07/02/88	G	10		
Omar Tomassoni	ITA	06/12/88	D	15	(1)	
Luca Zafferani		06/09/97	M	5	(3)	

SS Cosmos

1979 • no website
Major honours
San Marino League (1) 2001; San Marino Cup (4) 1980, 1981, 1995, 1999
Coach: Oscar Lasagni (ITA); (29/03/16) Francesco Donnini

2015

13/09	Cailungo	L	1-2	Venerucci
19/09	Faetano	L	1-2	Neri
26/09	La Fiorita	L	1-3	Pino
03/10	Juvenes/Dogana	D	2-2	Maurizi, Celli
16/10	Pennarossa	D	1-1	Neri
24/10	Libertas	D	0-0	
01/11	San Giovanni	W	2-1	Venerucci, Grassi
08/11	Virtus	L	1-2	Pari
28/11	Tre Fiori	L	1-3	Celli
05/12	Fiorentino	D	0-0	
13/12	Tre Penne	D	2-2	Maurizi, Neri

2016

06/02	Murata	D	1-1	Benedetti
13/02	Folgore	L	1-2	Neri (p)
21/02	Domagnano	W	3-1	Venerucci, Neri, Celli
27/02	Cailungo	L	1-2	Semprini
06/03	Faetano	D	0-0	
13/03	La Fiorita	L	0-5	
20/03	Juvenes/Dogana	D	2-2	Negri, Neri (p)
02/04	Pennarossa	L	1-3	Zaghini
09/04	Libertas	L	1-2	Neri
16/04	San Giovanni	W	3-1	Celli, Neri, Negri

Name	Nat	DoB	Pos	Aps	(s)	Gls
Michael Benedetti		30/04/00	A	2	(10)	1
Marco Casalboni	ITA	04/12/82	G	9		
Giuseppe Casali		08/07/73	G	10		
Alex Cavalli		26/02/92	D	17	(1)	
Alberto Celli		24/06/85	A	9	(5)	4
Rocco Di Filippo	ITA	07/01/84	D	8	(2)	
Alessandro Esposito	ITA	06/08/93	A		(1)	
Lorenzo Fortunato	ITA	13/12/98	A	1	(1)	
Matteo Giardi		14/04/97	A	1	(5)	
Alberto Girotti	ITA	28/04/63	G	2		
Daniel Giulianelli		12/01/95	D	11	(3)	
Fabiano Grassi		06/05/88	M	18		1
Giacomo Guerra		10/03/94	D	12	(1)	
Tommaso Guerra		22/08/90	M	14	(1)	
Francesco Maurizi	ITA	10/01/90	A	14	(2)	2
Nicola Moretti		20/04/84	M	17	(1)	
Cristian Negri		16/01/85	A	6	(2)	2
Roberto Neri	ITA	06/08/93	A	19		8
Stefano Pari		13/12/93	A	7	(9)	1
Facundo Pino	ARG	31/08/93	A	3	(1)	1
Alberto Semprini	ITA	13/02/90	D	18	(1)	1
Massimo Vagnetti		25/06/79	D	4	(7)	
Nicolò Venerucci		27/08/95	A	12	(5)	3
Denis Veronesi		17/07/88	M	1	(3)	
Guido Zaghini	ITA	06/12/88	M	16		1

FC Domagnano

1966 • no website

Major honours
San Marino League (4) 1989, 2002, 2003, 2005;
San Marino Cup (8) 1972, 1988, 1990, 1992, 1996,
2001, 2002, 2003
Coach: Cristian Protti (ITA)

2015

12/09	Virtus	W	2-0	*Chiarabini, Rossi (p)*
20/09	Murata	W	2-0	*Mami, Chiarabini*
27/09	Tre Fiori	L	2-4	*Chiarabini 2 (1p)*
04/10	Folgore	L	0-2	
18/10	Tre Penne	L	0-2	
30/10	Fiorentino	W	2-1	*Faetanini, Chiarabini*
07/11	Pennarossa	D	2-2	*Chiarabini, Rossi*
22/11	Juvenes/Dogana	D	2-2	*L Ceccaroli, Chiarabini (p)*
29/11	Cailungo	W	3-0	*Narducci, Chiarabini 2*
05/12	La Fiorita	L	2-4	*Narducci 2*
12/12	Libertas	D	1-1	*Chiarabini (p)*

2016

07/02	San Giovanni	W	5-2	*Chiarabini 3 (1p), Dolcini, Burioni*
13/02	Faetano	W	1-0	*Mami*
21/02	Cosmos	L	1-3	*Chiarabini*
27/02	Virtus	W	2-1	*Chiarabini, Rossi*
05/03	Murata	W	2-1	*Burioni 2*
12/03	Tre Fiori	L	0-2	
19/03	Folgore	W	2-1	*Narducci, Rossi*
02/04	Tre Penne	L	2-3	*Venerucci, Chiarabini (p)*
17/04	Fiorentino	L	0-1	

Name	Nat	DoB	Pos	Aps	(s)	Gls
Federico Buldrini	ITA	19/08/83	D	11		
Filippo Burioni	ITA	20/05/98	A	10	(6)	3
Luca Ceccaroli		05/07/95	M	14		1
Marco Ceccaroli		09/03/92	M		(2)	
Marco Cecchetti		03/02/77	M	3	(5)	
Carlo Chiarabini	ITA	27/04/76	A	19		16
Davide Dolcini		30/01/91	A	8	(7)	1
Alessio Faetanini		15/03/90	M	7	(7)	1
Francesco Gatti		09/02/98	M		(2)	
Matteo Giannoni		25/03/88	D	13	(3)	
Daniele Lusini	ITA	10/03/82	M	12		
Alessandro Mami	ITA	24/07/92	A	13	(3)	2
Alessandro Moraccini		30/04/96	M		(1)	
Michele Moretti		26/10/81	M	16	(1)	
Giacomo Muraccini		15/09/90	G	20		
Marco Narducci	ITA	16/09/89	M	18		4
Mirko Piscaglia		29/09/90	M	12	(4)	
Nicola Ranocchini		01/04/85	D	12		
Giovanni Righi		05/07/94	D	1	(6)	
Paolo Rossi	ITA	06/09/83	A	17		4
Luca Sensoli		07/03/91	A	1	(5)	
Andrea Venerucci		21/11/89	M	13	(1)	1

SC Faetano

1962 • faetanocalcio.sm

Major honours
San Marino League (3) 1986, 1991, 1999;
San Marino Cup (3) 1993, 1994, 1998
Coach: Pierluigi Angeloni (ITA)

2015

11/09	San Giovanni	W	1-0	*Ordonselli*
19/09	Cosmos	W	2-1	*Mosconi, Ordonselli*
27/09	Cailungo	W	2-1	*A Moroni, Franklin (p)*
04/10	Libertas	L	0-2	
18/10	La Fiorita	D	0-0	
24/10	Juvenes/Dogana	L	1-3	*Ordonselli*
31/10	Pennarossa	L	0-1	
07/11	Tre Penne	L	0-2	
22/11	Folgore	L	1-3	*og (Genestreti)*
06/12	Murata	L	0-2	
12/12	Tre Fiori	L	1-2	*Giardi*

2016

06/02	Virtus	L	2-4	*A Moroni, Ferrari*
13/02	Domagnano	L	0-1	
21/02	Fiorentino	D	2-2	*Giardi, Polanco*
28/02	San Giovanni	D	1-1	*Polanco (p)*
06/03	Cosmos	D	0-0	
12/03	Cailungo	D	1-1	*Ugolini*
19/03	Libertas	L	0-1	
02/04	La Fiorita	L	1-4	*Ferrari*
09/04	Juvenes/Dogana	L	0-1	
16/04	Pennarossa	D	3-3	*Ordonselli, A Della Valle, Guidi*

Name	Nat	DoB	Pos	Aps	(s)	Gls
Marco Becci	ITA	30/08/91	M	21		
Andrea Borgagni		21/10/93	M	9	(8)	
Sergio Carlucci	ITA	17/12/74	D	6	(8)	
Mattia Casali		06/05/97	M		(2)	
Alex Della Valle		13/06/90	D	11	(1)	1
Pier Marino Della Valle		10/07/63	D		(1)	
Nicolò Ferrari	ITA	03/02/91	D	21		2
Franklin	BRA	13/04/84	A	5	(1)	1
Mattia Giardi		15/12/91	M	20		2
Claudio Giustolisi	ITA	13/02/81	G	18		
Francesco Guidi		16/08/98	M		(2)	1
Samuel Lazzaro	ITA	10/08/91	G	3		
Andrea Moroni		10/10/85	A	16		2
Marco Moroni		30/12/85	D		(3)	
Massimo Moroni		17/02/90	A	2	(7)	
Luca Mosconi		28/06/82	D	1	(2)	1
Jacopo Ordonselli	ITA	07/07/94	M	18		4
Maurizio Pedrelli	ITA	26/02/68	D	4	(4)	
Emiliano Polanco	ITA	05/07/84	D	9		2
Enrico Raggini		30/07/90	M	10	(3)	
Giacomo Rinaldi		23/03/90	D	20		
Matteo Rossi		09/07/86	M	1	(2)	
Marian Tubrea	ROU	21/03/88	A		(4)	
Simone Ugolini		28/02/91	M	17	(3)	1
Vittorio Valentini		09/10/73	D	19		

FC Fiorentino

1974 • no website

Major honours
San Marino League (1) 1992
Coach: Massimo Campo (ITA)

2015

13/09	Tre Fiori	L	0-1	
19/09	Tre Penne	L	0-3	
03/10	Virtus	L	2-3	*Vicini, Jaupi*
17/10	Murata	W	3-1	*Maiani, Vicini 2*
25/10	Folgore	W	2-1	*Bernardi, Vicini*
30/10	Domagnano	L	1-2	*Jaupi*
07/11	Cailungo	W	2-0	*Baizan, Jaupi*
22/11	Pennarossa	L	0-1	
28/11	San Giovanni	W	3-1	*Maiani, Molinari, Biordi*
05/12	Cosmos	D	0-0	
13/12	La Fiorita	W	2-1	*Ceccoli, Paglialonga*

2016

07/02	Juvenes/Dogana	W	2-0	*Vicini, Baizan*
13/02	Libertas	W	1-0	*Jaupi*
21/02	Faetano	D	2-2	*Jaupi, Vicini*
27/02	Tre Fiori	W	3-1	*Vicini, Jaupi 2*
05/03	Tre Penne	L	0-3	
20/03	Virtus	W	3-0	*Jaupi 3*
03/04	Murata	W	3-1	*Vicini, Paglialonga, Jaupi*
10/04	Folgore	L	0-3	
17/04	Domagnano	W	1-0	*Bernardi*

Name	Nat	DoB	Pos	Aps	(s)	Gls
Maximiliano Baizan		23/03/93	M	19	(1)	2
Marco Benvenuti		09/12/95	M	2	(1)	
Michele Berardi		07/04/92	G	1	(1)	
Andrea Bernardi		08/11/88	D	20		2
Luca Bianchi	ITA	27/02/90	G	19		
Juri Biordi		01/01/95	D	17		1
Manuel Carlini		26/05/93	D	3	(3)	
Andrea Ceccoli		22/09/93	M	13	(5)	1
Federico Gennari		28/08/92	M	3	(4)	
Enea Jaupi	ALB	06/10/93	A	15	(1)	11
Evgeni Lipen	BLR	15/12/92	D	20		
Daniele Maiani		04/08/93	D	7	(3)	2
Elia Marchetti		26/01/95	M		(1)	
Alex Mattioli		14/06/95	M		(4)	
Alessandro Molinari	ITA	14/05/89	M	19		1
Mirko Paglialonga	ITA	19/09/83	D	19		2
Samuele Paoloni		18/01/97	A		(1)	
Massimiliano Pratelli	ITA	14/04/83	D	18		
Matteo Scarponi		28/09/91	M	4	(3)	
Fabio Vechiolla	ITA	23/02/82	M	2	(4)	
Emanuele Vicini	ITA	11/07/86	A	12		8
Adriano Zanotti		15/07/86	M		(2)	
Enrico Zanotti		15/05/97	D		(3)	
Donald Zenunay	ALB	11/01/91	M	2	(4)	
Gerhard Zenunay	ALB	12/06/89	M	5	(9)	

SS Folgore

1972 • folgorecalcio.com

Major honours
San Marino League (4) 1997, 1998, 2000, 2015;
San Marino Cup (1) 2015

Coach: Nicola Berardi

2015
12/09	Tre Penne	L	0-1	
20/09	Virtus	D	1-1	*Nucci*
25/09	Murata	W	2-1	*Hirsch, Rossi*
04/10	Domagnano	W	2-0	*Rossi, Hirsch*
17/10	Tre Fiori	L	1-2	*Hirsch*
25/10	Fiorentino	L	1-2	*Perrotta*
07/11	Juvenes/Dogana	W	3-2	*Perrotta (p), Hirsch, Domeniconi*
22/11	Faetano	W	3-1	*Ceschi, Hirsch 2*
28/11	La Fiorita	D	1-1	*Valeriani*
06/12	Libertas	W	4-0	*Perrotta 2 (1p), Domeniconi, Nucci*
12/12	San Giovanni	W	4-1	*Della Valle, Perrotta (p), Hirsch, Domeniconi*

2016
07/02	Cailungo	W	5-1	*Ceschi 2, Nucci, Genestreti, Hirsch*
13/02	Cosmos	W	2-1	*Genestreti, Della Valle*
20/02	Pennarossa	W	2-1	*Hirsch, Ceschi*
28/02	Tre Penne	L	0-2	
05/03	Virtus	W	3-2	*Hirsch 2, Genestreti*
12/03	Murata	D	3-3	*Valeriani, Muccini, Perrotta*
19/03	Domagnano	L	1-2	*Valeriani*
03/04	Tre Fiori	W	3-1	*Ceschi, Perrotta (p), Della Valle*
10/04	Fiorentino	W	3-0	*Perrotta, Hirsch 2*

Name	Nat	DoB	Pos	Aps	(s)	Gls
Riccardo Aluigi		29/03/94	A	2	(2)	
Nicola Antonelli		02/02/99	G	1		
Marco Berardi		12/02/93	D	18		
Davide Bicchiarelli	ITA	19/05/89	G	19		
Fabio Bollini		19/09/83	M	3	(3)	
Gian Luca Bollini		24/03/80	D	9	(6)	
Michele Casadei		24/01/92	M	3	(6)	
Fabio Ceschi	ITA	19/01/82	A	18	(1)	5
Andrea Contato	ITA	21/02/98	D		(1)	
Achille Della Valle		31/01/89	A	6	(10)	3
Marco Domeniconi		29/01/84	M	13	(1)	3
Christofer Genestreti	ITA	30/05/84	D	18		3
Tomas Guidi		04/09/92	D		(1)	
Adolfo Hirsch		31/01/86	A	19		13
Alberto Mazzola	ITA	21/07/84	D	11		
Manuel Muccini		24/11/89	M	19		1
Andrea Nucci	ITA	06/09/86	M	8	(4)	3
Simone Pacini	ITA	08/01/81	M	1	(1)	
Francesco Perrotta	ITA	27/08/81	A	12	(3)	8
Francsco Quintavalla	ITA	26/06/82	D	8	(1)	
Marco Rattini		31/12/84	M		(2)	
Luca Righi		01/04/95	D	14	(2)	
Luca Rossi	ITA	14/04/93	D	11	(5)	2
Luca Valeriani	ITA	15/05/91	M	7	(3)	3

AC Juvenes/Dogana

2000 • no website

Major honours
San Marino Cup (2) 2009, 2011

Coach: Fabrizio Costantini

2015
12/09	La Fiorita	L	0-2	
20/09	San Giovanni	W	2-0	*Battistini, Mantovani*
26/09	Pennarossa	W	1-0	*Santini*
03/10	Cosmos	D	2-2	*Mariotti 2*
18/10	Libertas	L	1-2	*Mariotti*
24/10	Faetano	W	3-1	*Maccagno 2 (1p), Santini*
31/10	Cailungo	W	3-0	*Mantovani 2, Zonzini*
07/11	Folgore	L	2-3	*Canini, Mantovani*
22/11	Domagnano	D	2-2	*Mariotti (p), Ugolini*
28/11	Murata	L	1-2	*Santini*
06/12	Tre Fiori	W	2-1	*Mantovani 2*

2016
07/02	Fiorentino	L	0-2	
13/02	Tre Penne	D	1-1	*Ugolini*
20/02	Virtus	L	1-2	*Mariotti*
28/02	La Fiorita	L	2-3	*Santini, og (Cavalli)*
05/03	San Giovanni	W	4-0	*Mariotti (p), Mantovani 2, Gasperoni*
13/03	Pennarossa	L	0-1	
20/03	Cosmos	D	2-2	*Mariotti (p), Zafferani*
02/04	Libertas	W	2-1	*Mantovani 2*
09/04	Faetano	W	1-0	*Zafferani*
16/04	Cailungo	W	2-0	*Zafferani, Zonzini*

Name	Nat	DoB	Pos	Aps	(s)	Gls
Giordo Bagli	ITA	15/01/81	M	18	(1)	
Manuel Battistini		22/07/94	M	18		1
Marco Bernardi		02/01/94	A	4	(6)	
Nicola Canini		14/08/88	M	12	(3)	1
Nicolas Cavalli	ITA	22/04/94	D	1	(5)	
Thomas Cavalli	ITA	17/01/88	D	13	(2)	
Eugenio Colombini		16/01/92	M	12	(6)	
Federico Costantini		11/09/95	D		(1)	
Mattia Dominici	ITA	29/07/94	D	6	(4)	
Lorenzo Francini		11/04/95	M		(3)	
Lorenzo Gasperoni		03/01/90	M	13	(1)	1
Cristian Maccagno	ITA	05/06/83	M	15		2
Mirko Mantovani	ITA	14/11/86	D	19	(1)	10
Mattia Manzaroli		03/10/91	G	21		
Giorgio Mariotti	ITA	06/05/86	A	13	(1)	7
Mattia Merlini		23/12/93	D	15		
Riccardo Santini	ITA	18/10/86	M	19		4
Marco Ugolini	ITA	23/12/86	A	8	(3)	2
Daniele Villa	ITA	24/05/82	D	17		
Nicola Zafferani		06/11/91	D	3	(13)	3
Alessandro Zonzini		11/10/94	D	4	(8)	2

SP La Fiorita

1933 • lafiorita.sm

Major honours
San Marino League (3) 1987, 1990, 2014;
San Marino Cup (4) 1986, 2012, 2013, 2016

Coach: Luigi Bizzotto (ITA)

2015
12/09	Juvenes/Dogana	W	2-0	*Rinaldi, Selva*
19/09	Pennarossa	W	1-0	*Mottola (p)*
26/09	Cosmos	W	3-1	*Casadei, Selva, M Martini*
03/10	Cailungo	W	5-0	*M Martini, T Zafferani, Selva 2 (1p), Gasperoni*
18/10	Faetano	D	0-0	
24/10	San Giovanni	W	5-0	*Selva 3 (1p), T Zafferani, M Martini*
31/10	Libertas	W	4-0	*A Martini, M Martini 2 (1p), Rinaldi*
08/11	Murata	L	1-3	*M Martini*
20/11	Virtus	L	3-4	*M Martini, Mottola, Selva*
28/11	Folgore	D	1-1	*M Martini*
05/12	Domagnano	W	4-2	*Selva, Rinaldi, Macerata, T Zafferani*
13/12	Fiorentino	L	1-2	*Selva*

2016
06/02	Tre Penne	L	0-3	
20/02	Tre Fiori	W	2-0	*M Martini 2 (1p)*
28/02	Juvenes/Dogana	W	3-2	*M Martini, Gasperoni 2*
06/03	Pennarossa	L	1-2	*Gasperoni*
13/03	Cosmos	W	5-0	*Selva 2, M Martini 3*
20/03	Cailungo	W	6-0	*M Martini 3, A Martini, Rinaldi, Gasperoni*
02/04	Faetano	W	4-1	*A Martini, Guidi 2, M Martini*
09/04	San Giovanni	W	4-2	*Selva, Guidi, M Martini, Gasperoni*
16/04	Libertas	L	1-2	*Rinaldi*

Name	Nat	DoB	Pos	Aps	(s)	Gls
Francesco Beinat		18/12/96	M	1	(1)	
Davide Bugli		23/12/84	D	19		
Alessio Cangini	ITA	05/01/91	M	19		
Nicola Casadei		24/01/89	D	9	(5)	1
Nicola Cavalli		15/12/86	M	10	(5)	
Thomas De Biagi		03/11/90	M	1	(3)	
Stefano Fraternali	ITA	13/04/86	M	7		
Marco Gasperoni	ITA	18/02/92	D	18	(1)	6
Alessandro Guidi		14/12/86	A	3	(10)	3
Sandro Macerata	ITA	08/10/69	D	12	(4)	1
Andrea Martini	ITA	24/12/81	D	18		3
Marco Martini	ITA	12/04/79	A	20		19
Tiziano Mottola	ITA	06/07/86	A	8	(3)	2
Filippo Muccioli		20/06/96	D	2	(5)	
Filippo Pensalfini	ITA	08/02/77	M	11		
Emanuele Quadrelli		12/10/81	G	1	(1)	
Andrea Righi		10/07/97	M	4	(8)	
Danilo Rinaldi		18/04/86	A	18	(2)	5
Nabila Samba	SEN	15/09/92	D	3	(1)	
Andy Selva		23/05/76	A	18		13
Samuel Toccaceli		09/11/96	A		(3)	
Gianluca Vivan		27/12/83	G	20		
Elia Zafferani		25/06/92	A		(1)	
Tommaso Zafferani		19/02/96	M	9	(1)	3

AC Libertas

1928 • polisportivalibertas.com

Major honours
San Marino League (1) 1996; San Marino Cup (11) 1937, 1950, 1954, 1958, 1959, 1961, 1987, 1989, 1991, 2006, 2014

Coach: Roberto Marcucci; (09/02/16) Angelo Affatigato (ITA)

2015

Date	Opponent		Score	Scorers
13/09	Pennarossa	D	1-1	*Valle*
19/09	Cailungo	D	1-1	*Valle*
26/09	San Giovanni	W	3-0	*Valle, Bianchi, Rocchi*
04/10	Faetano	W	2-0	*Valle, Bianchi*
18/10	Juvenes/Dogana	W	2-1	*Golinucci, Parma*
24/10	Cosmos	D	0-0	
31/10	La Fiorita	L	0-4	
08/11	Tre Fiori	L	0-1	
25/11	Murata	L	1-2	*Parma*
29/11	Virtus	D	1-1	*Parma*
06/12	Folgore	L	0-4	
12/12	Domagnano	D	1-1	*Valle*

2016

Date	Opponent		Score	Scorers
13/02	Fiorentino	L	0-1	
21/02	Tre Penne	L	0-3	
27/02	Pennarossa	L	0-1	
06/03	Cailungo	W	4-0	*Antonelli, Parma, Morelli 2*
13/03	San Giovanni	D	1-1	*Morelli*
19/03	Faetano	W	1-0	*Rocchi*
02/04	Juvenes/Dogana	L	1-2	*Morelli*
09/04	Cosmos	W	2-1	*Parma, Nanni*
16/04	La Fiorita	W	2-1	*Angeli, Rocchi*

Name	Nat	DoB	Pos	Aps	(s)	Gls
Daniele Angeli		29/07/92	D	10	(4)	1
Filippo Antonelli	ITA	28/01/83	M	16	(1)	1
Andrea Benvenuti		24/07/90	D	12	(3)	
Marco Bianchi	ITA	26/09/86	A	7	(1)	2
Michele Camillini		10/01/84	D	11	(1)	
Mirco Facondini	ITA	30/09/82	M	10	(3)	
Mirko Giardi		11/05/95	M	1	(5)	
Enrico Golinucci		16/07/91	M	16	(2)	1
Manuel Molinari		20/08/86	D	12	(1)	
Gian Luca Morelli	ITA	13/02/85	A	9		4
Federico Nanni		22/09/81	M	8	(6)	1
Simon Parma		20/03/83	A	14	(4)	5
Daniele Rocchi	ITA	23/06/82	D	18		3
Michele Rossi		26/01/95	D	16	(2)	
Aldo Simoncini		30/08/86	G	19		
Davide Simoncini		30/08/86	D	18		
Andrea Tamagnini		27/09/97	M	8	(6)	
Luca Valle	ITA	25/01/81	A	13		5
Andrea Zavoli		04/07/94	M	11	(5)	
Matteo Zavoli		06/07/96	G	2	(1)	

SS Murata

1966 • muratacalcio.com

Major honours
San Marino League (3) 2006, 2007, 2008; San Marino Cup (3) 1997, 2007, 2008

Coach: Matteo Cecchetti (ITA)

2015

Date	Opponent		Score	Scorers
20/09	Domagnano	L	0-2	
25/09	Folgore	L	1-2	*Domini*
04/10	Tre Fiori	L	1-4	*Valentini*
17/10	Fiorentino	L	1-3	*Rosti*
25/10	Virtus	W	1-0	*Berretti*
01/11	Tre Penne	L	1-4	*Rosti*
08/11	La Fiorita	W	3-1	*Friguglietti 2, Simoncini*
25/11	Libertas	W	2-1	*Sternini, Friguglietti*
28/11	Juvenes/Dogana	W	2-1	*Valentini, Domini*
06/12	Faetano	W	2-0	*Friguglietti 2*
12/12	Cailungo	L	3-5	*Casadei, Friguglietti 2*

2016

Date	Opponent		Score	Scorers
06/02	Cosmos	D	1-1	*Cuttone*
14/02	Pennarossa	D	3-3	*Angelini, Rosti, Berretti*
20/02	San Giovanni	W	4-0	*Angelini 2, Casadei, Rosti*
05/03	Domagnano	L	1-2	*Casadei*
12/03	Folgore	D	3-3	*Casadei, Angelini, Valentini*
19/03	Tre Fiori	L	0-4	
03/04	Fiorentino	L	1-3	*og (Lipen)*
10/04	Virtus	L	2-5	*Casadei (p), Marani (p)*
17/04	Tre Penne	W	3-1	*Valentini, Rosti, Rais*

Name	Nat	DoB	Pos	Aps	(s)	Gls
Nicola Albani		21/02/79	D		(4)	
Nicolò Angelini		15/03/92	A	6	(2)	4
Maicol Berretti		01/05/89	M	15	(2)	2
Lorenzo Buscarini		27/05/91	D	18		
Alfredo Cardinale	ITA	20/08/76	M	1	(1)	
Marco Casadei		20/09/85	A	18	(1)	5
Nicolò Catalano	ITA	15/01/89	M		(2)	
Alessandro Cuttone		24/03/84	M	15		1
Rocco Di Filippo	ITA	08/07/84	D	8	(1)	
Tommaso Domini	ITA	18/08/89	M	6		2
Angelo Faetanini		17/01/93	D	13	(3)	
Daniele Friguglietti	ITA	21/11/79	A	9	(2)	7
Domenico Giordani	ITA	25/03/83	D	9		
Marco Graziosi		26/08/89	G	19		
Manuel Marani		07/06/84	A	17	(2)	1
Alessandro Protti		28/07/81	M	3	(7)	
Adnan Rais	TUN	02/05/82	A	3		1
Marco Rosti		21/10/88	A	12	(7)	5
Michael Simoncini		01/02/87	A	9		1
Michael Simoncini		01/02/87	G	1		
Francesco Sternini	ITA	29/06/87	M	17		1
Alan Toccaceli		14/04/83	A		(2)	
Luca Tomassoni		21/11/94	M	5	(2)	
Davide Vagnetti		19/07/83	D	2	(6)	
Carlo Valentini		15/03/82	D	14		4
Giacomo Zonzini		20/09/90	A		(4)	

SS Pennarossa

1968 • pennarossa.com

Major honours
San Marino League (1) 2004; San Marino Cup (2) 2004, 2005

Coach: Alberto Manca (ITA)

2015

Date	Opponent		Score	Scorers
13/09	Libertas	D	1-1	*og (Antonelli)*
19/09	La Fiorita	L	0-1	
26/09	Juvenes/Dogana	L	0-1	
03/10	San Giovanni	W	4-1	*Nicolini 4*
16/10	Cosmos	D	1-1	*N Ciacci*
25/10	Cailungo	D	0-0	
31/10	Faetano	W	1-0	*Nicolini*
07/11	Domagnano	D	2-2	*N Ciacci 2*
22/11	Fiorentino	W	1-0	*Stradaioli*
29/11	Tre Penne	D	1-1	*N Ciacci*
13/12	Virtus	D	0-0	

2016

Date	Opponent		Score	Scorers
06/02	Tre Fiori	L	0-2	
14/02	Murata	D	3-3	*N Ciacci, Conti, Stradaioli*
20/02	Folgore	L	1-2	*Aissaoui*
27/02	Libertas	W	1-0	*Gualtieri*
06/03	La Fiorita	W	2-1	*Agostinelli, Toccaceli*
13/03	Juvenes/Dogana	W	1-0	*Agostinelli*
19/03	San Giovanni	W	4-0	*Del Pivo, N Ciacci, Agostinelli 2*
02/04	Cosmos	W	3-1	*Aissaoui, N Ciacci, Del Pivo*
09/04	Cailungo	W	3-0	*Agostinelli 2 (1p), Giunchi*
16/04	Faetano	D	3-3	*Stradaioli, A Ciacci, Toccaceli*

Name	Nat	DoB	Pos	Aps	(s)	Gls
Marco Agostinelli	ITA	22/04/78	A	9	(2)	6
Amir Aissaoui	ITA	30/11/92	A	17	(1)	2
Nicola Albani		15/04/81	D	17	(1)	
Nicholas Capozzi	ITA	12/12/87	A	7	(10)	
Michele Cervellini		14/04/88	M	19		
Alessandro Ciacci		15/07/96	A	1	(13)	1
Nicola Ciacci		07/07/82	A	20		7
Daniele Conti	ITA	06/06/90	M	9	(2)	1
Nicola Del Pivo	ITA	10/04/92	M	16		2
Andrea Farabegoli	ITA	01/08/76	D	14		
Marco Fariselli	ITA	17/05/87	A	12	(1)	
Luca Giunchi	ITA	07/12/85	M	17	(1)	1
Giacomo Gualtieri	ITA	21/12/82	A	3	(3)	1
Antonino Guidi		23/12/72	G	1		
Luca Lazzarini		08/04/86	D	18		
Paolo Mariotti		05/11/79	M	2	(1)	
Simone Montanari		11/03/80	G	20		
Mattia Nicolini	ITA	21/06/79	A	10		5
Nicholas Stradaioli		21/01/85	M	15	(3)	3
Samuel Toccaceli		09/11/96	A	2	(4)	2
Luca Tomassoni		21/11/94	M	2	(4)	

SAN MARINO

SS San Giovanni

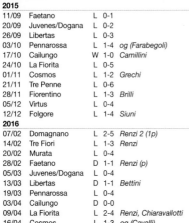

1948 • no website
Coach: Ermanno Zonzini

2015

11/09	Faetano	L 0-1	
20/09	Juvenes/Dogana	L 0-2	
26/09	Libertas	L 0-3	
03/10	Pennarossa	L 1-4	og (Farabegoli)
17/10	Cailungo	W 1-0	Camillini
24/10	La Fiorita	L 0-5	
01/11	Cosmos	L 1-2	Grechi
21/11	Tre Penne	L 0-6	
28/11	Fiorentino	L 1-3	Brilli
05/12	Virtus	L 0-4	
12/12	Folgore	L 1-4	Siuni
2016			
07/02	Domagnano	L 2-5	Renzi 2 (1p)
14/02	Tre Fiori	L 1-3	Renzi
20/02	Murata	L 0-4	
28/02	Faetano	D 1-1	Renzi (p)
05/03	Juvenes/Dogana	L 0-4	
13/03	Libertas	D 1-1	Bettini
19/03	Pennarossa	L 0-4	
03/04	Cailungo	D 0-0	
09/04	La Fiorita	L 2-4	Renzi, Chiaravallotti
16/04	Cosmos	L 1-3	og (Cavalli)

Name	Nat	DoB	Pos	Aps	(s)	Gls
Marco Balducci		07/01/77	M	2	(3)	
Riccardo Bettini	ITA	07/07/96	A	8		1
Marco Borgelli	ITA	19/01/81	D	12	(3)	
Nicholas Brilli	ITA	05/02/90	M	18		1
Matteo Bugli		10/03/83	M	8	(1)	
Matteo Camillini	ITA	10/01/84	M	20		1
Edoardo Cecchetti		14/07/93	M	15	(5)	
Valentino Chiaravallotti	ITA	14/02/89	M	20		1
Fabio Colonna		07/01/84	G	6		
Sam Fantini		17/09/92	M	11	(2)	
Thomas Felici		26/11/95	D	14	(5)	
Gabriele Genghini		07/10/90	D	9	(3)	
Fabio Giardi		15/03/71	D	1	(3)	
Nicola Grechi	ITA	05/01/89	D	18		1
Jacopo Manzari		06/03/88	A	3	(6)	
Andrea Manzaroli		12/02/95	G	8		
Nicola Montanari	ITA	30/05/82	G	2		
Alvaro Musta		10/11/89	A	4	(1)	
Diego Pasquali		15/11/89	D	7	(5)	
William Pierini		12/06/96	D		(3)	
Andrea Renzi		13/01/84	A	5	(1)	5
Matteo Siuni		15/02/89	A	9	(1)	1
Andrea Valentini		04/11/98	A	9	(8)	
Fabio Vecchiola	ITA	23/02/82	M	1	(4)	
Matteo Venerucci		16/12/80	G	5	(3)	
Loris Zafferani		14/08/83	D	6		
Davide Zonzini		01/04/84	D	10	(2)	

SP Tre Fiori

1949 • no website
Major honours
San Marino League (7) 1988, 1993, 1994, 1995, 2009, 2010, 2011; San Marino Cup (6) 1966, 1971, 1974, 1975, 1985, 2010
Coach: Floriano Sperindio

2015

13/09	Fiorentino	W 1-0	Maiani
27/09	Domagnano	W 4-2	Ferri 2, Vannoni, Lini
04/10	Murata	W 4-1	Romano 2, Fonte, Ferri (p)
17/10	Folgore	W 2-1	Della Valle, Ferri
24/10	Tre Penne	W 1-0	Ferri
01/11	Virtus	D 2-2	Ferri, Romano
08/11	Libertas	W 1-0	Ferri
21/11	Cailungo	L 1-4	Ferri
28/11	Cosmos	W 3-1	Liverani, Andreini, Ferri
06/12	Juvenes/Dogana	L 1-2	Amici
12/12	Faetano	W 2-1	Lini, Buda
2016			
06/02	Pennarossa	W 2-0	Ferri 2
14/02	San Giovanni	W 3-1	Lolli (p), Lini, Matteoni
20/02	La Fiorita	L 0-2	
27/02	Fiorentino	L 1-3	Lini
12/03	Domagnano	W 2-1	Lolli 2 (1p)
19/03	Murata	W 4-0	Lolli, Romano, og (Marani), Ferri
03/04	Folgore	L 1-3	Romano (p)
10/04	Tre Penne	L 0-4	
17/04	Virtus	W 2-0	Amici, Fonte

Name	Nat	DoB	Pos	Aps	(s)	Gls
Federico Amici		27/03/82	A	2	(6)	2
Matteo Andreini		10/10/81	D	16		1
Alberto Balducci	ITA	16/08/93	M	11	(2)	
Giacomo Benedettini		07/10/82	D	4		
Samuele Buda		04/07/86	M	18		1
Michele Ceccoli		04/12/73	G	13		
Stefano Conti		18/07/70	M	9	(5)	
Stefano De Mattia	ITA	26/02/98	M		(1)	
Nicola Della Valle		19/05/97	D	10	(6)	1
Daniele Ferri	ITA	07/03/92	A	16	(1)	12
Emanuele Fonte	ITA	06/08/92	D	13	(1)	2
Nicolò Grini		14/02/92	D		(1)	
Nicolò Lini	ITA	13/04/93	D	15		4
Altin Lisi	ALB	09/03/74	M	8		
Lorenzo Liverani		13/05/93	M	10	(4)	1
Nicolò Lolli	ITA	11/10/94	A	9		4
Federico Maiani		25/12/95	A	6	(2)	1
Filippo Matteoni		27/05/96	D	1	(6)	1
Simone Matteoni		26/04/92	M	4	(6)	
Luca Pelliccioni		10/01/96	M		(2)	
Alessandro Podeschi		04/05/97	A		(1)	
Antonio Romano	ITA	21/02/95	A	18		5
Alex Stimac	ITA	22/06/96	G	7		
Davide Succi	ITA	07/06/90	D	8	(5)	
Paolo Tarini	ITA	08/06/76	A		(1)	
Fabio Vannoni	ITA	07/10/77	M	7		1
Matteo Vendemini		18/01/82	D	15	(4)	

SP Tre Penne

1956 • trepenne.sm
Major honours
San Marino League (3) 2012, 2013, 2016; San Marino Cup (5) 1967, 1970, 1982, 1983, 2000
Coach: Marco Protti

2015

12/09	Folgore	W 1-0	Gai
19/09	Fiorentino	W 3-0	Valli, Simoncelli 2
27/09	Virtus	W 3-1	Gai, Cesarini, Simoncelli
18/10	Domagnano	W 2-0	Simoncelli 2
24/10	Tre Fiori	L 0-1	
01/11	Murata	W 4-1	Pignieri 2, Simoncelli 2 (1p)
07/11	Faetano	W 2-0	Lazzarini, Simoncelli
21/11	San Giovanni	W 6-0	Gai 2, Lazzarini 2, Simoncelli (p), og (Grechi)
29/11	Pennarossa	D 1-1	Chiaruzzi
05/12	Cailungo	W 2-1	Patregnani, A Rossi
13/12	Cosmos	D 2-2	Cesarini, Valli (p)
2016			
06/02	La Fiorita	W 3-0	Friguglietti 2, Calzolari
13/02	Juvenes/Dogana	D 1-1	Gai
21/02	Libertas	W 3-0	Calzolari, Gai, Rispoli
28/02	Folgore	W 2-0	Gai, Patregnani
05/03	Fiorentino	W 3-0	Lazzarini, Rispoli, Friguglietti
12/03	Virtus	W 4-1	Patregnani 2, Friguglietti, Gai
02/04	Domagnano	W 3-2	Friguglietti 2, Gai
10/04	Tre Fiori	W 4-0	Friguglietti 2, Rispoli, Gai
17/04	Murata	L 1-3	Gai

Name	Nat	DoB	Pos	Aps	(s)	Gls
Giovanni Bonini		05/09/86	M	4	(2)	
Pietro Calzolari		28/10/91	M	11	(5)	2
Lorenzo Capicchioni		27/01/89	D	8		
Mattia Censoni		31/03/96	D	7	(4)	
Davide Cesarini		16/02/95	D	10	(1)	2
Nicola Chiaruzzi		25/12/87	M	10	(3)	1
Alfredo Chierighini	ITA	07/02/66	G		(1)	
Matteo Colonna		10/05/90	D	1	(1)	
Enrico Fattori	ITA	12/06/78	D	11	(1)	
Daniele Friguglietti	ITA	21/11/79	A	5	(1)	8
Nicola Gai	ITA	06/12/87	M	19		11
Alex Gasperoni		30/06/84	M	13	(3)	
Michele Giuliani		26/08/93	M	4	(8)	
Andrea Lazzarini		08/04/86	A	9	(4)	4
Fabio Macaluso		05/08/86	G	4		
Dario Merendino	ITA	14/11/83	D	15		
Mattia Migani	ITA	10/03/92	G	8		
Mirko Palazzi		21/03/87	D	4	(3)	
Luca Patregnani	ITA	08/04/85	M	20		4
Daniele Pignieri	ITA	14/05/75	A	1	(3)	2
Simone Rispoli	ITA	08/01/80	A	8	(1)	3
Andrea Rossi	ITA	20/07/87	D	16		1
Matteo Rossi		09/07/86	M		(2)	
Michele Simoncelli	ITA	03/03/82	A	9		9
Kengie Valentini		05/06/96	G	8		
Matteo Valli		11/09/86	A	9	(2)	2
Giacomo Zafferani		16/07/96	M	1	(6)	
Michele Zanotti		05/11/88	D	5	(3)	

Virtus FC

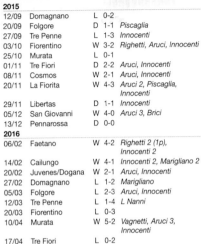

1964 • no website
Coach: Davide Nicolini (ITA)

2015

12/09	Domagnano	L	0-2	
20/09	Folgore	D	1-1	Piscaglia
27/09	Tre Penne	L	1-3	Innocenti
03/10	Fiorentino	W	3-2	Righetti, Aruci, Innocenti
25/10	Murata	L	0-1	
01/11	Tre Fiori	D	2-2	Aruci, Innocenti
08/11	Cosmos	W	2-1	Aruci, Innocenti
20/11	La Fiorita	W	4-3	Aruci 2, Piscaglia, Innocenti
29/11	Libertas	D	1-1	Innocenti
05/12	San Giovanni	W	4-0	Aruci 3, Brici
13/12	Pennarossa	D	0-0	

2016

06/02	Faetano	W	4-2	Righetti 2 (1p), Innocenti 2
14/02	Cailungo	W	4-1	Innocenti 2, Marigliano 2
20/02	Juvenes/Dogana	W	2-1	Aruci, Innocenti
27/02	Domagnano	L	1-2	Marigliano
05/03	Folgore	L	2-3	Aruci, Innocenti
12/03	Tre Penne	L	1-4	L Nanni
20/03	Fiorentino	L	0-3	
10/04	Murata	W	5-2	Vagnetti, Aruci 3, Innocenti
17/04	Tre Fiori	L	0-2	

Name	Nat	DoB	Pos	Aps	(s)	Gls
Armando Aruci	ITA	10/07/89	A	14	(1)	13
Gianmarco Baschetti		29/04/91	A	9	(6)	
Francesco Bonfé	ITA	27/05/94	D	4	(5)	
Luca Bonifazi		12/11/82	M	4	(1)	
Emanuele Brici	ITA	16/02/87	D	18		1
Denis Broccoli		10/08/88	G	5		
Vittorio Cesari	ITA	11/01/92	M	15	(1)	
Riccardo Ercolani		17/07/85	A		(1)	
Emanuele Giglietti		06/10/93	M	2	(2)	
Mattia Gualandi		08/04/94	D	10	(2)	
William Innocenti	ITA	30/04/87	A	17	(1)	13
Massimiliano La Monaca		26/04/95	G	15		
Kevin Marigliano	ITA	10/05/93	A	10	(4)	3
Nicola Moroni	FRA	05/05/97	M		(3)	
Luca Nanni		30/01/95	M	15	(2)	1
Matteo Nanni		07/03/93	M	5	(5)	
Daniel Piscaglia		06/12/92	D	11		2
Dalibor Riccardi		04/09/83	D	2	(4)	
Manuel Ricci	ITA	19/05/88	D	14	(3)	
Enea Righetti	ITA	08/10/86	M	11	(1)	3
Stefano Sacco		10/02/91	M	9	(1)	
Luca Tosi	ITA	23/07/94	M	5	(6)	
Massimo Vagnetti		19/07/83	D	6	(1)	1
Marco Zannoni		14/08/82	M	16	(1)	
Evert Zavoli		10/08/69	M	3		

Top goalscorers

(excluding Play-offs)

19	Marco Martini (La Fiorita)
16	Carlo Chiarabini (Domagnano)
15	Daniele Friguglietti (Murata/Tre Penne)
13	Adolfo Hirsch (Folgore)
	Andy Selva (La Fiorita)
	Armando Aruci (Virtus)
	William Innocenti (Virtus)
12	Daniele Ferri (Tre Fiori)
11	Enea Jaupi (Fiorentino)
	Nicola Gai (Tre Penne)
10	Mirko Mantovani (Juvenes/Dogana)

DOMESTIC CUP

Coppa Titano 2015/16

FIRST PHASE

(Played in Groups)

Group A

(15/09/15)
Tre Penne 2-2 Domagnano

(16/09/15)
Faetano 1-5 Murata

(30/09/15)
Domagnano 0-1 Faetano
Murata 1-4 Tre Penne

(21/10/15)
Domagnano 2-1 Murata
Tre Penne 1-1 Faetano

(23/01/16)
Murata 2-0 Faetano

(24/01/16)
Domagnano 2-1 Tre Penne

(30/01/16)
Faetano 0-1 Domagnano

(31/01/16)
Tre Penne 4-3 Murata

(29/03/16)
Faetano 0-0 Tre Penne

(30/03/16)
Murata 4-1 Domagnano

Final standings

Domagnano 10 pts *(qualified)*
Tre Penne 9 pts *(qualified)*
Murata 9 pts
Faetano 5 pts

Group B

(16/09/15)
Cosmos 1-1 Pennarossa
Libertas 1-0 Virtus

(30/09/15)
Pennarossa 1-2 Libertas
Virtus 2-1 Cosmos

(21/10/15)
Libertas 0-2 Cosmos
Virtus 1-4 Pennarossa

(23/01/16)
Pennarossa 0-0 Cosmos

(24/01/16)
Virtus 1-1 Libertas

(30/01/16)
Cosmos 1-6 Virtus

(31/01/16)
Libertas 0-1 Pennarossa

(30/03/16)
Cosmos 0-1 Libertas
Pennarossa 0-0 Virtus

Final standings

Libertas 10 pts *(qualified)*
Pennarossa 9 pts *(qualified)*
Virtus 8 pts
Cosmos 5 pts

Group C

(16/09/15)
Juvenes/Dogana 1-1 Fiorentino
La Fiorita 1-2 Cailungo

(29/09/15)
Fiorentino 1-2 La Fiorita

(30/09/15)
Cailungo 0-4 Juvenes/Dogana

(21/10/15)
Cailungo 0-1 Fiorentino
La Fiorita 2-0 Juvenes/Dogana

(23/01/16)
Cailungo 0-5 La Fiorita

(24/01/16)
Fiorentino 4-0 Juvenes/Dogana

(30/01/16)
Juvenes/Dogana 1-2 Cailungo
La Fiorita 1-0 Fiorentino

(30/03/16)
Fiorentino 2-0 Cailungo
Juvenes/Dogana 2-0 La Fiorita

Final standings

La Fiorita 12 pts *(qualified)*
Fiorentino 10 pts *(qualified)*
Juvenes/Dogana 7 pts
Cailungo 6 pts

Group D

(16/09/15)
Tre Fiori 5-1 San Giovanni

(30/09/15)
San Giovanni 0-2 Folgore

(20/10/15)
Folgore 3-3 Tre Fiori

(24/11/15)
San Giovanni 0-4 Tre Fiori

(23/01/16)
Folgore 4-0 San Giovanni

(31/01/16)
Tre Fiori 1-2 Folgore

(02/03/16)
San Giovanni 1-3 Tre Fiori

(09/03/16)
Folgore 2-4 San Giovanni

(30/03/16)
Tre Fiori 2-3 Folgore

Final standings

Folgore 13 pts *(qualified)*
Tre Fiori 10 pts *(qualified)*
San Giovanni 3 pts

QUARTER-FINALS

(21/04/16)
Domagnano 0-0 Pennarossa
(aet; 3-4 on pens)

Folgore 1-1 Tre Penne *(Hirsch 33; Rispoli 55) (aet; 3-5 on pens)*

La Fiorita 3-1 Tre Fiori *(Selva 42, M Martini 98, T Zafferani 108; Lolli 24p) (aet)*

Libertas 1-1 Fiorentino *(Camillini 54; Pratelli 37) (aet; 5-6 on pens)*

SEMI-FINALS

(26/04/16)
La Fiorita 1-0 Tre Penne
(Gasperoni 84)

Pennarossa 3-1 Fiorentino
(Fariselli 3, Agostinelli 45, N Ciacci 70; Jaupi 25)

FINAL

(01/05/16)
San Marino Stadium, Serravalle
SP LA FIORITA 2 *(Selva 53p, Rinaldi 59)*
SS PENNAROSSA 0
Referee: *Casanova*
LA FIORITA: *Vivan, Gasperoni, A Martini, Bugli, Cangini, Fraternali, T Zafferani (Macerata 76), Pensalfini (Cavalli 87), Selva, Rinaldi, M Martini (Guidi 44)*
PENNAROSSA: *Montanari, Lazzarini, Farabegoli (Capozzi 87), Albani, Cervellini, Del Pivo, Giunchi, Fariselli, Aissaoui (Toccaceli 87), Agostinelli, N Ciacci (Gualtieri 65)*

La Fiorita celebrate a third Coppa Titano triumph in five years

SCOTLAND
Scottish Football Association (SFA)

Address	Hampden Park	**President**	Alan McRae
	GB-Glasgow G42 9AY	**Chief executive**	Stewart Regan
Tel	+44 141 616 6000	**Media officer**	Darryl Broadfoot
Fax	+44 141 616 6001	**Year of formation**	1873
E-mail	info@scottishfa.co.uk	**National stadium**	Hampden Park,
Website	scottishfa.co.uk		Glasgow (52,063)

PREMIERSHIP CLUBS

 1 **Aberdeen FC**

 2 **Celtic FC**

 3 **Dundee FC**

 4 **Dundee United FC**

 5 **Hamilton Academical FC**

 6 **Heart of Midlothian FC**

 7 **Inverness Caledonian Thistle FC**

 8 **Kilmarnock FC**

9 **Motherwell FC**

 10 **Partick Thistle FC**

 11 **Ross County FC**

 12 **Saint Johnstone FC**

PROMOTED CLUB

 13 **Rangers FC**

OTHER CLUB

 14 **Hibernian FC**

KEY

- ● UEFA Champions League
- ● UEFA Europa League
- ● Promoted
- ● Relegated
- ■ Second level club in UEFA Europa League

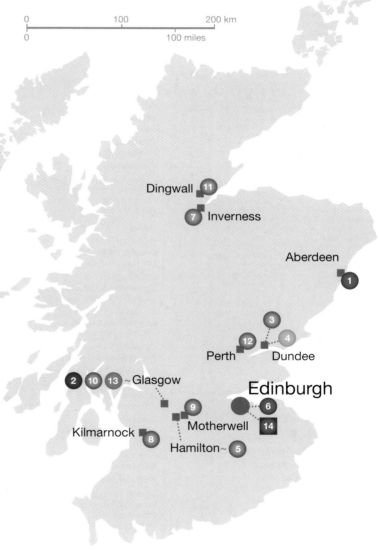

Bare minimum for Celtic

Celtic fulfilled the obligation of winning their 47th Scottish league title, outlasting sole challengers Aberdeen in a repeat of the previous season's contest, but there was no joy elsewhere for Ronny Deila's team as they failed twice over in Europe and lost in the semi-finals of both domestic cup competitions.

Instead, it was Ross County who collected their first major trophy by winning the League Cup, with their defeated final opponents Hibernian going on to win the Scottish Cup in an all second-tier final against Rangers, who won promotion back to the Premiership after a four-year exile.

| **Bhoys breeze to 47th league title** | **Unlikely cup glory for Ross County and Hibs** | **Rangers return from four-year exile** |

Domestic league

With arch-rivals Rangers still absent, Celtic duly won the league for the fifth season running – the club's longest sequence of success since the late 1960s and early '70s. As in 2014/15, they were challenged by Aberdeen for much of the campaign, only for Derek McInnes's team to run out of steam and end up 15 points in arrears. With results elsewhere not going to plan, Deila's second season at Celtic Park turned out to be his last. It was announced in late April that he would be stepping down, and while few Celtic fans shed a tear at his prospective departure, they did share in the Norwegian's celebrations a couple of weeks later when the Bhoys wrapped up the title with a 3-2 victory over Aberdeen at Celtic Park.

The Dons had been responsible for two of Celtic's three league defeats up to that point, winning both fixtures at Pittodrie, the first of them during a brilliant opening surge of eight successive victories. At that stage Celtic were five points back, but any hopes of an upset were effectively dashed by the rotten run of form from Aberdeen that followed – a draw and four defeats, the last of them 2-1 at home to Celtic. McInnes's men did recover well over the winter, reducing the gap back to three points with another 2-1 win against Celtic in early February, but in the final two months their challenge

petered out as defeats suddenly outnumbered victories. Celtic ended up with 93 goals, precisely a third of them scored by runaway golden boot winner Leigh Griffiths. No fewer than 20 other Celtic players chipped in with at least one goal, although none reached double figures.

While Aberdeen were always safe in second despite their late slide, Robbie Neilson's newly-promoted Hearts comfortably claimed third spot and a place in Europe. Dundee United, on the other hand, paid the price for selling off their best players – many of them to Celtic – by finishing bottom and vacating a place for the long-awaited return of Rangers, who, with Englishman Mark Warburton at the controls, were convincing winners of the Championship.

Domestic cups

Most of the season's high drama was provided by the two domestic cup competitions. Ross County stunned Celtic by beating them 3-1 in the League Cup semi-final before going on to lift the trophy – the first in their history – after scoring a 90th-minute winner to beat Hibernian at Hampden Park. Hibs, however, would score a memorable last-gasp goal of their own at the same stadium two months later, through captain David Gray, to claim a

sensational 3-2 win over Rangers – conquerors of Celtic on penalties in the semi-final – and lift the Scottish Cup for the first time in 114 years.

Europe

Once again, Celtic were the only Scottish club to extend their European campaign into the autumn. However, it was not in the competition they entered, a second successive UEFA Champions League play-off defeat – this time against Malmö FF – despatching them into the group stage of the UEFA Europa League, where they not only failed to win a game but also suffered further dismay against Scandinavian opposition, losing twice to Molde.

National team

There was also severe disappointment for the Scottish national team as they failed to seize an inviting opportunity to qualify for UEFA EURO 2016, losing unexpectedly in Georgia, then taking just one point at Hampden against Germany and Poland to end up fourth in their section behind those two teams and the Republic of Ireland. With England, Northern Ireland and Wales also qualifying for France, it was a hammer blow to the pride of Scotland and their manager Gordon Strachan, who, nevertheless, was handed a new two-year contract extension.

DOMESTIC SEASON AT A GLANCE

Premiership 2015/16 final table

		Pld	Home					Away					Total					Pts
			W	D	L	F	A	W	D	L	F	A	W	D	L	F	A	
1	**Celtic FC**	**38**	**14**	**4**	**1**	**55**	**12**	**12**	**4**	**3**	**38**	**19**	**26**	**8**	**4**	**93**	**31**	**86**
2	Aberdeen FC	38	12	4	3	30	19	10	1	8	32	29	22	5	11	62	48	71
3	Heart of Midlothian FC	38	11	5	3	37	22	7	6	6	22	18	18	11	9	59	40	65
4	Saint Johnstone FC	38	8	6	5	27	22	8	2	9	31	33	16	8	14	58	55	56
5	Motherwell FC	38	8	3	8	27	27	7	2	10	20	36	15	5	18	47	63	50
6	Ross County FC	38	9	0	10	29	33	5	6	8	26	28	14	6	18	55	61	48
7	Inverness Caledonian Thistle FC	38	7	5	7	25	20	7	5	7	29	28	14	10	14	54	48	52
8	Dundee FC	38	7	7	5	30	23	4	8	7	23	34	11	15	12	53	57	48
9	Partick Thistle FC	38	6	4	9	21	29	6	6	7	20	21	12	10	16	41	50	46
10	Hamilton Academical FC	38	4	6	9	21	28	7	4	8	21	35	11	10	17	42	63	43
11	Kilmarnock FC	38	4	4	11	19	37	5	5	9	22	27	9	9	20	41	64	36
12	Dundee United FC	38	3	4	12	22	35	5	3	11	23	35	8	7	23	45	70	28

NB League splits into top and bottom halves after 33 games, with each team playing a further five matches exclusively against clubs from its half of the table; Dundee United FC – 3 pts deducted.

European qualification 2016/17

Champion: Celtic FC (second qualifying round)

Cup winner: Hibernian FC (second qualifying round)
Aberdeen FC (first qualifying round)
Heart of Midlothian FC (first qualifying round)

Top scorer	Leigh Griffiths (Celtic), 31 goals
Relegated club	Dundee United FC
Promoted club	Rangers FC
Scottish Cup final	Hibernian FC 3-2 Rangers FC
League Cup final	Ross County FC 2-1 Hibernian FC

Team of the season
(4-3-3)

Manager: McInnes *(Aberdeen)*

Bain *(Dundee)*
Logan *(Aberdeen)* — Alim *(Hearts)* — Davies *(Ross County)* — Tierney *(Celtic)*
Hayes *(Aberdeen)* — McLean *(Aberdeen)* — Shinnie *(Aberdeen)*
Hemmings *(Dundee)* — Griffiths *(Celtic)* — Stewart *(Dundee)*

Player of the season

Leigh Griffiths
(Celtic FC)

The 2015/16 season will not go down as one of the most memorable in Celtic's history, but it was certainly the best in Griffiths' career to date as the 25-year-old striker scored 40 goals in all competitions – the first Celtic player to reach that mark since Henrik Larsson struck 53 in 2000/01 – and collected the golden boot for his 31-goal tally in the Premiership. Having signed a mid-season contract extension until 2021, he will be eager to continue in the same vein for new Celtic boss Brendan Rodgers.

Newcomer of the season

Kieran Tierney
(Celtic FC)

Born on the Isle of Man but brought up in Scotland, Tierney was the revelation of the 2015/16 Premiership season and a winner of both of the country's Young Player of the Year awards. Handed his chance in a UEFA Europa League encounter against Fenerbahçe because of Emilio Izaguirre's suspension, the 18-year-old left-back performed so well that he soon became a regular in Ronny Deila's first XI. He also won his first senior cap for Scotland, making his debut in a March 2016 friendly against Denmark.

NATIONAL TEAM

International tournament appearances
FIFA World Cup (8) 1954, 1958, 1974, 1978, 1982, 1986, 1990, 1998
UEFA European Championship (2) 1992, 1996

Top five all-time caps
Kenny Dalglish (102); Jim Leighton (91); Alex McLeish (77); Paul McStay (76); **Darren Fletcher** (73)

Top five all-time goals
Kenny Dalglish & Denis Law (30); Hughie Gallacher (23); Lawrie Reilly (22), Ally McCoist (19)

Results 2015/16

04/09/15	Georgia (ECQ)	A	Tbilisi	L	0-1	
07/09/15	Germany (ECQ)	H	Glasgow	L	2-3	Hummels (28og), McArthur (43)
08/10/15	Poland (ECQ)	H	Glasgow	D	2-2	Ritchie (45), S Fletcher (62)
11/10/15	Gibraltar (ECQ)	A	Faro (POR)	W	6-0	C Martin (25), Maloney (39), S Fletcher (52, 56, 85), Naismith (90+1)
24/03/16	Czech Republic	A	Prague	W	1-0	Anya (10)
29/03/16	Denmark	H	Glasgow	W	1-0	Ritchie (8)
29/05/16	Italy	N	Ta'Qali (MLT)	L	0-1	
04/06/16	France	A	Metz	L	0-3	

Appearances 2015/16

Coach: Gordon Strachan	09/02/57		GEO	GER	POL	GIB	Cze	Den	Ita	Fra	Caps	Goals
David Marshall	05/03/85	Cardiff (ENG)	G	G	G				G	G	24	-
Alan Hutton	30/11/84	Aston Villa (ENG)	D	D	D	D	D				50	-
Charlie Mulgrew	06/03/86	Celtic	D	D			M	s46	D	s46	24	2
Russell Martin	04/01/86	Norwich (ENG)	D	D	D		D		D	D	25	-
Andrew Robertson	11/03/94	Hull (ENG)	D59			D	D58			D46	10	1
Shaun Maloney	24/01/83	Hull (ENG)	M	M60	s69	M		M69		M46	47	7
Scott Brown	25/06/85	Celtic	M	M81	M	M63		M			50	4
James Morrison	25/05/86	West Brom (ENG)	M	M							41	3
Ikechi Anya	03/01/88	Watford (ENG)	M75	s60			M87	s46	M71	s46	21	3
Steven Naismith	14/09/86	Everton (ENG) /Norwich (ENG)	M59		M69	s76			s71	s58	43	6
Steven Fletcher	26/03/87	Sunderland (ENG) /Marseille (FRA)	A	A	A	A		A46	s46	A58	28	8
Grant Hanley	20/11/91	Blackburn (ENG)	s59	D	D			D	D	D	23	1
James Forrest	07/07/91	Celtic	s59	M81	M84						13	-
Leigh Griffiths	20/08/90	Celtic	s75					A60			7	-
James McArthur	07/10/87	Crystal Palace (ENG)		M	s74				M83	M84	24	2
Chris Martin	04/11/88	Derby (ENG)		s81		A76		s60			8	1
Matt Ritchie	10/09/89	Bournemouth (ENG)		s81	M	M63		M82	M	M	10	3
Steven Whittaker	16/06/84	Norwich (ENG)			D			D			31	-
Darren Fletcher	01/02/84	West Brom (ENG)			M74	s63	M		M	M	73	5
Graham Dorrans	05/05/87	Norwich (ENG)			s84		M				12	-
Allan McGregor	31/01/82	Hull (ENG)				G	G				35	-
Christophe Berra	31/01/85	Ipswich (ENG)				D	D		s46		33	3
Gordon Greer	14/12/80	Brighton (ENG)				D		D		D	11	-
Johnny Russell	08/04/90	Derby (ENG)				s63					4	-
Robert Snodgrass	07/09/87	Hull (ENG)					M			M66	17	3
Kenny McLean	08/01/92	Aberdeen					M58				1	-
Ross McCormack	18/08/86	Fulham (ENG)					A78		A46		13	2
Barry Bannan	01/12/89	Sheffield Wednesday (ENG)					s58				21	-
Matt Philipps	13/03/91	QPR (ENG)					s58		M71		4	-
Tony Watt	29/12/93	Blackburn (ENG)					s78				1	-
Paul Caddis	19/04/88	Birmingham (ENG)					s87				1	-
Craig Gordon	31/12/82	Celtic						G			44	-
Kieran Tierney	05/06/97	Celtic						D46			1	-
John McGinn	18/10/94	Hibernian						M			1	-
Liam Bridcutt	08/05/89	Leeds (ENG)						s69			2	-
Oliver Burke	07/04/97	Nottingham Forest (ENG)						s82	s71		2	-
Callum Paterson	13/10/94	Hearts							D46		1	-
Craig Bryson	06/11/86	Derby (ENG)							s83		3	-
Stephen Kingsley	23/07/94	Swansea (ENG)								s66	1	-
Barry McKay	30/12/94	Rangers								s84	1	-

EUROPE

Celtic FC

CHAMPIONS LEAGUE

Second qualifying round - Stjarnan (ISL)
H 2-0 *Boyata (44), Johansen (56)*
Gordon, Izaguirre, Biton, Nadir Çiftçi (Stokes 74), Brown, Armstrong, Boyata (Ambrose 82), Mulgrew, Lustig, Johansen, Forrest (Griffiths 58). Coach: Ronny Deila (NOR)
A 4-1 *Biton (33), Mulgrew (49), Griffiths (88), Johansen (90+3)*
Gordon, Van Dijk, Biton, Nadir Çiftçi (Rogic 82), Brown, Armstrong (Griffiths 62), Mackay-Steven, Boyata, Mulgrew, Lustig (Ambrose 52), Johansen. Coach: Ronny Deila (NOR)

Third qualifying round - Qarabağ FK (AZE)
H 1-0 *Boyata (82)*
Gordon, Izaguirre, Van Dijk, Biton (Griffiths 69), Nadir Çiftçi (Commons 80), Brown, Armstrong (Forrest 62), Mackay-Steven, Boyata, Lustig, Johansen. Coach: Ronny Deila (NOR)
A 0-0
Gordon, Izaguirre, Van Dijk, Biton, Nadir Çiftçi (Griffiths 67), Brown, Armstrong (Forrest 84), Mackay-Steven (Commons 79), Boyata, Lustig, Johansen. Coach: Ronny Deila (NOR)

Play-offs - Malmö FF (SWE)
H 3-2 *Griffiths (3, 61), Biton (10)*
Gordon, Izaguirre, Van Dijk, Biton, Brown, Griffiths (Nadir Çiftçi 74), Armstrong (Mackay-Steven 63), Boyata, Lustig (Ambrose 80), Johansen, Forrest. Coach: Ronny Deila (NOR)
A 0-2
Gordon, Van Dijk, Biton (Nadir Çiftçi 72), Brown, Griffiths, Armstrong (Commons 46), Boyata, Mulgrew, Janko, Johansen, Forrest (Mackay-Steven 79). Coach: Ronny Deila (NOR)

EUROPA LEAGUE

Group A
Match 1 - AFC Ajax (NED)
A 2-2 *Biton (8), Lustig (42)*
Gordon, Izaguirre, Šimunović, Biton, Brown, Griffiths, Commons (Janko 83), Boyata, Lustig (Ambrose 69), Johansen, Forrest (Blackett 75). Coach: Ronny Deila (NOR)
Red card: Izaguirre 74
Match 2 - Fenerbahçe SK (TUR)
H 2-2 *Griffiths (28), Commons (32)*
Gordon, Ambrose, Biton, Brown, Griffiths, Commons, Boyata, Lustig, Johansen (Rogic 82), Forrest (Armstrong 90), Tierney (Blackett 82). Coach: Ronny Deila (NOR)
Match 3 - Molde FK (NOR)
A 1-3 *Commons (55)*
Gordon, Izaguirre, Ambrose, Biton, Brown, Griffiths, Armstrong (Mackay-Steven 74), Commons (Nadir Çiftçi 76), Boyata, Lustig, Johansen. Coach: Ronny Deila (NOR)
Match 4 - Molde FK (NOR)
H 1-2 *Commons (26)*
Gordon, Šimunović (Blackett 9; Nadir Çiftçi 69), Biton, Griffiths, Armstrong, Commons (Forrest 46), Rogic, Boyata, Lustig, Johansen, Tierney. Coach: Ronny Deila (NOR)
Red card: Biton 77

Match 5 - AFC Ajax (NED)
H 1-2 *McGregor (4)*
Gordon, Šimunović, Griffiths, Armstrong, Mackay-Steven (Allan 72), Rogic (Mulgrew 66), Boyata, Lustig, McGregor, Forrest, Tierney (Izaguirre 78). Coach: Ronny Deila (NOR)
Match 6 - Fenerbahçe SK (TUR)
A 1-1 *Commons (75)*
Gordon, Šimunović, Biton, Nadir Çiftçi, Armstrong (Forrest 63), Allan (Commons 74), Boyata, Lustig, Johansen (Rogic 74), McGregor, Tierney. Coach: Ronny Deila (NOR)

Inverness Caledonian Thistle FC

EUROPA LEAGUE

Second qualifying round - FC Astra Giurgiu (ROU)
H 0-1
O Williams, Warren, Meekings (Raven 80), Dani López (Foran 84), Draper (Roberts 81), Doran, Devine, Wedderburn, Tansey, D Williams, Christie. Coach: John Hughes (SCO)
A 0-0
O Williams, Raven, Warren, Meekings, Dani López, Doran, Devine, Wedderburn (Draper 79), Tansey, D Williams (Foran 78), Christie. Coach: John Hughes (SCO)

Aberdeen FC

EUROPA LEAGUE

First qualifying round - KF Shkëndija (MKD)
A 1-1 *McGinn (79)*
Ward, Logan, Shinnie, Considine, Taylor, Reynolds (Quinn 69), Flood (Pawlett 65), Rooney (Goodwillie 65), McGinn, Hayes, Jack. Coach: Derek McInnes (SCO)
H 0-0
Ward, Logan, Shinnie, Considine, Taylor, McLean (Pawlett 68), Flood (Robson 80), Rooney, McGinn, Hayes (Goodwillie 79), Jack. Coach: Derek McInnes (SCO)

Second qualifying round - HNK Rijeka (CRO)
A 3-0 *Considine (38), Pawlett (52), McLean (75)*
Ward, Logan, Shinnie, Considine, Taylor, McGinn (McLean 69), Hayes, Pawlett (Flood 63), Goodwillie (Rooney 83), Quinn, Jack. Coach: Derek McInnes (SCO)
H 2-2 *McGinn (64), Hayes (72)*
Ward, Logan, Shinnie, Considine, Taylor, McLean (Pawlett 73), McGinn (Flood 83), Hayes, Goodwillie (Rooney 75), Quinn, Jack. Coach: Derek McInnes (SCO)

Third qualifying round - FC Kairat Almaty (KAZ)
A 1-2 *McLean (69)*
Ward, Logan, Shinnie, Considine, Taylor, McGinn, Hayes, Pawlett (Rooney 46), Goodwillie (McLean 64), Quinn (Robson 85), Jack. Coach: Derek McInnes (SCO)
H 1-1 *McLean (84)*
Ward, Logan, Shinnie, Considine, Taylor, McLean, McGinn, Hayes (Flood 81), Pawlett (Rooney 68), Goodwillie (Quinn 81), Jack. Coach: Derek McInnes (SCO)

Saint Johnstone FC

EUROPA LEAGUE

First qualifying round - Alashkert FC (ARM)
A 0-1
Mannus, Scobbie, Lappin, Davidson (Brown 44), MacLean, Wotherspoon, Sutton (Kane 60), Shaughnessy, McKay, Easton, O'Halloran. Coach: Tommy Wright (NIR)
H 2-1 *O'Halloran (34), McKay (87)*
Mannus, Scobbie, Wright (McKay 65), Anderson (Caddis 71), MacLean, Sutton (Cummins 80), Shaughnessy, Brown, Easton, Kane, O'Halloran. Coach: Tommy Wright (NIR)

DOMESTIC LEAGUE CLUB-BY-CLUB

Aberdeen FC

1903 • Pittodrie (20,897) • afc.co.uk

Major honours
*UEFA Cup Winners' Cup (1) 1983; UEFA Super Cup
(1) 1983; Scottish League (4) 1955, 1980, 1984,
1985; Scottish Cup (7) 1947, 1970, 1982, 1983,
1984, 1986, 1990; Scottish League Cup (6) 1956,
1977, 1986, 1990, 1996, 2014*

Manager: Derek McInnes

2015

02/08	a	Dundee United	W 1-0	McLean
09/08	h	Kilmarnock	W 2-0	Shinnie, Rooney (p)
15/08	a	Motherwell	W 2-1	McGinn, Taylor
22/08	h	Dundee	W 2-0	Rooney 2 (1p)
29/08	a	Partick	W 2-0	Rooney, McLean
12/09	h	Celtic	W 2-1	Rooney (p), Quinn
15/09	h	Hamilton	W 1-0	Rooney (p)
20/09	a	Hearts	W 3-1	Goodwillie 2, McGinn
26/09	a	Inverness	L 1-2	Taylor
03/10	h	St Johnstone	L 1-5	Taylor
17/10	a	Ross County	L 0-2	
24/10	h	Motherwell	D 1-1	Rooney
31/10	a	Celtic	L 1-3	Rooney
07/11	h	Dundee United	W 2-0	Rooney, Hayes
21/11	a	Hamilton	D 1-1	McLean
28/11	h	Ross County	W 3-1	Rooney, Hayes, McGinn
05/12	a	Dundee	W 2-0	McGinn, Rooney
12/12	h	Hearts	W 1-0	Rooney (p)
19/12	a	Kilmarnock	W 4-0	McGinn, Rooney, Hayes, Logan
26/12	h	Inverness	D 2-2	McGinn, Rooney (p)
30/12	h	Partick	D 0-0	

2016

17/01	a	Ross County	W 3-2	Rooney (p), Logan 2
22/01	h	Dundee	W 1-0	Rooney
03/02	h	Celtic	W 2-1	Hayes, Church
06/02	a	St Johnstone	W 4-3	Rooney 2, Pawlett, McGinn
15/02	a	Inverness	W 2-1	Rooney
27/02	h	St Johnstone	D 1-1	Church
02/03	a	Dundee United	W 1-0	Church
08/03	h	Partick	W 2-1	Considine, Church
12/03	h	Kilmarnock	W 2-1	Taylor, Logan
19/03	a	Motherwell	L 1-2	McLean
03/04	h	Hamilton	W 3-0	Church, McGinn, McLean
08/04	a	Hearts	L 1-2	Church
22/04	a	St Johnstone	L 0-3	
30/04	h	Motherwell	W 4-1	McLean (p), McGinn, Rooney, Hayes
08/05	a	Celtic	L 2-3	McGinn, Considine
12/05	h	Hearts	L 0-1	
15/05	h	Ross County	L 0-4	

No	Name	Nat	DoB	Pos	Aps	(s)	Gls
20	Scott Brown	ENG	26/04/85	G	13		
17	Simon Church	WAL	10/12/88	A	13		6
19	Adam Collin	ENG	09/12/84	G	3		
4	Andrew Considine		01/04/87	D	26	(6)	2
8	Willo Flood	IRL	10/04/85	M	18	(4)	
17	David Goodwillie		28/03/89	A	7	(10)	2
29	Daniel Harvie		14/07/98	D		(2)	
11	Jonny Hayes	IRL	09/07/87	M	35		5
7	Ryan Jack		27/02/92	M	26	(2)	
30	Aaron Lennox	AUS	19/02/93	G	1		
2	Shay Logan	ENG	29/01/88	D	35	(2)	4
10	Niall McGinn	NIR	20/07/87	M	33	(3)	10
26	Scott McKenna		12/11/96	D	2	(1)	
21	Ryan McLaughlin	NIR	30/09/94	D	1	(3)	
7	Kenny McLean		08/01/92	M	38		6
37	Connor McLennan		05/10/99	A		(1)	
41	Joe Nuttall	ENG	27/01/97	A		(2)	
32	Josh Parker	ATG	01/12/90	A	1	(6)	
16	Peter Pawlett		18/06/91	M	9	(9)	1
18	Paul Quinn		21/07/85	D	9	(4)	1
6	Mark Reynolds		07/05/87	D	19	(3)	
15	Barry Robson		07/11/78	M	3	(9)	
9	Adam Rooney	IRL	21/04/88	A	22	(5)	20
24	Michael Rose		11/10/95	D	1		
31	Frank Ross		18/02/98	M		(2)	
3	Graeme Shinnie		04/08/91	D	37		1
14	Cameron Smith		24/08/95	A	2	(12)	
23	Craig Storie		13/01/96	M	6	(4)	
5	Ash Taylor	WAL	02/09/90	D	36	(1)	4
19	Danny Ward	WAL	22/06/93	G	21		
27	Scott Wright		08/08/97	A	1	(3)	

Celtic FC

1888 • Celtic Park (60,355) • celticfc.net

Major honours
*European Champion Clubs' Cup (1) 1967;
Scottish League (47) 1893, 1894, 1896, 1898, 1905, 1906, 1907, 1908, 1909, 1910, 1914, 1915, 1916, 1917,
1919, 1922, 1926, 1936, 1938, 1954, 1966, 1967, 1968, 1969, 1970, 1971, 1972, 1973, 1974, 1977, 1979, 1981,
1982, 1986, 1988, 1998, 2001, 2002, 2004, 2006, 2007, 2008, 2012, 2013, 2014, 2015, 2016;
Scottish Cup (36) 1892, 1899, 1900, 1904, 1907, 1908, 1911, 1912, 1914, 1923, 1925, 1927, 1931, 1933, 1937,
1951, 1954, 1965, 1967, 1969, 1971, 1972, 1974, 1975, 1977, 1980, 1985, 1988, 1989, 1995, 2001, 2004, 2005,
2007, 2011, 2013;
Scottish League Cup (15) 1957, 1958, 1966, 1967, 1968, 1969, 1970, 1975, 1983, 1998, 2000, 2001, 2006,
2009, 2015*

Manager: Ronny Deila (NOR)

2015

01/08	h	Ross County	W 2-0	Griffiths (p), Johansen
09/08	a	Partick	W 2-0	Rogic, Commons
12/08	a	Kilmarnock	D 2-2	Griffiths, Biton
15/08	h	Inverness	W 4-2	Lustig, Griffiths, Armstrong 2
22/08	a	Dundee United	W 3-1	Griffiths, og (Durnan), McGregor
29/08	h	St Johnstone	W 3-1	Griffiths, Rogic, Mulgrew
12/09	a	Aberdeen	L 1-2	Griffiths (p)
20/09	h	Dundee	W 6-0	Rogic, Griffiths, Izaguirre 2, Brown, Nadir
26/09	h	Hearts	D 0-0	
04/10	a	Hamilton	W 2-1	Boyata, Griffiths
17/10	a	Motherwell	W 1-0	Nadir
25/10	h	Dundee United	W 5-0	Griffiths, Boyata, Commons 2 (1p), og (Kuhl)
31/10	h	Aberdeen	W 3-1	Griffiths 2 (1p), Forrest
08/11	a	Ross County	W 4-1	Rogic, Griffiths 2, Biton
21/11	h	Kilmarnock	D 0-0	
29/11	a	Inverness	W 3-1	McGregor, Griffiths, og (Devine)
13/12	a	St Johnstone	W 3-0	Nadir 2, Boyata
19/12	h	Motherwell	L 1-2	Biton
27/12	a	Hearts	D 2-2	Biton, Rogic

2016

02/01	h	Partick	W 1-0	Griffiths
15/01	a	Dundee United	W 4-1	Griffiths 2, Šimunović, Commons
19/01	h	Hamilton	W 8-1	Lustig, Biton, Rogic, Griffiths 3, Forrest, McGregor
23/01	h	St Johnstone	W 3-1	Mackay-Steven 2, Armstrong
03/02	a	Aberdeen	L 1-2	Griffiths
13/02	h	Ross County	W 2-0	Griffiths, Boyata
20/02	h	Inverness	W 3-0	Mackay-Steven, Griffiths 2
26/02	a	Hamilton	D 1-1	Griffiths (p)
02/03	h	Dundee	D 0-0	
12/03	a	Partick	W 2-1	Griffiths, McGregor
19/03	a	Kilmarnock	W 1-0	Rogic
02/04	h	Hearts	W 3-1	Mackay-Steven, Roberts 2
05/04	a	Dundee	D 0-0	
09/04	a	Motherwell	W 2-1	Griffiths 2
24/04	h	Ross County	D 1-1	Griffiths
30/04	a	Hearts	W 3-1	Kazim-Richards, Roberts, Griffiths
08/05	h	Aberdeen	W 3-2	Roberts 2, Lustig
11/05	a	St Johnstone	L 1-2	Griffiths
15/05	h	Motherwell	W 7-0	Tierney, Rogic, Lustig, Armstrong, Roberts, Christie, Aitchison

No	Name	Nat	DoB	Pos	Aps	(s)	Gls
99	Jack Aitchison		05/03/00	A		(1)	1
19	Scott Allan		28/11/91	M	2	(11)	
4	Efe Ambrose	NGA	18/10/88	D	15	(6)	
14	Stuart Armstrong		30/03/92	M	19	(6)	4
26	Logan Bailly	BEL	27/12/85	G	3		
6	Nir Biton	ISR	30/10/91	M	28	(2)	5
2	Tyler Blackett	ENG	02/04/94	D	3		
20	Dedryck Boyata	BEL	28/11/90	D	25	(1)	4
8	Scott Brown		25/06/85	M	22		1
17	Ryan Christie		28/04/95	M	2	(3)	1
24	Carlton Cole	ENG	12/11/83	A		(4)	
15	Kris Commons		30/08/83	M	16	(5)	4
49	James Forrest		07/07/91	M	10	(9)	2
1	Craig Gordon		31/12/82	G	35		
9	Leigh Griffiths		20/08/90	A	32	(2)	31
53	Liam Henderson		25/04/96	M		(1)	
3	Emilio Izaguirre	HON	10/05/86	D	14	(3)	2
22	Saidy Janko	SUI	22/10/95	D	6	(4)	
25	Stefan Johansen	NOR	08/01/91	M	22	(1)	1
13	Colin Kazim-Richards	TUR	26/08/86	A	4	(7)	1
23	Mikael Lustig	SWE	13/12/86	D	29	(1)	4
16	Gary Mackay-Steven		31/08/90	M	15	(10)	4
42	Callum McGregor		14/06/93	M	15	(12)	4
21	Charlie Mulgrew		06/03/86	D	8	(5)	1
7	Nadir Çiftçi	TUR	12/02/92	A	5	(6)	4
34	Eoghan O'Connell	IRL	13/08/95	D	1		
51	Anthony Ralston		16/11/98	M		(1)	
27	Patrick Roberts	ENG	05/02/97	M	9	(2)	6
10	Tom Rogic	AUS	16/12/92	M	24	(6)	8
12	Stefan Šćepović	SRB	10/01/90	A		(1)	
5	Jozo Šimunović	CRO	04/08/94	D	11		1
10	Anthony Stokes	IRL	25/07/88	A	1		
28	Erik Sviatchenko	DEN	04/10/91	D	14		
52	Joe Thomson		14/01/97	M		(1)	
63	Kieran Tierney		05/06/97	D	23		1
5	Virgil van Dijk	NED	08/07/91	D	5		

SCOTLAND

Dundee FC

1893 • Dens Park (11,506) • dundeefc.co.uk

Major honours
Scottish League (1) 1962; Scottish Cup (1) 1910; Scottish League Cup (3) 1952, 1953, 1974

Manager: Paul Hartley

2015

01/08	a	Kilmarnock	W	4-0	*Stewart 2, Loy 2*
08/08	h	Hearts	L	1-2	*Hemmings*
11/08	a	Dundee United	D	2-2	*Stewart, McPake*
15/08	h	St Johnstone	W	2-1	*McPake, Hemmings*
22/08	a	Aberdeen	L	0-2	
29/08	h	Inverness	D	1-1	*Hemmings*
12/09	a	Partick	W	1-0	*Stewart*
20/09	a	Celtic	L	0-6	
26/09	h	Ross County	D	3-3	*Stewart, Loy 2 (1p)*
03/10	h	Motherwell	W	2-1	*Loy, Holt*
17/10	a	Hamilton	D	1-1	*Holt*
24/10	h	Kilmarnock	L	1-2	*Healey*
31/10	a	Inverness	D	1-1	*Loy (p)*
07/11	h	Partick	D	1-1	*Hemmings*
21/11	a	Hearts	D	1-1	*Loy*
27/11	a	St Johnstone	D	1-1	*Hemmings*
05/12	h	Aberdeen	L	0-2	
12/12	a	Motherwell	L	1-3	*Harkins*
19/12	h	Hamilton	W	4-0	*Hemmings 3, Stewart*
26/12	a	Ross County	L	2-5	*Hemmings 2*

2016

02/01	h	Dundee United	W	2-1	*Hemmings, Ross*
16/01	a	Partick	W	4-2	*Hemmings (p), Harkins 2, Stewart*
22/01	a	Aberdeen	L	0-1	
30/01	h	Motherwell	D	2-2	*McGowan, Hemmings (p)*
12/02	h	St Johnstone	W	2-0	*Hemmings 2*
20/02	a	Kilmarnock	D	0-0	
27/02	h	Inverness	D	1-1	*Hemmings*
02/03	a	Celtic	D	0-0	
12/03	h	Hearts	L	0-1	
20/03	a	Dundee United	D	2-2	*Hemmings 2*
02/04	h	Ross County	W	5-2	*Stewart 2, Hemmings, Loy, Wighton*
05/04	h	Celtic	D	0-0	
09/04	a	Hamilton	L	1-2	*Harkins*
23/04	a	Partick	W	2-1	*Hemmings 2*
02/05	h	Dundee United	W	2-1	*Gadzhalov, Wighton*
07/05	h	Hamilton	L	0-1	
11/05	h	Kilmarnock	D	1-1	*Loy*
14/05	a	Inverness	L	0-4	

No	Name	Nat	DoB	Pos	Aps	(s)	Gls
22	Arturo Rodríguez	ESP	30/04/89	A		(3)	
1	Scott Bain		22/11/91	G	37		
24	Andrew Black		20/09/95	D		(1)	
20	Riccardo Calder	ENG	26/01/96	M	3	(8)	
28	Dylan Carreiro	CAN	20/01/95	M		(2)	
35	Calvin Colquhoun		25/07/96	M	2	(1)	
27	Jesse Curran	AUS	16/07/96	M		(3)	
16	Julen Extabeguren	ESP	07/03/91	D	20	(3)	
11	Simon Ferry		11/01/88	M		(1)	
26	Kostadin Gadzhalov	BUL	20/07/89	D	8	(6)	1
29	Gary Harkins		02/01/85	M	22	(8)	4
23	Rhys Healey	ENG	06/12/94	A	4	(3)	1
15	Kane Hemmings	ENG	08/04/91	A	34	(3)	21
3	Kevin Holt		25/01/93	D	34		2
2	Gary Irvine		17/03/85	D	6	(1)	
30	Cammy Kerr		10/09/95	D	7	(3)	
4	Thomas Konrad	GER	05/11/89	D	20	(7)	
8	Nicky Low		06/01/92	M	15	(6)	
9	Rory Loy		19/03/88	A	21	(8)	9
19	Paul McGinn		22/10/90	D	33	(1)	
18	Paul McGowan		07/10/87	M	27	(3)	1
5	James McPake	NIR	24/06/84	D	16		2
6	Daryll Meggatt		20/10/90	D	2	(4)	
12	David Mitchell		04/04/90	G	1	(1)	
21	Darren O'Dea	IRL	04/02/87	D	16		
17	Nick Ross		11/11/91	M	36	(1)	1
7	Greg Stewart		17/03/90	A	36	(1)	9
21	Luka Tankulic	GER	21/06/91	A		(1)	
10	Kevin Thomson		14/10/84	M	11	(1)	
33	Craig Wighton		27/07/97	A	7	(6)	2

Dundee United FC

1909 • Tannadice (14,229) • dufc.co

Major honours
Scottish League (1) 1983; Scottish Cup (2) 1994, 2010; Scottish League Cup (2) 1980, 1981

Manager: Jackie McNamara; (26/09/15) (Dave Bowman); (14/10/15) Mixu Paatelainen (FIN); (04/05/16) (Gordon Young)

2015

02/08	h	Aberdeen	L	0-1	
08/08	a	Motherwell	W	2-0	*og (Laing), Murray*
11/08	h	Dundee	D	2-2	*Spittal 2*
15/08	a	Hamilton	L	0-4	
22/08	h	Celtic	L	1-3	*Erskine (p)*
29/08	a	Ross County	L	1-2	*Dillon*
12/09	h	Kilmarnock	L	1-2	*McKay (p)*
19/09	h	Inverness	D	1-1	*McKay*
26/09	a	St Johnstone	L	1-2	*McKay (p)*
03/10	a	Partick	L	0-3	
18/10	h	Hearts	L	0-1	
25/10	a	Celtic	L	0-5	
31/10	h	Ross County	W	1-0	*McKay (p)*
07/11	a	Aberdeen	L	0-2	
21/11	h	St Johnstone	L	1-2	*McKay*
28/11	h	Hamilton	L	1-2	*McKay*
05/12	a	Kilmarnock	D	1-1	*McKay (p)*
12/12	h	Partick	L	0-1	
19/12	a	Inverness	D	2-2	*Rankin, McKay*
30/12	a	Hearts	L	2-3	*McKay (p), Fraser*

2016

02/01	a	Dundee	L	1-2	*Spittal*
15/01	h	Celtic	L	1-4	*Murray*
23/01	h	Kilmarnock	W	5-1	*Spittal 2, Durnan, Rankin, Dillon*
13/02	a	Hamilton	D	0-0	
16/02	h	Motherwell	L	0-3	
20/02	h	Hearts	W	2-1	*Demel, Paton*
27/02	a	Ross County	W	3-0	*Paton, McKay, Dow*
02/03	h	Aberdeen	L	0-1	
11/03	a	Motherwell	L	1-2	*Anier*
20/03	h	Dundee	D	2-2	*McKay 2 (1p)*
02/04	a	St Johnstone	W	1-0	*Dow*
05/04	a	Partick	L	0-1	
09/04	h	Inverness	L	0-2	
24/04	h	Hamilton	L	1-3	*Murray*
02/05	a	Dundee	L	1-2	*Ofere*
06/05	a	Inverness	W	3-2	*Murray, og (Meekings), Ofere*
10/05	h	Partick	D	3-3	*og (Frans), Ofere, Johnson*
14/05	a	Kilmarnock	W	4-2	*Durnan, Murray 2, H Souttar*

No	Name	Nat	DoB	Pos	Aps	(s)	Gls
26	Henri Anier	EST	17/12/90	A	5	(2)	1
36	Cammy Ballantyne		13/04/97	D		(2)	
19	Mario Bilate	NED	16/07/91	A	1	(1)	
30	Darko Bodul	CRO	11/01/89	A	7	(4)	
18	Aidan Connolly		15/08/95	A	1	(1)	
27	Ali Coote		11/06/98	M		(1)	
55	Guy Demel	CIV	13/06/81	D	12		1
2	Seán Dillon	IRL	30/07/83	D	22	(4)	2
3	Paul Dixon		22/11/86	D	27	(1)	
28	Coll Donaldson		09/04/95	D	15	(3)	
14	Ryan Dow		07/06/91	A	12	(6)	2
17	Mark Durnan		28/11/92	D	26	(2)	2
11	Chris Erskine		08/02/87	M	8	(7)	1
22	Scott Fraser		30/03/95	M	23	(9)	1
19	Gavin Gunning	IRL	26/01/91	D	19		
33	Justin Johnson	NED	27/08/96	A	1	(2)	1
1	Eiji Kawashima	JPN	20/03/83	G	16		
12	Kyle Knoyle	ENG	24/09/96	D	8	(1)	
25	Aaron Kuhl	ENG	30/01/96	M	5		
12	Ryan McGowan	AUS	15/08/89	D	22		
7	Billy McKay	NIR	22/10/88	A	28	(1)	12
5	Callum Morris	IRL	03/02/90	D	13		
10	Robbie Muirhead		08/03/89	A	1	(2)	
15	Simon Murray		15/03/92	A	9	(13)	6
9	Edward Ofere	NGA	13/02/95	A	6	(7)	3
6	Paul Paton	NIR	18/04/87	M	13	(1)	2
8	John Rankin		27/06/83	M	34	(1)	2
25	Riku Riski	FIN	16/08/89	M	1	(2)	
54	Florent Sinama-Pongolle	FRA	20/10/84	A	4		
35	Brad Smith		23/04/97	M		(2)	
43	Matty Smith		13/03/97	A	2		
7	Rodney Sneijder	NED	31/03/91	M		(1)	
38	Harry Souttar		22/10/98	D	1	(1)	1
4	John Souttar		25/09/96	D	17	(3)	
24	Euan Spark		29/11/96	D	1		
20	Blair Spittal		19/12/95	M	27	(6)	5
21	Michał Szromnik	POL	04/03/93	G	9		
29	Adam Taggart	AUS	02/06/93	A	4	(3)	
16	Charlie Telfer		04/07/95	M	5	(2)	
51	Luis Zwick	GER	24/05/94	G	13		

Hamilton Academical FC

1874 • New Douglas Park (6,078) • hamiltonacciesfc.co.uk

Manager: Martin Canning

2015

01/08	h	Partick	D	0-0	
08/08	a	Ross County	L	0-2	
15/08	h	Dundee United	W	4-0	*Crawford, Lucas, Morris, Nadé*
22/08	a	Inverness	W	2-0	*Morris, Longridge*
29/08	h	Hearts	W	3-2	*Kurtaj, Crawford, García Tena*
12/09	a	St Johnstone	L	1-4	*Lucas*
15/09	a	Aberdeen	L	0-1	
19/09	h	Motherwell	W	1-0	*Imrie*
26/09	a	Kilmarnock	W	2-1	*Imrie, Crawford*
04/10	h	Celtic	L	1-2	*Kurtaj*
17/10	h	Dundee	D	1-1	*Imrie*
24/10	a	Partick	D	1-1	*Imrie*
31/10	h	St Johnstone	L	2-4	*García Tena 2 (1p)*
07/11	a	Hearts	L	0-2	
22/11	h	Aberdeen	D	1-1	*Imrie*
28/11	a	Dundee United	W	2-1	*og (Gunning), Gordon*
12/12	h	Ross County	L	1-3	*Kurtaj*
19/12	a	Dundee	L	0-4	
26/12	h	Kilmarnock	L	0-1	
30/12	h	Inverness	L	3-4	*Morris, Gordon, Nadé*

2016

02/01	a	Motherwell	D	3-3	*Lucas, MacKinnon, Crawford (p)*
16/01	a	St Johnstone	D	0-0	
19/01	a	Celtic	L	1-8	*Brophy*
24/01	h	Hearts	D	0-0	
30/01	a	Kilmarnock	W	1-0	*Morris*
13/02	h	Dundee United	D	0-0	
20/02	a	Ross County	L	1-2	*Imrie*
26/02	h	Celtic	D	1-1	*Brophy*
05/03	h	Motherwell	L	0-1	
12/03	a	Inverness	W	1-0	*Morris*
19/03	h	Partick	L	1-2	*Docherty*
03/04	a	Aberdeen	L	0-3	
09/04	h	Dundee	W	2-1	*Crawford, García Tena (p)*
24/04	a	Dundee United	W	3-1	*Gillespie, Morris 2*
30/04	h	Kilmarnock	L	0-4	
07/05	a	Dundee	W	1-0	*Morris*
11/05	h	Inverness	L	0-1	
14/05	a	Partick	D	2-2	*Brophy 2 (1p)*

No	Name	Nat	DoB	Pos	Aps	(s)	Gls
15	Kemy Agustien	CUW	20/08/86	M	1	(1)	
9	Alexandre D'Acol	BRA	18/07/86	A	3	(12)	
30	Steven Boyd		12/04/97	A	2	(3)	
20	Eamonn Brophy		10/03/96	A	7	(7)	4
5	Martin Canning		03/12/81	D	1	(2)	
11	Ali Crawford		03/07/91	M	32	(1)	5
35	Ross Cunningham		23/05/98	M		(1)	
4	Michael Devlin		03/10/93	D	16		
8	Oumar Diaby	FRA	07/02/90	A	1	(5)	
21	Greg Docherty		10/09/96	M	16	(18)	1
24	Jesús García Tena	ESP	07/06/90	D	20	(3)	4
6	Grant Gillespie		02/07/91	M	28	(2)	1
2	Ziggy Gordon		23/04/93	D	38		2
33	Ronan Hughes		15/12/98	M		(2)	
7	Dougie Imrie		03/08/83	M	34	(1)	6
3	Antons Kurakins	LVA	01/01/90	D	35		
12	Gramoz Kurtaj	GER	30/04/91	M	28	(6)	3
17	Louis Longridge		05/07/91	A	6	(9)	1
44	Lucas	BRA	05/11/90	D	34		3
22	Darren Lyon		08/06/95	M	9	(3)	
18	Darian MacKinnon		09/10/85	M	30	(1)	1
26	Alan Martin		01/01/89	G	1		
1	Michael McGovern	NIR	12/07/84	G	37		
14	Carlton Morris	ENG	16/12/95	A	27	(5)	8
27	Christian Nadé	FRA	18/09/84	A	4	(13)	2
10	Daniel Redmond	ENG	03/02/91	M	1	(10)	
15	Jamie Sendles-White	NIR	10/04/94	D	4	(3)	
8	Chris Turner	NIR	03/01/87	M	3	(1)	
16	Craig Watson		13/02/95	M		(1)	

Heart of Midlothian FC

1874 • Tynecastle (17,529) • heartsfc.co.uk
Major honours
*Scottish League (4) 1895, 1897, 1958, 1960;
Scottish Cup (8) 1891, 1896, 1901, 1906, 1956,
1998, 2006, 2012; Scottish League Cup (4) 1955,
1959, 1960, 1963*
Manager: Robbie Neilson

2015

02/08	h	St Johnstone	W	4-3	Juanma, Walker, Paterson, Nicholson
08/08	a	Dundee	W	2-1	Juanma 2 (1p)
12/08	h	Motherwell	W	2-0	Reilly (p), King
15/08	a	Ross County	W	2-1	Sow, Alim
22/08	h	Partick	W	3-0	Sow, Nicholson, Juanma
29/08	a	Hamilton	L	2-3	King, Paterson
11/09	a	Inverness	L	0-2	
20/09	h	Aberdeen	L	1-3	Igor Rossi
26/09	a	Celtic	D	0-0	
03/10	a	Kilmarnock	D	1-1	Walker (p)
18/10	a	Dundee United	W	1-0	Juanma (p)
24/10	h	Ross County	D	2-2	Paterson, Sow
31/10	a	Partick	W	4-0	Juanma 2 (1p), Sow 2 (1p)
07/11	h	Hamilton	W	2-0	Buaben, Sutchuin Djoum
21/11	a	Dundee	D	1-1	Sutchuin Djoum
28/11	h	Motherwell	D	2-2	Juanma, Sow
12/12	a	Aberdeen	L	0-1	
19/12	a	St Johnstone	D	0-0	
27/12	h	Celtic	D	2-2	Nicholson, Sow
30/12	h	Dundee United	W	3-2	Reilly, Buaben, Sow (p)

2016

02/01	a	Kilmarnock	D	2-2	Reilly, Paterson
16/01	h	Motherwell	W	6-0	Igor Rossi, Sow, Reilly (p), Paterson, Juanma, Sutchuin Djoum
24/01	a	Hamilton	D	0-0	
10/02	a	Ross County	W	3-0	og (Davies), Dauda 2
20/02	a	Dundee United	L	1-2	Walker
27/02	h	Kilmarnock	W	1-0	Walker
01/03	h	Inverness	W	2-0	Walker, Dauda
05/03	a	Partick	W	1-0	Sutchuin Djoum
12/03	a	Dundee	W	1-0	Walker
19/03	h	St Johnstone	L	0-3	
02/04	a	Celtic	L	1-3	Walker
08/04	h	Aberdeen	W	2-1	Juanma 2
12/04	a	Inverness	D	0-0	
23/04	a	Motherwell	L	0-1	
30/04	h	Celtic	L	1-3	Dauda
07/05	h	Ross County	D	1-1	Juanma
12/05	a	Aberdeen	W	1-0	Dauda
15/05	h	St Johnstone	D	2-2	Sutchuin Djoum, og (Shaughnessy)

No	Name	Nat	DoB	Pos	Aps	(s)	Gls
1	Neil Alexander		10/03/78	G	35		
5	Alim Öztürk	TUR	17/11/92	D	24		1
4	Błażej Augustyn	POL	26/01/88	D	21	(1)	
8	Prince Buaben	GHA	23/04/88	M	33	(3)	2
21	Don Cowie		15/02/83	M	7	(3)	
25	Abiola Dauda	NGA	03/02/88	A	7	(6)	5
6	Morgaro Gomis	SEN	14/07/85	M	12	(5)	
13	Jack Hamilton		22/03/94	G	3		
18	Igor Rossi	BRA	10/03/89	D	28	(1)	2
19	Juanma	ESP	17/11/90	A	28	(5)	12
12	Billy King		12/05/94	A	7	(8)	2
23	Perry Kitchen	USA	29/02/92	M	9	(1)	
22	Jordan McGhee		24/07/96	D	10	(12)	
3	Kevin McHattie		15/07/93	D		(1)	
35	Sean McKirdy		12/04/98	M	1	(1)	
37	Lewis Moore		04/06/98	M	1		
41	Callum Morrison		05/07/99	M		(1)	
11	Sam Nicholson		20/01/95	M	28	(8)	3
16	Gary Oliver		14/07/95	A		(1)	
17	Juwon Oshaniwa	NGA	14/09/90	D	24		
14	Miguel Pallardó	ESP	05/09/86	M	10	(6)	
2	Callum Paterson		13/10/94	D	27	(2)	5
20	Gavin Reilly		10/05/93	A	11	(17)	4
28	Liam Smith		10/04/96	D	5	(5)	
24	John Souttar		25/09/96	D	14	(1)	
10	Osman Sow	SWE	22/04/90	A	22	(1)	9
16	Arnaud Sutchuin Djoum	BEL	02/05/89	M	24	(4)	5
23	Danny Swanson		28/12/86	M	4	(4)	
7	Jamie Walker		25/06/93	M	20	(2)	7
44	Dario Zanatta	CAN	24/05/97	A	3	(10)	

Inverness Caledonian Thistle FC

1994 • Caledonian Stadium (7,800) • ictfc.com
Major honours
Scottish Cup (1) 2015
Manager: John Hughes

2015

01/08	h	Motherwell	L	0-1	
08/08	a	St Johnstone	D	1-1	Christie
12/08	h	Partick	D	0-0	
15/08	a	Celtic	L	2-4	Christie, Dani López
22/08	h	Hamilton	L	0-2	
29/08	a	Dundee	D	1-1	Raven
11/09	h	Hearts	W	2-0	Vincent, Storey
19/09	a	Dundee United	D	1-1	Meekings
26/09	h	Aberdeen	W	2-1	Storey, Christie
03/10	a	Ross County	W	2-1	Storey, Vincent
17/10	a	Kilmarnock	L	0-2	
24/10	h	St Johnstone	L	0-1	
31/10	h	Dundee	D	1-1	Tansey (p)
07/11	a	Motherwell	W	3-1	Tansey (p), Storey, Vigurs
21/11	a	Partick	L	1-2	Storey
29/11	h	Celtic	L	1-3	Storey
12/12	h	Kilmarnock	W	2-1	Vigurs 2
19/12	a	Dundee United	D	2-2	Polworth, Horner
26/12	a	Aberdeen	D	2-2	Polworth, Tansey (p)
30/12	a	Hamilton	W	4-3	Tansey 2, Polworth 2

2016

02/01	h	Ross County	W	2-0	Storey, Tansey
16/01	h	Kilmarnock	L	1-2	Draper
23/01	h	Partick	D	0-0	
15/02	h	Aberdeen	W	3-1	Vigurs, Tansey (p), Tremarco
20/02	a	Celtic	L	0-3	
27/02	a	Dundee	D	1-1	Draper
01/03	a	Hearts	L	0-2	
09/03	a	St Johnstone	L	0-1	
12/03	h	Hamilton	L	0-1	
19/03	a	Ross County	W	3-0	Polworth, Draper, Storey
02/04	h	Motherwell	L	1-2	Vigurs (p)
09/04	a	Dundee United	W	2-0	Storey, Vigurs
12/04	h	Hearts	D	0-0	
24/04	h	Kilmarnock	W	3-1	Tansey (p), Draper, D Williams
30/04	a	Partick	W	4-1	Tremarco, Storey, Meekings, Roberts
06/05	h	Dundee United	L	2-3	Roberts, Polworth
11/05	a	Hamilton	W	1-0	Devine
14/05	h	Dundee	W	4-0	Storey, Devine, Draper, Foran (p)

No	Name	Nat	DoB	Pos	Aps	(s)	Gls
22	Ryan Christie		28/04/95	M	12	(1)	3
7	Dani López	ESP	25/10/85	A	5	(2)	1
12	Daniel Devine	NIR	07/09/92	D	37		2
8	Ross Draper	ENG	20/10/88	M	31	(1)	5
18	Alex Fisher	ENG	30/06/90	A		(1)	
9	Richie Foran	IRL	16/06/80	A		(7)	1
17	Lewis Horner	ENG	01/02/92	M	11	(5)	1
21	Liam Hughes	ENG	10/08/92	M	4	(5)	
28	Andréa Mbuyi-Mutombo	COD	10/06/90	M	12	(13)	
6	Josh Meekings	ENG	02/09/92	D	21		2
20	Liam Polworth		12/10/94	M	33	(3)	6
2	David Raven	ENG	10/03/85	D	18	(1)	1
11	Jordan Roberts	ENG	05/01/94	A	8	(1)	2
18	Tobi Sho-Silva	ENG	27/03/95	A		(5)	
39	Miles Storey	ENG	04/01/94	A	29	(1)	11
37	Alisdair Sutherland		19/09/96	A		(5)	
16	Greg Tansey	ENG	21/11/88	M	37		8
3	Carl Tremarco	ENG	11/10/85	D	28	(4)	2
27	Iain Vigurs		07/05/88	A	24	(6)	6
4	James Vincent	ENG	27/09/89	M	14	(2)	2
5	Gary Warren	ENG	16/08/84	D	23	(2)	
15	Nathaniel Wedderburn	ENG	30/06/91	D	8	(7)	
19	Danny Williams	ENG	25/01/88	M	25	(10)	1
25	Owain Fon Williams	WAL	17/03/87	G	38		
7	Ryan Williams	ENG	08/04/91	M		(8)	

Kilmarnock FC

1869 • Rugby Park (18,128) • kilmarnockfc.co.uk
Major honours
Scottish League (1) 1965; Scottish Cup (3) 1920, 1929, 1997; Scottish League Cup (1) 2012
Manager: Gary Locke; (30/01/16) (Lee McCulloch); (15/02/16) Lee Clark (ENG)

2015

01/08	h	Dundee	L	0-4	
09/08	a	Aberdeen	L	0-2	
12/08	h	Celtic	D	2-2	Magennis, Higginbotham (p)
15/08	a	Partick	D	2-2	McKenzie, Boyd
22/08	h	Ross County	L	0-4	
29/08	a	Motherwell	D	0-0	
12/09	h	Dundee United	W	2-1	Higginbotham (p), McHattie
19/09	h	St Johnstone	W	2-1	Magennis, og (Easton)
26/09	h	Hamilton	L	1-2	Kiltie
03/10	a	Hearts	D	1-1	Balatoni
17/10	h	Inverness	W	2-0	Kiltie, Magennis
24/10	a	Dundee	W	2-1	Magennis, Smith
31/10	h	Motherwell	L	0-1	
07/11	a	St Johnstone	L	1-2	Smith
21/11	a	Celtic	D	0-0	
28/11	h	Partick	L	2-5	Magennis, Connolly
05/12	h	Dundee United	D	1-1	Boyd
12/12	a	Inverness	L	1-2	Connolly
19/12	a	Aberdeen	L	0-4	
26/12	h	Hamilton	W	1-0	Obadeyi
29/12	a	Ross County	L	2-3	Obadeyi, Magennis

2016

02/01	h	Hearts	D	2-2	Balatoni, Magennis
16/01	h	Inverness	W	2-1	Kiltie, Slater
23/01	a	Dundee United	L	1-5	Magennis
30/01	h	Hamilton	L	0-1	
13/02	a	Motherwell	W	2-0	Kiltie, Slater
20/02	h	Dundee	D	0-0	
27/02	a	Hearts	L	0-1	
01/03	h	Ross County	L	0-2	
12/03	a	Aberdeen	L	1-2	Magennis
19/03	h	Celtic	L	0-1	
02/04	a	Partick	D	0-0	
09/04	h	St Johnstone	W	3-0	Boyd 2 (1p), Higginbotham
24/04	a	Inverness	L	1-3	Higginbotham
30/04	a	Hamilton	W	4-0	Kiltie 2, Boyd (p), Magennis
07/05	h	Partick	L	0-2	
11/05	a	Dundee	D	1-1	Balatoni
14/05	h	Dundee United	L	2-4	Higginbotham, Obadeyi

No	Name	Nat	DoB	Pos	Aps	(s)	Gls
4	Miles Addison	ENG	07/01/89	D	6		
18	Lee Ashcroft		29/08/93	D	14	(1)	
26	Conrad Balatoni	ENG	27/01/91	D	30		3
2	Ross Barbour		01/02/93	D	1	(1)	
9	Kris Boyd		18/08/83	A	15	(14)	5
13	Conor Brennan	NIR	30/03/94	G	1	(2)	
20	Dale Carrick		07/01/94	A	1	(10)	
43	Lewis Clark		01/07/99			(1)	
6	Mark Connolly	IRL	16/12/91	D	10		2
29	Gary Dicker	IRL	21/07/86	M	12		
36	Julien Faubert	FRA	01/08/83	M	7	(2)	
4	Stuart Findlay		14/09/95	D	21	(1)	
39	Adam Frizzell		22/01/98	M	6	(4)	
4	Jamie Hamill		29/07/86	M	14	(2)	
4	Alex Henshall	ENG	15/02/94	M	1	(1)	
11	Kallum Higginbotham	ENG	15/06/89	A	23	(4)	5
27	Lee Hodson	NIR	02/10/91	D	13		
10	Chris Johnston		03/09/94	M	1		
23	Greg Kiltie		18/01/97	M	30	(5)	6
21	Jamie MacDonald		17/04/86	G	37		
28	Josh Magennis	NIR	15/08/90	A	32	(2)	10
5	Lee McCulloch		14/05/78	M	1		
22	Kevin McHattie		15/07/93	D	18	(3)	1
7	Rory McKenzie		07/10/93	A	23	(5)	1
37	Scott McLean		30/08/97	A		(1)	
14	Mark O'Hara		12/12/95	M	23	(6)	
16	Tope Obadeyi	ENG	29/10/89	M	15	(15)	3
8	Scott Robinson		12/03/92	M	6	(6)	
19	Craig Slater		26/04/94	M	23	(3)	2
3	Steven Smith		30/08/85	D	21	(1)	2
17	Aaron Splaine		13/10/96	M	1		
24	David Syme		23/06/97	D	4	(1)	
32	Greg Taylor		05/11/98	M	1		
12	Darryl Westlake	ENG	01/03/91	D	7	(1)	

Motherwell FC

1886 • Fir Park (13,677) • motherwellfc.co.uk

Major honours
Scottish League (1) 1932; Scottish Cup (2) 1952,
1991; Scottish League Cup (1) 1951

Manager: Ian Baraclough (ENG);
(23/09/15) (Stephen Craigan)
(13/10/15) Mark McGhee

2015
01/08	a	Inverness	W	1-0	Fletcher
08/08	h	Dundee United	L	0-2	
12/08	h	Hearts	L	0-2	
15/08	h	Aberdeen	L	1-2	Johnson
22/08	a	St Johnstone	L	1-2	Moult
29/08	h	Kilmarnock	W	1-0	Moult (p)
12/09	h	Ross County	D	1-1	Moult
19/09	a	Hamilton	L	0-1	
26/09	h	Partick	W	2-1	og (Frans), McDonald
03/10	a	Dundee	L	1-2	Pearson
17/10	h	Celtic	L	0-1	
24/10	a	Aberdeen	D	1-1	McDonald
31/10	a	Kilmarnock	W	1-0	Moult
07/11	h	Inverness	L	1-3	Moult
21/11	a	Ross County	L	0-3	
28/11	h	Hearts	D	2-2	Moult, Johnson
12/12	a	Dundee	W	3-1	McDonald, Moult, Pearson
19/12	h	Celtic	W	2-1	Moult 2 (1p)
30/12	h	St Johnstone	W	2-0	Hall, Pearson

2016
02/01	h	Hamilton	D	3-3	McDonald 2, Moult
16/01	h	Hearts	L	0-6	
23/01	h	Ross County	L	1-2	Pearson
30/01	a	Dundee	D	2-2	Cadden, Pearson
02/02	a	Partick	L	0-1	
13/02	h	Kilmarnock	L	0-2	
16/02	a	Dundee United	W	3-0	McManus, McDonald 2
20/02	a	St Johnstone	L	1-2	Moult
27/02	h	Partick	W	3-1	Moult 2 (1p), Johnson
05/03	a	Hamilton	W	1-0	Laing
11/03	h	Dundee United	W	2-1	Johnson, Moult
19/03	h	Aberdeen	W	2-1	McDonald, Moult
02/04	a	Inverness	W	2-1	Ainsworth, Johnson
09/04	h	Celtic	L	1-2	McDonald
23/04	h	Hearts	W	1-0	Ainsworth
30/04	a	Aberdeen	L	1-4	Cadden
07/05	h	St Johnstone	L	1-2	McDonald
11/05	a	Ross County	W	3-1	Pearson 2, Lasley
15/05	a	Celtic	L	0-7	

No	Name	Nat	DoB	Pos	Aps	(s)	Gls
7	Lionel Ainsworth	ENG	01/10/87	M	17	(12)	2
26	Chris Cadden		19/09/96	M	16	(4)	2
15	Joe Chalmers		03/01/94	D	11	(6)	
19	David Clarkson		10/09/85	M		(7)	
9	Wes Fletcher	ENG	28/02/90	A	5	(9)	1
17	Morgaro Gomis	SEN	14/07/85	M	8	(2)	
4	Liam Grimshaw	ENG	02/02/95	M	13	(1)	
32	Ben Hall	NIR	16/01/97	D	16	(2)	1
3	Steven Hammell		18/02/82	D	25	(2)	
11	Marvin Johnson	ENG	01/12/90	M	34	(4)	5
17	Kieran Kennedy	ENG	23/09/93	D	18	(4)	
5	Louis Laing	ENG	06/03/93	D	13	(2)	1
14	Keith Lasley		21/09/79	M	30		1
18	Josh Law	ENG	20/07/89	D	28	(1)	
21	Jack Leitch		17/07/85	M	3	(8)	
34	Dylan Mackin		15/01/97	A		(1)	
77	Scott McDonald	AUS	21/08/83	A	34	(3)	10
24	James McFadden		14/04/83	A	2	(1)	
6	Stephen McManus		10/09/82	D	37		1
20	Louis Moult	ENG	14/05/92	A	34	(4)	15
8	Stephen Pearson		02/10/82	M	25	(1)	7
1	Connor Ripley	ENG	13/02/93	G	36		
17	Theo Robinson	JAM	22/01/89	A	2	(8)	
13	Craig Samson		01/04/84	G	2		
25	Jake Taylor	WAL	01/12/91	M	6	(1)	
23	Dom Thomas		14/02/86	M	2	(12)	
28	Luke Watt		20/06/97	D	1	(1)	

Partick Thistle FC

1876 • Firhill (10,102) • ptfc.co.uk

Major honours
Scottish Cup (1) 1921; Scottish League Cup (1) 1972

Manager: Alan Archibald

2015
01/08	a	Hamilton	D	0-0	
09/08	h	Celtic	L	0-2	
12/08	a	Inverness	D	0-0	
15/08	h	Kilmarnock	D	2-2	Doolan 2
22/08	a	Hearts	L	0-3	
29/08	h	Aberdeen	L	0-2	
12/09	h	Dundee	L	0-1	
19/09	a	Ross County	L	0-1	
26/09	a	Motherwell	L	1-2	Amoo
03/10	h	Dundee United	W	3-0	Amoo, Dumbuya, Bannigan
17/10	a	St Johnstone	W	2-1	Miller, Lawless
24/10	h	Hamilton	D	1-1	Pogba
31/10	h	Hearts	L	0-4	
07/11	a	Dundee	D	1-1	Lindsay
21/11	a	Inverness	W	2-1	Doolan, Stevenson
28/11	a	Kilmarnock	W	5-2	Doolan 2, Fraser, Muirhead 2
12/12	a	Dundee United	W	1-0	Doolan
19/12	h	Ross County	W	1-0	og (Davies)
30/12	a	Aberdeen	D	0-0	

2016
02/01	a	Celtic	L	0-1	
16/01	h	Dundee	L	2-4	Amoo, Doolan
23/01	a	Inverness	D	0-0	
02/02	a	Motherwell	W	1-0	Lawless
23/02	h	St Johnstone	W	2-0	Doolan, Amoo
27/02	a	Motherwell	L	1-3	Booth
02/03	a	St Johnstone	W	2-1	Booth, Lawless
05/03	a	Hearts	L	0-1	
08/03	h	Aberdeen	L	1-2	Lawless
12/03	h	Celtic	L	1-2	Welsh (p)
19/03	a	Hamilton	W	2-1	Pogba, Edwards
02/04	h	Kilmarnock	D	0-0	
05/04	h	Dundee United	W	1-0	Doolan
09/04	a	Ross County	L	0-1	
23/04	a	Dundee	L	1-2	Doolan
30/04	a	Inverness	L	1-4	Doolan
07/05	a	Kilmarnock	L	1-2	Lawless, Doolan
10/05	a	Dundee United	D	3-3	Frans, Doolan, Edwards
14/05	h	Hamilton	D	2-2	Doolan, Amoo

No	Name	Nat	DoB	Pos	Aps	(s)	Gls
7	David Amoo	ENG	13/04/91	M	27	(10)	5
8	Stuart Bannigan		17/09/92	M	26		1
5	Callum Booth		30/05/91	D	34		2
1	Tomáš Černý	CZE	10/04/85	G	28		
15	Kris Doolan		14/09/86	A	24	(12)	14
19	Mustapha Dumbuya	SLE	07/08/87	D	19	(2)	1
19	Ryan Edwards	AUS	18/11/93	M	10	(7)	2
14	Christie Elliott	ENG	26/05/91	M	5	(7)	
3	Frédéric Frans	BEL	03/01/89	D	17	(4)	1
22	Gary Fraser		20/06/83	M	7	(5)	1
35	Paul Gallacher		16/08/79	G	1		
10	Antonio German	ENG	26/12/91	A		(2)	
19	Jack Hendry		07/05/95	D	1	(2)	
11	Steven Lawless		12/04/91	M	36	(1)	5
17	Liam Lindsay		12/10/85	D	25		1
20	Declan McDaid		22/11/95	M	1	(3)	
25	Matthew McInally		02/08/97			(1)	
2	Gary Miller		15/04/87	D	20	(1)	1
23	Robbie Muirhead		08/03/96	A	4	(4)	2
16	Aidan Nesbitt		05/02/97	M		(8)	
27	Kevin Nisbit		08/03/97	A	4	(3)	
6	Abdul Osman	GHA	27/02/87	M	32	(1)	
29	James Penrice		22/12/98	D	2		
99	Mathias Pogba	GUI	19/08/90	A	13	(15)	2
12	Ryan Scully		29/10/92	G	9	(1)	
3	Danny Seaborne	ENG	05/03/87	D	31	(1)	
10	Ryan Stevenson		24/08/84	M	6	(4)	1
4	Sean Welsh		15/03/90	M	32	(2)	1
18	David Wilson		06/09/94	M	4	(7)	

Ross County FC

1929 • Victoria Park (6,541) •
rosscountyfootballclub.co.uk

Major honours
Scottish League Cup (1) 2016

Manager: Jim McIntyre

2015
01/08	a	Celtic	L	0-2	
08/08	h	Hamilton	W	2-0	Curran 2
11/08	a	St Johnstone	D	1-1	Curran
15/08	h	Hearts	L	1-2	Boyce (p)
22/08	a	Kilmarnock	W	4-0	Boyce 2, Franks, Davies
29/08	h	Dundee United	W	2-1	Boyce (p), Davies
12/09	a	Motherwell	D	1-1	Gardyne
19/09	h	Partick	W	1-0	Boyce
26/09	a	Dundee	D	3-3	Boyce, og (McPake), Gardyne
03/10	h	Inverness	L	1-2	Boyce
16/10	h	Aberdeen	W	2-0	Graham 2
24/10	a	Hearts	L	0-2	
31/10	a	Dundee United	L	0-1	
21/11	h	Celtic	L	1-4	Dingwall
21/11	h	Motherwell	W	3-0	Curran, Dingwall, Boyce (p)
28/11	a	Aberdeen	L	1-3	Curran
05/12	h	St Johnstone	W	3-1	Boyce, og (Davidson)
12/12	a	Hamilton	W	3-1	Curran, Murdoch, Boyce
19/12	a	Partick	L	0-1	
26/12	h	Dundee	W	5-2	Boyce 3, Gardyne, Irvine
29/12	h	Kilmarnock	W	3-2	Curran, Gardyne 2

2016
02/01	a	Inverness	L	0-2	
17/01	h	Aberdeen	L	2-3	McShane 2
23/01	a	Motherwell	W	2-1	Irvine, Graham
10/02	h	Hearts	L	0-3	
13/02	a	Celtic	L	0-3	
20/02	a	Hamilton	W	2-1	Schalk, McShane
27/02	a	Dundee United	L	0-3	
01/03	a	Kilmarnock	W	2-0	Schalk, Graham
16/03	a	St Johnstone	D	1-1	Graham (p)
19/03	h	Inverness	L	0-3	
02/04	a	Dundee	L	2-5	Davies, Schalk
09/04	h	Partick	W	1-0	Schalk
24/04	a	Celtic	D	1-1	Murdoch
30/04	a	St Johnstone	L	0-1	
07/05	a	Hearts	L	1-3	Goodwillie
11/05	h	Motherwell	L	1-3	Boyce
15/05	a	Aberdeen	W	4-0	Graham (p), Schalk, Boyce, M Woods

No	Name	Nat	DoB	Pos	Aps	(s)	Gls
21	Daniel Bachmann	AUT	09/07/94	G		(1)	
10	Liam Boyce	NIR	08/04/91	A	29	(6)	15
5	Scott Boyd		06/04/86	D	12	(3)	
11	Craig Curran	ENG	23/08/89	A	15	(4)	7
15	Andrew Davies	ENG	17/12/84	D	31		3
19	Raffaele De Vita	ITA	23/09/87	A	8	(11)	
19	Tony Dingwall		25/07/94	M	5	(7)	2
12	Ricky Foster		31/07/85	D	28	(1)	
1	Scott Fox		28/06/87	G	27		
17	Jonathan Franks	ENG	06/04/90	M	18	(11)	1
2	Marcus Fraser		23/06/94	D	29		
7	Michael Gardyne		23/01/86	M	34	(1)	5
25	David Goodwillie		28/03/89	A	4	(5)	1
9	Brian Graham		23/11/87	A	10	(13)	6
36	Jackson Irvine	AUS	07/03/93	M	34	(2)	2
44	Christopher McLaughlin		22/03/98	M	2		
8	Ian McShane		20/12/92	M	16	(2)	3
53	Greg Morrison		19/02/98	A		(2)	
18	Stewart Murdoch		17/12/90	M	14	(15)	2
43	Paul Quinn		07/09/86	D	14		
4	Rocco Quinn		21/07/85	M	5	(5)	
3	Jamie Reckord	ENG	09/03/92	D	14	(2)	
6	Chris Robertson		11/10/85	D	21	(2)	
23	Alex Schalk	NED	07/08/92	A	14	(10)	6
21	Gary Woods	ENG	01/10/90	G	11	(1)	
26	Martin Woods		26/04/92	M	23	(3)	1

Saint Johnstone FC

1884 • McDiarmid Park (10,696) •
perthstjohnstonefc.co.uk
Major honours
Scottish Cup (1) 2014
Manager: Tommy Wright (NIR)

2015

02/08	a	Hearts	L	3-4	Lappin, Sutton, Cummins
08/08	h	Inverness	D	1-1	Cummins
11/08	h	Ross County	D	1-1	Cummins
15/08	a	Dundee	L	1-2	MacLean
22/08	h	Motherwell	W	2-1	MacLean 2
29/08	a	Celtic	L	1-3	og (Boyata)
12/09	h	Hamilton	W	4-1	Craig, MacLean 3 (1p)
19/09	a	Kilmarnock	L	1-2	Wotherspoon
26/09	h	Dundee United	W	2-1	Cummins, Lappin
03/10	a	Aberdeen	W	5-1	Easton, Shaughnessy, Craig, MacLean 2
17/10	h	Partick	L	1-2	MacLean
24/10	a	Inverness	W	1-0	Craig (p)
31/10	a	Hamilton	W	4-2	Cummins 2, Wotherspoon, O'Halloran
07/11	h	Kilmarnock	W	2-1	O'Halloran, Kane
21/11	a	Dundee United	W	2-1	Kane, Davidson
27/11	h	Dundee	D	1-1	Wotherspoon
05/12	a	Ross County	W	3-2	Wotherspoon 2, Mackay
13/12	h	Celtic	L	0-3	
19/12	h	Hearts	D	0-0	
30/12	a	Motherwell	L	0-2	

2016

16/01	h	Hamilton	D	0-0	
23/01	a	Celtic	L	1-3	MacLean
06/02	a	Aberdeen	L	3-4	Wotherspoon, Anderson, Scobbie
12/02	a	Dundee	L	0-2	
20/02	h	Motherwell	W	2-1	Wotherspoon, Scobbie
23/02	h	Partick	L	0-2	
27/02	a	Aberdeen	D	1-1	Craig (p)
02/03	h	Partick	L	1-2	Kane
09/03	h	Inverness	W	1-0	Kane
16/03	h	Ross County	D	1-1	Wotherspoon
19/03	a	Hearts	W	3-0	Davidson 2, Fisher
02/04	a	Dundee United	L	0-1	
09/04	a	Kilmarnock	L	0-3	
22/04	h	Aberdeen	W	3-0	Wotherspoon, MacLean, Craig
30/04	a	Ross County	W	1-0	MacLean
07/05	a	Motherwell	W	2-1	MacLean, Swanson
11/05	h	Celtic	W	2-1	MacLean, Cummins
15/05	h	Hearts	D	2-2	Craig (p), Cummins

No	Name	Nat	DoB	Pos	Aps	(s)	Gls
6	Steven Anderson		19/12/85	D	23	(1)	1
20	Scott Brown		25/11/94	M	2	(3)	
16	Liam Caddis		20/09/93	M		(5)	
12	Zander Clark		26/06/92	G	5	(1)	
26	Liam Craig		27/12/86	M	24	(11)	6
18	Graham Cummins	IRL	29/12/87	A	23	(9)	8
8	Murray Davidson		07/03/88	M	30		3
5	Michael Doyle		01/08/91	D		(2)	
24	Brian Easton		05/03/88	D	26	(3)	1
22	Darnell Fisher	ENG	04/04/94	D	22	(1)	1
36	Liam Gordon		26/01/96	D	1		
31	Greg Hurst		08/04/97	M		(2)	
25	Chris Kane		05/09/94	A	10	(19)	4
66	Plamen Krachunov	BUL	11/01/89	D	1	(1)	
4	Simon Lappin		25/01/83	M	14	(9)	2
2	David Mackay		02/05/80	D	17		1
9	Steven MacLean		23/08/82	A	29	(4)	14
1	Alan Mannus	NIR	19/05/82	G	33		
15	Brad McKay		26/03/93	D	2		
7	Chris Millar		30/03/83	M	20		
29	Michael O'Halloran		06/01/91	A	19	(1)	2
3	Tam Scobbie		31/03/88	D	28	(2)	2
14	Joe Shaughnessy	IRL	06/07/92	D	35	(2)	1
11	John Sutton	ENG	26/12/83	A	5	(16)	1
16	Danny Swanson		28/12/86	M	14		1
27	Craig Thomson		10/03/95	M	2	(8)	
10	David Wotherspoon		16/01/90	M	32	(3)	9
5	Frazer Wright		23/12/79	D	1		

Top goalscorers

31	Leigh Griffiths (Celtic)
21	Kane Hemmings (Dundee)
20	Adam Rooney (Aberdeen)
15	Louis Moult (Motherwell)
	Liam Boyce (Ross County)
14	Kris Doolan (Partick)
	Steven MacLean (St Johnstone)
12	Billy McKay (Dundee United)
	Juanma (Hearts)
11	Miles Storey (Inverness)

Promoted club

Rangers FC

1872 • Ibrox Stadium (50,947) • rangers.co.uk
Major honours
UEFA Cup Winners' Cup (1) 1972; Scottish League (54) 1891 (joint), 1899, 1900, 1901, 1902, 1911, 1912, 1913, 1918, 1920, 1921, 1923, 1924, 1925, 1927, 1928, 1929, 1930, 1931, 1933, 1934, 1935, 1937, 1939, 1947, 1949, 1950, 1953, 1956, 1957, 1959, 1961, 1963, 1964, 1975, 1976, 1978, 1987, 1989, 1990, 1991, 1992, 1993, 1994, 1995, 1996, 1997, 1999, 2000, 2003, 2005, 2009, 2010, 2011; Scottish Cup (33) 1894, 1897, 1898, 1903, 1928, 1930, 1932, 1934, 1935, 1936, 1948, 1949, 1950, 1953, 1960, 1962, 1963, 1964, 1966, 1973, 1976, 1978, 1979, 1981, 1992, 1993, 1996, 1999, 2000, 2002, 2003, 2008, 2009; Scottish League Cup (27) 1947, 1949, 1961, 1962, 1964, 1965, 1971, 1976, 1978, 1979, 1982, 1984, 1985, 1987, 1988, 1989, 1991, 1993, 1994, 1997, 1999, 2002, 2003, 2005, 2008, 2010, 2011.
Manager: Mark Warburton (ENG)

Second level final table 2015/16

		Pld	W	D	L	F	A	Pts
1	Rangers FC	36	25	6	5	88	34	81
2	Falkirk FC	36	19	13	4	61	34	70
3	Hibernian FC	36	21	7	8	59	34	70
4	Raith Rovers FC	36	18	8	10	52	46	62
5	Greenock Morton FC	36	11	10	15	39	42	43
6	Saint Mirren FC	36	11	9	16	44	53	42
7	Queen of the South FC	36	12	6	18	46	56	42
8	Dumbarton FC	36	10	7	19	35	66	37
9	Livingston FC	36	8	7	21	37	51	31
10	Alloa Athletic FC	36	4	9	23	22	67	21

Promotion/Relegation play-offs

(04/05/16 & 07/05/16)
Raith Rovers 1-0 Hibernian
Hibernian 2-0 Raith Rovers
(Hibernian 2-1)

(10/05/16 & 13/05/16)
Hibernian 2-2 Falkirk
Falkirk 3-2 Hibernian
(Falkirk 5-4)

(19/05/16 & 22/05/16)
Falkirk 1-0 Kilmarnock
Kilmarnock 4-0 Falkirk
(Kilmarnock 4-1)

SCOTLAND

DOMESTIC CUPS

Scottish Cup 2015/16

FOURTH ROUND

(08/01/16)
St Mirren 1-2 Partick Thistle

(09/01/16)
Airdrieonians 0-1 Dundee United
Annan 4-1 Hamilton
Dumbarton 2-1 Queen of the South
Dunfermline 2-2 Ross County
Hearts 1-0 Aberdeen
Linlithgow 3-3 Forfar
Livingston 1-2 Morton
Motherwell 5-0 Cove Rangers
Raith 0-2 Hibernian
St Johnstone 0-1 Kilmarnock
Stirling 0-0 Inverness

(10/01/16)
Rangers 5-1 Cowdenbeath
Stranraer 0-3 Celtic

(20/01/16)
East Kilbride 2-0 Lothian/Hutchison

(26/01/16)
Dundee 3-1 Falkirk

David Gray – the first Hibernian captain to lift the
Scottish Cup since 1902

Replays

(12/01/16)
Ross County 1-0 Dunfermline

(19/01/16)
Inverness 2-0 Stirling

(26/01/16)
Forfar 0-1 Linlithgow *(aet)*

FIFTH ROUND

(06/02/16)
Annan 1-4 Morton
Dumbarton 0-0 Dundee
Dundee United 1-0 Partick Thistle
Motherwell 1-2 Inverness
Rangers 0-0 Kilmarnock
Ross County 4-2 Linlithgow

(07/02/16)
East Kilbride 0-2 Celtic
Hearts 2-2 Hibernian

Replays

(16/02/16)
Hibernian 1-0 Hearts
Kilmarnock 1-2 Rangers

(23/02/16)
Dundee 5-0 Dumbarton

QUARTER-FINALS

(05/03/16)
Rangers 4-0 Dundee *(Forrester 1, Holt 47, Halliday 54, Wallace 84)*

Ross County 2-3 Dundee United *(Boyce 24, Graham 60p; Anier 57, 65, McKay 89)*

(06/03/16)
Celtic 3-0 Morton *(Griffiths 14, Mackay-Steven 25, McGregor 35)*

Hibernian 1-1 Inverness *(Keatings 54; Mbuyi-Mutombo 77)*

Replay

(16/03/16)
Inverness 1-2 Hibernian *(Vigurs 77; Stokes 36, 41)*

SEMI-FINALS

(16/04/16)
Hibernian 0-0 Dundee United *(aet; 4-2 on pens)*

(17/04/16)
Rangers 2-2 Celtic *(Miller 16, McKay 96; Sviatchenko 50, Rogic 106) (aet; 5-4 on pens)*

FINAL

(21/05/16)
Hampden Park, Glasgow
HIBERNIAN FC 3 *(Stokes 3, 80, Gray 90+2)*
RANGERS FC 2 *(Miller 27, Halliday 64)*
Referee: *McLean*
HIBERNIAN: Logan, McGregor, Hanlon *(Gunnarson 83)*, Fontaine *(Henderson 70)*, Gray, Fyvie, McGeouch, McGinn, Stevenson, Stokes, Cummings *(Keatings 65)*
RANGERS: Foderingham, Tavernier, Kiernan, Wilson, Wallace, Zelalem *(Shiels 63)*, Halliday, Holt, Waghorn *(Clark 75)*, Miller, McKay

League Cup 2015/16

QUARTER-FINALS

(27/10/15)
Inverness 1-2 Ross County *(Tansey 78; Irvine 41, Gardyne 48)*

Morton 1-3 St Johnstone *(Johnstone 52; MacLean 61p, O'Halloran 63, Kane 83)*

(28/10/15)
Hearts 1-2 Celtic *(Sutchuin Djoum 90; Griffiths 71, Rogic 82)*

(04/11/15)
Hibernian 3-0 Dundee United *(Gray 20, Cummings 61p, Stevenson 90)*

SEMI-FINALS

(30/01/16)
Hibernian 2-1 St Johnstone *(Cummings 29p, McGinn 74; Shaughnessy 33)*

(31/01/16)
Ross County 3-1 Celtic *(M Woods 15p, P Quinn 48, Schalk 63; Mackay-Steven 1)*

FINAL

(13/03/16)
Hampden Park, Glasgow
ROSS COUNTY FC 2 *(Gardyne 25, Schalk 90)*
HIBERNIAN FC 1 *(Fontaine 45)*
Referee: *Clancy*
ROSS COUNTY: G Woods, Fraser, P Quinn, Davies, Foster *(Franks 85)*, Gardyne, Irvine, M Woods, McShane *(Murdoch 79)*, Boyce *(Graham 59)*, Schalk
HIBERNIAN: Oxley, Gray, McGregor, Fontaine, Stevenson, Henderson, Thomson *(Keatings 76)*, Bartley *(Boyle 90+4)*, McGinn, Stokes, Cummings

A first major trophy for the Highlanders of Ross County

SERBIA
Fudbalski savez Srbije (FSS)

Address	Terazije 35, CP 263
	RS-11000 Beograd
Tel	+381 11 323 4253
Fax	+381 11 323 3433
E-mail	office@fss.rs
Website	fss.rs

President	Slaviša Kokeza
General secretary	Nebojša Ivković
Media officer	Aleksandar
	Bošković
Year of formation	1919

SUPERLIGA CLUBS

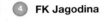

1. FK Borac Čačak
2. FK Crvena zvezda
3. FK Čukarički
4. FK Jagodina
5. FK Javor
6. FK Metalac
7. FK Mladost Lučani
8. FK Novi Pazar
9. OFK Beograd
10. FK Partizan
11. FK Rad
12. FK Radnički Niš
13. FK Radnik Surdulica
14. FK Spartak Subotica
15. FK Vojvodina
16. FK Voždovac

PROMOTED CLUBS

17. FK Napredak
18. FK Bačka

KEY
- UEFA Champions League
- UEFA Europa League
- Promoted
- Relegated

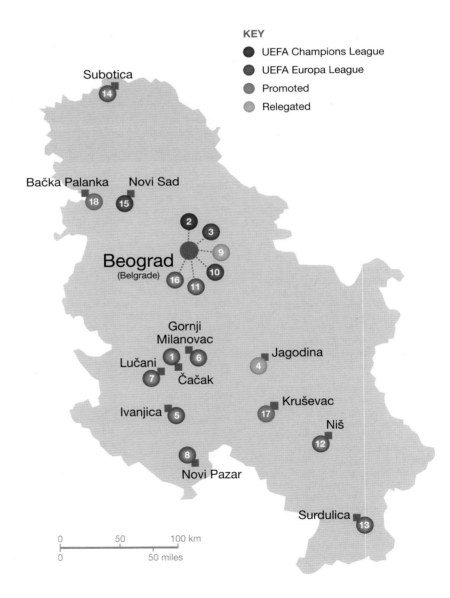

Crvena zvezda in cruise control

A remodelled and extended Superliga was designed to prolong the excitement in Serbia's top division, but Crvena zvezda, under new Montenegrin boss Miodrag Božović, prevented the theory from becoming reality by storming to a runaway victory in record-breaking style.

It was the Red-and-Whites' 27th league title, one more than deposed champions and eternal rivals Partizan, whose consolation for a largely forgettable league campaign was provided by a first Serbian Cup triumph in five years.

'Red Star' romp to record 27th league title

Partizan end five-year wait for cup win

Muslin appointed as national team coach

Domestic league

Eliminated early from Europe, Crvena zvezda were able to concentrate fully on removing Partizan from domestic power, but former defender Božović, who had returned to Serbia after an eight-year sojourn in Russia, had to withstand some early supporter unrest before he won over the fans with an incredible sequence of victories that would last from the beginning of August all the way through to the end of March – an unprecedented run of 24 successive three-pointers that turned the title race into a one-team procession.

Revitalised not only by Božović but also by the further development of exciting young guns such as Marko Grujić and Aleksandar Katai and a batch of new signings that included the foreign trio of Dutch midfielder Mitchell Donald, Argentinian left-back Luis Ibánez and Portuguese striker Hugo Vieira, Crvena zvezda were transformed into a team with no equal in the Superliga. The record-breaking run incorporated two derby victories against Partizan – 3-1 at home in September and 2-1 away in February – plus a sensational 7-2 win in December away to Čukarički, the low-budget Belgrade team that would be their closest challengers, at a distance of 25 points, when the Superleague shut down for the winter.

That lead had become even bigger when the 30-match split arrived, but because of the new rules, Crvena zvezda's 28-point advantage was reduced by half in advance of the seven-match second phase. Not that Božović and his players had anything to worry about. Although they drew at home to Partizan and then lost their unbeaten record against Čukarički, the championship was sewn up next time out as they defeated another Belgrade side, Voždovac, 1-0. The champions remained undefeated away from home at the finish with a winning margin that was listed as 14 points but in a conventional format would have been twice that amount.

Partizan ended up second, having lost 10 of their 37 games and used three coaches – Zoran Milinković, Ljubinko Drulović and, for the second half of the season, 40-year-old former midfielder Ivan Tomić. Čukarički, who finished a point behind Partizan, also changed their coach twice, while fourth-placed Vojvodina rose up the league after the November appointment of Nenad Lalatović, Božović's predecessor at Crvena zvezda.

Domestic cup

Partizan ended a lengthy wait for a victory in the Serbian Cup, defeating unlikely first-time finalists Javor 2-0 in the unlikelier setting of Metalac's 4,800-capacity stadium in Gornji Milanovac with goals from two even unlikelier scorers – defender Marko Jovanović and, in added time, 16-year-old Dušan Vlahović. Partizan's 13th domestic cup win was achieved without conceding a single goal in their entire campaign.

Europe

While Crvena zvezda, back from a European ban, crashed out of the UEFA Europa League first qualifying round after losing home and away to Kairat Almaty of Kazakhstan, Partizan had one of their more enterprising European campaigns. Having just missed out on a place in the UEFA Champions League group stage, they really should have reached the knockout phase of the UEFA Europa League, but all the good work of three group wins was frustratingly undone by a late meltdown at home to Augsburg.

National team

Despite a reasonable finish to an ill-fated UEFA EURO 2016 qualifying campaign, the contract of Serbia coach Radovan Čurčić was terminated by mutual consent and he was replaced by the vastly experienced Slavoljub Muslin. The expectation is that the 63-year-old will have the skill and knowhow to get the best out of a talented crop of youngsters and make Serbia competitive again in a 2018 FIFA World Cup qualifying group containing Wales, Austria, the Republic of Ireland, Moldova and Georgia.

DOMESTIC SEASON AT A GLANCE

Superliga 2015/16 final table

		Pld	Home					Away					Total					Pts
			W	D	L	F	A	W	D	L	F	A	W	D	L	F	A	
1	FK Crvena zvezda	37	15	2	2	45	14	15	3	0	52	13	30	5	2	97	27	54
2	FK Partizan	37	13	2	4	42	18	7	5	6	30	26	20	7	10	72	44	40
3	FK Čukarički	37	9	4	6	24	23	10	4	4	24	12	19	8	10	48	35	39
4	FK Vojvodina	37	10	4	4	32	20	6	7	6	25	24	16	11	10	57	44	36
5	FK Radnički Niš	37	8	6	4	18	11	8	3	8	22	24	16	9	12	40	35	35
6	FK Borac Čačak	37	10	5	4	32	21	4	6	8	14	22	14	11	12	46	43	30
7	FK Voždovac	37	8	2	8	21	19	3	10	6	13	17	11	12	14	34	36	25
8	FK Radnik Surdulica	37	8	6	4	22	23	3	5	11	19	42	11	11	15	41	65	25
9	FK Mladost Lučani	37	4	10	5	14	17	7	4	7	20	27	11	14	12	34	44	31
10	FK Spartak Subotica	37	7	4	4	24	20	4	7	8	13	22	11	11	15	37	42	29
11	FK Metalac	37	7	9	3	26	22	3	6	9	15	26	10	15	12	41	48	28
12	FK Rad	37	6	7	5	26	24	3	6	10	14	23	9	13	15	40	47	27
13	FK Javor	37	5	7	7	13	15	5	6	7	12	14	10	13	14	25	29	26
14	FK Novi Pazar	37	8	6	5	18	19	2	4	12	11	31	10	10	17	29	50	25
15	OFK Beograd	37	8	2	8	24	25	1	3	15	14	33	9	5	23	38	58	18
16	FK Jagodina	37	3	8	7	14	22	2	5	12	15	39	5	13	19	29	61	15

NB League splits into top and bottom halves after 30 games, after which the clubs play exclusively against teams in their group. Points obtained during the regular season are halved (and rounded upwards); FK Spartak Subotica – 2 pts deducted.

European qualification 2016/17

 Champion: FK Crvena zvezda (second qualifying round)

 Cup winner: FK Partizan (second qualifying round)
FK Čukarički (first qualifying round)
FK Vojvodina (first qualifying round)

Top scorer Hugo Vieira (Crvena zvezda) & Aleksandar Katai (Crvena zvezda), 21 goals
Relegated clubs FK Jagodina, OFK Beograd
Promoted clubs FK Napredak, FK Bačka
Cup final FK Partizan 2-0 FK Javor

Team of the season
(4-4-2)

Coach: Božović (Crvena zvezda)

Aleksandar S Jovanović (Radnički Niš)

Stojković (Čukarički) — Luković (Crvena zvezda) — Ostojić (Čukarički) — Ibáñez (Crvena zvezda)

Katai (Crvena zvezda) — Grujić (Crvena zvezda) — Sekulić (Vojvodina) — N Mihajlović (Rad/Partizan)

Hugo Vieira (Crvena zvezda) — Pavlović (Čukarički)

Player of the season

Hugo Vieira
(Crvena zvezda)

A Portuguese striker whose career appeared to be stagnating following a number of personal and professional issues, Hugo Vieira found the perfect stage for his talents in the Serbian Superliga. Not only did he score 21 goals in his first season to win the title with Crvena zvezda and share the league's top scorer prize with his team-mate Aleksandar Katai, he also won the hearts of the club's fans, supplementing his goals – which included 13 in nine games at the turn of the year - with his mazy dribbling and technical skills.

Newcomer of the season

Nemanja Mihajlović
(FK Rad/FK Partizan)

Partizan were a much-improved team in the second half of the 2015/16 season, and part of the reason for their resurgence in form was the mid-season signing from Belgrade rivals Rad of left-winger Mihajlović. The 20-year-old effectively took the place of FIFA U-20 World Cup-winning star Andrija Živjković, who was banished to Partizan's B team after refusing to sign a new contract. By the end of the season Mihajlović had a Serbian Cup winner's medal to go with a hail of adulation from the Partizan fans.

 **SERBIA**

NATIONAL TEAM

International tournament appearances*

FIFA World Cup (11) 1930 (semi-finals), 1950, 1954 (qtr-finals), 1958 (qtr-finals), 1962 (4th), 1974 (2nd phase), 1982, 1990 (qtr-finals), 1998 (2nd round), 2006, 2010 UEFA European Championship (5) 1960 (runners-up), 1968 (runners-up), 1976 (4th), 1984, 2000 (qtr-finals)

Top five all-time caps

Dejan Stanković (103); Savo Milošević (102); **Branislav Ivanović** (87); Dragan Džajić (85); Dragan Stojković (84)

Top five all-time goals

Stjepan Bobek (38); Milan Galić & Savo Milošević (37); Blagoje Marjanović (36); Rajko Mitić (32)

(* before 2006 as Yugoslavia; 2006 as Serbia & Montenegro.)

Results 2015/16

04/09/15	Armenia (ECQ)	H	Novi Sad	W	2-0	Hayrapetyan (22og), Ljajić (53)
07/09/15	France	A	Bordeaux	L	1-2	A Mitrović (40)
08/10/15	Albania (ECQ)	A	Elbasan	W	2-0	Kolarov (90+1), Ljajić (90+4)
11/10/15	Portugal (ECQ)	H	Belgrade	L	1-2	Z Tošić (65)
13/11/15	Czech Republic	A	Ostrava	L	1-4	Škuletić (78)
23/03/16	Poland	A	Poznan	L	0-1	
29/03/16	Estonia	A	Tallinn	W	1-0	Kolarov (81)
25/05/16	Cyprus	H	Uzice	W	2-1	A Mitrović (2), Tadić (10)
31/05/16	Israel	H	Novi Sad	W	3-1	Ivanović (33), Milunović (74), Tadić (88)
05/06/16	Russia	N	Monaco (FRA)	D	1-1	A Mitrović (88)

Appearances 2015/16

Coach: Radovan Ćurčić /(05/05/16) Slavoljub Muslin	10/01/72 15/06/53		ARM	Fra	ALB	POR	Cze	Pol	Est	Cyp	Isr	Rus	Caps	Goals
Vladimir Stojković	28/07/83	M. Haifa (ISR)	G		G	G	G	G	G			G	68	-
Nenad Tomović	30/08/87	Fiorentina (ITA)	D	D	D	D	D82						22	-
Branislav Ivanović	22/02/84	Chelsea (ENG)	D	D	D65		D	D	D	D46	D		87	11
Uroš Spajić	13/02/93	Toulouse (FRA)	D	D89			s90	s46		D46			5	-
Aleksandar Kolarov	10/11/85	Man. City (ENG)	D		D	D77 80*	D	D	D	s46	D	s46	64	8
Nemanja Matić	01/08/88	Chelsea (ENG)	M	M	M73	M 81*	M82	M85	M64	M46			29	1
Darko Brašanac	12/02/92	Partizan	M					s85	s64				3	-
Andrija Živković	11/07/96	Partizan	M59							s46		s79	5	-
Adem Ljajić	29/09/91	Internazionale (ITA)	M73	s56	M	M	M	M	M	s46			20	3
Filip Kostić	01/11/92	Stuttgart (GER)	M84	s46			s59	M78	M75	M46		M79	9	-
Aleksandar Mitrović	16/09/94	Newcastle (ENG)	A	A76	A	A85	A69		A90	A46	s79	A89	22	4
Zoran Tošić	28/04/87	CSKA Moskva (RUS)	s59	s58	M	M84	M59	M65	M87		M79	s65	74	11
Ljubomir Fejsa	14/08/88	Benfica (POR)	s73	M82	s73								22	-
Dušan Tadić	20/11/88	Southampton (ENG)	s84	M46	M54	M	M59			M46	s69	M	38	8
Predrag Rajković	31/10/95	M. Tel-Aviv (ISR)		G							G		3	-
Ivan Obradović	25/07/88	Anderlecht (BEL)		D		s77							22	1
Nemanja Gudelj	16/11/91	Ajax (NED)			M56			s69					11	1
Lazar Marković	02/03/94	Fenerbahçe (TUR)			M58								21	3
Petar Škuletić	29/06/90	Lokomotiv Moskva (RUS)			s76		s85	s69					6	1
Radosav Petrović	08/03/89	Dynamo Kyiv (UKR)			s82			s82					44	2
Miloš Kosanović	28/05/90	Mechelen (BEL)			s89								1	-
Stefan Mitrović	22/05/90	Gent (BEL)			D	D							8	-
Luka Milivojević	07/04/91	Olympiacos (GRE)			M	M	M69	M73	M82		M	M90	15	-
Miralem Sulejmani	05/12/88	Young Boys (SUI)			s54	s84		s65	s87				20	1
Duško Tošić	19/01/85	Beşiktaş (TUR)			s65	D	D						17	1
Aleksandar Katai	06/02/91	Crvena zvezda					s59						1	-
Marko Petković	03/09/92	Crvena zvezda					s82						1	-
Nikola Maksimović	25/11/91	Torino (ITA)					D90	D46	D	s46	s83		12	-
Slobodan Rajković	03/02/89	Darmstadt (GER)						D	D	D	s46	D83	19	-
Nikola Stojiljković	17/08/92	Braga (POR)						A56	s90		A	s89	4	-
Filip Đuričić	30/01/92	Anderlecht (BEL)						s56	s75				24	4
Nemanja Maksimović	26/01/95	Astana (KAZ)						s73	s82	M			3	-
Filip Mladenović	15/08/91	Köln (GER)						s78		D46		D65	4	-
Damir Kahriman	19/11/84	Crvena zvezda								G			8	-
Antonio Rukavina	26/01/84	Villareal (ESP)								D75	s46	D	33	-
Nemanja Milunović	31/05/89	BATE (BLR)								D	D	D	3	1
Andrija Pavlović	16/11/93	Čukarički								s46	A69		2	-
Marko Grujić	13/04/96	Crvena zvezda								s46	s46	M46	3	-
Aleksandar Sedlar	13/12/91	Metalac								s75	M46		2	-
Saša Zdjelar	20/03/95	Olympiacos (GRE)									M46	s90	2	-

EUROPE

FK Partizan

CHAMPIONS LEAGUE

Second qualifying round - FC Dila Gori (GEO)
H 1-0 Babović (83)
Ž Živković, Vulićević, Petrović, Balažic, Brašanac, Babović, Ninković (Ilić 72), Ćirković, Oumarou (A Živković 60), Jevtović, Bozhinov (Šaponjić 77). Coach: Zoran Milinković (SRB)
A 2-0 Brašanac (37), Oumarou (64)
Ž Živković, Vulićević, Petrović, Balažic, Brašanac (Ilić 80), Babović, Ćirković, Oumarou (Šaponjić 87), A Živković, Jevtović, Bozhinov (Ninković 68). Coach: Zoran Milinković (SRB)

Third qualifying round - FC Steaua Bucureşti (ROU)
A 1-1 Vulićević (62)
Ž Živković, Vulićević, Petrović, Balažic, Brašanac, Babović (Ilić 83), Oumarou (Ninković 70), A Živković, Jevtović, Fabrício, Bozhinov (Šaponjić 19). Coach: Zoran Milinković (SRB)
H 4-2 Babović (8), Jevtović (60), A Živković (70), Trujić (90+1)
Ž Živković, Vulićević, Petrović, Balažic, Brašanac, Babović (Trujić 90), Oumarou, A Živković, Jevtović, Fabrício, Bozhinov (Ilić 60). Coach: Zoran Milinković (SRB)

Play-offs - FC BATE Borisov (BLR)
A 0-1
Ž Živković, Vulićević, Petrović, Balažic, Brašanac, Babović, Oumarou, A Živković (Ilić 89), Jevtović, Fabrício, Bozhinov (Trujić 54). Coach: Zoran Milinković (SRB)
Red card: Jevtović 45+1
H 2-1 Zhavnerchik (74og), Šaponjić (90+3)
Ž Živković, Vulićević, Petrović, Balažic, Brašanac, Babović, Oumarou, A Živković, Lukić (Ilić 63), Fabrício, Bozhinov (Šaponjić 39). Coach: Zoran Milinković (SRB)

EUROPA LEAGUE

Group L
Match 1 - AZ Alkmaar (NED)
H 3-2 Oumarou (11, 40), A Živković (89)
Ž Živković, Leković, Vulićević, Petrović, Brašanac, Babović, Oumarou (Ilić 83), A Živković (Ninković 90), Jevtović, Šaponjić (Bozhinov 66), Fabrício. Coach: Zoran Milinković (SRB)
Match 2 - FC Augsburg (GER)
A 3-1 A Živković (31, 62), Fabrício (54)
Ž Živković, Vulićević, Balažic (Ostojić 46), Brašanac, Babović, Oumarou (Bozhinov 22; Petrović 66), A Živković, Subić, Jevtović, Fabrício, A Stevanović. Coach: Zoran Milinković (SRB)
Red card: Subić 64
Match 3 - Athletic Club (ESP)
H 0-2
Ž Živković, Leković, Vulićević, Petrović, Ninković (Trujić 84), A Živković, Lukić, Ostojić, Fabrício, Bozhinov (Grbić 64), A Stevanović (Šaponjić 79). Coach: Ljubinko Drulović (SRB)
Match 4 - Athletic Club (ESP)
A 1-5 Oumarou (17)
Kljajić, Vulićević, Balažic (Ćirković 26), Babović, Grbić, Oumarou (Šaponjić 46), Subić, Lukić, Jevtović, Fabrício, A Stevanović (Ninković 73). Coach: Ljubinko Drulović (SRB)

Match 5 - AZ Alkmaar (NED)
A 2-1 Oumarou (65), A Živković (89)
Kljajić, Bandalovski, Vulićević, Brašanac, Babović (Ilić 75), Ninković (Bozhinov 84), Ćirković, Oumarou, A Živković (Grbić 90+2), Subić, Jevtović. Coach: Ljubinko Drulović (SRB)
Match 6 - FC Augsburg (GER)
H 1-3 Oumarou (11)
Ž Živković, Bandalovski, Brašanac, Babović, Ninković (Grbić 83), Ćirković, Oumarou, A Živković, Subić (Petrović 64), Jevtović, Fabrício. Coach: Ljubinko Drulović (SRB)
Red card: A Živković 81

FK Čukarički

EUROPA LEAGUE

First qualifying round - NK Domžale (SVN)
A 1-0 Matić (43p)
Stevanović, Lucas, D Srnić, B Janković (Mirosavljević 89), Matić (Jovanović 82), Pavlović (Radovanović 90+4), S Srnić, Stojković, Ostojić, Bojić, Brežančić. Coach: Vladan Milojević (SRB)
H 0-0
Stevanović, Lucas, D Srnić, B Janković, Matić (Mandić 69), Pavlović (Stjoiljković 81), S Srnić, Stojković, Ostojić, Bojić (Mirosavljević 90), Brežančić. Coach: Vladan Milojević (SRB)

Second qualifying round - Qäbälä FK (AZE)
H 1-0 Stojiljković (53p)
Stevanović, Lucas, D Srnić, B Janković, Stojiljković (Mirosavljević 85), Pavlović (Mandić 67), S Srnić, Stojković, Ostojić, Bojić (Jovanović 90+1), Brežančić. Coach: Vladan Milojević (SRB)
A 0-2
Stevanović, Lucas, D Srnić (Regan 55), B Janković (Matić 76), Stojiljković, Pavlović, S Srnić (Mandić 81), Stojković, Ostojić, Bojić, Brežančić. Coach: Vladan Milojević (SRB)

FK Crvena zvezda

EUROPA LEAGUE

First qualifying round - FC Kairat Almaty (KAZ)
H 0-2
Rajković, Vered, Pavićević, Cvetković, Parker, Katai (Ristić 77), Savićević, Andjelković, Kovačević (Jovanović 5), Rendulić, Orlandić (Jović 60). Coach: Miodrag Božović (MNE)
Red card: Pavićević 3

A 1-2 Savićević (85p)
Rajković, Petković (Cvetković 46), S Stojanovic, Jović, Vered (Gavrić 70), Mbodj, Parker (Orlandić 60), Katai, Savićević, Andjelković, Rendulić. Coach: Miodrag Božović (MNE)

FK Vojvodina

EUROPA LEAGUE

First qualifying round - MTK Budapest (HUN)
A 0-0
Žakula, Vasilić, Ivanić (Š Kordić 90+3), Stanisavljević, Puškarić, Mrdaković (Maksimović 89), Paločević (Stamenić 64), Nastić, Djurić, Sekulić, Dinga. Coach: Zlatomir Zagorčić (BUL)
H 3-1 Stanisavljević (14), Mrdaković (40), Ivanić (51)
Žakula, Vasilić, Ivanić, Stanisavljević, Mrdaković (Paločević 90), Pankov, Nastić, Djurić, Sekulić, Maksimović (Puškarić 55), Stamenić (Babić 77). Coach: Zlatomir Zagorčić (BUL)

Second qualifying round - FK Spartaks Jūrmala (LVA)
H 3-0 Stanisavljević (6), Mrdaković (16), Mickevičs (88og)
Žakula, Vasilić, Ivanić, Stanisavljević, Mrdaković (Ožegović 74), Pankov, Nastić, Djurić, Sekulić, Maksimović (Puškarić 79), Stamenić (Paločević 72). Coach: Zlatomir Zagorčić (BUL)
A 1-1 Š Kordić (86)
Žakula, Ivanić (Paločević 69), Stanisavljević (Stamenić 73), Pankov, Lakićević, Nastić, Babić, Djurić, Sekulić, Maksimović, Ožegović (Š Kordić 80). Coach: Zlatomir Zagorčić (BUL)

Third qualifying round - UC Sampdoria (ITA)
A 4-0 Ivanić (4), Stanisavljević (49), Ožegović (58, 90+1)
Žakula, Vasilić, Ivanić (Babić 87), Stanisavljević (Stamenić 85), Puškarić (Paločević 71), Pankov, Nastić, Djurić, Sekulić, Maksimović, Ožegović. Coach: Zlatomir Zagorčić (BUL)
H 0-2
Žakula, Vasilić, Ivanić (Babić 90+3), Stanisavljević (Lakićević 87), Puškarić (Paločević 78), Pankov, Nastić, Djurić, Sekulić, Maksimović, Ožegović. Coach: Zlatomir Zagorčić (BUL)

Play-offs - FC Viktoria Plzeň (CZE)
A 0-3
Žakula, Vasilić, Ivanić, Stanisavljević (Babić 88), Puškarić (Paločević 68), Pankov, Nastić, Djurić, Sekulić, Maksimović, Ožegović (Pavkov 88). Coach: Zlatomir Zagorčić (BUL)
H 0-2
Žakula, Vasilić, Ivanić (Stamenić 80), Pekarić, Paločević, Nastić (Radović 66), Babić (Zoćević 64), Djurić, Sekulić, Maksimović, Ožegović. Coach: Zlatomir Zagorčić (BUL)

DOMESTIC LEAGUE CLUB-BY-CLUB

FK Borac Čačak

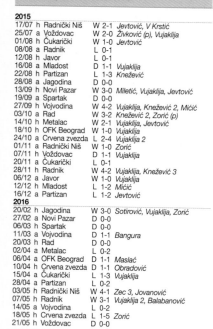

1928 • Gradski stadion (8,000) • boracfk.com

Coach: Nenad Lalatović;
(14/11/15) Milorad Kosanović;
(30/01/16) Ljubiša Stamenković;
(30/04/16) Milorad Kosanović

2015

17/07	h	Radnički Niš	W 2-1	*Jevtović, V Krstić*
25/07	a	Voždovac	W 2-0	*Živković (p), Vujaklija*
01/08	h	Čukarički	W 1-0	*Jevtović*
08/08	a	Radnik	L 0-1	
12/08	h	Javor	L 0-1	
16/08	a	Mladost	D 1-1	*Vujaklija*
22/08	h	Partizan	L 1-3	*Knežević*
28/08	a	Jagodina	D 0-0	
13/09	h	Novi Pazar	W 3-0	*Miletić, Vujaklija, Jevtović*
19/09	a	Spartak	D 0-0	
27/09	h	Vojvodina	W 4-2	*Vujaklija, Knežević 2, Mićić*
03/10	a	Rad	W 3-2	*Knežević 2, Zorić (p)*
14/10	h	Metalac	W 2-1	*Vujaklija, Jevtović*
18/10	h	OFK Beograd	W 1-0	*Vujaklija*
24/10	a	Crvena zvezda	L 2-4	*Vujaklija 2*
01/11	a	Radnički Niš	W 1-0	*Zorić*
07/11	h	Voždovac	D 1-1	*Vujaklija*
20/11	a	Čukarički	L 0-1	
28/11	h	Radnik	W 4-2	*Vujaklija, Knežević 3*
06/12	a	Javor	W 1-0	*Vujaklija*
12/12	h	Mladost	L 1-2	*Mićić*
16/12	a	Partizan	L 1-2	*Jevtović*

2016

20/02	h	Jagodina	W 3-0	*Sotirović, Vujaklija, Zorić*
27/02	a	Novi Pazar	D 0-0	
06/03	h	Spartak	D 0-0	
11/03	a	Vojvodina	D 1-1	*Bangura*
20/03	h	Rad	D 0-0	
02/04	a	Metalac	L 0-2	
06/04	a	OFK Beograd	D 1-1	*Maslać*
10/04	h	Crvena zvezda	D 1-1	*Obradović*
15/04	a	Čukarički	L 1-3	*Vujaklija*
28/04	a	Partizan	L 0-2	
03/05	h	Radnički Niš	W 4-1	*Zec 3, Jovanović*
07/05	h	Radnik	W 3-1	*Vujaklija 2, Balabanović*
14/05	a	Vojvodina	L 0-2	
18/05	h	Crvena zvezda	L 1-5	*Zorić*
21/05	h	Voždovac	D 0-0	

No	Name	Nat	DoB	Pos	Aps	(s)	Gls
94	Aldin Adžović	MNE	18/06/94	M	2	(4)	
30	Vladimir Bajić		28/11/87	G	36		
88	Milorad Balabanović		18/01/90	M	13		1
3	Mustapha Bangura	SLE	24/10/89	M	1	(9)	1
14	Uroš Djerić		28/05/92	A	1	(17)	
22	Dušan Djordjević		25/06/96	D	1		
25	Stefan Djordjević		13/03/91	D	1		
19	Stefan Drašković		27/07/89	D	9	(6)	
85	Miljan Jablan		30/01/85	D	20		
11	Milan Jevtović		13/06/93	A	21		5
5	Milan Jokić		21/03/95	M		(2)	
29	Dušan Jovančić		19/10/90	M	21		
73	Lazar Jovanović		13/07/93	A	14		1
80	Filip Knežević		08/11/91	M	18	(2)	8
15	Miroljub Kostić		05/06/88	M	14		
6	Miloš Krstić		19/11/88	D	12		
18	Vladimir Krstić		28/06/87	M	3	(5)	1
3	Djordje Lazović		01/10/90	D		(1)	
16	Milan Marčić		14/03/96	M		(1)	
17	Mario Maslać		09/09/90	D	14		1
23	Dušan Mićić		29/11/84	M	19		2
33	Nemanja Miletić		16/01/91	D	20		1
8	Stefan Milojević		29/01/89	M	7	(15)	
24	Saša Mišić		24/08/87	G	1		
5	Miljan Mutavdžić		03/02/86	M	1	1	
4	Lazar Obradović		05/12/92	D	6	(6)	1
7	Pedro Petrazzi	BRA	15/09/90	M	12		
80	Pavle Propadalo		24/11/94	M	1	(1)	
10	Igor Savić		31/01/97	M		(2)	
23	Vuk Sotirović		13/07/82	A	6	(6)	1
2	Aleksandar Tanasin		15/11/91	D	33		
31	Ivan Todorović		29/07/83	M	3		
21	Branislav Tomić		12/02/95	A		(6)	
34	Srdjan Vujaklija		21/03/88	A	34		15
26	Stefan Vukmirović		19/07/91	M	11	(15)	
11	Ilian Yordanov	BUL	03/04/89	A		(3)	
77	Djuro Zec		06/03/90	M	7	(4)	3
9	Darko Zorić	MNE	12/09/93	M	23	(2)	4
28	Stefan Živković		01/06/90	D	22		1

FK Crvena zvezda

1945 • Rajko Mitić (51,328) • crvenazvezdafk.com

Major honours
European Champion Clubs' Cup (1) 1991; European/South American Cup (1) 1991; Yugoslav/Serbian League (27) 1951, 1953, 1956, 1957, 1959, 1960, 1964, 1968, 1969, 1970, 1973, 1977, 1980, 1981, 1984, 1988, 1990, 1991, 1992, 1995, 2000, 2001, 2004, 2006, 2007, 2014, 2016; Yugoslav/Serbian Cup (24) 1948, 1949, 1950, 1958, 1959, 1964, 1968, 1970, 1971, 1982, 1985, 1990, 1993, 1995, 1996, 1997, 1999, 2000, 2002, 2004, 2006, 2007, 2010, 2012

Coach: Miodrag Božović (MNE)

2015

19/07	a	OFK Beograd	W 6-2	*Mbodj, Jović, Savićević 2 (1p), Parker 2*
26/07	a	Metalac	D 0-0	
31/07	h	Radnički Niš	D 1-1	*Jović*
09/08	a	Voždovac	W 3-2	*Katai, Hugo Vieira, Jović*
12/08	h	Čukarički	W 3-1	*Ibáñez 2 (1p), Katai*
16/08	a	Radnik	W 2-0	*Katai, S Stojanović*
23/08	h	Javor	W 1-0	*Katai*
30/08	a	Mladost	W 3-0	*Donald (p), Jovanović, Vered*
12/09	h	Partizan	W 3-1	*Hugo Vieira 2, Katai*
18/09	a	Jagodina	W 3-0	*Srnić, Plavšić, Hugo Vieira*
26/09	h	Novi Pazar	W 2-0	*Grujić, Katai*
03/10	a	Spartak	W 3-2	*Grujić, Katai, Jović*
17/10	a	Rad	W 3-0	*Grujić, Ristić, Katai*
21/10	h	Vojvodina	W 3-0	*Srnić 3*
24/10	h	Borac	W 4-2	*Katai 2, Grujić, Sikimić*
31/10	h	OFK Beograd	W 4-1	*Srnić 2, Jovanović, Hugo Vieira*
07/11	h	Metalac	W 2-0	*Bruno, Hugo Vieira*
22/11	a	Radnički Niš	W 2-1	*Katai, Ibáñez*
28/11	h	Voždovac	W 2-0	*Hugo Vieira 2*
06/12	a	Čukarički	W 7-2	*Grujić, Ibáñez 2 (1p), Srnić, Hugo Vieira 2, Jović*
12/12	h	Radnik	W 5-0	*Hugo Vieira 3, Katai, Srnić*
16/12	a	Javor	W 3-0	*Hugo Vieira, Plavšić, Katai*

2016

20/02	h	Mladost	W 2-1	*Le Tallec, Hugo Vieira*
27/02	a	Partizan	W 2-1	*Ibáñez, Hugo Vieira*
05/03	h	Jagodina	W 3-1	*Ibáñez, Katai, Hugo Vieira*
19/03	h	Spartak	W 4-0	*Ibáñez 2 (2p), Ristić, Hugo Vieira*
22/03	a	Novi Pazar	W 4-0	*Luković, Hugo Vieira, og (Trtovac), Le Tallec*
02/04	a	Vojvodina	D 0-0	
06/04	h	Rad	W 1-0	*Donald*
10/04	a	Borac	D 1-1	*Hugo Vieira*
16/04	h	Partizan	D 1-1	*Sikimić*
27/04	h	Čukarički	L 1-2	*Katai*
03/05	a	Voždovac	W 1-0	*Sikimić*
07/05	h	Vojvodina	L 1-3	*Grujić*
14/05	a	Radnik	W 4-1	*Katai 2, Hugo Vieira, Orlandić*
18/05	a	Borac	W 5-1	*og (Maslać), Katai 3, Orlandić*
21/05	h	Radnički Niš	W 2-0	*Orlandić, Katai*

No	Name	Nat	DoB	Pos	Aps	(s)	Gls
33	Dušan Andjelković		15/06/82	D	4	(1)	
18	David Babunski	MKD	01/03/94	M	3	(3)	
15	Bruno	BRA	05/06/90	M	3	(2)	1
19	Miloš Cvetković		06/01/90	D	6	(2)	
20	Mitchell Donald	NED	10/12/88	M	28		2
5	Édson Silva	BRA	09/05/86	D	7		
44	Nenad Gavrić		12/12/91	M	3	(4)	
8	Marko Grujić		13/04/96	M	27	(2)	6
70	Hugo Vieira	POR	25/07/88	A	30	(3)	21
88	Luis Ibáñez	ARG	15/07/88	D	31		9
6	Vukašin Jovanović		17/05/96	D	17	(2)	2
9	Luka Jović		23/12/97	A	4	(15)	5
1	Damir Kahriman		19/11/84	G	30		
10	Aleksandar Katai		06/02/91	M	32	(1)	21
55	Aleksandar Kovačević		09/01/92	M	4		
4	Damien Le Tallec	FRA	19/04/90	M	14		2
3	Aleksandar Luković		23/10/82	D	23	(5)	1
16	Mamadou Mbodj	SEN	12/03/93	D	4	(1)	1
99	Petar Orlandić	MNE	06/08/90	A	1	(5)	3
23	Josh Parker	ATG	01/12/90	A	2	(1)	2
14	Savo Pavićević	MNE	11/12/80	D	16	(1)	
2	Marko Petković		03/09/92	D	31	(2)	
17	Srdjan Plavšić		03/12/95	M	18	(13)	2
6	Uroš Račić		17/03/98	M		(1)	
95	Predrag Rajković		31/10/95	G	6		
77	Zoran Rendulić		22/05/84	D	7	(2)	
24	Mihailo Ristić		31/10/95	M	13	(16)	2
28	Vukan Savićević	MNE	29/01/94	M	3		2
81	Predrag Sikimić		29/08/92	A	4	(18)	3
55	Slavoljub Srnić		12/01/92	A	25	(2)	8
34	Miloš Stojanović		18/01/97	D	2	(1)	
7	Saša Stojanović		21/01/83	M	1	(4)	1
27	Nemanja Supić	BIH	01/12/82	G	1		
11	Idan Vered	ISR	25/05/89	M	7	(1)	1

FK Čukarički

1926 • FK Čukarički (4,070) • fkcukaricki.rs

Major honours
Serbian Cup (1) 2015

Coach: Vladan Milojević;
(05/10/15) Zoran Popović;
(04/03/16) Milan Lešnjak

2015

19/07	a	Vojvodina	W 4-0	*Pavlović 3, Stojiljković*
26/07	h	Rad	D 1-1	*Stojiljković*
01/08	a	Borac	L 0-1	
08/08	h	OFK Beograd	W 1-0	*Pavlović*
12/08	a	Crvena zvezda	L 1-3	*S Srnić*
16/08	h	Radnički Niš	L 0-1	
23/08	a	Voždovac	D 0-0	
30/08	a	Metalac	W 2-1	*Boljević, Lucas Piasentin (p)*
11/09	h	Radnik	W 2-0	*D Srnić 2*
19/09	a	Javor	D 0-0	
25/09	h	Mladost	L 0-1	
05/10	a	Partizan	W 1-0	*Lucas Piasentin*
15/10	h	Jagodina	W 2-0	*og (Filipović), N Janković*
18/10	a	Novi Pazar	D 0-0	
23/10	h	Spartak	W 3-0	*Matić, Thiago Galvão, og (Marinković)*
01/11	h	Vojvodina	D 1-1	*Bojić*
08/11	a	Rad	W 1-0	*Ostojić*
20/11	h	Borac	W 1-0	*Mirosavljević*
28/11	a	OFK Beograd	W 3-0	*Mirosavljević, Bojić, Pavlović*
06/12	h	Crvena zvezda	L 2-7	*Pavlović 2*
11/12	a	Radnički Niš	D 0-0	
16/12	h	Voždovac	D 0-0	

2016

19/02	h	Metalac	D 1-1	*Mirosavljević*
27/02	a	Radnik	L 1-2	*Lagator*
06/03	h	Javor	W 1-0	*Pavlović*
20/03	h	Partizan	L 1-2	*og (Bandalovski)*
27/03	a	Mladost	W 2-0	*Bojić, Radonjić*
02/04	a	Jagodina	W 3-1	*Djurić, Radonjić, Pavlović*
06/04	h	Novi Pazar	W 1-0	*Ostojić*
10/04	a	Spartak	W 2-0	*Pavlović 2*
15/04	h	Borac	W 3-1	*Pavlović 3*
23/04	a	Partizan	W 2-1	*B Janković, Pavlović*
27/04	a	Crvena zvezda	W 2-1	*Pavlović 2*
03/05	h	Vojvodina	L 1-2	*Jovanović*
07/05	h	Radnički Niš	L 1-5	*Jovanović*
14/05	a	Voždovac	L 0-2	
21/05	h	Radnik	W 2-1	*Jovanović, Pavlović*

No	Name	Nat	DoB	Pos	Aps	(s)	Gls
14	Lee Addy	GHA	07/07/90	D	6	(2)	
3	Djordje Bašanović		31/07/96	D	2		
24	Petar Bojić		04/09/91	M	26	(5)	3
25	Dejan Boljević	MNE	30/05/90	D	15	(2)	1
31	Rajko Brežančić		21/08/89	D	3		
26	Djordje Djurić		10/08/91	D	12		1
8	Branislav Janković	MNE	08/02/92	M	23	(6)	1
17	Nikola Janković		07/06/93	D	8	(6)	1
19	Saša Jovanović		30/08/93	M	11	(14)	3
95	Nikola Karaklajić		05/02/95	M		(1)	
77	Filip Knežević		08/11/91	M	8	(2)	
44	Dušan Lagator	MNE	29/03/94	M	4	(1)	1
4	Lucas Piasentin	BRA	17/03/86	D	16	(4)	2
7	Staniša Mandić	MNE	27/01/95	A	21	(7)	
55	Erhan Mašović		22/11/98	D	7	(4)	
10	Igor Matić		22/07/81	M	17	(6)	1
57	Zehrudin Mehmedović		15/03/98	M		(1)	
30	Nenad Mirosavljević		04/09/77	A	5	(19)	3
23	Bojan Ostojić		12/02/84	D	34		2
11	Andrija Pavlović		16/11/93	A	35	(1)	18
28	Nemanja Radonjić		15/02/96	A		(10)	2
5	Marko Randjelović		16/08/84	D	6	(2)	
20	Obeng Regan	GHA	15/08/94	M	17	(2)	
6	Dragoljub Srnić		12/01/92	M	31	(3)	2
55	Slavoljub Srnić		12/01/92	A	6		1
12	Nemanja Stevanović		08/05/92	G	37		
9	Nikola Stojiljković		17/08/92	A	1	(2)	2
22	Filip Stojković	MNE	22/01/93	D	34		
65	Stefan Šapić		26/02/97	D		(1)	
9	Thiago Galvão	BRA	24/08/89	A	8	(4)	1
33	Stefan Živković		01/06/90	D	14		

FK Jagodina

1918 • Pod Djurdjevim brdom (15,000) •
fkjagodina.org.rs
Major honours
Serbian Cup (1) 2013
Coach: Miljojko Gošić;
(23/02/16) Stevan Mojsilović;
(07/04/16) Aleksandar Janjić

2015
18/07	h	Mladost	L 0-3	
25/07	a	Partizan	L 0-6	
02/08	h	Metalac	L 0-1	
07/08	h	Novi Pazar	L 1-2	*Savković*
12/08	a	Spartak	D 0-0	
22/08	h	Rad	D 0-0	
28/08	h	Borac	D 0-0	
13/09	a	OFK Beograd	W 2-0	*Popović, Kyeremeh*
18/09	h	Crvena zvezda	L 0-3	
23/09	h	Vojvodina	D 1-1	*Ivanović*
27/09	h	Radnički Niš	D 0-0	
03/10	h	Voždovac	D 0-0	
15/10	a	Čukarički	L 0-2	
18/10	h	Radnik	D 1-1	*U Nikolić (p)*
24/10	a	Javor	D 1-1	*U Nikolić (p)*
01/11	a	Mladost	L 0-2	
08/11	h	Partizan	D 2-2	*U Nikolić, Popović*
20/11	h	Metalac	W 4-1	*U Nikolić 2, Kyeremeh, Gašić*
06/12	h	Spartak	D 1-1	*Martinović*
09/12	a	Novi Pazar	L 0-1	
12/12	a	Vojvodina	L 1-3	*Popović*
16/12	h	Rad	W 1-0	*Savković*

2016
20/02	a	Borac	L 0-3	
27/02	h	OFK Beograd	W 3-1	*Jevtić, Savković 2*
05/03	a	Crvena zvezda	L 1-3	*Jevtić*
12/03	h	Radnički Niš	L 1-2	*U Nikolić (p)*
19/03	a	Voždovac	L 0-1	
02/04	a	Čukarički	L 1-3	*Lečić (p)*
06/04	h	Radnik	D 0-0	
10/04	h	Javor	W 1-0	*Lečić*
16/04	a	Novi Pazar	L 2-3	*Kyeremeh, Lečić*
22/04	h	Mladost	L 0-1	
28/04	a	Metalac	L 1-2	*Martinović*
03/05	a	Spartak	L 1-5	*Lečić*
07/05	h	Rad	D 1-1	*Lečić*
15/05	h	Javor	D 0-0	
21/05	a	OFK Beograd	L 2-6	*Lečić, Filipović*

No	Name	Nat	DoB	Pos	Aps	(s)	Gls
23	Veljko Antonijević		28/05/92	D	1	(3)	
15	Jovan Baošić	MNE	07/07/96	D	6	(1)	
4	Aleksandar Cvetković		04/06/95	D	2		
99	Lazar Cvetković		13/10/95	M		(1)	
23	Stefan Čolović		22/07/94	M		(1)	
7	Miloš Deletić		14/10/93	A	8	(5)	
31	Nemanja Djekić		13/05/97	M	2	(3)	
2	Predrag Djordjević		30/06/90	D	14	(1)	
6	Aleksandar Filipović		20/12/94	D	35		1
5	Danijel Gašić		19/01/87	D	26	(3)	1
11	Igor Ivanović		28/07/97	A	8	(4)	1
7	Marko Janković		22/03/96	M	2	(1)	
50	Goran Jerkovic	FRA	10/11/86	A	3	(5)	
35	Aleksandar Jevtić		30/03/85	A	13	(2)	2
19	Zoran Knežević		15/08/86	M	15	(5)	
4	Mićo Kuzmanović	BIH	18/03/96	A		(1)	
38	Francis Kyeremeh	GHA	31/12/97	A	15	(8)	3
17	Miroslav Lečić		20/04/85	A	10	(3)	6
20	Slavko Marić		03/07/84	D	23		
18	Dušan Martinović		22/12/87	M	13	(4)	2
32	Zoran Mihailović		02/06/96	A	6	(5)	
20	Sladjan Mijatović		23/05/94	D	4		
3	Ivan Miladinović		14/08/94	D	21	(1)	
23	Milan Milinković		04/05/92	D	17		
44	Aleksa Milojević		08/01/00	G		(1)	
77	Nemanja Milošević		28/08/96	M	2	(7)	
50	Marko Mirkailo		20/06/98	D	4	(1)	
29	Vuk Mitošević		12/02/91	M	10	(1)	
36	Stefan Nedović		12/01/88	M	24	(6)	
13	Djordje Nikolić		13/04/97	G	19		
10	Uroš Nikolić		14/12/93	M	29	(4)	6
8	Miloš Ozegović		11/05/92	M	5	(3)	
9	Mladen Popović		29/08/88	A	15	(7)	3
50	Nikola Radović		10/07/92	A	1	(1)	
33	Lazar Sajčić		24/09/96	M	1	(2)	
21	Mile Savković		03/11/92	M	25	(5)	4
35	Mladen Stoicev		21/10/95	A		(6)	
30	Aleksandar Stojmirović		11/12/82	A	9	(7)	
9	Djordje Šušnjar	MNE	18/02/92	A	1	(1)	
1	Lazar Tatić		01/04/94	G	18	(1)	

FK Javor

1912 • Kraj Moravice (4,000) • fkjavor.com
Coach: Aleksandar Janjić;
(08/01/16) Mladen Dodić

2014
18/07	a	Novi Pazar	W 1-0	*Ajuru*
25/07	h	Spartak	W 2-0	*Dražić, Docić (p)*
02/08	a	Vojvodina	L 0-2	
08/08	h	Rad	W 3-0	*og (Maraš), Docić, Djokić*
12/08	a	Borac	W 1-0	*Josović*
16/08	h	OFK Beograd	W 2-1	*Gafurov, Docić*
23/08	a	Crvena zvezda	L 0-1	
29/08	h	Radnički Niš	D 0-0	
13/09	a	Voždovac	W 2-0	*Eliomar, Dražić*
19/09	h	Čukarički	D 0-0	
26/09	a	Radnik	D 1-1	*Gafurov*
02/10	a	Metalac	D 0-0	
14/10	h	Mladost	D 0-0	
18/10	a	Partizan	L 2-3	*Dražić, Kolaković*
24/10	h	Jagodina	D 1-1	*Dražić*
31/10	h	Novi Pazar	D 1-1	*Gafurov*
07/11	a	Spartak	D 0-0	
21/11	h	Vojvodina	L 0-1	
28/11	a	Rad	D 1-1	*Dražić*
06/12	h	Borac	L 0-1	
12/12	a	OFK Beograd	W 1-0	*Gafurov*
16/12	h	Crvena zvezda	L 0-3	

2015
21/02	h	Radnički Niš	L 0-2	
27/02	h	Voždovac	D 0-0	
06/03	a	Čukarički	L 0-1	
12/03	h	Radnik	L 0-1	
20/03	h	Metalac	W 1-0	*Djokić*
01/04	a	Mladost	D 1-1	*Docić*
06/04	h	Partizan	L 1-2	*Dražić*
10/04	a	Jagodina	L 0-1	
16/04	h	Spartak	L 0-2	
23/04	a	Rad	L 0-1	
28/04	h	OFK Beograd	W 1-0	*Gafurov*
03/05	a	Novi Pazar	D 2-2	*Dražić, Docić*
07/05	h	Metalac	D 1-1	*Ratković*
15/05	a	Jagodina	D 0-0	
21/05	h	Mladost	L 0-1	

No	Name	Nat	DoB	Pos	Aps	(s)	Gls
6	Nnaemeka Ajuru	NGA	28/09/86	M	20	(8)	1
24	Aleksa Amanovic	MKD	24/10/96	D	3	(3)	
25	Nikola Bjelanović		07/11/97	D	1		
15	Djordje Crnomarković		10/09/93	D	31		
16	Bojan Čečarić		10/10/93	A	4	(8)	
22	Aleksandar Dimitrić		29/02/96	D	2	(4)	
1	Vladan Djogatović		03/11/84	G	35		
19	Jovan Djokić		13/08/92	M	35		2
5	Marko Docić		21/04/93	A	32	(1)	5
9	Stefan Dražić		14/08/92	A	35	(1)	7
8	Eliomar	BRA	16/03/88	M	26	(1)	1
11	Husniddin Gafurov	UZB	29/07/94	A	33		5
26	Marko Gajić		10/03/92	D	32		
2	Petar Glintić		09/06/92	G	2		
3	Ivan Josović		27/12/89	D	14	(14)	1
14	Marko Kolaković		09/02/93	D	11	(2)	1
30	Miroslav Maričić		19/08/98	M		(2)	
8	Maksim Martusevich	RUS	07/03/95	M	1	(2)	
4	Mladen Milanović		02/12/96	M	1		
17	Nemanja Miletić		26/07/91	D	34		
20	Milovan Milović		27/10/80	D	22		
31	Andrija Ratković		14/11/97	A	1	(3)	1
10	Igor Stojaković		27/05/80	M	13	(10)	
21	Zoran Švonja		04/10/95	M	8	(14)	
18	Nikola Vujović		27/11/90	A	4	(4)	
33	Marko Zečević		06/08/90	A	7	(22)	

FK Metalac

1961 • Gradski stadion kraj Despotovice (4,600)
• fkmetalac.rs
Coach: Nenad Vanić

2015
17/07	a	Partizan	L 0-4	
26/07	h	Crvena zvezda	D 0-0	
02/08	a	Jagodina	W 1-0	*Merdović*
08/08	h	Radnički Niš	L 0-2	
12/08	a	Novi Pazar	D 2-2	*Merdović, Milovanović*
15/08	h	Voždovac	D 1-1	*Otašević*
22/08	a	Spartak	W 3-0	*Merdović, Stanojević, Sedlar*
30/08	h	Čukarički	L 1-1	*Milovanović*
13/09	a	Vojvodina	L 2-3	*Merdović, Sedlar*
19/09	h	Radnik	D 2-2	*Otašević, Bukorac*
27/09	a	Rad	W 1-0	*Mladenović*
02/10	h	Javor	D 0-0	
14/10	a	Borac	L 1-2	*Dimitrijević*
18/10	h	Mladost	D 0-0	
24/10	a	OFK Beograd	L 0-1	
01/11	h	Partizan	W 1-0	*Mladenović (p)*
07/11	a	Crvena zvezda	L 0-2	
20/11	h	Jagodina	L 1-4	*Dimitrijević*
27/11	a	Radnički Niš	L 1-2	*Mladenović (p)*
04/12	h	Novi Pazar	W 3-2	*Panić, Mladenović, Brkić*
12/12	a	Voždovac	D 0-0	
16/12	h	Spartak	W 1-0	*Dimitrijević*

2016
19/02	a	Čukarički	D 1-1	*Caicedo*
26/02	h	Vojvodina	D 0-0	
06/03	a	Radnik	D 0-0	
13/03	h	Rad	D 2-2	*Caicedo, Mladenović (p)*
20/03	a	Javor	L 0-1	
02/04	h	Borac	W 2-0	*Caicedo, Stojanović*
06/04	a	Mladost	D 0-0	
10/04	h	OFK Beograd	W 3-1	*Merdović, Stojanović, Milovanović*
16/04	h	OFK Beograd	D 1-1	*Merdović*
23/04	a	Spartak	L 1-5	*Caicedo*
28/04	h	Jagodina	W 2-1	*Mijić, Mladenović*
03/05	h	Mladost	D 2-2	*Stojanović, Milovanović*
07/05	a	Javor	D 1-1	*Milovanović*
15/05	a	Rad	D 1-1	*Caicedo*
21/05	h	Novi Pazar	W 4-2	*Panić, Stanojević 3*

No	Name	Nat	DoB	Pos	Aps	(s)	Gls
18	Milan Basrak		24/12/94	A		(2)	
33	Nemanja Belić		24/04/87	G	34		
12	Stevan Bojović		07/05/95	G	1		
4	Goran Brkić		28/04/91	M	6	(7)	1
21	Stefan Bukorac		15/02/91	M	13	(2)	1
99	Walberto Caicedo	ECU	23/08/92	A	11	(4)	5
21	Uroš Delić		10/08/87	M	2	(7)	
14	Nikola Dimitrijević		10/05/91	A	24	(5)	3
6	Dejan Djenić		02/06/86	A	18	(3)	
6	Bosko Dopudj		09/12/90	D	6	(3)	
8	Aleksandar Ivanović		20/11/88	M	11	(7)	
13	Stefan Lukačević		09/11/95	M	2		
20	Goran Luković		05/11/78	M	3	(15)	
7	Luka Merdović	MNE	14/03/89	A	30	(3)	6
32	Bojan Mijalović		28/08/95	D	4	(7)	
18	Miloš Mijić		01/11/89	M	14	(1)	1
9	Dragan Milovanović		03/01/86	A	11	(12)	5
11	Nemanja Mladenović		03/03/93	M	29	(4)	6
25	Saša Nikodijević		16/07/87	D	29	(1)	
15	Vladimir Otašević		08/06/86	D	30	(1)	2
3	Stefan Panić		20/09/92	M	24	(4)	2
23	Miloš Rnić		24/01/89	D	20		
22	Aleksandar Sedlar		13/12/91	D	33	(1)	2
4	Aleksandar Simov		05/02/87	D	9	(2)	
17	Srdjan Simović		17/07/85	D	10	(2)	
12	Igor Stanojević		24/10/91	M	8	(9)	4
24	Milan Stojanović		10/05/88	M	13	(2)	3
19	Nikola Stojković		02/02/95	D	9	(4)	
16	Nikola Vuković		05/10/96	A	1	(3)	
1	Bojan Zogović		16/02/89	G	2		

SERBIA

FK Mladost Lučani

1952 • SC Mladost (8,050) • fkmladostlucani.com

Coach: Nenad Milovanović

2014				
18/07	a	Jagodina	W 3-0	*Golemić (p), Mijić, L Jovanović*
25/07	h	Novi Pazar	D 1-1	*S Jovanović*
01/08	a	Spartak	L 0-2	
09/08	h	Vojvodina	L 1-2	*Pavlov*
12/08	a	Rad	L 2-4	*Gavrić, S Jovanović*
16/08	h	Borac	D 1-1	*Golemić (p)*
22/08	a	OFK Beograd	W 1-0	*S Jovanović*
30/08	h	Crvena zvezda	L 0-3	
13/09	a	Radnički Niš	D 1-1	*S Jovanović*
19/09	h	Voždovac	D 0-0	
25/09	a	Čukarički	W 1-0	*S Jovanović*
03/10	h	Radnik	D 0-0	
14/10	a	Javor	D 0-0	
18/10	a	Metalac	D 0-0	
25/10	h	Partizan	D 2-2	*Lepović, Gavrić*
01/11	h	Jagodina	W 2-0	*S Jovanović 2*
07/11	a	Novi Pazar	W 3-1	*Kitanovski 2, Mbiobe*
20/11	h	Spartak	D 0-0	
28/11	a	Vojvodina	L 0-3	
05/12	h	Rad	W 1-0	*Živadinović*
12/12	a	Borac	W 2-1	*Milosavljević, Golemić (p)*
16/12	h	OFK Beograd	D 0-0	
2015				
20/02	a	Crvena zvezda	L 1-2	*Luković*
27/02	h	Radnički Niš	L 0-1	
05/03	a	Voždovac	L 1-4	*Bajić*
19/03	a	Radnik	L 1-3	*Mbiobe*
27/03	h	Čukarički	L 0-2	
01/04	h	Javor	D 1-1	*S Jovanović*
06/04	h	Metalac	D 0-0	
10/04	a	Partizan	L 0-4	
17/04	h	Rad	L 1-3	*S Jovanović (p)*
22/04	a	Jagodina	W 1-0	*Kitanovski*
28/04	h	Spartak	D 0-0	
03/05	a	Metalac	D 2-2	*Saničanin, Kitanovski*
08/05	h	Novi Pazar	W 1-0	*Milosavljević*
15/05	h	OFK Beograd	W 3-1	*Čečarić, S Jovanović, Golubović*
21/05	a	Javor	W 1-0	*Milosavljević*

No	Name	Nat	DoB	Pos	Aps	(s)	Gls
8	Aleksandar Alempijević		25/07/88	M	4	(1)	
27	Miloš Bajić		27/04/94	M	4	(8)	1
22	Ognjen Čančarević		25/09/89	G	2		
16	Bojan Čečarić		10/10/93	A	5	(6)	1
55	Uroš Djerić		28/05/92	A	1	(2)	
33	Aleksandar Djoković		16/12/91	A	1	(4)	
11	Nebojša Gavrić		27/08/91	M	28	(5)	2
5	Vladimir Golemić		28/06/91	D	20		3
8	Stefan Golubović		01/08/96	M	2	(1)	1
14	Milan Jagodić		11/03/91	D		(6)	
32	Lazar Jovanović		13/07/93	A	4	(3)	1
7	Saša Jovanović		15/12/91	M	36		10
3	Tome Kitanovski	MKD	21/05/92	D	27	(2)	4
1	Nemanja Krznarić		29/05/84	G	35		
18	Aleksandar Lazevski	MKD	21/01/88	D	22		
28	Miloš Lepović		03/10/87	M	22	(5)	1
88	Predrag Luka		11/05/88	M	6	(5)	
77	Stevan Luković		16/03/93	M	13		1
58	Michel Mbiobe	CMR	03/02/96	A	10	(11)	2
31	Miloš Mijić		01/11/89	M	10	(4)	1
10	Radomir Milosavljević		30/07/92	M	26	(4)	3
13	Nemanja Milovanović		12/06/91	M	4	(2)	
8	Yevhen Pavlov	UKR	11/03/91	A	4	(2)	1
17	Ivan Pešić		07/07/89	D	19	(2)	
20	Matija Protić		05/03/94	M	2	(3)	
13	Darko Rakočević		13/09/81	D	9		
5	Siniša Saničanin	BIH	24/04/95	D	14		1
6	Miloš Stanojević		20/11/93	M	15	(4)	
93	Miloš Šatara	BIH	28/10/95	M	12	(11)	
28	Dušan Tešić		16/07/88	M	1	(3)	
14	Marko Zočević		19/05/93	M	1		
21	Predrag Živadinović		07/07/83	A	12	(10)	1
19	Aleksandar Živanović		08/04/87	D	36		

FK Novi Pazar

1928 • Gradski stadion – Abdulah Gegić Duce (6,500) • fknovipazar.rs

Coach: Petar Kurćubić; (25/08/15) Mladen Dodić; (01/11/15) Radmilo Ivančević; (10/01/16) Zoran Marić

2015				
18/07	h	Javor	L 0-1	
25/07	a	Mladost	D 1-1	*Predrag Pavlović*
01/08	h	Partizan	W 3-2	*Predrag Pavlović (p), Askovski 2*
07/08	a	Jagodina	W 2-1	*Predrag Pavlović, Askovski*
12/08	h	Metalac	D 2-2	*Radivojević, Predrag Pavlović*
16/08	h	Spartak	D 0-0	
23/08	a	Vojvodina	L 1-4	*Rušević*
29/08	h	Rad	W 1-0	*Radivojević*
13/09	a	Borac	L 0-3	
19/09	h	OFK Beograd	W 1-0	*Predrag Pavlović*
26/09	a	Crvena zvezda	L 0-2	
03/10	h	Radnički Niš	W 1-0	*Trtovac*
14/10	a	Voždovac	L 0-1	
18/10	h	Čukarički	D 0-0	
24/10	a	Radnik	L 0-2	
31/10	a	Javor	D 1-1	*Radivojević*
07/11	h	Mladost	L 1-3	*Radivojević*
21/11	a	Partizan	L 0-3	
04/12	a	Metalac	L 2-3	*Predrag Pavlović (p), Radivojević*
09/12	h	Jagodina	W 1-0	*Predrag Pavlović*
12/12	a	Spartak	L 0-2	
16/12	h	Vojvodina	D 1-1	*Osmanagić*
2016				
20/02	a	Rad	L 0-1	
27/02	h	Borac	D 0-0	
06/03	a	OFK Beograd	D 0-0	
18/03	a	Radnički Niš	D 0-0	
22/03	h	Crvena zvezda	L 0-4	
02/04	h	Voždovac	D 1-1	*Šarac*
06/04	a	Čukarički	L 0-1	
10/04	h	Radnik	W 2-0	*Ubiparip 2*
16/04	h	Jagodina	W 3-2	*Bruno, Ubiparip, Vasilić*
23/04	a	OFK Beograd	W 2-1	*Ubiparip 2*
28/04	h	Rad	W 1-0	*Ubiparip*
03/05	h	Javor	L 0-2	
08/05	a	Mladost	L 0-1	
15/05	h	Spartak	L 0-1	
21/05	a	Metalac	L 2-4	*Rušević, Pajović*

No	Name	Nat	DoB	Pos	Aps	(s)	Gls
92	Adriano	BRA	15/02/92	M		(1)	
6	Nemanja Ahčin		07/04/94	M		(3)	
3	Stefan Askovski	MKD	24/02/92	D	12	(2)	3
15	Ensar Bajramlić		16/02/97	M		(1)	
33	Denis Biševac		22/09/96	D	2	(2)	
18	Mirsad Brunčević		11/06/94	D		(2)	
15	Bruno	BRA	05/06/90	M	11		1
82	Jovan Damjanović		04/10/82	A	10	(1)	
86	Marko Djalović		19/05/86	D	14	(1)	
5	Miroljub Kostić		05/06/88	M	18	(3)	
88	Darko Micevski	MKD	12/04/92	M	13		
8	Ivan Obrovac		08/12/86	M	5	(8)	
17	John Okoye	NGA	01/01/95	A	2	(1)	
55	Amer Osmanagić	BIH	07/05/89	M	11	(7)	1
20	Kontoh Owusu-Ansah	GHA	24/08/93	M	1	(1)	
21	Lazar Pajović		26/08/91	D	5	(5)	1
8	Dušan Pantelić		15/03/93	M	4		
24	Petar Pavlović		03/03/87	D	6	(4)	
77	Predrag Pavlović		19/06/86	M	22		7
11	Radoš Protić		31/01/87	D	9	(1)	
27	Vladimir Radivojević		04/02/86	M	31	(3)	5
9	Anes Rušević		02/12/96	A	2	(19)	2
5	Milan Savić		04/04/94	D	11		
80	Edin Selimović		28/01/91	M		(5)	
2	Sinisa Stevanović		12/01/89	D	16		
22	Dino Šarac		06/09/90	M	16	(12)	1
99	Miloš Tintor		21/08/86	D	27	(2)	
6	Ivan Todorović		29/07/83	M	9	(1)	
4	Jasmin Trtovac		27/12/86	D	19	(1)	1
14	Vojo Ubiparip		10/05/88	A	14		6
2	Jovica Vasilić		08/07/90	D	10		1
44	Nemanja Vidić		06/08/89	M	11	(1)	
26	Slobodan Vuković		23/01/86	D	16		
7	Irfan Vusljanin		07/01/86	M	29		
1	Zlatko Zečević		10/08/83	G	19		
10	Almedin Zilkić		25/02/96	M	3	(19)	
77	Nemanja Zlatković		21/08/88	D	11		
23	Mladen Živković		26/08/89	G	18		

OFK Beograd

1911 • Omladinski stadion (13,900) • ofkbeograd.co.rs

Major honours

Yugoslav League (5) 1931, 1933, 1935, 1936, 1939; Yugoslav Cup (5) 1934, 1953, 1955, 1962, 1966

Coach: Dejan Djurdjević; (13/07/15) Vladimir Petrović; (24/08/15) Dragoljub Bekvalac; (11/11/15) Miodrag Radanović; (25/12/15) Dragan Radojičić

2015				
19/07	h	Crvena zvezda	L 2-6	*Andrić, Dražić*
24/07	a	Radnički Niš	L 0-1	
01/08	h	Voždovac	W 2-1	*Škrbić, Jovanović (p)*
08/08	a	Čukarički	L 0-1	
12/08	h	Radnik	W 3-0	*Jovanović, Liščević, Subašić*
16/08	a	Javor	L 1-2	*Sarajlin*
22/08	h	Mladost	L 0-1	
29/08	a	Partizan	L 1-2	*Ignjatijević*
13/09	h	Jagodina	L 0-2	
19/09	a	Novi Pazar	L 0-1	
26/09	h	Spartak	W 2-0	*Denković, Jovanović (p)*
03/10	a	Vojvodina	L 0-1	
14/10	h	Rad	W 2-0	*Mikić, Jovanović*
18/10	a	Borac	L 0-1	
24/10	h	Metalac	W 1-0	*Jovanović*
31/10	a	Crvena zvezda	L 1-4	*Simić*
07/11	h	Radnički Niš	L 0-2	
21/11	a	Voždovac	W 3-2	*Mikić, Pejović, Andrić*
28/11	h	Čukarički	L 0-3	
06/12	a	Radnik	L 1-2	*Rajevac*
12/12	h	Javor	L 0-1	
16/12	a	Mladost	D 0-0	
2016				
21/02	h	Partizan	W 2-1	*Jovović, Pavlovski*
27/02	a	Jagodina	L 1-3	*Andrić*
06/03	h	Novi Pazar	D 0-0	
12/03	a	Spartak	L 1-2	*Cuckić*
19/03	h	Vojvodina	W 1-0	*Martinović*
02/04	a	Rad	D 1-1	*Jovović*
06/04	h	Borac	D 1-1	*Planić*
10/04	a	Metalac	L 1-3	*Jovović*
16/04	a	Metalac	D 1-1	*Andrić*
23/04	h	Novi Pazar	L 1-2	*Jovović (p)*
28/04	a	Javor	L 0-1	
03/05	a	Rad	L 1-2	*Andrić*
08/05	h	Spartak	L 1-3	*Gigić*
15/05	a	Mladost	L 1-3	*Jovović*
21/05	h	Jagodina	W 6-2	*Pejović 2, Andrić 2, Vukobratović, D Stojković*

No	Name	Nat	DoB	Pos	Aps	(s)	Gls
9	Komnen Andrić		01/07/95	A	24	(2)	7
11	Miloš Antić		28/10/94	M	2		
90	Daniel Avramovski	MKD	20/02/95	M	18	(4)	
36	Marko Batinica		31/05/97	M	2	(2)	
33	Nemanja Belaković		08/01/97	A	2	(9)	
16	Nikola Cuckić		11/04/97	M	10	(8)	1
12	Ognjen Čančarević		25/09/89	G	1	(1)	
1	Stefan Čupić		07/05/94	G	36		
20	Dario Damjanović	BIH	23/07/81	M	6	(1)	
28	Aleksa Denković		21/03/97	M	2	(3)	1
19	Željko Dimitrov		19/02/94	A	1	(3)	
10	Dejan Dražić		26/09/95	M	3		1
17	Borko Duronjić		24/09/97	A	9	(10)	
99	Petar Gigić		07/03/97	A	3	(8)	1
30	Damjan Gojkov		02/01/98	M	7	(8)	
3	Nikola Ignjatijević		12/12/83	D	12	(1)	1
37	Stefan Janković		25/06/97	M	1	(2)	
7	Aleksandar Ješić		13/09/94	M	8	(1)	
12	Ivica Jovanović	MNE	04/12/87	A	21		5
8	Vladimir Jovović	MNE	26/10/94	M	12		5
55	Srdja Knežević		15/04/85	D	6	(2)	
13	Zlatko Liščević		08/03/91	M	25		1
19	Vuk Martinović	MNE	19/09/89	D	10		1
27	Filip Matović		06/02/95	D	3	(1)	
23	Andrija Mijailović		07/06/95	D		(1)	
66	Nikola Mikić		13/09/85	D	11		2
10	Marko Pavlovski		07/02/94	M	7	(2)	1
18	Aleksandar Pejović		28/12/90	M	27	(2)	3
6	Bogdan Planić		19/01/92	D	30		1
25	Aleksandar Radovanović		11/11/93	D	14	(1)	
2	Filip Rajevac		21/06/92	M	1	(6)	1
4	Ivan Rogač		08/06/92	M	4	(1)	
8	Mladen Sarajlin		17/04/95	M	1	(2)	1
5	Milan Savić		04/04/94	D	17	(2)	
14	Marko Simić		07/11/93	A	5	(6)	1
24	Ostoja Stjepanovic	MKD	17/01/85	M	11	(3)	
55	Arandjel Stojković		02/03/85	D	2		
5	Danijel Stojković		14/08/90	D	14		1
15	Branimir Subašić	AZE	07/04/82	A	12	(4)	1
99	Miljan Škrbić		18/09/95	A	1	(5)	1
11	Nemanja Vidaković		29/09/85	A	2	(3)	
15	Nemanja Vlahović	MNE	04/01/91	M		(1)	
4	Dragomir Vukobratović		12/05/88	M	13		1
21	Miloš Zlatković		01/01/97	D	11	(2)	

FK Partizan

1945 • FK Partizan (30,900) • partizan.rs

Major honours
Yugoslav/Serbian League (26) 1947, 1949, 1961, 1962, 1963, 1965, 1976, 1978, 1983, 1986, 1987, 1993, 1994, 1996, 1997, 1999, 2002, 2003, 2005, 2008, 2009, 2010, 2011, 2012, 2013, 2015;
Yugoslav/Serbian Cup (13) 1947, 1952, 1954, 1957, 1989, 1992, 1994, 1998, 2001, 2008, 2009, 2011, 2016

Coach: Zoran Milinković;
(16/10/15) Ljubinko Drulović;
(25/12/15) Ivan Tomić

2015

17/07 h Metalac W 4-0 *A Živković, Oumarou, Bozhinov, Ilić*
25/07 h Jagodina W 6-0 *Bozhinov 2 (1p), A Živković, Ninković, Šaponjić 2*
01/08 a Novi Pazar L 2-3 *Trujić, Kojić*
08/08 h Spartak W 2-1 *Bozhinov, Lukić*
13/08 a Vojvodina L 2-3 *Oumarou 2*
22/08 a Borac W 3-1 *Trujić, Balažic, Lukić*
29/08 h OFK Beograd W 2-1 *A Živković, Šaponjić*
12/09 a Crvena zvezda L 1-3 *A Stevanović*
20/09 h Radnički Niš D 0-0
23/09 h Rad D 1-1 *Bozhinov*
27/09 a Voždovac W 2-1 *A Živković, Babović (p)*
05/10 h Čukarički L 0-1
14/10 a Radnik D 2-2 *A Stevanović, Bozhinov*
18/10 h Javor W 3-2 *Ostojić, A Živković, Bozhinov*
25/10 a Mladost D 2-2 *Babović, Grbić*
01/11 a Metalac L 0-1
08/11 a Jagodina D 2-2 *Bozhinov, Babović*
21/11 h Novi Pazar W 3-0 *Bozhinov, Ninković 2*
29/11 a Spartak W 1-0 *A Živković*
05/12 h Vojvodina L 0-2
13/12 a Rad D 2-2 *Bozhinov 2*
16/12 h Borac W 2-1 *A Živković, Bozhinov*

2015

21/02 a OFK Beograd L 1-2 *Brašanac*
27/02 h Crvena zvezda L 1-2 *Gogoua*
06/03 a Radnički Niš W 1-0 *Ilić*
12/03 h Voždovac W 3-0 *Brašanac, A Stevanović (p), Kosović*
20/03 a Čukarički W 2-1 *M Stevanović, Bozhinov*
02/04 h Radnik W 3-2 *Vlahović, Ilić 2*
06/04 a Javor W 2-1 *Mihajlović, og (Crnomarković)*
10/04 h Mladost W 4-0 *Bozhinov 2 (1p), Ilić 2*
16/04 a Crvena zvezda D 1-1 *Everton Luiz*
23/04 h Čukarički L 1-2 *Bozhinov*
28/04 h Borac W 2-0 *Golubović, Brašanac (p)*
03/05 a Radnik W 4-0 *Bozhinov 2, Mihajlović 2*
07/05 h Voždovac W 2-1 *Golubović, Mihajlović*
15/05 a Radnički Niš L 0-1
21/05 h Vojvodina W 3-2 *Milenković, Mihajlović, og (Rosić)*

No	Name	Nat	DoB	Pos	Aps	(s)	Gls
10	Stefan Babović		07/01/87	M	13	(1)	3
6	Gregor Balažic	SVN	12/02/88	D	10		1
2	Ivan Bandalovski	BUL	23/11/86	D	22		
30	Veljko Birmančević		05/03/98	M	1	(2)	
23	Miroslav Bogosavac		14/10/96	D	15	(1)	
86	Valeri Bozhinov	BUL	15/02/86	A	26	(5)	18
8	Darko Brašanac		12/02/92	M	25		3
13	Lazar Ćirković		22/08/92	D	11	(2)	
25	Everton Luiz	BRA	24/05/88	M	9		1
44	Fabrício	BRA	20/02/90	D	13		
11	Ismaël Fofana	CIV	08/09/88	A	1		
18	Nemanja Glavčić		19/02/97	M	1	(1)	
51	Cédric Gogoua	CIV	10/07/94	D	8		1
80	Marko Golubović		20/09/95	M	6	(8)	2
14	Petar Grbić	MNE	07/08/88	M	6	(3)	1
22	Saša Ilić		30/12/77	M	20	(8)	6
21	Marko Jevtović		24/07/93	M	19	(3)	
23	Marko Jovanović		26/03/89	D	12		
61	Marko Jovičić		02/02/95	G	1		
12	Filip Kljajić		16/08/90	G	9		
9	Nemanja Kojić		03/02/90	A	1		1
27	Nebojša Kosović	MNE	24/02/95	M	9	(8)	1
3	Nikola Leković		19/12/89	D	5		
20	Saša Lukić		13/08/96	M	16	(9)	2
7	Nemanja Mihajlović		19/01/96	M	13	(1)	5
31	Nikola Milenković		12/10/97	D	4		1
11	Nikola Ninković		19/12/94	M	6	(8)	3
40	Miloš Ostojić		08/03/91	D	7		1
15	Aboubakar Oumarou	CMR	04/01/87	A	11	(2)	3
28	Ivan Petrović		03/07/93	M	1		
5	Nemanja Petrović		17/04/92	D	8	(3)	
91	Alen Stevanović		07/01/91	M	15	(5)	3
35	Miladin Stevanović		11/02/96	D	7		1
19	Aleksandar Subić	BIH	27/09/93	D	10		
33	Ivan Šaponjić		02/08/97	A	4	(13)	3
50	Bojan Šaranov		22/10/87	G	12		
92	Nikola Trujić		14/04/92	A	3	(6)	2
9	Dušan Vlahović		28/01/00	A		(14)	1
4	Miroslav Vulićević		29/05/85	D	18	(1)	
17	Andrija Živković		11/07/96	M	14	(1)	7
1	Živko Živković		14/04/89	G	15		

FK Rad

1958 • Kralj Petar I (6,000); Stadion na Vračaru (4,506) • fkrad.rs

Coach: Milan Milanović;
(10/04/16) Bogdan Korak

2015

18/07 h Voždovac L 0-2
26/07 a Čukarički D 1-1 *Dabić*
01/08 h Radnik W 4-1 *Dabić, Arsenijević (p), Nenadović, N Mihajlović*
08/08 a Javor L 0-3
12/08 h Mladost W 4-2 *N Mihajlović 2 (2p), Arsenijević 2*
22/08 h Jagodina D 0-0
29/08 a Novi Pazar L 0-1
13/09 h Spartak D 3-3 *Arsenijević 2 (1p), Nenadović*
19/09 a Vojvodina W 2-1 *Trninić, Lutovac*
23/09 a Partizan D 1-1 *Vidić*
27/09 h Metalac L 0-1
03/10 h Borac L 2-3 *Veselinović, Maraš*
14/10 a OFK Beograd L 0-2
17/10 h Crvena zvezda L 0-3
24/10 a Radnički Niš L 0-1
31/10 a Voždovac L 0-1
08/11 h Čukarički L 0-1
21/11 a Radnik D 1-1 *Milisavljević*
28/11 h Javor D 1-1 *Veselinović*
05/12 a Mladost L 0-1
13/12 h Partizan D 2-2 *Trninić, Denić*
16/12 a Jagodina L 0-1

2016

20/02 h Novi Pazar W 1-0 *Protić*
27/02 a Spartak L 1-2 *Maraš*
06/03 h Vojvodina D 2-2 *Maraš, Kaludjerović*
13/03 a Metalac D 2-2 *Ćulum, Kaludjerović*
20/03 a Borac D 0-0
02/04 h OFK Beograd D 1-1 *Bates*
06/04 a Crvena zvezda L 0-1
10/04 h Radnički Niš W 2-0 *Lutovac, Kaludjerović*
17/04 a Mladost W 3-1 *Lutovac 2, Kaludjerović*
23/04 h Javor W 1-0 *Maraš*
28/04 a Novi Pazar L 0-1
03/05 h OFK Beograd W 2-1 *Lutovac 2*
07/05 a Jagodina D 1-1 *Ćulum*
15/05 h Metalac D 1-1 *Kaludjerović*
21/05 a Spartak W 2-1 *Kaludjerović, Arsenijević*

No	Name	Nat	DoB	Pos	Aps	(s)	Gls
19	Nemanja Arsenijević		29/03/86	A	27	(2)	6
34	Filip Bainović		28/06/96	M		(1)	
3	Marko Bašanović		26/09/94	D	6	(4)	
55	Stevan Bates		29/11/81	D	12		1
66	Miloš Budaković		10/07/91	G	17		
8	Milan Ćulum		28/10/84	M	10		2
11	Miodrag Dabić	MNE	01/05/91	A	8	(1)	2
1	Darko Dejanović	BIH	17/03/95	G	10		
10	Djordje Denić		01/04/96	M	18	(6)	1
4	Nikola Djurić		06/11/89	D	19	(1)	
26	Nenad Filipović		24/04/87	G	10		
12	Ivica Jovanović	MNE	04/12/87	A	6	(6)	
44	Petar Jovanović	BIH	12/07/82	D	14		
9	Andrija Kaludjerović		05/07/87	A	15		6
23	Dušan Kolarević		19/04/87	M	7	(12)	
31	Ivan Kričak		19/07/96	D		(1)	
7	Miloš Krstić		07/03/87	M	3	(3)	
6	Zoran Ljubinković		07/12/81	D	24	(3)	
22	Matija Ljujić		28/01/93	M	5	(9)	
17	Aleksandar Lutovac		28/06/97	M	13	(10)	6
25	Nikola Maraš		19/12/95	D	34		4
7	Nemanja Mihajlović		19/01/96	M	7		3
69	Stefan Mihajlović		24/06/94	A		(1)	
8	Miloš Milisavljević		26/10/92	M	7	(10)	1
33	Bogdan Mladenović		04/04/96	M	6	(11)	
70	Uroš Nenadović		28/01/94	M	14	(11)	2
5	Miloš Obradović		30/03/87	D	12		
20	Marko Prljević		02/08/88	D	12	(1)	
3	Radoš Protić		21/01/87	D	12		1
20	Dejan Rusmir		28/01/80	M		(5)	
30	Branislav Stanić		30/07/88	M	4	(2)	
88	Marko Stanojević		22/06/88	M	13		
55	Aleksandar Trninić		27/03/87	M	12	(3)	2
77	Borko Veselinović		06/01/86	A	23	(4)	2
24	Stefan Vico		28/02/95	D	10	(2)	
44	Nemanja Vidić		06/08/89	M	17		1

FK Radnički Niš

1923 • Čair (18,151) • fkradnickinis.rs

Coach: Milan Rastavac

2015

17/07 a Borac L 1-2 *Zemlyanukhin*
24/07 h OFK Beograd W 1-0 *Djuričković (p)*
31/07 a Crvena zvezda D 1-1 *Rosić*
08/08 a Metalac W 2-0 *Zemlyanukhin, Tomić*
12/08 h Voždovac D 0-0
16/08 a Čukarički W 1-0 *Trifunović*
21/08 h Radnik D 1-1 *Trifunović*
29/08 a Javor D 0-0
13/09 h Mladost D 1-1 *Lakić Pešić*
20/09 a Partizan D 0-0
27/09 h Jagodina D 0-0
03/10 a Novi Pazar L 0-1
14/10 h Spartak W 1-0 *Aščerić*
17/10 a Vojvodina W 2-0 *Marjanović, Djuričković (p)*
24/10 h Rad W 1-0 *Marjanović*
01/11 h Borac L 0-1
07/11 a OFK Beograd W 2-0 *Zemlyanukhin, Aščerić*
22/11 h Crvena zvezda L 1-2 *Aleksandar M Jovanović*
27/11 h Metalac W 2-1 *Aščerić 2*
05/12 a Voždovac L 1-3 *Zemlyanukhin*
11/12 h Čukarički D 0-0
16/12 a Radnik L 1-2 *Djuričković*

2016

21/02 h Javor W 2-0 *Todorović, Marjanović*
27/02 a Mladost W 1-0 *Mrkić*
06/03 h Partizan L 0-1
12/03 a Jagodina W 2-1 *Marjanović, D Bulatović*
18/03 h Novi Pazar D 0-0
02/04 a Spartak W 2-1 *Mrkić, Aleksandar M Jovanović*
06/04 h Vojvodina L 0-3
10/04 a Rad L 0-2
16/04 a Vojvodina L 0-4
23/04 h Voždovac W 2-0 *Djuričković, R Bulatović*
28/04 h Radnik W 5-1 *Marjanović 5*
03/05 a Borac L 1-4 *D Bulatović*
07/05 a Čukarički W 5-1 *Lakić Pešić, Marjanović 2, Mrkić 2*
15/05 h Partizan W 1-0 *Marjanović*
21/05 a Crvena zvezda L 0-2

No	Name	Nat	DoB	Pos	Aps	(s)	Gls
70	Andreja Apostolović		16/06/96	M	22	(6)	
9	Nikola Aščerić		19/04/91	A	13	(5)	4
55	Marko Blažić		02/08/85	M	13	(4)	
32	Vladimir Bogdanović		05/10/86	M	16	(6)	
89	Darko Bulatović	MNE	05/09/89	D	35		2
4	Radoš Bulatović		05/06/84	D	32		1
2	Bojan Djordjević		05/04/84	D	2		
28	Vladimir Djordjević		25/12/82	D	4	(6)	
7	Petar Djuričković		20/06/91	M	33		4
1	Nenad Filipović		24/04/87	G	1		
3	Nikola Ignjatijević		12/12/83	D	1	(4)	
71	Aleksa Jovanović		27/05/99	M		(3)	
24	Aleksandar M Jovanović		17/12/84	M	27	(1)	2
26	Aleksandar S Jovanović		06/12/92	G	36		
23	Dušan Kolarević		19/04/87	M		(1)	
18	Ivan Konovalov	RUS	18/08/94	G		(1)	
27	Miloš Krstić		07/03/87	M	1	(6)	
54	Petar Krstić		03/09/97	M	4	(7)	
44	Nemanja Lakić Pešić		22/09/91	D	33	(2)	2
21	Saša Marjanović		13/11/87	M	35	(1)	12
27	Lazar Mitrović		18/08/98	A		(6)	
13	Mladen Mitrović		14/12/97	D		(1)	
67	Nikola Mitrović		14/12/97	M		(8)	
19	Marko Mrkić		20/08/96	A	14	(10)	4
91	Aleksandar Mrševič		25/07/96	D	1		
11	Ivan Pejčić		11/09/82	A	1	(4)	
50	Nikola Petković		14/10/97	A		(1)	
14	Miloš Petrović		05/05/90	D	29		
19	Lazar Rosić		29/06/93	D	2	(1)	1
5	Nikola Stevanović		13/09/98	D		(1)	
40	Miodrag Todorović		10/09/95	A	4	(10)	1
6	Marko Tomić		28/10/91	M	23	(8)	1
99	Miloš Trifunović		15/10/84	A	7		2
20	Anton Zemlyanukhin	KGZ	11/12/88	A	16		4
2	Miloš Živković		01/12/84	D	2		

SERBIA

FK Radnik Surdulica

1926 • Gradski stadion (3,312) • fk-radnik.com

Coach: Mladen Milinković; (03/09/15) Miloš Veselinović

2015

18/07	a	Spartak	D 0-0	
26/07	h	Vojvodina	D 2-2	*S Stojanović, Ćulum*
01/08	a	Rad	L 1-4	*Ćulum*
08/08	h	Borac	W 1-0	*S Stojanović (p)*
12/08	a	OFK Beograd	L 0-3	
16/08	h	Crvena zvezda	L 0-2	
21/08	a	Radnički Niš	D 1-1	*Ćulum*
29/08	h	Voždovac	L 1-3	*Arsić*
11/09	a	Čukarički	L 0-2	
19/09	a	Metalac	D 2-2	*Ćulum 2*
26/09	h	Javor	D 1-1	*Owusu*
03/10	a	Mladost	D 0-0	
14/10	h	Partizan	D 2-2	*Stanković 2*
18/10	a	Jagodina	D 1-1	*S Stojanović (p)*
24/10	h	Novi Pazar	W 2-0	*S Stojanović 2 (1p)*
01/11	h	Spartak	W 1-0	*Owusu*
06/11	a	Vojvodina	W 3-2	*Owusu, S Stojanović (p), Arsić*
21/11	h	Rad	D 1-1	*S Stojanović*
28/11	a	Borac	L 2-4	*F Stojanović, Arsić*
06/12	h	OFK Beograd	W 2-1	*Djordjević, Ćulum*
12/12	a	Crvena zvezda	L 0-5	
16/12	h	Radnički Niš	W 2-1	*S Stojanović, F Stojanović*

2016

21/02	a	Voždovac	L 1-2	Stanković
27/02	h	Čukarički	W 2-1	*S Stojanović, Arsić (p)*
06/03	h	Metalac	D 0-0	
12/03	a	Javor	W 1-0	*Owusu*
19/03	h	Mladost	W 3-1	*Vuković, Owusu, Stanković*
02/04	a	Partizan	L 2-3	*Owusu, Deletić*
06/04	h	Jagodina	D 0-0	
10/04	a	Novi Pazar	L 0-2	
16/04	a	Voždovac	W 2-1	*Arsić, Mutavdžić*
23/04	h	Vojvodina	W 1-0	*Owusu*
28/04	a	Radnički Niš	L 1-5	*Radovanović*
03/05	h	Partizan	L 0-4	
07/05	a	Borac	L 1-3	*Jovanović*
14/05	h	Crvena zvezda	L 1-4	*Deletić*
21/05	a	Čukarički	L 1-2	*Jovanović*

No	Name	Nat	DoB	Pos	Aps	(s)	Gls
10	Lazar Arsić		24/09/91	M	20	(9)	5
5	Ljubo Baranin		25/08/86	D	8	(3)	
22	Bojan Čukić		05/02/88	M		(1)	
24	Milan Ćulum		28/10/84	M	18	(2)	6
77	Miloš Deletić		14/10/93	A	8	(6)	2
2	Predrag Djordjević		30/06/90	D	4	(4)	1
15	Aleksandar Gojković		18/08/88	D	25		
1	Miroslav Grujičić		17/06/94	G	5		
16	Jovan Jovanović		02/10/85	A	7	(21)	2
6	Miloš Krstić		19/11/88	D	21		
21	Predrag Lazić		15/01/82	M	2	(2)	
86	Miloš Marković		10/12/86	D	28		
3	Miloš Milovanović		09/12/87	D	30		
9	Uroš Mirković		08/08/90	M	1	(8)	
22	Miljan Mutavdžić		03/02/86	M	5	(4)	1
19	Samuel Owusu	GHA	28/03/96	A	25	(5)	7
30	Vladan Pavlović		24/02/84	D	7	(9)	
17	Bratislav Pejčić		17/01/83	M	23	(5)	
23	Marko Putinčanin		16/12/87	D	31	(2)	
18	Stefan Radovanović		19/02/92	D	6		1
12	Borivoje Ristić		19/09/83	G	26		
6	Miloš Simonović		28/05/90	D	7	(4)	
18	Petar Stamatović		12/07/95	M		(1)	
7	Miloš Stanković		22/07/92	A	22	(7)	4
8	Filip Stojanović		19/05/88	M	30	(2)	2
20	Nikola Stojanović		06/11/83	D		(3)	
11	Slaviša Stojanović		27/01/89	A	27	(2)	9
14	Zakaria Suraka	GHA	17/01/96	A	2	(5)	
13	Bojan Šejić		14/07/83	G	5		
22	Vukašin Tomić		08/04/87	D		(1)	
31	Nikola Vasiljević		24/06/96	G	1		
9	Marko Vučetić		24/06/86	M	2	(1)	
4	Slobodan Vuković		23/01/86	D	11	(1)	1

FK Spartak Subotica

1945 • Gradski stadion (13,000) • fkspartak.com

Coach: Stevan Mojsilović; (01/11/15) Andrei Chernyshov (RUS)

2015

18/07	h	Radnik	D 0-0	
25/07	a	Javor	L 0-2	
01/08	h	Mladost	W 2-0	*Makarić, Milošević*
08/08	a	Partizan	L 1-2	*Torbica*
12/08	h	Jagodina	D 0-0	
16/08	a	Novi Pazar	D 0-0	
22/08	h	Metalac	L 0-3	
30/08	h	Vojvodina	W 2-1	*Makarić, Ilić*
13/09	a	Rad	D 3-3	*Makarić, Kovačević, Milić*
19/09	h	Borac	D 0-0	
26/09	a	OFK Beograd	L 0-2	
03/10	h	Crvena zvezda	L 2-3	*Milić, Makarić*
14/10	a	Radnički Niš	L 0-1	
18/10	h	Voždovac	L 0-2	
23/10	a	Čukarički	L 0-3	
01/11	a	Radnik	L 0-1	
07/11	h	Javor	D 0-0	
20/11	a	Mladost	D 0-0	
29/11	h	Partizan	L 0-1	
06/12	a	Jagodina	D 1-1	*Ilić*
12/12	h	Novi Pazar	W 2-0	*Ilić, Ivanović*
16/12	a	Metalac	L 0-1	

2016

20/02	a	Vojvodina	D 1-1	*Šljivić*
27/02	h	Rad	W 2-1	*Torbica, og (Ljubinković)*
06/03	a	Borac	D 0-0	
12/03	h	OFK Beograd	W 2-1	*Torbica (p), Antonić*
19/03	a	Crvena zvezda	L 0-4	
02/04	h	Radnički Niš	L 1-2	*Milošević*
06/04	a	Voždovac	W 1-0	*Milošević*
10/04	h	Čukarički	L 0-2	
16/04	a	Javor	W 2-0	*Mudrinski, Ivanović*
23/04	h	Metalac	W 5-1	*Ilić 3, Torbica (p), Ivanović*
28/04	a	Mladost	D 0-0	
03/05	h	Jagodina	W 5-1	*Farkaš, Milošević, Ivanović 2, Milić*
08/05	a	OFK Beograd	W 3-1	*Farkaš, Mudrinski, Ilić*
15/05	a	Novi Pazar	W 1-0	*Antonić*
21/05	h	Rad	L 1-2	*Milošević*

No	Name	Nat	DoB	Pos	Aps	(s)	Gls
30	Ermin Alić	MNE	23/02/92	D	1		
17	Goran Antonić		05/11/90	D	35		2
22	Nikola Banjac		18/09/96	D	2		
23	Miloš Bogunović		10/06/85	A	7	(3)	
40	Bojan Božović	MNE	03/02/85	A		(2)	
30	Vladimir Branković	BIH	22/09/85	D	1	(2)	
21	Daniel Farkaš		13/01/93	D	31		2
7	Maksim Fedin	KAZ	08/06/96	M	1	(4)	
9	Dejan Georgijević		19/01/94	A		(2)	
19	Stefan Ilić		07/04/95	A	22	(6)	7
10	Djordje Ivanović		20/11/95	A	17	(13)	5
1	Budimir Janošević		21/10/89	G	25		
4	Branimir Jočić		30/11/94	M	30	(1)	
5	Milan Jokić		21/03/95	M	1	(6)	
26	Marko Jondić		03/05/95	M	11	(11)	
66	Marko Klisura		15/10/92	D	1		
6	Vladimir Kovačević		11/11/92	D	33		1
27	Milan Makarić		04/10/95	M	18	(7)	4
29	Miloš Manojlović		25/10/95	A		(1)	
3	Marko Marinković		01/06/94	D	4	(1)	
14	Nebojša Mezei		15/02/91	M	9		
16	Nemanja Milić		25/05/90	A	12	(7)	3
11	Stefan Milošević		07/04/95	D	30		5
12	Nikola Mirković		26/07/91	G	12	(1)	
9	Andrej Mrkela		09/04/92	M	14	(10)	
28	Ognjen Mudrinski		15/11/91	A	8	(5)	2
15	Slobodan Novaković		15/10/86	M	4	(2)	
17	Srdjan Plavšić		03/12/95	M	3	(1)	
15	Stefan Spremo		18/05/97	M	1	(2)	
18	Nenad Šljivić		08/06/85	M	14		1
28	Dušan Tešić		16/07/88	M		(2)	
40	Vukašin Tomić		08/04/87	D	6	(3)	
20	Dimitrije Tomović		29/04/96	D	1		
8	Vladimir Torbica		20/09/80	M	23	(4)	4
24	Janko Tumbasević	MNE	14/01/85	M	21	(2)	
2	Eke Uzoma	NGA	11/08/89	M	7	(3)	
13	Danijel Zlatković		29/03/96	M		(2)	
18	Dušan Živković		31/07/96	M	2	(6)	

FK Vojvodina

1914 • Karadjordje (15,754) • fkvojvodina.rs

Major honours

Yugoslav League (2) 1966, 1989; Serbian Cup (1) 2014

Coach: Zlatomir Zagorčić (BUL); (23/10/15) (Goran Šaula); (08/11/15) (Milan Kosanović); (13/11/15) Nenad Lalatović

2015

19/07	h	Čukarički	L 0-4	
26/07	a	Radnik	D 2-2	*Ožegović, Ivanić*
02/08	h	Javor	W 2-0	*Stanisavljević, Ožegović*
09/08	a	Mladost	W 2-1	*Puškarić (p), Paločević*
13/08	h	Partizan	W 3-2	*Ivanić, Stanisavljević, Ožegović*
23/08	h	Novi Pazar	W 4-1	*Babić, Ivanić, Paločević, Stanisavljević (p)*
30/08	a	Spartak	L 1-2	*Ivanić*
13/09	h	Metalac	W 3-2	*Ožegović, Ivanić, Vukčević*
19/09	h	Rad	L 1-2	*Nastić*
23/09	a	Jagodina	D 1-1	*Sekulić*
27/09	a	Borac	L 2-4	*Paločević, Ivanić*
03/10	h	OFK Beograd	W 1-0	*og (Ignjatijević)*
17/10	h	Radnički Niš	L 0-2	
21/10	a	Crvena zvezda	L 0-3	
25/10	a	Voždovac	D 0-0	
01/11	a	Čukarički	D 1-1	*Ožegović*
06/11	h	Radnik	L 2-3	*Zličić, Stanisavljević (p)*
21/11	a	Javor	W 1-0	*Babić*
28/11	h	Mladost	W 3-0	*Babić, Ivanić, Stanisavljević*
05/12	a	Partizan	W 2-0	*Rosić, Stanisavljević*
12/12	h	Jagodina	W 3-1	*Rosić, Ožegović 2*
16/12	a	Novi Pazar	D 1-1	*Ivanić*

2016

20/02	h	Spartak	D 1-1	*Meleg (p)*
26/02	a	Metalac	D 0-0	
06/03	a	Rad	D 2-2	*Rosić, og (Stanojević)*
11/03	h	Borac	D 1-1	*Malbašić*
19/03	a	OFK Beograd	L 0-1	
02/04	h	Crvena zvezda	D 0-0	
06/04	a	Radnički Niš	W 3-0	*Meleg (p), Trujić 2*
10/04	h	Voždovac	W 2-1	*Meleg, Sekulić*
16/04	h	Radnički Niš	W 4-0	*Puškarić, Sekulić, Ašćerić, Trujić*
23/04	a	Radnik	L 0-1	
28/04	h	Voždovac	D 0-0	
03/05	a	Čukarički	W 2-1	*Miletić, Trujić*
07/05	a	Crvena zvezda	W 3-1	*Trujić 2, Paločević*
14/05	h	Borac	W 2-0	*Babić, Ašćerić*
21/05	a	Partizan	L 2-3	*Meleg 2*

No	Name	Nat	DoB	Pos	Aps	(s)	Gls
20	Nikola Antić		04/01/94	D	9	(1)	
9	Nikola Ašćerić		19/04/91	A	9	(3)	2
16	Siniša Babić		13/02/91	M	17	(12)	4
26	Dominik Dinga		07/04/98	D	4	(2)	
23	Igor Djurić		22/02/85	D	4		
4	Mirko Ivanić		13/09/93	M	20		8
29	Dušan Jovančić		19/10/90	M	4	(5)	
25	Marko Kordić	MNE	22/02/95	G	19	(1)	
19	Šaleta Kordić	MNE	19/04/93	A		(1)	
21	Nikola Kovačević		14/04/94	M	2	(2)	
14	Ivan Lakićević		27/07/93	D	17	(5)	
28	Novica Maksimović		04/04/88	M	25	(3)	
22	Filip Malbašić		18/11/92	M	13	(1)	1
99	John Mary	CMR	09/03/93	A		(1)	
7	Dejan Meleg		01/10/94	M	11	(3)	5
4	Dušan Mićić		29/11/84	M	6		
33	Nemanja Miletić		16/01/91	D	12		1
23	Milan Milinković		04/05/92	D	1		
9	Miljan Mrdaković		06/05/82	A	2	(4)	
15	Bojan Nastić		06/07/94	D	25		1
51	Ognjen Ožegović		09/06/94	A	17	(1)	7
10	Aleksandar Paločević		22/08/93	M	15	(12)	4
13	Radovan Pankov		05/08/95	D	27	(3)	
27	Milan Pavkov		09/02/94	A	4	(9)	
6	Nino Pekarić		16/08/82	D	5		
12	Nikola Perić		04/02/92	G	14		
8	Darko Puškarić		13/07/85	M	12	(2)	2
3	Slaviša Radović	BIH	08/10/93	D	3		
19	Lazar Rosić		29/06/93	D	25		3
24	Danilo Sekulić		18/04/90	M	29	(3)	3
31	Uroš Stamenić		14/10/96	A	3	(9)	
7	Aleksandar Stanisavljević		11/06/89	M	14	(5)	6
92	Nikola Trujić		14/04/92	A	13	(1)	6
2	Jovica Vasilić		08/07/90	D	9		
11	Marko Vukčević	MNE	07/06/93	A	12	(5)	1
18	Lazar Zličić		07/02/97	M	1	(1)	1
22	Marko Zoćević		19/05/93	M		(7)	
1	Srdjan Žakula		22/03/79	G	4		

FK Voždovac

1912 • SC Stadion - Bojan Majić (5,172);
Stadion na Vračaru (4,506) • fkvozdovac.rs
Coach: Bratislav Živković

2015

18/07	a	Rad	W 2-0	Adamović, Terzić
25/07	h	Borac	L 0-2	
01/08	a	OFK Beograd	L 1-2	Sikimić
09/08	h	Crvena zvezda	L 2-3	Mašović, Sikimić
12/08	a	Radnički Niš	D 0-0	
15/08	a	Metalac	D 1-1	Sikimić
23/08	h	Čukarički	D 0-0	
29/08	a	Radnik	W 3-1	Adamović, Odita 2 (1p)
13/09	h	Javor	L 0-2	
19/09	a	Mladost	D 0-0	
27/09	h	Partizan	L 1-2	Ćirković
03/10	a	Jagodina	D 0-0	
14/10	h	Novi Pazar	W 1-0	Marinković
18/10	a	Spartak	W 2-0	Asani, Stojanović
25/10	h	Vojvodina	D 0-0	
31/10	a	Rad	W 1-0	Marinković
07/11	a	Borac	D 1-1	Odita
21/11	h	OFK Beograd	L 2-3	Mihajlov, Odita
28/11	a	Crvena zvezda	L 0-2	
05/12	h	Radnički Niš	W 3-1	Marinković, Mihajlov, Radivojević
12/12	h	Metalac	W 1-0	Odita
16/12	a	Čukarički	D 0-0	
2016				
21/02	h	Radnik	W 2-1	Terzić, Mašović
27/02	a	Javor	D 0-0	
05/03	h	Mladost	W 4-1	Marinković 3, Odita
12/03	a	Partizan	L 0-3	
19/03	h	Jagodina	D 1-1	Damjanović
02/04	a	Novi Pazar	D 1-1	Marinković
06/04	h	Spartak	L 0-1	
10/04	a	Vojvodina	L 1-2	Marinković
16/04	h	Radnik	L 1-2	Ivković
23/04	a	Radnički Niš	L 0-2	
28/04	a	Vojvodina	D 0-0	
03/05	h	Crvena zvezda	L 0-1	
07/05	a	Partizan	L 1-2	Mihajlov
14/05	h	Čukarički	W 2-0	Stojanović, Krasić
21/05	a	Borac	D 0-0	

No	Name	Nat	DoB	Pos	Aps	(s)	Gls
10	Marko Adamović		11/03/91	M	16	(8)	2
14	Elmir Asani		15/09/95	M	8	(8)	1
7	Nikola Beljić		14/05/83	M	3	(3)	
26	Jovica Blagojević		27/08/98	M	2	(4)	
9	Nikola Ćirković		15/04/91	A	21	(3)	1
20	Jovan Damjanović		04/10/82	A	3	(6)	1
23	Vladan Grujić	BIH	17/05/81	M	6	(1)	
41	Saša Ivković		13/05/93	D	20	(4)	1
27	Marko Jovanović		26/03/89	D	10	(1)	
17	Petar Jovanović	BIH	12/07/82	D	16	(1)	
17	Ognjen Krasić		09/04/88	M	9	(3)	1
15	Nenad Marinković		28/09/88	M	21	(2)	8
44	Alen Mašović		07/08/94	A	21	(3)	2
3	Miloš Mihajlov		15/12/82	D	28		3
22	Marko Milošević		07/02/91	G	5		
18	Obiora Odita	NGA	14/05/83	A	27	(5)	6
21	Deni Pavlović		01/09/93	D	10		
25	Miloš Pavlović		27/11/83	M	31		
6	Todor Petrović		18/08/94	M	11	(7)	
1	Zoran Popović		28/05/88	G	32		
77	Bojan Puzigaća	BIH	10/05/85	D	10		
8	Dejan Račić	MNE	15/07/98	A		(1)	
29	Milan Radin		25/06/91	M	11	(2)	
5	Miloš Radivojević		05/04/90	D	21	(1)	1
8	Risto Ristović		05/05/88	M	9	(7)	
81	Predrag Sikimić		29/08/92	A	7		3
4	Uroš Sindjić		19/01/86	M	11	(8)	
26	Nikola Srećković		26/04/96	M	7	(9)	
11	Jovan Stojanović		25/04/92	A	10	(13)	2
50	Borislav Terzić		01/11/91	D	13	(6)	2
77	Nemanja Zlatković		21/08/88	D	8	(2)	

Top goalscorers

Hugo Vieira   Aleksandar Katai

21 Hugo Vieira (Crvena zvezda)
Aleksandar Katai (Crvena zvezda)

18 Andrija Pavlović (Čukarički)
Valeri Bozhinov (Partizan)

15 Srdjan Vujaklija (Borac)

12 Saša Marjanović (Radnički Niš)

10 Saša Jovanović (Mladost)

9 Luis Ibáñez (Crvena zvezda)
Slavoljub Srnić (Čukarički/Crvena zvezda)
Slaviša Stojanović (Radnik)

Promoted clubs

FK Napredak

1946 • Mladost (10,331) • fknapredak.rs
Coach: Bogić Bogićević

FK Bačka

1945 • Slavko Maletin – Vava (5,500) •
fkbacka.com
Coach: Spasoje Jelačić

Second level final table 2015/16

		Pld	W	D	L	F	A	Pts
1	FK Napredak	30	21	5	4	48	26	68
2	FK Bačka	30	16	8	6	52	30	56
3	FK ČSK Pivara	30	14	6	10	28	19	48
4	FK Indjija	30	12	9	9	46	28	45
5	FK Bežanija	30	11	10	9	35	27	43
6	FK Sindjelić	30	11	9	10	32	25	42
7	FK Kolubara	30	11	9	10	29	28	42
8	FK Proleter Novi Sad	30	9	13	8	32	29	40
9	FK BSK Borča	30	11	7	12	32	38	40
10	FK Sloga Petrovac	30	10	9	11	34	36	39
11	FK Zemun	30	9	11	10	29	33	39
12	FK Dinamo Vranje	30	11	5	14	27	38	38
13	FK Sloboda Užice	30	8	11	11	35	34	35
14	FK Donji Srem	30	8	10	12	24	38	34
15	FK Loznica	30	7	10	13	21	35	31
16	FK Radnički 1923	30	2	6	22	23	63	12

DOMESTIC CUP

Kup Srbije 2015/16

FIRST ROUND

(27/10/15)
ČSK Pivara 0-1 Borac

(28/10/15)
Bačka 1-3 Crvena zvezda
Bežanija 0-0 Radnički 1923 *(6-5 on pens)*
BSK Borča 3-1 Mladost
Indjija 1-0 Rad
Kolubara 0-0 Vojvodina *(4-5 on pens)*
Loznica 1-2 Radnički Niš
Metalac 3-3 OFK Beograd *(6-7 on pens)*
Mokra Gora 1-3 Čukarički
Moravac Orion 0-3 Napredak
Novi Pazar 0-2 Javor
Proleter 0-1 Jagodina
Radnik 0-0 Donji Srem *(3-4 on pens)*
Sindjelić Beograd 0-2 Partizan
Sloga Petrovac 0-0 Voždovac *(1-4 on pens)*
Zemun 0-1 Spartak

SECOND ROUND

(02/12/15)
Crvena zvezda 1-5 Borac
Jagodina 2-0 BSK Borča
Javor 1-1 Čukarički *(4-3 on pens)*
Napredak 0-2 Radnički Niš
OFK Beograd 5-0 Donji Srem
Spartak 3-2 Bežanija
Vojvodina 1-0 Indjija
Voždovac 0-1 Partizan

QUARTER-FINALS

(02/03/16)
Borac 2-0 OFK Beograd *(Maslać 63, Vujaklija 80)*
Jagodina 0-2 Spartak *(Mudrinski 89p, 90)*
Javor 2-2 Vojvodina *(Docić 23, Djokić 89;
Aščerić 48, Babić 68) (5-3 on pens)*
Partizan 2-0 Radnički Niš *(Mihajlović 18,
A Stevanović 79)*

SEMI-FINALS

(16/03/16 & 20/04/16)
Javor 2-1 Borac *(Eliomar 7, Dražić 49; Kostić 54)*
Borac 1-1 Javor *(Vujaklija 55p; Docić 63p)*
(Javor 3-2)

Partizan 0-0 Spartak
Spartak 0-3 Partizan *(Mihajlović 2, Vlahović 84,
Bandalovski 89)*
(Partizan 3-0)

FINAL

(11/05/16)
Gradski stadion kraj Despotovice, Gornji Milanovac
FK PARTIZAN 2 *(Jovanović 35, Vlahović 90+5)*
FK JAVOR 0
Referee: Mažić
PARTIZAN: Šaranov, Jovanović, Vulićević,
Bogosavac, Gogoua, Ilić, Everton Luiz, Brašanac,
Mihajlović, Golubović (A Stevanović 90+5),
Bozhinov (Vlahović 72)
JAVOR: Djogatović, Milović, Josović, Gajić (Vujović
78), Crnomarković, Miletić, Stojaković, Ajuru
(Eliomar 65), Djokić, Docić, Dražić

SLOVAKIA
Slovenský futbalový zväz (SFZ)

Address	Trnavská 100/II	**President**	Ján Kováčik
	SK-821 01 Bratislava	**General secretary**	Jozef Kliment
Tel	+421 2 4820 6000	**Media officer**	Juraj Čurný
Fax	+421 2 4820 6099	**Year of formation**	1938
E-mail	office@futbalsfz.sk		
Website	futbalsfz.sk		

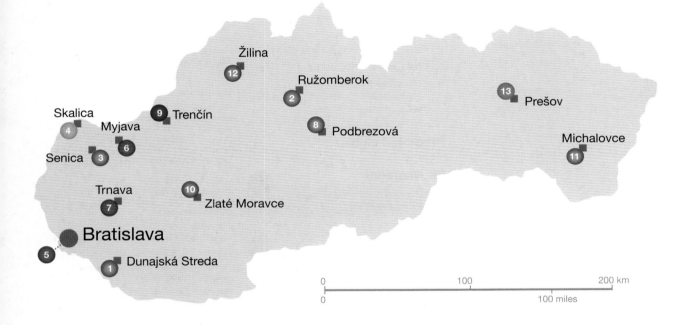

1. LIGA CLUBS

 1 FC DAC 1904 Dunajská Streda

2 MFK Ružomberok

 3 FK Senica

4 MFK Skalica

 5 ŠK Slovan Bratislava

 6 TJ Spartak Myjava

 7 FC Spartak Trnava

 8 ŽP Šport Podbrezová

 9 FK AS Trenčín

 10 FC ViOn Zlaté Moravce

 11 MFK Zemplín Michalovce

 12 MŠK Žilina

PROMOTED CLUB

 13 1. FC Tatran Prešov

KEY

⬤ UEFA Champions League

⬤ UEFA Europa League

⬤ Promoted

⬤ Relegated

Repeat double for Trenčín

Without a major honour to their name until 2014/15, FK AS Trenčín confirmed their status as a growing force in Slovakian football by winning the league and cup double for the second year in a row.

Martin Ševela's side, virtually unchanged from the previous campaign, simply carried on where they had left off, displaying particularly ruthless form away from home. Slovan Bratislava had to be content with two runners-up spots, while there was a disappointing mid-table finish in the league for MŠK Žilina.

Domestic league

Trenčín's first league title had come out of the blue, enabling them to catch the other 1. Liga teams off guard, but even though the opposition knew what was coming from Ševela's side in 2015/16, they were unable to withstand them. Right from the word go Trenčín had the bit between their teeth, and with seven wins and a draw from their opening eight fixtures, it was clear that they would once again be the team to beat.

In fact, only four teams would get the better of them all season, and with 26 wins from their other 29 games, Trenčín were never toppled from their perch. Eight straight wins enabled the defending champions to take a seven-point lead into the winter break, and although Slovan, led by their new Cypriot coach Nikodimos Papavasiliou, reduced that to four points by defeating them 2-0 in the first game after the resumption, Trenčín's consistency, enhanced by the brilliant form of 20-year-old Matúš Bero, enabled them to reconstruct another healthy lead without due concern.

Slovan's last hope was to beat Trenčín in the teams' final encounter of the season, in Bratislava on 8 May. What actually ensued in the Pasienky stadium was a masterclass from Ševela's side as they scored twice in each half to clinch the title with the biggest away win of the entire season. Curacao forward Gino van Kessel scored twice in that 4-0 win to end a long barren run in the league, and he added five more in Trenčín's last two fixtures to overtake team-mate Bero and Trnava's David Depetris and win the 1. Liga golden boot.

Slovan trailed the champions by 12 points in the final standings, but they were comfortable runners-up, with Spartak Myjava's late surge enabling them to finish higher than ever before in third. Trnava, who also enjoyed an impressive run-in following the appointment of Slovakia's record cap-holder Miroslav Karhan as coach, took fourth place ahead of underachieving 2014/15 runners-up Žilina. Skalica, meanwhile, suffered immediate relegation, their place taken by Tatran Prešov, who topped the second division after a three-point penalty was imposed on runners-up VSS Košice.

Domestic cup

Trenčín's 4-0 victory against Slovan in the league was preceded by another trophy-clinching win over the team from the capital. The Slovakian Cup final was a much tighter contest, and indeed Slovan were 1-0 up with 12 minutes to play, but Trenčín roared back to equalise through former Austria striker Stefan Maierhofer before Van Kessel took centre stage with two late goals to turn the game around and give his team an exhilarating 3-1 win.

Europe

Although they struggled in the league, Žilina were Slovakia's best performers in Europe, scoring in the last minute of extra time against Vorskla Poltava to reach the UEFA Europa League play-offs on the away goals rule. Unfortunately the same method was used to eliminate them in the next round after an excellent effort against Spain's Athletic Club.

National team

Impressive qualifiers for UEFA EURO 2016, Ján Kozák's Slovakia achieved their avowed objective of qualifying for the round of 16 in France before Germany, a team they had defeated 3-1 on a rain-soaked pitch in an Augsburg friendly just before the tournament, proved much too powerful for them in the Lille re-match. Kozák's men qualified for the knockout phase as the best of the third-placed teams after losing 2-1 to Wales, winning 2-1 against Russia – with a couple of cracking goals from Vladimír Weiss and skipper Marek Hamšík – and defending stoutly to get the 0-0 draw they needed against England, one of the teams they have been paired with in their 2018 FIFA World Cup qualifying group.

DOMESTIC SEASON AT A GLANCE

1. Liga 2015/16 final table

		Pld	Home					Away					Total					Pts
			W	D	L	F	A	W	D	L	F	A	W	D	L	F	A	
1	FK AS Trenčín	33	13	1	3	42	21	13	2	1	31	7	26	3	4	73	28	81
2	ŠK Slovan Bratislava	33	12	2	3	30	15	8	7	1	20	10	20	9	4	50	25	69
3	TJ Spartak Myjava	33	10	3	3	23	12	8	3	6	18	21	18	6	9	41	33	60
4	FC Spartak Trnava	33	12	3	2	30	10	4	3	9	19	31	16	6	11	49	41	54
5	MŠK Žilina	33	10	4	3	40	15	4	2	10	18	31	14	6	13	58	46	48
6	MFK Ružomberok	33	7	6	4	26	21	5	3	8	16	20	12	9	12	42	41	45
7	FC DAC 1904 Dunajská Streda	33	10	3	3	24	12	2	4	11	14	30	12	7	14	38	42	43
8	ŽP Šport Podbrezová	33	8	2	6	27	16	2	5	10	16	30	10	7	16	43	46	37
9	FC ViOn Zlaté Moravce	33	6	5	5	22	17	1	5	11	16	40	7	10	16	38	57	31
10	FK Senica	33	3	7	7	18	24	4	2	10	12	24	7	9	17	30	48	30
11	MFK Zemplín Michalovce	33	5	3	8	20	24	2	5	10	12	31	7	8	18	32	55	29
12	MFK Skalica	33	5	4	7	15	20	1	2	14	15	42	6	6	21	30	62	24

European qualification 2016/17

Champion/Cup winner: FK AS Trenčín (second qualifying round)

ŠK Slovan Bratislava (second qualifying round)
TJ Spartak Myjava (first qualifying round)
FC Spartak Trnava (first qualifying round)

Top scorer	Gino van Kessel (Trenčín), 17 goals
Relegated club	MFK Skalica
Promoted club	1. FC Tatran Prešov
Cup final	FK AS Trenčín 3-1 ŠK Slovan Bratislava

Team of the season
(3-4-3)

Coach: Ševela (Trenčín)

Šemrinec (Trenčín)

Šulek (Trenčín) — Saláta (Slovan) — Čonka (Trnava)

Hlohovský (Senica/Žilina) — Pečovský (Žilina) — Bero (Trenčín) — Milinković (Slovan)

Van Kessel (Trenčín) — Vittek (Slovan) — Zreľák (Slovan)

Player of the season

Gino van Kessel
(FK AS Trenčín)

Capped by Curacao but born in the Netherlands, Van Kessel received a part of his football education at the Ajax academy before moving on loan to Trenčín in 2013/14. He returned to the club on a permanent basis in January 2015 and 18 months later had two Slovakian league and cup winner's medals to treasure. The winger-cum-striker was particularly potent in front of goal in 2015/16, scoring twice in the cup final and winning the 1. Liga golden boot. To the dismay of the Trenčín fans, he left for Slavia Praha in the summer.

Newcomer of the season

Adam Zreľák
(ŠK Slovan Bratislava)

A gifted left-footed striker who joined Slovan in the 2014/15 winter break from Ružomberok, Zreľák's first full season in Bratislava brought no silverware but plenty of plaudits for both the quality of his play and his indefatigable spirit. He scored six goals in the league and one in the cup final for Slovan, adding another five in the 2017 UEFA European Under-21 Championship qualifiers to help Slovakia top their group at the halfway stage. He also scored for the senior side – on his second appearance – in a friendly against Georgia.

SLOVAKIA

International tournament appearances

FIFA World Cup (1) 2010 (2nd round)
UEFA European Championship (1) 2016 (round of 16)

Top five all-time caps

Miroslav Karhan (107); **Marek Hamšík** (91); **Martin Škrtel** (85); **Ján Ďurica** (83); **Róbert Vittek** (82)

Top five all-time goals

Róbert Vittek (23); Szilárd Németh (22); **Marek Hamšík** (19); Miroslav Karhan & Marek Mintál (14)

Results 2015/16

Date	Opponent	H/A	Venue	Result	Score	Scorers
05/09/15	Spain (ECQ)	A	Oviedo	L	0-2	
08/09/15	Ukraine (ECQ)	H	Zilina	D	0-0	
09/10/15	Belarus (ECQ)	H	Zilina	L	0-1	
12/10/15	Luxembourg (ECQ)	A	Luxembourg	W	4-2	Hamšík (24, 90+1), Nemec (29), Mak (30)
13/11/15	Switzerland	H	Trnava	W	3-2	Ďuriš (39, 49), Mak (55)
17/11/15	Iceland	H	Zilina	W	3-1	Mak (58, 61), Ďuriš (84)
25/03/16	Latvia	H	Trnava	D	0-0	
29/03/16	Republic of Ireland	A	Dublin	D	2-2	Stoch (14), McShane (45og)
27/05/16	Georgia	N	Wels (AUT)	W	3-1	Nemec (5, 57), Zrelák (70)
29/05/16	Germany	A	Augsburg	W	3-1	Hamšík (41), Ďuriš (44), Kucka (52)
04/06/16	Northern Ireland	H	Trnava	D	0-0	
11/06/16	Wales (ECF)	N	Bordeaux (FRA)	L	1-2	Duda (61)
15/06/16	Russia (ECF)	N	Lille (FRA)	W	2-1	Weiss (32), Hamšík (45)
20/06/16	England (ECF)	N	Saint-Etienne (FRA)	D	0-0	
26/06/16	Germany (ECF)	N	Lille (FRA)	L	0-3	

Appearances 2015/16

Coach: Ján Kozák — 17/04/54

Player	DOB	Club	ESP	UKR	BLR	LUX	Sui	Isl	Lva	Irl	Geo	Ger	Nir	WAL	RUS	ENG	GER	Caps	Goals
Matúš Kozáčik	27/12/83	Plzeň (CZE)	G	G	G	G				G		G	G	G	G	G	G	21	-
Peter Pekarík	30/10/86	Hertha (GER)	D	D51				D		D		D	D	D	D	D	D	71	2
Tomáš Hubočan	17/09/85	Dinamo Moskva (RUS)	D	D	D	D	D	D							D	D		46	-
Kornel Saláta	24/01/85	Slovan Bratislava	D	s51	D			D		D	D						s84	38	2
Lukáš Tesák	08/03/85	Arsenal Tula (RUS)/Kairat (KAZ)	D					D	s88		D							4	-
Patrik Hrošovský	22/04/92	Plzeň (CZE)	M73			M86		s46	M	s74	s79	M78	M	M60			M	14	-
Ján Greguš	29/01/91	Jablonec (CZE)	M			s86	M			M74	M87	s86				s46		8	-
Norbert Gyömbér	03/07/92	Roma (ITA)	M	D		D	D73	D			D					s66	D84	15	-
Marek Hamšík	27/07/87	Napoli (ITA)	M61	M	M	M	M88	M89		M		M86	M	M	M	M	M	91	19
Dušan Švento	01/08/85	Köln (GER)	M		D	D		s82		D88	s87	D	D	D	s72	s57		42	1
Róbert Mak	08/03/91	PAOK (GRE)	A46	M84	M79	M87	M73	M75	M	s64		M65	M	M80	M			30	7
Michal Ďuriš	01/06/88	Plzeň (CZE)	s46	M	A	A	A	s75		s70		A68	A66	A59	s80		A64	29	4
Ondrej Duda	05/12/94	Legia (POL)	s61		s79	s88	M	M		s64		M61	s66	s60	A67	A57		14	2
Erik Sabo	22/11/91	PAOK (GRE)	s73			s87	s73	s46	s89	M64	M66							9	-
Martin Škrtel	15/12/84	Liverpool (ENG)		D	D	D	D		D82	D		D	D	D	D	D		85	5
Juraj Kucka	26/02/87	Milan (ITA)		M	M	M	M73					M81	M82	M	M	M		51	5
Viktor Pečovský	24/05/83	Žilina		M	M60	M	s73	M46			M	s81			M	M66		34	1
Róbert Vittek	01/04/82	Slovan Bratislava		A66						A64								82	23
Martin Jakubko	26/02/80	Ružomberok		s66		s79	s73	s75										41	9
Miroslav Stoch	19/10/89	Bursaspor (TUR)	s84	s71						M64			s61	s65	s83			55	6
Vladimír Weiss	30/11/89	Lekhwiya (QAT)/Al-Gharafa (QAT)			M71	M72	M73	M	M		s64	M	M	M83	M72	M78	M46	56	5
Adam Nemec	02/09/85	Willem II (NED)			s60	A79		A75		s64	A70		s82	s59	s67			24	6
Stanislav Šesták	16/12/82	Ferencváros (HUN)			s72	s73				M64	s66	s68					s64	66	13
Ján Mucha	05/12/82	Slovan Bratislava					G		G		G63							46	-
Ján Ďurica	10/12/81	Lokomotiv Moskva (RUS)					D	D46	D			D	D	D	D		D	83	4
Ján Novota	29/11/83	Rapid Wien (AUT)						G			s63							3	-
Milan Škriniar	11/02/95	Sampdoria (ITA)									D		s78			s78	M	4	-
Matúš Bero	06/09/95	Trenčín									M79							1	-
Adam Zrelák	05/05/94	Slovan Bratislava									M							2	1

EUROPE

FK AS Trenčín

Second qualifying round - FC Steaua Bucureşti (ROU)
H 0-2
Šemrinec, Rundić, Van Kessel, Ibrahim (Koolwijk 79), Jairo, Madu, Čögley, Guba (Wesley 59), Bero, Ramón, Lobotka. Coach: Martin Ševela (SVK)
A 3-2 *Wesley (13, 84), Bero (21)*
Šemrinec, Rundić, Koolwijk, Van Kessel (Guba 64), Jairo (Kleščík 87), Madu, Čögley (Ibrahim 73), Bero, Ramón, Wesley, Lobotka. Coach: Martin Ševela (SVK)
Red card: Rundić 74

MŠK Žilina

First qualifying round - Glentoran FC (NIR)
A 4-1 *Jelić (13), Paur (20), Čmelík (59), Kane (81og)*
Voléšák, Škriniar, Káčer, Paur (Mihalík 63), Jelić (Willian 89), Pečovský, Čmelík (Špalek 78), Vavro, Letić, Bénes, Mabouka. Coach: Adrián Guľa (SVK)
H 3-0 *Jelić (44, 55, 66)*
Voléšák, Škriniar, Jelić (Paur 79), Špalek (Čmelík 59), Pečovský (Káčer 59), Vavro, Škvarka, Letić, Bénes, Mihalík, Mabouka. Coach: Adrián Guľa (SVK)

Second qualifying round - FC Dacia Chisinau (MDA)
A 2-1 *Jelić (53, 59)*
Voléšák, Škriniar, Káčer, Paur (Mihalík 66), Jelić, Pečovský, Čmelík (Špalek 85), Vavro, Letić, Bénes (Škvarka 89), Mabouka. Coach: Adrián Guľa (SVK)
H 4-2 *Vavro (15), Káčer (50), Škvarka (62), Paur (85)*
Voléšák, Škriniar, Káčer, Jelić, Pečovský, Čmelík (Paur 73), Vavro, Škvarka (Bénes 66), Letić, Mihalík (Špalek 81), Mabouka. Coach: Adrián Guľa (SVK)

Third qualifying round - FC Vorskla Poltava (UKR)
H 2-0 *Jelić (26), Paur (73)*
Voléšák, Škriniar, Káčer, Paur, Jelić, Pečovský, Vavro, Letić, Bénes (Škvarka 90+6), Mihalík (Willian 83), Mabouka (Špalek 20). Coach: Adrián Guľa (SVK)
A 1-3 (aet) *Willian (120+1)*
Voléšák, Škriniar, Káčer, Paur, Jelić, Špalek, Pečovský, Vavro, Letić (Hučko 118), Bénes (Škvarka 73), Mihalík (Willian 78). Coach: Adrián Guľa (SVK)
Red card: Špalek 99

Play-offs - Athletic Club (ESP)
H 3-2 *Paur (66), Willian (77, 90+4)*
Voléšák, Škriniar, Káčer, Paur, Jelić, Pečovský, Čmelík (Mihalík 72), Vavro, Letić, Bénes (Škvarka 88), Mabouka (Willian 57). Coach: Adrián Guľa (SVK)
A 0-1
Voléšák, Škriniar, Káčer (Špalek 88), Paur, Jelić (Čmelík 67), Willian, Pečovský, Mazáň, Vavro, Bénes, Mabouka (Mihalík 81). Coach: Adrián Guľa (SVK)

ŠK Slovan Bratislava

First qualifying round - Europa FC (GIB)
A 6-0 *Mészáros (5, 26, 31), Simović (33), Štefánik (41), Priskin (90+3)*
Krnáč, Sekulić, Dobrotka, Zrelák (Peltier 65), Milinković, Mészáros (Kubík 64), Štefánik (Oršula 70), Saláta, Priskin, Simović, Podaný. Coach: Ján Švehlík (SVK)
H 3-0 *Gorosito (21), Zrelák (35), Vittek (67p)*
Krnáč, Sekulić, Dobrotka, Kubík, Zrelák, Milinković, Gorosito (Saláta 43), Lásik (Mészáros 46), Simović, Vittek (Priskin 75), Podaný. Coach: Ján Švehlík (SVK)

Second qualifying round - University College Dublin AFC (IRL)
H 1-0 *Zrelák (84)*
Mucha, Sekulić, Zrelák, Milinković, Gorosito, Štefánik, Saláta, Priskin (Záhumenský 90+3), Simović (Hudák 44), Vittek (Kubík 46), Podaný. Coach: Ján Švehlík (SVK)
Red card: Gorosito 29
A 5-1 *Vittek (41, 90+1, 90+3), Milinković (49), Saláta (81)*
Mucha, Sekulić, Dobrotka (Hudák 69), Kubík (Oršula 67), Zrelák, Milinković (Gašparović 83), Štefánik, Lásik, Saláta, Vittek, Podaný. Coach: Ján Švehlík (SVK)

Third qualifying round - FC Krasnodar (RUS)
A 0-2
Mucha, Sekulić, Hudák, González (Štefánik 80), Zrelák (Kubík 73), Milinković, Mészáros (Oršula 60), Saláta, Kotula, Vittek, Podaný. Coach: Dušan Tittel (SVK)
H 3-3 *Vittek (54, 60, 77)*
Mucha, Sekulić, Hudák, Kubík (Oršula 74), González (Štefánik 81), Milinković, Gorosito, Saláta, Peltier (Mészáros 46), Vittek, Podaný. Coach: Dušan Tittel (SVK)

FC Spartak Trnava

First qualifying round - FK Olimpic Sarajevo (BIH)
A 1-1 *Halilović (70)*
Kneževic, Mikovič (Cléber 63), Vlasko, Bortel, Nikolić, Čonka, Godál, Sabo, Schranz (Halilović 70), Harba, Greššák (Casado 46). Coach: Juraj Jarábek (SVK)
H 0-0
Jakubech, Mikovič, Vlasko (Greššák 90), Casado, Nikolić, Tóth, Čonka, Godál, Sabo, Halilović (Schranz 58), Cléber (Harba 10). Coach: Juraj Jarábek (SVK)

Second qualifying round - Linfield FC (NIR)
H 2-1 *Sabo (16p), Mikovič (35)*
Jakubech, Baéz, Mikovič, Casado (Mikinič 64), Nikolić, Tóth (Greššák 70), Čonka, Godál, Sabo, Halilović, Harba (Bortel 46). Coach: Juraj Jarábek (SVK)
Red card: Nikolić 44
A 3-1 *Sabo (54, 84), Vojtuš (60)*
Jakubech, Vojtuš (Jirka 88), Mikovič, Casado, Bortel, Tóth, Čonka, Sabo, Halilović (Baéz 76), Harba (Mikinič 70), Greššák. Coach: Juraj Jarábek (SVK)
Red card: Bortel 80

Third qualifying round - PAOK FC (GRE)
A 0-1
Kamenár, Janečka, Vojtuš (Harba 74), Mikovič (Steinhübel 20), Casado, Nikolić, Tóth, Sabo, Halilović (Baéz 86), Mikinič, Greššák. Coach: Juraj Jarábek (SVK)
H 1-1 *Sabo (35p)*
Kamenár, Janečka, Vojtuš (Harba 62), Mikovič, Casado (Baéz 79), Bortel, Nikolić, Tóth, Sabo, Halilović (Mikinič 79), Greššák. Coach: Juraj Jarábek (SVK)

DOMESTIC LEAGUE CLUB-BY-CLUB

FC DAC 1904 Dunajská Streda

1904 • DAC (6,100) • fcdac.sk
Major honours
Czechoslovakian Cup (1) 1987
Coach: Tomislav Marić (CRO)

2015

18/07	h	Senica	W 2-0	Szarka, Pačinda (p)	
26/07	h	Spartak Trnava	W 2-1	Pačinda 2 (1p)	
02/08	h	Slovan	D 1-1	Kwin	
09/08	a	Žilina	D 1-1	Kwin	
15/08	h	Trenčín	L 0-2		
22/08	a	Michalovce	W 3-0	Szarka, Sarr, Ľupták	
29/08	h	Podbrezová	W 5-1	Ľupták, Szarka 4	
13/09	a	Zlaté Moravce	L 1-2	Pačinda (p)	
19/09	a	Spartak Myjava	L 0-1		
22/09	a	Skalica	D 2-2	Pačinda 2	
26/09	a	Ružomberok	L 0-1		
04/10	a	Senica	W 3-2	Štepanovský, Brašeň 2	
17/10	a	Spartak Trnava	L 0-2		
24/10	a	Slovan	L 0-2		
31/10	h	Žilina	W 1-0	Polievka (p)	
08/11	a	Trenčín	L 1-4	Szarka	
20/11	h	Michalovce	W 3-1	Pačinda (p), Szarka 2	
27/11	a	Podbrezová	D 0-0		
05/12	a	Zlaté Moravce	W 2-0	Ljubičić, Ľupták	

2016

28/02	h	Spartak Myjava	D 1-1	Sarr	
02/03	h	Skalica	W 1-0	Sarr	
05/03	h	Ružomberok	D 1-1	Horváth	
11/03	h	Senica	W 3-1	Sarr, Horváth, Stephens	
19/03	a	Spartak Trnava	L 0-1		
01/04	h	Slovan	L 0-2		
08/04	a	Žilina	L 1-4	Pačinda	
16/04	h	Trenčín	W 1-0	Pačinda	
19/04	a	Michalovce	D 1-1	Černák	
23/04	h	Podbrezová	W 1-0	Ljubičić	
30/04	a	Zlaté Moravce	L 0-1		
07/05	a	Spartak Myjava	L 0-3		
13/05	a	Skalica	L 1-2	Pačinda	
20/05	a	Ružomberok	L 0-3		

No	Name	Nat	DoB	Pos	Aps	(s)	Gls
2	Antonio Asanović	CRO	30/11/91	D		(11)	
21	Jakub Brašeň		02/05/89	M	26		2
23	Roland Černák		22/07/97	M	2	(8)	1
31	Erick Davis	PAN	31/03/91	D	15		
16	Dezider Egri		20/06/92	D	5		
11	Vojtech Horváth		28/06/94	M	4	(11)	2
5	Tomáš Huk		22/12/94	D	14		
29	Pavol Jurčo		12/02/86	A		(9)	
10	Dario Krišto	CRO	05/03/89	M		(3)	
14	Achile Kwin	CMR	14/01/90	D	27	(2)	2
4	Marin Ljubičić	CRO	15/06/88	M	30		2
9	Branislav Ľupták		05/06/91	M	22	(2)	3
15	András Meszáros		29/03/96	A		(5)	
6	Ľubomír Michalík		13/08/83	D	24	(1)	
30	Vojtech Milošovič		02/10/92	G	1		
8	Erik Pačinda		09/05/89	A	31		10
20	Yves Pambou	FRA	27/11/96	M	11	(4)	
26	Róbert Polievka		09/06/96	A	20	(13)	1
18	Pape Sarr	SEN	25/07/92	M	27	(3)	4
81	Alfredo Stephens	PAN	25/12/94	A	10	(7)	1
7	Gábor Straka		18/12/81	M	15	(2)	
27	Ákos Szarka		24/11/90	A	19	(1)	9
3	János Szepe		15/03/96	D	1		
24	Peter Štepanovský		12/01/88	M	19	(7)	1
1	Tomáš Tujvel		19/09/83	G	32		
19	Matúš Turňa		11/05/86	D	1	(2)	
28	Marko Živković	CRO	17/05/94	D	7	(2)	

MFK Ružomberok

1906 • Pod Čebraťom (4,817) •
mfkruzomberok.sk
Major honours
Slovakian League (1) 2006; Slovakian Cup (1) 2006
Coach: Ivan Galád;
(11/09/15) Ladislav Pecko

2015

18/07	h	Skalica	L 1-3	Jakubko	
24/07	a	Senica	D 1-1	Lovás	
19/08	h	Spartak Trnava	D 0-0		
09/08	a	Slovan	L 1-2	Masaryk	
16/08	h	Žilina	D 2-2	Ďubek, Faško	
23/08	a	Trenčín	D 1-1	Lovás	
29/08	h	Michalovce	D 2-2	Jakubko, Zošák	
12/09	a	Podbrezová	W 1-0	Lovás	
19/09	h	Zlaté Moravce	W 5-2	Kružliak, Jakubko, Ďubek (p), Lovás, Faško	
22/09	a	Spartak Myjava	L 1-2	Jakubko	
26/09	h	Dunajská Streda	W 1-0	Jakubko	
03/10	a	Skalica	W 1-0	Kružliak	
17/10	h	Senica	L 0-1		
23/10	a	Spartak Trnava	L 1-2	Ďubek (p)	
01/11	h	Slovan	D 1-1	Lačný	
07/11	a	Žilina	L 0-2		
21/11	h	Trenčín	L 0-3		
28/11	a	Michalovce	W 3-1	Boszorád, Jakubko, Faško	
05/12	h	Podbrezová	W 3-2	Daghbasyan 2, Lupták	

2016

27/02	a	Zlaté Moravce	W 2-0	Lačný, Sapara	
02/03	h	Spartak Myjava	W 1-0	Lačný	
05/03	a	Dunajská Streda	D 1-1	Lačný	
12/03	h	Skalica	W 3-1	Lupták, Lačný 2	
19/03	a	Senica	W 1-0	Lačný	
01/04	h	Spartak Trnava	W 3-1	Zošák, J Maslo, Lačný	
09/04	a	Slovan	L 1-3	Lačný (p)	
16/04	h	Žilina	L 0-2		
19/04	a	Trenčín	L 0-2		
23/04	a	Michalovce	D 0-0		
30/04	a	Podbrezová	L 1-3	og (Kostelný)	
07/05	h	Zlaté Moravce	D 1-1	Ďubek	
13/05	a	Spartak Myjava	L 0-1		
20/05	h	Dunajská Streda	W 3-0	Ďubek (p), Lačný (p), Zošák	

No	Name	Nat	DoB	Pos	Aps	(s)	Gls
24	Martin Boszorád		13/11/89	D	21	(7)	1
7	Anatol Cheptine	MDA	20/05/90	M	2	(6)	
19	Gagik Daghbasyan	ARM	19/10/90	D	3	(2)	2
9	Tomáš Ďubek		22/01/87	M	29	(4)	5
16	Michal Faško		24/08/94	M	17	(10)	3
7	Peter Gál-Andrezly		03/05/90	M	13		
8	Tomáš Gerát		15/06/93	M	5	(8)	
34	Ľuboš Hajdúch		06/03/80	G	3		
26	Martin Jakubko		26/02/80	A	17	(11)	6
2	Dominik Kružliak		10/07/96	D	25	(1)	2
21	Adam Kučera	CZE	25/02/93	A	1	(4)	
31	Miloš Lačný		08/03/88	A	17	(7)	10
12	Andrej Lovás		28/05/91	A	14	(10)	4
14	Lukáš Lupták		28/07/90	M	17	(3)	2
1	Matúš Macík		19/05/93	G	1		
21	Pavol Masaryk		11/02/80	A	3	(11)	1
3	Ján Maslo		05/02/86	D	28		1
17	Peter Maslo		02/02/87	D	27	(2)	
10	Martin Nagy		05/09/90	M	23	(1)	
16	Lukáš Ondrek		11/01/93	D	8	(4)	
22	Antonín Rosa	CZE	12/11/86	D	25		
27	Marek Sapara		31/07/82	M	5	(2)	1
35	Matej Šavol		14/04/84	G	2		
30	Darko Tofiloski	MKD	13/01/86	G	27		
13	Juraj Vavrík		09/02/91	M	2		
18	Štefan Zošák		03/04/84	M	17	(1)	(4)

FK Senica

1921 • OMS Arena (5,070) • fksenica.eu
Coach: Eduard Pagáč;
(08/09/15) Dušan Vrťo & Juraj Sabol

2015

18/07	a	Dunajská Streda	L 0-2		
24/07	h	Ružomberok	D 1-1	Pillár	
01/08	h	Skalica	W 2-1	Hlohovský 2	
09/08	h	Spartak Trnava	D 0-0		
15/08	h	Slovan	D 1-1	Mráz	
23/08	a	Žilina	L 1-4	Komara	
29/08	h	Trenčín	L 1-4	Hlohovský	
12/09	a	Michalovce	W 3-1	Hromada 2, Dolný	
19/09	h	Podbrezová	W 3-1	Klec, Dolný 2	
22/09	h	Zlaté Moravce	L 0-3		
26/09	h	Spartak Myjava	L 0-1		
04/10	a	Dunajská Streda	L 2-3	Hromada, Kalabiška	
17/10	a	Ružomberok	W 1-0	Hromada	
25/10	a	Skalica	W 3-0	Hromada, Klec, Kalabiška	
31/10	a	Spartak Trnava	W 1-0	Kalabiška (p)	
07/11	a	Slovan	L 1-2	Mráz	
21/11	h	Žilina	W 2-0	J Kosorín, Dolný	
29/11	a	Trenčín	L 0-2		
05/12	h	Michalovce	D 1-1	Klec	

2016

27/02	a	Podbrezová	L 0-1		
01/03	h	Zlaté Moravce	D 1-1	Pavlík	
06/03	a	Spartak Myjava	D 0-0		
11/03	a	Dunajská Streda	L 1-3	Leško	
19/03	h	Ružomberok	L 0-1		
02/04	h	Skalica	D 2-2	Pavlík, Pillár	
09/04	a	Spartak Trnava	L 0-1		
17/04	h	Slovan	L 1-3	Leško	
20/04	a	Žilina	D 0-0		
23/04	h	Trenčín	L 0-2		
30/04	a	Michalovce	L 1-2	Almási	
07/05	h	Podbrezová	L 0-1		
13/05	a	Zlaté Moravce	L 0-1		
20/05	h	Spartak Myjava	D 1-1	Dolný	

No	Name	Nat	DoB	Pos	Aps	(s)	Gls
12	Ladislav Almási		30/03/99	A	3	(3)	1
28	Pavol Cicman		30/01/85	A		(5)	
28	Jakub Čunta		28/08/96	A	25		
10	Jozef Dolný		13/05/92	M	23	(4)	5
15	Ivan Hladík		30/01/93	D	13	(6)	
13	Filip Hlohovský		13/06/88	M	7		3
13	Jakub Hromada		25/05/96	M	24	(1)	5
20	Ľuboš Hušek	CZE	26/01/84	M	28		
2	Viktor Jedinák		08/02/98	A		(1)	
39	Martin Junas		09/03/96	G	5	(1)	
19	Jan Kalabiška	CZE	22/12/86	A	15	(1)	3
9	Michal Klec		05/12/95	M	15	(6)	3
7	Tomáš Komara		23/05/94	M	13	(6)	1
2	Zoltán Kontár		07/11/93	D	18	(4)	
10	Jakub Kosorín		27/04/95	A	10	(5)	1
26	Matej Kosorín		03/04/97	M	2	(3)	
5	Jakub Krč		02/09/97	M	2	(8)	
23	Dávid Leško		04/06/88	A	14		2
3	Adi Mehremić	BIH	26/04/92	D	12	(1)	
24	Adam Morong		16/06/93	M	9	(5)	
15	Samuel Mráz		13/05/97	A	13	(8)	2
2	Denis Nemček		08/01/98	D		(1)	
3	Erik Otrísal		28/06/96	D	1	(1)	
4	Petr Pavlík	CZE	22/02/87	D	30	(1)	2
17	Róbert Pillár		27/05/91	D	28		2
18	František Plach		08/03/92	G	1	(2)	
16	Marek Rajník		22/09/96	M		(2)	
27	Šimon Šmehyl		09/02/94	M	12		
1	Michal Šulla		15/07/91	G	27		
22	Peter Varga		27/01/98	M	2	(8)	
23	Tomáš Vengřinek	CZE	08/06/92	D	9		
24	Denis Ventúra		01/08/95	M	2	(5)	

SLOVAKIA

MFK Skalica

1920 • Mestský štadión (1,500) •
mfkskalica.sk
**Coach: Aleš Křeček (CZE);
(28/10/15) Štefan Horný**

2015
18/07	a	Ružomberok	W 3-1	Gašparík (p), Lietava, Mazan (p)
25/07	h	Michalovce	W 1-0	Gašparík
01/08	a	Senica	L 1-2	Kurák
07/08	h	Podbrezová	D 0-0	
16/08	h	Spartak Trnava	L 2-3	Gašparík, Lietava
22/08	h	Zlaté Moravce	L 2-3	Kurák, Gašparík
29/08	a	Slovan	L 1-4	Šebesta
12/09	h	Spartak Myjava	D 0-0	
19/09	a	Žilina	D 2-2	Ulrich, Kurák
22/09	h	Dunajská Streda	D 2-2	Lietava, Ulrich
26/09	a	Trenčín	L 0-3	
03/10	a	Ružomberok	L 0-1	
18/10	a	Michalovce	L 1-3	Ulrich
25/10	h	Senica	L 0-3	
31/10	a	Podbrezová	L 0-3	
06/11	a	Spartak Trnava	L 1-2	Gašparík (p)
21/11	a	Zlaté Moravce	L 1-3	Ulrich
28/11	h	Slovan	L 0-3	
04/12	h	Spartak Myjava	L 0-3	

2016
26/02	h	Žilina	W 1-0	Jakubek
02/03	a	Dunajská Streda	L 0-1	
05/03	h	Trenčín	L 1-2	Masaryk (p)
12/03	a	Ružomberok	L 1-3	Hlavatovič
20/03	h	Michalovce	D 0-0	
02/04	a	Senica	D 2-2	Vaško, Jakubek
09/04	h	Podbrezová	W 2-1	Jakubek, Dobrotka
16/04	a	Spartak Trnava	L 1-5	Jakubek
19/04	h	Zlaté Moravce	W 1-0	Hlinka
24/04	a	Slovan	L 0-2	
01/05	h	Spartak Myjava	L 1-2	Jakubek
06/05	a	Žilina	L 0-1	
13/05	h	Dunajská Streda	W 2-1	Masaryk, Piroska
20/05	a	Trenčín	L 1-2	Dobrotka

No	Name	Nat	DoB	Pos	Aps	(s)	Gls
18	Damián Bariš		09/12/94	M	12		
14	Radoslav Ciprys		24/06/97	D	16	(4)	
7	Adrián Čermák		01/07/93	M	17	(6)	
3	Martin Dobrotka		22/01/85	D	14		2
4	Lukáš Fialka	CZE	19/09/95	D	1		
30	Andrej Fišan		08/01/85	G	11		
33	Michal Gašparík		19/12/81	M	13	(5)	5
21	Ľuboš Hajdúch		06/03/80	G	7		
46	Ikenna Hillary	NGA	17/04/91	M	3	(4)	
13	Lukáš Hlavatovič		22/04/87	D	14		1
17	Marek Hlinka		04/10/90	M	27		1
39	Dávid Hudák		21/03/93	D	9	(1)	
10	Michal Jakubek		01/06/90	A	8	(7)	5
3	Roman Konečný		25/07/83	D	14		
1	Martin Krnáč		30/01/85	G	13		
11	Mário Kurák		30/11/83	M	14	(1)	3
39	Ivan Lietava		20/07/83	A	14	(3)	3
24	Michal Lupač	CZE	15/05/84	G	2		
9	Pavol Majerník		31/12/78	D	27		
20	Pavol Masaryk		11/02/80	A	11	(3)	2
8	Peter Mazan		13/05/90	M	20	(7)	1
15	Ondrej Neoveský		10/09/86	M	14	(3)	
16	Andrej Petrovský		23/01/92	D	5	(2)	
33	Juraj Piroska		27/02/87	A	7	(1)	1
11	Daniel Šebesta		24/10/91	M	15	(14)	1
9	David Štrombach	CZE	09/01/96	M	1	(2)	
6	Lukáš Švrček		11/09/90	D	8	(5)	
12	Ľubomír Ulrich		01/02/89	A	11	(17)	4
5	Peter Vaško		19/05/87	M	16	(2)	1
28	Martin Vrablec		13/01/92	D	8	(6)	
44	Timotej Záhumenský		17/07/95	D	11		

ŠK Slovan Bratislava

1919 • Pasienky (11,907) • skslovan.com
Major honours
UEFA Cup Winners' Cup (1) 1969; Czechoslovakian League (8) 1949, 1950, 1951, 1955, 1970, 1974, 1975, 1992; Slovakian League (12) 1940, 1941, 1942, 1944, 1994, 1995, 1996, 1999, 2009, 2011, 2013, 2014; Czechoslovakian Cup (5) 1962, 1963, 1968, 1974, 1982; Slovakian Cup (6) 1994, 1997, 1999, 2010, 2011, 2013
**Coach: Dušan Tittel;
(21/08/15) Nikodimos Papavasiliou (CYP)**

2015
19/07	a	Zlaté Moravce	W 2-1	Priskin, Saláta
26/07	h	Spartak Myjava	W 1-0	
02/08	a	Dunajská Streda	D 1-1	Priskin
09/08	h	Ružomberok	W 2-1	Hudák, Priskin
15/08	a	Senica	D 1-1	Gorosito
25/08	h	Spartak Trnava	W 2-0	Milinković (p), Zrelák
29/08	a	Skalica	W 4-1	Milinković (p), Zrelák, Vittek, Oršula
12/09	a	Žilina	L 0-3	
20/09	h	Trenčín	D 0-0	
23/09	a	Michalovce	W 2-1	Milinković (p), og (Šimčák)
27/09	h	Podbrezová	W 3-1	González, Vittek, Priskin
02/10	h	Zlaté Moravce	W 2-0	Vittek, Milinković
17/10	a	Spartak Myjava	W 2-0	Vittek 2
24/10	h	Dunajská Streda	W 1-0	Zrelák
01/11	a	Ružomberok	D 1-1	Priskin
07/11	h	Senica	W 2-1	Saláta, Priskin
22/11	a	Spartak Trnava	D 0-0	
28/11	h	Skalica	W 2-0	Vittek, Milinković
06/12	h	Žilina	W 2-1	Milinković, Priskin

2016
27/02	a	Trenčín	W 2-0	Kubík, Priskin
09/03	h	Michalovce	W 1-0	Priskin
05/03	h	Podbrezová	W 1-0	Kubík
12/03	a	Zlaté Moravce	D 0-0	
20/03	h	Spartak Myjava	L 0-1	
02/04	a	Dunajská Streda	W 2-0	Savićević (p), Milinković (p)
09/04	h	Ružomberok	W 3-1	Crnkić, Vittek 2 (2p)
17/04	a	Senica	W 3-1	Zrelák, Saláta, Crnkić
20/04	h	Spartak Trnava	W 4-1	Vittek 2, Zrelák 2
24/04	h	Skalica	W 2-0	Kele, Savićević
02/05	a	Žilina	D 0-0	
08/05	h	Trenčín	L 0-4	
13/05	a	Michalovce	W 2-1	Priskin
20/05	h	Podbrezová	D 2-2	Šefčík, Priskin (p)

No	Name	Nat	DoB	Pos	Aps	(s)	Gls
92	Moise Adilehou	FRA	01/11/95	D		(1)	
17	Nermin Crnkić	USA	31/08/92	M	7	(2)	2
4	Erik Čikoš		31/07/88	D	10	(1)	
6	Joeri de Kamps	NED	10/02/92	M	12	(1)	
5	Claude Dielna	FRA	14/12/87	D	2	(2)	
8	Mauro González	ARG	31/08/96	M	12	(4)	1
16	Nicolás Gorosito	ARG	17/08/88	D	14	(1)	1
22	Dominik Greif		06/04/97	G	2		
5	Dávid Hudák		21/03/93	D	5	(1)	1
23	Kevin Kele		26/04/98	M	2	(2)	1
13	Adrián Kopičár		13/01/97	M		(1)	
28	Juraj Kotula		30/09/95	D	5	(1)	
30	Martin Krnáč		30/01/85	G	3		
7	František Kubík		14/03/89	M	22	(6)	2
26	František Lády		22/04/96	A		(1)	
18	Richard Lásik		18/08/92	M	2		
12	Karol Mészáros		25/07/93	A	6	(2)	
10	Marko Milinković	CRO	16/04/88	M	23	(3)	7
82	Ján Mucha		05/12/82	G	28		
11	Filip Oršula		25/02/93	M	2	(20)	1
23	Lester Peltier	TRI	13/09/88	A	3	(5)	
88	Vasilios Pliatsikas	GRE	14/04/88	D	11	(1)	
39	Jakub Podaný	CZE	15/06/87	D	24	(1)	
20	Tamás Priskin	HUN	27/09/86	A	21	(5)	11
13	Patrik Sabo		09/03/93	M		(1)	
19	Kornel Saláta		24/01/85	D	28	(1)	3
4	Vukan Savićević	MNE	29/01/94	M	15	(5)	2
12	Granwald Scott	RSA	01/07/87	M	7	(6)	
2	Boris Sekulić	SRB	21/10/91	D	31		
27	Slobodan Simović	SRB	22/05/89	M	15	(3)	
24	Samuel Šefčík		04/11/96	M	2		1
17	Samuel Štefánik		16/11/91	M	5	(8)	
33	Róbert Vittek		01/04/82	A	19	(6)	10
14	Timotej Záhumenský		17/07/95	D		(1)	
9	Adam Zrelák		05/05/94	A	25	(1)	6

TJ Spartak Myjava

1920 • Štadión Spartaka (2,728) •
spartakmyjava.sk
Coach: Norbert Hrnčár

2015
19/07	h	Spartak Trnava	W 4-2	Marček, Bílovský, Pekár, Sládek
26/07	a	Slovan	W 1-0	Sládek
02/08	h	Žilina	L 1-4	Bílovský
08/08	h	Trenčín	L 0-1	
15/08	h	Michalovce	W 2-1	Piroska, Daniel
22/08	a	Podbrezová	W 2-1	Kóňa, Daniel
29/08	h	Zlaté Moravce	D 0-0	
12/09	a	Skalica	D 0-0	
19/09	a	Dunajská Streda	W 1-0	Sládek
22/09	h	Ružomberok	W 2-1	Pekár, Sládek
26/09	a	Senica	W 1-0	Daniel
03/10	a	Spartak Trnava	L 1-2	Sládek (p)
17/10	h	Slovan	L 0-2	
25/10	a	Žilina	L 0-3	
30/10	a	Trenčín	L 1-2	og (Rundić)
07/11	a	Michalovce	W 2-1	Sládek, Daniel
21/11	h	Podbrezová	W 2-1	Škutka, Sládek
28/11	a	Zlaté Moravce	W 3-1	Kóňa, Bílovský, Duga
04/12	h	Skalica	W 3-0	Pekár 2, Kóňa

2016
28/02	a	Dunajská Streda	D 1-1	Kolár
02/03	a	Ružomberok	L 0-1	
06/03	h	Senica	D 0-0	
12/03	h	Spartak Trnava	W 1-0	Marček
20/03	a	Slovan	W 1-0	Sládek
02/04	h	Žilina	D 0-0	
10/04	a	Trenčín	L 1-3	Sládek
16/04	h	Michalovce	W 3-0	Daniel 2, Škutka
19/04	a	Podbrezová	L 0-2	
23/04	a	Zlaté Moravce	W 1-0	Sládek
01/05	a	Skalica	W 2-1	Sládek, Duga
07/05	h	Dunajská Streda	W 3-0	Pekár, Bílovský, Marček
13/05	h	Ružomberok	W 1-0	Sládek
20/05	a	Senica	D 1-1	Duga

No	Name	Nat	DoB	Pos	Aps	(s)	Gls
2	Patrik Banovič		13/11/91	D	22		
8	Lukáš Beňo		07/11/89	D	27	(1)	
19	Frederik Bílovský		03/03/92	M	26	(7)	4
11	Ján Chovanec		22/03/84	M	16	(6)	
22	Dávid Copko		03/07/96	M		(3)	
10	Martin Černáček		09/11/79	D	2	(6)	
23	Erik Daniel	CZE	04/02/92	M	31	(2)	6
18	Denis Duga		05/09/94	M	7	(12)	4
7	Dominik Ferenčič		29/05/96	A		(3)	
28	Matúš Hruška		17/09/94	G	23		
3	Peter Jánošík		02/01/88	D	5	(9)	
2	Marek Jastráb		16/07/93	M		(1)	
5	Karol Karlík		29/06/86	D	6	(6)	
14	Ľuboš Kolár		01/09/89	M	20	(11)	1
6	Tomáš Kóňa		01/03/84	M	33		3
3	Jaroslav Machovec		06/02/87	D	14		
20	Tomáš Marček		10/03/87	M	29	(2)	3
27	Ivan Múdry		03/08/92	D	1	(2)	
3	Ivan Ostojić	SRB	26/06/89	D	11		
9	Štefan Pekár		03/12/88	A	30	(1)	5
33	Juraj Piroska		27/02/87	M	8	(1)	1
26	Peter Sládek		07/07/89	A	29	(1)	11
27	Fabian Slančík		22/09/91	A	2	(11)	
1	Peter Solnička		14/06/82	G	10		
16	Dávid Škutka		25/05/88	A	11	(10)	2

FC Spartak Trnava

1923 • Antona Malatinského (19,200) • spartak.sk

Major honours
Czechoslovakian League (5) 1968, 1969, 1971, 1972, 1973; Czechoslovakian Cup (4) 1967, 1971, 1975, 1986; Slovakian Cup (1) 1998

Coach: Juraj Jarábek;
(28/08/15) (Branislav Mráz);
(01/09/15) Ivan Hucko
(21/04/16) Miroslav Karhan

2015
19/07	a	Spartak Myjava	L 2-4	Sabo 2 (1p)
26/07	h	Dunajská Streda	L 1-2	Mikovič
19/08	a	Ružomberok	D 0-0	
09/08	a	Senica	D 0-0	
16/08	h	Skalica	W 3-2	Casado, Mikovič, Vojtuš
25/08	a	Slovan	L 0-2	
30/08	h	Žilina	W 2-0	Janečka, Baéz
13/09	a	Trenčín	L 3-5	Harba, Depetris 2
19/09	h	Michalovce	L 0-1	
22/09	a	Podbrezová	W 2-0	Schranz, Majtán
25/09	h	Zlaté Moravce	W 2-1	Godál (p), Mikovič
03/10	h	Spartak Myjava	W 2-1	Schranz, og (Marček)
17/10	h	Dunajská Streda	W 2-0	Depetris 2
23/10	h	Ružomberok	W 2-1	Schranz, Nikolić
31/10	a	Senica	L 0-1	
06/11	h	Skalica	W 2-1	Depetris, Mikovič
22/11	h	Slovan	D 0-0	
28/11	a	Žilina	L 0-2	
05/12	h	Trenčín	D 1-1	Harba (p)

2016
27/02	a	Michalovce	W 1-0	Depetris
02/03	h	Podbrezová	D 0-0	
06/03	a	Zlaté Moravce	D 2-2	Mihálik, Depetris (p)
12/03	h	Spartak Myjava	L 0-1	
19/03	h	Dunajská Streda	W 1-0	Halilović
01/04	a	Ružomberok	L 1-3	Mikovič
09/04	h	Senica	W 2-0	Mikovič 2
16/04	h	Skalica	W 5-1	Depetris 3 (1p), Jež, Košťál
20/04	a	Slovan	L 1-4	Jež
24/04	h	Žilina	W 3-0	Depetris, Schranz, Halilović
02/05	a	Trenčín	W 3-1	Godál, Depetris, Schranz
07/05	h	Michalovce	W 3-0	Schranz, Depetris 2
13/05	a	Podbrezová	L 0-3	
20/05	h	Zlaté Moravce	W 3-2	Schranz 2, Depetris

No	Name	Nat	DoB	Pos	Aps	(s)	Gls
7	Bello Babatunde	BEN	06/10/89	M	8	(2)	
4	Aldo Baéz	ARG	05/09/88	M	23	(5)	1
24	Niaré Benogo	MLI	27/08/92	M	3	(3)	
13	Milan Bortel		07/04/87	D	6	(3)	
17	José David Casado	ESP	14/01/88	M	9	(7)	1
30	Cléber	BRA	03/06/86	M		(1)	
20	Matúš Čonka		15/10/90	D	28		
3	Filip Deket		01/05/93	D		(2)	
22	David Depetris		11/11/88	A	18	(3)	15
21	Boris Godál		27/05/87	D	25		2
34	Lukáš Greššák		23/01/89	D	22	(1)	
27	Emir Halilović	BIH	04/11/89	M	21	(7)	2
33	Ľuboš Hanzel		07/05/87	D	3		
28	Haris Harba	BIH	14/07/88	M	4	(10)	2
5	Denis Horník		13/07/97	D	12		
22	Adam Jakubech		02/01/97	G	13	(2)	
6	Marek Janečka		09/06/83	D	17		1
12	Róbert Jež		10/07/81	M	13		2
2	Andrej Kadlec		02/02/96	D	8	(1)	
71	Ľuboš Kamenár		17/06/87	G	19		
18	Martin Košťál		23/02/96	M		(7)	1
10	Tomáš Majtán		30/03/87	A	13	(6)	1
32	Lukáš Mihálik		10/02/97	M	4	(6)	1
32	Tomáš Mikinič		22/11/92	M	3	(2)	
8	Martin Mikovič		12/09/90	M	30		7
15	Miloš Nikolić	SRB	21/02/89	D	14	(3)	1
14	Ivan Pikulík		11/10/94	M		(1)	
25	Erik Sabo		22/11/91	M	3		2
26	Ivan Schranz		13/09/93	M	20	(1)	8
2	Christian Steinhübel		02/10/94	M		(1)	
41	Matej Strapák		28/06/93	G	1		
29	Robert Tambe	CMR	22/02/94	A	3	(8)	
19	Martin Tóth		13/10/86	D	14	(4)	
28	Jakub Vojtuš		22/10/93	A	6	(8)	1

ŽP Šport Podbrezová

1920 • ZELPO Aréna (4,061) • zpfutbal.sk

Coach: Zdenko Frťala;
(21/09/15) Marek Fabuľa

2015
25/07	h	Trenčín	L 0-2	
01/08	h	Michalovce	W 6-2	Melunović (p), Mehanović 2, Vaščák, Kupčík, Gál-Andrezly
07/08	a	Skalica	D 0-0	
15/08	a	Zlaté Moravce	D 2-2	Sabler, Almaský
22/08	h	Spartak Myjava	L 1-2	Pančík
29/08	a	Dunajská Streda	L 1-5	Mehanović (p)
12/09	h	Ružomberok	L 0-1	
15/09	h	Žilina	L 2-3	Sabler, Gál-Andrezly
19/09	a	Senica	L 1-3	Vajda
22/09	h	Spartak Trnava	L 0-2	
27/09	a	Slovan	L 1-3	Kupčík
03/10	a	Žilina	W 3-1	Kapor, Gál-Andrezly 2
17/10	a	Trenčín	L 1-2	Andrić
24/10	a	Michalovce	L 0-2	
31/10	h	Skalica	W 3-0	Rendla, Kochan, Pančík
07/11	h	Zlaté Moravce	D 2-2	Gál-Andrezly, Vajda
21/11	a	Spartak Myjava	L 1-2	Pančík
27/11	h	Dunajská Streda	D 0-0	
05/12	a	Ružomberok	L 2-3	Sabler, Viazanko

2016
27/02	h	Senica	W 1-0	Podio
02/03	a	Spartak Trnava	D 0-0	
05/03	h	Slovan	L 0-1	
12/03	h	Žilina	W 2-0	Kostelný, Podio (p)
19/03	a	Trenčín	L 0-2	
02/04	h	Michalovce	W 2-0	Šafranko, Rendla
09/04	a	Skalica	L 1-2	Kostelný
15/04	a	Zlaté Moravce	D 0-0	
19/04	h	Spartak Myjava	W 2-0	Podio, Vajda
23/04	a	Dunajská Streda	L 0-1	
30/04	h	Ružomberok	W 3-1	Podio, Dejen Pasevski 2
07/05	a	Senica	W 1-0	Rendla
13/05	h	Spartak Trnava	W 3-0	Vajda 2, Rendla
20/05	a	Slovan	D 2-2	Podio, Rendla

No	Name	Nat	DoB	Pos	Aps	(s)	Gls
16	Mário Almaský		25/06/91	M	7	(1)	1
10	Nikola Andrić	SRB	23/05/92	D	17	(1)	1
27	Juraj Baláž		12/06/80	G	2		
13	Bernardo Frizoni	BRA	12/03/90	D	3		
14	Lazar Djordjević	SRB	14/07/92	D	12		
6	René Duda		06/12/96	A		(6)	
3	Peter Gál-Andrezly		03/05/90	M	18	(1)	5
21	Václav Ježdík	CZE	03/07/87	D	3	(1)	
22	Milovan Kapor	CAN	05/08/91	D	6	(3)	1
11	Matej Kochan		21/11/92	M	24	(4)	1
4	Jaroslav Kostelný		19/04/85	D	14		2
20	Ján Krivák		10/11/93	D	14		
22	Martin Kuciak		15/03/82	G	34		
12	Ľuboš Kupčík		03/03/89	D	20	(3)	2
16	Adam Lipčák		19/03/97	D		(1)	
1	Patrik Lukáč		05/12/94	G	1		
13	Daniel Magda		25/11/97	D		(1)	
23	Mirzad Mehanović	BIH	05/01/93	A	6	(5)	3
10	Alen Melunović	SRB	26/01/90	A	5	(2)	1
7	Lukáš Migala		04/07/94	D	17	(7)	
6	Tomáš Mikinič		22/11/92	M	2		
17	Juraj Pančík		11/05/90	M	6	(11)	3
23	Dejen Pasevski	MKD	05/08/93	M	12	(2)	2
23	Jiří Pimpara	CZE	04/02/87	D	9		
9	Pablo Podio	ARG	08/08/89	M	23	(2)	5
25	Andrej Rendla		13/10/90	A	15	(3)	5
24	Roman Sabler		05/09/94	A	5	(18)	3
21	Július Szöke		01/08/95	M	6	(4)	
18	Pavol Šafranko		16/11/94	A	12	(1)	1
3	Matúš Turňa		11/05/86	D	14		
3	Patrik Vajda		20/03/89	D	30		5
8	Blažej Vaščák		21/11/83	A	16	(2)	1
2	Miroslav Viazanko		27/10/81	M	13		1
14	Adam Žilák		07/12/91	M		(6)	

FK AS Trenčín

1992 • Na Sihoti (3,500) • astrencin.sk

Major honours
Slovakian League (2) 2015, 2016; Slovakian Cup (2) 2015, 2016

Coach: Martin Ševela

2015
18/07	a	Michalovce	W 1-0	Koolwijk
25/07	a	Podbrezová	W 2-0	Bero, Van Kessel
01/08	a	Zlaté Moravce	W 1-0	Guba
08/08	a	Spartak Myjava	W 1-0	Rundić
15/08	a	Dunajská Streda	W 2-0	Van Kessel 2
23/08	h	Ružomberok	D 1-1	Koolwijk
29/08	a	Senica	W 4-1	Bero, Guba, Van Kessel, Bala
13/09	h	Spartak Trnava	W 5-3	Bero, Van Kessel, Ibrahim, Wesley, Schet
20/09	a	Slovan	D 0-0	
23/09	h	Žilina	L 1-4	Bero
26/09	h	Skalica	W 3-0	Bero 3
03/10	h	Michalovce	W 2-0	Ibrahim, Bero
17/10	h	Podbrezová	W 2-1	Van Kessel, Bero
24/10	h	Zlaté Moravce	W 4-1	Jančo, Wesley, Ibrahim, og (Tipuric)
30/10	h	Spartak Myjava	W 4-1	Schet, og (Beňo), Wesley, Van Kessel
08/11	h	Dunajská Streda	W 4-1	Madu, Koolwijk, Wesley 2
21/11	a	Ružomberok	W 3-0	Schet, Van Kessel 2
29/11	h	Senica	W 2-0	Van Kessel, Bero
05/12	a	Spartak Trnava	D 1-1	Wesley

2016
27/02	h	Slovan	L 0-2	
08/03	a	Žilina	W 3-2	Schet, Holúbek, Bero
05/03	a	Skalica	W 2-1	Maierhofer, Bero
13/03	a	Michalovce	W 3-1	Bero, Maierhofer, Opatovský
19/03	a	Podbrezová	W 2-0	Bero, Lawrence
03/04	a	Zlaté Moravce	W 2-0	Koolwijk, Schet
10/04	h	Spartak Myjava	W 3-1	Ibrahim, Kalu, Bero
16/04	a	Dunajská Streda	L 0-1	
19/04	h	Ružomberok	W 1-0	Kalu
23/04	a	Senica	W 2-0	Kalu, Koolwijk
02/05	h	Spartak Trnava	L 1-3	Ibrahim
08/05	a	Slovan	W 4-0	Van Kessel 2, Schet, Udeh
13/05	h	Žilina	W 5-2	Šulek, Van Kessel 4
20/05	h	Skalica	W 2-1	Van Kessel, Bala

No	Name	Nat	DoB	Pos	Aps	(s)	Gls
16	Aliko Bala	NGA	27/02/97	A	1	(14)	2
21	Matúš Bero		06/09/95	M	30		15
30	Adrián Chovan		08/10/95	G	2		
17	Peter Čögley		11/08/88	D	8		
14	Dávid Guba		29/06/91	M	16	(15)	2
14	Jakub Holúbek		12/01/91	M	3	(21)	1
10	Rabiu Ibrahim	NGA	15/03/91	M	24	(2)	5
11	Jairo	BRA	06/05/92	A	3		
17	Denis Jančo		01/08/97	M	4	(3)	1
17	Samuel Kalu	NGA	26/08/97	A	10	(3)	3
19	Peter Kleščík		09/08/88	D	28	(1)	
7	Ryan Koolwijk	NED	18/08/85	M	27	(3)	5
18	Jamie Lawrence	ENG	22/08/92	D	8	(7)	1
29	Stanislav Lobotka		25/11/94	M	6		
15	Kingsley Madu	NGA	11/12/95	D	30		1
9	Stefan Maierhofer	AUT	16/08/82	A	6	(4)	2
20	Matúš Opatovský		22/07/94	D	5	(8)	1
22	Ramón	BRA	22/08/90	D	2		
3	Milan Rundić	SRB	23/09/92	D	17		1
17	Mitchell Schet	NED	28/01/88	M	15	(3)	6
2	Lukáš Skovajsa		27/03/94	D	20	(4)	
24	Igor Šemrinec		22/11/87	G	31		
6	Martin Šulek		15/01/98	D	22		1
22	Christopher Udeh	NGA	03/09/97	D	1	(1)	1
9	Gino van Kessel	CUW	09/03/93	A	28	(5)	17
25	Wesley	BRA	26/11/96	A	15	(3)	6

SLOVAKIA

FC ViOn Zlaté Moravce

1995 • ViOn (3,300) • fcvion.sk
Major honours
Slovakian Cup (1) 2007
**Coach: Milko Gjurovski (MKD);
(27/08/15) Libor Fašiang**

2015

19/07	h	Slovan	L 1-2	Glavaš
26/07	a	Žilina	L 1-5	Krznarić
01/08	h	Trenčín	L 0-1	
08/08	a	Michalovce	L 1-2	Mance
15/08	h	Podbrezová	D 2-2	Tawamba (p), Bamba
22/08	a	Skalica	W 3-2	Orávik 2, Cebara
29/08	a	Spartak Myjava	D 0-0	
13/09	h	Dunajská Streda	W 2-1	Tipuric, Tawamba
19/09	a	Ružomberok	L 2-5	Tawamba 2 (p)
22/09	h	Senica	W 3-0	Jhonnes, Tawamba, Ploj
25/09	a	Spartak Trnava	L 1-2	Tawamba (p)
02/10	a	Slovan	L 0-2	
16/10	h	Žilina	W 4-0	Jhonnes, Orávik, Školnik, Tawamba
24/10	a	Trenčín	L 1-4	Jhonnes
31/10	h	Michalovce	D 1-1	Jhonnes
07/11	a	Podbrezová	D 2-2	Jhonnes, Tawamba
21/11	h	Skalica	W 3-1	Tawamba 3 (1p)
28/11	h	Spartak Myjava	L 1-3	Jhonnes
05/12	a	Dunajská Streda	L 0-2	

2016

27/02	h	Ružomberok	L 0-2	
01/03	a	Senica	D 1-1	Majkić
06/03	a	Spartak Trnava	D 2-2	Jhonnes, Cebara (p)
12/03	h	Slovan	D 0-0	
18/03	a	Žilina	L 0-6	
03/04	h	Trenčín	L 0-2	
09/04	a	Michalovce	D 1-1	Bamba
15/04	h	Podbrezová	D 0-0	
19/04	a	Skalica	L 0-1	
23/04	a	Spartak Myjava	L 0-1	
30/04	h	Dunajská Streda	W 1-0	Jhonnes
07/05	a	Ružomberok	D 1-1	Kuzma
13/05	h	Senica	W 2-0	Jhonnes (p), Perišić
20/05	a	Spartak Trnava	L 2-3	Kuzma, Orávik

No	Name	Nat	DoB	Pos	Aps	(s)	Gls
35	Mourukou Bamba	FRA	03/02/96	M	2	(9)	2
27	Damián Bariš		09/12/94	M	7	(1)	
10	Denis Bochl	CRO	30/08/93	D			
16	Mario Burić	CRO	25/10/91	D	15	(2)	
7	Stefan Cebara	CAN	12/04/91	M	12	(14)	2
20	Róbert Gešnábel		24/11/91	A	9	(3)	
92	Marin Glavaš	CRO	17/03/92	M	16	(2)	1
5	Jhonnes	BRA	22/04/84	D	28	(1)	9
23	Karol Karlík		29/06/96	D	9	(2)	
66	Patrik Klačan		10/11/97	A		(1)	
30	Pavol Kováč		12/08/74	G	16		
17	Marko Kovjenič	SVN	02/02/93	M	1		
21	Josip Krznarić	CRO	07/01/93	A	19	(13)	1
32	Šimon Kupec		11/02/96	D	15	(2)	
29	Marek Kuzma		22/06/88	A	6	(6)	2
6	Danijel Majkić	BIH	16/12/87	M	29		1
9	Armando Mance	CRO	27/10/92	A	3	(7)	1
77	Stefan Milojević	SRB	20/02/91	D	4		
15	Ivan Mršić	BIH	24/06/91	D	2		
24	Jozef Novota		24/01/86	G	3		
18	Peter Orávik		18/12/88	M	30	(1)	4
14	Marko Perišić	BIH	25/01/91	A	18	(8)	1
42	Michal Pintér		04/02/94	D	19	(1)	
19	Alen Ploj	SRB	30/06/92	A	1	(5)	1
25	Marko Ranilović	SVN	25/11/86	G	14	(1)	
8	Jozef Rejdovian		18/03/91	M	1	(7)	
45	Lamin Samateh	GAM	26/06/92	D	3		
22	Fabián Slančík		22/09/91	M	6	(3)	
40	Dejan Školnik	CRO	01/01/89	M	27	(1)	1
3	Leandre Tawamba	CMR	20/12/89	A	19		11
4	Toni Tipuric	AUT	10/09/90	D	29		1

MFK Zemplín Michalovce

1912 • Mestský futbalový štadión (4,440) • mfkzemplin.sk
**Coach: František Šturma (CZE);
(30/12/15) Stanislav Griga**

2015

18/07	h	Trenčín	L 0-1	
25/07	a	Skalica	L 0-1	
01/08	a	Podbrezová	L 2-6	Vernon, Hamuľák
08/08	h	Zlaté Moravce	W 2-1	Danko, Regáli
15/08	a	Spartak Myjava	L 1-2	Šimčák
22/08	h	Dunajská Streda	L 0-3	
29/08	a	Ružomberok	D 2-2	Regáli, Koscelník
12/09	h	Senica	L 1-3	og (Hromada)
19/09	a	Spartak Trnava	W 1-0	Danko
23/09	h	Slovan	L 1-2	Vernon
27/09	a	Žilina	L 0-2	
03/10	h	Trenčín	L 0-2	
18/10	h	Skalica	W 3-1	Samuel Bayón (p), Danko 2
24/10	h	Podbrezová	W 2-0	Vernon 2
31/10	a	Zlaté Moravce	D 1-1	Kunca
07/11	h	Spartak Myjava	L 1-2	Mensah
20/11	a	Dunajská Streda	L 1-3	Vernon
28/11	h	Ružomberok	L 1-3	Vernon
05/12	a	Senica	D 1-1	Kunca

2016

27/02	h	Spartak Trnava	L 0-1	
09/03	a	Slovan	L 0-1	
04/03	a	Žilina	W 3-2	Koscelník, Lukić 2
13/03	h	Trenčín	L 1-3	Lukić (p)
20/03	a	Skalica	D 0-0	
02/04	a	Podbrezová	L 0-2	
09/04	h	Zlaté Moravce	D 1-1	Hamuľák
16/04	a	Spartak Myjava	L 0-3	
19/04	h	Dunajská Streda	D 1-1	Hamuľák
23/04	a	Ružomberok	D 0-0	
30/04	h	Senica	W 2-1	Serečín, Kunca
07/05	a	Spartak Trnava	L 0-3	
13/05	h	Slovan	D 1-1	Kunca
20/05	h	Žilina	W 3-0	Kunca 2, Koscelník

No	Name	Nat	DoB	Pos	Aps	(s)	Gls
10	Martin Bednár		22/04/99	M		(2)	
28	Pavol Bellás		28/05/97	A		(2)	
15	Stanislav Danko		17/03/94	M	22	(3)	4
77	Panagiotis Deligiannidis	GRE	29/08/96	M		(1)	
26	Eric Barroso	ESP	04/10/90	D	6		
3	Michal Gallo		02/06/88	D	5	(2)	
8	Jakub Grič		05/07/96	M	18	(7)	
21	Michal Hamuľák		26/11/90	A	15	(10)	3
2	Joan Sánchez	ESP	26/09/92	D	1		
23	Marián Kelemen		07/12/79	G	26		
29	Andrej Kerić	CRO	11/02/86	A	1	(3)	
13	Akaki Khubutia	GEO	17/03/86	D	17		
22	Matúš Kira		10/10/94	G	6		
24	Martin Koscelník		02/03/95	M	33		3
11	Dominik Kunca		04/03/92	A	21	(11)	7
11	Adrián Leško		24/06/96	M	1	(2)	
90	Nikola Lukić	SRB	14/05/90	M	7	(2)	3
7	Marcos	ESP	09/04/93	D	24	(1)	
16	Emmanuel Mensah	GHA	30/06/94	M	7	(7)	1
25	Peter Nworah	NGA	15/12/90	A	11	(3)	
20	Oliver Podhorín		06/07/92	D	17		
1	Martin Raška	CZE	31/07/77	G	1		
14	Martin Regáli		18/03/93	A	6	(2)	2
19	Samuel Bayón	ESP	15/03/83	M	9	(11)	1
88	Kyriakos Savvidis	GRE	20/06/95	M	1	(2)	
7	Tomáš Sedlák		03/02/83	M	27		
89	Filip Serečín		04/10/89	A	6	(4)	1
44	Aleksandr Sverchinski	BLR	16/09/91	D	10	(2)	
2	Milan Šimčák		23/08/95	D	20	(3)	1
5	Toni García	ESP	07/08/91	M	2	(2)	
4	Lukáš Tóth		09/01/96	M		(5)	
12	Jozef Šimon Turík		19/07/95	M	10		
18	Vernon	ESP	18/11/92	D	27	(3)	5
99	Maksim Votinov	RUS	29/08/88	A	6	(2)	

MŠK Žilina

1908 • Pod Dubňom (11,313) • mskzilina.sk
Major honours
Slovakian League (6) 2002, 2003, 2004, 2007, 2010, 2012; Slovakian Cup (1) 2012
Coach: Adrián Guľa

2015

26/07	h	Zlaté Moravce	W 5-1	Káčer, Paur 2, Škvarka, Jelić
02/08	a	Spartak Myjava	W 4-1	Mihalík 2, Jelić, Willian
09/08	h	Dunajská Streda	D 1-1	Jelić
16/08	a	Ružomberok	D 2-2	Jelić 2
23/08	h	Senica	W 4-1	Škriniar (p), Jelić, Willian, Čmelík
30/08	a	Spartak Trnava	L 0-2	
12/09	h	Slovan	W 3-0	Willian, Bénes, Mihalík
15/09	h	Podbrezová	W 3-2	Mabouka, Škriniar (p), Willian
19/09	a	Skalica	D 2-2	Paur, Willian
23/09	a	Trenčín	W 4-1	Mihalík, Špalek, Káčer, Škriniar
27/09	h	Michalovce	W 2-0	Mihalík, Bénes
03/10	h	Podbrezová	L 1-3	Škriniar (p)
16/10	a	Zlaté Moravce	L 0-4	
25/10	h	Spartak Myjava	W 3-0	Mabouka, Mihalík, Haskić
31/10	a	Dunajská Streda	L 0-1	
07/11	h	Ružomberok	W 2-0	Paur, Willian
21/11	a	Senica	W 2-0	
28/11	h	Spartak Myjava	W 2-0	Špalek, og (Nikolić)
06/12	a	Slovan	L 1-2	Haskić

2016

26/02	a	Skalica	L 0-1	
08/03	h	Trenčín	L 2-3	Paur, Haskić
04/03	h	Michalovce	L 2-3	Paur, Vavro
12/03	a	Podbrezová	L 0-2	
18/03	h	Zlaté Moravce	W 6-0	Hlohovský 3, Králik, Letić, Michlík
02/04	a	Spartak Myjava	D 0-0	
08/04	h	Dunajská Streda	W 4-1	Díaz, Špalek, Haskić 2
16/04	a	Ružomberok	W 2-0	Haskić 2
20/04	h	Senica	D 0-0	
24/04	a	Spartak Trnava	L 0-3	
02/05	h	Slovan	D 0-0	
06/05	h	Skalica	W 1-0	Haskić
13/05	a	Trenčín	L 2-5	Špalek 2
20/05	a	Michalovce	L 0-3	

No	Name	Nat	DoB	Pos	Aps	(s)	Gls
22	László Bénes		09/09/97	M	19	(4)	2
16	Lukáš Čmelík		13/04/96	M	4	(4)	1
9	Iván Díaz	ARG	23/01/93	M	10		1
16	Dávid Hancko		13/12/97	M		(4)	
13	Nermin Haskić	BIH	27/06/89	A	12	(9)	8
13	Filip Hlohovský		13/06/88	M	14	(10)	3
3	Tomáš Hučko		03/10/85	D	5	(3)	
8	Lukáš Jánošík		05/03/94	D	2	(2)	
35	Matej Jelić	CRO	05/11/90	A	4	(2)	6
6	Miroslav Káčer		02/02/96	M	16	(8)	2
7	Andrej Kadlec		02/02/96	D	1	(1)	
33	Michal Klec		05/12/95	M	2		
24	Martin Králik		03/04/95	D	18		1
45	Bojan Letić	BIH	21/12/92	D	20	(2)	1
45	Ernest Mabouka	CMR	16/06/88	D	17	(1)	2
30	Aleš Mandous	CZE	21/04/92	G	2		
14	Róbert Mazáň		09/02/94	D	16	(1)	
10	Chigozie Mbah	NGA	18/09/97	A	1	(4)	
5	Jakub Michlík		10/09/97	M	5	(10)	1
33	Jaroslav Mihalík		27/07/94	A	16	(2)	6
29	Jakub Paur		04/07/92	M	24	(2)	6
12	Viktor Pečovský		24/05/83	M	26		
3	Peter Puček		09/09/95	M	2	(1)	
3	Milan Škriniar		11/02/95	D	18		4
20	Michal Škvarka		19/08/92	M	13	(12)	1
11	Nikolas Špalek		12/02/97	M	23	(4)	5
7	Branislav Šušolík		16/10/88	D	2		
4	Ondřej Švejdík	CZE	03/12/92	D	4		
15	Kristián Vallo		02/06/98	M		(2)	
9	Denis Vavro		10/04/96	D	23		1
1	Miloš Volešák		20/04/84	G	31		
10	Willian	BRA	07/12/91	A	15	(3)	6

Top goalscorers

17	Gino van Kessel (Trenčín)
15	David Depetris (Spartak Trnava)
	Matúš Bero (Trenčín)
11	Tamás Priskin (Slovan)
	Peter Sládek (Spartak Myjava)
	Leandre Tawamba (Zlaté Moravce)
10	Erik Pačinda (Dunajská Streda)
	Miloš Lačný (Ružomberok)
	Róbert Vittek (Slovan)
9	Ákos Szarka (Dunajská Streda)
	Jhonnes (Zlaté Moravce)

Promoted club

1. FC Tatran Prešov

1898 • FC Tatran (5,410) • 1fctatran.sk
Coach: Stanislav Varga

Second level final tables 2015/16

First stage

West		Pld	W	D	L	F	A	Pts
1	FK Iskra Borčice	22	13	3	6	40	19	42
2	FK Pohronie	22	12	4	6	29	23	40
3	FC Nitra	22	11	3	8	42	27	36
4	MŠK Žilina II	22	8	9	5	36	28	33
5	ŠK Slovan Bratislava II	22	10	3	9	36	37	33
6	ŠKF Sereď	22	10	3	9	25	28	33
7	FK Dukla Banská Bystrica	22	10	3	9	24	25	33
8	AFC Nové Mesto nad Váhom	22	9	4	9	25	25	31
9	OFK Dunajská Lužná	22	9	4	9	27	32	31
10	FK Slovan Duslo Šaľa	22	8	1	13	24	39	25
11	FC Spartak Trnava II	22	7	0	15	16	27	21
12	ŠK Senec	22	5	3	14	26	40	18

East		Pld	W	D	L	F	A	Pts
1	FC VSS Košice	20	13	3	4	36	15	42
2	1. FC Tatran Prešov	20	11	7	2	46	18	40
3	MFK Tatran Liptovský Mikuláš	20	10	6	4	32	18	36
4	MFK Lokomotíva Zvolen	20	10	3	7	25	22	33
5	FC Lokomotíva Košice	20	9	5	6	28	22	32
6	Partizán Bardejov	20	9	4	7	30	26	31
7	FK Poprad	20	9	4	7	33	24	31
8	FK Haniska	20	7	4	9	20	32	25
9	FK Spišská Nová Ves	20	4	3	13	16	37	15
10	OFK Teplička nad Váhom	20	3	4	13	14	38	13
11	MFK Rimavská Sobota	20	2	3	15	14	42	6
12	MFK Dolný Kubín	0	0	0	0	0	0	0

NB MFK Dolný Kubín withdrew after round 18 – all their matches were annulled; FK Rimavská Sobota – 3 pts deducted.

Promotion play-offs final table

		Pld	W	D	L	F	A	Pts
1	1. FC Tatran Prešov	30	16	10	4	61	26	58
2	FC VSS Košice	30	18	5	7	48	23	56
3	MFK Tatran Liptovský Mikuláš	30	16	8	6	52	29	56
4	Lokomotíva Košice	30	16	6	8	50	34	54
5	Partizán Bardejov	30	16	5	9	49	36	53
6	FK Pohronie	30	15	6	9	35	33	51
7	FC Nitra	30	13	7	10	54	36	46
8	MŠK Žilina II	30	11	8	11	41	36	41
9	MFK Lokomotíva Zvolen	30	11	6	13	30	34	39
10	ŠKF Sereď	30	11	5	14	35	44	38
11	ŠK Slovan Bratislava II	30	9	4	17	38	63	31
12	FK Iskra Borčice	0	0	0	0	0	0	0

NB FK Iskra Borčice withdrew after round 3 – all their matches were annulled; FC VSS Košice – 3 pts deducted.

NB The top six clubs from each regional group progress to the promotion play-offs, carrying forward their records against the top 10 or 11 teams, respectively, in the first stage. In the play-offs they play only against the qualified teams from the other regional group (home and away).

DOMESTIC CUP

Slovenský pohár 2015/16

SECOND ROUND

(11/08/15)
Komárno 1-6 Velký Meder
Lamač Bratislava 1-6 SFM Senec
Šamorín 0-3 Dunajská Lužná
Šenkvice 2-12 Podbrezová
Slovan Nemšová 2-0 Gabčíkovo
Tatran Krásno1-1 Skalica *(5-4 on pens)*

(12/08/15)
Bodva Moldava 0-0 Vranov nad Topľou *(1-3 on pens)*
Častkovce 0-1 Palárikovo
Detva 1-3 Teplička nad Váhom
Družstevník 1-0 Sokol Ľubotice
Galanta 6-2 Neded
Inter Bratislava 0-6 Sereď
Jesenské 1-2 Fomat Martin
Kalinkovo 3-3 Bernolákovo *(4-3 on pens)*
Kalná nad Hronom 2-0 Slovan Duslo Šaľa
Kolárovo 0-4 Spartak Trnava
Kráľová pri Senci 1-3 Borčice
Liptovský Hrádok 0-0 Poprad *(4-3 on pens)*
Lovča 0-3 Vinica
Malacky 5-0 Lozorno
Malženice 1-6 Nitra
Mocenok 0-5 Blava
Nevidzany 0-2 Nové Mesto
Nová Baňa 4-0 Bytča
Nová Dubnica 1-2 Nové Zámky
Partizán Domaniža 0-2 Senica
Pezinok 0-5 Trenčín
Podlavice Badín 0-1 Javorník Makov
Pokrok Krompachy 1-5 Lokomotíva Zvolen
Predmier 1-1 Partizán Bardejov *(4-2 on pens)*
Rožňava 1-2 Spišská Nová Ves
Rusovce 1-4 Svätý Jur
Ružinov 0-3 Rača
Šarišské Michaľany 1-0 Družstevník Velký Horeš
Slávia Staškov 2-5 Stráňavy
Slovan Most 1-2 Zlaté Moravce
Slovenský Grob 0-9 Pohronie
Sokol Bravácovo 0-8 Dolný Kubín
Sokol Medzibrod 1-2 Zemplín Michalovce
Stráža 1-0 Liptovská Štiavnica
Strážske 0-9 Žilina
Šurany 1-2 Topolčany
Svit 0-1 Snina
Tatran Kračúnovce 0-2 Haniska
Tatran Spišsk 1-1 Čaňa *(2-4 on pens)*
Tomášov 3-2 Rovinka
Trenčianske Stankovce 0-3 Spartak Myjava
Turčianska Štiavnička 4-0 Divín
Vajnory 2-3 Rohožník
Velké Ludince 3-0 Dubnica *(w/o)*
Viničné 3-3 Ivánka pri Dunaji *(3-4 on pens)*
Závod 1-0 Lokomotíva DNV

(18/08/15)
Ďarmoty 1-2 Lokomotíva Košice
Družstevník Perín 0-8 Tatran Prešov

(19/08/15)
Báhoň 0-5 Dukla Banská Bystrica
Fatran Varín 0-8 Slovan Bratislava
Mária Huta 1-5 Vyšné Opátske
Partizán Prečín 3-2 Baník Horná Nitra
Tesla Stropkov 0-3 Dunajská Streda

(25/08/15)
Oravské Veselé 3-1 Rimavská Sobota

Continued over the page

THIRD ROUND

(01/09/15)
Blava 2-1 Velké Ludince
Čaňa 2-1 Spišská Nová Ves
Družstevník 1-1 Dunajská Streda *(1-3 on pens)*
Galanta 1-2 Senica
Haniska 1-1 Tatran Prešov *(5-6 on pens)*
Ivánka pri Dunaji 2-6 Sereď
Javorník Makov 4-0 Tatran Krásno
Kalinkovo 1-2 Pohronie
Kalná nad Hronom 0-2 Nové Mesto
Liptovský Hrádok 0-1 Dolný Kubín
Malacky 0-6 Podbrezová
Medzev 0-4 VSS Košice
Predmier 0-4 Fomat Martin
Šarišské Michaľany 0-7 Ružomberok
SFM Senec 0-1 Borčice
Slovan Nemšová 0-2 Spartak Myjava
Snina 0-1 Lokomotíva Zvolen
Stráňavy 2-0 Oravské Veselé
Svatý Jur 1-3 Zlaté Moravce
Teplička nad Váhom 0-2 Zemplín Michalovce
Tomášov 1-0 Rača
Turčianska Štiavnička 0-4 Stráža
Vyšné Opátske 1-1 Vranov nad Topľou *(4-3 on pens)*

(02/09/15)
Nová Baňa 0-0 Lokomotiva Košice *(4-3 on pens)*
Palárikovo 1-3 Dunajská Lužná
Partizán Prečín 1-3 Topoľčany
Rohožník 1-1 Dukla Banská Bystrica *(5-3 on pens)*
Velký Meder 0-3 Nitra

(08/09/15)
Nové Zámky 0-4 Spartak Trnava

(15/09/15)
Vinica 0-8 Slovan Bratislava
Závod 0-11 Trenčín

(30/09/15)
Liptovský Mikuláš 0-4 Žilina

FOURTH ROUND

(13/10/15)
Blava 0-3 Trenčín
Fomat Martin 0-3 Zlaté Moravce
Lokomotíva Zvolen 0-2 Senica
Sereď 1-2 Spartak Myjava
VSS Košice 3-0 Spartak Trnava

(14/10/15)
Čaňa 2-6 Topoľčany
Dunajská Lužná 2-7 Ružomberok
Javorník Makov 3-10 Tatran Prešov
Nové Mesto 1-1 Podbrezová *(5-3 on pens)*
Rohožník 1-1 Zemplín Michalovce *(5-3 on pens)*
Stráňavy 0-3 Dunajská Streda
Stráža 1-1 Dolný Kubín *(3-5 on pens)*
Tomášov 2-3 Pohronie
Vyšné Opátske 1-0 Nová Baňa

(20/10/15)
Nitra 2-3 Slovan Bratislava

(28/10/15)
Borčice 0-3 Žilina

FIFTH ROUND

(03/11/15)
Vyšné Opátske 0-5 Žilina
Zlaté Moravce 4-2 Spartak Myjava

(04/11/15)
Dolný Kubín 1-4 Trenčín
Dunajská Streda 3-1 Tatran Prešov
Nové Mesto 1-1 Senica *(3-4 on pens)*
Rohožník 0-2 VSS Košice
Slovan Bratislava 1-0 Pohronie

(11/11/15)
Topoľčany 0-5 Ružomberok

QUARTER-FINALS

(15/03/16)
Senica 1-1 Slovan Bratislava *(Hromada 15; Priskin 44) (3-4 on pens)*

Zlaté Moravce 1-2 Ružomberok *(Slančík 28; Ďubek 11p, Lačný 39)*

Žilina 3-0 Dunajská Streda *(Špalek 34, Paur 64, Vavro 80)*

(16/03/16)
VSS Košice 1-2 Trenčín *(Janič 25; Koolwijk 18p, Konnsimbal 72og)*

SEMI-FINALS

(05/04/16 & 12/04/16)
Slovan Bratislava 0-0 Žilina
Žilina 1-1 Slovan Bratislava *(Hlohovský 42; Oršula 52)*
(1-1; Slovan Bratislava on away goal)

(06/04/16 & 13/04/16)
Trenčín 5-1 Ružomberok *(Kalu 3, Van Kessel 24, 68, 82, Skovajsa 66; Zošák 62p)*
Ružomberok 0-1 Trenčín *(Guba 77)*
(Trenčín 6-1)

FINAL

(29/04/16)
Štadion Antona Malatinského, Trnava
FK AS TRENČÍN 3 *(Maierhofer 78, Van Kessel 86, 90+3)*
ŠK SLOVAN BRATISLAVA 1 *(Zrelǎk 53)*
Referee: *Sedlák*
TRENČÍN: *Šemrinec, Šulek, Kleščík, Skovajsa, Madu, Koolwijk (Lawrence 90), Ibrahim, Guba (Schet 66), Bero, Van Kessel, Kalu (Maierhofer 66)*
SLOVAN BRATISLAVA: *Mucha, Pliatsikas, Saláta, Sekulić, Podaný, Scott (Savićević 90), De Kamps, Milinković (Crnkić 84), Kubík, Zrelǎk, Vittek*

Trenčín retained the Slovakian Cup with a 3-1 victory over Slovan Bratislava in Trnava

SLOVENIA
Nogometna zveza Slovenije (NZS)

Address Predoslje 40 a
pp 130
SI-4000 Kranj
Tel +386 4 27 59 400
Fax +386 4 27 59 456
E-mail fas@nzs.si
Website nzs.si

President Aleksander Čeferin
General secretary Aleš Zavrl
Media officer Matjaž Krajnik
Year of formation 1920

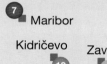

KEY
- UEFA Champions League
- UEFA Europa League
- Promoted
- Relegated

PRVA LIGA CLUBS

  1 NK Celje

  2 NK Domžale

  3 ND Gorica

  4 FC Koper

 5 NK Krka

  6 NK Krško

  7 NK Maribor

  **8** NK Olimpija Ljubljana

  **9** NK Rudar Velenje

 10 NK Zavrč

PROMOTED CLUBS

  11 NK Radomlje

 12 NK Aluminij

Olimpija end Maribor's reign

A new club – if not a new name - was added to the Slovenian Prva Liga roll of honour as Olimpija Ljubljana denied NK Maribor a sixth successive title following a season-long duel during which both clubs used three coaches.

With four-time championship-winning boss Darko Milanič back in charge, Maribor won a record ninth domestic cup, inflicting an eighth final defeat on NK Celje after a lengthy penalty shoot-out. It was a poor season internationally for Slovenian football, highlighted by a UEFA EURO 2016 play-off defeat against Ukraine.

| Ljubljana club hold nerve to claim first title | Champions of past five seasons win the cup | EURO qualifying hopes ended in play-offs |

Domestic league

Although the name, colours and fan base of the former Olimpija Ljubljana – a club that won the first four Slovenian titles in the early 1990s but was dissolved in 2005 – have remained, the new club, formed the same year under the original title of NK Bežigrad, has no official association with its predecessor. Therefore, in 2015/16, the 25th anniversary of the Prva Liga, the new Olimpija became the sixth different club to be crowned champions of Slovenia.

It was a deserved triumph for a team that topped the table from early September right through to the close of play in May, but the road to victory was nevertheless a rocky one. Olimpija had Maribor breathing down their necks throughout, and while they were able to stay out in front, they did not always make it easy for themselves.

They were the dominant force in the autumn, with new coach Marijan Pušnik sending out an exciting, attack-minded team in which striker Andraž Šporar flourished, scoring 17 goals in 18 starts, but both of those key individuals were gone when the campaign resumed after the winter break – Pušnik sacked after an internal dispute, while Šporar was sold to Swiss league leaders FC Basel.

Pušnik's replacement, Marko Nikolić, the former coach of Serbian giants FK Partizan, lasted only three months before he was dismissed. At the time of his departure, Olimpija were on the brink of title success, but under third coach Rodolfo Vanoli, an Italian formerly with FC Koper, they lost the big derby at home to Maribor – a result that put the two teams level on points with three games to go.

Fortunately for Olimpija, the 2-1 loss meant they still preserved a head-to-head advantage, and with Maribor losing next time out, at home to Rudar Velenje, while Olimpija won at Cejle, the frontrunners knew another victory in the penultimate round, away to Rudar, would clinch the title. They got it, but not until the fourth minute of added time, when star midfielder Rok Kronaveter made it 1-0 from the penalty spot. It was his 17th goal of the season, enabling him to match Šporar's total and join his former team-mate and Maribor's Jean-Philippe Mendy in a three-way tie for the Prva Liga golden boot.

Domestic cup

The end of Maribor's five-year reign as champions was a crushing disappointment as they had been eager to match or better their seven-year winning run from 1997-2003, but they did ensure an eighth successive season of domestic silverware by capturing the Slovenian Cup. Their record ninth triumph came at the end of an extended final in Koper against Celje, whose misfortune in the fixture continued as they lost out 7-6 on penalties after twice coming from behind to draw 2-2 in regular play. Celje's eighth defeat in nine finals was also their fourth in five years and their third (and second on penalties) during that time against Maribor.

Europe

After four successive seasons of European group stage football, the last of them in the UEFA Champions League, Maribor suffered a major setback in 2015/16 when their European season ended in July following a shock defeat by Kazakhstan's FC Astana. Slovenia's other three representatives were also knocked out early, with only Koper winning a tie.

National team

Slovenia's bid to qualify for UEFA EURO 2016 suffered a painful body blow when they surrendered a 2-0 lead and conceded three times in the last ten minutes to lose to Switzerland in Basel – a result that effectively condemned Srečko Katanec's side to the play-offs, where they battled gamely but ultimately lost 3-1 on aggregate to Ukraine.

DOMESTIC SEASON AT A GLANCE

Prva Liga 2015/16 final table

		Pld	Home					Away					Total					Pts
			W	D	L	F	A	W	D	L	F	A	W	D	L	F	A	
1	**NK Olimpija Ljubljana**	36	9	4	5	41	15	13	4	1	34	10	22	8	6	75	25	74
2	NK Maribor	36	8	6	4	43	25	11	5	2	35	12	19	11	6	78	37	68
3	NK Domžale	36	4	7	7	20	20	10	6	2	26	11	14	13	9	46	31	55
4	ND Gorica	36	7	3	8	20	23	8	4	6	28	26	15	7	14	48	49	52
5	NK Celje	36	5	6	7	17	24	6	6	6	15	22	11	12	13	32	46	45
6	NK Krško	36	5	6	7	12	16	5	5	8	12	32	10	11	15	24	48	41
7	NK Rudar Velenje	36	6	4	8	15	18	5	4	9	19	34	11	8	17	34	52	41
8	FC Koper	36	4	4	10	21	29	7	3	8	19	25	11	7	18	40	54	40
9	NK Zavrč	36	4	6	8	14	20	5	7	6	18	21	9	13	14	32	41	40
10	NK Krka	36	5	4	9	17	29	3	6	9	13	27	8	10	18	30	56	34

European qualification 2016/17

Champion: NK Olimpija Ljubljana (second qualifying round)

Cup winner: NK Maribor (second qualifying round)
NK Domžale (first qualifying round)
ND Gorica (first qualifying round)

Top scorer	Jean-Philippe Mendy (Maribor), Rok Kronaveter (Olimpija) & Andraž Šporar (Olimpija), 17 goals
Relegated clubs	NK Krka, NK Zavrč
Promoted clubs	NK Radomlje, NK Aluminij
Cup final	NK Maribor 2-2 NK Celje (aet; 7-6 on pens)

Team of the season
(4-3-3)

Coach: Srebrnič (Gorica)

Vidmar (Domžale/Olimpija)

Fink (Olimpija) · Mitrovič (Olimpija) · Datkovič (Zavrč/Koper) · Skubic (Domžale)

Vrhovec (Celje) · Kronaveter (Olimpija) · Zajc (Olimpija)

Mendy (Maribor) · Šporar (Olimpija) · Eleke (Gorica/Olimpija)

Player of the season

Rok Kronaveter
(NK Olimpija Ljubljana)

The man who arguably did most to end NK Maribor's long run of Slovenian titles was Maribor-born Kronaveter, a shining star throughout his debut season for champions Olimpija. A player of whom great things had been predicted in his youth, and a Hungarian champion in 2012/13 with Győr, the nifty midfielder was Olimpija's main creative spark as well as a regular supplier of goals, his final tally of 17, which included a nerveless title-clinching penalty, proving to be the joint highest in the division.

Newcomer of the season

Miha Zajc
(NK Olimpija Ljubljana)

Like team-mate Rok Kronaveter, Zajc was one of the few Prva Liga players to appear for the Slovenian national team during the 2015/16 season. The Under-21 regular was handed his first senior cap in a March friendly against FYR Macedonia – a fitting reward for a breakthrough club season with Olimpija that ended with the ex-Celje player landing his first championship winner's medal. A confident and elegant midfielder, the 22-year-old's accurate shooting from distance makes him a particular threat at free-kicks.

SLOVENIA

NATIONAL TEAM

International tournament appearances

FIFA World Cup (2) 2002, 2010
UEFA European Championship (1) 2000

Top five all-time caps

Boštjan Cesar (91); **Samir Handanovič** (81); **Valter Birsa** & Zlatko Zahovič (80); **Bojan Jokič** (79)

Top five all-time goals

Zlatko Zahovič (35); **Milivoje Novakovič** (31); Sašo Udovič (16); Ermin Šiljak (14); Milenko Ačimovič (13)

Results 2015/16

05/09/15	Switzerland (ECQ)	A	Basel	L	2-3	Novakovič (45), Cesar (48)
08/09/15	Estonia (ECQ)	H	Maribor	W	1-0	Berič (63)
09/10/15	Lithuania (ECQ)	H	Ljubljana	D	1-1	Birsa (45+1p)
12/10/15	San Marino (ECQ)	A	Serravalle	W	2-0	Cesar (54), Pečnik (75)
14/11/15	Ukraine (ECQ)	A	Lviv	L	0-2	
17/11/15	Ukraine (ECQ)	H	Maribor	D	1-1	Cesar (11)
23/03/16	FYR Macedonia	H	Koper	W	1-0	Bezjak (58)
28/03/16	Northern Ireland	A	Belfast	L	0-1	
30/05/16	Sweden	A	Malmo	D	0-0	
05/06/16	Turkey	H	Ljubljana	L	0-1	

Appearances 2015/16

Coach: Srečko Katanec	16/07/63		SUI	EST	LTU	SMR	UKR	UKR	Mkd	Nir	Swe	Tur	Caps	Goals
Samir Handanovič	14/07/84	Internazionale (ITA)	G	G	G		G	G					81	-
Andraž Struna	23/04/89	Giannina (GRE)	D	D	D	D					s90	D56	25	1
Boštjan Cesar	09/07/82	Chievo (ITA)	D	D	D	D	D	D	D	D80			91	9
Branko Ilič	06/02/83	Astana (KAZ)	D	D	D		D	D					63	1
Bojan Jokič	17/05/86	Villarreal (ESP) /Nottingham Forest (ENG)	D	D	D	D	D	D	D	D	D	D	79	1
Dalibor Stevanovič	27/09/84	Mordovia (RUS)	M										22	1
Jasmin Kurtič	10/01/89	Atalanta (ITA)	M	M	M	M	M		M	M46	s57	M	34	1
Valter Birsa	07/08/86	Chievo (ITA)	M83	M	M	M	M73	M80	s46	M			80	6
Kevin Kampl	09/10/90	Leverkusen (GER)	M	M			M	M			M	M86	23	2
Josip Iličič	29/01/88	Fiorentina (ITA)	M90	M55	M90	A46	A63	s67	M46	M46	M90	M77	39	2
Milivoje Novakovič	18/05/79	Nagoya Grampus (JPN) /Maribor	A58				A90	A	s70	s46	s60	s46	76	31
Nejc Pečnik	03/01/86	JEF United (JPN)	s58		s73	s46	s73	M67					32	6
Rene Krhin	21/05/90	Granada (ESP)	s83	M88	M	M	M	M	M89	M	M88		25	1
Miral Samardžič	17/02/87	Rijeka (CRO)	s90			D			s46	D			9	-
Robert Berič	17/06/91	St-Étienne (FRA)		A77	A62	A46					A60	A46	11	1
Zlatan Ljubijankič	15/12/83	Urawa Reds (JPN)		s55	s62		s90	s68					48	6
Dejan Lazarevič	15/02/90	Antalyaspor (TUR)		s77	M73	s70		s80					20	1
Rajko Rotman	19/03/89	İstanbul Başakşehir (TUR)		s88							s88		8	-
Tim Matavž	13/01/89	Augsburg (GER)		s90	s46								31	10
Jan Oblak	07/01/93	Atlético (ESP)					G			G	G		8	-
Andraž Kirm	06/09/84	Omonia (CYP)				M70				s63	s62		71	6
Mišo Brečko	01/05/84	Nürnberg (GER)					D	D 93*					77	-
Roman Bezjak	21/02/89	Rijeka (CRO)					s63	A68	A70	A75	M82	M46	12	1
Aljaž Struna	04/08/90	Palermo (ITA)							D46	s80	D	D	4	-
Nejc Skubic	13/06/89	Konyaspor (TUR)							D	D62	D85		3	-
Miha Zajc	01/07/94	Olimpija Ljubljana							M87			s77	2	-
Benjamin Verbič	27/11/93	København (DEN)							M63	M62		s46	4	-
Enej Jelenič	11/12/92	Livorno (ITA)							s87				1	-
Blaž Vrhovec	20/02/92	Celje							s89	s46		M	3	-
Petar Stojanovič	07/10/95	Dinamo Zagreb (CRO)								s62			4	-
Matic Črnic	12/06/92	Domžale								s75	s82		2	-
Vid Belec	06/06/90	Carpi (ITA)									G	G	3	-
Luka Krajnc	19/09/94	Cagliari (ITA)									D		2	-
Rok Kronaveter	07/12/86	Olimpija Ljubljana									M57		1	-
Boban Jovič	25/06/91	Wisła Kraków (POL)									s85	s56	2	-
Miha Mevlja	12/06/90	Dinamo Bucureşti (ROU)										D	1	-
Jure Matjašič	31/05/92	Zavrč										s86	1	-

EUROPE

NK Maribor

CHAMPIONS LEAGUE

Second qualifying round - FC Astana (KAZ)
H 1-0 *Šuler (5)*
Handanovič, Šuler, Marcos Tavares, Ibraimi, Volaš (Zahovič 74), Vršič (Bohar 66), Kabha (Filipovič 66), Rajčevič, Viler, Stojanovič, Mertelj. Coach: Ante Šimundža (SVN)
A 1-3 *Rajčevič (39)*
Handanovič, Šuler, Tavares, Ibraimi, Mendy, Kabha, Rajčevič, Viler, Stojanovič, Bohar (Vršič 77), Mertelj (Filipovič 60). Coach: Ante Šimundža (SVN)

FC Koper

EUROPA LEAGUE

First qualifying round - Víkingur Reykjavík (ISL)
A 1-0 *Pučko (77)*
Simčič, Šme, Guberac, Ivančić (Lotrič 82), Galešić (Blažič 90+1), Halilovič, Črnigoj, Hadžič, Tomić, Palčič (Rahmanovič 67), Pučko. Coach: Rodolfo Vanoli (ITA)
H 2-2 *Pučko (18), Palčič (61)*
Simčič, Šme, Blažič, Guberac, Ivančić (Štromajer 58), Galešić (Krivičič 90+2), Črnigoj, Hadžič, Tomić, Palčič, Pučko. Coach: Rodolfo Vanoli (ITA)

Second qualifying round - HNK Hajduk Split (CRO)
H 3-2 *Halilovič (7), Rahmanovič (17, 41)*
Simčič, Šme, Guberac, Rahmanovič (Pučko 60), Ivančić (Štromajer 71), Galešić, Halilovič, Črnigoj, Krivičič, Hadžič, Palčič. Coach: Rodolfo Vanoli (ITA)
A 1-4 *Palčič (45+2)*
Simčič, Šme (Pučko 71), Guberac, Rahmanovič (Radujko 77), Ivančić, Galešić, Halilovič, Črnigoj, Hadžič, Tomić (Vekić 81), Palčič. Coach: Rodolfo Vanoli (ITA)

NK Celje

EUROPA LEAGUE

First qualifying round - WKS Śląsk Wrocław (POL)
H 0-1
Kotnik, T Klemenčič, Firer, Miškić, Bajde (Vrhovec 63), Ahmedi (Omoregie 46), Jakolič, Mršić (Težak 70), Soria, Klapan, Vidmajer. Coach: Simon Rožman (SVN)
A 1-3 *Firer (80)*
Kotnik, Vrhovec, T Klemenčič, Firer, Miškić (Ahmedi 79), Omoregie (Bajde 58), Jakolič, Mršić (Spremo 70), Soria, Klapan, Vidmajer. Coach: Simon Rožman (SVN)

NK Domžale

EUROPA LEAGUE

First qualifying round - FK Čukarički (SRB)
H 0-1
Vidmar, Zec, Horić, Požeg Vancaš, Juninho (Horvat 46), Vuk (Podlogar 46), Trajkovski, Dobrovoljc, Majer (Kous 49), Morel, Korun. Coach: Luka Elsner (SVN)
Red card: Dobrovoljc 47
A 0-0
Vidmar, Skubic, Horić, Požeg Vancaš (Grvala 60), Podlogar, Horvat, Trajkovski, Majer (Vuk 67), Morel, Korun, Husmani (Šišić 81). Coach: Luka Elsner (SVN)
Red card: Korun 90+5

DOMESTIC LEAGUE CLUB-BY-CLUB

NK Celje

1919 • Petrol Arena (13,400) • nk-celje.si
Major honours
Slovenian Cup (1) 2005
Coach: Simon Rožman;
(07/09/15) Iztok Kapušin;
(09/04/16) Robert Pevnik

2015

Date	H/A	Opponent	Res	Score	Scorers
19/07	a	Krško	L	0-1	
26/07	h	Krka	D	1-1	Firer
02/08	a	Koper	D	1-1	Firer
07/08	h	Gorica	L	2-3	Erico Sousa, og (Jogan)
12/08	a	Maribor	L	0-1	
17/08	h	Zavrč	W	2-1	Vrhovec, Omoregie
23/08	a	Olimpija	L	0-6	
29/08	h	Domžale	L	0-3	
12/09	a	Rudar	L	0-4	
18/09	h	Krško	D	0-0	
23/09	a	Krka	L	0-1	
26/09	h	Koper	D	1-1	Djurković
03/10	a	Gorica	D	1-1	Miškić
17/10	h	Maribor	L	1-3	Djurković
24/10	a	Zavrč	W	1-0	Pajač
31/10	h	Olimpija	L	0-4	
08/11	a	Domžale	D	2-2	Pajač 2
22/11	h	Rudar	W	1-0	T Klemenčič
28/11	a	Krško	D	0-0	
02/12	h	Krka	W	1-0	T Klemenčič
05/12	a	Koper	W	2-1	Spremo, Omoregie
12/12	h	Gorica	D	2-2	Firer 2

2016

Date	H/A	Opponent	Res	Score	Scorers
27/02	a	Maribor	W	1-0	Spremo
05/03	h	Zavrč	D	0-0	
13/03	a	Olimpija	D	0-0	
19/03	h	Domžale	L	0-2	Erico Sousa
02/04	a	Rudar	L	0-2	
06/04	h	Krško	L	0-1	
10/04	a	Krka	D	1-1	Pajač
16/04	h	Koper	W	3-0	Podlogar, Omoregie, Pišek
23/04	a	Gorica	W	2-1	Podlogar 2
30/04	h	Maribor	D	0-0	
06/05	a	Zavrč	W	1-0	Hadžič
11/05	h	Olimpija	L	1-3	Čirjak
14/05	a	Domžale	W	3-0	Podlogar 2, Čirjak
21/05	h	Rudar	W	1-0	Pišek

No	Name	Nat	DoB	Pos	Aps	(s)	Gls
10	Valon Ahmedi	ALB	07/10/94	M	9	(5)	
20	Gregor Bajde		29/04/94	A	1		
21	Adnan Bašić	BIH	13/12/96	A		(4)	
20	Mario Brlečić	CRO	10/01/89	M	4	(4)	
25	Lovre Čirjak	CRO	02/11/91	M	9	(1)	2
26	Enis Djurković		24/05/89	M	9	(5)	2
9	Erico Sousa	POR	12/03/95	A	19	(11)	2
7	Ivan Firer		19/11/84	A	18	(1)	4
27	Damir Hadžič		01/10/84	D	9	(1)	1
37	Ivan Hosman	CRO	11/11/89	G	7		
30	Marko Jakolič		16/04/91	D	1	(1)	
29	Mihovil Klapan	CRO	27/03/95	M	15	(2)	
3	Marko Klemenčič		09/03/97	D	3		
6	Tilen Klemenčič		21/08/95	D	26	(2)	2
12	Matic Kotnik		23/07/90	G	26		
2	Žiga Kous		27/10/92	D	19	(2)	
5	Marko Krajcer		06/06/85	D	18		
17	Matic Marcius		01/02/97	A		(1)	
8	Danijel Miškić	CRO	11/10/93	M	24		1
25	Matej Mršić	CRO	13/01/94	M	1	(3)	
1	Amel Mujčinovič		20/11/73	G	3	(1)	
11	Sunny Omoregie	NGA	02/01/89	A	16	(11)	3
20	Abd Al-Rahman Osman Ali	AUT	02/06/86	A	9	(2)	
19	Marko Pajač	CRO	11/05/93	M	17	(2)	4
32	Janez Pišek		04/05/98	M	6	(6)	2
14	Matej Podlogar		23/02/91	A	13		5
10	Rudi Požeg Vancaš		15/03/94	M	6	(5)	
23	Nino Pungaršek		01/11/95	M	1	(3)	
27	Ramón Soria	ESP	07/03/89	D	18	(1)	
24	Milan Spremo	SRB	27/04/95	A	11	(16)	2
28	Karlo Težak	CRO	30/10/93	M	2	(4)	
16	Jure Travner		28/09/85	D	18	(1)	
30	Tadej Vidmajer		10/03/92	D	26	(2)	
4	Blaž Vrhovec		20/02/92	M	30		1

SLOVENIA

NK Domžale

1921 • Športni park (3,212) • nkdomzale.si

Major honours
Slovenian League (2) 2007, 2008; Slovenian Cup (1) 2011

Coach: Luka Elsner

2015					
19/07	a	Koper	W	3-2	*Majer, Skubic, Juninho*
25/07	h	Maribor	L	0-1	
01/08	a	Olimpija	W	2-0	*Trajkovski, Mance*
08/08	h	Rudar	L	0-2	
12/08	a	Krka	W	4-0	*Podlogar, Črnic 2, Mance*
15/08	h	Gorica	L	2-3	*Morel, Mance*
21/08	a	Zavrč	D	0-0	
29/08	a	Celje	W	3-0	*Husmani, Šišić, Dobrovoljc*
13/09	h	Krško	W	2-0	*Vuk 2*
20/09	h	Koper	W	1-0	*Črnic*
23/09	a	Maribor	D	1-1	*Vuk*
26/09	h	Olimpija	D	1-1	*Zec*
03/10	a	Rudar	D	0-0	
17/10	h	Krka	W	3-0	*Horvat 2, Vuk*
25/10	a	Gorica	W	1-0	*Blažič*
31/10	h	Zavrč	L	0-1	
08/11	h	Celje	D	2-2	*Mance, Vuk*
25/11	a	Krško	D	1-1	*Črnic*
28/11	a	Koper	W	2-0	*Požeg Vancaš, Morel*
02/12	h	Maribor	D	0-0	
06/12	a	Olimpija	D	0-0	
12/12	h	Rudar	W	4-0	*Črnic, Skubic (p), Mance, Zec*
2016					
28/02	a	Krka	L	1-3	*Jarovic*
06/03	h	Gorica	D	1-1	*Črnic*
11/03	a	Zavrč	W	1-0	*Mance*
19/03	a	Celje	W	2-1	*Črnic (p), Balkovec*
02/04	h	Krško	L	2-3	*Alvir, Mance*
06/04	h	Koper	D	1-1	*Dobrovoljc*
09/04	a	Maribor	L	1-2	*Mance*
16/04	h	Olimpija	L	0-1	
23/04	a	Rudar	W	2-1	*Repas, Mance*
30/04	h	Krka	D	1-1	*Mance*
08/05	a	Gorica	W	2-0	*Črnic, Mance*
11/05	h	Zavrč	D	0-0	
14/05	h	Celje	L	0-3	
21/05	a	Krško	D	0-0	

No	Name	Nat	DoB	Pos	Aps	(s)	Gls
77	Marko Alvir	CRO	19/04/94	M	8	(4)	1
29	Jure Balkovec		09/09/94	D	9	(2)	1
25	Miha Blažič		08/05/93	D	15		1
2	Álvaro Brachi	ESP	06/01/86	D	5	(1)	
11	Matic Črnic		12/06/92	M	28		8
27	Gaber Dobrovoljc		27/01/93	D	32		2
12	Adnan Golubović		22/07/95	G	1		
21	Ernest Grvala		11/10/96	M	1	(6)	
6	Kenan Horić	BIH	13/09/90	D	30		
23	Lucas Horvat	ARG	13/10/85	M	16	(7)	2
90	Zeni Husmani	MKD	28/11/90	M	12	(3)	1
14	Dominik Ivkič		31/07/97	D	1		
9	Filip Janković	SRB	17/01/95	M		(2)	
18	Senad Jarovic	GER	20/01/98	A	2	(3)	1
8	Juninho	BRA	15/03/84	M	13	(11)	1
16	Žan Kumer		16/05/96	D		(1)	
37	Žan Majer		25/07/92	M	26	(3)	1
95	Antonio Mance	CRO	07/08/95	A	21	(10)	11
35	Axel Maraval	FRA	20/10/93	G	13		
7	Samir Masimov	AZE	25/08/95	M	1	(4)	
87	Benjamin Morel	FRA	10/06/87	A	16		2
99	Ousseynou Ndiaye	SEN	13/12/92	A	1		
17	Matej Podlogar		23/02/91	A	6	(8)	1
7	Rudi Požeg Vancaš		15/03/94	A	2	(5)	1
15	Jan Repas		19/03/97	M	4	(4)	1
2	Nejc Skubic		13/06/89	D	22		2
20	Aladin Šišić	BIH	28/09/91	M	9	(13)	1
24	Dejan Trajkovski		14/04/92	D	28		1
4	Amedej Vetrih		16/09/90	M	22	(3)	
41	Nejc Vidmar		31/03/89	G	22		
10	Slobodan Vuk		15/09/89	A	12	(5)	5
5	Darko Zec		21/02/89	D	18	(5)	2
13	Žan Žužek		26/01/97	M		(3)	

ND Gorica

1947 • Športni park (5,000) • nd-gorica.com

Major honours
Slovenian League (4) 1996, 2004, 2005, 2006; Slovenian Cup (3) 2001, 2002, 2014

Coach: Miran Srebrnič

2015					
18/07	a	Olimpija	L	1-4	*Arčon*
24/07	h	Rudar	W	2-1	*Martinovič, Džuzdanovič*
02/08	a	Krka	W	2-1	*Džuzdanovič, Širok*
07/08	a	Celje	W	3-2	*Eleke, Džuzdanovič, Nunič*
11/08	h	Zavrč	W	3-0	*Eleke 2, Jogan*
15/08	a	Domžale	W	3-2	*Eleke 2, Širok*
23/08	h	Krško	W	3-1	*Nunič 2, Džuzdanovič*
29/08	a	Koper	W	3-1	*Eleke 2, Burgič*
12/09	h	Maribor	L	1-4	*Burgič*
19/09	h	Olimpija	L	0-3	
23/09	a	Rudar	L	0-1	
27/09	h	Krka	W	2-0	*Burgič, Eleke*
03/10	h	Celje	D	1-1	*Škarabot*
16/10	a	Zavrč	W	2-1	*Burgič, Eleke*
25/10	h	Domžale	L	0-1	
30/10	a	Krško	L	0-1	
08/11	h	Koper	L	1-2	*Eleke*
25/11	a	Maribor	L	2-4	*Eleke, Arčon*
29/11	a	Olimpija	W	2-0	*Džuzdanovič, Cvijanovič*
02/12	h	Rudar	W	1-0	*Eleke*
06/12	a	Krka	L	0-1	
12/12	a	Celje	D	2-2	*Širok, Jogan*
2016					
27/02	h	Zavrč	D	2-2	*Osuji, Nunič*
06/03	a	Domžale	D	1-1	*Humar*
12/03	h	Krško	W	1-0	*Burgič*
18/03	a	Koper	D	1-1	*Gregorič*
02/04	h	Maribor	L	0-2	
06/04	h	Olimpija	D	1-1	*Kotnik*
09/04	a	Rudar	L	0-1	
16/04	h	Krka	W	1-0	*Osuji*
23/04	h	Celje	L	1-2	*Kavčič*
29/04	a	Zavrč	D	1-1	*Kapić*
08/05	h	Domžale	L	0-2	
11/05	a	Krško	W	2-0	*Kotnik, Nunič*
14/05	h	Koper	L	0-1	
21/05	a	Maribor	W	3-2	*Burgič, Kotnik, Osuji*

No	Name	Nat	DoB	Pos	Aps	(s)	Gls
11	Sandi Arčon		06/01/91	A	23	(6)	2
42	Matija Boben		26/02/94	D	8	(1)	
10	Miran Burgič		25/09/84	A	28	(4)	6
3	Uroš Celcer		07/04/89	D	29	(2)	
29	Jani Curk		27/02/94	D	2		
21	Goran Cvijanovič		09/09/86	M	9		1
26	Amel Džuzdanović		26/08/94	M	19		5
19	Blessing Eleke	NGA	05/03/96	A	19		12
6	Miha Gregorič		22/08/89	D	13		1
24	Jan Humar		24/03/96	M	13	(12)	1
27	Alen Jogan		24/08/85	D	26		2
90	Marshal Johnson	NGA	12/12/89	M	19		
8	Rifet Kapić	BIH	03/07/95	A	6	(6)	1
23	Tine Kavčič		16/02/94	D	26		1
14	Jaka Kolenc		23/02/94	M	18	(5)	
7	Andrej Kotnik		04/08/95	M	11	(7)	3
30	Leon Marinič		21/11/97	A		(1)	
77	Dino Martinovič		20/07/90	M	15	(13)	1
31	Nejc Mevlja		12/06/90	D	13		
96	Tilen Nagode		21/03/96	A	9	(7)	
33	Marko Nunič		16/03/93	A	9	(18)	5
17	Bede Osuji	NGA	21/01/96	A	7	(6)	3
1	Gregor Sorčan		05/03/96	G	35		
8	Matija Širok		31/05/91	D	21		3
4	Matija Škarabot		04/02/88	D	17	(8)	1
91	Januš Štrukelj		08/04/91	G	1	(1)	

FC Koper

1920 • Bonifika (5,000) • fckoper.si

Major honours
Slovenian League (1) 2010; Slovenian Cup (3) 2006, 2007, 2015

Coach: Rodolfo Vanoli (ITA);
(01/09/15) Nedžad Okčič;
(07/10/15) Slavko Matić (SRB);
(22/03/16) Milan Obradović (SRB)

2015					
19/07	h	Domžale	L	2-3	*Štromajer, Rahmanović*
26/07	a	Krško	L	0-1	
02/08	h	Celje	D	1-1	*Halilovič*
07/08	h	Maribor	W	2-1	*Štromajer, Galešić*
12/08	a	Olimpija	L	1-4	*Rahmanović*
15/08	h	Rudar	D	1-1	*Palčič*
23/08	a	Krka	W	4-2	*Štromajer 2, Halilovič, Ivančić*
29/08	h	Gorica	L	1-3	*Ivančić*
11/09	a	Zavrč	L	0-1	
20/09	a	Domžale	L	0-1	
23/09	h	Krško	W	4-0	*Ivančić, Rahmanović (p), Štulac, Vekič*
26/09	a	Celje	D	1-1	*Štulac*
03/10	a	Maribor	L	0-4	
18/10	h	Olimpija	L	1-2	*Ivančić*
24/10	a	Rudar	L	0-1	
31/10	h	Krka	D	0-0	
08/11	a	Gorica	W	2-1	*Memolla, Štromajer*
21/11	h	Zavrč	W	3-1	*Vekič, Štulac 2*
28/11	h	Domžale	L	0-2	
02/12	a	Krško	W	1-0	*Štromajer*
05/12	h	Celje	L	1-2	*Memolla*
13/12	h	Maribor	L	0-5	
2016					
28/02	a	Olimpija	L	0-2	
05/03	h	Rudar	L	0-1	
13/03	a	Krka	W	1-0	*Lokaj*
18/03	h	Gorica	D	1-1	*Jurina*
03/04	a	Zavrč	W	3-1	*Datković 2, Belima*
06/04	a	Domžale	D	1-1	*Belima*
10/04	h	Krško	L	0-1	
16/04	a	Celje	L	0-3	
24/04	a	Maribor	D	2-2	*Štromajer, Andrejašič*
01/05	h	Olimpija	L	1-2	*Štromajer*
07/05	a	Rudar	W	2-0	*Valencia, Štulac*
11/05	h	Krka	L	2-3	*Datković, Jurina*
14/05	a	Gorica	W	1-0	*Horvat*
21/05	h	Zavrč	W	1-0	*Štulac*

No	Name	Nat	DoB	Pos	Aps	(s)	Gls
33	Mislav Andjelković	CRO	22/04/88	M	3	(2)	
2	Jan Andrejašič		16/09/95	D	19	(4)	1
44	Luka Batur	CRO	28/11/89	D	8	(2)	
7	Rubén Belima	EQG	11/02/92	M	8	(2)	2
6	Jakov Biljan	CRO	02/08/95	M	6	(1)	
39	Ivan Blatančić	CRO	14/01/98	M	1	(1)	
79	Mademba Cisse	MLI	04/05/95	A		(2)	
20	Domen Črnigoj		18/11/95	M	6	(1)	
4	Toni Datković	CRO	06/11/93	D	14		3
23	Sven Dedić	CRO	15/04/91	M	4	(1)	
28	Haris Dedič		06/07/97	M	6	(1)	
6	Cristian Del Toro	ESP	16/08/93	D	4	(1)	
77	Drago Gabrić	CRO	27/09/86	A	5		
15	Igor Gal	CRO	20/01/83	D	3		
7	Goran Galešić	BIH	11/03/89	M	3	(4)	1
14	Ivica Guberac		05/07/88	M	9		
27	Damir Hadžič		01/10/84	D	14	(1)	
16	Denis Halilovič		02/03/86	D	9		2
32	Ivor Horvat	CRO	19/08/91	D	9	(2)	1
9	Josip Ivančić	CRO	29/03/91	A	9	(5)	4
19	Tijan Jaiteh	GAM	31/12/88	M	1	(1)	
3	Jefthon	BRA	03/01/82	D	6	(1)	
88	Jony	ESP	02/04/85	M	4	(1)	
99	Marin Jurina	CRO	26/11/93	A	7	(3)	2
87	Kristijan Kahlina	CRO	24/07/92	G	11		
16	Žiga Kljun		12/10/97	M		(2)	
23	Marko Krivičič		01/02/96	M	7		
19	Luka Leko	CRO	17/02/94	M	3		
20	Fabian Lokaj	ALB	23/08/96	A	5	(4)	1
10	Mitja Lotrič		03/09/94	A	3	(4)	
21	Aleksander Maslič		08/11/97	D		(2)	
26	Hysen Memolla	ALB	03/07/92	D	17		2
21	Nik Mršič		07/03/96	M	1		
9	Zlatan Muslimović	BIH	06/03/81	A	3	(5)	
29	Matej Palčič		21/06/93	D	4		1
25	Antonio Pavić	CRO	18/11/94	D	20	(3)	
22	Patrik Posavac		14/03/95	M	9	(9)	
29	Rok Požrl		14/07/98	M	1	(1)	
49	Matej Pučko		06/10/93	A	3		
17	Dalibor Radujko		17/06/85	M	14	(5)	
8	Amar Rahmanović	BIH	13/05/94	M	15		3
11	Albert Riera	ESP	15/04/82	M		(1)	
83	Vasja Simčič		01/07/83	G	13		
5	Darnel Situ	FRA	18/03/92	D	3		
24	Ivan Šimurina	CRO	08/05/92	D	2	(1)	
15	Davor Škerjanc		07/01/86	A	2	(3)	
4	Denis Šme		22/03/94	D	12		
30	Jaka Štromajer		27/07/83	A	23	(11)	8
18	Leo Štulac		26/09/94	M	28	(1)	6
28	Ante Tomić	CRO	23/05/83	M	11	(3)	
35	Vjekoslav Tomić	CRO	19/07/83	G	12		
10	Joel Valencia	ECU	16/11/94	M	10	(3)	1
11	Luka Vekič		10/04/95	A	4	(6)	2
14	Boris Živanović	SRB	18/07/89	M	2	(2)	

NK Krka

1922 • Portoval (1,500) • nkkrka.com
**Coach: Andrej Kastrevec;
(08/04/16) Miloš Kostič**

2015

18/07	a	Rudar	W	1-0	Perić
26/07	a	Celje	D	1-1	Welbeck (p)
02/08	h	Gorica	L	1-2	Fuček
07/08	a	Zavrč	W	1-0	Ejup
12/08	h	Domžale	L	0-4	
15/08	a	Krško	D	0-0	
23/08	h	Koper	L	2-4	Fuček 2 (1p)
29/08	a	Maribor	D	2-2	Welbeck, Vučkič
11/09	h	Olimpija	L	1-3	Kastrevec
19/09	h	Rudar	D	0-0	
23/09	h	Celje	W	1-0	Perić
27/09	a	Gorica	L	0-2	
04/10	h	Zavrč	D	1-1	Perić
17/10	a	Domžale	L	0-3	
25/10	h	Krško	W	2-0	Dangubić, Novinić
31/10	a	Koper	D	0-0	
08/11	h	Maribor	L	0-2	
25/11	a	Olimpija	L	1-3	og (Kelhar)
28/11	a	Rudar	D	1-1	Welbeck (p)
02/12	h	Celje	L	0-1	
06/12	h	Gorica	W	1-0	Gliha
11/12	h	Zavrč	L	1-2	Mojstrović

2016

28/02	h	Domžale	W	3-1	Kostanjšek, Fuček 2 (1p)
06/03	h	Krško	L	0-3	
13/03	h	Koper	L	0-1	
19/03	a	Maribor	L	1-2	Kostanjšek
02/04	h	Olimpija	L	0-2	
06/04	h	Rudar	L	1-5	Fuček
10/04	h	Celje	D	1-1	Vučkič
16/04	a	Gorica	L	0-1	
24/04	a	Zavrč	W	2-0	Dangubić, Boccaccini
30/04	a	Domžale	D	1-1	Ejup
07/05	h	Krško	D	0-0	
11/05	a	Koper	W	3-2	Majcen 2, Boccaccini
14/05	h	Maribor	L	1-3	Fuček
21/05	a	Olimpija	L	0-3	

No	Name	Nat	DoB	Pos	Aps	(s)	Gls
8	Favour Aniekan	NGA	10/01/94	M		(11)	
22	Mateo Barukčić		27/07/94	G	3	(1)	
20	Matteo Boccaccini	ITA	08/02/93	D	8		2
4	Luka Bogdan	CRO	26/03/96	D	25		
6	Mario Brkljača		07/02/85	M	10	(1)	
21	Jamilu Collins	NGA	05/08/94	D	12	(1)	
90	Filip Dangubić	CRO	05/05/95	A	22	(9)	2
17	Danijel Dežman		31/03/88	D	12	(8)	
15	Leo Ejup		09/09/94	M	28	(1)	2
7	Josip Fuček	CRO	26/02/85	M	32	(1)	7
8	Erik Gliha		13/02/97	D	6	(9)	1
21	Mohammed Kabiru	NGA	18/08/97	D	1	(2)	
23	Luka Kambič		20/12/98	M		(1)	
77	Žiga Kastrevec		25/02/94	A	19	(2)	1
25	Grega Končar		21/01/96	M		(1)	
36	Miha Kostanjšek		23/06/94	M	13	(8)	2
19	Urban Kramar		03/10/90	M		(7)	
99	Luka Majcen		25/07/89	A	9	(5)	2
43	Damjan Marjanović		27/06/96	D	1	(10)	
18	Bruno Marotti	CRO	02/03/94	D	33		
31	Miodrag Mitrovic	SUI	14/07/91	G	33		
10	Denis Mojstrović		17/10/86	M	27	(6)	1
44	Jan Novak		04/10/97	A	3		
9	Enes Novinić	CRO	18/07/85	A	9	(7)	1
27	Marin Perić	CRO	17/10/90	A	25	(7)	3
55	Matej Potokar		19/10/96	M	8	(9)	
5	Alen Vučkič		01/02/90	D	23		2
24	Nana Welbeck	GHA	24/11/94	M	34		3

NK Krško

1922 • Matija Gubec (1,470) • nkkrsko.com
Coach: Tomaž Petrovič

2015

19/07	h	Celje	W	1-0	Rujović (p)
26/07	h	Koper	W	1-0	Poljanec
01/08	a	Maribor	L	1-4	Poljanec
08/08	h	Olimpija	L	0-2	
12/08	a	Rudar	D	1-1	Djukič
15/08	h	Krka	D	0-0	
23/08	a	Gorica	L	1-3	Urbanč (p)
29/08	h	Zavrč	L	0-1	
13/09	a	Domžale	L	0-2	
18/09	a	Celje	D	0-0	
23/09	a	Koper	L	0-1	
27/09	h	Maribor	L	1-3	Štefanec
04/10	a	Olimpija	L	0-5	
17/10	h	Rudar	D	0-0	
25/10	a	Krka	L	0-2	
30/10	h	Gorica	W	1-0	Štefanec
06/11	a	Zavrč	D	1-1	Čeh
25/11	h	Domžale	D	1-1	Čeh
28/11	h	Celje	D	0-0	
02/12	h	Koper	L	0-1	
05/12	a	Maribor	L	0-6	
12.12	h	Olimpija	W	2-1	Volarič, Žinko (p)

2016

27/02	a	Rudar	W	1-0	Volarič
06/03	h	Krka	W	3-0	Volarič, Urbanč, Djurkovič
12/03	a	Gorica	L	0-1	
19/03	h	Zavrč	L	0-1	
02/04	a	Domžale	W	3-2	Poljanec 2, Volarič
06/04	u	Celje	W	1-0	Djurkovič
10/04	a	Koper	W	1-0	Hotič
17/04	h	Maribor	L	1-3	Žinko (p)
23/04	a	Olimpija	W	1-0	Kramarič
27/04	a	Rudar	D	1-1	Vuklišević
07/05	h	Krka	D	0-0	
11/05	h	Domžale	L	0-1	
14/05	a	Zavrč	D	1-1	Gregov
21/05	h	Domžale	D	0-0	

No	Name	Nat	DoB	Pos	Aps	(s)	Gls
5	Jože Barkovič		02/01/86	D		(1)	
23	Igor Blažinčič		22/03/93	M		(6)	
11	David Bučar		08/02/94	A	2	(9)	
28	Tim Čeh		13/03/94	A	13	(6)	2
33	Bojan Djukič		06/11/86	D	8		1
89	Enis Djurkovič		24/05/89	A	12	(1)	2
19	Miha Drnovšek		14/01/87	M	19	(5)	
25	Marko Felja		19/10/96	M		(1)	
26	Šime Gregov	CRO	08/07/89	D	13		1
98	Dino Hotič		26/07/95	M	12	(1)	1
30	Marko Jakolič		16/04/91	D	18	(4)	
8	Žiga Jurečič		23/08/95	M	11	(6)	
8	Aleš Kožar		11/10/95	D	2	(5)	
97	Martin Kramarič		14/11/97	A	3	(3)	1
32	Rhema Obed	ENG	11/09/91	D	6	(2)	
20	Luka Pavič		23/11/94	M	8	(6)	
22	Marko Perkovič	CRO	30/08/91	D	13		
90	Petar Petranić	CRO	26/06/92	A	5	(8)	
4	Jure Petric		24/03/91	D	24	(1)	
9	David Poljanec		27/11/86	A	27	(4)	4
45	Robert Pušaver		09/05/95	D	12		
21	Enes Rujović		29/05/89	M	6	(2)	1
33	Dejan Rusič		05/12/82	A		(1)	
12	Gregor Sikošek		13/02/94	D	33		
10	Klemen Slivšek		30/07/89	M	1	(11)	
6	Jure Špiler		27/11/92	M	1	(4)	
7	Luka Štefanec	CRO	26/09/95	A	18	(7)	2
15	Dejan Urbanč		13/04/84	M	29	(1)	2
7	Luka Volarič		13/01/91	M	33		4
22	Damjan Vuklišević		28/06/95	D	8	(1)	1
1	Marko Zalokar		18/06/90	G	36		
70	Luka Žinko		23/03/83	M	23		2

NK Maribor

1960 • Ljudski vrt (12,432) • nkmaribor.com
Major honours
*Slovenian League (13) 1997, 1998, 1999, 2000,
2001, 2002, 2003, 2009, 2011, 2012, 2013, 2014,
2015; Slovenian Cup (9) 1992, 1994, 1997, 1999,
2004, 2010, 2012, 2013, 2016*
**Coach: Ante Šimundža;
(29/08/15) Krunoslav Jurčić (CRO);
(02/03/16) Darko Milanič**

2015

17/07	h	Zavrč	D	1-1	Zahović
25/07	a	Domžale	W	1-0	Marcos Tavares
01/08	h	Krško	W	4-1	Mendy, Vršič, Ibraimi 2
07/08	a	Koper	L	1-2	Vršič
12/08	h	Celje	W	1-0	Marcos Tavares
16/08	h	Olimpija	L	0-3	
22/08	a	Rudar	D	0-0	
29/08	h	Krka	D	2-2	Mendy, Ibraimi
12/09	a	Gorica	W	4-1	Mendy 2, Marcos Tavares, Bohar
19/09	a	Zavrč	L	1-2	Bohar
23/09	h	Domžale	D	1-1	Marcos Tavares
27/09	a	Krško	W	3-1	Šuler, Vršič, Bajde
03/10	h	Koper	W	4-0	Vršič, Marcos Tavares 2, Ibraimi
17/10	a	Celje	W	3-1	Ibraimi, Marcos Tavares (p), Sallalich
31/10	h	Rudar	W	7-1	Ibraimi, Bajde, Marcos Tavares 2, Filipović, Sallalich, Mendy
08/11	a	Krka	W	2-0	Marcos Tavares, Bajde
21/11	a	Olimpija	D	2-2	Bajde, Stojanović
25/11	h	Gorica	W	4-2	Ibraimi, Sallalich, og (Jogan), Bajde
28/11	h	Zavrč	D	3-3	Ibraimi, Mendy, Kabha
02/12	a	Domžale	D	0-0	
05/12	h	Krško	W	6-0	Mendy 3, Bajde 3
13/12	a	Luka Koper	W	5-0	Bajde, Ibraimi 2, Sallalich, Mendy

2016

27/02	h	Celje	L	0-1	
05/03	h	Olimpija	D	0-0	
12/03	a	Rudar	W	3-0	Derviševič, Bajde 2
19/03	h	Krka	W	2-1	Vršič, Marcos Tavares
02/04	a	Gorica	W	2-0	Mendy 2
06/04	a	Zavrč	W	0-0	
09/04	h	Domžale	W	2-1	Novaković, Rodrigo Defendi
17/04	a	Krško	W	3-1	Novaković, Mendy 2
24/04	a	Koper	D	2-2	Novaković 2 (1p)
30/04	a	Celje	W	0-0	
07/05	h	Olimpija	W	2-1	Novaković (p), Marcos Tavares
11/05	h	Rudar	L	2-3	Sallalich, Mendy
14/05	a	Krka	W	3-1	Mendy 2, Derviševič
21/05	h	Gorica	L	2-3	Bajde 2

No	Name	Nat	DoB	Pos	Aps	(s)	Gls
30	Valon Ahmedi	ALB	07/10/94	M		(1)	
44	Arghus	BRA	19/01/88	D	1		
20	Gregor Bajde		29/04/94	A	17	(10)	13
39	Damjan Bohar		18/10/91	M	11	(17)	2
99	Žan Celar		14/03/99	A	1		
1	Aljaž Cotman		26/04/94	G	1		
21	Amir Derviševič		04/07/92	M	5	(4)	2
5	Željko Filipović		03/10/88	M	30		1
13	Abel Gigli	ITA	16/08/90	D	10	(2)	
33	Jasmin Handanović		28/01/78	G	35		
2	Adis Hodžič		16/01/99	D	1		
23	Dino Hotič		26/07/95	M		(4)	
10	Agim Ibraimi	MKD	29/08/88	M	25	(2)	10
95	Marko Jankovič	MNE	09/07/95	M	5	(5)	
3	Erik Janža		21/06/93	D	10	(1)	
24	Marwan Kabha	ISR	07/03/91	M	27	(3)	1
9	Marcos Tavares	BRA	30/03/84	A	26	(7)	12
7	Aleš Mejač		18/03/83	D	3	(3)	
14	Jean-Philippe Mendy	FRA	04/03/87	A	20	(13)	17
70	Aleš Mertelj		22/03/87	M	27	(3)	
11	Milivoje Novaković		18/05/79	A	10	(1)	5
18	Sandi Ogrinec		05/06/98	M	1		
7	Amar Rahmanović	BIH	13/05/94	M	4	(3)	
26	Aleksander Rajčevič		17/11/86	D	2		
35	Rodrigo Defendi	BRA	17/06/86	D	10		1
8	Sintayehu Sallalich	ISR	20/06/91	M	17	(8)	5
30	Petar Stojanović		07/10/95	D	11		1
44	Denis Šme		22/03/94	D	10		
4	Marko Šuler		09/03/83	D	24	(1)	1
28	Mitja Viler		01/09/86	D	26		
17	Dalibor Volaš		27/02/87	A	1	(3)	
22	Dare Vršič		26/09/84	A	23	(5)	5
31	Daniel Vujčič		12/04/95	M	2	(3)	
11	Luka Zahović		15/11/95	A	2	(1)	1

 **SLOVENIA**

NK Olimpija Ljubljana

2005 • Stožice (16,038) • nkolimpija.si
Major honours
Slovenian League (1) 2016
Coach: Marijan Pušnik;
(11/01/16) Marko Nikolić (SRB);
(22/04/16) Rodolfo Vanoli (ITA)

2015
18/07	h	Gorica	W	4-1	Kapun, Kronaveter 2, Šporar
24/07	a	Zavrč	D	0-0	
01/08	h	Domžale	L	0-2	
08/08	a	Krško	W	2-0	Ricardo Alves, Šporar
12/08	h	Koper	W	4-1	Djermanovič, Kronaveter, Henty 2
16/08	a	Maribor	W	3-0	Henty 2, Šporar
23/08	h	Celje	W	6-0	Kronaveter 2, Kelhar, Ricardo Alves, Šporar, Djermanovič
30/08	h	Rudar	W	5-0	Kelhar, Šporar 3, Djermanovič
11/09	a	Krka	W	3-1	Henty, Zajc 2
19/09	a	Gorica	W	3-0	Kronaveter 2 (1p), Kapun
23/09	h	Zavrč	L	0-2	
26/09	a	Domžale	D	1-1	Šporar
04/10	h	Krško	W	5-0	Ontivero 2, Kapun 2, Šporar (p)
18/10	a	Koper	W	2-1	Henty 2
31/10	a	Celje	W	4-0	Šporar 4
07/11	a	Rudar	W	3-1	Šporar 2, Ontivero
21/11	h	Maribor	D	2-2	Šporar 2
25/11	h	Krka	W	3-1	og (Bogdan), Kronaveter 2
29/11	h	Gorica	L	0-2	
02/12	a	Zavrč	W	2-1	Ontivero, Henty
06/12	h	Domžale	L	0-2	
12/12	h	Krško	L	1-2	Kronaveter

2016
28/02	h	Koper	W	2-0	Zajc, Radović
05/03	a	Maribor	D	0-0	
13/03	h	Celje	D	0-0	
20/03	h	Rudar	W	5-0	Kronaveter 2 (1p), Wobay, og (Knezović), Ricardo Alves
02/04	a	Krka	W	2-0	Radović, Eleke
06/04	a	Gorica	D	1-1	Kronaveter (p)
10/04	a	Zavrč	D	1-1	Eleke
16/04	a	Domžale	W	1-0	Kronaveter
23/04	a	Krško	L	0-1	
01/05	a	Koper	W	2-1	Wobay, Klinar
07/05	h	Maribor	L	1-2	Kronaveter
11/05	a	Celje	W	3-1	Bajrić, Zajc, Kronaveter
14/05	a	Rudar	W	1-0	Kronaveter (p)
21/05	h	Krka	W	3-0	Zajc, Eleke, Delamea Mlinar

No	Name	Nat	DoB	Pos	Aps	(s)	Gls
24	Kenan Bajrić		20/12/94	D	13	(8)	1
29	Rok Baskera		26/05/93	M		(3)	
21	Darko Brljak		23/12/84	G	3		
25	Hrvoje Čale	CRO	04/03/85	D	12	(1)	
20	Antonio Delamea Mlinar		10/06/91	D	2	(2)	1
33	Dejan Djermanovič		17/06/88	A	3	(8)	3
9	Blessing Eleke	NGA	05/03/96	A	9	(3)	3
17	Matic Fink		27/02/90	D	31	(1)	
7	Josip Golubar	CRO	04/03/85	M		(5)	
55	Ezekiel Henty	NGA	13/05/93	A	21		8
23	Nik Kapun		09/01/94	M	18	(11)	4
4	Dejan Kelhar		05/04/84	D	31		2
2	Denis Klinar		21/02/92	D	15	(2)	1
19	Aljaž Krefl		20/02/94	D	7	(5)	
7	Rok Kronaveter		07/12/86	M	29	(1)	17
99	Mariotto	BRA	15/01/96	A		(4)	
8	Darijan Matić		28/05/83	M	34		
92	Martin Mimoun	FRA	11/06/92	M	14	(11)	
32	Nemanja Mitrovič		15/10/92	D	32		
18	Jakob Novak		04/03/98	M		(1)	
5	Lucas Ontivero	ARG	09/09/94	A	9	(2)	4
10	Miroslav Radović	SRB	16/01/84	M	13	(1)	2
16	Ricardo Alves	POR	25/03/93	M	12	(12)	3
1	Aleksander Šeliga		01/02/80	G	22		
10	Andraž Šporar		27/02/94	A	18		17
41	Nejc Vidmar		31/03/89	G	11		
15	Marko Vukčević	MNE	07/06/93	A		(2)	
11	Julius Wobay	SLE	07/06/93	A	5	(7)	2
6	Miha Zajc		01/07/94	M	24	(8)	5
27	Aris Zarifovič		02/06/88	D	8	(5)	

NK Rudar Velenje

1948 • Ob jezeru (7,000) • nkrudarvelenje.com
Major honours
Slovenian Cup (1) 1998
Coach: Jernej Javornik;
(10/05/16) Ramiz Smajlovič

2015
18/07	h	Krka	L	0-1	
24/07	a	Gorica	L	1-2	Prašnikar
01/08	h	Zavrč	L	1-3	Prašnikar
08/08	a	Domžale	W	2-0	Prašnikar, Krcič
12/08	h	Krško	D	1-1	Prašnikar
15/08	a	Koper	L	1-2	Kašnik
22/08	h	Maribor	D	0-0	
30/08	a	Olimpija	L	0-5	
12/09	h	Celje	W	4-0	Knezović, S Babić (p), Krcič, Kocič
19/09	a	Krka	D	0-0	
23/09	h	Gorica	W	1-0	M Babić
26/09	a	Zavrč	L	2-3	Knezović, Trifkovič
03/10	h	Domžale	D	0-0	
17/10	a	Krško	D	0-0	
24/10	h	Koper	W	1-0	Džinič
31/10	a	Maribor	L	1-7	Trifkovič
07/11	h	Olimpija	L	1-3	Eterović
22/11	a	Celje	L	0-1	
28/11	h	Krka	D	1-1	Eterović (p)
02/12	a	Gorica	L	0-1	
05/12	h	Zavrč	W	1-0	Kašnik
12/12	a	Domžale	L	0-4	

2016
27/02	h	Krško	L	0-1	
05/03	a	Koper	W	1-0	Bolha
12/03	h	Maribor	L	0-3	
20/03	a	Olimpija	L	0-5	
02/04	h	Celje	W	2-0	Eterović 2 (2p)
06/04	h	Krka	W	5-1	Črnčič, Eterović, Pišek, Džinič, Grbič
09/04	h	Gorica	W	1-0	Jahić
17/04	a	Zavrč	W	2-0	Eterović, Krcič
23/04	h	Domžale	L	1-2	S Babić
27/04	a	Krško	D	1-1	Eterović
07/05	h	Koper	L	0-2	
11/05	a	Maribor	W	3-2	Knezović, Črnčič, Tolimir
14/05	h	Olimpija	L	0-1	
21/05	a	Celje	L	0-1	

No	Name	Nat	DoB	Pos	Aps	(s)	Gls
33	Mario Babić	CRO	03/07/92	M	33	(1)	
12	Stjepan Babić	CRO	04/12/88	M	25	(3)	2
17	Erman Bevab	AUT	27/02/95	D	2		
1	Klemen Bolha		19/03/93	M	30	(1)	1
1	Matic Čretnik		02/03/91	G	1		
10	Leon Črnčič		02/03/90	M	17	(5)	2
27	Rusmin Dedić		11/09/82	D	1		
3	Elvedin Džinič		25/08/85	D	19	(4)	2
32	Mate Eterović	CRO	13/07/84	A	20	(3)	7
20	Denis Grbič		15/03/86	M	4	(10)	1
45	Damir Grgič	CRO	18/05/92	A	3	(12)	
31	Jaka Ihbeiseh	PLE	29/08/86	M	22	(4)	
31	Senad Jahić		13/05/87	D	18	(4)	1
4	David Kašnik		16/01/87	D	28		2
14	Ivan Knezović	CRO	25/09/82	D	22		3
14	Milan Kocič		16/02/90	A	21	(4)	1
7	Amer Krcič		23/05/89	M	8	(13)	3
2	Tilen Lešnik		03/05/96	D		(1)	
10	Mitja Lotrič		03/09/94	A	1	(6)	
6	Anže Pišek		06/10/96	M	9	(7)	1
11	Nejc Plesec		13/03/94	M		(1)	
11	Luka Prašnikar		11/06/87	A	14	(15)	4
13	Matej Radan		13/05/90	G	34		
21	Nikola Tolimir		01/04/89	M	22	(8)	1
8	Damjan Trifkovič		22/07/87	M	33		2
44	Matic Žitko		21/02/90	D	8	(4)	

NK Zavrč

1998 • Športni park (962) • nkzavrc.si
Coach: Ivica Solomun (CRO);
(04/08/16) Slavko Matić (SRB)

2015
17/07	a	Maribor	D	1-1	Matjašič
24/07	h	Olimpija	D	0-0	
01/08	a	Rudar	W	3-1	Polić, Glavica 2
07/08	h	Krka	L	0-1	
11/08	a	Gorica	L	0-3	
17/08	a	Celje	L	1-2	Pihler
21/08	h	Domžale	D	0-0	
29/08	a	Krško	W	1-0	Kokorović
11/09	h	Koper	W	1-0	Zorko
19/09	h	Maribor	W	2-1	og (Šuler), og (Kabha)
23/09	a	Olimpija	W	2-0	Batrović, Matjašič
26/09	h	Rudar	W	3-2	Cvek, Pihler 2
04/10	a	Krka	D	1-1	Batrović
16/10	h	Gorica	L	1-2	Batrović
24/10	h	Celje	L	0-1	
31/10	a	Domžale	W	1-0	Muslimović
06/11	h	Krško	D	1-1	Cvek
21/11	a	Koper	L	1-3	Golubar
28/11	a	Maribor	D	3-3	Glavica, Riera (p), Batrović
02/12	h	Olimpija	L	1-2	Golubar
05/12	a	Rudar	L	0-1	
11/12	h	Krka	W	2-1	og (Vučkič), Tahiraj

2016
27/02	a	Gorica	D	2-2	Batrović 2 (1p)
05/03	a	Celje	D	0-0	
11/03	h	Domžale	D	0-0	
19/03	h	Krško	W	1-0	Cvek
03/04	h	Koper	L	1-3	Tahiraj
06/04	h	Maribor	D	0-0	
10/04	a	Olimpija	D	1-1	og (Šeliga)
17/04	h	Rudar	L	0-2	
24/04	a	Krka	L	0-2	
29/04	a	Gorica	D	1-1	Golubar
06/05	h	Celje	L	0-1	
11/05	a	Domžale	L	0-1	
14/05	a	Krško	D	1-1	Golubar
21/05	a	Koper	L	0-1	

No	Name	Nat	DoB	Pos	Aps	(s)	Gls
14	Ovbokha Agboyi	NGA	14/12/94	M	6	(5)	
14	Aitor Ruano	ESP	13/08/94	D		(2)	
13	Sebastijan Antić	CRO	05/11/91	D	28		
91	Pavol Bajza	SVK	04/09/91	G	11		
94	Veljko Batrović	MNE	24/03/95	M	24	(1)	6
4	Luka Bogdan	CRO	26/03/96	D	1		
4	Lovro Cvek	CRO	06/07/95	M	24	(6)	3
18	Toni Datković	CRO	06/11/93	D	21		
89	Timotej Dodlek		23/11/89	M	8	(4)	
35	Josip Filipović	CRO	08/05/96	D	5	(1)	
10	Denis Glavica	CRO	20/08/91	M	18	(7)	3
3	Denis Glavina	CRO	03/03/86	D	6	(2)	
7	Josip Golubar	CRO	04/03/85	A	8	(9)	4
21	Nemanja Jakšić	SRB	11/07/95	D	9	(1)	
3	Tin Karamatić	CRO	01/03/93	D	8	(1)	
99	Ed Kevin Kokorović	CRO	04/01/95	M	20	(6)	1
12	Matija Kovačić	CRO	25/02/94	G	10	(1)	
11	Jure Matjašič		31/05/92	A	25	(5)	2
55	Matija Miketić	SRB	03/02/96	M	6	(1)	
19	Zlatan Muslimović	BIH	06/03/81	A	2	(8)	1
20	Mateo Mužek		29/04/95	D	11	(2)	
77	Luka Muženjak	CRO	04/07/93	D		(1)	
33	Ivan Novoselec	CRO	19/06/95	D	13		
35	Stefan Petrovic	AUT	30/08/93	D	8	(2)	
1	Dominik Picak	CRO	12/02/92	G	7		
23	Aleks Pihler		15/01/94	M	32	(1)	3
8	Dejan Polić	CRO	21/04/93	M	7	(3)	1
1	Marko Ranilović		25/11/86	G	8		
9	Albert Riera	ESP	15/04/82	M	8	(4)	1
9	Davor Rogač	CRO	15/05/90	D	29	(1)	
44	Stanislav Shtanenko	UKR	05/02/96	D	4		
9	Luka Šalamun		18/01/97	A		(1)	
7	Filip Škvorc	CRO	22/07/91	A		(1)	
73	Frančesko Tahiraj	ALB	21/09/96	M	14	(6)	2
19	Dean Tišma	CRO	24/02/95	M	5	(4)	
28	Patrik Tudjan	CRO	14/05/97	M		(7)	
17	Rok Zorko		20/10/93	A	10	(7)	1

Top goalscorers

Jean-Philippe
Mendy
Rok Kronaveter
Andraž Šporar

17 Jean-Philippe Mendy (Maribor)
Rok Kronaveter (Olimpija)
Andraž Šporar (Olimpija)

15 Blessing Eleke (Gorica/Olimpija)

13 Gregor Bajde (Maribor)

12 Marcos Tavares (Maribor)

11 Antonio Mance (Domžale)

10 Agim Ibraimi (Maribor)

8 Matic Črnic (Domžale)
Jaka Štromajer (Koper)
Ezekiel Henty (Olimpija)

Promoted clubs

NK Radomlje

1972 • Športni park (1,200) • nk-radomlje.si
Coach: Dejan Djuranovič

NK Aluminij

1946 • Športni park (2,570) • nkaluminij.net
**Coach: Simon Seslar;
(02/03/16) Bojan Špehonja**

Second level final table 2015/16

		Pld	W	D	L	F	A	Pts
1	NK Radomlje	27	16	7	4	51	24	55
2	NK Aluminij	27	14	8	5	61	29	50
3	NK Drava Ptuj	27	13	7	7	43	42	46
4	NK Triglav	27	12	8	7	43	25	44
5	NK Dob	27	9	5	13	42	44	32
6	NK Veržej	27	8	8	11	41	54	32
7	NK Zarica Kranj	27	8	7	12	27	46	31
8	NK Ankaran Hrvatini	27	8	7	12	33	45	31
9	NK Tolmin	27	6	8	13	36	43	26
10	NK Šenčur	27	5	7	15	38	63	22

Promotion/Relegation play-offs

(29/05/16 & 02/06/16)
Zavrč 3-2 Aluminij
Aluminij 1-1 Zavrč
(Zavrč 4-3)

NB Aluminij subsequently promoted as Zavrč were denied licence for Prva Liga.

DOMESTIC CUP

Pokal NZS 2015/16

FIRST ROUND

(19/08/15)
Brda 1-4 Zarica Kranj
Fužinar 1-3 Krka
Hotiza 1-2 Drava *(aet)*
Ilirija 2-1 Radomlje *(aet)*
Ivančna Gorica 6-0 Odranci
Izola 0-0 Veržej *(aet; 2-3 on pens)*
Mura 1-0 Gorica
Pesnica 0-7 Rudar
Olimpija w/o Rogaška
Šampion 0-2 Zavrč
Stojnci 0-1 Triglav
Tolmin 2-1 Ankaran

Byes - Celje, Domžale, Koper, Maribor

SECOND ROUND

(09/09/15)
Drava 1-1 Triglav *(aet; 5-3 on pens)*
Mura 0-3 Celje

(15/09/15)
Ivančna Gorica 1-3 Olimpija
Zarica Kranj 0-3 Koper

(16/09/15)
Ilirija 1-3 Domžale
Rudar 3-2 Krka
Tolmin 0-3 Maribor
Veržej 0-4 Zavrč

QUARTER-FINALS

(21/10/15 & 28/10/15)
Olimpija Ljubljana 2-2 Celje *(Mitrovič 32, 68; Firer 26, Pajač 36)*
Celje 3-1 Olimpija Ljubljana *(Firer 23, Spremo 33, Mitrovič 79og; Henty 88)*
(Celje 5-3)

Rudar 1-0 Maribor *(Jahić 80)*
Maribor 3-0 Rudar *(Kabha 60, Vršič 76, Marcos Tavares 86)*
(Maribor 3-1)

Zavrč 1-1 Drava Ptuj *(Batrović 37; Šalamun 57)*
Drava Ptuj 0-3 Zavrč *(Batrović 41, 77, Riera 68)*
(Zavrč 4-1)

(28/10/15 & 04/11/15)
Domžale 0-1 Koper *(Rahmanović 89)*
Koper 1-2 Domžale *(Ivančić 47; Črnic 3, Morel 90+2)*
(2-2; Domžale on away goals)

SEMI-FINALS

(13/04/16 & 20/04/16)
Celje 1-0 Domžale *(Omoregie 55)*
Domžale 0-1 Celje *(Omoregie 6)*
(Celje 2-0)

(14/04/16 & 20/04/16)
Zavrč 2-1 Maribor *(Golubar 11, Matjašič 43; Bajde 71)*
Maribor 5-1 Zavrč *(Mendy 30, Sallalich 72, 91, Novakovič 102, 105; Handanovič 43og) (aet)*
(Maribor 6-3)

FINAL

(25/05/16)
Bonifika, Koper
NK MARIBOR 2 *(Kabha 7, Vršič 107)*
NK CELJE 2 *(Podlogar 19, 111)*
(aet; 7-6 on pens)
Referee: *Jug*
MARIBOR: *Handanovič, Mertelj, Šme, Rodrigo Defendi, Viler, Sallalich (Vršič 69), Janković, Kabha, Filipovič, Mendy (Marcos Tavares 91), Bajde (Novakovič 74)*
CELJE: *Kotnik, Travner, T Klemenčič (Kous 88), Hadžić, Vidmajer, Pajač (Pungaršek 61), Vrhovec, Miškić, Čirjak (Erico Sousa 109), Podlogar, Omoregie*

Slovenian Cup joy once again for record nine-time winners Maribor

SPAIN
Real Federación Española de Fútbol (RFEF)

Address	Ramón y Cajal s/n Apartado postal 385 ES-28230 Las Rozas (Madrid)	**President**	Ángel María Villar Llona
Tel	+34 91 495 9800	**General secretary**	Jorge Juan Pérez Arias
Fax	+34 91 495 9801	**Media officer**	Antonio Bustillo Abella
E-mail	rfef@rfef.es	**Year of formation**	1909
Website	rfef.es		

Eibar ~ 7
Gijón
18 Bilbao
16
La Coruña
1
San Sebastián
6
21 ~Vitoria
23 Pamplona
Vigo
5
Barcelona
3 8
2
9
Madrid
14
Villarreal
20
22 15
Valencia
12 19

4 17
Granada
Sevilla
(Seville)
13 10
Málaga

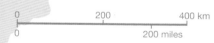

0   200   400 km
0   200 miles

LIGA CLUBS

 1 **Athletic Club**

 2 **Club Atlético de Madrid**

 3 **FC Barcelona**

 4 **Real Betis Balompié**

 5 **RC Celta de Vigo**

 6 **RC Deportivo La Coruña**

 7 **SD Eibar**

 8 **RCD Espanyol**

 9 **Getafe CF**

 10 **Granada CF**

 11 **UD Las Palmas**

 12 **Levante UD**

 13 **Málaga CF**

 14 **Rayo Vallecano de Madrid**

 15 **Real Madrid CF**

 16 **Real Sociedad de Fútbol**

17 **Sevilla FC**

18 **Real Sporting de Gijón**

19 **Valencia CF**

20 **Villarreal CF**

PROMOTED CLUBS

 21 **Deportivo Alavés**

 22 **CD Leganés**

 23 **CA Osasuna**

KEY
● UEFA Champions League
● UEFA Europa League
● Promoted
● Relegated

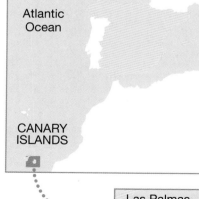

Atlantic
Ocean

CANARY
ISLANDS

Las Palmas
11
*GRAN
CANARIA*

Barcelona reign again in Spain

Luis Enrique's FC Barcelona were the top dogs in Spain for the second season in a row, retaining the Liga and Copa del Rey, but, like every UEFA Champions League winner before them, they were unable to make a successful defence of their continental crown.

Instead it was arch-rivals Real Madrid who replaced them as the kings of Europe, defeating Barça's conquerors Atlético Madrid on penalties in the final. Sevilla also completed a remarkable hat-trick of UEFA Europa League triumphs, but the national team's eight-year rule in Europe was brought to an end in France.

| League and cup retained by Catalan club | European trophies for Real Madrid and Sevilla | National team dethroned at UEFA EURO 2016 |

Domestic league

Barcelona's 24th Liga title was not acquired until the 38th and last match of the season, when a hat-trick by the division's leading marksman Luis Suárez defeated Granada 3-0 in southern Spain and ensured that they finished one point above Real Madrid, simultaneous victors a thousand or so kilometres away to the north at Deportivo La Coruña. Two points further back were Atlético, winners also on the final day, at home to Celta Vigo, but whose title hopes had been dashed a week earlier by a shock 2-1 defeat at bottom club Levante.

It was a surprise that Barça were run so close, because only a few weeks earlier they looked home and dry. Going into the second Clásico of the season, at Camp Nou in early April, they were ten points in front of Real Madrid and nine ahead of Atlético. Furthermore, Luis Enrique's men had gone 39 matches unbeaten in all competitions – a record run not just for Barcelona but for any Spanish club – and seemed well set for a second successive all-conquering campaign.

A two-goal lead surrendered in Barça's previous league match, a 2-2 draw at Villarreal, had ended a 13-match winning streak, but given the huge advantage they still held, and with

memories of a magnificent 4-0 win in November at the Santiago Bernabéu still fresh, it seemed fanciful to imagine that the champions would not go on to win a sixth Liga title in eight years. However, despite taking the lead against Madrid through defender Gerard Piqué, Barcelona would go on to lose the game, with Karim Benzema scoring a quick equaliser before Cristiano Ronaldo grabbed the winner five minutes before the end.

Barcelona were still in total command of the title race, but the frustration of losing to their great rivals at home left its mark, and suddenly all self-belief appeared to vanish when they lost their next two league games as well, 1-0 at Real Sociedad and 2-1 at home to Valencia (and in between were knocked out of the UEFA Champions League by Atlético). With Real Madrid taking confidence from their Camp Nou success and easily beating Eibar and Getafe – while Atlético surprisingly surrendered three points at Sporting Gijón – Barça now held first place only by virtue of their head-to-head superiority over Atlético (2-1 wins in both games), with Madrid just one point in arrears.

There were five games to go, and Barcelona knew that if they could regroup and win all five, against teams

in mid-table or lower down, they would be champions. It was a challenge to which they would rise in some style. Especially Suárez, who became the first player to score four goals in successive Liga games as he spearheaded brilliant 8-0 and 6-0 wins over Deportivo and Sporting, respectively, before adding one more in a 2-0 success at Real Betis, another two in a 5-0 victory at home to Espanyol and, finally, that all-important title-clinching hat-trick at Granada. To those 15 points required to secure first place Barça had added 24 goals, with their rampant Uruguayan scoring 14 of them – and boosting his end-of-season total to a formidable 40.

Suárez's South American strike partners Lionel Messi and Neymar contributed another 50 goals between them as Barcelona chalked up 112 for the season – two more than Madrid. En route to his tally of 26, Messi, who missed two months in the autumn with a knee injury, became the first Liga player to score 300 goals and he also passed the career milestone of 500 goals for club and country. Intriguingly, when he was sidelined in October and November, Suárez and Neymar scored 20 league goals in a row between them until skipper Andrés Iniesta ended that sequence with a stunning long-range strike in the 4-0 win at the Bernabéu

– where Messi returned from his lay-off as a second-half substitute.

While Barcelona's attacking trio inevitably hogged the headlines, praise for the title triumph was due also to stalwarts Iniesta, Piqué and Jordi Alba, while Croatian schemer Ivan Rakitić enjoyed a second season every bit as influential as his first. It was more or less the same personnel on show as in 2014/15, with new signings Arda Turan and Aleix Vidal not permitted to play until January and neither making a significant impact thereafter.

Real Madrid also stuck largely with the same team from the previous season, but they brought in a new coach, with Rafael Benítez replacing Carlo Ancelotti. Back in his home city, Benítez took Madrid to the top of the league in October, but a first defeat, 3-2 at Sevilla, was immediately followed by that calamitous Clásico in the Bernabéu, and despite leading the team to a 10-2 win over Rayo Vallecano just before Christmas, he was sacked early in the New Year, with the job passed on to B team coach and legendary former player Zinédine Zidane.

Zizou's only defeat in his first 20 Liga games came at home to Atlético at the end of February – when his fellow Frenchman Antoine Griezmann scored the only goal – and although that result ultimately proved costly, it was counterbalanced by the victory at Camp Nou and a closing 12-match winning run from March to May. Madrid's three-pronged attack was not quite as potent as Barcelona's, but Gareth Bale, Karim Benzema and Cristiano Ronaldo did manage 78 goals between them, with Ronaldo becoming the first player to score 30 or more in the Liga six seasons running. The Portuguese superstar also became Madrid's all-time record scorer during the campaign, overtaking Raúl, and he actually beat Messi to his 500th career goal by a few months – although the milestone was reached much later in terms of games played (749 as opposed to 632).

While Barcelona and Real Madrid thrilled Spanish crowds with their attacking play, Diego Simeone's Atlético accumulated points with similar regularity thanks to a finely-honed defend-and-counterattack style. Goalkeeper Jan Oblak's goal was

Real Madrid's Cristiano Ronaldo (right) is denied by Atlético goalkeeper Jan Oblak in a Liga derby at the Bernabéu

breached a mere 18 times, making him a clear winner of the Zamora trophy. Equally worthy of recognition were the players in front of him, notably central defensive linchpin Diego Godín, full-backs Juanfran and Filipe Luís and midfield grafters Gabi and Koke, while the Atlético attack was led with wonderful incision by Griezmann, who scored 22 Liga goals for the second straight season.

Atlético finished third with 88 points, which was 24 more than Villarreal chalked up to take fourth spot and book themselves a place in the UEFA Champions League play-offs. League leaders in early autumn after kicking off with five wins and a draw, Marcelino's team also enjoyed an excellent mid-season patch during which long-serving skipper Bruno Soriano and newly recruited striker Cédric Bakambu came to the fore.

Villarreal faded at the finish but had enough points in store to keep Athletic Club and Celta at arm's length and hold on to the position they had filled since Christmas. Ernesto Valverde's Athletic, who beat Barcelona 5-1 on aggregate in the Spanish Super Cup, were deeply indebted to the 20 goals of evergreen striker Aritz Aduriz for their fifth-place finish, while Celta, who inflicted a heaviest league defeat of the campaign on Barça when they overwhelmed them 4-1 in September, also possessed one of the stars of the season in 29-year-old winger Nolito.

Mid-table safety was all that Real Sociedad and Valencia could muster, the two clubs both dismissing British coaches during the campaign, with Scotsman David Moyes lasting one day short of a full year in San Sebastian and English TV pundit Gary Neville, the former Manchester United and England full-back, getting the sack less than four months after he was surprisingly appointed by Valencia in December. The battle to avoid relegation ended early for Levante, but Getafe and Rayo Vallecano maintained their hopes of survival until the final day, when Sporting rescued themselves with a win at home to Villarreal to ensure that none of the three newly promoted clubs went straight back down. Hoping to do likewise in 2016/17 were Segunda División champions Alavés, runners-up Leganes and play-off winners Osasuna.

Domestic cup

Six days after winning the league, Barcelona added a 28th Copa del Rey triumph to their honours list with a 2-0 extra-time victory over Sevilla at the Estadio Vicente Calderón. It was a hard-fought victory against the perennial UEFA Europa League winners, with Javier Mascherano seeing red in the first half and Barça holding out until the end of the regular 90 minutes, when Éver Banega was dismissed to make it ten against ten in the extra period. Messi set up both Jordi Alba and, in the final minute, Neymar to give Barça victory in a competition from which Real

Madrid had been expelled back in December when Benítez fielded an ineligible player, Russian midfielder Denis Cheryshev, in a fourth-round win at third-tier Cádiz.

Europe

Spain's dominance of European club football continued in 2015/16. For the third season in a row Liga sides won both the UEFA Champions League and UEFA Europa League, with Real Madrid succeeding Barcelona in the former and Unai Emery's Sevilla taking the spoils for the third successive year in the latter. With Barcelona also winning the UEFA Super Cup – 5-4 against Sevilla in a Tbilisi thriller – and the FIFA Club World Cup – 3-0 against River Plate in the Yokohama final – it was another season in which the rest of Europe could only look on in envy.

There were five Spanish clubs on the UEFA Champions League starting grid for the first time, so it was perhaps unsurprising that two of them should go on to contest the final, with Real Madrid piling further agony on Atlético as they defeated them on penalties in Milan – two years after snatching victory from the jaws of defeat against the same opponents in Lisbon. With his 16 goals, plus the winning penalty in the final, Cristiano Ronaldo deserved all the plaudits going as he inspired Madrid to their record-extending 11th European Cup triumph, but sympathy was widespread for Atlético, who had brilliantly upset the odds to eliminate holders Barcelona and Pep Guardiola's Bayern München in the two previous rounds.

While none of the Big Three were eliminated by non-Spanish opponents in the knockout phase of the UEFA Champions League, it was the same story in the UEFA Europa League until Villarreal felt the force of Jürgen Klopp's Liverpool in the second leg of their semi-final at Anfield. Sevilla, however, would extract Spanish revenge in the final, coming from behind to defeat the English side 3-1 in Basel and lift the trophy for an unprecedented third successive season. They also booked a return ticket to the UEFA Champions League, although coach Emery would not be around for that as he departed in the summer for Paris Saint-Germain, with ex-Chile coach Jorge Sampaoli recruited to replace him.

National team

Spain's quest to win the UEFA European Championship for a third successive tournament began brightly when, with Iniesta in top form, they beat the Czech Republic and Turkey in their opening two group fixtures to qualify for the knockout phase with a game to spare. But a 2-1 defeat to Croatia – in which they took the lead, with Álvaro Morata's third goal of the tournament, but then missed a penalty and conceded a late winner – thrust them into a last-16 engagement with Italy at the Stade de France.

Although they had defeated the Azzurri en route to their trophy successes in 2008 (on penalties in the quarter-final) and 2012 (4-0 in the final), they were a clear second-best to Antonio Conte's side in the rain of Saint-Denis, with only the heroics between the posts of David de Gea – selected ahead of the man who had just become Europe's most-capped footballer, Iker Casillas – keeping the score down to 2-0.

Coach Vicente del Bosque had announced long before the tournament that he would be stepping down at the end of it, and the man who led Spain to their 2010 FIFA World Cup and UEFA EURO 2012 victories duly departed. The reins were then passed on to Julen Lopetegui, a winning coach at European level with Spain's Under-19 and Under-21 sides but dismissed from his club job at FC Porto midway through the 2015/16 campaign. The 50-year-old's first task is to steer Spain safely through a 2018 World Cup qualifying campaign that will feature two further mouth-watering clashes with Italy.

Álvaro Morata (right) heads Spain into the lead in their UEFA EURO 2016 victory against Turkey

DOMESTIC SEASON AT A GLANCE

Liga 2015/16 final table

		Pld	Home					Away					Total					Pts
			W	D	L	F	A	W	D	L	F	A	W	D	L	F	A	
1	**FC Barcelona**	38	16	1	2	67	14	13	3	3	45	15	29	4	5	112	29	91
2	Real Madrid CF	38	16	1	2	70	16	12	5	2	40	18	28	6	4	110	34	90
3	Club Atlético de Madrid	38	15	3	1	33	7	13	1	5	30	11	28	4	6	63	18	88
4	Villarreal CF	38	12	4	3	26	12	6	6	7	18	23	18	10	10	44	35	64
5	Athletic Club	38	11	4	4	35	17	7	4	8	23	28	18	8	12	58	45	62
6	RC Celta de Vigo	38	9	6	4	29	25	8	3	8	22	34	17	9	12	51	59	60
7	Sevilla FC	38	14	1	4	38	21	0	9	10	13	29	14	10	14	51	50	52
8	Málaga CF	38	8	6	5	26	15	4	6	9	12	20	12	12	14	38	35	48
9	Real Sociedad de Fútbol	38	7	5	7	22	20	6	4	9	23	28	13	9	16	45	48	48
10	Real Betis Balompié	38	6	6	7	17	23	5	6	8	17	29	11	12	15	34	52	45
11	UD Las Palmas	38	8	5	6	25	17	4	3	12	20	36	12	8	18	45	53	44
12	Valencia CF	38	6	7	6	25	23	5	4	10	21	25	11	11	16	46	48	44
13	RCD Espanyol	38	9	5	5	22	28	3	2	14	18	46	12	7	19	40	74	43
14	SD Eibar	38	8	5	6	26	22	3	5	11	23	39	11	10	17	49	61	43
15	RC Deportivo La Coruña	38	4	8	7	25	34	4	10	5	20	27	8	18	12	45	61	42
16	Granada CF	38	6	5	8	26	31	4	4	11	20	38	10	9	19	46	69	39
17	Real Sporting de Gijón	38	7	4	8	28	28	3	5	11	12	34	10	9	19	40	62	39
18	Rayo Vallecano de Madrid	38	8	4	7	29	29	1	7	11	23	44	9	11	18	52	73	38
19	Getafe CF	38	6	7	6	23	20	3	2	14	14	47	9	9	20	37	67	36
20	Levante UD	38	7	5	7	23	26	1	3	15	14	44	8	8	22	37	70	32

European qualification 2016/17

Champion/Cup winner: FC Barcelona (group stage)
Real Madrid CF (group stage)
Club Atlético de Madrid (group stage)
Sevilla FC (group stage)
Villarreal CF (play-offs)

Athletic Club (group stage)
RC Celta de Vigo (group stage)

Top scorer	Luis Suárez (Barcelona), 40 goals
Relegated clubs	Levante UD, Getafe CF, Rayo Vallecano de Madrid
Promoted clubs	Deportivo Alavés, CD Leganés, CA Osasuna
Cup final	FC Barcelona 2-0 Sevilla FC (aet)

Player of the season

Luis Suárez
(FC Barcelona)

Suárez had long been renowned for his prolific goalscoring, but in 2015/16, his first complete season as a Barcelona player, his feats surpassed anything he had managed before – for Ajax, Liverpool or Uruguay. With his 40 Liga goals he became the first player for seven years other than Lionel Messi or Cristiano Ronaldo to win the prestigious Pichichi trophy, and he added a further 19 goals in other competitions, including eight in the UEFA Champions League and five in two matches at the FIFA Club World Cup.

Newcomer of the season

Cédric Bakambu
(Villarreal CF)

An impressive 2014/15 season in Turkey with Bursaspor brought Bakambu to Villarreal on a five-year contract. Although he arrived at El Madrigal as a relative unknown, by the end of the season the DR Congo international had made a name for himself not only as a scorer of important goals in the Liga, with 12 in total, but also as Villarreal's sharpest attacking weapon in their run to the UEFA Europa League semi-finals, scoring nine times and finishing second in the competition's goal charts behind Athletic Club's Aritz Aduriz.

Team of the season
(4-3-3)

Coach: Simeone *(Atlético)*

Oblak *(Atlético)*

Juanfran *(Atlético)* · Godín *(Atlético)* · Piqué *(Barcelona)* · Filipe Luís *(Atlético)*

Rakitić *(Barcelona)* · Koke *(Atlético)* · Iniesta *(Barcelona)*

Messi *(Barcelona)* · Suárez *(Barcelona)* · Cristiano Ronaldo *(Real Madrid)*

NATIONAL TEAM

International honours
FIFA World Cup (1) 2010
UEFA European Championship (3) 1964, 2008, 2012

International tournament appearances
FIFA World Cup (14) 1934, 1950 (4th), 1962, 1966, 1978, 1982 (2nd phase), 1986 (qtr-finals), 1990 (2nd round), 1994 (qtr-finals), 1998, 2002 (qtr-finals), 2006 (2nd round), 2010 (Winners), 2014
UEFA European Championship (10) 1964 (Winners), 1980, 1984 (runners-up), 1988, 1996 (qtr-finals), 2000 (qtr-finals), 2004, 2008 (Winners), 2012 (Winners), 2016 (round of 16)

Top five all-time caps
Iker Casillas (167); **Sergio Ramos** (136); Xavi Hernández (133); Andoni Zubizarreta (126); Xabi Alonso (114)

Top five all-time goals
David Villa (59); Raúl González (44); Fernando Torres (38); Fernando Hierro (29); Fernando Morientes (27)

Results 2015/16

Date	Opponent		Venue	Result		Scorers
05/09/15	Slovakia (ECQ)	H	Oviedo	W	2-0	Jordi Alba (5), Iniesta (30p)
08/09/15	FYR Macedonia (ECQ)	A	Skopje	W	1-0	Pacovski (8og)
09/10/15	Luxembourg (ECQ)	H	Logrono	W	4-0	Santi Cazorla (42, 85), Paco Alcácer (67, 80)
12/10/15	Ukraine (ECQ)	A	Kyiv	W	1-0	Mario (22)
13/11/15	England	H	Alicante	W	2-0	Mario (71), Santi Cazorla (84)
24/03/16	Italy	A	Udine	D	1-1	Aduriz (70)
27/03/16	Romania	A	Cluj-Napoca	D	0-0	
29/05/16	Bosnia & Herzegovina	N	St Gallen (SUI)	W	3-1	Nolito (11, 18), Pedro (90+4)
01/06/16	South Korea	N	Salzburg (AUT)	W	6-1	Silva (30), Fàbregas (32), Nolito (38, 54), Morata (50, 89)
07/06/16	Georgia	H	Getafe	L	0-1	
13/06/16	Czech Republic (ECF)	N	Toulouse (FRA)	W	1-0	Piqué (87)
17/06/16	Turkey (ECF)	N	Nice (FRA)	W	3-0	Morata (34, 48), Nolito (37)
21/06/16	Croatia (ECF)	N	Bordeaux (FRA)	L	1-2	Morata (7)
27/06/16	Italy (ECF)	N	Saint-Denis (FRA)	L	0-2	

Appearances 2015/16

Coach: Vicente del Bosque	23/12/50		SVK	MKD	LUX	UKR	Eng	Ita	Rou	Bih	Kor	Geo	CZE	TUR	CRO	ITA	Caps	Goals
Iker Casillas	20/05/81	Porto (POR)	G		G		G				G74						167	
Juanfran	09/01/85	Atlético	D		D			D79				D46	D	D	D	D	22	1
Gerard Piqué	02/02/87	Barcelona	D	D	D		D	D	D52		D59	D	D	D	D	D	81	5
Sergio Ramos	30/03/86	Real Madrid	D	D				D46				D46	D	D81	D	D	136	10
Jordi Alba	21/03/89	Barcelona	D		D	s75	D	s79	D		s46	D	D	D81	D		47	6
Sergio Busquets	16/07/88	Barcelona	M	M	M	s85	M78				s46	M76	M	M	M	M	88	2
Andrés Iniesta	11/05/84	Barcelona	M85	s78			M46				M46	s46	M	M	M	M	113	12
Cesc Fàbregas	04/05/87	Chelsea (ENG)	M67		M	M64	M	M	s59	M60	M46	M46	M70	M71	M84	M	110	15
David Silva	08/01/86	Man. City (ENG)	A	A	A11			s71	M79	M46	A46	s61	A	A64	A		103	24
Pedro Rodríguez	28/07/87	Chelsea (ENG)	A		A77		s74		M67	s46	s46	s76	s82			s81	60	17
Diego Costa	07/10/88	Chelsea (ENG)	A75	A61			A63										10	1
Santi Cazorla	13/12/84	Arsenal (ENG)	s67	M68	M		s27										77	14
Paco Alcácer	30/08/93	Valencia	s75	s61	s33	A85	A74	s86	A59								13	6
Koke	08/01/92	Atlético	s85	s68			s78	s46	M			s46		s71			24	
David de Gea	07/11/90	Man. United (ENG)		G		G	G					G	G	G	G	G	13	-
Daniel Carvajal	11/01/92	Real Madrid		D													5	-
Juan Bernat	01/03/93	Bayern (GER)		D													7	1
Isco	21/04/92	Real Madrid		M78		M		s61	s46								14	1
Juan Mata	28/04/88	Man. United (ENG)		A	s11	s64	s63	M46	s67								40	10
Marc Bartra	15/01/91	Barcelona		D		D82		D	D	D							10	-
Álvaro Morata	23/10/92	Juventus (ITA)		A33				M86	s79		A		A62	A	A67	A70	13	6
Nolito	15/10/86	Celta		s77	M75	s46		M46	M60	A	A	A82	A	A60	A46	13	5
Mario Gaspar	24/11/90	Villarreal		D	D		D										3	2
Xabier Etxeita	31/10/87	Athletic		D													1	-
Nacho	18/01/90	Real Madrid		D			s46	s52									4	-
César Azpilicueta	28/08/89	Chelsea (ENG)		D	s82	D		D	D46				s81				16	-
Mikel San José	30/05/89	Athletic		M		M		D83			s46						7	-
Thiago Alcántara	11/04/91	Bayern (GER)		M	M27	M61				s46	M46	s70		s84			12	-
Aritz Aduriz	11/02/81	Athletic		A71	s59	A46	s59	A	s62		s67	s46/81					9	1
Sergi Roberto	07/02/92	Barcelona			M59												1	-
Sergio Asenjo	28/06/89	Villarreal					G										1	-
Héctor Bellerín	19/03/95	Arsenal (ENG)				D	D	s46									3	-
Bruno Soriano	12/06/84	Villarreal				M	M			s64	s60						10	-
Marco Asensio	21/01/96	Espanyol					M60										1	-
Denis Suárez	06/01/94	Villarreal					s46										1	-
Diego Llorente	16/08/93	Rayo Vallecano					s60										1	-
Iñaki Williams	15/06/94	Athletic					s60										1	-
Mikel Oyarzabal	21/04/97	Real Sociedad					s60										1	-
Pablo Fornals	22/02/96	Málaga					s83										1	-
Sergio Rico	01/09/93	Sevilla						s74			G						1	-
Lucas Vázquez	01/07/91	Real Madrid										A61			s70		2	-

EUROPE

FC Barcelona

Group E
Match 1 - AS Roma (ITA)
A 1-1 *Suárez (21)*
Ter Stegen, Piqué, Rakitić (Rafinha 61; Mascherano 65), Busquets, Iniesta, Suárez, Messi, Neymar, Jordi Alba, Sergi Roberto, Mathieu. Coach: Luis Enrique (ESP)
Match 2 - Bayer 04 Leverkusen (GER)
H 2-1 *Sergi Roberto (80), Suárez (82)*
Ter Stegen, Piqué, Rakitić (Sergi Roberto 72), Busquets, Dani Alves, Iniesta (Jordi Alba 60), Suárez, Neymar, Mascherano, Sandro Ramírez (Munir 63), Mathieu. Coach: Luis Enrique (ESP)
Match 3 - FC BATE Borisov (BLR)
A 2-0 *Suárez (48, 64)*
Ter Stegen, Piqué, Busquets (Gerard Gumbau 72), Dani Alves, Suárez, Neymar, Mascherano, Bartra, Munir (Sandro Ramírez 70), Jordi Alba, Sergi Roberto (Rakitić 18). Coach: Luis Enrique (ESP)
Match 4 - FC BATE Borisov (BLR)
H 3-0 *Neymar (30p, 83), Suárez (60)*
Ter Stegen, Rakitić (Munir 20), Busquets (Gerard Gumbau 76), Dani Alves, Iniesta (Bartra 68), Suárez, Neymar, Mascherano, Sergi Roberto, Adriano, Vermaelen. Coach: Luis Enrique (ESP)
Match 5 - AS Roma (ITA)
H 6-1 *Suárez (15, 44), Messi (18, 60), Piqué (56), Adriano (77)*
Ter Stegen, Piqué (Bartra 56), Rakitić, Busquets (Sergi Samper 46), Dani Alves, Suárez, Messi, Neymar, Jordi Alba, Sergi Roberto (Adriano 64), Vermaelen. Coach: Luis Enrique (ESP)
Match 6 - Bayer 04 Leverkusen (GER)
A 1-1 *Messi (20)*
Ter Stegen, Rakitić, Messi, Bartra, Munir, Jordi Alba (Cámara 74), Sandro Ramírez, Adriano, Vermaelen, Sergi Samper, Kaptoum (Gerard Gumbau 62). Coach: Luis Enrique (ESP)

Round of 16 - Arsenal FC (ENG)
A 2-0 *Messi (71, 83p)*
Ter Stegen, Piqué, Rakitić, Busquets, Dani Alves, Iniesta, Suárez, Messi, Neymar, Mascherano, Jordi Alba. Coach: Luis Enrique (ESP)
H 3-1 *Neymar (18), Suárez (65), Messi (88)*
Ter Stegen, Rakitić (Arda Turan 77), Busquets, Dani Alves, Iniesta (Sergi Roberto 72), Suárez, Messi, Neymar, Mascherano, Jordi Alba, Mathieu. Coach: Luis Enrique (ESP)

Quarter-finals - Club Atlético de Madrid (ESP)
H 2-1 *Suárez (63, 74)*
Ter Stegen, Piqué, Rakitić (Rafinha 63), Busquets (Sergi Roberto 80), Dani Alves, Iniesta (Arda Turan 83), Suárez, Messi, Neymar, Jordi Alba. Coach: Luis Enrique (ESP)
A 0-2
Ter Stegen, Piqué, Rakitić (Arda Turan 64), Busquets, Dani Alves (Sergi Roberto 64), Iniesta, Suárez, Messi, Neymar, Jordi Alba. Coach: Luis Enrique (ESP)

Real Madrid CF

Group A
Match 1 - FC Shakhtar Donetsk (UKR)
H 4-0 *Benzema (30), Cristiano Ronaldo (55p, 63p, 81)*
Navas, Varane (Pepe 46), Sergio Ramos (Nacho 59), Cristiano Ronaldo, Kroos, Benzema, Bale (Kovačić 31), Marcelo, Carvajal, Modrić, Isco. Coach: Rafael Benítez (ESP)
Match 2 - Malmö FF (SWE)
A 2-0 *Cristiano Ronaldo (29, 90)*
Navas, Varane, Nacho, Cristiano Ronaldo, Kroos, Benzema (Modrić 67), Casemiro, Carvajal, Kovačić (Lucas Vázquez 73), Arbeloa, Isco (Cheryshev 83). Coach: Rafael Benítez (ESP)
Match 3 - Paris Saint-Germain (FRA)
A 0-0
Navas, Varane, Sergio Ramos, Cristiano Ronaldo, Kroos, Marcelo, Casemiro, Lucas Vázquez, Jesé (Cheryshev 73), Isco (Modrić 69), Danilo. Coach: Rafael Benítez (ESP)
Match 4 - Paris Saint-Germain (FRA)
H 1-0 *Nacho (35)*
Navas, Varane, Sergio Ramos, Cristiano Ronaldo, Kroos, Marcelo (Nacho 33), Casemiro, Modrić, Jesé (Lucas Vázquez 63), Isco (Kovačić 82), Danilo. Coach: Rafael Benítez (ESP)
Match 5 - FC Shakhtar Donetsk (UKR)
A 4-3 *Cristiano Ronaldo (18, 70), Modrić (50), Carvajal (52)*
Casilla, Varane (Danilo 32), Pepe, Nacho, Cristiano Ronaldo, Bale (Benzema 71), Casemiro, Carvajal, Kovačić, Modrić (Kroos 62), Isco. Coach: Rafael Benítez (ESP)
Match 6 - Malmö FF (SWE)
H 8-0 *Benzema (12, 24, 74), Cristiano Ronaldo (39, 47, 50, 59), Kovačić (70)*
Casilla, Pepe (Marcelo 53), Nacho, Cristiano Ronaldo, Benzema, James Rodríguez (Jesé 65), Casemiro, Kovačić (Cheryshev 76), Arbeloa, Isco, Danilo. Coach: Rafael Benítez (ESP)

Round of 16 - AS Roma (ITA)
A 2-0 *Cristiano Ronaldo (57), Jesé (86)*
Navas, Varane, Sergio Ramos, Cristiano Ronaldo (Casemiro 89), Kroos, Benzema, James Rodríguez (Jesé 82), Marcelo, Carvajal, Modrić, Isco (Kovačić 64). Coach: Zinédine Zidane (FRA)
H 2-0 *Cristiano Ronaldo (64), James Rodríguez (68)*
Navas, Pepe, Sergio Ramos, Cristiano Ronaldo, Kroos, James Rodríguez, Bale (Lucas Vázquez 61), Marcelo, Casemiro (Kovačić 84), Modrić (Jesé 76), Danilo. Coach: Zinédine Zidane (FRA)

Quarter-finals - VfL Wolfsburg (GER)
A 0-2
Navas, Pepe, Sergio Ramos, Cristiano Ronaldo, Kroos (James Rodríguez 85), Benzema (Jesé 41), Bale, Marcelo, Casemiro, Modrić (Isco 64), Danilo. Coach: Zinédine Zidane (FRA)
H 3-0 *Cristiano Ronaldo (15, 17, 77)*
Navas, Pepe, Sergio Ramos, Cristiano Ronaldo, Kroos, Benzema (Jesé 84), Bale, Marcelo, Casemiro, Carvajal, Modrić (Varane 90+2). Coach: Zinédine Zidane (FRA)

Semi-finals - Manchester City FC (ENG)
A 0-0
Navas, Pepe, Sergio Ramos, Kroos (Isco 90), Benzema (Jesé 46), Bale, Marcelo, Carvajal, Lucas Vázquez, Modrić. Coach: Zinédine Zidane (FRA)
H 1-0 *Fernando (20og)*
Navas, Pepe, Sergio Ramos, Cristiano Ronaldo, Kroos, Bale, Marcelo, Carvajal, Modrić (Kovačić 88), Jesé (Lucas Vázquez 56), Isco (James Rodríguez 67). Coach: Zinédine Zidane (FRA)

Final - Club Atlético de Madrid (ESP)
N 1-1 (aet; 5-3 on pens) *Sergio Ramos (15)*
Navas, Pepe, Sergio Ramos, Cristiano Ronaldo, Kroos (Isco 72), Benzema (Lucas Vázquez 77), Bale, Marcelo, Casemiro, Carvajal (Danilo 52), Modrić. Coach: Zinédine Zidane (FRA)

Club Atlético de Madrid

Group C
Match 1 - Galatasaray AŞ (TUR)
A 2-0 *Griezmann (18, 25)*
Oblak, Godín, Siqueira, Tiago, Koke, Griezmann, Martínez (Fernando Torres 60), Saúl Ñíguez (Óliver Torres 80), Juanfran, Vietto (Gabi 62), Giménez. Coach: Diego Simeone (ARG)
Match 2 - SL Benfica (POR)
H 1-2 *Correa (23)*
Oblak, Godín, Filipe Luís, Tiago, Griezmann (Vietto 71), Óliver Torres (Saúl Ñíguez 63), Martínez, Gabi, Correa (Fernando Torres 77), Juanfran, Carrasco. Coach: Diego Simeone (ARG)
Match 3 - FC Astana (KAZ)
H 4-0 *Saúl Ñíguez (23), Martínez (29), Óliver Torres (63), Dedechko (89og)*
Oblak, Godín, Siqueira, Tiago (Óliver Torres 46), Griezmann (Correa 58), Martínez (Fernando Torres 67), Gabi, Savić, Saúl Ñíguez, Juanfran, Carrasco. Coach: Diego Simeone (ARG)
Match 4 - FC Astana (KAZ)
A 0-0
Oblak, Godín, Siqueira, Tiago, Koke (Óliver Torres 82), Griezmann, Fernando Torres (Martínez 64), Gabi, Saúl Ñíguez (Carrasco 73), Juanfran, Giménez. Coach: Diego Simeone (ARG)
Match 5 - Galatasaray AŞ (TUR)
H 2-0 *Griezmann (13, 65)*
Oblak, Godín, Filipe Luís, Tiago (Saúl Ñíguez 75), Koke, Griezmann (Vietto 68), Fernando Torres, Gabi, Jesús Gámez, Carrasco (Óliver Torres 71), Giménez. Coach: Diego Simeone (ARG)
Match 6 - SL Benfica (POR)
A 2-1 *Saúl Ñíguez (33), Vietto (55)*
Oblak, Godín, Filipe Luís, Koke, Griezmann (Giménez 90+2), Gabi, Savić, Saúl Ñíguez, Juanfran, Carrasco (Óliver Torres 73), Vietto (Fernando Torres 63). Coach: Diego Simeone (ARG)

Round of 16 - PSV Eindhoven (NED)
A 0-0
Oblak, Godín, Filipe Luís, Koke, Griezmann, Óliver Torres, Gabi, Savić, Saúl Ñíguez (Correa 74), Juanfran, Vietto (Fernando Torres 61). Coach: Diego Simeone (ARG)
H 0-0 (aet; 8-7 on pens)
Oblak, Godín (Hernández 89), Filipe Luís, Koke, Griezmann, Fernández (Fernando Torres 56), Gabi, Saúl Ñíguez, Juanfran, Carrasco (Kranevitter 75), Giménez. Coach: Diego Simeone (ARG)

Quarter-finals - FC Barcelona (ESP)
A 1-2 *Fernando Torres (25)*
Oblak, Godín, Filipe Luís, Koke, Griezmann (Partey 76), Fernando Torres, Gabi, Saúl Ñíguez (Correa 90), Hernández, Juanfran, Carrasco (Fernández 53). Coach: Diego Simeone (ARG)
Red card: Fernando Torres 35
H 2-0 *Griezmann (36, 88p)*
Oblak, Godín, Filipe Luís, Koke, Griezmann (Correa 90), Fernández (Savić 90+3), Gabi, Saúl Ñíguez, Hernández, Juanfran, Carrasco (Partey 74). Coach: Diego Simeone (ARG)

Semi-finals - FC Bayern München (GER)
H 1-0 *Saúl Ñíguez (11)*
Oblak, Filipe Luís, Koke, Griezmann, Fernando Torres, Fernández, Gabi, Savić, Saúl Ñíguez (Partey 85), Juanfran, Giménez. Coach: Diego Simeone (ARG)
A 1-2 *Griezmann (54)*
Oblak, Godín, Filipe Luís, Koke (Savić 90+3), Griezmann (Partey 82), Fernando Torres, Fernández (Carrasco 46), Gabi, Saúl Ñíguez, Juanfran, Giménez. Coach: Diego Simeone (ARG)

Final - Real Madrid CF (ESP)
N 1-1 (aet; 3-5 on pens) *Carrasco (79)*
Oblak, Godín, Filipe Luís (Hernández 109), Koke (Partey 116), Griezmann, Fernando Torres, Fernández (Carrasco 46), Gabi, Savić, Saúl Ñíguez, Juanfran. Coach: Diego Simeone (ARG)

Sevilla FC

CHAMPIONS LEAGUE

Group D
Match 1 - VfL Borussia Mönchengladbach (GER)
H 3-0 *Gameiro (47p), Éver Banega (66p), Konoplyanka (84)*
Sergio Rico, Trémoulinas, Krychowiak, Kolodziejczak, Gameiro (Immobile 71), Reyes (Konoplyanka 83), N'Zonzi, Andreolli, Éver Banega (Krohn-Dehli 76), Vitolo, Coke. Coach: Unai Emery (ESP)
Match 2 – Juventus FC (ITA)
A 0-2
Sergio Rico, Trémoulinas, Krychowiak, Kolodziejczak, Krohn-Dehli, Gameiro (Immobile 66), Reyes (Juan Muñoz 79), N'Zonzi, Andreolli, Konoplyanka, Coke. Coach: Unai Emery (ESP)
Match 3 - Manchester City FC (ENG)
A 1-2 *Konoplyanka (30)*
Sergio Rico, Trémoulinas, Rami, Krychowiak, Kolodziejczak, Iborra, Gameiro, Éver Banega (Krohn-Dehli 66), Vitolo, Konoplyanka (N'Zonzi 78), Coke (Mariano 84). Coach: Unai Emery (ESP)
Match 4 - Manchester City FC (ENG)
H 1-3 *Trémoulinas (25)*
Sergio Rico, Trémoulinas, Rami, Krychowiak, Kolodziejczak, Iborra (Krohn-Dehli 46), Éver Banega, Vitolo, Konoplyanka, Coke (Mariano 55), Llorente (Immobile 65). Coach: Unai Emery (ESP)
Match 5 - VfL Borussia Mönchengladbach (GER)
A 2-4 *Vitolo (82), Éver Banega (90+1p)*
Sergio Rico, Trémoulinas, Rami, Krychowiak, Kolodziejczak, Krohn-Dehli (N'Zonzi 64), Gameiro (Llorente 76), Éver Banega, Vitolo, Konoplyanka, Coke (Mariano 82). Coach: Unai Emery (ESP)
Match 6 – Juventus FC (ITA)
H 1-0 *Llorente (65)*
Sergio Rico, Trémoulinas, Rami, Krychowiak, Kolodziejczak (Mariano 57), N'Zonzi, Éver Banega, Vitolo, Konoplyanka (Krohn-Dehli 68), Coke, Llorente (Gameiro 77). Coach: Unai Emery (ESP)

EUROPA LEAGUE

Round of 32 - Molde FK (NOR)
H 3-0 *Llorente (35, 49), Gameiro (72)*
Soria, Kolodziejczak, Daniel Carriço, Krohn-Dehli (Konoplyanka 73), Cristóforo (Iborra 69), N'Zonzi, Sergio Escudero, Éver Banega, Vitolo, Coke, Llorente (Gameiro 57). Coach: Unai Emery (ESP)
A 0-1
Soria, Kolodziejczak, Daniel Carriço, Iborra, Reyes (Krohn-Dehli 55), Sergio Escudero, Éver Banega, Konoplyanka (Figueiras 80), Llorente (Gameiro 62), Mariano, Fazio. Coach: Unai Emery (ESP)

Round of 16 - FC Basel 1893 (SUI)
A 0-0
Soria, Trémoulinas, Rami, Kolodziejczak, Krohn-Dehli, Gameiro (Llorente 73), Cristóforo, N'Zonzi, Éver Banega (Daniel Carriço 90+3), Vitolo (Konoplyanka 64), Coke. Coach: Unai Emery (ESP)
Red card: N'Zonzi 87
H 3-0 *Rami (35), Gameiro (44, 45)*
Soria, Trémoulinas, Rami, Kolodziejczak, Krohn-Dehli (Sergio Escudero 52), Iborra (Krychowiak 61), Gameiro (Llorente 69), Reyes, Cristóforo, Éver Banega, Mariano. Coach: Unai Emery (ESP)

Quarter-finals - Athletic Club (ESP)
A 2-1 *Kolodziejczak (56), Iborra (83)*
Soria, Trémoulinas (Fazio 12), Rami, Krychowiak, Kolodziejczak, Krohn-Dehli (Konoplyanka 68), Gameiro, N'Zonzi, Éver Banega (Iborra 74), Vitolo, Coke. Coach: Unai Emery (ESP)

H 1-2 (aet; 5-4 on pens) *Gameiro (59)*
Soria, Rami, Krychowiak, Kolodziejczak, Krohn-Dehli (Konoplyanka 51), Iborra (Cristóforo 66), Gameiro, N'Zonzi, Sergio Escudero, Vitolo, Mariano (Coke 100). Coach: Unai Emery (ESP)

Semi-finals - FC Shakhtar Donetsk (UKR)
A 2-2 *Vitolo (6), Gameiro (82p)*
Soria, Rami, Krychowiak, Daniel Carriço, Gameiro, N'Zonzi, Sergio Escudero, Éver Banega, Vitolo, Konoplyanka (Krohn-Dehli 59; Coke 72), Mariano. Coach: Unai Emery (ESP)
H 3-1 *Gameiro (9, 47), Mariano (59)*
Soria, Trémoulinas (Sergio Escudero 73), Rami, Krychowiak, Daniel Carriço, Gameiro (Iborra 82) N'Zonzi, Banega (Cristóforo 89), Vitolo, Coke, Mariano. Coach: Unai Emery (ESP)

Final - Liverpool FC (ENG)
N 3-1 *Gameiro (46), Coke (64, 70)*
Soria, Rami, Krychowiak, Daniel Carriço, Gameiro (Iborra 89), N'Zonzi, Sergio Escudero, Éver Banega (Cristóforo 90+3), Vitolo, Coke, Mariano. Coach: Unai Emery (ESP)

Valencia CF

CHAMPIONS LEAGUE

Play-offs - AS Monaco FC (FRA)
H 3-1 *Rodrigo (4), Parejo (59), Feghouli (86)*
Ryan, Rúben Vezo, Mustafi, Feghouli, Paco Alcácer (Javi Fuego 66), Parejo, Gayá, Pérez (Negredo 76), Rodrigo, Barragán, De Paul (Piatti 56). Coach: Nuno Espírito Santo (POR)
A 1-2 *Negredo (4)*
Ryan, Rúben Vezo, Mustafi, Negredo (Paco Alcácer 60), Feghouli, Parejo, Gayá, Pérez (Danilo 77), Rodrigo (Piatti 65), Javi Fuego, Barragán. Coach: Nuno Espírito Santo (POR)

Group H
Match 1 - FC Zenit (RUS)
H 2-3 *João Cancelo (55), André Gomes (73)*
Doménech, João Cancelo, Mustafi, Negredo, Feghouli (Rodrigo 71), Parejo, Piatti (André Gomes 46), Gayá, Pérez, Javi Fuego (Paco Alcácer 46), Abdennour. Coach: Nuno Espírito Santo (POR)
Match 2 - Olympique Lyonnais (FRA)
A 1-0 *Feghouli (42)*
Doménech, João Cancelo, Mustafi, Orbán, Negredo (Rodrigo 71), Feghouli, Parejo, Piatti, Pérez (Danilo 84), Javi Fuego, Abdennour (Aderlan Santos 59). Coach: Nuno Espírito Santo (POR)
Match 3 - KAA Gent (BEL)
H 2-1 *Feghouli (15), Mitrović (72og)*
Doménech, João Cancelo, Aderlan Santos, Mustafi, Feghouli, Paco Alcácer (Danilo 82), Parejo (Rodrigo 68), Gayá, Javi Fuego, André Gomes, Santi Mina (Piatti 61). Coach: Nuno Espírito Santo (POR)
Match 4 - KAA Gent (BEL)
A 0-1
Doménech, Aderlan Santos, Mustafi, Feghouli (João Cancelo 70), Paco Alcácer, Parejo, Gayá, Pérez, Javi Fuego (André Gomes 63), Barragán, Santi Mina (Piatti 46). Coach: Nuno Espírito Santo (POR)
Match 5 - FC Zenit (RUS)
A 0-2
Doménech, João Cancelo (De Paul 79), Rúben Vezo, Feghouli, Paco Alcácer, Parejo, Gayá, Pérez (Danilo 73), André Gomes, Abdennour, Mir (Santi Mina 56). Coach: Nuno Espírito Santo (POR)
Red card: Rúben Vezo 80
Match 6 - Olympique Lyonnais (FRA)
H 0-2
Doménech, João Cancelo, Mustafi, Paco Alcácer, Parejo, Danilo (Negredo 52), Gayá, Pérez (Javi Fuego 24), De Paul (Piatti 75), Santi Mina, Abdennour. Coach: Gary Neville (ENG)

EUROPA LEAGUE

Round of 32 - SK Rapid Wien (AUT)
H 6-0 *Santi Mina (4, 25), Parejo (10), Negredo (29), André Gomes (35), Rodrigo (89)*
Ryan, João Cancelo (Barragán 76), Rúben Vezo, Aderlan Santos, Negredo, Parejo (Javi Fuego 59), Piatti, Danilo, Gayá, André Gomes (Rodrigo 68), Santi Mina. Coach: Gary Neville (ENG)
A 4-0 *Rodrigo (59), Feghouli (64), Piatti (72), Rúben Vezo (88)*
Ryan, Rúben Vezo, Mustafi, Negredo (Mir 65), Feghouli, Piatti, Danilo, Gayá (Lato 46), Rodrigo, Javi Fuego (Tropi 79), Barragán. Coach: Gary Neville (ENG)

Round of 16 - Athletic Club (ESP)
A 0-1
Ryan, Mustafi, Negredo, Parejo (Paco Alcácer 82), Piatti (André Gomes 70), Danilo, Gayá, Rodrigo (Feghouli 86), Javi Fuego, Barragán, Abdennour. Coach: Gary Neville (ENG)
H 2-1 *Santi Mina (13), Aderlan Santos (37)*
Ryan, Rúben Vezo, Aderlan Santos, Mustafi, Negredo, Danilo, Gayá, Rodrigo (Feghouli 74), Javi Fuego (Parejo 68), André Gomes (Paco Alcácer 83), Santi Mina. Coach: Gary Neville (ENG)

Villarreal CF

EUROPA LEAGUE

Group E
Match 1 - SK Rapid Wien (AUT)
A 1-2 *Léo Baptistão (45)*
Barbosa, Jokič, Víctor Ruiz, Samuel (Samu Castillejo 46), Jonathan dos Santos, Léo Baptistão, Denis Suárez (Nahuel 79), Adrián López (Bakambu 68), Bruno Soriano, Rukavina, Bonera. Coach: Marcelino (ESP)
Match 2 - FC Viktoria Plzeň (CZE)
H 1-0 *Léo Baptistão (54)*
Barbosa, Víctor Ruiz, Jonathan dos Santos (Trigueros 76), Soldado, Léo Baptistão, Jaume Costa, Samu Castillejo, Bruno Soriano, Rukavina, Bailly, Nahuel (Samuel 83). Coach: Marcelino (ESP)
Match 3 - FC Dinamo Minsk (BLR)
H 4-0 *Bakambu (17, 32), Soldado (61), Bailly (71)*
Barbosa, Jokič, Pina (Trigueros 62), Víctor Ruiz, Samuel, Jonathan dos Santos, Soldado, Bakambu (Nahuel 46), Denis Suárez (Samu Castillejo 67), Rukavina, Bailly. Coach: Marcelino (ESP)
Match 4 - FC Dinamo Minsk (BLR)
A 2-1 *Soldado (72p), Politevich (86og)*
Barbosa, Mario Gaspar, Jokič, Pina (Jonathan dos Santos 62), Víctor Ruiz, Samuel, Trigueros, Bakambu, Samu Castillejo (Denis Suárez 73), Rukavina, Nahuel (Soldado 46). Coach: Marcelino (ESP)
Match 5 - SK Rapid Wien (AUT)
H 1-0 *Bruno Soriano (78)*
Barbosa, Mario Gaspar, Víctor Ruiz, Jonathan dos Santos (Trigueros 73), Soldado, Jaume Costa, Bakambu (Samu 52), Denis Suárez, Samu Castillejo (Nahuel 83), Bruno Soriano, Rukavina. Coach: Marcelino (ESP)
Match 6 - FC Viktoria Plzeň (CZE)
A 3-3 *Bakambu (40), Jonathan dos Santos (62), Bruno Soriano (90+4)*
Barbosa, Jokič (Adrián Marín 43), Musacchio, Víctor Ruiz, Samuel (Jonathan dos Santos 56), Soldado, Trigueros, Bakambu, Samu Castillejo (Denis Suárez 72), Bruno Soriano, Rukavina. Coach: Marcelino (ESP)

Round of 32 - SSC Napoli (ITA)
H 1-0 Denis Suárez (82)
Areola, Mario Gaspar, Musacchio, Víctor Ruiz, Jonathan dos Santos (Samu Castillejo 36), Soldado, Léo Baptistão (Bakambu 61), Jaume Costa, Trigueros (Pina 74), Denis Suárez, Bruno Soriano. Coach: Marcelino (ESP)
A 1-1 Pina (59)
Areola, Mario Gaspar, Pina (Trigueros 84), Musacchio, Víctor Ruiz, Soldado (Adrián López 71), Jaume Costa, Bakambu, Denis Suárez, Bruno Soriano, Rukavina (Samu Castillejo 77). Coach: Marcelino (ESP)

Round of 16 - Bayer 04 Leverkusen (GER)
H 2-0 Bakambu (4, 56)
Areola, Mario Gaspar, Víctor Ruiz, Soldado (Léo Baptistão 76), Trigueros, Bakambu (Adrián López 82), Denis Suárez, Samu Castillejo (Nahuel 80), Bruno Soriano, Rukavina, Bailly. Coach: Marcelino (ESP)
A 0-0
Asenjo, Mario Gaspar, Pina, Víctor Ruiz, Soldado (Adrián López 74), Bakambu, Denis Suárez (Alfonso Pedraza 89), Samu Castillejo (Trigueros 61), Bruno Soriano, Bailly. Coach: Marcelino (ESP)

Quarter-finals - AC Sparta Praha (CZE)
H 2-1 Bakambu (3, 63)
Asenjo, Mario Gaspar, Víctor Ruiz, Soldado, Jaume Costa (Adrián Marín 77), Trigueros, Bakambu (Adrián López 82), Denis Suárez, Samu Castillejo (Léo Baptistão 62), Bruno Soriano, Bailly. Coach: Marcelino (ESP)
A 4-2 Bakambu (5, 49), Samu Castillejo (43), Lafata (45+1og)
Aréola, Mario Gaspar (Jaume Costa 57), Víctor Ruiz, Soldado, Trigueros (Jonathan dos Santos 61), Bakambu, Denis Suárez (Léo Baptistão 66), Samu Castillejo, Bruno Soriano, Rukavina, Bailly. Coach: Marcelino (ESP)

Semi-finals - Liverpool FC (ENG)
H 1-0 Adrián López (90+2)
Asenjo, Mario Gaspar, Pina, Víctor Ruiz, Jonathan dos Santos (Samu Castillejo 72), Soldado (Adrián López 74), Jaume Costa, Bakambu, Denis Suárez, Bruno Soriano, Bailly (Musacchio 76). Coach: Marcelino (ESP)
A 0-3
Areola, Mario Gaspar, Pina (Trigueros 60), Musacchio, Víctor Ruiz, Jonathan dos Santos (Bonera 73), Soldado (Adrián López 68), Jaume Costa, Bakambu, Denis Suárez, Bruno Soriano. Coach: Marcelino (ESP)
Red card: Víctor Ruiz 71

Athletic Club

Third qualifying round - İnter Bakı PİK (AZE)
H 2-0 Eraso (12, 49)
Iago Herrerín, Eraso, Beñat Etxebarria, Iturraspe (Elustondo 46), De Marcos, Ibai Gómez (Aketxe 70), Susaeta (Viguera 81), Etxeita, Gurpegui, Aduriz, Balenziaga. Coach: Ernesto Valverde (ESP)
A 0-0
Iago Herrerín, Laporte, Eraso (Sabín Merino 67), San José, Beñat Etxebarria (Elustondo 90), De Marcos, Susaeta (Ibai Gómez 86), Etxeita, Aduriz, Aketxe, Balenziaga. Coach: Ernesto Valverde (ESP)

Play-offs - MŠK Žilina (SVK)
A 2-3 Sabín Merino (16), Kike Sola (33)
Iago Herrerín, Bóveda, Elustondo, Laporte, Kike Sola, Ibai Gómez, Mikel Rico (Beñat Etxebarria 70), Gurpegui, Aketxe, Sabín Merino (Iñaki Williams 74; De Marcos 82), Iñigo Lekue. Coach: Ernesto Valverde (ESP)
H 1-0 Elustondo (24)
Iago Herrerín, Elustondo, Laporte, Eraso (Aketxe 73), Beñat Etxebarria, De Marcos, Susaeta (Mikel Rico 85), Gurpegui, Aduriz, Viguera (Sabín Merino 57), Lekue. Coach: Ernesto Valverde (ESP)

Group L
Match 1 - FC Augsburg (GER)
H 3-1 Aduriz (55, 66), Susaeta (90)
Iago Herrerín, Elustondo (Mikel Rico 46), Laporte, Beñat Etxebarria, De Marcos, Ibai Gómez (Sabín Merino 64), Susaeta, Etxeita, Aduriz, Raúl García (Gurpegui 80), Lekue. Coach: Ernesto Valverde (ESP)
Match 2 - AZ Alkmaar (NED)
A 1-2 Aduriz (75)
Iago Herrerín, Bóveda, Laporte, Eraso, Iturraspe (Raúl García 63), Kike Sola (Aduriz 63), Mikel Rico, Gurpegui, Viguera, Aketxe (Iñaki Williams 57), Lekue. Coach: Ernesto Valverde (ESP)
Match 3 - FK Partizan (SRB)
A 2-0 Raúl García (32), Beñat Etxebarria (85)
Iago Herrerín, Laporte, San José, Beñat Etxebarria (Elustondo 90), De Marcos, Susaeta (Sabín Merino 55), Iñaki Williams (Bóveda 85), Etxeita, Aduriz, Raúl García, Balenziaga. Coach: Ernesto Valverde (ESP)
Match 4 - FK Partizan (SRB)
H 5-1 Iñaki Williams (15, 19), Beñat Etxebarria (40), Aduriz (71), Elustondo (81)
Iago Herrerín, Bóveda, Laporte, San José, Beñat Etxebarria (Elustondo 73), Susaeta, Iñaki Williams (De Marcos 63), Etxeita, Aduriz, Raúl García (Eraso 66), Balenziaga. Coach: Ernesto Valverde (ESP)
Match 5 - FC Augsburg (GER)
A 3-2 Susaeta (10), Aduriz (83, 86)
Iago Herrerín, Bóveda, Laporte, Eraso (Raúl García 58), San José (Iturraspe 73), Susaeta, Mikel Rico, Gurpegui, Aduriz, Balenziaga, Sabín Merino (Iñaki Williams 58). Coach: Ernesto Valverde (ESP)
Match 6 - AZ Alkmaar (NED)
H 2-2 Kike Sola (43), San José (47p)
Iago Herrerín, Bóveda, Elustondo, Eraso (Aketxe 81), San José (Iturraspe 70), Kike Sola (Viguera 77), Susaeta, Mikel Rico, Gurpegui, Enric Saborit, Sabín Merino. Coach: Ernesto Valverde (ESP)

Round of 32 - Olympique de Marseille (FRA)
A 1-0 Aduriz (54)
Iago Herrerín, Laporte, Eraso (Mikel Rico 58), San José, Beñat Etxebarria (Elustondo 90+1), De Marcos, Iñaki Williams, Etxeita, Aduriz, Balenziaga, Sabín Merino (Bóveda 75). Coach: Ernesto Valverde (ESP)
H 1-1 Merino (81)
Iago Herrerín, Laporte, San José, Iturraspe, De Marcos, Susaeta (Mikel Rico 88), Etxeita, Aduriz, Raúl García (Sabín Merino 76), Balenziaga, Lekue (Muniain 58). Coach: Ernesto Valverde (ESP)

Round of 16 - Valencia CF (ESP)
H 1-0 Raúl García (20)
Iago Herrerín, Laporte, Beñat Etxebarria, Iturraspe (Mikel Rico 82), De Marcos, Susaeta (Elustondo 73), Etxeita, Muniain (Sabín Merino 53), Aduriz, Raúl García, Balenziaga. Coach: Ernesto Valverde (ESP)
A 1-2 Aduriz (76)
Iago Herrerín, Laporte, San José, Beñat Etxebarria, De Marcos, Etxeita, Muniain (Susaeta 25), Aduriz, Raúl García, Balenziaga (Lekue 75), Sabín Merino (Iturraspe 75). Coach: Ernesto Valverde (ESP)

Quarter-finals - Sevilla FC (ESP)
H 1-2 Aduriz (48)
Iago Herrerín, Eneko Bóveda, Eraso (Viguera 69), San José, Beñat Etxebarria, De Marcos, Iñaki Williams (Susaeta 63), Etxeita, Muniain (Lekue 63), Aduriz, Balenziaga. Coach: Ernesto Valverde (ESP)
A 2-1 (aet; 4-5 on pens) Aduriz (57), Raúl García (80)
Iago Herrerín, Bóveda (Iturraspe 60), San José, Beñat Etxebarria, De Marcos, Susaeta, Etxeita, Aduriz (Viguera 70), Raúl García, Balenziaga, Lekue (Muniain 54). Coach: Ernesto Valverde (ESP)

DOMESTIC LEAGUE CLUB-BY-CLUB

Athletic Club

1898 • Nuevo San Mamés (53,332) • athletic-club.eus
Major honours
Spanish League (8) 1930, 1931, 1934, 1936, 1943, 1956, 1983, 1984; Spanish Cup (23) 1903, 1904, 1910, 1911, 1914, 1915, 1916, 1921, 1923, 1930, 1931, 1932, 1933, 1943, 1944, 1945, 1950, 1955, 1956, 1958, 1969, 1973, 1984
Coach: Ernesto Valverde

2015

23/08	h	Barcelona	L	0-1	
30/08	a	Eibar	L	0-2	
13/09	h	Getafe	W	3-1	Aduriz 2, Raúl García
19/09	a	Villarreal	L	1-3	Aduriz
23/09	h	Real Madrid	L	1-2	Sabín Merino
27/09	a	Real Sociedad	D	0-0	
04/10	h	Valencia	W	3-1	Laporte, Susaeta, Aduriz
18/10	a	Deportivo	D	2-2	Iñaki Williams, Aduriz
26/10	h	Sporting	W	3-0	Susaeta, Aduriz 2
01/11	h	Betis	W	3-1	Iñaki Williams 2, Raúl García
08/11	h	Espanyol	W	2-1	Iñaki Williams, Raúl García
22/11	a	Granada	L	0-2	
29/11	a	Rayo Vallecano	W	3-0	Aduriz 3 (1p)
06/12	h	Málaga	D	0-0	
13/12	a	Atlético	L	0-2	Laporte
20/12	h	Levante	W	2-0	San José, Iñaki Williams
30/12	a	Celta	W	1-0	Raúl García

2016

03/01	h	Las Palmas	D	2-2	Aduriz (p), Iñaki Williams
09/01	a	Sevilla	L	0-2	
17/01	h	Barcelona	L	0-6	
24/01	h	Eibar	W	5-2	Aduriz 2, Sabín Merino, Laporte, og (Mauro dos Santos)
30/01	a	Getafe	W	1-0	Iñaki Williams
06/02	h	Villarreal	D	0-0	
13/02	a	Real Madrid	L	2-4	Eraso, Elustondo
21/02	a	Real Sociedad	L	0-1	
28/02	a	Valencia	W	3-0	Sabín Merino, Muniain, Aduriz
02/03	h	Deportivo	W	4-1	Muniain, Aduriz 3
06/03	a	Sporting	W	2-0	Beñat, De Marcos
13/03	h	Betis	W	3-1	Sabín Merino 2, Mikel Rico
20/03	a	Espanyol	L	1-2	Eraso
03/04	h	Granada	D	1-1	Lekue
10/04	h	Rayo Vallecano	W	1-0	Iñaki Williams
17/04	a	Málaga	W	1-0	Raúl García
20/04	h	Atlético	L	0-1	
24/04	a	Levante	D	2-2	Susaeta, San José
01/05	h	Celta	W	2-1	Aduriz (p), Raúl García
08/05	a	Las Palmas	D	0-0	
14/05	h	Sevilla	W	3-1	Aduriz 2, Raúl García

No	Name	Nat	DoB	Pos	Aps	(s)	Gls
20	Aritz Aduriz		11/02/81	A	30	(4)	20
23	Ager Aketxe		30/12/93	M	2	(1)	
24	Mikel Balenziaga		29/02/88	D	33	(1)	
7	Beñat Etxebarria		19/02/87	M	32	(4)	1
2	Eneko Bóveda		14/12/88	D	15	(8)	
10	Óscar De Marcos		14/04/89	M	33	(1)	1
3	Gorka Elustondo		18/03/87	M	4	(7)	1
5	Javier Eraso		22/03/90	M	8	(8)	2
16	Xabier Etxeita		31/10/87	D	28	(2)	
1	Gorka Iraizoz		06/03/81	G	37		
18	Carlos Gurpegui		19/08/80	D	12	(3)	
13	Iago Herrerín		25/01/88	G	1	(1)	
11	Ibai Gómez		11/11/89	A	1	(4)	
15	Iñaki Williams		15/06/94	A	21	(4)	8
8	Ander Iturraspe		08/03/89	M	7	(9)	
9	Kike Sola		25/02/86	A	1	(4)	
4	Aymeric Laporte	FRA	27/05/94	D	25	(1)	3
30	Iñigo Lekue		04/05/93	D	12	(8)	1
17	Mikel Rico		04/11/84	M	8	(9)	1
19	Iker Muniain		19/12/92	M	13	(7)	2
22	Raúl García		11/07/86	M	27	(3)	7
25	Sabín Merino		04/01/92	A	13	(9)	5
6	Mikel San José		30/05/89	D	30	(4)	2
14	Markel Susaeta		14/12/87	M	22	(6)	3
21	Borja Viguera		26/03/87	A	3	(6)	

Club Atlético de Madrid

1903 • Vicente Calderón (54,851) • clubatleticodemadrid.com

Major honours
UEFA Cup Winners' Cup (1) 1962; UEFA Europa League (2) 2010, 2012; UEFA Super Cup (2) 2010, 2012; European/South American Cup (1) 1974; Spanish League (10) 1940, 1941, 1950, 1951, 1966, 1970, 1973, 1977, 1996, 2014; Spanish Cup (10) 1960, 1961, 1965, 1972, 1976, 1985, 1991, 1992, 1996, 2013

Coach: Diego Simeone (ARG)

2015

22/08	h	Las Palmas	W	1-0	*Griezmann*
30/08	a	Sevilla	W	3-0	*Koke, Gabi, Martínez*
12/09	h	Barcelona	L	1-2	*Fernando Torres*
19/09	a	Eibar	W	2-0	*Correa, Fernando Torres*
22/09	h	Getafe	W	2-0	*Griezmann 2*
26/09	a	Villarreal	L	0-1	
04/10	h	Real Madrid	D	1-1	*Vietto*
18/10	a	Real Sociedad	W	2-0	*Griezmann, Carrasco*
25/10	h	Valencia	W	2-1	*Martínez, Carrasco*
30/10	a	Deportivo	D	1-1	*Tiago*
08/11	h	Sporting	W	1-0	*Griezmann*
22/11	a	Betis	W	1-0	*Koke*
28/11	h	Espanyol	W	1-0	*Griezmann*
05/12	a	Granada	W	2-0	*Godín, Griezmann*
13/12	h	Athletic	W	2-1	*Saúl Ñíguez, Griezmann*
20/12	a	Málaga	L	0-1	
30/12	a	Rayo Vallecano	W	2-0	*Correa, Griezmann*

2015

02/01	h	Levante	W	1-0	*Partey*
10/01	a	Celta	W	2-0	*Griezmann, Carrasco*
17/01	a	Las Palmas	W	3-0	*Filipe Luís, Griezmann 2*
24/01	h	Sevilla	D	0-0	
30/01	a	Barcelona	L	1-2	*Koke*
06/02	h	Eibar	W	3-1	*Giménez, Saúl Ñíguez, Fernando Torres*
14/02	a	Getafe	W	1-0	*Fernando Torres*
21/02	h	Villarreal	D	0-0	
27/02	a	Real Madrid	W	1-0	*Griezmann*
01/03	h	Real Sociedad	W	3-0	*og (Reyes), Saúl Ñíguez, Griezmann (p)*
06/03	a	Valencia	W	3-1	*Griezmann, Fernando Torres, Carrasco*
12/03	h	Deportivo	W	3-0	*Saúl Ñíguez, Griezmann, Correa*
19/03	a	Sporting	L	1-2	*Griezmann*
02/04	h	Betis	W	5-1	*Fernando Torres, Griezmann 2, Juanfran, Partey*
09/04	a	Espanyol	W	3-1	*Fernando Torres, Griezmann, Koke*
17/04	h	Granada	W	3-0	*Koke, Fernando Torres, Correa*
20/04	a	Athletic	W	1-0	*Fernando Torres*
23/04	h	Málaga	W	1-0	*Correa*
30/04	h	Rayo Vallecano	W	1-0	*Griezmann*
08/05	a	Levante	L	1-2	*Fernando Torres*
14/05	h	Celta	W	2-0	*Fernando Torres, Griezmann*

No	Name	Nat	DoB	Pos	Aps	(s)	Gls
21	Yannick Carrasco	BEL	04/09/93	M	16	(13)	4
16	Ángel Correa	ARG	09/03/95	A	8	(18)	5
12	Augusto Fernández	ARG	10/04/86	M	11	(2)	
9	Fernando Torres		20/03/84	A	17	(13)	11
3	Filipe Luís	BRA	09/08/85	D	32		1
14	Gabi		10/07/83	M	34	(1)	1
24	José María Giménez	URU	20/01/95	D	27		1
2	Diego Godín	URU	16/02/86	D	31		1
7	Antoine Griezmann	FRA	21/03/91	A	36	(2)	22
19	Lucas Hernández	FRA	14/02/96	D	8	(2)	
18	Jesús Gámez		10/04/85	D	7	(3)	
20	Juanfran		09/01/85	D	34		1
6	Koke		08/01/92	M	34	(1)	5
8	Matías Kranevitter	ARG	21/05/93	M	3	(5)	
11	Jackson Martínez	COL	03/10/86	A	8	(7)	2
32	Nacho		27/04/94	D	1		
13	Jan Oblak	SVN	07/01/93	G	38		
10	Óliver Torres		10/11/94	M	9	(12)	
22	Thomas Partey	GHA	13/06/93	M	3	(10)	2
8	Raúl García		11/07/86	M		(1)	
17	Saúl Ñíguez		21/11/94	M	26	(5)	4
15	Stefan Savić	MNE	08/01/91	D	10	(2)	
4	Guilherme Siqueira	BRA	28/04/86	D	1		
5	Tiago	POR	02/05/81	M	12	(2)	1
23	Luciano Vietto	ARG	05/12/93	A	12	(7)	1

FC Barcelona

1899 • Camp Nou (98,772) • fcbarcelona.com

Major honours
European Champion Clubs' Cup/UEFA Champions League (5) 1992, 2006, 2009, 2011, 2015; UEFA Cup Winners' Cup (4) 1979, 1982, 1989, 1997; Inter Cities Fairs Cup (3) 1958, 1960, 1966; UEFA Super Cup (4) 1992, 1997, 2009, 2011; FIFA Club World Cup (2) 2009, 2011; Spanish League (24) 1929, 1945, 1948, 1949, 1952, 1953, 1959, 1960, 1974, 1985, 1991, 1992, 1993, 1994, 1998, 1999, 2005, 2006, 2009, 2010, 2011, 2013, 2015, 2016; Spanish Cup (28) 1910, 1912, 1913, 1920, 1922, 1925, 1926, 1928, 1942, 1951, 1952, 1953, 1957, 1959, 1963, 1968, 1971, 1978, 1981, 1983, 1988, 1990, 1997, 1998, 2009, 2012, 2015, 2016

Coach: Luis Enrique

2015

23/08	a	Athletic	W	1-0	*Suárez*
29/08	h	Málaga	W	1-0	*Vermaelen*
12/09	a	Atlético	W	2-1	*Neymar, Messi*
20/09	h	Levante	W	4-1	*Bartra, Neymar, Messi 2 (1p)*
23/09	a	Celta	L	1-4	*Neymar*
26/09	h	Las Palmas	W	2-1	*Suárez 2*
03/10	a	Sevilla	L	1-2	*Neymar (p)*
17/10	h	Rayo Vallecano	W	5-2	*Neymar 4 (2p), Suárez*
25/10	h	Eibar	W	3-1	*Suárez 3*
31/10	a	Getafe	W	2-0	*Suárez, Neymar*
08/11	h	Villarreal	W	3-0	*Neymar 2, Suárez (p)*
21/11	a	Real Madrid	W	4-0	*Suárez 2, Neymar, Iniesta*
28/11	h	Real Sociedad	W	4-0	*Neymar 2, Suárez, Messi*
05/12	a	Valencia	D	1-1	*Suárez*
12/12	h	Deportivo	D	2-2	*Messi, Rakitić*
30/12	h	Betis	W	4-0	*og (Westermann), Messi, Suárez 2*

2016

02/01	a	Espanyol	D	0-0	
09/01	h	Granada	W	4-0	*Messi 3, Neymar*
17/01	h	Athletic	W	6-0	*Messi (p), Neymar, Suárez 3, Rakitić*
23/01	a	Málaga	W	2-1	*Munir, Messi*
30/01	h	Atlético	W	2-1	*Messi, Suárez*
07/02	a	Levante	W	2-0	*og (David Navarro), Suárez*
14/02	h	Celta	W	6-1	*Messi, Suárez 3, Rakitić, Neymar*
17/02	a	Sporting	W	3-1	*Messi 2, Suárez*
20/02	a	Las Palmas	W	2-1	*Suárez, Neymar*
28/02	h	Sevilla	W	2-1	*Messi, Piqué*
03/03	a	Rayo Vallecano	W	5-1	*Rakitić, Messi 3, Arda*
06/03	a	Eibar	W	4-0	*Munir, Messi 2 (1p), Suárez*
12/03	h	Getafe	W	6-0	*og (Juan Rodríguez), Munir, Neymar 2, Messi, Arda*
20/03	a	Villarreal	D	2-2	*Rakitić, Neymar (p)*
02/04	h	Real Madrid	L	1-2	*Piqué*
09/04	a	Real Sociedad	L	0-1	
17/04	h	Valencia	L	1-2	*Messi*
20/04	a	Deportivo	W	8-0	*Suárez 4, Rakitić, Messi, Bartra, Neymar*
23/04	h	Sporting	W	6-0	*Messi, Suárez 4 (2p), Neymar (p)*
30/04	a	Betis	W	2-0	*Rakitić, Suárez*
08/05	h	Espanyol	W	5-0	*Messi, Suárez 2, Rafinha, Neymar*
14/05	a	Granada	W	3-0	*Suárez 3*

No	Name	Nat	DoB	Pos	Aps	(s)	Gls
21	Adriano	BRA	26/10/84	D	4	(4)	
22	Aleix Vidal		21/08/89	D	6	(3)	
7	Arda Turan	TUR	30/01/87	M	9	(9)	2
15	Marc Bartra		15/01/91	D	4	(9)	2
13	Claudio Bravo	CHI	13/04/83	G	32		
5	Sergio Busquets		16/07/88	M	34	(1)	
6	Dani Alves	BRA	06/05/83	D	24	(5)	
2	Douglas	BRA	06/08/90	D		(1)	
28	Gerard Gumbau		18/12/94	M		(3)	
8	Andrés Iniesta		11/05/84	M	25	(3)	1
18	Jordi Alba		21/03/89	D	29	(2)	
14	Javier Mascherano	ARG	08/06/84	D	31	(1)	
24	Jérémy Mathieu	FRA	29/10/83	D	12	(9)	
10	Lionel Messi	ARG	24/06/87	A	31	(2)	26
17	Munir El Haddadi		01/09/95	A	8	(7)	3
11	Neymar	BRA	05/02/92	A	34		24
3	Gerard Piqué		02/02/87	D	30		2
12	Rafinha	BRA	12/02/93	M	3	(3)	1
4	Ivan Rakitić	CRO	10/03/88	M	30	(6)	7
19	Sandro Ramírez		09/07/95	A	4	(6)	
20	Sergi Roberto		07/02/92	M	21	(10)	
26	Sergi Samper		20/01/95	M		(1)	
9	Luis Suárez	URU	24/01/87	A	35		40
1	Marc-André ter Stegen	GER	30/04/92	G	6	(1)	
23	Thomas Vermaelen	BEL	14/11/85	D	6	(4)	1

Real Betis Balompié

1907 • Benito Villamarín (55,000) • realbetisbalompie.es

Major honours
Spanish League (1) 1935; Spanish Cup (2) 1977, 2005

Coach: Pepe Mel;
(10/01/16) Juan Merino

2015

23/08	h	Villarreal	D	1-1	*Rubén Castro*
29/08	a	Real Madrid	L	0-5	
12/09	h	Real Sociedad	W	1-0	*Rubén Castro*
19/09	a	Valencia	D	0-0	
24/09	h	Deportivo	L	1-2	*Petros*
27/09	a	Sporting	W	2-1	*Joaquín, Rubén Castro*
04/10	a	Rayo Vallecano	W	2-0	*Westermann, Rubén Castro*
17/10	h	Espanyol	L	1-3	*Rennella*
24/10	a	Granada	D	1-1	*Rubén Castro (p)*
01/11	h	Athletic	L	1-3	*Rubén Castro (p)*
07/11	a	Málaga	W	1-0	*Rubén Castro*
22/11	h	Atlético	L	0-1	
27/11	a	Levante	W	1-0	*Rubén Castro*
05/12	h	Celta	D	1-1	*Jorge Molina*
12/12	a	Las Palmas	L	0-1	
19/12	h	Sevilla	D	0-0	
30/12	a	Barcelona	L	0-4	

2016

03/01	h	Eibar	L	0-4	
09/01	a	Getafe	L	0-1	
16/01	a	Villarreal	D	0-0	
24/01	h	Real Madrid	D	1-1	*Álvaro Cejudo*
30/01	a	Real Sociedad	L	1-2	*Rubén Castro*
07/02	h	Valencia	W	1-0	*Rubén Castro*
13/02	a	Deportivo	D	2-2	*Musonda, Vargas*
20/02	h	Sporting	D	1-1	*Pezzella*
27/02	h	Rayo Vallecano	D	2-2	*Rubén Castro 2*
03/03	a	Espanyol	W	3-0	*Rubén Castro, Pezzella, Vargas*
06/03	h	Granada	W	2-0	*N'Diaye, Rubén Castro*
13/03	a	Athletic	L	1-3	*Rubén Castro*
19/03	h	Málaga	L	0-1	
02/04	a	Atlético	L	1-5	*Rubén Castro*
09/04	h	Levante	W	1-0	*Rubén Castro*
16/04	a	Celta	D	1-1	*N'Diaye*
19/04	h	Las Palmas	W	1-0	*Van Wolfswinkel*
24/04	a	Sevilla	L	0-2	
30/04	h	Barcelona	L	0-2	
08/05	a	Eibar	D	1-1	*Rubén Castro*
15/05	h	Getafe	W	2-1	*Pezzella, Rubén Castro (p)*

No	Name	Nat	DoB	Pos	Aps	(s)	Gls
13	Antonio Adán		13/05/87	G	36		
16	Álvaro Cejudo		29/01/84	M	21	(9)	1
4	Bruno González		24/05/90	D	32		
10	Dani Ceballos		07/08/96	M	22	(12)	
1	Dani Giménez		30/07/83	G	2	(1)	
15	Didier Digard	FRA	12/07/86	M	2	(6)	
52	Fabián Ruiz		03/04/96	M	6	(6)	
7	Joaquín		21/07/81	A	22	(8)	1
6	Jordi Figueras		16/05/87	D	2	(1)	
19	Jorge Molina		22/04/82	A	10	(13)	1
5	Foued Kadir	ALG	05/12/83	M	6	(2)	
12	Leandro Damião	BRA	22/07/89	A	1	(2)	
2	Francisco José Molinero		26/07/85	D	15	(6)	
3	Martín Montoya		14/04/91	D	13		
8	Charly Musonda	BEL	15/10/96	M	13	(3)	1
18	Alfred N'Diaye	SEN	06/03/90	M	34		2
25	Petros	BRA	29/05/89	M	27	(3)	1
20	Germán Pezzella	ARG	27/06/91	D	23	(2)	3
12	Cristiano Piccini	ITA	26/09/92	D	16		
22	Francisco Portillo		13/06/90	M	11	(8)	
8	Vicenzo Rennella	FRA	08/10/88	A	2	(4)	1
24	Rubén Castro		27/06/81	A	38		19
21	Álvaro Vadillo		12/09/94	M	1	(2)	
23	Rafael van der Vaart	NED	11/02/83	M	2	(5)	
9	Ricky van Wolfswinkel	NED	27/01/89	A	5	(11)	1
6	Franciso Miguel Varela		26/10/94	D	10	(4)	
11	Juan Manuel Vargas	PER	05/10/83	D	20		2
17	Heiko Westermann	GER	10/08/83	D	20		1
14	Xavi Torres		21/11/86	M	6	(6)	

SPAIN

RC Celta de Vigo

1923 • Balaídos (29,000) • celtavigo.net
Coach: Eduardo Berizzo (ARG)

2015
23/08	a	Levante	W	2-1	Orellana, Iago Aspas
29/08	h	Rayo Vallecano	W	3-0	Nolito 2 (1p), Fontàs
13/09	h	Las Palmas	D	3-3	Orellana (p), Wass, Nolito
20/09	a	Sevilla	W	2-1	Nolito, Wass
23/09	a	Barcelona	W	4-1	Nolito, Iago Aspas 2, Guidetti
26/09	a	Eibar	D	1-1	Iago Aspas
02/10	h	Getafe	D	0-0	
18/10	a	Villarreal	W	2-1	Orellana, Nolito
24/10	h	Real Madrid	L	1-3	Nolito
31/10	a	Real Sociedad	W	3-2	Iago Aspas 2, Hernández
07/11	h	Valencia	L	1-5	Fernández
21/11	a	Deportivo	L	0-2	
28/11	h	Sporting	W	2-1	Orellana, Nolito
05/12	a	Betis	D	1-1	Bongonda
12/12	h	Espanyol	W	1-0	Iago Aspas
20/12	a	Granada	W	2-0	Orellana, Iago Aspas
30/12	a	Athletic	L	0-1	

2016
02/01	a	Málaga	L	0-2	
10/01	h	Atlético	L	0-2	
16/01	h	Levante	W	4-3	Guidetti 2, Iago Aspas, Orellana
23/01	a	Rayo Vallecano	L	0-3	
31/01	a	Las Palmas	L	1-2	Bongonda
07/02	h	Sevilla	D	1-1	Beauvue
14/02	a	Barcelona	L	1-6	Guidetti (p)
20/02	h	Eibar	W	3-2	Guidetti 2, Jonny
27/02	a	Getafe	W	1-0	Nolito
02/03	a	Villarreal	D	0-0	
05/03	a	Real Madrid	L	1-7	Iago Aspas
12/03	h	Real Sociedad	D	1-1	Iago Aspas
20/03	a	Valencia	W	2-0	Guidetti, Hugo Mallo
02/04	h	Deportivo	D	1-1	Nolito
10/04	a	Sporting	W	1-0	Nolito
16/04	h	Betis	D	1-1	Hernández
19/04	a	Espanyol	D	1-1	Iago Aspas
24/04	h	Granada	W	2-1	Iago Aspas 2 (1p)
01/05	a	Athletic	L	1-2	Orellana
08/05	h	Málaga	W	1-0	Nolito
14/05	a	Atlético	L	0-2	

No	Name	Nat	DoB	Pos	Aps	(s)	Gls
29	Diego Alende		25/08/97	D		(1)	
12	Claudio Beauvue	FRA	16/04/88	A	6	(4)	1
7	Theo Bongonda	BEL	20/11/95	A	14	(9)	2
28	Borja Fernández		16/08/95	M	1	(3)	
22	Gustavo Cabral	ARG	14/10/85	D	31		
5	Marcelo Díaz	CHI	30/12/86	M	10	(4)	
33	Pape Cheikh Diop		08/08/97	M		(6)	
16	Dejan Dražić	SRB	26/09/95	A	1	(5)	
24	Augusto Fernández	ARG	10/04/86	M	15		1
3	Andreu Fontàs		14/11/89	D	6	(1)	1
34	David Goldar		15/09/94	D	1		
11	John Guidetti	SWE	15/04/92	A	12	(23)	7
8	Pablo Hernández	ARG	24/10/86	M	28	(5)	2
2	Hugo Mallo		22/06/91	D	33	(1)	1
10	Iago Aspas		01/08/87	A	31	(4)	14
19	Jonny		03/03/94	D	34	(2)	1
17	Levy Madinda	GAB	22/06/92	M		(1)	
26	Néstor Díaz		26/06/92	G		(1)	
10	Nolito		15/10/86	A	27	(2)	12
14	Fabián Orellana	CHI	27/01/86	A	33		7
21	Carlos Planas		04/03/91	D	18	(8)	
6	Nemanja Radoja	SRB	06/02/93	M	15	(15)	
13	Rubén Blanco		25/07/95	G	8		
23	Josep Señé		10/12/91	M	4	(4)	
20	Sergi Gómez		28/07/92	D	29	(2)	
1	Sergio Álvarez		03/08/86	G	30	(1)	
18	Daniel Wass	DEN	31/05/89	M	31	(5)	2

RC Deportivo La Coruña

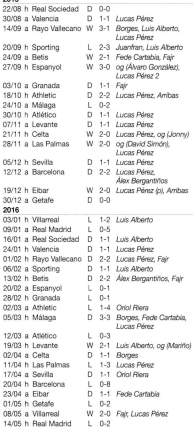

1906 • Riazor (33,091) • canaldeportivo.com
Major honours
Spanish League (1) 2000; Spanish Cup (2) 1995, 2002
Coach: Víctor Sánchez

2015
22/08	h	Real Sociedad	D	0-0	
30/08	a	Valencia	D	1-1	Lucas Pérez
14/09	a	Rayo Vallecano	W	3-1	Borges, Luis Alberto, Lucas Pérez
20/09	h	Sporting	L	2-3	Juanfran, Luis Alberto
24/09	a	Betis	W	2-1	Fede Cartabia, Fajr
27/09	h	Espanyol	W	3-0	og (Álvaro González), Lucas Pérez 2
03/10	a	Granada	D	1-1	Fajr
18/10	h	Athletic	D	2-2	Lucas Pérez, Arribas
24/10	a	Málaga	L	0-2	
30/10	h	Atlético	D	1-1	Lucas Pérez
07/11	h	Levante	D	1-1	Lucas Pérez
21/11	h	Celta	W	2-0	Lucas Pérez, og (Jonny)
28/11	a	Las Palmas	W	2-0	og (David Simón), Lucas Pérez
05/12	h	Sevilla	D	1-1	Lucas Pérez
12/12	h	Barcelona	D	2-2	Lucas Pérez, Álex Bergantiños
19/12	h	Eibar	W	2-0	Lucas Pérez (p), Arribas
30/12	a	Getafe	D	0-0	

2016
03/01	h	Villarreal	L	1-2	Luis Alberto
09/01	a	Real Madrid	L	0-5	
16/01	h	Real Sociedad	D	1-1	Luis Alberto
24/01	h	Valencia	D	1-1	Lucas Pérez
01/02	h	Rayo Vallecano	D	2-2	Lucas Pérez, Fajr
06/02	a	Sporting	D	1-1	Luis Alberto
13/02	h	Betis	D	2-2	Álex Bergantiños, Fajr
20/02	a	Espanyol	L	0-1	
28/02	h	Granada	L	0-1	
02/03	a	Athletic	L	1-4	Oriol Riera
05/03	h	Málaga	D	3-3	Borges, Fede Cartabia, Lucas Pérez
12/03	a	Atlético	L	0-3	
19/03	h	Levante	W	2-1	Luis Alberto, og (Mariño)
02/04	a	Celta	D	1-1	Borges
11/04	a	Las Palmas	L	1-3	Lucas Pérez
17/04	a	Sevilla	D	1-1	Oriol Riera
20/04	h	Barcelona	L	0-8	
23/04	a	Eibar	D	1-1	Fede Cartabia
01/05	h	Getafe	L	0-2	
08/05	h	Villarreal	W	2-0	Fajr, Lucas Pérez
14/05	h	Real Madrid	L	0-2	

No	Name	Nat	DoB	Pos	Aps	(s)	Gls
4	Álex Bergantiños		07/06/85	M	20	(2)	2
14	Alejandro Arribas		01/05/89	D	31		2
22	Celso Borges	CRC	27/05/88	M	21	(3)	3
6	Cani		03/08/81	M	12	(6)	
19	Fayçal Fajr	MAR	01/08/88	M	31	(7)	5
17	Fede Cartabia	ARG	20/01/93	M	15	(11)	3
3	Fernando Navarro		25/06/82	D	35		
24	Jonás Gutiérrez	ARG	05/07/83	M	3	(12)	
10	Juan Domínguez		08/01/90	M	2	(3)	
11	Juanfran		11/09/88	D	30	(5)	1
15	Laure		22/03/85	D	16	(7)	
23	Alberto Lopo		05/05/80	D	8	(2)	
7	Lucas Pérez		10/09/88	A	35	(1)	17
21	Luis Alberto		28/09/92	M	25	(4)	6
16	Luisinho	POR	05/05/85	D	11	(9)	
1	Germán Lux	ARG	07/06/82	G	29		
25	Manu		09/05/86	G	7	(1)	
2	Manuel Pablo		25/01/76	D	2	(1)	
30	Miguel Cardoso	POR	19/06/94	A		(3)	
5	Pedro Mosquera		21/04/88	M	37		
9	Oriol Riera		03/10/86	A	7	(15)	2
13	Stipe Pletikosa	CRO	08/01/79	G	2		
27	Róber		16/02/95	D		(2)	
20	Jonathan Rodríguez	URU	06/07/93	A	6	(7)	
12	Sidnei	BRA	23/06/89	D	33		

SD Eibar

1940 • Ipurúa (6,300) • sdeibar.com
Coach: José Luis Mendilíbar

2015
24/08	a	Granada	W	3-1	Adrián, Escalante, Arruabarrena
30/08	h	Athletic	W	2-0	Saúl Berjón (p), Adrián
13/09	h	Málaga	D	0-0	
19/09	h	Atlético	L	0-2	
23/09	a	Levante	D	2-2	Borja Bastón 2
26/09	h	Celta	D	1-1	Borja Bastón
03/10	h	Las Palmas	W	2-0	Saúl Berjón, Borja Bastón
17/10	h	Sevilla	D	1-1	Borja Bastón
25/10	a	Barcelona	L	1-3	Borja Bastón
01/11	h	Rayo Vallecano	W	1-0	og (Llorente)
07/11	h	Getafe	W	3-1	Sergi Enrich 2, Saúl Berjón (p)
22/11	a	Villarreal	D	1-1	Sergi Enrich
29/11	h	Real Madrid	L	0-2	
06/12	a	Real Sociedad	L	1-2	Borja Bastón
13/12	h	Valencia	D	1-1	Sergi Enrich
19/12	a	Deportivo	L	0-2	
30/12	h	Sporting	W	2-0	Keko, Borja Bastón

2016
03/01	a	Betis	W	4-0	Capa, Keko, Adrián, Borja Bastón
10/01	h	Espanyol	W	2-1	Inui, Borja Bastón (p)
18/01	h	Granada	W	5-1	Inui, Sergi Enrich 2, Borja Bastón 2
24/01	a	Athletic	L	2-5	Borja Bastón 2 (1p)
30/01	h	Málaga	L	1-2	Borja Bastón
06/02	a	Atlético	L	1-3	Keko
14/02	h	Levante	W	2-0	Borja Bastón, Adrián
20/02	a	Celta	L	2-3	Saúl Berjón (p), Inui
26/02	h	Las Palmas	D	0-1	
02/03	a	Sevilla	L	0-1	
06/03	h	Barcelona	L	0-4	
12/03	h	Rayo Vallecano	D	1-1	Escalante
18/03	a	Getafe	D	1-1	Borja Bastón
03/04	h	Villarreal	L	1-2	Capa
09/04	a	Real Madrid	L	0-4	
16/04	h	Real Sociedad	W	2-1	Sergi Enrich, Escalante
20/04	a	Valencia	L	0-4	
23/04	h	Deportivo	D	1-1	Adrián
29/04	a	Sporting	L	0-2	
08/05	h	Betis	D	1-1	Sergi Enrich
15/05	a	Espanyol	L	2-4	Borja Bastón (p), Sergi Enrich

No	Name	Nat	DoB	Pos	Aps	(s)	Gls
24	Adrián		25/05/88	M	26	(6)	5
2	Ion Ansotegi		13/07/82	D	6	(2)	
10	Mikel Arruabarrena		09/02/83	A		(6)	1
28	Iñigo Barrenetxea		10/01/94	A		(2)	
18	Borja Bastón		25/08/92	A	29	(7)	18
7	Ander Capa		08/02/92	D	34	(2)	2
33	Imanol Corral		19/03/94	D		(1)	
14	Dani García		24/05/90	M	35		
23	Borja Ekiza		30/03/88	D	2	(2)	
5	Gonzalo Escalante	ARG	27/03/93	M	32	(2)	3
32	Ander Gayoso		20/07/93	M		(1)	
11	Izet Hajrovic	BIH	04/08/91	A	2	(5)	
8	Takashi Inui	JPN	02/06/88	M	18	(9)	3
6	Eddy Ísrafilov	AZE	02/08/92	M	1	(5)	
22	Jota		16/06/91	M	8	(5)	
17	David Juncà		16/11/93	D	25	(6)	
20	Keko		27/12/91	M	27	(2)	3
16	Lillo		27/03/89	D	5	(5)	
19	Antonio Luna		03/03/91	D	12	(3)	
15	Mauro dos Santos	ARG	07/07/89	D	30	(1)	
3	Aleksandar Pantić	SRB	11/04/92	D	18	(2)	
6	Josip Radošević	CRO	03/04/94	M	5	(3)	
4	Iván Ramis		25/10/84	D	21	(2)	
13	Asier Riesgo		06/10/83	G	34		
21	Saúl Berjón		24/05/86	M	16	(13)	4
9	Sergi Enrich		26/02/90	A	25	(13)	9
2	Simone Verdi	ITA	12/07/92	M	3	(6)	
1	Xabi Irureta		21/03/86	G	4		

RCD Espanyol

1900 • Power8 (40,500) • rcdespanyol.com
Major honours
Spanish Cup (4) 1929, 1940, 2000, 2006
Coach: Sergio González;
(14/12/15) Constantin Gâlcă (ROU)

2015

22/08	h	Getafe	W	1-0	Salva Sevilla
28/08	a	Villarreal	L	1-3	Caicedo
12/09	h	Real Madrid	L	0-6	
19/09	a	Real Sociedad	W	3-2	Gerard Moreno (p), Roco, Pérez
22/09	h	Valencia	W	1-0	Víctor Álvarez
27/09	a	Deportivo	L	0-3	
03/10	h	Sporting	L	1-2	Caicedo
17/10	a	Betis	W	3-1	Roco, Caicedo, Víctor Sánchez
23/10	a	Rayo Vallecano	L	0-3	
01/11	h	Granada	D	1-1	Caicedo
08/11	a	Athletic	L	1-2	Pérez
21/11	h	Málaga	W	2-0	Pérez 2
28/11	a	Atlético	L	0-1	
07/12	h	Levante	D	1-1	Gerard Moreno
12/12	a	Celta	L	0-1	
19/12	a	Las Palmas	W	1-0	Caicedo
30/12	a	Sevilla	L	0-2	

2016

02/01	h	Barcelona	D	0-0	
10/01	a	Eibar	L	1-2	Joan Jordán
17/01	a	Getafe	L	1-3	Pérez
23/01	h	Villarreal	D	2-2	Caicedo, Gerard Moreno
31/01	a	Real Madrid	L	0-6	
08/02	h	Real Sociedad	L	0-5	
13/02	a	Valencia	L	1-2	Ó Duarte
20/02	h	Deportivo	W	1-0	Marco Asensio
27/02	a	Sporting	W	4-2	Burgui, Gerard Moreno 2, og (Luis Hernández)
03/03	h	Betis	L	0-3	
07/03	h	Rayo Vallecano	W	2-1	Abraham, Pérez
14/03	a	Granada	D	1-1	og (Miguel Lopes)
20/03	h	Athletic	W	2-1	Diop, Caicedo
03/04	a	Málaga	D	1-1	Diop
09/04	h	Atlético	L	1-3	Diop
15/04	h	Levante	L	1-2	Pérez
19/04	h	Celta	D	1-1	Marco Asensio
22/04	a	Las Palmas	L	0-4	
01/05	h	Sevilla	W	1-0	Caicedo
08/05	a	Barcelona	L	0-5	
15/05	h	Eibar	W	4-2	Gerard Moreno 2, Marco Asensio 2

No	Name	Nat	DoB	Pos	Aps	(s)	Gls
10	Abraham		16/07/85	M	13	(7)	1
22	Álvaro González		08/01/90	D	36		
23	Anaitz Arbilla		15/05/87	D	7		
1	Giedrius Arlauskis	LTU	01/12/87	G	3		
9	Burgui		29/10/93	A	8	(18)	1
20	Felipe Caicedo	ECU	05/09/88	A	26	(5)	8
25	José Cañas		27/05/87	M	7	(6)	
15	Michaël Ciani	FRA	06/04/84	D	2		
2	Roberto Correa		20/09/92	D	5	(2)	
12	Pape Diop	SEN	18/03/86	M	29	(1)	3
24	Óscar Duarte	CRC	03/06/89	D	13	(1)	1
3	Rubén Duarte		18/10/95	D	21	(1)	
18	Juan Fuentes		05/01/90	D	9	(1)	
7	Gerard Moreno		07/04/92	A	19	(13)	7
16	Javi López		21/01/86	D	28	(3)	
19	Joan Jordán		06/07/94	M	5	(4)	1
25	Marco Asensio		21/06/96	M	33	(1)	4
11	Paco Montañés		08/10/86	M	2	(5)	
13	Pau López		13/12/94	G	35	(1)	
17	Hernán Pérez	PAR	25/02/89	M	27	(5)	7
24	Antonio Raíllo		08/10/91	D	4		
6	Enzo Roco	CHI	16/08/92	D	26	(7)	2
8	Salva Sevilla		18/03/84	M	5	(10)	1
28	Mamadou Sylla	SEN	20/03/94	A	2	(12)	
5	Víctor Álvarez		14/03/93	M	25	(2)	1
4	Víctor Sánchez		08/09/87	M	28	(1)	1

Getafe CF

1983 • Coliseum Alfonso Pérez (16,800) • getafecf.com
Coach: Fran Escribá
(12/04/16) Juan Esnáider (ARG)

2015

22/08	a	Espanyol	L	0-1	
30/08	h	Granada	L	1-2	Lafita
13/09	a	Athletic	L	1-3	Velázquez
18/09	h	Málaga	W	1-0	Šćepović
22/09	a	Atlético	L	0-2	
27/09	h	Levante	W	3-0	Álvaro Vázquez 2, Emi Buendía
02/10	a	Celta	D	0-0	
18/10	h	Las Palmas	W	4-0	Víctor Rodríguez, Sarabia, Šćepović 2
24/10	a	Sevilla	L	0-5	
31/10	h	Barcelona	L	0-2	
07/11	h	Eibar	L	1-3	Víctor Rodríguez
23/11	h	Rayo Vallecano	D	1-1	og (Jozabed)
29/11	a	Villarreal	W	2-0	Lafita, Álvaro Vázquez
05/12	a	Real Madrid	L	1-4	Alexis
11/12	h	Real Sociedad	D	1-1	Sarabia
19/12	a	Valencia	D	2-2	Sarabia, Lafita
30/12	h	Deportivo	D	0-0	

2016

04/01	a	Sporting	W	2-1	Cala, Sarabia
09/01	h	Betis	W	1-0	Álvaro Vázquez
17/01	h	Espanyol	W	3-1	Pedro León, Sarabia, Moi Gómez
23/01	a	Granada	L	2-3	Šćepović, Moi Gómez
30/01	h	Athletic	L	0-1	
05/02	a	Málaga	L	0-3	
14/02	h	Atlético	L	0-1	
19/02	a	Levante	L	0-3	
27/02	h	Celta	L	0-1	
01/03	a	Las Palmas	L	0-4	
05/03	h	Sevilla	D	1-1	Velázquez
12/03	a	Barcelona	L	0-6	
18/03	h	Eibar	D	1-1	Velázquez
01/04	a	Rayo Vallecano	L	0-2	
10/04	a	Villarreal	L	0-2	
16/04	h	Real Madrid	L	1-5	Sarabia
21/04	a	Real Sociedad	W	2-1	Sarabia, Álvaro Vázquez (p)
24/04	a	Valencia	D	2-2	Álvaro Medrán, Šćepović
01/05	a	Deportivo	W	2-0	Pedro León, Vigaray
08/05	h	Sporting	D	1-1	Šćepović
15/05	a	Betis	L	1-2	Álvaro Medrán

No	Name	Nat	DoB	Pos	Aps	(s)	Gls
2	Alexis		04/08/85	D	15		1
23	Álvaro Medrán		15/03/94	M	16	(4)	2
9	Álvaro Vázquez		27/04/91	A	24	(10)	5
6	Cala		26/11/89	D	21	(1)	1
32	Emi Buendía	ARG	25/12/96	A	6	(11)	1
7	Henok Goitom	ERI	16/09/84	A	1	(1)	
13	Vicente Guaita		18/02/87	G	38		
26	Ian González		11/02/93	A		(1)	
27	Javi Noblejas		18/03/93	D	1		
22	Juan Rodríguez		01/04/82	M	30	(2)	
8	Mehdi Lacen	ALG	15/05/84	M	31		
7	Ángel Lafita		07/08/84	M	12	(2)	3
17	Bernard Mensah	GHA	17/10/94	M		(8)	
35	Miguel Muñoz		26/01/95	D	2	(1)	
21	Moi Gómez		23/06/94	M	9	(13)	2
14	Pedro León		24/11/86	M	23	(8)	2
2	Álvaro Pereira	URU	28/11/85	D	6		
3	Roberto Lago		30/08/85	D	17		
10	Pablo Sarabia		11/05/92	M	30	(1)	7
12	Stefan Šćepović	SRB	10/01/90	A	17	(17)	6
19	Damián Suárez	URU	27/04/88	D	30	(1)	
4	Emiliano Velázquez	URU	30/04/94	D	11		3
5	Santiago Vergini	ARG	03/08/88	D	24	(2)	
18	Víctor Rodríguez		23/07/89	M	26	(7)	2
15	Carlos Vigaray		07/05/94	D	14		1
30	Wamberto	BRA	07/10/94	A	6	(14)	
11	Abdoul Yoda	FRA	25/10/88	M	8	(10)	

Granada CF

1931 • Nuevo Los Cármenes (22,500) • granadacf.es
Coach: José Ramón Sandoval;
(22/02/16) José González

2015

24/08	h	Eibar	L	1-3	Rubén Rochina
30/08	a	Getafe	W	2-1	El-Arabi (p), Success
13/09	a	Villarreal	L	1-3	Fran Rico
19/09	a	Real Madrid	L	0-1	
22/09	h	Real Sociedad	L	0-3	
25/09	h	Valencia	L	0-1	
03/10	h	Deportivo	D	1-1	Piti
19/10	a	Sporting	D	3-3	Piti, Success, El-Arabi
24/10	h	Betis	D	1-1	Foulquier
01/11	a	Espanyol	D	1-1	Babin
07/11	a	Rayo Vallecano	L	1-2	Babin
22/11	h	Athletic	W	2-0	og (Laporte), Success
28/11	a	Málaga	D	2-2	El-Arabi, Rubén Rochina
05/12	h	Atlético	L	0-2	
12/12	a	Levante	W	2-1	Peñaranda 2
20/12	h	Celta	L	0-2	
30/12	a	Las Palmas	L	1-4	Peñaranda

2016

03/01	h	Sevilla	W	2-1	Success, Peñaranda
09/01	a	Barcelona	L	0-4	
18/01	a	Eibar	L	1-5	El-Arabi
23/01	h	Getafe	W	3-2	Fran Rico, El-Arabi, Rubén Rochina
30/01	a	Villarreal	L	0-1	
07/02	h	Real Madrid	L	1-2	El-Arabi
14/02	a	Real Sociedad	L	0-3	
21/02	h	Valencia	L	1-2	Édgar Méndez
28/02	a	Deportivo	W	1-0	El-Arabi (p)
03/03	a	Sporting	D	2-2	El-Arabi (p), Success
06/03	h	Betis	L	0-2	
14/03	h	Espanyol	D	1-1	Rubén Rochina
19/03	h	Rayo Vallecano	D	2-2	El-Arabi 2 (1p)
03/04	a	Athletic	D	1-1	Peñaranda
08/04	h	Málaga	D	0-0	
17/04	a	Atlético	D	0-0	
21/04	h	Levante	W	5-1	Success, El-Arabi 3 (2p), Rubén Rochina
25/04	a	Celta	L	0-2	
30/04	h	Las Palmas	W	3-2	Rubén Rochina, El-Arabi, Ricardo Costa
08/05	a	Sevilla	W	4-1	Cuenca 2, Babin, El-Arabi (p)
14/05	h	Barcelona	L	0-3	

No	Name	Nat	DoB	Pos	Aps	(s)	Gls
13	Andrés Fernández		16/12/86	G	37		
6	Jean-Sylvain Babin	MTQ	14/10/86	D	25		3
15	David Barral		10/05/83	A	3	(11)	
3	Cristiano Biraghi	ITA	01/09/92	D	32		
19	Isaac Cuenca		27/04/91	M	8	(4)	2
12	Dória	BRA	08/11/94	D	7	(1)	
16	Abdoulaye Doucouré	FRA	01/01/93	M	13	(2)	
17	Édgar Méndez		30/04/91	M	7	(8)	1
9	Youssef El-Arabi	MAR	03/02/87	A	27	(8)	16
22	Dimitri Foulquier	FRA	23/03/93	D	16	(5)	1
4	Fran Rico		03/08/87	M	15	(13)	2
7	Robert Ibáñez		22/03/93	A	7	(11)	
25	Jesús Fernández		11/06/88	G	1		
21	Rene Krhin	SVN	21/05/90	M	16	(8)	
2	David Lombán		05/06/87	D	29	(2)	
15	Nicolás López	URU	01/10/93	A	1	(7)	
5	Diego Mainz		29/12/82	D	4	(1)	
8	Javi Márquez		11/05/86	M	3	(6)	
18	Miguel Lopes	POR	19/12/86	D	23	(3)	
27	Adalberto Peñaranda	VEN	31/05/97	A	21	(2)	5
10	Piti		26/05/81	A	5	(3)	2
24	Ricardo Costa	POR	16/05/81	D	14		1
20	Rubén Pérez		26/04/89	M	30	(1)	
23	Rubén Rochina		23/03/91	A	29	(6)	6
14	Salva Ruiz		17/05/95	D	1	(1)	
11	Isaac Success	NGA	07/01/96	A	28	(2)	6
16	Thievy Bifouma	CGO	13/05/92	A		(7)	
26	Uche Agbo	NGA	04/12/95	M	3	(3)	

UD Las Palmas

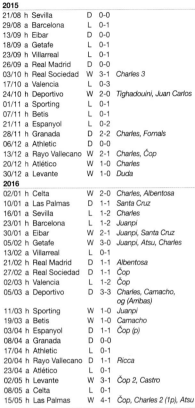

1949 • Gran Canaria (31,250) •
udlaspalmas.es
Coach: Paco Herrera;
(19/10/15) Quique Setién

2015

22/08	a	Atlético	L	0-1		
30/08	h	Levante	D	0-0		
13/09	a	Celta	D	3-3	Araujo, og (Hernández), David Simón	
20/09	h	Rayo Vallecano	L	0-1		
23/09	h	Sevilla	W	2-0	Roque Mesa, Alcaraz	
26/09	a	Barcelona	L	1-2	Jonathan Viera	
03/10	h	Eibar	L	0-2		
18/10	a	Getafe	L	0-4		
25/10	h	Villarreal	L	0-2		
31/10	a	Real Madrid	L	1-3	Hernán	
06/11	h	Real Sociedad	W	2-0	Jonathan Viera, Araujo	
21/11	a	Valencia	D	1-1	Jonathan Viera	
28/11	h	Deportivo	L	0-2		
06/12	a	Sporting	L	1-3	El Zhar	
12/12	h	Betis	W	1-0	Willian José	
19/12	h	Espanyol	L	0-1		
30/12	h	Granada	W	4-1	Tana, Araujo, Jonathan Viera (p), og (Lombán)	

2016

03/01	a	Athletic	D	2-2	Vicente Gómez, Tana	
10/01	h	Málaga	D	1-1	Tana	
17/01	a	Atlético	L	0-3		
25/01	a	Levante	L	2-3	Willian José 2	
31/01	h	Celta	W	2-1	Jonathan Viera (p), Willian José	
06/02	a	Rayo Vallecano	L	0-2		
14/02	a	Sevilla	L	0-2		
20/02	h	Barcelona	L	1-2	Willian José	
26/02	a	Eibar	W	1-0	Bigas	
01/03	h	Getafe	W	4-0	Willian José, Jonathan Viera (p), Tana 2	
05/03	a	Villarreal	W	1-0	David García	
13/03	h	Real Madrid	L	1-2	Willian José	
19/03	a	Real Sociedad	W	1-0	Willian José	
02/04	h	Valencia	W	2-1	Jonathan Viera (p), og (Mustafi)	
11/04	a	Deportivo	W	3-1	Araujo 2, David García	
16/04	h	Sporting	D	1-1	Bigas	
19/04	a	Betis	L	0-1		
22/04	h	Espanyol	W	4-0	El Zhar, Jonathan Viera, Bigas, Wakaso	
30/04	a	Granada	L	2-3	Jonathan Viera 2	
08/05	h	Athletic	D	0-0		
15/05	a	Málaga	L	1-4	Willian José	

No	Name	Nat	DoB	Pos	Aps	(s)	Gls
3	Antolín Alcaraz	PAR	30/07/82	D	6		1
6	Ángel López		10/03/81	D		(3)	
10	Sergio Araujo	ARG	28/01/92	A	20	(10)	5
16	Aythami		02/04/86	D	30	(1)	
17	Pedro Bigas		15/05/90	D	26	(1)	3
19	Juan Emmanuel Culio	ARG	30/08/83	M	6	(6)	
23	Dani Castellano		02/11/87	D	25	(2)	
5	David García		25/02/82	D	18	(1)	2
2	David Simón		31/12/89	D	24	(3)	1
25	Nabil El Zhar	MAR	27/08/86	M	17	(13)	2
22	Javier Garrido		15/03/85	D	18		
14	Hernán		26/08/90	M	11	(7)	1
18	Javi Castellano		02/11/87	M	1		
13	Javi Varas		10/09/82	G	31		
20	Jonathan Viera		21/10/89	A	36		10
3	Mauricio Lemos	URU	28/12/95	D	8	(2)	
1	Raúl Lizoaín		27/01/91	G	7	(1)	
11	Momo		15/07/82	M	15	(8)	
18	Ángel Montoro		25/06/88	M	5	(4)	
7	Nauzet Alemán		25/02/85	M	2	(8)	
29	Nili		18/02/94	M	4	(4)	
15	Roque Mesa		07/06/89	M	34		1
24	Tana		20/09/90	A	26	(1)	5
21	Juan Carlos Valerón		17/06/75	M	3	(10)	
4	Vicente Gómez		31/08/88	M	16	(5)	1
12	Wakaso Mubarak	GHA	25/07/90	M	10	(10)	1
8	Willian José	BRA	23/11/91	A	19	(11)	9

Levante UD

1939 • Ciutat de València (25,354) •
levanteud.com
Coach: Lucas Alcaraz;
(26/10/15) Rubi

2015

23/08	h	Celta	L	1-2	Verza	
30/08	a	Las Palmas	D	0-0		
11/09	h	Sevilla	D	1-1	Camarasa	
20/09	a	Barcelona	L	1-4	Víctor Casadesús	
23/09	h	Eibar	D	2-2	Morales, Deyverson	
27/09	a	Getafe	L	0-3		
04/10	h	Villarreal	W	1-0	Deyverson	
17/10	a	Real Madrid	L	0-3		
25/10	h	Real Sociedad	L	0-4		
31/10	a	Valencia	L	0-3		
07/11	h	Deportivo	D	1-1	Camarasa	
22/11	a	Sporting	W	3-0	Deyverson 2, Feddal	
27/11	h	Betis	L	0-1		
07/12	a	Espanyol	D	1-1	Lerma	
12/12	h	Granada	L	1-2	Simão	
20/12	a	Athletic	L	0-1		
30/12	h	Málaga	L	0-1		

2016

02/01	a	Atlético	L	0-1		
09/01	h	Rayo Vallecano	W	2-1	Deyverson, Morales	
16/01	a	Celta	L	3-4	Deyverson, Pedro López, Morales	
25/01	h	Las Palmas	W	3-2	Morales 2, Deyverson	
31/01	h	Sevilla	L	1-3	Rossi	
07/02	a	Barcelona	L	0-2		
14/02	a	Eibar	L	0-2		
19/02	h	Getafe	W	3-0	Morales, Rossi (p), Joan Verdú	
28/02	a	Villarreal	L	0-3		
02/03	h	Real Madrid	L	1-3	Deyverson	
06/03	a	Real Sociedad	D	1-1	Deyverson	
13/03	h	Valencia	W	1-0	Rossi	
19/03	a	Deportivo	L	1-2	Rossi	
04/04	h	Sporting	D	0-0		
09/04	a	Betis	L	0-1		
15/04	h	Espanyol	W	2-1	Rossi, Medjani	
21/04	a	Granada	L	1-5	Rubén García	
24/04	h	Athletic	D	2-2	Víctor Casadesús, og (Etxeita)	
02/05	a	Málaga	L	1-3	Morales	
08/05	h	Atlético	W	2-1	Víctor Casadesús, Rossi	
15/05	a	Rayo Vallecano	L	1-3	Verza (p)	

No	Name	Nat	DoB	Pos	Aps	(s)	Gls
6	Víctor Camarasa		28/05/94	M	21	(13)	2
9	Mauricio Cuero	COL	28/01/93	A	5	(8)	
4	David Navarro		25/05/80	D	20		
20	Deyverson	BRA	08/05/91	A	24	(9)	9
24	Zouhair Feddal	MAR	01/01/89	D	28		1
23	Nabil Ghilas	ALG	20/04/90	A	10	(10)	
2	Iván López		23/08/93	D	10	(3)	
25	José Verdú		05/05/83	M	10	(3)	1
22	José Mari		06/12/87	M	10	(2)	
12	Juanfran		15/07/76	D	19	(1)	
15	Nikolaos Karabelas	GRE	20/12/84	D	1		
8	Jefferson Lerma	COL	25/10/94	M	31	(2)	1
1	Diego Mariño		09/05/90	G	23		
14	Carl Medjani	ALG	15/05/85	M	14		1
11	José Luis Morales		23/07/87	M	31	(4)	7
15	Lucas Orbán	ARG	03/02/89	D	3		
19	Pedro López		01/11/83	D	16	(6)	1
14	Roger		03/01/91	A	7	(9)	
21	Giuseppe Rossi	ITA	01/02/87	A	15	(2)	6
13	Rubén		22/06/84	G	15		
10	Rubén García		14/07/93	M	9	(13)	1
5	Simão	MOZ	23/07/88	M	26	(4)	1
3	Toño		11/07/89	D	26	(1)	
16	Ángel Trujillo		08/09/87	D	8		
7	Verza		29/09/86	M	23	(6)	2
18	Víctor Casadesús		28/02/85	A	8	(15)	3
17	Jordi Xumetra		24/10/85	M	5	(8)	

Málaga CF

1994 • La Rosaleda (30,044) • malagacf.com
Coach: Javier Gracia

2015

21/08	h	Sevilla	D	0-0		
29/08	a	Barcelona	L	0-1		
13/09	h	Eibar	D	0-0		
18/09	a	Getafe	L	0-1		
23/09	h	Villarreal	L	0-1		
26/09	a	Real Madrid	D	0-0		
03/10	h	Real Sociedad	W	3-1	Charles 3	
17/10	a	Valencia	D	0-0		
24/10	h	Deportivo	W	2-0	Tighadouini, Juan Carlos	
01/11	a	Sporting	L	0-1		
07/11	h	Betis	L	0-1		
21/11	a	Espanyol	L	0-2		
28/11	h	Granada	D	2-2	Charles, Fornals	
06/12	a	Athletic	D	0-0		
13/12	h	Rayo Vallecano	W	2-1	Charles, Čop	
20/12	a	Atlético	L	0-1		
30/12	a	Levante	W	1-0	Duda	

2016

02/01	h	Celta	W	2-0	Charles, Albentosa	
10/01	h	Las Palmas	D	1-1	Santa Cruz	
16/01	a	Sevilla	L	1-2	Charles	
23/01	h	Barcelona	L	1-2	Juanpi	
30/01	a	Eibar	W	2-1	Juanpi, Santa Cruz	
05/02	h	Getafe	W	3-0	Juanpi, Atsu, Charles	
13/02	a	Villarreal	L	0-1		
21/02	h	Real Madrid	D	1-1	Albentosa	
27/02	a	Real Sociedad	D	1-1	Čop	
02/03	h	Valencia	L	1-2	Čop	
05/03	a	Deportivo	D	3-3	Charles, Camacho, og (Arribas)	
11/03	h	Sporting	W	1-0	Juanpi	
19/03	h	Betis	W	1-0	Camacho	
03/04	h	Espanyol	D	1-1	Čop (p)	
08/04	a	Granada	D	0-0		
17/04	a	Athletic	L	0-1		
20/04	h	Rayo Vallecano	D	1-1	Ricca	
23/04	a	Atlético	L	0-1		
02/05	h	Levante	W	3-1	Čop 2, Castro	
08/05	a	Celta	L	0-1		
15/05	h	Las Palmas	W	4-1	Čop, Charles 2 (1p), Atsu	

No	Name	Nat	DoB	Pos	Aps	(s)	Gls
2	Raúl Albentosa		07/09/88	D	27	(2)	2
11	Nordin Amrabat	MAR	31/03/87	A	13		
15	Marcos Angeleri	ARG	07/04/83	D	13		
11	Christian Atsu	GHA	10/01/92	M	3	(9)	2
19	Arthur Boka	CIV	02/04/83	D	12	(2)	
6	Ignacio Camacho		04/05/90	M	23		2
5	Gonzalo Castro	URU	14/09/84	M	15	(1)	1
9	Charles	BRA	04/04/84	A	33	(2)	12
20	Duje Čop	CRO	01/02/90	A	25	(6)	7
30	Sergi Darder		22/12/93	M	1		
17	Duda	POR	27/06/80	M	10	(15)	1
8	Fábio Espinho	POR	18/08/85	M		(2)	
21	Yegor Filipenko	BLR	10/04/88	D	6	(2)	
31	Pablo Fornals		22/02/96	M	12	(15)	1
7	Juan Carlos		20/03/90	D	14	(5)	1
28	Juanpi	VEN	24/01/94	M	18	(11)	4
1	Carlos Kameni	CMR	18/02/84	G	28		
16	Hachim Mastour	MAR	15/06/98	A		(1)	
23	Miguel Torres		28/01/86	D	22	(1)	
13	Guillermo Ochoa	MEX	13/07/85	G	10	(1)	
39	Javier Ontiveros		09/09/97	M		(4)	
10	Recio		11/10/91	M	32	(1)	
10	Ricardo Horta	POR	15/09/94	A	9	(8)	
15	Federico Ricca	URU	01/12/94	D	7	(1)	1
18	Roberto Rosales	VEN	20/11/88	D	35		
24	Roque Santa Cruz	PAR	16/08/81	A	3	(14)	2
22	Adnane Tighadouini	MAR	30/10/92	A	4	(6)	1
12	Fernando Tissone	ARG	24/07/86	M	12		
8	Ikechukwu Uche	NGA	05/01/84	A	1	(2)	
3	Weligton	BRA	26/08/79	D	30		

Rayo Vallecano de Madrid

1924 • Vallecas (14,708) • rayovallecano.es
Coach: Paco Jémez

2015

Date		Opponent	Res	Score	Scorers
22/08	h	Valencia	D	0-0	
29/08	a	Celta	L	0-3	
14/09	h	Deportivo	L	1-3	Embarba
20/09	a	Las Palmas	W	1-0	Javi Guerra
23/09	h	Sporting	W	2-1	Trashorras (p), Javi Guerra
26/09	a	Sevilla	L	2-3	Bebé, Javi Guerra
04/10	h	Betis	L	0-2	
17/10	a	Barcelona	L	2-5	Javi Guerra, Jozabed
23/10	h	Espanyol	W	3-0	Trashorras (p), Javi Guerra 2
01/11	a	Eibar	L	0-1	
07/11	h	Granada	W	2-1	Javi Guerra 2
23/11	a	Getafe	D	1-1	Jozabed
29/11	h	Athletic	L	0-3	
06/12	h	Villarreal	L	1-2	Jozabed
13/12	h	Málaga	L	1-2	Javi Guerra
20/12	a	Real Madrid	L	2-10	Amaya, Jozabed
30/12	h	Atlético	L	0-2	

2016

Date		Opponent	Res	Score	Scorers
03/01	h	Real Sociedad	D	2-2	Llorente, Jozabed
09/01	a	Levante	L	1-2	Pablo Hernández
17/01	a	Valencia	D	2-2	Jozabed, Llorente
23/01	h	Celta	W	3-0	Miku, Tito, Jozabed
01/02	a	Deportivo	D	2-2	Miku, Jozabed
06/02	h	Las Palmas	W	2-0	Miku, Bebé
12/02	a	Sporting	D	2-2	Miku, Jozabed
21/02	h	Sevilla	D	2-2	Manucho, Miku
27/02	a	Betis	D	2-2	Manucho 2
03/03	h	Barcelona	L	1-5	Manucho
07/03	a	Espanyol	L	1-2	Bebé
12/03	h	Eibar	D	1-1	Zé Castro
19/03	a	Granada	D	2-2	Pablo Hernández, Zé Castro
01/04	h	Getafe	W	2-0	Javi Guerra, Miku
10/04	a	Athletic	L	0-1	
17/04	h	Villarreal	W	2-1	Javi Guerra, Miku
20/04	a	Málaga	D	1-1	Baena
23/04	h	Real Madrid	L	2-3	Embarba, Miku
30/04	a	Atlético	L	0-1	
08/05	a	Real Sociedad	L	1-2	Javi Guerra
15/05	h	Levante	W	3-1	Pablo Hernández, Jozabed, Miku

No	Name	Nat	DoB	Pos	Aps	(s)	Gls
4	Antonio Amaya		31/05/83	D	10	(7)	1
8	Raúl Baena		02/03/89	M	22	(2)	1
19	Alhassane "Lass" Bangoura	GUI	30/03/92	A	7	(9)	
23	Bebé	POR	12/07/90	A	27	(7)	3
22	José Ángel Crespo		09/02/87	D	9		
5	José Antonio Dorado		10/07/82	D	4	(6)	
20	Patrick Ebert	GER	17/03/87	M	7	(2)	
11	Adrián Embarba		07/05/92	M	19	(9)	2
12	Luis Fariña	ARG	20/04/91	M		(3)	
6	Manuel Iturra	CHI	23/06/84	M	4	(2)	
24	Javi Guerra		15/03/82	A	23	(7)	12
26	Jonathan Caballero		03/09/98	M	1	(7)	
21	Jozabed		08/03/91	M	24	(3)	10
13	Juan Carlos		20/01/88	G	19	(2)	
27	Diego Llorente		16/08/93	D	33		2
9	Manucho	ANG	07/03/83	A	5	(23)	4
7	Miku	VEN	19/08/85	A	18	(4)	9
3	Nacho		07/03/89	D	22		
16	Aras Özbiliz	ARM	09/03/90	M	1	(2)	
14	Pablo Hernández		11/04/85	M	24	(3)	3
12	Piti		26/05/81	M	4	(4)	
17	Quini		01/01/90	D	22	(5)	
15	Răzvan Raţ	ROU	26/05/81	D	8	(2)	
2	Tito		11/07/85	D	29		1
25	Toño		17/12/79	G	10		
10	Roberto Trashorras		28/02/81	M	35	(1)	2
25	Yoel		28/08/88	G	5		
18	Zé Castro	POR	13/01/83	D	22		2
16	Zhang Chengdong	CHN	09/02/89	M		(1)	

Real Madrid CF

1902 • Santiago Bernabéu (80,354) • realmadrid.com

Major honours
European Champion Clubs' Cup/UEFA Champions League (11) 1956, 1957, 1958, 1959, 1960, 1966, 1998, 2000, 2002, 2014, 2016;
UEFA Cup (2) 1985, 1986;
UEFA Super Cup (2) 2002, 2014;
European/South American Cup (3) 1960, 1998, 2002; FIFA Club World Cup (1) 2014;
Spanish League (32) 1932, 1933, 1954, 1955, 1957, 1958, 1961, 1962, 1963, 1964, 1965, 1967, 1968, 1969, 1972, 1975, 1976, 1978, 1979, 1980, 1986, 1987, 1988, 1989, 1990, 1995, 1997, 2001, 2003, 2007, 2008, 2012;
Spanish Cup (19) 1905, 1906, 1907, 1908, 1917, 1934, 1936, 1946, 1947, 1962, 1970, 1974, 1975, 1980, 1982, 1989, 1993, 2011, 2014

Coach: Rafael Benítez;
(04/01/16) Zinédine Zidane (FRA)

2015

Date		Opponent	Res	Score	Scorers
23/08	a	Sporting	D	0-0	
29/08	h	Betis	W	5-0	Bale 2, James Rodríguez 2, Benzema
12/09	h	Espanyol	W	6-0	Cristiano Ronaldo 5 (1p), Benzema
19/09	h	Granada	W	1-0	Benzema
23/09	a	Athletic	W	2-1	Benzema 2
26/09	h	Málaga	D	0-0	
04/10	a	Atlético	D	1-1	Benzema
17/10	h	Levante	W	3-0	Marcelo, Cristiano Ronaldo, Jesé
24/10	a	Celta	W	3-1	Cristiano Ronaldo, Danilo, Marcelo
31/10	h	Las Palmas	W	3-1	Isco, Cristiano Ronaldo, Jesé
08/11	a	Sevilla	L	2-3	Sergio Ramos, James Rodríguez
21/11	h	Barcelona	L	0-4	
29/11	a	Eibar	W	2-0	Bale, Cristiano Ronaldo (p)
05/12	h	Getafe	W	4-1	Benzema 2, Bale, Cristiano Ronaldo
13/12	a	Villarreal	L	0-1	
20/12	h	Rayo Vallecano	W	10-2	Danilo, Bale 4, Cristiano Ronaldo 2 (1p), Benzema 3
30/12	h	Real Sociedad	W	3-1	Cristiano Ronaldo 2 (1p), Lucas Vázquez

2016

Date		Opponent	Res	Score	Scorers
03/01	a	Valencia	D	2-2	Benzema, Bale
09/01	h	Deportivo	W	5-0	Benzema 2, Bale 3
17/01	h	Sporting	W	5-1	Bale, Cristiano Ronaldo 2, Benzema 2
24/01	a	Betis	D	1-1	Benzema
31/01	h	Espanyol	W	6-0	Benzema, Cristiano Ronaldo 3 (1p), James Rodríguez, og (Ó Duarte)
07/02	a	Granada	W	2-1	Benzema, Modrić
13/02	h	Athletic	W	4-2	Cristiano Ronaldo 2, James Rodríguez, Kroos
21/02	a	Málaga	D	1-1	Cristiano Ronaldo
27/02	a	Atlético	L	0-1	
02/03	h	Levante	W	3-1	Cristiano Ronaldo (p), og (Mariño), Isco
05/03	h	Celta	W	7-1	Pepe, Cristiano Ronaldo 4, Jesé, Bale
13/03	a	Las Palmas	W	2-1	Sergio Ramos, Casemiro
20/03	h	Sevilla	W	4-0	Benzema, Cristiano Ronaldo, Bale, Jesé
02/04	a	Barcelona	W	2-1	Benzema, Cristiano Ronaldo
09/04	h	Eibar	W	4-0	James Rodríguez, Lucas Vázquez, Cristiano Ronaldo, Jesé
16/04	h	Getafe	W	5-1	Benzema, Isco, Bale, James Rodríguez, Cristiano Ronaldo
20/04	h	Villarreal	W	3-0	Benzema, Lucas Vázquez, Modrić
23/04	a	Rayo Vallecano	W	3-2	Bale 2, Lucas Vázquez
30/04	a	Real Sociedad	W	1-0	Bale
08/05	h	Valencia	W	3-2	Cristiano Ronaldo 2, Benzema
14/05	a	Deportivo	W	2-0	Cristiano Ronaldo 2

No	Name	Nat	DoB	Pos	Aps	(s)	Gls
17	Álvaro Arbeloa		17/01/83	D	2	(4)	
11	Gareth Bale	WAL	16/07/89	A	21	(2)	19
9	Karim Benzema	FRA	19/12/87	A	26	(1)	24
29	Borja Mayoral		05/04/97	A	3	(3)	
15	Daniel Carvajal		11/01/92	D	19	(3)	
14	Casemiro	BRA	20/02/92	M	17	(6)	1
13	Kiko Casilla		02/10/86	G	4		
21	Denis Cheryshev	RUS	26/12/90	M		(2)	
7	Cristiano Ronaldo	POR	05/02/85	A	36		35
23	Danilo	BRA	15/07/91	D	23	(1)	2
22	Isco		21/04/92	M	21	(10)	4
10	James Rodríguez	COL	12/07/91	M	19	(9)	7
20	Jesé		26/02/93	A	7	(21)	5
16	Mateo Kovačić	CRO	06/05/94	M	8	(17)	
8	Toni Kroos	GER	04/01/90	M	32		1
28	Marcos Llorente		30/01/95	M		(2)	
18	Lucas Vázquez		01/07/91	M	10	(15)	4
12	Marcelo	BRA	12/05/88	D	28	(2)	2
19	Luka Modrić	CRO	09/09/85	M	31	(1)	2
6	Nacho		18/01/90	D	12	(4)	
1	Keylor Navas	CRC	15/12/86	G	34		
3	Pepe	POR	26/02/83	D	21		1
4	Sergio Ramos		30/03/86	D	23		2
2	Raphaël Varane	FRA	25/04/93	D	23	(3)	

SPAIN

Real Sociedad de Fútbol

1909 • Anoeta (32,076) • realsociedad.com
Major honours
Spanish League (2) 1981, 1982; Spanish Cup (2) 1909, 1987
Coach: David Moyes (SCO); (10/11/15) Eusebio Sacristán

2015

22/08	a Deportivo	D	0-0	
29/08	h Sporting	D	0-0	
12/09	h Betis	L	0-1	
19/09	a Espanyol	L	2-3	Agirretxe, Jonathas
22/09	a Granada	W	3-0	Agirretxe 3
27/09	h Athletic	D	0-0	
03/10	a Málaga	L	1-3	Agirretxe
18/10	h Atlético	L	0-2	
25/10	h Levante	W	4-0	Vela 2, Agirretxe, Illarramendi
31/10	h Celta	L	2-3	Agirretxe 2
06/11	a Las Palmas	L	0-2	
21/11	h Sevilla	W	2-0	Agirretxe, Xabi Prieto
28/11	a Barcelona	L	0-4	
06/12	h Eibar	W	2-1	Agirretxe 2
11/12	a Getafe	D	1-1	Agirretxe
20/12	h Villarreal	L	0-2	
30/12	a Real Madrid	L	1-3	Bruma

2016

03/01	a Rayo Vallecano	D	2-2	Aritz Elustondo, Bruma
10/01	h Valencia	W	2-0	Jonathas 2
16/01	h Deportivo	D	1-1	Xabi Prieto (p)
22/01	a Sporting	L	1-5	Vela
30/01	h Betis	W	2-1	Xabi Prieto, Íñigo Martínez
08/02	a Espanyol	W	5-0	Jonathas 2, Vela, Oyarzábal, Reyes
14/02	h Granada	W	3-0	Oyarzábal 2, Jonathas
21/02	h Athletic	W	1-0	Jonathas
27/02	h Málaga	D	1-1	Agirretxe
01/03	a Atlético	L	0-3	
06/03	h Levante	D	1-1	Reyes
12/03	a Celta	L	0-1	
19/03	h Las Palmas	L	0-1	
03/04	a Sevilla	W	2-1	Markel Bergara, og (Krychowiak)
09/04	h Barcelona	W	1-0	Oyarzábal
16/04	a Eibar	L	1-2	Zurutuza
21/04	h Getafe	L	1-2	Vela
24/04	a Villarreal	D	0-0	
30/04	h Real Madrid	L	0-1	
08/05	h Rayo Vallecano	W	2-1	Oyarzábal, Jon Bautista
13/05	a Valencia	W	1-0	Oyarzábal

No	Name	Nat	DoB	Pos	Aps	(s)	Gls
9	Imanol Agirretxe		24/02/87	A	14	(2)	13
30	Aritz Elustondo		28/03/84	D	30	(1)	1
7	Bruma	POR	24/10/94	A	14	(18)	2
16	Sergio Canales		16/02/91	M	11	(5)	
34	Eneko Capilla		13/06/95	M		(1)	
2	Carlos Martínez		09/04/86	D	6	(4)	
18	Gonzalo Castro	URU	14/09/84	M	1	(7)	
24	Alberto de la Bella		02/12/85	D	14	(1)	
8	Esteban Granero		02/07/87	M	9	(6)	
21	Héctor Hernández		23/05/91	D	4	(9)	
4	Asier Illarramendi		08/03/90	M	32	(1)	1
6	Íñigo Martínez		17/05/91	D	30		1
35	Jon Bautista		03/07/95	A	1	(3)	1
22	Jonathas	BRA	06/03/89	A	17	(10)	7
5	Markel Bergara		05/05/86	M	15	(5)	1
28	Mikel González		24/09/85	D	17	(2)	
13	Oier Olazábal		14/09/89	G	2	(1)	
28	Mikel Oyarzábal		21/04/97	A	16	(6)	6
23	Diego Reyes	MEX	19/09/92	D	26	(1)	2
14	Rubén Pardo		22/10/92	M	19	(9)	
1	Gerónimo Rulli	ARG	20/05/92	G	36		
10	Carlos Vela	MEX	01/03/89	A	32	(3)	5
7	Xabi Prieto		29/08/83	M	27	(9)	3
19	Yuri Berchiche		10/02/90	D	21		
20	Joseba Zaldúa		24/06/92	D	10	(3)	
29	Igor Zubeldia		30/03/97	M		(1)	
17	David Zurutuza		19/07/86	M	14	(2)	1

Sevilla FC

1905 • Ramón Sánchez Pizjuán (45,500) • sevillafc.es
Major honours
UEFA Cup (2) 2006, 2007; UEFA Europa League (3) 2014, 2015, 2016; UEFA Super Cup (1) 2006; Spanish League (1) 1946; Spanish Cup (5) 1935, 1939, 1948, 2007, 2010
Coach: Unai Emery

2015

21/08	a Málaga	D	0-0	
30/08	h Atlético	L	0-3	
11/09	a Levante	D	1-1	N'Zonzi
20/09	h Celta	L	1-2	Llorente
23/09	a Las Palmas	L	0-2	
26/09	h Rayo Vallecano	W	3-2	Gameiro, N'Zonzi, Konoplyanka
03/10	h Barcelona	W	2-1	Krohn-Dehli, Iborra
17/10	a Eibar	D	1-1	Gameiro
24/10	h Getafe	W	5-0	Gameiro 3 (1p), Éver Banega (p), Konoplyanka (p)
31/10	a Villarreal	L	1-2	Llorente
08/11	h Real Madrid	W	3-2	Immobile, Éver Banega, Llorente
21/11	a Real Sociedad	L	0-2	
29/11	h Valencia	W	1-0	Sergio Escudero
05/12	a Deportivo	D	1-1	Iborra
12/12	h Sporting	W	2-0	Gameiro 2 (1p)
19/12	a Betis	D	0-0	
30/12	h Espanyol	W	2-0	Immobile, Éver Banega

2016

03/01	a Granada	L	1-2	Vítolo
09/01	h Athletic	W	2-0	Gameiro 2 (1p)
16/01	h Málaga	W	2-1	Gameiro 2
24/01	a Atlético	D	0-0	
31/01	h Levante	W	3-1	Gameiro, Iborra, Konoplyanka
07/02	a Celta	D	1-1	Daniel Carriço
14/02	h Las Palmas	W	2-0	Éver Banega, Gameiro
21/02	a Rayo Vallecano	D	2-2	N'Zonzi, Iborra
28/02	a Barcelona	L	1-2	Vítolo
02/03	h Eibar	W	1-0	Llorente
05/03	a Getafe	D	1-1	Éver Banega
13/03	h Villarreal	W	4-2	Iborra, og (Víctor Ruiz), Konoplyanka, Reyes
20/03	a Real Madrid	L	0-4	
03/04	h Real Sociedad	L	1-2	Gameiro (p)
10/04	a Valencia	L	1-2	Gameiro
17/04	h Deportivo	D	1-1	Iborra
20/04	a Sporting	L	1-2	Iborra
24/04	h Betis	W	2-0	Gameiro, Coke
01/05	a Espanyol	L	0-1	
08/05	h Granada	L	1-4	Diego González
14/05	a Athletic	L	1-3	Juan Muñoz

No	Name	Nat	DoB	Pos	Aps	(s)	Gls
17	Marco Andreolli	ITA	10/06/86	D	7		
13	Beto	POR	01/05/82	G	4		
28	Carlos Fernández		22/05/96	A		(1)	
26	David Carmona		11/07/97	D	1		
23	Coke		26/04/87	D	20	(1)	1
27	Antonio Cotán		19/09/95	M	1		
17	Sebastián Cristóforo	URU	23/08/93	M	17	(4)	
36	Curro Sánchez		03/01/96	M	3	(1)	
6	Daniel Carriço	POR	04/08/88	D	11	(3)	1
38	Diego González		28/01/95	D	1	(1)	1
17	Diogo Figueiras	POR	01/07/91	D	4		
19	Éver Banega	ARG	29/06/88	M	20	(5)	5
16	Federico Fazio	ARG	17/03/87	D	4		
9	Kevin Gameiro	FRA	09/05/87	A	22	(9)	16
8	Vicente Iborra		16/01/88	M	21	(8)	7
11	Ciro Immobile	ITA	20/02/90	A	4	(4)	2
11	Juan Muñoz		12/11/95	A	3	(5)	1
12	Gaël Kakuta	FRA	21/06/91	M	1	(1)	
5	Timothée Kolodziejczak	FRA	01/10/91	D	26	(3)	
22	Yevhen Konoplyanka	UKR	29/09/89	M	15	(17)	4
7	Michael Krohn-Dehli	DEN	06/06/83	M	16	(11)	1
4	Grzegorz Krychowiak	POL	29/01/90	M	25	(1)	
24	Fernando Llorente		26/02/85	A	14	(9)	4
25	Mariano	BRA	23/06/86	D	18	(5)	
29	José Matos		06/05/95	D	1		
15	Steven N'Zonzi	FRA	15/12/88	M	22	(6)	3
21	Nicolás Pareja	ARG	19/01/84	D	1	(1)	
3	Adil Rami	FRA	27/12/85	D	28		
10	José Antonio Reyes		01/09/83	M	14	(10)	1
18	Sergio Escudero		02/09/89	D	13	(2)	1
1	Sergio Rico		01/09/93	G	34		
2	Benoît Trémoulinas	FRA	28/12/85	D	24		
20	Vítolo		02/11/89	M	23	(5)	4

Real Sporting de Gijón

1905 • El Molinón (29,000) • realsporting.com
Coach: Abelardo Fernández

2015

23/08	h Real Madrid	D	0-0	
29/08	a Real Sociedad	D	0-0	
12/09	h Valencia	L	0-1	
20/09	a Deportivo	W	3-2	Sanabria 2, Álex Menéndez
23/09	h Rayo Vallecano	L	1-2	Jony
27/09	h Betis	L	1-2	Carlos Castro
03/10	a Espanyol	W	2-1	Halilović, Álex Menéndez
19/10	h Granada	D	3-3	Espinosa, Nacho Cases, Guerrero
26/10	a Athletic	L	0-3	
01/11	h Málaga	W	1-0	Halilović
08/11	h Atlético	L	0-1	
22/11	h Levante	L	0-3	
28/11	a Celta	L	1-2	Carlos Castro
06/12	h Las Palmas	W	3-1	Sanabria 3
12/12	a Sevilla	L	0-2	
30/12	a Eibar	L	0-2	

2016

04/01	h Getafe	L	1-2	Sanabria
10/01	a Villarreal	L	0-2	
17/01	h Real Madrid	L	1-5	Isma López
22/01	h Real Sociedad	W	5-1	Carmona, N'Di, Sanabria 3
31/01	a Valencia	W	1-0	Sanabria (p)
06/02	h Deportivo	D	1-1	Jony
12/02	h Rayo Vallecano	D	2-2	Guerrero, Halilović
17/02	h Barcelona	L	1-3	Carlos Castro
20/02	h Betis	D	1-1	Carlos Castro
27/02	h Espanyol	L	2-4	Carlos Castro 2
03/03	a Granada	L	0-2	
06/03	h Athletic	L	0-2	
11/03	a Málaga	L	0-1	
19/03	h Atlético	W	2-1	Sanabria, Carlos Castro
04/04	a Levante	D	0-0	
10/04	h Celta	L	0-1	
16/04	a Las Palmas	D	1-1	Jony
20/04	h Sevilla	W	2-1	og (Krychowiak), Isma López
23/04	a Barcelona	L	0-6	
29/04	h Eibar	W	2-0	Carmona, Jony
08/05	a Getafe	D	1-1	Sergio Álvarez
15/05	h Villarreal	W	2-0	Jony, Sergio Álvarez

No	Name	Nat	DoB	Pos	Aps	(s)	Gls
24	Rachid Aït-Atmane	FRA	04/02/93	M	11	(7)	
13	Alberto García		09/02/85	G	6		
8	Álex Barrera		12/05/91	M		(5)	
3	Álex Menéndez		15/07/91	M	11	(10)	2
15	Roberto Canella		07/02/88	D	8	(1)	
16	Carlos Castro		01/06/95	A	7	(18)	7
19	Carlos Carmona		05/07/87	M	16	(4)	2
1	Iván Cuéllar		27/05/84	G	32		
5	Bernardo Espinosa	COL	11/07/89	D	16		1
9	Miguel Ángel Guerrero		12/07/90	A	13	(10)	2
14	Alberto Guitián		29/07/90	D	1		
25	Alen Halilović	CRO	18/06/96	M	24	(12)	3
21	Hugo Fraile		16/03/87	M	1	(2)	
18	Isma López		29/01/90	D	28	(3)	2
23	Jony		09/07/91	M	33	(3)	5
28	Jorge Meré		17/04/97	D	24	(1)	
7	Juan Muñiz		14/03/92	D		(4)	
4	Igor Lichnovsky	CHI	07/03/94	D	2		
11	Alberto Lora		25/03/87	D	26	(5)	
2	Luis Hernández		14/04/89	D	36		
17	Omar Mascarell	EQG	02/02/93	M	20	(6)	
27	Mendi		12/06/93	A		(1)	
33	Dani N'Di	CMR	18/08/95	M	10	(5)	1
10	Nacho Cases		22/12/87	M	21	(3)	1
22	Pablo Pérez		09/05/90	M	9	(9)	
20	Antonio Sanabria	PAR	04/03/96	A	27	(2)	11
6	Sergio Álvarez		23/01/92	M	26	(1)	2
21	Ognjen Vranješ	BIH	24/10/89	D	10	(1)	

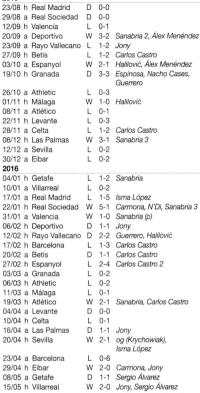

Valencia CF

1919 • Mestalla (55,000) • valenciacf.com

Major honours
UEFA Cup Winners' Cup (1) 1980; UEFA Cup (1)
2004; Inter Cities Fairs Cup (2) 1962, 1963;
UEFA Super Cup (2) 1980, 2004; Spanish League (6)
1942, 1944, 1947, 1971, 2002, 2004; Spanish Cup (7)
1941, 1949, 1954, 1967, 1979, 1999, 2008

Coach: Nuno Espírito Santo (POR);
(30/11/15) (Voro);
(02/12/15) Gary Neville (ENG);
(30/03/16) Pako Ayestarán

2015

22/08	a	Rayo Vallecano	D	0-0	
30/08	h	Deportivo	D	1-1	Negredo
12/09	a	Sporting	W	1-0	Paco Alcácer
19/09	h	Betis	D	0-0	
22/09	a	Espanyol	L	0-1	
25/09	h	Granada	W	1-0	Mustafi
04/10	a	Athletic	L	1-3	Parejo
17/10	h	Málaga	W	3-0	og (Charles), André Gomes, Parejo (p)
25/10	a	Atlético	L	1-2	Paco Alcácer (p)
31/10	h	Levante	W	3-0	Paco Alcácer (p), Feghouli, Bakkali
07/11	a	Celta	W	5-1	Paco Alcácer 2, Parejo 2, Mustafi
21/11	h	Las Palmas	D	1-1	Paco Alcácer
29/11	a	Sevilla	L	0-1	
05/12	h	Barcelona	D	1-1	Santi Mina
13/12	a	Eibar	D	1-1	André Gomes
19/12	h	Getafe	D	2-2	Paco Alcácer, Santi Mina
31/12	a	Villarreal	L	0-1	

2016

03/01	h	Real Madrid	D	2-2	Parejo (p), Paco Alcácer
10/01	a	Real Sociedad	L	0-2	
17/01	h	Rayo Vallecano	D	2-2	Negredo, Paco Alcácer
24/01	a	Deportivo	D	1-1	Negredo
31/01	h	Sporting	L	0-1	
07/02	a	Betis	L	0-1	
13/02	h	Espanyol	W	2-1	Negredo, Cheryshev
21/02	a	Granada	W	2-1	Parejo, Santi Mina
28/02	h	Athletic	L	0-3	
02/03	a	Málaga	W	2-1	og (Kameni), Cheryshev
06/03	h	Atlético	L	1-3	Cheryshev
13/03	a	Levante	L	0-1	
20/03	h	Celta	L	0-2	
02/04	a	Las Palmas	L	1-2	Rodrigo
10/04	h	Sevilla	W	2-1	Parejo, Negredo
17/04	a	Barcelona	W	2-1	og (Rakitić), Santi Mina
20/04	h	Eibar	W	4-0	Paco Alcácer 3, Joâo Cancelo
24/04	a	Getafe	D	2-2	Parejo, Paco Alcácer
01/05	h	Villarreal	L	0-2	
08/05	a	Real Madrid	L	2-3	Rodrigo, André Gomes
13/05	h	Real Sociedad	L	0-1	

No	Name	Nat	DoB	Pos	Aps	(s)	Gls
23	Aymen Abdennour	TUN	06/10/89	D	22		
4	Aderlan Santos	BRA	09/04/89	D	17		
21	André Gomes	POR	30/07/93	M	27	(3)	3
16	Zakaria Bakkali	BEL	26/01/96	M	4	(12)	1
19	Antonio Barragán		12/06/87	D	19	(5)	
24	Denis Cheryshev	RUS	26/12/90	M	6	(1)	3
12	Danilo	BRA	28/02/96	M	16	(3)	
20	Rodrigo de Paul	ARG	24/05/94	A	6	(3)	
1	Diego Alves	BRA	24/06/85	G	13		
8	Sofiane Feghouli	ALG	26/12/89	M	13	(8)	1
30	Fran Villalba		11/05/98	M		(1)	
14	José Gayá		25/05/95	D	15	(5)	
13	Jaume Doménech		05/11/90	G	17		
18	Javi Fuego		04/01/84	M	23	(3)	
2	Joâo Cancelo	POR	27/05/94	D	25	(3)	1
5	Shkodran Mustafi	GER	17/04/92	D	30		2
7	Álvaro Negredo		20/08/85	A	12	(13)	5
6	Lucas Orbán	ARG	03/02/89	D	6	(1)	
9	Paco Alcácer		30/08/93	A	25	(9)	13
10	Daniel Parejo		16/04/89	M	30	(3)	8
15	Enzo Pérez	ARG	22/02/86	M	16	(4)	
11	Pablo Piatti	ARG	31/03/89	A	9	(12)	
17	Rodrigo		06/03/91	A	15	(10)	2
3	Rúben Vezo	POR	25/04/94	D	10	(5)	
25	Mathew Ryan	AUS	08/04/92	G	8		
22	Santi Mina		07/12/95	A	18	(8)	4
6	Guilherme Siqueira	BRA	28/04/86	D	14		
34	Sito Pascual		18/11/96	M		(1)	
28	Tropi		12/05/95	M		(1)	
29	Wilfried Zahibo	FRA	21/08/93	M	2		

Villarreal CF

1923 • El Madrigal (24,500) • villarrealcf.es

Coach: Marcelino

2015

23/08	a	Betis	D	1-1	Soldado
28/08	h	Espanyol	W	3-1	Soldado, Bakambu 2
13/09	a	Granada	W	3-1	Trigueros, Bakambu, Samuel
20/09	h	Athletic	W	3-1	Bruno Soriano (p), Mario, Léo Baptistão
23/09	a	Málaga	W	1-0	og (Tissone)
26/09	h	Atlético	W	1-0	Léo Baptistão
04/10	a	Levante	L	0-1	
18/10	h	Celta	L	1-2	Denis Suárez
25/10	a	Las Palmas	D	0-0	
31/10	h	Sevilla	W	2-1	Mario, Bakambu
08/11	a	Barcelona	L	0-3	
22/11	h	Eibar	D	1-1	Jaume Costa
29/11	h	Getafe	L	0-2	
06/12	h	Rayo Vallecano	W	2-1	Bakambu 2
13/12	h	Real Madrid	W	1-0	Soldado
20/12	a	Real Sociedad	W	2-0	Denis Suárez 2
31/12	h	Valencia	W	1-0	Bruno Soriano

2016

03/01	h	Deportivo	W	2-1	Bruno Soriano 2 (1p)
10/01	h	Sporting	W	2-0	Bakambu 2
16/01	h	Betis	D	0-0	
23/01	a	Espanyol	D	2-2	Trigueros, Musacchio
30/01	h	Granada	W	1-0	Bruno Soriano (p)
06/02	a	Athletic	D	0-0	
13/02	h	Málaga	W	1-0	Soldado
21/02	a	Atlético	D	0-0	
28/02	h	Levante	W	3-0	Léo Baptistão, Samu Castillejo, Adrián López
02/03	a	Celta	D	0-0	
05/03	h	Las Palmas	L	0-1	
13/03	a	Sevilla	L	2-4	Bakambu 2
20/03	h	Barcelona	D	2-2	Bakambu, og (Mathieu)
03/04	a	Eibar	D	1-1	Adrián López, Soldado
10/04	h	Getafe	W	2-0	Denis Suárez, Bakambu
17/04	a	Rayo Vallecano	L	1-2	Adrián López
20/04	a	Real Madrid	L	0-3	
24/04	h	Real Sociedad	D	0-0	
01/05	a	Valencia	W	2-0	Samuel, Adrián López
08/05	h	Deportivo	L	0-2	
15/05	a	Sporting	L	0-2	

No	Name	Nat	DoB	Pos	Aps	(s)	Gls
20	Adrián López		08/01/88	A	10	(6)	4
28	Adrián Marín		09/01/97	D	10	(1)	
28	Alfonso Pedraza		09/04/96	M	2		
13	Alphonse Areola	FRA	27/02/93	G	32		
1	Sergio Asenjo		28/06/89	G	4		
24	Eric Bailly	CIV	12/04/94	D	25		
17	Cédric Bakambu	COD	11/04/91	A	21	(13)	12
25	Mariano Barbosa	ARG	27/07/84	G	2		
23	Daniele Bonera	ITA	31/05/81	D	10	(4)	
21	Bruno Soriano		12/06/84	M	28	(3)	5
18	Denis Suárez		06/01/94	M	25	(8)	4
11	Jaume Costa		18/03/88	D	17	(1)	1
3	Bojan Jokič	SVN	17/05/86	D	2		
8	Jonathan dos Santos	MEX	26/04/90	M	20	(6)	
10	Léo Baptistão	BRA	26/08/92	A	12	(14)	3
2	Mario Gaspar		24/11/90	D	32	(1)	2
5	Mateo Musacchio	ARG	26/08/90	D	12	(1)	1
26	Nahuel		22/10/96	M	11	(9)	
4	Tomás Pina		14/10/87	M	19	(8)	
29	Rodri Hernández		22/06/96	M	1	(2)	
22	Antonio Rukavina	SRB	26/01/84	D	14	(4)	
19	Samu Castillejo		18/01/95	M	19	(9)	1
7	Samuel		13/07/90	M	7	(9)	2
9	Roberto Soldado		27/05/85	A	27	(1)	5
14	Manu Trigueros		17/10/91	M	24	(7)	2
6	Víctor Ruiz		25/01/89	D	32	(3)	

Top goalscorers

40	Luis Suárez (Barcelona)
35	Cristiano Ronaldo (Real Madrid)
26	Lionel Messi (Barcelona)
24	Neymar (Barcelona)
	Karim Benzema (Real Madrid)
22	Antoine Griezmann (Atlético)
20	Aritz Aduriz (Athletic)
19	Rubén Castro (Betis)
	Gareth Bale (Real Madrid)
18	Borja Bastón (Eibar)

Promoted clubs

Deportivo Alavés

1921 • Mendizorroza (19,840) •
deportivoalaves.com
Coach: José Bordalás

CD Leganés

1928 • Butarque (8,158) •
deportivoleganes.com
Coach: Asier Garitano

CA Osasuna

1920 • El Sadar (19,800) • osasuna.es
Coach: Enrique Martín

Second level final table 2015/16

		Pld	W	D	L	F	A	Pts
1	Deportivo Alavés	42	21	12	9	49	35	75
2	CD Leganés	42	20	14	8	59	34	74
3	Gimnàstic de Tarragona	42	18	17	7	57	41	71
4	Girona FC	42	17	15	10	46	28	66
5	Córdoba CF	42	19	8	15	59	52	65
6	CA Osasuna	42	17	13	12	47	40	64
7	AD Alcorcón	42	18	10	14	48	44	64
8	Real Zaragoza	42	17	13	12	50	44	64
9	Real Oviedo	42	16	11	15	52	51	59
10	CD Numancia de Soria	42	13	18	11	57	51	57
11	Elche CF	42	13	18	11	40	46	57
12	SD Huesca	42	14	13	15	48	49	55
13	CD Tenerife	42	13	16	13	45	46	55
14	CD Lugo	42	13	15	14	44	50	54
15	CD Mirandés	42	13	13	16	55	56	52
16	Real Valladolid CF	42	12	15	15	47	52	51
17	RCD Mallorca	42	12	13	17	39	45	49
18	UD Almería	42	10	18	14	44	51	48
19	SD Ponferradina	42	12	11	19	39	54	47
20	UE Llagostera	42	12	8	22	44	54	44
21	Albacete Balompié	42	10	9	23	39	61	39
22	Athletic Club B	42	8	8	26	35	59	32

Promotion/Relegation play-offs

(08/06/16 & 11/06/16)
Osasuna 3-1 Gimnàstic
Gimnàstic 2-3 Osasuna
(Osasuna 6-3)

(09/06/16 & 12/06/16)
Córdoba 2-1 Girona
Girona 3-1 Córdoba *(aet)*
(Girona 4-3)

(15/06/16 &18/06/16)
Osasuna 2-1 Girona
Girona 0-1 Osasuna
(Osasuna 3-1)

DOMESTIC CUP

Copa del Rey 2015/16

FOURTH ROUND

(28/10/15 & 02/12/15)
Villanovense 0-0, 1-6 Barcelona *(1-6)*

(01/12/15 & 17/12/15)
Leganés 2-1, 0-1 Granada *(2-2; Granada on away goal)*
Reus 1-2, 0-1 Atlético *(1-3)*

(02/12/15 & 15/12/15)
Betis 2-0, 3-3 Sporting *(5-3)*
Llagostera 1-2, 1-1 Deportivo *(2-3)*
Logroñés 0-3, 0-2 Sevilla *(0-5)*

(02/12/15 & 16/12/15)
Barakaldo 1-3, 0-2 Valencia *(1-5)*
Cádiz 1-3, (w/o) Real Madrid *(Real Madrid disqualified after 1st leg)*
Rayo Vallecano 2-0, 1-3 Getafe *(3-3; Rayo Vallecano on away goal)*

(02/12/15 & 17/12/15)
Almería 1-3, 0-1 Celta *(1-4)*

(03/12/15 & 15/12/15)
Levante 1-1, 1-2 Espanyol *(2-3)*

(03/12/15 & 16/12/15)
Las Palmas 2-1, 1-1 Real Sociedad *(3-2)*
Linense 0-2, 0-6 Athletic *(0-8)*
Mirandés 2-1, 1-0 Málaga *(3-1)*
Ponferradina 3-0, 0-4 Eibar *(3-4)*

(03/12/15 & 17/12/15)
Huesca 3-2, 0-2 Villarreal *(3-4)*

FIFTH ROUND

(06/01/16 & 12/01/16)
Betis 0-2, 0-4 Sevilla *(0-6)*
Mirandés 1-1, 3-0 Deportivo *(4-1)*

(06/01/16 & 13/01/16)
Athletic 3-2, 1-0 Villarreal *(4-2)*
Barcelona 4-1, 2-0 Espanyol *(6-1)*

(06/01/16 & 14/01/16)
Rayo Vallecano 1-1, 0-3 Atlético *(1-4)*
Valencia 4-0, 3-0 Granada *(7-0)*

(07/01/16 & 13/01/16)
Cádiz 0-3, 0-2 Celta *(0-5)*
Eibar 2-3, 2-3 Las Palmas *(4-6)*

QUARTER-FINALS

(20/01/16 & 27/01/16)
Athletic 1-2 Barcelona *(Aduriz 88; Munir 17, Neymar 24)*
Barcelona 3-1 Athletic *(Suárez 53, Piqué 81, Neymar 90; Iñaki Williams 12)*
(Barcelona 5-2)

Celta 0-0 Atlético
Atlético 2-3 Celta *(Griezmann 28, Correa 81; Hernández 21, 63, Guidetti 55)*
(Celta 3-2)

(21/01/16 & 28/01/16)
Sevilla 2-0 Mirandés *(N'Zonzi 20, Vitolo 90)*
Mirandés 0-3 Sevilla *(Iborra 8p, Juan Muñoz 71, Coke 90)*
(Sevilla 5-0)

Valencia 1-1 Las Palmas *(Paco Alcácer 61; Zahibo 39og)*
Las Palmas 0-1 Valencia *(Rodrigo 20)*
(Valencia 2-1)

SEMI-FINALS

(03/02/16 & 10/02/16)
Barcelona 7-0 Valencia *(Suárez 7, 11, 83, 88, Messi 29, 58, 74)*
Valencia 1-1 Barcelona *(Negredo 39; Kaptoum 84)*
(Barcelona 8-1)

(04/02/16 & 11/02/16)
Sevilla 4-0 Celta *(Rami 45, Gameiro 59, 62, Krohn-Dehli 89)*
Celta 2-2 Sevilla *(Iago Aspas 35, 55; Éver Banega 57, Konoplyanka 87)*
(Sevilla 6-2)

FINAL

(21/05/16)
Vicente Calderón, Madrid
FC BARCELONA 2 *(Jordi Alba 97, Neymar 120+2)*
SEVILLA FC 0
(aet)
Referee: Del Cerro Grande
BARCELONA: Ter Stegen, Dani Alves, Piqué, Mascherano, Jordi Alba (Sergi Roberto 120), Rakitić (Mathieu 46), Busquets, Iniesta, Messi, Suárez (Rafinha 57), Neymar
Red card: Mascherano (37)
SEVILLA: Sergio Rico, Mariano (Konoplyanka 79), Daniel Carriço, Rami, Sergio Escudero, Krychowiak, Iborra (Llorente 105), Coke, Éver Banega, Vitolo, Gameiro
Red cards: Éver Banega (90+3), Daniel Carriço (120+1)

Barcelona retained the Copa del Rey after a feisty extra-time victory over Sevilla in Madrid

SWEDEN
Svenska Fotbollförbundet (SvFF)

Address	Evenemangsgatan 31	**President**	Karl-Erik Nilsson
	SE-171 23 Solna	**General secretary**	Håkan Sjöstrand
Tel	+46 8 7350900	**Media officer**	Camilla Hagman
Fax	+46 8 7350901	**Year of formation**	1904
E-Mail	svff@svenskfotboll.se	**National stadium**	Friends Arena, Solna
Website	svenskfotboll.se		(54,329)

ALLSVENSKAN CLUBS

 1 **AIK Solna**

 2 **Djurgårdens IF**

 3 **IF Elfsborg**

 4 **Falkenbergs FF**

 5 **Gefle IF**

 6 **IFK Göteborg**

 7 **Halmstads BK**

 8 **Hammarby Fotboll**

 9 **Helsingborgs IF**

 10 **BK Häcken**

 11 **Kalmar FF**

 12 **Malmö FF**

 13 **IFK Norrköping**

 14 **GIF Sundsvall**

 15 **Åtvidabergs FF**

 16 **Örebro SK**

PROMOTED CLUBS

 17 **Jönköpings Södra IF**

 18 **Östersunds FK**

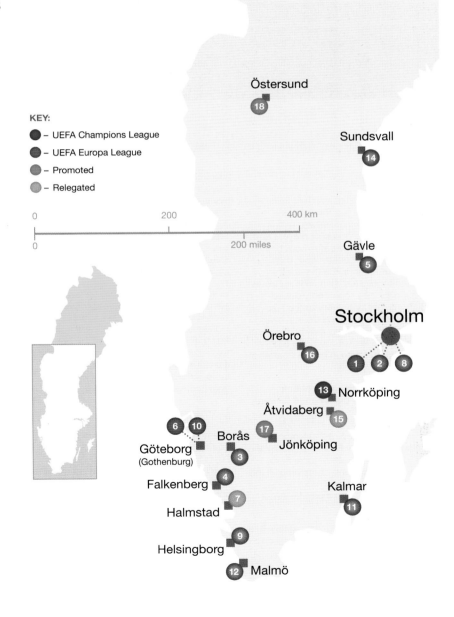

KEY:
- – UEFA Champions League
- – UEFA Europa League
- – Promoted
- – Relegated

Norrköping shock the nation

Once the most decorated club in Sweden, IFK Norrköping emerged from a long spell in the wilderness to re-capture the Allsvenskan title they had last won in 1989. It was an against-the-odds triumph secured only on the final day at the expense of long-time frontrunners IFK Göteborg.

BK Häcken caused another surprise by winning the Swedish Cup after a penalty shoot-out success against Malmö FF, but there was little to celebrate for the Swedish national team at UEFA EURO 2016 as they exited early with a solitary point.

SVENSKA MÄSTARE 2015

| Thirteenth title ends 26-year wait | Häcken win Svenska Cupen for first time | Ibrahimović retires from international duty |

Domestic league

Relegation candidates in 2014, Norrköping looked set for another angst-ridden campaign when, with a largely unchanged group of players and, in Jan Andersson, the same coach, they picked up just four points from their opening four fixtures. On the contrary, they were to lose just two further games all season as they repeatedly defied predictions, not only mounting a concerted challenge to historical rivals Göteborg but eventually overtaking them and claiming Swedish football's biggest prize for the first time in over a quarter of a century.

The consistent goalscoring of Emir Kujovic, the team's giant centre forward, was the key to their success. It was he who opened the scoring in the title-clinching last-day win, a 2-0 victory at outgoing champions Malmö aided by the fifth-minute sending-off of local hero Markus Rosenberg and completed in the final minute, against nine men, by Kujovic's Icelandic strike partner Arnór Ingvi Traustason.

Norrköping had gone into that game with a one-point lead over Jörgen Lennartsson's Göteborg, who had effectively put third-placed AIK out of contention by winning 2-1 in Solna – and therefore leapfrogging them back into second place – in the penultimate round. At the outset a win was imperative for Andersson's men, but with Göteborg falling 2-0 behind at home to Kalmar FF, the afternoon turned out to be relatively stress-free. Göteborg fought back to draw 2-2 but the record-breaking 19th league title that had looked theirs for the taking from May to September ultimately escaped their clutches on the last day of October.

Göteborg, AIK and Elfsborg ended up second, third and fourth, respectively, for the second season running, which highlighted Malmö's dramatic fall from first to fifth, the champions of the previous two seasons having failed both to build on a promising start, when they topped the table, and to recover sufficiently from an unexpected mid-season slump.

Domestic cup

Malmö maintained their hope of re-qualifying for Europe by reaching the 2015/16 Swedish Cup final. It was the club's first appearance for 20 years, and a first win since 1989 was widely anticipated – not just because their opponents, Häcken, had never won a major trophy, but because the fixture took place in their home stadium. But as with the 2015 Allsvenskan, the Svenska Cupen served up a surprise as the underdogs from Gothenburg not only recovered a two-goal deficit to take the match into extra time but also came from behind in the penalty shoot-out to win 6-5.

Europe

Malmö's failure to qualify for Europe was keenly felt as they had carried the flag for Sweden into the UEFA Champions League group stage for the second season running in 2015/16. Second-leg comebacks in the Swedbank Stadion against Salzburg and Celtic restored their place among Europe's elite, but it was an unhappy return for Åge Hareide's side as they lost five times without scoring and checked out with a record-equalling 8-0 defeat at Real Madrid.

National team

Twelve months on from becoming European Under-21 champions, Sweden never threatened to do the same with their seniors at UEFA EURO 2016. Having qualified via the play-offs with a Zlatan Ibrahimović-inspired victory over Denmark, Erik Hamrén's team huffed and puffed without reward in France. They defended well enough, conceding just once against the Republic of Ireland, Italy and Belgium, but the only goal they scored came off an opposition player and although Ibrahimović set that one up to earn a point against Ireland, the great man could not add to his record 62 goals and, at 34, announced his international retirement. On the evidence of Sweden's showing in France, a rocky road would appear to lie ahead without him.

DOMESTIC SEASON AT A GLANCE

Allsvenskan 2015 final table

		Pld	Home					Away					Total					Pts
			W	D	L	F	A	W	D	L	F	A	W	D	L	F	A	
1	**IFK Norrköping**	30	11	2	2	36	20	9	4	2	24	13	20	6	4	60	33	66
2	IFK Göteborg	30	10	4	1	30	8	8	5	2	22	14	18	9	3	52	22	63
3	AIK Solna	30	13	1	1	36	16	5	6	4	18	18	18	7	5	54	34	61
4	IF Elfsborg	30	10	4	1	34	18	6	3	6	25	24	16	7	7	59	42	55
5	Malmö FF	30	9	4	2	30	16	6	5	4	24	18	15	9	6	54	34	54
6	Djurgårdens IF	30	7	6	2	31	20	7	3	5	21	17	14	9	7	52	37	51
7	BK Häcken	30	8	4	3	30	17	5	2	8	15	22	13	6	11	45	39	45
8	Helsingborgs IF	30	7	1	7	20	17	4	3	8	23	28	11	4	15	43	45	37
9	Örebro SK	30	6	5	4	20	19	3	5	7	16	31	9	10	11	36	50	37
10	Gefle IF	30	7	4	4	22	16	3	2	10	13	34	10	6	14	35	50	36
11	Hammarby Fotboll	30	6	3	6	18	15	2	6	7	17	24	8	9	13	35	39	33
12	GIF Sundsvall	30	4	4	7	13	18	5	1	9	21	34	9	5	16	34	52	32
13	Kalmar FF	30	6	3	6	18	18	2	4	9	13	24	8	7	15	31	42	31
14	Falkenbergs FF	30	4	3	8	22	24	3	1	11	16	32	7	4	19	38	56	25
15	Halmstads BK	30	4	3	8	11	18	0	6	9	10	26	4	9	17	21	44	21
16	Åtvidabergs FF	30	1	7	7	18	25	1	2	12	7	30	2	9	19	25	55	15

European qualification 2016/17

Champion: IFK Norrköping (second qualifying round)

Cup winner: BK Hácken (second qualifying round)
IFK Göteborg (first qualifying round)
AIK Solna (first qualifying round)

Top scorer	Emir Kujovic (Norrköping), 21 goals
Relegated clubs	Åtvidabergs FF, Halmstads BK
Promoted clubs	Jönköpings Södra IF, Östersunds FK
Cup final	BK Häcken 2-2 Malmö FF *(aet; 6-5 on pens)*

Team of the season
(4-4-2)

Coach: Andersson *(Norrköping)*

Alvbåge *(Göteborg)*

Tinnerholm *(Malmö)* — Johansson *(Norrköping)* — Bjärsmyr *(Göteborg)* — Aleesami *(Göteborg)*

Ofori *(AIK)* — Sjölund *(Norrköping)* — Claesson *(Elfsborg)* — Lewicki *(Malmö)*

Kujovic *(Norrköping)* — Goitom *(AIK)*

Player of the season

Emir Kujovic
(IFK Norrköping)

Born in Montenegro but raised in Sweden, Kujovic's career was at a crossroads when he returned home from Turkey in August 2013 to join forces once again with his ex-Halmstad coach Jan Andersson at Norrköping. A promising, albeit injury-affected, 2014 season was followed by a magnificent one in 2015. The big target man not only scored 21 goals to win the Allsvenskan golden boot. He found the net in 19 of Norrköping's games, 18 of which contributed points towards the club's title-winning total.

Newcomer of the season

Kerim Mrabti
(Djurgårdens IF)

Djurgården did not supply too many headlines during the 2015 Allsvenskan campaign, but the Stockholm side did provide the league's official newcomer of the season in 21-year-old Mrabti. The club's pre-season signing from second-tier Sirius shot to prominence when he scored both of his team's goals in the big derby at home to AIK (2-2), and his cultured midfield play was to earn him a first senior cap for Sweden, only for a serious knee injury to cut short his debut against Estonia in Abu Dhabi.

International tournament appearances
FIFA World Cup (11) 1934 (2nd round), 1938 (4th), 1950 (3rd), 1958 (runners-up), 1970, 1974 (2nd phase), 1978, 1990, 1994 (3rd), 2002 (2nd round), 2006 (2nd round)
UEFA European Championship (6) 1992 (semi-finals), 2000, 2004 (qtr-finals), 2008, 2012, 2016

Top five all-time caps
Anders Svensson (148); Thomas Ravelli (143); **Andreas Isaksson** (133); **Kim Källström** (131); Olof Mellberg (117)

Top five all-time goals
Zlatan Ibrahimović (62); Sven Rydell (49); Gunnar Nordahl (43); Henrik Larsson (37); Gunnar Gren (32)

Results 2015/16

Date	Opponent		Venue	Result	Scorers
05/09/15	Russia (ECQ)	A	Moscow	L 0-1	
08/09/15	Austria (ECQ)	H	Solna	L 1-4	Ibrahimović (90+1)
09/10/15	Liechtenstein (ECQ)	A	Vaduz	W 2-0	Berg (18), Ibrahimović (55)
12/10/15	Moldova (ECQ)	H	Solna	W 2-0	Ibrahimović (24), Zengin (47)
14/11/15	Denmark (ECQ)	H	Solna	W 2-1	Forsberg (45), Ibrahimović (50p)
17/11/15	Denmark (ECQ)	A	Copenhagen	D 2-2	Ibrahimović (19, 76)
06/01/16	Estonia	N	Abu Dhabi (UAE)	D 1-1	Ishak (70)
10/01/16	Finland	N	Abu Dhabi (UAE)	W 3-0	Salomonsson (45+1p), Hallberg (46), Kujovic (59)
24/03/16	Turkey	A	Antalya	L 1-2	Granqvist (74)
29/03/16	Czech Republic	H	Solna	D 1-1	Berg (14)
30/05/16	Slovenia	H	Malmo	D 0-0	
05/06/16	Wales	H	Solna	W 3-0	Forsberg (40), Lustig (57), Guidetti (87)
13/06/16	Republic of Ireland (ECF)	N	Saint-Denis (FRA)	D 1-1	Clark (71og)
17/06/16	Italy (ECF)	N	Toulouse (FRA)	L 0-1	
22/06/16	Belgium (ECF)	N	Nice (FRA)	L 0-1	

Appearances 2015/16

Coach: Erik Hamrén	27/06/57		RUS	AUT	LIE	MDA	DEN	DEN	Est	Fin	Tur	Cze	Svn	Wal	IRL	ITA	BEL	Caps	Goals
Andreas Isaksson	03/10/81	Kasımpaşa (TUR)	G	G	G	G	G	G			G	G	G	G46	G	G	G	133	-
Pierre Bengtsson	12/04/88	Mainz (GER)	D60					D86										24	-
Mikael Antonsson	31/05/81	København (DEN)		D	D	D	D29											28	-
Andreas Granqvist	16/04/85	Krasnodar (RUS)	D	D	D	D	D	D			D	D	D	D	D	D	D	55	3
Martin Olsson	17/05/88	Norwich (ENG)	D	D82	D	D	D	s86				D		D46	D	D	D	38	5
Sebastian Larsson	06/06/85	Sunderland (ENG)	M	D	s69	M	s68	M81			s46	s46	M	M	M	M	M70	87	6
Albin Ekdal	28/07/89	Hamburg (GER)	M82	M86	M66					M80			s61	s86	M79			25	-
Pontus Wernbloom	25/06/86	CSKA Moskva (RUS)	M								s71	s63	M71					51	2
Jimmy Durmaz	22/03/89	Olympiacos (GRE)	M	s82	M69		M68				M46	M46	D	s61		s79	s70	34	2
Emil Forsberg	23/10/91	RB Leipzig (GER)	M	M			M	M			s62	M	M46	M61	M	M79	M82	20	2
Zlatan Ibrahimović	03/10/81	Paris (FRA)	A46	A	A	A57	A82	A			A			A61	A	A	A	116	62
Ola Toivonen	03/07/86	Sunderland (ENG)	s46			s57												45	9
Marcus Berg	17/08/86	Panathinaikos (GRE)	s60	A	A62		A	A			A	A46		A76	A59	s85	A63	41	10
Isaac Kiese Thelin	24/06/92	Bordeaux (FRA)	s82	s62									A					8	-
Erkan Zengin	05/08/81	Trabzonspor (TUR)		M62							M62		s46				s82	21	3
Kim Källström	24/08/82	Grasshoppers (SUI)	M	M	M57	M	M69				M71	M46		M	M	M	M	131	16
Abdul Khalili	07/06/92	Mersin (TUR)		s86														1	-
Mikael Lustig	13/12/86	Celtic (SCO)				D	D83	D			D	s81	D46	D	D45			53	3
John Guidetti	15/04/92	Celta (ESP)		s62	A	s82					A62	s46	A	s76	s59	A85	s63	12	1
Oscar Lewicki	14/07/92	Malmö			s66	M	M	M				M63		M61	M86	s79		12	-
Gustav Svensson	07/02/87	Göteborg				s57		s69	M61	M46								6	-
Anton Tinnerholm	26/02/91	Malmö				s83			D46	s46								6	-
Erik Johansson	30/12/88	Gent (BEL) /København (DEN)				s29	D							D	s45	D	D	12	-
Oscar Hiljemark	28/06/92	Palermo (ITA)					s81				s80	s46	M					10	1
Karl-Johan Johnsson	28/01/90	Randers (DEN)							G									3	-
Sebastian Holmén	29/04/92	Elfsborg							D	D62								4	-
Emil Bergström	19/05/93	Djurgården							D83	D								3	-
Adam Lundqvist	20/03/94	Elfsborg							D46	s46								2	-
Markus Rohdén	11/05/91	Elfsborg							M46	M				s71				6	1
Alexander Fransson	02/04/94	Norrköping							M55	s62								2	-
Viktor Claesson	02/01/92	Elfsborg							M46	M62								6	1
Emir Kujovic	22/06/88	Norrköping							A46	s46	s62			s61				4	1
Christoffer Nyman	05/10/92	Norrköping							A46	s62								4	-
Emil Salomonsson	28/04/89	Göteborg							s46	D46			D81					6	1
Pa Konate	25/04/94	Malmö							s46	D46								2	-
Nicklas Bärkroth	19/01/92	Norrköping							s46	M46								4	-
Kerim Mrabti	20/05/94	Djurgården							s46/70									1	-
Gustav Engvall	29/04/96	Göteborg							s46	A46								2	-
Mikael Ishak	31/03/93	Randers (DEN)							s46	A62								4	1
Sebastian Eriksson	31/01/89	Göteborg							s55	s46								7	-
Melker Hallberg	20/10/95	Vålerenga (NOR)							s61	s46								2	1
Joakim Nilsson	06/02/94	Sundsvall							s70									1	-
Linus Wahlqvist	11/11/96	Norrköping							s83	s62								2	-
Patrik Carlgren	08/01/92	AIK								G62								1	-
Jacob Rinne	20/06/93	Örebro								s62								1	-
Robin Olsen	08/01/90	København (DEN)									G			s46				4	-
Victor Nilsson-Lindelöf	17/07/94	Benfica (POR)									D	D65	D		D	D	D	6	-
Ludwig Augustinsson	21/04/94	København (DEN)									D		s46					4	-
Alexander Milosevic	30/01/92	Hannover (GER)										s65						5	-
Pontus Jansson	13/02/91	Torino (ITA)											s46					8	-

EUROPE

Malmö FF

CHAMPIONS LEAGUE

Second qualifying round - FK Žalgiris (LTU)
H 0-0
Azinovic, Tinnerholm, Lewicki, Kroon (Rakip 69), Rosenberg, Yotún, Cibicki (Sana 46), Bengtsson, Eikrem (Mehmeti 82), Berget, Brorsson. Coach: Åge Hareide (NOR)
A 1-0 Tinnerholm (55)
Azinovic (M Johansson 50), Tinnerholm, Rakip, Lewicki, Rosenberg, Yotún, Bengtsson, Eikrem (Vindheim 90+3), Sana (Adu 75), Berget, Brorsson. Coach: Åge Hareide (NOR)

Third qualifying round - FC Salzburg (AUT)
A 0-2
Wiland, Tinnerholm, Lewicki, Adu, Rosenberg, Yotún, Rodić (Eikrem 77), Árnason, Sana (Berget 61), Carvalho, Djurdjić. Coach: Åge Hareide (NOR)
H 3-0 Djurdjić (7), Rosenberg (14), Rodić (42)
Wiland, Tinnerholm, Lewicki, Adu, Rosenberg, Yotún, Bengtsson, Rodić (Carvalho 55), Árnason, Berget, Djurdjić (Rakip 69). Coach: Åge Hareide (NOR)
Red card: Adu 64

Play-offs - Celtic FC (SCO)
A 2-3 Berget (52, 90+5)
Wiland, Tinnerholm, Rakip (Sana 81), Lewicki, Yotún, Bengtsson, Eikrem (Carvalho 72), Rodić, Árnason, Berget, Djurdjić. Coach: Åge Hareide (NOR)
H 2-0 Rosenberg (23), Boyata (54og)
Wiland, Tinnerholm, Lewicki, Adu, Rosenberg, Yotún, Bengtsson (Carvalho 46), Rodić (Rakip 83), Árnason, Berget (Mehmeti 90+3), Djurdjić. Coach: Åge Hareide (NOR)

Group A
Match 1 - Paris Saint-Germain (FRA)
A 0-2
Wiland, Tinnerholm, Adu (Rakip 85), Rosenberg, Yotún, Bengtsson, Árnason, Berget, Carvalho (Rodić 46), Djurdjić. Coach: Åge Hareide (NOR)
Match 2 - Real Madrid CF (ESP)
H 0-2
Wiland, Tinnerholm, Lewicki, Adu, Rosenberg, Yotún, Bengtsson, Rodić (Eikrem 67), Árnason, Berget, Djurdjić (Carvalho 81). Coach: Åge Hareide (NOR)
Red card: Yotún 78
Match 3 - FC Shakhtar Donetsk (UKR)
H 1-0 Rosenberg (17)
Wiland, Konate, Tinnerholm, Lewicki, Adu, Rosenberg, Bengtsson, Rodić (Rakip 79), Árnason, Berget (Mehmeti 88). Coach: Åge Hareide (NOR)
Match 4 - FC Shakhtar Donetsk (UKR)
A 0-4
Wiland, Konate, Tinnerholm, Lewicki (Rakip 11), Adu, Rosenberg, Bengtsson, Rodić, Árnason, Berget (Yotún 46), Djurdjić (Eikrem 74). Coach: Åge Hareide (NOR)
Red card: Árnason 89
Match 5 - Paris Saint-Germain (FRA)
H 0-5
Wiland, Konate, Tinnerholm, Lewicki, Adu (Rakip 81), Rosenberg, Bengtsson, Rodić (Eikrem 60), Berget, Djurdjić (Kroon 70), Brorsson. Coach: Åge Hareide (NOR)
Match 6 - Real Madrid CF (ESP)
A 0-8
Wiland, Tinnerholm, Rakip (Kroon 76), Lewicki, Adu, Yotún, Árnason, Sana (Mehmeti 64), Berget, Carvalho, Djurdjić (Rodić 46). Coach: Åge Hareide (NOR)

IFK Göteborg

UEFA EUROPA LEAGUE

Second qualifying round - WKS Śląsk Wrocław (POL)
A 0-0
Alvbåge, Salomonsson, Aleesami, Eriksson, Ankersen, Smedberg-Dalence (Rieks 78), Svensson, Boman (Engvall 78), Rogne (Jónsson 86), Vibe, Bjärsmyr. Coach: Jörgen Lennartsson (SWE)
H 2-0 Engvall (55), Boman (59)
Alvbåge, Salomonsson, Aleesami, Eriksson, Rieks, Ankersen, Svensson, Boman (Smedberg-Dalence 79), Engvall (Pettersson 86), Rogne, Bjärsmyr. Coach: Jörgen Lennartsson (SWE)

Third qualifying round - Os Belenenses (POR)
A 1-2 Aleesami (58)
Alvbåge, Salomonsson, Aleesami, Eriksson, Rieks, Smedberg-Dalence (Ankersen 46), Svensson, Boman (Pettersson 72), Engvall (Sköld 81), Rogne, Bjärsmyr. Coach: Jörgen Lennartsson (SWE)
H 0-0
Alvbåge, Salomonsson, Aleesami, Eriksson (Pettersson 75), Rieks, Ankersen, Svensson, Boman (Smedberg-Dalence 75), Engvall, Rogne, Bjärsmyr. Coach: Jörgen Lennartsson (SWE)

AIK Solna

UEFA EUROPA LEAGUE

First qualifying round - VPS Vaasa (FIN)
A 2-2 Bahoui (70, 83p)
Carlgren (Linnér 29), Karlsson, Johansson, Brustad (Bangura 64), Blomberg, Goitom, Bahoui, Hauksson, Ofori, Sonko Sundberg, Etuhu (Salétros 78). Coach: Andreas Alm (SWE)
H 4-0 Goitom (14, 59), Bangura (54), Ofori (85)
Linnér, Johansson, Blomberg, Goitom (Nikolic 77), Hauksson (Lundholm 70), Alex Pereira (Salétros 71), Ofori, Sonko Sundberg, Etuhu, Bangura, Eliasson. Coach: Andreas Alm (SWE)

Second qualifying round - FC Shirak (ARM)
H 2-0 Goitom (29, 83p)
Stamatopoulos, Karlsson (Lundholm 89), Johansson, Goitom, Pavey, Ofori, Sonko Sundberg, Etuhu, Bangura (Brustad 67), Ishizaki, Eliasson (Blomberg 67). Coach: Andreas Alm (SWE)
A 2-0 Goitom (14), Ishizaki (25)
Stamatopoulos, Karlsson (Alex Pereira 13), Johansson, Brustad (Eliasson 46), Blomberg, Goitom, Hauksson, Ofori, Sonko Sundberg, Etuhu (Salétros 59), Ishizaki. Coach: Andreas Alm (SWE)

Third qualifying round - Atromitos FC (GRE)
H 1-3 Goitom (70p)
Carlgren, Johansson, Brustad (Goitom 57), Blomberg (Eliasson 57), Pavey, Alex Pereira, Ofori, Sonko Sundberg, Etuhu, Bangura, Ishizaki. Coach: Andreas Alm (SWE)
Red card: Sonko Sundberg 79
A 0-1
Carlgren, Johansson, Brustad (Nikolic 79), Goitom, Hauksson, Pavey, Alex Pereira (Blomberg 11), Etuhu, Ishizaki, Eliasson (Bangura 46), Salétros. Coach: Andreas Alm (SWE)

IF Elfsborg

UEFA EUROPA LEAGUE

First qualifying round - FC Lahti (FIN)
A 2-2 Rohdén (15), Prodell (59)
Stuhr Ellegaard, Lundqvist, Jönsson, Rohdén, Svensson, Hauger, Lundevall, Klarström (Manns 74), Claesson, Hedlund, Prodell (Frick 69). Coach: Magnus Haglund (SWE)
H 5-0 Svensson (11), Claesson (21p), Rohdén (33), Prodell (70), L Nilsson (81)
Stuhr Ellegaard, Lundqvist, Rohdén (Jönsson 59), Svensson, Holmén, Zeneli, Klarström, Claesson, Frick (L Nilsson 68), Hedlund (Lundevall 68), Prodell. Coach: Magnus Haglund (SWE)

Second qualifying round - Randers FC (DEN)
A 0-0
Stuhr Ellegaard, Manns (Klarström 19), Lundqvist, Rohdén, Svensson, Holmén, Zeneli (Lundevall 61), Claesson, Frick, Hedlund (L Nilsson 75), Hauger. Coach: Magnus Haglund (SWE)
H 1-0 (aet) Lundevall (94)
Stuhr Ellegaard, Lundqvist, Rohdén, Svensson, Holmén, Zeneli (Prodell 72), Klarström (Lundevall 90), Claesson, Frick (L Nilsson 106), Hedlund, Hauger. Coach: Magnus Haglund (SWE)

Third qualifying round - Odds BK (NOR)
H 2-1 Prodell (43), Lundevall (76)
Stuhr Ellegaard, Lundqvist, Rohdén, Svensson, Holmén, Zeneli, Klarström, Claesson (L Nilsson 87), Hedlund (Lundevall 69), Hauger, Prodell (Frick 80). Coach: Magnus Haglund (SWE)
A 0-2
Stuhr Ellegaard, Lundqvist, Rohdén, Svensson, Holmén, Zeneli, Klarström (Lans 46), Claesson, Hedlund (Frick 79), Hauger, Prodell (L Nilsson 78). Coach: Magnus Haglund (SWE)

DOMESTIC LEAGUE CLUB-BY-CLUB

AIK Solna

1891 • Friends Arena (54,329) • aikfotboll.se

Major honours
Swedish League (11) 1900, 1901, 1911, 1914, 1916, 1923, 1932, 1937, 1992, 1998, 2009; Swedish Cup (8) 1949, 1950, 1976, 1985, 1996, 1997, 1999, 2009

Coach: Andreas Alm

2015

06/04	h	Halmstad	W	2-1	Goitom, Blomberg
09/04	a	Malmö	D	0-0	
12/04	h	Gefle	W	3-1	Blomberg, Goitom, Bangura
21/04	a	Elfsborg	L	2-3	Bahoui 2
26/04	h	Örebro	W	3-0	Bahoui, Goitom, Brustad
29/04	a	Åtvidaberg	D	1-1	Brustad
04/05	h	Hammarby	W	2-0	Goitom, Sonko Sundberg
10/05	h	Norrköping	D	2-2	Goitom, Väisänen
21/05	a	Göteborg	L	0-3	
25/05	a	Djurgården	D	2-2	Johansson, Bangura
31/05	h	Helsingborg	W	3-1	Bahoui 2 (1p), Bangura
03/06	h	Falkenberg	W	4-3	Etuhu, Blomberg, Goitom 2
06/06	h	Häcken	D	0-0	
05/07	a	Kalmar	D	0-0	
12/07	h	Sundsvall	W	4-1	Goitom 2, Bangura, Brustad
19/07	a	Helsingborg	L	1-3	Goitom
26/07	h	Elfsborg	W	4-2	Goitom 2, Bangura, Alex Pereira
02/08	a	Norrköping	W	2-1	Bangura, Goitom
10/08	h	Djurgården	W	1-0	Bangura
16/08	h	Kalmar	W	2-1	Blomberg 2
23/08	a	Gefle	W	2-1	Johansson, Blomberg
30/08	h	Åtvidaberg	W	1-0	Johansson
12/09	a	Falkenberg	W	4-2	Brustad, Goitom 2, Bangura
19/09	h	Häcken	W	2-1	Brustad, Etuhu
23/09	a	Sundsvall	W	2-0	Alex Pereira, Hooiveld
27/09	a	Hammarby	L	0-1	
04/10	h	Malmö	W	2-1	Goitom, Ishizaki
18/10	a	Halmstad	W	1-0	og (Ali Khan)
26/10	h	Göteborg	L	1-2	Goitom
31/10	a	Örebro	D	1-1	Goitom

No	Name	Nat	DoB	Pos	Aps	(s)	Gls
16	Alex Pereira	BRA	15/05/82	D	9	(5)	2
11	Nabil Bahoui		05/02/91	M	9		5
23	Mohamed Bangura	SLE	27/07/89	A	26	(4)	8
8	Johan Blomberg		14/06/87	M	25	(5)	6
7	Fredrik Brustad	NOR	22/06/89	A	12	(14)	5
35	Patrik Carlgren		08/01/92	G	25		
5	Panajotis Dimitriadis		12/08/86	M	9		
28	Niclas Eliasson		07/12/95	M	3	(7)	
20	Dickson Etuhu	NGA	08/06/82	M	18	(3)	2
10	Henok Goitom	ERI	22/09/84	A	28	(1)	18
31	Christos Gravius		14/10/97	A		(1)	
12	Haukur Heidar Hauksson	ISL	01/09/91	D	23		
26	Jos Hooiveld	NED	22/04/83	D	11		1
24	Stefan Ishizaki		15/05/82	M	9		1
4	Nils-Eric Johansson		13/01/80	D	29		3
3	Per Karlsson		02/01/86	D	24		
34	Oscar Linnér		23/02/97	G	2		
25	Sam Lundholm		01/07/94	M	7	(6)	
9	Marko Nikolic		17/09/97	M		(3)	
17	Ebenezer Ofori	GHA	01/07/95	M	27		
14	Kenny Pavey	ENG	23/08/79	M	5	(11)	
29	Anton Jönsson Salétros		12/04/96	M	6	(14)	
18	Noah Sonko Sundberg		06/06/96	D	16	(8)	1
13	Kenny Stamatopoulos	CAN	28/08/79	G	3		
2	Sauli Väisänen	FIN	05/06/94	D	4	(2)	1

Djurgårdens IF

1891 • Tele2Arena (33,000) • dif.se

Major honours
Swedish League (11) 1912, 1915, 1917, 1920, 1955, 1959, 1964, 1966, 2002, 2003, 2005; Swedish Cup (4) 1990, 2002, 2004, 2005

Coach: Per Olsson

2015

05/04	h	Elfsborg	L	1-2	Berntsen
09/04	a	Häcken	D	1-1	Mushekwi
13/04	a	Hammarby	L	1-2	Johnson
17/04	h	Kalmar	W	1-0	Mushekwi
24/04	a	Sundsvall	W	2-0	Colley, Mushekwi
29/04	h	Falkenberg	W	3-1	Mushekwi 2, Berntsen
03/05	h	Gefle	W	5-1	Arvidsson, Berntsen, Walker, Colley, Andersson
11/05	a	Åtvidaberg	W	3-2	Berntsen, Mushekwi 2
18/05	h	Halmstad	W	3-2	Bergström, Mushekwi 2
25/05	h	AIK	D	2-2	Mrabti 2
01/06	a	Göteborg	D	0-0	
04/06	h	Norrköping	D	1-1	Johnson
07/06	a	Malmö	D	1-1	Mushekwi
04/07	h	Örebro	W	2-0	Berntsen, Johnson
13/07	a	Helsingborg	W	1-0	Mushekwi
20/07	a	Åtvidaberg	D	0-0	
27/07	a	Örebro	W	1-0	Arvidsson
01/08	h	Häcken	W	2-1	Johnson 2
10/08	a	AIK	L	0-1	
16/08	a	Elfsborg	L	0-2	
24/08	h	Hammarby	D	2-2	Arvidsson (p), Mushekwi
29/08	h	Halmstad	W	4-2	Andersson, Moon, Johnson, Berntsen
14/09	a	Gefle	L	1-2	Bergström
20/09	h	Malmö	L	0-2	
23/09	h	Norrköping	L	2-4	Andersson, Arvidsson (p)
28/09	h	Helsingborg	D	2-2	Mrabti, Johnson
04/10	a	Kalmar	W	3-0	Johnson, Mrabti, Karlström
19/10	h	Göteborg	D	2-2	Johnson, Walker (p)
24/10	a	Falkenberg	W	2-0	Colley, Andersson
31/10	h	Sundsvall	W	4-2	Andersson 3, Johnson

No	Name	Nat	DoB	Pos	Aps	(s)	Gls
16	Sebastian Andersson		15/07/91	A	11	(11)	7
2	Jesper Arvidsson		01/01/85	D	23	(3)	4
3	Emil Bergström		19/05/93	D	29		2
10	Daniel Berntsen	NOR	04/04/93	M	23	(5)	6
17	Tim Björkström		08/01/91	D	24	(1)	
15	Omar Colley	GAM	24/10/92	D	27		3
6	Alexander Faltsetas		04/07/87	M	22	(2)	
12	Kenneth Høie	NOR	11/09/79	G	28		
4	Amadou Jawo		26/09/84	A	3	(8)	
20	Sam Johnson	LBR	06/05/93	A	24	(5)	10
24	Tino Kadewere	ZIM	05/01/96	A		(5)	
5	Stefan Karlsson		15/12/88	D	6	(3)	
22	Jesper Karlström		21/06/95	M	13	(14)	1
14	Elliot Käck		18/09/89	D	9	(10)	
7	Moon Seon-min	KOR	09/06/92	M	4	(6)	1
16	Kerim Mrabti		20/05/94	M	27	(1)	4
21	Nyasha Mushekwi	ZIM	21/08/87	A	18	(3)	12
23	Hampus Nilsson		17/07/90	G	2		
3	Haris Radetinac	SRB	28/10/85	M	12	(2)	
3	Fredrik Stenman		02/06/83	D	4	(2)	
8	Kevin Walker		03/08/89	M	21	(2)	2

IF Elfsborg

1904 • Borås Arena (16,284) • elfsborg.se

Major honours
Swedish League (6) 1936, 1939, 1940, 1961, 2006, 2012; Swedish Cup (3) 2001, 2003, 2014

Coach: Magnus Haglund

2015

05/04	a	Djurgården	W	2-1	Frick, Zeneli
08/04	h	Hammarby	D	1-1	Hedlund
13/04	a	Norrköping	W	4-0	Hedlund, Claesson, Rohdén, Zeneli
21/04	h	AIK	W	3-2	Claesson, Frick, Zeneli
26/04	a	Halmstad	L	0-1	
29/04	h	Kalmar	W	2-1	Claesson, Zeneli
03/05	a	Sundsvall	W	1-0	Prodell
11/05	h	Malmö	D	2-2	Rohdén 2
20/05	h	Helsingborg	W	2-1	Claesson, L Nilsson
24/05	a	Åtvidaberg	W	2-1	Claesson, Frick
31/05	h	Örebro	D	2-2	L Nilsson, Hauger
04/06	a	Göteborg	L	0-1	
07/06	h	Gefle	W	5-1	Claesson, Zeneli, Prodell 2, Hedlund
05/07	a	Falkenberg	D	2-2	Rohdén, Prodell
12/07	h	Häcken	W	1-0	Hedlund
26/07	a	AIK	L	2-4	Prodell, Lundevall
02/08	a	Halmstad	W	2-0	Prodell 2
09/08	a	Hammarby	D	0-0	
12/08	h	Gefle	W	3-2	Prodell, Gunnarsson, Rohdén (p)
16/08	h	Djurgården	W	2-0	Prodell 2
23/08	h	Kalmar	W	3-0	Hedlund 2, Zeneli
30/08	h	Sundsvall	L	1-2	Rohdén
12/09	a	Malmö	D	1-1	Lundqvist
21/09	a	Örebro	L	2-4	Svensson, Frick
23/09	h	Göteborg	D	1-1	Svensson
28/09	a	Åtvidaberg	W	3-1	Frick, Lundevall, Zeneli
04/10	a	Helsingborg	L	1-2	Claesson
19/10	h	Norrköping	W	3-2	Zeneli, Claesson 2 (1p)
25/10	a	Häcken	L	2-5	Rohdén (p), Claesson
31/10	h	Falkenberg	W	4-2	Claesson, Zeneli 2, Lundevall

No	Name	Nat	DoB	Pos	Aps	(s)	Gls
14	Anton Andreasson		26/07/93	M		(4)	
16	Viktor Claesson		02/01/92	M	28	(1)	11
17	Per Frick		14/04/92	A	22	(2)	5
25	Niklas Gunnarsson	NOR	27/04/91	D	11		1
23	Abbas Hassan	LIB	10/05/85	G	1		
21	Henning Hauger	NOR	17/07/85	M	27	(2)	1
19	Simon Hedlund		11/03/93	M	21	(4)	6
12	Sebastian Holmén		29/04/92	D	29		
6	Jon Jönsson		08/07/83	D	4	(1)	
15	Andreas Klarström		23/12/77	D	15	(2)	
5	Anton Lans		17/04/91	D	3	(1)	
10	Simon Lundevall		23/09/88	M	14	(16)	3
3	Adam Lundqvist		20/03/94	D	29		1
2	Jesper Manns		05/08/90	D	5	(1)	
9	Lasse Nilsson		03/01/82	A	3	(13)	2
18	Viktor Nilsson		15/08/96	D		(1)	
22	Viktor Prodell		29/02/88	M	8	(14)	10
7	Marcus Rohdén		11/05/91	M	27		7
1	Kevin Stuhr Ellegaard	DEN	23/05/86	G	29		
8	Anders Svensson		17/07/76	M	27	(1)	2
13	Arber Zeneli		25/02/95	A	27	(3)	10

Falkenbergs FF

1928 • Falkenbergs IP (6,000) •
falkenbergsff.se
Coach: Hans Eklund

2015

05/04	h	Gefle	L	0-2
08/04	a	Helsingborg	D	0-0
12/04	h	Örebro	W	2-0 Eriksson, Vall
19/04	a	Åtvidaberg	L	1-3 Mustafa
24/04	h	Malmö	D	3-3 Carlsson, Rodevåg, Araba
29/04	a	Djurgården	L	1-3 Araba
04/05	a	Göteborg	L	1-2 Araba
10/05	h	Halmstad	W	1-0 Araba
19/05	h	Kalmar	L	1-3 Araba
25/05	a	Häcken	W	2-0 Rodevåg, Araba
30/05	h	Sundsvall	D	1-1 Wede
03/06	a	AIK	L	3-4 Rodevåg, Vall, Keat
07/06	a	Norrköping	L	0-2
05/07	h	Elfsborg	D	2-2 Svensson, P Karlsson
13/07	a	Hammarby	L	0-3
18/07	a	Kalmar	L	0-4
26/07	h	Göteborg	W	1-0 Nilsson
01/08	a	Gefle	L	0-1
08/08	h	Helsingborg	L	2-3 Nilsson 2
17/08	h	Hammarby	L	0-1
24/08	a	Sundsvall	W	1-0 Jacobsen
29/08	h	Norrköping	L	0-1
12/09	h	AIK	L	2-4 Svensson, Rodevåg
18/09	a	Halmstad	W	1-0 Rodevåg
23/09	a	Malmö	L	3-4 Donyoh, Araba, Vall
27/09	h	Häcken	L	1-2 Araba
03/10	a	Örebro	L	1-2 Nilsson
18/10	h	Åtvidaberg	W	6-0 Nilsson 2 (1p), Jacobsen, Donyoh, Rodevåg, Wede
24/10	h	Djurgården	L	0-2
31/10	a	Elfsborg	L	2-4 Svensson, Svahn

No	Name	Nat	DoB	Pos	Aps	(s)	Gls
6	Rasmus Andersson		17/04/93	M	1	(2)	
18	Hakeem Araba	ENG	12/02/91	A	19	(8)	8
12	Christoffer Carlsson		15/01/89	M	28	(1)	1
22	Godsway Donyoh	GHA	14/10/94	A	10	(3)	2
13	Adam Eriksson		02/02/88	D	30		1
70	Alexander Jacobsen	DEN	18/03/94	A	9	(8)	2
4	Daniel Johansson		28/07/87	D	27	(1)	
33	Tibor Joza		10/08/86	D	17		
14	Per Karlsson		20/04/89	D	15	(2)	1
8	Tobias Karlsson		25/02/75	D	12	(1)	
21	Dan Keat	NZL	28/09/87	M	21	(2)	1
23	Enock Kwakwa	GHA		A		(3)	
1	Otto Martler		14/04/87	G	30		
77	Kamal Mustafa		22/07/91	M		(6)	1
29	Gustaf Nilsson		23/05/97	A	11	(10)	6
15	Stefan Rodevåg		11/06/80	A	18	(7)	6
2	Rasmus Sjöstedt		28/02/92	D	20		
19	Johan Svahn		01/04/88	M		(3)	1
7	David Svensson		09/04/84	M	28		3
11	Johannes Vall		19/10/92	M	6	(20)	3
20	Carl Wede		20/04/90	M	28	(1)	2

Gefle IF

1882 • Strömvallen (7,302);
Gavlevallen (6,500) • gefleiffotboll.se
Coach: Roger Sandberg

2015

05/04	a	Falkenberg	W	2-0 Oremo, Williams
08/04	h	Kalmar	W	2-0 Oremo 2 (1p)
12/04	a	AIK	L	1-3 og (Johansson)
18/04	h	Halmstad	D	0-0
27/04	h	Norrköping	L	1-4 Oremo
30/04	h	Göteborg	D	0-0
03/05	a	Djurgården	L	1-5 Bertilsson
09/05	a	Helsingborg	W	2-1 Bertilsson, Oremo
20/05	h	Sundsvall	W	3-1 Bertilsson, Williams, Oremo
24/05	a	Örebro	L	0-1
29/05	h	Häcken	W	2-0 Nilsson, Oremo
03/06	h	Malmö	L	1-2 Bertilsson
07/06	a	Elfsborg	L	1-5 Berisha
06/07	h	Hammarby	D	1-1 Fällman
11/07	a	Åtvidaberg	D	1-1 Williams
27/07	a	Halmstad	W	1-0 Bååth
01/08	h	Falkenberg	W	1-0 Bertilsson
08/08	a	Häcken	D	1-1 Bertilsson
12/08	h	Elfsborg	L	2-3 Lantto, Bertilsson
15/08	a	Malmö	L	0-2
23/08	h	AIK	L	1-2 Williams
30/08	a	Göteborg	L	0-3
14/09	h	Djurgården	W	2-1 Oremo 2
20/09	h	Helsingborg	W	2-1 Williams 2
23/09	a	Hammarby	L	0-3
27/09	h	Norrköping	L	1-2 Lantto
03/10	a	Sundsvall	L	1-2 Oremo
19/10	h	Örebro	D	2-2 Lantto, Oremo
26/10	a	Kalmar	L	1-3 Oremo
31/10	a	Åtvidaberg	W	2-1 Berisha, Tshakasua

No	Name	Nat	DoB	Pos	Aps	(s)	Gls
19	Christoffer Aspgren		20/09/95	M	1	(2)	
20	Emil Bellander		05/01/94	A	2	(5)	
2	Ilir Berisha	KOS	25/06/91	D	3	(4)	2
13	Johan Bertilsson		15/02/88	M	30		7
21	Kwame Bonsu	GHA	25/09/94	M	10	(4)	
12	Anders Bååth		13/04/91	M	21	(1)	1
5	Jacob Ericsson		17/09/93	D	11	(10)	
6	Jesper Florén		11/09/90	D	28		
10	David Fällman		04/02/90	D	30		1
1	Emil Hedvall		09/06/83	G	30		
15	Jacob Hjelte		11/08/96	M	1	(13)	
17	Jonas Lantto		22/05/87	M	30		3
11	Dardan Mustafa		05/02/92	A	3	(18)	
7	Robin Nilsson		15/09/88	M	28	(1)	1
9	Johan Oremo		24/10/86	A	21	(1)	12
14	Jens Portin	FIN	13/12/84	D	26	(2)	
29	Martin Rauschenberg	DEN	15/01/92	D	28		
24	Tshutshu Tshakasua		15/05/97	M		(10)	1
4	Anders Wikström		14/12/81	D		(1)	
10	Dioh Williams	LBR	08/01/84	A	27		6

IFK Göteborg

1904 • Nya Gamla Ullevi (19,000) •
ifkgoteborg.se
Major honours
UEFA Cup (2) 1982, 1987; Swedish League (18)
1908, 1910, 1918, 1935, 1942, 1958, 1969, 1982,
1983, 1984, 1987, 1990, 1991, 1993, 1994, 1995,
1996, 2007; Swedish Cup (7) 1979, 1982, 1983,
1991 (autumn), 2008, 2013, 2015
Coach: Jörgen Lennartsson

2015

05/04	h	Åtvidaberg	W	1-0 Rogne
08/04	a	Örebro	W	2-0 Salomonsson, Vibe
12/04	h	Malmö	L	0-1
19/04	a	Häcken	W	2-1 Eriksson (p), Boman
27/04	h	Helsingborg	W	3-1 Vibe, Eriksson (p), Pettersson
30/04	a	Gefle	D	0-0
04/05	h	Falkenberg	W	2-1 Rieks 2
08/05	a	Kalmar	W	2-0 Bjärsmyr, Vibe
21/05	h	AIK	W	3-0 Vibe, og (Karlsson), Boman
24/05	a	Halmstad	W	2-1 Ankersen 2
01/06	h	Djurgården	D	0-0
04/06	h	Elfsborg	W	1-0 Vibe
07/06	a	Hammarby	W	1-0 Mikkelsen
05/07	a	Sundsvall	D	2-2 Boman, Vibe
12/07	h	Norrköping	D	0-0
19/07	a	Norrköping	D	2-2 Svensson, Rieks
26/07	a	Falkenberg	L	0-1
02/08	h	Örebro	W	6-0 Engvall 2, Boman, Ankersen 2, Rieks
09/08	a	Malmö	L	1-2 Salomonsson (p)
16/08	h	Häcken	W	4-0 Rieks 3, Aleesami
23/08	a	Åtvidaberg	W	1-0 Boman
30/08	h	Gefle	W	3-0 Rieks, Riski, Salomonsson
13/09	a	Helsingborg	W	2-1 Ankersen, Rieks
20/09	h	Hammarby	W	1-0 Rieks
24/09	a	Elfsborg	D	1-1 Salomonsson (p)
28/09	h	Sundsvall	W	3-2 Salomonsson (p), Boman, Albæk
04/10	h	Halmstad	D	1-1 Aleesami
19/10	a	Djurgården	D	2-2 Engvall, Ankersen
26/10	a	AIK	W	2-1 Engvall 2
31/10	h	Kalmar	D	2-2 Albæk 2

No	Name	Nat	DoB	Pos	Aps	(s)	Gls
7	Mads Albæk	DEN	14/01/90	M	11		3
4	Haitam Aleesami	NOR	31/07/91	D	30		2
1	John Alvbåge		10/08/82	G	30		
9	Jakob Ankersen	DEN	22/11/90	M	27	(1)	6
30	Mattias Bjärsmyr		03/01/86	D	23		1
26	Karl Bohm		24/08/95	M		(1)	
16	Mikael Boman		14/07/88	A	17	(9)	6
19	Gustav Engvall		29/04/96	A	17	(8)	5
6	Sebastian Eriksson		31/01/89	M	20	(7)	2
22	Adam Johansson		21/02/83	D		(1)	
14	Hjálmar Jónsson	ISL	29/07/80	D	18	(1)	
15	Thomas Mikkelsen	DEN	29/01/90	A	1	(8)	1
27	Billy Nordström		18/09/95	D		(1)	
24	Tom Pettersson		25/05/90	D	7	(18)	1
8	Søren Rieks	DEN	07/04/87	M	28		10
10	Riku Riski	FIN	16/08/89	A	7	(4)	1
28	Thomas Rogne	NOR	29/06/90	D	19		1
2	Emil Salomonsson		28/04/89	D	30		6
20	Victor Sköld		31/07/89	A		(6)	
11	Martin Smedberg-Dalence	BOL	10/05/84	M	1	(14)	
13	Gustav Svensson		07/02/87	M	28		1
29	Lasse Vibe	DEN	22/02/87	M	16		6

Halmstads BK

1914 • Örjans Vall (15,500) • hbk.se
Major honours
*Swedish League (4) 1976, 1979, 1997, 2000;
Swedish Cup (1) 1995*
Coach: Jan Jönsson

2015

06/04	a	AIK	L	1-2	Fagercrantz
09/04	h	Norrköping	L	0-3	
12/04	h	Helsingborg	L	1-2	Barny
18/04	a	Gefle	D	0-0	
26/04	h	Elfsborg	W	1-0	Karikari
29/04	a	Malmö	L	1-3	Karikari
04/05	h	Häcken	L	0-2	
10/05	a	Falkenberg	L	0-1	
18/05	h	Djurgården	L	2-3	Barny, Keene
24/05	h	Göteborg	L	1-2	Keene
30/05	a	Hammarby	D	2-2	Andersson 2
03/06	h	Sundsvall	W	1-0	Barny
06/06	h	Örebro	D	1-1	Gyan
04/07	a	Åtvidaberg	D	0-0	
11/07	h	Kalmar	W	1-0	Keene
18/07	a	Sundsvall	D	0-0	
27/07	h	Gefle	L	0-1	
02/08	a	Elfsborg	L	0-2	
09/08	a	Åtvidaberg	D	0-0	
17/08	h	Helsingborg	L	0-2	
23/08	h	Örebro	D	2-2	Rusike, Rojas
29/08	a	Djurgården	L	2-4	Rusike 2
14/09	a	Häcken	L	1-4	og (Abubakari)
18/09	h	Falkenberg	L	0-1	
23/09	a	Kalmar	L	0-1	
26/09	h	Malmö	D	0-0	
04/10	a	Göteborg	D	1-1	Keene
18/10	h	AIK	L	0-1	
25/10	a	Norrköping	L	1-3	Barny
31/10	h	Hammarby	W	2-1	Henningsson, Rusike

No	Name	Nat	DoB	Pos	Aps	(s)	Gls
6	Mohamed Ali Khan	LIB	01/11/88	D	29		
5	Christoffer Andersson		22/10/78	D	23	(4)	2
4	Joseph Baffo		07/11/92	D	5	(2)	
7	Junes Barny		04/11/89	A	29	(1)	4
21	Andreas Bengtsson		22/02/96	D	4	(1)	
15	Perparim Beqaj		03/08/95	A		(1)	
26	Alexander Berntsson		30/03/96	D	2	(17)	
8	Kristoffer Fagercrantz		09/10/86	M	6	(9)	1
11	King Osei Gyan	GHA	22/12/88	M	17		1
17	Sead Haksabanovic		04/05/99	M	5	(5)	
14	Alexander Henningsson		14/05/90	M	3	(5)	1
27	Marcus Johansson		24/08/93	D	1	(1)	
14	Kwame Karikari	GHA	21/01/92	A	7	(2)	2
9	James Keene	ENG	26/12/85	A	21	(1)	4
19	Snorre Krogsgård	NOR	25/01/91	M	24	(2)	
3	Fredrik Liverstam		04/03/88	D	28		
2	Viktor Ljung		19/04/91	D	14		
1	Stojan Lukic		28/12/79	G	29		
18	Shkodran Maholli		10/04/93	A	2	(10)	
30	Malkolm Nilsson		03/08/93	G	1		
10	Antonio Rojas	PAR	27/03/84	M	21	(4)	1
23	Matthew Rusike	ZIM	28/06/90	A	10	(1)	4
24	Simon Silverholt		17/06/93	M	3	(7)	
16	Eric Smith		08/01/97	M	17	(10)	
28	Jesper Westerberg		01/02/86	D	29		

Hammarby Fotboll

1915 • Tele2Arena (33,000) •
hammarbyfotboll.se
Major honours
Swedish League (1) 2001
Coach: Nanne Bergstrand

2015

04/04	h	Häcken	W	2-0	Bakircioglü (p), Söderqvist
08/04	a	Elfsborg	D	1-1	Hallenius
13/04	h	Djurgården	W	2-1	Bakircioglü, Besara
20/04	a	Malmö	L	1-3	Bakircioglü
25/04	h	Åtvidaberg	W	2-1	Hallenius, Besara
30/04	a	Örebro	D	2-2	Solheim, Sævarsson
04/05	a	AIK	L	0-2	
11/05	h	Sundsvall	L	1-2	Persson
20/04	a	Norrköping	L	0-1	
25/05	a	Helsingborg	L	0-1	
30/05	h	Halmstad	D	2-2	Israelsson, Solli
04/06	a	Kalmar	D	2-2	Söderqvist, Hallenius
07/06	h	Göteborg	L	0-1	
06/07	a	Gefle	D	1-1	Besara
13/07	h	Falkenberg	W	3-0	Besara 2, Israelsson
20/07	a	Häcken	D	3-3	Torsteinbø, Persson, Israelsson
27/07	h	Norrköping	L	0-1	
03/08	a	Sundsvall	L	0-3	
09/08	h	Elfsborg	D	0-0	
17/08	a	Falkenberg	W	1-0	Torsteinbø
24/08	h	Djurgården	D	2-2	Torsteinbø, Israelsson
28/08	h	Kalmar	D	0-0	
13/09	h	Örebro	L	1-2	Orlov
20/09	a	Göteborg	L	0-1	
23/09	h	Gefle	W	3-0	Orlov, Bakircioglü (p), Israelsson
27/09	h	AIK	W	1-0	Israelsson
02/10	a	Åtvidaberg	W	3-0	Solheim, Torsteinbø 2
18/10	h	Helsingborg	L	1-4	Sævarsson
25/10	h	Malmö	L	0-1	
31/10	a	Halmstad	L	1-2	Sætra

No	Name	Nat	DoB	Pos	Aps	(s)	Gls
6	Joseph Aidoo	GHA	29/09/95	D	1		
10	Kennedy Bakircioglü		02/11/80	M	18	(4)	4
9	Stefan Batan		20/03/85	D	18	(1)	
7	Nahir Besara		25/02/91	M	12	(3)	5
22	Lars Fuhre	NOR	29/09/89	M	1	(13)	
5	Philip Haglund		22/03/87	M	20	(6)	
17	Linus Hallenius		01/04/89	A	16	(7)	3
16	Johannes Hopf		16/06/87	G	11		
4	Erik Israelsson		25/02/89	M	19	(3)	6
26	Dusan Jajic		04/07/98	M	1	(1)	
55	Imad Khalili	PLE	03/04/87	A	6	(6)	
1	Ögmundur Kristinsson	ISL	19/06/89	G	14		
27	Isac Lidberg		08/09/98	A		(2)	
3	Richard Magyar		03/05/91	D	11		
25	Tim Markström		09/10/86	G	5		
15	Viktor Nordin		18/01/96	M	1		
7	Jakob Orlov		15/03/86	A	11		2
8	Johan Persson		20/06/84	M	25		2
11	Pablo Piñones-Arce		27/08/81	A	3	(8)	
20	Amadaiya Rennie	LBR	17/03/90	M	3	(6)	
18	Oliver Silverholt		22/06/94	D	10	(5)	
77	Mats Solheim	NOR	03/12/87	D	25	(1)	2
21	Jan Gunnar Solli	NOR	19/04/81	M	6	(11)	1
23	Lars Sætra	NOR	24/07/91	D	29		1
2	Birkir Már Sævarsson	ISL	11/11/84	D	28		2
34	Måns Söderqvist		08/02/93	A	22	(4)	2
14	Fredrik Torsteinbø	NOR	13/03/91	M	14	(7)	5

Helsingborgs IF

1907 • Olympia (17,200) • hif.se
Major honours
*Swedish League (5) 1933, 1934, 1941, 1999, 2011;
Swedish Cup (5) 1941, 1998, 2006, 2010, 2011*
Coach: Henrik Larsson

2015

04/04	a	Kalmar	D	0-0	
08/04	h	Falkenberg	D	0-0	
12/04	a	Halmstad	W	2-1	Wede, Lindström
20/04	h	Norrköping	W	3-1	Atakora 2, Simovic
27/04	a	Göteborg	L	1-3	Simovic
30/04	h	Sundsvall	W	2-0	Simovic, Boateng
03/05	a	Malmö	L	1-3	Simovic
09/05	h	Gefle	L	1-2	Ajdarevic
20/05	a	Elfsborg	L	1-2	Krafth
25/05	h	Hammarby	W	1-0	Simovic
31/05	a	AIK	L	1-3	Simovic
03/06	h	Örebro	D	0-0	
06/06	h	Åtvidaberg	W	3-0	J Larsson, P Larsson, Boateng
05/07	a	Häcken	L	2-3	Simovic, Pálsson
13/07	h	Djurgården	L	0-1	
19/07	h	AIK	W	3-1	J Larsson 2, Smárason
25/07	a	Åtvidaberg	W	2-1	Simovic 2
31/07	h	Kalmar	L	1-2	Boateng
08/08	a	Falkenberg	W	3-2	Bojanic 2, Boateng
17/08	h	Halmstad	W	2-0	Uronen, Smárason
24/08	a	Norrköping	L	2-3	Bojanic, Simovic
30/08	h	Malmö	L	0-3	
13/09	h	Göteborg	L	1-2	Simovic
20/09	a	Gefle	L	1-2	Smárason
24/09	h	Örebro	L	0-2	
28/09	a	Djurgården	D	2-2	Prica, Smárason
04/10	h	Elfsborg	W	2-1	Prica, Wede, Uronen, og (Gunnarsson)
18/10	a	Hammarby	W	4-1	Prica, Wede, Uronen, Simovic
25/10	a	Sundsvall	L	1-2	Uronen
31/10	h	Häcken	L	1-2	Johansson

No	Name	Nat	DoB	Pos	Aps	(s)	Gls
13	Alexander Achinioti-Jönsson		17/04/96	M		(1)	
42	Astrit Ajdarevic		17/04/90	A	9	(4)	1
39	Daniel Andersson		18/12/72	G	1		
14	Lalawele Atakora	TOG	09/11/90	M	24	(3)	2
29	Jesper Björkman		29/04/93	D		(2)	
20	Emmanuel Boateng	GHA	17/01/94	M	5	(16)	4
19	Darijan Bojanic		28/12/94	M	17	(8)	3
16	Mikael Dahlberg		16/03/85	A	1	(11)	
30	Pär Hansson		22/06/86	G	23		
3	Frederik Helstrup	DEN	16/03/93	D	30		
2	Carl Johansson		23/05/94	D	10	(5)	1
24	Anton Kinnander		23/02/96	A		(2)	
15	Emil Krafth		02/08/94	D	12		1
6	Andreas Landgren		17/03/89	D	20	(5)	
18	Jordan Larsson		27/06/97	A	24	(1)	3
26	Peter Larsson		30/04/84	D	8	(2)	1
7	Mattias Lindström		18/04/80	M	8	(7)	1
9	Johan Mårtensson		16/02/89	M	28		
8	Gudlaugur Victor Pálsson	ISL	30/04/91	M	20	(1)	1
22	Rade Prica		30/06/80	A	6	(3)	2
1	Matt Pyzdrowski	USA	17/08/86	G	6	(2)	
21	Mohamed Ramadan		04/04/91	A		(1)	
9	Robin Simovic		29/05/91	A	23	(2)	12
11	Arnór Smárason	ISL	07/09/88	M	10	(4)	5
28	Jere Uronen	FIN	13/07/94	D	27		3
10	Anton Wede		20/04/90	M	18	(1)	2

BK Häcken

1940 • Rambergsvallen (8,480);
Nya Gamla Ullevi (19,000); Bravida Arena (6,500) •
bkhacken.se
Major honours
Swedish Cup (1) 2016
Coach: Peter Gerhardsson

2015

04/04	a Hammarby	L	0-2	
09/04	h Djurgården	D	1-1	Makondele
13/04	a Sundsvall	D	1-1	Makondele
19/04	a Göteborg	L	1-2	Simon Gustafsson
26/04	a Kalmar	W	1-0	Ericsson
30/04	h Norrköping	L	0-2	
04/05	a Halmstad	W	2-0	Thorvaldsson, J Andersson
10/05	h Örebro	W	2-0	Mohammed, Samuel Gustafsson
21/05	a Malmö	W	3-0	Samuel Gustafsson, Mohammed, Binaku
25/05	h Falkenberg	L	0-2	
29/05	h Gefle	L	0-2	
03/06	a Åtvidaberg	D	1-1	Samuel Gustafsson
06/06	h AIK	D	0-0	
05/07	h Helsingborg	W	3-2	Simon Gustafsson, Sudic, Jeremejeff
12/07	a Elfsborg	L	0-1	
20/07	h Hammarby	D	3-3	Abubakari, Paulinho 2
25/07	h Kalmar	W	3-0	Mohammed 2, J Andersson
01/08	a Djurgården	L	1-2	Hemmen
08/08	a Gefle	D	1-1	Paulinho (p)
16/08	a Göteborg	L	0-4	
22/08	h Malmö	W	1-0	Ericsson
29/08	a Örebro	L	0-2	
14/09	h Halmstad	W	4-1	Paulinho 3, Jeremejeff
19/09	a AIK	L	1-2	Jeremejeff
24/09	a Åtvidaberg	W	3-0	Jeremejeff 2, Makondele
27/09	a Falkenberg	W	2-1	Ericsson (p), Paulinho
04/10	a Norrköping	L	1-3	Paulinho
19/10	h Sundsvall	W	3-1	Samuel Gustafsson, Hemmen, Rexhepi
25/10	h Elfsborg	W	5-2	Paulinho 3, Samuel Gustafsson, Jeremejeff
31/10	a Helsingborg	W	2-1	Makondele 2

No	Name	Nat	DoB	Pos	Aps	(s)	Gls
26	Peter Abrahamsson		18/07/88	G	17		
12	Mohammed Abubakari	GHA	15/02/86	M	21	(2)	1
28	Adam Andersson		11/11/96	M	1	(5)	
27	Joel Andersson		11/11/96	D	14	(9)	2
15	Kari Arkivuo	FIN	23/06/83	D	19	(1)	
25	Egzon Binaku		28/08/95	D	5	(6)	1
14	Martin Ericsson		04/09/80	M	10	(5)	3
6	David Frölund		04/06/79	M	2	(1)	
22	Samuel Gustafsson		11/01/95	M	24	(3)	5
7	Simon Gustafsson		11/01/95	M	14		2
31	Michiel Hemmen	NED	28/06/87	A	2	(5)	2
18	Alexander Jeremejeff		12/10/91	A	10	(3)	6
1	Christoffer Källqvist		26/08/83	G	13		
2	Diego Lugano	URU	02/11/80	D	11		
24	René Makondele	COD	20/04/82	M	10	(15)	5
4	Tefu Mashamaite	RSA	27/09/84	D	7		
21	Nasiru Mohammed	GHA	06/06/94	M	30		4
13	Sebastian Ohlsson		31/12/92	M		(6)	
16	Joachim Olausson		14/04/95	M		(1)	
10	Paulinho	BRA	09/03/86	A	14		11
20	Ivo Pekalski		03/11/90	M	14	(3)	
9	Dardan Rexhepi		16/02/92	A	8	(13)	1
23	Simon Sandberg		25/03/94	D	23		
4	Albin Skoglund		01/02/97	A		(1)	
3	Jasmin Sudic		24/11/90	D	19		1
11	Gunnar Heidar Thorvaldsson	ISL	01/04/82	A	7	(3)	1
7	Niels Vorthoren	NED	21/02/88	M	3		
5	Emil Wahlström		02/03/87	D	11	(3)	
19	Leonard Zuta	MKD	09/08/92	D	21		

Kalmar FF

1910 • Guldfågeln Arena (12,105) •
kalmarff.se
Major honours
Swedish League (1) 2008; Swedish Cup (3) 1981, 1987, 2007
Coach: Peter Swärdh

2015

04/04	h Helsingborg	D	0-0	
08/04	a Gefle	L	0-2	
13/04	a Åtvidaberg	W	2-1	V Elm 2
17/04	a Djurgården	L	0-1	
26/04	h Häcken	L	0-1	
29/04	h Elfsborg	L	1-2	D Elm
04/05	a Örebro	W	3-0	Eriksson (p), Antonsson, V Elm
08/05	h Göteborg	L	0-2	
19/05	a Falkenberg	W	3-1	Eriksson, Antonsson, Sachpekidis
24/05	h Malmö	W	2-1	D Elm, Antonsson
30/05	a Norrköping	L	1-2	Antonsson
04/06	h Hammarby	D	2-2	Antonsson 2
07/06	a Sundsvall	D	1-1	D Elm
05/07	h AIK	D	0-0	
11/07	a Halmstad	L	0-1	
18/07	h Falkenberg	W	4-0	Ring, Antonsson 2, Ismael
25/07	a Häcken	L	0-3	
31/07	a Helsingborg	W	2-1	Eriksson, Sachpekidis
10/08	h Sundsvall	L	0-2	
16/08	a AIK	L	1-2	Eriksson
23/08	h Elfsborg	L	0-3	
28/08	h Hammarby	D	0-0	
11/09	h Norrköping	L	1-2	Antonsson
20/09	a Åtvidaberg	D	1-1	Antonsson
23/09	h Halmstad	W	1-0	Romarinho
28/09	a Örebro	L	1-2	Romarinho
04/10	h Djurgården	L	0-3	
17/10	a Malmö	L	0-3	
26/10	h Gefle	W	3-1	Antonsson 2 (2p), Diouf
31/10	a Göteborg	D	2-2	Eriksson, Diouf

No	Name	Nat	DoB	Pos	Aps	(s)	Gls
5	Viktor Agardius		23/10/89	D	24		
9	Marcus Antonsson		08/05/91	A	25	(4)	12
77	Lars Cramer	NOR	25/05/91	G	19		
27	Pape Alioune Diouf	SEN	22/06/89	A	20	(6)	2
80	Nenad Djordjević	SRB	07/08/79	D	7	(1)	
16	David Elm		10/01/83	A	13	(5)	3
6	Rasmus Elm		17/03/88	M	1	(11)	
23	Viktor Elm		13/11/85	M	27		3
26	Pär Ericsson		21/07/88	A	3	(5)	
10	Tobias Eriksson		19/03/85	M	23	(3)	5
18	Tor Øyvind Hovda	NOR	24/09/89	M	1	(5)	
26	Svante Ingelsson		04/06/98	D		(4)	
21	Ismael	BRA	01/12/94	M	23	(4)	1
14	Stefan Larsson		21/01/83	D	6	(5)	
3	Marcus Nilsson		26/02/88	D	23		
21	Emin Nouri	AZE	22/07/85	D	21		
22	Måns Olström		01/11/96	D		(2)	
33	Johan Ramhorn		03/05/96	D	3		
31	Sebastian Ramhorn		03/05/96	D	2		
11	Jonathan Ring		05/12/91	M	15	(4)	1
29	Romarinho	BRA	10/08/85	M	14	(7)	2
24	Filip Sachpekidis		03/07/97	M	15	(9)	2
1	Ole Söderberg		20/07/90	G	11		
2	Markus Thorbjörnsson		01/10/87	M	19	(5)	
4	Ludvig Öhman		09/10/91	D	15	(4)	

Malmö FF

1910 • Swedbank Stadion (24,000) • mff.se
Major honours
Swedish League (18) 1944, 1949, 1950, 1951, 1953, 1965, 1967, 1970, 1971, 1974, 1975, 1977, 1986, 1988, 2004, 2010, 2013, 2014; Swedish Cup (14) 1944, 1946, 1947, 1951, 1953, 1967, 1973, 1974, 1975, 1978, 1980, 1984, 1986, 1989
Coach: Åge Hareide (NOR)

2015

06/04	a Sundsvall	W	4-1	Berget 2, Rosenberg, Lewicki
09/04	h AIK	D	0-0	
12/04	a Göteborg	W	1-0	Yotún
20/04	h Hammarby	W	3-1	Rosenberg, Lewicki, Mehmeti
24/04	a Falkenberg	D	3-3	Berget, Cibicki, Adu
29/04	h Halmstad	W	3-1	Cibicki, Berget 2
03/05	h Helsingborg	W	3-1	Eikrem 2, Berget
11/05	a Elfsborg	D	2-2	Eikrem 2
21/05	h Häcken	L	0-3	
24/05	a Kalmar	L	1-2	Berget
31/05	a Åtvidaberg	W	3-0	Rosenberg, Eikrem, Johansson
03/06	a Gefle	W	2-1	Rakip, Johansson
07/06	h Djurgården	D	1-1	Eikrem
04/07	a Norrköping	L	1-3	Kroon
11/07	a Örebro	D	2-2	Cibicki, Mehmeti
18/07	a Örebro	D	1-1	Rosenberg
25/07	h Sundsvall	W	3-0	Djurdjić, Rodić, Rosenberg
01/08	a Åtvidaberg	D	2-2	Djurdjić 2 (1p)
09/08	h Göteborg	W	2-1	Árnason, Rosenberg (p)
15/08	h Gefle	W	2-0	Rodić, Rosenberg
22/08	h Häcken	L	0-1	
30/08	h Helsingborg	W	3-0	Berget, Carvalho, Rosenberg
12/09	h Elfsborg	D	1-1	Adu
20/09	h Djurgården	W	2-0	Eikrem, Carvalho
23/09	h Falkenberg	W	4-3	Rosenberg, Djurdjić 2, Rodić
26/09	a Halmstad	D	0-0	
04/10	h AIK	L	1-2	Rodić
17/10	h Kalmar	W	3-0	Rosenberg 2, Berget
25/10	h Hammarby	W	1-0	Bengtsson
31/10	h Norrköping	L	0-2	

No	Name	Nat	DoB	Pos	Aps	(s)	Gls
8	Enoch Kofi Adu	GHA	14/09/90	M	24	(3)	2
21	Kári Árnason	ISL	13/10/82	D	13		1
27	Zlatan Azinovic		31/01/88	G	3		
17	Rasmus Bengtsson		26/06/86	D	15	(1)	1
23	Jo Inge Berget	NOR	11/09/90	A	24	(3)	9
31	Franz Brorsson		30/01/96	D	3	(5)	
25	Felipe Carvalho	URU	18/09/93	D	7	(4)	2
15	Paweł Cibicki		09/01/94	M	5	(4)	3
28	Nikola Djurdjić	SRB	01/04/86	A	12		5
19	Magnus Wolff Eikrem	NOR	08/08/90	M	22	(6)	7
4	Filip Helander		22/04/93	D	10	(2)	
21	Erik Johansson		30/12/88	D	13		2
2	Pa Konate		25/04/94	D	7	(3)	
7	Simon Kroon		16/06/93	M	3	(3)	1
6	Oscar Lewicki		14/07/92	M	25	(2)	2
11	Agon Mehmeti	ALB	20/11/89	A	4	(11)	2
10	Guillermo Molins		26/09/88	M		(7)	
25	Robin Olsen		08/01/90	G	13		
5	Erdal Rakip		13/02/96	M	10	(10)	1
20	Vladimir Rodić	MNE	07/09/93	M	11	(2)	4
9	Markus Rosenberg		27/09/82	A	26	(2)	11
22	Tobias Sana		11/07/89	M	11	(8)	
3	Anton Tinnerholm		26/02/91	D	26	(2)	
26	Andreas Vindheim	NOR	14/08/95	D	5	(5)	
1	Johan Wiland		24/01/81	G	14		
13	Yoshimar Yotún	PER	07/04/90	D	24		1

SWEDEN

IFK Norrköping

1897• Nya Parken (17,234) • ifknorrkoping.se

Major honours
Swedish League (13) 1943, 1945, 1946, 1947, 1948, 1952, 1956, 1957, 1960, 1962, 1963, 1989, 2015; Swedish Cup (6) 1943, 1945, 1969, 1988, 1991 (spring), 1994

Coach: Jan Andersson

2015

04/04	h	Örebro	D	1-1	Nyman
09/04	a	Halmstad	W	3-0	Dagerstål, Kujovic 2
13/04	h	Elfsborg	L	0-4	
20/04	a	Helsingborg	L	1-3	Kujovic
27/04	h	Gefle	W	4-1	Nyman 2, Traustason 2
30/04	a	Häcken	W	2-0	Kujovic, Lawan
03/05	h	Åtvidaberg	W	2-1	Traustason, Nyman
10/05	a	AIK	D	2-2	Fransson, Kujovic
20/05	h	Hammarby	W	1-0	Kujovic
25/05	a	Sundsvall	W	1-0	Kujovic
30/05	h	Kalmar	W	2-1	Kujovic, Nyman
04/06	a	Djurgården	D	1-1	Tkalčić
07/06	h	Falkenberg	W	2-0	Tkalčić, Kujovic
04/07	h	Malmö	W	3-1	Wahlqvist, Kujovic (p), Fransson
12/07	a	Göteborg	D	0-0	
19/07	h	Göteborg	D	2-2	Kujovic, Fransson
27/07	a	Hammarby	W	1-0	Kujovic
02/08	h	AIK	L	1-2	Wahlqvist
10/08	a	Örebro	W	3-1	Traustason, Nyman, Kujovic
17/08	a	Åtvidaberg	D	1-1	Kamara
24/08	h	Helsingborg	W	3-2	Traustason, Sjölund, Johansson
29/08	a	Falkenberg	W	1-0	Nyman
11/09	a	Kalmar	W	2-1	Kujovic, Fransson
20/09	h	Sundsvall	W	5-1	Nyman 2, Kujovic, Johansson, Fransson
23/09	h	Djurgården	W	4-2	Traustason, Sjölund, Wahlqvist, Kujovic
27/09	a	Gefle	W	2-1	Nyman, Kujovic
04/10	h	Häcken	W	3-1	Kujovic 2 (1p), Kamara
19/10	a	Elfsborg	L	2-3	Kamara 2
25/10	h	Halmstad	W	3-1	Kamara 2, Kujovic
31/10	a	Malmö	W	2-0	Kujovic, Traustason

No	Name	Nat	DoB	Pos	Aps	(s)	Gls
14	Nicklas Bärkroth		19/01/92	M	15	(3)	
24	Gentrit Citaku		25/02/96	M	1	(6)	
25	Filip Dagerstål		01/02/97	M	4	(2)	1
10	Joel Enarsson		27/06/93	A	1	(12)	
15	Marcus Falk-Olander		21/05/87	D	2	(3)	
26	Alexander Fransson		02/04/94	M	29		5
21	Andreas Hadenius		18/03/91	D	6	(7)	
19	Mirza Halvadzic		15/02/96	M		(1)	
4	Andreas Johansson		10/03/82	D	29		2
17	Al-Hadji Kamara	SLE	16/04/94	A	3	(11)	6
10	Emir Kujovic		22/06/88	A	29		21
8	Rawez Lawan		04/10/87	M	1	(20)	1
91	David Mitov Nilsson	MKD	12/01/91	G	30		
5	Christoffer Nyman		05/10/92	A	29		10
20	Daniel Sjölund	FIN	22/04/83	M	28		2
27	Tesfaldet Tekie		04/06/97	M	2	(4)	
11	Christopher Telo		04/11/89	M	18	(5)	
30	Nikola Tkalčić	CRO	03/12/89	D	23	(4)	2
9	Arnór Ingvi Traustason	ISL	30/04/93	M	29		7
28	Linus Wahlqvist		11/11/96	D	29		3
23	David Boo Wiklander		03/10/84	D	22	(1)	

GIF Sundsvall

1903 • Norrporten Arena (8,500) • gifsundsvall.se

Coach: Joel Cedergren & Roger Franzén

2015

06/04	h	Malmö	L	1-4	Eklund (p)
09/04	a	Åtvidaberg	W	3-2	Eklund, Nilsson, Dibba
13/04	h	Häcken	D	1-1	Englund
20/04	a	Örebro	W	3-1	Dibba, Sellin, Helg
26/04	h	Djurgården	L	0-2	
30/04	a	Helsingborg	L	0-2	
03/05	h	Elfsborg	L	0-1	
11/05	a	Hammarby	W	2-1	Lundström, Sigurjónsson
20/05	a	Gefle	L	1-3	Eklund
25/05	h	Norrköping	L	0-1	
30/05	a	Falkenberg	D	1-1	Chennoufi
03/06	h	Halmstad	L	0-1	
07/06	h	Kalmar	D	1-1	Ålander
05/07	h	Göteborg	D	2-2	Nilsson, Sigurjónsson
12/07	a	AIK	L	1-4	Dibba
18/07	h	Halmstad	D	0-0	
25/07	a	Malmö	L	0-3	
03/08	h	Hammarby	W	3-0	Sigurjónsson, Dibba, Sliper
10/08	a	Kalmar	W	2-0	Sellin, Helg
15/08	h	Örebro	W	1-0	Sigurjónsson
24/08	h	Falkenberg	L	0-1	
30/08	a	Elfsborg	W	2-1	Dibba, Gerson
14/09	h	Åtvidaberg	L	0-1	
20/09	a	Norrköping	L	1-5	Dibba
23/09	h	AIK	L	0-2	
28/09	a	Göteborg	L	2-3	og (Alvbåge), Rajalakso
03/10	h	Gefle	W	2-1	Olsson, Dibba
19/10	a	Häcken	L	1-3	Dibba
25/10	h	Helsingborg	W	2-1	Fjóluson, Hasani
31/10	a	Djurgården	L	2-4	Eklund, Chennoufi

No	Name	Nat	DoB	Pos	Aps	(s)	Gls
19	Adam Chennoufi		04/07/88	M	17	(9)	2
22	Marcus Danielsson		08/04/89	D	6	(2)	
14	Pa Dibba	GAM	15/10/87	A	30		8
9	Johan Eklund		30/05/84	A	19	(6)	4
91	Leo Englund		16/04/91	A	6	(14)	1
5	Jón Gudni Fjóluson	ISL	10/04/89	D	27	(2)	1
8	Lars Gerson	LUX	05/02/90	M	29		1
26	Erik Granat		09/08/95	M		(4)	
12	Shpetim Hasani	KOS	10/08/82	A	5	(5)	1
16	Simon Helg		10/04/90	M	3	(12)	4
21	Eric Larsson		15/07/91	D	24		
15	Robert Lundström		01/11/89	D	17		1
17	Tommy Naurin		17/05/84	G	1		
2	Joakim Nilsson		06/02/94	D	20		2
3	Dennis Olsson		03/10/94	M	17	(1)	1
11	Sebastian Rajalakso		23/09/88	M	16	(9)	1
1	Lloyd Saxton	ENG	18/04/90	G	2		
18	Robin Sellin		12/04/90	M	28		2
6	Rúnar Már Sigurjónsson	ISL	18/06/90	M	25	(2)	4
7	Daniel Sliper		23/04/87	M		(11)	1
20	Smajl Suljevic		15/07/94	M		(3)	
30	Peter Wilson		09/10/96	M		(2)	
4	Stefan Ålander		25/04/83	D	11	(4)	1

Åtvidabergs FF

1907 • Kopparvallen (8,600) • atvidabergsff.se

Major honours
Swedish League (2) 1972, 1973; Swedish Cup (2) 1970, 1971

Coach: Roar Hansen

2015

05/04	a	Göteborg	L	0-1	
09/04	h	Sundsvall	L	2-3	Owoeri, Jelavić
13/04	a	Kalmar	L	1-2	Sköld
19/04	h	Falkenberg	W	3-1	Albornoz, Bergström, Sköld
25/04	a	Hammarby	L	1-2	Owoeri
29/04	h	AIK	D	1-1	Owoeri (p)
03/05	a	Norrköping	L	1-2	Sköld
11/05	h	Djurgården	L	2-3	Bergström, Owoeri
20/05	a	Örebro	L	1-2	Skrabb
24/05	h	Elfsborg	L	1-2	Sköld
31/05	a	Malmö	L	0-3	
03/06	h	Häcken	D	1-1	Owoeri
06/06	a	Helsingborg	L	0-3	
04/07	h	Halmstad	D	0-0	
11/07	h	Gefle	D	1-1	Skrabb
20/07	a	Djurgården	D	0-0	
25/07	h	Helsingborg	L	1-2	Hovda
01/08	h	Malmö	D	2-2	Bergström, Albornoz
09/08	a	Halmstad	D	0-0	
17/08	h	Norrköping	D	1-1	Dahlén
23/08	h	Göteborg	L	0-1	
30/08	a	AIK	L	0-1	
14/09	a	Sundsvall	W	1-0	Albornoz
20/09	a	Kalmar	D	1-1	Hovda
24/09	a	Häcken	L	0-3	
28/09	a	Elfsborg	L	1-3	Ahmed
02/10	h	Hammarby	L	0-3	
19/10	a	Falkenberg	L	0-6	
26/10	h	Örebro	L	2-3	Skrabb, Owoeri (p)
31/10	a	Gefle	L	1-2	Skrabb

No	Name	Nat	DoB	Pos	Aps	(s)	Gls
6	Ammar Ahmed		03/07/88	M	19	(9)	1
13	Álberis Silva	BRA	02/12/84	D	10	(6)	
10	Mauricio Albornoz		10/03/88	M	28		3
7	Kristian Bergström		08/01/74	M	30		3
12	Bruno Marinho	BRA	05/07/84	M		(1)	
32	Martin Christensen	DEN	23/12/87	M	27	(2)	
2	Andreas Dahlén		11/12/82	D	19	(2)	1
8	Petter Gustafsson		16/09/85	M		(2)	
1	Henrik Gustavsson		21/10/76	G	19		
5	Daniel Hallingström		10/02/81	D	19	(2)	
13	Kenny Hildeby		07/03/97	M		(2)	
17	Hampus Holmgren	FIN	14/11/95	D	7	(3)	
18	Tor Øyvind Hovda	NOR	24/09/89	M	14		2
20	Gustav Jansson		24/02/86	G	11		
11	Mario Jelavić	CRO	20/08/93	A	1	(18)	1
3	Månz Karlsson		04/04/89	D	20	(3)	
9	Ajsel Kujovic		01/03/86	A		(10)	
28	Martin Lorentzson		21/07/84	D	17		
15	David Lundgren		14/08/96	M		(1)	
12	Simon Marklund		14/09/99	M		(1)	
16	Pontus Nordenberg		16/02/95	D	11	(8)	
19	John Owoeri	NGA	13/01/87	A	29		6
28	Sebastian Ramhorn		03/05/96	D	12		
23	Rúben Lameiras	POR	22/12/94	M	4	(6)	
14	Simon Skrabb	FIN	19/01/95	M	22	(6)	4
9	Victor Sköld		31/07/89	A	11	(4)	4
22	Lucas Öhrn		27/09/97	D		(1)	

Örebro SK

1908 • Behrn Arena (12,674) • oskfotboll.se
Coach: Alexander Axén

2015

04/04	a	Norrköping	D	1-1	Åhman Persson
08/04	h	Göteborg	L	0-2	
12/04	a	Falkenberg	L	0-2	
20/04	h	Sundsvall	L	1-3	Yasin (p)
26/04	a	AIK	L	0-3	
30/04	h	Hammarby	D	2-2	Haginge, Yasin (p)
04/05	a	Kalmar	L	0-3	
10/05	a	Häcken	L	0-2	
20/05	h	Åtvidaberg	W	2-1	Gustafsson, Sigurbjörnsson
24/05	h	Gefle	W	1-0	Gustafsson
31/05	a	Elfsborg	D	2-2	Pode, Gustafsson
03/06	h	Helsingborg	D	0-0	
06/06	h	Halmstad	D	1-1	Gerzic
04/07	a	Djurgården	L	0-2	
11/07	a	Malmö	D	2-2	Gustafsson, Holmberg
18/07	h	Malmö	D	1-1	Nordmark
27/07	h	Djurgården	L	0-1	
02/08	a	Göteborg	L	0-6	
10/08	h	Norrköping	L	1-3	Broberg
15/08	a	Sundsvall	L	0-1	
23/08	a	Halmstad	D	2-2	Broberg, Eriksson
29/08	h	Häcken	W	2-0	Broberg, Gustafsson
13/09	a	Hammarby	W	2-1	Eriksson, Ajdarevic
21/09	h	Elfsborg	W	4-2	Broberg 3, Gustafsson
24/09	a	Helsingborg	W	2-0	Eriksson, Nordmark
28/09	h	Kalmar	W	2-1	Broberg 2
03/10	h	Falkenberg	W	2-1	Holmberg, Broberg
19/10	a	Gefle	D	2-2	Holmberg 2
26/10	a	Åtvidaberg	W	3-2	Ajdarevic, Gustafsson, Moberg
31/10	h	AIK	D	1-1	Broberg

No	Name	Nat	DoB	Pos	Aps	(s)	Gls
8	Astrit Ajdarevic		17/04/90	M	10		2
12	Daniel Björnkvist		08/01/89	D	28	(1)	
7	Martin Broberg		24/09/90	M	13	(2)	10
18	Pär Eriksson		21/07/88	A	8	(5)	3
25	Nordin Gerzic		09/11/83	M	27	(1)	1
90	Daniel Gustafsson		29/08/90	M	27	(3)	7
2	Patrik Haginge		02/04/85	D	10	(7)	1
17	Karl Holmberg		03/03/93	A	17	(13)	4
1	Oscar Jansson		23/12/90	G	16	(1)	
13	Jonathan Lundberg		27/10/97	A		(3)	
23	Samuel Mensah	GHA	19/05/89	D		(2)	
20	Erik Moberg		05/07/86	D	23		1
3	Ayanda Nkili	RSA	11/09/90	D	8	(7)	
16	Daniel Nordmark		04/01/88	M	12	(13)	2
11	Marcus Pode		27/03/86	A	16	(8)	1
19	Sebastian Ring		18/04/95	D	1		
30	Jakob Rinne		20/06/93	G	14		
7	Michael Seaton	JAM	01/05/96	A	2	(2)	
27	Eidur Aron Sigurbjörnsson	ISL	26/02/90	D	27	(1)	1
4	Hjörtur Logi Valgardsson	ISL	27/09/88	D	22	(6)	
21	Christoffer Wiktorsson		22/03/89	D	8	(8)	
9	Ahmed Yasin	IRQ	21/04/91	M	14		2
6	Robert Åhman Persson		26/03/87	M	27		1

Top goalscorers

21	Emir Kujovic (Norrköping)
18	Henok Goitom (AIK)
12	Nyasha Mushekwi (Djurgården)
	Johan Oremo (Gefle)
	Robin Simovic (Helsingborg)
	Marcus Antonsson (Kalmar)
11	Viktor Claesson (Elfsborg)
	Paulinho (Häcken)
	Markus Rosenberg (Malmö)
10	Sam Johnson (Djurgården)
	Viktor Prodell (Elfsborg)
	Arber Zeneli (Elfsborg)
	Søren Rieks (Göteborg)
	Christoffer Nyman (Norrköping)
	Martin Broberg (Örebro)

Promoted clubs

Jönköpings Södra IF

1922 • Stadsparksvallen (5,500) • j-sodra.com
Coach: Jimmy Thelin

Östersunds FK

1996 • Jämtkraft Arena (6,200) •
ostersundsfotbollsklubb.se
Coach: Graham Potter (ENG)

Second level final table 2015

		Pld	W	D	L	F	A	Pts
1	Jönköpings Södra IF	30	19	6	5	54	28	63
2	Östersunds FK	30	18	8	4	56	25	62
3	IK Sirius FK	30	15	13	2	53	25	58
4	Assyriska FF	30	14	5	11	46	37	47
5	Varbergs BoIS FC	30	12	11	7	34	27	47
6	Ljungskile SK	30	11	10	9	44	37	43
7	Syrianska FC	30	11	10	9	37	30	43
8	Athletic FC United	30	10	10	10	43	44	40
9	Degerfors IF	30	10	8	12	36	38	38
10	IFK Värnamo	30	10	8	12	40	40	38
11	GAIS Göteborg	30	10	5	15	37	44	35
12	Ängelholms FF	30	8	9	13	31	47	33
13	Mjällby AIF	30	8	6	16	23	43	30
14	IK Frej Täby	30	7	8	15	22	44	29
15	Utsiktens BK	30	7	5	18	28	56	26
16	IF Brommapojkarna	30	5	8	17	30	46	23

Promotion/Relegation play-offs

(05/11/15 & 08/11/15)
Sirius 2-2 Falkenberg
Falkenberg 1-1 Sirius
(3-3; Falkenberg on away goals)

DOMESTIC CUP

Svenska Cupen 2015/16

SECOND ROUND

(19/08/15)
BKV Norrtälje 0-3 Örebro
Brage 0-2 Frej Täby
Ekerö 0-6 AIK
Enskede 0-4 Sundsvall
Eskilsminne 1-2 Varberg
Gute 2-4 Degerfors (aet)
Hittarp 0-3 Ljungskile
Husqvarna 2-3 Häcken
Härnösand 1-3 Syrianska
Höllviken 0-2 Ängelholm
Kristianstad 1-6 Göteborg
Nacka 1-2 Sirius
Oskarshamn 0-1 Jönköpings Södra
Sollentuna 1-2 Assyriska
Somaliska 0-1 Elfsborg
Söderhamn 1-2 Östersund
Team TG 0-4 Gefle
Tenhult 2-0 Mjällby
Trollhättan 4-3 Utsikten (aet)
Örgryte 0-2 Värnamo (aet)

(20/08/15)
Akropolis 0-5 Norrköping
Assyriska BK 0-4 Falkenberg
Carlstad United 2-3 Hammarby
Halmia 1-1 Kalmar (aet; 2-4 on pens)
Lunden Överås 1-8 Helsingborg
Norrby 3-3 GAIS (aet; 5-6 on pens)
Sylvia 0-3 Brommapojkarna
Torstorp 1-5 Djurgården
Trelleborg 1-2 Halmstad
Västerås 3-3 Athletic United (aet; 3-4 on pens)

(26/08/15)
Forward 2-1 Åtvidaberg

(08/11/15)
Götene 0-5 Malmö

THIRD ROUND

Group 1

(20/02/16)
Jönköpings Södra 0-1 Athletic United
Norrköping 4-0 Östersund

(27/02/16)
Athletic United 0-1 Norrköping
Jönköpings Södra 1-0 Östersund

(06/03/16)
Norrköping 1-1 Jönköpings Södra
Östersund 3-0 Athletic United

Final standings
1 Norrköping 7 pts *(qualified)*
2 Jönköpings Södra 4 pts; 3 Östersund 3 pts;
4 Athletic United 3 pts *(eliminated)*

Group 2

(20/02/16)
Halmstad 2-0 Frej Täby

(21/02/16)
Göteborg 1-1 Degerfors

(27/02/16)
Halmstad 3-0 Degerfors

(28/02/16)
Frej Täby 1-1 Göteborg

(06/03/16)
Degerfors 1-1 Frej Täby
Göteborg 3-0 Halmstad

Final standings
1 Halmstad 6 pts *(qualified)*
2 Göteborg 5 pts; Frej 2 pts; 4 Degerfors 2 pts
(eliminated)

Continued over the page

Group 3

(20/02/16)
AIK 2-1 Varberg
(21/02/16)
Tenhult 0-2 Falkenberg
(27/02/16)
Falkenberg 1-1 Varberg
(28/02/16)
Tenhult 0-6 AIK
(05/03/16)
AIK 2-1 Falkenberg
Varberg 1-0 Tenhult

Final standings
1 AIK 9 pts *(qualified)*
2 Falkenberg 4 pts; 2 Varberg 4 pts; 4 Tenhult 0 pts *(eliminated)*

Group 4

(20/02/16)
Elfsborg 3-2 Assyriska
Kalmar 2-1 Värnamo
(27/02/16)
Kalmar 3-1 Assyriska
Värnamo 3-3 Elfsborg
(05/03/16)
Assyriska 1-0 Värnamo
Elfsborg 0-1 Kalmar

Final standings
1 Kalmar 9 pts *(qualified)*
2 Elfsborg 4 pts; 2 Assyriska 3 pts; 4 Värnamo 1 pt *(eliminated)*

Group 5

(20/02/16)
Malmö 2-1 Sirius
Sundsvall 1-0 Ängelholm
(27/02/16)
Sundsvall 0-1 Sirius
(28/02/16)
Ängelholm 1-4 Malmö
(05/03/16)
Malmö 4-0 Sundsvall
Sirius 1-1 Ängelholm

Final standings
1 Malmö 9 pts *(qualified)*
2 Sirius 4 pts; 2 Sundsvall 3 pts; 4 Ängelholm 1 pt *(eliminated)*

Group 6

(21/02/16)
Hammarby 0-0 Syrianska
(22/02/16)
Djurgården 2-1 Ljungskile
(28/02/16)
Syrianska 1-0 Djurgården
(29/02/16)
Hammarby 4-2 Ljungskile
(06/03/16)
Djurgården 1-3 Hammarby
Ljungskile 0-1 Syrianska

Final standings
1 Hammarby 7 pts *(qualified)*
2 Syrianska 7 pts; 2 Djurgården 3 pts;
4 Ljungskile 0 pts *(eliminated)*

Group 7

(20/02/16)
Häcken 0-0 Brommapojkarna
Trollhättan 2-1 Gefle
(27/02/16)
Gefle 4-2 Brommapojkarna
Trollhättan 2-6 Häcken
(05/03/16)
Brommapojkarna 1-1 Trollhättan
Häcken 4-0 Gefle

Final standings
1 Häcken 7 pts *(qualified)*
2 Trollhättan 4 pts; 2 Gefle 3 pts;
4 Brommapojkarna 2 pts *(eliminated)*

Group 8

(20/02/16)
Helsingborg 3-1 GAIS
(21/02/16)
Forward 2-2 Örebro
(27/02/16)
Örebro 3-1 GAIS
(28/02/16)
Forward 0-1 Helsingborg
(05/03/16)
GAIS 1-5 Forward
Helsingborg 1-1 Örebro

Final standings
1 Helsingborg 7 pts *(qualified)*
2 Örebro 5 pts; 2 Forward 4 pts; 4 GAIS 0 pts *(eliminated)*

QUARTER-FINALS

(12/03/16)
Häcken 1-0 Halmstad *(Jeremejeff 90+3)*
(13/03/16)
Kalmar 0-0 Helsingborg *(aet; 5-4 on pens)*
Malmö 1-0 Norrköping *(Kjartansson 47)*
(15/03/16)
AIK 1-1 Hammarby *(Hooiveld 61; Smárason 45)*
(aet; 2-4 on pens)

SEMI-FINALS

(19/03/16)
Kalmar 2-3 Malmö *(Romarinho 19, Antonsson 90; Rosenberg 57p, 60, Berget 63)*
(20/03/16)
Hammarby 2-3 Häcken *(Alex 3, Hallberg 86; Paulinho 58, 67, Mohammed 89)*

FINAL

(05/05/16)
Swedbank Stadion, Malmo
BK HÄCKEN 2 *(Savage 61, Mohammed 66)*
MALMÖ FF 2 *(Rosenberg 39, Eikrem 44)*
(aet; 6-5 on pens)
Referee: *Ekberg*
HÄCKEN: *Abrahamsson, Sandberg, Sudic, Wahlström, Arkivuo, Samuel Gustafsson, Abubakari (Makondele 90+2), Ericsson (Paulinho 62), Mohammed, Jeremejeff (Owoeri 91), Savage*
MALMÖ: *Wiland, Tinnerholm, Árnason, Brorsson, Konate, Eikrem (Sana 79), Lewicki, Christiansen, Berget, Kjartansson (Molins 100), Rosenberg (Rakip 64)*
Red card: *Lewicki (51)*

Svenska Cupen winners Häcken lift their first major trophy

SWITZERLAND
Schweizerischer Fussballverband/Association Suisse de Football (SFV/ASF)

Address	Worbstrasse 48, Postfach CH-3000 Bern 15	**President**	Peter Gilliéron
Tel	+41 31 950 8111	**General secretary**	Alex Miescher
Fax	+41 31 950 8181	**Media officer**	Marco von Ah
E-mail	sfv.asf@football.ch	**Year of formation**	1895
Website	football.ch		

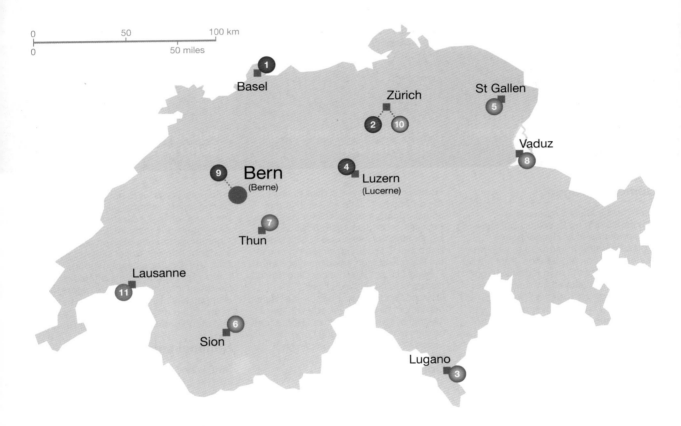

SUPER LEAGUE CLUBS

  **1** FC Basel 1893

 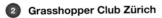 **2** Grasshopper Club Zürich

  3 FC Lugano

  4 FC Luzern

 5 FC St Gallen

  6 FC Sion

  7 FC Thun

  8 FC Vaduz

  **9** BSC Young Boys

 10 FC Zürich

PROMOTED CLUB

 11 FC Lausanne-Sport

KEY

● UEFA Champions League

● UEFA Europa League

● Promoted

● Relegated club in UEFA Europa League

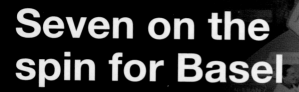

Seven on the spin for Basel

The Swiss Super League title was won for the seventh successive season by FC Basel, who, with new coach Urs Fischer at the helm, took maximum points from their first eight fixtures and were never challenged, wrapping up proceedings with an unprecedented five games to spare.

As in 2014/15, Young Boys trailed in a distant but comfortable second, while FC Zürich experienced both the agony of relegation and the ecstasy of winning the Swiss Cup. Mixed feelings also marked the Swiss national team's efforts at UEFA EURO 2016.

| Runaway title triumph for serial champions | FC Zürich go down but win the Swiss Cup | Penalty defeat ends best EURO performance |

Domestic league

There was initially a measure of resistance among Basel's supporters to the appointment of Fischer as the replacement for Paulo Sousa, who after just one season at St Jakob-Park left for Fiorentina. But the man recruited from FC Thun soon allayed any fears as he masterminded an opening burst of entertaining victories over every one of Basel's Super League opponents bar Young Boys, who halted their run with a 4-3 victory at the Stade de Suisse.

By the winter break Basel's lead was up to ten points. Furthermore, they had scored in all 18 games, with new signing Marc Janko topping the goal charts, teenager Breel Embolo pleasing the crowds, and other key men such as goalkeeper Tomáš Vaclík, centre-back Marek Suchý and midfielder Luca Zuffi all thriving under the new regime. The pre-season loss of Swiss internationals Fabian Schär and Fabian Frei had barely been noticed, and it was the same story in the spring as Basel continued to play well and prosper, a 2-1 win at home to FC Sion ensuring the club's 19th Swiss title on the last day of April.

Basel racked up 83 points – five more than in 2014/15 – to finish 14 ahead of a Young Boys side who, with ex-Salzburg boss Adi Hütter in charge and former Paris Saint-Germain striker Guillaume

Hoarau on fire, played so well during the second half of the season that they actually outpointed Basel. Indeed, the gap between second and third position was bigger than the one above it, with Markus Babbel's FC Luzern coming on strong at the finish to snatch a podium place from Pierluigi Tami's Grasshopper Club, Basel's closest challengers at halfway. Grasshoppers' second-half-of-the-season decline did not, however, prevent their 19-goal Israeli striker Munas Dabbur from beating Hoarau, Janko and Luzern's Marco Schneuwly to the golden boot.

Domestic cup

Like their city rivals, FC Zürich's form crashed in the spring – to such an extent that they were relegated, ending a 26-year stint in the top flight. Uli Forte had replaced Sami Hyypiä as coach during the disastrous run-in, so he was on duty for the Swiss Cup final, which took place just four days after the club's relegation. FCZ's opponents were FC Lugano, the team that had finished a point above them, and revenge of a kind was gained as Forte's men survived a missed penalty to win 1-0, lift the cup for the ninth time, and qualify for the group stage of the UEFA Europa League.

Europe

The 2015/16 final of that competition took place at St Jakob-Park but the

stadium's hosts were not present, having lost to eventual winners Sevilla in the round of 16. Frustrated victims of the away goals rule in their UEFA Champions League play-off against Maccabi Tel-Aviv, Basel skated through their UEFA Europa League group, merrily taking four points off Paulo Sousa's Fiorentina en route, before dramatically overcoming Saint-Étienne in the round of 32. Sion also reached that stage before bowing out to Braga.

National team

Switzerland qualified for UEFA EURO 2016 as group runners-up, and they were second also in their section at the final tournament, which brought a first ever qualification for the knockout phase. An opening 1-0 win over Albania was supplemented by draws against Romania and hosts France, earning Vladimir Petković's side a last-16 encounter with Poland.

A spectacular late equaliser by Xherdan Shaqiri earned Switzerland a penalty shoot-out, but, as in the FIFA World Cup against Ukraine a decade earlier, spot kicks would be their undoing, with Granit Xhaka, one of their best performers at the tournament, putting his effort wide and goalkeeper Yann Sommer, another star turn, failing to save any of Poland's five expertly converted kicks.

DOMESTIC SEASON AT A GLANCE

Super League 2015/16 final table

		Pld	Home					Away					Total					Pts
			W	D	L	F	A	W	D	L	F	A	W	D	L	F	A	
1	**FC Basel 1893**	36	14	2	2	44	15	12	3	3	44	23	26	5	5	88	38	83
2	BSC Young Boys	36	12	4	2	50	24	8	5	5	28	23	20	9	7	78	47	69
3	FC Luzern	36	8	5	5	36	23	7	4	7	23	27	15	9	12	59	50	54
4	Grasshopper Club Zürich	36	9	3	6	35	21	6	5	7	30	35	15	8	13	65	56	53
5	FC Sion	36	11	2	5	31	20	3	6	9	21	29	14	8	14	52	49	50
6	FC Thun	36	6	5	7	26	27	4	6	8	19	27	10	11	15	45	54	41
7	FC St Gallen	36	7	4	7	25	32	3	4	11	16	34	10	8	18	41	66	38
8	FC Vaduz	36	3	11	4	20	20	4	4	10	24	40	7	15	14	44	60	36
9	FC Lugano	36	6	4	8	25	31	3	4	11	21	44	9	8	19	46	75	35
10	FC Zürich	36	4	7	7	29	32	3	6	9	19	39	7	13	16	48	71	34

European qualification 2016/17

Champion: FC Basel 1893 (group stage)
BSC Young Boys (third qualifying round)

Cup winner: FC Zürich (group stage)
FC Luzern (third qualifying round)
Grasshopper Club Zürich (second qualifying round)

Top scorer   Munas Dabbur (Grasshoppers), 19 goals
Relegated club   FC Zürich
Promoted club   FC Lausanne-Sport
Cup final   FC Zürich 1-0 FC Lugano

Team of the season
(4-4-2)

Coach: Tami (Grasshoppers)

Vaclík (Basel)

Lang (Basel) — Gelmi (St Gallen) — Suchý (Basel) — Modou (Sion)

Carlitos (Sion) — Källström (Grasshoppers) — Zuffi (Basel) — Caio (Grasshoppers)

Dabbur (Grasshoppers) — Embolo (Basel)

Player of the season

Breel Embolo
(FC Basel 1893)

Building on the high promise of his debut season, Embolo was the Swiss Super League's most eye-catching individual in 2015/16 and duly scooped the official player of the season prize, beating Grasshoppers duo Munas Dabbur and Kim Källström into second and third place, respectively. Quick, skilful and a composed finisher, the 19-year-old scored ten league goals to help Basel to another title, and shortly after appearing for Switzerland at UEFA EURO 2016, he signed a five-year contract for Schalke.

Newcomer of the season

Shani Tarashaj
(Grasshopper Club Zürich)

A place in Switzerland's 23-man squad for UEFA EURO 2016 was the end-of-season reward for 21-year-old Tarashaj after a season of rapid development that brought him 11 Super League goals and a move to English Premier League club Everton. Off to a flying start in the Super League with five goals in Grasshoppers' first four games, the robust young striker who cites Wayne Rooney as his idol was signed by the England striker's former club in January but allowed to see out the second half of the season back in Zurich on loan.

SWITZERLAND

NATIONAL TEAM

International tournament appearances

FIFA World Cup (10) 1934, 1938 (qtr-finals), 1950, 1954 (qtr-finals), 1962, 1966, 1994 (2nd round), 2006 (2nd round), 2010, 2014 (2nd round)
UEFA European Championship (4) 1996, 2004, 2008, 2016 (round of 16)

Top five all-time caps

Heinz Hermann (118); Alain Geiger (112); Stéphane Chapuisat (103); Johann Vogel (94); **Gökhan Inler** (89)

Top five all-time goals

Alexander Frei (42); Xam Abegglen & Kubilay Türkyilmaz (34); André Abegglen & Jacky Fatton (29)

Results 2015/16

Date	Opponent		Venue		Score	Scorers
05/09/15	Slovenia (ECQ)	H	Basel	W	3-2	Drmic (80, 90+4), Stocker (84)
08/09/15	England (ECQ)	A	London	L	0-2	
09/10/15	San Marino (ECQ)	H	St Gallen	W	7-0	Lang (17), Inler (55p), Mehmedi (65), Djourou (72p), Kasami (75), Embolo (80p), Derdiyok (89)
12/10/15	Estonia (ECQ)	A	Tallinn	W	1-0	Klavan (90+4og)
13/11/15	Slovakia	A	Trnava	L	2-3	Derdiyok (63), Drmic (67)
17/11/15	Austria	A	Vienna	W	2-1	Seferovic (9, 38)
25/03/16	Republic of Ireland	A	Dublin	L	0-1	
29/03/16	Bosnia & Herzegovina	H	Zurich	L	0-2	
28/05/16	Belgium	H	Geneva	L	1-2	Dzemaili (32)
03/06/16	Moldova	H	Lugano	W	2-1	Dzemaili (12), Mehmedi (70)
11/06/16	Albania (ECF)	N	Lens (FRA)	W	1-0	Schär (5)
15/06/16	Romania (ECF)	N	Paris (FRA)	D	1-1	Mehmedi (57)
19/06/16	France (ECF)	N	Lille (FRA)	D	0-0	
25/06/16	Poland (ECF)	N	Saint-Etienne (FRA)	D	1-1	Shaqiri (82) (aet; 4-5 on pens)

Appearances 2015/16

Coach: Vladimir Petković 15/08/63

Player	DOB	Club	SVN	ENG	SMR	EST	Svk	Aut	Irl	Bih	Bel	Mda	ALB	ROU	FRA	POL	Caps	Goals
Yann Sommer	17/12/88	Mönchengladbach (GER)	G	G				G	G	G	G		G	G	G	G	22	-
Stephan Lichtsteiner	16/01/84	Juventus (ITA)	D	D			D58	D19		D65		D64	D	D	D	D	85	5
Fabian Schär	20/12/91	Hoffenheim (GER)	D	D	D		D		D	D46		D	D	D	D	D	24	6
Timm Klose	09/05/88	Wolfsburg (GER)/Norwich (ENG)	D	D			D			D	s46						14	-
Ricardo Rodriguez	25/08/92	Wolfsburg (GER)	D	D	D62			D78	D65	D	D63	D	D	D	D		41	-
Valon Behrami	19/04/85	Watford (ENG)	M	M79			s58	M	M71		M	M	M	M	M	M77	70	2
Granit Xhaka	27/09/92	Mönchengladbach (GER)	M	M		M80			M	M	M	M70	M	M	M	M	47	6
Xherdan Shaqiri	10/10/91	Stoke (ENG)	M	M		M46	M	M88		M	M	M88	M91	M79	M	57	18	
Blerim Dzemaili	12/04/86	Genoa (ITA)	M64	s79		M			M71		M78	M77	M75	M83	M58	M52	52	7
Admir Mehmedi	16/03/91	Leverkusen (GER)	M56		M68	M71	s58	M60	M71	M46	M64	M61	M61		M86	M70	46	5
Haris Seferovic	22/02/92	Eintracht Frankfurt (GER)	A80	s71			s74	A75	A62	A	s40 81*		A	A63	s74	A	34	7
Breel Embolo	14/02/97	Basel	s56	s63	M	s46				M	s46	M63	s61	s63	A74	s58	14	1
Josip Drmic	08/08/92	Mönchengladbach (GER)	s64	A63	A78		s58	A70									25	8
Valentin Stocker	12/04/89	Hertha (GER)	s80	M71			M58	s60									33	5
Gökhan Inler	27/06/84	Leicester (ENG)		M	M	M	M74	M60									89	7
Roman Bürki	14/11/90	Dortmund (GER)			G		G*										5	-
Michael Lang	08/02/91	Basel			D	D	s58	s19	D81	s65	D64	s64		s83	s86		19	2
Johan Djourou	18/01/87	Hamburg (GER)			D	D	D	D			D84		D	D	D	D	64	2
Luca Zuffi	27/03/90	Basel			M		s74	s60		s46							4	-
Pajtim Kasami	02/06/92	Olympiacos (GRE)			M	s80	M58		s71	M72							12	2
François Moubandje	21/06/90	Toulouse (FRA)			s62	D	D	D	s78	s65		s63					11	-
Eren Derdiyok	12/06/88	Kasımpaşa (TUR)			s68	A	A74	s75			A40	A46				s70	53	10
Renato Steffen	03/11/91	Young Boys/Basel			s78	s71				s62	M						4	-
Marwin Hitz	18/09/87	Augsburg (GER)				G											2	-
Fabian Lustenberger	02/05/88	Hertha (GER)				D		s70									3	-
Gelson Fernandes	02/09/86	Rennes (FRA)					M58		s71	M46	s84		s88		s79	s77	59	2
Silvan Widmer	05/03/93	Udinese (ITA)						s88	s81		s64						7	-
Shani Tarashaj	07/02/95	Grasshoppers						s71	s72		s64	s63		s91			5	-
Philippe Senderos	14/02/85	Grasshoppers								D	D64						57	5
Nico Elvedi	30/09/96	Mönchengladbach (GER)									s64						1	-
Denis Zakaria	20/11/96	Young Boys									s78	s77					2	-
Steve von Bergen	10/06/83	Young Boys										D					50	-
Fabian Frei	08/01/89	Mainz (GER)											s70	s75			9	1

EUROPE

FC Basel 1893

Third qualifying round - KKS Lech Poznań (POL)
A 3-1 *Lang (34), Janko (77), Callà (90+2)*
Vaclík, Lang, Zuffi, Bjarnason, Gashi (Callà 75), Suchý, Safari, Kuzmanović (Elneny 86), Høegh, Xhaka, Embolo (Janko 61). Coach: Urs Fischer (SUI)
Red card: Xhaka 90+3
H 1-0 *Bjarnason (90+1)*
Vaclík, Lang, Bjarnason, Delgado (Zuffi 77), Suchý, Safari (Traoré 89), Janko (Embolo 70), Kuzmanović, Høegh, Callà. Coach: Urs Fischer (SUI)

Play-offs - Maccabi Tel-Aviv FC (ISR)
H 2-2 *Delgado (39p), Embolo (88)*
Vaclík, Lang, Zuffi, Bjarnason, Delgado (Boëtius 68), Suchý, Safari (Degen 74), Janko (Gashi 15), Høegh, Elneny, Embolo. Coach: Urs Fischer (SUI)
A 1-1 *Zuffi (11)*
Vaclík, Lang, Samuel, Zuffi, Bjarnason (Boëtius 68), Suchý, Safari, Elneny (Gashi 76), Xhaka, Embolo, Callà (Albian Ajeti 83). Coach: Urs Fischer (SUI)

Group I
Match 1 - ACF Fiorentina (ITA)
A 2-1 *Bjarnason (71), Elneny (79)*
Vaclík, Lang, Zuffi, Bjarnason, Suchý, Janko (Callà 87), Høegh, Elneny, Xhaka, Embolo, Boëtius (Delgado 72). Coach: Urs Fischer (SUI)
Match 2 - KKS Lech Poznań (POL)
H 2-0 *Bjarnason (55), Embolo (90)*
Vaclík, Lang, Samuel, Zuffi, Bjarnason, Suchý, Janko, Elneny, Xhaka, Embolo, Callà (Gashi 80). Coach: Urs Fischer (SUI)
Match 3 - Os Belenenses (POR)
H 1-2 *Lang (15)*
Vailati, Lang, Samuel, Delgado (Zuffi 67), Gashi, Suchý, Safari, Janko, Kuzmanović (Albian Ajeti 77), Xhaka, Embolo (Bjarnason 58). Coach: Urs Fischer (SUI)
Match 4 - Os Belenenses (POR)
A 2-0 *Janko (45+1p), Embolo (64)*
Vaclík, Lang, Zuffi, Bjarnason, Akanji, Suchý, Safari, Janko, Elneny, Xhaka, Embolo. Coach: Urs Fischer (SUI)
Match 5 - ACF Fiorentina (ITA)
H 2-2 *Suchý (40), Elneny (74)*
Vailati, Lang, Zuffi, Bjarnason (Kuzmanović 88), Suchý, Safari, Janko, Elneny, Xhaka, Embolo, Boëtius (Callà 60). Coach: Urs Fischer (SUI)
Match 6 - KKS Lech Poznań (POL)
A 1-0 *Boëtius (50)*
Vailati (Salvi 45+1), Traoré, Lang (Adonis Ajeti 46), Samuel, Zuffi, Bjarnason (Huser 79), Elneny, Xhaka, Albian Ajeti, Callà, Boëtius. Coach: Urs Fischer (SUI)

Round of 32 - AS Saint-Étienne (FRA)
A 2-3 *Samuel (44), Janko (56p)*
Vaclík, Lang, Samuel, Zuffi, Bjarnason, Suchý, Safari, Janko, Steffen (Boëtius 64), Xhaka, Embolo (Callà 89). Coach: Urs Fischer (SUI)
H 2-1 *Zuffi (15, 90+2)*
Vaclík, Lang, Samuel (Fransson 90+2), Zuffi, Bjarnason, Delgado (Steffen 68), Suchý, Safari (Traoré 72), Janko, Xhaka, Embolo. Coach: Urs Fischer (SUI)
Red card: Embolo 84

Round of 16 - Sevilla FC (ESP)
H 0-0
Vaclík, Lang (Traoré 46), Samuel (Høegh 90), Zuffi, Bjarnason, Delgado (Fransson 83), Suchý, Safari, Janko, Steffen, Xhaka. Coach: Urs Fischer (SUI)
A 0-3
Vaclík, Lang, Zuffi, Bjarnason (Fransson 61), Delgado (Embolo 61), Suchý, Safari, Janko (Itten 71), Steffen, Høegh, Xhaka. Coach: Urs Fischer (SUI)

BSC Young Boys

Third qualifying round - AS Monaco FC (FRA)
H 1-3 *Nuzzolo (74)*
Mvogo, Vilotić, Von Bergen, Sulejmani, Gajić, Sutter, Nuzzolo, Kubo, Sanogo (Zakaria 60), Benito (Lecjaks 51), Hoarau (Afum 76). Coach: Uli Forte (SUI)
A 0-4
Mvogo, Vilotić (Rochat 46), Von Bergen, Bertone, Sulejmani, Lecjaks, Gajić, Sutter (Hadergjonaj 65), Nuzzolo (González 71), Kubo, Afum. Coach: Uli Forte (SUI)

Play-offs - Qarabağ FK (AZE)
H 0-1
Mvogo, Vilotić, Von Bergen, Bertone (Zakaria 80), Sulejmani, Lecjaks, Gajić, Sutter, Nuzzolo (González 69), Kubo (Tabakovic 85), Hoarau. Coach: Harald Gämperle (SUI)
A 0-3
Mvogo, Hadergjonaj, Vilotić, Von Bergen, Bertone, Sulejmani (Nuzzolo 65), Sutter, Zakaria, González , Kubo (Gajić 80), Hoarau (Afum 54). Coach: Harald Gämperle (SUI)
Red card: Von Bergen 4

FC Sion

Group B
Match 1 - FC Rubin (RUS)
H 2-1 *Konaté (11, 82)*
Vanins, Ziegler, Lacroix, Kouassi, Fernandes, Salatic, Carlitos, Konaté (N'Doye 90), Modou, Assifuah (Mujangi Bia 68), Zverotić. Coach: Didier Tholot (FRA)
Match 2 - Liverpool FC (ENG)
A 1-1 *Assifuah (18)*
Vanins, Ziegler, Lacroix, Kouassi, Fernandes, Salatic, Carlitos, Konaté (Mujangi Bia 89), Modou, Assifuah (N'Doye 86), Zverotić. Coach: Didier Tholot (FRA)
Match 3 - FC Girondins de Bordeaux (FRA)
A 1-0 *Lacroix (21)*
Vanins, Ziegler, Lacroix, Fernandes, Salatic, Carlitos, Konaté, Modou, Assifuah (Follonier 77), Zverotić, N'Doye. Coach: Didier Tholot (FRA)
Match 4 - FC Girondins de Bordeaux (FRA)
H 1-1 *Chantôme (90+4og)*
Vanins, Ziegler, Lacroix, Fernandes, Salatic, Carlitos (Zeman 73), Konaté, Assifuah (Karlen 87), Rüfli, Zverotić, N'Doye (Follonier 87). Coach: Amar Boumilat (FRA)
Match 5 - FC Rubin (RUS)
A 0-2
Vanins, Ziegler, Lacroix, Fernandes, Salatic (Mujangi Bia 88), Carlitos, Konaté (Karlen 81), Assifuah (Follonier 81), Rüfli, Zverotić, N'Doye. Coach: Didier Tholot (FRA)
Red card: N'Doye 34
Match 6 - Liverpool FC (ENG)
H 0-0
Vanins, Ziegler, Lacroix, Kouassi, Fernandes, Salatic, Carlitos, Modou, Assifuah (Mujangi Bia 73), Rüfli (Joaquim Adão 90+4), Zverotić. Coach: Didier Tholot (FRA)

Round of 32 - SC Braga (POR)
H 1-2 *Konaté (53)*
Vanins, Ziegler, Lacroix (Assifuah 24), Fernandes, Salatic, Carlitos, Konaté (Gekas 77), Modou, Rüfli, N'Doye, Mujangi Bia (Follonier 70). Coach: Didier Tholot (FRA)
A 2-2 *Gekas (16, 29)*
Vanins, Fernandes, Salatic, Carlitos, Konaté, Modou, Vanczák, Assifuah (Mujangi Bia 76), Rüfli, Gekas (Zeman 88), N'Doye. Coach: Didier Tholot (FRA)

DOMESTIC LEAGUE CLUB-BY-CLUB

FC Zürich

Third qualifying round - FC Dinamo Minsk (BLR)
H 0-1
Brecher, Djimsiti, Cabral, Schneuwly, Chermiti (Gavranovic 66), Chiumiento (Chikhaoui 46), Sadiku, Nef, Buff, Koch, Kleiber (Brunner 12). Coach: Urs Meier (SUI)
A 1-1 (aet) *Chermiti (4)*
Brecher, Djimsiti, Cabral, Gavranovic (Sarr 110), Schneuwly (Simonyan 102), Chermiti, Nef, Buff (Sadiku 73), Koch, Kukeli, Grgic. Coach: Massimo Rizzo (SUI)

FC Thun

Second qualifying round - Hapoel Beer Sheva FC (ISR)
A 1-1 *Frontino (87p)*
Faivre, Bürki, Sulmoni, Frontino, Siegfried (Sutter 18; Schirinzi 67), Buess (Rapp 62), Rojas, Hediger, Nélson Ferreira, Wittwer, Glarner. Coach: Ciriaco Sforza (SUI)
H 2-1 *Nélson Ferreira (40, 72)*
Faivre, Sulmoni, Frontino (Munsy 85), Rojas (Bürki 90+4), Rapp, Zino, Hediger, Nélson Ferreira, Reinmann, Wittwer, Glarner (Schirinzi 60). Coach: Ciriaco Sforza (SUI)

Third qualifying round - FC Vaduz (LIE)
H 0-0
Faivre, Sulmoni, Wieser, Frontino (Buess 56), Rojas (Munsy 89), Rapp, Hediger, Nélson Ferreira, Reinmann, Schirinzi, Wittwer. Coach: Ciriaco Sforza (SUI)
A 2-2 *Rojas (38), Buess (65)*
Faivre, Sulmoni, Wieser, Frontino (Sutter 80), Buess, Rojas (Schindelholz 90+1), Hediger, Reinmann, Schirinzi (Rapp 58), Wittwer. Coach: Ciriaco Sforza (SUI)

Play-offs - AC Sparta Praha (CZE)
A 1-3 *Sutter (5)*
Faivre, Sulmoni, Frontino, Buess (Zárate 56), Rapp (Munsy 82), Hediger, Nélson Ferreira (Rojas 72), Bigler, Reinmann, Wittwer, Sutter. Coach: Ciriaco Sforza (SUI)
H 3-3 *Nélson Ferreira (33, 81), Munsy (50)*
Faivre, Sulmoni, Frontino (Munsy 46), Rojas (Schirinzi 46), Rapp, Schindelholz, Zino (Zárate 55), Hediger, Nélson Ferreira, Bigler, Wittwer. Coach: Ciriaco Sforza (SUI)

FC Basel 1893

1893 • St Jakob-Park (37,994) • fcb.ch
Major honours
Swiss League (19) 1953, 1967, 1969, 1970, 1972, 1973, 1977, 1980, 2002, 2004, 2005, 2008, 2010, 2011, 2012, 2013, 2014, 2015, 2016; Swiss Cup (11) 1933, 1947, 1963, 1967, 1975, 2002, 2003, 2007, 2008, 2010, 2012
Coach: Urs Fischer

2015
19/07	h	Vaduz	W 2-0	Delgado (p), Kakitani
25/07	a	Grasshoppers	W 3-2	Gashi, Janko, Lang
01/08	h	Sion	W 3-0	Delgado, Traoré, og (Lacroix)
08/08	a	Luzern	W 3-1	Embolo 2, Delgado
12/08	h	Thun	W 3-1	Janko 2, Gashi
22/08	a	Lugano	W 3-1	Callà 2 (1p), Elneny
30/08	h	Zürich	W 3-1	Lang, Gashi, Janko (p)
12/09	h	St Gallen	W 2-1	Delgado (p), Janko
23/09	a	Young Boys	L 3-4	Embolo, Suchý, Janko
26/09	h	Lugano	W 3-1	Zuffi 2, Bjarnason
04/10	a	Zürich	D 2-2	Janko, Ajeti
18/10	a	Sion	W 2-0	Janko 2
25/10	h	Young Boys	W 1-0	Embolo
31/10	a	Vaduz	W 2-1	Bjarnason, Janko
08/11	h	Grasshoppers	L 2-3	Callà, Embolo
22/11	a	St Gallen	L 1-2	Janko
29/11	h	Luzern	W 3-0	Bjarnason, Callà, Elneny
06/12	a	Thun	W 2-0	Janko 2
2016				
07/02	h	Luzern	W 3-0	Bjarnason, Delgado (p), Steffen
14/02	a	Grasshoppers	W 4-0	Lang 2, Suchý, Zuffi
21/02	h	Vaduz	W 5-1	Lang, Fransson, Zuffi, Bjarnason 2
28/02	a	Thun	D 1-1	Steffen
13/03	h	St Gallen	W 4-2	Janko 3, Steffen
20/03	a	Sion	W 1-0	Delgado (p)
03/04	h	Young Boys	W 2-0	Embolo, Steffen
10/04	h	Zürich	D 2-2	Delgado (p), Bjarnason
13/04	a	Lugano	W 4-1	Bjarnason, Samuel, Delgado (p), Itten
17/04	a	St Gallen	W 7-0	Steffen 3, og (Angha), og (Gaudino), Callà, Embolo
20/04	h	Lugano	W 3-0	Embolo 2, Boëtius
24/04	a	Vaduz	D 0-0	
30/04	h	Sion	W 2-1	Delgado (p), Bjarnason
07/05	a	Zürich	W 3-2	Delgado, Callà, Embolo
10/05	h	Thun	D 1-1	Bjarnason
16/05	a	Luzern	L 0-4	
22/05	a	Young Boys	W 3-2	Delgado, Boëtius 2
25/05	h	Grasshoppers	L 0-1	

No	Name	Nat	DoB	Pos	Aps	(s)	Gls
38	Albian Ajeti		26/02/97	A	1	(4)	1
16	Manuel Akanji		19/07/95	D	5	(3)	
27	Naser Aliji	ALB	27/12/93	D	10	(5)	
8	Birkir Bjarnason	ISL	27/05/88	M	21	(8)	10
77	Jean-Paul Boëtius	NED	22/03/94	M	6	(6)	3
39	Davide Callà		06/10/84	M	14	(14)	6
41	Eray Cümart		04/02/98	D	4	(1)	
7	Philipp Degen		15/02/83	D	6	(2)	
10	Matías Delgado	ARG	15/12/82	M	26	(2)	11
33	Mohamed Elneny	EGY	11/07/92	M	11	(5)	2
36	Breel Embolo		14/02/97	A	26	(1)	10
15	Alexander Fransson	SWE	02/04/94	M	14	(2)	1
11	Shkëlzen Gashi	ALB	15/07/88	A	7	(3)	3
26	Daniel Høegh	DEN	06/01/91	D	10	(2)	
35	Nicolas Hunziker		23/02/96	A		(3)	
30	Cédric Itten		27/12/96	A	4	(7)	1
21	Marc Janko	AUT	25/06/83	A	18	(2)	16
14	Yōichirō Kakitani	JPN	03/01/90	A	4	(1)	1
22	Zdravko Kuzmanović	SRB	22/09/87	M	8	(4)	
5	Michael Lang		08/02/91	D	22		5
42	Charles Pickel		15/05/97	M	1	(1)	
6	Behrang Safari	SWE	09/02/85	D	16	(2)	
6	Walter Samuel	ARG	23/03/78	D	15	(2)	1
9	Andraž Šporar	SVN	27/02/94	A		(1)	
24	Renato Steffen		03/11/91	M	12	(4)	7
17	Marek Suchý	CZE	29/03/88	D	34		2
4	Adama Traoré	CIV	03/02/90	D	16	(8)	1
1	Tomáš Vaclík	CZE	29/03/89	G	30		
18	Germano Vailati		30/08/80	G	6		
34	Taulant Xhaka	ALB	28/03/91	M	21	(3)	
7	Luca Zuffi		27/03/90	M	28	(8)	4

Grasshopper Club Zürich

1886 • Letzigrund (26,104) • gcz.ch
Major honours
Swiss League (27) 1898, 1900, 1901, 1905, 1921, 1927, 1928, 1931, 1937, 1939, 1942, 1943, 1945, 1952, 1956, 1971, 1978, 1982, 1983, 1984, 1990, 1991, 1995, 1996, 1998, 2001, 2003; Swiss Cup (19) 1926, 1927, 1932, 1934, 1937, 1938, 1940, 1941, 1942, 1943, 1946, 1952, 1956, 1983, 1988, 1989, 1990, 1994, 2013
Coach: Pierluigi Tami

2015
19/07	a	Thun	W 5-3	Caio, Ravet, Bašić, Dabbur (p), Tarashaj
25/07	h	Basel	L 2-3	Dabbur, Caio
02/08	a	Zürich	W 3-2	Tarashaj 2, Kamberi
08/08	h	Lugano	W 6-1	Caio, Ravet, Tarashaj 2, Dabbur (p), Bašić
13/08	a	Vaduz	D 3-3	Dabbur, Ravet, Gjorgjev
23/08	a	St Gallen	W 2-0	Caio, Dabbur
30/08	h	Young Boys	W 3-2	Ravet, Tarashaj, Caio
13/09	a	Luzern	D 3-3	Ravet, Pnishi, Dabbur
23/09	h	Sion	W 2-0	Caio, Ravet
26/09	h	St Gallen	D 1-1	Tarashaj
04/10	a	Young Boys	L 1-3	Dabbur
17/10	h	Luzern	W 1-0	Dabbur
25/10	a	Sion	L 2-3	Caio, Dabbur
31/10	h	Thun	L 1-2	Brahimi
08/11	a	Basel	W 3-2	Ravet, og (Suchý), Dabbur
21/11	h	Vaduz	W 2-0	Caio, Kamberi
29/11	h	Zürich	W 5-0	Dabbur, Ravet, Tarashaj, Caio, Källström
06/12	a	Lugano	L 1-4	og (Russo)
2016				
06/02	a	Young Boys	D 1-1	Kamberi
14/02	h	Basel	L 0-4	
21/02	h	Sion	W 3-0	Dabbur, Tarashaj 2
28/02	a	Vaduz	D 1-1	Dabbur
07/03	a	St Gallen	L 0-2	
13/03	h	Zürich	W 4-2	Dabbur, Caio, Tarashaj, Bašić
20/03	a	Lugano	L 0-1	
10/04	a	Thun	L 1-2	Dabbur
09/04	h	Luzern	D 1-1	Caio
16/04	a	Sion	L 1-2	Dabbur
19/04	a	Zürich	D 1-1	Caio
23/04	h	St Gallen	W 2-0	Tabakovic, Dabbur
30/04	h	Young Boys	L 1-2	Dabbur
08/05	a	Lugano	W 1-0	Caio
11/05	a	Luzern	L 0-3	
16/05	h	Vaduz	L 1-2	Dabbur (p)
22/05	h	Thun	D 0-0	
25/05	a	Basel	W 1-0	og (Traoré)

No	Name	Nat	DoB	Pos	Aps	(s)	Gls
31	Harun Alpsoy		03/03/97	M	6	(7)	
3	Nemanja Antonov	SRB	06/05/95	D	16	(5)	
24	Jan Bamert		09/03/98	D	16		
5	Alexandre Barthe	FRA	03/03/86	D	10	(1)	
8	Marko Bašić	CRO	08/05/91	M	27	(2)	3
34	Moritz Bauer		25/01/92	D	32	(1)	
11	Mërgim Brahimi	KOS	08/08/92	M	10	(12)	1
21	Caio	BRA	29/05/86	M	34	(1)	13
9	Munas Dabbur	ISR	14/05/92	A	35		19
35	Nikola Gjorgjev	MKD	22/08/97	M	2	(10)	1
29	Levent Gülen		24/02/94	D	13	(1)	
4	Kim Källström	SWE	24/08/82	M	33		1
26	Florian Kamberi		08/03/95	A	10	(18)	3
25	Sherko Kareem	IRN	25/05/96	A	1	(10)	
16	Manuel Kubli		09/04/95	M		(1)	
32	Noah Loosli		23/01/97	D	1		
22	Benjamin Lüthi		30/11/88	D	23	(3)	
18	Joël Mall		05/04/91	G	19		
17	Georgi Milanov	BUL	19/02/92	M	10	(1)	
6	Alban Pnishi	KOS	20/10/90	D	21	(5)	1
14	Yoric Ravet	FRA	12/09/89	A	18		8
14	Philippe Senderos		14/02/85	D	14		
19	Haris Tabakovic		20/06/94	A	2	(13)	1
30	Shani Tarashaj		07/02/95	A	26	(7)	11
1	Vaso Vasić	SRB	26/04/90	G	17	(1)	

FC Lugano

1908 • Cornaredo (6,330) • fclugano.com
Major honours
Swiss League (3) 1938, 1941, 1949; Swiss Cup (3) 1931, 1968, 1993
Coach: Zdeněk Zeman (CZE)

2015

19/07	a St Gallen	L	0-2	
26/07	h Thun	L	2-3	Bottani (p), Rossini (p)
02/08	h Vaduz	W	1-0	Josipovic
08/08	a Grasshoppers	L	1-6	Bottani (p)
12/08	a Young Boys	L	0-1	Rossini
22/08	h Basel	L	1-3	Piccinocchi
29/08	h Luzern	L	0-1	
13/09	a Sion	L	0-3	
22/09	h Zürich	D	0-0	
26/09	a Basel	L	1-3	Čulina
03/10	a Luzern	D	2-2	Rossini, Čulina
18/10	h St Gallen	W	3-1	Bottani, Čulina, Datković
25/10	a Thun	L	1-2	Čulina
01/11	h Sion	W	3-0	Datković, Sabbatini 2
07/11	h Young Boys	D	1-1	Rossini
22/11	a Zürich	L	3-5	Čulina 2, Urbano
28/11	a Vaduz	D	1-1	Sabbatini
06/12	h Grasshoppers	W	4-1	Čulina (p), Črnigoj, Tosetti, Šušnjar

2016

06/02	h Vaduz	L	2-5	Sabbatini, Bottani
13/02	a Thun	L	1-2	Tosetti
20/02	h Zürich	D	0-0	
28/02	a St Gallen	D	3-3	Črnigoj, Sabbatini, Čulina
12/03	a Luzern	L	1-2	Sabbatini
20/03	a Grasshoppers	W	1-0	Čulina
03/04	h Sion	L	0-6	
09/04	a Young Boys	L	0-7	
13/04	h Basel	L	1-4	Čulina
17/04	h Thun	W	2-1	A Donis 2
20/04	a Basel	L	0-3	
23/04	a Sion	L	1-3	Bottani
01/05	h Luzern	D	1-1	A Donis
08/05	h Grasshoppers	L	0-1	
11/05	a Zürich	W	4-0	Alioski 2, Bottani 2
16/05	h Young Boys	L	1-3	Alioski
22/05	a Vaduz	D	0-0	
25/05	h St Gallen	W	3-0	Črnigoj, Bottani (p), A Donis

No	Name	Nat	DoB	Pos	Aps	(s)	Gls
7	Ezgjan Alioski	MKD	12/02/92	M	10	(6)	3
10	Mattia Bottani		24/05/91	M	28	(1)	8
33	Domen Črnigoj	SVN	18/11/95	M	12	(14)	3
9	Antonini Čulina	CRO	27/01/92	M	22	(4)	10
20	Niko Datković	CRO	21/04/93	D	27		2
5	Igor Djuric		30/08/88	D	5	(5)	
22	Anastasios Donis	GRE	29/08/96	A	15	(10)	4
16	Christos Donis	GRE	09/10/94	M	1		
11	Zoran Josipovic		25/08/95	A	1	(8)	1
3	Goran Jozinović	CRO	27/08/90	D	15	(7)	
12	Sandro Lombardi		20/07/86	M	5	(1)	
12	Matías Malvino	URU	20/01/92	D	8	(2)	
31	Denis Markaj	KOS	20/02/91	D	9	(2)	
21	Nikola Milosavljevic		24/04/96	M	1	(2)	
4	Marco Padalino		08/12/83	M	12	(7)	
18	Mario Piccinocchi	ITA	21/02/95	M	30	(1)	1
8	Domagoj Pušić	CRO	24/10/91	M	4	(13)	
18	Antoine Rey		25/08/86	M	31	(1)	
11	Karim Rossi		01/05/94	A	1	(2)	
7	Patrick Rossini		02/04/88	A	15		4
21	Francesco Russo	ITA	23/12/81	G	14	(1)	
14	Jonathan Sabbatini	URU	31/03/88	M	30	(3)	6
23	Mirko Salvi		14/02/94	G	11		
99	Djordje Šušnjar	SRB	18/02/92	A	6	(2)	1
99	Matteo Tosetti		15/02/92	M	9	(10)	2
6	Orlando Urbano	ITA	09/06/84	M	30	(2)	1
1	Alex Valentini	ITA	05/04/88	G	11		
13	Frederic Veseli	ALB	20/11/92	D	33		

FC Luzern

1901 • swissporarena (16,520) • fcl.ch
Major honours
Swiss League (1) 1989; Swiss Cup (2) 1960, 1992
Coach: Markus Babbel (GER)

2015

18/07	h Sion	D	2-2	M Schneuwly, Hyka
25/07	a Young Boys	D	1-1	Lezcano
02/08	a Thun	W	1-0	Lezcano
08/08	h Basel	L	1-3	Lezcano
12/08	h St Gallen	L	0-1	
22/08	a Zürich	W	5-2	Jantscher, Lezcano 3 (2p), Kryeziu
29/08	a Lugano	W	1-0	Lezcano
13/09	h Grasshoppers	D	3-3	Lezcano 2 (1p), M Schneuwly
23/09	a Vaduz	W	2-1	M Schneuwly, Affolter
27/09	h Zürich	W	1-0	Yeşil
03/10	h Lugano	D	2-2	Thiesson, M Schneuwly
17/10	a Grasshoppers	L	0-1	
24/10	h Vaduz	D	1-1	M Schneuwly
01/11	a St Gallen	L	0-1	
08/11	a Sion	L	0-2	
21/11	h Thun	W	1-0	Schachten
29/11	a Basel	L	0-3	
05/12	h Young Boys	W	3-1	M Schneuwly, og (Wüthrich), Freuler

2016

07/02	a Basel	L	0-3	
14/02	h Zürich	L	1-2	Schachten
21/02	h St Gallen	L	0-1	
27/02	a Sion	L	1-3	Puljić
06/03	h Young Boys	L	2-5	M Schneuwly, Hyka
12/03	h Lugano	W	2-1	Frey, C Schneuwly
19/03	a Thun	D	1-1	M Schneuwly
02/04	a Vaduz	W	5-1	Neumayr 2 (2p), M Schneuwly, C Schneuwly, Hyka
09/04	a Grasshoppers	D	1-1	Neumayr
16/04	a Zürich	W	1-0	M Schneuwly
20/04	h Young Boys	L	2-3	Frey, M Schneuwly
24/04	a Thun	W	3-0	M Schneuwly, Neumayr (p), og (Sulmoni)
01/05	a Lugano	D	1-1	Neumayr
08/05	h Vaduz	W	2-1	Jantscher (p), M Schneuwly
11/05	h Grasshoppers	W	3-0	Jantscher 2 (2p), Frey
16/05	h Basel	W	4-0	M Schneuwly, Jantscher (p), Hyka, Haas
22/05	a St Gallen	W	4-1	Puljić, Frey, M Schneuwly, Jantscher
25/05	h Sion	D	2-2	og (Zverotić), M Schneuwly

No	Name	Nat	DoB	Pos	Aps	(s)	Gls
16	François Affolter		13/03/91	D	32		1
6	Remo Arnold		17/01/97	M	4	(3)	
11	Migjen Basha	ALB	05/01/87	M	4	(3)	
6	Frane Čirjak	CRO	23/06/95	M		(1)	
6	Thierry Doubai	CIV	01/07/88	M	1		
28	Clemens Fandrich	GER	10/01/91	M	11	(11)	
9	Remo Freuler		15/04/92	M	18		1
9	Michael Frey		19/07/94	A	14	(2)	4
32	Nicolas Haas		23/01/96	M	14	(10)	1
8	Jahmir Hyka	ALB	08/03/88	M	23	(12)	4
10	Jakob Jantscher	AUT	08/01/89	M	21	(13)	6
31	Hekiran Kryeziu	KOS	12/02/93	M	23	(4)	1
21	Darío Lezcano	PAR	30/06/90	A	12		9
7	Claudio Lustenberger		06/01/87	D	22	(3)	
77	Markus Neumayr	GER	26/03/86	M	11	(1)	5
37	João Oliveira		06/01/96	M		(16)	
13	Tomislav Puljić	CRO	21/03/83	D	26	(2)	2
5	Kaja Rogulj	CRO	15/06/86	D	6		
23	Sally Sarr	FRA	06/05/86	D	11		
4	Sebastian Schachten	GER	06/11/84	D	14	(5)	2
35	Yannick Schmid		11/05/95	D	1	(2)	
20	Christian Schneuwly		07/02/88	M	18		2
15	Marco Schneuwly		27/03/85	A	35		16
61	Jérôme Thiesson		06/08/87	D	34		1
61	Samed Yeşil	GER	25/05/94	A	3	(11)	1
1	David Zibung		10/01/84	G	36		

FC St Gallen

1879 • AFG Arena (19,456) • fcsg.ch
Major honours
Swiss League (2) 1904, 2000; Swiss Cup (1) 1969
Coach: Jeff Saibene (LUX);
(01/09/15) (Christian Stübi & Daniel Tarone);
(16/09/15) Joe Zinnbauer (GER)

2015

19/07	h Lugano	W	2-0	Aleksić 2
26/07	a Sion	L	0-1	
01/08	h Young Boys	D	1-1	Bunjaku
09/08	h Zürich	L	0-2	
12/08	a Luzern	W	1-0	Tréand
23/08	h Grasshoppers	D	1-1	
29/08	a Vaduz	L	0-1	
12/09	a Basel	L	1-2	Aratore
22/09	h Thun	W	1-0	Gelmi
26/09	a Grasshoppers	D	1-1	Mutsch
04/10	h Sion	D	1-1	Aleksić
18/10	a Lugano	L	1-3	Tafer
24/10	a Zürich	D	2-2	Salli, Čavušević
01/11	h Luzern	W	1-0	Salli
08/11	a Thun	W	2-0	Salli, Aleksić
22/11	h Basel	W	2-1	Tafer 2
28/11	a Young Boys	L	1-2	Tréand
06/12	h Vaduz	D	2-2	Tafer 2

2016

07/02	h Thun	L	1-2	Aleksić
21/02	h Luzern	W	1-0	Aleksić
28/02	h Lugano	D	3-3	Bunjaku, Aleksić 2
07/03	h Grasshoppers	W	2-0	Bunjaku, Aleksić
13/03	a Basel	L	2-4	Salli, Angha
19/03	h Young Boys	L	2-3	Leitgeb, Lang
02/04	a Zürich	L	0-4	
10/04	a Vaduz	L	0-3	
13/04	a Sion	D	1-1	Aleksić
17/04	a Basel	L	0-7	
20/04	h Sion	W	2-1	Salli 2
23/04	a Grasshoppers	L	0-2	
01/05	h Vaduz	L	1-3	Salli
07/05	a Thun	D	2-2	Bunjaku, Aleksić
11/05	a Young Boys	L	1-3	Aratore
16/05	h Zürich	W	3-0	Aleksić (p), Aratore 2
22/05	h Luzern	L	1-4	Salli
25/05	a Lugano	L	0-3	

No	Name	Nat	DoB	Pos	Aps	(s)	Gls
23	Danijel Aleksić	SRB	30/04/91	A	30	3	12
4	Martin Angha		22/01/94	D	28	1	1
22	Marco Aratore		04/06/91	M	21	12	4
94	Batuhan Karadeniz	TUR	24/04/91	A		(7)	
10	Albert Bunjaku	KOS	29/11/83	A	19	(4)	4
20	Džengis Čavušević	SVN	26/11/87	A	11	(11)	1
13	Lucas Cueto	GER	24/05/88	M	2	(6)	
25	Michael Eisenring		29/03/93	D	1	(1)	
5	Everton Luiz	BRA	24/05/88	M	11	(4)	
3	Mickaël Facchinetti		15/02/91	D	12		
28	Gianluca Gaudino	GER	11/11/96	M	14	(1)	
9	Roy Gelmi		21/02/95	D	27	(1)	1
11	Sandro Gotal	AUT	09/09/91	A	3	(4)	
29	Florent Hanin	FRA	04/02/90	D	17		
36	Silvan Hefti		25/10/97	D	22	(1)	
18	Marcel Herzog		28/06/80	G	2		
31	Dejan Janjatovic	GER	25/02/92	M	5	(2)	
50	Sanijel Kucani	SRB	14/03/96	M		(1)	
8	Steven Lang		03/09/87	M	14	(13)	1
32	Mario Leitgeb	AUT	30/06/88	M	8	(6)	1
1	Daniel Lopar		19/04/85	G	34		
27	Marco Mathys		05/07/87	M	9	(6)	
19	Mario Mutsch	LUX	03/09/84	D	30	(1)	1
33	Daniele Russo		03/11/85	D		(2)	
21	Edgar Salli	CMR	17/08/92	M	22	(4)	8
9	Yannis Tafer	FRA	17/02/91	A	13	(3)	5
16	Pascal Thrier		04/11/84	D	10	(4)	
7	Geoffrey Tréand	FRA	16/01/86	M	13	(5)	2
6	Alain Wiss		21/08/90	D	18	(2)	

SWITZERLAND

FC Sion

1909 • Tourbillon (14,283) • fc-sion.ch
Major honours
Swiss League (2) 1992, 1997; Swiss Cup (13) 1965, 1974, 1980, 1982, 1986, 1991, 1995, 1996, 1997, 2006, 2009, 2011, 2015
Coach: Didier Tholot (FRA)

2015
18/07	a	Luzern	D	2-2	Konaté, Assifuah
26/07	h	St Gallen	W	1-0	Salatic (p)
01/08	a	Basel	L	0-3	
09/08	a	Vaduz	D	1-1	Carlitos
13/08	h	Zürich	W	3-1	Konaté 2, Carlitos
23/08	h	Young Boys	L	1-3	Konaté
30/08	a	Thun	W	2-0	Carlitos, Konaté
13/09	a	Lugano	W	3-0	Salatic (p), Fernandes, Mujangi Bia
23/09	a	Grasshoppers	L	0-2	
27/09	h	Vaduz	L	0-1	
04/10	a	St Gallen	D	1-1	Follonier
18/10	a	Basel	L	0-2	
25/10	h	Grasshoppers	W	3-2	Assifuah, Ziegler (p), Karlen
01/11	a	Lugano	L	0-3	
08/11	h	Luzern	W	2-0	Carlitos, Assifuah
22/11	a	Young Boys	D	1-1	Mujangi Bia
29/11	h	Thun	L	1-2	og (Reinmann)
05/12	a	Zürich	L	0-1	

2016
07/02	a	Zürich	W	1-0	Konaté
21/02	a	Grasshoppers	L	0-3	
27/02	h	Luzern	W	3-1	Gekas 2, Assifuah
06/03	h	Vaduz	W	2-0	Léo Itaperuna, Karlen
13/03	h	Young Boys	L	2-3	Assifuah, Gekas
20/03	h	Basel	L	0-1	
03/04	a	Lugano	W	6-0	Gekas 2, Konaté 2, Follonier, Assifuah
10/04	h	Thun	W	2-1	Sierro, Mujangi Bia
13/04	h	St Gallen	D	1-1	Mujangi Bia
16/04	h	Grasshoppers	W	2-1	Mujangi Bia, Sierro
20/04	a	St Gallen	L	1-2	Konaté
23/04	a	Lugano	W	3-1	Gekas 3
30/04	a	Basel	L	1-2	Salatic
08/05	h	Young Boys	W	2-1	Ziegler, Mujangi Bia
11/05	a	Vaduz	L	0-2	
16/05	a	Thun	D	1-1	Mujangi Bia
22/05	h	Zürich	D	2-2	Konaté, Ziegler
25/05	a	Luzern	D	2-2	Gekas 2

No	Name	Nat	DoB	Pos	Aps	(s)	Gls
13	Chadrac Akolo	CGO	01/04/95	A	2	(5)	
21	Ebenezer Assifuah	GHA	03/07/93	A	28	(6)	6
10	Carlitos	POR	06/09/82	M	23	(2)	4
77	Dimitris Christofi	CYP	28/09/88	A		(2)	
66	Gabriel Cichero	VEN	03/04/84	D	3	(5)	
7	Edimilson Fernandes		15/04/96	M	22	(4)	1
18	Kevin Fickentscher		06/07/88	G	1	(1)	
94	Daniel Follonier		18/01/94	M	6	(15)	2
33	Theofanis Gekas	GRE	23/05/80	A	11	(7)	10
42	Ibrahima Gueye	SEN	08/10/96	A		(1)	
92	Joaquim Adão	ANG	14/07/92	M	1	(1)	
12	Grégory Karlen		30/01/95	A		(5)	2
14	Moussa Konaté	SEN	03/04/93	A	26	(3)	10
6	Xavier Kouassi	CIV	28/12/89	M	10	(1)	
4	Léo Lacroix		27/02/92	D	20		
30	Léo Itaperuna	BRA	12/04/89	A	6	(5)	1
40	Quentin Maceiras		10/10/95	D		(1)	
17	Pa Modou	GAM	26/12/89	D	17	(1)	
63	Geoffrey Mujangi Bia	BEL	12/08/89	M	11	(8)	7
16	Anton Mitryushkin	RUS	08/02/96	G	7		
34	Birama N'Doye	SEN	27/03/94	M	16	(5)	
22	Vincent Rüfli		22/01/88	D	21	(7)	
8	Veroljub Salatic		14/11/85	M	32		3
19	Vincent Sierro		08/10/95	M	13	(3)	2
20	Vilmos Vanczák	HUN	20/06/83	D	13	(2)	
15	Kay Voser		04/01/87	D	3	(1)	
11	Martin Zeman	CZE	28/03/89	M	14	(10)	
3	Reto Ziegler		16/01/86	D	30		3
31	Elsad Zverotić	MNE	31/10/86	D	32		

FC Thun

1898 • Stockhorn Arena (10,014) • fcthun.ch
**Coach: Ciriaco Sforza;
(30/09/15) (Marc Schneider);
(06/10/15) Jeff Saibene (LUX)**

2015
19/07	h	Grasshoppers	L	3-5	Buess, Munsy, og (Barthe)
26/07	a	Lugano	W	3-2	Rapp, Rojas, Buess
02/08	h	Luzern	L	0-1	
09/08	a	Young Boys	L	1-3	Rapp
12/08	a	Basel	L	1-3	Frontino (p)
23/08	h	Vaduz	W	1-0	Frontino (p)
30/08	h	Sion	L	0-2	
13/09	a	Zürich	D	3-3	Buess, Nélson Ferreira, Rapp
22/09	a	St Gallen	L	0-1	
27/09	h	Young Boys	L	0-1	
03/10	a	Vaduz	D	1-1	Sulmoni
18/10	h	Zürich	W	5-1	Buess 3, Schirinzi (p), Munsy
25/10	h	Lugano	W	2-1	Wieser, Munsy
31/10	a	Grasshoppers	W	2-1	Munsy, Schirinzi
08/11	h	St Gallen	L	0-2	
21/11	a	Luzern	L	0-1	
29/11	a	Sion	W	2-1	Wieser, Munsy
06/12	h	Basel	L	0-2	

2016
07/02	a	St Gallen	W	2-1	Buess, og (Hanin)
13/02	h	Lugano	W	2-1	Buess (p), Munsy
20/02	a	Young Boys	L	1-2	Buess (p)
28/02	h	Basel	D	1-1	Munsy
05/03	a	Zürich	D	0-0	
12/03	a	Vaduz	D	0-0	
19/03	h	Luzern	D	1-1	Wittwer
03/04	h	Grasshoppers	W	2-1	Munsy (p), Rapp
10/04	a	Sion	L	1-2	Rapp
17/04	a	Lugano	L	1-2	Rapp
20/04	h	Vaduz	D	2-2	Munsy, Rapp (p)
24/04	a	Luzern	L	0-3	
01/05	h	Zürich	W	4-0	Joss, Hediger, Munsy 2
07/05	a	St Gallen	D	2-2	Schirinzi (p), Rojas
10/05	a	Basel	D	1-1	Schirinzi
16/05	h	Sion	D	1-1	Sulmoni
22/05	a	Grasshoppers	D	0-0	
25/05	h	Young Boys	L	0-3	

No	Name	Nat	DoB	Pos	Aps	(s)	Gls
25	Kevin Bigler		05/10/92	M	14	(1)	
9	Roman Buess		21/09/92	A	27	(4)	9
4	Marco Bürki		10/07/93	D	20	(2)	
19	Omer Dzonlagic		25/05/95	M		(1)	
1	Guillaume Faivre		20/02/87	G	28		
7	Gianluca Frontino		29/11/89	M	8	(5)	2
31	Stefan Glarner		21/11/87	D	9	(2)	
17	Dennis Hediger		22/09/86	M	33		1
29	Alejandro Henzi		27/04/95	M		(1)	
39	Sven Joss		18/07/94	D	24	(1)	1
30	Sandro Lauper		25/10/96	M	3	(3)	
20	Ridge Munsy	COD	09/07/89	A	19	(13)	11
21	Nélson Ferreira	POR	26/03/87	M	13	(4)	1
23	Norman Peyretti	FRA	06/02/94	M	1	(12)	
13	Simone Rapp		01/10/92	M	21	(9)	7
26	Thomas Reinmann		09/04/83	D	17	(2)	
10	Marco Rojas	NZL	05/11/91	M	13	(7)	2
18	Francesco Ruberto		19/03/93	G	8	(1)	
14	Nicolas Schindelholz		12/02/88	D	12	(2)	
27	Enrico Schirinzi	ITA	14/11/84	D	23	(8)	4
8	Michael Siegfried		18/02/88	D	8	(4)	
5	Fulvio Sulmoni		04/01/86	D	24	(1)	2
34	Nicola Sutter		08/05/95	M	4	(4)	
3	Colin Trachsel		28/09/97	D	1	(1)	
6	Sandro Wieser	LIE	03/02/93	M	21	(1)	2
28	Andreas Wittwer		05/10/90	M	17	(3)	1
33	Gonzalo Zárate	ARG	06/08/84	M	26	(1)	
15	Lotem Zino	ISR	16/03/92	M	2	(4)	

FC Vaduz

1932 • Rheinpark (7,584) • fcvaduz.li
Major honours
Liechtenstein Cup (44) 1949, 1952, 1953, 1954, 1956, 1957, 1958, 1959, 1960, 1961, 1962, 1966, 1967, 1968, 1969, 1970, 1971, 1974, 1980, 1985, 1986, 1988, 1990, 1992, 1995, 1996, 1998, 1999, 2000, 2001, 2002, 2003, 2004, 2005, 2006, 2007, 2008, 2009, 2010, 2011, 2013, 2014, 2015, 2016
Coach: Giorgio Contini

2015
19/07	a	Basel	L	0-2	
26/07	h	Zürich	D	2-2	Muntwiler 2
02/08	a	Lugano	L	0-1	
09/08	h	Sion	D	1-1	Costanzo
13/08	h	Grasshoppers	D	3-3	Costanzo, Messaoud, Burgmeier
23/08	a	Thun	L	0-1	
29/08	h	St Gallen	W	1-0	Kukuruzović
12/09	a	Young Boys	L	0-4	
23/09	h	Luzern	L	1-2	Grippo
27/09	a	Sion	W	1-0	Kukuruzović
03/10	h	Thun	D	1-1	og (Reinmann)
17/10	h	Young Boys	D	1-1	Neumayr
24/10	a	Luzern	D	1-1	Kukuruzović
31/10	h	Basel	L	1-2	Avdijaj
07/11	a	Zürich	D	1-1	Avdijaj
21/11	a	Grasshoppers	L	0-2	
28/11	h	Lugano	D	1-1	Neumayr (p)
06/12	a	St Gallen	D	2-2	Burgmeier, Avdijaj

2016
06/02	a	Lugano	W	5-2	Grippo, Sadiku 2, Kukuruzović, Janjatovic
13/02	h	Young Boys	D	1-1	Bühler
21/02	h	Basel	L	1-5	Bühler
27/02	h	Grasshoppers	D	1-1	Sadiku
06/03	a	Sion	L	0-2	
12/03	h	Thun	D	0-0	
19/03	h	Zürich	L	0-3	
02/04	a	Luzern	L	1-5	Bühler
10/04	h	St Gallen	W	3-0	Costanzo, Sadiku, Janjatovic
17/04	a	Young Boys	L	4-5	og (Lecjaks), Sadiku, Stahel, Grippo
20/04	a	Thun	D	2-2	Ciccone, Stahel
24/04	h	Basel	D	0-0	
01/05	a	St Gallen	W	3-1	Costanzo 2, Von Niederhäusern
08/05	h	Luzern	L	1-2	Janjatovic
11/05	h	Sion	W	2-0	Sadiku 2 (1p)
16/05	a	Grasshoppers	W	2-1	Costanzo, Muntwiler
22/05	h	Lugano	D	0-0	
25/05	a	Zürich	L	1-3	Avdijaj

No	Name	Nat	DoB	Pos	Aps	(s)	Gls
30	Naser Aliji	ALB	27/12/93	D	7		
7	Albion Avdijaj	ALB	12/01/94	A	14	(9)	4
21	Axel Borgmann	GER	08/07/94	D	19	(1)	
11	Franz Burgmeier	LIE	07/04/82	M	5	(13)	2
29	Mario Bühler		05/01/92	D	20	(3)	3
33	Mauro Caballero	PAR	08/10/94	A	7	(7)	
12	Ramon Cecchini		30/08/90	M	2	(3)	
8	Diego Ciccone		21/07/87	M	31	(2)	1
16	Moreno Costanzo		20/02/88	M	28	(5)	6
14	Thomas Fekete		19/09/95	D	2		
3	Simone Grippo		12/12/88	D	34		3
5	Levent Gülen		24/02/94	D	14	(3)	
20	Nicolas Hasler	LIE	04/05/91	M	5	(4)	
37	Dejan Janjatovic	GER	25/02/92	M	12	(3)	3
1	Peter Jehle	LIE	22/01/82	G	34		
36	Robin Kamber		15/02/96	M	6	(10)	
4	Daniel Kaufmann	LIE	22/12/90	D	5	(4)	
35	Oliver Klaus		04/05/90	G	2		
25	Stjepan Kukuruzović	CRO	07/06/89	M	30	(5)	4
7	Steven Lang		03/09/87	M	1		
10	Ali Messaoud	FRA	13/04/91	M	7	(15)	1
27	Philipp Muntwiler		25/02/87	M	25		3
23	Markus Neumayr	GER	26/03/86	M	13	(1)	2
5	Pavel Pergl	CZE	14/11/77	D	2	(2)	
32	Armando Sadiku	ALB	27/05/91	A	16		7
22	Florian Stahel		10/03/85	D	16	(4)	2
9	Manuel Sutter	AUT	08/03/91	A	2	(5)	
17	Joel Untersee		11/02/94	D	19	(2)	
19	Nick von Niederhäusern		28/09/89	D	18	(6)	1

BSC Young Boys

1898 • Stade de Suisse (31,789) • bscyb.ch
Major honours
Swiss League (11) 1903, 1909, 1910, 1911, 1920, 1929, 1957, 1958, 1959, 1960, 1986; Swiss Cup (6) 1930, 1945, 1953, 1958, 1977, 1987
Coach: Uli Forte;
(06/08/15) (Harald Gämperle);
(03/09/15) Adi Hütter (AUT)

2015
18/07	a	Zürich	D	1-1	Hoarau
25/07	h	Luzern	D	1-1	Bertone
01/08	a	St Gallen	D	1-1	Gajić (p)
09/08	h	Thun	W	3-1	Vilotić, Gajić, Tabakovic
12/08	h	Lugano	L	0-1	
23/08	a	Sion	W	3-1	Kubo, González, Sulejmani
30/08	a	Grasshoppers	L	2-3	Vilotić, Kubo
12/09	h	Vaduz	W	4-0	Bertone, Steffen, Kubo, Nuzzolo
23/09	h	Basel	W	4-3	Sulejmani 2, Gerndt 2
27/09	a	Thun	W	1-0	Steffen
04/10	h	Grasshoppers	W	3-1	Bertone, Sulejmani, Steffen
17/10	a	Vaduz	D	1-1	Sulejmani
25/10	a	Basel	L	0-1	
01/11	h	Zürich	D	1-1	Kubo
07/11	a	Lugano	D	1-1	og (Urbano)
22/11	h	Sion	D	1-1	Gerndt
28/11	h	St Gallen	W	2-1	Zakaria, Gerndt
05/12	a	Luzern	L	1-3	Gerndt

2016
06/02	h	Grasshoppers	D	1-1	Hoarau
13/02	a	Vaduz	D	1-1	Gerndt
20/02	h	Thun	W	2-1	Hoarau (p), Kubo
27/02	a	Zürich	W	1-0	Hoarau
06/03	h	Luzern	W	5-2	Rochat, Hoarau 3, Sulejmani
13/03	h	Sion	W	3-2	Hoarau 2 (2p), Gerndt
19/03	a	St Gallen	W	3-2	Ravet 2, Kubo
03/04	a	Basel	L	0-2	
09/04	h	Lugano	W	7-0	Sulejmani, Gajić, Kubo, Ravet, Hoarau, Nuzzolo, Bertone
17/04	h	Vaduz	W	5-4	Hoarau 3 (1p), Ravet, Vilotić
20/04	a	Luzern	W	3-2	Lecjaks, Kubo 2
24/04	h	Zürich	W	3-0	Sulejmani, Hoarau, Gerndt
30/04	a	Grasshoppers	W	2-1	Ravet, Bertone
08/05	a	Sion	L	1-2	Hoarau (p)
11/05	h	St Gallen	W	3-1	Gerndt 2, Sanogo
16/05	a	Lugano	W	3-1	Gerndt 2, Hoarau
22/05	h	Basel	L	2-3	Nuzzolo, Hoarau
25/05	h	Thun	W	3-0	Sutter, Sanogo, Hoarau

No	Name	Nat	DoB	Pos	Aps	(s)	Gls
77	Samuel Afum	GHA	24/12/90	A	3	(4)	
80	Loris Benito		07/01/92	D	10		
6	Leonardo Bertone		14/03/94	M	25	(5)	5
27	Miguel Castroman		17/03/95	M		(5)	
14	Milan Gajić	SRB	17/11/86	M	19	(10)	3
9	Alexander Gerndt	SWE	14/07/86	A	23	(6)	12
30	Alexander González	VEN	13/09/92	M	3	(3)	1
3	Florent Hadergjonaj		31/07/94	D	29	(3)	
99	Guillaume Hoarau	FRA	05/03/84	A	21	(1)	18
17	Benjamin Kololli		15/05/92	M		(1)	
31	Yuya Kubo	JPN	24/12/93	A	23	(6)	9
8	Jan Lecjaks	CZE	09/08/90	D	26	(3)	1
18	Yvon Mvogo		06/06/94	G	34		
29	Raphael Nuzzolo		05/07/83	M	7	(18)	3
32	Linus Obexer		05/06/97	D	2	(1)	
10	Yoric Ravet	FRA	12/09/89	A	16	(2)	5
21	Alain Rochat		31/08/83	D	12	(1)	1
35	Sekou Sanogo	CIV	05/05/89	M	7	(4)	2
11	Renato Steffen		03/11/91	M	12		3
7	Miralem Sulejmani	SRB	05/12/88	M	30	(1)	8
23	Scott Sutter		13/05/86	D	8	(1)	1
31	Haris Tabakovic		20/06/94	D	1	(10)	1
4	Milan Vilotić	SRB	21/10/86	D	23	(1)	3
	Steve von Bergen		10/06/83	D	27		
1	Marco Wölfli		22/08/82	G	2		
22	Gregory Wüthrich		04/12/94	D	11	(1)	
22	Denis Zakaria		20/11/96	M	21	(6)	1
44	Philipp Zulechner	AUT	12/04/90	A	1	(7)	

FC Zürich

1896 • Letzigrund (26,104) • fcz.ch
Major honours
Swiss League (12) 1902, 1924, 1963, 1966, 1968, 1974, 1975, 1976, 1981, 2006, 2007, 2009; Swiss Cup (9) 1966, 1970, 1972, 1973, 1976, 2000, 2005, 2014, 2016
Coach: Urs Meier;
(03/08/15) (Massimo Rizzo & Alex Kern);
(21/08/15) Sami Hyypiä (FIN);
(13/05/16) Uli Forte

2015
18/07	h	Young Boys	D	1-1	Koch
26/07	a	Vaduz	D	2-2	Sadiku (p), Etoundi
02/08	h	Grasshoppers	L	2-3	Simonyan, Buff
09/08	a	St Gallen	W	2-0	Buff, Di Gregorio
13/08	a	Sion	L	1-3	Sadiku
22/08	h	Luzern	L	2-5	Schneuwly, Sadiku
30/08	a	Basel	L	1-3	Kecojević
13/09	h	Thun	D	3-3	Etoundi, Buff, Yapi Yapo
22/09	a	Lugano	D	0-0	
27/09	a	Luzern	L	0-1	
04/10	h	Basel	D	2-2	Gavranovic, Sadiku
18/10	a	Thun	L	1-5	Sadiku
24/10	h	St Gallen	D	2-2	Gavranovic, Bua
01/11	a	Young Boys	D	1-1	Buff
07/11	h	Vaduz	D	1-1	Nef
22/11	h	Lugano	W	5-3	Yapi Yapo, Djimsiti, Grgic, Bua, Gavranovic
29/11	a	Grasshoppers	L	0-5	
05/12	h	Sion	W	1-0	Etoundi

2016
07/02	h	Sion	L	0-1	
14/02	a	Luzern	W	2-1	Grgic, Kerzhakov
20/02	a	Lugano	D	0-0	
27/02	h	Young Boys	L	0-1	
05/03	h	Thun	D	0-0	
13/03	a	Grasshoppers	L	2-4	Kerzhakov, Bua
19/03	a	Vaduz	W	3-0	Chiumiento, Bua, Buff
02/04	h	St Gallen	W	4-0	Grgic, Kukeli, Bua, Kerzhakov
10/04	a	Basel	D	2-2	Kerzhakov, Bua
16/04	h	Luzern	L	0-1	
19/04	h	Grasshoppers	D	1-1	Grgic (p)
24/04	a	Young Boys	L	0-3	
01/05	a	Thun	L	0-4	
07/05	h	Basel	L	2-3	Koch, Buff
11/05	h	Lugano	L	0-4	
16/05	a	St Gallen	L	0-3	
22/05	a	Sion	D	2-2	Buff, Kerzhakov
25/05	h	Vaduz	W	3-1	Kecojević, Buff, Koch

No	Name	Nat	DoB	Pos	Aps	(s)	Gls
19	Armin Alesevic		06/03/94	D		(1)	
1	Yanick Brecher		25/05/93	G	22		
26	Cédric Brunner		17/02/94	D	23		
33	Kevin Bua		11/08/93	M	19	(11)	6
15	Oliver Buff		03/08/92	M	27	(4)	8
6	Cabral	CPV	22/10/88	M	13	(2)	
4	Amine Chermiti	TUN	26/12/87	A	6	(4)	
10	Davide Chiumiento		22/11/84	M	15	(3)	1
2	Leandro Di Gregorio		18/03/92	D	1	(6)	1
5	Berat Djimsiti	ALB	19/02/93	D	12	(3)	1
34	Maxime Dominguez		01/02/96	M	2		
14	Franck Etoundi	CMR	30/08/90	A	16	(6)	3
32	Anthony Favre		01/02/84	G	14		
7	Mario Gavranovic		24/11/89	A	10	(6)	3
22	Anton Grgic		28/11/96	M	20	(4)	4
25	Ivan Kecojević	MNE	10/04/88	D	21		2
35	Michael Kempter		12/01/95	D	1	(1)	
72	Aleksandr Kerzhakov	RUS	27/11/82	A	17		5
21	Mike Kleiber		04/02/93	M		(1)	
16	Philippe Koch		08/02/91	D	34		3
4	Moussa Koné	SEN	30/12/96	A	1	(3)	
20	Burim Kukeli	ALB	16/01/84	M	19	(3)	1
13	Alain Nef		06/02/82	D	30	(1)	1
12	Avi Rikan	ISR	10/08/88	M		(1)	
11	Armando Sadiku	ALB	27/05/91	A	6	(8)	5
6	Leonardo Sánchez	ARG	02/08/86	D	11		
29	Sangoné Sarr	SEN	07/02/92	M	6	(7)	
8	Christian Schneuwly		07/02/88	M	11	(1)	1
23	Artem Simonyan	ARM	20/02/95	M	4	(8)	1
30	Aldin Turkes		22/04/96	A	1	(6)	
17	Vinícius	BRA	07/03/93	D	15	(5)	
37	Gilles Yapi Yapo	CIV	30/01/82	M	19	(1)	2

Top goalscorers

19 Munas Dabbur (Grasshoppers)

18 Guillaume Hoarau (Young Boys)

16 Marc Janko (Basel)
Marco Schneuwly (Luzern)

13 Caio (Grasshoppers)
Yoric Ravet (Young Boys/Grasshoppers)

12 Danijel Aleksić (St Gallen)
Alexander Gerndt (Young Boys)
Armando Sadiku (Zürich/Vaduz)

11 Matías Delgado (Basel)
Shani Tarashaj (Grasshoppers)
Ridge Munsy (Thun)

Promoted club

FC Lausanne-Sport

1896 • Olympique de la Pontaise (15,700) • lausanne-sport.ch
Major honours
Swiss League (7) 1913, 1932, 1935, 1936, 1944, 1951, 1965; Swiss Cup (9) 1935, 1939, 1944, 1950, 1962, 1964, 1981, 1998, 1999
Coach: Fabio Celestini

Second level final table 2015/16

		Pld	W	D	L	F	A	Pts
1	FC Lausanne-Sport	34	19	8	7	61	39	65
2	Neuchâtel Xamax FCS	34	15	9	10	53	42	54
3	FC Wil 1900	34	14	11	9	60	49	53
4	FC Aarau	34	12	14	8	44	39	50
5	FC Schaffhausen	34	14	5	15	43	45	47
6	FC Winterthur	34	12	7	15	40	49	43
7	FC Chiasso	34	7	16	11	39	44	37
8	FC Wohlen	34	9	9	16	35	52	36
9	FC Le Mont	34	7	11	16	36	50	32
10	FC Biel-Bienne	18	5	6	7	28	30	16

NB FC Biel-Bienne withdrew after round 29 – their results until round 18 stood; FC Biel-Bienne – 5 pts deducted.

SWITZERLAND

DOMESTIC CUP

Schweizer Cup/Coupe de Suisse 2015/16

FIRST ROUND

(15/08/15)
Bavois 1-3 Wil
Bulle 2-1 Dardania Lausanne
Buochs 0-2 Le Mont *(aet)*
Castello 0-2 Lugano
Hausen am Albis 0-9 St Gallen
Konolfingen 1-1 Martigny-Sports *(aet; 1-4 on pens)*
Kriens 1-2 Young Boys
Küsnacht 2-9 Wohlen
La Chaux-de-Fonds 3-1 Zug *(aet)*
Länggasse 1-2 Wettswil-Bonstetten
Meyrin 0-4 Basel
Pied du Jura 1-3 Münsingen
Pratteln 2-3 Muttenz *(aet)*
Red Star Zürich 1-0 Oberwallis Naters
Rheineck 1-7 König
Solothurn 0-4 Thun
Uzwil 0-0 Sierre *(aet; 4-5 on pens)*

(16/08/15)
Arbon 05 1-4 YF Juventus
Brunnen 0-2 Sion
Brühl 1-5 Neuchâtel Xamax
Cham 1-4 Grasshoppers
Delémont 0-1 Winterthur
Gontenschwil 0-2 Azzurri 90
Grand-Saconnex 1-10 Biel-Bienne
Härkingen 0-4 Breitenrain
Matran 1-4 Bellinzona
Old Boys 1-2 Schaffhausen
Servette 2-5 Luzern
Stade Nyonnais 2-2 Chiasso *(aet; 1-4 on pens)*
Tavannes/Tramelan 1-6 Zürich
Ticino 0-3 Lausanne-Sport
United Zürich 0-5 Aarau

SECOND ROUND

(18/09/15)
Köniz 3-1 Grasshoppers
Lausanne-Sport 0-1 Thun

(19/09/15)
Bellinzona 2-3 Lugano *(aet)*
Breitenrain 0-2 St Gallen
La Chaux-de-Fonds 0-3 Aarau
Red Star Zürich 1-1 Azzurri 90 *(aet; 4-3 on pens)*
Schaffhausen 2-1 Wil *(aet)*
Sierre 0-3 Wettswil-Bonstetten
Winterthur 1-1 Biel-Bienne *(aet; 5-4 on pens)*
Wohlen 0-1 Zürich

(20/09/15)
Bulle 0-3 Muttenz
Chiasso 0-2 Young Boys
Martigny-Sports 0-1 Le Mont
Münsingen 0-2 Sion
Neuchâtel Xamax 2-4 Luzern
YF Juventus 1-4 Basel

THIRD ROUND

(28/10/15)
Muttenz 1-5 Basel
Red Star Zürich 1-2 Köniz
St Gallen 2-3 Luzern
Wettswil-Bonstetten 1-2 Thun

(29/10/15)
Aarau 2-0 Le Mont
Schaffhausen 2-3 Sion *(aet)*
Winterthur 0-2 Lugano
Young Boys 1-3 Zürich

QUARTER-FINALS

(12/12/15)
Aarau 3-4 Luzern *(Nganga 4, 90+3, Romano 55; M Schneuwly 9, 79, Hyka 60, Lezcano 76)*
Thun 1-4 Zürich *(Wittwer 11; Etoundi 50, 71, Grgic 57, Koch 79)*

(13/12/15)
Lugano 2-0 Köniz *(Črnigoj 110, A Donis 116) (aet)*
Sion 2-2 Basel *(Modou 37, Assifuah 66; Elneny 79, Janko 89) (aet; 4-3 on pens)*

SEMI-FINALS

(02/03/16)
Luzern 1-2 Lugano *(M Schneuwly 45p; A Donis 2, 51)*
Sion 0-3 Zürich *(Kerzhakov 10, 43, Buff 50)*

FINAL

(29/05/16)
Letzigrund, Zurich
FC ZÜRICH 1 *(Sarr 41)*
FC LUGANO 0
Referee: *Bieri*
ZÜRICH: *Favre, Koch, Kecojević, Nef, Vinícius, Yapi Yapo (Cabral 52), Sarr, Kukeli (Grgic 20), Buff (Chiumiento 74), Bua, Kerzhakov*
LUGANO: *Salvi, Veseli, Datković, Urbano, Jozinović, Sabbatini (Črnigoj 60), Piccinocchi, Rey, Alioski (Tosetti 56), Bottani, A Donis (Rossi 70)*
Red card: *Veseli (90+5)*

FC Zürich's Swiss Cup win helped to soften the blow of relegation from the Super League

TURKEY

Türkiye Futbol Federasyönü (TFF)

Address	Hasan Doğan Milli Takımlar Kamp ve Eğitim Tesisleri Riva, Beykoz TR-İstanbul	**President**	Yıldırım Demirören
		General secretary	Kadir Kardaş
		Media officer	İlker Uğur
		Year of formation	1923
Tel	+90 216 554 5100		
Fax	+90 216 319 1945		
E-mail	intdept@tff.org		
Website	tff.org		

16 Rize
18 Trabzon

Karabük
20

3 6 7 10 11

İstanbul
Bursa

9 Sivas
17
5

12
4 Kayseri
Eskişehir

Ankara
15

Manisa
1

Konya
13 Gaziantep
8

Mersin 19
14 Adana

Antalya
2 21
Alanya

0   200   400 km
0   200 miles

SÜPER LIG CLUBS

 1 **Akhisar Belediyespor**

 2 **Antalyaspor**

 3 **Beşiktaş JK**

 4 **Bursaspor**

 5 **Eskişehirspor**

 6 **Fenerbahçe SK**

 7 **Galatasaray AŞ**

 8 **Gaziantepspor**

 9 **Gençlerbirliği SK**

 10 **İstanbul Başakşehir**

 11 **Kasımpaşa SK**

 12 **Kayserispor**

 13 **Konyaspor**

 14 **Mersin İdman Yurdu**

 15 **Osmanlıspor**

 16 **Rizespor**

 17 **Sivasspor**

18 **Trabzonspor AŞ**

PROMOTED CLUBS

 19 **Adanaspor**

 20 **Kardemir Karabükspor**

 21 **Alanyaspor**

KEY

● UEFA Champions League

● UEFA Europa League

● Promoted

● Relegated

Beşiktaş back in business

Beşiktaş scratched a seven-year itch to become champions of Turkey for the 14th time, holding off a protracted challenge from Istanbul rivals Fenerbahçe before finishing off the job in their newly constructed stadium with a game to spare.

Fenerbahçe were runners-up also in the Turkish Cup, going down 1-0 in the final to Süper Lig also-rans Galatasaray, who therefore completed a hat-trick of wins in the competition. The Turkish national side did well to qualify for UEFA EURO 2016 but underperformed in France and headed home after the group stage.

ŞAMPİYON

2015-201

Black Eagles swoop to 14th league title

Galatasaray beat Fenerbahçe in cup final

Fatih Terim's side found wanting in France

Domestic league

After a dramatic 2014/15 Süper Lig season during which all of Istanbul's Big Three had a say in the title race, there were just two contenders in 2015/16. While defending champions Galatasaray stumbled from one lean spell to the next, eventually finishing sixth, Beşiktaş and Fenerbahçe, both led by new coaches, duelled long and hard in a quest for their crown.

Fenerbahçe, boosted by the arrival of Portuguese coach Vítor Pereira and a trio of high-profile new attackers in Robin van Persie, Nani and Fernandão, made the better start, but when Beşiktaş ended their unbeaten run with a 3-2 win, it was the Black Eagles, now led by the experienced Şenol Güneş, who soared to the Süper Lig summit. Once perched and nested, they proved extremely difficult to dislodge.

Beşiktaş played fluent, high-tempo football. Their midfield was beautifully balanced, with Atiba Hutchinson and Oğuzhan Özyakup dovetailing well behind playmaker José Sosa, and with a resurgent Mario Gomez, on loan from Fiorentina, returning to the scoring form of his Bayern München pomp, they were both efficient and fun to watch. They were undefeated away until Fenerbahçe defeated them 2-0 at the Şükrü Saraçoğlu in late February. That result set up a

potentially thrilling climax, but while the Yellow Canaries went through an untimely dry spell, their rivals bounced back with nine wins in their next 11 games, three of them at their new Vodafone Arena home, the last of which, 3-1 against Osmanlıspor, clinched the title.

For Şenol Güneş, the man who led Turkey to bronze medals at the 2002 FIFA World Cup, it was a first national title – following four spells with Trabzonspor and an impressive 2014/15 campaign with Bursaspor. However, there would be no Turkish championship crown to add to those won in Portugal and Greece for his opposite number at Fenerbahçe. One of Vítor Pereira's predecessors at the Şükrü Saraçoğlu, Aykut Kocaman, steered Konyaspor to third place – the club's highest ever final position - and they were joined in the 2016/17 UEFA Europa League by İstanbul Başakşehir and newly-promoted Osmanlıspor.

Domestic cup

Galatasaray had a proud record to protect when they met Fenerbahçe in the final of the Turkish Cup. The two teams had met four previous times in the fixture, and on each occasion Gala had prevailed. History would repeat itself in 2016 as a 30th-minute header from Lukas Podolski decided the outcome at a packed-out Antalya Arena, giving Cimbom a record-extending 17th cup success. However,

there would be no bonus UEFA Europa League place for the winners as a breach of Financial Fair Play regulations resulted in a one-year European ban.

Europe

Galatasaray played UEFA Champions League football in 2015/16 but could finish only third in their group, thus hopping across to the UEFA Europa League, where Beşiktas had exited in the group stage despite having an identical record in Group H to that of Group A qualifiers Fenerbahçe. Vítor Pereira's side were Turkey's last team standing, although the end, when it came, was brutal – a 4-1 defeat at Braga in which three of their players saw red.

National team

A magical late free-kick from Selçuk İnan against Iceland qualified Turkey directly for UEFA EURO 2016 as the best of the third-placed teams. But it was as one of the worst in that category that they exited the final tournament, a late goal for the Republic of Ireland against already-qualified Italy eliminating them after they had closed their group programme with a 2-0 win against Czech Republic following two defeats by Croatia (0-1) and Spain (0-3). It was a frustrating third EURO, therefore, for coach Fatih Terim, who had steered Turkey to the semi-finals in 2008.

DOMESTIC SEASON AT A GLANCE

Süper Lig 2015/16 final table

			Home				Away					Total					
		Pld	W	D	L	F	A	W	D	L	F	A	W	D	L	F	A	Pts
1	Beşiktaş JK	34	14	1	2	38	14	11	3	3	37	21	25	4	5	75	35	79
2	Fenerbahçe SK	34	14	3	0	32	10	8	5	4	28	17	22	8	4	60	27	74
3	Konyaspor	34	12	4	1	29	16	7	5	5	15	17	19	9	6	44	33	66
4	İstanbul Başakşehir	34	11	3	3	33	17	5	8	4	21	19	16	11	7	54	36	59
5	Osmanlıspor	34	7	4	6	28	21	7	6	4	24	15	14	10	10	52	36	52
6	Galatasaray AŞ	34	9	6	2	40	18	4	6	7	29	31	13	12	9	69	49	51
7	Kasımpaşa SK	34	8	4	5	27	18	6	4	7	23	22	14	8	12	50	40	50
8	Akhisar Belediyespor	34	7	6	4	18	16	4	7	6	24	25	11	13	10	42	41	46
9	Antalyaspor	34	9	6	2	36	20	3	3	11	17	32	12	9	13	53	52	45
10	Gençlerbirliği SK	34	8	5	4	23	14	5	1	11	19	28	13	6	15	42	42	45
11	Bursaspor	34	7	4	6	23	23	6	1	10	24	32	13	5	16	47	55	44
12	Trabzonspor AŞ	34	8	3	6	25	24	4	1	12	15	35	12	4	18	40	59	40
13	Rizespor	34	7	5	5	27	19	2	5	10	12	29	9	10	15	39	48	37
14	Gaziantepspor	34	6	2	9	16	22	3	7	7	15	28	9	9	16	31	50	36
15	Kayserispor	34	3	8	6	12	16	4	5	8	13	25	7	13	14	25	41	34
16	Sivasspor	34	4	9	4	21	20	2	4	11	13	28	6	13	15	34	48	31
17	Eskişehirspor	34	6	2	9	26	33	2	4	11	13	31	8	6	20	39	64	30
18	Mersin İdman Yurdu	34	4	3	10	19	33	1	3	13	12	38	5	6	23	31	71	21

European qualification 2016/17

Champion: Beşiktaş JK (group stage)
Fenerbahçe SK (third qualifying round)

Konyaspor (group stage)
İstanbul Başakşehir (third qualifying round)
Osmanlıspor (second qualifying round)
NB Cup winner Galatasaray AŞ banned.

Top scorer	Mario Gomez (Beşiktaş), 27 goals
Relegated clubs	Mersin İdman Yurdu, Eskişehirspor, Sivasspor
Promoted clubs	Adanaspor, Kardemir Karabükspor, Alanyaspor
Cup final	Galatasaray AŞ 1-0 Fenerbahçe SK

Team of the season
(4-2-3-1)

Coach: Şenol Güneş (Beşiktaş)

Volkan Demirel (Fenerbahçe)
Beck (Beşiktaş) · Yalçın (İstanbul Başakşehir) · Hakan (Galatasaray) · Hasan Ali (Fenerbahçe)
Hutchinson (Beşiktaş) · Oğuzhan (Beşiktaş)
Višća (İstanbul Başakşehir) · Sosa (Beşiktaş) · Volkan Şen (Fenerbahçe)
Gomez (Beşiktaş)

Player of the season

Oğuzhan Özyakup
(Beşiktaş JK)

Once on the books of Arsenal, Oğuzhan has evolved into one of the best midfielders in Turkey. His fourth season at Beşiktaş was unquestionably his best as he helped the Istanbul club claim a first Süper Lig title in seven years with a succession of high-grade performances, which he embellished with a career-best tally of nine goals. The 23-year-old also took up permanent residence in Fatih Terim's national side, scoring his first international goal with an excellent breakaway strike in a 3-0 victory against the Netherlands.

Newcomer of the season

Sinan Gümüş
(Galatasaray AŞ)

Born in Germany and a graduate of the VfB Stuttgart academy, Sinan had only a bit-part role in Galatasaray's 2014/15 Turkish league and cup double success, but the exciting 22-year-old winger-cum-striker became much more involved as his second season with Cimbom progressed, particularly in the Turkish Cup triumph, during which he found the net six times and started the final against Fenerbahçe. He closed the league campaign with a hat-trick against Kayserispor, offering the promise of greater things to come.

TURKEY

NATIONAL TEAM

Results 2015/16

03/09/15	Latvia (ECQ)	H	Konya	D	1-1	Selçuk (77)
06/09/15	Netherlands (ECQ)	H	Konya	W	3-0	Oğuzhan (8), Arda (26), Burak (86)
10/10/15	Czech Republic (ECQ)	A	Prague	W	2-0	Selçuk (62p), Hakan Çalhanoğlu (79)
13/10/15	Iceland (ECQ)	H	Konya	W	1-0	Selçuk (89)
13/11/15	Qatar	A	Doha	W	2-1	Arda (70), Cenk (73)
17/11/15	Greece	H	Istanbul	D	0-0	
24/03/16	Sweden	H	Antalya	W	2-1	Cenk (32, 81)
29/03/16	Austria	A	Vienna	W	2-1	Hakan Çalhanoğlu (43), Arda (56)
22/05/16	England	A	Manchester	L	1-2	Hakan Çalhanoğlu (14)
29/05/16	Montenegro	H	Antalya	W	1-0	Mehmet (90+4)
05/06/16	Slovenia	A	Ljubljana	W	1-0	Burak (5)
12/06/16	Croatia (ECF)	N	Paris (FRA)	L	0-1	
17/06/16	Spain (ECF)	N	Nice (FRA)	L	0-3	
21/06/16	Czech Republic (ECF)	N	Lens (FRA)	W	2-0	Burak (10), Ozan (65)

Appearances 2015/16

Coach: Fatih Terim	04/09/53		LVA	NED	CZE	ISL	Qat	Gre	Swe	Aut	Eng	Mne	Svn	CRO	ESP	CZE	Caps	Goals
Volkan Babacan	11/08/88	İstanbul Başakşehir	G	G	G	G	G	G	G	G	G	G	G	G	G	G	20	-
Ozan Tufan	23/03/95	Fenerbahçe	D	M	M	M	M	M86	M90	M	M87	M83	M	M	M	M	27	2
Hakan Balta	23/03/83	Galatasaray	D	D	D	D		D38		D			D	D	D	D	49	2
Serdar Aziz	23/10/90	Bursaspor	D	D	D	D	D43										9	1
Caner Erkin	04/10/88	Fenerbahçe	D	D	D	D			D	D69	D70	D72	D64	D	D		49	2
Selçuk İnan	10/02/85	Galatasaray	M	M	M	M			M	M	M		M83	M	M70	M	55	8
Hakan Çalhanoğlu	08/02/94	Leverkusen (GER)	M	M65	M	A72	M59	M81		M73	M78	M58	M46	M	M46		21	6
Arda Turan	30/01/87	Barcelona (ESP)	M	M57	M86	M	M	M90	M90	M		M	M74	M65	M	M	94	17
Gökhan Töre	20/01/92	Beşiktaş	M58		s86	s62 78*											26	-
Volkan Şen	07/07/87	Fenerbahçe	M55	s57	s64	M75			M65	s46 /80	M83	M46	s46	s46		M61	19	-
Burak Yılmaz	15/07/85	Galatasaray /Beijing Guoan (CHN)	A84	A								s58	A90	s65	A	A90	47	21
Umut Bulut	15/03/83	Galatasaray	s55			s75											38	10
Şener Özbayraklı	23/01/90	Fenerbahçe	s58	D	D	D	D63			s46		D					8	-
Mehmet Topal	03/03/86	Fenerbahçe	s84	s65	s87		M	D	D	D	D	D	D	D	D	D	62	1
Oğuzhan Özyakup	23/09/92	Beşiktaş		M83	M87	M62	M46	M63	M63	M46	M70	M58	M46	M46	M62	s61	23	1
Olcay Şahan	26/05/87	Beşiktaş		s83			s43	M74	s90		s78		s90		s62	s69	26	2
Cenk Tosun	07/06/91	Beşiktaş			A64	s72	A83	A63	A82	A86	A	A70		A69		s90	11	3
Atınç Nukan	20/07/93	RB Leipzig (GER)					D										1	-
Emre Taşdemir	08/08/95	Bursaspor					D73	s81									4	-
Yunus Mallı	24/02/92	Mainz (GER)						s46	s63	s82	s73		s70	s83		s70	7	-
Yasin Öztekin	19/03/87	Galatasaray						s59	s90		s80	s83					5	-
Gökhan Gönül	04/01/85	Fenerbahçe						s63	D	D46	D		D	D	D	D	60	1
İsmail Köybaşı	10/07/89	Beşiktaş						s73	D		s69	s70	s72	s64		D	20	-
Alper Potuk	08/04/91	Fenerbahçe						s83	s86	s63			s83				15	-
Ahmet Çalık	26/02/94	Gençlerbirliği						D	s38	D		D					4	-
Emre Çolak	20/05/91	Galatasaray							s63								2	-
Okay Yokuşlu	09/03/94	Trabzonspor							s74								1	-
Kerim Koyunlu	19/11/93	Beşiktaş							s63								5	-
Çağlar Söyüncü	23/05/96	Altınordu							s90								1	-
Nuri Şahin	05/09/88	Dortmund (GER)							s86			s58	s74		s46		50	2
Mahmut Tekdemir	20/01/88	İstanbul Başakşehir							s70								2	-
Mevlüt Erdinç	25/02/87	Guingamp (FRA)							s87								34	8
Emre Mor	24/07/97	Nordsjælland (DEN)										s46	s46	s69		M69	4	-

Galatasaray AŞ

Group C
Match 1 - Club Atlético de Madrid (ESP)
H 0-2
Muslera, Selçuk İnan, Sneijder, Podolski (Sinan Gümüş 71), Burak Yılmaz, Hakan Balta, Carole, Semih Kaya, Emre Çolak (Umut Bulut 32), Sabri Sarıoğlu (Yasin Öztekin 46), Denayer. Coach: Hamza Hamzaoğlu (TUR)
Match 2 - FC Astana (KAZ)
A 2-2 Bilal Kısa (31), Erić (86og)
Muslera, Bilal Kısa (Sinan Gümüş 81), Yasin Öztekin (Sabri Sarıoğlu 90+1), Selçuk İnan, Umut Bulut, Sneijder, Podolski (José Rodríguez 68), Hakan Balta, Carole, Semih Kaya, Denayer. Coach: Hamza Hamzaoğlu (TUR)
Match 3 - SL Benfica (POR)
H 2-1 Selçuk İnan (19p), Podolski (33)
Muslera, Bilal Kısa (José Rodríguez 90+4), Yasin Öztekin (Olcan Adın 59), Selçuk İnan, Umut Bulut (Burak Yılmaz 78), Sneijder, Podolski, Chedjou, Hakan Balta, Sabri Sarıoğlu. Coach: Hamza Hamzaoğlu (TUR)
Match 4 - SL Benfica (POR)
A 1-2 Podolski (58)
Muslera, Bilal Kısa (Yasin Öztekin 69), Selçuk İnan, Sneijder, Podolski, Burak Yılmaz (Umut Bulut 74), Chedjou, Hakan Balta, Olcan Adın, Sabri Sarıoğlu, Denayer (Emre Çolak 74). Coach: Hamza Hamzaoğlu (TUR)
Match 5 - Club Atlético de Madrid (ESP)
A 0-2
Muslera, Bilal Kısa (Umut Bulut 63), Jem Karacan, Yasin Öztekin, Sneijder, Podolski, Chedjou, Hakan Balta (Sinan Gümüş 78), Semih Kaya, Sabri Sarıoğlu, Denayer (Olcan Adın 25). Coach: Cláudio Taffarel (BRA)
Match 6 - FC Astana (KAZ)
H 1-1 Selçuk İnan (64)
Muslera, Yasin Öztekin (Umut Bulut 88), Selçuk İnan, Sneijder, Podolski, Burak Yılmaz, Chedjou, Hakan Balta, Semih Kaya, Olcan Adın (José Rodríguez 82), Sabri Sarıoğlu. Coach: Mustafa Denizli (TUR)

Round of 32 - SS Lazio (ITA)
H 1-1 Sabri Sarıoğlu (12)
Muslera, Selçuk İnan, Sneijder (Yasin Öztekin 89), Podolski, Donk, Chedjou, Hakan Balta, Carole (Olcan Adın 71), Günter, Sabri Sarıoğlu (Umut Bulut 78), Denayer. Coach: Mustafa Denizli (TUR)
A 1-3 Yasin Öztekin (62)
Muslera, Yasin Öztekin (Olcan Adın 76), Selçuk İnan, Sneijder, Podolski, Donk (Bilal Kısa 85), Chedjou, Hakan Balta, Carole, Sabri Sarıoğlu (Umut Bulut 66), Denayer. Coach: Mustafa Denizli (TUR)

Fenerbahçe SK

Third qualifying round - FC Shakhtar Donetsk (UKR)
H 0-0
Volkan Demirel, Hasan Ali Kaldırım, Kjær, Mehmet Topal (Raul Meireles 64), Souza, Sow (Van Persie 68), Fernandão, Diego (Stoch 84), Nani, Bruno Alves, Caner Erkin. Coach: Vítor Pereira (POR)
A 0-3
Volkan Demirel, Kjær, Souza, Sow, Fernandão, Diego, Raul Meireles (Alper Potuk 78), Nani (Stoch 88), Şener Özbayraklı (Mehmet Topal 88), Bruno Alves, Caner Erkin. Coach: Vítor Pereira (POR)
Red card: Kjær 90+3

Play-offs - Atromitos FC (GRE)
A 1-0 Van Persie (90)
Volkan Demirel, Souza, Sow (Van Persie 80), Fernandão, Diego, Raul Meireles (Mehmet Topal 71), Nani (Volkan Şen 87), Şener Özbayraklı, Bruno Alves, Ba, Caner Erkin. Coach: Vítor Pereira (POR)
H 3-0 Fernandão (7, 78), Gorbunov (59og)
Volkan Demirel, Kjær, Mehmet Topal (Volkan Şen 77), Souza, Fernandão, Diego (Raul Meireles 67), Van Persie (Alper Potuk 67), Nani, Şener Özbayraklı, Ba, Caner Erkin. Coach: Vítor Pereira (POR)

Group A
Match 1 - Molde FK (NOR)
H 1-3 Nani (42)
Fabiano, Mehmet Topal (Fernandão 58), Ozan Tufan, Van Persie (Alper Potuk 69), Raul Meireles (Uygar Mert Zeybek 69), Nani, Şener Özbayraklı, Volkan Şen, Bruno Alves, Kadlec, Caner Erkin. Coach: Vítor Pereira (POR)
Match 2 - Celtic FC (SCO)
A 2-2 Fernandão (43, 48)
Fabiano, Hasan Ali Kaldırım, Kjær, Mehmet Topal, Ozan Tufan (Diego 46), Van Persie, Raul Meireles (Ba 78), Nani, Şener Özbayraklı, Volkan Şen (Fernandão 40), Bruno Alves. Coach: Vítor Pereira (POR)
Match 3 - AFC Ajax (NED)
H 1-0 Fernandão (89)
Fabiano, Kjær, Mehmet Topal, Souza, Diego (Ozan Tufan 72), Van Persie (Fernandão 72), Nani, Marković (Alper Potuk 84), Ba, Gökhan Gönül, Caner Erkin. Coach: Vítor Pereira (POR)
Match 4 - AFC Ajax (NED)
A 0-0
Volkan Demirel, Hasan Ali Kaldırım, Kjær, Mehmet Topal, Souza, Diego (Ozan Tufan 74), Van Persie (Volkan Şen 80), Nani (Fernandão 63), Bruno Alves, Alper Potuk, Gökhan Gönül. Coach: Vítor Pereira (POR)
Match 5 - Molde FK (NOR)
A 2-0 Fernandão (68), Ozan Tufan (84)
Fabiano, Hasan Ali Kaldırım (Kadlec 84), Kjær, Souza, Ozan Tufan, Fernandão (Van Persie 86), Diego, Nani (Volkan Şen 82), Bruno Alves, Alper Potuk, Gökhan Gönül. Coach: Vítor Pereira (POR)
Match 6 - Celtic FC (SCO)
H 1-1 Marković (39)
Fabiano, Hasan Ali Kaldırım, Mehmet Topal, Souza, Fernandão (Caner Erkin 86), Diego, Bruno Alves, Alper Potuk, Marković (Ozan Tufan 83), Ba, Gökhan Gönül. Coach: Vítor Pereira (POR)
Red card: Diego 67

Round of 32 - FC Lokomotiv Moskva (RUS)
H 2-0 Souza (18, 72)
Fabiano, Kjær, Mehmet Topal, Souza (Kadlec 84), Ozan Tufan, Van Persie (Fernandão 78), Nani, Volkan Şen (Alper Potuk 78), Bruno Alves, Gökhan Gönül, Caner Erkin. Coach: Vítor Pereira (POR)
A 1-1 Mehmet Topal (83)
Fabiano, Hasan Ali Kaldırım, Kjær, Mehmet Topal, Souza, Ozan Tufan (Kadlec 74), Van Persie, Nani (Alper Potuk 79), Volkan Şen, Bruno Alves, Gökhan Gönül (Şener Özbayraklı 44). Coach: Vítor Pereira (POR)

Round of 16 - SC Braga (POR)
H 1-0 Mehmet Topal (82)
Volkan Demirel, Kjær, Mehmet Topal, Souza, Ozan Tufan (Raul Meireles 72), Van Persie, Şener Özbayraklı, Volkan Şen (Nani 65), Bruno Alves, Alper Potuk (Fernandão 79), Caner Erkin. Coach: Vítor Pereira (POR)
A 1-4 Alper Potuk (45+3)
Volkan Demirel, Kjær, Mehmet Topal, Souza, Diego (Kadlec 73), Van Persie (Fernandão 78), Nani (Volkan Şen 72), Şener Özbayraklı, Bruno Alves, Alper Potuk, Caner Erkin. Coach: Vítor Pereira (POR)
Red cards: Mehmet Topal 66, Alper Potuk 87, Volkan Şen 90+7

Beşiktaş JK

Group H
Match 1 - KF Skënderbeu (ALB)
A 1-0 Sosa (28)
Tolga Zengin, İsmail Köybaşı, Sosa, Hutchinson, Ricardo Quaresma (Mustafa Pektemek 83), Necip Uysal, Kerim Koyunlu (Gökhan Töre 54), Ersan Gülüm, Cenk Tosun (Gomez 61), Beck, Rhodolfo. Coach: Şenol Güneş (TUR)
Match 2 - Sporting Clube de Portugal (POR)
H 1-1 Gökhan Töre (61)
Tolga Zengin, İsmail Köybaşı, Sosa (Cenk Tosun 68), Gökhan Töre, Hutchinson, Ricardo Quaresma (Kerim Koyunlu 90), Necip Uysal (Oğuzhan Özyakup 46), Ersan Gülüm, Beck, Gomez, Rhodolfo. Coach: Şenol Güneş (TUR)
Match 3 - FC Lokomotiv Moskva (RUS)
A 1-1 Gomez (64)
Tolga Zengin, İsmail Köybaşı, Sosa (Necip Uysal 57), Gökhan Töre (Cenk Tosun 65), Hutchinson, Oğuzhan Özyakup, Ricardo Quaresma (Kerim Koyunlu 87), Ersan Gülüm, Beck, Gomez, Rhodolfo. Coach: Şenol Güneş (TUR)
Match 4 - FC Lokomotiv Moskva (RUS)
H 1-1 Ricardo Quaresma (58)
Tolga Zengin, İsmail Köybaşı, Sosa (Necip Uysal 72), Gökhan Töre, Olcay Şahan (Ricardo Quaresma 46), Hutchinson, Oğuzhan Özyakup (Cenk Tosun 83), Ersan Gülüm, Beck, Gomez, Rhodolfo. Coach: Şenol Güneş (TUR)
Match 5 - KF Skënderbeu (ALB)
H 2-0 Cenk Tosun (35, 78)
Tolga Zengin, İsmail Köybaşı, Gökhan Töre (Olcay Şahan 84), Hutchinson, Oğuzhan Özyakup, Necip Uysal, Kerim Koyunlu (Ricardo Quaresma 68), Ersan Gülüm (Tošić 33), Cenk Tosun, Beck, Rhodolfo. Coach: Şenol Güneş (TUR)
Match 6 - Sporting Clube de Portugal (POR)
A 1-3 Gomez (58)
Tolga Zengin, İsmail Köybaşı (Kerim Koyunlu 85), Sosa (Cenk Tosun 79), Tošić, Olcay Şahan (Necip Uysal 71), Hutchinson, Oğuzhan Özyakup, Ricardo Quaresma, Beck, Gomez, Rhodolfo. Coach: Şenol Güneş (TUR)

DOMESTIC LEAGUE CLUB-BY-CLUB

İstanbul Başakşehir

Third qualifying round - AZ Alkmaar (NED)
A 0-2
Volkan Babacan, Yalçın Ayhan, Mahmut Tekdemir, Višća, Mossoró (Ufuk Ceylan 15), Doka Madureira (Cenk Ahmet Alkılıç 77), Badji, Uğur Uçar, Gençer Cansev (Emre Belözoğlu 65), Ferhat Öztorun, Çikalleshi. Coach: Abdullah Avcı (TUR)
Red card: Volkan Babacan 14
H 1-2 Doka (45)
Ufuk Ceylan, Yalçın Ayhan, Višća, Mossoró (Mehmet Batdal 74), Doka Madureira, Badji, Emre Belözoğlu (Mahmut Tekdemir 64), Uğur Uçar (Cenk Ahmet Alkılıç 46), Gençer Cansev, Ferhat Öztorun, Çikalleshi. Coach: Abdullah Avcı (TUR)

Trabzonspor AŞ

Second qualifying round - FC Differdange 03 (LUX)
H 1-0 Mehmet Ekici (44)
Onur Kıvrak, Medjani, Mehmet Ekici (Fatih Atik 84), Sefa Yılmaz, Uğur Demirok, Soner Aydoğdu, Erkan Zengin (Yusuf Erdoğan 64), Mustafa Yumlu, Salih Dursun, Waris (Zeki Yavru 81), Musa Nizam. Coach: Shota Arveladze (GEO)
A 2-1 Salih Dursun (19), Soner Aydoğdu (90+3)
Onur Kıvrak, Medjani (Aytaç Kara 90+4), Mehmet Ekici (Soner Aydoğdu 59), Sefa Yılmaz, Constant, Uğur Demirok, Mustafa Yumlu, Salih Dursun, Waris, Yusuf Erdoğan (Erkan Zengin 72), Musa Nizam. Coach: Shota Arveladze (GEO)

Third qualifying round - FK Rabotnicki (MKD)
A 0-1
Uğurcan Çakır, Aykut Demir (Okay Yokuşlu 75), Medjani, Cardozo, Sefa Yılmaz (Özer Hurmacı 62), Constant, Mustafa Yumlu, Salih Dursun, Waris (Erkan Zengin 80), Yusuf Erdoğan, Alper Uludağ. Coach: Shota Arveladze (GEO)
H 1-1 (aet) Okay Yokuşlu (55)
Onur Kıvrak, Okay Yokuşlu (Aytaç Kara 86), Medjani, Cardozo, Özer Hurmacı (Deniz Yılmaz 77), Constant, Erkan Zengin, Mustafa Yumlu, Mbia, Yusuf Erdoğan (Sefa Yılmaz 105+1), Cavanda . Coach: Shota Arveladze (GEO)

Akhisar Belediyespor

1970 • 19 Mayıs, Manisa (16,597) • akhisarbelediyespor.com
Coach: Cihat Arslan

2015
16/08	a	Konyaspor	D 1-1	Custódio
22/08	h	Mersin	W 2-0	Rodallega, Güray
30/08	a	Trabzonspor	D 2-2	Hasan (p), Rodallega
12/09	h	Gaziantepspor	D 0-0	
18/09	a	İstanbul Başakşehir	L 0-2	
26/09	h	Gençlerbirliği	W 1-0	Rodallega
04/10	a	Fenerbahçe	D 2-2	Güray (p), Douglão
18/10	h	Eskişehirspor	W 1-0	Güray
23/10	a	Rizespor	W 2-0	Güray (p), Rodallega
30/10	a	Antalyaspor	W 2-1	Rodallega, Douglão
07/11	a	Kasımpaşa	L 1-2	Rodallega
21/11	h	Bursaspor	W 3-1	Rodallega 2, Bruno Mezenga
29/11	a	Beşiktaş	W 2-0	Güray, Sami
07/12	h	Sivasspor	W 1-0	Douglão
13/12	a	Kayserispor	L 2-3	Rodallega 2
20/12	a	Galatasaray	L 2-3	N'Guémo, Rodallega
27/12	h	Osmanlıspor	D 0-0	

2016
16/01	h	Konyaspor	L 0-2	
23/01	a	Mersin	D 0-0	
07/02	h	Trabzonspor	W 2-1	Douglão, Rodallega
14/02	a	Gaziantepspor	W 1-0	Rodallega
21/02	h	İstanbul Başakşehir	D 0-0	
28/02	a	Gençlerbirliği	L 1-3	Onur
06/03	h	Fenerbahçe	L 0-3	
13/03	a	Eskişehirspor	D 3-3	Rodallega 2, Onur
19/03	h	Rizespor	D 1-1	Orhan
03/04	a	Antalyaspor	D 2-2	Vaz Té, Rodallega
11/04	h	Kasımpaşa	L 0-1	
17/04	a	Bursaspor	W 2-0	Grbić, N'Guémo
23/04	h	Beşiktaş	D 3-3	Rodallega 3
01/05	a	Sivasspor	D 1-1	Bruno Mezenga
08/05	h	Kayserispor	D 1-1	Sami
15/05	h	Galatasaray	L 1-2	Douglão
19/05	a	Osmanlıspor	L 0-1	

No	Name	Nat	DoB	Pos	Aps	(s)	Gls
8	Abdülkadir Özdemir		25/03/91	M	1	(1)	
20	Ahmet Cebe		02/03/83	M	23		
19	Alper Uludağ		11/12/90	D	3		
18	Aykut Çeviker		03/01/90	M	3	(14)	
35	Bora Körk		09/06/80	G	1		
80	Bruno Mezenga	BRA	08/08/88	A	6	(16)	2
88	Caner Osmanpaşa		15/01/88	D	33		
27	Mervan Celik	SWE	28/05/90	M	2	(3)	
40	Custódio	POR	24/05/83	M	33		1
44	Douglão	BRA	15/08/96	D	25		5
10	Fatih Öztürk		22/12/86	G	9		
7	Petar Grbić	MNE	07/08/88	M	4	(6)	1
99	Güray Vural		11/06/88	M	18	(5)	
23	Halil Çolak		29/01/88	M	2	(5)	
4	Hasan Kabze		26/05/82	A	5	(5)	1
89	İsmail Konuk		16/01/88	D	10	(2)	
21	Kadir Keleş		01/01/88	D	15		
32	Lomana LuaLua	COD	28/12/80	A	4	(6)	
6	Milan Lukač	SRB	04/10/85	G	24		
90	Merter Yüce		18/02/85	M	27		
1	Muğdat Çelik		03/01/90	M	4	(3)	
24	Landry N'Guémo	CMR	28/11/85	M	27	(2)	2
11	Onur Ayık		28/01/90	M	4	(18)	2
22	Orhan Taşdelen		06/02/87	D	13	(1)	1
12	Hugo Rodallega	COL	25/07/85	A	32	(2)	19
17	Sami	GNB	18/12/88	A	24	(3)	2
30	Soner Aydoğdu		05/01/91	M	4	(8)	
14	Tolga Ünlü		10/09/89	D	11		
29	Ricardo Vaz Té	POR	01/10/86	A	7	(7)	1

Antalyaspor

1966 • Akdeniz Üniversitesi (7,083); Antalya Arena (32,539) • antalyaspor.com.tr
Coach: Yusuf Şimşek; (07/12/15) (Mehmet Uğurlu); (06/01/16) José Morais (POR)

2015
15/08	a	İstanbul Başakşehir	W 3-2	Emrah, Eto'o 2
23/08	h	Gençlerbirliği	W 3-1	Lazarevič, Etame, Eto'o
30/08	a	Fenerbahçe	L 1-2	Guilherme
12/09	h	Eskişehirspor	W 2-0	Eto'o 2 (1p)
19/09	a	Rizespor	L 1-5	Emrah
27/09	h	Sivasspor	D 1-1	Lazarevič
04/10	a	Kasımpaşa	D 0-0	
17/10	a	Bursaspor	W 2-0	Eto'o, Emrah
26/10	h	Beşiktaş	L 1-5	Eto'o
30/10	a	Akhisar	L 1-2	Eto'o (p)
07/11	h	Kayserispor	D 1-1	Eto'o (p)
21/11	a	Galatasaray	D 3-3	Sezer, Eto'o (p), Etame
27/11	h	Osmanlıspor	D 1-1	Eto'o
05/12	a	Konyaspor	L 2-3	Emrah, Eto'o
12/12	h	Mersin	W 3-2	Etame, Eto'o, Lokman
19/12	a	Trabzonspor	L 0-3	
26/12	h	Gaziantepspor	D 0-0	

2016
17/01	h	İstanbul Başakşehir	L 1-2	Etame
24/01	a	Gençlerbirliği	L 0-1	
05/02	h	Fenerbahçe	W 4-2	Eto'o, Danilo, Makoun, Sakıb
14/02	a	Eskişehirspor	L 2-3	og (Hadžić), Ömer Şişmanoğlu
20/02	h	Rizespor	W 2-1	Danilo (p), Ömer Şişmanoğlu
28/02	a	Sivasspor	D 0-0	
06/03	a	Kasımpaşa	L 1-2	Ömer Şişmanoğlu
14/03	h	Bursaspor	W 3-0	Diego Ângelo, Eto'o 2
19/03	a	Beşiktaş	L 0-1	
03/04	h	Akhisar	D 2-2	Makoun, Eto'o
10/04	a	Kayserispor	D 0-0	
16/04	h	Galatasaray	W 4-2	Eto'o 2, Emrah, Rıdvan
23/04	a	Osmanlıspor	L 0-3	
01/05	h	Konyaspor	W 1-0	Eto'o
08/05	a	Mersin	W 1-0	Etame
13/05	h	Trabzonspor	W 7-0	Ömer Şişmanoğlu 3, Charles, Makoun, Etame 2
19/05	a	Gaziantepspor	L 0-2	

No	Name	Nat	DoB	Pos	Aps	(s)	Gls
39	Ahmet Aras		13/12/87	A		(1)	
75	Birkan Öksüz		19/03/96	D		(3)	
2	Can Arat		21/01/84	D	2	(1)	
28	Ondřej Čelůstka	CZE	18/06/89	D	28	(2)	
70	Charles	BRA	14/02/85	M	5	(9)	1
20	Chico	BRA	02/02/87	M	7	(4)	
90	Danilo	BRA	13/01/90	M	8	(4)	2
10	Lamine Diarra	SEN	20/12/83	A	5	(3)	
33	Diego Ângelo	BRA	17/02/86	D	25		1
15	Doğukan Sinik		21/01/99	M		(1)	
11	Emrah Başşan		17/04/92	M	10	(9)	5
80	Emre Akbaba		04/10/92	M	3	(5)	
24	Lionel Enguene	CMR	07/01/86	M	3	(3)	
35	Erman Kılıç		25/04/86	M	2		
99	Mbilla Etame	CMR	22/06/88	A	12	(9)	7
9	Samuel Eto'o	CMR	10/03/81	A	31		20
32	Sašo Fornezzi	SVN	11/12/82	G	20	(1)	
13	Gökhan Yılmaz		19/01/91	D	3		
12	Guilherme	BRA	23/01/90	M	10	(2)	1
22	Samuel Inkoom	GHA	01/06/89	D	12	(2)	
8	Kadir Bekmezci		05/07/85	M	11	(6)	
3	Josip Kvesić	BIH	21/09/90	D	6		
27	Dejan Lazarevič	SVN	15/02/90	A	13	(4)	2
53	Lokman Gör		15/12/90	D	10	(1)	1
17	Jean II Makoun	CMR	29/05/83	M	20	(4)	3
92	Rais M'Bolhi	ALG	25/04/86	G	12		
55	Oktay Delibalta		27/10/85	M	1		
65	Ömer Kandemir		03/07/93	D	9		
77	Ömer Şişmanoğlu		01/08/89	A	4	(6)	6
20	Osman Çelik		27/11/91	D	1		
1	Ozan Evrim Özenç		07/01/93	G	2	(1)	
14	Ozan İpek		10/10/86	M	1		
31	Ramon	BRA	06/05/88	D	14		
25	Rıdvan Şimşek		17/01/91	D	10	(1)	1
22	Sakıb Aytaç	TUE	24/11/91	D	18	(2)	1
21	Serdar Özkan		01/01/87	M	18	(12)	
5	Sezer Badur		20/06/84	M	8	(2)	1
18	Yekta Kurtuluş		11/12/85	M	11		
7	Zeki Yıldırım		15/01/91	M	19	(2)	

Beşiktaş JK

1903 • Atatürk Olimpiyat (76,092); Başakşehir
Fatih Terim (17,300); Vodafone Arena (41,903)
• bjk.com.tr

Major honours
Turkish League (14) 1957, 1958, 1960, 1966, 1967,
1982, 1986, 1990, 1991, 1992, 1995, 2003, 2009,
2016; Turkish Cup (9) 1975, 1989, 1990, 1994, 1998,
2006, 2007, 2009, 2011

Coach: Şenol Güneş

2015

16/08	a	Mersin	W 5-2	Cenk 3, Olcay, Kerim
22/08	h	Trabzonspor	L 1-2	Ricardo Quaresma
28/08	a	Gaziantepspor	W 4-0	Oğuzhan, Cenk (p), Olcay, Kerim
13/09	h	İstanbul Başakşehir	W 2-0	Gomez 2
21/09	a	Gençlerbirliği	D 1-1	Gökhan
27/09	h	Fenerbahçe	W 3-2	og (Kjær), Gomez 2
04/10	a	Eskişehirspor	W 2-1	Gomez 2
18/10	h	Rizespor	W 1-0	Ricardo Quaresma
26/10	a	Antalyaspor	W 5-1	Necip, Ricardo Quaresma, Gomez, Olcay, Cenk
30/10	h	Kasımpaşa	D 3-3	Rhodolfo, Gomez, Oğuzhan (p)
08/11	a	Bursaspor	W 1-0	Oğuzhan
22/11	h	Sivasspor	W 2-0	Gomez (p), Oğuzhan
29/11	h	Akhisar	L 0-2	
05/12	a	Kayserispor	W 2-1	Gomez, Sosa
14/12	h	Galatasaray	W 2-1	Gomez, Gökhan
21/12	a	Osmanlıspor	W 3-2	Gomez, Sosa 2
27/12	h	Konyaspor	W 4-0	Oğuzhan, Gomez, Gökhan, Kerim

2016

07/02	h	Gaziantepspor	W 4-0	Gökhan, Oğuzhan, Gomez 2
14/02	a	İstanbul Başakşehir	D 2-2	Cenk, Hutchinson
17/02	h	Mersin	W 1-0	Sosa
22/02	h	Gençlerbirliği	W 1-0	Gomez
29/02	a	Fenerbahçe	L 0-2	
07/03	h	Eskişehirspor	W 3-1	Hutchinson, Gomez 2
12/03	a	Rizespor	W 2-1	Sosa, Kerim
15/03	a	Trabzonspor	W 2-0	Gomez, Olcay
19/03	h	Antalyaspor	W 1-0	Oğuzhan
04/04	h	Kasımpaşa	L 1-2	Sosa
11/04	h	Bursaspor	W 3-2	Gomez 2, Alexis
16/04	a	Sivasspor	W 2-1	Gomez, Oğuzhan
23/04	h	Akhisar	D 3-3	Gomez, Olcay, Cenk
30/04	h	Kayserispor	W 4-0	Gomez, Oğuzhan, Ricardo Quaresma, Cenk
08/05	a	Galatasaray	W 1-0	Gomez
15/05	h	Osmanlıspor	W 3-1	Marcelo 2, Gomez
18/05	a	Konyaspor	L 1-2	Sosa

No	Name	Nat	DoB	Pos	Aps	(s)	Gls
12	Alexis	ESP	04/08/85	D	9	(1)	1
18	Tolgay Arslan	GER	16/08/90	M	1	(5)	
32	Andreas Beck	GER	13/03/87	D	31	(1)	
71	Denys Boyko	UKR	29/01/88	G	3		
23	Cenk Tosun		07/06/91	A	3	(26)	8
22	Ersan Gülüm		17/05/87	D	14		
7	Gökhan Töre		20/01/92	M	15	(9)	4
33	Mario Gomez	GER	10/07/85	A	31	(2)	26
27	Günay Güvenç		25/06/91	G	1	(1)	
13	Atiba Hutchinson	CAN	08/02/83	M	33	(1)	2
3	İsmail Köybaşı		09/07/89	D	26	(1)	
45	Veli Kavlak	AUT	03/11/88	M		(1)	
21	Kerim Koyunlu		19/11/93	M	6	(17)	4
30	Marcelo	BRA	20/05/87	D	14		2
4	Alexander Milosevic	SWE	30/01/92	D	1		
11	Mustafa Pektemek		11/08/88	A		(4)	
20	Necip Uysal		24/01/91	M	9	(20)	1
15	Oğuzhan Özyakup		23/09/92	M	31		9
10	Olcay Şahan		26/05/87	M	27	(6)	5
31	Ramon	BRA	06/05/88	D	1		
44	Rhodolfo	BRA	11/08/86	D	18		1
17	Ricardo Quaresma	POR	26/09/83	M	23	(3)	4
2	Serdar Kurtuluş		23/07/87	D	3		
8	José Sosa	ARG	19/06/85	M	30	(1)	7
29	Tolga Zengin		10/10/83	G	30		
6	Duško Tošić	SRB	19/01/85	D	14	(1)	

Bursaspor

1963 • Atatürk (25,661); Timsah Arena
(43,331) • bursaspor.org.tr

Major honours
Turkish League (1) 2010; Turkish Cup (1) 1986

Coach: Ertuğrul Sağlam;
(27/11/13) (Ersel Uzgur);
(17/12/15) Hamza Hamzaoğlu

2015

15/08	a	Trabzonspor	L 0-1	
23/08	h	Gaziantepspor	L 0-1	
29/08	a	İstanbul Başakşehir	L 1-2	Bekir
12/09	h	Gençlerbirliği	W 3-2	Dzsudzsák 2 (1p), Necid
20/09	a	Fenerbahçe	L 0-2	Necid
28/09	h	Eskişehirspor	W 2-0	Necid, Faty
04/10	a	Rizespor	W 3-2	Necid 3
17/10	h	Antalyaspor	L 0-2	
24/10	a	Kasımpaşa	W 1-0	Necid
28/10	h	Sivasspor	W 1-0	Cuenca
08/11	h	Beşiktaş	L 0-1	
21/11	a	Akhisar	L 1-3	Dzsudzsák
27/11	h	Kayserispor	L 1-2	Nounkeu
04/12	a	Galatasaray	L 0-3	
11/12	h	Osmanlıspor	L 0-4	
19/12	a	Konyaspor	L 0-1	
27/12	h	Mersin	W 2-1	Necid, Sercan

2016

17/01	h	Trabzonspor	W 4-2	Sercan, Necid (p), Sivok, Serdar
24/01	a	Gaziantepspor	W 3-2	Necid (p), Bekir, Jorquera
06/02	h	İstanbul Başakşehir	D 3-3	Necid, Sercan, Behich
13/02	a	Gençlerbirliği	L 0-2	
20/02	h	Fenerbahçe	D 0-0	
27/02	a	Eskişehirspor	W 1-0	Batalla
05/03	h	Rizespor	W 1-0	Deniz
14/03	a	Antalyaspor	L 0-3	
20/03	h	Kasımpaşa	W 4-1	Deniz 2, Sercan, og (Popov)
03/04	a	Sivasspor	W 2-1	Deniz 2
13/04	a	Beşiktaş	L 2-3	Traoré, Stoch
17/04	h	Akhisar	L 0-2	
22/04	a	Kayserispor	L 1-2	Serdar
29/04	h	Galatasaray	D 1-1	Sivok
07/05	a	Osmanlıspor	D 3-3	Batalla, Faty, Jorquera
14/05	h	Konyaspor	D 1-1	Deniz
18/05	a	Mersin	W 5-2	Kubilay 2, Batalla, Talha, Furkan Emre

No	Name	Nat	DoB	Pos	Aps	(s)	Gls
82	Luis Advíncula	PER	02/03/90	D	12		
20	Aydın Karabulut		25/01/88	M		(2)	
23	Pablo Batalla	ARG	01/01/84	M	14		3
23	Aziz Behich	AUS	16/12/90	D	24	(2)	1
5	Bekir Yılmaz		06/03/88	M	13	(9)	2
29	Bünyamin Kasal		13/01/97	D	1		
98	Isaac Cuenca	ESP	27/04/81	M	5	(7)	1
19	Tom De Sutter	BEL	03/07/85	A	4	(7)	
88	Deniz Yılmaz		26/02/88	A	12	(1)	6
27	Balázs Dzsudzsák	HUN	23/12/86	M	21	(2)	3
98	Emirhan Aydoğan		26/06/97	D		(3)	
3	Emre Taşdemir		08/08/95	D	18	(4)	
82	Erdem Özgenç		22/08/84	D	11	(1)	
91	Ricardo Faty	SEN	04/08/86	M	22	(2)	2
95	Furkan Emre Ünver		30/01/97	D	1		1
11	Furkan Soyalp		12/06/95	A	1	(3)	
1	Harun Tekin		17/06/89	G	14		
21	Hajime Hosogai	JPN	10/06/86	M	17	(3)	
68	Jem Karacan		21/02/89	M	6	(3)	
14	Cristóbal Jorquera	CHI	04/08/88	M	13	(9)	2
10	Josué	POR	17/09/90	M	14		
90	Kubilay Kanatsızkuş		28/03/97	A	3	(1)	2
17	Mert Günok		01/03/89	G	20		
97	Mert Örnek		12/02/97	M	1	(4)	
15	Tomáš Necid	CZE	13/08/89	A	23	(5)	11
13	Dany Nounkeu	CMR	11/04/86	D	11	(4)	1
6	Şamil Çinaz		08/03/84	M	16	(5)	
99	Sercan Yıldırım		05/04/90	A	12	(7)	4
4	Serdar Aziz		23/10/90	D	21		2
66	Tomáš Sivok	CZE	15/09/83	D	23	(1)	2
89	Miroslav Stoch	SVK	19/10/89	M	13	(12)	1
93	Talha Çalışkan		10/01/96	M		(1)	
8	Bakaye Traoré	MLI	06/03/85	M	8		1
27	Utku Türk		20/01/97	M		(1)	

Eskişehirspor

1965 • Atatürk (13,520) • eskisehirspor.org.tr

Major honours
Turkish Cup (1) 1971

Coach: Michael Skibbe (GER);
(11/10/15) İsmail Kartal;
(17/11/15) Samet Aybaba

2015

14/08	a	Fenerbahçe	L 0-2	
23/08	h	Sivasspor	W 4-2	Gekas 3, Kaan
30/08	h	Rizespor	D 1-1	Emre Güral (p)
12/09	a	Antalyaspor	L 0-2	
19/09	h	Kasımpaşa	L 0-3	
28/09	a	Bursaspor	L 0-2	
04/10	h	Beşiktaş	L 1-2	Gekas
18/10	a	Akhisar	L 0-1	
23/10	h	Kayserispor	L 1-3	Gekas
29/10	a	Galatasaray	L 0-4	
06/11	h	Osmanlıspor	L 0-1	
22/11	a	Konyaspor	L 2-3	Emre Güral, Engin
28/11	h	Mersin	W 3-2	og (Mitrović), Emre Güral, Engin
07/12	a	Trabzonspor	L 1-3	Pinto
12/12	h	Gaziantepspor	L 1-2	Emre Güral
20/12	a	İstanbul Başakşehir	L 1-2	Emre Güral
28/12	h	Gençlerbirliği	W 2-0	Engin, Emre Güral

2016

18/01	h	Fenerbahçe	L 0-3	
24/01	a	Sivasspor	W 2-1	Méyé, Engin
07/02	a	Rizespor	D 1-1	Emre Güral (p)
14/02	h	Antalyaspor	W 3-2	Kaan, Emre Güral (p), Méyé
20/02	a	Kasımpaşa	L 1-2	Emre Güral
27/02	h	Bursaspor	L 0-1	
07/03	a	Beşiktaş	L 1-3	Hadžić
13/03	h	Akhisar	D 3-3	Nadir, Engin 2
18/03	a	Kayserispor	D 0-0	
02/04	h	Galatasaray	W 4-3	Bokila, Nadir, Hadžić, Kaan
09/04	a	Osmanlıspor	D 0-0	
16/04	h	Konyaspor	L 1-2	Nadir
24/04	a	Mersin	W 2-1	Murat, Okriashvili
30/04	h	Trabzonspor	W 1-0	Engin (p)
07/05	a	Gaziantepspor	D 1-1	Nadir (p)
14/05	h	İstanbul Başakşehir	W 1-0	Okriashvili
19/05	a	Gençlerbirliği	L 1-3	Murat

No	Name	Nat	DoB	Pos	Aps	(s)	Gls
30	Jerry Akaminko	GHA	02/05/88	D	4	(1)	
1	Ali Şaşal Vural		10/07/90	G	4	(1)	
6	Alpaslan Öztürk		16/07/93	M	9	(6)	
3	Anıl Karaer		04/07/88	D	15	(3)	
13	Nassim Ben Khalifa	SUI	13/01/92	A	8	(3)	
4	Birol Parlak		01/03/90	D	11	(2)	
25	Ruud Boffin	BEL	05/11/87	G	30		
35	Jeremy Bokila	COD	14/11/88	A	4	(9)	1
92	Goran Čaušić	SRB	05/05/92	M	20	(3)	
11	Matias Defederico	ARG	23/08/89	M	7	(4)	
7	Dorukhan Toköz		21/05/96	D	2	(2)	
22	Dossa Júnior	CYP	28/07/86	D	5		
23	Emre Güngör		01/08/84	D	17	(1)	
7	Emre Güral		05/04/89	A	13	(8)	9
9	Engin Bekdemir		07/02/92	M	23	(4)	7
18	Theofanis Gekas	GRE	23/05/80	A	10		5
88	Anel Hadžić	BIH	16/08/89	M	13	(2)	2
68	İshak Doğan		09/08/90	D	2		
21	Jordi Figueras	ESP	16/05/87	D	16		
17	Kaan Kanak		06/10/90	D	25	(5)	3
65	Kamil Ahmet Çörekçi		01/02/92	D	25	(1)	
66	Kıvanç Karakaş		03/03/85	M	9	(4)	
45	Vladyslav Kulach	UKR	07/05/93	A	2	(2)	
10	Raheem Lawal	NGA	04/05/90	M	10	(1)	
96	Mehmet Feyzi Yıldırım		30/01/98	M	1	(1)	
99	Axel Méyé	GAB	06/06/95	A	11	(5)	2
94	Cédric Mongongu	COD	22/06/89	D		(1)	
9	Muarem Muarem	MKD	22/10/88	M		(1)	
77	Murat Uçar		01/08/91	A	4	(3)	2
27	Nadir Çiftçi		12/02/92	A	11	(1)	4
80	Tornike Okriashvili	GEO	01/02/92	M	6	(5)	2
8	Onur Bayramoğlu		04/01/90	M	6	(4)	
60	Özgür Çek		03/01/91	M	3	(1)	
15	Sebastián Pinto	CHI	02/02/86	A	5	(8)	1
5	Sezgin Coşkun		23/08/84	D	20	(1)	
28	Nzuzi Toko	COD	20/12/90	M	18		

TURKEY

Fenerbahçe SK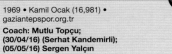

1907 • Şükrü Saraçoğlu (50,509) •
fenerbahce.org
Major honours
*Turkish League (19) 1959, 1961, 1964, 1965, 1968,
1970, 1974, 1975, 1978, 1983, 1985, 1989, 1996,
2001, 2004, 2005, 2007, 2011, 2014; Turkish Cup (6)
1968, 1974, 1979, 1983, 2012, 2013*
Coach: Vítor Pereira (POR)

2015

14/08	h	Eskişehirspor	W 2-0	Sow, Fernandão
23/08	a	Rizespor	D 1-1	Van Persie
30/08	h	Antalyaspor	W 2-1	Nani 2
13/09	a	Kasımpaşa	W 1-0	Souza
20/09	h	Bursaspor	W 2-1	Nani, Van Persie
27/09	a	Beşiktaş	L 2-3	og (Tošić), Van Persie
04/10	h	Akhisar	D 2-2	Fernandão 2
18/10	a	Kayserispor	W 1-0	Van Persie
25/10	h	Galatasaray	D 1-1	Diego
29/10	a	Osmanlıspor	W 1-0	Alper
08/11	h	Konyaspor	W 1-0	Fernandão
21/11	a	Mersin	W 3-1	Hasan Ali, Nani, Van Persie
30/11	h	Trabzonspor	W 2-0	Nani, Fernandão
06/12	a	Gaziantepspor	D 2-2	Gökhan, Alper
13/12	h	İstanbul Başakşehir	W 1-0	Nani
20/12	a	Gençlerbirliği	W 1-0	Fernandão
28/12	h	Sivasspor	W 2-1	Van Persie, Kjær

2016

18/01	a	Eskişehirspor	W 3-0	Fernandão 2 (1p), Van Persie
24/01	h	Rizespor	W 2-1	Fernandão 2 (2p)
05/02	a	Antalyaspor	L 2-4	Bruno Alves, Van Persie (p)
12/02	h	Kasımpaşa	W 3-1	Diego, Van Persie (p), Alper
20/02	a	Bursaspor	D 0-0	
29/02	h	Beşiktaş	W 2-0	Volkan Şen, Nani
06/03	a	Akhisar	W 3-0	Şener, Volkan Şen, Fernandão
13/03	h	Kayserispor	W 1-0	Van Persie
03/04	h	Osmanlıspor	D 0-0	
09/04	a	Konyaspor	L 1-2	Fernandão
13/04	a	Galatasaray	D 0-0	
17/04	h	Mersin	W 4-1	Volkan Şen 2, Fernandão, Van Persie
24/04	a	Trabzonspor	W 4-0	Alper, Volkan Şen, Nani, Van Persie
01/05	h	Gaziantepspor	W 3-0	Kjær, Van Persie 2
09/05	a	İstanbul Başakşehir	L 1-2	Mehmet Topal
15/05	h	Gençlerbirliği	W 2-1	Alper, Van Persie 2
19/05	a	Sivasspor	D 2-2	Ba, Raul Meireles

No	Name	Nat	DoB	Pos	Aps	(s)	Gls
26	Alper Potuk		08/04/91	M	17	(10)	4
53	Abdoulaye Ba	SEN	01/01/91	D	6		1
22	Bruno Alves	POR	27/11/81	D	26		1
88	Caner Erkin		04/10/88	D	9	(4)	
10	Diego	BRA	28/02/85	M	19	(9)	2
40	Fabiano	BRA	29/02/88	G	2		
9	Fernandão	BRA	27/03/87	A	20	(12)	13
77	Gökhan Gönül		04/01/85	D	21	(1)	1
41	Hakan Çinemre		14/02/94	D			
3	Hasan Ali Kaldırım		09/12/89	D	25	(1)	1
24	Michal Kadlec	CZE	13/12/84	D	9	(1)	
4	Simon Kjær	DEN	26/03/89	D	28		2
50	Lazar Marković	SRB	02/03/94	M	10	(4)	
5	Mehmet Topal		03/03/86	M	31	(2)	1
38	Mehmet Topuz		07/09/83	M		(3)	
35	Melih Okutan		01/07/96	M		(1)	
17	Nani	POR	17/11/86	A	25	(3)	8
8	Ozan Tufan		23/03/95	M	9	(17)	
28	Ramazan Civelek		22/01/96	M	1	(1)	
14	Raul Meireles	POR	17/03/83	M	5	(6)	1
19	Şener Özbayraklı		23/01/90	D	13	(1)	1
6	Souza	BRA	11/02/89	M	30	(1)	1
7	Moussa Sow	SEN	19/01/86	A	1	(1)	1
15	Uygar Mert Zeybek		04/06/95	M		(1)	
11	Robin van Persie	NED	06/08/83	A	20	(11)	16
1	Volkan Demirel		27/10/81	G	32		
20	Volkan Şen		07/07/87	M	15	(10)	5

Galatasaray AŞ

1905 • Türk Telekom Arena (52,600) •
galatasaray.org
Major honours
*UEFA Cup (1) 2000; UEFA Super Cup (1) 2000; Turkish
League (20) 1962, 1963, 1969, 1971, 1972, 1973,
1987, 1988, 1993, 1994, 1997, 1998, 1999, 2000,
2002, 2006, 2008, 2012, 2013, 2015; Turkish Cup (17)
1963, 1964, 1965, 1966, 1973, 1976, 1982, 1985, 1991,
1993, 1996, 1999, 2000, 2005, 2014, 2015, 2016*
**Coach: Hamza Hamzaoğlu;
(19/11/15) (Cláudio Taffarel (BRA));
(26/11/15) Mustafa Denizli;
(01/03/16) (Orhan Atik);
(16/03/16) Jan Olde Riekerink (NED)**

2015

15/08	a	Sivasspor	D 2-2	Burak, Podolski
24/08	h	Osmanlıspor	L 1-2	Selçuk
29/08	a	Konyaspor	W 4-1	Burak, Semih, Sneijder 2
12/09	h	Mersin	D 1-1	Podolski
19/09	a	Trabzonspor	W 1-0	og (Mbia)
26/09	h	Gaziantepspor	W 2-1	Podolski, Umut
03/10	a	İstanbul Başakşehir	W 2-0	Podolski, Umut
17/10	h	Gençlerbirliği	W 4-1	Bilal, Chedjou, Yasin, Burak (1)
25/10	a	Fenerbahçe	D 1-1	Olcan
29/10	h	Eskişehirspor	W 4-0	Selçuk, Burak 2 (1p), Bilal
07/11	a	Rizespor	L 3-4	Sneijder, Podolski, Olcan
21/11	h	Antalyaspor	D 3-3	Yasin, Podolski, Selçuk
29/11	a	Kasımpaşa	D 2-2	Burak, Hakan
04/12	h	Bursaspor	W 3-0	Podolski, Yasin, Burak
14/12	a	Beşiktaş	L 1-2	Sneijder
20/12	h	Akhisar	W 3-2	Umut, Podolski, Yasin
27/12	a	Kayserispor	D 1-1	Sinan

2016

16/01	h	Sivasspor	W 3-1	Selçuk (p), Sinan, Burak (p)
23/01	a	Osmanlıspor	L 2-3	Burak, Sneijder
06/02	h	Konyaspor	D 0-0	
13/02	a	Mersin	L 1-2	Podolski
21/02	h	Trabzonspor	W 2-1	Podolski, Selçuk (p)
28/02	a	Gaziantepspor	L 0-2	
06/03	h	İstanbul Başakşehir	D 3-3	Yasin 2, Selçuk, Semih
13/03	a	Gençlerbirliği	D 1-1	Selçuk (p)
02/04	a	Eskişehirspor	L 3-4	Bilal, Yasin, Semih
09/04	h	Rizespor	D 1-1	Emre
13/04	h	Fenerbahçe	D 0-0	
16/04	a	Antalyaspor	L 2-4	og (Diego Ângelo), Umut
24/04	h	Kasımpaşa	W 4-1	Bilal, Podolski 2, Selçuk
29/04	a	Bursaspor	D 1-1	Olcan
08/05	h	Beşiktaş	L 0-1	
15/05	a	Akhisar	W 2-1	Selçuk 2 (2p)
19/05	h	Kayserispor	W 6-0	Podolski, Sinan 3, Bilal, Selçuk

No	Name	Nat	DoB	Pos	Aps	(s)	Gls
13	Alex Telles	BRA	15/12/92	D	2		
5	Bilal Kısa		22/06/83	M	13	(9)	5
17	Burak Yılmaz		15/07/85	A	12	(3)	9
23	Lionel Carole	FRA	12/04/91	D	16	(3)	
99	Cenk Gönen		21/02/88	G	1		
21	Aurélien Chedjou	CMR	20/06/85	D	18	(1)	1
64	Jason Denayer	BEL	28/06/95	D	15	(2)	
15	Ryan Donk	NED	30/03/86	M	8	(6)	
52	Emre Çolak		20/05/91	M	13	(5)	1
3	Felipe Melo	BRA	26/06/83	M	1	(1)	
16	Koray Günter	GER	16/08/94	D	6	(3)	
22	Hakan Balta		23/03/83	D	27		1
6	Jem Karacan		21/02/89	M	1	(1)	
12	José Rodríguez	ESP	16/12/94	M	9	(5)	
27	Martin Linnes	NOR	20/09/91	D	9	(1)	
1	Fernando Muslera	URU	16/06/86	G	33		
29	Olcan Adın		30/09/85	M	21	(6)	3
11	Lukas Podolski	GER	04/06/85	A	29	(1)	13
55	Sabri Sarıoğlu		26/07/84	D	20	(7)	
8	Selçuk İnan		10/02/85	M	28		11
26	Semih Kaya		24/02/91	D	18	(3)	2
19	Sinan Gümüş		15/01/94	M	5	(10)	5
10	Wesley Sneijder	NED	09/06/84	M	24	(1)	5
38	Tarık Çamdal		24/03/91	D	2	(6)	
9	Umut Bulut		15/03/83	A	17	(10)	4
34	Volkan Pala		24/02/97	A		(3)	
7	Yasin Öztekin		19/03/87	M	26	(1)	7

Gaziantepspor

1969 • Kamil Ocak (16,981) •
gaziantepspor.org.tr
**Coach: Mutlu Topçu;
(30/04/16) (Serhat Kandemirli);
(05/05/16) Sergen Yalçın**

2015

16/08	h	Kasımpaşa	L 0-3	
23/08	a	Bursaspor	W 1-0	Muhammet
28/08	h	Beşiktaş	L 0-4	
12/09	a	Akhisar	D 0-0	
20/09	h	Kayserispor	W 1-0	Muhammet (p)
26/09	a	Galatasaray	L 1-2	Muhammet
03/10	h	Osmanlıspor	W 2-1	Muhammet, Chibuike
17/10	a	Konyaspor	L 1-2	Erdem
24/10	h	Mersin	W 1-0	Larsson
28/10	a	Trabzonspor	D 2-2	Orkan, Larsson
01/11	h	Sivasspor	L 0-3	
23/11	h	İstanbul Başakşehir	L 0-1	
29/11	a	Gençlerbirliği	D 2-2	Muhammet, Camara
06/12	h	Fenerbahçe	D 2-2	Camara, Muhammet (p)
12/12	a	Eskişehirspor	W 2-1	Chibuike, Mustafa
19/12	h	Rizespor	W 2-0	Larsson, Orkan
26/12	a	Antalyaspor	D 0-0	

2016

16/01	a	Kasımpaşa	W 2-1	Chibuike (p), Muhammet
24/01	h	Bursaspor	L 2-3	Chibuike 2
07/02	a	Beşiktaş	L 0-4	
14/02	h	Akhisar	L 0-1	
21/02	a	Kayserispor	D 2-2	Putilo, İlhan
28/02	h	Galatasaray	W 2-0	Emre, Larsson
05/03	a	Osmanlıspor	D 1-1	Orkan
12/03	h	Konyaspor	D 0-1	
20/03	h	Mersin	D 0-1	
02/04	h	Trabzonspor	L 0-1	
08/04	h	Sivasspor	L 0-1	
17/04	a	İstanbul Başakşehir	L 1-4	Arokoyo
25/04	h	Gençlerbirliği	L 1-3	Putilo
01/05	a	Fenerbahçe	L 0-3	
07/05	h	Eskişehirspor	D 1-1	Elyasa
14/05	a	Rizespor	L 0-1	
19/05	h	Antalyaspor	W 2-0	İldiz, Abdülkadir

No	Name	Nat	DoB	Pos	Aps	(s)	Gls
5	Abdülkadir Kayalı		30/01/91	M	15	(7)	1
22	Abuda	BRA	22/01/89	M	25	(3)	
67	Alpay Koçaklı		19/09/98	M		(1)	
68	Alperen Uysal		01/01/94	G	1		
15	Gbenga Arokoyo	NGA	01/11/92	D	12	(3)	1
26	Barış Yardımcı		16/08/92	D	31		
91	Bora Sevim		17/02/84	G	1	(1)	
9	Demba Camara	GUI	07/11/94	A	7	(5)	2
11	John Chibuike	NGA	10/10/89	M	27	(5)	5
55	Doğanay Kılıç		08/06/96	M	1	(1)	
3	Elyasa Süme		13/08/83	D	31	1	1
6	Emre Nefiz		24/11/94	M	5	(6)	1
6	Erdem Şen		05/01/89	M	14	(1)	1
16	Ferhat Ayaz		04/10/94	M		(3)	
33	Prince Gouano	FRA	24/12/93	D	12		
44	Habib Habibou	CTA	16/04/87	A	6	(3)	
41	Hakan Çinemre		14/02/94	D	1	(4)	
78	Hürriyet Güçer		25/10/81	M	3	(6)	
20	Muhammet İldiz	AUT	14/05/91	M	5	(7)	1
32	İlhan Parlak		18/01/87	A	3	(11)	1
35	İsmail Haktan Odabaşı		07/08/91	D		(2)	
1	Žydrūnas Karčemarskas	LTU	24/05/83	G	32		
51	Koray Arslan		01/10/83	D	10	(1)	
12	Daniel Larsson	SWE	15/01/87	M	31		4
50	Marçal	BRA	19/02/89	D	21		
2	Mehmet Sedef		05/08/87	D	4	(1)	
9	Muhammet Demir		10/01/92	A	17	(1)	7
21	Mustafa Durak		13/08/88	A	9	(9)	1
17	Orkan Çınar		29/01/96	M	20	(11)	3
24	Anton Putilo	BLR	10/06/87	M	14	(4)	2
45	Süleyman Özdamar		25/02/93	D		(1)	
4	Ognjen Vranješ	BIH	24/10/89	D	12		

Gençlerbirliği SK

1923 • 19 Mayıs (19,209) • genclerbirligi.org.tr

Major honours
Turkish Cup (2) 1987, 2001

Coach: Stuart Baxter (SCO);
(25/08/15) Naci Şensoy;
(01/09/15) Mehmet Özdilek;
(13/12/15) Mustafa Kaplan);
(24/12/15) Yılmaz Vural;
(31/12/15) İbrahim Üzülmez

2015

17/08	h	Rizespor	L	2-3	Tomić, Dimitriadis
23/08	a	Antalyaspor	L	1-3	El Kabir
29/08	h	Kasımpaşa	W	1-0	İrfan Can
12/09	a	Bursaspor	L	2-3	Djalma, El Kabir
21/09	h	Beşiktaş	D	1-1	og (Tošić)
26/09	a	Akhisar	L	0-1	
03/10	h	Kayserispor	W	2-0	El Kabir 2
17/10	a	Galatasaray	L	1-4	El Kabir
24/10	h	Osmanlıspor	W	1-0	Kulušić
30/10	a	Konyaspor	D	0-0	
06/11	h	Mersin	D	1-1	Stancu
22/11	a	Trabzonspor	L	0-1	
29/11	h	Gaziantepspor	D	2-2	Stancu, El Kabir
06/12	a	İstanbul Başakşehir	L	0-2	
13/12	a	Sivasspor	L	0-1	
20/12	h	Fenerbahçe	L	0-1	
28/12	a	Eskişehirspor	L	0-2	

2016

17/01	h	Rizespor	W	3-2	Stancu, Ahmet Çalık, Djalma
24/01	a	Antalyaspor	W	1-0	Kulušić
08/02	a	Kasımpaşa	W	1-0	İrfan Can
13/02	h	Bursaspor	W	2-0	Kulušić, El Kabir
22/02	a	Beşiktaş	L	0-1	
28/02	h	Akhisar	W	3-1	Stancu 2 (1p), Djalma
05/03	a	Kayserispor	W	2-0	Stancu (p), Djalma
13/03	h	Galatasaray	D	1-1	Stancu (p)
19/03	a	Osmanlıspor	L	1-3	Selçuk
02/04	h	Konyaspor	L	0-1	
10/04	a	Mersin	W	3-1	Stancu, Djalma 2
18/04	h	Trabzonspor	W	3-1	Politevich, Stancu, İrfan Can
25/04	a	Gaziantepspor	W	3-1	El Kabir, Selçuk, Stancu
30/04	h	İstanbul Başakşehir	D	0-0	
07/05	a	Sivasspor	L	1-2	Ahmet Çalık
15/05	a	Fenerbahçe	L	1-2	Serdar
19/05	h	Eskişehirspor	W	3-1	og (Jordi Figueras), Ahmet Oğuz, Djalma

No	Name	Nat	DoB	Pos	Aps	(s)	Gls
3	Ahmet Çalık		26/02/94	D	30		2
2	Ahmet Oğuz		16/01/93	D	29	(1)	1
99	Atabey Çiçek		24/07/95	A		(1)	
26	Walid Atta	ETH	28/08/86	D	4		
82	Aydın Karabulut		25/01/88	M	4	(7)	
9	Berat Tosun		01/01/94	A	1	(9)	
8	Panajotis Dimitriadis	SWE	12/08/86	M	6	(7)	1
30	Djalma	ANG	30/05/87	A	27		7
20	Doğa Kaya		30/06/84	M	10	(6)	
11	Moestafa El Kabir	MAR	05/10/88	A	25	(3)	8
4	Ferhat Görgülü		28/10/91	D	3	(1)	
1	Ferhat Kaplan		07/01/89	G	5		
25	Guido Koçer		15/09/88	M	2	(6)	
42	Hakan Aslantaş		26/08/85	D	2	(6)	
33	Halil İbrahim Pehlivan		21/08/93	D	2	(1)	
45	Hikmet Balioğlu		04/08/90	D		(1)	
34	Aleksandr Hleb	BLR	01/05/81	M	9	(3)	
34	Johannes Hopf	SWE	16/06/87	G	29		
17	İrfan Can Kahveci		15/07/95	M	22	(10)	3
66	Ante Kulušić	CRO	06/06/86	D	27		3
16	Guy-Michel Landel	GUI	07/07/90	M	15	(6)	
14	Iasmin Latovlevici	ROU	11/05/86	D	10		
15	Sergei Politevich	BLR	09/04/90	D	5	(1)	1
21	Selçuk Şahin		31/01/81	M	16		2
67	Serdar Gürler		14/09/91	M	4	(8)	1
22	Ólafur Ingi Skúlason	ISL	01/04/83	M	21	(4)	
88	Martin Spelmann	DEN	21/03/87	M	9	(5)	
10	Bogdan Stancu	ROU	28/06/87	A	29		10
7	Nemanja Tomić	SRB	21/01/88	M	4	(8)	1
36	Turgut Doğan Şahin		02/02/88	A		(3)	
3	Uğur Çiftçi		04/05/92	D	24	(1)	

İstanbul Başakşehir

2014 • Başakşehir Fatih Terim (17,300) •
ibfk.com.tr

Coach: Abdullah Avcı

2015

15/08	h	Antalyaspor	L	2-3	Doka Madureira, Çikalleshi
21/08	a	Kasımpaşa	L	0-1	
29/08	h	Bursaspor	W	2-1	Višća 2
13/09	a	Beşiktaş	L	0-2	
18/09	h	Akhisar	W	2-0	Mehmet, Višća
28/09	a	Kayserispor	W	1-0	Yalçın
03/10	a	Galatasaray	L	0-2	
19/10	a	Osmanlıspor	W	3-0	Yalçın, Višća, Doka Madureira
25/10	h	Konyaspor	W	4-0	Bekir, Višća 2, Mehmet
29/10	a	Mersin	D	1-1	Mehmet
07/11	h	Trabzonspor	W	1-0	Yalçın
23/11	a	Gaziantepspor	W	1-0	Çikalleshi
28/11	a	Sivasspor	D	2-2	Yalçın, Mehmet
06/12	h	Gençlerbirliği	W	2-0	Bekir, Mossoró
13/12	a	Fenerbahçe	L	0-1	
20/12	h	Eskişehirspor	W	2-1	Mehmet, Emre (p)
26/12	a	Rizespor	L	1-2	Doka Madureira

2016

17/01	a	Antalyaspor	W	2-1	Višća, Mehmet
25/01	h	Kasımpaşa	D	1-1	Višća
06/02	a	Bursaspor	D	3-3	Çikalleshi 2, og (Sivok)
14/02	h	Beşiktaş	D	2-2	Višća, Mahmut
21/02	a	Akhisar	D	0-0	
26/02	h	Kayserispor	W	1-0	Bekir
06/03	a	Galatasaray	D	3-3	Višća 2, Mehmet
12/03	h	Osmanlıspor	L	2-3	Mehmet, Višća
20/03	a	Konyaspor	D	1-1	Çikalleshi
03/04	h	Mersin	W	3-0	Višća (p), Mossoró, Hakan
10/04	a	Trabzonspor	D	1-1	Yalçın
17/04	a	Gaziantepspor	W	4-1	Mehmet, Yalçın, Emre (p), Višća (p)
23/04	h	Sivasspor	D	2-2	Emre (p), Napoleoni
30/04	a	Gençlerbirliği	D	0-0	
09/05	h	Fenerbahçe	W	2-1	Višća 2
14/05	a	Eskişehirspor	W	2-1	Napoleoni, Çikalleshi
18/05	h	Rizespor	W	1-0	Višća

No	Name	Nat	DoB	Pos	Aps	(s)	Gls
39	Alparslan Erdem		11/12/88	D	22	(2)	
17	Stéphane Badji	SEN	29/05/90	M	11	(5)	
14	Bekir Irtegün		20/04/84	D	31		3
34	Cenk Ahmet Alkılıç		09/12/87	M	7	(9)	
10	Sokol Çikalleshi	ALB	27/07/90	A	8	(19)	6
25	Doka Madureira	BRA	11/02/84	A	25	(7)	3
25	Emre Belözoğlu		07/09/80	M	21	(5)	3
67	Enver Cenk Şahin		30/04/95	M	8	(9)	
4	Alexandru Epureanu	MDA	27/09/86	D	13	(1)	
87	Ferhat Öztorun		08/05/87	D	12	(1)	
66	Gençer Cansev		04/01/89	D	1		
20	Hakan Özmert		03/06/85	M	2	(4)	1
11	Hüseyin Altuğ Taş		10/01/94	A		(1)	
5	Mahmut Tekdemir		20/01/88	D	31		1
9	Mehmet Batdal		24/02/86	A	26	(5)	9
8	Mossoró	BRA	04/07/83	M	29	(5)	2
18	Stefano Napoleoni	ITA	26/06/86	A	2	(8)	2
4	Rajko Rotman	SVN	19/03/89	M	6	(10)	
4	Sedat Ağçay		22/09/81	M	1		
23	Semih Şentürk		29/04/83	A		(8)	
33	Uğur Uçar		05/04/87	D	16	(3)	
7	Edin Višća	BIH	17/02/90	M	34		17
1	Volkan Babacan		11/08/88	G	34		
2	Yalçın Ayhan		01/05/82	D	34		6

Kasımpaşa SK

1921 • Recep Tayyip Erdoğan (14,234) •
kasimpasaspor.org.tr

Coach: Rıza Çalımbay

2015

16/08	a	Gaziantepspor	W	3-0	Adem, og (Barış), Del Valle
21/08	h	İstanbul Başakşehir	W	1-0	Scarione
29/08	a	Gençlerbirliği	L	0-1	
13/09	h	Fenerbahçe	L	0-1	
19/09	a	Eskişehirspor	W	3-0	Titi, Scarione, Derdiyok
28/09	h	Rizespor	D	1-1	Scarione
04/10	a	Antalyaspor	D	0-0	
18/10	h	Sivasspor	W	2-1	Derdiyok, André Castro
24/10	h	Bursaspor	L	0-1	
30/10	h	Beşiktaş	D	3-3	Derdiyok 2, Donk
07/11	h	Akhisar	W	2-1	Scarione, Del Valle
21/11	a	Kayserispor	D	0-0	
29/11	h	Galatasaray	D	2-2	Hakan, Titi
05/12	a	Osmanlıspor	W	1-0	Tunay
12/12	h	Konyaspor	W	2-1	Derdiyok 2
19/12	a	Mersin	W	2-1	Derdiyok, Donk
26/12	h	Trabzonspor	D	1-1	Derdiyok (p)

2016

16/01	h	Gaziantepspor	L	1-2	Del Valle
25/01	a	İstanbul Başakşehir	D	1-1	Derdiyok
08/02	h	Gençlerbirliği	L	0-1	
12/02	a	Fenerbahçe	L	1-3	Malki
20/02	h	Eskişehirspor	W	2-1	Tunay, Derdiyok
27/02	a	Rizespor	L	0-2	
06/03	h	Antalyaspor	W	2-1	Hakan 2
14/03	a	Sivasspor	L	0-1	
20/03	a	Bursaspor	L	1-4	André Castro
04/04	h	Beşiktaş	W	2-1	Del Valle, Scarione
11/04	a	Akhisar	W	1-0	Scarione
17/04	h	Kayserispor	L	1-2	Derdiyok
24/04	a	Galatasaray	L	1-4	Scarione
02/05	h	Osmanlıspor	D	1-1	André Castro
09/05	a	Konyaspor	L	0-2	
15/05	h	Mersin	W	7-0	Adem, Koita, Scarione 3, André Castro, Hakan
19/05	a	Trabzonspor	W	6-0	Derdiyok 2, Del Valle, Scarione, Adem, Titi

No	Name	Nat	DoB	Pos	Aps	(s)	Gls
87	Abdullah Durak		01/04/87	M	8	(12)	
10	Adem Büyük		30/08/87	A	25	(6)	3
8	André Castro	POR	02/04/88	M	32	(1)	4
17	Aydın Yılmaz		29/01/88	M	3	(4)	
3	Vasil Bozhikov	BUL	02/06/88	D	11	(3)	
28	Yonathan Del Valle	VEN	28/05/90	M	20	(13)	5
9	Eren Derdiyok	SUI	12/06/88	A	24	(7)	13
6	Ryan Donk	NED	30/03/86	M	15	(1)	2
34	Eray Birniçan		20/07/88	G	4		
20	Erhan Kartal		01/03/93	D	6		
14	Ferhat Kiraz		02/01/89	A	3	(10)	
37	Hakan Arslan		18/07/88	D	16	(13)	4
15	Andreas Isaksson	SWE	03/10/81	G	13		
99	Bengali-Fodé Koita	FRA	21/10/90	A	4	(7)	1
16	Sanharib Malki	SYR	01/03/84	A	1	(8)	1
22	Kennem Omeruo	NGA	17/10/93	D	25		
12	David Pavelka	CZE	18/05/91	M	6	(3)	
6	Strahil Popov	BUL	31/08/90	D	13		
1	Ramazan Köse		12/05/88	G	17		
11	Ezequiel Scarione	ARG	14/07/85	A	27	(1)	11
4	Titi	BRA	12/03/88	D	33		3
7	Tunay Torun		21/04/90	M	23	(8)	2
31	Olivier Veigneau	FRA	16/07/85	D	28	(2)	
88	Veysel Sarı		25/07/88	D	17	(3)	

Kayserispor

1966 • Kadir Has (32,864) • kayserispor.org.tr
Major honours
Turkish Cup (1) 2008
Coach: Tolunay Kafkas;
(03/03/16) (Ertuğrul Seçme);
(10/03/16) Hakan Kutlu

2015

16/08	a	Osmanlıspor	D	1-1	Sinan
22/08	h	Konyaspor	D	1-1	Deniz
29/08	a	Mersin	W	2-1	Ömer, Zeki
14/09	h	Trabzonspor	L	0-1	
20/09	a	Gaziantepspor	L	0-1	
28/09	h	İstanbul Başakşehir	L	0-1	
03/10	a	Gençlerbirliği	L	0-2	
18/10	h	Fenerbahçe	L	0-1	
23/10	a	Eskişehirspor	W	3-1	Biseswar (p), Derley, Oğulcan
28/10	h	Rizespor	D	0-0	
07/11	a	Antalyaspor	D	1-1	Sow
21/11	h	Kasımpaşa	D	0-0	
27/11	a	Bursaspor	W	2-1	Derley, Zeki
05/12	h	Beşiktaş	L	1-2	Biseswar
13/12	h	Akhisar	W	3-2	Biseswar 2, Derley
20/12	a	Sivasspor	D	0-0	
27/12	h	Galatasaray	D	1-1	Mabiala

2016

16/01	h	Osmanlıspor	W	1-0	Derley
23/01	a	Konyaspor	L	0-1	
06/02	h	Mersin	L	0-1	
15/02	a	Trabzonspor	L	1-2	Zeki
21/02	h	Gaziantepspor	D	2-2	Deniz, Simić
26/02	a	İstanbul Başakşehir	L	0-1	
05/03	h	Gençlerbirliği	L	0-2	
13/03	a	Fenerbahçe	L	0-1	
18/03	h	Eskişehirspor	D	0-0	
04/04	a	Rizespor	D	0-0	
10/04	h	Antalyaspor	D	0-0	
17/04	a	Kasımpaşa	W	2-1	og (Ramazan), Sinan
22/04	h	Bursaspor	W	2-1	Sinan, Furkan
30/04	h	Beşiktaş	L	0-4	
08/05	a	Akhisar	D	1-1	Derley
14/05	h	Sivasspor	D	1-1	Biseswar
19/05	a	Galatasaray	L	0-6	

No	Name	Nat	DoB	Pos	Aps	(s)	Gls
25	Abdülaziz Demircan		05/02/91	G	6		
16	Ali Ahamada	FRA	19/08/91	G	13		
24	Yakubu Aiyegbeni	NGA	22/11/82	A	3	(9)	
8	Barış Özbek		14/09/86	M	1	(3)	
3	Berkan Emir		06/02/88	D	15	(4)	
2	Birol Parlak		01/03/90	D	3		
21	Diego Biseswar	NED	08/03/88	M	30	(2)	5
40	Cem Can		01/04/81	D	7	(6)	
11	Deniz Türüç		29/01/93	M	23	(8)	2
33	Derley	BRA	29/12/87	A	19	(4)	5
10	Diego Lopes	BRA	03/05/94	M	18	(5)	
20	Furkan Özçal		05/09/90	M	26	(3)	1
1	Hakan Arıkan		17/08/82	G	8		
5	İbrahim Dağaşan		15/06/84	M	5		
27	Kayacan Erdoğan		21/03/88	G	7		
6	Larrys Mabiala	COD	08/10/87	D	28	(2)	1
30	Mert Özyıldırım		28/02/95	D		(1)	
35	Srdjan Mijailović	SRB	10/11/93	M	23	(5)	
17	Mustafa Akbaş		30/05/90	D	26	(2)	
19	Oğulcan Çağlayan		22/03/96	A	12	(13)	1
38	Ömer Bayram		27/07/91	M	27	(2)	1
22	Marko Simić	MNE	16/06/87	D	17	(7)	1
23	Samba Sow	MLI	29/04/89	M	16		1
92	Adnane Tighadouini	MAR	30/11/92	M		(7)	
9	Willian	BRA	07/12/91	A	7	(1)	
61	Zeki Yavru		05/09/91	D	30		3

Konyaspor

1981 • Büyükşehir (41,981) • konyaspor.org.tr
Coach: Aykut Kocaman

2015

16/08	h	Akhisar	D	1-1	Dossa Júnior
22/08	a	Kayserispor	D	1-1	Vuković
29/08	h	Galatasaray	L	1-4	Meha
13/09	a	Osmanlıspor	W	2-1	Sissoko, Meha
19/09	h	Sivasspor	D	0-0	
27/09	h	Mersin	W	2-0	Traoré, Holmén
02/10	a	Trabzonspor	W	2-1	Meha (p), Traoré
17/10	h	Gaziantepspor	W	2-1	Bajić, Holmén
25/10	a	İstanbul Başakşehir	L	0-4	
30/10	h	Gençlerbirliği	D	0-0	
08/11	a	Fenerbahçe	L	0-1	
22/11	h	Eskişehirspor	W	3-2	Abdülkerim, Holmén, Meha
27/11	a	Rizespor	D	0-0	
05/12	h	Antalyaspor	W	3-2	Mbamba, Bajić, Ali Çamdalı
12/12	a	Kasımpaşa	L	1-2	Ömer Ali
19/12	h	Bursaspor	W	1-0	Bajić
27/12	a	Beşiktaş	L	0-4	

2016

16/01	h	Akhisar	W	2-0	Vuković, Rangelov
23/01	h	Kayserispor	W	1-0	Vuković (p)
06/02	a	Galatasaray	D	0-0	
13/02	h	Osmanlıspor	D	1-1	Ömer Ali
19/02	h	Sivasspor	W	2-1	Traoré, Skubic
27/02	a	Mersin	W	2-0	Traoré, Bajić
06/03	h	Trabzonspor	W	2-0	Traoré, Ömer Ali
12/03	a	Gaziantepspor	W	1-0	Holmén
20/03	h	İstanbul Başakşehir	D	1-1	Volkan
02/04	a	Gençlerbirliği	W	1-0	Rangelov
09/04	h	Fenerbahçe	W	2-1	Rangelov, Ali Çamdalı
16/04	a	Eskişehirspor	W	2-1	Bajić (p), Volkan
24/04	h	Rizespor	W	3-1	Halil İbrahim, Vuković, Rangelov
01/05	a	Antalyaspor	L	0-1	
09/05	h	Kasımpaşa	W	2-0	og (Omeruo), Traoré
14/05	a	Bursaspor	D	1-1	Halil İbrahim
18/05	h	Beşiktaş	W	2-1	Traoré, Holmén

No	Name	Nat	DoB	Pos	Aps	(s)	Gls
42	Abdülkerim Bardakçı		04/09/94	D	4	(3)	1
8	Ali Çamdalı		22/02/84	M	33		2
4	Ali Turan		06/09/83	D	28	(1)	
25	Riad Bajić	BIH	06/05/94	A	19	(13)	5
3	Dossa Júnior	CYP	28/07/86	D	4		1
21	Barry Douglas	SCO	04/09/89	D	11	(1)	
18	Amir Hadziahmetović	BIH	08/03/97	M	2	(3)	
61	Halil İbrahim Sönmez		01/10/90	A	4	(14)	2
6	Samuel Holmén	SWE	28/06/84	M	26	(4)	5
1	Kaya Tarakçı		23/04/81	G	3		
11	Kenan Özer		16/08/87	M		(1)	
10	Ciprian Marica	ROU	02/10/85	A		(1)	
14	Marc Mbamba	CMR	15/10/88	M	7	(6)	1
17	Alban Meha	ALB	26/04/86	M	24		4
54	Mehmet Uslu		25/02/88	D	20	(1)	
7	Ömer Ali Şahiner		02/01/92	M	28	(5)	3
77	Ömer Şişmanoğlu		01/08/89	A	3	(8)	
9	Dimitar Rangelov	BUL	09/02/83	A	22	(7)	4
23	Selçuk Alibaz		03/12/89	M		(5)	
5	Selim Ay		31/07/91	D	4	(8)	
30	Serkan Kırıntılı		15/02/85	G	31		
33	Ibrahim Sissoko	CIV	29/11/91	A	5	(3)	1
89	Nejc Skubic	SVN	13/06/89	D	17		1
12	Abdou Traoré	BFA	28/12/88	M	25	(5)	7
80	Uğur İnceman		25/05/81	M	6	(5)	
20	Vedat Bora		27/01/95	M	4	(3)	
2	Volkan Fındıklı		13/10/90	D	12	(4)	2
26	Jagoš Vuković	SRB	10/06/88	D	32		4

Mersin İdman Yurdu

1925 • Mersin Arena (25,497) •
mersinidmanyurdu.org.tr
Coach: Mesut Bakkal;
(22/09/15) Bülent Korkmaz;
(05/01/16) Hakan Kutlu;
(12/01/16) Nurullah Sağlam;
(17/01/16) Ümit Özat;
(06/05/16) Serkan Damla

2015

16/08	h	Beşiktaş	L	2-5	Nakoulma 2
22/08	a	Akhisar	L	0-2	
29/08	h	Kayserispor	L	1-2	Welliton
12/09	a	Galatasaray	D	1-1	Welliton
18/09	h	Osmanlıspor	L	0-4	
27/09	a	Konyaspor	L	0-2	
02/10	a	Sivasspor	D	2-2	Gökçek Vederson (p), Pedriel
19/10	h	Trabzonspor	W	3-2	Nakoulma 2, Gökçek Vederson
24/10	a	Gaziantepspor	L	0-1	
29/10	h	İstanbul Başakşehir	D	1-1	Pedriel
06/11	a	Gençlerbirliği	D	1-1	Pedriel
21/11	h	Fenerbahçe	L	1-3	Nakoulma
28/11	a	Eskişehirspor	L	2-3	Welliton, Mitrović
06/12	h	Rizespor	W	3-0	Gökçek Vederson (p), Serkan, Welliton
12/12	a	Antalyaspor	L	2-3	Mitrović (p), Pedriel
19/12	a	Kasımpaşa	L	1-2	Servet
27/12	a	Bursaspor	L	1-2	Welliton

2016

23/01	h	Akhisar	D	0-0	
06/02	a	Kayserispor	W	1-0	Gökçek Vederson (p)
13/02	h	Galatasaray	W	2-1	Nakoulma, Güven
17/02	a	Beşiktaş	L	0-1	
21/02	h	Osmanlıspor	L	1-3	Khalili
27/02	h	Konyaspor	L	0-2	
04/03	h	Sivasspor	W	1-0	Welliton
11/03	a	Trabzonspor	L	0-1	
20/03	h	Gaziantepspor	D	0-0	
03/04	a	İstanbul Başakşehir	L	0-3	
10/04	h	Gençlerbirliği	L	1-3	Pedriel
17/04	a	Fenerbahçe	l	1-4	Güven
24/04	h	Eskişehirspor	L	1-2	Mehmet Taş
29/04	a	Rizespor	l	0-2	
08/05	h	Antalyaspor	L	0-1	
15/05	a	Kasımpaşa	L	0-7	
18/05	h	Bursaspor	L	2-5	Mahmut, Gökhan

No	Name	Nat	DoB	Pos	Aps	(s)	Gls
96	Ahmet Taner Çukadar		04/08/98	D		(4)	
42	Berkan Afşarlı		01/03/91	M	1	(4)	
33	Efe Özarslan		29/03/90	D	1	(1)	
94	Emrah Özyaylız		01/12/94	M		(2)	
39	Eren Tozlu		27/12/90	A	13	(5)	
99	Márkó Futács	HUN	22/02/90	A	1	(3)	
6	Gökçek Vederson		22/07/81	D	26		4
66	Gökhan Akkan		30/08/98	D	5	(2)	1
7	Güven Varol		02/06/81	M	23	(4)	2
92	Hakan Olkan		09/01/92	D	4	(1)	
95	Hasan Daş		04/01/95	G		(1)	
55	Abdul Khalili	SWE	07/06/92	M	22	(1)	1
98	Mahmut Metin		12/07/94	M	4		1
46	Mehmet Ali Kaçar		18/01/98	A		(1)	
4	Mehmet Enes Sığırcı		24/02/93	D	2	(2)	
25	Mehmet Taş		20/03/91	M	13	(8)	1
1	Nikolay Mihaylov	BUL	28/06/88	G	3		
15	Milan Mitrović	SRB	02/07/88	D	25	(4)	2
90	Muammer Yıldırım		14/09/90	G	26		
5	Murat Ceylan		02/03/88	M	25	(2)	
22	Prejuce Nakoulma	BFA	21/04/87	A	25	(2)	6
23	Nihat Şahin		15/09/89	G	5		
72	Nurullah Kaya		20/07/86	A	7	(2)	
13	Oktay Delibalta		27/10/85	M	11	(4)	
58	Ricardo Pedriel	BOL	19/01/87	M	16	(11)	5
3	Loret Sadiku	KOS	28/07/91	D	29		
30	Serkan Balcı		22/08/83	D	28		1
88	Serol Demirhan		05/12/88	M	7	(3)	
76	Servet Çetin		17/03/81	D	14		1
17	Sinan Kaloğlu		10/06/81	A	2	(14)	
47	Tekin Oğrak		13/04/94	M	3		
10	Tita	BRA	20/07/81	M	14	(11)	
11	Welliton	BRA	22/10/86	A	19	(2)	6

Osmanlıspor

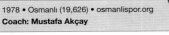

1978 • Osmanlı (19,626) • osmanlispor.org
Coach: Mustafa Akçay

2015

16/08	h	Kayserispor	D	1-1	Umut
24/08	a	Galatasaray	W	2-1	Serdar, Torje
30/08	a	Sivasspor	D	1-1	Ndiaye
13/09	h	Konyaspor	L	1-2	Ndiaye
18/09	a	Mersin	W	4-0	Webó, Ndiaye 3
26/09	h	Trabzonspor	W	3-1	Torje, Erdal, Serdar
03/10	a	Gaziantepspor	L	1-2	Erdal (p)
19/10	h	İstanbul Başakşehir	L	0-3	
24/10	a	Gençlerbirliği	L	0-1	
29/10	h	Fenerbahçe	L	0-1	
06/11	a	Eskişehirspor	W	2-0	Tiago Pinto, Serdar
22/11	h	Rizespor	L	0-1	
27/11	a	Antalyaspor	D	1-1	Ndiaye
05/12	h	Kasımpaşa	L	0-1	
11/12	a	Bursaspor	W	4-0	Ndiaye 2, Rusescu, Umar
21/12	h	Beşiktaş	L	2-3	Rusescu, Ndiaye
27/12	a	Akhisar	D	0-0	

2016

16/01	a	Kayserispor	L	0-1	
23/01	h	Galatasaray	W	3-2	Umar 2, Musa
05/02	h	Sivasspor	W	4-0	Rusescu, Torje, Ndiaye, Mehmet
13/02	a	Konyaspor	D	1-1	Rusescu
21/02	h	Mersin	W	3-1	Rusescu, Musa, Lawal
27/02	a	Trabzonspor	W	2-1	Rusescu 2
05/03	a	Gaziantepspor	D	1-1	Rusescu
12/03	a	İstanbul Başakşehir	W	3-2	Umar 2, Ndiaye
19/03	h	Gençlerbirliği	W	3-1	Musa, Umar, og (Uğur)
03/04	a	Fenerbahçe	D	0-0	
09/04	h	Eskişehirspor	D	0-0	
16/04	a	Rizespor	W	1-0	Rusescu
23/04	h	Antalyaspor	W	3-0	Webó 2, Erdal
02/05	a	Kasımpaşa	D	1-1	Uğur (p)
07/05	h	Bursaspor	D	3-3	Webó 2, Umar
15/05	a	Beşiktaş	L	1-3	Webó
19/05	h	Akhisar	W	1-0	Umar

No	Name	Nat	DoB	Pos	Aps	(s)	Gls
78	Ahmet Şahin		22/03/78	G	28		
1	Artur	BRA	25/01/81	G	4		
7	Bilal Aziz Özer		01/07/85	M	4	(1)	
28	Dzon Delarge	CGO	24/06/90	A	10	(5)	
11	Erdal Kılıçaslan		23/08/84	M	12	(12)	3
5	Galip Güzel		10/01/87	M		(5)	
25	Hakan Arıkan		17/08/82	G	1		
42	Hakan Aslantaş		26/08/85	D	10	(1)	
99	Hakan Canbazoğlu		28/11/87	G	1	(1)	
23	Raheem Lawal	NGA	04/05/90	M	13	(2)	1
6	Mehmet Güven		30/07/87	M	27	(4)	1
33	Muhammet Bayır		05/02/89	D	22		
35	Musa Çağıran		17/11/92	M	29		3
10	Pape Alioune Ndiaye	SEN	27/10/90	M	30	(3)	11
61	Numan Çürüksu		02/12/84	D	24	(1)	
21	Václav Procházka	CZE	08/05/84	D	1	(5)	
24	Raul Rusescu	ROU	09/07/88	A	17	(7)	9
23	Serdar Deliktaş		04/08/86	A	10	(7)	3
48	Takayuki Seto	JPN	05/02/86	M	2	(5)	
52	Bakary Soro	CIV	05/12/85	D	7	(1)	
4	Łukasz Szukała	POL	26/05/84	D	10		
15	Tiago Pinto	POR	01/02/88	D	19	(7)	1
20	Tonia Tisdell	LBR	20/03/92	M	1	(2)	
22	Gabriel Torje	ROU	22/11/89	M	19	(6)	3
17	Uğur Demirok		08/07/88	D	26		1
30	Aminu Umar	NGA	06/03/95	M	27	(1)	8
18	Umut Nayir		06/06/93	A		(7)	1
8	Avdija Vršajević	BIH	06/03/86	D	13	(3)	
9	Pierre Webó	CMR	20/01/82	A	7	(13)	6

Rizespor

1953 • Yeni Rize Şehir (15,485) •
caykurrizespor.org.tr
Coach: Hikmet Karaman

2015

17/08	a	Gençlerbirliği	W	3-2	Ahmet İlhan, Kweuke 2 (1p)
23/08	h	Fenerbahçe	D	1-1	og (Kjær)
30/08	a	Eskişehirspor	D	1-1	Kweuke
13/09	h	Sivasspor	D	1-1	Kweuke
19/09	h	Antalyaspor	W	5-1	Oboabona, Ahmet İlhan, Deniz 3
28/09	a	Kasımpaşa	D	1-1	Kweuke (p)
04/10	h	Bursaspor	L	2-3	Deniz, Kweuke (p)
18/10	a	Beşiktaş	L	0-1	
23/10	h	Akhisar	L	0-2	
28/10	a	Kayserispor	D	0-0	
07/11	h	Galatasaray	W	4-3	Mehmet 2, Kweuke, Deniz
22/11	h	Osmanlıspor	W	1-0	Kweuke
27/11	h	Konyaspor	D	0-0	
06/12	a	Mersin	L	0-3	
12/12	h	Trabzonspor	W	3-0	Kweuke, Murat, Deniz
19/12	a	Gaziantepspor	L	0-2	
26/12	h	İstanbul Başakşehir	W	2-1	Deniz, Tuszyński

2016

17/01	h	Gençlerbirliği	L	2-3	Sercan, Kweuke (p)
24/01	a	Fenerbahçe	L	1-2	Sylvestre (p)
07/02	h	Eskişehirspor	L	1-1	Mehmet
14/02	a	Sivasspor	L	1-2	Mehmet
20/02	h	Antalyaspor	L	1-2	Viera
27/02	h	Kasımpaşa	W	2-0	Deniz 2
05/03	a	Bursaspor	L	0-1	
12/03	h	Beşiktaş	L	1-2	Chevalier
18/03	a	Akhisar	D	1-1	Deniz
04/04	h	Kayserispor	D	0-0	
09/04	a	Galatasaray	D	1-1	Tuszyński
16/04	h	Osmanlıspor	L	0-1	
24/04	a	Konyaspor	L	1-3	Sylvestre (p)
29/04	h	Mersin	W	2-0	Ahmet İlhan, Mehmet
08/05	a	Trabzonspor	L	0-6	
14/05	h	Gaziantepspor	W	1-0	Deniz
18/05	a	İstanbul Başakşehir	L	0-1	

No	Name	Nat	DoB	Pos	Aps	(s)	Gls
78	Ahmet İlhan Özek		01/01/88	M	28	(5)	3
99	Teddy Chevalier	FRA	28/06/87	A	10	(13)	1
63	Deniz Kadah		02/03/86	A	27	(6)	11
10	Nika Dzalamidze	GEO	06/01/92	M	1	(4)	
11	Eren Albayrak		23/04/91	D	18	(3)	
5	Ertuğrul Ersoy		13/02/97	D	9	(2)	
23	Gökhan Akkan		01/05/95	G	1		
53	Dhurgham Ismail	IRQ	23/05/94	D	13	(7)	
1	Charles Itandje	CMR	02/11/82	G	33		
4	Koray Altınay		11/10/91	D	27	(3)	
55	Ümit Korkmaz	AUT	17/09/85	M	1	(8)	
9	Leonard Kweuke	CMR	12/07/87	A	17		10
16	Cédric Makiadi	COD	02/03/84	M	19	(1)	
17	Mehmet Akyüz		02/01/86	M	14	(18)	5
21	Murat Duruer		15/01/88	M	14	(4)	1
2	Godfrey Oboabona	NGA	16/08/90	D	31	(1)	
77	Orhan Ovacıklı		23/11/88	D	24	(2)	
6	Robin Yalçın		25/01/94	M	18	(2)	
7	Sercan Kaya		15/03/88	M	18	(4)	1
14	Ludovic Sylvestre	FRA	05/02/84	M	15	(10)	2
8	Patryk Tuszyński	POL	13/12/89	A	9	(9)	2
80	Ümit Kurt		02/05/91	D	3		
3	Ousmane Viera	CIV	21/12/86	D	25		1

Sivasspor

1967 • Sivas 4 Eylül (14,998) • sivasspor.org.tr
**Coach: Sergen Yalçın;
(25/10/15) Okan Buruk;
(06/02/16) Mesut Bakkal**

2015

15/08	h	Galatasaray	D	2-2	Chahéchouche 2 (1p)
23/08	a	Eskişehirspor	L	2-4	Dani Abalo, Batuhan
30/08	h	Osmanlıspor	D	1-1	Boye
13/09	a	Rizespor	D	1-1	Ziya
19/09	h	Konyaspor	D	0-0	
27/09	a	Antalyaspor	D	1-1	Erkan
02/10	h	Mersin	D	2-2	Boye, Koné
18/10	a	Kasımpaşa	L	1-2	Boye
24/10	h	Trabzonspor	L	0-2	
28/10	a	Bursaspor	L	0-1	
08/11	h	Gaziantepspor	W	3-0	Burhan, Eneramo, Chahéchouche
22/11	a	Beşiktaş	L	0-2	
28/11	h	İstanbul Başakşehir	D	2-2	Beykan, Chahéchouche
07/12	a	Akhisar	L	0-1	
13/12	a	Gençlerbirliği	W	1-0	Boye
20/12	h	Kayserispor	D	0-0	
28/12	a	Fenerbahçe	L	1-2	Beykan

2016

16/01	a	Galatasaray	L	1-3	Texeira
24/01	a	Eskişehirspor	L	1-2	Chahéchouche
05/02	a	Osmanlıspor	L	0-4	
14/02	h	Rizespor	W	2-1	Texeira, Hasan
19/02	a	Konyaspor	L	1-2	Burhan
28/02	h	Antalyaspor	D	0-0	
04/03	a	Mersin	L	0-1	
14/03	h	Kasımpaşa	W	1-0	Yiğit
19/03	a	Trabzonspor	L	0-1	
03/04	h	Bursaspor	L	1-2	Burhan
08/04	a	Gaziantepspor	W	1-0	Chahéchouche
16/04	h	Beşiktaş	L	1-2	Chahéchouche
23/04	a	İstanbul Başakşehir	D	2-2	Beykan 2
01/05	h	Akhisar	D	1-1	Chahéchouche
07/05	h	Gençlerbirliği	W	2-1	Chahéchouche 2 (1p)
14/05	a	Kayserispor	D	1-1	Chahéchouche
19/05	h	Fenerbahçe	D	2-2	Chahéchouche, Oumari

No	Name	Nat	DoB	Pos	Aps	(s)	Gls
66	Adem Koçak		01/09/83	M	21	(5)	
19	Jerónimo Barrales	ARG	28/01/87	A	5	(1)	
9	Batuhan Karadeniz		24/04/91	A	3	(1)	1
28	Beykan Şimşek		01/01/95	M	20	(5)	4
15	John Boye	GHA	23/04/87	D	26		4
21	Burhan Eşer		01/01/85	M	25	(3)	3
2	Çağatay Çeken		18/05/92	D	3		
92	Aatif Chahéchouche	MAR	02/07/86	M	33		12
12	Cicinho	BRA	24/06/80	D	25	(2)	
7	Dani Abalo	ESP	29/09/87	A	3	(8)	1
3	Emre Öztürk		08/08/92	D	1	(4)	
14	Michael Eneramo	NGA	26/11/85	A	8	(2)	1
39	Erkan Kaş		10/09/91	M	10	(3)	1
26	Gökhan Süzen		12/07/87	D	3	(1)	
8	Hakan Özmert		03/06/85	M	3	(4)	
99	Hasan Kabze		26/05/82	A	7	(9)	1
23	Etzaz Hussain	NOR	27/01/93	M	3	(5)	
11	İbrahim Akın		04/01/84	A	2	(10)	
16	İbrahim Öztürk		21/06/81	D	22	(4)	
6	Djakaridja Koné	BFA	22/07/86	M	16	(2)	1
1	Korcan Çelikay		31/12/87	G	3		
4	Orhan Gülle		15/01/92	M	1	(3)	
17	Joan Oumari	LIB	19/08/88	D	17		1
13	Ernestas Šetkus	LTU	25/05/85	G	31	(1)	
20	Cristian Tănase	ROU	18/02/87	M	9	(5)	
91	Mehdi Taouil	MAR	20/05/83	M	11	(5)	
27	David Texeira	URU	27/02/81	A	11	(4)	2
80	Ümit Kurt		02/05/91	M	6		
25	Yekta Kurtuluş		11/12/85	M	3	(6)	
5	Yiğit İncedemir		09/03/85	M	18	(4)	1
58	Ziya Erdal		05/01/88	D	25	(2)	1

TURKEY

Trabzonspor AŞ

1967 • Hüseyin Avni Aker (24,169) •
trabzonspor.org.tr
Major honours
Turkish League (6) 1976, 1977, 1979, 1980, 1981,
1984; Turkish Cup (8) 1977, 1978, 1984, 1992, 1995,
2003, 2004, 2010
Coach: Shota Arveladze (GEO);
(11/11/15) (Sadi Tekelioğlu);
(21/01/16) Hami Mandıralı;
(13/05/16) (Taner Yılmaz)

2015
15/08	h	Bursaspor	W	1-0	Zengin
22/08	a	Beşiktaş	W	2-1	Yusuf Erdoğan, Zengin
30/08	h	Akhisar	D	2-2	Yusuf Erdoğan, Cardozo
14/09	a	Kayserispor	W	1-0	Cardozo
19/09	h	Galatasaray	L	0-1	
26/09	a	Osmanlıspor	L	1-3	Marin
02/10	h	Konyaspor	L	1-2	Medjani
19/10	a	Mersin	L	2-3	Cardozo, Mbia
24/10	a	Sivasspor	W	2-0	Okay 2
28/10	h	Gaziantepspor	D	2-2	Aykut, Cardozo
07/11	a	İstanbul Başakşehir	L	0-1	
22/11	h	Gençlerbirliği	W	1-0	Mehmet Ekici
30/11	a	Fenerbahçe	L	0-2	
07/12	h	Eskişehirspor	W	3-1	Cardozo, Mehmet Ekici (p), Muhammet Beşir
12/12	a	Rizespor	L	0-3	
19/12	h	Antalyaspor	W	3-0	Cardozo, Mehmet Ekici (p), Mbia
26/12	a	Kasımpaşa	D	1-1	Mustafa

2016
17/01	a	Bursaspor	L	2-4	Musa, Cardozo
07/02	a	Akhisar	L	1-2	Muhammet Demir
15/02	h	Kayserispor	W	2-1	Marin, Sefa
21/02	a	Galatasaray	L	1-2	Zengin (p)
27/02	h	Osmanlıspor	L	1-2	Sefa
06/03	a	Konyaspor	L	0-2	
11/03	h	Mersin	W	1-0	Cardozo
15/03	h	Beşiktaş	L	0-2	
19/03	h	Sivasspor	W	1-0	Aytaç
02/04	a	Gaziantepspor	W	1-0	Mustafa
10/04	h	İstanbul Başakşehir	D	1-1	Akakpo
18/04	a	Gençlerbirliği	L	1-3	Muhammet Demir
24/04	h	Fenerbahçe	L	0-4	
30/04	a	Eskişehirspor	L	0-1	
08/05	h	Rizespor	W	6-0	Yusuf Yazıcı 2, Mehmet Ekici, Muhammet Demir 2, Yusuf Erdoğan
13/05	a	Antalyaspor	L	0-7	
19/05	h	Kasımpaşa	L	0-6	

No	Name	Nat	DoB	Pos	Aps	(s)	Gls
33	Serge Akakpo	TOG	15/10/87	D	7	(2)	1
64	Alper Uludağ		11/12/90	D	5	(1)	
23	Esteban Alvarado	CRC	28/04/89	G	14		
4	Aykut Demir		22/10/88	D	19	(1)	1
35	Aytaç Kara		28/03/93	M	13	(5)	1
3	José Bosingwa	POR	24/08/82	D	12		
7	Óscar Cardozo	PAR	20/05/83	A	14	(7)	8
39	Luis Cavanda	BEL	02/01/91	D	24		
11	Kévin Constant	GUI	10/05/87	D	8		
18	Deniz Yılmaz		26/02/88	A	2	(2)	
2	Douglas	BRA	12/01/88	D	15	(1)	
66	Fatih Atik		25/06/84	M	2	(1)	
88	Güray Vural		11/06/88	M	5	(1)	
19	Marko Marin	GER	13/03/89	M	18	(5)	2
25	Stéphane Mbia	CMR	20/05/86	M	17		2
6	Carl Medjani	ALG	15/05/85	M	4	(4)	1
8	Mehmet Ekici		25/03/90	M	16	(2)	4
98	Mehmet Yeşil		31/05/95	D	1		
57	Melih Kabasakal		18/02/96	D	1	(6)	
17	Muhammet Beşir		21/01/97	A	1	(6)	1
92	Muhammet Demir		10/01/92	A	11	(1)	4
77	Musa Nizam		08/09/90	D	7	(1)	1
22	Mustafa Yumlu		25/09/87	D	24	(1)	2
14	Dame N'Doye	SEN	21/02/85	A	7	(5)	
5	Okay Yokuşlu		09/03/94	M	24	(3)	2
1	Onur Kıvrak		01/01/88	G	20		
10	Özer Hurmacı		20/11/86	M	19	(4)	
38	Ramazan Övüç		16/03/94	M	2	(1)	
24	Salih Dursun		12/07/91	D	6	(4)	
29	Savaş Çakır		17/06/96	A	2	(1)	
9	Sefa Yılmaz		14/02/90	M	7	(5)	2
27	Semih Karadeniz		02/07/96	D	4	(1)	
20	Soner Aydoğdu		05/01/91	M		(1)	
80	Yağızcan Erdem		13/02/97	G		(1)	
26	Yavuz Aygün		27/06/96	D		(1)	
32	Yusuf Erdoğan		07/08/92	M	18	(9)	3
97	Yusuf Yazıcı		29/01/97	A	3	(4)	2
21	Erkan Zengin	SWE	05/08/85	M	22	(2)	3

Top goalscorers

26	Mario Gomez (Beşiktaş)
20	Samuel Eto'o (Antalyaspor)
19	Hugo Rodallega (Akhisar)
17	Edin Višća (İstanbul Başakşehir)
16	Robin van Persie (Fenerbahçe)
13	Fernandão (Fenerbahçe)
	Lukas Podolski (Galatasaray)
	Eren Derdiyok (Kasımpaşa)
12	Aatif Chahéchouche (Sivasspor)
11	Tomáš Necid (Bursaspor)
	Selçuk İnan (Galatasaray)
	Muhammet Demir (Gaziantepspor/ Trabzonspor)
	Ezequiel Scarione (Kasımpaşa)
	Pape Alioune Ndiaye (Osmanlıspor)
	Deniz Kadah (Rizespor)

Promoted clubs

Adanaspor

1954 • 5 Ocak Fatih Terim (16,095) •
adanaspor.com.tr
Coach: Eyüp Arın;
(18/11/15) Engin İpekoğlu

Kardemir Karabükspor

1969 • Dr Necmettin Şeyhoğlu (14,078) •
kardemirkarabukspor.org.tr
Coach: Hüseyin Kalpar;
(30/09/15) (Levent Açıkgöz);
(07/10/15) Elvir Baljić (BIH);
(21/12/15) (Levent Açıkgöz);
(30/12/15) Yücel İldiz

Alanyaspor

1948 • Oba (10,842) • alanyaspor.org.tr
Coach: Erhan Altın;
(30/09/15) (Mustafa Camunak);
(08/10/15) Hüseyin Kalpar

Second level final table 2015/16

		Pld	W	D	L	F	A	Pts
1	Adanaspor	34	20	5	9	53	36	65
2	Kardemir Karabükspor	34	17	11	6	41	27	62
3	Alanyaspor	34	17	10	7	59	37	61
4	Adana Demirspor	34	15	9	10	53	40	54
5	Elazığspor	34	13	13	8	45	38	52
6	Balıkesirspor	34	13	13	8	41	30	52
7	Giresunspor	34	14	9	11	49	40	51
8	Gaziantep BB	34	11	15	8	38	33	48
9	Samsunspor	34	13	8	13	45	39	44
10	Altınordu	34	11	11	12	39	43	44
11	Yeni Malatyaspor	34	12	7	15	36	42	43
12	Boluspor	34	10	12	12	36	46	42
13	Göztepe SK	34	9	11	14	38	40	38
14	Şanlıurfaspor	34	10	8	16	34	45	38
15	Denizlispor	34	10	9	15	41	52	36
16	1461 Trabzon	34	9	7	18	31	52	34
17	Kayseri Erciyesspor	34	8	9	17	35	54	33
18	Karşıyaka	34	6	9	19	33	53	27

NB Denizlispor & Samsunspor – 3 pts deducted.

Promotion play-offs

(19/05/16 & 23/05/16)
Balıkesirspor 0-0 Alanyaspor
Alanyaspor 1-0 Balıkesirspor
(Alanyaspor 1-0)

Elazığspor 3-2 Adana Demirspor
Adana Demirspor 2-1 Elazığspor
(4-4; Adana Demirspor on away goals)

(27/05/16)
Alanyaspor 1-1 Adana Demirspor *(aet; 3-1 on pens)*

DOMESTIC CUP

Türkiye Kupası 2015/16

SECOND ROUND

(22/09/15)
1461 Trabzon 4-0 Tarsus İdman Yurdu
Amed Sportif Faaliyetler 2-1 Karaman
Akhisar 2-0 Yomraspor
Ankaragücü 0-2 Payasspor
Antalyaspor 1-0 Çorum Belediyespor
Bandırmaspor 1-1 Keçiörengücü *(aet; 7-6 on pens)*
Büyükçekmece Tepecik Spor 2-1 Samsunspor
Denizlispor 0-0 Fethiyespor *(aet; 3-0 on pens)*
Göztepe 1-1 BB Erzurumspor *(aet; 3-0 on pens)*
Kahramanmaraş BB 0-1 Adanaspor
Kilis Belediye Spor 1-3 Ümraniyespor
Manisa BB Spor 2-3 Balıkesirspor *(aet)*
Osmanlıspor 6-0 Kızılcabölükspor
Sivasspor 0-1 Diyarbekir Spor
Yeni Amasya Spor 1-2 Karagümrük

(23/09/15)
Ankara Demirspor 1-2 Sarıyer
Aydınspor 3-1 Anadolu Üsküdar 1908 Spor
Bodrumspor 0-5 Menemen Belediye Spor
Boluspor 3-0 Çatalca Spor
Bucaspor 1-0 Sancaktepe Belediye Spor
Cizre Spor 1-2 Nazilli Belediyespor
Dardanelspor 5-4 Tokatspor
Düzcespor 1-1 Kocaeli Birlik Spor *(aet; 2-4 on pens)*
Elazığspor 1-0 Bursa Nilüferspor
Eskişehirspor 1-0 Körfez İskenderun Spor
Etimesgut Belediye Spor 2-0 Hatayspor
Gaziantep BB 1-1 Tuzlaspor *(aet; 3-4 on pens)*
Giresunspor 2-0 Eyüpspor
Gölcükspor 1-0 Kayseri Erciyesspor
Hacettepe Spor 1-1 Çine Madranspor *(aet; 3-4 on pens)*
Iğdır Aras Spor 1-0 Altınordu *(aet)*
İnegölspor 1-0 Gümüşhanespor *(aet)*
İstanbulspor 0-1 Manisaspor
Kahramanmaraşspor 0-1 Pazarspor
Karabükspor 2-0 Arsinspor
Kartalspor 3-1 Düzyurtspor
Kasımpaşa 3-0 Tire 1922 Spor
Kastamonuspor 3-0 Konya Anadolu Selçukspor
Kırklarelispor 2-1 Bugsaş Spor
Kurtalan Spor 0-3 Karşıyaka *(w/o)*
Manavgatspor 0-1 Adana Demirspor *(aet)*
Orhangazispor 1-0 Yeni Malatyaspor
Pendikspor 0-1 24 Erzincanspor
Rizespor 2-0 Adliyespor
Sivas Belediye Spor 2-2 Alanyaspor *(aet; 5-4 on pens)*
Sultanbeyli Belediyespor 1-3 Şanlıurfaspor
Tekirdağspor 2-0 Orduspor
Uşakspor 1-0 Bayrampaşa
Zonguldak Kömürspor 0-1 Kayserispor

THIRD ROUND
(01/12/15)
24 Erzincanspor 1-1 Antalyaspor *(aet; 4-5 on pens)*
Amed Sportif Faaliyetler 2-1 Elazığspor *(aet)*
Aydınspor 1-0 Denizlispor
Bursaspor 3-0 Uşakspor
Konyaspor 4-1 Kocaeli Birlik Spor
Osmanlıspor 0-1 Büyükçekmece Tepecik Spor
Sarıyer 2-7 Kayserispor

(02/12/15)
1461 Trabzon 3-0 Pazarspor
Adana Demirspor 2-4 Sivas Belediye Spor
Boluspor 4-1 Ümraniyespor
Çine Madranspor 1-2 Bucaspor
Etimesgut Belediye Spor 1-0 Gençlerbirliği
Iğdır Aras Spor 1-3 Bandırmaspor
İnegölspor 1-1 Balıkesirspor *(aet; 3-1 on pens)*

Karabükspor 5-2 Payasspor *(aet)*
Karagümrük 3-3 Mersin *(aet; 4-5 on pens)*
Karşıyaka 3-2 Tekirdağspor
Kastamonuspor 3-3 Kasımpaşa *(aet; 7-6 on pens)*
Rizespor 1-0 Orhangazispor
Şanlıurfaspor 1-0 Kırklarelispor
Tuzlaspor 1-0 Manisaspor

(03/12/15)
Adanaspor 3-1 Diyarbekir Spor
Akhisar 5-0 Dardanel Spor
Gaziantepspor 3-2 Gölcükspor *(aet)*
Göztepe 1-2 Nazilli Belediyespor *(aet)*
Kartalspor 0-2 Giresunspor
Menemen Spor 0-1 Eskişehirspor

GROUP STAGE

Group A
(16/12/15)
Bandırmaspor 1-2 Amed Sportif Faaliyetler
İstanbul Başakşehir 4-1 Şanlıurfaspor

(23/12/15)
Amed Sportif Faaliyetler 2-2 İstanbul Başakşehir
Şanlıurfaspor 0-2 Bandırmaspor

(10/01/16)
İstanbul Başakşehir 3-2 Bandırmaspor

(11/01/16)
Şanlıurfaspor 0-2 Amed Sportif Faaliyetler

(13/01/16)
Bandırmaspor 0-2 İstanbul Başakşehir

(14/01/16)
Amed Sportif Faaliyetler 1-0 Şanlıurfaspor

(21/01/16)
Amed Sportif Faaliyetler 3-3 Bandırmaspor
Şanlıurfaspor 0-3 İstanbul Başakşehir

(27/01/16)
Bandırmaspor 0-0 Şanlıurfaspor

(28/01/16)
İstanbul Başakşehir 2-2 Amed Sportif Faaliyetler

Final standings
1 İstanbul Başakşehir 14 pts; 2 Amed Sportif
Faaliyetler 12 pts *(qualified)*
3 Bandırmaspor 5 pts; Şanlıurfaspor 1 pt
(eliminated)

Group B
(15/12/15)
Büyükçekmece Tepecik Spor 2-3 Bursaspor
Eskişehirspor 2-0 Boluspor

(22/12/15)
Boluspor 3-1 Büyükçekmece Tepecik Spor

(24/12/15)
Bursaspor 4-1 Eskişehirspor

(10/01/16)
Bursaspor 3-0 Boluspor

(11/01/16)
Büyükçekmece Tepecik Spor 2-1 Eskişehirspor

(13/01/16)
Boluspor 0-1 Bursaspor

(14/01/16)
Eskişehirspor 2-2 Büyükçekmece Tepecik Spor

(20/01/16)
Bursaspor 4-2 Büyükçekmece Tepecik Spor

(21/02/16)
Boluspor 0-2 Eskişehirspor

(28/01/16)
Büyükçekmece Tepecik Spor 2-1 Boluspor
Eskişehirspor 2-3 Bursaspor

Final standings
1 Bursaspor 18 pts; 2 Büyükçekmece Tepecik
Spor 7 pts *(qualified)*
3 Eskişehirspor 7 pts; Boluspor 3 pts *(eliminated)*

Group C
(17/12/15)
1461 Trabzon 7-1 Sivas Belediye Spor
Beşiktaş 3-0 Karabükspor

(24/12/15)
Karabükspor 0-5 1461 Trabzon
Sivas Belediye Spor 0-2 Beşiktaş

(10/01/16)
1461 Trabzon 1-1 Beşiktaş
Sivas Belediye Spor 5-0 Karabükspor

(14/01/16)
Beşiktaş 1-0 1461 Trabzon
Karabükspor 1-2 Sivas Belediye Spor

(20/01/16)
Karabükspor 2-0 Beşiktaş
Sivas Belediye Spor 1-0 1461 Trabzon

(27/01/16)
1461 Trabzon 2-0 Karabükspor

(28/01/16)
Beşiktaş 3-4 Sivas Belediye Spor

Final standings
1 Sivas Belediye Spor 12 pts; 2 Beşiktaş 10 pts
(qualified)
3 1461 Trabzon 10 pts; 4 Karabükspor 3 pts
(eliminated)

Group D
(16/12/15)
Aydınspor 4-0 Mersin
Rizespor 4-1 Bucaspor

(22/12/15)
Mersin 2-2 Rizespor

(23/12/15)
Bucaspor 2-0 Aydınspor

(09/01/16)
Bucaspor 1-0 Mersin

(10/01/16)
Rizespor 3-1 Aydınspor

(13/01/16)
Aydınspor 1-3 Rizespor
Mersin 1-2 Bucaspor

(20/01/16)
Bucaspor 3-2 Rizespor
Mersin 4-0 Aydınspor

(27/01/16)
Aydınspor 0-1 Bucaspor

(28/01/16)
Rizespor 1-0 Mersin

Final standings
1 Bucaspor 15 pts; 2 Rizespor 13 pts *(qualified)*
3 Mersin 4 pts; 4 Aydınspor 3 pts *(eliminated)*

Continued over the page

TURKEY

Group E

(17/12/15)
Galatasaray 2-1 Akhisar
Karşıyaka 2-1 Kastamonuspor

(23/12/15)
Akhisar 0-2 Karşıyaka
Kastamonuspor 1-2 Galatasaray

(09/01/16)
Akhisar 0-0 Kastamonuspor
Galatasaray 3-1 Karşıyaka

(12/01/16)
Karşıyaka 1-3 Galatasaray
Kastamonuspor 1-2 Akhisar

(19/01/16)
Akhisar 1-1 Galatasaray
Kastamonuspor 2-1 Karşıyaka

(26/01/16)
Galatasaray 4-1 Kastamonuspor

(28/01/16)
Karşıyaka 0-2 Akhisar

Final standings
1 Galatasaray 16 pts; 2 Akhisar 8 pts *(qualified)*
3 Karşıyaka 6 pts; 4 Kastamonuspor 4 pts
(eliminated)

Group F

(15/12/15)
Gaziantepspor 1-1 Adanaspor
Nazilli Belediyespor 0-2 Trabzonspor

(22/12/15)
Trabzonspor 2-1 Gaziantepspor

(24/12/15)
Adanaspor 2-1 Nazilli Belediyespor

(09/01/16)
Nazilli Belediyespor 0-0 Gaziantepspor
Trabzonspor 3-0 Adanaspor

(12/01/16)
Adanaspor 1-4 Trabzonspor
Gaziantepspor 1-0 Nazilli Belediyespor

(20/01/16)
Adanaspor 2-3 Gaziantepspor
Trabzonspor 1-0 Nazilli Belediyespor

(26/01/16)
Nazilli Belediyespor 1-2 Adanaspor

(27/01/16)
Gaziantepspor 2-0 Trabzonspor

Final standings
1 Trabzonspor 15 pts; 2 Gaziantepspor 11 pts
(qualified)
3 Adanaspor 7 pts; 4 Nazilli Belediyespor 1 pt
(eliminated)

Group G

(16/12/15)
İnegölspor 3-0 Etimesgut Belediye Spor
Konyaspor 1-0 Kayserispor

(22/12/15)
Etimesgut Belediye Spor 0-1 Konyaspor

(24/12/15)
Kayserispor 1-0 İnegölspor

(09/01/16)
Etimesgut Belediye Spor 2-5 Kayserispor
İnegölspor 1-1 Konyaspor

(12/01/16)
Kayserispor 3-0 Etimesgut Belediye Spor
Konyaspor 2-0 İnegölspor

(19/01/16)
Etimesgut Belediye Spor 0-1 İnegölspor
Kayserispor 0-1 Konyaspor

(26/01/16)
İnegölspor 0-3 Kayserispor
Konyaspor 2-1 Etimesgut Belediye Spor

Final standings
1 Konyaspor 16 pts; 2 Kayserispor 12 pts
(qualified)
3 İnegölspor 7 pts; 4 Etimesgut Belediye Spor 0 pts
(eliminated)

Group H

(15/12/15)
Antalyaspor 2-1 Giresunspor

(16/12/15)
Tuzlaspor 1-2 Fenerbahçe

(23/12/15)
Fenerbahçe 4-2 Antalyaspor

(24/12/15)
Giresunspor 0-1 Tuzlaspor

(10/01/16)
Giresunspor 0-2 Fenerbahçe

(11/01/16)
Antalyaspor 1-0 Tuzlaspor

(13/01/16)
Fenerbahçe 6-1 Giresunspor

(14/01/16)
Tuzlaspor 1-1 Antalyaspor

(21/01/16)
Fenerbahçe 1-0 Tuzlaspor
Giresunspor 0-1 Antalyaspor

(27/01/16)
Antalyaspor 0-0 Fenerbahçe
Tuzlaspor 2-0 Giresunspor

Final standings
1 Fenerbahçe 16 pts; 2 Antalyaspor 11 pts
(qualified)
3 Tuzlaspor 7 pts; 4 Giresunspor 0 pts *(eliminated)*

1/8 FINALS

(30/01/16)
Fenerbahçe 1-0 Kayserispor *(aet)*

(31/01/16)
Bucaspor 0-2 Beşiktaş
Bursaspor 1-2 Amed Sportif Faaliyetler
Galatasaray 3-1 Gaziantepspor
Konyaspor 1-0 Antalyaspor
Sivas Belediye Spor 0-2 Rizespor

(01/02/16)
İstanbul Başakşehir 4-0 Büyükçekmece Tepecik Spor
Trabzonspor 0-1 Akhisar

QUARTER-FINALS

(09/02/16 & 03/03/16)
Amed 3-3 Fenerbahçe *(Şehmus 10, İbrahim 68, Yusuf 70; Ramazan 14, Fernandão 44, Volkan Şen 76)*
Fenerbahçe 3-1 Amed *(Mehmet Topuz 31, Fernandão 40, Nani 88; Kamil 27)*
(Fenerbahçe 6-4)

(10/02/16 & 02/03/16)
Akhisar 1-2 Galatasaray *(Rodallega 53; Sneijder 70, Selçuk 72)*
Galatasaray 1-1 Akhisar *(Douglão 10og; Rodallega 47)*
(Galatasaray 3-2)

(10/02/16 & 03/03/16)
Beşiktaş 1-2 Konyaspor *(Cenk 31; Bajić 65, Volkan 79)*
Konyaspor 1-0 Beşiktaş *(Meha 85)*
(Konyaspor 3-1)

(11/02/16 & 01/03/16)
İstanbul Başakşehir 0-2 Rizespor *(Robin 6, Mehmet 70)*
Rizespor 1-0 İstanbul Başakşehir *(Murat 90+2)*
(Rizespor 3-0)

SEMI-FINALS

(20/04/16 & 04/05/16)
Rizespor 1-3 Galatasaray *(Ahmet İlhan 76; Emre 15, Yasin 61, Podolski 90+4)*
Galatasaray 0-0 Rizespor
(Galatasaray 3-1)

(20/04/16 & 05/05/16)
Konyaspor 0-3 Fenerbahçe *(Volkan Şen 39, Nani 45, Van Persie 89)*
Fenerbahçe 2-0 Konyaspor *(Fernandão 47, 71p)*
(Fenerbahçe 5-0)

FINAL

(26/05/16)
Antalya Arena, Antalya
GALATASARAY AŞ 1 *(Podolski 30)*
FENERBAHÇE SK 0
Referee: *Mete Kalkavan*
GALATASARAY: *Muslera, Semih, Denayer, Hakan, Carole, Selçuk, Emre (Linnes 89), Sinan (Sabri 65), Sneijder (Chedjou 46), Yasin, Podolski*
FENERBAHÇE: *Fabiano, Şener (Gökhan 79), Kjær, Ba, Hasan Ali, Mehmet Topal, Souza, Alper (Marković 68), Volkan Şen, Nani, Van Persie (Fernandão 46)*
Red card: *Nani (90)*

Galatasaray celebrate their Turkish Cup final win against arch-rivals Fenerbahçe

UKRAINE
Federatsiya Futbola Ukrainy (FFU)

Address	Provulok Laboratorniy 7-A	**President**	Andriy Pavelko
	PO Box 55	**General secretary**	Yuriy Zapisotskiy
	UA-01133 Kyiv	**Media officer**	Olexandr Hlyvynskiy
Tel	+380 44 521 0521	**Year of formation**	1989
Fax	+380 44 521 0550	**National stadium**	NSK Olimpiyskiy,
E-mail	info@ffu.org.ua		Kyiv (70,050)
Website	ffu.org.ua		

PREMIER LEAGUE CLUBS

 1 **FC Chornomorets Odesa**

2 **FC Dnipro Dnipropetrovsk**

 3 **FC Dynamo Kyiv**

 4 **FC Hoverla Uzhhorod**

5 **FC Karpaty Lviv**

6 **FC Metalist Kharkiv**

 7 **FC Metalurh Zaporizhya**

 8 **FC Olexandriya**

 9 **FC Olimpik Donetsk**

 10 **FC Shakhtar Donetsk**

 11 **FC Stal Dniprodzerzhynsk**

 12 **FC Volyn Lutsk**

 13 **FC Vorskla Poltava**

 14 **FC Zorya Luhansk**

PROMOTED CLUB

 15 **FC Zirka Kirovohrad**

KEY
- ● UEFA Champions League
- ● UEFA Europa League
- ● Promoted
- ● Relegated

Dynamo Kyiv deliver again

Former Ukraine striker Serhiy Rebrov made it two league titles in as many seasons as Dynamo Kyiv head coach, the country's record champions emerging triumphant once again from another engaging duel with Shakhtar Donetsk.

Still unable to play at their Donbass Arena home, Shakhtar performed creditably across all competitions, reaching the UEFA Europa League semi-finals and winning the Ukrainian Cup in what turned out to be the last season of Romanian coach Mircea Lucescu's highly successful 12-year reign.

Two league titles in two seasons for Rebrov	**Shakhtar end Lucescu's long reign with cup win**	**National team draw blanks at UEFA EURO 2016**

Domestic league

Undefeated in winning the 2014/15 Premier League title, Dynamo were unable to replicate that achievement 12 months on, but Rebrov's side were equally impressive, finishing up with 70 points, an increase of four on the previous season. Shakhtar actually beat them twice, 3-0 both times, but the second of those defeats came after the title had already been secured, with a 1-0 win at home to Vorskla Poltava. That was Dynamo's 12th straight victory – a sequence in which they collected three points from every other club in the division bar Shakhtar.

While Dynamo found the rank and file of the Premier League easy to beat, Shakhtar occasionally slipped up in matches they were expected to win. Dnipro Dnipropetrovsk, who finished third, defeated Lucescu's men twice, while draws in the spring against Stal Dniprodzerzhynsk and Chornomorets Odesa proved decisive. It was to Shakhtar's credit, however, that they troubled their rivals for so long. Not only did they have a crowded fixture schedule, they also had to negotiate it without Douglas Costa and Luiz Adriano, sold the previous summer to Bayern München and AC Milan respectively, and – in the second half of the season – another Brazilian star, Alex Teixeira, who scored a golden boot-winning 22 goals before jetting off to China in January.

At the time of his departure, Shakhtar actually led the table, on goal difference, having won 11 games in a row. But it was Dynamo who delivered when it mattered, skipper Andriy Yarmolenko inspiring the team from the front and Domagoj Vida and Aleksandar Dragovic holding the fort at the back to steer the club to their 28th national title. Although the runners-up comprehensively outscored the champions, 76 goals to 54, Dynamo conceded a mere 11 goals – more than half of those against Shakhtar.

The top five teams in the final table were unchanged from the previous season, but as Dnipro were banned from Europe, sixth-placed Olexandriya were invited to join the two teams above them, Zorya Luhansk and Vorskla, in the UEFA Europa League. Financial problems had led to the mid-season exclusion of Metalurh Zaporizhya, and two other clubs – Metalist Kharkiv and Hoverla Uzhhorod – were demoted for similar reasons at the season's end, leaving a 12-team Premier League (including newcomers Zirka Kirovohrad) for 2016/17.

Domestic cup

Newly-promoted Olexandriya ended Dynamo's Ukrainian Cup defence with a shock quarter-final victory, but then lost to Shakhtar, who went on to lift the trophy for the tenth time – and sixth under Lucescu – with a comfortable 2-0 win over Zorya in the final thanks to a double from striker Olexandr Gladkiy.

Europe

Although 2014/15 UEFA Europa League runners-up Dnipro could not get past the group stage on their return to the competition, Shakhtar, having finished third in their UEFA Champions League group, powered their way undefeated to the semi-finals, only to fall victim, like Dnipro before them, to Sevilla. Lucescu's last European campaign with the Pitmen lasted a club-record 18 matches, while Rebrov achieved something no Dynamo boss had managed for 16 years by steering the club into the last 16 of the UEFA Champions League.

National team

Rebrov's former Dynamo strike partner, Andriy Shevchenko, was appointed as the new head coach of the Ukrainian national team a few weeks after assisting Mikhail Fomenko at UEFA EURO 2016. Fomenko, the first coach to qualify Ukraine for a major tournament via the play-offs, was unable to get any more from his players in France as they became the first side eliminated following 2-0 defeats against Germany and Northern Ireland. Another loss, 1-0 to Poland, left Ukraine as the only team to depart without a point or a goal.

DOMESTIC SEASON AT A GLANCE

Premier League 2015/16 final table

		Pld	W	D	L	F	A	W	D	L	F	A	W	D	L	F	A	Pts
				Home					**Away**					**Total**				
1	**FC Dynamo Kyiv**	26	12	0	1	23	4	11	1	1	31	7	23	1	2	54	11	70
2	FC Shakhtar Donetsk	26	11	0	2	36	7	9	3	1	40	18	20	3	3	76	25	63
3	FC Dnipro Dnipropetrovsk	26	8	1	4	23	12	8	4	1	27	10	16	5	5	50	22	53
4	FC Zorya Luhansk	26	6	4	3	25	17	8	2	3	26	9	14	6	6	51	26	48
5	FC Vorskla Poltava	26	6	4	3	14	13	5	5	3	18	13	11	9	6	32	26	42
6	FC Olexandriya	26	6	3	4	17	13	4	5	4	13	16	10	8	8	30	29	38
7	FC Karpaty Lviv	26	5	3	5	20	15	3	3	7	6	22	8	6	12	26	37	30
8	FC Stal Dniprodzerzhynsk	26	4	4	5	16	19	3	4	6	6	12	7	8	11	22	31	29
9	FC Olimpik Donetsk	26	3	5	5	12	16	3	2	8	11	19	6	7	13	23	35	25
10	FC Metalist Kharkiv	26	4	4	5	14	21	1	5	7	5	25	5	9	12	19	46	24
11	FC Chornomorets Odesa	26	2	5	6	12	15	2	5	6	10	24	4	10	12	22	39	22
12	FC Volyn Lutsk	26	4	5	4	19	17	6	3	4	17	19	10	8	8	36	36	20
13	FC Hoverla Uzhhorod	26	1	5	7	8	27	2	2	9	5	21	3	7	16	13	48	7
14	FC Metalurh Zaporizhya	26	0	2	11	2	24	0	1	12	5	26	0	3	23	7	50	3

NB FC Metalurh Zaporizhya excluded after round 16 – their remaining matches were awarded as goalless defeats;
FC Volyn Lutsk – 18 pts deducted; FC Hoverla Uzhhorod – 9 pts deducted.

European qualification 2016/17

Champion: FC Dynamo Kyiv (group stage)
Cup winner: FC Shakhtar Donetsk (third qualifying round)

FC Zorya Luhansk (group stage)
FC Vorskla Poltava (third qualifying round)
FC Olexandriya (third qualifying round)

Top scorer	Alex Teixeira (Shakhtar), 22 goals
Relegated clubs	FC Metalurh Zaporizhya (excluded), FC Hoverla Uzhhorod (excluded), FC Metalist Kharkiv (excluded)
Promoted club	FC Zirka Kirovohrad
Cup final	FC Shakhtar Donetsk 2-0 FC Zorya Luhansk

Team of the season
(4-2-3-1)

Coach: Rebrov (Dynamo)

M Shevchenko (Zorya)

Srna (Shakhtar)   Khacheridi (Dynamo)   Rakitskiy (Shakhtar)   Kamenyuka (Zorya)

Rybalka (Dynamo)   Stepanenko (Shakhtar)

Yarmolenko (Dynamo)   Marlos (Shakhtar)   Matheus (Dnipro)

Alex Teixeira (Shakhtar)

Player of the season

Andriy Yarmolenko
(FC Dynamo Kyiv)

Retained by Dynamo in 2015/16 despite considerable interest from abroad, Yarmolenko was once again a pivotal figure in the club's Ukrainian Premier League triumph. He started 23 matches – more than any other Dynamo player – and contributed 13 goals and 12 assists. Tall, powerful and armed with an explosive left foot, the 26-year-old winger was also Ukraine's hero in their UEFA EURO 2016 play-off win against Slovenia. Like his team-mates, though, he was disappointingly off-colour at the finals.

Newcomer of the season

Viktor Kovalenko
(FC Shakhtar Donetsk)

Having excelled for Shakhtar in the 2014/15 UEFA Youth League – he struck three goals in the final tournament – and for Ukraine at the 2015 FIFA U-20 World Cup in New Zealand – where he won the golden boot with five goals – 20-year-old Kovalenko made the breakthrough for both club and country at senior level in 2015/16. The dynamic midfielder played in the UEFA Champions League and UEFA Europa League for Shakhtar and appeared in all three games at UEFA EURO 2016 for Ukraine.

 **UKRAINE**

NATIONAL TEAM

International tournament appearances

FIFA World Cup (1) 2006 (qtr-finals)
UEFA European Championship (2) 2012, 2016

Top five all-time caps

Anatoliy Tymoshchuk (144); Andriy Shevchenko (111); Oleh Gusev (98); Olexandr Shovkovskiy (92); **Ruslan Rotan** (89)

Top five all-time goals

Andriy Shevchenko (48); **Andriy Yarmolenko** (25); Serhiy Rebrov (15); **Oleh Gusev** & **Yevhen Konoplyanka** (13)

Results 2015/16

05/09/15	Belarus (ECQ)	H	Lviv	W	3-1	*Kravets (7), Yarmolenko (30), Konoplyanka (40p)*
08/09/15	Slovakia (ECQ)	A	Zilina	D	0-0	
09/10/15	FYR Macedonia (ECQ)	A	Skopje	W	2-0	*Seleznyov (59p), Kravets (87)*
12/10/15	Spain (ECQ)	H	Kyiv	L	0-1	
14/11/15	Slovenia (ECQ)	H	Lviv	W	2-0	*Yarmolenko (22), Seleznyov (54)*
17/11/15	Slovenia (ECQ)	A	Maribor	D	1-1	*Yarmolenko (90+7)*
24/03/16	Cyprus	H	Odesa	W	1-0	*Stepanenko (40)*
28/03/16	Wales	H	Kyiv	W	1-0	*Yarmolenko (28)*
29/05/16	Romania	N	Turin (ITA)	W	4-3	*Zozulya (43), Zinchenko (48), Konoplyanka (54), Yarmolenko (59)*
03/06/16	Albania	N	Bergamo (ITA)	W	3-1	*Stepanenko (8), Yarmolenko (49), Konoplyanka (87)*
12/06/16	Germany (ECF)	N	Lille (FRA)	L	0-2	
16/06/16	Northern Ireland (ECF)	N	Lyon (FRA)	L	0-2	
21/06/16	Poland (ECF)	N	Marseille (FRA)	L	0-1	

Appearances 2015/16

Coach: Mykhailo Fomenko	19/09/48		BLR	SVK	MKD	ESP	SVN	SVN	Cyp	Wal	Rou	Alb	GER	NIR	POL	Caps	Goals
Andriy Pyatov	28/06/84	Shakhtar Donetsk	G	G	G	G	G	G		G	G	G	G	G	G	67	-
Artem Fedetskiy	26/04/85	Dnipro	D	D	D	D	D	D	D	D	D46	D	D	D	D	52	2
Yevhen Khacheridi	28/07/87	Dynamo Kyiv	D	D	D		D	D		D	D46	D	D	D	D	45	3
Yaroslav Rakitskiy	03/08/89	Shakhtar Donetsk	D	D	D	D	D	D			D	D	D	D		42	4
Vyacheslav Shevchuk	13/05/79	Shakhtar Donetsk	D	D	D	D	D	D	D81	D	D71	D46	D	D		56	-
Ruslan Rotan	29/10/81	Dnipro	M75	M	M90	M87			M46	M59	s67	s67			M	89	7
Taras Stepanenko	08/08/89	Shakhtar Donetsk	M	M		M		M	M72	M	M	M90	M	M	M	32	3
Andriy Yarmolenko	23/10/89	Dynamo Kyiv	M69	M	M86	M	M90	M	M	M	M	M76	M	M	M	62	25
Denys Garmash	19/04/90	Dynamo Kyiv	M 92*			M58	M79	s61	M46	M		M46		s76		28	2
Yevhen Konoplyanka	29/09/89	Sevilla (ESP)	M	M	M	M	M	M96			M	M	M	M		56	13
Artem Kravets	03/06/89	Dynamo Kyiv /Stuttgart (GER)	A86	A91	s74	A87	s84	s80	s63							13	4
Oleh Gusev	25/04/83	Dynamo Kyiv	s69						M46							98	13
Serhiy Rybalka	01/04/90	Dynamo Kyiv	s75	M	M	s58	M	M			M46					9	-
Olexandr Gladkiy	24/08/87	Shakhtar Donetsk	s86	s91												11	1
Serhiy Sydorchuk	02/05/91	Dynamo Kyiv			M		M	M61		s59	M67	M67	M	M76		14	2
Yevhen Seleznyov	20/07/85	Dnipro /Shakhtar Donetsk		A74	s87	A84	A80				s46	s63	s66	A71		52	11
Olexandr Karavayev	02/06/92	Zorya			s86		s90				s71					3	-
Ruslan Malinovskiy	04/05/93	Zorya			s90		s79									3	-
Olexandr Kucher	22/10/82	Shakhtar Donetsk				D			D	D	s46				D	51	2
Olexandr Zinchenko	15/12/96	Ufa (RUS)				s87					s46	s76	s73	s83	M73	6	1
Anatoliy Tymoshchuk	30/03/79	Kairat (KAZ)					s96	s72			s90			s92		144	4
Denys Boyko	29/01/88	Beşiktaş (TUR)							G							4	-
Artem Putivtsev	29/08/88	Nieciecza (POL)							D							1	-
Roman Zozulya	17/11/89	Dnipro							A63	A	A46	A63	A66	s71	A92	29	4
Viktor Kovalenko	14/02/96	Shakhtar Donetsk							s46	M		s46	M73	M83	s73	6	-
Maxym Malyshev	24/12/92	Shakhtar Donetsk							s46							1	-
Ivan Petryak	13/03/94	Zorya							s46							1	-
Mykyta Kamenyuka	03/06/85	Zorya							s81							1	-
Bohdan Butko	13/01/91	Amkar (RUS)									s46	s46			D	18	-

EUROPE

FC Dynamo Kyiv

Group G
Match 1 - FC Porto (POR)
H 2-2 *Gusev (20), Buyalskiy (89)*
Rybka, Danilo Silva, Miguel Veloso (Kravets 86), Antunes, Dragovic, Júnior Moraes, Rybalka, Garmash, Gusev (Buyalskiy 67), González (Belhanda 70), Khacheridi. Coach: Serhiy Rebrov (UKR)

Match 2 - Maccabi Tel-Aviv FC (ISR)
A 2-0 *Yarmolenko (4), Júnior Moraes (50)*
Shovkovskiy, Danilo Silva, Miguel Veloso (Buyalskiy 69), Antunes, Dragovic, Yarmolenko, Júnior Moraes (Kravets 81), Sydorchuk, Rybalka, González (Vida 78), Khacheridi. Coach: Serhiy Rebrov (UKR)

Match 3 - Chelsea FC (ENG)
H 0-0
Shovkovskiy, Danilo Silva, Dragovic, Yarmolenko, Sydorchuk, Rybalka, Kravets (Júnior Moraes 78), Vida, González, Buyalskiy (Garmash 83), Khacheridi. Coach: Serhiy Rebrov (UKR)

Match 4 - Chelsea FC (ENG)
A 1-2 *Dragovic (78)*
Shovkovskiy, Antunes, Dragovic, Yarmolenko, Sydorchuk (Garmash 46), Rybalka, Kravets (Júnior Moraes 56), Vida, González, Buyalskiy , Khacheridi. Coach: Serhiy Rebrov (UKR)

Match 5 - FC Porto (POR)
A 2-0 *Yarmolenko (35p), González (64)*
Shovkovskiy, Danilo Silva, Antunes, Dragovic, Yarmolenko, Júnior Moraes (Teodorczyk 86), Sydorchuk (Buyalskiy 84), Rybalka, Garmash, González (Belhanda 78), Khacheridi. Coach: Serhiy Rebrov (UKR)

Match 6 - Maccabi Tel-Aviv FC (ISR)
H 1-0 *Garmash (16)*
Shovkovskiy, Danilo Silva, Antunes, Dragovic, Yarmolenko (Gusev 18), Júnior Moraes (Teodorczyk 89), Sydorchuk, Rybalka, Garmash (Miguel Veloso 64), González, Khacheridi. Coach: Serhiy Rebrov (UKR)

Round of 16 - Manchester City FC (ENG)
H 1-3 *Buyalskiy (59)*
Shovkovskiy, Danilo Silva (Makarenko 66), Dragovic, Yarmolenko, Rybalka, Garmash (Miguel Veloso 31), Vida, González, Buyalskiy , Khacheridi, Teodorczyk (Júnior Moraes 46). Coach: Serhiy Rebrov (UKR)

A 0-0
Shovkovskiy, Miguel Veloso, Antunes, Dragovic, Yarmolenko, Garmash (Sydorchuk 64), Gusev (Yakovenko 62), Vida, Buyalskiy , Khacheridi, Teodorczyk (González 46). Coach: Serhiy Rebrov (UKR)

FC Shakhtar Donetsk

Third qualifying round - Fenerbahçe SK (TUR)
A 0-0
Pyatov, Stepanenko, Fred (Malyshev 90), Marlos (Eduardo 77), Shevchuk, Ordets, Gladkiy, Taison (Kovalenko 79), Alex Teixeira, Srna, Rakitskiy. Coach: Mircea Lucescu (ROU)

H 3-0 *Gladkiy (25), Srna (65p), Alex Teixeira (68)*
Pyatov, Stepanenko, Fred, Marlos (Kovalenko 87), Shevchuk, Ordets (Kucher 83), Gladkiy (Eduardo 82), Taison, Alex Teixeira, Srna, Rakitskiy. Coach: Mircea Lucescu (ROU)

Play-offs - SK Rapid Wien (AUT)
A 1-0 *Marlos (44)*
Pyatov, Kucher, Stepanenko (Malyshev 46), Fred, Marlos (Eduardo 80), Gladkiy, Taison (Bernard 86), Alex Teixeira, Srna, Rakitskiy, Márcio Azevedo. Coach: Mircea Lucescu (ROU)

H 2-2 *Marlos (10), Gladkiy (27)*
Pyatov, Stepanenko, Fred, Marlos, Gladkiy (Eduardo 83), Taison (Bernard 87), Alex Teixeira, Srna, Kryvtsov, Rakitskiy, Márcio Azevedo. Coach: Mircea Lucescu (ROU)

Group A
Match 1 - Real Madrid CF (ESP)
A 0-4
Pyatov, Kucher, Stepanenko, Fred, Marlos (Kovalenko 74), Gladkiy (Bernard 82), Taison (Malyshev 67), Alex Teixeira, Srna, Rakitskiy, Márcio Azevedo. Coach: Mircea Lucescu (ROU)
Red card: Stepanenko 50

Match 2 - Paris Saint-Germain (FRA)
H 0-3
Pyatov, Kucher, Fred, Marlos (Kovalenko 71), Shevchuk, Malyshev, Gladkiy (Dentinho 85), Taison (Bernard 71), Alex Teixeira, Srna, Rakitskiy. Coach: Mircea Lucescu (ROU)

Match 3 - Malmö FF (SWE)
A 0-1
Pyatov, Kucher, Stepanenko, Fred, Bernard, Marlos (Eduardo 71), Gladkiy (Kovalenko 81), Alex Teixeira, Ismaily, Srna, Rakitskiy. Coach: Mircea Lucescu (ROU)

Match 4 - Malmö FF (SWE)
H 4-0 *Gladkiy (29), Srna (48p), Eduardo (55), Alex Teixeira (73)*
Kanibolotskiy, Kucher, Stepanenko, Fred (Taison 68), Bernard (Kovalenko 75), Marlos, Gladkiy (Eduardo 46), Alex Teixeira, Srna, Rakitskiy, Ismaily. Coach: Mircea Lucescu (ROU)

Match 5 - Real Madrid CF (ESP)
H 3-4 *Alex Teixeira (77p, 88), Dentinho (83)*
Pyatov, Stepanenko, Fred, Bernard, Marlos (Taison 62), Kobin, Ordets, Gladkiy (Ferreyra 74), Alex Teixeira, Rakitskiy, Márcio Azevedo (Dentinho 64). Coach: Mircea Lucescu (ROU)

Match 6 - Paris Saint-Germain (FRA)
A 0-2
Kanibolotskiy, Kucher, Stepanenko, Fred, Marlos (Kovalenko 74), Eduardo (Dentinho 78), Taison (Bernard 69), Alex Teixeira, Ismaily, Srna, Rakitskiy. Coach: Mircea Lucescu (ROU)

Round of 32 - FC Schalke 04 (GER)
H 0-0
Pyatov, Kucher, Stepanenko, Marlos (Wellington Nem 74), Malyshev (Kryvtsov 89), Gladkiy, Taison (Eduardo 79), Ismaily, Srna, Rakitskiy, Kovalenko. Coach: Mircea Lucescu (ROU)
Red card: Kucher 86

A 3-0 *Marlos (27), Ferreyra (63), Kovalenko (77)*
Pyatov, Stepanenko, Marlos (Wellington Nem 74), Malyshev, Ferreyra (Boryachuk 89), Taison (Eduardo 80), Ismaily, Srna, Kryvtsov, Rakitskiy, Kovalenko. Coach: Mircea Lucescu (ROU)

Round of 16 - RSC Anderlecht (BEL)
H 3-1 *Taison (21), Kucher (24), Eduardo (79)*
Pyatov, Kucher, Marlos (Wellington Nem 74), Malyshev, Ferreyra, Eduardo (Dentinho 88), Taison (Bernard 46), Ismaily, Srna, Rakitskiy, Kovalenko. Coach: Mircea Lucescu (ROU)

A 1-0 *Eduardo (90+3)*
Pyatov, Kucher, Stepanenko, Marlos (Eduardo 90+1), Malyshev, Ferreyra, Taison (Dentinho 83), Ismaily, Srna, Rakitskiy, Kovalenko (Ordets 88). Coach: Mircea Lucescu (ROU)
Red card: Kucher 84

Quarter-finals - SC Braga (POR)
A 2-1 *Rakitskiy (45), Ferreyra (75)*
Pyatov, Stepanenko, Marlos (Eduardo 82), Malyshev, Ordets, Ferreyra, Taison (Dentinho 79), Ismaily, Srna, Rakitskiy, Kovalenko (Bernard 88). Coach: Mircea Lucescu (ROU)

H 4-0 *Srna (25p), Ricardo Ferreira (43og, 73og), Kovalenko (50)*
Pyatov, Kucher, Stepanenko, Marlos (Eduardo 77), Malyshev, Ordets, Ferreyra, Taison (Dentinho 78), Ismaily, Srna, Kovalenko (Bernard 86). Coach: Mircea Lucescu (ROU)

Semi-finals - Sevilla FC (ESP)
H 2-2 *Marlos (23), Stepanenko (36)*
Pyatov, Kucher, Stepanenko, Marlos (Bernard 90+2), Malyshev, Ferreyra (Eduardo 90+1), Taison (Wellington Nem 90+1), Ismaily, Srna, Rakitskiy, Kovalenko. Coach: Mircea Lucescu (ROU)

A 1-3 *Eduardo (44)*
Pyatov, Kucher, Stepanenko, Marlos (Wellington Nem 84), Malyshev, Eduardo (Dentinho 84), Taison (Bernard 76), Ismaily, Srna, Rakitskiy, Kovalenko. Coach: Mircea Lucescu (ROU)

FC Dnipro Dnipropetrovsk

Group G
Match 1 - SS Lazio (ITA)
H 1-1 *Seleznyov (90+4)*
Boyko, Edmar (Bruno Gama 85), Seleznyov, Léo Matos, Douglas, Fedorchuk (Danilo 46), Rotan, Gueye, Anderson Pico, Fedetskiy (Ruiz 61), Matheus. Coach: Myron Markevych (UKR)

Match 2 - Rosenborg BK (NOR)
A 1-0 *Seleznyov (80)*
Boyko, Edmar, Seleznyov (Bruno Gama 84), Léo Matos, Tomečak (Luchkevych 72), Douglas, Fedorchuk, Rotan, Gueye, Fedetskiy, Matheus (Cheberyachko 90+1). Coach: Myron Markevych (UKR)

Match 3 - AS Saint-Étienne (FRA)
H 0-1
Boyko, Edmar, Seleznyov, Léo Matos, Tomečak, Douglas, Fedorchuk (Bezus 59), Rotan, Gueye, Fedetskiy (Bruno Gama 46), Matheus (Anderson Pico 78). Coach: Myron Markevych (UKR)

Match 4 - AS Saint-Étienne (FRA)
A 0-3
Boyko, Edmar, Seleznyov (Bruno Gama 78), Léo Matos, Cheberyachko (Bezus 46), Tomečak (Luchkevych 63), Douglas, Rotan, Gueye, Fedetskiy, Matheus. Coach: Myron Markevych (UKR)

DOMESTIC LEAGUE CLUB-BY-CLUB

Match 5 - SS Lazio (ITA)
A 1-3 *Bruno Gama (65)*
Boyko, Danilo, Bezus (Zozulya 57), Seleznyov, Léo Matos, Chygrynskiy, Bruno Gama, Douglas, Gueye, Fedetskiy (Shakhov 74), Matheus (Anderson Pico 41). Coach: Myron Markevych (UKR)
Match 6 - Rosenborg BK (NOR)
H 3-0 *Matheus (35, 60), Shakhov (79)*
Boyko, Ruiz (Tomeček 85), Edmar, Léo Matos, Cheberyachko, Chygrynskiy, Bruno Gama (Luchkevych 77), Shakhov (Bezus 80), Gueye, Fedetskiy, Matheus. Coach: Myron Markevych (UKR)

FC Zorya Luhansk

Third qualifying round - R. Charleroi SC (BEL)
A 2-0 *Malinovskiy (70, 89)*
Shevchenko, Sivakov, Chaikovskiy (Grechishkin 81), Hordiyenko (Ljubenović 63), Kamenyuka, Malinovskiy, Karavayev (Petryak 78), Budkivskiy, Khomchenovskiy, Opanasenko, Pylyavskiy. Coach: Yuriy Vernydub (UKR)
H 3-0 *Ljubenović (58, 68p), Malinovskiy (90+3)*
Shevchenko, Sivakov, Chaikovskiy (Ljubenović 46), Hordiyenko, Kamenyuka, Malinovskiy, Karavayev (Grechishkin 59), Budkivskiy (Petryak 70), Khomchenovskiy, Opanasenko, Pylyavskiy. Coach: Yuriy Vernydub (UKR)

Play-offs - Legia Warszawa (POL)
H 0-1
Shevchenko, Sivakov, Chaikovskiy (Ljubenović 46), Hordiyenko, Kamenyuka, Malinovskiy, Karavayev (Lipartia 70), Budkivskiy, Petryak (Khomchenovskiy 46), Opanasenko, Pylyavskiy. Coach: Yuriy Vernydub (UKR)
A 2-3 *Khomchenovskiy (39), Malinovskiy (66)*
Shevchenko, Sivakov, Hordiyenko, Kamenyuka, Malinovskiy, Karavayev, Ljubenović (Lipartia 87), Petryak, Khomchenovskiy (Budkivskiy 58), Opanasenko, Pylyavskiy (Checher 83). Coach: Yuriy Vernydub (UKR)

FC Vorskla Poltava

Third qualifying round - MŠK Žilina (SVK)
A 0-2
Bohush, Siminin, Dallku, Sklyar (A Tkachuk 85), Gromov (Bartulović 77), Shinder, Chesnakov, Sapai, Tkachuk, Kovpak (Barannyk 80), Tursunov. Coach: Vasyl Sachko (UKR)
Red card: Bohush 90
H 3-1 *Shinder (67), Y Tkachuk (90+1), Tursunov (101p)*
Nepogodov, Siminin (Perduta 46), Dallku, Sklyar (Mishchenko 87), A Tkachuk, Shinder, Sapai, Bartulović (Barannyk 60), Y Tkachuk, Kovpak, Tursunov. Coach: Vasyl Sachko (UKR)

FC Chornomorets Odesa

1936 • Chornomorets (34,164) • chernomorets.odessa.ua
Major honours
Ukrainian Cup (2) 1992, 1994
Coach: Olexandr Babych

2015
18/07	a	Olimpik	D	2-2	*Kalitvintsev, Martynenko*
26/07	a	Dnipro	L	2-4	*Kalitvintsev, Khocholava*
02/08	h	Dynamo	L	0-2	
08/08	a	Karpaty	L	0-4	
16/08	h	Zorya	L	0-2	
30/08	a	Olexandriya	D	0-0	
13/09	h	Volyn	L	1-2	*Petko*
20/09	a	Hoverla	D	1-1	*Starikov*
27/09	a	Vorskla	D	0-0	
03/10	a	Shakhtar	L	0-2	
18/10	h	Metalurh	W	5-2	*Kabayev, Starikov, Kutsenko, Kalitvintsev, Murashov*
14/11	h	Stal	D	1-1	*Kalitvintsev (p)*
07/11	a	Olimpik	L	0-2	
21/11	h	Dnipro	D	0-0	
29/11	a	Dynamo	L	1-2	*Kovalets*
06/12	a	Metalist	D	2-2	*Smirnov, Korkishko*

2016
05/03	h	Karpaty	D	0-0	
12/03	a	Zorya	L	0-4	
19/03	h	Olexandriya	L	1-2	*Martynenko*
03/04	a	Volyn	D	1-1	*Smirnov*
09/04	h	Hoverla	W	3-0	*(w/o; original result 1-0 Azatskiy)*
17/04	a	Vorskla	L	0-2	
23/04	h	Shakhtar	D	1-1	*Kalitvintsev*
30/04	a	Metalurh	W	0-0	*(w/o)*
07/05	h	Metalist	L	0-1	
15/05	a	Stal	W	1-0	*Khoblenko*

No	Name	Nat	DoB	Pos	Aps	(s)	Gls
2	Olexandr Azatskiy		13/01/94	D	8		1
86	Volodymyr Barylko		29/01/94	D	2	(5)	
71	Dmytro Bezruk		30/03/96	G	7		
12	Yevhen Borovyk		02/03/85	G	18		
94	Oleh Danchenko		01/08/94	M	20	(1)	
16	Artem Filimonov		21/02/94	M	18		
15	Giorgi Gadrani	GEO	30/09/94	D	6	(1)	
22	Vladyslav Kabayev		01/09/95	A	12	(6)	1
19	Olexandr Kalitov		29/09/93	D	3	(3)	
10	Vladyslav Kalitvintsev		04/01/93	M	20		5
4	Olexiy Khoblenko		04/04/94	A	4	(3)	1
5	David Khocholava	GEO	08/02/93	D	18		1
7	Dmytro Korkishko		04/05/90	D	15	(1)	1
6	Kyrylo Kovalets		02/07/93	M	11	(5)	1
20	Valeriy Kutsenko		02/11/86	M	19		1
25	Yevheniy Martynenko		25/06/93	D	22	(2)	2
61	Mateus	BRA	22/01/92	D	4	(1)	
14	Yevhen Murashov		09/05/95	A	6	(7)	1
52	Navid Nasimi		01/03/95	M		(7)	
23	Dmytro Nemchaninov		27/01/90	D	5		
21	Petro Pereverza		10/07/94	A	5	(6)	
32	Serhiy Petko		23/01/94	D	11	(1)	1
18	Serhiy Shapoval		07/02/90	M	6	(1)	
18	Silvio	BRA	04/05/94	A		(2)	
33	Andriy Slinkin		19/02/91	D	9	(5)	
11	Yevhen Smirnov		16/04/93	M	12	(5)	2
78	Yuriy Solomka		04/01/90	A		(3)	
87	Yevhen Starikov		17/11/88	A	7	(3)	2
17	Mykyta Tatarkov		04/01/95	A	6	(3)	
99	Vadym Yavorskiy		26/06/94	A	1	(2)	

FC Dnipro Dnipropetrovsk

1918 • Dnipro-Arena (31,003) • fcdnipro.ua
Major honours
USSR League (2) 1983, 1988; USSR Cup (1) 1989
Coach: Myron Markevych

2015
19/07	a	Hoverla	D	1-1	*Bezus*
26/07	h	Chornomorets	W	4-2	*Rotan, Bezus, Kalinić 2*
02/08	a	Vorskla	D	1-1	*Kalinić*
09/08	h	Dynamo	L	1-2	*Fedorchuk*
14/08	a	Shakhtar	W	2-0	*Matheus, Seleznyov*
30/08	h	Karpaty	W	2-0	*Seleznyov 2*
12/09	a	Metalurh	W	4-1	*Seleznyov 2 (1p), Rotan, Edmar*
20/09	h	Zorya	L	0-3	
27/09	a	Metalist	W	2-1	*og (Ryzhuk), Matheus*
04/10	h	Olexandriya	W	2-1	*Chygrynskiy, Matheus*
17/10	a	Stal	W	6-0	*Rotan, Matheus, Seleznyov 4 (1p)*
31/10	a	Olimpik	D	1-1	*Léo Matos*
08/11	h	Hoverla	W	2-0	*Matheus, Seleznyov*
21/11	a	Chornomorets	D	0-0	
30/11	h	Vorskla	L	0-2	
05/12	h	Volyn	L	0-1	

2016
05/03	a	Dynamo	L	0-2	
13/03	h	Shakhtar	W	4-1	*Ruiz, Shakhov, Zozulya, Bezus*
20/03	a	Karpaty	W	1-0	*Zozulya*
02/04	h	Metalurh	W	0-0	*(w/o)*
10/04	a	Zorya	W	2-1	*Shakhov, Anderson Pico*
16/04	h	Metalist	W	5-0	*Shakhov, Ruiz 2, Luchkevych, Zozulya (p)*
24/04	a	Olexandriya	W	4-0	*Anderson Pico, Rotan, Ruiz, Bruno Gama*
30/04	h	Stal	W	2-0	*Ruiz, Matheus*
07/05	a	Volyn	W	3-2	*Ruiz, Bezus, Matheus*
15/05	h	Olimpik	D	1-1	*Shakhov*

No	Name	Nat	DoB	Pos	Aps	(s)	Gls
3	Volodymyr Adamyuk		17/07/91	M	3		
36	Anderson Pico	BRA	04/11/88	D	11	(1)	2
79	Michel Babatunde	NGA	24/12/92	M		(2)	
19	Roman Bezus		26/09/90	M	10	(10)	4
97	Andriy Blyznychenko		24/07/94	M	1	(1)	
71	Denys Boyko		29/01/88	G	15		
20	Bruno Gama	POR	15/11/87	M	13	(10)	1
14	Yevhen Cheberyachko		19/06/83	M	5	(1)	
15	Dmytro Chygrynskiy		07/11/86	D	12	(1)	1
6	Danilo	BRA	13/01/90	M	5	(7)	
8	Douglas	BRA	04/04/90	D	13		
8	Edmar		16/06/80	M	7	(3)	1
44	Artem Fedetskiy		26/04/85	D	11	(2)	
25	Valeriy Fedorchuk		05/10/88	M	8	(2)	1
30	Papa Gueye	SEN	07/06/84	D	22		
9	Nikola Kalinić	CRO	05/01/88	A	2	(2)	3
7	Jaba Kankava	GEO	18/03/86	M	3	(1)	
19	Aleksandre Kobakhidze	GEO	11/02/87	M	1		
38	Oleh Kozhushko		17/02/98	M	1		
13	Danylo Kucher		25/01/97	G	1		
16	Jan Laštůvka	CZE	07/07/82	G	9		
12	Léo Matos	BRA	02/04/86	D	17	(2)	1
24	Valeriy Luchkevych		11/01/96	M	11	(9)	1
99	Matheus	BRA	15/01/83	A	20	(3)	7
9	Serhiy Nazarenko		16/02/80	M		(2)	
89	Serhiy Politylo		09/01/89	M	4	(2)	
29	Ruslan Rotan		29/10/81	M	19	(2)	4
7	John Jairo Ruiz	CRC	10/01/94	M	8	(6)	6
11	Yevhen Seleznyov		20/07/85	A	15	(1)	10
28	Yevhen Shakhov		30/11/90	M	9	(1)	4
39	Olexandr Svatok		27/09/94	D	3		
22	Ivan Tomeček	CRO	07/12/89	M	9		
18	Roman Zozulya		17/11/89	A	7	(3)	3

FC Dynamo Kyiv

1927 • NSK Olimpiyskiy (70,050) • fcdynamo.kiev.ua

Major honours
UEFA Cup Winners' Cup (2) 1975, 1986; UEFA Super Cup (1) 1975; USSR League (13) 1961, 1966, 1967, 1968, 1971, 1974, 1975, 1977, 1980, 1981, 1985, 1986, 1990; Ukrainian League (15) 1993, 1994, 1995, 1996, 1997, 1998, 1999, 2000, 2001, 2003, 2004, 2007, 2009, 2015, 2016; USSR Cup (9) 1954, 1964, 1966, 1974, 1978, 1982, 1985, 1987, 1990; Ukrainian Cup (11) 1993, 1996, 1998, 1999, 2000, 2003, 2005, 2006, 2007, 2014, 2015

Coach: Serhiy Rebrov

2015
19/07	a	Stal	W	2-1	Buyalskiy, Gusev (p)
25/07	h	Olimpik	W	2-0	Yarmolenko, Júnior Moraes
02/08	a	Chornomorets	W	2-0	Júnior Moraes, Yarmolenko
09/08	a	Dnipro	W	2-1	og (Douglas), Miguel Veloso
15/08	h	Karpaty	W	3-0	Miguel Veloso, Yarmolenko, Júnior Moraes
30/08	a	Zorya	D	0-0	
12/09	h	Olexandriya	W	3-0	Garmash, Vida, Danilo Silva
20/09	a	Volyn	W	2-0	Kravets, Gusev (p)
26/09	h	Hoverla	W	2-0	Kravets, Gusev
04/10	a	Vorskla	W	4-0	Buyalskiy, Antunes, González, Yarmolenko
16/10	h	Shakhtar	L	0-3	
31/10	h	Metalist	W	2-0	Sydorchuk, Júnior Moraes
08/11	h	Stal	W	2-0	Yarmolenko 2
20/11	a	Olimpik	W	3-0	Júnior Moraes, Garmash, Gusev (p)
29/11	h	Chornomorets	W	2-1	González, Yarmolenko (p)
04/12	a	Metalurh	W	6-0	Yarmolenko, Petrović, Garmash, Teodorczyk, Gusev 2 (1p)

2016
05/03	h	Dnipro	W	2-0	Yarmolenko, Gusev
11/03	a	Karpaty	W	2-1	Teodorczyk, Yarmolenko
20/03	h	Zorya	W	1-0	Júnior Moraes
02/04	a	Olexandriya	W	2-0	Vida, Gusev
10/04	h	Volyn	W	3-0	Júnior Moraes 2, Gusev
16/04	a	Hoverla	W	3-0	Yarmolenko, Khacheridi
24/04	h	Vorskla	W	1-0	Júnior Moraes
01/05	a	Shakhtar	L	0-3	
07/05	h	Metalurh	W		(w/o)
14/05	a	Metalist	W	4-1	Teodorczyk 3, Gusev (p)

No	Name	Nat	DoB	Pos	Aps	(s)	Gls
5	Antunes	POR	01/04/87	D	22		1
90	Younes Belhanda	MAR	25/02/90	M	5	(5)	
2	Artem Besedin		31/03/96	A		(1)	
29	Vitaliy Buyalskiy		06/01/93	M	9	(9)	2
2	Danilo Silva	BRA	24/11/86	D	17		1
6	Aleksandar Dragovic	AUT	06/03/91	D	17		
19	Denys Garmash		19/04/90	M	12	(7)	3
25	Derlis González	PAR	20/03/94	M	5	(9)	2
20	Oleh Gusev		25/04/83	M	18	(6)	10
11	Júnior Moraes	BRA	04/04/87	A	18	(4)	7
34	Yevhen Khacheridi		28/07/87	D	15		1
18	Nikita Korzun	BLR	06/03/95	M	1		
22	Artem Kravets		03/06/89	A	4	(8)	2
27	Yevhen Makarenko		21/05/91	D	3		
4	Miguel Veloso	POR	11/05/86	M	19	(1)	2
9	Mykola Morozyuk		17/01/88	D	4	(3)	
88	Serhiy Myakushko		15/04/93	M	1	(3)	
48	Pavlo Orikhovskiy		13/05/96	M		(1)	
8	Radosav Petrović	SRB	08/03/89	M	6	(1)	1
72	Artur Rudko		07/05/92	G	1		
17	Serhiy Rybalka		01/04/90	M	17		
23	Olexandr Rybka		10/04/87	G	6		
1	Olexandr Shovkovskiy		02/01/75	G	18		
16	Serhiy Sydorchuk		02/05/91	M	11	(8)	1
91	Łukasz Teodorczyk	POL	03/06/91	A	4	(7)	5
24	Domagoj Vida	CRO	29/04/89	D	18		2
7	Olexandr Yakovenko		23/06/87	M	1	(3)	
10	Andriy Yarmolenko		23/10/89	M	23		13

FC Hoverla Uzhhorod

1925 • Avanhard (12,000) • fcgoverla.uz.ua

Coach: Vyacheslav Hrozniy

2015
19/07	h	Dnipro	D	1-1	Hemeha
25/07	h	Vorskla	D	1-1	Khlebas
01/08	a	Shakhtar	L	0-2	
08/08	h	Metalurh	D	1-1	Tsurikov (p)
16/08	h	Metalist	D	2-2	Jagodinskas, Khlebas
29/08	h	Stal	D	0-0	
12/09	a	Olimpik	W	1-0	Serhiychuk
20/09	h	Chornomorets	D	1-1	Kuzyk
26/09	a	Dynamo	L	0-2	
04/10	h	Karpaty	L	0-2	
18/10	a	Zorya	L	1-2	Ivanov
01/11	a	Volyn	D	0-0	
08/11	a	Dnipro	L	0-2	
21/11	a	Vorskla	L	1-2	Serhiychuk
29/11	h	Shakhtar	L	1-6	Khlebas
05/12	h	Olexandriya	L	1-2	Khlebas

2016
05/03	h	Metalurh	W	0-0	(w/o)
13/03	h	Metalist	W	1-0	Honchar
19/03	a	Stal	L	0-1	
03/04	h	Olimpik	L	0-3	(w/o; original result 0-2)
09/04	a	Chornomorets	L	0-3	(w/o; original result 0-1)
16/04	h	Dynamo	L	0-3	
23/04	h	Karpaty	L	0-3	
30/04	a	Zorya	L	0-4	
07/05	a	Olexandriya	L	0-4	
14/05	h	Volyn	L	1-4	Kuzyk

No	Name	Nat	DoB	Pos	Aps	(s)	Gls
33	Dmytro Babenko		28/06/78	G	10		
31	Andriy Cherepko		17/01/97	G		(1)	
28	Yevhen Chumak		25/08/95	M	9	(2)	
32	Yevhen Dobrovolskiy		10/02/95	M		(3)	
14	Vitaliy Gavrysh		18/03/86	M	7	(5)	
2	Viktor Hei		02/02/96	M	2	(2)	
11	Vitaliy Hemeha		10/10/94	M	23		1
21	Ihor Honchar		10/01/93	M	11	(5)	1
30	Pavlo Ivanov		28/09/84	D	11	(3)	1
20	Vitālijs Jagodinskis	LVA	28/02/92	D	19		1
24	Vitaliy Kaverin		04/09/90	M	2	(3)	
7	Dmytro Khlebas		09/05/94	A	15		4
9	Olexiy Khoblenko		04/04/94	A	6	(6)	
25	Olexiy Khomenko		28/08/94	M	2	(2)	
10	Ihor Khudobyak		05/04/87	A	10	(3)	
5	Stanislav Kotyo		06/04/94	D		(1)	
77	Pavlo Kutas		03/09/82	D	13	(1)	
17	Orest Kuzyk		17/05/95	M	20	(4)	2
3	Vyacheslav Lukhtanov		12/02/95	D	16		
23	Serhiy Lyulka		22/02/90	D	16		
18	Pavlo Polehenko		06/01/95	D		(3)	
12	Artur Rudko		07/05/92	G	15		
5	Mykhailo Ryashko		05/11/96	D	11	(6)	
8	Olexiy Savchenko		27/09/93	M	21		
29	Mykhailo Serhiychuk		29/07/91	A	15	(2)	2
22	Yuriy Toma		27/04/96	M	3	(3)	
27	Andriy Tsurikov		05/10/92	M	15		1
6	Dmytro Yeremenko		20/06/90	M	3	(6)	

FC Karpaty Lviv

1963 • Ukraina (27,925) • fckarpaty.lviv.ua

Major honours
USSR Cup (1) 1969

**Coach: Igor Jovićević (CRO);
(18/01/16) Volodymyr Bezubyak**

2015
18/07	a	Metalist	L	0-2	
25/07	h	Stal	W	1-0	Karnoza (p)
01/08	h	Olimpik	W	1-0	Kozhanov
08/08	h	Chornomorets	W	4-0	Karnoza, Holodyuk, Strashkevych, Daushvili (p)
15/08	a	Dynamo	L	0-3	
30/08	a	Dnipro	L	0-2	
13/09	h	Zorya	D	1-1	Khudobyak
20/09	a	Olexandriya	L	1-4	Strashkevych
27/09	h	Volyn	L	0-2	
04/10	a	Hoverla	W	2-0	og (Savchenko), Plastun
18/10	h	Vorskla	L	1-3	og (Tursunov)
31/10	h	Metalurh	W	1-0	Kostevych
07/11	h	Metalist	D	1-1	Holodyuk
22/11	a	Stal	D	1-1	Hutsulyak
28/11	h	Olimpik	W	4-1	Kozhanov (p), Chachua, Khudobyak, Klyots
03/12	a	Shakhtar	L	0-3	

2016
05/03	a	Chornomorets	D	0-0	
11/03	h	Dynamo	L	1-2	Chachua
20/03	h	Dnipro	L	0-1	
02/04	h	Zorya	L	1-4	Okechukwu
10/04	h	Olexandriya	D	2-2	Karnoza 2
17/04	a	Volyn	D	0-0	
23/04	h	Hoverla	W	3-0	Miroshnychenko, Hutsulyak, Blanco
30/04	a	Vorskla	L	0-3	
08/05	h	Shakhtar	L	1-2	Blanco
15/05	a	Metalurh	W	0-0	(w/o)

No	Name	Nat	DoB	Pos	Aps	(s)	Gls
29	Gustavo Blanco	ARG	05/11/91	A	9		2
11	Ambrosiy Chachua		02/04/94	M	10	(6)	2
77	Murtaz Daushvili	GEO	01/05/89	M	12	(6)	1
5	Andriy Hitchenko		02/10/84	D	19	(1)	
17	Oleh Holodyuk		02/01/88	M	23		2
97	Oleksiy Hutsulyak		25/12/97	A	3	(12)	2
92	Gegam Kadimyan	ARM	19/10/92	M	4		
10	Artur Karnoza		02/08/90	M	13	(7)	4
16	Ihor Khudobyak		20/02/85	M	22	(1)	2
18	Dmytro Klyots		15/04/96	M	6	(12)	1
8	Volodymyr Kostevych		23/10/92	D	23	(1)	1
9	Denys Kozhanov		13/06/87	M	14	(3)	2
3	Vasyl Kravets		20/08/97	D	8	(7)	
19	Pavlo Ksionz		02/01/87	M	16	(2)	
79	Andriy Markovych		25/06/95	D	2		
94	Denys Miroshnychenko		11/10/94	D	22	(1)	1
23	Roman Mysak		09/09/91	G	22		
21	Yevhen Neplyakh		11/05/92	D	1		
26	Artur Novotryasov		19/07/92	D	10	(3)	
98	Gabriel Okechukwu	NGA	28/08/95	A	1	(3)	1
1	Roman Pidkivka		09/05/95	G	3		
2	Ihor Plastun		20/08/90	D	25		1
35	Maryan Shved		16/07/97	A		(2)	
27	Vadym Strashkevych		21/04/94	A	3	(8)	2

FC Metalist Kharkiv

1925 • Metalist Stadium (41,307) • metalist.ua
Major honours
USSR Cup (1) 1988
Coach: Olexandr Sevidov;
(18/04/16) (Olexandr Pryzetko)

2015

18/07	h	Karpaty	W	2-0	Priyomov 2 (1p)
25/07	a	Zorya	D	0-0	
02/08	h	Olexandriya	D	1-1	Dovhiy
07/08	a	Volyn	D	2-2	Putivtsev, Churko
16/08	h	Hoverla	D	2-2	Rudyka, Ryzhuk
29/08	a	Vorskla	L	0-1	
11/09	h	Shakhtar	L	0-5	
19/09	h	Metalurh	D	0-0	
27/09	a	Dnipro	L	1-2	Priyomov
03/10	h	Stal	D	1-1	Priyomov
18/10	a	Olimpik	L	0-3	
31/10	a	Dynamo	L	0-2	
07/11	a	Karpaty	D	1-1	Priyomov
22/11	h	Zorya	L	0-1	
28/11	a	Olexandriya	L	0-2	
06/12	h	Chornomorets	D	2-2	Rodić, Priyomov

2016

06/03	h	Volyn	W	3-0	Polyanskiy, Priyomov, Rodić
13/03	a	Hoverla	L	0-1	
19/03	h	Vorskla	L	0-3	
01/04	a	Shakhtar	L	1-8	Kornev
09/04	h	Metalurh	W	0-0	(w/o)
16/04	a	Dnipro	L	0-5	
23/04	a	Stal	D	0-0	
30/04	h	Olimpik	W	1-0	Ryzhuk
07/05	a	Chornomorets	W	1-0	Zotko
14/05	h	Dynamo	L	1-4	Napolov

No	Name	Nat	DoB	Pos	Aps	(s)	Gls
8	Serhiy Barylko		05/01/87	M	4	(2)	
21	Artem Besedin		31/03/96	A	8	(3)	
7	Ivan Bobko		10/12/90	M	7	(6)	
10	Vyacheslav Churko		10/05/93	M	12	(2)	1
94	Semen Datsenko		10/05/94	D	1	(1)	
4	Olexiy Dovhiy		02/11/89	M	14		1
35	Olexandr Ilyushchenkov		23/03/90	G	3		
1	Danylo Kanevtsev		26/07/96	G	2		
20	Olexandr Kapliyenko		07/03/96	D	7	(1)	
12	Artem Kasiyanov		20/04/83	M	5		
21	Ihor Kharatin		02/02/95	M	8		
12	Rustam Khudzhamov		05/10/82	G	6		
52	Yuriy Kopyna		04/07/82	M		(1)	
19	Illya Kornev		01/11/96	A	3	(1)	1
56	Ihor Koshman		07/03/95	M		(1)	
5	Kyrylo Kovalchuk		11/06/86	M	13		
54	Vladyslav Krayev		05/02/95	M	3	(1)	
9	Stanislav Kulish		08/02/89	A	2	(7)	
88	Olexiy Kurilov		24/04/88	D	12		
11	Dmytro Liopa		23/11/88	M	10	(2)	
53	Serhiy Napolov		27/01/96	M	1	(3)	1
28	Serhiy Nazarenko		16/02/80	M	2	(4)	
18	Olexandr Noyok		15/05/92	M	7	(4)	
23	Serhiy Pohoriliy		28/07/86	G	14		
2	Olexiy Polyanskiy		12/04/86	M	14		1
80	Volodymyr Priyomov		02/01/86	A	21	(1)	7
77	Artem Putivtsev		29/08/88	D	11	(3)	1
49	Andriy Ralyuchenko		08/06/95	M	5	(2)	
55	Ivan Rodić	CRO	11/11/85	A	4	(7)	2
19	Serhiy Rudyka		14/06/88	M	12		1
15	Dmytro Ryzhuk		05/04/92	D	14	(5)	2
95	Eduard Sobol		20/04/95	D	19	(2)	
44	Oleh Synytsya		20/03/96	M	1	(3)	
43	Yuriy Tkachuk		18/04/95	M		(3)	
11	Maxym Tretyakov		06/03/93	M	7	(1)	
13	Ivan Zotko		09/07/96	D	7	(1)	1
42	Yevhen Zubeiko		30/09/89	D	16	(1)	

FC Metalurh Zaporizhya

1935 • Slavutych Arena (11,756) • fcmetalurg.com
Coach: Anatoliy Chantsev

2015

17/07	h	Zorya	L	0-6	
26/07	a	Olexandriya	L	0-1	
02/08	h	Volyn	L	0-2	
08/08	a	Hoverla	D	1-1	Kapliyenko
15/08	a	Vorskla	D	1-1	Kornev
28/08	a	Shakhtar	L	0-2	
12/09	h	Dnipro	L	1-4	Gvilia
19/09	a	Metalist	D	0-0	
27/09	a	Stal	L	0-3	
03/10	h	Olimpik	L	0-3	
18/10	a	Chornomorets	L	2-5	Platon 2
31/10	a	Karpaty	L	0-1	
07/11	a	Zorya	L	1-4	Zhurakhovskiy
22/11	h	Olexandriya	L	0-2	
29/11	a	Volyn	L	1-9	Ihnatenko
04/12	h	Dynamo	L	0-6	

2016

05/03	h	Hoverla	L	0-0	(w/o)
12/03	a	Vorskla	L	0-0	(w/o)
19/03	h	Shakhtar	L	0-0	(w/o)
02/04	a	Dnipro	L	0-0	(w/o)
09/04	a	Metalist	L	0-0	(w/o)
16/04	h	Stal	L	0-0	(w/o)
23/04	a	Olimpik	L	0-0	(w/o)
30/04	h	Chornomorets	L	0-0	(w/o)
07/05	a	Dynamo	L	0-0	(w/o)
15/05	h	Karpaty	L	0-0	(w/o)

No	Name	Nat	DoB	Pos	Aps	(s)	Gls
35	Maxym Babiychuk		28/04/94	M	4		
7	Yehor Demchenko		25/07/97	M	3	(3)	
37	Kyrylo Demidov		18/08/96	M	1		
50	Ali Farid		11/02/92	A		(1)	
10	Valerian Gvilia	GEO	24/05/94	M	14		1
2	Dmytro Haponchuk		08/11/95	D	2	(1)	
77	Vladyslav Ignatiyev		25/10/97	M		(1)	
97	Danylo Ihnatenko		13/03/97	M	3	(7)	1
3	Yevhen Izdebskiy		03/06/95	D	3	(1)	
18	Olexandr Kapliyenko		07/03/96	D	14		1
60	Yehor Klymenko		11/11/97	M	3	(1)	
5	Semen Klyuchyk		23/12/97	D	1	(1)	
19	Ihor Kornev		01/11/96	A	11		1
89	Yan Kovalevskiy		26/06/93	A	3		
27	Serhiy Kulinich		09/01/95	D	15		
15	Artur Kuznetsov		09/03/95	D	3		
22	Vitaliy Lysytskiy		16/04/82	D	11		
88	Nurudeen Orelesi	NGA	10/04/89	M	12		
20	Pavlo Paşayev	AZE	04/01/88	D	7		
17	Dmytro Plakhtyr		14/02/96	M		(3)	
24	Ruslan Platon		12/01/82	A	2	(8)	2
6	Roman Pomazan		05/09/94	D	8	(2)	
95	Roman Popov		29/06/95	M	10	(4)	
16	Tymofiy Sheremeta		06/10/95	G	4	(1)	
1	Maxym Startsev		20/01/80	G	8		
11	Roman Stefurak		17/04/96	M		(4)	
4	Mykyta Tatarkov		04/01/95	A	14		
44	Dmytro Yusov		11/05/93	M	8	(1)	
70	Artem Zakharov		19/06/96	M		(1)	
25	Ihor Zhurakhovskiy		19/09/94	M	12	(1)	1

FC Olexandriya
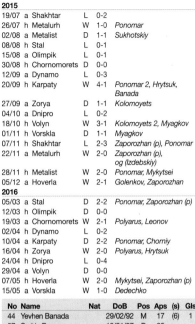

1948 • KSK Nika (7,000) • fco.com.ua
Coach: Volodymyr Sharan

2015

19/07	a	Shakhtar	L	0-2	
26/07	h	Metalurh	W	1-0	Ponomar
02/08	a	Metalist	D	1-1	Sukhotskiy
08/08	h	Stal	L	0-1	
15/08	a	Olimpik	L	0-1	
30/08	h	Chornomorets	D	0-0	
12/09	a	Dynamo	L	0-3	
20/09	h	Karpaty	W	4-1	Ponomar 2, Hrytsuk, Banada
27/09	a	Zorya	D	1-1	Kolomoyets
04/10	a	Dnipro	L	0-2	
18/10	h	Volyn	W	3-1	Kolomoyets 2, Myagkov
01/11	a	Vorskla	D	1-1	Myagkov
07/11	h	Shakhtar	L	2-3	Zaporozhan (p), Ponomar
22/11	a	Metalurh	W	2-0	Zaporozhan (p), og (Izdebskiy)
28/11	h	Metalist	W	2-0	Ponomar, Mykytsei
05/12	a	Hoverla	W	2-1	Golenkov, Zaporozhan

2016

05/03	a	Stal	D	2-2	Ponomar, Zaporozhan (p)
12/03	h	Olimpik	D	0-0	
19/03	h	Chornomorets	W	2-1	Polyarus, Leonov
02/04	h	Dynamo	L	0-2	
10/04	a	Karpaty	D	2-2	Ponomar, Chorniy
16/04	h	Zorya	W	2-0	Polyarus, Hrytsuk
24/04	a	Dnipro	L	0-4	
29/04	a	Volyn	D	0-0	
07/05	h	Metalurh	W	2-0	Mykytsei, Zaporozhan (p)
15/05	a	Vorskla	W	1-0	Dedechko

No	Name	Nat	DoB	Pos	Aps	(s)	Gls
44	Yevhen Banada		29/02/92	M	17	(6)	1
87	Serhiy Basov		19/01/87	D	25		
25	Serhiy Chebotayev		07/03/88	D	14		
13	Artem Chorniy		23/10/89	M	9	(10)	1
31	Denys Dedechko		02/07/87	M	3		1
45	Aderinsola Eseola		28/06/91	A		(2)	
17	Anton Golenkov		17/12/89	M	12	(1)	1
22	Vasyl Hrytsuk		21/11/87	M	13	(5)	2
32	Maxym Imerekov		23/01/91	D	8	(1)	
29	Yuriy Kolomoyets		22/03/90	A	7	(4)	3
72	Mykhailo Kozak		20/01/91	M	6	(15)	
7	Stanislav Kulish		08/02/89	A	6	(1)	
6	Dmytro Leonov		06/11/88	M	4	(10)	1
24	Vladyslav Levanidov		23/02/93	G	12	(1)	
5	Olexandr Matveyev		11/02/89	D	1	(2)	
77	Yevhen Morozenko		16/12/91	M		(1)	
3	Pavlo Myagkov		30/12/92	M	9	(1)	2
3	Stanislav Mykytsei		07/09/89	D	15	(1)	2
54	Andriy Novak		06/12/88	G	14		
14	Artem Polyarus		05/07/92	M	10	(2)	2
40	Yuriy Putrash		29/01/90	D	5		
26	Anton Shendryk		26/05/86	D	19	(2)	
27	Serhiy Starenkiy		20/09/84	M	5	(6)	
2	Ruslan Stepanyuk		16/01/92	M		(3)	
2	Artem Sukhotskiy		06/12/92	D	16		1
11	David Targamadze	GEO	22/08/89	M	7	(3)	
15	Andriy Zaporozhan		21/03/83	M	25		5

FC Olimpik Donetsk

2001 • NTK FFU im. V. Bannikov, Kyiv (1,678); Dynamo im. Valeriy Lobanovskiy, Kyiv (16,873) • olimpik.com.ua

Coach: Roman Sanzhar

2015

18/07	h	Chornomorets	D	2-2	Semenyna, Borzenko
25/07	a	Dynamo	L	0-2	
01/08	h	Karpaty	L	0-1	
09/08	h	Zorya	L	0-4	
15/08	h	Olexandriya	W	1-0	Kadymyan
29/08	a	Volyn	L	0-1	
12/09	h	Hoverla	L	0-1	
19/09	a	Vorskla	L	1-2	Rhasalla
26/09	h	Shakhtar	L	2-3	Kadymyan, Lysenko
03/10	a	Metalurh	W	3-0	Hryshko, Kadymyan, Tanchyk
18/10	h	Metalist	W	3-0	Rhasalla, Lysenko, Matyazh
31/10	h	Dnipro	D	1-1	Tanchyk
07/11	a	Chornomorets	W	2-0	Drachenko, Rhasalla
20/11	h	Dynamo	L	0-3	
28/11	a	Karpaty	L	1-4	Matyazh
06/12	a	Stal	L	0-1	

2016

06/03	h	Zorya	D	1-1	Postupalenko
12/03	a	Olexandriya	D	0-0	
20/03	h	Volyn	D	1-1	Matyazh
03/04	a	Hoverla	W	3-0	(w/o; original result 2-0 Hoshkoderya, Rhasalla)
09/04	h	Vorskla	D	1-1	Matyazh (p)
17/04	a	Shakhtar	L	0-3	
23/04	a	Metalurh	W	0-0	(w/o)
30/04	a	Metalist	L	0-1	
08/05	h	Stal	L	0-2	
15/05	a	Dnipro	D	1-1	Lysenko

No	Name	Nat	DoB	Pos	Aps	(s)	Gls
33	Serhiy Borzenko		22/06/86	D	15	(2)	1
50	Sekou Conde	GUI	09/06/93	D	8	(5)	
8	Volodymyr Doronin		15/01/93	D	4	(6)	
7	Maxym Drachenko		28/01/90	M	12	(10)	1
24	Vitaliy Fedoriv		21/10/87	D	7	(3)	
27	Denys Galenkov		13/10/95	A		(2)	
10	Vladyslav Gelzin		27/08/73	A	1	(1)	
9	Vitaliy Hoshkoderya		08/01/88	D	22	(1)	1
4	Dmytro Hryshko		02/12/85	D	20	(1)	1
32	Vladis-Emmerson Illoy-Ayyet		07/10/95	D	2	(1)	
23	Sheriff Isa	NGA	10/11/90	M	5		
77	Gegam Kadymyan	ARM	19/10/92	A	14	(1)	3
45	Vladyslav Khomutov		04/06/98	M		(1)	
15	Valeriy Lebid		05/01/89	M	6		
21	Volodymyr Lysenko		20/04/88	A	3	(11)	3
16	Serhiy Lytovchenko		04/10/87	G	6	(1)	
1	Zauri Makharadze		24/03/93	G	19		
20	Ivan Matyazh		15/02/88	A	11	(6)	4
23	Dmytro Nemchaninov		27/01/90	D	7		
13	Kelvin Nwamora	NGA	31/10/90	A		(2)	
5	Vladyslav Ohyrya		03/04/90	M	23		
3	Temur Partsveniya		06/07/91	D	17		
26	Kyrylo Petrov		22/06/90	D	7		
14	Anton Postupalenko		28/08/88	M	15	(1)	
11	Mohammed Rhasalla	MAR	15/09/93	A	20	(1)	4
18	Ihor Semenyna		01/01/89	M	1	(5)	1
17	Serhiy Shestakov		12/04/90	M	5	(6)	
25	Ruslan Stepanyuk		16/01/92	M	1	(3)	
23	Volodymyr Tanchyk		17/10/91	M	20	(1)	2
19	Ihor Tyshchenko		11/05/89	M	3		
89	Olexandr Volkov		07/02/89	A	1	(2)	

FC Shakhtar Donetsk

1936 • Arena Lviv, Lviv (34,915); NTK FFU im. V. Bannikov, Kyiv (1,678); Slavutych Arena, Zaporizhya (11,756); Chornomorets, Odesa (34,164) • shakhtar.com

Major honours

UEFA Cup (1) 2009; Ukrainian League (9) 2002, 2005, 2006, 2008, 2010, 2011, 2012, 2013, 2014; USSR Cup (4) 1961, 1962, 1980, 1983; Ukrainian Cup (10) 1995, 1997, 2001, 2002, 2004, 2008, 2011, 2012, 2013, 2016

Coach: Mircea Lucescu (ROU)

2015

19/07	h	Olexandriya	W	2-0	Alex Teixeira 2
23/07	a	Volyn	W	4-1	Taison, Alex Teixeira 2, Eduardo
01/08	h	Hoverla	W	2-0	Alex Teixeira, Eduardo
09/08	a	Vorskla	D	2-2	Marlos, Eduardo
14/08	h	Dnipro	L	0-2	
28/08	h	Metalurh	W	2-0	Alex Teixeira 2 (1p)
11/09	a	Metalist	W	5-0	Rakitskiy, Alex Teixeira 2 (1p), Kucher, Gladkiy
19/09	h	Stal	W	2-0	Fred, Alex Teixeira
26/09	a	Olimpik	W	3-2	Alex Teixeira 2 (1p), Srna (p)
03/10	a	Chornomorets	W	2-0	Alex Teixeira 2 (1p)
16/10	a	Dynamo	W	3-0	Marlos, Alex Teixeira 2
30/10	a	Zorya	W	7-1	Fred, Stepanenko 2, Alex Teixeira 2, Eduardo 2
07/11	a	Olexandriya	W	3-2	Dentinho, Gladkiy, Alex Teixeira
21/11	h	Volyn	W	4-0	Marlos 2, Ismaily, Gladkiy
29/11	a	Hoverla	W	6-1	Rakitskiy, Taison, Marlos, Ferreyra, Alex Teixeira 2 (1p)
03/12	h	Karpaty	W	3-0	Eduardo, Ismaily, Alex Teixeira

2016

06/03	h	Vorskla	W	3-1	Srna, Taison, Eduardo
13/03	a	Dnipro	L	1-4	Malyshev
19/03	a	Metalurh	W	0-0	(w/o)
01/04	h	Metalist	W	8-1	Taison 3, Ismaily, Ferreyra, Marlos, Eduardo, Bernard
10/04	a	Stal	D	3-3	Eduardo, Dentinho, Malyshev
17/04	h	Olimpik	W	3-0	Wellington Nem, Marlos (p), Eduardo
23/04	a	Chornomorets	D	1-1	Bernard
01/05	h	Dynamo	W	3-0	Eduardo 2, Wellington Nem
08/05	a	Karpaty	W	2-1	og (Hitchenko), Marlos (p)
15/05	h	Zorya	L	2-3	Ferreyra, Gladkiy

No	Name	Nat	DoB	Pos	Aps	(s)	Gls
29	Alex Teixeira	BRA	06/01/90	M	15		22
20	Giorgi Arabidze	GEO	04/03/98	A		(2)	
10	Bernard	BRA	08/09/92	M	15	(6)	2
9	Dentinho	BRA	19/01/89	M	8	(6)	2
22	Eduardo	CRO	25/02/83	A	6	(13)	12
19	Facundo Ferreyra	ARG	14/03/91	A	8	(3)	3
8	Fred	BRA	05/03/93	M	12		2
21	Olexandr Gladkiy		24/08/87	A	13	(4)	4
31	Ismaily	BRA	11/01/90	D	10		3
32	Anton Kanibolotskiy		16/05/88	G	9		
14	Vasyl Kobin		24/05/85	D	6		
58	Andriy Korobenko		28/05/97	M		(1)	
74	Viktor Kovalenko		14/02/96	M	11	(12)	
38	Serhiy Krivtsov		15/03/91	D	7		
5	Olexandr Kucher		22/10/82	D	10	(1)	1
17	Maxym Malyshev		24/12/92	M	13	(2)	2
66	Márcio Azevedo	BRA	05/02/86	D	6		
11	Marlos	BRA	07/06/88	M	17	(7)	8
25	Mykola Matviyenko		02/05/96	D	1	(1)	
18	Ivan Ordets		08/07/92	D	15	(1)	
30	Andriy Pyatov		28/06/84	G	14		
44	Yaroslav Rakitskiy		03/08/89	D	17	(1)	2
23	Bohdan Sarnavskiy		29/01/95	G	2		
13	Vyacheslav Shevchuk		13/05/79	D	9		
33	Darijo Srna	CRO	01/05/82	D	19		2
6	Taras Stepanenko		08/08/89	M	18		2
28	Taison	BRA	13/01/88	A	9	(9)	6
7	Wellington Nem	BRA	06/02/92	A	5	(4)	2
59	Olexandr Zubkov		03/08/96	A		(1)	

FC Stal Dniprodzerzhynsk

1926 • Meteor, Dnipropetrovsk (24,381) • fcstal.com.ua

Coach: Volodymyr Mazyar; (16/01/16) Erik van der Meer (NED)

2015

19/07	h	Dynamo	L	1-2	og (Miguel Veloso)
25/07	a	Karpaty	L	0-1	
02/08	h	Zorya	W	2-0	Putrash 2
08/08	a	Olexandriya	W	1-0	og (Banada)
16/08	h	Volyn	L	1-2	Kulach
29/08	a	Hoverla	D	0-0	
13/09	h	Vorskla	L	1-2	Babenko
19/09	a	Shakhtar	L	0-2	
27/09	h	Metalurh	W	3-0	Kulach 2, Debelko
03/10	a	Metalist	D	1-1	Kulach
17/10	h	Dnipro	L	0-6	
01/11	a	Chornomorets	D	1-1	Kotlyar (p)
08/11	a	Dynamo	L	0-2	
22/11	h	Karpaty	D	1-1	Adamyuk
28/11	a	Zorya	L	1-2	Kulach
06/12	h	Olimpik	W	1-0	Kucherov

2016

05/03	h	Olexandriya	D	2-2	Kravchenko, Debelko
13/03	a	Volyn	L	0-1	
19/03	h	Hoverla	W	1-0	Lazić (p)
02/04	a	Vorskla	D	0-0	
10/04	a	Shakhtar	D	3-3	Kalenchuk, Lazić, Ishchenko
16/04	a	Metalurh	W	0-0	(w/o)
23/04	h	Metalist	D	0-0	
30/04	a	Dnipro	L	0-2	
08/05	h	Olimpik	W	2-0	Vasin 2
14/05	h	Chornomorets	L	0-1	

No	Name	Nat	DoB	Pos	Aps	(s)	Gls
3	Volodymyr Adamyuk		17/07/91	D	16		1
29	Ruslan Babenko		08/07/92	M	4	(5)	1
42	Rostyslav Bagdasarov		24/05/93	D	1		
12	Olexandr Bandura		30/05/86	G	5		
2	Artem Baranovskiy		17/03/90	D	7	(5)	
11	Yevhen Budnyk		04/09/90	A	2	(16)	
51	Artur Daneliyan		09/02/98	D		(1)	
93	Roman Debelko		08/08/93	A	10	(8)	2
99	Guyon Fernandez	NED	04/08/86	A	2		
8	Volodymyr Homenyuk		19/07/85	A	5	(2)	
22	Rumyan Hovsepyan	ARM	13/11/91	M	1	(2)	
32	Mykola Ishchenko		09/03/83	D	15	(1)	1
6	Maxym Kalenchuk		05/12/89	M	18	(1)	1
91	Roman Karasyuk		27/03/91	M	25		
14	Anton Kotlyar		07/03/93	M	6	(11)	1
25	Olexandr Kozak		25/07/94	M	4	(2)	
4	Anton Kravchenko		23/03/97	D	17	(2)	1
21	Valeriy Kucherov		11/08/93	M	6	(6)	1
10	Vladyslav Kulach		07/05/93	A	14	(1)	5
17	Akeem Latifu	NGA	16/11/89	D	6		
10	Djordje Lazić	SRB	18/06/83	M	8		2
18	Edgar Malakyan	ARM	22/09/90	M	9		
8	Gor Malakyan	ARM	12/06/94	M	9		
88	Maryan Mysyk		02/10/96	M		(3)	
79	Yuriy Pankiv		03/11/84	G	20	(1)	
17	Anton Postupalenko		28/08/88	M		(1)	
19	Serhiy Pshenychnykh		19/11/81	D	17	(1)	
44	Yuriy Putrash		29/01/90	M	7	(3)	2
39	Denys Vasin		04/03/89	A	21	(1)	2
7	Serhiy Voronin		24/03/87	D	20		

FC Volyn Lutsk

1960 • Avanhard (10,792) • fcvolyn.net
Coach: Vitaliy Kvartsyaniy

2015

18/07	a	Vorskla	D	1-1	Kobakhidze
23/07	h	Shakhtar	L	1-4	Matei (p)
02/08	a	Metalurh	W	2-0	Žunić, Didenko
07/08	h	Metalist	D	2-2	Matei (p), Didenko
16/08	a	Stal	W	2-1	og (Pshenychnykh), Kobakhidze
29/08	h	Olimpik	W	1-0	Sharpar
13/09	a	Chornomorets	W	2-1	Matei, Didenko
20/09	a	Dynamo	L	0-2	
27/09	a	Karpaty	W	2-0	Kravchenko, og (Hitchenko)
04/10	h	Zorya	L	0-3	
18/10	a	Olexandriya	L	1-3	Matei (p)
01/11	h	Hoverla	W	2-1	Politylo, Kozban
08/11	h	Vorskla	W	2-1	Politylo, Kozban
21/11	a	Shakhtar	L	0-4	
29/11	h	Metalurh	W	9-1	Kozban, Kobakhidze 2, Matei 2 (2p), Sharpar 3 (1p), Herasymyuk
05/12	a	Dnipro	W	1-0	Sharpar

2016

06/03	a	Metalist	L	0-3	
13/03	h	Stal	W	1-0	Khomchenko
20/03	a	Olimpik	D	1-1	Polyoviy
03/04	h	Chornomorets	D	1-1	Dudyk
10/04	a	Dynamo	L	0-3	
17/04	a	Karpaty	D	0-0	
24/04	a	Zorya	D	1-1	Didenko
29/04	h	Olexandriya	D	0-0	
07/05	h	Dnipro	L	2-3	Žunić, Goropevšek
14/05	a	Hoverla	W	4-1	Žunić 2, Didenko 2

No	Name	Nat	DoB	Pos	Aps	(s)	Gls
90	Andriy Bogdanov		21/01/90	M	16		
17	Yevheniy Bokhashvili		05/01/93	A		(2)	
48	Olexandr Chepelyuk		05/09/97	M		(4)	
59	Yaroslav Deda		28/05/99	A	2	(1)	
29	Anatoliy Didenko		09/06/82	A	16	(1)	6
69	Artem Dudyk		02/01/97	A		(4)	1
24	Miha Goropevšek	SVN	12/03/91	D	8	(5)	1
7	Oleh Herasymyuk		25/09/86	M	14	(3)	1
30	Oleh Humenyuk		03/05/83	D	9	(2)	
94	Viktor Khomchenko		11/11/94	A	7	(5)	1
19	Aleksandre Kobakhidze	GEO	11/02/87	M	13		4
89	Dmytro Kozban		27/04/89	A	7	(6)	2
4	Serhiy Kravchenko		24/04/83	M	24		1
74	Artem Kychak		16/05/89	G	3		
18	Serhiy Loginov		24/08/90	D	7	(5)	
10	Florentin Matei	ROU	15/04/93	M	15		6
9	Redvan Memeshev		15/08/93	M	15	(10)	
23	Oleksandr Nasonov		28/04/92	D	9	(1)	
42	Vitaliy Nedilko		21/08/82	G	4	(1)	
68	Andriy Nykytyuk		16/08/94	M		(1)	
26	Roman Nykytyuk		09/09/93	D	1	(3)	
38	Serhiy Petrov		21/05/97	A	1	(7)	
8	Serhiy Politylo		09/01/89	M	15	(1)	1
14	Volodymyr Polyoviy		28/07/85	D	16		1
93	Vitaliy Pryndeta		02/02/93	D		(1)	
47	Yuriy Romanyuk		06/05/94	M	2	(2)	
13	Artem Shabanov		07/03/92	D	21		
45	Vladyslav Shapoval		08/09/95	D	3	(3)	
11	Vyacheslav Sharpar		02/06/87	M	9	(1)	5
16	Gal Shish	ISR	28/01/89	D	5	(4)	
1	Bohdan Shust		04/03/86	G	19	(1)	
15	Ivica Žunić	CRO	11/09/88	D	25		4

FC Vorskla Poltava

1955 • Vorskla im. Olexiy Butovskiy (24,795) • vorskla.com.ua
Major honours
Ukrainian Cup (1) 2009
Coach: Vasyl Sachko

2015

18/07	h	Volyn	D	1-1	Shinder
25/07	a	Hoverla	D	1-1	Kovpak
02/08	a	Dnipro	D	1-1	og (Fedetskiy)
09/08	h	Shakhtar	D	2-2	Barannyk, Kovpak
15/08	a	Metalurh	D	1-1	Dityatyev
29/08	h	Metalist	W	1-0	Dityatyev
13/09	a	Stal	W	2-1	Chesnakov, Bartulović
19/09	h	Olimpik	W	2-1	Gromov, Tursunov (p)
27/09	a	Chornomorets	D	0-0	
04/10	h	Dynamo	L	0-4	
18/10	a	Karpaty	W	3-1	Barannyk 2, A Tkachuk
01/11	a	Olexandriya	D	1-1	Shinder
08/11	h	Volyn	L	1-2	Dityatyev
21/11	h	Hoverla	W	2-1	Shinder 2
30/11	a	Dnipro	W	2-0	Tursunov, Shinder
05/12	h	Zorya	L	0-2	

2016

06/03	a	Shakhtar	L	1-3	Gromov
12/03	h	Metalurh	W	0-0	(w/o)
19/03	a	Metalist	W	3-0	Khlebas, Shinder 2 (1p)
02/04	h	Stal	D	0-0	
09/04	a	Olimpik	W	1-0	Gromov
17/04	h	Chornomorets	W	2-0	A Tkachuk, Kolomoyets
24/04	a	Dynamo	L	0-1	
30/04	h	Karpaty	W	3-0	Sklyar, Khlebas, Kolomoyets
07/05	a	Zorya	W	2-1	Khlebas, Shinder
15/05	h	Olexandriya	L	0-1	

No	Name	Nat	DoB	Pos	Aps	(s)	Gls
24	Oleh Barannyk		20/03/92	A	2	(13)	3
30	Mladen Bartulović	CRO	05/10/86	M	12	(8)	1
31	Stanislav Bohush		25/10/83	G	9		
17	Volodymyr Chesnakov		12/02/88	D	16	(4)	1
4	Armend Dallku	ALB	16/06/83	D	22		
54	Olexiy Dityatyev		07/11/88	D	20		3
33	Olexiy Dovhiy		02/11/89	M	1	(4)	
7	Artem Gromov		14/01/90	M	18	(1)	3
77	Dmytro Khlebas		09/05/94	A	8		3
26	Yuriy Kolomoyets		22/03/90	A	6	(2)	2
39	Olexandr Kovpak		02/02/83	A	8	(9)	2
20	Mykola Kvasniy		04/01/95	D		(3)	
39	Bohdan Melnyk		04/01/97	M		(1)	
99	Oleh Mishchenko		10/10/89	A	2	(5)	
12	Dmytro Nepogodov		17/02/88	G	8		
19	Volodymyr Odaryuk		13/02/94	M		(1)	
40	Ihor Perduta		15/11/90	M	12	(1)	
82	Pavlo Rebenok		23/07/85	M	4	(4)	
23	Vadym Sapai		07/02/86	D	13	(6)	
11	Anton Shinder		13/06/87	A	21		8
3	Serhiy Siminin		09/10/87	D	23		
6	Olexandr Sklyar		26/02/91	M	17	(3)	1
21	Olexandr Tkachenko		19/02/93	G	8		
8	Andriy Tkachuk		18/11/87	M	24		2
34	Yevhen Tkachuk		27/06/90	D	6	(1)	
77	Sanzhar Tursunov	UZB	29/12/86	M	15	(1)	2
50	Yan Vichniy		27/02/97	G		(1)	

FC Zorya Luhansk

1923 • Slavutych Arena, Zaporizhya (11,756) • zarya-lugansk.com
Major honours
USSR League (1) 1972
Coach: Yuriy Vernydub

2015

17/07	a	Metalurh	W	6-0	Khomchenovskiy, Ljubenović, Malinovskiy, Karavayev, Kamenyuka, Sivakov
25/07	h	Metalist	D	0-0	
02/08	a	Stal	L	0-2	
09/08	h	Olimpik	W	4-0	Lipartia, Petryak, Budkivskiy 2
16/08	a	Chornomorets	W	2-0	Petryak, Karavayev
30/08	h	Dynamo	D	0-0	
13/09	a	Karpaty	D	1-1	Karavayev
20/09	a	Dnipro	W	3-0	Hordiyenko, Karavayev, Lipartia
27/09	a	Olexandriya	D	1-1	Budkivskiy
04/10	a	Volyn	W	3-0	Malinovskiy, Budkivskiy, Lipartia (p)
18/10	h	Hoverla	W	2-1	Budkivskiy, Kamenyuka (p)
30/10	h	Shakhtar	L	1-7	Kamenyuka (p)
07/11	h	Metalurh	W	4-1	Karavayev 2, Malinovskiy, Budkivskiy
22/11	h	Metalist	W	1-0	Ljubenović (p)
28/11	h	Stal	W	2-1	og (Kravchenko), Budkivskiy
05/12	a	Vorskla	W	2-0	Budkivskiy, Hordiyenko

2016

06/03	a	Olimpik	D	1-1	Budkivskiy
12/03	h	Chornomorets	W	4-0	Karavayev, Totovytskiy, Budkivskiy, Ljubenović
20/03	a	Dynamo	L	0-1	
02/04	h	Karpaty	W	4-1	Ljubenović, Budkivskiy, Totovytskiy, Chaikovskiy
10/04	h	Dnipro	L	1-2	Hordiyenko
16/04	a	Olexandriya	L	0-1	
24/04	h	Volyn	D	1-1	Paulinho
30/04	h	Hoverla	W	4-0	Opanasenko, Budkivskiy 2, Karavayev
07/05	h	Vorskla	L	1-2	Budkivskiy
15/05	a	Shakhtar	W	3-2	Totovytskiy 3

No	Name	Nat	DoB	Pos	Aps	(s)	Gls
59	Drnys Bezborodko		31/05/94	A		(3)	
28	Pylyp Budkivskiy		10/03/92	A	22	(1)	14
4	Ihor Chaikovskiy		07/10/91	M	9	(6)	1
44	Vyacheslav Checher		15/12/80	D	10		
3	Kyrylo Doroshenko		17/11/87	M		(1)	
24	Dmytro Grechishkin		22/09/91	M	12	(6)	
5	Artem Hordiyenko		04/03/91	M	19	(2)	3
27	Ihor Kalinin		11/11/95	D	1		
6	Mykyta Kamenyuka		03/06/85	D	23	(1)	3
20	Olexandr Karavayev		02/06/92	M	25		8
34	Dmytro Khomchenovskiy		16/04/90	M	3		1
17	Yaroslav Kvasov		05/03/92	A		(2)	
91	Ihor Levchenko		21/02/91	G	3		
49	Jaba Lipartia	GEO	16/11/87	A	11	(10)	3
22	Željko Ljubenović	SRB	09/07/81	M	11	(14)	4
49	Dmytro Lunyaka		02/03/95	A		(1)	
18	Ruslan Malinovskiy		04/05/93	M	11	(2)	3
39	Yevhen Opanasenko		25/08/90	D	23		1
11	Paulinho	BRA	29/05/93	A	2	(3)	1
34	Ivan Petryak		13/03/94	M	21		2
99	Andriy Pylyavskiy		04/12/88	D	12	(1)	
12	Rafael Forster	BRA	23/07/90	D	8		
1	Krševan Santini	CRO	11/04/87	G	1		
30	Mykyta Shevchenko		26/01/93	G	21		
1	Olexiy Shevchenko		24/02/92	G	1		
3	Mikhail Sivakov	BLR	16/01/88	D	20	(2)	1
2	Artem Sukhovskiy		06/12/92	D	2	(4)	
8	Vyacheslav Tankovskiy		16/08/95	M	6	(7)	
29	Andriy Totovytskiy		20/01/93	M	7	(8)	5
16	Hryhoriy Yarmash		04/01/85	D	2	(1)	
9	Artur Zahorulko		13/02/93	A		(1)	

Top goalscorers

22	Alex Teixeira (Shakhtar)
14	Pylyp Budkivskiy (Zorya)
13	Andriy Yarmolenko (Dynamo)
12	Eduardo (Shakhtar)
10	Yevhen Seleznyov (Dnipro)
	Oleh Gusev (Dynamo)
8	Marlos (Shakhtar)
	Anton Shinder (Vorskla)
	Olexandr Karavayev (Zorya)
7	Matheus (Dnipro)
	Júnior Moraes (Dynamo)
	Volodymyr Priyomov (Metalist)
	Vitaliy Ponomar (Olexandria)
	Dmytro Khlebas (Hoverla/Vorskla)

Promoted club

FC Zirka Kirovohrad

1911 • Zirka (14,628) • fczirka.com.ua
Coach: Serhiy Lavrynenko

Second level final table 2015/16

		Pld	W	D	L	F	A	Pts
1	FC Zirka Kirovohrad	30	20	5	5	49	22	65
2	FC Obolon-Brovar Kyiv	30	16	7	7	45	27	55
3	FC Cherkaskiy Dnipro Cherkasy	30	16	6	8	45	35	54
4	FC Illychivets Mariupil	30	14	11	5	34	24	53
5	FC Hirnyk Kryvyi Rih	30	13	12	5	33	24	51
6	FC Helios Kharkiv	30	13	10	7	39	27	49
7	MFC Mykolaiv	30	13	8	9	35	27	44
8	FC Desna Chernihiv	30	11	7	12	30	30	40
9	FC Naftovyk-Ukrnafta Okhtyrka	30	11	7	12	31	33	40
10	FC Poltava	30	10	8	12	29	32	38
11	FC Dynamo-2 Kyiv	30	9	9	12	27	34	36
12	FC Hirnyk-Sport Komsomolsk	30	8	9	13	30	35	33
13	FC Avanhard Kramatorsk	30	8	8	14	29	42	32
14	FC Sumy	30	8	6	16	35	54	30
15	FC Ternopil	30	6	7	17	18	47	22
16	FC Nyva Ternopil	30	2	4	24	10	26	7

NB FC Nyva Ternopil withdrew after round 18 – their remaining matches were awarded as goalless defeats; MFC Mykolaiv, FC Nyva Ternopil & FC Ternopil – 3 pts deducted.

DOMESTIC CUP

Kubok Ukraïny 2015/16

SECOND ROUND

(21/08/15)
Cherkaskiy Dnipro Cherkasy 1-3 Stal Dniprodzerzhynsk

(22/08/15)
Arsenal Kyiv 0-3 Shakhtar Donetsk
Avanhard Kramatorsk 1-3 Olexandriya
Balkany Zorya 0-1 Dnipro Dnipropetrovsk
Desna Chernihiv 1-1 Vorskla Poltava *(aet; 2-4 on pens)*
Helios Kharkiv 1-0 Hoverla Uzhhorod
Hirnyk Kryvyi Rih 3-0 Illychivets Mariupil
Hirnyk-Sport Komsomolsk 0-6 Dynamo Kyiv
Inhulets 0-2 Volyn Lutsk
Mykolaiv 2-1 Metalist Kharkiv
Myr Hornostaivka 0-2 Chornomorets Odesa
Naftovyk-Ukrnafta Okhtyrka 0-2 Olimpik Donetsk
Sumy 0-1 Obolon-Brovar Kyiv
FC Ternopil 3-1 Metalurh Zaporizhya
Zirka Kirovohrad 1-1 Karpaty Lviv *(aet; 5-4 on pens)*

(23/08/15)
Krystal Kherson 0-5 Zorya Luhansk

THIRD ROUND

(23/09/15 & 27/10/15)
Chornomorets Odesa 0-1, 0-0 Vorskla Poltava *(0-1)*
Helios Kharkiv 0-2, 1-3 Zorya Luhansk *(1-5)*
Obolon-Brovar Kyiv 0-2, 0-5 Dynamo Kyiv *(0-7)*
FC Ternopil 0-5, 0-4 Shakhtar Donetsk *(0-9)*

(23/09/15 & 28/10/15)
Hirnyk Kryvyi Rih 1-1, 1-2 Stal Dniprodzerzhynsk *(2-3)*
Mykolaiv 0-2, 0-5 Volyn Lutsk *(0-7)*
Olimpik Donetsk 0-2, 2-3 Dnipro Dnipropetrovsk *(2-5)*
Zirka Kirovohrad 1-1, 0-2 FC Olexandriya *(1-3)*

QUARTER-FINALS

(01/03/16 & 06/04/16)
Olexandriya 1-1 Dynamo Kyiv *(Basov 30; Yarmolenko 67)*
Dynamo Kyiv 0-1 Olexandriya *(Chorniy 25)*
(Olexandriya 2-1)

Stal Dniprodzerzhynsk 0-3 Dnipro Dnipropetrovsk *(Matheus 32p, Bruno Gama 70, Léo Matos 90+2)*
Dnipro Dnipropetrovsk 4-1 Stal Dniprodzerzhynsk *(Léo Matos 29, Matheus 48, 61, Luchkevych 64; Vasin 85)*
(Dnipro Dnipropetrovsk 7-1)

(02/03/16 & 27/03/16)
Vorskla Poltava 0-4 Shakhtar Donetsk *(Kovalenko 4, Ferreyra 55, Kucher 58, Wellington Nem 80)*
Shakhtar Donetsk 1-2 Vorskla Poltava *(Bernard 67p; Khlebas 28, 88)*
(Shakhtar Donetsk 5-2)

(02/03/16 & 06/04/16)
Volyn Lutsk 1-1 Zorya Luhansk *(Bogdanov 18; Totovytskiy 23)*
Zorya Luhansk 5-0 Volyn Lutsk *(Hordiyenko 22, Petryak 49, Karavayev 78, 87, Opanasenko 90+2)*
(Zorya Luhansk 6-1)

SEMI-FINALS

(20/04/16 & 11/05/16)
Dnipro Dnipropetrovsk 1-0 Zorya Luhansk *(Zozulya 17)*
Zorya Luhansk 2-0 Dnipro Dnipropetrovsk *(Lipartia 8, Totovytskiy 90+5)*
(Zorya Luhansk 2-1)

Olexandriya 1-1 Shakhtar Donetsk *(Hrytsuk 36; Eduardo 54)*
Shakhtar Donetsk 2-0 Olexandriya *(Malyshev 15, Wellington Nem 90+2)*
(Shakhtar Donetsk 3-1)

FINAL

(21/05/16)
Arena Lviv, Lviv
FC SHAKHTAR DONETSK 2 *(Gladkiy 42, 57)*
FC ZORYA LUHANSK 0
Referee: *Aranovskiy*
SHAKHTAR: *Kanibolotskiy, Srna, Kucher, Rakitskiy, Ismaily, Stepanenko, Malyshev, Marlos, Kovalenko (Eduardo 59), Taison (Ferreyra 81), Gladkiy (Wellington Nem 74)*
ZORYA: *M Shevchenko, Opanasenko (Yarmash 64), Sivakov, Rafael Forster, Kamenyuka, Hordiyenko (Lipartia 58), Chaikovskiy, Karavayev, Ljubenović, Petryak (Totovytskiy 46), Budkivskiy*

Shakhtar Donetsk pose with the Ukrainian Cup after their 2-0 win against Zorya

WALES

Cymdeithas Bêl-droed Cymru /
Football Association of Wales (FAW)

Address	11/12 Neptune Court, Vanguard Way GB-Cardiff CF24 5PJ	**President**	David Griffiths
		General secretary	Jonathan Ford
Tel	+44 29 2043 5830	**Media officer**	Ian Gwyn Hughes
Fax	+44 29 2049 6953	**Year of formation**	1876
E-mail	info@faw.co.uk	**National stadium**	Cardiff City Stadium,
Website	faw.org.uk		Cardiff (28,018)

PREMIER LEAGUE CLUBS

 1 **Aberystwyth Town FC**

 2 **AUK Broughton FC**

 3 **Bala Town FC**

 4 **Bangor City FC**

 5 **Carmarthen Town AFC**

 6 **Connah's Quay FC**

 7 **Haverfordwest County AFC**

 8 **Llandudno FC**

 9 **Newtown AFC**

 10 **Port Talbot Town FC**

 11 **Rhyl FC**

 12 **The New Saints FC**

PROMOTED CLUBS

 13 **Cefn Druids AFC**

 14 **Cardiff Metropolitan University FC**

KEY

● UEFA Champions League

● UEFA Europa League

● Promoted

● Relegated

Another clean sweep for TNS

The remarkable exploits of Chris Coleman and his Wales team at UEFA EURO 2016 transported football to a new level of popularity in the Principality, but there were no shocks or surprises before that on the domestic front as The New Saints swept all before them for the second season in a row.

A fifth successive Premier League title made it ten in total for the club based in the English border town of Oswestry. They also retained the Welsh Cup, at the expense of AUK Broughton, after defeating second-tier Denbigh Town 2-0 in the League Cup final.

Border club claim back-to-back trebles

Bala Town retain runners-up spot

Heroic EURO effort from national team

Domestic league

Runaway champions in 2014/15, Craig Harrison's side were once again a cut above the rest, their ownership of the Premier League title never seriously threatened after they cruised undefeated through their first 21 matches. By the time they finally lost, away to Connah's Quay in mid-January, they had a ten-point lead at the top of the table.

Newly-promoted Llandudno were TNS's closest challengers at the time, but they could not string two wins together thereafter and although Bala Town collected a sufficient number of points during the run-in to overtake Llandudno and claim the runners-up spot for the second successive season, their last hope of stealing the title from under the perennial champions' noses was extinguished when TNS beat them 2-0 at The Venue in the all-important head-to-head.

Bala had held TNS to draws in each of their previous three meetings, but Harrison's team came out on top when it mattered most, second-half goals from Ryan Brobbel and Aaron Edwards bringing a victory that was not witnessed by many – 623 was the official attendance – but nevertheless enabled the home club to make history by becoming the first team to be crowned Welsh champions five years in a row. With the most wins, the fewest defeats,

the most goals scored and the fewest conceded, TNS's latest title was as clear-cut as those that had preceded it – although Bala did trim the final points deficit from 18 in 2014/15 to a much more palatable seven. TNS's 72 goals were shared among 17 players, with only their Polish import Adrian Cieślewicz reaching double figures – thanks to a final-day hat-trick against Llandudno.

Chris Venables also signed off with a treble to reach 20 and win the golden boot for the third successive season, but his Aberystwyth Town side failed to reach the UEFA Europa League qualifying play-offs, which were won by Connah's Quay, who thus joined third-placed Llandudno as European first-time qualifiers. There was good news too for another northern team as Rhyl were rescued from relegation – alongside Haverfordwest County – after Port Talbot Town were denied a top-division licence for 2016/17.

Domestic cup

TNS completed the last leg of their treble by overcoming AUK Broughton 2-0 in the final of the Welsh Cup in nearby Wrexham. As in the league decider, Brobbel opened the scoring, with fellow Englishman Scott Quigley doubling the lead early in the second half. They were the first goals conceded by Broughton, who had scored 15 times without reply en route to their first final.

Europe

TNS won a European tie for only the third time in 18 campaigns, defeating Cieślewicz's former club B36 Tórshavn on away goals in the first qualifying round of the UEFA Champions League. They nearly made it past Videoton, too, only to lose out narrowly after extra time in Hungary.

National team

Wales supporters lived an improbable dream at UEFA EURO 2016. The country's first participation at a major tournament since the 1958 FIFA World Cup – before the UEFA European Championship even came into being – turned out far better than any of their followers could have dared to imagine.

Although Coleman's charges lost the game they probably most wanted to win – against England – they more than made amends by not only topping Group B but also progressing all the way to the semi-finals. Slovakia, Russia, Northern Ireland and, most memorably, Belgium were all overcome in impressive fashion before eventual winners Portugal halted their victory charge in Lyon. It was not the predicted one-man show, either, with superstar Gareth Bale scoring in all three group games but sharing equal billing with several of his colleagues in a heroic, and historic, all-round team effort.

DOMESTIC SEASON AT A GLANCE

Premier League 2015/16 final table

		Pld	Home					Away					Total					Pts
			W	D	L	F	A	W	D	L	F	A	W	D	L	F	A	
1	**The New Saints FC**	32	10	5	1	34	9	8	5	3	38	15	18	10	4	72	24	64
2	Bala Town FC	32	10	5	1	28	10	5	7	4	20	17	15	12	5	48	27	57
3	Llandudno FC	32	7	3	6	22	25	8	4	4	31	21	15	7	10	53	46	52
4	Connah's Quay FC	32	10	1	5	30	18	5	2	9	20	24	15	3	14	50	42	48
5	Newtown AFC	32	4	5	7	23	34	7	4	5	23	20	11	9	12	46	54	42
6	AUK Broughton FC	32	7	3	6	27	27	5	3	8	19	28	12	6	14	46	55	42
7	Carmarthen Town AFC	32	6	3	7	19	25	8	2	6	26	27	14	5	13	45	52	47
8	Aberystwyth Town FC	32	6	2	8	28	28	7	5	4	23	19	13	7	12	51	47	46
9	Bangor City FC	32	7	3	6	27	24	6	3	7	22	28	13	6	13	49	52	45
10	Port Talbot Town FC	32	4	5	7	20	27	6	4	6	19	29	10	9	13	39	56	39
11	Rhyl FC	32	3	6	7	20	23	2	6	8	16	27	5	12	15	36	50	27
12	Haverfordwest County AFC	32	2	5	9	11	23	3	1	12	16	34	5	6	21	27	57	21

NB League splits into top and bottom halves after First Phase of 22 games, with each team playing a further ten matches (home and away) exclusively against clubs from its half of the table. Port Talbot Town FC did not receive licence for 2016/17 Premier League, enabling Rhyl FC to avoid relegation.

European qualification 2016/17

 Champion/Cup winner: The New Saints FC (first qualifying round)

 Bala Town FC (first qualifying round)
Llandudno FC (first qualifying round)
Connah's Quay FC (first qualifying round)

Top scorer	Chris Venables (Aberystwyth), 20 goals
Relegated clubs	Haverfordwest County AFC, Port Talbot Town FC (excluded)
Promoted clubs	Cefn Druids AFC, Cardiff Metropolitan University FC
Cup final	The New Saints FC 2-0 AUK Broughton FC

Team of the season
(4-3-3)

Coach: Morgan (Llandudno)

Morris (Bala)

Spender (TNS) — Pearson (Broughton) — K Edwards (TNS) — Marriott (TNS)

A Edwards (TNS) — Venables (Aberystwyth) — Mullan (TNS)

Marc Williams (Llandudno) — Hunt (Bala) — Gray (Broughton)

Player of the season

Marc Williams
(Llandudno FC)

After several years playing in English football, notably at Wrexham and Chester, Williams decided to try his hand in the Welsh Premier League, and the 27-year-old striker's conversion proved so successful that he not only helped newly-promoted Llandudno qualify for a first tilt at Europe with a third-place finish but also scooped the division's official player of the year award. The former Wales youth and Under-21 international started all 32 games for the northern seaside club and scored 16 goals.

Newcomer of the season

Matty Owen
(Newtown AFC)

One of the more memorable individual performances of the 2015/16 Welsh Premier League season was provided by 21-year-old Newtown midfielder Owen as he scored both goals for his club in a 2-1 victory away to local rivals and champions-elect The New Saints in late March that suggested the title might still be up for grabs. It was not the only game in which the young midfielder excelled, his vital goal in Malta several months earlier having taken Newtown past Valletta in the UEFA Europa League.

NATIONAL TEAM

International tournament appearances

FIFA World Cup (1) 1958 (qtr-finals)
UEFA European Championship (1) 2016 (semi-finals)

Top five all-time caps

Neville Southall (92); Gary Speed (85); Craig Bellamy (78) Dean Saunders (75); **Chris Gunter**, Peter Nicholas & Ian Rush (73)

Top five all-time goals

Ian Rush (28); Ivor Allchurch & Trevor Ford (23); **Gareth Bale** & Dean Saunders (22)

Results 2015/16

03/09/15	Cyprus (ECQ)	A	Nicosia	W	1-0	*Bale (82)*
06/09/15	Israel (ECQ)	H	Cardiff	D	0-0	
10/10/15	Bosnia & Herzegovina (ECQ)	A	Zenica	L	0-2	
13/10/15	Andorra (ECQ)	H	Cardiff	W	2-0	*Ramsey (50), Bale (86)*
13/11/15	Netherlands	H	Cardiff	L	2-3	*Ledley (45+3), Huws (70)*
24/03/16	Northern Ireland	H	Cardiff	D	1-1	*Church (86p)*
28/03/16	Ukraine	A	Kyiv	L	0-1	
05/06/16	Sweden	A	Solna	L	0-3	
11/06/16	Slovakia (ECF)	N	Bordeaux (FRA)	W	2-1	*Bale (10), Robson-Kanu (81)*
16/06/16	England (ECF)	N	Lens (FRA)	L	1-2	*Bale (42)*
20/06/16	Russia (ECF)	N	Toulouse (FRA)	W	3-0	*Ramsey (11), Taylor (20), Bale (67)*
25/06/16	Northern Ireland (ECF)	N	Paris (FRA)	W	1-0	*McAuley (75og)*
01/07/16	Belgium (ECF)	N	Lille (FRA)	W	3-1	*A Williams (31), Robson-Kanu (55), Vokes (86)*
06/07/16	Portugal (ECF)	N	Lyon (FRA)	L	0-2	

Appearances 2015/16

Coach: Chris Coleman 10/06/70		CYP	ISR	BIH	AND	Ned	Nir	Ukr	Swe	SVK	ENG	RUS	NIR	BEL	POR	Caps	Goals
Wayne Hennessey	24/01/87 Crystal Palace (ENG)	G	G	G	G	G74	G46	G	G46		G	G	G	G	G	62	-
Ashley Richards	12/04/91 Fulham (ENG)	D	D	D				s65		s88						10	-
Chris Gunter	21/07/89 Reading (ENG)	D	D	D	D	D66	D	D	D	D	D	D	D	D	D	73	-
Ashley Williams	23/08/84 Swansea (ENG)	D	D	D	D	D46	D	D65	D	D	D	D	D	D	D	65	2
Ben Davies	24/04/93 Tottenham (ENG)	D	D	D	D	D		D	D	D	D	D	D	D		25	-
Neil Taylor	07/02/89 Swansea (ENG)	D	D	D		D65		D72	D	D	D	D	D	D	D	34	1
Andy King	29/10/88 Leicester (ENG)	M	M86			M			M64			s76		s78	M	36	2
David Edwards	03/02/86 Wolves (ENG)	M	M	s85	s23/46				s64	M69	s67	s74				35	3
Gareth Bale	16/07/89 Real Madrid (ESP)	M90	M	M	M				s64	A	M	M83	M	M	M	61	22
Aaron Ramsey	26/12/90 Arsenal (ENG)	M93	M	M	M				M	M88	M	M	M	M90		44	11
Hal Robson-Kanu	21/05/89 Reading (ENG)	A68	A79	A84	A23				s71	A72		s55	A80	A63		35	4
Sam Vokes	21/10/89 Burnley (ENG)	s68	s86	s75	A	A76	s61	A73		A	A55	s80	s58			44	7
Simon Church	10/12/88 MK Dons (ENG)/Aberdeen (SCO)	s90	s79	s84	s86		s76	A61	s73		s83		s63			38	3
Shaun MacDonald	17/06/88 Bournemouth (ENG)	s93					s61									4	-
Joe Allen	14/03/90 Liverpool (ENG)			M85		M	s71	M		M	M	M74	M	M	M	31	-
Joe Ledley	23/01/87 Crystal Palace (ENG)			M75		M56	M46	s79		s69	M67	M76	M63	M78	M58	67	4
James Chester	23/01/89 West Brom (ENG)				D	D	D	D	D64	D	D	D	D	D	D	17	-
Jonathan Williams	09/10/93 Nottingham Forest (ENG)/MK Dons (ENG)/Crystal Palace (ENG)				M86	M60		s62	M61		M74	M71	s72		s63	s66	16	-
David Vaughan	18/02/83 Nottingham Forest (ENG)				M		M71		M64							42	1
Tom Lawrence	13/01/94 Blackburn (ENG)/Cardiff (ENG)				s46	A		M62	A72							4	-
James Collins	23/08/83 West Ham (ENG)					s46			s64				s90	D66		49	3
Emyr Huws	30/09/93 Huddersfield (ENG)/Wigan (ENG)					s56		M79		s74						7	1
George Williams	07/09/95 Fulham (ENG)/Gillingham (ENG)					s60	M62									7	-
Paul Dummett	26/09/91 Newcastle (ENG)					s65										2	-
Adam Henley	14/06/94 Blackburn (ENG)					s66		s72								2	-
Owain Fon Williams	17/03/87 Inverness (SCO)					s74										1	-
Adam Matthews	13/01/92 Bristol City (ENG)						D									13	-
David Cotterill	04/12/87 Birmingham (ENG)						M									23	2
Danny Ward	22/06/93 Liverpool (ENG)						s46		s46	G						3	-
Andrew Crofts	29/05/84 Gillingham (ENG)						s46									28	-
Lloyd Isgrove	12/01/93 Barnsley (ENG)						s62									1	-
Tom Bradshaw	27/07/92 Walsall (ENG)							s72								1	-

WALES

EUROPE

DOMESTIC LEAGUE CLUB-BY-CLUB

The New Saints FC

CHAMPIONS LEAGUE

First qualifying round - B36 Tórshavn (FRO)
A 2-1 *Quigley (9), Wilde (90)*
Harrison, Spender, Marriott, K Edwards, Seargeant, Finley (Williams 81), Rawlinson, Wilde, Cieślewicz (Mullan 75), Quigley (Draper 84), A Edwards. Coach: Craig Harrison (ENG)
H 4-1 *Wilde (15, 27, 47), Williams (89)*
Harrison, Spender, Marriott, K Edwards, Seargeant, Finley, Rawlinson, Wilde (Draper 74), Cieślewicz (Mullan 62), Quigley, A Edwards (Williams 83). Coach: Craig Harrison (ENG)

Second qualifying round - Videoton FC (HUN)
H 0-1
Harrison, Spender, Marriott, K Edwards, Seargeant (Williams 81), Finley, Rawlinson, Wilde (Draper 84), Cieślewicz (Mullan 57), Quigley, A Edwards. Coach: Craig Harrison (ENG)
A 1-1 (aet) *Williams (78)*
Harrison, Spender, Marriott, K Edwards, Seargeant (Williams 72), Finley, Mullan (Draper 109), Rawlinson, Wilde, Cieślewicz (Quigley 66), A Edwards. Coach: Craig Harrison (ENG)
Red card: Finley 118

Bala Town FC

EUROPA LEAGUE

First qualifying round - FC Differdange 03 (LUX)
A 1-3 *Sheridan (38)*
Morris, Valentine, Stephens, Artell, Murtagh, Connolly (Brown 82), M Jones, Sheridan, Smith, Pearson (Hayes 46), Bell. Coach: Stephen O'Shaughnessy (WAL)
Red card: Hayes 83
H 2-1 *Murtagh (49), Sheridan (83)*
Morris, Valentine, Stephens, Murtagh, Connolly, M Jones (Lunt 90+2), Sheridan, Smith, Pearson, Davies, Thompson. Coach: Stephen O'Shaughnessy (WAL)

AUK Broughton FC

EUROPA LEAGUE

First qualifying round - NK Lokomotiva Zagreb (CRO)
H 1-3 *Riley (28)*
Coates, Pearson, Field, A Jones, Budrys (Evans 83), Riley, Gray (Wade 75), Wignall (Healing 84), Owen, McGinn, Owens. Coach: Andy Preece (ENG)
A 2-2 *Budrys (46), A Jones (75)*
Coates, Pearson, Field (Barrow 65), A Jones, Budrys, Riley (Spittle 90+2), Gray (Wade 74), Wignall, Owen, McGinn, Owens. Coach: Andy Preece (ENG)

Newtown AFC

EUROPA LEAGUE

First qualifying round - Valletta FC (MLT)
H 2-1 *Boundford (40), Oswell (90+1)*
Jones, Edwards, Owen (Evans 78), Mills-Evans, Sutton (Cadwallader 90+3), Hearsey, Boundford, Oswell, Mitchell (Price 70), C Williams, Goodwin. Coach: Chris Hughes (WAL)
A 2-1 *Oswell (7), Owen (85)*
Jones, Edwards, Owen (Price 89), Mills-Evans, Sutton, Hearsey (Cook 68), Boundford, Oswell, Mitchell (Partridge 88), C Williams, Goodwin. Coach: Chris Hughes (WAL)
Red card: Cook 87

Second qualifying round - FC København (DEN)
A 0-2
Jones, Edwards, Owen (Price 80), Mills-Evans (Cadwallader 78), Sutton, Hearsey (Evans 69), Boundford, Oswell, Mitchell, C Williams, Goodwin. Coach: Chris Hughes (WAL)
H 1-3 *Goodwin (70)*
Jones, Edwards, Owen (Price 73), Mills-Evans, Sutton, Hearsey (Harris 82), Boundford, Oswell, Mitchell, C Williams, Goodwin (Cook 73). Coach: Chris Hughes (WAL)

Aberystwyth Town FC

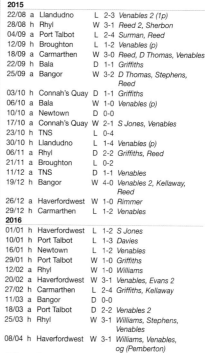

1884 • Park Avenue (3,000) • atfc.org.uk
Major honours
Welsh Cup (1) 1900
Manager: Ian Hughes

2015

22/08	a	Llandudno	L	2-3	*Venables 2 (1p)*
28/08	h	Rhyl	W	3-1	*Reed 2, Sherbon*
04/09	a	Port Talbot	L	2-4	*Surman, Reed*
12/09	h	Broughton	L	1-2	*Venables (p)*
18/09	a	Carmarthen	W	3-0	*Reed, D Thomas, Venables*
22/09	h	Bala	D	1-1	*Griffiths*
25/09	a	Bangor	W	3-2	*D Thomas, Stephens, Reed*
03/10	h	Connah's Quay	D	1-1	*Griffiths*
06/10	a	Bala	W	1-0	*Venables (p)*
10/10	a	Newtown	D	0-0	
17/10	a	Connah's Quay	W	2-1	*S Jones, Venables*
23/10	h	TNS	L	0-4	
30/10	a	Llandudno	L	1-4	*Venables (p)*
06/11	a	Rhyl	D	2-2	*Griffiths, Reed*
21/11	a	Broughton	L	0-2	
11/12	a	TNS	D	1-1	*Venables*
19/12	h	Bangor	W	4-0	*Venables 2, Kellaway, Reed*
26/12	a	Haverfordwest	W	1-0	*Rimmer*
29/12	h	Carmarthen	L	1-2	*Venables*

2016

01/01	h	Haverfordwest	L	1-2	*S Jones*
10/01	h	Port Talbot	L	1-3	*Davies*
16/01	h	Newtown	L	1-2	*Venables*
29/01	h	Port Talbot	W	1-0	*Griffiths*
12/02	h	Rhyl	W	1-0	*Williams*
20/02	a	Haverfordwest	W	3-1	*Venables, Evans 2*
27/02	h	Carmarthen	L	2-4	*Griffiths, Kellaway*
11/03	a	Bangor	D	0-0	
18/03	a	Port Talbot	D	2-2	*Venables 2*
25/03	h	Rhyl	W	3-1	*Williams, Stephens, Venables*
08/04	h	Haverfordwest	W	3-1	*Williams, Venables, og (Pemberton)*
16/04	a	Carmarthen	L	0-1	
23/04	h	Bangor	W	4-0	*Venables 3, Stephens*

No	Name	Nat	DoB	Pos	Aps	(s)	Gls
21	Ryan Batley	ENG	17/11/91	D		(5)	
22	Nashawn Blake		14/12/96	M		(1)	
2	Antonio Corbisiero	ENG	17/11/84	D	28		
3	Cledan Davies		10/03/90	D	17	(12)	1
15	Jonathan Evans		10/03/93	A	8	(1)	2
26	Rhys Griffiths		01/03/80	A	17	(4)	5
12	Sion James		03/02/80	D	27	(3)	
19	Liam Jaques		21/11/97	M	3	(11)	
5	Stuart Jones		14/03/84	D	32		2
7	Tom Jones		14/01/99	D		(1)	
7	Geoff Kellaway		07/04/86	M	23	(1)	2
1	Mike Lewis		04/04/89	G	29		
21	Chris Mullock		16/09/88	G	3		
23	Kane Owen		22/10/94	D	1	(5)	
9	Jamie Reed		13/08/87	A	17		7
16	Jack Rimmer		29/03/99	D	1	(8)	1
8	Luke Sherbon		06/06/86	M	18	(2)	1
4	Ross Stephens		28/05/85	M	25	(2)	2
6	Lee Surman		03/04/86	D	32		1
15	Darren Thomas		20/01/87	A	11	(1)	2
14	Wyn Thomas		11/01/79	D		(2)	
10	Chris Venables		23/07/85	M	29	(2)	20
11	Craig Williams		28/01/83	M	31	(1)	3

AUK Broughton FC

1946 • The Airfield (4,000) • airbusfc.com
Manager: Andy Preece (ENG)

2015

22/08	h	Carmarthen	W	5-1	McGinn, Gray 2, Wade, A Jones
31/08	a	Bala	L	1-2	Gray
04/09	h	Bangor	L	1-4	Field (p)
12/09	a	Aberystwyth	W	2-1	Murphy, Budrys
19/09	h	TNS	D	1-1	Gray
22/09	a	Newtown	W	3-0	Gray 2, McGinn
26/09	h	Haverfordwest	W	2-1	Gray, McGinn
03/10	a	Llandudno	L	0-1	
06/10	h	Newtown	L	1-4	Riley
10/10	h	Port Talbot	W	2-0	Gray 2
16/10	h	Llandudno	L	0-2	
23/10	a	Rhyl	L	0-1	
31/10	a	Carmarthen	W	3-2	Gray (p), A Jones, Wade
06/11	h	Bala	W	2-0	Gray, McGinn
15/11	a	Bangor	L	0-3	
21/11	h	Aberystwyth	W	2-0	Wade 2
28/11	a	TNS	L	0-4	
11/12	h	Rhyl	D	0-0	
19/12	a	Haverfordwest	W	1-0	Gray
26/12	a	Connah's Quay	D	1-1	Gray
2016					
01/01	h	Connah's Quay	W	3-2	Kearney, Murphy, Gray
16/01	a	Port Talbot	D	2-2	Budrys, Gray
30/01	a	Llandudno	D	1-1	Barrow
13/02	h	Bala	L	0-3	
20/02	h	Connah's Quay	L	0-1	
27/02	a	TNS	L	0-5	
12/03	a	Newtown	W	3-0	Monteiro, Wignall, Gray
19/03	h	Llandudno	L	3-4	Barrow, Gray, Wignall
25/03	a	Bala	L	1-3	Blake
08/04	a	Connah's Quay	L	1-2	Kearney
16/04	h	TNS	W	3-2	Budrys 2, Murphy
23/04	h	Newtown	D	2-2	Budrys, Gray

No	Name	Nat	DoB	Pos	Aps	(s)	Gls
33	Arnaldo Mendes	POR	08/07/93	M	3	(3)	
12	Jordan Barrow	ENG	18/10/93	A	31		2
6	Liam Blake	ENG	07/05/96	M	3	(2)	1
9	Chris Budrys	SCO	13/08/85	A	25	(2)	5
21	James Coates	ENG	28/02/85	G	29		
32	Zebb Edwards		08/05/99	M		(2)	
24	Ricky Evans		24/09/76	M		(3)	
6	Tom Field	ENG	02/08/85	M	15	(3)	1
8	Ryan Fraughan	ENG	11/02/91	M	6	(10)	
11	Tony Gray	ENG	06/12/84	A	29		18
3	Bailey Jackson	ENG	22/02/97	D	9	(8)	
7	Andy Jones	ENG	23/03/85	A	17	(2)	2
30	Keighan Jones		04/04/97	G	3		
5	Ian Kearney	ENG	15/06/87	D	9		2
22	Matty McGinn	ENG	27/06/83	D	24	(2)	4
34	Kevin Monteiro	FRA	21/03/94	D	4	(1)	1
31	James Murphy	ENG	31/01/97	M	17	(10)	3
18	James Owen		14/01/91	M	21	(2)	
26	Lee Owens	ENG	29/06/86	D	22	(2)	
4	Mike Pearson		19/01/87	D	19	(1)	
10	Wayne Riley	ENG	26/09/89	M	7	(6)	1
34	Charles Short	ENG	21/04/98	M		(1)	
30	Liam Smith	ENG	14/09/96	M	1	(1)	
19	Jonny Spittle	ENG	13/08/94	D	5		
14	Ryan Wade	ENG	22/01/88	A	20	(6)	4
16	Ryan Wignall	ENG	28/03/89	M	10	(2)	2
17	Ashley Williams	ENG	08/10/87	M	23		

Bala Town FC

1880 • Maes Tegid (2,000) • balatownfc.co.uk
Manager: Colin Caton

2015

22/08	a	Port Talbot	D	0-0	
31/08	h	Broughton	W	2-1	Stephens 2 (1p)
05/09	a	Carmarthen	D	0-0	
11/09	h	Connah's Quay	W	2-0	Irving, Artell
18/09	a	Bangor	W	3-0	M Jones 2, Thompson
22/09	a	Aberystwyth	D	1-1	Hunt
26/09	h	TNS	D	0-0	
03/10	a	Newtown	W	3-2	Connolly 2, M Jones
06/10	h	Aberystwyth	L	0-1	
10/10	a	Llandudno	D	0-0	
16/10	h	Newtown	W	1-0	Thompson
24/10	a	Haverfordwest	W	2-0	Connolly 2
31/10	h	Port Talbot	W	5-2	Hunt 3, Sheridan 2
06/11	a	Broughton	L	0-2	
21/11	h	Connah's Quay	L	1-2	Hunt
15/12	a	Bangor	D	1-1	Sheridan
18/12	a	TNS	D	1-1	Pearson
29/12	h	Rhyl	W	3-1	Smith, Sheridan, Hayes
2016					
01/01	h	Rhyl	D	0-0	
05/01	h	Carmarthen	W	2-1	Sheridan, Hunt (p)
09/01	a	Haverfordwest	W	3-2	og (Morris), og (Rodon), og (Walters)
16/01	h	Llandudno	W	3-0	Hunt 2, Hayes
29/01	h	Newtown	D	1-1	Hunt
13/02	a	Broughton	W	3-0	Murtagh, Connolly, Hayes
26/02	a	Llandudno	L	2-3	Hayes, Hunt
11/03	a	Connah's Quay	W	3-1	S Jones, M Jones, Hunt
15/03	h	TNS	D	0-0	
19/03	a	Newtown	D	2-2	Hunt, S Jones
25/03	h	Broughton	W	3-1	Connolly, S Jones, Sheridan
09/04	a	TNS	L	0-2	
16/04	h	Llandudno	D	0-0	
23/04	a	Connah's Quay	W	1-0	Hunt (p)

No	Name	Nat	DoB	Pos	Aps	(s)	Gls
5	David Artell	ENG	22/11/80	D	16	(1)	1
15	Will Bell	ENG	29/09/94	M		(1)	
17	Stephen Brown	ENG	11/08/84	M	1	(3)	
88	Nathan Burke	ENG	19/09/95	M	9	(1)	
7	Mark Connolly	ENG	02/07/84	M	21	(5)	6
9	Mike Hayes	ENG	21/11/87	A	14	(13)	4
18	Lee Hunt	ENG	05/06/82	A	28	(4)	13
26	John Irving	ENG	17/09/88	D	29	(1)	1
8	Mark Jones		15/08/84	M	17	(11)	4
4	Stuart Jones	ENG	28/08/86	D	20	(1)	3
20	Kenny Lunt	ENG	20/11/79	M		(1)	
1	Ashley Morris		31/03/84	G	32		
6	Conall Murtagh	NIR	29/06/85	M	28	(1)	1
14	Rob Pearson	ENG	16/11/90	M	19	(2)	1
22	Christian Platt	ENG	15/12/91	D	5	(11)	
10	Ian Sheridan	ENG	12/03/89	A	24	(1)	6
11	Kieran Smith	ENG	06/03/92	A	23	(3)	1
3	Anthony Stephens	ENG	21/01/94	D	30		2
27	Dave Thompson	ENG	27/02/91	M	15	(8)	2
2	Ryan Valentine		19/08/82	D	21	(2)	

Bangor City FC

1876 • Nantporth (1,800) • bangorcityfc.co.uk
Major honours
Welsh League (3) 1994, 1995, 2011; Welsh Cup (8) 1889, 1896, 1962, 1998, 2000, 2008, 2009, 2010
Manager: Nev Powell

2015

21/08	a	Rhyl	D	1-1	Hart (p)
29/08	h	Port Talbot	L	1-2	R Edwards
04/09	a	Broughton	W	4-1	S Edwards, Allen, Jones, Williams
12/09	h	Carmarthen	L	1-2	Ahmadi
18/09	a	Bala	L	0-3	
22/09	h	Connah's Quay	W	2-1	Ahmadi, Hart
25/09	a	Aberystwyth	L	2-3	Hart, Clowes
02/10	a	TNS	L	0-2	
06/10	h	Connah's Quay	W	3-1	Miley, Jones, S Edwards
10/10	a	Haverfordwest	L	1-2	Williams
16/10	h	TNS	L	0-2	
24/10	a	Newtown	W	3-0	Allen, Ahmadi, Cummins
30/10	a	Rhyl	W	1-0	Ahmadi
07/11	a	Port Talbot	L	0-2	
15/11	h	Broughton	W	3-0	Hart (p), S Edwards, Allen
21/11	a	Carmarthen	L	1-2	Jones
15/12	h	Bala	D	1-1	Cavanagh
19/12	a	Aberystwyth	L	0-4	
28/12	a	Llandudno	W	2-1	Hart (p), Miley
2016					
01/01	h	Llandudno	L	0-3	
08/01	h	Newtown	W	3-0	S Edwards, R Edwards, Ahmadi
16/01	a	Haverfordwest	W	2-1	Allen, Ahmadi
29/01	a	Rhyl	W	4-3	Lewis 3 (1p), Ahmadi
13/02	a	Haverfordwest	D	1-1	S Edwards
27/02	a	Port Talbot	L	0-2	
05/03	a	Carmarthen	W	1-0	Elstone
11/03	a	Aberystwyth	D	0-0	
19/03	a	Rhyl	W	4-3	Hart (p), Elstone, Ahmadi 2
02/04	a	Haverfordwest	W	5-2	Cavanagh 2, Walker, Lewis, Allen
09/04	h	Carmarthen	D	2-2	Elstone, Miley
16/04	a	Port Talbot	D	1-1	S Edwards
23/04	a	Aberystwyth	L	0-4	

No	Name	Nat	DoB	Pos	Aps	(s)	Gls
9	Porya Ahmadi	IRN	08/01/93	A	20	(8)	8
8	Damien Allen	ENG	01/08/86	M	30		5
17	Shaun Cavanagh		18/12/97	A	8	(12)	3
4	Leon Clowes	ENG	27/02/92	D	27		1
16	Adam Cummins	ENG	03/03/93	D	28	(1)	1
20	Ryan Edwards		22/06/88	M	24		2
11	Sion Edwards		01/08/87	M	31		6
25	Michael Elstone	ENG	04/10/98	A	7	(8)	3
14	Sam Faulkner		25/09/96	M		(3)	
3	Sam Hart	ENG	29/11/91	D	31		6
16	Iolo Hughes		12/10/95	D	2	(2)	
18	Caio Hywel		08/09/96	D		(1)	
7	Chris Jones		09/10/85	M	16	(9)	3
22	Christian Langos	CGO	09/03/94	A	14	(13)	
32	Steve Lewis	ENG	10/11/87	A	10		4
6	Anthony Miley	ENG	30/08/92	D	23	(2)	4
13	Cai Owen		12/07/98	D		(1)	
5	Chris Roberts		14/08/85	D			
27	Connor Roberts		08/12/92	G	31		
1	Antoni Sarnowski	POL	18/04/98	G	1	(1)	
2	Declan Walker	IRL	01/03/92	D	7		1
15	Phil Warrington		21/12/95	M		(3)	
24	Joe Williams		22/12/96	A	2	(9)	4
19	Matthew Woodward	ENG	14/06/83	D	10		
23	Ashley Young	ENG	14/07/90	M	30		

 **WALES**

Carmarthen Town AFC

1896 • Richmond Park (3,000) •
carmarthentownafc.com
Major honours
Welsh Cup (1) 2007
Manager: Mark Aizlewood

2015

22/08	a	Broughton	L	1-5	*Jones*
29/08	h	Connah's Quay	W	1-0	*Harling*
05/09	h	Bala	D	0-0	
12/09	a	Bangor	W	2-1	*L Thomas, Jones*
18/09	a	Aberystwyth	L	0-3	
22/09	a	TNS	L	0-2	
26/09	h	Newtown	L	0-2	
03/10	a	Haverfordwest	D	0-0	
06/10	h	TNS	L	1-6	*Jones*
10/10	a	Rhyl	W	4-1	*Jones, C Thomas, Bassett, Harling*
16/10	h	Haverfordwest	W	4-1	*Jones 2, L Thomas 2 (1p)*
24/10	a	Llandudno	W	2-1	*L Thomas, Walters*
31/10	h	Broughton	L	2-3	*L Thomas 2*
07/11	a	Connah's Quay	L	0-4	
21/11	a	Bangor	W	2-1	*og (Clowes), L Thomas*
12/12	a	Llandudno	L	2-4	*L Thomas, Prosser*
19/12	a	Newtown	L	1-4	*Prosser*
26/12	a	Port Talbot	W	3-0	*L Thomas 2, Cummings*
29/12	a	Aberystwyth	W	2-1	*Cummings 2*

2016

02/01	h	Port Talbot	D	0-0	
05/01	a	Bala	L	1-2	*Jones*
16/01	a	Rhyl	D	1-1	*Lewis*
12/02	a	Port Talbot	W	2-0	*Lewis, White*
27/02	a	Aberystwyth	W	4-2	*Jones 3 (2p), Knott*
05/03	h	Bangor	L	0-1	
12/03	h	Rhyl	W	2-0	*Jones 2*
19/03	a	Haverfordwest	W	2-1	*Lewis, Vincent*
25/03	a	Port Talbot	L	2-3	*Bassett, Jones*
05/04	h	Haverfordwest	W	1-0	*Sheehan*
09/04	a	Bangor	D	2-2	*L Thomas 2 (1p)*
16/04	a	Aberystwyth	W	1-0	*Lewis*
23/04	a	Rhyl	L	0-1	

No	Name	Nat	DoB	Pos	Aps	(s)	Gls
19	Dwaine Bailey		24/04/92	M	26	(5)	
11	Kyle Bassett		10/09/88	A	24	(3)	2
2	Luke Cummings		25/10/91	D	26	(1)	3
23	Glenn Fearn		02/12/96	M		(4)	
3	Craig Hanford		08/07/84	D	20	(3)	
10	Lewis Harling		11/06/92	M	27	(2)	2
1	Lee Idzi		08/02/88	G	32		
9	Mark Jones		01/05/89	A	29	(3)	13
5	Jordan Knott		13/09/93	D	21	(7)	1
25	Kieran Lewis		26/06/93	M	28		4
14	Ceri Morgan		22/01/91	M	18	(8)	
8	Luke Prosser		08/01/91	A	9	(14)	2
12	Dan Sheehan		22/12/90	D	29	(1)	1
6	Chris Thomas		16/01/83	D	19	(1)	1
20	Danny Thomas		13/05/85	M	1	(4)	
18	Liam Thomas		06/11/91	M	32		12
4	Dave Vincent		17/06/90	D	9	(1)	1
22	Sacha Walters		20/06/84	A	1	(15)	1
17	Jeff White		18/01/86	A	1	(10)	1

Connah's Quay FC

1946 • Deeside Stadium (4,000) •
the-nomads.co.uk
Manager: Alan Bickerstaffe (ENG);
(02/11/15) Andy Morrison (SCO)

2015

22/08	h	Newtown	L	0-2	
29/08	a	Carmarthen	L	0-1	
05/09	h	Haverfordwest	W	2-1	*Davies, Ruane*
11/09	a	Bala	L	0-2	
19/09	h	Llandudno	W	2-1	*Morris, Rimmer*
22/09	a	Bangor	L	1-2	*Baynes*
26/09	h	Rhyl	W	3-1	*Morris, Ruane, N Rushton*
03/10	a	Aberystwyth	D	1-1	*N Rushton*
06/10	h	Bangor	L	1-3	*Ruane*
09/10	a	TNS	L	0-2	
17/10	a	Aberystwyth	L	1-2	*Davies*
25/10	a	Port Talbot	W	4-0	*N Rushton, Morris, Ruane 2*
31/10	a	Newtown	L	2-4	*Morris, Davies*
07/11	h	Carmarthen	W	4-0	*N Rushton 3, Ruane*
14/11	a	Haverfordwest	W	2-0	*Horan 2*
21/11	h	Bala	W	2-1	*Crowther, Davies*
28/11	a	Llandudno	L	0-1	
12/12	h	Port Talbot	W	5-0	*Parry, Linwood, Davies, Morris (p), Miller*
19/12	a	Rhyl	W	2-1	*Baynes, Miller*
26/12	h	Broughton	D	1-1	*Ruane*

2016

01/01	a	Broughton	L	2-3	*Parry, Linwood*
16/01	h	TNS	W	2-0	*Morris (p), Davies*
29/01	a	TNS	D	0-0	
13/02	a	Llandudno	L	2-3	*Crowther, Morris*
20/02	a	Broughton	W	1-0	*Woolfe*
27/02	h	Newtown	W	1-0	*Morris (p)*
11/03	a	Bala	L	1-3	*Morris (p)*
19/03	h	TNS	W	2-1	*Davies, Morris*
26/03	a	Llandudno	W	2-1	*og (Roberts), Woolfe*
08/04	h	Broughton	W	2-1	*N Rushton 2*
16/04	a	Newtown	L	2-3	*Woolfe, Linwood*
23/04	h	Bala	L	0-1	

No	Name	Nat	DoB	Pos	Aps	(s)	Gls
20	Wes Baynes	ENG	12/10/88	D	29		2
27	Thomas Bibby	ENG	17/03/88	M	1	(2)	
25	Jack Chambers		31/10/97	A		(6)	
21	Chris Churchman	ENG	13/06/95	M	2		
4	Jamie Crowther		10/02/92	M	28	(2)	2
1	John Danby	ENG	15/08/83	G	30		
10	Leslie Davies		29/10/84	A	30		7
22	George Deniz		29/08/96	G	1		
2	John Disney	ENG	15/05/92	D	4		
18	Kieran Gaul	ENG	30/01/97	M		(1)	
18	Danny Harrison		04/11/82	M	25	(1)	
5	George Horan		19/02/82	D	25		2
3	Paul Linwood		24/10/83	D	28	(1)	3
14	Kevin McIntyre		23/12/77	D	14	(8)	
7	Sean Miller	ENG	09/05/95	M	18	(9)	2
8	Callum Morris	ENG	12/09/92	M	30		10
26	Ben Nash	ENG	23/07/98	D	1		
19	Robert Parry		18/10/94	M	6	(1)	2
12	Jack Riley		06/03/97	D	2		
17	Chris Rimmer	ENG	02/07/92	D	11	(13)	1
16	Corey Roper	ENG	13/09/95	M		(5)	
9	Ashley Ruane	ENG	26/06/85	A	15	(14)	7
28	Jon Rushton		17/05/90	G	1	(1)	
11	Nicky Rushton		03/02/92	A	20	(5)	8
15	Sean Smith	ENG	12/12/94	D	23	(4)	
19	Callum Terrell	ENG	26/10/95	A		(1)	
2	Michael Wilson	ENG	24/01/95	D	2		
16	Nathan Woolfe	ENG	06/10/88	M	6	(2)	3

Haverfordwest County AFC

1899 • New Bridge Meadow Stadium (2,500)
• haverfordwestcounty.co.uk
Manager: Wayne Jones

2015

22/08	h	TNS	L	0-4	
29/08	h	Newtown	L	0-3	
05/09	a	Connah's Quay	L	1-2	*Christopher*
12/09	h	Llandudno	W	2-0	*Steffan Williams, Griffiths*
19/09	h	Rhyl	W	2-1	*Batley (p), Griffiths*
22/09	h	Port Talbot	L	1-2	*Borrelli*
26/09	a	Broughton	L	1-2	*Rodon*
03/10	a	Carmarthen	D	0-0	
06/10	h	Port Talbot	W	2-1	*Follows, Borrelli*
10/10	h	Bangor	W	2-1	*Christopher, Howard*
16/10	a	Carmarthen	L	1-4	*Pemberton*
24/10	h	Bala	L	0-2	
31/10	a	TNS	L	0-2	
07/11	h	Newtown	L	0-1	
14/11	h	Connah's Quay	L	0-2	
21/11	a	Llandudno	L	0-1	
28/11	a	Rhyl	D	1-1	*Borrelli (p)*
19/12	h	Broughton	L	0-1	
26/12	h	Aberystwyth	L	0-1	

2016

01/01	a	Aberystwyth	W	2-1	*Borrelli 2*
09/01	a	Bala	L	2-3	*Howard, Walters*
16/01	a	Bangor	L	1-2	*Borrelli*
13/02	h	Bangor	D	1-1	*Bertorelli*
20/02	a	Aberystwyth	L	1-3	*Walters*
27/02	a	Rhyl	D	1-1	*Rodon*
12/03	h	Port Talbot	D	1-1	*Borrelli*
19/03	a	Carmarthen	L	1-2	*Watts*
02/04	a	Bangor	L	2-5	*Spencer Williams, Carroll*
05/04	a	Carmarthen	L	0-1	
08/04	a	Aberystwyth	L	1-3	*Borrelli*
16/04	h	Rhyl	D	1-1	*Rodon*
23/04	a	Port Talbot	L	0-2	

No	Name	Nat	DoB	Pos	Aps	(s)	Gls
3	Ryan Batley		17/11/91	D	12	(2)	1
25	Jason Bertorelli		04/03/86	A	10	(1)	1
7	Luke Borrelli		28/03/91	A	29	(3)	8
10	Declan Carroll		04/07/93	A	19	(9)	1
17	Jack Christopher		18/05/87	A	8	(6)	2
1	Alex Connell	AUS	23/11/89	G	4		
22	Glen Fitini		29/01/97	A		(1)	
9	Jordan Follows		23/03/90	A	12	(10)	1
5	Dale Griffiths		02/11/85	D	24		2
14	Kieran Howard		17/01/91	M	27	(3)	2
12	Liam Hutchinson		11/02/91	M	1	(2)	
1	Scott James		29/08/89	G	15		
19	Scott McCoubrey		20/04/88	M		(1)	
13	Craig Morris		27/07/81	D	13		
16	Craig Moses		12/04/88	A		(4)	
18	Nicky Palmer		11/06/81	M	19	(1)	
4	Sean Pemberton		15/12/85	D	25	(5)	1
15	John Roberts	ENG	18/06/93	A	6	(10)	
6	Sam Rodon		27/05/93	D	30		3
12	Kristian Speake		23/05/91	M	3	(5)	
23	Alfie Stottor		30/12/98	M		(3)	
8	Greg Walters		10/01/95	M	31	(2)	2
2	Ricky Watts		07/11/91	D	30		1
21	Tomas Wellington		20/11/88	N	5	(3)	
20	Spencer Williams		19/10/96	D	19	(4)	1
11	Steffan Williams		08/06/92	A	10	(6)	1

Llandudno FC

1878 • Parc Maesdu (1,503) •
llandudnotownfc.co.uk
Manager: Alan Morgan

2015

Date		Opponent	Result	Scorers
22/08	h	Aberystwyth	W 3-2	Evans, Marc Williams, Hughes
28/08	a	TNS	D 1-1	Joyce
04/09	h	Newtown	L 0-2	
12/09	a	Haverfordwest	L 0-2	
19/09	a	Connah's Quay	L 1-2	Hughes
22/09	h	Rhyl	W 1-0	Buckley
26/09	a	Port Talbot	W 4-1	Marc Williams 3, Taylor
03/10	h	Broughton	W 1-0	Buckley
06/10	h	Rhyl	D 1-1	Marc Williams
10/10	a	Bala	D 0-0	
16/10	a	Broughton	W 2-0	Marc Williams, Buckley
24/10	a	Carmarthen	L 1-2	Joyce (p)
30/10	a	Aberystwyth	W 4-1	Thomas, og (Surman), Hughes, Buckley
07/11	h	TNS	L 3-4	Marc Williams 2, Buckley
14/11	a	Newtown	W 3-0	Thomas, Buckley, Dawson
21/11	h	Haverfordwest	W 1-0	Riley
28/11	h	Connah's Quay	W 1-0	Marc Williams
12/12	a	Carmarthen	W 4-2	Riley, Marc Williams 2, Thomas
19/12	h	Port Talbot	D 1-1	Marc Williams
28/12	h	Bangor	L 1-2	Marc Williams
2016				
01/01	a	Bangor	W 3-0	Marc Williams, Hughes, Bull
16/01	h	Bala	L 0-3	
30/01	h	Broughton	D 1-1	Thomas
13/02	a	Connah's Quay	W 3-2	Marc Williams, Thomas (p), Mike Williams
20/02	a	Newtown	D 1-1	Reed
26/02	h	Bala	W 3-2	Shaw, Joyce, Reed
11/03	a	TNS	L 0-2	
19/03	a	Broughton	W 4-3	Dawson 2, Reed, Shaw
26/03	h	Connah's Quay	L 1-2	Mike Williams
08/04	h	Newtown	W 3-2	Marc Williams, Thomas (p), Buckley
16/04	a	Bala	D 0-0	
23/04	h	TNS	L 1-5	Dawson

No	Name	Nat	DoB	Pos	Aps	(s)	Gls
23	Lewis Buckley		10/12/91	M	20	(12)	7
16	Alan Bull	ENG	25/11/87	A	7	(8)	1
19	Liam Dawson	ENG	12/01/91	A	9	(13)	4
20	Thomas Dix	ENG	13/10/91	M	30		
7	Gareth Evans		29/04/87	M	13	(4)	1
8	Danny Hughes		28/05/88	M	32		4
6	Michael Johnston		16/12/87	D	15	(2)	
11	Peter Jones		21/09/96	A		(2)	
3	James Joyce		03/11/94	D	30		3
22	Sean McCaffery		19/06/98	M		(3)	
17	Lewis Moynes	ENG	09/10/96	M		(2)	
15	Jamie Reed		13/08/87	A	5	(4)	3
15	Jordan Rico	ENG	03/03/94	M	1	(2)	
14	Leo Riley	ENG	09/01/96	M	12	(7)	2
1	David Roberts	ENG	10/12/88	G	32		
12	Daniel Shaw	ENG	19/04/96	M	21	(8)	2
4	Jonny Spittle	ENG	13/08/94	D	10	(4)	
2	Danny Taylor	ENG	01/09/91	D	22	(1)	1
9	Lee Thomas		14/06/84	A	29	(1)	6
21	Anthony Tierney		09/02/87	D	2	(9)	
10	Marc Williams		27/07/88	A	32		16
18	Mike Williams		27/10/86	D	30		2

Newtown AFC

1875 • Latham Park (6,000) •
newtownafc.co.uk
Major honours
Welsh Cup (2) 1879, 1895
Manager: Chris Hughes

2015

Date		Opponent	Result	Scorers
22/08	a	Connah's Quay	W 2-0	Mitchell, og (Linwood)
29/08	h	Haverfordwest	W 3-0	Mitchell 2, Oswell
04/09	a	Llandudno	W 2-0	Owen, Sutton
12/09	h	Rhyl	L 1-2	Boundford
20/09	a	Port Talbot	D 1-1	Boundford
22/09	h	Broughton	L 0-3	
26/09	a	Carmarthen	W 2-0	og (Bailey), Mitchell
03/10	h	Bala	L 2-3	Mitchell 2 (1p)
06/10	h	Broughton	W 4-1	Oswell, Owen, Price, Boundford
10/10	h	Aberystwyth	D 0-0	
16/10	a	Bala	L 0-1	
24/10	a	Bangor	L 0-3	
31/10	a	Connah's Quay	W 4-2	Oswell, Mitchell, Mills-Evans, Boundford
07/11	a	Haverfordwest	W 1-0	Oswell
14/11	h	Llandudno	L 0-3	
21/11	a	Rhyl	D 1-1	Evans (p)
28/11	h	Port Talbot	D 1-1	Evans (p)
19/12	a	Carmarthen	W 4-1	Oswell, Boundford 2, Mitchell (p)
26/12	h	TNS	D 2-2	Mitchell (p), Boundford
2016				
01/01	a	TNS	L 1-4	Mitchell
08/01	a	Bangor	L 0-3	
16/01	a	Aberystwyth	W 2-1	Mitchell, Evans
29/01	a	Bala	D 1-1	Owen
13/02	h	TNS	L 0-6	
20/02	h	Llandudno	D 1-1	Owen
27/02	a	Connah's Quay	L 0-1	
12/03	h	Broughton	L 0-3	
19/03	h	Bala	D 2-2	Mitchell, Ryan
26/03	a	TNS	W 2-1	Owen 2
08/04	a	Llandudno	L 2-3	Oswell 2
16/04	h	Connah's Quay	W 3-2	Oswell 3
23/04	a	Broughton	D 2-2	Sutton, Owen

No	Name	Nat	DoB	Pos	Aps	(s)	Gls
9	Luke Boundford		30/01/88	D	28	(1)	7
16	Gavin Cadwallader	ENG	18/04/86	D	13		
8	Matthew Cook	ENG	07/09/85	M	19	(7)	
3	Stefan Edwards		10/10/89	D	26	(4)	
18	Sean Evans		25/09/87	M	11	(10)	3
20	Tom Goodwin		12/01/90	M	26	(3)	
26	Mark Griffiths		04/08/87	A	1	(9)	
24	Craig Harris	ENG	15/04/96	M		(8)	
7	Matthew Hearsey	ENG	25/02/91	A	7		
22	Jack Steven Hughes		12/02/90	D	5	(7)	
1	David Jones		03/02/90	G	32		
5	Kieran Mills-Evans	ENG	11/10/92	D	25	(3)	1
11	Neil Mitchell	ENG	01/04/88	A	31	(1)	12
10	Jason Oswell	ENG	07/10/92	A	28		10
4	Matty Owen	ENG	23/06/94	M	30	(2)	7
15	Jamie Price	ENG	22/07/88	M	11	(9)	1
17	Scott Ryan	ENG	04/11/95	A	4	(3)	1
6	Shane Sutton		31/01/89	D	10		2
27	Jamie Tolley	ENG	05/12/83	M	7	(4)	
14	Jordan Wells	ENG	18/10/96	D	6	(1)	
19	Craig Williams		21/12/87	M	28		
2	Rob Williams	ENG	06/07/87	D	4		

Port Talbot Town FC

1901 • GenQuip stadium (3,000) •
porttalbottown.co.uk
Manager: Andy Dyer

2015

Date		Opponent	Result	Scorers
22/08	h	Bala	D 0-0	
29/08	a	Bangor	W 2-1	Clarke, Hood
04/09	h	Aberystwyth	W 4-2	Rose, Mohamed, Hood 2
12/09	a	TNS	L 1-3	Chris Jones
20/09	h	Newtown	D 1-1	J Jones
22/09	a	Haverfordwest	W 2-1	Fowler, Rose
26/09	h	Llandudno	L 1-4	Hood
03/10	a	Rhyl	W 1-0	Belle
06/10	h	Haverfordwest	L 1-2	Rose
10/10	a	Broughton	L 0-2	
17/10	h	Rhyl	L 0-3	
25/10	h	Connah's Quay	L 0-4	
31/10	a	Bala	L 2-5	Chris Jones, Hood
07/11	h	Bangor	W 2-0	Rose, og (Hart)
22/11	h	TNS	L 0-1	
28/11	a	Newtown	D 1-1	Hood
12/12	a	Connah's Quay	L 0-5	
19/12	a	Llandudno	D 1-1	Long
26/12	h	Carmarthen	L 0-3	
2016				
02/01	a	Carmarthen	D 0-0	
10/01	a	Aberystwyth	W 3-1	Hood, Georgievsky, Chris Jones
16/01	h	Broughton	D 2-2	Chris Jones, Rose
29/01	a	Aberystwyth	L 0-1	
12/02	h	Carmarthen	L 0-2	
27/02	a	Bangor	W 2-0	Bowen 2
12/03	a	Haverfordwest	D 1-1	Clarke
18/03	a	Aberystwyth	D 2-2	Bowen, Fowler
25/03	a	Carmarthen	W 3-2	Clarke, Artell, Latham
28/03	h	Rhyl	W 4-0	Bishop-Wisdom, Chris Jones (p), Latham, Morgan
09/04	a	Rhyl	L 0-5	
16/04	h	Bangor	D 1-1	Latham
23/04	h	Haverfordwest	W 2-0	Bishop-Wisdom, Bowen

No	Name	Nat	DoB	Pos	Aps	(s)	Gls
2	David Artell	GIB	22/11/80	D	7		1
5	Cortez Belle	ENG	27/08/83	D	9		1
24	Marley Bishop-Wisdom		12/11/96	A	5	(1)	2
10	Luke Bowen		07/03/88	A	10	(1)	4
1	Steven Cann		20/01/88	G	28		
6	Joe Clarke		13/09/91	M	29		3
15	Tom De Silva		26/11/92	A		(1)	
21	Leigh De-Vulgt		10/03/81	D	8	(6)	
4	Paul Fowler		02/08/85	M	22	(2)	2
17	Kostya Georgievsky		28/06/96	M	7	(5)	1
23	James Hartson		20/10/94	A	1	(11)	
16	Jonathan Hood		07/02/91	M	18	(1)	7
11	Leon Jeanne		17/11/80	A	4	(2)	
7	Chris Jones		14/02/90	M	25	(1)	5
2	Craig Jones		26/03/87	D	11	(2)	
15	Joseph Jones		14/07/96	D	14	(1)	1
25	Ryan Kostromin		19/09/96	M	5	(3)	
20	Jordan Langley		22/09/96	A		(4)	
17	Jamie Latham		08/12/96	M	5	(3)	3
23	Matthew Long	ENG	31/01/97	D	24	(1)	
11	James Loveridge		16/05/94	A	10	(10)	
12	Kurtis March		30/04/93	M	26	(4)	
8	Liam McCreesh		09/05/85	M	7		
13	Conah McFenton		18/05/96	G	4	(3)	
24	Kaid Mohamed		23/07/84	A	1		1
14	Kerry Morgan		31/10/88	M	8	(1)	1
3	James Parry		27/05/95	D	16	(5)	
9	Martin Rose	ENG	29/02/84	A	23	(1)	5
19	Duane Saunders		22/09/86	M		(3)	
5	Alan Tate		02/09/82	D	9		
14	Dave Vincent		17/06/90	D	8	(1)	
18	Kieran Williams		08/10/96	M	5	(1)	

WALES

Rhyl FC

1879 • Belle Vue Stadium (3,000) • rhylfc.co.uk

Major honours
Welsh League (2) 2004, 2009; Welsh Cup (4) 1952, 1953, 2004, 2006

Manager: Gareth Owen;
(16/02/16) Niall McGuinness

2015

21/08	h	Bangor	D	1-1	Bowen
28/08	a	Aberystwyth	L	1-3	Keates
05/09	h	TNS	D	0-0	
12/09	h	Newtown	W	2-1	D Taylor, Bowen
19/09	h	Haverfordwest	L	1-2	Owen
22/09	a	Llandudno	L	0-1	
26/09	a	Connah's Quay	L	1-3	D Taylor
03/10	h	Port Talbot	L	0-1	
06/10	h	Llandudno	D	1-1	Bell
10/10	a	Carmarthen	L	1-4	Bell
17/10	a	Port Talbot	W	3-0	Bell 3
23/10	h	Broughton	W	1-0	Bell
30/10	a	Bangor	L	0-1	
06/11	a	Aberystwyth	D	2-2	Hughes, Owen
13/11	a	TNS	D	2-2	Owen 2
21/11	h	Newtown	D	1-1	Owen
28/11	a	Haverfordwest	D	1-1	Bell
11/12	a	Broughton	D	0-0	
19/12	h	Connah's Quay	L	1-2	Bell
29/12	a	Bala	L	1-3	D Taylor

2016

01/01	a	Bala	D	0-0	
16/01	a	Carmarthen	D	1-1	Corbett
29/01	a	Bangor	L	3-4	og (Clowes), Wright, Mackin
12/02	h	Aberystwyth	L	0-1	
27/02	h	Haverfordwest	D	1-1	Bell
12/03	a	Carmarthen	L	0-2	
19/03	h	Bangor	L	3-4	Owen 2, Hughes
25/03	a	Aberystwyth	L	1-3	Corbett
28/03	a	Port Talbot	L	0-4	
09/04	h	Port Talbot	W	5-0	Corbett, Touray 2, Owen 2
16/04	a	Haverfordwest	D	1-1	Gossett
23/04	h	Carmarthen	W	1-0	Wandless

No	Name	Nat	DoB	Pos	Aps	(s)	Gls
1	Michael Askew	ENG	15/08/96	G	7	(1)	
22	Connor Bell	ENG	15/07/96	A	26		9
2	Liam Benson	ENG	25/02/92	D	8		
9	Aaron Bowen	ENG	30/03/91	A	6	(2)	2
8	Jamie Brewerton		17/11/79	D	5	(1)	
2	Phil Clarke	ENG	20/10/88	D	11	(1)	
10	Zac Corbett	ENG	14/05/96	M	7	(3)	3
10	Tom Donegan	ENG	15/09/92	M	8	(1)	
13	Chay Dysart		03/12/85	D	21	(1)	
5	Luke Fitzpatrick		13/11/98	M	1	(2)	
21	Josh Gordon	ENG	10/10/94	A		(1)	
15	Danny Gossett		30/09/94	M	6		1
11	Robert Hughes		22/04/92	M	14	(12)	2
12	Tom Jones		29/11/96	M		(3)	
12	Dean Keates	ENG	14/06/88	M	22		1
3	Curtis Langton	ENG	21/09/95	D	2		
4	Levi Mackin	ENG	04/04/86	A	18	(5)	1
27	Ben Maher		01/07/94	D	11	(5)	
8	David Mannix	ENG	24/09/85	M	13	(5)	
25	Terry McCormick	ENG	25/08/83	G	25		
5	Jordan Miller		29/02/92	M		(1)	
20	John Owen		18/08/92	A	27	(3)	9
31	Aaron Rey	ENG	25/07/84	A		(10)	
23	Greg Stones	ENG	04/05/82	D	27	(2)	
17	Corey Taylor		23/11/97	M		(2)	
7	Derek Taylor	ENG	29/06/92	M	17	(1)	3
16	Ibou Touray	GAM	24/12/94	D	28	(1)	2
6	Michael Walsh	ENG	30/05/86	M	16	(4)	
14	Luke Wandless	ENG	07/12/94	M	4	(1)	1
26	Jamie Whitehouse		04/03/96	M	2	(1)	
18	Corey Williams		26/09/95	M	3		
29	Stephen Wright	ENG	08/02/80	D	17		1

The New Saints FC

1959 • The Venue (3,000) • tnsfc.co.uk

Major honours
Welsh League (10) 2000, 2005, 2006, 2007, 2010, 2012, 2013, 2014, 2015, 2016; Welsh Cup (6) 1996, 2005, 2012, 2014, 2015, 2016

Manager: Craig Harrison (ENG)

2015

22/08	a	Haverfordwest	W	4-0	Darlington 2, Seargeant, Draper
28/08	h	Llandudno	D	1-1	Wilde
05/09	a	Rhyl	D	0-0	
12/09	h	Port Talbot	W	3-1	A Edwards, Marriott, Wilde
19/09	a	Broughton	D	1-1	Wilde
22/09	h	Carmarthen	W	2-0	Seargeant (p), Draper
26/09	a	Bala	D	0-0	
02/10	h	Bangor	W	2-0	Seargeant (p), Marriott
06/10	a	Carmarthen	W	6-1	K Edwards, Quigley 3 (1p), Mullan, Marriott
09/10	h	Connah's Quay	W	2-0	Quigley 2
16/10	a	Bangor	W	2-0	R Edwards, A Edwards
23/10	a	Aberystwyth	W	4-0	Quigley 2, Darlington, Cieślewicz
31/10	h	Haverfordwest	W	2-0	Draper 2
07/11	a	Llandudno	W	4-3	Cieślewicz, Evans, Wilde, Seargeant (p)
13/11	h	Rhyl	D	2-2	Wilde, Evans
22/11	a	Port Talbot	W	1-0	Mullan
28/11	h	Broughton	W	4-0	Cieślewicz 2, A Edwards, Quigley
11/12	h	Aberystwyth	D	1-1	Williams
18/12	h	Bala	D	1-1	A Edwards
26/12	a	Newtown	D	2-2	Marriott, Spender

2016

01/01	h	Newtown	W	4-1	Cieślewicz, Mullan, R Edwards, Wilde
16/01	a	Connah's Quay	L	0-2	
29/01	h	Connah's Quay	D	0-0	
13/02	a	Newtown	W	6-0	Cieślewicz, Draper 3, Wilde, K Edwards
27/02	h	Broughton	W	5-0	Draper 2, Baker, Mullan, Quigley
11/03	h	Llandudno	W	2-0	Mullan, Cieślewicz
13/03	a	Bala	D	0-0	
19/03	a	Connah's Quay	L	1-2	Seargeant (p)
26/03	h	Newtown	L	1-2	Mullan
09/04	h	Bala	W	2-0	Brobbel, A Edwards
16/04	a	Broughton	L	2-3	R Edwards, Seargeant
23/04	a	Llandudno	W	5-1	Cieślewicz 3, A Edwards, Parry

No	Name	Nat	DoB	Pos	Aps	(s)	Gls
4	Phil Baker	ENG	04/11/82	D	26		1
8	Ryan Brobbel	ENG	05/03/93	M	5	(3)	1
21	Adrian Cieślewicz	POL	16/11/90	M	24	(7)	10
20	Alex Darlington		26/12/88	A	8	(5)	3
9	Greg Draper	NZL	13/08/89	A	11	(11)	9
23	Aeron Edwards		16/02/88	M	30		6
6	Kai Edwards		29/01/91	D	32		2
17	Ryan Edwards		25/05/94	M	10	(8)	3
5	Steve Evans		26/02/79	D	3	(6)	2
15	Danny Gossett		30/09/94	M	1	(3)	
1	Paul Harrison	ENG	18/12/84	G	31		
27	James Jones		13/03/87	D		(1)	
3	Chris Marriott	ENG	24/09/89	D	27		4
14	Jamie Mullan	ENG	10/02/88	M	17	(4)	6
25	Chris Mullock		16/09/88	G	1		
11	Robbie Parry		18/10/94	A		(5)	1
26	Ryan Pryce	ENG	30/06/97	D	6	(1)	
22	Scott Quigley	ENG	02/09/92	A	19	(9)	9
16	Connell Rawlinson		22/09/91	D	10	(2)	
12	Christian Seargeant	ENG	13/09/86	M	29	(1)	6
2	Simon Spender		15/11/85	D	27		1
18	Michael Wilde	ENG	27/08/83	A	16	(8)	7
10	Matty Williams		05/11/82	A	19	(5)	1

Top goalscorers

20	Chris Venables (Aberystwyth)
18	Tony Gray (Broughton)
16	Marc Williams (Llandudno)
13	Lee Hunt (Bala)
	Mark Jones (Carmarthen)
12	Liam Thomas (Carmarthen)
	Neil Mitchell (Newtown)
10	Jamie Reed (Aberystwyth/Llandudno)
	Callum Morris (Connah's Quay)
	Jason Oswell (Newtown)
	Adrian Cieślewicz (TNS)

UEFA Europa League qualification play-offs

SEMI-FINALS

(07/05/16)
Newtown 1-2 Broughton (Sutton 36; McGinn 14p, 38p)

(08/05/16)
Connah's Quay 2-0 Carmarthen (N Rushton 5, Baynes 63)

FINAL

(14/05/16)
Connah's Quay 1-0 Broughton (Baynes 79)

Promoted clubs

Cefn Druids AFC

1869 • The Rock (2,000) • cefndruidsafc.co.uk

Major Honours
Welsh Cup (8) 1880, 1881, 1882, 1885, 1886, 1898, 1899, 1904
Manager: Huw Griffiths

Cardiff Metropolitan University FC

2000 • Cyncoed Stadium (1,620) • no website
Manager: Robyn Jones

Second level final tables 2015/16

North		Pld	W	D	L	F	A	Pts
1	Caernarfon Town FC	30	24	3	3	95	23	75
2	Cefn Druids AFC	30	21	3	6	62	33	66
3	Denbigh Town FC	30	20	3	7	72	46	63
4	Guilsfield FC	30	17	2	11	60	44	53
5	Holywell Town FC	30	15	7	8	55	34	52
6	Gresford Athletic FC	30	15	4	11	45	44	49
7	Holyhead Hotspur FC	30	13	7	10	44	40	46
8	Prestatyn Town FC	30	14	3	13	61	50	45
9	Flint Town United FC	30	13	3	14	54	45	42
10	CPD Porthmadog FC	30	13	2	15	47	54	41
11	Conwy Borough FC	30	11	3	16	47	54	36
12	Buckley Town FC	30	9	5	16	45	65	32
13	Mold Alexandra FC	30	9	4	17	38	59	31
14	Caersws FC	30	8	2	20	40	67	26
15	Llanfair United FC	30	7	0	23	35	70	21
16	Rhayader Town FC	30	4	3	23	24	96	15

NB Caernarfon Town FC did not obtain licence for Premier League; Cefn Druids AFC promoted instead.

South		Pld	W	D	L	F	A	Pts
1	Cardiff Metropolitan University FC	30	19	5	6	63	26	62
2	Barry Town United FC	30	16	10	4	62	33	58
3	Goytre AFC	30	17	5	8	72	36	56
4	Caerau (Ely) FC	30	15	5	10	59	43	50
5	Cambrian & Clydach Vale BGC	30	15	5	10	48	39	50
6	Taffs Well AFC	30	14	5	11	57	51	47
7	Goytre United AFC	30	13	4	13	45	47	43
8	Afan Lido FC	30	11	9	10	53	53	42
9	Ton Pentre AFC	30	12	4	14	45	52	40
10	Risca United FC	30	12	3	15	48	48	39
11	Penybont FC	30	11	6	13	53	56	39
12	Monmouth Town FC	30	10	9	11	56	60	39
13	Briton Ferry Llansawel AFC	30	10	9	11	41	49	39
14	Aberdare Town FC	30	11	4	15	34	56	37
15	Aberbargoed Buds FC	30	8	3	19	42	63	27
16	Garden Village AFC	30	1	4	25	27	93	7

DOMESTIC CUP

Welsh Cup 2015/16

THIRD ROUND

(04/12/15)
Port Talbot 2-1 Cambrian & Clydach Vale *(aet)*

(05/12/15)
Afan Lido 1-0 Holywell
Barry 6-1 Denbigh
Caerau (Ely) 4-0 Brecon
Cardiff Metropolitan 2-0 STM
Carmarthen 1-3 Bala
Cefn Druids 1-0 Rhyl *(aet)*
Flint 0-2 Newtown
Haverfordwest 0-2 Broughton
Llandudno FC 0-0 Buckley *(aet; 3-4 on pens)*
Penrhyncoch 2-3 Cwmbran Celtic
Prestatyn 0-3 Connah's Quay
TNS 2-0 Aberystwyth

(08/12/15)
Holyhead 2-1 Bangor

(12/12/15)
Goytre AFC 4-2 Caernarfon

(19/12/15)
Cwmamman 0-3 Guilsfield

FOURTH ROUND

(05/02/16)
Connah's Quay 4-1 Buckley

(06/02/16)
Barry 2-5 TNS
Holyhead 1-3 Bala
Newtown 6-0 Cefn Druids
Port Talbot 3-0 Caerau (Ely)

(10/02/16)
Afan Lido 0-2 Cardiff Metropolitan

(13/02/16)
Cwmbran Celtic 5-3 Goytre AFC

(16/02/16)
Guilsfield 0-3 Broughton

QUARTER-FINALS

(05/03/16)
Broughton 3-0 Bala *(Murphy 8, McGinn 17, Monteiro 39)*
Cardiff Metropolitan 0-2 Connah's Quay *(Woolfe 45, Morris 56)*
Cwmbran Celtic 1-2 Port Talbot *(R Williams 61; Bowen 32, 66)*
TNS 1-0 Newtown *(Mullan 8)*

SEMI-FINALS

(02/04/16)
Broughton 7-0 Port Talbot *(Gray 4, 74, 88, Wignall 9, Monteiro 35, Murphy 51, 58)*
TNS 5-0 Connah's Quay *(Quigley 22, 57, 66, Williams 23, Mullan 41)*

FINAL

(02/05/16)
Glyndwr University Stadium, Wrexham
THE NEW SAINTS FC 2 *(Brobbel 33, Quigley 51)*
AUK BROUGHTON FC 0
Referee: Markham-Jones
TNS: Harrison, Spender, Marriott, K Edwards, Rawlinson, Seargeant (Baker 66), Brobbel, Cieślewicz, A Edwards, Williams (Wilde 46), Quigley
BROUGHTON: Coates, Pearson, Kearney, Owens, McGinn (Jackson 60), Wignall, Williams, Owen (Barrow 61), Murphy (Fraughan 81), Budrys, Gray

TNS spray the champagne in celebration of a third successive Welsh Cup triumph

UEFA Events Calendar 2016/17

National team

2018 FIFA World Cup European Qualifiers

04-06/09/2016	Qualifying round matches
06-11/10/2016	Qualifying round matches
11-13/11/2016	Qualifying round matches
24-26/03/2017	Qualifying round matches
09-11/06/2017	Qualifying round matches

2017 UEFA European Under-21 Championship

01/09-06/09/2016	Qualifying round matches
05-11/10/2016	Qualifying round matches
14/10/2016	Play-off round draw (Nyon, Switzerland)
07-15/11/2016	Play-off round matches
24/11/2016	Final tournament draw (Krakow, Poland)
16-30/06/2017	Final tournament (Poland)

Club

2016/17 UEFA Champions League

25/08/2016	Group stage draw (Monaco)
13-14/09/2016	Group stage, Matchday 1
27-28/09/2016	Group stage, Matchday 2
18-19/10/2016	Group stage, Matchday 3
01-02/11/2016	Group stage, Matchday 4
22-23/11/2016	Group stage, Matchday 5
06-07/12/2016	Group stage, Matchday 6
12/12/2016	Round of 16 draw (Nyon, Switzerland)
14-15/02/2017	Round of 16, first leg
21-22/02/2017	Round of 16, first leg
07-08/03/2017	Round of 16, second leg
14-15/03/2017	Round of 16, second leg
17/03/2017	Quarter-final draw (Nyon, Switzerland)
11-12/04/2017	Quarter-finals, first leg
18-19/04/2017	Quarter-finals, second leg
14/04/2017	Semi-final and Final draw (Nyon, Switzerland)
02-03/05/2017	Semi-final, first leg
09-10/05/2017	Semi-final, second leg
03/06/2017	Final (Cardiff, Wales)

2016 FIFA Club World Cup

08-18/12/2016	Final tournament (Japan)

2016/17 UEFA Europa League

26/08/2016	Group stage draw (Monaco)
15/09/2016	Group stage, Matchday 1
29/09/2016	Group stage, Matchday 2
20/10/2016	Group stage, Matchday 3
03/11/2016	Group stage, Matchday 4
24/11/2016	Group stage, Matchday 5
08/12/2016	Group stage, Matchday 6
12/12/2016	Round of 32 draw (Nyon, Switzerland)
16/02/2017	Round of 32, first leg
23/02/2017	Round of 32, second leg
24/02/2017	Round of 16 draw (Nyon, Switzerland)
09/03/2017	Round of 16, first leg
16/03/2017	Round of 16, second leg
17/03/2017	Quarter-final draw (Nyon, Switzerland)
13/04/2017	Quarter-finals, first leg
20/04/2017	Quarter-finals, second leg
21/04/2017	Semi-final draw (Nyon, Switzerland)
04/05/2017	Semi-final, first leg
11/05/2017	Semi-final, second leg
24/05/2017	Final (Stockholm, Sweden)

2016/17 UEFA Youth League

25/08/2016	Group stage draw (Monaco)
30/08/2016	Domestic champions path draw (Nyon)
13-14/09/2016	Group stage, Matchday 1
27-28/09/2016	Group stage, Matchday 2
28/09/2016	Round 1, Domestic champions path, first leg matches
18-19/10/2016	Group stage, Matchday 3
19/10/2016	Round 1, Domestic champions path, second leg matches
01-02/11/2016	Group stage, Matchday 4
02/11/2016	Round 2, Domestic champions path, first leg matches
22-23/11/2016	Group stage, Matchday 5
23/11/2016	Round 2, Domestic champions path, second leg matches
06-07/12/2016	Group stage, Matchday 6
12/12/2016	Knockout play-off round draw (Nyon, Switzerland)
07-08/02/2017	Knockout round play-off matches
13/02/2017	Knockout round draw (Nyon, Switzerland)
21-22/02/2017	Round of 16 matches
07-08/03/2017	Quarter-final matches
21-24/04/2017	Final Four (Nyon, Switzerland)

Youth & Amateur

2016/17 UEFA European Under-19 Championship

04/10-14/11/2016	Qualifying round matches
13/12/2016	Elite round draw (Nyon, Switzerland)
20-28/03/2017	Elite round matches
19/06/2017	Final tournament draw (tbd, Georgia)
02-15/07/2017	Final tournament (Georgia)

2017/18 UEFA European Under-19 Championship

13/12/2016	Qualifying round draw (Nyon, Switzerland)

2016/17 UEFA European Under-17 Championship

16/09-06/11/2016	Qualifying round matches
13/12/2016	Elite round draw (Nyon, Switzerland)
01-31/03/2017	Elite round matches
05/04/2017	Final tournament draw (tbd, Croatia)
01-17/05/2017	Final tournament (Croatia)

2017/18 UEFA European Under-17 Championship

13/12/2016	Qualifying round draw (Nyon, Switzerland)

2017 UEFA Regions' Cup

20/09-18/11/2016	Intermediate round matches
21/12/2016	Host appointment
12/04/2017	Final tournament draw (tbd)
12-20/06/2017	Final tournament (Venue tbd)

Women's

UEFA Women's EURO 2017

15-20/09/2016	Qualifying round matches
23/09/2016	Play-off round draw (Nyon, Switzerland)
17-25/10 2016	Play-off round matches
08/11/2016	Final tournament draw (The Netherlands)
16/07-06/08/2017	Final tournament (The Netherlands)

2016/17 UEFA Women's Champions League

05-06/10/2016	Round of 32, first leg
12-13/10/2016	Round of 32, second leg
17/10/2016	Round of 16 draw (Nyon, Switzerland)
09-10/11/2016	Round of 16, first leg
16-17/11/2016	Round of 16, second leg
25/11/2016	Quarter-finals, Semi-finals and Final draw (Nyon, Switzerland)
22-23/03/2017	Quarter-finals, first leg
29-30/03/2017	Quarter-finals, second leg
22-23/04/2017	Semi-finals, first leg
29-30/04/2017	Semi-finals, second leg
01/06/2017	Final (Cardiff, Wales)

2016/17 UEFA European Women's Under-19 Championship

08/09-25/10/2016	Qualifying round matches
11/11/2016	Elite round draw (Nyon, Switzerland)
04-09/04/2017	Elite round matches
23/05/2017	Final tournament draw (Northern Ireland, exact venue tbd)
08-20/08/2017	Final tournament (Northern Ireland)

2017/18 UEFA European Women's Under-19 Championship

11/11/2016	Qualifying round draw (Nyon, Switzerland)

2016/17 UEFA European Women's Under-17 Championship

20/09-15/10/2016	Qualifying round matches
11/11/2016	Elite round draw (Nyon, Switzerland)
01/02-14/04/2017	Elite round matches
25/04/2017	Final tournament draw (Czech Republic, exact venue tbd)
02-14/05/2017	Final tournament (Czech Republic)

2017/18 UEFA European Women's Under-17 Championship

11/11/2016	Qualifying round draw (Nyon, Switzerland)

Futsal

UEFA Futsal EURO 2018

21/10/2016	Preliminary & Main round draws
16-22/01/2017	Preliminary round matches
27/03-02/04/2017	Main round matches
06/07/2017	Play-off round draw

2016/17 UEFA Futsal Cup

11-16/10/2016	Main round matches
21/10/2016	Elite round draw
22-27/11/2016	Elite round matches
19/03/2017	Final tournament draw (venue tbd)
27-30/04/2017	Final tournament (venue tbd)

tbd = to be decided

2018 FIFA World Cup Preliminary Competition

Group A (Netherlands, France, Sweden, Bulgaria, Belarus, Luxembourg)	Group B (Portugal, Switzerland, Hungary, Faroe Islands, Latvia, Andorra)
06/09/16	*06/09/16*
Belarus - France	**Andorra - Latvia**
Bulgaria - Luxembourg	**Faroe Islands - Hungary**
Sweden - Netherlands	**Switzerland - Portugal**
07/10/16	*07/10/16*
France - Bulgaria	**Hungary - Switzerland**
Luxembourg - Sweden	**Latvia - Faroe Islands**
Netherlands - Belarus	**Portugal - Andorra**
10/10/16	*10/10/16*
Belarus - Luxembourg	**Andorra - Switzerland**
Netherlands - France	**Faroe Islands - Portugal**
Sweden - Bulgaria	**Latvia - Hungary**
13/11/16	*13/11/16*
Bulgaria - Belarus	**Hungary - Andorra**
France - Sweden	**Portugal - Latvia**
Luxembourg - Netherlands	**Switzerland - Faroe Islands**
25/03/17	*25/03/17*
Bulgaria - Netherlands	**Andorra - Faroe Islands**
Luxembourg - France	**Portugal - Hungary**
Sweden - Belarus	**Switzerland - Latvia**
09/06/17	*09/06/17*
Belarus - Bulgaria	**Andorra - Hungary**
Netherlands - Luxembourg	**Faroe Islands - Switzerland**
Sweden - France	**Latvia - Portugal**
31/08/17	*31/08/17*
Bulgaria - Sweden	**Hungary - Latvia**
France - Netherlands	**Portugal - Faroe Islands**
Luxembourg - Belarus	**Switzerland - Andorra**
03/09/17	*03/09/17*
Belarus - Sweden	**Faroe Islands - Islands**
France - Luxembourg	**Hungary - Portugal**
Netherlands - Bulgaria	**Latvia - Switzerland**
07/10/17	*07/10/17*
Belarus - Netherlands	**Andorra - Portugal**
Bulgaria - France	**Faroe Islands - Latvia**
Sweden - Luxembourg	**Switzerland - Hungary**
10/10/17	*10/10/17*
France - Belarus	**Hungary - Faroe Islands**
Luxembourg - Bulgaria	**Latvia - Andorra**
Netherlands - Sweden	**Portugal - Switzerland**

Continued over the page

2018 FIFA World Cup Preliminary Competition

EUROPEAN QUALIFIERS

Group C

(Germany, Czech Republic, Northern Ireland, Norway, Azerbaijan, San Marino)

04/09/16
Czech Republic - Northern Ireland
Norway - Germany
San Marino - Azerbaijan

08/10/16
Azerbaijan - Norway
Germany - Czech Republic
Northern Ireland - San Marino

11/10/16
Czech Republic - Azerbaijan
Germany - Northern Ireland
Norway - San Marino

11/11/16
Czech Republic - Norway
Northern Ireland - Azerbaijan
San Marino - Germany

26/03/17
Azerbaijan - Germany
Northern Ireland - Norway
San Marino - Czech Republic

10/06/17
Azerbaijan - Northern Ireland
Germany - San Marino
Norway - Czech Republic

01/09/17
Czech Republic - Germany
Norway - Azerbaijan
San Marino - Northern Ireland

04/09/17
Azerbaijan - San Marino
Germany - Norway
Northern Ireland - Czech Republic

05/10/17
Azerbaijan - Czech Republic
Northern Ireland - Germany
San Marino - Norway

08/10/17
Czech Republic - San Marino
Germany - Azerbaijan
Norway - Northern Ireland

Group D

(Wales, Austria, Serbia, Republic of Ireland, Moldova, Georgia)

05/09/16
Georgia - Austria
Serbia - Republic of Ireland
Wales - Moldova

06/10/16
Austria - Wales
Moldova - Serbia
Republic of Ireland - Georgia

09/10/16
Moldova - Republic of Ireland
Serbia - Austria
Wales - Georgia

12/11/16
Austria - Republic of Ireland
Georgia - Moldova
Wales - Serbia

24/03/17
Austria - Moldova
Georgia - Serbia
Republic of Ireland - Wales

11/06/17
Moldova - Georgia
Republic of Ireland - Austria
Serbia - Wales

02/09/17
Georgia - Republic of Ireland
Serbia - Moldova
Wales - Austria

05/09/17
Austria - Georgia
Moldova - Wales
Republic of Ireland - Serbia

06/10/17
Austria - Serbia
Georgia - Wales
Republic of Ireland - Moldova

09/10/17
Moldova - Austria
Serbia - Georgia
Wales - Republic of Ireland

Group E

(Romania, Denmark, Poland, Montenegro, Armenia, Kazakhstan)

04/09/16
Denmark - Armenia
Kazakhstan - Poland
Romania - Montenegro

08/10/16
Armenia - Romania
Montenegro - Kazakhstan
Poland - Denmark

11/10/16
Denmark - Montenegro
Kazakhstan - Romania
Poland - Armenia

11/11/16
Armenia - Montenegro
Denmark - Kazakhstan
Romania - Poland

26/03/17
Armenia - Kazakhstan
Montenegro - Poland
Romania - Denmark

10/06/17
Kazakhstan - Denmark
Montenegro - Armenia
Poland - Romania

01/09/17
Denmark - Poland
Kazakhstan - Montenegro
Romania - Armenia

04/09/17
Armenia - Denmark
Montenegro - Romania
Poland - Kazakhstan

05/10/17
Armenia - Poland
Montenegro - Denmark
Romania - Kazakhstan

08/10/17
Denmark - Romania
Kazakhstan - Armenia
Poland - Montenegro

Group F

(England, Slovakia, Scotland, Slovenia, Lithuania, Malta)

04/09/16
Lithuania - Slovenia
Malta - Scotland
Slovakia - England

08/10/16
England - Malta
Scotland - Lithuania
Slovenia - Slovakia

11/10/16
Lithuania - Malta
Slovakia - Scotland
Slovenia - England

11/11/16
England - Scotland
Malta - Slovenia
Slovakia - Lithuania

26/03/17
England - Lithuania
Malta - Slovakia
Scotland - Slovenia

10/06/17
Lithuania - Slovakia
Scotland - England
Slovenia - Malta

01/09/17
Lithuania - Scotland
Malta - England
Slovakia - Slovenia

04/09/17
England - Slovakia
Scotland - Malta
Slovenia - Lithuania

05/10/17
England - Slovenia
Malta - Lithuania
Scotland - Slovakia

08/10/17
Lithuania - England
Slovakia - Malta
Slovenia - Scotland

Group G

(Spain, Italy, Albania, Israel, FYR Macedonia, Liechtenstein)

05/09/16
Albania - FYR Macedonia
Israel - Italy
Spain - Liechtenstein

06/10/16
Italy - Spain
Liechtenstein - Albania
FYR Macedonia - Israel

09/10/16
Albania - Spain
Israel - Liechtenstein
FYR Macedonia - Italy

12/11/16
Albania - Israel
Liechtenstein - Italy
Spain - FYR Macedonia

24/03/17
Italy - Albania
Liechtenstein - FYR Macedonia
Spain - Israel

11/06/17
Israel - Albania
Italy - Liechtenstein
FYR Macedonia - Spain

02/09/17
Albania - Liechtenstein
Israel - FYR Macedonia
Spain - Italy

05/09/17
Italy - Israel
Liechtenstein - Spain
FYR Macedonia - Albania

06/10/17
Italy - FYR Macedonia
Liechtenstein - Israel
Spain - Albania

09/10/17
Albania - Italy
Israel - Spain
FYR Macedonia - Liechtenstein

Group H

(Belgium, Bosnia & Herzegovina, Greece, Estonia, Cyprus, Gibraltar)

06/09/16
Bosnia & Herzegovina - Estonia
Cyprus - Belgium
Gibraltar - Greece

07/10/16
Belgium - Bosnia & Herzegovina
Estonia - Gibraltar
Greece - Cyprus

10/10/16
Bosnia & Herzegovina - Cyprus
Estonia - Greece
Gibraltar - Belgium

13/11/16
Belgium - Estonia
Cyprus - Gibraltar
Greece - Bosnia & Herzegovina

25/03/17
Belgium - Greece
Bosnia & Herzegovina - Gibraltar
Cyprus - Estonia

09/06/17
Bosnia & Herzegovina - Greece
Estonia - Belgium
Gibraltar - Cyprus

31/08/17
Belgium - Gibraltar
Cyprus - Bosnia & Herzegovina
Greece - Estonia

03/09/17
Estonia - Cyprus
Gibraltar - Bosnia & Herzegovina
Greece - Belgium

07/10/17
Bosnia & Herzegovina - Belgium
Cyprus - Greece
Gibraltar - Estonia

Group I

(Croatia, Iceland, Ukraine, Turkey, Finland, Kosovo)

05/09/16
Croatia - Turkey
Finland - Kosovo
Ukraine - Iceland

06/10/16
Iceland - Finland
Kosovo - Croatia
Turkey - Ukraine

09/10/16
Finland - Croatia
Iceland - Turkey
Ukraine - Kosovo

12/11/16
Croatia - Iceland
Turkey - Kosovo
Ukraine - Finland

24/03/17
Croatia - Ukraine
Kosovo - Iceland
Turkey - Finland

11/06/17
Finland - Ukraine
Iceland - Croatia
Kosovo - Turkey

02/09/17
Croatia - Kosovo
Finland - Iceland
Ukraine - Turkey

05/09/17
Iceland - Ukraine
Kosovo - Finland
Turkey - Croatia

06/10/17
Croatia - Finland
Kosovo - Ukraine
Turkey - Iceland

09/10/17
Finland - Turkey
Iceland - Kosovo
Ukraine - Croatia

NB The nine group winners will advance directly to the final tournament. The eight best runners-up will proceed to play-offs to decide the remaining four European berths. Russia, as tournament hosts, are exempt from qualification.

Play-off first leg:
9–11 November 2017

Play-off second leg:
12–14 November 2017

Final tournament (Russia):
14 June–15 July 2018